France

written and researched by

**David Abram, Ruth Blackmore, Brian Catlos, Hugh
Cleary, Samantha Cook, Ella Davies, Jan Dodd,
Marc Dubin, Donald Eastwood, Mike Kielty,
Alexander Larman, James McConnachie, Kate
Turner, Neville Walker, Greg Ward and Lucy White**

ROUGH
GUIDES

Contents

Bars, Bistros and Brasseries colour section following p.312

Walking in France colour section following p.600

Festive France colour section following p.1064

3

◄◄ Lavender field, Provence ◄ Divers at the Pont du Gard, Languedoc

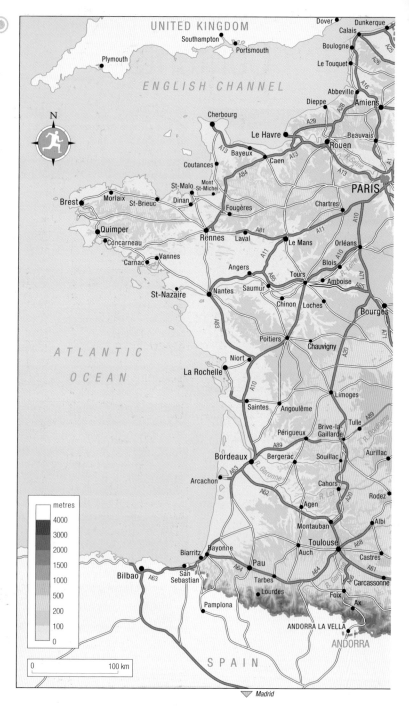

UNITED KINGDOM

Dover
Dunkerque
Calais
Southampton
Portsmouth
Boulogne
Plymouth
Le Touquet

ENGLISH CHANNEL

Abbeville
Dieppe A28 Amiens A1
A29
Cherbourg
Le Havre Beauvais
Rouen R. Seine
A13 Bayeux A13
Coutances Caen
A84 A13
St-Malo Mont St-Michel PARIS
Dinan Fougères
Brest Morlaix St-Brieuc Chartres
A10
Quimper Rennes Laval Le Mans Orléans
Concarneau A81 A11 A10
Vannes Blois R. Loire A71
Carnac Angers Tours Amboise A85
A85 Saumur A85
St-Nazaire Nantes Chinon Loches Bourges
Chauvigny A71
A83
Poitiers

ATLANTIC
OCEAN
Niort
La Rochelle A20
A10
Limoges
Saintes Angoulême
Tulle A89
Brive-la- R. Dordogne
Périgueux Gaillarde
A89
Souillac Aurillac
Bordeaux Bergerac
A63 R. Garonne
Arcachon Cahors R. Lot
A62 A20 Rodez
Agen
Montauban Albi
Toulouse A68
Biarritz Bayonne Auch A61
Bilbao A63 San Pau Castres
Sebastian A64 A64 A61
Tarbes R. Garonne Carcassonne
Lourdes Foix
Pamplona Ax
ANDORRA LA VELLA
ANDORRA
SPAIN
Madrid

metres
4000
3000
2000
1500
1000
500
200
100
0

N

0 — 100 km

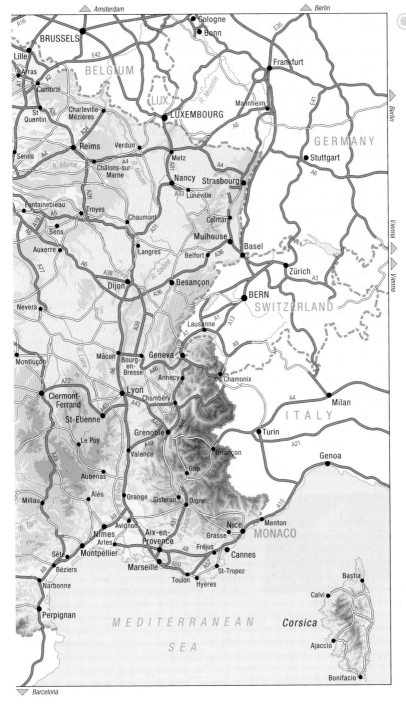

Introduction to
France

The sheer physical diversity of France would be hard to exhaust in a lifetime of visits. Landscapes range from the fretted coasts of Brittany and the limestone hills of Provence to the canyons of the Pyrenees and the half-moon bays of Corsica, and from the lushly wooded valleys of the Dordogne and the gentle meadows of the Loire valley to the glaciated peaks of the Alps. Each region looks and feels different, has its own style of architecture, its own characteristic food and often its own dialect. Though the French word *pays* is the term for a whole country, people frequently refer to their own region as *mon pays* – my country – and this strong sense of regional identity has persisted despite centuries of centralizing governments, from Louis XIV to de Gaulle.

Industrialization came relatively late to France, and for all the millions of French people that live in cities, the idea persists that theirs is a rural country. The importance of the land reverberates throughout French culture, manifesting itself in areas as diverse as regional pride in local cuisine and the state's fierce defence of Europe's agricultural subsidies. Perhaps the most striking feature of the French **countryside** is the sense of space. There are huge tracts of woodland and undeveloped land without a house in sight, and, away from the main urban centres, hundreds of towns and villages have changed only slowly and organically over the years, their old houses and streets intact, as

▲ Olive grove, Corsica

much a part of the natural landscape as the rivers, hills and fields.

Despite this image of pastoral tranquillity, France's history is notable for its extraordinary vigour. For more than a thousand years the country has been in the vanguard of European development, and the accumulation of wealth and experience is evident everywhere in the astonishing variety of **things to see**, from the Dordogne's prehistoric cave-paintings and the Roman monuments of the south, to the Gothic cathedrals of the north, the châteaux of the Loire, and the cutting-edge architecture of the *grands projets* in Paris. This legacy of history and culture – **la patrimoine** – is so widely dispersed across the land that even the briefest of stays will leave the visitor with a powerful sense of France's past.

Fact file

• With a land area of 547,000 square kilometres, France is the **second largest country** in Europe; its population of around 60 million is less only than its European neighbours, Germany and the UK.

• Now in its Fifth Republic, France has a long **secular republican tradition** dating back to the Revolution of 1789. Yet the majority of the population is Roman Catholic – notionally, at least – and there's a substantial Muslim minority of around 5–10 percent.

• **The government** consists of a directly elected president and a two-house parliament. As a nuclear power and G8 member, and with a permanent seat on the United Nations Security Council, France retains a strong international profile.

• **Annual GDP** per capita is around US$30,000, making France one of the world's richer countries, but unemployment is a persistent problem, at around 9 percent. Taxes are high, at around 45 percent of GDP, but so is social spending, at almost 30 percent.

• France remains by far the **most popular tourist destination** in the world, with some 75 million visitors each year.

▲ Galleries Lafayette, Paris

The importance of these traditions is felt deeply by the French state, which fights to preserve and develop its national **culture** perhaps harder than any other country in the world, and private companies, which also strive to maintain French traditions in arenas as diverse as *haute couture*, pottery and, of course, food. The fruits of these efforts are evident in the subsidized **arts**, notably the film industry, and in the lavishly endowed and innovative **museums and galleries**. From colonial history to fishing techniques, aeroplane design to textiles, and migrant shepherds to manicure, these collections can be found across the nation, but, inevitably, first place must go to the fabulous displays of fine art in Paris, a city which has nurtured more than its share of the finest creative artists of the last century and a half, both French – Monet and Matisse for example – and foreign, such as Picasso and Van Gogh.

There are all kinds of pegs on which to hang a holiday in France: a city, a region, a river, a mountain range, gastronomy, cathedrals, châteaux. All that open space means there's endless scope for outdoor activities – from walking, canoeing and cycling to skiing and sailing – but if you need more urban stimuli – clubs, shops, fashion, movies, music – then the great cities provide them in abundance.

Where to go

ravelling around France is easy. Restaurants and hotels proliferate, many of them relatively inexpensive when compared with other developed Western European countries. Train services are admirably efficient, as is the road network – especially the (toll-paying) autoroutes – and cyclists are much admired and encouraged. **Information** is highly organized and available from tourist offices across the country, as well as from specialist organizations for walkers, cyclists, campers and so on.

As for specific destinations, **Paris**, of course, is the outstanding cultural centre, with its impressive buildings and atmospheric backstreets, its art, nightlife and ethnic diversity, though the great **provincial cities** – Lyon, Bordeaux, Toulouse, Marseille – all now vie with the capital and each other for prestige in the arts, ascendancy in sport and innovation in attracting visitors.

For most people, however, it's the unique characters of the **regions** – and not least their cuisines – that will define a trip. Few holiday-makers stay long in the largely flat, industrial **north**, but there are some fine cathedrals and energetic cities to leaven the mix. The picture is similar in **Alsace–Lorraine** where Germanic influences are strong, notably in the food. On the northern Atlantic coast, **Normandy** has a rich heritage of cathedrals, castles, battle-fields and beaches – and, with its cream-based sauces, an equally rich cuisine. To the west, **Brittany** is more renowned for its Celtic links, beautiful coastline, prehistoric

> Hundreds of towns and villages have changed only slowly and organically over the years... as much a part of the natural landscape as the rivers, hills and fields

sites and seafood, while the **Loire** valley, extending inland towards Paris, is famed for soft, fertile countryside and a marvellous parade of châteaux. Further east, the green valleys of **Burgundy** shelter a wealth of Roman-esque churches, and the wines and food are among the finest in France. More Romanesque churches follow the pilgrim routes through rural

▼ Canoeing, Dordogne

Poitou–Charentes and down the Atlantic coast to **Bordeaux**, where the wines rival those of Burgundy. Inland from Bordeaux, visitors flock to the gorges, prehistoric sites and picturesque fortified villages of the **Dordogne** and neighbouring **Limousin**, drawn too by the truffles and duck and goose dishes of Périgord cuisine. To the south, the great mountain chain of the **Pyrenees** rears up along the Spanish border, running from the Basque country on the Atlantic to the Catalan lands of **Roussillon** on the Mediterranean; there's fine walking and skiing to be had, as well as beaches at either end. Further along the Mediterranean coast, **Languedoc** offers dramatic landscapes, medieval towns and Cathar castles, as well as more beaches, while the **Massif Central**, in the centre of the country, is undeveloped and little visited, but beautiful nonetheless, with its rivers, forests and the wild volcanic uplands of the **Auvergne**. The **Alps**, of course, are prime skiing territory, but a network of signposted paths makes walking a great way to explore too; to the north, the wooded mountains of the **Jura**

> The great provincial cities – Lyon, Bordeaux, Toulouse, Marseille – all now vie with the capital and each other for prestige in the arts, ascendancy in sport and innovation in attracting visitors.

Food and drink

The power and influence of French culture is evident anywhere that people read, wear clothes, vote or go to the cinema, but nowhere is the country's contribution greater than in culinary affairs. In France, a picnic could be a simple crusty baguette with cheese, washed

down by an inexpensive red wine, or a gourmet feast of cold meats and prepared salads, as available from practically any charcuterie; either way it's likely to be as good as you'll find anywhere in the world. The same is true of eating out, whether that means a perfect *steak-frites* at a railway-station brasserie, a lovingly prepared set menu in a provincial restaurant, featuring the homeliest of regional specialities, or the most exquisite refinements of a Parisian chef.

There's an endless variety of cheeses, cakes and pastries to match, as well as wines – and not just those from the renowned vineyards of Bordeaux, Burgundy and Champagne. Whether choosing a good local vintage or pondering some obscure regional speciality, never be afraid to ask advice – most French people are true enthusiasts, ever ready to convert the uninitiated.

provide further scope for outdoor pursuits. Stretching down from the Alps to the Mediterranean is **Provence**, which, as generations of travellers have discovered, seems to have everything: Roman ruins, picturesque villages, vineyards and lavender fields – and legions of visitors. Its cuisine is similarly diverse, encompassing fruit, olives, herbs, seafood, lamb and an unusual emphasis on vegetables. Along the Provençal coast, the beaches, towns and chic resorts of the **Côte d'Azur** form a giant smile extending from the down-at-heel but vibrant city of **Marseille** to the super-rich Riviera hotspots of Nice and Monaco. For truly fabulous beaches, however, head for the rugged island of **Corsica**, birthplace of Napoleon and home to an Italian-leaning culture and cuisine and some fascinating Neolithic sculptures.

When to go

The single most important factor in deciding when to visit France is tourism itself. As most French people take their holidays in their own country, it's as well to consider avoiding the main **French holiday periods** – mid-July to the end of August. At this time almost the entire country closes down, except for the tourist industry itself. You can easily walk a kilometre and more in Paris, for example, in search of

The French

According to the clichés, the French are stylish, romantic and passionate. They also have a reputation for rudeness – and yet they are courteous with each other to the point of formality. It's common for someone entering a shop to wish customers and shopkeeper alike a general "good morning", and foreigners on business quickly learn the importance of shaking hands, asking the right questions and maintaining respectful eye contact. At the same time, if they want something, many French people can be direct in ways that are disconcerting for Anglo-Saxons. To foreigners stumbling over the language, never mind the cultural gap, this can seem like rudeness; it isn't. It's fairer to say that the French are proud. Opinions tend to be held and argued strongly – it's not for nothing that so many revolutions have shaken the political landscape. Culture, too, is a source of great pride, and artists, writers and thinkers are held in high esteem even beyond elite circles. And French people everywhere are proud of their locality. Whether it's for a village shopfront, a civic floral display or another landmark building for the French state, no effort is too great.

▼ Dinan, Brittany

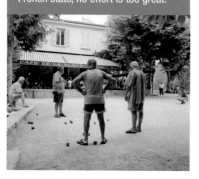

an open boulangerie, and the city sometimes seems deserted by all except fellow tourists. Prices in the resorts rise to take full advantage and often you can't find a room for love nor money, and on the Côte d'Azur not even a space in the campsites. The seaside is the most crowded, but the mountains and popular regions like the Dordogne are not far behind. Easter, too, is a bad time for Paris: half of Europe's schoolchildren seem to descend on the city. For the same reasons, ski buffs should keep in mind the February school ski break. And no one who values life, limb and sanity should ever be caught on the roads during the last weekend of July or August, and least of all on the weekend of August 15.

Generally speaking, **climate** needn't be a major consideration in planning when to go. If you're a skier, of course, you wouldn't choose the mountains between May and November; and if you want a beach holiday, you wouldn't head for the seaside out of summer – except for the Mediterranean coast, which is at its most attractive in spring. **Northern France**, like nearby Britain, is wet and unpredictable. **Paris** has a marginally better climate than New York, rarely reaching the extremes of heat and cold of that city, but only **south of the Loire** does the weather become significantly warmer. **West coast** weather, even in the south, is tempered by the proximity of the Atlantic, subject to violent storms and close thundery days even in summer. The **centre** and **east**, as you leave the coasts behind, have a more continental climate, with colder winters and hotter summers. The most reliable weather is along and behind the **Mediterranean** coastline and on **Corsica**, where winter is short and summer long and hot.

Average daily maximum temperatures

For a recorded weather forecast you can phone the main forecasting line on ☏08.92.68.08.08, or check online at ⓦwww.meteofrance.com.

	Jan	Feb	Mar	Apr	May	Jun	Jul	Aug	Sep	Oct	Nov	Dec
Paris												
Max/min (C)	6/2	7/2	11/4	14/6	18/9	21/12	24/14	23/14	20/12	16/9	10/5	7/2
Max/min (F)	43/35	45/35	51/39	57/42	64/49	70/54	74/58	74/57	68/53	60/47	49/40	44/36
Rainfall mm	54	46	52	45	62	57	54	51	57	59	59	55
St-Malo												
Max/min (C)	8/3	9/3	11/4	13/6	17/9	20/11	22/13	22/13	20/12	16/10	12/6	9/4
Max/min (F)	47/38	48/38	52/40	56/43	62/48	67/53	71/56	71/56	68/54	61/49	53/43	48/40
Rainfall mm	82	68	63	50	57	48	41	48	62	75	95	89
Lyon												
Max/min (C)	6/0	8/1	12/3	15/6	19/9	23/13	27/15	26/14	23/12	17/8	10/4	6/1
Max/min (F)	42/32	47/34	53/37	60/42	67/49	74/55	80/59	78/58	73/53	62/46	50/38	43/33
Rainfall mm	58	58	66	69	89	78	61	77	78	79	73	64
Toulouse												
Max/min (C)	9/2	11/3	14/4	16/7	20/10	24/13	28/15	27/15	24/13	19/10	13/5	10/3
Max/min (F)	49/35	52/37	56/39	61/44	68/49	75/55	82/60	80/59	76/55	67/49	56/41	49/37
Rainfall mm	59	59	57	67	77	71	44	57	67	58	63	69
Nice												
Max/min (C)	11/3	11/4	13/6	15/8	19/12	22/15	26/18	26/18	23/16	19/12	14/7	12/5
Max/min (F)	51/38	52/39	55/42	60/47	66/53	72/59	78/64	78/64	73/60	67/54	58/45	53/40
Rainfall mm	77	79	74	66	61	46	22	43	65	104	101	78

things not to miss

I ACTIVITIES I CONSUME I EVENTS I NATURE I SIGHTS I

It's not possible to see everything that France has to offer in one trip – and we don't suggest you try. What follows is a selective taste of the country's highlights: natural wonders and outstanding sights, plus the best activities and experiences. They're arranged in five colour-coded categories, so you can browse through to find the very best things to see and do. All highlights have a page reference to take you straight into the Guide, where you can find out more.

14

01 Les Gorges du Verdon Page **1007** • The mighty gorges are Europe's answer to the Grand Canyon, and offer stunning views, a range of hikes, and colours and scents that are uniquely, gorgeously Provençal.

02 The Louvre Page **100** • The palace of the Louvre cuts a grand Classical swathe through the centre of Paris and houses what is nothing less than the gold standard of France's artistic tradition.

03 Bordeaux Page **586** • Stylish and lively Bordeaux became the principal English stronghold in France for three hundred years, and is still known for the refined red wines – claret – which the English popularized.

04 Amiens cathedral Page **210** • The largest Gothic building in all France, this lofty cathedral has a clever evening light show that gives a vivid idea of how the west front would have looked when it rejoiced in coloured paint.

05 **Annecy** Page **895** • One of the prettiest towns in the Alps, Annecy has a picture-postcard quality which even the crowds can't mar.

06 **The Issenheim altarpiece** Page **278** • The village of Colmar might be excessively twee, but it's still worth a visit for Grünewald's amazing altarpiece, one of the most extraordinary works of art in the country.

07 **Mont St-Michel** Page **346** • Second only to the Eiffel Tower as France's best-loved landmark, the *merveille* of Mont St-Michel is a splendid union of nature and architecture.

09 **St-Ouen** Page **140** • It's easy to lose track of an entire weekend morning browsing the acres of fine antiques, covetable curios and general bric-a-brac at St-Ouen, the mother of Paris's flea markets.

08 **Bastille Day** Page **50** & *Festive France* colour section • July 14 sees national celebrations commemorating the beginning of the French Revolution, with fireworks and parties across the whole country.

10 **Medieval Provençal villages** Page **980** & Page **995** • Provence's hilltop villages attract visitors by the score. Though Gordes is one of the most famous, there are others less well known but equally beautiful.

11 **Tour de France** Page **52** ● One of the world's greatest sporting events, this gruelling, three-week bike race follows a different route around the country every year, always ending on the Champs-Élysées.

12 **Carnac** Page **415** ● Archeologically, Brittany is one of the richest regions in the world and the alignments at Carnac rival Stonehenge.

13 **Canal du Midi** Page **789** • A calm, watery avenue, stretching from beyond Toulouse to the Mediterranean. Cycling, walking or drifting along its tree-shaded course is the most atmospheric way of savouring France's southwest.

14 **Gorges de l'Ardèche** Page **854** • The fantastic gorges begin at the Pont d'Arc and cut their way through limestone cliffs before emptying into the Rhône valley.

15 **Cathar castles** Page **738** • Languedoc's mountains are dotted with these gaunt fortresses, grim but fascinating relics of the brutal crusade launched by the Catholic church and northern French nobility against the heretic Cathars.

19

16 Bayeux Tapestry Page **336** • This 70-metre-long tapestry is an astonishingly detailed depiction of the 1066 Norman invasion of England, and one of the finest artistic works of the early medieval era.

17 Dining out in a Lyon bouchon
Page **941** • Famed for its gastronomy and home to super chefs such as Paul Bocuse, Lyon offers no end of wonderful eating places, not least the old-fashioned *bouchons*, traditional colourful bistros, where you can sample *quenelles* (pike sausages), *andouillettes* (chunky sausages made from chitterlings) and other local specialities.

18 Fontenay Abbey Page **513** • One of the most complete monastic complexes anywhere, this Burgundian monastery has a serene setting in a stream-filled valley.

19 **Jardin du Luxembourg** Page **123** • Paris's most beautiful park, in the heart of the laid-back Left Bank, is the ideal spot for relaxing.

21 **Champagne tasting at Épernay** Page **244** • Dom Pérignon might be the most famous, but there are plenty of other bubblies to try in the atmospheric cellars of Épernay's *maisons*.

22 **War memorials** Page **333** • World Wars I and II left permanent scars on the French countryside – and on its psyche. The dead are remembered in solemn, sometimes overwhelming cemeteries, such as the one at Ryes in Normandy.

20 **Les Calanques** Page **1036** • The limestone cliffs on the stretch of coast between Marseille and Cassis offer excellent hiking, and you can scramble down to isolated coves that are perfect for swimming.

24 The GR20 Page 1119 & *Walking in France* colour section • Arguably France's most dramatic – and most demanding – long-distance footpath climbs through and over Corsica's precipitous mountains for some 170km.

23 Châteaux of the Loire
Page **467** • The River Loire is lined with gracious châteaux, of which Chambord is surely the most staggeringly impressive, both for its size and the double-spiral staircase designed by Leonardo da Vinci.

25 Carcassonne Page **787** • So atmospheric is this medieval fortress town that it manages to resist even relentless commercialization and summer's throng of visitors.

26 Corsican beaches Page **1113** • Some of the best of France's many beautiful beaches are found on Corsica, including the plage de Saleccia, with its soft white shell sand, turquoise water and not a building or road in sight.

27 Prehistoric cave art Page **642** • Prehistoric art can be seen in several places around France, but perhaps the most impressive paintings are those at Lascaux in the Dordogne.

23

28 **Winter sports in the Alps** Page **877** • The French Alps are home to some of the world's most prestigious ski resorts, offering a wide range of winter sports.

29 **Aix-en-Provence** Page **997** • Marseille may be the biggest city in Provence, but aristocratic Aix is the region's capital, and it's a wonderful place to shop, eat and linger under the plane trees with a *pastis*.

30 **Bastide towns** Page **633** • Monpazier is one of the best preserved of the fortified towns – *bastides* – built in the Dordogne region during the turbulent medieval period when there was almost constant conflict between the French and English.

Basics

Basics

Getting there

The quickest way of reaching France from most parts of the United Kingdom and Ireland is by air. From southern England, however, the Eurostar provides a viable alternative, making the journey from London to Paris in under three hours. The Channel Tunnel is the most flexible option if you want to take your car to France, though cross-Channel ferries are often cheaper. It's also worth bearing in mind that if you live west of London, the ferry services to Roscoff, St-Malo, Cherbourg, Caen and Le Havre can save a lot of driving time. From the US and Canada a number of airlines fly direct to Paris, from where you can pick up onward connections. You can also fly direct to Paris from South Africa, while the best fares from Australia and New Zealand are generally via Asia.

Whether you are travelling by air, sea or rail, prices increasingly depend on how far in advance you book, but will also depend on the **season**. Fares are at their highest from around early June to the end of August, when the weather is best, drop during the "shoulder" seasons – roughly September to October and April to May – and are at their cheapest during the low season, November to March (excluding Christmas and New Year when prices are hiked up and seats are at a premium). Note also that flying at weekends can be more expensive; price ranges quoted below assume midweek travel, and include all taxes and surcharges.

Flights from the UK and Ireland

With the rapid increase in the number of **budget airlines** between the UK, Ireland and France, flying is becoming ever cheaper, particularly if you're leaving from or heading to one of the regional airports. The main budget airlines are bmibaby, easyJet, flyBE and Ryanair, which between them cover over thirty airports across France, including Ajaccio (March–Sept), Avignon, Bergerac, Chambéry, La Rochelle, Nantes, Pau, Rennes, Toulon and Tours, as well as more established hubs such as Paris, Lyon and Nice. Bear in mind though that routes and destinations change regularly, so it's wise to keep an eye on the airlines' websites (see p.31). It's also worth double-checking exactly where the airport is in relation to where you want to be; Ryanair claims to fly to Paris, for example, but in reality

flies to the airport in Beauvais, a ninety-minute coach drive from the city centre. **Tickets** work on a quota system, and it's wise to book as early as possible for the really cheap seats, which can, if you're lucky work out to as little as £5–30/€5–45 each way, including taxes.

It's worth checking out the **traditional carriers**, such as Air France, British Airways and Aer Lingus, which have lowered their prices in recent years in the face of stiff competition from budget airlines. Again, the further ahead you book the better, but low-season return fares to Paris start at around £120 from London, £130 from Edinburgh and €220 from Dublin; to Nice you'll pay upwards of £130, £200 and €240 respectively.

Air France, along with its partners, offers the widest regional coverage. It flies to Paris Charles-de-Gaulle (CDG) several times daily from London Heathrow, Dublin and regional airports such as Birmingham, Manchester, Southampton and Newcastle. It also operates flights from Heathrow and other UK airports direct to French regional airports such as Lyon, Nice and Strasbourg. Flights to Corsica – into Ajaccio, Bastia or Calvi – involve a change in Paris. **British Airways** has several flights a day to Paris CDG from London Heathrow and at least one direct from Birmingham and Manchester. BA also operates flights from London to Bordeaux, Lyon, Marseille, Nice and Toulouse. In Ireland, **Aer Lingus** offers nonstop flights from Dublin and Cork to Paris CDG; from Dublin to Bordeaux, Lyon, Marseille, Nice, Rennes and Toulouse; and from Cork to Nice.

Flights from the US and Canada

Most major airlines operate scheduled flights to Paris from the US and Canada. Air France has the most frequent service, with good onward regional connections, but their fares tend to be on the expensive side. Other airlines offering **nonstop** services to Paris from a variety of US cities include: American Airlines from New York, Boston, Chicago, Dallas and Miami; Continental from Newark and Houston; Delta from Atlanta, Boston, Chicago, Cincinnati, Houston, Los Angeles, Miami, New York, Philadelphia and Washington DC; Northwest from Detroit; and United from Chicago, Philadelphia and Washington DC. Air Canada offers nonstop services to Paris from Montréal and Toronto, while Air Transat offers good-value scheduled and **charter flights** from a number of bases. Another option is to take one of the other

European carriers, such as British Airways, bmi, Iberia or Lufthansa, from the US or Canada to their home base and then continue on to Paris or a regional French airport. If you have a specific French destination in mind outside Paris and you're in a hurry – and are prepared to pay extra – it's possible to be ticketed straight through to any of more than a dozen regional airports. Most of these entail changing planes in Paris, and check to make sure there's no inconvenient transfer between the city's two main airports, Charles-de-Gaulle and Orly.

Thanks to intense competition, transatlantic **fares** to France are still pretty reasonable. A typical return fare for a midweek flight to Paris is around US$850 from New York, US$1100 from Los Angeles and US$950 from Houston. From Canada, prices to Paris are in the region of CAN$1000 from Montréal and Toronto, and CAN$1300 from Vancouver.

Six steps to a better kind of travel

At Rough Guides we are passionately committed to travel. We feel strongly that only through travelling do we truly come to understand the world we live in and the people we share it with – plus tourism has brought a great deal of benefit to developing economies around the world over the last few decades. But the extraordinary growth in tourism has also damaged some places irreparably, and of course climate change is exacerbated by most forms of transport, especially flying. This means that now more than ever it's important to travel thoughtfully and responsibly, with respect for the cultures you're visiting – not only to derive the most benefit from your trip but also in order to preserve the best bits of the planet for everyone to enjoy. At Rough Guides we feel there are six main areas in which you can make a difference:

• Consider what you're contributing to the local economy, and indeed how much the services you use do the same, whether it's through employing local workers and guides or sourcing locally grown produce and local services.

• Consider the environment on holiday as well as at home. Water is scarce in many developing destinations, and the biodiversity of local flora and fauna can be adversely affected by tourism. Patronise businesses that take account of this rather than those that trash the local environment for short-term gain.

• Give thought to how often you fly and what you can do to redress any harm that your trips create. Reduce the amount you travel by air; avoid short hops by air and more harmful night flights.

• Consider alternatives to flying, travelling instead by bus, train, boat and even by bike or on foot where possible. Take time to enjoy the journey itself as well as your final destination.

• Think about making all the trips you take "climate neutral" via a reputable carbon offset scheme. All Rough Guide flights are offset, and every year we donate money to a variety of charities devoted to combating the effects of climate change.

• Travel with a purpose, not just to tick off experiences. Consider spending longer in a place, and really getting to know it and its people – you'll find it much more rewarding than dashing from place to place.

Flights from Australia, New Zealand and South Africa

Most travellers from **Australia and New Zealand** choose to fly to France via London, although the majority of airlines can add a Paris leg (or a flight to any other major French city) to an Australia/New Zealand–Europe ticket. Flights via Asia or the Gulf States, with a transfer or overnight stop at the airline's home port, are generally the cheapest option; those routed through the US tend to be slightly pricier. Return **fares** start at around AUS$2100 from Sydney, AUS$1900 from Perth, AUS$2300 from Melbourne and NZ$2000 from Auckland.

From **South Africa**, Johannesburg is the best place to start, with Air France flying direct to Paris from around R8000 return; from Cape Town, they fly via Amsterdam and are more expensive, starting at around R11,000. BA, flying via London, costs upwards of R11,000 from Johannesburg and R12,000 from Cape Town.

By train

Eurostar operates high-speed passenger trains daily from St Pancras International to France through the **Channel Tunnel**; most but not all services stop at either Ebbsfleet or Ashford, both in Kent (15min and 30min from London, respectively). There are 1–2 services an hour (from around 5.30am to 8pm for Paris Gare du Nord (2hr 15min–2hr 26min), a few of which stop at Calais (1hr) and Lille (1hr 30min), where you can connect with TGV trains heading south to Bordeaux, Lyon and Nice. In addition, Eurostar runs direct trains from London to Disneyland Paris (daily; 2hr 35min), to Avignon (mid-July to mid-Sept; Sat; 6hr), and a special twice-weekly ski service to Moutiers, Aime-la-Plagne and Bourg-St-Maurice in the French Alps (mid-Dec to mid-April; around 8hr); skis are carried free.

Standard **fares** from London to Paris start at £59 (£55 to Lille and £99 to Avignon) for a non-refundable, non-exchangeable return. The next option is the changeable "semi-flexible" ticket (from £135/130/189 respectively), where you can change the dates but is non-refundable and must include a Saturday night. Both these deals have limited availability, so it

pays to plan ahead; tickets go on sale 120 days before the date of travel. Otherwise, you're looking at £309/270/290 for a fully refundable ticket with no restrictions. Return fares to Disneyland Paris start at £59 for adults (£44 for children aged 4–11) and those on the Eurostar ski train at £179 (£130 for children under 12). Under-4s travel for free.

Tickets can be bought online or by phone from Eurostar, as well as through travel agents and mainline stations, and it's possible to get through-ticketing from stations around Britain – including the tube journey across London to St Pancras. InterRail, Eurail and **rail passes** (see below) entitle you to discounts on Eurostar trains. For information about taking your bike on Eurostar, see p.40. For rail contacts, see p.32.

By car via the Channel Tunnel

The simplest way of taking your car across to France from the UK is to load it on one of the drive-on drive-off shuttle trains operated by **Eurotunnel**. The service runs continuously between Folkestone and Coquelles, near Calais, with up to three departures per hour (one every 2hr from midnight–6am) and takes 35 minutes (slightly longer at night departures). It is possible to turn up and buy your ticket at the check-in booths, though you'll pay a premium rate and at busy times booking is strongly recommended; if you have a booking, you must arrive at least thirty minutes before departure. Note that Eurotunnel is not allowed to transport cars fitted with LPG or CNG tanks.

Standard **fares** start at £49 one-way if you book far enough ahead and/or travel offpeak, rising to £155. Fully refundable and change-able FlexiPlus fares cost £149 each way for a short stay (up to 5 days) and £199 for longer periods. There's room for only six **bicycles** on any departure, so book ahead in high season – a standard return costs £32 for a bike plus rider.

Rail passes

There are a number of international rail passes useful for travel within France, many of which need to be bought in your home country (for details of railcards that you can buy in France, see p.36). **Rail Europe**, the umbrella company for all national and international rail purchases, is the most useful source of information on which passes are available and how much they cost. For information on where to buy InterRail, Eurail and France Rail passes, see p.30.

InterRail Pass

InterRail Passes are only available to European residents, or those who have lived in a European country for at least six months, and you will be asked to provide proof of residency (and long-stay visa if applicable) before being allowed to purchase one. They come in over-26 and (cheaper) under-26 versions, and cover thirty European countries. Children from 4-12 years pay half price, and those under 4 travel for free.

There are two types of passes: global and one-country. The global pass covers all thirty countries and comes in various options: five days of travel in a ten-day period (£135 for under-26s/£212 for over-26s); ten days of travel within a 22-day period (£203/305); 22 days continuous travel (£262/398); and one month (£339/508) continuous travel. Similarly, the one-country pass allows you to opt for various periods, ranging from three days in one month (£106/161) to eight days in one month (£165/254). In each case, first-class passes are also available.

Inter-Rail Passes do not include travel within your country of residence, though pass holders are eligible for discounts on rail fares to and from the border of the relevant zone as well as reductions on Eurostar and some cross-Channel ferries.

Eurail Pass

Eurail Passes are not available to European residents and must be purchased before arrival in Europe. Again, there are various options, of which the most useful are likely to be one of the five **regional passes**, covering France with the Benelux countries, Germany, Italy, Spain or Switzerland, or the **France Railpass**. The latter offers three days of unlimited train travel within a month for US$278/AUS$287/NZ$376/R2180 travelling second class, with the option of buying up to six additional days' travel at US$40/AUS$42/NZ$54/R314 per day. The Saverpass offers the same for two-five people travelling together. First-class passes and child, youth and senior passes are also available, as well as a Rail'n Drive Pass combining two days' unlimited train travel in France with two days' car rental.

By ferry

Though slower than travelling by plane or via the Channel Tunnel, the ferries and catamarans plying between Dover and Calais offer the cheapest means of travelling to France **from the UK** and are particularly convenient if you live in southeast England. If you're coming from the north of England or Scotland, you could consider the overnight crossings from Hull (13hr) and Rosyth (18hr) to Zeebrugge (Belgium) operated by P&O Ferries and Superfast Ferries, respectively. **From Ireland**, putting the car on the ferry from Cork or Rosslare (near Wexford) to Cherbourg and Roscoff (14hr) in Brittany or Le Havre (21hr) in Normandy cuts out the drive across Britain to the Channel.

Ferry **prices** are seasonal and, for motorists, depend on the size of your vehicle. In general, the further you book ahead, the cheaper the fare and it's well worth playing around with dates and times to find the best deals: midweek, midday sailings are usually cheapest. At the time of writing, one-way fares for a car and up to five passengers are available for as little as £25 with Norfolkline on the Dover–Dunkerque route, while one-way fares on the Dover–Calais crossing start at around £40. One-way fares from Ireland

---

Travelling with pets from the UK

If you wish to take your dog (or cat) to France, the **Pet Travel Scheme (PETS)** enables you to avoid putting it in quarantine when re-entering the UK as long as certain conditions are met. Current regulations are available on the Department for Environment, Food and Rural Affairs (DEFRA) website Ⓦ www.defra.gov.uk/animalh /quarantine/index.htm or through the PETS Helpline (℡ 0870 241 1710).

(Cork–Roscoff) kick off at around €180 for a car and two adults.

Most ferry companies also offer fares for **foot passengers**, typically around £20 return on cross-Channel routes; accompanying **bicycles** can usually be carried free in low season, though there may be a small charge during peak periods.

By bus

Eurolines runs regular services from London Victoria to over forty French cities, including up to eight a day to Paris, crossing the Channel by ferry or Eurotunnel. Prices are lower than for the same journey by train and comparable with discount airlines, with adult return "Promo" fares (must be booked at least seven days in advance) starting at around £40 to Paris and £46 to Lille, and "Value" fares (at least four days in advance) at £100 each to Bordeaux and Toulouse. Regional fares from the rest of England and from Wales are available, as are student, youth, over-60s and family discounts. The Eurolines pass offers unlimited Europe-wide travel for fifteen or thirty days. Prices range from £139 for an adult fifteen-day pass in low season (£119 for under-26s) to £299 for a peak-season thirty-day pass (£249 for under-26s). From December to early April Eurolines runs an overnight "ski bus" service on Fridays to the major Alpine resorts; return fares start at around £115.

Airlines, agents and operators

There are a vast number of travel agents and tour operators offering holidays in France, with options varying from luxury, château-based breaks to adventure trips involving skiing and hiking. The following pages list the most useful contacts.

Online booking

Ⓦ www.cheapflights.com
Ⓦ www.ebookers.com
Ⓦ www.expedia.com
Ⓦ www.flightcentre.com
Ⓦ www.lastminute.com
Ⓦ www.opodo.com
Ⓦ www.orbitz.com
Ⓦ www.priceline.com
Ⓦ www.sta-travel.com

Ⓦ www.travel-kelkoo.co.uk (UK)
Ⓦ www.travelocity.com
Ⓦ www.travelzoo.com
Ⓦ www.zuji.com (Australia & New Zealand)

Airlines

Aer Arann UK ☎ 0870 876 7676, Republic of Ireland ☎ 0818/210 210; Ⓦ www.aerarann.com.
Aer Lingus UK ☎ 0870 876 5000, Republic of Ireland ☎ 0818/365 000, US & Canada ☎ 1-800-474-7424; Ⓦ www.aerlingus.com.
Air Canada ☎ 1-888-247-2262, Ⓦ www .aircanada.com.
Air France UK ☎ 0871 6633 777, US ☎ 1-800-237-2747, Canada ☎ 1-800-667-2747, Australia ☎ 1300 390 190, South Africa ☎ 0861 340 340; Ⓦ www.airfrance.com.
Air Transat Canada ☎ 1-877-872-6728, Ⓦ www .airtransat.com.
American Airlines US ☎ 1-800-433-7300, Ⓦ www.aa.com.
bmi UK ☎ 0870 607 0555, Republic of Ireland ☎ 01/407 3036, US ☎ 1-800-788-0555; Ⓦ www .flybmi.com.
bmibaby UK ☎ 0871 224 0224, Ⓦ www.bmibaby .com.
British Airways UK ☎ 0844 493 0787, Republic of Ireland ☎ 1890 626 747, US & Canada ☎ 1-800-247-9297, Australia ☎ 1300 767 177, New Zealand ☎ 09/966 9777, South Africa ☎ 011/441 8600; Ⓦ www.ba.com.
Cathay Pacific Australia ☎ 131-747, New Zealand ☎ 09/379 0861; Ⓦ www.cathaypacific.com.
Continental Airlines ☎ 1-800-231-0856, Ⓦ www.continental.com.
Delta US & Canada ☎ 1-800-241-4141, Ⓦ www .delta.com.
easyJet UK Ⓦ www.easyjet.com.
Emirates Australia ☎ 1300 303 777, New Zealand ☎ 09/968 2208, South Africa ☎ 0861/364 728; Ⓦ www.emirates.com.
flyBE UK ☎ 0871 700 2000, Republic of Ireland ☎ +44 1392/268 500; Ⓦ www.flybe.com.
Jet2 UK ☎ 0871 226 1737, Republic of Ireland ☎ 0818 200 017; Ⓦ www.jet2.com.
KLM Australia ☎ 1300 392 192, New Zealand ☎ 09/921 6040, South Africa ☎ 0860 247 747; Ⓦ www.klm.com.
Lufthansa US ☎ 1-800-645-3880, Canada ☎ 1-800-563-5954, Australia ☎ 1300 655 727, New Zealand ☎ 0800 945 220, South Africa ☎ 0861/842 538; Ⓦ www.lufthansa.com. From major cities in the US, plus Canada, New Zealand and South Africa, to airports across France, all via Frankfurt.
Northwest US ☎ 1-800-225-2525, Ⓦ www .nwa.com.

31

Qantas Australia ☎13 13 13, New Zealand ☎0800 808 767; ⊛www.qantas.com.

Ryanair UK ☎0871 246 0000, Republic of Ireland ☎0818 303 030; ⊛www.ryanair.com.

Singapore Airlines Australia ☎13 1011, New Zealand ☎0800 808 909; ⊛www.singaporeair.com.

South African Airways South Africa ☎0861 359 722, ⊛www.flysaa.com.

Thomsonfly.com UK ☎0871 231 4691, ⊛www .thomsonfly.com.

United Airlines US ☎1-800-538-2929, ⊛www .united.com.

US Airways US & Canada ☎1-800-622-1015, ⊛www.usair.com.

Agents and operators

Allez France ⊛www.allezfrance.com. UK tour operator offering accommodation only as well as fly-drive and other holiday packages throughout France.

Belle France UK ☎01580/214 010, ⊛www .bellefrance.co.uk. Walking, cycling and boating holidays throughout France.

Bonnes Vacances Direct UK ☎0870 760 7071; ⊛www.bvdirect.co.uk. Agent for property owners in France for self-catering and B&B accommodation.

Canvas Holidays UK ☎0870 192 1154, ⊛www .canvas.co.uk. Tailor-made caravan and camping holidays.

Chez Nous UK ☎0870 197 1000, ⊛www .cheznous.com. Search over seven thousand self-catering and B&B properties online, including ski rentals.

Corsican Places UK ☎0845 330 2059, ⊛www .corsica.co.uk. Corsica specialists.

Crown Blue Line France ☎+33 (0)4.68.94.52.72, ⊛www.crownblueline.com. Good-value self-drive canal holidays all over France.

Cycling for Softies UK ☎0161/248 8282, ⊛www.cycling-for-softies.co.uk. Easy-going cycle holiday operator to rural France.

Discover France US ☎1-800-960-2221, ⊛www. discoverfrance.com. Self-guided cycling and walking holidays throughout France.

Euro-Bike & Walking Tours US & Canada ☎1-800-321-6060, ⊛www.eurobike.com. Good range of bike and walking tours all over France for family groups or solo travellers.

Eurocamp UK ☎0844 406 0402, ⊛www .eurocamp.co.uk. Camping holidays with kids' activities and single-parent deals.

Fields Fairway France ☎+33 (0)3.21.33.65.64, ⊛www.fieldsfairway.co.uk. British-run, France-based company offering all-inclusive golfing holidays.

France Afloat UK ☎0870 011 0538, ⊛www .franceafloat.com. Canal and river cruises across France.

France Holiday Store ⊛www.fr-holidaystore .co.uk. Search engine for tour operators offering holidays in France.

French Affair UK ☎020/7381 8519, ⊛www .frenchaffair.com. Wide range of self-catering accommodation in southern France and Corsica.

French Travel Connection Australia ☎02/9966 1177, ⊛www.frenchtravel.com.au. Offers large range of holidays to France.

Headwater UK ☎01606/720 033, Republic of Ireland through Leopardstown Tours ☎01/295 8901, US & Canada through Breakaway Adventures ☎1-800-567-6286, Australia & New Zealand through Adventure World, Australia ☎02/8913 0700, New Zealand ☎09/524 5118; ⊛www. headwater.com. UK-based operator offering walking, cycling and canoeing tours throughout France, and cross-country skiing.

Holiday France ⊛www.holidayfrance.org.uk. Website that allows you to search for French tour operators by holiday type and location.

Inntravel UK ☎01653/617 949, ⊛www.inntravel .co.uk. Broad range of activity holidays, including riding, skiing, walking and cycling, as well as property rental.

Keycamp Holidays UK ☎0844 406 0200, ⊛www.keycamp.com. Caravan and camping holidays, including transport to France.

Locaboat UK ☎01279/505 097, Republic of Ireland ☎071/964 5923, US ☎1-866-606-5278; ⊛www.locaboat.com. French company specializing in holidays on *pénichettes* (scaled-down replicas of commercial barges).

North South Travel UK ☎01245/608 291, ⊛www.northsouthtravel.co.uk. Friendly, competitive travel agency, offering discounted fares worldwide. Profits are used to support projects in the developing world, especially the promotion of sustainable tourism.

STA Travel UK ☎0871 2300 040, US & Canada ☎1-800-781-4040, Australia ☎134-782, New Zealand ☎0800 474 400, South Africa ☎0861/781 781; ⊛www.statravel.com. Worldwide specialists in independent travel; also student IDs, travel insurance, car rental, rail and bus passes, and more. Good discounts for students and under-26s.

Trailfinders UK ☎0845 058 5858, Republic of Ireland ☎01/677 7888, Australia ☎1300 780 212; ⊛www.trailfinders.com. One of the best-informed and most efficient agents for independent travellers.

Rail, Channel Tunnel and bus contacts

Eurolines UK ☎0871 781 8181, ⊛www .eurolines.co.uk

European Rail UK ☎020/7619 1083, ⊛www .europeanrail.com.

Eurostar UK ☎0870 518 6186, ⊛www.eurostar .com.

Eurotunnel UK ☎0870 535 3535, ⓦwww
.eurotunnel.com.
International Rail UK ☎0870 084 1410, ⓦwww
.international-rail.com.
Rail Europe (SNCF French Railways) UK ☎0844
848 4064, ⓦwww.raileurope.co.uk; US ☎1-
888-382-7245, ⓦwww.raileurope.com; Canada
☎1-800-361-7245, ⓦwww.raileurope.ca.
Rail Plus Australia ☎1300 555 003, New
Zealand ☎09/377 5415; ⓦwww.railplus.com.au.
Trainseurope UK ☎0871 700 7722, ⓦwww
.trainseurope.co.uk.
World Travel South Africa ☎011/628 2300,
ⓦwww.world-travelco.za.

Ferry contacts

Brittany Ferries UK ☎0871 244 0744,
ⓦwww.brittanyferries.co.uk; Republic of Ireland
☎021/4277 801, ⓦwww.brittanyferries.ie.

Condor Ferries UK ☎0845 609 1024, ⓦwww
.condorferries.co.uk.
EuroDrive UK ☎0844 576 8835, ⓦwww
.eurodrive.co.uk.
Ferry Savers UK ☎0870 066 9612, ⓦwww
.ferrysavers.com.
Irish Ferries Republic of Ireland ☎0818/300 400,
ⓦwww.irishferries.com.
LD Lines UK ☎0844 576 8836, ⓦwww.ldlines
.com.
Norfolkline UK ☎0844 847 5007, ⓦwww
.norfolkline.com.
P&O Ferries UK ☎08716 645 645, ⓦwww
.poferries.com.
Sea France UK ☎0871 423 7119, ⓦwww
.seafrance.com.
Superfast Ferries UK ☎01383/608 003, ⓦwww
.superfast.com.

Getting around

With the most extensive train network in Western Europe, France is a great
country in which to travel by rail. The nationally owned French train company,
SNCF (Société Nationale des Chemins de Fer), runs fast, efficient trains between
the main towns. Buses cover the rural areas, but services can be rather sporadic,
with departures often at awkward times. If you really want to get off the beaten
track, by far the best option is to have your own transport. Approximate journey
times and frequencies of the main train, bus, plane and ferry services can be
found in the "Travel details" at the end of each chapter.

By train

SNCF (☎36.35, €0.34 per minute; ⓦwww
.voyages-sncf.com) has pioneered one of
the most efficient, comfortable and user-
friendly railway systems in the world. Its staff
are generally courteous and helpful, and its
trains – for the most part, fast, clean and
reliable – continue, in spite of the closure of
some rural lines, to serve the vast part of the
country.

Trains

Pride and joy of the French rail system is the
high-speed **TGV** (*train à grande vitesse*),

capable of speeds of up to 300kph, and its
offspring Eurostar. The continually expanding
TGV network has its main hub at Paris, from
where main lines head north to Lille, east to
Strasbourg and two head south: one to
Marseille and the Mediterranean, the other
west to Bordeaux and the Spanish frontier.
Spur lines service Brittany and Normandy,
the Alps, Pyrenees and Jura.

A new-style high-speed train, the **iDTGV**
(ⓦwww.idtgv.com), was introduced in 2004
in order to compete with the budget airlines.
The trains come with all mod cons, such as
facilities to watch DVDs and play computer
games on board. Currently available on

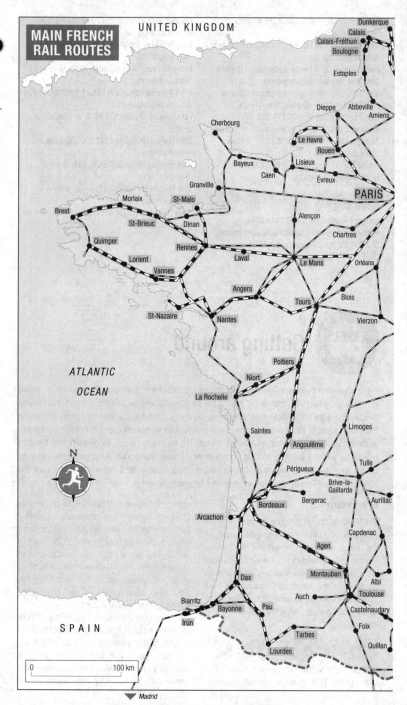

MAIN FRENCH RAIL ROUTES

UNITED KINGDOM

Dunkerque
Calais
Calais-Fréthun
Boulogne
Estaples
Dieppe
Abbeville
Amiens
Cherbourg
Le Havre
Rouen
Bayeux
Caen
Lisieux
Évreux
Granville
PARIS
Morlaix
St-Malo
Brest
St-Brieuc
Dinan
Alençon
Chartres
Quimper
Rennes
Lorient
Laval
Le Mans
Orléans
Vannes
Angers
Blois
St-Nazaire
Tours
Nantes
Vierzon
Poitiers
ATLANTIC
OCEAN
Niort
La Rochelle
Saintes
Limoges
Angoulême
Périgueux
Tulle
Brive-la-Gaillarde
Bergerac
Aurillac
Bordeaux
Arcachon
Capdenac
Agen
Montauban
Albi
Dax
Auch
Toulouse
Biarritz
Bayonne
Pau
Castelnaudary
Irún
Foix
SPAIN
Tarbes
Quillan
Lourdes

N

0   100 km

Madrid

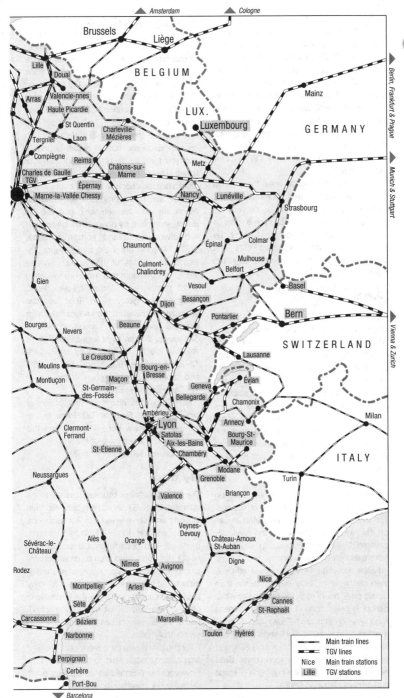

▲ Amsterdam   ▲ Cologne

Brussels
Liège

Lille
Douai
Arras
Valencie-nnes
Haute Picardie
St Quentin
Tergnier   Laon
Compiègne
Reims
Charles de Gaulle TGV
Épernay
Marne-la-Vallée Chessy

BELGIUM

LUX.
Luxembourg

Mainz

GERMANY

Charleville-Mézières
Châlons-sur-Marne
Metz
Nancy   Lunéville
Strasbourg

Berlin, Frankfurt & Prague

Munich & Stuttgart

Chaumont
Épinal   Colmar
Mulhouse
Culmont-Chalindrey   Belfort
Vesoul
Gien   Dijon   Besançon   Basel
Bourges   Beaune   Pontarlier   Bern
Nevers
Le Creusot
Moulins   Lausanne
Montluçon   Maçon   Bourg-en-Bresse
St-Germain-des-Fossés   Geneva   Évian
Ambérieu   Bellegarde   Chamonix
Clermont-Ferrand   Lyon   Annecy   Milan
St-Étienne   Satolas   Bourg-St-Maurice
Aix-les-Bains
Chambéry
Neussargues   Modane   ITALY
Valence   Grenoble   Briançon   Turin

Vienna & Zurich

SWITZERLAND

Veynes-Devouy
Alès   Orange   Château-Arnoux St-Auban
Sévérac-le-Château   Nîmes   Avignon   Digne
Rodez
Montpellier   Arles   Nice
Sète   Cannes St-Raphaël
Carcassonne   Béziers   Marseille
Narbonne   Toulon   Hyères
Perpignan
Cerbère
Port-Bou

▼ Barcelona

	Main train lines
	TGV lines
Nice	Main train stations
Lille	TGV stations

routes from Paris to Mulhouse, Marseille, Nice, Perpignan, Toulouse and Hendaye, tickets are sold online only and are non-refundable. SNCF's **Corail** trains provide the main intercity service. Though not as fast as the TGV, they have good facilities, particularly Corail Téoz trains, which link Paris to Clermont-Ferrand, Bordeaux, Toulouse and Nice and have child-friendly carriages with roomy changing areas and bottle warmers. Corail Lunéa are comfortable sleeper trains. Local services are covered by **TER** regional express trains.

Aside from the regular lines there are a number of special **tourist trains**, usually not part of the SNCF system or covered by normal rail passes, though some offer a discount to rail pass holders. One of the most popular is the spectacular Petite Train Jaune, which winds its way up through the Pyrenees (see p.752).

Tickets and fares

Tickets for all SNCF trains can be bought online (see p.33) or at any train station (*gare SNCF*). At stations, it's easiest to use the counter service; if you have language problems or there are long queues, use one of the touch-screen vending machines with instructions in English, which are available in most stations. All tickets – but not passes or computerized tickets printed out at home – must be validated in the orange machines located beside the entrance to the platforms, and it's an offence not to follow the instruction *Compostez votre billet* ("validate your ticket").

Regional **timetables** and leaflets covering particular lines are available free at stations. The word *Autocar* (often abbreviated to *car*) on the timetable signifies that the service is covered by an SNCF bus, on which rail tickets and passes are valid.

Fares are cheaper if you travel off-peak (*période bleue* or blue period) rather than during peak hours (*période blanche* or white period); peak period generally means Monday mornings and Friday and Sunday evenings. One-way "Loisir" fares from Paris to Toulouse by TGV start at around €53, and from Paris to Nice €59 in second class. **Seat reservations** are obligatory on all TGV trains and are included in the price.

Discounts and rail passes

On certain mainline routes a limited number of **discount tickets**, known as *tarifs Prem's* (one-way fares from €20 on regional trains and €22 on TGVs), can be bought online up to ninety days in advance; these are non-refundable and cannot be changed. Even cheaper, internet-only TGV fares (from €19 one-way) are available on iDTGVs; tickets go on sale up to six months before departure and you have to be able to print out your ticket. These discount fares carry certain restrictions, so check when you book.

SNCF also offers a range of **travel cards**, which are valid for one year, and can be purchased online, by phone, through accredited travel agents and from main *gares SNCF*. Anyone aged 26 to 59 years, for example, is eligible for the *Carte Escapades* (€85). This guarantees a minimum reduction of 25 percent on standard off-peak fares, rising to 40 percent on Téoz services according to availability, on return tickets for journeys over 200km which include a Saturday or Sunday night away. Similar deals are available for 12 to 25-year olds (*Carte 12–25*; €49), over-60s (*Carte Senior*; €56) and families with children under the age of 12 (*Carte Enfant +*; €70).

Non-Europeans also have the option of picking up the **France Rail Pass** before arriving in France. For information on this and other passes available outside the country, see "Getting there" (p.29).

By bus

The most convenient **bus services** are those operated by SNCF, which run between train stations and serve areas not accessible by rail. In addition to SNCF buses, private, municipal and departmental buses can be useful for local and some cross-country journeys, though if you want to see much outside the main towns be prepared for early starts and careful planning – the timetable is often constructed to suit market and school hours. As a rule, buses are cheaper and slower than trains.

Larger towns usually have a *gare routière* (bus station), often next to the *gare SNCF*. However, the private bus companies don't always work together and you'll frequently find them leaving from an array of different points (the local tourist office should be able to help locate the stop you need).

In addition to the SNCF, Eurolines (see p.31) runs a number of routes through France.

By ferry

The majority of France's coastal islands, which are concentrated around Brittany and the Côte d'Azur, can only be reached by **ferry**. Small local companies run services, with timetables and prices varying according to season. Some routes have a reduced schedule or cease to operate completely in winter months, while in high season booking ahead is recommended on all but the most frequent services. Information on these local companies is listed in the Brittany and Normandy and Côte d'Azur chapters in the Guide. For details of ferry services from the mainland to Corsica, see p.1100.

By air

Arriving by air from outside Europe, you may be able to get a good deal on add-on **domestic flights**. Air France operates the most routes within the country, although competition is hotting up, with the likes of easyJet running internal discount flights from Paris to Biarritz, Toulouse, Nice and Geneva. You may also be able to pick up an internal flight on some of the foreign airlines (such as Lufthansa) whose routes include intermediate stops within France. For details of airlines operating within France, see "Getting there" p.31.

By car

Driving in France can be a real pleasure, with a magnificent network of autoroutes which provide huge, sweeping views of the countryside. Outside the peak holiday periods and if you're in a hurry, it's well worth paying the motorway tolls to avoid the slow and frequently congested toll-free national roads (marked, for example, RN116 or N116 on signs and maps). The smaller *routes départementales* (marked with a D) are generally uncongested and make for a more scenic drive, though may occasionally be in relatively poor condition.

Of course, there are times when it's wiser not to drive: most obviously in big cities; around major seaside resorts in high season; and at peak holiday migrations such as the beginning and end of the month-long August holiday, and the notoriously congested weekends nearest July 14 and August 15.

Practicalities

US, Canadian, Australian, New Zealand, South African and all EU **driving licences** are valid in France, though an International Driver's Licence makes life easier. The minimum driving age is 18 and you must hold a full (not a provisional) licence. Drivers are required to carry their licence with them when driving, and you should also have the insurance papers with you in the car. If the vehicle is rented, its registration document (*carte grise*) must also be carried.

All the major car manufacturers have garages and service stations in France, which can help if you run into mechanical difficulties. You'll find them listed in the Yellow Pages of the phone book under "*Garages d'automobiles*"; for breakdowns, look under "*Dépannages*". If you have an accident or theft, contact the local police – and keep a copy of their report in order to file an insurance claim. Within Europe, most car **insurance policies** cover taking your car to France; check with your insurer. However, you're advised to take out extra cover for motoring assistance in case your car breaks down.

Note that **petrol stations** in rural areas tend to be few and far between, and those that do exist usually open only during normal shop hours – don't count on being able to buy petrol at night and on Sunday. An increasing number of stations are equipped with automated 24-hour pumps, but many of these only accept French bank cards. At the time of writing, **petrol prices** were around €1.15 a litre for unleaded (*sans plomb*), €1 for diesel (*gazole* or *gasoil*) and €1.80 for four-star (*super*); you'll find prices lowest at out-of-town hypermarkets.

Most autoroutes have **tolls**: rates vary, but to give you an idea, travelling by motorway from Calais to Montpellier costs roughly €60; pay in cash or by credit card (get in a lane marked CB at the toll-gates).

You can work out routes and costs of both petrol and tolls online at the useful ⓦwww .viamichelin.com.

Rules of the road

Since the French **drive on the right**, drivers of right-hand-drive cars must adjust their **headlights** to dip to the right. This is most easily done by sticking on black glare deflectors, which can be bought at most motor accessory shops and at the Channel ferry ports or the Eurostar terminal. It's more complicated if your car is fitted with High-Intensity Discharge (HID) or halogen-type lights; check with your dealer about how to adjust these well in advance.

All non-French vehicles must display their **national identification letters** (GB, etc) either on the number plate or by means of a sticker, and all vehicles must carry a **red warning triangle** and a **reflective safety jacket**. You are also strongly advised to carry a spare set of bulbs, a fire extinguisher and a first-aid kit. **Seat belts** are compulsory and children under 10 years are not allowed to sit in the front of the car. It's illegal to use a hand-held **mobile phone** while driving.

The law of *priorité à droite* – **giving way** to traffic coming from your right, even when it is coming from a minor road – has largely been phased out. However, it still applies on some roads in built-up areas and the occasional roundabout, so it pays to be vigilant at junctions. A sign showing a yellow diamond on a white background indicates that you have right of way, while the same sign with a diagonal black slash across it warns you that vehicles emerging from the right have priority. *Cédez le passage* means "Give way".

If you have an **accident** while driving, you must fill in and sign a *constat d'accident* (declaration form) or, if another car is also involved, a *constat aimable* (jointly agreed declaration); in the case of a hire car, these forms should be provided with the car's insurance documents.

Unless otherwise indicated **speed limits** are: 130kph (80mph) on *autoroutes*; 110kph (68mph) on dual carriageways; 90kph (55mph) on other roads; and 50kph (31mph) in towns. In wet weather, and for drivers with less than two years' experience, these limits are 110kph (68mph), 100kph (62mph) and 80kph (50mph), respectively, while the town limit remains constant. Fixed and mobile radars are now widely used. The **alcohol limit** is 0.05 percent (0.5 grams per litre of blood), and random breath tests and saliva tests for drugs are common. There are increasingly stiff **penalties** for driving violations, which range from on-the-spot **fines** for minor infringements up to €75,000, the immediate confiscation of your licence and a prison sentence in the most serious cases.

Car rental

Car rental in France costs upwards of €70 a day and €250 for a week, but can be cheaper if arranged before you leave home or online. You'll find the big firms represented at airports and in most major towns and cities; renting from airports normally includes a surcharge. Local firms can be cheaper but most don't offer one-way rentals and you need to check the small print carefully. It's difficult – and expensive – to rent cars with **automatic transmission** in France. You'll need to book well in advance.

The cost of car rental includes the minimum car **insurance** required by law. Under the standard contract you are liable for an excess (*franchise*) for any damage to the vehicle. This starts at around €500 for the smallest car and can be covered by credit card. You

Road information

Up-to-the-minute information regarding traffic jams and road works throughout France can be obtained from the Bison Futé free-dial recorded information service (☎08.00.10.02.00; French only) or their website ⓦwww.bison-fute.equipement .gouv.fr. For information regarding autoroutes, you can also consult the bilingual website ⓦwww.autoroutes.fr.

Buy-back leasing schemes

If you are not resident in an EU country and will be touring France for between 17 days (21 in the case of Renault) and six months, it's worth investigating the special **buy-back leasing schemes** operated by Peugeot ("Peugeot Open Europe"), Citroën ("Citroën DriveEurope" and Renault ("Renault Eurodrive"). Under these deals, you purchase a new car tax-free and the manufacturer guarantees to buy it back from you for an agreed price at the end of the period. In general, the difference between the purchase and repurchase price works out considerably less per day than the equivalent cost of car hire. Further details are available from Peugeot, Citroën and Renault dealers and online at ⓦ www.peugeot-openeurope. com, ⓦ www.citroendriveeurope.com and ⓦ www.eurodrive.renault.com.

should return the car with a full tank of fuel to avoid paying an exorbitant fuel charge.

To rent a car in France you must be over 21 and have driven for at least one year; some companies stipulate two. Most companies charge **drivers under 25** an extra insurance premium, typically €25 per day.

Car-rental agencies

Alamo US ☏ 1-800-462-5266, ⓦ www.alamo.com.
Argus Car Hire UK ☏ 0870 625 1234, Republic of Ireland ☏ 01/499 9601; ⓦ www.arguscarhire.com.
Auto Europe US & Canada ☏ 1-888-223-5555, ⓦ www.autoeurope.com.
Avis UK ☏ 0844 581 8181, Republic of Ireland ☏ 021/428 1111, US ☏ 1-800-331-1212, Canada ☏ 1-800-879-2847, Australia ☏ 136 333 or 02/9353 9000, New Zealand ☏ 09/526 2847 or 0800 655 111, South Africa ☏ 011/923 3660; ⓦ www.avis.com.
Budget UK ☏ 08701 565 656, US ☏ 1-800-527-0700, Canada ☏ 1-800-268-8900, Australia ☏ 1300 362 848, New Zealand ☏ 0800 283 438; ⓦ www.budget.com.
Dollar UK ☏ 0808 234 7524, US ☏ 1-800-800-6000, Canada ☏ 1-800-848-8268; ⓦ www.dollar .com.
Europcar UK ☏ 0870 607 5000, Republic of Ireland ☏ 01/614 2800, US & Canada ☏ 1-877-940-6900; ⓦ www.europcar.com.
Europe by Car US ☏ 1-800-223-1516, ⓦ www .europebycar.com.
Hertz UK ☏ 0870 844 8844, Republic of Ireland ☏ 01/870 5777, US & Canada ☏ 1-800-654-3001, Australia ☏ 03/9698 2555, New Zealand ☏ 0800 654 321, South Africa ☏ 021/935 4800; ⓦ www .hertz.com.
Holiday Autos UK & Republic of Ireland ☏ 0871 472 5229 or 01483/909 056, US & Canada ☏ 1-866-392-9288, Australia ☏ 1300 554 432, New Zealand ☏ 0800 144 040, South Africa ☏ 011/234 0597; ⓦ www.holidayautos.com.

National UK ☏ 0870 400 4581, Republic of Ireland ☏ 021/432 0755, US & Canada ☏ 1-800-227-2876, Australia & New Zealand ☏ 03/8336 6601, South Africa ☏ 011/574 4324; ⓦ www.nationalcar.com.
SIXT UK ☏ 0870 010 3040, Republic of Ireland ☏ 61/206 088, US & Canada ☏ 1-888-749-8227, Australia ☏ 1300 660 660, South Africa ☏ 11/396 1080; ⓦ www.sixt.com.
Suncars UK ☏ 0870 902 8021, Republic of Ireland ☏ 1850/201 416; ⓦ www.suncars.com.
Thrifty UK ☏ 0808/234 7642, US & Canada ☏ 1-800-847-4389; ⓦ www.thrifty.com.

By scooter and motorbike

Scooters are ideal for pottering around local areas. They're relatively easy to rent – places offering bicycles often also rent out scooters. Expect to pay in the region of €40 a day for a 50cc machine, less for longer periods. You don't need a licence, just a passport or some other form of ID.

For anything over 125cc you'll need to have held a full **motorbike** licence for at least two years. Rental prices are around €60 a day for a 125cc bike and expect to leave a hefty deposit by cash or credit card – over €1000 is the norm – which you may lose in the event of damage or theft. Crash helmets are compulsory on all bikes, and the headlight must be switched on at all times. It is recommended to carry a first-aid kit and a set of spare bulbs.

By bicycle

Bicycles (*vélos*) have high status in France, where cyclists are given respect both on the roads and as customers at restaurants and hotels. In addition, local authorities are

Canal and river trips

With over 7000km of navigable rivers and canals, **boating** can be one of the best and most relaxed ways of exploring France. Expect to pay between €800 and €2000 per week, depending on the season and level of comfort, for a four- to six-person boat. Details of firms offering canal and river holidays can be found on p.32, or contact the Fédération des Industries Nautiques (℡01.44.37.04.00, ⓦwww.france-nautic.com). If you want to bring your own boat, Voies Navigables de France (VNF) (℡03.21.63.24.24, ⓦwww.vnf.fr) can provide information in English on maximum dimensions, documentation, regulations and so forth.

The **principal areas** for boating are Brittany, Burgundy, Picardy-Flanders, Alsace and Champagne. Brittany's canals join up with the Loire, but this is only navigable as far as Angers. Other waterways permit numerous permutations, including joining up via the Rhône and Saône with the Canal du Midi in Languedoc and then northwestwards to Bordeaux and the Atlantic. The eighteenth-century Canal de Bourgogne and 300-year-old Canal du Midi are fascinating examples of early canal engineering. The latter, together with its continuation the Canal du Sète à Rhône, passes within easy reach of several interesting areas.

The through-journey from the Channel to the Mediterranean requires some planning. The Canal de Bourgogne has an inordinate number of locks, while other waterways demand considerable skill and experience – the Rhône and Saône rivers, for example, have tricky currents. The most direct route is from Le Havre to just beyond Paris, then south along either Canal du Loing and de Briare or Canal du Nivernais to the Canal Latéral à la Loire, which you follow as far as Digoin in southern Burgundy, where it crosses the River Loire and meets the Canal du Centre. You follow the latter as far as Châlon, from where you continue south on the Saône and Rhône until you reach the Mediterranean at Port St-Louis in the Camargue.

actively promoting cycling, not only with urban cycle lanes, but also with comprehensive networks in rural areas (often on disused railways). Most towns have well-stocked repair shops, but if you're using a foreign-made bike with non-standard wheels, it's a good idea to carry spare tyres.

The **train network** runs various schemes for cyclists. Trains marked with a bicycle on the timetable allow you to take a bike in the dedicated bike racks (packed in a carrier 90cm by 120cm) for free. Alternatively, you can put it in the luggage van (€10) – reservations are obligatory and space is limited, so make sure you buy your ticket well in advance. Another option is to send your bike parcelled up as registered baggage for a fee of €39; delivery should take two days, bearing in mind the service doesn't operate at weekends.

Eurostar allows you to take your bicycle as part of your baggage allowance provided it's dismantled and packed in a bag no more than 120cm by 90cm. Alternatively, if you are travelling to Paris, you can put it in

the luggage van of the same train you are travelling on at a cost of £20 one way; space is limited, so reserve well in advance by calling Esprit Europe (℡08705 850 850, ⓦwww.espriteurope.co.uk). For the same price, you can also send it registered baggage to Paris or Lille with the same company, with a guaranteed arrival time of 24 hours. **Ferries** usually carry bikes free (though you may need to register it), as do some **airlines** such as British Airways, while others now charge – check when making your booking.

Bikes – usually mountain bikes (*vélos tout-terrain* or VTT) or hybrid bikes (*vélos tout-chemin* or VTC) – are often available to **rent** from campsites and hostels, as well as from specialist cycle shops and some tourist offices for around €10–15 per day. The bikes are often not insured, however, and you will be presented with the bill for a replacement if it's stolen or damaged; check your travel insurance policy for cover.

As for **maps**, a minimum requirement is the IGN 1:100,000 series (see p.62) – the smallest scale that marks contours. The UK's national cyclists' association, the CTC (☏0844 736 8450, ⦿www.ctc.org.uk), can suggest routes and supply advice for members (£35 a year or £57 for a family of four, and £12 for under-18s and full-time students under 26 years). They run a particularly good **insurance** scheme. Companies offering specialist bike touring holidays are listed on p.32.

Accommodation

At most times of the year, you can turn up in any French town and find a room or a place in a campsite. Booking a couple of nights in advance can be reassuring, however, as it saves you the effort of trudging round and ensures that you know what you'll be paying; many hoteliers, campsite managers and hostel managers speak at least a little English. In most places, you'll be able to get a simple double for €35–40, though expect to pay at least €50 for a reasonable level of comfort. Paris and the Côte d'Azur are more expensive, however, with equivalent rates of roughly €60 and €100. We've detailed a selection of hotels throughout the Guide, and given a price range for each (see box, p.42); as a general rule the areas around train stations have the highest density of cheap hotels.

Problems may arise between mid-July and the end of August, when the French take their own vacations en masse. During this period, hotel and hostel accommodation can be hard to come by, particularly in the coastal resorts, and you may find yourself falling back on local tourist offices for help.

All **tourist offices** can provide lists of hotels, hostels, campsites and bed-and-breakfast possibilities, and some offer a booking service, though they can't guarantee rooms at a particular price. With campsites, you can be more relaxed about finding an empty pitch, though it may be more difficult with a caravan or camper van or if you're looking for a place on the Côte d'Azur.

Hotels

French hotels are graded from zero to four stars, though there is talk of adding a fifth band for luxury hotels. The price more or less corresponds to the number of stars, though the system is a little haphazard, having more to do with ratios of bathrooms per guest and so forth than genuine quality, and some unclassified and single-star hotels can actually be very good. A new label,

HotelCert (⦿www.hotelcert.org), has been introduced to fill the gap, focusing on cleanliness and the quality of the service in general. What you get for your money varies enormously between establishments; for a general guide see the box on p.42. Single rooms – if the hotel has any – are only marginally cheaper than doubles, so sharing always slashes costs, especially since most hotels willingly provide rooms with extra beds for three or more people at good discounts.

Big cities tend to have a good variety of cheap establishments; in small towns and rural areas, you may not be so lucky, particularly as the cheaper, family-run hotels find it increasingly hard to survive. Swanky resorts, particularly those on the Côte d'Azur, have very high **prices** in July and August, but even these are still cheaper than Paris, which is far more expensive than the rest of the country. If you're staying for more than three nights in a hotel it's often possible to negotiate a lower price, particularly out of season.

Breakfast, which is never included in the quoted price, will add between €6 and €15 per person to a bill, sometimes more –

Accommodation price categories

All the hotels and guesthouses listed in this book have been price coded according to the scale below. The prices quoted are for the cheapest available double room in high season, although remember that many of the cheap places will also have more expensive rooms with more facilities. For accommodation in the ❶ bracket, expect simple rooms, occasionally with communal (*dans le palier*) showers (*douches*) and toilets (WC or *toilettes*). ❷ will probably guarantee you a separate bathroom (*salle de bain*), while ❸ should get you a TV, phone and better furnishings. At around ❹, the rooms will be more spacious and attractively decorated, if not state of the art; anything from ❺ upwards tends towards luxury, with all the mod cons you would expect, except in the larger cities, where luxury rooms tend to start at around ❻. Rooms from ❼ upwards will be increasingly plush and by the time they get to a ❾, sumptuous rooms will often be accompanied by a sauna, gym, swimming pool and many other services.

❶ €40 and under
❷ €41–50
❸ €51–65

❹ €66–80
❺ €81–100
❻ €101–120

❼ €121–150
❽ €151–200
❾ €201 and over

though there is no obligation to take it. It's actually illegal for hotels to insist on your taking half board (*demi-pension*), though you'll come across some that do, especially during the summer peak. This is not always such a bad thing, however, since the food may be excellent and you can sometimes get a real bargain.

Note that many **family-run hotels** close for two or three weeks a year in low season. In smaller towns and villages they may also close for one or two nights a week, usually Sunday or Monday. Details are given where relevant in the Guide, but dates change from year to year and some places may decide to close for a few days in low season if they have no bookings. The best precaution is to phone ahead to be sure.

A very useful option, especially if you're driving and are looking for somewhere late at night, are the **chain hotels** located at motorway exits and on the outskirts of major towns. They may be soulless, but you can usually count on a decent and reliable standard. Among the cheapest (from around €30 for a three-person room with communal toilets and showers) is the one-star Formule 1 chain (℡08.92.68.56.85, ⓦwww.hotelformule1.com). Other budget chains include B&B (℡01.72.36.51.06, ⓦwww.hotel-bb.com), the slightly more comfortable Première Classe (℡08.25.02.80.38, ⓦwww.premiereclasse.fr) and Etap Hôtel (℡08.92.68.89.00, ⓦwww.etaphotel.com). Slightly more upmarket are

Ibis (℡01.61.61.61.62, ⓦwww.ibishotel.com) and Campanile (℡08.25.02.80.38, ⓦwww.campanile.fr), where en-suite rooms with satellite TV and often broadband internet access cost from around €50–60.

There are a number of well-respected **hotel federations** in France. The biggest and most useful of these is Logis de France (℡01.45.84.83.84, ⓦwww.logis-de-france.fr), an association of over three thousand hotels nationwide. They produce a free annual guide, available in French tourist offices, from Logis de France itself and from member hotels. Two other, more upmarket federations worth mentioning are Châteaux & Hôtels de France (℡01.72.72.92.02, ⓦwww.chateauxhotels.com) and the Relais du Silence (℡01.44.49.90.00, ⓦwww.silencehotel.com), both of which offer high-class accommodation in beautiful older properties, often in rural locations.

Bed and breakfast and self-catering

In country areas, in addition to standard hotels, you will come across **chambres d'hôtes** – bed-and-breakfast accommodation in someone's house, château or farm. Though the quality varies widely, on the whole standards have improved dramatically in recent years and the best can offer more character and greater value for money than an equivalently priced hotel. If you're lucky, the owners may also provide traditional home cooking and a great insight into French life. Prices generally range between €40 and €80 for two people including breakfast; payment is almost always expected in cash. Some offer meals on request (*tables d'hôtes*), usually evenings only.

If you're planning to stay a week or more in any one place it's worth considering renting self-catering accommodation. This will generally consist of self-contained country cottages known as **gîtes**. Many *gîtes* are in converted barns or farm outbuildings, though some can be quite grand. "Gîtes Panda" are *gîtes* located in a national park or other protected area and are run on environmentally friendly lines.

You can get lists of both *gîtes* and *chambres d'hôtes* from the government-funded agency Gîtes de France (℡01.49.70.75.75, ⊛www .gites-de-france.fr), or search on their website for accommodation by location or theme (for example, *gîtes* near fishing or riding opportunities). In addition, every year the organization publishes a number of national guides, such as *Nouveaux Gîtes Ruraux* (listing new addresses), *Chambres et Tables d'Hôtes* and *Chambres d'Hôtes de Charme* (€20–22), and more comprehensive departmental guides which include photos (€5–20). All these guides are available online or from departmental offices of Gîtes de France, as well as from bookstores and tourist offices. Tourist offices will also have lists of places in their area which are not affiliated to Gîtes de France.

Hostels and student accommodation

At between €12 and €16 per night for a **dormitory bed**, sometimes with breakfast thrown in, youth hostels – *auberges de jeunesse* – are invaluable for single travellers of any age on a budget. Some now offer rooms, occasionally en suite, but they don't necessarily work out cheaper than hotels – particularly if you've had to pay a taxi fare to reach them. However, many allow you to cut costs by eating in the hostels' cheap canteens, while in a few you can prepare your own meals in the communal kitchens. In the Guide we give the cost of a dormitory bed.

In addition to those belonging to the two French hostelling associations listed below, there are now also several independent hostels, particularly in Paris. At these, dorm beds cost upwards of €20 with breakfast included, though these tend to be party places with an emphasis on good times rather than a good night's sleep.

A few large towns provide hostel accommodation in Foyers des Jeunes Travailleurs, **residential hostels** for young workers and students, where you can usually get a private room for upwards of €12. On the whole they are more luxurious than youth hostels and normally have a good cafeteria or canteen. These are listed in the Guide, or ask at local tourist offices. In July and August, there's also the possibility of staying in **student accommodation** in university towns and cities at prices similar to hostels. Contact CROUS (℡01.40.51.37.65, ⊛www .crous-paris.fr) for further information.

Youth hostel associations

Slightly confusingly, there are two rival **French hostelling associations** – the Fédération Unie des Auberges de Jeunesse and the much smaller Ligue Française (see below). In either case, you normally have to show a current Hostelling International (HI) **membership card**. It's usually cheaper and easier to join before you leave home, provided your national youth hostel association is a full member of HI. Alternatively, you can purchase an HI card in certain French hostels for €16 (€11 for those under 26), or buy individual "welcome stamps" at a rate of €2.90 per night; after six nights you are entitled to the HI card.

France

Fédération Unie des Auberges de Jeunesse (FUAJ) ℡01.44.89.87.27, ⊛www.fuaj.org.
Ligue Française pour les Auberges de Jeunesse (LFAJ) ℡01.44.16.78.78, ⊛www .auberges-de-jeunesse.com.

UK and Ireland

Youth Hostel Association (YHA) England and Wales ℡01629/592 700, ⊛www.yha.org.uk.
Scottish Youth Hostel Association ℡01786/891 400, ⊛www.syha.org.uk.
Irish Youth Hostel Association Republic of Ireland ℡01/830 4555, ⊛www.aoinge.org.

Hostelling International Northern Ireland
☎028/9032 4733, ⊛www.hini.org.uk.

US and Canada

Hostelling International USA ☎1-301-495-1240, ⊛www.hiayh.org.
Hostelling International Canada ☎1-800-663-5777, ⊛www.hihostels.ca.

Australia and New Zealand

Australia Youth Hostels Association Australia ☎02/9283 7195, ⊛www.yha.com.au.
Youth Hostelling Association New Zealand ☎03/379 9970, ⊛www.yha.co.nz.

Gîtes d'étape and refuges

In the countryside, another hostel-style option exists in the form of **gîtes d'étape**. Aimed primarily at hikers and long-distance bikers, *gîtes d'étape* are often run by the local village or municipality and are less formal than hostels, providing bunk beds and primitive kitchen and washing facilities from around €10 per person. They are marked on the large-scale IGN walkers' maps and listed in the individual Topo guides (see "Walking and climbing" p.54). In addition, mountain areas are well supplied with **refuge huts**, mostly run by the Fédération Français des Clubs Alpins et de Montagne (FFCAM; ☎01.53.72.87.00, ⊛www.ffcam.fr). These huts, generally only open in summer, offer dorm accommodation and meals, and are the only available shelter once you are above the villages. Costs range from €12 to €25 for the night, or half of this if you're a member of a climbing organization affiliated to FFCAM, plus around €18–20 for breakfast and dinner, which is good value when you consider that in some cases supplies have to be brought up by mule or helicopter.

More information can be found either online or in the guides *Gîtes d'Étape et de Séjours* (€10), published by Gîtes de France (see above).

Camping

Practically every village and town in France has at least one **campsite** to cater for the thousands of people who spend their holiday under canvas. Most sites open from around Easter to September or October. The vast majority are graded into four categories, from one to four stars, by the local authority. One- and two-star sites are very basic, with toilets and showers (not necessarily with hot water) but little else, and standards of cleanliness are not always brilliant. At the other extreme, four-star sites are far more spacious, have hot-water showers and electrical hook-ups; most will also have a swimming pool (sometimes heated), washing machines, a shop and sports facilities, and will provide refreshments or meals in high season. At three-star sites you can expect a selection of these facilities and less spacious plots. A further designation, **Camping Qualité** (⊛www.campingqualite.com), indicates campsites with particularly high standards of hygiene, service and privacy, while the **Clef Verte** (⊛www.laclefverte.org) label is awarded to sites run along environmentally friendly lines. For those who really like to get away from it all, camping **à la ferme** – on somebody's farm – is a good, simple option. Lists of sites are available at local tourist offices or from Gîtes de France (see p.43).

The Fédération Française de Camping et de Caravaning (☎01.42.72.84.08, ⊛www.ffcc.fr) publishes an annual **guide** (€16.30) covering over ten thousand campsites, details of which can also be found online on the excellent Camping France website (⊛www.campingfrance.com). If you'd rather have everything organized for you, a number of companies specialize in camping holidays; see "Getting there" p.32 for details.

Though **charging systems** vary, most places charge per site and per person, usually including a car, while others apply a global figure. As a rough guide, a family of four with a tent and car should expect to pay from €12 per day at a one-star site, rising to €40 or more at a four-star. In peak season it's wise to book ahead, and note that many of the big sites now have caravans and even chalet bungalows for rent.

If you're plan to do a lot of camping, it's worth investing in an **international camping carnet (CCI)**, which gives discounts at member sites and serves as useful identification. Many campsites will take it instead of making you surrender your passport during your stay, and it covers you for third-party insurance when camping. You can buy it from national motoring organizations or, in the UK, from the Camping and Caravanning Club (☎0845/130 7631, ⊛www.campingand caravanningclub.co.uk). Lastly, a word of caution: always ask permission before **camping rough** (*camping sauvage*) on anyone's land. If the dogs don't get you,

the guns might – farm̲ to shoot first, and a̲ hand, a politely phra̲ sion to camp will positive results. Ca̲ not officially per̲ practised by the̲ discreet you're u̲n̲ᵣᵣᵥₑ ̲. On beaches, it's best to camp ̲ where other people are doing so.

Food and drink

France is famous for producing some of the most sublime food in the world, whether you're talking about the rarefied delicacies of haute cuisine or the robust, no-nonsense fare served up at country inns. Nevertheless, French cuisine has taken a bit of a knocking in recent years. The wonderful ingredients are still there, as every town and village market testifies, but those little family restaurants serving classic dishes that celebrate the region's produce – and where the bill is less than €15 – are increasingly hard to find. Don't be afraid to ask locals for their recommendations; this will usually elicit strong views and sound advice. For more on where to eat in France, see the "Cafés, bistros and brasseries" colour section.

In the rarefied world of **haute cuisine**, where the top chefs are national celebrities, a battle has long been raging between traditionalists, determined to preserve the purity of French cuisine, and those who experiment with different flavours from around the world to create novel combinations. At this level, French food is still brilliant – in both camps – and need not cost a fortune: many gourmet places offer weekday lunchtime menus where you can sample culinary genius for under €40.

France is also a great place for **foreign cuisine**, in particular North African, Caribbean (known as *Antillais*) and Asiatic.

Breakfast and lunch

A croissant or *pain au chocolat* (a chocolate-filled, light pastry) in a café or bar, with tea, hot chocolate or coffee, is generally the most economical way to eat breakfast, costing around €4 to €5. If there are no croissants left, it's perfectly acceptable to go and buy

your own at the nearest baker or patisserie. The standard hotel breakfast comprises bread and/or pastries, jam and a jug of coffee or tea, and orange juice if you're lucky, from around €6. More expensive places might offer a buffet comprising cereals, fruit, yoghurt and the works.

The main meal of the day is traditionally eaten at **lunchtime**, usually between noon and 2pm. Midday, and sometimes in the evening, you'll find places offering a *plat du jour* (daily special) for €8–12, or *formules*, limited menus typically offering a main dish and either a starter or a dessert for a set price. **Crêpes**, or pancakes with fillings, served at ubiquitous crêperies, are popular lunchtime food. The savoury buckwheat variety (*galettes*) provide the main course; sweet, white-flour crêpes are dessert. **Pizzerias**, usually *au feu du bois* (baked in wood-fired ovens), are also very common. They are somewhat better value than crêperies, but quality and quantity vary greatly.

45

...ics, the local outdoor market or ...rket will provide you with almost ...thing you need from tomatoes and ...cados to cheese and pâté. Cooked ...eat, prepared snacks, ready-made dishes and assorted salads can be bought at charcuteries (delicatessens), which you'll find even in most small villages, and at supermarket cold-food counters. You purchase by weight, or you can ask for *une tranche* (a slice), *une barquette* (a carton) or *une part* (a portion) as appropriate.

Snacks

Food snobs may say this is where French cuisine falls short, and where American-influenced fast food culture is taking over. There is, however, a large range of choice when it comes to eating on the run, or snacking between meals. *Croques-monsieur* or *croques-madame* (variations on the toasted cheese-and-ham sandwich) are on sale at cafés, brasseries and many street stands, along with *frites* (fries), crêpes, *galettes*, *gauffres* (waffles), *glaces* (ice creams) and all kinds of fresh-filled baguettes (which usually cost between €3 and €5 to take away). For variety, in main towns and cities you can find Tunisian snacks like *brik à l'œuf* (a fried pastry with an egg inside), *merguez* (spicy North African sausage), Greek *souvlaki* (kebabs) and Middle Eastern falafel (deep-fried chickpea balls served in flat bread with salad) and kebab shops. Wine bars are good for regional sausages and cheese, usually served with brown bread (*pain de campagne*).

Regional dishes

French cooking is as varied as its landscape, and differs vastly from region to region. In **Provence**, in close proximity to Italy, local dishes make heavy use of olive oils, garlic and tomatoes, as well as Mediterranean vegetables such as aubergines (eggplant) and peppers. In keeping with its proximity to the sea, the region's most famous dish is without doubt *bouillabaisse*, a hearty fish stew from Marseille. To the southwest, in **Languedoc** and **Pays Basque**, hearty *cassoulet* stews and heavier meals are in order, more in common with Spanish cuisine. **Alsace**, in the northeast, features Germanic influences in its cuisine, specializing in dishes such as *choucroute* (sauerkraut), and a hearty array of sausages. **Burgundy**, famous for its wines, is the home of what many people consider classic French dishes such as *coq au vin* and *boeuf bourguignon*. In the northwest, **Normandy** and **Brittany** are about the best places you could head for seafood, as well as for sweet and savoury crêpes and *galettes*. Finally, if you're in the **Dordogne**, make sure to sample its famous foie gras or pricey truffles (*truffes*).

For more on which regional dishes to try, see the boxes at the start of each chapter in the Guide.

Vegetarian food

On the whole, **vegetarians** can expect a somewhat lean time in France. Most cities now have at least one specifically vegetarian restaurant, but elsewhere your best bet will probably be a crêperie, pizzeria or Chinese or North African restaurant. Otherwise you may have to fall back on an omelette or a plate of vegetables (often tinned) in an ordinary restaurant. Sometimes restaurants are willing to replace a meat dish on the fixed-price menu (*menu fixe*); at other times you'll have to pick your way through the *carte*. Remember the phrase *Je suis végétarien(ne); est-ce qu'il y a quelques plats sans viande?* ("I'm a vegetarian; are there any non-meat dishes?"). **Vegans**, however, should probably forget about eating in restaurants and stick to self-catering.

Drinking

In France, drinking is done at a leisurely pace whether it's a prelude to food (*apéritif*) or a sequel (*digestif*), and **café-bars** are the standard places to do it. By law the full price list, including service charges, must be clearly displayed. You normally pay when you leave, and it's perfectly acceptable to sit for hours over just one cup of coffee, though in this case a small tip will be appreciated.

Wine

French **wines** (*vin*), drunk at just about every meal or social occasion, are unrivalled in the world for their range, sophistication, diversity and status. With the exception of the

Cheese

Charles de Gaulle famously commented "How can you govern a country that has 246 kinds of cheese?" For serious **cheese**-lovers, France is the ultimate paradise. Other countries may produce individual cheeses which are as good as, or even better than, the best of the French, but no country offers a range that comes anywhere near them in terms of sheer inventiveness. In fact, there are officially over 350 types of French cheese, and the way they are made are jealously guarded secrets. Many cheese-makers have successfully protected their products by gaining the right to label their produce **AOC** (*appellation d'origine contrôlée*), covered by laws similar to those for wines, which – among other things – controls the amount of cheese that a particular area can produce. As a result, the subtle differences between French local cheeses have not been overwhelmed by the industrialized uniformity that has plagued other countries.

The best, or most traditional, restaurants offer a well-stocked *plateau de fromages* (cheeseboard), served at room temperature with bread, but not butter. Apart from the ubiquitous Brie, Camembert and numerous varieties of goat's cheese (*chèvre*), there will usually be one or two local cheeses on offer – these are the ones to go for. If you want to buy cheese, local markets are always the best bet, while in larger towns you'll generally find a *fromagerie*, a shop with dozens of varieties to choose from. We've indicated the best regional cheeses throughout the Guide.

northwest of the country and the mountains, wine is produced just about everywhere. The famous wine-producing **regions** are Champagne, Bordeaux and Burgundy, closely followed by the Loire and Rhône valleys. Alsace also has some great wines, and there are many good ones to be had in the lesser wine **regions** of Bergerac, Languedoc, Roussillon, Provence and Savoie. Even within each region, there's enormous diversity, with differences generated by the varying types of soil, the lie of the land, the type of grape grown – there are over sixty varieties – the ability of the wine to age, and the individual skills of the producer.

The **quality** of wine can also vary enormously. *Vin de table* or *vin ordinaire* – table wine – is generally drinkable and always cheap, although it may be disguised and priced-up as the house wine, or *cuvée*. Local *vins de pays* can vary in quality but they are still exceptional for the price. The best-quality wines are denoted by the **AOC** (*appellation d'origine contrôlée*) label, which means that the wine comes from an area (known in this case as an *appellation*) where the amount of wine produced is strictly controlled. You can buy a very decent bottle of AOC wine for €6 in a shop or from the producer, while over €10 will get you something worth savouring.

By the time restaurants have added their considerable mark-up, wine can constitute an alarming proportion of the bill. A glass of wine in a bar will typically cost around €3–6.

Choosing wine is an extremely complex business and it's hard not to feel intimidated by the seemingly innate expertise of all French people. Many *appellations* are mentioned in the text, but trusting your own taste is the best way to go. Knowing the grape types that you particularly like (or dislike), whether you like wines very fruity, dry, light or heavy, is all useful when discussing your choice with a waiter, producer or wine merchant. The more interest you show, the more helpful advice you're likely to receive. The only thing the French cannot tolerate is people ordering Coke or the like to accompany a gourmet meal.

The best way of **buying wine** is directly from the producers (*vignerons*) at their vineyards or at Maisons or Syndicats du Vin (representing a group of wine-producers), or Coopératifs Vinicoles (producers' co-ops). At all these places you can usually sample the wines first. It's best to make clear at the start how much you want to buy (particularly if it's only one or two bottles) and you'll not be popular if you drink several glasses and then fail to make a purchase. The most economical option is to buy *en vrac*, which you can do at some wine shops (*caves*), filling an easily obtainable plastic five- or ten-litre container (usually sold on the premises) straight from the barrel. Supermarkets often have good bargains, too.

The basic wine terms are: *brut*, very dry; *sec*, dry; *demi-sec*, sweet; *doux*, very sweet; *mousseux*, sparkling; *méthode champenoise*, mature and sparkling.

Beer and spirits

Familiar light Belgian and German brands, plus French brands from Alsace, account for most of the **beer** you'll find. Draught beer (*à la pression*) – very often Kronenbourg – is the cheapest drink you can have next to coffee and wine; *un pression* or *un demi* (0.33 litre) will cost around €3. For a wider choice of draught and bottled beer you need to go to the special beer-drinking establishments such as the English- and Irish-style pubs found in larger towns and cities. A small bottle at one of these places can set you back double what you'd pay in an ordinary café-bar. Buying bottled or canned bear in supermarkets is, of course, much cheaper.

Spirits, such as cognac and armagnac, and liqueurs are consumed at any time of day, though in far smaller quantities these days thanks to the clampdown on drink-driving. *Pastis* – the generic name of aniseed drinks such as Pernod and Ricard – is served diluted with water and ice (*glace* or *glaçons*). It's very refreshing and not expensive. Among less familiar names, try Poire William (pear brandy) or Marc (a spirit distilled from grape pulp). Measures are generous, but they don't come cheap: the same applies for imported spirits like whisky (*Scotch*). Two drinks designed to stimulate the appetite – *un apéritif* – are *pineau* (cognac and grape juice) and kir (white wine with a dash of Cassis – blackcurrant liqueur – or with champagne instead of wine for a Kir Royal). Cognac, armagnac and Chartreuse are among the many aids to digestion – *un digestif* – to relax over after a meal. Cocktails are served at most late-night bars, discos and clubs, as well as upmarket hotel bars and at every seaside promenade café; they usually cost at least €5.

Soft drinks, tea and coffee

You can buy cartons of unsweetened **fruit juice** in supermarkets, although in cafés the bottled (sweetened) nectars such as apricot (*jus d'abricot*) and blackcurrant (*cassis*) still hold sway. Fresh orange (*jus d'orange*) or lemon juice (*citron pressé*) is a much more refreshing choice on a hot day – for the latter, the juice is served in the bottom of a long ice-filled glass, with a jug of water and a sugar bowl to sweeten it to your taste. Other soft drinks to try are syrups (*sirops*) – mint or grenadine, for example, mixed with water. The standard fizzy drinks of lemonade (*limonade*), Coke (*coca*) and so forth are all available, and there's no shortage of bottled mineral **water** (*eau minérale*) or spring water (*eau de source*) – whether sparkling (*gazeuse*) or still (*plate*) – either, from the big brand names to the most obscure spa product. But there's not much wrong with the tap water (*l'eau de robinet*), which will always be brought free to your table if you ask for it. The only time you shouldn't drink the tap water is if the tap is labelled *eau non potable*.

Coffee is invariably espresso – small, black and very strong. *Un café* or *un express* is the regular; *un crème* is with milk; *un grand café* or *un grand crème* are large versions. *Un déca* is decaffeinated, now widely available. Ordinary **tea** (*thé*) – Lipton's nine times out of ten – is normally served black (*nature*) or with a slice of lemon (*limon*); to have milk with it, ask for *un peu de lait frais* (some fresh milk). *Chocolat chaud* – **hot chocolate** – unlike tea, lives up to the high standards of French food and drink and can be had in any café. After meals, herb teas (*infusions* or *tisanes*), offered by most restaurants, can be soothing. The more common ones are *verveine* (verbena), *tilleul* (lime blossom), *menthe* (mint) and *camomille* (camomile).

The media

French newspapers and magazines are available from newsagents (*maisons de la presse*) or any of the ubiquitous street-side kiosks, while TV, satellite and otherwise, is easy to track down in most forms of accommodation. A limited range of British and US newspapers and magazines is widely available in cities and occasionally in even quite small towns.

Newspapers and magazines

Of the **French daily papers**, *Le Monde* (@www.lemonde.fr) is the most intellectual; it's widely respected, and somewhat austere, though it does now carry such frivolities as colour photos. Conservative, and at times controversial, *Le Figaro* (@www.lefigaro.fr) is the most highly regarded of the more right-wing papers. *Libération* (@www.liberation .com), founded by Jean-Paul Sartre in the 1960s, is moderately left-wing, pro-European, independent and more colloquial, while rigorous left-wing criticism of the government comes from *L'Humanité* (@www.humanite.presse.fr), the Communist Party paper, though it is struggling to survive. The top-selling **tabloid**, predictably more readable and a good source of news, is *Aujourd'hui* (published in Paris as *Le Parisien*), while *L'Équipe* (@www.lequipe.fr) is dedicated to sports coverage. The widest circulations are enjoyed by the **regional dailies**, of which the most important is the Rennes-based *Ouest-France* (@www.ouest-france.fr). For visitors, these are mainly of interest for their listings.

Weekly **magazines** of the *Newsweek*/*Time* model include the wide-ranging and left-leaning *Le Nouvel Observateur* (@www.nouvelobs.com), its right-wing counterpart *L'Express* (@www.lexpress.fr) and the centrist with bite, *Marianne* (@www.marianne-en-ligne.fr). Comprising mainly translated articles, *Courrier International* (@www.courrierinternational.com) offers an overview of what's being discussed in media around the globe. The best investigative journalism is to be found in the weekly satirical paper *Le Canard Enchaîné* (@www.lecanardenchaine.fr), while *Charlie Hebdo* is roughly equivalent to the UK's *Private Eye*. There's also Paris Match (@www.parismatch.com), for gossip about stars and royalty, and, of course, the French versions of *Vogue*, *Elle* and *Marie-Claire*, and the relentlessly urban *Biba*, for women's fashion and lifestyle.

English-language newspapers which are printed locally, such as the *International Herald Tribune*, are available on the day of publication. Others usually arrive the following day, and the prices are all heavily marked up.

Moral censorship of the press is rare. On the newsstands you'll find pornography of every shade alongside knitting patterns and DIY. You'll also find French **comics** (*bandes dessinées*), many of which are aimed at the adult market, with wild and wonderful illustrations; they're considered to be quite an art form and whole museums are devoted to them.

Television and radio

French **terrestrial TV** has six channels: three public (France 2, France 3 and Arte/France 5); one subscription (Canal Plus – with some unencrypted programmes); and two commercial (TF1 and M6). Of these, TF1 (@www.tf1.fr) and France 2 (@www.france2.fr) are the most popular channels, showing a broad mix of programmes.

In addition there are any number of **cable and satellite channels**, including CNN, BBC World, BBC Prime, Eurosport, MTV, Planète (which specializes in documentaries), Ciné Première and Canal Jimmy (*Friends* and the like in French). The main French-run music channel is MCM.

Radio France (@www.radio-france.fr) operates seven stations. These include

France Culture for arts, France Info for news and France Musique for classical music. Other major stations include Europe 1 (⊛www.europe1.fr) for news, debate and

sport. Radio France International (RFI, ⊛www.rfi.fr) broadcasts in French and various foreign languages, including English, on 89 FM and 738 MW.

Festivals

It's hard to beat the experience of arriving in a small French village, expecting no more than a bed for the night, to discover the streets decked out with flags and streamers, a band playing in the square and the entire population out celebrating the feast of their patron saint. As well as nationwide celebrations such as the Fête de la Musique (around June 21, the summer solstice; ⊛www .fetedelamusique.culture.fr), Bastille Day (July 14) and the Assumption of the Virgin Mary (Aug 15), there are any number of festivals – both traditional and of more recent origin – held in towns and villages throughout France. For a detailed account of some of the major ones, see the *Festive France* colour section; also see ⊛www.culture.fr and ⊛www.viafrance.com.

Festival calender

January

Nantes La Folle Journée (late Jan to early Feb; ⊛www.follejournee.fr).
Nice Carnival (Jan–Feb; ⊛www.nicecarnaval .com).

February to April

Menton Fête du Citron (two weeks following Mardi Gras, forty days before Easter; ⊛www .feteducitron.com); parades, concerts and fireworks.
Nîmes La Féria de Nîmes (Pentecost, seven weeks after Easter); bullfights.

May

Cannes Festival de Cannes (⊛www.festival -cannes.com); international film festival.

Les Saintes-Maries-de-la-Mer Fête de Ste Sarah (May 24–25); Romany festival.
Paris Festival de St-Denis (May–June; ⊛www .festival-saint-denis.com); classical and world music festival.

June

Annecy Festival International du Film d'Animation (early June; ⊛www.annecy.org); animated films.
Bordeaux Fête le Vin (late June in even-numbered years; ⊛www.bordeaux-fete-le-vin.com).
Châlons-en-Campagne Festival Furies (early June; ⊛www.festival-furies.com); street theatre.
Lyon Les Nuits de Fourvière (early June to early Aug; ⊛www.nuitsdefourviere.fr); performance arts.
Montpellier Montpellier Danse (late June to early July; ⊛www.montpellierdanse.com).
Paris La Marche des Fiertés Lesbienne, Gai, Bi & Trans (late June; ⊛www.inter-lgbt.org).
Paris Festival Django Reinhardt (late June; ⊛www .festivaldjangoreinhardt.com); jazz.
Strasbourg Festival de Musique de Strasbourg (⊛www.festival-strasbourg.com); classical music.
Uzès Uzès Danse (⊛www.uzesdanse.fr); contemporary dance.
Vienne Jazz à Vienne (late June to mid-July; ⊛www.jazzavienne.com).

July

Aix-en-Provence Festival International d'Art Lyrique (⊛www.festival-aix.com); classical music. Danse à Aix (late July/early Aug; ⊛www .aixenprovencetourism.com/uk/aix-danse.htm).
Alès Cratère/Surfaces (early July; ⊛www .lecratere.fr); street theatre.
Arles Les Suds à Arles (mid-July; ⊛www .suds-arles.com); world music.
Avignon Festival d'Avignon (⊛www.festival -avignon.com); contemporary dance and theatre.

Beaune Festival International d'Opéra Baroque (🕸www.festivalbeaune.com).

Belfort Eurockéennes (early July; 🕸www .eurockeennes.fr); rock and indie music.

Carhaix Festival des Vieilles Charrues (mid-July; 🕸www.vieillescharrues.asso.fr/festival); contemporary music festival.

Chalon-sur-Saône Chalon dans la Rue (third week July; 🕸www.chalondanslarue.com); street theatre.

Colmar Festival International de Colmar (early July; 🕸www.festival-colmar.com); classical music.

Gannat (near Vichy) Les Cultures du Monde (late July; 🕸www.gannat.com).

Grenoble Rencontres du Jeune Théâtre Européen (early July); contemporary theatre.

Juan-les-Pins Jazz à Juan (mid-July).

La Rochelle Festival International du Film (early July; 🕸www.festival-larochelle.org). Francofolies (mid-July; 🕸www.francofolies.fr); contemporary French music.

La Roque d'Anthéron Festival International de Piano (mid-July to mid-Aug; 🕸www.festival-piano .com).

Nice Jazz Festival (late July; 🕸www .nicejazzfestival.fr).

Orange Chorégies d'Orange (mid-July to early Aug; 🕸www.choregies.asso.fr); opera.

Périgueux Mimos (late July to early Aug; 🕸www .mimos.fr); international mime festival.

Prades Festival Pablo Casals (late July to mid-Aug; 🕸www.prades-festival-casals.com); chamber music.

Reims Flâneries Musicales d'Été (🕸www .flaneriesreims.com); open-air concerts.

Rennes Les Tombées de la Nuit (early July; 🕸www.lestombeesdelanuit.com); concerts, cinema and performance arts.

Saintes Festival de Saintes (mid-July; 🕸www .abbayeauxdames.org); classical music.

Vaison-la-Romaine Vaison Danse (mid-July; 🕸www.vaison-festival.com); contemporary dance.

August

Aurillac Festival International de Théâtre de Rue (🕸www.aurillac.net); street theatre.

Lorient Festival Interceltique (early Aug; 🕸www .festival-interceltique.com); Celtic folk festival.

Menton Festival de Musique (🕸www .festivalmusiquementon.com); chamber music.

Mulhouse Festival du Jazz (mid- to late Aug; 🕸www.jazz-mulhouse.org).

Paris Rock en Seine (late Aug; 🕸www .rockenseine.com).

Quimper Semaines Musicales (🕸www.semaines -musicales-quimper.org); classical, jazz and folk music.

St-Malo La Route du Rock (mid-Aug; 🕸www .laroutedurock.com).

September

Amiens Festival des Cathédrales de Picardie (Sept–Oct; 🕸www.festivaldescathedrales.com); Baroque and Renaissance music.

Limoges Les Francophonies en Limousin (late Sept to early Oct; 🕸www.lesfrancophonies.com); contemporary theatre.

Lyon Bienniale de la Dance (next in 2010; 🕸www .biennale-delyon.org).

Paris Biennial des Antiquaires (next in 2010) antiques fair; Jazz à la Villette (early Sept); Festival d'Automne (mid-Sept to mid-Dec; 🕸www.festival -automne.com); theatre, concerts, dance, films and exhibitions.

Perpignan Visa pour l'Image (early to mid-Sept; 🕸www.visapourlimage.com); international photojournalism.

Puy-en-Velay Fête Renaissance du Roi de l'Oiseau (mid-Sept; 🕸www.roideloiseau.com); historical pageants, fireworks and re-creations.

Strasbourg Musica (late Sept to early Oct; 🕸www.festival-musica.org); contemporary music.

October

Bastia Les Musicales (🕸www.musicales-de -bastia.com); sacred and world music.

Nancy Jazz Pulsations (🕸www .nancyjazzpulsations.com).

Paris Foire International d'Art Contemporain (late Oct; 🕸www.fiac.com).

November and December

Rennes Rencontres Transmusicales (early Dec; 🕸www.lestrans.com); contemporary music.

Strasbourg Jazz d'Or (Nov; 🕸www.jazzdor.com).

Sports and outdoor activities

France has a wide range of sports on offer, both for the spectator and the partici-pant. It's not difficult to get tickets for domestic and international football and rugby matches, while the biggest event of all, the Tour de France, is free. And if you're interested in expending some energy yourself, there's a whole host of activities and adventure sports available.

Spectator sports

More than any of the cultural jamborees, it's **sporting events** that really excite the French – particularly cycling, football, rugby and tennis. In the south, bullfighting and the Basque game of pelota are also popular. At the local, everyday level, the rather less gripping game of *boules* is the sport of choice, played in every town and village.

Cycling

The sport the French are truly mad about is **cycling**. It was, after all, in Paris's Palais Royale gardens in 1791 that the precursor of the modern bicycle, the *célerifière*, was presented, and in the same city seventy years later that father and son team Pierre and Ernest Michaux constructed the *véloci-pede* (from which comes the French term *vélo* for bicycle), the first really efficient bicycle. The French can also legitimately claim the sport of cycle racing as their own, with the first event, a 1200-metre sprint, held in Paris's Parc St-Cloud in 1868 – although the first champion was an Englishman.

The world's premier cycling race is the **Tour de France**, held over three weeks in July and covering around 3500 kilometres. The course changes each year, but always includes some truly arduous mountain stages and time trials, and ends on the Champs-Élysées. An aggregate of each rider's times is made daily the overall leader wearing the coveted yellow jersey (*maillot jaune*). Huge crowds turn out to cheer on the cyclists and the French president himself presents the jersey to the overall winner. The last French cyclist to win the Tour, however, was Bernard Hinault in 1985.

Other classic long-distance bike races include the **Paris–Roubaix**, instigated in 1896 and held in April, which is reputed to be the most exacting one-day race in the world; the **Paris–Brussels** (Sept), held since 1893; and the rugged seven-day **Paris–Nice** event (March). Details for all the above can be found at ⓦ www.letour.fr.

Football

As in most countries, **football** is France's number-one team sport. Football fever reached a pitch when the French team won the **World Cup** in front of their home crowd in **1998** and in 2000 became the first side ever to add a **European Championships** title to the world crown. The team has found it hard to live up to expectations since then. They were eliminated in the first round of the 2002 World Cup without scoring a single goal, but then reached the final in **2006**, only to lose out to Italy on penalties. Sadly that game will be best remembered for national hero **Zinedine Zidane**, representing France for the last time, being sent off for headbutting an Italian defender. And France performed dismally again in the **2008 European Championships**, when it failed to make even the quarter finals, scoring only one goal in the tournament and coming bottom of its group.

The **domestic game** has been on the up in recent years, and average attendances have improved. Almost all clubs now have sound financial backing, and the biggest clubs, such as Monaco, Marseille and Paris St-Germain (PSG), have all performed well in European competitions. For the latest information visit the website of the *Ligue de Football Professionel* at ⓦ www.lfp.fr.

Sporting calendar

January Monte Carlo Car Rally (ⓦwww.acm.mc).

February–April Six Nations rugby tournament (Paris; ⓦwww.6-nations-rugby.com).

April Paris Marathon (ⓦwww.parismarathon.com); Le Mans 24-hour motorcycle rally (ⓦwww.lemans.org).

May Roland Garros International Tennis Championship (Paris; ⓦwww.rolandgarros .com); Monaco Formula 1 Grand Prix (ⓦwww.monaco-formula1.com).

June Le Mans 24-hour car rally (ⓦwww.lemans.org); Grand Prix de France Formula (Nevers; ⓦwww.gpfrancef1.com).

July Tour de France (ⓦwww.letour.fr).

October Grand Prix de l'Arc de Triomphe (Paris; ⓦwww.prixarcdetriomphe.com).

Tickets to see domestic clubs are available either from specific club websites, or in the towns where they are playing; ask at local tourist offices. To watch the national team, you can get tickets online at ⓦwww.fff.fr (Fédération Française de Football), or try ⓦwww.francebillet.com. Prices tend to start at around €10–15.

Rugby

Although most popular in the southwest, **rugby** enjoys a passionate following throughout France. French rugby's greatest moment to date came in the 1999 World Cup, when they trounced the favourites New Zealand in the semi-finals, though then lost to an Australian side that never had to rouse itself out of second gear. They also made it to the semi-finals in 2003 and 2007, losing to England on both occasions.

More international fare is provided by the **Six Nations** tournament – the other five nations being England, Wales, Scotland, Ireland and Italy. France has been the most consistent team in recent years, clinching Grand Slams in 2002 and 2004, and winning again in 2006 and 2007.

Domestic clubs to watch for include Toulouse (winner of the French Championship in 2008), Paris's Stade Français, Perpignan and Brive (all past winners or runners up in the Europe-wide Heineken Cup), Agen, and the Basque teams of Bayonne and Biarritz, which still retain their reputation as keepers of the game's soul.

Tickets for local games can be bought through the clubs themselves, with prices starting around €10. For bigger domestic and international games, they are available online at ⓦwww.francebillet.com; prices start at around €15. Information can be found on the Fédération Française de Rugby's website (ⓦwww.ffr.fr).

Pelota

In the Basque country (and also in the nearby Landes), the main draw for crowds is **pelota**, a lethally (sometimes literally) fast variety of team handball or raquetball played in a walled court with a ball of solid wood. The most popular form today is played with bare hands in a two-walled court called a *fronton*. In other varieties wooden bats are used or wicker slings strapped to the players' arms. Ask at local tourist offices for details of where to see the game played.

Bullfighting

In and around the Camargue, the number-one sport is **bullfighting**. Different from the Spanish version, the *course camarguaise* involves variations on the theme of removing cockades from the base of the bull's horns, and it's generally the fighters, rather than the bulls, who get hurt. Further west, particularly in the Landes *département*, you'll come across the similar *courses landaises*, where men perform acrobatics with the by no means docile local cows.

Spanish bullfights, known as *corridas*, do take place – and draw capacity crowds – in southern France. The major events of the year are the Féria de Nîmes (see p.763) at Pentecost (Whitsun) and the Easter *féria* at Arles (p.985). See the local press or ask at tourist offices for details of where to pick up tickets.

Boules

In every town or village square, particularly in the south, you'll see beret-clad men playing *boules* or its variant, *pétanque* (in which contestants must keep both feet on the ground when throwing). Although more women are taking up *boules*, at competition level it remains very male-dominated: there are café or village teams and endless championships. There's even talk – not all of it in jest – of getting *boules* recognized as an Olympic sport.

Outdoor activities

In addition to the perennial favourites – walking, cycling and skiing – France provides a fantastically wide range of outdoor activities. Most have a national federation (listed in the text where relevant), which can provide information on local clubs.

Walking and climbing

France is covered by a network of some 60,000km of long-distance footpaths, known as *sentiers de grande randonnée* or **GRs**. They're signposted and equipped with campsites, refuges and hostels (*gîtes d'étape*) along the way. Some are real marathons, like the GR5 from the coast of Holland to Nice, the trans-Pyrenean GR10, the Grande Traversée des Alpes (the GTA) and the magnificent GR20 in Corsica (see box, p.1119). Other famous hikes include the Chemin de St-Jacques (GR65), which follows the pilgrim route from Le Puy in the Auvergne to the Spanish border above St-Jean-Pied-de-Port and on to the shrine of Santiago de Compostela, and the GR3, which traces the Loire from source to sea. There are also thousands of shorter *sentiers de promenade et de randonnée*, the **PRs**, as well as nature walks and many other local footpaths.

Each GR and many PRs are described in the **Topo-guide series** (available outside France in good travel bookshops), which give a detailed account of each route, including maps, campsites, refuges, sources of provisions, and so on. In France, the guides are available from bookshops and some tourist offices, or direct from the principal French walkers' association, the Fédération Française de la Randonnée Pédestre (☎01.44.89.93.90, ⓦwww.ffrandonnee.fr). In addition, many tourist offices have guides to local footpaths.

Mountain climbing is possible all year round, although bear in mind that some higher routes will be snowbound until quite late in the year, and require special equipment such as crampons and ice axes; these shouldn't be attempted without experience or at least a local guide. See p.44 for information about staying in mountain refuges.

No matter where you are walking, make sure you have your own water supplies, or find out locally if you'll be able to fill up your water bottles on the way. You'll also need decent footwear, waterproofs and a map, compass and possibly GPS system. Finally, don't forget sunblock, sunglasses and a hat.

In mountain areas associations of professional **mountain guides**, often located in the tourist office, organize walking expeditions for all levels of experience. In these and more low land areas, particularly the limestone cliffs of the south and west, you'll also find possibilities for **rock climbing** (*escalade*). For more information you could contact the Fédération Française de la Montagne et de l'Escalade (☎01.40.18.75.50, ⓦwww.ffme.fr).

Details of tour operators specializing in walking holidays are listed on p.32.

Cycling

Cyclists have around 50,000km of marked cycle paths (*pistes cyclables*) in France. Many towns and cities have established cycle lanes, while in the countryside there are an increasing number of specially designated **long-distance cycle routes** (*véloroutes* and *voies vertes*). Burgundy is particularly well served, with an 800km circuit nearing completion, while the Loire à Vélo cycle route will eventually run almost the complete length of the Loire valley. The Fédération Française de Cyclisme (☎01.49.35.69.00, ⓦwww.ffc.fr) produces a guide to mountain-biking sites and tourist offices can provide details of local cycle ways; the Fédération Française de Cyclotourisme (☎01.56.20.88.88, ⓦwww.ffct.org) provides links to local cycling clubs, and lists local trips.

IGN produces a number of departmental "Cycloguides", with maps at 1:25,000, specially aimed at cyclists. Otherwise, their France-wide 1:100,000 maps are the best option (see p.62).

For information on the practicalities of cycling in France, see "Getting around", p.39. Details of tour operators specializing in cycling holidays are on p.32.

Skiing and snowboarding

Millions of visitors come to France to go **skiing** and **snowboarding**, whether its downhill, cross-country or ski-mountaineering. It can be an expensive sport to arrange independently, however, and the best deals are often to be had from package operators (see p.32). These can be arranged in France or before you leave (most travel agents sell all-in packages). Though it's possible to ski from early November through to the end of April at high altitudes, peak season is February and March.

The best skiing and boarding is generally to be had in the **Alps**. The higher the resort the longer the season, and the fewer the anxieties you'll have about there being enough snow. For a brief rundown of all the main Alpine skiing areas, see the box on p.877. The foothills of the Alps in **Provence** have the same mix of old and new on a smaller scale. The clientele are Riviera residents and prices are not cheap, though at least you can nip down to the coast when you're bored with snow. The **Pyrenees** are a friendlier range of mountains, less developed (though that can be a drawback if you want to get in as many different runs as possible per day) and warmer, which means a shorter season and less reliable snow.

Cross-country skiing (*ski de fond*) is being promoted hard, especially in the smaller ranges of the Jura and Massif Central. It's easier on the joints, but don't be fooled into thinking it's any less athletic. For the really experienced and fit, though, it's a good way of getting about, using snowbound GR routes to discover villages still relatively uncommercialized. Several independent operators organize **ski-mountaineering courses** in the French mountains (see p.32).

Practicalities

Lift **passes** start at around €25 a day in most resorts, but can reach almost €50 in the pricier spots; six-day passes cost from €150 to around €250. **Equipment** hire is available at most resorts, and comes in at around €20 per day for skis and boots, while a week's hire will set you back anything from €80–100, but can climb to €150 for the most high-tech or stylish gear.

The vast majority of skiiers **book** from home through tour operators offering all-in deals, though there are also plenty of local hotels and B&Bs which offer independent ski deals; see the Guide for details. If you are going to the Alps, however, you should consider organizing at least your accommodation in advance; many hotels are booked months ahead in high season, whilst others allocate their rooms to tour operators or only accept bookings on a strict Saturday-to-Saturday basis, though nowadays more offer flexible stays. If you do decide to book ahead, it's worth choosing a specalized operator that can also give ATOL protection, such as Momentum Ski (☎020/7371 9111, ⓦwww.momentum.uk.com).

Independent travellers might consider joining the Ski Club of Great Britain (☎020/8410 2000, ⓦwww.skiclub.co.uk), which offers in-resort assistance, guiding and an advice service. The Fédération Française de Ski (☎04.50.51.40.34, ⓦwww.ffs.fr) provides links to local clubs, while ⓦwww.skifrance.fr is a good overall source of **information**, with links to all the country's ski resorts.

Adventure sports

Hang-gliding and **paragliding** are popular in the Hautes-Alpes of Provence, the Pyrenees and Corsica. Prices start at around €50 for a single trip; contact local tourist offices for more information.

Caving is practised in the limestone caverns of southwest France and in the gorges and ravines of the Pyrenees, the Alps and the Massif Central. You'll need to make an arrangement through a local club; they usually organize beginner courses as well as half- or full-day outings. For more information, contact the Fédération Française de Spéléologie (☏04.72.56.09.63, ⊛www.ffspeleo.fr).

As for all adventure sports, it is important to make sure that your **insurance** covers you for these rather more risky activities. See p.61 for details.

Horseriding

Horseriding is an excellent way to explore the French countryside. The most famous and romantic region for riding is the flat and windswept Camargue at the Rhône Delta, but practically every town has an equestrian centre (*centre équestre*) where you can ride with a guide or unaccompanied. **Mule-** and **donkey-trekking** are also increasingly popular, particularly along the trails of the Pyrenees and Alps. A day's horse- or donkey-trekking will cost upwards of €30.

Lists of **riding centres** and events are available from the Comité National de Tourisme Équestre (☏02.54.94.46.80, ⊛www.tourisme-equestre.fr), or from local tourist offices.

Watersports and activities

France's extensive coastline has been well developed for recreational activities, especially in the south. Although in summer you can swim just about anywhere, from Normandy to the Mediterranean, the Côte d'Azur and Corsica undoubtedly have the best beaches.

In the towns and resorts of the Mediterranean coast, you'll find every conceivable sort of beachside activity, including boating, sea-fishing and diving, and if you don't mind high prices and crowds, the too-blue waters and sandy coves are unbeatable. The wind-battered western Mediterranean is where **windsurfers** head to enjoy the calm saltwater inlets (*étangs*) that typify the area.

The Atlantic coast is good for **sailing**, particularly around Brittany, while the best conditions for **surfing** (Fédération Française de Surf; ⊛www.surfingfrance.com) are to be found around Biarritz, something of a Mecca for the sport; further north, Anglet, Hossegor and Lacanau regularly host international competitions. Corsica is the most popular destination for **diving** and snorkelling; contact the Fédération Française d'Études et de Sports Sous-Marins (☏04.91.33.99.31, ⊛www.ffessm.com) for more information.

Most towns have a **swimming pool** (*piscine*), though outdoor pools tend to open only in the height of summer. You may be requested to wear a bathing cap and men to wear trunks (not shorts), so come prepared. You can also swim at many river beaches (usually signposted) and in the real and artificial lakes that pepper France. Many lakes have leisure centres (*bases de plein airs* or *centres de loisirs*) at which you can rent pedaloes, windsurfers and dinghies, as well as larger boats and, on the bigger reservoirs, jet-skis.

Canoeing (Fédération Française de Canoë-Kayak; ⊛www.ffck.org) is hugely popular in France, and in summer practically every navigable stretch of river has outfits renting out boats and organizing excursions. The rivers of the southwest (the Dordogne, Vézère, Lot and Tarn) in particular offer tremendous variety.

For information on **canal-boating**, see the box on p.40 in "Getting around".

Practicalities

Tourist offices will be able to put you in touch with local companies to help you arrange activities, or contact the national federations listed in the text. For tour operators organizing holidays around these activities, see p.32.

Shopping

France in general is a paradise for shoppers. Even outside Paris, which is crammed with international clothing chains, fashion boutiques and antique shops, most main towns have a range of excellent department stores, such as Printemps and Galeries Lafayette, as well as a host of independent shops which make superb targets for window-shopping (known as *lèche-vitrines*, or literally "window-licking" in French).

Food is a particular joy to shop for; well-stocked supermarkets are easy to find, while on the outskirts of most towns of any size you'll come across at least one *hypermarché*, enormous supermarkets selling everything from food to clothes and garden furniture. The most well-known chains include Carrefour, Leclerc and Casino. Every French town worth its salt holds at least one **market** (*marché*) a week. These tend to be vibrant, mostly morning affairs when local producers gather to sell speciality goods such as honey, cheese and alcohol, alongside excellent quality vegetable, meat and fish stalls. Boulangeries are the best places to buy bread, while patisseries offer a broader range of pastries, cakes and sometimes also sandwiches and other snacks.

Regional specialities are mostly of the edible kind. If you're travelling in Brittany, be sure to pick up some of the local cider (*cidre*), while Normandy is famous for its calvados, and the south for its *pastis*.

Provence is well known for its superb olive oil (*huile d'olive*) and pricey truffles (*truffes*), as is the Dordogne. No matter where you go, each region will produce at least one local cheese, and wine of course also varies from region to region. Cognac (p.580) and the Champagne region (pp.236–250) are also obvious destinations if you're looking to stock up.

Other items to look out for include **lace** (*dentelle*) in the north, **pottery** in Brittany and **ceramics** in Limoges. The northeast, especially Lorraine, is renowned for its **crystal** production, while Provence, particularly the town of Grasse (pp.1065–1067), is *the* place in France to buy **perfume**.

Non-EU residents are able to claim back **VAT** (*TVA*) on purchases that come to over €175. To do this, make sure the shop you're buying from fills out the correct paperwork, and present this to customs before check in at the airport for your return flight.

Travel essentials

Costs

Although prices have been rising steadily in recent years, France is not an expensive place to visit, at least compared to other northern European countries, largely because of the relatively low cost of accommodation and eating out. When and where you go, however, will make a difference: in prime tourist spots hotel prices can go up by a third during July and August, while places like Paris and the Côte d'Azur are always more expensive than other regions.

For a reasonably comfortable existence – staying in hotels, eating lunch and dinner in restaurants, plus moving around, café stops and museum visits – you need to allow a **budget** of around €100 (£79/$156) a day per person, assuming two people sharing a mid-range room. By counting the pennies – staying at youth hostels or camping and being strong-willed about extra cups of coffee and doses of culture – you could manage on €55 (£43/$86) a day, or even less if you're surviving on street snacks and market food.

Admission charges to museums and monuments can also eat into your budget, though many state-owned museums have one day of the week when they're free or half-price. Reductions are often available for those over 60 and under 18 (for which you'll need your passport as proof of age) and for students under 26, while many are free for children under 12, and almost always for kids under 4. Several towns and regions offer multi-entry tickets covering a number of sights (detailed in the Guide).

Discount cards

Once obtained, various official and quasi-official youth/student ID cards soon pay for themselves in savings. Full-time students are eligible for the **International Student ID Card** (ISIC, Ⓦwww.isiccard.com, or Ⓦwww .isic.org in the US and Canada), which entitles you to special air, rail and bus fares and discounts at museums, theatres and other attractions. Holders also have access to a 24-hour hotline to call in the event of a medical, legal or financial emergency.

You only have to be 26 or younger to qualify for the **International Youth Travel Card (IYTC)**, while teachers are eligible for the **International Teacher Card (ITIC)**. See Ⓦwww.istc.com or Ⓦwww.isic.org for further details, and your nearest outlet. Several other travel organizations and accommodation groups also sell their own cards, good for various discounts. A **university photo ID** might open some doors, but is not always as easily recognizable as the above cards.

Most museums and other tourist sites give discounts to the **over-60s** (usually the same as the student reduction) while SNCF offers special deals on train tickets (see p.36), although proof of age will usually be required.

Crime and personal safety

Theft

While violent crime involving tourists is rare in France, **petty theft** is endemic in all the big cities, along the Côte d'Azur, on beaches and at major tourist sights. In Paris, be especially wary of pickpockets at train stations and on the métro and RER lines; RER line B, serving Charles de Gaulle airport and Gare du Nord, and subway line number 1 are particularly notorious. Cars with foreign numberplates face a high risk of break-ins; vehicles are rarely stolen, but luggage makes a tempting target. Motorbike thieves operate in big cities and along the Mediterranean coast, often stealing from cars at traffic lights or in jams; don't leave valuables on the seats and keep car windows shut and doors locked at all times.

It obviously makes sense to take the normal **precautions**: don't flash wads of notes around; carry your bag or wallet securely and be especially careful in crowds; never leave valuables lying around; and park

Emergency numbers

Police ☎17
Medical emergencies/ambulance ☎15
Fire brigade/paramedics ☎18
Rape crisis (Viols Femmes Informations) ☎08.00.05.95.95
All emergency numbers are toll-free.

your car overnight in a monitored parking garage or, at the very least, on a busy and well-lit street. It's wise to keep a separate record of cheque and credit card numbers and the phone numbers for cancelling them. Finally, make sure you have a good insurance policy (see p.61).

To **report a theft**, go to the local gendarmerie or Commissariat de Police (addresses are given in the Guide for major cities), where they will fill out a *constat de vol*. Remember to take your passport, and vehicle documents if relevant. The duty officer will usually find someone who speaks English if they don't themselves.

Drugs

Drug use is just as prevalent in France as anywhere else in Europe – and just as risky. People caught smuggling or possessing drugs, even just a few grams of marijuana, are liable to find themselves in jail. Should you be arrested on any charge, you have the right to contact your consulate (addresses given in the Guide), though don't expect much sympathy.

Racism

Though the self-proclaimed home of "liberté, égalité, fraternité", France has an unfortunate reputation for **racism and anti-Semitism**. The majority of racist incidents are focused against the Arab community, although black and Asian visitors may also encounter an unwelcome degree of curiosity or suspicion from shopkeepers, hoteliers and the like. It is not unknown for hotels to claim they are fully booked when they're not, for example, and the police are far more likely to stop Arab and black people and demand to see their ID. In the worst cases, you might be unlucky

enough to experience outright hostility. If you suffer a **racial assault**, contact the police, your consulate or one of the local anti-racism organizations (though they may not have English-speakers); SOS Racism (⊛www.sos-racisme.org) and Mouvement contre le Racisme et pour l'Amitié entre les Peuples (MRAP; ⊛www.mrap.asso.fr) have offices in most regions of France. Alternatively, you could contact the **English-speaking helpline** SOS Help (☎01.46.21.46.46, daily 3–11pm; ⊛www.soshelpline.org). The service is staffed by trained volunteers who not only provide a confidential listening service, but also offer practical information for foreigners facing problems in France.

Safety

Pedestrians should take great care when crossing roads. Although the authorities are trying to improve matters, many French drivers pay little heed to pedestrian/zebra crossings. Never step out onto a crossing assuming that drivers will stop. Also be wary at traffic lights: check cars are not still speeding towards you even when the green man is showing.

Electricity

Voltage is almost always 220V, using **plugs** with two round pins. If you need an adapter, it's best to buy one before leaving home, though you can find them in big department stores in France.

Entry requirements

Citizens of **EU countries** can enter France freely, while those from many **non-EU countries**, including Australia, Canada, New Zealand and the United States, among others, do not need a visa for a stay of **up to ninety days**. South African citizens require a short-stay visa for up to ninety days, which should be applied for in advance, and costs €60.

All non-EU citizens who wish to remain **longer than ninety days** must apply for a long-stay visa, for which you'll have to show proof of – among other things – a regular income or sufficient funds to support yourself and medical insurance. Be aware, however, that the situation can change and it's advisable to check with your nearest French embassy or consulate before departure. For further information about visa regulations consult the Ministry of Foreign Affairs website: ⓦwww.diplomatie.gouv.fr.

French embassies and consulates

Australia Canberra ☏02/6216 0100, ⓦwww .ambafrance-au.org.
Britain London ☏020/7073 1000, ⓦwww .ambafrance-uk.org; Edinburgh ☏0131/225 7954; ⓦwww.consulfrance-edimbourg.org.
Canada Ottawa ☏613/789 1795, ⓦwww .ambafrance-ca.org; Montréal ☏514/878 4385, ⓦwww.consulfrance-montreal.org; Toronto ☏416/847 1900, ⓦwww.consulfrance-toronto.org.
Ireland Dublin ☏01/277 5000, ⓦwww .ambafrance-ie.org.
New Zealand Wellington ☏04/384 2555, ⓦwww .ambafrance-nz.org.
South Africa Johannesburg ☏011/778 5600, ⓦwww.consulfrance-jhb.org.
USA Wasington ☏202/944 6000, ⓦwww .ambafrance-us.org.

Gay and lesbian France

In general, France is more liberal on **homosexuality** than most other European countries. The age of consent is 16, and same-sex couples have been able to form civil partnerships, called PACs, since 1999. Gay marriage, however, along with the right to adopt, remains illegal, despite the fact that the controversial mayor of Bègles, near Bordeaux, conducted the country's first and only gay marriage in 2004 (it was later declared invalid).

Gay male communities thrive, especially in Paris and southern towns such as Toulouse and Nice. Nevertheless, gays tend to keep a low profile outside communities and specific gay venues, parades, and the prime gay areas of Paris and the coastal resorts. Lesbian life is rather less upfront, although Toulouse has a particularly lively lesbian community. The biggest annual event is the Gay Pride march in Paris (ⓦwww.gaypride .fr), which takes place every June.

In **Corsica**, attitudes remain much more conservative than on the mainland. Women can get away with holding hands and walking with arms around each other, but gay men can expect hostile comments if they do the same. At the same time, the island has long been a popular destination for discreet gay couples and no one is likely to raise much more than an eyebrow when gay couples checks in to a hotel.

Addresses of local gay and/or lesbian establishments are listed in the Guide. Also useful is the French tourist board website with their online magazine *FranceGuide for the Gay Traveller*, and the *France Gay et Lesbian* guide published by Petit Futé (ⓦwww.petitfute.com).

Useful contacts

Dykeplanet ⓦwww.dykeplanet.com. Sells *Le dykeGuide*, a guidebook (last published 2006, in French) listing primarily lesbian-friendly places across France. It's also available from FNAC and other bookstores.
Spartacus ⓦwww.spartacusworld.com. Site selling the English-language *Spartacus International Gay Guide*, which has an extensive section on France and contains some information for lesbians.
Têtu ⓦwww.tetu.com. France's best-selling gay/lesbian magazine with events listings and contact addresses; you can buy it in bookshops or through their website, which is also an excellent source of information.

Health

Visitors to France have little to worry about as far as health is concerned. No vaccinations are required, there are no nasty diseases and tap water is safe to drink. The worst that's likely to happen to you is a case of sunburn or an upset stomach from eating too much rich food. If you do need treatment, however, you should be in good hands: the French healthcare system is rated one of the best in the world.

Under the French health system, all services, including doctors' consultations, prescribed medicines, hospital stays and ambulance call-outs, incur a charge which you have to pay upfront. **EU citizens** are entitled to a refund (usually between seventy and one hundred percent) of medical and dental expenses, providing the doctor is government-registered (*un médecin conventionné*) and provided you have a European Health Insurance Card (EHIC; *Carte Européenne d'Assurance Maladie*). Note that everyone in the family, including children, must have their own card, which are free. In the UK, you can apply for them through the Department of Health website (🌐 www.dh.gov.uk), by phone (☎ 0845/606 2030) or by post – forms are available at post offices. Even with the EHIC card, however, you might want to take out some additional insurance to cover the shortfall. All **non-EU visitors** should ensure they have adequate medical insurance cover. For minor complaints go to a **pharmacie**, signalled by an illuminated green cross. You'll find at least one in every small town and even in some villages. They keep normal shop hours (roughly 9am–noon & 3–6pm), though some stay open late and in larger towns at least one (known as the *pharmacie de garde*) is open 24 hours according to a rota; details are displayed in all pharmacy windows, or the local police will have information.

Condoms (*préservatifs*) are widely available in pharmacies, supermarkets and coin-operated street dispensers. The pill (*la pilule*), and the morning-after pill (*la pilule du lendemain*) are available only on prescription.

For anything more serious you can get the name of a **doctor** from a pharmacy, local police station, tourist office or your hotel. Alternatively, look under "Médecins" in the Yellow Pages of the phone directory. The consultation fee is in the region of €21 to €25, and you'll be given a *Feuille de Soins* (Statement of Treatment) for later insurance claims. Any prescriptions will be fulfilled by the pharmacy and must be paid for; little price stickers (*vignettes*) from each medicine will be stuck on the *Feuille de Soins*.

In serious **emergencies** you will always be admitted to the nearest general hospital (*centre hospitalier*). Phone numbers and addresses of hospitals in all the main cities are given in the Guide. The national number for calling an ambulance is ☎ 15.

Insurance

Even though EU citizens are entitled to health-care privileges in France, they would do well to take out an **insurance policy** before travelling in order to cover against theft, loss, illness or injury. Before paying for a new policy, however, it's worth checking whether you are already covered: some all-risks home insurance policies may cover your possessions when overseas, and many private medical schemes include cover when abroad. In Canada, provincial health plans usually provide partial cover for medical mishaps overseas. **Students** will often find that their student health coverage extends during the vacations and for one term beyond the date of last enrolment.

After investigating these possibilities above, you might want to contact a **specialist travel insurance** company, or consider the Rough Guides travel insurance deal outlined below. A typical travel insurance policy usually provides cover for the loss of baggage, tickets and – up to a certain limit – cash or cheques, as well as cancellation or curtailment of your journey. Most exclude so-called **dangerous sports** unless an extra premium is paid; in France this can mean skiing, whitewater rafting, rock climbing and potholing. Many policies can be chopped and changed to exclude coverage you don't need – for example, sickness and accident benefits can often be excluded or included at will.

If you need to **make a claim**, you should keep receipts for medicines and medical treatment, and in the event you have anything stolen, you must obtain an official statement from the police (called a *constat de vol*; see p.59).

Rough Guides has teamed up with Columbus Direct to offer you **travel insurance** that can be tailored to suit your needs. Products include a low-cost **backpacker** option for long stays; a **short break** option for city getaways; a typical **holiday package** option; and others. There are also annual **multi-trip** policies for those who travel regularly.

See our website (🌐 www.roughguides.com /website/shop) for eligibility and purchasing options. Alternatively, UK residents should call ☎ 08700 339 988, Australians ☎ 1300 669 999 and New Zealanders ☎ 0800/55 9911. All other nationalities should call ☎ +44 870 890 2843.

Laundry

Self-service **laundries** are common in French towns – just ask in your hotel or the tourist office, or look in the phone book under "*Laveries automatiques*" or "*Laveries en libre-service*". Machines are graded for different wash sizes; a 7kg load, for example, will cost around €4. Most **hotels** forbid doing laundry in your room, though you should get away with just one or two items.

Mail

French **post offices**, known as La Poste and identified by bright yellow-and-blue signs, are generally open from around 9am to 6pm Monday to Friday, and 9am to noon on Saturday. However, these hours aren't set in stone: smaller branches and those in rural areas are likely to close for lunch (generally noon to 2pm) and finish at 5pm.

You can **receive letters** using the poste restante system available at the central post office in every town. They should be addressed (preferably with the surname first and in capitals) "Poste Restante, Poste Centrale, Town x, post code". You'll need your passport to collect your mail and there'll be a charge of €0.55 per item. Items are usually only kept for 15 days.

For **sending mail**, standard letters (20g or less) and postcards within France cost €0.55; €0.65 to other European Union countries; and €0.85 to all other countries. You can also buy stamps from *tabacs* and newsagents. To post your letter on the street, look for the bright yellow postboxes.

For **further information** on postal rates, among other things, log on to the post office website ⓦ www.laposte.fr.

Maps

In addition to the maps in this guide and the various free town plans and regional maps you'll be offered along the way, the one extra map you might want is a good, up-to-date **road map** of France. The best are those produced by Michelin (1:200,000; ⓦ www .viamichelin.fr) and the Institut Géographique National (IGN; 1:250,000; ⓦ www.ign.fr), either as individual sheets or in one large spiral-bound *atlas routier*.

If **walking or cycling**, it's worth investing in the more detailed IGN maps. Their Carte de Randonnée and Carte de Promenade series (1:25,000) are specifically designed for walkers and cyclists, while the Cycloguides (1:25,000) are a new series of maps detailing cycle routes in certain departments. See "Contexts" (p.1213) for details of walking guides.

Rough Guides also produces a national map of France, a city map of Paris, and

regional maps of Brittany, Corsica and the Pyrenees.

Money

France's **currency** is the euro, which is divided into 100 cents (often still referred to as *centimes*). There are seven notes – in denominations of 5, 10, 20, 50, 100, 200 and 500 euros – and eight different coins – 1, 2, 5, 10, 20 and 50 cents, and 1 and 2 euros. At the time of writing, the **exchange rate** for the euro was around €1.12 to the pound sterling (or £0.90 to €1) and €0.75 to the dollar (or $1.33 to €1). See ⓦ www.xe .com for current rates.

You can change cash at most **banks** and main **post offices**, though only the latter will change traveller's cheques. In either case, you'll typically be charged a flat rate of around €5, but rates and commission vary, so it's worth shopping around. There are **money-exchange counters** (*bureaux de change*) at French airports, major train stations and usually one or two in city centres as well, though they don't always offer the best exchange rates.

By far the easiest way to access money in France is to use your credit or debit card to withdraw cash from an **ATM** (known as a *distributeur* or *point argent*); most machines give instructions in several European languages. Note that there is often a trans-action fee, so it's more efficient to take out a sizeable sum each time rather than making lots of small withdrawals.

Credit and debit cards are also widely accepted in shops, hotels and restaurants, although some smaller establishments don't accept cards, or only for sums above a certain threshold. Visa – called Carte Bleue in France – is almost universally recognized, followed by MasterCard (also known as EuroCard). American Express ranks a bit lower.

Opening hours and public holidays

Basic **hours of business** are Monday to Saturday 9am to noon and 2 to 6pm. In big cities, **shops** and other businesses stay open throughout the day, as do most **tourist offices** and museums in July and August. In rural areas and throughout southern France places tend to close for at least a couple of

Public holidays

January 1 New Year's Day
Easter Monday
Ascension Day (forty days after Easter)
Whit Monday (seventh Monday after Easter)
May 1 Labour Day
May 8 Victory in Europe (VE) Day 1945
July 14 Bastille Day
August 15 Assumption of the Virgin Mary
November 1 All Saints' Day
November 11 Armistice Day
December 25 Christmas Day

hours at lunchtime. Small food shops may not reopen till halfway through the afternoon, closing around 7.30 or 8pm, just before the evening meal. The standard **closing day** is Sunday, even in larger towns and cities, though some food shops and newsagents are open in the morning. Some shops and businesses, particularly in rural areas, also close on Mondays.

Core **banking hours** are Monday to Friday 9am to noon and 2 to 4.30pm. Some branches, especially those in rural areas, close on Monday, while those in big cities may remain open at midday and may also open on Saturday morning. All are closed on Sunday and public holidays.

Museums tend to open from 9 or 10am to noon and from 2 or 3pm to 5 or 6pm, though in the big cities some stay open all day and opening hours tend to be longer in summer. Museum closing days are usually Monday or Tuesday, sometimes both. **Churches** are generally open from around 8am to dusk, but may close at lunchtime and are reserved for worshippers during services (times of which will be posted on the door).

France celebrates eleven **public holidays** (*jours fériés*), when most shops and businesses (though not necessarily restaurants), and some museums, are closed.

Phones

You can make domestic and international **phone calls** from any telephone box (*cabine*)

and can also receive calls – look for the number in the top right-hand corner of the information panel. The vast majority of public phones require a phone card (*télécarte*), available from *tabacs* and newsagents; they come in units of 50 and 120 units (€7.50 and €15 respectively). Alternatively, a more flexible option is one of the many phone cards which operate with a unique code (*cartes télépho-niques*) on sale at post offices, *tabacs*, newsagents and many supermarkets, which can be used from both private and public phones. The post office, for example, sells e.Ticket pre paid cards for domestic and European calls (€5 and €10) and for international calls (€7.50 and €15); the €15 card buys up to 858 minutes to the US and Canada. You can also use credit cards in many call boxes. Coin-operated phones have almost completely disappeared except in cafés and bars.

Calling within France

For **calls within France** – local or long distance – simply dial all ten digits of the number. Numbers beginning ☎08.0 are free-dial numbers; those beginning ☎08.1 and ☎08.6 are charged as a local call; anything else beginning ☎08 is premium-rated. Note that none of these ☎08 numbers can be accessed from abroad. Numbers starting ☎06 are mobile numbers and therefore also expensive to call.

Mobile phones

If you want to use your **mobile/cell phone**, contact your phone provider to check whether it will work in France and what the call charges are – they tend to be pretty exorbitant, and remember you're likely to be charged extra for receiving calls. French mobile phones operate on the European GSM standard, so US cellphones won't work in France unless you have a tri-band phone. If you are going to be in France for any length of time and will be making and receiving a lot of local calls, it may be worth buying a **French SIM card** and pre paid recharge cards (*mobicartes*) from any of the big mobile providers (Orange, SFR and Boygues Telecom), all of which have high-street outlets. They cost around €30, including a certain amount of credit, and you need to give an address in France to register – that of your hotel or a friend will usually suffice.

Smoking

Smoking is now banned in all public places, including public transport, museums, cafés, restaurants and nightclubs.

Time

France is in the Central European Time Zone (GMT+1). This means it is one hour ahead of the UK, six hours ahead of Eastern Standard Time and nine hours ahead of Pacific Standard Time. Between March and October France is one hour behind South Africa, eight hours behind eastern Australia and ten hours behind New Zealand; from October to March it is the same time as in South Africa, 10 hours behind southeastern Australia and 12 hours behind New Zealand. Daylight Saving Time (GMT+2) in France lasts from the last Sunday in March to the last Sunday in October.

Tipping

At restaurants you only need to leave an additional cash **tip** if you feel you have received service out of the ordinary, since restaurant prices always include a service charge. It's customary to tip porters, tour guides, taxi drivers and hairdressers a couple of euros.

Tourist information

The **French Government Tourist Office** (Maison de la France; Ⓦ www.franceguide .com) generally refers you to their website for information, though they still produce a useful practical guide for young travellers to France, and dispense items including maps and the Logis de France book (see "Accommodation" p.41). For more detailed information, such as hotels, campsites, activities and festivals in a specific location, it's best to contact the relevant regional or departmental tourist offices; contact details can be found online at Ⓦ www.fncrt.com and Ⓦ www .fncdt.net respectively.

In France itself you'll find a tourist office – usually an **Office du Tourisme** (OT) but sometimes a **Syndicat d'Initiative** (SI, run by local businesses) – in practically every town

and many villages. Addresses, contact details and opening hours are detailed in the Guide, or try Ⓦ www.tourisme.fr. All local tourist offices provide specific information on the area, including hotel and restaurant listings, leisure activities, car and bike rental, bus times, laundries and countless other things; many can also book accommodation for you. If asked, most offices will provide a town plan (for which you may be charged a nominal fee), and will have maps and local walking guides on sale. In mountain regions they display daily meteorological information and often share premises with the local hiking and climbing organizations. In the big cities you can usually pick up free *What's On* guides.

Tourist offices and government sites

Australia and New Zealand Level 13, 25 Bligh St, Sydney, NSW 2000 ☎ 02/9231 5244, Ⓦ au .franceguide.com.
Canada 1800 Ave McGill College, Suite 1010, Montréal, QC H3A 3J6 ☎ 514/288 2026, Ⓦ ca-en.franceguide.com.
Ireland ☎ 1560 235 235, Ⓦ ie.franceguide.com.
South Africa 3rd Floor, Village Walk Office Tower, corner of Maude and Rivonia, Sandton ☎ 11/523 8292, Ⓦ za.franceguide.com.
UK Lincoln House, High Holborn, London WV1V 7JH ☎ 09068 244 123, Ⓦ uk.franceguide.com.
USA ☎ 514-288-1904; 9454 Wilshire Blvd, Suite 210, Beverly Hills, CA 90212; 205 North Michigan Ave, Suite 3770, Chicago, IL 60601; 825 Third Avenue, 29th Floor, New York, NY 10022; Ⓦ us .franceguide.com.

Travellers with disabilities

The French authorities have been making a concerted effort to improve facilities for **disabled travellers**. Though haphazard parking habits and stepped village streets remain serious obstacles for anyone with mobility problems, ramps or other forms of access are gradually being added to hotels, museums and other public buildings. All but the oldest hotels are required to adapt at least one room to be wheelchair accessible and a growing number of *chambres d'hôtes* are doing likewise. Accessible hotels, sights and other facilities are gradually being inspected and, if they fulfil certain criteria, issued with a "Tourisme & Handicap" certificate and logo; follow-up inspections take place every five years. Tourist offices can provide lists of recognized establishments, now numbering more than 2000, and you can also find them in the "Voyageurs" section of the national tourist office site ⓦwww.fr.franceguide.com.

For **getting to France**, Eurotunnel (see p.29) offers the simplest option for travellers from the UK, since you can remain in your car. Alternatively, Eurostar trains have a limited number of wheelchair spaces at a fixed price of £59 return (a companion can also travel for the same fare); it's wise to reserve well in advance, when you might also like to enquire about the special assistance that Eurostar offers. If you're flying, it's worth noting that, while airlines are required to offer access to travellers with mobility problems, the level of service provided by some discount airlines may be fairly basic. All cross-Channel ferries have lifts for getting to and from the car deck, but moving between the different passenger decks may be more difficult.

Within France, most train stations now make provision for travellers with reduced mobility. Spaces for wheelchairs are available in first-class carriages of all TGVs for the price of the standard second-class fare; note that these must be booked in advance. For other trains, a wheelchair symbol in the timetable indicates services offering special on-board facilities, though it's best to double-check when booking. SNCF produces a free booklet, *Carnet pour un voyage serein*, outlining its services, which is available from main stations and you'll also find information online at ⓦwww .voyages-sncf.com/voyageurs_handicapes /handicap _moteur.html.

Drivers of **taxis** are legally obliged to help passengers in and out of the vehicle and to carry guide dogs. Specially adapted taxi services are available in some towns: contact the local tourist office for further information or one of the organizations listed opposite. All the big **car hire** agencies can provide automatic cars if you reserve sufficiently far in advance, while Hertz offers cars with hand controls on request – again, make sure you give them plenty of notice.

As for finding suitable **accommodation**, guides produced by Logis de France (see p.42) and Gîtes de France (see p.43) indicate places with specially adapted rooms, though it's essential to double-check when booking that the facilities meet to your needs.

Up-to-date **information** about accessibility, special programmes and discounts is best obtained before you leave home from the organizations listed below. French readers might want to get hold of the *Handi-tourisme* guide, published by Petit Futé (ⓦwww.petitfute.com), available online or from major bookstores. You should also visit the French tourist board website at ⓦwww .franceguide.com.

(see p.29)

Useful contacts

Access in Paris ⓦwww.accessinparis.org. Comprehensive information on accessible Paris in book form or as downloadable pdfs (donation of €10–15 requested).

Association des Paralysés de France (APF) France ⓣ01.40.78.69.00, ⓦwww.apf.asso .fr. National association which can answer general enquiries and put you in touch with their departmental offices.

Door to Door ⓦwww.dptac.gov.uk/door-to-door /index.htm. General online travel information from the UK's Disabled Persons Transport Advisory Committee.

Fédération Française Handisport ⓣ01.40.31.45.00, ⓦwww.handisport.org. Among other things, this federation provides information on sports and leisure facilities for people with disabilities.

Irish Wheelchair Association Ireland ⓣ01/818 6400, ⓦwww.iwa.ie. Usefull information about travelling abroad with a wheelchair, and good links.

Le Guide Accessible ⓦwww.guide-accessible .com. Database of accessible accommodation, activities, restaurants etc.

Mobile en Ville France ⓣ06.82.91.72.16, ⓦwww.mobile-en-ville.asso.fr. Information on getting around, mainly in Paris but also other cities and towns (French only).

Mobility International USA US ⓣ541/343-1284, ⓦwww.miusa.org. Provides information and referral services and international exchange programmes.

Tourism for All UK ⓣ0845 124 9971, ⓦwww .toursimforall.org.uk. Masses of useful information, including a comprehensive travel pack on France with details of facilities in hotels, resorts and so on (£5).

Travelling with children

France is a relatively easy country in which to travel with children. They're generally welcome everywhere and young children and babies in particular will be fussed over. There are masses of family-oriented theme parks and no end of leisure activities geared towards kids, while most public parks contain children's play areas.

Local **tourist offices** will have details of specific activities for children, which might include anything from farm visits, nature walks or treasure hunts to paintball and forest ropeways for older children. In summer most seaside resorts organize clubs for children on the beach, while bigger campsites put on extensive programmes of activities and entertainments. Children under 4 years travel free on public transport, while those between 4 and 12 pay half-fare. Museums and the like are generally free to under-12s and half-price up to the age of 18.

Hotels charge by the room, with a small supplement for an additional bed or cot, and family-run places will usually babysit or offer a listening service while you eat or go out. Some youth hostels also now offer family rooms. Nearly all **restaurants** offer children's menus. Disposable **nappies/ diapers** (*couches à jeter*) are available at most pharmacies and supermarkets, alongside a vast range of **baby foods**, though many have added sugar and salt. **Milk powders** also tend to be sweet, so bring your own if this is likely to be a concern. Note that **breastfeeding** in public tends to be frowned on

Further information

Baby Centre ⓦ www.babycentre.co.uk/baby /travel. Covers everything you need to know about going on holiday with young babies, including the most family-friendly tour operators and airlines, and country-specific reports.

Family Travel ⓦ www.family-travel.co.uk. Slightly outdated but useful for basic information on where to go, health and what to pack.

The Rough Guide to Travel with Babies and Young Children. Comprehensive guide to hassle-free family travel.

Women travellers

Despite a relatively strong feminist movement, France can still feel like a very male-dominated country, with many men still holding rather strong chauvinist ideas.

While change is in the air, with female politicians starting to take a higher profile and giving the male ruling class a run for their money, for the moment many women still suffer the double burden of being housewife and earner.

French men tend to be on the predatory side, but are usually easily brushed off if you don't want the attention. It's not unusual, however, to be chatted up regularly, or have men (more often boys) call at you from cars in the street, and make comments as they pass you. The best way to deal with this is simply to avoid making eye contact and fail to react, and they'll soon get the message. On the beaches, especially on the Riviera, women young and old tend to go **topless**. Be sensitive though; if on the rare occasion you find you're the only one baring all on the beach, do cover up.

Work and study in France

EU citizens are able to work in France on the same basis as a French citizen. This means that you don't have to apply for a residence or work permit except in very rare cases – contact your nearest French consulate for further information (see "Entry requirements", p.59). **Non-EU citizens** need a work permit (*autorisation de travail*) and a residence permit; again, contact your nearest French consulate or, if already in France, your local *mairie* or *préfecture* to check what rules apply in your particular situation.

When **looking for a job**, a good starting point is to read one of the books on working abroad published by Vacation Work (ⓦ www .vacationwork.co.uk). You might also want to search the online recruitment resource Monster (ⓦ www.monster.fr) and Job Etudiant (ⓦ www.jobetudiant.net) and Jobs d'Eté (ⓦ www.jobs-ete.com), which focus on jobs for students and summer jobs respectively. In France, try the youth information agency CIDJ (ⓦ www.cidj.com), or CIJ (Centre d'Information Jeunesse) offices in main cities, which have information about temporary jobs and about working in France. The national employment agency, ANPE (Agence Nationale pour l'Emploi; ⓦ www .anpe.fr), advertises temporary jobs and offers a whole range of services to job-seekers from all over the EU. Non-EU citizens will have to show a work permit to apply for any of the jobs they list.

A degree and a TEFL (Teaching English as a Foreign Language) or similar qualification are normally required for **English-language teaching** posts. The annual *EL Gazette Guide to English Language Teaching Around the World* (🖲 www.elgazette.com) provides lists of schools and other practical information. Other useful resources are *Teaching English Abroad* published by Vacation Work and the TEFL website (🖲 www.tefl.com), with its database of English-teaching vacancies.

Foreign **students** pay the same as French nationals to enrol for a course, and you'll be eligible for subsidized accommodation, meals and all the student reductions. French universities are relatively informal, but there are strict entry requirements, including an exam in French for undergraduate courses. For full details and prospectuses, contact the Cultural Service of any French embassy or consulate (see p.60).

Embassies and consulates can also provide details of **language courses** at French universities and colleges, which are often combined with lectures on French "civilization" and usually very costly. Alternatively, you can sign up to one of the hundreds of language-learning courses offered by private organizations – contact the tourist board for details. It's also worth noting that if you're a full-time non-EU student in France, you can get a temporary **work permit** enabling you to work in vacations, including the summer after you qualify, as long as your visa is still valid.

Further contacts

AFS Interncultural Programs 🖲 www.afs.org. Opportunities for high-school students to study in France for a term or full academic year, living with host families.

American Institute for Foreign Study US ☎ 866-906-2437, 🖲 www.aifs.com. Language study and cultural immersion for the summer or school year.

Council on International Educational Exchange (CIEE) US ☎ 1-800-40-STUDY, 🖲 www .ciee.org. A non-profit organization with summer, semester and academic-year programmes in France.

Erasmus UK ☎ 029/2039 7405, 🖲 www .britishcouncil.org/erasmus. EU-run student exchange programme enabling students at participating EU universities to study in another European member country.

Experiment in International Living US ☎ 1-800-345-2929, 🖲 www.usexperiment.org. Summer programmes for high-school students.

World Wide Opportunities on Organic Farms (WWOOF) 🖲 www.wwoof.fr. Volunteer to work on organic farm in return for board and lodging.

Guide

Guide

Paris and around

CHAPTER 1 # Highlights

✳ **Sainte-Chapelle** The stunning stained-glass windows of the Sainte-Chapelle rank among the finest achievements of French High Gothic. See p.94

✳ **Musée Jacquemart-André** One-time sumptuous residence of a wealthy Second- Empire couple, who built up a choice collection of Italian, Dutch and French masters. See p.98

✳ **The Louvre** One of the world's greatest museums, containing a vast display of French and Italian paintings and notable Ancient Egyptian, Roman and Greek collections. See p.100

✳ **Marais** Arguably the city's most lively and attractive district, characterized by narrow streets, fine Renaissance mansions and trendy bars. See p.109

✳ **Jardin du Luxembourg** The haunt of old men playing *boules*, children riding donkeys, students reading textbooks and couples kissing, these gardens capture Paris at its most warm-hearted. See p.123

✳ **Palais de Tokyo** This cool 1930s structure houses two of Paris's most exciting art spaces. See p.130

✳ **Musée Rodin** Rodin's intense sculptures are displayed to powerful effect in his eighteenth-century town house. See p.134

✳ **Puces de St-Ouen** Even if it's less of a flea market now, and more of a mega-emporium for arty bric-a-brac and antiques, the St-Ouen market is a wonderful place for relaxed weekend browsing. See p.140

▲ The Louvre

Paris and around

Long considered the paragon of style, **PARIS** is perhaps the most glamorous city in Europe. It is at once deeply traditional – a village-like metropolis whose inhabitants continue to be notorious for their hauteur – and famously cosmopolitan. The city's reputation as a magnet for writers, artists and dissidents lives on, and it remains at the forefront of Western intellectual, artistic and literary life. At the same time the cultural contributions of its large immigrant populations, particularly from Algeria and West and Central Africa, have sparked unprecedented social transformation in the past few decades. While such contradictions and contrasts may be the reality of any city, they are the makings of Paris: consider the tiny lanes and alleyways of the Quartier Latin or Montmartre against the monumental vistas of the Louvre and La Défense; the multiplicity of markets and old-fashioned pedestrian arcades against the giant underground commercial complexes of Montparnasse, the Louvre and Les Halles; or the obsession with refashioning old buildings and creating ground-breaking architecture against the old ladies who still iron sheets by hand in the laundries of Auteil.

The most tangible and immediate pleasures of Paris are to be found in its street life and along the banks and bridges of the River Seine. Few cities can compete with the cafés, bars and restaurants that line every street and boulevard, and the city's compactness makes it possible to experience the individual feel of the different *quartiers*. You can move easily, even on foot, from the calm, almost small-town atmosphere of **Montmartre** and parts of the **Quartier Latin** to the busy commercial centres of the **Bourse** and **Opéra–Garnier** or the aristocratic mansions of the **Marais**. The city's lack of open space is redeemed by unexpected havens like the **Mosque, Arènes de Lutèce** and the **place des Vosges**, and courtyards of grand houses like the **Hôtel de Sully**. The gravelled paths and formal beauty of the **Tuileries** create the backdrop for the ultimate Parisian Sunday promenade, while the islands and quaysides of the Left and Right Banks of the **River Seine** and the Quartier Latin's two splendid parks, the **Luxembourg** and the **Jardin des Plantes**, make for a wonderful wander. Paris's architectural spirit resides in the elegant streets and boulevards begun in the nineteenth century under Baron Haussmann. The mansion blocks that line them are at once grand and perfectly human in scale, a triumph in city planning proved by the fact that so many remain residential to this day. Rising above these harmonious buildings are the more arrogant monuments that define the French capital. For centuries, an imposing Classical style prevailed with great set pieces such as the **Louvre, Panthéon** and **Arc de Triomphe**, but the last hundred years or so has seen the architectural mould repeatedly broken in a succession of ambitious structures, the industrial chic of the **Eiffel Tower** and **Pompidou**

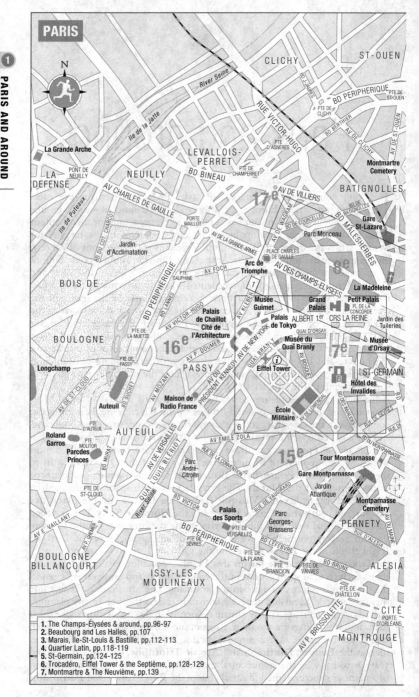

PARIS

N

CLICHY   ST-OUEN

River Seine

BD PERIPHERIQUE   PTE DE ST-OUEN

RUE VICTOR HUGO

PTE DE CLICHY

BD BERTHIER

AV DE CLICHY

AV DE ST-OUEN

Île de la Jatte

La Grande Arche

PONT DE NEUILLY

LA DÉFENSE

NEUILLY

LEVALLOIS-PERRET

BD BINEAU

PTE D'ASNÈRES

PTE DE CHAMPERRET

Montmartre Cemetery

BATIGNOLLES

AV CHARLES DE GAULLE

Île de Puteaux

BD DU CDT CHARCOT

PORTE MAILLOT

AV DE LA GRANDE-ARMÉE

17e

AV DE VILLIERS

AV DE WAGRAM

AV DE COURCELLES

BD MALESHERBES

Gare St-Lazare

Jardin d'Acclimatation

Parc Monceau

BOIS DE

AV FOCH

PTE DAUPHINE

PLACE CHARLES DE GAULLE

Arc de Triomphe

AV DES CHAMPS-ELYSÉES

8e

La Madeleine

BOULOGNE

BD LANNES

AV VICTOR-HUGO

PTE DE LA MUETTE

16e

AV KLEBER

Musée Guimet

Grand Palais

Petit Palais

PL DE LA CONCORDE

CRS LA REINE

Jardin des Tuileries

Palais de Chaillot

Cité de l'Architecture

Palais de Tokyo

ALBERT 1er

QUAI D'ORSAY

Musée du Quai Branly

7e

Musée d'Orsay

AV P. DOUMER

PASSY

AV DE NEW YORK

QUAI BRANLY

Eiffel Tower

ST-GERMAIN

Longchamp

PTE DE PASSY

AV DU PRESIDENT KENNEDY

AV BOSQUET

Hôtel des Invalides

AV MOZART

Maison de Radio France

Auteuil

AV DE ST-CLOUD

BD SUCHET

École Militaire

AV DE LOWENDAL

BD DES INVALIDES

RUE DE SEVRES

Roland Garros

PTE D'AUTEUIL

AUTEUIL

PTE MOLITOR

Parc des Princes

BD MURAT

AV EMILE ZOLA

BD DU MONTPARNASSE

QUAI LOUIS BLERIOT

AV DE VERSAILLES

RUE DE LA CONVENTION

15e

Tour Montparnasse

Gare Montparnasse

PTE DE ST-CLOUD

Parc André-Citroën

RUE DE VAUGIRARD

Jardin Atlantique

Montparnasse Cemetery

AV DU MAINE

AV E. VAILLANT

Palais des Sports

BD VICTOR

Parc Georges-Brassens

PERNETY

RUE D'ALESIA

AV P. GRENIER

River Seine

BD PERIPHERIQUE

PTE DE VERSAILLES

BD LEFEBVRE

PTE DE SEVRES

PTE DE LA PLAINE

PTE BRANCION

BD BRUNE

PTE DE VANVES

ALESIA

BOULOGNE BILLANCOURT

ISSY-LES-MOULINEAUX

PTE DE CHÂTILLON

CITÉ

PORTE D'ORLÉANS

AV P. BROSSOLETTE

MONTROUGE

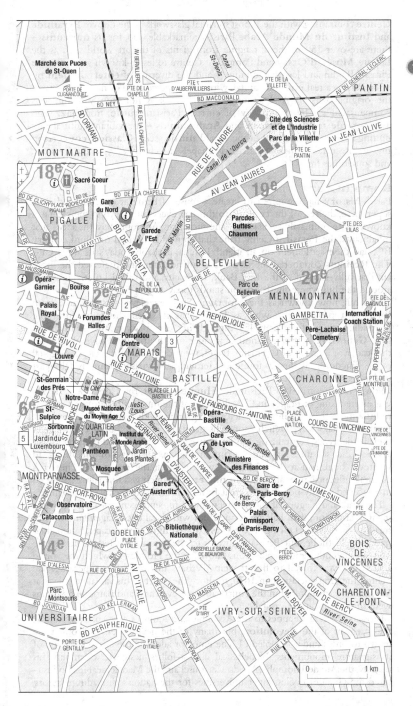

Marché aux Puces
de St-Ouen

PORTE DE
CLIGNANCOURT

PTE DE LA
CHAPELLE

PTE
D'AUBERVILLIERS

PTE DE LA
VILLETTE

AV DU GENERAL-LECLERC

PANTIN

AV BERVILLIERS

Canal
St-Denis

BD NEY

BD MACDONALD

RUE DE LA CHAPELLE

RUE DE FLANDRE

Canal de L'Ourcq

Cité des Sciences
et de L'Industrie
Parc de la Villette

PTE DE
PANTIN

AV JEAN LOLIVE

BD ORNANO

MONTMARTRE

18e

Sacré Coeur

BD DE CLICHY

PLACE ROCHECHOUART

PIGALLE

7

PIGALLE

9e

BD DE LA CHAPELLE

Gare
du Nord

AV JEAN JAURES

19e

Parcdes
Buttes-
Chaumont

PTE DES
LILAS

BD HAUSSMANN

Opéra-
Garnier

Bourse

Gare de
l'Est

BD DE MAGENTA

Canal St-Martin

BD DE LA VILLETTE

10e

BELLEVILLE

RUE DE PYRENES

BELLEVILLE

20e

PTE DE
BAGNOLET

RUE LAFAYETTE

RUE DE CLICHY

BD ST-MARTIN

2e

PL DE LA
RÉPUBLIQUE

RUE DE

Parc de
Belleville

MÉNILMONTANT

Palais
Royal

RUE

REAUMUR

2

3e

AV DE LA REPUBLIQUE

BD DE MENILMONTANT

AV GAMBETTA

International
Coach Station

Forumdes
Halles

Pompidou
Centre

3

11e

Père-Lachaise
Cemetery

BD PERIPHERIQUE

RUE DE RIVOLI

Louvre

1er

MARAIS

4e

RUE ST-ANTOINE

BASTILLE

CHARONNE

PTE DE
MONTREUIL

St-Germain
des Prés

Ile de
la Cité

PLACE DE LA
BASTILLE

RUE DU FAUBOURG ST-ANTOINE

BD DAVOUT

RUE D'AVRON

Notre-Dame

Musée Nationale
du Moyen Age

IleSt-
Louis

RUE DE
LYON

Opéra-
Bastille

PLACE
DE LA
NATION

COURS DE VINCENNES

PTE DE
VINCENNES

6e

BD ST-GERMAIN

St-
Sulpice

Sorbonne

QUARTIER
LATIN

ST-BERNARD

River Seine

Q. HENRI IV

AV AUSTERLITZ

Gare
de Lyon

Promenade Plantée

PTE DE
ST-MANDE

VAUGIRARD

5

Jardindu
Luxembourg

Institut du
Monde Arabe

12e

Panthéon

5e

Jardin
des Plantes

Ministère
des Finances

AV DAUMESNIL

MONTPARNASSE

Mosquée

4

BD DE PORT-ROYAL

Gared'
Austerlitz

QUAI D'AUSTERLITZ

BD DE BERCY

Gare de
Paris-Bercy

PTE
DOREE

Observatoire

Catacombs

QUAI DE LA RAPEE

Parc
de Bercy

Palais
Omnisport
de Paris-Bercy

BOIS
DE
VINCENNES

14e

BD AUGUSTE

GOBELINS

PLACE
D'ITALIE

13e

Bibliothèque
Nationale

QUAI DE LA GARE

QUAI PANHARD
ET LASSOUR

PTE DE
BERCY

CHARENTON-
LE-PONT

RUE D'ALESIA

RUE DE TOLBIAC

RUE DE TOLBIAC

PASSERELLE SIMONE
DE BEAUVOIR

QUAI DE BERCY

Parc
Montsouris

BD JOURDAN

BD KELLERMAN

AV D'ITALIE

BD MASSENA

PTE
D'IVRY

IVRY-SUR-SEINE

QUAI M. BOYER

River Seine

RUE LENINE

UNIVERSITAIRE

BD PERIPHERIQUE

PORTE DE
GENTILLY

PTE
D'ITALIE

0   1 km

Centre contrasting with the almost spiritual glasswork of the Louvre **Pyramide** and **Institut du Monde Arabe**.Paris is remarkable, too, for its **museums** – there are over 150 of them, ranging from giants of the art world such as the Louvre, **Musée d'Orsay** and Pompidou Centre to lesser-known gems like the Picasso, Rodin and Jewish museums – and the diversity of **entertainment** on offer. Paris is a real **cinema** capital, with a large percentage of films on show in the original version. And although French rock is notoriously awful, it is compensated for by the quality of current Parisian **music**, from **jazz** and **avant-garde** to **West African** and **Arab sounds** – the vibrant cultural mix putting Paris at the forefront of the **world music** scene. **Classical concerts** in fine architectural settings – particularly chapels and churches – are also frequent, and sometimes free.

Some history

Paris's **history** has conspired to create a sense of being apart from, and even superior to, the rest of the country. To this day, everything beyond the capital is known quite ordinarily as *province* – the provinces. Appropriately, the city's first inhabitants, the **Parisii**, a Celtic tribe that arrived in around the third century BC, had their settlement on an island: Lutetia, probably today's Île de la Cité. The **Romans** conquered the city two centuries later, and preferred the more familiar hilly ground of the Left Bank. Their city, also called Lutetia, grew up around the hill where the Panthéon stands today.

This hill, now known as the Montagne Ste-Geneviève, gets its name from Paris's first patron saint, who, as legend has it, saved the town from the marauding army of Attila in 451 through her exemplary holiness. Fifty years later **Geneviève** converted another invader to Christianity: Clovis the Frank, the leader of a group of Germanic tribes, went on to make the city the capital of his kingdom. His newly founded Merovingian dynasty promptly fell apart under his son Childéric II.

Power only returned to Paris under **Hugues Capet**, the Count of Paris. He was elected king of France in 987, although at the time his territory amounted to little more than the Île de France, the region immediately surrounding Paris. From this shaky start French monarchs gradually extended their control over their feudal rivals, centralizing administrative, legal, financial and political power as they did so, until anyone seeking influence, publicity or credibility, in whatever field, had to be in Paris – which is still the case today. The city's cultural influence grew alongside its **university**, which was formally established in 1215 and swiftly became the great European centre for scholastic learning.

The wars and plagues of the fourteenth and fifteenth centuries left Paris half in ruins and more than half abandoned, but with royal encouragement, the city steadily recovered. During the **Wars of Religion** the capital remained staunchly Catholic, but Parisians' loyalty to the throne was tested during the mid-seventeenth-century rebellions known as the Frondes, in which the young Louis XIV was forced to flee the city. Perhaps this traumatic experience lay behind the king's decision, in 1670, to move the court to his vast new palace at **Versailles**. Paris suffered in the court's absence, even as grand Baroque buildings were thrown up in the capital.

Parisians, both as deputies to the Assembly and mobs of sans-culottes, were at the forefront of the **Revolution**, but many of the new citizens welcomed the return to order under Napoleon I. The emperor adorned the city with many of its signature monuments, Neoclassical almost-follies designed to amplify his majesty: the Arc de Triomphe, Arc du Carrousel and the Madeleine. He also instituted the Grandes Écoles, super-universities for the nation's elite administrators, engineers and teachers. At the fall of the Empire, in 1814, Paris was saved from destruction by the arch-diplomat Talleyrand, who delivered the city to the Russians with hardly a shot fired. Nationalists grumbled that the occupation continued well into the Restoration regime, as the city once again became the playground of the rich of Europe, the ultimate tourist destination.

The greatest shocks to the fabric of the city came under Napoléon III. He finally completed the Louvre, rebuilding much of the facade in the process, but it was his Prefect of the Seine, **Baron Haussmann**, who truly transformed the city, smashing through the slums to create wide boulevards that could be easily controlled by rifle-toting troops – not that it succeeded in preventing the **1871 Commune**, the most determined insurrection since 1789. In the process of slum clearance, Haussmann created the uniquely Parisian aesthetic that survives today, of long geometrical boulevards lined with rows of grey bourgeois residences. It was down these boulevards that **Nazi troops** paraded in June 1940, followed by the Allies, led by General Leclerc, in August 1944.

Although riotous street protests are still a feature of modern Parisian life – most famously in **May 1968**, when students burst onto the streets of the Quartier Latin – the traditional barricade-builders have long since been booted into the suburban factory-land or depressing satellite towns, alongside the under-served populations of immigrants and their descendants. Many Parisians see the economic and cultural integration of these communities as the greatest challenge facing the contemporary city, and there's a strong undercurrent of **racism** in Paris, as throughout France.

The city continues to expand outward, but offices are steadily elbowing out apartments in the centre, even in this most village-like of cities. **Housing** remains a problem – trying to find an apartment in Paris is a notoriously difficult affair – and yet the decaying parts of the city, especially in the east and north, are gradually being rebuilt, and grand-scale new developments such as La Défense and the Paris Rive Gauche area attest to the vitality of the city's commercial life.

The interests of business and the bourgeoisie – not to mention those of the mayor's family and friends – flourished under the rule of **Jacques Chirac**, Paris's mayor from 1977 to 1995, and his successor Jean Tiberi, but since 2001, socialist politician Bertrand Delanoë has held the reins. It's the first time the Left has controlled Paris since the 1871 Commune, and the first time that the city has had an openly gay mayor – not that many Parisians seem to think it matters. Delanoë has focused on easing the capital's traffic problems, creating new green spaces and fighting the "museumification" of Paris, with some measure of success. Two of his most popular innovations have been the introduction of the Velib', inexpensive bikes for rent dotted all round the city, and Paris Plage, which sees a swathe of the Seine's *quais* converted into a beach every summer. Delanoë now has his sights on the Elysée Palace – at the time of writing, he was pitching for leadership of the socialist party and could be running against Sarkozy in 2012.

Arrival

Many British travellers to Paris arrive by Eurostar at the central **Gare du Nord train station**, while more far-flung visitors are likely to land at one of Paris's two main airports: Charles de Gaulle and Orly. Trains from other parts of France or continental Europe arrive at one of the six central mainline stations. Almost all the **buses** coming into Paris – whether international or domestic – arrive at the main *gare routière* at 28 avenue du Général-de-Gaulle, Bagnolet, at the eastern edge of the city; métro Gallieni (line 3) links it to the centre. If you're **driving** in yourself, don't try to go straight across the city to your destination. Use the ring road – the *boulevard périphérique* – to get around to the nearest *porte*: it's much quicker, except at rush hour, and far easier to navigate, albeit pretty terrifying.

By air

The two main Paris airports that deal with international flights are **Roissy-Charles de Gaulle** and **Orly**, both well connected to the centre. Detailed information in English can be found online at Ⓦ www.adp.fr. The more distant **Beauvais** airport is used by some budget airlines, including Ryanair.

Roissy-Charles de Gaulle Airport

Roissy-Charles de Gaulle Airport (24hr information in English ☏ 01.48.62.22.80), usually referred to as Charles de Gaulle and abbreviated to CDG or Paris CDG, is 23km northeast of the city. The airport has two main **terminals**, CDG 1 and CDG 2. A third terminal, CDG 3 (sometimes called CDG-T3), handles various low-cost airlines, including easyJet. Make sure you know which terminal your flight is departing from when it's time to leave Paris, so you take the correct bus or get off at the right train station. A TGV station links the airport (CDG 2) with Bordeaux, Brussels, Lille, Lyon, Nantes, Marseille and Rennes, among other places.

The least expensive and probably quickest way into the centre of Paris is to take the suburban train line **RER B3**, sometimes called Roissy-Rail, which runs every ten to fifteen minutes from 5am until midnight; the journey time is thirty minutes and tickets cost €8.20 one way (no return tickets). To get to the RER station from CDG 1 you have to take a free shuttle bus (*navette*) to the RER station, but from CDG 2 and CDG-T3 it's simpler to take the pedestrian walkway, though the station is also served by a shuttle bus. The RER train stops at stations including Gare du Nord, Châtelet–Les Halles and St-Michel, at all of which you can transfer to the ordinary métro system – your ticket is valid through to any métro station in central Paris.

Various bus companies provide services from the airport direct to various city-centre locations, but they're slightly more expensive than Roissy-Rail, and may take longer. A more useful alternative is the Blue Vans door-to-door minibus service, which costs from €36 for two people, with no extra charge for luggage. Bookings must be made at least 24 hours in advance on ☏ 01.30.11.13.00 or, for the best rates, online at Ⓦ www.paris-blue-airport-shuttle.fr/.

Taxis into central Paris from CDG cost around €50 on the meter, plus a small luggage supplement (€1 per item), and should take between fifty minutes and one hour. Note that if your flight gets in after midnight your only means of transport is a taxi.

Orly Airport

Orly Airport (information in English daily 6am–11.30pm; ☏ 01.49.75.15.15), 14km south of Paris, has **two terminals**, Orly Sud and Orly Ouest, linked by shuttle bus but easily walkable; Ouest (West) is used for domestic flights while Sud (South) handles international flights.

The easiest way into the centre is via Orlyval, a fast **train shuttle** link to the suburban RER station Antony, where you can pick up RER line B trains to the central RER/métro stations Denfert-Rochereau, St-Michel and Châtelet-Les Halles; Orlyval runs every four to seven minutes from 6.10am to 11pm (€9.30 one way; 35min to Châtelet). A useful alternative is the **Orlybus**: a shuttle bus takes you direct to RER line B station Denfert-Rochereau, on the Left Bank, with good onward métro connections; Orlybus runs every fifteen to twenty minutes from roughly 6am to 11.20pm (€6.10 one way; total journey around 30min). **Taxis** take about 35 minutes to reach the centre of Paris and cost around €35.

Beauvais Airport

Ryanair passengers arrive at Beauvais Airport (℡08.92.68.20.66, ⓦwww .aeroportbeauvais.com), some 65km northwest of Paris. **Coaches** (€13 one way) shuttle between the airport and Porte Maillot, at the northwestern edge of Paris, where you can pick up métro line 1 to the centre. Coaches take about an hour, and leave between fifteen and thirty minutes after the flight has arrived and about three hours before the flight departs on the way back.

By train

Paris has six mainline train stations. **Eurostar** (℡08.92.35.35.39, ⓦwww .eurostar.com) terminates at the busy **Gare du Nord**, rue Dunkerque, in the northeast of the city. Coming off the train, turn left for the métro and the RER, and right for taxis (expect to pay around €10 to central Paris). Just short of the taxi exit, head down the escalators for left luggage (*consignes*) and the various car rental desks. Two bureaux de change (neither offer a good deal) allow you to change money at the station, or you can use your card in one of the ATM cash machines. The Gare du Nord is also the arrival point for trains from Calais and other north European countries.

Nearby, the **Gare de l'Est** (place du 11-Novembre-1918, 10ᵉ) serves eastern France and central and eastern Europe. The **Gare St-Lazare** (place du Havre, 8ᵉ), serving the Normandy coast and Dieppe, is the most central, close to the Madeleine and the Opéra-Garnier. Still on the Right Bank but towards the southeast corner is the **Gare de Lyon** (place Louis-Armand, 12ᵉ), for trains to Italy and Switzerland and TGV lines to southeast France. South of the river, **Gare Montparnasse** (boulevard de Vaugirard, 15ᵉ) is the terminus for Chartres, Brittany, the Atlantic coast and TGV lines to Tours and southwest France. **Gare d'Austerlitz** (boulevard de l'Hôpital, 13ᵉ) serves the Loire Valley and the Dordogne. The **motorail station**, Gare de Paris-Bercy, is down the tracks from the Gare de Lyon on boulevard de Bercy, 12ᵉ.

Orientation

Finding your way around Paris is remarkably easy, as the centre is fairly small for a major capital city, and very **walkable**. The city proper is divided into twenty arrondissements, or districts. These are marked on the map on pp.74–75 and are included as an integral part of addresses throughout the chapter. Arrondissements are abbreviated as 1ᵉʳ (premier = first), 2ᵉ (deuxième = second), 3ᵉ, 4ᵉ and so on; the numbering is confusing until you work out that it spirals out from the centre.

The **Seine** flows in a downturned arc from east to west, cutting the city in two. In the middle of the Seine lie two islands, while north of the river is the busy, commercial **Right Bank**, or *rive droite*. Most of the city's sights are found here, within the historic central arrondissements (1ᵉʳ to 4ᵉ). South of the river is the relatively laid-back **Left Bank**, or *rive gauche* (5ᵉ to 7ᵉ). The outer arrondissements (8ᵉ to 20ᵉ) were mostly incorporated into the city in the nineteenth century. Generally speaking, those to the east accommodated the working classes while those to the west were, and still are, the addresses for the aristocracy and new rich. For a brief rundown of Paris's different quarters, see the introduction to the city on p.93.

Paris proper is encircled by the *boulevard périphérique* ring road. The sprawling conurbation beyond is known as the **banlieue**, or suburbs. There are few sights for the tourist here, and only one of significant interest: St-Denis, with its historic cathedral.

Information

At Paris's tourist offices (Ⓦwww.parisinfo.com) you can pick up **maps** and information, book accommodation and buy travel passes and the Paris Museum Pass (see box below). The most usefully located branches are at 25 rue Pyramides, 1ᵉʳ (June–Oct daily 9am–7pm; Nov–May Mon–Sat 10am–7pm, Sun 11am–7pm; Mᵒ Pyramides), and in the Carrousel du Louvre, accessed from 99 rue de Rivoli, 1ᵉʳ (daily 10am–6pm; Mᵒ Palais Royal-Musée du Louvre). The last also has information on the region around Paris, the Île de France. Montmartre has its own little office on place du Tertre, 18ᵉʳ (daily 7am–10pm; Mᵒ Anvers) and there are booths at the Gare du Nord (daily 8am–6pm) and Gare de Lyon (Mon–Sat 8am–6pm).

Of Paris's inexpensive weekly **listings magazines,** sold at newsagents and kiosks, *Pariscope* has the edge, with a comprehensive section on films. On Wednesdays, *Le Monde* and *Le Figaro* also bring out free listings supplements, while for more detail, the **Webzines** *Paris Voice* (Ⓦwww.parisvoice.com) and *GoGo Paris* (Ⓦgogoparis.com) cover the latest events and trends. For a comprehensive A–Z map, your best bet is one of the pocket-sized "*L'indispensable*" series booklets, sold throughout the city.

City transport

While walking is undoubtedly the best way to discover Paris, the city's integrated **public transport system** of bus, métro and trains – the RATP (Régie Autonome des Transports Parisiens) – is cheap, fast and meticulously

---

Reductions and the Museum Pass

The permanent collections at all municipal museums are free all year round, while all national museums (including the Louvre, Musée d'Orsay and Pompidou Centre) – see Ⓦwww.rmn.fr for a full list – are free on the first Sunday of the month and to under-18s. Elsewhere, the cut-off age for free admission varies between 18, 12 and 4. Reduced admission is usually available for 18 to 26-year-olds and for those over 60 or 65; you'll need to carry your passport or ID card around with you as proof of age. Some discounts are available for students with an ISIC Card (International Student Identity Card; Ⓦwww.isiccard.com). If you're planning to visit a great many museums in a short time – on some kind of marathon museum binge – it might be worth buying the **Paris Museum Pass** (€30 two-day, €45 four-day, €60 six-day; Ⓦwww.parismuseumpass.fr). Available from the tourist office and participating museums, it's valid for 35 or so of the most important museums and monuments including the Louvre (but not special exhibitions) inside Paris, and allows you to bypass ticket queues (though not the security checkpoints).

Tickets and passes

For a short stay in the city, **carnets** of ten tickets can be bought from any station or *tabac* (€11.10, as opposed to €1.50 for an individual ticket). The city's integrated transport system, the RATP (ⓦ www.ratp.fr), is divided into **five zones**, and the métro system itself more or less fits into zones 1 and 2. The same tickets are valid for the buses (including the night bus), métro and, within the city limits and immediate suburbs (zones 1 and 2), the RER express rail lines, which also extend far out into the Île de France. Only one ticket is ever needed on the métro system, and within zones 1 and 2 for any RER or bus journey, but you can't switch between buses or between bus and métro/RER on the same ticket. For RER journeys beyond zones 1 and 2 you must buy an RER ticket. In order to get to La Défense on the RER rather than on the métro, for example, you need to buy a RER ticket, as La Défense is in zone 3. Children under 4 travel free and from ages 4 to 10 at half-price. Don't buy from the touts who hang round the main stations – you may pay well over the odds, quite often for a used ticket – and be sure to keep your ticket until the end of the journey as you'll be fined on the spot if you can't produce one.

If you're doing a fair number of journeys in one day, it might be worth getting a **Mobilis day pass** (€5.60 for zones 1 & 2; €7.50 zones 1–3), which offers unlimited access to the métro, buses and, depending on which zones you choose, the RER. Other possibilities are the **Paris Visite** passes (ⓦ www.ratp.fr/touristes/), one-, two-, three- and five-day visitors' passes at €8.50, €14, €19 and €27.50 for Paris and close suburbs, or €18, €27.50, €38.50 and €47 to include the airports, Versailles and Disney-land Paris (make sure you buy this one when you arrive at Roissy-Charles de Gaulle or Orly to get maximum value). A half-price child's version is also available. You can buy them from métro and RER stations, tourist offices and online from ⓦ www.allo-france .com. Paris Visite passes can begin on any day and entitle you to unlimited travel (in the zones you have chosen) on bus, métro, RER, SNCF and the Montmartre funicular; they also allow you discounts at certain monuments and museums.

signposted. Free métro and bus **maps** of varying sizes and detail are available at most stations, bus terminals and tourist offices: the largest and most useful is the *Grand Plan de Paris numéro 2*, which overlays the métro, RER and bus routes on a map of the city so you can see exactly how transport lines and streets match up. If you just want a handy pocket-sized métro/bus map ask for the *Petit Plan de Paris* or the smaller *Paris Plan de Poche*. You can also **download maps**, including a wallet-sized version of the métro map and a very useful searchable interactive online version of *Grand Plan de Paris numéro 2* at ⓦ www.ratp.fr.

The métro and RER

The métro, combined with the RER (Réseau Express Régional) suburban express lines, is the simplest way of getting around. The métro runs from 5.20am to 1.20am, RER trains from 4.45am to 1.30am. Stations (abbreviated: M° Concorde, RER Luxembourg, etc) are evenly spaced and you'll rarely find yourself more than 500m from one in the centre, though the interchanges can involve a lot of legwork, including many stairs. In addition to the free maps available (see above), every station has a big plan of the network outside the entrance and several inside, as well as a map of the local area. The lines are colour-coded and designated by numbers for the métro and by letters for the RER, although they are signposted within the system with the names of the terminus stations: for example, travelling from Montparnasse to Châtelet, you follow the sign "Direction Porte-de-Clignancourt"; from Gare d'Austerlitz to

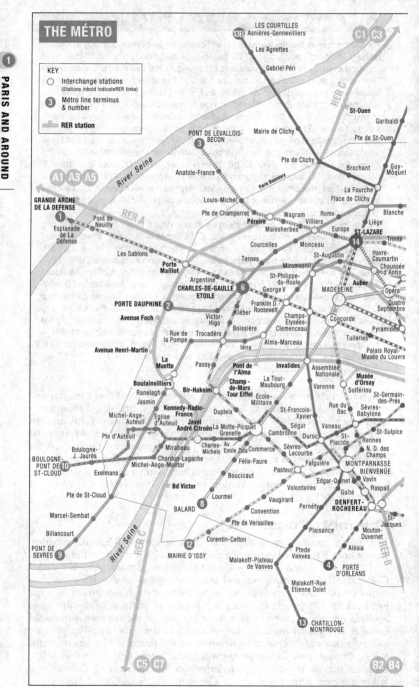

THE MÉTRO

KEY
○ Interchange stations
(Stations in bold indicate RER links)
❸ Métro line terminus & number
▨ RER station

LES COURTILLES
13B Asnières-Gennevilliers
Les Agnettes
Gabriel Péri
Mairie de Clichy

C1 C3

RER C

St-Ouen
Garibaldi
Pte de St-Ouen
Brochant
Guy-Môquet
La Fourche
Place de Clichy
Blanche
Liège
ST-LAZARE
Trinité

PONT DE LEVALLOIS-BECON
3
Anatole-France
Paris Boundary
Louis-Michel
Pte de Champerret
Wagram
Rome
Péreire
Villiers
Malesherbes
Europe
Courcelles
St-Augustin
Monceau
Ternes
Miromesnil
St-Philippe-du-Roule

A1 A3 A5

River Seine

RER A

GRANDE ARCHE DE LA DEFENSE
1
Esplanade de La Défense
Pont de Neuilly
Les Sablons
Porte Maillot
Argentine
CHARLES-DE-GAULLE ETOILE
6
George V
Franklin D.-Roosevelt
Champs-Elysées-Clemenceau
Concorde

Havre-Caumartin
Chaussée d'Antin
Auber
MADELEINE
Opéra
Quatre Septembre
Pyramides
Tuileries
Palais Royal-Musée du Louvre

PORTE DAUPHINE
2
Avenue Foch
Victor-Higo
Kléber
Boissière
Rue de la Pompe
Trocadéro
Iéna
Alma-Marceau

Avenue Henri-Martin
La Muette
Passy
Pont de l'Alma
Champ-de-Mars Tour Eiffel
La Tour-Maubourg
Invalides
Assemblée Nationale
Musée d'Orsay
Solférino
St-Germain-des-Prés

Boulainvilliers
Ranelagh
Jasmin
Bir-Hakeim
Dupleix
Ecole-Militaire
St-Francois-Xavier
Varenne
Rue du Bac
Sèvres-Babylone

Michel-Ange-Auteuil
Eglise d'Auteuil
Kennedy-Radio-France
Javel André Citroën
La Motte-Picquet Grenelle
Ségur
Cambronne
Duroc
Vaneau
St-Placide
St-Sulpice
Rennes
N. D. des Champs

Pte d'Auteuil
Mirabeau
Charles-Michels
Av. Emile Zola
Commerce
Sèvres-Lecourbe
Pasteur
Falguière
MONTPARNASSE BIENVENÜE

BOULOGNE-PONT DE ST-CLOUD
10
Boulogne-J. Jaurès
Chardon-Lagache
Michel-Ange-Molitor
Félix-Faure
Boucicaut
Volontaires
Edgar-Quinet
Gaîté
Vavin
Raspail

Exelmans
Bd Victor
Lourmel
Vaugirard
Pernéty
DENFERT-ROCHEREAU

Pte de St-Cloud
BALARD
8
Convention
Pte de Versailles
Plaisance
Mouton-Duvernet
St-Jacques

Marcel-Sembat
12
Corentin-Celton
MAIRIE D'ISSY
Ptede Vanves
Alésia

Billancourt
PONT DE SEVRES
9
River Seine
RER C
Malakoff-Plateau de Vanves
4
PORTE D'ORLEANS
RER B

Malakoff-Rue Etienne Dolet
13
CHATILLON-MONTROUGE

C5 C7
B2 B4

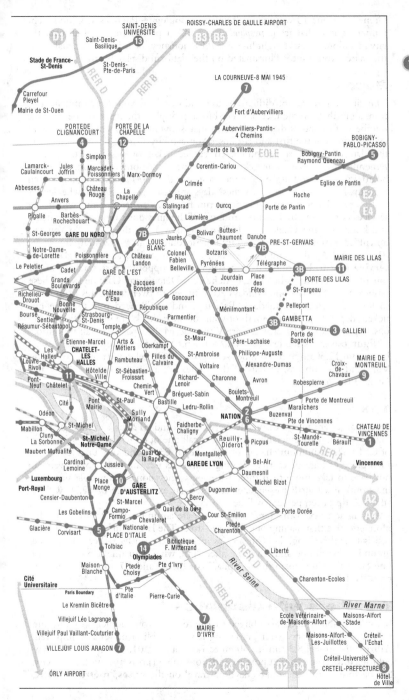

Grenelle on line 10 you follow "Direction Boulogne–Pont-de-St-Cloud". The numerous interchanges (*correspondances*) make it possible to travel all over the city in a more or less straight line. For RER journeys beyond the city, make sure the station you want is illuminated on the platform display board.

Buses

The city's buses are not difficult to use, and of course you do see much more from a bus than on the métro. Every bus stop displays the name of the stop, the numbers of the buses that stop there, a map showing all the stops on the route, and the times of the first and last buses. You can buy a single ticket (€1.50 from the driver), or use a pre-purchased carnet ticket or pass (see box, p.81); remember to validate your ticket by inserting it into one of the machines on board. Press the red button to request a stop and an *arrêt demandé* sign will then light up. More and more buses these days are easily accessible for wheelchairs and prams. Generally speaking, buses run from 5.30am to 8.30pm with some services continuing to 1.30am. Around half the lines don't operate on Sundays and holidays – the *Grand Plan de Paris* (see above) lists those that do. You can download a **map** of the most useful tourist routes from Ⓦ www.ratp.fr.

From mid-April to mid-September, a special orange-and-white **Balabus service** (not to be confused with Batobus, see opposite) passes all the major tourist sights between the Grande Arche de la Défense and Gare de Lyon. These buses run on Sundays and holidays every fifteen to twenty minutes from noon to 9pm. Bus stops are marked "Balabus", and you'll need one to three bus tickets, depending on the length of your journey: check the information at the bus stop or ask the driver. The Paris Visite and Mobilis passes are all valid too.

Night buses (Noctilien; Ⓦ www.noctilien.fr) ply forty routes at least every hour from 12.30am to 5.30am between place du Châtelet, west of the Hôtel de Ville, and the suburbs. Details of the routes are available online and on the Grand Plan de Paris.

Taxis

Taxi charges are fairly reasonable: between €7 and €12 for a central daytime journey, though considerably more if you call one out; there's a pick-up charge of €2.10. The minimum charge for a journey is €5.60, and you'll pay €0.90 for each piece of luggage carried. Waiting time costs €25 an hour. Taxi drivers do not have to take more than three passengers (they don't like people sitting in the front); if a fourth passenger is accepted, an extra charge of €2.70 will be added. A tip of ten percent will be expected.

Waiting at a **taxi rank** (*arrêt taxi* – there are around 470 of them) is usually more effective than hailing one from the street. The large white light signals the taxi is free; the orange light means it's in use. Taxis can be rather thin on the ground at lunchtime and any time after 7pm, when you might prefer to **call** one out – the three main firms, Alpha, Taxis Bleues and G7, can all be reached on ⓣ 01.45.30.30.30.

Travellers with disabilities

If you're disabled, **taxis** are obliged by law to carry you and help you into the vehicle – and to carry your guide dog if you are blind or visually impaired. **Aihrop** (Mon–Fri 8.30am–12.30pm & 1.30–6pm; ⓣ 01.41.29.01.29, Ⓦ www .aihrop.com) arranges transport to and from the airports and within the city, but be sure to call ahead. For daytime travel on the **buses**, **métro** or **RER**, the RATP offers accompanied journeys for disabled people not in wheelchairs (Les compagnons du voyage; ⓦwww.compagnons.com), which costs €15 an hour. You have to book on ☎01.58.76.08.53 at least a day in advance. Blind and visually impaired passengers can request a free companion from the volunteer organization Auxiliaires des Aveugles (☎01.43.06.39.68, ⓦwww .lesauxiliairesdesaveugles.asso.fr).

Métro line 14 and RER line E are currently the only lines fully accessible to **wheelchair** users; an increasing number of stations on other lines are accessible with assistance. The interactive map at ⓦwww.ratp.fr shows which ones. More extensive information, in French only, on getting around the city can be found on ⓦwww.infomobi.com.

Driving and parking

Travelling around Paris by **car** – in the daytime at least – is hardly worth it because of the difficulty of finding parking spaces. You're better off finding a motel-style place on the edge of the city and using public transport. But if you're determined to use the **pay-and-display** parking system you must first buy a *Paris Carte* (€10) from a *tabac*, then look for the blue "P" signs alongside grey parking meters. Put the card into the meter – in the centre you'll pay €3 an hour for a maximum of two hours. Covered car parks cost around €2.50 per hour. Whatever you do, don't park in a bus lane or the Axe Rouge **express routes** (marked with a red square). Should you be towed away, you'll find your car in the pound (*fourrière*) belonging to that particular arrondissement – check with the local *mairie* for the address. For more on car parks in Paris, see ⓦwww .parkingsdeparis.com.

In the event of a **breakdown** call SOS Dépannage (☎01.47.07.99.99) or Dan Dépann Auto (☎01.40.06.09.64) for round-the-clock assistance. Alternatively, ask the police. See p.172 for details of **car rental**.

Cycling

Parisians took enthusiastically to **Velib'** (ⓦwww.velib.paris.fr), the self-service bike scheme set up in 2007. More than 20,000 sleek, modern – and heavy – bicycles are stationed at some 1500 locations around the city; you simply pick one up at one rack, or *borne*, ride to your destination, and drop it off again.

Passes – one-day €1, weekly €5 – are sold from meters at each *borne*; plug in your credit card details (which will also secure a €150 deposit, not cashed unless you damage the bike). The first thirty minutes on top of the cost of the pass are free, but after that costs mount; €1 for the next half-hour, €3 for the next, and €4 for every further half hour. Helmets are not provided. There are between twelve and twenty bike stands at each *borne*, which are around 300m apart – so if the *borne* you come to is full, or empty, you shouldn't have too far to walk. Maps of the network are displayed at the *bornes*, and available to print in advance from the Velib' website. Incidentally, if you're caught running a red light while cycling in Paris, you'll be fined €100 on the spot.

Boats

One of the most enjoyable ways to get around Paris is on the Batobus (ⓦwww .batobus.com), which operates all year round, apart from January, stopping at eight points along the Seine, from the Eiffel Tower to the Jardin des Plantes. Boats run every 15–30 minutes (mid-Dec to Jan 10.30am–5pm; Feb to mid-March & mid-Nov to mid-Dec 10.30am–4.30pm; mid-March to May & Sept to mid-Nov 10am–7pm; June–Aug 10am–9.30pm). The total journey time from one end to the other is around thirty minutes and you can hop on and off as many times as you like – a day pass costs €12, two days €14 and five days €17 (there are no single tickets).

Accommodation

Paris has some two thousand hotels offering a wide range of comfort, price and location. Hotels in the budget and mid-range category **are reasonably priced** and cheaper than those in many other European capitals. By contrast, the city's four- and five-star hotels, some of them truly luxurious, are among Europe's most expensive. Smaller two-star hotels often charge between €60 and €90 (❸–❺) for a double room, though for something with a bit of style you'll probably have to pay upwards of €100 (❻), and €120 or more (❼) in swankier areas. It's possible to find a double room with a basin, in a decent central location, for around €45 (❷), and bargains exist in the 10ᵉ, especially around place de la République. You can also get good deals in quieter areas further out, in the 13ᵉ and 14ᵉ, south of Montparnasse, and the 17ᵉ, around Place de Clichy. Wherever you stay, and in whatever price range, don't be surprised if your room is knee- and head-bangingly small; and especially in the less expensive hotels don't take it for granted that there will be an elevator.

If you want to secure a really good room it's worth **booking** a couple of months or more in advance, as even the nicer hotels often leave their pokiest rooms at the back for last-minute reservations, and the best places will sell out

---

Boat trips

Most tourists are keen, rightly, to take a **boat trip** on the Seine. The faithful old Bateaux-Mouches is the best-known operator. Leaving from the Embarcadère du Pont de l'Alma on the Right Bank in the 8ᵉ (reservations and information ☏01.42.25.96.10; Mᵒ Alma-Marceau), the rides last 1hour 10 minutes, cost €10 (€5 for children and over-65s) and take you past the major Seine-side sights, such as Notre-Dame and the Louvre. From April to September boats leave every 45 minutes from 10.15am to 3.15pm, then every twenty minutes from 4 to 11pm; winter departures are less frequent. The night-time cruises use lights to illuminate the streetscapes that are so bright they almost blind passers-by – much more fun on board than off – and at all times a narration in several languages blares out. The outrageously priced lunch and dinner trips, for which "correct" dress is mandatory, are probably best avoided. Bateaux-Mouches has many competitors, all much of a muchness and detailed in *Pariscope* under "Croisières" in the "Promenades et Loisirs" section.

Another option, which takes you past less-visited sights, is to take a **canal boat trip** run by Canauxrama (ⓦwww.canauxrama.com; ☏01.42.39.15.00) on the Canal St-Martin in the east of the city. Departing daily at 9.45am and 2.30pm from the Bastille (Mᵒ Bastille, exit Opera), and, in high season only, at 9.45am and 2.45pm from the Bassin de la Villette (Mᵒ Jaurès), the ride lasts 2 hours 30 minutes and costs €15 (children €8); reservations are not always necessary. The **catamaran** Paris-Canal also plies the canal St-Martin, running two-and-a-half-hour trips between the Musée d'Orsay, quai Anatole-France, 7ᵉ (Mᵒ Solferino), and the Parc de la Villette, 19ᵉ ("Folie des Visites du Parc"; Mᵒ Porte-de-Pantin); boats operate in both directions daily from the end of March to mid-November, leaving the museum at 9.30am and the park at 2.30pm (reservations required; ☏01.42.40.96.97; ⓦwww.pariscanal.com, €17, children €10).

▲ The Seine

well in advance in all but the coldest months. If you find yourself stuck on arrival, the main **tourist office** at rue des Pyramides and the branches at the Gare de Lyon and Eiffel Tower will find you a room in a hotel or hostel free of charge. The tourist office also offers a free **online** reservation service (ⓦ www .paris-info.com), with discounts on some hotels.

Our hotel recommendations are divided by area (see map on pp.74–75). Hostels and student accommodation are listed separately on pp.91–92.

The Champs-Élysées and around

See map, pp.96–97.

Des Champs-Élysées 2 rue Artois, 8ᵉ ℡01.43.59.11.42, ⓦ www.champselysees-paris -hotel.com/; Mᵒ St-Philippe-du-Roule. The rooms at this two-star hotel are small but nicely decorated in warm reds and yellows and come with shower or bath, plus satellite TV, minibar, hairdryer and safe. Breakfast is served in a cool, relaxing converted stone cellar. Good value for the location, just off the Champs Élysées. ❻

De L'Élysée Faubourg Saint Honoré 12 rue des Saussaies, 8ᵉ ℡01.42.65.29.25, ⓦ www.france -hotel-guide.com/h75008efsh.htm; Mᵒ Champs-Élysées-Clemenceau. This comfy three-star, a mere chandelier swing from the Élysée Palace, has sixty rooms decorated in traditional style, with *toile de jouy* wallpaper, solid mahogany furniture and jacquard bedspreads. ❽

Lancaster 7 rue de Berri, 8ᵉ ℡01.40.76.40.76, ⓦ www.hotel-lancaster.fr; Mᵒ George-V. Once the pied-à-terre for the likes of Garbo, Dietrich and Sir Alec Guinness, this elegantly restored nineteenth-century town house is still a favourite hide-out today for those fleeing the paparazzi. The rooms retain original features and are chock-full of Louis XVI and rococo antiques, but with a touch of contemporary chic. To top it all off, there's a Michelin-starred restaurant and zen-style interior garden. Doubles start at €490. ❾

De Sers 41 av Pierre 1ᵉʳ Serbie, 8ᵉ ℡01.53.23.75.75, ⓦ www.hoteldesers.com; Mᵒ George-V. A seriously chic boutique hotel, just off the Champs Elysées, offering rooms in minimalist style, with rosewood furnishings and decor in white, grey, deep reds and pinks; facilities include CD/DVD player and huge TV. The two suites on the top floor have fabulous panoramic terraces. Doubles from €480. ❾

The Louvre and Tuileries

See map, pp.96–97.

Brighton 218 rue de Rivoli, 1er
☎01.47.03.61.61, ⓦwww.paris-hotel
-brighton.com; Mo Tuileries. An elegant hotel dating
back to the late nineteenth century and affording
magnificent views of the Tuileries gardens from the
front-facing rooms on the upper floors. The 65
rooms have recently been renovated, retaining
period charm and ambience. ⓭

Hôtel de Lille 8 rue du Pélican, 1er
☎01.42.33.33.42; Mo Palais-Royal-Musée-du-
Louvre. A small, old-fashioned budget hotel on a
quiet street, just a couple of blocks from the Louvre.
The rooms, some en suite, are very basic, decorated
with a nod to *belle époque* style. Non-en-suite
rooms have access to a shower on the landing for
an extra €2. There's no lift to serve the five floors,
and no breakfast, and the walls are rather thin. ⓭

Relais St-Honoré 308 rue St-Honoré, 1er
☎01.42.96.06.06, ⓦsainthonore.free.fr; Mo
Tuileries. A snug little hotel set in a stylishly
renovated seventeenth-century town house. The
pretty wood-beamed rooms are decorated in warm
colours and rich fabrics. Facilities include free
broadband internet access and flat-screen TVs. ⓭

Thérèse 5–7 rue Thérèse, 1er ☎01.42.96.10.01,
ⓦwww.hoteltherese.com; Mo Palais-Royal-Musée-
du-Louvre. A very attractive boutique hotel, set on
a quiet street within easy walking distance of the
Louvre. The small, contemporary-styled rooms are
decorated in soothing beige, pale greens or reds,
dark woods and prints, and equipped with marble
bathrooms. ⓭

Grands Boulevards and around

See map, pp.96–97.

Chopin 46 passage Jouffroy, entrance on bd
Montmartre, near rue du Faubourg-Montmartre,
9e ☎01.47.70.58.10, ⓦwww.bretonnerie.com;
Mo Grands-Boulevards. A lovely period building
hidden away at the end of an elegant *passage*,
with quiet and pleasantly furnished rooms,
though the cheaper ones are on the small side
and a little dark. ⓭

Mansart 5 rue des Capucines 1er
☎01.42.61.50.28, ⓦwww.paris-hotel-mansart
.com; Mo Opéra/Madeleine. This gracious hotel is
situated on the corner of place Vendôme, just a
stone's throw from the *Ritz*, but with rooms at a
fraction of the price, and while they're not quite in
the luxury bracket they're very agreeably decorated
in Louis XIV style, with plenty of antique furniture,
old prints and quality fabrics, and most are fairly
spacious by Parisian standards. ⓭

Vivienne 40 rue Vivienne, 2e
☎01.42.33.13.26, ⓔparis@hotel-vivienne
.com; Mo Grands-Boulevards. A 10min walk from
the Louvre, this is a friendly, family-run place, with
good-sized, cheery rooms and modern bathrooms
– a pretty good deal considering the location. ⓭

Beaubourg and Les Halles

See map, p.107.

Relais du Louvre 19 rue des Prêtres St-Germain
l'Auxerrois, 1er ☎01.40.41.96.42, ⓦwww.relais
dulouvre.com; Mo Palais-Royal-Musée-du-Louvre.
A small, discreet hotel set on a quiet back street
opposite the church of St-Germain l'Auxerrois. The
decor is traditional but not stuffy, with rich, quality
fabrics, old prints, Turkish rugs and solid furniture.
All rooms have cable TV and wi-fi access; the
cheaper ones are rather small. ⓭

De Roubaix 6 rue Greneta, 3e ☎01.42.72.89.91,
ⓦwww.hotel-de-roubaix.com; Mo Réaumur-Sébas-
topol or Mo Arts-et-Métiers. An old-fashioned two-
star hotel run by a pleasant elderly couple, who
don't speak much English. The 53 rooms are small
and done out with floral wallpaper and rickety
furniture, but they're pretty good value when you
consider the location, just 5min walk from the
Pompidou Centre. Breakfast – a hunk of crusty
bread and a hot drink – is included in the price
whether you want it or not. ⓭

Tiquetonne 6 rue Tiquetonne, 2e ☎01.42.36.94.58;
Mo Etienne-Marcel. Located on a characterful,
pedestrianized street a block away from
Montorgueil street market and around the corner
from the rue Saint Denis red light district, this
excellent-value budget hotel dates back to the
1920s and looks as though it's probably changed
little since. The simple rooms are well maintained,
many quite spacious, though walls are thin.
Non-en-suite rooms are equipped with a sink and
bidet. There are no TVs and breakfast is served in
your room. ⓭

The Marais, islands and Bastille

See map, pp.112–113.

Caron de Beaumarchais 12 rue Vieille-du-
Temple, 4e ☎01.42.72.34.12, ⓦwww
.carondebeaumarchais.com; Mo Hôtel-de-Ville. A
pretty boutique hotel, named after the eighteenth-
century French playwright Beaumarchais, who lived
just up the road. Everything – down to the original
engravings and Louis XVI-style furniture, not to
mention the pianoforte in the foyer – evokes the
refined tastes of high-society pre-Revolutionary
Paris. Rooms overlooking the courtyard are small

but cosy, while those on the street are more spacious, some with a balcony. **7**

Grand Hôtel du Loiret 8 rue des Mauvais Garçons, 4ᵉ ☎01.48.87.77.00, ☻www.hotel-loiret .fr; Mᵒ Hôtel-de-Ville. A budget hotel, grand in name only. The rooms are essentially uneventful, but acceptable for the price; cheaper ones have washbasin only, all have TV and telephone. **3**

De Lutèce 65 rue St-Louis-en-l'Île, 4ᵉ ☎01.43.26.23.52, ☻www.paris-hotel-lutece.com; Mᵒ Pont-Mairie. Twenty-three tiny but appealing rooms, decorated in contemporary style and equipped with sparkling-white bathrooms, are eked out of this old wood-beamed town house situated on the most desirable island in France. **6**

Marais Bastille 36 bd Richard-Lenoir, 11ᵉ ☎01.48.05.75.00, ☻www.paris-hotel-marais -bastille.com; Mᵒ Bréguet-Sabin. A pleasant three-star, part of the Best Western chain, located on a fairly quiet road near the Bastille. Rooms are equipped with minibar, TV and internet point and are attractively furnished in light oak and pastel colours. **7**

Pavillon de la Reine 28 place des Vosges, 3ᵉ ☎01.40.29.19.19, ☻www.pavillon-de-la-reine .com; Mᵒ Bastille. A perfect honeymoon or romantic-weekend hotel in a beautiful ivy-covered mansion secreted away off the place des Vosges. It preserves an intimate ambience, with friendly, personable staff. The rooms mostly have a distinctly 1990s "hip hotel" feel, and could probably use another makeover. Doubles from €370. **9**

Du Petit Moulin 29–31 rue du Poitou, 3ᵉ ☎01.42.74.10.10, ☻www.paris-hotel-petitmoulin .com; Mᵒ Saint-Sébastien-Froissart/Filles du Calvaire. An ultra-stylish boutique hotel, set in an old bakery and designed top to bottom by Christian Lacroix. Each room bears the designer's hallmark flamboyancy and is a fusion of different styles, from elegant Baroque to Sixties kitsch. **9**

Hôtel St-Louis Marais 1 rue Charles-V, 4ᵉ ☎01.48.87.87.04, ☻www.saintlouismarais .com; Mᵒ Sully-Morland. Formerly part of the seventeenth-century Célestins Convent, this characterful place retains its period feel, with stone walls, exposed beams and tiled floors. Rooms are cosily done out with terracotta-coloured fabrics and old maps of Paris, and have wi-fi access. A major plus is its location on a very quiet road, just a short walk from all the Marais action further north, and the Left Bank is easily reached over the Pont de Sully. The cheaper rooms are very small. **7**

Sévigné 2 rue Malher, 4ᵉ ☎01.42.72.76.17, ☻www.le-sevigne.com; Mᵒ St-Paul. A pleasant family-run hotel set in a narrow town house, with small, simple rooms in shades of pale yellow and red, and modern tiled bathrooms. Double glazing

helps muffle the traffic noise from nearby rue de Rivoli. Good value for the area. **5**

Quartier Latin

See map, pp.118–119.

See map, pp.118–119.

Le Central 6 rue Descartes, 5ᵉ ☎01.46.33.57.93; Mᵒ Maubert-Mutualité/Cardinal-Lemoine. Tiny, classic backpacker place: shabbily furnished, in a typically Parisian house above a café on a little square, run rather sleepily by an on-site couple. The double rooms facing the street are good value – avoid the sombre rooms on the internal courtyard. Most are singles (€36); you'll need to book months in advance for a double. **2**

Du Commerce 14 rue de la Montagne-Ste-Geneviève, 5ᵉ ☎01.43.54.89.69, ☻www .commerce-paris-hotel.com; Mᵒ Maubert-Mutualité. Business-like budget hotel with a range of rooms from washbasin-only cheapies (€49, €39 for one person) up to modern en suites (€70) and family rooms (€70–100). The communal kitchen and dining area are handy, there's free internet access, and the location is excellent. No credit cards. **3–6**

Esmeralda 4 rue St-Julien-le-Pauvre, 5ᵉ ☎01.43.54.19.20, ☎01.40.51.00.68; Mᵒ St-Michel/Maubert-Mutualité. Right next to Shakespeare and Co (see p.168) in a seventeenth-century house on square Viviani, this rickety hotel offers cosily unmodernized en-suite rooms – some are done up in faded red velvet. The priciest have superb views of Notre-Dame (€95), and there are a few very basic washbasin-only singles (€35). **5**

Des Grandes Écoles 75 rue du Cardinal-Lemoine, 5ᵉ ☎01.43.26.79.23, ☻www .hotel-grandes-ecoles.com; Mᵒ Cardinal-Lemoine. Follow the cobbled alleyway to a large, peaceful garden – in the heart of the *quartier* – and this welcoming, tranquil hotel with its modest, pretty and old-fashioned rooms. Reservations are taken three and a half months in advance. **6**

Marignan 13 rue du Sommerard, 5ᵉ ☎01.43.54.63.81, ☻www.hotel-marignan.com; Mᵒ Maubert-Mutualité. Great value place, totally sympa-thetic to the needs of rucksack-toting foreigners, with free wi-fi, laundry, ironing and kitchen facilities, a library of guidebooks – and rooms for up to five people. The cheapest have shares bathrooms with one other room. No credit cards. **4**

Select 1 place de la Sorbonne, 5ᵉ ☎01.46.34.14.80, ☻www.selecthotel.fr; Mᵒ Cluny-La Sorbonne. This designer-styled but un-snooty three-star sits right on the *place*. Standard doubles begin at €169, but it's probably worth paying the extra thirty-odd euros for a *supérieure*. **8**

St-Germain
See map, pp.124–125.

Delhy's 22 rue de l'Hirondelle, 6ᵉ
℡01.43.26.58.25; Mº St-Michel. The superb
location – in an old house on a pedestrianized lane
just off place St-Michel – is the big draw here;
rooms are clean but nothing special. Some come
with shower and TV; toilets are down the hall. ⑤
Ferrandi St-Germain 92 rue du Cherche-Midi, 6ᵉ
℡01.42.22.97.40, ⓦwww.hotel-ferrandi-paris
.com; Mº Vaneau/St-Placide. Genteel three-star
with a timeless feel, hidden away in a quiet street
but near the bustle of St-Germain. Rooms are
homely, and cost €140–190, depending on size.
Good deals available online. ⑦
Du Globe 15 rue des Quatre-Vents, 6ᵉ
℡01.43.26.35.50, ⓦwww.hotel-du-globe.fr;
Mº Odéon. Welcoming hotel in a tall, narrow, seventeenth-century building decked out with four-posters,
stone walls, roof beams and the like. Rooms can be
small, but aren't expensive for the location. ⑥
Grand Hôtel des Balcons 3 rue Casimir-Delavigne,
6ᵉ ℡01.46.34.78.50, ⓦwww.balcons.com;
Mº Odéon. Appealing, comfortable hotel with a few
Art Deco motifs in the modern rooms. Lovely location
near the Odéon and Luxembourg gardens. ⑥
Des Marronniers 21 rue Jacob, 6ᵉ
℡01.43.25.30.60, ⓦwww.hotel-marronniers.com;
Mº St-Germain-des-Prés. A romantic hotel, with
small rooms swathed in expensive fabrics. The
breakfast room gives onto a courtyard garden.
Online discounts. ⑧
Michelet-Odéon 6 place de l'Odéon, 6ᵉ
℡01.53.10.05.60, ⓦwww.hotelmicheletodeon.com;
Mº Odéon. €120 for a double is good value when
you're this close to the Jardin de Luxembourg –
rooms are largeish and with some style; those on the
corner facing the *place* are particularly attractive. ⑦
De Nesle 7 rue de Nesle, 6ᵉ ℡01.43.54.62.41,
ⓦwww.hoteldenesleparis.com; Mº St-Michel.
Offbeat, good-value and friendly hotel in a quiet
side street near Pont Neuf. The colourful rooms,
with historical or literary themes, are decorated
with wacky murals; some share bathrooms. ④
Relais Saint-Sulpice 3 rue Garancière, 6ᵉ
℡01.46.33.99.00, ⓦwww.relais-saint-sulpice.com;
Mº St-Sulpice/St-Germain-des-Prés. Set in an aristocratic town house immediately behind St-Sulpice's
apse, this is a discreetly classy hotel with well-
furnished rooms. Mod cons include a sauna. ⑧

Trocadéro, Eiffel Tower and the Septième
See map, pp.128–129.

Du Champs-de-Mars 7 rue du
Champs-de-Mars, 7ᵉ ℡01.45.51.52.30,
ⓦwww.hotelduchampdemars.com; Mº École-
Militaire. Cosy, colourful and excellent value rooms
in a friendly, well-run hotel. The neighbourhood is
great, too, just off the lively rue Cler market. ⑤
Eiffel Rive-Gauche 6 rue du Gros-Caillou, 7ᵉ
℡01.45.51.24.56, ⓦwww.hotel-eiffel.com;
Mº Ecole-Militaire. Traditional, family-run two-star
with decent rooms – those at the top have amazing
views of the Eiffel Tower. The street is dingy, but
there's a tiny, cheerful covered courtyard. ⑥
Du Palais Bourbon 49 rue de Bourgogne, 7ᵉ
℡01.44.11.30.70, ⓦwww.hotel-palais-bourbon
.com; Mº Varenne. This handsome old building in
the hushed, posh district near the Musée Rodin
offers spacious, comfortable accommodation,
including homely family rooms (€170), and simple
singles (€50), with a good breakfast included. ⑦
Saint Dominique 62 rue Saint-Dominique, 7ᵉ
℡01.47.05.51.44, ⓦwww.hotelstdominique.com;
Mº Invalides/La Tour-Maubourg. Welcoming hotel in
an upmarket, villagey neighbourhood near the Eiffel
Tower. Smallish but tastefully decorated rooms are
arranged around a bright little courtyard. ⑥

Montmartre and Northern Paris
See map, p.139.

Bonséjour Montmartre 11 rue Burq, 18ᵉ
℡01.42.54.22.53, ⓦwww.hotel-bonsejour
-montmartre.fr; Mº Abbesses. The location is a
dream – on a quiet untouristy street on the slopes of
Montmartre, footsteps away from great neighbourhood bars and restaurants – and the rooms, which
are basic, clean and spacious, are an unbelievable
bargain (with shower, WC down the hall). Those on
the corners have delightful balconies. ③
Caulaincourt Square 2 sq Caulaincourt, by 63 rue
Caulaincourt, 18ᵉ ℡01.46.06.46.06, ⓦwww
.caulaincourt.com; Mº Lamarck-Caulaincourt. You
can have shower-only or en-suite rooms at this
friendly budget hotel/hostel on the heights of
Montmartre. Dorm beds are €25 a night. Rooms are
small and faintly shabby but decent enough, and
breakfast is free. Free wi-fi; bike rental available. ③
Eldorado 18 rue des Dames, 17ᵉ
℡01.45.22.35.21, ⓦwww.eldoradohotel.fr;
Mº Place-de-Clichy. Idiosyncratic and enjoyable
Batignolles hotel with bright colour schemes, funky
furnishings, a wine bar and a lovely annexe at the
back of the courtyard garden. ④
Ermitage 24 rue Lamarck, 18ᵉ ℡01.42.64.79.22,
ⓦwww.ermitagesacrecoeur.fr; Mº Anvers. A
discreet, family-run hotel on the lofty heights
behind Sacré-Coeur. Rooms are old-fashioned in
the classic French manner; some have views out
across northern Paris. Free breakfast served in your

room. Approach via the *funiculaire* to avoid a steep climb. No credit cards. ⑤

Langlois 63 rue St-Lazare, 9ᵉ ☎01.48.74.78.24, ⓦwww.hotel-langlois.com; Mᵒ Trinité. Though it has all the facilities you'd expect of a two-star, this genteel hotel has barely changed in the last century, with antique furnishings and some unusually large, handsome rooms. ⑦

Perfect 39 rue Rodier, 9ᵉ ☎01.42.81.18.86, ⓕ01.42.85.01.38; Mᵒ Anvers. Popular budget hotel on a lively street lined with restaurants. Simple, well-kept rooms (with paper-thin walls) – some with shared bathroom – and a warm welcome. ①

Regyns Montmartre 13 place des Abbesses, 18ᵉ ☎01.42.54.45.21, ⓦwww.paris-hotels -montmartre.com; Mᵒ Abbesses. Friendly, tidy rooms with country-style decor, a number of which give onto the lively place des Abbesses. The more expensive top-floor rooms have grand views. Good online offers. ⑤

Style Hôtel 8 rue Ganneron (av Clichy end), 18ᵉ ☎01.45.22.37.59, ⓕ01.45.22.81.03; Mᵒ Place-de-Clichy. Wooden floors, marble fireplaces, a secluded internal courtyard, and very nice people. Great value, especially the rooms with shared bathrooms. ③

Eastern Paris

Beaumarchais 3 rue Oberkampf, 11ᵉ ☎01.43.38.16.16, ⓦwww.hotelbeaumarchais .com; Mᵒ Filles-du-Calvaire/Oberkampf. A fashionable, gay-friendly hotel with personal service and colourful 1950s-inspired decor; all rooms are en suite with a/c, individual safes and cable TV. ⑥

Mondia 22 rue du Grand Prieuré, 10ᵉ ☎01.47.00.93.44, ⓦwww.hotel-mondia.com; Mᵒ République/Oberkampf. The 23 rooms of this old-fashioned budget hotel are modestly furnished in pastel colours and floral prints; those facing the street on the fifth floor have little balconies, and the two attic hideaways (nos. 602 and 603) have a certain charm. For stays of three nights or more in quieter periods you'll get a ten-percent reduction on presentation of your Rough Guide. ⑤

De Nevers 53 rue de Malte, 11ᵉ ☎01.47.00.56.18, ⓦwww.hoteldenevers.com; Mᵒ République /Oberkampf. A hospitable budget hotel with very simple but cheerfully decorated rooms – the best are the en-suite doubles at the front; courtyard-facing rooms are dark and poky. ②

Southern Paris

De la Loire 39bis rue du Moulin Vert, 14ᵉ ☎01.45.40.66.88, ⓦwww.hoteldelaloire -paris.com; Mᵒ Pernety/Alésia. Behind the pretty blue shutters lies a delightful family hotel with a garden and a homely feel. Rooms all have charming personal touches and spotless bathrooms; a real bargain for Montparnasse. Free wi-fi. ③

Résidence Les Gobelins 9 rue des Gobelins, 13ᵉ ☎01.47.07.26.90, ⓦwww.hotelgobelins.com; Mᵒ Gobelins. Nicely old-fashioned and quiet place on a narrow street an easy walk away from the Quartier Latin's rue Mouffetard. Its large, simple, comfortable rooms are a well-known bargain, so book in advance. ⑤

Tolbiac 122 rue de Tolbiac, 13ᵉ ☎01.44.24.25.54, ⓦwww.hotel-tolbiac.com; Mᵒ Tolbiac/Place du Italie. Situated on a noisy junction, this big, friendly budget hotel has a bright colour scheme, free internet and wi-fi, and good prices. In July and Aug you can rent small studios by the week (€120 for two per week). ③

Le Vert-Galant 41 rue Croulebarbe, 13ᵉ ☎01.44.08.83.50, ⓦwww.vertgalant.com; Mᵒ Gobelins. Set on a quiet, green square, with a large garden behind and the *Auberge Etchegorry* below (see p.156), this could be a family-run provincial hotel. Rooms are modern and pleasantly airy; the bigger ones give on to the garden and have kitchenettes. ⑤

Des Voyageurs 22 rue Boulard, 14ᵉ ☎01.43.21.08.20, ⓦhotelvoyageursparis.free.fr; Mᵒ Denfert-Rochereau. In a nice, old-fashioned Montparnasse street near rue Daguerre, this budget hotel has a warm spirit – paintings on the walls and cultural events on the back deck. Don't be put off by the grim exterior – rooms are comfortable and modern, with air conditioning, TV and free wi-fi. ③

Hostels and student accommodation

Paris is well supplied with **hostel** accommodation. You can book in advance for most hostels. In addition to the **Fédération Unie des Auberges de Jeunesse** (FUAJ; ⓦwww.fuaj.fr), for which you need Hostelling International (HI) membership (available on the spot, no age limit), and LFAJ (Ligue Française pour les Auberges de Jeunesse; ⓦwww.auberges-de-jeunesse.com), the smaller MIJE (Maison Internationale de la Jeunesse et des Étudiants; ⓦwww.mije.com), which runs three hostels in historic buildings in the Marais district, with dorm beds from €29. A handful of privately run hostels also exist, most of which cost upwards of €20, depending on season. Except where indicated below, there is no effective age limit.

If there are two of you and you don't want to sleep in a dorm, note that **double rooms**, where available, may not offer better value than Paris's cheaper hotels; unless you are particularly keen to stay in a hostel, you should compare prices with the budget hotels we've reviewed above. Most hostels impose a stay limit, which can be negotiable, depending on the season, and bear in mind, too, that some places have a curfew – usually around 11pm – though you may be given a key or entry code.

Student accommodation is let out during the summer vacation. Rooms are spartan, part of large modern university complexes, often complete with self-service kitchen facilities and shared bathrooms. Space tends to fill up quickly with international students, school groups and young travellers, so it's best to make plans well in advance. Expect to pay €15–30 per night for a room. The organization to contact for information and reservations is CROUS (ⓦ www.crous-paris.fr).

Hostels

BVJ Paris Louvre 20 rue Jean-Jacques-Rousseau, 1ᵉʳ ⓣ 01.53.00.90.90, ⓦ www.bvjhotel .com; Mᵒ Louvre/Châtelet-Les Halles; see map, pp.96–97. Clean, modern and efficiently run independent hostel for 18- to 35-year-olds. Bookings should be made by phone at least fifteen days prior to your stay. Accommodation ranges from single rooms to dorms sleeping eight. From €28 per person, including breakfast.

BVJ Paris Quartier Latin 44 rue des Bernardins, 5ᵉ ⓣ 01.43.29.34.80, ⓦ www.bvjhotel.com; Mᵒ Maubert-Mutualité; see map, pp.118–119. Typically institutional hostel, but spick and span and in a good location. Dorm beds (€28) and single rooms (€42) are good; for double rooms (€64) you can do better elsewhere.

Le Fauconnier 11 rue du Fauconnier, 4ᵉ ⓣ 01.42.74.23.45, ⓕ 01.40.27.81.64; Mᵒ St-Paul /Pont-Marie; see map, pp.112–113. A MIJE hostel in a superbly renovated seventeenth-century building with a courtyard. Dorms (€29 per person) sleep four to eight, and there are some single (€47) and double rooms (€34) with en-suite showers. Breakfast is included.

Le Fourcy 6 rue de Fourcy, 4ᵉ ⓣ 01.42.74.23.45; Mᵒ St-Paul; see map, pp.112–113. Another MIJE hostel (same prices as *Le Fauconnier*, above) housed in a beautiful mansion. This one has a small garden and an inexpensive restaurant. Doubles and triples are available as well as dorms.

Maubuisson 12 rue des Barres, 4ᵉ ⓣ 01.42.74.23.45; Mᵒ Pont-Marie/Hôtel-de-Ville; see map, pp.112–113. A MIJE hostel in a medieval timbered mansion on a quiet street. Accommodation is in dorms only, sleeping four (€29 per person). Breakfast is included.

Three Ducks Hostel 6 place Étienne-Pernet, 15ᵉ ⓣ 01.48.42.04.05, ⓦ www.3ducks.fr; Mᵒ Commerce/Félix-Faure. A private youth hostel with kitchen and internet facilities, a cheap bar and no age limit. In high season, beds cost €23 in dorms (four to eight people), and double rooms cost €54; there are discounts in winter. Book ahead between May and Oct. Lockout noon–4pm, curfew at 2am.

Le Village Hostel 20 rue d'Orsel, 18ᵉ ⓣ 01.42.64.22.02, ⓦ www.villagehostel.fr; Mᵒ Anvers; see map, p.139. Attractive hostel in a handsome old building, with good facilities such as phones in the rooms. There's a view of Sacré-Coeur from the terrace. Dorms cost €24, doubles €30 and triples €27 per person, including breakfast. Small discounts in winter.

Woodstock Hostel 48 rue Rodier, 9ᵉ ⓣ 01.48.78.87.76, ⓦ www.woodstock.fr; Mᵒ Anvers/St-Georges; see map, p.139. A reliable hostel in the *Three Ducks* stable, with its own bar, set in a great location on a pretty street not far from Montmartre. Dorm beds €19–22, twin rooms €22–25 per person, breakfast included. Book ahead.

Young and Happy Hostel 80 rue Mouffetard, 5ᵉ ⓣ 01.47.07.47.07, ⓦ www.youngandhappy.fr; Mᵒ Monge/Censier-Daubenton; see map, pp.118–119. Noisy, basic and studenty independent hostel in a lively, touristy location. Dorms, with shower, sleep four (€23 per person), and there are a few doubles (€26 per person). Curfew at 2am; lockout 11am–4pm.

The City

Rather than slavishly following the boundaries of the official twenty arrondissements (see map pp.74–75), this book divides Paris into several quarters, each with their own distinct identities. The account begins with the **Île de la Cité**, the ancient heart of Paris and home of the cathedral of **Notre-Dame**. Heading north onto the **Right Bank**, we take in the Arc de Triomphe and follow the Voie Triomphale through the glamorous **Champs-Élysées** area to the Louvre palace. Immediately north is the expensive **Opéra district**, home of the shopping arcades of the *passages*, ritzy Place Vendôme and the tranquil gardens of the Palais Royal. East, the bustle and tacky shops of **Les Halles** and **Beaubourg** give way to the aristocratic and fashionable **Marais** and still-trendier **Bastille** quarters. Detouring via the Île St-Louis, Paris's second island, we cross the Seine onto the (southern) **Left Bank**, moving west from the studenty **Quartier Latin** through elegant and international **St-Germain** and into the aristocratic, museum-rich area around the **Eiffel Tower**, taking in the **Trocadéro** quarter, immediately across the river. We then explore outlying areas of the city, visiting first **Montparnasse** and southern Paris, then heading out west to the wealthy **Beaux Quartiers**, the green space of the Bois de Boulogne and the outlying business district of La Défense. Lastly, we move up to **Montmartre** and the northern arrondissements before finishing in the grittier eastern end of the city, which incorporates the vast Père-Lachaise cemetery.

Île de la Cité

The **Île de la Cité** is where Paris began. The earliest settlements were built here, followed by the small Gallic town of Lutetia, overrun by Julius Caesar's troops in 52 BC. A natural defensive site commanding a major east–west river trade route, it was an obvious candidate for a bright future. In 508 it became the stronghold of the Merovingian kings, then of the counts of Paris, who in 987 became kings of France.

The Frankish kings built themselves a splendid palace at the western tip of the island, of which the **Sainte-Chapelle** and **Conciergerie** survive today. At the other end of the island, they erected the great cathedral of **Notre-Dame**. By the early thirteenth century this tiny island had become the bustling heart of the capital, accommodating twelve parishes, not to mention numerous chapels and convents. It's hard to imagine this today: virtually the whole medieval city was erased by heavy-handed nineteenth-century demolition and much of it replaced by four vast edifices largely given over to housing the law. The warren of narrow streets around the cathedral was swept away and replaced with a huge, rather soulless square, but it does at least afford uncluttered views of the cathedral.

Pont-Neuf and the quais, Sainte-Chapelle and the Conciergerie

One of the most popular approaches to the island is via the graceful, twelve-arched **Pont-Neuf**, which despite its name is Paris's oldest surviving bridge, built in 1607 by Henri IV. It takes its name ("new") from the fact that it was the first in the city to be built of stone. Henri is commemorated with an equestrian statue halfway across, and also lends his nickname to the **square du Vert-Galant**, enclosed within the triangular stern of the island and reached via steps leading down behind the statue. "Vert-Galant", meaning a "green" or "lusty gentleman", is a reference to Henri's legendary amorous exploits, and he would no doubt have approved of this tranquil, tree-lined garden, a popular haunt of lovers.

Back on Pont-Neuf, opposite the square du Vert-Galant, red-bricked seventeenth-century houses flank the entrance to **place Dauphine**, one of the city's most appealing squares. Traffic noise recedes in favour of the gentle tap of *boules* being played in the shade of the chestnuts. At the further end looms the huge facade of the **Palais de Justice**, which swallowed up the palace that was home to the French kings until Étienne Marcel's bloody revolt in 1358 frightened them off to the greater security of the Louvre.

A survivor of the old palace complex is the magnificent **Sainte-Chapelle** (daily: March–Oct 9.30am–6pm; Nov–Feb 9am–5pm; €7.50, combined admission to the Conciergerie €10; M° Cité), accessed from the boulevard du Palais. It was built by Louis IX between 1242 and 1248 to house a collection of holy relics, including Christ's crown of thorns and a fragment of the True Cross, bought at extortionate rates from the bankrupt empire of Byzantium. Though much restored, the chapel remains one of the finest achievements of French High Gothic. Its most radical feature is its seeming fragility – created by reducing the structural masonry to a minimum to make way for a huge expanse of exquisite stained glass. The impression inside is of being enclosed within the wings of a myriad brilliant butterflies.

Further along boulevard du Palais is the entrance to the **Conciergerie** (same hours as Sainte-Chapelle; €6.50, combined ticket with Ste-Chapelle €10; M° Cité), Paris's oldest prison, where Marie-Antoinette and, in their turn, the leading figures of the Revolution were incarcerated before execution. Inside are several splendidly vaulted late-Gothic halls, vestiges of the old Capetian kings' palace. The most impressive is the Salle des Gens d'armes, originally the canteen and recreation room of the royal household staff. A number of rooms and prisoners' cells, including Marie-Antoinette's, have been reconstructed to show what they might have been like at the time of the Revolution.

Heading east from here, along the north side of the island, you come to **place Lépine**, named after the police boss who gave Paris's cops their white truncheons and whistles. The old police headquarters, better known as the Quai des Orfèvres to readers of Georges Simenon's Maigret novels, stands on one side of the square, while the other side is enlivened by an exuberant **flower market**, held daily and augmented by a chirruping bird market on Sundays.

Cathédrale de Notre-Dame

One of the masterpieces of the Gothic age, the **Cathédrale de Notre-Dame** (daily 7.45am–6.45pm; free; M° St-Michel/Cité) rears up from the Île de la Cité's southeast corner like a ship moored by huge flying buttresses. It was among the first of the great Gothic cathedrals built in northern France and one of the most ambitious, its nave reaching an unprecedented 33m.

Built on the site of the old Merovingian cathedral of Saint-Étienne, Notre-Dame was begun in 1160 under the auspices of Bishop de Sully and completed around 1345. In the seventeenth and eighteenth centuries it fell into decline, suffering its worst depredations during the French Revolution when the frieze of Old Testament kings on the facade was damaged by enthusiasts who mistook them for the kings of France. It was only in the 1820s that the cathedral was at last given a much-needed restoration, a task entrusted to the great architect-restorer, Viollet-le-Duc, who carried out a thorough – some would say too thorough – renovation, including remaking most of the statuary on the facade (the originals can be seen in the Musée National du Moyen Âge, see p.120) – and adding the steeple and baleful-looking gargoyles, which you can see close up if you brave the ascent of the **towers** (daily: April–Sept 10am–6.30pm, till 11pm Sat & Sun June–Aug; Oct–March 10am–5.30pm; €7.50). Queues for the towers often start before they open, so it pays to get here early or to come in the evening, when it's often quieter. The same goes for visiting the cathedral itself.

The cathedral's **facade** is one of its most impressive exterior features; the Romanesque influence is still visible, not least in its solid H-shape, but the overriding impression is one of lightness and grace, created in part by the delicate filigree work of the central rose window and gallery above. Of the facade's magnificent **carvings**, the oldest, dating from the twelfth century, are those in the right portal, depicting the Virgin Enthroned, elegantly executed and displaying all the majesty of a royal procession.

The interior

Inside Notre-Dame, the immediately striking feature is the dramatic contrast between the darkness of the nave and the light falling on the first great clustered pillars of the choir. It's the end walls of the transepts that admit all this light: they are nearly two-thirds glass, including two magnificent rose windows coloured in imperial purple. These, the vaulting and the soaring columns are all definite Gothic elements, though there remains a strong sense of Romanesque in the stout round pillars of the nave. Free guided tours (1hr–1hr 30min) take place in English on Wednesdays and Thursdays at 2pm and on Saturdays at 2.30pm; the gathering point is the welcome desk near the entrance. There are free organ concerts every Sunday, usually at 4.30pm, plus four Masses on Sunday morning and one at 6.30pm.

The kilomètre zéro and crypte archéologique

On the pavement by the west door of the cathedral is a spot known as **kilomètre zéro**, the symbolic heart of France, from which all main road distances in the country are calculated. At the far end of the *place* is the entrance to the atmospheric **crypte archéologique** (Tues–Sun 10am–6pm; €3.30), a large excavated area under the square revealing the remains of the original cathedral, as well as remnants of the streets and houses that once clustered around Notre-Dame: most are medieval, but some date as far back as Gallo-Roman times and include parts of a Roman hypocaust (heating system).

Le Mémorial de la Déportation

At the eastern tip of the island is the symbolic tomb of the 200,000 French who died in Nazi concentration camps during World War II – Resistance fighters, Jews and forced labourers among them. The stark and moving **Mémorial de la Déportation** (daily 10am–noon & 2–7pm, closes 5pm in winter; free) is scarcely visible above ground; stairs hardly shoulder-wide descend into a space like a prison yard and then into the crypt, off which is a long, narrow, stifling corridor, its wall covered in thousands of points of light representing the dead. Floor and ceiling are black, and it ends in a raw hole, with a single naked bulb hanging in the middle. Above the exit are the words "Pardonne, n'oublie pas" ("Forgive, do not forget").

The Champs-Élysées and around

Synonymous with Parisian glitz and glamour, the **Champs-Élysées** cuts through one of the city's most exclusive districts, studded with luxury hotels and top fashion boutiques. The avenue forms part of a grand, nine-kilometre

THE CHAMPS-ÉLYSÉES & AROUND

CAFÉS & BARS

Angelina	10
L'Arbre à Cannelle	1
Bar Costes	7
Juveniles	5
Ladurée	12
Musée Jacquemart-André	4
Le Rubis	6
Verlet	9

RESTAURANTS

Gallopin	3
Aux Lyonnais	2
Pierre Gagnaire	11
Le Relais de l'Entrecôte	13
Taillevent	8

axis that extends from the Louvre, at the heart of the city, to the Grande Arche de la Défense, in the west. Often referred to as the Voie Triomphale, or Triumphal Way, it offers impressive vistas all along its length and incorporates some of the city's most famous landmarks – the **Tuileries** gardens, **place de la Concorde**, the **Champs-Élysées** avenue and the **Arc de Triomphe**. The whole ensemble is so regular and geometrical it looks as though it was laid out by a single town planner rather than by successive kings, emperors and presidents, all keen to add their stamp and promote French power and prestige.

The Arc de Triomphe

The best view of the Voie Triomphale is from the top of the **Arc de Triomphe** (daily: April–Sept 10am–11pm; Oct–March 10am–10.30pm; €9; Mº Charles-de-Gaulle-Étoile), towering above the traffic in the middle of **place Charles-de-Gaulle**, better known as l'Étoile ("star") on account of the twelve avenues radiating out from it. Access is via underground stairs from the north corner of the Champs-Élysées. The arch was started by Napoleon

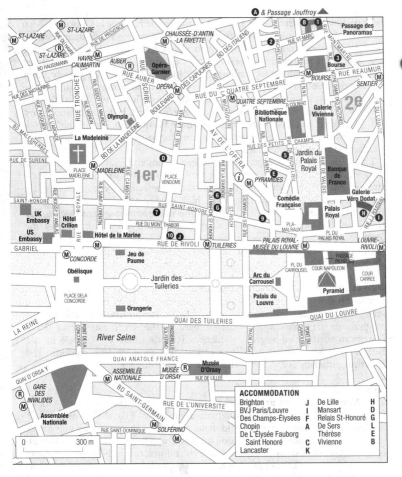

as a homage to the armies of France and himself, but it wasn't actually finished until 1836 by Louis-Philippe, who dedicated it to the French army in general. The names of 660 generals and numerous French battles are engraved on the inside of the arch, and reliefs adorn the exterior: the best is François Rude's extraordinarily dramatic *Marseillaise*, in which an Amazon-type figure personifying the Revolution charges forward with a sword, her face contorted in a fierce rallying cry. A quiet reminder of the less glorious side of war is the **tomb of the unknown soldier** placed beneath the arch and marked by an eternal flame that is stoked up every evening at 6.30pm by war veterans. If you're up for climbing the 280 steps to the top you'll be amply rewarded by the panoramic views; the best time to come is towards dusk on a sunny day, when the marble of the Grande Arche de la Défense sparkles in the setting sun and the Louvre is bathed in warm light.

The Champs-Élysées

The celebrated **avenue des Champs-Élysées**, a popular rallying point at times of national crisis and the scene of big military parades on Bastille Day, sweeps down from the Arc de Triomphe towards the place de la Concorde. Seen from a distance it's an impressive sight, but close up can be a little disappointing, with its constant stream of traffic, fast-food outlets and chain stores. Over the last few years, however, it's been steadily regaining something of its former cachet as a chic address: top fashion stores have moved in, once dowdy shops such as the Publicis ad agency and the Renault car showroom have undergone stylish makeovers and acquired cool bar-restaurants, while new, fashionable cafés and restaurants in the streets around have injected fresh buzz and glamour. Just off the avenue, **rue Francois 1er** and **avenue Montaigne**, part of the "*triangle d'or*" (golden triangle), are home to the most exclusive names in fashion: Dior, Prada, Chanel and many others.

The Champs-Élysées began life as a leafy promenade, an extension of the Tuileries gardens. It was transformed into a fashionable thoroughfare during the Second Empire when members of the *haute bourgeoisie* built themselves splendid mansions along its length and high society would come to stroll and frequent the cafés and theatres. Most of the mansions subsequently gave way to office blocks and the *beau monde* moved elsewhere, but remnants of the avenue's glitzy heyday live on at the *Lido* cabaret, *Fouquet's* café-restaurant, the perfumier Guerlain's shop and the former *Claridges* hotel, now a swanky shopping arcade.

North of the Champs-Élysées

Just north of the Champs-Élysées are a number of *hôtels particuliers* housing select museums, the best of which is the **Musée Jacquemart-André**, with its magnificent art collection. North of here is the small and formal **Parc Monceau**, surrounded by grand residences. **Rue de Lévis** (a few blocks up rue Berger from Mº Monceau) has one of the city's most strident, colourful and appetizing markets every day of the week except Monday.

Musée Jacquemart-André

The **Musée Jacquemart-André** at 158 boulevard Haussmann, 8e (daily 10am–6pm; Ⓦwww.musee-jacquemart-andre.com; €10; Mº Miromesnil/ St-Philippe-du-Roule), is a splendid mansion laden with the outstanding works of art which its owners, banker Édouard André and his wife Nélie Jacquemart, collected on their extensive trips abroad. Free, informative audioguides (available in English) take you through sumptuous *salons*, mainly decorated in Louis XV and Louis XVI style, among them a room open to the floor above and surrounded by a carved wooden balcony from which musicians would have entertained guests at the glittering soirees that the Jacquemart-Andrés were renowned for. The pride of the couple's collection was their early Italian Renaissance paintings, on the upper floor. At the top of the stairs is a huge, animated fresco by Tiepolo depicting the French king Henri III being received by Frederigo Contarini in Venice. Other highlights are Uccello's *St George and the Dragon*, a haunting *Virgin and Child* by Mantegna, and another by Botticelli. An excellent way to finish off a visit is a reviving halt at the museum's **salon de thé**, with its lavish interior and ceiling frescoes by Tiepolo.

South of the Rond-Point des Champs-Élysées

The lower stretch of the Champs-Élysées, between the Rond-Point des Champs-Élysées and place de la Concorde, is bordered by chestnut trees and flowerbeds and is the most pleasant part of the avenue for a stroll. The gigantic Neoclassical building topped with a glass cupola that rises above the greenery to the south is the **Grand Palais** (Ⓦwww.grandpalais.fr), created with its neighbour, the Petit

Palais, for the 1900 Exposition Universelle. The cupola forms the centrepiece of the *nef* (nave), a huge, impressive exhibition space, used for large-scale installations, fashion shows and trade fairs. In the Grand Palais' north wing is the **Galeries nationales** (W www.rmn.fr/galeriesnationalesdugrandpalais), the city's prime venue for blockbuster art exhibitions.

The **Petit Palais**, facing the Grand Palais on avenue Winston-Churchill, is hardly "petit" but certainly palatial, boasting beautiful spiral wrought-iron staircases, stained-glass windows, ceiling frescoes and a grand gallery on the lines of Versailles' Hall of Mirrors. A recent revamp has freed up more space for the museum's extensive holdings of paintings, sculpture and decorative artworks, ranging from the ancient Greek and Roman period up to the early twentieth century. At first sight it looks like it's mopped up the leftovers after the other city's galleries have taken their pick, but there are some real gems here, such as Monet's *Sunset at Lavacourt* and Courbet's provocative *Young Ladies on the Bank of the Seine*.

On the other side of the avenue, to the north of place Clemenceau, combat police guard the high walls round the presidential **Palais de l'Élysée** and the line of ministries and embassies ending with the US in prime position on the corner of place de la Concorde. On Thursdays and at weekends you can see more national branding in the **postage-stamp market** at the corner of avenues Gabriel and Marigny.

Place de la Concorde and the Tuileries

At the lower end of the Champs is the vast **place de la Concorde**, where crazed traffic makes crossing over to the middle a death-defying task. As it happens, some 1300 people did die here between 1793 and 1795, beneath the Revolutionary guillotine – Louis XVI, Marie-Antoinette, Danton and Robespierre among them. The centrepiece of the square is a stunning gold-tipped **obelisk** from the temple of Luxor, offered as a favour-currying gesture by the viceroy of Egypt in 1829. From here there are sweeping vistas in all directions; the Champs-Élysées looks particularly impressive, and you can admire the alignment of the Assemblée Nationale in the south with the church of the Madeleine – sporting an identical Neoclassical facade – to the north.

The symmetry continues beyond place de la Concorde in the formal layout of the **Jardin des Tuileries**, the formal French garden *par excellence*. It dates back to the 1570s, when Catherine de Médicis had the site cleared of the medieval warren of tilemakers (*tuileries*) to make way for a palace and grounds. One hundred years later, Louis XIV commissioned renowned landscape artist Le Nôtre to redesign them and the results are largely what you see today: straight avenues, formal flowerbeds and splendid vistas. Shady tree-lined paths flank the grand central alley, and ornamental ponds frame both ends. The much-sought-after chairs strewn around the ponds are a good spot from which to admire the landscaped surroundings and contemplate the superb statues executed by the likes of Coustou and Coysevox, many of them now replaced by copies, the originals transferred to the Louvre.

The two buildings flanking the garden at the Concorde end are the **Jeu de Paume** (Tues noon–9pm, Wed–Fri noon–7pm, Sat & Sun 10am–7pm; W www .jeudepaume.org; €7; M° Concorde), by rue de Rivoli, once a royal tennis court and now a venue for major photographic exhibitions, and the **Orangerie**. Originally designed to protect the Tuileries' orange trees, the Orangerie (daily except Tues 9am–6pm; €7.50; W www.musee-orangerie.fr), an elegant Neoclassical-style building, now houses a private art collection including eight of Monet's giant water-lily paintings, vast, mesmerizing

▲ Jardin des Tuileries

canvases executed in the last years of the artist's life. On the lower floor of the museum is a fine collection of paintings by Monet's contemporaries. Highlights include a number of Cézanne still lifes, sensuous nudes by Renoir and vibrant landscapes by Derain.

The Louvre

The palace of the **Louvre** cuts a magnificent Classical swathe right through the centre of the city – a fitting setting for one of the world's grandest and most gracious art galleries. Originally little more than a feudal fortress, begun by Philippe-Auguste in the 1190s, the castle was enlarged by Charles V in the 1360s. However, it wasn't until 1546 that the first stones of the Louvre we see today were laid. Over the next century and a half, France's rulers continued to enlarge and aggrandize their palace without significantly altering its style, and the result is an architecturally harmonious building entirely suited to its role as the most historic of Parisian landmarks.

The origins of the Musée du Louvre lie in the personal art collection of François I. While the royal academy mounted exhibitions, known as salons, in the palace as early as 1725, the Louvre was only opened as an **art gallery** in 1793, the year of Louis XVI's execution. Within a decade, Napoleon's wagon-loads of war booty transformed the Louvre's art collection into the world's largest – and not all the loot has been returned.

Napoleon's pink marble Arc du Carrousel has always looked a bit out of place at the end of the main courtyard, but the emperor's nephew, Napoléon III, returned to form in the late nineteenth century, with the conservative courtyard facades of the Richelieu and Denon wings. It was only in 1989, when I.M. Pei's controversial **Pyramide** erupted from the centre of the Cour Napoléon like a visitor from another architectural planet, that the Louvre received its first radical makeover. Since then, the museum has palpably basked in its status as a truly first-class art gallery.

Quite separate from the Louvre proper, but still within the palace, are three museums under the aegis of **Les Arts Décoratifs**, dedicated to fashion and textiles, decorative arts and advertising. The entrance to the **Musée de la Mode et du Textile**, the **Musée des Arts Décoratifs** and the **Musée de la Publicité** can be found at 107 rue de Rivoli.

The Musée du Louvre

It's easy to be put off by tales of long queues outside the Pyramide, miles of foot-wearing corridors or multilingual jostles in front of the *Mona Lisa*, but there are ways around such hassles – you can use a back entrance, stop at one of the cafés or make for a less well-known section – and ultimately, the draw of the mighty collections of the **Musée du Louvre** is irresistible.

Orientation

From the Hall Napoléon under the **Pyramide**, stairs lead into each of the three wings: Denon (south), Richelieu (north) and Sully (east, around the giant quadrangle of the Cour Carré). Few visitors will be able to resist the allure of the *Mona Lisa*, in the **Denon** wing, housed along with the rest of the Louvre's Italian paintings and sculptures and its large-scale French nineteenth-century canvases. A relatively peaceful alternative would be to focus on the grand chronologies of French painting and sculpture, in the **Richelieu** wing. For a complete change of scene, descend to the **Medieval Louvre** section on the lower ground floor of Sully where you'll find the dramatic stump of Philippe-Auguste's keep and vestiges of Charles V's medieval palace walls.

A **floor plan**, available free from the information booth in the Hall Napoléon, will help you find your way around. It's wise not to attempt to see too much – even if you spent the entire day here you'd only see a fraction of the collection. The museum's size does at least make it easy to get away from the crowds – beyond the Denon wing you can explore the Louvre in relative peace. You can always step outside for a break, but three moderately expensive **cafés** are

Access and opening hours

The Pyramide is the main **entrance** to the Musée du Louvre, although the often lengthy lines can be avoided by using one of the alternative entrances: at the Porte des Lions, just east of the Pont Royal; at the Arc du Carrousel, at 99 rue de Rivoli; or directly from the métro station Palais Royal-Musée du Louvre (line 1 platform). If you've already got a ticket or a museum pass (see p.80) you can also enter from the passage Richelieu.

The permanent collection is open every day except Tuesday, from 9am to 6pm. On Wednesdays and Fridays, it stays open till 9.45pm – these **"nocturnes"** are an excellent time to visit. Note that almost a quarter of the museum's rooms are closed one day a week on a rotating basis, though the most popular rooms are always open. See ⓦ www.louvre.fr for details of current exhibitions. The **entry fee** is €9, reduced to €6 for the twice-weekly evening openings. Admission is free on the first Sunday of each month, and to under-18s at all times. Under-26s get in free on the Friday **nocturne**, ie after 6pm. Tickets can be bought in advance from branches of FNAC (see p.168) Virgin Megastore (conveniently, there's one right outside the entrance under the Arc du Carrousel) and the big Parisian department stores. All tickets allow you to leave and re-enter as many times as you like throughout the day.

enticing and open all day. *Café Richelieu* (first floor, Richelieu), elegant and relatively quiet, has a summer-only terrace, with views of the Pyramide. *Café Denon* (lower ground floor, Denon) is cosily romantic, while *Café Mollien* (first floor, Denon) has a summer terrace and some inexpensive snacks. The various cafés and restaurants under the Pyramide are mostly noisy and overpriced.

Antiquities

Oriental Antiquities covers the sculptures, stone-carved writings, pottery and other relics of the ancient Middle and Near East, including the Mesopotamian, Sumerian, Babylonian, Assyrian and Phoenician civilizations, plus the art of ancient Persia. The highlight of this section is the boldly sculpted stonework, much of it in relief. Watch out for the statues and busts depicting the young Sumerian prince Gudea, and the black, two-metre-high Code of Hammurabi, a hugely important find from the Mesopotamian civilization, dating from around 1800 BC. The utterly refined **Arts of Islam** collection is next door.

Egyptian Antiquities contains jewellery, domestic objects, sandals, sarcophagi and dozens of examples of the delicate naturalism of Egyptian decorative technique, such as the wall tiles depicting a piebald calf galloping through fields of papyrus, and a duck taking off from a marsh. Among the major exhibits are the Great Sphinx, carved from a single block of pink granite, the polychrome Seated Scribe statue, the striking, life-size wooden statue of Chancellor Nakhti, a bust of Amenophis IV and a low-relief sculpture of Sethi I and the goddess Hathor.

The collection of **Greek and Roman Antiquities**, mostly statues, is one of the finest in the world. The biggest crowd-pullers in the museum, after the *Mona Lisa*, are here: the *Winged Victory of Samothrace*, at the top of Denon's great staircase, and the *Venus de Milo*. Venus is surrounded by hordes of antecedent Aphrodites, from the graceful marble head known as the "Kaufmann Head" and the delightful *Venus of Arles* – both early copies of the work of the great sculptor Praxiteles – to the strange *Dame d'Auxerre*. In the Roman section a sterner style takes over, but there are some very attractive mosaics from Asia Minor and luminous frescoes from Pompeii and Herculaneum.

Sculpture

The **French Sculpture** section is arranged on the lowest two levels of the Richelieu wing, with the more monumental pieces housed in two grand, glass-roofed courtyards: the four triumphal *Marly Horses* grace the Cour Marly, while Cour Puget has Puget's dynamic *Milon de Crotone* as its centrepiece. The surrounding rooms trace the development of sculpture in France from painful Romanesque Crucifixions to the lofty public works of David d'Angers. The startlingly realistic Gothic pieces – notably the Burgundian *Tomb of Philippe Pot*, complete with hooded mourners – and the experimental Mannerist works are particularly rewarding, but towards the end of the course you may find yourself crying out for an end to all those gracefully perfect nudes and grandiose busts of noblemen. You'll have to leave the Louvre for Rodin, but an alternative antidote lies in the smaller, more intense **Italian and northern European** sections, on the lower two floors of Denon, where you'll find such bold masterpieces as two of Michelangelo's writhing *Slaves*, Duccio's virtuoso *Virgin and Child Surrounded by Angels*, and some severely Gothic Virgins from Flanders and Germany.

Objets d'Art

The vast **Objets d'Art** section, on the first floor of the Richelieu wing, presents the finest tapestries, ceramics, jewellery and furniture commissioned by France's wealthiest and most influential patrons. Walking through the entire 81-room chronology affords a powerful sense of the evolution of aesthetic taste at its most refined and opulent. The exception is the **Middle Ages** section, which is of a decidedly pious nature, while the apotheosis of the whole experience comes towards the end, as the circuit passes through the breathtakingly plush **apartments** of Napoléon III's Minister of State.

Painting

The largest section by far is **Painting**. A good place to start a tour of **French painting** is in the Sully wing with the master of French Classicism, Poussin; his profound themes, taken from antiquity, the Bible and mythology, together with his harmonious style, were to influence generations of artists. You'll need a healthy appetite for Classical grandeur in the next suite of rooms, with large-scale works by the likes of Lorrain, Le Brun and Rigaud. The more intimate paintings of Watteau come as a relief, followed by Chardin's intense still lifes and the inspired Rococo sketches by Fragonard known as the *Figures of Fantasy*. From the southern wing of Sully to the end of this section, the chilly wind of Neoclassicism blows through the paintings of Gros, Gérard, Prud'hon, David and Ingres, contrasting with the more sentimental style that begins with Greuze and continues into the Romanticism of Géricault and Delacroix. The final set of rooms takes in Millet, Corot and the Barbizon school of painting.

The nineteenth century is most dramatically represented in the second area of the Louvre devoted to painting, on the first floor of the Denon wing. A pair of giant rooms is dedicated to Nationalism and Romanticism, respectively, featuring some of France's best-known works including such gigantic, epic canvases as David's *Coronation of Napoleon in Notre Dame*, Géricault's *The Raft of the Medusa*, and Delacroix's *Liberty Leading the People*, the icon of nineteenth-century revolution.

Denon also houses the frankly staggering **Italian collection**. The high-ceilinged Salon Carré – which has been used to exhibit paintings since the first "salon" of the Royal Academy in 1725 – displays the so-called Primitives, with works by Giotto, Cimabue and Fra Angelico, as well as one of Uccello's bizarrely theoretical panels of the *Battle of San Romano*. To the west of the Salon, the famous Grande Galerie stretches into the distance, parading all the great names of the Italian Renaissance – Mantegna, Filippo Lippi, Leonardo da Vinci, Raphael, Coreggio, Titian. The playfully troubled Mannerists kick in about halfway along, but the second half of the Galerie dwindles in quality and representativeness as it moves towards the eighteenth century. Leonardo's *Mona Lisa*, along with Paolo Veronese's huge *Marriage at Cana*, hangs in the Salle des États, a room halfway along the Galerie between the two rooms of Nationalist and Romantic French art. If you want to catch *La Joconde* – as she's known to the French – without a swarm of admirers, go first or last thing in the day. At the far end of Denon, the relatively small but worthwhile **Spanish** collection has some notable Goya portraits.

The western end of Richelieu's second floor is given over to a more selective collection of **German**, **Flemish** and **Dutch** paintings, with a brilliant set of works by Rubens and twelve Rembrandts, including some powerful self-portraits. Interspersed throughout the painting section are rooms dedicated to the Louvre's impressive collection of **prints and drawings**, exhibited in rotation.

Les Arts Décoratifs

The westernmost wing of the Louvre palace houses a separate museum, **Les Arts Décoratifs** ("applied arts"; entrance at 107 rue de Rivoli; Tues–Fri

11am–6pm, Sat & Sun 10am–6pm; €8; www.lesartsdecoratifs.fr). The core of the collection is the recently revamped **Musée des Arts Décoratifs**, while the Musée de la Mode et du Textile and the Musée de la Publicité showcase fashion and advertising, respectively.

The eclectic collection of art objects and superbly crafted furnishing at the **Musée des Arts Décoratifs** certainly fits the "design" theme. The works in the "historical" rooms, running from the medieval period through to Art Deco and Art Nouveau, may seem humble in comparison with those in the Louvre's Objets d'Art section, but most of those here were made to be lived with or actually used, and feel more accessible as a result. There are curiously shaped and beautifully carved chairs, dressers and tables, religious paintings, Venetian glass and some wonderful tapestries. A number of "period rooms" have been reconstituted top-to-toe in the style of different eras, giving a powerful flavour of the ethos behind design trends, while separate galleries focus on jewellery and toys. Perhaps the most exciting part of the museum is the brand-new contemporary section, on the topmost floors, with rooms dedicated to each decade from the 1940s through to the present day. There are brilliant works by French, Italian and Japanese designers, including some great examples from the prince of French design, Philippe Starck.

The **Musée de la Mode et du Textile** holds high-quality exhibitions demonstrating the most brilliant and cutting edge of Paris fashions from all eras. Recent exhibitions have included Jean-Paul Gaultier's designs for the ballet choreographer Régine Chopinot. Immediately above, the **Musée de la Publicité** shows off its collection of advertising posters through cleverly themed, temporary exhibitions. Designed by the French über-architect Jean Nouvel, the space is appropriately trendy: half exposed brickwork and steel panelling, half crumbling Louvre finery. There's even a bar and a dozen computers from which you can freely access the archive.

The Opéra district

Between the Louvre and **boulevards Haussmann**, **Montmartre**, **Poissonnière** and **Bonne-Nouvelle** to the north lies the city's main **commercial and financial district**. Right at its heart stand the solid institutions of the Banque de France and the Bourse, while just to the north, beyond the glittering **Opéra-Garnier**, are the large department stores **Galeries Lafayette** and **Printemps**. More well-heeled shopping is concentrated on the rue **St-Honoré** in the west and the streets around aristocratic place Vendôme, lined with top couturiers, jewellers and art dealers. Scattered around the whole area are the delightful, secretive **passages** – nineteenth-century arcades that hark back to shopping from a different era.

The passages

Among the most attractive of the *passages* is the **Galerie Vivienne**, between rue Vivienne and rue des Petits-Champs, its decor of Grecian and marine motifs providing a suitably flamboyant backdrop for its smart shops, such as a branch of Jean-Paul Gaultier. But the most stylish examples are the three-storey **passage du Grand-Cerf**, between rue St-Denis and rue Dussoubs, and **Galerie Véro-Dodat**, between rue Croix-des-Petits-Champs and rue Jean-Jacques-Rousseau, named after the two pork butchers who set it up in 1824. This last is the most homogeneous and aristocratic *passage*, with painted ceilings and faux marble columns. North of rue St-Marc, the several arcades making up the **passage des Panoramas** are more workaday, although they do retain a great deal of character: there's an old brasserie with carved wood panelling (now a tea shop, *L'Arbre à Cannelle*, see p.149) and a printshop with its original 1867 fittings, as well as bric-a-brac shops, and stamp and secondhand postcard dealers. **Passage Jouffroy**, across boulevard Montmartre, harbours a number of quirky shops, including one selling antique walking sticks and another stocking exquisite dolls' house furniture.

The Madeleine and the Opéra-Garnier

Set back from the boulevard des Capucines and crowning the avenue de l'Opéra is the dazzling **Opéra-Garnier**, which was constructed from 1860 to 1875 as part of Napoléon III's new vision of Paris. The building's architect, Charles Garnier, whose golden bust by Carpeaux can be seen on the rue Auber side of his edifice, pulled out all the stops to provide a suitably grand space in which Second Empire high society could parade and be seen. The facade is a fabulous extravaganza of white, pink and green marble, colonnades, rearing horses, winged angels and niches holding gleaming gold busts of composers. You can look round the equally sumptuous **interior** (daily 10am–5pm; €8), including the plush auditorium – rehearsals permitting – the colourful ceiling of which is the work of Chagall, depicting scenes from well-known operas and ballets. The visit includes the **Bibliothèque-Musée de l'Opéra**, dedicated to the artists connected with the Opéra throughout its history, and containing model sets, dreadful nineteenth-century paintings and rather better temporary exhibitions on operatic themes.

West of the Opéra, occupying nearly the whole of the place de la Madeleine, the imperious-looking **Église de la Madeleine** is the parish church of the cream of Parisian high society. Modelled on a Greek classical temple, it's surrounded by 52 Corinthian columns and fronted by a huge pediment depicting the Last Judgement. Originally intended as a monument to Napoleon's army, it narrowly escaped being turned into a railway station before finally being consecrated to Mary Magdalene in 1845. Inside, a wonderfully theatrical sculpture, *Mary Magdalene Ascending to Heaven,* draws your eye to the high altar. In the half-dome above, a fresco entitled *The History of Christianity* commemorates the concordat signed between the church and the state after the Revolution and depicts all the major figures in Christendom, with Napoleon centre stage, naturally.

If the Madeleine caters to spiritual needs, the rest of the square is given over to nourishment of quite a different kind, for this is where Paris's top gourmet food stores Fauchon and Hédiard are located. Their remarkable displays are a feast for the eyes, and both have restaurants where you can sample some of their epicurean treats. On the east side of the Madeleine church is one of the city's oldest **flower markets** dating back to 1832, open every day except Monday while, nearby, some rather fine Art Nouveau public toilets are definitely worth inspecting.

Place Vendôme

A short walk east of the Madeleine along ancient rue St-Honoré, a preserve of top fashion designers and art galleries, lies **place Vendôme**, one of the city's most impressive set pieces. Built by Versailles' architect Hardouin-Mansart, it's a pleasingly symmetrical, eight-sided *place*, enclosed by a harmonious ensemble of elegant mansions, graced with Corinthian pilasters, *mascarons* and steeply pitched roofs. Once the grand residences of tax collectors and financiers, they now house such luxury establishments as the *Ritz* hotel, Cartier, Bulgari and other top-flight jewellers, lending the square a decidedly exclusive air. No. 12, now occupied by Chaumet jewellers, is where Chopin died in 1849.

Somewhat out of proportion with the rest of the square, the centrepiece is a towering triumphal **column**, surmounted by a statue of Napoleon dressed as Caesar, raised in 1806 to celebrate the Battle of Austerlitz – bronze reliefs of scenes of the battle, cast from 1200 recycled Austro-Russian cannons, spiral their way up the column.

The Palais Royal and Bibliothèque Nationale

At the eastern end of rue St-Honoré stands the handsome, colonnaded **Palais Royal**, built for Cardinal Richelieu in 1624, though much modified and renovated since. The current building houses various governmental bodies and the **Comédie Française**, a long-standing venue for the classics of French theatre. To its rear lie gardens lined with stately three-storey houses built over arcades housing quirky antique and designer shops. It's an attractive and peaceful oasis, with avenues of limes, fountains and flowerbeds. You'd hardly guess that this was a site of gambling dens, brothels and funfair attractions until the Grands Boulevards took up the baton in the 1830s. Folly, some might say, has returned in the form of Daniel Buren's art installation, which consists of black and white striped pillars, rather like sticks of Brighton rock, all of varying heights, dotted about the palace's main courtyard.

The gardens are a handy short cut from the rue de Rivoli to the **Bibliothèque Nationale** (Tues–Sat 10am–7pm, Sun noon–7pm; ⓦ www.bnf.fr) on the north side; you can enter free of charge and peer into the atmospheric reading rooms, though some look rather bereft, as many books have now been transferred to the new François Mitterrand site on the Left Bank. Visiting the library's temporary exhibitions (closed Mon) will give you access to the beautiful **Galerie Mazarine**, with its panelled ceilings painted by Romanelli (1617–62). It's also worth calling into the **Cabinet des Monnaies, Médailles et Antiques** (daily 1–5/6pm; free), a permanent display of coins and ancient treasures built up by successive kings from Philippe-Auguste onwards; Charlemagne's ivory chess set is a particular highlight.

Les Halles and around

Les Halles was the city's main food market for over eight hundred years. It was moved out to the suburbs in 1969, despite widespread opposition, and replaced by a large underground shopping and leisure complex, known as the Forum des Halles, and an RER/métro interchange. Unsightly, run down, even unsavoury in parts, the complex is now widely acknowledged as an architectural disaster – so much so that steps are under way to give it a major facelift. The French architect David Mangin, who won the competition to redevelop the site, plans to suspend a **vast glass roof** over the forum, allowing light to flood in, while also redesigning the gardens and creating a wide promenade on the model of Barcelona's Ramblas. Work is due to be completed by 2012.

The **Forum des Halles** centre stretches underground from the Bourse du Commerce rotunda to rue Pierre-Lescot and is spread over four levels. The overground section comprises aquarium-like arcades of shops, arranged around a sunken patio, and landscaped gardens. The shops are mostly devoted to high-street fashion and there's also a large FNAC bookshop and the Forum des Créateurs, an outlet for young fashion designers. It's not all commerce, however: there's scope for various diversions including swimming, billiards and movie-going.

Although little now remains of the former working-class quarter, you can still catch a flavour of the old Les Halles atmosphere in some of the surrounding bars and bistros and on the lively market street of **rue**

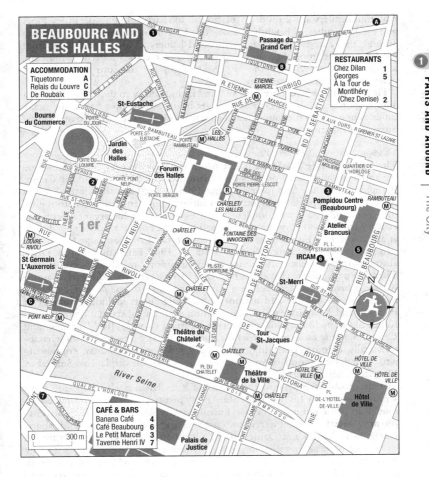

BEAUBOURG AND LES HALLES

ACCOMMODATION
Tiquetonne	A
Relais du Louvre	C
De Roubaix	B

RESTAURANTS
Chez Dilan	1
Georges	5
À la Tour de Montlhéry (Chez Denise)	2

CAFÉ & BARS
Banana Café	4
Café Beaubourg	6
Le Petit Marcel	3
Taverne Henri IV	7

0   300 m

Montorgueil to the north, where traditional grocers, horse butchers and fishmongers continue to ply their trade.

At the foot of rue Montorgueil stands another survivor from the past, the beautiful, gracefully buttressed church of **St-Eustache**. Built between 1532 and 1637, it's a glorious fusion of Gothic and Renaissance styles, with soaring vaults, Corinthian pilasters and arcades. It was the scene of Molière's baptism, and Rameau and Marivaux are buried here.

Centre Georges Pompidou

The **Centre Georges Pompidou** (aka Beaubourg; Ⓦ www.centrepompidou .fr; Mº Rambuteau/Hôtel-de-Ville), housing the Musée National d'Art Moderne, is one of the twentieth century's most radical buildings and its opening in 1977 gave rise to some violent reactions. Since then, however, it has won over critics and public alike, and has become one of the city's most recognizable landmarks. Architects Renzo Piano and Richard Rogers freed up maximum gallery space inside by placing all infrastructure outside: utility pipes and escalator tubes, all brightly colour-coded according to their function, climb around the exterior in crazy snakes-and-ladders fashion. The transparent escalator on the front of the building, giving access to the modern art museum, affords superb views over the city. Aside from the museum there are two cinemas, performance spaces and a library.

Tickets for the museum cost €10 and include entry to the Atelier Brancusi and temporary exhibitions. Under-18s get in free – pick up a pass at the ticket office. Admission to the museum and exhibitions is free for everyone on the first Sunday of the month.

Musée National d'Art Moderne

The superb **Musée National d'Art Moderne** (daily except Tues 11am–9pm; see above for admission) presides over the fourth and fifth floors of the Centre Pompidou, with the fifth floor covering 1905 to 1960 and the fourth 1960 to the present day. Thanks to an astute acquisitions policy and some generous gifts, the collection is a near-complete visual essay on the history of twentieth-century art and is so large that only a fraction of the 50,000 works are on display at any one time. The paintings are frequently rotated and rearranged.

In the section covering the years **1905 to 1960** Fauvism, Cubism, Dada, abstract art, Surrealism and abstract expressionism are all well represented. There's a particularly rich collection of Matisses, ranging from early Fauvist works to his late masterpieces – a stand-out is his *Tristesse du Roi*, a moving meditation on old age and memory. Other highlights include a number of Picasso's and Braque's early Cubist paintings and a substantial collection of Kandinskys, including his pioneering abstract works *Avec l'arc noir* and *Composition à la tache rouge*. A whole room is usually devoted to the characteristically colourful paintings of Robert and Sonia Delaunay, contrasting with the darker mood of more unsettling works on display by Surrealists Magritte, Dalí and Ernst.

In the post-1960s section the works of Yves Klein are perhaps the most arresting, especially his luminous blue "body prints", made by covering female models in paint and using them as human paintbrushes. Established **contemporary artists** you're likely to come across include Claes Oldenburg, Christian Boltanski and Daniel Buren. Christian Boltanski is known for his large *mise-en-scène* installations, often containing veiled allusions to the Holocaust. Daniel Buren's works are easy to spot: they all bear his trademark stripes, exactly 8.7cm in width. Some space is dedicated to **video art**, with changing installations by artists such as Jean-Luc Vilmout, Dominique Gonzalez-Foerster, the up-and-coming Melik Ohanian and current star of the scene Pierre Huyghe, who in 2006 had solo exhibitions at London's Tate Modern and Paris's Musée de l'Art Moderne de la Ville de Paris.

Atelier Brancusi

On the northern edge of the Pompidou Centre, down some steps off the sloping piazza, in a small separate one-level building, is the **Atelier Brancusi** (daily except Tues 2–6pm), the reconstructed home and studio of Constantin Brancusi. The sculptor bequeathed the contents of his workshop to the state on condition that the rooms be arranged exactly as he left them, and they provide a fascinating insight into how he lived and worked. Studios one and two are crowded with Brancusi's trademark abstract bird and column shapes in highly polished brass and marble, while studios three and four comprise the artist's private quarters.

Quartier Beaubourg and the Hôtel de Ville

The *quartier* around the Centre Pompidou, known as **Beaubourg**, is home to more contemporary art. Jean Tinguely and Niki de St-Phalle created the colourful moving sculptures and fountains in the pool in front of Église St-Merri on **place Igor Stravinsky**. This squirting waterworks pays homage to Stravinsky – each fountain corresponds to one of his compositions (*The Firebird*, *The Rite of Spring* and so on) – and shows scant respect for passers-by. On the west side of the square is the entrance to **IRCAM**, a research centre for contemporary music founded by the composer Pierre Boulez and an occasional venue for concerts; much of it is underground, with an overground extension by Renzo Piano. To the north are numerous commercial art galleries, occupying the attractive old *hôtels particuliers* on pedestrianized **rue Quincampoix**.

Heading back towards the river along rue Renard will bring you to the **Hôtel de Ville**, the seat of the city's government. It's a mansion of gargantuan proportions in florid neo-Renaissance style, modelled pretty much on the previous building burned down in the Commune. Those opposed to the establishments of kings and emperors created their alternative municipal governments on this spot in 1789, 1848 and 1870. But with the defeat of the Commune in 1871, the conservatives concluded that the Parisian municipal authority had to go if order was to be maintained and the working class kept in their place. Thereafter Paris was ruled directly by the ministry of the interior. Eventually, in 1977 the city was allowed to run its own affairs again and Jacques Chirac was elected mayor. In front of the Hôtel de Ville, the huge square – a notorious guillotine site in the French Revolution – becomes the location of a popular ice-skating rink from December to March.

The Marais, the Île St-Louis and the Bastille

Jack Kerouac translated **rue des Francs-Bourgeois**, the Marais' main east–west axis along with rue Rivoli/rue St-Antoine, as "street of the outspoken middle classes", though the original owners of the mansions lining its length would not have taken kindly to such a slight on their blue-bloodedness. The name's origin is medieval and actually means "people exempt from tax" in reference to the penurious inmates of an almshouse that stood on the site of no. 34. It was not until the sixteenth and seventeenth centuries that the **Marais**, as the area between the Pompidou Centre and the Bastille is known, became a fashionable aristocratic district. After the Revolution it was abandoned to the masses, who, up until some fifty years ago, were living ten to a room on unserviced, squalid streets. Since then, gentrification has proceeded apace and the middle classes are finally ensconced – mostly media, arty or gay, and definitely outspoken.

The renovated **mansions**, their grandeur concealed by the narrow streets, have become museums, libraries, offices and chic apartments, flanked by trendy fashion outlets, interior design shops and art galleries. Though cornered by Haussmann's boulevards, the Marais itself was spared the baron's heavy touch and has been left pretty much unspoilt. This is Paris at its most seductive – old, secluded, as lively by night as it is by day, and with as many alluring shops, bars and places to eat as you could wish for.

Rue des Francs-Bourgeois

Rue des Francs-Bourgeois begins with the eighteenth-century magnificence of the **Palais Soubise**, which houses the Archives Nationales de

France and the **Musée de l'Histoire de France**. The palace's fabulous rococo interiors are the setting for changing exhibitions (Mon & Wed–Fri 10am–12.30pm & 2–5.30pm, Sat & Sun 2–5.30pm; €3) drawn from the archives. The adjacent Hôtel de Rohan is also occasionally used for exhibitions from the archives and has more sumptuous interiors, notably the charming Chinese-inspired Cabinet des Singes, whose walls are painted with monkeys acting out various aristocratic scenes.

Further down the street are two of the grandest Marais *hôtels*, **Carnavalet** and **Lamoignon**, housing respectively the Musée Carnavalet and the Bibliothèque Historique de la Ville de Paris.

Musée Carnavalet

The **Musée Carnavalet**, whose entrance is off rue des Francs-Bourgeois at 23 rue de Sévigné (Tues–Sun 10am–6pm; free; M° St-Paul), presents the history of Paris from its origins up to the Belle Époque through an extraordinary collection of paintings, sculptures, decorative arts and archeological finds. The museum's setting in two beautiful Renaissance mansions, Hôtel Carnavalet and Hôtel Le Peletier, surrounded by attractive gardens, makes a visit worthwhile in itself. There are 140 rooms in all, with hardly a dull one among them. The **collection** begins with nineteenth- and early twentieth-century shop and inn signs (beautiful objects in themselves) and fascinating models of Paris through the ages. Other highlights on the ground floor include the renovated orangery, which houses a significant collection of Neolithic finds such as wooden pirogues which were unearthed during the 1990s redevelopment of the Bercy riverside area.

On the **first floor** is a succession of richly decorated Louis XV and Louis XVI salons and boudoirs rescued from buildings destroyed to make way for Haussmann's boulevards, and remounted here more or less intact. Rooms 128 to 148 are largely devoted to the *belle epoque*, evoked through vivid paintings of the period and some wonderful Art Nouveau interiors, among which is the sumptuous peacock-green interior designed by Alphonse Mucha for Fouquet's jewellery shop in the rue Royal. José-Maria Sert's Art Deco ballroom, with its extravagant gold-leaf decor and grand-scale paintings, including one of the Queen of Sheba with a train of elephants, is also well preserved. Nearby is a section on literary life at the beginning of the twentieth century, including a reconstruction of Proust's cork-lined bedroom. The **second floor** has rooms full of mementos of the **French Revolution**: models of the Bastille, the original *Declaration of the Rights of Man and the Citizen*, tricolours and liberty caps, sculpted allegories of Reason, crockery with Revolutionary slogans, models of the guillotine and execution orders to make you shed a tear for royalists as well as revolutionaries.

Musée Picasso

To the north of the rue des Francs-Bourgeois, at 5 rue de Thorigny, is the **Musée Picasso** (daily except Tues: April–Sept 9.30am–6pm; Oct–March 9.30am–5.30pm; €6.50; free first Sun of the month; ⓦ www.musee-picasso.fr; M° Filles du Calvaire/St-Paul), housed in the magnificent seventeenth-century Hôtel Salé. It's the largest collection of Picassos anywhere, representing almost all the major periods of the artist's life from 1905 onwards. Many of the works were owned by Picasso and on his death in 1973 were seized by the state in lieu of taxes owed. The result is an unedited body of work, which, although not including the most recognizable of Picasso's masterpieces, does provide a sense of the artist's development and an insight into the person behind the myth. In addition, the collection includes paintings Picasso bought or was given by contemporaries such as Matisse and Cézanne, his African masks and sculptures and photographs of him in his studio taken by Brassaï.

The **exhibition** starts with the artist's blue period, his experiments with Cubism and Surrealism, and moves on to his larger-scale works on themes of war and peace and his later preoccupations with love and death, reflected in his Minotaur and bullfighting paintings. Perhaps some of the most striking works on display are Picasso's more personal ones – those of his children, wives and lovers – such as *Olga Pensive* (1923), in which his first wife is shown lost in thought, the deep blue of her dress reflecting her mood. Portraits of later lovers, Dora Maar and Marie-Thérèse, show how the two women inspired Picasso in very different ways: Dora Maar is painted with strong lines and vibrant colours, suggesting a passionate, vivacious personality, while Marie-Thérèse's muted colours and soft contours convey serenity and peace.

The museum also holds a substantial number of Picasso's **engravings**, **ceramics** and **sculpture**, reflecting the remarkable ease with which the artist moved from one medium to another. Some of the most arresting sculptures are those he created from recycled household objects, such as the endearing *La Chèvre* (Goat), whose stomach is made from a basket, and *Tête de Taureau*, an ingenious pairing of a bicycle seat and handlebars.

The Jewish quarter

One block south of the rue des Francs-Bourgeois, the area around narrow **rue des Rosiers** has traditionally been the **Jewish quarter** of the city, though recent incursions by trendy fashion boutiques are threatening to change the character of the quarter. Some Jewish shops survive, however, especially falafel takeaways, testimony to the influence of the North African *Sephardim*, who replenished Paris's Jewish population, depleted when its *Ashkenazim* were rounded up by the Nazis and the French police and transported to the concentration camps.

That fate befell some of the inhabitants who once lived in the Hôtel de St-Aignan, at 71 rue de Temple, just northeast of the Centre Pompidou, now fittingly home to the **Musée d'Art et d'Histoire du Judaisme** (Mon–Fri 11am–6pm, Sun 10am–6pm; €6.80, ⓦ www.mahj.org; Mº Rambuteau), tracing the culture, history and artistic endeavours of the Jewish people from the Middle Ages to the present day. The focus is on the history of Jews in France, but there are also many artefacts from the rest of Europe and North Africa. Some of the most notable exhibits are a Gothic-style Hanukkah lamp, one of the very few French Jewish artefacts to survive from the period before the expulsion of the Jews from France in 1394; an Italian gilded circumcision chair from the seventeenth century; and a completely intact late nineteenth-century Austrian *sukkah*, a brightly painted wooden hut built as a temporary dwelling for the celebration of the harvest. Other artefacts include Moroccan wedding garments, highly decorated marriage contracts from eighteenth-century Modena and gorgeous, almost whimsical, spice containers. One room is devoted to the **Dreyfus affair**, documented with letters, postcards and press clippings. There's also a significant collection of paintings and sculpture by Jewish artists, such as Soutine and Chagall, who came to live in Paris at the beginning of the twentieth century. Events beyond the early twentieth century are taken up at the Mémorial de la Shoah's museum (see p.114).

Place des Vosges

A vast square of symmetrical pink brick and stone mansions built over arcades, the **place des Vosges**, at the eastern end of rue des Francs-Bourgeois, is a

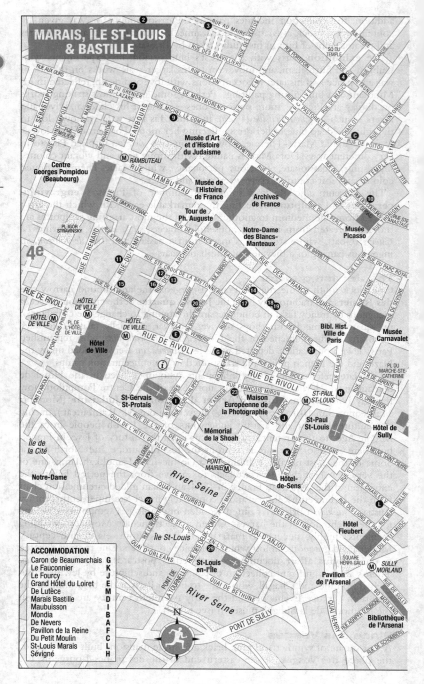

MARAIS, ÎLE ST-LOUIS & BASTILLE

4e

Île de la Cité

Notre-Dame

Centre Georges Pompidou (Beaubourg)

PL IGOR STRAVINSKY

Musée d'Art et d'Histoire du Judaisme

Musée de l'Histoire de France

Tour de Ph. Auguste

Notre-Dame des Blancs-Manteaux

Archives de France

Musée Picasso

Hôtel de Ville

Hôtel de Ville

St-Gervais St-Protais

Maison Européenne de la Photographie

Mémorial de la Shoah

Bibl. Hist. Ville de Paris

Musée Carnavalet

St-Paul St-Louis

Hôtel de Sully

Hôtel-de-Sens

Île St-Louis

St-Louis en-l'Île

Hôtel Fieubert

Pavillon de l'Arsenal

Bibliothèque de l'Arsenal

River Seine

PONT DE SULLY

PONT DE LA TOURNELLE

N

ACCOMMODATION

Caron de Beaumarchais	G
Le Fauconnier	K
Le Fourcy	J
Grand Hôtel du Loiret	E
De Lutèce	M
Marais Bastille	D
Maubuisson	I
Mondia	B
De Nevers	A
Pavillon de la Reine	F
Du Petit Moulin	C
St-Louis Marais	L
Sévigné	H

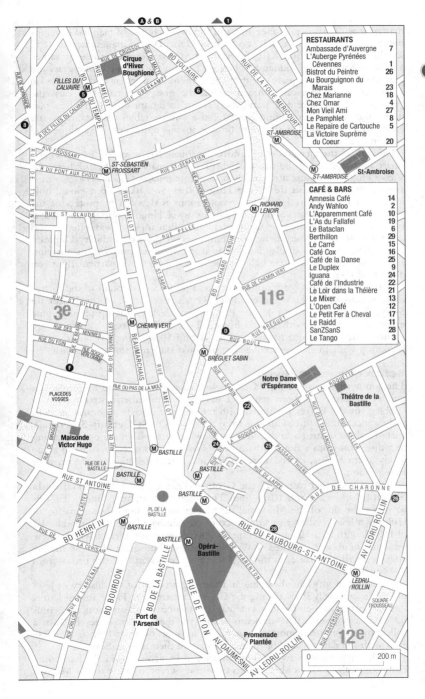

RESTAURANTS

Ambassade d'Auvergne	7
L'Auberge Pyrénées Cévennes	1
Bistrot du Peintre	26
Au Bourguignon du Marais	23
Chez Marianne	18
Chez Omar	4
Mon Vieil Ami	27
Le Pamphlet	8
Le Repaire de Cartouche	5
La Victoire Suprême du Coeur	20

CAFÉ & BARS

Amnesia Café	14
Andy Wahloo	2
L'Apparement Café	10
L'As du Fallafel	19
Le Bataclan	6
Berthillon	29
Le Carré	15
Café Cox	16
Café de la Danse	25
Le Duplex	9
Iguana	24
Café de l'Industrie	22
Le Loir dans la Théière	21
Le Mixer	13
L'Open Café	12
Le Petit Fer à Cheval	17
Le Raidd	11
SanZSanS	28
Le Tango	3

masterpiece of aristocratic elegance and the first example of planned development in the history of Paris. It was built by Henri IV and inaugurated in 1612 for the wedding of Louis XIII and Anne of Austria; Louis's statue – or, rather, a replica of it – stands hidden by chestnut trees in the middle of the grass and gravel gardens at the square's centre. The gardens are popular with families on weekends – children can run around on the grass (unusually for Paris the "pelouse" is not "interdite") and mess about in sandpits. Buskers often play under the arcades, serenading diners at the outside tables of restaurants and cafés, while well-heeled shoppers browse in the upmarket art, antique and fashion boutiques.

Through all the vicissitudes of history, the square has never lost its cachet as a smart address. Among the many celebrities who made their homes here was Victor Hugo: his house, at no. 6, where he wrote much of *Les Misérables*, is now a museum, the **Maison de Victor Hugo** (Tues–Sun 10am–6pm; closed hols; free; M° Chemin-Vert/Bastille); a whole room is devoted to posters of the various stage adaptations of his most famous novel. Hugo was multi-talented: as well as writing, he drew – many of his ink drawings are exhibited – and designed his own furniture; he even put together the extraordinary Chinese-style dining room on display here. That apart, the usual portraits, manuscripts and memorabilia shed sparse light on the man and his work, particularly if you don't read French.

From the southwest corner of the square, a door leads through to the formal château garden, orangery and exquisite Renaissance facade of the **Hôtel de Sully**, the sister site to the Jeu de Paume (see p.99). Changing photographic exhibitions, usually with social, historical or anthropological themes, are mounted here (Tues–Fri noon–7pm, Sat & Sun 10am–7pm; €5), and there's a bookshop with an extensive collection of books on Paris, some in English.

South of rue de Rivoli

The southern section of the Marais, below rues de Rivoli and St-Antoine, is quieter than the northern part and has some atmospheric streets, such as cobbled rue des Barres, perfumed with the scent of roses from nearby gardens and the occasional waft of incense from the church of **St-Gervais-St-Protais**, a late Gothic construction that looks somewhat battered on the outside owing to a direct hit from a Big Bertha howitzer in 1918. Its interior contains some lovely stained glass, carved misericords and a seventeenth-century organ – Paris's oldest.

One block further east, at 17 rue Geoffroy-l'Asnier, is the **Mémorial de la Shoah** (Mon–Fri & Sun 10am–6pm, Thurs until 10pm; free). Since 1956 this has been the site of the Mémorial du Martyr Juif Inconnu (Memorial to an Unknown Jewish Martyr), a sombre crypt containing a large black marble star of David, with a candle at its centre. In 2005 President Chirac opened a new museum here and unveiled a Wall of Names: four giant slabs of marble engraved with the names of the 76,000 French Jews sent to death camps from 1942 to 1944.

The museum gives an absorbing and moving account of the history of Jews in France, especially Paris, during the German occupation. There are last letters from deportees to their families, videotaped testimony from survivors, numerous ID cards and photos. The museum ends with the Mémorial des Enfants, a collection of photos, almost unbearable to look at, of 2500 French children, each with the date of their birth and the date of their deportation.

A little further east, between rues Fourcy and François-Miron, the handsome Hôtel Hénault de Cantoube, with its two-storey crypt, is home to the **Maison**

Européenne de la Photographie (Wed–Sun 11am–8pm; €6, free Wed after 5pm; ⓦ www.mep-fr.org; M° St-Paul/Pont-Marie) and hosts excellent exhibitions of contemporary photography; the entrance is at 5/7 rue du Fourcy.

The Île St-Louis

Often considered the most romantic part of Paris, the peaceful **Île St-Louis** is prime strolling territory. Unlike its larger neighbour, the Île de la Cité, the Île St-Louis has no heavyweight sights, just austerely handsome seventeenth-century houses on single-lane streets, tree-lined *quais*, a school, church, restaurants, cafés, interesting little shops, and the best sorbets in the world at *Berthillon*, 31 rue St-Louis-en-l'Île (see p.148). The island is particularly atmospheric in the evening, and an arm-in-arm wander along the *quais* is a must in any lover's itinerary.

Bastille

The landmark column topped with the gilded "Spirit of Liberty" on **place de la Bastille** was erected not to commemorate the surrender in 1789 of the prison – whose only visible remains have been transported to square Henri-Galli at the end of boulevard Henri-IV – but the July Revolution of 1830 that replaced the autocratic Charles X with the "Citizen King" Louis-Philippe. When Louis-Philippe fled in the more significant 1848 Revolution, his throne was burnt beside the column and a new inscription added. Four months later, the workers again took to the streets. All of eastern Paris was barricaded, with the fiercest fighting on rue du Faubourg-St-Antoine, until the rebellion was quelled with the usual massacres and deportation of survivors. However, it is the events of July 14, 1789, symbol of the end of feudalism in Europe, that France celebrates every year on Bastille Day.

The Bicentennial in 1989 was marked by the inauguration of the **Opéra-Bastille**, President Mitterrand's pet project. Filling almost the entire block between rues de Lyon, Charenton and Moreau, it has shifted the focus of place de la Bastille, so that the column is no longer the pivotal point; in fact, it's easy to miss it altogether when dazzled by the night-time glare of lights emanating from this "hippopotamus in a bathtub", as one critic dubbed the Opéra.

The building's construction destroyed no small amount of low-rent housing, but, as with most speculative developments, the pace of change is uneven, and cobblers and ironmongers still survive alongside cocktail haunts and sushi bars, making the **quartier de la Bastille** a simultaneously gritty and trendy quarter. **Place** and **rue d'Aligre**, east of square Trousseau, still have their raucous daily market and, on **rue de Lappe**, *Balajo* is one remnant of a very Parisian tradition: the *bals musettes*, or music halls of 1930s *gai Paris*, frequented between the wars by Piaf, Jean Gabin and Rita Hayworth. It was founded by one Jo de France, who introduced glitter and spectacle into what were then seedy gangster dives, and brought Parisians from the other side of the city to the rue de Lappe lowlife. Now the street is crammed with bars drawing a largely teen crowd. Bars and cafés have also sprung up in the surrounding streets, especially on rue de **Charonne**, also home to fashion boutiques and whacky interior designers, while alternative, hippy outfits cluster on **rues Keller** and **de la Roquette**.

Just south of here you can find quiet havens in the courtyards of **rue du Faubourg-St-Antoine**. Since the fifteenth century, this has been the principal artisan and working-class *quartier* of Paris, the cradle of revolutions and mother of street-fighters. From its beginnings the principal trade associated with it has been **furniture-making**, and the maze of interconnecting yards and *passages* are still full of the workshops of the related trades: marquetry, stainers, polishers and inlayers.

Quartier Latin

South of the river, the **Rive Gauche** (Left Bank) has long maintained an "alternative" identity, opposed to the formal, businesslike ambience of the Right Bank – as much left wing as left bank. The Left Bank – generally understood to describe the 5ᵉ and 6ᵉ arrondissements – was at the heart of *les évènements*, the revolutionary political "events" of May 1968, which grew from leftist student demonstrations to factory occupations and massive national strikes and culminated in the near-overthrow of de Gaulle's presidency.

Since that infamous summer, however, conservatives have certainly had their vengeance on the spirit of the Left Bank, with rampant gentrification transforming the artists' garrets and beatnik cafés into designer pads and top-end restaurants. What is left of the alternative image is mostly kept up by the student population of the **Quartier Latin**, which first settled on the high ground of the Montagne Ste-Geneviève in the twelfth century. No one knows if it was the learned Latin of the medieval scholars or the ruins of the Roman city of Lutetia that gave the area its name. The pivotal point of this "Latin quarter" is **place St-Michel**, where the tree-lined **boulevard St-Michel** begins. The famous *boul' Mich* has long since changed from radical student heartland to busy commercial thoroughfare, but the universities on all sides give an intellectual air to the place, and the cafés and shops are still jammed with people, mainly young and – in summer – largely from overseas.

Around St-Séverin

The touristy scrum is at its most intense around **rue de la Huchette**, just east of the place St-Michel. Hemmed in by cheap bars and indifferent Greek restaurants

▲ Church of St-Séverin, Quartier Latin

the Théâtre de la Huchette is the last bastion of the area's postwar beatnik heyday, still showing Ionesco's absurdist *La Cantatrice Chauve* ("The Bald Prima Donna") and *La Leçon* more than fifty years on. Connecting rue de la Huchette to the riverside is **rue du Chat-qui-Pêche**, a narrow slice of medieval Paris as it was before Haussmann got to work.

At the end of rue de la Huchette, **rue St-Jacques** is aligned on the main street of Roman Paris, and was the road up which millions of medieval pilgrims trudged at the start of their long march to Santiago de Compostela in Spain. One block south of rue de la Huchette, just west of rue St-Jacques, is the mainly fifteenth-century church of **St-Séverin**, whose entrance is on rue des Prêtres St-Séverin (Mon–Sat 11am–7.30pm, Sun 9am–8.30pm; Mº St-Michel/Cluny–La Sorbonne). It's one of the city's more intense churches, its Flamboyant (distinguished by *flamboyant*, or flame-like, carving) choir resting on a virtuoso spiralling central pillar and its windows filled with edgy stained glass by the modern French painter Jean Bazaine. East of rue St-Jacques, and back towards the river, **square Viviani** provides a perfect view of Notre-Dame and a pleasant patch of green. The mutilated church behind is **St-Julien-le-Pauvre** (daily 9.30am–12.30pm & 3–6.30pm; Mº St-Michel/Maubert Mutualité). The same age as Notre-Dame, it used to be the venue for university assemblies until rumbustious students tore it apart in 1524. Across rue Lagrange from the square, rue de la Bûcherie is the home of the celebrated English-language bookshop **Shakespeare and Co** (see p.168), which acts as an informal hostel for wannabe Hemingways who sleep on lumpy divans on the top floor. If not buying, you can pen a few words on the typewriter upstairs or join the earnest youths thinking deep thoughts in the upper floor "library". The original site – owned by Sylvia Beach, the first publisher of Joyce's *Ulysses* – was on rue de l'Odéon.

The riverbank and Institut du Monde Arabe

A short walk from square Viviani on the riverbank, you'll find old books, postcards and prints on sale from the **bouquinistes**, whose green boxes line the parapets of the **riverside quais**. It's a pleasant walk upstream to **Pont de Sully**, which leads across to the Île St-Louis and offers a dramatic view of Notre-Dame.

Opposite Pont de Sully, you can't miss the bold glass and aluminium mass of the **Institut du Monde Arabe** (Tues–Sun 10am–6pm; ⓦ www.imarabe.org; Mº Jussieu/Cardinal-Lemoine), a cultural centre built to further understanding of the Arab world. Designed by Paris's architect of the moment, Jean Nouvel, its broad southern façade, which mimics a *moucharabiyah*, or traditional Arab latticework, is made up of thousands of tiny metallic shutters. Originally designed to be light-sensitive, they now open and close just once an hour, and though the institute's exterior is stunning, the exhibition spaces are quite gloomy. Inside, a **museum** (€5) winds down from the seventh floor as it traces the evolution of art in the Islamic world; intriguing temporary exhibitions (€10) go into more detail. There's also a library and multimedia centre for scholars, an auditorium, and a specialist bookshop with a good selection of CDs from the Arab world. The **café-restaurant** on the ninth floor is a great place to enjoy a mint tea and the view towards the apse of Notre-Dame.

The Musée National du Moyen Age and the Sorbonne

The nearby area around the slopes of the **Montagne Ste-Geneviève**, the hill on which the Panthéon stands, is good for a stroll. The best approach is from **place Maubert** (which has a market on Tues, Thurs & Sat mornings) or from the St-Michel/St-Germain crossroads, where the walls of the third-century

QUARTIER LATIN

Île de la Cité

R DE LUTÈCE
RUE DE LA CITÉ

RUE SAINT...

RUE ST-ANDRÉ-DES-ARTS

RUE ST-SÉVERIN

RUE DE LA HUCHETTE

PONT ST-MICHEL
QUAI ST-MICHEL
ST-MICHEL NOTRE-DAME
PONT AU DOUBLE

PLACE ST-MICHEL
PL ST-ANDRÉ-DES-ARTS
ST-MICHEL

RUE DE LA HARPE

RUE DANTON

RUE HAUTEFEUILLE

Shakespeare & Co

St-Séverin

R DE LA PARCHEMINERIE

St-Julien-le-Pauvre

SQUARE VIVIANI

RUE GALANDE

RUE DANTE

RUE LAGRANGE

RUE FRÉD SAUTON

QUAI DE MONTEBELLO

PONT DE L'ARCHEVÊCHÉ

PONT AU DOUBLE

Notre-Dame

6e

ODÉON

Université Paris V

RUE DE L'ÉCOLE DE MÉDECINE

RUE DE L'ODÉON

École de Médecine

CLUNY-LA SORBONNE

BD SAINT-GERMAIN

Musée Nat. du Moyen-Age Thermes de Cluny

MAUBERT-MUTUALITÉ

RUE DU SOMMERARD

PL MAUBERT

RUE DES BERNARDINS

RUEDES GRANDS DEGRÉS

RUE DE BIÈVRE

RUE DE PONTOISE

BD SAINT-

RUE RACINE

RUE DES ÉCOLES

RUE DES CARMES

RUE MONGE

RUE SAINT-VICTOR

RUE DE POISSY

Lycée St-Louis

BD ST-MICHEL

RUE CHAMPOLLION

RUE DE LA SORBONNE

Collège de France

RUE DE L'ÉCOLE POLYTECHNIQUE

RUE DE LA MONTAGNE-STE-GENEVIÈVE

RUE DES ÉCOLES

Odéon

PL D'ODÉON

RUE VAL-GIRARD

RUE DE MÉDICIS

PL DE LA SORBONNE

Sorbonne

RUE SAINT-JACQUES

Lycée Louis-le-Grand

RUE VALETTE

RUE DE L'ÉCOLE POLYTECHNIQUE

Bibliothèque Ste Geneviève

St-Étienne-du-Mont

CARDINAL LEMOINE

Jardin du Luxembourg

PL. EDMOND ROSTAND

RUE VICTOR COUSIN

RUE CUJAS

RUE TOULLIER

RUE SOUFFLOT

PL. DU PANTHÉON

RUE CLOVIS

RUE DESCARTES

5e

LUXEMBOURG

RUE ROYER-COLLARD

GAY-LUSSAC

Panthéon

RUE DES FOSSÉS ST-JACQUES

RUE DE L'ESTRAPADE

Lycée Henri IV

RUE DU CARDINAL LEMOINE

RUE ROLLIN

RUE MONGE

LUXEMBOURG

RUE P. ET M. CURIE

SAINT-JACQUES

GAY-LUSSAC

PL. DE LA CONTRESCARPE

RUE LACEPEDE

RUE SAINT-MÉDARD

MONGE

BD ST-MICHEL

RUE HENRI BARBUSSE

RUE

RUE GAY-LUSSAC

St-Jacques-du-Haut-Pas

École Nat. Sup. de Chimie

RUE D'ULM

Institut Curie

École Nat. Sup. des Arts Decoratifs

RUE L'HOMOND

RUE TOURNEFORT

RUE CARDINALE

RUE MOUFFETARD

MONGE

PL MONGE

RUE DU POT-DE-FER

École Normale Supérieure (E.N.S.)

École Nat. Sup. de Physique

PL. L. KERR

RUE J. CALVIN

RUE DE L'ÉPÉE DE BOIS

RUE MONGE

Val-de-Grâce

RUE CLAUDE

BERNARD

RUE VAUGELIN

RUE L'HOMOND

RUE DAUBENTON

RUE DES PATRIARCHES

PL DES PATRIARCHES

CENSIER-DAUBENTON

Musée du Service de Santé des Armées

RUE BERTHOLLET

RUE DE L'ARBALÈTE

RUE MOUFFETARD

RUE MANGE

St-Médard

0   200 m

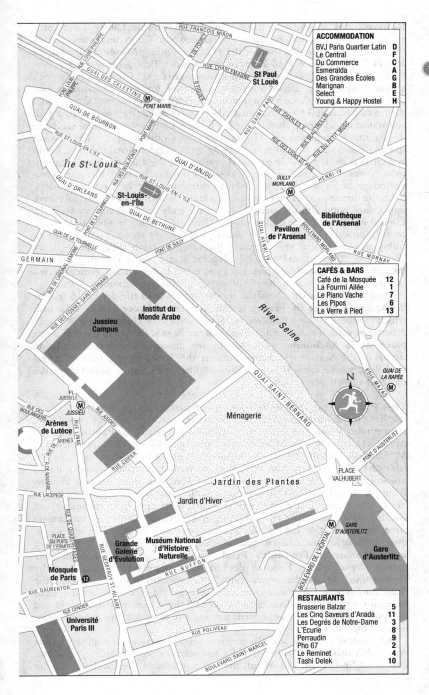

ACCOMMODATION

BVJ Paris Quartier Latin	**D**
Le Central	**F**
Du Commerce	**C**
Esmeralda	**A**
Des Grandes Écoles	**G**
Marignan	**B**
Select	**E**
Young & Happy Hostel	**H**

CAFÉS & BARS

Café de la Mosquée	12
La Fourmi Ailée	1
Le Piano Vache	7
Les Pipos	6
Le Verre à Pied	13

RESTAURANTS

Brasserie Balzar	5
Les Cinq Saveurs d'Anada	11
Les Degrés de Notre-Dame	3
L'Ecurie	8
Perraudin	9
Pho 67	2
Le Reminet	4
Tashi Delek	10

Roman baths are visible in the garden of the **Hôtel de Cluny**, a sixteenth-century mansion built by the abbots of the powerful Cluny monastery as their Paris pied-à-terre. It now houses the richly rewarding **Musée National du Moyen Age**, 6 place Paul-Painlevé, off rue des Écoles (daily except Tues 9.15am–5.45pm; €7.50; ⓦ www.musee-moyenage.fr; Mº Cluny-La Sorbonne), a treasure house of medieval art. The vaults of the former cold room, or *frigidarium*, are intact – though temporarily protected by corrugated sheets – and shelter two beautiful Roman capitals; the *Pillar of St-Landry* has animated gods and musicians adorning three of its faces. There's a feast of medieval sculpture throughout – including the Flamboyant little Gothic chapel, with its vault splaying out from a central pillar – along with wonderful stained glass, books and curious *objets d'art* – but the real beauties are the **tapestries** that hang in most rooms. Conjuring up scenes from the medieval world, there are vivid depictions of a grape harvest, a woman spinning while her servant patiently holds the threads, a lover making advances and a woman in a bath that overflows into a duck pond. But the greatest of all is the truly stunning tapestry series *La Dame à la Licorne* ("The Lady with the Unicorn"). Made in the late fifteenth century, probably in Brussels, the set depicts the five senses – along with an ambiguous image that may represent the virtue in controlling them – in six luxuriantly coloured and detailed allegoric scenes, each featuring a richly dressed woman flanked by a lion and a unicorn. Medieval music **concerts** (€6) are held on Friday lunchtimes (12.30pm) and Saturday afternoons (4pm).

The forbidding-looking buildings on the other side of rue des Écoles are the **Sorbonne**, **Collège de France** and the prestigious **Lycée Louis-le-Grand**, which numbers Molière, Robespierre, Sartre and Victor Hugo among its pupils. A better aspect can be found if you head up rue de la Sorbonne to the traffic-free **place de la Sorbonne**, overlooked by the dramatic Counter-Reformation facade of the Sorbonne's chapel, built in the 1640s by the great Cardinal Richelieu, whose tomb it houses. With its lime trees, fountains and cafés, the square is a lovely place to sit.

The Panthéon, St-Étienne-du-Mont and around

Further up the Montagne Ste-Geneviève, the broad rue Soufflot provides an appropriately grand perspective on the domed and porticoed **Panthéon** (daily: April–Sept 10am–6.30pm; Oct–March 10am–6pm; €7.50; RER Luxembourg/Mº Cardinal-Lemoine), Louis XV's grateful response to Ste-Geneviève, patron saint of Paris, for curing him of illness. The Revolution transformed it into a mausoleum, and the remains of giants of French culture such as Voltaire, Rousseau, Hugo and Zola are entombed in the vast, barrel-vaulted crypt below, along with Marie Curie (the only woman), writer, political adventurer and Gaullist culture minister André Malraux, and Alexandre Dumas, of musketeers fame, who was the last to be "panthéonized", in 2002. The interior is overwhelmingly monumental, bombastically Classical in design – and has a working model of **Foucault's Pendulum** swinging from the dome. The French physicist Léon Foucault devised the experiment, conducted at the Panthéon in 1851, to demonstrate vividly the rotation of the earth: while the pendulum appeared to rotate over a 24-hour period, it was in fact the earth beneath it turning. The demonstration wowed the scientific establishment and the public alike, with huge crowds turning up to watch the ground move beneath their feet.

The remains of Pascal and Racine, two seventeenth-century literary giants who didn't make the Panthéon, and a few relics of Ste-Geneviève, lie in the church of **St-Étienne-du-Mont**, immediately behind the Panthéon on the corner of rue Clovis. The church's garbled facade conceals a stunning and highly unexpected interior. The sudden transition from Flamboyant Gothic choir to sixteenth-century nave is smoothed over by a remarkable narrow catwalk which runs right round the interior, twisting down the pillars of the crossing in two spiral staircases before arching across the width of the church in the broad span of the rood screen. This last feature is highly unusual in itself, as most others in France have fallen victim to Protestant iconoclasts, reformers or revolutionaries. Exceptionally tall windows at the triforium level fill the church with light, and there is also some beautiful seventeenth-century glass in the cloister. Further down rue Clovis, a huge piece of Philippe-Auguste's twelfth-century **city walls** emerges from among the houses.

Place Maubert to the rue Mouffetard

North of St-Étienne-du-Mont, the villagey **rue de la Montagne-Ste-Geneviève** descends towards place Maubert, passing the pleasant cafés and restaurants around rue de l'École-Polytechnique. Heading uphill, rue Descartes runs into the tiny **place de la Contrescarpe**, once an arty hangout where Hemingway wrote – in the café *La Chope* – and Georges Brassens sang, but now a dog-eared student meeting-place. The ancient **rue Mouffetard** – rue Mouff' to locals – begins here. Most of the upper half of the street is given over to rather touristy eating places but the lower half, a cobbled lane winding downhill to the church of **St-Médard**, still offers a taste of the quintessentially Parisian market street that once thrived here, with a few grocers' stalls, butchers and speciality cheese shops, and a fruit-and-veg market on Tuesday and Saturday mornings.

The Paris mosque and Jardin des Plantes

A little further east, across rue Monge, are some of the city's most agreeable surprises. Just past place du Puits de l'Ermite stand the crenellated walls of the **Mosquée de Paris** (daily except Fri & Muslim holidays 9am–noon & 2–6pm; ⓦ www.mosquee-de-paris.org; €3; Mº Jussieu), built by Morocoan craftsmen in the early 1920s. You can walk in the sunken garden and patios with their polychrome tiles and carved ceilings, but not the prayer room. There's also a lovely courtyard **tearoom/restaurant** (see p.151), which is open to all, and an atmospheric **hamam** (Turkish bath, bathing here is one of the most enjoyable things to do in this part of the city.

Behind the mosque is the **Jardin des Plantes** (daily 7.30am–7.45pm; free; Mº Austerlitz/Jussieu/Censier Daubenton), which was founded as a medicinal herb garden in 1626 and gradually evolved into Paris's botanical gardens, with shady avenues of trees, lawns to sprawl on, hothouses, museums and a zoo. By the rue Cuvier exit is a fine Lebanon Cedar, planted in 1734, raised from a seed from the Oxford Botanical Gardens, and a slice of an American sequoia more than 2000 years old. In the nearby physics labs, Henri Becquerel discovered radioactivity in 1896, and two years later the Curies discovered radium.

Magnificent floral beds make a fine approach to the collection of buildings that forms the **Muséum National d'Histoire Naturelle** (ⓦ www.mnhn.fr). Best of the lot is the **Grand Galerie de l'Évolution** (daily except Tues 10am–6pm; €8), housed in a dramatically restored nineteenth-century glass-domed building (the entrance is off rue Buffon). Though it doesn't actually tell the story of evolution as such, it does feature a huge cast of life-size animals, some of them striding dramatically across the central space.

Real animals can be seen in the small **menagerie** across the park to the northeast near rue Cuvier (summer Mon–Sat 9am–6.30pm, Sun 9am–6pm; winter daily 9am–5pm; €7). Founded here just after the Revolution, it is

France's oldest zoo – and looks it. The old-fashioned iron cages of the big cats' *fauverie*, the stinky vivarium and the glazed primate house are depressing, though these animals are at least spared the fate of their predecessors during the starvation months of the 1870 Prussian siege. Most of the zoo is pleasantly park-like, however, and given over to deer, antelope, goats, buffaloes and other beasts that seem happy enough in their outdoor enclosures. The **Microzoo** allows you to inspect headlice and other minuscule wonders.

A short distance away to the northwest, with entrances in rue de Navarre, rue des Arènes and through a passage on rue Monge, is the **Arènes de Lutèce**, an unexpected backwater hidden from the street, and, along with the Roman baths (see p.120), Paris's only Roman remains. A few ghostly rows of stone seats are all that's left of an amphitheatre that once seated ten thousand; old men playing *boules* in the sand provide the only show.

St-Germain

The northern half of the 6ᵉ arrondissement, centred on **place St-Germain-des-Prés**, is one of the most attractive, lively and wealthy square kilometres in the city – and one of the best places to shop for clothes. The most dramatic approach is to cross the river from the Louvre by the footbridge, the **Pont des Arts**, from where there's a classic upstream view of the Île de la Cité, with barges moored at the quai de Conti, the Tour St-Jacques and Hôtel de Ville breaking the skyline of the Right Bank. The dome and pediment at the end of the bridge belong to the **Institut de France**, seat of the Académie Française, an august body of writers and scholars whose mission is to safeguard the purity of the French language. This is the most grandiose part of the Left Bank riverfront: to the left is the **Hôtel des Monnaies**, redesigned as the Mint in the late eighteenth century; to the right is the **Beaux-Arts**, the School of Fine Art, whose students throng the *quais* on sunny days, sketchpads on knees. More students can be found relaxing in the **Jardin du Luxembourg**, bordering the Quartier Latin towards the southern end of the *sixième*, which is one of the largest, loveliest and best-loved green spaces in the city.

The riverside

The riverside chunk of the 6ᵉ arrondissement is cut lengthwise by rue St-André-des-Arts and rue Jacob. It's an area full of bookshops, commercial art galleries, antique shops, cafés and restaurants, and if you poke your nose into the courtyards and side streets, you'll find foliage, fountains and peaceful enclaves removed from the bustle of the city. The houses are four to six storeys high, seventeenth- and eighteenth-century, some noble, some bulging and skew, all painted in infinite gradations of grey, pearl and off-white. Broadly speaking, the further west you go the posher the houses get.

Historical associations are legion: Picasso painted *Guernica* in rue des Grands-Augustins; Molière started his career in rue Mazarine; Robespierre et al split ideological hairs at the *Café Procope* in rue de l'Ancienne-Comédie. In rue Visconti, Racine died, Delacroix painted and Balzac's printing business went bust. In the parallel rue des Beaux-Arts, Oscar Wilde died, Corot and Ampère (father of amps) lived and the poet Gérard de Nerval went walking with a lobster on a lead.

If you're looking to eat, you'll find numerous places on **place** and **rue St-André-des-Arts** and along **rue de Buci**, up towards boulevard St-Germain. Rue de Buci preserves a strong flavour of its origins as a market street, with food shops, delis and some excellent cafés and brasseries. Before you get to rue de Buci, there is an intriguing little passage on the left, **Cour du Commerce St-André**, where Marat had a printing press and Dr Guillotin perfected his notorious machine by lopping off sheep's heads. A couple of smaller courtyards open off it, revealing another stretch of Philippe-Auguste's twelfth-century city wall.

A delightful corner for a quiet picnic is around rue de l'Abbaye and rue du Furstemberg. Halfway down rue du Furstemburg at no. 6, opposite a tiny square and backing onto a secret garden, Delacroix's old studio is now the **Musée Delacroix** (daily except Tues 9.30am–5pm; €5; M° Mabillon/St-Germain-des-Prés), with a small collection of the artist's personal belongings as well as minor exhibitions of his work. This is also the beginning of some very upmarket shopping territory, in rue Jacob, rue de Seine and rue Bonaparte in particular.

St-Germain-des-Prés to St-Sulpice

Place St-Germain-des-Prés, the hub of the *quartier*, is only a stone's throw away from the Musée Delacroix, with the *Deux Magots* café (see p.152) on the corner of the square, *Flore* (see p.152) adjacent and *Lipp* (see p.152) across the boulevard St-Germain. All three are renowned for the number of philosophico-politico-literary backsides that have shined – and continue to shine – their seats, along with plenty of celebrity-hunters. Picasso's bust of a woman, dedicated to the poet Apollinaire, recalls the district's creative heyday. The tower opposite the *Deux Magots* belongs to the church of St-Germain, all that remains of an enormous Benedictine monastery. Inside, the transformation from Romanesque to early Gothic is just about visible under the heavy green and gold nineteenth-century paintwork. The last chapel on the south side contains the tomb of the philosopher René Descartes.

South of boulevard St-Germain, the streets round St-Sulpice are calm and classy. **Rue Mabillon** is pretty, with a row of old houses set back below the level of the modern street. On the left are the shops of the **Halles St-Germain**, on the site of a nineteenth-century market. Rue St-Sulpice leads through to the front of the enormous, early eighteenth-century church of **St-Sulpice** (daily 7am–7.30pm; M° St-Sulpice), an austerely Classical building with Doric and Ionic colonnades and Corinthian pilasters in the towers. The north tower will be under reconstruction work until 2011, spoiling the aspect of the square somewhat; ironically on the south tower you'll see centuries-old uncut masonry blocks protruding from the top, still awaiting the sculptor's chisel. Three Delacroix murals can be seen in the first chapel on the right, but most visitors these days come to see the **gnomon**, a kind of solar clock whose origins and purpose were so compellingly garbled by *The Da Vinci Code*.

All is expensive elegance around **place St-Sulpice**, but if you're heading east towards boulevard St-Michel, the glitzy shops quickly fade into the worthy bookshops and inexpensive restaurants around the École de Médecine.

Jardin du Luxembourg

The **Jardin du Luxembourg** – with formal lawns and floral parterres dotted with trees in giant pots that are taken inside in winter – is a welcome green space in the heart of the city. The gardens get fantastically crowded on summer days, when the most contested spots are the shady **Fontaine de Médicis** in the northeast corner and the lawns of the southernmost strip – the latter being the only place where you're allowed to sit on the grass. Everywhere else you'll have to settle yourself on the heavy, sage-green metal chairs, which are liberally distributed around the gravel paths. Alternatively, there's a delightful tree-shaded **café** roughly 100m northeast of the central pond.

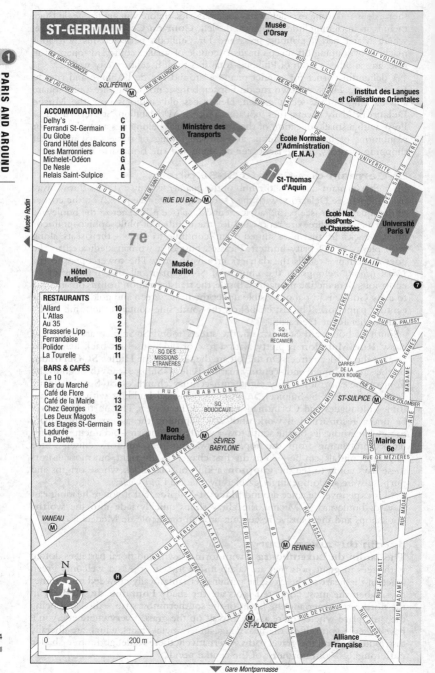

ST-GERMAIN

Musée d'Orsay

RUE SAINT-DOMINIQUE
RUE LAS CASES
SOLIFÉRINO Ⓜ
RUE DE VILLERSEXEL
RUE DE LILLE
QUAI VOLTAIRE
RUE DE VERNEUIL
BD ST-GERMAIN

Institut des Langues
et Civilisations Orientales

ACCOMMODATION
Delhy's	C
Ferrandi St-Germain	H
Du Globe	D
Grand Hôtel des Balcons	F
Des Marronniers	B
Michelet-Odéon	G
De Nesle	A
Relais Saint-Sulpice	E

Ministère des Transports

École Normale
d'Administration
(E.N.A.)

St-Thomas
d'Aquin

RUE SAINT-SIMON

RUE DE GRENELLE

RUE DU BAC Ⓜ

7e

RUE DU BAC

RUE DE LIPNES

École Nat.
desPonts-
et-Chaussées

Université
Paris V

BD ST-GERMAIN

Hôtel
Matignon

RUE DE VARENNE

Musée
Maillol

RUE DE GRENELLE

RUE SAINT-GUILLAUME

BD RASPAIL

❼

RESTAURANTS
Allard	10
L'Atlas	8
Au 35	2
Brasserie Lipp	7
Ferrandaise	16
Polidor	15
La Tourelle	11

BARS & CAFÉS
Le 10	14
Bar du Marché	6
Café de Flore	4
Café de la Mairie	13
Chez Georges	12
Les Deux Magots	5
Les Etages St-Germain	9
Ladurée	1
La Palette	3

SQ DES
MISSIONS
ETRANGÈRES

RUE CHOMEL

RUE DE BABYLONE

SQ
BOUCICAUT

Bon
Marché

Ⓜ
SÈVRES
BABYLONE

RUE DE SÈVRES

RUE DES SAINTS-PÈRES

RUE DU DRAGON

RUE B. PALISSY

SQ
CHAISE-
RECAMIER

CARREF.
DE LA
CROIX ROUGE

RUE DU
CHERCHE MIDI

ST-SULPICE Ⓜ

RUE MADAME

RUE
VIEUX-COLOMBIER

Mairie du
6e

CASSETTE

RENNES

RUE DE MÉZIÈRES

VANEAU
Ⓜ

RUE DU CHERCHE MIDI

R. DUPIN

RUE SAINT-PLACIDE

RUE DU REGARD

BD RASPAIL

Ⓜ RENNES

RUE D'ASSAS

RUE MADAME

N

Ⓗ

RUE DE L'ABBÉ GRÉGOIRE

RUE DE VAUGIRARD

RUE JEAN BAET

RUE MADAME

RUE DE FLEURUS

RUE D'ASSAS

ST-PLACIDE
Ⓜ

Alliance
Française

Musée Rodin ◀

0 _____ 200 m

▼ Gare Montparnasse

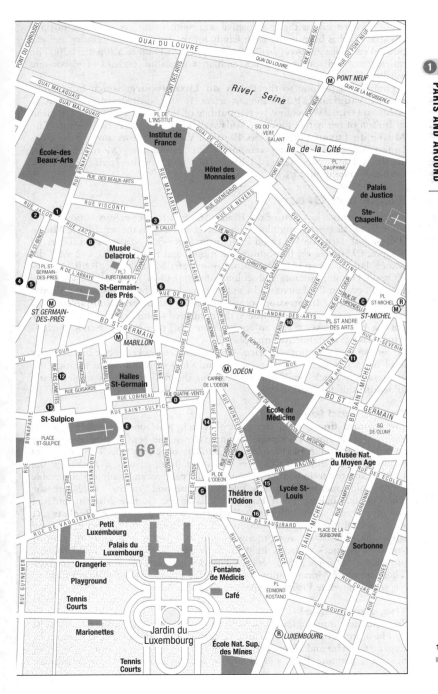

QUAI DU LOUVRE

QUAI DU LOUVRE

RUE DE L'ARBRE SEC

RUE DU PONT NEUF

Ⓜ PONT NEUF

QUAI DE LA MÉGISSERIE

River Seine

QUAI MALAQUAIS

QUAI MALAQUAIS

PONT DES ARTS

PL DE L'INSTITUT

SQ DU VERT GALANT

Île de la Cité

PONT NEUF

PL DAUPHINE

École-des Beaux-Arts

RUE DES BEAUX-ARTS

RUE BONAPARTE

Institut de France

QUAI DE CONTI

Hôtel des Monnaies

Palais de Justice

RUE VISCONTI

RUE JACOB

RUE DE NEVERS

QUAI DES GRANDS AUGUSTINS

Ste-Chapelle

❷ ❶

RUE JACOB

RUE MAZARINE

RUE GUÉNÉGAUD

R DE NESLE

RUE ST-BENOIT

Ⓐ

RUE DAUPHINE

❸ R CALLOT

Ⓑ

Musée Delacroix

RUE DE SEINE

RUE CHRISTINE

RUE DES GRANDS-AUGUSTINS

R DE L'ABBAYE

(PL) FURSTEMBERG

RUE DE L'EPERON

RUE SÉGUIER

PL ST-MICHEL Ⓡ

PL ST-GERMAIN-DES-PRÉS

St-Germain-des Prés

❹ ❺

❻ RUE DE BUCI

R DU ANCIENNE COMÉDIE

RUE SAINT-ANDRÉ-DES-ARTS

ST-MICHEL Ⓜ

Ⓒ

❽ ❾

Ⓜ ST GERMAIN-DES-PRÉS

RUE DE L'HIRONDELLE

RUE DE L'ÉCOLE

BD ST-GERMAIN

PL ST ANDRE DES ARTS

❿

RUE SERPENTE

Ⓜ MABILLON

RUE GRÉGOIRE DE TOURS

RUE DE L'EPERON

RUE ST-SÉVERIN

DU

FOUR

RUE MABILLON

RUE DE SEINE

COUR DU COM. ST ANDRE

DANTON

RUE

⓫

RUE DES CANETTES

RUE PRINCESSE

RUE GUISARDE

Halles St-Germain

RUE QUATRE-VENTS

Ⓜ ODÉON

RUE HAUTEFEUILLE

BD SAINT-MICHEL

⓬

RUE LOBINEAU

CARREF. DE L'ODÉON

BD ST GERMAIN

⓭

RUE SAINT-SULPICE

Ⓓ

RUE MONSIEUR-LE-PRINCE

École de Médecine

SQ DE CLUNY

St-Sulpice

Ⓔ

6e

⓮

RUE DE L'ODÉON

ÉCOLE DE MÉDECINE

RUE BONAPARTE

RUE GARANCIÈRE

RUE TOURNON

RUE CASIMIR-DELAVIGNE

Ⓕ

RUE RACINE

Musée Nat. du Moyen Age

PLACE ST-SULPICE

RUE SERVANDONI

RUE DE CONDÉ

Lycée St-Louis

RUE DES ÉCOLES

RUE FÉROU

PL DE L'ODÉON

Ⓖ

⓯

RUE CHAMPOLLION

RUE DE VAUGIRARD

Théâtre de l'Odéon

⓰

RUE DE VAUGIRARD

BD SAINT-MICHEL

RUE DE LA SORBONNE

Sorbonne

Petit Luxembourg

Palais du Luxembourg

LE PRINCE

PLACE DE LA SORBONNE

RUE GUYNEMER

Orangerie

RUE DE MÉDICIS

Fontaine de Médicis

Café

PL EDMOND ROSTAND

RUE CUJAS

Playground

Tennis Courts

RUE SOUFFLOT

RUE SAINT-JACQUES

Marionettes

Jardin du Luxembourg

Ⓡ LUXEMBOURG

Tennis Courts

École Nat. Sup. des Mines

The western side is the more active area, with tennis courts and a **puppet theatre** that has been in the same family for the best part of a century, and still puts on enthralling shows (Wed & Sat 3.30pm, Sun 11am & 3.30pm; €4.20). The quieter, wooded southeast corner ends in a miniature orchard of elaborately espaliered pear trees.

The gardens belong to the **Palais du Luxembourg**, which fronts onto **rue de Vaugirard**, Paris's longest street. It was constructed for Marie de Médicis, Henri IV's widow, to remind her of the Palazzo Pitti and Giardino di Boboli of her native Florence. Today, it's the seat of the French Senate. The **Musée du Luxembourg**, at no. 19 rue de Vaugirard, hosts some of the city's largest and most exciting temporary art exhibitions (Mon, Fri & Sat 10.30am–10pm, Tues–Thurs 10.30am–7pm, Sun 9.30am–7pm; €11; Ⓦ www .museeduluxembourg.fr).

Musée d'Orsay

On the riverfront just west of the Beaux-Arts, in a former railway station whose stone facade disguises a stunning vault of steel and glass, is the remarkable **Musée d'Orsay**, at 1 rue de la Légion d'Honneur (Tues–Sun 9.30am–6pm, Thurs till 9.45pm; €9.50, free on first Sun of the month and to under-18s; €12 with the Musée Rodin, see p.134; Ⓦ www.musee-orsay.fr; Mᵒ Solférino/RER Musée-d'Orsay). Housing painting and sculpture from 1848 to 1914, and thus bridging the gap between the Louvre and Centre Pompidou, its highlights are the electrifying works of the **Impressionists** and so-called **Post-Impressionists**. You could spend half a day meandering through the numbered rooms in chronological order, but the layout makes it easy to confine your visit to a specific section, each of which has a very distinctive atmosphere.

The two **cafés** are fine – if pricey – places to take stock: the one on the upper level has a summer terrace and wonderful view of Montmartre through the giant railway clock, while the tearoom on the middle level is resplendently gilded in authentic period style.

The ground level

The **ground floor**, under the great glass arch, is devoted to pre-1870 work, with a double row of sculptures running down the central aisle like railway tracks, and paintings in the odd little bunkers on either side. The first set of rooms (1–3) is dedicated to Ingres, Delacroix (most of whose work is in the Louvre) and the serious-minded works of the painters and sculptors acceptable to the mid-nineteenth century salons; just beyond (rooms 11–13) are the relatively unusual works of Puvis de Chavannes, Gustave Moreau and the younger Degas. The influential **Barbizon school** and the **Realists** are showcased on the Seine side (rooms 4–7), with works by Daumier, Corot and Millet. Just a few steps away, rooms 14 and 18 explode with the early controversies of Monet's violently light-filled *Femmes au Jardin* (1867) and Manet's provocative *Olympia* (1863), which heralded the arrival of **Impressionism**. There are more Monet paintings in room 20, including his well-loved *Coquelicots* (*Poppies*), while Pissarro dominates room 22.

The upper level

To continue chronologically you have to go straight to the **upper level**, done up like a suite of attic studios. After the shock of the ghostly, realist portraits by Eugéne Carriére and Henri Fantin-Latour in room 29 – not everybody at this time was painting light and colour – you arrive in deep **Impressionist** territory. From this point on, you'll have to fight off a persistent sense of famili-arity or recognition – Manet's waterlilies, Degas' *Au Café du L'Absinthe*, Renoir's *Bal du Moulin de la Galette*, Monet's *Femme à l'Ombrelle* – in order to appreciate Impressionism's vibrant, experimental vigour. There's a host of small-scale landscapes and outdoor scenes by Renoir, Sisley, Pissarro and Monet, paintings which owed much of their brilliance to the novel practice of setting up easels in the open to capture the light. Degas' ballet-dancers demonstrate his principal interest in movement and line as opposed to the more common Impressionist concern with light, while his domestic scenes of ordinary working life are touchingly humane Berthe Morisot, the first woman to join the early Impres-sionists, is represented by her famous *Le Berceau* (1872), among others. More heavyweight masterpieces can be found in rooms 34 and 39, devoted to **Monet** and **Renoir** in their middle and late periods – the development of Monet's obsession with light is shown with five of his extraordinary Rouen Cathedral series, each painted in different light conditions. Room 35 explodes with the fervid colours and disturbing rhythms of **Van Gogh**, while **Cézanne**, another step removed from the preoccupations of the mainstream Impressionists, is wonderfully displayed in room 36. Room 36bis is dominated by **Toulouse-Lautrec**'s deliciously smoky caricatures, including *Dance Mauresque* depicting celebrated cancan dancer La Goulue.

Passing the **café** you arrive at a dimly lit, melancholy chamber (40) devoted to **pastels** by Redon, Mondrian and others. The next and final suite of rooms on this level is given over to the various offspring of Impressionism, and has an edgier, more modern feel, with a much greater emphasis on psychology. It begins with Rousseau's dreamlike *La Charmeuse de Serpents* (1907) and continues past **Gauguin**'s ambivalent Tahitian paintings to **Pointillist** works by Seurat (the famous *Cirque, 1891*), Signac and others.

The middle level

The Kaganovitch collection (room 50) – Bonnard, Gauguin, Van Gogh, Sisley – leads you down to the **middle level**, where the flow of the painting section continues with Vuillard and Bonnard (rooms 71 & 72). On the far side, in rooms 55 and 58, overlooking the Seine, you can see a less familiar side of late nineteenth-century painting, with epic, naturalist works such as Detaille's stirring *Le Rêve* (1888) and Cormon's *Caïn* (1880). On the parallel sculpture terraces, nineteenth-century marbles on the Seine side face early twentieth-century pieces across the divide, while the **Rodin terrace** bridging the two puts almost everything else to shame. If you've energy to spare, don't skip the last half-dozen rooms, which contain superb Art Nouveau furniture and *objets*.

The Trocadéro, Eiffel Tower and the Septième

As examples of landmark architecture, the **Palais de Tokyo** and **Palais de Chaillot**, on the heights of the Trocadéro, on the north bank of the river, are hard to love. They do, however, hold a couple of exciting museums – in partic-ular the **Site de Création Contemporaine** and the **Cité de l'Architecture** – the latter offering the bonus of breathtaking views of the Eiffel Tower, across the river. The area at the tower's feet, to the east, is the **septième** (7ᵉ) arrondis-sement, worth exploring for the classy, villagey shops and restaurants around the **rue Cler** and the lavish museum of non-Western art, the Musée du Quai Branly. Much of the rest of the quarter is dominated by monumental military and government buildings, most imposingly the **École Militaire** and **Hôtel**

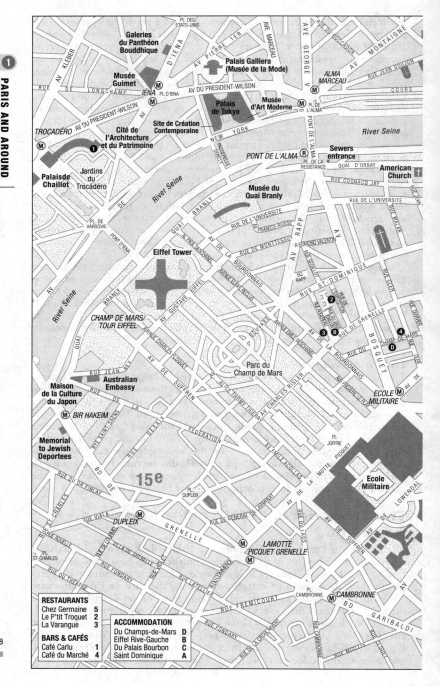

RESTAURANTS
Chez Germaine 5
Le P'tit Troquet 2
La Varangue 3

BARS & CAFÉS
Café Carlu 1
Café du Marché 4

ACCOMMODATION
Du Champs-de-Mars **D**
Eiffel Rive-Gauche **B**
Du Palais Bourbon **C**
Saint Dominique **A**

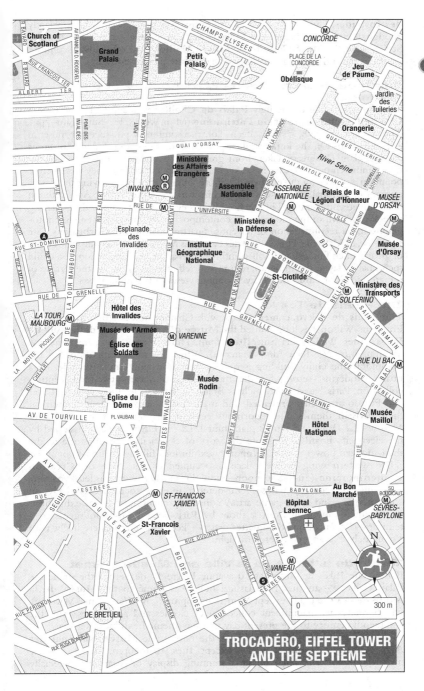

TROCADÉRO, EIFFEL TOWER AND THE SEPTIÈME

des Invalides. The latter houses an impressive war museum and, appropriately enough, the tomb of Napoleon. Tucked away in the streets to the east, towards St-Germain, the **Musée Rodin** and **Musée Maillol** show off the two sculptors' works in the intimate surroundings of handsome private houses.

Palais de Chaillot: Cité de l'Architecture et du Patrimoine

The northern wing of the ugly **Palais de Chaillot** is occupied by the superb **Cité de l'Architecture et du Patrimoine** (Mon, Wed & Fri–Sun 11am–7pm, Thurs 11am–9pm; €8; ⓦwww.citechaillot.fr), a stunningly put-together museum of architecture. On the loftily vaulted ground floor, the **Galerie des Moulages** displays giant plastercasts taken from great French buildings at the end of the nineteenth century. The carvings, seen here as crisp and clear as they were before pollution and erosion dulled their detail, are vibrant, vividly displaying the development of national (mainly church) architecture from the Middle Ages through to the nineteenth century. The top floor brings everything slap up to date, offering a sleek rundown of the modern and contemporary, with models, designs, photographs and a reconstruction of an entire apartment from **Le Corbusier**'s Cité Radieuse, in Marseille. The Galerie des Peintures Murales, with its full-scale copies of great French frescoes and wall-paintings, fades a little in comparison. You could spend half a day at the museum; restore yourself afterwards on the the terrace of the ground-floor **café**, with its eye-popping views of the Eiffel Tower.

The Palais de Tokyo

The **Palais de Tokyo**, contemporary with Chaillot, and nearby on avenue du Président-Wilson, has long housed the **Musée d'Art Moderne de la Ville de Paris** (Tues, Wed & Fri–Sun 10am–6pm, Thurs 10am–10pm; free; ⓦwww .mam.paris.fr; M° Iéna/Alma-Marceau). While it's no competition for the Pompidou, the chilly building is quieter and more contemplative, offering a fitting Modernist setting for the museum's strong early twentieth-century collection. Paris-based artists such as Braque, Chagall, Delaunay, Derain, Léger and Picasso are well represented, and many works were expressly chosen for their Parisian themes. The enormous centrepieces are the two versions of Matisse's *La Danse* and Dufy's giant mural, *La Fée Électricité*, commissioned by the electricity board to illustrate the story of electricity from Aristotle to the then-modern power station. Temporary exhibitions fill the ground-floor space.

The western wing of the palace is occupied by the **Site de Création Contemporaine** (Tues–Sun noon–midnight; €6; ⓦwww.palaisdetokyo.com), a cutting-edge gallery whose semi-derelict interior focuses exclusively on contemporary and avant-garde art. A constantly changing flow of exhibitions and events – anything from a show by Paris-born Louise Bourgeois to a temporary "occupation" by squatter-artists – keeps the atmosphere lively, with a genuinely exciting, countercultural, buzz.

Musée de la Mode de la Ville and Musée Guimet

Behind the Palais de Tokyo, at 10 avenue Pierre 1ᵉʳ de Serbie, the grandiose Palais Galliera – another Neoclassical hulk – is home to the **Musée de la Mode de la Ville** (daily except Mon 10am–6pm; €7; M° Iéna/Alma-Marceau), which rotates its magnificent collection of clothes and accessories from the eighteenth century to the present day in a few themed exhibitions a year.

A short way away, on place d'Iéna, the remarkable **Musée National des Arts Asiatiques-Guimet** (daily except Tues 10am–6pm; €6.50; ⓦwww .museeguimet.fr; M° Iéna) boasts a stunning display of Asian and especially

Buddhist art. Four floors groan under the weight of imaginatively displayed statues of Buddhas and gods, some fierce, some meditative. A roofed-in courtyard provides an airy space in which to show off the museum's world-renowned collection of **Khmer sculpture**. The Buddhist statues of the **Gandhara civilization**, on the first floor, betray a fascinating debt to Greek sculpture, while the fierce demons from Nepal, the many-armed gold gods of South India, the Tang ceramic statuettes and the pot-bellied Chinese Buddhas are stunningly exotic. Oddly enough, one of the most moving exhibits is one of the simplest: a two-thousand-year-old blown-glass fish from Afghanistan.

The Eiffel Tower
It's hard to believe that the **Eiffel Tower**, the quintessential symbol both of Paris and of the brilliance of industrial engineering, was designed to be a temporary structure for a fair. Late nineteenth-century Europe had a decadent taste for such giant-scale, colonialist-capitalist extravaganzas, but the 1889 Exposition was particularly ambitious, and when completed the tower, at 300m, was the tallest building in the world. Reactions were violent. Outraged critics protested "in the name of menaced French art and history" against this "useless and monstrous" tower. "Is Paris", they asked, "going to be associated with the grotesque, mercantile imaginings of a constructor of machines?"

Curiously, Paris's most famous landmark was only saved from demolition by the sudden need for "wireless telegraphy" aerials in the first decade of the twentieth century. The tower's role in telecommunications – its only function apart from tourism – has become increasingly important, and the original crown is now masked by an efflorescence of antennae. Over the last century, the tower has needed few structural adjustments, but it has seen some cosmetic changes: the original deep-red paint-scheme, for example, has been covered up with a dusty-chocolate brown since the late 1960s. After dark, however, the

▲ The Eiffel Tower

tower is spectacular, an urban lighthouse illuminated by a double searchlight. For the first ten minutes of every hour thousands of effervescent lights fizz across its gridlines, defining the famous silhouette in luminescent champagne.

Though you may have to grit your teeth and wait a while, it's arguable that you simply haven't seen Paris until you've seen it from the top (daily: mid-June to Sept 9am–12.45am; Sept to mid-June 9.30am–11.45pm; last entry 45min before closing time. Top level €12; second level €7.80, or €4 by stairs [access closes 6pm Sept to mid-June]; first level €4.80). While the views are almost better from the second level, especially on hazier days, there's something irresistible about taking the lift all the way, looking down over the surreally microscopic city below.

Stretching back from the legs of the Eiffel Tower, the long rectangular gardens of the **Champs de Mars** lead to the eighteenth-century buildings of the **École Militaire**, originally founded in 1751 by Louis XV for the training of aristocratic army officers, and attended by Napoleon, among other fledgling leaders. The surrounding *quartier* may be expensive and sought after as an address, but it's mostly uninspiring to visit.

Musée du Quai Branly

A short distance upstream of the Eiffel Tower, on quai Branly, stands the intriguing **Musée du Quai Branly** (Tues, Wed & Sun 11am–7pm, Thurs–Sat 11am–9pm; €8.50, €13 including temporary exhibits; Ⓦ www.quaibranly.fr; Mº Iéna/RER Pont de l'Alma). Designed by the French state's favourite architect, Jean Nouvel, the museum – which gathers together hundreds of thousands of non-European objects bought or purloined by France over the centuries – was the brainchild of President Chirac, whose passion for what he would no doubt call *arts primitifs* or *arts premiers* helped secure funding. Nouvel's elaborate design, which aims to blur the divide between structure and environment, unfurls in a long curve through the middle of an enormous garden. Inside, areas devoted to Asia, Africa, the Americas and the Pacific ("Oceania") snake through semi-dark rooms lined by curving "mud" walls in brown leather. The 3500 **folk artefacts** on display at any one time are as fascinating as they are beautiful; the tone of the place, however, is muddled. While the objects are predominantly displayed – and easily experienced – as works of art, there's an uneasy sense that they are being presented above all in terms of their exotic "otherness". This is not helped when the museum loses the courage of its convictions, shifting into outdated anthropological mode, using written (and often poorly translated) panels to give lofty cultural context.

The riverside

Just beyond the museum, opposite the Pont d'Alma on the northeast side of the busy junction of place de la Résistance, is the entrance to the **sewers**, or *les égouts* (Sat–Wed: May–Sept 11am–5pm; Oct–April 11am–4pm; €4.20). Once you're underground it's dark, damp and noisy from the gushing water; the main exhibition, which runs along a gantry walk poised above a main sewer, renders the history of the city's water supply and waste management surprisingly fascinating. Children, however, may be disappointed to find that it's not all that smelly.

A little further upstream still, the **American Church** on quai d'Orsay, together with the American College nearby at 31 avenue Bosquet, is a focal point in the well-organized life of Paris's large American community. Immediately to the south lies a villagey wedge of early nineteenth-century streets. This tiny neighbourhood, between rue St-Dominique and rue de Grenelle, is full of appealingly bijou shops, hotels and restaurants, with the lively market street of **rue Cler** at the centre of it all.

Les Invalides

The **Esplanade des Invalides**, striking due south from Pont Alexandre III, is a more attractive vista than the one from the Palais de Chaillot to the École Militaire. The proud dome and heavy facade of the Hôtel des Invalides, built as a home for soldiers on the orders of Louis XIV, looms at the further end of the Esplanade. Under the dome are two churches, one for the soldiers, the other intended as a mausoleum for the king but now containing the mortal remains of Napoleon.

Les Invalides today houses the vast **Musée de l'Armée** (daily: April–Sept 10am–5.45pm; Oct–March 10am–4.45pm; €8 ticket also valid for Napoleon's tomb; Ⓦwww.invalides.org; Mᵒ La Tour-Maubourg/Varenne), an enormous national war museum. The most interesting section covers the two world wars, beginning with Prussia's annexation of Alsace-Lorraine in 1871 and ending with the defeat of the Third Reich. The battles, the resistance and the slow liberation are documented through imaginatively displayed war memorabilia combined with stirring contemporary news reels, most of which have an English-language option. The simplest artefacts – a rag doll found on a battle-field, plaster casts of mutilated faces, an overcoat caked in mud from the trenches – tell a stirring human story, while un-narrated footage, from the Somme, from Dunkirk and from a bomb attack on a small French town, flicker across bare white walls in grim, almost unbearable silence. The collection of medieval and Renaissance armour in the west wing of the royal courtyard is worth admiring, along with the super-scale models of French ports and fortified cities in the **Musée des Plans-Reliefs** under the roof of the east wing. Essentially giant three-dimensional maps, they were created to plan defences or plot potential artillery positions. The eerie green glow of their landscapes only just illuminates the long, tunnel-like attic; the effect is rather chilling. The remainder of the museum, dedicated to the history of the French army from Louis XIV up to the 1870s, is closed for restoration until at least 2010.

The Invalides churches and Napoleon's tomb

The two Invalides churches have separate entrances. The lofty **Église des Soldats** (free; entrance from main courtyard of Les Invalides) is the spiritual home of the French army. The walls are hung with almost one hundred enemy standards captured on the battlefield, the rump of a collection of some three thousand that once adorned Notre-Dame. The proud simplicity of this "Soldiers' Church" stands in stark contrast to the lavish **Église du Dôme** (same hours and ticket as Musée de l'Armée above; entrance from south side of Les Invalides), which lies on the other side of a dividing glass wall – a design innova-tion that allowed worshippers to share the same high altar without the risk of coming into social contact. The domed "Royal church" is a supreme example of the architectural pomposity of Louis XIV's day, with grandiose frescoes and an abundance of Corinthian columns and pilasters. **Napoleon**, or rather his ashes, lies in a hole in the floor in a cold, smooth sarcophagus of red porphyry, installed there on December 14, 1840. Freshly returned from St Helena, his remains were carried through the streets from the newly completed Arc de Triomphe to the Invalides. As many as half a million people came out to watch the emperor's last journey, and Victor Hugo commented that "it felt as if the whole of Paris had been poured to one side of the city, like liquid in a vase which has been tilted".

Musée Rodin

Immediately east of Les Invalides is the lovely **Musée Rodin**, on the corner of rue de Varenne (Tues–Sun: April–Sept 9.30am–5.45pm, garden closes 6.45pm; Oct–March 9.30am–4.45pm, garden closes 5pm; house and gardens €6, €12 with the Musée d'Orsay, see p.126, garden only €1; Ⓦ www.musee-rodin.fr; M° Varenne), elegantly presented in a beautiful eighteenth-century mansion which the sculptor leased from the state in return for the gift of all his work at his death. Major projects like *The Burghers of Calais*, *The Thinker*, *The Gate of Hell* and *Ugolini* are exhibited in the extensive garden – the latter forming the centrepiece of the ornamental pond. Indoors, where the vigour of the sculptures sits beautifully with the time-worn wooden panelling of the *boiseries*, can get very crowded. Well-loved works like the touchingly erotic *The Kiss* and *The Hand of God* share space with vibrant surprises like *Romeo and Juliet* and *The Centaur*, which seem only half-created, not wholly liberated from their raw blocks of stone.

Musée Maillol and around

The rest of rue de Varenne and the parallel rue de Grenelle is full of aristocratic mansions, including the Hôtel Matignon, the prime minister's residence. At 61 rue de Grenelle, a handsome eighteenth-century house has been turned into the Musée Maillol (daily except Tues 11am–5.15pm; €8; Ⓦ www.museemaillol .com; M° Rue-du-Bac), overstuffed with Aristide Maillol's endlessly buxom sculpted female nudes, copies of which can be seen to better effect in the Louvre's Jardin du Carrousel. His paintings follow a similar theme, and there are also minor works by contemporaries like Picasso, Degas, Cezanne, Gauguin and Suzanne Valadon.

From here, **rue du Bac** leads south to rue de Sèvres, cutting across **rue de Babylone**, another of the *quartier*'s livelier streets. Don't miss **La Pagode** at no. 57bis (M° François Xavier). Built in 1895 for the wife of a director of Paris's elegant Le Bon Marché department store, this Orientalist folly was turned into an arts cinema in the 1930s – in 1959 it premiered Jean Cocteau's *Le Testament d'Orphée*, and it remains one of Paris' classic art-house venues.

Montparnasse and southern Paris

The entertainment nexus of **Montparnasse** divides the well-heeled opinion-formers and powerbrokers of St-Germain and the 7ᵉ from the relatively anonymous populations to the south. The three arrondissements to the south have suffered from large-scale housing developments, most notably along the riverfronts to both east and west, but villagey areas such as **rue du Commerce** in the 15ᵉ, **Pernety** in the 14ᵉ and the **Buttes-aux-Cailles** in the 13ᵉ are well worth a foray. On the fringes of the city proper, hard up against the *périphérique* ring road, are three fantastic parks: André Citroën, Georges-Brassens and Montsouris.

Like other Left Bank *quartiers*, Montparnasse trades on its association with the wild characters of the inter-war artistic and literary boom. Many were *habitués* of the cafés *Select*, *Coupole*, *Dôme*, *Rotonde* and *Closerie des Lilas*. The cafés are all still going strong on **boulevard du Montparnasse**, while the glitterati have mostly ended up in the nearby **Montparnasse cemetery**. The quarter's artistic traditions are maintained in a couple of second-tier, but fascinating, art museums, while elsewhere you can ascend the **Tour Montparnasse**, Paris's first and ugliest skyscraper, and descend into the bone-lined **catacombs**.

Around Montparnasse station

Most of the life of the quarter is concentrated between the junction with boulevard Raspail, where Rodin's *Balzac* broods over the traffic, and at the station end of boulevard du Montparnasse, where the colossal **Tour Montparnasse** has become one of the city's principal and most despised landmarks. Although central Paris is more distant, the view from the top is better than the one from the Eiffel Tower in that it includes the Eiffel Tower – and excludes the Tour Montparnasse. It also costs less to ascend (daily: May–Sept 9.30am–11.30pm; Oct–April 9.30am–10.30pm; €10). Alternatively, you could sit down for an expensive drink in the 56th-storey café-gallery, from where you get a tremendous view westwards. Sunset is the best time to visit. Asbestos is being stripped out level by level over the next few years, so check to see if the top floors are open (Ⓦ www.tourmontparnasse56.com).

One block northwest of the tower, on rue Antoine-Bourdelle, a garden of sculptures invites you into the fascinating **Musée Bourdelle** (Tues–Sun 10am–6pm; €6; Mᵒ Montparnasse-Bienvenüe/Falguière), which has been built around the sculptor's atmospheric, musty and slightly ghostly old studio. As Rodin's pupil and Giacometti's teacher, Bourdelle's bronze and stone works move from a naturalistic style – as in the wonderful series of Beethoven busts – towards a more geometric, Modernist style, seen in his better-known, monumental sculptures, some of which are dotted around the overgrown garden.

Montparnasse station was once the great arrival and departure point for travellers heading across the Atlantic, a connection commemorated in the unexpected **Jardin Atlantique**, suspended above the train tracks behind the station. Hemmed in by cliff-like high-rise apartment blocks, the park is a wonderful example of French design, with fields of Atlantic-coast grasses, wave-like undulations in the lawns (to cover the irregularly placed concrete struts below) – and well-hidden ventilation holes that reveal sudden glimpses of TGV roofs and rail sleepers below.

Montparnasse cemetery and the Fondation Henri Cartier-Bresson

Just south of boulevard Edgar-Quinet (which has a good food market) is the main entrance to the **Montparnasse cemetery** (mid-March to Nov 5 Mon–Fri 8am–6pm, Sat 8.30am–6pm, Sun 9am–6pm; Nov 6 to mid-March closes 5.30pm; free; Mᵒ Raspail/Gaîté/Edgar Quinet). Second in size and celebrity to Père Lachaise, its ranks of miniature temples pay homage to illustrious names from Baudelaire to Beckett and Gainsbourg to Saint-Saëns; pick up a free map at the entrance gate to track down your favourites. The simple joint grave of Jean-Paul Sartre and Simone de Beauvoir lies immediately right of the main entrance; a couple of poignant monuments are marked by artist Niki de Saint-Phalle's distinctive mosaic sculptures. In the southwest corner is an old windmill, remains of one of the seventeenth-century taverns frequented by the carousing students who caused the district to be named after Mount Parnassus, the legendary home of the muses of poetry and song, and of Bacchus's drunken revels.

Cutting across Avenue du Maine to the west, you come to the tiny Impasse Lebouis, where the slender steel-and-glass front of the **Fondation Henri Cartier-Bresson** (Tues, Thurs, Fri & Sun 1–6.30pm, Wed 1–8.30pm, Sat 11am–6.45pm; closed Aug; €6; Ⓦ www.henricartierbresson.org; Mᵒ Gaîté) is hidden away. The foundation houses the archive of the grand old photographer of Paris, who died shortly after its opening, in August 2004. Shows of the work of Cartier-Bresson and his contemporaries alternate with exhibitions promoting younger photographers.

The catacombs, the Fondation Cartier and the Observatoire

For a surreal, somewhat chilling experience, head down into the **catacombs** (Tues–Sun 10am–4pm; €7; M° Denfert-Rochereau) in nearby **place Denfert-Rochereau**, formerly place d'Enfer (Hell Square). Abandoned quarries stacked with millions of bones, which were cleared from overstocked charnel houses and cemeteries between 1785 and 1871, the catacombs are said to hold the remains of around six million Parisians. Lining the gloomy passageways, long thigh bones are stacked end-on, forming a wall to keep in the smaller bones and shards, which can just be seen in dusty, higgledy-piggledy heaps behind. These high femoral walls are further inset with gaping, hollow-eyed skulls and plaques carrying macabre quotations. It's undeniably a fascinating place, but note that there are a good couple of kilometres to walk – it's 500m through dark, damp, narrow passageways before you even get to the ossuary – and it can quickly become claustrophobic in the extreme.

Rue Schoelcher and boulevard Raspail, on the east side of Montparnasse cemetery, have some interesting examples of twentieth-century architecture, from Art Nouveau to the modern glass-and-steel façade of the **Fondation Cartier pour l'Art Contemporain** at 261 boulevard Raspail (Tues 11am–10pm, Wed–Sun 11am–8pm; €6.50; ⓦ www.fondation.cartier.fr; M° Raspail). Built in 1994 by Jean Nouvel, this presents contemporary installations, videos and multimedia in high-quality temporary exhibitions. About 500m to the east, on avenue de l'Observatoire, the classical **Observatoire de Paris** sat on France's zero meridian line from the 1660s, when it was constructed, until 1884. After that date, they reluctantly agreed that 0° longitude should pass through a small village in Normandy that happens to be due south of Greenwich. You can see one of the bronze markers of the "Arago line" – which has nothing to do with any mystical "rose line", notwithstanding the claims of a certain best-selling conspiracy thriller – set into the cobbles of the observatory's courtyard.

The 14ᵉ below Montparnasse

The jokey quasi-Classical Ricardo Bofill apartment complex around place de Catalogne gives way to a walkway along the old rue Vercingétorix and to the cosy district of **Pernety**, which was long an artists' haunt. Wandering around Cité Bauer, rue des Thermopyles and rue Didot reveals adorable houses, secluded courtyards and quiet mews, and on the corner of rue du Moulin Vert and rue Hippolyte-Maindron you'll find Giacometti's old ramshackle studio and home. There are more artistic associations south of rue d'Alésia near the junction with avenue Réné-Coty: Dalí, Lurcat, Miller and Durrell lived in the tiny cobbled street of Villa Seurat off rue de la Tombe-Issoire; Lenin and his wife lodged across the street at 4 rue Marie-Rose; Le Corbusier built the studio at 53 avenue Reille, close to the secretive and verdant square du Montsouris which links with rue Nansouty; and Georges Braque's home was in the cul-de-sac now named after him off this street.

The nearby **Parc Montsouris** (RER Cité-Universitaire) is a pleasant place to wander, with its unlikely contours, winding paths and waterfall above the lake – even the RER tracks cutting right through it fail to dent its charm.

The 15ᵉ arrondissement

Though it's the largest and most populous of them all, the **15ᵉ arrondissement** falls off the agenda for most visitors as it lacks a single important building or monument. The western edge fronts the Seine from the **Porte de Javel** to the Eiffel Tower. From Pont Mirabeau northwards, the riverbank is marred by a sort of mini-Défense development of half-cocked futuristic towers rising out of a litter-blown pedestrian platform some 10m above street level. Far pleasanter riverside strolling is to be had on the narrow midstream island, the **Allée des Cygnes**, which you can reach from the Pont de Grenelle. South of Pont Mirabeau, between rue Balard and the river, is the hyper-designed **Parc André-Citroën** (M° Balard), so named because the site used to be the Citroën motor works. Its best features are the glasshouses full of exotic-smelling shrubs, the dancing fountains – which bolder park-goers run through on hot days – and the tethered **balloon** (fine days only: 9am to roughly one hour before dusk; Mon–Fri €10, Sat & Sun €12), which offers spectacular views.

It is in the **rue du Commerce**, running down the middle of the arrondissement from M° La Motte Piquet-Grenelle, that George Orwell worked as a dishwasher, an experience described in *Down and Out in Paris and London*. These days it's a lively, old-fashioned high street full of small shops and peeling, shuttered houses, with one fine old brasserie, the *Café du Commerce* (see p.89).

The **Parc Georges-Brassens**, in the southeast corner of the arrondissement (M° Convention/Porte-de-Vanves), is a delight, with a garden of scented herbs and shrubs (best in late spring), puppets and rocks and merry-go-rounds for kids, a mountain stream with pine and birch trees, beehives and a tiny terraced vineyard. On the west side of the park, in a secluded garden in passage Dantzig, off rue Dantzig, stands an unusual polygonal studio space known as **La Ruche**. Home to Fernand Léger, Modigliani, Chagall, Soutine and many other artists at the start of the century, it's still used by creative types. In the sheds of the old horse market between the park and rue Brançion, a **book market** is held every Saturday and Sunday morning.

The 13e arrondissement

The 13ᵉ is one of the most disparate areas of the city. Place d'Italie, with the ornate *mairie* and vast Gaumont cinema, is the hub, with each of the major roads radiating out into very different *quartiers*. North of the mega-roundabout of **Place d'Italie**, the genteel neighbourhood around the ancient **Gobelins** tapestry works has more in common with the adjacent Quartier Latin. Between boulevard Auguste-Blanqui and rue Bobillot, meanwhile, is the lively hilltop quarter of the Butte-aux-Cailles. If you're looking for unpretentious, youthful and vaguely lefty restaurants and nightlife, it's well worth the short métro ride out from the centre. The easiest route is to walk up rue Bobillot from place d'Italie.

Over to the east, in the middle of a swathe of high-rise social housing, is the **Chinese quarter** of Paris. Avenues de Choisy and d'Ivry are full of Vietnamese, Chinese, Thai, Cambodian and Laotian restaurants and food shops, as is **Les Olympiades**, a weird semi-derelict pedestrian area seemingly suspended between giant tower blocks.

Following rue Tolbiac or boulevard Vincent-Auriol to the river, you reach the new district of **Paris Rive Gauche**, whose star attraction is the impressive **Bibliothèque Nationale de France** (Tues–Sat 10am–8pm, Sun 1–7pm; €3.30 for a reading room pass; Ⓦwww.bnf.fr). Accessible from its northern and southern corners (M° Quai-de-la-Gare or Bibliothèque-François-Mitterrand), it has four enormous towers – intended to look like open books – framing a sunken pine copse. Glass walls alongside the trees allow dappled light to filter through to the underground library spaces. Jaw-dropping as it is, architect Dominique Perrault's design attracted widespread derision after shutters had to be added to the towers to protect the books and manuscripts from sunlight. It's worth wandering around inside, to see the pair of wonderful globes that belonged to Louis XIV and occasional small-scale exhibitions; the garden level is reserved for accredited researchers only. From the Bibliothèque Nationale down to the *boulevard périphérique*, almost every stick of street furniture and square metre of tarmac is shiny and new. The still-under-populated cafés and apartment blocks, and the **Passerelle Simone de Beauvoir**, a €21-million footbridge that crosses the Seine in a hyper-modern double-ribbon structure, give the area a futuristic frontier-town feel. Between the bridge and the pont de Bercy, several tethered **barges** have made the area a nightlife attraction in its own right (see p.157); among them, the floating swimming pool **Piscine Josephine Baker**, on its own barge, is wonderful, but often closed down for mysterious repairs. Immediately south of rue Tolbiac, the giant, decaying warehouse of **Les Frigos** was once used for cold-storage of meat and fish destined for Les Halles, but was taken over immediately after the market's closure by artists and musicians. It has been run as an anarchic studio space ever since, with a bar-restaurant on site and open-door exhibitions once or twice a year.

Newest of all, the former warehouses on the bleak Quai d'Austerlitz are currently being transformed into **Docks en Seine**, an ultra-modern fashion, shopping and entertainment complex with lots of glass and open space, including a "vegetalized" terrace. A projected fashion institute inside is still in development.

Montmartre and northern Paris

Perched on Paris's highest hill, towards the northern edge of the city, **Montmartre** was famously the home and playground of artists such as Renoir, Degas, Picasso and Toulouse-Lautrec. The crown of the Butte Montmartre, around place du Tertre, is a scrum, overrun with tourists these days, but the steep streets around **Abbesses** métro preserve an attractively festive, village-like atmosphere – and seem to become more gentrified and more fashionable every year. **Pigalle**, by contrast, at the southern foot of the Butte, remains brassy and seedy, while the **Goutte d'Or**, to the east, is vibrantly multi-ethnic. Out at the northern city limits, the mammoth **St-Ouen market** hawks everything from extravagant antiques to the cheapest flea-market hand-me-downs.

Place des Abbesses and up to the Butte

In spite of being one of the city's chief tourist attractions, the **Butte Montmartre** manages to retain the quiet, almost secretive, air of its rural origins. The most popular access route is via the rue de Steinkerque and the steps below the Sacré-Coeur (the funicular railway from place Suzanne-Valadon is covered by normal métro tickets). For a quieter approach, wind your way up via place des Abbesses or rue Lepic.

Place des Abbesses, featuring one of the few complete surviving Guimard métro entrances, is the hub of a lively neighborhood. To the east, at the Chapelle des Auxiliatrices in rue Yvonne-Le-Tac, Ignatius Loyola founded the Jesuit movement in 1534. It's also supposed to be the place where St-Denis, the first bishop of Paris, was beheaded by the Romans around 250 AD. He is said to have carried it until he dropped, where the cathedral of St-Denis now stands north of the city. Today, the streets are full of trendy clothes shops, buzzing wine bars and laid-back restaurants.

One quiet and attractive way to get from place des Abbesses to the top of the Butte is to climb up rue de la Vieuville and the rue Drevet stairs to the

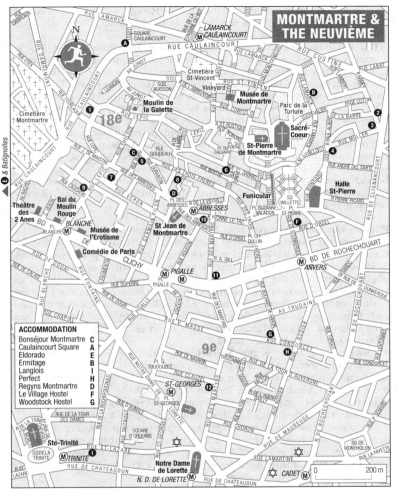

**MONTMARTRE &
THE NEUVIÈME**

ACCOMMODATION

Bonséjour Montmartre	C
Caulaincourt Square	A
Eldorado	E
Ermitage	B
Langlois	I
Perfect	H
Regyns Montmartre	D
Le Village Hostel	F
Woodstock Hostel	G

BARS & CAFÉS					
Au Clair de la Lune	2	Chez Camille	8		
Au Rendez-Vous des Amis	6	L'Eté en Pente Douce	4		
Café des Deux Moulins	9	La Fourmi	11		

RESTAURANTS			
Le XVIIIème Barathym	3	Le Mono	7
Café Burq	5	Le Relais Gascon	10
Haynes	12	Au Virage Lepic	1

minuscule **place du Calvaire**, with a lovely view back over the city; you could also head up rue Tholozé, turning right below the **Moulin de la Galette** – the last survivor of Montmartre's forty-odd windmills, immortalized by Renoir – into rue des Norvins.

Artistic associations abound hereabouts. Zola, Berlioz, Turgenev, Seurat, Degas and Van Gogh lived in the area. Picasso, Braque and Gris invented Cubism in an old piano factory in place Émile-Goudeau, known as the **Bateau-Lavoir**, still serving as artists' studios, though the original building burnt down years ago. Toulouse-Lautrec's inspiration, the **Moulin Rouge**, survives too, albeit as a shadow of its former self, on the corner of boulevard de Clichy and place Blanche (see p.159).

The intriguing little **Musée de Montmartre**, in a quiet spot at 12 rue Cortot (Wed–Sun 11am–6pm; €7; ⓦ www.museedemontmartre.fr; M° Lamarck-Caulaincourt), recaptures something of the feel of those bohemian days with old posters, paintings and photos and recreations of period rooms. The house, rented at various times by Renoir, Dufy, Suzanne Valadon and her alcoholic son Utrillo, also offers views over the neat terraces of the tiny **Montmartre vineyard** – which produces some 1500 bottles a year – on the north side of the Butte. You can walk round to the vineyard, where the steep rue de Saules falls away past the infamous cabaret club **Le Lapin Agile** at no. 22. Famously painted and patronized by Picasso, Utrillo and other leading lights of the early twentieth-century Montmartre scene, it's an adorable little building, hidden behind shutters and a pretty garden, and still puts on arty cabaret shows featuring French chanson and poetry (Tues–Sun 9pm–2am; €24; ⓦ www .au-lapin-agile.com).

Place du Tertre and the Sacré-Coeur

The **place du Tertre**, the core of old Montmartre, is today best avoided. It's been sucked dry of all interest, clotted with tour groups, overpriced restaurants, tacky souvenir stalls and jaded artists knocking out garish paintings. Between place du Tertre and the Sacré-Coeur, the old church of St-Pierre is all that remains of the Benedictine abbey that occupied the Butte Montmartre from the twelfth century on. Though much altered, it still retains its Romanesque and early Gothic feel. In it are four ancient columns, two by the door, two in the choir, leftovers from a Roman shrine that stood on the hill – *mons mercurii* (Mercury's Hill), the Romans called it.

Crowning the Butte is the **Sacré-Coeur** (daily 6.45am–10.30pm; free; M° Abbesses/Anvers) with its iconic ice-cream-scoop dome. Construction of this French–Byzantine confection was started in the 1870s on the initiative of the Catholic Church to atone for the "crimes" of the Commune. **Square Willette**, the space at the foot of the monumental staircase, is named after the local artist who turned out on inauguration day to shout "Long live the devil!". Today the staircase acts as impromptu seating for visitors enjoying the views over Paris, munching on picnics and watching the street entertainers; the crowds only increase as night falls. You can also get stunning **views** from the top of the dome (daily: April–Sept 9am–7pm; Oct–March 9am–6pm; €5), which takes you almost as high as the Eiffel Tower.

Montmartre cemetery

West of the Butte, with its entrance on avenue Rachel under rue Caulaincourt, lies the **Montmartre cemetery** (mid-March to Nov 5 Mon–Fri 8am–6pm, Sat 8.30am–6pm, Sun 9am–6pm; Nov to mid-March closes 5.30pm; free; M° Blanche/Place-de-Clichy). It's a melancholy place, tucked down below street level in the hollow of an old quarry, its steep tomb-dotted hills creating a sombre ravine of the dead. The graves of Nijinsky, Zola, Stendhal, Berlioz, Degas, Feydeau, Offenbach and Truffaut, among others, are marked on a free map available at the entrance.

St-Ouen flea market

Officially (many stands are closed on Monday) open Saturday to Monday from 9am to 6.30pm – unofficially, from 5am – **the puces de St-Ouen**

(M° Porte-de-Clignancourt) claims to be the largest flea market in the world. Nowadays it's predominantly a proper – and expensive – antiques market (mainly furniture, but including old café-bar counters, telephones, traffic lights, jukeboxes and the like), with many quirky treasures to be found. Of the twelve or so individual markets, you could concentrate on Marché **Dauphine**, good for movie posters, chanson and jazz records, comics and books, and Marché **Vernaison** for curios and bric-a-brac. Under the flyover of the *périphérique*, along rue J.H. Fabre, vendors hawk counterfeit clothing, sunglasses and pirated DVDs, while cup-and-ball scam merchants try their luck on hapless tourists.

Pigalle

From place Clichy in the west to Barbès-Rochechouart in the east, the hill of Montmartre is underlined by the sleazy **boulevards de Clichy and Rochechouart**. At the Barbès end of boulevard Rochechouart, where the métro clatters by on iron trestles, crowds teem round the Tati department stores, the city's cheapest, while the pavements are lined with West and North African street vendors selling textiles, watches and trinkets. At the place Clichy end, tour buses from all over Europe feed their contents into massive hotels. In the middle, between place Blanche and place Pigalle, **sex shows**, sex shops, girly bars and streetwalkers (both male and female) vie for the custom of *solitaires* and couples alike.

   In this appropriate setting you'll find the rather classy **Musée de l'Erotisme**, 72 boulevard Clichy (daily 10am–2am; €8; Ⓦ www.musee-erotisme.com; M° Blanche), which explores different cultures' approaches to sex. The ground floor and first floor are brimming with sacred and ethnographic art – displaying proud phalluses and well-practised positions from Asia, Africa and pre-Colombian Latin America, plus satirical European curiosities – and feature a fascinating history of Parisian brothels. The remaining five floors are devoted to high-quality temporary exhibitions.

Goutte d'Or

Along the north side of the grotty boulevard de la Chapelle, between boulevard Barbès and the Gare du Nord rail lines, stretches the *quartier* of the **Goutte d'Or** ("Drop of Gold"), a name that derives from the medieval vineyard that occupied this site. After World War I, when large numbers of North Africans were first imported to replenish the ranks of Frenchmen dying in the trenches, the area gradually became an immigrant ghetto. Today, while the *quartier* remains poor, it is a vibrant place, home to a host of mini-communities, predominantly West African and Congolese, but with pockets of South Asian, Haitian, Turkish and other ethnicities as well. Countless shops sell ethnic music and fabrics, but the main sight for visitors is on rue Dejean, a few steps east of métro Château-Rouge, where the **Marché Dejean** (closed Sun afternoon and Mon) heaves with African groceries and thrums with shoppers. Another, more general market takes place in the mornings twice weekly (Wed & Sat) underneath the métro viaduct on the **boulevard de la Chapelle**.

Canal St-Martin and La Villette

The **Bassin de la Villette** and the **canals** at the northeastern gate of the city were for generations the centre of a densely populated working-class district, whose main source of employment were the La Villette abattoirs and meat market. These have long gone, replaced by the huge complex of La Villette, a postmodern park of science and technology.

The Villette complex stands at the junction of the **Ourcq** and **St-Denis canals**. The first was built by Napoleon to bring fresh water into the city; the second is an extension of the Canal St-Martin built as a short cut to the great western loop of the Seine around Paris. The canals have undergone extensive renovation, and derelict sections of the *quais* have been made more appealing to cyclists, rollerbladers and pedestrians.

Canal St-Martin and place de Stalingrad

The **Canal St-Martin** runs underground at the Bastille to surface again in boulevard Jules-Ferry by rue du Faubourg-du-Temple. The canal still has a slightly industrial feel, especially along its upper stretch. The lower part is more attractive, with plane trees, cobbled *quais* and elegant, high-arched footbridges, as well as lively bars and stylish boutiques frequented by artsy, media folk. The area is particularly lively on Sunday afternoons, when the *quais* are closed to traffic, and pedestrians, cyclists and rollerbladers take over the streets; on sunny days a young crowd hangs out along the canal's edge, nursing beers or softly strumming guitars.

The canal disappears underground again further north at **place de Stalingrad**. To one side of the square stands the beautifully restored Palladian-style Rotonde de la Villette, one of Ledoux's tollhouses in Louis XVI's tax wall, where taxes were levied on all goods coming into the city – a major bone of contention in the lead-up to the 1789 Revolution. The *rotonde* is currently being converted into a cultural space and restaurant.

Beyond the square is the renovated **Bassin de la Villette** dock, once France's premier port. It's been recobbled and the dockside buildings have been converted into brasseries and a multiplex cinema (the MK2), which has screens on both banks, linked by a boat shuttle. In August, as part of the Paris Plage scheme (see p.77), there are canoes, pedaloes for children and other boating activities. At rue de Crimée a unique hydraulic bridge marks the end of the dock and the beginning of the Canal de l'Ourcq. If you keep to the south bank on quai de la Marne, you can cross directly into the Parc de la Villette.

The Parc de la Villette

The **Parc de la Villette** (daily 6am–1am; free; Ⓦwww.villette.com) music, art and science complex, between avenues Corentin-Cariou and Jean-Jaurès, has so many disparate and disconnected elements that it's hard to know where to start. To help you get your bearings, it's worth picking up a map at the **information centre** at the entrance by Mº Porte-de-Pantin, to the south.

The main attraction is the enormous **Cité des Sciences et de l'Industrie** (Tues–Sat 10am–6pm, Sun 10am–7pm; €8 or €11 with the planetarium; Ⓦwww.cite-sciences.fr; Mº Porte-de-la-Villette). This high-tech museum devoted to science and all its applications is built into the concrete hulk of the abandoned abattoirs on the north side of the Canal de l'Ourcq. Four times the size of the Pompidou Centre, it's a colossal glass-walled building, surrounded by a moat. Inside are crow's-nests, cantilevered platforms, bridges and suspended walkways, the different levels linked by lifts and escalators around a huge central space open to the full forty-metre height of the roof. The permanent exhibition, called Explora, covers subjects such as sound, robotics, energy, light, ecology, maths, medicine, space and language. As the name suggests, the emphasis is on exploring, encouraged through interactive computers, videos, holograms, animated models and games.

When all the interrogation and stimulation becomes too much, you can relax in cafés within Explora, before joining the queue for the **planetarium**. Back on the ground floor there's the **Louis-Lumière Cinema**, which shows 3-D films (included in Cité des Sciences et de l'Industrie ticket), and the **Cité des Enfants** for children (see p.166), as well as a whole programme of excellent **temporary exhibitions**.

In front of the complex floats the **Géode** (hourly shows Tues–Sun 10.30am–8.30pm; €10.50), a bubble of reflecting steel that looks as though it's been dropped from an intergalactic *boules* game into a pool of water. Inside is a screen for Imax films, not noted for their plots, but a great visual experience. There's also the **Cinaxe**, between the Cité and the Canal St-Denis (screenings every 15min Tues–Sun 11am–1pm & 2–5pm; €4.80), combining 70mm film shot at thirty frames a second with seats that move. Beside the Géode is a real 1957 French **submarine**, the **Argonaute** (Tues–Sat 10am–5.30pm, Sun 10am–6.30pm; €3). South of the canal are bizarrely landscaped **themed gardens** of "mirrors", "mists", "winds and dunes" and "islands", and over to the east is the **Zénith** inflatable rock music venue. To the south, the largest of the old **market halls** is now a vast and brilliant exhibition space, the **Grande Salle**.

South of the Grande Salle stands the **Cité de la Musique** (Ⓦ www.cite -musique.fr), in two fine contemporary buildings to either side of the Porte-de-Pantin entrance. To the west is the national music academy, while to the east are a concert hall, the chic *Café de la Musique*, a music and dance information centre and the excellent **Musée de la Musique** (Tues–Sat noon–6pm, Sun 10am–6pm; €7), presenting the history of music from the end of the Renaissance to the present day, both visually – through a collection of 4500 instruments – and aurally, with headsets and interactive displays.

Belleville, Ménilmontant and Père-Lachaise

Traditionally working class, with a history of radical and revolutionary activity, the gritty **eastern districts** of Paris, particularly the old villages of **Belleville** and **Ménilmontant**, are nowadays some of the most diverse and vibrant parts of the city, home to sizeable ethnic populations, as well as students and artists, attracted by the low rents. The main visitor attraction in the area is the **Père-Lachaise cemetery**, final resting place of many well-known artists and writers. Visiting the modern **Parc de Belleville** will reveal the area's other main asset – wonderful views of the city below. Another park well worth seeing is the fairytale-like **Parc des Buttes–Chaumont**.

Parc des Buttes-Chaumont

At the northern end of the Belleville heights, a short walk from La Villette, is the **parc des Buttes–Chaumont** (M° Buttes-Chaumont/Botzaris), constructed by Haussmann in the 1860s to camouflage what until then had been a desolate warren of disused quarries and miserable shacks. Out of this rather unlikely setting a wonderfully romantic park was created – there'a a grotto with a cascade and artificial stalactites, and a picturesque lake from which a huge rock rises up topped with a delicate Corinthian temple. From the temple you get fine views of Sacré-Coeur and beyond. The park stays open all night and, equally rarely for Paris, you're not cautioned off the grass.

Belleville and Ménilmontant

The route from Buttes-Chaumont to Père-Lachaise will take you through the one-time villages of **Belleville** and **Ménilmontant**. Absorbed into Paris in the 1860s and subsequently built up with high-rise blocks to house migrants from rural districts and the ex-colonies, this area might not be exactly "belle", but it's certainly vibrant and happening. The main street, rue de Belleville, abounds with Vietnamese, Thai and Chinese shops and restaurants, and numerous artists live and work in the area, attracted by the availability of affordable and large spaces; the best time to view their work is during the **Journées portes ouvertes ateliers d'artistes de Belleville** in mid-May (for exact dates see ⓦwww.ateliers-artistes-belleville.org).

You get fantastic views down onto the city centre from the higher reaches of Belleville and Ménilmontant: the best place to watch the sun set is the **Parc de Belleville** (M° Couronnes/Pyrénées), which descends in a series of terraces and waterfalls from rue Piat. And from **rue de Ménilmontant**, by rues de l'Ermitage and Boyer, you can look straight down to the Pompidou Centre. On rue de Ménilmontant, and particularly its extension **rue Oberkampf**, trendsetting bars and cafés jostle for space alongside the ethnic bakeries, cheap goods stores and grocers.

Père-Lachaise cemetery

Père-Lachaise cemetery (Mon–Fri 8am–5.30pm, Sat 8.30am–5.30pm, Sun 9am–5.30pm; M° Gambetta/Père-Lachaise/Alexandre-Dumas/Phillipe-Auguste), final resting place of numerous notables, is an atmospheric, eerily beautiful haven, with little cobbled footpaths, terraced slopes and magnificent old trees which spread their branches over the tombs as though shading them from the outside world. The cemetery was opened in 1804, after an urgent stop had been put to further burials in the overflowing city cemeteries and churchyards. The civil authorities had Molière, La Fontaine, Abelard and Héloïse reburied here, and to be interred in Père-Lachaise quickly acquired cachet. A free **map** of the cemetery is available at all the entrances or you can buy a more detailed one for around €2 at nearby newsagents and florists.

Among the most visited graves is that of **Chopin** (Division 11), often attended by Poles bearing red-and-white wreaths and flowers. Fans also flock to the ex-Doors lead singer **Jim Morrison** (Division 6), who died in Paris at the age of 27.

Femme fatale Colette's tomb, close to the main entrance in Division 4, is very plain, though always covered in flowers. The same holds true for those of Sarah Bernhardt (Division 44) and Edith Piaf (Division 97). Marcel Proust lies in his family's black-marble, conventional tomb (Division 85).

Cutting a rather romantic figure, French president Félix Faure (Division 4), who died in the arms of his mistress in the Elysée palace in 1899, lies draped in a French flag, his head to one side. Corot (division 24) and Balzac (division 48) both have superb busts, while Géricault reclines on cushions of stone (division 12), paint palette in hand. One of the most impressive of the individual tombs is Oscar Wilde's (Division 89), topped with a sculpture by Jacob Epstein of a mysterious Pharaonic winged messenger (sadly vandalized of its once prominent member, last seen being used as a paperweight by the director of the cemetery). Nearby, in division 96, is the grave of **Modigliani** and his lover Jeanne Herbuterne, who killed herself in crazed grief a few days after the artist died in agony from meningitis.

In Division 97 are the memorials to the victims of the Nazi concentration camps and executed Resistance fighters. The sculptures are relentless in their images of inhumanity, of people forced to collaborate in their own degradation and death. Marking one of the bloodiest episodes in French history is the Mur des Fédérés (Division 76), the wall where the last troops of the Paris Commune were lined up and shot in the final days of the battle in 1871. The man who ordered their execution, Adolphe Thiers, lies in the centre of the cemetery in division 55.

Bercy, the Promenade Plantée and Bois de Vincennes

The riverside **Bercy** *quartier*, which extends southeast from the Gare de Lyon, was where the capital's wine supplies used to be unloaded from river barges. Much of the area has now been turned into a welcome green space, the extensive **Parc de Bercy** (M° Bercy), cleverly incorporating elements of the old warehouse district such as disused railway tracks and cobbled lanes.

The impressive building resembling a pack of falling cards that overlooks the east side of the park, at 51 rue de Bercy, was designed by Bilbao's Guggenheim architect Frank O. Gehry and houses the **Cinémathèque** (ⓦwww.cinematheque.fr; M° Bercy), the repository for a huge archive of films dating back to the earliest days of cinema. Regular retrospectives of French and foreign films are screened in the four cinemas and it also has an engaging museum (Mon & Wed–Fri noon–7pm, Thurs till 10pm, Sat & Sun 10am–8pm; €5), with lots of early cinematic equipment and silent-film clips, as well as the dress that Vivien Leigh wore in *Gone with the Wind*.

Continuing eastwards through the Parc de Bercy, you come to **Bercy Village** (M° Cour Saint-Émilion), another new development, the main thoroughfare of which is the Cour Saint Émilion, a pedestrianized street lined with former wine warehouses converted into cafés, restaurants and shops. The ochre-coloured stone and the homogeneity of the buildings make for an attractive ensemble and it's an agreeable spot for a wander.

Even better for a stroll, especially if you feel like escaping from the bustle of the city for a bit, is the **Promenade Plantée** (M° Bastille/Ledru-Rollin), a stretch of disused railway line, much of it along a viaduct, that has been converted into an elevated walkway and planted with a profusion of trees and flowers. The walkway starts near the beginning of avenue Daumesnil, just south of the Bastille opera house, and is reached via a flight of stone steps – or lifts – with a number of similar access points all the way along. It takes you to the Parc de Reuilly, then descends to ground level and continues nearly as far as the *périphérique*, from where you can follow signs to the Bois de Vincennes. The whole walk is around 4.5km long, but if you don't feel like doing the entire thing you could just walk the first part – along the viaduct – which also happens to be the most attractive stretch, running past venerable old mansion blocks and giving a bird's-eye view of the area below and of small architectural details not seen from street level. What's more, the arches of the viaduct itself have been ingeniously converted into spaces for artisans' *ateliers* and craftshops, collectively known as the **Viaduc des Arts**. There are 51 of them, including furniture restorers, interior designers, cabinet makers and fashion and jewellery boutiques.

The Bois de Vincennes

The **Bois de Vincennes** is a favourite family Sunday retreat and the largest green space that the city has to offer, aside from the Bois de Boulogne in the west. It's rather crisscrossed with roads, but there are some very pleasant corners, including the picturesque Lac Daumesnil, where you can hire boats, and the **Parc Floral** (daily: summer 9.30am–8pm; winter 9.30am–dusk; €1; ⓦwww .parcfloraldeparis.com; M° Château-de-Vincennes then bus #112 or a 15min walk), perhaps Paris's best gardens, with an adventure playground attached. Flowers are always in bloom in the Jardin des Quatres Saisons; you can picnic amid pines and rhododendrons, then wander through concentrations of camellias, cacti, ferns, irises and bonsai trees. Just north of Lac Daumesnil is the city's largest **zoo**, currently closed for major renovation and due to reopen in 2012.

On the northern edge of the *bois* lies the **Château de Vincennes** (daily 10am–5pm; €7.50; M° Château-de-Vincennes), the country's only surviving medieval royal residence, **built by Charles V**, subsequently turned into a state prison, then porcelain factory, weapons dump and military training school. Enclosed by a high defensive wall and still preserving the feel of a military barracks, it presents a rather austere aspect on first sight, but it's worth visiting for its Gothic **Chapelle Royale** (currently being restored and due to reopen in 2009), decorated with superb Renaissance stained-glass windows; and the restored fourteenth-century *keep*, where you can see some fine vaulted ceilings, Charles V's bedchamber and graffiti left by prisoners, whose number included one Marquis de Sade.

Eating and drinking

Eating and drinking are among the chief delights of Paris, as they are in France as a whole. An incredible number of restaurants remain defiantly traditional, offering the classic *cuisine bourgeoise* based on well-sauced meat dishes, but you can find a tremendous variety of foods, from Senegalese to Vietnamese,

▲ Flo Brasserie

and from eastern European to North African. Regional French cuisines, notably from the southwest, are always popular, as is contemporary French gastronomy – spices and ingredients from the Asia-Pacific region are current fads. There is a huge diversity of places to eat: luxurious, hushed **restaurants** decked with crystal and white linen; noisy, elbow-to-elbow bench-and-trestle-table joints; intimate neighbourhood **bistros** with specials on the blackboard; grand seafood **brasseries** with splendid, historic interiors; and artfully distressed **cafés** serving dishes of the day. Relatively inexpensive offshoots of top restaurants are something of a fashion at the moment, as are the more commercial equivalents – the spin-off bistros of celebrity chefs like Alain Ducasse and Guy Savoy, often focusing on a speciality such as rotisserie or Basque food.

Though the cost of eating out in Paris has gone up markedly in recent years, it's still possible to eat cheaply and well, especially at lunchtime, when set menus (known as menus or *formules*) can be as little as €12–16. In the evening, however, around €30 is fairly typical, though you can often easily pay a lot more. For true, starred gastronomy you'll pay something in the region of €150 or more. The big boulevard cafés and brasseries are always more expensive than those a little further removed, and addresses in the smarter or more touristy arrondissements set prices soaring. A snack or drink on the Champs-Élysées or place St-Germain-des-Prés, for instance, will be double or triple the price of one in Belleville or Batignolles.

It's worth budgeting for at least one meal in one of Paris's truly spectacular **gourmet restaurants**, such as *Pierre Gagnaire* (see p.148), famed for his experimental "molecular cuisine", or *L'Arpège,* where Alain Passard largely eschews meat in favour of superb fish and vegetable dishes. At almost all of these restaurants you'll need to dress smartly; most prefer men to wear a jacket and tie. Prices are often cheaper if you go at midday during the week, and some offer a set lunch menu for around €75–90. Otherwise count on €100 as a bare minimum – the top menus soar above €200, and there's no limit on the amount you can pay for wine.

Drinking venues range from the many **cafés** that move seamlessly from coffees to cocktails as evening approaches, to the tiny, dedicated **wine bars** offering little-known vintages from every region of France. There are cavernous **beer cellars**, designer **bars** with DJ *soirées* at weekends and the ubiquitous Irish/British/Canadian **pubs**. You can take coffee and cakes in a chintzy **salon de thé**, in a bookshop or gallery, or even in the courtyard of a mosque. Many bars have happy hours, but prices can double after 10pm, and any clearly trendy, glitzy or stylish place is bound to be expensive.

The different **eating** and **drinking establishments** are listed here by area. They are divided into restaurants, including brasseries and bistros, and bars and cafés, a term used to incorporate anywhere you might go for a drink or a lighter meal – cafés, ice-cream parlours and *salons de thé*. You'll also find boxes listing vegetarian (see p.154) and student (see p.155) restaurants. Restaurant **opening times** are typically noon–2/2.30pm and 7.30–10.30/11pm; exceptions to this are noted in the text. Where possible, we have marked restaurants listed on the maps. It's best to **book ahead** for evening meals, especially from Thursday to Saturday; for most places it's usually enough to book on the day, though for the top gourmet restaurants you'll need to book at least two or three weeks in advance. Note that a surprising number of places don't accept credit cards.

The Islands

See maps, p.107 and pp.112–113.

Berthillon 31 rue St-Louis-en-l'Île, 4ᵉ; M° Pont-Marie. You may well have to queue for one of *Berthillon*'s exquisite ice creams or sorbets – arguably the best in Paris. Wed–Sun 10am–8pm.

🏃 **Mon Vieil Ami** 69 rue St-Louis-en-l'Île, 4ᵉ ☎01.40.46.01.35; M° Pont-Marie. Charming little bistro, with appealing contemporary decor of chocolate browns and frosted-glass panels. The excellent cuisine is bold and zesty, using seasonal ingredients, and the wine list includes some choice vintages. Three courses cost around €40. Closed Mon & Tues, and three weeks in Jan & Aug.

Taverne Henri IV 13 place du Pont-Neuf, Île de la Cité, 1ᵉʳ; M° Pont-Neuf. An old-style wine bar that's probably changed little since Yves Montand used to come here with Simone Signoret. It's especially lively at lunchtime when lawyers from the nearby Palais de Justice drop in for generous platters of meats and cheeses (for around €12) and toasted sandwiches. Mon–Fri 11.30am–9.30pm, Sat noon–5pm; closed Sun & Aug.

The Champs-Élysées and around

See map, pp.96–97.

Bars and cafés

Ladurée 75 av des Champs-Élysées, 8ᵉ; M° George-V. This Champs-Élysées branch of the *Ladurée* tearooms, with its luxurious gold and green decor, is perfect for a shopping break. Try the delicious macaroons or the thick hot chocolate. Daily 7.30am–11.30pm.

Musée Jacquemart-André 158 bd Haussmann, 8ᵉ ☎01.45.62.11.59; M° St-Philippe-du-Roule/Miromesnil. Part of the Musée Jacquemart-André but with independent access, this is the most sumptuously appointed *salon de thé* in the city. Admire the ceiling frescoes by Tiepolo while savouring fine pastries or salads. Daily 11.45am–5.30pm.

Restaurants

Pierre Gagnaire *Hôtel Balzac*, 6 rue Balzac, 8ᵉ ☎01.58.36.12.50, ⓦwww.pierre-gagnaire.com; M° George-V. Regularly rated as one of the top ten restaurants in the world by *Restaurant* magazine, *Pierre Gagnaire* is a gastronomic adventure. The lunch menu costs €95, dinner around €245. Mon–Fri noon–1.30pm & 7.30–9.30pm, Sun 7.30–9.30pm.

Le Relais de l'Entrecôte 15 rue Marbeuf, 8ᵉ; M° Franklin-D.-Roosevelt. No reservations are taken at this bustling diner, so you may have to queue for the single main course on the menu: steak and *frites*. This is no ordinary steak though – the secret is in the delicious, buttery sauce. Around €30 for three courses. Daily; closed Aug.

La Table du Lauriston 129 rue Lauriston, 16ᵉ ☎01.47.27.00.07; M° Trocadéro. A slightly older, well-off crowd from the neighbourhood usually dines at this traditional bistro run by chef-to-the-stars Serge Rabey. Game terrine with chanterelle mushrooms and *poularde fondante au vin jaune* (chicken croquettes with Arbois wine) are indicative of the upscale dishes here, and be sure to taste their famed Baba au Rhum. You'll easily spend €40–50 per person, but the *cuisine bourgeoise* is excellent. Closed Sat lunch & all day Sun.

Taillevent 15 rue Lamennais, 8ᵉ ☎01.44.95.15.01; M° Charles-de-Gaulle. One of Paris's finest gourmet restaurants. The Provencal-influenced cuisine and wine list are exceptional, the decor classy and refined. There's a set menu for €80 at lunch only, otherwise reckon on an average of €150 a head, excluding wine, and book well in advance. Closed Sat, Sun & Aug.

The Louvre, Tuileries and Palais Royal

See map, pp.96–97.

Angelina 226 rue de Rivoli, 1ᵉʳ; M° Tuileries. This elegant old *salon de thé*, with its murals, gilded stuccowork and comfy leather armchairs, does the best hot chocolate in town – a generous jugful with whipped cream on the side is enough for two. Mon–Fri 8am–7pm, Sat & Sun 9.15am–7pm; closed Tues in July & Aug.

Bar Costes *Hotel Costes*, 239 rue St-Honoré, 8ᵉ; M° Concorde/Tuileries. A favourite haunt of fashionistas and celebs, this is a romantic place for an aperitif or late-night drinks amid decadent nineteenth-century decor of red velvet, swags and columns, set around an Italianate courtyard. Cocktails around €16. Daily until 2am.

Juveniles 47 rue de Richelieu, 2ᵉ; M° Palais-Royal. A very popular tiny wine bar run by a Scot. There are usually around ten different wines available by the glass (from €3); *plats du jour* cost €12, cheese plates and other light dishes €8. Tues–Sat 11am–11pm, Sun noon–2pm, Mon 7.30–11pm.

🏃 **Verlet** 56 rue St-Honoré, 1ᵉʳ; M° Palais-Royal/Musée du Louvre. A heady aroma of coffee greets you as you enter this charming old-world coffee merchant's and café done out with wood furnishings and green-leather benches. You can dither over 25 varieties of coffee, and there's a selection of teas and light snacks, too. Mon–Sat 9am–7pm.

The Grands Boulevards and around
See map, pp.96–97.

Bars and cafés

L'Arbre à Cannelle 57 passage des Panoramas, 2ᵉ; Mᵒ Grands Boulevards. Tucked away in an attractive *passage*, this *salon de thé* with exquisite wood panelling, frescoes and painted ceilings makes an excellent spot to treat yourself to salads and tarts both savoury and sweet. Mon–Sat 11.30am–6pm.

Delaville Café 34 bd de la Bonne Nouvelle, 10ᵉ; Mᵒ Bonne-Nouvelle. This ex-bordello, with grand staircase, gilded mosaics and marble columns, draws in crowds of hipsters, who sling back a mojito or two before moving on to one of the area's clubs. Daily 11am–2am.

Le Rubis 10 rue du Marché-St-Honoré, 1ᵉʳ; Mᵒ Pyramides. This very small and very crowded wine bar is one of the oldest in Paris, known for its excellent wines – mostly from the Beaujolais and Loire regions – and home-made *rillettes* (a kind of pork pâté). Mon–Fri 7.30am–9pm, Sat 9am–3pm; closed mid-Aug.

Restaurants

Gallopin 40 rue Notre-Dame-des-Victoires, 2ᵉ ☎01.42.36.45.38; Mᵒ Bourse. An utterly endearing old brasserie, with all its original brass and mahogany fittings and a beautiful painted glass roof in the back room. The classic French dishes, especially the *foie gras maison*, are well above par, and menus range from €23 to €33.50. Daily noon–midnight.

Aux Lyonnais 32 rue St-Marc, 2ᵉ ☎01.42.96.65.04; Mᵒ Bourse/Richelieu-Drouot. This revamped old bistro, with lovely *belle époque* tiles and mirrored walls, serves up delicious Lyonnais fare – try the *quenelles* (light and delicate fish dumplings) followed by the heavenly Cointreau soufflé for dessert. Three-course set menu €30. Closed Sat lunch, Sun & Mon.

Beaubourg and Les Halles
See map, p.107.

Bars and cafés

Café Beaubourg 43 rue St-Merri, 4ᵉ; Mᵒ Rambuteau/Hôtel-de-Ville. Seats under the expansive awnings of this stylish café command frontline views of the Pompidou piazza and are great for people-watching. It's also good for a relaxing Sunday brunch (around €20). Daily 8am–1am.

Le Petit Marcel 63 rue Rambuteau, 4ᵉ; Mᵒ Rambuteau. Speckled tabletops, mirrors and Art Nouveau tiles, a cracked and faded ceiling and about eight square metres of drinking space. There's a small dining area, too, where you can get reasonably cheap and filling bistro fare such as *frites* and omelette or steak tartare. Mon–Sat till 2am.

Restaurants

Chez Dilan 13 rue Mandar, 2ᵉ ☎01.42.21.14.88; Mᵒ Les Halles/Sentier. An excellent-value Kurdish restaurant, strewn with kilims and playing taped Kurdish music. Starters include melt-in-your mouth *babaqunuc* (stuffed aubergines) and mains *beyti* (spiced minced beef wrapped in pastry, with yoghurt, tomato sauce and bulgar wheat). Around €18 for two courses. Closed Sun.

Georges Centre Georges Pompidou, 4ᵉ ☎01.44.78.47.99; Mᵒ Rambuteau/Hôtel-de-Ville. On the top floor of the Pompidou Centre, this trendy minimalist restaurant with outdoor terrace commands stunning views over Paris and makes a stylish place for lunch or dinner. The international cuisine is pretty good, if overpriced. Count on around €50–60 per head. Daily except Tues noon–midnight.

À la Tour de Montlhéry (Chez Denise) 5 rue des Prouvaires, 1ᵉʳ ☎01.42.36.21.82; Mᵒ Louvre-Rivoli/Châtelet. A quintessential old-style Parisian bistro, going back to the Les Halles market days. Diners sit elbow to elbow at long tables in a narrow dining room and tuck into substantial meaty dishes, such as *andouillette* (tripe sausage), offal and steak, accompanied by perfectly cooked *frites*. Mains cost around €23. Mon–Fri noon–3pm & 7.30pm–5am. Closed mid-July to mid-Aug.

The Marais
See map, pp.112–113.

Bars and cafés

Andy Wahloo 69 rue des Gravilliers, 3ᵉ ☎01.42.71.20.38; Mᵒ Arts-et-Métiers. A very popular bar decked out in original Pop Art-inspired Arabic decor. Yummy mezze appetizers are available until midnight and the bar serves a few original cocktails, including the Wahloo Special (rum, lime, ginger, banana and cinnamon; €10). DJs play a wide range of dance music. Tues–Sat noon–2am.

L'Apparement Café 18 rue des Coutures-St-Gervais, 3ᵉ; Mᵒ St-Sébastien-Froissart. A chic and cosy café resembling a series of comfortable sitting rooms, with quiet corners and deep sofas. The salads, which you compose yourself by ticking off your chosen ingredients and handing your order to the waiter, are recommended, as is the popular Sunday brunch (€20). Mon–Fri noon–2am, Sat 4pm–2am, Sun 12.30pm–midnight.

L'As du Fallafel 34 rue des Rosiers, 4ᵉ ☏ 01.48.87.63.60; Mᵒ St-Paul. The best falafel shop in the Jewish quarter. Falafels to take away cost only €4, or you can pay a bit more and sit in the little dining room. Daily noon–midnight; closed Fri evening & Sat.

Le Loir dans la Théière 3 rue des Rosiers, 4ᵉ; Mᵒ Saint-Paul. A laid-back and very popular *salon de thé* where you can sink into comfy sofas and feast on enormous portions of home-made cakes and vegetarian quiches. Come early for the popular Sunday brunch (€16–22). Mon–Fri 11am–7pm, Sat & Sun 10am–7pm.

Le Petit Fer à Cheval 30 rue Vieille-du-Temple, 4ᵉ; Mᵒ St-Paul. A very attractive small drinking spot with original *fin-de-siècle* decor, including a marble-topped bar in the shape of a horseshoe (*fer à cheval*). You can snack on sandwiches or something more substantial in the little back room furnished with old wooden métro seats. Mon–Fri 9am–2am, Sat & Sun 11am–2am; food noon–midnight.

Restaurants

Ambassade d'Auvergne 22 rue de Grenier St-Lazare, 3ᵉ ☏ 01.42.72.31.22; Mᵒ Rambuteau. Suited, mustachioed waiters serve scrumptious Auvergnat cuisine that would have made Vercingétorix proud. There's a set menu for €30, but you may well be tempted by some of the house specialities, like the roast guinea fowl with garlic. Open daily; closed last two weeks in Aug.

Au Bourguignon du Marais 52 rue François Miron, 4ᵉ ☏ 01.48.87.15.40; Mᵒ St-Paul. A warm, relaxed restaurant, with attractive contemporary decor and tables outside in summer, serving excellent Burgundian cuisine with carefully selected wines to match. Mains cost around €20. Mon–Fri noon–3pm & 8–11pm; closed three weeks in Aug.

Chez Marianne 2 rue des Hospitalières-St-Gervais, 4ᵉ ☏ 01.42.72.18.86; Mᵒ St-Paul. You can eat very well and cheaply at this homely restaurant specializing in Middle Eastern and Jewish delicacies. A platter of mezzes that might include tabbouleh, aubergine purée, chopped liver and hummus starts from €12, and the wines are reasonably priced too. Daily noon–midnight.

Chez Omar 47 rue de Bretagne, 3ᵉ; Mᵒ Arts-et-Métiers. No reservations are taken at this popular North African couscous restaurant, so it's best to arrive early, though it's no hardship to wait at the bar for a table, taking in the handsome old brasserie decor and the buzzy atmosphere. Portions are copious and the couscous light and fluffy. The *merguez* (spicy sausage) costs €13, or go all out for the *royal* (€23). No credit cards. Daily except Sun lunch noon–2.30pm & 7–11.30pm.

Le Pamphlet 38 rue Debelleyme, 3ᵉ; Mᵒ Filles du Calvaire. This is one of the Marais' best restaurants, where the cuisine is *haute*, but the prices aren't. The excellent-value three-course menu of €35 might include such delicacies as duck croquettes, smoked *magret de canard* and tomato with cumin for starters, and pork fillet, chorizo and prunes with lentil salad for mains. Though billed as a bistro, it's more like a comfy restaurant, with upholstered chairs, soothing taupe and rust-red decor and plenty of elbow room. Mon 8–10.30pm, Tues–Fri noon–2pm & 8–10.30pm, Sat 8–10.30pm. Closed two weeks mid-Aug.

La Victoire Suprème du Coeur 27–31 rue du Bourg Tibourg, 4ᵉ ☏ 01.40.41.95.03; Mᵒ Hotel de Ville. Arguably the best vegetarian restaurant in the city, with sunny contemporary decor and childed ambience. You can get salads (€8), quiches or more substantial dishes (€14) such as mushroom roast with blackberry sauce. Mon–Fri noon–3pm & 6.30–10.30pm, Sat noon–11pm, Sun noon–10.30pm.

Bastille
See map, pp.112–113.

Bars and cafés

Iguana 15 rue de la Roquette, corner of rue Daval, 11ᵉ; Mᵒ Bastille. A place to be seen in with a decor of trellises, colonial fans and a brushed bronze bar. By day, the clientele studies recherché art reviews over excellent coffee, while things hot up at night with a youngish, high-spirited crowd. DJ on Thurs. Cocktails around €9. Daily 9am–5am.

Café de l'Industrie 16 rue St-Sabin, 11ᵉ; Mᵒ Bastille. Rugs on the floor around solid old wooden tables, miscellaneous objects – from stuffed crocodiles to atmospheric black-and-white photos – on the walls, and a young, unpretentious crowd enjoying the comfortable absence of minimalism. One of the best Bastille cafés, packed out every evening. Daily 10am–2am.

SanZSanS 49 rue du Faubourg-St-Antoine, 11ᵉ; Mᵒ Bastille. Gothic getup of red velvet, oil paintings and chandeliers, popular with a young crowd, especially on Fri & Sat evenings, when DJs play funk, Brazilian beats and house. Drinks are reasonably priced. Daily 9am–5am.

Restaurants

L'Auberge Pyrénées Cévennes 106 rue de la Folie Méricourt, 11ᵉ ☎01.43.57.33.78; Mᵒ République. Make sure you come hungry to this homely little place serving hearty portions of country cuisine. The garlicky *moules marinières* and the wonderful cassoulet, served in its own copper pot, are highly recommended. Around €30 a head. Closed Sat lunch and all day Sun.

Bistrot du Peintre 116 av Ledru Rollin, 11ᵉ ☎01.47.00.34.39; Mᵒ Faidherbe-Chaligny. A traditional neighbourhood bistro, where small tables are jammed together beneath faded Art Nouveau frescoes and wood panelling. The emphasis is on traditional cuisine, with dishes such as beef tartare and *confit de canard* for around €15. Mon–Sat 7am–2am, Sun 10am–1am.

Le Repaire de Cartouche 8 bd des Filles du Calvaire, 11ᵉ ☎01.47.00.25.86; Mᵒ Filles du Calvaire. Supposedly the house where eighteenth-century brigand Cartouche once hid away, this cosy, rustic restaurant is a popular bolthole with locals, who come for the excellent classic French cuisine and the exceptional wine list of over 400 vintages. Around €50 a head for three courses and wine. Closed Mon & Sun.

Quartier Latin
See map, pp.118–119.

Bars and cafés

La Fourmi Ailée 8 rue du Fouarre, 5ᵉ; Mᵒ Maubert-Mutualité. Simple, classically French food and speciality teas are served in this former feminist bookshop, now a relaxed *salon de thé* with a pretty, tiled exterior. The high, cloud-painted ceiling, book-lined walls and background jazz contribute to the atmosphere. Around €10 for a *plat du jour*. Daily noon–3pm & 7–11pm, Fri & Sat till midnight.

Café de la Mosquée 39 rue Geoffroy-St-Hilaire, 5ᵉ; Mᵒ Monge. Drink mint tea and eat sweet cakes beside the courtyard fountain and fig trees of the Paris mosque – a haven of calm (except on weekend lunchtimes when it's a popular spot for festive families). The indoor salon has a beautiful Arabic interior, where tasty tagines and couscous are served for €15 and up. Daily 9am–midnight.

Le Piano Vache 8 rue Laplace, 5ᵉ; Mᵒ Cardinal-Lemoine. Venerable bar crammed with students drinking at little tables, with cool music and a laid-back atmosphere. Mon–Fri noon–2am, Sat & Sun 9pm–2am.

Les Pipos 2 rue de l'Ecole-Polytechnique, 5ᵉ; Mᵒ Maubert-Mutualité/Cardinal-Lemoine. Cosy old bar

with rustic decor and a local clientele. Order a glasss of wine and a simple plate of Auvergnat charcuterie or cheese (€5–10). Mon–Sat 8.30pm–2am; closed 2 weeks in Aug.

Le Verre à Pied 118bis rue Mouffetard, 5ᵉ; Mᵒ Monge. Deeply old-fashioned little market bar where traders take their morning glass of wine at the bar, or sit down to eat a delicious *plat du jour* for €11 and engage in lively conversation. Simple *formules* €13. Tues–Sat 9am–8.30pm, Sun 9am–3.30pm.

Restaurants

Brasserie Balzar 49 rue des Ecoles 5ᵉ ☎01.43.54.13.67; Mᵒ Maubert-Mutualité. Classic, high-ceilinged brasserie, long frequented by the literary intelligentsia of the Quartier Latin – along with hordes of delighted tourists. It's not cheap: steak tartare, roast chicken or sauerkraut garnished with sausage cost around €18, but there are menus from €24. Daily 8am–11.30pm.

Les Cinq Saveurs d'Anada 72 rue du Cardinal-Lemoine, 5ᵉ ☎01.43.29.58.54; Mᵒ Cardinal-Lemoine. Informal restaurant serving macrobiotic, vegetarian food. Salads are tasty, and there are creative meat-substitute dishes (around €14–18), such as tofu soufflé or *confit* of tempeh with ginger. Tues–Sun noon–2.30pm & 7–10.30pm.

Les Degrés de Notre-Dame 10 rue des Grands Degrés, 5ᵉ ☎01.55.42.88.88; Mᵒ Maubert-Mutualité. Reliable, substantial and home-made French food – plus lots of couscous dishes and tagines – in a cosy bistro setting, or out on the *terrasse*. Good-value lunch menu €12.50; dinner menu €26.50. Closed Sun.

L'Ecurie 58 rue de la Montagne Ste-Geneviève, corner of rue Laplace, 5ᵉ ☎01.46.33.68.49; Mᵒ Maubert-Mutualité/Cardinal-Lemoine. Shoe-horned into a former stables on a lovely corner of the Montagne Ste-Geneviève, this quirky family-run restaurant is very lovable. Expect well-cooked meat dishes served grilled with chips for less than €20. Book ahead. Mon–Sat noon–3pm & 7pm–midnight, Sun 7pm–midnight.

Perraudin 157 rue St-Jacques, 5ᵉ ☎01.46.33.15.75; RER Luxembourg. Quintessential Left Bank bistro, featuring solid, homely cooking and an atmosphere thick with Parisian chatter floating above packed tables. Menus €18 (lunch) and €28 (dinner). Mon–Fri noon–2pm & 7.30–10.15pm; closed Aug.

Pho 67 59 rue Galande, 5ᵉ ☎01.43.25.56.69; Mᵒ Maubert-Mutualité. A beacon of South Asian authenticity in this touristy area. The Vietnamese proprietors work in an open kitchen, preparing a good range of inexpensive dishes including fried eels and sweet and sour pig ears; the less adventurous should go for the famous and filling *pho* soup (€9), or one of the four good-value menus. Tues–Sun noon–3pm & 7–11pm.

Le Reminet 3 rue des Grands-Degrés, 5ᵉ ☎01.44.07.04.24; Mᵒ Maubert-Mutualité. This postage-stamp-sized *bistrot* is effortlessly stylish, with gilded mirrors and brass candlesticks at every table, and French windows opening out onto a leafy square. It's a relaxed place to eat classy food – lots of quality French ingredients and imaginative sauces. The €14 lunch *formule* is an astonishing bargain. Evenings are pricier, and can get crowded. Mon & Thurs–Sun noon–3pm & 7.30–11pm; closed 2 weeks in Aug.

Tashi Delek 4 rue des Fossés-St-Jacques, 5ᵉ ☎01.43.26.55.55; RER Luxembourg. Cheery Tibetan restaurant serving Himalayan dishes – hearty noodle soups; addictive, ravioli-like *momok*; yak-butter tea and suchlike. There's a good evening menu at €21, but you can eat well for much less. Mon–Sat noon–2.30pm & 7.30–11pm; closed 2 weeks in Aug.

St-Germain

See map, pp.124–125.

Bars and cafés

Le 10 10 rue de l'Odéon, 6ᵉ; Mᵒ Odéon. Classic Art Deco-era posters line the walls of this small, dark, studenty bar and its vaulted cellar. Daily 6pm–2am.

Chez Georges 11 rue des Canettes, 6ᵉ; Mᵒ Mabillon. This delapidated wine bar, with its venerable counter, attracts a young, studenty crowd and stays lively well into the small hours at weekends. The cellar bar is rowdier. Tues–Sat noon–2am; closed Aug.

Les Deux Magots 170 bd St-Germain, 6ᵉ; Mᵒ St-Germain-des-Prés. Beautifully set on the corner of the *place*, this historic hang out of Left Bank intellectuals has fallen victim to its own fame. Prices are ridiculous, but it's still an irresistible place for people-watching. Try coming for breakfast (€20). Daily 7.30am–1am; closed one week in Jan.

Les Etages St-Germain 5 rue de Buci, 6ᵉ; Mᵒ Mabillon. Bastion of boho trendiness at the edge of the Buci street market, with pop-retro banquettes outside and dog-eared armchairs inside. Great for a coffee watching the street bustle and, later on, for people-watching over a drink. Daily noon–2am.

Café de Flore 172 bd St-Germain, 6ᵉ; Mᵒ St-Germain-des-Prés. The rival and neighbour of *Les Deux Magots*, with a trendier and more local clientele. Sartre, De Beauvoir, Camus et al used to hang out here – and there's still the odd reading or

debate. Come for the famous morning hot chocolate, a late-afternoon coffee or an after-dinner drink. Daily 7am–1.30am.

Ladurée 21 rue Bonaparte, 6ᵉ; Mᵒ St-Germain-des-Prés. Deliciously elegant outpost of *Ladurée*'s tearoom mini-empire with a lovely pale-green muralled conservatory at the back of the shop and a lounge upstairs, all lush velvets and Second Empire decadence. The *macarons*, of course, are out of this world, but they also do a good, if pricey, brunch. Mon–Sat 8.30am–7.30pm, Sun 10am–7.30pm.

Café de la Mairie 8 place St-Sulpice, 6ᵉ; Mᵒ St-Sulpice. A pleasant café on the sunny north side of the square, opposite the church of St-Sulpice. Mon–Sat 7am–2am.

Bar du Marché 75 rue de Seine, 6ᵉ; Mᵒ Mabillon. Thrumming café in the heart of the Buci market bustle, with *serveurs* kitted out in flat caps and dungarees. Expect animated conversation rather than banging techno, and kir rather than cocktails. Daily 7am–2am.

La Palette 43 rue de Seine, 6ᵉ; Mᵒ Odéon. This former Beaux Arts student hang out is now a relaxed haunt for art dealers and their customers. The decor is witty, including, of course, a large selection of paint-spattered palettes. There's a roomy *terrasse* and a short menu of lunchtime specials. Mon–Sat 9am–2am.

Restaurants

Allard 41 rue St-André-des-Arts, 6ᵉ ☎01.43.26.48.23; Mᵒ Odéon. Proudly unreconstructed restaurant serving meaty, rich standards. If it wasn't for the almost exclusively international clientele, you could be dining in another century. Menus from €25 (lunch) and €34 (dinner). Daily noon–3pm & 7.30–11pm.

L'Atlas 11 rue de Buci, 6ᵉ ☎01.40.51.26.30; Mᵒ Mabillon. Art Deco details are the only fuss at this unpretentious market brasserie, which serves good seafood, and simple, meaty dishes from €14. Daily 6.30am–1am.

Au 35 35 rue Jacob, 6ᵉ ☎01.42.60.23.24; Mᵒ St-Germain-des-Prés. The food is superb at this adorable bistro, filled with Art Deco lamps, mirrors and old posters. Try a rich *pastilla d'agneau* (lamb in pastry with honey and spices), or a simple duck breast. Lunch menu €22; around €38 à la carte without wine. Mon–Fri noon–2.30pm & 7.30–11pm, Sat 7.30–11pm.

Brasserie Lipp 151 bd St-Germain, 6ᵉ ☎01.45.48.53.91; Mᵒ St-Germain-des-Prés. One of the most celebrated of all the classic Paris brasseries, the haunt of the very successful and very famous, with a wonderful 1900s wood-and-glass interior. Decent *plats du jour*, including the famous *choucroute* (sauerkraut), are around €20. Daily 11.45am–12.45am.

Ferrandaise 8 rue de Vaugirard, 6ᵉ ℡01.43.26.36.36; M° St-Germain-des-Prés. Beef is the theme here, with arty photos of cows on the flagstoned walls and veal dominating the menu – along with dishes such as minced cod with ratatouille or caramelized pork ribs – all fresh from the market. The ambience may be rustic, but this is an excellent, modern restaurant. Lunch menus €24/€32, €32/€40 at dinner. Mon–Thurs noon–2pm & 7.30–11pm, Fri noon–2pm & 7.30pm–midnight, Sat 7.30pm–midnight.

Polidor 41 rue Monsieur-le-Prince, 6ᵉ ℡01.43.26.95.34; M° Odéon. A Left Bank classic, open since 1845, this bright, easy-going place bustles with aproned, middle-aged waitresses and gets packed elbow-to-elbow with noisy diners. Good, solid French classics like *confit de canard* or guinea fowl, with *plats* from €11. Menus €22 and €32. Mon–Sat noon–2.30pm & 7–12.30pm, Sun noon–2.30pm & 7–11pm.

La Tourelle 5 rue Hautefeuille, 6ᵉ ℡01.46.33.12.47; M° St-Michel. This little bistro, named for the stone tower outside, is packed into a low-ceilinged, stone-walled, convivial room. The meaty cuisine is fresh, simple and traditional, and service is great. Good value €21 menu. Mon–Fri noon–3pm & 7–10.30pm, Sat 7–11.30pm; closed Aug.

Trocadéro, Eiffel Tower and the Septième

See map, pp.128–129.

Bars and cafés

Café Carlu Palais de Chaillot, 1 place du Trocadéro; M° Trocadéro. It's well worth the slightly inflated prices at this little museum café to enjoy the phenomenal close-up views of the Eiffel Tower from the outdoor terrace – you could sit here all day grazing on light snacks, coffees and juices. only; closed Tues.

Café du Marché 38 rue Cler, 7ᵉ; M° La-Tour-Maubourg. Big, busy café-brasserie in the rue Cler market serving reasonably priced meals, with hearty salads (€9.50) and market-fresh *plats du jour* for €11. Outdoor seating, with a covered terrace in winter. Mon–Sat 7am–midnight.

Restaurants

Chez Germaine 30 rue Pierre-Leroux, 7ᵉ ℡01.42.73.28.34; M° Duroc/Vaneau. A charming little family restaurant offering simple, perfectly prepared classics like anchovy fillets on potato

salad and a meaty pikeperch steak. Good-value lunchtime *formule* (€14) and a menu for €15. Mon–Fri noon–2.30pm & 7–10pm, Sat noon–2.30pm; closed Aug.

Le P'tit Troquet 28 rue de l'Exposition, 7ᵉ ℡01.47.05.80.39; M° Ecole Militaire. This tiny family restaurant has a discreetly nostalgic feel with its marble tables, tiled floor and ornate zinc bar. The well-judged, traditional cuisine changes seasonally; on a summer *menu du marché* (€33) for example, you might find tabbouleh with herbs, grapefruit and prawns, followed by rabbit with mustard. Mon & Sat 6.30–10.15pm, Tues–Fri also noon–2pm.

La Varangue 27 rue Augereau, 7ᵉ ℡01.47.05.51.22; M° Ecole-Militaire. Also known as *Philippe's*, after the proprietor who presides over the simple dining room from his minuscule open kitchen. Food ranges from good salads and veggie choices – popular with the loyal American clientele – to more traditional mains (around €12) such as *boeuf bourguignonne*. Two-course *formule* €17.10. Mon–Fri noon–2.30pm & 5.30–9pm (from 6.15pm Wed), Sat & Sun 5.30–9pm.

Montmartre and le Neuvième

See map, p.139.

Bars and cafés

Chez Camille 8 rue Ravignan, 18ᵉ; M° Abbesses. *Très chouette* (very cool) little neighbourhood bar that never tries too hard. With a simple list of drinks, and an effortlessly stylish decor – creamy walls, ceiling fans, a few old mirrors, mismatched seating – it pulls a local crowd of all ages who could as easily be enjoying a quiet chat as sponta-neously dancing to anything from Elvis to *raï*. Tues–Sat 9am–2am, Sun 9am–8pm.

Au Clair de la Lune 1 rue Ramey, 18ᵉ; M° Jules-Joffrin. Scruffily hip bar – all neglected Art Deco styling, 1970s shaggy pouffes and peeling movie posters – a million miles away, in spirit, from the touristy Montmartre hubbub. Huge picture windows allow you to watch the rough-edged street scene on rue Clignancourt. Daily 8am–2am.

Café des Deux Moulins 15 rue Lepic, 18ᵉ; M° Blanche. Having seen its heyday of fans on the *Amélie* trail (she waited tables here in the film), this comfortably shabby retro diner is back to what it always was: a down-to-earth neighbourhood hang-out. Sunday brunch is popular; the place is sweetly candlelit at night. Mon–Sat 7am–2am, Sun 9am–2am.

L'Eté en Pente Douce 23 rue Muller, 18ᵉ (cnr rue Paul-Albert); M° Château-Rouge. A handy refueling spot, with a terrace alongside the steps leading up to Sacré-Cœur. The giant salads and traditional French *plats* (around €14) are good, and the atmosphere is pure Montmartre. Daily noon–midnight.

La Fourmi 74 rue des Martyrs, 18e; M° Pigalle/Abbesses. Artfully distressed, high-ceilinged café-bar full of beautiful young Parisian bohos drinking coffee and cocktails and thinking deep thoughts. Snacks and light meals available during the day. Mon–Thurs 8am–2am, Fri & Sat 8am–4am, Sun 10am–2am.

Au Rendez-Vous des Amis 23 rue Gabrielle, 18e; M° Abbesses. Everything a Parisian bar should be: in a quiet spot halfway up the Butte, this welcoming hang out is a favourite for locals who gather to chat, drink, play board games, and dance to occasional gypsy and Latin bands. The crowd, though predominantly artsy and alternative-leaning, is mixed – in age, sex and colour – and always interesting. Happy hour 8–10pm; inexpensive cheese and charcuterie plates served all day. Daily 8.30am–2am.

Restaurants

Le XVIIIème Barathym 2 rue Ramey, 18e ☎01.42.54.61.31; M° Jules-Joffrin. Appetizing Provençal salads, meats and *tartes tatins* in this cosy, shabby chic restaurant on the funkier edge of Montmartre. They host occasional live music – jazz, groove or local *chanteuses* – and do a good Sunday brunch. Lunch menu €12.50 (Mon–Fri); evenings à la carte dishes from around €16. Daily noon–2.30pm & 7pm–2am.

Café Burq 6 rue Burq, 18e ☎01.42.52.81.27; M° Blanche/Abbesses. Contemporary neighbourhood bistro offering simple, delicious food – guacamole of peas and chorizo, dorade with asparagus pesto – in a pared-down space. It's a special occasion, noisy kind of place, the only decoration provided by the unfailingly beautiful – not unfriendly – crowd, with whom you will be pressed elbow to elbow. Menus €15/€19 at lunch, €28/€32 at dinner. Daily noon–2.30pm & 6pm–2am.

Haynes 3 rue Clauzel, 9e ☎01.48.78.40.63; M° St-Georges. Cosy soul food restaurant that's been going since the 1940s, serving delicious fried chicken, gumbo and the like from around €13. There's blues or jazz most nights from around 8pm (€5). À la carte only. Tues–Sat 7pm–midnight.

Le Mono 40 rue Véron, 18e ☎01.46.06.99.20; M° Abbesses. Welcoming, family-run Togolese restaurant with soukous on the stereo and Togolese carvings on the walls. Delicious mains (from €10) are mostly grilled fish or meat served with sour, hot sauces and rice or cassava meal. Starters include a Scotch Bonnet-rich stuffed crab. Daily except Wed 7am–1am.

Le Relais Gascon 6 rue des Abbesses, 18e ☎01.42.58.58.22; M° Abbesses. Serving filling meals all day, this noisy two-storey restaurant provides a welcome blast of Gascon heartiness. Enormous hot salads start at €11.50, tasty *plats* around €12, and there's a good-value lunch menu at €15.50. Daily 10.30am–2am.

Au Virage Lepic 61 rue Lepic, 18e ☎01.42.52.46.79; M° Blanche/Abbesses. The gingham napkins draped over the lamps, the photos of movie stars on the walls and the soul music quietly playing on the hi-fi give this old bistro a quirky edge. The warm welcome is old-fashioned, however, as is the cosy atmosphere and satisfying *cuisine bourgeoise* – cassoulet, a delicious *choucroute*, *escargots* – from €7. Daily except Tues 7–11.30pm.

Northern Paris

Restaurants

Bistral 80 rue Lemercier, 17e ☎01.42.63.59.61; M° Place-de-Clichy. Carefully sourced foods, imaginatively cooked – the blackboard menu changes daily but you might find lamb loin with a shrimp crust (delicious) or roast *lotte* with chorizo. *Plats* from €15 and menus at €35, €40 and €60. Tues–Sat noon–2.30pm & 8–11.15pm.

Wepler 14 place de Clichy, 18e ☎01.45.22.53.24; M° Place-de-Clichy. Its clientele has moved

Paris for vegetarians

The chances of finding vegetarian main dishes on the menus of traditional French restaurants are not good, though these days some of the newer, more innovative establishments will often have one or two on offer. It's also possible to put together a meal from vegetarian starters, omelettes and salads. Your other option is to go for a Middle Eastern or Indian restaurant or head for one of the city's handful of proper **vegetarian restaurants** – they do tend to be based on a healthy diet principle rather than *haute cuisine*, but at least you get a choice. Try **Les Cinq Saveurs d'Anada** (see p.151), **Aquarius** (see p.156) and **La Victoire Suprême du Coeur** (see p.150).

Student restaurants

Students of any age – with an ISIC card – are eligible to apply for meal tickets for university cafeterias and restaurants. The tickets, which cost €4.80, have to be obtained from the particular restaurant of your choice (opening hours generally 11.30am–2pm & 6–8pm). Though the food isn't wonderful, you can't complain about the price. The most central venues are all on the Left Bank, and some of the most usefully located include: *Châtelet*, 10 rue Jean-Calvin, 5ᵉ (Mᵒ Censier-Daubenton; closed Sat & Sun); *Mabillon*, 3 rue Mabillon, 6ᵉ (Mᵒ Mabillon); and *Mazet*, rue André Mazet, 6ᵉ (Mᵒ Odéon; lunch only). Not all serve both midday and evening meals, and most are closed on the weekend and only operate during term-time; the exception is *Bullier*, 39 avenue Georges-Bernanos, 5ᵉ (Mᵒ Port-Royal), which is open every day, including during vacations. A full list of venues is available from ⊛ www.crous-paris.fr.

upmarket since it was depicted in Truffaut's *Les 400 Coups*, but as giant old-fashioned brasseries go, the century-old *Wepler* has remained unashamedly *populaire*, serving honest brasserie food and classic seafood platters (€35–50 à la carte). Menus €20 and €26. Daily noon–1am, café from 8am.

Eastern Paris

Bars and cafés

Le Baron Rouge 1 rue Théophile-Roussel, corner of place d'Aligre market, 12ᵉ; Mᵒ Ledru-Rollin. This traditional *bar à vins* is perfect for a light lunch or aperitif after shopping at the place d'Aligre market. If it's crowded inside (as it often is), join the locals standing around the wine barrels on the pavement lunching on *saucisson* or mussels washed down with a glass of Muscadet. Tues–Sat 10am–2pm & 5–9.30pm, Sun 10am–2pm.

Café Charbon 109 rue Oberkampf, 11ᵉ; Mᵒ St-Maur/Parmentier. The place that pioneered the rise of the Oberkampf bar scene is still going strong and continues to draw in a fashionable mixed crowd. Part of the allure is the attractively restored *fin-de-siècle* decor. Beer €2.50; full-blown meals (set menu €18) also available. Thurs–Sat 9am–4am, Sun–Wed 9am–2am.

Le Cannibale 93 rue Jean-Pierre Timbaud, 11ᵉ; Mᵒ Couronnes. A cool retro café-bar, where nattily dressed locals sit at their laptops or chill out at the bar against a soundtrack of electro lounge. Classic dishes such as *blanquette de veau* are served in the dining area, and there's live music (chanson, jazz funk, Cuban) most Sun at 6pm. Demi €2.60, cocktails €6.50. Daily 8am–2am.

Aux Folies 8 rue de Belleville, 20ᵉ; Mᵒ Belleville. *Aux Folies* offers a real slice of Belleville life: its outside terrace and 1930s long brass bar, with mirrored tiles and red neon lights, are packed day and night with a mixed crowd of North Africans,

Chinese, students and artists. Beer €3.50, cocktails €4.50. Daily 6.30am–1am.

Pause Café 41 rue de Charonne, corner of rue Keller, 11ᵉ; Mᵒ Ledru-Rollin. Or maybe "Pose Café" – given its popularity with the *quartier's* young and fashionable who bag the pavement tables at lunch and aperitif time. *Plats du jour* around €11. Mon–Sat 8am–2am, Sun 8.45am–8pm.

Tribal Café cour des Petites-Écuries, 10ᵉ; Mᵒ Château-d'Eau. Tucked down an atmospheric side street, this North African-tinged café-bar pulls in the new bohemians of the quarter with loud music, cheap beer and mojitos, outside tables and, before 8pm, free couscous on Fri & Sat nights (or free *moules frites* on Wed and Thurs). Daily noon–2am.

Restaurants

Bistrot Paul Bert 18 rue Paul Bert, 11ᵉ ☏ 01.43.72.24.01; Mᵒ Faidherbe-Chaligny. A quintessential Parisian bistro, patronized by a mix of locals and visitors drawn by the cosy, friendly ambience and high-quality simple fare such as *poulet rôti* as well as more sophisticated dishes such as guinea fowl and morel mushrooms. There's a lunch set menu at €16 and dinner at €32, and the wine list is reasonably priced, with an excellent selection of familiar and rarer vintages. Closed Mon & Sun and three weeks in Aug.

Flo 7 cour des Petites-Écuries, 10ᵉ ☏ 01.47.70.13.59; Mᵒ Château-d'Eau. Tucked away down a secret side alley, this is a dark, handsome and extremely atmospheric old-time brasserie. Fish and seafood are the specialities, but the food is generally excellent – if not cheap, from around €30. Daily 11am–1am.

Julien 16 rue du Faubourg-St-Denis, 10ᵉ ☏ 01.47.70.12.06; Mᵒ Strasbourg-St-Denis. Part of the same enterprise as *Flo* (see above), with an even more splendid decor of globe lamps, brass, murals, white linen and polished wood – if not such a romantic situation. Similar high-quality brasserie cuisine at the same prices. Daily until 1am.

Lao Siam 49 rue de Belleville, 19ᵉ ☎01.40.40.09.68; Mᵒ Belleville. The surroundings are nothing special, but the excellent Thai and Laotian food, popular with locals, makes up for it. From around €20 a head. Mon–Fri noon–3pm & 6–11.30pm, Sat & Sun noon–12.30am.

Pooja 91 passage Brady, 10ᵉ ☎01.48.24.00.83; Mᵒ Strasbourg-St-Denis/Château-d'Eau. Not quite London, let alone Bombay, but friendly and located in a glazed passage that is lined with Indian restaurants, all offering good if rather similar fare. Costs around €20 in the evening. Daily noon–3pm & 6–11pm; closed Mon lunchtime.

Le Train Bleu Gare de Lyon, 12ᵉ ☎01.43.43.09.06; Mᵒ Gare de Lyon. The sumptuous decor of what must be the world's most luxurious station buffet is straight out of a bygone golden era – everything drips with gilt, and chandeliers hang from high ceilings frescoed with scenes from the Paris–Lyon–Marseilles train route. The traditional French cuisine has a hard time living up to all this, but is still pretty good, if a tad overpriced. The set menu costs €48, including half a bottle of wine; for à la carte reckon on around €70. Daily 11.30am–3pm & 7–11pm.

Waly Fay 6 rue Godefroy-Cavaignac, 11ᵉ ☎01.40.24.17.79; Mᵒ Charonne. A moderately priced West African restaurant with a cosy, stylish atmosphere, the dim lighting, rattan and old, faded photographs creating an intimate, faintly colonial ambience. Smart young black and white Parisians come here to dine on perfumed, richly spiced stews and other West African delicacies. Mon–Sat noon–2pm & 7.30–11pm, Sun 11am–5pm; closed last two weeks of Aug.

Southern Paris

Bars and cafés

L'Entrepôt 7–9 rue Francis-de-Pressensé, 14ᵉ; Mᵒ Pernety. Arty cinema with a spacious, relaxed café and courtyard seating. Great Sunday brunch (€25), *plats* for around €15–19, and occasional evening concerts. Mon–Sat noon–2am.

La Folie en Tête 33 rue Butte-aux-Cailles, 13ᵉ; Mᵒ Place-d'Italie/Corvisart. Vibrant, friendly and distinctly lefty bar littered with bric-a-brac. Cheap drinks and snacks in the daytime and a wide-ranging soundtrack at night. Mon–Sat 5pm–2am, Sun 5pm–midnight. Happy hour 6–8pm.

Le Merle Moqueur 11 rue Butte-aux-Cailles, 13ᵉ; Mᵒ Place-d'Italie/Corvisart. This narrow, noisy bar – which saw the Parisian debut of Manu Chao – serves home-made flavoured rums and 1980s French rock to young Parisians. Daily 5pm–2am.

Le Rosebud 11bis rue Delambre, 14ᵉ; Mᵒ Vavin. A hushed, faintly exclusive Art Nouveau bar just off the bd Montparnasse – Sartre and his crew used to drink here. The barmen, who seem to date from the same era as the decor, serve wonderful Martinis from €12. Daily 7pm–2am.

Le Select 99 bd du Montparnasse, 6ᵉ; Mᵒ Vavin. The best of the great old Montparnasse cafés as frequented by Picasso, Matisse, Henry Miller et al. It's the least spoilt, with the best prices, and it's on the sunny side of the street. Only the food is disappointing. Daily 7pm–2am, Fri & Sat till 4am.

Restaurants

Aquarius 40 rue de Gergovie, 14ᵉ ☎01.45.41.36.88; Mᵒ Pernety/Plaisance. Homely vegetarian restaurant serving wholesome if unspectacular meals. Nut roast, chilli and lasagne cost around €12, and there's a menu at €15 (€12 at lunch). Mon–Sat noon–2.30pm & 7.30–11pm; closed 3 weeks in Aug.

Auberge Etchegorry 41 rue Croulebarbe, 13ᵉ ☎01.44.08.83.51; Mᵒ Gobelins. Once a *guinguette* on the banks of the Bièvre, this old-fashioned Basque restaurant is convivial and relaxed with great food. Menus from €21; from €35 a head à la carte. Tues–Fri noon–3pm & 7.30–10.30pm, Sat 7.30–10.30pm.

Chez Gladines 30 rue des Cinq-Diamants, 13ᵉ ☎01.45.80.70.10; Mᵒ Corvisart. Warm, welcoming and packed, this tiny corner *bistro* serves hearty Basque and southwestern dishes – try mashed/fried potato with *magret de canard* or a giant salad for under €9. Mon & Tues noon–3pm & 7pm–midnight, Wed–Sun noon–3pm & 7pm–1am.

Le Café du Commerce 51 rue du Commerce, 15ᵉ ☎01.45.75.03.27; Mᵒ Emile-Zola. This huge, former workers' brasserie is a buzzing, dramatic place to eat, set on three levels around a patio. Honest, high-quality meat is the speciality; expect to pay €15–20 for a *plat* (€29.50 for the *menu gourmet*). The lunch menu is a bargain at €15. Daily noon–3pm & 7pm–midnight.

La Coupole 102 bd du Montparnasse, 14ᵉ ☎01.43.20.14.20; Mᵒ Vavin. The largest and most splendid of the old Montparnasse brasseries. Now part of the Flo chain, it remains a genuine institution, its lovely interior buzzing with atmosphere. The choice runs from oysters to Welsh rarebit, with plenty of classics in between; menus €19.90 and €31. Daily 8am–1am.

L'Os à Moëlle 3 rue Vasco da Gama, 15ᵉ ☎01.45.57.27.27; Mᵒ Lourmel. The highlight of chef Thierry Faucher's relaxed bistro is the €40 menu, which brings you six courses of superb French cuisine. *La Cave de l'Os à Moelle*

(℡01.45.57.28.88), across the road, is a no-frills offshoot with communal tables groaning with homely food. Reserve well in advance at either. Tues–Sun noon–3pm & 7.30pm–midnight; closed 3 weeks in Aug.

Tricotin Kiosque de Choisy, 15 av de Choisy, 13ᵉ ℡01.45.85.51.52 and 01.45.84.74.44; Mᵒ Porte-de-Choisy. Glazed in like a pair of fish tanks, set back from the avenue at the south end of Chinatown, *Tricotin* is in fact two restaurants: no. 1 (closed Tues) specializes in Thai and grilled dishes,

while no. 2 has a longer list of Vietnamese, Cambodian and steamed foods. *Plats* from €7. Daily 9am–11.30pm.

Au Vin des Rues 21 rue Boulard, 14ᵉ ℡01.43.22.19.78; Mᵒ Denfert-Rochereau. Charmingly unreconstructed bistro, which offers French classics – *andouillette*, *pavé* of salmon and so on – and excellent wines. Convivial atmosphere, especially on the rowdy accordion and *pot-au-feu* evenings (Thurs). Main courses around €17. Mon–Sat noon–3pm & 7.30–11pm, Sun 7.30–11pm.

Music and nightlife

The strength of the Paris **music scene** is its diversity – a reputation gained mainly from its absorption of immigrant and exile populations. The city has no rival in Europe for the variety of **world music**: Algerian, West and Central African, Caribbean and Latin American sounds are represented in force. You'll have to look out for individual gigs in one of the listings magazines (see map, p.80), as most venues don't specialize but instead pursue eclectic programmes that might feature Congolese hip-hop cheek-by-jowl with home-grown pop-rock. For the quintessentially Parisian experience try to find a chanson night – the song style long associated with the city through wartime cabaret artists such as Edith Piaf, Maurice Chevalier and Charles Trenet and 1960s poet-musicians ranging from Georges Brassens to Serge Gainsbourg. Jazz fans are in for a treat, with all styles from New Orleans to current experimental to be heard, although in most clubs admission and drinks prices are high.

Nightlife recommendations for **clubs** are listed separately from live venues, though many clubs also showcase live acts on certain nights, and many concert venues hold DJ-led sessions after hours. Most clubs play *électro*, which covers anything from lounge to house and techno, mixed in with goodtime Mediterranean, Latin and African flavours. Places that cater for a primarily **gay or lesbian** clientele are listed in the "Gay and lesbian Paris" section on p.162.

Classical music, as you might expect in this Neoclassical city, is in vibrant form. The **Paris Opéra**, with its two homes – the Opéra-Garnier and Opéra-Bastille – puts on a fine selection of opera and ballet. The need for advance reservations (except sometimes for the concerts held in churches) rather than the price is the major inhibiting factor here. On June 21 the **Fête de la Musique** sees live bands and free concerts of every kind of music throughout the city.

Information and tickets

See p.80 for **listings magazines**. The best places to get **tickets** for concerts, whether rock, jazz, chansons or classical, is at the **FNAC** chain of book and music stores (ⓦwww.fnac.fr; ℡08.92.68.36.22; Mon–Sat 9am–1pm & 2–6pm): the main branch is at Forum des Halles, 1–5 rue Pierre-Lescot, 1ᵉʳ (Mon–Sat 10am–7.30pm; Mᵒ Chatelet-Les Halles), for other branches (see p.168).

Music venues

Most of the **music venues** below double up as clubs on certain nights, or after hours. A few will have live music all week, but the majority host bands on just a couple of nights. Admission prices vary depending on who's playing.

Note also that the most interesting **clubs** tend to host gigs earlier on; watch out for the programmes at *Le Nouveau Casino*, for example. Jazz venues, too, often branch into other genres such as world music and folk – *New Morning* (see p.160) is a classic example.

Rock and world music venues

Le Bataclan 50 bd Voltaire, 11ᵉ ☏ 01.43.14.00.30, ⊛ www.bataclan.fr; Mᵒ Oberkampf see map pp.112–113. Pagoda-styled ex-music-hall venue with one of the best and most eclectic line-ups, ranging from big-name international and local musicians – Francis Cabrel, George Clinton, Khaled, Stereophonics – to chanson, comedy and techno nights.

La Cigale 120 bd de Rochechouart, 18ᵉ ☏ 01.49.25.81.75, ⊛ www.lacigale.fr; Mᵒ Pigalle. Formerly hosting the likes of Mistinguett and Maurice Chevalier, since 1987 – and a Philippe Starck renovation – this historic, 1400-seater Pigalle theatre has become a leading venue for cutting-edge rock and indie acts from France and continental Europe.

🏃 **La Dame de Canton** quai François Mauriac, 13ᵉ ☏ 01.45.84.41.71, ⊛ www .damedecanton.com; Mᵒ Quai-de-la-Gare. Beautiful Chinese junk, moored alongside the quay in front of the Bibliothèque Nationale, hosting relaxed but upbeat world music, chanson and DJ nights, along with edgy music hall and kids' shows. This stretch of the river, in the developing Paris Rive Gauche area, is a veritable nightlife corridor: *Batofar* (see p.159), moored nearby, is another excellent floating venue, with a hip programme of gigs and club nights.

Café de la Danse 5 passage Louis-Philippe, 11ᵉ ☏ 01.47.00.57.59, ⊛ www.chez.com/cafedela danse; Mᵒ Bastille. Rock, pop, world, folk and jazz music played in an intimate and attractive space.

Le Divan du Monde 75 rue des Martyrs, 18ᵉ ☏ 01.40.05.06.99, ⊛ www.divandumonde.com; Mᵒ Anvers. A youthful venue in a café whose regulars once included Toulouse-Lautrec. One of the city's most exciting programmes, ranging from poetry slams through swing nights to Congolese rumba, with dancing till dawn on weekend nights.

Elysée Montmartre 72 bd de Rochechouart, 18ᵉ ☏ 01.44.92.45.47, ⊛ www.elyseemontmartre .com; Mᵒ Anvers. Historic Montmartre nightspot that pulls in a young, excitable crowd with its rock and dance acts – Redman, the Pharcyde, Chic, the Wombats. Also hosts good-time club nights – the music may be fairly unsophisticated but the giant dancefloor under a huge, arching roof guarantees plenty of space.

Le Nouveau Casino 109 rue Oberkampf, 11ᵉ ☏ 01.43.57.57.40, ⊛ www.nouveaucasino.net; Mᵒ Parmentier. An eclectic line-up makes way for a relaxed club night later on, with music ranging from electro-pop or house to rock. There's a good sound system and ventilation, but not all that much space.

Olympia 28 bd des Capucines, 9ᵉ ☏ 08.92.68.33.68, ⊛ www.olympiahall.com; Mᵒ Madeleine/Opéra. The classic Paris venue, a renovated old-style music hall hosting top international rock and pop acts, with a good programme of domestic stars as well.

Trabendo Parc de la Villette, 19ᵉ ☏ 01.49.25.89.99, ⊛ www.trabendo.fr; Mᵒ Porte-de-Pantin. Despite its moderate size, this place attracts some big French and international names in the world, jazz and rock fields.

Zenith Parc de la Villette, 211 av Jean-Jaurès, 20ᵉ ☏ 01.42.08.60.00; Mᵒ Porte-de-Pantin. Seating for 6000 in a giant tent designed exclusively for rock and pop concerts, with a good programme including acts like the Kooks and Scissor Sisters.

Clubs

Paris's **club** scene varies between monster-clubs rammed with techno-heads to smaller, edgier venues hosting esoteric programmes. The clubs listed below attract some of the trendiest or biggest crowds, but the style of music and the general vibe will depend on who's running the "*soirée*" on a particular night.

Bear in mind that **live music** venues (see above) often hold DJ-led sessions after hours, and that some of the hipper **bars** (see pp.146–157) bring in DJs for

Cabaret

Paris's **cabaret clubs** are still high-kicking along, but if you're looking for an atmosphere of sexy, bohemian exuberance you're better off in the gay bars of the Marais (see p.149) and if it's titillation you're after try the sex clubs of Pigalle. That said, the cabaret shows listed below provide a certain glitzy good time, and the dancers are superbly professional. Audiences are mostly groups of international tourists, paying top dollar. You can also choose to have dinner before the show, but you'll pay heavily for the privilege. To get away from the crowds, as long as you don't mind roughing it, you could visit the tiny transvestite cabaret on rue des Martyrs, just up from Pigalle métro.

Chez Michou 80 rue des Martyrs, 18ᵉ ☎01.46.06.16.04, ⓦ www.michou.com. At its best this is like a scene from an Almodóvar film, with transvestites masquerading as various female celebrities, lip-syncing to classic songs and teasing the audience – but you'll need to know your French pop culture to get the most out of it, and it can be rather desperate on a quiet night. Show €35, not including the various dinner menus.

Crazy Horse 12 av George-V, 8ᵉ ☎01.47.23.32.32, ⓦ www.lecrazyhorseparis.com; Mᵒ George-V. At the sexier end of the scene, with lots of provocative "dancing". Two shows daily at 8.30pm and 11pm (or three shows squeezed in on Sat at 8pm, 10.15pm and 12.15am). €80, or €120 including two drinks.

Le Lido 116bis av des Champs-Élysées, 8ᵉ ☎01.40.76.56.10, ⓦwww.lido.fr; Mᵒ George-V. The most spectacular show, with expensive lighting and sound effects, lots of professional, Vegas-style glitz. Two shows daily at 9.30pm (€100) and 11.30pm (€90).

Le Moulin Rouge 82 bd de Clichy, 18ᵉ ☎01.53.09.82.82, ⓦwww.moulinrouge.fr; Mᵒ Blanche. The traditional Paris show, with the serried ranks of the sixty Doriss Girls' frilly knickers as the highlight. Shows at 9pm (€99) and 11pm (Thurs–Sun only; €89). Book up to two months in advance at weekends.

weekend nights. Check the listings for **gay and lesbian** clubs (see p.162), too, most of which attract huge and mixed crowds.

Clubs tend to **open** around 11pm and midnight, sometimes earlier if they follow on from a gig, but things rarely warm up before 1am. At the most fashionable places you'll need to look good to avoid hanging around at the velvet rope, but at least racism, these days, is rare. Most **entry prices** include one free drink (*consommation*), and may vary from night to night. Given the difficulty of finding a **taxi after hours**, many Parisian clubbers just keep going until the métro starts up at around 5.30am, or even later, moving on to one of the city's famous *after* events.

Batofar quai François Mauriac, 13ᵉ ☎01.53.60.17.30, ⓦwww.batofar.org; Mᵒ Quai-de-la-Gare. Old lighthouse boat moored at the foot of the Bibliothèque Nationale, offering a quirky space for electro, house, techno, hip-hop, whatever – with the odd experimental funk night or the like thrown in. Entry €8–13.

Le Cab 2 place du Palais-Royal, 1ᵉ ☎01.58.62.56.25, ⓦ www.cabaret.fr; Mᵒ Palais-Royal. Slick, fashionable club that sucks the beautiful and designer-clad away from the Champs-Élysées – you'll need to look good to get in, though dining beforehand at the glitzy supper club helps. Designer retro-meets-futuristic lounge decor, with a similar music policy. Entry €28–30.

Favela Chic 18 rue du Faubourg du Temple, 11ᵉ ☎01.40.03.02.66, ⓦ www.favelachic.com;

Mᵒ République. Parisian hip meets an amped-up carnival spirit as a very up-for-it and unpretentious crowd enjoy a wildly eclectic samba-soul-hip-hop-afro-jazz-funk-pop fusion in sexy, fun surroundings. Entry €10–15.

La Loco 90 bd de Clichy, 18ᵉ ☎01.53.41.88.89, ⓦwww.laloco.com; Mᵒ Blanche. High-tech monster club with three dancefloors, playing mostly house and techno, though you can find all kinds of musical styles on weekday nights. Not particularly cool, but almost always busy. Entry €12–20.

Point Ephemere 200 quai de Valmy, 10ᵉ ☎01.40.34.02.48, ⓦ www.pointephemer.org; Mᵒ Jaurès. Very cool radical arts centre on the St Martin canal, with an underground music policy that focuses on anything from hard-core electronica. The lease runs out in 2009, so make the most of it now.

Rex Club 5 bd Poissonnière, 2ᵉ ☎01.42.36.10.96, ⓦwww.rexclub.com; Mᵒ Bonne-Nouvelle. The clubbers' club: spacious and serious about its music, which is strictly electronic, notably techno. Attracts big-name DJs. Entry €10–13.

WAGG 62 rue Mazarine, 6ᵉ ☎01.55.42.22.01, ⓦwww.wagg.fr; Mᵒ Odéon. Adjoining Terence Conran's flashy *Alcazar* restaurant and bar, the *WAGG* pulls in a yuppie Left Bank crowd for 1980s music, Latin beats, and the Seventies-themed "Carwash" nights on Fri. Entry €12. Closed Aug.

Jazz venues

Le Baiser Salé 58 rue des Lombards, 1ᵉ ☎01.42.33.37.71, ⓦwww.lebaisersale.com; Mᵒ Châtelet. Small, crowded upstairs room with live music every night from 10pm – usually jazz, rhythm & blues, fusion, reggae or Brazilian. The downstairs bar is great for just chilling out. Admission €18. Mon–Sat 5.30pm–6am.

Caveau de la Huchette 5 rue de la Huchette, 5ᵉ ☎01.43.26.65.05, ⓦwww.caveaudelahuchette .fr; Mᵒ St-Michel. One of the city's oldest jazz clubs dating back to the mid-1940s. Both Lionel Hampton and Sidney Bechet played here. Live jazz, usually trad and big band, to dance to on a floor surrounded by tiers of benches. Popular with students. Admission Sun–Thurs €11, Fri & Sat €13; drinks around €6. Daily 9.30pm–2am or later.

New Morning 7–9 rue des Petites-Écuries, 10ᵉ ☎01.45.23.51.41, ⓦwww.newmorning.com; Mᵒ Château-d'Eau. This cavernous, somewhat spartan venue, an ex-printing press, is the place to hear the big international names on the circuit. It's often standing room only unless you get here

early. Admission €20. Usually Mon–Sat 8pm–1.30am (concerts start around 9pm).

Le Sunside/Le Sunset 60 rue des Lombards, 1ᵉʳ ☎01.40.26.46.60, ⓦwww.sunset-sunside.com; Mᵒ Châtelet-Les Halles. Two clubs in one: *Le Sunside* on the ground floor features mostly traditional jazz, whereas the downstairs *Sunset* is a venue for electric and fusion jazz. The *Sunside* concert usually starts at 9 or 9.30pm and the *Sunset* at 10pm, so you can sample a bit of both. Admission around €20. Daily 9pm–2.30am.

Chanson venues

Casino de Paris 16 rue de Clichy, 9ᵉ ☎01.49.95.99.99, ⓦwww.casinodeparis.fr; Mᵒ Trinité. This decaying, once-plush former casino in one of the seediest streets in Paris is a venue for all sorts of performances – including chansons, poetry combined with flamenco guitar and cabaret. Check the listings magazines under "*Variétés*" and "*Chansons*". Most performances start at 8.30pm. Tickets start at €27.50.

Au Limonaire 18 Cité Bergère, 9ᵉ ☎01.45.23.33.33, ⓦlimonaire.free.fr; Mᵒ Grands Boulevards. Tiny backstreet venue, perfect for Parisian chanson nights showcasing young singers and zany music/poetry/performance acts. Dinner beforehand – traditional, inexpensive and fairly good – guarantees a seat for the show at 10pm (Tues–Sat) – otherwise you'll be crammed up against the bar, if you can get in at all.

Au Magique 42 rue de Gergovie, 14ᵉ ☎01.45.42.26.10, ⓦwww.aumagique.com; Mᵒ Pernety. A bar and "chanson cellar" with traditional French chanson performances by lesser-known stars during the week. At weekends the owner takes to the piano. Admission is free, payment for the show is at your discretion, and drinks are very reasonably priced. Wed–Sat 8pm–2am.

Classical music

Paris is a stimulating environment for **classical music**, both established and contemporary. The former is well represented in performances within churches – sometimes free or very cheap – and in an enormous choice of commercially promoted concerts held every day of the week. Contemporary and experimental computer-based work also flourishes.

Concert venues

Some of the city's most dynamic and eclectic programming is to be found at the **Cité de la Musique** at La Villette (ⓦwww.cite-musique.fr; Mᵒ Porte-de-Pantin). Ancient music, contemporary works, jazz, chanson and music from all over the world can be heard at the complex's two major concert venues: the **Conservatoire** (the national music academy) at 209 avenue Jean-Jaurès, 19ᵉ (☎01.40.40.46.46); and the **Salle des Concerts** at 221 avenue Jean-Jaurès, 19ᵉ (☎01.44.84.44.84). Soon these will be eclipsed however by a new state-of-the-art 2400-seater auditorium that's being built on the same site and is due to be completed in 2012.

The city's other top **concert halls** are the Salle Pleyel, 252 rue du Faubourg-St-Honoré, 8ᵉ (℡08.25.00.02.52, ⓦwww.pleyel.com; Mº Concorde); the Salle Gaveau, 45 rue de la Boëtie, 8ᵉ (℡01.49.53.05.07, ⓦwww.sallegaveau.com; Mº Miromesnil); Théâtre des Champs-Élysées, 15 avenue Montaigne, 8ᵉ (℡01.49.52.50.50, ⓦwww.theatrechampselysees.fr; Mº Alma-Marceau); and the Théâtre Musical de Paris (ⓦwww.chatelet-theatre.com; Mº Châtelet). **Tickets** are best bought at the box offices, though for big names you may find overnight queues, and a large number of seats are always booked by subscribers. The price range is very reasonable.

Churches and **museums** are also good places to hear classical music. Regular concerts can be caught at the Église St-Séverin, 1 rue des Prêtres St-Séverin, 5ᵉ (℡01.48.24.16.97; Mº St-Michel); the Église St-Julien le Pauvre, 23 quai de Montebello, 5ᵉ (℡01.42.26.00.00; Mº St-Michel); and the Sainte-Chapelle, 4 boulevard du Palais, 1ᵉʳ (℡01.42.77.65.65; Mº Cité).

The Musée du Louvre, the Musée d'Orsay and Musée Carnvalet host chamber music recitals in their auditoriums, while the Musée National du Moyen-Âge regularly holds recitals of medieval music. Radio France lunchtime concerts are held every Thursday (12.30pm Sept–June) in the Petit Palais' auditorium – turn up half an hour or so in advance to claim a free ticket.

Opera

The city's main opera house is the **Opéra-Bastille**, Mitterrand's most extravagant legacy to the city, opened in 1989. Opinions differ over the acoustics, but the orchestra is first-rate and nearly every performance is a sell out. The current, rather controversial, director, Belgian Gérard Mortier, whose production of Mozart's *Magic Flute* featured punks skating on stage, breasts beamed on video screens and swinging acrobats, is being replaced in 2009 with the more conservative Nicolas Joël. Tickets (€5–160) can be bought online (ⓦwww.opera-de-paris.fr), the date that tickets go on sale varies with each production and is given on the site. You can also book by phone (Mon–Fri 9am–6pm, Saturday 9am–1pm; ℡08.92.89.90.90 or 331.72.29.35.35 from abroad), or at the ticket office (Mon–Sat 11am–6.30pm). Unfilled seats are sold at a discount to students fifteen minutes before the curtain goes up, and 62 standing tickets at €5 are available for Opéra-Bastille performances one and a half hours before the curtain goes up.

The Opéra-Bastille enjoys a friendly rivalry with the **Théâtre du Châtelet**, 1 place du Châtelet, 1ᵉʳ (℡01.40.28.28.40; Mº Châtelet), which also puts on large-scale productions. Operas are still staged at the old **Opéra-Garnier**, place de l'Opéra, 9ᵉ (℡08.92.89.90.90, ⓦwww.opera-de-paris.fr; Mº Opéra), though these days it hosts mostly ballets; the procedure for getting tickets for the latter is the same as for the Opéra-Bastille above. Operetta, as well as more daring modern operas, are performed at the **Opéra-Comique**, Salle Favart, 5 rue Favart, 2ᵉ (℡01.42.44.45.46, ⓦwww.opera-comique.com; Mº Richelieu-Drouot).

Festivals

Festivals are plentiful in all the diverse fields that come under the far too general term of "classical". The **Festival d'Art Sacré** consists mainly of concerts and recitals of early sacred music (end of Nov to mid-Dec; ⓦwww.festivaldartsacre .new.fr); concerts feature in the general arts **Festival d'Automne** (mid-Sept to end Dec; ⓦwww.festival-automne.com); and a **Festival Chopin** is held in the lovely setting of the Bois de Boulogne's Orangerie (mid-June to mid-July; ⓦwww.frederic-chopin.com).

For details of these and more, the current year's **festival schedule** is available from tourist offices or their website (Ⓦ www.parisinfo.com).

Gay and lesbian Paris

Paris is one of Europe's major centres for **gay men**, with numerous bars, clubs, restaurants, saunas and shops catering for a gay clientele. The scene's focal point is the **Marais**, and especially rue Sainte-Croix-de-la-Bretonnerie. **Lesbians** have fewer dedicated addresses, but there are a handful of women-only places. The high spots of the calendar are the annual **Marche des Fiertés LGBT**, or gay pride march, which normally takes place on the last Saturday in June, and the **Bastille Day Ball** – open to all – held on the quai de Tournelle, 5ᵉ (Mº Pont-Marie) on July 13.

Information and contacts

The gay and lesbian community is well catered for by the media, the best source of information being *Têtu* (Ⓦ www.tetu.com), France's main gay monthly magazine – the name means "headstrong". Alternatively, have a look at Ⓦ www.paris-gay.com, a major portal for gay tourists visiting the city.

Centre Lesbien, Gay, Bi et Trans de Paris 63 rue Beaubourg, 3ᵉ ℡ 01.43.57.21.47, Ⓦ www.centrelgbtparis.org; Mº Rambuteau. Fights for political rights and acts as a first port of call for information and advice – legal, social, psychological and medical. Also puts on small exhibitions. Open Mon 6–8pm, Tues 4–8pm, Wed, Fri & Sat 12.30–8pm, Thurs 3–8pm, Sun 4–7pm.
Maison des Femmes 163 rue de Charenton, 12ᵉ Ⓔ maisondesfemmesdeparis@orange.fr, Ⓦ maisondesfemmes.free.fr; Mº Reuilly-Diderot. Feminist campaigning centre that organizes

workshops, meetings and gay/straight lunches and parties. Mon–Fri 7am–7pm.
Les Mots à la Bouche 6 rue Ste-Croix-de-la-Bretonnerie, 4ᵉ ℡ 01.42.78.88.30, Ⓦ www.motsbouche.com; Mº Hôtel-de-Ville. The main gay and lesbian bookshop, with a selection of literature in English and lots of free info (maps, flyers) to pick up. Mon–Sat 11am–11pm, Sun 1–9pm.
SOS Homophobie ℡ 01.48.06.42.41, Ⓦ www.sos-homophobie.org. First-stop helpline for victims of homophobia. Based in the centre LGBT.

Bars and clubs

In terms of **nightlife**, the key centre is the "gay village" of the Marais – the selection below only scratches the surface. **Lesbians** are less well served, but there are a few great women-only addresses, and women are welcome in some of the predominantly male clubs.

The promise of wild hedonism in Paris's gay **clubs** has attracted heterosexuals in search of a good time; straights are welcome in some gay establishments, especially when in gay company. Indeed, some gay clubs have all but abandoned a gay policy and many of the more mainstream clubs have started doing gay *soirées*. Check *Têtu* for a complete rundown.

Amnesia Café 42 rue Vieille-du-Temple, 4ᵉ ℡ 01.42.72.16.94; Mº St-Paul. Pleasantly trashy, friendly gay bar with a relaxed clientele lounging around on sofas. Later on, the tiny dancefloor pulls in happy good-timers with a noisy, camp playlist. Daily 11am–2am.
Banana Café 13 rue de la Ferronnerie, 1ᵉʳ ℡ 01.42.33.35.31; Mº Châtelet. Somewhat away

from the main scene, right beside Les Halles, but a historic and friendly gay address. By day it's a café, with furiously camp tropical decor and *terrasse*; at night it gets more hedonistic and trendy. Daily 6pm–5am.
Le Carré 18 rue du Temple, 4ᵉ ℡ 01.44.59.38.57; Mº Hôtel-de-Ville. Sophisticated, good-looking Parisians and the occasional clued-up tourist head

for this stylish, comfortable café with good food, an excellent *terrasse*, and occasional party events. Daily 10am–4am.

Café Cox 15 rue des Archives, 3ᵉ ☎01.42.72.08.00; M° Hôtel-de-Ville. Lively Marais bar filled with honed and toned, shaven-headed beauties. Friendly – if your face fits – with DJs on weekend nights. Daily noon–2am.

Le Duplex 25 rue Michel-le-Comte, 3ᵉ ☎01.42.72.80.86; M° Rambuteau. Popular with intellectual or media types for its relatively relaxed and chatty atmosphere. Friendly rather than cruisy – the barmen know the regulars by name. Sun–Thurs 8pm–2am, Fri & Sat 8pm–4am.

Le Mixer 23 rue Ste-Croix de la Bretonnerie, 4ᵉ ☎01.42.78.26.20; M° Hôtel-de-Ville. Popular and crowded high-tech Marais bar with a mezzanine. DJs play techno and house to a genuinely mixed clientele – gay, straight, black, white, whatever. Daily 5pm–2am.

L'Open Café 17 rue des Archives, 3ᵉ ☎01.42.72.26.18; M° Arts-et-Métiers. *The* most famous gay bar/café in Paris and, as such, expensive and quite touristy, but still fairly cool, with sidewalk seating and a loungey ambience

inside. Sun–Thurs 11am–2am, Fri & Sat 11am–4am.

La Petite Vertu 15 rue des Vertus, 3ᵉ ☎01.48.04.77.09; M° Arts-et-Métiers. Welcoming, inventive Marais address pulling in gay, lesbian and straight punters alike. Frequent special events. Tues–Sun noon–2am.

Le Raidd 23 rue du Temple, 4ᵉ ☎01.48.87.80.25; M° Hôtel-de-Ville. One of the city's gayest gay bars, famous for its beautiful staff, topless waiters and go-go boys' shower shows. Daily 5pm–2am.

Le Redlight 34 rue du Départ, 14ᵉ ☎01.42.79.94.53; M° Montparnasse-Bienvenue. Huge hard and deep house club with a serious sound system, two dance-floors, post-industrial decor and impressive light shows. Thurs & Sun midnight–6am, Fri & Sat midnight–noon. Cover €20.

Le Tango/La Boîte à Frissons 13 rue au-Maire, 3ᵉ ☎01.42.72.17.78; M° Arts-et-Métiers. Delightful old dance hall with gay and lesbian *bals* featuring anything from tango to polka and line dancing; traditional tea dances on Sun. Full-on club nights start after midnight. Fri & Sat 10.30pm–5am, Sun 5pm–5am. €6.50.

Film, theatre and dance

Cinema-goers have a choice of around three hundred films showing in Paris in any one week. The city's plethora of little arts cinemas screen unrivalled programmes of classic and contemporary films, and you can find mainstream movies at almost any time of the day or night. The city also has a vibrant **theatre** scene. Several superstar directors are based here, including Peter Brook and Ariane Mnouchkine. **Dance** enjoys a high profile, enhanced by the opening of the Centre National de la Danse, Europe's largest dance academy, in 2004.

The main **festivals** include the **Festival de Films des Femmes** (March; ☎01.49.80.38.98, ⓦwww.filmsdefemmes.com) at the Maison des Arts in Créteil, just southeast of Paris (M° Créteil-Préfecture); the **Festival Exit** (March; ⓦwww.maccreteil.com), which features international contemporary dance, performance and theatre, at the same venue; **Paris Quartier d'Été** (mid-July to mid-Aug; ⓦwww.quartierdete.com), with music, theatre and cinema events around the city; the **Festival d'Automne** (Sept–Dec; ⓦwww.festival-automne.com), with traditional and experimental theatrical, musical, dance and multimedia productions from all over the world; and the **Festival du Cinéma en Plein Air** (July to mid-Aug; ⓦwww.cinema.arbo.com) at Parc de la Villette, showing free films in the park.

Information and tickets

The most comprehensive **film listings** are given in the inexpensive weekly *Pariscope*. Watch out for the smaller Reprises section, where you'll usually find a number of British or American classics listed, though often enough these turn out to be one-off screenings at an unlikely hour of the afternoon. You rarely need to book in advance; programmes (*séances*) often start around midday and continue through to the early hours. The average price is around €8, but many smaller cinemas have lower rates on Monday or Wednesday and for earlier *séances*, and student reductions are available from Monday to Thursday. Almost all of the huge selection of foreign films will be shown at some cinemas in the original language – *version originale* or *v.o.* in the listings. Dubbed films will be listed as *v.f.* and English versions of co-productions as *version anglaise* or *v.a.*

Stage productions are detailed in *Pariscope* and *L'Officiel des Spectacles* with brief résumés or reviews. Ticket prices are often around €15–30, though you may pay less in smaller venues, and more for many commercial and major state productions (most closed Sun & Mon). Half-price previews are advertised in *Pariscope* and *L'Officiel des Spectacles*, and there are weekday student discounts. Tickets can be bought directly from the theatres, from FNAC shops and the Virgin Megastore (see p.171), or at the **ticket kiosks** on place de la Madeleine, 8ᵉ, opposite no. 15, and on the parvis of the Gare du Montparnasse, 15ᵉ (Tues–Sat 12.30–7.45pm, Sun 12.30–3.45pm). They sell half-price same-day tickets and charge a small commission, but be prepared to queue.

Film

Cinephiles have an unbeatable choice of non-mainstream films in Paris, covering every region and period. Even in the multiplexes you can find Senegalese, Taiwanese, Brazilian or Finnish films, for example, that would never be shown in Britain or the US, while you can find Hollywood classics having a Sunday morning airing in the little old independent cinemas or watch the entire careers of individual directors in the city's many mini-festivals. The Latin Quarter, around the Sorbonne, has a particularly high concentration of **arts cinemas** showing an amazing repertoire of classic films, while the area around the Gare Montparnasse is chock-full with big-screen movie-houses offering the latest glossy releases.

Classic venues

L'Arlequin 76 rue de Rennes, 6ᵉ ☎01.45.44.28.80; Mᵒ St-Sulpice. Owned by Jacques Tati in the 1950s, then by the Soviet Union (as the Cosmos) until 1990, L'Arlequin is one of the Latin Quarter's favourite art house venues. Classic Sun 11am screenings are followed by debates in the café opposite.

Cinémathèque Française 51 rue de Bercy, 12ᵉ ⓦwww.cinemathequefrancaise.com; Mᵒ Bercy. This dedicated museum of cinema, in an incredible Frank Gehry building, shows a huge variety of films and shorts every week, many of which you would never see commercially. Closed Aug.

L'Entrepôt 7–9 rue Francis-de-Pressensé, 14ᵉ ⓦwww.lentrepot.fr; Mᵒ Pernety. One of Paris's best alternative cinemas, which has been keeping ciné-addicts happy for years with its three screens dedicated to the obscure, the subversive and the brilliant.

Forum des Images 2 Grande Galerie, Porte St-Eustache, Forum des Halles, 1ᵉ ⓦwww.forumdesimages.net; Mᵒ Les Halles. Following a major renovation, this huge temple to cinema screens a huge variety of films (and videos), hosts festivals of all colours, and provides access to an intriguing library of Paris-related footage.

Max Linder Panorama 24 bd Poissonnière, 9ᵉ ⓦwww.maxlinder.com; Mᵒ Grands Boulevards. Opposite Le Grand Rex, and with almost as big a screen, this Art Deco cinema always shows films in the original and has state-of-the-art sound.

La Pagode 57bis rue de Babylone, 7ᵉ ☎01.45.55.48.48; Mᵒ St-François-Xavier. The most beautiful of the city's cinemas, built in Japanese style at the turn of the last century for a rich Parisienne socialite. The walls of the Salle Japonaise auditorium are swathed in silk; golden dragons and elephants hold up the candelabra; and warriors battle on the ceiling. Art films, documentaries and commercial movies in *v.o.*

Reflet Medicis 3, 5, 7 & 9 rue Champollion ☎01.43.54.42.34, and **Le Champo** 51 rue des

Écoles ☎01.43.54.51.60, 5ᵉ; Mᵒ Cluny-La-Sorbonne/Odéon. A cluster of Latin Quarter art house cinemas offering rare screenings and classics, including directors' retrospectives (always in *v.o.*). The small, boho cinema café *Le Reflet*, at 6 Champollion, is a cult classic in itself.
Le Studio 28 10 rue de Tholozé, 18ᵉ 🕸www .cinemastudio28.com; Mᵒ Blanche/Abbesses. In its early days, after a screening of Buñuel's *L'Age d'Or*, extreme right-wing Catholics destroyed the screen and the paintings by Dalí and Ernst in the foyer. The Montmartre cinema still hosts avant-garde premières, directors' Q&A sessions, and regular festivals.

Theatre

Bourgeois farces, postwar classics, Shakespeare, Racine and Molière are all staged with the same range of talent or lack of it that you'd find in London or New York. What is rare are home-grown, socially concerned and realist dramas, though touring foreign companies make up for that. Exciting contemporary work is provided by the superstar breed of directors such as Peter Brook and Ariane Mnouchkine; spectacular and dazzling sensation tends to take precedence over speech in their productions, which often feature huge casts, extraordinary sets and overwhelming sound and light effects – an experience, even if you haven't understood a word.

Bouffes du Nord 37bis bd de la Chapelle, 10ᵉ ☎01.46.07.34.50, 🕸www.bouffesdunord.com; Mᵒ La Chapelle. Peter Brook resurrected the derelict Bouffes du Nord in 1974 and has been based there ever since. The theatre also hosts top-notch chamber music recitals.
Cartoucherie rte du Champ-de-Manoeuvre, 12ᵉ; Mᵒ Château-de-Vincennes. Home to several interesting theatre companies including workers' co-op Théâtre du Soleil, set up by Ariane Mnouchkine (☎01.43.74.24.08, 🕸www.theatre-du-soleil.fr).
Comédie Française 2 rue de Richelieu, 1ᵉʳ ☎01.44.58.15.15, 🕸www.comedie-francaise.fr; Mᵒ Palais-Royal. This venerable national theatre stages mainly Racine, Molière and other classics, but also twentieth-century greats such as Anouilh and Genet.
Odéon Théâtre de l'Europe 1 place Paul-Claudel, 6ᵉ ☎01.44.41.36.36, 🕸www.theatre-odeon.fr; Mᵒ Odéon. Contemporary plays and foreign-language productions in the theatre that became an open parliament during May 1968.
Théâtre de la Huchette 23 rue de la Huchette, 5ᵉ ☎01.43.26.38.99; Mᵒ Saint-Michel. Fifty years on, this small theatre is still showing Ionesco's *Cantatrice Chauve* (*The Bald Prima Donna*; 7pm) and *La Leçon* (8pm), two classics of the Theatre of the Absurd. Reserve by phone or at the door from 5pm; tickets €19 for one play or €29 for two.
Théâtre National de Chaillot Palais de Chaillot, place du Trocadéro, 16ᵉ ☎01.53.65.30.00, 🕸www .theatre-chaillot.fr; Mᵒ Trocadéro. Puts on an exciting programme and often hosts foreign productions; Deborah Warner and Robert Lepage are regular visitors.

Dance

The status of dance in the capital received a major boost with the inauguration in 2004 of the **Centre National de la Danse**, committed to promoting every possible dance form from classical to contemporary, and including ethnic traditions. While Paris itself has few home-grown companies (government subsidies go to regional companies expressly to decentralize the arts) it makes up for this by regularly hosting all the best contemporary practitioners. Names to look out for are Régine Chopinot's troupe from La Rochelle, Maguy Marin's from Rilleux-le-Pape and Angelin Preljocaj's from Aix-en-Provence. Plenty of space and critical attention are also given to tango, folk and visiting traditional dance troupes from all over the world. As for ballet, the principal stage is at the Palais Garnier, home to the Ballet de l'Opéra National de Paris, directed by Brigitte Lefèvre. It still bears the influence of **Rudolf Nureyev**, its charismatic, if controversial, director from 1983 to 1989, and frequently revives his productions, such as *Swan Lake* and *La Bayadère*. Many of the venues listed above under "Theatre" also host dance productions.

Centre National de la Danse 1 rue Victor Hugo, Pantin ☏01.41.83.27.27, ⓦwww.cnd.fr; M° Hoche/RER Pantin. The capital's major new dance centre occupies an impressively large building, ingeniously converted from a disused 1970s monolith into an airy high-tech space. Though several of its eleven studios are used for performances, the main emphasis of the centre is to promote dance through training, workshops and exhibitions.

Opéra-Garnier place de l'Opéra, 9ᵉ ☏08.36.69.78.68, ⓦwww.opera-de-paris.fr; M° Opéra. Main home of the Ballet de l'Opéra National de Paris.

Théâtre des Abbesses 31 rue des Abbesses, 18ᵉ; M° Abbesses. The Théâtre de la Ville's sister company, where you'll find slightly more offbeat performances by the likes of provocative choreographers Robyn Orlin and Jan Fabre.

Théâtre Musical de Paris place du Châtelet, 4ᵉ ☏01.40.28.28.40, ⓦwww.chatelet-theatre.com; M° Châtelet. A major ballet venue where, in 1910, Diaghilev put on the first season of Russian ballet. Though mainly used for classical concerts and opera, it also hosts top-notch visiting ballet companies such as the Mariinsky.

Théâtre de la Ville 2 place du Châtelet, 4ᵉ ☏01.42.74.22.77, ⓦwww.theatredelaville-paris .com; M° Châtelet. The height of success for contemporary dance productions is to end up here. Works by Karine Saporta, Maguy Marin and Pina Bausch are regularly featured, along with modern theatre classics, comedy and concerts.

Kids' Paris

For most **kids** the biggest attraction for miles around is **Disneyland Paris** (see p.178), though within the city there are plenty of less expensive and more educational possibilities for keeping them entertained. Wednesday afternoons, when primary school children have free time, and Saturdays are the big times for children's activities and entertainments; Wednesdays continue to be child-centred even during the school holidays. The tours around the **sewers** and the **catacombs** will delight some older children, while smaller ones can enjoy performances of **Guignol** (the equivalent of Punch and Judy) in the city's parks. Many of the **museums** and **amusements** already detailed will appeal, especially the **Cité des Sciences et de l'Industrie** (see p.142) and its special section for children, the **Cité des Enfants** (see below), in the Parc de la Villette. A number of museums have children's activities on Wednesdays and Saturdays, details of which are carried in the free booklet *Objectif Musée*, available from the museums. Otherwise, the most useful **sources of information** for current shows, exhibitions and events are the special sections in the listings magazines ("Enfants" in *Pariscope*, and "Jeunes" in *L'Officiel des Spectacles*) and the Kiosque Paris-Jeunes at the Direction Jeunesse et Sports, 25 boulevard Bourdon, 4ᵉ (Mon–Fri noon–7pm; ☏01.42.76.22.60; M° Bastille), and at the CIDJ (Centre Information et Documentation Jeunesse), 101 quai Branly, 15ᵉ (Mon–Fri 9.30am–6pm, Sat 9.30am–1pm; ☏01.44.49.12.00; M° Bir-Hakeim). The tourist office also publishes a free booklet in French, *Paris-Île-de-France avec des Yeux' Enfants*, with lots of ideas and contacts.

Cité des Enfants

The **Cité des Enfants**, which has areas for 3-to 5-year-olds and 6-to12-year-olds, is a hugely engaging special section of the Cité des Sciences et de l'Industrie in the Parc de la Villette (Tues–Sat 10am–6pm, Sun 10am–7pm). The kids can touch, smell and feel things, play about with water, construct buildings on a miniature construction site, experiment with sound and light, manipulate robots, put together their own television news and race their own shadows. It's beautifully organized and managed, and if you haven't got a child it's worth borrowing one to get in here. Sessions run for an hour and a half (Tues, Thurs & Fri 11.30am, 1.30pm & 3.30pm; Wed, Sat, Sun & public holidays 10.30am, 12.30pm, 2.30pm & 4.30pm; adults and children €6; children must be accompanied by at least one adult). It's worth booking in advance during busy holiday periods at the Cité des Sciences ticket office on ☎08.92.69.70.72 or via the website (Ⓦ www.cite-sciences.fr).

The rest of the museum is also pretty good for kids, particularly the **planetarium**, the various film shows, the *Argonaute* submarine and the frequent temporary exhibitions designed for the young. And in the park, there's lots of green space, a dragon slide and seven themed gardens featuring mirrors, trampolines, water jets and spooky music.

Jardin d'Acclimatation

The **Jardin d'Acclimatation**, in the Bois de Boulogne by Porte des Sablons (daily: June–Sept 10am–7pm; Oct–May 10am–6pm; adults and children €2.70; Ⓦ www.jardindacclimatation.fr; M° Les Sablons/Porte-Maillot) is a children's paradise: a cross between a funfair, zoo and amusement park. Temptations range from bumper cars, go-karts and pony and camel rides to sea lions, birds, bears and monkeys; plus there's a magical mini-canal ride (*la rivière enchantée*), distorting mirrors, scaled-down farm buildings and a puppet theatre. Rides do cost extra – around €2.50 a time, or you can buy a carnet of fifteen tickets for €32. The best way to get to the park is via the *petit train* (€5.40 return, including entrance fee) which leaves every fifteen minutes from behind the *L'Orée du Bois* restaurant near Porte Maillot métro station.

Parc Floral

Fun and games are always to be had at the **Parc Floral**, in the Bois de Vincennes, route de la Pyramide (M° Château-de-Vincennes, then a 7min walk via the Château de Vincennes, or bus #112; daily: March–Sept 9.30am–7pm; Oct–Feb 9.30am–5pm; €1, children €0.50 plus supplements for some activities, under-7s free; Ⓦ www.parcfloraldeparis.com). The excellent playground has slides, swings, ping-pong, pedal carts, miniature golf modelled on Paris monuments (from 2pm), an electric car circuit and a *petit train* touring all the gardens (April–Oct daily 1–5pm; €1). Tickets for the activities are sold at the playground between 2 and 5.30pm weekdays and until 7pm on weekends; activities stop fifteen minutes afterwards. Note that many of these activities are available from March/April to August only and on Wednesdays and weekends only in September and October. On Wednesdays at 2.30pm (May–Sept) there are free performances by clowns, puppets and magicians. Also in the park is a children's theatre, the **Théâtre Astral**, which puts on mime and other not-too-verbal shows for small children aged 3 to 8 (Wed, Sun & during school holidays Mon–Fri 3pm; ☎01.43.71.31.10; €6).

Parc Zoologique

Paris's main zoo, in the Bois de Vincennes at 53 avenue de St-Maurice, 12ᵉ, is currently undergoing major renovation and will remain closed until 2012.

Funfairs and the circus

The Tuileries gardens normally have a **funfair** in July, and there's usually a **merry-go-round** at the Forum des Halles and beneath Tour St-Jacques at Châtelet, with carousels for smaller children on place de la République and at the Rond-Point des Champs-Élysées, by avenue Matignon. Circus shows are put on from October to January at the **Cirque d'Hiver Bouglione**, 110 rue Amelot, 11ᵉ (Mᵒ Filles-du-Calvaire; ⓦ www.cirquedhiver.com).

Shopping

Even if you don't plan to buy, browsing Paris's **shops and markets** is one of the chief delights of a visit to the city. The Parisian love of style and fierce attachment to small local traders have kept alive a wonderful variety of speciality shops. Among specific areas, the nineteenth-century **arcades**, or *passages*, in the **2ᵉ and 9ᵉ arrondissements** harbour the kind of outlets that make shopping an exciting expedition rather than a chore, while the square kilometre around **place St-Germain-des-Prés** is hard to beat, packed with books, antiques, gorgeous garments and artworks. **Les Halles** is good for high-street fashion, while the aristocratic **Marais**, the **Bastille quartier**, **Abbesses in Montmartre**, and northeastern Paris (**Oberkampf** and the **Canal Saint-Martin**) specialize in dinky little boutiques, specialist shops and galleries. For **haute couture** the traditional bastions are avenue Montaigne, rue François 1ᵉʳ and the upper end of **rue du Faubourg-St-Honoré** in the 8ᵉ.

Books

The most atmospheric areas for **book** shopping are the Seine *quais*, with their rows of new and secondhand bookstalls perched against the river parapet, and the narrow streets of the Quartier Latin.

Artcurial 9 av Matignon, 8ᵉ; Mᵒ Franklin-D.-Roosevelt. The best art bookshop in Paris, set in an elegant town house. Sells French and foreign editions, and there's also a gallery and stylish café. Mon–Sat 10.30am–7pm; closed two weeks in Aug.
FNAC 74 av des Champs-Élysées, 8ᵉ; Mᵒ George-V; Forum des Halles, niveau 2, Porte Pierre-Lescot, 1ᵉʳ; Mᵒ/RER Châtelet-Les Halles; 136 rue de Rennes, 6ᵉ; Mᵒ Montparnasse; ⓦ www.fnac.com. Not the most congenial of bookshops, but it's the biggest and covers everything. Mon–Sat 10am–7.30pm; the Champs-Élysées branch is open till midnight daily.
Gibert Jeune 5 place St-Michel and around, 5ᵉ ⓦ www.gibertjeune.fr; Mᵒ St-Michel. A Latin Quarter institution for student/academic books, with nine, slightly chaotic, stores on and around Place St-Michel. There's a second-hand selection at 2 pl St-Michel, and foreign-language titles at 10 pl St-Michel. Mon–Sat 9.30am–7.30pm.

Parallèles 47 rue St-Honoré, 1ᵉʳ; Mᵒ Châtelet-Les Halles. An alternative bookshop, with everything from anarchism to New Age. Good for info on current events and gigs. Mon–Sat 10am–7pm.
Shakespeare & Co 37 rue de la Bûcherie, 5ᵉ ⓦ www.shakespeareandcompany.com; Mᵒ Maubert-Mutualité. Cosy, crowded literary haunt (see p.117), staffed by earnest young wannabe Hemingways, selling the best selection of English-language books in town. Readings Mon 7pm. Daily 10am–11pm.
Village Voice 6 rue Princesse, 6ᵉ ⓦ www.villagevoicebookshop.com; Mᵒ Mabillon. A welcoming neighbourhood bookstore in St-Germain, with a good selection of contemporary titles and British and American classics. Frequent readings and author signings. Mon 2–7.30pm, Tues–Sat 10am–7.30pm, Sun noon–6pm.

Clothes

For designer prêt-à-porter, the **department stores** Galeries Lafayette and Printemps have unrivalled selections. Alternatively, the streets around **St-Sulpice** métro, on the Left Bank, are lined with clothing shops of all kinds. You'll find rich pickings if you wander down rues du Vieux Colombier, de Rennes, Madame, de Grenelle and du Cherche-Midi; the relatively compact size and relaxed, Left Bank atmosphere make this one of the most appealing of

Paris's shopping quarters. The historic Bon Marché department store, on rue de Sèvres, is another good reason to begin your shopping trip in this part of the Left Bank, while rues du Cherche-Midi and de Grenelle are good for shoes, and rue des Saints-Pères is known for its underwear shops.

For couture and seriously expensive designer wear, make for the wealthy, manicured streets around the **Champs-Élysées**, especially avenue François 1er, avenue Montaigne and **rue du Faubourg-St-Honoré**. Younger designers have colonized the lower reaches of the latter street, between rue Cambon and rue des Pyramides. In the heart of this area, luxurious **place Vendôme** is the place for serious jewellery.

On the eastern side of the city, chic boutiques line the Marais' main shopping street, **rue des Francs-Bourgeois**, and young, trendy designers and hippie outfits congregate on Bastille streets **rue de Charonne** and **rue Keller**.

At the more alternative end of the spectrum, one-off designer boutiques cluster around **Abbesses** métro, at the foot of Montmartre – try rues des Martyrs, des Trois Frères, de la Vieuville, Houdon and Durantin. The **Forum des Halles** and surrounding streets is a good place to browse for street gear – though you'll have to sift through a fair bit of cheap tat. **Rue Etienne-Marcel** and pedestrianized **rue Tiquetonne** are good for young, trendy fashion boutiques.

As long as there's a strong euro, visitors from outside the eurozone will find shopping relatively expensive. The **sales** are officially held twice a year, beginning in mid-January and mid-July and lasting a month. Ends of lines and old stock of the couturiers are sold year round in "*stock*" **discount** shops, listed below, or out at the vast, American-style **La Vallée Outlet**, inside the frontiers of Disneyland (Mon–Fri & Sun 10am–7pm, Sat 10am–8pm; ⓦ www .lavalleevillage.com; RER Val d'Europe–Serris–Montévrain).

agnès b 6 rue du Jour, 1er (M° Châtelet-Les Halles), 6 & 10 rue du Vieux Colombier, 6e (M° St-Sulpice). The queen of classic understatement, for men and women of all persuasions. Relatively affordable for designer gear.
Anne Willi 13 rue Keller, 11e; M° Ledru-Rollin/ Voltaire. Original pieces of clothing in gorgeous fabrics that respect classic French sartorial design. Prices from around €60 upwards. Mon 2–8pm, Tues–Sat 11.30am–8pm.
APC 3 & 4 rue de Fleurus, 6e; M° St-Placide. Young and urban, but still effortlessly classic in that Parisian way. The men's and women's shops face each other across the road. Mon, Fri & Sat

Department stores

Le Bon Marché 38 rue de Sèvres, 7e, ⓦ www.lebonmarche.fr; M° Sèvres-Babylone. The world's oldest department store, founded in 1852, is a beautiful building and a classy place to shop, with a legendary food hall. Mon–Wed & Fri 9.30am–7pm, Thurs 10am–9pm, Sat 9.30am–8pm.

Galeries Lafayette 40 bd Haussmann, 9e, ⓦ www.galerieslafayette.com; M° Havre-Caumartin. The store's forte is high fashion. Three floors are given over to the latest creations by leading designers for women, while an adjoining three-storey store is devoted to men's fashion. Then there's a huge *parfumerie* and a host of big names in mens and women's accessories – all under a superb 1900 dome. Lafayette Maison, the huge, impressive home store, is just up the road at 35 bd Haussmann. Mon–Sat 9.30am–7.30pm, Thurs till 9pm.

Printemps 64 bd Haussmann, 9^e, ⓦ www.printemps.com; M° Havre-Caumartin. Printemps has an excellent fashion collection for men and women and a *parfumerie* even bigger than that of rival Galeries Lafayette. The store is set to undergo a major revamp: its fine Art Nouveau decor will be fully restored and it will stock more luxury brands. Mon–Sat 9.35am–7pm, Thurs till 10pm.

11am–7pm, Tues–Thurs 9am–7.30pm. There's a branch in the Marais at 112 rue Vieille du Temple, 3ᵉ; Mᵒ St-Paul.

Comptoir des Cotonniers 30 rue de Buci & 59ter rue Bonaparte, 6ᵉ; Mᵒ Mabillon/St-Germain-des-Prés. Reliable, stylish chain stocking comfortable, well-cut women's basics that nod to contemporary fashions without being modish. Trousers, shirts and dresses for around €100. Mon 11am–7pm, Tues–Sat 10am–7.30pm. Around thirty branches in Paris.

Heaven 83 rue des Martyrs, 18ᵉ; Mᵒ Abbesses. Luxurious – sometimes brash, sometimes elegant – clothing and accessories for men and women designed by English-bred Lea-Anne Wallis. Tues–Sat 11am–7.30pm, Sun 2–7.30pm. There's another branch in the 4ᵉ at 16 rue du Pont Louis-Philippe; Mᵒ Hotel-de-Ville.

Isabel Marant 16 rue de Charonne, 11ᵉ; Mᵒ Bastille. Marant excels in feminine and flattering clothes in quality fabrics such as silk and cashmere. Prices from around €90 upwards. Mon–Sat 10.30am–7.30pm.

Jacques Le Corre 193 rue Saint-Honoré, 1ᵉʳ; Mᵒ Tuileries. Creative, original hats, footwear and handbags. The stylish, unisex hats here come in interesting colours and shapes; Jacques is famed for his classic cotton *cloche*, perfecting the vagrant-chic look. Mon–Sat 11am–7pm.

Le Mouton à Cinq Pattes 138 bd St-Germain, 6ᵉ; Mᵒ Odéon/Mabillon. You might just find a Helmut Lang or a Gaultier among the racks of discounted end-of-line and last-season's bargains – though often the labels are cut out so you'll have to trust your judgement. Mon–Sat 10.30am–7.30pm. There's a branch at 18 rue St-Placide, 6ᵉ, and one just for women's clothes at 8 rue St-Placide, 6ᵉ (both Mon–Sat 10am–7pm; Mᵒ Sèvres-Babylone).

Sabbia Rosa 71–73 rue des Saints-Pères, 6ᵉ; Mᵒ St-Germain-des-Près. Supermodels' knickers – literally, they all shop here – at supermodel prices in this famed Parisian store. Exquisite lingerie in buttery silk and Calais lace. Mon–Sat 10am–7pm.

Sonia/Sonia Rykiel 61 rue des Saints-Pères, 6ᵉ; Mᵒ Sèvres-Babylone. Sonia Rykiel has been a St-Germain institution since opening a store on bd St-Germain in 1968; this is a younger, less expensive offshoot. Mon–Sat 10.30am–7pm. Further branches around town.

Spree 16 rue de la Vieuville, 18ᵉ; Mᵒ Abbesses. Funky, feminine clothing store/gallery led by designers such as Vanessa Bruno, Isabel Marant and Christian Wijnants. Also vintage pieces, accessories, furniture and beauty products. Mon 2–7pm, Tues–Sat 11am–7.30pm. Another branch at 1 rue St-Simon, 7ᵉ.

Vanessa Bruno 25 rue St-Sulpice, 6ᵉ; Mᵒ Odéon. Effortlessly beautiful women's fashions with a hint of updated hippy chic. Mon–Sat 10.30am–7.30pm. Branches at 12 rue Castiglione, 1ᵉʳ (Mᵒ Tuileries), and 100 rue Vieille du Temple, 4ᵉʳ (Mᵒ St-Sébastien/Froissart).

YSL Rive Gauche men: 6 place St-Sulpice, 6ᵉ (Mᵒ St-Sulpice/Mabillon), women: 32–38 rue du Faubourg-Saint-Honoré, 8ᵉ (Mᵒ Concorde). Ready-to-wear spin-off from the designer label. Skinny monochrome chic remains the staple for men; the lines for women are more colourful but no less distinctively YSL.

Zadig & Voltaire 1 & 3 rue du Vieux Colombier, 6ᵉ; Mᵒ St-Sulpice. The women's clothes at this small, moderately expensive Parisian chain are pretty and feminine, not a million miles from agnès b, but with a more wayward flair. Mon–Sat 10.30am–7.30pm. Other branches include 15 rue du Jour, 1ᵉʳ (Mᵒ Les Halles); 9 rue du 29 Juillet, 1ᵉʳ (Mᵒ Tuileries); 11 rue Montmartre, 1ᵉʳ (Mᵒ Les Halles); and 3 rue des Rosiers (Mᵒ St-Paul-St Louis).

Food and drink

Almost every Parisian *quartier* has its own charcuterie, boulangerie and weekly market, while some **streets**, such as rue Cler, in the 7ᵉ, rue des Martyrs, in the 9ᵉ, and rue Lepic, in Montmartre, are crammed with delis, patisseries, cheese shops and wine merchants where shopping is as much a feast for the eyes as the palate. **Place de la Madeleine** in the 8ᵉ has the finest **luxury food** stores, but there are plenty of others: we've listed **some of the best** below. Tasty **picnic food** can be picked up at the **street markets** or **supermarkets**; the least expensive supermarket chain is Ed l'Epicier. Food markets are detailed at the end of this section.

Arnaud Delmontel 39 rue des Martyrs, 9ᵉ; Mᵒ St-Georges. Exquisite Parisian patisserie with a funky twist, its *bavaroises*, *macarons* and tarts decorated in fresh candy colours. The award-winning bread is outstanding, too. Mon & Wed–Sun 7am–8.30pm.

Barthélémy 51 rue de Grenelle, 7ᵉ ☎01.45.48.56.75; Mᵒ Bac. Purveyors of carefully ripened and meticulously stored seasonal cheeses to the rich and powerful. Delivery available. Tues–Sat 8.30am–1pm & 4–7.15pm; closed Aug.

Les Caves Augé 116 bd Haussmann, 8ᵉ; Mᵒ St-Augustin. This old-fasioned, wood-panelled shop is the oldest *cave* in Paris and sells not only fine wines, but also a wide selection of port, armagnac, cognac and champagne. Mon 1–7.30pm, Tues–Sat 9am–7.30pm.

Debauve and Gallais 30 rue des Sts-Pères, 7ᵉ; Mᵒ St-Germain-des-Prés/Sèvres-Babylone. A beautiful, ancient shop specializing in ambrosial chocolates. Mon–Sat 9.30am–7pm.

Fauchon 26 place de la Madeleine, 8ᵉ; Mᵒ Madeleine. A dazzling range of exquisite groceries and wine; just the place for presents of tea, jam, truffles, chocolates, exotic vinegars and mustards etc. There's a *traiteur* which stays open until 9pm and a newly opened swish restaurant. Mon–Sat 9am–7pm.

Hédiard 21 place de la Madeleine, 8ᵉ; Mᵒ Madeleine. The aristocrat's grocer since 1850;

there are several other branches throughout the city. Mon–Sat 9am–10pm.

La Maison de l'Escargot 79 rue Fondary, 15ᵉ; Mᵒ Dupleix. As the name suggests, this place is all about snails: they'll sauce them and shell them while you wait. Tues–Sat 9.30am–7pm; closed mid-July to Sept.

Mariage Frères 30 rue du Bourg-Tibourg, 4ᵉ; Mᵒ Hôtel-de-Ville. Hundreds of teas, neatly packed in tins, line the floor-to-ceiling shelves of this 100-year-old emporium. There's a *salon de thé* in the back with exquisite pastries (daily noon–7pm). Daily 10.30am–7.30pm.

Poilâne 8 rue du Cherche-Midi, 6ᵉ ⓦ ww.poilane .fr; Mᵒ Sèvres-Babylone. You can order the famous, traditionally made sourdough pain Poilâne online, or visit the delicious-smelling store for loaves and baked goods. Mon–Sat 7.15am–8.15pm. There's a second branch at 49 bd de Grenelle, 15ᵉ (Mᵒ Duplex), open Tues–Sun.

Music

New **CDs** are not particularly cheap in Paris, but there are plenty of second-hand bargains, and anyone looking for world music and jazz rarities are in luck. The **flea markets** (St-Ouen especially) and the *bouquinistes* along the Seine are good places to look for old records.

Crocodisc 40–42 Rue des Écoles; Mᵒ Maubert-Mutualité. Everything from folk and Afro-Antillais to salsa and movie soundtracks, new and used, at good prices. **Crocojazz**, nearby at 64 rue de la Montagne-Ste-Geneviève, offers jazz and blues imports, with some inexpensive used titles. Mᵒ Maubert-Mutualité. Both Tues–Sat 11am–7pm; Crocodisc closed Aug.

FNAC Musique 4 place de la Bastille, 12ᵉ; Mᵒ Bastille. Extremely stylish shop in black, grey and chrome, with computerized catalogues, books, every variety of music and a concert booking agency. Mon–Sat 10am–8pm.

Paul Beuscher 15–29 bd Beaumarchais, 4ᵉ; Mᵒ Bastille. A music department store that's been going strong for over 100 years, selling instruments, scores, books and recording equipment. Mon–Fri 9.45am–12.30pm & 2–7pm, Sat 9.45am–7pm.

Virgin Megastore 52–60 av des Champs-Élysées, 8ᵉ; Mᵒ Franklin-D.-Roosevelt (Mon–Sat 10am–midnight, Sun noon–midnight); and 99 rue de Rivoli, 1ᵉʳ; Mᵒ Palais-Royal (Wed–Sat 10am–10pm, Sun & Mon 10am–8pm). The biggest and trendiest of Paris's music shops, with a concert booking agency.

Markets

Paris's **food markets**, like its shops, are grand spectacles. Mouthwatering arrays of produce from around the globe assail the senses in even the drabbest parts of town. In Belleville and the Goutte d'Or, North Africa predominates; Southeast Asia in the 13ᵉ arrondissement. There are also street markets dedicated to junk (the *marchés aux puces*), clothes and textiles, flowers, birds, books, stamps and art. Markets are traditionally **morning** affairs, usually starting between 7am and 8am and tailing off sometime between 1pm and 2.30pm. However, in a break with Parisian tradition a few afternoon-only markets have recently opened.

Flea markets

Paris's **flea markets**, or *marchés aux puces*, are increasingly oriented towards genuine antiques rather than junk, but you can still find some quirky bargains, and the festive atmosphere is unbeatable. Arrive early.

Place d'Aligre 12ᵉ; Mᵒ Ledru-Rollin. A small flea market and the only one located in the city proper, peddling secondhand clothes and bric-a-brac – anything from old gramophone players to odd bits of crockery. Tues–Sun 7.30am–12.30pm.

Porte de Montreuil 20ᵉ; Mᵒ Porte-de-Montreuil. The most junkyard-like of them all, and the best for secondhand clothes – it's cheapest on Mon when leftovers from the weekend are sold off. Also good for old furniture and household goods. Sat, Sun & Mon 7am–7.30pm.

Porte de Vanves av Georges-Lafenestre/av Marc-Sangnier, 14ᵉ; Mᵒ Porte-de-Vanves. The best for bric-a-brac and Parisian knick-knacks. Sat & Sun 7am–1pm (Marc-Sangnier), all day (Georges-Lafenestre).

St-Ouen/Porte de Clignancourt 18ᵉ; Mᵒ Porte-de-Clignancourt. The biggest and most touristy flea market, with nearly a thousand stalls selling new and used clothes, shoes, records, books and junk of all sorts, along with expensive antiques. Mon, Sat & Sun 7.30am–6pm.

Food markets

Belleville bd de Belleville, 20ᵉ; Mᵒ Belleville/Ménilmontant. Tues & Fri 7am–2pm.

Dejean place du Château-Rouge, 18ᵉ; Mᵒ Château-Rouge. African foods. Tues–Sun.

Enfants-Rouges 39 rue de Bretagne, 3ᵉ; Mᵒ Filles-du-Calvaire. Tues–Sat 8am–1pm & 4–7pm, Sun 8am–2pm.

Maubert place Maubert, 5ᵉ; Mᵒ Maubert-Mutualité. Tues, Thurs & Sat 7am–2.30pm.

Monge place Monge, 5ᵉ. Mᵒ Monge. Wed & Fri 7am–2.30pm, Sun 7am–3pm.

Montorgueil rue Montorgueil & rue Montmartre, 1ᵉʳ; Mᵒ Châtelet-Les Halles/Sentier. Tues–Sat 8am–1pm & 4–7pm, Sun 9am–1pm.

Mouffetard rue Mouffetard, 5ᵉ; Mᵒ Censier-Daubenton. Tues–Sun.

Place d'Aligre 12ᵉ; Mᵒ Ledru-Rollin. Tues–Sun until 12.30pm.

Porte-St-Martin rue du Château-d'Eau, 10ᵉ, Mᵒ Château-d'Eau. Tues–Sat 8am–1pm & 4–7.30pm, Sun 8am–1pm.

Raspail bd Raspail, between rue du Cherche-Midi & rue de Rennes, 6ᵉ; Mᵒ Rennes. Tues & Fri, plus celebrated organic market on Sun.

Richard Lenoir bd Richard Lenoir, 11ᵉ; Mᵒ Bastille/Richard Lenoir. Thurs & Sun.

Rue Cler 7ᵉ; Mᵒ Ecole-Militaire. Tues–Sun 8.30am–noon.

Ternes rue Lemercier, 17ᵉ; Mᵒ Ternes. Specializes in flowers. Tues–Sun 8am–7.30pm.

Listings

Airlines Aer Lingus ☎08.21.23.02.67, ⊛www.aerlingus.com; Air Canada ☎08.25.88.08.81, ⊛www.aircanada.com; Air France ☎08.20.82.08.20 ⊛www.airfrance.com; bmibaby ☎08.90.71.00.81, ⊛www.bmibaby.co.uk; British Airways ☎08.25.82.54.00, ⊛www.ba.com; Delta ☎08.11.64.00.05, ⊛www.delta.com; easyJet ☎08.25.08.25.08, ⊛www.easyjet.co.uk; Qantas ☎08.11.98.00.02, ⊛www.qantas.com; Ryanair ☎08.92.23.23.75, ⊛www.ryanair.com.

Ambulance service ☎15 (operators can put you through to an English-speaker).

Banks and exchange Cash machines (ATMs) can be found at all airports and mainline train stations, and at most of the banks in town. Beware of money-exchange bureaux and automatic exchange machines, however, which may advertise the selling rather than buying rate and add on hefty commission fees.

Buses For national and international buses, including Eurolines (☎08.92.89.90.91), you can get information and tickets at the main terminus, 28 av du Général-de-Gaulle, Bagnolet (Mᵒ Gallieni).

Car rental The big international car rental companies have offices at the airports, at the Gare du Nord and at various points around the city. Two reliable local firms are Buchard, 99 bd Auguste-Blanqui (Mᵒ Place-d'Italie) ☎01.45.80.15.15; and Locabest ☎01.48.31.77.05, ⊛www.locabest.fr, with offices at 3 rue Abel, 12ᵉ (Mᵒ Gare-de-Lyon) ☎01.43.46.05.05, and 104 bd Magenta, 10ᵉ (Mᵒ Gare-du-Nord) ☎01.44.72.08.05.

Dental treatment A useful (private) emergency service is SOS Dentaire, 87 bd Port-Royal, 5ᵉ ℡01.43.37.51.00; Mᵒ Port-Royal.

Doctor callout The private association SOS Médecins ℡08.20.33.24.24 offers 24hr medical help.

Embassies/Consulates Australia, 4 rue Jean-Rey, 15ᵉ ℡01.40.59.33.00, ⓦwww.france.embassy .gov.au, Mᵒ Bir-Hakeim; Canada, 35 av Montaigne, 8ᵉ ℡01.44.43.29.00, ⓦwww.amb-canada.fr, Mᵒ Franklin-D.-Roosevelt; Germany, 28 rue Marbeau, 16ᵉ ℡01.53.83.45.00, ⓦwww.amb-allemagne.fr, Mᵒ Porte Maillot/Porte Dauphine; Ireland, 4 rue Rude, 16ᵉ ℡01.44.17.67.00, Mᵒ Charles-de-Gaulle-Étoile; New Zealand, 7ter, rue Léonardo-de-Vinci, 16ᵉ ℡01.45.01.43.43, ⓦwww.nzembassy.com, Mᵒ Victor-Hugo; South Africa, 59 Quai d'Orsay, 7ᵉ ℡01.53.59.23.23, ⓦwww.afriquesud.net, Mᵒ Invalides; UK, 35 rue du Faubourg-St-Honoré, 8ᵉ ℡01.44.51.31.00, ⓦwww.amb-grandebretagne.fr, Mᵒ Concorde; US, 2 av Gabriel, 8ᵉ ℡01.43.12.22.22, ⓦfrance.usembassy.gov, Mᵒ Concorde.

Festivals There are free concerts and street performers all over Paris for the Fête de la Musique, which coincides with the summer solstice (June 21; ⓦwww.fetedelamusique.culture.fr). Gay Pride follows swiftly afterwards, on the last Sat of June. July 14 (Bastille Day) is celebrated with official pomp in parades of tanks down the Champs-Élysées, firework displays, concerts and *bals pompiers* in the fire stations (head for rue Blanche and rue des Vieux-Colombiers). For a month afterwards, the *quais* are transformed into a sandy beach along the Seine as part of the wildly popular Paris Plages scheme. The Tour de France finishes along the Champs-Élysées on the third or fourth Sun of July. In early Oct, the Nuit Blanche ("sleepless night") persuades Parisians to stay up all night for an energetic programme of arts events and parties all over the city. For further details on these and many others, see "*Sorties & événements*" on the tourist board website ⓦwww .parisinfo.com.

Hospitals In emergencies, call an ambulance on ℡15. If you require longer-term out-patient care, perhaps, or if you prefer not to avail yourself of France's superb healthcare system, then consider one of the English-speaking private, not-for-profit hospitals. These include the Hertford British Hospital, 3 rue Barbès, Levallois-Perret (℡01.46.39.22.22, ⓦwww.british-hospital.org; Mᵒ Anatole-France) and the American Hospital, 63 bd Victor-Hugo, Neuilly-sur-Seine (℡01.46.41.25.25, ⓦwww.american-hospital.org; Mᵒ Porte-Maillot then bus #82 to terminus).

Internet Internet access is everywhere in Paris – if it's not in your hotel it'll be in a café nearby, and there are lots of *points internet* around the city. Most post offices offer online access, too.

Laundries There's bound to be a self-service laundromat (*laverie self-service* or *libre-service*) somewhere near where you're staying – just ask locally. They're generally open from 7am to around 8pm.

Left luggage Lockers are available at all train stations.

Lost property Your first port of call should be the Commissariat de Police for the arrondissement where you think the loss took place; the next step is the central police Bureau des Objets Trouvés, 36 rue des Morillons, 15ᵉ (℡08.21.00.25.25; Mᵒ Convention; Mon–Thurs 8.30am–5pm, Fri 8.30am–4.30pm). For property lost on métro/RER and bus services, try the station where you might have lost it first, then call ℡08.92.68.77.14. If you lose your passport, report it to a police station and then your embassy.

Pharmacies 24hr service at: Dhery, 84 av des Champs-Élysées, 8ᵉ ℡01.45.62.02.41 (Mᵒ George-V); 6 place Clichy, 9ᵉ ℡01.48.74.65.18. There's a British pharmacy, SNC, at 62 av des Champs-Élysées, 8ᵉ ℡01.43.59.22.52; it's open daily from 8am to midnight. All pharmacies, if closed, post the address of one nearby that stays open late (*pharmacie de garde*).

Police ℡17 (℡112 from a mobile) for emergencies. To report a theft, go to the Commissariat de Police of the arrondissement in which the theft took place.

Post office Main office at 52 rue du Louvre 1ᵉʳ; Mᵒ Châtelet-Les-Halles. Open daily 24hr for letters, poste restante, faxes, telegrams and phone calls. Other offices are usually open Mon–Fri 8am–7pm, Sat 8am–noon.

Telephones To call within Paris, even if you're already in the city, you need to dial the ℡01 code. ℡08.92 numbers cost €0.34 a minute from any (landline) phone in France; ℡08.21 numbers cost €0.12; neither work from abroad. Public phones accept phonecards (*télécartes*), sold at *tabacs*, and sometimes credit cards – rarely coins. If you plan to make a lot of calls, consider buying a French phone using pre-paid charge-up cards (*mobicartes*); deals are often available for around €30 – less than the cost of just a few international calls on a foreign mobile. Note that France operates on the European GSM standard, so US cellphones won't work in France unless you've got a tri-band phone. Numbers for mobile phones (*portables*) begin ℡06.

Around Paris

The region around the capital – the **Île de France** – and the borders of the neighbouring provinces are studded with large-scale **châteaux**. Many were royal or noble retreats for hunting and other leisured pursuits, while some – like **Versailles** – were for more serious state show. All are impressive, especially **Vaux-le-Vicomte** for its harmonious architecture and **Chantilly** for its masterpiece-studded art collection. If you have even the slightest curiosity about church buildings the **cathedral of Chartres** more than fulfils expectations. Closer in, on the edge of Paris itself, **St-Denis** boasts a cathedral second only to Notre-Dame – a visit which can be combined with a wander back into the centre of the city along the banks of the St-Denis canal. Other **waterside walks** include the Marne-side towns, which, when they were small villages, were frequented by the carousing, carefree painters and musicians of the early 1900s. **Auvers-Sur-Oise**, Van Gogh's final resting place, has a museum that transports you back to Impressionist days. Various suburban museums cover specific interests – china at **Sèvres**, Napoleon at **Malmaison** or horses at **Chantilly,** for example. The biggest pull for kids is without question **Disneyland Paris**, out beyond the satellite town of **Marne-la-Vallée**, but they might also like the air and space museum at **Le Bourget**.

All of the attractions detailed here are easily accessible by public transport. We have arranged the accounts geographically, moving clockwise around Paris from St-Denis in the north to Malmaison in the west.

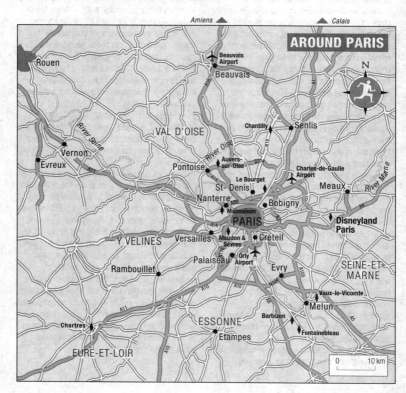

St-Denis

For most of the twentieth century, **ST-DENIS**, 10km north of the centre of Paris (M° St-Denis-Basilique), was one of the most heavily industrialized communities in France, and a bastion of the Communist party. Since then, factories have closed, unemployment is rife and immigration has radically altered the ethnic mix. Visitors will find a poor but buoyant community, its pride buttressed by the town's twin attractions: the ancient **basilica of St-Denis** and the hyper-modern **Stade-de-France**, seat of the 1998 World Cup final (Ⓦwww.stadedefrance.fr). The **tourist office**, close to the St-Denis-Basilique metro and opposite the basilica (April–Sept Mon–Sat 9.30am–1pm & 2–6pm, Sun 10am–1pm & 2–4pm; Oct–March Mon–Sat 9.30am–1pm & 2–6pm, Sun 10am–2pm; Ⓣ01.55.87.08.70; Ⓦwww.saint-denis-tourisme.com) can provide **maps**.

The centre of St-Denis retains traces of small-town origins, but the area abutting its cathedral has been transformed into a fortress-like housing and shopping complex. A **market**, in the place Jean-Jaurès (Tues, Fri & Sun mornings) peddles vegetables at half the price of Parisian markets, as well as cheap curios, clothes and fabrics. Adjacent, off rue Dupont, are the covered *halles*, an exuberant multi-ethnic affair.

The town's chief claim to fame, though, is its magnificent cathedral, the burial place of the kings of France. Begun by Abbot Suger, friend and adviser to royalty, in the first half of the twelfth century, the **Basilique St-Denis** (April–Sept Mon–Sat 10am–6.15pm, Sun noon–6.15pm; Oct–March Mon–Sat 10am–5pm, Sun noon–5.15pm) is generally regarded as the birthplace of the Gothic style in European architecture. With its two towers (the northern one collapsed in 1837), three large sculpted portals and high rose window, the west front set the pattern of Gothic facades to come, but it's in the choir that you best see the emergence of the new style: the use of the pointed arch, the ribbed vault and the long shafts of half-column rising from pillar to roof. It's beautifully lit, thanks to the transept windows – so big that they occupy their entire end walls – and the clerestory, which is almost entirely made of glass – another first.

Legend holds that the first church here was founded by a mid-third-century Parisian bishop, later known as St-Denis. The story goes that after he was beheaded for his beliefs at Montmartre (Mount of the Martyr), he picked up his head and walked to St-Denis, thereby establishing the abbey. The site's **royal history** began with the coronation of Pepin the Short in 754, but it wasn't until the reign of Hugues Capet, in 996, that it became the customary burial place of the kings of France. Since then, all but three of France's kings have been interred here, and their fine tombs and effigies are distributed about the **necropolis** (€6.50; closed during services) in the transepts and ambulatory.

Immediately on the left of the entrance, in the south transept, is one of the most bizarre sights: the bare feet of **François 1ᵉʳ** and his wife Claude de France peeking out of their enormous Renaissance memorial. Beside the steps to the ambulatory lies **Charles V**, the first king to have his funeral effigy carved from life, on the day of his coronation in 1364. Alongside him is his wife Jeanne de Bourbon, who clutches the sack of her own entrails to her chest – a reminder that royalty was traditionally eviscerated at death, the flesh boiled away from the bones and buried separately. Up the steps and round to the right, a florid Louis XVI and busty **Marie-Antoinette** – often graced by bouquets of flowers – kneel in prayer. The pious scene was sculpted in 1830, long after their execution.

Five minutes' south of the basilica, in a former Carmelite convent at 22 rue Gabriel-Péri, the **Musée d'Art et d'Histoire** (Mon, Wed & Fri 10am–5.30pm, Thurs 10am–8pm, Sat & Sun 2–6.30pm; €4; ⓦ www.musee-saint-denis.fr) has a good archaeology collection, interesting paintings of nineteenth- and twentieth-century industrial landscapes, and posters, cartoons, broadsheets and paintings relating to the Commune.

You can **walk back to Paris** along the **canal towpath** from the northern side of the stadium's footbridge. Parts of the canalside are being rehabilitated and may necessitate a slight detour, and there are decaying, semi-abandoned stretches that can feel eerie, but keep going and you'll arrive at Porte de la Villette in a couple of hours. The walk is only conventionally picturesque in patches, but it's a fascinating way to experience Paris's forgotten, rusting underbelly.

Chantilly

CHANTILLY, a small town 40km north of Paris, is associated mainly with horses. Scores of thoroughbreds can be seen thundering along the forest rides of a morning, and two of the season's classiest flat races, the Jockey Club and the Prix de Diane, are held here. The old château stables are given over to a horse museum.

Trains run almost every hour from Paris's Gare du Nord to Chantilly (30min). Free shuttle buses to the château meet some but not all trains – in any case it's a pleasant two-kilometre stroll through the forest; turn right outside the station, then left at the major roundabout on the signposted **footpath**.

The château and the Musée Vivant du Cheval

The Chantilly estate used to belong to two of the most powerful clans in France: first the Montmorencys, then, through marriage, to the Condés. The present **Château** (daily except Tues: château April–Oct 10am–6pm, Nov–March 10.30am–5pm; park April–Oct 10am–8pm, Nov–March 10.30am–6pm; château and park €10, park only €5; ⓦ www.chateaudechantilly.com) was built in the late nineteenth century on the ruins of the Grand Château, built for the Grand Condé, who helped Louis XIV smash Spanish power in the mid-seventeenth century. It's a beautiful structure, graceful and romantic, surrounded by water and looking out over a formal arrangement of pools and pathways designed by Le Nôtre, Louis XIV's gardener. A major restoration, funded by local resident the Aga Khan, is now in progress, so expect certain areas of the château and park to be closed for works – and, as time goes on, expect new rooms to open for the first time.

The entrance is across a moat, past two realistic bronzes of hunting hounds. The bulk of what you'll see in the château is from the enormous collection of **paintings and drawings** owned by the Institut de France. Stipulated to remain as organized by Henri d'Orléans (the donor of the château), the arrangement is haphazard but immensely satisfying. Some highlights can be found in the Rotunda of the picture gallery – Piero di Cosimo's *Simonetta Vespucci* and Raphael's *La Vierge de Lorette* – and in the so-called Sanctuary, with Raphael's *Three Graces* displayed alongside Filippo Lippi's *Esther et Assuerius* and forty miniatures from a fifteenth-century Book of Hours attributed to the great French Renaissance artist Jean Fouquet. Pass through the Galerie de Psyche, with its series of sepia stained glass illustrating Apuleius' *Golden Ass*, to the room known as the Tribune, where Italian art, including Botticelli's *Autumn*, takes up two walls, and Ingres and Delacroix have a wall each.

The countryside around Paris began to take a primary role for painters in search of inspiration in the late nineteenth century. The towns along the banks of the Seine read like a roll call of Musée d'Orsay paintings, and pockets of unchanged scenery remain.

Auvers-sur-Oise

On the banks of the River Oise, about 35km northwest of Paris, **AUVERS** makes an attractive rural excursion. **Van Gogh** spent the last two months of his life here, in a frenzy of painting activity. The church at Auvers, the portrait of Dr Gachet, black crows flapping across a wheat field – many of Van Gogh's best-known works belong to this period. He died in his brother's arms, after an incompetent attempt to shoot himself, in the attic room he rented in the **Auberge Ravoux**. The *auberge* still stands on the main street, and you can visit Van Gogh's room (March–Oct Wed–Sun 10am–6pm; €5). The **Musée de l'Absinthe** (June–Sept Wed–Sun 2–6pm, Oct, Nov & March–May Sat & Sun 2–6pm; €4.50) nearby is devoted to the wormwood-based liqueur much loved by Van Gogh and his ilk for its supposed stimulation of creativity.

The **Château d'Auvers** offers a fascinating multimedia tour of the world the Impressionists inhabited (April–Sept Tues–Fri 10.30am–6pm, Sat & Sun till 6.30pm; Oct–March Tues–Fri 10.30am–4.30pm, Sat & Sun till 5.30pm; €11.50; Ⓦwww .chateau-auvers.fr). Most evocative of all, however, is to walk through the old part of the village, past the church and the red lane into the famous wheat field and up the hill to the cemetery where, against the far left wall in a humble ivy-covered grave, the Van Gogh brothers lie side by side. Auvers boasts a further artistic connection in Van Gogh's predecessor, **Daubigny** – contemporary of Corot and Daumier – who is celebrated, with others, in a small **museum** above the tourist office (April–Oct Wed–Fri 2–6pm, Sat & Sun 10.30am–12.30pm & 2–6pm; Nov–March Wed–Fri 2–5pm, Sat & Sun 10.30am–12.30pm & 2–5.30pm; €5). You can visit his studio-house (April–Oct Thurs–Sun 2–6pm; €5) at 61 rue Daubigny, from where he would set off in his boat for weeks at a time to paint his famed Seine riverscapes.

Hourly trains for Auvers leave from Gare du Nord; usually you have to change at Valmondois (1hr–1hr 15min).

Barbizon

The landscape and country life around Barbizon, 60km southeast of Paris and 10km from Fontainebleau, inspired painters such as **Rousseau** and **Millet** to set up camp here, initiating an artistic movement known as the Barbizon group. More painters followed, as well as writers and musicians. The **Auberge du Père Ganne**, on the main road, became the place to stay, with the generous owner accepting the artists' decorations of his inn and furniture as payment. Now home to a museum (daily except Tues 10am–12.30pm & 2–5.30pm; €3), the Impressionist inn still contains the original painted furniture as well as many Barbizon paintings. To get to Barbizon, you'll need your own car; an infrequent bus service connects with Fontainebleau (see p.180), but is limited to summer Sundays.

Meudon

The tranquil suburb of Meudon, 10km southwest of Paris, was where **Rodin** spent his last years. His house and studio, the **Villa des Brillants**, 19 avenue Rodin (April–Sept Fri–Sun 1–6pm; €4), is worth a visit for its preparatory sketches, plaster casts and studies. Here he lived with his companion, Rose Beuret, and married her, after fifty years together, just a fortnight before her death in February 1917. His own death followed in November, and they are buried together on the terrace below the house, beneath a bronze version of *The Thinker*. The classical facade behind masks an enormous pavilion containing plaster casts of many of Rodin's most famous works. To get there, take RER line C to Meudon-Val Fleury, from where it's a fifteen-minute walk along avenues Barbusse and Rodin, or a short ride by bus (#169; Paul Bert stop).

The sixteenth-century wing known as the Petit Château includes the well-stocked **library**, where a facsimile of the museum's single greatest treasure is on display, *Les Très Riches Heures du Duc de Berry*, the most celebrated of all the Books of Hours. The remaining half-dozen rooms on the tour mostly show off superb furnishings, with exquisite *boiseries* panelling the walls of the Monkey Gallery, wittily painted with allegorical stories in a pseudo-Chinese style. A grand parade of canvases in the long gallery depicts the many battles won by the Grand Condé.

Five-minutes' walk back towards town along the château drive, the colossal stable block has been transformed into a museum of horses and horsemanship, the **Musée Vivant du Cheval** (April–Oct daily except Tues 10am–6pm; Nov Mon & Wed–Fri 1–5pm, Sat & Sun 10.30am–5.30pm; Dec–March Mon & Wed–Fri 1–5pm, Sat & Sun 1–6pm; €9, €17 combined ticket with château and park; Ⓦwww.museevivantducheval.fr). The building was erected at the beginning of the eighteenth century by the incumbent Condé prince, who believed he would be reincarnated as a horse and wished to provide accommodation for 240 of his future relatives. Breeds from around the world are stalled in the vast main hall, with a central ring for equestrian **demonstrations**. The lush **Potager des Princes**, or "kitchen garden of the princes" (April–Oct daily except Tues 2–7pm; €7.50; Ⓦwww.potagerdesprinces.com), a few hundred metres down from the stables, is a horticultural haven of herbs, salad plants and meticulously planted vegetables. Designed for the Grand Condé by the ubiquitous Le Nôtre, the orchard is almost restored to its former glory, complete with period poetry piped into the centre of the garden.

Disneyland Paris

There are no two ways about it – children will love **Disneyland Paris** (Ⓦwww.disneylandparis.co.uk), and the young at heart will find much to enjoy. Quite why American parents might bring their charges here is hard to fathom, though; even British parents might deem it better to buy a family package to Florida, where sunshine is assured, the rides are bigger and better, and where the conflict between enchanted kingdom and enchanting city does not arise.

Carping aside, at a distance of just 25km east of Paris, it's easy to visit in a day-trip from the capital, and there's a far wider choice of things to do than at a funfair or ordinary theme park. The complex is divided into three areas: **Disneyland Park**, with most of the big rides; **Walt Disney Studios Park**, a more technology-based attempt to re-create the world of cartoon film-making; and **Disney Village**, with its expensive hotels.

Arrival, information and accommodation

To reach Disneyland from Paris, take RER line A from Châtelet-Les Halles, Gare-de-Lyon or Nation to Marne-la-Vallée/Chessy station, which is opposite the main park gates. The journey takes around 35 minutes. If you're coming straight **from the airport**, there are shuttle buses from both Charles de Gaulle and Orly, taking 45 minutes from each (every 30min–1hr from 8.30am; check Ⓦwww.vea.fr/uk for timetables and pickup points). Tickets cost €17 one-way, but children under 12 pay €13, and under-3s go free. Marne-la-Vallée/Chessy also has its own TGV train station, linked to Lille, Lyon – and London via special Eurostar trains. By car, the park is a 32-kilometre drive east of Paris along the A4: take the "Porte de Bercy" exit off the *périphérique*, then follow "direction Metz/Nancy", leaving at exit 14. From Calais follow the A26, changing to the A1, the A104 and finally the A4.

Most people buy their Disney **admission passes** online, but you can also get them, along with the relevant train tickets, at all Paris's RER line A and B stations, tourist offices and major metro stations. A "1-day/1-Park" ticket costs €49 for an adult or €41 for a child (aged 3–11); the ticket allows entry to either the Disneyland Park or Walt Disney Studios Park, not both. One-day "Hopper" tickets, allowing access to both parks, cost €59/51; two- and three-day Hopper tickets are also available. The website details various seasonal offers. **Opening hours** vary, and should be checked when you buy your ticket, but are usually 9/10am–6/8pm, or until 11pm in high summer.

Disney's six themed, heavily designed **hotels** are a mixed bag, and incredibly expensive; they're only worth staying in as part of a multi-day package booked through an agent, or through Disneyland. To really economize, you could camp at the nearby *Camping du Parc de la Colline*, route de Lagny, 77200 Torcy (ⓦ www.camping-de-la-colline.com), which is open all year and provides minibus service to the parks.

Disneyland Park

Disneyland Park has a variety of good thrill rides, though the majority of attractions remain relatively sedate. The Magic Kingdom is divided into four "lands" radiating out from **Main Street USA**. **Fantasyland** appeals to the tinies, with "It's a Small World", Sleeping Beauty's Castle, Peter Pan's Flight and Dumbo the Flying Elephant among its attractions. **Adventureland** has the most outlandish sets and two of the best rides – Pirates of the Caribbean and Indiana Jones and the Temple of Peril. **Frontierland**, loosely set in the Wild West, features the hair-raising roller coaster Big Thunder Mountain, modelled on a runaway mine train, and the gothic Phantom Manor. In **Discoveryland** there's a high-tech 3-D experience called "Honey, I Shrunk The Audience", an interactive Buzz Lightyear laser battle, and the terrifyingly fast Space Mountain roller coasters. The grand **parade** of floats representing all your favourite characters sallies down Main Street USA at about 7pm every day, with smaller events, special shows and fireworks displays occurring regularly.

Walt Disney Studios Park

Though it has its share of big rides – among them the Rock 'n' Roller Coaster Starring Aerosmith, a corkscrew-looping, metal-playing white-knuckler, and the Twilight Zone Tower of Terror, with its gut-churning elevator drop – the **Walt Disney Studios Park** largely focuses on what Disney was and is still renowned for – animation. You can try your hand at drawing, be part of the audience in a mocked up film or TV set, and enjoy special effects and stunt shows. The virtual-reality Armageddon ride is genuinely thrilling – your space-station is bombarded by meteors – the tram tour through the collapsing Catastrophe Canyon is good fun, and smaller children will be bowled over by their live interactions with that alarmingly crazed blue alien, Stitch.

Vaux-le-Vicomte

Of all the great mansions within reach of a day's outing from Paris, the classical **Château of Vaux-le-Vicomte** (April to mid-Nov Mon–Fri 10am–1pm & 2–6pm, Sat & Sun 10am–6pm; €12.50; ⓦ www.vaux-le-vicomte.com), 46km southeast of Paris, is the most architecturally harmonious and aesthetically pleasing – and the most human in scale.

To get there, take a train from Gare de Lyon to Melun (25min), from where a sparse shuttle-bus service (April–Oct Sat & Sun; €7 return) heads the 7km to the château. Otherwise, a taxi costs roughly €15.

The château

Louis XIV's finance minister, Nicholas Fouquet, had the **château** built between 1656 and 1661 at colossal expense, using the top designers of the day – architect Le Vau, painter Le Brun and landscape gardener Le Nôtre. The result was magnificence and precision in perfect proportion, and a bill that could only be paid by someone who occasionally confused the state's accounts with his own. In September 1661, weeks after his sumptuous and showy housewarming party, he was arrested – by d'Artagnan of **Musketeer** fame – charged with embezzlement, of which he was certainly guilty, and clapped into jail for life. Thereupon, the design trio was carted off to build the king's own piece of one-upmanship, the palace of Versailles.

Seen from the entrance, the château is an austere grey pile surrounded by an artificial moat. It's only when you go through to the south side – where clipped box and yew, fountains and statuary stand in formal gardens – that you can look back and appreciate the very harmonious and very French combination of steep, tall roof and central dome with classical pediment and pilasters.

Inside, the main artistic interest lies in the work of Le Brun. He was responsible for the two fine **tapestries** in the entrance, made in the local workshops set up by Fouquet specifically to adorn his house, and **painted ceilings** including the Salon des Muses, *Sleep* in the Cabinet des Jeux and the so-called King's Bedroom, whose decor is the first example of the style that became known as "Louis Quatorze".

Other points of interest are the **kitchens**, which have not been altered since construction, and a room displaying letters in the hand of Fouquet, Louis XIV and other notables. One, dated November 1794 (mid-Revolution), addresses the incumbent Duc de Choiseul-Praslin as *tu*. "Citizen," it says, "you've got a week to hand over one hundred thousand pounds …", and signs off with "Cheers and brotherhood".

The **Musée des Equipages** in the stables comprises a collection of horse-drawn vehicles, complete with model horses. On summer evenings (May–Sept Sat 8pm–midnight; July & Aug also Fri 8pm–midnight; €15.50) the **state rooms** are illuminated with a thousand candles, as they probably were on the occasion of Fouquet's fateful party, with classical music in the gardens adding to the effect. The **fountains** can be seen in action on the second and last Saturdays of each month (3–6pm).

Fontainebleau

From the Gare de Lyon it's a forty-minute train ride to **FONTAINEBLEAU**, famous for its vast, rambling **Château** (daily except Tues: June–Sept 9.30am–6pm; Oct–May 9.30am–5pm; €8; ⓦ www.musee-chateau-fontainebleau.fr). The connecting buses #A and #B from Fontainebleau-Avon station take you to the château gates in fifteen minutes.

The château owes its existence to its situation in the middle of a magnificent forest, which made it the perfect base for royal hunting expeditions. A lodge was built here as early as the twelfth century, but it only began its transformation into a luxurious palace during the 1500s on the initiative of François I, who imported a colony of Italian artists – most notably Rosso il Fiorentino and Niccolò dell'Abate – to carry out the decoration. Their work is best seen in the celebrated **Galerie François I** – which had a seminal influence on the development of French aristocratic art and design – and the dazzlingly frescoed **Salle de Bal**. The palace continued to enjoy royal favour well into the nineteenth century; Napoleon spent huge amounts of money on it, as did Louis-Philippe.

The sober elegance of Napoleon's **Petits Appartements**, the private rooms of the emperor, his wife, and their intimate entourage, makes a dramatic contrast

Museums around Paris

Though they may sound a little specialist, the museums of **ceramics** at Sèvres and **aviation** at Le Bourget are both well worth a look.

Musée de l'Air et d'Espace
The French were always pioneering aviators and **LE BOURGET**, a short hop up the A1 motorway from St-Denis, is intimately connected with their earliest exploits. Lindbergh landed here after his epic first flight across the Atlantic and, until the development of Orly in the 1950s, this was Paris's principal airport. The superb **museum** (Tues–Sun: April–Sept 10am–6pm; Oct–March 10am–5pm; free, €5 for the Boeing 747 and Concorde; ⓦ www.mae.org) has displays including early flying machines, fighter planes, a Concorde prototype and space capsules. Things set off with the Montgolfier brothers, inventors of the first successful hot-air balloon, and come up to date with two Ariane space-launchers. Everything is accompanied by good explanatory panels – in French only. **To get there**, take RER line B from Gare du Nord to Gare du Bourget, or metro line 7 to La Courneuve; bus #152 connects both stations to the museum. Alternatively, take bus #350 from the Gare du Nord, Gare de l'Est or Porte de la Chapelle, or #152 from Porte de la Villette.

Musée National de la Céramique
The **Musée National de la Céramique** (daily except Tues 10am–5pm; €4.50; ⓦ www .musee-ceramique-sevres.fr) in **SÈVRES** possesses one of the world's greatest collections of pottery and china. There's a vast quantity to savour here, including Islamic, Chinese, Italian, German, Dutch and English pieces, with a comprehensive collection of French Sèvres porcelain, as beloved by Louis XV's mistress, Madame de Pompadour. Right by the museum is the **Parc de St-Cloud**, with a geometrical sequence of pools and fountains; if you take a train from St-Lazare to St-Cloud you can head south through the park to the museum. A more direct route would be to take the metro to the Pont-de-Sèvres terminus, then cross the bridge and spaghetti junction; the museum is the massive building facing the river bank on your right. Alternatively, Meudon (see p.177) and Sèvres are connected by bus #389 (from stop "Paul Besnard" to "Pont-de-Sèvres"; 20min) making a combined afternoon or day-trip a possibility.

to the Italian interiors. Along with the **Musée Napoléon**, which displays a wide variety of personal and official souvenirs, they can only be visited as part of a **guided tour** (€12.50 including château admission). The **Musée Chinois** (included in château admission), which is only sporadically open, displays the Empress Eugénie's private collection of Chinese and Thai *objets d'art* in their original Second Empire setting.

The **gardens** are equally splendid, but if you want to escape to the relative wilds, the surrounding **forest** of Fontainebleau is full of walking and cycling trails, all marked on Michelin map #196 (*Environs de Paris*).

Versailles
Twenty kilometres southwest of Paris, the royal town of **VERSAILLES** is renowned for Louis XIV's extraordinary **Château de Versailles** (Tues–Sun: April–Oct 9am–6.30pm; Nov–March 9am–5.30pm; ⓦ www.chateauversailles .fr). With 700 rooms, 67 staircases and 352 fireplaces alone, Versailles is, without doubt, the apotheosis of French regal indulgence. While it's possible to see the whole complex in one day, it's undeniably tiring. The best plan to avoid the worst of the crowds is to head in the morning through the glorious **gardens**

(free), with their perfectly symmetrical lawns, grand vistas, statuary, fountains and pools, to **Marie Antoinette's estate**, leaving the main palace to the tour buses. You can then work your way backwards, leaving the palace, and in particular the Hall of Mirrors, till as late as possible.

Distances are considerable, so at some point you may want to make use of the **petit train** (€3.50; every 15min–1hr, depending on season) that shuttles between the terrace in front of the château and the Trianons. You could also rent a **buggy** (you'll need a driving licence) or a **bike** to get around. There are a number of cafés and restaurants dotted around the gardens, should you need to refuel.

The palace

Driven by envy of his finance minister's château at Vaux-le-Vicomte (see p.179), the young Louis XIV recruited the same design team – architect Le Vau, painter Le Brun and gardener Le Nôtre – to create a **palace** a hundred times bigger. Construction began in 1664 and lasted virtually until Louis XIV's death in 1715. Second only to God, and the head of an immensely powerful state, Louis was an institution rather than a private individual. His risings and sittings, comings and goings, were minutely regulated and rigidly encased in ceremony, attendance at which was an honour much sought after by courtiers. Versailles was the headquarters of every arm of the state, and the entire court of around 3500 nobles lived in the palace (in a state of squalor, according to contemporary accounts).

Following the king's death, the château was abandoned for a few years before being reoccupied by Louis XV in 1722. It remained a residence of the royal family until the Revolution of 1789, when the furniture was sold and the pictures dispatched to the Louvre. Thereafter Versailles fell into ruin until Louis-Philippe established his giant museum of French Glory here – it still exists, though most is mothballed. In 1871, during the Paris Commune, the château

▲ Hall of Mirrors, Versailles

Versailles practicalities

To **get to Versailles**, take the RER line C5 from Champs de Mar or another Left Bank station to Versailles-Rive Gauche; the palace is an eight-minute walk away.

The cheapest way to visit Versailles, if you want to see as much as possible, is to buy a **combined rail and Passeport Versailles ticket** (April–Oct Tues–Fri €21.65, Sat & Sun €27; Nov–March €18; under-18s free) from the RER station itself. If you don't do this, you will pay €2.90 train fare on top of whichever admission ticket you choose.

The **Passeport Versailles** (April–Oct Tues–Fri €20, Sat & Sun €25; Nov–March €16; under-18s free) is a one-day pass that gives you access to all the main sights, including the Grandes Eaux Musicales, and includes audioguides. Tickets for the **château alone** cost €13.50 (€10 after 3pm), including audioguide, while admission to **Marie-Antoinette's estate** is €9. All tickets, including the Passeport, are available in advance from branches of FNAC (see p.157), the tourist office at the Carrousel du Louvre (see p.80) and the tourist office in Versailles town, which is near the entrance to the palace.

You can also buy the Passeport at the château itself up until 3pm on the day, though this of course means queuing with everyone else.

A number of **guided tours** (prices vary) are available, including English-language tours, which take you to wings that you wouldn't otherwise get to see; they can be booked in the morning at the information point – turn up early to make sure of a place.

became the seat of the nationalist government, and the French parliament continued to meet in Louis XV's opera building until 1879.

Without a guide you can visit the **State Apartments**, used for the king's official business. A procession of gilded drawing rooms leads to the dazzling **Galerie des Glaces** (Hall of Mirrors), where the Treaty of Versailles was signed after World War I. More fabulously rich rooms, this time belonging to the **queen's apartments**, line the northern wing, beginning with the queen's bedchamber, which has been restored exactly as it was in its last refit, of 1787, with hardly a surface unadorned with gold leaf.

The Domaine de Marie-Antoinette

Hidden away in the northern reaches of the gardens is the **Domaine de Marie-Antoinette** (daily: April–Oct noon–7pm; Nov–March noon–5.30pm), the young queen's country retreat, where she found relief from the stifling etiquette of the court. Here she commissioned some dozen or so buildings, sparing no expense and imposing her own style and tastes throughout (and gaining herself a reputation for extravagance that did her no favours).

The centrepiece is the elegant Neoclassical **Petit Trianon** palace, built by Gabriel in the 1760s for Louis XV's mistress, Mme de Pompadour, and given to Marie-Antoinette by her husband Louis XVI as a wedding gift. The interior boasts an intriguing *cabinet des glaces montantes*, a pale-blue salon fitted with sliding mirrors that could be moved to conceal the windows, creating a more intimate space. West of the palace, in the formal **Jardin français**, is the **Petit Théâtre** where Marie-Antoinette would regularly perform, often as a maid or shepherdess, before the king and members of her inner circle.

On the other side of the palace lies the bucolic **Jardin anglais**, impossibly picturesque with its little winding stream, grassy banks and grotto, and the enchanting, if bizarre, **Hameau de la Reine**, a play village and farm where the queen indulged her fashionable Rousseau-inspired fantasy of returning to the "natural" life.

The Italianate **Grand Trianon** palace, designed by Hardouin-Mansart in 1687 as a country retreat for Louis XIV, was refurbished in Empire style by Napoleon, who stayed here intermittently between 1805 and 1813.

Chartres

About 80km southwest of Paris, **CHARTRES** is a modest but charming market town whose existence is almost entirely overshadowed by its extraordinary Gothic **cathedral** (daily 8.30am–7.30pm; free). Built between 1194 and 1260, it was one of the quickest ever constructed and, as a result, preserves a uniquely harmonious design. The cathedral's official name, Notre-Dame (Our Lady), and its staggering size and architectural richness are owed to its holiest relic, the **Sancta Camisia** – supposed to have been the robe Mary wore when she gave birth to Jesus – which was discovered here, miraculously unharmed, three days after an earlier Romanesque structure burnt down in 1194. In the heyday of the pilgrimage to Santiago de Compostela hordes of medieval pilgrims would stop here on their way to Spain – note the sloping floor, which allowed it to be washed down more easily. The Sancta Camisia still exists, though it has been rolled up and put into storage.

The geometry of the building is unique in being almost unaltered since its consecration, and virtually all of the magnificent **stained glass** is original thirteenth-century work. But the paint and gilt that once brought the portal sculptures to life has vanished, while the walls have lost the whitewash that reflected the vivid colours of the stained glass. Worse still, the high altar has been brought down into the body of the church, among the hoi polloi, and chairs usually cover the thirteenth-century **labyrinth** on the floor of the nave. The cathedral's **stonework**, however, is still captivating, particularly the **choir**

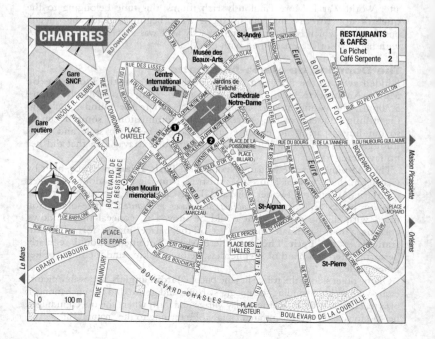

screen, which curves around the ambulatory. Like the south tower and spire that abuts it, the mid-twelfth-century **Royal Portal** actually survives from the earlier Romanesque church. You have to pay extra to visit the crypt and treasury, though these are relatively unimpressive. Crowds permitting, it's worth climbing the **north tower** for its bird's-eye view of the sculptures and structure of the cathedral.

The **Musée des Beaux Arts** (May–Oct Mon & Wed–Sat 10am–noon & 2–6pm, Sun 2–6pm; Nov–April Mon & Wed–Sat 10am–noon & 2–5pm, Sun 2–5pm; €2.90; €6 with the Maison Picassiette), in the former episcopal palace just north of the cathedral, has some beautiful tapestries, work by the French Fauvist Vlaminck, and the Spanish Baroque painter Zurbarán's *Sainte Lucie*. Behind the museum, rue Chantault leads past old town houses to the River Eure and Pont du Massacre. You can follow the river upstream, passing ancient wash houses. A left turn at the end of rue de la Tannerie, then third right, will bring you to the **Maison Picassiette**, at 22 rue du Repos (May, June, Sept & Oct Mon & Wed–Sat 10am–noon & 2–6pm, Sun 2–6pm; July & Aug Mon & Wed–Sat 10am–6pm, Sun 2–6pm; April & Nov Mon & Wed–Sat 10am–noon & 2–5pm, Sun 2–5pm; €4.50, €6 with the **Musée des Beaux Arts**), a house entirely decorated with mosaics by a local road-mender and cemetery-caretaker, Raymond Isidore. Back at the end of rue de la Tannerie, the bridge over the river brings you back to the medieval town. A food **market** takes place on place Billard and rue des Changes, and there's a flower market on place du Cygne (Tues, Thurs & Sat).

Practicalities

Trains run from Paris's Gare du Montparnasse at least hourly on weekdays (1hr). The station is just five-minutes' walk from the **tourist office** (April–Sept Mon–Sat 9am–7pm, Sun 9.30am–5.30pm; Oct–March Mon–Sat 9am–6pm, Sun 9.30am–5.30pm; ☎02.37.18.26.26), which is right by the cathedral. For a **snack**, there are lots of places with outside tables on rue Cloître-Notre-Dame, opposite the south side of the cathedral: try the *Café Serpente*. For a **restaurant** meal, *Le Pichet*, 19 rue de Cheval Blanc, almost under the northwest spire (☎02.37.21.08.35, ⓦle-pichet.com), has a cosy interior full of gingham and bric-a-brac, with waiters, inexplicably trussed up in Renaissance-style gear, serving simple, tasty dishes like steak or Greek salad.

Malmaison

The **Château of Malmaison** (April–Sept Mon & Wed–Fri 10am–noon & 1.30–5pm, Sat & Sun 10am–noon & 1.30–5.30pm; Oct–March Mon & Wed–Fri 10am–noon & 1.30–4.30pm, Sat & Sun 10am–noon & 1.30–5pm; €5; ⓦwww.chateau-malmaison.fr), set in the beautiful grounds of the **Bois-Préau**, about 15km west of central Paris, is a relatively small and enjoyable place to visit. It was the home of the Empress Josephine, and – during the 1800–04 Consulate – of Napoleon, too. According to his secretary, "it was the only place next to the battlefield where he was truly himself". After their divorce, Josephine stayed on, building up her superb rose garden and occasionally receiving visits from the emperor until her death in 1814. Visitors can see the official apartments, which perfectly preserve the First Empire style, as well as Josephine's clothes, china and personal possessions. There are other Napoleonic bits in the nearby Bois-Préau museum, currently closed for renovation with no opening date in sight.

To **reach** Malmaison, take the metro line 1 (or RER A) to La Défense, then the fairly frequent bus #258 to Malmaison-Château.

Travel details

Trains

Gare de'Austerlitz to: Tours (18 daily; 1hr–2hr 30min).

Gare de l'Est to: Metz (14 daily; 1hr 25min–2hr 45min); Nancy (12 daily; 1hr 30–2hr 20min); Reims (12 daily; 45min–2hr); Strasbourg (17 daily; 2hr 20min–3hr).

Gare de Lyon to: Avignon (21 daily; 2hr 40min–4hr); Besançon (15 daily; 2hr 30min–3hr 50min); Dijon (18 daily; 1hr 40min); Grenoble (hourly; 2hr 50min–4hr 30min); Lyon (hourly; 2hr); Marseille (hourly; 3–4hr); Nice (15 daily; 5hr 30min–13hr 35min).

Gare Montparnasse to: Bayonne (6 daily; 4hr 45min–6hr 30min); Bordeaux (at least hourly; 3hr–3hr 30min); Brest (8 daily; 4hr 20min–5hr 20min); Nantes (11 daily; 2hr); Pau (7 daily; 5hr 15min–7hr 20min); Poitiers (14 daily; 1hr 40min); Rennes (at least hourly; 2hr 15min); Toulouse (10 daily; 5hr–6hr 30min); Tours (hourly; 1hr–1hr 30min).

Gare du Nord to: Amiens (at least hourly; 1hr 45min); Arras (roughly every 2hr; 50min); Boulogne (at least hourly; 2hr 10min); Lille (hourly; 1hr).

Gare St-Lazare to: Caen (hourly; 1hr 50min–2hr 30min); Cherbourg (roughly every 2hr; 3hr–3hr 30min); Dieppe (2 daily; 2hr 15min); Le Havre (every 2–3hr; 2hr–2hr 30min); Rouen (hourly; 1hr 15min).

2

The north

CHAPTER 2

Highlights

* **Marquenterre Bird Sanctuary** From geese and godwits to storks and spoonbills, a huge variety of birds make their home amid briny meres and tamarisk-fringed dunes. See p.208

* **Son et lumière at Amiens Cathedral** The biggest Gothic building in France, brought to life by sound and light on summer evenings, transporting you back to a truly medieval experience. See p.211

* **Lillois cuisine** Eat anything from the ubiquitous *moules-frites*, washed down with micro-brewed beer, to fried *escargots* with onions roasted in lavender oil in the historic centre of Lille, the cultural capital of northern France. See p.219

* **World War I monuments in the Somme** Moving memorials by Lutyens and others to the victims of the trenches. See p.228

* **The towers of Laon cathedral** Weird stone carvings adorning one of the great wonders of French Gothic. See p.231

* **Champagne tasting at Épernay or Reims** Taste vintage bubbly in the atmospheric cellars of world-famous sparkling wine emporia. See p.242 & p.244

▲ Lutyens' Memorial to the Missing, Thiepval

The north

When conjuring up exotic holiday locations, you're unlikely to light upon the **north** of France. Even among the French, the most enthusiastic tourists of their own country, it has few adherents. Largely flat Artois and Flanders include some of the most heavily industrialized parts of the country, still feeling the effects of post-industrial depression, while across the giant fields of sparsely populated Picardy and Champagne a few drops of rain are all that is required for total gloom to descend. Coming from Britain it's likely, however, that you'll arrive and leave France via this region, and there are good reasons to stop within easy reach of Dunkerque with it's bustling, university atmosphere and poignant war memorials, and the busy ferry port of Calais. Just inland the delightful village of **Cassel** is a rare example of a Flemish hill settlement, while **St-Omer** and **Montreuil-sur-Mer** are also strong contenders in terms of charm and interest.

Northern France has been on the path of various invaders into the country, from northern Europe as well as from Britain, and the events that have taken place in Flanders, Artois and Picardy have shaped French and world history. The bloodiest battles were those of World War I, above all the **Battle of the Somme**, which took place north of Amiens, and **Vimy Ridge**, near Arras, where the trenches have been preserved in perpetuity; a visit to any of these is highly recommended to understand the sacrifice and futility of war.

On a more cheerful note, **Picardy** boasts some of France's finest cathedrals, including those at **Amiens**, **Beauvais** and **Laon**. Further south, the vineyards and cellars of the world-famous **Champagne** region are the main draw, for which the best bases are **Épernay** and **Reims**, the latter with another fine cathedral. Other attractions include the bird sanctuary of **Marquenterre**; the wooded wilderness of the **Ardennes**; industrial archeology in the coalfields around **Douai**, where Zola's *Germinal* was set; the great medieval castle of **Coucy-le-Château**; and the battle sites of the Middle Ages, **Agincourt** and **Crécy**, familiar names in the long history of Anglo–French rivalry.

In city centres from **Lille** to **Troyes**, you'll find your fill of food, culture and entertainment in the company of locals similarly intent on having a good time.

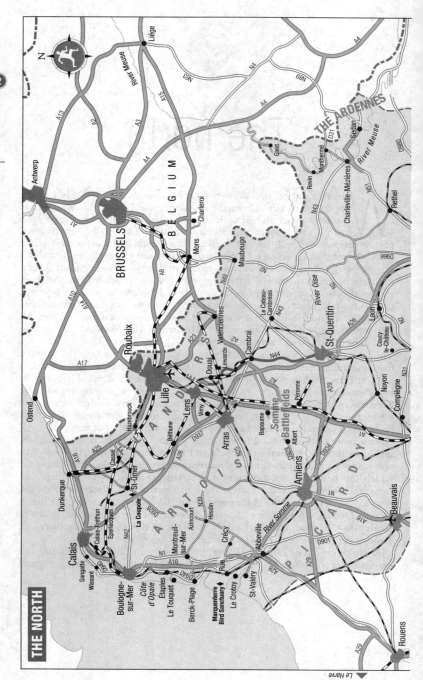

THE NORTH

Le Havre ▲

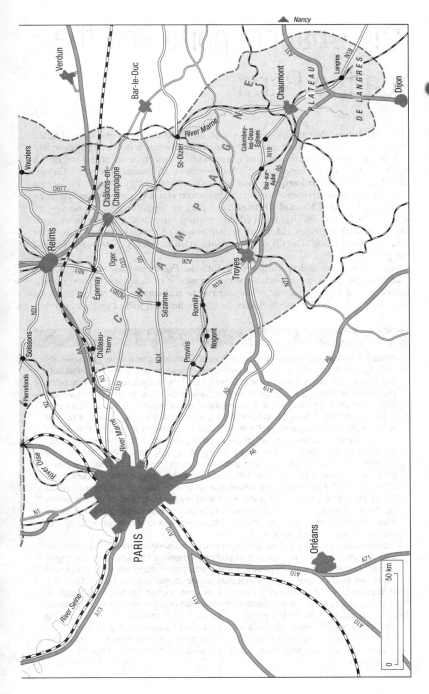

The Channel ports and the road to Paris

The millions of British day-trippers who come to the northern tip of France every year are mostly after a sniff of something foreign: a meal, a shopping bag full of produce, or a few crates of cheap wine. Until the end of the twentieth century the chief function of the northern Channel ports – **Calais**, **Boulogne**, and **Dunkerque** – was to provide cheap, efficient points of access into France from Britain. Since then, however, serious competition has been provided by the **Channel Tunnel**, emerging at Sangatte, 5km southwest of Calais. The "Chunnel" has reduced the crossing time to just half an hour, with the efficient but pricey autoroute system waiting to whisk you away to your ultimate destination. Details of the various train and ferry crossings are listed on p.29 and p.30.

For a more immediate immersion into *la France profonde* – little towns, idiosyncratic farms, a comfortable verge on which to sleep off the first cheese, baguette and *vin rouge* picnic – the old **route nationale N1**, which shadows the coast from Dunkerque to Abbeville before heading inland to Paris, is more

---

Regional food and drink

French Flanders has one of the north of France's richest regional cuisines. Especially on the coast the **seafood** – oysters, shrimps and scallops and **fish** – above all sole and turbot – are outstanding, while in Lille *moules-frites* are appreciated every bit as much as in neighbouring Belgium. Here, too, **beer** is the favourite drink, with pale and brown Pelforth the local brew. Traditional *estaminets* or brasseries also serve a range of dishes cooked in beer, most famously *carbonades à la flamande*, a kind of beef stew; rabbit, chicken, game and fish may also be prepared *à la bière*. Other pot-cooked dishes include *hochepot* (a meaty broth), *waterzooi* (chicken in a creamy sauce) and *potjevlesch* (white meats in a rich sauce). In addition to *boulette d'Avesnes*, the Flemish **cheese** *par excellence* is the strong-flavoured *maroilles*, used to make *flamiche*, a kind of open tart of cheese pastry also made with leeks (*aux poireaux*). For the sweet toothed, *crêpes à la cassonade* (pancakes with muscovado sugar) are often on menus, but **waffles** (*gaufres*) are the local speciality and come in two basic varieties: the thick honeycomb type served with sugar or cream, or the wafer-like biscuit filled with jam or syrup. Charles de Gaulle, who was from Lille, was apparently particularly fond of the latter.

Champagne's cuisine is dominated by the famous **sparkling wine**, large quantities of which are sloshed in sauces or over sorbets. Otherwise the province's cooking is known for little apart from its **cheeses** – sharp-tasting, creamy white Chaource and orange-skinned Langres – and Champagne's main contribution to French food, the **andouillette**, for which Troyes is famed. Translated euphemistically into English as "chitterling sausage", it is an intestine crammed full of more intestines, all chopped up. An acquired taste (and texture), it's better than it sounds – look out for the notation AAAAA, a seal of approval awarded by the Association of Amateurs of the Authentic Andouillette. Game looms large on menus in the Ardennes, with *pâté d'Ardennes* being the most famous dish and juniper berries used to flavour food *à l'ardennaise*.

sedate than the A16 autoroute. Interesting things to see on the way include: the cathedrals at **Amiens** and **Beauvais**; the hilltop fortress at **Montreuil**; the remains of Hitler's Atlantic Wall along the **Côte d'Opale**; and the **Marquenterre Bird Sanctuary** at the mouth of the River Somme. Immediately south of Dunkerque is the Flemish hilltop settlement of **Cassel**, a minor gem, while **St-Omer** is definitely day-trip material for the visitor over from Britain; its remaining old buildings and treasures make it far preferable to dreary Calais.

Dunkerque and around

Less reliant than either Boulogne or Calais on the cross-channel ferry trade, **DUNKERQUE** is the liveliest of the three big Channel ports, a university town with fewer empty shops than central Calais and busy streets that out-bustle modest Boulogne. It has an appealing, boat-filled inner harbour, the **Bassin du Commerce**, and an attractive beachfront suburb, **Malo-les-Bains**, from whose vast sandy beach the evacuation of Allied troops took place in 1940. It remains France's third largest port and a massive industrial centre, its oil refineries and steelworks producing a quarter of the total French output. Devastated during World War II, Dunkerque is not exactly beautiful; although its postwar rebuild was more ambitious and stylish than those of Calais or Boulogne, these days its 1950s architecture could do with a good scrub.

Arrival, information and accommodation

From Dunkerque's **gare SNCF** – where **buses** also stop – it's a short walk to rue de l'Amiral Ronarc'h and the **tourist office** (Mon–Sat 9.30am–12.30pm & 1.30–6.30pm, Sun & public holidays 10am–noon & 2–4pm; ☏03.28.66.79.21, Ⓦwww.ot-dunkerque.fr) housed in a fifteenth-century belfry. If you're looking to rent a **car**, there's a branch of Avis at the station (☏03.28.66.67.95). **Accommodation** is split between the business-oriented town-centre offerings and more individual options in Malo-les-Bains. There's also a **campsite**, *La Licorne*, close to the beach at 1005 boulevard de l'Europe in Malo (☏03.28.69.26.68, Ⓦwww.campinglalicorne-dunkerque.fr).

Hotels and hostel
Au Bon Coin 49 av Kleber, Malo-les-Bains ☏03.28.69.12.63, Ⓦwww.restaurantauboncoin .com. More a "restaurant with rooms" than a hotel, but comfortable, characterful and convenient for the beach. ❺

Borel 6 rue L'Hermite ☏03.28.66.51.80, Ⓦwww .hotelborel.fr. Right on the Bassin du Commerce, a comfortable but slightly anonymous three-star option. ❹

Hirondelle 46/48 av Faidherbe, Malo-les-Bains ☏03.28.63.17.65, Ⓦwww.hotelhirondelle.com.

Bright modern Logis de France hotel with a good restaurant and comfortable en-suite rooms, including three adapted for people of limited mobility. ❺

Select 25/27 place de la Gare ☏03.28.66.64.47, Ⓦwww.leselect-hotel.fr.st. Reasonably priced two-star hotel with just nine rooms, right opposite the train station. ❷

Youth Hostel place Paul Asseman ☏03.28.63.36.34, Ⓦwww.fuaj.org. HI hostel just east of the centre and close to the beach; from €15.50, breakfast included. Bus #3, stop "Piscine".

The town centre and the Bassin du Commerce

Central Dunkerque is largely the brick-built product of postwar reconstruction, much of it fairly utilitarian but with occasional stylistic flourishes, particularly on prominent corner sites where some buildings affect a sculptural, almost Art Deco look. Among the few buildings of any significance to have survived World War II (or at least to have been rebuilt afterwards) are the tall medieval brick **belfry**, the town's chief landmark (guided tours: April–Sept Mon–Sat 10am, 11am & hourly 2–5pm; July & Aug also Sun & holidays 10am, 11am, 2pm & 3pm; Oct–March Sat hourly 2–5pm; €2.80); the impressive, bullet-ridden fifteenth-century **church of St-Éloi** opposite, to which the belfry belonged; and, a few blocks north of the church on place Charles-Valentin, the early twentieth-century **Hôtel de Ville**, a giant Flemish fancy to rival that of Calais.

Dunkerque does have a few worthwhile museums too. The **Mémorial du Souvenir** (April–Sept daily 10am–noon & 2–5pm; €3.50), north of the centre at 32 Courtines du Bastion is the place to go if you want to find out more about the 1940 evacuations; it has an important collection of photographs as well as maps, uniforms and military equipment relating to the period. In the park just to the south of the Mémorial du Souvenir, the **LAAC (Lieu d'Art et Action Contemporaine)**, or Modern Art Museum (April–Oct daily 10am–12.15pm & 2–6.30pm, Thurs until 8.30pm; Nov–March Tue–Sun 10am–12.15pm & 2–5.30pm; €4.50), specializes in the period from 1950 to 1980 and features Andy Warhol, Pierre Soulages and César in its collection. More interesting, especially for children, is the **Musée Portuaire** (daily except Tues: July & Aug 10am–6pm; Sept–June 10am–12.45pm & 1.30–6pm; €4), housed in a restored brick warehouse at 9 quai de la Citadelle on the Bassin du Commerce, which illustrates the history of Dunkerque from its beginnings as a fishing hamlet, using ship models, panoramas and tools of the various trades associated with the port, as well as period film footage. It also mounts engrossing temporary exhibitions on related themes, such as the ocean liners that were once built at Dunkerque.

The **Bassin du Commerce** itself is a lively and attractive stretch of water, housing not just fishing boats and yachts but a miscellany of preserved historic ships, including the three-masted sailing ship **Duchesse Anne**, built as a training sail ship in Germany in 1901. It and several other vessels can be visited as part of the **Musée à Flot** (daily July–Aug; guided visits, afternoons only otherwise guided tours Sun at 3.30pm; €7.50, or €9 joint ticket with Musée Portuaire) – the "floating" half of the city's maritime museum. The spindly fifteenth-century **Tour de Leughenaer**, a surviving remnant of the city's medieval defences, overshadows the fish stalls on the northeast side of the dock.

Malo-les-Bains

MALO-LES-BAINS is a pleasant nineteenth-century seaside suburb on the east side of Dunkerque (buses #3 & #9), from whose vast sandy beach the Allied troops embarked in 1940. Digue des Alliés is the urban end of an extensive beachfront promenade lined with cafés and restaurants; things are however rather nicer further east along Digue de Mer, which is away from Dunkerque's industrial inferno. Much of the promenade's attractive architecture somehow survived wartime destruction; there's more *fin-de-siècle* charm away from the seafront, a few blocks inland along avenue Faidherbe and its continuation avenue Kléber, with leafy place Turenne sandwiched in between and centred on a dainty old-fashioned bandstand.

Eating and drinking

Dunkerque's best options for **eating and drinking** are never far from the water: there's a decent line-up of restaurants and bars along quai de la Citadelle on the Bassin du Commerce, with plenty more in Malo-les-Bains.

The evacuation of 350,000 Allied troops from the beaches of **Dunkerque** from May 27 to June 4, 1940, has become a legend, conveniently concealing the fact that the Allies, through their own incompetence, almost lost their entire armed forces in the first weeks of the war.

The German army had taken just ten days to reach the English Channel and could easily have cut off the Allied armies. Unable to believe the ease with which he had overcome a numerically superior enemy, however, Hitler ordered his generals to halt their advance, giving Allied forces trapped in the Pas-de-Calais time to organize **Operation Dynamo**, the largest wartime evacuation ever undertaken. Initially it was hoped that around 10,000 men would be saved, but thanks to low-lying cloud and the help of more than 1750 vessels – including pleasure cruisers, fishing boats and river ferries – 140,000 French and more than 200,000 British soldiers were successfully shipped back to England. The heroism of the boatmen and the relief at saving so many British soldiers were the cause of national celebration.

In France, however, the ratio of British to French evacuees caused bitter resentment, since Churchill had promised that the two sides would go *bras dessus, bras dessous* ("arm in arm"). Meanwhile, the British media played up the "remarkable discipline" of the troops as they waited to embark, the "victory" of the RAF over the Luftwaffe and the "disintegration" of the French army all around. In fact, there was widespread indiscipline in the early stages as men fought for places on board; the battle for the skies was evenly matched; and the French fought long and hard to cover the whole operation, some 150,000 of them remaining behind to become prisoners of war. In addition, the Allies lost seven destroyers and 177 fighter planes and were forced to abandon more than 60,000 vehicles. After 1940 Dunkerque remained occupied by Germans until the bitter end of the war. It was the last French town to be liberated in 1945.

L'Auberge de Jules 9 rue de la Poudrière ☎03.28.63.68.80. Funky, informal modern restaurant just off the Bassin du Commerce, Michelin-listed and with plenty of fish on its *carte*; *plats* from €17. Closed Sun.

Au Bon Coin 49 av Kleber, Malo-les-Bains ☎03.28.69.12.63. Oysters, lobster and a big selection of *plateaux de fruits de mer* from €33 to €112 grace the menu of this plush Malo restaurant. Closed Sun evening & Mon.

Les Boucaniers 2 rue de la Tranquilité ☎03.28.65.01.71. The over-the-top decor of this snug quayside bar/restaurant is more nautical than the menu, which offers rather more non-fish options than most Dunkerque restaurants. *Plats* around €18; closed Sat evening & Sun.

Le Corsaire 6 quai de la Citadelle ☎03.28.59.03.61. There's plenty of fish on the menu of this plush, comfortable dockside restaurant with a €26 *menu* and views of the *Duchesse Anne*. Closed Wed & Sun evening.

Hirondelle 46/48 av Faidherbe, Malo-les-Bains ☎03.28.63.17.65. There's a heavy seafood emphasis on the menu here, with everything from marinated herrings to poached turbot in hollandaise; menus at €18.30 and €25. Closed Sun evening & Mon lunch.

La Marie-Jane 13 quai de la Citadelle. Lively portside bar with nautical theme and regular live music.

La Moule Rit 175 Digue de Mer, Malo-les-Bains ☎03.28.29.06.07. More than fifty dishes with *moules* plus sea views through the huge windows greet visitors to this beachfront place in Malo.

Cassel

Barely 30km southeast of Dunkerque and just off the A25 autoroute to Lille, is the tiny hilltop town of **CASSEL**. Hills are rare in Flanders, and consequently Cassel was much fought over from Roman times onwards. During World War I, Marshal Foch spent "some of the most distressing hours" of his life here, and it was supposedly to the top of Cassel's hill that the "Grand Old Duke of York" marched his ten thousand men in 1793, though, as hinted at in the nursery rhyme, he failed to take the town.

As its name suggests, Cassel was originally a Flemish-speaking community – until use of the language was suppressed by the authorities – and it still boasts a very Flemish **Grand'Place**, lined with some magnificent mansions, from which narrow cobbled streets fan out to the ramparts. From the public gardens in the upper town, you have an unrivalled view over Flanders, with Belgium just 10km away. Here among the trees is eighteenth-century **Kasteel Meulen**, the last of Cassel's wooden windmills (April–Sept daily except Mon 10am–12.30pm & 2–6pm; Oct–March Sat, Sun & school hols; €3), which once numbered 29 across the town, still pounding out flour and linseed oil for educational purposes.

Practicalities

There's no bus into town from Cassel's **gare SNCF** (a regular train service on the Dunkerque–Lille line), a full 3km west. The town's **tourist office** is on the Grand'Place (Mon–Fri 8.30am–noon & 1.30–5.30pm, also Sat & Sun 10am–12.30pm & 2–6pm in peak season; ☎03.28.40.52.55, ⓦwww.cassel-horizons .com); it houses a small but enjoyable exhibition, **Cassel Horizons**, on the history of the town (same hours as tourist office; €3), and can offer a list of bed-and-breakfasts, *gîtes* and other **places to stay** in or near Cassel. An upmarket option is the very smart *Châtellerie de Schoebeque* at 32 rue Foch (☎03.28.42.42.67, ⓦwww.schoebeque.com; ❽).

On the southern side of the Grand'Place many of the **cafés and restaurants** have a fabulous view over the surrounding countryside. *La Taverne Flamande* at no. 34 (closed Tues evening & Wed; from €15.50) specializes in Flemish cuisine, while *Le Sauvage*, no. 38 (☎03.28.42.40.88), offers classic French fare at similar prices. Up near the windmill at 8 rue St Nicolas, *Kasteel Hof* (☎03.28.40.59.29; from €9.50) oozes local ambience and has a variety of beers to go with the simple cuisine, which includes a delicious *carbonade*; its popularity makes bookings advisable at weekends. Cassel's big annual event is its annual Easter Monday **Carnival**, when giant effigies are paraded through the town's streets.

Calais and around

CALAIS is less than 40km from Dover – the Channel's shortest crossing – and is by far the busiest French passenger port. The port, petrochemical industries and out-of-town shopping dominate the place; in fact, there's not much else here. In World War II the British destroyed it to prevent it being used as a base for a German invasion, but the French still refer to it as "the most English town in France", an influence that began after the battle of Crécy in 1346, when Edward III seized it for use as a beachhead in the Hundred Years War. It remained in English hands for over two hundred years until 1558, when its loss caused Mary Tudor famously to say: "When I am dead and opened, you shall find Calais lying in my heart." The association has been maintained by various Brits across the centuries: Lady Emma Hamilton, Lord Nelson's mistress; Nottingham lacemakers who set up business in the early nineteenth century; and, nowadays, nine million British travellers per year, plus another million-odd day-trippers. One dispiriting side-effect of globalisation and conflict is the sight

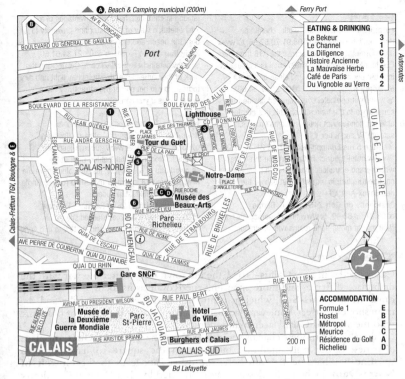

EATING & DRINKING

Le Bekeur	3
Le Channel	1
La Diligence	C
Histoire Ancienne	6
La Mauvaise Herbe	5
Café de Paris	4
Du Vignoble au Verre	2

ACCOMMODATION

Formule 1	E
Hostel	B
Métropol	F
Meurice	C
Résidence du Golf	A
Richelieu	D

of miserable-looking would-be migrants roaming the town aimlessly, or huddled under blankets in the neatly manicured parks.

Arrival, information and accommodation

There's a daytime **bus** (€1 one way) from the **ferry terminal** to place d'Armes and the central Calais-Ville **gare SNCF**, from which **buses** depart for Dunkerque, Boulogne and the out-of-town shopping centres. To get to the outlying **gare TGV** for Eurostar trains to London and Paris, take the *navette*, usually a shuttle bus, occasionally a TER train. It's free on demonstration of a SNCF ticket. Alternatively, a few Lille-bound regional trains stop at Calais-Fréthun. If you're driving and intent on skipping Calais in favour of Paris, take a left out of the ferry terminal – the *autoroute* bypass begins almost immediately, leading to the A26 and the N1. If you plan to **rent a car**, try Avis (☎03.21.34.66.50) in place d'Armes and at the car ferry terminal, or Budget (☎03.55.33.14.34) at the ferry terminal; a cheaper option, also at the ferry terminal, is National/Citer (☎03.21.34.58.45). For details of ferry crossings, see p.30. Via the **tunnel**, road connections to Calais and the autoroutes are well signposted and straightforward.

If you decide to stay in Calais, plenty of **accommodation** is available, though it's wise to book ahead in the high season. The **tourist office** at 12 boulevard Clémenceau, the continuation of rue Royale (Mon–Sat 10am–1pm & 2–6.30pm; ☎03.21.96.62.40, ⓦwww.calais-cotedopale.com), has a free accommodation booking service as well as a list of *gîtes* and hotels in the region.

Hotels

Formule 1 av Charles-de-Gaulle, chemin de Bergnieulles, Coquelles ☎08.91.70.52.06, ⓦwww .hotelformule1.com. Just across the A16 from the Eurotunnel terminal, this chain hotel is a character-less but perfectly modern and clean option. ❶

Métropol 45 quai du Rhin ☎03.21.97.54.00, ⓦwww.metropolhotel.com. Situated beside the canal close to the train station, this is a comfortable but nondescript hotel with small rooms, satellite TV and a bar. ❹

Meurice 5 rue Edmond-Roche ☎03.21.34.57.03, ⓦwww.hotel-meurice.fr. Comfortable three-star with a grand entrance, luxurious high beds and antique furniture in a quiet street behind the Musée des Beaux-Arts. ❺

Résidence du Golf 745 Digue G. Berthe ☎03.21.96.88.99, ⓦwww.hoteldugolf-calais.com. Neat, bright motel-style rooms which, although lacking in character, have the advantages of a kitchenette, a view of the water and proximity to both the beach and the centre of town. ❹

Richelieu 17 rue Richelieu ☎03.21.34.61.60, ⓦwww.hotelrichelieu-calais.com. Overlooking the park of the same name, this hotel has light and airy rooms – try to get one of the attractively refurbished ones if you can. ❸

Hostel and campsite

Hostel av du Maréchal-de-Lattre-de-Tassigny ☎03.21.34.70.20, ⓦwww.auberge-jeunesse -calais.fr. Modern hostel located right at the seaward end of rue Royale, just one block from the beach. From €18 in two-or three-bed rooms; single rooms €24; breakfast included.

Camping municipal 26 av Raymond-Poincaré ☎03.21.97.89.79. A large, exposed site at the harbour end of Calais' beach; closed Nov to mid April.

The Town

Calais divides in two: **Calais–Nord**, the old town rebuilt after the war with the drab place d'Armes and more appealing rue Royale as its focus, is separated by canals from **Calais–Sud**, which is centred around the Hôtel de Ville and the main shopping street, boulevard Jacquard. It's named after the inventor of looms, who mechanized Calais' lacemaking industry.

Calais–Nord's modest charms soon wear thin. The **Tour du Guet**, on place d'Armes, is the only medieval building on the square to have survived wartime bombardment. From here, rue de la Paix leads to the **church of Notre-Dame**, where Charles de Gaulle married local girl Yvonne Vendroux in 1921. Allegedly the only English Perpendicular church on the continent, it's not a particularly good example of the style. There is an unusual lacemaking exhibition, plus a small but interesting collection of sixteenth- to twentieth-century art, including paintings by Picasso and Dubuffet, and a Rodin sculpture, in the **Musée des Beaux-Arts et de la Dentelle** on rue Richelieu (Mon & Wed–Fri 10am–noon & 2–5.30pm, Sat 10am–noon & 2–6.30pm, Sun 2–6.30pm; free), which fringes Parc Richelieu at the southern, inland end of Calais-Nord. At the opposite end of rue Royale, cross the bridge over the Bassin Ouest to reach the city's **beach**, where the waters are chilly but swimmable, and from which on a fine day the English shore is visible; or take rue des Thermes to visit the 59-metre **lighthouse** at place Henri-Barbusse, with 271 steps to a panoramic view (June–Sept daily; Oct–May Wed, Sat & Sun: weekdays 2–6.30pm, weekends and holidays 10am–noon & 2–6.30pm; €4).

Calais–Sud is scarcely more exciting. Just over the canal bridge, the town's landmark, the **Hôtel de Ville**, raises its belfry over 60m into the sky; this Flemish extravaganza was finished in 1926, and miraculously survived World War II. Somewhat dwarfed by the building, Rodin's famous bronze, the *Burghers of Calais*, records for ever the self-sacrifice of local dignitaries, who offered their lives to assuage the blood lust of the victor at Crécy, Edward III – only to be spared at the last minute by the intervention of Queen Philippa, Edward's wife. For a record of Calais' wartime travails, visit the fascinating **Musée de la Seconde Guerre Mondiale** (Feb–April & Oct–Nov daily

Shopping in Calais

For truly epic cross-border shopping it's best to head out of town, either to the **hypermarkets**, or *grandes surfaces*, to one of the many **wine and beer** stores, or to a mall. The best hypermarket is **Auchan** on avenue Roger Salengro west of town (Mon–Sat 8.3am–10pm; bus #5), closely followed by **Carrefour/Mi-Voix**, on the east side of town, on avenue Georges-Guynemer (Mon–Sat 8.30am–9pm; bus #2 or #4). **Cité Europe**, a vast shopping mall on boulevard du Kent by the Channel Tunnel terminal (bus #5), offers another Carrefour (Mon–Sat 8.30am–10pm) plus high–street clothing and food shops (Mon–Thurs 10am–8pm, Fri 10am–9pm, Sat 9am–8pm). You could also visit the nearby **Marques Avenue** outlet centre on boulevard du Parc (Mon–Sat 10am–7pm; bus #5), where the discounted brands include Adidas, Nike and Puma. For cheap wine, head for the British-run **Wine & Beer World** on the eastern side of town at rue de Judee, Zone Marcel Doret (daily 8am–9pm; bus #7) with another branch close to the Channel Tunnel terminal in the *zone industrielle,* La Francaise (daily 8am–7pm; bus #5); alternatively, head for the more Francophile **Franglais Vins** at junction 44 of the A16 (Mon–Sat 9am–7pm, Sun 10am–7pm).

Central Calais has not been unaffected by all this out-of-town activity. Still, in Calais-Nord, La Maison du Fromage et des Vins (daily except Tues and Sun pm) just off **place d'Armes** is worth a visit for a good selection of cheeses and wine. In Calais-Sud, the **Les 4 Boulevards** complex (Mon–Sat 9.30am–7.30pm) on boulevard Jacquard represents the town centre's fight back against the big malls, though more colourful are the markets around place d'Armes (Wed & Sat am) and place Crève-coeur (Thurs & Sat am).

except Tues 11am–5pm; May–Sept daily 10am–6pm; €6) in a former German *Blockhaus* in the Parc St-Pierre across the street, with exhibits of uniforms, weapons and models from World War II and a small section devoted to World War I.

Eating and drinking

Calais is full of **restaurants** catering for its transient visitors, but there are enough decent ones to make eating one of the best uses of your time here. Place d'Armes and rue Royale are where the concentration is thickest. **Drinking** establishments range from Gaelic theme pubs to trendier offerings, with a concentration on rue Royale and its continuation, rue de la Mer. *La Mauvaise Herbe* on rue Royale is about the hippest of Calais-Nord's watering holes, while *Le Bekeur* is a **gay bar** just east of place d'Armes at 40 rue de Thermes.

Le Channel 3 bd de la Résistance ℡03.21.34.42.30. Generous menus – ranging from €21.50 to €58 – and stylish decor. Beautifully prepared but safely unadventurous food, with a wide range of delicious desserts, and views over the yacht basin. Closed Sun evening. Tues, Christmas & two weeks in summer; booking recommended.

La Diligence 7 rue Edmond-Roche ℡03.21.34.57.03. The well-regarded restaurant of the *Meurice* hotel is snug and atmospheric, with wood-panelled walls, beamed ceilings and menus at €25–35.

Histoire Ancienne 20 rue Royale ℡03.21.34.11.20. Greek-run brasserie with a charming, vaguely Art Deco interior; the good, mainly French menu includes a separate list for vegetarians. Menus from €11.50 for lunch and early dinner; otherwise from €18.50.

Café de Paris 72 rue Royale ℡03.21.34.76.84. This lively Calais-Nord brasserie is popular with locals and tourists alike for its cheap dishes; *plats du jour* from €10, menu at €13.

Du Vignoble au Verre 43 place d'Armes ℡03.21.34.83.29. The cosy interior matches the traditional French cooking – including paté made on the premises – and there's an emphasis on wine, including a reasonable selection by the glass. Menus from €14.50.

Around Calais

Most tourists travel straight through the **Pas-de-Calais** – Calais' hinterland – but if you're on a short break from across the Channel, it's worth making the effort to venture inland to the likes of **St-Omer** and its surrounding World War II museums.

St-Omer

Away from the ports, the landscape becomes more rural and the roads straighter and quieter. The first stop inland for many is **ST-OMER**, an attractive old Flemish town of yellow-brick houses 43km southeast of Calais. The Hôtel de Ville on place Foch and the chapel of the former Jesuit college on rue du Lycée are genuine flights of architectural fancy, but for the most part the style is simple but handsome, though some parts of the town are rather run-down. The Gothic **Basilique Notre-Dame** (April–Sept Mon–Sat 8am–6pm, Sun 9am–5pm; Oct–March Thurs & Sun 8am–5pm) contains some fine statues and the fascinating **Musée de l'Hôtel Sandelin** at 14 rue Carnot (Wed–Sun 10am–noon & 2–6pm; €4.50) is worth a stop. The centrepiece of this eighteenth-century town mansion is the suite of panelled rooms on the ground floor. The museum displays are grouped according to three themes: history, covering the arts in Flanders and the Artois from the 11th to 15th centuries; fine arts, with a remarkable seletion of French, Dutch and Flemish paintings including a Breughel; and ceramics. The museum's treasures include a glorious piece of medieval goldsmithing known as the *Pied de Croix de St-Bertin*.

It's also worth visiting the pleasant **public gardens** to the west of town and you can explore the nearby **marais**, a network of Flemish waterways cut between plots of land on reclaimed marshes east of town along the river. Boat trips, or *bateaux-promenade*, run by Isnor Location (℡03.21.39.15.15, Ⓦwww.isnor.fr), leave from the church in nearby Clairmarais. For further information, including times, plus details of kayak and canoe rental, contact the tourist office (see below).

Practicalities

To get to the centre of town from the exuberant 1903 **gare SNCF**, cross over the canal and walk down rue F.-Ringot, which leads through place Vainquai and rue Faidherbe into rue Carnot. The **tourist office** is in the western end of town near the park at 4 rue Lion d'Or (Easter–Sept Mon–Sat 9am–6pm, Sun 10am–1pm; Oct–Easter Mon–Sat 9am–12.30pm & 2–6pm; ℡03.21.98.08.51, Ⓦwww.tourisme-saintomer.com).

For **accommodation**, try the pretty, old, *Hôtel St-Louis* at 25 rue d'Arras (℡03.21.38.35.21, Ⓦwww.hotel-saintlouis.com; ❹; *Le Flaubert* restaurant from €15.50) or the *Bretagne*, 2 place du Vainquai, near the train station (℡03.21.38.25.78, Ⓦwww.hotellebretagne.com; ❹; *Le Vainquai* restaurant from €14.70). The closest **campsite** is *Le Clair Marais* on rue du Romelaër near the Forêt de Clairmarais, 4.5km east of St-Omer (℡03.21.38.34.80, Ⓦwww.camping-clairmarais.com; closed mid-Dec to end Jan), although there's no transport out there. For **places to eat** other than the hotels, try the establishments around place Foch: *Les Trois Caves*, at no. 18 has the best reputation and specializes in local dishes (menu €25; ℡03.21.39.72.52; closed Mon & Wed).

The Blockhaus at Eperlecques

In the Forêt d'Eperlecques, 12km north of St-Omer off the D300, you can visit the largest ever **Blockhaus**, or concrete bunker, built in 1943–44 by the Germans – or rather by six thousand of their half-starved prisoners of war (daily: March & Nov 10am–5pm; April & Oct 10am–6pm; May–Sept 10am–7pm;

closed Dec–Feb; €7). It was designed to launch V2 rockets against London, but fortunately the RAF and French Resistance prevented it ever being ready for use by bombing it during construction – unfortunately killing many of the Allied prisoners at the same time. As well as the Blockhaus, you will see remnants of weapons that were used to attack (or were built with the purpose of attacking) London, including a 45-metre ramp for launching V1 rockets.

The Blockhaus is hard to reach without your own transport: it's a four-kilometre walk from the station at Watten, on the eastern edge of the forest, to which there are several trains daily from Calais.

La Coupole

Of all the converted World War II bunker museums, **La Coupole** (daily: July & Aug 10am–7pm; Sept–June 9am–6pm; closed for two weeks over Christmas and New Year; Ⓦ www.lacoupole-france.com; €9), 5km southwest of St-Omer, is the most modern and stimulating. As you walk around the site of an intended V2 rocket launch pad, you can listen on multilingual infrared headphones to a discussion of the occupation of northern France by the Nazis, the use of prisoners as slave labour, and the technology and ethics of the first liquid-fuelled rocket – advanced by Hitler and taken at the end of the war by the Soviets, the French and the Americans and developed in the space race. Visits last two and a half hours: films, models and photographs, all with accompanying text in four different languages, help to develop each theme. Getting there by car is easy: it's just off the D928 (A26 junctions 3 & 4), but there are only a few buses running from St-Omer train station (ring La Coupole or St-Omer tourist office for times).

The Côte d'Opale

The **Côte d'Opale** is the stretch of Channel coast between Calais and the mouth of the River Somme, characterized by huge, windswept beaches more attractive than anything to be found in the port cities. In the northern part, as far as Boulogne, the beaches are fringed, as on the English side of the Channel, by white chalk cliffs. Here, between the prominent headlands of **Cap Blanc-Nez** and **Cap Gris-Nez**, the D940 coast road winds high above the sea, allowing you to appreciate the "opal" in the name – the sea and sky merging in an opalescent, oyster-grey continuum. The southern part of the coast is flatter, and the beach, uninterrupted for 40km, is backed by pine-anchored dunes and brackish tarns, punctuated by German pillboxes toppled on their noses by the shifting sands. An organization called Eden 62 (℡03.21.32.13.74, Ⓦ www .eden62.fr) offers **guided walks** all year round.

South from Calais: the Channel Tunnel and Wissant

On the western outskirts of Calais, **Blériot-Plage** was named for Louis Blériot's epic first cross-Channel flight in 1909. Six kilometres west by the sedate seaside village of Sangatte, the Channel Tunnel comes ashore; the actual terminal is 5km to the east outside the village of Fréthun. Thereafter, the D940 winds up onto the grassy windswept heights of **Cap Blanc-Nez**, topped by an obelisk commemorating the Dover Patrol, who kept the Channel free from U-boats during World War I. From here, 130m above sea level, you can spot the Channel craft plying the water to the north, while to the south you look down on Wissant and its enormous beach from which Julius Caesar sailed for Britain in 55 BC. Before arriving in Wissant, you pass through the beachside village of **Escalles**, where you can stay at the smart, appropriately named *Escale* (T03.21.85.25.00, W www.hotel-lescale.com; ❸; restaurant from €16.50).

WISSANT itself is a small, quietly attractive place, popular with windsurfers and weekending Britons. The **tourist office** (May–Sept Mon–Sat 9am–noon & 2–6pm, Sun 10am–1pm & 3–6pm; Oct–April Mon–Sat 9am–noon & 3–6pm; T08.20.20.76.00, W www.terredes2caps.fr) is on place de la Mairie. **Hotels** here include the picturesque old *Hôtel de la Plage*, 1 place Edouard-Houssin (T03.21.35.91.87, W www.hotelplage-wissant.com; ❷–❹; good restaurant from €16), whose rooms are arranged around a wide courtyard, and the two-star *Bellevue*, rue P. Crampel (T03.21.35.91.07, W www.wissant-hotel-bellevue.com; ❹). Wissant also has a **campsite**, *La Source* (T03.21.35.92.46; closed Dec–March).

To Cap Gris-Nez and the Blockhaus at Audinghen

The GR du Littoral footpath passes through Wissant and continues up to **Cap Gris-Nez**, just 28km from the English coast. To get to the cape by road, take the turn-off north 1km outside **AUDINGHEN**, from which it's another three kilometres. Just after the Cap Gris-Nez turn-off beside the D940 is one of the many massive concrete **Blockhäuser** that stud the length of the Côte d'Opale though those with a real interest in the subject should visit the Blockhaus at Eperlecques (see p.200). The remainder of the drive along the D940 towards Boulogne-sur-Mer is lined with beautiful and undeveloped dunes with frequent turn-offs for **walking paths** to the shore, each of which is tempting on a fine day.

Boulogne-sur-Mer

BOULOGNE-SUR-MER is the smallest of the three main channel ports and although the **ville basse** is pretty unprepossessing, rising above the lower town is a diminutive medieval quarter, the **ville haute**, contained within the old town walls and dominated by a grand, domed basilica.

Shopping in Boulogne

For the serious **hypermarkets**, catch bus #20 for the Leclerc or bus #8 for the huge Auchan complex, 8km along the N42 towards St-Omer – certainly the most convenient place for large-scale food and wine shopping. More fastidious foodies should stay in town and head for the **Grande-Rue** and streets leading off it, but be aware that most are closed all day Monday. For charcuterie, locals' favourite Bourgeois is at 1 Grande–Rue; for chocolates and other goodies, head for Timmerman at no. 40. Check out the fabulous fish displays at Aux Pêcheurs d'Étaples, at no. 31; you can also sample the seafood at the brasserie tucked behind. A shop definitely not to be missed is Philippe Olivier's famous *fromagerie*, just around the corner at 43 rue Thiers, which has a selection of over two hundred cheeses in various states of maturation. To go with it you'll find a great choice of wines at Les Vins de France, 10 rue Nationale, but for buying wine in bulk try Le Chais at 49 rue des Deux-Ponts, in the Bréquerecque district by the train station. On Wednesday and Saturday mornings place Dalton hosts a **market**, or for basic groceries and a cheap cafeteria head for the Centre Commercial Liane on the corner of boulevards Diderot and Daunou.

Arrival, information and accommodation

It is only a fifteen-minute walk across the river from the **ferry terminal** into town; there is no bus. The centre is a ten–minute walk from the **gare SNCF** (Boulogne-Ville), down boulevard Voltaire then right along boulevard Diderot. The **tourist office** (July & Aug Mon–Sat 9am–7pm, Sun 10.30am–1pm & 2.30–5pm; Sept–June Mon–Sat 9.30am–12.30pm & 1.45–6pm, Sun 10am–1pm; Nov–Jan closed Sun; ℡03.21.10.88.10, Ⓦwww.tourisme-boulognesurmer .com), at Pont Marguet, can advise on rooms – which, in summer, get taken early. There's plenty of inexpensive **accommodation** in Boulogne, plus a couple of upmarket places around the centre.

Hotels

Enclos de L'Evêché 6 rue de Pressy ℡03.91.90.05.90, Ⓦwww.enclosde leveche.com. Five individually designed rooms, in a fine town house in the heart of the medieval ville haute. ❹–❻

Faidherbe 12 rue Faidherbe ℡03.21.31.60.93, Ⓦwww.hotelfaidherbe.fr. Great value two-star near the water and shops, with elegant rooms and friendly proprietors. ❹

Hamiot 1 rue Faidherbe at corner with bd Gambetta ℡03.21.31.44.20, Ⓦwww.hotelhamiot .com. Harbour-side hotel over a popular bistro.

Renovated rooms have bath and double-glazing; some have a balcony. ❺

Hostel (HI) place Rouget-de-Lisle ℡03.21.99.15.30, Ⓦwww.fuaj.org, opposite the *gare SNCF* in the middle of a housing estate. Friendly hostel with rooms for 3–4 people at €18.50 per person, breakfast included; €2.90 extra for non-members. Also has en-suite double rooms. ❶

La Matelote 80 bd Ste-Beuve ℡03.21.30.33.33, Ⓦwww.la-matelote.com. Very smart rooms on the seafront, opposite Nausicaá and above famed restaurant; minibar, a/c, cable TV and tasteful decor in all rooms. ❺

The Town

Boulogne's number one attraction – and one of the most visited in northern France – is the Centre National de la Mer, or **Nausicaá**, on boulevard Ste-Beuve (daily: July & Aug 9.30am–7.30pm; Sept–June 9.30am–6.30pm; closed for 3 weeks in Jan; Ⓦwww.nausicaa.fr; €16.50), though in May and June all of the floors are crawling with French and British school groups, and you may find it best to stay away. With ultraviolet lighting and New Age music creating a suitably weird ambience, you wander from tank to tank while hammerhead sharks circle overhead, a shoal of tuna lurks in a diamond-shaped aquarium, and giant conger eels conceal themselves in rusty pipes. Compared with the startling colours of the tropical fish and the clownish antics of the sea lions at feeding time, some of the educational stuff (in French and English throughout – one in five visitors is British) is rather dull. Environmental issues are touched on in some of the display materials and as you'd expect in France, the sea as a source of food is given a high level of importance – witness the chic bistro, where you can sample suitably fresh fish and wine.

The quiet cobbled streets of the **ville haute**, southeast of Nausicaá and uphill along Grande Rue, make a pleasant respite from the noise and drabness of the *ville basse*. The most impressive sight here is the **medieval walls** themselves, which are decked out with rose beds, gravel paths and benches, and provide impressive views of the city below; it takes about 45 minutes to complete the walk around them. Within the square walls, the domed **Basilique Notre-Dame** (April–Aug 9am–noon & 2–6pm; Sept–Mar 10am–noon 2–5pm) is an odd building – raised in the nineteenth century by the town's vicar without any architectural knowledge or advice – yet it seems to work. In the vast **crypt** (Tues–Sun 2–5pm; €2) you can see frescoed remains of the Romanesque building and relics of a Roman temple to Diana. In the main part of the church sits a bizarre white statue of the Virgin and Child on a boat-chariot, drawn here on its own wheels from Lourdes over the course of six years during a pilgrimage in the 1940s.

Nearby, the **Château Musée** (Mon & Wed–Sat 10am–12.30pm & 2–5pm, Sun 10am–12.30pm & 2.30–5.30pm; €2) contains Egyptian funerary objects donated by a local-born Egyptologist, an unusual set of Eskimo masks and a sizeable collection of Greek pots. A short walk down the main tourist street, **rue de Lille**, will bring you to the **Hôtel de Ville**, whose twelfth-century belfry is the most ancient monument in the old town, but is only accessible by arranging a guided tour with the tourist office.

Three kilometres north of Boulogne on the N1 stands the **Colonne de la Grande Armée** where, in 1803, Napoleon is said to have changed his mind about invading Britain and turned his troops east towards Austria. The column was originally topped by a bronze figure of Napoleon symbolically clad in Roman garb – though his head, equally symbolically, was shot off by the British navy during World War II; a replacement statue now tops the column. The original is displayed in the little museum near the entrance to the column (mid-June to Sept Wed–Sun 10.30am–noon & 2.30–5.45pm; Oct to mid-June Fri–Sun 10am–noon & 2–4pm).

Eating and drinking

As a fishing port, Boulogne is a good spot to **eat** fish and seafood, with plenty of possibilities around place Dalton and a scattering in the *ville haute* (mostly the rue de Lille). If you're just after a **drink**, there is a handful of bars in the *ville haute* and a rather livelier selection in place Dalton, with *Au Bureau* and the smart *Welsh Pub* being the most popular.

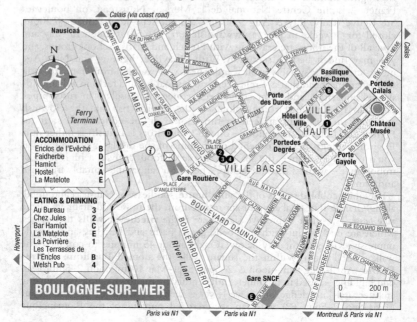

▲ Nausicaá, Boulogne

Bar Hamiot 1 rue Faidherbe ☎ 03.21.31.44.20. Under the hotel of the same name, this brasserie remains as popular as ever with locals and tourists alike, offering a large range of dishes from €8 omelettes and €14 fish dishes to €18–32 menus.

Chez Jules 8–10 place Dalton ☎ 03.21.31.54.12. On the square of the *ville basse* and a great place to watch the Wed & Sat markets. Typical brasserie fare with menus from €18.50.

La Matelote 80 bd Ste-Beuve ☎ 03.21.30.17.97. The best restaurant near the water, located opposite Nausicaá, featuring a *dégustation* menu at €75. If you'd rather not spend that much, you could go for the €33 menu or à la carte fish from €30. Loving care is taken over the food and service, but it can be rather snooty.

La Poivrière 15 rue de Lille ☎ 03.21.80.18.18. Set in a parade of rather mediocre eateries in the prettiest part of the *ville haute*, offering traditional French cuisine with a very reasonable €19.50 menu. Closed Wed.

Les Terrasses de l'Enclos 6 rue de Pressy ☎ 03.91.90.05.90. This is the smartest restaurant in the *ville haute*, focusing on freshness, with excellent meat and fish. Menus €19.50–46. Closed Sun evening. Mon & Tues lunch.

South to Amiens

South of Boulogne the coast is just as wild and magnificent as it is further north, but without your own transport it's hard to get down to the beach: a band of unstable dunes forces the D940 coast road and the Calais–Paris railway inland. With the exception of **Étaples**, the seaside towns are artificial resorts of twentieth-century creation – only of interest in that they provide access to the beaches. These, however, really are worth getting to, and their eerie beauty is best experienced by walking the coastal GR path or any one of the several marked trails that the local tourist offices promote, or by visiting the **Marquenterre Bird Sanctuary**. For car-drivers, the D119 between Boulogne and just north of Dannes is a little closer to the water with turn-offs directly into the dunes.

The quickest route south is the A16 Boulogne–Abbeville autoroute, which continues all the way to Paris. More interesting, if you want to take in the battlefield of **Agincourt**, is a winding cross–country route exploring some of the English-looking side valleys on the north side of the River Canche – such as the Crequoise, Planquette and Ternoise. For more information on the region consult ⓦ www.somme–tourisme.com.

Le Touquet and around

Situated among dunes and wind–flattened tamarisks and pines, leafy **LE TOUQUET** (officially called Le Touquet–Paris–Plage) is not so different to some of the snootier places on the English south coast, which is no real surprise, given its interwar popularity with the British smart set: Noel Coward spent weekends here, while the author P.G. Wodehouse lived in the town for a period from 1934. In 1940, Wodehouse, surprised by the rapidity of the German advance, was captured here, and interned, later making his notorious wartime broadcasts from Berlin. Though Le Touquet's seafront has been colonized by modern apartments, back from the sea magnificent villas still hide behind its trees. One treat worth indulging in – especially if you've got kids – is Le Touquet's **Aqualud** swimming complex right on the beach (July & Aug daily 10.15am–7pm; €16.95; rest of year mostly 10.15am–8pm but days of opening vary; closed mid-Nov to mid-Feb; €14.95), which boasts three giant water slides and a series of indoor and outdoor themed pools; there's also the vast **Bagatelle** amusement park, 10km south of town on the D940 (April–Sept daily 10.30am–7pm; evenings until 9.30pm in high season; €20, or €22.50 from late July to the end of August).

Practicalities

To get to Le Touquet, either take the train from Boulogne to Étaples, from where a local bus covers the last four kilometres, or take the infrequent, slow bus (Mon–Sat only; timetable from local tourist offices) directly from Boulogne; it heads down the coast through Le Touquet to Berck-sur-Mer. Le Touquet's **tourist office** is in the Palais de l'Europe on place de l'Hermitage (April–Sept Mon–Sat 9am–7pm, Sun 10am–7pm; Oct–March Mon–Sat 9am–6pm, Sun 10am–6pm; ⓣ 03.21.06.72.00, ⓦ www.letouquet.com), which also houses the casino.

If you're looking for somewhere reasonable to **stay**, try the hostel *Riva Bella* just 30m from the sandy beach at 12 rue Léon–Garet (ⓣ 03.21.05.08.22, ⓦ www.rivabella-touquet.com; €20–40), or the two-star *Armide*, 56 rue Léon-Garet (ⓣ 03.21.05.21.76, ⓦ www.hotelarmide.com; ❸). If you fancy splashing out, there's plenty of choice including the very English-looking *Le Manoir* on avenue du Golf (ⓣ 03.21.06.28.28, ⓦ www.opengolfclub.com; ❻) and *Le Westminster*, avenue du Verger (ⓣ 03.21.05.48.48, ⓦ www.westminster.fr; ❻). There's also a **caravan site**, the *Stoneham* (ⓣ 03.21.05.16.55, ⓔ caravaning .stoneham@letouquet.com; closed mid-Nov to mid-Feb), on avenue François-Godin, 1km from the centre and the beach. Places to **eat** can also be expensive in Le Touquet. For an affordable treat, visit *Le Café des Arts*, 80 rue de Paris, which specializes in fish dishes (menus from €18; ⓣ 03.21.05.21.55; closed Tues & Wed), or for more traditional cuisine try the *Auberge de la Dune aux Loups* on the avenue of the same name (menus from €24.50; ⓣ 03.21.05.42.54; closed Tues evening & Wed out of season), where you can eat on the terrace. Slightly less expensive is *Les Sports*, 22 rue St-Jean (ⓣ 03.21.05.05.22), a classic brasserie with a menu at €17.

Étaples

On the other side of the River Canche is the much more workaday **ÉTAPLES**, a picturesque fishing port whose charm lies in its relaxed air. Between April and

September **boat trips** departing from the port can be booked via the **tourist office** (April–June & Sept daily 9.30am–12.30pm & 2–6pm; July–Aug daily 9.30am–6pm, Oct–March Mon–Sat 10am–12.30pm & 2–5pm; ℡ 03.21.09.56.94) at La Corderie, a former fish filleting plant on boulevard Bigot–Descelers. You can choose between a 45-minute sea jaunt (€6.40) and a more rigorous twelve-hour fishing stint with experienced fishermen (€45.80). If you've still not had your fill of fish afterwards, you can visit the Centre de Découverte de la Pêche en Mer (**Sea Fishing Discovery Centre**: April–Sept daily 10am–1pm & 2–7pm; Oct–March Tue–Sun 2–6pm; €6) in the same building as the tourist office. The village also boasts a good seafood **restaurant**, *Aux Pêcheurs d'Étaples*, situated upstairs from the bustling and well-stocked **fish market** on quai de la Canche (from €16; ℡ 03.21.94.06.90).

Montreuil-sur-Mer

Once a port, **MONTREUIL-SUR-MER** is now stranded 13km inland, owing to the silting up of the River Canche. Perched on a hilltop above the river and surrounded by ancient walls, it's an appealing place. Quite compact, it's easily walkable, with its hilltop ramparts offering fine views. Laurence Sterne spent a night here on his *Sentimental Journey*, and it was the scene of much of the action in Victor Hugo's *Les Misérables*, perhaps best evoked by the steep cobbled street of pavée St-Firmin, first left after the Porte de Boulogne, a short climb from the *gare SNCF*.

Two heavily damaged Gothic churches grace the main square: the **church of St-Saulve** and a tiny wood-panelled **chapelle** tucked into the side of the red-brick hospital, now a three-star hotel (see below). To the south there are numerous cobbled lanes to wander down, all lined with tiny artisan houses. In the northwestern corner of the walls lies Vauban's **Citadelle** (mid-April to mid-Oct daily 10am–noon & 2–6pm; March to mid-April & mid-Oct to end Nov daily except Tues; €2.50) – ruined, overgrown and, after dark, pretty atmospheric, with subterranean gun emplacements and a fourteenth-century tower that records the coats of arms of the French noblemen killed at Agincourt. A path following the top of the walls provides views out across the Canche estuary.

In mid-August, Montreuil puts on a surprisingly lively mini-arts **festival** of opera, theatre and dance, Les Malins Plaisirs.

Practicalities

The **tourist office** is by the citadelle at 21 rue Carnot (April–June, Sept & Oct Mon–Sat 10am–12.30pm & 2–6pm, Sun 10am–12.30pm; July–Aug also open Sun afternoons 2–6pm; Nov–Feb Mon–Sat 10am–12.30pm & 2–5pm; ℡ 03.21.06.04.27, 🌐 www.tourisme-montreuillois.com). For an **accommodation** treat, there's the classy, expensive *Château de Montreuil* (℡ 03.21.81.53.04, 🌐 www.chateaudemontreuil.com; ❾), which overlooks the citadelle. It contains a top-class restaurant (closed Mon outside high season; menus €70. For good food and accommodation at more manageable prices, try *Le Darnétal*, in place Darnétal (℡ 03.21.06.04.87; ❷; closed Mon & Tues; restaurant from €22). Another good bet is the *Clos des Capucins* on the wide place de Gaulle (℡ 03.21.06.08.65, 📧 clos-des-capucins@orange.fr; ❸; menu from €17). There's also a **youth hostel** (℡ 03.21.06.10.83; closed Nov–Feb; €10.30; reception open 10am–6pm) in one of the citadelle's outbuildings, and a **campsite**, *La Fontaine des Clercs*, (℡ 03.21.06.07.28, 📠 03.21.86.15.10; open all year), below the walls, by the Canche on rue d'Église.

The Agincourt and Crécy battlefields

Agincourt and Crécy, two of the bloodiest Anglo–French battles of the Middle Ages, took place near the attractive little town of **HESDIN** (familiar to Simenon fans from the TV series *Inspector Maigret*). Getting to either is difficult without your own transport; by car, it takes around an hour from Boulogne.

Twenty kilometres southwest of Hesdin, at the **Battle of Crécy**, Edward III inflicted the first of his many defeats of the French in 1346. This was the first appearance on the continent of the new English weapon, the six-foot longbow, and the first use in European history of gunpowder. There's not a lot to see today: just the **Moulin Édouard III** (now a watchtower), 1km northeast of **Crécy-en-Ponthieu** on the D111 to Wadicourt, site of the windmill from which Edward watched the hurly-burly of battle. Further south, on the D56 to Fontaine, the battered **croix de Bohème** marks the place where King John of Bohemia – fighting for the French – died, having insisted on leading his men into the fight despite his blindness.

Ten thousand more died in the heaviest defeat ever of France's feudal knight-hood at the **Battle of Agincourt** on October 25, 1415. Forced by muddy conditions to fight on foot in heavy armour, the French, though more than three times as numerous, were sitting ducks to the lighter, mobile English archers. The rout took place near present-day **AZINCOURT**, about 12km northeast of Hesdin off the D928, and a colourful, well-organized museum in the village, the **Centre Historique Médiéval Azincourt** (April–June & Sept–Oct daily 10am–6pm; July–Aug daily 9.30am–6.30pm; Nov–March daily except Tues 10am–5pm; €7.50) uses video and interactive facilities to bring the story to life. The museum can give you a map indicating the position of the English and French lines, and south-east of the village, by the crossroads of the D104 and the road to Maisoncelle, there's an informative orientation point at the foot of a stone obelisk.

The Marquenterre Bird Sanctuary

Even if you know nothing about birds, the **Parc ornithologique du Marquenterre** (daily: mid-Feb, March & Oct to mid-Nov 10am–3.30pm; April–Sept 10am–5pm; mid-Nov to mid-Feb 10am–3pm; €10), situated 30km south of Étaples off the D940 between the estuaries of the rivers Canche and Somme, will still be a revelation. The landscape is beautiful and strange: all dunes, tamarisks and pine forest, full of salty meres and ponds thick with water plants. Marquenterre is a haven in an area not known for valuing the fowl that pass through each year – almost all species are prey to local hunters, and between September and January the sound of gunshot is common.

Binoculars can be hired (€4); otherwise, rely on the guides posted at some of the observation huts, who set up portable telescopes and will tell you about the nesting birds. There's a choice of itineraries – two longer, more interesting walks (2–3hr) and a shorter one (roughly 1hr 30min); you can expect to see dozens of species – ducks, geese, oyster-catchers, terns, egrets, redshanks, greenshanks, spoonbills, herons, storks, godwits – some of them residents, most taking a breather from their epic migratory flights. In April and May they head north, returning from the end of August to October, while in early summer the young chicks can be seen.

Keen natural historians might also want to drop into the **Maison de la baie de Somme et de l'Oiseau** on the other side of the bay, between St-Valéry-sur-Somme and Cayeux-sur-Mer (daily: April–Sept 9.30am–7pm; Oct–March 10am–5pm; ☎03.22.26.93.93; €7), which has displays relating to birds and to the seals of the bay of the Somme and organizes seal excursions.

The Somme estuary

After Marquenterre, the D940 meanders through yet more silted-up fishing hamlets, whose crouching cottages are reminders of their former poverty. Some, like **LE CROTOY**, have enough sea still to attract the yachties, and have enjoyed a boom in second homes. Le Crotoy's south–facing beach has attracted numerous writers and painters over the years: Jules Verne wrote *Twenty Thousand Leagues under the Sea* here.

Across the bay lies **ST-VALÉRY-SUR-SOMME**, accessible in summer by a **steam train** (mid-March & Oct Sat & Sun; April Tues, Wed, Thurs, Sat & Sun; May–Sept daily; ⓦ www.chemin-fer-baie-somme.asso.fr; €7–10) from Le Crotoy and Noyelles, and by six buses a day from Noyelles. This is the place from which William, Duke of Normandy, set sail to conquer England in 1066. With its intact medieval citadelle and brightly painted quays, St-Valéry is the jewel of the coast. The only notable sight is the **Écomusée Picarvie** at 5 quai du Romerel (April–Sept Wed–Sun 10am–12.30pm & 1.30–6pm; €5.70), with its interesting collection of tools and artefacts relating to vanished trades and ways of life. Otherwise, there are plenty of **activities**, including boat trips from €9 (☎03.22.60.74.68), cycling (guided cycle rides from €15; ☎03.22.29.07.51) and guided walks (☎03.22.26.92.30). Digging for shellfish is also popular, but you have to be extremely careful about the tide. When it's high it reaches up to the quays, but withdraws 14km at low tide, creating a dangerous current; equally, it returns very suddenly, cutting off the unwary.

The town's **tourist office** (June–Aug daily 9.30am–noon & 2.30–6pm; Sept–May Tues–Sun 9.30am–noon & 2.30–6pm; ☎03.22.60.93.50) is situated on the quayside. There are two attractive **hotel-restaurants**: the three-star *Hôtel du Port et des Bains* (☎03.22.60.80.09, ⓦ www.hotelhpb.fr; ❹; restaurant menu from €16), right on the quayside by the tourist office; and the two-star *Les Pilotes* (☎03.22.60.80.39, ⓦ www.lespilotes.com; ❹), which fronts both rue la Ferté and the quayside and has over thirty different ways of serving mussels, with most under €14.

Abbeville

ABBEVILLE lies about halfway from Calais to Paris and makes a convenient stop-off on the N1. Until hit by a German air raid in May 1940, it was a very beautiful town. Remnants of its small-scale charm can still be found in the pretty, winding streets north and east of the tourist office, especially along rue des Teinturiers. The town's chief glory however is the splendid late Gothic **church of St-Vulfran**, marooned now amid the regimented postwar shopping streets that replaced the destroyed historic centre. Restoration work on the church, which was badly scarred during the war, only finished in 1993; the nave retains a real feeling of dusty antiquity but the restorers' touches are obvious in the choir. As at Beauvais, the original builders' ambitions exceeded their reach; funds ran out, and the grandiose nave and modest choir seem to belong to different churches.

The **tourist office** is at 1 place de l'Amiral–Courbet (summer Mon–Sat 9.30am–7pm, Sun 10am–1pm; winter Mon–Sat 9.30am–12.30pm & 1.30–5.30pm, Sun 10am–1pm; ☎03.22.24.27.92, ⓦ www.ot-abbeville.fr). For those who want to **stay**, Abbeville has few establishments with individual charm. The most comfortable and central of the chains is the *Mercure Hôtel de France*, in place du Pilori in the town centre (☎03.22.24.00.42, ⓦ www.mercure.com; ❺; menus from €11.50), while a cheap local option is the neat but basic *Le Liberty*, 5 rue St-Catherine (☎&℉03.22.24.21.71; ❶). For a **meal**, *L'Escale en Picardie*, at

15 rue des Teinturiers (menus from €25; ☎03.22.24.21.51), specializes in fresh fish with crisp white wines, while the pizzeria *Le Célavone*, 30 place du Grand Marché, is pastel plush and full of locals, with pasta dishes from under €8.

Amiens and the route south

AMIENS was badly scarred during both world wars, but restored sensitively afterwards. The cathedral is the main reason to visit, but **St-Leu**, the renovated medieval artisans' quarter north of the cathedral with its network of canals, has considerable charm, while a few-minutes' walk from the train station the *hortillonnages* (see p.212) transport you into a peaceful rural landscape. Amiens has an unmistakably northern feel; some parts of the city look rather Flemish, while the redbrick nineteenth-century workers' houses beyond the centre are reminiscent of the English Midlands and North. The student presence ensures there's enough life in the evening to make an overnight stay worthwhile.

Arrival and information

The main **gare SNCF** (Amiens-Nord) is on the place A.-Fiquet; the **gare routière** is concealed beneath the Amiens 2 shopping complex, which is connected to the train station and useful for its supermarket and public toilets. Much of central Amiens is traffic-free – the rest of it is full of cars circling endlessly in search of non existent parking spaces. The **tourist office** is next to the cathedral on place Notre Dame (April–Sept Mon–Sat 9.30am–6.30pm, Sun 10am–noon & 2–5pm; Oct–March Mon–Sat 9.30am–6pm, Sun 10am–noon & 2–5pm; ☎03.22.71.60.50, ⓦwww.amiens-tourisme.com). If you're intending spending much time in Amiens it's worth considering the **Pass Amiens**, which for €8 entitles the holder to a string of reductions on everything from museum entry to city transport, bicycle hire and restaurants.

Accommodation

Amiens has many two-star **hotels**, all with similar prices, which tend to fill up fairly fast.

Central et Anzac 17 rue Alexandre-Fatton ☎03.22.91.34.08, ⓦwww.hotelcentraletanzac .com. Fewer creature comforts than its neighbour, but perfectly decent and in a good, central location. ❷

Hôtel de Normandie 1 bis rue Lamartine ☎03.22.91.74.99, ⓦwww.hotelnormandie-80 .com; comfortable two-star hotel in a quiet side street close to the *gare SNCF*. ❶–❹

Le Prieuré 17 rue Porion ☎03.22.71.16.71, ⓦwww.hotelrestaurantleprieure.com. Comfortable hotel close to the cathedral, slightly upmarket of the *Victor Hugo*. ❸

Spatial 15 rue Alexandre-Fatton ☎03.22.91.53.23, ⓦwww.hotelspatial.com. Slightly more comfortable of two neighbouring hotels in a side street opposite the *gare SNCF*. ❷–❸

Victor Hugo 2 rue de l'Oratoire ☎03.22.91.57.91, ⓦwww.hotel-a-amiens.com. Good value, renovated hotel near the cathedral with the feel of a country bed and breakfast. ❷

The City

The **Cathédrale Notre-Dame** (daily: April–Sept 8.30am–6.30pm; Oct–March 8.30am–5.30pm) dominates the city by sheer size – it's the biggest Gothic building in France – but its appeal lies mainly in its unusual uniformity of style. Begun in 1220 under architect Robert de Luzarches, it was effectively finished by 1269, and so the building escaped the influence of succeeding architectural

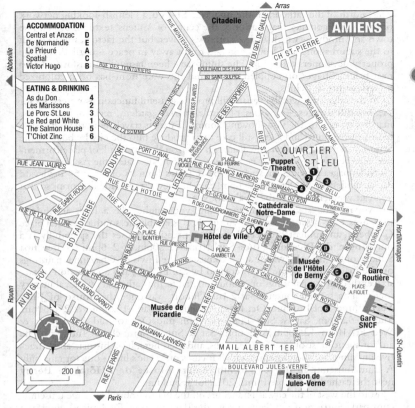

ACCOMMODATION
Central et Anzac   D
De Normandie   E
Le Prieuré   A
Spatial   C
Victor Hugo   B

EATING & DRINKING
As du Don   4
Les Marissons   2
Le Porc St Leu   3
Le Red and White   1
The Salmon House   5
T'Chiot Zinc   6

THE NORTH | Amiens and the route south

fads that marred the "purity" of some of its more leisurely built sisters. A laser scrub, used on the west front, has revealed traces of the original polychrome exterior, in stark contrast to its sombre, grey modern appearance. An evening **light show** (daily: June 15 to June 30 10.45pm, July 10.30pm, Aug 10pm, Sept 9.45pm, Dec 1 to Jan 1 7pm; free) gives a vivid idea of how the west front would have looked when coloured, with music added to create atmosphere, and an explanation of the various statues on the facade first in French and then in English. By way of contrast, the interior is all vertical lines and no fuss: a light, calm and unaffected space. Ruskin thought the apse "not only the best, but the very first thing done perfectly in its manner by northern Christendom". The later embellishments, like the sixteenth-century choir stalls, are works of breathtaking virtuosity. The same goes for the sculpted panels depicting the life of St Firmin, Amiens' first bishop, on the right side of the choir screen. The choir itself can be visited at 3.30pm daily but is otherwise locked. Those with strong legs can mount the cathedral's front **towers** (April–June & Sept Mon & Wed–Fri at 3pm & 4.30pm, weekends 2.30–5.15pm; July–August daily except Tues & Sun 11am, daily except Tues 2.30–5.15pm; Oct–March Mon & Wed–Sat at 3.45pm; €4.50). One of the most atmospheric ways of seeing the cathedral is to attend a Sunday morning Mass (10am or 10.30am, depending on time of year), when there's sublime Gregorian chanting.

Just north of the cathedral is the **quartier St-Leu**, a Flemish-looking network of canals and cottages that was once the centre of Amiens' textile industry. The town still produces much of the country's velvet, but the factories moved out to the suburbs long ago, leaving St-Leu to rot away in peace – until, that is, the property developers moved in. The slums have been tastefully transformed into neat brick cottages on cobbled streets, and the waterfront has been colonized by restaurants and clubs.

On the edge of town, the canals still provide a useful function as waterways for the **hortillonnages** – a series of fertile market gardens, reclaimed from the marshes created by the slow-flowing Somme. Farmers travel about them in black, high-prowed punts and a few still take their produce into the city by boat for the Saturday morning **market**, the *marché sur l'eau*, on the riverbank of place Parmentier. The best way to see the *hortillonnages* is from the water: the Association des Hortillonnages provides inexpensive **boat tours** from its office at 54 bovlevard de Beauvillé (April–Oct daily 2–6pm; €5.50). They also provide free maps so that you can wander some of the area's footpaths.

If you're interested in Picardy culture, you might take a look at Amiens' museums. Five-minutes' walk down rue de la République, south of central place Gambetta, an opulent nineteenth-century mansion houses the splendidly laid out **Musée de Picardie** (Tues–Sun 10am–12.30pm & 2–6pm; €5; free first Sunday of the month), whose star exhibits are the Puvis de Chavannes paintings on the main stairwell, the room created by Sol LeWitt, and a collection of rare sixteenth-century paintings on wood donated to the cathedral by a local literary society. The second museum, at 2 rue Dubois, was once the **house of Jules Verne** (mid-April to mid-Oct Mon & Wed–Fri 10am–12.30pm & 2–6.30pm, Tues 2–6.30pm, Sat & Sun 11am–6.30pm; mid-Oct to mid-April Mon & Wed–Fri 10am–12.30pm & 2–6pm, Sat & Sun 2–6pm; closed Tues; €5). The author spent most of his life in Amiens, and died here. It's a historic and attractive building, but the museum, which focuses on Verne's life, is one for fans only. A third museum, in the seventeenth-century **Musée de l'Hôtel de Berny** near the cathedral, is closed until 2012 for rebuilding.

Just to the west of the city, at Tirancourt off the N1 to Abbeville, a large museum-cum-park, **Samara** (from Samarobriva, the Roman name for Amiens), re-creates the life of prehistoric man in northern Europe with reconstructions of dwellings and displays illustrating the way of life, trades and so on (mid-March to June & Sept to mid-Nov Mon–Fri 9.30am–5.30pm, Sat & Sun 10am–6pm; July & Aug daily 10am–6.30pm; closed mid-Nov to mid-March; Ⓦwww.samara.fr; €9).

Eating, drinking and entertainment

By far the most attractive area to eat is around **St-Leu**, where many of the **restaurants** have outdoor seating overlooking a canal and the cathedral, especially on quai Belu.

As du Don, 1 place Don. On a pretty, cobbled square below the cathedral, with a *formule* for €16 and a heated terrace.

Les Marissons 69 rue Marissons ☎03.22.92.96.66. Just by the canal at the Pont de la Dodane, this is Amiens' best gourmet restaurant. Lunch menu €18.50, tasting menu €40; closed Wed & Sat lunch & all day Sun.

Le Porc St Leu 45/47 quai Belu ☎03.22.80.00.73. More traditional than its trendy neighbours, with *cochon de lait* and menus at €24–29.

The Salmon House 14/16 rue Cormont ☎03.22.91.27.83. Right by the south door of the cathedral, this restaurant offers salmon in every conceivable form, plus a few meat dishes. *Plats* from €12; closed Sun.

T'chiot Zinc 18 rue Noyon. Handsome, diminutive place with menus at €13 & €22, serving traditional country fare.

Bars and pubs abound in the area, especially on quai Belu, and there is a trendy late-night gay bar *Le Red and White* at 9 rue de la Dodane.

In late March and early April Amiens bursts into life for its annual international **jazz festival**; on the third weekend in June, the local costumes come out for the **Fête d'Amiens**, which is the best time of year to visit the *hortillonnages*. Traditional Picardy **marionette** (*cabotans*) performances take place at the Théâtre de Marionnettes Chés Cabotans d'Amiens, 31 rue Edouard-David (☎03.22.22.30.90, ⒲www.ches-cabotans-damiens.com; tickets €10). To purchase or take a look at hand-made marionettes, visit the workshop of Jean-Pierre Facquier at 67 rue du Don.

Beauvais

As you head south from Amiens towards Paris, the countryside becomes broad and flat; **BEAUVAIS**, 60km south of Amiens, seems to fit into this landscape. Rebuilt in tasteful but dull fashion after World War II, it's not a town that repays aimless wandering, but it is redeemed by its audacious, eccentric Gothic cathedral, the **Cathédrale St-Pierre** (daily: July–Aug 9am–6.30pm; Sept–June 9am–12.15pm & 2–5.30pm), which rises above the town. It's a building that perhaps more than any other in northern France demonstrates the religious materialism of the Middle Ages – its main intention was to be taller and larger than its rivals. The choir, completed in 1272, was once 5m higher than that of Amiens, though only briefly, as it collapsed in 1284. Its replacement, only completed three centuries later, was raised by the sale of indulgences – a right granted to the local bishops by Pope Leo X. This, too, fell within a few years, and, the authorities having overreached themselves financially, the church remained as it is today: unfinished, mutilated and really rather odd. At over 155m high, the interior vaults are undeniably impressive, giving the impression that the cathedral is of a larger scale than at Amiens; at the same time, the network of props and brackets that reinforce the structure internally attests to its fragility. The building's real beauty lies in its glass, its sculpted doorways and the remnants of the so-called Basse-Oeuvre, a ninth-century Carolingian church incorporated into (and dwarfed by) the Gothic structure. It also contains a couple of remarkable **clocks**: one, a twelve-metre high astronomical clock built in 1865, above which on the hour 68 figures mimic scenes from the Last Judgement; the other, a medieval clock that's been working for seven hundred years. Ongoing restoration work means much of the exterior is likely to be shrouded in scaffolding for some time to come.

Though the cathedral is the town's only remarkable sight, the church of **St-Étienne**, a few blocks to the south of the cathedral on rue de Malherbe, is worth a look for yet more spectacular Renaissance stained-glass windows. There are also the **Galerie Nationale de la Tapisserie** alongside the cathedral (April–Sept Tues–Sun 9.30am–12.30pm & 2–6pm; Oct–March Tues–Sun 10am–12.30pm & 2–5pm; free), a museum of the tapestry for which Beauvais was once renowned, housing a collection ranging from the fifteenth century to the present day; and the **Musée Départemental de l'Oise** (daily except Tues: July–Sept 10am–6pm; Oct–June 10am–noon & 2–6pm; free), devoted to painting, local history and archeology, in the sharp, black-towered building west of the cathedral.

Practicalities

Beauvais is just over an hour by train from Paris, and the **gare SNCF** is a short walk from the centre of town – take avenue de la République, then turn right up rue de Malherbe. Paris-Beauvais **airport** – served by Ryanair from the UK and Ireland – is just outside the town (shuttle bus €4; 8 daily; 17min to cathedral). The **tourist office** (Mon–Sat 9.30am–12.30pm & 1.30–6pm; April–Oct also Sun 10am–5pm; ☎03.44.15.30.30, ⓦwww.beauvaistourisme.fr) is just across from the Galerie Nationale de Tapisserie, at 1 rue Beauregard.

If you want to **stay**, plump for the modest *Hôtel du Palais Bleu*, within sight of the cathedral at 9 rue St-Nicolas (☎03.44.45.18.58, ⓦwww.hoteldupalaisbeauvais .com; ❷), or try the *Cygne*, 24 rue Carnot (☎03.44.48.68.40, ⓦwww .hoteleducygne-beauvais.com; ❸).There's a **campsite** (☎03.44.02.00.22; July–Aug only) just out of town on the Paris road. Beauvais' best **food** is served just south of the town centre at *La Maison Haute*, 128 rue de Paris (☎03.44.02.61.60), which has menus from €29 and offers cookery classes. Less expensive is the charming *L'Auberge de la Meule*, 8 rue du 27 Juin (closed Sun & Mon), situated in one of Beauvais' few surviving streets of half–timbered houses and specializing in fondues and salads; *plats* from €7.

The Flemish cities and world war battlefields

From the Middle Ages until the late twentieth century great Flemish cities like **Lille**, **Roubaix**, **Douai** and **Cambrai** flourished, mainly thanks to their textile industries. The other dominating – now virtually extinct – presence in this part of northern France was the **coalfields** and related industries, which, at their peak in the nineteenth century, formed a continuous stretch from Béthune in the west to Valenciennes in the east. At **Lewarde** you can visit one of the pits, while in the region's big industrial cities you can see what the masters built with their profits: noble town houses, magnificent city halls, ornate churches and some of the country's finest art collections. Lille is a major trans-European communications hub, with a thriving centre of interest to locals and tourists alike.

On a more sombre note, Picardy, Artois and Flanders are littered with the monuments, battlefields and cemeteries of the two world wars, and nowhere as intensely as the region northeast of Amiens, between **Albert** and the appealing market town of **Arras**. It was here, among the fields and villages of the Somme, that the main battle lines of World War I were drawn. They can be visited most spectacularly at **Vimy Ridge**, just off the A26 north of Arras, where the trenches have been left *in situ*. Lesser sites, often more poignant, dot the countryside around Albert along the **Circuit de Souvenir**.

Lille and around

LILLE (Rijsel in Flemish), northern France's largest city, surprises many visitors with its impressive architecture, the winding streets of its tastefully restored old quarter (Vieux Lille), its plethora of excellent restaurants, and bustling nightlife. It boasts a large university, a modern métro system, and a very serious attitude

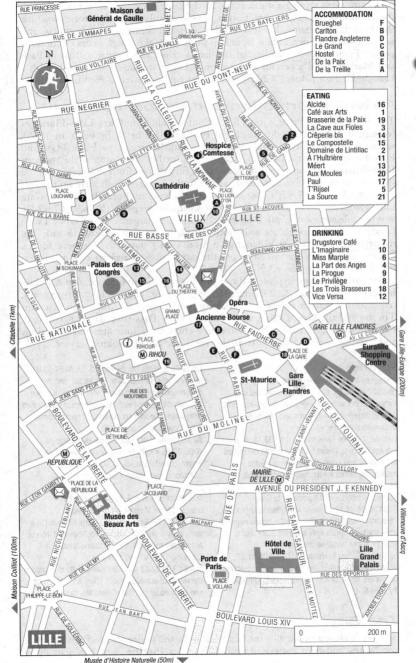

RUE PRINCESSE

Maison du
Général de Gaulle

RUE DE JEMMAPES

SQ. GRIMOMPREZ

RUE METZ

RUE DE LA HALLE

RUE DES BATELIERS

AVENUE DU PEUPLE BELGE

RUE VOLTAIRE

RUE DU PONT-NEUF

N

RUE DE LA COLLEGIALE

R. PHARAON DE WINTER

RUE MARACCI

AVENUE DU PEUPLE BELGE

RUE DE THIONVILLE

ACCOMMODATION

Brueghel	F
Carlton	B
Flandre Angleterre	D
Le Grand	C
Hostel	G
De la Paix	E
De la Treille	A

RUE NEGRIER

RUE D'ANGLETERRE

RUE DES CELESTINS

EATING

Alcide	16
Café aux Arts	1
Brasserie de la Paix	19
La Cave aux Fioles	3
Crêperie bis	14
Le Compostelle	15
Domaine de Lintillac	2
À l'Huîtrière	11
Méert	13
Aux Moules	20
Paul	17
T'Rijsel	5
La Source	21

RUE SAINTE-CATHERINE

RUE ROYALE

Hospice
Comtesse

RUE LEONARD DANEL

RUE DE LA MONNAIE

RUE DE GAND

PLACE L. DE BETTIGNIES

PLACE LOUCHARD

Cathédrale

RUE DOUDIN

PLACE DU LION D'OR

RUE ST-JACQUES

RUE DE LA BARRE

RUE J.J. ROUSSEAU

VIEUX LILLE

RUE DES CHATS BOSSUS

RUE DE LA CLEF

RUE DE LA HALLOTERIE

RUE ESQUERMOISE

RUE BASSE

RUE DES CHATS BOSSUS

BOULEVARD CARNOT

RUE DES CANONNIERS

DRINKING

Drugstore Café	7
L'Imaginaire	10
Miss Marple	6
La Part des Anges	4
La Pirogue	9
Le Privilège	8
Les Trois Brasseurs	18
Vice Versa	12

PLACE M SCHUMANN

Palais des
Congrès

RUE LE PELLETIER

RUE DES ARTS

AV. FOCH

RUE ST-ETIENNE

PLACE DU THÉÂTRE

Opéra

RUE DE L'HOPITAL MILITAIRE

GRAND PLACE

Ancienne Bourse

RUE FAIDHERBE

GARE LILLE FLANDRES

M AV. LE CORBUSIER

Euralille
Shopping
Centre

RUE NATIONALE

PLACE RIHOUR

M RIHOU

RUE NEUVE

RUE DE PARIS

PLACE DE LA GARE

RUE DES FOSSES

St-Maurice

Gare
Lille-
Flandres

RUE DE TOURNAI

RUE JEAN SANS PEUR

RUE DES MOLFONDS

RUE DE BÉTHUNE

RUE DES TANNEURS

RUE DU MOLINEL

AVENUE CHARLES SAINT-VENANT

PLACE DE BÉTHUNE

RUE D'AMIENS

RUE GUSTAVE DELORY

BOULEVARD DE LA LIBERTÉ

M
RÉPUBLIQUE

MAIRIE
DE LILLE M

RUE LEON GAMBETTA

PLACE DE LA RÉPUBLIQUE

PLACE JACQUARD

RUE DE PARIS

AVENUE DU PRESIDENT J. F KENNEDY

RUE NICOLAS LEBLANC

RUE JACQUEMARS GIÉLÉE

Musée des
Beaux Arts

RUE MALPART

RUE LYDERIC

RUE SAINT-SAUVEUR

RUE CHARLES DEBIERRE

Hôtel de
Ville

Lille
Grand
Palais

RUE DE VALMY

BOULEVARD DE LA LIBERTÉ

Porte de
Paris

PLACE S. VOLLANT

RUE DES DEPORTES

RUE F. MOTTEZ

AVENUE EUGENE

PLACE PHILIPPE-LE-BON

RUE JEAN BART

RUE DE SOLFERINO

BOULEVARD LOUIS XIV

0   200 m

LILLE

Citadelle (1km)

Maison Coilliot (100m)

Gare Lille-Europe (200m)

Villeneuve d'Ascq

Musée d'Histoire Naturelle (50m)

to culture, with some great museums. At the same time, the city spreads far into the countryside in every direction, a jumble of suburbs and factories, and for the French it remains the very symbol of the country's heavy industry and working-class politics. Lille is facing up to many of the tough issues of contemporary France: poverty and racial conflict, a crime rate similar to that of Paris and Marseille, and a certain regionalism – Lillois sprinkle their speech with a French–Flemish patois ("Ch'ti") and to some extent assert a Flemish identity.

Arrival, information and accommodation

The central Grand'Place is just a few-minutes' walk from **Gare Lille-Flandres** (originally Paris's Gare du Nord, but brought here brick by brick in 1865), served by regional trains plus the hourly shuttle service to Paris. TGV and Eurostar services from London, Brussels and further afield stop at the modern **Lille-Europe** station, a few-minutes' walk further out from the centre, or one stop on the métro. If you arrive by air, a shuttle-bus service (hourly on the half hour; ☎03.20.49.67.47; €5 one way) whisks you to Euralille, just by Gare Lille-Flandres, in twenty minutes from **Lesquin airport** (☎08.91.67.32.10, ⊛www.lille.aeroport.com). Despite being the fifth-largest city in France, Lille's centre is small enough to walk round and, unless you choose to visit the modern art museum at Villeneuve-d'Ascq, or to travel to Roubaix for La Piscine, you won't even need to use the city's efficient **métro** system (tickets €1.25 per trip; day pass €3.50).

The **tourist office** in place Rihour (Mon–Sat 9.30am–6.30pm, Sun & public holidays 10am–noon & 2–5pm; ☎03.59.57.94.00, ⊛www.lilletourism.com), ten-minutes' walk from the station along rue Faidherbe and through place du Théâtre and the Grand'Place, will sell you a **City Pass** (one day €18, two days €30 and three days €45), which offers free entry to various sites and attractions and free use of public transport. It also has a free **hotel** booking service.

Hotels

Brueghel 3–5 parvis St-Maurice ☎03.20.06.06.69, ⊛www.hotel-brueghel.com. Very attractive and typically Flemish two-star hotel with antique-furnished rooms and charming, understated service. ❺

Carlton 3 rue de Paris ☎03.20.13.33.13, ⊛www.carltonlille.com. Smart four-star rooms decorated in Louis XV and Louis XVI style with marble bathrooms. Noted for its magnificent reception halls. ❽

Flandre Angleterre 13 place de la Gare ☎03.20.06.04.12, ⊛www.hotel-flandreangleterre-lille.com. Much the classiest of the hotels near the train station: impressively large en-suite rooms with TV & free wireless internet. ❹

Le Grand 51 rue Faidherbe ☎03.20.06.31.57, ⊛www.legrandhotel.com. Comfortable two-star; rooms are en-suite and soundproofed, with satellite TV & wi-fi. ❹

De la Paix 46bis rue de Paris ☎03.20.54.63.93, ⊛www.hotel-la-paix.com. The nicest, and most expensive, two-star in town, with a great location, a gleaming wooden staircase, and rooms decorated with classy modern art posters. All rooms come with shower, toilet and TV. ❺

De la Treille 7–9 place Louise-de-Bettignies ☎03.20.55.45.46, ⊛www.hoteldelatreille.com. Bright, cheerful Vieux Lille hotel, with marble bathrooms and pastel-walled bedrooms. ❻

Hostel and campsite

Hostel 12 rue Malpart, off rue de Paris ☎03.20.57.08.94, ⊛www.fuaj.org. HI hostel in a fairly central position. Kitchen facilities and internet access are available. €17 including breakfast.

Camping Les Ramiers Bondues ☎&℻03.20.23.13.42. Lille's nearest site is located in the village of Bondues, about 10km north of the city and is linked by bus #35. Closed Nov to mid-April.

The City

The city's museums are all a bit of a walk from the pedestrianized centre, while the hottest museum associated with Lille is **La Piscine**, which is actually in

Roubaix (see p.221). The focal point of central Lille is the **Grand'Place** (officially known as place du Général-de-Gaulle and often referred to as the **place de la Déesse**), which marks the southern boundary of the old quarter, **Vieux Lille**. To the south is the central pedestrianized shopping area, which extends along rue de Béthune as far as the adjacent squares of place Béthune and place de la République.

Vieux Lille

The east side of the Grand'Place is dominated by the lavishly ornate **Ancienne Bourse**, as perfect a representative of its age as could be imagined. To the merchants of seventeenth-century Lille, all things Flemish were the epitome of wealth and taste; they were not men to stint on detail, either here or on the imposing surrounding mansions. The courtyard of the Bourse is now a **flea market**, with stalls selling books in the afternoons. A favourite Lillois pastime is lounging around the fountain at the centre of the square, in the middle of which is a **column** commemorating the city's resistance to the Austrian siege of 1792, topped by *La Déesse* (the goddess), modelled on the wife of the mayor at the time – hence the square's alternative moniker.

In the adjacent **place du Théâtre**, you can see how Flemish Renaissance architecture was assimilated and Frenchified in grand flights of Baroque extravagance – above all at the **Opéra** (℡08.20.48.90.40, ⓦwww.opera-lille.fr; closed July & Aug), built at the turn of the twentieth century by Louis-Marie Cordonnier, who also designed the extravagant **belfry** of the neighbouring Nouvelle Bourse – now the regional chamber of commerce.

From the north side of these two squares, the smart shopping streets, rues Esquermoise and Lepelletier, lead towards the heart of **Vieux Lille**, a warren of red-brick terraces on cobbled lanes and passages. It's an area of great character and charm, successfully reclaimed and reintegrated into the mainstream of the city's life, having been for years a dilapidated North African ghetto. To experience the atmosphere of Vieux Lille, head up towards rue d'Angleterre, rue du

▲ Grand'Place, Lille

Pont-Neuf and the Porte de Gand, rue de la Monnaie and place Lion-d'Or. Places to eat and drink are everywhere, interspersed with chic boutiques.

Vieux Lille's main sight is the **Hospice Comtesse** at 32 rue de la Monnaie. Twelfth century in origin, though much reconstructed in the eighteenth, it served as a hospital before becoming an orphanage after World War I, and its medicinal garden, a riot of poppies and verbena, is a delight. The Hospice is the setting for a collection of paintings, tapestries and porcelain of the region, re-creating the ambiance of a seventeenth century Flemish convent (Mon 2–6pm, Wed–Sun 10am–12.30pm & 2–6pm; €3).

Charles de Gaulle was born in this part of the town, at 9 rue Princesse, in 1890. His house is now a **museum** (Wed–Sun 10am–noon & 2–5.15pm; €5), which normally exhibits, among de Gaulle's effects, the bullet–riddled Citroën in which he was driving when the OAS attempted to assassinate him in 1962. Another must for military buffs is the **citadelle** that overlooks the old town to the northwest, constructed in familiar star-shaped fashion by Vauban in the seventeenth century. Still in military hands, it can be visited on Sundays between May and August by guided tour (€7.50; tours depart from the citadelle's Porte Royale at 3pm). To get there, go along rue de la Barre from Vieux Lille.

Amid the city's secular pomp, Lille's ecclesiastical architecture can seem rather subdued. Exceptions include the facade of the cathedral, **Notre-Dame-de-la -Treille**, just off rue de la Monnaie. The body of the cathedral is a Neo-Gothic construction begun in 1854, but the new facade, completed in 1999, is a trans-lucent marble skin supported by steel wires, best appreciated from inside, or at night when lit up from within. More traditional, but also impressive, is the **church of St-Maurice**, close to the station on rue de Paris, whose white stone front hides a classic Flemish Hallekerke, with the five aisles characteristic of the style.

South of the Grand'Place

Just south of the Grand'Place is **place Rihour**, a largely modern square flanked by brasseries and the remains of an old palace that now houses the tourist office, hidden behind a war memorial of gigantic proportions. Close by, the busiest shopping street, rue de Béthune, leads into place de Béthune, home to some excellent cafés, and beyond to the **Musée des Beaux-Arts** on place de la République (Mon 2–6pm, Wed–Sun 10am–6pm; €5). The late 1990s redesign is almost too sleek and spacious, but the museum does contain some important works. Flemish painters form the core of the collection, from "primitives" like Dirck Bouts, through the northern Renaissance to Ruisdael, de Hooch and the seventeenth-century greats, including several painted by Rubens for the Capuchin convent in Lille. French works include paintings by Delcroix, Courbet and Monet. The museum's temporary exhibitions cost extra, but can be worthwhile.

A few hundred metres south of the museum, near the green avenue Jean-Baptiste Lebas, is the **Musée d'Histoire Naturelle**, 19 rue de Bruxelles (Mon–Sat 9am–noon & 2–5pm, Sun 10am–5pm; €2.50). It's a small museum, a manageable size for children, with a lovely collection of dinosaur bones, fossils, and an impressive array of stuffed birds, including a dodo.

West of the Musée des Beaux-Arts, on rue de Fleurus, lies **Maison Coilliot**, one of the few houses built by Hector Guimard, who made his name designing the Art Nouveau entrances to the Paris métro – it's worth taking a look at the facade. Built at the height of the Art Nouveau movement, it's as striking today as it obviously was to the conservative burghers of Lille (there are no other such buildings in the city), but it also displays the somewhat muddled eclecticism of the style, coming over as half brick-faced mansion, half timber-framed cottage. East of the museum, near the triumphal arch of Porte de Paris, is the city's odd but serviceable **Hôtel de Ville**, executed in a Flemish–modernist style not unlike German *jugendstil*, with an extremely tall belfry.

Euralille

Thanks to Eurostar and the international extension of the TGV network, Lille has become the transport hub of northern Europe, a position it is trying to exploit to turn itself into an international business centre: hence **Euralille**, the burgeoning complex behind the old *gare SNCF*. Some of the structures are by big-name architects like Rem Koolhaas and Jean Nouvel, yet even as construction continues some of the glitter is coming off this "new" Lille: the TGV station is bustling and audacious, but the shopping mall opposite is dull, the brutal concrete expanse between the two stations is popular only with drunks and vagrants, and the weed-infested kerbs and dirty fountains point to a lack of adequate maintenance.

Villeneuve d'Ascq: the Musée d'Art Moderne

The suburb of Villeneuve d'Ascq is a mark of Lille's cultural ambition. Acres of parkland, an old windmill or two, and a whole series of mini-lakes form the setting for the **Musée d'Art Moderne** (closed for refurbishment; contact tourist office for latest information, scheduled to reopen during 2009), which houses an unusually good, if small, collection in its uninviting red-brick buildings. The ground floor is generally given over to exhibitions of varying quality by contemporary French artists, while the permanent collection, on the first floor, contains canvases by Picasso, Braque, Modigliani, Miró and a whole room devoted to Fernand Léger and Georges Rouault.

Eating, drinking and entertainment

A Flemish flavour and a taste for mussels characterize the city's traditional cuisine, with the main central concentration of cafés, **brasseries** and **restaurants** around **place Rihour** and along rue de Béthune. Vieux Lille has also gained a reputation for gastronomic excellence, and for something more innovative or atmospheric it's here, particularly on the eastern side towards and along **rue de Gand**, where you'll find the thickest concentration of worthwhile places. The **student quarter** along rues Solférino and Masséna is good for ethnic eating – the former mostly Chinese or Japanese, the latter dominated by cheap kebab shops. Foodies should make a pilgrimage to Philippe Olivier's *fromagerie* with its three hundred cheeses on 3 rue du Curé-St-Étienne.

The **cafés** around the Grand'Place and place Rihour are always buzzing with life. Up near the cathedral in Vieux Lille, rue Royale, rue de la Barre, rue Basse and place Louise-de-Bettignies have trendier spots, with a few stretched out along rue de la Monnaie too. West of the centre, celtic-style pubs predominate in studenty rue Masséna, and attract a young crowd. For **gay bars**, of which there are several, try *Vice Versa* on rue de la Barre or *Le Privilège* opposite and, for lesbians, *Miss Marple* at 18 rue de Gand. Art and music events are always worth checking up on – there's a particularly lively **jazz** scene. Pick up a copy of the free weekly listings magazine, *Sortir*, from the tourist office, or look in the local paper, *La Voix du Nord*.

Restaurants and cafés

Alcide 5 rue Débris St-Étienne ☏ 03.20.12.06.95. A Lillois institution, an upmarket brasserie tucked down a narrow alleyway near the Grand'Place. Reliable, hearty fare (*flamiche*, fish, *crêpes à la cassonade*) and home-made ice creams served in a wood-panelled dining room. Menus from €19. Open daily, closed Sunday evening.

Café aux Arts 1 place du Concert. Good old-fashioned café with wicker chairs on its terrace, in an unbeatable vantage point over the market.

Brasserie de la Paix 25 place Rihour ☏ 03.20.54.70.41. Sumptuous brasserie, unrelated to its namesake hotel, specializing in mussels and seafood. Menus from €18. Closed Sun.

La Cave aux Fioles 39 rue de Gand ☏ 03.20.55.18.43. The jazz–related decor is backed by the music and mellow ambience. Food ranges from classics and Flemish specials to more adventurous fare. Menus from €19 or *plats* from €16. Closed Sat lunch, Sun & Mon.

Le Compostelle 4 rue St-Étienne ☏ 03.28.38.08.30. In a much renovated Knights Templar Renaissance palace, this airy restaurant with indoor trees offers refined versions of traditional French specialities, including vegetarian options. Menus from €29.

Crêperie bis 4 rue Débris St-Étienne ☏ 03.20.42.12.16. Stylish modern crêperie with a good choice of sweet and savoury pancakes plus *tartines* & salads; *plats* around €11. There's another branch on rue de Gand.

Domaine de Lintillac 43 rue de Gand ☏ 03.20.06.53.51. Unpretentious, old-fashioned French cuisine specializing in foie gras, cassoulet and other *produits du terroir* from the owner's farm (the *produits* can also be purchased). Mains from €9.50. Closed lunch Sun–Wed.

🏃 **A l'Huîtrière** 3 rue des Chats-Bossus ☏ 03.20.55.43.41. A wonderful shop (worth a visit just to look at the mosaics and stained glass) with an expensive, chandelier-hung restaurant at the back – acclaimed as Lille's best – specializing in fish and oysters at

€30-plus a dish; there's an impressive €105 menu. Closed Sun evening.

Méert 25–27 rue Esquermoise ☏ 03.20.57.07.44. Decorated with mirrors and chandeliers, this is Lille's most famous (and expensive) *salon de thé* specializing in *gaufres* as well as excellent cakes and teas. Closed Mon.

Aux Moules 34 rue de Béthune ☏ 03.20.57.12.46. The best place to eat mussels; it's been serving them since 1930 in its Art Deco-style interior. Nothing costs much over €12, including the other brasserie fare and it's all excellent value. Daily noon–11pm (until 12 on Sat); closed Sun evening.

Paul place du Théâtre, corner of rue Faidherbe *Paul* is an institution in Lille; though it's now becoming a bit of a chain, it started here with the boulangerie, patisserie and *salon de thé* all under one roof.

La Source 13 rue du Plat ☏ 03.20.57.53.07. Vegetarian restaurant and healthfood store, best at lunchtime. From €9.

T'Rijsel 25 rue de Gand ☏ 03.20.15.01.59. Traditional Flemish *estaminet*, serving the whole gamut of regional dishes and over 40 beers. *Plats* from €10. Closed Sun & Mon.

Bars and clubs

Drugstore Café 21 rue Royale. Trendy Vieux Lille bar on three levels, with 1970s–style decor and an eclectic music policy playing everything from oldies and jazz to electro.

L'Imaginaire place Louise-de-Bettignies, next door to the *Hôtel Treille*. Arty young bar with paintings adorning the walls. Mon–Sat 11pm–3am.

La Part des Anges 50 rue de la Monnaie. Trendy wine bar with an enviable cellar, serving simple meals and snacks to accompany the wine.

La Pirogue 16 rue J.-J.-Rousseau. Antilles-themed bar with reasonably priced cocktails, especially popular with local students.

Les Trois Brasseurs 22 place de la Gare. Dark, smoke-stained dining stalls surround copper cauldrons in this genuine brasserie that brews its own beer. Food is also served but it's the beer that's the main attraction.

Listings

Banks Several major banks have branches on rue Nationale, and they're mostly open on Sat until lunchtime.

Books Le Furet du Nord, 11 place Général-de-Gaulle, is a huge bookshop on eight floors with a wide selection of books in English.

Car rental is mostly from the two train stations: Avis, Gare Flandres ☏ 03.20.06.35.55, Gare Europe ☏ 03.20.51.12.31; Europcar, Gare Flandres

☏ 03.20.06.10.04, Gare Europe ☏ 03.20.06.01.46; Hertz, Gare Flandres ☏ 03.28.36.28.70, Gare Europe ☏ 03.28.36.25.90.

Cinema Lille's two main cinemas, Le Majestic and UGC, are along the rue de Béthune; UGC at no. 40 shows blockbusters with usually at least one film in English, Le Majestic at nos. 54–56 is more arty and sometimes runs festivals.

Doctors SOS Médecins ☏ 03.20.29.91.91.

Festivals The major festival of the year, the Grande Braderie, takes place over the first weekend of Sept, when a big street parade and vast flea market fill the streets of the old town by day, and the evenings see a *moules-frites* frenzy in all the restaurants.

Laundry There are several outlets of Lavotec, the most central being at 57 rue des Postes and 137 rue Solférino, open daily 7am–9pm. There's another, unnamed laundry close to the youth hostel on the corner of rue Ovigneur and rue Monnoyer.

Markets The loud and colourful Wazemmes flea market, selling food and clothes, spills around place de la Nouvelle Aventure, to the west of central Lille. Main day Sun but also open Tues and Thurs (7am–2pm). A smaller food market takes place in Vieux Lille on place du Concert (Wed, Fri & Sun 7am–2pm).

Post office 8 place de la République (℡03.28.36.10.20; Mon–Fri 8am–7pm, Sat 8.30am–12.30pm) and 13–15 rue Nationale (℡03.28.38.18.40; Mon 10am–6.30pm, Tues–Fri 9am–6.30pm, Sat 10am–1pm & 2–4pm).

Taxi Gare ℡03.20.06.64.00; Taxi Union ℡03.20.06.06.06.

Roubaix

Just 15km northeast of Lille, right up against the Belgian border, **ROUBAIX** is a once-great Flemish textile city that fell into decline and is striving to rejuvenate itself. The city centre is not especially attractive: even the outlet shopping mall on its southern fringe is somehow dispiriting, its modest collection of brand names outclassed by Troyes' more impressive offering. Nevertheless Roubaix is worth a quick visit to see **La Piscine**, or the **Musée d'Art et d'Industrie** (Tues–Thurs 11am–6pm, Fri 11am–8pm, Sat & Sun 1–6pm; temporary and permanent collection €6; permanent collection only €3.50), halfway between the *gare SNCF* and the Grand'Place at 23 rue de l'Espérance. This fascinating museum opened its doors in 2001 in the improbable setting of one of France's most beautiful swimming pools, originally built in the early 1930s. Architect Paul Philippon's contemporary conversion retains various aspects of the baths – part of the pool, the shower-cubicles, the changing-rooms and the bathhouses – and uses each part of the complex to display a splendid collection of mostly nineteenth- and early twentieth-century sculpture and painting, plus *haute couture* clothing, textiles and photographs of the pool in its heyday.

A short way southeast of central Roubaix, at 25 rue de la Prudence, is the **Manufacture des Flandres**, a working tapestry factory, where you'll find the **Musée du Jacquard** (Tues–Sun 1.30–6pm; €6). One-hour guided tours take you round an interesting collection of looms and other machinery, plus tapestries from the Middle Ages to the present day, and end up in a boutique selling the factory's wares. The quickest way to Roubaix is by **métro** from Lille, which stops at Roubaix Gare/Jean-Baptiste-Lebas, Grand'Place and Eurotéléport, the last of which, just east of Grand'Place, is also the terminus of the tram from Lille's Eurostar station.

Douai and around

Right at the heart of mining country, 40km south of Lille, and badly damaged in both world wars, **DOUAI** is an unpretentious, surprisingly attractive town, its handsome streets of eighteenth-century houses cut through by both the River Scarpe and a canal. Once a haven for English Catholics fleeing Protestant oppression in Tudor England, Douai later became the seat of Flemish local government under Louis XIV, an aristocratic past evoked in the novels of Balzac.

The Town

Most of what's worth seeing in Douai is west of the central **place d'Armes**, from which rue de la Mairie leads to the splendid fifteenth-century Gothic **Hôtel de Ville** (guided tours: July & Aug daily 10am, 11am & hourly 2–6pm; Sept–June Mon 3pm, 4pm & 5pm Tues–Sun 11am, 3pm, 4pm & 5pm; €3.50), topped by a belfry of fairy-tale fabulousness, popularized by Victor Hugo and renowned for its carillon of 62 bells – the largest single collection in Europe. There are concerts every Saturday at 11am.

One block north of the town hall, on **rue Bellegambe**, is an outrageous Art Nouveau facade fronting a very ordinary children's store. At the end of the street, rising above the old town, is the **church of St-Pierre**, its Baroque nave bracketed by a stone west tower begun in 1513 but not finished until 1690, and by a dumpy round tower and dome at the opposite end. The church contains – among other treasures – a spectacular carved Baroque organ case. With the exception of the 1970s extension to the old Flemish Parliament, the riverfront west of the town hall is pleasant to wander along; across the river to the west are quiet streets of handsome two-storey houses. Here, at 130 rue des Chartreux, the **Ancienne Chartreuse** has been converted into a wonderful **museum** (daily except Tues: 10am–noon & 2–6pm; €3; free first Sun of the month), with a fine collection of paintings by Flemish, Dutch and French masters, including Van Dyck, Jordaens, Rubens and Douai's own Jean Bellegambe. The adjacent chapel displays an array of sculptures including a poignant *Enfant prodige* by Rodin.

Practicalities

The **gare SNCF** is a five–minute walk from the centre – from the station head straight along avenue G. Clémenceau, cross place Carnot and turn left down rue Saint Jacques, the main shopping street, to reach place d'Armes. The **tourist office** (April–Sept Mon–Sat 10am–1pm & 2–6.30pm, Sun 3–6pm; Oct–March Mon–Sat 10am–12.30pm & 2–6.30pm; ☎03.27.88.26.79, ⓦwww.ville-douai .fr) is at no. 70.

For **accommodation** there's the classy *La Terrasse* at 36 terrasse St-Pierre (☎03.27.88.70.04, ⓦwww.laterrasse.fr; ❺), to one side of the church of St-Pierre; alternatively, try the *Ibis* (☎03.27.98.31.64, ⓦwww.ibishotel.com; ❸) on pretty place St Amé, housed in a historic mansion. **Eating** in Douai tends towards the cheap and informal – kebabs, crêpes, pizza – but the restaurant at *La Terrasse* is an exception, with a superb €27 menu including wine; also worth trying is *Au Turbotin* (☎03.27.87.04.16, menus from €24), west of the river at 9 rue de la Massue. Douai's best **drinking** is in the relaxed bars fringing place Saint Amé; *Taverne les Grès* is atmospheric, with occasional live bands.

Lewarde

A visit to the colliery at **LEWARDE**, 7km east of Douai, is a must for admirers of Zola's *Germinal*. Bus #1 from Douai (direction Aniche) heads east across flat, featureless beet fields, down a road lined with dour brick dwellings and intersected by streets named after Pablo Neruda, Jean-Jacques Rousseau, Georges Brassens and other luminaries of the Left. This is the traditional heart of France's coal-mining country, though you'll look in vain for winding towers or slag heaps hereabouts, demolition and landscaping having removed almost all visible traces.

The bus drops you at the main square, leaving a fifteen-minute walk down the D132 towards Erchin to get to the colliery. **The Centre Historique Minier** (guided tours: March–Oct daily 9am–5.30pm; Nov–Feb Mon–Sat 1–5pm, Sun 10am–5pm; 2hr; €10.90) is on the left in the old Fosse Delloye. Visitors can tour the exhibition and surface installations with an English-language audioguide, but the tours of the mine itself are guided by retired miners, many of whom are not French, but Polish, Italian or North African. These pits were deep and hot, with steeply inclined narrow seams that forced the miners to work on slopes of 55 degrees and more, just as Étienne and the Maheu family do in Zola's story. They also had a poor safety record; the worst disaster occurred at Courrières in 1906, when 1100 men were killed. Incredibly, although the owners made little effort to search for survivors, thirteen men emerged after twenty days without food, water or light. The first person they met thought that they were ghosts and fainted in fright. More incredible still, a fourteenth man surfaced alone four days later.

Cambrai and around

Despite the tank battle of November 1917 (see box below) and the fact that the heavily defended Hindenburg Line ran through the town centre for most of World War I, **CAMBRAI** has kept enough of its character to make a fleeting visit worthwhile, though it is less attractive than either Douai, 27km to the north, or Arras to the northwest.

The huge, cobbled main square, **place Aristide-Briand**, is dominated by the Neoclassical Hôtel de Ville, and still suggests the town's former wealth, which was based on textiles and agriculture. Cambrai's chief ecclesiastical treasure is the **Church of St-Géry**, off rue St-Aubert west of the main square, worth a visit for a celebrated *Mise au Tombeau* by Rubens. The appealingly presented **Musée de Cambrai** (Wed–Sun 10am–noon & 2–6pm; €3.10; free entry first weekend of the month) at 15 rue de l'Épée, a short way south of the town square, is also worthwhile. Paintings by Velázquez, Utrillo and Ingres feature prominently alongside works by various Flemish old masters, plus great twentieth-century artists like Zadkine and Van Dongen. Don't turn down the audio-guided tour and be sure to check out out the archeological display in the basement, where you can see some fascinating exhibits including elegant statues rescued from Cambrai's cathedral, decimated after the Revolution. Look out for the *gourde eucharistique de Concevreux*, an amazingly well-preserved sixth-century bronze hipflask.

Cambrai 1917

At dawn on November 20, 1917, the first full-scale **tank battle** in history began at Cambrai, when over four hundred British tanks poured over the Hindenburg Line. In just 24 hours, the Royal Tank Corps and British Third Army made the biggest advance by either side since the trenches were dug in 1914. A fortnight later, however, casualties had reached 50,000, and the armies were back where they'd started.

Although the tanks were ahead of their time, they still relied on cavalry and plodding infantry as back-up. The tanks were primitive, operated by a crew of eight who endured almost intolerable conditions – with no ventilation, the temperature inside could reach 48°C. The steering alone required three men, each on separate gearboxes, communicating by hand signals through the mechanical din. Maximum speed (6kph) dropped to barely 1kph over rough terrain, and refuelling was necessary every 55km. Of the 179 tanks lost at Cambrai, few were destroyed by the enemy; most broke down and were abandoned by their crews.

Cambrai's **tourist office** is housed in the Maison Espagnole on the corner of avenue de la Victoire at 48 rue de Noyon (Mon–Sat 9.30am–12.30pm & 2–6pm, Sun 2.30–5.30pm; ☎03.27.78.36.15, ⓦwww.tourisme-cambrai.fr). Central **accommodation** includes *Le Mouton Blanc*, 33 rue d'Alsace-Lorraine (☎03.27.81.30.16, ⓦwww.mouton-blanc.com; ❹), convenient, moderately priced and close to the station, with a posh **restaurant** inside (from €23.50; closed Sun evening & Mon, plus last week of July & 1st week Aug), and the very pleasant *Hotel de France* nearby at 37 rue de Lille (☎03.27.81.38.80, ⓕ03.27.78.13.88; ❹), which also has a good restaurant. The nearest **campsite** is *Les Colombes* at Aubencheul-au-Bac (April–Oct; ☎03.27.89.25.90), 10km away off the N43 to Douai.

Le Cateau-Cambrésis

Twenty-two kilometres east of Cambrai along an old Roman road, the small town of **LE CATEAU-CAMBRÉSIS** is the birthplace of Henri Matisse (1869–1954), and as a gift to his home town, the artist bequeathed it a collection of his works. Some of them are displayed in the **Musée Matisse** (daily except Tues 10am–6pm; €4.50, free first Sun of month), housed in Palais Fénelon in the centre of town. Although no major works are displayed, this is the third-largest Matisse collection in France, and the paintings here are no less attractive and interesting than the better-known ones exhibited elsewhere. The collection includes several studies for the chapel in Vence, plus a whole series of his characteristically simple pen-and-ink sketches. Also worth a look is the work of local Cubist Auguste Herbin, particularly his psychedelic upright piano. For somewhere to **stay** and **eat** there's the simple but comfortable *Hostellerie du Marché* at 9 rue Landrecies (☎03.27.84.09.32, ⓦwww.hostelleriedumarche.com; ❸; menus €18.50).

Arras, Albert and the Somme battlefields

Some of the fiercest and most futile battles of World War I took place around **Arras** and **Albert**. The beautiful town of Arras, easily accessible from Paris and Lille by TGV, is the best base for exploring the battlefields. Nearby to the north, at **Vimy Ridge**, Canadians fell in their thousands, while at Notre-Dame de Lorette, the French suffered the same fate; the battlefields and cemeteries of the Somme lie to the south, around **Albert** and **Péronne**.

Arras

ARRAS, with its fine old centre, is one of the prettiest towns in northern France. It was renowned for its tapestries in the Middle Ages, giving its name to the hangings behind which Shakespeare's Polonius was killed by Hamlet. The town later fell under Spanish control, and many of its citizens today claim that Spanish blood runs in their veins. Only in 1640 was Arras returned to French control, with the help of Cyrano de Bergerac. During World War I, the British dug tunnels under the town to try to surprise the Germans to the northeast, while the Germans bombarded the town.

Arrival, information and accommodation

From the **gare SNCF** it's a ten–minute walk up rue Gambetta then traffic-free rue Ronville and its extension, to place des Héros and the **tourist office**, located in the Hôtel de Ville (April to mid-Sept Mon–Sat 9am–6.30pm, Sun 10am–1pm & 2.30–6.30pm; mid-Sept to March Mon 10am–noon & 2–6pm, Tues–Sat 9am–noon & 2–6pm, Sun 10am–12.30pm & 2.30–6.30pm; ☎03.21.51.26.95, Ⓦwww.ot-arras.fr); they have details of transport and tours of local battlefields (see "Vimy Ridge and around", p.226). To reach the Vimy memorial and the cemeteries around Neuville–St–Vlaast, you can also rent a car from Hertz, boulevard Carnot (☎03.21.23.11.14).

There are two good **hotels** on the beautiful central squares: the *Diamant*, 5 place des Héros (☎03.21.71.23.23, Ⓦwww.arras-hotel-diamant.com; ❹), a comfortable, reliable two-star; and *Ostel Les Trois Luppars*, 49 Grand'Place (☎03.21.60.02.03, Ⓦwww.ostel-les-3luppars.com; ❹), a friendly place with modern facilities in a characterful old building. For a more luxurious night, go to the *Univers*, a beautiful former monastery around a courtyard at 3 place de la Croix-Rouge, near the Abbaye St-Vaast (☎03.21.71.34.01, Ⓦwww .hotel-univers-arras.com; ❺; restaurant menu €47). Facing the train station there are more hotels in nearly every price range.

The Town

Reconstruction after the war was careful and stylish, and two grand arcaded Flemish- and Dutch-style squares in the centre – **Grand'Place** and the smaller **Place des Héros** – preserve their historic, harmonious character, though both resemble large car parks today. On every side are restored seventeenth- and eighteenth-century mansions and, on place des Héros, there's a grandly ornate **Hôtel de Ville**, its entrance hall housing a photographic display documenting its wartime destruction and subsequent reconstruction.

Also inside the town hall is the entrance to the **belfry** viewing platform, 150m high – to which a lift takes you up almost all the way (€2.70) – and **les souterrains** (or *les boves*) – cold, dark passageways and spacious vaults tunnelled since the Middle Ages, and completed by the British during World War I, beneath the centre of the city (frequent bilingual guided tours – ask for times in the tourist office; €4.70). Once down, you're escorted on a forty-minute tour and given an interesting survey of local history. The rooms – many of which have fine, tiled floors and lovely pillars and stairways – were used as a British barracks and hospital. Pictures from this period are on display, as is a bilingual newspaper published for the soldiers. Arras boasts a further subterranean attraction in the newly-opened **Carrière Wellington**, just off the Bapaume road southeast of the centre at rue Delétoile (daily 10am–12.30pm & 1.30–6pm; €6.50). It's a network of medieval chalk quarries adapted by New Zealand engineers to create secret underground quarters for the 24,000 allied troops awaiting the start of the Battle of Arras, which was conceived in 1916 as a diversionary attack in preparation for the Chemin des Dames assaults. The troops emerged to mount their surprise attack on 9 April 1917; the visit is accompanied but there are also individual audioguides, and there's a film on the battle at the end of the tour.

Next to its enormous cathedral is Arras's other main above-ground sight, the **Benedictine Abbaye St-Vaast**, a grey-stone classical building – still pockmarked by wartime shrapnel – erected in the eighteenth century by Cardinal Rohen. The abbey now houses the **Musée des Beaux–Arts**, with its entrance at 22 rue Paul-Donnier (daily except Tues 9.30am–noon & 2–5.30pm; €4), which contains a motley collection of paintings, including a couple of Jordaens and Brueghels, plus fragments of sculpture and local porcelain. Only one of the tapestries or *arras* that made the town famous in medieval times survived the wartime bombardments. Figuring among the highlights are a pair of delicately sculpted thirteenth-century angels, the *Anges de Saudemont*, and a room on the first floor filled with vivid seventeenth-century paintings by Philippe de Champaigne and his contemporaries, including his own *Présentation de la Vierge au Temple*.

Thirty minutes away by foot on the mournful south-western edge of town, along boulevard Général-de-Gaulle from the Vauban barracks (which although a citadelle was monikered "*la belle inutile*" because it served no purpose in protecting the city, even when it was built in 1668), is a **war cemetery** and memorial by the British architect Sir Edwin Lutyens. It's a movingly elegiac, classical colonnade of pristine brick and stone, commemorating 35,928 missing soldiers, their names inscribed on the walls. Around the back of the barracks, alongside an overgrown moat, is the **Mémorial des Fusillés**, a stark wall accessed via the avenue of the same name; its plaques commemorate two hundred Resistance fighters shot by firing squad in World War II – many of them of Polish descent, nearly all of them miners, and most of them Communists.

On a lighter note, on the last Sunday of August the town transforms itself into an open-air bistro for **La Fête de l'Andouillette**, with parades, colourful costumes and tasting of the sausage itself.

Eating

Restaurants worth trying include *La Rapière*, 44 Grand'Place (☎03.21.55.09.92), with excellent regional food and menus from €19; and, for a splurge, the gourmet *La Faisanderie*, across the square at no. 45 (☎03.21.48.20.76; from €39). Nearer the station at 26 boulevard de Strasbourg is an attractive, old-fashioned brasserie, *La Coupole*, where you'll find locals and tourists eating oysters and other fresh seafood, as well as traditional brasserie dishes (☎03.21.71.88.44; €34 menu; closed Sun).

There's a good *fromagerie*, on the corner of place des Héros and rue de la Taillerie. Saturdays are the best day for food and wine, when the squares are taken up with a morning **market**.

Vimy Ridge and around

Eight kilometres north of Arras on the D49, **Vimy Ridge**, or Hill 145, was the scene of some of the worst trench warfare of World War I: almost two full years of battle, culminating in its capture by the Canadian Corps in April 1917. It's a vast site, given in perpetuity to the Canadian people out of respect for their sacrifices, and the churned land has been preserved, in part, as it was during the conflict. You really need your own transport to get there as the Arras–Lens bus will get you no closer than the N17, which is still a long walk from the ridge (for details contact the tourist office in Arras). Alternatively, book a private taxi tour with Mr Ishak (☎06.16.20.34.38), whose father and grandfather fought with the Canadian forces. It is well worth the journey – of all the battlefields, it is perhaps easiest here to gain an impression of the lay of the land, and of how it may actually have felt to be part of a World War I battle.

There's a **visitor centre** (daily: April–Oct 10am–6pm; Nov–March 9am–5pm; ☎03.21.50.68.68; free) supervised by friendly, bilingual Canadian students, who run free guided **tours** (May–Nov: call to pre-book, as tours are heavily over-subscribed; office is only open Mon–Fri). Tours are available of the "subway", the Canadian term for the series of interlinking underground tunnels used as secret passageways and to hoard ammunition and equipment, or of the cemeteries and battlefields. The visitor centre's exhibition illustrates the well-planned Canadian attack and its importance for the Canadians. This was the first time that they were recognized as fighting separarately from the British, thus adding to their growing sense of nationhood.

▲ Canadian Memorial, Vimy Ridge

Near the information centre, long worms of neat, sanitized **trenches** meander over the now grassy ground, still heavily pitted by shell bursts beneath the planted pines. Beneath the ground lie countless rounds of unexploded ammunition – visitors are warned not to stray from the paths.

On the brow of the ridge to the north, overlooking the slag-heap-dotted plain of Artois, a great white **monument** reaches for the heavens, inscribed with the names of 11,285 Canadians and Newfoundlanders whose bodies were never found. It must have been an unenviable task to design a fitting memorial to such slaughter, but this one, aided by its setting, succeeds with great drama. It has recently been extensively restored. Back from the ridge lies a memorial to the **Moroccan Division** who also fought at Vimy, and in the woods behind, on the headstones of another exquisitely maintained **cemetery**, you can read the names of half the counties of rural England.

La Targette, Neuville-St-Vaast and Notre-Dame de Lorette

At the crossroads (D937/D49) of **LA TARGETTE**, 8km north of Arras, the **Musée de la Targette** (irregular hours: officially 9am–8pm daily; €4) contains an interesting collection of World War I and II artefacts. It's the private collection of one David Bardiaux, inspired by his grandfather, a veteran of Verdun. Its appeal lies in the precision with which the mannequins of British, French, Canadian and German soldiers are dressed and equipped, down to their sweet and tobacco tins and such rarities as a 1915 British cap with earflaps – very comfortable for the troops but withdrawn because the top brass thought it made their men look like yokels. All the pieces exhibited have been under fire; some have stitched-up tears of old wounds.

North and south of La Targette along the D937 are several **cemeteries**. There's a small British one, a huge French one, and south of the crossroads an equally vast and moving German one, containing the remains of 44,833 Germans, four to a cross or singly under a Star of David. To the north a Polish memorial – among the Poles who died in action here was the sculptor Henri Gaudier-Brzeska, in 1915 – and a Czech cemetery face each other across the D937 between La Targette and Souchez.

On a bleak hill a few kilometres further north in the village of Ablain-Nazaire (and 5km north of La Targette) is the church of **Notre–Dame de Lorette**, scene of a costly French offensive in May 1915. The original church was blasted to bits during the war – its ruins can be seen in the village below the cemetery; afterwards a Neo-Byzantine church was built, grey and dour outside but rich and bejewelled within. It stands at the centre of a vast graveyard with over 20,000 crosses laid out in pairs, back to back, each separated by a cluster of roses. There are 20,000 more buried in the ossuary, and there's a small **Musée Vivant 1914–1918** (daily 9am–8pm; €5) behind the church, displaying photographs, uniforms and other paraphernalia.

Albert and around

The church at **ALBERT**, 40km south of Arras and 30km northeast of Amiens, was one of the minor landmarks of World War I. Its tall tower was hit by German bombing early on in the campaign, leaving the statue of the Madonna on top leaning at a precarious angle. The British, entrenched over three years in the region, came to know it as the "Leaning Virgin". Superstition had it that when she fell the war would end, a myth inspiring frequent pot shots by disgruntled troops. Before visiting the battle sites and war cemeteries along as the Circuit de Souvenir (see opposite), you might want to stop in at the **Musée "Somme 1916"** (daily: Feb–May & Oct to mid–Dec 9am–noon & 2–6pm; June–Sept 9am–6pm; €5), an underground museum which has re-enactments of fifteen different scenes from life in the trenches of the Somme in 1916. The mannequins look slightly too jolly and eager but it does go some way to bringing the props to life. The final section recreates the actual battle, complete with flashing lights and the sound of exploding shells.

The Battle of the Somme

On July 1, 1916, the British and French launched the **Battle of the Somme** to relieve pressure on the French army defending Verdun. The front ran roughly northwest–southeast, 6km east of Albert across the valley of the Ancre and over the almost treeless high ground north of the Somme – huge hedgeless fields now. The windy terrain had no intrinsic value, nor was there any long-term strategic objective – the region around Albert was the battle-site simply because it was where the two Allied armies met.

There were 57,000 British casualties on the first day alone, approximately 20,000 of them dead, making it the costliest defeat the British army has ever suffered. **Sir Douglas Haig** is the usual scapegoat, yet he was only following the military thinking of the day, which is where the real problem lay. As historian A.J.P. Taylor put it, "Defence was mechanized: attack was not." Machine guns were efficient, barbed wire effective, and, most important of all, the rail lines could move defensive reserves far faster than the attacking army could march. The often ineffective heavy bombardment that presaged an advance only made matters worse, warning the enemy of an offensive and churning the trenches into a giant muddy quagmire.

Despite the bloody disaster of the first day, the battle wore on until bad weather in November made further attacks impossible. The cost of this futile struggle was roughly 415,000 British, 195,000 French and 600,000 German casualties.

As you arrive (trains from Amiens or Arras), the town's "new" church tower, capped by an equally improbably posed statue, is the first thing that catches your eye. The **tourist office** is close by at 9 rue Gambetta (April–Sept Mon–Fri 9am–12.30pm & 1.30–6.30pm, Sat 9am–noon & 2–6.30pm, Sun 10am–12.30pm; Oct–March Mon–Sat 10am–12.30pm & 3–5pm; ⓣ03.22.75.16.42). Of the town's **hotels**, *La Paix*, a friendly establishment with a decent restaurant, at 43 rue Victor-Hugo (ⓣ03.22.75.01.64, ⓕ03.22.75.44.17; ❸; menus from €16.50), is the best choice.

The Circuit de Souvenir

Was it for this the clay grew tall?
O what made fatuous sunbeams toil
To break earth's sleep at all?

Wilfred Owen, *Futility*

The **Circuit de Souvenir** conducts you from graveyard to mine crater, trench to memorial. There's little to show the scale of the destruction that happened here less than a century ago. Nor do you get much sense of battle tactics. But you will find that, no matter what the level of your interest in the Great War, you have embarked on a sort of pilgrimage, as each successive step becomes more harrowing.

The **cemeteries** are deeply moving – beautiful, with the grass perfectly mown and flowers at the foot of every gravestone. There are tens of thousands of them, all identical, with a man's name, if it's known (nearly half the British dead have never been found), his rank and regiment and, often, a personal message chosen by the bereaved family. In the lanes between Albert and Bapaume you'll see cemeteries everywhere: at the angle of copses, halfway across a field, in the middle of a wood.

The circuit can be explored by either car or bicycle. Both Albert to the west and Péronne to the southeast (see p.230) make good starting points, their tourist offices and museums offering free **maps** of the circuit. The route is marked (somewhat intermittently) by arrows and poppy symbols, with Commonwealth graves also indicated in English. It would be difficult to see all four hundred Commonwealth cemeteries in the area, though visiting one or two small ones can be rewarding. What follows is a selection of some of the better-known sites.

The Circuit du Souvenir heads east from Albert to the giant mine crater of **Lochnagar** at La Boisselle before swinging north to **BEAUMONT-HAMEL**, where, pipes playing, the 51st Highland Division walked abreast to their deaths. Here, on the hill where most of them died, a series of trenches, now grassed over and eroding, is preserved – you'll get a good overview of the slaughter at the visitor centre at the **Newfoundland Memorial** (daily 10am–6pm), a few-minutes' walk to the south; of 800 Newfoundlanders who took part in the push, just 86 returned. Across the river, near the village of **THIEPVAL**, the 5000 Ulstermen who died in the Battle of the Somme are commemorated by the **Ulster Memorial**, a replica of Helen's Tower at Clandeboyne near Belfast (café and exhibition open May–Sept Tues–Sun 10am–6pm; March–April & Oct–Nov Tues–Sun 10am–5pm; closed Dec–Feb). Probably the most famous of Edwin Lutyens' many memorials is also at Thiepval: the colossal **Memorial to the Missing**, inscribed with the names of the 73,367 British troops whose bodies were never recovered at the Somme, is visible for miles around. Here, too, there's an informative **visitor centre** (daily 10am–6pm), with a poignant photo wall of some of the missing, an exhibition on the Somme Offensive and short films in English on related themes.

Delville Wood, known as "**Devil's Wood**", lies some 10km to the east at **LONGUEVAL**. Here, thousands of **South Africans** lost their lives, and a memorial to the dead from both world wars has been erected, as well as a

museum (daily except Mon: April–Oct 10am–5.30pm; Nov & March 10am–3.45pm) relating not just the battle in France but also the longest march of the war, undertaken thousands of kilometres away, when South African troops walked 800km to drive the Germans out of East Africa (now Tanzania). The display is brought up to date with a short section documenting the armed struggle against apartheid.

The most informative of the museums is at **PÉRONNE**, on the River Somme some 25km east of Albert – the **Historial de la Grande Guerre** (mid-Jan to mid-Dec 10am–6pm; €7.50). Newsreel and film footage, commemorative plates and Otto Dix drawings, artificial limbs and displays of hardware together provide a broad, modern view of the catastrophe, including the political and cultural tensions that led to war.

There's a **TGV** station about 15km from Péronne – the **Gare Haute Picardie** – which is thirty minutes from the Eurostar stop at Lille-Europe; for a taxi to or from the station, call Confort Taxi (☎03.22.84.15.83) or Taxi Nico (☎03.22.84.59.22). The **tourist office** is at place Andé Audinot, opposite the museum (July–Aug Mon–Sat 9am–noon & 2–6.30pm, Sun 10am–noon & 2–5pm; April–June & Sept Mon–Sat 10am–noon & 2–6.30pm; Oct–March Mon–Sat 10am–noon & 2–5pm; May closed Sun; ☎03.22.84.42.38, ⓦwww.ville -peronne.fr). **Accommodation** includes the pricey *Saint Claude*, on the main square at 42 place Louis Daubré (☎03.22.79.49.49, ⓦwww.hotel-saintclaude .com; ❻; restaurant from €15), or the better value *Campanile* (☎03.22.84.22.22, ⓦwww.campanile.fr; ❸), just out of town on the N17 to Roye and Paris.

To the southwest of the main circuit near **VILLERS-BRETONNEUX**, 18km from Albert near the River Somme, stands another fine Lutyens memorial. As at Vimy, the landscaping of the **Australian Memorial** here is dramatic – for the full effect, climb up to the viewing platform of the stark white central tower. The monument was one of the last to be inaugurated, in July 1938, when the prospects for peace were again looking bleak, and it was damaged during fighting not long afterwards – the bullet holes are still visible. There's a small **Franco–Australian Museum** (Tues–Sat 10am–12.30pm & 2–6pm, also first and third Sun afternoon of the month; €4) on the first floor of the school in the village, just to the south of the memorial.

Aisne and Oise

To the southeast of the Somme, away from the coast and the main Paris through-routes, the often rainwashed and dull province of Picardy becomes considerably more inviting. In the *départements* of **Aisne** and **Oise**, where the region merges with neighbouring Champagne, there are some real attractions amid the lush wooded hills. **Laon**, **Soissons** and **Noyon** all have handsome Gothic cathedrals, while at **Compiègne**, Napoleon Bonaparte and Napoléon III enjoyed the luxury of a magnificent château. The most rewarding overnight stop is off the beaten track in the tiny fortified town of **Coucy-le-Château-Auffrique**, in the forest and on a hill between Soissons and Laon. **Transport** is good, too, with a network of bus connections from Amiens and good train links with Paris.

Laon

Looking out over the plains of Champagne and Picardy from the spine of a high narrow ridge, still protected by its gated medieval walls, **LAON** (pronounced "Lon") is one of the highlights of the region. Dominating the town, and visible for miles around, are the five great towers of one of the earliest and finest Gothic cathedrals in the country. Of all the cathedral towns in the Aisne, Laon is the one to head for.

Arrival, information and accommodation

Arriving by train or road, you'll find yourself in the dreary lower town, or **ville basse**. To get to the upper town – **ville haute** – without your own transport, you can make the stiff climb up the steps at the end of avenue Carnot, or take the **Poma 2000** (Mon–Sat 7am–8pm every 5 min; one-day return ticket €1), a fully automated, rubber-tyred cable railway; you board next to the train station and alight by the town hall (Terminus "Hôtel de Ville") on place Général-Leclerc; from there a left turn down rue Sérurier brings you nose to nose with the cathedral.

The **tourist office** (April–Sept daily 9.30am–1pm & 2–6.30pm; Oct–March Mon–Sat 9.30am–12.30pm & 2–5.30pm, Sun noon–5pm; ☎03.23.20.28.62, ⓦ www.tourisme-paysdelaon.com) is right by the western end of the cathedral, housed in the impressive Gothic Hôtel-Dieu, built in 1209; ask for information about local *gîtes* and guesthouses. If you need **accommodation** in the *ville basse* (if you arrive too late to take the Poma), try *HôtelWelcome* (☎03.23.23.06.11, Ⓔels hotel-welcome.laon@orange.fr; ❶), at 12 avenue Carnot, a few-minutes' walk from the *gare SNCF*. Otherwise, in the *ville haute*, try the charming, characterful *Les Chevaliers*, at 3–5 rue Sérurier, near the Poma stop (☎03.23.27.17.50, Ⓔhotelchevaliers@aol.com; ❹), or the three-star *Hôtel de la Bannière de France*, 11 rue Franklin-Roosevelt (☎03.23.23.21.44, ⓦwww .hoteldelabannieredefrance.com; ❺; decent traditional restaurant from €18). *La Chênaie* (☎03.23.20.25.56; May–Sept), Laon's **campsite**, is on allée de la Chênaie, on the northwest side of town.

The Town

Laon really only has one attraction, its magnificent **Cathédrale Notre-Dame** (daily 9am–7pm; guided tours at 3pm or 4pm; frequency varies – enquire at tourist office). Built in the second half of the twelfth century, the cathedral was a trendsetter in its day, elements of its design – the gabled porches, the imposing towers and the gallery of arcades above the west front – being repeated at Chartres, Reims and Notre-Dame in Paris. When wrapped in thick mist, the towers seem otherworldly. The creatures craning from the uppermost ledges, looking like reckless mountain goats borrowed from a medieval bestiary, are reputed to have been carved in memory of the valiant horned steers who lugged the cathedral's masonry up from the plains below. Inside, the effects are no less dramatic – the high white nave is lit by the dense ruby, sapphire and emerald tones of the stained glass, which at close range reveals the appealing scratchy, smoky quality of medieval glass.

Crowded in the cathedral's lee is a quiet, rather sad jumble of grey stone streets; for all its beauty, Laon is no chic weekenders' haunt and even the lunchtime bustle along rue Châtelaine can't disguise the number of vacant commercial premises. South of the cathedral on rue Ermant is the crumbly little twelfth-century octagonal **Chapelle des Templiers** – the Knights Templar – set in a secluded garden. Next door is the **Musée de l'Art et de l'Archéologie**,

32 rue Georges-Ermant (June–Sept Tues–Sun 11am–6pm; Oct–May Tues–Sun 2–6pm; €3.50), which contains a rather stuffy collection of classical antiquities, albeit with some fine Grecian ceramics among them, and a jumble of furniture and paintings, including an acclaimed seventeenth-century work, *Le Concert*, by local lad Mathieu Le Nain. The rest of the *ville haute*, which rambles along the ridge to the west of the cathedral into the Le Bourg quarter around the early Gothic church of St-Martin, is enjoyable to wander round, with sweeping views north from the **ramparts**.

Eating, drinking and entertainment

Eating and drinking in Laon is inexpensive, if not particularly fancy, provided a few of the more obviously tourist-oriented spots are avoided. *Crêperie L'Agora*, on place du Marché opposite the cathedral, is a cheap Breton place (open until 11pm; closed Mon & Wed eves; menu €11); at *Le Chant des Voyelles*, midway along rue Châtelaine, you can tuck into omelettes for less than €7 or more substantial *plats du jour* for around €8. Even fancy **restaurants** in Laon tend to be good value: Michelin-listed *La Petite Auberge*, at 45 boulevard Pierre-Brossolette in the *ville basse* near the station, falls into this category, serving a five-course *menu gourmand* using the freshest ingredients for a remarkable €36 (T03.23.23.02.38, booking recommended; closed Sun and Mon evening). They also own the adjacent bistro, which offers simpler fare. There's a basic selection of snack outlets, boulangeries and *traiteurs* along pedestrianized rue Châtelaine, in the *ville haute*.

There's usually something going on at the **Maison des Arts de Laon** (MAL), based in a theatre on the place Aubry to the north of the cathedral – including a concentration of events during Les Médiévales de Laon in May and big-name classical concerts during the Festival de Laon in October, either in the cathedral or MAL venues (details from the tourist office).

Soissons and around

Half an hour by train, or 30km down the N2, southwest of Laon, **SOISSONS** can lay claim to a long and highly strategic history. Before the Romans arrived it was already a town, and in 486 AD the last Roman ruler, Syagrius, suffered a decisive defeat here at the hands of Clovis the Frank, making Soissons one of the first real centres of the Frankish kingdom. Napoleon, too, considered it a crucial military base, a judgement borne out in the twentieth century by extensive war damage.

The town boasts the fine, if shell-pocked and battered, **Cathédrale St Gervais-St Protais** – thirteenth century for the most part with majestic glass and vaulting – at the west end of the oversized main square, place F.–Marquigny. More impressive still is the ruined **Abbaye de St-Jean-des-Vignes**, to the south of place Marquigny down rue St-Martin and then right down avenue Thiers. The gaping west front of the tremendous Gothic abbey rises sheer and grand, impervious to the empty space behind it – you get a superb view of it from the peaceful abbey precincts, but the ruin itself is in crumbly condition and fenced off. The rest of the complex, save for remnants of a **cloister** and **refectory** (free to visit), was dismantled in 1804. North of place Marquigny on the river is the town's impressive eighteenth-century **Hôtel de Ville**.

Practicalities

Soissons is relatively compact. From the **gare SNCF** (good services to Laon and Paris) the main square is a fifteen-minute walk along avenue du Général-de-Gaulle, which becomes rue St-Martin. The **gare routière** is closer to the centre by the river on avenue de l'Aisne; buses leave for Compiègne early in the morning, at lunchtime and at the end of the afternoon during school term times, but otherwise less frequently. The **tourist office** is on place F-Marquigny near the cathedral (April–Sept daily 9.30am–7pm; Oct–March Mon–Sat 9.30am–5.30pm; ☎03.23.53.17.37, ⓦwww.tourisme-soissons.fr).

The town is more of a place to stop en route than to **stay** but if you're keen to explore the nearby forest or are just stuck, try the reasonably priced two–star hotel *Terminus* above a bar by the station at 56 avenue du Général-de-Gaulle (☎03.23.53.33.59; ❸), or the **campsite** (☎03.23.74.52.69), north of the centre on avenue du Mail. An excellent place for *galettes* is *La Galetière* (closed Sun & Mon) at 1 rue du Beffroi by the cathedral: there's a good Tunisian **restaurant**, the *Sidi Bou*, at 4 rue de la Bannière down towards the river and a pretty **salon de thé**, l'Arthé, nearby.

Coucy-le-Château-Auffrique

About 30km west of Laon, and just over 15km north of Soissons, in hilly countryside on the far side of the forest of St-Gobain, lie the straggling ruins of one of the greatest castles of the Middle Ages, **Coucy-le-Château** (daily: May to early Sept 10am–1pm & 2–6.30pm; early Sept to April 10am–1pm & 2–5.30pm; €5). The castle's walls still stand, and encircle the attractive village of **COUCY-LE-CHÂTEAU-AUFFRIQUE**. In the past this was a seat of great power and the influence of its lords, the Sires de Coucy, rivalled and often even exceeded that of the king – "King I am not, neither Prince, Duke nor Count. I am the Sire of Coucy" was Enguerrand III's proud boast. The retreating Germans capped the destruction of World War I battles by blowing up the castle's keep as they left in 1917, but enough remains, crowning a wooded spur, to be extremely evocative.

Enter the village through one of three original gates, squeezed between powerful, round flanking towers – there's a footpath around the outside which is open even when the castle is closed. A small museum, the **Tour de Coucy Musée Panorama** (no fixed hours: ask at tourist office to gain entry; free) at the **Porte de Soissons** on the south side of the walled part of town, has a display of photographs showing how it looked pre-1917, which can be compared with today's remains from the vantage point of the roof.

Practicalities

It's hard to get to Coucy-le-Château without a car, though several Laon–Soissons trains stop at Chauny, from where there are around four buses per day; there is a similarly infrequent bus from Soissons. The **tourist office** is in the central square (Mon–Fri 9am–6pm, Sat & Sun 2–6pm; ☎03.23.52.44.55), just north of the Porte de Soissons. There are lots of medieval spectacles offered in this magical town, so it's worth checking ⓦwww.coucy.com in advance of your visit to book tickets.

Staying the night here, especially if you have children, is something special: try the *Hôtel Le Belle Vue* within the walls, although the bedrooms have seen better days (☎03.23.52.69.70, ⓦwww.hotel-bellevue-coucy.com; ❷; closed Fri & Sat in Dec). Its restaurant specializes in Picardy cuisine (menus from €19), and serves special "medieval" meals (€18) on certain summer nights, when medieval re-enactments are held across the city.

Compiègne and around

Thirty-eight kilometres west of Soissons lies **COMPIÈGNE**, whose reputation
as a tourist centre rests on the presence of a vast royal palace, built at the edge
of the Forêt de Compiègne in order that generations of French kings could play
at "being peasants", in Louis XIV's words. It's also worth a visit to see the sites
associated with the two world wars and as a good base for walks in the
surrounding forest.

Arrival, information and accommodation

The **gares routière** and **SNCF** are adjacent to each other, just a few
minutes' walk from the centre of town: cross the wide River Oise and go up
rue Solférino to place de l'Hôtel-de-Ville. The **tourist office** (April–Sept
Mon–Sat 9.15am–12.15pm & 1.45–6.15pm; Oct–March Mon 1.45–5.15pm,
Tues–Sat 9.15am–12.15pm & 1.45–5.15pm; open Sun Easter–Oct 10am–
12.15pm & 2.15–5pm; ☎03.44.40.01.00, ⓦwww.compiegne-tourisme.fr)
takes up part of the ornate Hôtel de Ville. It offers free hotel bookings, and
will provide you with a plan of the town, on which is conveniently marked
an exhaustive visitors' route, including the forest paths (see opposite).

As for **accommodation**, there are cheap but comfortable en-suite rooms at
the centrally –located *Etap*, 1 rue Pierre Sauvage (☎08.92.68.31.04; ❶). Not
necessarily any more expensive but altogether more characterful, the *Hôtel de
Flandre*, at 16 quai de la République (☎03.44.83.24.40, ⓦwww.hoteldeflandre
.com; ❶–❸), has some good-value, simple doubles with hall showers alongside
its more expensive and plusher offerings. It's near the train station and overlooks
the river.

The Town

Compiègne itself is a handsome, lively if traffic-choked place of pale stone
houses, white shutters and dark slate roofs, though there's no doubt the entire
town merely plays foil to its star attraction, the large and opulent **Château de
Compiègne**, with its extensive gardens, which make excellent picnicking
territory. The eighteenth-century Château stands two blocks east of the Hôtel
de Ville along rue des Minimes, and for all its pompous excess, inspires a
certain fascination, particularly its interior, which can be visited on a self-
guided tour (daily except Tues: March–Oct 10am–6pm, last admission 5.15;
Nov–Feb 10am–3.45pm; €7.70, more during temporary exhibitions). Napoléon
commissioned repairs and redecoration of the former royal palace in 1807, and
the work was carried out in time for the emperor to welcome his second wife,
Marie-Louise of Austria – a relative of Marie-Antoinette, no less – here in
1810. The ostentatious post–revolutionary apartments are in marked contrast
to the more sober neoclassicism of the few surviving late royal interiors, and
are a monument to the unseemly haste with which Napoléon I moved in,
scarcely a dozen years after the Revolution. The self-guided tour also takes in
the temporary exhibitions of the Musée du Second Empire, but if you also
want to see the **Musée de la Voiture** (same ticket) you have to join a one-
hour guided tour. It contains a wonderful array of antique bicycles, tricycles
and fancy aristocratic carriages, as well as the world's first steam coach. The
Théâtre Impérial, planned (but never finished) by Napoléon III, was finally
completed in 1991 at a cost of some thirty million francs. Originally designed
with just two seats for Napoléon and his wife, it now seats nine hundred and
is regularly used for concerts.

You can visit the palace gardens (daily: March to mid-April & mid-Sept to Oct 8am–6pm; mid-April to mid-Sept 8am–7pm; Nov–Feb 8am–5pm; free) separately. Much of the original French-style garden was replanted on Napoléon's orders after 1811. The result is informal but monumental; the great avenue that extends 4.5km into the Forêt de Compiègne (see below) was inspired by the Austrian imperial summer residence at Schönbrunn on the outskirts of Vienna.

The centre of town is handsome rather than picturesque, though several half-timbered buildings remain on rue Napoléon and rue des Lombards, south of the main place de l'Hôtel-de-Ville. The **Hôtel de Ville** itself – Louis XII Gothic – has ebullient nineteenth-century statuary including the image of Joan of Arc, who was captured in this town by the Burgundians before being handed to the English. By the side of the town hall is the **Musée de la Figurine Historique** (Tues–Sat 9am–noon & 2–6pm, Sun 2–6pm; closes at 5pm in winter; €2), which features reputedly the world's largest collection of toy soldiers in mock-up battles; the huge diorama of the Battle of Waterloo is the most impressive.

South west of the town centre at 2bis avenue des Martyrs de la Liberté, the sombre **Mémorial de l'Internement et de la Déportation** (daily except Tues 10am–6pm; €5) occupies the former barracks of Royallieu, transformed into a prisoner of war camp by the German army in 1940 and later used as a transit camp for political prisoners, Jews and others; it was from here in March 1942 that the first deportation from France to Auschwitz took place.

Eating and drinking

Compiègne lacks a wide variety of good places to **eat**. Notable places include: *Le Cordelier*, 1 rue des Cordeliers (from €12; ☎03.44.40.23.38; closed all day Sun plus Tues and Weds eves), and *Le Bistrot de Flandre*, on the ground floor of the hotel of the same name. One of Compiègne's best restaurants is the *Bistrot des Arts* at 35 cours Guynemer, serving traditional bistro food with a twist, accompanied by excellent wines, for around €25 a head (☎03.44.20.10.10). *Le Saint Clair*, 6 rue des Lombards (☎03.44.40.58.18; from €12), guarantees a good meal, a big selection of Belgian beers and a warm welcome for gay travellers. There is an **internet** café, *L'Évasion*, at 5 rue St-Martin.

The Forêt de Compiègne and the Clairière de l'Armistice

Very ancient, and cut by a succession of hills, streams and valleys, the **Forêt de Compiègne**, with the GR12 running through it, is ideal for walkers and cyclists. East of Compiègne, some 6km into the forest and not far from the banks of the Aisne, is the green, sandy clearing known as the **Clairière de l'Armistice**. Here, in what was a rail siding for rail-mounted artillery, World War I was brought to an end on November 11, 1918. A plaque commemorates the deed: "Here the criminal pride of the German empire was brought low, vanquished by the free peoples whom it had sought to enslave." To avenge this humiliation, Hitler had the French sign their capitulation on June 22, 1940, on the same spot, in the same rail carriage. The original car was taken to Berlin and destroyed by fire in the last days of the war. Its replacement, housed in a small **museum** (daily except Tues: May to mid-Oct 10am–6pm; mid-Oct to April 9am–noon & 2–5.30pm; last admission 30min before closing; €4), is similar, and the objects inside are the originals.

Vieux-Moulin and St-Jean-aux-Bois are picturesque villages right in the heart of the forest, the latter retaining part of its twelfth-century fortifications; while 13km southeast of Compiègne at **PIERREFONDS** there's a classic medieval **château** (May–Aug daily 10am–6.30pm; Sept–April 10am–1pm 2–5.30pm; €6.50), built in the twelfth century, dismantled in the seventeenth and restored by order of Napoléon III in the nineteenth to create a fantastic fairy-tale affair of turrets, towers and moat.

Noyon

Further up the Oise, and a possible day-trip from Compiègne, is **NOYON**, another of Picardy's cathedral towns. Its quiet provinciality belies a long, illustrious history, first as a Roman prefecture, then as seat of a bishopric from 531. Here, in 768, Charlemagne was crowned king of Neustria, largest of the Frankish kingdoms; in 987, Hugues Capet was crowned king of France; and John Calvin was born here in 1509.

Rowing along the Oise on his *Inland Journey* of 1876, Robert Louis Stevenson stopped briefly at Noyon, which he described as "a stack of brown roofs at the best, where I believe people live very respectably in a quiet way". It's still like that, though the **cathedral**, to which Stevenson warmed, is impressive enough. Spacious and a little stark, it successfully blends Romanesque and Gothic, and is flanked by the ruins of thirteenth-century cloisters and a strange, exquisitely shaped Renaissance library. On the south side of the cathedral, the old episcopal palace houses the **Musée du Noyonnais** (Tues–Sun 10am–noon & 2–6pm; Nov–March closes 5pm; €3), a small, well-presented collection of local archeological finds and cathedral treasure. Close by, signs direct you to the **Musée Calvin** (same hours and ticket), ostensibly on the site of the reformer's birthplace. The respectable citizens of Noyon were never among their local boy's adherents and tore down the original building long before its tourist potential was appreciated.

The **tourist office** is in the Hôtel de Ville on place Bertrand Labarre (Nov–March Mon 2–6.15pm, Tue–Fri 9am–noon & 2–6.15pm, Sat 9am–noon & 2–6/5pm); also Sun 10am–noon in June–Sept; ☎03.44.44.21.88, Ⓦwww.noyon –tourisme.com). The best **accommodation** option is *Le St Eloi*, at 81 boulevard Carnot (☎03.44.44.01.49, Ⓦwww.hotelsainteloi.fr; Ⓢ; restaurant €38), just off the roundabout between the train station and cathedral.

Champagne and the Ardennes

The bubbly stuff is the reason most people visit **Champagne**. The cultivation of vines was already well established in Roman times, when Reims was the capital of the Roman province of Belgae (Belgium), and by the seventeenth century still wines from the region had gained a considerable reputation. Contrary to popular myth, however, it was not Dom Pérignon, cellar master of the Abbaye de Hautvillers near Épernay, who then "invented" champagne. He was probably responsible for the innovation of mixing grapes from different vineyards, but the wine's well-known tendency to re-ferment within the bottle was not controllable until eighteenth-century glass-moulding techniques (developed in Britain) produced vessels strong enough to contain the natural effervescence.

Away from the hillsides with their ranks of vines, the region's monotonous plains grow more wheat and cabbages per hectare than any other region of France, though it seems to bring the run-down villages little benefit.

At least the region's capital, the cathedral city of **Reims**, is worth a visit, and has a reasonably full cultural calendar. Some of the most extravagant champagne houses are here, the *caves* beneath them notable for their vaulted ceilings and kilometres of bottles. **Épernay**, a smaller town set in the scenic heart of the region, is dominated by an avenue of champagne *maisons*, where visitors can float from one to another like so many bubbles. The region's other major attraction is **Troyes**, some way to the southwest, a great place of cobbled streets, half-timbered houses and cut-price shopping. Further south still, the small, far-flung towns of **Chaumont** and **Langres** also merit a stop, if only for an hour or two.

Reims

Laid flat by the shells of World War I, **REIMS** (pronounced like a nasal "Rance", and traditionally spelled Rheims in English) was rebuilt afterwards with tact and touches of Art Nouveau and Art Deco, but consequently lacks any great sense of antiquity. It makes up for this with a walkable centre, beneath which lies its real treasure – kilometre upon kilometre of bottles of fermenting champagne. Its status as champagne capital of the world aside, Reims possesses one of the most impressive Gothic cathedrals in France – formerly the coronation church of dynasties of French monarchs going back to Clovis, first king of the Franks, and later painted obsessively by Monet. These attractions, plus a handful of interesting museums and a big city buzz unusual in this part of France, make it worth a day or two's stopover.

Arrival, information and accommodation

The cathedral is less than ten-minutes' walk from the **gare SNCF** and **gare routière**. The **tourist office**, 2 rue Guillaume-de-Machault (May to mid–Oct Mon–Sat 9am–7pm, Sun 10am–6pm; mid-Oct to April Mon–Sat 9am–6pm, Sun 11am–4pm; ☎08.92.70.13.51, ⊛www.reims–tourisme.com), is next to the cathedral in a picturesque ruin; for €5 you can hire an English audioguide to the city from them, though note that if you want to do the circuit more than once you'll have to pay again. **Internet access** is available at *Clique et Croque*, 19 rue Chanzy (Mon–Sat 10am–midnight, Sun 2–8pm).

Rooms are fairly easy to come by in Reims, though as the city is an easy day-trip from Paris it may not be necessary to stay at all.

Hotels

De la Cathédrale 20 rue Libergier
☎03.26.47.28.46, ⊛www.hotel-cathedrale
-reims.fr. Old-fashioned but comfortable two-star near, as the name suggests, the cathedral. ❸

Château Les Crayères 64 bd Henry-Vasnier
☎03.26.82.80.80, ⊛www.lescrayeres.com. Ideal for a special occasion, this refined hotel in a restored eighteenth-century château has a beautiful garden, luxurious rooms and impec-

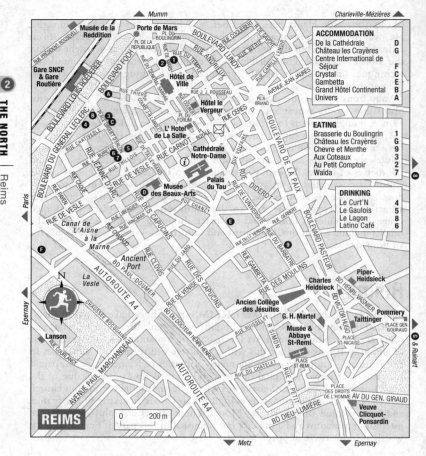

Mumm ▲   Charleville-Mézières ▲

ACCOMMODATION

De la Cathédrale	D
Château les Crayères	G
Centre International de Séjour	F
Crystal	C
Gambetta	E
Grand Hôtel Continental	B
Univers	A

EATING

Brasserie du Boulingrin	1
Château les Crayères	G
Chevre et Menthe	9
Aux Coteaux	3
Au Petit Comptoir	2
Waïda	7

DRINKING

Le Curt'N	4
Le Gaulois	5
Le Lagon	8
Latino Café	6

REIMS   0   200 m

Metz ▼   Epernay ▼

Paris ◀   Epernay ◀

cable service, as well as one of the region's most sophisticated restaurants (see p.241). **9**

Crystal 86 place Drouet-d'Erlon ☎03.26.88.44.44, ⓦwww.hotel-crystal.fr. Small rooms, charming service and a pretty courtyard garden which blocks out much of noise from the local nightlife. **1–2**

Gambetta 9–13 rue Gambetta ☎03.26.47.22.00, ⓦwww.hotel-gambetta-reims.fr. Neat, well-designed, modern rooms, all with shower and toilet above a pleasant café across the street from the conservatoire of music and dance. **3**

Grand Hôtel Continental 93 place Drouet-d'Erlon ☎03.26.40.39.35, ⓦwww.grandhotelcontinental .com. Very central hotel, with rather grand public areas and quiet rooms, all with bathroom and TV. **3**

Univers 41 bd Foch ☎03.26.88.68.08, ⓦwww.hotel-univers-reims.com. Handsomely located on the tree-lined Hautes Promenades, this smart neo–Art Deco-style establishment, with double-glazing, is the best mid-range hotel in the city. **5**

Hostel

Centre International de Séjour 1 chaussée Bocquaine, Parc Léo Lagrange ☎03.26.40.52.60, ⓦwww.cis-reims.com. HI hostel with 3–5 bed dorms plus doubles & singles (dorm bed €16.40, doubles **1**). Bus H from theatre to "Charles de Gaulle", or a 15min walk from the station on the other side of the A4 autoroute: cross the big roundabout in front of the station, turn right down bd du Général-Leclerc to Pont de Vesle; chaussée Bocquaine is the first left after the bridge.

The City

The old centre of Reims stretches from the **cathedral** north to place de la République's triumphal Roman arch, the **Porte de Mars**, punctuated by the grand squares of place Royale, place du Forum and place de l'Hôtel-de-Ville. To the west, place Drouet d'Erlon is the focus of the city's nightlife and an almost-complete example of the city's 1920s reconstruction. To the south, about fifteen-minutes' walk from the cathedral, is the other historical focus of the town, the **Abbaye St-Remi**, and nearby the Jesuits' College. To the east of here are most of the **champagne maisons** and, further east still, a museum of cars.

The cathedral and around

The glorious Gothic thirteenth-century **Cathédrale Notre-Dame** (daily 7.30am–7.30pm) features prominently in French history: in 1429 Joan of Arc managed to get the Dauphin crowned here as Charles VII – an act of immense

Champagne: the facts

Nowhere else in the world, are you allowed to make a drink called **champagne**, though many people do, calling it "champan", "shampanskoye" and all manner of variants. You can blend grape juice harvested from chalk–soil vineyards, double-ferment it, store the result for years at the requisite constant temperature and high humidity in sweating underground *caves*, turn and tilt the bottles little by little to clear the sediment, add some vintage liqueur, and finally produce a bubbling golden (or pink) liquid; but according to international law you may refer to it only as "*méthode champenoise*". The jealously-guarded monopoly helps keep the region's sparkling wines in the luxury class, although the locals will tell you the difference comes from the squid fossils in the chalk, the lay of the land and its climate, the evolution of the grapes, the regulated pruning methods and the legally enforced quantity of juice pressed.

Three authorized **grape varieties** are used: chardonnay, the only white grape, growing best on the Côte des Blancs and contributing a light and elegant element; pinot noir, grown mainly on the Montagne de Reims slopes, giving body and long life; and pinot meunier, cultivated primarily in the Marne valley, adding flowery aromas.

The **vineyards** are owned either by *maisons*, who produce the *grande marque* champagne, or by small cultivators called *vignerons*, who sell the grapes to the *maisons*. The *vignerons* also make their own champagne and will happily offer you a glass and sell you a bottle at two-thirds the price of a *grande marque* (ask at any tourist office in the Champagne region for a list of addresses). The difference between the two comes down to capital. The *maisons* can afford to blend grapes from up to sixty different vineyards and to tie up their investment while their champagne matures for several years longer than the legal minimum (one year for non-vintage, three years vintage). So the wine they produce is undoubtedly superior – and not a lot cheaper here than in a good discount off-licence/liquor store in Britain or the US.

If you could visit the head offices of Cartier or Dior, the atmosphere would probably be similar to that in the champagne *maisons*, whose palaces are divided between Épernay and Reims. Visits to the handful that organize regular **tours** are not free, and most require appointments, but don't be put off – their staff all speak English and a generous *dégustation* is generally thrown in. Their audiovisuals and (cold) cellar tours are on the whole very informative, and do more than merely plug brand names. Local tourist offices can provide full lists of addresses and times of visits.

If you want to work on the **harvest**, contact any of the smaller *maisons* direct; the Agence Nationale pour l'Emploi, 30 rue de Sézanne, Épernay (☎03.26.51.01.33); or one of the offices in Rheims – see the site ⓦwww.anpe.fr for details.

significance when France was more or less wiped off the map by the English and their allies. In all, 26 French kings were crowned here.

The chief draw inside the cathedral is the kaleidoscopic patterns in the stained glass, with fantastic Marc **Chagall** designs in the east chapel and champagne processes glorified in the south transept. But the greatest appeal is outside: an inexplicable joke runs around the restored but still badly mutilated statuary on the west front – the giggling angels who seem to be responsible for disseminating the prank are a delight. Not all the figures on the cathedral's west front are originals – some have been removed to spare them further erosion and are now at the former bishop's palace, the Palais du Tau. The **towers** of the cathedral are open to the public (mid-March to early May & early Sept to end Oct Sat at 10 & 11am, Sat & Sun at 2, 3 & 4pm; early May to early Sept Tues–Sat every half hour 10–11.30am & 2–5.30pm, Sun every half hour 2–5.30pm; €6.50, or combined ticket with the Palais du Tau €8.50); as well as a walk round the transepts and chevet, you get to see inside the framework of the cathedral roof; tickets available from the Palais du Tau.

At the **Palais du Tau** (daily: early May to early Sept 9.30am–6.30pm; early Sept to early May 9.30am–12.30pm & 2–5.30pm; €6.50, or combined ticket with the towers €8.50), next door to the cathedral, you can appreciate the expressiveness of the statuary from close up – a view that would never have been possible in their intended monumental positions on the cathedral. Apart from the grinning angels, there is also a superb Eve, shiftily clutching the monster of sin, while embroidered tapestries of the Song of Songs line the walls. The palace also preserves the paraphernalia of Charles X's coronation in 1824, right down to the dauphin's hat box.

West of the cathedral on rue Chanzy, the **Musée des Beaux-Arts** (daily except Tues & public holidays 10am–noon & 2–6pm; entry with Pass Découverte) is the city's principal art museum, which, though ill-suited to its ancient building, effectively covers French art from the Renaissance to the present. Few of the works are among the artists' best but the collection includes one of David's replicas of his famous Marat death scene, a set of 27 Corots, two great Gauguin still lifes, and some beautifully observed sixteenth-century portraits by the German artists Lucas Cranach the Elder and Younger.

Just north of the cathedral, the **Musée-Hôtel Le Vergeur**, 36 place du Forum (Tues–Sun 2–6pm; €4) is a stuffed treasure house of all kinds of beautiful objects, including two sets of Dürer engravings – an *Apocalypse* and *Passion of Christ* – but you have to go through a long guided tour to see it. Opposite the museum there's access to sections of the partly submerged arcades of the **crypto portique Gallo–Romain** (June to mid-Oct Tues–Sun 2–6pm; free), which date back to 200 AD. Reims' other Roman monument, the quadruple-arched **Porte de Mars**, on place de la République, belongs to the same era.

West of the Porte, behind the station in rue Franklin-Roosevelt, is the **Musée de la Reddition** ("Museum of the Surrender"; daily except Tues & public holidays 10am–noon & 2–6pm; entry with Pass Découverte), based around an old schoolroom that served as Eisenhower's HQ from February 1945. In the early hours of May 7, 1945, General Jodl agreed to the unconditional surrender of the German army here, thus ending World War II in Europe. The room has been left exactly as it was (minus the ashtrays and carpet), with the Allies' battle maps on the walls.

The Abbaye St-Remi, Jesuits' College and surrounding museums

Most of the early French kings were buried in Reims' oldest building, the eleventh-century **Basilique St-Remi**, fifteen-minutes' walk from the cathedral on rue Simon (daily 8am–dusk, closed during services; music & light show July–Sept Sat 9.30pm; free), part of a former Benedictine abbey named after the 22-year-old bishop who baptized Clovis and three thousand of his warriors. An immensely spacious building, it preserves its Romanesque transept walls and ambulatory chapels, some of them with modern stained glass that works beautifully. Albert Nicart, the bellringer of St Remi, was the inspiration for Victor Hugo's fictional Quasimodo in *The Hunchback of Notre Dame;* Hugo met Nicart and the gypsy girl Esméralda in 1825 while visiting Reims to attend Charles X's coronation. The spectacular abbey buildings alongside the church house the **Musée St-Remi** (Mon–Fri 2–6.30pm, Sat & Sun 2–7pm; entry with Pass Découverte) the city's rather dry archaeological and historical museum. The collection includes some fine tapestries on St Remi's life, plus the reconstructed façade of a thirteenth-century house, the Maison des Musiciens, which was destroyed by World War I German shelling. The museum's twelfth- to thirteenth-century chapterhouse has been listed as a UNESCO World Heritage Site.

The **Ancien Collège des Jésuites** (closed for renovation: temporary exhibitions open daily 2–6pm; free), a short walk north on rue du Grand-Cerf, was founded in Reims in 1606, and the building completed in 1678. Extensive renovation work, likely to continue until 2012, means it is currently only possible to visit the temporary exhibitions of modern art, just inside the main entrance.

If you have even a passing interest in old cars you should not miss the **Musée de l'Automobile**, 84 avenue Georges-Clemenceau (April to mid-Nov daily 10am–noon & 2–6pm; mid-Nov to March daily except Tues 10am–noon & 2–5pm; €7), fifteen-minutes' walk southeast of the cathedral. The collection contains many prototypes and rarities; highlights include a string of sleek, powerful Delahaye coupés designed by Philippe Charbonneaux in the 1940s and 1950s, though top spot in the looks department goes to a stunning Panhard et Levassor Dynamic 130 Coupé from 1936, which is pure Art Deco on wheels.

Eating and drinking

Place Drouet-d'Erlon, a wide pedestrianized boulevard lined with **bars** and **restaurants**, is where you'll find most of the city's nightlife, which is geared more to pavement café lounging and brasserie idling than high-octane partying. For self-catering, there's a big Saturday **market** in place du Boulingrin (6am–1pm).

Brasserie du Boulingrin 48 rue de Mars ☎03.26.40.96.22. Charming and good-value brasserie, dating back to 1925, famed for its seafood platters and *fondant au chocolat*. Weekday menus at €18.50 and €25, including wine. Closed Sun.

Château les Crayères 64 bd Henry-Vasnier ☎03.26.82.80.80. Reputed to be one of France's finest gastronomic restaurants – with prices and style to match. Closed Mon & Tues lunch; à la carte around €200.

Champagne tasting in Reims

Tours of the Reims champagne houses and *caves* generally need to be pre-booked. Those in the southern part of town near the Abbaye St-Remi tend to have the most impressive cellars – some have been carved in cathedral-esque formations from the Gallo–Roman quarries used to build the city, long before champagne was invented.

Non-appointment houses

Taittinger 9 place St-Niçaise ☏03.26.85.84.33, ⓦwww.taittinger.com. Starts with a film show before a guided stroll through the ancient cellars, some of which have doodles and carvings added by more recent workers; there are also statues of St Vincent and St Jean, patron saints respectively of *vignerons* and cellar hands. Mid-March to mid-Nov daily 9.30am–1pm & 2–5.30pm (last tour at 4.30); mid-Nov to mid-March Mon–Fri same hours; closed Sat & Sun; tour 1hr; €10.

Appointment-only houses

Most houses nowadays prefer that you call or email in advance, but in summer it may be worth showing up on the off chance. This is not a comprehensive list of all the *maisons* in the city, but includes the most visitor-friendly.

Lanson 66 rue de Courlancy ☏03.26.78.50.17, ⓦwww.lanson.fr. Worth the trip across the river because the in-depth tours here actually bring you into the factory, and demonstrate the mechanized process of champagne making. Most days you'll see the machines degorging the bottles, as well as labelling and filling them in preparation for the second fermentation. A refreshing change from those houses that just talk about the process and show their cellars. Mon–Fri only; closed Aug; €8.

G.H.Martel & Co 17 rue des Créneaux, near the Basilique St-Remi ☏03.26.82.70.67, ⓦwww.champagnemartel.com. At €8, this is a good-value tour, with a *dégustation* of three champagnes as well as a film show and guided visit. Open daily year round (10am–7pm, but last tour at 5.30).

Mumm 34 rue du Champ-de-Mars ☏03.26.49.59.70, ⓦwww.mumm.com. Known by its red–slashed Cordon Rouge label, Mumm's un-French-sounding name is the legacy of its founders, affluent German wine-makers from the Rhine Valley who established the business in 1827. The tour is guided and includes a short film. It all ends with a generous glass of either Cordon Rouge, the populist choice; the sweeter Cordon Vert; or their Extra Dry. March–Oct daily 9–11am & 2–5pm; Nov–Feb by appointment only; €8.

Pommery 5 place du Général-Gouraud ☏03.26.61.62.55, ⓦwww.pommery.fr. The creator of the cute one-eighth size "Pop" bottles has excavated Roman quarries for its cellars – it claims to have been the first *maison* to do so. April to mid-Nov daily 9.30am–7pm; mid-Nov to March 10am–6pm; from €10.

Ruinart 4 rue des Crayères ☏03.26.77.51.51, ⓦwww.ruinart.com. The fanciest of the champagne houses, in a swanky mansion. Reserved and upmarket, the tours are nonetheless informative.

Veuve Clicquot-Ponsardin 1 place des Droits-de-l'Homme ☏03.26.89.53.90, ⓦwww.veuve-cliquot.com. In 1805 the widowed Mme Clicquot not only took over her husband's business – *veuve* means "widow" in French – but also later bequeathed it to her business manager rather than to her children, a radical break with tradition. The *maison* is one of the least pompous, and its *caves* some of the most spectacular, sited in ancient Gallo–Roman quarries, with high vaulted ceilings. Tours last 1hr 30min with tasting; 10am–6pm (last tour at 4.15pm); April–Oct Mon–Sat; Nov–Mar Mon–Fri; €8.50.

Chèvre et Menthe 63 rue de Barbâtre
☎03.26.05.17.03. A homely, inexpensive establishment recommended for vegetarians with a range of gourmet salads from €6.20. Daily *carte* dishes (some of which contain meat) plus the eponymous goat's cheese and fresh mint quiche. Closed Sun & Mon.

Aux Coteaux 86–88 place Drouet d'Erlon
☎03.26.47.08.79. Dependable cheapie on Reims' main café strip, with a wide range of pizzas and salads from under €8. Closed Sun & Mon.

Au Petit Comptoir 17 rue de Mars
☎03.26.40.58.58. Close to the Marché du Boulingrin, with traditional and inventive dishes from €20 and a menu at €29, served in modern surroundings – a subtle grey decor with white leather chairs. Closed Sun & Mon.

Waïda 3–5 place Drouet-d'Erlon. Beautiful *patissier-glacier* and *salon de thé*, with pastries and ice cream made on the premises, plus one of the best original Art Deco interiors in Reims. Closed Mon.

Nightlife and entertainment

For **drinking** into the early hours there are plenty of large terrace cafés on place Drouet-d'Erlon; try *Le Gaulois*, at nos. 2–4, which serves excellent cocktails. One of Drouet-d'Erlon's livelier spots is *Latino Café* at no. 33, open until 2.30am, with hispanic food and music, plus occasional live entertainment. If you want to **dance**, try *Le Curt'N* at 7 boulevard Général-Leclerc (daily from 10pm; admission charge with drink Fri & Sat) or *Le Lagon* at 1 rue de Nice (☎03.26.07.61.34), the city's best **gay club**.

The Opéra Cinema, 3 rue T.-Dubois (☎08.91.68.01.22), shows some undubbed films. From mid-June to early August, over a hundred classical concerts – many of them free – take place as part of **Les Flâneries Musicales d'Été**; pick up a leaflet at the tourist office.

Épernay and around

ÉPERNAY, 26km south of Reims, is a single-industry town of no particular charm or beauty. But it's beautifully situated below rolling, vine-covered hills, and the industry in question – champagne – is a compelling reason for a visit. The town contains some of the most famous champagne *maisons* as well as several smaller houses, and makes a sensible base for exploring the surrounding villages and vineyards.

Arrival, information and accommodation

Épernay's **gare SNCF** and **gare routière** are next to each other, a five-minute walk north of the central place de la République, which is reached via rue Jean-Moët. The **tourist office** is at 7 avenue de Champagne (mid-April to mid–Oct Mon–Sat 9.30am–12.30pm & 1.30–7pm, Sun 11am–4pm; mid-Oct to mid-April Mon–Sat 9.30am–12.30pm & 1.30–5.30pm; ⓦ www.ot-epernay .fr) and has information about a huge selection of tours ranging from minibuses to hot-air balloons. If you feel like touring the vineyards by **mountain bike** (**VTT**), either independently or in an organized group, contact Bulleo, in Parc Roger Menu (☎03.26.53.35.60; from €10 per half day).

The best of the cheap **hotels** in Épernay is the one-star *St-Pierre*, 1 rue Jeanne-d'Arc (☎03.26.54.40.80, ⓦ www.villasaintpierre.fr; ❶–❷), in a quiet street away from the centre. More comfort is to be had at the excellent *Les Berceaux*, at 13 rue des Berceaux (☎03.26.55.28.84, ⓦ www.lesberceaux.com; ❺), which also has one of the best restaurants in town (see p.245); or failing that the Best Western-run *Hôtel de Champagne*, 30 rue E.-Mercier (☎03.26.53.10.60, ⓦ www.bw-hotel -champagne.com; ❺). Classiest of all in town is the elegant *Clos Raymi*, 3 rue

▲ Champagne cellar

Joseph-de-Venoge (℡03.26.51.00.58, Ⓦwww.closraymi-hotel.com; Ⓖ), in a beautiful red-brick house once belonging to the Chandon family. For even more luxury out of town, head for the *Royal Champagne*, 5km north on the N2051 to Champillon (℡03.26.52.87.11, Ⓦwww.royalchampagne.com; Ⓞ). At the opposite end of the scale, the local **campsite** is 2km to the north on route de Cumières in the Parc des Sports, on the south bank of the Marne (℡03.26.55.32.14; closed Oct–April).

The Town

Since you're only here for the alcohol, you may as well make a beeline for the appropriately named **avenue de Champagne**, running east from place de la République. Dubbed "the most drinkable street in the world" by Winston Churchill, it's worth strolling for its imposing eighteenth- and nineteenth-century champagne *maisons*; it may, in effect, be no more than an exalted industrial zone – as a short detour down one of the side streets will prove – but it's pretty showy for all that. You can tour some of the *maisons*, and many others welcome visitors to taste and buy. The Epernay tourist office's *guide touristique* has details.

The largest, and probably the most famous *maison*, though neither the most beautiful nor necessarily the most interesting to tour, is **Moët et Chandon**, 18 avenue de Champagne (9.30–11.30am & 2–4.30pm; mid-Nov to March closed Sat & Sun; from €13 including *dégustation* of the brut Impérial); one of the keystones of the LVMH (Louis Vuitton, Moët and Hennessy) empire which owns Mercier, Veuve Clicquot, Krug and Ruinart, and a variety of other concerns, including Dior perfumes. The house is also the creator of the iconic **Dom Pérignon** label. The tour is rather generic, beginning with a mawkish video, followed by a walk through the cellars, which are adorned with mementos of Napoleon (a good friend of the original M. Moët), and concluding with a tasting of their truly excellent champagne.

Further up the street, **Mercier**, at 70 avenue de Champagne, runs a fairly rewarding tour around its cellars in an electric train (mid-March to mid-Nov 9.30–11.30am & 2–4.30pm; closed Tues & Wed out of season and mid-Dec to mid-Feb; €8, including *dégustation*). Nowadays Mercier is known as the lower-end champagne of French supermarkets, showing that M. Mercier was successful in his goal: he founded the house, aged 20, in 1858 with a plan to make champagne more accessible to the French people. In 1889 he carted a giant barrel that held 200,000 bottles' worth to the Paris Exposition, with the help of 24 oxen – only to be upstaged by the Eiffel Tower. The barrel is on display in the lobby.

Castellane, by the station at 57 rue de Verdun (March–Dec daily 10am–noon & 2–6pm; €8 including *dégustation*), provides Épernay with its chief landmark: a tower looking like a kind of Neoclassical signal box. As well as the inevitable cellars, the visit shows off the working assembly lines that fill the champagne bottles, and the huge vats that hold the grape juice prior to fermentation. After the tour you can wander the little museum freely and climb the tower, which reveals a great view of the surrounding vineyards.

Épernay has a few other *grandes maisons* that can be visited by appointment, but perhaps more worthwhile are the many smaller houses. Since these houses have fewer employees it's best to call or email well in advance. Try **Leclerc-Briant** at 67 rue Chaude-Ruelle, west of the town centre (☎03.26.54.45.33, ⓦwww .leclercbriant.com); for €8 they give a tour of their presshouse, museum and cellars, as well as a tasting of three vintages and a souvenir champagne glass.

Eating and drinking

Restaurants in Épernay are not necessarily cheap. There is good value to be had at *Les Berceaux*, 13 rue des Berceaux (☎03.26.55.28.84; closed Mon, Tues, two weeks of August & three weeks in Feb; menus from €26), while *La Table Kobus*, 3 rue Dr-Rousseau, is good for traditional French fare (☎03.26.51.53.53; €28). Call in advance to squeeze into *La Cave à Champagne* at 16 rue Gambetta (☎03.26.55.50.70; from €17, closed Tues & Wed). For a major blowout, the *Royal Champagne*, north of town (see opposite), serves menus at €65 and €110.

Around Épernay

The villages in the appealing **vineyards** of the Montagne de Reims, Côte des Blancs and Vallée de la Marne which surround Épernay promote a range of curiosities: the world's largest champagne bottle and cork in **Mardeuil** and a tradi-tional *vigneron*'s house and early twentieth-century school room at **Oeuilly**. Many of the villages have a sleepy, old stone charm: **Vertus**, 16km south of Épernay, is particularly pretty, and so too is **Hautvillers**, 6km north of town, where you can see the abbey of Dom Pérignon fame (though it is closed to the public).

The best reason for venturing out into the countryside is simply to view the vines and taste less well-known but often delicious champagnes. One such house is Charlier & Fils, set in an attractive *maison* surrounded by flowers at 4 rue des Pervenches, **MONTIGNY-SOUS-CHATILLON**, 15km west of Épernay (☎03.26.58.35.18, ⓦwww.champagne-charlier.com).

For somewhere to **stay** that offers a real treat in an atmosphere of faded elegance, base yourself at *Château d'Etoges*, 4 rue Richebourg, **Etoges** (☎03.26.59.30.08, ⓦwww.etoges.com; ❼). This small château offers 28 characterful bedrooms, and a top-notch restaurant.

Troyes

It is easy to find charm in the leaning medieval half–timbered houses and many churches of **TROYES**, the ancient capital of the Champagne region. The town also offers top-quality museums and shopping outlets, and is a good place to try the regional speciality, *andouillette* (see box, p.192).

Arrival and information

The **gare SNCF** and **gare routière** are side by side off boulevard Carnot (part of the ring road). Not all buses use the main station, though, and if you're heading for the outlet stores or the countryside it's best to check first with the **tourist office** (Ⓦ www.tourisme-troyes.com). There are two branches: the station branch is at 16 boulevard Carnot (Mon–Sat 9am–12.30pm & 2–6.30pm; also open Sun Nov–March 10am–1pm; Ⓣ 03.25.82.62.70); and the town-centre branch is on rue Mignard facing the Église St-Jean (April–June & mid-Sept to Oct Mon–Sat 9am–12.30pm & 2–6.30pm, Sun 10am–noon and 2–5pm; July to mid-Sept daily 10am–7pm; Nov–March closed; Ⓣ 03.25.73.36.88). For information concerning the Aube *département*, of which Troyes is the capital, consult Ⓦ www.aube-champagne.com or visit the Aube tourist office on place de la Libération (Mon–Fri 9.30am–12.30pm & 1.30–6pm). If you want to **rent a car** try Hertz at 28 rue Voltaire, near the station (Ⓣ 03.25.71.35.50).

Accommodation

Places to stay around the station are plentiful, though for not much more you can find **accommodation** in the old town – the tourist office has details, along with information about *chambres d'hôtes* and places to stay in the wine villages around Troyes.

Hotels

Les Comptes de Champagne 54 rue de la Monnaie Ⓣ 03.25.73.11.70, Ⓦ www.comtes dechampagne.com. Central and charming two-star in a twelfth-century house with slanted floors. Friendly proprietors and covered parking. ❶–❸
Grand Hôtel/Patiotel 4 av Mal-Joffre Ⓣ 03.25.79.90.90, Ⓦ www.grand-hotel-troyes.com. Right opposite the station, a big three-star hotel with a garden; rooms in the "Patiotel" annexe are less grand (only two-star) and accordingly cheaper. ❷–❸
La Maison de Rhodes 18 rue Linard-Gonthier Ⓣ 03.25.43.11.11, Ⓦ www.maisonderhodes.com.

A fine Renaissance house, with Templar links, near the cathedral, which has been transformed into a four-star boutique hotel with contemporary interior decor and an abundance of medieval wooden beams. The lovely internal courtyard is a tranquil place for a quality evening meal. ❺
Le Relais St–Jean 51 rue Paillot-de-Montabert Ⓣ 03.25.73.89.90, Ⓦ www.relais-st-jean.com. Posh hotel in a half-timbered building right in the centre, though the modern interior comes as a surprise. ❺
Royal 22 bd Carnot Ⓣ 03.25.73.19.99, Ⓦ www .royal-hotel-troyes.com. Decent, pleasantly restored hotel behind a stern facade near the station; spacious bathrooms and a copious breakfast. ❹

Museum pass

The museum pass (€12) to visit all of the city's museums is well worth buying if you plan to visit the **Musée d'Art Moderne**, **La Maison de l'Outil et de la Pensée Ouvrière** and one other. It also includes a *dégustation* of two champagnes from a local shop, an hour's free parking, thirty minutes of internet use, and discount vouchers for the factory outlets. It's only valid for one visit to each establishment, but can be used over the course of a year. Buy it from the tourist office or in some of the city's museums.

Hostel and campsite

Camping municipal 7 rue Roger-Salengro, Pont Ste–Marie ⓣ&ⓕ 03.25.81.02.64, ⓦ www .troyescamping.net. Attractive grassy campsite, situated 5km out on the N60 to Châlons, on the left, with good facilities including washing machines and children's play area. Minimum two-night reservation, closed mid-Oct to March.

HI hostel chemin Ste-Scholastique, Rosières ⓣ 03.25.82.00.65, ⓦ www.fuaj.org/aj/troyes. Decent hostel located in a former fourteenth-century priory, 5.5km out of town on the Dijon road; take bus #8 direction "Rosières", stop "Liberté". Open year round; HI card required. Dorm beds €15.70, including breakfast.

The Town

The centre of Troyes between the station and cathedral is scattered with marvellous **churches**, four of which are open to the public. The first you come to is the sumptuous, high-naved **St-Pantaléon** (Mon–Sat 9.30am–12.30pm & 2–5.30pm, Sun 2–5.30pm) on rue de Vauluisant, almost a museum of sculpture. A short walk to the north is Troyes' oldest church, twelfth-century **Ste-Madeleine**, on the road of the same name (same hours as St-Pantaléon) and remodelled in the sixteenth century, when the delicate stonework rood screen (*jubé*) – used to keep the priest separate from the congregation – was added. A short way to the southeast, between rues Émile-Zola and Champeaux and opposite the tourist office, is **St-Jean-au-Marché**, the church where Henry V of England married Catherine of France after being recognized as heir to the French throne in the 1420 Treaty of Troyes. Between it and the cathedral is the elegant Gothic **Basilique St-Urbain**, on place Vernier (same hours as St–Pantaléon), its exterior dramatizing the Day of Judgement.

Across the Canal de la Haute Seine lies the city's most outstanding museum, the **Musée d'Art Moderne** (Tues–Sun 10am–1pm & 2–6pm; €5, or part of the museum pass, see box opposite), housed in the old bishops' palace next to the cathedral on place St-Pierre. The museum displays the private collection built up by Alsace-born industrialist Pierre Lévy (1907–2002) and his wife Denise, who died in 1994. Lévy developed a strong friendship with the Fauvist André Derain, and it's this artist's work (including the famous paintings of Hyde Park and Big Ben) that forms the collection's core. For the rest, there are works by Degas, Courbet, Gauguin, Bonnard, Robert Delaunay and Max Ernst, but it's in no sense a greatest hits of modern art and therein lies its charm: entire rooms are devoted to a particular theme or to the works of lesser-known artists such as Maurice Marinot or Roger de la Fresnaye. Another room is given over to a beautiful collection of African carvings.

This is the ancient **quartier de la Cité**, an area with many of the city's oldest buildings. These all huddle around the **Cathédrale St-Pierre-et-St-Paul** (Mon–Sat 9.15am–noon & 1–5.45pm Sun 10am–4.45pm), whose pale Gothic nave is stroked with reflections from wonderful stained-glass. On the other side of the cathedral from the Musée d'Art Moderne, at 1 rue Chrétien-de-Troyes, the once glorious **Abbaye St-Loup** houses the **Musée Saint-Loup** (Tues–Sun 9am–noon & 1–5pm; €4, or part of museum pass scheme, see box opposite), seemingly endless galleries of mostly French paintings, including a couple by Watteau, an impressive collection of medieval sculpture, and some dismally displayed natural history and archeological exhibits. Down rue de la Cité, but with its entrance round the corner on quai des Comtes de Champagne, is the **apothicairerie**, a richly decorated sixteenth-century pharmacy (Tues–Sun 9am–noon & 1–5pm; €2, or part of museum pass scheme, see box opposite) occupying a corner of the majestic eighteenth-century **Hôtel-Dieu-le-Comte**; rows of painted wooden "simple" boxes dating from the eighteenth century adorn its shelves.

Clothes shopping in Troyes

Troyes made its name in the clothing trade, and today the industry still accounts for more than half of the town's employment. Buying clothes from **factory outlets** is one of the chief attractions: designer-label clothes can be picked up at two-thirds or less of the normal shop price. The best array is in the four giant sheds of **Marques Avenue**, avenue de la Maille, St-Julien-les-Villas, a couple of kilometres south of the city on the N71 to Dijon or on bus #2 (Mon–Fri 10am–7pm, Sat 9.30am–7pm, plus some Sun; ⓦwww.marquesavenue.com); there's also a special "shed" for household goods at 230 Faubourg Croncels, including luxury glass- and chinaware. At Pont–Ste-Marie, a short way to the northeast of Troyes between the D677 to Reims and the D960 to Nancy, are **Marques City** (Mon–Fri 10am–7pm, Sat 9.30am–7pm; ⓦwww.marquescity.com), and **McArthur Glen** (same hours as Marques City; ⓦwww.mcarthurglen.fr). Buses for the outlets on the outskirts of town depart from the bus stops by Marché les Halles (ask at the tourist offices for details).

Despite being raked by numerous fires since the Middle Ages, Troyes' old town has retained many timber-framed buildings. The most famous fire, in 1524, led to a massive rebuilding scheme that resulted in Troyes' wealth of Renaissance palaces. An outstanding example, just east of the church of St Pantaléon, is the sixteenth-century Hôtel de Mauroy, 7 rue de la Trinité, once an orphanage, then a textile factory, but now the **Maison de l'Outil et de la Pensée Ouvrière** (10am–6pm; €6.50, or part of the museum pass scheme, see box, p.246). Troyes' most original museum exhibits traditional tools of a myriad of trades, from chair caning to blacksmiths and from glove makers to coopers. Its beautifully lit displays provide a window into the world of workers who used them and the people who crafted them; video monitors throughout the museum demonstrate how they were used. Be sure to pick up the English language guide at the entrance – and to return it after your visit.

As tourist pamphlets point out, the ring of boulevards round the town is shaped like a champagne cork. It also looks a bit like a sock – rather appropriately, since hosiery ("bonneterie") and woollens have been Troyes' most important industry since the late Middle Ages. In the seventeenth century Louis XIII decreed that charitable houses had to be self-supporting and the orphanage of the Hôpital de la Trinité (the Hôtel de Mauroy) set its charges to knitting stockings. Some of the old machines and products used for creating garments can be seen in the sixteenth-century palace, the **Hôtel de Vauluisant**, at 4 rue de Vauluisant, part of which houses the rather dry **Musée de la Bonneterie** (Tues–Sun 9am–noon & 1–5pm; €3, or part of the museum pass scheme, see box, p.246); it houses an array of looms, sewing machines and the like as well as historic photographs and a collection of socks and stockings from the nineteenth and twentieth centuries. The palace also houses the more compelling **Musée Historique de Troyes et de la Champagne Méridionale** (same hours and ticket – English language leaflet available at entrance), which contains some gorgeous sixteenth-century sculptures of the Troyes school as well as some fine winged triptychs.

Eating, drinking and entertainment

Self-caterers should head for the Marché les Halles, a daily covered **market** on the corner of rue Général-de-Gaulle and place St-Rémy, close to the Hôtel de Ville. Central Troyes is sprinkled with **places to eat**, but quality is uneven and there's a preponderance of crêperies above anything more substantial. Most of the places worth tracking down cluster in the narrow streets around St Jean. *Le Tricasse* is a perennially popular **bar** at 2 rue Charbonnet, on the corner with narrow rue Paillot-de-Montabert – which is where you'll find the the tiny and consistently packed-out *Bar des Bougnets des Pouilles*. Back on rue Charbonnet, *Cotton Club* at no. 8 has a busy programme of DJ nights and live music, including jazz.

From late June to late July, the city organizes free **Ville en Musique** concerts in three or four picturesque locations in the historic centre; the programme ranges from classical and jazz to rock and hip–hop - pick up a schedule at the tourist office.

Bistroquet place Langevin ☎ 03.25.73.65.65. A classic place to try the regional speciality of *andouillette* (see box on "Regional food and drink", p.192), along with delicious home-style cooking; menus from €20.90; closed Sun evening.

Aux Crieurs de Vins 4 place Jean-Jaurès. Delightfully uncomplicated wine bar with *andouillettes* on the menu and a jumble of different furniture; *plats du jour* from €10.

Le Gaulois 12 rue Champeaux, ☎ 03.25.43.90.27. Bar/restaurant serving skewers of grilled meat with bowls of sauces for around €13.

La Mignardise 1 ruelle des Chats ☎ 03.25.73.15.30. Troyes' best restaurant, set in a sixteenth-century building with a quiet courtyard and serving a traditional French menu from €27. Closed Sun evening and Mon.

Le Valentino 35 rue Paillot de Montabert (entrance cours de la Rencontre); ☎ 03.25.73.14.14. Chic, intimate place serving gastronomic delights at reasonable prices. Reservations essential; closed Sun & Mon, & 3 weeks in Aug; menus €25 for lunch, from €33 for dinner.

The Plateau de Langres

The Seine, Marne, Aube and several other lesser rivers rise in the **Plateau de Langres** between Troyes and Dijon, with main routes from the former to the Burgundian capital skirting this area. To the east, the N19 (which the train follows) takes in **Chaumont** and **Langres**, two towns that could briefly slow your progress if you're in no hurry, and the home village of Charles de Gaulle, **Colombey-les-Deux-Églises**.

Chaumont

Situated on a steep ridge between the Marne and Suize valleys, **CHAUMONT** (Chaumont-en-Bassigny to give its full name), 93km east of Troyes, is best approached by train, which enables you to cross the town's stupendous mid-nineteenth-century viaduct, which took an average of 2500 labourers working night and day two years to construct. It's possible to walk across the viaduct, which gives you fine views of the Suize valley.

The town's most interesting historic building is the **Basilique St-Jean-Baptiste**. Though built with the same dour, grey stone of most Champagne churches, it has a wonderful Renaissance addition to the Gothic transept of balconies and turreted stairway, and a superb church organ of terrifying, earth–shattering power. The decoration includes an *Arbre de Jessé* of the early sixteenth-century Troyes school, in which all the characters are sitting in the tree, dressed in the style of the day.

You shouldn't leave without taking a look at **Les Silos**, 7–9 avenue Foch, near the *gare SNCF* (Tues, Thurs & Fri 2–7pm, Wed & Sat 10am–6pm; free), a 1930s agricultural co-op transformed into a graphic arts centre and *média-thèque*. As well as hosting temporary exhibitions, it's the main venue for

Chaumont's international **poster festival** (Festival de l'Affiche), held every year from mid-May to mid-June. As for the rest of the old town, there's not much to do except admire the twelfth-century castle keep of the Comtes de Champagne, the delightfully-named Tour d'Arse at the foot of the Vieille Ville – which is all that remains of the thirteenth-century town gate – and the strange, bulging stair towers of the houses.

The **tourist office** is opposite the *gare SNCF* on place du Général-Charles-de-Gaulle (Mon–Sat 9.30am–12.30pm & 2.30–6pm; ℡03.25.03.80.80), which is also where you'll find *Le Terminus Reine* (℡03.25.03.66.66, ⓦwww.relais-sud-champagne.com; ❹), an old-fashioned hotel with great charm; its *restaurant gastronomique* is the best place to eat.

Colombey-les-Deux-Églises

Twenty-seven kilometres northwest of Chaumont, on the N19 to Troyes, is **COLOMBEY-LES-DEUX-ÉGLISES**, the village where Gaullist leaders come to pay their respects at the grave of **General Charles de Gaulle**. The former president's family home, **La Boisserie**, opens its ground floor to the public (May–Sept daily 10am–7.30pm; Oct–April daily except Tues 10am–5.30pm; €4), but more impressive are the pink-granite **Cross of Lorraine**, symbol of the French Resistance movement, standing over 40m high on a hill just west of the village, signposted off the N19, and the spanking (and pricey) new **Mémorial Charles de Gaulle** (May–Sept daily 10am–7.30pm; Oct–April daily except Tues 10am–5.30pm; €12.50), an exhaustive chronicle of the man's life and times housed in an ultra-sleek museum building on the hillside beneath the cross. It was inaugurated in 2008 with much pomp by Nicolas Sarkozy and German Chancellor Angela Merkel on the fiftieth anniversary of the rapprochement between de Gaulle and then-German Chancellor Konrad Adenauer.

The best place to **stay** here is the splendid *Hostellerie La Montagne-Restaurant Natali*, rue de Pisseloup (℡03.25.01.51.69, ⓦwww.hostellerielamontagne.com; ❽; menus from €50), where the rooms are individually designed and truly top-notch. Run by a father and son team, it's really a restaurant with rooms – chef Jean-Baptiste Natali worked previously at the two-star restaurant at the Martinez in Cannes. A more modest option, with a simple country dining room and smartly renovated rooms with hi-tech bathrooms, is *La Grange du Relais* (℡03.25.02.03.89, ⓦwww.lagrangedurelais.fr; ❷; menus from €20) on the RN19 at the bottom of the town.

Langres

LANGRES, 35km south of Chaumont and just as spectacularly situated above the Marne, retains its near-complete encirclement of gateways, towers and ramparts. Walking this circuit, which gives views east to the hills of Alsace and southwest across the Plateau de Langres, is the best thing to do if you're just stopping for an hour or so. Don't miss the **St-Ferjeux tower** with its beautiful metal sculpture, *Air and Dreams*. Wandering inside the walls is also rewarding – Renaissance houses and narrow streets give the feel of a place time has left behind, swathed in the mists of southern Champagne. Langres was home to the eighteenth-century Enlightenment philosopher **Diderot** for the first sixteen years of his life, and people like to make the point that, if he were to return to Langres today, he'd have no trouble finding his way around.

The **Hôtel du Breuil de St-Germain**, at 2 rue Chambrûlard, is one of the best of the town's sixteenth-century mansions, though it can only be viewed from outside. The **Musée d'Art et Histoire** on place du Centenaire, near the cathedral (daily except Tues: April–Oct 10am–noon & 2–6pm; until 5pm in winter; €4) has a section devoted to Diderot, with his encyclopedias and various other first editions of his works, a portrait by Van Loos and collections of local archeology. The highlight of the museum is the superbly restored Romanesque **chapel of St Didier** in the old wing, housing a fourteenth-century painted ivory *Annunciation*. Sets of dining knives, a craft for which this area was famous for several centuries, are also on display along with other decorative arts. Local faïence – glazed terracotta – is featured, though these nicely crafted pieces are upstaged by the sixteenth-century tiles from Rouen in one of the nave chapels of the **Cathédrale St-Mammès**. This grey-stone edifice was not improved by the eighteenth-century addition of a new facade, but there's an amusing sixteenth-century relief of the Raising of Lazarus, in which the apostles watch, totally blasé, while other characters look like kids at a good horror movie.

Practicalities

The **tourist office** is just inside the town's main gate, the Porte des Moulins, on place Bel'Air (April–Aug Mon–Sat 9am–noon & 1.30–6.30pm, Sun 10am–12.15pm & 1.45–6pm; Oct Mon–Fri 9am–noon & 1.30–6pm, Sat 9.30am–noon & 1.30–6pm; Nov–March Mon–Fri 9am–noon & 1.30–5.30pm; Sat from 9.30am; ☏03.25.87.67.67, ⓦwww.tourisme-langres.com), on the other side of town from the **gare SNCF** (infrequent connections to Reims and Dijon); staff can give you a useful map of the main sights in town, and also have information on the four lakes in the surrounding region. The **bus** timetable from the train station to the Porte des Moulins is loosely based on the train timetable; note though that the last bus leaves before 7pm, although there are later train arrivals.

For **accommodation**, there's a **hostel** close by the Porte des Moulins on place Bel'Air (☏03.25.87.09.69, ⒻThis03.25.87.76.74; book ahead for Sat & Sun as the reception closes at weekends; ❶, breakfast and bedding extra), and the reasonable *Auberge Jeanne d'Arc*, 26 rue Gambetta (☏03.25.86.87.88; ❶), in the centre of town. More comfortable rooms can be had at the characterful *Cheval Blanc*, in a converted church at 4 rue de l'Estrés (☏03.25.87.07.00, ⓦwww .hotel-langres.com; ❺), or in the seventeenth-century, though rather less elegant, *Grand Hôtel de l'Europe*, 23–25 rue Diderot (☏03.25.87.10.88, ⓦwww .relais-sud-champagne.com; ❺). For good but expensive **food**, try *Restaurant Diderot* at the *Cheval Blanc* (closed Sun evening). Better value is to be had at the *Lion d'Or* (☏03.25.87.03.30), a restaurant and hotel just outside the town on the route de Vesoul with views of the surrounding lakes. Langres has its own highly flavourful, strong-smelling – and excellent – cheese, which you can buy at the Friday **market** on place Bel'Air.

The Ardennes

To the northeast of Reims, the scenery of the **Ardennes** region along the Meuse valley knocks spots off any landscape in Champagne. Most of the hills lie over the border in Belgium, but there's enough of interest on the French side to make it well worth exploring.

In war after war, the people of the Ardennes have been engaged in protracted last-ditch battles down the valley of the Meuse, which, once lost, gave invading armies a clear path to Paris. The rugged, hilly terrain and deep forests (frightening even to Julius Caesar's legionnaires) gave some advantage to World War II's

Resistance fighters when the Ardennes was annexed to Germany, but even during peace time life has never been easy. The land is unsuitable for crops, and the slate and ironworks, which were the main source of employment during the nineteenth century, closed in the 1980s. The only major investment in the region has been a nuclear power station in the loop of the Meuse at Chooz, to which locals responded by etching "Nuke the Élysée!" high on a half-cut cliff of slate just downstream.

This said, tourism, the main growth industry, is developing apace – there are walking and boating possibilities, plus good train and bus connections – though the eerie, isolated atmosphere of this region lingers.

Charleville-Mézières

The twin towns of **CHARLEVILLE** and **MÉZIÈRES** – the former a planned new town which in the seventeenth century more or less sucked the life out of the latter – provide a good base for exploring the northern part of the region, which spreads across the meandering Meuse before the valley closes in and the forests take over. Of the two, Charleville is the one to head for.

The splendid seventeenth-century **place Ducale**, in the centre of Charleville, was the result of the local duke's envy of the contemporary place des Vosges in Paris, which it somewhat resembles. Despite the posh setting, the shops in the arcades remain very down-to-earth and the cafés charge reasonable prices to sit outside: a very good position on Tuesdays, Thursdays and Saturdays, when the **market** is held here. From 31 place Ducale you can reach the complex of old and new buildings that house the **Musée de l'Ardenne** (Tues–Sun 10am–noon & 2–6pm; €4, combined ticket with Musée Arthur Rimbaud; free on first Sun of the month), a typically eclectic local museum which includes archeological finds from a local Merovingian cemetery, fascinating historic models of Charleville and Mézières in the seventeenth century and paintings on nineteenth-century industrial and political themes by Paul Gondrexon.

The most famous person to emerge from the town was Arthur Rimbaud (1854–91), who ran away from Charleville four times before he was 17, so desperate was he to escape its provincialism. He is honoured in the **Musée Arthur Rimbaud**, housed in a very grand stone windmill – a contemporary of the place Ducale – on quai Arthur-Rimbaud, two blocks north of the main square (same hours and ticket as Musée de l'Ardenne). It contains a host of pictures of him and people he hung out with, including his lover Verlaine, as well as facsimiles of his writings and related documents. A few steps down the quayside is the spot where he composed his most famous poem, *Le Bateau Ivre*. After penning poetry in Paris, journeying to the Far East and trading in Ethiopia and Yemen, Rimbaud died in a Marseille hospital. His body was brought back to his home town – probably the last place he would have wanted to be buried – and true Rimbaud fanatics can visit his **tomb** in the cemetery west of the place Ducale at the end of avenue Charles Boutet.

Charleville is a major international puppetry centre (its school is justly famous), and every three years it hosts one of the largest puppet festivals in the world, the **Festival Mondial des Théâtres de Marionnettes** (Ⓦwww .marionnette.com). Up to 150 professional troupes – some from as far away as Mali and Burma – put on something like fifty shows a day on the streets and in every available space in town. Tickets are cheap, and there are shows for adults as well as the usual stuff aimed at kids. If you miss the festival you can still catch one of the puppet performances in the summer months every year (Ⓣ03.24.33.72.50 for booking and information; tickets around €12), or if you're passing by the **Institut de la Marionnette** between 10am and 9pm, you can see one of the automated episodes of the *Four Sons of Aymon* enacted on the facade's clock every hour, or all twelve scenes on Saturday at 9.15am.

Practicalities

From the **gare SNCF**, place Ducale is a ten-minute walk; the **gare routière** is a couple of blocks west of the square, by the Marché Couvert. The **regional tourist office** for the Ardennes is at 22 place Ducale (July & Aug Mon–Sat 9am–7pm, Sun 10am–7pm; Sept–June Mon–Wed, Fri & Sat 9.30am–noon & 1.30–6pm, Thurs 10am–noon & 1.30–6pm; ☎03.24.56.06.08), with Charleville-Mézières' **tourist office** at no. 4 (June–Sept Mon–Fri 9.30am–noon & 1.30–7pm, Sat until 6pm, Sun until 5pm; April, May & Sept–Dec Mon–Sat 9.30am–noon & 1.30–6pm; Jan–Mar closes at 5pm; ☎03.24.55.69.90, ⓦwww.charleville-tourisme.com).

Three fairly central **hotels** that are worth trying are: the *Hôtel de Paris*, 24 avenue G.-Corneau, which offers free internet access (☎03.24.33.34.38, ⓦwww.hoteldeparis08.fr; ❷); the *Cesar*, 23 avenue du Maréchal–Leclerc (☎03.24.26.12.00, ⓦwww.cesar-hotel.fr; ❷); and *Le Relais du Square*, 3 place de la Gare (☎03.24.33.38.76, ⓦwww.hotel-charleville-mezieres.com; ❸), a two-star hotel in a tree-filled square near the station. The town's **campsite**, *Camping du Mont Olympe* (☎03.24.33.23.60, ⓔcamping-charlevillemezieres @orange.fr; open May to mid-Oct), is north of place Ducale, over the river and left along rue des Paquis. There are plenty of places to **eat and drink**. For something a bit special, *La Côte à l'Os*, at 11 cours Aristide-Briand (☎03.24.59.20.16), specializes in *fruits de mer* and local cuisine; daily menus start at €13. At 33 rue du Moulin, the Michelin-listed *La Clef des Champs* (☎03.24.56.17.50) offers menus from €35.

North of Charleville

George Sand wrote of the stretch of the Meuse that winds through the Ardennes that "its high wooded cliffs, strangely solid and compact, are like some inexorable destiny that encloses, pushes and twists the river without permitting it a single whim or any escape". What all the tourist literature emphasizes, however, are the legends of medieval struggles between Good and Evil whose characters have given names to some of the curious rocks and crests. The grandest of these, where the schist formations have taken the most peculiar turns, is the **Roc de la Tour**, also known as the "Devil's Castle", up a path off the D31, 3.5km out of **Monthermé**, itself a slate-roofed little town with nothing of great interest except a twelfth-century church with late medieval frescoes.

The journey through this frontier country should ideally be done on foot or skis, or **by boat**. The alternatives for the latter are good old *bateau-mouche*-type cruises or live-in pleasure boats – not wildly expensive if you can split the cost four or six ways; the regional tourist office at Charleville (see above) can provide information on hiking, canoeing, biking or riding. For **public transport** from Charleville, trains follow the Meuse towards Belgium, while local Charleville buses run as far as **Nouzonville**.

The **GR12** is a good walking route, circling the **Lac des Vieilles Forges**, 17km northwest of Charleville, then meeting the Meuse at Bogny and crossing over to Hautes-Rivières in the even more sinuous **Semoy Valley**. There are plenty of other tracks, too, though beware of *chasse* (hunting) signs – French hunters tend to hack through the undergrowth with their safety catches off and are notoriously trigger-happy. Wild boar are the main quarry – they are nowhere near as dangerous as their pursuers, and would seem to be more intelligent, too, rooting about near the crosses of the Resistance memorial near **Revin**, while hunters stalk the forest. A good place to stay, overlooking the river at Revin, is the *Hôtel François-1er*, 46 quai Camille-Desmoulins (℡03.24.40.15.88, ⓦ www.francois1.fr; ❶).

The abundance of wild boar is partly explained when you rummage around on the forest floor yourself and discover, between the trees to either side of the river, an astonishing variety of mushrooms, and, in late summer, wild strawberries and bilberries. For a quaint insight into life in the forest, stop at the **Musée de la Forêt**, situated right on the edge of the Ardennes, 2km north of **Renwez** on the D40 (daily: Jan–May 9am–noon & 2–6pm; June–Sept 9am–7pm; Oct–Dec 9am–noon & 2–5pm; €8). All manner of wood-cutting, gathering and transporting is enacted by wooden dummies along with displays of utensils and flora and fauna of the forest; it's also a tranquil spot for a picnic.

Travel details

Trains

Amiens to: Albert (frequent; 20min); Arras (frequent; 40–50min); Compiègne (5 daily; 1hr 30min); Laon (5 daily; 1hr 40min); Lille (frequent; 1hr 25min); Paris (every 30min–1hr; 1hr 20min); Reims (2 daily; 2hr 30min).

Arras to: Albert (approx. every 1–2hr; 25min); Calais (2 daily, 1hr 45min); Etaples (4 daily; 1hr 30min); Boulogne (4 daily; 1 hr 50min); Douai (frequent; 15–20min); Lille (approx. every 1–2hr; 45min); Paris (frequent; 50min–1hr).

Beauvais to: Paris (every 45min–1hr; 1hr 10min).

Boulogne–Ville to: Abbeville (8 daily; 1 hr); Amiens (frequent; 1hr 20min); Arras (5 daily; 2hr); Calais-Ville (approx. hourly; 30min); Étaples–Le Touquet (8 daily; 20–30min); Lille (6 daily; 1hr); Montreuil–sur-Mer (8 daily; 40min); Paris (9 daily; 2hr 40min).

Calais–Ville to: Abbeville (4 daily; hr 30min); Boulogne-Ville (approx. hourly; 30min); Dunkerque (4 daily; 40–55min); Étaples–Le Touquet (6 daily; 1hr) Paris (2 daily; 1hr 40min).

Calais–Fréthun to: Lille (6 daily; 30min); Paris (3 daily; 1hr 30min).

Compiègne to: Paris (frequent; 40–50min).

Dunkerque to: Calais-Ville (5 daily; 50–55min); Cassel (approx. hourly; 25min).

Laon to: Paris (9 daily; 1hr 30min–2hr); Soissons (approx. every 1–2hr; 30min).

Lille to: Arras (approx. every 1–2hr; 40min); Boulogne (6 daily; 55min); Brussels (TGV 6 daily; 40min); Charleville Mézières (6 daily; 2hr 30min); Dunkerque (approx. hourly; 1hr); Lyon (TGV 10 daily; 3hr–3hr 50min); Marseille (TGV 6 daily; 4–5hr, via Lyon); Paris (TGV frequent; 50min–1hr); TGV Haute Picardie (9 daily; 25min).

Reims to: Charleville-Mézières (almost hourly; 50min); Épernay (7 daily; 35min); Laon (8 daily; 35–45min); Paris (6 daily; 45min).

Troyes to: Chaumont (9 daily; 50min); Langres (8 daily; 1hr 15min); Paris (frequent; 1hr 30min).

Buses

Amiens to: Abbeville (2 daily; 1hr 25min); Albert (4 daily; 45min–1hr 8min); Beauvais (3 daily; 1hr 45min).

Boulogne to: Calais (5 daily; 40min); Dunkerque (2–4 daily; 1hr 20min); Le Touquet (5 daily; 1hr 20min).

Calais to: Boulogne (5 daily; 40min).

Dunkerque to: Boulogne (2–5 daily; 1hr 40min); Calais (11 daily; 45min).

Reims to: Laon (2–3 daily; 1hr 30min).

Soissons to: Coucy (7 daily; 25min).

Alsace and Lorraine

CHAPTER 3 **Highlights**

* **Strasbourg Cathedral**
  Climb the lofty spire of this magnificent Gothic cathedral for stunning views as far as the Black Forest. See p.263

* **The Route du Vin**
  Surrounded by a sea of vines, Alsace's picturesque wine villages are overlooked by a wealth of ruined castles, perched on pine-clad fringes of the Vosges. See p.272

* **The Issenheim Altarpiece, Colmar** Luridly expressive, this Renaissance masterpiece alone makes quaint Colmar worth a visit. See p.278

* **Bugattis at Mulhouse's Cité de l'Automobile** A unique collection of vintage motors in the city where the French car industry was set in motion. See p.282

* **Place Stanislas, Nancy** Along with some outstanding Art Nouveau, elegant Nancy is home to one of the most grandiose eighteenth-century squares in all France. See p.286

* **Chagall windows, Metz Cathedral** Moses and co. captured in glorious technicolour glass. See p.289

▲ Hôtel de Ville, Nancy

Alsace and Lorraine

Disputed for centuries by French kings and the princes of the Holy Roman Empire, and subsequently embroiled in a bloody tug-of-war between France and Germany, France's easternmost provinces share a tumultuous history. Visiting Alsace and Lorraine, you'll find a host of ruined castles, poignant war memorials and France's only Nazi concentration camp.

The people of **Alsace** tend to display a Mitteleuropa taste for Hansel-and-Gretel-type decoration – oriel windows, carved timberwork, toy-town gables and window boxes overflowing with geraniums. This distinct combination of French and German influences is seen at its most vivid in the numerous wine villages that punctuate the **Route du Vin**, along the eastern margin of the forests of the Vosges mountains. The region's white wines are an attraction in themselves; they accompany a cuisine more Germanic than French, which revolves around pork, cabbage and pungent cheese. The handsome regional capital, **Strasbourg**, and smaller, more postcardish **Colmar**, are home to some outstanding museums and churches. A noticeably wealthy province, Alsace has historically churned out cars and textiles, not to mention half the beer in France.

Alsace's less prosperous rival, **Lorraine**, shares borders with Luxembourg, Germany and Belgium, and is part farmland, part rust belt. Although less scenic than Alsace, the elegant former capital, **Nancy**, home to a major school of Art Nouveau, is well worth a visit, as is leafy **Metz**, the current capital. The bloody World War I battlefields around **Verdun** also attract a large number of visitors. Gastronomically less renowned than other French provinces, Lorraine has nonetheless bequeathed to the world one of its favourite savoury pies – the *quiche lorraine*.

Alsace

Although it can sometimes seem unfeasibly quaint, there's no denying that **Alsace** is charming, thanks to its old stone and half-timbered towns and villages set along the fertile Rhine valley and amid the thickly wooded hills of the Vosges. **Strasbourg**, the capital of Alsace, is undoubtedly one of the most attractive cities in France. The pretty market towns of **Saverne** and **Wissembourg**, to the north,

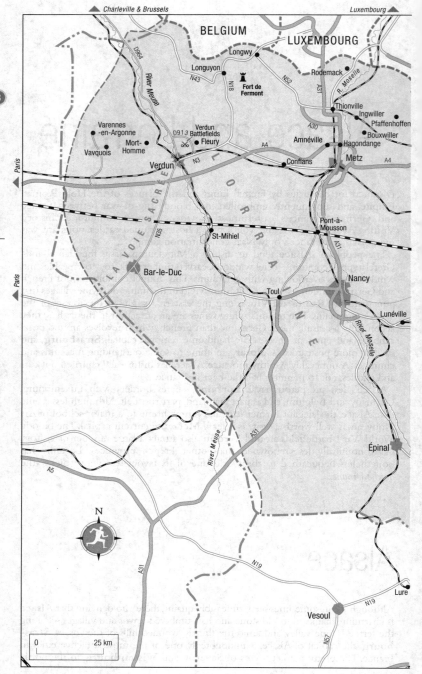

Charleville & Brussels

Luxembourg

BELGIUM

LUXEMBOURG

Longwy

Longuyon

N43

Rodemack

R. Moselle

N18

Fort de
Fermont

N52

A31

D964

River Meuse

Thionville

Ingwiller

A30

Pfaffenhoffen

Varennes
-en-Argonne

Verdun
Battlefields

Bouxwiller

Mort-
Homme

D913

Fleury

Amnéville

Hagondange

Vavquois

Verdun

N3

Conflans

Metz

A4

A4

Paris

L O R R A I N E

LA VOIE SACRÉE

N35

Pont-à-
Mousson

A31

St-Mihiel

Bar-le-Duc

Nancy

Paris

Toul

River Moselle

Lunéville

River Meuse

A37

Épinal

A5

N

A31

N19

Lure

Vesoul

N19

N57

0   25 km

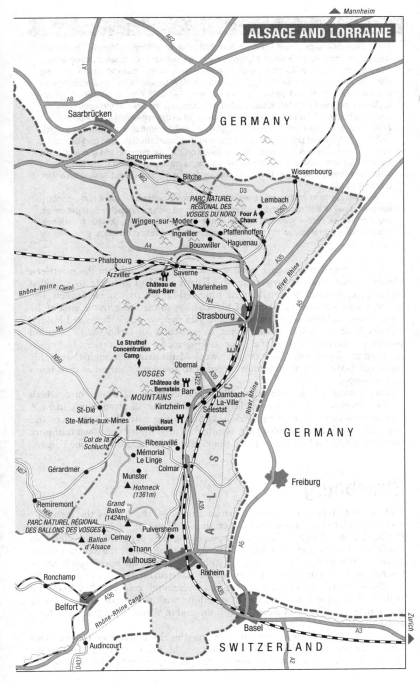

ALSACE AND LORRAINE

Mannheim

Saarbrücken

GERMANY

Sarreguemines

Bitche

Wissembourg

PARC NATUREL
RÉGIONAL DES
VOSGES DU NORD

Lembach

Four À
Chaux

Wingen-sur-Moder

Ingwiller

Pfaffenhoffen

Bouxwiller

Haguenau

Phalsbourg

Arzviller

Saverne

Château de
Haut-Barr

Marlenheim

Strasbourg

River Rhine

Le Struthof
Concentration
Camp

VOSGES

Obernai

Château de
Bernstein

Barr

MOUNTAINS

Kintzheim

Dambach-
La-Ville

Sélestat

St-Dié

Ste-Marie-aux-Mines

Haut
Koenigsbourg

GERMANY

Col de la
Schlucht

Ribeauvillé

Mémorial
Le Linge

Gérardmer

Colmar

Munster

Hohneck
(1361m)

Freiburg

Grand
Ballon
(1424m)

Remiremont

PARC NATUREL RÉGIONAL
DES BALLONS DES VOSGES

Pulversheim

Ballon
d'Alsace

Cernay

Thann

Mulhouse

Ronchamp

Rixheim

Belfort

Rhône-Rhine Canal

Basel

Zurich

Audincourt

SWITZERLAND

Rhône-Rhine Canal

Alsatian food

The cuisine of Alsace is quite distinct from that of other regions of France. The classic dish is *choucroute*, the aromatic pickled cabbage known in German as **sauerkraut**. The secret here is the inclusion of juniper berries in the pickling stage and the addition of goose grease or lard. Traditionally it's served with large helpings of smoked pork, ham and sausages, but some restaurants offer a succulent variant replacing the meat with fish (*choucroute aux poissons*), usually salmon and monkfish. The qualification *à l'alsacienne* after the name of a dish means "with *choucroute*". **Foie gras** is another prized local speciality, as is **baeckoffe**, a three-meat hotpot, comprising layers of potato, pork, mutton and beef marinated in wine and baked for several hours. **Onions**, too, crop up frequently on menus, either in the guise of a tart (*tarte à l'oignon*), made with a béchamel sauce, or as *flammeküche* (*tarte flambée*), a mixture of onion, cream and pieces of chopped smoked pork breast, baked on a thin, pizza-like base.

Alsatians are fond of their **pastries**. In almost every patisserie, you'll find a mouth-watering array of fruit tarts made with rhubarb (topped with meringue), wild blueberries, red cherries or yellow *mirabelle* plums. Cake-lovers should try *kugelhopf*, a dome-shaped cake with a hollow in the middle made with raisins and almonds.

are a good base for exploring some spectacular ruined castles in the **northern Vosges**, while south of Strasbourg, the **Route du Vin** is home to countless picturesque medieval hamlets, all with timbered houses and cobbled streets. The concentration camp of **Le Struthof**, hidden away in the forest, to the west of the wine village of **Barr**, is a sobering reminder of the province's chequered history.

Pretty **Colmar** is well worth a visit, in particular for Grünewald's beautiful Issenheim altarpiece, one of the most striking pieces of religious art in France. By contrast, less-visited (and far less twee) **Mulhouse**, although thoroughly industrial, boasts eclectic museums devoted to subjects as varied as cars, trains and wallpaper.

Every town has its own **tourist office** (🌐 www.tourisme-alsace.com), which is often housed in the *mairie* or Hôtel de Ville; almost all provide free maps. A comprehensive TER **train** network links Strasbourg with all major towns and many of the wine villages along the Route du Vin. Without your own transport, however, you'll find it hard to reach the castles and hiking trails in the Vosges.

Strasbourg

STRASBOURG owes both its Germanic name – "the City of the Roads" – and its wealth to its strategic position on the west bank of the Rhine. Self-styled *le Carrefour de l'Europe* ("Europe's Crossroads"), it is geographically closer to Frankfurt, Zurich and even Milan than to Paris, although the much-awaited TGV has placed the French capital within two and a half hours' reach. Strasbourg's medieval commercial pre-eminence was damaged by its involvement in the religious struggles of the sixteenth and seventeenth centuries, but recovered with its absorption into France in 1681. Along with the rest of Alsace, the city was annexed by Germany from 1871 to the end of World War I and again from 1940 to 1944.

Today, old animosities have been submerged in the **European Union**, with Strasbourg the seat of the Council of Europe, the European Court of Human Rights and the European Parliament. Prosperous, beautiful and easy to get around, Strasbourg has a metropolitan air without being in the least overwhelming. Boasting one of the loveliest cathedrals in France and one of the oldest and most active universities, it is a leading destination in its own right.

Arrival and information

The **gare SNCF** lies on the west side of the city centre, fifteen-minutes' walk from the cathedral along rue du Maire-Kuss and rue du 22-Novembre. The **airport shuttle bus** (*navette*), departing Entzheim international airport every twenty minutes (5.20am–11.20pm), drops off at Baggersee, south of the centre, from where you can catch the tram into central Strasbourg (€5.20 single combined ticket).

The main **tourist office** is at 17 place de la Cathédrale (daily 9am–7pm; ℡03.88.52.28.28, ⓦwww.otstrasbourg.fr), with the regional office for the Bas-Rhin *département* (northern Alsace) nearby at 9 rue du Dôme (Mon–Fri 9am–noon & 1–5pm; ℡03.88.15.45.85/88). The tourist office can provide you with a map (€1 for one with museums and sights marked on it; free otherwise). There's also a tourist office in the underground shopping complex just in front of the train station (daily 9am–7pm). Depending on your itinerary, it may be worth investing in a **Strasbourg Pass** (€11.40), which entitles you to one free museum entry, one half-price museum entry, a boat tour, a full day of bike hire and the cathedral tower and clock.

With much of the city centre pedestrian-only, several car parks (ⓦwww .parcus.com) cater for drivers. While the compact centre can easily be explored on foot, the city boasts an efficient public transport system, which includes five tram lines (€1.30 single or €2.50 return; ⓦwww.cts-strasbourg .fr). Strasbourg must also be a strong contender for France's most **bicycle**-friendly city; 300km of cycle lanes make bicycle hire a tempting option (see "Listings", p.268).

Accommodation

When looking for a place to **stay**, do bear in mind that once a month (except Aug, but twice in Oct) the European Parliament is in session for the best part of a week, bringing hundreds of MEPs and their entourages into town. To find out in advance when the parliament is sitting, contact the main tourist office.

Hotels

Beaucour Romantik 5 rue des Bouchers ℡03.88.76.72.00, ⓦwww.hotel-beaucour.com. Central but rather overpriced hotel in a handsome old house just off place du Corbeau. Rooms are furnished in a cosy Alsatian style; the more expensive come with Jacuzzi baths. **❼**

Cathédrale 12–13 place de la Cathédrale ℡03.88.22.12.12, ⓦwww.hotel-cathedrale .fr. Upmarket hotel with comfortable, if unimaginative rooms, the priciest of which boast unrivalled views of the cathedral. **❼**

Cerf d'Or 6 place de l'Hôpital ℡03.88.36.20.05, ⓦwww.cerf-dor.com. Attractive, family-run place, housed in a sixteenth-century building, with a small swimming pool/ sauna and its own restaurant (lunch menu €34). Closed mid-Dec to mid-Jan and last two weeks of July. **❹**

Diana Dauphine 30 rue de la 1ᵉʳ-Armée ℡03.88.36.26.61, ⓦwww.hotel-diana-dauphine .com. Large, designer hotel a short walk south of the Ill, with contemporary rooms and a chic breakfast café, albeit in a building you wouldn't look twice at. **❼**

Dragon 2 rue de l'Écarlate ℡03.88.35.79.80, ⓦwww.dragon.fr. Seventeenth-century house with a paved courtyard, completely renovated to create a luxurious modern hotel with attractive rooms, decorated in soothing light grey shades. **❺**

Le Grillon 2 rue Thiergarten ℡03.88.32.71.88, ⓦwww.grillon.com. Great budget option just a few-minutes' walk from the train station; homely rooms with creaky wooden floors above the lively *Perestroïka* vodka bar. Shared bathrooms **❷**; or rooms with showers **❸**

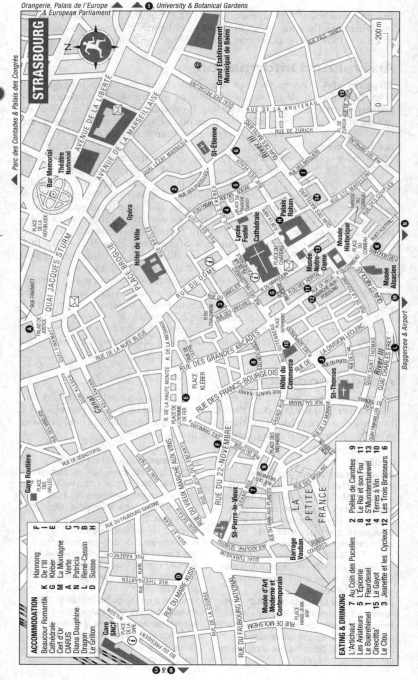

STRASBOURG

Orangerie, Palais de l'Europe & European Parliament ▲ ▲ ❶ University & Botanical Gardens

Parc des Contades & Palais des Congrès

Grand Etablissement Municipal de Bains

RUE PAUL TASET
RUE DE LA KRUTENAU
RUE DES PECHEURS
QUAI DES PECHEURS
RUE DE ZÜRICH
PL. DE ZÜRICH RUE DE ZÜRICH ❶❺
QUAI DES BATELIERS

St-Etienne ❻
River III
QUAI DES PECHEURS

AVENUE DE LA MARSEILLAISE
AVENUE DE LA LIBERTÉ
QUAI LEZAY MARNESIA
RUE DES PUCELLES
RUE DES FRÈRES
RUE DES SOEURS
PLACE DU MARCHÉ GAYOT
RUE DE LA RAPE
QUAI DES BATELIERS ❶
RUE DES BATELIERS

Bar Memorial
Théâtre National

Opéra

Hôtel de Ville

PLACE DE LA RÉPUBLIQUE
QUAI JACQUES STURM
PLACE BROGLIE
RUE BRÛLÉE
RUE DU DÔME

❷ RUE DES PUCELLES
❹ ❺
Lycée Fustel
Cathédrale
PLACE DU CHÂTEAU
Palais Rohan
Musée Notre-Dame ❶❸
Musée Historique
PLACE DU CORBEAU ❶❹
Musée Alsacien

RUE FINKMATT
RUE DE LA NUÉE BLEUE
PALAIS DE JUSTICE ❶

QUAI FINKMATT
Canal
QUAI KLÉBER
RUE KUHN

RUE DE LA MESANGE
R. DE LA HAUTE MONTÉE
PLACE DE L'HOMME DE FER
R. DE LA TOUR

❶ RUE DU SANGLIER
RUE DES ORFÈVRES ❸
R. DU CHAUDRON
RUE DES ORFÈVRES
RUE DU MAROQUIN
R. DU VIEUX HÔPITAL ❶❷ RUE DU MARCHÉ AUX POISSONS

RUE DES GRANDES ARCADES
PLACE KLÉBER
RUE GUTENBERG ❶⓿
RUE DES FRANCS-BOURGEOIS
Hôtel du Commerce
RUE DE LA DIVISION LECLERC
St-Thomas
RUE DU PUITS ❾
RUE SAINTE-BARBE
GRAND RUE
RUE SAINTE-BARBE

PLACE DES HALLES
Gare Routière
RUE DE SÉBASTOPOL
RUE DU JEU DES ENFANTS ❺
RUE DU VIEUX MARCHÉ AUX VINS
RUE DES TANNEURS ❼ ❻
RUE DU 22-NOVEMBRE
St-Pierre-le-Vieux
PLACE DES MEUNIERS
RUE DES MEUNIERS

Gare SNCF
PLACE DE LA GARE
RUE DU MAIRE-KUSS
RUE DU FAUBOURG NATIONAL
RUE DU FAUBOURG SAVERNE

Musée d'Art Moderne et Contemporain
PLACE HANS-JEAN ARP
RUE DE MOLSHEIM
QUAI TURCKHEIM
QUAI CHARLES FREY
Barrage Vauban
LA PETITE FRANCE
PONTS COUVERTS
PONT ST-THOMAS
QUAI ST-THOMAS
QUAI FINKWILLER
River III
RUE DE LA MONNAIE
RUE DES MOULINS
QUAI DE LA COURSE
BD DU PRÉSIDENT WILSON

Baggersee & Airport

200 m
0

▲ Orangerie, Palais de l'Europe

ACCOMMODATION

Beaucour Romantik	K
Cathédrale	G
Cerf d'Or	M
CARUS	A
Diana Dauphine	J
Dragon	B
Le Grillon	H
Hannong	F
De l'Ill	I
Kléber	E
La Montagne	C
Verte	A
Patricia	J
René-Cassin	L
Suisse	D

EATING & DRINKING

L'Artichaut	7	Au Coin des Pucelles	2
Les Aviateurs	5	L'Epicerie	8
Le Buerehiesel	1	Fleurdesel	14
Cinecitta'	15	Le Gayot	4
Le Clou	3	Jeanette et les Cycleux	12
Poêles de Carottes	9		
Le Roi et son Fou	11		
S'Munsterstuewel	13		
Terres à Vin	10		
Les Trois Brasseurs	6		

Hannong 15 rue du 22-Novembre
ⓣ 03.88.32.16.22, ⓦ www.hotel-hannong.com.
Beautiful parquet floors and tasteful furnishings in
the rooms go some way to justifying the room
rates; the bar is open late and has live jazz. ⓺–⓼
De l'Ill 8 rue des Bateliers ⓣ 03.88.36.20.01,
ⓦ www.hotel-ill.com. Immaculate rooms over several
stories of an old town house, on a quiet street just
50m from the river; the only drawback is the absence
of a lift. Closed end of Dec to mid-Jan. ⓷
Kléber 29 place Kléber ⓣ 03.88.32.09.53, ⓦ www
.hotel-kleber.com. Quirky, bijou rooms, themed
around spices and fruits, such as cardamom and
strawberry; there's even a room inspired by the
ubiquitous local *kugelhopf*. ⓸
Patricia 1a rue du Puits ⓣ 03.88.32.14.60,
ⓦ www.hotelpatricia.fr. Decent sized rooms, up an
old wooden staircase bedecked in oriental rugs, in
a great location in the backstreets of the old town.
Reception has limited opening hours. ⓶
Suisse 2–4 rue de la Râpe ⓣ 03.88.35.22.11,
ⓦ www.hotel-suisse.com. Friendly hotel in a
labyrinthine old house just a stone's throw from the
cathedral. It's a superb location, although the
rooms (with the exception of the family rooms) are
rather cramped. ⓸

Hostels and campsite

CIARUS 7 rue Finkmatt ⓣ 03.88.15.27.88/90,
ⓦ www.ciarus.com. By far the most central hostel;
it's just behind the Palais de Justice, 15min walk
around the river from the train station. 8 bed dorms
€18.50 including breakfast, single rooms ⓶, twin
rooms ⓷.
La Montagne Verte 2 rue Robert-Forrer
ⓣ 03.88.30.25.46, ⓦ www.camping-montagne
-verte-strasbourg.com. Well-equipped campsite
behind the *René-Cassin* hostel; take bus #2 from
train station, direction "Campus d'Illkirch", to "Nid
des Cigognes", or tram B or C from Place Homme
de Fer to "Montagne Verte" then bus #2, #13 or
#15 to "Nid des Cigognes". Open mid-March to
Oct & Dec.
René-Cassin 9 rue de l'Auberge-de-Jeunesse
ⓣ 03.88.30.26.46, ⓔ strasbourg.rene-cassin
@fuaj.org. Large, fully-equipped HI hostel in a
tranquil spot 3km southwest of the city centre.
Bus #2 from the station (direction "Campus
d'Illkirch") to "Auberge de Jeunesse", or tram
then bus from Homme de Fer as for the campsite.
3–12 bed dorms €19 including breakfast, private
rooms ⓶.

The City

It isn't difficult to find your way around Strasbourg on foot, as the flat city centre
is concentrated on a small island encircled by the **River Ill** and an old canal. The
magnificent filigree spire of the pink-sandstone **cathedral** is visible throughout
the city, though its silhouette was deformed by scaffolding at the time of writing.
Immediately south of the cathedral are the best of the museums, while to the
northwest, **place Kléber** is the heart of the commercial district. The more
attractive **place Gutenberg** to the south is nominally the city's main square.
About a ten-minute walk west, on the tip of the island, is picturesque **La Petite
France**, where timber-framed houses and canals hark back to the city's medieval
trades of tanning and dyeing. Across the canal to the east of the centre is the late
nineteenth-century **German quarter** and the city's **European institutions**.

The cathedral and place Gutenberg

The **Cathédrale de Notre-Dame** (daily 7–11.30am & 12.40–7pm; closed
during services; free) soars out of the close huddle of medieval houses at its
feet with a single spire of such delicate, flaky lightness that it seems the work
of confectioners rather than masons. It's worth slogging up the 332 steps to
the spire's **viewing platform** (daily, April–Sept 9am–7.15pm; Oct–March
10am–5.15pm; June & July open until 9.45pm on Fri and Sat; €4.60) for the
superb view of the old town, and, in the distance, the Vosges to the west and
the Black Forest to the east.

The **interior**, too, is magnificent, the high nave a model of proportion
enhanced by a glorious sequence of stained-glass windows. The finest are in the
south aisle next to the door, depicting the life of Christ and the Creation, but
the modern glass in the apse designed in 1956 by Max Ingrand to commemorate the city's first European institutions is also beautiful. On the left of the nave,

The Alsatian language

Travelling through the province, you'll hear locals converse in **Elsässisch** – a High German dialect known to philologists as Alemannic. There are two versions – High and Low Alemannic, plus an obscure Frankish dialect spoken in the Wissembourg region and a Romance one (*Welche*) in the valleys around Orbey.

Given the province's turbulent history, it's in many ways a miracle that these dialects have survived. **Elsässisch** was suppressed during the French Revolution only for French to be ousted by German after the Prussian victory in 1870, and again under the Nazi occupation.

Nowadays, most daily transactions are conducted in French. Yet Elsässisch remains a living language and is still spoken by young and old throughout Alsace. A renaissance of regional identity has meant that it's beginning to reappear on signs, too.

the cathedral's organ perches precariously above one of the arches, while further down on the same side is the late fifteenth-century pulpit, a masterpiece of intricacy in stone by the aptly named Hans Hammer.

In the south transept are the cathedral's two most popular sights. The **Pilier des Anges** is a slender triple-tiered central column, decorated with some of the most graceful and expressive statuary of the thirteenth century. The huge and enormously complicated **astrological clock** (tickets can be bought from the postcard stand 9am–11am, then at the cash desk at the south door 11.35am–noon; €2) was built by Schwilgué of Strasbourg in 1842. It is a favourite with the tour-group operators, whose customers roll up in droves at midday to witness the clock's crowning performance of the day, striking the hour of noon, which it does with unerring accuracy at 12.30pm – that being 12 o'clock "Strasbourg time".

Narrow rue Mercière, busy with cathedral-gazers, funnels west to **place Gutenberg**, with its steep-pitched roofs and brightly painted facades. It was named after the printer and pioneer of moveable type who lived in the city in the early fifteenth century and whose statue occupies the middle of the square. On the west side stands the sixteenth-century **Hôtel de Commerce**.

South of the cathedral

Most of Strasbourg's **museums** are to the south of the cathedral, between the tree-lined place du Château and the river. Check with the tourist office for museum passes/discounts if you're planning to visit them all. Entry is free on the first Sunday of the month.

Next to the cathedral, place du Château is enclosed to the south by the imposing **Palais Rohan**, designed for the immensely powerful Rohan family, who, for several generations, cornered the market in cardinals' hats. It now contains three museums (Mon & Wed–Fri noon–6pm, Sat & Sun 10am–6pm; closed Tues and public hols; €4 each): the **Musée des Arts Décoratifs**; the **Musée des Beaux-Arts**; and the rather specialist **Musée Archéologique**. Of the three collections, the Arts Décoratifs stands out; its collections include some fine eighteenth-century faïence tiles crafted in the city by Paul Hannong and some impressive trompe l'oeil crockery. The palace itself fell victim to the vicissitudes of the Revolution, following which the original furnishings were sold off. Although refurnished in period style, its vast, ostentatious rooms are not especially interesting.

Next door, the excellent **Musée de l'Oeuvre Notre-Dame** (Tues–Fri noon–6pm, Sat & Sun 10am–6pm; closed Mon & public hols; €4) houses the original sculptures from the cathedral exterior, damaged in the Revolution and replaced today by copies. Other treasures here include the eleventh-century Wissembourg Christ, said to be the oldest representation of a human figure in stained glass, and the architect's original parchment drawings for the statuary, which are fascinatingly detailed.

Past the picturesque place du Marché-aux-Cochons-de-Lait is the much refurbished **Musée Historique** (Sept–June Tues–Fri noon–6pm, Sat & Sun 10am–6pm; July & Aug daily except Mon 10am–6pm; closed public hols; €4). Interactive exhibits guide you through Strasbourg's political and social history, as a prosperous free city of the Holy Roman Empire, through the theological controversies of the Reformation to French annexation by Louis XIV and the revolutionary fervour of 1789. The prize exhibit is an enormous 3D relief map of the city, commissioned in the 1720s to show the state of the city's fortifications. At the time of writing, the narrative ended rather abruptly in the 1830s; exhibits on the nineteenth and twentieth centuries are due to open in 2009. Across the river, in a typically Alsatian house on quai St-Nicolas, the **Musée Alsacien** (Mon & Wed–Fri noon–6pm, Sat & Sun 10am–6pm; closed public hols; €4) contains elaborately painted furniture and other quaint local artefacts.

Musée d'Art Moderne et Contemporain

Housed in a purpose-built, glass-fronted building overlooking the river and Vauban's dam (see below), the light and airy **Musée d'Art Moderne et Contemporain** (Tues, Wed & Fri noon–7pm, Thurs noon–9pm, Sat & Sun 10am–6pm; closed Mon & public hols; €5) hosts temporary exhibitions, alongside its well-presented permanent collections, which include a sprinkling of minor works by some of the most celebrated twentieth-century French artists. Most interesting is the ground floor, which confronts the themes of modern European art from the late nineteenth century through to the 1950s. Starting with a small group of impressionist paintings, by the likes of Pissarro, Sisley and Monet, the collection features Kandinsky's studies for the ceramic *salon de musique*, a couple of Picassos, plus a good section on Surrealism, with plenty of folkloric, mystical paintings by Brauner. There's a room devoted to the voluptuous, smooth curves sculpted by Strasbourg's own Jean Arp, who was influenced by Dada and Surrealism before turning to sculpture. The collections are not extensive – but there are some interesting works by lesser known artists. Upstairs, the emphasis switches to more conceptual "contemporary art", primarily Arte Povera, before finishing up with stripey creations by Daniel Buren and temporary installations.

La Petite France and the rest of the old city

On the south side of the Pont du Corbeau, the medieval street **Impasse du Corbeau** still looks much as it must have done in the fourteenth century. Heading west along the quai, the Pont St-Thomas leads to the **church of St-Thomas** (Feb Sat & Sun 2–5pm; March, Nov & Dec daily 10am–5pm; April–Oct daily 10am–6pm; closed Sun morning for services; ☎03.88.32.14.46), with a Romanesque facade and Gothic towers. Since 1549 it has been the principal Protestant church of the city.

A short walk upstream, the Pont St-Martin marks the beginning of the district known as **La Petite France**, where the city's millers, tanners and fishermen used to live. At the far end of a series of canals are the so-called **Ponts Couverts** (they are in fact no longer covered), built as part of the fourteenth-century city fortifications. Just beyond is a **dam** built by Vauban (daily 9am–7.30pm; free) to protect the city from waterborne assault. The whole area is picture-postcard pretty, with winding streets – most notably rue du Bain-aux-Plantes – bordered by sixteenth- and seventeenth-century houses adorned with flowers and elaborately carved woodwork.

The area east of the cathedral, where rue des Frères leads to place St-Étienne, is good for a stroll, too. **Place du Marché-Gayot**, off rue des Frères behind the cathedral, is a lively cobbled square, lined with café-bars and one of the city's top nightspots. From the north side of the cathedral, rue du Dôme leads to the eighteenth-century **place Broglie**, with the Hôtel de Ville, the bijou **Opéra** and some imposing eighteenth-century mansions.

The German quarter (Neustadt) and the European institutions

Across the canal from place Broglie, **place de la République** is surrounded by vast German Neo-Gothic edifices erected during the Prussian occupation, one example being the main **post office** on avenue de la Marseillaise. At the centre of the square, amid the magnolias, is a **war memorial** showing a mother holding two dead sons in her arms, neither of which, unusually for such monuments, wears a military uniform. At the other end of avenue de la Liberté, across the confluence of the Ill and Aar, is the city's **university**, where Goethe studied.

From in front of the university, allée de la Robertsau, flanked by confident *fin-de-siècle* bourgeois residences, leads to the headquarters of three major European institutions: the bunker-like **Palais de l'Europe**, the 1970s-built home of the 44-member Council of Europe; the glass and steel curvilinear **European Parliament building**, opened in 1999; and the glass entrance and silver towers of Richard Rogers' **European Court of Human Rights**, completed in 1995. Individuals can arrange to visit the European Parliament during plenary sessions (℡03.88.17.51.84, 🌐www.europarl.europa.eu; free); the European Court of Human Rights has public court hearings (℡03.90.21.52.17, 🌐www.echr.coe.int; free). Booking is also required to visit the Council of Europe (℡03.90.21.49.40, 📧visites@coe.int; free).

Opposite the Palais de l'Europe, the **Orangerie**, Strasbourg's best bit of greenery, hosts a variety of exhibitions and free concerts. There's also a small zoo with monkeys and exotic birds.

Eating and drinking

For the classic Alsatian eating experience, you should go to a **winstub**, loosely translated as a "wine bar", a cosy establishment with bare beams, panels and benches and a convivial atmosphere. The food revolves around Alsatian classics, such as *choucroute*, all accompanied by local wines (or, in a *bierstub*, beer). Traffic-free place du Marché-Gayot ("PMG") near the cathedral is one of the best spots for **café-bars**, most of which stay open until 1.30am. In summer, when the sun comes out, the floating cafés and deckchairs along the **Quai des Pêcheurs** are also popular hang outs. There's a good selection of less touristy **restaurants**, ranging from upmarket *winstubs* to simple neighbourhood eateries, along the Quai des Pêcheurs and on surrounding streets, such as rue de Zürich and rue de la Krutenau.

Restaurants

Le Buerehiesel 4 parc de l'Orangerie ℡03.88.45.56.65, 🌐www.buerehiesel.com. Formerly under the helm of Michelin lauded chef Antoine Westermann, who recently handed over control of the kitchen to his son, *Buerehiesel* is delightfully housed in a rustic farmhouse in the Parc de l'Orangerie. Best value is the lunchtime €35 set menu; otherwise count on almost double that. Try the Alsatian pigeon stuffed with celery tagine with fricasée of vegetables and fruits, €28. Closed Sun & Mon.

Cinecitta' 42 Rue de Zurich. Lively, local pizzeria near the university district, one of several cheap spots in this area offering something a little different from the standard Alsatian fare; pizzas €8. Closed Sat & Sun lunch and Mon.

Le Clou 3 rue du Chaudron ℡03.88.32.11.67, Ⓦwww.le-clou.com. Reliable, ever-popular *winstub* tucked away close to the cathedral, serving good Alsatian classics, such as *choucroute* (€17). Closed Wed lunch & Sun.

Au Coin des Pucelles 12 rue des Pucelles ℡03.88.35.35.14. Atmospheric little *winstub* in a cosy, panelled old house, serving mounds of *choucroute* and other hearty dishes until

1am, alongside a good selection of local wines. *Mignon de porc* with Munster *spaetzles* €16. Closed Sun & Mon.

Fleurdesel 22 quai des Bateliers ℡03.88.36.01.54. Stylish restaurant in an old house beside the river. Imaginative, beautifully presented cuisine, with an emphasis on exotic flavours and combinations. Main dishes €16. Closed Sun & Mon.

Poêles de Carottes 2 place des Meuniers ℡03.88.32.33.23, Ⓦwww.poelesdecarottes.com. Strasbourg's best vegetarian and organic restaurant, in a quiet square near picturesque Petite France. Daily €12 set menu or a selection of

▲ Bierstub, Strasbourg

vegetarian pastas, gratins and burritos from €10. Closed Sun & Mon.

🏃 **S'Munsterstuewel** 8 place du Marché-aux-Cochons-de-Lait ☎ 03.88.32.17.63. Set on an attractive square and renowned as one of Strasbourg's finest *winstubs*; traditional and more unusual dishes, accompanied by excellent local wines. Coq au Riesling €20; full meals around €45. Closed Mon.

Cafés and bars

L'Artichaut 56 Grande Rue. Lively café-bar serving organic snacks; the regular Thurs night jazz jam attracts a young, arty crowd. Closed Mon.

Les Aviateurs 12 rue des Soeurs. "*Les Aviat*", as it's known locally, is regularly packed with Strasbourg's fashionable intelligentsia sipping cocktails or draught Guinness until 4am. Evenings only.

🏃 **L'Épicerie** 6 rue du Vieux Seigle. This homely café is a reconstruction of an old-fashioned grocer's shop, with wooden tables, old boxes and jars. Substantial, very reasonably priced *tartines* (open sandwiches), served daily until midnight. *Tartine* with brie, honey and walnuts €5.

Le Gayot 6 Place du Marché-Gayot. One of the most frequented café-bars on this animated square. Open daily till 1.30am.

Jeanette et les Cycleux 30 rue des Tonneliers. A cycling theme predominates here, with canteen-style furnishings and bric-a-brac décor. Trendy little bar with cocktails, milkshakes and wines by the glass.

Le Roi et Son Fou 37 rue du Vieil-Hôpital. Appealing café and brasserie with a sunny terrace in a quiet square, popular with locals for its good value lunch menu (salads €10) and decent breakfasts (€7).

Terres à Vin 1 rue du Miroir, ⚈ www.terresavin .com. Excellent boutique wine shop/bar stocking over 1600 different wines from high-quality producers around France, with an emphasis on bio-dynamic wines. One of the few places in Strasbourg where you can taste top-notch wines by the glass (from €4). Lunchtime menu €14. Closed after 7.30pm and all day Sun & Mon.

Les Trois Brasseurs 22 rue des Veaux. Convivial *bierstub*, which brews its own beers. *Tarte flambée* from €5. Happy hour 5–7pm. Open daily till 1am.

Entertainment

Strasbourg usually has lots going on, particularly when it comes to music. Pick up the free monthly magazine *Spectacles à Strasbourg et alentours* (⚈ www.spectacles -publications.com) for entertainment info and **listings**. In summer months, the tourist office also stocks a free '*programme des animations*' brochure. **Free concerts** are held regularly in the Parc des Contades and Parc de l'Orangerie.

The best of the annual **festivals** focus on classical music in mid-June, jazz in July, and "contemporary classical" music – Musica – from mid-September to early October. In addition, there's **Les Nuits de Strasbourg**, a firework, light and music display at the Ponts Couverts during July and August, and the impressive illumination of the cathedral facade with music during July and the first week of August (10.30pm–1am). At the **Marché de Noël** (late Nov to Dec 24), an increasingly commercial event dating back over 400 years, central Strasbourg is taken over by wooden stalls selling mulled wine, crafts of varying quality and spicy Christmas cookies known as *bredele*.

Listings

Bike rental Bikes can be hired from the Gare SNCF (☎ 03.88.23.56.75) or 10, rue des Bouchers (☎ 03.88.24.05.61) for €8 a day/€5 half a day; see ⚈ www.velocation.net.

Boat trips Batorama (☎ 03.88.84.13.13, ⚈ www .batorama.fr) runs cruises on the Ill, which depart from in front of the Palais Rohan (daily: April–Oct every 30min 9.30am–9pm; Dec every 30min 9.30am–5pm; Nov & Jan–March four departures 10.30am–4pm). The itinerary includes Petite-France, the Vauban dam, the European Parliament

and the Palais de l'Europe. Evening cruises depart at 9.30 & 10pm May–Sept only. The trip lasts 1hr 10min and costs €7.60 (discounts for students and children).

Books FNAC, 22 place Kléber, for a huge selection of books, records and concert tickets; Librairie Internationale Kléber, 1 rue des Francs-Bourgeois, sells new books, some in English; La Librocase, 2 quai des Pêcheurs, sells second-hand books; Quai des Brumes, 120 Grand'Rue, also has a good selection.

Buses Eurolines has an office at place d'Austerlitz (☎03.90.22.14.60); its international coaches depart from the southern outskirts of the city (tram stop "Couffignal"). Buses to destinations in Alsace leave from the place des Halles.

Car rental Europcar, airport ☎08.25.00.41.01; 16 place de la Gare ☎08.25.85.74.79; Avis, airport ☎08.20.61.17.00; Galérie Marchande, place de la Gare ☎08.20.61.16.98; Hertz, 6 bd de Metz by the *gare SNCF* ☎03.88.32.57.62.

Cinemas Le Star, 27 rue du Jeu-des-Enfants and Le Star St Exupéry, 18 rue du 22-novembre (☎ 03.88.32.67.77); L'Odyssée, 3 rue des Francs-Bourgeois (☎03.88.75.11.52), a sumptuous restored cinema with red velvet seats, shows a combination of classic and contemporary films, many in *v.o.*

Internet NET SUR COUR, 18 quai des Pêcheurs.

Markets Place Broglie hosts a large market of produce and bric-a-brac every Wed & Fri (7am–6pm); there are fruit, vegetable and local produce markets every Tues and Sat morning on bd de la Marne and in the place du Vieux-Marché aux poissons on Sat. The flea market is on Wed and Sat on rue du Vieil-Hôpital (near the cathedral).

Post offices 5 av de la Marseillaise and place de la Cathédrale.

Taxis Taxis 13 ☎03.88.36.13.13.

The northern Vosges

The **northern Vosges** begin at the Saverne gap northwest of Strasbourg and run up to the German border, where they continue as the Pfälzerwald. They don't reach the same heights as the southern Vosges (see p.272), nor do they boast particularly quaint villages or famous vineyards but, as a result, they're spared the mass tourism of the southern range. Much of the region comes under the auspices of the Parc Régional des Vosges du Nord, and there are numerous hiking possibilities, plus a couple of attractive towns – **Saverne** and **Wissembourg** – built in the characteristic red sandstone of the area.

Transport here is erratic, though not hopeless. SNCF buses wind their way through the villages and orchards around Haguenau, and the Strasbourg–Sarreguemines and Hagenau–Bitche train lines cut across the range. Even so, the ideal way to explore the region is with your own transport – hilly but rewarding work, if it's a bike.

Saverne and around

SAVERNE, seat of the exiled Catholic prince-bishops of Strasbourg during the Reformation, commands the only easy route across the Vosges into Alsace, at a point where the hills are pinched to a narrow waist. The best launch pad from which to explore the northern Vosges, it's a small town, with plenty of the region's characteristic steep-pitched roofs and window boxes full of geraniums.

The vast red-sandstone Château des Rohan, on place de Gaulle, was built in rather austere classical style by one of the Rohans who was prince-bishop at the time, and now houses the youth hostel and the **Musées du Château des Rohan** (Jan to mid-June & mid-Sept to Dec daily except Tues 2–6pm; mid-June to mid-Sept, daily except Tues 10am–noon & 2–6pm; Dec–March Sun only 2–5pm; €2.50). The museum contains a rather motley selection of local artefacts; including, in the basement, archaeological fragments from the Gallo-Roman period. Upstairs, by far the most interesting section of the museum presents the life and work of the writer and feminist Louise Weiss (1893–1983), who, after founding the political journal *l'Europe Nouvelle* in 1918 to campaign for peace, wrote prolifically on women's suffrage and international affairs, until her election as an MEP in 1979.

The River Zorn and the Marne–Rhine canal both weave their way through the town, the latter framing the château's formal gardens in a graceful right-angle bend. Alongside the château, the **church of Notre-Dame-de-la-Nativité** contains another finely carved pulpit by Hans Hammer. Horticultural distraction can be found in the town's famed rose garden, **La Roseraie** (June to mid-Sept daily 10am–7pm; ℡03.88.71.21.33; Ⓦwww.roseraie-saverne.fr; €2.50) to the west of the centre by the river.

There are several relatively easy **walks** around Saverne (the tourist office can provide details). The most popular trail, to the ruined **Château du Haut-Barr**, is no more than one hour each way. Follow rue du Haut-Barr southeast along the canal past the leafy suburban villas until you reach the forest. Take the path marked "Haut-Barr" through woods and you'll see the castle standing dramatically on a narrow sandstone ridge, with fearsome drops on both sides and views across the wooded hills. Approaching by road you'll pass the reconstruction of a late eighteenth-century **relay tower** (June to mid-Sept Wed–Sun 1–6pm; ℡03.88.52.98.99; €1.50), part of the optical telegraph link between Paris and Strasbourg until the middle of the nineteenth century.

Practicalities

It's only a couple of minutes' walk from the *gare SNCF* into the centre of Saverne; as you exit the station, take rue de la Gare, then turn up the Grand' Rue, where the **tourist office** is at number 37 (Jan–April & Oct–Nov Mon–Sat 10am–noon & 2–6pm; May, June, Sept & Dec Mon–Sat 10am–noon & 2–6pm, Sun 10am–noon & 2–5pm; July & Aug Mon–Sat 10am–noon & 2–6pm, Sun 10am–noon & 2–6pm; ℡03.88.91.80.47, Ⓦwww.ot-saverne.fr). For **accommodation** in town, *Europe*, at 7 rue de la Gare (℡03.88.71.12.07, Ⓦwww .hotel-europe-fr.com; ❹), has bright, spacious rooms with shiny modern bathrooms. Alternatively, there's the friendly *Hotel/Restaurant Chez Jean*, 3 rue de la Gare (℡03.88.91.10.19, Ⓦwww.chez-jean.com; ❺), with homely, wood-panelled rooms and it own restaurant serving traditional Alsatian cuisine (€15 lunch menu), or the **HI hostel** in the Château Rohan (℡03.88.91.14.84, Ⓔsaverne@fuaj.org; cardholders only; 4 bed dorms €12.60).

As for **food**, Saverne has more than its fair share of patisseries and *salons de thé*, the majority to be found along the Grand' Rue. Gourmets will appreciate the ☖ *Taverne Katz* on the main street, 80 Grand' Rue (℡03.88.71.16.56, Ⓦwww .tavernekatz.com; closed Tues evening & Wed; menu €15–25): occupying a beautiful old house with an ornately carved facade, beams and elaborate décor, it offers refined, well-presented traditional cuisine (taster menu €54; *carte* mains €13–20) with a selection of divine sorbets and ice creams for dessert. *Restaurant Staeffele*, 1 rue Poincaré (℡03.88.91.63.94; closed Wed, Thurs lunch & Sun eve; menus €38–55), also offers impeccably prepared Alsatian fare. More modest, the *Restaurant de la Marne*, 5 rue du Griffon (℡03.88.91.19.18; closed Thurs & Sun evening in winter), has a large terrace overlooking the canal and serves copious salads and pizzas (from €7.90).

Wissembourg and around

WISSEMBOURG, 60km north of Strasbourg and right on the German border, is a small cobbled town of higgledy-piggledy prettiness. The linguistically anomalous townspeople speak an ancient dialect derived from Frankish, unlike their fellow Alsatians whose language is closer to modern German.

At the end of rue Nationale, the town's main commercial street, stands the Gothic **church of St-Paul-et-St-Pierre**, with a Romanesque belfry and some fine twelfth- and thirteenth-century stained glass, once attached to the town's abbey. Beneath the apse, the River Lauter flows under the Pont du Sel beside the town's first hospital, the **Maison du Sel** (1450), in a part of town

The Maginot Line

Like the Séré de Rivières forts constructed after the 1870–71 war, the objective of the **Maginot line** was to keep the Germans out of France. A vast network of defensive fortifications spanning the entire length of the French–German border (plus a section of the French–Belgian border) was constructed between 1930 and 1940, the brainchild of André Maginot, French Minister of War (1929–31). The main section of the line consisted of a continuous chain of underground strong points linked by anti-tank obstacles and equipped with state-of-the-art machinery. When put to the test in 1940, it proved to be worse than useless: the Germans simply violated Belgian neutrality and attacked through the Ardennes.

dubbed **la Petite Venise** (Little Venice). A few-minutes' walk away, at 3 rue du Musée, another fine old building, with beautifully carved woodwork round its windows, houses the **Musée Westercamp** (closed for structural renovations until 2013). Along the southern edge of town, following the riverbank from the Tour des Husgenossen in the western corner, a long section of the red sandstone **medieval walls** survives intact.

Tucked away in the forest just outside the village of Lembach, some 13km southwest of Wissembourg, is the **Four à Chaux** (℡03.88.94.43.16, ⓦwww .lignemaginot.fr; guided tours daily: April & Oct 2pm & 3pm; May–Sept 10.30am, 2pm, 3pm & 4pm; €5). This vast subterranean fort, with its own ventilation, heating systems and command headquarters, was constructed between 1930 and 1935 as part of the infamous **Maginot line** (see box above). In the first months of World War II, it housed more than five hundred soldiers, each of whom did a monthly stint underground. The multilingual (usually French and German) guided tour lasts between one and a half and two hours and takes you through the extensive soldiers' quarters and on to the munitions stores and combat blocs at the northern end of the fort. There's also a small museum containing munitions, uniforms and some fascinating anti-allied propaganda. Take a sweater though – the bunker is atmospherically chilly, with an average temperature of just 13°C.

Practicalities

Wissembourg's **tourist office** is at 9 place de la République (May–Sept Mon–Sat 9am–12.30pm & 2–6pm, Sun 2–5.30pm; Oct–April Mon–Sat 9am–noon & 2–5.30pm; ℡03.88.94.10.11, ⓦwww.ot-wissembourg.fr). From the **gare SNCF** the "Office du Tourisme" signs are for cars – if you're on foot the quickest route is to turn left out of the station and walk to the roundabout. Turn right and you're in town.

For **accommodation**, the most attractive hotel is the *Hostellerie au Cygne*, 3 rue du Sel (℡03.88.94.00.16, ⓦwww.hostellerie-cygne.com; ❹ closed one week in Nov, two weeks in Feb & two weeks in July; restaurant €20–54, closed Sun evening, Thurs lunch and Wed). *L'Escargot*, 40 rue Nationale (℡03.88.94.90.29, ℡03.88.54.25.00; ❷), also has clean, simple rooms above a confectioner's.

One of the best **places to eat** on the main drag is *Au Petit Dominicain*, 36 rue Nationale (℡03.88.94.90.87; closed Mon and Tues; set menu €25). A much fancier establishment, with more inventive variations on the regional cuisine, is *De l'Ange*, 2 rue de la République (℡03.88.94.12.11; closed Mon & Tues), in a beautiful old house by the stream next to place du Marché-aux-Choux; the cheapest menu is the lunchtime €28, otherwise you're looking at twice that. For simple *tartes flambées* (from €6), *Au Saumon*, behind the Maison du Sel, is open daily and has pleasant outdoor seating.

The southern Vosges

Flanked to the west by the rising forests of the **southern Vosges,** which stretch all the way down to Belfort, Alsace's picturesque **Route du Vin** ("Wine Route") follows the foot of the mountains along the western edge of the wide and flat Rhine valley; surrounded by striped terraces of vines, you'll find a series of exquisitely preserved medieval towns and villages. Many of these, notably **Colmar,** suffer from an unfortunate overdose of visitors. To escape from the crowds, you need to head for the hills proper, along the scenic **Route des Crêtes,** which traces the central ridge of the Vosges to the west.

The Route du Vin

Set against the strategic "blue line of the Vosges", the **Route du Vin** winds from Marlenheim, west of Strasbourg, to Thann, near Mulhouse, through endless terraced vineyards which produce the region's famous white wines (see below). Tasting opportunities are plentiful, particularly during the region's countless wine festivals, which mainly coincide with the October harvest. For a closer look at the vines themselves you can follow various *sentiers vinicoles* (vineyard paths); ask at local tourist offices for information. In the midst of this sea of vines are dozens of picturesque villages, which outdo each other to have the biggest display of window-box geraniums. Many are dominated from the nearby craggy heights by an extraordinary number of ancient ruined castles, testimony to the province's turbulent past.

Obernai and around

Picturesque little **OBERNAI**, on the D422 (or the Strasbourg–Molsheim–Sélestat train line) is the first place most people head for when travelling south

---

The wines of Alsace

Despite the long, tall bottles and Germanic names, Alsatian wines are unmistakably French in their ability to compliment the region's traditional cuisine. This is white-wine country – if you do spot a local red, it will be light-bodied, fresh and often served chilled. Winemakers take advantage of the long, dry autumns to pick extremely ripe grapes producing wines with a little more sweetness than elsewhere in France, but good wines will have a refreshing natural acidity, too. Each of the three main grape varieties listed below can be made with a sweetness level ranging from off-dry right through to *"Sélection des Grains Nobles"* for the most highly-prized dessert wines (*vendages tardives* being the label for the slightly less sweet late-harvested wines). *Grand Cru* labelled wines come from the best vineyard sites.

Riesling – the ultimate thirst-quencher, limey, often peachy, excellent with fish dishes (most obviously trout).

Gewurztraminer – Alsace's most aromatic grape, with roses, lychees, honey, spice and all manner of exotic flavours. Try with pungent Munster cheese or rich paté.

Pinot Gris – rich, fruity, smoky and more understated than Gewurztraminer. A versatile food wine; try with white meat in creamy sauces and milder cheeses.

Other wines you're likely to come across include the grapey **Muscat**, straightforward **Sylvaner**, and delicate **Pinot Blanc/Auxerrois**, which also forms the base of the region's excellent sparkling **Cremant d'Alsace**. **Pinot Noir** is used for light, fruity reds and rosés.

To taste wine, it's best to visit the *caveaux* of local wine-growers, though you'll be expected to buy at least a couple of bottles.

from Strasbourg. Miraculously unscathed by the last two world wars, Obernai has retained almost its entire **rampart system**, including no fewer than fifteen towers, along with street after street of carefully maintained medieval houses. Not surprisingly, it gets more than its fair share of visitors. The **tourist office**, on place du Beffroi (April–June, Sept & Oct daily 9am–noon & 2–6pm, July & Aug daily 9.30am–12.30pm & 2–7pm; Nov–March Mon–Sat 9am–noon & 2–5pm; ☏03.88.95.64.13) is well-stocked with information about the region. If you wish to stay, *La Diligence*, 23 place de la Mairie (☏03.88.95.55.69, Ⓦ www.hotel-diligence.com;❸) is comfortable, if somewhat prim rooms, above a charming *salon de thé*. For something more special, you could try the stylish boutique hotel *Le Colombier* (☏03.88.47.63.33, Ⓦ www.hotel-colombier .com; ❻), at 6–8 rue Dietrich. *La Halle au Blé* on the Place du Marché has a large terrace and is a good **café** for a hot chocolate after a hard day's hiking.

ROSHEIM, 7km north of Obernai and up in the hills a little to the west of the D422, is relatively off the beaten track, but also accessible by train from Strasbourg or Seléstat. It's a 2km walk from the *gare* SNCF into the village centre. There are two main sights: the Romanesque **church of St–Pierre-et–St–Paul**, whose roof is peppered with comical sculptured figures, and the twelfth-century **Heidenhüs**, at 24 rue de la Principale, thought to be the oldest building in Alsace. Accommodation options are somewhat limited. *Hostellerie du Rosenmeer* by the train station at 45 Ave de la Gare (☏03.88.50.43.29, Ⓦ www.le-rosenmeer.com; ❹) has clean, cheerful rooms, plus a *winstub* (plat du jour €8; closed Sun & Mon) and a prestigious gastronomic restaurant (mains €25; closed Sun, Mon & Wed evening), presided over by Alsatian celebrity chef Hubert Maetz.

South west of Rosheim, **Ottrott,** which produces one of the few red wines of Alsace, brings you within hiking distance – 6km – of **Mont Ste-Odile** (763m), whose summit is surrounded by a mysterious prehistoric wall (known as the **Mur Païen**, or Pagan Wall), originally built in the tenth century BC. The wall is almost 10km in length and in parts reaches a height of 3.5m. St Odilia herself is buried in the small **chapel** on top of the hill, a pilgrimage site even today. According to legend, she was cast out by her father at birth on account of her blindness, but miraculously regained her sight during childhood and returned to found the convent on Mont Ste-Odile, where she cured thousands of cases of blindness and leprosy.

Barr

For some reason, **BARR**, west of the main road, is overlooked by mass tourism. Every bit as charming as Obernai, it's easy to while away a couple of hours wandering its twisting cobbled streets, at their busiest during the lively mid-July **wine festival**, when you can taste over two hundred local wines in the town hall. Barr has just one specific sight, **La Folie Marco**, at 30 rue du Docteur-Sultzer (June & Oct Sat & Sun 10am–noon & 2–6pm; July–Sept daily except Tues 10am–noon & 2–6pm; Dec Sat & Sun 2–6pm; €4), an eighteenth-century house on the outskirts of town along the road to Obernai, which has displays of period furniture. The restaurant in its cellar serves Alsatian specialities (☏03.88.08.22.71; €8 lunch menu or €25 in the evening). Several walks begin behind the Hôtel de Ville, including one to Mont Ste-Odile (14km; 3–4 hours), or there are shorter trails around the local *Grand Cru* vineyards.

The nicest **place to stay** is the charming ⚘ *Hôtel Le Manoir*, 11 rue St-Marc (☏03.88.08.03.40, Ⓦ www.hotel-manoir; ❺), housed in a nineteenth-century winemaker's villa. Light and spacious rooms are individually furnished with elegant drapes and antiques. Alternatively, a family-friendly option is the

Hôtel/Restaurant Maison Rouge 1, Ave de la Gare (℡03.88.08.90.40, ⓦwww .maison-rouge-barr.com; ❸), which has a *bierstub* boasting over 60 different types of beer and a restaurant serving excellent *tartes flambées* for €7 (closed Wed). If you're under canvas, there's a pick of two **campsites**: the central, but fairly basic *Camping St-Martin*, at rue de l'Ill (℡03.88.08.00.45, ⓦwww.pays-de-barr.com /saint-martin; June to mid-Oct), and the more swish municipal **campsite**, *Mont Ste-Odile "Wepfermatt"*, 4km north of town at 137 rue de la Vallée (℡03.88.08.02.38, ⓦwww.les-reflets.com; April–Nov). *Winstub S'Barrer Stubbel*, 5 place de l'Hôtel-de-Ville (℡03.88.08.57.44), has a homely, festive interior and serves good local specialities at reasonable prices (*baeckoffe* €15). Anyone with a sweet tooth will find it hard to resist ℀ *J Oster*, a superb patisserie and *salon de thé* at 31 rue du Collège – it has a dazzling window display featuring rows of mouth-watering pastries and cakes, from glistening strawberry tarts to lemon meringue pies, sticky caramels and bulbous *kugelhopf.*

Le Struthof concentration camp

Deep in the forests and hills of the Vosges, over 20km west of Barr, **Le Struthof-Natzwiller** (daily: March, April & mid-Sept to Dec 10am–5pm; May to mid-Sept 9am–6pm; closed Jan & Feb; ℡03.88.47.44.67, ⓦwww.struthof.fr; €5) was the only Nazi concentration camp to be built on French soil.

The site is almost perversely beautiful, its stepped terraces cut into hillside, giving fantastic views across the Bruche valley. Set up shortly after Hitler's occupation of Alsace-Lorraine, it is thought that over 10,000 people died here. When the Allies liberated the camp on November 23, 1944, they found it empty – the remaining prisoners had already been transported to Dachau.

The barbed wire and watchtowers are as they were, though only two of the prisoners' barracks remain, one of which is now a **museum**. An arson attack on the museum by neo-Nazis in 1976 only served to underline the need for such displays; captions are in French only, but the pictures suffice to tell the story. At the foot of the camp is the crematorium with its ovens still intact, while a couple of kilometres down the road to the west, towards Schirmeck, the Germans built a gas chamber. To the east are the two main granite quarries worked by the internees.

Sélestat and around

Back on the Route du Vin, **SÉLESTAT**, midway between Strasbourg and Colmar, is a delightful old town and a good base for exploring the most popular section of the route. Sélestat itself also contains a couple of interesting churches and a great museum for bibliophiles.

Alsace under the Nazi occupation

After the conclusion of the **Armistice** on June 22, 1940, the Bas-Rhin, Haut Rhin and Moselle *départements* were annexed to the German Reich. Over the next four years, Alsace experienced a sustained programme of **Nazification**; the use of French was prohibited; town, street and personal names were translated into German; children were indoctrinated by the Hitler Youth; and thousands of "undesirables", Jews and "francophiles" were expelled from the region. Most unpalatable to the local population, from August 1942, Hitler imposed **conscription** all eligible Alsatian men of "German race"; the vast majority of these 130,000 young men – the *Malgré Nous"* (against our will), as they were known – were sent to fight Stalin's forces on the inhospitable Eastern Front, where more than 40,000 of them perished.

The oldest of the two churches is the romanesque **church of Ste-Foy**, much restored since its construction by the monks of Conques. Close by, the attractive gothic **church of St-Georges** sports spectacularly multicoloured roof tiles and some very beautiful stained glass. For a brief period in the late fifteenth and early sixteenth centuries, Sélestat was the intellectual centre of Alsace; its Latin School attracted a group of humanists led by Beatus Rhenanus, whose personal library was one of the most impressive collections of its time. Rhenanus's library is now on display in the **Bibliothèque Humaniste**, housed in the town's former corn exchange (July & Aug Mon & Wed–Fri 9am–noon & 2–6pm, Sat 9am–noon & 2–5pm, Sun 2–5pm; Sept–June Mon & Wed–Fri 9am–noon & 2–6pm, Sat 9am–noon; €4). Alongside Rhenanus's humanist texts, the library holds rare books and manuscripts dating back to the seventh century, including the 1507 *Cosmographiae Introductio*, the first document ever to use the word "America". On the southern edge of the town, not a great deal remains of Sélestat's ramparts, originally designed by Vauban. Constructed between 1675 and 1691 on the orders of Louis XIV, they were dismantled in 1874 after the capture of the town by the Prussians; the surviving section now features an incongruous modern art piece.

Sélestat is well served transport-wise, with frequent train connections to Strasbourg and Colmar; the **gare SNCF** is west of the town centre down avenue de la Liberté. Information is available from the **tourist office** on boulevard du Général-Leclerc (Sept–June Mon–Fri 9am–noon & 2–5.45pm, Sat 9am–noon & 2–5pm; July & Aug Mon–Fri 9.30am–noon & 1.30–6.45pm, Sat 9am–12.30pm & 2–5pm, Sun and public holidays 10.30am–3pm; ☎03.88.58.87.20, ⓦwww.selestat-tourisme.com). For a **place to stay**, there's none better than the friendly *Auberge des Alliés*, 39 rue des Chevaliers (☎03.88.92.09.34, ⓦwww.auberge-des-allies.fr; ❸); its restaurant is worth a look for its splendid tiled stove (set menus from €23; closed Sun Oct–June, or Mon lunch July–Sept). Alternatively, family-run *Hôtel de l'Il*, 13 rue des Bateliers (☎03.88.92.91.09; ❷), has fifteen simple, comfortable rooms. There's also a **campsite**, *Les Cigognes* (☎03.88.92.03.98; May to mid-Oct), just south of the centre behind the ramparts.

Castles around Sélestat

Within easy range of Sélestat is a whole host of **ruined castles**. Seven kilometres north, and accessible by train, the village of **DAMBACH-LA-VILLE**, with its walls and three fortified gates all intact, is one of the highlights of the route. Thirty to forty-five minutes' climb west of the village brings you to the formidable **Castle of Bernstein**, with its typically Germanic narrow mountain keep. You can also go on a mini-train **tour** of the town and local vineyards (July & Aug Mon, Thurs & Sat 5pm; €5), leaving from the main square. *À la Couronne*, on 13 place du Marché (☎03.88.92.40.85; closed Thurs, mid-Feb to early March & the last week of Nov), is an attractive and inexpensive restaurant, with mains for €11–15, plus *tartes flambées* from €8.

The best cluster of castles, though, is southwest of Sélestat. **KINTZHEIM** boasts a small but wonderful ruined castle built around a cylindrical refuge-tower. Today it's an aviary, the **Volerie des Aigles**, for birds of prey, with magnificent displays of aerial prowess by eagles and vultures (open April–Nov demonstrations 2–5pm; July to mid-Aug 10am–5pm; ☎03.88.92.84.33; consult ⓦwww.voleriedesaigles.com for details of demonstration times; adults €9, under 15s €6). 3km further west at the **Montagne des Singes** you can watch barbary apes at play in the Vosgian jungle (daily: April, Oct & Nov 10am–noon & 1–5pm; May, June & Sept 10am–noon & 1–6pm; July & Aug 10am–6pm; ⓦwww.montagnedessinges.com; €8, children €5).

▲ Haut-Koenigsbourg Castle

Another 5km on from Kintzheim, the massive **Haut-Koenigsbourg** (daily: March & Oct 9.45am–4.30pm; April, May & Sept 9.30am–5pm; June, July & Aug 9.30am–6pm; Nov–Feb 9.45am–noon & 1–4.30pm; ℡03.88.82.50.60, Ⓦwww.haut-koenigsbourg.net; €7.50) is one of the biggest, most visited castles in Alsace, and – astride its 757-metre bluff – by far the highest. Ruined after an assault in 1633, it was heavily restored in the early years of the twentieth century for Kaiser Wilhelm II. It's easy to criticize some of the detail of the restoration, but it's situated in a stunning spot with fantastic views on a clear day.

Ribeauvillé and around

RIBEAUVILLÉ is the largest town between Sélestat and Colmar – not as pretty as some of its immediate neighbours, but well placed for exploring the many ruined fortresses and villages that surround it. If you wish to **stay**, you could try *Hôtel de la Tour*, in a converted winery at 1 rue de la Mairie (℡03.89.73.72.73, Ⓦwww.hotel-la-tour.com; ❹–❺; closed Dec 15 to end of Mar). To the south of the village, the friendly *Pierre-de-Courbertin* campsite (℡03.89.73.66.71, Ⓔcamping.ribeauville@orange.fr; mid-March to mid-Nov) is well equipped and has free wi-fi.

The charming little village of **BERGHEIM**, 3.5km northeast of Ribeauvillé, retains a good part of its old fortifications. Despite being extremely picturesque, it remains surprisingly tranquil. Also within easy walking range of Ribeauvillé, this time to the south, the beguiling hamlet of **HUNAWIHR** has a fourteenth-century walled church standing out amid the green vines. Hunawihr is at the forefront of the Alsatian ecological movement aimed at protecting the stork – the *cigogne* – of the region, and there's a **reserve** for them along with otters (*loutres*) to the east of the village; the **Centre de Réintroduction des Cigognes et des Loutres** (March–Nov Sat, Sun & public holidays 10am–noon & 2–4.30pm;

April daily 10am–12.30pm & 2–5.30pm; May & Sept daily 10am–12.30pm & 2–6pm; June daily 10am–6pm; July daily 10am–6.30pm; Aug daily 10am–7pm and late opening the first three Thurs; call to check show times, ℡03.89.73.72.62, ⓦwww.cigogne-loutre.com; €8).

Lastly, closer to Colmar are a couple of very busy tourist targets, best visited midweek or out of season. A couple of kilometres south of Hunawihr, **RIQUEWIHR** is exceptionally well preserved, with plenty of medieval houses and a château containing a postal museum – the **Musée de la Communication en Alsace** (April–Oct & Dec daily except Mon 10am–5.30pm; €4). **KAYSERS-BERG**, still further southwest, also suffers a deluge of visitors thanks to its pretty Hansel and Gretel houses, fortified **bridge** and sixteenth-century altarpiece. The town's principal renown is as the birthplace of Nobel Peace Prize-winner Albert Schweitzer, who founded a leprosy hospital at Lambaréné in French Equatorial Africa. He is honoured with the **Centre Culturel Albert Schweitzer**, 126 rue du Général-de-Gaulle (Easter & May–Oct daily 9am–noon & 2–6pm; €2).

Colmar

The old centre of **COLMAR**, a fifty-minute train ride south of Strasbourg, is totally *echt* Alsatian, with picturesque crooked half-timbered and painted houses. As the proud home of Mathias Grünewald's magnificent Issenheim altarpiece, the town is a magnet for tourists all year round.

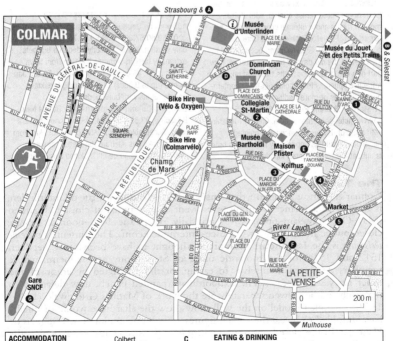

ACCOMMODATION		Colbert	C	EATING & DRINKING		À la Ville de Paris	1
Auberge de Jeunesse		Le Colombier	F	Jadis et Gourmande	3	Winstub Brenner	6
Mittelhardt	A	Grand Hôtel Bristol	G	Le Petit Gourmand	5		
Camping Colmar-		St-Martin	E	Le Restaurant du Marché	2		
Horbourg-Wihr	B	Les Têtes	D	Le Streusel	4		

Arrival and information

From the **gare SNCF** it's a ten-minute walk down avenue de la République to the **tourist office** on place d'Unterlinden (April–June, Sept & Oct Mon–Sat 9am–6pm, Sun 10am–2pm; July & Aug Mon–Sat 9am–7pm, Sun 9.30am–2pm; Nov–March Mon–Sat 9am–noon & 2–6pm, Sun 10am–2pm; ☎03.89.20.68.92, ⊛www.ot-colmar.fr). **Bikes** can be rented from Colmarvélo in Place Rapp (April–Oct daily 8.30am–12.15pm & 13.15–19.15pm; €6 per day) or Vélo & Oxygen, 6 boulevard du Champ de Mars (Tues–Sat 8.30am–noon & 2–6pm; €11 per day).

Accommodation

Accommodation is not overpriced, with a wide range of places to stay, including an excellent boutique hotel. If you have a car, one good option is to contact the tourist office and ask for a list of *gîtes* and *chambres d'hôtes* in attractive nearby wine villages, such as **Eguisheim**.

Hotels

Colbert 2 rue des Trois-Épis ☎03.89.41.31.05, ⊛www.le-colbert.fr. A run-of-the-mill place with functional, affordable rooms, outside the old town. ❸

🏃 **Le Colombier** 7 rue Turenne ☎03.89.23.96.00, ⊛www.hotel-le-colombier.fr. Colmar's only boutique hotel, in the heart of the Petite Venise quarter, with stylish, modern rooms and a internal courtyard. ❺–❻

Grand Hôtel Bristol 7 place de la Gare ☎03.89.23.59.59, ⊛www.grand-hotel-bristol.fr. This relic of the old days of pre-war tourism, now part of a chain, is opposite the train station; it's an attractive option, with a choice of stylish contemporary doubles or more traditional rooms. ❺–❽

St-Martin 38 Grand'Rue ☎03.89.24.11.51, ⊛www.hotel-saint-martin.com. Chintzy furnishings with a riot of flowers, flounces and painted headboards, but this impeccably maintained hotel is unbeatable for its central location. ❺

Les Têtes 19 rue des Têtes ☎03.89.24.43.43, ⊛www.maisondestetes.com. Well-appointed hotel in a beautiful seventeeth-century stone house. Like its gourmet restaurant set in the atmospheric courtyard, the hotel verges on the starchy, but it's still an obvious choice for a special visit. ❻

Hostel and campsite

Auberge de Jeunesse Mittelhardt 2 rue Pasteur ☎03.89.80.57.39, ☏03.89.80.76.16. The town's only youth hostel is perfectly adequate but gets extremely busy in summer. It's 1km from town; take bus #4, #5 or #15 to Pont Rouge. Closed Jan. Dorms (up to 9 beds) €13, including breakfast; private rooms with bunk beds. ❶

Camping Colmar-Horbourg-Wihr Rte de Neuf-Brisach ☎03.89.41.15.94, ⊛www.campingdelill.com. Acceptable, inexpensive campsite 2km from Colmar. Take bus #1 from the station, direction "Wihr", stop "Plage de l'Ill". Closed Jan & Feb.

The Town

Colmar's foremost attraction, the **Musée d'Unterlinden** at 1 rue d'Unterlinden, is housed in a former Dominican convent with a peaceful cloistered garden (May–Oct daily 9am–6pm; Nov–April daily except Tues 9am–noon & 2–5pm; closed public hols; €7; ⊛www.musee-unterlinden.com). The museum's *pièce de résistance* is the **Issenheim altarpiece**, thought to have been made between 1512 and 1516 for the monastic order of St Anthony at Issenheim, whose members dedicated themselves to caring for those afflicted by ergotism and other nasty skin diseases. The extraordinary painted panels, now detached so that each can be viewed separately, are the work of Mathias Grünewald (1480–1528); a wooden model on the wall shows how the altarpiece would originally have unfolded to reveal the carved figures at its centre, sculpted by Nicholas de Hagenau. In the closed position, the luridly expressive centre panel depicts the Crucifixion: a tortured Christ of exaggerated dimensions turns his outsize hands upwards, fingers splayed in pain, flanked by his pale, fainting mother and saints John and Mary Magdalene. The face of St Sebastian, on one of the side wings, is believed to have been modelled on Grünewald's own likeness. The reverse panels – which would have been revealed when the altarpiece opened – depict the annunciation, Christ's resurrection, the nativity and a vivid, flamboyant orchestra of angels; all splendidly bathed in transcendental light. On the final set of painted panels, you'll find a truly disturbing representation of the temptation of St Anthony, who is engulfed by a grotesque pack of demons; note the figure afflicted with the disfiguring symptoms of ergotism. Altarpieces by Martin Schongauer, in the same room as the *Issenheim*, are also worth a quick look, as is the museum's collection of modern paintings, also on the ground floor, which includes a couple of Picassos.

A short walk away, the austere **Dominican church** on rue des Serruriers (April–Dec daily 10am–1pm & 3–6pm; €1.50) has some fine glass and a beautiful altarpiece known as *The Virgin in a Bower of Roses*, painted in 1473 by Schongauer. At the other end of the street you reach the **Collégiale St–Martin** (daily except Sun mornings 8.30am–6pm; free) on a busy café-lined square. Known locally as "the cathedral", it's worth a quick peek for its stonework and stained glass, as is the sixteenth-century **Maison Pfister**, on the south side of the church, for its external painted panels. Frédéric Auguste Bartholdi, the sculptor responsible for New York's Statue of Liberty, was born at 30 rue des Marchands. This now houses the **Musée Bartholdi** (March–Dec daily except Tues 10am–noon & 2–6pm; closed public hols; €4.50), containing Bartholdi's personal effects and the original designs for the statue, along with sundry Colmarabilia.

Rue des Marchands continues south to the Ancienne Douane or **Koïfhus**, its gaily painted roof tiles loudly proclaiming the town's medieval prosperity. This is the heart of Colmar's old town, a short step away from the picturesque quarter down the Grand'Rue known as **La Petite Venise** (Little Venice). The dolly-mixture colours of the old fishing cottages on quai de la Poissonnerie contrast with the much taller, black-and-white, half-timbered tanners' houses on **rue des Tanneurs**, which leads off from the Koïfhus.

Eating and drinking

There is no lack of **cafés** in Colmar, dotted all around the central streets and squares, but **restaurants** are generally overpriced. A tempting alternative is to amass a sumptuous picnic from the town's patisseries and charcuteries.

Jadis et Gourmande 8 Place du Marché aux Fruits. *Salon de thé* with cosy wooden interior, serving daytime *plats* for under €13 and generous slabs of cakes for €4.50. Closed evenings.

Le Petit Gourmand quai de la Poissonnerie ☎03.89.41.09.32. Traditional Alsatian cuisine with a degree of finesse and a delightful little terrace overlooking the canal, for which it's advisable to book. Set menu €25; *baeckoffe* €14.50. Closed Sun evening & Mon.

Le Restaurant du Marché 20 place de la Cathédrale ☎03.89.24.93.88. Creative modern French cuisine, stylishly presented. More sophisticated flavours than elsewhere, with the occasional oriental twist. A welcome (if pricey) change from Alsatian staples. Fixed menu €26 for two courses or €34 for three. Closed Sun.

Le Streusel 4 passage de l'Ancienne Douane. Friendly little café, slightly hidden away, despite being close to the touristy Grand'Rue. Relatively varied menu including salads and some veggie options.

À la Ville de Paris 4 place Jeanne-d'Arc. This atmospheric little *winstub* is a preferred haunt of locals; Alsatian classics €12–16. Closed Tues.

Winstub Brenner 1 rue Turenne. Traditional mainstay Petite Venise *winstub* serving generous portions, with a lovely waterside terrace; €21 for starter and main. Closed Tues & Wed.

Munster and the Route des Crêtes

MUNSTER owes its existence and its name to a band of Irish monks who founded a monastery here in the seventh century, some 19km west of Colmar up the narrowing valley of the River Fecht, and overlooked by Le Petit Ballon

Hiking in the southern Vosges

There's no shortage of scenic hiking paths in the **southern Vosges**. Six **GRs** cross the Vosges and are a good way to see the less-frequented castles:

GR7: Ballon d'Alsace to Remiremont.

GR53: Wissembourg to Belfort (part of the route coincides with GR5).

GR59: Ballon d'Alsace to Besançon.

GR531: Wissembourg to the Ballon d'Alsace.

GR532: Soultz-sous-Forêts to Belfort.

GR533: Sarrebourg to Belfort, along the west flank of the Vosges.

In the centre of the Parc Régional des Ballons des Vosges, the 1427m-high Ballon d'Alsace is the meeting point of the GR5, GR7 and GR59; a short "discovery trail" has been marked out around the summit and a number of rambles commence here. Detailed hiking maps are published by the Club Vosgien (ⓦwww.club-vosgien.com) and can be easily obtained in local tourist offices or bookshops. The Office Départemental du Tourisme du Bas-Rhin, 9 rue du Dôme, 67000 Strasbourg (☎03.88.15.45.85, ⓦwww.tourisme67.com), publishes a free brochure (which you can download online) *Hiking through Northern Alsace*, with information on trekking routes from 2 to 17 days, together with some shorter hikes of 11– 25km, plus details of accommodation. The Association Départementale du Tourisme du Haut-Rhin (☎03.89.20.10.62/68, ⓦwww.tourisme68.com) has similar brochures for the Haut-Rhin region.

(1267m) and Le Hohneck (1362m), among the highest peaks of the Vosges. Today its name is associated with a rich, creamy and exceedingly smelly **cheese**, the crowning glory of many an Alsatian meal. The town itself is not as picturesque as the wine villages further east, but makes a peaceful and verdant base for exploring the Parc Régional des Ballons des Vosges. In May each year, it hosts a **jazz festival** (ⓦjazzmunster.onlc.fr).

Munster is accessible by **train** from Colmar. From the station, walk up rue de la Gare and turn right down rue Sébastopol to reach the centre. The **tourist office**, 1 rue du Couvnet (July & Aug Mon–Sat 9.30am–12.30pm & 1.30– 6.30pm; Sept–June Mon–Fri 9.30am–12.30pm & 2–6pm, Sat 10am–noon & 2–6pm; ☎03.89.77.31.80, ⓦwww.la-vallee-de-munster.com), can provide information about hiking in the Munster valley and the *parc régional*, as can the Maison du Parc, 1 cour de l'Abbaye (mid-June to Sept daily except Mon 10am–noon & 2–6pm; Oct–June Mon–Fri 2–6pm; closed public holidays ☎03.89.77.70.34, ⓔinfo@parc-ballon-vosges.fr).

If you want to **stay**, the friendly *Hôtel Bar des Vosges*, 58 Grand Rue (☎03.89.77.31.41, ⓦwww.hotelbardesvosges.fr; ❷), has comfortable, rooms above a café-bar. Alternatively, you could try the large, modern but rather bland *Hôtel Verte-Vallée*, 10 rue Alfred-Hartmann (☎03.89.77.15.15, ⓦwww.verte-vallee.com; ❺), just outside town, which has four-star facilities including a spa and swimming pool, plus a restaurant specializing in traditional French dishes (closed most of Jan; set menus €20–50). Munster's **campsite**, *Camping municipal du Parc de la Fecht*, is on the route de Gunsbach, 1km from the centre (☎03.89.77.31.08; May to mid-Sept).

The Route des Crêtes

Above Munster the main road west to Gérardmer crosses the mountains by the principal pass, the Col de la Schlucht, where it intersects the "Route des Crêtes" (crest road), built for strategic purposes during World War I to facilitate the movement of munitions and supplies. It's a spectacular road traversing thick forest and open pasture; in winter it becomes one long cross-country ski route. Starting in **Cernay**, 15km west of Mulhouse, it follows the main ridge of the Vosges, including the highest peak of the range, the Grand Ballon (1424m), north as far as **Ste–Marie–aux–Mines**, 20km west of Sélestat, once at the heart of a silver-mining district. From Munster it's also accessible by a twisting minor road through Hohrodberg, which takes you past beautiful glacial lakes and the eerie World War I battlefield of **Linge**, where the French and German trenches, once separated by just a few metres, are still clearly visible.

Mulhouse and around

A large, sprawling, industrial city 35km south of Colmar, **MULHOUSE** was Swiss until 1798 when, at the peak of its prosperity (founded on printed textiles), it voted to become part of France. It's also the birthplace of Alfred Dreyfus, the unfortunate Jewish army officer erroneously convicted of espionage in 1894, provoking a national furore (see p.1165). Not being endowed with an especially picturesque old town, Mulhouse attracts less tourists than Colmar or Strasbourg, but there are nevertheless a handful of rather unusual museums in and around the town that delve into the region's manufacturing past: wallpaper, printed fabrics, locomotives and automobiles are all given their platform. At the beginning of August vintage cars from the Musée de l'Automobile are on display as part of a **Grande Parade**, and in late August, Mulhouse hosts the region's hottest **jazz festival** (T03.89.45.63.95, Wwww .jazz-mulhouse.fr).

Arrival, information and accommodation

The main square, place de la Réunion, is five-minutes' walk north of the **gare SNCF**. The main **tourist office** is on the ground floor of Hôtel de Ville (July, Aug & Dec daily 10am–7pm; Jan–June & Sept–Nov Mon–Sat 10am–6pm, Sun and public holidays 10am–noon & 2–6pm; T03.89.66.93.13, Wwww.tourisme-mulhouse.com). Two new tram lines have revolutionized the city's public **transport** network; (Wwww.solea.info) has routes and timetables.

For **accommodation**, an affordable, central option is *St-Bernard*, 3 rue des Fleurs (T03.89.45.82.32, Wwww.hotel-saint-bernard.com; ❶–❸), where an enormous St Bernard is in permanent residence. Rooms in this big, wonky house have high ceilings, although some of the cheaper ones are on the poky side. An alternative budget option is the respectable *Hôtel de Bâle*, 19–21 Passage Central (T03.89.46.19.87, Wwww.hoteldebale.fr; ❷). For something more luxurious *Hôtel du Parc*, at 26 rue de la Sinne (T03.89.66.12.22, Wwww .hotelduparc-mulhouse.com; ❻–❽), has elegant, spacious rooms and its own jazz club. The **HI hostel** has 3-, 4- and 6-bed dorms for €14 including breakfast; it is located west of the centre at 37 rue de l'Illberg (T03.89.42.63.28, Emulhouse@fuaj.org; tram #2, stop "Palais des Sports"; closed mid-Dec to start of Feb). There's a well-equipped **campsite** with a heated pool – *Camping de l'Ill* – at 1 rue Pierre-de-Coubertin, near the suburb of Dornach, 4km from the centre (T03.89.06.20.66, Wwww.camping-de-lill.com; April–Oct); take tram #2 from place Porte-Jeune to "Université" then walk across the canal, down rue de Dornach.

The Town

Close to the *gare SNCF* is the **Musée de l'Impression sur Étoffes**, 14 rue Jean-Jacques-Henner (daily except Mon 10am–noon & 2–6pm; Ⓦwww .musee-impression.com; €6 or €10 for a combined ticket with the **Musée du Papier-Peint** – wallpaper museum – in the village of Rixheim, 6km east; bus #18 direction "Chemin–Vert", stop "Temple"; same hours, closed Tues Oct–May). Mostly displayed in temporary exhibitions, the museum's vast collection of sumptuous fabrics includes the eighteenth-century Indian and Persian imports that revolutionized the European ready-to-wear market and made Mulhouse a prosperous manufacturing centre. It's worth trying to coincide with one of the daily demonstrations of fabric printing (consult the website). The **Hôtel de Ville** on central place de la Réunion contains a beautifully presented history of the city in the **Musée Historique** (daily except Tues: July & Aug 10am–noon & 2–6.30pm; Sept–June 10am–noon & 2–6pm; free).

Some way to the west of the centre, in the direction of the A36 autoroute, is the revamped **Cité du Train – Musée Français du Chemin de Fer**, 2 rue Alfred-de-Glehn (daily 10am–5/6pm, Jan closed weekday afternoons; €10, combined ticket with Cité de l'Automobile, €17.50; take bus #20 from *gare SNCF* to stop "Musées"; Ⓦwww.citedutrain.com). Slick and interactive, the museum has impressive railway rolling stock on display, including Napoléon III's aide-de-camp's drawing room and a luxuriously appointed 1926 diner from the *Golden Arrow*.

A couple of kilometres north of the city centre the **Cité de l'Automobile, Musée National-Collection Schlumpf**, 192 avenue de Colmar (daily 10am–5/6pm, Jan closed weekday mornings; €10.50, combined ticket with Cité du Train, €17.50; take tram #1 from *gare SNCF* or place Porte-Jeune to stop "Musée Auto"; Ⓦwww.collection-schlumpf.com), houses an overwhelming collection of over six hundred cars, originally belonging to local brothers Hans and Fritz Schlumpf, who made their fortunes running a nearby spinning mill.

▲ Cité de l'Automobile, Mulhouse

Lined up in endless rows, the impeccably preserved vehicles range from the industry's earliest attempts, like the extraordinary wooden-wheeled Jacquot steam "car" of 1878, to 1968 Porsche racing vehicles and contemporary factory prototypes. The highlight is locally made Bugatti models: dozens of alluringly displayed, glorious racing cars, coupés and limousines, the pride of them being the two Bugatti Royales, out of only seven that were constructed – one of them Ettore Bugatti's own, with bodywork designed by his son. Car enthusiasts will want to spend hours here.

Eating and drinking

There are plenty of options for **eating** in Mulhouse. *Winstub Henriette,* at 9 rue Henriette (☏03.89.46.27.83; closed Sun & Mon), situated on a lively little street, serves good Alsatian standards (€8 *plat du jour*; mains €14–17). For something different, the *Crêperie Crampous Mad*, 14 impasse des Tondeurs, just off rue des Tondeurs, is often packed to the rafters (*galettes* from €5; closed Sun and Mon & Tues eve; also closed Wed and Thurs evening May–Sept). A popular' watering hole with outside seating is *Gambrinus*, 5 rue des Franciscians, northwest of place de la Réunion (*plat du jour* €11; closed Sun lunch), which boasts over thirty **beers** on tap.

To find out what's going on by way of entertainment, pick up a free copy of *Spectacles* or *L'Echo Mulhousien* from the tourist office.

Lorraine

Lorraine derives its name from the Latin, *Lotharii regnum*, "the kingdom of Lothar", one of the three grandsons of Charlemagne, among whom his empire was divided in 843 AD. Much of the province is a rolling plateau of dull farmland; that said, **Nancy**, its smart former capital, has a harmoniously proportioned Neoclassical square regarded by many as the finest in France. The École de Nancy added to the city's attractions with some sumptuous Art Nouveau furniture and glassware. North of Nancy, the harmonious present-day capital of **Metz** is justly famed for its magnificent cathedral.

West of Metz, several sites connected with the province's bloody history make an interesting detour. During World War II, when de Gaulle and the Free French chose Lorraine's double-barred cross as their emblem, they were making a powerful point. For over a thousand years Lorraine had been the principal route of invasion from across the Rhine. Long the cause of disputes between France and the dukes of Burgundy, the duchy of Lorraine was only fully subsumed into France in 1766. It was on the heights above Metz that Napoléon III's troops suffered their humiliating defeat at the hands of the Prussians in 1870, precipitating the annexation of Alsace and the Moselle. During the twentieth century, Lorraine became once again the site of horrific fighting; of all the battles, **Verdun** remains etched in national memory as one of the most costly and protracted conflicts of the First World War. If you intend to visit the poignant **battlefields** surrounding Verdun, you need your own transport. The SNCF network will take you to and between Nancy, Metz and Verdun – but little further.

Nancy

The city of **NANCY**, on the River Meurthe, is justly famed for the magnificent place Stanislas, cited as a paragon of eighteenth-century Neoclassical urban planning. The city also has on offer some impressive examples of Art Nouveau furniture and glassware. For its spectacularly grand centre, Nancy has the last of the independent dukes of Lorraine to thank, the dethroned king of Poland and father-in-law of Louis XV, Stanislas Leszczynski. During the twenty-odd years of his office in the mid-eighteenth century, he ordered some of the most successful construction of the period in all France.

Arrival, information and accommodation

The part of Nancy you're likely to want to see extends to no more than a ten- or fifteen-minute walk either side of **rue Stanislas**, the main axis

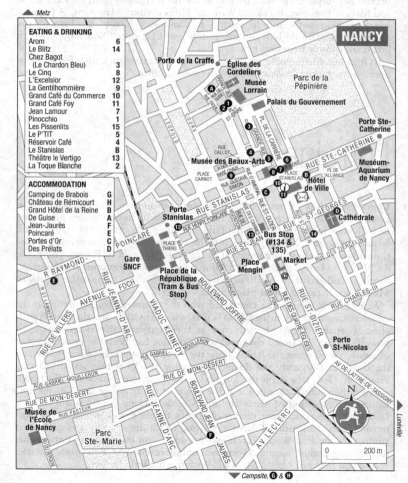

▲ Metz

EATING & DRINKING

Arom	6
Le Blitz	14
Chez Bagot (Le Chardon Bleu)	3
Le Cinq	8
L'Excelsior	12
La Gentilhommière	9
Grand Café du Commerce	10
Grand Café Foy	11
Jean Lamour	7
Pinocchio	1
Les Pissenlits	15
Le P'TIT	5
Réservoir Café	A
Le Stanislas	B
Théâtre le Vertigo	13
La Toque Blanche	2

ACCOMMODATION

Camping de Brabois	G
Château de Rémicourt	H
Grand Hôtel de la Reine	B
De Guise	A
Jean-Jaurès	F
Poincaré	E
Portes d'Or	C
Des Prélats	D

NANCY

▼ Campsite, **G** & **H**

▼ Lunéville

0   200 m

connecting the **gare SNCF** and **place Stanislas**. The **tourist office**, on the south side of place Stanislas in the Hôtel de Ville (April–Oct Mon–Sat 9am–7pm, Sun & holidays 10am–5pm; Nov–March Mon–Sat 9am–6pm, Sun 10am–1pm; ℡03.83.35.22.41, Ⓦwww.ot-nancy.fr), is well stocked with information about both the city and the region. **Internet** access is available at the excellent *e-café* at 11 rue des Quatre-Églises (daily, except Sun am, till 9pm). Nancy's main **public transport** hub is place de la République, just around the corner from the train station; the STAN information centre there (Ⓦwww.reseau-stan.com; Mon–Sat 7am–7.30pm) has timetables and tickets for local bus and tram routes.

Reasonable **accommodation** is not hard to find in Nancy. For somewhere special out of town, try the *Château d'Adoménil* near Lunéville, 37km southeast by the A33 autoroute (℡03.83.74.04.81, Ⓦwww.adomenil.com; ❽–❾), which has beautifully furnished rooms and a highly rated gourmet restaurant (cheapest menu €47, *carte* mains upwards of €40; closed Sun Nov–April).

Hotels

Grand Hôtel de la Reine 2 place Stanislas ℡03.83.35.03.01, Ⓦwww .hoteldelareine.com. The grandest hotel in Nancy, situated on the elegant main square; you'll have to shell out €290 upwards for a room overlooking place Stanislas, though. The gastronomic restaurant serves an extravagant dinner menu for €52 or a more modest business lunch at €27 (closed Mon & Sat lunch, all day Sun Oct–Apr and Sun evening May–Sept). ❼–❾

De Guise rue de Guise, just off Grande-Rue ℡03.83.32.24.68, Ⓦwww.hoteldeguise.com. Characterful hotel in an eighteenth-century seigneurial residence, atmospherically furnished with antiques, tucked away on a quiet side street off the Grande-Rue. ❹–❻

Jean-Jaurès 14 bd Jean-Jaurès ℡03.83.27.74.14, Ⓦwww.hotel-jeanjaures.fr. Small, friendly hotel 5min walk south of the station in a homely, four-storey house; a solid budget option. ❸

Poincaré 81 rue Raymond-Poincaré ℡03.83.40.25.99, ℮poincare.hotel@orange.fr. 10min walk from Porte Stanislas; rooms are on the shabby side, but for the price you can't really complain. If you book at least 8 days in advance and stay Fri and Sat night, you get Sun night for free. ❷

Portes d'Or 21 rue Stanislas ℡03.83.35.42.34, Ⓦwww.hotel-lesportesdor.com. Located just a few steps from Place Stanislas, this is an absolute bargain; recently refurbished doubles in cheerful colours. ❸

Des Prélats 56 place du Monseigneur-Ruch ℡03.83.30.20.20, Ⓦwww.hoteldesprelats .com. Attractive, classic rooms in a neatly converted seventeenth-century house with luxurious drapes and four-poster beds. Breakfast is served in the elegant conservatory. ❻

Hostel and campsite

Camping de Brabois ℡03.83.27.18.28 Ⓦwww .camping-brabois.com. Set in a large park near the hostel. To get there take bus #126 direction "Villers Clairlieu", stop "Camping". April to mid-Oct.

Château de Rémicourt 149 rue de Vandoeuvre ℡03.83.27.73.67, ℮aubergeremicourt @mairie-nancy.fr. Spacious and pretty hostel, set in a sixteenth-century castle, but a fair trek from the centre in the suburb of Villers-lès-Nancy. To get there, take tram #1 from the station to "Le Reclus", then it's a 10min walk; bus #134 or #135 to terminus "Lycée Stanislas", or bus #126 on direction "Villers Clairlieu", stop "Fiacre". €15 including breakfast in 4- or 3-bed dorm; 2-bed private rooms. ❶

The Town

From the *gare SNCF*, walk through Neoclassical **Porte Stanislas**, straight down rue Stanislas to reach **place Stanislas**. Both this gate and porte St Catherine opposite are meticulously aligned with place Stanislas's solitary statue – that of the portly Stanislas **Leszczynski**, who commissioned architect Emmanuel Héré to design the square in the 1750s. On the south side of the square stands the imposing **Hôtel de Ville**, its roof topped by a balustrade ornamented with florid urns and winged cupids. Along its walls lozenge-shaped lanterns dangle from the beaks of gilded cockerels; similar motifs adorn the other buildings bordering the square – look out for the fake, two-dimensional replacements. The square's entrances are enclosed by magnificent wrought-iron gates; the particularly impressive railings on the northern corners frame fountains dominated by statues of Neptune and Amphitrite.

In the corner where rue Stanislas joins the square, the **Musée des Beaux-Arts** (daily except Tues 10am–6pm; €6) presents some excellent nineteenth- and twentieth-century French art, including a number of paintings by Émile Friant and Nancy's own Victor Prouvé on the ground floor. The rest of the collection upstairs, encompassing Italian, German, northern European and more French painting, is less interesting. Time is better spent in the basement, where works from Nancy's glass company, Daum, are beautifully lit in black rooms. The layout of the basement follows the shape of fortifications constructed from the fifteenth century through to Vauban's seventeenth-century alterations, discovered during the museum's 1990s renovation. For a glimpse of Daum's contemporary creations you can visit their shop on place Stanislas. A short walk east of the square is the **Muséum–Aquarium de Nancy**, at 34 rue Ste-Cathérine (daily 10am–noon & 2–6pm; €3.80). Upstairs is a colossal collection of stuffed animals and birds, while downstairs is a startling aquarium of exotic fish whose colours surpass even the daring of Matisse.

On its north side, place Stanislas opens into the long, tree-lined **place de la Carrière**. Its far end is enclosed by the classical colonnades of the **Palais du Gouvernement**, former residence of the governor of Lorraine. Behind it, housed in the fifteenth-century Palais Ducal is the **Musée Lorrain**, 64 Grande-Rue (daily except Mon 10am–12.30pm & 2–6pm, closed public hols; €4 or €5.50 combined ticket with the Musée des Cordeliers). It contains, among other local treasures, a room full of superb etchings by the Nancy-born seven-teenth-century artist, Jacques Callot, whose concern with social issues, evident in series such as *The Miseries of War,* presaged much nineteenth and twentieth-century art. Next door, in the Église des Cordeliers and Chapelle Ducale, the **Musée des Cordeliers** (same hours as Musée Lorrain; €3.50, €5.50 combined ticket with the Musée Lorrain), illustrates the history of rural life in the region. On the other side of the Palais du Gouvernement, you can collapse with

Stanislas Leszczynski

Stanislas Leszczynski, born in the Polish–Ukrainian city of Lemberg (now Lviv) in 1677, lasted just five years as the king of Poland before being forced into exile by Tsar Peter the Great. For the next twenty-odd years he lived on a French pension in Wissembourg, along with a motley entourage of Polish expats. After fifteen years Stanislas' luck changed when he managed, against all odds, to get his daughter, Marie, betrothed to the 15-year-old king of France, **Louis XV**. Marie was not so fortunate: married by proxy in Strasbourg Cathedral, having never set eyes on the groom, she gave birth to ten children, only to be rejected by Louis, who preferred the company of his mistresses, Mme de Pompadour and Mme du Barry. Bolstered by his daughter's marriage, Stanislas had another spell on the Polish throne from 1733 to 1736, but gave it up in favour of the comfortable dukedom of Barr and Lorraine. He lived out his final years in aristocratic style in the capital, Nancy, which he trans-formed into one of France's most beautiful towns.

exhaustion on the green grass of the attractive **Parc de la Pépinière**, which also contains a free zoo.

A half-hour walk southwest of the train station, the **Musée de l'École de Nancy**, 36 rue Sergent-Blandan (Wed–Sun 10.30am–6pm; €6), is housed in a 1909 villa built for the Corbin family, founders of the Magasins Réunis chain of department stores. Even if you're not into Art Nouveau, this collection is exciting. Although not all of it belonged to the Corbins, the museum is arranged as if it were a private house. The furniture is outstanding – all swirling curvilinear forms – and the standards of workmanship are superlative. In particular, there's some extraordinary glassware by Emile Gallé (1846–1904), the founder of the Nancy School, whose expressive naturalistic motifs and experimental glass-making techniques, particularly in colouring and etching, brought him international recognition from the 1880s. Some of Gallé's marquetry and furniture is also on display – look out for the *Aube et Crépuscle* (Dawn and Dusk) bed, with its beautifully curvaceous headboard and exotic moths, inlaid with mother of pearl. The **garden**, planted with irises, magnolias, saxifrages and all kinds of plants that inspired the School of Nancy's creations, is also worth exploring.

Eating and drinking

There are plenty of places to eat and drink in Nancy, led by the respected gastronomic restaurant *Le Stanislas* in the *Grand Hôtel de la Reine*. There's a cluster of **restaurants** around the Grande-Rue, rue des Maréchaux (nicknamed "rue Gourmande") and the rue des Ponts, although some of those on the rue des Maréchaux cater primarily to tourists. For coffee, *Grand Café du Commerce, Jean Lamour, Le Cinq* and the sumptuous *Grand Café Foy,* all on place Stanislas, make great vantage points for watching Nancy go by. At night, head up the Grande-Rue towards lively Place St-Epvre. The tourist office stocks the free listings magazine *Spectacles à Nancy*; whilst ⓦwww.nancybynight.com has information on nightlife and entertainment.

Restaurants

Arom 26 rue Héré, ☎03.85.35.08.24. One of several restaurants with an outdoor terrace along this stumpy street, offering a vantage point of place Stanislas. The food, served on square glass plates, is modish but delicious all the same. Set menus €25/30/38. Closed Sun evening & Wed.

Chez Bagot (Le Chardon Bleu) 45 Grande-Rue ☎03.83.37.42.43. Fresh fish dishes cooked to Breton recipes served up in an appropriately decorated restaurant. Menus from €14. Closed Mon & Tues lunch.

L'Excelsior 50 rue Henri-Poincaré, opposite the train station. A wonderfully *fin-de-siècle* Art Nouveau brasserie; now part of the *Flo* brasserie chain, but managing to retain its good classic food (mains €18–32). It's an atmospheric place to linger over a morning coffee.

La Gentilhommière 29 Rue des Maréchaux, ☎03.83.32.26.44. One of the more trendy establishments on this street of eateries, with a busy terrace, generous portions and lots of freebies in between courses; €22/26 three-course set-menu with tasty dessert options, including a three chocolate mousse. Closed Sun & Sat lunch.

Les Pissenlits 25bis rue des Ponts. Real old-fashioned bistro fare in a less touristy spot; lunch menu €9.30. Closed Sun & Mon.

La Toque Blanche 1 rue Mgr-Trouillet, just off place St-Epvre ☎03.83.30.17.20, ⓦwww .latoqueblanche.fr. One of the finest gourmet restaurants in Nancy, serving inventive, seasonal cuisine. The cheapest set menu, the "*retour du marché*", is a very reasonable €18 (2 courses; Tues and Fri lunch only); otherwise, menus €26/38/55 & 70. Closed Sun evening & Mon.

Cafés and bars

Le Blitz 76 rue St-Julien. Relaxed little bar, which comes alive at the weekend with danceable music; lurid plastic seats outside and a hip, youthful clientele.

Pinocchio 9 place St-Epvre. Features attractive wooden interior furnishings and has a busy terrace, facing the church of St-Epvre; good for drinks at all hours.

Le P'TIT 8 Grande Rue. Tiny beer bar, regularly packed with a crowd which spills out onto the street. Open till 2am. Closed Sun & Mon.

Réservoir Café 13 rue Callot. Leather armchairs and mellow music add to the cosiness of this fashionable café-bar known for its stiff cocktails. Closed Mon.

Théâtre le Vertigo 29 rue de la Visitation. Postmodern gargoyles contribute to its interesting theatrical atmosphere. Bands and other performances regularly. Open till 5am at weekends. Closed Sun & Mon.

Metz and around

METZ (pronounced "Mess"), the capital of Lorraine, lies on the east bank of the River Moselle, close to the Autoroute de l'Est, linking Paris and Strasbourg, and the main Strasbourg–Brussels train line. Its origins go back at least to Roman times, when, as now, it stood astride major trade routes. On the death of Charlemagne it became the capital of Lothar's portion of his empire. By the Middle Ages it had sufficient wealth and strength to proclaim itself an independent republic, which it remained until its absorption into France in 1552. Caught between warring influences, Metz has endured more than its share of historical hand-changing; reluctantly ceded to Germany in 1870, it recovered its liberty at the end of World War I, only to be re-annexed by Hitler until the Liberation.

Although the only really important sight is the magnificent **cathedral**, beautifully lit at night, Metz deserves its self-styled title of *Ville jardin* or Garden City; impeccable flowerbeds, the warm hues of mustard-yellow stone buildings and the waters of the Moselle all make for a seductive cityscape.

Arrival, information and accommodation

The huge granite **gare SNCF** stands opposite the **post office** at the end of rue Gambetta. The **gare routière**, where regional buses depart, is east of the train station on avenue de l'Amphithéâtre. The **tourist office** (April–Sept Mon–Sat 9am–7pm, Sun 10am–5pm; Oct–March Mon–Sat 9am–7pm, Sun 10am–3pm; ℡03.87.55.53.76, ⓦtourisme.mairie-metz.fr) is located by the side of the Hôtel de Ville on place d'Armes in the old town. Almost any bus from the station will take you there.

Metz offers a good range of hotels and budget **accommodation**, including an HI hostel and campsite, plus a couple of more ritzy establishments.

Hotels

De la Cathédrale 25 place de Chambre ℡03.87.75.00.02, ⓦwww.hotelcathedrale -metz.fr. Lovely hotel in a seventeenth-century townhouse, wonderfully located opposite the cathedral. Parquet floors, original beams and elegant furnishings give this place bags of character. ❹–❻

Cécil 14 rue Pasteur ℡03.87.66.66.13, ⓦwww .cecilhotel-metz.com. Part of a large chain, with welcoming staff and functional, spacious rooms, 5min walk from the train station. ❸

La Citadelle 5 av Ney ℡03.87.17.17.17, ⓦwww.citadelle-metz.com. This stylish four-star hotel opened in 2005 in an impeccably converted fifteenth-century military buildiing, overlooking a park, with chic, contemporary rooms. ❾

Grand-Hôtel de Metz 3 rue des Clercs ℡03.87.36.16.33, ⓦwww.grandhotelmetz.com. A characterful old establishment, with friendly staff; the more expensive rooms are surprisingly spacious, although the decor is on the prissy side. ❸–❺

Du Théâtre 3 rue du Pont-St-Marcel ℡03.87.31.10.10, ⓦwww.port-saint-marcel .com. Upmarket hotel with pastel-hued decor, less charming than some of its rivals, but in a pretty location on the Île de la Comedie. There's an outdoor swimming pool, fitness centre and sauna. ⑤–⑦

Hostels and campsite

Camping municipal allée de Metz-Plage ☎03.87.68.26.48, ℮campingmetz@mairie-metz .fr. Quiet, very central campsite right next door to *Metz Plage,* within 10 minutes, walk of the historic centre. May–Sept.

Carrefour 6 rue Marchant ☎03.87.75.07.26, ℮ascarrefour@orange.fr. Large, exemplary HI hostel, just 5 minutes, walk north of the museums and cathedral; it's packed with teenagers in summer. Four bed dorms €15.90; the en-suite private rooms are excellent value. ❶

Metz Plage 1 allée de Metz-Plage ☎03.87.30.44.02, ☎03.87.33.19.80. Friendly hostel on the picturesque Île Chambière, though a little further from town than *Carrefour.* Bus #3 or #11 (stop "Pontiffroy") from the *gare SNCF.* Eight bed dorms €15.20 including breakfast; 2-bed room with shared bathroom ❶

The City

Metz in effect is two towns: the original French quarters, gathered round the cathedral, and the *ville allemande,* undertaken as part of a once-and-for-all process of Germanification after the Prussian occupation in 1870. To the south the latter, unmistakably Teutonic in style, has considerable elegance and grandeur. The **gare SNCF** sets the tone, a vast and splendid granite structure of 1870 in Rhenish Romanesque, a bizarre cross between a Scottish laird's hunting lodge and a dungeon. Its gigantic dimensions reflect the Germans' long-term intention to use it as the fulcrum of their military transport system. It's matched in style by the **post office** opposite and by some imposing bourgeois apartment buildings on the surrounding streets. The whole quarter was meant to serve as a model of superior town planning, in contrast to the squalid Latin hugger-mugger of the old French neighbourhoods further north.

To the south of the train station, as you head towards the **gare routière** a futuristic building, designed by Shigeru Ban and Jean de Gastines, is currently under construction; this will open its doors as a branch of the **Centre Pompidou** in 2010.

To the north west of the *gare SNCF,* the place de la République is a major parking area, bounded on the east side by shops and cafés, with army barracks to the south and the formal gardens of the **Esplanade,** overlooking the Moselle, to the west. To the right, as you look down the esplanade from the square, is the handsome **Palais de Justice** in the city's characteristic yellow stone. To the left, a gravel drive leads past the old arsenal, now converted into a prestigious concert hall (**L'Arsenal**).

From the north side of place de la République, **rue des Clercs** cuts through the attractive, bustling and largely pedestrianized heart of the old city. Past the **place St-Jacques,** with its numerous outdoor cafés, you come to the eighteenth-century **place d'Armes,** where the lofty Gothic **Cathedral of St-Étienne** towers above the colonnaded classical facade of the Hôtel de Ville. Its nave is the tallest in France – after Beauvais and Amiens cathedrals – but its best feature is without doubt the stained glass (*vitraux*), both medieval and modern, including windows dating from the thirteenth century. Pride of place, however, goes to **Chagall**'s 1963 masterpiece in the western wall of the north transept, representing the Garden of Eden, while his slightly earlier works in the ambulatory vividly depict Old Testament scenes – Moses and David, Abraham's Sacrifice and Jacob's Dream.

From the cathedral, a short walk up rue du Chanoine Collin brings you to the city's main museum complex, the **Musées de la Cour d'Or,** 2 rue du Haut-Poirier (Mon & Wed–Fri 9am–5pm, Sat & Sun 10am–5pm; €4.60, free first Sun of month), a treasure house of Gallo-Roman sculpture, which contains

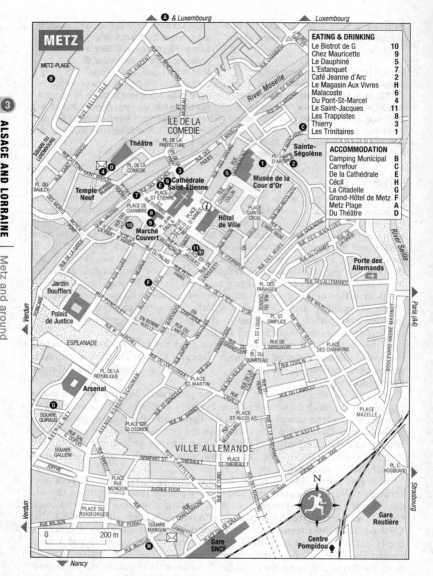

METZ

EATING & DRINKING

Le Bistrot de G	10
Chez Mauricette	9
Le Dauphiné	5
L'Estanquet	7
Café Jeanne d'Arc	2
Le Magasin Aux Vivres	H
Malacoste	6
Du Pont-St-Marcel	4
Le Saint-Jacques	11
Les Trappistes	8
Thierry	3
Les Trinitaires	1

ACCOMMODATION

Camping Municipal	B
Carrefour	C
De la Cathédrale	E
Cécil	H
La Citadelle	G
Grand-Hôtel de Metz	F
Metz Plage	A
Du Théâtre	D

the remains of the city's Roman baths, excavated during the museum's extension in the 1930s.

For the city's most compelling townscape, you have only to go down to the riverbank and cross to the tiny **Île de la Comédie**, dominated by its classical eighteenth-century square and theatre (the oldest in France) and a rather striking Protestant church erected under the German occupation. An older, equally beautiful square and a popular drinking spot is the **place St-Louis** with its Gothic arcades some ten-minutes' walk to the east of the cathedral along En-Fournirue. On the way, wander up the Italianate streets climbing the **hill of Sainte-Croix** to your left, the legacy of the Lombard bankers who came to run the city's finances in the thirteenth century. It's also worth continuing east down the rue des Allemands to have a look at the **Porte des Allemands** – a massive, fortified double gate that once barred the eastern entrances to the medieval city.

Eating and drinking

Finding somewhere **to eat** in Metz is not difficult; there's a cluster of cafés and restaurants between the cathedral and Île de la Comédie. At night, place St-Jacques attracts drinkers of all ages. For a picnic or snack lunch, one excellent option is to visit the city's **covered market** (Tues–Sat 8am–6pm); inside, the superb ⚜ *Chez Mauricette* serves vast sandwiches, made with the finest local cheese and charcuterie on crusty rustic bread (eat in or take away from €2.80). On Saturday mornings, nearby place Jean Paul II is taken over by the weekly fruit and vegetable market.

Restaurants

🎣 **Le Bistrot de G** 9 Rue du Faisan ☏ 03.87.37.06.44, ⊛ www.restaurant -bistrotdeg.com. Atmospheric, Parisian-style bistro, very popular with locals for its lively ambience and good value set lunch menu (€11–13). In the evening *carte* mains are €17 or €18.50 and there's a selection of classic French deserts for €6, including a heavenly chocolate mousse. Closed Sun.

Le Dauphiné 8 rue du Chanoine-Collin. Spruce little place in a handy location, popular for its reasonable lunchtime menus (€8 for the *plat du jour*), the more expensive ones featuring delicacies such as frogs' legs and duck breast. Closed Sun & Mon–Thurs evening.

Le Magasin Aux Vivres ☏ 03.87.17.17.17. Upmarket restaurant in the *Citadelle* hotel serving creative, seasonal cuisine, which has won prestigious awards. Menus €40 upwards. Closed Sat lunch, Sun evening & Mon.

Malacoste 23 Place de Chambre ☏ 03.87.32.15.34. Small, intimate *bar à vins* with an attractive wooden interior, knowledgeable staff and a small terrace out

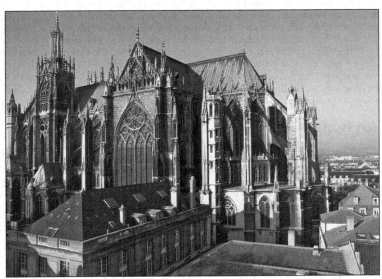

▲ Saint-Étienne Cathedral

the front, blessed with a magnificent view of the Cathedral. There's a good selection of wines available by the glass and a Mediterranean influenced daily menu for €15–23. Closed Sun; no food served Mon & Tues evening.

Du Pont-St-Marcel 1 rue du Pont-St-Marcel ☏03.87.30.12.29. On the twee side, admittedly, but this seventeenth-century establishment, where the staff don regional costume, is renowned for its excellent local specialities and fine Moselle wines. Menus at €18 and €29.

Thierry 5 rue des Piques ☏03.87.74.01.23. Modern decor and a charming patio combined with some adventurous fusion cuisine and an intelligent wine list. Menu €22. Closed Sun & Wed.

Cafés and bars

L'Estanquet 27 rue des Roches. Friendly riverside bar open daily with live music at weekends and lots of outside seating in summer, serving snacks from €6.50.

Café Jeanne d'Arc place Jeanne-d'Arc. Medieval beams and frescoes inside, and an attractive balmy-weather terrace on the square, dominated by the lofty towers of Ste-Ségolène church. An ideal spot to catch one of the free jazz concerts which take place in the square every Thurs evening in summer. Closed Sun.

Le Saint-Jacques 10 place Saint-Jacques. Less trendy than the neighbouring cafés on this happening square, but with wi-fi and internet access (€1 per hour).

Les Trappistes 20 Place de Chambre. Outside seating in a prime people-watching spot, in an attractive cobbled square. Food at lunchtime only; *plat du jour* €9.50. Closed Sun & Mon.

Les Trinitaires 10–12 rue des Trinitaires ☏03.87.20.03.03, ⓦ www.lestrinitaires.com. The place to go for serious jazz, rock, folk and chanson, enhanced by the Gothic cellars. Live music generally Thurs–Sat 8.30pm; consult the website for programmes.

Verdun and the battlefield

VERDUN lies in a bend of the River Meuse, some 70km west of Metz. Of no great interest in itself, what makes this sleepy provincial town remarkable is its association with the ghastly battle that took place on the bleak uplands to its north between 1916 and 1918.

In the aftermath of German victory in the 1870–71 war, Verdun and its environs became the lynch-pin of France's northeastern defences. In 1916, aiming to break the stalemate of trench warfare, the German General Erich von Falkenhayn chose Verdun as the target for an offensive that ranked among the most devastating ever launched in the annals of war. His troops advanced to within 5km of Verdun, but never captured the town. Gradually the French clawed back the lost ground, but final victory came only in the last months of the war with the aid of US troops. The price was high: hundreds of thousands of men died on both sides. To this day, memorials in every village, hamlet and town of France are inscribed with the names of men slaughtered at Verdun.

Arrival, information and accommodation

The **gare SNCF** is on avenue Garibaldi. The official **tourist office** (Jan, Feb & Dec Mon–Sat 10am–12.30pm & 2–5pm, Sun & public holidays 10am–12.30pm; March–June & Sept–Nov Mon–Sat 9.30am–12.30pm & 1.30–6pm, Sun & public holidays 10am–noon & 2.30–5pm; July & Aug Mon–Sat 9am–7pm, Sun & public holidays 10am–noon & 2–6pm; ☏03.29.84.55.55, ⓦ www .tourisme-verdun.fr) lies just across the River Meuse from the Porte Chaussée and is well stocked with free information on the battlefields. Opposite, the Maison du Tourisme (☏03.29.86.14.18, ⓦ www.verdun-tourisme.com) runs daily four-hour minibus **tours of the battlefield** (in French only, booking advisable; May–Sept 2pm; €29).

As for **accommodation**, there's much more to choose from in Metz or Nancy. However, if you do wish to spend the night in Verdun, head for the friendly *Hôtel St-Paul*, 17 rue du Général Sarrail (☎03.29.86.02.16, ⓔhotelspaul @orange.fr ❷; closed Dec 7 – Jan 7) or the simple family-run *Hôtel Montaulbain*, 4 rue de la Vieille-Prison (☎03.29.86.00.47; ❶–❷).The *Auberge de Jeunesse* (☎03.29.86.28.28, ⓔverdun@fuaj.org; closed Jan) is between the cathedral and Centre Mondial (5-, 6- or 7-bed dorms €12.10), with a splendid panoramic view of the town.

The Town

Perhaps surprisingly, given the pounding it received during the course of two world wars, Verdun's centre is not entirely unattractive. Memorials to the town's unfortunate history aside, however, there's not a vast amount to see or do.

Near the railway station, the **Rodin memorial**, a disturbing statue of winged Victory, stands beside a handsome eighteenth-century gateway at the northern end of rue St-Paul, where it joins avenue Garibaldi. Nearby, a simple engraving lists all the years between 450 and 1916 that Verdun has been involved in conflict. The fourteenth-century **Porte Chaussée** guards the river-crossing in the middle of town. Beyond it, further along rue Mazel, a flight of steps climbs up to the **Monument de la Victoire**, where a helmeted warrior leans on his sword in commemoration of the 1916 battle, while in the crypt below a roll is kept of all the soldiers, French and American, who took part. Beyond the monument, on rue de la Belle Vierge, is the **Musée de la Princerie** (April–Oct daily except Tues 9.30am–noon & 2–6pm; €2), which exhibits ceramics, furniture and paintings.

The rue de la Belle Vierge leads round to the **Cathedral of Notre-Dame**, whose outward characteristics are Gothic; its earlier Romanesque origins were only uncovered by shell damage in 1916. The elegant **bishop's palace** behind it has been converted into the **Centre Mondial de la Paix et des Droits de l'Homme** (Jan to mid-June & mid-Sept to Dec daily except Mon 9.30am–noon & 2–6pm; mid-June to mid-Sept daily 9.30am–7pm; €3) hosting exhibitions on themes such as peacekeeping and human rights.

Rue du Rû, the continuation of rue Mazel, takes you to the underground galleries of the **Citadelle** (daily Dec, Feb & Mar 10am–noon & 2–5pm; April–June & Sept 9am–6pm; Jul & Aug 9am–7pm; Oct & Nov 9.30am–12.30pm & 1.30–5.30pm; €6), used as shelter for thousands of soldiers during the battle. The Unknown Soldier, whose remains now lie under the Arc de Triomphe in Paris, was chosen from among the dead who lie here.

Eating

You shouldn't have trouble finding somewhere to **eat**: there are plenty of cafés along the river. For a galette or crêpe, *Marie la Crepe* at 54 rue des Royers is a cheap and cheerful (from €3; closed Sun & Mon in winter). *L'Estaminet*, opposite, has a great selection of beers and is open until late.

The battlefield

The **Battle of Verdun** opened on the morning of February 21, 1916, with a German artillery barrage that lasted ten hours and expended two million shells. The battle concentrated on the forts of Vaux and Douaumont, which the French had built after the 1870 Franco–Prussian War. By the time the main battle ended ten months later, nine villages had been pounded into oblivion; not a single trace of them is detectable in aerial photos taken at the time.

The most visited part of the battlefield extends along the hills north of Verdun, but the fighting also spread to the west of the Meuse, to the hills of Mort-Homme and Hill 304, to Vauquois and the Argonne, and south along the Meuse to St-Mihiel, where the Germans held an important salient until dislodged by US forces in 1918. Unless you take an organised tour, the only viable way to explore the area is with your own transport. The main sights are reached via two minor roads that snake through the battlefields, forming a crossroads northeast of Verdun: the D913 and D112.

The monument to André Maginot and the Fort de Souville

The D913 branches left from the main N3 to Metz, 5km east of Verdun; the D112 leaves the same N3 opposite the Cimetière du Faubourg-Pavé on the eastern outskirts of Verdun and is soon enclosed by gloomy conifer plantations.

If you take the D112, on the right you pass a **monument to André Maginot**, later French Minister of War, who was wounded in the battle. Shortly afterwards, a sign points out a forest ride to the **Fort de Souville**, the furthest point of the German advance in 1916. The site is not on the main tourist beat, and is a very moving, if rather frightening, twenty-minute walk over ground absolutely shattered by artillery fire, with pools of black water standing in the now grassy shell-holes. The fort itself lies half-hidden among the scrub, the armoured gun turrets still louring in their pits. A little way beyond the fort, where the D112 intersects the D913, a **stone lion** marks the spot at which the German advance was checked. To the left the D913 continues to Fleury, 1km from the crossroads, and on to Douaumont, before curling back round to the D964.

Fleury and the Fort de Vaux

The full horror of the battle is graphically documented at **FLEURY**, in the **Memorial de Verdun** (℡03.29.84.35.34, ⓦ www.memorial-de-verdun.fr; daily: Feb, March & mid-Nov to mid-Dec 9am–noon & 2–6pm; April to mid-Sept 9am–6pm; mid-Sept to mid-Nov 9am–noon & 2–6pm; €7), where, alongside contemporary newsreels and photos, a section of the shell-torn terrain that was once the village of Fleury has been reconstructed as the battle left it.

Another major monument is the **Fort de Vaux**, 4km east of Fleury (daily: Feb, March, Nov & Dec 10am–noon & 1–5pm; April–Aug 9am–6.30pm; Sept & Oct 10am–noon & 1–5.30pm; €3). After six days' hand-to-hand combat in the gas-filled tunnels, the French garrison were left with no alternative but to surrender. On the exterior wall, a plaque commemorates the last messenger pigeon sent to the command post in Verdun asking, in vain, for reinforce-

St-Mihiel and the Voie Sacrée

As early as 1914, the Germans captured the town of **St-Mihiel** on the River Meuse to the south, which gave them control of the main supply route into Verdun. The only route left open to the French was the N35, winding north from Bar-le-Duc over the open hills and wheat fields. In memory of all those who kept the supplies going, the road is called **La Voie Sacrée** (The Sacred Way) and marked with milestones capped with the helmet of the *poilu* (the slang term for infantryman). In St-Mihiel itself, the **Église St-Michel** contains the **Sépulcre** or *Entombment of Christ*, by local sculptor **Ligier Richier** – a set of thirteen stone figures, carved in the mid-sixteeenth century and regarded as one of the masterpieces of the French Renaissance. Just beyond the town to the east, on the Butte de Montsec, is a **memorial** to the Americans who died here in 1918 and a US **cemetery** at Thiancourt on the main road.

ments. Having delivered its message, the pigeon expired, poisoned by the gas-filled air above the battlefield. It was posthumously awarded the Légion d'Honneur.

Douaumont

The principal memorial to the carnage stands in the middle of the battlefield a short distance along the D913 beyond Fleury. The **Ossuaire de Douaumont** (daily: March & Oct 9am–noon & 2–5.30pm; April 9am–6pm; May–Aug 9am–6.30pm; Sept 9am–noon & 2–6pm; Nov 9am–noon & 2–5pm; Dec 2–5pm; €3.50) is a vast and surreal structure, with a central tower shaped like a projectile aimed at the heavens. Its vaults contain the bones of thousands upon thousands of unidentified soldiers, some of them visible through windows set in the base of the building. When the battle ended in 1918, the ground was covered in fragments of corpses; 120,000 French bodies were identified, perhaps a third of the total killed. Across the road, a **cemetery** contains the graves of 15,000 men, including Muslims of the French colonial regiments; while a nearby wall, beneath an eerily tree-less ridge top, commemorates the Jewish dead.

The **Fort de Douaumont** (daily: Feb, March, Nov & Dec 10am–1pm & 2–5pm; April–Aug 10am–6.30pm; Sept & Oct 10am–5.30pm; closed Jan; €3) is 900m down the road from the cemetery. Completed in 1912, it was the strongest of the 38 forts built to defend Verdun. Inexplicably, however, the armament of these forts was greatly reduced in 1915, and when the Germans attacked in 1916, twenty men were enough to overrun the garrison. The fort is on three levels and its claustrophobic, dungeon-like galleries are hung with stalactites. The Germans held the fort for eight months while under continuous siege, housing 3000 men in these cramped, unventilated, quarters, infested with fleas and lice and plagued by rats that attacked the sleeping and the dead indiscriminately.

Travel details

Trains

Barr to: Dambach-la-ville (12 daily; 15min); Obernai (13 daily; 14 min); Rosheim (12 daily; 20min); Sélestat (12 daily; 25min); Strasbourg (14 daily; 45min).
Colmar to: Mulhouse (every 30min; 20min); Munster (hourly; 30min); Sélestat (every 30min; 11min); Strasbourg (every 40min; 40–50min).
Dambach-la-ville to: Obernai (8 daily; 30min); Rosheim (7 daily; 40min); Sélestat (12 daily; 10min); Strasbourg (8 daily; 1hr).
Metz to: Luxembourg (every 30min–1hr; 55min) Nancy (hourly; 30min–1hr); Paris-Est (TGV 12 daily; 1hr 30min); Saverne (every 1–2hr; 1hr 15min); Verdun (3 daily; 1hr 30min).
Mulhouse to: Basel (every 20min; 20min); Belfort (every 30min; 35min); Sélestat (every 40min; 30min); Strasbourg (every 30–40min; 50min).

Nancy to: Longuyon (6 daily; 1hr 20min); Paris-Est (TGV 12 daily; 1hr 30min); Saverne (every 1–2hr; 1 hr); Strasbourg (every 1–2hr; 1hr 20min).
Obernai to: Rosheim (every 30–50 min; 7min); Sélestat (10 daily; 30min); Strasbourg (14 daily; 30min).
Rosheim to: Barr (12 daily; 20min); Dambach-la-ville; Obernai (every 30–40min; 7min); Sélestat (10 daily; 40min); Strasbourg (every 40–60min; 20min).
Saverne to: Paris-Est (2 daily; 2hr 30min).
Sélestat to: Obernai (10 daily; every 30min); Rosheim (10 daily; 40min); Strasbourg (every 40min; 20min).
Strasbourg to: Barr (14 daily; 45min); Basel (hourly; 1hr 20min); Colmar (every 40min; 40–50min); Dambach-la-ville (8 daily; 1hr); Ingwiller (12 daily; 30min); Kehl, Germany (hourly; 10min); Lille (TGV 3 daily; 3hr 40min); Lyon (12 daily;

5hr 20min); Metz (every 1–2hr; 1hr 30min); Mulhouse (every 30–40 min; 50min); Nancy (every 1–2hr; 1hr 20min); Nantes (TGV 1 daily; 5hr 15min); Obernai (14 daily; 40min); Paris-Est (TGV hourly; 2hr 20min); Rosheim (every 40-60min; 20min); Rennes (TGV 1 daily; 5hr 15min); Saverne (every 15–40min; 30–40min); Sélestat (every 40min; 20min); Wissembourg (every 1–2hr; 1hr).
Verdun to: Metz (3 daily; 1hr 30min).
Wissembourg to: Strasbourg (every 1–2hr; 1hr).

Buses

Colmar to: Mulhouse (4 daily; 1hr 15min); Freiburg, Germany (11 daily; 1hr 20min). Ribeauvillé (3 daily; 30min).
Metz to: Verdun (4 daily Mon–Fri; 1hr 30min).
Mulhouse to: Freiburg (2 daily; 1hr 30min).
Sélestat to: Ribeauvillé (5 daily; 30min); Ste-Marie -aux-Mines (hourly; 35min).
Strasbourg to: Obernai (11 daily; 50min), Ottrot (11 daily; 1hr 10min).

4

Normandy

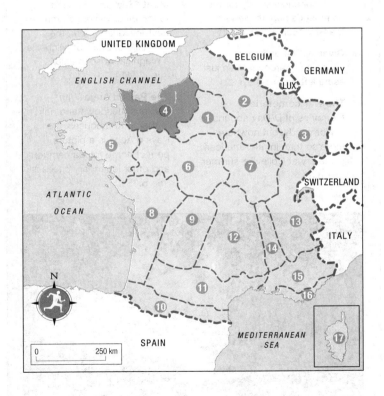

CHAPTER 4 # Highlights

✳ **Rouen** This fine old medieval city would still seem familiar to Joan of Arc, whose life came to a tragic end in its main square. See p.313

✳ **Château Gaillard** Richard the Lionheart's sturdy fortress commands superb views of the River Seine. See p.321

✳ **Giverny** Claude Monet's house and garden remain just as he left them. See p.321

✳ **The war cemeteries** Memories of D-Day abound in Normandy, but nowhere more so than in the American cemetery at Colleville-sur-mer. See p.333

✳ **The Bayeux Tapestry** One of the world's most extraordinary historical documents, embroidering the saga of William the Conqueror in every colourful detail. See p.336

✳ **Mont St-Michel** Second only to the Eiffel Tower as France's best-loved landmark, the *merveille* of Mont St-Michel is a magnificent spectacle. See p.346

✳ **The Pays d'Auge** With luscious meadows and half-timbered farmhouses, the Pays d'Auge is a picture-perfect home for Camembert and other legendary cheeses. See p.351

▲ Monet's garden at Giverny

Normandy

Though firmly incorporated into the French mainstream, the seaboard province of **Normandy** has a history of prosperous independence as one of the crucial powers of medieval Europe. Colonized by Scandinavian Vikings (or Norsemen) from the ninth century onwards, it in turn began to colonize during the eleventh and twelfth centuries, with military expeditions conquering not only England but as far afield as Sicily and areas of the Near East. Later, as part of France, it was instrumental in the settlement of Canada.

Normandy has always had large ports: **Rouen**, on the Seine, is the nearest navigable point to Paris, while **Dieppe**, **Le Havre** and **Cherbourg** have important transatlantic trade. Inland, it is overwhelmingly agricultural – a fertile belt of tranquil pastureland, where the chief interest for most visitors will be the groaning restaurant tables of regions such as the **Pays d'Auge**. Significant portions of the seaside are overdeveloped, whether because of industry, as with the huge sprawl of Le Havre, or tourism – in the second half of the nineteenth century, the last French emperor created a "Norman Riviera" around **Trouville** and **Deauville**, and an air of pretension still hangs about their elegant promenades. However, more ancient harbours such as **Honfleur** and **Barfleur** remain visually irresistible, and there are numerous seaside villages with few crowds or affectations. The banks of the Seine, too, hold several delightful little communities, including Caudebec and Jumièges.

Normandy also boasts extraordinary Romanesque and Gothic architectural treasures, although only the much-restored capital, Rouen, retains a complete medieval centre. Elsewhere, the attractions are more often single buildings than entire towns. Most famous of all is the spectacular *merveille* on the island of **Mont St-Michel**, but there are also the monasteries at **Jumièges** and **Caen**, the cathedrals of **Bayeux** and **Coutances**, and Richard the Lionheart's castle above the Seine at **Les Andelys**. In addition, **Bayeux** has its vivid and astonishing tapestry, while among more recent creations are Monet's garden at **Giverny** and, at Le Havre, a fabulous collection of paintings by Dufy and Boudin, as well as other Impressionists. Furthermore, Normandy's vernacular architecture makes it well worth exploring inland – the back roads through the countryside are lined with splendid centuries-old half-timbered manor houses. It's remarkable how much has survived – or, less surprisingly, been restored – since the Allied landings in 1944 and the subsequent **Battle of Normandy**, which has its own legacy in a series of war museums, memorials and cemeteries.

To the French, at least, the essence of Normandy is its produce. This is the land of Camembert and Calvados, cider and seafood, and a butter- and cream-based

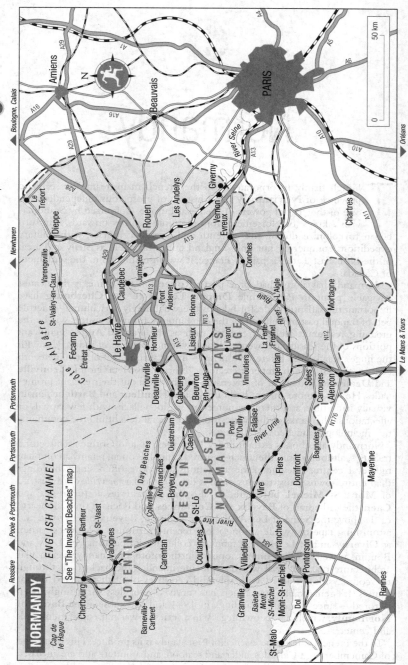

NORMANDY

Cap de la Hague

ENGLISH CHANNEL

◄ Rosslare ◄ Poole & Portsmouth ◄ Portsmouth ◄ Portsmouth ◄ Newhaven ◄ Boulogne, Calais

Cherbourg
Barfleur
St-Vaast
Barneville-
Carteret
Valognes
COTENTIN
Granville
Baie de
Mont
St-Michel
Mont-St-Michel
St-Malo
Dol
Pontorson
Rennes

Le Tréport
Dieppe
Varengeville
St-Valéry-en-Caux
Côte d'Albâtre
Fécamp
Étretat
Le Havre
Honfleur
Trouville
Deauville
Cabourg
Beuvron-
en-Auge
Caudebec
Jumièges
Pont
Audemer
Brionne
Lisieux
PAYS
D'AUGE
Livarot
La Ferté-
Fresnel
L'Aigle
River Risle
Risle

Amiens
Beauvais
N
Rouen
Les Andelys
Vernon
Giverny
Évreux
Conches
River Seine
PARIS
Chartres
A11

A4
A29
A16
A28
A29
A13
A13
A13
A28
A13
A6
A5
A10
A10

50 km
0

D Day Beaches
Colleville
Arromanches
Bayeux
BESSIN
St-Lô
Carentan
Coutances
Villedieu
Avranches
Flers
Vire
Domfront
Mayenne

Ouistreham
Caen
NORMANDE
SUISSE
River Orme
River Orme
Pont
D'Ouilly
Falaise
Argentan
Séez
Carrouges
Alençon
Bagnoles
Vimoutiers
Mortagne
N13
N12
N176
A84

River Vire

See "The Invasion Beaches" map

◄ Le Mans & Tours ◄ Orléans

4

The main towns and cities of Normandy are well served by **rail links**, although changes at Rouen are quite common on many routes in Haute Normandie (for example, Dieppe to Le Havre), and services are much less frequent at weekends. **Bus services** vary by *département*, by far the best served is Calvados, whose Bus Verts (🌐www.busverts.fr) provide many useful services, such as those linking Le Havre and Honfleur, and routes from Caen to the D-Day beaches. For those wanting to explore the countryside, a **car** is a necessity, as bus services to rural areas such as villages in the Pays d'Auge are at best infrequent, more likely non existent. A car also makes it much easier to explore the coast, which is home to the D-Day beaches, although tours from Bayeux and Caen are also a good option.

cuisine with a proud disdain for most things *nouvelle*. Economically, however, the richness of the dairy pastures has been Normandy's downfall in recent years. EU milk quotas have liquidated many small farms, and stringent sanitary regulations have forced many small-scale traditional cheese factories to close. Parts of inland Normandy are now among the most depressed in the whole country, and in the forested areas to the south, where life has never been easy, things have not improved.

Seine Maritime

The *département* of Seine Maritime comprises three very distinct sections: Normandy's dramatic **northern coastline**, home not only to major ports like Dieppe and Le Havre but also to such delightful resorts as **Étretat**; the meandering course of the **River Seine**, where unchanged villages stand both up- and downstream of the provincial capital of Rouen; and the flat, chalky **Caux plateau**, which makes for pleasant cycling country but holds little of note to detain visitors.

Dieppe in particular offers a much more appealing introduction to France than its counterparts further north in Picardy, and with the impressive white cliffs of the aptly named **Côte d'Albâtre** (Alabaster Coast) stretching away to either side it could easily serve as the base for a long stay. The most direct route to Rouen from here is simply to head due south, but it's well worth tracing the shore all the way west to **Le Havre**, and then following the Seine inland.

Driving along the D982 along the northern bank of the Seine, you'll often find your course paralleled by mighty container ships out on the water. Potential stops en route include the medieval abbeys of **Jumièges** and **St-Wandrille**, but **Rouen** itself is the prime destination, its association with the execution of Joan of Arc merely the most compelling episode in its fascinating history. Further upstream, Monet's wonderful house and garden at **Giverny** and the English frontier stronghold of Château Gaillard at **Les Andelys** also justify taking a slow route into Paris.

Dieppe

Squeezed between high cliff headlands, **DIEPPE** is an enjoyably small-scale port that used to be more of a resort. During the nineteenth century, Parisians came here by train to take the sea air, promenading along the front while the English indulged in the peculiar pastime of swimming. These days, it may not be a place many travellers go out of their way to visit, but it's certainly one of the nicer ferry ports in northern France, and makes a pleasant spot for a relaxing break or a last night stop over prior to crossing the Channel. Saturday's bustling market on the Grand Rue is a definite attraction, but those visiting on other days won't be disappointed by Dieppe's compact town centre, filled with pretty old buildings, or its strip of pebble beach flanked by extravagant seafront lawns. The business of the port goes on as ever, with Dieppe's commercial docks

The food of Normandy

The **food of Normandy** owes its most distinctive characteristic – its gut-bursting, heart-pounding richness – to the lush orchards and dairy herds of its agricultural heartland, especially the area southeast of Caen known as the Pays d'Auge. Menus abound in **meat** such as veal (*veau*) cooked in *vallée d'Auge* style, which consists largely of the profligate addition of cream and butter. Many dishes also feature orchard fruit, either in its natural state or in successively more alcoholic forms – either as apple or pear cider, or perhaps further distilled to produce brandies.

Normans have a great propensity for blood and guts. In addition to gamier meat and fowl such as rabbit and duck (a speciality in Rouen, where the birds are strangled to ensure that all their blood gets into the sauce), they enjoy such intestinal preparations as *andouilles*, the sausages known in English as chitterlings, and *tripes*, stewed for hours *à la mode de Caen*. A full blowout at a country restaurant in one of the small towns of inland Normandy will also traditionally entail one or two pauses between courses for the *trou normand*: a glass of the apple brandy Calvados that lets you catch your breath before struggling on with the feast.

Normandy's long coastline ensures that it is also a wonderful region for **seafood**. Many of the larger ports and resorts have long waterfront lines of restaurants competing for attention, each with its *"copieuse" assiette de fruits de mer*. **Honfleur** is probably the most enjoyable of these, but **Dieppe**, **Étretat** and **Cherbourg** also offer endless eating opportunities. The menus tend to be much the same as those on offer in Brittany, if perhaps slightly more expensive.

The most famous products of Normandy's meadow-munching cows are, of course, their **cheeses**. The tradition of cheese-making in the Pays d'Auge is thought to have started in the monasteries during the Dark Ages. By the eleventh century the local products were already well defined; in 1236, the *Roman de la Rose* referred to Angelot cheese, identified with a small coin depicting a young angel killing a dragon. The principal modern varieties began to emerge in the seventeenth century – Pont l'Evêque, which is square with a washed crust, soft but not runny, and Livarot, which is round, thick and firm, and has a stronger flavour. Although Marie Herel is generally credited with having invented Camembert in the 1790s, a smaller and stodgier version of that cheese had already existed for some time. A priest fleeing the Revolution seems to have stayed in Mme Herel's farmhouse at Camembert, and suggested modifications in her cheese-making in line with the techniques he'd seen employed to manufacture Brie de Meaux – a slower process, gentler on the curd and with more thorough drainage. The rich full cheese thus created was an instant success in the market at Vimoutiers, and the development of the railways (and the invention of the chipboard cheesebox in 1880) helped to give it a worldwide popularity.

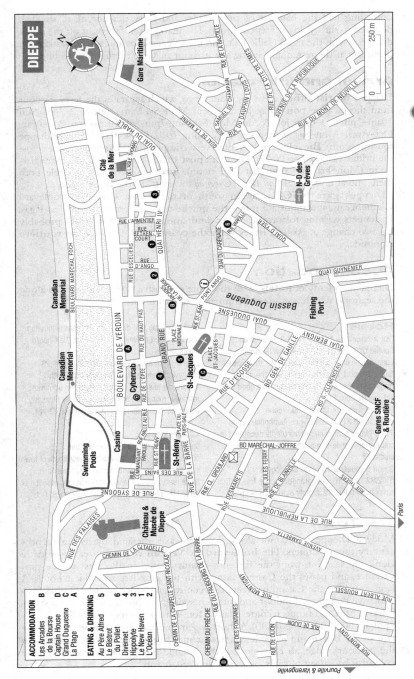

DIEPPE

ACCOMMODATION
Les Arcades
de la Bourse   **B**
Captain House   **D**
Grand Duquesne   **C**
La Plage   **A**

EATING & DRINKING
Au Père Alfred   **5**
Le Bistrot
du Pollet   **6**
Divernet   **4**
Hippolyte   **3**
Le New Haven   **1**
L'Océan   **2**

Gare Maritime

Cité
de la Mer

Canadian
Memorial

Canadian
Memorial

N-D des
Grèves

Swimming
Pools

Casino

St-Jacques

St-Rémy

Château & Musée de Dieppe

Bassin Duquesne

Fishing
Port

Gares SNCF
& Routière

@ Cybercab

RUE DE LA BASTILLE
RUE DE LA CITÉ DE LIMES
AVENUE DE LA RÉPUBLIQUE
RUE DU MONT DE NEUVILLE
RUE SAMUEL DE CHAMPLAIN
RUE DU DAUPHIN LOUIS X
QUAI DE LA MARNE
QUAI DU HÂBLE
RUE DE L'ABBÉ THOMAS
RUE L'ARMENTIER
RUE BETHENCOURT
QUAI HENRI IV
RUE DESCELIERS
RUE D'ANGO
BOULEVARD MARÉCHAL FOCH
BOULEVARD DE VERDUN
RUE DU HAUT-PAS
GRAND RUE
RUE SAINTE-CATHERINE
RUE ST-JEAN
PLACE NATIONALE
QUAI DU CARENAGE
RUE DE L'EPÉE
RUE NALLE AU BLÉ
RUE ST-RÉMY
PLACE DU PUITS-SALÉ
RUE DE LA BARRE
RUE DES BAINS
RUE DU COMMANDANT FAYOLLE
PLACE ST-JACQUES
PLACE ST-RÉMY
RUE D'ÉCOSSE
QUAI DUQUESNE
QUAI BÉRIGNY
BD GÉN. DE GAULLE
BD G. CLÉMENCEAU
BD MARÉCHAL-JOFFRE
RUE CL. GROULARD
RUE DESMARETS
RUE JULES FERRY
RUE DE BLAINVILLE
RUE THIERS
RUE DE LA RÉPUBLIQUE
CHEMIN DE LA CITADELLE
CHEMIN DE LA CHAPELLE SAINT-NICOLAS
CHEMIN DU PRÊCHE
RUE DU FAUBOURG DE LA BARRE
AVENUE GAMBETTA
RUE MONTIGNY
RUE DES FONTAINES
RUE DE DIJON
RUE MONTIGNY
RUE ALBERT ROUSSEL
RUE DE SYGOGNE
RUE DES FALAISES
QUAI GUYNEMER
QUAI D'YSER
PONT ANGO
QUAI DU CARENAGE
RUE DE LA BOURSE

0   250 m

▲ Pourville & Varengeville

▼ Paris

unloading half the bananas of the Antilles and forty percent of all shellfish destined to slither down French throats. The markets sell fish right off the boats, displayed with the usual Gallic flair, and the sole, scallops and turbot available in profusion at the restaurants lining the harbour may well tempt you to linger.

Arrival and information

Dieppe's **tourist office** is on the pont Ango, which separates the ferry harbour from the pleasure port (May, June & Sept Mon–Sat 9am–1pm & 2–7pm, Sun 10am–1pm & 3–6pm; July & Aug Mon–Sat 9am–7pm, Sun 10am–1pm & 3–6pm; Oct–April Mon–Sat 9am–noon & 2–6pm; ☏02.32.14.40.60, ⓦwww.dieppe tourisme.com). **Bicycles** can be rented very cheaply from Vélo Service, just across the bridge (☏06.24.56.06.27). The main **post office** is at 2 boulevard Maréchal-Joffre (Mon–Fri 8am–6pm, Sat 8am–noon); **internet access** is available both there, and at *Cybercafé Art au Bar – Cybercab* for short, 19 rue de Sygogne.

Dieppe's **gare SNCF** is 500m south of the tourist office, on boulevard Clemenceau, and trains are much the quickest way to get to Rouen or Paris. Passengers wishing to travel to other destinations in Normandy will probably have to change at Rouen. Buses along the coast leave from the **gare routière** alongside.

Accommodation

Dieppe has plenty of **hotels**, with the more expensive ones concentrated along the seafront, which is among the quietest areas of town.

Hotels

Les Arcades de la Bourse 1–3 arcades de la Bourse ☏02.35.84.14.12, ⓦwww.lesarcades.fr. Long-established central hotel, under the arcades facing the port. Cheaper rooms face the street rather than the port. The restaurant has good value set menus from €18. ④

Captain House 4 Chemin du Prêche ☏02.35.40.31.96, ⓦwww.captainhousedieppe .com. Two spacious *chambres d'hôte* decorated in country-chic style in a pretty old house below the castle. ④

Grand Duquesne 15 place St-Jacques ☏02.32.14.61.10, ⓦaugrandduquesne.free.fr. This small hotel offers 12 slightly old-fashioned plain rooms, but the real draws are the central location and the smart downstairs restaurant. Half-board available. ③

La Plage 20 bd de Verdun ☏02.35.84.18.28 ⓦwww.plagehotel.fr.st. Seafront hotel with something to suit all budgets, from the upmarket sea view rooms to smaller but perfectly pleasant courtyard-facing doubles. No restaurant. ④–⑤

Campsite

Camping Vitamin Chemin des Vertus ☏02.35.82.11.11. Three-star site, well south of town in an unremarkable setting in St-Aubin-sur-Scie that's really only convenient for motorists, even if it is served by the #2 bus route. Open Apri to mid Oct.

The Town

Modern Dieppe is laid out along the three axes dictated by its eighteenth-century town planners. The **boulevard de Verdun** runs for over a kilometre along the seafront, from the fifteenth-century castle in the west to the port entrance, and passes the Casino, along with the grandest and oldest hotels. A large area near the Casino has recently been re-landscaped to hold "Les Bains", a massive complex of indoor and outdoor swimming pools, along with a sauna, Turkish bath and fitness facilities (daily Mon–Fri 10am–8pm, Sat & Sun 10am–7pm; €5.60; ☏02.35.82.80.90). A short way inland, parallel to the seafront, is the **rue de la Barre** and its pedestrianized continuation, the Grande Rue. Along the harbour's edge, an extension of the Grande Rue, **quai Henri IV**, has a colourful backdrop of cafés, brasseries and restaurants.

The **place du Puits Salé**, at the centre of the old town, is dominated by the huge, restored **Café des Tribunaux**, built as an inn towards the end of the seventeenth century. Two hundred years later, it was favoured by painters and writers such as Renoir, Monet, Sickert, Whistler and Pissarro. For English visitors, its most evocative association is with the exiled and unhappy Oscar Wilde, who drank here regularly. It's now a cavernous café, popular with college students and open until after midnight.

As for monuments, the obvious place to start is the medieval **castle** overlooking the seafront from the west, home of the **Musée de Dieppe** and temporary exhibitions (June–Sep daily 10am–noon & 2–6pm; Oct–May daily except Tues 10am–noon & 2–5pm; €3.50). The museum's permanent collection includes a display of carved ivories – virtuoso pieces of sawing, filing and chipping of the plundered riches of Africa, shipped back to the town by early Dieppe explorers. Other exhibits include paintings of local scenes by artists such as Pissarro, Renoir, Dufy, Sickert and Boudin, and a number of works by Georges Braque, the co-founder of **Cubism**, who went to school in Le Havre, spent summers in Dieppe and is buried just west of the town at Varengeville-sur-Mer. A separate, much newer wing of the castle stages temporary exhibitions.

An exit from the western side of the castle takes you out onto a path up to the **cliffs**, from where there are impressive views of Dieppe and beyond. On the other side, a flight of steps leads down to the **square du Canada**, originally named in commemoration of the role played by Dieppe sailors in the colonization of Canada. Now a small plaque is dedicated to the Canadian soldiers who died in the suicidal 1942 raid on Dieppe, justified later as a trial run for the 1944 Normandy landings.

On the eastern end of town just back from the harbour, the **Cité de la Mer**, at 37 rue de l'Asile-Thomas, is a museum and scientific research centre for all things sea-related (daily 10am–noon & 2–6pm; Ⓦestrancitedelamer.free.fr; €5.50). Unless you are a maritime history or marine biology enthusiast, you are unlikely to find much to hold your attention for long: the small museum features a quick romp through the history of seagoing vessels, the highlight of which is a Viking *drakkar* under construction, following methods depicted in the Bayeux Tapestry, and an exhibition detailing Dieppe's relationship with the sea, which somewhat bizarrely includes a rather pungent display of dried, salted fish. Visits culminate with large **aquariums** filled with the marine life of the Channel, including eels, dogfish and cod.

Eating

The most promising area to look for **restaurants** in Dieppe is along the quai Henri IV, which makes a lovely place to stroll and compare menus of a summer's evening. The café-lined Place St-Jacques, dominated by the Gothic Église St-Jacques, is an ideal spot for a relaxed drink.

The sea front isn't home to any restaurants, but it does have a couple of open-air cafés selling mussels, sandwiches and so on, and plenty of crêpe stands. As well as the daily spectacle of the fish on sale in the **fishing port**, there's an all-day open-air **market** in the place Nationale and Grande Rue on Saturday.

Le Bistrot du Pollet 23 rue du Tête du Boeuf Ⓣ02.35.84.68.57. Little local restaurant just east of Pont Ango, especially cosy on a winter's evening, which sells fresh seafood at low prices. Closed Mon, Sun, two weeks in March & all Aug.

Diverne Traiteur 138 Grand Rue Ⓣ02.35.84.13.87. Chic patisserie and tearoom serving a variety of delicious cakes.

Hippolyte 57–59 Quai Henri IV Ⓣ02.35.84.59.81, Popular seafood restaurant by the port which serves tasty mussels in a variety of sauces, from Provençal to curry. Set menus from €14.

Le New Haven 53 quai Henri IV ☎02.35.84.89.72. Reliable seafood specialist, towards the quieter end of the quayside, with good menus from €16. Closed Tues evening. plus Mon & Wed in winter.

L'Océan 23 quai Henri IV ☎02.32.90.97.80. Large family-friendly restaurant with a wide variety of set menus featuring both fish and meat, including a bargain €10 option.

Au Père Alfred 4 Rue de la Boucherie ☎ 02.35.89.56.23 This boulangerie offers an excellent value €4.50 take-away lunch deal, consisting of a filled baguette, a cake and a drink.

The Côte d'Albâtre

The shoreline of the Côte d'Albâtre is eroding at a ferocious rate, and it's conceivable that the small resorts here, tucked in among the cliffs at the ends of a succession of valleys, may not last more than another century or so. For the moment, however, they are quietly prospering, with casinos, sports centres and yacht marinas ensuring a modest but steady summer trade. From Dieppe, the obvious direction to head is west, where both **Fécamp** and **Étretat** make attractive places to base yourself.

Varengeville

If the museum in Dieppe (see p.305) awakened your interest in **Georges Braque**, you may be interested in visiting his grave in the clifftop church further up the coast at **VARENGEVILLE**, 8km west of Dieppe (25min ride on bus #311 or #312, afternoon only). Braque's marble **tomb** is topped by a sadly decaying mosaic of a white dove in flight. More impressive is his vivid blue *Tree of Jesse* stained-glass window inside the church, through which the sun rises in summer.

Back along the road towards Dieppe from the church, the house at the **Bois des Moutiers**, built for Guillaume Mallet from 1898 onwards and un-French in almost every respect, was one of architect Edwin Lutyens' first commissions. Lutyens, then aged just 29, was at the start of a career that was to culminate during the 1920s when he laid out most of New Delhi. The real reason to visit, however, is to enjoy the magnificent **gardens**, designed by Mallet in conjunction with Gertrude Jekyll, which are at their most spectacular in May (house open mid-March to mid-Nov daily 10am–noon & 2–6pm; gardens open April–Oct 10am–8pm; €8 entry to house & gardens during May & June, otherwise €7). Enthusiastic guides lead you through the highly innovative engineering of the house and grounds – you must take the tour of the house, but can walk freely through the gardens. The colours of the tapestry by British painter Edward Burne-Jones hanging in the stairwell were copied from Renaissance cloth in William Morris's studio; the rhododendrons were chosen from similar samples. Outside, paths lead through vistas based on paintings by Poussin, Lorrain and other seventeenth-century artists.

While Varengeville offers no choice of **accommodation**, its one available option is irresistible – the lovely *Hôtel de la Terrasse*, set amid the pines on the route de Vastérival (☎02.35.85.12.54, ☎www.hotel-restaurant-la-terrasse.com; open mid-March to mid-Oct; ❸). Reached via a right turn off the main road as you head west of town, it's perched high above the cliffs, with great sea views. Fish menus in its panoramic dining room cost from €22, and you can follow footpaths down through narrow cracks in the cliffs to reach the rocky beach below.

Fécamp

FÉCAMP, just over halfway from Dieppe to Le Havre, is a serious fishing port with an attractive seafront promenade. One compelling reason to visit is to see the **Benedictine Distillery** (Ⓦ www.benedictine.fr) on rue Alexandre-le-Grand, in the narrow strip of streets running parallel to the port towards the town centre. Tours (daily: early Feb to March & Oct–Dec 10.30–11.45am & 2–5pm; April to early July & early Sept to Oct 10am–noon & 2–5.30pm; early July to early Sept 10am–6pm; admission by 90min guided tours only; €6) start with a small **museum**, set firmly in the Middle Ages with props of manuscripts, locks, testaments, lamps and religious paintings beneath a nightmarish mock-Gothic roof. The first whiff of Benedictine – a sweet herby liqueur often combined with brandy – comes in the grim rust-and-grey-coloured Salle des Abbés, and at this point the script abruptly changes – from mysterious monks to PR for an exclusive product. The boxes of ingredients are a rare treat for the nose (take it easy with the myrrh), and there's further theatricality in the old distillery, where boxes of herbs are flung with gusto into copper vats and alembics, though commercial production has long since moved to an out-of-town site. Finally you're offered a *dégustation* in their bar across the road – neat, in a cocktail, or on crêpes; make sure you hold onto your ticket to qualify.

If your aesthetic sensibilities need soothing after this, head for the soaring medieval nave and Renaissance carved screens of the **church of the Trinité**, up in the town centre, or the modern **Musée des Terres-Neuvas et de la Pêche**, on the seafront at 27 boulevard Albert 1er (July & Aug daily 10am–7pm; Sept–June daily except Tues 10am–noon & 2–5.30pm; €3). Spreading across two floors, with lots of miniature model boats and amateur paintings, it focuses on the long tradition whereby the fishermen of Fécamp decamp en masse each year to catch cod in the cold, foggy waters off Newfoundland. Sailing vessels continued to make the trek from the sixteenth century right up until 1931; today vast refrigerated container ships have taken their place.

Practicalities

Fécamp's main **tourist office** is opposite the distillery at 113 rue Alexandre-le-Grand (Sept–March Mon–Fri 9am–6pm, Sat 9.30am–12.30pm & 2–6pm; April–June Mon–Fri 9am–6pm, Sat & Sun 10am–6.30pm; July & Aug daily 9am–6.30pm; Ⓣ 02.35.28.51.01, Ⓦ www.fecamptourisme.com). Most of the **hotels** are set on side streets away from the sea, but there are a couple of good options near the waterfront. Only the higher rooms at the rather genteel *Hôtel de la Plage*, 87 rue de la Plage (Ⓣ 02.35.29.76.51; ❷), have sea views, but all are comfortable and the location is quiet. The *De la Mer*, on the seafront at 89 boulevard Albert 1er (Ⓣ 02.35.28.24.64, Ⓦ www.hotel-dela-mer.com; ❷), is good value, and nicer inside than it looks from the outside. There's also a superb **campsite,** the *Camping de Renneville* (Ⓣ 02.35.28.20.97, Ⓦ www.camping derenneville.com; open mid-March to mid-Oct), five-minutes' walk up from the seafront, in a dramatic location on the western cliffs, with magnificent views.

There are a number of well-priced fish **restaurants**: *La Marée*, 75 quai Bérigny (Ⓣ 02.35.29.39.15; closed Sun evening & Mon), is attached to a fish shop and offers menus from €18; and the friendly little *Marine*, 23 quai de la Vicomté (Ⓣ 02.35.28.15.94), is open daily for €15 lunches.

Étretat

Here the alabaster cliffs are at their most spectacular – their arches, tunnels and the solitary "needle" will doubtless be familiar from tourist brochures – and the town

▲ Étretat

itself has become a pleasure resort. There isn't even a port of any kind: the seafront consists of a sweeping unbroken curve of concrete above a shingle beach.

Thanks partly to its superb setting, and the lovely architectural ensemble that surrounds its central **place Foch**, Étretat is a very pretty little place. The old wooden market *halles* still dominate the main square, the ground floor now converted into souvenir shops, but the beams of the balcony and roof are bare and ancient. As soon as you step onto the beach you'll see the cliff formations to either side. To the west, on the **Falaise d'Aval**, a straightforward walk – made unnerving by the scary drops nearby – leads up the crumbling side of the cliff, with lush lawns and pastures to the inland side, and German fortifications on the shore side extending to the point where the turf abruptly stops, occasionally ripped by the latest rock fall. From the windswept top you can see further rock formations and sometimes even glimpse Le Havre, but the views back to the town sheltered in the valley, and the **Falaise d'Amont** – which Maupassant compared to an elephant dipping its trunk into the ocean – on its eastern side, are what stick in the memory. The cliff itself presents an idyllic rural scene, with a gentle footpath winding up the green hillside to the little chapel of Notre-Dame.

Practicalities

Étretat's **tourist office** is alongside the main road through the centre of town, on place M. Guillard (mid-March to mid-June & mid-Sept to mid-Nov Mon–Sat 10am–noon & 2–6pm; mid-June to mid-Sept daily 10am–7pm; mid-Nov to mid-March Fri & Sat 10am–noon & 2–6pm; ☎02.35.27.05.21, ⓦwww .etretat.net). The main hub for hotels is the area arround place Foch; the *Hôtel des Falaises*, at 1 boulevard René-Coty (☎02.35.27.02.77; ❸), is a reliable choice, with modernized en-suite bedrooms. *L'Escale*, on place Foch itself (☎02.35.27.03.69; ❸), has simple but pleasant rooms, and a snack restaurant downstairs specializing in *moules-frites* and crêpes. The grand, modern *Dormy House*, perched above town

on the coastal route du Havre to the west (☎02.35.27.07.88, ⓦwww.dormy
-house.com; ❺–❾), offers comfortable rooms with superlative views, and a good
restaurant. Campers will find the municipal **campsite** 1km out on rue Guy-de-
Maupassant (☎02.35.27.07.67; open mid-March to mid-Oct).

The top **restaurant** in town is the *Galion*, distinct from the adjoining *Résidence*
at 4 boulevard René-Coty (☎02.35.29.48.74; closed Tues & Wed in low season),
where the €22 menu makes a definitive introduction to Norman cuisine.

Le Havre

Most ferry passengers head straight out of the port of **LE HAVRE** as quickly
as the traffic will allow to escape a city that is regularly dismissed as a dismal
transport hub. While it's hardly picturesque or tranquil, however, it's not such a
soulless urban sprawl, even if the port – the largest in France after Marseille –
does take up half the Seine estuary, extending way beyond the town. The city
was originally built in 1517 to replace the ancient ports of Harfleur and
Honfleur, then silting up. Under the simple name of Le Havre – "The Harbour",
it became the principal trading post of France's northern coast, prospering
especially during the American War of Independence and thereafter, importing
cotton, sugar and tobacco. In the years before 1939, it was the European home
of the great luxury liners such as the *Normandie*, *Île de France* and *France*.

Le Havre suffered heavier damage than any other port in Europe during World
War II. Following its near-total destruction, it was rebuilt to the specifications of
a single architect, **Auguste Perret**, between 1946 and 1964, an enterprise
circumscribed by constraints of time and money. The sheer sense of space can be
exhilarating: the showpiece monuments have a winning self-confidence, and the

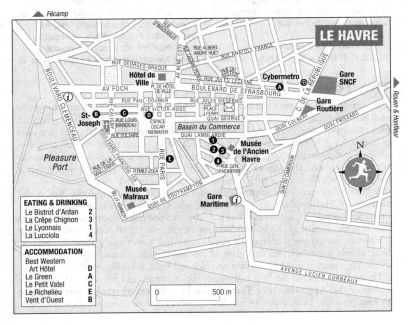

EATING & DRINKING

Le Bistrot d'Antan	2
La Crêpe Chignon	3
Le Lyonnais	1
La Lucciola	4

ACCOMMODATION

Best Western Art Hôtel	D
Le Green	A
Le Petit Vatel	C
Le Richelieu	E
Vent d'Ouest	B

few surviving relics of the old city have been sensitively integrated into the whole. Admittedly, the endless mundane residential blocks can be dispiriting, but with open public space and expanses of water at every turn, even those visitors who fail to agree with Perret's famous dictum that "concrete is beautiful" should enjoy a stroll around his city.

Arrival and information

Le Havre's **gare SNCF** and adjoining **gare routière** are close to the ferry port, and a ten-minute walk from the town centre down the Boulevard de Strasbourg. The town's large **tourist office** is on the main seafront drag, at 186 boulevard Clemenceau (May–Oct Mon–Sat 9am–7pm, Sun 10am–12.30pm & 2.30–6pm; Nov–April Mon–Fri 9am–6.30pm, Sat 9am–12.30pm & 2–6.30pm, Sun 10am–1pm; ☏ 02.32.74.04.04, ⓦ www.lehavretourisme.com). The **post office** at 62 rue Jules-Siegfried (Mon–Fri 8am–7pm, Sat 8am–noon) offers **internet** access, as does Cybermetro, facing the **gare SNCF** at 15 cours de la République (Mon–Sat 7am–midnight; ☏ 02.32.73.04.28).

Accommodation

Le Havre holds two main concentrations of **hotels**: one group faces the *gare SNCF*, while most of the rest lie within walking distance of the ferry terminal.

Best Western Art Hôtel 147 rue Louis Brindeau ☏ 02.35.22.69.44, ⓦ www.art-hotel.fr. Very smart, comfortable hotel on the north side of the Espace Oscar Niemeyer, facing the Volcano cultural centre. All rooms have flat-screen LCD TVs and wi-fi access. ❻

Le Green 209 bd de Strasbourg ☏ 02.35.22.63.10, ⓦ www.hotel-le-green.fr. A decent, if slightly faded, budget option near the train station. En suite ❷, shared bathroom. ❶

Le Petit Vatel 86 rue Louis Brindeau ☏ 02.35.21.37.86. Friendly small hotel with clean, spacious rooms, including a family room which sleeps 4. ❸

Le Richelieu 135 rue de Paris ☏ 02.35.42.38.71, ⓔ hotel.lerichelieu@orange.fr. For a mid-priced hotel in a very central location with bright, comfortable rooms, this hotel is hard to beat. ❸

Vent d'Ouest 4 rue de Caligny ☏ 02.35.42.50.69, ⓦ www.ventdouest.fr. Le Havre's smartest hotel is a stylishly designed boutique affair, with comfortable, well-equipped rooms decorated with a nautical or mountain theme. Apartments sleeping 4 are also available. ❻

The Town

One reason visitors often dismiss Le Havre out of hand is that it's easy to get to and from the city without ever seeing its downtown area. For those who do make the effort, the Perret-designed central **Hôtel de Ville** is a logical first port of call, a long, low, flat-roofed building topped by a seventeen-storey concrete tower. Surrounded by pergola walkways, flowerbeds and water flowing from an array of fountains, the square in which it sits is an attractive, lively place, while the Hôtel de Ville itself is often the venue for imaginative exhibitions.

Perret's other major creation, clearly visible southwest of the town hall, is the **church of St-Joseph**, built on a cross of which all four arms are equally short. From the outside it's a mass of speckled concrete, the main doors thrown open to hint at dark interior spaces within. When you get inside it all makes sense: the altar is right in the centre, with the hundred-metre bell tower rising directly above it. Very simple patterns of stained glass, all around the church and right the way up the tower, create a bright interplay of coloured light, focusing on the altar.

Those interested in finding out more about Perret and his work should take a tour of the **Appartement Témoin de la ville reconstruite par Auguste Perret** (meet at 1 place de l'Hôtel de Ville; Weds, Sat and Sun at 2, 3, 4 and 5pm;

€3), one of the apartments which he designed in the 1950s. The informative tours of the period-decor apartment explain more about the architect's vision for Le Havre and for modern living.

Le Havre's boldest specimen of modern architecture is a post-Perret creation – the cultural centre known as the **Volcano** (or less reverentially as the "yoghurt pot"), dominating the Espace Oscar Niemeyer. Niemeyer, a Brazilian architect, is best known for overseeing the construction of Brasilia, and was still hard at work – at the age of 100 – at the time of writing. He designed this slightly asymmetrical smooth gleaming white cone during the 1970s, and now it plays host to a variety of shows, including theatre performances and concerts.

The **Bassin du Commerce**, which stretches away from the complex, is of minimal commercial significance. Kayaks and rowing boats can be rented to explore its regular contours, and a couple of larger boats are moored permanently to serve as clubs or restaurants, but it's all disconcertingly quiet, serving mainly as an appropriate stretch of water for the graceful white footbridge of the Passerelle du Commerce to cross.

Overlooking the harbour entrance, the modern **Musée Malraux** (Mon & Wed–Fri 11am–6pm, Sat & Sun 11am–7pm; €5) ranks among the best-designed art galleries in France, making full use of natural light to display an enjoyable assortment of nineteenth- and twentieth-century French paintings. Its principal highlights are over two hundred canvases by Eugène Boudin, including greyish landscapes produced all along the Norman coastline with views of Trouville, Honfleur and Étretat, as well an entire wall of miniature cows and a lovely set of works by Raoul Dufy (1877–1953), which make Le Havre seem positively radiant, whatever the weather outside.

If you have time to spare, you might like to see what old Le Havre looked like in the prewar days when Jean-Paul Sartre wrote *La Nausée* here. He taught philosophy for five years during the 1930s in a local school, and his almost transcendent disgust with the place cannot obscure the fascination he felt in exploring the formerly seedy dockside quarter of St-François, in those moments when he wasn't visiting Simone de Beauvoir in Rouen. Little survives of the city Sartre knew, but pictures and artefacts gathered from the rubble are on display in one of the few buildings that escaped World War II intact, the **Musée de l'Ancien Havre** at 1 rue Jérôme-Bellarmato, just south of the Bassin du Commerce (Wed–Sun 10am–noon & 2–6pm; €1.50).

Eating and drinking

Le Havre's restaurants are concentrated in the same areas as its hotels, with plenty of **bars**, **cafés** and **brasseries** around the *gare SNCF*, and all sorts of restaurants, from traditional French to Japanese, in the backstreets of the waterside St-François district, opposite the Bassin du Commerce.

Le Bistrot d'Antan 5 rue St Louis ☎02.35.19.06.88. Smart restaurant close to the Bassin du Commerce serving traditional French cooking, with set menus from €15.

La Crêpe Chignon 28 rue de Bretagne ☎02.35.21.42.20. Bustling crêperie offering a variety of savoury gallettes and sweet crêpes at reasonable prices.

La Lucciola 8 rue de la Crique ☎02.35.43.27.48. Large Italian restaurant with an extensive menu of pasta, pizza and meat dishes, including an €12.50 three-course menu. The outdoor terrace is pleasant in summer.

Le Lyonnais 7–9 rue de Bretagne ☎02.35.22.07.31. Small, cosy restaurant with chequered tablecloths and a welcoming atmosphere. The house speciality is baked fish, though dishes from Lyon, such as *andouillettes*, are also available. Menus from €12.50 for lunch, €16 for dinner. Closed Sun.

Along the Seine to Rouen

Until relatively recently, no bridges crossed the Seine any lower than Rouen, which made the river an all but impassable barrier for motorists heading between Upper and Lower Normandy. Since 1995, however, the enormous **Pont de Normandie** has spanned the rivermouth, enabling motorists to zip across from Le Havre to Honfleur (for a hefty €5 toll), while further inland the immense **Tancarville** suspension bridge and magnificent **Pont de Brotonne**, just upstream from Caudebec, offer alternative routes across the river. If Rouen is your destination from Le Havre, stick to the north bank of the river. A succession of quiet roads follow the Seine's every loop, leading through sleepy towns and past intriguing ruins like the abbey of **Jumièges**.

Abbaye de St-Wandrille

Just beyond the Pont de Brotonne as you continue towards Rouen, the medieval abbey in **ST-WANDRILLE** was founded – so legend has it – by a seventh-century count who, with his wife, renounced all earthly pleasures on the day of their wedding. The abbey's buildings make an attractive if curious architectural ensemble: part ruin, part restoration and, in the case of the main buildings, part transplant – a fifteenth-century barn brought in a few years ago from another Norman village miles away.

St-Wandrille remains an active monastery, home to fifty Benedictine monks who in addition to their spiritual duties turn their hands to money-making tasks that range from candle-making to running a reprographic studio; they also show visitors around the abbey on **guided tours** (Easter–Oct Mon & Wed–Sat 3.30pm, Sun 11.30am & 3.30pm; €3.50; Ⓦ www.st-wandrille.com). You can wander through the **grounds** (daily 5.15am–1pm & 2–9.15pm) for no charge, and you can also listen to the monks' **Gregorian chanting** in their new church (Mon–Sat 5.25am, 7.30am, 9.45am, 12.45pm, 2.15pm, 5.30pm & 8.35pm; Sun 5.25am, 7.30am, 10am, 12.45pm, 2.30pm, 5pm & 8.35pm).

There's a crêperie opposite the abbey, and, a few doors along in the place de l'Église, the more upmarket *Deux Coronnes* **restaurant** (Ⓣ 02.35.96.11.44; closed Sun evening & Mon), a seventeenth-century inn – half-timbered, naturally – serving delicious menus priced at €15 for lunch and €25 for dinner.

Abbaye de Jumièges

In the next loop of the Seine, 12km on from St-Wandrille, comes the highlight of the Seine valley: the majestic **abbey** in **JUMIÈGES** (mid-April to June and first fortnight of Sept Mon–Fri 9.30am–1pm & 2.30–6.30pm, Sat & Sun 9.30am–6.30pm; July Mon–Fri & Sun 9.30am–6.30pm, Sat 9.30am–6.30pm & 10.30pm–12.30am; Aug Mon–Fri & Sun 9.30am–6.30pm, Sat 9.30am–6.30pm & 9.30pm–12.30am; mid-Sept to mid-April daily 9.30am–1pm & 2.30–5.30pm; €5), said to have been founded by St Philibert in 654 AD, just five years after St-Wandrille. A haunting ruin, the abbey was burned by marauding Vikings in 841, rebuilt a century later, then destroyed again – as a deliberate act – during the Revolution. Its main surviving outline, as far as it can still be discerned, dates from the eleventh century – William the Conqueror himself attended its re-consecration in 1067. The twin towers, 52m high, are still standing, as is one arch of the roofless nave, while a one-sided yew tree stands in the centre of what were once the cloisters. The *Auberge des Ruines*, across from the abbey at 17 place

Bars, Bistros and Brasseries

France is famous for its cuisine, of course, but how do you decide exactly where to eat it? What's the difference between a bistro and a brasserie? What does *gastronomique* mean and where can you get a simple sandwich? Read on. Just like anywhere in the world, France has its share of fast-food outlets and takeaways, but if you want to sit down to eat in reasonable comfort you'll be able to choose from a variety of alluring establishments.

Cafés and wine bars

For breakfast or a simple snack, your best bet is a **café-bar**, where you can lounge for hours, watching the world go by. In addition to an extensive drinks list, most offer morning croissants and can rustle up filled baguettes, toasted sandwiches and the like at lunchtime, possibly all day. Some might run to more substantial fare, along the lines of a couple of **plats du jour**, maybe even a basic menu (see box overleaf), but nothing too elaborate.

For a sophisticated, night-time feel, drop into a **wine bar**, which you'll generally find in larger towns and cities. At the top end, these can be very refined establishments catering to serious wine connoisseurs; others are small and convivial. Some offer excellent cuisine, as good as any in a quality bistro, or at the very least they'll have cheese or cold meat platters.

Brasserie de l'Isle St Louis, Paris ▲
Goose farm, Pompougnac ▼

Brasseries vs Bistros

Brasseries, the quintessential urban French eateries, are typically large and bustling, with lots of mirrors and brasswork, whereas **bistros** tend to be small, casual and inexpensive neighbourhood restaurants. Most bistros open for lunch and dinner; brasseries generally serve meals all day – a few city-centre places may keep going until midnight – and double as café-bars outside regular meal times. Standard brasserie fare consists of salads, omelettes, grills and a smattering of fish dishes, plus seafood platters at more upmarket places. Don't expect any fireworks, but the food should be quick and wholesome.

If it's something more homely you're after, you'll probably be better off in a

Café de l'Industrie, Paris ▼

▲ La Cigale Brasserie, Nantes

▼ Lapérouse, Paris

bistro, where the daily dishes could be a selection of fuss-free classics, such as *boeuf bourguignon* or quiche and salad. Though most bistros remain traditional, you'll find some now offering more contemporary, eye-catching cuisine.

All the restos

If it offers meals and doesn't fall into any of the above categories, it must be a **restaurant**. From the lowly truckers' *routiers* up through family-run country inns (usually called *auberges* or sometimes *relais*) and hotel dining rooms to Michelin-starred establishments serving the very highest *haute cuisine*, restaurants cover a broad range. In general, however, they're more formal than café-bars or brasseries and stick to the traditional meal times of noon–2pm and 7–9pm, sometimes later in larger towns and during the summer months. The food could be traditional or

Menu board ▲

Magret de canard in a Bordeaux restaurant ▼

modern, hearty home cooking or classic and refined, international or resolutely French.

Restaurant etiquette

Bread and tap water are provided free of charge in France. If there's no side-plate, just put your bread on the table. It's fine to tear it into pieces and mop your plate with it. Elbows on the table is fine, too. In fact, you should keep your hands visible at all times.

In touristy areas in high season, and for all the more upmarket places, it's wise to reserve. Prices, and what you get for them, must be posted outside. There's usually a service charge of 15 percent – in which case it should say *service compris* (*s.c.*) or *prix net*. Very occasionally you'll see *service non compris* (*s.n.c.*) or *servis en sus*, which means it's up to you whether you leave a tip or not.

Menu primer

▶▶ **Plat du jour** A reasonably priced "daily special", commonly served at lunchtime.

▶▶ **Menu fixe or menu du jour** A fixed-price menu – often referred to simply as "menu" – comprising a set number of courses and a limited choice. Lunchtime menus are cheaper than those at dinner and often represent excellent value.

▶▶ **Formule** Usually available only at lunchtime, a *formule* is a trimmed-down menu, typically offering just two courses for a set price.

▶▶ **Carte** Choosing from the *carte* (the full menu) naturally offers a greater choice – though you'll pay more for the privilege.

▶▶ **Menu carte** Choose freely from the *carte* but pay a fixed price according to whether you opt for one, two or three courses.

de la Mairie (☎02.35.37.24.05; closed Sun and Tues evening, Wed and over Christmas and New Year), is a truly superb **restaurant**, with outdoor seating on a shaded terrace. Menus start at €18 for lunch and go up to €55 for a gastronomic evening feast.

Rouen

ROUEN, the capital of Upper Normandy, is one of France's most ancient cities. Standing on the site of Roman Rotomagus, the lowest point on the river then capable of being bridged, it was laid out by the Viking Rollo shortly after he became Duke of Normandy in 911. Captured by the English in 1419, it was the scene in 1431 of the trial and execution of Joan of Arc, and returned to French control in 1449.

Over the centuries, Rouen has suffered repeated devastation; there were 45 major fires in the first half of the thirteenth century alone. It has had to be almost entirely rebuilt during the last sixty years, and now you could spend a whole day wandering around the city without realizing that the Seine ran through its centre. Wartime bombs destroyed all its bridges, the area between the cathedral and the *quais*, and much of the industrial quarter. The riverside area has never been adequately restored, and what you might expect to be the most beautiful part of the city is in fact something of a disappointment.

Enormous sums have, however, been lavished on an upmarket restoration job on the streets a few hundred metres north of the river, which turned the centre into the closest approximation to a medieval city that modern imaginations could come up with. The suggestion that for historical authenticity the houses should be painted in bright, clashing colours was not deemed appropriate, but so far as it goes, the whole of this inner core can be very seductive, and its churches are impressive by any standards.

Arrival and information

Vehicle access to Rouen has been improved somewhat by the construction of the new Pont Gustave Flaubert, the city's sixth and largest bridge across the Seine, which connects the motorways just west of the city. Many of the central streets, north of the river, have in any case been pedestrianized, so it's best to park as soon as you can – there are plenty of central underground **car parks**, especially near the cathedral and the place du Vieux-Marché – and explore the city on foot.

The main **gare SNCF**, Gare Rive Droite, stands at the north end of rue Jeanne-d'Arc. It's connected to the centre by a **métro** system, which follows the line of the rue Jeanne-d'Arc, making two stops before it resurfaces to cross the river by bridge. Individual journeys cost €1.40 and a book is €10.50. One-, two- and three-day passes are also available, priced €3.70, €5.40 and €7 respectively. All **buses** from the *gare SNCF* except #2A run down rue Jeanne-d'Arc to the centre, which takes five minutes. From the fifth stop, the "Théâtre des Arts" by the river, the **gare routière** is one block west in rue des Charettes, tucked away behind the riverfront buildings (☎02.35.52.92.00).

Rouen's **tourist office** stands opposite the cathedral at 25 place de la Cathédrale (May–Sept Mon–Sat 9am–7pm, Sun 9.30am–12.30pm & 2–6pm; Oct–April Mon–Sat 9am–6pm, Sun 10am–1pm; ☎02.32.08.32.40, ⓦwww.rouentourisme .com). It serves as the starting point for a motorized **petit train**, which makes a forty-minute tour of Rouen's main sights at regular intervals (April–Oct daily

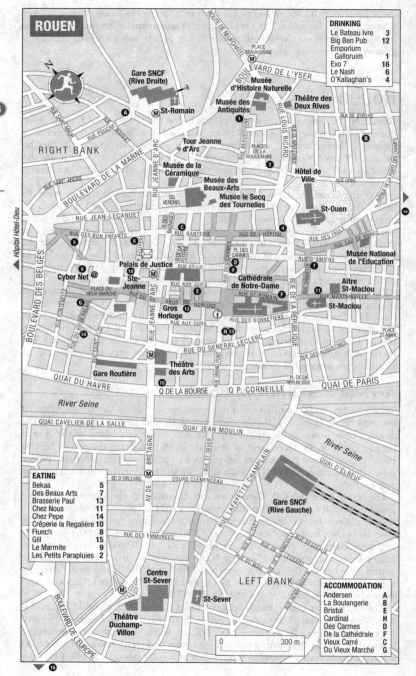

ROUEN

NORMANDY

DRINKING

Le Bateau Ivre	3
Big Ben Pub	12
Emporium Galloruim	1
Exo 7	16
Le Nash	6
O'Kallaghan's	4

Gare SNCF (Rive Droite)

Musée d'Histoire Naturelle

St-Romain

Musée des Antiquités

Théâtre des Deux Rives

RUE DE JOYEUSE

BOULEVARD DE L'YSER

ROUTE DE NEUFCHATEL

PLACE BEAUVOISINE

RUE SAINT-HILAIRE

ILE LACROIX

RUE POUCHET BEUVILLE

RUE JEANNE D'ARC

RIGHT BANK

Tour Jeanne d'Arc

Musée de la Céramique

Musée des Beaux-Arts

Musée le Secq des Tournelles

RUE SAINT-ANDRÉ

BOULEVARD DE LA MARNE

PLACES DE LA ROUGEMARE

RUE BEAUVOISINE

RUE LOUIS RICARD

RUE DE MALPOLET

Hôtel de Ville

RUE ORBE

St-Ouen

RUE DE LA PORTE DES CHAMPS

RUE JEAN-LECANUET

SQ VERDREL

RUE DES FAULX

RUE EAU DE ROBEC

Hôpital Hôtel-Dieu

RUE DES BON ENFANTS

RUE GANTERIE

RUE DE L'HÔPITAL

Musée National de l'Education

RUE D'AMIENS

RUES BASNAGES

RUE DE LA POTERNE

Palais de Justice

RUE ST-LÔ

PL. DES CARMES

RUE DES CARMES

RUE DAMIETTE

Aître St-Maclou

RUE MARTAINVILLE

St-Maclou

Cyber Net

Ste-Jeanne

RUE AUX JUIFS

Cathédrale de Notre-Dame

RUE ST-ROMAIN

RUE DE LA RÉPUBLIQUE

BOULEVARD DES BELGES

BOULEVARD DES BELGES

RUE DU FARDEAU

PLACE DU VIEUX-MARCHÉ

RUE JEANNE D'ARC

GROS HORLOGE

Gros Horloge

RUE DES BONNETIERS

RUE AUX OURS

PLACE ST-MARC

RUE CONTRELINE

RUE DU GENERAL LECLERC

RUE DES AUGUSTINES

PL DE LA RÉPUBLIQUE

Gare Routière

RUE SAINT-ELOI

Théâtre des Arts

QUAI DU HAVRE

QUAI DE PARIS

Q DE LA BOURSE

Q P. CORNEILLE

River Seine

QUAI CAVELIER DE LA SALLE

QUAI JEAN MOULIN

River Seine

QUAI D'ELBEUF

BRETAGNE

BD D'ORLEANS

COURS CLEMENCEAU

RUE ST-SEVER

RUE LAFAYETTE CHAMPLAIN

Gare SNCF (Rive Gauche)

EATING

Bekaa	5
Des Beaux Arts	7
Brasserie Paul	13
Chez Nous	11
Chez Pepe	14
Crêperie la Regalière	10
Flunch	8
Gill	15
Le Marmite	9
Les Petits Parapluies	2

AV DE

RUE DES EMMUREES

RUE DU MAIL

RUE DE L'ESSARD

RUE MALOUIN

RUE BAUDRIVILLE

RUE DESSEAUX

RUE HENRI MARTIN

Centre St-Sever

St-Sever

LEFT BANK

ACCOMMODATION

Andersen	A
La Boulangerie	B
Bristol	E
Cardinal	H
Des Carmes	D
De la Cathédrale	F
Vieux Carré	C
Du Vieux Marché	G

Théâtre Duchamp-Villon

BOULEVARD DE L'EUROPE

0   300 m

10am–5pm; €5.50). Those wishing to explore the city on foot can hire an audio guide from the tourist office (€5).

You can rent **bicycles** from Rouen Cycles, 45 rue St-Éloi (Tues–Sat 9am–noon & 2–7pm; ☏02.35.71.34.30). The **post office** is at 45 rue Jeanne-d'Arc, in the centre of town (Mon–Fri 8am–7pm, Sat 8am–noon). For **internet** access, head to *Cyber Net*, 47 place du Vieux-Marché (daily 10am–11pm).

Accommodation

With over three thousand **hotel** rooms in town, there should be no difficulty in finding accommodation in Rouen, even at the busiest times. Few of the hotels have restaurants, largely because the city boasts a wide array of eateries.

Hotels

Andersen 4 rue Pouchet ☏02.35.71.88.51, ⓦwww .hotelandersen.com. Very friendly place with plenty of character close to the Gare Rive Droite, set behind a small gravel yard. Bathrooms are a little basic, but the bedrooms are large, light and colourful. ❸

La Boulangerie 59 rue Saint Nicaise ☏06.12.94.53.15, ⓦwww.laboulangerie.fr. Two spacious rooms and a suite – ideal for families – above a half-timbered bakery in a residential area of Rouen. Good breakfasts and a warm welcome. ❹

Bristol 45 rue aux Juifs ☏02.35.71.54.21. Clean, pretty nine-room hotel, above its own little brasserie in a half-timbered house overlooking the Palais de Justice. All rooms are en suite, and have TV. Closed Sun, plus 3 weeks in Aug. ❷

Cardinal 1 place de la Cathédrale ☏02.35.70.24.42, ⓦwww.cardinal-hotel.fr. Well-priced hotel in a stunning location facing the cathedral. Rooms are spacious and clean, with flat-screen TVs and wi-fi access. Two family rooms are available. ❹

Des Carmes 33 place des Carmes ☏02.35.71.92.31, ⓦwww.hoteldescarmes.com. Twelve-room hotel in a beautiful nineteenth-century house on a quiet central square, a short walk north from the cathedral. The rooms are slightly old-fashioned, but comfortable. ❸

Le Clos Jouvenet 42 rue Hyacinthe Langlois ☏02.35.89.80.66, ⓦwww .leclosjouvenet.com. Four beautifully decorated, comfortable rooms in an immaculate nineteenth-century house 10min walk from the train station.

Breakfast is served in the conservatory, overlooking the enclosed garden. ❺

De la Cathédrale 12 rue St-Romain ☏02.35.71.57.95, ⓦwww.hotel-de-la-cathedrale .fr. Conveniently located hotel with a pleasantly olde-worlde theme which even extends to the *toile de jouy* wallpaper. Has a pleasant breakfast room and a flower-filled courtyard. Set in a quiet pedestrianized street – close to a public car park – lined with fourteenth-century timber-framed houses. ❹

Vieux Carré 34 rue Ganterie ☏02.35.71.67.70, ⓦwww.vieux-carre.fr. Petite but pleasant rooms in a half-timbered house in a pedestrianized central street. The nice little tea shop below doubles as the breakfast room. ❸

Du Vieux Marché 15 rue de la Pie ☏02.35.71.00.88, ⓦwww.bestwestern-hotel -vieuxmarche.com. Very modern place, set around a venerable old courtyard, just a few steps from the place du Vieux-Marché. A high standard of comfort has quickly made this the most popular upmarket hotel in town. ❼

Campsites

Camping de l'Aubette 23 Vert Buisson in St-Léger du Bourg-Denis ☏02.35.08.47.69. Basic site in a more rural, but much less accessible setting than the *Camping municipal*, 4km east of town on bus route #8.

Camping municipal rue Jules-Ferry in Déville-lès-Rouen ☏02.35.74.07.59. Surprisingly small site, 4km northwest of town, that's geared towards caravans rather than tents; bus #2.

The Town

Rouen has traditionally spent a bigger slice of its civic budget on monuments than any other provincial town, which maddens many a Rouennais. As a tourist, however, your one complaint may be the lack of time to visit them all.

Place du Vieux-Marché to the cathedral

The obvious place to start sightseeing is the **place du Vieux-Marché**, where a small plaque and a huge cross (nearly 20m high) mark the spot on which Joan of

▲ Rouen Cathedral

Arc (see box opposite) was burnt to death on May 30, 1431. A modern memorial **church** to the saint was dedicated in the square in 1979 (Mon–Sat 10am–12.30pm & 2–6pm, Sun 2–6pm); it's a wacky, spiky-looking thing and an architectural triumph, incorporating some sixteenth-century stained glass and said to represent either an upturned boat or the flames that consumed Joan. It forms part of an ensemble that incorporates a covered food market in similar style. The theme of the church's fish-shaped windows is continued in the scaly tiles that adorn its roof, which is elongated to form a walkway across the square. The outline of its predecessor's foundations is visible on the adjacent lawns, which also mark the precise spot of Joan's martyrdom. The square itself is surrounded by fine old brown-and-white half-timbered houses, many of those on the south side now serving as restaurants. The private **Musée Jeanne d'Arc**, tucked in among them in an ancient cellar in the back of a gift shop, draws the crowds to its collection of tawdry waxworks and facsimile manuscripts (daily: mid-April to mid-Sept 9.30am–7pm; mid-Sept to mid-April 10am–noon & 2–6.30pm; €5).

From place du Vieux-Marché, **rue du Gros-Horloge** leads east towards the cathedral. Just across the intersection with rue Jeanne-d'Arc you come to the **Gros Horloge** itself, returned to public view in 2007 after ten years of renovation. A colourful one-handed clock, it used to be on the adjacent Gothic **belfry** until it was moved down by popular demand in 1529, so that people could see it better.

Despite the addition of all sorts of different towers, spires and vertical extensions, the **Cathédrale de Notre-Dame** (Mon 2–7pm, Tues–Sat 7.45am–7pm, Sun 8am–6pm) remains at heart the Gothic masterpiece that was built in the twelfth and thirteenth centuries. The west facade of the cathedral, intricately sculpted like the rest of the exterior, was Monet's subject for over thirty studies of changing light, which now hang in the Musée d'Orsay in Paris. Monet might not recognize it now, however – in the last few years, it's been scrubbed a gleaming white, free from the centuries of accreted dirt he so carefully recorded.

In recent summers, the town has laid on a thirty-minute light show, **La Cathédrale de Monet aux Pixels** (daily: July 11pm, August 10.30pm; free), whereby colours inspired by Monet's cathedral paintings are projected onto the

Joan of Arc

When the 17-year-old peasant girl known to history as **Joan of Arc** (Jeanne d'Arc in French) arrived at the French court early in 1429, the Hundred Years War had already dragged on for over ninety years. Most of northern France was in the grip of an Anglo–Burgundian alliance, but Joan, who had been hearing voices since 1425, was certain she could save the country, and came to present her case to the as-yet-uncrowned Dauphin. Partly through recognizing him despite a simple disguise he wore to fool her at their first meeting, she convinced him of her divine guidance; and after a remarkable three-week examination by a tribunal of the French *parlement*, she went on to secure command of the armies of France. In a whirlwind **campaign**, which culminated in the raising of the siege of Orléans on May 8, 1429, she broke the English hold on the Loire Valley. She then escorted the Dauphin deep into enemy territory so that, in accordance with ancient tradition, he could be crowned King Charles VII of France in the cathedral at Reims, on July 17.

Within a year of her greatest triumph, Joan was **captured** by the Burgundian army at Compiègne in May 1430, and held to ransom. Chivalry dictated that any offer of payment from the vacillating Charles must be accepted, but in the absence of such an offer Joan was handed over to the English for 10,000 ducats. On Christmas Day 1430, she was imprisoned in the château of Philippe-Auguste at Rouen.

Charged with heresy, on account of her "false and diabolical" visions and refusal to give up wearing men's clothing, Joan was put on trial for her life on February 21, 1431. For three months, a changing panel of 131 assessors – only eight of whom were English-born – heard the evidence against her. Condemned, inevitably, to death, Joan recanted on the scaffold in St-Ouen cemetery on May 24, and her sentence was commuted to life imprisonment. The presiding judge, Bishop Pierre Cauchon of Beauvais, reassured disappointed English representatives that "we will get her yet". The next Sunday, Joan was tricked into breaking her vow and putting on male clothing, and taken to the archbishop's chapel in rue St-Romain to be condemned to death for the second time. On May 30, 1431, she was burned at the stake in the place du Vieux-Marché; her ashes, together with her unburned heart, were thrown into the Seine.

Joan passed into legend, until the discovery and publication of the full transcript of her trial in the 1840s. The forbearance and devout humility she displayed throughout her ordeal added to her status as France's greatest religious heroine. She was canonized as recently as 1920, and soon afterwards became the country's patron saint.

church's facade, transforming it quite magnificently into a series of giant Monet-esque canvases. Inside the cathedral, the **ambulatory** and **crypt** – closed on Sundays and during services – hold the assorted tombs of various recumbent royalty, stretching back as far as Duke Rollo, who died "enfeebled by toil" in 933 AD, and the actual heart of Richard the Lionheart.

St-Ouen and around

The **church of St-Ouen**, next to the Hôtel de Ville (which itself occupies buildings that were once part of the abbey), is larger than the cathedral and has far less decoration, so from the outside there's nothing to diminish the instant impact of its vast Gothic proportions and the purity of its lines. Inside (mid-Jan to mid-March and Nov to mid-Dec Tues, Sat & Sun 10am–noon & 2–5pm; mid-March to Oct Tues–Sat 10am–12.15pm & 2–6pm, Sun 9am–12.15pm & 2–6pm), it holds some stunning fourteenth-century stained glass, though much was destroyed during the Revolution. The world that produced it – and, nearer the end of the era, the light and grace of the **church of St-Maclou** not far to the south – was one of mass death from the plague: thus the **Aître St-Maclou** immediately to the east, a cemetery for the victims, was an integral part of the St-Maclou complex (daily: mid-March to Oct 8am–8pm; Nov to mid-March 8am–7pm; entrance between 184 & 186 rue Martainville; free). It's now the tranquil garden courtyard of the Fine Arts school, but if you examine the one open lower storey of the surrounding buildings you'll discover the original deathly decorations and a mummified cat.

The **rue Eau de Robec**, which runs east from rue Damiette just south of St-Ouen, was described by one of Flaubert's characters in an earlier age as a "degraded little Venice". It's now a textbook example of how Rouen has been restored. Where once a shallow stream flowed beneath the raised doorsteps of venerable half-timbered houses, a thin trickle now makes its way along a stylized cement bed crossed by concrete walkways. In a fine old mansion at no. 185, the **Musée National de l'Éducation** (Mon & Wed–Fri 10am–12.30pm & 1.30–6pm, Sat & Sun 2–6pm; €3) tells the story of the last five centuries of schooling in France, with photos, paintings, ancient textbooks and a mocked-up schoolroom. Audio guides in English provide an informative commentary, but unless you have a particular interest in education, you may prefer to head north past the Hôtel de Ville to the **Musée des Antiquités**, which occupies a seventeenth-century convent on rue Beauvoisine (Mon & Wed–Sat 10am–12.15pm & 1.30–5.30pm, Sun 2–6pm; €3): its tapestries and medieval collection are particularly good.

The Musée des Beaux-Arts and around

Rouen's imposing **Musée des Beaux-Arts** commands the square Verdrel from just east of the central rue Jeanne-d'Arc (daily except Tues 10am–6pm; €3, combined ticket for Musée de la Céramique and Musée Le Secq des Tournelles €5.35). The grand edifice is home to a varied and absorbing permanent collection, as well as regular temporary exhibitions, for which there is sometimes an extra charge. Unexpected highlights include dazzling Russian icons from the sixteenth century onwards, and an entertaining three-dimensional eighteenth-century *Nativity* from Naples. Many of the biggest names among the painters – Caravaggio (the centrepiece *Flagellation of Christ*), Velázquez, Rubens – tend to be represented by a single minor work, but there are several Modiglianis and a number of Monets, including *Rouen Cathedral* (1894), the *Vue Générale de Rouen* and *Brume sur la Seine* (1894). The central sculpture court, roofed over but very light, is dominated by a wonderful three-part mural of the course of the Seine from Paris to Le Havre, prepared by Raoul Dufy in 1937 for the Palais de Chaillot in Paris.

Rouen's history as a centre for *faïencerie*, or earthenware pottery, is recorded in the **Musée de la Céramique**, facing the Beaux-Arts from the north (daily except Tues 10am–1pm & 2–6pm; €2.50). A series of beautiful rooms, some of which incorporate sixteenth-century wood panelling rescued from a demolished nunnery of St-Amand, display specimens from the 1600s onwards. Assorted tiles and plates reflect the eighteenth-century craze for *chinoiserie*, although the genuine Chinese and Japanese pieces nearby possess a sophistication contemporary French craftsmen could only dream of emulating.

Behind the Beaux-Arts, housed in the old, barely altered church of St-Laurent on rue Jacques-Villon, the **Musée Le Secq des Tournelles** (daily except Tues 10am–1pm & 2–6pm; €2.50) consists of a gloriously eccentric and uncategorizable collection of wrought-iron objects of all dates and descriptions, among them nutcrackers and door knockers, spiral staircases that lead nowhere and hideous implements of torture.

The Tour Jeanne d'Arc

The **Tour Jeanne d'Arc** (daily except Tues: Mon–Sat 10am–noon & 2–6pm, Sun 2–6.30pm; €1.50), a short way southeast of the *gare SNCF*, is all that remains of the castle of Philippe-Auguste, built in 1205 and scene of the imprisonment and trial of Joan of Arc. It served as the castle's keep and entrance-way, and was itself fully surrounded by a moat. It was not, however, Joan's actual prison – that was the Tour de la Pucelle, demolished in 1809 – while the trial took place first of all in the castle's St-Romain chapel, and then later in its great central hall, both of which were destroyed in 1590. The tall, sharp-pointed tower was bought by public subscription in 1860, and restored to its present state. After seeing a small collection of Joan-related memorabilia, you can climb a steep spiral staircase to the very top, but you can't see out over the city, let alone step outside into the open air.

Eating, drinking and nightlife

Rouen's bars and restaurants are largely concentrated around the streets which radiate out from the place du Vieux-Marché, with rue Martainville offering some excellent, often less touristy alternatives.

Restaurants

Des Beaux Arts 34 rue Damiette ☏02.35.70.17.15. Very good-value Algerian cuisine, on a pretty pedestrianized street north of St-Maclou church: couscous from €8 or tagine from €10, with all kinds of sausages and assorted meats. Closed Mon & Tues evening.

Bekaa 60 rue de Fontenelle ☏02.35.15.58.58. If all the Norman cuisine gets too much, head to this cosy Lebanese restaurant close to the place du Vieux-Marché. A variety of *mezze* menus are on offer, including an €16 vegetarian option.

Brasserie Paul 1 place de la Cathédrale ☏02.35.71.86.07. The definitive address for Rouen's definitive bistro, an attractive *belle-époque* place with seating both indoors and on a terrace in full view of the cathedral. Daily lunch specials, such as the goat's cheese and smoked duck salad that was Simone de Beauvoir's favourite in the 1930s, cost around €11.

Chez Nous 234 rue Martainville ☏02.35.89.50.02. Deservedly popular bistro with a cosy interior and some outdoor seating. The small daily menu of modern French dishes offers a choice of four starters, main courses and desserts. 2 courses €6.50, 3 courses €19.50.

Chez Pepe 10–12 rue du Vieux Palais ☏02.35.07.44.94. Rather smart pizza restaurant with a wide choice of tasty pizzas for two, making it an excellent option for those on a budget. Also has a children's menu.

Crêperie la Regalière 12 rue Massacre ☏02.35.15.33.33. Quaint country-style crêperie near the Gros Horloge, whose excellent *galettes* and crêpes draw crowds of locals. Closed Sun.

Dame Cakes 70 rue St Romain ☏02.35.07.49.31. Elegant tearoom on a quiet street next to the cathedral, tempting the tastebuds with delicious desserts, savoury tarts and salads.

Flunch 60 rue des Carmes ☎02.35.71.81.81.
Efficient, popular self-service on a street running
north from the cathedral, with many fresh dishes,
starters and desserts, and a €5.60 daily *formule*.
Unlimited vegetables with any hot dish, or an all-
you-can-eat salad for €4.40.

Gill 9 quai de la Bourse ☎02.35.71.16.14. Absolutely
definitive French restaurant with specialities such as
lobster grilled with asparagus and pigeon baked in
puff pastry. Weekday lunch menus start at €40 (not
bad value considering the quality), while the most
expensive dinner menu will set you back €85. Closed
Sun & Mon, plus three weeks in Aug.

Le Marmite 3 rue de Florence ☎02.35.71.75.55.
Romantic little place just west of the place du
Vieux-Marché, offering beautiful, elegantly
presented gourmet dishes as part of well-priced
menus at €25, €35 (featuring hot foie gras) and
€50. Closed Sun evening, Mon, & Tues lunch.

Les Petits Parapluies 46 rue Bourg l'Abbé, place de
la Rougemare ☎02.35.88.55.26. Chic and secluded
half-timbered restaurant not far north of the Hôtel de
Ville. The place to go to splash out: set menus start at
€28, but the quality of the rather fancy food is high.
Closed Sat lunch, Sun evening & Mon.

Bars

Le Bateau Ivre 17 rue des Sapins
☎02.35.70.09.05. This low-key but atmospheric
hangout a long way northeast of the centre puts on
a rock-oriented programme of music and performance, with an open-mic night on Thurs. Tues & Wed

10pm–2am, Thurs–Sat 10pm–4am. Closed Sun,
Mon & all Aug.

Big Ben Pub 95 rue du Gros-Horloge
☎02.35.88.44.50. Right under the big clock, this
busy pub in a splendid half-timbered house has the
air of a medieval tavern, even if it does feature
karaoke on Thurs, Fri and Sat evenings (except
during summer). There are two floors inside and
some tables on the busy street outside. Mon
6pm–2am, Tues–Sat noon–2am.

Emporium Gallorum 151 rue Beauvoisine
☎02.35.71.76.95. Busy half-timbered bar, a short
walk north of the centre, that's especially popular
with students, which often puts on small-scale gigs
and theatrical productions. Tues & Wed 8pm–2am,
Thurs–Sat 6pm–4am. Closed Aug.

Exo 7 13 place des Chartreux ☎02.35.03.32.30,
Ⓦwww.exo7.net. Traditionally the centre of Rouen's
heavy-rock scene, a long way south of the centre, the
Exo 7 (pronounced "Exocet") is nowadays a bit more
eclectic, with varied gigs and dance nights as well.
Fri & Sat 11pm–5am. Closed first 3 weeks of Aug.

Le Nash 97 rue Écuyère ☎02.35.98.25.24.
Relaxed bar popular with locals. With its moody
lighting and zebra-striped upholstery, the interior
has a lounge-like feel, while the outdoor terrace is
much more akin to a classic French café and
serves light snacks. Mon–Fri 11.30am–2pm &
6pm–2am, Sat 6pm–2am. O'Kallaghan's Place du
Général de Gaulle "Irish" bar with a large outdoor
terrace, which gets particularly packed on
summer weekends.

Entertainment

As you would expect in a conurbation of 400,000, there's always plenty going
on in Rouen, from classical concerts in churches to alternative events in
community and commercial centres. The city has several **theatres**, which
mainly work to winter seasons. The most highbrow venue for big spectacles is
the **Théâtre des Arts**, 7 rue de Dr-Rambert (☎08.10.81.11.16, Ⓦwww
.operaderouen.com), which puts on opera, ballet and concerts. The more
adventurous repertory company of the **Théâtre des Deux Rives**
(☎02.35.70.22.82), based opposite the Antiquités museum at the junction of
rue Louis-Ricard and rue de Joyeuse, presents work by playwrights such as
Beaumarchais, Shakespeare, Beckett and Gorky.

Major **concerts** often take place in the **Théâtre Duchamp-Villon** in the
St-Sever complex (☎02.32.18.28.10, Ⓦwww.theatreduchampvillon.com),
accessible by métro (stop "St-Sever"). Also south of the river and on the
métro (direction "Georges Braque"), albeit considerably further out, is the
Théâtre Charles Dullin, allée des Arcades, Grand Quévilly (☎02.35.69.51.18,
Ⓦwww.theatre-charles-dullin.com). There are two multi-screen **cinemas**
just north of the river (at 28 rue de la République and 75 rue du
Général-Leclerc).

Upstream from Rouen

Upstream from Rouen towards Paris, high cliffs on the north bank of the Seine imitate the coast, looking down on waves of green and scattered river islands. By the time you reach **Les Andelys**, 25km southeast of Rouen, you're within 100km of the capital, meaning that accommodation and eating prices tend to be geared towards affluent weekend and day-trippers. Large country estates abound in this agreeable countryside, and public transport is minimal. However, infrequent buses run from Rouen to Les Andelys, and trains from Rouen call at **Vernon**, just across the river from one of Normandy's most visited tourist attractions, the village of **Giverny**.

Les Andelys

The most dramatic sight anywhere along the Seine has to be Richard the Lionheart's **Château Gaillard**, perched high above **LES ANDELYS**. Constructed in a position of impregnable power, it looked down over any movement on the river at the frontier of the English king's domains. Built in less than a year (1196–97), the castle might have survived intact had Henri IV not ordered its destruction in 1603 in the aftermath of the War of Religion between Catholics and Protestants. As it is, the dominant outline remains. Visits to the château are permitted between mid-March and mid-November only (daily except Tues 10am–1pm & 2–6pm; €3). On foot, you can make the steep climb up via a path that leads off rue Richard-Coeur-de-Lion in Petit Andely. The only route for motorists is extraordinarily convoluted, following a long-winded one-way system that starts opposite the church in Grand Andely.

The **tourist office** for Les Andelys is in Petit Andely, at 24 rue Philippe-Auguste (Oct–May Mon–Fri 2–6pm, Sat & Sun 10am–noon & 2–5pm; June–Sept Mon–Fri 10am–noon & 2–6pm, Sat & Sun 10am–noon & 2–7pm; ☎02.32.54.41.93, ⓦwww.ville-andelys.fr). One of the nicest **hotels** is the eighteenth-century *Chaîne d'Or*, on the banks of the Seine opposite the thirteenth-century church of St-Sauveur at 27 rue Grande (☎02.32.54.00.31, ⓦwww.hotel-lachainedor.com; ⑤; restaurant closed in winter all Mon & Tues lunch). Some of the large, rather stately rooms have views of the river; the one drawback is that though the food in its **restaurant** is undeniably delicious, the cheapest dinner menu costs €44, and even breakfast costs €12. There's also a lovely, well-equipped riverside **campsite**, far below the château, the *Île des Trois Rois* (☎02.32.54.23.79, ⓦwww.camping-troisrois.com; open mid-March to mid-Nov).

Giverny

Roughly 15km south of Les Andelys, on the north bank of the river, you come to **Monet's house and gardens** – complete with water-lily pond – at **GIVERNY** (gardens and house April–Oct Tues–Sun 9.30am–6pm; last entrance 5.30pm, no advance sales; ☎02.32.51.28.21, ⓦwww.fondation-monet.com; €5.50 house and gardens, €4 gardens only). Monet lived here from 1883 till his death in 1926, and the gardens that he laid out were considered by many of his friends to be his masterpiece. In fact art lovers who make the pilgrimage here tend to be outnumbered by garden enthusiasts. None of Monet's original paintings is on display – most are in the Orangerie and Musée d'Orsay in Paris – whereas the gardens are still lovingly tended in all their glory. The house and gardens attract a great number of visitors, so be prepared to queue during the summer months.

You enter the house through the huge studio, built in 1915, where Monet painted the last and largest of his canvases depicting water lilies (*nymphéas*). It now serves as a book and gift shop. A gravel footpath leads to the house itself, a long two-storey structure facing down to the river. Monet's bedroom is bedecked with family photos and paintings by friends and family, while his salon holds further washed-out reproductions. Many of the other main rooms are crammed floor-to-ceiling with his collection of **Japanese** prints, especially works by Hokusai and Hiroshige. Most of the original furnishings are gone, but you do get a real sense of how the dining room used to be, with all its walls and fittings painted a glorious bright yellow; Monet designed his own yellow crockery to harmonize with the surroundings. By contrast, the stairs and upstairs rooms are a pale blue.

Colourful flower gardens, with trellised walkways and shady bowers, stretch down from the house. At the bottom, a dank underpass beneath the road leads to the *jardin d'eau*, focused around the narrow **water-lily pond**. Footpaths around the perimeter and arching Japanese footbridges offer differing views of the water lilies themselves, nurtured by gardeners in rowing boats. May and June, when the rhododendrons flower around the pond and the wisteria that winds over the Japanese bridge is in bloom, are the best times to visit.

A few-minutes' walk up Giverny's village street, the **Musée d'Art Américain** is an unattractive edifice that hides a spacious and well-lit gallery devoted to American artists resident in France between 1865 and 1915 (April–Oct Tues–Sun 10am–6pm; Ⓦ www.maag.org; €5.50, free first Sun of each month). Some took their admiration of Monet to a point that now seems embarrassing, painting many of the same scenes, but there are some interesting works by John Singer Sargent, Winslow Homer and, especially, Mary Cassatt.

Giverny's one **hotel**, the *Musardière*, stands not far beyond Monet's house at 123 rue Claude-Monet (Ⓣ 02.32.21.03.18, Ⓦ www.lamusardiere.fr; open April–Oct ❹); dinner menus in its restaurant start at €26. The nearest inexpensive accommodation is the *Hôtel d'Évreux*, 11 place d'Évreux (Ⓣ 02.32.21.16.12; Ⓦ www.hoteldevreux.fr; ❷), across the river in the heart of the town of **VERNON**. Connecting buses from outside Vernon's **gare SNCF** run to a car park close to the gardens in Giverny (€4 return) and are timed to coincide with the arrivals and departures of trains between Paris and Rouen.

Basse Normandie

As you head west along the coast of Basse Normandie from Le Havre, a succession of somewhat exclusive resorts – of which only **Honfleur** is especially memorable – is followed first by the beaches where the Allied armies landed in 1944, and then by the wilder, and in places deserted, shore around the **Cotentin Peninsula**.

The Norman Riviera

The only section of the Norman coast to have serious delusions of grandeur is the stretch that lies immediately west of the mouth of the Seine. The **Pont de Normandie** across the river estuary from Le Havre has made such places as

Trouville and Deauville busier than ever, though only Honfleur could be said to have had all that much to lose.

Honfleur

HONFLEUR, the best preserved of the old ports of Normandy and the most easterly on the Calvados coast, is a near-perfect seaside town that lacks only a beach. It used to have one, but with the accumulation of silt from the Seine the sea has steadily withdrawn, leaving the eighteenth-century waterfront houses of boulevard Charles-V stranded and a little surreal. The ancient port, however, still functions – the channel to the beautiful Vieux Bassin is kept open by regular dredging – and though only pleasure craft now use the moorings in the harbour basin, fishing boats tie up alongside the pier nearby, and you can usually buy fish either directly from the boats or from stands on the pier, still by right run by fishermen's wives.

Honfleur is highly picturesque, and has moved significantly upmarket since the opening of the Pont de Normandie. Despite now being just a few minutes' drive from Le Havre, the old port has strong echoes of the fishing village that appealed so greatly to artists in the second half of the nineteenth century. Its compact size, quaint waterside setting and abundance of restaurants make Honfleur an ideal location for a weekend break.

Arrival and information

Honfleur's **gare routière**, to the east of the Vieux Bassin, is served by over a dozen direct daily **buses** to and from Caen (#20), and up to eight express services from Le Havre (Bus Verts; ☎08.01.21.42.14, ⓦ www.busverts.fr). There are also regular buses to Deauville and Trouville (#20). The nearest **gare SNCF** is the Trouville-Deauville station, a twenty-minute bus ride away.

The well-stocked **tourist office** adjoins the glass-fronted Mediathèque on quai Le Paulmier, between the Vieux Bassin and the *gare routière* (Easter–June & Sept Mon–Sat 9.30am–12.30pm & 2–6.30pm, Sun 10am–5pm; July & Aug Mon–Sat 9.30am–7pm, Sun 10am–5pm; Oct–Easter Mon–Sat 10am–12.30pm & 2–6pm; ☎02.31.89.23.30, ⓦ www.ot-honfleur.fr). Ask about their summer programme of **guided tours** of the town, which range from two-hour walkabouts to full-day excursions including meals.

Accommodation

If finding budget **accommodation** is one of your main priorities, Honfleur itself may not be an ideal choice, but there are plenty of reasonably priced *chambres d'hôte* along the coastal road towards Trouville (the tourist office can provide details). The two-star **Camping du Phare** (☎02.31.89.10.26; open April–Sept) is on place Jean-de-Vienne at the western end of boulevard Charles-V.

Belvédère 36 rte Emile-Renouf ☎02.31.89.08.13, ⓦ www.hotel-belvedere -honfleur.com. Peaceful, traditional Logis de France, with garden and terrace, roughly 10min walk east of (and up from) the harbour. All nine rooms are en suite; some are in a cottage in the grounds that has views of the Pont de Normandie, and there's a good restaurant, with menus from €16.90. Closed Jan. ❹

Cascades 17 place Thiers ☎02.31.89.05.83. Seventeen-room hotel-restaurant opening onto both place Thiers and the cobbled rue de la Ville behind. Rooms are quite large for the price, and some have beamed ceilings. Good value. Closed mid-Nov to early Feb. ❸

La Cour Sainte Catherine 74 rue du Puits ☎02.31.89.42.40, ⓦ www.giaglis.com. Beautiful B&B tucked away down a quiet street beyond the St Catherine church. The comfortable, well-decorated rooms are set around a plant-filled courtyard, and breakfast is served in the old cider press. ④

Hotel du Dauphin 10 Place Pierre Berthelot ☎02.31.89.15.53, ⓦwww.hoteldudauphin.com. Pleasant and friendly 34-room hotel close to the St Catherine church. The communal areas are significantly more modern than most of the bedrooms, but further renovations are planned. Street view rooms are cheaper than those with a church view. ④

Monet Charrière du Puits ☎02.31.89.00.90, ⓦwww.motelmonet.fr. This old ivy-covered house is in a very quiet location 10min walk up a moderately steep hill from the centre and offers modern, en-suite rooms and plenty of courtyard parking. ④

The Town

Visitors to Honfleur inevitably gravitate towards the old centre, around the **Vieux Bassin**. At the *bassin*, slate-fronted houses, each of them one or two storeys higher than seems possible, harmonize – despite their tottering and ill-matched forms – into a backdrop that is only excelled by the **Lieutenance** at the harbour entrance. The latter was the dwelling of the King's Lieutenant, and has been the gateway to the inner town since at least 1608, when Samuel Champlain sailed from Honfleur to found Québec. The **church of St-Étienne** nearby is now the **Musée de la Marine**, which combines a collection of model ships with several rooms of antique Norman furnishings (mid-Feb to March & Oct to mid-Nov Tues–Fri 2.30–5.30pm; Sat & Sun 10am–noon; April–Sept Tues–Sun 10am–noon & 2–6.30pm; €3.20, or €4.50 with Musée de Vieux Honfleur). Just behind it, two seventeenth-century **salt stores** that used to contain the precious commodity during the days of the much-hated *gabelle*, or salt tax, now serve as the **Musée du Vieux Honfleur** (same hours and entrance fee), filled with everyday artefacts from old Honfleur.

The town's artistic past – and its present concentration of galleries and painters – owes most to Eugène Boudin, forerunner of Impressionism. He was born and worked in the town, trained the 18-year-old Monet and was joined for various periods by Pissarro, Renoir and Cézanne. Boudin was among the founders of what's now the **Musée Eugène Boudin** (mid-March to Sep daily except Tues 10am–noon & 2–6pm; Oct to mid-March Mon & Wed–Fri 2.30–5pm, Sat & Sun 10am–noon & 2.30–5pm; €5.40), west of the port on place Erik-Satie, and left 53 works to it after his death in 1898. His pastel seascapes and sunsets in particular are quite appealing here in context, and they're accompanied by changing temporary exhibitions and a few ethnographic displays.

Admission to the museum also gives you access to the detached belfry of the **church of Sainte-Catherine** (daily 9am–6pm). Both church and belfry are built almost entirely of wood. The church itself makes a change from the usual Norman stone constructions, and has the added peculiarity of being divided into twin naves, with one balcony running around both.

Just down the hill from the Musée Boudin, at 67 boulevard Charles-V, is **Les Maisons Satie** (daily except Tues: May–Sept 10am–7pm; mid-Feb to April & Oct–Dec 11am–6pm; last entrance 1hr before closing time; €5.10), the red-timbered house of Erik Satie. From the outside it looks unchanged since the composer was born there in 1866. Step inside, however, and you'll find yourself in Normandy's most unusual and eccentric museum. It's worth finding out a little about Satie before visiting, as the unconventional exhibits don't provide much in the way of facts. As befits a close associate of the Surrealists, Satie is commemorated by all sorts of weird and wonderful interactive surprises. It would be a shame to give too many of them away here; suffice it to say that you're immediately confronted by a giant pear, bouncing into the air on huge wings to the strains of his best-known piano piece, *Gymnopédies*. You also get to see a filmed reconstruction of *Parade*, a ballet on which Satie collaborated with Picasso, Stravinsky and Cocteau, which created a furore in Paris in 1917.

Eating

With its abundance of day-trippers and hotel guests, Honfleur supports an astonishing number of **restaurants**, many specializing in seafood. Most don't face onto the harbour itself; the majority of the narrow buildings around the edge are home to crêperies, cafés and ice-cream parlours.

Le Bouillon Normand 7 rue de la Ville ☎02.31.89.02.41. Old-fashioned bistro, with indoor and outdoor seating, set just back from the basin behind St-Étienne church. Fish, cider and cheese are prominent on simple, good-value menus at €16 and €23. Closed Wed, Sun evening. & Jan.

La Cidrerie 26 place Hamelin ☎02.31.87.23.12. Traditional crêperie serving good value sweet and savoury pancakes washed down with jugs of local cider.

Le Hamelin 16 place Hamelin ☎02.31.89.16.25. Small restaurant with some outdoor seating near the harbour. The three-course *menu terroir* is an

excellent introduction to Norman cooking, while a few euros more will buy you an *assiette de fruits de mer*.

La Tortue 36 rue de l'Homme de Bois ☎02.31.89.04.93. A smart but welcoming place near the Musée Boudin, with lunch menus of modern French cooking from €14 and dinner from €19. Closed Mon evening & Tues, Oct–March only.

Le Vieux Honfleur 13 quai St-Étienne ☎02.31.89.15.31. The best of the restaurants around the harbour itself, with spacious alfresco dining – in shade at lunchtime – on its pedestrian-ized eastern side. Simple menus, but the seafood is very good, as befits prices starting at €29.

Trouville and Deauville

Heading west along the corniche from Honfleur, green fields and fruit trees lull the land's edge, and cliffs rise from sandy beaches all the way to Trouville, 15km away. The resorts aren't exactly cheap but they're relatively undeveloped, and if you want to stop along the coast this is a good place to do it. The next stretch, from Trouville to Cabourg, is what you might call the Riviera of Normandy: with Trouville as "Nice" and Deauville as "Cannes," within a stone's throw of each other.

TROUVILLE is perhaps more of a real town, with a constant population and industries other than tourism. But it's still a resort, with a tangle of pedestrian streets just back from the beach that are alive with restaurants and hotels, and a busy boardwalk running along a sandy beach. On Wednesday mornings, a lively market selling everything from fluorescent underpants to local produce runs along the quayside. Although Trouville has been a chic destination ever since Napoléon III started bringing his court here every summer in the 1860s, its glamour has faded somewhat, while next-door Deauville's has only grown. One of Napoleon's dukes, looking across the river that now separates the two towns, saw, instead of marshlands, money – and lots of it, in the form of a racetrack. His vision materialized, and villas appeared between the racetrack and the sea to become Deauville. Deauville is slightly larger than its neighbour, and significantly smarter, its sleek streets lined with designer boutiques and chic cafés. During the summer, life revolves around the beach and the *planches*, 650m of boardwalk, beyond which rows of primary-coloured parasols obscure the view of the sea.

Deauville's **American Film Festival** (@www.festival-deauville.com), held in the first week of September, is the antithesis of Cannes, with public admission to a wide selection of previews.

Practicalities

Trouville and Deauville share their **gare SNCF** and **gare routière**, located in between the two just south of the marina. Each day, thirteen of the hourly buses from Caen continue along the coast to Honfleur. Plenty of lavish brochures can be found at the helpful **tourist office** on place de la Mairie in Deauville (May & June Mon–Fri 9am–12.30pm & 2–6.30pm, Sat 9am–6.30pm, Sun 10am–1pm & 2–5pm; July & Aug Mon–Sat 9am–7pm, Sun 10am–1pm & 3–6pm; Sept–April Mon–Sat 9am–12.30pm & 2–6.30pm, Sun 10am–1pm & 2–5pm; ☎02.31.14.40.00, ⓦwww.deauville.org), or the one at 32 quai F. Moureaux in Trouville (April–June, Sept & Oct Mon–Sat 9.30am–noon & 2–6.30pm, Sun 10am–1pm; July & Aug Mon–Sat 9.30am–7pm, Sun 10am–4pm; Nov–March Mon–Sat 9.30am–noon & 1.30–6.30pm, Sun 10am–1pm; ☎02.31.14.60.70, ⓦwww.trouvillesurmer.org).

As you might imagine, **hotels** here tend to be luxurious, overpriced or both. If you fancy staying right on the seafront, it's hard to beat the *Flaubert*, rue Gustave-Flaubert (☎02.31.88.37.23, ⓦwww.flaubert.fr; ❺), a grand, faux-timbered mansion with spacious, comfortable rooms at the start of Trouville's boardwalk. Cheaper options include the *Hôtel des Sports*, behind Deauville's fish market at 27 rue Gambetta (☎02.31.88.22.67; ❸; closed Feb & Nov, plus Sun in winter), and Trouville's closest equivalent, *Le Trouville*, 50m from the beach at 1 rue Thiers (☎02.31.98.45.48, ⓦwww.hotelletrouville.com; ❸; closed Jan). Deauville, meanwhile, has a **campsite**, *La Vallée de Deauville*, 3km from the centre on route de Beaumont-en-Auge in St-Arnoult (☎02.31.88.58.17, ⓦwww.camping-deauville.com; open April–Oct).

A good **place to eat** in Deauville is *Chez Miocque* at 81 rue Eugène-Colas (☎02.31.88.09.52; closed Tues in winter, plus all Jan), a top-quality Parisian-style bistro where a three-course meal costs around €40. Trouville also has its fair share of good fish restaurants, including *La Petite Auberge*, 7 rue Carnot (☎02.31.88.11.07; closed Tues all year, plus Wed except in Aug). Those wishing to sample café society in Deauville should head for the long-established *Dupont Salon du thé* at 20 place Morny, where cakes and snacks are served until late in summer, while Trouville's modern *Tutti Frutti* restaurant (☎02.31.81.29.00; closed Jan), opposite the casino at 16 place Maréchal-Foch, is a good choice for families or those looking for a light lunch.

Houlgate

A hundred years ago, **HOULGATE**, 15km west of Deauville, was every bit as glamorous and sophisticated a destination as its immediate neighbours. What makes it different today is that it has barely changed since then. Its long straight beach remains lined with a stately procession of nineteenth-century villas, while the town's handful of commercial enterprises are confined to the narrow parallel street, the **rue des Bains**, fifty metres inland. As a result, Houlgate is the most relaxed of the local resorts, ideal if you're looking for a peaceful family break where the only stress is deciding whether to paddle or play mini-golf.

The **tourist office** is well back from the sea on boulevard des Belges (April–June Sept & Oct Mon–Sat 10am–1pm & 2–6pm, Sun 10.30am–1pm & 2–4pm; July & Aug daily 10am–1pm & 2–6.30pm; Nov–March Mon–Sat 10am–1pm & 2–6pm; ☎02.31.24.34.79, ⓦwww.ville-houlgate.fr). The *Hostellerie Normande*, just off the rue des Bains at 11 rue E.-Deschanel (☎02.31.24.85.50; ❹), is a pretty but rather impersonal little **hotel** covered with ivy and creeping flowers, with a €15 lunch menu on which you can follow fish soup with a plate of *moules-frites* or tripe. Above the Vaches Noires ("Black Cows") cliffs on the corniche road east of town, *La Ferme Auberge des Aulnettes* (℡02.31.28.00.28; ❸; closed Dec & Jan), is a lovely half-timbered country house in pleasant gardens, where the cheapest rooms have a shower but share a WC. A pleasant restaurant with outdoor seating serves menus from €18. The best **campsite** in the area, the four-star *Les Falaises* (℡02.31.24.81.09, Ⓦwww.lesfalaises.com; open April to mid Oct), is close by, at Gonneville sur mer.

Caen

CAEN, capital and largest city of Basse Normandie, may not be a place that many tourists go out of their way to visit: in the months of fighting in 1944, it was completely devastated. Nonetheless, the city that nine hundred years ago was the favoured residence of William the Conqueror remains impressive in parts, and makes a convenient and pleasant base for exploring the D-day beaches and the rest of the region.

Its central feature is a ring of ramparts that no longer have a castle to protect, and, though there are the scattered spires and buttresses of two abbeys and eight old churches, roads and roundabouts fill the wide spaces where prewar houses stood. The city centre remains attractive on the whole, though, with some pretty pedestrianized shopping streets and a restaurant-lined marina.

Arrival and information

Caen's small, modern **airport**, 7km west just outside **Carpiquet** (℡02.31.71.20.10), is served by **buses** (€1.30) connecting with all services, taking 25 minutes to run to and from the Tour-le-Roi stop in place Courtonne. Avis (℡02.31.34.88.89), Budget (℡02.31.83.70.47) and Rent A Car (℡02.31.84.10.10) provide **car hire** both in the terminal and in town.

The **gare SNCF** (℡08.36.35.35.35) is a kilometre's walk south of the town centre across the river, with the **gare routière** alongside. An extensive network of local **buses** and **trams** is run by TWISTO (℡02.31.15.55.55, Ⓦwww.twisto .fr), which has ticket and information centres at 15 rue de Geôle (just north of the tourist office), and on boulevard Maréchal-Leclerc. The main tram route connects the southern and northern suburbs, running through the heart of the city from the *gare SNCF* up avenue de 6-Juin to the university and beyond. To get from the train station to the centre, take trams #1 or #11 (€1.27).

Caen's **tourist office** is on place St-Pierre across from the church of St-Pierre (April–June & Sept Mon–Sat 9.30am–1pm & 2–6.30pm, Sun 10am–1pm; July & Aug Mon–Sat 9am–7pm, Sun 10am–1pm & 2–5pm; Oct–March Mon–Sat 9.30am–1pm & 2–6pm, Sun 10am–1pm; ℡02.31.27.14.14, Ⓦwww.caen.fr /tourisme). It's worth dropping in to pick up the "Passe Tourisme", a booklet filled with discount coupons for sights in and around Caen. You can go **online** at Espace Micro, on place Courtonne at 1 rue Basse, or the main **post office** on place Gambetta (Mon–Fri 8am–7pm, Sat 8am–noon).

Accommodation

Caen has a great number of **hotels**, though, as ever in the rebuilt bomb-damaged cities of Normandy, few could be called attractive. They're not particularly concentrated in any one area, either, though you'll find clusters just west of the castle and tourist office – a convenient location for motorists heading to or from the ferry – as well as around the pleasure port, and a handful facing the *gare SNCF*.

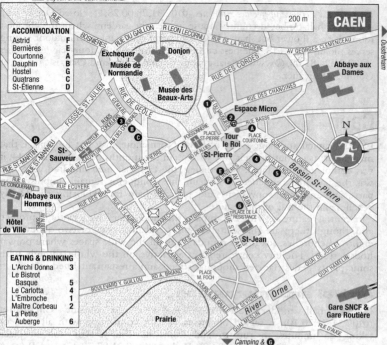

▲ Bayeux & the Caen Memorial

CAEN

0   200 m

ACCOMMODATION
Astrid   F
Bernières   E
Courtonne   A
Dauphin   B
Hostel   G
Quatrans   C
St-Étienne   D

Exchequer

Musée de Normandie

Donjon

Abbaye aux Dames

Musée des Beaux-Arts

Espace Micro

Tour le Roi

St-Pierre

St-Sauveur

Bassin St-Pierre

Abbaye aux Hommes

Hôtel de Ville

St-Jean

EATING & DRINKING
L'Archi Donna   3
Le Bistrot
   Basque   5
Le Carlotta   4
L'Embroche   1
Maître Corbeau   2
La Petite
   Auberge   6

Prairie

River Orne

Gare SNCF & Gare Routière

▼ Camping & G

NORMANDY | Caen

Hotels

Astrid 39 rue de Bernières ☎02.31.85.48.67,
ⓦhotel_astrid.club.fr. Recently renovated two-star
hotel with spacious rooms but rather compact
bathrooms. The friendly staff provide tourist information. ❸

Bernières 50 rue de Bernières ☎02.31.86.01.26,
ⓦwww.hotelbernieres.com. This bright, central
hotel offers decent en-suite rooms halfway
between the churches of St-Pierre and St-Jean. ❷

Courtonne 5 rue des Prairies St-Gilles
☎02.31.93.47.83, ⓦhttp://hotelcourtonne.com. A
very welcoming, modernized hotel overlooking the
place Courtonne and the pleasure port, though the
building is so narrow it's easy to miss. All rooms
have bath or shower, phone and TV. ❹

Dauphin 29 rue Gémare ☎02.31.86.22.26,
ⓦwww.le-dauphin-normandie.com. Upmarket
hotel, tucked away behind the tourist office. Part of
it was a priory during the eighteenth century,
although this isn't immediately obvious. The public
areas are impressive, while the rooms are comfortable but relatively compact, at least at the lower
end of the price scale. Sauna and fitness facilities
and free wi-fi access. Grand restaurant, with an

€19 weekday dinner menu; weekend menus €30
and €52 (restaurant closed Sat lunch & Sun all
year, and open for dinner only June–Sept). ❺

Quatrans 17 rue Gémare ☎02.31.86.25.57,
ⓦwww.hotel-des-quatrans.com. Recently
renovated medium-size hotel close to the tourist
office and château. The rooms may not be as
high-tech as the lobby, but they are all spacious,
clean and en suite. Several family rooms are
available. ❸–❹

St-Étienne 2 rue de l'Académie ☎02.31.86.35.82,
ⓦwww.hotel-saint-etienne.com. Friendly budget
hotel housed an old stone house in the characterful
St-Martin district, not far from the Abbaye des
Hommes. The cheaper rooms share bathrooms, but
en-suite ones cost little more. ❷

Hostel

HI hostel Foyer Robert-Remé, 68bis rue E.-
Restout, Grâce-de-Dieu ☎02.31.52.19.96. Lively
and welcoming hostel, situated in an otherwise
sleepy area about 500m southwest of the *gare
SNCF*. Beds in both four-bed dorms or two-bed
private rooms cost €14 per person. Reception open
5–9pm. Open June–Oct.

The Town

A virtue was made of the postwar necessity of clearing away the rubble of Caen's medieval houses, which formerly pressed up against its ancient **château ramparts**. The resulting open green space means that those walls are now fully visible for the first time in centuries. A stroll around the ramparts gives a good overview of the city, with a particularly fine prospect of the reconstructed fourteenth-century facade of the nearby **church of St-Pierre**.

Most of Caen's centre is taken up with shopping streets and pedestrian precincts, featuring branches of the big Parisian stores and local rivals. The main city **market** takes place on Friday, spreading along both sides of Fosse St-Julien, and there's also a Sunday market in place Courtonne. The **Bassin St-Pierre**, the pleasure port at the end of the canal that links Caen to the sea, is the liveliest area during the summer months.

Castle grounds

Within the castle walls, it's possible to visit the former **Exchequer** – which dates from shortly after the Norman conquest of England, and was the scene of a banquet thrown by Richard the Lionheart en route to the Crusades – and inspect a garden planted with herbs and medicinal plants that were cultivated here during the Middle Ages. Also inside the precinct, though not in original structures, are two museums. Perhaps more interesting is the **Musée des Beaux-Arts** (daily except Tues 9.30am–6pm; permanent collection free, special exhibitions €3 or €5), which traces a potted history of European art from Renaissance Italy through such Dutch masters as Brueghel the Younger up to grand portraits from eighteenth-century France in the upstairs galleries. Downstairs brings things up to date with some powerful twentieth-century art, though there are few big-name works. The other museum, the **Musée de Normandie** (June–Sept daily 9.30am–6pm; Oct–March daily except Tues 9.30am–6pm; permanent collection free, special exhibitions €3 or €5), provides a cursory overview of Norman history, ranging from archaeological finds like stone tools from the region's megalithic period and glass jewellery from Gallo-Roman Rouen up to the impact of the Industrial Revolution. It also hosts two or three temporary exhibitions per year, covering particular themes in much greater detail.

Abbaye aux Hommes

The impressive **Abbaye aux Hommes**, at the west end of rue St-Pierre, was founded by William the Conqueror and designed to hold his tomb within the huge, austere Romanesque church of St-Étienne (Mon–Sat 8.30am–12.30pm & 1.30–7pm, Sun 8.30am–12.30pm & 2.30–7pm; free; 1hr 15min guided tours leave adjacent Hôtel de Ville daily 9.30am, 11am, 2.30pm & 4pm; tours in English mid-July to Aug only, times vary, ask at tourist office; €2.20, free on Sun). However, his burial here, in 1087, was hopelessly undignified. The funeral procession first caught fire and was then held to ransom, as various factions squabbled over his rotting corpse for any spoils they could grab. A further interruption came when a man halted the service to object that the grave had been constructed without compensation on the site of his family house, and the assembled nobles had to pay him off before William could be laid to rest. During the Revolution the tomb was again ransacked, and it now holds a solitary thigh-bone rescued from the river. Still, the building itself is a spectacular Romanesque monument. Adjoining the church are the abbey buildings, designed during the eighteenth century and now housing the Hôtel de Ville.

The Caen Memorial

Just north of Caen, at the end of avenue Marshal–Montgomery in the Folie Couvrechef area, the **Caen Memorial** (Jan 2–5 & Jan 29 to Feb 10 & 12 Nov to 31 Dec 9.30am–6pm, Feb 11 to Nov 11 9am–7pm; ☏02.31.06.06.44, ⊛www .memorial-caen.fr; March–Sept €17.50, Oct–Feb €16.50, tickets valid for 24hr), which describes itself as a "museum for peace", stands on a plateau named after General Eisenhower on a clifftop beneath which the Germans had their HQ in June and July 1944.

The museum is a typically French high-tech, novel-architecture conception, with excellent displays divided into several distinct sections; allow two hours at the very least for a visit. The first section deals with the rise of fascism in Germany, the next with resistance and collaboration in France, while a third charts all the major battles of World War II. Most of the captions, though not always the written exhibits themselves, are translated into English. Further areas examine the course of the Cold War and the prospects for global peace, with the former German bunkers below housing the Nobel Peace Prize Winners' Gallery. In addition to the permanent displays, there are also regular temporary exhibitions which often extend the focus into the personal realm or the modern day; recent topics include "The Righteous in France" and "World Trade Centre: a global moment". There's also a good-value self-service restaurant upstairs. The memorial is served by bus #2 from the "Tour le Roi" stop in the centre of town.

Eating

Caen's town centre offers two major areas for **eating**: with cosmopolitan restaurants in the pedestrianized **quartier Vaugueux** and more traditional French restaurants on the streets off **rue de Geôle**, near the western ramparts, particularly rue des Croisiers and rue Gémare.

L'Archi Dona 8 rue des Croisiers ☏ 02.31.85.30.30. Smart restaurant which belies its stately setting by serving fresh and zestful Mediterranean-influenced cuisine, ranging from simple entrée-plus-dessert meals at €20 up to the €32 "seduction" menu. Closed Sun, Mon & three weeks in Aug.

Le Bistrot Basque 24 Quai Vendeuvre ☏ 02.31.38.21.26. Atmospheric restaurant with a bright interior, serving tasty Basque-influenced cooking, such as grilled cod with chorizo (€14.50).

Le Carlotta 16 quai Vendeuvre ☏ 02.31.86.68.99, ⊛www.lecarlotta.fr. Busy and fashionable Paris-style brasserie beside the pleasure port, which serves good Norman cooking both à la carte and on menus from €22. Closed Sun.

L'Embroche 17 rue Porte au Berger ☏ 02.31.93.71.31. Cosy little place in a busy restaurant district, where the open kitchen whips up simple regional specialities in full view of appreciative diners, with lunch from €18 and dinner from €22. Closed Sat lunch, Sun & Mon lunch.

Maître Corbeau 8 rue Buquet ☏ 02.31.93.93.00. Large restaurant with an entirely cheese-related menu featuring fondue, *raclette*, *tartiflette* to name but a few. The kitsch decor ties in with the theme, too – cow print and dairy iconography feature strongly. A typical fondue costs around €14, while non-fondue menus start from €18.50. Closed Sat lunch, Sun, Mon lunch & three weeks in Aug.

La Petite Auberge 17 rue des Équipes-d'Urgence ☏ 02.31.86.43.30. Plain and simple restaurant, with a nice view of the St-Jean church. Very well-priced Norman specialities served on a €12 menu (daily except Sat evening) that doesn't force you to eat tripe, or a wide-ranging €19 one. Closed Sun, Mon & first three weeks of Aug.

The D-Day beaches

Despite the best efforts of Steven Spielberg, it's all but impossible now to picture the scene at dawn on **D-Day**, June 6, 1944, when Allied troops landed along the Norman coast between the mouth of the Orne and Les

Normandie Pass

If you're planning to visit several D-Day related sights, it's worth paying an extra €1 on top of your first admission to a participating attraction (see ⓦ www.normandiepass .com for details) to purchase a Normandie Pass. The card offers a range of discounts, from €0.30 to €4.50, for entry to 26 museums and sights on the D-Day circuit, including the Caen Memorial, the Musée du Débarquement at Arromanches and the Pegasus Memorial. It can also be used at a number of other attractions in Basse Normandie, such as the Bayeux Tapestry and Cherbourg's Cité de la Mer.

Dunes de Varneville on the Cotentin Peninsula. For the most part, these are innocuous beaches backed by gentle dunes, and yet this foothold in Europe was won at the cost of 100,000 soldiers' lives. That the invasion happened here and not nearer to Germany was partly a result of the disastrous Canadian raid on Dieppe in 1942, which showed the perils of attacking fortified positions without strong air and artillery support. The ensuing **Battle of Normandy** killed thousands of civilians and reduced nearly six hundred towns and villages to rubble but, within a week of its eventual conclusion, Paris was liberated.

The **beaches** are still often referred to by their wartime code names: from east to west, Sword, Juno, Gold, Omaha and Utah. Substantial traces of the fighting are rare, the most remarkable being the remains of the astounding **Mulberry Harbour** at **Arromanches**, 10km northeast of Bayeux. Further west, at **Pointe du Hoc** on Omaha Beach, the cliff heights are deeply pitted with German bunkers and shell holes, while the church at **Ste-Mère-Église**, from whose steeple the US paratrooper dangled during heavy fighting throughout *The Longest Day*, still stands, and now has a model parachute permanently fastened to the roof. Note that **Utah Beach**, the westernmost of the Invasion Beaches, is on the Cotentin Peninsula, and covered on p.342 onwards.

Just about every coastal town has its **war museum**. These tend as a rule to shy away from the unbearable reality of war in favour of *Boy's Own*-style heroics, but the wealth of incidental human detail can nonetheless be overpowering. Veterans and their descendants apart, visitors these days come to this stretch of coast for its **seaside**: sand and seafood (the best oysters are at Courseulles), plenty of campsites and no Deauville chic.

Bus Verts (☎08.10.21.42.14, ⓦ www.busverts.fr) run all along this coast. From Bayeux, bus #75 goes to Arromanches, Courseulles, and Ouistreham, and bus #70 to the Pointe du Hoc, the US cemetery at Colleville-sur-mer, and Port-en-Bessin. From Caen, bus #30 runs inland to Isigny via Bayeux, express bus #1 to Ouistreham, and express bus #3 to Courseulles. Visitors without their own transport may prefer the convenience of a **guided tour**, and a wide range of companies are happy to oblige, with a variety of half- and full-day itineraries. Notable tours include the bilingual ones organized by the Caen Memorial (see opposite), with four or five hours on the road and a visit to the Memorial at your own pace (end Jan to March & Oct–Dec daily 1pm; April–Sept daily 9am & 2pm; ☎02.31.06.06.45, ⓦ www.memorial-caen.fr; €69). Other popular tour operators include Battlebus (☎02.31.22.28.82 ⓦ www.battlebus.fr), which takes groups of up to eight people on tours which depart from Bayeux, and D-Day tours (☎ 02.31.22.75.80, ⓦ www.dday-tours .fr), also based out of Bayeux.

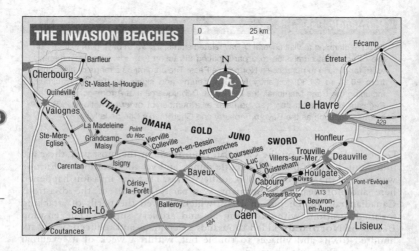

THE INVASION BEACHES

0   25 km

N

Fécamp

Barfleur

Étretat

Cherbourg

St-Vaast-la-Hougue

Quinéville

Le Havre

Valognes

UTAH

A29

Ste-Mère-
Eglise

La Madeleine

OMAHA

Point
du Hoc

GOLD

Vierville

JUNO

Grandcamp-
Maisy

Colleville

Honfleur

SWORD

Port-en-Bessin

Arromanches

Trouville

Courseulles

Villers-sur-Mer

Deauville

Isigny

Luc

Lion

Carentan

Ouistreham

Houlgate

Bayeux

Cabourg

Dives

Pont-l'Evêque

Cérisy-
la-Forêt

Pegasus Bridge

A13

Beuvron-
en-Auge

Balleroy

Caen

Saint-Lô

A84

Lisieux

Coutances

Ouistreham and around

The sleepy town of **OUISTREHAM**, on the coast 15km north of Caen and connected to it by a dual carriageway, gives the impression that it can barely believe its luck at having become a major ferry port. Ferry services began here in 1986, and the easternmost of the D-Day resorts has developed an array of reasonable hotels and restaurants.

If, instead of setting off for Caen, you head directly west along the coast from the ferry terminal, after a few hundred metres you come to the long straight main drag of beach – the **Riva Bella**. This is progressively shedding its run-down image; the large casino has been remodelled as a 1930s passenger liner, housing an expensive restaurant and cocktail bar, and even the old-fashioned bathing huts have had a fresh lick of paint.

Nearby, the **Musée du Mur de l'Atlantique** (daily: Oct–March 10am–6pm; April–Sept 9am–7pm; €7) is housed in a lofty bunker – hence its alternative name, the Grand Bunker. This was the headquarters of the several German batteries that defended the mouth of the River Orne; after brief resistance, it fell to Allied forces on June 9, 1944. Inside the heavily restored bunker, displays re-create living quarters and explain what happened here, with newspapers, cutlery and packets of cigarettes adding a welcome human touch to the moderately interesting explanations of the workings of the generators, gas filters and radio room.

The **tourist office**, alongside the casino on the beach (daily 10am–1pm & 2–7pm; ☎02.31.97.18.63, ⓦwww.ville-ouistreham.fr), provides **internet access** at €0.10 per minute. The main concentrations of cafés and restaurants are the place Courbonne, immediately outside the *gare maritime*, and the Avenue de la Mer, Ouistreham's main drag. Those looking for decent food and accommodation should make for *Le Normandie*, close to the ferry port at 71 avenue Michel-Cabieu (☎02.31.97.19.57, ⓦwww.lenormandie.com; ❹; closed mid-Dec to mid-Jan, plus Sun evening & Mon Nov–March), a smart Logis de France with pleasant, quiet rooms. Its restaurant features menus from €16.50 to €33.50, with plenty of meat options alongside the usual seafood choices.

Pegasus Bridge

Roughly 5km south of Ouistreham, the main road towards Caen passes close by the site now known as **Pegasus Bridge**. On the night before D-Day, the twin bridges here that cross the Caen canal and the River Orne were a crucial Allied objective, and were the target of a daring but successful glider assault just

The war cemeteries

The **World War II** cemeteries that dot the Norman countryside are filled with foreigners – most of the French dead are buried in the churchyards of their home towns. After the war, some felt that the soldiers should remain buried in the original makeshift graves that were dug where they fell. Instead, commissions gathered the remains into purpose-built cemeteries devoted to the separate warring nations.

▲ US Military Cemetery, Colleville-sur-Mer

The **British** and **Commonwealth** cemeteries are magnificently maintained. They tend not to be screened off with hedges or walls, or to be forbidding expanses of manicured lawn, but are instead intimate, punctuated with bright flowers. The family of each soldier was invited to suggest an inscription for his tomb, making each grave very personal, and yet part of a common attempt to bring meaning to the carnage. Some epitaphs are questioning – "One day we will understand"; some are accepting – "Our lad at rest"; some matter-of-fact, simply giving the home address; some patriotic, quoting the "corner of a foreign field that is forever England". And interspersed among them all is the chilling refrain of the anonymous "A soldier … known unto God". Thus the cemetery at **Ryes**, where so many of the graves bear the date of D-Day, and so many of the victims are under 20, remains immediate and accessible – each grave clearly contains a unique individual. Even the monumental sculpture is subdued, a very British sort of fumbling for the decent thing to say. The understatement of the memorial at **Bayeux**, with its painfully contrived Latin epigram commemorating the return as liberators of "those whom William conquered", conveys an entirely appropriate humility and deep sadness.

An even more eloquent testimony to the futility of war is afforded by the **German** cemeteries, filled with soldiers who served a cause so despicable as to render any talk of "nobility" or "sacrifice" obscene. They are sombre places, inconspicuous to minimize the bitterness they still arouse. At **Orglandes** ten thousand are buried, three to each of the plain headstones set in the long flat lawn, almost hidden behind an anonymous wall. There are no noble slogans and the plain entrance is without a dedicatory monument. At the site of **Mont d'Huisnes** near Mont St-Michel, the circular mausoleum holds another ten thousand, filed away in cold concrete tiers. Though no attempt is made to defend the indefensible, there's still an overpowering sense of sorrow – that there is nothing to be said in such a place bitterly underlines the sheer waste and stupidity.

The largest **American** cemetery, at **Colleville-sur-Mer** near the Pointe du Hoc, may already be familiar from the opening sequences of *Saving Private Ryan*. Here, by contrast, neat rows of crosses cover the tranquil clifftop lawns, with no individual epitaphs, just gold lettering for a few exceptional warriors. At one end, a muscular giant dominates a huge array of battlefield plans and diagrams, covered with surging arrows and pincer movements.

after midnight. The original bridge was replaced in 1994, but is now the focus of the **Mémorial Pegasus** immediately to the east (daily: Feb–March & Oct–Nov 10am–1pm & 2–5pm; April–Sept 9.30am–6.30pm; ⓦ www.normandy1944 .com; €6). This vaguely glider-shaped museum explains the attack in detail, accompanied by the expected array of helmets, goggles, medals and other memorabilia, most captioned in English, as well as photographs and various model bridges used in planning the attack. The museum also features the world's only full-size replica of a Horsa glider.

Arromanches

At **ARROMANCHES**, 10km northeast of Bayeux, an artificial **Mulberry harbour**, "Port Winston", protected the landings of 2,500,000 men and 500,000 vehicles during the invasion. Two of these prefab concrete constructions were built in Britain, while "doodlebugs" blitzed overhead; they were then submerged in rivers away from the prying eyes of German aircraft, and finally towed across the Channel at 6kph as the invasion began. The seafront **Musée du Débarquement**, in Arromanches' main square (daily Feb–Dec: winter 10am–12.30pm & 1.30–5pm, summer 9am–7pm; €6.50; ⓦ www.normandy1944 .com), recounts the whole story by means of models, machinery and movies. A huge picture window runs the length of the museum, enabling you to look straight out to where the bulky remains of the harbour, whose sheer scale is impossible to appreciate at this distance, make a strange intrusion on the beach and shallow sea bed (the other one, slightly further west on Omaha Beach, was destroyed by a ferocious storm within a few weeks). Note that the museum can be very crowded in summer months. There are war memorials throughout Arromanches, and statues of Jesus and Mary high up on the cliffs above the invasion site.

Nonetheless, Arromanches somehow manages to be quite a cheerful place to stay, with a lively pedestrian street of **bars** and **brasseries**, and a long expanse of sand where you can rent windsurfing boards. The spacious three-star municipal **campsite** is 200m back from the seafront (ⓣ 02.31.22.36.78; closed Nov–March). *La Marine*, at 2 quai Canada (ⓣ 02.31.22.34.19, ⓦ www .hotel-de-la-marine.fr; open Feb 11 to Nov 11; ❹–❺), is a smart but slightly pricy **hotel**, with large, relatively modern en-suite bedrooms and an excellent sea-view restaurant serving fishy menus from €22. The half-board option (from €70 per person) increases value for money considerably. For a more informal dining experience, rue M. Joffre is lined with seafood restaurants, including the relaxed *Bistro d'Arromanches* at number 23 (ⓣ 02.31.22.31.32), which serves up generous portions of *moules frites*.

Coleville-sur-Mer

This tiny seaside town's main attraction for visitors is the vast **Normandy American Cemetery and Memorial**, perched on a grassy clifftop above the expanse of Omaha beach, a stretch of sand so secluded and beautiful that it is impossible to imagine the events that took place here. In addition to the cemetery described on p.333, the site is also home to an impressive visitor centre (daily 9am–6pm; free; ⓦ www.abmc.gov), a modern, high-tech construction which features clear explanations of the events of 1944 and the American role in them. The multimedia displays are often touching, many focusing on the personal angle by highlighting the stories of both casualties and survivors. Particularly haunting is the corridor which speaks the names of all those whose lives were lost on French soil. Among the resources available at the centre is a computer search facility which enables visitors to locate graves by name.

Bayeux and around

BAYEUX, with its perfectly preserved medieval ensemble, magnificent cathedral and world-famous tapestry, is 23km west of Caen – a mere twenty-minute train ride. It's a smaller and much more intimate place, and, despite the large crowds of summer tourists, an enjoyable place to visit.

Arrival and information

The **gare SNCF** is fifteen-minutes' walk south of the town centre, just outside the ring road, while the **gare routière** is on the north side of place St-Patrice. For information on local **buses**, contact BusVerts du Calvados (☏08.10.21.42.14, Ⓦwww.busverts.fr), whose services stop at both the *gare SNCF* and the *gare routière*. Travellers without cars who plan to visit the landing beaches and/or the war cemeteries are better advised to join a **minibus trip** with a local operator (see p.331 for details). Bayeux's **tourist office** stands in the centre of town, on the arched Pont St-Jean (Jan–March & Nov–Dec Mon–Sat 9.30am–12.30pm & 2–5.30pm; April–May & Sept–Oct daily 9.30am–12.30pm & 2–6pm; June–Aug Mon–Sat 9am–7pm, Sun 9am–1pm & 2–6pm; ☏02.31.51.28.28, Ⓦwww .bayeux-bessin-tourism.com). Internet access is available at *Un p'tit bout de Normandie*, opposite the tourist office at 6 rue Saint Jean (☏02.31.51.74.74).

Accommodation

As one of Normandy's most important tourist destinations, Bayeux is well equipped with **accommodation**. However, hotels here tend to be more expensive than elsewhere in Normandy. There's a large three-star **campsite** on boulevard d'Eindhoven (☏02.31.92.08.43; open April–Oct), on the northern ring road (RN13) near the river.

D'Argouges 21 rue St-Patrice ☏02.31.92.88.86, Ⓦwww.hotel-dargouges.com. Quiet, central eighteenth-century building, with an imposing courtyard entered via an archway on the west side of place St-Patrice. Several rooms are rather grand, with magnificent exposed wooden beams; all are decorated in classic period style, as is the wooden-floored breakfast room. Ⓖ

Churchill 14–16 rue St-Jean ☏02.31.21.31.80, Ⓦwww.hotel-churchill.fr. Relatively large, completely renovated 32-room hotel, whose size does not preclude friendly service. Perfectly situated in the heart of the town centre, with free parking directly behind the hotel. Closed mid-Nov to mid-Feb. Ⓖ

Family Home 39 rue du Général-de-Dias ☏02.31.92.15.22. This hostel is conveniently central, in a seventeenth-century house. Prices are a little high – dorm beds cost €18 for members, €20 for non-members, while private doubles are €30 – but rates include breakfast. Communal dinners, served at 7.30pm nightly at a long table, cost €12 per person. They also offer bike hire and can find you a bed in their other property *Les Sablons*, about 1km from the centre, if the *Family Home* is full – which it often is during summer. Ⓞ

De la Gare 26 place de la Gare ☏02.31.92.10.70. Old but perfectly adequate basic hotel, with a simple brasserie, beside the station, on the ring road 15min walk from the cathedral. Ⓞ

Lion d'Or 71 rue St-Jean ☏02.31.92.06.90, Ⓦwww.liondor-bayeux.fr. Grand old coaching inn, dating from 1734 and affiliated to the quiet "Relais du Silence" organization, that's set back behind a courtyard just beyond the pedestrianized section of rue St-Jean. The rooms themselves are brighter and newer than the exterior suggests. Closed mid-Dec to late Jan. Menus from €26. Ⓖ

Reine Mathilde 23 rue Larcher ☏02.31.92.08.13, Ⓦwww.hotel-reinemathilde.com. Simple but well-equipped rooms, next to the canal, between the tapestry and the cathedral. A full refurbishment is planned for winter 2008. Good value. The downstairs brasserie, *Le Guillaume,* is open all day. ❸

Hotel Sainte Croix Place St Patrice 12 rue du marché ☎ 06.08.09.62.69 , ⓦwww .hotel-de-sainte-croix.com. Three large, comfortable B&B rooms in a charming old house next to Bayeux's central square. The abundant breakfasts vary daily. ❹

The Town

Housed in an impressive eighteenth-century seminary on rue de Nesmond, the **Bayeux Tapestry** (daily: mid-March to April & Sept–Oct 9am–6.30pm; May–Aug 9am–7pm; Nov to mid-March 9.30am–12.30pm & 2–6pm; last admission 45 minutes before closing; €7.70) – also known to the French as the Tapisserie de la Reine Mathilde – is a seventy-metre strip of embroidered linen that recounts the story of the Norman conquest of England. Although created over nine centuries ago, the brilliance of its coloured wools has barely faded, and the tale is enlivened throughout with parallel scenes of medieval life, popular fables and mythical beasts; the skill of its draughtsmanship, and the sheer vigour and detail, are stunning. The work is thought to have been carried out by monks or nuns in England, commissioned by Bishop Odo, William's half-brother, in time for the inauguration of Bayeux cathedral in 1077.

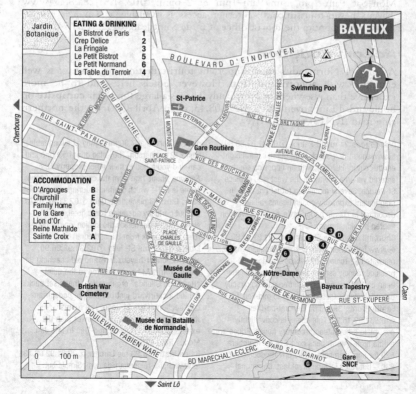

EATING & DRINKING
Le Bistrot de Paris   1
Crep Delice   2
La Fringale   3
Le Petit Bistrot   5
Le Petit Normand   6
La Table du Terroir   4

ACCOMMODATION
D'Argouges   B
Churchill   E
Family Home   C
De la Gare   G
Lion d'Or   D
Reine Mathilde   F
Sainte Croix   A

Visits are well planned and highly atmospheric, although the order of them changes frequently. At the time of writing, visits began with a look at the tapestry itself, with an interesting audio-guided commentary explaining the events depicted so vividly on the canvas. The tapestry looks – and reads – like a modern comic strip. Harold is every inch the villain, with his dastardly little moustache and shifty eyes. He looks extremely self-satisfied as he breaks his oath to accept William as king of England and seizes the throne for himself, but his come-uppance swiftly follows, as William, the noble hero, crosses the Channel and defeats the English armies at Hastings. After this comes an exhibition detailing the theories surrounding the whys and wherefores of the tapestry's creation, and explaining more about its turbulent history, followed by a film – which it would make far more sense to see before the tapestry itself – (shown in English at least once an hour during the summer months) giving some of the historical background and bringing the events of the tapestry to life.

The **Cathédrale Notre-Dame** (daily: Jan–March 8.30am–5pm; April–June & Oct–Dec 8.30am–6pm; July–Sept 8.30am–7pm; free) was the first home of the tapestry and is just a short walk away from its latest resting-place. The original Romanesque plan of the building is still intact, although only the crypt and towers date from the original work of 1077. The crypt is a beauty, its columns graced with frescoes of angels playing trumpets and bagpipes, looking exhausted by their performance for eternity. On the southern side of the cathedral, the **Musée Baron Gerard** on rue Lambert-Forestier displays a large collection of beautifully decorated porcelain and intricate lacework, donated by local families over the centuries to the archbishops of Bayeux (daily: July & Aug 10am–12.30pm & 2–7pm; Sept–June 10am–12.30pm & 2–6pm; €3.50, free with ticket for the tapestry).

Set behind massive guns next to the ring road on the southwest side of town, Bayeux's **Musée de la Bataille de Normandie** (daily: May to mid-Sept 9.30am–6.30pm; mid-Sept to April 10am–12.30pm & 2–6pm; €6.50) is one of the old school of war museums, with its emphasis firmly on hardware rather than humans. By way of contrast, the understated and touching **British War Cemetery** stands immediately across the road (see box, p.333).

Although the **Musée-Mémorial Général de Gaulle**, at 10 rue de Bourbes-neur near place de Gaulle (daily 10am–noon & 2–6pm; €3.50, free with ticket from Musée de la Bataille de Normandie), is aimed squarely at French devotees of the great man, it does make an interesting detour for foreign visitors. The sheer obsessiveness of the displays, which focus on the three separate day-trips De Gaulle made to Bayeux during the course of his long life, somehow illuminates the extent to which he came to epitomize the very essence of a certain kind of Frenchness, which seems scarcely removed from self-parody.

Eating

Some of Bayeux's hotels have good dining rooms, while most **restaurants** are on rue St-Jean and the aptly named rue des Cuisiniers. Many eateries close on Sunday evenings.

Le Bistrot de Paris 3 rue du docteur Guillet ℡02.31.92.00.82. Inexpensive bistro at the west end of place St Patrice, serving good quality French cooking on menus from €17.50.

Crep' Delice 16 rue des Cuisiniers ℡02.31.51.71.16. Cheap but chic crêperie serving an imaginative variety of savoury *galettes* followed by sweet crêpes.

La Fringale 43 rue St-Jean ℡02.31.21.34.40. The nicest of the many pavement restaurants along rue St-Jean, offering lunch menus from €14.50, generous salads and snacks and more formal fish dinners. Closed Wed and mid-Dec to mid-Feb.

Le Petit Bistrot 2 rue Bienvenue ℡ 02.31.51.85.40. Tiny old place opposite the cathedral, where the menus from €25 upwards boast a fine assortment of terrines and foie gras. Closed Sun & Mon.

Le Petit Normand 35 rue Larcher ℡ 02.31.22.88.66. Below the cathedral, offering

good traditional cooking, with seafood specialities and local cider. Lunch menus from €11, dinner from €19. Closed mid-Dec to Jan.

La Table du Terroir 42 rue St-Jean ℡ 02.31.92.05.53. Meat is the order of the day at this small restaurant tucked away behind a butcher's shop, with seating at communal tables. Menus from €16. Closed Sun evening in low season.

Cerisy and Balleroy

Heading southwest from Bayeux towards St-Lô, you pass close to the remarkable Romanesque **Abbaye de Cerisy-la-Forêt** (access to church Easter–Oct daily 9am–6.30pm; €2; guided tours Easter–Sept daily 10.30am–12.30pm & 2.30–6.30pm; Oct Sat & Sun 10.30am–noon & 2.30–6pm; €4), halfway along the D572 and 5km to the north of it. Its triple tiers of windows and arches and the delicate workmanship of its nave and choir are testimony to the breathtaking skills of medieval Norman masons.

No less notable is the **Château de Balleroy** (château and museum mid-March to mid-Oct daily 10am–6pm; mid-Oct to mid-March daily 10am–noon & 2–5pm; ⓦ www.chateau-balleroy.com; château €6.50, museum €4.50, both €8), 3km southeast of the same junction, where you switch to an era when architects ruled over craftsmen. The main street of the village leads straight to the brick-and-stone château, a masterpiece of François Mansart, the celebrated seventeenth-century architect, which stands like a faultlessly reasoned and dogmatic argument for the power of its owners and their class. It belongs to the family of the late American press magnate Malcolm Forbes, owner of *Forbes* magazine, keen balloonist and pal of Nixon, Ford and Nancy Reagan. In the former stables is a **hot-air balloon museum** with exhibits detailing the history of ballooning.

The Cotentin Peninsula

Hard against the frontier with Brittany, and cut off from the rest of Normandy by difficult marshy terrain, the **Cotentin Peninsula** has traditionally been seen as something of a backwater, far removed from the French mainstream. It nonetheless makes a surprisingly rewarding goal for travellers, and one that by sea at least is very easily accessible. Regular ferries from both England and Ireland dock at the peninsula's major port, **Cherbourg**, a city turned resolutely seaward. Nearby are a plethora of attractive little villages, such as **Barfleur** and **St-Vaast**, nestled amid the hills to the east, and the handsome landscapes of heather-clad cliffs and stone-wall-divided patchwork fields to be found in La Hague to the west.

For many visitors the Cotentin's long western flank, with its flat beaches, serves primarily as a prelude to **Mont St-Michel**, with hill towns such as **Coutances** and **Avranches** cherishing architectural and historical relics associated with the abbey. Halfway down, however, the walled port of **Granville**, an extremely popular destination with French holiday-makers, is a sort of small-scale mirror-image of Brittany's St-Malo.

Cherbourg

If you are arriving from Britain or Ireland, **CHERBOURG** may well be your port of arrival. Many people head straight out and on, yet the town offers a busy network of pedestrian streets lined with appealing stone facades, the labyrinth of alleyways known as *boëls*, some lively bars, and an impressive maritime museum in a converted Art Deco station. Napoleon inaugurated the transformation of what had been a rather poor, but perfectly situated, natural harbour into a major transatlantic port, by means of massive artificial breakwaters. An equestrian statue commemorates his boast that in Cherbourg he would "recreate the wonders of Egypt"; although there are as yet no pyramids nearer than the Louvre, he succeeded in providing the city with one of the biggest fortified harbours in the world.

Arrival and information

The days of the great transatlantic liners may be over, but cross-Channel ferries still sail into Cherbourg's **gare maritime** (daily 5.30am–11.30pm; ☎02.33.44.20.13), not far east of the town centre. Regular €1.20 shuttle buses connect the terminal with the tourist office and **gare SNCF**.

Cherbourg's **tourist office** is at 2 quai Alexandre III (June Mon–Sat 9am–12.30pm & 2–6.30pm; July & Aug Mon–Sat 9am–6.30pm, Sun 10am–12.30pm;

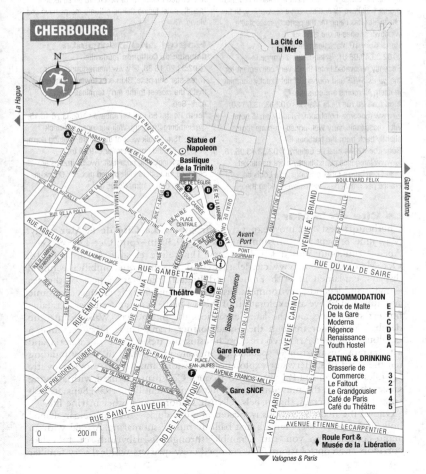

CHERBOURG

La Cité de la Mer

N

La Hague

Gare Maritime

Statue of Napoleon

Basilique de la Trinité

Avant Port

PONT TOURNANT

RUE GAMBETTA

Théâtre

Bassin du Commerce

Gare Routière

PLACE JEAN-JAURES

AVENUE FRANCIS-MILLET

Gare SNCF

0   200 m

AVENUE ETIENNE LECARPENTIER

Roule Fort & Musée de la Libération

Valognes & Paris

ACCOMMODATION	
Croix de Malte	E
De la Gare	F
Moderna	C
Régence	D
Renaissance	B
Youth Hostel	A

EATING & DRINKING	
Brasserie de Commerce	3
Le Faitout	2
Le Grandgousier	1
Café de Paris	4
Café du Théâtre	5

Sept–May Mon–Fri 9am–noon & 2–6pm Sat, 9am–12.30pm & 2–6pm; ℡02.33.93.52.02, Ⓦwww.ot-cherbourg-cotentin.fr). The **gare SNCF**, on avenue François-Miller/place Jean-Jaurès, is served by regular trains to Paris, Bayeux and Caen. Tourisme Verney (℡02.33.44.32.22) run buses to Barfleur, Valognes, Coutances, St-Lô, Granville and other destinations from the **gare routière** opposite.

Accommodation

By usual Norman standards, **room rates** in Cherbourg are very reasonable and there's no reason for ferry passengers to avoid spending a night here, though traffic and the lack of parking space can be problematic.

Hotels

Croix de Malte 5 rue des Halles ℡02.33.43.19.16, Ⓦwww.hotelcroixmalte.com. Simple hotel on three upstairs floors, one block back from the harbour and around the corner from the theatre. Clean renovated rooms – all have TV and at least a shower – with the cheapest rates being for the perfectly acceptable, windowless ones in the attic. ❷

De la Gare 10 place Jean-Jaurès ℡02.33.43.06.81, Ⓔluc-fleury@orange.fr. Recently renovated hotel that's very convenient for the *gares SNCF* and *routière*, if not exactly stunning in itself. All rooms are en-suite. ❷

Moderna 28 rue de la Marine ℡02.33.43.05.30, Ⓦwww.moderna-hotel.com. Friendly small hotel with reasonable, very well-priced en-suite rooms, slightly back from the harbour. ❷

Régence 42–44 quai de Caligny ℡02.33.43.05.16, Ⓦwww.laregence.com. Slightly more upmarket than Cherbourg's other offerings, this Logis de France has small, neat rooms overlooking the

harbour. The restaurant downstairs has menus from €19. ❸–❹

Renaissance 4 rue de l'Église ℡02.33.43.23.90, Ⓦwww. hotel-renaissance-cherbourg.com. Large, refurbished rooms, all of which are en suite, in a friendly hotel facing the port. Some rooms have sea views. ❸

Hostel and campsite

Camping de Collignon Tourlaville ℡02.33.20.16.88, Ⓦwww.mairie-tourlaville.fr. Three-star campsite, 3km east towards Barfleur, that's the closest to the ferry terminal. Open April–Sep.

Youth Hostel 55 rue de l'Abbaye ℡02.33.78.15.15, Ⓔcherbourg@fuaj.org. Well-equipped red-brick hostel, 15min walk west of the centre, offering dorm beds for €16.60 (members) or €19.50 (non-members), including breakfast. Two bedrooms are designed for visitors with limited mobility. Check-in 9am–1pm or 6–11pm, closed Jan.

La Cité de la Mer

Cherbourg's best, and most expensive, attraction is **La Cité de la Mer** (daily: May, June & Sept 9.30am–6pm; July & Aug 9.30am–7pm; Oct–Dec & Feb–April 10am–6pm; closed Jan; last entry 1hr before closing; April–Sept €18, Oct–March €15.50; Ⓦwww.citedelamer.com). The museum combines technical displays, explained in both French and English, on every aspect of the sea – myths and legends, environmental issues including climatic change, economic activities and, above all, exploration of the sea bed – with aquariums, a visitable nuclear submarine, and the latest attraction, the interactive "Walking into the depths". You enter through the grand former Transatlantic ferry terminal, a fabulously restored Art Deco treasure, housing the ticket offices, a cafeteria, and a restaurant unsurprisingly specializing in seafood. Displays in a new building tell the story of underwater exploration in history and fiction, moving swiftly via Jules Verne and H.P. Lovecraft to Jacques Cousteau, pictured with a diving saucer shaped, as the museum claims, "like a giant lentil" in 1959. Separate fish tanks hold giant crabs, sharks, eels, jellyfish, seahorses and other marine life.

One of the main attractions is located in a dry dock – the dark, cigar-shaped hulk of *Le Redoutable*, France's first ballistic missile submarine. Armed with an audio-commentary you can scramble through its labyrinth of tube-like corridors and control rooms. The cramped crew quarters will feel very familiar if you've just shared a cabin on an overnight ferry crossing, while the plush carpeting and moulded chairs in the living room are remarkably reminiscent of Elvis's Graceland.

La Cité de la Mer's new "Walking into the depths" experience is primarily aimed at children, although they do a good job of keeping exactly what it entails under wraps. Entry is by timed admission, and once inside, visitors are divided into teams; make sure to ask staff for a headset with an English commentary. Then you are ushered into a showing of an over-long film which explains your "mission": to help an underwater explorer in his latest expedition. This is followed by some rather silly "training" exercises, and a ride in a submarine simulator. Although the whole experience is pretty long (approximately 45 minutes), the final "surprise" is undeniably amusing.

The Town

If you're waiting for a boat, the best way to kill time is to settle into a café or restaurant or do some last-minute shopping. Try the excellent Thursday **market**, held on and off rue des Halles, near the majestic theatre with its *belle-époque* facade, or the tempting array of small shops and boutiques clustered round the place Centrale – including a place to buy the city's most famous product, the genuine **Cherbourg umbrella**, at 30 rue des Portes.

As for walking off lunch, the only area in the centre that really encourages a ramble is over by the **Basilique de la Trinité**, worth a quick look inside for its English alabaster decorations dating from the Hundred Years War, and the former town **beach**, now grassed over to form the "Plage Verte". Over to the south, you could alternatively climb up to **Roule Fort** for an impressive view of the whole port. The fort itself contains a **Musée de la Libération** (June–Sept Mon & Sun 2–6pm; Tues–Sat 10am–noon & 2–6pm; Oct–May Wed–Sun 2–6pm; €3), with the usual dry maps and diagrams but plenty of contemporary newsreel – much of it, for once, in English – commemorating the period in 1944 when Cherbourg was briefly the busiest port in the world.

Eating

Restaurants in Cherbourg divide readily into the glass-fronted seafood places along the quai de Caligny, each with its "copious" *assiette de fruits de mer*, and the more varied, less expensive little places tucked away in the pedestrianized streets and alleyways of the old town. This is also where you'll find some animated **bars**, especially along rue de l'Union.

Le Commerce 42 rue François-la-Vieille ⊕02.33.53.18.20. If you're tired of white table-cloths and over-attentive service, this central brasserie, larger than it looks from the outside, serves huge portions of good food from 11am until late, with cheap menus from €13 and plenty of à la carte options. Closed Sun.
Le Faitout 25 rue Tour-Carrée ⊕02.33.04.25.04. Shopping-district restaurant that offers traditional French cuisine, including bowls of mussels, prepared with celery, apples and the like. Most dishes are à la carte with meat and fish dishes priced around €10–13. Closed Sat lunch, Sun evening & Mon.
Le Grandgousier 21 rue de l'Abbaye ⊕02.33.53.19.43. Formal, definitive French fish restaurant, worth the walk to its unprepossessing location at the west end of town. Menus start at €16,

but this is a place to expect to spend a lot and dine well, with lobster, for example, featuring on the €38 option. Closed Sun evening & Mon in low season.
Café de Paris 40 quai de Caligny ⊕02.33.43.12.36. Work your way up through the ranks of *assiettes de fruits de mer*, from the €18.50 *Matelot* to the *Amiral* at €110 for two; there's also a selection of menus from €21, featuring a few meat dishes along with the predominately fishy selection. Closed Sun evening, plus Mon lunch in low season.
Café du Théâtre 8 place de Gaulle ⊕02.33.43.01.49. Attractive setup adjoining the theatre, with a café on the ground floor and a full-scale brasserie upstairs. Popular with locals. The varied menus, from €14, offer more than just seafood. Closed Sun.

Around the Cotentin

Once you get away from the industrial harbour city of Cherbourg, the largely rural Cotentin Peninsula is geographically an area of transition. Little ports such as **Barfleur** on the indented northern headland presage the rocky Breton coast, while inland the meadows resemble the farmlands of the Bocage and the Bessin. **La Hague** is a little-explored gem, where all manner of activities, from sailing and diving to riding and rambling, can be practised. In any case, the temptation to race south towards Mont St-Michel is likely to be thwarted by slow traffic on the peninsula's narrow roads, though the Cherbourg–St-Lô route is now mostly four-lane, so you might as well stop off in your pick of the towns and resorts that line its western shore, such as **Granville** and **Avranches**.

Barfleur

The pleasant little harbour village of **BARFLEUR**, 25km east of Cherbourg, was the biggest port in Normandy seven centuries ago. The population has since dwindled, and fortunes have diminished – most recently through the invasion of a strain of plankton that poisoned the mussels. It's now a surprisingly low-key place, where the sweeping crescent of the picturesque grey-granite quayside sees little tourist activity.

Barfleur has two fine **hotels**. *Le Conquérant* stands a short distance back from the sea at 16–18 rue St-Thomas-à-Becket (℡02.33.54.00.82 ⓦwww .hotel-leconquerant.com; closed mid-Nov to mid-March; ❹); behind its stern stone facade lies a gorgeous, rambling and very welcoming old town house, where the nicest rooms face onto a lovely garden, and there's a summer-only crêperie. *Le Moderne* is tucked away south of the main road at 1 place de Gaulle (℡02.33.23.12.44, ⓦwww.hotel-restaurant-moderne-barfleur.com; closed Tues evening & Wed mid-Sept to mid-July, plus all Jan to mid-Feb; ❸); some of the rooms are very inexpensive, while the restaurant is superb, with menus from €19. A nice, albeit basic **campsite** stands a couple of kilometres north of town in Le Crabec. *La Ferme du Bord du Mer* (℡02.33.54.01.77), true to its name, is a farm beside the sea, where grassy meadows hold donkeys as well as tents and caravans, and there's a scruffy flat beach.

Surprisingly, no hotels, and barely any bars or other businesses face the harbour itself, but there is another excellent restaurant on the waterfront, the friendly and very charming *Comptoir de la Presqu'île*, 30 quai Henri-Chardon (℡02.33.20.37.51), which as well as its outdoor tables has an upstairs dining room with good views of the port. The cuisine is all à la carte and dominated by fish, with a deliciously simple whole grilled bream costing the amazing price of €10.50.

St-Vaast

Pretty **ST-VAAST-LA-HOUGUE**, 11km south of Barfleur, is more of a resort, with lots of tiny Channel-crossing yachts moored in the bay where Edward III landed on his way to Crécy and a string of fortifications from Vauban's time. The *Hôtel de France et des Fuchsias*, just back from the sea at 18 rue du Maréchal-Foch (℡02.33.54.42.26, ⓦwww.france-fuchsias.com; closed Jan–Feb, plus Mon in winter; ❸–❼), has splendid gardens and an excellent restaurant. It makes for an ideal stopover for ferry passengers – in fact both it and the annexe at the end of the garden are packed throughout the season with British visitors.

Utah Beach

The westernmost of the main Invasion Beaches, **Utah Beach** stretches for approximately thirty kilometres south from St-Vaast. From 6.30am onwards on

D-Day, 23,000 men and 1700 vehicles landed here. A minor coast road, the D241, traces the edge of the dunes and enables visitors to follow the course of the fighting, though in truth there's precious little to see these days. Ships deliberately sunk to create artificial breakwaters are still visible at low tide, while markers along the seafront commemorate individual fallen heroes.

Two museums now tell the story: the **Mémorial de la Liberté** in **QUINÉVILLE** (April to mid-Nov daily 10am–7pm; Ⓦwww.memorial -quineville.com; €6), which focuses on everyday life for the people of Normandy under Nazi occupation, and the much more comprehensive **Musée du Débarquement d'Utah-Beach** in **STE-MARIE-DU-MONT** (Feb, March & first two weeks of Nov daily 10am–12.30pm & 2–5.30pm; April, May & Oct daily 10am–6pm; June–Sept daily 9.30am–7pm; mid-Nov to Dec Sat, Sun & holidays 10am–12.30pm & 2–5.30pm; closed Jan; Ⓦwww.utah-beach.com; €5.50), which explains the operations in exhaustive detail, with huge sea-view windows to lend immediacy to the copious models, maps, films and diagrams.

La Hague

If you go west from Cherbourg to **La Hague**, the northern tip of the peninsula, you'll find wild and isolated countryside where you can lean into the wind, watch waves smashing against rocks in secluded inlets or sunbathe amid a profusion of wild flowers, while a whole range of activities are on offer. The area's main **tourist office**, at 45 rue Jallot in the village of Beaumont-Hague, 14km out of Cherbourg on the D901, can supply the details (June Mon–Sat 9am–12.30pm & 2–6.30pm; July–Aug Mon–Sat 9am–6.30pm, Sun 10am–12.30pm; Sept–May Mon–Sat 9am–12.30pm & 2–6pm; ℡02.33.52.74.94, Ⓦwww.lahague.org).

Attractions on the cape include some of the highest cliffs in Europe at the **Nez de Jobourg**, reachable by the Sentier des Douaniers, a well-marked ramblers' path that hugs the coast for 43km between Urville-Nacqueville, on the north coast, to the dunes at Biville, in the far south of the region. Crêperies, bars and little restaurants dot the headland, as do *gîtes-rurales* (information also from the tourist office), many in the area's handsome, immaculately kept stone cottages, with their slate roofs and pretty gardens.

Art and poetry fans might like to visit the houses where Jean-François Millet and Jacques Prévert were born and died respectively. The painter of poster-favourite *Les Glaneuses* was born at Hameau Gruchy (daily: April & May 2–6pm; June & Sept 11am–6pm; July & Aug 11am–7pm; €4), at **GRÉVILLE-HAGUE**, where temporary exhibitions are held, while the great twentieth-century writer's workshop and garden at the home he retired to in the 1970s can be visited at Le Val, **OMONVILLE-LA-PETITE** (same opening hours and fee as the Millet house). Two other interests, star-gazing and botany, are catered for at the Ludiver planetarium at the village of **TONNEVILLE**, in the east of the promontory (July & Aug daily 11am–6.30pm; Sept–June Mon–Fri & Sun 2–6pm; closed Sat & all Jan; see website for schedules of planetarium shows; tour €3.60, tour and show €7.25; Ⓦwww.ludiver.com), and the tropical-looking garden at the Château de Vauville, in the especially picturesque village of **VAUVILLE** to the west (March & April Sat & Sun 2–6pm; May–Sept daily 2–6pm; Oct Tue & Fri–Sun 2–6pm; €6 (tour optional); Ⓦwww.jardin-vauville.fr), is famed for its huge palm-grove, a sign of the area's mild microclimate.

South of La Hague a great curve of sand – some of it military training ground – takes the land's edge to **Flamanville** and another nuclear installation. But the next two sweeps of beach down to **Carteret**, with sand dunes like mini-mountain ranges, are probably the best beaches in Normandy: there are no resorts, no hotels and just two campsites – at **Le Rozel** (*Le Ranch*; ☎02.33.10.07.10, ⓦ www.camping-leranch.com; open April–Sep) and **Surtain-ville** (*Les Mielles*; ☎02.33.04.31.04, ⓦ www.surtainville.new.fr).

Coutances

The old hill town of **COUTANCES**, 65km south of Cherbourg, confined by its site to just one main street, has on its summit a landmark for all the surrounding countryside, the **Cathédrale de Notre-Dame**. Essentially Gothic, it is still very Norman in its unconventional blending of architectural traditions, and the octagonal lantern crowning the crossing in the nave is nothing short of divinely inspired. The son et lumière on Sunday evenings and throughout the summer is for once a true complement to the light stone building. Also illuminated on summer nights (and left open) are the formal fountained **public gardens**.

Coutances' **gare SNCF**, about 1.5km southeast of the town centre (at the bottom of the hill), also serves as the stop for **buses** heading north and south. The local **tourist office** is housed behind the Hôtel de Ville in place Georges-Léclerc (July & Aug Mon–Fri 9.30am–6pm, Sat 10am–noon & 2–6pm, Sun 10am–1pm; Sept–June Mon–Wed & Fri 9.30am–12.30pm & 2–6pm, Thurs 9.30am–6pm, Sat 10am–12.30pm & 2–5pm; ☎02.33.19.08.10, ⓦ www.ville-coutances.fr). Central Coutances is very short of **hotels**. In the cathedral square, the *Hôtel du Parvis* (☎02.33.45.13.55; ❸; restaurant closed Sun), has unexciting but adequate rooms, above a reasonable brasserie. A more comfortable alternative is the large *Cositel* (☎02.33.19.15.00, ⓦ www .hotelcositel.com; ❹), halfway up the hill west of town that's climbed by the D44 towards Agon. It stands next to an excellent year-round municipal **campsite**, *Les Vignettes* (☎02.33.45.43.13).

Granville

From Coutances, the D971 runs down to the coast to **GRANVILLE**, the Norman equivalent of Brittany's St-Malo, with a history of piracy and the severe citadel of the **haute ville** guarding the approaches to the bay of Mont St-Michel. Thanks in part to the long beach that stretches away north of town, and disappears almost completely at low tide, it's the most lively town and most popular resort in the area. However, with its nightmarish traffic and hordes of tourists milling around in summer in the vain hope of finding some way of amusing themselves, it doesn't quite match the appeal of its Breton rival.

The great difference between Granville and St-Malo is that in Granville the fortified citadel contains little of interest, just three or four long, narrow, parallel streets of forbidding grey-granite eighteenth-century houses, although the views up and down the coast, across to Mont St-Michel and out to the Îles Chausey, whose granite was quarried for the Mont St-Michel buildings, are dramatic. In pride of place at the inland end of the haute ville is the **Musée d'Art Moderne Richard Anacréon** (April–Sept daily except Mon 11am–6pm; Oct–March Wed–Sun 2–6pm; €2.60), housing art accumulated by a Parisian bookseller from 1940 onwards. Filled with sketches and autographs from the likes of Jean Cocteau and André Derain, it's not all that compelling, but the gallery itself is impressive, and hosts interesting temporary exhibitions.

The **tourist office** is below the citadel at 4 cours Jonville (July & Aug Mon–Sat 9am–1pm & 2–7pm, Sun 10am–1pm; Sept–June Mon–Sat 9am–noon & 2–6pm; ☎02.33.91.30.03, ⓦ www.ville-granville.fr). Trains between Paris and Cherbourg arrive well to the east at the **gare SNCF** on avenue Maréchal-Leclerc, which also serves as the **gare routière**. **Ferries** run from Granville to the Channel Islands and the Îles Chausey.

With so many visitors in summer, it's well worth booking **accommodation** in advance. Most of it is concentrated in the new town that sprawls below the citadel, either beneath the walls on the seaward side, or near the station. The *Michelet*, 5 rue Jules-Michelet (☎02.33.50.06.55, ⓦwww.hotel-michelet -granville.com; ❷), offers good value, comfortable rooms, while the *Des Bains*, closer to the tourist office at 19 rue G-Clemenceau (☎02.33.50.17.31; ❸), has a reasonable restaurant. An option nearer the station is the *Terminus* at 5 place de la Gare (☎02.33.50.02.05, ⓦwww.hotel-granville-france.com; ❷). The modern, oceanfront *Centre Régional de Nautisme* (☎02.33.91.22.62, ⓦwww .crng.fr; closed Sat & Sun Nov–Feb; €12.50 per dorm bed), a kilometre south of the station in the town centre, serves as Granville's **hostel**.

Where Granville really does excel is in its waterfront **restaurants**, below the citadel walls, though be warned that the views here are of a commercial port rather than a delightful harbour. The best are the 🍴 *Restaurant du Port*, 19 rue du Port (☎02.33.50.00.55; closed Sun evening. plus Mon in low season), with its mouth-watering assortment of very fishy menus, and the *Phare*, nearby at no. 11 (☎02.33.50.12.94; closed Tues & Wed), which has the standard mussels and *panaché de poissons* on its €19 menu and a superb *assiette des fruits de mer* on the €29.50 equivalent. Up in the old town, *L'Échauguette*, 24 rue St-Jean (☎02.33.50.51.87), serves good crêpes and simple meals, cooked over an open fire.

Avranches

AVRANCHES is the nearest large town to Mont St-Michel, and it has always had close connections with the abbey. The Mont's original church was founded by a bishop of Avranches, spurred on by the Archangel Michael, who suppos-edly became so impatient with the lack of progress that he prodded a hole in the bishop's skull – still to be seen in Avranches' **St-Gervais basilica**. Robert of Torigny, a subsequent abbot of St-Michel, played host in the town on several occasions to Henry II of England, the most memorable being when Henry was obliged, barefoot and bareheaded, to do public penance for the murder of Thomas Becket, on May 22, 1172.

A more vivid evocation of the area's medieval splendours comes from the illuminated manuscripts, mostly created on the Mont, on display in a state-of-the-art new museum in the place d'Estouteville, the **Scriptorial d'Avranches** (Feb–April & Oct–Dec Tues–Fri 10am–12.30pm & 2–5pm, Sat & Sun 10am–12.30pm & 2–6pm; May, June & Sept daily except Mon 10am–6pm; July & Aug daily 10–7pm; closed Jan; €7). Additional exhibits trace the history of Avranches, and bring the story up to date by covering modern book-production techniques.

The **gare SNCF** is about a mile downhill from the town centre. In high summer, one bus per day runs to Mont St-Michel from the **tourist office** on place Général-de-Gaulle (July & Aug Mon–Sat 9.30am–12.30pm & 2–7pm, Sun 9.30am–12.30pm & 2–6pm; Sept–June Mon–Fri 9.30am–12.30pm & 2–6pm, Sat 10am–12.30pm & 2–6pm; ☎02.33.58.00.22, ⓦwww.ot-avranches .com). The nicest **hotel** has to be the gloriously old-fashioned *Croix d'Or*, near the Patton monument at 83 rue de la Constitution (☎02.33.58.04.88, ⓦwww .hoteldelacroixdor.fr; closed Jan, plus Sun evening in winter; ❹), which boasts beautiful hydrangea-filled gardens and the best **restaurant** in town. Reasonable alternatives include *Le Jardin des Plantes*, across town at 10 place Carnot (☎02.33.58.03.68; ⓦwww.le-jardin-des-plantes.fr; ❸), where the restaurant is more basic but still good value.

Mont St-Michel

The island of **MONT ST-MICHEL** was once known as the "Mount in Peril from the Sea", as many pilgrims in medieval times drowned or were sucked under by quicksand while trying to cross the bay to the eighty-metre-high rocky outcrop. The Archangel Michael was its vigorous protector, the most militant spirit of the Church Militant, with a marked tendency to leap from rock to rock in titanic struggles against Paganism and Evil. The abbey dates back to the eighth century, when the archangel supposedly appeared to a bishop of Avranches, Aubert, who duly founded a monastery on the island poking out of the Baie du Mont St-Michel. Since the eleventh century – when work on the sturdy church at the peak commenced – new buildings have been grafted onto the island to produce a fortified hotchpotch of Romanesque and Gothic buildings clambering to the pinnacle of the graceful church, forming probably the most recognizable silhouette in France after the Eiffel Tower.

Although it was such a prominent **religious community**, there were never more than forty monks resident on the Mont up to the time of the Revolution, when it was converted into a prison. In 1966, exactly a thousand years after Duke Richard the First originally brought the order to the Mont, the Benedictines were invited to return, but they departed again in 2001, after finding that the present-day island does not exactly lend itself to a life of quiet contemplation. In their place, a dozen nuns and monks from the Monastic Fraternity of Jerusalem now maintain a presence.

For many years, the Mont has not, strictly speaking, been an island – the causeway (*digue*) that leads to it is never submerged, and is continuing to silt up to either side. Current plans envisage that the causeway will soon be cut away and replaced by a pedestrian bridge, which should not only make tourist numbers easier to control but also enable the sea to wash away much of the accumulated silt. For the latest news on the project, contact Ⓦwww.projetmontsaintmichel.org.

Visiting Mont St-Michel

Access to the island of Mont St-Michel is free and unrestricted, although there's a €4 fee to park on either the causeway or the sands below it (which are submerged by the tides). If you're visiting by car in summer, you might prefer to park on the mainland well short of the Mont, both to enjoy the walk across the causeway and to avoid the dense traffic jams.

Between May and August, the **abbey** is open daily from 9am to 7pm, with last admission at 6pm; from September to April, it's open daily from 9.30am until 6pm, last admission at 5pm. It's closed on Jan 1, May 1 and Dec 25. Owing to the volume of visitors the abbey receives, be prepared to queue. The same **admission fee** (adults €8.50, ages 18–25 €5, under-18s free) is charged whether you choose to wander the generally accessible areas on your own, or to join an expert-led **guided tour**. The tours last 45 minutes between mid-June and mid-Sept, and a full hour the rest of the year, and are available in French and English year round, as well as other languages in summer; the daily schedule for each language is displayed at the entrance to the abbey and at the tourist office. Audio guides are available for €4.

In some recent years, the Mont has stayed open **after hours** during July and August, both in the early evening when visitors can stroll freely in the gardens, and at night when the abbey itself has reopened for musical and video installations. Whether it does so in any particular year seems to be unpredictable, however; contact the tourist office or access Ⓦwww.monum.fr for the latest information.

▲ Mont St-Michel

The abbey

The **abbey**, an architectural ensemble incorporating the high-spired, archangel-topped church and the magnificent Gothic buildings known since 1228 as the **Merveille** ("The Marvel") – which in turn includes the entire north face, with the cloister, Knights' Hall, Refectory, Guest Hall and cellars – is visible from all around the bay, but it becomes if anything more awe-inspiring the closer you approach. In Maupassant's words:

I reached the huge pile of rocks which bears the little city dominated by the great church. Climbing the steep narrow street, I entered the most wonderful Gothic dwelling ever made for God on this earth, a building as vast as a town, full of low rooms under oppressive ceilings and lofty galleries supported by frail pillars. I entered that gigantic granite jewel, which is as delicate as a piece of lacework, thronged with towers and slender belfries which thrust into the blue sky of day and the black sky of night their strange heads bristling with chimeras, devils, fantastic beasts and monstrous flowers, and which are linked together by carved arches of intricate design.

The Mont's rock comes to a sharp point just below what is now the transept of the **church**, a building where the transition from Romanesque to Gothic is only too evident in the vaulting of the nave. In order to lay out the church's ground plan in the traditional shape of the cross, supporting crypts had to be built up from the surrounding hillside, and in all construction work the Chausey granite has had to be sculpted to match the exact contours of the hill. Space was always limited, and yet the building has grown through the centuries, with an architectural ingenuity that constantly surprises in its geometry – witness the shock of emerging into the light of the cloisters from the sombre Great Hall.

Not surprisingly, the building of the **monastery** was no smooth progression: the original church, choir, nave and tower all had to be replaced after collapsing. The style of decoration has varied, too, along with the architecture. That you now walk through halls of plain grey stone is a reflection of modern taste. In the Middle Ages, the walls of public areas such as the refectory would have been festooned with tapestries and frescoes, while the original coloured tiles of the cloisters have long since been stripped away to reveal bare walls.

The rest of the island

The base of Mont St-Michel rests on a primeval slime of sand and mud. Just above that, you pass through the heavily fortified **Porte du Roi** onto the narrow **Grande Rue**, climbing steadily around the base of the rock and lined with medieval gabled houses and a jumble of overpriced postcard and souvenir shops, maintaining the ancient tradition of parting pilgrims from their money.

The rather dry **Musée Maritime** offers an insight into the island's ties with the sea, while the Archangel Michael manages in just fifteen minutes to lead visitors on a voyage through space and time in the **Archéoscope**, with the full majestic panoply of multimedia mumbo jumbo. Further along the Grande Rue and up the steps towards the abbey church, next door to the eleventh-century **church of St-Pierre**, the absurd **Musée Grévin** contains such edifying specimens as a wax model of a woman drowning in a sea of mud (open Feb to mid-Nov daily 9am–6pm; €15 for all, or €7 each one).

Large crowds gather each day at the **North Tower**, to watch the tide sweep in across the bay. Seagulls wheel away in alarm, and those foolish enough to be wandering too late on the sands have to sprint to safety.

Practicalities

Mont St-Michel has its own **tourist office**, in the lowest gateway (April–June & Sept Mon–Sat 9am–12.30pm & 2–6.30pm, Sun 9am–noon & 2–6pm; July & Aug daily 9am–7pm; Oct–March Mon–Sat 9am–noon & 2–6pm, Sun 10am–noon & 2–5pm; ☎02.33.60.14.30, ⓦwww.ot-montsaintmichel.com). Regular buses connect it with the SNCF stations at Pontorson (see opposite), Rennes and St-Malo.

The island holds a surprising number of **hotels** and **restaurants**, albeit nothing likely enough to cope with the sheer number of visitors. Most are predictably expensive, though virtually all seem to keep a few cheaper rooms. The tourist hordes which descend daily make Mont St Michel a far from relaxing place to lay your head, so a better option is to head for one of the many *chambres d'hôtes* that (ⓦwww.chambresdhotefrance.com or ⓦwww.chambresdhotes.fr) that line the country road that leads from the motorway to the mount; this way you also get a room with a spectacular view. If you have your heart set on staying on the island, note that the most famous hotel is *La Mère Poulard* (☎02.33.89.68.68,

@ www.mere-poulard.com; **❼–❾**), which uses the time-honoured legend of its fluffy omelettes, as enjoyed by Leon Trotsky and Margaret Thatcher (not simultaneously), to justify extortionate charges. Higher up the Mont, room prices fall to more realistic levels. The cheapest option is the *Du Guesclin* (☎ 02.33.60.14.10, @ www.hotelduguesclin.com; closed Nov–March; **❹**), a Logis de France where all the rooms have been reasonably spruced up, and five have sea views; the nicest is the *Hôtel La Croix Blanche* (☎ 02.33.60.14.04; closed mid-Nov to mid-Feb; **❻**), with its small but exquisite rooms; and the *Mouton Blanc* (☎ 02.33.60.14.08, @ www.lemoutonblanc.com; **❺**) falls somewhere in between.

The three-star, 350-pitch *Camping du Mont-St-Michel* (☎ 02.33.60.22.10; open mid-Feb to mid-Nov) is also on the mainland just short of the causeway.

Many visitors to Mont St-Michel choose instead to stay at **PONTORSON**, 6km inland, which has the nearest **gare SNCF**, connected to the Mont by a bus service. The **hotels** here are not especially interesting, but the *Montgomery* is housed in a fine old ivy-covered mansion at 13 rue du Couesnon (☎ 02.33.60.00.09, @ www.hotel-montgomery.com; closed two weeks in Feb & Nov; **❹–❺**), and has fairly appealing rooms and a good restaurant, as does the *Tour Brette*, 8 rue du Couesnon (☎ 02.33.60.10.69, @ www.latourbrette.fr.st; **❷**; restaurant closed Wed in low season).

Inland Normandy

Seeking out specific highlights is not really the point when you're exploring **inland Normandy**. The pleasure of a visit lies not so much in show-stopping sights or individual towns as in the feel of the landscape – the lush meadows, orchards and forests of the Norman countryside. **Gastronomy** is, of course, a major motivation for coming here. The cheeses, creams, apple and pear brandies and ciders for which the region is famous are at their best in the **Pays d'Auge**, south of Lisieux, and the **Vire Valley** to the west. The **Suisse Normande** is canoeing and rock-climbing country, and there are endless good walks in the stretch along the southern border of the province designated as the **Parc Naturel Régional de Normandie-Maine**. Of the towns, **Conches** is the most charming, **Falaise** has William the Conqueror as a constant fall-back attraction, and **Lisieux** has its religious significance.

South of the Seine

Heading south from the Seine you can follow the River Risle from the estuary just east of Honfleur, or the Eure and its tributaries from upstream of Rouen. Between the two stretches the long featureless **Neubourg Plain**. The lowest major crossing point over the Risle is at **PONT-AUDEMER**, where medieval houses lean out at alarming angles over the crisscrossing roads, rivers and canals. From here, perfect cycling roads lined with timbered farmhouses follow the river south.

Le Bec-Hellouin

The size and tranquillity of the **Abbaye de Bec-Hellouin**, upstream from Pont-Audemer just before Brionne, give a monastic feel to the whole Risle valley. Bells echo across the water and white-robed monks go soberly about their business. From the eleventh century onwards, the abbey was one of the most important centres of intellectual learning in the Christian world; the philosopher Anselm was abbot here before becoming Archbishop of Canterbury in 1093. Owing to the Revolution, most of the monastery buildings are recent – the monks only returned in 1948 – but there are some survivors and appealing clusters of stone ruins, including the fifteenth-century **bell tower of St-Nicholas** and the cloister. Visitors are welcome to wander through the grounds for no charge, though you can also join regular **guided tours** (June–Sept Mon & Wed–Sat 10.30am, 3pm, 4pm & 5pm, Sun & holidays noon, 3pm & 4pm; Oct–May Mon & Wed–Sat 10.30am, 3pm & 4pm, Sun & holidays noon, 3pm & 4pm; €4.60; ⓦwww.abbayedubec.com).

The tiny and rather twee adjacent village of **Bec-Hellouin** is home to **riding stables**, the Centre Equestre du Bec-Hellouin, where horses can be booked by the hour or the day (☎02.32.44.86.31). There are also a couple of **restaurants**. Try the ivy-covered *Canterbury* (☎02.32.44.14.59; closed Sun & Tues eves, Wed & all Feb), which serves regional specialities on menus from €18 up to €38, and the rather cheaper *Restaurant de la Tour* on place Guillaume-le-Conquérant (☎02.32.44.86.15; closed Wed evening & Thurs, plus two weeks in Nov), which has some outdoor tables.

Conches-en-Ouche

Fourteen kilometres east of La Ferrière across the wild and open woodland of the **Forêt de Conches**, standing above the River Rouloir on an abrupt and narrow spur, is **CONCHES-EN-OUCHE**, many a Norman's favourite heartland town. At the highest point, in the middle of a row of medieval houses, is the **church of Ste-Foy**, its windows a stunning sequence of Renaissance stained glass. Behind are the gardens of the **Hôtel de Ville**, where a robust, if anatomically odd stone boar gazes proudly out over a spectacular view. Next to that, you can scramble up the slippery steps of the ruined twelfth-century **castle**. Conches is given a certain edge over other towns with historic relics by the pieces of modern sculpture that seem to lie around every other corner.

The town's **tourist office** is close to the castle, 200m south of the church in place Aristide-Briand (July & Aug Tues–Sat 10am–12.30pm & 2–6pm, Sun 10am–noon; Sept–June Tues–Sat 10am–12.30pm & 2–6pm; ☎02.32.30.76.42, ⓦwww.conches-en-ouche.fr), and hires out mountain bikes. The best **accommodation** option is *Le Cygne*, a Logis de France at 2 rue Paul-Guilbaud at the north end of town (☎02.32.30.20.60, ⓦwww.lecygne.fr; ❷; restaurant closed Sun evening & Mon), which has a good restaurant where menus start at €18. There's also a two-star municipal **campsite**, *La Forêt* (☎02.32.30.22.49; open April-Sep), while on Thursday the whole town is taken up by a **market**.

Lisieux and the Pays d'Auge

The rolling hills and green twisting valleys of the **Pays d'Auge** stretch south of **Lisieux** and are scattered with magnificent manor houses. The pastures here are the lushest in the province, their produce the world-famous cheeses of

Camembert, Livarot and Pont L'Evêque. They are intermingled with hectares of orchards, which yield the best of Norman ciders, both apple and pear (*poiré*), as well as Calvados apple brandy.

Lisieux

LISIEUX, 35 minutes by train from Caen, is the main town of the Pays d'Auge, and the large street **market** on Wednesday and Saturday is a good place to get acquainted with its cheeses and ciders. Most people, however, come to Lisieux in pilgrimage. St Thérèse, the most popular French spiritual figure of the last hundred years, was born here in 1873 and lived just 24 years. Passivity, self-effacement and a self-denial that verged on masochism were her trademarks, and she is honoured by the gaudy and gigantic **Basilique de Ste-Thérèse**, completed in 1954 on a slope to the southwest of the town centre. The huge modern mosaics that decorate the nave are undeniably impressive, but the overall impression is of a quasi-medieval hagiography. The faithful can ride on a white, flag-bedecked fairground train around the holiest sites, which include the infinitely restrained and sober **Cathédrale St-Pierre**.

Lisieux's **tourist office**, 11 rue d'Alençon, is the best place to gather information on the rural areas further inland (June–Sept Mon–Sat 8.30am–6.30pm, Sun 10am–12.30pm & 2–5pm; Oct–May Mon–Sat 8.30am–noon & 1.30–6pm; ☎02.31.48.18.10, ⓦwww.lisieux-tourisme.com). The quantity of pilgrims means the town is full of good-value **hotels**, such as the *Terrasse*, near the basilica at 25 avenue Ste-Thérèse (☎02.31.62.17.65; ❷; closed mid-Jan to mid-Feb, plus Mon in winter), and the smart, central *Azur Hôtel*, just north of the Église St-Jacques at 15 rue au Char (☎02.31.62.09.14, ⓦwww.azur-hotel .com; ❹; closed mid-Dec to mid-Jan). There's also a large two-star **campsite**, *de la Vallée* (☎02.31.62.00.40; open early April to Sept), but campers would probably be better off somewhere more rural, such as Livarot or Orbec.

Into the Pays d'Auge

For really good, solid Norman cooking this is the perfect area to look out for *fermes auberges*, working farms which welcome paying visitors to share their meals. Local tourist offices can provide copious lists of these and of local producers from whom you can buy your cheese and booze.

Crèvecoeur-en-Auge

While it's always fun to stumble across dilapidated old half-timbered farms in the Pays d'Auge, here and there it's possible to visit prime specimens that have been beautifully restored and preserved. An especially fine assortment has been gathered just west of **CRÈVECOEUR-EN-AUGE**, 17km west of Lisieux on the N14, in the grounds of a small twelfth-century **château** (April–June & Sept daily 11am–6pm; July & Aug daily 11am–7pm; Oct Sun 2–6pm; ⓦwww .chateau-de-crevecoeur.com; €5). Around the pristine lawns of a re-created village green, circled by a shallow moat, this photogenic group of golden adobe structures includes a manor house, a barn and a tall thin dovecote that date from the fifteenth century. The little twelfth-century chapel that adjoins the château holds a fascinating exhibition on the music and instruments of the Middle Ages, although almost all the explanatory captions are in French.

Beuvron-en-Auge

By far the prettiest of the Pays d'Auge villages is **BEUVRON-EN-AUGE**, 7km north of the N13 halfway between Lisieux and Caen. It consists of an oval central *place*, ringed by a glorious ensemble of multicoloured half-timbered houses, including the yellow-and-brown sixteenth-century Vieux Manoir. The very centre of the square is taken up by the *Pavé d'Auge* restaurant (☎02.31.79.26.71; closed Mon, plus Tues Sept–June), where regularly changing menus start at €29.50.

Orbec and Livarot

The town of **ORBEC**, 19km southeast of Lisieux, epitomizes the simple pleasures of the Pays d'Auge. Along the rue Grande, you'll see several houses in which the gaps between the timbers are filled with intricate patterns of coloured tiles and bricks. Debussy composed *Jardin sous la Pluie* in one of these, and the oldest and prettiest of the lot – a tanner's house dating back to 1568, known as the **Vieux Manoir** – holds a museum of local history. On the whole, though, it's more fun just to walk down behind the church to the river, and its watermill and paddocks.

The centre of the cheese country is the old town of **LIVAROT**, with the appealing **hotel** and restaurant *Du Vivier* in its heart (☎02.31.32.04.10; ❸; Oct–May, restaurant closed Fri and Sun evening & Mon lunch). The **Fromagerie Graindorge,** on the route de Vimoutiers (Mon–Fri 9.30am–noon & 1.30–5pm, Sat 9.30am–noon; free), gives you a closer look at how Livarot's eponymous cheese is made, with free samples doled out at the end of each visit. For superb views of the valley, climb up to the thirteenth-century church of **St-Michel de Livet**, just above the town.

Vimoutiers and Camembert

The pretty little town of **VIMOUTIERS**, due south of Livarot, is home to the **Musée du Camembert**, at 10 avenue Général-de-Gaulle (April–Sept Mon 2–6pm, Tues–Sat 9am–noon & 2–6pm, Sun 10am–noon & 2–6pm; Nov–March Mon 2–5.30pm, Tues–Sat 10am–noon & 2.30–6pm; €3), a rather homespun affair which explains the production process of the famous cheese, with tastings at the end.

A statue in the town's main square honours Marie Harel, who, at the nearby village of Camembert, developed the original cheese early in the nineteenth century, promoting it with a skilful campaign that included sending free samples to Napoleon. Marie is confronted across the main street by what might be called the statue of the Unknown Cow.

Vimoutiers is the venue of a **market** on Monday afternoons. The **tourist office**, close to the cheese museum at 21 place de Mackau (April–Oct Mon 2–6pm, Tue–Sat 9.30am–12.30 pm & 2–6pm, Sun 10am–12.30pm; Nov–March Mon 2–5.30pm, Tue–Sat 10am–12.30pm & 2–5.30pm, closed Sun; ☎02.33.39.30.29, ⓦwww.mairie-vimoutiers.fr), has plenty of information on local cheese-related attractions. Of its small number of **hotels**, the central *Soleil d'Or*, 3 rue de Chatelet (☎02.33.39.07.15; ❷; hotel closed two weeks in Feb & two weeks in Oct; restaurant closed Fri & Sun evening), has decent rooms and good set menus from €18.

A short way south of Vimoutiers, en route to Camembert, the beautifully sited lake known as the **Escale du Vitou** offers everything you need for windsurfing, swimming and horseriding, as well as its own comfortable, rural **hotel**, *L'Escale du Vitou* (☎02.33.39.12.04, ⓦgite-normandie.ifrance.com/hotel.htm; ❷). There's also a clean and very cheap **campsite** nearby on boulevard Docteur-Dentu, the two-star *La Campière* (☎02.33.39.18.86; closed Nov–Feb).

CAMEMBERT itself, 3km southeast of Vimoutiers, is tiny, hilly and very rural, home to far more cows than humans. On one side of its little central square, the largest camembert producers, **La Ferme Président**, run their own, surprisingly amateurish, museum (April–Oct Mon 2–6pm, Tue–Sat 9am–noon & 2–6pm, Sun 10am–noon & 2.30–6pm; Ⓦwww.fermepresident.com; €3), which whirls through the history of the cheese and the methods, both traditional and modern, used to make it. Some of the multimedia elements are moderately interesting, but continual mentions of the Président brand and EU regulations give it a rather corporate feel. Afterwards comes a cheese tasting at **Le Maison du Camembert** on the other side of the square, which also serves as an information centre and café (Feb–April & Sept Wed–Sun 10am–6pm; May–Aug daily 10am–6pm; Ⓦwww.maisonducamembert.com).

The **Fromagerie Durand**, below Camembert on the road towards Trun (Ferme de la Hérronière; daily except Sun 9.30am–12.30pm & 3–6pm; free) offers an alternative experience: a visit to the last farm in the region which produces camembert made the traditional way, using unpasteurized milk. Visitors can watch an interesting film which explains – you've guessed it – the cheese production process, plus a little about its producers, before heading outside to see a short exhibition with more information. Four windows allow you to glimpse the cheese at various stages in its life, and you're also likely to catch a glimpse of the artisan at work. The end product and other local produce are on sale in the shop.

Falaise

William the Conqueror, or William the Bastard as he is more commonly known here, was born in **FALAISE**, 40km southwest of Lisieux. His mother, Arlette, a laundrywoman, was spotted by his father, Duke Robert of Normandy, at the washing place below the château. She was a shrewd woman, scorning secrecy in her eventual assignation by riding publicly through the main entrance to meet him. During her pregnancy, she is said to have dreamed of bearing a mighty tree that cast its shade over Normandy and England.

Falaise's **castle** keep, firmly planted on the massive rocks of the cliff (*falaise*) that gave the town its name, and towering over the **Fontaine d'Arlette** down by the river, is one of the most evocative historic sights imaginable. Nonetheless, it was so heavily damaged during the war that it took over fifty years to reopen for regular visits (Feb–June & Sept–Dec daily 10am–6pm; July & Aug daily 10am–7pm; English-language tours daily 11.30am, with another at 3.30pm in July & Aug; Ⓦwww.chateau-guillaume-leconquerant.fr; €6.50). Huge resources have been lavished on restoring the central **donjon**, reminiscent of the Tower of London with its cream-coloured Caen stone. Steel slabs, concrete blocks, glass floors and tent-like canvas awnings have been slapped down atop the bare ruins, and metal staircases squeezed into the wall cavities. The raw structure of the keep, down to its very foundations, lies exposed to view, while the newly created rooms are used for changing exhibitions that focus on the castle's fascinating past.

The whole of Falaise was devastated in the struggle to close the "Falaise Gap" in August 1944 – the climax of the **Battle of Normandy**, as the Allied armies sought to encircle the Germans and cut off their retreat. By the time the Canadians entered the town on August 17, they could no longer tell where the roads had been and had to bulldoze a new four-metre strip straight through the middle. The full bloody story is told in horrific detail at the **Musée Août 44**, beyond the château in a former cheese factory, on the chemin des Rochers (early April to mid-Nov 10am–noon & 2–6pm; €5.50).

Practicalities

The **tourist office** can be found on the boulevard de la Libération (May to mid-June Mon–Sat 9.30am–12.30pm & 1.30–6.30pm; mid-June to Sept same hours plus Sun 10am–noon & 3–5pm; Oct–April Mon–Sat 9.30am–12.30pm & 1.30–5.30pm; ℡02.31.90.17.26, ⓦwww.otsifalaise.com). Most of Falaise's few **hotels** stand along the main Caen–Argentan road, which can make them rather noisy. The *Poste*, not far from the tourist office at 38 rue Georges-Clemenceau (℡02.31.90.13.14, ⓔhotel.delaposte@orange.fr; ❷; hotel closed Jan, restaurant closed Jan, Sun evening & Mon), offers large, clean rooms and serves good food on menus from €15, while rooms at the *Hôtel de la Place*, next to the church at 1 place St-Gervais (℡02.31.40.19.00; ❷; closed Sun evening & Wed), are significantly cheaper. The three-star **campsite**, *Camping du Château* (℡02.31.90.16.55; closed Oct–April), next to Arlette's fountain and the municipal swimming pool, is in a much better location.

The Suisse Normande

The area known as the **Suisse Normande** lies roughly 25km south of Caen, along the gorge of the River Orne, between Thury-Harcourt and Putanges. While the name is a little far-fetched – there are certainly no mountains – it is quite distinctive, with cliffs, crags and wooded hills at every turn. There are plenty of opportunities for outdoor pursuits: you can race along the Orne in canoes and kayaks, cruise more sedately on pedaloes, or dangle on ropes from the sheer rock-faces high above. For mere walkers the Orne can be frustrating: footpaths along the river are few and far between, and often entirely overgrown.

The Suisse Normande is usually approached from Caen or Falaise and contrasts dramatically with the prairie-like expanse of wheat fields en route. On wheels, the best access is via the D235 from Caen (signed to Falaise then right through Ifs). Bus Verts #34 will take you to **Thury-Harcourt** or **Clécy** on its way from Caen to Flers.

Thury-Harcourt and Clécy

At **THURY-HARCOURT**, the **tourist office** on place St-Sauveur (Jan–April & Oct–Dec Mon 2.30–5pm, Tues–Fri 10am–12.30pm & 2.30–5pm, Sat 10am–12.30pm; May, June–Sept Tues–Sat 10am–12.30pm & 2.30–6.30pm, Sun 10am–12.30pm; July & Aug also open Mon 10am–12.30pm & 2.30–6.30pm; ℡02.31.79.70.45, ⓦwww.ot-suisse-normande.com) can suggest walks, rides and *gîtes d'étape* throughout the Suisse Normande. Hotels are for the most part overpriced, but there is an attractive four-star **campsite**, the *Vallée du Traspy* (℡02.31.79.61.80; open April–Sept), beside the river on the rue du Pont-Benoit.

CLÉCY, 10km to the south, is a slightly better bet for finding a room, although visitors outnumber residents in peak season. The **hotel** facing the church in the village centre, *Au Site Normand*, 1 rue des Châtelets (℡02.31.69.71.05, ⓦwww.ausitenormand.com; ❷; closed mid-Dec to mid-Feb), has pleasant, comfortable rooms in a modern annexe, and an old-fashioned and good-value dining room in the main timber-framed building itself. The river is a kilometre away, down the hill. En route, in the Parc des Loisirs, is a **Musée du Chemin de Fer Miniature** (March to mid-April Sun 2–5.30pm; mid-April to mid-June daily 10am–noon & 2–6pm; second half of June & all

Sept daily except Mon 10am–noon & 2–6pm; July & Aug daily 10am–noon & 2–6.30pm; Oct to early Nov Sun 2–5pm; €5), featuring a gigantic model railway certain to appeal to children.

Set in spacious grounds on the far bank of the river, the ✱ *Moulin du Vey* (☎02.31.69.71.08, ⓦwww.moulinduvey.com; ❺; hotel closed Dec, restaurant closed Sun in winter) is a beautifully positioned, luxuriously appointed hotel that takes its name from the restored watermill by the bridge, which is itself, confusingly, now a restaurant. The western riverbank is lined with restaurants, takeaways and snack bars as far as the two-star municipal **campsite** (☎02.31.69.70.36, ⓦwww.ocampings.com/campingclecy; open March to mid-Oct).

Pont d'Ouilly

If you're planning on walking or cycling, a good central spot in which to base yourself is **PONT D'OUILLY**, at the point where the main road from Vire to Falaise crosses the river. It's a small town, with a few shops, an old market hall and a promenade slightly upstream alongside the weir. Continuing upstream, a pleasant walk leads for 3.5km alongside the river to the pretty little village of Le Mesnil Villement.

As well as a **campsite** overlooking the river (☎02.31.69.46.12; open Easter –Sept), Pont d'Ouilly offers an attractive **hotel**, the *Du Commerce* (☎02.31.69.80.16; ❷; closed Sun evening & Mon), the quintessential French village hotel, with a friendly welcome and attentive service. Its **restaurant** is very popular with locals, serving superb, definitive Norman cooking, with plenty of creamy Pays d'Auge sauces, on menus that start at €16. About a kilometre north, the more upmarket *Auberge St-Christophe* (☎02.31.69.81.23; ❸; closed Sun evening. Mon & three weeks in Feb) stands, covered with ivy and geraniums, in a beautiful setting on the right bank of the Orne.

A short distance south of Pont-d'Ouilly is the **Roche d'Oëtre**, a high rock with a tremendous view into the deep and totally wooded gorge of the Rouvre, a tributary of the Orne. The river widens soon afterwards into the **Lac du Rabodanges**, formed by the many-arched Rabodanges Dam.

Southern Normandy

As an alternative to following the more northerly routes across Normandy, motorists heading west from Paris towards Brittany may prefer to cut directly across the province by following the line of the N12 through **Alençon** and then heading northwest on the N176. Much of the terrain along Normandy's southern border is taken up by the dense woodlands of the **Forêt d'Écouves** and the **Forêt des Andaines**, so there's plenty of good walking to be had, while the hill towns of **Carrouges** and **Domfront** make great stopovers.

Alençon and around

ALENÇON, a medium-sized and lively town, is known for its traditional – and now pretty much defunct – lacemaking industry. The **Musée des Beaux-Arts et de la Dentelle** (July & Aug daily 10am–noon & 2–6pm; Sept–June daily except Mon 10am–noon & 2–6pm; €3.10) is housed in a former Jesuit school and has all the best trappings of a modern museum. The highly informative history of lacemaking upstairs, with examples of numerous different techniques, can, however, be tedious for anyone not already riveted by the subject. It also contains an unexpected collection of gruesome Cambodian artefacts like spears and lances, tiger skulls and elephants' feet, gathered by the militant socialist governor of Alençon at the end of the nineteenth century. The paintings in the adjoining Beaux-Arts section are nondescript, except for a few works by Courbet and Géricault. Wandering around the town might also take you to St Thérèse's birthplace on rue St-Blaise, just in front of the **gare routière**.

The **Forêt d'Écouves**, north of Alençon and inaccessible by public transport, is a dense mixture of spruce, pine, oak and beech, unfortunately a favoured spot of the military – and, in autumn, deer hunters, too. You can usually ramble along the cool paths, happening on wild mushrooms and even the odd wild boar.

Practicalities

The **tourist office** is housed in the fifteenth-century Maison d'Ozé on place La Magdelaine (July & Aug Mon–Sat 9.30am–7pm, Sun 10am–12.30pm & 2–5pm; Sept–June Mon–Sat 9.30am–noon & 2–6pm; ☎02.33.80.66.33, ⓦwww.paysdalencontourisme.com). The **gare routière** and the **gare SNCF** are both northeast of the centre, in an area that holds Alençon's prime concentration of **hotels**. The *Hôtel de Paris*, above a bar at 26 rue de Denis-Papin (☎02.33.29.01.64; ❶), offers simple rooms at very good rates, while the *Hotel des Ducs* at 50 Avenue Wilson (☎02.33.29.03.93, ⓦwww.hoteldesducs-alencon.fr; ❷) offers a similar standard of accommodation at a slightly higher price. Good restaurants include *Le Bistrot* at 21 rue de Sarthe (☎02.33.26.51.69), which serves menus of traditional French cooking from €12. Alençon has good shops and **cafés** in a few pedestrianized streets at the heart of its one-way traffic system. A good place to sample the thriving local **bar** scene is the half-timbered *Café des Sept Colonnes* at 2 rue du Château.

Le Perche

Famous for the percheron horses who derive their name from this rural region, **Le Perche** is a pleasant spot for a few days' relaxation, or as a base to explore the countryside of southern Normandy. An obvious place to stay is the region's capital, the pretty town of **Mortagne-au-Perche**, 38km east of Alençon. The tourist office (Mon 10am–12.30pm & 2.30–6pm, Tues–Sat 9.30am–12.30pm & 2.30–6pm, Sun 10am–12.30pm; ☎02.33.85.11.18, ⓦwww.ot-mortagneauperche.fr) is situated in the former Halle aux Grains in the café-lined central square, the place Général de Gaulle. The town's historical centre includes the sixteenth-century Église Notre Dame, and an impressive Hôtel de Ville set in some lovely formal gardens, which have an excellent view of the countryside beyond. A good hotel option is the *Hostellerie Genty-Home* at 4 rue Notre Dame (☎02.33.25.11.33; ❷), which also has a decent restaurant, while for something a bit different, try the modern, comfortable B&B rooms on offer at the ⚑ *Ferme du Gros Chêne*, just outside Mortagne on the D8 towards Logny-au-Perche (☎02.33.25.02.72, ⓦwww.fermedugroschene.com; ❸). This working farm has five guest rooms in a converted barn, and offers self-catering facilities plus the option of a three-course dinner with the hosts for €18 (by reservation only).

The Perche is also home to a beautiful, chateau-studded natural park, which has its own visitor centre, the Maison du Parc, housed in the impressive old Manoir de Courboyer in Nocé (daily 10.30am–7pm; ☎02.33.85.36.36, ⓦwww .parc-naturel-perche.fr). The manor itself can be visited during these hours (€2/€3 including a guided tour), and the centre can provide information on walks, attractions and events in the area. There are also occasional equestrian displays featuring the percheron horses who graze nearby.

Carrouges

An alternative base to Alençon, at the western end of the Forêt d'Écouves, is the hill town of **CARROUGES**, with its impressive moat-encircled **château** set in spacious grounds at the foot of the hill (daily: April to mid-June & Sept 10am–noon & 2–6pm; mid-June to Aug 9.30am–noon & 2–6.30pm; Oct–March 10am–noon & 2–5pm; €6.50). The interesting guided tours are in French, but leaflets are available in other languages with a summary of the key information. The rooms, including a large kitchen and a beautiful wood-panelled bedroom, have been brought to life with period and reproduction furniture. A highlight is the room containing portraits of fourteen successive generations of the Le Veneur family, an extraordinary illustration of the processes of heredity. On the narrow rue Ste-Marguerite that runs through the heart of Carrouges – a noisier location than it might look – the *Hôtel du Nord* (☎02.33.27.20.14; ❶; closed mid-Dec to mid-Jan, plus Fri evening & Sun evening Sept–June) offers a handful of reasonably large en-suite **rooms** at low rates, and delicious local cuisine on menus that start at €10.

Bagnoles-de-l'Orne

West of Carrouges, the quaint spa town of **BAGNOLES-DE-L'ORNE** is quite unlike anywhere else in this part of the world, attracting the moneyed sick and convalescent from all over France to its thermal baths, along with mainly elderly visitors wanting to indulge themselves in the various spas. The layout is formal and spacious, centring on a lake surrounded by well-tended gardens. With so many visitors to keep entertained, and spending money, there are also innumerable cultural events of a restrained and stressless nature, such as tea dances and stage shows. Those wishing for slightly more active pursuits have the choice of mini golf or a pedalo trip around the lake.

Whether you'd actually want to spend time in Bagnoles depends on your disposable income as well as your health. Furthermore, the town as a whole operates to a season that lasts roughly from early April to the end of October; arrive in winter, and you may find everything shut. The numerous hotels are, on the whole, expensive and sedate places, and the three-star **campsite**, *De la Vée* (☎02.33.37.87.45; open mid-March to Oct), south of town, is rather forlorn.

The **tourist office** on place du Marché (April–Oct Mon–Sat 9.30am–12.30pm & 2–6pm, Sun 10am–12.30pm & 2.30–6.30pm; Nov–March Mon–Sat 9.30am–12.30pm & 2–6pm; ☎02.33.37.85.66; ⓦwww.bagnolesdelorne.com) will give details on accommodation in Bagnoles and its less exclusive sister town of **TESSE-MADELEINE**.

Among the cheaper options in Bagnoles proper is the excellent ⚑ *ô Gayot* (☎02.33.38.44.01; ⓔcontact@ogayot.com; closed Jan–March; ❸), close to the tourist office at 2 avenue de la Ferté Macé, whose stylish, modern rooms are a definite cut above the average French two-star hotel. Despite its ugly would-be-Deco exterior, the *Hôtel du Béryl*, on rue des Casinos (☎02.33.38.44.44, ⓦwww.groupe-emeraude.com; ❺), is probably the best of the larger establishments, bedecked with balconies and terraces overlooking the lake. It also boasts its own spa and swimming pool.

Domfront

The road through the forest from Bagnoles, the D335 and then the D908, climbs above the lush woodlands and progressively narrows before entering the pretty hill-top town of **DOMFRONT**.

A public park, near the long-abandoned former train station, leads up to some redoubtable castle ruins perched on an isolated rock. Eleanor of Aquitaine was born in this **castle** in October 1162, and Thomas Becket came to stay for Christmas 1166, saying Mass in the **Notre-Dame-sur-l'Eau** church down by the river, which has sadly been ruined by vandals. The views from the flower-filled gardens that surround the mangled keep are spectacular, including a very graphic panorama of the ascent you've made to get up. A slender footbridge connects the castle with the narrow little village itself, which boasts an abundance of half-timbered houses. Near its sweet central square, the neo-Byzantine **St Julien church**, constructed out of concrete segments during the 1920s, is bursting with exciting mosaics. The church is currently closed for restorations, which sadly may never be completed due to a lack of funds, but visitors can still have a look inside.

On summer afternoons (July & Aug Tues & Thurs 4.30pm), free **guided tours** (in French; there are several tours a year in English, enquire at the tourist office) of old Domfront leave from the **tourist office**, facing the castle entrance at 12 place de la Roirie (Mon–Sat 9.30am–12.30pm & 2.30–6pm; ℡02.33.38.53.97, Ⓦwww.domfront.com). The tourist office displays a list of available accommodation, updated daily, for visitors arriving out of hours without a reservation. An excellent choice is the welcoming ⚿ *Normandy Town and Country,* a four bedroom B&B in a nineteenth-century house located opposite the *gendarmerie* at 1 rue Georges Clemenceau (℡02.33.30.14.69, Ⓦwww.normandytownandcountry .com; ❸). The spacious rooms are excellent value for money, and the continental breakfast is extensive. In terms of hotels, two Logis de France stand side by side at the foot of the hill below the old town: the *Relais St-Michel*, 5 rue du Mont-St-Michel (℡02.33.38.64.99, Ⓦwww.hotellerelaisstmichel.com; ❶–❸; closed Fri & Sun evening), has rooms with and without en-suite facilities, plus menus from €15, while the similarly priced *Hôtel de France*, 7 rue du Mont-St-Michel (℡02.33.38.51.44, Ⓦwww.hoteldefrance-fr.com; ❷), has a nice bar and garden. Campers should note that the two-star local **campsite**, *du Champs Passais* (℡02.33.37.37.66; open April–Sept), is exceptionally small. Delicious and well-priced traditional cooking is available at the smart *Auberge du Grand Gousier,* in the medieval centre at 1 place de la Liberté. Three-course menus start at €18.50.

The Bocage

The region that centres on **St-Lô**, just south of the Cotentin, is known as the **Bocage**, from a word that refers to a type of cultivated countryside common in the west of France, where fields are cut by tight hedgerows rooted into walls of earth well over a metre high. An effective form of smallhold farming in pre-industrial days, it also proved to be a perfect system of anti-tank barricades. When the Allied troops tried to advance through the region in 1944, it was almost impenetrable – certainly bearing no resemblance to the East Anglian plains where they had trained. The war here was hand-to-hand slaughter, and the destruction of villages was often wholesale.

St-Lô

The city of **ST-LÔ**, 60km south of Cherbourg and 36km southwest of Bayeux, is still known as the "Capital of the Ruins". Memorial sites are everywhere and what is new speaks as tellingly of the destruction as the ruins that have been preserved. In the main square, the gate of the old prison commemorates Resistance members executed by the Nazis, people deported east to the concentration camps and soldiers killed in action. When the bombardment of St-Lô was at its fiercest, the Germans refused to take any measures to protect the prisoners and the gate was all that survived. Samuel Beckett was here during and after the battle, working for the Irish Red Cross as interpreter, driver and provision-seeker – for such things as rat poison for the maternity hospitals.

All the trees in the city are the same height, planted to replace the battle's mutilated stumps. But the most visible – and brilliant – reconstruction is the **Cathédrale de Notre-Dame**. Its main body, with a strange southward-veering nave, has been conventionally repaired and rebuilt. But the shattered west front and the base of the collapsed north tower have been joined by a startling sheer wall of icy green stone that makes no attempt to mask the destruction.

By way of contrast, a lighthouse-like 1950s folly spirals to nowhere on the main square. Should you feel the urge, you can climb its staircase and make your way into the new and even more pointless labyrinth of glass at its feet for a €1.50 admission fee. More compelling is the **Musée des Beaux-Arts** (Wed–Sun 10am–noon & 2–6pm; €2), behind the Mairie, which is full of treasures: a Boudin sunset; a Lurçat tapestry of his dog, *Nadir and the Pirates*; works by Corot, van Loo, Moreau; a Léger watercolour; a fine series of unfaded sixteenth-century Flemish tapestries on the lives of two peasants; and sad bombardment relics of the town.

St-Lô's **tourist office** adjoins the "lighthouse" on the main square (July & Aug Mon–Sat 9am–6pm; Sept–June Mon 2–6pm, Tues–Fri 10am–12.30pm & 2–6pm, Sat 10am–1pm; ☎02.33.77.60.35, Ⓦwww.mairie-saint-lo.fr). Most of the **hotels**, restaurants and bars are across the river, near the **gare SNCF**. Overlooking the river from the brow of a ridge beside the station, the upmarket *Hôtel des Voyageurs*, 5–7 avenue Brivère (☎02.33.05.08.63; ④) is home to the *Tocqueville*, which has menus from €19. If you'd rather be up in town, *La Crémaillère*, at 8 rue de la Chancellerie (☎02.33.57.14.68; ②; closed Fri evening & Sat in low season), has a good restaurant with menus starting at €9.50 for lunch and €12.50 for dinner.

The Vire Valley

Once St-Lô was taken in the Battle of Normandy, the armies speedily moved on southwestwards for their next confrontation. The **Vire Valley**, trailing south from St-Lô, saw little action – and its towns and villages seem to have been rarely touched by any historic or cultural mainstream. The motivation in coming to this landscape of rolling hills and occasional gorges is essentially to consume the region's cider, Calvados apple brandy (much of it bootleg), fruit pastries and sausages made from pigs' intestines.

From St-Lô to Tessy-sur-Vire

The best section of the valley is south of St-Lô through the Roches de Ham to Tessy-sur-Vire. The **Roches de Ham** are a pair of sheer rocky promontories high above the river. Though these are promoted as "viewing tables", the pleasure lies as much in the walk up, through lanes lined with blackberries, hazelnuts and rich orchards. Downstream from the Roches at **LA CHAPELLE-SUR-VIRE**, the church that towers majestically above the river has been an object of pilgrimage since the twelfth century. According to legend, in the Middle Ages a shepherd tending his flock noticed a lamb rooted to the spot; after digging he unearthed a statue of the Virgin Mary, since revered as a miraculous relic.

Five kilometres northeast of La Chapelle, **TORIGNI-SUR-VIRE** was the base of the Grimaldi family before they achieved quasi-royal status on moving on to the principality of Monaco. A spacious country town, it boasts a few grand buildings and an attractive **campsite**, *Camping du Lac* (T 02.33.56.91.74). The *Auberge de l'Orangerie*, 3 rue Victor-Hugo (T 02.33.56.70.64, W www .auberge-orangerie.abcsalles.com; hotel closed mid-Nov to mid-Feb; restaurant closed Sun evening & Mon; ❷), is a good **restaurant**, with menus starting at €15, and also offers five rooms.

❹ Travel details

Trains

Alençon to: Caen (6 daily; 1hr 15min), via Sées (13min) and Argentan (30min); Le Mans (10 daily; 50min).

Caen to: Cherbourg (10 daily; 1hr 15min), via Bayeux (20min) and Valognes (1hr); Lisieux (hourly; 30min); Le Mans (5 daily; 2hr), via Argentan (45min) and Alençon (1hr 15min); Paris-St-Lazare (up to 10 daily; 2hr 10min); Rennes (4 daily; 3hr), via St-Lô (50min), Coutances (1hr 15min) and Pontorson (2hr); Rouen (6 daily; 2hr).

Cherbourg to: Paris (8 daily; 3hr), via Valognes (15min) and Caen (1hr 15min).

Dieppe to: Paris-St-Lazare (10 daily; 2hr 10min), via Rouen (50min).

Granville to: Coutances (7 daily; 30min).

Le Havre to: Paris (11 daily; 2hr 15min); Rouen (15 daily; 1hr).

Rouen to: Caen (6 daily; 2hr); Paris-St-Lazare (19 daily; 1hr 15min); Vernon (12 daily; 30min).

St-Lô to: Caen (4 daily; 50min), via Bayeux (30min); Rennes (4 daily; 2hr 10min), via Coutances (20min) and Pontorson (1hr 15min).

Trouville-Deauville to: Lisieux (6 daily in winter, much more frequently in summer; 20min); Paris (6 daily in winter, much more frequently in summer; 2hr).

Buses

Alençon to: Bagnoles (3 daily; 1hr); Bellême (1–2 daily; 1hr); Évreux (1 daily; 2hr), via L'Aigle

(1hr 40min); Mortagne (1–3 daily; 1hr); Vimoutiers (1–3 daily; 1hr 30min), via Sées (30min).

Bayeux to: Arromanches (4 daily; 30min); Ouistreham (3 daily; 1hr 15min).

Caen to: Arromanches (1 daily; 1hr 10min); Bayeux (3 daily; 50min); Clécy (4 daily; 50min); Falaise (7 daily; 1hr); Honfleur (13 daily; 2hr), via Cabourg (50min), Houlgate (55min) and Deauville (1hr 5min), of which 5 continue to Le Havre (2hr 30min); Le Havre (2 daily bus #80 express services; 1hr 25min), via Honfleur (1hr); Ouistreham (20 daily; 30min); Pont L'Evêque (3 daily; 1hr 10min); Thury-Harcourt (5 daily; 40min).

Cherbourg to: St-Lô (3 daily; 1hr 45min); St-Vaast (3 daily; 50min) via Barfleur (30min).

Dieppe to: Fécamp (4 daily; 2hr 20min); Le Tréport (4 daily; 30min); St-Valery (5 daily; 1hr).

Le Havre to: Caen (2 daily express services; 1hr 25min); Étretat (9 daily; 50min); Fécamp (8 daily; 1hr 30min); Honfleur (7 daily; 30min).

Mont St-Michel to: Rennes (5 daily; 1hr 20min); St-Malo (4 daily; 1hr 30min).

Rouen to: Clères (6 daily; 45min); Évreux (hourly; 1hr); Le Havre (hourly; 2hr 45min), via Jumièges and Caudebec; Lisieux (2 daily; 2hr 30min).

St-Lô to: Bayeux (8 daily; 30min); Cherbourg (3 daily; 1hr 45min); Coutances (5 daily; 30min).

Brittany

CHAPTER 5 **Highlights**

✱ **The Côte de Granit Rose** With its bizarre pink rock formations and gem-like beaches, this memorable stretch of coastline is perfect for kids. See p.365

✱ **Cancale** If you love oysters, the stalls and restaurants in Cancale's little harbour will have you in raptures. See p.377

✱ **Hôtel de la Baie des Tréspassés** Brittany holds no more romantic destination than this land's-end hotel, facing its own colossal beach in splendid isolation. See p.402

✱ **Île de Sein** Misty and mysterious island, barely rising from the Atlantic, which makes a great day-trip from western Finistère. See p.402

✱ **The Inter-Celtic Festival** Celebrate the music and culture of the Celtic nations at Brittany's best-loved summer festival. See p.415

✱ **Carnac** France's most extraordinary megalithic monuments, predating even the Egyptian pyramids. See p.417

✱ **Belle-Île** The well-named island offers a microcosm of Brittany, with wild coast in the south, beaches in the north, beautiful countryside between and centuries-old fortifications at Le Palais. See p.421

✱ **Les Machines de L'Île, Nantes** A thrilling new art and engineering project at the forefront of Nantes' revitalized tourism industry, offering rides on a twelve-metre walking mechanical elephant. See p.431

▲ Les Machines de L'Ile, Nantes

Brittany

No one area – and certainly no one city or town – in **Brittany** encapsulates the character of the province; that lies in its people and in its geographical unity. For generations Bretons risked their lives fishing and trading on the violent seas and struggled with the arid soil of the interior. This toughness and resilience is tinged with **Celtic** culture: mystical, musical, sometimes morbid and defeatist, sometimes vital and inspired.

Though archeologically Brittany is one of the richest regions in the world – the alignments at **Carnac** rival Stonehenge – its first appearance in recorded history is as the quasi-mythical "Little Britain" of Arthurian legend. In the days when to travel by sea was safer and easier than by land, it was intimately connected with "Great Britain" across the water. Settlements such as St-Malo, St-Pol and Quimper were founded by Welsh and Irish missionary "saints" whose names are not to be found in any official breviary. Brittany remained **independent** until the sixteenth century, its last ruler, Duchess Anne, only managing to protect the province's autonomy through marriage to two consecutive French monarchs. After her death, in 1532, François I took her daughter and lands, and sealed the **union with France** with an act supposedly enshrining certain privileges. These included a veto over taxes by the local *parlement* and the people's right to be tried, or conscripted to fight, only in their province. The successive violations of this treaty by Paris, and subsequent revolts, form the core of Breton history since the Middle Ages.

As their language has been steadily eradicated, and the interior of the province severely depopulated, many Bretons continue to treat France as a separate

Getting to Brittany

There are plenty of different options for how to get to Brittany, with six international airports; Brest, Lorient, Dinard and Rennes have flights across France and to the UK, Quimper serves Spain and Northern Africa while the biggest airport, at Nantes, has flights across Europe, Asia, North America and Africa. The two **deep-sea ports** at Roscoff and St Malo both run to Britain and Ireland, on top of the excellent French train network. Two TGV lines from Paris serve the major cities on the north and south coasts, ending at Brest and Quimper, respectively, while there are also direct high-speed lines from Lyon to Nantes and from Lille to Rennes or Nantes. Many visitors choose to **drive**, however, either arriving via car ferry to one of the seaports listed above, or making the five-hour trip from the channel tunnel. There are no tolls on Brittany's autoroutes and some of the remote coastal villages towards the western tip are inaccessible by public transport, even in the July and August high season.

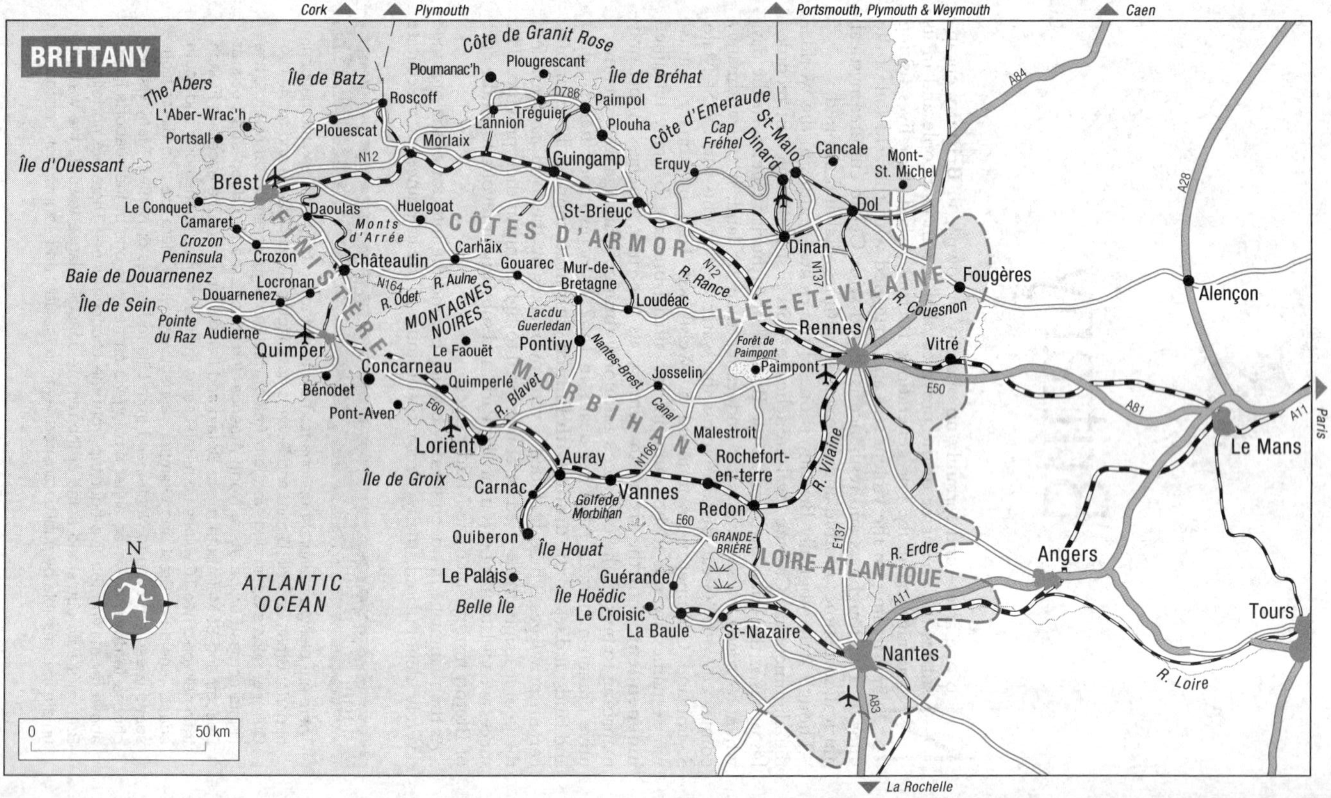
BRITTANY
Cork
Plymouth
Portsmouth, Plymouth & Weymouth
Caen
Paris
La Rochelle
Côte de Granit Rose
Île de Bréhat
Côte d'Emeraude
The Abers
Île de Batz
Île d'Ouessant
Ploumanac'h
Plougrescant
Roscoff
L'Aber-Wrac'h
Portsall
Plouescat
Lannion
Tréguier
Paimpol
Plouha
Morlaix
Guingamp
Cap Fréhel
St-Malo
Dinard
Cancale
Mont-St. Michel
Erquy
Brest
Le Conquet
Camaret
Crozon Peninsula
Crozon
Daoulas
Huelgoat
Monts d'Arrée
Châteaulin
Carhaix
Gouarec
St-Brieuc
Dol
Dinan
CÔTES D'ARMOR
FINISTÈRE
ILLE-ET-VILAINE
MORBIHAN
LOIRE ATLANTIQUE
Baie de Douarnenez
Locronan
Douarnenez
Île de Sein
Pointe du Raz
Audierne
Quimper
Bénodet
Concarneau
Pont-Aven
Quimperlé
MONTAGNES NOIRES
Le Faouët
R. Aulne
R. Odet
Mur-de-Bretagne
Loudéac
Lacdu Guerledan
Pontivy
R. Rance
R. Couesnon
Fougères
Alençon
Rennes
Vitré
Forêt de Paimpont
Paimpont
Josselin
Nantes-Brest Canal
Malestroit
Rochefort-en-terre
R. Vilaine
R. Blavet
Lorient
Île de Groix
Auray
Carnac
Vannes
Golfede Morbihan
Redon
Quiberon
Île Houat
Le Palais
Belle Île
ATLANTIC OCEAN
GRANDE-BRIÈRE
Guérande
Île Hoëdic
Le Croisic
La Baule
St-Nazaire
Nantes
R. Erdre
Angers
Le Mans
Tours
R. Loire
N12
N137
N164
N166
D786
E50
E60
E137
A11
A28
A81
A83
A84
0
50 km
N

country. Few, however, actively support Breton nationalism (which it's a criminal offence to advocate) much beyond putting Breizh (Breton for "Brittany") stickers on their cars. But there have been many successes in reviving the language, and the economic resurgence of the last three decades, helped partly by summer tourism, has largely been due to local initiatives, like Brittany Ferries re-establishing an old trading link, carrying produce and passengers across to Britain and Ireland. At the same time a Celtic artistic identity has consciously been revived, and local festivals – above all August's **Inter-Celtic Festival** at Lorient – celebrate traditional Breton music, poetry and dance, with fellow Celts treated as comrades.

If you're looking for traditional Breton fun, and you can't make the Lorient festival (or the smaller *Quinzaine Celtique* at Nantes in June/July), look out for gatherings organized by **Celtic folklore groups** – *Circles* or *Bagadou*. You may also be interested by the **pardons**, pilgrimage festivals commemorating local saints, which guidebooks (and tourist offices) tend to promote as

Food in Brittany

Brittany's proudest addition to the great cuisines of the world has to be the **crêpe** and its savoury equivalent the **galette**; crêperies throughout the region attempt to pass them off as satisfying meals, serving them with every imaginable filling. However, few people plan their holidays specifically around eating pancakes, and gourmets are more likely to be enticed to Brittany by its magnificent array of **seafood**. Restaurants in resorts such as St-Malo and Quiberon jostle to attract fish connoisseurs, while some smaller towns – like Cancale, widely regarded as the best place in France for oysters (*huîtres*), and Erquy, with its scallops (*coquilles St-Jacques*) – depend wholly on one specific mollusc for their livelihood.

Although they can't claim to be uniquely Breton, two appetizers feature on every self-respecting menu. These are **moules marinières**, giant bowls of succulent orange mussels steamed in a combination of white wine, shallots and parsley (and perhaps enriched with cream or crème fraîche to become *moules à la crème*), and **soupe de poissons** (fish soup), traditionally served with a pot of the garlicky mayonnaise known as *rouille* (coloured with pulverized sweet red pepper), a mound of grated *gruyère*, and a bowl of croutons. Jars of fresh *soupe de poissons* – or even crab or lobster – are always on sale in seaside *poissonneries*, and make an ideal way to take a taste of France home with you. Paying a bit more in a restaurant – typically on menus costing €25 or more – brings you into the realm of the **assiette de fruits de mer**, a mountainous heap of langoustines, crabs, oysters, mussels, clams, whelks and cockles, most raw and all delicious. **Main courses** tend to be plainer than in Normandy, with fresh local fish being prepared with relatively simple sauces. Skate served with capers, or salmon baked with a mustard or cheese sauce, are typical dishes, while even the **cotriade**, a stew containing sole, turbot or bass, as well as shellfish, is distinctly less rich than its Mediterranean equivalent, the *bouillabaisse*. Brittany is also better than much of France in maintaining its respect for fresh **vegetables**, thanks to the extensive local production of peas, cauliflowers, artichokes and the like. Only with the **desserts** can things get a little heavy; **far Breton**, considered a great delicacy, is a baked concoction of sponge and custard dotted with chopped plums, while *îles flottantes* are soft meringue icebergs adrift in a sea of *crème anglaise*, a light egg custard.

Strictly speaking, no **wine** is produced in Brittany. However, along the lower Loire valley, the *département* of Loire-Atlantique, centred on Nantes, is still generally regarded as "belonging" to Brittany – and is treated as such in this chapter. Vineyards here are responsible for the dry white Muscadet – normally used in *moules marinières* – and the even drier Gros-Plant.

exciting spectacles. In truth, unlike most French festivals, these are not phoney affairs kept alive for tourists, but deeply serious and rather gloomy religious occasions.

For most visitors, however, the Breton **coast** is the dominant feature. Apart from the Côte d'Azur, this is the most popular resort area in France, for both French and foreign tourists. Its attractions are obvious: warm white-sand beaches, towering cliffs, rock formations and offshore islands and islets, and everywhere the stone dolmens and menhirs of a prehistoric past. The most frequented areas are the **Côte d'Émeraude** around **St-Malo**; the **Côte de Granit Rose** in the north; the **Crozon peninsula** in far western **Finistère**; the family resorts such as **Bénodet** just to the south; and the **Morbihan coast** below **Vannes**. Accommodation and campsites here are plentiful, if pushed to their limits from mid-June to the end of August. Be aware, though, that out of season, many of the coastal resorts close down completely.

Whenever you come, don't leave Brittany without visiting one of its scores of **islands** – such as the **Île de Bréhat**, the **Île de Sein**, or **Belle-Île** – or taking in cities like **Quimper** or **Morlaix**, testimony to the riches of the medieval duchy. Allow time, too, to leave the coast and explore the interior, even if the price you pay for the solitude is sketchy transport and a shortage of hotels and campsites.

Eastern Brittany and the north coast

All roads in Brittany curl eventually inland to **Rennes**, the capital, which lies a short way northeast of the legendary **Forêt de Paimpont**. East of Rennes, the fortified citadels of **Fougères** and **Vitré** protected the eastern approaches to medieval Brittany, which vigorously defended its independence against incursors. Along the north coast, west of Normandy's Mont St-Michel, stand some of Brittany's finest old towns. A spectacular introduction to the province greets ferry passengers from Portsmouth: the **River Rance**, guarded by magnificently preserved **St–Malo** on its estuary, and beautiful medieval **Dinan** 20km upstream. Further west stretches a varied coastline that culminates in the seductive **Île de Bréhat**, and the colourful chaos of the **Côte de Granit Rose**.

Rennes and around

For a city that has been the capital and power centre of Brittany since the 1532 union with France, **Rennes** is – outwardly at least – uncharacteristic of the province, with its Neoclassical layout and pompous major buildings. What potential it had to be a picturesque tourist spot was destroyed in 1720,

A Breton glossary

Estimates of the number of **Breton-speakers** range from 400,000 to 800,000. You may well encounter it spoken as a first, day-to-day language by the very old and the young in parts of Finistère and the Morbihan. Learning Breton is not really a viable prospect for visitors without a grounding in Welsh, Gaelic or some other Celtic language. However, as you travel through the province, it's interesting to note the roots of Breton place names, many of which have a simple meaning in the language. Below are some of the most common:

aber	estuary	lann	heath
argoat	land	lech	flat stone
armor	sea	mario	dead
avel	wind	men	stone
bihan	little	menez	(rounded) mountain
bran	hill	menhir	long stone
braz	big	meur	big
coat	forest	nevez	new
cromlech	stone circle	parc	field
dol	table	penn	end, head
dolmen	stone table	plou	parish
du	black	pors	port, farmyard
enez	island	roc'h	ridge
goaz	stream	ster	river
gwenn	white	stivel	fountain, spring
hir	long	traez henn	beach
ker	village or house	trou	valley
kozh	old	ty	house
lan	holy place	wrach	witch

when a drunken carpenter managed to set light to virtually the whole city. Only the area known as **Les Lices**, at the junction of the canalized Ille and the River Vilaine, was undamaged. The remodelling of the rest of the city was handed over to Parisian architects, not in deference to the capital but in an attempt to rival it. The result, on the north side of the river at any rate, is something of a patchwork quilt, consisting of grand eighteenth-century public squares interspersed with intimate little alleys of half-timbered houses. It's quite a pleasant city to stroll around for half a day, but it lacks a cohesive personality.

Arrival and information

Rennes' **gare SNCF** (☎08.36.35.35.35), with TGVs to Paris and Brest, is south of the Vilaine, twenty-minutes' walk from the tourist office and a little more from the medieval quarter. A fast, efficient and ultra-clean **métro** system (Mon–Sat 5am–12.45am, Sun 7.15am–12.45am); connects the *gare SNCF*, the place de la République and the place Ste-Anne, as well as other destinations of less interest to visitors. Any one-way journey costs €1.20, or you can ride all day for €3.20.

Although the **gare routière** stands alongside the *gare SNCF* on boulevard Solferino, most **local buses** (Ⓦ www.star.fr) start and finish by the canal in the heart of town, on or near place de la République; the tourist office can supply a map of the bus routes. Rennes is a busy junction, with direct Illenoo services to Paimpont, Vitré, Fougères, St-Malo, Cancale, Dinan and Dinard

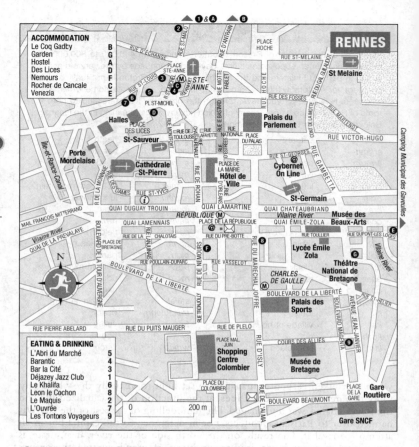

ACCOMMODATION
Le Coq Gadby	B
Garden	G
Hostel	A
Des Lices	D
Nemours	F
Rocher de Cancale	C
Venezia	E

St Melaine

PLACE HOCHE

RUE ST-MELAINE

RUE ST-MALO

RUE D'ANTRAIN

RUE D'ECHANGE

PLACE STE-ANNE

RUE ST-LOUIS

M STE-ANNE

RUE MOTTE FABLET

RUE DES FOSSES

RUE MARIENOT

RUE VICTOR-HUGO

PL ST-MICHEL

Halles

Palais du Parlement

PLACE DES LICES

St-Sauveur

RUE NATIONALE

PLACE DU PALAIS

Porte Mordelaise

Île-et-Rance-Canal

Cathédrale St-Pierre

Cybernet On Line

RUE ST-GEORGES

RUE DE ROHAN

Hôtel de Ville

PLACE DE LA MAIRIE

St-Germain

RUE ST-YVES

R DE LA MONNAIE

QUAI DUGUAY TROUIN

QUAI LAMARTINE

QUAI CHATEAUBRIAND

Musée des Beaux-Arts

RÉPUBLIQUE M

Vilaine River

QUAI ÉMILE-ZOLA

MAIL FRANÇOIS MITTERRAND

PLACE DE LA RÉPUBLIQUE

QUAI LAMENNAIS

QUAI DE LA PRÉVALAYE

Vilaine River

RUE DUPONT-LES-LOGES

RUE DE LA CHALOTAIS

RUE DU PRÉ-BOTTÉ

RUE TOULLIER

Lycée Émile Zola

PLACE DE BRETAGNE

RUE DES JAUNAIS

RUE POULLAIN-DUPARC

RUE VASSELOT

Théâtre National de Bretagne

BOULEVARD DE LA TOUR D'AUVERGNE

BOULEVARD DE LA LIBERTÉ

CHARLES DE GAULLE M

BOULEVARD DE LA LIBERTÉ

RUE ST-HELIER

Palais des Sports

AVENUE JEAN-JANVIER

BOULEVARD MAGENTA

RUE PIERRE ABELARD

RUE DU PUITS MAUGER

RUE DE PLELO

COURS DES ALLIÉS

PLACE MAL JUIN

Shopping Centre Colombier

Musée de Bretagne

RUE D'ISLY

RUE DE L'ALMA

PLACE DU COLOMBIER

Gare Routière

PLACE DE LA GARE

BOULEVARD BEAUMONT

Gare SNCF

Camping Municipal des Gavelilles

EATING & DRINKING
L'Abri du Marché	5
Barantic	4
Bar la Cité	3
Déjazey Jazz Club	1
Le Khalifa	6
Leon le Cochon	8
Le Maquis	2
L'Ouvrée	7
Les Tontons Voyageurs	9

0   200 m

(☎02.99.26.16.00, ⓦwww.illenoo.fr) and three or four Keolis Emeraude services to Mont St-Michel daily (☎02.99.19.70.80, ⓦwww.keolis-emeraude .com), departing Rennes' *gare routière* and timed to connect with arriving TGVs from Paris.

The **tourist office** stands in a disused medieval church, the Chapelle St-Yves, just north of the river at 11 rue St-Yves (April–Sept Mon–Sat 9am–7pm, Sun 11am–1pm & 2–6pm; Oct–March Mon 1–6pm, Tues–Sat 10am–6pm, Sun 11am–1pm & 2–6pm; ☎02.99.67.11.11, ⓦwww.tourisme-rennes.com). **Internet access** is available at Cybernet Online, 22 rue St-Georges (Mon 2–8pm, Tues–Fri 10.30am–8pm).

Accommodation

There is a fair smattering of **hotels** about the river and in old Rennes, the most convenient area for restaurants and nightlife. There is, however, a wider choice of options further out, and the excellent public transport system means you won't miss out by staying away from the centre.

Hotels

Le Coq Gadby 156 rue d'Antrain
⊤02.99.38.05.55, ⓦwww.lecoq-gadby
.com. This exceptional fourth generation family-run hotel with seventeenth-century period rooms, open fire lounge, on-site spa and Michelin-starred restaurant has recently become an "urban resort". It also boasts a beautiful sustainable extension providing sixty percent of its power through solar panels, rainwater collection and four more spa cabins. Full suites from (€450). ❽
Garden 3 rue Duhamel ⊤02.99.65.45.06, ⓦwww
.hotel-garden.fr. Comfortable, clean and very personal Logis de France, that's north of the *gare SNCF* not far from the river and with a pleasant garden café. The very cheapest rooms aren't en suite. ❸
Des Lices 7 place des Lices ⊤02.99.79.14.81, ⓦwww.hotel-des-lices.com. Forty-five rooms, all with TV and balcony, in a very comfortable and friendly modern hotel on the edge of the prettiest part of old Rennes, very convenient for the place des Lices car park. ❸
Hotel Nemours 5 rue de Nemours
⊤02.99.78.26.26, ⓦwww.hotelnemours.com. The pick of the central hotels has spotless, stylish and well-lit rooms in white and green tones and comfortable beds. The service is friendly and professional and you can take good continental breakfasts (€9.50) in bed. Reservations recommended. ❹
Le Rocher de Cancale 10 rue St-Michel
⊤02.99.79.20.83. Four-room hotel on the delightful, medieval rue St-Michel, also known as the *rue de soif* (thirsty street) and there are bars and cafés literally on the doorstep. The frontage and ground floor are beautifully restored, though the cosy rooms have slightly foamy beds. The friendly owner also does a good foie gras in the equally appealing ground-floor restaurant. ❷
Venezia 27 rue Dupont-les-Loges
⊤02.99.30.36.56, ⓔhotel.venezia@orange.fr. The friendly hostess of this budget hotel offers slightly musty but lovingly decorated, spacious rooms, some overlooking the canalized Vilaine River. The lowest-priced rooms only have a toilet, but it costs just €6 extra to get one with a shower as well. ❶

Hostel and campsite

Centre International de Séjour 10–12 Canal St-Martin ⊤02.99.33.22.33, ⓔrennes@fuaj.org. Welcoming, attractively positioned HI hostel, 3km north of the centre beside the Canal d'Ille et Rance. Charging €17 per person per night for a dorm bed, it has a cafeteria and a laundry, and operates a 1am curfew; membership of a hostelling association is compulsory. Bus #18 runs there from the place Ste-Anne métro station, direction "St-Gregoire". Open all year.
Camping Municipal des Gayeulles, rue de Professeur-Maurice-Audin ⊤02.99.36.91.22. An appealingly verdant site 1km east of central Rennes in a park that offers good shade and a pool and sporting facilities nearby; take bus #3 to the centre – last bus runs at 12.30am. Open all year, with pitches costing up to €14 in season.

The City

Rennes' surviving **medieval quarter**, bordered by the canal to the west and the river to the south, radiates from **Porte Mordelaise**, the old ceremonial entrance to the city. Just to the northeast of the *porte*, the **place des Lices** is dominated by two usually empty market halls but comes alive every Saturday for one of France's largest **street markets**. The place was originally the venue for jousting tournaments, and it was on this spot in 1337 that the hitherto unknown Bertrand du Guesclin, then aged 17, fought and defeated several older opponents. This set him on his career as a soldier, during which he was to save Rennes when it was under siege by the English. However, after the Bretons were defeated at Auray in 1364, he fought for the French, and twice invaded Brittany.

The one central building to escape the 1720 fire was the **Palais du Parlement** on rue Hoche downtown. Ironically, however, the Palais was all but ruined by a mysterious conflagration in 1994, thought to have been sparked by a flare during a demonstration by Breton fishermen. Since then, the entire structure has been rebuilt and restored, and is once more topped by an impressive array of gleaming gilded statues. Inside, its lobby stages temporary exhibitions.

If you head south from the Palais, you'll soon reach the **River Vilaine**, which flows through the centre of Rennes, narrowly confined into a steep-sided

369

channel. The south bank is every bit as busy as, if not busier than, the north, with the **Musée des Beaux-Arts** at 20 quai Émile-Zola (daily except Mon 10am–noon & 2–6pm; ⓦ www.mbar.org; €5.30). Unfortunately many of its finest artworks – which include drawings by Leonardo da Vinci, Botticelli, Fra Lippo Lippi and Dürer – are not usually on public display. Instead you'll find indifferent Impressionist views of Normandy by the likes of Boudin and Sisley, interspersed with the occasional treasure.

The showpiece **Musée de Bretagne**, housed in the new edifice Champs Libres, five hundred metres south on the cours des Alliés, provides a high-tech overview of Breton history and culture (Tues noon–9pm, Wed–Fri noon–7pm, Sat & Sun 2–7pm; €4, or €7 for museum and Éspace des Sciences; ⓦ www .musee-bretagne.fr). It starts at the very beginning, with a hearth used by humans in a Finistère seacave half a million years ago that ranks among the oldest signs of fire in the world. From there on, a quick, entertaining skate through regional history covers the dolmens and menhirs of the megalith builders, some magnificent jadeite axes and Bronze Age swords, and the arrival of first the Celts, next the Romans, and later still the spread of Christianity from the fifth century onwards. With labels in English as well as French and Breton, it makes a good introduction to the region, but unless some compelling temporary exhibition is on it's not really unmissable. Under the same roof, and sharing the same hours and entrance fees, the **Éspace des Sciences** is a peculiar sort of scaly volcano that contains two floors of rather dry scientific displays, this time with no English captions.

Eating and drinking

Most of Rennes' more interesting **bars** and **restaurants** are in the streets just south of the **place Ste-Anne**, towards the place des Lices, with the bar-lined **rue St-Michel** and rue Penhoët, each with a fine assemblage of ancient wooden buildings, as the epicentre. Ethnic alternatives are concentrated along **rue St-Malo** just to the north, and also on **rue St-Georges** near the place du Palais. Rue Vasselot is the nearest equivalent south of the river.

L'Abri du Marché 9 place des Lices ☎02.99.79.73.87. Nothing but the Breton staples of mussels (€9–10) and *galettes* (savoury pancakes, €3–9) are served at this local favourite, which sources fresh market produce every morning and serves it in a pleasant dining room smothered in old Breton trinkets.

Barantic 4 rue St-Michel. One of the city's favourite bars, putting on occasional live music for a mixed crowd of Breton nationalists and boisterous students; if it's too full, try one of half a dozen similar alternatives within spitting distance.

Bar la Cité 5 rue St-Louis. This great little bar, with art on the walls and friendly staff and clientele, is the ideal place for a cider, or some of their stronger house brews (€2). They host live music to suit a range of tastes on Sat nights, and the staff favour electro on the stereo. Open until 2pm.

Déjazey Jazz Club 54 rue St-Malo ☎02.99.38.70.72. Good quality live jazz and other gigs take place twice weekly here and the late closing makes it the popular "after" spot, despite the prices being a little steep (€7 for a large beer on tap). Open until 5am, closed Sun.

Le Khalifa 20 haut de la place des Lices ☎02.99.30.87.30. Assorted Moroccan dishes, served outside or in an atmospheric dining room. Couscous and *brochettes* from €10, tagine €11.50, as well as various set *formules,* including lunch and a glass of wine for €9. Closed all Mon, & Tues lunch.

Leon le Cochon 1 rue Maréchal-Joffre ☎02.99.79.37.54. Tasteful, contemporary but classically French restaurant, where the simple lunch menu costs just €12.50. It's best to reserve to enjoy dinner menus that start at €26. Closed Sun in July & Aug.

Le Maquis 13 rue St-Malo ☎02.99.63.83.06. Very lively, friendly African restaurant, serving lots of Senegalese marinated chicken and fish dishes for around €9, plus a €16.50 vegetarian set menu. Dinner only. Closed Mon.

L'Ouvrée 18 place des Lices ☎02.99.30.16.38. Formal but very friendly gourmet restaurant, spread through two dining rooms decorated in warm reds and yellows. Menus range from €14.50–32, and feature small but tasty portions with an emphasis on fish, as for example with the *flan de langoustines*, plus wonderful desserts. Closed Sat lunch, Sun evening & Mon.

Les Tontons Voyageurs 4 av Janvier ☎02.99.30.09.20. Lively, eclectic place that incorporates a piano bar and a cigar room, and puts on live music, while also serving inexpensive, high-quality brasserie lunches, and dinner menus up to €31. Closed Sat lunch, all Sun, & Mon evening.

Festivals and theatre

Rennes is at its best in the first ten days of July, when the **Festival des Tombées de la Nuit** celebrates Breton culture with music, theatre, film, mime and poetry (☎02.99.32.56.56, ⓦwww.lestombeesdelanuit.com). In the first week of December, the **Transmusicales** rock festival attracts big-name acts from all over France and the world at large, while retaining a Breton emphasis (☎02.99.31.12.10, ⓦwww.lestrans.com). The **Théâtre National de Bretagne**, 1 rue St-Helier (☎02.99.31.12.31, ⓦwww.t-n-b.fr), puts on varied events throughout the year, except in July and August. All year round, in a different auditorium on the same premises, *Club Ubu* (☎02.99.31.12.00, ⓦwww.ubu-rennes.com) puts on large-scale gigs.

The Forêt de Paimpont

Thirty kilometres west of Rennes, the **Forêt de Paimpont**, known also by its ancient name of Brocéliande, is – according to song and legend – the forest of the wizard Merlin. Medieval Breton minstrels, like their Welsh counterparts, set the tales of King Arthur and the Holy Grail both in Grande Bretagne and here in Petite Bretagne. For all the magic of these shared legends, however, and a succession of likely sites, few people come out here.

Roaming around for a day is easy, with **MAURON**, reachable by bus from Rennes, a good place to start. First stop should be **L'Étang et le Chateau de Comper**, at the eastern edge of the town of Concoret (Apr–June, Sept & Oct, Thurs–Mon 10am–5.30pm; July & Aug, Thurs–Tues 10am–7pm; €5), where an ever-changing series of exhibits on Arturian history and legend entertain visitors to the chateau, whose swamp is said to be the very one from which Excalibur emerged. From the hamlet of Folle Pensée, just south, a circuitous but enjoyable twenty-minute walk leads to **La Fontaine de Barenton** – Merlin's spring. The path leads off from the end of the road at Folle Pensée, turning to the right, running through pines and gorse to a junction of forest tracks: here, take the track straight ahead for about 100m, where an unobvious path to the left goes into the woods and turns back north to the spring – walled, and filled by the most delicious water imaginable. After drinking, stroke the great stone slab beside the spring to call up a storm, roaring lions and a horseman in black armour. Here Merlin first set eyes on Vivianne, who bound him willingly in a prison of air. Back in town, **L'Église de Tréhorenteuc**, famed for its mixture of Pagan and Christian symbolism, holds a representation of Morgane, along with a mosaic taken from one of the Arturian legends.

Practicalities

The **bus** from Rennes runs around the north corner to Mauron twice a day. Information on the forest can be picked up from the **tourist office** next to the lakeside abbey in the little market village of **PAIMPONT** (Feb–June &

Sept–Dec Tues–Sat 10am–noon & 2–5pm; July & Aug daily 10am–noon & 2–6pm; ℡02.99.07.84.23). Paimpont makes the most obvious base for explorations: it's right at the centre of the woods, has mountain bike rental at Brécilien (℡02.99.07.81.13; €8/half-day, €12/day) on the main street through town, and has some excellent **accommodation**. At the 🍴 *Relais de Brocéliande* in town, 7 rue des Forges (℡02.99.07.84.94, ⓦwww.le-relais-de-broceliande .fr; ❸), a flower-bedecked delight, you can fill up for €26.50, or much more, in the restaurant under the gaze of stuffed animal heads. There's also a two-star municipal **campsite** on the edge of the village (℡02.97.07.89.16; closed Oct–April), with green pitches and clean facilities for €8.50. Other accommodation in the forest includes a *gîte d'étape*-cum-*chambre d'hôte* in tiny Trudeau on the D40 (℡02.99.07.81.40; dorm beds €9.70, B&B ❷) and a beautifully situated **hostel**, at Le Choucan-en-Brocéliande, 5km out on the Concoret road (℡02.97.22.76.75; dorm beds €9.70; closed June & mid-Sept to Dec).

Vitré

VITRÉ, just north of the Le Mans–Rennes motorway, 30km east of Rennes, rivals Dinan as the best-preserved medieval town in Brittany. While its walls are not quite complete, the thickets of medieval stone cottages that lie outside them have hardly changed. The towers of the **castle**, which dominates the western end of the ramparts, have pointed slate-grey roofs in best fairy-tale fashion, looking like freshly sharpened pencils, but sadly the municipal offices and **museum** of shells, birds, bugs and local history inside are not exactly thrilling.

Vitré's principal **market** is held on Mondays in the square in front of **Notre-Dame church**. The old city is full of twisting streets of half-timbered houses, a good proportion of which are bars – **rue Beaudrairie** in particular has a fine selection.

The local **gare SNCF** is on the southern edge of the centre, where the ramparts have disappeared and the town blends into its newer sectors. Just across the square from the station you'll find the **tourist office** (July & Aug Mon–Sat 9.30am–12.30pm & 2–6.30pm, Sun 10am–12.30 & 3–6pm; Sept–June Mon 2.30–6pm, Tues–Fri 9.30am–12.30pm & 2.30–6pm, Sat 10am–12.30pm & 3–5pm; ℡02.99.75.04.46, ⓦwww.ot-vitre.fr). Most of the **hotels** are nearby. The *Petit Billot*, 5bis place du Général-Leclerc (℡02.99.75.02.10, ⓦwww.petit -billot.com; ❷), is good value, while rooms on the higher floors of the *Hôtel du Château*, 5 rue Rallon (℡02.99.74.58.59; ❷–❸; closed Sun in low season), on a quiet road just below the castle, have views of the ramparts. Of the **restaurants**, *Le St-Yves*, immediately below the castle at 1 place St-Yves (℡02.99.74.68.76; closed all Mon evening. plus Tues, Thurs & Sun eves), serves menus from €17 to €28, while *La Soupe aux Choux*, a little higher up at 32 rue Notre-Dame (℡02.99.75.10.86; closed Sat lunch, plus Sun in low season), prepares simple but classic French food, with a duo of frogs' legs and a pork main costing €12.

St-Malo and around

Walled and built with the same grey granite stone as Mont St-Michel, **ST-MALO** was originally a fortified island at the mouth of the Rance, controlling not only the estuary but the open sea beyond. Now inseparably attached to the mainland, it's the most visited place in Brittany – thanks more

ST-MALO

Tour Quic-en-Groigne

Porte St-Thomas

Château

PLACE VAUBAN

Keep

Ramparts

CHAUSSÉE DU SILLON

RUE CHATEAUBRIAND

Musée de la Ville

RUE DE LA VICTOIRE

RUE ST-BENOIT

RUE DU GRAS

RUE SAINT-THOMAS

RUE STE-BARBE

Gare Routière

Porte St-Vincent

Porte des Champs Vauverts

Plage de Bons Secours

R. GROUT ST-GEORGES

RUE STE-ANNE

PLACE DES FRÈRES-LAMMENNAIS

RUE DU BOYER

RUE DU MOLLET

CORPS DE GARDE

POISSON ERIE

RUE JACQUES-CARTIER

R. MARGUERITE

AV LOUIS-MARTIN

Cathédrale St-Vincent

GRANDE RUE

RUE DU BOYER

R VINCENT DE GOURNAY

LE PACIFIE

RUE THEVENARD

PL AUX HERBES

RUE BROUSSAIS

RUE DE LA BOUCHERIE

RUE PUITS AUX BRAIES

PLACE AUX POIDS-DU-ROI

Grande Porte

Bassin de Vauban

Porte St-Pierre

PLACE DU GUET

RUE DE LA PIE QUI BOIT

RUE DE LA FOSSE

RUE DE LA HERSE

Halle au Blé

RUE DES CORDIERS

CHAUSSÉE ERIC TABARLY

Porte St-Louis

RUE ST-SAUVEUR

RUE D'ESTRÉES

RUE DE DINAN

RUE DE TOULOUSE

RUE VAUBOREL

RUE DE TOULOUSE

Poterne D'Estrée

Plage du Môle

Porte de Dinan

Ramparts

QUAI DE DINAN

Quai Dinan

CHAUSSÉE ERIC TABARLY

Moving Bridges

N

Terminal Ferry du Naye

ACCOMMODATION	
Le Beaufort	B
Centre Patrick Varangot	A
Le Croiseur	E
De L'Europe	G
De France et Chateaubriand	C
Le Mont-Fleury	F
La Rance	J
San Pédro	H
Aux Vielles Pierres	I
L'Univers	D

EATING & DRINKING	
Le 109	8
L'Alchemiste	1
Bistrot de Rocher	9
Le Chalut	2
Le Corps de Garde	6
Cunningham's	10
Duchesse Anne	3
Chez Gilles	7
La Java	4
Tanpopo	5

0   100 m

Grand-Bé

Dinard

Paramé

5

BRITTANY | St-Malo and around

Gare SNCF (2km)

St-Servan, Camping la Cite d'Aleth, Camping la Ville Huchet, Tar Solidor & Grand Aquarium

to its superb **old citadelle** than to the ferry terminal that's tucked into the harbour behind. *Intra-muros* ("within the walls") is a busy, lively and very characterful town, packed with restaurants, bars and shops. Yes, the summer crowds can be oppressive, but even then a stroll atop the ramparts should restore your equilibrium, and vast, clean beaches beyond the walls are a huge bonus if you're travelling with kids in tow.

Arrival and information

St-Malo is always busy with **boats**. From the **Terminal Ferry du Naye**, Brittany Ferries (T02.99.40.64.41, Wwww.brittanyferries.com) sails to Portsmouth, while Condor Ferries (T02.99.20.03.00, Wwww.condorferries .co.uk) connects with both Weymouth (via Jersey or Guernsey) and Poole during spring and summer; for details, see p.30. Between April and early November, regular passenger **ferries to Dinard** operate from the **quai Dinan**, just outside the southernmost point of the ramparts (Compagnie Corsaire; T08.25.13.80.35, Wwww.compagniecorsaire.com; €4 single, €6 return, bikes €4.50 or €7.50 return); the trip across the estuary takes an all-too-short ten minutes.

The **gare routière** is the expanse of concrete right in front of the city walls on the Port des Yachts, though almost all St-Malo buses also stop at the **gare SNCF** – 2km out from the citadelle, set back from square Jean-Coquelin. Illenoo (T02.99.82.26.26, Wwww.illenoo.fr) run services to Dinard, Cancale, Dol, Rennes and, in summer, Mont St-Michel. TIBUS (T0810.22.22.22; Wwww .tibus.fr) runs a line to Dinan, which also calls in at Cap Fréhel in summer.

St-Malo's helpful **tourist office** is alongside the *gare routière* (April–June & Sept Mon–Sat 9am–12.30pm & 1.30–6.30pm, Sun 10am–12.30pm & 2.30–6pm; July & Aug Mon–Sat 9am–7.30pm, Sun 10am–6pm; Oct–March Mon–Sat 9am–12.30pm & 1.30–6pm; T08.25.13.52.00, Wwww.saint-malo-tourisme .com). For **internet access**, head to Cop' Imprim, just west of the *gare SNCF* at 29bis boulevard des Talards (Mon–Fri 9am–7pm, Sat 9am–noon; T02.99.56.05.83, Wwww.cybermalo.com).

Bicycles can be rented from Les Velos Bleus, 19 rue Alphonse-Thébault (T02.99.40.31.63, Wwww.velos-bleus.fr), or for brilliant leisurely low-riders head to Electra Breizh, 5bis avenue John Kennedy, Paramé (T02.99.56.11.06, Wwww.electra-breizh.fr).

Accommodation

St-Malo boasts over a hundred **hotels**, including the seaside boarding houses just off the beach, along with several **campsites** and a **hostel** – in high season it needs every one of them, so make reservations well in advance. Unfortunately, some *intra-muros* hotels tend to take advantage of high summer demand by insisting that you eat in their own restaurants. Cheaper rates can be found by the *gare SNCF*, or in suburban Paramé (bus #2 or #5). The hostel is notoriously busy, while campsites also tend to be full in July and August.

Hotels in the citadelle

Le Croiseur 2 place de la Poissonnerie T02.99.40.80.40, Wwww.hotel-le-croiseur.com. A new, contemporary-style hotel overlooking the fish market, with sleek and spotless rooms, wi-fi throughout and a great bar and terrace on the ground floor. Friendly and very good value. ❸

De France et Chateaubriand 12 place Chateaubriand T02.99.56.66.52, Wwww.hotel-fr -chateaubriand.com. Elegant rooms at surprisingly reasonable prices in the imposing birthplace of the writer Chateaubriand, approached via a courtyard from the main square. Higher rooms have sea views; breakfast is €10 and parking €12. ❺–❻ with sea view.

San Pédro 1 rue Ste-Anne T02.99.40.88.57, Wwww.sanpedro-hotel.com. Twelve compact but stylishly refurbished rooms in a nice quiet setting, just inside the walls in the north of the citadelle. The bubbly owner makes great breakfasts and is thrilled to offer advice on the town. Rooms on the higher floors (reached via a minuscule lift) enjoy sea views. Closed mid-Nov to Feb. ❸

L'Univers place Chateaubriand T02.99.40.89.52. This Saint Malo institution swings in favour, but with a great bar, good value restaurant and huge old rooms in an ideal spot, it is very hard to ignore. ❺

Aux Vieilles Pierres 9 rue Thévenard T02.99.56.46.80. Six-room hotel, near place aux

Herbes, which remains one of the better bargains within the walls, even if a room with a shower costs €16 extra. Menus at the restaurant cost €24 or €32. Open all year. ❷–❸

Hotels outside the walls

Le Beaufort 25 chaussée du Sillon, Coutoisville ☎02.99.40.99.99, 🖳www.hotel-beaufort.com. Grand sea-view hotel situated on the beach (ideal for a bracing morning dip) along which it is a 30min walk to the citadelle. Rooms are beautifully restored – some with lovely balconies – and there is a fine restaurant. ❼

De l'Europe 44 bd de la République ☎02.99.56.13.42, 🖳www.hotels-st-malo.com /europe. Year-round cheap but clean rooms (the cheaper ones don't have en-suite facilities) in a genuinely friendly (if noisy) hotel near the *gare SNCF*, with a cosy café serving breakfast for €5.50. There are rooms up to 6 person; if you are 4 or more, it'll work out cheaper than the hostel. ❶

Le Mont-Fleury 2 rue du Mont-Fleury ☎02.23.52.28.85, 🖳www.lemontfleury.com. Bed and breakfast in a beautiful seventeenth-century house and park couched in the suburbs of Paramé. There's a big fire in the living room and the owner, a former pilot, has decorated the four rooms in travelling themes from Oriental to American. ❹

La Rance 15 quai Sébastopol, St-Servan ☎02.99.81.78.63, 🖳www.larancehotel.com. Small, tasteful and airy option in sight of the Tour Solidor,

that boasts eleven spacious rooms and a much more tranquil atmosphere than St-Malo itself. ❹

Hostel and campsites

Centre Patrick Varangot 37 av du Père-Umbricht, Paramé ☎02.99.40.29.80, 🖳www.centrevarangot .com. Dominated as a rule by lively young travellers, this is one of France's busiest hostels, 2km northeast of the *gare SNCF* in the suburb of Paramé, not far from the beach. Dorm beds from €17.10 April–Sept, €6.10 Oct–March; hostelling association membership required. Rates include breakfast, and there's also a cut-price cafeteria, as well as kitchen facilities and tennis courts. No curfew, open all year.

🏃 **La Cité d'Aleth** allée Gaston Buy, St-Servan ☎02.99.81.60.91 🖳www .ville-saint-malo.fr/campings. By far the nearest campsite to the citadelle and best spot to camp, in a dramatic location on the headland southwest of St-Malo, overlooking the city from within the wartime German fortified stronghold. Closed Nov–April, pitches around €12 in high season.

Les Nielles av John-Kennedy, Paramé ☎02.99.40.26.35. On the beach at the smaller of Paramé's strands, the plage du Minhic, just a short walk from the town's facilities. Closed Sept–June, pitches under €12

La Ville Huchet route de la Passagère ☎02.99.81.11.83, 🖳www.lavillehuchet.com. Located south of St-Malo on the road to Rennes, this four-star campsite is in the grounds of a chateau, with an aquatic park, pool and bike rental on offer, too. Pitches around €25.

The Town

The **citadelle** of St-Malo, very much the prime destination for visitors, was for many years joined to the mainland only by a long causeway, before the original line of the coast was hidden forever by the construction of the harbour basin. Although its streets of restored seventeenth- and eighteenth-century houses can be crowded to the point of absurdity in summer, away from the more popular thoroughfares random exploration is fun, and you can always surface on the **ramparts** – first erected in the fourteenth century – to escape the claustrophobia and enjoy wonderful all-round views.

Owing to the limitations of space, **buildings** within the walls tend to be higher-rise than you might expect. Ancient as they look, they are almost entirely reconstructed; following the two-week bombardment that forced the German surrender in 1944, eighty percent of the city had to be lovingly and precisely rebuilt, stone by stone. One notable survivor of this, and the fire in 1661, is the **Maison International des Poètes et Écrivains** at 5 rue Pélicot (Tues-Sat 2–6pm; 🖳www.mipe.asso.fr), which holds ongoing exhibitions and literary events and stocks a growing library of world poetry.

Besides the prominent **Grande Porte**, the main gate of the citadelle is the **Porte St-Vincent**. To the right is the town's **castle**, which houses the **Musée de la Ville** (April–Sept daily 10am–12.30pm & 2–6pm; Oct–March Tues–Sun

10am–noon & 2–6pm; €5.10). The museum is something of a hymn to the "prodigious prosperity" enjoyed by St-Malo during its days of piracy, colonialism and slave trading. Climbing the 169 steps of the castle keep, you pass a fascinating mixture of maps, diagrams and exhibits – chilling handbills from the Nazi occupation, accounts of the "infernal machine" used by the English to blow up the port in 1693, and savage four-pronged *chausse-trappes* (a kind of early version of barbed wire), thrown by pirates onto the decks of ships being boarded to immobilize their crews.

You can pass under the ramparts at several points to reach the open shore, where a huge **beach** stretches away east beyond the rather featureless resort-suburb of **Paramé**. When the tide is low, it's safe to walk out to the small island of **Grand-Bé** – the walk is so popular that sometimes you even need to queue to get onto the short causeway. Solemn warnings are posted of the dangers of attempting to return from the island when the tide has risen too far – if you're caught there, there you have to stay. The island's "sight" is the tomb of the nineteenth-century writer-politician **Chateaubriand** (1768–1848).

The **St-Servan** district, within walking distance along the corniche south of the citadelle, was the city's original settlement, converted to Christianity by St Malou (or Maclou) in the sixth century; later, in the twelfth century, the townspeople moved to the impregnable island now called St-Malo. St-Servan is dominated by the distinctive **Tour Solidor**, which consists of three linked towers built in 1382, and in cross-section looks just like an ace of clubs. It now holds a **museum** of Cape Horn clipper ships, open for ninety-minute guided visits (April–Sept daily 10am–12.30pm & 2–6pm; Oct–March Tues–Sun 10am–noon & 2–6pm; €5.10). Most of the great European explorers of the Pacific are covered, from Magellan onwards, but naturally the emphasis is on French heroes like Bougainville. Tours culminate with a superb view from the topmost ramparts.

If you follow the main road due south from St-Servan, ignoring signs for the Barrage de la Rance – or take bus #5 from the *gare SNCF* – you'll come to the **Grand Aquarium**, on a roundabout high above town (daily: April–June & Sept 10am–7pm; July & Aug 9.30am–8/10pm; Oct–March 10am–6pm; €15.50, under-18s €10.50; ☎02.99.21.19.00, ⓦwww.aquarium-st-malo.com). The highly involving aquarium is an entertaining place to be, with the setup itself as much a thing of wonder as the fish. Its eight distinct fish tanks include one shaped so that visitors stand in the hole in the middle as myriad fish whirl around them; you can even spend a night sleeping with the sharks. (€100 for three people, bring sleeping bag and reserve at least a week in advance). Don't confuse with St-Malo's other aquarium, the logically named **Petit Aquarium**, set into the walls of the old city, as it is much less interesting.

For last-minute **shopping**, St-Malo's citadelle contains a few specialists, and **markets** are held in the Halle au Blé within the walls of St-Malo on Tuesdays and Fridays, in St-Servan on Mondays and Fridays, and in Paramé on Wednesdays and Saturdays. The fish market is on Saturdays in the place de la Poissonerie, also within the walls.

Eating and drinking

Intra-muros St-Malo boasts even more **restaurants and bars** than hotels, but prices are probably higher than anywhere else in Brittany, especially on the open café terraces – apart from the *Duchesse Anne*, avoid all those around rue Jacques-Cartier and Porte St Vincent. Bear in mind that most of the crêperies also serve *moules* and similar snacks.

Le 109 5 rue des Cordiers ℡02.99.56.81.09,
ⓦwww.le-109.com. St Malo's young and smart
nightspot, hosting live music and DJs with a funk
and electro persuasion. Open until 3.30am, entry
free before midnight, €10 after.

L'Alchemiste 7 rue St-Thomas ℡02.23.18.10.06.
A mellow and atmospheric bar with great book-
filled decor and good music. The beers and
cocktails are well priced and it is open until at
least 1am.

Bistrot de Rocher 19 rue de Toulouse
℡02.99.40.82.05. Great seasonal cuisine fresh
from the market in this wood-panelled little restaurant, hidden away from the main bustle. An evening
menu costs under €20 and the service and wine
are also commendable. Last sitting 9.30pm.

🏃 Le Chalut 8 rue de la Corne-du-Cerf
℡02.99.56.71.58. This quality establishment, whose *carte* is dominated by freshly caught
fish, is the finest dining in St Malo at the moment –
make sure you try the scallop and truffle oil salad.
Lunchtime menus €24, dinner €68.

Le Corps de Garde 3 montée Notre-Dame
℡02.99.40.91.46. The only restaurant that's right
up on St-Malo's ramparts is unfortunately an
ordinary crêperie, serving standard €3.50–8.50
crêpes. However, the views from its large open-air
terrace are sensational, looking out over the beach
to the myriad little islets.

Cunningham's 2 rue des Hauts-Sabons
℡02.99.81.48.08. A chestnut and mahogany bar
ending in bay windows looking out to sea at St
Servan, that gives this lively pub the feeling of
being in the stern cabin of a galleon. Drinks are

well priced, there's a good atmosphere and if you
have too much there are inexpensive (❷) rooms to
rent above. Until 3.30am.

Duchesse Anne 5–7 place Guy-la-Chambre
℡02.99.40.85.33. Situated right next to the Porte St-
Vincent, the best known of St-Malo's upmarket
restaurants continues to work hard to keep up its
reputation – and its prices. The only set menu is a
€70 lobster option or an entire *turbotin* costing €131
for four diners. Sneak in at lunch, though, when there
is a set menu for just €20. Closed Wed & Mon lunch,
Sun evening in low season, plus all Dec & Jan.

Chez Gilles 2 rue de la Pie-qui-Boit
℡02.99.40.97.25. Bright, modern, good-value
restaurant, just off the central pedestrian axis. The
basic €20 menu is fine; alternatively, €22.50
brings you oysters or mussel soup and a rabbit
cuissot with cider and camembert. Well worth it.
Closed Wed.

🏃 Le café du coin d'en bas de la rue du
bout de la ville d'en face du port... La
Java 3 rue Ste-Barbe ℡02.99.56.41.90, ⓦwww
.lajavacafe.com. Swings at the bar, old dolls on the
wall, an elevator door into the toilet; there is
absolutely no unity in the decor of this entertaining
and unique cider bar, whose personality is matched
by its cheeky owners. Opening hours are as errartic
as the name.

Tanpopo 5 place de la Poissonerie
℡02.99.40.87.53. Japanese restaurant which
offers just one menu at a set price of €35 a night.
A relief then that the dishes are cooked and
arranged with minute care and offer exceptional
subtlety of flavour.

The Pointe du Grouin and Cancale

Along the coast east of St-Malo is the **Pointe du Grouin**, a perilous and
windy height which offers spectacular views of the pinnacle of Mont
St-Michel and the bird sanctuary of the **Îles des Landes** to the east. Just south
of the *pointe*, and less than 15km from St-Malo across the peninsula,
CANCALE is France's most renowned spot for **oysters**. In the old church of
St-Méen at the top of the hill, the town's obsession is documented with
meticulous precision by the small **Musée des Arts et Traditions Populaires**
(June & Sept Mon & Fri–Sun 2.30–6.30pm; July & Aug Mon 2.30–6.30pm,
Tues–Sun 10am–noon & 2.30–6.30pm; €4). Cancale oysters were found in the
camps of Julius Caesar, taken daily to Versailles for Louis XIV and even accom-
panied Napoleon on the march to Moscow.

From the rue des Parcs next to the jetty of the port, you can see at low tide
the *parcs* where the oysters are grown. The rocks of the cliff behind are streaked
and shiny like mother-of-pearl; underfoot the beach is littered with countless
generations of empty shells. The port area is pretty and very smart, with a long
line of upmarket glass-fronted hotels and restaurants. Cancale's **hotels** mostly
insist that you eat in if you want to stay; among the best value are 🏃 *La Houle*,
with its highly desirable balconies overlooking the middle of the port at 18

▲ Oysters, Cancale

quai Gambetta (☎02.99.89.62.38; ❶), and large, light and well-decorated rooms of *Le Querrien*, above its own restaurant at 7 quai Duguey-Trouin (☎02.99.89.64.56, ⓦwww.le-querrien.com; ❹–❻ with sea view). Budget travellers can head instead for the **hostel** 2km north of town at Port Picain (☎02.99.89.62.62, Ⓔcancale@fuaj.org; closed Jan), where a dorm bed costs just €12.50 and camping is available for even less. ✖ *Au Pied de Cheval*, 10 quai Gambetta (☎02.99.89.76.95), is a ramshackle, gloriously atmospheric little place to sample a few oysters, with great baskets of them spread across its wooden quayside tables. A dozen raw oysters on a bed of seaweed can cost just €5. More upmarket is the *Côté Mer* on route de la Corniche (☎02.99.89.66.08) with well-prepared seafood.

Dinan

The wonderful citadel of **DINAN** has preserved almost intact its three-kilometre encirclement of protective masonry, with street upon colourful street of late medieval houses within. Like St-Malo, just 25km to the north, it's best seen when arriving by boat up the River Rance, which allows you to appreciate its castle and fortifications to their best advantage. Behind the houses on the left-bank quay where the boats tie up, a steep and cobbled street with fields and bramble thickets on either side climbs up to the thirteenth-century ramparts, partly hidden by trees.

Arrival and information

Both the Art Deco **gare SNCF** and the **gare routière** (☎08.10.22.22.22; ⓦwww.tibus.fr) are in the rather gloomy modern quarter, on place du 11-Novembre, ten-minutes' walk west of the walled town. The **tourist office** can be found at the southwest corner of the place du Guesclin, at 9 rue du

Château (July & Aug Mon–Sat 9am–7pm, Sun 10am–12.30pm & 2.30–6pm; Sept–June Mon–Sat 9am–12.30pm & 2–6pm; ☎02.96.87.69.76, ⓦwww .dinan-tourisme.com). **Internet access** is available at Zonzon.com, just outside the walled town at 9 rue des Rouairies (closed Thurs).

Between April and September, **boats** along the Rance sail between the port downstream and Dinard and St-Malo. The trip takes 2 hours 45 minutes, with the exact schedule varying according to the tides (adults €22.50, under-13s €13.50). It's only possible to do a day return by boat (adults €28.50, under-13s €17) if you start from St-Malo or Dinard; starting from Dinan, you'd have to come back by bus or train. For details and timings, contact Compagnie Corsaire on the quai de la Rance (☎08.25.13.80.35, ⓦwww.compagniecorsaire.com).

Accommodation

Dinan has a surprising shortage of the kind of welcoming mid-range hotel-restaurant **accommodation** that characterizes so many Breton towns, so if that's what you're looking for you might do best to visit only as a day-trip. There are, however, plenty of budget options including a hostel, and a couple of boutique hotels if you're after something a little classier.

Hotels and B&Bs

D'Avaugour 1 place du Champ ☎02.96.39.07.49, ⓦwww.avaugourhotel.com. Smart, elegant hotel, entered from the main square but backing onto the

ramparts, with very tasteful renovated rooms and lovely gardens. ❼

Le Challonge 29 place du Guesclin ☎02.96.87.16.30, ⓦwww.hotel-dinan.fr. Modern,

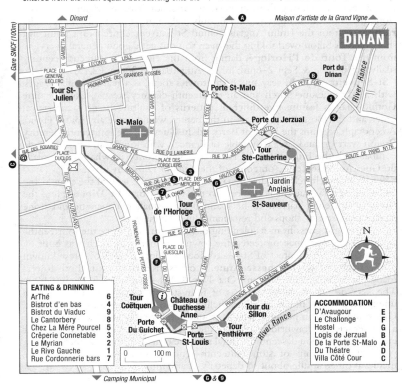

▲ Dinard ▲ Ⓐ Maison d'artiste de la Grand Vigne ▲

Gare SNCF (100m)

DINAN

PLACE DU GENERAL LECLERC
RUE GAMBETTA D766
RUE LECONTE DE LISLE
PROMENADE DES GRANDES FOSSÉS
RUE DE LA GARAYE
Tour St-Julien
Porte St-Malo
Ⓑ
Port du Dinan
RUE DU PETIT FORT
River Rance
❶
St-Malo
RUE DE L'ÉCOLE
Porte du Jerzual
❷
RUE THIERS
GRANDE RUE
RUE DU JERZUAL
Tour Ste-Catherine
ROUTE DE PARIS N176
RUE DES ROUAIRIES
Ⓒ
PLACE DUCLOS
RUE DE MARCHIX
RUE DU LAINERIE
PLACE DES CORDELIERS
HAUTEVILLE
RUE DU G. DE GAULLE
RUE DU PORT
RUE CHATEAUBRIAND
RUE DE LA CORDONNERIE
❸
❺ PLACE DES MERCIERS
❻
❹
Jardin Anglais
RUE LA CHAUX
Tour de l'Horloge
RUE DE L'HORLOGE
St-Sauveur
❽ Ⓓ
Ⓔ
RUE ST-CLAIRE
PROMENADE DES PETITES FOSSÉS
PLACE DU GUESCLIN
Ⓕ
RUE DU CHÂTEAU
RUE DE LÉHON
RUE W. ROUSSEAU
N
PROMENADE DE LA DUCHESSE ANNE
Tour Coëtquen
ⓘ Château de Duchesse Anne
Porte Du Guichet
Tour du Sillon
Porte Penthièvre
Porte St-Louis
River Rance

EATING & DRINKING	
ArThé	6
Bistrot d'en bas	4
Bistrot du Viaduc	9
Le Cantorbery	8
Chez La Mère Pourcel	5
Crêperie Connetable	3
Le Myrian	2
Le Rive Gauche	1
Rue Cordonnerie bars	7

0   100 m

ACCOMMODATION	
D'Avaugour	E
Le Challonge	F
Hostel	G
Logis de Jerzual	B
De la Porte St-Malo	A
Du Théâtre	D
Villa Côté Cour	C

▼ Camping Municipal ▼ ❻ & ❾

spotless rooms have slightly busy decor, but many have balconies, and it's above a good brasserie overlooking Dinan's main square. ❹

Logis de Jerzual 25–27 rue du Petit Fort ☎02.96.85.46.54, ⓦwww.logis-du-jerzual.com. *Chambre d'hôte* halfway up the exquisite little lane that leads from the port. The five rooms have wonderful character, with four-poster beds, modern bathrooms and romantic views over the rooftops. The house is surrounded by a lovely garden terrace and the friendly owner serves tasty breakfasts. ❹

De la Porte St-Malo 35 rue St-Malo ☎02.96.39.19.76, ⓦwww.hotelportemalo.com. Very comfortable rooms in a tasteful small hotel just outside the walls, beyond the Porte St-Malo, away from the bustle of the centre. ❸

Du Théâtre 2 rue Ste-Claire ☎02.96.39.06.91. Nine basic rooms above a bar (which closes early), opposite the Théâtre des Jacobins; the cheapest come only with a sink, but even those with en-suite bathrooms still cost under €30. Run by the same efficient management as the nearby *Le Restaurant Cantorbery* (see p.381). ❶

Hostel and campsite

HI hostel Moulin de Méen, Vallée de la Fontaine-des-Eaux ☎02.96.39.10.83, ⓔdinan@fuaj.org. Attractive, rural inn set in green fields below the town centre. Unfortunately it's not on any bus route: to walk there, follow the quay downstream from the port on the town side. Dorm bed €12.10, double room same price per person, breakfast €3.50 and camping is permitted in the grounds. Closed Jan.

Camping Municipal 103 rue Châteaubriand ☎02.96.39.11.96. In a quiet spot just outside the western ramparts, with just fifty pitches. Closed late Sept to late May.

The Town

For all its slightly unreal perfection, Dinan is not excessively overrun with tourists. There are no great museums; the monument is the town itself, and time is best spent wandering from crêperie to café, admiring overhanging houses along the way. Unfortunately, you can only walk along one small stretch of the **ramparts**, from the Jardin Anglais behind St-Sauveur church to a point just short of Tour Sillon overlooking the river. You can get a good general overview from the **Tour de l'Horloge**, dating from the end of the fifteenth century (daily: April–June & Sept 2–6pm; July & Aug 10am–6.30pm; €2.75).

St-Sauveur church, very much the town's focus, is a real mixture of ages, with a Romanesque porch and an eighteenth-century steeple. Even its nine Gothic chapels feature five different patterns of vaulting in no symmetrical order, and the most complex pair, in the centre, would make any spider proud. A cenotaph contains the heart of Bertrand du Guesclin, the fourteenth-century Breton warrior (and later Constable of France), who fought and won a single combat with the English knight Thomas of Canterbury, in what is now place du Guesclin, to settle the outcome of the siege of Dinan in 1364.

North of the church, rue du Jerzual leads down to the gate of the same name and on down (as rue du Petit-Fort) to the lovely **port du Dinan**. Here the river is sufficiently narrow to be spanned by a small but majestic old stone bridge, and artisans' shops and restaurants line the quay.

As you might guess from its blending of two separate towers, the fourteenth-century keep that once protected the town's southern approach was built by Estienne Le Tour, architect of St-Malo's Tour Solidor (see p.376). Now known as the **Château de Duchesse Anne**, it offers visitors access to both towers (daily: June–Sept 10am–6.30pm; Oct–Dec & Feb–May 1.30–5.30pm; €4.20). The keep itself, or *donjon*, consists of four storeys, each of which holds an unexpected hotch potch of items, including two big old looms and assorted Greek and Etruscan perfume jars; at ground level, well below the walls, there's a slender, closed drawbridge. Nearby, the ancient **Tour Coëtquen** is all but empty, though if you descend the spiral staircase to its waterlogged bottom floor, you'll find a group of stone fifteenth-century notables resembling some medieval time capsule, about to depetrify at any moment.

On the third weekend of July, every other (even-numbered) year, the **Fête des Remparts** is celebrated with medieval-style jousting, banquets, fairs and processions, culminating in an immense fireworks display. There's a **market** every Thursday in the places du Champ and du Guesclin (the original medieval fairground).

Eating and drinking

All sorts of specialist **restaurants**, including several ethnic alternatives, are tucked away in the old streets of Dinan. Stroll of an evening through the town and down to the port, and you'll pass at least twenty places. For **bars**, explore the series of tiny parallel alleyways between place des Merciers and rue de Marchix. Along **rue de la Cordonnerie**, you can really take your pick: *À la Truye qui File* at no. 14 is a contemporary folky Breton dive, while *Lulu Berlu*, next door at no. 12 (closed Sun & Mon), and *Chez Maryvonne* at no. 7, are considerably more raucous.

ArThé 19 rue de l'Apport ☎02.96.87.48.45. A pleasant surrounding of books and trinkets in which to sip from a wide collection of teas of the world, matched only by their even larger collection of antique teapots. It's busy, so get there early afternoon for a table.

Bistrot d'en bas 20 rue Haute Voie ☎02.96.85.44.00. The lively atmosphere spreads from behind the bar to its jazz and folk performances in this great little pub and wine bar, which serves salads and *tartines* which, too. Closed Sun evening & Mon.

Bistrot du Viaduc 22 rue du Lion d'Or ☎02.96.85.95.00. Traditional French cuisine and good wine served with the best view in town over the port and the Rance valley. Lunch menu €17.50; closed Sat lunch, Sun evening & Mon.

Le Cantorbery 6 rue Ste-Claire ☎02.96.39.02.52. Seasonal food served in an old stone house with rafters, a spiral staircase and a real wood fire. Lunch from €12, while traditional dinner menus start with a good €24 option that includes fish soup

and roast lamb. Closed Sun evening & Wed in low season.

Chez la Mère Pourcel 3 place des Merciers ☎02.96.39.03.80. Beautiful half-timbered fifteenth-century house in the central square. Good à la carte options are served all day, while the dinner menus (€18–33) are gourmet class. Closed Sun evening & Mon in low season.

Crêperie Connetable 1 rue de l'Apport. Magnificent old house, opposite the *Mère Pourcel* beside the place des Merciers, with crêpes for around €5 and snacks. The perfect spot for people-watching.

Le Myrian 3 rue du Port ☎02.96.87.93.36. Attractive and inexpensive pizzeria in a waterfront cottage down by the port, serving €7–12 pizzas, plus assorted salads and wine by the carafe, on its shady terrace.

Le Rive Gauche 4–6 rue du Port ☎02.96.87.56.77. A late running bar for a younger crowd, with a dancefloor and guest DJs, live music and themed nights, and serving well priced cocktails (€5). Closed Mon & Tues.

The north coast from Dinard to Lannion

The coast that stretches from the resort town of **Dinard** to Finistère at the far western end of Brittany is divided into two distinct regions, either side of the bay of **St-Brieuc**. Between Dinard and St-Brieuc are the exposed green headlands of the **Côte d'Émeraude**, while beyond St-Brieuc, along the **Côte de Goëlo**, the shore becomes more extravagantly indented, with a succession of secluded little bays and an increasing proliferation of huge pink-granite boulders, seen at their best on the **Côte de Granit Rose** near Treguier.

Dinard

The former fishing village of **DINARD** sprawls around the western approaches to the Rance estuary, just across from St-Malo but a good twenty minutes away by road. Known as the "Nice of the North", with its casino, spacious villas and social calendar of regattas and ballet - mementos of affluent nineteenth-century English and American tastes – it sticks out like a sore thumb in Brittany. Furthermore, despite undulating over a succession of pretty little coastal inlets, it attracts great numbers of the elderly; as a result, prices tend to be high, and pleasures sedate.

Central Dinard faces north to the open sea, across the curving bay that holds the attractive **plage de l'Écluse**. Hemmed in by venerable Victorian villas rather than hotels or shops, the beach itself has a low-key atmosphere, despite the casino and summer crowds. An unexpected statue of **Alfred Hitchcock** dominates its main access point. Standing on a giant egg, with a ferocious-looking bird perched on each shoulder, he was placed here to commemorate the town's annual festival of English-language films. Enjoyable **coastal footpaths** lead off in either direction from the principal beach, enlivened by notice boards holding reproductions of paintings produced at points along the way. Surprisingly Pablo Picasso's *Deux Femmes courants sur la Plage* and *Baigneuses sur la Plage*, both of which look quintessentially Mediterranean with their blue skies and golden sands, were in fact painted here in Dinard during his annual summer visits throughout the 1920s.

Practicalities

Dinard's small **airport**, 4km southeast of the town centre, off the D168 near **Pleurtuit**, is served by Ryanair flights from London Stansted. The connecting Illenoo bus #990 runs via Dinard's tourist office to St-Malo for a €4 flat fare. Many visitors simply come over for the day on one of the regular Companie Corsaire **boats** from St-Malo (℡08.25.13.81.30 Ⓦwww.compagniecorsaire .com; €6 return). A couple of hundred metres west is the **tourist office**, in the centre at 2 boulevard Féart (July & Aug Mon–Sat 9.30am–1pm & 2–7pm Sun 10am–12.15pm & 2.15–6.30pm; Sept–June Mon–Sat 9am–12.30pm & 2–6pm; ℡02.99.46.94.12, Ⓦwww.ot-dinard.com).

Dinard tends to be an expensive place to stay, but it does have a wide selection of **hotels** to choose from, many of which can be found at Ⓦwww.dinard-hotel -plus.com. Options include two good mid-ranges: the *Hôtel-Restaurant Printania*, 5 avenue George-V (℡02.99.46.13.07, Ⓦwww.printaniahotel.com; ❹; closed mid-Nov to mid-March), on a quiet street as it drops down to the port with a magnificent terrace restaurant looking towards St-Malo; and the *Didier Méril*, 1 place du Général-de-Gaulle (℡02.99.46.95.74; ❺), with tasteful decor and a great restaurant – if you call ahead you can be picked up from the station in an old black cab. The best local **campsite** is the municipal *Port Blanc*, with shady pitches right by the plage du Port-Blanc for under €20, on rue du Sergent-Boulanger (℡02.99.46.10.74; closed Oct–March).

The Côte d'Émeraude

To the west of the Rance, beyond Dinard, begins the green of the **Côte d'Émeraude**. Though composed mainly of developed family resorts, it also offers wonderful camping, at its best around the heather-backed beaches near **Cap Fréhel**, a high, warm expanse of heath and cliffs with views extending on good days as far as Jersey and the Île de Bréhat – camping is, however, forbidden within 5km of the headland itself. The **Fort la Latte**, to the east, is used regularly as a film set. Its tower, containing a cannonball factory, is accessible only over two drawbridges, and can only be visited on guided tours (early July to late Aug daily 10am–7pm; April to early July, and late Aug to Sept daily 10am–12.30pm & 2–6pm; Oct–March Sat, Sun & holidays 2–6pm; €4.50; ℡02.99.30.38.84, Ⓦwww.castlelalatte.com).

The nearest places to stay are the ideal, isolated **campsite** at Pléherel, the *Camping des Grèves d'En Bas* (☎02.96.41.43.34, ✉mairie.cap.frehel@orange.fr; closed Oct–May), and a basic **hostel** on the D16 just outside Plévenon en route towards the cape at Kérivet-en-Fréhel, *La Ville Hardrieux* (☎02.96.41.48.98, ✉capfrehel@fuaj.org; dorm beds €8; open April–Sept) – which also offers horseriding and rents out bicycles. Visit ⓦwww.pays-de-frehel.com for more information on the area.

Erquy

Further round the headland, the perfect crescent of beach at **ERQUY** curves through more than 180 degrees. At low tide, the sea disappears way beyond the harbour entrance, leaving gentle ripples of paddling sand. Equipped with suitable boots, you can walk right across its mouth, from the grassy wooded headland on the left side over to the picturesque little lighthouse at the end of the jetty on the right.

Tibus's Bus line 2 (ⓦwww.tibus.fr) goes from St Brieuc to Fréhel, also calling at the TGV station in Lamballe, and stopping at the place du Centre in Erquy. The tourist office, just north on 3 rue du 19 Mars (Apr–June Mon–Sat 9.30am–12.30pm & 2–6pm, Sun 10am–12.30pm; July & Aug Mon–Sat 9.30am–1pm & 2–7pm, Sun 10am–1pm & 4–6pm; Oct–April Mon–Sat 9.30am–12.30pm & 2–5pm; ☎02.96.72.30.12, ⓦwww.erquy-tourisme.com), coordinates information for the surrounding area. The best place in town is the excellently decorated *chambre d'hôte* 🏆 *La Villa Nazado* on 2 rue des Patriotes (☎02.96.63.67.14, ⓦwww.villanazado.com; 4) at the southern end of the beach. The stately *Hôtel Beauséjour*, perching at 21 rue de la Corniche (☎02.96.72.30.39, ⓦwww.beausejour-erquy.com; ❸; closed Mon evening in low season), has a good view of the bay, and excellent fish dinners from €18.50, while the more upmarket restaurant *l'Escurial* (☎02.96.72.31.56; closed Sun evening & Mon) by the seafront serves a five-course menu that consists entirely of scallops, the town's speciality. There are several campsites on the promontory (dotted with tiny coves) that leads to the Cap d'Erquy north of town, including the three-star *St-Pabu* (☎02.96.72.24.65, ⓦwww.saintpabu.com; closed mid-Oct to March) right beside the sea.

The Côte de Goëlo

Moving northwest towards Paimpol along the **Côte de Goëlo**, the shoreline becomes wilder and harsher and the seaside towns tend to be crammed into narrow rocky inlets or set well back in river estuaries. The sedate family resort of **ST-QUAY-PORTRIEUX** is the most appealing place to stay along the coast, with the small and characterful *Gerbot d'Avoine* as the best option beside the beach (☎02.96.70.40.09, ⓦwww.gerbotdavoine.com; ❸; closed Jan & mid-Nov to mid-Dec).

Paimpol and around

At the top of the Côte de Goëlo, **PAIMPOL** is an attractive town with a tangle of cobbled alleyways and fine grey-granite houses, though stripped of some character from its transition from working fishing port to pleasure harbour. It was once the centre of a cod and whaling fleet, which sailed to Iceland each February after being sent off with a ceremony marked by a famous *pardon*. From then until September the town would be empty of its young men. Thanks to naval shipyards and the like, the open sea is not visible from Paimpol; a maze of waterways leads to its two separate **harbours**. Both are usually filled with the high masts of yachts, but are still also used by the fishing vessels that keep a fish market and a plethora of *poissonneries* busy.

A couple of kilometres short of town, in a superbly romantic setting, the D786 passes the substantial ruins of the **Abbaye de Beauport** (daily: mid-June to mid-Sept 10am–7pm, with regular 1hr 30min guided tours; mid-Sept to mid-June 10am–noon & 2–5pm; Ⓦwww.abbaye-beauport.com; €4.50/€5 in season), established in 1202 by Count Alain de Goëlo. Its stone walls are covered with wild flowers and ivy, the central cloisters are engulfed by a huge tree, and birds fly everywhere. The Norman Gothic chapterhouse is the most noteworthy building to survive, and its roofless halls hold relics from all periods of its history. In summer, the abbey reopens for late-night visits, with imaginative lighting effects (July & Aug Wed & Sun 10pm–1am; €8), and also hosts weekly Breton music concerts (mid-July to mid-Aug Thurs 9pm; €12).

The **Gare SNCF**, with connections to the TGV at Guingamp, and the **Gare Routière**, from where line 9 serves the Côte de Goëlo, St Brieuc and the Pointe de l'Arcouest, are on Avenue du Générale de Gaulle. Places to **stay** in Paimpol include the grand old ⚓ *Hôtel K'Loys*, overlooking the small-boat harbour from 21 quai Morand (Ⓣ02.96.20.50.13, Ⓦwww.k-loys.com; ❸–❻), whose comfortable rooms vary in price according to size and view, the most expensive with a glass roof to sleep under the stars; the very hospitable *Hôtel Berthelot* at 1 rue du Port (Ⓣ02.96.20.88.66; ❶) is a little kitch, but good for the price. As for **restaurants**, *La Cotriade*, on the far side of the harbour on the quai Armand-Dayot (Ⓣ02.96.20.81.08; closed all day Mon, Fri evening & Sat lunch), is the best bet for authentic fish dishes, with menus from €21.

The Île de Bréhat

Two kilometres off the coast at Pointe de l'Arcouest, 6km northwest of Paimpol, the **ÎLE DE BRÉHAT** – in reality two islands joined by a tiny bridge – gives the appearance of spanning great latitudes. On its north side are windswept meadows of hemlock and yarrow, sloping down to chaotic erosions of rock; on the south, you're in the midst of palm trees, mimosa and eucalyptus. All around is a multitude of little islets – some accessible at low tide, others *propriété privée*, most just pink-orange rocks. All in all, it is one of the most beautiful places in Brittany, renowned as a sanctuary not only for rare species of wild flowers – especially blue acanthus – but also for birds of all kinds.

Boats to Bréhat (see opposite) arrive at the small harbour of **PORT-CLOS**, though depending on the tide passengers may have to walk several hundred metres before setting foot on terra firma. No **cars** are permitted on the island, so many visitors rent **bikes** at the port, for €15 per day. However, it's easy enough to explore the whole place on foot; walking from one end to the other takes less than an hour.

Each batch of new arrivals heads first to Bréhat's village, **LE BOURG**, five hundred metres up from the port. As well as a handful of hotels, restaurants and bars, it also holds a limited array of shops, a post office, a bank and an ATM, and hosts a small **market** most days. In high season, the attractive central square tends to be packed fit to burst, with exasperated holiday-home owners pushing their little hand-wagons through the throngs of day-trippers.

Continue a short distance north of Le Bourg, however, and you'll soon cross over the slender **Pont ar Prat** bridge to the northern island, where the crowds thin out, and countless little coves offer opportunities to sprawl on the tough grass or clamber across the rugged boulders. At the northmost tip, where the Paon lighthouse stands erect over the rock-scattered waters, young girls of the island used to throw rocks into the wash, believing that if it landed in the water without hitting a rock they would marry their love, but if it hit a rock, it would be a cold bed for another year. Though the coastal footpath around this northern half offers the most attractive walking on the island, the best **beaches** line the southern shores, with the **Grève du Guerzido** at its southeastern corner, being the pick of the crop.

Practicalities

Bréhat is connected regularly by **ferry** from the Pointe de l'Arcouest, 6km northwest of Paimpol, and served by summer buses from the *gare SNCF* there. Roughly speaking, sailings, with Les Vedettes de Bréhat (℡02.96.55.79.50, Ⓦwww.vedettesdebrehat.com), are half-hourly in July & Aug, hourly between April and June and in September, and every 1hr 30min otherwise, with the first boat out to Bréhat at 8.30am in summer, and the last boat back at 7.45pm. The return trip costs €8.50 (bikes, €15 extra, are only allowed outside peak crossing times). The same company also operates boats in summer from Erquy and St-Quay-Portrieux, as well as doing boat tours of the island (daily Sept–Mar; €15).

Bréhat's **tourist office** is in the main square in Le Bourg (July & Aug Mon–Sat 10am–5pm; Sept–June, call for current hours; ℡02.96.20.04.15, Ⓦwww.brehat-infos.fr). All the **hotels** on the island get booked through the summer, and close for at least part of the winter. The *Bellevue* in Port-Clos (℡02.96.20.00.05, Ⓦwww.hotel-bellevue-brehat.com; ❼; open mid-Feb to mid-Nov), insists on *demi-pension* in high season, despite its restaurant being interminally packed with newcomers from the ferry. The smaller *Aux Pêcheurs* (℡02.96.20.00.14; ❻; closed Jan), on the main square in Le Bourg, has a nice little garden terrace. The standout, and best value, place to stay is the ⚓ *Men-Joliguet* bed and breakfast (℡02.96.20.08.29; ❹), right beside the *Bellevue* in the Port-Clos, whose refitted, bright and sleek interior is more chilled than a yoga studio. There's also a wonderful municipal **campsite** in the woods high above the sea west of the port (℡02.96.20.00.36; closed mid-Sept to mid-June; €11 for a spot).

The Côte de Granit Rose

The entire northernmost stretch of the Breton coast, from Bréhat to **Ploumanac'h**, has loosely come to be known as the **Côte de Granit Rose**. There are indeed great granite boulders scattered in the sea around the island of Bréhat, and at the various headlands to the west, but the most memorable stretch of coast lies north of **Treguier**, where the pink-granite rocks are eroded into fantastic shapes.

La petite maison de Plougrescant

Perhaps the best-known photographic image of Brittany is of a small seafront cottage, known fairly unimaginatively as the *Petite maison de Plougrescant*, somehow squeezed between two mighty pink-granite boulders. Surprisingly few visitors, however, manage to see the house in real life. It stands 10km north of Tréguier, 2km out from the village of **PLOUGRESCANT**. The precise spot tends to be marked on regional maps as either **Le Gouffre** or Le Gouffre du Castel-Meur, and is signposted off the coastal road a short way west of the Pointe du Château. Although you can't visit the cottage itself, which actually faces inland across a small sheltered bay, the shoreline nearby offers superb short walks, and there's a little summer-only café selling snacks and ice creams. Bus 16 runs from Treguier to Plougrescent (Ⓦwww.tibus.fr).

Tréguier

The D786 turns west from Paimpol, passing over a green *ria* on the bridge outside Lézardrieux before arriving at **TRÉGUIER**, one of the very few hill-towns in Brittany. Its central feature is the **Cathédrale de St-Tugdual** (July & Aug daily 9am–7pm; Sept–June 10am–noon & 2–6pm), which contains the tomb of St Yves, a native of the town who died in 1303 and – for his incorruptibility – became the patron saint of lawyers. Attempts to bribe him continue to this day; his tomb is surrounded by marble plaques and an inferno of candles invoking his aid. Out of town to the south, near Trédarzec, the **Jardins de Kerdalo** (July & Aug Mon–Sat 2–6pm; April–June & Sept Mon & Sat 2–6pm; €8), brainchild of the aristocratic Russian artist and plantsman Peter Wolkonsky, and now in the care of his talented daughter, are unquestionably among the best in France. Rare and exotic breeds ramble through the grounds, given the care and space to express themselves through conscientious gardening; it is a joyful change from the exacting straight line gardening of so many châteaux and a rare treat to behold.

Buses run from the town centre to Paimpol and Lannion (line 7) and along the Côte de Granit Rose (line 16). **The tourist office** is at 67 rue Ernest-Renan (July & Aug Mon–Sat 10am–6pm, Sun 10am–1pm; Sept–June Tues–Sat 9.30am–1pm & 2–6pm; ℡02.96.92.22.33, ⓦwww.ot-cotedesajoncs.com). It's best to **stay** down by the port, at either the fancy new *Hôtel Aigue-Marine*, close to the bridge and boasting a heated pool, sauna, Jacuzzi and excellent restaurant (℡02.96.92.97.00, ⓦwww.aiguemarine.fr; ⑤), or the much more basic *Hôtel-Restaurant d'Estuaire* (℡02.96.92.30.25; ①), which has great views from its upstairs dining room and serves a reasonable €13 menu. At the *Poissonnerie Moulinet*, above a fish shop just below the cathedral at 2 rue Ernest-Renan (℡02.96.92.30.27), you can buy superb seafood platters at low prices, to take away and eat in the square. During the **market** each Wednesday, clothes are spread out in the square by the cathedral, with food and fresh fish down by the port.

Château de la Roche-Jagu

About 10km inland from Tréguier, on a heavily wooded slope above the Trieux River, stands the fifteenth-century **Château de la Roche-Jagu** (daily: mid-June to mid-Sept 10am–7pm; mid-Sept to Nov & Feb to mid-June 10.30am–12.30pm & 2–6pm; park access free, château €3, or more during special exhibitions). It's a gorgeous building – a harmonious combination of fortress and home – and plays host to lavish annual exhibitions, usually on some sort of Celtic theme. The rooms within are bare, but if you climb to the top, you can admire the beautiful woodwork of the restored eaves, and walk the two long indoor galleries, offering tremendous views over the river.

Ploumanac'h

A great walk along the **Sentier des Douaniers** pathway winds round the clifftops from plage Trestraou at the missable town of Perros-Guirec to the tiny resort of **PLOUMANAC'H**, past an astonishing succession of deformed and water-sculpted rocks. Birds wheel overhead towards the offshore bird sanctuary of **Sept-Îles**, and battered boats shelter in the narrow inlets or bob uncontrollably out on the waves. There are patches and brief causeways of grass, clumps of purple heather and yellow gorse. The small golden yellow beach here is a surreal treat, in an alcove of soft shaped and smooth pink granite formations protected by numerous other outcrops in the bay, one of which barely separates a glorious private house from the waves.

▲ Lighthouse on the Sentier des Douaniers

Ploumanac'h offers the *St-Guirec et de la Plage* (℡02.96.91.40.89, Ⓦwww
.hotelsaint-guirec.com; ❸–❺ obligatory half board in July & Aug; closed Nov–
March), which has some lovely sea-view rooms at bargain rates; eat either at the
adjoining *Coste-Mor* (℡02.96.91.65.55) – where good menus start at €14, with
a lovely seafood *pot au feu* on the €26 one, and the terrace is right above the
beach – or the simpler, cheaper dining room reserved for *pensionnaire* guests.
Immediately across the road, with an equally superb prospect of the beach, the
Castel Beau Site, plage du St-Guirec (℡02.96.91.40.87, Ⓦwww.castelbeausite
.com; ❽), is a much more lavish alternative, with a delicious, expensive restaurant into the bargain. The nicest place to **camp** is the four-star *Le Ranolien*
(℡02.96.91.65.65, Ⓦwww.leranolien.com; closed mid-Nov to March; €17–35
depending on the season), in a superb position backing onto the Sentier des
Douaniers near a little beach about halfway round, but directly accessible on the
other side by road, and boasting a great array of swimming pools, waterslides, a
spa and a cinema.

The Bay of Lannion

Despite being set significantly back from the sea on the estuary of the River
Léguer, **Lannion** gives its name to the next bay west along the Breton coast –
and it's the bay rather than the town that is most likely to impress visitors. One
enormous beach stretches from **St-Michel-en-Grève**, which is little more than
a bend in the road, as far as **Locquirec**; at low tide you can walk hundreds of
metres out on the sands.

Lannion

LANNION, set amid plummeting hills and stairways, is a historic city with
streets of medieval housing and a couple of interesting old churches – but it's
also a centre for a burgeoning and extremely high-tech telecommunications
industry, and one of modern Brittany's real success stories. Hence its rather self-
satisfied nickname, *ville heureuse* or "happy town". In addition to admiring the

half-timbered houses around the **place de Général-Leclerc** and along **rue des Chapeliers**, it's well worth climbing from the town up the 142 granite steps which lead to the twelfth-century Templar **Église de Brélévenez**. The views from its terrace are stupendous.

Lannion's **tourist office** is at 2 quai d'Aiguillon (July & Aug Mon–Sat 9am–7pm, Sun 10am–1pm; Sept–June Mon–Sat 9.30am–12.30pm & 2–6pm; ☎02.96.46.41.00, Ⓦwww.ot-lannion.fr). There's a **hostel** in the centre, at 6 rue du 73ᵉ Territorial (☎02.96.37.91.28; €17), recently done up and with a restaurant and bar on site; they also arrange birdwatching and similar expeditions and rent out bikes. You can eat good cheap seafood cuisine at *La Flambée*, 67 rue Georges-Pompidou (☎02.96.48.04.85; closed Mon).

The Cairn du Barnenez

In a glorious position at the mouth of the Morlaix estuary, 13km north of Morlaix itself, the prehistoric stone **Cairn du Barnenez** surveys the waters from the summit of a hill (May–Aug daily 10am–6.30pm; Sept–April Tues–Sun 10am–12.30pm & 2–5.30pm; €5). As on the island of Gavrinis in the Morbihan, its ancient masonry was exposed by quarrying activities around thirty years ago, and provides a stunning sense of the architectural prowess of the megalith builders. Radiocarbon testing has shown the work here to date back to around 4500 BC, which makes this one of the oldest large-scale monuments in the world.

The two distinct stepped pyramids rise in successive tiers, built of large flat stones chinked with pebbles; the second was added onto the side of the first, and the two are encircled by a series of terraces and ramps. The whole thing measures roughly 70m long by 15–25m wide and 6m high. Both pyramids were long buried under the same eighty-metre-long earthen mound. While the actual cairns are completely exposed to view, most of the passages and chambers that lie within them are sealed off. The two minor corridors that are open simply cut through the edifice from one side to the other but visitors are not permitted to pass through. Local tradition has it that one tunnel runs right through this "home of the fairies", and continues out deep under the sea, but recent findings suggest that this may not, in fact, be the case.

Finistère

It's hard to resist the appeal of the **Finistère coast**, with its ocean-fronting cliffs and headlands. Summer crowds may detract from the best parts of the **Crozon peninsula** and the **Pointe de Raz**, but there are many kilometres of coast where you can enjoy near solitude. If you have transport, explore the semi-wilderness beyond Brest and the little fishing village of **Le Conquet**, or take a ferry trip to the misty offshore islands of **Ouessant** and **Sein**. From the top of **Ménez-Hom** you can admire the anarchic limits of western France, while the cities of **Morlaix** and **Quimper** display modern Breton life as well as ancient splendours, and the **parish closes** south of Morlaix reveal much about the beliefs of the past.

Léon

Memories of the days when Brittany was "Petite Bretagne", as opposed to "Grande Bretagne" across the water, linger in the names of Finistère's two main areas, **Léon** (once Lyonesse), the northern peninsula, and its southern neighbour Cornouaille (Cornwall). Both feature prominently in Arthurian legend. In the north of Léon, the ragged **coastline** is the prime attraction, indented with a succession of estuaries or **abers**, each of which shelters its own tiny harbour: heading west from either the thriving historic town of **Morlaix** or the appealing little Channel port of **Roscoff**, there are possible stopping places all the way to **Le Conquet**. From Le Conquet, you can reach the island of **Ouessant** across a treacherous stretch of ocean. Inland, by contrast, the ornate medieval village churches known as **parish closes** hold some of Brittany's finest religious architecture.

Morlaix

MORLAIX, one of the great old Breton ports, thrived on trade with England in between wars during the "Golden Period" of the late Middle Ages. Built up the slopes of a steep valley with sober stone houses, the town was originally protected by an eleventh-century castle and a circuit of walls. Little is left of either, but the old centre remains in part medieval with its cobbled streets and half-timbered houses. The present grandeur comes from the pink-granite **viaduct** carrying trains from Paris to Brest towering above the town centre. Coming by road from the north, the opening view is of shiny yacht masts paralleling the pillars of the viaduct.

The **Jacobin convent** that fronts place des Jacobins, which once housed the five-year old Mary Queen of Scots on her way to the French court, now houses the **Musée de Morlaix**, a reasonably entertaining assortment of Roman wine jars, bits that have fallen off medieval churches, cannons and kitchen utensils, and a few modern paintings (April, May & Sept Mon & Wed–Sat 10am–noon & 2–6pm, Sun 2–6pm; July & Aug daily 10am–12.30pm & 2–6.30pm; Oct–March & June Mon & Wed–Sat 10am–noon & 2–5pm; €4). The same ticket entitles you to a guided tour of the fabulously restored, sixteenth-century **Maison à Pondalez**, at 9 Grand-Rue (same hours), an example of the fifteenth century 'maisons à lanterne' (lantern houses) unique to Morlaix and discernable by their increasingly jutting storeys and ornate exterior staircases in the courtyards.

Practicalities

The **tourist office** in Morlaix is in a solitary but central one-storey building, almost under the viaduct in place des Otages (July & Aug Mon–Sat 9am–12.30pm & 1.30–7pm, Sun 10.30am–12.30pm; Sept–June Mon 9.30am–12.30pm & 2–6pm, Tues–Sat 9am–12.30pm & 2–6pm; ☎02.98.62.14.94, Ⓦwww.morlaix tourisme.fr). All **buses** conveniently depart from place Cornic, right under the viaduct, but the **gare SNCF** is on rue Armand-Rousseau, high above the town at the western end of the viaduct. To reach it on foot, you have to climb the steep steps of Venelle de la Roche.

On the whole, Morlaix's **hotels** are fairly uninspiring, but the eccentric old *De l'Europe*, above a simple but good brasserie at 1 rue d'Aiguillon (☎02.98.62.11.99, Ⓦwww.hotel-europe-com.fr; ❺), holds well-equipped modern rooms. Less expensive options include the *Hôtel de la Gare*, 25 place St-Martin close to the *gare SNCF* (☎02.98.88.03.29; ❸). The best bet, if you don't mind the walk, is the English-owned ⚘ *Manoir Coatamour*, 1km southeast of the centre along the route de Paris (℡02.98.88.57.02, Ⓦwww.gites-morlaix .com; ❺) with lavish rooms in a manor house with large gardens and a pool.

The best hunting ground for **restaurants** is to be found between St-Melaine church and place des Jacobins. Choices include *La Marée Bleue*, 3 rampe Ste-Mélaine (℡02.98.63.24.21; closed Oct, plus Sun evening & Mon), a well-respected seafood restaurant – splash out on the €27 menu for a superb *assiette de fruits de mer* – and *Le Tempo* (℡02.98.63.29.11; closed Sat lunch & Sun), which serves big salads (€8) and has a good bar with seaviews, at their best in the evenings.

The parish closes

Morlaix makes an excellent base for visiting the countryside towards Brest, where **parish closes**, or *enclos paroissiaux* (walled churchyards incorporating cemetery, calvary and ossuary), celebrate the distinctive character of Breton Catholicism – closer to the Celtic past than to Rome – in elaborately sculpted scenes. Stone calvaries are covered in detailed scenes of the Crucifixion above a crowd of saints, Gospel stories and legends; in richer parishes, a high stone arch leads into the churchyard, adjoining an equally majestic ossuary, where bones would be taken when the tiny cemeteries filled up. Most of the parish closes date from the two centuries either side of the union with France in 1532, Brittany's wealthiest period.

The most famous *enclos* are in three neighbouring parishes off the N12 between Morlaix and Landivisiau, on a clearly signposted route that's served by an SNCF bus. At **ST-THÉGONNEC**, the church **pulpit**, carved by two brothers in 1683, is the acknowledged masterpiece, albeit so swamped with detail – symbolic saints, sibyls and arcane figures – that it is almost too intricate to take in. At the pretty flower-filled village of **GUIMILIAU**, 6km southwest, the **calvary** is an incredible ensemble of over two hundred granite figures, depicting scenes from the life of Christ and rendered all the more dramatic by being covered with what has been called "secular lichen". A uniquely Breton illustration, just above the Last Supper, depicts the unfortunate Katell Gollet – Katherine the Damned, a figure from local myth who stole consecrated wafers to give to her lover, who naturally turned out to be the Devil – being torn to shreds by demons. At **LAMPAUL–GUIMILIAU**, the painted wooden baptistry, the dragons on the beams and the suitably wicked faces of the robbers on the calvary are the key components.

Katell Gollet is said to have lived in the ruined castle above the Elhorn estuary at **LA ROCHE–MAURICE**, 15km on towards Brest. In legend, she danced all her suitors to death until the reaper-figure Ankou stepped in to whirl her to eternal damnation; Ankou is depicted on the ossuary of the nearby church with the inscription "I kill you all". Another five-kilometre detour southeast brings further variations at **LA MARTYRE** (where Ankou clutches his disembodied head) and its adjoining parish **PLOUDIRY**, the sculpting of its ossuary affirming the equality of social classes – in the eyes of Ankou.

In St-Thégonnec the ⚘ *Auberge de St-Thégonnec*, 6 place de la Mairie (℡02.98.79.61.18, Ⓦwww.aubergesaintthegonnec.com; ❺; restaurant closed Sat lunch, Sun evening & Mon lunch in July & Aug; Sun, Mon lunch & Sat lunch Sept–June, plus all Jan), is a surprisingly smart **hotel** for such a small village, and has a superb **restaurant**.

Roscoff

The opening of the deep-water port at **ROSCOFF** in 1973 was part of a general attempt to revitalize the Breton economy. The **ferry services** to

Plymouth and to Cork aim not just to bring tourists, but also to revive the traditional trading links between the Celtic nations of Brittany, Ireland and southwest England. In fact, Roscoff had already long been a significant port. Mary Queen of Scots landed here in 1548 on her way to Paris to be engaged to François, the son of Henri II of France, as did Bonnie Prince Charlie, the Young Pretender, in 1746, after his defeat at Culloden.

Arrival and information

Boats from Plymouth, Cork and Rosslare, run by Brittany Ferries (☎08.25.82.88.28, ⓦwww.brittany-ferries.fr), dock at the Port de Bloscon, a couple of kilometres to the east (and just out of sight) of Roscoff. In summer, a direct **bus** service to Morlaix and Quimper leaves from the ferry terminal (Tues, Wed, Fri & Sat 7.30am, Mon, Thurs & Sun 3.30pm; CAT; ☎02.98.44.46.73). From the **gare SNCF**, a few hundred metres south of the town proper, a restricted rail service (often replaced by buses) runs to Morlaix. Most **local buses** also go from here, including a direct service to Brest run by Bihan Voyages (☎02.98.83.45.80, ⓦwww.bihan.com).

The **tourist office** is at 46 rue Gambetta in town (July & Aug Mon–Sat 9am–12.30pm & 1.30–7pm, Sun 10am–12.30pm; Sept–June Mon–Sat 9am–noon & 2–6pm; ☎02.98.61.12.13, ⓦwww.roscoff-tourisme.com).

Accommodation

For a small town, Roscoff is well equipped with **hotels**, which are accustomed to late-night arrivals from the ferries. Most, however, are relatively expensive and closed for some or all of the winter. Cheaper options on the Île de Batz (see p.392) are easy to commute from by ferry. The campsite *Aux Quatre Saisons,* 2km west in Perharidy, offers standard facilities for under €13 just off the route de Santec (☎02.98.69.70.86, ⓔcamping-perharidy@orange.fr; closed mid-Oct to March).

Les Chardons Bleus 4 rue Amiral-Réveillère ☎02.98.69.72.03, ⓦwww.chardonsbleus.fr.st. A comfortable and very friendly hotel in the heart of the old town, with a good restaurant (closed Thurs & Sun evening Sept–June) where dinner menus start at €19. Closed mid-Feb to mid-March. ❸
Chez Lucie Quémeneur 27B rue Le Mat ☎02.98.69.71.36. The best value option in town, this B&B has fine and clean rooms, with a lovely garden and very friendly owner. ❷
Du Centre 5 rue Gambetta ☎02.98.61.24.25, ⓦwww.chezjanie.com. Family hotel above the café-bar *Chez Janie*, entered via the main street but looking out on the port. The rooms are modern and tastefully furnished; those with sea views cost €19 extra. The ground floor bar is one of the liveliest spots in town. Closed mid-Dec to mid-Feb. ❹
Le Temps de Vivre 19 place Lacaze-Duthiers ☎02.98.19.33.19, ⓦwww.letempsdevivre.net. This design-concious newcomer to Roscoff's hotel scene, near the Notre-Dame church in the heart of town, offers luxuriously spacious rooms with designer bathrooms, and wonderful sea views. Off-season rates are over €50 lower. ❼

The Town

Roscoff itself, nonetheless, remains a small resort, where almost all activity is confined to **rue Gambetta** and to the old port. The town's sixteenth-century church, **Notre-Dame-de-Croas-Batz**, at the far end of rue Gambetta, is embellished with an ornate Renaissance belfry, complete with sculpted ships and a protruding stone cannon. From the side, rows of bells can be seen hanging in galleries, one above the other like some kind of Disney wedding cake. Some way beyond is Roscoff's best **beach**, at Laber, surrounded by expensive hotels and apartments.

The old **harbour** is livelier, mixing an economy based on fishing with relatively low-key pleasure trips to the **Île de Batz**. The **Criée de Roscoff** (fish auction) on port de Bloscon (Apr–Jun & Sept–Oct Wed 3pm; July & Aug Mon–Thurs 11am, 3pm, 5pm; €4) opens up the fisherman's life from catch to sale, with exhibitions films, games and knot-tying to hoover up the kids' attention.

In 1828, Henri Ollivier took **onions** to England from Roscoff, thereby founding a trade that flourished until the 1930s. The story of the "Johnnies" – that classic French image of men in black berets with strings of onions hanging over the handlebars of their bicycles – is told at **La Maison des Johnnies et de l'Oignon Rosé de Roscoff**, 48 rue Brizeux, near the *gare SNCF* (mid-June to mid-Sept Mon–Fri 11am, 2pm, 3.30pm & 5pm, Sun 2pm, 3.30pm & 5pm; mid-Feb to mid-June & mid-Sept to Dec Mon, Tues, Thurs, Fri & Sun 2.30pm; €4).

Eating

The obvious places to **eat** in Roscoff are the dining rooms of the hotels themselves – *Le Temps de Vivre* is especially recommended – but the town does hold a few specialist **restaurants** as well, plus a bunch of appealing crêperies around the old harbour. If you're arriving on an evening ferry out of season, be aware that it can be difficult to find a restaurant still serving any later than 9.15pm.

Les Alizés 37 rue Amiral-Courbet
☎ 02.98.69.75.90. Good meat dishes, as well as fish, may come as a slight relief for those leaving Brittany from Roscoff. There is also a terrace on the quai-side and good value €12 lunch menus. Closed Sun evening & Mon out of season.
Crêperie de la Poste 12 rue Gambetta
☎ 02.98.69.72.81. Central crêperie, open from 11.30am until late, where an à la carte meal of sweet and savoury pancakes should work out cheaply; more exotic seafood options cost up to

€8.50. They also serve fish soup, mussels and other simple meals. Closed Wed Sept–June, or Tues July & Aug.
L'Écume des Jours quai d'Auxerre
☎ 02.98.61.22.83. Cosy restaurant in a grand old house facing the port, offering good-value set lunches for €12.50 on weekdays, plus dinner menus from €20, featuring such delights as braised oysters or scallops with local pink onions. Closed Dec & Jan, and Tues & Wed in low season.

The Île de Batz

The long, narrow **ÎLE DE BATZ** (pronounced "Ba") mirrors Roscoff across the water, separated from it by a sea channel that's barely 200m wide at low tide but perhaps five times that when the tide is high. Appearances from the mainland are somewhat deceptive: the island's old town fills much of its southern shoreline, but those parts of Batz not visible from Roscoff are much wilder and more windswept. With no cars permitted, and some great expanses of sandy beach, it makes a wonderfully quiet retreat for families in particular.

Ferries from Roscoff arrive at the quayside of the old town. There's a nice small beach along the edge of the harbour, but it turns into a morass of slimy seaweed at low tide. You may well spot the island's best beach from the boat – it's the white-sand **Grève Blanche** towards its eastern end. Walking in that direction also brings you to the hostel (see opposite), the 44-metre lighthouse that stands on the island's peak, all of 23m above sea level (second half of June daily except Wed 2–5pm; July to mid-Sept daily 1–5.30pm; €1.70) and the **Jardin exotique Georges-Delaselle** (Apr–June & Sept–Oct Wed–Mon 2–6pm; July & Aug daily 1–6pm; € 4.50) is a 75-year-old garden that takes advantage of the island's temperate microclimate to sustain its palm trees and other non-native flora.

Practicalities

Three different companies operate fifteen-minute **ferry** services to the Île de Batz from Roscoff's long pier. Between late June and mid-September, the service is pretty much nonstop between 8am and 8pm daily, while at other times of year there are eight to ten trips daily between 8.30am and 7pm. The return fare is €7, with a €5 charge for bikes; alternatively you can rent a bike at *La Cassonnade* (below).

The island's nicest **hotel**, at the centre of the harbour, is the *Grand Hôtel Morvan* (☎02.98.61.78.06, ⓦwww.grand-hotel-morvan.com; ❷; closed Dec to mid-March), which serves good meals on its large seafront terraces. There's a **hostel** in a beautiful setting by the beach at the evocatively named Creach ar Bolloc'h (☎02.98.61.77.69, ⓦwww.aj-iledebatz.org; closed Nov–March; €11.90). The best B&B is *Ti Va Zadou* (☎02.98.61.76.91; ❸), with comfortable rooms, a good view and big breakfasts. As for **eating** and **drinking**, *La Cassonade* (☎02.98.61.75.25) makes hearty *galettes*, largely from produce grown on the island itself, and rents out bikes for €10 per day, and ⚓ *Le Bigorneau Langoureux* (☎02.98.61.74.50) is a very pleasant spot to be languorous over a bottle from the good selection of Basque wines.

The abers

The coast west of Roscoff is among the most dramatic in Brittany, a jagged series of **abers** – deep, narrow estuaries – that hold a succession of small, isolated resorts. It's a little on the bracing side, especially if you're making use of the numerous **campsites**, but that just has to be counted as part of the appeal. In summer, at least, the temperatures are mild enough, and things get progressively more sheltered as you move around towards Le Conquet and Brest.

Around the abers

If you're dependent on public transport, bear in mind that the only stop on the Roscoff–Brest bus before it turns inland is **PLOUESCAT**. It's not quite on the sea itself, but there are campsites nearby on each of three adjacent beaches; of the **hotels**, best value is the *Roc'h-Ar-Mor*, right on the beach at Porsmeur with hearty meals too (☎02.98.69.63.01, ⓔroch.ar.mor@orange.fr; ❶; closed Oct–Easter).

BRIGNOGAN-PLAGE, on the *aber*, has a small natural harbour, once the lair of wreckers, with beaches and weather-beaten rocks to either side, as well as its own menhir. The two high-season **campsites** are the central municipal site at Kéravezan, the *Côte des Legendes* (☎02.98.83.41.65, ⓦwww.campingcotedes legendes.com; closed Nov–Easter), and the *Du Phare*, east of town (☎02.98.83.45.06, ⓦwww.camping-du-phare.com; open March–Oct). There are also schools of sailing and riding.

The *aber* between Plouguerneau and **L'ABER-WRAC'H** has a stepping-stone crossing just upstream from the bridge at Llanellis, built in Gallo-Roman times, and its long cut stones still cross the three channels of water (access off the D28 signposted "Rascoll"). L'Aber-Wrac'h itself, perched over the western side of the vast mouth of the Baie des Anges, is a small and attractive resort within reach of a whole range of sandy beaches. At the start of the bay, commanding this stunning view, the elegant ⚓ *Hôtel la Baie des Anges*, 350 route des Anges (☎02.98.04.90.04, ⓦwww.lesanges.fr; ❻; closed Jan), makes a peaceful and exceptionally comfortable place to stay, while its second house La Villa des Anges gives unparalleled sea views for a similar price to the main hotel's town-side views. It has no dining room, but there's a classy bar with a small waterfront terrace, reserved for guests only. The best local **restaurant**, *Le Brennig* (☎02.98.04.81.12; closed Tues & Nov–Feb), is back at the other end of the coastal road through town.

Just past the next *aber*, l'Aber-Benoît, a defining moment in local history for the small harbour of **PORTSALL** is commemorated at the **Espace Amoco**

Cadiz (July & Aug Tues–Sun 2.30–6.30pm; Sept–June Sat & Sun 2.30–6.30pm; free). On March 17, 1978, the sinking of the *Amoco Cadiz* supertanker resulted in an oil spill that devastated 350km of the Breton coastline, and threatened to ruin the local economy. Displays and films document not only the immense task of cleaning up the mess, but also the long legal battle to obtain compensation from the "multinational monster" responsible. If you need to **stay**, go for the surprisingly good *Demeure Océane*, 20 rue Bar-Al-Lan (☎02.98.48.77.42; ❸).

Five kilometres west of Portsall, at the least populated and most wild point of the coast is **TRÉMAZAN**, whose ruined castle was the point of arrival in Brittany for Tristan and Iseult. From here a beautiful corniche road leads further along the coast. Odd little chapels dot the route, and the views of sea and rocks are unhindered before turning inland just before Le Conquet.

Le Conquet

LE CONQUET, at the far western tip of Brittany 24km beyond Brest, is a wonderful place, scarcely developed, with a long beach of clean white sand, protected from the winds by the narrow spit of the Kermorvan peninsula. It's very much a working fishing village, with grey-stone houses leading down to the stone jetties of a cramped harbour. It occasionally floods, causing great amusement to locals who watch the waves wash over cars left there by tourists taking the ferry out to Ouessant. A good walk 5km south brings you to the lighthouse at **Pointe St–Mathieu**, with its much-photographed view out to the islands from its site among the ruins of a Benedictine abbey.

The *Relais du Vieux Port*, 1 quai Drellac'h (☎02.98.89.15.91; ❷; closed Jan), offers inexpensive but attractive **rooms** right by the jetty in Le Conquet, and has a simple crêperie downstairs. There's also a well-equipped two-star **campsite** over on the Kermorvan peninsula, *Les Blancs Sablon* (☎02.98.89.06.90, ⓦwww.lescledelles.com; closed mid-Nov to mid-March), with pool, bar and close access to the beach. For eating, *Les Boucaniers* on 3 rue Poncelin (☎02.98.89.06.25) is the local *galette* and *moules* favourite.

The Îles d'Ouessant

The **Île d'Ouessant** ("Ushant" to the English) lies 30km northwest of Le Conquet, and its lighthouse at **Creac'h** (said to be the strongest in the world)

Getting to Ouessant

Penn Ar Bed (☎02.98.80.80.80, ⓦwww.pennarbed.fr) boats sail to Ouessant and Molène all year, with one to six daily departures from **Le Conquet** (first sailing at 8am daily July to late Aug, 9am May to early July and late Aug to mid-Sept, 9.45am otherwise; Ouessant return €29.20, to Molène €25.80), and one to three daily from **Brest**, always including one at 8.30am, which is the only one that stops at Molène (Ouessant return €33.40; Molène return €30.10). They also depart from **Camaret** to Ouessant at 8.40am on Wednesday from early April until mid-Sept, and daily at 8.40am from early July until the end of Aug (return €27.50). Only on Fridays between early July and late Aug is it possible to sail from Camaret to Molène, at 8.40am (return €25.80).

In addition, you can **fly** to Ouessant with **Finist'Air** (☎02.98.84.64.87, ⓦwww.finistair.fr). The fifteen-minute flights leave Brest's Guipavas airport daily at 8.30am and 4.45pm, and make the return journey at 9am and 5.15pm with an adult one-way fare of €63 and groups of three or more adults costing €52 each, and return fare for three or more days at €89 is regarded as the entrance to the English Channel. The island is the last in a chain of smaller islands and half-submerged granite rocks. Most are uninhabited, or like Beniguet the preserve only of rabbits, but the **Île de Molène**, midway, has a village. Ouessant is served by at least one ferry each day from Le Conquet and Brest; however, to get the full experience it's not worth staying the night on the island.

Île d'Ouessant

You arrive on the **Île d'Ouessant** at the modern **harbour** in the ominous-sounding Baie du Stiff. There's a scattering of houses here, but the single town is 4km away at **LAMPAUL**, where the vast majority of wayfarers will head, either by the bus that meets each ferry or on the (advisable) bicycles rented from one of the many waiting entrepreneurs.

There's not a lot to Lampaul. The best beaches are sprawled around its bay, and, in case you should forget the perils of the sea, the town cemetery's **war memorial** lists all the ships in which townsfolk were lost, alongside graves of unknown sailors washed ashore and a chapel of wax "*proëlla* crosses" symbolizing the many islanders who never returned.

Two kilometres to the west, past **NIOU**, stands the **Creac'h lighthouse**, in 1939 the most powerful in the world, with a 500-million-candlepower beam capable of being seen from England's Cape Lizard. You can't visit the lighthouse tower itself, but the complex at its base holds the **Musée des Phares et Balises** (Easter–Sept Tues–Sun 10.30am–6.30pm; Oct–Easter Tues–Sun 1.30–5.30pm; €4.10), a large museum about lighthouses and buoys. As well as providing a history of lighthouses from the Pharos of Alexandria and Roman examples, it's crammed with assorted lenses and mirrors, and has detailed displays on shipwrecks in the vicinity. None of the information is in English, however, and photography is not permitted.

The Creac'h lighthouse makes a good starting point from which to set out along the barren and exposed rocks of the north coast. Particularly in September and other times of migration, it's a remarkable spot for birdwatching, frequented by puffins, storm petrels and cormorants. The violent currents and innumerable shipwrecks, including the 350metre long supertanker Olympic Bravery, around the island make for some pretty thrilling diving; *Ouessant Subaqua*, in the port de Lampaul (☎02.98.48.83.84, ✉santsubaqua@yahoo.fr) guide dives or take lessons for under €30 a go.

General information is available from Lampaul's central **tourist office** (Mon–Sat 10am–noon & 1.30–6pm, Sun 10am–noon; ☎02.98.48.85.83, ⓦwww.ot-ouessant.fr). The town boasts a small **hostel**, La Croix Rouge, north towards Niou (☎02.98.48.84.53, ✉ajouessant@club-internet.fr; closed Jan), where a dorm bed plus breakfast costs €15. Another bargain is the scrupulously cared for *chambre d'hôte Chez Odile et Victor Le Guen* (☎02.98.48.81.21; ❶) near the port at Pen Ar Land, while the best hotel is the colourful and comfortable *Ti Jan Ar C'hafé* (☎02.98.48.82.64; ❹), with a fine terrace, too. There's also a small official **campsite**, the *Penn ar Bed*, just outside town (☎02.98.48.84.65; closed Oct–March) whose €9 pitches are protected from the wind by the surrounding relics of a military installation. For **eating** *Hôtel Fromveur*, by the church in Lampaul (☎02.98.48.81.30), does good traditional island cooking; expect to pay around €20 for a set lunch. *Le Ty Korn* (☎02.98.48.87.33) has good value Breton menus, and is a fine place for a drink or two and occasional live music as well.

Brest

Set in a magnificent natural harbour, known as the Rade de Brest, the city of **BREST** is doubly sheltered from ocean storms by the bulk of Léon to the north and by the Crozon peninsula to the south. During World War II, Brest was continually bombed to prevent the Germans from using it as a submarine base. When liberated on September 18, 1944, after a six-week siege, the town was devastated beyond recognition. The architecture of the postwar town is raw and bleak and though there have been attempts to green the city, it has proved too windswept to respond.

Arrival and information

The **gare SNCF**, and end of the four-hour TGV line from Paris, and the **gare routière** (℡02.98.44.46.73) stand in line on place du 19ème RI at the bottom of avenue Clemenceau. **Bus** services include those to Plouescat and Roscoff, the Crozon peninsula via Le Faou, and to Le Conquet.

Brest's **airport** (℡02.98.32.01.00), 9km northeast of the centre at Guipavas, is served by numerous flights from across the channel, and also offers local connections to Ouessant (see p.394). An **airport shuttle** bus runs from the *gare SNCF* and the tourist office (6–11 daily; 25min; ℡02.98.32.01.00). All the major international **car rental** chains are represented at the airport.

As well as trips to Ouessant in summer **boats** run from Océanoplis to Brest's Port de Commerce and on the 25-minute journey to Le Fret on the Crozon peninsula (Société Azenor; July–Sept 2–3 daily; €17 return; ℡02.98.41.46.23, Ⓦwww.azenor.com). The same company also sails to Camaret (July & Aug daily except Sat 2–3 daily; €17 return).

Brest's **tourist office** on avenue Clemenceau is helpful, rents out bikes for €8 per day and boasts an excellent website (July & Aug Mon–Sat 9.30am–7pm, Sun 10am–noon; Sept–June Mon–Sat 9.30am–6pm; ℡02.98.44.24.96, Ⓦwww.brest-metropole-tourisme.fr).

Accommodation

Beneficiaries more of business trips than tourism, the vast majority of Brest's **hotels** remain open throughout the year; only a few, however, bother to maintain their own restaurants. Several lie within easy walking distance of the stations, near the central place de la Liberté.

Astoria 9 rue Traverse ℡02.98.80.19.10, Ⓦwww.hotel-astoria-brest.com. Peaceful central hotel with a cheerful ambience and decor, not far up from the port. Some rooms have sea views, while the four cheapest only have a sink. Closed 3 weeks Dec–Jan. ❶–❸

Citôtel de la Gare 4 bd Gambetta ℡02.98.44.47.01, Ⓦwww.hotelgare.com. En-suite rooms opposite the stations; you can pay a little extra for an uninterrupted view of the Rade de Brest from the upper storeys. Internet access for guests. ❸

Continental place de la Tour d'Auvergne ℡02.98.80.50.40, Ⓦwww.hotel-sofibra.com.

Brest's business tourism orientation is reflected by the ubiquity of chain hotels. This grand luxury hotel, with helpful staff and spotlessly clean rooms, several of them with fine Art Deco features, is the pick of them; rooms on the fourth floor have large balconies. ❾

Hostel Ethic Étapes, at 5 rue de Kerbriant ℡02.98.41.90.41, Ⓦwww.aj-brest.org. The town's hostel, set in a wooded park, is modern, clean and serves inexpensive meals. It's 3km east of the *gare SNCF* just by the beach and Océanop-olis – take bus #7 or #15. €15.70 including breakfast.

The Town

For the casual tourist, Brest has little to offer, and few relics of the past remain. The fifteenth-century **castle** looks impressive on its headland and offers a superb panorama of the city, but inside the **Musée National de la Marine** (daily: April to mid-Sept 10am–6.30pm; mid-Sept to March 1.30–6.30pm; €5; Ⓦ www.musee-marine.fr) are not especially interesting ship trinkets. The fourteenth-century **Tour Tanguy** on the opposite bank of the River Penfeld, with its conical slate roof, serves as a history museum of Brest before 1939 (June–Sept daily 10am–noon & 2–7pm; Oct–May Wed & Thurs 2–5pm, Sat & Sun 2–6pm; free).

Brest's most up-to-the-minute attraction is **Océanopolis**, a couple of kilometres east of the city centre (take bus 3) beside the Port de Plaisance du Moulin-Blanc (daily: April to early Sept 9am–6pm; early Sept to March Tues–Sun 10am–5pm; €16.20; Ⓦ www.oceanopolis.com). This futuristic complex currently consists of three distinct aquariums and a 3-D cinema. The aquarium in the main white dome, known as the Temperate Pavilion, focuses on the Breton littoral and Finistère's fishing industry. The emphasis is very much on the edible, with the displays on the life-cycle of a scallop, for example, culminating in a detailed recipe. Alongside, the Tropical Pavilion has tanks of ferocious-looking sharks and rainbow-hued smaller fish that populate a highly convincing coral reef, and a Polar Pavilion, complete with polar bears and penguins. Everything's very high-tech, and at times a little earnest, but entertaining none the less.

Eating

As well as several low-priced places near the stations, Brest offers a wide assortment of **restaurants**. Rue Jean-Jaurès, climbing east from the place de la Liberté, has plenty of bistros and bars, while place Guérin to the north is the centre of the student-dominated quartier St-Martin.

Le Bistro de Gaëtan 3 place Maurice-Gillet ☎02.98.43.44.10. Much-loved local restaurant in the St-Martin district, which serves a great-value €7.50 lunch menu but is most renowned for its many variations on the classic *kig ha farz* Breton stew, starting at €12.90. Closed Sun evening & Mon.

La Fleur de Sel 15bis rue de Lyon ☎02.98.44.38.65, Ⓦ www.lafleurdesel .com. The finest restaurant in Brest serving largely traditional cuisine in highly sophisticated combinations of flavour. The results are simply delicious, but the biggest shock is the price, with lunch menus for just €21 or dinner for €40.

Ma Petite Folie plage du Moulin-Blanc ☎02.98.42.44.42. Converted fishing boat, moored in the pleasure port, which serves a wonderfully fishy €20 set menu and also offers a wide range of à la carte dishes and daily specials. Reserve at weekends.

The Crozon peninsula

The **Crozon peninsula**, a craggy outcrop of land shaped like a long-robed giant, arms outstretched to defend bay and roadstead, is the central feature of Finistère's torn chaos of estuaries and promontories. Much the easiest way for cyclists and travellers relying on public transport to reach the peninsula from Brest is via the **ferries** to Le Fret (see p.396).

As you approach the Crozon peninsula, it's well worth making a slight detour to climb the hill of **Ménez-Hom** ("at the giant's feet") for a fabulous preview of the alternating land and water across the southern side of the peninsula out to the ocean. Getting down to the coastal headlands themselves can be a bit of a disappointment after this vision: you won't be the only person seeking a quiet

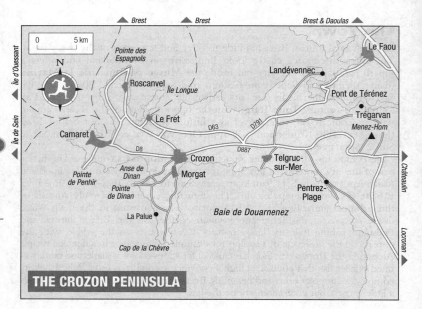

▲ Brest   ▲ Brest   Brest & Daoulas ▲

Le Faou

Landévennec

Pointe des
Espagnols

Roscanvel
Île Longue

Pont de Térénec

Le Frét   D63   D791   Trégarvan
Menez-Hom

Camaret   D8   Crozon   D887   Telgruc-
sur-Mer

Anse de
Dinan   Morgat

Pointe
de Penhir   Pointe
de Dinan   Pentrez-
Plage

Baie de Douarnenez

La Palue

Cap de la Chèvre

Île d'Ouessant   Île de Sein   Châteaulin   Locronan

0   5 km   N

THE CROZON PENINSULA

spot here. But it is the cliffs that tourists head for here, and some of the **beaches**,
like **La Palue** on the southern arm, are almost deserted.

Crozon and Morgat

The first town on the peninsula proper, **CROZON** is a busy nuisance of
tourists scurrying off to the various resorts – though it does keep a market
running most of the week, and the **tourist office** for the whole peninsula is
here, in the *gare routière* (June & Sept Mon–Fri 9.15am–noon & 2–5.30pm, Sat
9.15am–noon & 2–5pm; July & Aug Mon–Sat 9.15am–7pm, Sun 10am–1pm;
Oct–March Mon–Sat 9.15am–noon & 2–5.30pm; ☎02.98.27.07.92, ⓦwww
.crozon.com). **MORGAT**, just down the hill, is a more enticing base. It has a
long crescent beach that ends in a pine slope, and a well-sheltered harbour full
of pleasure boats on the short haul from England and Ireland. The main attractions are **boat trips** around the various headlands, such as the **Cap de la
Chèvre** (which is a good clifftop walk if you'd rather make your own way). The
most popular is the 45-minute tour of the **Grottes** with Vedettes Rosmeur
(daily April to late Sept; ☎02.98.27.10.71; €9). From these multicoloured caves
in the cliffs, accessible only by sea but with steep "chimneys" up to the clifftops,
saints are said to have emerged in bygone days to rescue the shipwrecked. For
some land-based amazement, the wooden maze at Peninsula Labyrinthe, 4km
southwest of town on the road to Pointe de Dinan (Apr–June & Sept daily
2–6pm; July–Aug daily 10am–7pm; Oct–Mar Wed, Sat & Sun 2–6pm; €7), is fun
for the young and justifies itself with a small history of labyrinths alongside.

    The pick of the **accommodation** in Morgat, with its garden leading onto
the beach, is *Kermaria* (☎02.98.26.20.02, ⓦwww.kermaria.com; ❺), a luxury
guest house with high ceilings and leather armchairs, while *Ar Kastell Dinn*
(☎02.98.27.26.40, ⓦwww.gite-rando-bretagne.com; ❷) is a great value *gîte
d'étape* along the GR34 hiking trail – try to get one of the garden rooms, which

feature upturned fishing boats as roofs. For hotels, *Julia*, 400m from the beach at 43 rue de Tréflez (☎02.98.27.05.89, ⓦwww.hoteljulia.fr; ❸–❼ obligatory half board in July–Aug; closed Nov–Feb except Christmas), is the best bet. For **campers** the best option is the three-star site at *Plage de Goulien* (☎02.98.26.23.16, ⓔcamping.delaplage.degoulien@presquile-crozon.com; closed mid-Sept to mid-June; under €15).

A flowery stone cottage near the port at 24 quai du Kador holds *Au Pied du Port* (☎02.98.26.12.63; closed Oct–Easter), Morgat's best **restaurant**, which serves refined menus from €24; what's on offer very much depends on the day's catch, but the €36 *menu tentation* is consistently wonderful. Overlooking the beach, *Kerguelen* (☎02.98.27.12.24) has a great selection of rums, and does good pizzas in the first floor restaurant.

Camaret

At **CAMARET** – another sheltered port, at the very tip of the peninsula – the most prominent building is the pink-orange **château de Vauban**, standing foursquare at the end of the long jetty that runs parallel to the main town water-front. Walled, moated, and accessible via a little gatehouse reached by means of a drawbridge, it was built in 1689 to guard the approaches to Brest; these days it guards no more than a motley assortment of decaying half-submerged fishing boats, abandoned to rot beside the jetty. There are two beaches nearby – a small one to the north and another, larger and more attractive, in the low-lying (and rather marshy) Anse de Dinan. There are also some good wreck dives and submerged islands for scuba-diving enthusiasts – head to *Léo-Lagrange* at 2 rue du Stade (ⓦwww.club-leo-camaret.net). In summer, **ferries** run from Camaret to the islands of Ouessant (see p.394) and Sein (see p.402).

Camaret has its own little **tourist office** at 15 quai Kleber (July & Aug Mon–Sat 9am–7pm, Sun 10am–1pm; Sept–June Mon–Sat 9am–noon & 2–6pm; ☎02.98.27.93.60, ⓦwww.camaret-sur-mer.com). A little walk away from the centre, around the port towards the protective jetty, the quai du Styvel contains a row of excellent **hotels**. Both the *Vauban* (☎02.98.27.91.36; ❶; closed Dec & Jan) and *Du Styvel* (☎02.98.27.92.74; ❶; closed Jan) are excep-tionally hospitable, with rooms that look right out across the bay; only the *Styvel* has a restaurant, but the *Vauban* does barbeques in its garden throughout the summer. There are also several **campsites** nearby, such as the four-star *Grand Large* (☎02.98.27.91.41, ⓦwww.campinglegrandlarge.com; closed Oct–March; around €25) boasting a water slide in its pool and great views, and the two-star municipal *Lannic* (☎02.98.27.91.31; open April–Sept; under €10).

Back along the quayside in the centre of town, the quai Toudouze, you'll find a succession of excellent **fish restaurants**, the best of which are *Les Frères de la Côte* at no. 11 (☎02.98.27.95.42; closed late Sept to April), and the *Côté Mer* at no. 12 (☎02.98.27.93.79; closed Wed & Thurs in low season). *Rhum*, rather than *cidre* is the drink of choice in this part of Finistére; *Rhumerie La Goel,* further along the quai at no. 36, has a good selection.

South towards Quimper

Moving south of the Crozon peninsula, you soon enter the ancient kingdom of **Cornouaille**. The most direct route to the region's principal city, **Quimper**, leaves the sea behind and heads due south, passing close to the unchanged medieval village of **Locronan**. However, if you can spare the time, it's worth following the supremely isolated coastline instead around the Baie de Douarnenez to the **Pointe du Raz**, the western tip of Finistère. With a few exceptions – most notably its "land's end" capes – this stretch of coast has kept out of the tourist mainstream, and nowhere does that hold more true than on the remarkable, remote **Île de Sein**.

Locronan

LOCRONAN, a short way from the sea on the minor road that leads down from the Crozon peninsula, is a rare example of architectural unity. From 1469 through to the seventeenth century, rich medieval houses built up in the centre as the town thrived on woven "lin" (linen), supplying sails to the French, English and Spanish navies. It was first rivalled by Vitré and Rennes, before suffering the "agony and ruin" so graphically described in its small **museum** (Feb–June & Sept Mon–Fri 10am–noon & 2–6pm; July & Aug Mon–Sat 10am–1pm & 2–7pm, Sun 2–7pm; €2). Film directors love this sense of time warp, even if Roman Polanski, filming *Tess*, deemed it necessary to change all the porches, put new windows on the Renaissance houses, and bury the main square in mud to make it all look a bit more English.

Today Locronan prospers on tourism, but this commercialization shouldn't put you off making at least a passing visit, as the town itself is genuinely remarkable, centred around the focal **Église St-Ronan**. Be sure to take the time to walk down the hill of the **rue Moal**, to the lovely little stone chapel of Nôtre-Dame de Bonne Nouvelle.

The **tourist office** is next to the museum (same hours; ⓣ02.98.91.70.14, ⓦwww.locronan.org). The one **hotel**, *du Prieuré*, at 11 rue du Prieuré on the main approach street (ⓣ02.98.91.70.89, ⓦwww.hotel-le-prieure.com; ❸; closed Feb, plus Fri evening & Sat lunch in low season) is not particularly attractive, but offers well-equipped rooms and a good restaurant.

Douarnenez

The catch at the sheltered port of **DOUARNENEZ**, home to the largest fish canneries in Europe, has been steadily declining since 1923, when 100 million sardines left the town in little tin coffins. In the last twenty years, realizing the fishing port was becoming a relic, a municipal initiative bought up over two hundred retirement-aged boats at controversial expense and has made a superb living museum of the port, and the maritime history to which it has born witness.

Since 1993, **Port-Rhû**, on the west side of town, has been designated as the **Port-Musée**, with its entire waterfront taken up with fishing and other vessels gathered from throughout northern Europe, five of which you can roam through. Its centrepiece, the **Musée du Bateau** (Boat Museum) in place de l'Enfer (April to mid-June & mid-Sept to early Nov daily except Mon 10am–12.30pm & 2–6pm; mid-June to mid-Sept daily 10am–7pm; €6.20), houses slightly smaller vessels, such as Gallic coracles and a Portugese *moliceiro*, and displays exhaustive explanations on boat construction techniques and a strong emphasis on fishing.

Of the three separate harbour areas still in operation, by far the most appealing is the rough-and-ready **port du Rosmeur**, on the east side, which is nominally the fishing port used by the smaller local craft. Its quayside, still far from commercialized, holds a reasonable number of relaxed waterside cafés and restaurants.

The **tourist office** in Douarnenez is at 2 rue du Dr-Mével (July & Aug Mon–Fri 10am–7pm, Sat 10am–noon & 4–6.30pm; Sept–June Mon–Sat

10am–noon & 2–5pm; ☎02.98.92.13.35, ⓦwww.douarnenez-tourisme.
com), a short walk up from the Port-Musée. Among the good-value **hotels**
are *Le Bretagne*, nearby at 23 rue Duguay-Trouin (☎02.98.92.30.44, ⓦwww
.le-bretagne.fr; ❷), above a restaurant serving reasonable Tex-Mex dishes for
around €12, and the tastefully decorated ⚘ *Ty Mad*, on plage Saint-Jean
(☎02.98.74.00.53, ⓦwww.hoteltymad.com; ❹–❻), where Picasso used to
stay. It's a real bargain if you're travelling out of season. There are a few
campsites by the beach at Les Sables Blancs; *Croas Men* (☎02.98.74.00.18,
ⓦwww.croas-men.com; closed Oct–March) is the best bet. In addition to the
hotel **restaurants**, *Les Bigorneaux Amoureux*, 2 boulevard Richepin
(☎02.98.92.35.55; closed Mon), is a good seafood place with a terrace
overlooking the plage des Dames.

The Baie des Trépassés and the Pointe du Raz

Thirty kilometres west of Douarnenez, the **Pointe du Raz** – the Land's End
of both Finistère and France – is designated a "Grand Site National", and makes
a magnificent spectacle. Buffeted by wind and waves and peppered with deep
gurgling fissures, it's quite a wild experience to walk to the end and back. Don't
expect to have the place to yourself; with three million visitors every year,
they've had to build a huge car park 1km short of the actual headland (€5 cars,
€3 motorcycles), alongside a new information complex (April–June & Sept
daily 10.30am–6pm; July & Aug daily 9.30am–7pm; ☎02.98.70.67.18, ⓦwww
.pointeduraz.com). To get to the *pointe*, take the free *navette*, then walk the most
direct route, along an undulating, arrow-straight track or take a longer stroll
along the footpath that skirts the top of the cliffs.

The **Baie des Trépassés** (Bay of the Dead), along the coast to the north,
gets its grim name from the shipwrecked bodies that used to be washed up
there, and is a possible site of the lost city of Ys (see p.403). However, it's
actually a very attractive spot; green meadows, too exposed to support trees,

▲ Pointe du Raz

end abruptly on the low cliffs to either side; there's a huge expanse of flat sand (in fact little else at low tide); and out in the crashing waves surfers and windsurfers get thrashed to within an inch of their lives. Beyond them, you can usually make out the white-painted houses along the harbour on the Île de Sein, while the various uninhabited rocks in between hold a veritable forest of lighthouses.

In total, less than half a dozen scattered buildings intrude upon the emptiness, including the two building of a single **hotel**, both with tremendous views. The pink ⚓ *Hôtel de la Baie des Trépassés* (☎02.98.70.61.34, ⓦ www.baiedestrepasses .com; ❶–❸; closed mid-Nov to mid-Feb) is a truly romantic hideaway, sitting alone on the grass just behind its wide, fine-sand beach. The rooms are simply decorated and comfortable – there is one cheaper room without en-suite facilities, and serves menus of wonderfully fresh seafood from €17.50.

The Île de Sein

Of all the Breton islands, the tiny **Île de Sein**, just 8km off the end of the Pointe du Raz, has to be the most extraordinary. Its very grip on existence seems so tenuous that it's hard to believe anyone could truly survive here; nowhere does it rise more than six metres above the surrounding ocean, and for much of its 2.5-kilometre length it's barely broader than the breakwater wall of bricks that serves as its central spine. In fact, the island has been inhabited since prehistoric times, and it was reputed to have been the very last refuge of the druids in Brittany. It also became famous during World War II, when its entire male population answered General de Gaulle's call to join him in exile in England. Today, over three hundred islanders continue to make their living from the sea, gathering rainwater and seaweed, and fishing for scallops, lobster and crayfish.

Never mind cars, not even bicycles are permitted here. Depending on the tide, boats pull in at one or other of the two adjoining harbours that constitute Sein's one tight-knit village, in front of which a little beach appears at low tide. There is a **museum** of local history here (June & Sept daily 10am– noon & 2–4pm; July & Aug daily 10am–noon & 2–6pm; €2.50), packed with black-and-white photos and press clippings, and displaying a long list of shipwrecks from 1476 onwards. The basic activity for visitors, however, is to take a bracing walk, preferably to the far end of the island, from where you can see the famous **Phare Ar-men**, peeking out of the waves 12km further west into the Atlantic.

Practicalities

The principal departure point for **boats** to Sein is Ste-Evette beach, just outside **Audierne**; the crossing takes around an hour. Penn Ar Bed has a 9.30am service out to Sein daily all year round, with a 4pm return; service increases to three daily each way in July and Aug (☎02.98.70.90.37, ⓦ www.pennarbed.fr; €26.70 return). On Sundays from mid-June to mid-September, a service runs from **Brest** (departs 9am, returns 5.30pm; 1hr 30min; €34.30 return) via **Camaret** (9.30am; 1hr; €31 return).

Sein is hardly bursting with facilities, but it does have two **hotels**: the simple *Trois Dauphins*, looking out over the beach from the middle of the port (☎02.98.70.92.09; ❷), and the *Hôtel-Restaurant d'Ar-men* (☎02.98.70.90.77, ⓦ www.hotel-armen.net; ❸), the very last building you come to as you walk west out of town – all its rooms face the sea, and it serves good food. Another good **restaurant**, and bar, is *Chez Brigitte* on the quai des Paimpolais – it's popular with fishermen, so the seafood is a good bet.

Quimper

QUIMPER, capital of the ancient diocese, kingdom and later duchy of Cornouaille, is the oldest Breton city. According to legend, the first bishop of Quimper, St Corentin, came with the early Bretons across the Channel to the place they named Little Britain. He lived by eating a regenerating and immortal fish, and was made bishop by one King Gradlon, whose life he later saved when the sea-bed city of **Ys** was destroyed. Gradlon had built Ys in the Baie de Douarnenez, protected from the water by gates and locks to which only he and his daughter had keys. However, St Corentin suspected her of evil doings, and was proven right: at the urging of the Devil, the princess unlocked the gates, the city flooded and Gradlon escaped only by obeying Corentin and throwing his daughter into the sea. Back on dry land and in need of a new capital, Gradlon founded Quimper. Ys remains on the sea floor; it will rise again when Paris ("*Par-Ys*", "equal to Ys") sinks. According to tradition, on feast days sailors can still hear church bells and hymns under the water.

The town's name comes from "kemper", denoting the junction of the two rivers, the Steir and the Odet, around which cram the cobbled streets (now mainly pedestrianized) of the **medieval quarter**, dominated by the cathedral nearby. As the Odet curves from east to southwest it's crossed by numerous low, flat bridges, bedecked with geraniums and chrysanthemums in autumn. Overlooking all are the wooded slopes of **Mont Frugy**. There's no great pressure in Quimper to rush around monuments or museums, and the most enjoyable option may be to take a boat and drift down "the prettiest river in France" to the open sea at Bénodet.

Arrival and information

The **gare SNCF** and **gare routière** (℡02.98.90.88.89) are next to each other on avenue de la Gare, 1km east of the town centre. Both are connected to the centre by bus #6, and all city buses pass the tourist office, via either place de la Résistance or along rue du Parc on the other side of the river, depending on which direction you are going. There's no train to the coast, Compagnie Amoricaine de Transport, or CAT, 10 rue Jules-Verne (℡02.98.90.88.89, Ⓦwww.cat29.fr), runs **buses** from the *gare routière* to Bénodet (#16), Pointe du Raz (#7 or 8) and Douarnez (#9). The international airport, 7km to the north of Quimper, is connected by #25 to the city centre.

Between June and September you can **cruise** from Quimper down the Odet to Bénodet, which takes about 1hr 15min each way, on Vedettes de l'Odet (Bénodet ℡02.98.57.00.58, Quimper ℡02.98.52.98.41, Ⓦwww.vedettes-odet .com; €25 return). The tourist office (which also sells tickets) is the best place to ask about the schedules and the precise departure points – they vary according to the tide and season.

Quimper's **tourist office** is housed in a small single-storey building on the south bank of the Odet at 7 rue de la Déesse, place de la Résistance (Apr–June & Sept Mon–Sat 9.30am–12.30pm & 1.30–6.30pm; July & Aug Mon–Sat 9am–7pm, Sun 10am–1pm & 3–5.45pm; Oct to March Mon–Sat 9.30am–12.30pm & 1.30–6pm; ℡02.98.53.04.05, Ⓦwww.quimper-tourisme.com). For **internet access**, call in at Cybercopy, 3 boulevard de Kerguélen (Mon 1–7pm, Tues–Fri 9am–7pm, Sat 9am–3pm; closed mid-July to mid-Aug; ℡02.98.64.33.99).

QUIMPER

ACCOMMODATION

Escale Océania	C
De la Gare	E
Gradlon	A
Hostel	G
Kregenn	B
Logis de Stang	D
TGV	F

EATING & DRINKING

Bistrot à Lire	2
La Brasserie de l'Epée	5
Le Ceili	4
La Couscouserie	6
Fleur de Sel	7
La Krampouzerie	1
Le XXIe	3

Gare SNCF

Gare Routière

Musée des Beaux-Arts

Cathédrale St-Corentin

Musée Breton

Amphithéâtre

Halles St-Francis

St-Mathieu

Musée de la Faïence

Bois du Mont-Frugy

River Odet

Odet Ferries & Faïencerie H.-B. Henriot

6 & Camping

200 m

RUE DE CONCARNEAU
RUE DE L'HIPPODROME
RUE JACQUES CARTIER
AV DE LA GARE
RUE LE DÉAN
RUE ARISTIDE BRIAND
RUE DE BREST
RUE GOURMELEN
RUE DES RÉGUAIRES
BD DE KERGUÉLEN
BD DUPLEIX
RUE DE CRAC'H AL LAN
BD Pt A MASSE
RUE LUZEL
RUE LUZEL
RUE AMVILLE
RUE LE HARS
RUE JEAN JAURÈS
RUE PEN AR STANG
RUE DES DOUVES
PLACE DE LA TOURBIE
RUE VERGELÉ
RUE DU FROUT
RUE FRÉRON
RUE DU GUÉODET
PLACE AU BEURRE
RUE DU SALLE
PLACE ST-CORENTIN
RUE DES BOUCHERIES
BD DUPLEIX
RUE DES GENTILS HOMMES
RUE KÉRÉON
RUE ASTOR
RUE DU PARC
RUE DU STEIR
RUE BRIZEUX
RUE DU PICHERY
RUE DE PEN AR STEIR
RUE MADEC
BOULEVARD DU MOULIN AU DUC
RUE LAËNNEC
RUE DE CHAPEAU ROUGE
PLACE DE LA RÉSISTANCE
RUE DE LA DÉESSE
RUE YAN DARGENT
RUE AMIRAL
RUE VIS
ALLÉES DE LOCMARIA
RUE DE FALKIRK
RUE DU PALAIS
PLACE DE LOCRONAN
RUE SAINT MARC
RUE DE DOUARNENEZ
RUE DOMPREL
RUE QUAI DE L'ODET
RUE LOUS HÉMON
RUE DE ROSMADEC
RUE DE KERLEREC
RUE DE KEN YS
VENELLE DE KERGOS
RUE BOURG LES BOURGS
QUAI NEUF
RUE DE PONT L'ABBÉ

Accommodation

There are remarkably few **hotels** in the old streets in the centre of Quimper, and those close-by are mostly pricey chains, though several cheaper options can be found near the station.

Hotels

Escale Océania 6 rue Théodore-Le-Hars ☎02.98.53.37.37, ⓦwww.oceaniahotels.com. The best bargain in the centre of town, with slightly characterless, but reliably clean and quiet rooms and very helpful and polite service. ❹

De la Gare 17 av de la Gare ☎02.98.90.00.81, ⓦwww.hoteldelagarequimper.com. Simple rooms, all with TV, shower and phone, arranged around a quiet, floral patio and above a no-nonsense snack bar across from the station. Parking. ❸

Gradlon 30 rue du Brest ☎02.98.95.04.39, ⓦwww.hotel-gradlon.com. Central but quiet (with a pleasant garden), and exceptionally friendly. The rooms may not be cheap, but they're tastefully decorated even for the price bracket in mid-twentieth-century-style. Also boasts a good bar, around an open fire in the cooler months. ❻

Kregenn 11–15 rue de Réguaires ☎02.98.95.08.70, ⓦwww.hotel-kregenn.fr. Smartly designed and low-lit luxury hotel right in the centre of town. The more expensive rooms have Jacuzzis in the bathrooms. ❻

Logis de Stang Allée du Stang-Youen ☎02.98.52.00.55, ⓦwww.logis-du-stang .com. A delightful bed and breakfast away from the bustle of the centre in a nineteenth-century residence set in a hortensia-filled garden and with well furnished en suites at a great price. ❸

TGV 4 rue de Concarneau ☎02.98.90.54.00, ⓦwww.hoteltgv.com. Another cheap option near the station, this time offering plain but clean rooms with shower and TV at bargain rates, though steer clear of the first floor ones, as they get a bit noisy. ❶

Hostel and Camping

Hostel 6 av des Oiseaux ☎02.98.64.97.97, Ⓔquimper@fuaj.org. An unremarkable but clean hostel within walking distance of the centre to the west. Sheets are included in the price but breakfast (€3) is not. €11.50.

Orangerie de Lannion. ☎98.90.62.02, ⓦwww .lanniron.com. A four-star campsite, with swimming pool and tennis court 4km out of the centre on the route de Bénodet. Closed mid-Sept to mid-May. Around €25 a pitch.

The Town

The enormous **Cathédrale St-Corentin**, the focal point of Quimper, is said to be the most complete Gothic cathedral in Brittany, though its neo-Gothic spires date from 1856. When the nave was being added to the old chancel in the fifteenth century, the extension would either have hit existing buildings or the swampy edge of the then-unchannelled river. So the nave was placed at a slight angle – a peculiarity which, once noticed, makes it hard to concentrate on the other Gothic splendours within. The exterior, however, gives no hint of the deviation, with King Gradlon now mounted in perfect symmetry between the spires.

The **Musée des Beaux-Arts** faces the cathedral on its north side, at 4 place St-Corentin (April–June, Sept & Oct Mon & Wed–Sun 10am–noon & 2–6pm; July & Aug daily 10am–7pm; Nov–March Mon & Wed–Sat 10am–noon & 2–6pm, Sun 2–6pm; €4.50; ⓦwww.musee-beauxarts.quimper.fr). Refurbished to very classy effect, with new floors and suspended walkways, it focuses especially on an amazing assemblage of drawings by Max Jacob – who was born in Quimper – and his contemporaries. Jean-Julien Lemordant's vibrant murals of Breton scenes, commissioned in 1907 for Quimper's *Hôtel de l'Epée* (which closed in 1974), get a room to themselves, and there's also quite a selection of nineteenth- and twentieth-century paintings from the Pont-Aven school, though you'd hardly notice the only Gauguin, a goose he painted on the door of Marie Henry's inn in Pont-Aven itself.

The heart of **old Quimper** lies in and to the west of place St-Corentin, in front of the cathedral. This is where you'll find the liveliest shops and cafés, housed in old half-timbered buildings, such as the Breton Keltia-Musique record shop at 1 place au Beurre, and the Celtic shop, Ar Bed Keltiek, between the cathedral and the river at 2 rue du Roi-Gradlon. The **Halles St-Francis** marketplace, on rue Astor, is quite a delight, not just for the food, but for the view past the upturned boat rafters through the roof to the cathedral's twin spires. It's open from Monday to Saturday, with an extra-large market spreading into the surrounding streets on Saturdays.

South of the covered market, on the opposite bank of the Odet at 14 rue Jean-Baptiste-Bosquet, is the excellent **Musée de la Faïence Jules Verlinque** (mid-April to mid-Oct Mon–Sat 10am–6pm; €4; ⓦ www.quimper-faiences .com). The museum tells the story of Quimper's long association with **faïence** – tin-glazed earthenware – which has been made in and around the town since 1690, and its consequent decline into the medium of souvenirs. If you are interested in some good quality glazed ceramics, visit the **gift shops** at major atelier **H.-B. Henriot**, in the allées de Locmaria just behind the museum (July & Aug Mon–Sat 9.15–11.15am & 1.30–4.15pm; Sept–June Mon–Fri 9.15–11.15am & 2–4.15pm; ☏ 02.98.90.09.36, ⓦ www.hb-henriot.com; €5 for tours), where prices are standard, and the selection is superb.

Eating and drinking

Although the pedestrian streets west of the cathedral are unexpectedly short on places to eat, there are quite a few **restaurants** further east on the north side of the river, en route towards the *gare SNCF*. For crêperies, the place au Beurre, a short walk northwest of the cathedral, is a good bet.

Bistrot à Lire 18 rue Boucheries ☏ 02.98.95.30.86. A café that specializes in two things: desserts and detective thrillers. The fruit crumbles are an excellent choice for the former; you can pick the latter off the bookshelves and read while you eat. There are also *plats du jour* at lunch for €7.50. 9am–7.30pm, closed Sun & Mon.

La Brasserie de l'Epée 14 rue du Parc ☏ 02.98.95.28.97. Lovely Art Nouveau brasserie, facing the river not far from the cathedral, which serves good-value menus in all price ranges, and stays open late – you can still get a meal at 11pm, which is rare indeed for Brittany. Closed Sun & Mon.

Le Ceili 4 rue Aristide-Briand ☏ 02.98.95.17.61. A lively and convivial bar that hosts live traditional Celtic bands and occasionally jazz on Sunday nights. Open until 1am.

La Couscousserie 1 bd de Kerguélen ☏ 02.98.95.46.50. Plush, enjoyable Middle Eastern restaurant by the river, serving couscous platters at €11–22, and tagines for around €15, in two Arabian Nights-themed rooms decked out with hookahs and the like. Closed Aug.

Fleur de Sel 1 quai Neuf ☏ 02.98.55.04.71. Gourmet French cooking at very good prices not far west of the town centre opposite the Musée de la Faïence on the north bank of the river, with largely fish menus ranging from €19.50 to €26.50. Closed Sat lunch & all Sun.

La Krampouzerie 9 rue du Sallé ☏ 02.98.95.13.08. One of the best of Quimper's many crêperies, with some outdoor seating on the place au Beurre. Most crêpes, such as the one with Roscoff onions and seaweed, cost around €3.50, though a wholewheat *galette* with smoked salmon and cream cheese is €5.80. Closed Sun, plus Mon in winter.

Le XXIe 38 pl Saint-Corentin ☏ 02.98.95.92.34. Trendy brasserie that does salads and dishes of the day each for under €10, and has a good terrace for an evening glass of wine. Closed Sun out of season.

Entertainment

Quimper's **Festival de Cornouaille** started in 1923 and has gone from strength to strength since. This great jamboree of Breton music, costumes, theatre and dance is held in the week before the fourth Sunday in July, attracting guest performers from the other Celtic countries and a scattering of other, sometimes highly unusual, ethnic-cultural ensembles. The whole thing culminates in an incredible Sunday parade through the town. Details can be found at the tourist office or at Ⓦ www.festival-cornouaille.com. Accommodation is at a premium in Quimper while the festival is on.

Not so widely known are the **Semaines Musicales** (Ⓦ www.semaines -musicales-quimper.org), which breathe life into the rather stuffy nineteenth-century theatre on boulevard Dupleix during the first three weeks of August. The music is predominantly classical and tends to favour French composers such as Berlioz, Debussy, Bizet and Poulenc.

South from Quimper

More tourists flock to Finistère's southern coast than to any other part of the region, with the busiest segment of all in summer centring on the family-friendly resort of **Bénodet**. The beaches between here and **La Forêt-Fouesnant** to the east rank among the finest in Brittany. A little further along the coast, the walled, sea-circled old town of **Concarneau** makes a perfect day-trip destination, though a prettier place to spend a night or two would be the flowery village of **Pont-Aven**, immortalized by Paul Gauguin, slightly further to the east still.

Bénodet and around

Once out of its city channel, the Odet spreads out to lake proportions then turns narrow corners between gorges until it reaches **BÉNODET** at the mouth of the river. This partially redeveloped family resort has a long, sheltered beach on the ocean side that's packed in summer but good fun for children. A good **hotel** near the port and beach is *Les Bains de Mer*, 11 rue du Kerguélen (☎02.98.57.03.41, Ⓦ www.lesbainsdemer.com; ❹; closed Jan), which has comfortable rooms and the added attraction of an outdoor heated swimming pool.

The coast that continues east of Bénodet is rocky and repeatedly cut by deep valleys. After 12km, clustered along the waterfront at the foot of a hill so steep that caravans are banned from even approaching, **LA FORÊT-FOUESNANT**, is known for its beaches and cider, though holds little of cultural interest. The community holds an assortment of attractive hotels such as the *Hôtel de l'Espérance*, place de l'Église (☎02.98.56.96.58, Ⓦ www .hotel-esperance.org; ❷; closed mid-Nov to March), and the pricier *Aux Cerisiers*, 3 rue des Cerisiers (☎02.98.56.97.24, Ⓦ www.auxcerisiers.com; ❸; closed all day Sat and Sun evening. plus mid-Dec to mid-Jan). Sample award-winning cider at *Cidre Séhédic* (☎02.98.56.85.18, Ⓦ www.cidre-sehedic.fr) on the road to Bénodet.

Concarneau

The first sizeable town you come to east of Bénodet is **CONCARNEAU**, where the third most important fishing port in France does a reasonable job of passing itself off as a holiday resort.

Arrival and information

There's no rail service to Concarneau, but SNCF **buses** connect the town with Quimper and Rosporden, next to the **tourist office** (May, June & Sept Mon–Sat 9am–12.30pm & 1.45–6.30pm, Sun 10am–1pm; July & Aug daily 9am–7pm; Oct–April Mon–Sat 9am–noon & 2–6pm; ☎02.98.97.01.44, Ⓦ www .tourismeconcarneau.fr) on the quai d'Aiguillon.

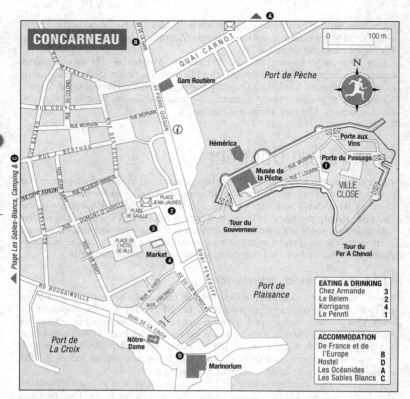

CONCARNEAU

Port de Pêche

Gare Routière

Hémérica

Musée de la Pêche

Porte aux Vins

Porte du Passage

VILLE CLOSE

Tour du Gouverneur

Tour du Fer A Cheval

PLACE JEAN-JAURÈS

PLACE DE GAULLE

PLACE DE L'HÔTEL DE VILLE

Market

Port de Plaisance

Port de La Croix

Nôtre-Dame

Marinorium

EATING & DRINKING
Chez Armande	3
Le Belem	2
Korrigans	4
Le Pennti	1

ACCOMMODATION
De France et de l'Europe	B
Hostel	D
Les Océanides	A
Les Sables Blancs	C

Accommodation

There are some lovely **campsites** close to the Sables-Blancs beach; the spacious *Prés Verts* spreads through verdant fields at Kernous Plage at the far end (☎02.98.97.09.74, 🌐www.presverts.com; closed late Sept to April). With no **hotels** in the *ville close*, your choices are restricted to the mainland.

Hôtel de France et d'Europe 9 av de la Gare ☎02.98.97.00.64, 🌐www.hotel-france-europe .com. Small, bright and modern hotel with clean rooms and a quiet courtyard terrace tucked away inside. Closed Sat in winter. ④

Hôtel-Restaurant les Océanides 3 rue du Lin ☎02.98.97.08.61, 🌐www.lesoceanides.free.fr. A Logis de France with comfortable rooms set over three floors, very helpful owners and a far-from-expensive restaurant. ③

Les Sables Blancs ☎02.98.50.10.12, 🌐www .hotel-les-sables-blancs.com. Jutting its wooden

decking right over the plage les Sables-Blancs, 2km west round the headland, this luxury hotel has brilliant white rooms, with large windows that get the best sunset view in town. It also has a truly excellent restaurant, *Le Nautile*. ⑥

Hostel ☎02.98.97.03.47, 🖂concarneau.aj.cis @orange.fr. Budget travellers will like this very central hostel, which enjoys magnificent ocean views at the south tip of the headland and has a windsurfing shop nearby. €14.50; open all year.

The Town

Concarneau's greatest asset is its **ville close**, the small and very well-fortified old city located a few metres offshore on an irregular rocky island in the bay, connected to the mainland by a narrow bridge. This can get too crowded for comfort in high summer, but otherwise it's a real delight. Like those of the citadelle at Le Palais on Belle-Île, its ramparts were completed by Vauban in the seventeenth century. The island itself, however, had been inhabited for at least a thousand years before that, and is first recorded as the site of a priory founded by King Gradlon of Quimper.

Concarneau boasts that it is a *ville fleurie*, and the flowers are most in evidence inside the walls, where climbing roses and clematis swarm all over the various gift shops, restaurants and crêperies. Walk the central pedestrianized street to the far end, and you can pass through a gateway to the shoreline to watch the fishing boats go by. The best views of all come from the (incomplete) promenade on top of the **ramparts** (daily 9am–7.30pm; mid-June to mid-Sept €1; mid-Sept to mid-June free). The absence of a railing means it's unsafe for children.

By exploring the history of fishing all over the world, the **Musée de la Pêche**, immediately inside the *ville close* (daily: July & Aug 9.30am–8pm; June & Sept 10am–6pm; Oct–May 10am–noon & 2–6pm; €6), provides an insight into the traditional life Concarneau shared with so many other Breton ports. Oddities on show include a three-thousand-year-old anchor from Crete, the swords of swordfish and the saws of sawfish, and a genuine trawler, moored on the other side of the city walls behind the museum.

Eating and drinking

Eating options in the ville close are generally overpriced and generic, with far better equivalents around the market just over the road.

Chez Armande 15bis av du Dr-Nicholas ☎02.98.97.00.76. A favourite with Concarneau natives, this wooden-beamed, Breton-style fish restaurant serves excellent seafood, fresh from the market. Closed Wed all year, plus Tues in winter.
Le Bélem place Jean-Jaurès ☎02.98.97.02.78. A pretty little indoor restaurant, next to the market, serving mussels for €9.20 and good seafood menus from €17.90. Closed Wed.

Korrigans ☎02.98.97.02.37. An authentic Celtic pub serving cider and ale, and hosting live jazz on the first Sun of the month.
Le Pennti place Guénolé ☎02.98.97.46.02. An exception to the rule in the *ville close*, this characterful little establishment serves good *galettes* as part of its €10 menus and has a sweet little garden out back.

Pont-Aven

PONT-AVEN, 14km east of Concarneau and just inland from the tip of the Aven estuary, is a small port packed with art galleries – and tourists. This was where Gauguin came to paint in the 1880s before he left for Tahiti, and inspired the **Pont-Aven School** of fellow artists, including Émile Bernard. For all the local hype, however, the town has no permanent collection of his work: the **Musée Municipal** (daily: Feb, March, Nov & Dec 10am–12.30pm & 2–6pm; April–June, Sept & Oct 10am–12.30pm & 2–6.30pm; July & Aug 10am–7pm; €4) in the *mairie* holds changing exhibitions of the school and other artists active during the same period. With the sheer density of art galleries in the town, you can guarantee a variety of work on offer, but you can't count on paintings by the man himself.

Gauguin aside, Pont-Aven is pleasant in its own right. Just upstream of the little granite bridge at the heart of town, the **promenade Xavier-Grall** crisscrosses the tiny river itself on landscaped walkways, offering glimpses of the backs of venerable mansions, dripping with ivy, and a little "chaos" of rocks in the stream itself. A longer walk – allow an hour – leads into the romantically named **Bois d'Amour**, wooded gardens which have long provided inspiration to painters, poets and musicians.

Practicalities

Pont-Aven's **tourist office**, 5 place de l'Hôtel-de-Ville (April–June & Sept Mon–Sat 10am–12.30pm & 2–6pm, Sun 3–6pm; July & Aug Mon–Sat 9.30am–7pm, Sun 10am–1pm & 3–6.30pm; Oct–March Mon–Sat 10am–12.30pm & 2–6pm; ℡ 02.98.06.04.70, Ⓦ www.pontaven.com), sells an excellent English-language booklet on the town that includes route maps of local walks. Much the best of the three relatively expensive **hotels** is the central *Hôtel des Ajoncs d'Or*, 1 place de l'Hôtel-de-Ville (℡ 02.98.06.02.06; ❸; closed Jan, plus Mon & Sun evening in low season), where gourmet menus start at €25. *Castel Braz*, a great new *maison d'hôte*, has opened at 12 rue du Bois d'Amour (℡ 02.98.06.07.81, Ⓦ www.castelbraz.com; ❸) with eclectic decoration and an arboreous pebble garden. The nicest of the local **campsites** is the four-star *Domaine de Kerlann* (℡ 02.98.06.01.77, Ⓦ www.camping-kerlann.fr; closed Oct–March), set in a large wooded park with a swimming pool, tennis courts and mini-golf.

Inland Brittany: the Nantes–Brest canal

The **Nantes–Brest canal** is a meandering chain of waterways from Finistère to the Loire, interweaving rivers with stretches of canal built at Napoleon's instigation to bypass the belligerent English fleets off the coast. Finally completed in 1836, it came into its own at the end of the nineteenth century as a coal, slate and fertilizer route. The building of the dam at **Lac Guerlédan** in the 1920s chopped the canal in two, leaving a whole section un-navigable by barge. Road transport had by then already superseded water haulage, but modern tourism has breathed life back into the area.

The canal passes through riverside towns, such as **Josselin**, that long predate its construction; the old port of **Redon**, a patchwork of water, where the canal crosses the River Vilaine; and a sequence of scenic splendours, including the string of lakes around the **Barrage de Guerlédan**, near Mur-de-Bretagne. As a focus for exploring **inland Brittany**, whether by barge, bike, foot, or all three, the canal is ideal. Not every stretch is accessible, but there are detours to be made away from it, such as into the wild and desolate **Monts d'Arrée** to the north of the canal in Finistère.

The Finistère stretch

As late as the 1920s, steamers would make their way across the Rade de Brest and down the Aulne River to **Châteaulin**, the first real town on the canal route. If you're walking the canal seriously, **Pont-Coblant** and **Pleyben** are just 10km further away on the map, but be warned that the meanders make it a several-hour hike. Pick your side of the water, too: there are no bridges between Châteaulin and Pont-Coblant.

Châteaulin and Carhaix

CHÂTEAULIN is a quiet place ideal for fishing and walking. Most bars sell permits for local salmon and trout **fishing** (as do fishing shops, some of which rent out tackle). Within a couple of minutes' walk upstream from the statue to Jean Moulin – the Resistance leader who was *sous-préfet* here from 1930 to 1933 – and the town centre, you'll find yourself on towpaths full of rabbits and squirrels. Hotel *Le Christmas*, 33 Grande-Rue (☏02.98.86.01.24, ✉le-chrismas @orange.fr; ❸), serves excellent food. There's little reason to visit **CARHAIX**, a further 25km east, other than for the third weekend of July, when it hosts the biggest **music festival** in France, *les Vieilles Charrues* (🌐www.vieillescharrues .asso.fr). The most interesting building in town is the granite Renaissance **Maison de Sénéchal** on rue Brisieux, which houses the **tourist office** (July & Aug Mon–Sat 9am–12.30pm & 1.30–7pm, Sun 10am–1pm; June & Sept Mon–Sat 9am–noon & 2–6pm; Oct–May Mon 2–6pm, Wed–Sat 10am–noon & 2–5.30pm; ☏02.98.93.04.42, 🌐www.poher.com).

Huelgoat and its forest

HUELGOAT, next to its own small **lake** halfway between Morlaix and Carhaix on the minor road D769, makes a pleasant overnight stop. Spreading north and east from the village is the **Forêt de Huelgoat**, a landscape of trees, giant boulders and waterfalls tangled together in primeval chaos. Various paths lead into the depths of the woods, allowing for long walks amid spectacularly wild scenery.

The *Hôtel du Lac*, beside the lake at 9 rue du Général-de-Gaulle (☏02.98.99.71.14; ❸; closed Mon Sept–June, plus mid-Jan to mid-Feb), offers well-refurbished rooms and hearty food. Also beside the lake, on the road towards Brest, the two-star *Camping du Lac* (☏02.98.99.78.80; closed Sept–June) comes complete with swimming pool.

The central stretch

Although the canal is limited to canoeists between Carhaix and Pontivy, it's worth some effort to follow on land, particularly for the scenery around the long, narrow **Lac de Guerlédan**, created by the construction of a dam near **Mur-de-Bretagne**. Approaching by road, the canal path is most easily joined at **Gouarec**, served by five daily buses between Carhaix and Loudéac.

Le lac de Guerlédan

For the 15km between Gouarec and Mur-de-Bretagne, the N164 skirts the edge of **Quénécan Forest**, within which is the artificial **Lac de Guerlédan** created by the dam of the same name completed in 1928. It's a beautiful stretch of river, peaceful enough despite the summer influx of campers and caravans.

Just off the N164, at the western end of the lake, at the tiny village of **BON REPOS**, the ravishing ⌘ *Les Jardins de l'Abbaye* (☏02.96.24.95.77; ❷; closed Tues evening & Wed in low season) is an irresistible (and inexpensive) **hotel-restaurant**, nestling beside the water at the end of an impressive avenue of ancient trees, and housed in the cosy slate outbuildings of a twelfth-century

Cistercian abbey. At the town of **MÛR-DE-BRETAGNE**, at the western end, can be found the **tourist office** for the area (July–Aug Mon–Sat 10am–12.30pm & 2–6.30pm; Sept–June Mon–Fri 10am–noon & 2–5pm; ℡02.96.28.51.41), which can help with organizing bike rides, horseriding, canoeing and jet-skiing on the lake. The *Auberge Grand'Maison,* on the left as you climb to the centre at 1 rue Léon-le-Cerf (℡02.96.28.51.10, ⓦwww.auberge-grand-maison.com; ➌), has clean and homely rooms, and the best restaurant in the region downstairs. If you want to eat by the lake, get one of the thick wooden tables at *Merlin les Pieds dans l'Eau* (℡02.97.27.52.36) one the south shore of the lake at Saint Aignan, where there is also camping and pedalo rental.

Josselin

From the Barrage de Guerlédan at the eastern end of the lake, the canal passes the three Rapunzel towers of the **château** in **JOSSELIN**, and continues unbroken to the Loire. The residents of the château, the Rohan family, used to own a third of Brittany, but the present duke contents himself with the position of local mayor. The pompous apartments of his residence are not very interesting, even if they do contain the table on which the Edict of Nantes was signed in 1598, but the duchess's collection of dolls, housed in the **Musée des Poupées**, behind the castle, is something special (château & doll museum open April, May & Oct Sat, Sun & holidays 2–6pm; June to mid-July & Sept daily 2–6pm; mid-July to Aug daily 10am–6pm; each €7, combined ticket €12).

The town is full of medieval splendours, from the gargoyles of the **basilica**, Notre-Dame-du-Roncier, to the castle **ramparts**, and the half-timbered houses in between. Josselin's **tourist office** is in a superb old house on the place de la Congrégation, by the castle entrance (April–June & Sept Mon–Sat 10am–noon & 2–6pm, Sun 2–6pm; July & Aug daily 10am–6.30pm; Oct–March Mon–Thurs 10am–noon & 2–6pm, Sat 10am–noon; ℡02.97.22.36.43, ⓦwww.paysdejosselin-tourisme.com). Practically opposite, the English Language Book Shop (℡02.97.75.62.55) buys, sells and swaps books in English. The lovely *Hôtel du Château,* a Logis de France facing the castle from across the river at 1 rue du Général-de-Gaulle (℡02.97.22.20.11, ⓦwww.hotel-chateau.com; ➌; closed Feb), makes a perfect place to **stay**. Rooms with views of the château are slightly more expensive, but worth it, and the food, with dinner menus from €15, is first rate. The nearest good campsite is the three-star *Bas de la Lande* (℡02.97.22.22.20, Ⓔcampingbassedelalande@orange.fr; closed Nov–March; under €15 a pitch), half an hour's walk from the castle, south of the river and west of town.

Rochefort-en-Terre

Commanding a high eminence 41km southeast of Josselin, **ROCHEFORT-EN-TERRE** ranks among the most delightful villages in Brittany. Every available stone surface, from the window ledges to the picturesque wishing well, is festooned with colourful geraniums, a tradition that originated with the painter Alfred Klots, who was born in France to a wealthy American family in 1875, and bought Rochefort's ruined **château** in 1907. Perched on the town's highest point, the castle is now open for guided tours (April & May Sat & Sun 2–6.30pm; June & Sept daily 2–6.30pm; July & Aug daily 10am–6.30pm; €4), though not until you go through its dramatic gateway do you find out that in fact that gateway is all that survives of the original fifteenth-century structure.

Rochefort's **tourist office**, in the central place du Puits (mid-June to mid-Sept Mon–Fri 10am–12.30pm & 2–6.30pm, Sat & Sun 2–6.30pm; mid-Sept to mid-June Mon–Fri 10am–12.30pm & 2–6pm; ☎02.97.43.33.57, ⓦwww .rochefort-en-terre.com), operates the three-star municipal **campsite**, *Le Moulin Neuf*, in the chemin de Bogeais (☎02.97.43.37.52; closed mid-Sept to mid-May). The one **hotel** stands in the place des Halles: *Le Pélican* (☎02.97.43.38.48, ⓦwww.hotel-pelican-rochefort.com; ❹; closed mid-Jan to mid-Feb) offers reasonable rooms and good food, with dinner menus starting at around €17.50.

Redon

Situated at the junction not only of the rivers Oust and Vilaine and the canal, but also of the train lines to Rennes, Vannes and Nantes, and of six major roads, **REDON** is not easy to avoid. And you shouldn't try to, either. A wonderful grouping of water and locks, it's a town with history, charm and life.

Until World War I, Redon was the seaport for Rennes. Its industrial docks – or what remains of them – are therefore on the Vilaine, while the canal, even in the very centre of town, is almost totally rural, its towpaths shaded avenues. Shipowners' houses from the seventeenth and eighteenth centuries can be seen along quai Jean-Bart by the *bassin* and quai Duguay-Truin next to the river. A rusted wrought-iron workbridge, equipped with a gantry, still crosses the river, but the main users of the port now are cruise ships heading down the Vilaine to La Roche-Bernard.

Redon was once also a religious centre, its first abbey founded in 832 by St Conwoion. The most prominent church today is **St-Sauveur**. Its unique four-storeyed Romanesque belfry is squat, almost obscured by later roofs and the high choir, and best seen from the adjacent cloisters; the Gothic tower was entirely separated from the main building by a fire. In the crypt, you'll find the tomb of the judge who tried the legendary Bluebeard – Joan of Arc's friend, Gilles de Rais.

Redon's **gare SNCF** is five-minutes' walk west from the **tourist office** in the place de la République (July & Aug Mon–Sat 9am–7pm, Sun 10am–1pm & 4–6pm; Sept–June Mon & Wed–Fri 9.30am–noon & 2–6pm, Tues 2–6pm, Sat 10am–12.30pm & 3–5pm; ☎02.99.71.06.04, ⓦwww.tourisme-pays-redon .com), north across the railway tracks from the town centre. Most of the **hotels** are concentrated in town and near the *gare SNCF* rather than in the port area. Near the station, the *Hôtel Chandouineau*, 1 rue Thiers (☎02.99.71.02.04; ❺; closed Sat & Sun evening), is an upmarket establishment with just seven bedrooms, where the restaurant serves gourmet menus from €23. If you're looking to eat, try *L'Akène* at 10 rue de Jeu de Paume (☎02.99.71.25.15), where they do a mean rhubarb jam crêpe.

The southern coast

Brittany's **southern coast** is best known for the province's – and indeed mainland Europe's – most famous prehistoric site, the alignments of **Carnac**, with the associated megaliths of the beautiful, island-studded **Golfe de Morbihan**. The beaches are not as spectacular as in Finistère, but there are more safe places to swim and the water is warmer. Of the cities, **Lorient** has Brittany's most compelling **festival** and **Vannes** has one of the liveliest medieval town centres. Further east you can escape to the islands of **Belle-Île**, **Hoëdic** and **Houat**. Inevitably it's popular, and in summer you can be hard-pressed to find a room, but if you're prepared to make reservations, or you're camping, there shouldn't be much problem.

Lorient and around

Brittany's fourth largest city, **LORIENT**, lies on an immense natural harbour protected from the ocean by the Île de Groix and strategically located at the junction of the rivers Scorff, Ter and Blavet. A functional, rather depressing port today, it was once a key base for French colonialism, and was founded in the mid-seventeenth century for trading operations by the Compagnie des Indes, an equivalent of the Dutch and English East India Companies. Apart from the name, little else remains to suggest the plundered wealth that once arrived here. During the last war, its naval value caused it to be relentlessly bombed by the Allies, and clung to by the Germans until the bitter end, almost completely destroying the city. The only substantial remains were the U-boat pens, now expanded to hold French nuclear submarines.

Opened on the fiftieth anniversary of Lorient's liberation, the **Abri 400 places**, a bomb shelter under place Alsace-Lorraine, pays homage to the quarter of a million inhabitants that "disappeared" during the raids, with tours and exhibits on Lorient within the context of the war (July–Aug 4 & 5pm; €4). A former fishing trawler moored in the pleasure port, **La Thalassa**, now serves as an interactive museum of the ocean-going experience (July & Aug daily 10am–7.30pm; Sept–June Mon & Sun 2–6pm, Tues–Fri 10am–1pm & 2–6pm; €6.60). Different areas of its various decks aim to illustrate the lives of the ship's captain, and crew. Across the estuary in **Port-Louis**, the **Musée de la Compagnie des Indes** is a dismal temple to imperialist exploitation; better to take the boat out to the **Île de Groix**, a smaller and wilder version of Belle-Île, with SMN (Mon–Sat 9.40am, Sun 10.30am; ☎08.20.05.60.00, ⓦwww .smn-navigation.fr; €15 return).

Practicalities

Lorient's **tourist office**, beside the pleasure port on the quai de Rohan (mid-May to mid-July and late Aug to late Sept Mon–Fri 10am–noon & 2–6pm, Sat 10am–noon & 2–5pm; mid-July to late Aug Mon–Sat 9.30am–1pm & 2–7pm, Sun 10am–1pm, except during festival, when it's daily 9am–8pm; late Sept to mid-May Mon–Fri 10am–noon & 2–5pm, Sat 10am–1pm; ☎02.97.21.07.84, ⓦwww.lorient-tourisme.fr), can provide full details on local boat trips and organizes some excursions itself. There's a huge choice of **hotels**, though they are in high demand during the Inter-Celtic Festival. There is a choice of cheap rooms or more expensive en-suite versions at the central *Victor Hugo Hôtel* at 36 rue Lazare-Carnot (☎02.97.21.16.24, ⓦwww.hotelvictorhugo-lorient.com; ❷–❸), which offers a filling €18 menu. *The Rex* is at 28 cours de Chazelles (☎02.97.64.25.60, ⓦwww.rex-hotel-lorient.com). There's also a **hostel** (☎02.97.37.11.65, ⓔlorient@fuaj.fr; €12.10), next to the River Ter at 41 rue Victor-Schoelcher, 3km out on bus line C1 from the *gare SNCF*, which, on top of table tennis and a small bar, has space for **camping** in summer. A good central **restaurant** is *Le Café Leffe* (☎02.97.21.21.30; closed Jan), in the same building as the tourist office, facing the port, which is particularly strong on seafood. Celts are

The Inter-Celtic Festival

The overriding reason people come to Lorient is for the **Inter-Celtic Festival**, held for ten days from the first Friday to the second Sunday in August. This is the biggest Celtic event in Brittany, or anywhere else for that matter, with representation from all the Celtic nations of Europe – Brittany, Ireland, Scotland, Wales, Cornwall, the Isle of Man, Asturias and Galicia. In a genuine celebration of cultural solidarity, well over a quarter of a million people come to more than a hundred different shows, five languages mingle, and Scotch and Guinness flow with French and Spanish wines and ciders. There is a certain competitive element, with championships in various categories, but the feeling of mutual enthusiasm and conviviality is paramount. Most of the activities – embracing music, dance and literature – take place around the central place Jules-Ferry, where most people end up sleeping, too.

For **schedules** of the festival, and further details of temporary accommodation, contact the Festival Interceltique de Lorient, 8 rue Nayal in Lorient (☎02.97.21.24.29, ⓦ www.festival-interceltique.com), bearing in mind that the festival programme is not finalized until June each year. For certain events you need to reserve tickets well in advance.

famed for their **pubs**, and there's a fine selection in Lorient: you can get good, hearty meat and fish dishes at *Tavarn ar Boue Morvan* on place Polig-Monjarret (☎02.97.21.61.57), as well as home-made cider and live traditional music; *Galway Inn* on 18 rue Belgique (☎02.97.64.50.77) is the Irish–Celtic alternative, with Guinness and rock instead.

Carnac and around

The **alignments** at **CARNAC** – rows of two thousand or so menhirs, or standing stones, stretching for over 4km to the north of the village – constitute the most important prehistoric site in Europe, long predating Knossos, the Pyramids, Stonehenge or the great Egyptian temples of the same name at Karnak. Mercifully, they now stand a few kilometres in from the sea, meaning you can combine a reasonably tranquil visit to the stones with a stay in the popular, modern seaside resort, pretty hectic by Brittany's mild standards.

Arrival and information

In July and August, when the Tire Bouchon **rail** link runs between Auray and Quiberon, trains call at Plouharnel, 4km northwest of Carnac. The main **tourist office**, where **buses** from Auray, Quiberon and Vannes stop, is slightly back from the main beach at 74 avenue des Druides (July & Aug daily 9am–7pm, Sun 3–7pm; Sept–June Mon–Sat 9.30am–12.30pm & 2–6pm; ☎02.97.52.13.52, ⓦ www.ot-carnac.fr). **Bicycles** can be rented from several local campsites, or from Le Randonneur, 20 avenue des Druides, Carnac-Plage (☎02.97.52.02.55). The *Grande Métairie* site (see p.416) also arranges horseback tours. There's a **market** in Carnac-Ville on Wednesday and Sunday mornings.

Accommodation

Hotels in Carnac are at a premium in July and August, when you can expect higher prices or half board (*demi-pension*). As befits such a family-oriented place, Carnac features as many as twenty **campsites**. Among the best are the two-star

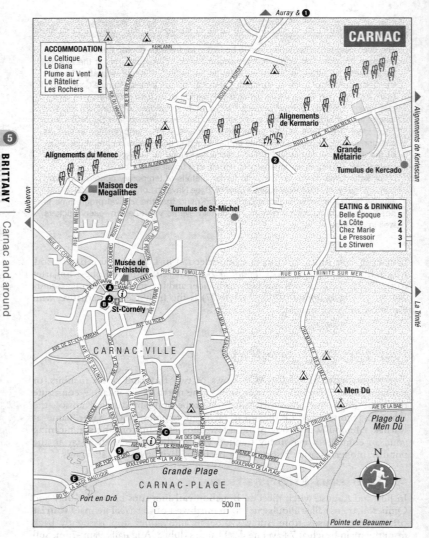

CARNAC

ACCOMMODATION
Le Celtique	C
Le Diana	D
Plume au Vent	A
Le Râtelier	B
Les Rochers	E

EATING & DRINKING
Belle Époque	5
La Côte	2
Chez Marie	4
Le Pressoir	3
Le Stirwen	1

Auray & ❶

Alignements de Kerlescan

Alignements de Kermario

Grande Métairie

Tumulus de Kercado

Alignements du Menec

Quiberon

Maison des Megalithes

Tumulus de St-Michel

❸

Musée de Préhistoire

RUE DU TUMULUS

RUE DE LA TRINITE SUR MER

La Trinité

❹

St-Cornély

AVE DU ROER

CARNAC-VILLE

Men Dû

Plage du Men Dû

AVE DE LA BAIE

❺

C

D

AVE DES DRUIDES

Grande Plage

CARNAC-PLAGE

E

Port en Drô

Pointe de Beaumer

N

0   500 m

Men Dû (☎02.97.52.04.23, ⓦwww.camping-mendu.fr; closed Oct–March; up to €23), near the sea, or the more expensive four-star *Grande Métairie* (☎02.97.52.24.01, ⓦwww.lagrandemetairie.com; closed early Sept to March; up to €28.10), near the Kercado tumulus.

Hôtel Celtique at 82 av des Druides ☎02.97.52.14.15, ⓦwww.hotel-celtique.com. One of the best luxury options by the beach at Carnac-Plage, largely because of its facilities, including an indoor pool, spa and billiard room. ⑥–⑦

Diana ☎02.97.52.05.38, ⓦwww.lediana.com. An big four-star hotel on the grand plage, whose rich, dark-wood rooms open out onto sea-view balconies. Facilities include pool, Jacuzzi, sauna and a great rum bar. ⑧

Plume de Vent 4 venelle Notre-Dame
☏06.16.98.34.79, ✉rabot.carnac
@orange.fr. Brilliantly decorated *chambres d'hôte*,
drawing tastefully on the nautical theme (for once)
with pastel colours and a great collection of found
artefacts. It also has a very warm welcome and a
prized location in the heart of Carnac-Ville. ❹
Hôtel le Râtelier 4 chemin de Douët, Carnac-Ville
☏02.97.52.05.04, ⓦwww.le-ratelier.com. An old

ivy-clad stone hotel with comfortable rooms
characterized by rustic colours and open wooden
beams; top-quality food on menus that start from
€17; restaurant closed Tues & Wed Oct–March. ❸
Les Rochers, 6 bd de la Base Nautique, Carnac-
Plage ☏02.97.52.10.09, ⓦwww.les-rochers.com. A
well-kept and family-friendly hotel offering the best
value by the beach, especially if you are looking for
sea-view balconies. Closed Nov–Easter. ❺

The Town

Carnac itself, divided between the original **Carnac-Ville** and the seaside resort
of **Carnac-Plage**, is extremely popular and swarms with holiday-makers in
July and August. For most of these, the alignments are, if anything, only a
sideshow. As a holiday centre, Carnac has a special charm, especially in late
spring and early autumn when it is less crowded – and cheaper. The town and

The megaliths of Brittany

Along with Newgrange in Ireland, Stonehenge in England and the Ring of Brodgar in
the Orkneys, the tumuli, alignments and single standing stones of Brittany are of pre-
eminent importance among the **Megalithic sites** of Europe, found principally around
the Mediterranean, and along the Atlantic seaboard. Archaeological evidence
suggests that late **Stone Age settlements** existed along the Breton coast until around
6000 BC, when they evolved into, or were replaced by, megalith builders. Dated at
5700 BC, the tumulus of Kercado at Carnac is the earliest known stone construction
in Europe. Each megalithic centre had its own distinct styles and traditions. Brittany
has relatively few stone circles, or **cromlechs**, and a greater proportion of free-
standing stones, **menhirs**; fewer burial chambers, known as **dolmens**, and more
evidence of ritual fires; and different styles of carving. The alignments are unique in
their sheer complexity. Little is known of their creators; the few skeletons found in
graves there indicate a short, dark, hairy race with a life expectancy of no more than
the mid-30s. What is certain is that the civilization was a long-lasting one; the earliest
and the latest constructions at Carnac are over five thousand years apart.

As for the actual **purpose** of the megaliths, the most fashionable theory these days
sees them as part of a vast astronomical compass, stretching across the lagoon and
low peninsulas of The Golfe de Morbihan. Centred on the fallen Grand Menhir of
Locmariaquer, eight other sites correspond to the eight extreme points of the rising
and setting of the moon during its 18.61-year cycle, recorded, presumably, over
hundreds of years of careful observation and using elevated fires at trial points on the
crucial nights every nine years. However, this has been hotly disputed. Controversy
rages as to whether the Grand Menhir ever stood at all, or, even if it did, whether it
fell or was broken up before the eight sites came into being. Moreover, sceptics say,
these measurements ignore the fact that the sea level in southern Brittany 6600 years
ago was 10m lower than it is today.

An alternative sociological approach argues that the stones date from the period of
transition when humankind was changing from a predatory role to a productive one,
and that they can only have been put in place by the coordinated efforts of a large
and stable **community**. This interprets the menhirs as a series of territorial or
memorial markers. This annual or occasional setting-up of a new stone is easier to
envisage than the vast effort required to erect them all at once – in which case the
fact that they were arranged in lines, mounds and circles might have been of periph-
eral importance.

seafront remain well wooded, and the tree-lined avenues and gardens are a delight, the climate being mild enough for evergreen oak and Mediterranean mimosa to grow alongside native stone pine and cypress.

The town's five **beaches** extend for nearly 3km in total. The two most attractive, usually counted as one of the five, are **plages Men Dû** and **Beaumer**, which lie to the east towards La Trinité beyond Pointe Churchill. They're especially popular these days with **kite surfers**.

The alignments

The **megaliths** of Carnac make up three distinct major alignments, running roughly in the same northeast–southwest direction, but each with a slightly separate orientation. These are the **Alignements de Menec**, "the place of stones" or "place of remembrance", with 1169 stones in eleven rows; the **Alignements de Kermario**, "the place of the dead", with 1029 stones in ten rows; and the **Alignements de Kerlescan**, "the place of burning", with 555 stones in thirteen lines. All three are sited parallel to the sea alongside the **Route des Alignements**, 1km or so to the north of Carnac-Ville.

The principal alignments are unpopularly fenced off, part of a long-term plan to protect and revegetate the over-trampled area, but plans are in the pipeline for sustainable bicycle and footpaths to go in. Currently you are allowed to walk freely around the best-preserved sites from October to March (daily 10am–5pm); between April and September access is on guided tours only (€4), run by the **Maison des Mégalithes**, across the road from the Alignements de Menec (daily: May–Aug 9am–7pm; Sept–April 10am–5.15pm; ☎02.97.52.29.81). You can also find maps, books and a model of the prehistoric site.

The stones themselves are clearly visible behind the fences, though thanks to generations of meddling by human hands, and a few millennia of Breton frost, many look like no more than stumps in the heather. Without any background, it is tempting to feel that you are just looking at some rocks in a field, so it is disappointing that **Musée de Préhistoire**, at 10 place de la Chapelle in town

▲ Megalithic remains near Carnac

(April–June & Sept Wed–Mon 10am–12.30pm & 2–5pm; July & Aug daily 10am–6pm; Oct–March Wed–Mon 10am–12.30pm & 2–5pm; €5; ⓦwww .museedecarnac.com), still only exhibits in French. It traces the history of the area from earliest times, starting with 450,000-year-old chipping tools and leading by way of the Neanderthals to the megalith builders and beyond. As well as authentic physical relics, it holds reproductions and casts of the carvings at Locmariaquer, a scale model of the Alignements de Menec and diagrams of how the stones may have been moved into place.

Eating and drinking

As well as the good hotel **restaurants** (see pp.416–417), Carnac has a range of eating options – the better ones found away from the beach – and a busy nightlife fuelled by the large seasonal-worker population.

Belle-Époque 43 av Port-en-Dro ☎02.97.52.73.25. Does an excellent couscous, amongst other dishes, and later turns into one of the town's favourite bars, with a penchant for fancy dress and themed nights.

La Côte 3 impasse Parc-er-Forn ☎02.97.52.02.80. An old stone building, but with inventive, modern gourmet cuisine, which you can try at lunch for just €24 a head (around €84 in the evenings). Closed all Mon and Tues lunch.

Chez Marie 3 place de l'Église ☎02.97.52.07.93. A old favourite in Carnac-Ville, this busystone-clad,

crêperie does good €11 menus, which include a full *galette*. Closed Nov–Easter.

Le Pressoir by the Ménec alignments ☎02.97.52.01.86. Good crêperie that prides itself on natural ingredients and serves moreish local cider. Closed Sept–Easter.

Le Stirwen ☎02.97.52.80.80. Nightclub institution in the woods just north of town, which draws heavily on the crowd of seasonal workers. Try to get catch their two big nights of the summer, the Kenavo and the allegedly better Super-Kenavo. Open weekends in season, until 4am.

Locmariaquer

With its complex patterning, the stone of the roof on Gavrinis (see p.426) has been identified as part of the same piece as the dolmen known as the **Table des Marchands** at **LOCMARIAQUER**, 12km east of Carnac. Locmariaquer also has the **Grand Menhir Brisé**, supposedly the crucial central point of the megalithic observatory of Carnac. Thought to have been toppled deliberately around the time the Table des Marchands was erected, it was by far the largest known menhir – 22m high and weighing more than a full jumbo jet at 347 tonnes. It now lies on the ground in four pieces, with a possible fifth missing, and is visited in conjunction with the Table des Marchands (daily: May–Sept 10am–7pm; Sept–April 10am–12.30pm & 2–5.15pm; €5, under-18s free; €7 with tour of Carnac).

Campsites in Locmariaquer include the excellent *Ferme Fleurie* (☎02.97.57.34.06; open Feb–Nov), 1km towards Kerinis, and the *Lann Brick* (☎02.97.57.32.79, ⓦwww.camping-lannbrick.com; open mid-March to Oct), 1.5km further on, nearer the beach.

The Presqu'île de Quiberon

The **Presqu'île de Quiberon**, south of Carnac, is well worth visiting on its own merits; **Quiberon** is quite a lively port, and you can get boats out to the islands or walk the shores of this narrow peninsula. The ocean-facing shore, known as the **Côte Sauvage**, is a wild and highly unswimmable stretch, where the stormy seas look like flashing scenes of snowy mountain tops. The sheltered eastern side has safe and calm sandy beaches, and plenty of campsites.

Quiberon

Despite recent construction on the peninsula, **QUIBERON**, at the peninsula's southern tip, is still the only real town. Its most active area, **Port-Maria**, is home to the **gare maritime** for the islands of Belle-Île, Houat and Hoëdic, and also has a sardine-fishing harbour of former glory.

Arrival and information

In July and August, the special Tire Bouchon train links Quiberon's *gare SNCF*, which is a short way above the town proper, with Auray. Bus #1 (TIM; ☎02.97.24.26.20) runs right to the *gare maritime* from Vannes, via Auray and Carnac.

The **tourist office** at 14 rue de Verdun in Quiberon (July & Aug daily 9am–1pm & 2–7pm; Sept–June Mon–Sat 9am–12.30pm & 2–5.30pm; ☎08.25.13.56.00, charge €0.30 per min, ⓦwww.quiberon.com) has a 24-hour computer terminal outside showing which hotels are full, hour by hour. In the summer a train service (July–Aug; 45min) known as the *Tire-Bouchon* – "corkscrew" connects to the mainline **train station** at Auray and a slower coach service does the journey from June to September. The #1 and #2 **buses** run around the peninsula between 9am and 7.10pm, or you can rent bikes at *Cycl'omar* at place Hoche (☎02.97.50.26.00).

Accommodation

For most of the year, it's hard to get a **room** in Quiberon. In July and August, the whole peninsula is packed, while in winter it's so quiet that virtually all its facilities close down. The nicest area to stay is along the seafront in Port-Maria, where several good hotel-restaurants face the Belle-Île ferry terminal.

Filets Bleus 45 rue du Roc'h-Priol ☎02.97.50.15.54, ⓔquiberon@fuaj.org. Well situated but fairly basic hostel, in which some rooms don't have a window. Better to camp under the pine trees in the back. €10.70, camping €5.70 or €7.50 if you use the tents they provide. Open April–Sept.

🏃 **Le Neptune** 4 quai de Houat ☎02.97.50.09.62. The best value around. All the rooms have either sea or garden views –

some with private balconies – and there's a very good restaurant (see opposite) with terrace overlooking the water. Closed Jan & Mon in low season. ❹

L'Océan 7 quai de l'Océan ☎02.97.50.07.58, ⓦwww.hotel-de-locean.com. Attractive little hotel in the port, with multicoloured pastel shutters, reasonable rooms and views over the port. The owners are friendly and rent out bikes. Closed Oct–March. ❸–❹

The Town

At Quiberon's centre is a busy little park and miniature golf course, but few of the streets further back hold anything of great interest. The exception is the little hill that leads down to the port from the **gare SNCF**, where browsing around is rewarded with some surprisingly good clothes and antique shops. Stretching away to the east of the harbour is a long curve of fine sandy **beach**, lined for several hundred yards with bars, cafés and restaurants.

Eating and drinking

The Port-Maria is the place for diners, where a line of seafood **restaurants** compete to attract ferry passengers. For **cafés**, those by the long bathing beach are the most enjoyable.

La Chaumine 36 place de Manémeur ☎02.97.50.17.67. Set close to the menhir in the main square of the next community west (800m northwest of the port), this lovely little fish restaurant serves menus from €16, with a €25 option featuring salmon braised in champagne. Closed Sun evening & Mon, plus mid-Nov to March.

De la Criée 11 quai de l'Océan ☎02.97.30.53.09. A truly superb local and seasonal fish restaurant; make your choice from the morning's catch, arranged in baskets along the front. Dishes include ling and sea bass, for example, and fish smoked on the premises, or a great seafood couscous. Closed Sun evening & Mon in low season, plus Jan.

Le Neptune 4 quai de Houat ☎02.97.50.09.62. Hotel dining room that serves exceptionally good seafood menus at €20 and €29. The portions are small, but the food is exquisite. Closed Jan & Mon in low season.

Belle-Île

The island of **BELLE-ÎLE**, 45 minutes by ferry from Quiberon, has its own Côte Sauvage on its Atlantic coast, while the landward side is fertile, cultivated ground, interrupted by deep estuaries with tiny ports. At different times in its turbulent history the island belonged to the monks of Redon, the English – who in 1761 swapped it for Menorca – and Lorient's Companie des Indes. Docking at Le Palais, the abrupt star-shaped fortifications of the **citadelle** are the first thing you see (daily: April–June, Sept & Oct 9.30am–6pm; July & Aug 9am–7pm; Nov–March 9.30am–noon & 2–5pm; €6.10). Built along stylish and ordered lines by the great fortress-builder, Vauban, it is startling in size – filled with doorways leading to mysterious cellars and underground passages and deserted cells. It only ceased being a prison in 1961, having numbered a succession of state enemies and revolutionaries among its inmates, including Ben Bella of Algeria. The island's charming wilderness also attracted painters such as Monet and Matisse, the writers Flaubert, Proust and presumably Dumas, too – Porthos's death, in *The Three Musketeers*, takes place here. A **museum** in the citadelle documents the island's history, in fiction as much as in fact.

The island is far too large to stroll round, but a coastal footpath runs on bare soil for the length of the **Côte Sauvage**. To appreciate the island's contrasts, some form of transport is advisable – you can **rent bikes** at the port and main town of **LE PALAIS**, and if you're in a (small) car the ferry fare is relatively low.

Getting to Belle-Île, Houat and Hoëdic

Four operators offer services to the islands of Belle-Île, Houat and Hoëdic, with departure options from Quiberon, Vannes, Lorient, Trinité-sur-mer, Locmariaquer and Le Croisec. Most operate only in the summer season; however, Compagnie-Océane (☎08.20.05.61.56, ⊛www.compagnie-oceane.fr) runs the cheap public services all year between **Quiberon** and **Le Palais** on Belle-Île (5 daily; 45min; €14 return), Houat (2 daily; 45min; €14 return) and Hoedic (daily; 1hr 15min; €14 return), with added services to **Sauzon** and a fast service between **Lorient** and Le Palais in July and August. Cars can also be taken across on the Quiberon to Belle-Île route, though with prices starting at €160 and such a small island it's not really worth it. Compagnie des Îles (☎02.97.46.18.19, ⊛www.compagniedesiles.com) supplements the Quiberon to Le Palais service from mid-April to September (3 daily; 40min; €25 return), and from July to August offers departures from Vannes to the smaller islands, via Locmariaquer (2 daily; 1hr 45min/2hr 15min; €28/32), and from **Le Croisec** to Le Palais (daily; 1hr 45min; €36 return) and to the Houat and Hoëdic (daily; 1hr 30min; €28/32 return). on the Quiberon peninsula, to **Le Palais**. Navix (☎02.97.46.60.00, ⊛www.navix.fr) also operates day-trips to the island from **Vannes** (daily; 2hr 10min; €31) calling at **Port-Navalo** and **La Trinité** along the way.

Near the west end you'll find the **Grotte de l'Apothicairerie**, so called because it was once full of cormorants' nests, arranged like the jars on a pharmacist's shelves. Inland, on the D25 back towards Le Palais, you pass the two **menhirs**, Jean and Jeanne, said to be lovers petrified as punishment for wanting to meet before their marriage. Another larger menhir used to lie near these two; it was broken up to help construct the road that separates them.

If you're staying any length of time, Belle-Île's second town, **SAUZON**, a beautiful little village arrayed along one side of a long estuary, or inland town of **Bangor** present less touristy places to base yourself.

Practicalities

The island's **tourist office** is next to the **gare maritime** in Le Palais (July & Aug Mon–Sat 8.45am–7.30pm, Sun 8.45am–1pm; Sept–June Mon–Sat 9am–12.30pm & 2–6pm; ℡02.97.31.81.93, ⓦwww.belle-ile.com). **Bikes** can be rented at *Roue Libre* on quai Jacques-Leblanc (℡02.97.31.49.81) and they'll also drop them off at the place you're staying. **Scooter** rental guys should be waiting for you as you walk off the ferry, but go to *Reversade,* 14 rue de l'Église (℡02.97.31.84.19) if not.

Accommodation in Le Palais includes the simple *Frégate*, above a nice little bar on the quayside (℡02.97.31.54.16; ❶; closed mid-Nov to March), and the comfortable *Atlantique* (℡02.97.31.80.11, ⓦwww.hotel-atlantique.com; ❸), with an excellent sea-view **restaurant**. A delightful luxury bed and breakfast, *Château Bordénéo* (℡02.97.31.53.00, ⓦwww.chateau-bordeneo.fr; ❽), is just out of town, and has a lovely garden and indoor pool. There are also three **campsites**, including the three-star *Camping de l'Océan* (℡02.97.31.83.86, ⓦwww.camping-ocean-belle-ile.com; open April to mid-Nov), and an often fully booked **hostel** (℡02.97.31.81.33, ⓔbelle-ile@fuaj.org; €12.10; closed Oct), a short way out of town along the clifftops from the citadelle at Haute-Boulogne.

Sauzon has one good hotel in a magnificent setting, the *Du Phare* (℡02.97.31.60.36; ❸; closed Oct–March), where guests must eat its delicious fish dinners, and the two-star **campsite** *La Source* (℡02.97.31.60.95, ⓦwww.belleile-lasource.com; open March to late Sept). The *Désirade* (℡02.97.31.70.70, ⓦwww.hotel-la-desirade.com; ❼) in Bangor is the island's best luxury and family option, with a little village of houses around a pool, sauna and gym and delightfully friendly owners.

Houat and Hoëdic

You can't take your car to these two smaller sisters of Belle-Île; known as the *'îles de silence'*, both islands have a feeling of being left behind by the passing centuries. However, the younger fishermen of Houat have revived the island's fortunes by establishing a successful fishing cooperative, and this island in particular has excellent **beaches** – as ever on its sheltered (eastern) side – that fill up with campers in the summer (even though camping is not strictly legal). The more traditional and less developed Hoëdic on the other hand has a large municipal **campsite**, overlooking the port (℡02.97.52.48.88; open June–Sept; €6 for a pitch). There are a couple of small **hotels** on Houat – *L'Ezenn* (℡02.97.30.69.73; ❷; closed Feb) and the pricier *Hôtel-Restaurant des Îles* (℡02.97.30.68.02; ❸; closed Nov–Easter) – and one on Hoëdic, *Les Cardinaux* (℡02.97.52.37.27, ⓔlescardinaux@aol.com; ❹; closed Sun pm & Mon in winter, all Feb).

Vannes

At the head of the Golfe de Morbihan, **VANNES**, southern Brittany's major tourist town, is such a large and thriving community that the size of the small walled town at its core, **Vieux Vannes**, may well come as a surprise. Its focal point, the old gateway of the **Porte St-Vincent**, commands a busy little square at the northern end of a canalized port leading to the gulf itself. Inside the ramparts, the winding car-free streets – crammed around the cathedral, and enclosed by gardens and a tiny stream – are great strolling territory.

Arrival and information

Vannes' **gare SNCF** is 25-minutes' walk north of the town centre. Buses to Auray, Carnac, Quiberon and other destinations leave from the **gare routière** alongside. The **tourist office** is at 1 rue Thiers (July & Aug daily 9am–7pm; Sept–June Mon–Sat 9.30am–12.30pm & 1.30–6pm; ☏08.25.13.56.10, ⊛www.tourisme-vannes.com), near place Gambetta. **Internet access** is available at Futur I-Media, 14 rue de la Boucherie (Mon–Fri noon–1am, Sat & Sun 2pm–1am; ☏02.97.01.84.09; €4 per hr).

Accommodation

In peak season, Vannes can get claustrophobic, but there is a wider choice of **hotels** than anywhere else around the gulf. The nearest **campsite** is the three-star *Camping Conleau* at the far end of avenue du Maréchal-Juin, alongside the

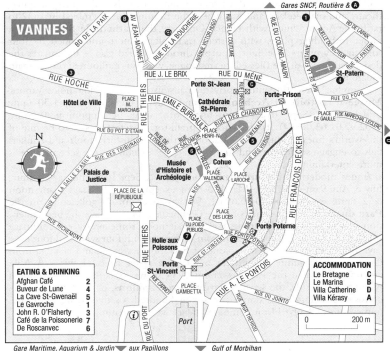

VANNES

EATING & DRINKING
Afghan Café 2
Buveur de Lune 4
La Cave St-Gwenaël 5
Le Gavroche 1
John R. O'Flaherty 3
Café de la Poissonerie 7
De Roscanvec 6

ACCOMMODATION
Le Bretagne C
Le Marina B
Villa Catherine D
Villa Kérasy A

0   200 m

Gare Maritime, Aquarium & Jardin ▼ *aux Papillons*   ▼ *Gulf of Morbihan*

gulf beyond the aquarium (☎02.97.63.13.88, ✉camping@mairie-vannes.fr; open April–Sept; up to €15).

Hotels

Le Bretagne 36 rue du Méné ☎02.97.47.20.21, ⓦwww.hotel-lebretagne-vannes.com. Reasonable and friendly hotel just outside the walls, around the corner from the Porte-Prison. The rooms have had a recent facelift, and all have showers or bath and TV. **②**

Le Marina 4 place Gambetta ☎02.97.47.00.10, ✉lemarinahotel@aol.com. Fifteen pleasantly refurbished rooms – double glazed to keep the noise out – and a downstairs bar, right by the port with sea views and morning sun. En-suite facilities cost €5 extra. **②**

Villa Catherine 89 av du president Édouard-Herriot ☎02.97.42.48.59, ⓦwww.villa-catherine.fr. A charming four-room bed and breakfast, in a late nineteenth-century town house that has been recently redone exclusively with ecologically sustainable materials, and serving an entirely organic breakfast. Good for the soul. **⑤**

Villa Kerasy 20 av Favrel-et-Lancy ☎02.97.68.36.83, ⓦwww.villakerasy.com. A top of the range luxury hotel and Indian spa, with the best rooms leading onto a Japanese garden. Service and surroundings are very good, though there's no restaurant. **⑧**

The Town

Modern Vannes centres on **place de la République**; the focus was shifted outside the medieval city in the nineteenth-century craze for urbanization. The grandest of the public buildings here, guarded by a pair of sleek and dignified bronze lions, is the **Hôtel de Ville** at the top of rue Thiers. By day, however, the streets of the old city, with their overhanging, witch-hatted houses and busy commercial life, are the chief source of pleasure.

La Cohue, an impressive building on place St-Pierre, has served over the past 750 years as High Court and assembly room, prison, Revolutionary tribunal, theatre and marketplace, and was where the Breton *États* assembled in 1532 to ratify the Act of Union with France. Opposite, the **Cathédrale St-Pierre** is a rather forbidding place, with a stern main altar almost imprisoned by four solemn grey pillars. The light – purple through stained glass – illuminates the desiccated finger of the Blessed Pierre Rogue, who was guillotined on the main square in 1796.

A sombre fifteenth-century private mansion at 2 rue Noé holds Vannes' **Musée d'Histoire et Archéologie** (mid-May to mid-June daily 1.30–6pm; mid-June to Sept daily 10am–6pm; otherwise by appointment only, ☎02.97.01.63.00; €4). Its collection of prehistoric artefacts is said to be one of the world's finest, though the curation of these prehistoric tools and trinkets fails to engage somewhat, and the Middle Ages exhibit on the second floor is more entertaining.

Vannes' modern **aquarium** (daily: April–June & Sept 10am–noon & 2–6pm; July & Aug 9am–7pm; Oct–March 2–6pm, except school holidays 10am–noon & 2–6pm; €9.50; ☎08.10.40.69.01, ⓦwww.aquarium-du-golfe.com), in the **Parc du Golfe**, 500m south of place Gambetta, claims to have the best collection of tropical fish in Europe. Certainly it holds some pretty extraordinary specimens, including a type of fish from Venezuela with four sexes and four eyes; cave fish from Mexico that by contrast have no eyes at all; and *arowana* from Guyana, which jump two metres out of the water to catch birds. A Nile crocodile found in the Paris sewers in 1984 shares its tank with a group of piranhas. Alongside, the separate **Jardin aux Papillons**, or Butterfly Garden, consists of a huge glass dome containing hundreds of free-flying butterflies (same hours; €8, or €14 for combined ticket with aquarium).

Eating, drinking and entertainment

Dining out in old Vannes can be an expensive experience, whether you eat in the intimate little restaurants along the rue des Halles, or down by the port. If you're just looking for a snack, try the area outside the walls in the northeast, towards the *gare SNCF*. At the end of July, the open-air concerts of the **Vannes Jazz Festival** take place in the Théâtre de Verdure.

Afghan Café 12 rue de la Fontaine ☎02.97.42.77.77. An excellent restaurant providing the rare opportunity to try good Afghan cuisine, which centres around rice with fish, meat or vegetarian dishes and cardamon tea. Count on €25 a head, and it is regularly in high demand, so book ahead. Closed Mon.

Buveur de Lune 8 rue Saint-Patern ☎02.97.54.32.32. A relaxed and good-natured spot for a drink with the night sky across the ceiling and fairly priced drinks. Closed Mon & Tues.

La Cave St-Gwenaël 23 rue St-Gwenaël ☎02.97.47.47.94. Atmospheric, good-value crêperie in the cellar of a lovely old house, facing the cathedral. Closed Sun, plus Mon Sept–June, & all Jan.

Le Gavroche 17 rue de la Fontaine Pasteur ☎02.97.54.03.54. A true godsend for meat-lovers, where you can feast on excellent meat-packed menus starting at a mere €15. The steaks are cooked to perfection, while starters such as pigs' trotters will put hairs on your chest. Closed Sun, Mon & Wed evening.

John R. O'Flaherty 22 rue Hoche ☎02.97.42.40.11. A real Irish pub with the right ales on tap, various bits of junk on the walls and traditional Irish folk live on Friday nights. closed Sun.

De Roscanvec 17 rue des Halles ☎02.97.47.15.96. Absolutely superb formal gourmet restaurant, in a lovely half-timbered house in the old town, with dining on two levels and also outdoors. Lunch at €20 is a bargain, while even the cheapest dinner menu, at €27, features unusual dishes such as *carbonara d'huîtres*, beautifully prepared and presented. For the standard, even the €74 menu is a bargain. Closed Sun in summer, Sun evening & all Mon Sept–June.

The Golfe de Morbihan

Immediately below Vannes, the ragged-edged **Golfe de Morbihan** – *mor bihan* means "little sea" in Breton – hides behind the peninsulas of **Rhuys** and **Locmariaquer**. By popular tradition the **islands** used to number the days of the year, but rising seas have left fewer than one for each week. Of these, thirty are owned by film stars and the like, while two – the **Île aux Moines** and **Île d'Arz** – have regular populations and ferry services and end up extremely crowded in summer. The rest are the best, and a **boat tour** around them, or at

Gulf tours

In season, dozens of boats leave on **gulf tours** each day from Vannes, Port Navalo, La Trinité, Locmariaquer, Auray, Le Bono and Larmor-Baden. Among the options are:

Navix ⓦwww.navix.fr. Up to five deluxe half-day (€22) and full-day (€29) tours around the gulf from Vannes (☎08.25.13.21.00) every day between March and October with the first leaving at 9.30am. During the same period, similar tours also depart from Port Navalo (☎08.25.13.21.20) and Locmariaquer (☎08.25.13.21.30), while trips leave from La Trinité (☎08.25.13.21.50) between early July and late August only.

Izenah Croisières ☎02.97.57.23.24 or 02.97.26.31.45, ⓦwww.izenah-croisieres .com. The best value gulf tours, leaving half-hourly from Port Blanc at Baden in summer (April–Sept; €15–23) and a year-round ferry service, with departures every half-hour, to the Île aux Moines (daily: July & Aug 7am–10pm; Sept–June 7am–7.30pm; €4.20 return).

least a trip out to **Gavrinis** near the mouth of the gulf, is a compelling attraction, with megalithic ruins and stone circles dotted around the beguiling maze of channels and solitary menhirs look down from small hillocks.

Gavrinis

The reason to visit the island of **Gavrinis**, which can only be reached on guided boat tours from Larmor-Baden, is its **megalithic site**. The most impressive and remarkable in Brittany, it stands comparison with Newgrange in Ireland and – in shape as well as size and age – with the earliest pyramids of Egypt.

The megalithic structure is essentially a **tumulus**, an earth mound covering a stone cairn and "passage grave". However, half of the mound has been peeled back and the side of the cairn that faces the water was reconstructed to make a facade resembling a step-pyramid. Inside, every stone of both passage and chamber is covered in carvings, with a restricted "alphabet" of fingerprint whorls, axe-heads and other conventional signs, including the spirals familiar in Ireland but seen only here in Brittany.

Gavrinis can be reached between March and November only. Tides permitting, **ferries** leave Larmor-Baden at half-hourly intervals, and the cost includes a 45-minute guided tour of the cairn (April, June & Sept daily 9.30am–12.30pm & 1.30–6.30pm; May Mon–Fri 1.30–6.30pm, Sat & Sun 9.30am–12.30pm & 1.30–6.30pm; July & Aug daily 9.30am–12.30pm & 1.30–7pm; March, Oct &

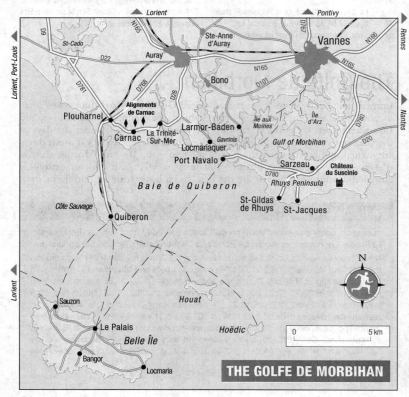

THE GOLFE DE MORBIHAN

Nov daily except Wed 1.30–5pm; ☎02.97.57.19.38, ⓦ www.gavrinis.info; €10). The last boats of the morning and afternoon leave Larmor-Baden an hour and a half before the closing time.

South to the Loire

When you cross the **Vilaine** on the way south, you're not only leaving the Morbihan *département* but also technically leaving Brittany itself. The roads veer firmly east and west, avoiding the marshes of the **Grande-Brière**. For centuries these 20,000 acres of peat bog have been deemed to be the common property of all who lived in them. The scattered population, the *Brièrois*, still make their living by fishing for eels in the streams, gathering reeds and – on the nine days permitted each year – cutting peat. Tourism has arrived relatively recently, and is resented. The touted attraction is renting a punt to get yourself lost for a few hours with your pole tangled in the rushes.

Guérande

On the edge of the marshes of the Grande-Brière, just before you come to the sea, stands the tiny, gorgeous walled town of **GUÉRANDE**. It gave its name to this peninsula, and to its famed delicately flavoured sea salt. This "white country" is chequered with bizarre-looking *oeillets* (salt pans) each seventy to eighty square metres in extent, in which sea water has been collected and evaporated since Roman times.

Guérande today is still entirely enclosed by its stout fifteenth-century ramparts. Although you can't walk along them, a spacious promenade leads right the way around the outside, passing four fortified gateways. The main entrance, the **Porte St-Michel** on the east side of town, now holds a small **museum** of local history (April–Sept Mon 2.30–7pm, Tues–Sun 10am–12.30pm & 2.30–7pm; Oct Mon 2–6pm, Tues–Sun 10am–noon & 2–6pm; €4).

Guérande's **tourist office** is just outside the Porte St-Michel at 1 place du Marché au Bois (June & Sept Mon–Sat 9.30am–12.30pm & 1.30–6pm, Sun 10am–1pm; July & Aug Mon–Sat 9.30am–7pm, Sun 10am–1pm & 3–5pm; Oct–May Mon–Sat 9.30am–12.30pm & 1.30–6pm; ☎02.40.24.96.71, ⓦ www.ot-guerande.fr). Tucked out of sight behind the market, the pretty *Roc-Maria*, 1 rue des Halles (☎02.40.24.90.51, ⓦ www.hotelcreperierocmaria.com; ❸), offers cosy **rooms** above a crêperie in a fifteenth-century town house. Also in the old town by the Porte Vannetaise, the hugely attractive 🌿*La Guérandière* (☎02.40.62.17.15, ⓦ www.guerande.fr; ❹) is a beautifully restored and decorated manor house – with pleasant garden to breakfast in.

Le Croisic

The small port of **LE CROISIC**, sheltering from the ocean around the corner of the headland, but stretching right across the peninsula, is a more attractive place to stay than La Baule. These days it's basically a pleasure port, but fishing boats do still sail from its harbour, near the very slender mouth of the bay, and there's a modern **fish market** near the long Tréhic jetty, where you can watch the day's catch being auctioned. The hills on either side of the harbour, Mont Lenigo and Mont Esprit, are not natural; they were formed from the ballast left by the ships of the salt trade. If you're staying, choose between the **hotels** *Castel Moor*, 500m beyond the town centre towards the end of the headland, on the sheltered side (☎02.40.23.24.18, ⊛www.castel-moor.com; ❸; closed Jan), or *Les Nids*, set slightly back from the ocean side of the peninsula at 15 rue Pasteur (☎02.40.23.00.63, ⊛www.hotellesnids.com; ❹; closed mid-Nov to early April), which has its own small indoor swimming pool. Both have good restaurants.

Close by, all around the rocky sea coast known as the **Grande Côte**, are a range of **campsites**, including the *Océan* (☎02.40.23.07.69, ⊛www.camping-ocean.com; closed Oct–March; around €18). For equally good beaches you could go east to the upmarket resort of La Baule, further west to **Pornichet** (though preferably keeping away from the plush marina) or to the tiny **St-Marc**, where in 1953 Jacques Tati filmed *Monsieur Hulot's Holiday*.

Nantes

NANTES, the former capital of Brittany, is no longer officially part of the province: it was transferred to the Pays de la Loire in 1962 when the modern administrative regions were established. Nonetheless, such bureaucracy is not taken too seriously in a city whose history is so intimately bound up with Breton fortunes. A considerable medieval centre, it later achieved great wealth from colonial expeditions, the slave trade and shipbuilding – activities in turn

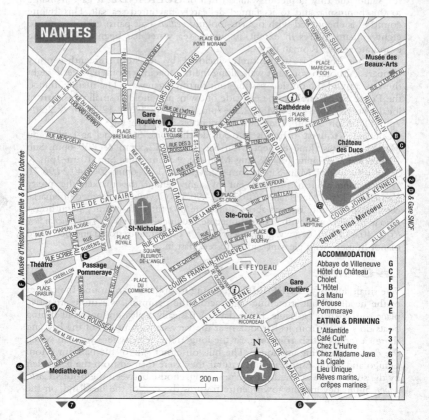

ACCOMMODATION

Abbaye de Villeneuve	G
Hôtel du Château	C
Cholet	F
L'Hôtel	B
La Manu	D
Pérouse	A
Pommaraye	E

EATING & DRINKING

L'Atlantide	7
Café Cult'	3
Chez L'Huitre	4
Chez Madame Java	6
La Cigale	5
Lieu Unique	2
Rêves marins, crêpes marines	1

surpassed by more recent industrial growth. Although much of the former provincial character of the city has been lost, thanks to such recent accretions as the tower blocks masking the Loire and motorways tearing past the city, it remains to its inhabitants an integral part of Brittany.

Arrival and information

Nantes' **gare SNCF**, with regular TGVs to Paris, Lyon and Bordeaux, has two exits; for most facilities (tramway, buses, hotels) use Accès Nord. There are two main **bus** stations. The one just south of the centre on allée Baco, near place Ricordeau, is used by buses heading south and southwest, while the one where the cours des 50 Ôtages meets rue de l'Hôtel de Ville serves routes that stay north of the river. **Trams** run along the old riverfront, past the *gare SNCF* and the two bus stations. Flat-fare tickets, at €1.50, are valid for one hour, rather than just a single journey, though one-day tickets are also available for €3.50.

Nantes' **tourist office** is between the medieval city and the nineteenth-century town at 3 cours Olivier-de-Clisson (Mon, Tues & Wed–Sun 10am–6pm; Thurs 10.30am–6pm; ☏08.92.46.40.44, ⓦwww.nantes-tourisme.com); it provides free book-size guides to local hotels and restaurants, and runs various guided tours of the city. It also sells the **Pass Nantes**, available in 24-hour (€16), 48-hour (€27) and 72-hour (€32) versions, which grants unrestricted use of local transport, including river cruises, and free admission to a wide range of museums and the chateau. Cyber Cité, 14 rue de Strasbourg, offers **internet access** (daily 1pm–1am; ☏02.40.89.57.92; €4 per hr).

Accommodation

Nantes has plenty of **hotels** to suit all budgets; the two hotspots are in the immediate vicinity of the *gare SNCF*, and the narrow streets around the place Greslin. The tourist office runs a booking service (☏08.92.46.40.44).

Hotels

Abbaye de Villeneuve route des Sables d'Olonne, 7km north of town ☏02.40.04.40.25, ⓦwww .abbayedevilleneuve.com. The only four star in the Nantes region and home to one of the best restaurants, housed in a restored eighteenth-century *abbaye*, with gorgeously lavish rooms and a circular swimming pool and spa. ❼–❽

Hôtel du Chateau 5 place de la Duchesse-Anne ☏02.40.74.17.16, ⓦwww.hotelduchateau-nantes .fr. Well-kept and friendly, if basic, budget option in town. The top rooms offer by far the cheapest view over the Chateau des Ducs in town. ❶

Cholet 10 rue Gresset ☏02.40.73.31.04, ⓦwww .hotelcholet-nantes.com. Quiet, friendly option very close to place Graslin, with a wide assortment of rooms, all with en-suite facilities. Mon–Fri ❸, Sat & Sun ❷

L'Hôtel 6 rue Henri-IV ☏02.40.29.30.31, ⓦwww .nanteshotel.com. An insouciant name for one of the city's finest options, a very grand modern edifice

facing the château with a high standard of comfort. Buffet breakfasts cost €9.90; parking is €9. ❺

La Manu 2 place de la Manufacture ☏02.40.29.29.20, ⓔnanteslamanu@fuaj.org. The hostel, with internet and public kitchen, is housed in a postmodern former tobacco factory a few hundred metres east of the *gare SNCF*, and five minutes from the centre by taking tramway #1. €15.65 per night.

La Pérouse 3 allée Duquesne ☏02.40.89.75.00, ⓦwww.hotel-laperouse .fr. Superb contemporary building ingeniously integrated with the older architecture that surrounds it. The interior is decorated with 1930s furniture, stucco walls and ultramodern touches such as high-tech TVs and wireless internet access in the rooms. Mon–Fri ❻, Sat & Sun ❹

Pommeraye 2 rue Boileau ☏02.40.48.78.79, ⓦwww.hotel-pommeraye.com. Extremely good-value modern boutique hotel with large, designer-decor rooms, beautiful bathrooms and free parking; good buffet breakfast. Mon–Fri ❺, Sat & Sun ❸

The City

The Loire, the source of Nantes' riches, has dwindled from the centre. As recently as the 1930s, the river crossed the city in seven separate channels, but German labour as part of reparations for World War I filled in five. What are still called "islands" in the centre are now surrounded and isolated, not by water, but by difficult-to-cross dual carriageways. These separate Nantes' districts: the older **medieval city** is concentrated around the cathedral, with the château prominent in its southeast corner, while the elegant **nineteenth-century town** lies to the west, across the cours des 50-Otages.

The old town

Though no longer on the waterfront, the **Château des Ducs** still preserves the form in which it was built by two of the last rulers of independent Brittany, François II, and his daughter Duchess Anne, born here in 1477. The list of famous people who have been guests or prisoners, defenders or belligerents, of the castle includes Gilles de Rais (Bluebeard), publicly executed in 1440; Machiavelli, in 1498; John Knox as a galley-slave in 1547–49; and Bonnie Prince Charlie preparing for Culloden in 1745. In addition, the **Edict of Nantes** was signed here in 1598 by Henri IV, ending the Wars of Religion by granting a degree of toleration to the Protestants. It had far more crucial consequences when it was revoked, by Louis XIV, in 1685.

The stout **ramparts** of the château remain pretty much intact, surrounded by well-tended lawns – ideal for picnickers. These ramparts opened up to the public last year, making available their vertiginous views down over the city. Within the walls is the new and well-arranged **Musée d'Histoire de Nantes** (July & Aug, daily 9.30am–7pm; Sept–June daily 10am–6pm; €5, €8 combined with temporary exhibitions; Ⓦ www.chateau-nantes.fr), whose lively curation adds interest to the potentially dry subject of local history and hosts an ambitious programme of cultural events.

In 1800 the Spaniards Tower, the castle's arsenal, exploded, shattering the stained glass of the **Cathédrale de St-Pierre-et-St-Paul** over 200m away. This was just one of many disasters that have befallen the unlucky church. It was used as a barn during the Revolution, bombed during World War II, and damaged by fire in 1972. Restored and finally reopened, its soaring height and lightness are emphasized by its clean white stone. It contains the tomb of François II and his wife Margaret – with somewhat grating symbols of Power, Strength and Justice for him and Fidelity, Prudence and Temperance for her. Nantes' **Musée des Beaux-Arts**, east of the cathedral on rue Clemenceau, has a respectable collection and good temporary exhibitions (Mon, Wed & Fri–Sun 10am–6pm, Thurs 10am–8pm; €3.50, €2 after 4.30pm). Not all its Renaissance and contemporary works are on display at any one time, but try to catch *David Triumphant* by Delaunay, Chagall's *Le Cheval Rouge* and Monet's *Nymphéas*.

The nineteenth-century town

The financier Graslin took charge of the development of the western part of the city in the 1780s, when Nantes' prosperity was at a high due to the sugar and slave trades. **Place Royale**, with its distinctive fountain, was first laid out in the closing years of the eighteenth century, and has been rebuilt since it was bombed in 1943; the 1780s also produced the nearby **place Graslin**, named after its creator, with the elaborately styled **Grand Théâtre**, whose Corinthian portico contrasts with the 1895 Art Nouveau of the not-to-be-missed *La Cigale* brasserie (see opposite) on the corner.

Rue Voltaire runs west of the place Graslin, leading to the **Musée d'Histoire Naturelle** at no. 12 (daily except Tues 10am–6pm, ⓦwww.museum.nantes.fr; €3.50). This holds an eccentric assortment of oddities, including tatty taxidermy, plus rhinoceros toenails, a coelecanth, an aepyornis egg and an Egyptian mummy. There's even a complete tanned human skin, taken in 1793 from the body of a soldier whose dying wish was to be made into a drum. Further along is Viollet-le-Duc's **Palais Dobrée** (Tues–Fri 1.30–5.30pm, Sat & Sun 2.30–5.30pm; €3, free on Sun), a nineteenth-century mansion given over to two museums, one of which claims to feature Duchess Anne's heart in a box.

Across the river on Île de Nantes is the town's most outlandish and delightful new attraction. The recently opened workshops of **Les Machines de Île** (July–Aug daily 10am–8pm; mid-April to June, Sept & Oct Tues–Sun 10am–6pm; Nov, Dec & mid-Feb to mid-April Wed–Sun 2–6pm; €6 gallery tour, €6 elephant ride; ⓦwww.lesmachines-nantes.fr) offer the flabbergasting opportunity to ride on a twelve metre high mechanical elephant as it paces up and down an old shipping warehouse spraying onlookers from its trunk. A gallery alongside presents more madcap inventions from the team of artist, engineers whose oeuvre draws heavily on the aesthetics of Jules Verne and Leonardo de Vinci. Reports that the elephant will be released on the town for city tours had yet to materialize at the time of writing.

Eating and drinking

Restaurants fill the winding lanes of the old city and it shouldn't take long to come up with something if you wander the pedestrian streets in the centre. Bars can be found around place du Commerce and place du Bouffay, and you could do worse than to head on to Lieu Unique (below) afterwards.

L'Atlantide Centre des Salorges, 16 quai Ernest-Renaud ℡02.40.73.23.23. Designer restaurant, with big views from the fourth floor of a modern block, that serves the contemporary French cuisine of chef Jean-Yves Gueho. Fish is the speciality, but expect quirky twists like the bananas braised in beer. Menus at €30 and €72. Closed Sat lunch & all Sun, plus first 3 weeks of Aug.

Chez L'Huître 5 rue des Petites-Écuries ℡02.51.82.02.02. Much as the name suggests, this lovely little restaurant specializes in oysters of all sizes and provenance; the "*apérihuître*" consists of six oysters and a glass of Muscadet for €8.50; you can also get smoked fish, fish soup and other simple dishes. Open until late nightly, closed Sun lunch.

Chez Madame Java 118 rue Basse-Île ℡02.40.04.20.88. A colourful and laid-back wine bar, with different food on offer most days and a garden out back for the summer. Live samba and reggae every second Sun in the winter.

La Cigale 4 place Graslin ℡02.51.84.94.94. Fabulous late nineteenth-century brasserie, offering fine meals in opulent surroundings, with seating at terrace tables or in a more formal indoor dining room. Fish is a speciality, with lunch options like the €16.90 *tartare de thon*. Also serves good breakfasts.

Café Cult' 2 rue des Carnes ℡02.40.47.18.49. A friendly, good value café housed in a beautiful old beamed house. They serve two-course lunches for just €11 and cheap drinks later on, when it becomes a lively bar. Until 2am, closed Sunday.

Lieu Unique quai Ferdinand Favre ℡02.51.82.15.00, ⓦwww.lelieuunique.com. A truly unique place, this former LU biscuit factory now plays host to concerts, theatre, dance, art exhibitions, a book shop, a fair brasserie and a great bar, open until late. Check the website for event details.

Rêves marins, crêpes marines 2 rue de Roi Albert ℡02.40.47.00.96. A boat-themed crêperie with a frequently changing menu of seriously original *galettes*, including braised duck and lobster in saffron. Closed Sun, Mon & 2–7pm daily.

Travel details

Trains

Brest to: Le Mans (2 daily; 3hr 50min); Morlaix (16 daily; 35min); Paris-Montparnasse (7 TGVs daily; 4hr); Quimper (5 daily; 1hr 10min); Rennes (7 daily; 2hr 15min).

Guingamp to: Paimpol (June–Sept only, 4–5 daily; 45min).

Nantes to: Bordeaux (2 daily; 4hr 20min); Le Croisic (5 daily; 40min); Nantes (5 daily; 1hr 30min); Paris-Montparnasse (6 TGVs daily; 2hr 10min);

Quimper to: Lorient (12 daily; 40min); Nantes (10 daily; 2hr 30min); Paris-Montparnasse (7 TGVs daily; 4hr 15min); Redon (6 daily; 1hr 30min); Vannes (12 daily; 1hr 15min).

Rennes to: Brest (5 TGVs daily; 2hr 15min, plus 6 daily slower services, 2hr 40min); Caen (4 daily; 3hr) and Pontorson (1hr); Lille (2 daily; 3hr 45min); Morlaix (10 daily; 1hr 45min), via Lamballe (40min); Nantes (5 daily; 1hr 30min); Paris-Montparnasse (20 TGVs daily; 2hr 10min); Quimper (9 daily; 2hr 30min); Vannes (6 daily; 1hr); Vitré (10 daily; 35min).

Roscoff to: Morlaix (4 daily; 35min).

St-Malo to: Rennes (6 daily; 50min; connections for Paris on TGV).

Buses

Brest to: Brignogan (6 daily; 1hr); Camaret (6 daily; 1hr 10min); Le Conquet (7 daily; 40min);

Quimper (5 daily; 1hr 15min); Roscoff (3 daily; 1hr 45min).

Quimper to: Bénodet (3–8 daily; 30min); Camaret (3 daily; 1hr 20min); Concarneau (7 daily; 30min); Crozon (3 daily; 1hr 15min); Douarnenez (10 daily; 40min); Fouesnant (8 daily; 30min); Locronan (3 daily; 20min); Pointe du Raz (5 daily; 1hr 30 min); Roscoff (1 daily; 2hr 45min).

Rennes to: Dinan (6 daily; 1hr 20min); Dinard (5 daily; 1hr 40min); Fougères (10 daily; 1hr); Mont St-Michel (5 daily; 1hr 20min).

Roscoff to: Brest (3 daily; 2hr); Morlaix (5 daily; 1hr); Quimper (1 daily; 2hr 30min).

St-Malo to: Cancale (6 daily; 45min); Combourg (2 daily; 1hr); Dinan (6 daily; 45min); Dinard (10 daily; 30min); Fougères (3 daily; 2hr 15min); Mont St-Michel (4 daily; 1hr 30min); Pontorson (4 daily; 1hr 15min); Rennes (3 daily; 1hr 30min).

Vannes to: Auray (8 daily; 30min); Carnac (7 daily; 1hr 20min); Quiberon (7 daily; 2hr).

Ferries

For details of ferries to Ouessant, see p.394; to Bréhat, see p.385; to Batz, see p.392; to Sein, see p.402; to Belle-Île, see p.421; and for tours of the Gulf of Morbihan see p.425.

The Loire

UNITED KINGDOM

BELGIUM

GERMANY

ENGLISH CHANNEL

LUX.

ATLANTIC
OCEAN

SWITZERLAND

ITALY

N

SPAIN

MEDITERRANEAN
SEA

0   250 km

CHAPTER 6 # Highlights

* **Stained glass at Bourges cathedral** Some of France's finest stained-glass windows are preserved in Bourges' extravagant Gothic cathedral. See p.452

* **Château de Chenonceau** The most graceful of all the Loire châteaux bridges the River Cher. See p.456

* **Château de Blois** An epic and brilliantly conceived building, and a must-visit for anyone. See p.462

* **Amboise** Beautiful, archetypal Loire Valley town, and a brilliant base for an exploration of the outlying regions. See p.475

* **The gardens at Villandry** These superb gardens are home to allegorical Renaissance hedge-work. See p.478

* **The Tapestry of the Apocalypse** Dramatically displayed in Angers' half-ruined château, this is an astonishingly well-preserved piece of medieval doom-mongering. See p.490

▲ Château de Chenonceau

The Loire

T
he Loire has a justifiable reputation as one of the greatest, grandest and most striking rivers anywhere in Europe. In its most characteristic stretch, from the hills of Sancerre to the city of Angers, it flows past an extraordinary parade of castles, palaces and fine mansions; unsurprisingly, when it came to choosing which should be awarded the title of World Heritage Site, UNESCO just bestowed the label on the entire valley. Although the most striking feature is the beautiful views, there are simpler pleasures, such as the outstanding food and drink and the noticeably gentler pace of life.

The region's heartland, **Touraine**, long known as "the garden of France", has some of the best wines, the tastiest goat's cheese, and the most regal history in France, including one of the finest châteaux in **Chenonceau**. Touraine also takes in three of the Loire's pleasantest tributaries: the **Cher**, **Indre** and **Vienne**. If you have just a week to spare for the region, then these are the parts to concentrate on. The attractive towns of **Blois** and **Amboise**, each with their own exceptional châteaux, make good bases for visiting the area upstream of Tours. Numerous grand châteaux dot the wooded country immediately south and east of Blois, including **Chambord**, the grandest of them all, while the wild and watery region of the **Sologne** stretches away further to the southeast.

The Loire by bike

Thanks to the **Loire à Vélo** scheme (🌐 www.loire-a-velo.fr), the Loire valley is now one of the most charming places in the world to have a cycling holiday or take a day out on a hired bike. A mix of dedicated cycle paths and meticulously signposted routes along minor roads now runs all the way along the Loire from Orléans to beyond Angers – a distance of more than 300km. Or almost all the way: a single gap upstream of Tours means you'll have to follow ordinary roads for 50km between Tours and Candé-sur-Beuvron, 14km downstream of Blois – or work out a much lengthier route on back roads. Work is still under way to extend the network further up- and downstream; it is hoped that this will be complete by mid-2009. The region around Blois offers an additional, 300km network, **Châteaux à vélo** (🌐 www.chateauxavelo.com; see p.465). These routes thread inland among the forests, linking the area's many châteaux.

Tourist offices provide detailed maps and other information, and you can download most details, including maps, online. French villages are accustomed to cyclists, and all larger towns have at least one hire agency. Bikes can also be hired at hotels, campsites, tourist offices, train stations and even restaurants along the way. Many have signed up to the **Détours de Loire scheme** (☎ 02.47.61.22.23, 🌐 www.locationdevelos.com), which allows you to pick up a bike in one place and drop it off in another, paying inexpensive drop-off costs per zone crossed – on top of the bike rental charge.

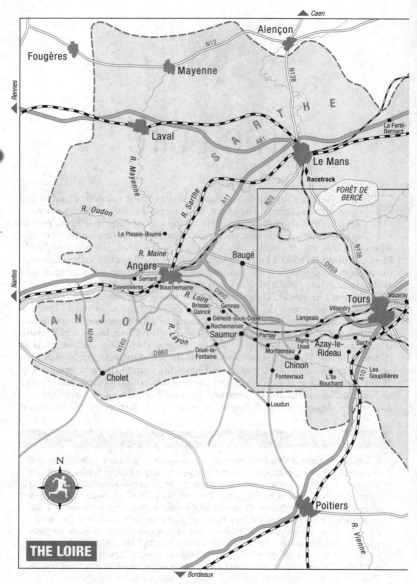

THE LOIRE

Downstream of Tours, around handsome **Saumur**, quirky troglodyte dwellings have been carved out of the rock faces.

As well as the many châteaux, the region has a few unexpected sights, most compelling of which are the gardens at **Villandry**, outside Tours, and the abbey at **Fontevraud**. The major towns of Angers, Tours, Le Mans and Orleans seem disappointing in comparison, though each has its charms, from Tours' astonishing cathedral to the apocalyptic tapestry sequence at Angers.

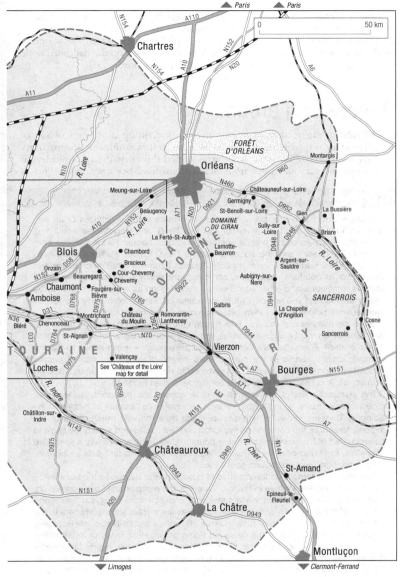

The Loire itself is often called the last wild river in France, mostly because unpredictable currents and shallow water brought an end to commercial river traffic as soon as the railways arrived, and the many quays remain largely forgotten, except by the occasional tour boat. The river's wildness also takes shape in dramatic floods, but for most of the year it meanders gently past its shifting sandbanks, shaded by reeds and willows, and punctuated by long, sandy islands beloved by birds.

Though most sites are accessible by public transport, buses and trains can be rather limiting, so it's a good idea to hire some means of transport, at least for occasional forays away from the crowds. Hiring a bike is perhaps the most enjoyable option of all: this is wonderful and easy **cycling** country, especially on the dedicated cycle routes that make up the new Loire à Vélo network (see box, p.435).

Orléans and around

ORLÉANS is the northernmost city on the Loire, sitting at the apex of a huge arc in the river as it switches direction and starts to flow southwest. Its proximity to Paris, just over 100km away, has always shaped this ancient city. Nowadays, it is far from its glory days, but nonetheless there have been welcome signs of

The food and drink of the Loire

The **Loire** is renowned for the softness of its climate and the richness of its soil, qualities that help produce some of the best **fruit** and **vegetables** you'll find anywhere. From Anjou's orchards come greengages, named *Reine Claudes* after François I's queen, and the succulent Anjou pear. Market stalls overflow with seasonal fruits, particularly local apricots. Tours is famous for its French beans and Saumur for its potatoes. Asparagus, particularly the fleshy white variety, appears in soufflés, omelettes and other egg dishes as well as on its own, accompanied by vinaigrette made (if you're lucky) with local walnut oil. Finally, from Berry, comes the humble lentil, whose green variety often accompanies salmon or trout.

Given the number of rivers that flow through the region, it's hardly surprising that **fish** features on most restaurant menus, though this doesn't guarantee that it's from the Loire itself. Favourites are *filet de sandre* (pike-perch – a fish native to Central Europe), usually served in the classic Loire *beurre blanc* sauce; stuffed bream; *matelote* (a kind of stew) of local eels softened in red wine; salmon (often flavoured with sorrel); and little smelt-like fishes served deep-fried (*la friture*).

The favoured meat of the eastern Loire is **game**, and pheasant, guinea fowl, pigeon, duck, quails, young rabbit, venison and even wild boar are all hunted in the Sologne. They are served in rich sauces made from the wild **mushrooms** of the region's forests or the common *champignon de Paris*, cultivated on a huge scale in caves cut out of the limestone rock near Saumur. Both Tours and Le Mans specialize in *rillettes*, or potted **pork**; in Touraine charcuteries you'll also find *pâté au biquion*, made from pork, veal and young goat's meat.

Though not as famous as the produce of Bordeaux and Burgundy, the Loire valley has some of the finest **wines** in France. Sancerre, the easternmost Loire *appellation*, produces perhaps the finest white wines in the region from the great Sauvignon grape, and the whites of Muscadet around Nantes are a great accompaniment to the local shellfish. Touraine's finest reds – Chinon, Bourgueil and St-Nicolas de Bourgueil – get their ruby colour from the Cabernet Franc grape, while many of its attractive white wines are made from the Chenin Blanc including the highly fashionable Jasnières. At the other end of the spectrum is the honeyed complexity of Côteaux du Layon's so-called dessert wines – best with blue cheese or foie gras rather than pudding – and Vouvray's still, sweet and semi-sweet whites, which only release the best of the Chenin Blanc grape after decades in the bottle.

Touraine makes something of a cult of its **goat's cheese**, and a local *chèvre fermier* (farm-produced goat's cheese) can be a revelation. Four named goats' cheeses are found on most boards: Ste-Maure is a long cylinder with a piece of straw running through the middle; Pouligny-St-Pierre and Valençay are pyramid-shaped; and Selles-sur-Cher is flat and round.

Château and monument pass

The handy **Passeport Val de Loire** "la clef des temps" (€25, free to under-18s) allows you to visit ten national monuments in the Loire valley over the course of a year. You can purchase it at any participating site, including the châteaux at Angers, Azay-le-Rideau, Chambord and Chaumont, the Cloître de la Psalette at Tours cathedral, and the Abbaye de Fontevraud. However, it's probably only worth it if you plan on having a lengthy stay in the region.

progress lately; high-speed train and motorway links to the capital and a rash of cosmetics factories set up in the suburbs have brought new jobs and prosperity. The ancient riverside quays have been redeveloped and ultramodern trams have been introduced – a perfect foil to the handsome eighteenth- and nineteenth-century streets of the old centre.

The city is deservedly most famous for its heroine **Joan of Arc** and her deliverance of the city in May 1429. This was the turning point in the Hundred Years War (1339–1453), when Paris had been captured by the English and Orléans, as the key city in central France, was under siege. Joan, a 17-year-old peasant girl in men's clothing, had talked her way into meeting Charles, the heir to the French throne, and persuaded him to reconquer his kingdom. Her legend has probably coloured her actual achievements, but it's undeniable that she was an important symbolic figure. Less than three years later she was captured in battle, tried as a heretic, and burnt at the stake. Today, the Maid of Orléans is an omnipresent feature, whether in museums, hotels or in the stained glass of the vast Neo-Gothic cathedral. One of the best times to visit is the evening before and the day of May 8 (**Joan of Arc Day**), when the city is filled with parades, fireworks and a medieval fair.

Arrival and information

The **gare SNCF** leads straight into the modern shopping centre on place d'Arc, which fronts onto a huge swathe of busy roads; the old town centre lies on the far side of the traffic. The **gare routière**, on rue Marcel-Proust, is just north of place d'Arc. The main **tourist office**, 2 place de l'Étape (Mon–Sat: April & May 9.30am–1pm & 2–6.30pm; June & Sept 9am–1pm & 2–7pm; July & Aug 9am–7pm, also Sun 10am–1pm; Oct–March 10am–1pm & 2–6pm; ☎02.38.24.05.05, ⊛www.tourisme-orleans.com;), is in the old centre, opposite the cathedral.

Accommodation

Accommodation in Orléans is notoriously boring; one wonders why some enterprising hotelier hasn't opened somewhere of a higher standard than the universally mediocre options. If you must spend the night here, these are probably the most acceptable. Avoid most of the places round the station, they're neither clean nor even a bargain.

D'Arc 37 rue de la République ☎02.38.53.10.94, ⊛www.hoteldarc.fr. This long-established Art Nouveau hotel has touches of grandeur, alas mainly faded and unkempt. The most attractive rooms have small balconies with window boxes, looking down onto the tramlines and pedestrianized street below. ❻
Auberge de Jeunesse d'Orléans-La Source Stade Omnisports, 7 av Beaumarchais

☎02.38.53.60.06, ⓔauberge.crjs@orange.fr. Clean, decent hostel, with friendly management and very modern rooms and facilities. The major downside is the suburban location, underneath a stand of Orléans' stadium: take tram A from the train station, get off at "Université l'indien" (30min), then walk 500m east down av du Président-Kennedy. Closed at weekends; reception open Mon–Fri 8am–7pm. €9 per night with HI membership, the purchase

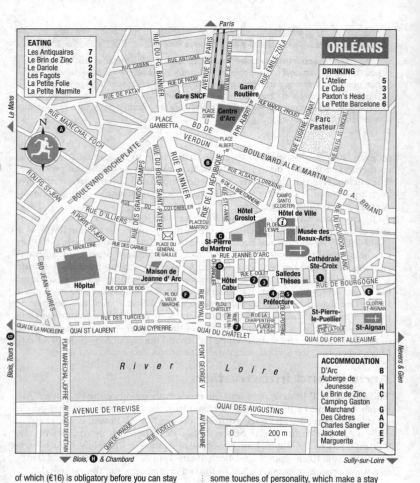

EATING

Les Antiquaires	7
Le Brin de Zinc	C
Le Dariole	2
Les Fagots	6
La Petite Folie	4
La Petite Marmite	1

ORLÉANS

DRINKING

L'Atelier	5
Le Club	3
Paxton's Head	3
Le Petite Barcelone	6

ACCOMMODATION

D'Arc	B
Auberge de Jeunesse	H
Le Brin de Zinc	C
Camping Gaston Marchand	G
Des Cèdres	A
Charles Sanglier	D
Jackotel	E
Marguerite	F

of which (€16) is obligatory before you can stay
in a hostel.

Le Brin de Zinc 62 rue Ste-Catherine
☏02.38.53.88.77, ⊛www.brindezinc.fr. Half a
dozen sparsely furnished but decent enough, and
cheap, rooms in an old building above a popular
and very central restaurant. The marble chimneys
add a welcome note of class. ❷

Camping Gaston Marchand chemin de la Roche,
St-Jean-de-la-Ruelle ☏02.38.88.39.39. The
municipal campsite, and the closest to Orléans,
3km away out on the Blois road, beside the Loire;
bus #26, stop "Petite Espère". Showers and a shop
on site. Closed Sept–June.

Des Cèdres 17 rue Maréchal-Foch
☏02.38.62.22.92, ⊛www.hoteldescedres.com.
The best hotel in town; faint praise, admittedly, but
this one is at least comfortable, clean and has

some touches of personality, which make a stay
here less of a burden. ❺

Charles Sanglier 8 rue Charles-Sanglier
☏02.38.53.38.50, ⓔhotelsanglier@orange.fr. Very
central, so tends to get booked up. The modern
building is unprepossessing, and the rooms are
small and a little shabby, but it's a friendly place,
and comfortable enough. ❸

Jackotel 18 Cloître-St-Aignan ☏02.38.54.48.48,
☏02.38.77.17.59. Unrivalled location overlooking
the church of St-Aignan across a shaded square,
but the decor is anonymous 1980s-style. ❹

Marguerite 14 place du Vieux-Marché
☏02.38.53.74.32, ⓔhotel.marguerite@orange.fr.
Central, friendly and well run. Large, immaculate
rooms painted in cheery modern colours – a few
unrenovated rooms are cheaper. ❹

The City

In pride of place in the large, central **place du Martroi,** a mostly pedestrian-ized square at the end of rue de la République, rises an unflattering mid-nineteenth-century likeness of St Joan on horseback. Just beyond place du Martroi, the grand nineteenth-century stretch of rue Jeanne-d'Arc marches arrow-straight up to the doors of the **Cathédrale Sainte-Croix** (daily 9.15am–noon & 2–6pm), where Joan celebrated her victory over the English – although the uniformly Gothic structure actually dates from well after her death. Huguenot iconoclasts destroyed the transepts in 1568, and in 1601 Henri IV inaugurated a rebuilding programme that lasted until the nineteenth century. The lofty towers of the west front, which culminate in a delicate stone palisade, were only completed at the time of the Revolution. Inside, skeletal columns of stone extend in a single vertical sweep from the cathedral floor to the vault. Joan's canonization in 1920 is marked by a garish monumental altar next to the north transept, supported by two jagged and golden leopards that represent the English. In the nave, the late nineteenth-century stained-glass windows tell the story of her life, starting from the north transept. In a series of cartoon-like images, *L'Anglois Perfide*, or perfid-ious Albion, gets a rough ride, while the role of the Burgundians in her capture and the French clergy in her trial is rather brushed over. Across place d'Étape from the cathedral, outside the red brick Renaissance **Hôtel Groslot**, the old Hôtel de Ville, Joan appears again, in pensive mood, her skirt now shredded by World War II bullets.

The interesting **Musée des Beaux-Arts** (Tues–Sat 10am–12.15pm & 1.30–5.45pm, Sun 2–6.30pm, €3), opposite the Hôtel Groslot, is probably the cultural high point of the city. The highlights of the main French collection on the first floor include Claude Deruet's *Four Elements*, the Le Nain brothers' dream-like and compelling *Bacchus Discovering Ariane on Naxos*, and the exquisite collection of eighteenth-century pastel portraits in room eight. The suite of rooms on the mezzanine level leads from nineteenth-century Neoclas-sicism through Romanticism and on to a large chamber devoted to the early Realists, dominated by Antigna's taut, melodramatic *The Fire*. Foreign art, mainly Flemish and Italian sixteenth- and seventeenth-century works, is on the second floor – look out for Correggio's renowned *Holy Family* (1522) and Velázquez's *St Thomas*. Twentieth-century art lurks in the basement, where the big names include Picasso and Gauguin; a small inner chamber has a number of African-influenced sculptures by Henri Gaudier-Brzeska (1891–1915), who was born just outside Orléans at St-Jean-de-Braye. English explanation sheets are supplied in each room.

If you follow rue Jeanne-d'Arc east from the cathedral and turn left down rue Charles-Sanglier, you'll find the ornate **Hôtel Cabu** (May, June & Sept Tues–Sat 1.30–5.45pm, Sun 2–6.30pm; July & Aug Tues–Sat 9.30am–12.15pm & 1.30–5.45pm, Sun 2–6.30pm; Oct–April Wed & Sat 1.30–5.45pm, Sun 2–5.45pm; same ticket as Musée des Beaux-Arts), whose three tiers faithfully follow the three main classical orders in strict Renaissance style. Inside, a small historical and archeological museum houses the extraordinary **Treasure of Neuvy-en-Sullias**, a collection of bronze animals and figurines found near Orléans in 1861. The cache was probably buried in the second half of the third century AD, either to protect it from Germanic invaders or to stop it being melted down for coinage at a time of rampant inflation, and possibly represents the last flourishing of Celtic religion at the end of the Gallo-Roman period. The floors above house various medieval oddities and Joan-related pieces, as well as exhibits on the history of Orléans. The entrance is on square Abbé-Desnoyers.

If you haven't had enough of Jeanne d'Arc by this stage, head to place Général-de-Gaulle, where you'll find the semi-timbered **Maison de Jeanne d'Arc** (Tues–Sun: May–Oct 10am–12.30pm & 1.30–6pm; Nov–April 1.30–6pm; €2), a 1960s reconstruction of the house where Joan stayed, an entertaining enough diversion for an hour. Despite the consistency in artists' renderings of the saint, it seems the pageboy haircut and demure little face are part of the myth – there is no contemporary portrait of her, save for a clerk's doodle in the margin of her trial proceedings, kept in the National Archives in Paris.

The riverfront and around

The scattered vestiges of the old city are to the east, down towards the river. **Rue de Bourgogne** was the Gallo-Roman main street, and is now lined with lively bars and restaurants. The **Salles des Thèses** is all that remains of the medieval university of Orléans where the hardline Reformation theologian Calvin studied Roman law. A short distance west on rue de Bourgogne, the circular Greek Revival-style **Protestant chapel** dates from the 1830s.

To the south, the attractive narrow streets of the old industrial area slope gently down towards the river. Once semi-derelict, it is now the focus of a campaign to make the riverfront once more the focus of the city. On the **place de la Loire**, which slopes down to the river from a nine-screen cinema complex, the flagstones are inset with a pattern that's supposed to suggest waves. At least two of the quarter's churches are on the list of precious monuments: the remains of **St-Aignan** and its well-preserved eleventh-century crypt; and the Romanesque **St-Pierre-le-Puellier**, a former university church now used for concerts and exhibitions. St-Aignan was destroyed during the English siege, rebuilt by the Dauphin and extended into one of the greatest churches in France by Louis XII. More sieges of the city during the Wars of Religion took their toll, leaving just the choir and transepts standing. Tours of the **crypt**, which was built in the early eleventh century to house the relics of St-Aignan, are occasionally conducted by the tourist office.

Eating and drinking

Rue de Bourgogne is the main street for **restaurants** and **nightlife**. You can choose from among French, Spanish, North African, Middle Eastern, Indian and Asian cuisines, all of which can be sampled at very reasonable prices. For buying your own provisions there are the covered **market halls** on place du Châtelet, near the river.

Restaurants

Les Antiquaires 2 & 4 rue au Lin ☎02.38.53.52.35. Run by a renowned chef, Philippe Bardau, this is Orléans' best restaurant and is well worth a visit. Lobster consommé, wild turbot with girolle mushrooms and pike perch steak are some of its delights. Menus begin at €46, but there's an excellent €38 menu (not available Sat evening or Sun) which includes selected wines. Closed Sun evening & Mon.

Le Brin de Zinc 62 rue Ste-Catherine. Bustling bistro just off place du Martroi in hotel of the same name. The outside tables are packed with a noisy crowd tucking into huge seafood platters (€14–28) and *plats du jour* (€7.40).

Le Dariole 25 rue Étienne Dolet ☎02.38.77.26.67. Tearoom-cum-restaurant in a picture-postcard half-timbered building that serves good quality food at inexpensive prices (mains from around €10).

Les Fagots 32 rue du Poirier ☎02.38.62.22.79. Wonderfully convivial place that looks as if it has been crammed into someone's grandmother's kitchen. Traditional main courses and grilled meats feature on the €11 and €15 menus. Closed Sun & Mon.

La Petite Folie 223 rue de Bourgogne ☎02.38.53.39.87. Youthful, designer bar-restaurant serving fresh, light and exciting food – you might have asparagus flan, chicken with *sauce*

Canadienne, then strawberry soup with wine – all for around €20 for the set menu. Closed Sun; closed at lunchtime Oct–April.

La Petite Marmite 178 rue de Bourgogne ☎02.38.54.23.83. The most highly regarded restaurant on this busy street combines a stylish but homely feel with excellent regional cuisine. The excellent €22 *menu du terroir* features local products such as rabbit and guinea fowl from the Sologne. Closed Tues & Wed.

Bars and nightlife

L'Atelier 203 rue de Bourgogne. Arty, studenty place, with regular concerts and exhibitions. Possibly slightly too insular if you don't speak the language as well as the bohemian regulars, but quite fun if you do.

Le Club 266 rue de Bourgogne. Cellar club-bar with a tiny dance floor overlooked by a little mezzanine seating level. Nothing special but a friendly choice if you're out late at the weekend and want to push on past 2am. Entry €10 with a drink.

Paxton's Head 264–266 rue de Bourgogne. If you're homesick for an archetypal English pub, this will just about fit the bill. Not the cheapest place in town, though. Daily 3pm–3am.

Le Petit Barcelone 218 rue de Bourgogne Friendly, informal student bar with cheap enough drinks (around €3-4 for a pint or glass of wine) and meals served from April to December.

Listings

Bike hire The only central option is CAD, 95 rue Faubourg-Bannier ☎02.38.81.23.00.Otherwise, try Kit Loisirs, 1720 rue Marcel-Belot (☎02.38.63.44.34, ⓦwww.kitloisirs.com), out in the suburb of Olivet.

Must see châteaux

First things first; though it is tempting to try and pack in as many châteaux as you can in a short period of time, this is counter-productive and frustrating, leading only to fatigue and overload. It's far better to aim to visit three or four of the best in the area in which you're staying, possibly with a one-day trip to one of the most spectacular set-piece châteaux in the region.

Of the most famous, **Azay-le-Rideau** (see p.479) and **Chenonceau** (see p.456) both belong exclusively to the Renaissance period, and their settings in the middle of moat and river respectively are very beautiful, rivalled only by the wonderful Renaissance gardens of **Villandry** (see p.478). Azay-le-Rideau, in particular, is a marvellous encapsulation of a long-gone period of grandeur and power, in a beautifully serene setting, conveniently hidden from public view. **Blois** (see p.461), with its four wings representing four distinct eras, is extremely impressive, as is the monstrously huge **Chambord** (see p.467), the triumph of François I's Renaissance. The latter is something of an acquired taste, not least because it's always busy. The key feature here is the dual-spiral staircase, which legend has it was designed by Leonardo da Vinci. At **Valençay** (see p.459), the interior of the Renaissance château is Napoleonic, while **Cheverny** (see p.466) is the prime example of seventeenth-century magnificence.

For an urban château, **Amboise** (see p.475), which rears above the Loire like a cliff, is one of the most compelling and striking, even if the interior decoration leaves something to be desired. For an evocation of medieval times, the citadel of **Loches** (see p.495) is hard to beat.

Other châteaux are more compelling for their contents than for their architecture: **Beauregard** (see p.466) is most famous for its portrait gallery while **La Bussière** (see p.448) for its obsessive nineteenth-century decoration, entirely dedicated to freshwater fishing, and **La Ferté-St-Aubin** is a living aristocratic home. At **Angers** (see p.490) the stark, largely ruined medieval castle houses the Tapestry of the Apocalypse, the greatest work of art in the Loire valley, and worth a visit in itself.

Entry prices are undeniably steep, particularly for the châteaux that have remained in private hands – and there are a surprising number of French aristocrats still living in their family homes. This means that picking and choosing the best really will help you. There is no consistency in concessions offered, and children rarely go free. If you're over 65, under 25, a student or still at school, check for any reductions and make sure you've got proof of age or a student card with you.

Car rental Avis, Gare SNCF ☎02.38.62.27.04; Rent-a-Car, 3 rue Sansonnières ☎02.38.62.22.44; Europcar, 17 av de Paris ☎02.38.73.00.40.

Festivals Fête de Jeanne d'Arc is a series of period-costume parades held on April 29, May 1 and May 7–8, with the big set-pieces occurring in front of the cathedral on the night of the 7th and morning of the 8th May. The Festival de Jazz d'Orléans is held right through June, culminating in concerts held in the Campo Santo (ⓦwww.ville-orleans.fr/orleansjazz).

Every Sept in odd years, the Loire Festival takes place, with five days of concerts and shows beside the Châtelet quay.

Internet Leader Best Phone, 196 rue de Bourgogne (July & Aug 9.30am–11.30pm; Sept–June 11am–11.30pm; €3 per hour).

Medical assistance Centre Hospitalier, 1 rue Porte-Madeleine ☎02.38.51.44.44; emergencies ☎15.

Police 63 rue du Faubourg-St-Jean ☎02.38.24.30.00; emergencies ☎17.

Château de Meung

Little streams known as *les mauves* flow between the houses in the village of **MEUNG-SUR-LOIRE**, 14km southwest of Orléans on the Blois rail line. During the summer months they leave slimy green high-water marks, but the sound of water is always pleasant, and Meung is an agreeable place to spend an afternoon, having also accumulated a number of literary associations over the centuries.

In the late thirteenth century, Jean de Meun, or de Meung, added eighteen thousand lines to the already four thousand line-long *Roman de la Rose*, a poetic hymn to sexuality written half a century earlier (by Guillaume de Lorris, from the town of the same name in the nearby Forêt d'Orléans). Inspired by the philosophical spirit of the times, de Meun transformed the poem into a finely argued disquisition on the nature of love, and inspired generations of European writers. Most recently, the town featured in the works of Georges Simenon – his fictional hero, Maigret, takes his holidays here.

Looming at the western edge of the old town centre, the **Château de Meung** (March–Oct daily 10am–7pm; Nov–Feb Sat & Sun 2–6pm; €7.50; ⓦwww.chateaudemeung.com) remained in the hands of the bishops of Orléans from its construction in the twelfth century right up to the Revolution, since when it has passed through seven or eight private hands. The exterior of the château on the side facing the old drawbridge looks grimly defensive, retaining its thirteenth-century pepper-pot towers, while the side facing the park presents a much warmer facade, its eighteenth-century windows framed by salmon-pink stucco. You can explore the older part on your own, even poking around under the roof but most of this pleasantly shambolic section of the building was remodelled in the nineteenth century, and little sense of the building's history remains. More impressive is the eighteenth-century wing, where the bishops entertained their guests in relative comfort. Below here are the **cellars** where criminals condemned by the Episcopal courts were imprisoned. The most famous of the detainees was the poet François Villon, who was kept under lock and key between May and October 1461.

Beaugency

Six kilometres southwest of Meung along the Loire, **BEAUGENCY** is a pretty little town, which, in contrast to its innocuous appearance today, played its part in the conniving games of early medieval politics. In 1152 the marriage of Louis VII of France and Eleanor of Aquitaine was annulled by the Council of Beaugency in the church of Notre-Dame, allowing Eleanor to marry Henry Plantagenet, the future Henry II of England. Her huge land holdings in southwest France thus passed to the English crown – which already controlled Normandy, Maine, Anjou and Touraine – and the struggles between the French and English kings over their claims to these territories, and to the French throne itself, lasted for centuries.

Liberated by the indefatigable Joan of Arc on her way to Orléans in 1429, Beaugency was a constant battleground in the Hundred Years War due to its strategic significance as the only bridge crossing point of the Loire between Orléans and Blois. Remarkably, the 26-arch **bridge** still stands and gives an excellent view of the once heavily fortified medieval heart of the town, which clusters tightly around a handful of central squares. **Place St-Firmin**, with its statue of Joan, is overlooked by a tower of a church destroyed during the Revolution, while **place Dunois** is bordered by the massive eleventh-century **Tour de César**, formerly part of the rather plain, fifteenth-century **Château Dunois**, which is closed to visitors for major structural works, probably until 2009. The square is completed by the rather severe Romanesque **abbey church of Notre-Dame**, the venue for the council's fateful matrimonial decision in 1152. Shady place du Docteur-Hyvernaud, two blocks north of place Dunois, is dominated by the elaborate sixteenth-century facade of the **Hôtel de Ville**. Inside, the main council chamber is graced by eight fine **embroidered wall hangings** from the era of Louis XIII, but you'll have to ask at the tourist office (on the same square) to be allowed inside to have a look. One set illustrates the four continents as perceived in the seventeenth century, with the rest dramatizing pagan rites such as gathering mistletoe and sacrificing animals.

Practicalities

A small **tourist office** (May–Sept Mon–Sat 10am–12.30pm & 2.30–6.30pm, Sun 10am–noon; Oct–April Mon–Sat 9.30am–noon & 2.30–6pm; ☏02.38.44.54.42, Ⓦwww.beaugency.fr) is on place Docteur-Hyvernaud. Two charming **hotels** make the most of Beaugency's atmosphere of genteel charm: the ✻ *Hôtel de l'Abbaye*, 2 quai de l'Abbaye (☏02.38.44.67.35, www.hotel-abbaye-beaugency.com; ❼), is set in a beautiful seventeenth-century abbey with painted ceilings and beds on raised platforms, offering traditional luxury at an inexpensive price; while the small, delightful *Hôtel de la Sologne*, 6 place St-Firmin (closed Dec 20 to Jan 15; ☏02.38.44.50.27, Ⓦwww.hoteldelasologne.com; ❹), has some rooms with views of the Tour de César. The family-run *Relais de Templiers*, 68 rue du Pont (☏02.38.44.53.78, Ⓦwww.hotelrelaistempliers.com; ❸) is relatively inexpensive, and ideal for those on a tighter budget.

Le Relais du Château, 8 rue du Pont (closed Wed; ☏02.38.44.55.10), is a decent, traditional **restaurant** with menus from €14; alternatively, *Le P'tit Bateau*, 54 rue du Pont (closed Mon; ☏02.38.44.56.38), has a pleasant terrace that is ideal for summer dining, and slightly more elevated gastronomic ambitions, with menus from €20 upwards. Midway between the two, *La Crep'zeria*, 32 rue du Pont, serves decent pizzas and crêpes on its sunny terrace.

Château de la Ferté-St-Aubin and around

The **Château de la Ferté-St-Aubin** lies 20km south of Orléans (mid-Feb to mid-Nov daily 10am–7pm; €7, children aged 4–15 €4.50; Ⓦwww.chateau-ferte-st-aubin.com), at the north end of the village of the same name. The late sixteenth- and early seventeenth-century building presents an enticing combination of salmon-coloured brick, creamy limestone and dark roof slates, while the interior is a real nineteenth-century home – and you are invited to treat it as such, which makes a real change from the stuffier attitudes of most grand homes. You can wander freely into almost every room, playing billiards or the piano, picking up the old telephone, sitting on the worn armchairs or washing your hands in a porcelain sink; only the rather fancier grand salon is cordoned off. Roughly every hour there are demonstrations down in the kitchens of how to make Madeleine cakes – the sweet spongy biscuit that so inspired Proust. At the rear of the château, also enclosed by the moat, there's a play fort with sponge balls supplied for storming it, little cabins with dummies acting out fairy tales, and a toy farm.

The **gare SNCF** is roughly 200m southwest of the village square; around nine trains arrive daily from Orléans and continue south to Vierzon and Bourges. For **eating**, an inexpensive option is the *Auberge Solognote*, 50 rue des Poulies (closed Tues evening & Wed), behind the covered market on La Ferté's main square.

East to the Burgundy border

Upstream from Orléans, the rambling Forêt d'Orléans spreads to the north. Beyond it, a bland, treeless wheat plain stretches to Paris, and the immediate countryside to the south is similarly drab: sticking to the Loire itself is the best advice. Along the river are plenty of lesser-known attractions, most notably the **abbey at St-Benoît**, the **château at Sully-sur-Loire**, the small town of **Gien**, the **aqueduct at Briare** and the hilltop town of **Sancerre**, right on the Burgundy border, where the famous dry white wines are produced.

Germigny-des-Près and St-Benoît-sur-Loire

Heading east of Orléans on the D960, you pass through **Châteauneuf-sur-Loire** – whose château has very pleasant gardens of rhododendrons and magnolias and a small museum of traditional Loire shipping – en route to **GERMIGNY-DES-PRÈS**, 30km from the city. It's a pleasant afternoon's bike ride. The small, plain **church** (daily: April–Oct 8.30am–7.30pm; Nov–March 8.30am–6pm; €2 coin needed for lighting) incorporates at its east end one of the few surviving buildings from the Carolingian Renaissance, a tiny, perfectly formed church in the shape of a Greek cross. The oratory's sheer antiquity is spoiled by too-perfect restoration work, but the unique gold and silver mosaic on the dome of the eastern chapel preserves all its rare beauty. Covered by distemper, it was only discovered by accident in the middle of the nineteenth century when children were found playing with coloured glass cubes in the church.

Five kilometres further upstream, along the D60, **ST-BENOÎT-SUR-LOIRE** offers the striking edifice of the Romanesque **Abbaye de Fleury** (daily: April–Oct 7am–9pm; Nov–March 9am–7pm; Ⓦ www.abbaye-fleury.com), which is still populated by a small community of some forty Benedictine monks, who still observe the original Rule – poverty, chastity and obedience – and can be heard singing Gregorian chant at the daily midday mass (11am on Sun).

Built in warm, cream-coloured stone between 1020 and 1218, the church dates from the abbey's greatest epoch. The oldest part, the porch tower, illustrates St John's vision of the New Jerusalem in Revelation – foursquare, with open gates on each side. The fantastically sculpted capitals of the heavy pillars are alive with acanthus leaves, birds and exotic animals. Three of them depict scenes from the Apocalypse, while another shows Mary's flight into Egypt.

Inside, the choir is split into two levels: above, a marble mosaic of Roman origin covers the chancel floor; below, in the ancient crypt, the relics of St-Benoît lie buried at the very root of the church's forest of columns and arches.

Sully-sur-Loire and around

SULLY-SUR-LOIRE lies on the south bank of the Loire, 7km east of St-Benoît and accessible by bus from Orléans. The grand **château** here is pure fantasy, despite savage wartime bombing that destroyed the nearby bridge. From the outside, rising massively out of its gigantic moat, it has all the picture-book requirements of pointed towers, machicolations and drawbridge. The interior is slowly being refurnished by its owners – the *département* of the Loiret – and has begun to reopen, although not entirely as of yet. Sully's **international Music Festival** (ⓦ www.festival-sully.com) runs right through June, featuring classical concerts held in a huge marquee in the château grounds.

The **village** of Sully itself is uninteresting, but the quiet riverbank roads are worth exploring by bike, or you can venture north into the Forêt d'Orléans, on the far bank. From the village of **Les Bordes**, 6km north of Sully on the D948/D961, a seven-kilometre forest road will take you due east to the Carrefour de la Résistance, a crossroads in the heart of the wood surrounded by stands of giant oaks and sequoias.

Practicalities

The **gare SNCF**, on the Bourges–Étampes line, is 500m from the centre of the village. The **tourist office** can be found on central place de Gaulle (ⓦ www .ot.sully.sur.loire.fr; May–Sept Mon–Sat 9.45am–12.15pm & 2.30–6.30pm, Sun 10.30am–1pm; Oct–April Mon 10am–noon, Tues, Wed, Fri & Sat 10am–noon & 2–6pm, Thurs 2–6pm; ⓣ02.38.36.23.70). Bikes can be hired from Passion Deux Roues, 10 rue des Epinettes (ⓣ02.38.35.13.13).

Two decent **hotels** both lie in the centre: the *Hôtel de la Poste*, 11 rue Faubourg-St-Germain (ⓣ02.38.36.26.22; ❹), is a reliable choice with a decent restaurant (menus from €15); while the rambling *Hôtel de la Tour*, above a bar at 21 rue Porte de Sologne (ⓣ02.38.36.21.72, ⓕ02.38.36.37.63; ❸), has simple rooms freshly done up in a modern style. For camping, *Camping Hortus* (closed Nov–April; ⓣ02.38.36.35.94, ⓦ www.camping-hortus.com) is on the opposite side of the Loire. For **eating** out, *Côtes et Jardin*, 8 rue du Grand Sully (closed Sun & Tues eves, Wed & last 2 weeks in Sept; ⓣ02.38.36.35.89), on the château side of the village, is the best bet, with an exceptionally good-value lunchtime menu for €13.

Gien and around

The pretty town of **GIEN** has been restored to its late fifteenth-century quaint-ness after extensive wartime bombing, and the sixteenth-century stone **bridge** spanning the river gives excellent views as you approach from the south. The fifteenth-century **château** in the town centre – where the young Louis XIV and his mother, Anne of Austria, hid during the revolts against taxation known as the *Frondes* (see p.1160) – has been turned over to the **Musée international de la Chasse et de la Nature** (Feb, March & Oct–Dec Mon, Wed–Sun 10am–noon & 2–5pm; April–June & Sept Mon, Wed–Sun 10am–6pm; July & Aug daily 10am–6pm; closed Jan; €5). Perhaps unsurprisingly, the emphasis lies more on *la chasse* – hunting horns, tapestries, exquisite watercolours of horseback hunts, guns and falconers' gear – than *la nature*. The château itself is modest, but unusual in its brick construction, a pattern of dark red interrupted by geometric inlays of grey; the interior is similarly striking, with its warm combination of brick and timber. Although the exhibits here are dominated by depictions of royal and aristocratic hunting as a sport, it's worth remembering that one of the significant consequences of the French Revolution for rural people was the right to hunt; a right still jealously guarded today.

Gien has also long been known in France for its fine china, if you're a fan it's worth paying a visit to the **Musée de la Faïencerie**, immediately adjacent to the factory shop (Jan & Feb Mon–Fri 2–6pm, Sat 9am–noon & 2–6pm; March–Dec Mon–Sat 9am–noon & 2–6pm, Sun 10am–noon & 2–6pm; €3.50), which displays the more extravagant ceramic knick-knacks produced over the last 180-odd years, ranging from exquisitely worked vases to some monstrously pretentious *objets d'art*. A video shows current fabrication techniques, which you can sometimes see for real in the **factory** (by appointment only; closed July, Aug & Dec; ☏02.38.67.44.92).

Practicalities

Gien's **tourist office** is on place Jean-Jaurès, between the château and the river (June & Sept Mon–Sat 9am–12.30pm & 2–6.30pm; July & Aug Mon–Sat 9.30am–6.30pm, Sun 10am–noon; Oct–May Mon–Sat 9.30am–noon & 2–6pm; ☏02.38.67.25.28, ⓦwww.gien.fr). **Bus** #3, which runs between Briare and Orléans, stops at place Leclerc, at the north end of the bridge. For **accommodation**, *La Poularde*, 13 quai de Nice (☏02.38.67.36.05, ⓔlapoularde2 @orange.fr; ❸), on the way out of town on the road to Briare, has some lovely rooms looking out onto the river, and an excellent restaurant (menus €29–50). Adjacent is the **campsite** (☏02.38.67.12.50, ⓦwww.camping-gien .com; closed mid-Nov to Feb), which has a swimming pool and lays on outdoor activities, including bike hire and canoe trips. For an alternative to the **restaurant** at *La Poularde*, make for the small strip of decent places on quai Lenoir, by the bridge; the pick of the bunch is the *Restaurant de la Loire*, at no. 18 (☏02.38.67.00.75; closed Mon), which is a refined place serving a wide variety of fish on menus from €18.50.

La Bussière

Twelve kilometres northeast of Gien is another château dedicated to country pursuits – this time fishing. The so-called **Château des Pêcheurs** at **LA BUSSIÈRE** (April–June & Sept to mid-Nov Mon & Wed–Sat 10am–noon & 2–6pm; July & Aug daily 10am–6pm; €7) is moored like a ship on its enormous, six-hectare fishpond, connected to a formal arrangement on its mainland of gardens and huge outbuildings. Initially a fortress, the château was turned into a luxurious residence at the end of the sixteenth century, but only the gateway and one pepper-pot tower are recognizably medieval. Guided tours are available, but you're free to wander around, soaking up the genteel atmosphere evoked by the handsome, largely nineteenth-century furnishings and the eccentrically huge collection of freshwater fishing memorabilia bequeathed by Count Henri de Chasseval, whose widow lives in an apartment in one of the outbuildings. Paintings, models, stuffed fish, engravings, flies and rods are scattered throughout the house, while a huge coelacanth (a giant prehistoric relic discovered in the Comoros islands) lurks in a formaldehyde tank in the basement.

Briare

The small town of **BRIARE**, 10km southeast of Gien on the Orléans–Nevers road and the Paris–Nevers rail line, is notable for its *belle-époque* iron aqueduct, the **Pont Canal**, linking the Canal de Briare to the north with the Canal

Lateral à la Loire, making it the longest bridge-canal in Europe. The design of the Pont Canal came from the workshops of Gustav Eiffel (of Tower fame), but parts of the canal scheme date back to the early seventeenth century, when internal waterways linking the Mediterranean, Atlantic and Channel coasts were devised. Poised high above the Loire, you can walk along the aqueduct's extraordinary 625-metre span, with its wrought-iron crested lamps and railings, hopefully without a *bâteau-mouche* spoiling the effect.

On the opposite side of town from the canal, at the northern end, the tiny **Maison des Deux Marines** (daily: March–Sept 10am–12.30pm & 2–6.30pm; Oct to mid-Nov 2–6pm; €5, or €8 with Musée de la Mosaïque) is dedicated to the rival boatmen who plied the Loire and the Canal Lateral; its basement houses a modest aquarium of Loire species. Just across the street, the **Musée de la Mosaïque et des Emaux** (daily: Feb–Sept 10am–6.30pm; Oct–Dec 2–6pm; €5), has a small collection of reproduction and contemporary mosaics made using locally manufactured tiles – Briare's wares adorn sites as prestigious and varied as the mosque at Medina and Paris's RER stations.

The **tourist office**, 1 place Charles-de-Gaulle (April–Sept Mon–Sat 10am–noon & 2–6pm, Sun 10am–noon; Oct–March Mon 2–5pm, Tues–Sat 10am–noon & 2–5pm; ☎02.38.31.24.51, ⓦwww.briare-le-canal.com), can provide details of canal boats and canoe rental as well as maps of footpaths, towpaths and the locks (the one at Chatillon-sur-Loire, 4km upstream, is particularly charming). For **accommodation**, the modern *Auberge du Pont Canal* at 19 rue du Pont-Canal (☎02.38.31.24.24, Ⓔnicolas.rou@orange.fr; ❷) is right next to the bridge.

Sancerre and around

Huddled at the top of a steep, round hill with the vineyards below, **SANCERRE** could almost be in Tuscany. The village trades heavily on its famous wines – there are endless *caves* offering tastings – rather than any particular sights or attractions, but it's certainly picturesque and the rolling hills of the Sancerrois, to the northwest, make an attractive venue for walks and cycle rides. First port of call for wine enthusiasts should be the **Maison de Sancerre**, 3 rue du Méridien (April, May, Oct & Nov 10am–6pm; June–Sept 10am–7pm; €5; ⓦwww.maison-des-sancerre.com), which has an elaborate permanent exhibition on winemaking in Sancerre, and a garden of aromatic plants that represent the sixty key flavours found in Sancerre wines. The building itself is a fine

---

The vineyards of Sancerre

If you're going to be staying in Sancerre, your first priority is probably going to be the wine, and so it makes sense during your visit to have an idea of which are the best **vineyards** in the area. There are numerous quirks of wine production here that may come as something of a surprise; for instance, wines here aren't allowed to carry an individual vineyard's name, instead being sold under the name of the producer or, very occasionally, the *cuvée*, which means that seeking out good local vineyards is best done with the help of a guide.

The Daumy family, based in Crézancy-en-Sancerre (☎02.48.79.05.75), has been making excellent **organic wines** for three generations, including the wonderful but much less commonly made red Sancerre. For a more unusual buy than the well-known white Sancerre, it's well worth exploring the neighbouring areas of **Menetou-Salon** and **Pouilly-Fumé**. The informative Aronde Sancerroise, at 4 rue de la Tour, just off the central Nouvelle Place (☎02.48.78.05.72), offers excellent, free tastings as well as tours of local vineyards by minibus.

fourteenth-century town house, the top of whose tower offers a great view over the rolling, vine-clad hills around.

Wine outlets in the village itself tend to belong to the most famous names, with prices to match, but the tourist office can supply a list. Well suited to the wines is the local *crottin de Chavignol*, a goat's cheese named after the neighbouring village in which it's made; signs in Chavignol direct you to **fromageries** open to visitors.

Practicalities

The town is difficult to access by public transport, save for an occasional bus service that connects with the trains from Gien station and then heads to Sancerre, and one to three buses a day to and from Bourges, depending on the time of year. Private transport, such as a car or chartered bus, is more convenient, especially as this makes visiting the vineyards far easier. The **tourist office**, on Nouvelle Place (daily: June–Sept 10am–6pm; Oct–May 10am–12.30pm & 2.30–5.30pm; ☎02.48.54.08.21, ⓦwww.sancerre.fr), is an invaluable source of local information, especially when it comes to wine.

The choice of **hotels** in Sancerre is surprisingly poor, but two charming *chambres d'hôtes* more than make up for it: *Le Logis du Grillon*, 3 rue du Chantre (☎02.48.78.09.45;❹); and *La Belle Époque*, rue St-André (☎02.48.78.00.04;❸). The best hotel in the area is by the river in St-Satur, at the antique-furnished, extremely comfortable and picturesque ⚑ *Hôtel de la Loire*, 2 quai de la Loire (☎02.48.78.22.22, ⓦwww.hotel-de-la-loire.com; ❹). The welcoming youth hostel *Auberge de St-Thibault*, 37 rue J.-Combes (☎02.48.78.04.10; ❶), a block away from the river, has the best value rooms in the area. An excellent **campsite** (☎02.48.54.04.67; closed Oct–April) is found a little further along the quay, beyond the kayak shop.

There are two fine **restaurants** in Sancerre: *La Pomme d'Or*, 1 rue de la Panneterie (☎02.48.54.13.30; closed Tues & Wed evening), and the more formal *La Tour*, 31 place de la Halle (☎02.48.54.00.81), both with menus (around €25) to suit all pockets. *Auberge Joseph Mellot*, Nouvelle Place (☎02.48.54.20.53; closed Sun, Tues evening & Wed) serves good, simple meals that are designed to complement its own top notch wines.

Bourges

BOURGES, the chief town of the rather distant region of Berry, is some way from the Loire valley proper but linked to it historically. The presence of one of the finest Gothic cathedrals in France, rising gloriously out of the unpretentious and handsome medieval quarter, provides enough reason for making a detour, but the city also offers an impressive mansion belonging to the Dauphin's financial adviser, Jacques Coeur.

Bourges's **festival** programme is excellent. Les Printemps de Bourges (ⓦwww.printemps-bourges.com) features hundreds of contemporary music acts from rock to rap, and lasts for one week during the French Easter holidays. Atmospheric ambient lighting transforms the streets of the old town every evening in July and August (and from Thurs–Sat in May, June & Sept).

Arrival and information

The **gare routière** is west of the city beyond boulevard Juranville on rue du Prado. The **gare SNCF** lies 1km north of the centre; it's a straightforward-enough walk

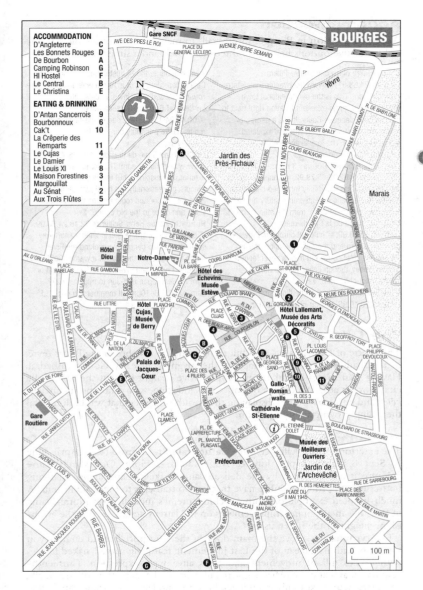

BOURGES

ACCOMMODATION

D'Angleterre	C
Les Bonnets Rouges	D
De Bourbon	A
Camping Robinson	G
HI Hostel	F
Le Central	B
Le Christina	E

EATING & DRINKING

D'Antan Sancerrois	9
Bourbonnoux	6
Cak't	10
La Crêperie des Remparts	11
Le Cujas	4
Le Damier	7
Le Louis XI	8
Maison Forestines	3
Margouillat	1
Au Sénat	2
Aux Trois Flûtes	5

along avenues Henri Lauder and Jean-Jaurès to place Planchat, from where rue du Commerce connects with the main street, **rue Moyenne**. The **tourist office** is just off the top end of rue Moyenne, at 21 rue Victor-Hugo (April–Sept Mon–Sat 9am–7pm, Sun 10am–7pm; Oct–March Mon–Sat 9am–6pm, Sun 2–5pm; ☏02.48.23.02.60, ⌘www.bourges-tourisme.com), facing the south facade of the cathedral. The old medieval quarter falls away to the east, below the cathedral.

Accommodation

Accommodation in Bourges mostly fails to make the best of the old city, the only attractive options being two three-star hotels and a superb *chambre d'hôte*.

D'Angleterre place des Quatre-Piliers ℡02.48.24.68.51, Ⓦwww.bestwestern-angleterre -bourges.com. This is the old, traditional town-centre hotel, with an excellent location right next to the Palais de Jacques-Coeur. It has a degree of old-fashioned charm, along with the expected modern facilities. The less expensive rooms are very small for the price. ⑥–⑦

Les Bonnets Rouges 3 rue de la Thaumas-sière ℡02.48.65.79.92, Ⓦbonnets-rouges .bourges.net. Five beautifully furnished *chambres d'hôtes* in a striking seventeenth-century house with views of the cathedral from the attic rooms. ⑤

De Bourbon bd de la République ℡02.48.70.70.00, Ⓦhoteldebourbon.fr. Between the town centre and the railway station, this is a luxurious hotel converted from a seventeenth-century abbey, though inside it's standard luxury-hotel-chain fare. ⑦

Camping Robinson 26 bd de l'industrie ℡02.48.20.16.85. Decent-sized three-star site located south of the Hi hostel. Bus #1 from place Cujas, stop "Joffre", or a 10min walk from the *gare routière*. Closed mid-Nov to mid-March.

Le Central 6 rue du Docteur-Témoin ℡02.48.24.10.25. Tiny, deeply old-fashioned rooms above a friendly bar just off rue Moyenne. ⑦

Le Christina 5 rue de la Halle ℡02.48.70.56.50, Ⓦwww.le-christina.com. The six-storey modern exterior is uninspiring, but inside you'll find a friendly, professionally run hotel with seventy cheerfully decorated rooms, some with a/c. Good value and close to the old centre. ③

HI hostel 22 rue Henri-Sellier ℡02.48.24.58.09, Ⓔbourges@fuaj.org. Hostel located a short way southwest of the centre, overlooking the River Auron. Bus #1 from the station towards "Golf", stop "Europe"; or a 10min walk from the cathedral or *gare routière*. Open mid-Jan to mid-Dec daily 8am–noon & 6–10pm. HI membership required.

The City

The centre of **Bourges** sits on a hill rising from the marshes of the River Yèvre, in the shadow of its main attraction, the magnificent early Gothic cathedral. Having seen the cathedral, many people move straight on, but the rest of the city is worth at least a couple of hours of wandering, with a number of ancient *hôtels* and burghers' houses displaying the wealth of a place that was built to rival the ruling provincial city of Dijon.

The cathedral

The exterior of the twelfth-century **Cathédrale St-Étienne** (daily: April–June & Sept 8.30am–7.15pm; July & Aug 8.30am–7.45pm; Oct–March 9am–5.45pm) is characterized by the delicate, almost skeletal appearance of flying buttresses supporting an entire nave that has no transepts to break up its bulk. A much-vaunted example of Gothic architecture, it's modelled on Notre-Dame in Paris but incorporates improvements on the latter's design, such as the aston-ishing height of the inner aisles.

The **tympanum** above the main door of the west portal could engross you for hours with its tableau of the Last Judgement, featuring carved, naked figures with bodies full of movement and faces alive with expression. Thirteenth-century imagination has been given full rein in the depiction of the devils, complete with snakes' tails and winged bottoms and faces appearing from below the waist, symbolic of the soul in the service of sinful appetites.

The interior's best feature is the twelfth- to thirteenth-century **stained glass**. There are geometric designs in the main body of the cathedral, but the most glorious windows, with astonishing deep colours, are around the choir, all created between 1215 and 1225. You can follow the stories of the Prodigal Son, the Rich Man and Lazarus, the life of Mary, Joseph in Egypt, the Good

Samaritan, Christ's Crucifixion, the Last Judgement and the Apocalypse – binoculars come in handy for picking up the exquisite detail. On either side of the central absidal chapel, polychrome figures kneel in prayer; these are **Jean de Berry**, the great artistic patron of late fourteenth-century Bourges, and his wife. The painted decoration of the **astronomical clock** in the nave celebrates the wedding of Charles VII, who married Marie d'Anjou here on April 22, 1422.

On the northwest side of the nave aisle is the door to the **Tour de Beurre** (daily except Sun morning: April & Sept 9.45–11.45am & 2–5.30pm; May & June 9.30–11.30am & 2–6pm; July & Aug 9.30am–6.15pm; Oct–March 9.30–11.30am & 2–4.45pm; €5, or €9 with the crypt and Palais de Jacques-Coeur), which you can climb unsupervised for fantastic views over the old city, the marshes and the countryside beyond. You can also join a guided tour of the **crypt** (same hours and ticket; tours roughly every hour), where you can see the alabaster statue of a puggish Jean de Berry, a small bear, symbol of strength, lying asleep at his feet. Alongside are fragments of the cathedral's original rood screen, which survived the Protestant siege of 1562 but not the modernizers of the mid-eighteenth century, while a wonderful polychrome *Entombment* from the 1530s adorns the dark centre of the crypt. The same ticket allows you to climb unsupervised to the top of the north **tower**, rebuilt in flamboyant style after the original collapsed in 1506.

Next to the cathedral in place E.-Dolet, the **Musée des Meilleurs Ouvriers de France** (Tues–Sat 10am–noon & 2–5pm, Sun 2–5pm; free) displays show-off pieces by French artisans. The theme changes each year, and recent features have included glassblowing, woodwork and pastry making.

The rest of the city

Bourges's museums may be modest, but they are housed in some beautiful medieval buildings, the finest of which are all within a stone's throw of the north end of rue Moyenne. Rue Bourbonnoux, parallel to rue Moyenne to the east of the cathedral, is worth a wander for the early Renaissance **Hôtel Lallemant**, richly decorated in an Italianate style. It houses the **Musée des Arts Décoratifs** (Tues–Sat 10am–noon & 2–5pm, Sun 2–5pm; free), a diverting enough museum of paintings, tapestries, furniture and *objets d'art*, including works by the Berrichon artist Jean Boucher (1575–1633). The coffered ceiling of the oratory is carved with alchemical symbols. Halfway along the street, you can take a narrow passage up to the remains of the Gallo-Roman town **ramparts**, lined with old houses and trees. On rue Edouard-Branly, you'll find the fifteenth-century **Hôtel des Échevins**, home to the **Musée de Maurice Estève** (Mon & Wed–Sat 10am–noon & 2–5pm, Sun 2–5pm; free), dedicated to the highly coloured, mostly abstract paintings and tapestries by the locally born artist, who died in 2001.

The continuation of rue Edouard-Branly, **rue Jacques-Coeur**, was the site of the head office, stock exchange, dealing rooms, bank safes and home of Charles VII's finance minister, Jacques Coeur (1400–56), a medieval shipping magnate, moneylender and arms dealer who dominates Bourges as Joan of Arc does Orléans – Charles VII doesn't get a look-in. The **Palais de Jacques-Coeur** (daily: May & June 9.45–11am & 2–5.15pm; July & Aug 9.45–11.30am & 2–5.45pm; Sept–April 9.45–11am & 2–4.15pm; €6.10; guided tours every 30min–1hr, depending on the season) is one of the most remarkable examples of fifteenth-century domestic architecture in France. The visit starts with the fake windows on the entrance front from which two realistically sculpted half-figures look down. There are hardly any furnishings, but the decoration of the house's stonework recalls the man who had it built, including a pair of bas-reliefs on the courtyard tower that may represent Jacques and his wife, and numerous hearts and scallop shells inside that playfully allude to his name. On the first floor, a wonderful bas-relief of a *galleasse*, with its oars and sails spread, symbolizes Jacques' trading empire. The house is unusually modern for its time, with latrines, a steam room, and a rationally planned design that predates the symmetries of French Renaissance architecture. A reconstruction of the tomb of Jean de Berry dominates one of the rooms on the upper floor.

Steps lead down beside the palace to rue des Arènes, where the sixteenth-century **Hôtel Cujas** houses the **Musée du Berry** (Mon & Wed–Sat 10am–noon & 2–5pm, Sun 2–5pm; free), which has an interesting collection of local artefacts, most notably ten of the forty *pleurants* that survived the breaking up of Jean de Berry's tomb; Rodin considered these weeping statues so beautiful that he paid six thousand francs for one shortly before his death. Etruscan bronzes and Roman funerary monuments bear witness to Bourges's ancient history, while an exhibition on the theme of traditional rural life occupies the first floor. Close by is the pleasant **place Notre-Dame**, with its church clearly showing the shift from Gothic to Renaissance.

Eating and drinking

Bourges's main centre for **eating** is along rue Bourbonnoux, which runs between place Gordaine and the cathedral. Those with a sweet tooth should head for the excellent **patisserie**, Aux Trois Flûtes, on the corner of rues Joyeuse and Bourbonnoux; for chocolates and the local sweet speciality of *fourrées au praliné*, try the imposing Maison Forestines, on place Cujas, at the foot of rue Porte Jaune. On warm nights, place Cujas is also a great spot for a **drink**; the bar *Le Cujas* has plenty of outside seating. Another good option is the cocktail bar *Le Damier*, on 5 rue Emile Deschamps.

D'Antan Sancerrois 50 ☎02.48.65.96.26. Excellent local dishes, specializing in fish and game (à la carte mains around €18); closed Sun & Mon lunch.

Bourbonnoux 44 rue Bourbonnoux ☎02.48.24.14.76. A friendly place offering some ambitious regional menus (€13–30). Closed Sat lunch, Fri & Sun evening out of season.

Cak't promenade des Remparts ☎02.48.24.94.60. Just off rue Borbonnoux, this deliciously refined tea room serves home-made quiches and tarts at lunchtime and afternoon tea. Closed Sun & Mon.

La Crêperie des Remparts 59 rue Bourbonnoux ☎02.48.24.55.44. A better-than-usual range of crêpes and salads. Those with the local goat's cheese are especially good. Closed Sun & Mon lunch.

Le Louis XI 11 rue Porte Jaune ☎02.48.70.92.14. Just 200m down from the cathedral, *Le Louis XI* serves impeccable steaks and chargrilled meats in a small, informal dining room (menus €17–26). Closed Sun.

Margouillat 53 rue Edouard Vaillant, beyond place Gordaine ☎02.48.24.08.13. For a complete change, this friendly restaurant offers delicious, reasonably priced food from Réunion such as giant prawns or pork and beans served with hot dips, plus delicious tropical desserts and cocktails. Closed Sun, plus Sat & Mon lunch.

Au Sénat 8 rue de la Poissonnerie ☎02.48.24.02.56. Just off attractive, medieval place Gordaine, this smart Bourges institution cooks excellent traditional dishes, and has tables out on the street (menus €17–33). Closed Wed & Thurs.

The Cher and upper Indre

Of all the Loire's many tributaries, the slow-moving **Cher** and **Indre** are closest to the heart of the region, watering a host of châteaux as they flow northwest from the little-visited region to the south. Twenty kilometres southeast of Tours, spanning the Cher, the **Château de Chenonceau** is

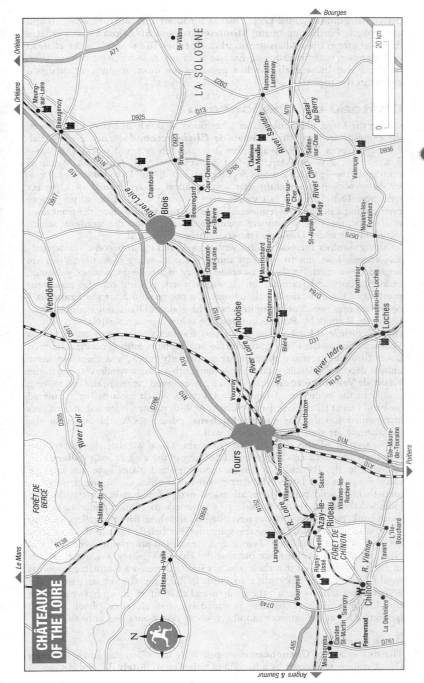

perhaps the quintessential Loire château for its architecture, site, contents and atmosphere. Further upstream, **Montrichard** and **St-Aignan** make quieter diversions from the endless stream of castle tours. To the south is the château of **Valençay**, with its exquisite Empire interiors. A short drive west of here, on the River Indre itself, **Loches** possesses the most magnificent medieval citadel in the region.

Château de Chenonceau

Unlike the Loire, the gentle River Cher flows so slowly and passively between the exquisite arches of the **Château de Chenonceau** (daily: first 2 weeks Feb & first 2 weeks Nov 9am–5pm; last 2 weeks Feb & last 2 weeks Oct 9am–5.30pm; first 2 weeks March & first 2 weeks Oct 9am–6pm; mid-March to mid-Sept 9am–7pm; last 2 weeks Sept 9am–6.30pm; Nov 16 to Jan 9am–4.30pm; €9; Ⓦwww.chenonceau.com) that you're almost always assured of a perfect reflection. The château is not visible from the road so you have to pay before even getting a peek at the residence. While the tree-lined path to the front door is dramatic, for a more intimate approach, head through the **gardens**, which were laid out under Diane de Poitiers, mistress of Henri II.

During summer the place teems with people, and it can become uncomfortably crowded, so aim to visit first thing in the morning if possible. Visits are unguided – a relief, for there's an endless array of arresting tapestries, paintings, ceilings, floors and furniture on show. It's worth seeking out the numerous portraits of the château's female owners. On the ground floor the **François I room** features two contrasting images of the goddess Diana; one is a portrait of Diane de Poitiers by Primaticcio, and the other represents a relatively aristocratic Gabrielle d'Estrées. The room also features works by or attributed to Veronese, Tintoretto, Correggio, Murillo and Rubens, among others. The tiled floors throughout, many original, are particularly lovely, and there are some unique decorative details, such as the seventeenth-century window-frame in the **César de Vendôme room**, supported by two carved caryatids, and the moving ceiling in the bedroom of Louise de Lorraine, which mourns her murdered husband Henri III in black paint picked out with painted tears and the couple's intertwined initials. The vaulted **kitchens**, poised above the water in the foundations, are well worth a look as well.

The section of the château that spans the Cher is relatively empty. The seemingly incongruous chequerboard flooring of the elegant long **gallery** is in fact true to the Renaissance design, though potted plants have replaced the classical statues that Louis XIV carried off to Versailles. Catherine de Médicis used to hold wild parties here, all naked nymphs and Italian fireworks. She intended the door on the far side to continue into another building on the south bank, but the project was never begun, and these days the gallery leads to quiet, wooded gardens. During the war, the Cher briefly formed the boundary between occupied and "free" France, and the current proprietors, who rode out Nazi occupation, like to make out that the château's gallery was much used as an escape route. Given that their adjacent farm quartered a German garrison, it would have been a risky place to cross. In July and August, as part of the "Nocturne à Chenonceau", the gardens and château are lit up between 10pm and 11.30pm, with atmosphere provided by classical music played through speakers. Also in the summer months, you can take **boats** out onto the Cher.

Practicalities

The tiny village of **Chenonceaux** – spelt with an "x" on the end – has been almost entirely taken over by a handful of rather swish **hotels**. All of them are on rue du Docteur-Bretonneau, within easy reach of the **gare SNCF** and the château. The *Hostel du Roy* at no. 9 (T)02.47.23.90.17, (W)www.hostelduroy.com; ❸) is comfortable and relatively inexpensive; while *La Roseraie*, at no. 7 ((T)02.47.23.90.09, (W)www.charmingroseraie.com; ❹), is very welcoming, with good food, extensive grounds and a swimming pool; and at no. 6, the luxurious *Auberge du Bon Laboureur* ((T)02.47.23.90.02, (W)www.bonlaboureur.com; ❼) is spread around five former village houses. For **camping**, the municipal site (closed Oct–March; (T)02.47.23.90.13) is between the railway line and the river.

Montrichard and Bourré

In many ways just a laid-back market town, **MONTRICHARD** also happens to have a full complement of medieval and Renaissance buildings, plus a hilltop **fortress**, of which just the keep remains after Henri IV broke down the rest of the defences at the end of the sixteenth century. Between mid-July and mid-August costumed medieval spectacles (daily at 4.30pm and around 9pm; €15) in the former château grounds entertain mainly younger audiences. At any time, you can climb up the hill for the view of the Cher – though the keep itself is out of bounds. Montrichard's Romanesque **church** was where the disabled 12-year-old princess, Jeanne de Valois, who would never be able to have children, married her cousin the Duc d'Orléans. When he became King Louis XII, after the unlikely death of Charles VIII at Amboise, politics dictated that he marry Charles VIII's widow, Anne of Brittany. Poor Jeanne was divorced and sent off to govern Bourges, where she founded a new religious order and eventually took the veil herself, before dying in 1505. It's not all gloom: in summer, you can rent pedalos and **kayaks** (July & Aug; (T)02.54.71.49.48) at the pleasant artificial **beach** on the opposite bank of the Cher. Some hardy locals swim from here, but be sure to seek advice before entering the water.

Three kilometres to the east of Montrichard, the hills around **BOURRÉ** are riddled with enormous, cave-like quarries, dug deep to get at the famous château-building stone that gets whiter as it weathers. Some of the caves are now used to cultivate mushrooms – big business in the Loire – a peculiar process that you can witness at the **Caves Champignonnières**, 40 route des Roches (Easter to mid-Nov guided visits daily at 10am, 11am, 2pm, 3pm, 4pm & 5pm; €6; (W)www.le-champignon.com). A second tour takes you to a "subterranean city" (€6, or €10 for both tours) sculpted in recent years as a tourist attraction, and there's an excellent shop including rare varieties of mushroom and various mushroom products. You can visit a fascinating troglodyte dwelling at **La Magnanerie**, 4 chemin de la Croix-Bardin (guided visits only: Easter–Aug daily except Tues at 11am, 3pm, 4pm & 5pm; Sept Sun–Thurs at 3pm, 4pm & 5pm; Oct Fri–Sun at 4pm; €6). The owner demonstrates how his family and their ancestors lived a troglodyte life here, quarrying the soft stone using huge saws, and producing silk in a chamber riddled with pigeonhole-like niches and stocked with living silkworms.

Practicalities

Montrichard's **tourist office** is in the Maison Ave Maria (April–Sept Mon–Sat 9am–noon & 2–6pm, Sun 10am–noon; (T)02.54.32.05.10, (W)www.office tourisme-montrichard.com), an ancient house with saints and beasties sculpted down its beams, on rue du Pont. The only enticing **hotel** is *La Tête Noir*, 24 rue de Tours ((T)02.54.32.05.55, (E)g.galimard@orange.fr; ❹), with its terrace on the river, though the atmospheric *Manoir de la Salle du Roc*, 69 route de Vierzon ((T)02.54.32.73.54, (W)manoirdelasalleduroc.monsite.orange .fr; ❺), offers grand *chambres d'hôtes* set in an ancient manor house above the main road leading west from Bourré. There's also a **campsite**, *L'Étourneau* (closed mid-Sept to May; ☎02.54.32.10.16), right in town, on the banks of the Cher. Decent meals can be had at *Les Tuffeaux*, a straightforward brasserie on Montrichard's main square, place Bartélémy-Gilbert.

St-Aignan

ST-AIGNAN, 15km southeast of Montrichard, is a small town comprising a cluster of houses below a huge Romanesque collegiate church and sixteenth-century private château. The lofty **Collégiale de St-Aignan** (Mon–Sat 9am–7pm, Sun 1–7pm) features some fine capitals carved in the twelfth century, though many more are nineteenth-century recreations. The crypt is renowned for its remarkably preserved, brightly coloured twelfth- and thirteenth-century frescoes, some of which show the beginnings of naturalistic Gothic tendencies. A flight of 144 steps climbs from the *collégiale* to the grand gravelled terrace of the **château**, enclosed on one side by the L-shape of the Renaissance *logis*, and on the other by the remnants of the eleventh-century fortress. Private ownership means it's closed to visitors, but you're free to stroll around – the far corner of the terrace leads through to a great **view** of the river, and you can continue down some steep steps to the river. You can ask at the tourist office for details of **boat trips** on the Cher, or hire windsurfers, canoes and sail boats at the lake a couple of kilometres upstream, in **Seigy**. The Maison du Vin, on place Wilson (July & Aug daily 10am–noon & 3–6pm; Sept–June Tues & Thurs 8am–noon), is open for tastings and sales of Côteaux du Cher wines.

One of the region's biggest tourist attractions is the excellent **Zoo Parc Beauval** (daily: 9am–dusk; €17, children aged 3–12 €12; ⒲www.zoobeauval .com), 2km to the south of town on the D675. The space given to the animals is ample, and it's part of a Europe-wide programme for breeding threatened species in captivity. Sumptuous flowerbeds give way to little streams and lakes where islands provide natural enclosures for some of the monkeys. Two hothouses with tropical flowers and greenery are home to an extraordinary collection of birds as well as a large group of chimpanzees and two families of orang-utans.

Practicalities

The **tourist office**, 60 rue Constant-Ragot (June & Sept Mon–Sat 10am– 12.30pm & 2–6.30pm, Sun 10am–noon & 3–6pm; July & Aug Mon–Sat 9.30am–12.30pm & 2–6.30pm, Sun 10am–noon & 3–6pm; Oct–May Mon–Sat 10am–12.30pm & 2–6pm; ☎02.54.75.22.85, ⒲www.tourisme -valdecher-staignan.com), is just off the car-park-like place Président-Wilson, in the upper part of town. The only two **hotels** are both alongside the river, on either side of the bridge: *Hôtel du Moulin*, 7 rue Novilliers (closed Sun; ☎02.54.75.15.54; ❷), is fairly basic but friendly, while *Le Grand Hôtel St-Aignan*, 7–9 quai J.-J.-Delorme (☎02.54.75.18.04, ⒠grand.hotel.st .aignan@orange.fr; ❸), is a hushed, well-furnished affair, with a good restaurant (menus €13–36). St-Aignan has an excellent **campsite** on the bank of the river near Seigy, the *Camping des Cochards* (☎02.54.75.15.59; closed mid-Oct to March). For an alternative to the hotel **restaurants**, the *Mange-Grenouille*, 10 rue Paul-Boncour (☎02.54.71.74.91; closed Tues evening & Wed; menus €14–28), has delightful sixteenth-century decor and outside seating in its courtyard. The welcoming *L'Amarena*, place de la Paix (closed Mon lunch; ☎02.54.75.47.98), serves inexpensive Italian food on an attractive square.

Château de Valençay

There is nothing medieval about the fittings and furnishings of the **Château de Valençay**, 20km southeast of St-Aignan on the main Blois–Châteauroux road (daily: April, May & Sept 10.30am–6pm; June 9.30am–6pm; July & Aug 9.30am–7.30pm; Oct 10.30am–5.30pm; €9; ⓦ www.chateau-valencay.com), for all its huge pepper-pot towers and turreted, decorated keep. This refined castle was originally built to show off the wealth of a sixteenth-century financier, but the lasting impression of a visit today is the imperial legacy of its greatest owner, the **Prince de Talleyrand**.

One of the great political operators and survivors, Talleyrand owes his greatest fame to his post as Napoleon's foreign minister. A bishop before the Revolution, with a reputation for having the most desirable mistresses, he proposed the nationalization of church property, renounced his bishopric, escaped to America during the Terror, backed Napoleon and continued to serve the state under the restored Bourbons. One of his tasks for the emperor was keeping Ferdinand VII of Spain entertained for six years here after the king had been forced to abdicate in favour of Napoleon's brother Joseph. The Treaty of Valençay, signed in the château in 1813, put an end to Ferdinand's forced guest status, giving him back his throne. The interior consequently is largely First Empire: elaborately embroidered chairs, Chinese vases, ornate inlays to all the tables, faux-Egyptian details, finicky clocks and chandeliers. A single discordant note is struck by the leg-brace and shoe displayed in a glass cabinet along with Talleyrand's uniforms – the statesman's deformed foot was concealed in every painting of the man, including the one displayed in the portrait gallery that runs the length of the graceful Neoclassical wing.

The château **park** (same hours as above) keeps a collection of unhappy-looking camels, zebras, llamas and goats, and there's a small, imaginative maze. In the village, about 100m from the château gates, a **car museum** (daily: April–June, Sept & Oct 10am–12.30pm & 1.30–6pm; July & Aug closes 7.30pm; €3) houses an excellent collection of sixty-odd mostly pre-war cars.

Loches and around

LOCHES, 42km southeast of Tours, is the obvious place to head for in the Indre valley. Its walled **citadel** is by far the most impressive of the Loire valley fortresses, with its unbreached ramparts and the Renaissance houses below still partly enclosed by the outer wall of the medieval town. Tours is only an hour away by bus, but Loches makes for a quiet, relatively untouristy base for exploring the Cher valley, or the much lesser-known country south, up the Indre.

The **old town** is dominated by the Tour St-Antoine belfry, close to the handsome place du Marché, which links rue St-Antoine with Grande Rue. Two fifteenth-century gates to the old town still stand: the **Porte des Cordeliers**, by the river at the end of Grande Rue, and the **Porte Picois** to the west, at the end of rue St-Antoine. Rue du Château, lined with Renaissance buildings, leads to the twelfth-century towers of **Porte Royale**, the main entrance to the citadel.

Arrival and information

From Tours, trains and buses alike arrive at the **gare SNCF** on the east side of the Indre, just up from place de la Marne, where the **tourist office** is housed in a little wooden chalet (April–June & Sept Mon–Sat 9.30am–12.30pm & 1.30–6.30pm, Sun 10am–12.30pm & 1.30–6pm; July & Aug Mon–Sat 9am–7pm, Sun 10am–12.30pm & 1.30–6pm; Oct–March Mon–Sat 10am–12.30pm & 2.30–6pm; ⓣ 02.47.91.82.82, ⓦ www.loches-tourainecotesud.com).

The best **accommodation** option is the old-fashioned and characterful *Hôtel de France*, 6 rue Picois (T 02.47.59.00.32, W www.hoteldefranceloches.com; ❸), which has a good restaurant. The *Hôtel George Sand*, 37 rue Quintefol (T 02.47.59.39.74, W www.hotelrestaurant-georgesand.com; ❺), just below the eastern ramparts, has its best rooms at the back, looking onto the river; its restaurant has a lovely terrace overlooking the Indre. Inexpensive rooms can be found at the charmingly tumbledown *Hôtel de Beaulieu*, 3 rue Foulques-Nerra (T 02.47.91.60.80; ❷), right next to the abbey in Beaulieu-les-Loches, 1km across the river. The municipal **campsite** *La Citadelle* (closed mid-Oct to mid-March; T 02.47.59.05.91) is between two branches of the Indre by the swimming pool and stadium.

The citadel

Behind the Porte Royale, the **Musée Lansyer** (April–Oct daily except Tues 10.30am–12.30pm & 2.30–5pm; €3) occupies the house of local nineteenth-century landscape painter Emmanuel Lansyer, done up in period style. Straight ahead is the Romanesque church, the **Collégiale de St-Ours**, with its distinctively odd roofline – the nave bays are capped by two octagonal stone pyramids, sandwiched between two more conventional spires. The porch has some entertainingly grotesque twelfth-century monster carvings, and the stoup, or basin for holy water, is a Gallo-Roman altar. But the church's highlight is the shining white **tomb of Agnès Sorel**, the mistress of the Dauphin Charles VII. It's a beautiful recumbent figure tenderly watched over by angels. The alabaster is rather more pristine than it should be, as it had to be restored after anticlerical revolutionary soldiers mistook her for a saint – an easy error to make.

The northern end of the citadel is taken up by the **Logis Royal**, or Royal Lodgings, of Charles VII and his three successors (daily: Jan–March & Oct–Dec 9.30am–5pm; April–Sept 9am–7pm; €5, €7 including the donjon). It has two distinct halves, similar at first glance, but separated by a century in which the medieval need for defence began to give way to a more courtly, luxurious lifestyle. The first section was built in the late fourteenth century as a kind of pleasure palace for the Dauphin Charles and Agnès Sorel. A copy of Charles's portrait by Fouquet can be seen in the antechamber to the Grande Salle, where the Dauphin met the second woman of importance in his life between June 3 and June 5, 1429 – Joan of Arc, who came here victorious from Orléans to give the defeatist Dauphin another pep talk about coronations.

From the Logis Royal, cobbled streets overlooked by handsome town houses wind through to the far end of the elevated citadel, where the **donjon** (same hours and ticket as Logis Royal) begun by Foulques Nerra, the eleventh-century count of Anjou, stands in grim ruin. Vertiginous gantry stairways climb up through the empty shell of the massive keep to its very top, but the main interest lies in the dungeons and lesser towers. The Tour Ronde was built under Louis XI to provide a platform for artillery and also served as a prison for his adviser, Cardinal Balue, who was kept locked up in a wooden cage in one of the upper rooms. Perhaps he was kept in the extraordinary graffiti chamber on the second floor, which is decorated with an enigmatic series of deeply carved, soldier-like figures that may date from the thirteenth century. From the courtyard, steps lead down into the bowels of the Martelet, which became the home of a more famous prisoner: Ludovico "il Moro" Sforza, duke of Milan, patron of Leonardo da Vinci and captive of Louis XII. In the four years he was imprisoned here, from 1500, he found time to decorate his cave-like cell with ruddy wall paintings, still faintly visible. The dungeons peter out into quarried-out galleries which produced the stone for the keep.

Eating and drinking

For an alternative to the hotel **restaurants**, *L'Entracte*, 4 Grande-Rue (℡02.47.94.05.70; closed Sun; menus from €10), does hearty and generous bistro food, and has a lovely courtyard out back. The recreations of medieval recipes at *Le Vicariat*, next to the château on place Charles-VII (℡02.47.59.08.79; closed Mon & Sun eve; menus €19–43), can be fun, and there is a great outside terrace. The best option of all is to stock up at the superb **market**, held in the winding streets just above the château gate on Wednesday and Saturday mornings.

Blois and around

The château at **BLOIS**, the handsome former seat of the dukes of Orléans, is magnificent, and the main reason for visiting the town. Its great facade rises above the modern town like an Italianate cliff, with the dramatic esplanade and courtyard behind and the rooms within steeped in, sometimes bloody, history. There are several stretches of woodland within striking distance including the **Forêt de Blois** to the west of the town on the north bank of the Loire, and the **Parc de Chambord** and **Forêt de Boulogne**, further upstream. To the south and east, the forested, watery, game-rich area known as the **Sologne** lies between the Loire and Cher, stretching beyond Orléans almost as far as Gien.

Arrival and information

Blois is easy to get around: avenue Jean-Laigret is the main street leading south from the **gare SNCF** to place Victor-Hugo and the château, and past it to the town centre. The **gare routière** is directly in front of the *gare SNCF*, with **buses** leaving up to three times a day for Cheverny and Chambord. The **tourist office**, 23 place du Château, the château esplanade (May–Sept Mon & Sun 10am–7pm, Tues–Sat 9am–7pm; Oct–April Mon–Sat 9am–12.30pm & 2–6pm, Sun 9.30am–12.30pm; ℡02.54.90.41.41, ⓦwww.loiredeschateaux.com), organizes hotel rooms for a small fee and has information on day coach tours of Chambord and Cheverny. It also sells a combined ticket (€15) to the château, son et lumière and Maison de la Magie. Regional information is available online at ⓦwww .chambordcountry.com. **Bikes** can be hired from Cycles Leblond, 44 levée des Tuileries (℡02.54.74.30.13, ⓦcycles.leblond.free.fr), and Bike in Blois, 8 rue Henri Drussy (℡02.54.56.07.73, ⓦwww.locationdevelos.com).

Accommodation

The hotels in Blois are acceptable enough, but you may want to think about staying overnight unless you need to.

Anne de Bretagne 31 av Dr Jean Laigret. ℡02.54.78.05.38, ⓦannedebretagne.free.fr. Charming, vine-covered hotel set a little way back from the station, but more peaceful than many others in its category. ❹

Du Bellay 12 rue des Minimes ℡02.54.78.23.62, ⓦhoteldubellay.free.fr. Comfortable budget option with twelve well-worn but clean little rooms, much cheered up by pictures of local sights and the odd

wooden beam. Good location at the top of the hill, above the town centre. ❷

Camping Rives de Loire Vineuil ℡08.00.30.04.10. On the south bank of the river, 4km from the town centre. Bus #3C (stop "Mairie Vineuil") only runs four times daily, but the campsite offers bike hire. Closed Oct–May.

Côté Loire 2 place de la Grève ℡02.54.78.07.86, ⓦwww.coteloire.com.

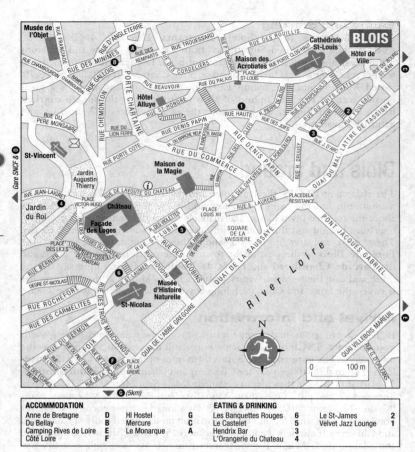

BLOIS

Musée de l'Objet
RUE FRANCIADE
RUE D'ANGLETERRE
RUE DES MINIMES
RAMPE CHAMBOURDIN
RUE CHAMBOURDIN
RUE GALLOIS
RUE DES REMPARTS
RUE DES CORDELIERS
RUE TROUESSARD
RUE DES ROUILLIS
RUE P. RENOUARD
RUE PORTE CLOS-HAUT
Cathédrale St-Louis
Hôtel de Ville
RUE DU BOURG ST-JEAN
Maison des Acrobates
PLACE ST-LOUIS
PORTE CHARTRAINE
RUE CHEMONTON
RUE BEAUVOIR
RUE DU PALAIS
Hôtel Alluye
RUE ST-HONORE
RUE PIERRE DE BLOIS
RUE DES PAPEGAULTS
RUE DU PUITS CHATEL
RUE FOULERIE
RUE DU PERE MONSABRE
RUE DU LION FERRE
RUE DENIS PAPIN
RUE HAUTE
RUE DES JUIFS
R. VANNER
R. J. D'ARC
RUE DE TASSIGNY
St-Vincent
RUE PORTE COTE
R. DU MARCHE NEUF
R. FOR BASSE
R. PARDESSUS
R. PIERRE LESUEUR
R. H. DRUSSY
RUE DU MAL. DE LATTRE DE TASSIGNY
Gare SNCF & D
AVE JEAN-LAIGRET
Jardin Augustin Thierry
RUE DE LAVOUTE DU CHATEAU
Maison de la Magie
RUE DU COMMERCE
RUE DENIS PAPIN
R. ST-MARTIN
RUE DES ORFEVRES
RUE E. LAURENS
QUAI DU MAL. DE LATTRE DE TASSIGNY
PLACE DE LA RESISTANCE
Jardin du Roi
PLACE VICTOR-HUGO
Château
Façade des Loges
RUE DES FOSSES DU CHATEAU
R. DES VIOLETTES
R. ST-LUBIN
PLACE LOUIS XII
SQUARE DE LA VAISSIERE
PONT JACQUES GABRIEL
PLACE DES LICES
RAMPES FOSSES DU CHATEAU
RUE BERNIER
RUE ST-LAUMER
RUE DES JACOBINS
RUE HOUDIN
RUE ANNE DE BRETAGNE
QUAI DE LA SAUSSAYE
River Loire
DEGRE ST-NICOLAS
RUE ROCHEFORT
RUE DES CARMELITES
RUE DES TROIS MARCHANDS
Musée d'Histoire Naturelle
St-Nicolas
QUAI DE L'ABBE GREGOIRE
RUE DU SERMON
RUE FOIX
RUE PUITS DE BEL AIR
RUE DE LA GREVE
PLACE DE LA GREVE
QUAI VILLEBOIS MAREUIL
RUE C. D'ORLEANS
RUE DES ECURIES
RUE DU ROI
N
0   100 m

G (5km)

ACCOMMODATION				EATING & DRINKING			
Anne de Bretagne	D	HI Hostel	G	Les Banquettes Rouges	6	Le St-James	2
Du Bellay	B	Mercure	C	Le Castelet	5	Velvet Jazz Lounge	1
Camping Rives de Loire	E	Le Monarque	A	Hendrix Bar	3		
Côté Loire	F			L'Orangerie du Chateau	4		

Charming boutique hotel, tucked away in a quiet corner by the river. Rooms have antique furnishings and brand-new bathrooms – those on the front have views of the river. ④

HI Hostel 18 rue de l'Hôtel-Pasquier ℡02.54.78 27.21, ℮blois@fuaj.org. Five kilometres downstream from Blois, between the Forêt de Blois and the river. Bus #4 runs at least once an hour, but stops at around 7pm. Showers are provided. Closed mid-Nov to Feb.

Mercure 28 quai St-Jean ℡02.54.56.66.66, ⓦwww.mercure.com. The best place to stay in town if all you want is clean, faintly soulless efficiency at a reasonable price; a decent location overlooking the river helps. ⑦

Le Monarque 61 rue Porte Chartraine ℡02.54.78.02.35, ⓦannedebretagne.free.fr. Professional and energetically managed hotel with rooms cheerfully renovated in a modern style. Usefully located at the top end of town. ③

The château

The **Château de Blois** (daily: April–Oct 9am–6.30pm; Nov–March 9am–12.30pm & 2–5.30pm; €7) was home to six kings, and countless more aristocratic and noble visitors. The impression given is one of grandiloquent splendour, mixed with not a little awe-inspiring spectacle, especially the way in which the predominantly Renaissance north wing is dominated by a superb spiral staircase. The grandly Classical west wing was built in the 1630s by François Mansart for Gaston d'Orléans, the brother of Louis XIII. Turning to the south side, you go back in time 140-odd years to Louis XII's St-Calais chapel, which contrasts with the more exuberant brickwork of his flamboyant Gothic east wing.

The signposts point you straight ahead and up Mansart's breathtaking staircase, which leads you round to the less interesting **François I wing**; the garish decor dates from Félix Duban's mid-nineteenth-century efforts to turn an empty barn of a château into a showcase for sixteenth-century decorative motifs. One of the largest rooms is given over to paintings of the notorious murder of the Duke of Guise and his brother, the Cardinal of Lorraine, by Henri III. As leaders of the radical Catholic League, the Guises were responsible for the summary execution of Huguenots at Amboise. The king had summoned the States-General to a meeting in the Grande Salle, only to find that an overwhelming majority supported the Duke, along with the stringing up of Protestants, and aristocratic rather than royal power. Henri had the duke summoned to his bedroom in the palace, where he was ambushed and hacked to death, and the cardinal was murdered in prison the next day. Their deaths were avenged a year later when a monk assassinated the king himself.

The château was also home to Henri III's mother and manipulator, Catherine de Médicis, who died here a few days after the murders in 1589. The most famous of her suite of rooms is the study, where, according to Alexandre Dumas' novel, *La Reine Margot*, she kept poison hidden in secret caches in the skirting boards and behind some of the 237 narrow carved wooden panels; they now contain small Renaissance *objets d'art*. In the nineteenth century, revolutionaries were tried in the Grande Salle for conspiring to assassinate Napoléon III, a year before the Paris Commune of 1870. You can return to the courtyard via the vast space of the Salle des États, where the arches, pillars and fireplaces are another riot of nineteenth-century colour.

A thorough examination would take several hours, but if you're still not flagging, you can head back across the courtyard to the ground floor of the François I wing, where an **archaeological museum** displays original

▲ The Château de Blois

stonework from the staircase and dormer windows, as well as carved details rescued from other châteaux.

French-speakers may want to take the two-hour guided **visite privilégiée** (July & Aug daily at 3pm; €7.50), which explores parts of the château you won't normally see, such as the roof and cellars. You can usually just turn up at the gate for the **son et lumière** (mid-April to mid-Sept daily; €6.50, or €10 including château entrance; in English on Wed), which takes place at dusk on summer evenings. It's one of the best in the region, rising above the usual mix of melodrama, light and musical effects by making the most of the château's fascinating history and lovely courtyard setting, and thrillingly re-creates the Duc de Guise's murder.

The rest of the town

Just below the château on rue St-Laumer, the **church of St Nicholas** (daily 9am–6.30pm) once belonged to an abbey, and the choir is a handsome example of the humble Benedictine treatment of the Romanesque style. The **Maison de la Magie**, facing the château on the far side of the esplanade (April–Sept daily 10am–12.30pm & 2–6pm; €7.50 or €12 with château entry; Ⓦ www .maisondelamagie.fr); sounds interesting but is rather boring; slightly more instructive is the **Musée d'Histoire Naturelle**, rue Anne-de-Bretagne (daily except Mon 2–6pm; €2.50), with some good dioramas showing the different environments of the region, and the birds and animals that live in them.

At the top of town, the superb **Musée de l'Objet**, 6 rue Franciade (March–June & Sept–Nov Sat & Sun 1.30–6.30pm; July & Aug Wed–Sun 1.30–6.30pm; €4), celebrates modern sculptures created from found objects rather than traditional materials. A forest of hammers hanging from the staircase ceiling gradually morphs into handbags, and the two long, spacious galleries are filled with similarly witty or alarming artworks, including some by major figures in modern art.

At the east end of town, on the handsome **place St-Louis**, look out for the half-timbered and sculpted facade of the **Maison des Acrobates**. The Gothic **cathédrale St-Louis** (daily 7.30am–6pm), at the west end of the square, leans against a weighty bell tower whose lowest storey is twelfth century. The interior is unexceptional, but the most interesting feature is the modern **stained-glass windows**, completed in 2003 by the Dutch artist Jan Dibbets. Leading off place St-Louis, rue du Palais traverses above the town centre, passing the long stairs at the head of rue Denis-Papin and leading into rue St-Honoré. At no. 8, the elaborate **Hôtel Alluye**, the private house of the royal treasurer Florimond Robertet, is a rare survival of Blois' golden years under Louis XII.

Eating and drinking

Most of Blois' traditional **restaurants** can be found on or around rue Saint-Lubin, between the château and the river. *Le Castelet*, 40 rue Saint-Lubin (☎02.54.74.66.09; closed Wed & Sun; meals from €15), specializes in homely Loire cuisine, using regional produce. The house wines by the carafe are excellent; avoid the throat-stripping cognac. A little further along the same street, *Les Banquettes Rouges*, 16 rue des Trois Marchands (☎02.54.78.74.92; closed Sun & Mon), serves modern French, Mediterranean-influenced food, with evening menus from €21. The best gastronomic experience in town is *L'Orangerie du Château*, 1 avenue Jean-Laigret (☎02.54.78.05.36; menus €30–68), with acclaimed Michelin-starred cuisine, although the atmosphere can be snooty.

The small square at the end of rue Vauvert, on the east side of town, has a number of crêperies and pizzerias with tables set out under the trees; the *Hendrix Bar* is a fun place to grab a drink. Immediately below, rue de la Foulerie is the best place for ethnic food – Portuguese, Moroccan and Indian – and for late-night **bars** as well. The cocktail bar *Le St-James*, 50 rue de la Foulerie, is a good bet, as is the *Velvet Jazz Lounge*, nearby at 15bis rue Haute.

Around Blois

A good reason to have Blois as a base is for visiting nearby **châteaux**. By car you could call at all of them in a couple of days, but they also make ideal cycling or walking targets if you arm yourself with a map and strike out along minor roads and woodland rides. It's particularly pleasant to be able to visit them by bicycle, as local **public transport** in the area is very poor, with even the main routes served by only a couple of commuter buses a day. Note, however, that the local bus company TLC (☎02.54.58.55.55, ⓦ www.tlcinfo.net) runs **coach trips** to Chambord and Cheverny, with two morning and one lunchtime departure from Blois' *gare SNCF* (mid-May to Aug; €10.75); tickets can be bought at the tourist office. Staff may also be able to find places on a chartered taxi or minibus tour, which will not be cheap; expect to pay a minimum of €45 for a half-day tour.

Château de Chaumont

Catherine de Médicis forced Diane de Poitiers to hand over Chenonceau in return for the **Château de Chaumont** (daily: April & late Sept 10.30am–5.30pm; May to mid-Sept 9.30am–6.30pm; Oct–March 10am–12.30pm & 1.30–5pm; €7; grounds open daily 9.30am–dusk; free), 20km downstream from Blois. Diane got a bad deal but this is still one of the lovelier châteaux.

The original fortress was destroyed by Louis XI in the mid-fifteenth century in revenge for the part its owner, Pierre d'Amboise, played in the "League of Public Weal", an alliance of powerful nobles against the ever-increasing power of the monarch. But Pierre found his way back into the king's favour, and with his son Charles I built much of the quintessentially medieval castle that stands today. Proto-Renaissance design is more obvious in the courtyard, which today forms three sides of a square, the fourth side having been demolished in 1739 to improve views over the river, which are spectacular. Inside, the heavy nineteenth-century decor of the ground-floor rooms dates from the ownership of the Broglie family, but a few rooms on the first floor have been remodelled in the Renaissance style. The large council chamber is particularly fine, with seventeenth-century majolica tiles on the floor and its walls adorned with wonderfully busy sixteenth-century tapestries showing the gods of each of the seven planets known at the time.

The Broglie family also transformed the 21-hectare landscaped **park** into the fashionable English style and built the remarkable *belle époque* **stables**, with their porcelain troughs and elegant electric lamps for the benefit of the horses at a time before the château itself was wired – let alone the rest of the country. A corner of the château grounds now plays host to an annual **Festival des Jardins** (May to mid-Oct daily 9.30am to dusk; €8.50, or €11 with château entry), which shows off the extravagant efforts of contemporary garden designers.

On weekends in summer, you can secure the best view of the château from the deck of a traditional Loire boat. Contact the Association Millière Raboton (☎06.88.76.57.14, ⓦ www.milliere-raboton.net), whose **boat trips** (€12–15) leave from the quay immediately below the château, and last roughly an hour and a half. Best for wildlife are the regular dawn excursions, and you can organize longer trips – even camping out overnight on an island sandbank.

Château de Cheverny

Fifteen kilometres southeast of Blois, the **Château de Cheverny** (daily: April–June & Sept 9.15am–6.15pm; July & Aug 9.15am–6.45pm; Oct–March 9.45am–5pm; ⓦ www.chateau-cheverny.fr; €6.50) is the quintessential seventeenth-century château. Built between 1604 and 1634 and little changed since, it presents an immaculate picture of symmetry, harmony and the aristocratic good life. This continuity may well be because descendants of the first owners still own, live in and go hunting from Cheverny today. Its stone, from Bourré on the River Cher, lightens with age, and the château gleams like a great white brick in its acres of rolling parkland. The interior decoration has only been added to, never destroyed, and the extravagant display of paintings, furniture, tapestries and armour against the gilded, sculpted and carved walls and ceilings is extremely impressive. The most precious objects are hard to pick out from the sumptuous whole, but some highlights are the painted wall panels in the dining room telling stories from *Don Quixote*; the vibrant, unfaded colours of the Gobelin tapestry in the arms room; and the three rare family portraits by François I's court painter, François Clouet, in the gallery.

You can explore the elegant **grounds** on foot, or take a sedate tour by golf buggy and boat (April to mid-Nov; €11.20 including château entry). The **kennels** near the main entrance are certainly worth a look: a hundred lithe hounds mill and loll about while they wait for the next stag; feeding time (5pm) is something to be seen. Cheverny's hunt culls around thirty deer a year, a figure set by the National Forestry Office.

You can **stay** in the rustic *Hôtel des Trois Marchands* (☎02.54.79.96.44, ⓦ www .hoteldes3marchands.com; ❸), in **COUR-CHEVERNY**, Cheverny's larger neighbour, 1km north. The hotel's restaurant is rather smart, or there's the inexpensive bar and grill next door.

Château de Beauregard

A pleasant cycle ride from Blois, the little-visited **Château de Beauregard** (Feb 8 to end March, Oct, Nov & Dec 20 to end Dec daily except Wed 9.30am–noon & 2–5pm; April–June & Sept daily 9.30am–noon & 2–7.30pm; July & Aug daily 9.30am–6.30pm; €6.50; ⓦ www.beauregard-loire.com), 7km south of Blois on the D956 to Contres, lies amid the Forêt de Russy. It was – like Chambord – one of François I's hunting lodges, but its transformation in the sixteenth century involved beautification rather than aggrandizement. It was added to in the seventeenth century and the result is sober and serene, very much at ease in its manicured geometric park.

The highlight of the château is a richly decorated, long **portrait gallery**, whose floor of Delft tiling depicts an army on the march. The walls are entirely panelled with 327 portraits of kings, queens and great nobles, including European celebrities such as Francis Drake, Anne Boleyn and Charles V of Spain. All of France's kings are represented, from Philippe VI (1328–50), who precipitated the Hundred Years War, to Louis XIII (1610–43), who occupied the throne when the gallery was created. Kings, nobles and executed wives alike are given equal billing – except for Louis XIII, whose portrait is exactly nine times the size of any other. It's worth strolling down through the grounds to the sunken **Jardin des Portraits**, a Renaissance-influenced creation by contemporary landscaper Gilles Clément, who was responsible for Paris's futuristic Parc André Citroën (see p.137). It could be better tended, but the garden's formal arrangement – by colour of flower and foliage – is fascinating.

Château de Chambord

The **Château de Chambord** (daily: April to mid-July & mid-Aug to end Sept 9am–6.15pm; mid-July to mid-Aug 9am–7.30pm; Oct–March 9am–5.15pm; July & Aug €9.50, Sept–June €8.50; ℡02.54.50.50.00, ⓦwww.chambord.org), François I's little "hunting lodge", is the largest and most popular of the Loire châteaux and one of the most extravagant commissions of its age. If you are going to visit – and it's one of the region's absolute highlights - try to arrive early, and avoid weekends, when the crush of visitors can be both unpleasant and overwhelming. Its patron's principal object – to outshine the Holy Roman Emperor Charles V – would, he claimed, leave him renowned as "one of the greatest builders in the universe"; posterity has judged it well.

Before you even get close, the sheer gargantuan scale of the place is awe-inspiring: there are more than 440 rooms and 85 staircases, and a petrified forest of 365 chimneys runs wild on the roof. In architectural terms, the mixture of styles is as outrageous as the size. The Italian architect Domenico da Cortona was chosen to design the château in 1519 in an effort to establish prestigious Italian Renaissance art forms in France, though the labour was supplied by French masons. The château's plan (attributed, fancifully, to da Vinci) is pure Renaissance: rational, symmetrical and totally designed to express a single idea – the central power of its owner. Four hallways run crossways through the central keep, at the heart of which the Great Staircase rises up in two unconnected spirals before opening out into the great lantern tower, which draws together the confusion on the roof like a great crown.

The cold, draughty size of the château made it unpopular as an actual residence – François I himself stayed there for just 42 days in total – and Chambord's role in history is slight. A number of rooms on the first floor were fitted out by Louis XIV and his son, the Comte de Chambord, and as reconstructed today they feel like separate apartments within the unmanageable whole. You can explore them freely, along with the adjacent eighteenth-century apartments, where the château was made habitable by lowering ceilings, building small fireplaces within the larger ones, and cladding the walls with the fashionable wooden panelling known as *boiseries*. The second floor houses a rambling **Museum of Hunting** where, among the endless guns and paintings that glorify hunting, are two superb seventeenth-century tapestry cycles: one depicts Diana, goddess of the hunt; another, based on cartoons by Lebrun, tells the story of Meleager, the heroic huntsman from Ovid's *Metamorphoses*.

The **events and festivals** calendar is a busy one, with evening lighting displays, guided nature walks, cycle rides and jeep tours in the forest, costumed tours for children and a twice-daily dressage display, among other attractions. A free leaflet available at the château gives details.

The **Parc de Chambord** around the château is an enormous walled game reserve – the largest in Europe. Wild boars roam freely, though red deer are the beasts you're most likely to spot. You can explore on foot, or by bike or boat – both rentable from the jetty where the Cosson passes alongside the main facade of the château.

Accommodation in the village of **Chambord** itself can be found opposite the château (and beside the cafeterias and postcard stalls) at the *Hôtel du Grand St-Michel* (℡02.54.20.31.31, ⓦwww.saintmichel-chambord.com; ❸–❻). What it gains in ease of location it loses in charm and value for money. In **BRACIEUX**, a small village just beyond the southern wall of the Parc de Chambord, 8km from the château, the *Hôtel de la Bonnheure*, 9bis rue R.-Masson (℡02.54.46.41.57, ⓦwww.hoteldelabonnheur.com; ❹) has various rooms and apartments set around floral gardens. Bracieux also has an excellent

restaurant, *Le Relais de Bracieux* (☎02.54.46.41.22; €38–140; closed Tues &
Wed), and a large **campsite** (☎02.54.46.41.84; closed Nov to mid-March)
with a summer-only pool.

The Sologne

Stretching southeast of Blois, **the Sologne** is one of those traditionally rural
regions of France that help keep alive the national self-image. Depending on the
weather and the season, it can be one of the most dismal areas in central France:
damp, flat, featureless and foggy. But at other times its forests, lakes, ponds and
marshes have a quiet magic – in summer, for example, when the heather is in
bloom and the ponds are full of water lilies, or in early autumn when you can
collect mushrooms. Wild boar and deer roam here, not to mention the ducks,
geese, quails and pheasants, who far outnumber the small human population. The
Sologne remains the refuge of the French aristocracy, along with the descendants
of rich industrialists who bought land and built châteaux here in the latter part
of the nineteenth century. Hunting is the thing, not tourism, and much of the
region is out of bounds or simply physically impenetrable. It's worth passing
through on a fine day's bike ride, but there's little to see otherwise.

Two *grandes randonnées* lead through the Sologne, both variants of the main
GR3 along the Loire. The northern **GR3C** runs through Chambord and east
mostly along forest roads to Thoury and La Ferté-St-Cyr, where it rejoins the
southern branch, the **GR31**, which has taken a more attractive route through
Bracieux and along footpaths through the southern part of the Forêt de
Chambord. There are numerous other well-signposted paths, and tourist
offices in most of Sologne's towns and villages can provide maps and details
of bike rental or horse riding, as well as accommodation details. If you're
exploring the Sologne during the hunting season (Oct 1 to March 1), don't
stray from the marked paths: there are depressingly frequent stories of people
being accidentally shot.

Tours and around

Straddling a spit of land between the rivers Loire and Cher, the ancient
cathedral city of **TOURS** is the chief town of the Loire valley. It has the
usual feel of a mid-sized provincial city, with uneasy shifts between the strikingly grand and depressingly modern. However, for all that, it has its charms,

with some good bars and cafés, and some fine restaurants. It has a prettified and animated **old quarter**, some unusual **museums** – of wine, crafts, stained glass and an above-average Beaux-Arts museum – and a great many fine buildings, not least **St Gatien cathedral**. It's also the main transport link to the great châteaux of **Villandry, Langeais, Azay-le-Rideau** and **Amboise**.

Arrival and information

The **gare routière** and **gare SNCF** are situated a short way southeast of the cathedral district, facing the futuristic Centre de Congrès Vinci, which was hugely expensive and has proved to be something of a local white elephant. Most TGVs stop at **St-Pierre-des-Corps** station, in an industrial estate outside the city, but frequent shuttles (or sometimes buses) provide a link to the main station. The excellent **tourist office** is on the corner of rue Bernard-Palissy and busy boulevard Heurteloup (mid-April to mid-Oct Mon–Sat 8.30am–7pm, Sun 10am–12.30pm & 2.30–5pm; mid-Oct to mid-April Mon–Sat 9am–12.30pm & 1.30–6pm, Sun 10am–1pm; ℡02.47.70.37.37, ⓦwww.ligeris.com), just across the square from the train and bus stations. It sells a **museum pass** (*carte multi-visites*; €7.50) that lets you into the five city museums, and can give information on **château tours**.

Accommodation

Tours has some great budget and two-star hotels in the area just west of the cathedral, though there's less choice at the higher end of the market. It's worth booking in advance at almost all times of the year.

Des Arts 40 rue de la Préfecture ℡02.47.05.05.00, Ⓔhoteldesartstours@orange.fr. Warmly decorated hotel with a choice of rooms, including inexpensive ones in the garret, and larger rooms on the lower floors. All are en suite. ❷–❸
Central 21 rue Berthelot ℡02.47.05.46.44, ⓦwww.bestwesterncentralhoteltours.com. It's overpriced and part of a business-oriented chain (Best Western), but the rooms are large and high-ceilinged, and there's a small garden and garage parking for €9 a night. ❻
Colbert 78 rue Colbert ℡02.47.66.61.56, Ⓔhotel-colbert@club-internet.fr. Pleasant, well-furnished hotel in a good location near the cathedral. Rooms overlooking the small back garden are a little more expensive. ❸

Château tours

It's possible to get to most of the more-visited châteaux by public transport but if you're short of time it's worth considering a minibus trip. The main drawback is that you're usually limited to fairly brief visits. A number of companies run **excursions** from Tours, and on most schedules you'll find the following châteaux: Amboise, Azay-le-Rideau, Blois, Chambord, Chenonceau, Cheverny, Clos-Lucé (in Amboise), Fougères-sur-Bièvre, Langeais, Ussé and Villandry. **Ticket** prices are steep: usually around €19 for a morning trip, taking in a couple of châteaux, and €40–50 for a full-day tour. These prices do not usually include entrance fees or lunch. Ask at tourist offices or contact the following Touraine-based **agencies** directly: Acco Dispo (℡06.82.00.64.51, ⓦwww.accodispo-tours.com); Saint-Eloi Excursions (℡06.70.82.78.75, ⓦwww.chateauxexcursions.com); Alienor Excursions (℡06.10.85.35.39, ⓦwww.alienortours.com); and Quart de Tours (℡06.30.65.52.01, ⓦwww.quartdetours.com). There's little to choose between them, and most pick up from the tourist office in Tours or from your hotel. Alternatively, some packages offered by tour operators will include some châteaux visits; the question of whether it's worth the premium you will undoubtedly be charged is up to you.

▲ Orléans   ▲ St-Pierre-des-Corps

◄ Le Mans, Saumur & Angers

► River Cher & Loches

▼ Prieuré de St-Cosme

TOURS

Musée des Beaux-Arts

Logis des Gouverneurs

Château

Cathédrale St-Gatien

RUE DES URSELINES

RUE JULES-SIMON

RUE A. THOMAS

QUAI D'ORLÉANS

RUE LAVOISIER

RUE DES AMANDIERS

RUE DE LA BARRE

RUE DU CYGNE

RUE DES JACOBINS

RUE COLBERT

RUE DES CORDELIERS

RUE FOIRE LE ROI

RUE DE LA SCELLERIE

RUE CORNEILLE

AV ANDRÉ MALRAUX

RUE VOLTAIRE

Musée de Compagnonnage

Musée des Vins

St-Julien

Jardin de Beaune-Semblançay

RUE NATIONALE

RUE JULES-FAVRE

Grand Théâtre

RUE ÉMILE-ZOLA

Église Réformée

RUE BERNARD-PALISSY

Jardin de la Préfecture

Préfecture

RUE BUFFON

Hôtel de Ville

Palais de Justice

RUE NATIONALE

PLACE JEAN-JAURÈS

AV DE GRAMONT

RUE MARCEAU

RUE G-SAND

RUE MARCEAU

RUE DES DÉPORTÉS

RUE DES HALLES

RUE DE JÉRUSALEM

Basilique de St-Martin

RUE NÉRICAULT-DESTOUCHES

RUE DE LA GRANDIÈRE

BOULEVARD BÉRANGER

RUE CHANNOINEAU

Halles

PLACE DES HALLES

Tour de Charlemagne

RUE DE LA MONNAIE

RUE DU COMMERCE

Hôtel Gouin

RUE DE CONSTANTINE

RUE DES TANNEURS

RUE DE LA PAIX

R BRIÇONNET

VIEILLE VILLE

RUE BRETONNEAU

RUE ÉTIENNE MARCEL

RUE DES QUATREVENTS

PLACE DE VICTOIRE

RUE DE LA VICTOIRE

River Loire

PONT WILSON

PLACE ANATOLE-FRANCE

PONT NAPOLÉON

Gare SNCF

Gare Routière

BOULEVARD HEURTELOUP

RUE E. VAILLANT

RUE TRAVERSIÈRE

N

0   200 m

Du Cygne 6 rue du Cygne ☎02.47.66.66.41, ⓦwww.hotel-cygne-tours.com. Pleasantly old-fashioned and well-run hotel on a quiet street. The rooms are dated but comfortable and preserve the flavour of the house. Garage parking available. ④

HI Hostel 5 rue Bretonneau ☎02.47.37.81.58, ⓔtours@fuaj.org. Large, modern youth hostel with an excellent central location near place Plumereau. Singles or twin-bed rooms available. Bicycles are hired out inexpensively, too. Reception 8am–noon & 6–11pm.

Du Manoir 2 rue Traversière ☎02.47.05.37.37, ⓦsite.voila.fr/hotel.manoir.tours. Set in an over-modernized nineteenth-century town house, but friendly, comfortable and in a peaceful location between the cathedral and train station. ③

Regina 2 rue Pimbert ☎02.47.05.25.36, ⓕ02.47.66.08.72. Friendly and well-run budget place right in the town centre. Popular with backpackers, with a range of room prices. ①

St-Éloi 79 bd Béranger ☎02.47.37.67.34. Excellent-value, intimate hotel run by a friendly young couple. ②

Du Théâtre 57 rue de la Scellerie ☎02.47.05.31.29, ⓦwww.hotel-du-theatre37 .com. Charming, friendly hotel set in a tastefully restored medieval town house in the cathedral quarter. ④

De l'Univers 5 bd Heurteloup ☎02.47.05.37.12, ⓦwww.hotel-univers-loirevalley.com. The grandest and most historic hotel in town, with an enviable list of past guests including Churchill, Georges Sand and Pete Townshend, this was once great but now considerably down at heel and catering mainly to tour groups. It is believed that a forthcoming renovation should re-establish its former glory. ⑨

Val de Loire 33 bd Heurteloup ☎02.47.05.37.86. Charming, antiques-laden town house hotel close to the station, and a real bargain at the price. Noisy, but double glazing does help. ③

The City

The centre of Tours lies between the Loire and its tributary, the Cher, but the city has spread far across both banks, with industrial Tours north of the Loire. Neither river is a particular feature of the town, though there are parks on islands in both and an attractive new footbridge leads across the Loire from the site of the old castle on quai d'Orléans. The city's two distinct old quarters lie on either side of **rue Nationale**, which forms the town's main axis. The quieter of the areas lies around the **cathedral**, while the main tourist area lies around picturesque **place Plumereau**, some 600m to the west. It was once a major pilgrimage site; these days, the pilgrimage is more likely to be to one of the many bars lying around.

The cathedral quarter

The great west towers of the **Cathédrale St–Gatien**, standing on the square of the same name, are visible all over the city. Their surfaces crawl with decorated stone in the flamboyant Gothic style, and even the Renaissance belfries that cap them share the same spirit of refined exuberance. Inside, the style moves back in time, ending with relatively severe High Gothic east end – built in the thirteenth century – and its glorious stained-glass windows.

A door in the north aisle leads to the **Cloître de la Psalette** (April–Sept Mon–Sat 9.30am–12.30pm & 2–6pm, Sun 2–6pm; Oct–March Wed–Sun closes 5pm; €2.30), which has an unfinished air, with the great foot of a flying buttress planted in the southeast corner and the missing south arcade – lost when a road was driven through in 1802 by the same progressive, anticlerical prefect who destroyed the basilica of St-Martin. The area behind the cathedral and museum, to the east, is good for a short stroll. There's a fine view of the spidery buttresses supporting the cathedral's painfully thin-walled apse from **place Grégoire de Tours**. Overlooking the square is the oldest wing of the **archbishop's palace**, whose end wall is a mongrel of Romanesque and eighteenth-century work, with an early sixteenth-century projecting balcony once used by clerics to address their flock.

Just south of the cathedral, the **Musée des Beaux-Arts** (daily except Tues 9am–12.45pm & 2–6pm; €4) is housed in the former archbishop's palace. Other than Mantegna's intense, unmissable *Agony in the Garden* (1457–59), in the basement, there are few celebrity works in the large collection. Even Rembrandt's much-advertised *Flight into Egypt* is a small oil study rather than a finished work. But the stately, loosely chronological progression of palatial seventeenth- and eighteenth-century rooms, each furnished and decorated to match the era of the paintings it displays, is extremely attractive. Local gems include Boulanger's portrait of Balzac, and the engravings *The Five Senses* by the locally born Abraham Bosse, which have been interpreted as full-size canvases in the handsome Louis XIII room. It's also worth a look at the utterly out of place remnants of an elephant in the old stables, acquired from P. T. Barnum in faintly mysterious circumstances in the nineteenth century.

On the other side of the cathedral, between rue Albert-Thomas and the river, just two towers remain of the ancient royal **château** of Tours. You can get inside when an exhibition is being held but there's nothing much left of the interior. In the fifteenth-century **Logis des Gouverneurs** alongside (Wed & Sat 2–6pm, sometimes closed during school holidays; free), across the remnants of the city's Gallo-Roman wall, there's an exhibition of historical artefacts called "Vivre à Tours" (Life in Tours) that gives a good sense of how the city has developed over the centuries.

The old quarter

To the west, the pulse of the city quickens as you approach **place Plumereau** – or place Plum' as it's known locally. The square's tightly clustered, ancient houses have been carefully restored as the city's showpiece, transforming what was once a slum into the epicentre of social life. On sunny days, the square is packed almost end to end with café tables, and students and families drink and dine out until late in the evening.

If you're looking for peace, slip down **rue Briçonnet** into a miniature maze of quiet, ancient streets. Opposite an oddly Venetian-looking, fourteenth-century house, at no. 41 rue Briçonnet, a passageway leads past a palm tree and an ancient outdoor staircase to the quiet and insulated **Jardin de St-Pierre-le-Puellier**, laid out around the dug-out ruins of a conventual church. Further down rue Briçonnet, at no. 16, just before the heavily modernized riverfront, is the Gothic **Maison de Tristan**.

To the south lay the pilgrim city once known as **Martinopolis** after St Martin, the ex-soldier who became bishop of Tours in the fourth century and went on to be a key figure in the spread of Christianity through France. Among Catholics he is usually remembered for giving half his cloak to a beggar, an image repeated on capitals and in stained-glass windows all over the region. The Romanesque **basilica** stretched along rue des Halles from rue des Trois-Pavées-Ronds almost to place de Châteauneuf: the outline is traced out in the street, but only the north tower, the Tour de Charlemagne, and the western clock tower survived the iconoclastic Huguenot riots of 1562. The new **Basilique de St-Martin**, on rue Descartes, is a late nineteenth-century neo-Byzantine affair built to honour the relics of St Martin, rediscovered in 1860. They are now housed in the crypt, watched over by hundreds of votive prayers carved into the walls. St Martin's day, November 11, is still celebrated. A short distance away, down rue des Halles, lies the huge, modern **Halles**, or covered market – an excellent place to browse for a picnic in the morning.

Around rue Nationale

At the head of **rue Nationale**, Tours' main street, statues of Descartes and Rabelais – both Touraine-born – overlook the scruffy walkways that run along the bank of the Loire. A short walk back from the river and you come to the Benedictine **church of St Julien**, whose old monastic buildings are home to two fairly missable museums. The surprisingly boring **Musée des Vins**, 16 rue Nationale (daily except Tues 9am–noon & 2–6pm; €4.20), has a great location, but that's about it; all the exhibits are in French, and there is no opportunity to taste wines either. Behind the museum, a Gallo-Roman winepress from Cheillé sits in the former cloisters of the church. The **Musée de Compagnonnage**, at 8 rue Nationale (mid-June to mid-Sept daily 9am–noon & 2–6pm; mid-Sept to mid-June closed Tues; €4), is housed in the eleventh-century guesthouse and sixteenth-century monks' dormitory. It honours the peculiarly French cult of the artisan, displaying the "master-pieces" that craftsmen had to create in order to join their guild (*compagnonnage*) as a master craftsman. The skills are unquestionable but many of these showpieces are breathtakingly vulgar, displaying arts as diverse as cake making, carpentry, clog-making and cooperage.

A few steps west of rue Nationale, the **Hôtel Gouin**, 25 rue du Commerce, has a Renaissance facade to stop you in your tracks, but the **museum** inside (Tues–Sun 10am–1pm & 2–6pm; €4.50) is a dull collection of archeological oddities and the remnants of a private scientific laboratory from Chenonceau, which is less compelling than it sounds.

At the southern end of rue Nationale, the huge, traffic-ridden place Jean-Jaurès is the site of the grandiose Hôtel de Ville and Palais de Justice. To the west of place Jean-Jaurès, a giant **flower market** takes over boulevard Béranger on Wednesdays and Saturdays, lasting from 8am into the early evening.

St-Cosme

In May, when the roses are in full bloom, the **Prieuré de St-Cosme**, 3km west of the centre (mid-March to April & Sept to mid-Oct daily 10am–6pm; May–Aug daily 10am–7pm; mid-Oct to mid-March daily except Tues 10am–12.30pm & 2–5pm; €5), is one of the most appealing sights in the area even if it is hemmed in by suburbs and barred off from the nearby Loire by a trunk road. Once an island priory, now a semi-ruin, it was here that Pierre de Ronsard, France's greatest Renaissance poet, lived as prior from 1565 until his death in 1585. Vestiges of many monastic buildings survive but the most affecting sight is the lovingly tended garden of roses, which has some two thousand rose bushes, and 250 varieties – including the tightly rounded, pink rose called "Pierre de Ronsard". To get there by public transport, take **bus** #7 from immediately outside the Palais de Justice, on place Jean-Jaurès, towards La Riche-Petit Plessis, getting off at the La Pléiade stop.

Eating

The streets around place Plumereau, especially rue du Grand-Marché, are overrun with cafés, bars and **bistros**, and if don't mind paying a little extra for the bustling atmosphere and an outside table, this is the area to head for. Don't expect too many culinary fireworks though. On the cathedral side of rue Nationale, rue Colbert is lined with much less touristy bars and ethnic eateries, as well as a few good restaurants serving regional cuisine. For a drink or a **snack**, make for the pleasant (if overpriced) café-patisserie *Aux Délices de Michel Colombe*, 1 place François-Sicard, near the cathedral, or *Scarlett*, a relaxed tearoom at 70 rue Colbert. Unfortunately, Tours' best restaurant, *Jean Bardet*, recently closed, and as of yet nowhere has filled the gap at the highest end of the market.

Au Bureau place Plumereau. One of a number of places serving pizzas and simple dishes on the square, but of a slightly higher calibre than its competitors.

Chez Jean-Michel 123 rue Colbert ☎02.47.20.80.20. Intimate wine bar and restaurant that manages to be elegant and relaxed at the same time. Serves good regional dishes to go along with the excellent local wines. Main courses at around €15. Closed Sat & Sun.

Comme Autre-Fouée 11 rue de la Monnaie ☎02.47.05.94.78. The food served here is a revival of the archaic *fouace* (or *fouée*) breads immortalized by Rabelais, served hot and heavily garnished with local titbits. An excellent option for a quick lunch. Closed Sun, Mon & Tues lunch.

Au Lapin qui Fume 90 rue Colbert ☎02.47.66.95.49. Tiny, relaxed but elegant restaurant serving a good menu that's half Loire and half south of France. Lots of *lapin* (rabbit) – it comes as a terrine, as a fricassée with rosemary, or *confit* – but it's not obligatory. Evening menus around the €20 mark.

🏃 **Le Petit Patrimoine** 58 rue Colbert ☎02.47.66.05.81. Romantic little place serving rich, lovingly prepared Loire dishes and good Loire wines, including the famous red Sancerre. Menus €14–26.

Drinking and nightlife

Packed with tables and chairs, place Plumereau is *the* place to start the evening with an open-air aperitif and to finish it with a restorative coffee. There's a slightly depressing absence of bars and pubs with really individual character in the area, but there are plenty of less commercial places to be found in the streets around, with some good **café–bars** on rue du Commerce – try *Les Frères Berthom*, which has lots of outside tables. In the cathedral quarter, the bars on rue Colbert are overpriced and unfriendly to non-locals, with the exception of the *Académie de la Bière*, just up from the cathedral at 43 rue Lavoisier, which is a lively, student-friendly place, with an excellent range of beers and plenty of outdoor seating for good weather. If you're around during the university term, it might be worth a visit to *Le Palais* on 15 place Jean Jaurès on a Monday night, where the *Café des langues* allows you to speak in a variety of different languages to the students.

Even in summer, when local students are away, the **nightclubs** just off place Plumereau fill up with backpackers, locals and language students, though things don't usually get going until past midnight. Try *Les Trois Orfèvres*, 6 rue des Orfèvres, or *L'Excalibur*, which has a medieval theme. For details of **classical music** concerts, ask at the tourist office which provides a free monthly magazine of exhibitions, concerts and events in Touraine, *Détours et des nuits*.

Listings

Airport Aéroport Tours Val de Loire ☎02.47.49.37.00, ⊛www.tours-aeroport.com. A shuttle bus runs to the airport from the centre of town, costing €5.

Bike hire Store Trek, 31 bd Heurteloup, opposite the tourist office ☎02.47.61.22.35, ⊛www .locationdevelos.com. Runs the Détours de Loire scheme (see p.435), which allows you to drop off the bike at various locations along the river, for a small extra charge.

Car hire Avis, gare de Tours ☎02.47.20.53.27; Budget, 194 av André-Maginot ☎02.47.88.00.50; Europcar, 76 rue Bernard-Palissy ☎02.47.64.47.76; Hertz, 57 rue Marcel-Tribut ☎02.47.75.50.00. All offer pick up and drop off at Tours airport, at St-Pierre-des-Corps TGV station or near the *gare SNCF* in Tours.

Emergencies Ambulance ☎15; different hospital departments are spread around the city – call ☎02.47.47.47.47 to check where to head.

Internet Alliance Arena, 32bis rue Briçonnet (Mon–Sat 11am–7pm, Sun 1–8pm), is good value. Otherwise try L'Alexandra, 106 rue du Commerce (daily 3pm–1am or 2am); or Globilis Communication, 30 rue Michelet (Mon–Sat 9am–11pm, Sun 2–11pm).

Police Commisariat Général, 70–72 rue Marceau ☎02.47.70.88.88.

One of the great privileges of visiting the Loire is that there are a variety of châteaux that allow visitors to stay in them, and, by so doing, re-create a bygone way of life. Obviously, the standards range enormously. At the top end of the market, you are guaranteed de luxe accommodation, with room service, all mod cons, excellent food and all the amenities you would expect from a top-class hotel. At the other end, you are effectively staying in a bed and breakfast in someone's house, which can be pot luck; some of these places are wonderful, others badly dated and in need of sympathetic refurbishment.

The following are the pick of the hotels in the Tours area:

Chateau D'Artigny Nr Montbazon (take D17 from there) ☏02.47.34.30.39, ⓦwww .grandesetapes.fr/en/Chateau-hotel-artigny/index.html. Stunning, beautifully restored château originally owned by the perfumier François Coty, and decorated in a Neo-Classical style. The rooms are all large, lavishly appointed and very comfortable, and the excellent restaurant has sweeping views across the Loire valley. ❻

Domaine de Beauvois Nr Luynes ☏02.47.55.50.11, ⓦwww.grandesetapes.fr/en /Chateau-hotel-beauvois/index.html. Much of the appeal of this beautiful sixteenth-century mansion comes from its peaceful seclusion, with long country walks and beautiful bike rides the order of the day. There are some lovely, quirky touches in the rooms, too, which have beamed ceilings and painted frescoes, as well as excellent cooking. ❽

Domaine de la Tortinière Nr Montbazon ☏02.47.34.35.00, ⓦwww.tortiniere.com. Delightful family-run hotel, with friendly and bilingual owners. Rooms range from the modestly comfortable to the spectacularly luxurious (such as the suites in the turrets, complete with circular bedrooms) and very good food is served in the dining room, overlooking an open-air swimming pool. ❼

Amboise

Twenty kilometres upstream of Tours, **AMBOISE** is one of the highlights of the Loire region, with a beguiling mix of beauty, excellent food and drink and a genuine sense of history. The **château** dominates the town, but there are many other attractions, most famously Leonardo da Vinci's residence of **Clos-Lucé**, with its exhibition of the great man's inventions. Amboise draws a busy tourist trade that may detract from the quieter pleasures of strolling around town, but makes it a good destination for children. In July and August, **son et lumière** shows are held around 10pm at the château (Wed & Sat; adults from €14, children 6–14 from €7; ⓦwww.renaissance-amboise.com), with Leonardo images projected on the walls and costumed actors prancing about to loud Renaissance-style music.

Arrival and information

The **gare SNCF** is on the north bank of the river, at the end of rue Jules-Ferry, about 1km from the château. There are frequent connections to Tours and Blois. Information on Amboise and its environs, including the vineyards of the Touraine-Amboise *appellation*, is available at the **tourist office** on quai du Général-de-Gaulle, on the riverfront (June & Sept Mon–Sat 9.30am–1pm & 2–6.30pm, Sun 10am–1pm & 3–6pm; July & Aug Mon–Sat 9am–8pm, Sun 10am–6pm; Oct–May Mon–Sat 10am–1pm & 2–6pm; ☏02.47.57.09.28, ⓦwww.amboise-valdeloire.com).

Bikes can be hired from Cycles Richard, 2 rue Nazelles, near the station (☏02.47.57.01.79), or Locacycle, on rue Jean-Jacques-Rousseau (April–Oct; ☏02.47.57.00.28). **Canoes** are available from the Club de Canoë-Kayak, at the

Base de l'Île d'Or (☎02.47.23.26.52, ⑩www.loire-aventure.com), which also runs guided trips.

Accommodation

Hotels in Amboise vary enormously in price, but tend to be of a good standard.

Le Belle Vue 12 quai Charles-Guinot ☎02.47.57.02.26, ⑥bellevuehotel.amboise @orange.fr. Long-established Logis de France three-star just below the château, with comfortable, old-fashioned bedrooms. Some rooms at the front overlook the Loire – and the main road. Worth it if your budget won't stretch to more expensive accommodation. Closed mid-Nov to mid-March. ❹

Le Blason 11 place Richelieu ☎02.47.23.22.41, ⑩www.leblason.fr. Very smartly kept but homely hotel in a quiet corner. The furnishings are modern, but all rooms have pretty, exposed beams. Triples and quads available. Parking and internet access free. ❸

Café des Arts place Michel-Debré ☎02.47.57.25.04. Simple but friendly backpacker-oriented place – think pine bunkbeds and hard-wearing carpet – set up above an inexpensive café. ❶

Camping de l'Île d'Or Île d'Or ☎02.47.57.23.37. Pleasant, leafy campsite alongside the hostel, with access to the pool. Closed Oct–March.

Centre Charles Péguy Île d'Or ☎02.47.30.60.90, ⑥cis.amboise@orange.fr. Ordinary but clean and relatively comfortable hostel in a pleasant location on the midstream island, halfway across the town bridge, with a small summer swimming pool. It's best to reserve in advance. Prices vary, but beds cost no more than €11.50 a night. Closed at weekends; reception is open Mon–Fri 3–8pm.

🏃 **Le Choiseul** 36 quai Charles-Guinot ☎02.47.30.45.45, ⑩www.le-choiseul.com. Widely acknowledged to be the best hotel in Amboise, this luxurious place has grandly appointed and very comfortable rooms, an excellent restaurant and all the other touches you'd expect. ❾

🏃 **Le Vieux Manoir** 13 rue Rabelais ☎02.47.30.41.27, ⑩www.le-vieux-manoir .com. Run by an utterly charming American couple, this lovingly restored manor house is the best bed and breakfast in the region, some might say the country. Lots of lovely touches abound, whether it's the glass of Loire wine waiting on your arrival, the cleverly themed rooms or the self-contained cottages. ❽

Château d'Amboise

Rising above the river is the remains of the **château** (daily: Feb to mid-March 9am–noon & 1.30–5.30pm; last 2 weeks March & Sept to mid-Nov 9am–6pm; April–June 9am–6.30pm; July & Aug 9am–7pm; mid-Nov to Jan 9am–noon & 2–4.45pm; ⑩www.chateau-amboise.com; €9), once five times its present size, but much reduced by wars and lack of finance; it still represents a highly impressive accomplishment. It was in the late fifteenth century, following his marriage to Anne of Brittany at Langeais, that Charles VIII decided to turn the old castle of his childhood days into an extravagant palace, adding the flamboyant Gothic wing that overlooks the river and the **chapelle de St-Hubert**, which perches incongruously atop a buttress of the defensive walls. But not long after the work was completed, he managed to hit his head, fatally, on a door frame. He left the kingdom to his cousin, Louis XII, who spent most of his time at Blois but built a new wing at Amboise (at right angles to the main body) to house his nearest male relative, the young François d'Angoulême, thereby keeping him within easy reach. When the young heir acceded to the throne as François I he didn't forget his childhood home. He embellished it with classical stonework (visible on the east facade of the Louis XII wing), invited Leonardo da Vinci to work in Amboise under his protection, and eventually died in the château's collegiate church.

Henri II continued to add to the château, but it was during the reign of his sickly son, François II, that it achieved notoriety. The Tumult of Amboise was one of the first skirmishes in the Wars of Religion. Persecuted by the young king's powerful advisers, the Guise brothers, Huguenot conspirators set out for

▲ Château d'Amboise

Amboise in 1560 to "rescue" their king and establish a more tolerant monarchy under their tutelage. But they were ambushed by royal troops in woods outside the town, rounded up and summarily tried in the Salle des Conseils. Some were drowned in the Loire below the château, some were beheaded in the grounds, and others were hung from the château's balconies.

After such a history, the interior of the château is comparatively restrained, though the various rooms still retain some sense of their historical grandeur. The last French king, Louis-Philippe, also stayed in the château, hence the abrupt switch from the solid Gothic furnishings of the ground floor to the 1830s post-First Empire style of the first-floor apartments. The **Tour des Minimes**, the original fifteenth-century entrance, is architecturally the most exciting part of the castle. With its massive internal ramp, it was designed for the maximum number of fully armoured men on horseback to get in and out as quickly as possible. These days it leads down to the pleasant gardens, which in turn lead to the exit.

Clos-Lucé

Following his campaigns in Lombardy, François I decided that the best way to bring back the ideas of the Italian Renaissance was to import one of the finest exponents of the new arts. In 1516, **Leonardo da Vinci** ventured across the Alps in response to the royal invitation, carrying with him the *Mona Lisa* among other paintings. For three years before his death in 1519, he made his home at the **Clos-Lucé**, at the end of rue Victor-Hugo (daily: Jan 10am–5pm; Feb, March, Nov & Dec 9am–6pm; April–June, Sept & Oct 9am–7pm; July & Aug 9am–8pm; April–Oct €12, Nov–March €9). Leonardo seems to have enjoyed a semi-retirement at Amboise, devoting himself to inventions of varying brilliance and impracticability, and enjoying conversations with his royal patron, but it seems that no work of any great stature was produced there. The house – an attractive brick mansion with Italianate details added by Charles VIII – is now a museum to Leonardo. The gardens are over-designed, but it's nevertheless interesting to browse through the forty models of his mechanical inventions.

From the suspension bridge to the paddle-wheel boat and turbine, they are all meticulously constructed according to Leonardo's plans and sketches.

Beyond the town centre

If you take the main road south out of Amboise and turn right just before the junction with the D31, you'll come to an eighteenth-century **pagoda**, once part of the enormous but now demolished château of Chanteloup. You can climb to the top for an expansive view and explore the grounds of the surrounding park (April Mon–Fri 10am–noon & 2–6pm, Sat & Sun 10am–6pm; May & Sept daily 10am–6.30pm; June daily 10am–7pm; July & Aug daily 9.30am–7.30pm; Oct to mid-Nov Sat & Sun 10am–5pm; €6.90). Just south of town on the D751 to Chenonceaux, near the pagoda, the park **Mini-Châteaux** (daily: April–June, Sept & Oct 10am–6pm; July & Aug closes 7pm; €12, children 4–15 years €8) houses more than forty surprisingly good scale models of the chief Loire châteaux.

At Lussault, 5km west towards Tours, the mammoth **Aquarium du Val de Loire** (daily: July & Aug 10am–7pm; Sept–June 10am–6pm; closed last 2 weeks Jan & last 2 weeks Nov; adults €12, children 4–15 years €8; ⓦwww.aquariumduvaldeloire.com) boasts ten thousand fish, along with turtles, alligators and a tunnel through a large shark tank.

Eating and drinking

The best restaurant in town is Pascal Bouvier's Michelin-starred dining room at the hotel ☂ Le *Choiseul* (☎02.47.30.45.45; menus at €59 & €90), where the excellence of the food is matched by the stunning views over the Loire. *L'Épicerie*, 46 place Michel-Debré (☎02.47.57.08.94; menus €11–37; closed Mon & Tues except July & Aug), is overlooked by the chapelle St-Hubert and serves good country cuisine, with an good-value set lunch at €10 including wine. Another good restaurant is *L'Alliance,* 14 rue Joyeuse (☎02.47.30.52.13; menus €18–43; closed Wed & Jan), which serves mainly fish; in summer, both restaurants need to be booked in advance. *Chez Hippeau*, 1 rue François-I (☎02.47.57.26.30; menus €11–30), is a bustling brasserie next to the Hôtel de Ville, with good lunchtime menus and pleasant outdoor seating out back. If you fancy a late drink, head over to the Île d'Or, where you'll find the cocktail **bar** *Le Shaker* (6pm–2am; closed Mon), whose outside terrace has great views across to the château. The *Caveau des Vignerons d'Amboise* at the base of the château offers a wide variety of local wines to taste.

Château de Villandry

Even if gardens aren't normally your thing, those at the **Château de Villandry** (daily: Jan, Nov & Dec 9am–5pm; Feb 9am–5.30pm; March 9am–6pm; April–June & Sept 9am–7pm; July & Aug 9am–7.30pm; Oct 9am–6.30pm; château closes 30min–1hr earlier, plus mid-Nov to mid-Dec; €10 château and gardens, €6 gardens only; ⓦwww.chateauvillandry.com) are unmissable. Thirteen kilometres west of Tours along the Cher, this re-created Renaissance garden is as much symbolic as ornamental or practical. At the topmost level and in the elevated Classical spirit is a large, formal water garden. Next down, beside the château itself, is the ornamental garden, which features geometrical arrangements of box hedges symbolizing different kinds of love: tender, passionate, fickle and tragic. But the highlight, spread out at the lowest level across 12,500 square metres, is the potager, or Renaissance kitchen garden. Carrots, cabbages and aubergines are arranged into intricate patterns, while rose bowers and miniature box hedges form a kind of frame. Even in winter, there is almost always something to see, as the entire area is replanted twice a year. At the far end of the garden, overlooked by the squat tower of the village church, beautiful vine-shaded paths run past the medieval herb garden and the maze.

The elegant **château** was erected in the 1530s by one of François I's royal financiers, Jean le Breton, though the keep – from which there's a fine view of the gardens – dates back to a twelfth-century feudal castle. It's worth a quick visit, but pales in comparison to its gardens. Le Breton's Renaissance structure is arranged around three sides of a *cour d'honneur*, the fourth wing having been demolished in the eighteenth century. In summer you can take a **minibus** directly from Tours (☎02.47.70.37.37); the service leaves from the tourist office at 10am and 2.30pm and costs €16 return.

There are some top-class options for **eating** out in and around Villandry. In the centre of the tiny village, just down from the château, the wine bar, deli and restaurant, 🍴 *L'Épicerie Gourmande* (☎02.47.43.37.49) matches Loire wines with delicious delicatessen specialities, served all day. For something hearty, head 1km down the D121 towards Druye, where you'll find a farmhouse restaurant, the *Étape Gourmande* at the Domaine de la Giraudière (☎02.47.50.08.60; menus €15–30; closed mid-Nov to mid-March); its courtyard throngs with families enjoying honest home-cooked fare, with the farm's own goat's cheese featuring prominently. Right beside the Loire in Berthenay, a tiny village across the Cher from Villandry – you have to make a 7km round trip via Savonnières – 🍴 *Au Bout du Monde* (☎02.47.43.51.50; evening menus €28–52; closed Sun evening, Mon evening & Tues) serves fresh, light, imaginative cuisine in a lovely garden setting.

Château de Langeais

Twenty-three kilometres west of Tours, the small riverside town of **LANGEAIS** huddles in the shadow of its forbidding **château** (daily: Feb–June & Sept to mid-Nov; July & Aug 9am–7pm; mid-Nov to Jan 10am–5pm; €7.20), which was built to stop any incursions up the Loire by the Bretons. This threat ended with the marriage of Charles VIII and Duchess Anne of Brittany in 1491, which was celebrated in the castle, and a diptych of the couple portrays them looking less than joyous at their union – Anne had little choice in giving up her independence. The event is also recreated in waxworks in the chapel.

The main appeal here is in the way that the interior has resisted modernization to give a genuine sense of what life would have been like in the fifteenth century. There are fascinating tapestries, some rare paintings, cots and beds, a number of *chaires*, or seigneurial chairs, and in the huge marriage chamber, the gilded and bejewelled wedding coffer of Charles and Anne, carved with a miniature scene of the Annunciation and figures of the apostles, the wise and foolish virgins depicted on the lid.

Langeais has a pleasant **hotel**, the *Errard-Hosten*, 2 rue Gambetta (☎02.47.96.82.12, ⓦwww.errard.com; ❺), with a good but expensive restaurant. The *Anne de Bretagne*, 27 rue Anne de Bretagne (☎02.47.96.08.52; ❸), offers some exceptional *chambres d'hôtes* in a restored early nineteenth-century home. Sixteen kilometres north along the D57, just outside the village of Hommes, the *Vieux Château d'Hommes* (☎02.47.24.95.13, ⓦwww.le-vieux -chateau-de-hommes.com; ❼), offers well-furnished rooms in a fifteenth-century outhouse of the main château.

Azay-le-Rideau and around

Even without its striking **château** (daily: April–June & Sept 9.30am–6pm; July & Aug 9.30am–7pm; Oct–March 10am–12.30pm & 2–5.30pm; €7.50), the quiet village of **AZAY-LE-RIDEAU** would bask in its serene setting, complete with an old mill by the bridge and curious, doll-like Carolingian statues embedded in the facade of the church of St Symphorien. Perhaps unsurprisingly, it has become a magnet for tourists, and much of its charm is being gradually eroded by the sheer number of visitors it attracts. On its little island in the Indre, the château is one of the loveliest in the Loire: perfect turreted early Renaissance, pure in style right down to the blood-red paint of its window frames. Visiting the interior, furnished in mostly period style, doesn't add much to the experience although the grand staircase is worth seeing, and it's fun to look out through the mullioned windows across the moat and park and imagine yourself the *seigneur*. In summer, the château's grounds are the setting for a restrained and rather lovely **son et lumière** (July & Aug daily; early Sept Fri & Sat only; start time between 9 and 9.45pm; €9, or €12 with daytime château entry).

Practicalities

Azay's **tourist office** sits just off the village's main square, place de la République (May, June & Sept Mon–Sat 9am–1pm & 2–6pm, Sun 10am–1pm & 2–5pm; July & Aug Mon–Sat 9am–7pm, Sun 10am–6pm; Oct–April Mon–Sat 9am–1pm & 2–6pm; ℡02.47.45.44.40, ⓦwww.ot-paysazaylerideau.fr). The **bus stop** is next to the tourist office on the main road, but the **gare SNCF** is awkwardly situated a fifteen-minute walk west of the centre, along avenue Adélaïde-Riché – trains from Tours call at Azay-le-Rideau on their way to Chinon roughly every two hours (some services are replaced by *SNCF* buses). You can hire **bikes** from Cycles Leprovost, 13 rue Carnot (℡02.47.45.40.94), and in summer **canoes** can be hired from beside the bridge on the road out towards Chinon (daily 11am–7pm; ℡06.61.21.80.29).

Azay-le-Rideau has some of the best **accommodation** in the area, with two very pleasant hotels on or just off the main square. The *Hôtel de Biencourt*, 7 rue Balzac (closed mid-Nov to Feb; ℡02.47.45.20.75, ⓦwww.hotelbiencourt .com; ❸), is attractive and friendly, while *Le Grand Monarque*, 3 place de la République (℡02.47.45.40.08, ⓦwww.legrandmonarque.com; ❹–❾), is indeed rather grand, and has a wide range of rooms. But the best options are all *chambres d'hôtes*: the welcoming ⚘ *Manoir de la Rémonière* (℡02.47.45.24.88, ⓦwww .manoirdelaremoniere.com; ❼–❾), 1km from Azay on the opposite side of the Indre, on the road to Saché, was once the château's fifteenth-century hunting lodge and the two rooms offered by ⚘ *M. et Mme Sarrazin*, 9 chemin des Caves Mecquelines (℡02.47.45.31.25, ⓦwww.troglododo.fr; ❹) are both in troglodyte chambers hollowed out of the rock. Every hotel gets booked up a fair way in advance; don't even think about turning up in summer without a reservation. Upstream from the château is a large **campsite**, the *Camping du Sabot* (closed Nov–March; ℡02.47.45.42.72), signposted off the D84 to Saché.

For **restaurants**, *La Ridelloise*, 24 rue Nationale (℡02.47.45.46.53; menus €11–33), has a family atmosphere and inexpensive but decent cooking. In summer, *L'Aigle d'Or*, 10 avenue Adélaïde-Riché (℡02.47.45.24.58; closed Wed & Sun evening), serves elegant cuisine in its delightful garden, with menus from €24 to 60. The more commercial *Les Grottes*, 23ᵉʳ rue Pineau (℡02.47.45.21 04; menus from €16) offers the novel sensation of dining in a cave; the food does not match up to the experience.

Château d'Ussé

Fourteen kilometres west of Azay-le-Rideau, as the Indre approaches its confluence with the Loire, is the **Château d'Ussé** in **RIGNY-USSÉ** (daily: mid-Feb

to March & Oct to mid-Nov 10am–noon & 2–5pm; April–Sept 9.30am–
6.30pm; €10). With its shimmering white towers and terraced gardens, this is
the ultimate fairy-tale château – so much so that it's supposed to have inspired
Charles Perrault's classic retelling of the Sleeping Beauty myth. Whether you
find it an unmissable spectacle or a faintly embarrassing testament to kitsch
depends entirely on personal taste. The exterior resembles nothing so much as
a Disney fantasy; you half expect to see Beauty and the Beast emerge. Inside,
things are more restrained, apart from the tacky tableaux telling the story of
Sleeping Beauty, but the **gardens**, designed by Le Nôtre, are pleasant to wander.
The loveliest feature of all is the Renaissance **chapel** in the grounds, shaded
by ancient cedars.

The tiny village of Rigny-Ussé has a welcoming, family-run **hotel-restaurant**, *Le Clos d'Ussé* (☎&℉02.47.95.55.47; ❸), with eight simple rooms.
Behind the château, in a tranquil, wooded fold of the valley, the *Domaine de
la Juranvillerie*, 15 rue des Fougères (☎02.47.95.57.85, ⓦwww.lajuranvillerie
.com; ❸), is a charming little group of cottages, one housing a simple, attractive
chambres d'hôte. The friendly owners are enthusiastic naturalists and can advise
on walks in the Forêt de Chinon.

Chinon and around

CHINON lies on the north bank of the Vienne, 12km from its confluence
with the Loire, and is surrounded by some of the best vineyards in the Loire
valley. While spectacular to look at, with the cobbled medieval streets giving a
marvellous sense of history, there is surprisingly little to occupy you here.

Arrival and information

The **gare SNCF** lies to the east of the town, from where rue du Dr-P.-
Labussière and rue du 11-Novembre lead to the **gare routière** on place
Jeanne-d'Arc, where Joan is sculptured in mid-battle charge. Keep heading
west, either along the riverbank or across place Mirabeau into rue Rabelais,
and you'll soon reach the old quarter. The **tourist office** is on place
d'Hofheim, on the central rue Jean-Jacques-Rousseau (May–Sept daily
10am–7pm; Oct–April Mon–Sat 10am–noon & 2–6pm; ☎02.47.93.17.85,
ⓦwww.chinon.com), and can provide addresses of local vineyards where you
can taste Chinon's famous red wine. Just beside the campsite, Chinon Loisirs
Activités Nature (☎06.23.82.96.33) hires out **canoes** and kayaks, and runs
half-day and full-day guided trips in summer.

Accommodation

Most of the hotels in Chinon are decent and inexpensive, but for the more
extravagant, it's worth visiting one of the nearby châteaux.

Agnès Sorel 4 quai Pasteur ☎02.47.93.04.37,
ⓦwww.agnes-sorel.com. The situation down by
the main road, at the western edge of the old town,
lacks atmosphere and is awkward for the train
station, but it's very clean and welcoming inside.
Bikes are rented to all-comers. ❸
Camping de l'Île Auger ☎02.47.93.08.35.
Overlooks the old town and château from the south

bank of the Vienne; turn right from the bridge along
quai Danton. Closed mid-Oct to mid-March.
🏃 **Château de Danzay** near Avoine, 5km
north of Chinon ☎02.47.98.44.51, ⓦwww
.chateaudedanzay.com. Without a doubt the most
impressive, and expensive, hotel in the area, this is
a wonderful place if you fancy a touch of decadent
luxury. Prices begin at €180. Closed Oct–April. ❾

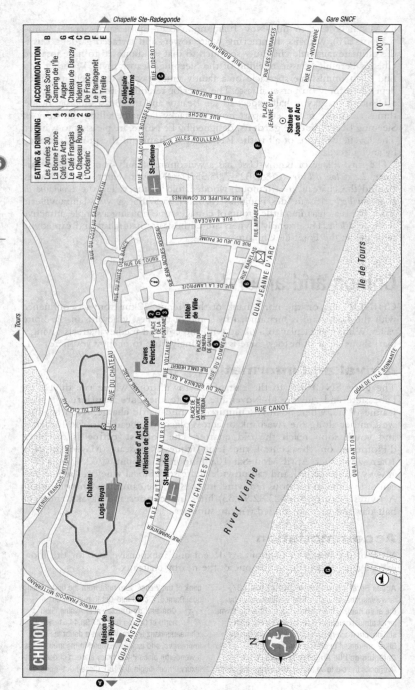

CHINON

▲ Chapelle Ste-Radegonde   ▲ Gare SNCF

ACCOMMODATION
Agnès Sorel   B
Camping de l'Île   1
Auger   G
Château de Danzay   A
Diderot   C
De France   D
Le Plantagenêt   F
La Treille   E

EATING & DRINKING
Les Années 30   1
La Bonne France   4
Café des Arts   5
Le Café Français   3
Au Chapeau Rouge   2
L'Océanic   6

Collégiale
St-Mexme

Statue of
Joan of Arc

PLACE
JEANNE D'ARC

RUE DES COURANCES

RUE DU 11-NOVEMBRE

RUE BONSARD

RUE DIDEROT

RUE DE BUFFON

RUE HOCHE

RUE JULES ROULLEAU

RUE JEAN-JACQUES ROUSSEAU

St-Étienne

RUE PHILIPPE DE COMMINES

RUE MARCEAU

RUE DU JEU DE PAUME

RUE MIRABEAU

RUE DU PUITS DES BANCS

RUE DE TOURS

RUE DU CÔTÉ AU SAINT-MARTIN

RUE JEAN-JACQUES ROUSSEAU

RUE RABELAIS

QUAI JEANNE D'ARC

RUE DE LA LAMPROIE

Hôtel
de Ville

PLACE
DE LA
FONTAINE

Caves
Peinctes

RUE DU CHÂTEAU

RUE VOLTAIRE

PLACE DU
GÉNÉRAL
DE GAULLE

RUE DU COMMERCE

RUE ÉMILE HÉBERT

RUE DU GRENIER À SEL

RUE CANOT

QUAI DE L'ÎLE SONNANTE

Île de Tours

QUAI DANTON

River Vienne

PLACE DE
LA VICTOIRE
DE VERDUN

RUE JEANNE D'ARC

Château
Logis Royal

AVENUE FRANÇOIS MITTERRAND

Musée d'Art et
d'Histoire de Chinon

St-Maurice

RUE HAUTE SAINT-MAURICE

QUAI CHARLES VII

RUE PARMENTIER

Maison de
la Rivière

AVENUE FRANÇOIS MITTERRAND

QUAI PASTEUR

▲ Tours

N

0   100 m

Diderot 7 rue Diderot ☎02.47.93.18.87, ⓦ www
.hoteldiderot.com. Solidly bourgeois hotel with an
old-fashioned welcome in a venerable town house.
Has some grand old rooms with antique furnishings
in the main building, and some brighter modern
ones in the annexe. ❸–❹
De France 47–49 place du Général-de-Gaulle
☎02.47.93.33.91, ⓦwww.bestwestern.com/fr/hotel
defrancechinon. Historic hotel overlooking the leafy
main square. Rooms are attractive and cosy, with big
comfy beds, beams and exposed stone walls. ❹

Le Plantagenêt 12 place Jeanne-d'Arc
☎02.47.93.36.92, ⓦwww.hotel-plantagenet.com.
Decent, welcoming two-star hotel on the large
market square on the eastern edge of town.
Rooms in the main, nineteenth-century house are
pleasantly decorated; those in the garden annexe
are characterless but have a/c. Family rooms
available. ❸
La Treille 4 place Jeanne-d'Arc ☎02.47.93.07.71.
Tiny, spartan and full of character, with four basic
rooms shoe-horned into an ancient building. ❷

The Town

A fortress of one kind or another existed at Chinon from the Stone Age until
the time of Louis XIV, the age of the most recent of its ruins. It was a favourite
residence of Henry Plantagenet, who held title to it long before he inherited
the throne of England. He added a new castle to the first medieval fortress on
the site, built by his ancestor Foulques Nerra, and died here, crying vengeance
on his son Richard, who had treacherously allied himself with the French king
Philippe-Auguste. Henry's youngest son, John, with no English inheritance,
stayed in Chinon off and on but after a year's siege in 1204–05, Philippe-
Auguste finally took the castle and put an end to the Plantagenet rule over
Touraine and Anjou.

Over two hundred years later, Chinon was one of the few places where the
Dauphin Charles, later Charles VII, could safely stay while Henry V of England
held Paris and the title to the French throne. Charles's situation changed with
the arrival here in 1429 of Joan of Arc from Domrémy in Lorraine, who
was able to talk her way into meeting him. The usual story – as depicted in
a tapestry on display on the site – is that as Joan entered the great hall, the
Dauphin remained hidden anonymously among the assembled nobles, as a test,
but that Joan picked him out straight away. Joan herself told a different story,
claiming that an angel had appeared before the court, bearing a crown. Either
way, it is clear that she begged him to allow her to rally her army against the
English. To the horror of the courtiers, Charles said yes.

Today, the **château** (currently daily, though times may vary during ongoing
works: April–Sept 9am–7pm; Oct–March 9.30–11.30am & 2–5.30pm; €3) is
little more than a ring of tumbledown walls and broken towers, and probably
better admired from the outside. The scene of Joan's encounter, the **Logis
Royal**, is being partially rebuilt under a new roof, with works expected to
continue at least until mid-2009. Access is permitted throughout, however, so
you will be able to watch traditional artisans at work, and an exhibition will
explain the techniques involved.

Below, the medieval streets with their half-timbered and sculpted town
houses are pleasant enough to wander through, or you could duck into one of
the town's low-key museums – but avoid the tacky wine- and barrel-making
Musée du Vin. The **Musée d'Art et d'Histoire de Chinon**, 44 rue Haute
St-Maurice (June–Sept daily 10.30am–12.30pm & 2–6pm; Oct–May Mon–Fri
2.15–6pm; €3), has some diverting oddments of sculpture, pottery and paintings
related to the town's history. The **Maison de la Rivière**, on the riverbank at
12 quai Pasteur (July & Aug Tues–Fri 10am–12.30pm & 2–5.30pm, Sat & Sun
3–5.30pm; €3; ☎02.47.93.21.34, ⓦwww.cpie-val-de-loire.org), displays models
of the many kinds of Loire river vessels, and on weekend afternoons in summer
you can take a short river trip on a traditional *fûtreau* or *toue* (€6); staff also lead

The troglodyte saint

A rewarding excursion out of Chinon starts along the road that leads east through town from rue Jean-Jacques-Rousseau, passing the Romanesque church of **St-Mexme** and then continuing along the cliffs past numerous **troglodyte dwellings**, some of which are still inhabited. After a kilometre or so the path runs out at the **Chapelle Ste-Radegonde**, a rock-cut church which is part of a complex of cave dwellings in which St Radegonde lived with her followers. The sixth-century German princess renounced the world and her husband – probably not a great sacrifice, since he eventually murdered her brother – in order to devote her life to God. The chapel's guardian has lived in the troglodyte home next door for nearly thirty years and often takes visitors into the chapel and caves behind – check with the tourist office in advance, or ask politely.

regular guided nature walks. Though it's better with a good meal, if you want to try a glass of Chinon you could visit the **Caves Peinctes**, off rue Voltaire, a deep cellar carved out of the rock where a fancy local winegrowers' guild runs **tastings** (July to mid-Sept daily except Mon 11am, 3pm, 4.30pm & 6pm; €3). The name of the *cave* supposedly derives from Rabelais, who was born at the manor farm of **La Devinière**, 6km southwest of town, where there's a good but rather dry museum. An antiques and flea market takes place every third Sunday of the month, while regular **market day** is Thursday.

Eating and drinking

Chinon's main square, place du Général-de-Gaulle, is enticingly filled with outdoor tables. Among the **restaurants** on the square, *Au Chapeau Rouge* (☎02.47.98.08.08) serves top-quality regional cuisine with menus from €26, while the *Café des Arts* offers reliable and reasonably priced brasserie fare. A more intimate square a short walk west, place de la Victoire de Verdun, conceals a good, homely restaurant, *La Bonne France* (☎02.47.98.01.34; closed Thurs evening & Wed). The cosy and old-fashioned *Les Années 30*. 78 rue Voltaire (☎02.47.93.37.18), has some adventurous dishes on its menus (€23 and €36). If you're in the mood for some local fish, you're unlikely to be disappointed by *L'Océanic* at 13 rue Rabelais (☎02.47.93.44.55; closed Sun dinner). Chinon is not overburdened with places to drink, though *Le Café Français* (37 place Général de Gaulle, ☎02.47.93.32.78) is a reasonably traditional option.

Forêt de Chinon

Northeast of Chinon, the elevated terrain of the *landes* is covered by the ancient **Forêt de Chinon**, which makes for great cycling or walking territory. If you want to **stay** in the area, there's a good *chambres d'hôte* near Rigny-Ussé (see p.481). Just outside St-Benoît-la-Forêt, the village in the heart of the forest, is a woodland adventure park, **Saint-Benoît Aventure** (Easter school holidays daily 1.30–7pm; May & June Sat & Sun 10am–7pm; July & Aug daily 10am–8pm; Sept & Oct Sat & Sun 1.30–7pm; adults €18, children aged 5–8 €8, aged 9–12 €12, aged 13–15 €15; ☎06.89.07.18.96, ⓦwww.stbenoitaventure.new.fr). It offers a chance to let kids off the leash – or rather attach them to it, in the form of an alarming aerial ropeway assault course that threads its way through the trees. There's also a mountain bike circuit and a nature walk.

Tavant

Sixteen kilometres southeast of Chinon, the village of **TAVANT** hides the great **St-Nicolas church** (March–Nov Wed–Sun 10am–12.30pm & 1.30–6pm, closed first Sun of every month; €3). The appeal lies in the twelfth-century, Romanesque **wall paintings** in its **crypt**, which rank among the finest in Europe. It's not clear why this crypt was so richly painted, as it hasn't been identified with any major relic cult or tomb. It's thought that the entire structure, inside and out, would once have been painted in bright colours, but today just fragments survive in the upper church, as well as a giant figure of Christ in Majesty on the half-dome of the apse. If the chapel isn't open when you arrive, ask for the guardian at the nearby *mairie*.

Saumur and around

SAUMUR is a civilized town notable for two things in particular, the excellent sparkling wine (some would say as good as Champagne) and the wealth of aristocratic military associations, based on its status as home to the French Cavalry Academy and its successor, the Armoured Corps Academy.

The stretch of the Loire from Chinon to Angers, which passes through Saumur, is particularly lovely, with the bizarre added draw of **troglodyte dwellings** carved out of the cliffs. The land on the south bank, under grapes and sunflowers, gradually rises away from the river, with long-inactive windmills still standing. Across the water cows graze in wooded pastures.

Arrival and information

Saumur spreads along both banks of the Loire and over the small Île d'Offard in the middle of the river too. Arriving at the **gare SNCF**, you'll find yourself on the north bank: turn right onto avenue David-d'Angers and either take bus #30 to the centre or cross the bridge to the island on foot. From the island the old **Pont Cessart** leads across to the main part of the town on the south bank, where you'll find the **gare routière**, a couple of blocks west of the bridge on place St-Nicolas, and the **tourist office**, next to the bridge on place de la Bilange (mid-May to mid-Oct Mon–Sat 9.15am–7pm, Sun 10.30am–5.30pm; mid-Oct to mid-May Mon–Sat 9.15am–12.30pm & 2–6pm, Sun 10am–noon; ☎02.41.40.20.60, ⓦwww.saumur-tourisme.com). The **old quarter**, around St-Pierre and the castle, lies immediately behind the Hôtel de Ville, on the riverbank 100m east of the bridge.

Accommodation

Accommodation in Saumur is mostly of nondescript quality and overpriced, with one very notable exception.

Anne d'Anjou 32 quai Mayaud ☎02.41.67.30.30, ⓦwww.hotel-anneanjou.com. Comfortable hotel, with a wide range of attractively decorated, if uniform, rooms in a grand, eighteenth-century listed building. ❺
La Bouère-Salée rue Grange-Couronne ☎02.41.67.38.85, ⓦwww.ifrance.com/labouere. Delightful bed and breakfast in a handsome nineteenth-century town house, though it's two

blocks north of the train station, on the far side of the river from the historic centre. ❸
Camping de l'Île d'Offard rue de Verden, Île d'Offard ☎02.41.40.30.00, ⓦwww.cvtloisirs.com. Big, well-run site right next door to the hostel.
🏃 **Chateau de Verrieres** 53 rue Alsace, ☎02.41.38.05.15, ⓦwww.chateau -verrieres.com. One of the finest buildings in the town is given over to this exceptional bed and

breakfast, with the friendly and dynamic owners dedicated to making your stay a special one. The rooms are ornate and lavish, the atmosphere luxurious. No restaurant, but meals are prepared for groups by special request. ❽

Cristal 10–12 place de la République ☎02.41.51.09.54, ⓦwww.cristal-hotel.fr. One of the nicer hotels in town, with a great situation on the riverfront, and friendly proprietors. Rooms on the side street can be noisy, but those with river or château views are usually fine. Some inexpensive attic rooms are also available. ❷–❸

Hostel rue de Verden, Île d'Offard ☎02.41.40.30.00, ⓦwww.hebergement-international-saumur.com. Large hostel at the east end of the island with laundry facilities, swimming-pool access and views

of the château. Reception 9am–noon & 2–7pm. Boat and bike hire available. Closed Nov–Feb.

De Londres ☎02.41.51.23.98, ⓦwww.lelondres .com. This sprawling but comfortable old town-centre hotel has been spotlessly renovated in recent years, but retains some period charm. ❸

St-Pierre 3 rue Haute-St-Pierre ☎02.41.50.33.00, ⓦwww.saintpierresaumur.com. Charming boutique hotel, slightly in need of updating. The main appeal lies in the convenient and picturesque location; the rooms remain fairly ordinary. ❺–❼

Le Volney 1 rue Volney ☎02.41.51.25.41, ⓦwww.levolney.com. This simple, budget hotel on the south side of town is a bit tired round the edges, but has friendly management and some inexpensive but cosy little rooms under the roof. ❷

The Town

Set high above town, Saumur's impressive **château** (interior closed for restoration works; exterior daily except Tues 10am–1pm & 2–5.30pm; €2) may seem oddly familiar, but then its famous depiction in *Les Très Riches Heures du Duc de Berry*, the most celebrated of all the medieval illuminated prayer books, is reproduced all over the region. It was largely built in the latter half of the fourteenth century by Louis I, Duc d'Anjou, who wanted to compete with his brothers Jean de Berry and Charles V. The threat of marauding bands of English soldiers made the masons work flat out – they weren't even allowed to stop for feast days. The château has been closed since April 2001, when a huge chunk of the star-shaped outer fortifications collapsed down the hill towards the river. In the aftermath, the alarmed authorities decided to embark on a major renovation programme, which looks likely to continue until at least mid-2009. Until works are complete, large parts of the interior will remain closed to visitors, including the formerly excellent Musée des Arts Décoratifs and Musée du Cheval.

Down by the public gardens south of the château, Saumur's oldest church, **Notre-Dame de Nantilly** (daily 9am–6pm), houses a large tapestry collection in its Romanesque nave. The original Gothic **church of St Pierre**, in the centre of the old town (daily 9am–noon & 2–5pm), hides behind a Counter-Reformation facade built as part of the church's efforts to overawe its persistently Protestant population – Louise de Bourbon, abbess of Fontevraud, called the town a "second Geneva", horrified at the thought that Saumur might become a similarly radical Calvinist power-base.

For relief from military and ecclesiastical history, try a glass of the famous Saumur *méthode champenoise* wines at the **Maison du Vin** on quai Lucien-Gautier (April–Sept Mon 2–7pm, Tues–Sat 9am–1pm & 2–7pm, Sun 9.30am–1pm; Oct–March Tues–Sat 10.30am–12.30pm & 2–6pm; ⓦwww.interloire.com), which can also provide addresses of wine-growers and *caves* that you can visit. Alternatively, make for the Caves des Vignerons at St-Cyr-en-Bourg (☎02.41.53.06.06), a short train hop south of Saumur and near the station, where there are kilometres of cellars.

Beyond the town centre

Saumur's cavalry traditions are displayed in all their glory at the **École Nationale d'Équitation**, in St-Hilaire-St-Florent, a suburb to the east of the centre (if you don't have your own transport, take bus #31 from the south end

▲ Grape harvest, Saumur

of rue Franklin-Roosevelt to the "Alouette" stop, then continue down the route de Marson, turning right at the signpost; it's a walk of a little over 1km). The Riding School (April–Sept Mon 2–6pm, Tues–Fri 9am–6pm, Sat 9am–12.30pm; €8) provides guided tours in which you can watch training sessions (mornings are best) and view the stables. Displays of dressage and anachronistic battle manoeuvres by the crackshot Cadre Noir, the former cavalry trainers, are regular events (programme details from the tourist office or online at Ⓦ www .cadrenoir.fr). The history of the tank – traditionally considered as cavalry not infantry – is covered in the separate **Musée des Blindés**, at 1043 rue Fricotelle, to the southeast of the centre (daily: May–Sept 9.30am–6.30pm; Oct–April 10am–5pm; €6).

The main activity in the suburb of St-Hilaire-St-Florent, especially along the main stretch of the riverside road, along rue Ackerman and rue Leopold-Palustre, is making **sparkling wine**. You can visit the impressive rock-carved cellars of any of Ackerman-Laurance, Bouvet-Ladubay, Langlois-Château, Gratien & Meyer, Louis de Grenelle and Veuve Amiot. Choosing between them is a matter of personal taste, and possibly a question of opening hours, though most are open all day every day throughout the warmer months (generally 10am–6pm, though most close for a couple of hours at lunchtime out of season). Buy a couple of bottles to take away, if you can, and you'll probably be impressed by both the taste and the price difference between the inexpensive wine and Champagne.

Eating and drinking

There are several reasonably inexpensive places around place St-Pierre, many of which offer a chance to enjoy a glass of sparkling Saumur brut at an outside table.

Les Ardilliers 35 rue Rabelais ☎ 02.41.67.12.86. Relaxed, contemporary bistro-restaurant on the way out towards Notre-Dame des Ardilliers. There's a sleek bar area, a pleasant summer terrace and some modern twists on the classic dishes – three fish and three meat, every day. Menus €15–30; closed Tues lunch, Sun evening & Mon.

Auberge Reine de Sicile 71 rue Waldeck-Rousseau Île d'Offard. ☎ 02.41.67.30.48. Over the bridge, on the Île d'Offard, with an atmospherically ancient dining room. Stick to the excellent local fish, and you're unlikely to be disappointed. Menus at €19 and €33; closed Mon & Sun evening. plus for the last week in Aug and first week in Sept.

Les Forges de St-Pierre 1 place St-Pierre ☎ 02.41.38.21.79. Specializing in grilled meats, this is one of the busy, tourist-oriented but relatively good value restaurants on the atmospheric old square. Steaks around €10–15; closed Tues evening & Sun.

Le Grand Bleu 6 rue du Marché ☎ 02.41.67.41.83. Specializes in sea fish – Brittany is, after all, not so

far away. Pleasant situation on a miniature square, with outside seating in summer. Menus €14–26; closed Wed.

Les Ménéstrels At the *Hôtel Anne d'Anjou*, 32 quai Mayaud ☎ 02.41.67.71.10. Saumur's best place for serious, formal gastronomy, though the stone walls and exposed beams add a note of rustic relaxation. Be wary of the *menu du jour*, which is a pale shadow of some of the more interesting things offered on the à la carte menu.

The Abbaye de Fontevraud

At the heart of the stunning Romanesque complex of the **Abbaye de Fontevraud** (daily: June–Sept 9am–6.30pm; Oct–May 10am–5.30pm; €6.50; ☎ 02.41.51.73.52, ⓦ www.abbaye-fontevraud.com), 13km southeast of Saumur, are the tombs of the Plantagenet royal family, eerily lifelike works of funereal art that powerfully evoke the historical bonds between England and France. A religious community was established in around 1100 as both a nunnery and a monastery with an abbess in charge – an unconventional move, even if the post was filled solely by queens and princesses. The remaining buildings date from the twelfth century and are immense, built as they were to house and separate not only the nuns and monks but also the sick, lepers and repentant prostitutes. There were originally five separate institutions, of which three still stand in graceful Romanesque solidity. Used as a prison from the Revolution until 1963, it was an inspiration for the writer Jean Genet, whose book *Miracle of the Rose* was partly based on the recollections of a prisoner incarcerated here.

The **abbey church** is an impressive space, not least for the four tombstone effigies: Henry II, his wife Eleanor of Aquitaine, who died here, their son Richard the Lionheart and daughter-in-law Isabelle of Angoulême, King John's queen. Carved as they were at the time of their deaths, the figures are eerily lifelike. The strange domed roof, the great cream-coloured columns of the choir and the graceful capitals of the nave add to the atmosphere. Elsewhere in the complex you can explore the magnificent **cloisters**, the **chapterhouse**, decorated with sixteenth-century murals, and the vast **refectory**. All the cooking for the religious community, which would have numbered several hundred, was done in the – now perfectly restored – Romanesque **kitchen**, an octagonal building as extraordinary from the outside (with its 21 spiky chimneys) as it is from within.

The abbey is now the **Centre Culturel de l'Ouest** (CCO), the cultural centre for western France, and one of Europe's most important centres of medieval archeology, and is used for a great many activities, from concerts to lectures, art exhibitions and theatre. Programme details are available at the abbey or from the Saumur tourist office. **Bus** #1 runs from Saumur to Fontevraud, but it's not a frequent service and the timetable varies throughout the year, so check with the tourist office in advance.

Angers and around

ANGERS, capital of the ancient county of Anjou, is an oddly depressing place. Although undoubtedly majestic, dominated by its monolithic château, the town seems a less welcoming and friendly destination that many others around it. The main reason for coming here is to see its two stunning **tapestry** series, the fourteenth-century *Apocalypse* and the twentieth-century *Le Chant du Monde*.

Arrival and information

The **gare SNCF** is south of the centre. Bus #6 (#25 on Sun) makes the 1km journey to the tourist office and château, while buses #1 and #16 will take you to central place du Railliement, which is roughly twice as far away; a flat-rate **bus** ticket, which you can buy on board, costs €1.10. The **gare routière** is down by the river, just past the Pont de Verdun on place Molière. The main **tourist office** is on place Kennedy, facing the château (May–Sept Mon–Sat 9am–7pm, Sun 10am–6pm; Oct–April Mon 2–6pm, Tues–Sat 9am–6pm, Sun 10am–1pm; ℡02.41.23.50.00, ⓦwww.angersloiretourisme.com); it sells a **city pass** (€14 for 24 hours, €21 for 48), which allows access to the tapestries as well as the city's museums and galleries.

Accommodation

There's a wide range of **accommodation** on offer, and finding a room shouldn't present too many problems, though it's still wise to book ahead in summer.

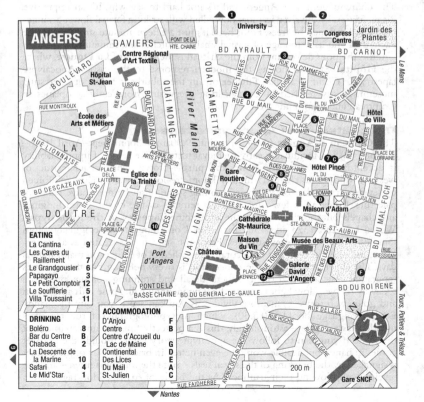

ANGERS

EATING

La Cantina	9
Les Caves du Railliement	7
Le Grandgousier	6
Papagayo	3
Le Petit Comptoir	12
Le Soufflerie	5
Villa Toussaint	11

DRINKING

Boléro	8
Bar du Centre	B
Chabada	2
La Descente de la Marine	10
Safari	4
Le Mid'Star	1

ACCOMMODATION

D'Anjou	F
Centre	B
Centre d'Accueil du Lac de Maine	G
Continental	D
Des Lices	E
Du Mail	A
St-Julien	C

D'Anjou 1 blvd du Maréchal Foch ℡ 02.41.21.12.11, ⍟ www.hoteldanjou.fr. An adequate Best Western option, with all the usual comforts and mod cons of the chain. ❺
Centre 12 rue St-Laud ℡ 02.41.87.45.07. Reasonably comfortable hotel above a lively bar. Double-glazing keeps out the worst of the street noise. ❸
Centre d'Accueil du Lac de Maine 49 av du Lac de Maine ℡ 02.41.22.32.10, ⍟ www .lacdemaine.fr. Rather swish hostel-style accommodation, complete with extensive sports facilities, a 20min ride southwest of the town; bus #6 (bus #11 from 7.30pm–midnight, bus #26 on Sun) either from the train station or bd Général-de-Gaulle. Single rooms €35, dorms €17. There's also a campsite here (℡ 02.41.73.05.03, ✉ camping@lacdemaine.fr; closed Oct–March), agreeably situated next to the lake.

Continental 12–14 rue Louis-de-Romain ℡ 02.41.86.94.94, ⍟ www.hotellecontinental.com. Well-equipped and well-run hotel with good service and a/c. Gets busy during the week with a mainly business crowd. ❹
Des Lices 25 rue des Lices ℡ 02.41.87.44.10. A real bargain in a balustraded town house on a distinctly posh, town-centre street. Closed Aug 1–15. ❷
🏃 **Du Mail** 8 rue des Ursules ℡ 02.41.25.05.25, ⍟ www.hotel-du-mail.com. The best hotel in the town by miles, with comfortable, inexpensive rooms, a friendly welcome, a beautiful situation and a good breakfast. Parking available. ❹
St-Julien 9 place du Ralliement ℡ 02.41.88.41.62, ⍟ www.hotelsaintjulien.com. Large hotel right in the centre of the city, offering a good spread of modernized rooms. Some of the pretty little ones under the roof have views over town. ❹

The City

The **château** dominates Angers, and it's not hard to see why. It's an impressive, sturdy fortress by the river, its moat now filled with striking formal flower arrangements and softened by trees. From here, it's just a fifteen-minute stroll east to the **cathedral** and its entourage of several smaller churches and museums.

Across the pont de Verdun from the château is the suburb of **La Doutre**, where the **Hôpital St-Jean** houses the modern response to the castle's Apocalypse tapestry, *Le Chant du Monde*. Further out in the suburbs is a rash of interesting museums, easily reached by bus, exalting everything from early aeroplanes to Cointreau and communication methods.

The château and Apocalypse tapestry

The **Château d'Angers** (daily: May–Aug 9.30am–6.30pm; Sept–April 10am–5.30pm; €8) is a formidable early medieval fortress. The sense of impregnability is accentuated by its dark stone, the purple-brown schist characteristic of western Anjou. The château's mighty kilometre-long curtain wall is reinforced by seventeen circular towers, their brooding stone offset by decorative bands of pale tufa. Inside are a few miscellaneous remains of the counts' royal lodgings and chapels, but the chief focus is the astonishing **Tapestry of the Apocalypse**. Woven between 1373 and 1382 for Louis I of Anjou, it was originally 140m long, of which 100m now survives. From the start, it was treated as a masterpiece, and only brought out to decorate the cathedral of Angers on major festival days. The sheer grandeur of the conception is overwhelming but the tapestry's reputation rests as much on its superb detail and stunning colours, preserved today by the very low light levels in the long viewing hall. These reds and greens and golds were once even more vivid – as you can see if you buy the handy English-language booklet (€5.30), which uses photographs of the tapestry's unfaded reverse side – astonishingly, this is a perfectly finished mirror-image of the front. If you plan to follow the apocalypse story right through, the booklet comes in handy but a Bible would be even better. In brief: the Day of Judgement is signalled by the breaking of the seven seals – note the four horsemen – and the seven angels blowing their trumpets. As the battle of Armageddon rages, Satan appears first as a seven-headed red dragon, then as the seven-headed lion-like Beast. The holy forces break the seven vials of plagues, whereupon the Whore of Babylon appears mounted on the Beast. She is challenged by the Word of God, seen riding a galloping horse, who chases the hordes of Satan into the lake of fire, allowing the establishment of the heavenly Jerusalem. It's spellbinding, operatic stuff, and will appeal whatever your religious views.

Those feeling in need of a drink can head straight out of the castle and into the **Maison du Vin de l'Anjou**, 5bis place Kennedy (May–Sept Tues–Sat 9am–1pm & 3–6.30pm, Sun 9am–1pm; Oct–April Tues–Sat 9.30am–1pm & 3–6.30pm), where the helpful staff will offer you wine to taste before you buy, and can provide lists of wine-growers to visit.

The cathedral and around

The most dramatic approach to the **Cathédrale St-Maurice** is via the quayside, from where a long flight of steps leads straight up to the mid-twelfth-century portal – which shows another version of the apocalypse. Built in the 1150s and 1160s, the cathedral exemplifies the Plantagenet style – in fact, it's probably the earliest example in France of this influential architectural development. The interior is somewhat prosaic, but the fifteenth-century windows are impressive.

Arguably the greatest stoneworks in Angers are the creations of the famous local sculptor David d'Angers (1788–1856), whose Calvary adorns the cathedral. His great civic commissions can be seen all over France, but these large-scale marbles and bronzes are almost all copies of the smaller plaster of Paris works created by the artist himself. It's mostly these plaster originals that are exhibited in the **Galerie David d'Angers**, 37bis rue Toussaint (June–Sept daily 10am–7pm; Oct–May Tues–Sun 10am–noon & 2–6pm; €4), set impressively in the glazed-over nave of a ruined thirteenth-century church, the **Église Toussaint**.

The **Musée des Beaux-Arts**, 10 rue du Musée (June–Sept daily 10am–7pm; Oct–May Tues–Sun 1–6pm; €4), is housed in the **Logis Barrault**, a proudly decorated mansion built by a wealthy late fifteenth-century mayor. Years of extensive restoration have cleaned up – and in some places entirely remade – the flamboyant Gothic stone carving. Eighteenth- and nineteenth-century paintings dominate the collection, with works by Watteau, Chardin and Fragonard, as well as Ingres' operatic *Paolo et Francesca* – the same subject depicted by Rodin in *The Kiss* – and a small collection devoted to Boucher's *Génie des Arts*.

La Doutre

The district facing the château across the Maine is known as **La Doutre** (literally, "the other side"), and still has a few mansions and houses dating from the medieval period, despite redevelopment over the years.

In the north of the area, a short way from the Pont de la Haute-Chaine (and just under 2km from the château), the **Hôpital St-Jean**, 4 boulevard Arago, was built by Henry Plantagenet in 1174 as a hospital for the poor, a function it continued to fulfil until 1854. Today it houses the **Musée Jean Lurçat et de la Tapisserie Contemporaine** (June–Sept daily 10am–7pm; Oct–May Tues–Sun 10am–noon & 2–6pm; €4), which contains the city's great twentieth-century tapestry, **Le Chant du Monde**. The tapestry sequence was designed by Jean Lurçat in 1957 in response to the Apocalypse tapestry, though he died nine years later, before its completion. It hangs in a vast vaulted space, the original ward for the sick, or Salle des Malades. The first four tapestries deal with *La Grande Menace*, the threat of nuclear war: first the bomb itself; then *Hiroshima Man*, flayed and burnt with the broken symbols of belief dropping from him; then the collective massacre of the *Great Charnel House*; and the last dying rose falling with the post-Holocaust ash through black space – the *End of Everything*. From then on, the tapestries celebrate the joys of life: *Man in Glory in Peace*; *Water and Fire*; *Champagne* – "that blissful ejaculation", according to Lurçat; *Conquest of Space*; *Poetry*; and *Sacred Ornaments*. Subject matter and treatment are intense, and the setting helps: it's a huge echoey space, with rows of columns supporting soaring Angevin vaulting. The artist's own commentary is available in English. The Romanesque cloisters at the back, with their graceful double columns, are also worth a peek.

There are more modern tapestries in the building adjoining the Salle des Malades, where the collection is built up around the donation by Lurçat's widow of several of his paintings, ceramics and tapestries, along with the highly tactile but more muted abstract tapestries of Thomas Gleb, who died in Angers in 1991, and Josep Grau Garriga. With four local *ateliers*, Angers is a leading centre for contemporary tapestry, and the neighbouring **Centre Régional d'Art Textile**, 3 boulevard Daviers (Mon–Fri 10am–noon & 2–4pm), can put you in touch with local artists and let you know where to find private exhibitions.

South of the Hôpital St-Jean, on La Doutre's central square, place de la Laiterie, the ancient buildings of the **Abbaye de Ronceray** are now occupied by one of France's elite *grandes écoles*, the **École des Arts et Métiers**, which trains the leading students of aerospace technology, among others. The abbey church is used to mount art exhibitions, worth visiting just to see the Romanesque galleries of the old abbey and admire their beautiful murals. When there's no exhibition, you can only visit as part of the tourist office's weekly tour of La Doutre. Inside the adjacent twelfth-century **Église de la Trinité**, an exquisite Renaissance wooden spiral staircase fails to mask a great piece of medieval bodging used to fit the wall of the church around a part of the abbey that juts into it.

Eating

The streets around place du Ralliement and place Romain have a wide variety of **cafés** and **restaurants**, many of them very inexpensive.

La Cantina 9 rue de l'Oisellerie ☏02.41.87.36.34. Relaxed café-bistro serving southwestern dishes such as *magret de canard* (duck steak). Good value for lunch, with straightforward fish and meat *plats* and salads for around €15. Closed Mon.

Les Caves du Ralliement 9 place du Ralliement ☏02.41.88.47.77. Busy brasserie underneath the posh and well-regarded *Provence Caffè*. Good for inexpensive *moules*- or *steak-frites* at lunchtime, and oysters or eels with a glass of wine in the evening, sitting at an outside table on the square. Closed Mon evening.

Le Grandgousier 7 rue St-Laud ☏02.41.87.81.47. Serves meats grilled on the wood fire, complemented by so-so local wines, which are included in the price of the €15 and €24 menus. Closed Sun.

Papagayo 44 bd Ayrault ☏02.41.87.03.35. Friendly bar-bistro near the university campus, with a great atmosphere during term-time and a conservatory room for summer. Serves decent, inexpensive traditional French food. Closed Mon lunch, Sat lunch & Sun.

🏃 **Le Petit Comptoir** 40 rue David d'Angers ☏02.41.88.81.57. Impressive restaurant specializing in local dishes with both a traditional and modernist focus; the €17 lunch menu is excellent value. Closed Mon.

Le Soufflerie 8 place Pilori ☏02.41.87.45.32. Popular café specializing in soufflés, both large and savoury (at around €11) and small and sweet (around €8). Closed Sun, Mon & 4 weeks in July/Aug.

Villa Toussaint 43 rue Toussaint ☏02.41.88.15.64. Currently the hippest place in town, specializing in sushi and seafood. The leafy terrace is a lovely spot in summer. Closed Sun.

Drinking and nightlife

Late-opening **bars** congregate around rue St-Laud: *Bar du Centre*, below *Hôtel Centre* is full of students, and there's a cluster of popular Irish-type places at the bottom end of the road, around place Romain. Just beyond the square, *Safari*,

23 rue du Mail (closed Mon), is a trendy bar with DJs playing salsa, reggae or hip-hop. Over in La Doutre, *La Descente de la Marine*, at 28 quai des Carmes, is an old-time bar with a strong nautical flavour, attracting lots of students and young people who come down for an outdoor, early evening *apéro* on the quay. Among Angers' numerous **clubs**, *Boléro*, 38 rue St-Laud, is popular and central, with an unpretentious, sometimes cheesy music policy. *Le Mid'Star*, 25 quai Félix-Faure, is the biggest and best-known clubbing venue, with a more serious playlist. *Chabada*, 56 boulevard du Doyenné, in the Monplaisir quarter just north of St-Serge (take a taxi), puts on live music.

Listings

Bike hire A desk in the tourist office hires out bikes.

Boat hire Numerous companies hire out canoes and run guided kayak trips on the five rivers in the vicinity of Angers. Try: Canoe Kayak Club d'Angers, 75 av du lac de Maine (on the Maine and Lac de Maine) ☎02.41.72.07.04, ⓦ ckcac.free.fr; Club Nautique d'Écouflant, rue de l'île St-Aubin, Écouflant (Sarthe, Mayenne, Loire, Maine) ☎02.41.34.56.38, ⓦ www.kayakecouflant.com; and Club de Canoe Kayak les Ponts de Cé, 30 rue Maximin-Gelineau, Les Ponts de Cé (on the Loire) ☎02.41.44.65.15, ⓦ www.canoelespontsdece .new.fr. The tourist office has details of more sedate trips on sightseeing boats.

Car hire Anjou Auto Location, 100 av Victor-Chatenay ☎02.41.18.59.18; Budget 14 rue Denis-Papin ☎02.41.24.96.18; Europcar, 10 rue Fulton ☎02.41.24.05.89; Hertz, place de la Gare ☎02.41.88.15.16.

Emergencies Ambulance ☎15; Centre Hospitalier, 4 rue Larrey (☎02.41.35.36.37); for

late-night pharmacies, phone the police on ☎02.41.57.52.00.

Festivals At the end of May, the Tour de Scènes festival (ⓦ www.tourdescenes.com) brings rock and world music acts to the city centre for four days of concerts. The Festival Angers l'Été features jazz and world music gigs in the atmospheric Cloître Toussaint, the cloisters behind the Galerie David d'Angers, on Tues & Thurs evenings throughout July and Aug; book through the tourist office. In early Sept, the festival Les Accroche Coeurs brings a host of theatrical companies, musicians and street performers for three days of surreal entertainment.

Internet Go online at 48 rue Plantagenêt, near Les Halles; 37 rue Bressigny, near bd Foch; and 25 rue de la Roë, just east of place de la République.

Market There's a flower market on place Leclerc and an organic produce market on rue Saint-Laud, both on Sat.

Police Commissariat, 15 rue Dupetit-Thouars ☎02.41.66.86.35.

Around Angers

Angers can be a good base, as long as you have your own transport. You can easily reach the château of **Le Plessis-Bourré** near Ecuillé (impossible to get to by public transport), 17km to the north or, for a more accessible glimpse of a real monster of a mansion, head for the **Château de Serrant**, just outside St-Georges-sur-Loire, on bus routes #7 and #18 from Angers.

Château du Plessis-Bourré

Five years' work at the end of the fifteenth century produced the fortress of **Le Plessis-Bourré** (guided tours only: mid-Feb to end March, Oct & Nov daily except Wed 2–6pm; April–June & Sept Mon, Tues & Fri–Sun 10am–noon & 2–6pm; Thurs 2–6pm; July & Aug daily 10am–6pm; closed Jan to mid-Feb & Dec; €10; ⓦ www.plessis-bourre.com), 17km north of Angers, between the Sarthe and Mayenne rivers. Despite the vast, full moat, spanned by an arched bridge with a still-functioning drawbridge, it was built as a luxurious residence rather than a defensive castle. The treasurer of France at the time, Jean Bourré, received important visitors here, among them Louis XI and Charles VIII.

Given the powerful, medieval exterior, the first three rooms on the ground floor are a surprise, being beautifully decorated and furnished in the Louis XVI, XV and Régence styles, respectively, though things revert to type in the Gothic Salle du Parlement. The highlight of the tour comes in the Salle des Gardes, just above, where the original, deeply coffered ceiling stems from Bourré's fashionable interest in alchemy. Every inch is painted with allegorical scenes: sixteen panels depict alchemical symbols such as the phoenix, the pregnant siren and the donkey singing Mass, while eight cartoon-like paintings come with morals attached – look out for "Chicheface", the hungry wolf that only eats faithful women, whose victim is supposed to be Jean Bourré's wife.

Château de Serrant

At the **Château de Serrant**, 15km west of Angers beside the N23 near **ST-GEORGES-SUR-LOIRE**, the combination of dark-brown schist and creamy tufa give a rather pleasant cake-like effect to the outside (guided tours only, departing on the hour; mid-March to June & Sept to mid-Nov daily except Tues 9.45am–noon & 2–5.15pm; July & Aug daily 9.45am–5.15pm; €9.50; @www.chateau-serrant.net). But with its heavy slate bell-shaped cupolas pressing down on massive towers, the exterior is grandiose rather than graceful. The building was begun in the sixteenth century and added to up until the eighteenth century. In 1755 it belonged to an Irishman, Francis Walsh, to whom Louis XV had given the title Count of Serrant as a reward for Walsh's help against the old enemy, the English. The Walsh family married into the ancient La Trémoille clan, whose descendants – via a Belgian offshoot – still own the château. The massive rooms of the interior are packed with all the trappings of old wealth. Much of the decor dates from the late nineteenth and early twentieth centuries, but it's tastefully – and expensively – done, and you are also shown the Renaissance staircase, the sombre private chapel designed by Mansart, a bedroom prepared for Napoleon (who only stopped here for a couple of hours), and the attractive vaulted kitchens.

Le Mans and around

LE MANS, the historic capital of the Maine region, is synonymous with its famous 24-hour car race in June. During the rest of the year, it's a much quieter place; what it lacks in obvious beauty it makes up for in historical background, being the favourite home of the Plantagenet family, the counts of Anjou, Touraine and Maine. The old quarter, in the shadow of the magnificent cathedral, is unusually well preserved, while outside town you can visit the serene Cistercian abbey of Epau and, of course, the racetrack, a must-see pilgrimage for petrolheads.

Arrival and information

The hub of Le Mans today is **place de la République**, beneath which, in the underground shopping centre, is the city **bus terminal**. At the time of writing, bus #16 ran between here and the **gare SNCF** via avenue Général-Leclerc, where the **gare routière** is located – a new tram system is to be up and running by early 2009. From place de la République, rue Bolton leads east into rue de l'Étoile, where the **tourist office** (July & Aug Mon–Sat 9am–6pm, Sun 10am–12.30pm & 2.30–5pm; Sept–June same hours except closed Sat noon–2pm and all day Sun; ☎02.43.28.17.22, @www.lemanstourisme.com) is situated. To hire a **bike**, make your way to the northern suburb of La-Chapelle-St-Aubin, where you'll find Veloland at 1 rue du Moulin-aux-Moines (℡02.43.51.16.00, Ⓦwww.veloland.com) – take bus #8 to its terminus, "Moulin aux Moines".

Accommodation

Unless your visit coincides with one of the big **racing events** during April, June or September – when hotel rates can quadruple – you should be able to find **accommodation** easily without having to book, though there's nothing very special to be found.

Chantecler 50 rue de la Pelouse ℡02.43.14.40.00, Ⓦwww.hotelchantecler.fr. Quiet, professionally run hotel, offering dull but well-fitted-out rooms and parking. ⑤

Le Flore 23 rue Maupertuis ℡02.43.81.27.55, Ⓔflorefjt@noos.fr. Mainly a workers' hostel, but reserves some beds for HI members. Has 24hr reception and a cheap canteen. The location is fairly central: take av du Général-de-Gaulle from place de la République, continue along av Bollée; rue Maupertuis is the third on the left; or catch the "Citadine" bus from the station or place de la République to stop "Flore". Beds €12.

Levasseur 5–7 bd René-Levasseur ℡02.43.39.61.61, Ⓔhotellevasseur@orange.fr. Well located just off place de la République, if rambling and functional in feel. Closed Aug. ④

Select 13 rue du Père-Mersenne, off av du Général-Leclerc ℡02.43.24.17.74. Clean and comfortable budget hotel – especially good value for families, which can have a room with a double bed and two bunks for under €50. ②

The City

The complicated web of the **old quarter** lies atop a minor hill above the River Sarthe, to the north of the central place de la République. Its medieval streets, a hotchpotch of intricate Renaissance stonework, medieval half-timbering, sculpted pillars and beams and grand classical facades, are still encircled by the original third- and fourth-century **Gallo-Roman walls**, supposedly the best preserved in Europe and running for several hundred metres. Steep, walled steps lead up from the river, and longer flights descend on the southern side of the enclosure, using old Gallo-Roman entrances. If intrigued, you can see pictures, maps and plans of the old quarter, Vieux Mans, plus examples of the city's ancient arts and crafts, in the rather dull **Musée de la Reine Bérengère** (Tues–Sun: May–Sept 10am–12.30pm & 2–6.30pm; Oct–April 2–6pm; €2.80, or €6 with Musée de Tessé), housed in a beautiful fifteenth-century construction on rue de la Reine-Bérengère. The **Maison des Deux-Amis**, opposite, gets its name for the carving of two men (the "two friends") supporting a coat of arms between the doors of nos. 18 and 20. Heading away from the cathedral, you enter the equally ancient **Grande Rue**.

The high ground of the old town has been sacred since ancient times, as testified by a strangely human, pink-tinted menhir now propped up against the southwest corner of the very impressive **Cathédrale St-Julien**, which crowns the hilltop. The nave of the cathedral was only just completed when Geoffroi Plantagenet, the count of Maine and Anjou, married Matilda, daughter of Henry I of England, in 1129, thus founding the English dynastic line. Inside, for all the power and measured beauty of this Romanesque structure, it's impossible not to be drawn towards the vertiginous High Gothic choir, filled with coloured light filtering through the stained-glass windows. At the easternmost end of the choir, the vault of the chapelle de la Vierge is painted with angels singing, dancing and playing medieval musical instruments.

In the 1850s a road was tunnelled under the old quarter – a slum at the time – helping to preserve its self-contained unity. On the north side of the quarter, the road tunnel comes out by an impressive **monument to Wilbur Wright**

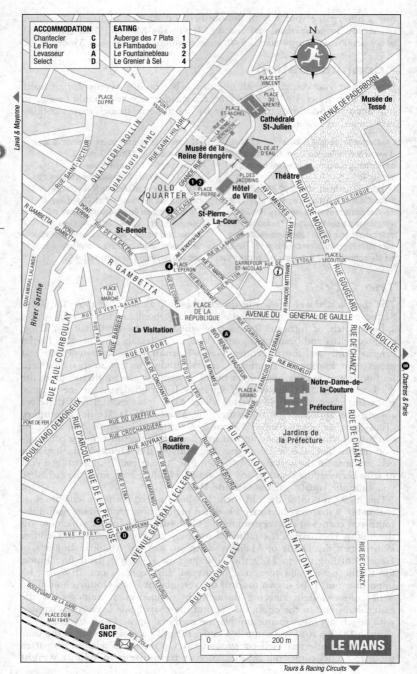

ACCOMMODATION
Chantecler   C
Le Flore   B
Levasseur   A
Select   D

EATING
Auberge des 7 Plats   1
Le Flambadou   3
Le Fountainebleau   2
Le Grenier à Sel   4

N

◄ Laval & Mayenne

PLACE ST-VINCENT

AVENUE DE PADERBORN

PLACE DU PRE

PLACE DU GRENTE

PLACE ST-MICHEL

Musée de Tessé

PONT YSSOIR

RUE SAINT-HILAIRE

RUE DE LA REINE BÉRENGÈRE

Cathédrale St-Julien

QUAI LEDRU ROLLIN

QUAI LOUIS BLANC

GRANDE RUE

Musée de la Reine Bérengère

PL DE JET D'EAU

RUE SAINT-VICTEUR

PL DES JACOBINS

Théâtre

AV P MENDES - FRANCE

RUE DU 33E MOBILES

RUE DU CIRQUE

R GAMBETTA

PONT PERRIN

RUE DE LA GALÈRE

OLD QUARTER

1 2

PLACE ST-PIERRE

St-Pierre-La-Cour

RUE F FLACEAU

3

RUE DES PANS DE GORRON

Hôtel de Ville

St-Benoît

PONT GAMBETTA

QUAI AMIRAL LALANDE

River Sarthe

R GAMBETTA

AVE DE PRÉFONTAINE LEON

RUE ST-MARTIN

RUE DE LA BARILLERIE

CARREFOUR ST-NICOLAS

RUE DE L'ÉTOILE

PLACE L. LECOUTEUX

RUE GOUGEARD

4

PLACE L'ÉPERON

RUE DU CORNET

RUE BONTEMPS

RUE BOLTON

RUE DE NICOLAS

AV FRANÇOIS MITTERRAND

i

PLACE DU MARCHÉ

RUE DU VERT-GALANT

PLACE DE LA RÉPUBLIQUE

AVENUE DU

GENERAL DE GAULLE

AV L BOLLÉE

Chartres & Paris ►

La Visitation

RUE BARBIER

RUE PASTEUR

A

RUE COURTHARDY

AVENUE FRANÇOIS MITTERRAND

RUE BERTHELOT

RUE DE CHANZY

RUE PAUL COURBOULAY

RUE DU PORT

RUE DES MINIMES

BVD RENÉ - LEVASSEUR

RUE DU DR LEROY

PLACE A BRIAND

Notre-Dame-de-la-Couture

Préfecture

RUE DE CHANZY

RUE DE CONSTANTINE

AVENUE

RUE NATIONALE

Jardins de la Préfecture

PONT DE FER

BOULEVARD DEMORIEUX

RUE D'ARCOLE

RUE DU GREFFIER

RUE CROCHARDIÈRE

RUE AUVRAY

Gare Routière

RUE DE RICHEBOURG

RUE DU CHANOINE LEFEBVRE

RUE DE WAGRAM

RUE DE LA PELOUSE

RUE D'IÉNA

RUE DE MARENGO

AVENUE GÉNÉRAL-LECLERC

RUE DE WAGRAM

RUE NATIONALE

RUE DE CHANZY

C

R P MERSENNE

RUE FOISY

D

RUE DE FLEURUS

RUE DU BOURG BÉLÉ

BOULEVARD DE LA GARE

PLACE DU 8 MAI 1945

Gare SNCF

BD E. ZOLA

0   200 m

LE MANS

Tours & Racing Circuits ▼

– who tested an early flying machine in Le Mans – which points you into place des Jacobins, the vantage point for St-Julien's double-tiered flying buttresses and apse. From here, you can walk northeast alongside the park to the **Musée de Tessé**, on avenue de Paderborn (July & Aug Tues–Sat 10am–12.30pm & 2–6.30pm; Sept–June Tues–Sat 9am–noon & 2–6pm, Sun 10am–noon & 2–6pm; €4 or €6 with Musée de la Reine Bérengère), where the highlight is an exquisite enamel portrait of Henry II's father, Geoffroi Le Bel, which was originally part of his tomb in the cathedral. Otherwise it's a mixed bag of paintings, furnishings and sculptures, while in the basement there's a full-scale reconstruction of the ancient Egyptian tomb of Queen Nefertari.

The modern centre of Le Mans is place de la République, bordered by a mixture of *belle époque* buildings and more modern office blocks, and the Baroque bulk of the **church of the Visitation**, built in 1730, with a balustrade inside designed by one of the sisters of the order.

On summer nights, the cathedral and various other buildings in the old town are illuminated in Le Mans' **son et lumière** show, called *La Nuit des Chimères*. The displays are free and take place daily, starting at 11pm in July and 10.30pm in August. The highlight is a parade of mythical monsters projected along the length of the Gallo-Roman walls.

Eating and drinking

In the centre of town, the **cafés** and **brasseries** on place de la République stay open till late, while on nearby place l'Éperon there's the best restaurant in town, ★ *Le Grenier à Sel* (☎02.43.23.26.30; closed Sun & Mon; menus

---

Le Mans racing

The first big race at Le Mans was in 1906, and two years later aviator **Wilbur Wright** took off here, remaining in the air for a record-breaking one hour and 31 minutes and 30 seconds. The first 24-hour car race was run as early as 1923, on the present 13.6-kilometre Sarthe circuit, with average speeds of 92kph (57mph) – these days, the drivers average around 210kph (130mph). The Sarthe circuit, on which the now world-renowned **24 Heures du Mans** car race takes place every year in mid-June, stretches south from the outskirts of the city, along ordinary roads. During the race weekend, you'll need a ticket to get anywhere near the circuit. These can be bought direct from the organizers at ⓦwww.lemans.org, or via the tourist office, and cost €61 for all three days, €25 for trial days (Fri & Sat), and €39 for race day, which is always on a Sunday. You'll need a separate ticket (€61–102) to get access to the grandstands, and be sure to book well in advance. Many enthusiasts' clubs and ticket agencies offer tour packages including accommodation – otherwise impossible to find at race times – and the crucial parking passes; try ⓦwww.clubarnage.com or ⓦwww.pageandmoy.com, or look through the adverts in a motor-sports magazine. True petrolheads book themselves a place at one of the circuit-side campsites.

At other times of year, you can watch practice sessions, or there's the bikers' **24 Heures Moto** in early April or the **Le Mans Classic** in September. Outside race days, the simplest way to get a taste of the action is just to take the main road south of the city towards Tours, a stretch of ordinary highway which follows the famous **Mulsanne straight** for 5.7km – a distance that saw race cars reach speeds of up to 375kph, until two chicanes were introduced in 1989. Alternatively, visit the **Musée de l'Automobile** (daily: Feb–May & Oct–Dec 10am–6pm; June–Sept 10am–7pm; €7), on the edge of the Bugatti circuit – the dedicated track section of the main Sarthe circuit, where the race starts and finishes. It parades some 150 vehicles, ranging from the humble 2CV to classic Lotus and Porsche race cars.

from €18), which is particularly good at local game dishes. The most atmospheric restaurants, however, are located in the old quarter. The *Auberge des 7 Plats*, 79 Grande-Rue (℡02.43.24.57.77; closed Sun & Mon), does a good range of good-value *plats* and menus. For a special occasion, make for the rustically styled *Le Flambadou*, 14bis rue St-Flaceau (℡02.43.24.88.38; closed Sat lunch & Sun), which offers a very meaty menu from Périgord and the Landes with mains from around €15. Nearby on place St-Pierre, *Le Fontainebleau* (℡02.43.14.25.74; closed Mon & Tues) has pleasant outside seating facing the Hôtel de Ville and serves moderately priced classic French cuisine. There's a daily **market** in the covered halls on place du Marché, plus a bric-a-brac market on Wednesday, Friday (when there's also food) and Sunday mornings on place du Jet-d'Eau, below the cathedral on the new town side.

The Abbaye de L'Epau

If car racing holds no romance, there's another outing from Le Mans of a much quieter nature, to the Cistercian **Abbaye de l'Epau** (daily 9.30–11.30am & 2–5.30pm; opening hours may vary in summer to accommodate exhibitions; ℡02.43.84.22.29; €3), 4km out of town off the Chartres–Paris road (bus #14 from place de la République in Le Mans, stop "Pologne", then a walk of some 500 metres). The abbey was founded in 1229 by Queen Berengaria, consort of Richard the Lionheart, and it stands in a rural setting on the outskirts of the Bois de Changé more or less unaltered since its fifteenth-century restoration after a fire. The visit includes the dormitory, with the remains of a fourteenth-century fresco, the abbey church and the scriptorium, or writing room. The church contains the recumbent figure of Queen Berengaria over her tomb.

Travel details

Trains

Angers to: Le Mans (frequent; 40min–1hr 20min); Nantes (frequent; 45min); Paris (frequent; 1hr 40min); Saumur (frequent; 20–30min); Tours (frequent; 1hr–1hr 30min).

Bourges to: Nevers (8–12 daily; 50min); Orléans (9 daily; 1hr–1hr 40min); Tours (12 daily; 1hr 40min).

Le Mans to: Angers (frequent, 40min–1hr 20min); Nantes (frequent, 55min–1hr 45min); Paris (frequent; 1hr); Rennes (frequent; 2hr); Saumur (3 daily; 2hr); Tours (frequent; 1hr).

Orléans to: Beaugency (frequent; 20min); Blois (frequent; 40min); La Ferté-St-Aubin (frequent; 15–25min); Meung-sur-Loire (frequent; 15min); Paris (at least hourly; 1hr); Romorantin-Lanthenay (change at Salbris; 7 daily; 1hr 30min); Tours (frequent; 1hr–1hr 30min).

Tours to: Amboise (frequent; 20min); Azay-le-Rideau (7 daily; 30min); Blois (frequent; 40min); Chenonceaux (6 daily; 35min); Chinon (7 daily; 45min); Langeais (8 daily; 25min); Le Mans (7 daily; 1hr); Montrichard (10 daily; 30min); Orléans (frequent; 1hr–1hr 30min); Paris (hourly; 2hr 30min, TGVs via St-Pierre-des-Corps 1hr); Saumur (frequent; 45min).

Buses

Angers to: Brissac-Quincé (5–7 daily; 30min).

Blois to: Chambord (1–3 daily; 45min); Cour-Cheverny (3 daily; 35min); Romorantin-Lanthenay (3 daily; 1hr); St-Aignan (2–3 daily; 1hr 10min); Valençay (3 daily; 1hr 30min).

Bourges to: Sancerre (1–3 daily; 1hr 15min).

Orléans to: Beaugency (4–6 daily; 45min); Chartres (9 daily; 1hr 10min–1hr 45min); Germigny-des-Près (3 daily; 1hr); Gien (3 daily; 1hr 50min); Meung-sur-Loire (8 daily; 35min); St-Benoît-sur-Loire (3 daily; 1hr); Sully-sur-Loire (2–3 daily; 45min–1hr 20min).

Saumur to: Fontevraud (4–6 daily; 35min).

Tours to: Amboise (7 daily; 50min); Azay-le-Rideau (2 daily; 50min); Chinon (2 daily; 1hr 10min); Loches (12 daily; 40min); Richelieu (1–4 daily; 1hr 50min).

Burgundy

CHAPTER 7 # Highlights

* **À la bourguignonne**
Voluptuaries, prepare
to indulge – Burgundy's
ambrosial sauces are based
on its full-flavoured red wines.
Snails meanwhile are stewed
in dry, white Chablis.
See p.501

* **Noyers-sur-Serein** Buried
in beautiful countryside east
of Auxerre, this stunningly
unspoilt medieval town has
the added bonuses of an
impressive museum and a
great place to sleep and dine.
See p.509

* **Château d'Ancy-le-Franc**
Utterly refined, still sumptuous;
a textbook Renaissance villa
designed by the great theorist
Sebastiano Serlio. See p.511

* **Fontenay Abbey** Stunningly
simple, serene and austere
Fontenay perfectly evokes
the stark atmosphere of a
Cistercian community.
See p.513

* **Autun cathedral** The
striking exterior serves as a
mere appetizer before the
magnificent beauty of the
capitals inside, all sculpted by
the renowned Romanesque
craftsman Gislebertus.
See p.522

* **Beaune's Hôtel-Dieu** Topped
by a myriad of glazed,
multicoloured tiles, the
medieval hospice at Beaune
also houses Rogier van der
Weyden's *Last Judgement*.
See p.535

▲ Château d'Ancy-le-Franc

Burgundy

P eaceful, rural **Burgundy** is one of the most prosperous regions in modern France, but for centuries its powerful dukes remained independent of the French crown. During the Hundred Years War, they even sided with the English, selling them the captured Joan of Arc. By the fifteenth century their power extended over all of Franche-Comté, Alsace and Lorraine, Belgium, Holland, Picardy and Flanders, and their state was the best organized and richest in Europe, its revenues equalled only by Venice. It finally fell to the French kings only when Duke Charles le Téméraire (the Bold) was killed besieging Nancy in 1477.

There's evidence everywhere of this former wealth and power, both secular and religious: in the dukes' capital of **Dijon**, in the great abbeys of **Vézelay** and **Fontenay**, in the ruins of the monastery of **Cluny** (whose abbots' influence was second only to the pope's), and in the châteaux of **Tanlay** and **Ancy**.

The food of Burgundy

The **cuisine** of Burgundy is known for its richness, due in large part to two factors: the region's heavy red wines and its possession of one of the world's finest breeds of beef cattle, the Charollais. The **wines** used in the preparation of the sauces earn a dish the designation of *à la bourguignonne*. Essentially, this means cooked in a red wine sauce to which baby onions, mushrooms and *lardons* (pieces of bacon) are added. The classic Burgundy dishes cooked in this manner are *bœuf bourguignon* and *coq au vin*. Another term which frequently appears on menus is *meurette*, also a red wine sauce but made without mushrooms and flambéed with a touch of marc brandy. It's used with eggs, fish and poultry as well as red meat.

Snails (*escargots*) are hard to avoid in Burgundy, and the local style of cooking them involves stewing for several hours in the white wine of Chablis with shallots, carrots and onions, then stuffing them with garlic and parsley butter and finishing them off in the oven. **Other specialities** include the parsley-flavoured ham (*jambon persillé*); hams from the Morvan hills cooked in a cream *saupiquet* sauce; calf's head (*tête de veau*, or *sansiot*); a *pauchouse* of river fish (that is, poached in white wine with onions, butter, garlic and *lardons*); a *poussin* (tender chicken) from Bresse; a saddle of hare (*rable de lièvre à la Piron*); and a *potée bourguignonne*, or soup of vegetables cooked in the juices of long-simmered bacon and pork bits.

Like other regions of France, Burgundy produces a variety of **cheeses**. The best known are the creamy white Chaource, the soft St-Florentin from the Yonne valley, the orange-skinned Époisses and the delicious goat's cheeses from the Morvan. And then there is *gougère*, a kind of cheesecake, best eaten warm with a glass of Chablis.

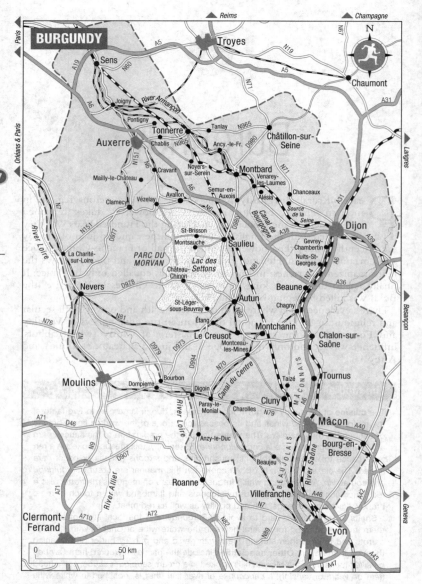

Because of its monastic foundations, Burgundy became – along with
Poitou and Provence – one of the great church-building areas in the Middle
Ages. Practically every village has its Romanesque church, especially in
the country around Cluny and Paray-le-Monial, and where the Catholic
Church built, so had the Romans before, with their legacy visible in the
substantial Roman remains at **Autun**. And the history goes back further:
Bibracte, on the vast, windswept hill of Mont-Beuvray, was an important

Gallic capital, and **Alésia** was the scene of Julius Caesar's epic victory over the Gauls in 52 BC.

For voluptuaries, **wine** is, of course, the region's most obvious attraction, and devotees head straight for the great **vineyards**, whose produce has played the key role in the local economy since Louis XIV's doctor prescribed wine as a palliative for the royal dyspepsia. If you lack the funds to indulge your taste for expensive drink, go in September or October when the *vignerons* are recruiting harvesters.

Between bouts of gastronomic indulgence, you can engage in some moderate activity: for **walkers** there's a wide range of hikes, from the gentle to the relatively demanding, in the **Parc Régional du Morvan** and the **Côte d'Or**. The region's many canals can be explored by rented barge, while their towpaths often form part of a rapidly expanding network of **cycle paths** (Ⓦ www.la-bourgogne-a-velo.com).

Burgundy has a pretty good **public transport** network, with buses filling in most of the gaps left by the SNCF, albeit with the usual skeletal timetables.

The road to Dijon

The old **road to Dijon**, the Nationale 6 runs from Paris down to the Côte d'Azur, the route taken by the National Guardsmen of Marseille when they marched on Paris singing the *Marseillaise* in 1792. It enters the province of Burgundy just south of Fontainebleau, near where the River Yonne joins the Seine, and follows the Yonne valley through the historic towns of **Sens**, **Joigny** and **Auxerre**. Scattered in a broad corridor to the west and east of the road, in the valleys of the Yonne's tributaries, the Armançon, Serein, Cure and Cousin rivers, is a fascinating collection of abbeys, châteaux, towns, villages and other sites as ancient as the history of France. It makes for a far more interesting, albeit slower route, than speeding around the bland curves of its modern replacement, the **Autoroute du Soleil** (A6), entrance to which requires a modest toll payment.

Sens

The name of **SENS**, the northernmost town in Burgundy, commemorates the Senones, the Gallic tribe whose shaggy troops all but captured Rome in 390 BC; they were only thwarted by the Capitoline geese cackling and waking the garrison. Its heyday as a major ecclesiastical centre was in the twelfth and thirteenth centuries, but it lost its pre-eminence in the ensuing centuries largely through damage caused by the Hundred Years War and the Wars of Religion. Nowadays, it is a quiet, relaxed place on the banks of the River Yonne – although the cathedral, its treasury and the adjacent museum make a stop worthwhile.

The Town

Contained within a ring of tree-lined boulevards where the city walls once stood, the town's ancient centre is still dominated by the **Cathédrale**

St-Étienne. Begun around 1130, it was the first of the great French Gothic cathedrals, and having been built without flying buttresses – these were added later for stability – its profile is relatively wide and squat. The architect who completed it, William of Sens, went on to rebuild the choir of Canterbury Cathedral in England – the other spiritual home of Thomas Becket, who had previously spent several years in exile around Sens. The story of Thomas's murder is told in the twelfth-century windows in the north aisle of the choir. From late June to September you can enjoy free **organ recitals** in this grand setting on Sunday afternoons (ⓦ www.portaildusenonais.com).

Next door is the thirteenth-century **Palais Synodal**, with its roof of Burgundian glazed tiles restored by the nineteenth-century "purist" Viollet-le-Duc, as were those of so many other buildings in this region. Originally designed to accommodate the ecclesiastical courts, it now houses part of the **Musée de Sens** (June–Sept daily except Tues 10am–noon & 2–6pm; Oct–May Wed, Sat & Sun 10am–noon & 2–6pm, Mon, Thurs & Fri 2–6pm; €4), whose collections are the envy of many a larger provincial town. Downstairs are prehistoric and Gallo-Roman **archeological finds**, whose highlights include the Villethierry treasure (867 items of bronze jewellery thought to be a craftsman's hoard), some impressive mosaics, and second-century ruins discovered beneath the cathedral. Upstairs is an extensive **art collection** donated in 2002 by the Marrey brothers (wealthy Parisians with a soft spot for Sens), which includes a tremendous statue by Rodin and a typically lively crowd scene by Brueghel the younger. Finally, the museum ticket gives access to the cathedral's **treasury**, containing some rich tapestries and vestments – among them those of the evidently rather corpulent Thomas Becket. In summer there are guided tours of the cathedral, treasury and museum (lasting 1hr each; July & Aug Mon–Sat from 2.30pm; €5 per tour or €9 for all three).

Facing the cathedral across the central place de la République are fine wood and iron *halles*, where a **market** is held on Monday and Friday mornings. Nearby, **rue de la République** and **Grande-Rue**, which cross to neatly quarter the centre, are lined with old houses now converted into shops, and mainly reserved for pedestrians. There are three particularly finely carved and timbered houses on the corner of rue Jean-Cousin one block south of the square.

Practicalities

From the **gare SNCF**, avenue Vauban leads to a bridge over the two broad arms of the River Yonne and then blends into Grande-Rue, bringing you straight to place de la République and the cathedral – about fifteen-minutes' walk. Just to the north is the **tourist office**, an octagonal building in place Jean-Jaurès (July & Aug Mon–Sat 9am–7pm, Sun 10am–5pm; Sept–June Mon–Fri 9am–noon & 1.30–6.15pm, Sat 9am–noon & 1.30–5.15pm; ☎ 03.86.65.19.49, ⓦ www .office-de-tourisme-sens.com).

For a central **place to stay**, try the simple but spotless *Esplanade*, (☎ 03.86.83.14.70, ⓕ 03.86.83.14.71; closed Sun & Aug; ❶), 2 boulevard du Mail, above a bar at the east end of place Jean-Jaurès, whose cheapest rooms (€25) have shared bathrooms. Just round the corner at 21 rue de Trois Croissants, the *Hôtel Brennus* (☎ 03.86.64.04.40, ⓦ www.hotel-brennus.fr; ❷) is better-equipped, with a/c and internet access, and more characterful – some rooms have exposed beams or offer top views of the cathedral. The old-time-feel *Hôtel de Paris et de la Poste* (☎ 03.86.65.17.43, ⓦ www.hotel-paris-poste. com; ❹), at 97 rue de la République, opposite the elaborate facade of the town hall, is grander still and has a respected but expensive restaurant (from €28). The local **campsite**, *Entre-deux-Vannes*, is at 191 avenue de Sénigallia (℡03.86.65.64.71 , @espacesverts@mairie-sens.fr; mid-May to mid Sept), twenty-minutes' walk south of town.

The café terraces on place de la République, between market and cathedral, are a great spot for a drink or light meal. For more substantial **dining**, try the friendly, bustling crêperie *Au P'tit Creux*, on the doorstep of the cathedral at 3 rue de Brennus (℡03.86.64,99.29; closed Tues & Wed), where you can enjoy excellent home-made desserts. Superb seafood can be found at *Le Soleil Levant*, 51 rue Emile-Zola (℡03.86.65.71.82; closed Wed, Sun evening & Aug; menus €16.50–38), near the train station.

Joigny

As you travel from Sens towards Auxerre, the next place of any size on the Yonne is the modest town of **JOIGNY**, its elegant old houses ranged up the slope above the river. The first fort here was constructed at the end of the tenth century, with houses built beneath it, though much of the original settlement was destroyed by a fire in 1530. The town is not worth a prolonged visit, but makes a pleasant rest stop, particularly on market days (Wed & Sat). Buildings worthy of attention are the **Château des Gondi**, built by Cardinal Gondi in the sixteenth century and wilfully classical, and the remains of the twelfth-century **ramparts** on Chemin de la Guimbard. A few half-timbered houses that somehow escaped the 1530 fire can be seen on **rue Montant-au-Palais**, the street leading up to the church of St-Jean, including the best known, **Maison du Pilori**, combining Gothic and Renaissance styles, with some carvings strangely reminiscent of crocodile heads.

From the **gare SNCF** it's a long, straight walk up avenues de Gaulle and Gambetta to the bridge over the river to the old town. By the bridge, you'll find a well-stocked **tourist office** (July & Aug Mon–Sat 9am–12.30pm & 2–7pm, Sun 10am–1pm; Sept–June Tues–Sat 9am–noon & 2–5/6pm, Mon 2–5/6pm; ℡03.86.62.11.05, @www.tourisme–joigny.fr) and the market halls. The nicest place to stay and eat is 6km west of town along the D182 in Thèmes. *Le P'tit Claridge* (℡03.86.63.10.92, @www.lepetitclaridge.com; ❷; closed Jan & Feb) has rooms full of charm and a restaurant offering a very good-value menu at €16 (closed Sun evening & Mon).

An interesting side trip from Joigny, located about 45 minutes away by car, is the village of **ST-SAUVEUR-EN-PUISAYE** and the birthplace, in 1873, of the French writer Colette. The **Musée Colette** is in the château (April–Oct daily except Tues 10am–6pm; Nov–March Sat & Sun 2–6pm; €5) and includes a reconstruction of her apartment in Paris, as well as personal items and original manuscripts.

Auxerre and around

A pretty old town of narrow lanes and unexpected open squares, **AUXERRE** stands on a hill a further 15km up the Yonne from Joigny. It looks its best from Pont Paul-Bert and the riverside **quais**, where houseboats and barges moor, its churches soaring dramatically and harmoniously above the surrounding rooftops.

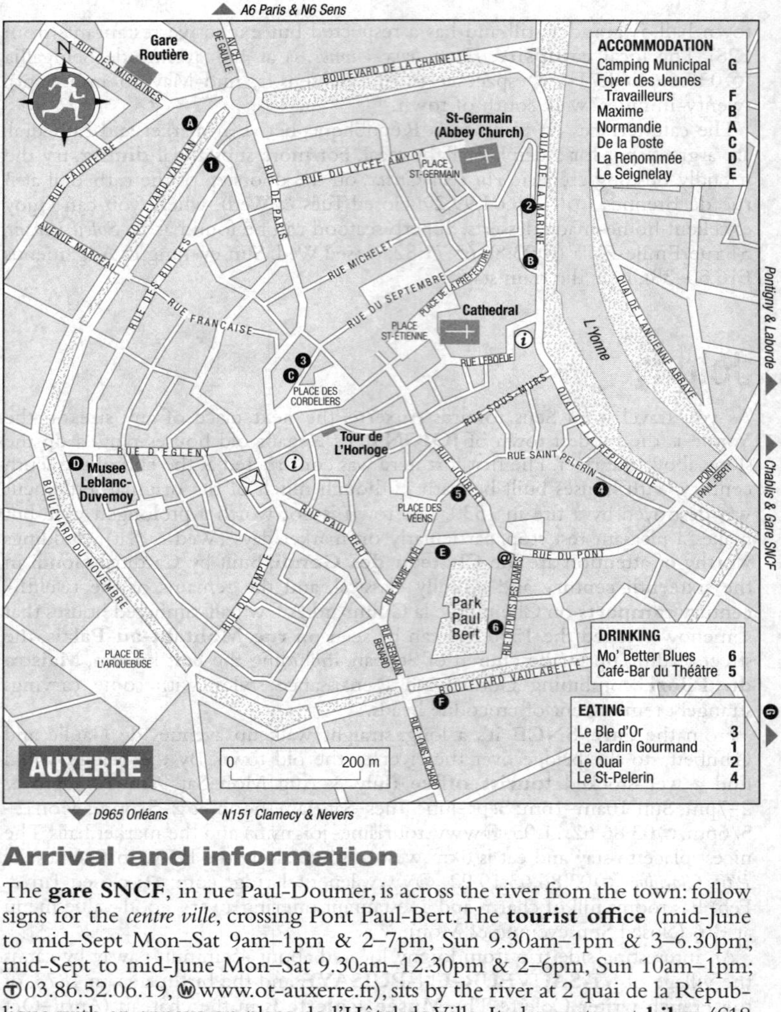
A6 Paris & N6 Sens
ACCOMMODATION
Camping Municipal G
Foyer des Jeunes Travailleurs F
Maxime B
Normandie A
De la Poste C
La Renommée D
Le Seignelay E
DRINKING
Mo' Better Blues 6
Café-Bar du Théâtre 5
EATING
Le Ble d'Or 3
Le Jardin Gourmand 1
Le Quai 2
Le St-Pelerin 4
Gare Routière
St-Germain (Abbey Church)
Cathedral
Tour de L'Horloge
Musee Leblanc-Duvemoy
Park Paul Bert
L'Yonne
PLACE ST-GERMAIN
PLACE ST-ETIENNE
PLACE DES CORDELIERS
PLACE DES VEENS
PLACE DE L'ARQUEBUSE
RUE DES MIGRAINES
AV CH DE GAULLE
BOULEVARD DE LA CHAINETTE
RUE FAIDHERBE
BOULEVARD VAUBAN
AVENUE MARCEAU
RUE DES BUTTES
RUE FRANCAISE
RUE DU LYCEE AMYOT
RUE DE PARIS
RUE MICHELET
RUE DU SEPTEMBRE
PLACE DE LA PREFECTURE
QUAI DE LA MARINE
QUAI DE L'ANCIENNE ABBAYE
RUE LEBOEUF
RUE SOUS MURS
QUAI DE LA REPUBLIQUE
RUE SAINT PELERIN
RUE JOUBERT
RUE D'EGLENY
BOULEVARD DU NOVEMBRE
RUE PAUL BERT
RUE DU TEMPLE
RUE MARIE NOIR
RUE DU PONT
RUE DU PUITS DES DAMES
RUE GERMAIN BENARD
BOULEVARD VAULABELLE
RUE LOUIS RICHARD
PONT PAUL BERT
Pontigny & Laborde
Chablis & Gare SNCF
AUXERRE
0 200 m
D965 Orléans
N151 Clamecy & Nevers

Arrival and information

The **gare SNCF**, in rue Paul-Doumer, is across the river from the town: follow signs for the *centre ville*, crossing Pont Paul-Bert. The **tourist office** (mid-June to mid–Sept Mon–Sat 9am–1pm & 2–7pm, Sun 9.30am–1pm & 3–6.30pm; mid-Sept to mid-June Mon–Sat 9.30am–12.30pm & 2–6pm, Sun 10am–1pm; ⓣ 03.86.52.06.19, ⓦ www.ot-auxerre.fr), sits by the river at 2 quai de la République with an annexe on place de l'Hôtel de Ville. It also rents out **bikes** (€18 per day) and small **electric boats** on the river (€20 per hour), and sell a **pass** (€4) giving reductions to all the sights in and around Auxerre. To enjoy some local colour, and local produce, try the **market** in place de l'Arquebuse (Tues & Fri morning). **Internet access** is easiest at Speed Informatique, 32 rue du Pont (Mon–Sat 2–9pm; €5 per hour), while **car hire** firms line the roads near the station: Avis (ⓣ 03.86.46.83.47) is closest at 3 rue Paul Doumer.

Accommodation

Maxime 2 quai de la Marine ⓣ 03.86.52.14.19, ⓦ www.lemaxime.com. Rooms here are stylishly monotone and luxurious (all have a/c, wireless internet and modern furnishings. Ask for one with river views as they are not necessarily more expensive; instead it's the size that matters. ❺

Normandie 41 bd Vauban ☏03.86.52.57.80, Ⓦwww.hotelnormandie.fr. Just outside the old town centre, this fairly swanky, creeper-covered chain hotel occupies a former nineteenth-century country house, though the rooms boast all modern trimmings. Other facilities include a sauna and a billiards room. ❹

De la Poste 9 rue d'Orbandelle ☏03.86.52.12.02, Ⓔhotel.de.la.poste@orange.fr. Don't be put off by the bizarre coconut-matting-clad walls of the corridors – they lead to charmingly decorated, airy, modern rooms which represent the best value in town. A great central location and a tempting, high-quality restaurant (three courses €29; closed Sun & Mon lunch) to boot. ❸

De la Renommée 27 rue d'Egleny ☏03.86.51.31.45. A reliable, family-run budget option, though it's a good half-hour uphill walk from the train station. Restaurant from €11. Closed Sun. ❶

Le Seignelay 2 rue du Pont ☏03.86.52.03.48, Ⓦwww.leseignelay.com. A popular mid-range choice with friendly staff, a hearty buffet breakfast and a restaurant (closed Sun & Mon) in its courtyard, where you can have a good *menu bourguignon* for €22. Closed mid-Feb to mid-March. ❸

Hostel and campsite

Foyer Auxerrois des Jeunes Travailleurs 16 bd Vaulabelle ☏03.86.52.45.38. Hard to find (it's behind a block of flats just to the right of the Citroen garage), this hostel offers single rooms reminiscent of prison cells. Exceptionally friendly staff and a tremendous canteen – four tasty courses for just €8.20 – more than make amends, though. €15.80 including breakfast.

Camping Municipal D'Auxerre 8 rte de Vaux ☏03.86.52.11.15, Ⓔcamping.mairie@auxerre .com. Next to the riverside football ground, a pleasant site on the south side of town. Mid-April to Sept.

The Town

The most interesting of Auxerre's many churches is the abbey church of **St Germain** (daily except Tues: June–Sept 10am–noon & 2–6pm; €4.50). The monks' former dormitories, around a classical cloister, now house a historical and archeological **museum**, but the real highlight is the **crypt**, one of the few surviving examples of Carolingian architecture, with its plain barrel vaults still resting on their thousand-year-old oak beams. Deep inside, the wonderfully vivid and expressive ochre frescoes of St Stephen (St-Étienne) are among the most ancient in France, dating back to around 850 AD. A ticket costing €6.30 also grants you entry to the **Musée Leblanc–Duvernoy** (daily except Tues 2–6pm; €2.20), which has some historically significant ceramics from the late 1700s.

The **cathedral** itself (7.30am–5/6pm) took from 1215 to 1560 to build, but still remains unfinished: the southernmost of the two west front towers has never been completed. Look out for the richly detailed sculpture of the porches and the glorious colours of the original thirteenth-century glass that still fills the windows of the choir, despite the savagery of the Wars of Religion and the Revolution. There has been a church on the site since about 400 AD, though nothing visible survives earlier than the eleventh-century **crypt** (€3). Among its frescoes is a unique depiction of a warrior Christ mounted on a white charger, accompanied by four mounted angels.

In front of the cathedral, rue Fourier leads to place des Cordeliers and off left to the Hôtel de Ville and the old city gateway known as the **Tour de l'Horloge**, with its fifteenth-century coloured clock face. The whole quarter, from place Surugue through rue Joubert and down to the river, is full of attractive old houses.

For an altogether different activity, more commonplace but less dusty than the crypts – and almost certainly more of a hit with youngsters – drive the 5km to Laborde, where the **Forêt de l'Aventure** (daily July & Aug; €20; Ⓦwww.foret-aventure-auxerre.com) offers a course of high wires, rope ladders and zip lines around the tree tops.

Eating, drinking and entertainment

Auxerre boasts some good **restaurants**, some revelling in, others diverging from, the much-loved Burgundian staples.

Later in the evening the *Mo'Better Blues* jazz bar, rue du Puits des Dames, often has live music (Wed–Sat 9pm; ⓦ www.addim89.org). For a quieter **drink**, the tiny corner bar *Café du Théâtre*, on rue Joubert, is popular and does light meals. In summer, be sure to pick up a programme for the "Garcon la Note" series of **free concerts**, held on different café terraces every evening in July and August.

Le Ble d'or 5 rue d'Orbandelle ⓣ 03.86.48.16.84. A good little crêperie, slightly light on atmosphere, but offering excellent, filling, tasty food at fair prices: salads, *galettes* and crêpes all €7–8.

🏃 **Le Jardin Gourmand** 56 bd Vauban ⓣ 03.86.51.53.52. Polished glass, crisp linen and immaculate decor; this is truly fine dining. Gastronomic dishes, with ingredients mainly sourced locally, one possibility being Morvan rabbit in a truffle sauce. Menus start at €55 and you get the full works, including wine, for €90. Closed Tues & Wed.

Le Quai place St-Nicholas ⓣ 03.86.51.66.67. Grab a seat on the outdoor terrace of this popular brasserie, which overlooks a pretty square. Reasonably-priced *plats* and pizzas (€10–12) have a light, modern feel, with more salad and less rich Burgundy sauce.

Le Saint Pelerin 56 rue St-Pélerin ⓣ 03.86.52.77.05. The centrepiece of this quiet, relaxed dining room is the wood fire on which the restaurant's speciality *grillades* are prepared. Good choice of meats and fish; menu for €21. Closed Sun & Mon.

Around Auxerre

On or close to the D965, in the open, rolling country east of Auxerre and particularly along the valley of the aptly named **Serein River**, lie several towns deserving of a visit, for reasons ranging from architecture to wine to sheer secluded beauty.

Pontigny

The ravages of time – in particular the 1789 Revolution – have destroyed most of the great monastic buildings of the Cistercian order of monks. Their rigorous insistence on simplicity and manual labour under their most influential twelfth-century leader, St Bernard, was a revolutionary response to the worldliness and luxury of the Benedictine abbots of Cluny. The only places in Burgundy where you can get an idea of how Cistercian ideas translated into bricks and mortar are at Pontigny and Fontenay.

PONTIGNY lies 18km northeast of Auxerre, and its beautifully preserved twelfth-century **abbey church** (daily: May–Sept 9am–7pm; Oct–April 10am–5pm; free), stands on the edge of the village, where its functional mass rises from the meadows. There's no tower, no stained glass and no statuary to distract from its austere, harmonious lines, though the effect is marred by the seventeenth-century choir that occupies much of the nave.

Three Englishmen played a major role in the abbey's early history, all of them archbishops of Canterbury: Thomas Becket took refuge from Henry II in the abbey in 1164, Stephen Langton similarly hid here during an argument over his eligibility for the primacy from 1207 to 1213, and Edmund Rich retired here in 1240 after unsuccessfully trying to stand up to Henry III. The abbey was also the origin of an attraction with which a nearby village is more often associated: the famous **Chablis wine**, for it was the monks of Pontigny who originally developed and refined the variety.

One **restaurant** with a decent wine list is the *Moulin de Pontigny* (ⓣ 03.86.47.44.98; closed Mon & Tues; regional menu at €20), just off the N77, on a leafy terrace surrounded by water. To **stay** the night, though, head to

Ligny-le-Chatel, 4km away, which has a comfortable hotel, the *Relais St-Vincent* (☏03.86.47.53.38; ❷) at 14 Grande-Rue, and a **campsite** by the Serein off the D8 Auxerre road (☏03.86.47.56.99; mid–May to Sept).

Chablis

Sixteen kilometres to the south of Pontigny on winding, rural D965, the pretty red-roofed village of **CHABLIS** is home to the region's famous light dry white wines. It lies in the valley of the River Serein between the wide and mainly treeless upland wheat fields typical of this corner of Burgundy. As you head into town you'll notice rows of vines etching the hills, interspersed by the yellow splashes of fields full of sunflowers. While wandering around the village you could take a look at the side door of the **church of St-Martin**, decorated with ancient horseshoes and other bits of rustic ironwork left as *ex votos* by visiting pilgrims. Legend has it that Joan of Arc was one of them.

For public transport users, there are two **buses** per day from Auxerre and Tonnerre, but in summer they must be reserved by phone by 5pm the day before you want to travel (☏08.00.30.33.09). The **tourist office** is just over the Serein bridge at 1 rue du Maréchal de Lattre de Tassigny (daily 10am–12.30pm & 1.30–6pm; Nov–March closed Sun; ☏03.86.42.80.80, ⓦ www.chablis.net). If you want to **stay** the night, a superb choice is the nearby *Relais de la Belle Etoile* (☏03.86.18.96.08, ⓦ www.chablis-france.fr; ❺; closed mid-Dec to mid-Jan) at 4 rue des Moulins, a charming bed-and-breakfast-style hotel, its rooms are beautifully and individually decorated. Cheaper, but still pleasant rooms are available above a bar at the *Hôtel de la Poste*, 24 rue Auxerroise (☏03.86.42.11.94, ⓦ www.hotel-poste-chablis.com; ❸), though some have shared facilities. An attractive **campsite**, the *Camping de Chablis* (☏03.86.42.44.39, ⓔ ot-chablis @chablis.net; June–Sept), lies beside the river just outside the village.

For **food**, *À vins du Domaine Laroche*, 18 rue des Moulins (☏03.86.42.47.30; open for lunch Tues–Sun, dinner Thurs–Sat), is a good, stylish restaurant (*plats* from €20) where they'll happily advise you on a choice of wine from their extensive list. Alternatively, *Bistro des Grand Crus* (☏03.86.42.19.41), 8 rue Jules-Rathier, has a very affordable *plat*-plus-wine deal at €9.50 and a menu full of local touches, offering, for example, guinea fowl or Charollais beef in rich Chablis sauces.

To buy **wine**, *caves* abound in Chablis, where you can taste and purchase a good bottle from €10 upwards. The best choice is *La Chablisienne,* ten-minutes' walk south of the centre (daily 9am–12.30pm & 2–6pm; ⓦ www.chablisienne .com), a cooperative in existence since 1923 which offers a fine, representative selection of the area's wines, free tastings and competitive prices. With that exception, however, the town does rather milk its product for all it's worth and you'll find prices lower – and restaurants less snooty about the cheaper vintages – in neighbouring villages like Pontigny or Maligny.

Noyers–sur–Serein

Twenty-three kilometres to the southeast of Chablis, you come to the beautiful little town of **NOYERS–SUR–SEREIN**. With no public transport, it's sealed from the modern world in a medieval time warp. Half-timbered and arcaded houses, ornamented with rustic carvings – particularly those on place de la Petite-Étape-aux-Vins and round place de l'Hôtel-de-Ville – are corralled inside a loop of the river and the town walls, and pleasant hours can be passed wandering the path between the river and the irregular walls, with their robust towers. The Serein here is as pretty as in Chablis, but Noyers, being remarkably free of commercialism, has more charm.

Considering that it is based in such a small town, the **Musée de Noyers** (Feb–May & Oct–Dec Sat & Sun 2.30–6.30pm; June–Sept daily except Tues 11am–6.30pm; €4) certainly punches above its weight. It comprises one of the best collections in the country of the Naive painters, who had no formal training and were often workers lacking academic education (one, Augustine Lesage, worked as a miner for sixty years before he started painting). Some star exhibits include Gérard Lattier's morbid comic-strip-style work, the excellent collages of Louis Quilici and dreamy early twentieth-century paintings of Jacques Lagrange. If you're in shape, you might want to attempt the hike up to the hill behind the town, at the top of which are a ruined twelfth-century **castle** and a beautiful panorama over the town. To find the path up, turn left just outside the southern gateway to the town.

The best place to **stay** and **eat** is the ivy-covered seventeenth-century 🍴 *La Vieille Tour* (April–Aug only; ☎03.86.82.87.69, 🖂03.86.82.66.04; ❸) in place du Grenier-à-Sel in the town centre. The five beautifully furnished and charmingly rustic *chambres d'hôte* are rife with personality and views across the gardens to the river. Their restaurant (☎03.86.82.87.36; closed Thurs; reservations essential), just down the road, offers wonderful meals, featuring all the regional classics plus a vegetarian option, for €15, with an equally good-value wine list to accompany them.

The valley of the Yonne

If you're travelling south from Auxerre and want a break from the main roads, head along the D163, a twisting minor road which follows the course of the **River Yonne** through a score of peaceful rural villages. Several have places both to stay and eat, making for a much more restful overnight stop than the towns.

VAUX and **ESCOLIVES-STE-CAMILLE**, the first villages you come to, both have attractive Romanesque churches. **VINCELOTTES** and **IRANCY**, on the opposite bank of the river, are flower-decked and picturesque: Irancy produces the only red wine in this area, much loved by Louis XIV, while Vincelottes was the port for shipping it.

A nice **place to stay** hereabouts is *Le Castel* (☎03.86.81.43.06, 🌐www .lecastelmailly.com; ❹), a *chambre d'hôte* on place de l'Église in **MAILLY-LE-CHÂTEAU**, a further 10km along the river which offers an excellent *table d'hôte* for €35, including wine. The main part of the village is on high ground above the river, but there's also a lovely riverside quarter, with ancient houses huddling under cliffs.

The Canal de Bourgogne

From Migennes near Joigny on the N6, the River Armançon, in tandem with the **Canal de Bourgogne**, branches off to the north of the River Yonne. Along or close to its valley are several places of interest: the Renaissance châteaux of **Ancy-le-Franc** and **Tanlay**, **Fontenay Abbey**, and the site of Julius Caesar's victory over the Gauls at **Alésia**. Just east of the Canal, perched above the River Armançon as it flows through a miniature gorge, is the exquisitely picturesque town of **Semur-en-Auxois**. Further east the Canal encompasses the upper reaches of the River Seine: at **Châtillon-sur-Seine** is the famous Celtic Treasure of Vix.

There are signed **cycle routes**, partly but not wholly on the traffic-free canal towpath, which run all the way from Tonnerre to Dijon and make for a

pleasant and flattish ride. Rudimentary maps and info are available at Ⓦwww
.tourisme-yonne.com.

Tonnerre and around

On the Paris–Sens–Dijon TGV train route, **TONNERRE** is a useful, though
not that inspiring, base for exploring this corner of the region. Though clearly
not as prosperous as its neighbour Chablis, it nonetheless has a few sights worth
a look.

The best of these is the huge medieval hospice (entrance through the tourist
office; €4.50) which hosts a wonderfully realistic sculpture of the Entombment
of Christ in the Burgundian style. Around the corner you can see the appropriately elaborate façade of the **Hôtel d'Uzès**, birthplace of Tonnerre's quirkiest
claim to fame, a gentleman with the fittingly excessive moniker Charles-
Geneviève-Louis-Auguste-André-Timothé Déon de Beaumont (b.1728). He
tickled his contemporaries' prurience by going about his important diplomatic
missions for King Louis XV dressed in women's clothes. Bookmakers took bets
on his real sex and the results of the autopsy after his death were eagerly awaited
by the gossip columnists of the day.

Another unlikely attraction sits at the foot of the steep hill crowned by the
Église Saint Pierre. The **Fosse Dionne** is a fascinating – and more than slightly
spooky – blue-green pool encircled by an eighteenth-century *lavoir*, or washing
place. A number of legends are attached to the spring (the name derives from
Divona, Celtic goddess of water), including suggestions that it was a gateway to
hell or the lair of a ferocious serpent slain by a local saint – a tale which may
refer to the draining of the malarial marshes. Divers have penetrated 360m
along a narrow underwater passageway with no end in sight, and further exploration is now banned as three have died in attempts.

The super-friendly **tourist office** is on place Marguerite-de-Bourgogne
(April–Sept daily 9.30am–noon & 2–6pm; Oct–March closed Sun & Wed;
Ⓣ03.86.55.14.48, Ⓦwww.tonnerre.fr). Here you can hire **bikes** (€18 per day),
use the **internet** (€4 per hour) and pick up an interesting, free, town history-
trail leaflet. Directly opposite is the least expensive **accommodation** in town,
the *Hôtel du Centre* (Ⓣ03.86.55.10.56, Ⓔhotelducentre.tonnerre@orange.fr; ❶),
65 rue de l'Hôpital, a relaxed, old-fashioned provincial hotel with a reasonable
little restaurant (menus from €10.50). Directly overlooking the spring, the *Ferme
de la Fosse Dionne*, 11 rue de la Fosse Dionne (Ⓣ03.86.54.82.62, Ⓦwww
.fermefossedionne.fr; ❹, breakfast included), is a tiny, sensitively restored former
farm, with lovely rooms in bright colours and a beamed, covered balcony
overlooking a small courtyard. The friendly owners also offer a *table d'hôte* for
€20 in the evening.

The local **campsite**, *La Cascade* (Ⓣ03.86.55.15.44; April to mid-Nov), is
between the River Armançon and the Canal de Bourgogne.

The châteaux of Ancy-le-Franc and Tanlay

Close to Tonnerre are two of the finest, though least-known and least-visited,
châteaux in France: **Ancy-le-Franc** and **Tanlay**. The former has the edge for
architectural purity, the latter for romantic appeal. The SNCF offers a **taxi** from
Tonnerre to either château for the same price as a train journey of equivalent
length – it's a hassle, though: you need to book by phone the day before (Ancy
Ⓣ03.80.89.31.30; Tanlay Ⓣ03.86.92.77.24).

The **Château d'Ancy-le-Franc** (guided tours only, April to mid-Nov Tues–
Sun at 10.30am, 11.30am & 2, 3 & 4pm; plus April–Sept 5pm; €9) is 25km from

Tonnerre and was built in the mid-sixteenth century for the brother-in-law of the notorious Diane de Poitiers, mistress of Henri II. More Italian than French, with its textbook classical countenance, it is the only accepted work of the Italian Sebastiano Serlio, one of the most important architectural theorists of the Renaissance, who was brought to France in 1540 by François I to work on his palace at Fontainebleau. The exterior is rather austere and forbidding, but the inner courtyard is a refined embodiment of the principles of classical architecture. Some of the apartments are sumptuous, decorated by the Italian artists Primaticcio and Niccolò dell'Abbate, who also worked at Fontainebleau. There are occasional concerts in the courtyard in summer, as well as atmospheric evening tours; Ⓦ www.chateau-ancy.com has the programme.

Ancy has a small **hotel**, the modernized *Hostellerie du Centre*, 34 Grande-Rue (Ⓣ 03.86.75.15.11, Ⓦ www.diaphora.com/hostellerieducentre; ❸; good restaurant from €17), which boasts a tiny, indoor, heated swimming pool.

The **Château de Tanlay** (April to mid-Nov, guided tours daily except Tues: 10am, 11.30am & hourly 2.15–5.15pm; €8) is a pleasant 8km walk or cycle along the canal from Tonnerre. This 1559 construction, very French in feel and full of ambience, is only slightly later in date than its near-neighbour, but those extra few years were enough for the purer Italian influences visible in Ancy to have become Frenchified. Encircling the château are water-filled moats and standing guard over the entrance to the first grassy courtyard is the grand lodge, from where you enter the château across a stone drawbridge.

For a bite to **eat**, *Le Bonheur Gourmand* (Ⓣ 03.86.75.82.18; €12–38), just next to the château entrance, has ample menus.

Châtillon-sur-Seine

For those interested in pre-Roman France, there is one compelling reason for going to **CHÂTILLON-SUR-SEINE**: the so-called **Treasure of Vix**. It consists of the finds from the sixth-century BC tomb of a Celtic princess buried in a four-wheeled chariot at **Vix**, 6km northwest of Châtillon. In addition to pieces of the chariot, the finds include exquisite jewellery and Etruscan bowls. But the best objects on display are the starkly beautiful heavy gold torc that she was wearing and the largest bronze vase (*krater*) of Greek origin known from antiquity. It stands an incredible 1.64m high on triple tripod legs, and around its rim is a superbly modelled high-relief frieze depicting naked hoplites and horse-drawn chariots, with Gorgons' heads for handles. It is an indication of the princess' status that items of such value were buried with her. At the time of writing the collection was being moved to a new and grander location on rue de la Libération, set to open in June 2009.

Archaeology aside, Châtillon makes for a very picturesque stop. Here the Seine embarks on a gloriously complex series of tangents and S-bends, many spanned by ancient, flower-decked bridges that make ideal photographs. Set against this – on the rocky bluff overlooking the steep-pitched roofs of the old quarter – are the ruins of a **castle** and the beautifully spare, early Romanesque **church of St Vorles**. At its foot in a luxuriantly verdant spot, a **spring** swells out of the rock forming an enchanting pool before tumbling off to join the infant Seine.

The **tourist office** is on place Marmont (Mon–Sat 9am–noon & 2–6pm; May–Sept also Sun 10am–noon; Ⓣ 03.80.91.13.19, Ⓦ www.pays-chatillonais.fr), and can provide an English-language town history-trail leaflet. If you decide to **stay**, try *Sylvia* (Ⓣ 03.80.91.02.44, Ⓦ www.sylvia-hotel.com; ❷), north of the centre at 9 avenue de la Gare – here you'll find charming rooms and great breakfasts, which include home-made jam and *brioche*. In the middle of town at 2 rue Charles-Ronot there's the *Hôtel de la Côte d'Or* (Ⓣ 03.80.91.13.29,

ⓕ 03.80.91.29.15; ❸; closed Jan & Feb), a wonderfully atmospheric old post-house, complete with hunting trophies on the walls. It also has a very good **restaurant** (from €18). Otherwise *O Chapo ron* (ⓣ 03.80.91.32.41), 21 rue de la Liberation, is a great place, with a large (heated if necessary) terrace and a blazing cooking fire (grilled dishes from €9; *galettes* around €7). Or you can kick back with a pint of Belgian draught and scoff down a baguette (€3) along the banks of the river at *Pub le Splendide*, on quai de Seine by the bridge.

Montbard and Fontenay Abbey

One base worth knowing about if you're counting on **public transport** in the area is the pretty but otherwise unexciting hillside town of **MONTBARD**, which is on the main railway between Dijon and Sens and where buses leave for both Chatillon and Semur. It has well-priced accommodation options, including *La Sirène*, on avenue Leclerc (ⓣ 03.80.92.07.21; ❶–❷), with simple rooms above a bar in a nice spot by the canal.

6km away, along the GR213 footpath, the privately owned **Abbey of Fontenay** (ⓦ www.abbayedefontenay.com; daily: April to mid-Nov 10am–6pm; mid-Nov to March 10am–noon & 2–5pm; €8.90, under 26 years €4.20) is probably the biggest draw in the area. Founded in 1118, it's the only Burgundian monastery to survive intact, despite conversion to a paper mill in the early nineteenth century. It was restored in the early 1900s to its original form and is one of the world's most complete monastic complexes, comprising caretaker's lodge, guesthouse and chapel, dormitory, hospital, prison, bakery, kennels and abbot's house, as well as a church, cloister, chapterhouse and even a forge.

On top of all this, the abbey's physical setting, at the head of a quiet stream-filled valley enclosed by woods of pine, fir, sycamore and beech, is superb. There's a bucolic calm about the place, particularly in the graceful cloister, and in these surroundings the spartan simplicity of Cistercian life seems utterly attractive. Hardly a scrap of decoration softens the church: even the carving on the capitals is reduced to the barest-bones outline of an acanthus leaf – the motherly statue of the Virgin arrived after St Bernard's death. There's no direct lighting in the nave, just an other-worldly glow from the square-ended apse. The effect is beautiful but daunting, the perfect structural embodiment of St Bernard's ascetic principles.

Alésia and around

A few kilometers south of Montbard is the site of the 52 BC **Battle of Alésia**, at which the Gauls, united for once under the leadership of Vercingétorix, made their last stand against the military might of Rome. Julius Caesar himself commanded the Roman army, surrounding the final Gallic stronghold with a huge double ditch and earthworks and starving the Gauls out, bloodily defeating any and all attempts at escape. Vercingétorix surrendered to save his people, was imprisoned in Rome for six years until Caesar's formal triumph and then strangled. The battle was a fundamental turning point in the fortunes of the region. Thereafter, Gaul remained under Roman rule for four hundred years.

The **site** of Alésia (mid-March to mid-Nov daily 9/10am–5/6pm; €3), treeless and exposed, is on Mont Auxois, above the village of **ALISE-STE-REINE**. You can re-create the scenes of the battle in your mind's eye as well as visit the excavations of the town, including the theatre and a Gallo-Roman house.

On the hilltop oposite, and visible for miles around, is a great bronze **statue of Vercingétorix**. Erected by Napoléon III, whose influence popularized the rediscovery of France's pre-Roman roots, the statue represents Vercingétorix as a romantic Celt, half virginal Christ, half long-haired 1970s matinee idol. On the plinth is inscribed a quotation from Vercingétorix's address to the Gauls as imagined by Julius Caesar: "United and forming a single nation inspired by a single ideal, Gaul can defy the world." Napoléon signs his dedication, "Emperor of the French", inspired by a vain desire to gain legitimacy by linking his own name to that of a "legendary" Celt.

The whole site looks set to be revolutionized over the coming years by the construction of a brand new, hi-tech **Muséoparc**, comprising two new buildings, due to open in 2010 and 2011 (Ⓦwww.alesia.com).

Practicalities

Trains from Dijon or Montbard will get you as far as the station of "Les Laumes – Alésia", but from there it's a 3km ascent to the real centre of interest. The most attractive stopover is in Alise-Ste-Reine at the *Hôtel-Restaurant Alésia* (Ⓣ03.80.96.19.67; ❷), 16 rue du Miroir, a welcoming, family-run hotel with a simple restaurant; all rooms have shared baths. A little further up the street at no. 9, *L'Auberge du Cheval Blanc* (Ⓣ03.80.96.01.55; closed Mon & Tues) serves excellent regional cuisine, with wonderful menus at €19–43 (choices include snails, rabbit and *foie gras de canard*).

The Château de Bussy-Rabutin

Eight kilometres east of Alésia, on the D954, stands the handsome **Château de Bussy-Rabutin** (Tues–Sun 9.15am–noon & 2–5/6pm; €6.50). It was built for Roger de Rabutin, a member of the Academy in the reign of Louis XIV and a notorious womanizer. The scurrilous tales of life at the royal court told in his book *Histoires Amoureuses des Gaules* earned him a spell in the Bastille, followed by years of exile in this château, which contains some interesting portraits of great characters of the age, including its famous female beauties, each underlined by an acerbic little comment such as: "The most beautiful woman of her day, less renowned for her beauty than the uses she put it to".

The source of the Seine

You'll need your own car to get to the **source of the Seine**, which lies some 15km southeast of Alésia. No more than a trickle here, it rises in a tight little vale of beech woods. The spring is now covered by an artificial grotto complete with a languid nymph, Sequana, spirit of the Seine. In Celtic times it was a place of worship, as is clear from the numerous votive offerings discovered there, including a neat bronze of Sequana standing in a bird-shaped boat, now in the Dijon archaeological museum.

Semur-en-Auxois

Extraordinarily beautiful, the small fortress town of **SEMUR-EN-AUXOIS** sits on a rocky bluff – a place of cobbled lanes, medieval gateways and ancient gardens tumbling down to the River Armançon. Thirteen kilometres west of Alésia, all roads here lead to place Notre-Dame, a handsome square dominated by the large thirteenth-century **church of Notre-Dame** (another Viollet-le-Duc restoration) characterized by its huge entrance porch and the narrowness of its nave. Inside, the windows of the second chapel on the left commemorates the dead of World War I – Semur was the general headquarters of the American 78th division, and the battlefields were not far away.

Down the street in front of the church you come to the four sturdy towers of Semur's once-powerful **castle**, all that remains after the body of the fortress was dismantled in 1602 because of its utility to enemies of the French crown. You can explore the winding streets around the castle – there's scarcely a lane in town without some building of note – and continue down to the delightful stretch of river between the Pont des Minimes and the Pont Joly, from where there's a dramatic view of town.

Cheese connoisseurs might like to take a twelve-kilometre hop **further** west on the Avallon road to **ÉPOISSES**, not just for its village and château (gardens open daily; €2; castle open July & Aug daily except Tues 10am–noon & 3–6pm; €6), but for its distinctive, soft orange-skinned cheese of the same name, washed in *marc de Bourgogne*.

Practicalities

Semur's **tourist office** is on the small place Gaveau (July & Aug 9.30am–1pm & 1.45–7pm; Sept–June 9am–noon & 2–6pm; ℡03.80.97.05.96, Ⓦwww .ville-semur-en-auxois.fr), at the junction of rues de l'Ancienne-Comédie, de la Liberté and Buffon, where the medieval Porte Sauvigny and Porte Guillier combine to form a single long, covered gateway.

The least expensive **hotel** is *Le Commerce* at 19 rue de la Liberté (℡03.80.96.64.40, Ⓔcyber21@free.fr; ❷), which has recently renovated rooms, though in a rather spartan style. Downstairs is a bar-restaurant with **internet** access (€6 per hour) and a quirky menu featuring shark, kangaroo and ostrich (from €19). Inside the medieval city proper is the more traditionally charming *Hôtel des Cymaises* (℡03.80.97.21.44, Ⓦwww.hotelcymaises.com; ❸; closed Nov & Feb), in a grand old mansion with a walled courtyard at 7 rue du Renaudot. The local **campsite** is at Lac-de-Pont (℡03.80.97.01.26; May–Sept), 3km south of town.

A bustling old-fashioned bistrot, *Le Saint-Vernier* (℡03.80.97.32.96), at 13 rue Févret, offers a filling *menu de jour* for €12, alongside its speciality *tartiflettes*. For something really special, though, it is well worth wandering down to the river and the Pont des Minimes, where the 🍴 *Maison Dieu Les Minimes*

▲ Semur-en-Auxois

(☎03.80.97.26.86; menus €16–27; closed Sun evening & Mon) is a great find: excellent food, a warm atmosphere and an extremely good price – look out for their great-value recommended wines. In the heart of the old town, the patisserie-**chocolaterie** at 14 rue Buffon (closed Mon) specializes in local *semurettes*, addictive little nuggets of chocolate made without butter.

The Morvan to the Loire

The **Morvan** region lies smack in the middle of Burgundy between the valleys of the Loire and the Saône, stretching roughly from **Clamecy**, **Vézelay** and **Avallon** in the north to **Autun** and **Le Creusot** in the south. It's a land of wooded hills, close and rounded rather than mountainous, although they rise to 900m above Autun. With poor soil and pastures only good for a few cattle, villages and farms are few and far between. In the old days, wood was the main business – supplying firewood and charcoal to Paris – and large tracts of hillside are now covered in coniferous plantations. But the region's chief export has been its escaping young, helping it earn a reputation as one of the poorest and most backward regions in the country, with few resources to trade on and little inspiration for outside investment.

The creation of a **parc naturel régional** in 1970 did something to promote the area as a place for outdoor activities and refuge from commuterdom, but more than anything it was the election of François Mitterrand, local politician and mayor of **Château-Chinon** for years, as president of the Republic that rescued the Morvan from oblivion. In addition to lending it some of the glamour of his office, he took concrete steps to beef up the local economy. Plentiful local information can be found **online** at Ⓦwww.morvan.com.

West of the Morvan, the landscape softens as it descends towards the River Loire and the fine medieval town of **Nevers**, on Burgundy's western border.

Avallon

Approaching **AVALLON** along the N6 from the north, you wouldn't give the place a second look. That, though, would be a mistake; the southern aspect is altogether more promising, clustered high on a ridge above the wooded valley of the River Cousin, looking out over the hilly, sparsely populated country of the Morvan regional park. Once a staging post on the Romans' *Via Agrippa* from Lyon to Boulogne, it's a small and ancient town of stone facades and sleepy cobbled streets.

The Town

Bisecting the town north to south, the narrow **Grande-Rue-Aristide-Briand** leads under the straddling arch of the fifteenth-century **Tour de l'Horloge** – the spire of which dominates the town – to the pilgrim **church of St Lazare**, on whose battered Romanesque facade you can still decipher the graceful carvings of the zodiac signs. Almost opposite, in a fifteenth-century house, is the tourist office, with the municipal **museum** (July–Sept daily except Tues 2–6pm; Oct–June Sat & Sun 2–6pm; free) behind it. The archeological section includes a second-century mosaic from a Gallo-Roman villa, while the highlight of the fine arts department is Alfred Boucher's sculpture of a very life-like Jason pinching the Golden Fleece. There is also the **Musée du Costume** at 6 rue Belgrand (April–Nov daily 10.30am–12.30pm & 1.30–5.30pm; €4), just off Grande-Rue, with a collection of regional dress.

Continuing from St-Lazare down what's now called rue Bocquillot brings you to the lime-shaded **Promenade de la Petite Porte**, with precipitous views across the plunging valley of the Cousin. From here, you can walk the perimeter of the outside walls. From the **Parc des Chaumes**, on the east side of town, there's a great view back to the old quarter, snug within its walls, with garden terraces descending on the slope beneath.

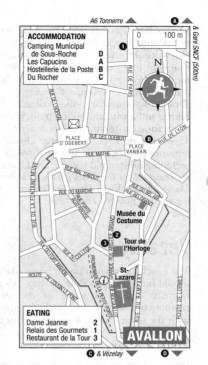

Practicalities

The **tourist office** is at 6 rue Bocquillot (June–Sept daily 9.30am–1pm & 2.30–7pm; Oct–May Mon 2.30–6pm, Tues–Sat 9.30am–12.30pm & 2.30–6pm; ☏03.86.34.14.19, Ⓦwww.avallonnais-tourisme.com), between the clock tower and the church and has **internet access** (€4 per hour). **Bikes** can be hired from 26 rue de Paris (☏03.86.34.28.11; closed Sun & Mon) or, a few minutes' drive along the road to Vézelay, from Loisirs en Morvan at the **Parc Aventure des Chatelaines** (☏03.86.31.90.10, Ⓦwww.loisirsenmorvan.com) which also organizes canoeing, paintballing and climbing, and has a series of graded treetop obstacle courses on their site (€24).

For **accommodation**, *Les Capucins* (☏03.86.34.06.52, Ⓦwww .avallonlescapucins.com; ❷), at 6 avenue Doumer, is a few-minutes' walk from the train station and a delightful mid-range choice with newly renovated rooms, all boasting air conditioning, en-suite bathrooms and wireless internet. For true luxury, however, make for the charming ⚑ *Hostellerie de la Poste* (☏03.86.34.16.16, Ⓦwww.hostelleriedelaposte.com; closed Jan & Feb; ❼), at 13 place Vauban – a former coaching inn with sumptuous, exquisitely furnished rooms set around a cobbled courtyard lined with wooden balconies. It also has a restaurant (from €25; closed Sun & Mon), which is the place for a real blow-out meal – seven courses, each with its own wine, for €85. Humbler but cosy are the well-kept, simple rooms of the *Hôtel du Rocher* (☏03.86.34.19.03; ❶), 11 rue des Îles Labaume. From the train station it's a thirty-minute hike through the city walls and down a steep staircase alongside intricately farmed plots of land. Further along the scenic riverside road to Vézelay are other attractive possibilities, including the ivy-clad *Moulin des Templiers* (T 03.86.34.10.80, W www.hotel-moulin-des-templiers.com; ❸), which huddles romantically round an inner courtyard right on the bank of the Cousin. The owners offer meals for €19.50 (reservation required).

The attractive, riverside *Camping Municipal de Sous-Roche* (T 03.86.34.10.39; E campingsousroche@ville-avallon.fr; April–Oct), which connects well with hiking and mountain biking trails, is to the south of town.

For **food** in town, the *Relais des Gourmets* (T 03.86.34.18.90; closed Mon), 45–47 rue de Paris, has a large choice of menus. For under €20 you get the regional classics, snails and beef, while €48 produces more gastronomic fare, including lobster and pigeon. On Grande Rue, in the heart of the old town, the *Restaurant de la Tour* does pizzas and plats for €8–10, while the refined tea room *Dame Jeanne* (closed Thurs) offers great, light, predominantly vegetarian lunches for €7 in a flowery courtyard.

Vézelay

The coach buses winding their way like ants up the steep incline to **VÉZELAY** should not deter you from visiting this attractive hilltop hamlet, surrounded by ramparts and with some of the most picturesque, winding streets and crumbly buildings in Burgundy. It's also a significant destination for pilgrims – with the town and its shops geared up for their presence.

The Town

Pilgrims journey here to venerate the relics of Mary Magdalene, housed in one of the seminal buildings of the Romanesque period, the **Basilica of Ste-Mary La Madeleine** (daily sunrise–sunset).

The church's restored west front begins with the colossal narthex, added to the nave around 1150 to accommodate the swelling numbers of pilgrims. Inside, your eye is first drawn to the superlative sculptures of the central doorway, on whose tympanum a Pentecostal Christ is shown swathed in exquisitely figured drapery. From Christ's outstretched hands, the message of the Gospel shoots out to the apostles in the form of beams of fire, while the frieze below depicts the converted and the pagan peoples – among those featured are giants, pygmies (one mounting his horse with a ladder), a man with breasts and huge ears, and dog-headed heathens. Better preserved are the charming small-scale medallions of zodiacal signs and the labours of the months in the outermost arch.

The arcades and arches are edged with fretted mouldings, and the supporting pillars are crowned with 99 finely cut capitals, depicting scenes from the Bible, classical mythology, allegories and morality stories.

In subsequent centuries, however, the abbey declined, first due to rumours that Mary Magdalene's bones were false relics, then pillaging by protestants in the sixteenth-century Wars of Religion, and finally the dismantling of much of the complex during the Revolution. Today, a significant Franciscan community has been re-established, and pilgrims stream here to view different relics of Mary Magdalene, given to Vézelay in the 1870s, at an intensely atmospheric shrine in the crypt.

The village is also home to one of the greatest **restaurants** in the land, *L'Espérance* (T 03.86.33.39.10, W www.marc-meneau-esperance.com; lunch menus from €65, dinner €160), where you can also sleep amid antiques in the exquisite luxury of the adjoining **hotel** (🔵). By the river here you can rent **canoes** for trips along the Cure from AB Loisirs; it's safest to reserve (☎03.86.33.38.38, 🌐www.abloisirs.com).

Practicalities

In summer, you can get here by **bus** from Clamecy or Avallon; alternatively, it's a manageable 20km cycle from the latter. Vézelay's small **tourist office** (daily 10am–1pm & 2–6pm; Oct–May closed Sun & Thurs; ☎03.86.33.23.69, 🌐www.vezelaytourisme.com), on the right of the only significant street, rue St-Pierre, as you go up towards the abbey, provides various services, including taking reservations for **hot-air balloon** flights over the town and surrounding countryside (from €185 per person; 🌐www.france-montgolfiere.com).

For **accommodation** you'll need to book far in advance at weekends and in high season. In a beautiful old building above an art gallery *Au Porc Épic* (☎03.86.33.32.16, 🌐www.le-porc-epic.com; closed Dec–Feb; 🔵), at 80 rue St-Pierre, has two delightful rooms, lined with exposed stone, wood and tapestries. There's also a raised courtyard-terrace for the excellent breakfast, which is included in the price.

Most of the town's hotels cluster round the bustling place Champ-du-Foire, just outside the walls at the foot of town and still a very pleasant location. *Le Compostelle* (☎03.86.33.28.63, 🌐www.lecompostellevezelay.com; 🔵–🔵) has comfortable, if not enormous rooms, all with private bathrooms. Just opposite, real grandeur is on offer at the *De la Poste et du Lion d'Or* (☎03.86.33.21.23, 🌐www.laposte-liondor.com; closed Jan & Feb; 🔵; restaurant from €25), whose rooms are plush and characterful, with imposing old wooden furniture and great views either of the old town or the sweeping valley behind. The youth hostel is about 1km along the route de l'Étang (☎03.86.33.24.18; closed Nov–March; beds €10); it also offers camping space.

Vézelay's **restaurants** can be rather touristy and overpriced. One great option is 🍴 *Auberge de la Coquille* (☎03.86.33.35.57), 81 rue St-Pierre. Deservedly popular with a lovely courtyard, they serve a huge range of dishes from crêpes to delicious Burgundian specialities. Their *menu de jour* (€15.90) is a good bet – but their five-course *menu gastronomique* (€28.50) is certainly worth the extra euros. Lower down the main street at no. 28, *Le Bougainville* (☎03.86.33.27.57; closed Tues, Wed, Dec & Jan; menus €22–28) serves good regional cuisine in a genteel dining room.

Clamecy

In sharp contrast to its rustic neighbours, **CLAMECY**, 23km to the west of Vézelay on the banks of the River Yonne, has a distinctly industrial feel. It was the centre of the Morvan's logging trade from the sixteenth century to the completion of the Canal du Nivernais in 1834. Individual woodcutting gangs working in the hills floated their logs down the Yonne and its tributaries as far as Clamecy, where they were made up into great rafts for shipment on to Paris.

There's nothing special to see in town, apart from the many fifteenth- to eighteenth-century buildings in the centre, but should you be in the mood for some strenuous activity, drive 17km south to **Varzy**, departure point for the local **Vélorail** – a new mode of transport all the rage in France, where you pedal a metal frame along abandoned railway tracks (on reservation; ☎03.86.45.70.05, 🌐www.cyclorail.com; €15 per hour for a four-person contraption). It's a fun novelty, but the strikingly high level of energy input required to achieve a very modest velocity will frustrate some. The same company also operates two other lines in the region.

To stay in Clamecy, try the *Hostellerie de la Poste*, on place Émile-Zola not far from the bridge (T03.86.27.01.55, Wwww.hostelleriedelaposte.fr; ❸; restaurant from €24), which has a faded facade oozing pedigree, and great-value, comfy rooms inside. There's also a good riverside **campsite** on the edge of town on the route de Chevroches (T03.86.27.05.97; May–Sept). If you're travelling south towards Nevers, the 🍴 *Ferme-Auberge du Vieux Château* (T03.86.68.06.77, Wwww.vieuxchateau.com; ❷–❹; dinner at €18) is 20km from Clamecy near the village of Oulon and just off the D977. It makes an ideal place to taste the good life, Burgundy-style, amid bucolic luxury and beautiful surroundings; meals are served exclusively with ingredients from the château's garden and farm.

Saulieu

SAULIEU suffered something of a decline with both the depopulation of the Morvan and then the construction of the A6 autoroute that took away the traffic from the old N6. These days, however, it's a highly engaging old market town, with a reputation for its gastronomy. Every year the town waits hungrily for its Charollais **festival** on the third weekend of August – a super-gourmet festival featuring mountains of meat and other local produce, and there's a festival of produce from the Morvan on the Ascension Day weekend. Saulieu is also a good springboard for the cycling, hiking and riding possibilities of the Parc du Morvan (see opposite). The town also makes for an excellent stopping point, halfway between Paris and Lyon.

The old town – on the west side of the N6 – is pretty enough and ideal for an after-dinner stroll. Its main sight is the twelfth-century **Basilique St-Andoche** (closed Sun morning & Mon), noted for its lovely capitals (probably carved by a disciple of Gislebertus, the master sculptor of Autun), but little else. Next door, the **Musée François-Pompon** (Mon 10.30–noon, Wed–Sun 10am–12.30pm & 2–5pm; closed Jan & Feb; €4) is surprisingly interesting, with good local folklore displays and a large collection of works by the local nineteenth-century animal sculptor, François Pompon.

From the **train station**, walking up avenue de la Gare brings you to a wide market place (market Sat morning), around which you'll find the **tourist office** (mid-June to mid-Sept Mon–Sat 9.30am–12.30pm & 2–7pm, Sun 9.30am– 12.30pm & 2–5pm; mid-Sept to mid-June Tues–Sat 9am–noon & 2–5/6pm; T03.80.64.00.21, Wwww.saulieu.fr) and some nine or ten hotel-restaurants.

Among the best options is *La Borne Imperiale*, 14–16 rue d'Argentine (T03.80.64.19.76, Wwww.borne-imperiale.com; ❸; closed Thurs). Run by a charming couple, it has rooms facing a peaceful garden and a great restaurant with an attractive terrace and classic Burgundian menus from €23. Should your trust fund mature while in Saulieu, head for *Le Relais Bernard Loiseau* (T03.80.90.53.53, Wwww.bernard-loiseau.com; ❼), practically next door. This hotel-restaurant-spa was created by the famed chef Bernard Loiseau (and made even more famous after his suicide in 2003 following a long bout with depression). It is an enchanting, elegant, beyond-luxurious place of rich woods, stone arches and plush furnishings which exudes wealth. Unfortunately it'll also drain yours; the cheapest rooms are €145, while the restaurant costs €98 at lunch time and *starts* at €145 for dinner. Alternatively, there is a **campsite** (☏ 03.80.64.16.19, ✉ camping.saulieu@orange.fr; April–Sept), 1km out along the Paris road, which also rents out mini chalets.

The Parc du Morvan

Carpeted with forest and etched by cascading streams, the **Parc Régional du Morvan** was only officially designated in 1970, when 170,000 hectares of hilly countryside were set aside in an attempt to protect the local cultural and physical environment with a series of nature trails, animal reserves, museums and local craft shops. The Maison du Parc, its official **information centre** (April–Oct Mon–Sat 9.30am–12.30pm & 2–5pm, Sun 10am–1pm & 3–5.30pm; Nov–March Mon–Fri 9.30am–12.30pm & 2–5pm; ☏ 03.86.78.79.57, ⓦ www .parcdumorvan.org), is located 13km from Saulieu in beautiful grounds about a kilometre outside **ST-BRISSON** on the D6. Although there's no public transport to get you there, if you're walking or cycling it's a good place to head for, as they have all available information on routes and facilities in the park. There's also a small **museum** (April to mid-Nov daily except Tues 10am–1pm & 2–5/6pm, also Tues July & Aug; €4), devoted to the region's World War II **Resistance** movement, which was particularly active in this hard-to-patrol forested backwater.

There is a plethora of **cycle** routes in the park, and tourist offices sell a pack of large-scale maps for €10. For **walkers** the most challenging trip is the three to four-day hike along the **GR13** footpath, crossing the park from Vézelay to Mont Beuvray and taking in the major lakes, which are among the park's most developed attractions. There are also hosts of less strenuous possibilities (ask at any of the local tourist offices for suggestions) including the four-kilometre walk from Saulieu to Lac Chamboux. **Riding** is a fairly popular way of seeing the park, and numerous *gîtes d'étape* offer pony-trekking facilities – again tourist offices can advise.

Every other village in the park seems to have its own **campsite** (most of which are open from April or May to Sept), and the larger ones often have a couple of simple **hotels** as well. There are several campsites and small, beach-resortish hotels round the large, wooded **Lac des Settons**, which basks at the heart of the park and makes for a good break from more strenuous activities with its watersports, café-restaurants and small beach areas. The plain, modern village of **MONTSAUCHE**, 4km to the northwest of the lake, is a good bet for provisions, including camping gas, and has a municipal campsite; **MOUX**, a similar distance to the southeast, can provide the same facilities, and also has a couple of decent hotels. **Bikes** are available from most campsites in the area: for a complete list ask at any tourist office, or check online for VTT (mountain bikes) at ⓦ www.morvan.com.

Château-Chinon

The most substantial community in the park – approximately 2500 residents – and accessible by bus from Autun, is the rather ugly village of **CHÂTEAU-CHINON**. It nestles though in contrastingly beautiful countryside dotted with evergreens, lakes and limestone deposits. President Mitterrand was mayor here from 1959 to 1981, and the town was the home base of his political life for half a century. Thanks largely to him, it now boasts a major hosiery factory and military printing works, both of which have provided much needed employment to an isolated and often forgotten region.

Atop the town in the **Musée du Septennat** (July & Aug daily 10am–1pm & 2–7pm; March–June & Sept–Dec daily except Tues 10am–noon & 2–6pm; €4), you can see the extraordinary variety of gifts Mitterrand received as head of state: carpets from the Middle East, ivory from Togo, Japanese puppets, beaded spears from Burundi and the bizarre table decorated with butterfly wings. Another of the town's attractions is the **Musée du Costume**, 4 rue du Château (same times and price), featuring a collection of over five thousand articles, allowing you to trace developments in French provincial fashion from the eighteenth century to the present.

Mitterrand's preferred **hotel** was *Le Vieux Morvan* (☎03.86.85.05.01, Ⓦwww .auvieuxmorvan.com; ❸; closed mid-Nov to Jan), just past the main drag at 8 place Gudin, with a nice restaurant (from €17). Cheaper is the cosy and comfortable *Lion d'Or* (☎03.86.85.13.56, Ⓕ03.86.79.42.22; ❶; restaurant from €12, closed Sun evening & Mon) at 10 rue des Fossés; be sure to ask for one of the rooms with views to the hillside surrounding Château-Chinon. There's also a **campsite** here, *Le Perthuy d'Oiseau* (☎03.86.85.08.17; May–Sept).

Autun

With its Gothic spire rising against a backdrop of Morvan hills, **AUTUN**, even today, is scarcely bigger than the circumference of its medieval **walls**, which follow the line of earlier Roman fortifications. The emperor Augustus founded the town in about 10 BC as part of a massive and, in the long term, highly successful campaign to pacify and Romanize the brooding Celts of defeated Vercingétorix. Augustodunum, as it was called, was designed to eclipse by its splendour the memory of **Bibracte** (see p.502), the neighbouring capital of the powerful tribe of the Aedui. And it did indeed become one of the leading cities of Roman Gaul.

The Town

This city's Roman past is still present – and very tangible. Two of its four Roman gates survive: **Porte St-André**, spanning rue de la Croix-Blanche in the northeast, and **Porte d'Arroux** in Faubourg d'Arroux in the northwest. In a field just across the River Arroux stands a lofty section of wall known as the **Temple of Janus**, which was probably part of the sanctuary of a Gallic deity, while on the east side of the town, on avenue du 2ème-Dragon just off the Dijon road, you can see the remains of what was the largest **Roman theatre** in Gaul, with a capacity of fifteen thousand – in itself a measure of Autun's importance at that time. It's not a totally evocative site – the remaining seats now overlook a football pitch – but in July and August its authenticity is enhanced by the performances of a play in which six hundred locals, dressed in period costume, reconstruct the Gallo-Roman past of the town. An artificial lake below the football pitch, the **Plan d'eau du Vallon**, provides the usual watersports.

The most enigmatic of the Gallo-Roman remains in the region is the **Pierre de Couhard**, off Faubourg St-Pancrace to the southeast of the town. It's a 27-metre-tall stone pyramid situated on the site of one of the city's necropolises, thought to date from the first century, and most probably either a tomb or a cenotaph.

The Cathédrale St-Lazare and around

Autun's great twelfth-century **Cathédrale St-Lazare** was built nearly a thousand years after the Romans had gone and stands in the highest and

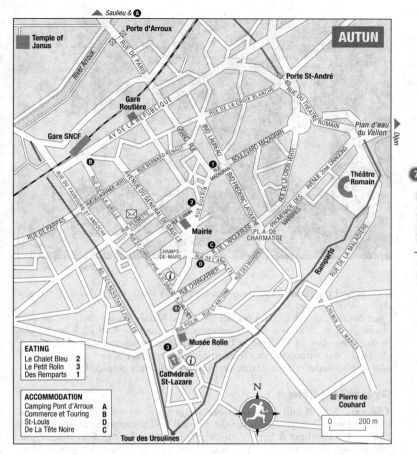

Saulieu & Ⓐ

AUTUN

Temple of Janus

Porte d'Arroux

Porte St-André

Gare Routière

Gare SNCF

RIVER ARROUX

RUE DE PARIS

AV DE LA RÉPUBLIQUE

GRAND RUE

RUE BERNARD RENAUT

RUE DE LA CROIX BLANCHE

RUE DU THÉÂTRE ROMAIN

BD LAUREAU

BOULEVARD MAZAGRAN

RUE MAZAGRAN

BD FRÉDÉRIC LATOUCHE

RUE GUÉRIN

RUE DE LA CROIX VERTE

AVENUE 2ème DRAGONS

Plan d'eau du Vallon

Dijon

Théâtre Romain

RUE DU FAUBOURG ST-ANDOCHE

RUE DE LAGRANGE-VEHU

RUE DE LA GRILLE

AVENUE DU GÉNÉRAL DE GAULLE

RUE JEANIN

RUE PERNETTE

Mairie

RUE DE L'ARQUEBUSE

PROMENADE DES MARBRES

PL A-DE CHARMASSE

RUE DE PARPAS

RUE ST-CHRISTOPHE

R ST-SALEUR

R DAGUIN

CHAMPS-DE-MARS

RUE DE L'ARBALÈTE

RUE CHANGARNIER

RUE DES MARBRES

Ramparts

RUE DE LA MALADIÈRE

BD DESFRESSIAN ST-JULES

RUE PIOLIN

RUE ST-ANTOINE

CHEMIN DES MARIES

Ⓑ

Ⓘ

❶

❷

Ⓒ

Ⓘ

Ⓓ

Ⓘ

Ⓘ

❸

Musée Rolin

Cathédrale St-Lazare

Pierre de Couhard

N

Tour des Ursulines

0   200 m

EATING

Le Chalet Bleu	2
Le Petit Rolin	3
Des Remparts	1

ACCOMMODATION

Camping Pont d'Arroux	A
Commerce et Touring	B
St-Louis	D
De La Tête Noire	C

best-fortified corner of the town. Its greatest claim to artistic fame lies in its sculptures, the work of Gislebertus, generally accepted as one of the most outstanding Romanesque sculptors.

The tympanum of the **Last Judgement** above the west door bears his signature – *Gislebertus hoc fecit* ("Gislebertus made this") – beneath the feet of Christ. To his left are depicted the Virgin Mary, the saints and the apostles, with the saved rejoicing below them; to the right the Archangel Michael disputes souls with Satan, who tries to cheat by leaning on the scales, while the damned despair beneath. During the eighteenth century the local clergy decided the tympanum was an inferior work and plastered it over, saving it from almost certain destruction during the Revolution. The head of Christ, however, had been hacked off, and was only rediscovered – hiding anonymously in the collection of the Musée Rolin – in 1948.

The interior of the cathedral, whose pilasters and arcading were modelled on the Roman architecture of the city's gates, was also decorated by Gislebertus, who carved most of the capitals himself. Conveniently for anyone wanting a close look, some of the finest are now exhibited in the old chapter library, up

▲ Porte St-Andre, Autun

the stairs on the right of the choir, among them a beautiful *Flight into Egypt* and *Adoration of the Magi*.

Just outside the cathedral on rue des Bancs, the **Musée Rolin** (daily except Tues 10am–noon & 2–5/6pm; €3.40) occupies a Renaissance *hôtel* built by Nicolas Rolin, chancellor of Philippe le Bon. In addition to interesting Gallo-Roman pieces, the star attractions are Gislebertus's representation of Eve as an unashamedly sensual nude, and the Maître de Moulins' brilliantly coloured *Nativity*.

Practicalities

The **gare SNCF** and **gare routière** are just a short walk from the central square of the Champs-de-Mars, where you'll find the main **tourist office** at 13 rue Demetz (June & Sept Mon–Sat 9am–1pm & 2–7pm, Sun 10am–1pm; July & Aug Mon–Sat 9am–7pm, Sun 10am–1pm & 3–6pm; Oct–May Mon 2–6pm, Tues–Sat 9.30am–12.30pm & 2–6pm; ☎03.85.86.80.38, ⓦwww.autun-tourisme.com). **Internet** aaccess is available at *Elge*, 10 Grande-rue Chauchien (€4 per hour; closed Sun).

Three inexpensive **hotels** line the main road opposite the station, including the *Commerce et Touring* (☎03.85.52.17.90, ⓦwww.hotelrestaurant-commerce-touring.com; ❶; closed Jan), which provides quiet, en-suite rooms. For something classier, try one of the old coaching inns just off the Champs-de-Mars. Napoleon twice slept at the now slightly faded but once magnificent *St-Louis* (☎03.85.52.01.01, ⓦwww.hotelsaintlouis.net; ❺), 6 rue de l'Arbalète. For €250, you can even sleep in the emperor's suite itself, still containing much of its original furniture. The comfortable *Hôtel de La Tête Noire*, opposite at no. 3 (☎03.85.86.59.99, ⓦwww.hoteltetenoire.fr; ❹; posh restaurant from €17) has less memorable rooms, on the whole, though those on the top floor are very pretty and have excellent views. There's also a **campsite** just across the river on the road to Saulieu, *Camping Porte d'Arroux* (☎03.85.52.10.82, ⓦwww.camping-autun.com; April–Oct), which offers **bike hire**.

For traditional French **cuisine** your best options lie behind the Hôtel de Ville: *Le Chalet Bleu*, 3 rue Jeannin (☎03.85.86.27.30; menus €18–58; closed Mon evening & Tues) is innovative and distinctly stylish, while at 17 rue Mazagran the *Restaurant des Remparts* (☎03.85.52.54.02; lunch €13.50, dinner from €21; closed Wed): is a convivial place – there's much kissing of cheeks between the regulars – with great value menus on which Burgundian specialities line up alongside some excellent fish dishes. You'll find lighter meals and more picturesque outside seating around the cathedral on place St-Louis, with a pair of pizzerias and *Le Petit Rolin* (☎03.85.86.15.55), serving *grillades* (€12) in a cosy downstairs dining room.

Mont-Beuvray

The base for the climb up Mont-Beuvray to the 2000-year-old site of the Gallic capital of Bibracte is **ST-LÉGER-SOUS-BEUVRAY**, about 26km southwest of Autun and reached along the N81 and D61 through typical Morvan countryside of wooded hills and scattered farms, coarse marshy pastures and brown streams. There's the odd bus from Autun, but the schedules won't allow you to come here for a day-trip. Convenient, then, that the *Hôtel-Restaurant du Morvan* (☎03.85.82.51.06, ⊚www.hoteldumorvan.com; ❶), at place de la Marie, has old-fashioned but decent rooms, and serves local food menus at €13.50.

Le Creusot

LE CREUSOT (not to be confused with Le Creuset, the northern French town of cast-iron cookware fame) means one thing to French ears: the **Schneider iron and steelworks**, maker of the first French locomotive in 1838, the first steamship in 1839, the 75mm field gun – mainstay of World War I artillery – and the ironwork of the Pont Alexandre-III and the Gare d'Austerlitz in Paris. The last Schneider died in 1960, whereupon the company was broken up, and a number of different firms now carry on the tradition: Creusot-Loire manufactures specialized steels for the French military and nuclear industry, while Alstom manufactures parts of the TGV.

The town's main attraction is the **Écomusée le Creusot-Montceau** in the Château de la Verrerie on place Schneider (same hours as tourist office; €6). Built as a glassworks in 1786–87 – Louis XVI was a shareholder before losing his head – the château was sold to the Schneider family in 1838 and transformed into their private home and the administrative centre of their business empire. The Schneiders were paternalistic but despotic employers, providing housing, schools and health care for their workers, but expecting "gratitude and obedience" in return.

Today, the château houses a museum dedicated to the iron and steel industry, with paintings of various Schneiders, mock-ups of workers' quarters, and giant model trains. The peculiar cone-shaped constructions in the courtyard of the château were glass furnaces; one of them was transformed into a tiny Neoclassical theatre where plays were put on to entertain the Schneiders' wealthy and influential guests, and can be visited on regular tours.

A more recent development in town is the huge **Parc Touristique des Combes** (March–June, Sept & Oct Sat & Sun 2–7pm; July & Aug daily 11am–7pm; ⊚www.parcdescombes.com), which boasts a narrow-gauge steam train (€6.40), a karting track, a 435-metre-long dry luge piste (€2.70) and an unusual panorama over the steelworks, the gleaming white Château de la Verrerie and the terraces of old workers' houses, all set against the northeastern bulwark of the Massif Central.

Practicalities

The **tourist office**, in the gatehouse of the Château de la Verrerie (Mon–Fri 10am–noon & 1–5/6pm, Sat & Sun 2.30–6/7pm; ℡03.85.55.02.46, ⓦwww .le-creusot.fr), sells tickets to the Écomusée and can provide information about a mining museum in nearby Blanzy. The local station is a short walk away down rue Leclerc, but the grander **TGV station** is 6km away in Montchanin and only served by a couple of buses per day; a taxi (℡03.85.80.97.18) will cost about €15. Eminently presentable if unexciting **rooms** are on offer at *Le Bourgogne* on place Schneider (℡03.85.80.32.02; ❸), which has a decent brasserie downstairs. If on a budget, try *Le Bodsonn* (℡03.85.55.03.34; ❶), 26 rue de l'Yser, with comfy rooms a fifteen-minute walk from the centre – cross the railway tracks then follow avenue de Verdun and rue Foch.

Nevers

Some sixty kilometres west of the Parc du Morvan, at the western confines of Burgundy, **NEVERS** is a small provincial city on the confluence of the rivers Loire and Nièvre. The town is known for its *nougatine* sweets and fine porcelain, hand-painted with a deep blue colour known as *bleue de Nevers*. **Faïence**, as it's also called, has been a hallmark of Nevers since the seventeenth century and is now something of a growth industry – you can see artisans at work (and buy their products) in the shops on rue du 14-Juillet.

Place Carnot is the hub of the centre, and it's here that you'll find the fifteenth-century **Palais Ducal**, former home of the dukes of Nevers, with octagonal turrets and a central tower adorned with elegantly carved hunting scenes. That aside, Nevers' main draws are its religious monuments. The stunning **Cathédrale de St-Cyr**, with its wonderful display of jutting gargoyles, displays French architectural styles from the tenth to the sixteenth centuries; it even manages to have two opposite apses, one Gothic, the other Romanesque. On the far side of the agreeable pedestrian precinct around rue Mitterand, which is where most of the shops are, is the even more interesting and aesthetically satis-fying late eleventh-century **church of St-Étienne**. Behind its plain exterior lies one of the prototype pilgrim churches, with galleries above the aisles, ambulatory and three radiating chapels around the apse.

Of spiritual rather than architectural appeal is the **convent of St-Gildard**, where Bernadette of Lourdes ended her days. A steady flow of pilgrims come to visit her tiny, embalmed body, displayed in a glass-fronted **shrine** (daily 7.30am–noon & 2–6pm) in the convent chapel. Next door a small but very engaging free **museum** displays some of her belongings and correspondence.

Practicalities

Avenue de Gaulle leads from the train and bus stations straight to place Carnot and the **tourist office** (April–Sept Mon–Sat 9am–6.30pm, Sun 10am–1pm & 3–6pm; Oct–March Mon–Sat 9am–noon & 2–6pm; ℡03.86.68.46.00, ⓦwww .nevers-tourisme.com). On the near bank of the Loire, next to the railway bridge, an excellent base for outdoor activities awaits you: Le Bureau des Guides de Loire rents out **bikes** (€15 per day) and organizes canoe trips from a few hours to several days (April–Sept; ℡03.86.57.69.76, ⓦwww.l-o-i-r-e.com).

A comfortable, central **hotel** is the traditional *Hôtel de Cleves*, 8 rue St Didier (☎03.86.61.15.87, ⓦwww.hoteldecleves.fr; ❷), with charming owners and rooms. For a marginally cheaper stay, go for the quiet and friendly *Hôtel Thermidor* (☎03.86.57.15.47; ❶), right opposite the train station at 14 rue Claude-Tillier. The municipal **campsite** (☎06.84.98.69.79, ⓦwww.campingnevers.com; mid-April to mid-Oct) lies just across the Pont de Loire, beside the river at rue de la Jonction.

For **restaurants**, a good place to look is avenue de Gaulle, where *La Mange'oir*, no. 24 (☎03.86.57.28.61; closed Sat & Sun lunch, & all day Mon), offers an excellent choice of grills, salads, pizzas and cheesy Savoie specialities (*plats* €8–15), and *Le Bistrot de Chloé*, no. 25 (☎03.86.36.72.70; closed Sun & Mon), represents a more formal, classic option, with a good, fresh *menu du marché* for €22. At the other end of town, *La Cour St-Étienne*, 33 rue St-Étienne (☎03.86.36.74.57; closed Sun evening. Mon & Tues evening), serves high-quality, traditional food (around €25) in a cheery, half-timbered dining room. A couple of brasseries around rue Mitterand and the posse of *kebaberies* by the station provide lighter – and cheaper – bites.

Dijon and southern Burgundy

If the much-touted image of "rural Burgundy" has got you anticipating a slightly ramshackle rustic charm, you'll have to do some adjusting when you encounter the slick prosperity of **Dijon** and the wine-producing country to the south, known as the **Côte d'Or**. It may look peacefully pastoral, but there's nothing medieval about the methods or the profits made in today's wine business. For any trace of the older traditions you have to head into the south-western corner of the region, into the wine-producing regions of the **Mâconnais** and **Beaujolais**, and the cattle country of the **Charollais**.

Dijon

DIJON owes its origins to its strategic position in Celtic times on the tin merchants' route from Britain up the Seine and across the Alps to the Adriatic. It became the capital of the dukes of Burgundy around 1000 AD, but its golden age occurred in the fourteenth and fifteenth centuries under the auspices of dukes Philippe le Hardi (the Bold), who as a boy had fought the English at Poitiers and been taken prisoner, Jean sans Peur (the Fearless), Philippe le Bon (the Good), who sold Joan of Arc to the English, and Charles le Téméraire (also the Bold). They used their tremendous wealth and power – especially their control of Flanders, the dominant manufacturing region of the age – to make Dijon one of the greatest centres of art, learning and science in Europe. It lost its capital status

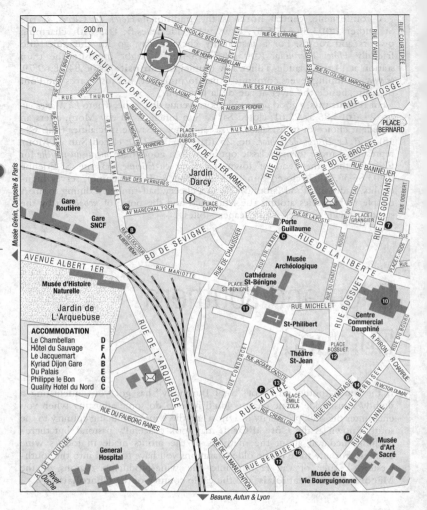

ACCOMMODATION
Le Chambellan	D
Hôtel du Sauvage	F
Le Jacquemart	A
Kyriad Dijon Gare	B
Du Palais	E
Philippe le Bon	G
Quality Hotel du Nord	C

▼ Beaune, Autun & Lyon

on incorporation into the kingdom of France in 1477, but has remained one of
the country's pre-eminent provincial cities, especially since the rail and industrial
booms of the mid-nineteenth century. Today, it's an affluent university town:
smart, modern and young, especially when the students are around.

Arrival and information

Dijon is not an enormous city and the area you'll want to see is neatly confined
to the eminently walkable centre. The **gare SNCF**, with the **gare routière**
next door, is a five-minute walk away from place Darcy and the city centre –
just head down avenue Maréchal-Foch.

The main **tourist office** is in the heart of the city at 11 rue des Forges (May–
Oct Mon–Sat 9am–7pm, Sun 9am–12.30pm & 2.30–5pm; Nov–April Mon–Sat

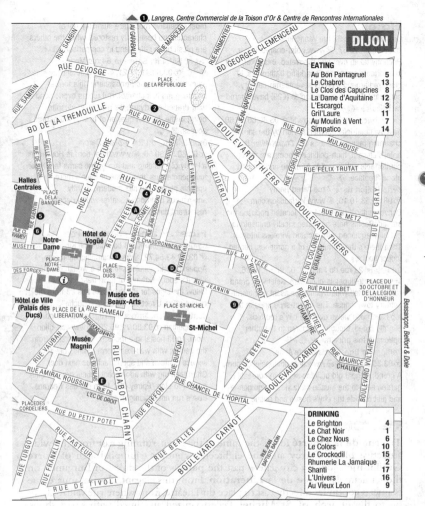

▲ ●, Langres, Centre Commercial de la Toison d'Or & Centre de Rencontres Internationales

DIJON

EATING

Au Bon Pantagruel	5
Le Chabrot	13
Le Clos des Capucines	8
La Dame d'Aquitaine	12
L'Escargot	3
Gril'Laure	11
Au Moulin à Vent	7
Simpatico	14

DRINKING

Le Brighton	4
Le Chat Noir	1
Le Chez Nous	6
Le Colors	10
Le Crockodil	15
Rhumerie La Jamaique	2
Shanti	17
L'Univers	16
Au Vieux Léon	9

7

BURGUNDY | Dijon

▶ Beasançon, Belfort & Dole

10am–noon & 2–6pm, Sun 2.30–5.30pm; ☎08.92.70.05.58, ⓦwww
.dijon-tourism.com) and organizes lots of guided tours. If you're planning a heavy
programme of museum and vineyard visits in the area, it might be worth investing
in the **Dijon Pass** (from €10), which gives significant reductions. There's a second
office on place Darcy (Mon–Sat 9am–12.30pm & 2.30–6pm), which is handier
if coming from the station and can also help with room reservations.

Accommodation

Dijon has no shortage of reasonably priced **hotels** in the centre of town, but
it's worth booking at least a week in advance if you plan to stay in the busy
months of May, June, September and October.

Hotels

Le Chambellan 92 rue Vannerie
⊕03.80.67.12.67, ⓦwww.hotel-chambellan.fr.
Recently taken over and renovated, this hotel, with comfortable rooms and sparkling bathrooms, is clustered around a pretty seventeenth-century courtyard. The cheapest singles (€29) have shared facilities. ❶–❸

Le Jacquemart 32 rue Verrerie ⊕03.80.60.09.60, ⓦwww.hotel-lejacquemart.fr. Run by the same charming management as the *Chambellan*, the hotel's elegant, high-ceilinged rooms are full of comfortable antique-style furniture and the odd stone fireplace. ❶–❸

Kyriad Dijon Gare 7 rue Albert Remy
⊕03.80.53.10.10, ⓦwww.kyriaddijon.com.
Conveniently, if unappealingly located opposite the station. Rooms here are categorically uninspiring, but fully-equipped with a/c and wireless internet. Then there's the trumpcard of a gorgeous, heated indoor pool. ❹

Du Palais 23 rue du Palais ⊕03.80.67.16.26, ⓦwww.hoteldupalais-dijon.com. Relatively grand rooms with tall windows in a pleasant eighteenth-century town house. The garret-style ones at the top have good views over the city's rooftops. Slightly faded, though, compared to the other options in this price range. ❷–❹

Philippe le Bon 18 rue Sainte Anne
⊕03.80.30.73.52, ⓦwww.hotelphilippelebon.com.
A grand, elegant old building set in an agreeable garden next to the Musée da la vie Bourguigonne and just outside the city's hustle and bustle. The most expensive rooms are stunning; full of character and beautifully restored, while the others are plush but a little bland in comparison. ❻–❽

Hôtel du Sauvage 64 rue Monge
⊕03.80.41.31.21, ⓦwww.hotellesauvage .com. Delightful and atmospheric, this former coaching inn has characterful rooms overlooking a vine-draped courtyard. It's also quiet, despite being in the liveliest quarter of town. Paid garage access. ❷–❹

Quality Hotel du Nord place Darcy
⊕03.80.50.80.50, ⓦwww.hotel-nord.fr. Housed in a lovely old building and run by the same family for four generations, this is one of Dijon's more upscale places, but has modern, slightly anonymous bedrooms. Central with a decent restaurant downstairs. ❺

Hostel and campsite

Camping du Lac Kir 3 bd Chanoine Kir,
⊕03.80.43.54.72, ⓦwww.camping-dijon.com.
Appealing and popular site with a wealth of activities. It's about 1km out of town near Lake Kir: follow the signs for Paris, or take bus #3 from the train station, direction "Fontaine d'Ouche".

Centre de Rencontres Internationales 1 bd Champollion ⊕03.80.72.95.20, ⓦwww.cri-dijon .com. An HI hostel in a modern complex 2km from the centre, with well-kept dorm rooms, a self-service canteen and sports facilities next door. Often teeming with adolescent school groups. Take bus #4 to stop "Épirey CRI" from rue des Godrans. Buses run until midnight.

The City

The **rue de la Liberté** forms the spine of the town, running east from the wide, attractive **place Darcy** and the eighteenth-century triumphal arch of **Porte Guillaume** – once a city gate – past the **palace** of the dukes of Burgundy on the semicircular **place de la Libération**. From this elegant, classical square, rue Rameau continues directly east to place du Théâtre, from where rue Vaillant leads on to the **church of St Michel**. Pedestrianized and lined with smart shops, mammoth department stores and elegant old houses, most places of interest are within ten-minutes' walk to the north or south of this main axis.

The Palais des Ducs

The geographical focus of a visit to Dijon is inevitably the seat of its former rulers, the **Palais des Ducs**, which stands at the hub of the city. Facing the main courtyard, Mansart's serene **place de la Libération** was built towards the end of the seventeenth century to show off a statue of the Sun King; it's now something of a sun trap on a good day, and a decision to close it to traffic has stimulated a boom in café trade. The fourteenth-century **Tour de Bar** dominates the courtyard in front of the east wing, which now houses the Musée des Beaux-Arts, while the loftier, fifteenth-century **Tour Philippe–le-Bon** can be visited only on guided tours (April–Nov, 11 tours daily; Dec–March on Wed, tours at 1.30pm, 2.30pm & 3.30pm; Sat & Sun six tours; €2.30). The view from the top is particularly worthwhile for the unobstructed views of the glazed Burgundian tiles of the Hôtel de Vogüé and the cathedral; on a clear day the Alps loom on the horizon.

Given the dukes' possessions in the Netherlands, it's hardly surprising that the **Musée des Beaux-Arts** (daily except Tues 10am–5pm; free) boasts a Flemish collection. Among the highlights is the *Nativity* by the so-called Master of Flémalle, a shadowy figure who may have been the teacher of Rogier van der Weyden and who ranks with van Eyck as one of the first artists to break from the chilly stranglehold of International Gothic.

Visiting the museum also provides the opportunity to see the surviving portions of the original ducal palace, including the vast **kitchen** and the magnificent **Salle des Gardes**, richly appointed with panelling, tapestries and a minstrels' gallery. Here are displayed the lavish, almost decadent **tombs** from the Chartreuse de Champmol of Philippe le Hardi and Jean sans Peur and his wife, Marguerite de Bavière, with their startling, painted effigies of the dead, surrounded by gold-plated angels.

The Quartier Notre-Dame

Architecturally more interesting than the palace, and much more suggestive of the city's former glories, are the lavish town houses of the rich burghers. These abound in the streets behind the palace: rue Verrerie, rue Vannerie, rue des Forges, rue Chaudronnière (look out for no. 28, **Maison des Cariatides**). Some are half-timbered, with storeys projecting over the street, others are in more formal and imposing Renaissance stone. Particularly fine are the Renaissance **Hôtel de Vogüé**, 12 rue de la Chouette, and at no. 34, the **Hôtel Chambellan** (1490).

Also in this quarter behind the dukes' palace, in the angle between rue de la Chouette and rue de la Préfecture, is the **church of Notre-Dame**, built in the early thirteenth century in the Burgundian Gothic style. In the south transept there is a ninth-century wooden "black" Virgin, one of the oldest in France. Known as "Our Lady of Good Hope", she is credited with twice miraculously saving the city from fighting, most recently when German troops left peacefully in 1944. Outside on rue de la Chouette, in the north wall of the church, is a small sculpted owl – *chouette* – polished by the hands of passers-by who for centuries have touched it for luck.

From here rue Musette leads west, passing just south of the **market square** and the covered *halles*. The whole area is full of sumptuous displays of food and attractive cafés and restaurants, and is thronged with people on market days (Tues, Thurs, Fri & Sat).

South of the place de la Libération

On the south side of the place Darcy–church of St-Michel axis, and especially in the *quartier* behind place de la Libération, there's a concentration of magnificent hotels from the seventeenth and eighteenth centuries. These were built for the most part by men who had bought themselves offices and privileges with the Parliament of Burgundy, established by Louis XI in 1477 after the death of Duke Charles le Téméraire (the Bold) as a concession designed to win the compliance of this newly acquired frontier province. One of them, 4 rue des Bons-Enfants, houses the **Musée Magnin** (Tues–Sun 10am–noon & 2–6pm; €3.50), the building – a seventeenth-century *hôtel particulier* – complete with its original furnishings, is more interesting than the exhibition of paintings by good but lesser-known artists. Other noteworthy houses are to be found nearby in rue Vauban, some showing the marks of Hugues Sambin's influence in their decorative details (lions' heads, garlands of fruit, tendrils of ivy and his famous *chou bourguignon*, or "Burgundy cabbage"), notably, nos. 3, 12, 21 and 23.

Continuing south from Musée Magnin, rue Ste-Anne, near place des Cordeliers, is home to two museums. The **Musée de la Vie Bourguignonne** at no. 17 (daily except Tues 9am–noon & 2–6pm; free) highlights nineteenth-century Burgundian life, featuring costumes, furniture and domestic industries like butter-, cheese- and bread-making, along with a reconstructed kitchen. Practically next door at no. 15, the **Musée d'Art Sacré** (same hours; free) contains an important collection of church treasures, including a seventeenth-century statue of St Paul, the first in the world to be restored using an extraordinary technique that involves injecting the stone with resin and then solidifying the resulting compound using gamma rays. Formerly crumbling to dust, the guinea-pig saint is now completely firm.

Eating, drinking and entertainment

Dijon has an inordinate number of **patisseries**, full of high-quality, tempting confectionery in which marzipan and fruit feature prominently. Some also promote the Dijon specialities: *pain d'épices*, a gingerbread made with honey and spices and eaten with butter or jam (from *Mulot et Petitjean*, 13 place Bossuet and other branches all over town), and *cassissines* – blackcurrant candies. **Chocolate**, best made on the premises, is another speciality – try *Au Parrain Généreux*, 21 rue du Bourg, southwest of the Palais. You can hardly forget that Dijon is also the high temple of **mustard** – the shop of leading producer Maille is at 30 rue de la Liberté, selling a range from mild to cauterizing. To buy good but affordable **wine**, head to *Au Vieux Millésime*, 82 rue Monge (closed Sun & Mon), where Ludovic Flexas offers helpful advice on wines from the region and further afield and prices start at around €10.

There are a large number of excellent **restaurants** throughout the city, particularly around rue Monge, while pretty place Émile Zola is packed with the open-air tables of reasonably priced pizzerias.

Restaurants

Au Bon Pantagruel place du Marché, 20 rue Quentin ☎ 03.80.30.68.69. A popular, lively bistro decorated with cartoons and located alongside the market. Beef, duck, veal and pork all appear on a menu that changes with healthy frequency. Menus from €23, set lunch €11.80.

Le Chabrot 36 rue Monge ☎ 03.80.30.69.61. Atmospheric, friendly restaurant on the west side of place Émile-Zola. It has a good-value lunch for €13.50, while Burgundian classics and more refined offerings mingle on the more expensive menus (from €28). Doubles as a wine bar-cum-cellar; the superb wine list offers lots of help for amateurs.

Le Clos des Capucines 3 rue Jeannin, at the end of rue Jean-Jacques-Rousseau ☎ 03.80.65.83.03. Housed in a beautiful medieval building, this restaurant serves very good traditional, rich Burgundy cuisine (*jambon persillé, escargots, boeuf bourguignon*) at very reasonable prices. Midday from €14.50, evenings from €18.50. Closed Sat lunch & Sun.

La Dame d'Aquitaine 23 place Bossuet ☎ 03.80.30.45.65. If the menus (€29–45) are nothing extraordinary, composed of the usual regional suspects, the setting most certainly is: a handful of tables set spaciously beneath the stone vaults of a twelfth-century crypt, in a refined atmosphere of classical music. Closed Sun & Mon.

L'Escargot 43 rue Rousseau ☎ 03.80.73.33.85. Attractive, red-fronted restaurant with surprisingly low prices, making it a great place to try the local classics. Menus from €20, closed Sun.

Gril'Laure 8 place St-Bénigne ☎ 03.80.41.86.76. Popular with the business lunch crowd for its convenient cathedral-side location, and pizzas, pasta and grilled dishes hot out of the wood-fired oven. Menu at €24, *plats* €12.

Au Moulin à Vent 8 place François Rude ☎ 03.80.30.81.43. A popular brasserie in a colourful, timbered house on one of the city's prettiest squares. *Boeuf bourguignon* and *oeufs meurette* are both on the menu. The room upstairs houses a more formal restaurant.

Simpatico 30 rue Berbisey ☎ 03.80.30.53.53. Excellent Italian restaurant with stylish, modern decor and an almost defiantly Italian wine list. Three courses for €18. Closed Sun, Mon & Aug.

Cafés, bars and nightclubs

Dijon is an important university city as well as one of France's main conference centres, so **nightspots** and cultural centres at both ends of the range are worth exploring. Rue Berbisey is a good place to start a night out. The English/Irish theme pubs are predictably popular, but there are plenty of alternatives. For **information** on bands and DJs, pick up a free *Mag de la Nuit* (ⓦwww.magdelanuit.net) at the tourist office or various establishments around the city.

Le Brighton 33 rue Auguste-Comte. English pub with 200 different kinds of beer, and dancing. Daily till around 3am or later.

Le Chat Noir 20 av Garibaldi. Just off place de la République, this is Dijon's most serious clubbing venue but not always its friendliest – especially if you're a group of young men. €10 entry includes a drink. Usually Thurs–Sat, but ⓦwww.lechatnoir.fr has the up-to-date programme.

Le Chez Nous just behind rue Quentin. Tucked down a tiny alleyway just off rue Quentin, this is an authentic community bar with a proudly alternative ethos and a genuine atmosphere. Expect strip lighting, mismatched old tables, exhibitions and impromptu performances. Also does cheap bar snacks and fine wines by the glass.

Le Colors Centre Commercial Dauphine. Probably the most popular student club, with the added advantage that it's dead central. Themed nights are organized regularly during term. ⓦwww.lecolors .net has full details of the programme.

Le Crockodil 88 rue Berbisey. Inside is an attempted pub decor, though the electric dartboard doesn't quite convince. Outside is a very continental café terrace. A good place for an afternoon coffee leading into an early evening drink. Mon–Sat till 2am.

Rhumerie la Jamaïque 14 place de la République. Popular with a trendy late-20s/early-30s crowd for its pricey cocktails and rock-opera decor; they have live bands most nights at 11pm, playing music ranging from rock to salsa to jazz. There's a younger vibe at weekends for the dancefloor and DJ downstairs. Open Tues–Sat till 5am.

Shanti 69 rue Berbisey. Great little hookah joint, decked out with divans in transcendental South Asian decor, serving delicious teas, non-alcoholic cocktails and flavoured *sheesha* (€8 for a tobacco pipe). Closed Sun & Mon.

L'Univers 47 rue Berbisey. Trendy and dark, this popular pub-bar has frequent student-run blues, jazz and rock concerts in the cellar. Open till midnight and later.

Au Vieux Léon 52 rue Jeannin. Tiny, noisy, friendly little bar that's positively jumping with students. Decorated like an old-fashioned French café on acid. Mon–Sat 6pm–2am.

Listings

Bike hire Available at the central tourist office for €18 per day.

Car hire Numerous outlets on the square outside the station, like Hertz (☏03.80.53.14.00) or Europcar (☏08.21.80.58.07).

Cinemas L'Eldorado, 21 rue Alfred-de-Musset (☏08.92.68.01.74, ⓦwww.cinema-eldorado.fr), is a three-screen arts cinema showing all films in original language with a concentration of foreign films. Devosge, 6 rue Devosge (☏08.92.68.73.33, ⓦwww.cinealpes.fr), shows most films in the original, and tries to deviate from the obvious blockbusters.

Festivals The city has a good summer music season, with classical concerts throughout June in its Été Musical programme. L'Estivade, which takes place at various locations around the city between late June and mid-Aug, puts on endless music, dance and street theatre performances. The Fête de la Vigne, in the last week of Aug, is a traditional costume/folklore jamboree; while the Foire gastronomique, during the first two weeks of Nov, celebrates all things edible.

Internet Cybersp@ce21 (46 rue Monge; Mon–Sat 11am–midnight, Sun 2pm–midnight; €4/hr) is a good option in the centre of the old town.

Laundry 41 rue Auguste-Comte; daily 6am–9pm.

Pharmacy Junction of rue Berbisey and rue Charrue Mon–Sat 8.45am–7pm.

Swimming pool Oxygène-Parc Aquatique, Centre Commercial de la Toison d'Or (closed Nov–March; ☏03.80.74.16.16; adults €9, children €7.50; bus #2 or #7). Has a wave machine, Jacuzzi and water slides.

The Côte d'Or

South of Dijon, the attractive countryside of the **Côte d'Or** is characterized by the steep scarp of the *côte*, wooded along the top and cut by sheer little valleys called *combes*, where local rock climbers hone their skills (footpaths **GR7** and **GR76** run the whole length of the wine country as far south as Lyon). Spring is a good time to visit this region, when you can avoid the crowds and the landscape is a dramatic symphony of browns – trees, earth and vines, along with millions of bone-coloured vine stakes wheeling past as you travel through, like crosses in a vast war cemetery.

The place names that line the N74 – Gevrey-Chambertin, Vougeot, Vosne-Romanée, Nuits-St-Georges, Pommard, Volnay, Meursault Beaune – are music to the ears of wine buffs. These places are certainly prosperous, but apart from the busy tourist centre of **Beaune**, they don't offer much of interest to the visitor. You can taste and buy direct from source at most of the **vineyards** by just turning up and asking (tourist offices can provide you with a good map), though few have regular opening hours. One that does is the **Château de Meursault** (daily 9.30–12 & 2–6pm; ⓦ www.chateau-meursault.com), which has extensive and beautiful grounds and is the most prestigious producer of white wine. The visit costs €15, though, before you've bought a single bottle.

The wines of Burgundy

Burgundy farmers have been growing grapes since Roman times, and their rulers, the dukes, frequently put their **wines** to effective use as a tool of diplomacy. Like other regions of France, though, Burgundy's vineyards have had a rough last decade due to competition from the southern hemisphere. Because of stringent legal restrictions banning watering and other interference, however, French wines, more than others, remain a faithful reflection of the *terroir* where they are produced, and Burgundy experts remain confident that the climate and soil of their region will fight off any temporary economic challenges.

Burgundy's best wines come from a narrow strip of hillside called the **Côte d'Or** that runs southwest from Dijon to Santenay, and is divided into two regions, Côte de Nuits (the better reds) and Côte de Beaune (the better whites). High-quality wine is certainly produced further south as well, though, in the **Mâconnais** and on the **Côtes Chalonnaises**, while **Beaujolais** is famous (some might say notorious) for its cheap, fruity *nouveau,* which is drunk very young. Reds from the region are made almost exclusively from the Pinot Noir grape, while whites are largely from Chardonnay. Of the latter, particularly renowned are the light, dry vintages of **Chablis**, which are divided into *Grands Crus* (the most prestigious, and therefore dearest), *Premiers Crus* (the next level down) and the still very drinkable *Petit Chablis.* Fans of bubbly should look out for the often highly regarded **sparkling** whites, which crop up across the region and won't set you back half as much as a bottle of Champagne.

The single most important factor determining the "character" of wines is the **soil**. In both the Côte d'Or and Chablis, its character varies over very short distances, making for an enormous variety of taste. Chalky soil makes a wine *virile* or *corsé*, in other words "heady" – *il y a de la mâche*, they say, "something to bite on" – while clay makes it *féminin*, more *agréable*.

For an **apéritif** in Burgundy, you should try *kir*, named after the man who was both mayor and MP for Dijon for many years after World War II – two parts dry white wine, traditionally *aligoté*, and one part *cassis* or blackcurrant liqueur. To round the evening off there are many **liqueurs** to choose from, but Burgundy is particularly famous for its marcs, of which the best are matured for years in oak casks.

Alternatively, there are countless *caves* in the towns, where you can get good advice on different vintages. Be prepared to pay for your tasting if you don't go on to make a significant purchase.

Beaune

BEAUNE, the principal town of the Côte d'Or, manages to maintain its attractively ancient air, despite a near constant stream of tourists and rampant commercialism – this must be one of the few towns in France where most of the shops stay open at lunchtime. Narrow cobbled streets and sunny squares dotted with cafés make it a lovely spot to sample the region's wine, though you may find it cheaper and easier to use Dijon as a base for getting around in the area, as there are good connections by train and Transco buses (Ⓦwww.cg21.fr for timetables), which serve all the villages down the N74.

Beaune's town centre is a tightly clustered, rampart-enclosed *vieille ville*, and its chief attraction is the fifteenth-century hospital, the **Hôtel-Dieu** (daily: April to mid-Nov 9am–6.30pm; mid-Nov to March 9–11.30am & 2–5.30pm; €6), on the corner of place de la Halle. The cobbled courtyard is surrounded by a wooden gallery overhung by a massive roof patterned with diamonds of gaudy tiles – green, burnt sienna, black and yellow – and similarly multicoloured steep-pitched dormers and turrets. Inside is a vast paved hall with a glorious arched timber roof, the Grande Salle des Malades, with the original heavy, enclosed wooden beds. Passing through two smaller, furnished wards, one with some stunning seventeenth-century frescos, then the kitchen and the pharmacy, you reach a dark chamber housing the splendid fifteenth-century altarpiece of the *Last Judgement* by Rogier van der Weyden.

The private residence of the dukes of Burgundy on rue d'Enfer now contains the **Musée du Vin** (April–Oct daily 9.30am–6pm; Nov–March daily except Tues 9.30am–5pm; €5.40), with giant winepresses, a collection of traditional tools of the trade and a relief map of the vineyards that begins to make sense of it all. If you feel like visiting all three museums in one day, a **combined ticket** into the Musée du Vin, the Hôtel-Dieu and the town's **Musée de Beaux-Arts** costs €10.

Practicalities

Beaune's **gare SNCF** is five-minutes' walk away from the old walls to the east of the centre on avenue du 8-Septembre; buses into town also stop there. The **tourist office**, 6 boulevard Perpreuil (April–Oct daily 9am–7pm; Nov–March Mon–Sat 9am–6pm, Sun 10am–12.30pm & 1.30–5pm; Ⓣ03.80.26.21.30, Ⓦwww .ot-beaune.fr), offers **internet access** (€5 per hour) and a vast array of tours and visits in the area. You can rent **bikes** from Bourgogne Randonnées at avenue de 8 Septembre by the *gare* (Ⓣ03.80.22.06.53; €4 per hour, €17 per day).

If you're going to **stay** in Beaune, be prepared to book well in advance and pay over €50. Within the town walls, one of the less extravagantly priced hotels is the *Central*, 2 rue Victor-Millot (Ⓣ03.80.24.77.24, Ⓦwww.hotelcentral -beaune.com; ⑤; good restaurant from €24), with unspectacular rooms that are cheered up by pretty window boxes. The delightful ⚘ *Hôtel des Remparts*, at 48 rue Thiers (Ⓣ03.80.24.94.94, Ⓦwww.hotel-remparts-beaune.com; ⑤–⑥), is a wonderful place, sensitively restored and full of old beams and ancient stone. You can still see the ramparts that give it its name in some of the (admittedly more expensive) rooms. Most of Beaune's hotels are found just outside the town walls to the southeast; *La Cloche*, at 40 rue du Faubourg Madeleine (Ⓣ03.80.24.66.33, Ⓦwww.hotel-lacloche-beaune.com; ③–⑤), has benefitted

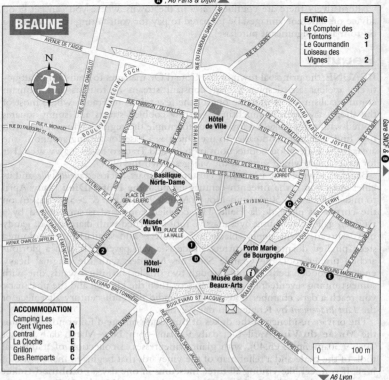

BEAUNE

EATING

Le Comptoir des Tontons	3
Le Gourmandin	1
Loiseau des Vignes	2

ACCOMMODATION

Camping Les Cent Vignes	A
Central	D
La Cloche	E
Grillon	B
Des Remparts	C

0   100 m

▼ A6 Lyon

from a bright refurbishment which complements the elegant old building. Further out, *Hôtel Grillon*, 21 route de Seurre (☎03.80.22.44.25, ⓦwww.hotel -grillon.fr; ❸), is set in gardens about 1km east of town, and has a small heated swimming pool. The pretty *Les Cent Vignes* **campsite**, 10 rue Auguste Dubois (☎03.80.22.03.91; mid-March to Oct), is about 1km north out of town, off rue du Faubourg-St-Nicolas (the N74 to Dijon), before the bridge over the autoroute; booking is advisable.

Eating out is an expensive business here, although good value is offered at lunchtime by the row of brasseries on place Carnot, which all have a *plat du jour* for under €10. For something more sophisticated, try *Le Gourmandin*, 8 place Carnot (☎03.80.24.07.88), with an excellent *menu bourguignon* for €37 and lunch at €18. There's also the decidedly upscale *Loiseau des Vignes*, 31 rue Maufoux (☎03.80.24.12.06; closed Sun & Mon; menus €23 midweek lunch, €48–98 evenings), with high ceilings, a delightful courtyard and an atmosphere of quiet refinement. Wine is served by the glass and accompanied by advice and recommendations. Just outside the town walls, *Le Comptoir des Tontons*, at 22 rue du Faubourg Madeleine (☎03.80.24.19.64; closed Sun & Mon), is a more down-to-earth place, working with lots of organic products. To taste and buy **wine** in Beaune, pay expert Bernard Gras (ⓦwww.vinsbernardgras.com) a visit at 20 rue Faubourg Madeleine. His wide-ranging selection begins with some very reasonably priced bottles (from €10), and tasting is free as long as you're purchasing.

Château du Clos-de-Vougeot

If you find French wine culture fascinating, it's worth visiting the **Château du Clos-de-Vougeot** to see the wine-making process (daily: April–Sept 9am–6.30pm; Oct–March 9–11.30am & 2–5.30pm, Sat closes 5pm; €3.80), 21km north of Beaune between Gévry-Chambertin and Nuits-St-Georges. Mammoth thirteenth-century winepresses, installed by the Cistercian monks to whom these vineyards belonged for nearly seven hundred years until the Revolution, are still here. The château today is the home of a chivalrous order founded in 1934, the Confrèrie des Chevaliers du Tastevin. Chivalrous or not, the new monks continue the good wine work. There's a three-day wine **festival**, Les Trois Glorieuses, on the third Saturday in November, starting in Vougeot and continuing in Beaune, with an important auction at the *Hôtel-Dieu*, and then Meursault.

The Saône valley

The **Saône valley** is prosperous and modern, nourished by the autoroute, tourism, industry (especially metal-working in Chalon and Mâcon), and the wine trade. But turn your back on the river and head west and immediately you enter a different Burgundy: of hilly pasture and woodland, utterly rural and more populated by cattle than people. This is the hinterland – the Deep South – of Burgundy, where every village clusters under the tower of a Romanesque church, spawned by the influence of Cluny in the 1000s and 1100s. It is only when you reach the Loire and encounter the main traffic routes again that you re-enter the modern world.

Its beautiful country for **cycling**, though there are few places from which to actually rent a bike. There are, however, plenty of bus and train connections.

Chalon-sur-Saône

CHALON, a sizeable port and bustling industrial centre on a broad meander of the Saône, is not normally worth a stop in itself, though its old riverside quarter does have an easy charm, and it makes a good base for exploring the more expensive areas of the Côte d'Or. You may be tempted to stay for the pre-Lent carnival (Feb or March), which features a parade of giant masks and a confetti battle, or the national festival of street artists and theatre in July (ⓦ www.chalondanslarue.com).

The highlight of the **old town**, set just back from the river, is the stunning **place St-Vincent**, where you can sit out at cafés beneath the twin towers of the cathedral, gleaming like new pins after their recent restoration, surrounded by medieval timber-framed houses.

Also here is the unusual **Musée Niépce**, 28 quai des Messageries (daily except Tues: July & Aug 10am–6pm; Sept–June 9.30–11.45am & 2–5.45pm; €3.10, free on Wed & first Sun of the month), just downstream from Pont St-Laurent. Nicéphore Niépce, who was born in Chalon, is credited with inventing photography in 1816 – though he named it "heliography". The museum possesses a fascinating range of cameras, from the first machine ever to the Apollo moon mission's equipment, plus a number of 007-type spy-camera devices, all attractively displayed.

You should also make a beeline for the ⚜ **Maison des Vins** on Promenade Ste-Marie (Mon–Sat 9am–7pm), where you can taste and buy a carefully selected range of Côte Chalonnaise wines at low prices – starting at €7, but rising to four figures for the most exclusive vineyards.

Practicalities

The **gares SNCF** and **routière** are well out of the action, but a fifteen-minute walk up avenue Jaurès and boulevard de la République brings you to the town centre. Then bear right towards the attractive riverfront and its **tourist office**, 4 place du Port Villiers (July & Aug Mon–Sat 9am–7pm, Sun 10am–noon & 4–7pm; Sept–June Mon–Sat 9am–12.30pm & 2–6pm; ☎03.85.48.37.97, Ⓦwww.chalon-sur-saone.net).

Accommodation options in the town centre are limited, the nicest undoubtedly being the *St-Jean*, right on the riverbank at 24 quai Gambetta (☎03.85.48.45.65, Ⓦwww.hotelsaintjean.fr; ❸), with classical-style rooms being energetically improved by the friendly owner. Greater luxuries like air conditioning and flat-screen TVS, should you desire them, are on offer at the *Hôtel Kyriad*, 35 place de Beaune (☎03.85.90.08.00, Ⓦwww.kyriad.com; ❹), which has a couple of less standardized oak-panelled rooms – try asking for no. 10. The cheapest hotel is the *Des Jacobines*, 10 rue des Jacobines (☎03.85.48.12.24, Ⓦwww.les-jacobines.fr; ❶), on a quiet street near the centre; or you could walk twenty minutes east out of town to the *Residences Chalon Jeunes* at 18 avenue Pierre Nugue (☎03.85.46.44.90, Ⓦwww.etudiant -chalon.com), which has rooms for €16.50 a night and a cafeteria-style restaurant. *Camping du Pont de Bourgogne* (☎03.85.48.26.86, Ⓦwww.camping -chalon.com; April–Sept) is 1km out of town on the south bank of the Saône in St-Marcel (cross a bridge and head east).

Rue de Strasbourg, across Pont St-Laurent on the so-called *île aux restos*, is lined with excellent **places to eat**, including Italian and Indian as well as French. At no. 31 is the bright-red *Le Bistrot* (☎03.85.93.22.01; closed Sat & Sun), chic to an almost Parisian degree, offering serious quality for around €30. *Chez Jules* at no. 11 (☎03.85.48.08.34; menus €18.50; closed Sat lunch and Sun) represents a good choice for traditional favourites. Back on the mainland is a rare treat for vegetarians: *La Pierre Vive,* 33 rue de Lyon (☎03.85.93.26.50; closed evenings and weekends), where menus are just €12.50 and diners choose from the home-made vegetable dishes listed daily on the slate. A handful of late-night **bars** can be found just off rue de Strasbourg, including the *Boogie Blues Bar* (closed Sun), with a jazzy atmosphere, in rue d'Uxelles. There are food **markets** in place de l'Hôtel de Ville (Wed) and place St-Vincent (Fri & Sun).

Tournus

Graced by ancient, golden buildings **TOURNUS** is a beautiful little town of narrow, huddled streets on the banks of the Saône, 27km south of Chalon. From the N6 you enter the town through a **gateway** flanked by medieval towers and are confronted by the old **abbey church of St-Philibert**, one of the earliest and most influential Romanesque buildings in Burgundy. Construction dates back to around 900 AD; the church was founded by monks fleeing Norman raids on their home community of Noirmoutier off the Atlantic coast. The present building dates to the first half of the eleventh century.

The facade of the church, with its powerful towers and simple decoration of Lombard arcading, has the massive qualities and clean, pared-down lines more associated with a fortress. A narrow staircase opposite the main entrance in the west front leads up to a **high chapel** whose main arch is inset with two extraordinary sculptures. They may represent the abbot responsible for the rebuilding (on the right, holding a hammer and giving a blessing) and possibly the sculptor himself (on the left, full-face), who may even be the "Gerlamus" of the inscription – in which case this may be one of the earliest self-portraits of the medieval period. In 2002, restoration work revealed one further treasure: some twelfth-century, but very Roman-looking, **mosaics**, to be seen in the ambulatory.

To the south of town the **Hôtel Dieu** (April–Oct daily except Tues 10am–1pm & 2–6pm; €5.40) is one of the region's many charity hospitals run by nuns. You can still see the rows of solid but unhygienic oak beds, in which patients, fleas and lice cohabited until 1978, but the real highlight is the elaborate dispensary, complete with a host of faïence pots and hand-blown glass jars.

Practicalities

The **gare SNCF** is on avenue Gambetta, across the road from the old town and a ten-minute walk from the **tourist office** at 2 place de l'Abbaye (June–Sept daily 10am–1pm & 2–7pm; Oct–May Mon–Sat 9.30am–1pm & 2–5pm; ℡03.85.27.00.20, ⓦ www.tournugeois.fr), where staff will reserve accommodation for you (€2.50) and let you use the **internet** (€1 for 15min).

Tournus' **hotels** are the best places to **eat**, as well as sleep, at both ends of the budgetary scale. A stone's throw from the abbey church, the *Hôtel Gras*, 2 rue Fénelon (℡03.85.51.07.25; ❶; restaurant closed Sun), has basic, but charmingly old-fashioned, rooms and an authentic café downstairs which serves delicious home-cooked meals for €13.50. Similarly named, but an altogether different proposition, is the turreted mansion *Hôtel de Greuze*, 5 place de l'Abbaye (℡03.85.51.77.77, ⓦ www.hotel-de-greuze-bourgogne.com; ❽). The plush rooms won't blow you away in themselves, so it's only really worth it if you go the whole hog and pay €225 for a stunning view straight onto the abbey. The restaurant (℡03.85.51.13.52; closed Tues, Wed & Thurs lunch; menus €35–80) is truly outstanding, and run by the highly regarded chef Yohann Chapuis. Alternatively, on the other side of the river, the *Hôtel-Restaurant de Saône* (℡03.85.51.20.65, ⓔ hotelrestaurantdesaone@orange.fr; ❷) has cheerful, modern rooms in a splendidly tranquil riverside location. The restaurant here (from €18; closed Tues & Wed) has standard dishes but a fine view back to the town. **Campers** should head for the municipal site on the river bank (℡03.85.94.16.90, ⓦ www.camping-tournus.com; May–Sept), a fifteen-minute walk north out of town, up rue René-Cassin.

Mâcon and around

MÂCON is a lively, prosperous place on the banks of the River Saône, 58km south of Chalon and 68km north of Lyon, with excellent transport connections between the two. It has no great sights, but despite being a centre for the wine trade it does have a surprisingly sunny, seaside feel, thanks to its long café-lined **riverbank** and free outdoor jazz concerts in late July to early August.

Lamartine, the nineteenth-century French Romantic poet (see box, p.540), was born here in 1790 and his name is much in evidence. He is remembered in the handsome eighteenth-century mansion, the Hôtel Senecé, 41 rue Sigorgne, which houses the **Musée Lamartine** (Tues–Sat 10am–noon & 2–6pm, Sun 2–6pm; €2.50), part of which is dedicated to documents and other memorabilia to do with his personal, political and poetic lives. Nearby, on the corner of place des Herbes where a summertime fruit and veg market is held, stands the town's main tourist curiosity, an incredibly elaborately carved wooden house built around 1500 and known as the **Maison du Bois Doré**, with a wonderful bar/café downstairs that serves cocktails until 2 or 3am.

On the far side of the St-Laurent bridge over the Saône you'll find the embarcation point for a more restful couple of hours: **cruises**, to be reserved at the tourist office (April–Oct: Tues, Thurs & Sat 3pm; €10), allow you to see the waterfront from a new perspective.

Alphonse Lamartine (1790–1869)

Often referred to as the French Byron, **Alphonse Lamartine** is one of the best-known of the French Romantic poets. He was born and grew up in Milly, about 15km west of Mâcon, and published his first poetic work, *Méditations poétiques*, in 1820. In 1825 he published *Le Dernier Chant du Pélérinage d'Harold* as a tribute to Byron.

After the 1830 Revolution in Paris, he became involved in politics, being elected to the Chambre des Députés in 1833 and quickly acquiring a reputation as a powerful orator on the weighty questions of the day, like the abolition of slavery and capital punishment. His finest hour was as the leading figure in the provisional government of the Second Republic, which was proclaimed from the Hôtel de Ville in Paris on February 23, 1848. He withdrew from politics when reactionary forces, under the leadership of General Cavaignac, let the army loose on the protesting workers of Paris and Marseille in June 1848, after which he retired to St-Point, continuing to write and publish until his death in 1869.

The most enjoyable way to bone up on the Mâcon, Beaujolais and Chalonnais **wines** is to head off on one of the much-signposted wine roads (Ⓦwww.bourgogne-tourisme.com), which extend north into the Maconnais, and south into the Beaujolais, sampling as you go. If you're without transport, however, you could make do with the **Maison Mâconnaise des Vins**, 484 avenue Lattre-de-Tassigny (Ⓣ03.85.22.91.11; daily 9am–7pm), on the riverbank ten-minutes' walk north of the centre. It has a selection of reasonably priced wines from around the region, starting at €7. The staff will offer free tastings, as long as you look likely to purchase.

Practicalities

The **gare SNCF** (adjacent to the **gare routière**) lies on rue Bigonnet at the southern end of rue Victor-Hugo, but TGV trains leave from Mâcon-Loché station 6km out of town – there are half a dozen buses daily, or it's a short taxi ride. The **tourist office**, 1 place St Pierre (Mon–Sat 10am–12.30pm; Ⓣ03.85.21.07.07, Ⓦwww.macon-tourism.com), is well stocked with info on the area. In summer a second office opens on the riverfront (June–Sept daily 10am–1pm & 3–7pm).

There should be no difficulty finding a **place to stay**. For a touch of only-slightly-faded grandeur go for the *Hôtel d'Europe et d'Angleterre*, on the river at 92 quai Jean-Jaurès (Ⓣ03.85.38.27.94, Ⓦwww.hotel-europeangleterre-macon.com; ❸). Rooms are finely furnished and have high ceilings, while the hotel lays claim to an illustrious history, on which the engaging director M. Racle is an expert. Nearer the station, the *Inter-Hôtel de Bourgogne*, 6 rue Victor-Hugo (Ⓣ03.85.21.10.23, Ⓦwww.hoteldebourgogne.com; ❹; restaurant from €19), offers a more standardized kind of luxury. Cheaper rooms, but still perfectly pleasant, fully-equipped ones, are available just across the river at the *Hôtel du Beaujolais*, 86 place République (Ⓣ03.85.38.42.06, Ⓕ03.85.38.78.02; ❷). There's a **campsite** 3km north out of town on the N6 (Ⓣ03.85.38.16.22; mid-March to Oct).

Restaurants are plentiful down by the river. On the west bank, the elegant *Le Carline*, 266 quai Lamartine (Ⓣ03.85.38.07.50; from €18; closed Sun), has classic menus in a laid-back atmosphere, while the rustic but high-quality *Au Cancale*, 393 quai Jean-Jaurès (Ⓣ03.85.38.07.50; closed Sun evening & Mon), offers an excellent-value lunch for €15 including wine. If you want to sit outside, though, it's worth crossing the old bridge to the traffic-free east bank and the classy fish restaurant *St Laurent*, on quai Bouchacourt (☎03.85.39.29.19), which has great views and dishes from around €15.

Brou

BROU is an uninteresting suburban village outside Bourg-en-Bresse, 32km east of Mâcon, which happens to have an early sixteenth-century **church** (daily 9am–noon & 2–5pm; €7). If you're heading east to Geneva or the Alps, take a look, but don't lose a lift or miss a train for it. Aldous Huxley found it "a horrible little architectural nightmare", its monuments "positively and piercingly vulgar". Certainly, it was a very rich woman's expensive folly – it was undertaken by Margaret of Austria after the death of her husband, Philibert, Duke of Savoy, as a mausoleum for the two of them and Philibert's mother. The level of detail and frilly ornamentation on their tombs constitutes a breathtaking display of craftsmanship, but the artistic whole is soulless, without a trace of vision or inspiration.

The Mâconnais, Beaujolais and Charollais

West of the valley of the Saône lies a tract of hilly country that is best known for its produce: the white wines of the **Mâconnais** are justly renowned, while the fashion for drinking the young red wine of **Beaujolais** has spread far beyond France. Further west still, the handsome white cattle that luxuriate in the green fields of the **Charollais** are an obvious sign that this is serious beef country.

In the past, however, the region was famed for its religion, and many large and powerful abbeys were established in the eleventh and twelfth centuries under the influence of the great monastery at Cluny. Few monks remain, and **Cluny** itself is largely destroyed, but Romanesque churches are almost as thick on the ground as cattle, and few are more impressive than the great basilica at **Paray-le-Monial**.

The Mâconnais

The **Mâconnais** wine-producing country lies to the west of the Saône, a strip hardly 20km wide, stretching from Mâcon to Tournus. The land rises sharply into steep little hills and valleys, at its prettiest in the south, where the region's best white wines come from, around the villages of **POUILLY**, **VINZELLES**, **PRISSÉ** and **FUISSÉ**. Should you yearn for rustic rest, the *Hôtel La Vigne Blanche* in Fuissé (☎03.85.35.60.50, ⓦwww.vigne-blanche.com; ❸) will provide just the setting you're looking for, with simple rooms, good regional cooking (menus from €13.50) and of course the chance to sample some of the local wines.

Directly above these villages rises the distinctive and precipitous 500-metre rock of **Solutré**, which in prehistoric times – around 20,000 BC – served as an ambush site for hunters after migrating animals: the bones of 100,000 horses have been found in the soil beneath the rock, along with mammoth, bison and reindeer carcasses. The history and results of the excavations are displayed in a museum at the foot of the rock, the **Musée Départemental de Préhistoire** (daily: Jan–March, Oct & Nov 10am–noon & 2–5pm; April–Sept 10am–6pm; €3.50). A steep path climbs to the top of the rock, where you get a superb view as far as Mont Blanc and the Matterhorn on a clear day, as well as looking down on the huddled roofs of **SOLUTRÉ-POUILLY**, the slopes beneath you covered with the vines of the Chardonnay grape, which makes the exquisite greenish Pouilly-Fuissé wine. The area is at its most enchanting in early spring when the earth still shows its *terre-cuite* colours, punctuated by bursts of white cherry blossom and the blue drift of bonfire smoke from prunings amid the neatly staked rows of vines.

Aside from the sheer pleasure of wandering about in such reposeful landscapes – not so, however, if you're trying to tackle this very hilly country on a bike – there are some specific places to make for. One is the sleepy hamlet of **ST-POINT**, where the poet Lamartine (see box, p.540) spent much of his life in the little medieval **Château de St-Point**, now a museum dedicated to him (guided visits 10am–noon & 2–6pm: weekends only April–June, Sept & Oct; daily July & Aug; ⊤03.85.50.50.30, Ⓦ www.chateaulamartine.com; €5), next to the Romanesque church where he's buried. If you continue up the road behind the château you come to an utterly rural farm where you can buy fresh goat's cheese.

Cluny and around

The abbey of **CLUNY** is the major tourist destination of the region. The voice of its abbot once made monarchs tremble, as his power in the Christian world was second only to that of the pope. The monastery was founded in 910 in response to the corruption of the existing church, and it took only a couple of vigorous early abbots to build the power of Cluny into a veritable empire. Gradually its spiritual influence declined, and Cluny became a royal gift. Both Richelieu and Mazarin did stints in the monastery as abbot.

Now, although the reputation of the place still pulls in the tourist coaches, little remains apart from the very attractive village. Hugues de Semur's vast and influential eleventh-century **church**, the largest building in Christendom until the construction of St Peter's in Rome, was dismantled in the destruction that followed the Revolution. Now what you see of the former **abbey** (daily: May–Aug 9.30am–6.30pm; Sept–April 9.30am–noon & 1.30–5pm; €6.50 combined ticket with museum) is an octagonal belfry and the huge south transept. Standing amid this fragment of a huge construction gives a tangible and poignant insight into the Revolution's enormous powers of transformation. Access to the belfry leads through the Grand École des Ingénieurs, one of France's elite higher-education institutions, and you can often see the students in their gowns decorated with cabalistic signs. At the back of the abbey is one of France's national stud farms, **Haras de Cluny** (⊤06.22.94.52.69; April–Sept Tues–Sun 2pm, 3.30pm & 5pm; Oct–March Tues–Fri 2pm; €5), which you can visit but only on a guided tour. The **Musée d'Art et d'Archaeologie** (same hours and ticket as abbey), in the fifteenth-century palace of the last freely elected abbot, helps to flesh out the ruins with reconstructions and fragments of sculpture, while from the top of the **Tour des Fromages** (entrance through the tourist office; €1.75) you can picture it in the landscape below.

The **tourist office** is beside the Tours des Fromages, at 6 rue Mercière (April–June & Sept Mon–Sat 10am–12.30pm & 2.30–6.45pm; July & Aug daily 10am–6.45pm; Oct–March Mon 2.30–5pm, Tues–Sat 10am–12.30pm & 2.30–5pm; ⊤03.85.59.05.34, Ⓦ www.cluny-tourisme.com). **Bikes** can be hired from Ludisport (⊤03.85.22.10.62, Ⓦ www.ludisport.com) next to the abandoned train station.

Cluny makes an excellent place to **stay**, boasting two really wonderful hotels and some great-value budget possibilities. The *Hôtel de Bourgogne*, place de l'Abbaye (☎03.85.59.00.58, ⓦwww.hotel-cluny.com; ❺–❼; closed Dec & Jan), with beautiful antique furniture in rooms which look onto either the abbey or the pretty breakfast garden, also has a top-notch restaurant working gastronomic wonders with local produce (menus €25–45). Even better value, though, is the charming ⚜*Le Potin Gourmand*, at 4 place du Champ de Foire (☎03.85.59.02.06, ⓦwww.potingourmand.com; ❸; closed Dec & Jan), whose seven beguiling rooms somehow manage to blend French rustic with nuances of a different style, from four-poster medieval to Byzantine. The delightful country restaurant here is just as enticing (evenings only; menus €22–48). In a lower price range, you can choose between the spotless *Hôtel du Commerce*, 8 place du Commerce (☎03.85.59.03.09, ⓦwww.hotelducommerce-cluny.com; ❶), where the cheaper rooms have shared facilities and start at €21, and the **hostel**, *Cluny Séjour*, right by the town bus stop at 22 rue Porte-de-Paris (☎03.85.59.08.83, ⓔclunysejour@orange.fr; closed Dec to mid-Jan; beds €16). There's also a **campsite**, *St-Vital* (☎03.85.59.08.34, ⓔcamping.st.vital@orange.fr; May–Sept), across Pont de la Levée in the direction of Tournus.

For **meals**, you can't beat the two hotels (see above), but the bustling *Café du Centre* in rue Municipale is a fine old-fashioned bistro whose *plats* from €8.50 deserve a mention.

The Beaujolais

Imperceptibly, as you continue south, the Mâconnais becomes the **Beaujolais**, a larger area of terraced hills producing lighter, fruity red wines, which it is now fashionable to drink very early. The Beaujolais grape is the Gamay, which, unlike in other parts of Burgundy, thrives here on this granite soil. Of the four *appellations* of Beaujolais, the best are the *crus*, which come from the northern part of the region between St-Amour and Brouilly. If you have transport, you can follow the *cru* trail south from Mâcon by turning right at Crêches-sur-Saône up the D31 to St-Amour, and then south along the D68. Beaujolais Villages, which produces the most highly regarded *nouveau*, comes from the middle of the Beaujolais region, south of the *cru* belt, while plain Beaujolais and Beaujolais Supérieur are produced in the vineyards southwest of Villefranche.

The well-marked **route de Beaujolais** winds down through the wine villages to **VILLEFRANCHE**, not far from Lyon and a good base for the route. Here, the **tourist office** at 96 rue de la Préfecture (Mon–Sat: May–Sept 9am–12.30pm & 2–6pm; Oct–April 9am–noon & 1.30–5.30pm; ☎04.74.07.27.40, ⓦwww .villefranche-beaujolais.fr) has information about *caves*, visits and wine tours. Hotels are clustered on the far side of town, near the **gare SNCF**. A pleasant and reasonably priced one is *Liberty's*, at 61 rue d'Anse above a lively Irish pub (☎04.74.68.36.13; ❷).

Rue Nationale is the central axis of the town where you'll find, as well as most of the shops, the striking **church** of Notre-Dame, which boasts some original fifteenth-century stained glass. This is also the area to head for the most popular **cafés**: *Le Saladier* (☎04.74.62.34.19), within a walled terrace at no. 579, offers tasty menus (from €15.80) and a good list of local wines.

Paray-le-Monial

Fifty kilometres west of Cluny, across countryside that becomes ever gentler and flatter as you approach the broad valley of the Loire, is **PARAY-LE-MONIAL**, whose major attraction is its **Basilique du Sacré-Coeur** (daily 9am–7pm). Not only is it an exquisite building in its own right, with a marvellously satisfying arrangement of apses and chapels stacking up in sturdy symmetry to its fine octagonal belfry, it's the best place to get an idea of what the abbey of Cluny looked like, as it was built shortly afterwards in devoted imitation of the mother church.

One secular building definitely worth a look, aside from just browsing down the main street – rue de la République/rue des Deux-Ponts/rue Victor-Hugo – is the highly ornamented **Maison Jayet**, now the Hôtel de Ville on place Guignault, built in the 1520s.

Practicalities

The **tourist office** is right outside the Basilica (July & Aug daily 9am–7pm; Sept–June Mon–Sat 9am–noon & 1.30–6pm; also Sun April–June & Sept–Oct; Ⓣ03.85.81.10.92, Ⓦwww.paraylemonial.fr) and rents out **bikes** (€9 per day) as well as offering **internet** access (€1 for 15 min).

For **accommodation**, an excellent bet is the pleasantly old-fashioned yet well-appointed *Grand Hôtel de la Basilique*, 18 rue de la Visitation (Ⓣ03.85.81.11.13, Ⓦwww.hotelbasilique.com; ❷; closed Nov–March; fine restaurant from €15), with some rooms overlooking the basilica. Rather swankier, but still not overpriced, the *Hostellerie des Trois Pigeons*, 2 rue Daugard, just beyond the Hôtel de Ville (Ⓣ03.85.81.03.77, Ⓦwww.h-3-p .com; ❸; closed Dec–Feb), boasts plusher rooms and a classy restaurant offering gourmet dishes like swordfish steak garnished with crayfish in a tomato and olive sauce, or the more local duck breast stuffed with figs (menus €19–47). If you want to immerse yourself in the religious atmosphere of this town try the cavernous *Au Foyer de Sacré Coeur*, at 14 rue de la Visitation (Ⓣ03.85.81.11.01, Ⓦwww.foyerdusacrecoeur.com), where single beds cost €21–36 depending on how many people you share a room with. The *Mambré* **campsite** is on route Gué-Léger (Ⓣ03.85.88.89.20; May to late Sept). For **food**, as well as the hotel-restaurants above, rue Victor Hugo and place Guignault provide options for light meals.

To explore the little villages throughout the Mâconnais, there's no better base than the Merle family's organic farm at Vitry-en-Charollais (Ⓣ03.85.81.30.62; ❷; dinner has to be booked ahead), with delicious home cooking, about 6km southwest of Paray.

The Charollais

The **Charollais** is cattle country, taking its name from the pretty little water-enclosed market town of **CHAROLLES**, with its 32 bridges, on the main N79 road, and in turn giving its name to one of the world's most illustrious breeds of cattle: the white, curly-haired, stocky Charollais, bred for its lean meat. Throughout this landscape, scattered across the rich farmland along the River Arconce, are dozens of small villages, all with more or less remarkable Romanesque churches, offspring of Cluny in its vigorous youth.

ANZY-LE-DUC, about 15km south of Paray off the main D982 to Roanne, boasts an exquisite complex of buildings: a perfect Romanesque church with jackdaw chatter echoing off the octagonal belfry, side by side with the remains of the old priory incorporated into a sort of fortified farm looking out over the Arconce valley, the whole built in a rich, warm stone. **MONTCEAUX-L'ÉTOILE**, a little nearer to Paray, has its special charm too: a quiet, worn church with beautiful sculptures adorning the porch, standing likewise above the Arconce valley, and, a little way down the village street, a curious tower-like house where a Marquis of Vichy is said to have practised alchemy with the notorious Italian wizard, Cagliostro.

▲ Cattle country, Charollais

Travel details

Trains

Autun to: Avallon (Mon–Sat 1–3 daily; 1hr 45min); Chalon-sur-Saône (1–2 daily; 1hr 10min–1hr 50min); Le Creusot-Ville (2–4 daily; 45min); Saulieu (2–6 daily; 50min).

Auxerre to: Avallon (4–6 daily; 1hr); Clamecy (3–5 daily; 1hr 20min); Dijon (8–10 daily; 1hr 50min–2hr 20min); Joigny (9–11 daily; 35min); Paris (6–8 daily; 1hr 50min–2hr 30min); Sens (6–8 daily; 1hr).

Avallon to: Autun (1–2 daily; 1hr 45min); Auxerre (5–8 daily; 1hr 5min); Saulieu (4 daily; 50min–1hr).

Beaune to: Dijon (frequent; 25min); Lyon (10–12 daily; 1hr 50min–2hr 10min).

Dijon to: Auxerre (8–11 daily; 1hr 50min–2hr 20min); Chalon-sur-Saône (frequent; 40min); Laroche-Migennes (8–11 daily; 1hr 30min); Les Laumes-Alésia (frequent; 30–50min); Lyon (10–15 daily; 1hr 35min–2hr 10min); Mâcon (frequent; 1hr–1hr 20min); Nevers (3–6 daily; 2hr 10min–2hr 50min); Paris (frequent; 1hr 40min–3hr 15min); Sens (6–9 daily; 1hr 45min–2hr 10min); Tonnerre (8–11 daily; 1hr–1hr 30min); Tournus (10 daily; 1hr); Villefranche (Mon–Sat frequent, Sun 5; 1hr 40min–2hr).

Laroche-Migennes to: Auxerre (7–10 daily; 15min).

Mâcon to: Bourg-en-Bresse (10 daily; 30–50min); Dijon (frequent; 1hr–1hr 20min); Geneva (8–12 daily; 2hr 30min–3hr 30min); Lyon (frequent; 30min–1hr).

Montbard to: Dijon (6–8 daily; 50min); Laroche-Migennes (5–7 daily; 1hr).

Montchanin to: Le Creusot (4–6 daily; 10min); Paray-le-Monial (2–3 daily; 50min).

Nevers to: Autun (2–4 daily; 1hr 40min–2hr 20min); Chalon-sur-Saône (3 daily; 2hr 45min); Clermont-Ferrand (7–8 daily; 1hr 30min–2hr 10min); Le Creusot (5–7 daily; 1hr 30min); Dijon (5–7 daily; 2hr 30min); Paris (frequent; 2–3hr).

Paray-le-Monial to: Dijon (2–6 daily; 1hr 50min); Lyon (2–3 daily; 2hr).

Sens to: Auxerre (4–6 daily; 30min–1hr 10min); Avallon (2–4 daily; 2hr); Dijon (9 daily; 1hr 50min–2hr 30min); Joigny (7–10 daily; 20min); Paris (9 daily; 1hr–1hr 30min); Tonnerre (9 daily; 1hr).

Tournus to: Chalon-sur-Saône (11–14 daily; 15min); Mâcon (10 daily; 15min).

Buses

Autun to: Beaune (Mon–Fri 1 daily; 1hr 10min); Chalon-sur-Saône (2 daily; 2hr); Château-Chinon (Mon–Fri 1 daily; 1hr); Le Creusot (3–5 daily; 45min); St-Léger-sous-Beuvray (1–5 weekly; 1hr).

Avallon to: Dijon (1–3 daily; 2hr–2hr 30min); Montbard (2–3 daily; 50min); Vézelay (summer only 1–3 daily; 30min).

Chablis to: Auxerre (winter Mon–Sat 1 daily, summer has to be booked; 35min); Tonnerre (winter 1–2 daily, summer has to be booked; 1hr).

Châtillon-sur-Seine to: Dijon (3 daily; 1hr 30min–2hr); Montbard (3–6 daily; 40min).

Cluny to: Chalon-sur-Saône (2–4 daily; 1hr 30min); Charolles (2–5 daily; 45min); Mâcon (2–7 daily; 45min); Paray-le-Monial (1–5 daily; 1hr); Taizé (1–7 daily; 15min).

Dijon to: Autun (1 daily; 2hr 30min); Avallon (2–3 daily; 2hr 30min); Beaune (3–7 daily; 30min–1hr 30min); Châtillon-sur-Seine (2–4 daily; 1hr 30min–2hr); Saulieu (3 daily; 1hr 30min).

Mâcon to: Charolles (2–5 daily; 2hr); Cluny (2–7 daily; 45min); Paray-le-Monial (2–5 daily; 2hr 20min).

Semur-en-Auxois to: Montbard (2–4 daily; 20min); Saulieu (2–4 daily; 30min).

Poitou-Charentes and the Atlantic coast

CHAPTER 8

Highlights

✳ Romanesque churches The facade of Notre-Dame in Poitiers is one of the most absorbingly intricate, but other humbler churches throughout the region are just as beautiful. See p.555

✳ Marais Poitevin The "green Venice", an intricate network of land and water that's perfect to explore by bike. See p.559

✳ La Rochelle This charming and unspoilt port town is the jewel of the west coast, with a well-preserved historic centre and some exquisite seafood restaurants. See p.562

✳ Île d'Oléron France's second biggest island is a centre for oysters, birds and hollyhocks and has some fantastic beaches. See p.574

✳ Angoulême Wholly underrated, this enchanting old-school town hosts an animated nightlife and some fine restaurants, and is an essential pilgrimage for any fan of comics. See p.582

✳ Bordeaux Lively, stylish city surrounded by some of the world's best vineyards. See p.586

▲ Marais Poitevin

Poitou-Charentes and the Atlantic coast

ewsstands selling *Sud-Ouest* remind you where you are: this is not the Mediterranean, certainly, but in summer the quality of the light, the warm air, the fields of sunflowers and the shuttered siesta-silence of the farmhouses give you the first exciting promises of the south. The coast, on the other hand, remains unmistakably Atlantic – dunes, pine forest, reclaimed marshland and misty mud flats. While it has great charm in places, particularly out of season on the islands of **Noirmoutier**, **Ré** and **Oléron**, it's a family, camper-caravanner seaside, lacking the glamour and excitement of the Côte d'Azur. The principal port in the north, **La Rochelle**, is one of the prettiest and most distinctive towns in France. The sandy beaches are beautiful everywhere, though can occasionally be disappointing, especially the northern stretches, where the water is murky and shallow for a long way out. On the dune-backed **Côte d'Argent**, south of Bordeaux, however, the sea can be outright dangerous.

Inland, the valley of the slow and green **River Charente** epitomizes blue-overalled, Gauloise-smoking, peasant France. The towpath is accessible for long stretches, on foot or mountain bike, and there are boat trips from **Saintes** and **Cognac**. The **Marais Poitevin**, too, with its groves of poplars and island fields reticulated by countless canals and ditches, is both an unusual landscape and easy-going walking or cycling country.

But perhaps the most memorable aspect of the countryside – and indeed of towns like **Poitiers** and **Angoulême** – is the presence of exquisite Roman-esque churches. This region formed a significant stretch of the medieval pilgrim routes across France and from Britain and northern Europe to the shrine of St Jacques (St James, or Santiago as the Spanish know him) at Compostela in northwest Spain, and was well endowed by its followers. The finest of the churches, among the best in all of France, are to be found in the countryside around Saintes and Poitiers: informal, highly individual and so integrated with their landscape they often seem as rooted as the trees.

Lastly, of course, remember that this is a region of seafood – fresh and cheap in every market for miles inland – and, around the modern, charismatic urban centre that is **Bordeaux**, some of the world's top vineyards.

Public transport users will find all the main urban centres covered here well connected by trains, with most of the smaller towns and villages also accessible

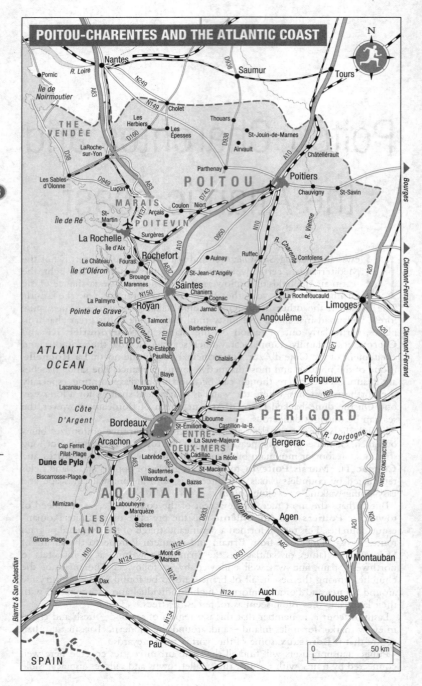

POITOU-CHARENTES AND THE ATLANTIC COAST

N

Pornic
R. Loire
Nantes
Saumur
Tours
Île de
Noirmoutier
A83
N249
D938

THE
VENDÉE
Cholet
NT49
Les
Herbiers
Thouars
St-Jouin-de-Marnes
Les
Épesses
D160
Airvault
Châtellérault
LaRoche-
sur-Yon
D38
Parthenay
A10
POITOU
Les Sables-
d'Olonne
D949
Luçon
A83
Poitiers
Bourges
MARAIS
Coulon
Niort
D143
Chauvigny
St-Savin
Arçais
N11
Île de Ré
St-
Martin
POITEVIN
Surgères
D950
N10
R. Vienne
La Rochelle
Île d'Aix
Rochefort
Aulnay
Ruffec
Confolens
Clermont-Ferrand
Le Château
Fouras
A837
St-Jean-d'Angély
R. Charente
A20
Île d'Oléron
Brouage
Marennes
Saintes
Chaniers
La Rochefoucauld
Limoges
Clermont-Ferrand
N150
Cognac
La Palmyre
Royan
Talmont
Jarnac
Angoulême
Pointe de Grave
Soulac
Gironde
Barbezieux
N10
MÉDOC
Chalais
Périgueux
N21
ATLANTIC
OCEAN
St-Estèphe
Pauillac
A10
Lacanau-Océan
Blaye
N89
N89
Margaux
PERIGORD
Côte
D'Argent
Bordeaux
Libourne
St-Émilion
Castillon-la-B.
R. Dordogne
Cap Ferret
Arcachon
ENTRE-
DEUX-MERS
La Sauve-Majeure
Bergerac
UNDER CONSTRUCTION
Pilat-Plage
Labrède
Cadillac
Dune de Pyla
A62
La Réole
Biscarrosse-Plage
Sauternes
St-Macaire
Villandraut
Bazas
AQUITAINE
R. Garonne
Mimizan
Labouheyre
Agen
A62
A20
A20
LES
Marquèze
LANDES
Sabres
D933
Girons-Plage
N124
Montauban
N10
Mont de
Marsan
D931
Biarritz & San Sebastian
Dax
N124
N124
Auch
Toulouse
N134
0   50 km
SPAIN
Pau

by regular, if infrequent, bus services. Off the main routes, though, particularly in the Bordeaux wine region and on the islands, having your own transport can be a major advantage – although cycling is often an attractive alternative.

Poitou

Most of the old province of **Poitou** comprises a huge expanse of rolling wheat fields and sunflower and maize plantations where the combines crawl and giant sprinklers shoot great arcs of white water over the fields in summertime, and villages are strung out along the valley floors. Heartland of the domains of Eleanor, Duchess of Aquitaine, whose marriage to King Henry II in 1152 brought the whole of southwest France under English control for three hundred years, it is also the northern limit of the *langue d'oc*-speaking part of the country, whose Occitan dialect survives among the older generations even today.

Poitiers

Heading south from Tours on the Autoroute de l'Aquitaine, you'd hardly be tempted by the cluster of towers and office blocks rising from the plain, which is all you see of **POITIERS**. But draw nearer and things look very different. Sitting on a hilltop overlooking two rivers, Poitiers is a country town with a unique charm that comes from a long and sometimes influential history – as the seat of the dukes of Aquitaine, for instance – discernible in the winding lines of the streets and the breadth of civic, domestic and ecclesiastical architectural fashions represented in its buildings. Its pedestrian precincts and wonderful central gardens make for comfortable sightseeing, while the large student population ensures a lively atmosphere in the restaurants and pavement cafés.

Arrival and information

It's a short taxi ride (around €7) into the centre from Poitiers-Biard **airport**, located to the west of town, while the **gare SNCF** is on boulevard du Grand Cerf, part of the ring-road system that encircles the base of the hill on which Poitiers is built. The *gare routière* is on the ground floor of the brand new conference centre just next door. The **tourist office** (mid-June to Aug daily 10am–11pm; Sept to mid-June Mon–Sat 10am–6pm; ☎05.49.41.21.24, ⓦ www.ot-poitiers.fr) is a fifteen-minute walk away, up the hill at 45 place Charles-de-Gaulle, and can supply **walkers** and cyclists with various guides to the regional opportunities: the GR364 sets out from here, reaching the Vendée coast via Parthenay.

You can hire **Bikes** from Cyclamen, 60 boulevard Pont-Achard (☎05.49.88.13.25; closed Sun & Mon), and **cars** from outlets near the train station on boulevard du Grand Cerf, such as National/Citer at no. 48 (☎05.49.58.51.58). Cybercorner, 18 rue Charles-Gide (daily 10am–late; €2 per hr), has a fast **internet** connection and

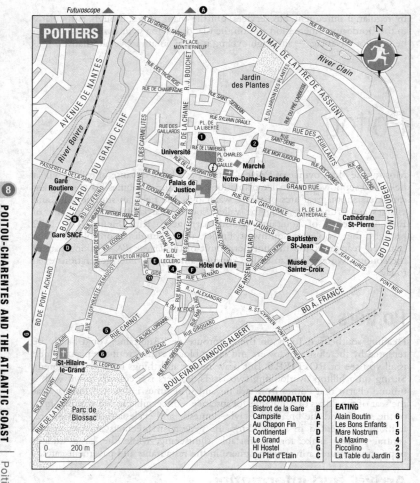

POITIERS

ACCOMMODATION	
Bistrot de la Gare	B
Campsite	A
Au Chapon Fin	F
Continental	D
Le Grand	E
HI Hostel	G
Du Plat d'Etain	C

EATING	
Alain Boutin	6
Les Bons Enfants	1
Mare Nostrum	5
Le Maxime	4
Piccolino	2
La Table du Jardin	3

long opening hours. The art house and independent **films** featured at Le Théâtre, place du Maréchal-Leclerc (Ⓦ www.letheatre-poitiers.com), are shown in their original language with French subtitles.

Accommodation

There are plenty of **hotels** along boulevard du Grand Cerf by the train station, but the area is not particularly salubrious; for more agreeable surroundings it's only a short uphill walk to the town centre.

Hotels

Bistrot de la Gare 131 bd du Grand Cerf
Ⓣ 05.49.58.56.30. Cheapest of the station hotels, up a dingy staircase behind a bar. The rooms are very pleasant for the price, but it can be noisy at the front. ❶

Au Chapon Fin place du Maréchal Leclerc
Ⓣ 05.49.88.02.97, Ⓦ www.hotel-chaponfin .com. A bargain, in a most central location – some rooms look out onto place Maréchal-Leclerc. Cheaper rooms have shower rather than bath. ❶–❸

Continental 2 bd Solférino ℡ 05.49.37.93.93, Ⓦ www.continental-poitiers.com. Comfortable chain two-star opposite the station, whose sound-proofed rooms are fully equipped. It's worth paying an extra couple of euros for a quiet room at the back. ❸

Le Grand 28 rue Carnot ℡ 05.49.60.90.60, Ⓦ www.grandhotelpoitiers.fr. The classiest hotel in Poitiers, with Art Deco-style furnishings and a swanky bar complete with sun terrace. The large rooms all have TV and minibar; most are a/c. ❹

Du Plat d'Étain 7 rue du Plat d'Étain ℡ 05.49.41.04.80, Ⓦ www.poitiers-leplatdetain.com.

An attractive, well-run hotel in a central, quiet street just off the main shopping precinct. ❸

Hostel and campsite

HI Hostel 1 allée Roger-Tagault ℡ 05.49.30.09.70, Ⓔ poitiers@fuaj.org. Large, modern hostel next to a swimming pool, often overrun with school groups. Take bus #7 from the *station* to "Bellejouanne", 3km away. Well signposted, it's to the right off the N10 Angoulême road.

Camping municipal rue du Porteau ℡ 05.49.41.44.88. Grassy site with clean facilities situated 2km north of town; bus #7 towards Le Porteau. June–Aug.

The Town

The two poles of communal life in Poitiers are the tree-lined **place du Maréchal-Leclerc**, with its popular cafés and lively outdoor culture, and **place Charles-de-Gaulle** to the north, where a big and bustling food and clothes **market** takes place (Mon–Sat 7am–1pm). Between the two is a warren of prosperous streets – as far along as the half-timbered medieval houses of **rue de la Chaine**. Rue Gambetta cuts north past the old **Palais de Justice** (Mon–Fri 9am–6pm; free), whose nineteenth-century facade hides a much older core, including the magnificent thirteenth-century Gothic grand hall.

The church of Notre-Dame-la-Grande

The Palais de Justice looks down on one of the greatest and most idiosyncratic churches in France, **Notre-Dame-la-Grande**, begun in the twelfth-century reign of Eleanor and renovated most recently in the mid-1990s – the lower parts of the facade had suffered considerable erosion due to salt from the market stalls of fishmongers seeping up into the stone over centuries.

The most exceptional thing about the church is the west front, which is wonderfully transformed into a display of coloured lights at 10.30pm every evening in summer. You can't call the facade beautiful, at least not in a conventional sense, squat and loaded as it is with detail to a degree that the modern eye could regard as fussy. And yet it's this detail which is enthralling, ranging from the domestic to the disturbingly anarchic. Such elaborate sculpted facades – and domes like pine cones on turret and belfry – are the hallmarks of the Poitou brand of Romanesque. The interior, which is crudely overlaid with nineteenth-century frescoes, is not nearly as interesting.

The cathedral and around

At the eastern edge of the old town stands the **Cathédrale St-Pierre**, an enormous building on whose broad, pale facade pigeons roost and plants take root. Some of the stained glass dates from the twelfth century, notably the Cruci-fixion in the central window of the apse, in which the features of Henry II and Eleanor are supposedly discernible. The choir stalls, too, are full of characteristic medieval detail: a coquettish Mary and Child, a peasant killing a boar, the architect at work with his dividers, a baker with a basket of loaves. But it's the grand eighteenth-century organ, the Orgue Clicquot, which is the cathedral's most striking feature, often playing deafening tunes, with concerts in summer.

Opposite – literally in the middle of rue Jean-Jaurès – you come upon a chunky, square edifice with the air of a second-rate Roman temple. It's actually the mid-fourth-century **Baptistère St-Jean** (April–June & Sept daily except Tues 10.30am–12.30pm & 3–6pm; July & Aug daily 10.30am–12.30pm & 3–6pm; Oct–March daily except Tues 2.30–4.30pm; €1.50), reputedly the oldest Christian building in France and, until the seventeenth century, the only place in town you could have a proper baptism. The "font" was the octagonal pool sunk into the floor. Water pipes uncovered in the bottom show the water could not have been more than 30–40cm deep, which casts doubt on the popular belief that early Christian baptism was by total immersion. There are also some very ancient and faded frescoes on the walls, including one of the emperor Constantine on horseback, and a collection of Merovingian sarcophagi.

Next to the baptistery is the town museum, the **Musée Sainte-Croix**, 3bis rue Jean-Jaurès (June–Sept Mon 2–6pm, Tues–Sun 10am–noon & 2–6pm; Oct–May Tues–Fri 10am–noon & 1.15–5pm, Mon, Sat & Sun 1.15–5pm; €3.70, free on Tues and 1st Sun of the month; Ⓦwww.musees-poitiers.org), featuring an interesting collection of farming implements. There's also a good Gallo-Roman section with some handsome glass, pottery and sculpture, notably a white marble Minerva of the first century. Another possibility is to take a more relaxed walk along the **riverside path** – on the right across Pont Neuf – upstream to Pont St-Cyprien. On the far bank, you'll see a characteristic feature of every French provincial town: neat, well-manured *potagers* – vegetable gardens – coming down to the water's edge with a little mud quay at the end and a moored punt.

Eating and drinking

Poitiers offers good opportunities for fine **food** whatever your culinary persuasions – there's a good range of ethnic options to try if you're bored with French cuisine. The most formal gastronomic palaces are on rue Carnot, but there's often a friendlier atmosphere, if less grandeur, in the smaller restaurants around place de la Liberté, where the town's student population also assures the liveliest **nightlife**. If you're really keen to make your money last, you can ask about student/youth offers at the Centre Information Jeunesse (CIJ), 64 rue Gambetta (☏05.49.60.68.68).

Alain Boutin 65 rue Carnot ☏05.49.88.25.53. A good bet for regional dishes like *cailles au pineau* (quails cooked in a brandy liqueur), with a small, carefully chosen selection; menus from €25. Closed Sun.

Les Bons Enfants 11bis rue Cloche Perse ☏05.49.41.49.82. No more than twenty spaces in a simple, timeless dining room and scrumptious home cooking like the house speciality of *escargots* melted in a parsley-buttered baked potato; you need to reserve. Closed Sun & Mon.

Mare Nostrum 74 rue Carnot ☏05.49.41.58.80. Mediterranean specialities including moussaka and *kawage*, a baked ratatouille-style dish with aubergine and *haricots verts*. Menus are from €15.

Le Maxime 4 rue St-Nicolas ☏05.49.41.09.55. *Gastronomique* cuisine at its finest: delicious dishes served in an elegant setting. Lunch here is popular with the well-to-do business crowd. Evening menus upwards of €25. Closed Sat and Sun.

Piccolino 37 rue Augouard ☏05.49.01.84.53. Friendly Italian serving pizzas from a wood fire in a large, open dining room. Popular with families. Closed Sun.

La Table du Jardin 42 rue du Moulin au Vent ☏05.49.41.68.46. Traditional and creative cooking with fresh ingredients, served in a relaxed atmosphere with outside seating on a pretty square. The *menu du marché* is good value at €20. Closed Sun & Mon.

Around Poitiers

The area immediately surrounding Poitiers is dominated by the post-modern cinema theme park **Futuroscope**, to the north. Families are also catered for by the recent explosion in *parcs animaliers*, reserves for various exotic species which distinguish themselves from zoos by an absence of cages. The best is the **Vallée des Singes** ("Valley of the Apes"), thirty-minutes' drive to the south near Romagne (daily March–Nov 10am–6pm; Ⓦwww.la-vallee-des-singes.fr; €13.50), where monkeys of all sizes roam in relative freedom. Information and cut-price tickets for this and similar attractions (snakes, birds of prey and crocodiles are all within reach) are available at the Maison du Tourisme, the tourist office for the Vienne region, on place Charles-de-Gaulle in Poitiers (Ⓣ.05.49.37.48.48, Ⓦwww.tourisme-vienne.com). More traditional attractions can be found at **Chauvigny** and **St-Savin**, which boast medieval centres and two fine Romanesque churches, with some great sculpture and frescoes. Less inspired are the small town of **Parthenay** and the larger city of **Niort**, neither of which is worth a special trip, though both make useful stopovers for provisions before you head further west into the verdant marshes of the **Marais Poitevin**.

Futuroscope

Poitiers' best-known attraction is the giant high-tech film theme park called **Futuroscope: Le Parc Européen de l'Image** (Ⓦwww.futuroscope.com), 8km north of the city, a collection of virtual-reality rides which draw onlookers into the action on screen, with the result that you feel you're being flung around or catapulted through the solar system in a vertigo-inducing 3-D nightmare. Futuroscope opens new attractions every year; recent additions include robots and more conventional rides, to supplement the virtual-reality films that are the park's *raison d'être*.

Futuroscope practicalities and attractions

The Paris Montparnasse–Poitiers TGV stops at Futuroscope; there are also regular buses (line #9; €1.30) from Poitiers' Hôtel de Ville or *gare SNCF*. The park is open all year apart from January, from 10am until shortly after sunset, when the laser show has finished. **Tickets** are valid for one or two days (adult one-day pass €33, child aged 5–16 €25; adult two-day pass €63, child €45) and to avoid queues at the park it's best to purchase tickets in advance from the Maison de Tourisme in Poitiers (see p.551). **Food** is predictably expensive inside, and bringing a picnic lunch can cut costs substantially. There are various deals available that include admission, plus a wide selection of accommodation on site, the cheapest of which costs €79 per adult in a four-bed room (Ⓦwww.futuroscope.com).

Attractions

Le Cinéma 360° Spain's contribution to Seville Expo '92 is now housed here permanently.

La Citadelle de la Vertige A tour of a virtual universe from the unusual perspective of walking on the ceiling.

Danse avec les Robots Strapped in to the arm of a giant robot, fly around the room to a waltz or rock-and-roll rhythm of your choice.

Destination Cosmos A vast planetarium brings the universe to life using images from the Hubble telescope.

Imax Solido An enormous screen, measuring 540 square metres, in conjunction with 3-D vision glasses brings you face to face with dinosaurs or stunning sea creatures – depending on which film is showing.

Laponie Express A high-octane joy-ride around a mountainous landscape in an all-terrain snowmobile.

The futuristic **cinema pavilions** are set in several acres of greenery around a series of undulating lakes, and the 24 attractions take some getting around, with plenty of walking between them, so it's wise to arrive early to beat the huge queues. To see everything in the park in one day, with time off for lunch, takes about ten exhausting hours, and as well as taking in the screen entertainment, you should give yourself time to ride the oversized floating bicycles on the park's lakes. To orientate yourself, head first for **La Gyrotour** where a lift takes you to the top of the high rotating tower and you can get the full effect of the futuristic scenario.

All the films are in French, with English commentaries on headphones often available, but as these are not very effective, and as it's the visual impact that's most important anyway, it's better to do without. Apart from the films and robots, there's a **laser show**, "La Forêt des Rêves", a display of music, colour and effects focused on the park's dancing fountains (shows start daily just after sunset).

Chauvigny and St-Savin

East of Poitiers, the towns of **CHAUVIGNY** and **ST-SAVIN** are both accessible by bus, though you'll need an early start if you want to see both in one day.

Chauvigny is a busy market town on the banks of the Vienne which boasts five **medieval castles** whose imposing ruins stand atop a precipitous rock spur. Its pride and joy, however, are the sculpted capitals in the Romanesque **church of St-Pierre**. If you take rue du Château, which winds up the spur from the central place de la Poste, you'll pass the ruins of the Château Baronnial, which belonged to the bishops of Poitiers and now hosts displays by birds of prey, then the better-preserved Château d'Harcourt, before coming to the attractive and unusual east end of St-Pierre.

Inside, the church of St-Pierre is damp and a little shabby, but the choir capitals are a visual treat. Each one is different, evoking a terrifying, nightmarish world. Graphically illustrated monsters – bearded, moustached, winged, scaly, human-headed with manes of flame – grab hapless mortals – naked, upside-down and puny – ripping their bowels out and crunching their heads. The only escape offered is in the naively serene events of the Nativity. On the second capital on the south side of the choir, for instance, the Angel Gabriel announces Christ's birth to the shepherds while just around the corner the Archangel Michael weighs souls in hand-held scales and a devil tries to grab one for his dinner.

Coinciding your visit with the Saturday or Thursday **market** gives an extra dimension to a day-trip here. Held between the church of Notre-Dame and the river, it offers a mouthwatering selection of food – oysters, prawns, crayfish, cheeses galore and pâtés in aspic. The cafés are fun, too, bursting with noisy wine-flushed farmers.

St-Savin is scarcely more than a hamlet in comparison with bustling Chauvigny, but it is worth a visit for its **abbey church** alone, now listed as a UNESCO monument of universal importance. Built in the eleventh century, possibly on the site of a church founded by Charlemagne, it rises strong and severe above the gazebos, vegetable gardens and lichened tile roofs of the houses at its feet. Inside, the entire vault is covered with paintings and, though colours are few, they're full of light and grace, depicting scenes from the stories of Genesis and Exodus. Some are instantly recognizable: Noah's three-decked ark, or Pharaoh's horses rearing at the engulfing waves of the Red Sea.

Attached to the abbey is a fascinating multimedia **museum** (in French; Feb–June & Sept–Dec daily except Sun morning 10am–noon & 2–5pm; July & Aug daily 10am–7pm; Ⓦ www.abbaye-saint-savin.com; €6) of Romanesque art history with a number of innovative exhibits about medieval monastic life and architecture.

Parthenay and around

Directly west of Poitiers, and served by regular SNCF buses, the attractive small town of **PARTHENAY** was once an important stop on the pilgrim routes to Compostela and is now the site of a major cattle market every Wednesday. It's not a place to make a special detour for, but its medieval heart is worth a stopover if you're heading north to Brittany or west to the sea.

The most appealing streets are on the far side of town from the abandoned train station where the buses now arrive. Avenue de Gaulle leads straight to the central place du Drapeau, from which you can cut through a largely pedestrianized shopping district to the Gothic **Porte de l'Horloge**, the fortified gateway to the old citadelle on a steep-sided neck of land above a loop of the River Thouet.

Through the gateway, on rue de la Citadelle, the plain but imposing Romanesque **church of Sainte-Croix** faces the *mairie* across a small garden, which offers views over the ramparts and the **gully of St-Jacques**, with its medieval houses and vegetable plots climbing the opposite slope. Further along rue de la Citadelle is a handsome but badly damaged Romanesque door, all that remains of the castle chapel of **Notre-Dame-de-la-Couldre**. Of the castle itself, practically nothing is left, but from the tip of the spur where it once stood you can look down on the twin-towered **gateway** and the **Pont St-Jacques**, a thirteenth-century bridge through which the nightly flocks of pilgrims poured into the town for shelter and security. To reach it, turn left under the Tour de l'Horloge and down the medieval lane known as **Vaux St-Jacques**. The lane is highly evocative of that period, with crooked half-timbered dwellings crowding up to the bridge.

Practicalities

The **tourist office** (May–Sept Mon–Fri 8.30am–12.30pm & 2–6pm, Sat 2.30–6.30pm; Oct–April Mon 2–6pm, Tues–Fri 9.30am–12.30pm & 2–6pm, Sat 9.30am–12.30pm; Ⓣ05.49.64.24.24, Ⓦ www.cc-parthenay.fr) is at 8 rue de la Vaux Saint-Jacques, right next to the old bridge. Nearby, at no. 10 place du Vauvert, is the town's most attractive **accommodation**, the extremely welcoming ⚜ *chambre d'hôte* run by M. and Mme Giboury (Ⓣ05.49.64.12.33; ❶). The rooms are wonderfully characterful, set in an old house in the heart of the medieval quarter. If convenience is a higher priority than romance, try the smart two-star *Hôtel du Nord* right opposite the station (Ⓣ05.49.94.29.11, Ⓦ www.hotelnordparthenay.com; ❸; restaurant from €14). **Campers** have to head to the four-star site at *Le Bois Vert* (Ⓣ05.49.64.78.43; April–Oct), part of the huge Base de Loisirs riverbank recreation area, about 3km west of Parthenay on the D949.

The best of Parthenay's restaurants is *Le Fin Gourmet*, 28 rue Ganne (Ⓣ05.49.64.04.53; closed Sun evening. Mon & Wed lunch), where high-quality cuisine combines with a jovial atmosphere; menus range from €26 to €45. Place du Drapeau also features several good-value brasseries with outside seating, of which *L'Esplanade* has a menu for €9.30 at lunch and does ice cream and drinks all day.

Around Parthenay

There are three more beautiful **Romanesque churches** within easy reach of Parthenay. One – with a sculpted facade depicting a mounted knight hawking – is only a twenty-minute walk away on the Niort road, at **Parthenay-le-Vieux**. The others are at **Airvault**, 20km northeast of Parthenay and easily accessible on the Parthenay–Thouars SNCF bus route, and **St-Jouin-de-Marnes**, 9km northeast of Airvault (no public transport). A trip to St-Jouin can easily be combined with a visit to the sixteenth-century **Château d'Oiron**, 8.5km to the northwest. Alternatively, you could go on north to **Thouars**, 21km from Airvault or 16km from St-Jouin, to see the abbey church of St-Laon; here there are accommodation options in the form of cheap hotels and a municipal **campsite**.

Niort

NIORT, 50km southwest of Poitiers, and connected to it by regular trains, makes a useful stopover if your goal is the Marais Poitevin (see opposite). The town itself has enough of interest to fill a pleasant morning's stroll, and it's the last place before the marshes to get a really wide choice of provisions. The most interesting part of the town is the mainly pedestrian area around **rue Victor-Hugo** and **rue St-Jean**, full of stone-fronted or half-timbered medieval houses. Coming from the *gare SNCF*, take rue de la Gare as far as avenue de Verdun, with the post office on the corner, then turn right into place de la Brèche. Rue Ricard leaves the square on the left; rue Victor-Hugo is its continuation, following the line of the medieval market in a gully separating the two small hills on which Niort is built. Up to the left, opposite the end of rue St-Jean, is the old **town hall**, a triangular building of the early sixteenth century with lantern, belfry and ornamental machicolations, perhaps capable of repelling drunken revellers but no match for catapult or sledgehammer.

At the end of the street is the river, the **Sèvre Niortaise**, with gardens and trees along the bank and, over the bridge, the ruins of a glove factory, the last vestige of Niort's once thriving leather industry. At the time of the Revolution, it kept more than thirty cavalry regiments in breeches. Today Niort's biggest industry is insurance: the most bourgeois town in France, so it's said, because of the prosperity brought by the large number of major insurance firms making their headquarters here. Accordingly, restaurants are usually packed at lunchtime, and well-heeled shoppers throng the pedestrianized streets, giving it a fairly lively, affluent feel.

Just downstream is the **market hall** and, beyond, vast and unmistakable on a slight rise, the keep of a **castle** (currently closed) begun by Henry II of England.

Practicalities

The **gare SNCF** is on rue Mazagran, with the **gare routière** just next door. The excellent **tourist office** at 16 rue de Petit St-Jean (July & Aug Mon–Fri 9.30am–7pm, Sun 10am–1pm; Sept–June Mon–Fri 9.30am–6.30pm, Sat 9.30am–12.30pm; ☏05.49.24.18.79, ⊛www.niortourisme.com) has plenty of information about walking itineraries around the Marais, sells large-scale maps of cycle routes (€1) and also rents out bikes in summer (€13 per day). For rustic accommodation in the Marais itself, contact Gîtes de France, at 15 rue Thiers (☏05.49.24.00.42). You can rent cars at any of the agencies that line rue de la Gare by the station, including Avis at no. 89 (☏05.49.24.36.98).

There are plenty of **hotels** in Niort; by far the best value is the *Hôtel Saint-Jean*, 21 avenue St-Jean d'Angély (☎05.49.79.20.76, ☏05.49.35.03.27; ❶), a budget hotel with welcoming, helpful owners, not far from the medieval quarter. Closer to the station is the impeccably smart *Ambassadeur*, 82 rue de la Gare (☎05.49.24.00.38; ⓦwww.ambassadeur-hotel.com; ❸), while the greatest luxury is to be found at the *Grand Hôtel*, 32 avenue de Paris (☎05.49.24.22.21, ⓦwww.grandhotelniort.com; ❺), whose back rooms look onto a peaceful garden.

Restaurants are congregated around place de la Brèche, but if you don't mind walking a quarter of an hour it's worth heading out to *L'Adress,* at 247 avenue de la Rochelle (☎05.49.79.41.06; closed Sun & Mon; menus from €24), which has distinctively local menus. For lunches, *Sucrée Salée*, at 2 rue du Temple (☎05.49.24.77.16), specializes in tarts and crumbles *à l'anglaise*; menus from €10.50.

The Marais Poitevin

The **Marais Poitevin** is a strange, lazy landscape of fens and meadows, shielded by poplar trees and crisscrossed by an elaborate system of canals, dykes and slow-flowing rivers. Recently declared a regional park, it is known as "La Venise Verte" – the Green Venice – and indeed, farmers in this area frequently travel through the marshes in flat-bottomed punts as their fields lack dry-land access. The area has proved a big hit with tourists in recent years, but away from the main villages peace and tranquility still abound. Whether walking or cycling, it's best to stick to the marked paths, as shortcuts invariably end in fields surrounded by water.

Access to the eastern edge of the marsh is easiest at the whitewashed village of **COULON**, on the River Sèvre, just 11km from Niort. The #20 bus from place Brèche in Niort sets you down outside the **tourist office** on rue Gabriel-Auchier (April–Oct Mon–Sat 10am–1pm & 2–6pm, Sun 10am–1pm; Nov–March Mon–Fri 10am–1pm & 2–5pm; ☎05.49.35.99.29, ⓦwww.marais -poitevin.fr). From there it's a short walk to the central place de L'Eglise where **punts** can be rented, with or without a guide, from La Trigale (☎05.49.35.14.14; from €13 per boat), while **bikes**, tandems and pedal-powered family vehicles are all available from La Libellule (☎05.49.35.83.42; €18 per day), also on place de L'Eglise.

The best **hotel** in the village is the family-run 🎋 *Central*, 4 rue d'Autremont (☎05.49.35.90.20, ⓦwww.hotel-lecentral-coulon.com;❸), which has charming rooms and an excellent, traditionally rustic restaurant for which it's wise to reserve (menus €19–40; closed Sun & Mon). If you're **camping**, head for the attractively sited *Camping Venise Verte* (☎05.49.35.90.36, ⓦwww.camping -laveniseverte.com; April–Oct), in a meadow about 2km downstream (a 25min walk). The tourist office can provide details of other campsites and *chambres d'hôtes* further into the marshes. Of the latter, *Le Paradis*, in Le Vanneau (☎05.49.35.33.95; ⓦwww.gite-le-paradis.com; ❸), is a particularly good deal.

Ten kilometres west of Coulon you arrive at the village of **ARÇAIS**, with a simple nineteenth-century church and a substantial port which is testimony to the earlier role of the canals as a serious means of agricultural transportation. Nowadays, it is another spot from which to hire canoes or punts. Beyond Arçais, there's practically no traffic, just meadows and cows. At the seaward end of the marsh – the area south of **LUÇON** – the landscape changes, becoming all straight lines and open fields of wheat and sunflowers. The villages cap low mounds that were once islands.

The Vendée

The northwest of the Poitou region falls within the rural *département* of the **Vendée**, whose main attraction is the 80km stretch of coast between chic **Les Sables-d'Olonne** and the northernmost tip of the scenic **Île de Noirmoutier**. Inland, the main focus of interest is the marvellous summertime *spectacle* at **Les Épesses**.

Les Sables-d'Olonne

The area around **LES SABLES-D'OLONNE** and northwards has been heavily developed with Costa-style apartment blocks. If you're passing through, though, it's worth having a look at the surprisingly good modern art section in the **Musée de l'Abbaye Sainte-Croix** on rue Verdun (mid-June to Sept Tues–Sun 10am–noon & 2.30–6.30pm; Oct to mid-June Tues–Sun 2.30–5.30pm; €4.60) and the collection of 150 classic autos and other vehicles at the **Musée d'Automobile**, 8km southeast of town on the road to Talmont (April, May, Sept & Oct daily 9.30am–noon & 2–6.30pm; June–Aug daily 9.30am–7pm; Ⓦwww.musee-auto-vendee.com; €8.50). The **tourist office** in the middle of the seafront (July & Aug daily 9am–7pm; Sept–June Mon–Sat 9am–noon & 1.30–5pm; Ⓣ02.5196.85.85) can provide information on a range of higher-octane **activities** in the area, from go-karting and canoeing to helicopter trips. The main reason to stay, though, is the town's vast curve of clean, beautiful **beach**, which lures hordes in the summer.

Hotels get booked up well in advance for July and August, but if you're staying a few days you could go for half board at the *Hôtel Antoine*, 60 rue Napoléon (Ⓣ02.51.95.08.36, Ⓦwww.antoinehotel.com; March–Oct; ❻), with spacious, comfortable rooms and a traditional restaurant. The cheapest rooms available are those at the welcoming but basic *Relais des Voyageurs*, 84 avenue Alcide Gabaret, between the station and the beach (Ⓣ02.51.95.15.96, Ⓕ02.51.21.37.19; ❶–❷) while the modern *Arundel* (Ⓣ02.51.32.03.77, Ⓦwww.arundel-hotel.fr; ❻) at 8 boulevard Franklin-Roosevelt has some rooms with sea views and Jacuzzis. The closest **campsite** to the centre is the four-star *Les Roses* (Ⓣ02.51.95.10.42, Ⓦwww.chadotel.com; April–Oct) on rue des Roses, 500m from the beach.

Good-quality fish **restaurants** line the port on quai Guiné and opposite on quai des Boucanniers, reached via the shuttle ferry which crosses the port channel (daily 6am–midnight; €0.90).

The Île de Noirmoutier

The twenty-kilometre-long **Île de Noirmoutier**, 60km north of Les Sables-d'Olonne on the D38, was an early monastic settlement of the seventh century; now it has bowed to pilgrims of a different type, serving as a relatively plush tourist resort. Although tourism is the island's main economy, it doesn't dominate everything. Salt marshes here are still worked, spring potatoes sown and fishes fished. The island can be reached in two hours by bus from La Roche-sur-Yon or Nantes, and is connected to the shore by both bridge and the *passage de gois*, a channel across which you can drive your car when the tides are low. Once you've arrived, cycling is the ideal way to explore: there are paths around almost the entire perimeter, and it's perfectly flat.

Noirmoutier-en-l'Île

The island town **NOIRMOUTIER-EN-L'ÎLE** is a low-key place that can get crowded in summer. It has a twelfth-century **castle**, a **church** with a Romanesque crypt, an **aquarium**, an excellent **market** (Tues, Fri & Sun) in place de la République and most of the island's **nightlife** in the form of piano bars with longer-than-usual café hours. The **tourist office** (April–June & Sept Mon–Sat 9.30am–12.30pm & 2–7pm; July & Aug daily 9am–7pm & 2.30–6.30pm; closed winter; ☎02.51.39.12.42, ⓦwww.ile-noirmoutier.com) on rue du Général Passaga has lists of campsites on the island and can give you a rudimentary map of cycle paths. **Bikes** can be rented from Vel-hop, 55 avenue Joseph-Pineau (☎02.51.39.01.34, ⓦwww.cyclhop.fr; €13 per day).

Hotels need to be booked in advance in summer. The cheapest in town is also a very agreeable one: *Bamboo*, 37 avenue Joseph Pineau (☎02.51.39.08.97; ❷), has brand new rooms decorated in light colours of sea and sand. Closer to the beach is the modern *Bois de la Chaize*, 23 avenue Victoire (☎02.51.39.04.62, ⓦwww.hotel-noirmoutier.com; ❹), while there are more luxurious surroundings at the *Général d'Elbée* (☎02.51.39.10.29, ⓦwww.generaldelbee.com; mid-March to Oct; ❼) in an atmospheric eighteenth-century building right opposite the castle.

The pedestrianized centre around the Grande Rue is packed with overpriced pizzerias and crêperies. The town's finer **restaurants** are to be found beneath the curtain wall and sparkling white keep of the château, like the long-standing *Le Grand Four*, 1 rue de la Cure (☎02.51.39.61.97), with traditional menus from €19.

The rest of the island

As for exploring the island, the western coast, with its great curves of sand, resembles the mainland, while the northern side dips in and out of little bays with rocky promontories between. Inland, were it not for the saltwater dykes, the horizon would suggest that you were far away from the sea. One beautiful beach, the Plage des Dames, is just thirty-minutes' walk east of Noirmoutier town, but the stretches in the south of the island are likely to be less crowded. The more southerly resorts, though built up, have not been the main targets for developers; for accommodation in this part of the island, head for the village of Barbatre and *Le Goéland*, 15 route du Gois (☎02.51.39.68.66, ⓦwww.hotel-legoeland.fr.st; ❹). In the village centres there are still the one-storey houses that you see throughout La Vendée and southern Brittany – whitewashed and ochre-tiled with decorative brickwork around the windows and S- or Z-shaped coloured bars on the shutters. During the spring, the weather is fickle – sunny one moment, stormy the next – and the heat of the summer cultivates a vicious mosquito population.

Les Épesses

Some 80km inland from Les Sables (on the N160 if you're driving), at the ruined **Château du Puy du Fou** in the village of **LES ÉPESSES**, a remarkable lakeside extravaganza takes place during the summer months (June–Sept Fri & Sat 10.30pm; 1hr 40min; booking essential; ☎02.51.64.11.11, ⓦwww.puydufou.com; €24). It's a weird affair: the enactment of the life of a local peasant from the Middle Ages to World War II, complete with fireworks, lasers, dances on the lake and Comédie Française voice-overs. The story, available in English through a headset translation (€7) is interesting but incidental – the massive spectacle itself is the real attraction.

To get to Les Épesses by public **transport**, you'll need to venture to **Cholet** (connected by train from Nantes) and take a bus south from there; Puy du Fou itself is 2.5km from Les Épesses on the D27 to Chambretaud. The tourist office in Cholet (☎02.41.49.80.00) can provide information about transport. There is one reasonably priced **hotel** in Les Épesses, *La Crémaillère*, 2 rue de la Libération (☎&℉02.51.57.30.01; ❷), and further accommodation options 10km west in **Les Herbiers**.

The coast around La Rochelle

The coast around **La Rochelle** – especially the **islands** – is great for young families, with miles of safe sandy beaches and shallow water. Be aware, however, that in August, unless you're camping or book in advance, accommodation is a near-insuperable problem. Out of season you can't rely on sunny weather, but that shouldn't deter you since the quiet misty seascapes and working fishing ports have a melancholy romance all their own. La Rochelle and **Royan** are the largest urban centres but **Rochefort**, cheaper than the former and more attractive than the latter, makes an excellent base. All three are connected by regular trains, while elsewhere you'll have to take pot luck with the rather quirky bus routes.

La Rochelle and around

LA ROCHELLE is the most attractive and unspoilt seaside town in France. Thanks to the foresight of 1970s mayor Michel Crépeau, its historic seventeenth- to eighteenth-century centre and waterfront were plucked from the clutches of the developers and its streets freed of traffic for the delectation of pedestrians. A real shock-horror outrage at the time, the policy has become standard practice for preserving old town centres across the country – even more successful than Crépeau's picturesque yellow bicycle plan, since imitated in Paris and elsewhere.

La Rochelle has a long history, as you would expect of such a sheltered Atlantic port. Eleanor of Aquitaine gave it a charter in 1199, which released it from its feudal obligations, and it rapidly became a port of major importance, trading in salt and wine and skillfully exploiting the Anglo–French quarrels. The Wars of Religion, however, were particularly destructive for La Rochelle. It turned Protestant and, because of its strategic importance, drew the remorseless enmity of Cardinal Richelieu, who laid siege to it in 1627. To the dismay of the towns-people, who reasoned that no one could effectively blockade seasoned mariners like themselves, he succeeded in sealing the harbour approaches with a dyke. The English dispatched the Duke of Buckingham to their aid, but he was caught napping on the Île de Ré and badly defeated. By the end of 1628 Richelieu had starved the city into submission. Out of the pre-siege population of 28,000, only 5000 survived. The walls were demolished and the city's privileges revoked. La

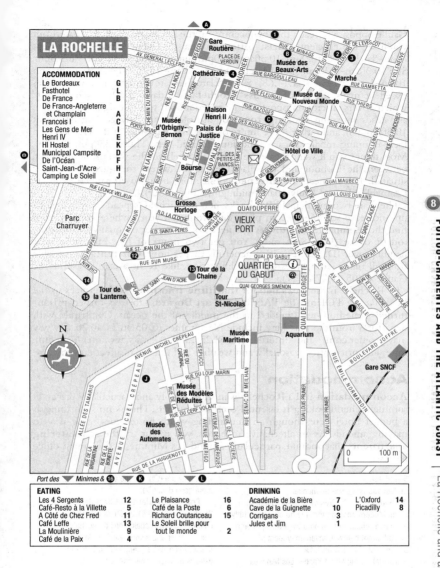

LA ROCHELLE

ACCOMMODATION

Le Bordeaux	G
Fasthotel	L
De France	B
De France-Angleterre et Champlain	A
Francois I	C
Les Gens de Mer	I
Henri IV	E
HI Hostel	K
Municipal Campsite	D
De l'Océan	F
Saint-Jean-d'Acre	H
Camping Le Soleil	J

EATING			
Les 4 Sergents	12	Le Plaisance	16
Café-Resto à la Villette	5	Café de la Poste	6
A Côté de Chez Fred	11	Richard Coutanceau	15
Café Leffe	13	Le Soleil brille pour	
La Moulinière	9	tout le monde	2
Café de la Paix	4		

DRINKING			
Académie de la Bière	7	L'Oxford	14
Cave de la Guignette	10	Picadilly	8
Corrigans	3		
Jules et Jim	1		

Rochelle later became the principal port for trade with the French colonies in the Caribbean Antilles and Canada. Indeed, many of the settlers, especially in Canada, came from this part of France.

Arrival, information and transport

Ryanair now runs daily flights here from London's Stansted airport, which accounts for the large number of Brits who visit. Bus #7 runs every twenty minutes between the **airport** and town centre (Mon–Sat 7am–7.20pm; €1.20; 10min). From the grandiose **gare SNCF** on boulevard Joffre, take avenue de

Gaulle opposite to reach the town centre; on the left as you reach the waterfront you'll see the efficient **tourist office**, on quai du Gabut (April–June & Sept Mon–Sat 9am–6pm, Sun 10.30am–5.30pm; July & Aug Mon–Sat 9am–8pm, Sun 10.30am–5.30pm; Oct–March Mon–Sat 10am–12.30pm & 1.30–6pm, Sun 10am–1pm; ☎05.46.41.14.68, ⊛www.larochelle-tourisme.com), which has excellent maps and sells the **Pass' Rochelais** (2 days €5.60; 1 week €8.40), which covers all city transport and gives reductions to most sights. The office also leads morning **walking tours** of the old town (July & Aug Mon–Sat 10.30am; €6), and rather more fun two-hour evening tours of the city, led by a local donning medieval garb (mid-June to mid-Sept Thurs 8.30pm; €10.50). Most things you'll want to see are in the area behind the waterfront; in effect, between the harbour and the place de Verdun, where the **gare routière** is situated. If you need an **internet** connection, head to Akromicro, rue de l'Aimable Nanette (daily 10am–midnight; €2 per hour).

There are two municipal **bike parks**, heir to Michel Crépeau's original pick-up-and-leave scheme: one in place de Verdun (all year), where you will also find the terminal for the town's bus network, the other on quai Valin near the tourist office (May–Sept only). You get two hours of free bike time after handing over ID; after this it's a generous €1 per hour. **Car rental** is available from all major companies outside the station, like Rent-a-car, 29 avenue de Gaulle (☎05.46.27.27.27).

La Rochelle is the area's hub for **maritime transport**, with services to the Île de Ré, Île d'Oléron, Île d'Aix and to **Fort Boyard**, a fortress-turned-prison-turned-gameshow-set, stranded in the middle of the ocean. Companies with departures from the port here include Navipromer (☎05.46.34.40.20, ⊛www.navipromer.com) and Interîles (☎08.25.13.55.00, ⊛www.inter-iles.com); times and prices vary seasonally, and weather and tides may affect crossings.

Accommodation

Accommodation in La Rochelle is in short supply and particularly pricey in summer, when booking is essential even for campers. There's no such thing as a budget hotel here, though an outstanding youth hostel goes some way to making amends. As an alternative to hotels, you might try the **self-catering apartments** that abound, particularly around Les Minimes – the tourist office has lists.

Hotels

Le Bordeaux 43 rue St-Nicolas ☎05.46.41.31.22, ⊛www.hotel-bordeaux-fr.com. Modern and comfortable hotel, whose fully-equipped rooms all look onto the lively, pedestrianized street below. Conveniently located between station and port. ❹

Fasthotel 20 rue Alfred-Kastler, Les Minimes ☎05.46.45.46.00, ⊛www.3y.fr/larochelle. Excellent-value hotel made up of modern bungalows. It's well out of the action, though, 15min walk from the port des Minimes. Larger rooms are available for families. ❷

De France 43 rue du Minage ☎05.46.28.06.00, ⊛www.hotel-larochelle.com. A hidden pocket of grandeur right in the town centre. The calm, luxurious rooms here surround an ivy-covered courtyard. Rooms and suites are expensive for

what they are (❽), but the very similar "studios" are a good deal (❻).

De France-Angleterre et Champlain 20 rue Rambaud ☎05.46.41.23.99, ⊛www.hotel champlain.com. A chain hotel of two halves: the elegant foyer and some rooms are in an old town house, while less exciting ones are in a modern extension. Surprisingly one of the best deals in town, though the older rooms are dearer. ❹–❺

François I 15 rue Bazoges ☎05.46.41.28.46, ⊛www.hotelfrancois1er.fr. A touch expensive, but characterful and well situated in a historic building within a walled courtyard. It's been modernized since François himself used to stop off here, with wireless internet and other mod cons now standard. ❺

Les Gens de Mer 20 av du Général-de-Gaulle ☎05.46.41.26.24, ⊛www.lesgensdemer.fr.

Business-like hotel, but relatively good-value. Rooms are fully kitted-out, and it's in a handy spot for the station. **❸**

Henri IV 31 rue des Gentilhommes
℡05.46.41.25.79, ✉henri-iv@orange.fr. Recently renovated, this popular hotel has sparkling rooms right in the town centre in a sixteenth-century building on place de la Caille, a short stroll from the harbour front. **❺**

De l'Océan 36 cours des Dames
℡05.46.41.31.97, ⓦwww.hotel-ocean-larochelle .com. Comfortable two-star hotel in an enviable location, with a/c rooms – many with views of the port. **❸**

Saint-Jean-d'Acre 4 place de la Chaine
℡05.46.41.73.33, ⓦwww.hotel-la-rochelle.com. This modern, luxurious chain hotel offers good-sized rooms with probably the city's best views of the towers and harbour from the more expensive ones. **❺–❼**

Hostel and campsites

HI Hostel av des Minimes
℡05.46.44.43.11, ⓦwww.fuaj-aj -larochelle.com. A big modern hostel with a veranda overlooking the marina at Port des Minimes. It has all facilities, including a bar and cafeteria serving decent grub for €5 in the evening. Dorm-beds €17, single rooms €25. Bus #10 or walk from the train station, following the signs to the left.

Camping municipal de Port-Neuf on the northwest side of town ℡05.46.43.81.20. Well-kept and shaded campsite about 40min walk from the town centre. Take bus #20 from place Verdun, direction "Port-Neuf". Open all year.

Camping Le Soleil av Michel Crépeau
℡05.46.44.42.53. In a great location near the hostel and close to the beaches, this site is often crowded with raucous young holiday-makers. Take bus #10 from place Verdun to Les Minimes. Open late June to late Sept.

The Town

The **Vieux Port** is very much the focus of the town, with pleasure boats moored in serried ranks in front of the two impressive towers guarding the entrance to the port. Leading north from the **Porte de la Grosse Horloge**, the **rue du Palais** runs towards the cathedral and several of the museums on rue Thiers. You can stroll very pleasantly for an hour or more along the seafront in either direction from the harbour, down to the **Port des Minimes**, a huge modern marina development 2km south of the centre, or west along an attractive promenade and through a beautiful strip of parkland towards the **Port Neuf**.

▲ Vieux Port, La Rochelle

POITOU-CHARENTES AND THE ATLANTIC COAST | La Rochelle and around

Dominating the inner harbour, the heavy Gothic gateway of the **Porte de la Grosse Horloge** straddles the entrance to the old town. The quays in front of it are too full of traffic to encourage loitering; for that, it's best to head out along the tree-lined cours des Dames, where sailors' wives used to anxiously await the return of their husbands from the high seas. There is a view here of all three of the famous **towers**, which can be visited with a combined ticket (daily: April–Sept 10am–6.30pm; Oct–March 10am–1pm & 2.15–5.30pm; €7.50 for two towers, €10.50 for all three). Architecturally speaking, the **Tour St-Nicolas** is the most interesting, boasting two spiral staircases which intertwine but never meet. Opposite, the **Tour de la Chaine**, from which a chain used to be slung across to close the harbour at night, now houses a gently informative exhibition on seventeenth-century emigration from La Rochelle to French Canada. You can then climb along the old city walls to the third tower, known as the **Tour de la Lanterne** or Tour des Quatre Sergents, named after four sergeants imprisoned and executed for defying the Restoration monarchy in 1822. All three towers have fine views back to the port, and the entry ticket also includes a trip on the nifty **electric ferry**, the *passeur*, which crosses all day from one side of the water to the other (€0.60).

The rue du Palais and around

The real charm of La Rochelle lies on the city's main shopping street, **rue du Palais**, leading up from the Vieux Port to place de Verdun. Lining the street are eighteenth-century houses, some grey-stone, some half-timbered, with distinctive Rochelais-style slates overlapped like fish scales, while the shopfronts are set back beneath the ground-floor arcades. Among the finest are the **Hôtel de la Bourse** – actually the Chamber of Commerce – and the **Palais de Justice** with its colonnaded facade, both on the left-hand side. A few metres further on, in **rue des Augustins**, there is another grandiose affair built for a wealthy Rochelais in 1555, the so-called **Maison Henri II**, complete with loggia, gallery and slated turrets, where the regional tourist board has its offices. Place de Verdun itself is dull and characterless, with an uninspiring, humpbacked, eighteenth-century classical **cathedral** on the corner.

To the west of rue du Palais, especially in **rue de l'Escale**, paved with granite setts brought back from Canada as ballast in the Rochelais cargo vessels, you get the discreet residences of the eighteenth-century shipowners and chandlers, veiling their wealth with high walls and classical restraint. A rather less modest gentleman once installed himself on the corner of **rue Fromentin**: a seventeenth-century doctor who adorned his house front with the statues of famous medical men – Hippocrates, Galen and others. East of rue du Palais, and starting out from place des Petits-Bancs, rue du Temple takes you up alongside the **Hôtel de Ville** (guided tours daily 3pm & 4pm; €4), protected by a decorative but seriously fortified wall. It was begun around 1600 in the reign of Henri IV, whose initials, intertwined with those of Marie de Médicis, are carved on the ground-floor gallery. It's a beautiful specimen of Frenchified Italian taste, adorned with niches and statues and coffered ceilings, all done in a stone the colour of ripe barley. Just up rue des Merciers, the other main shopping area, is the cramped and noisy **market square**, where a food market takes place every morning.

Various **museums** are concealed in the town houses around rue du Palais. The **Musée des Beaux-Arts** in rue Gargoulleau (Mon & Wed–Fri 1.30–5pm; Sat & Sun 2.30–6.30pm; €4) has a modest collection, whose highlights are the exotic works of Eugène Fromentin, one of the town's most beloved sons, whose statue you can admire beneath the Grosse Horloge. More out of the ordinary is the

Musée du Nouveau Monde (Mon & Wed–Fri 9.30am–12.30pm & 1.30–5pm, Sat & Sun 2.30–6pm; €4), whose entrance is in rue Fleuriau. It occupies the former residence of the Fleuriau family, rich shipowners and traders who, like many of their fellow Rochelais, made fortunes out of the slave trade and Caribbean sugar, spices and coffee. There's a fine collection of prints, paintings and photos of the old West Indian plantations; seventeenth- and eighteenth-century maps of America; and an interesting display of aquatint illustrations for Marmontel's novel *Les Incas* – an amazing mixture of sentimentality and coy salaciousness.

The quartier du Gabut and south to the Port des Minimes

On the east side of the old harbour behind the Tour St-Nicolas is the **quartier du Gabut**, the one-time fishermen's quarter of wooden cabins and sheds, now converted into bars, shops and eating places. Right on the quayside is the spectacular **aquarium** (daily: April–June & Sept 9am–8pm; July & Aug 9am–11pm; Oct–March 10am–8pm; Ⓦ www.aquarium-larochelle.com; adults €13, children €10), whose pride and joy are its twenty species of shark. Also worth recommending is the impressive panorama from the building's rooftop café. Opposite the aquarium is the **Musée Maritime** (April–Oct 10am–6.30pm; Ⓦ www.museemaritimelarochelle.fr; €8), consisting of two ships: an old weather station and a trawler whose working days are behind it.

A further ten-minute walk brings you to the **Musée des Automates** (daily: July & Aug 9.30am–7pm; Sept–June 10am–noon & 2–6pm; Ⓦ www .museedesautomates.com; adults €7.50, children €5, or joint ticket with Musée des Modèles Réduits, adults €11, children €6.50) on rue de la Désirée, a fascinating collection of three hundred automated puppets, drawing you into an irresistible fantasy world. Some of the puppets are interesting from a historical angle; others, like one that writes the name "Pierrot", from a mechanical viewpoint. Further down the same street is the **Musée des Modèles Réduits** (same hours and ticket prices as the Automates). Scale models of every variety and era are on show, starting with cars and including models of a submerged shipwreck and La Rochelle train station.

The **Port des Minimes** itself houses thousands of yachts and also has a beautiful beach, where the young and gorgeous flock out to parade at weekends and on summer evenings. You can get here on bus #10 from place Verdun, or more entertainingly on the **bus de mer**, a small boat which runs from the old port (April–June & Sept hourly 10am–7pm except 1pm; July & Aug half-hourly 9am–11.30pm; Oct–March Sat & Sun hourly 10am–6pm except 1pm; €1.75 one way).

Eating

For eating, the best place to look is the attractive rue St-Jean-du-Pérot, where the highest-quality traditional restaurants are to be found, as well as a couple of ethnic eateries. More relaxed and less touristy are a handful of authentic little places further inland around the market square. Particularly worth seeking out are the town's many excellent **fish restaurants**. *Ernest Le Glacier*, 15 rue du Port, and *Olivier Glacier*, 21 rue St- Jean-du-Pérot, both serve excellent **ice cream** well into the evening.

Les 4 Sergents 49 rue St-Jean-du-Pérot ☎05.46.41.35.80. Despite its smart appearance, the food here is not quite *haute cuisine*, but it's tasty nonetheless, and the restaurant has its own wine *cave* two doors down. Menus from €17. Closed Mon.

A Côté de Chez Fred 30–32 rue St-Nicolas ☎05.46.41.65.76. A characterful corner restaurant with simple wooden tables and watercolours of seaside scenes. A blackboard *carte* changes daily to reveal what yesterday's catch brought in. The excellent *menu de la mer* costs €27. Booking advisable. Closed Sun.

Café Leffe 48 cours des Dames. Brilliantly situated next to the Tour de la Chaine, this brasserie is popular from breakfast through to late evening, serving drinks and its speciality *moules-frites*.

La Moulinière 24 rue St-Sauveur ☏ 05.46.41.18.16. This is the place to come for mussels, which are served in a dozen different ways (from €8). It's in a pleasant spot, too, right opposite the recently restored church of St-Sauveur. Closed Sun, and Mon evening out of season.

Café de la Paix place de Verdun. A superbly decadent *belle-époque* café that is the highlight of an otherwise dull square. All mirrors, gilt and plush, La Rochelle's ladies of means come here to sip lemon tea and nibble daintily at sticky cakes. The *plats du jour* are also in the finest French brasserie tradition.

Le Plaisance 27 av des Minimes ☏ 05.46.44.41.51. One of a row of good-value options near the beach in Les Minimes. Fish menus for just €12, to be enjoyed on a covered terrace, from which you can watch the sun go down behind the marina.

Café de la Poste place de l'Hôtel de Ville. An ideal spot to admire the ornate town hall over a late breakfast or a drink in the afternoon. Brasserie staples all on offer, like the classic *steak-frites* for around €12.

Richard Coutanceau plage de la Concurrence ☏ 05.46.41.48.19. Unquestionably a great place to splash out. Located on the seafront just to the west of the old harbour, with a perfect view out over the beach and sea, this is a veritable palace of gastronomic excellence, renowned for its fish and seafood specialities. Menus €52–95; closed Sun.

Le soleil brille pour tout le monde 13 rue des Cloutiers ☏ 05.46.41.11.42. Cheerful and colourful home cooking in friendly surroundings. The vegetarian *tartes* (€8) are outstanding and, like everything else here, are made from fresh ingredients from the market down the road. Seafood and meat feature on the *plats du jour*. Very popular, so book or get here early. Closed Sun & Mon.

Café-Resto à la Villette 4 rue de la Forme, behind the market. Tiny, authentic place popular with locals; good *plats du jour* from €7.70. Lunch only, Mon–Sat.

Bars, nightlife and entertainment

As well as the numerous brasseries round the old harbour, one popular place for a daytime **drink** is the old-school watering hole *Cave de la Guignette* at 8 rue St-Nicolas, which might be called dingy or atmospheric depending on your taste, but serves great wine. The bars on the **quai du Gabut**, in behind the tourist office, are a notorious meeting point for students and youngsters on nights out during term-time, though they can be a bit dead in summer. **Rue St-Nicolas** is lively all year round. For a slower-paced atmosphere, head further inland to rue des Templiers and the agreeable *Académie de la Bière*. By far the most authentic of La Rochelle's numerous **Irish pubs** is *Corrigan's* at 20 rue des Cloutiers (ⓦ www.corrigans.fr), which has a relaxed and familiar mood, enjoyed by a mainly local clientele. Barry, the affable owner, organizes regular live music, including Irish folk evenings on Sundays.

La Rochelle's nightclubs tend to stick to a good-times rather than cutting-edge music policy. The places to go for are the *Picadilly*, on rue des Templiers, and the larger *Oxford*, plage de la Concurrence (ⓦ www.club-oxford.com), which often organizes themed nights. On rue Rambaud, meanwhile, is the friendly cabaret bar *Jules et Jim*, where there are often concerts and salsa nights.

The monthly **magazine** *Sortir* has listings for mainstream and classical music events, as well as for theatre and film. The town is blessed with some excellent independent arthouse cinemas, showing films in the original language with subtitles. Try the Dragon right on the harbour, or the Coursive, 4 rue St-Jean-du-Pérot (ⓦ www.la-coursive.com), which is also the town theatre.

In mid-July La Rochelle hosts the major **festival** of French-language music, Les Francofolies (ⓦ www.francofolies.fr), which features musicians from overseas as well as France and attracts the best part of 100,000 fans to the city.

The Île de Ré

A half-hour drive west from La Rochelle, the **Île de Ré** is a low, narrow island some 30km long, fringed by sandy beaches to the southwest and salt marshes and oyster beds to the northeast, with the interior a motley mix of small-scale vine, asparagus and wheat cultivation. All the buildings on Ré must abide by height restrictions and incorporate the typical local features of whitewashed walls, curly orange tiles and green-painted shutters, which gives the island villages a southern holiday atmosphere.

Out of season the island has a slow, misty charm, and life in its little ports revolves exclusively around the cultivation of oysters and mussels. In season, though, it's extraordinarily crowded, with upwards of 400,000 visitors passing through. The crowds mainly head for the **southern beaches**; those to the northeast are covered in rocks and seaweed, and the sea is too shallow for bathing.

ST-MARTIN, the island's capital, is an atmospheric fishing port with whitewashed houses clustered around the stone quays of a well-protected harbour, from where trawlers and flat-bottomed oyster boats, piled high with cage-like devices used for "growing" oysters, slip out every morning on the muddy tide. The military adventures of the Duke of Buckingham, who attacked the island unsuccessfully in 1627, are now only recalled by signs to the backstreet nightclub *Le Boucquingam*. However, to the east of the harbour, you can walk along the almost perfectly preserved **fortifications** – redesigned by Vauban in the late seventeenth century after Buckingham's attentions – to the citadelle, long used as a prison. From 1860 until 1938, it served as departure point for the *bagnards* – prisoners sentenced to hard labour in the penal colonies of French Guiana and New Caledonia.

As well as in the presence of its working fishing vessels, the island's pre-tourism existence can also be glimpsed near the village of **LOIX**, at the **Écomusée du Marais Salant** (daily mid-Feb to May & Oct 2–6pm; June–Sept 10am–12.30pm & 2–7pm; €4.30; @www.marais-salant.com), where the still satisfyingly unmodernized process of salt-harvesting is explained. A little further into the island, you come to the pretty village of **ARS-EN-RÉ**, easily recognizable by its distinctive black and white steeple. This belongs to a rather beautiful church, lower parts of which date from the twelfth century, including a grand but now somewhat weather-beaten Romanesque tympanum.

Practicalities

A great way to explore the island is on the excellent network of cycle paths which crisscross it. **Bikes** can be rented from Cyclosurf (℡05.46.09.08.28, @www.cyclo-surf.com) or Cycland (℡05.46.09.08.66, @www.cycland.fr), both of which have shops in all the towns on Ré and charge around €12 per day. To get to the island in the first place, there are **buses** which leave regularly from place de Verdun in La Rochelle, or you could drive over the **toll bridge** (€16.50 in summer, €9 in winter) which begins at the once significant commercial port of **La Pallice**. Alternatively, the cruise companies in La Rochelle (see p.564) do boat trips to St-Martin (1hr; €17).

Hotels are plentiful in all the island's villages, though packed in July and August. Most reasonably priced are the grand and green-shuttered *Le Sénéchal*, 6 rue Gambetta opposite the church in Ars-en-Ré (℡05.46.29.40.42, @www.hotel-le-senechal.com; ❹; closed Jan); *L'Océan*, 172 rue St-Martin in Le-Bois-Plage (℡05.46.09.23.07, @www.re-hotel-ocean.com; ❺; closed Jan); and, in La Flotte, *Le Français*, 1 cours Félix-Faure (℡05.46.09.60.06, @www.hotellefrancais.com; ❹; closed mid-Nov to March), with its own restaurant. For more pampering, try the very stylish but not-quite-luxury *La Jetée* on the quayside in St-Martin (☎05.46.09.36.36, ⓦwww.hotel-lajetee .com; ⑥).

There are even more **campsites** on the island than there are hotels, and it shouldn't be difficult finding a place, except perhaps in desirable locations near the southern beaches at the height of the summer. A few names, if you want to book ahead, are the *Camp du Soleil* in Ars-en-Ré (☎05.46.29.40.62, ⓦwww .campdusoleil.com; mid-March to mid-Nov); *L'Océan*, 50 route d'Ars in La Couarde (☎05.46.29.87.70, ⓦwww.campingocean.com; April–Sept); and the four-star *L'Île Blanche* in La Flotte (☎05.46.09.52.43, ⓦwww.ileblanche.com; April–Sept), with an outdoor heated pool and restaurant. Other options are listed at ⓦwww.campings-ile-de-re.com.

Good-value **food** is available on the quayside in St-Martin at *La Merine*, 31 quai de la Poitheviniere (☎05.46.09.20.39), with outdoor heated seating and a seafood menu for €24.50. The airy *La Salicorne*, 16 rue de l'Olivette in La Couarde (☎05.46.29.82.37), has a high standard of cuisine starting at €25, while the *K'Ré d'Ars*, 9 quai de la Criée in Ars-en-Ré (☎05.46.29.94.94), is another seafood specialist. Though not quite local cuisine, *Le Bar Basque*, on the port in La Flotte, serves excellent Basque dishes from as little as €5, best accompanied by a glass of their sangria.

Rochefort and around

ROCHEFORT dates from the seventeenth century, when it was created by Colbert, Louis XIV's navy minister, to protect the coast from English raids and to keep an eye on troublesome La Rochelle. It remained an important naval base until modern times with its shipyards, sail-makers, munitions factories and hospital. Built on a grid plan with regular ranks of identical houses, the town is a monument to the tidiness of the military mind, but is not without charm for all that. The central **place Colbert** is very pretty and nearby **rue Courbet** is exactly as the seventeenth century left it, complete with lime trees, and cobblestones brought from Canada as ships' ballast. The banks of the **Charente** are particularly beautiful here, too, dominated by the eighteenth-century royal ropeworks, while the unique and extraordinary house of explorer and novelist Pierre Loti is worth the trip in its own right.

Arrival and information

The **gare SNCF** is located at the northern end of avenue du Président-Wilson, about a fifteen-minute walk from the centre of town. The efficient **tourist office** (Mon–Sat: July & Aug 9.30am–7pm; Sept–June 9.30am–12.30pm & 2–6pm; ☎05.46.99.08.60, ⓦwww.pays-rochefortais.com) is on avenue Sadi-Carnot, two blocks north of the **gare routière**, where, in July and August, you can also hire **bikes** for just €1 per hour.

The municipal **campsite** (☎05.46.82.67.70; March–Nov) is a long haul if you've arrived at the *gare SNCF*: take avenue du Président-Wilson and keep going straight, until you reach the bottom of rue Toufaire, where you turn right, then left – about half an hour all the way. **Internet** access is available at Cybernet Copy 17, 38 rue du Dr-Peltier (Mon–Sat 9am–noon & 2–6pm; €4 per hour).

Accommodation

Rochefort's **hotels** are good value, and the town is a more relaxed, as well as more economical place to stay than neighbouring La Rochelle.

Caravelle 34 rue Jaurès ℡ 05.46.99.02.53, Ⓦ www.hotel-lacaravelle-rochefort.com. This central hotel offers brightly coloured comfortable rooms, many of them around a flowery inner courtyard. All equipped with TV and shower. ❹

La Corderie Royale rue Audebert ℡ 05.46.99.35.35, Ⓦ www.corderieroyale.com. The smartest hotel in Rochefort, with luxurious rooms and its own swimming pool. It's situated in the lovely grounds of the ropeworks, of which the top-end rooms have views. Closed Feb. ❻–❽

La Fayette 10 av Lafayette ℡ 05.46.99.03.31, Ⓦ www.hotel-lafayette.fr. A really good deal right in the town centre. Rooms have been renovated in a simple style, with modern fittings. ❸

HI Hostel 20 rue de la République ℡ 05.46.99.74.62. A basic hostel with clean rooms, communal kitchen and a pleasant garden area; no breakfast though. Dorm beds cost €13.

Le Welcome place Françoise-Dorléac ℡ 05.46.99.00.90, Ⓦ www.le-hotel-welcome.com. A budget hotel opposite the station, but rooms are more than acceptable; all have TV and you pay a touch more for a private bathroom. There's also a garden and a good brasserie. ❶

The Town

If you have a taste for the bizarre, there's no excuse to miss the house of the novelist Julien Viaud (1850–1923), alias Pierre Loti. Forty years a naval officer, he wrote numerous bestselling romances with exotic oriental settings and characters. The **Maison Pierre Loti**, at 141 rue Pierre-Loti (guided tours: daily except Tues 10–11.30am & 2–5pm; reservations essential; ℡ 05.46.99.16.88; €7.90), is part of a row of modestly proportioned grey-stone houses, outwardly a model of petit-bourgeois conformity and respectability, inside an outrageous and fantastical series of rooms decorated to exotic themes, from medieval gothic to an Arabian room complete with minaret. You can see how the house suited Loti's private life: he threw extravagant fancy dress parties and, rather more scandalously, kept an Oriental mistress in a separate part of the house from his more sober French wife.

Loti is in further evidence, along with the town's other explorer sons the Lesson brothers, at the nearby **Musée d'Art et d'Histoire**, 63 rue de Gaulle (mid-June to mid-Sept Tues–Sun 10.30am–7pm; mid-Sept to mid-June Tues–Sat 10.30am–12.30pm & 2–6pm, Sun 2–6pm; free), which has various objects brought back from far-flung places and some nautically themed works of art.

Down by the river, the **Corderie Royale** or royal ropeworks (July & Aug 9am–8pm; Sept–June 10am–noon & 2–5pm; Ⓦ www.corderie-royale.com; €6), off rue Toufaire, is the longest building in France and a rare and splendid example of seventeenth-century industrial architecture, substantially restored after damage in World War II. From 1660 until the Revolution, it furnished the entire French navy with rope. Inside is an exhibition on the building's history, but the main thing is the visual impact from the exterior. From here, you can stroll along an enchanting path through gardens by the river and examine the rest of the admirably restored **Arsenal**. After a few minutes, you come to Rochefort's latest pride and joy: a shipyard, rebuilding plank for plank the **Hermione**, the frigate aboard which La Fayette set sail from here in 1780 to assist the American bid for independence from the British. In the yard (daily: April–Sept 9am–7pm; Oct–March 10am–12.30pm & 2–6pm; €7.50) you can watch craftsman making slow but steady progress on the vessel.

Eating and drinking

Strolling through Rochefort, you should have no trouble finding somewhere to **eat**, though few establishments are culinary standouts. One lovely spot is the terrace of *Le Galion* (☏05.46.87.03.77), on rue Toufaire opposite the entrance to the Arsenal, where there are fish dishes and a couple of classic *plats du jour* on menus from €14.50. More formal is *Les Quatres Saisons*, 76 rue Grimaux (☏05.46.83.95.12; closed Sun & Mon), with menus from €23.

Fouras and the Île d'Aix

FOURAS, some 30km south of La Rochelle and accessible by the regular bus G from Rochefort, is the main embarkation point for the tiny Île d'Aix (see p.606), where Napoleon spent his last days in Europe. It's an uninspiring town, redeemed only by a clutch of popular beaches. The ferry dock, **Pointe de la Fumée**, is at the tip of the 3km long peninsula which is bordered by oyster beds. Off its westernmost tip at low tide can be seen the *bouchots à moules*, lines of mussel-encrusted stumps of wood, while at high tide this is a popular place to fish for *crevettes* (shrimp). The finger of land is hemmed by sea-dashed fortresses, originally intended to protect the Charente, and particularly La Rochelle, against Norman attack, and later employed against the Dutch in the seventeenth century and English in the eighteenth. The seventeenth-century **Fort Vauban** (daily 10am–7pm) now houses a small local history museum (€2.50), but its esplanade offers a magnificent panorama of neighbouring forts and islands, including the lesser visited **Île Madame**, which is accessible at low tide from Port des Barques, via the Passe aux Boeufs causeway. A rather desolate-looking place, especially at low tide, the island also has a grim history as the site of the internment, and in most cases death, of scores of priests from the region, victims of the anti-clerical terror unleashed in the 1790s.

Fouras's **tourist office**, which also serves the Île d'Aix, is situated on avenue du Bois Vert on the peninsula (Mon–Sat 9am–noon & 2–6pm, Sun 10am–noon & 3–6pm; ☏05.46.84.60.69, ⊛www.fouras.net). Fouras has a couple of reasonably priced **hotels**: the *Roseraie*, at 2 rue Eric-Tabarly on the peninsula (☏05.46.84.64.89, ⊛www.hotel-fouras.com; ❸), has bright rooms and friendly owners, while a few paces from the beach and the fort the *Commerce du Courreau*, 20 rue Bruncher (☏05.46.84.22.62, ⊛www.hotellecommerce.17 -flash.com; ❸), has the bonus of a good restaurant (menus €16.50).

Île d'Aix

Less frequented than the bigger islands, the crescent-shaped **Île d'Aix** (pronounced "eel-dex") is small enough – just 2km long – to be walked around in about three hours, giving a greater sense of its island status than is felt on the Île de Ré.

The island is well defended, with a pair of forts and ramparts around its southern tip; the whole island, particularly **Fort Liédot**, served as a prison for members of the Paris Commune and later held prisoners of war in the Crimean and First World Wars. There's a **museum** (daily except Tues: 9.30am–12.30pm & 2–6pm; €4.50 with Musée Africain; ⊛www.musees-nationaux-napoleoniens .org) in the house constructed to Napoleon's orders. He lived in it for a week in 1815 while he was planning his escape to America, only to find himself en route to St Helena and exile, via Portsmouth. Extensive displays fill ten rooms with the emperor's works of art, clothing, portraits and arms. The white dromedary from which he conducted his Egyptian campaign is lodged nearby in the **Musée Africain** (same hours and ticket as Musée Napoléon), with its entire collection devoted to African wildlife.

Access to the island is by frequent ferry (half-hourly in summer, five daily in winter, according to tide schedule – check ⊛www.service-maritime-iledaix .com) from Pointe de la Fumée (☏05.46.84.26.77), or with Interîles from

La Rochelle (May–Sept 2–4 daily). The island's long-standing hotel was closing for a long-term renovation at the time of writing so, for the time being at least, the only **accommodation** is the *Fort de la Rade* campsite (℡05.46.84.28.28; May–Sept).

Brouage and Marennes

Eighteen kilometres southwest of Rochefort, **BROUAGE** is another seven-teenth-century military base, this time created by Richelieu after the siege of La Rochelle.

The way into Brouage is through the **Porte Royale** in the north wall of the mid-seventeenth-century fortifications, which remain totally intact. Locked within its 400 square metres, the town now seems abandoned and somnolent; even the sea has retreated, and all that's left of the harbour are the partly fresh-water pools, or *claires*, where oysters are fattened in the last stage of their rearing (see box below).

Within the walls, the streets are laid out on a grid pattern, lined with low two-storey houses. On the second cross-street to the right is a **memorial** to Samuel de Champlain, the local boy who founded the French colony of Québec in 1608. In the same century, Brouage witnessed the last painful pangs of a royal romance: here, Cardinal Mazarin, successor to Richelieu, locked up his niece, Marie Mancini, to keep her from her youthful sweetheart, Louis XIV. The politics of the time made the Infanta of Spain a more suitable consort for the King of France than his daughter – in his own judgement. Louis gave in, while Marie pined and sighed on the walls of Brouage. Returning from his marriage in St-Jean-de-Luz, Louis dodged his escort and stole away to see her. Finding her gone, he slept in her room and paced the walls in her footsteps.

Half a dozen kilometres south, you come to the village of **MARENNES**. This is the centre of oyster production for an area that supplies over sixty percent of France's requirements. There are various opportunities to visit the oyster beds and learn about the business, either on foot or by boat; enquire at the **tourist office** on place Chasseloup-Laubat (April–June & Sept Tues–Sat 9.30am–noon & 2–5pm; July & Aug Mon–Sat 9.30am–6.30pm; Oct–March Tues–Sat 10am–noon & 2–4pm; ℡05.46.85.04.36).

For **accommodation** in Marennes, try the inexpensive *Hôtel du Commerce* at 9 rue de la République (℡05.46.85.00.09; ❷), with a restaurant where you can

Oysters

Marennes' speciality is fattening the **oysters** known as *creuses*. It's a lucrative but precarious business, extremely vulnerable to storm damage, changes of tempera-ture or salinity in the water, the ravages of starfish and umpteen other improbable natural disasters.

Oysters begin life as minuscule larvae, which are "born" about three times a year. When a birth happens, the oystermen are alerted by a special radio service, and they all rush out to place their "collectors" – usually arrangements of roofing tiles – for the larvae to cling to. There the immature oysters remain for eight or nine months, after which they are scraped off and moved to *parcs* in the tidal waters of the sea: sometimes covered, sometimes uncovered. Their last move is to the *claires* – shallow rectangular pools where they are kept permanently covered by water less salty than normal sea water. Here they fatten up and acquire the greenish colour the market expects. With "improved" modern oysters, the whole cycle takes about two years, as opposed to four or five with the old varieties.

eat generously and well from €18. A good alternative for **eating** is *La Verte Ostréa* at the end of the pier at La Cayenne, where oysters and shellfish form the basis of every menu (from €13).

The Île d'Oléron

The **Île d'Oléron** is France's largest island after Corsica and a favourite of day-trippers and families in the summer months for its beautiful sandy beaches. It's up the road from Marennes, joined to the mainland by a bridge and reachable in an hour on **bus** #6 from Rochefort. In July and August, nippy minibuses also connect the main towns on the island, see Ⓦwww.lesmouettes-transport.com for timetables.

Flat and more wooded than the Île de Ré, Oléron has plenty of greenery, with the extensive pine-studded **Forêt des Saumonards** in the northeast of the island; here you can eyeball a dazzling panorama of the surrounding *parcs à huîtres* and the mighty **Fort Boyard**. At the island's southern tip, the larger **Forêt de St-Trojan** creeps up the western coast along **La Grande Plage**, a popular spot but far enough from the main towns not to be too crowded. The island interior is pretty and distinctive. Waterways wind right into the land, their gleaming muddy banks overhung by round fishing nets suspended from ranks of piers. There are so many oyster *claires* that, from above, the island must look like an Afghan mirrored cushion; the stretch from Boyardville to St-Pierre – with its pines, tamarisks and woods of evergreen oak – is the most attractive.

The island's most interesting attraction is off the D126 between St-Pierre and Dolus, right in the middle of the island. The bird park of **Le Marais aux Oiseaux** (daily: April–June & Sept 10am–1pm & 2–6pm; July & Aug 10am–7pm; Ⓦwww .centre-sauvegarde-oleron.com; €4.50) was originally established as a hospital for injured birds found in the wild, but is now a breeding centre with many examples of rare or endangered species. Most of the little towns on the island have inevitably suffered from the development of hundreds of holiday homes – and it can be a real battle in the summer season to find a place to stay. There are a few places that still retain some amount of charm, however, not least of which is the main town in the south of the island, **LE CHÂTEAU**, named after the **citadel** that still stands, along with some seventeenth-century **fortifications**. The town thrives on its traditional oyster farming and boat building, and there's a lively **market** in place de la Répub-lique every morning. The chief town in the north – and most picturesque of the island's settlements – is **ST-PIERRE**, whose market square has an unusual thirteenth-century monument, **La Lanterne des Morts**. The best beach, meanwhile, is at **LA BRÉE LES BAINS**, in the northeast.

Practicalities

The main **tourist office** is on place de la République in Le Château (July & Aug Mon–Sat 9.30am–12.30pm & 2.30–7pm, Sun 10am–12.30pm; Sept–June Mon–Sat 9.30am–12.30pm & 2.30–7pm; ℡05.46.47.60.51, Ⓦwww .oleron.org). **Bikes** can be rented from Vélos 17 (℡05.46.47.14.05, Ⓦwww .velos17loisirs.com), which has outlets in all the towns on the island.

In St-Pierre, the best **accommodation** is the friendly hotel *Le Square*, place des Anciens Combattants (℡05.46.47.00.35, Ⓦwww.le-square-hotel.fr; ❹), where you should ask for a room at the back next to the pretty pool. In St-Trojan-les-Bains there's good value at *L'Albatros*, 11 boulevard du Dr-Pineau (℡05.46.76.00.08, Ⓦwww.albatros-hotel-oleron.com; ❸; closed Oct–Feb), right on the rocky shore, and extreme luxury at the *Novotel Thalassa Oléron*, Plage de Gatseau (℡05.46.76.02.46, Ⓦthalasso-oleron.info; ❾), a hotel-cum-spa offering every amenity under the sun to pacify body and mind. A nicely situated, small hotel on the harbour in the pretty fishing village of **LA COTINIÈRE**, ⚓ *L'Écailler* (☎05.46.47.10.31, ⓦwww.ecailler-oleron.com; ❺; closed Dec & Jan) is also an outstanding place to **eat**, with super-fresh seafood menus for under €20. Otherwise, the greatest choice of restaurants is in St-Pierre's pedestrian streets.

There are **campsites** all over the island: at La Brée, where the best beaches are, there's *Pertuis d'Antioche* (☎05.46.47.92.00; April–Sept), 150m from the beach off the D273. Further down the east coast, *Signol* at Boyardville (☎05.46.47.01.22, ⓦwww.signol.com; April–Sept) is pleasantly sited near pine forests. For stays of a week or longer, the tourist offices have lists of **holiday apartments** for rent.

Royan and around

Before World War II, **ROYAN**, at the mouth of the Gironde, was a fashionable resort for the bourgeoisie. It's still popular, but the prestige of its heyday lies very palpably in the past. The modern town has lost its elegance to the dreary rationalism of 1950s town planning: broad boulevards, car parks, shopping centres and planned greenery have shorn the town of its glamour and left the seafront crowded and uninspiring. The occasion for this planners' romp was provided by Allied bombing, an attempt to dislodge a large contingent of German troops who had withdrawn into the area after the D-Day landings. The **beaches** remain one good reason to come here, though. Particularly out towards the northern suburb of Pontaillac, they are enticingly beautiful expanses of fine pale sand, meticulously harrowed and raked.

Arrival and information

The **gare routière** and **gare SNCF** are located on cours de l'Europe. The **tourist office** (mid-June to Aug Mon–Sat 9am–7.30pm, Sun 10am–1pm & 3–6pm; Sept to mid-June Mon–Sat 9am–12.30pm & 2–6pm; ☎05.46.05.04.71, ⓦwww.royan-tourisme.com) and **PTT** lie on the Rond-Point-de-la-Poste at the east end of the seafront. You can hire **bikes** for €12 per day from Cycles Horseau at 107 cours de l'Europe (☎05.46.39.96.43) and **cars** from most major firms also near the station.

Accommodation

Accommodation in Royan is expensive and in short supply in season, when your best bet is to visit for the day from Saintes or Rochefort. There are a number of **campsites** in the region and around Royan itself, including the *Clairefontaine* (☎05.46.39.08.11 ⓦwww.camping-clairefontaine.com; May to mid-Oct), a fairly pricey site on Allée des Peupliers towards Pontaillac, and the municipal *La Triloterie* (☎05.46.05.26.91, ⓦwww.campingroyan.com) off avenue d'Aquitaine – the road to Bordeaux.

Les Bleuets 21 façade de Foncillon ☎05.46.38.51.79, ⓦwww.hotel-les-bleuets.com. A nautically themed hotel right on the seafront. All rooms have shower and TV, while for a little more money you can have a small balcony with a sea view. ❹

La Colinette 16 av de la Grande Plage, Saint-Georges de Didonne ☎05.46.05.15.75, ⓔinfo @colinette.fr. Situated 100m from the sea 3km southeast of Royan. It has its own restaurant and, in summer, the owners may expect all guests to take meals here. ❹

The Town

One sight worth seeing in Royan, and arguably the only positive contribution made by post war development to the town's aesthetic, is the 1950s **church of Notre-Dame**, designed by Gillet and Hébrard, in a tatty square behind the main waterfront. Though the concrete has weathered badly, the overall effect is dramatic and surprising. Tall V-sectioned columns rise dramatically to culminate in a 65-metre bell tower, like the prow of a giant vessel. The interior is even more striking: using uncompromisingly modern materials and designs, the architects have succeeded in out-Gothicking Gothic. The stained-glass panels, in each of which a different tone predominates, borrow their colours from the local seascapes – oyster, sea, mist and murk – before a sudden explosion of colour in the Christ figure above the altar.

The most attractive area in Royan is around **boulevard Garnier**, which leads southeast from Rond-Point-de-la-Poste along the beach, and once housed Parisian high society in purpose-built, *belle-époque* holiday villas. Some of these have survived, including **Le Rêve**, 58 boulevard Garnier, where Émile Zola lived and wrote; **Kosiki**, 100 avenue du Parc (running parallel to boulevard Garnier), a nineteenth-century folly of Japanese inspiration; and **Tanagra**, 34 avenue du Parc, whose facade is covered in sculptures and balconies.

Various **cruises** are organized from Royan in season, including one to the **Cordouan lighthouse**, erected by Edward III's son, the Black Prince, and commanding the mouth of the Gironde River. There's a frequent thirty-minute **ferry** crossing (one way: pedestrians €3.10, bikes €1.60, motorbikes €10, cars €21.90) to the headland on the other side of the Gironde, the **Pointe de Grave**, from where a **bicycle trail** and the **GR8** head down the coast through the pines and dunes to the bay of Arcachon.

Eating and drinking

The seafront itself is lined with brasseries, all serving fresh fish dishes at reasonable prices, so you can't go too far wrong. That said, the better **restaurants** are at least a few paces off the touristy thoroughfare. The bars along the front are certainly the best place for an evening **drink**, though, and some occasionally have live music.

Les Filets Bleus 14 rue Notre-Dame ℗ 05.46.05.74.00. Near the cathedral, this place serves up French specialities from seafood to foie gras; the decor has a muted maritime feel. A treat for all budgets, with menus from €14 to €45. Closed Sat lunch and Mon.

Le Régent Front de Mer. Long-standing ice-cream specialist which also does standard brasserie meals. A fine spot for a drink in the evening with occasional live jazz.

Le Relais de la Mairie 1 rue du Chay ℗ 05.46.39.03.15. A bit of a walk from town off av de Pontaillac, this restaurant is more of a local secret, offering lavish seafood dishes, like hake with shrimps, on menus from €16.50. Closed Sun evening. Mon & Thurs evening.

Le Tiki You can't miss this rather unsightly, touristy-looking establishment right on the beach. No denying, though, that it has monopolized the best views of the sea, and its various brasseries serve cheap menus non-stop from 11am to 11pm.

La Palmyre and Talmont

It's worth knowing about the **zoo park** in **La PALMYRE** (daily: April–Sept 9am–7pm; Oct–March 9am–6pm; Ⓦ www.zoo-palmyre.fr; €14), 10km northwest of Royan up the D25 coast road, especially if you're travelling with children; an exciting range of exotic species belies the slightly tacky advertising. To reach it, there are **buses** all day from Royan's *gare routière* and the place Charles-de-Gaulle.

An ideal bicycle or picnic excursion just over an hour's ride from Royan is to **TALMONT**, 16km up the Gironde on the GR360 – apart from a few ups and downs through the woods outside Royan, it's all level terrain. The low-crouching village clusters about the twelfth-century **church of Ste-Radegonde**, standing at the edge of a cliff above the Gironde. With gabled transepts, a squat tower and an apse simply but elegantly decorated with blind arcading – all in weathered tawny stone and pocked like a sponge – it stands magnificently against the forlorn browny-grey seascapes typical of the Gironde. The inside is as unpretentiously beautiful as the exterior.

The Charente

It's hard to believe that the tranquil, fertile valley of the **River Charente** was once a busy industrial waterway, bringing armaments from **Angoulême** to the naval shipyards at Rochefort. Today peaceful, low, ochre-coloured farms crown the valley slopes, with green swathes of vineyard sweeping up to the walls, and the graceful turrets of minor châteaux – properties of wealthy cognac-producers – poke up from out of the woods. The towns and villages may look old-fashioned, but the prosperous shops and classy new villas are proof that where the grape grows, money and modernity are not far behind.

The **valley** itself is easy to travel as the main road and train lines to Limoges run this way. North and south, Poitiers, Périgueux (for the Dordogne) and Bordeaux are also easily reached by train. Otherwise, for cross-country journeys, you're heavily reliant on your own transport.

Saintes and around

SAINTES was formerly much more important than its present size suggests. Today a busy market town for the surrounding region, it was capital of the old province of Saintonge and a major administrative and cultural centre in Roman times. It still retains some impressive remains from that period, as well as two beautiful Romanesque pilgrim churches and an attractive centre of narrow lanes and medieval houses. The town also hosts a highly regarded classical music festival in mid-July, when concerts are held in the atmospheric Abbaye aux Dames (Ⓦ www.abbayeauxdames.org; tickets from €10). If you're here at the right time, it's not to be missed.

Arrival and information

Saintes' **gare SNCF** is on avenue de la Marne at the east end of the main road, avenue Gambetta. The **tourist office** is housed in grand old Villa Musso, 62 cours National (Mon–Sat 9.30am–12.30pm & 2–5.30pm; ☎05.46.74.23.82, ⓦwww.ot-saintes.fr), organizes **boat trips** on the Charente during the summer (from €4) and also regular guided tours to many of the sites described below.

The municipal **campsite** (☎05.46.93.08.00; mid-April to mid-Oct) is by the river, along quai de l'Yser. Saintes' **hotels**, meanwhile, are inexpensive, and a couple are in really prime position to make the most of the old town.

Accommodation

Bleu Nuit 1 rue Pasteur ☎05.46.93.01.72, ⓦwww.hotelbleunuit.com. Newly taken over and renovated by a friendly couple, this long-established hotel is a good deal. Rooms at the front have small balconies, although the view over the roundabout outside is nothing to write home about. ❸

De France 56 rue Frédéric-Mestreau ☎05.46.93.01.16, ⓦwww.hoteldefrance-17.com. The best of the options near the train station, with comfortable rooms. Quieter ones at the back look out over a pretty garden. ❷

Les Messageries rue des Messageries ☎05.46.93.64.99, ⓦwww.hotel-les-messageries.com. In a seventeenth-century building, set back on a quiet courtyard in the middle of the pedestrianised old town, this is a good place for more

comfort: most rooms are air-conditioned and all have TV and minibar. ❹

🏃 **Saveurs de l'Abbaye** 1 place St-Pallais ☎05.46.94.17.91, ⓦwww.saveurs-abbaye .com. Right opposite the abbey, a stylish and welcoming hotel with parquet floors and very attractive rooms – particularly those on the top floor. Downstairs is a super restaurant (closed Sun & Mon) with excellent-value menus from €15. ❷

Hostel

HI Hostel 2 place Geoffroy-Martel ☎05.46.92.14.92, ⓔsaintes@fuaj.org. In a superb position in behind the Abbaye aux Dames, the facilities are modern and breakfast is included. Dorm beds are €15.80. Reception open 8am–noon & 5–10pm.

The Town

The abbey church, the **Abbaye aux Dames** (daily: April–Sept 10am–12.30pm & 2–7pm; Oct–March 2–6pm; entry €2, guided tour €3.50), is as quirky as Notre-Dame in Poitiers. An sculpted doorway conceals the plain, domed interior. Its rarest feature is the eleventh-century tower, by turns square, octagonal and lantern-shaped, flanked with pinnacles and capped with the Poitou pine cone.

Nearby on the riverbank is the imposing **Arc de Germanicus**, which originally stood on the bridge until 1843, when it was demolished to make way for

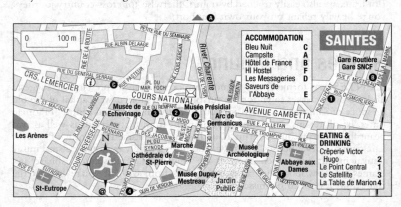

the modern crossing and rebuilt here. The arch was dedicated to the emperor Tiberius, his son Drusus and nephew Germanicus in 19 AD. In a stone building next door is an **archeological museum** (April–Sept Tues–Sat 10am–12.30pm & 1.30–6pm, Sun 1.30–6pm; Oct–March Tues–Sun 2–5pm; €1.70), with a great many more Roman bits and pieces strewn about, mostly rescued from the fifth-century city walls into which they had been incorporated.

A footbridge crosses from the archeological museum to the covered market on the west bank of the river and place du Marché at the foot of the rather uninspiring **Cathédrale de St-Pierre**, which began life as a Romanesque church but was significantly altered in the aftermath of damage inflicted during the Wars of Religion, when Saintes was a Huguenot stronghold. North of the cathedral, an early seventeenth-century mansion on rue Victor-Hugo houses the **Musée Présidial** (same hours and price as archeological museum), containing a collection of local pottery and some decent fifteenth- to eighteenth-century paintings. Just down the road is the **Musée de l'Echevinage** (same hours), with nineteenth- and twentieth-century paintings, mainly by local artists of the Saintongaise and Bordelaise schools. A ticket costing €4.20 will get you into both galleries, the archeological museum and the **Musée Dupuy-Mestreau (same hours)** down on the riverbank, which houses a vast personal collection of turn-of-the-century objects ranging from model ships to headdresses.

Saintes' Roman heritage is best seen at **Les Arènes** (June–Sept daily 10am–8pm; Oct–May Mon–Sat 10am–5pm, Sun 1.30–5pm; €2), an amphitheatre whose ruins lie at the head of a leafy little valley reached by a footpath which begins by 54 cours Reverseaux. The amphitheatre was dug into the end of the valley in around 40 AD, making it one of the oldest surviving examples in France. Although most of the seats are now grassed over, it's still an evocative spot.

On the way back from the amphitheatre, it's no extra trouble to take in the eleventh-century **church of St-Eutrope**. The upper church, which lost its nave in 1803, has some brilliant capital carving in the old choir, best seen from the gallery. But it's the crypt – entered from the street – which is most atmospheric and primitive: here massive pillars carved with stylized vegetation support the vaulting in semi-darkness, and there's a huge old font and the third-century tomb of Saintes' first bishop, Eutropius himself.

Eating and drinking

Saintes' best **restaurant** is *La Table de Marion* (☎05.46.74.16.38; closed Tues evening & Wed), by the river at 10 place Blair, with a daily menu from the market for €26, though you have to pay a bit more to see the distinguished chef at his best. For less formal surroundings, try the popular *Crêperie de Victor Hugo* at 20 rue Victor-Hugo. 10km upstream at **Chaniers**, you can sample the beautifully situated *Moulin de la Baine* (☎05.46.91.12.92; April–Sept daily; Oct–March weekends only; from €18).

POITOU-CHARENTES AND THE ATLANTIC COAST | Saintes and around

Saintes is no party town, but if you fancy a **drink**, check out the social hub that is *Le Point Central* on the corner of Cours National and rue Alsace-Lorraine, or one of the bars on quai de la République, with views across the river of the Arc de Germanicus. The bar *Le Satellite*, at 45 rue Berthonnière, has the added bonus of cheap **internet** access until late in the evening.

Around Saintes

If you have a car, you could explore several of the marvellous Romanesque churches within easy reach of Saintes. In **FENIOUX**, 29km to the north towards St-Jean-d'Angély, there's superb St-Eutrope with its mighty spire, while the church at **RIOUX**, 12km to the south, is well worth visiting for its detailed facade. There's also the fine **Château of Roche-Courbon**, 18km northwest off the Rochefort road – once described by Pierre Loti (see p.571) as the Sleeping Beauty's castle – with some stylish interiors and gardens.

One place worth any amount of trouble to get to is the twelfth-century pilgrim **church of St-Pierre** at **AULNAY**, 37km northeast of Saintes, and sadly not served by public transport. Aulnay church's finest sculpture is on the west front, the south transept and apse, with some more fine work inside. On the building's main facade, two blind arches flank the central portal. The tympanum of the right depicts Christ in Majesty; the left, St Peter, crucified upside down with two extraordinarily lithe and graceful soldiers balancing on the arms of his cross to get a better swing at the nails in his feet. The apse, too, is a beauty, framed by five slender columns and lit by three perfectly arched windows, the centre one enclosed by figures wrapped in the finest twining foliage. Inside, there is more extraordinary carving: capitals depicting Delilah cutting Samson's hair, devils pulling a man's beard, and human-eared elephants bearing the Latin inscription *Hic sunt elephants* – "Here are elephants" – presumably for the edification of ignorant locals.

You might also like to visit **Nuaillé-sur-Boutonne**, 9km west of Aulnay, which boasts another remarkable church; and, even nearer just down the D129 east of Aulnay, you can walk to **Salles-les-Aulnay** (20min), or **St-Mandé** (1hr), which has humbler churches of the same period.

Cognac and around

Anyone who does not already know what **COGNAC** is about will quickly nose its quintessential air as they stroll about the medieval lanes of the town's riverside quarter. For here is the greatest concentration of *chais* (warehouses), where the high-quality brandy is matured, its fumes blackening the walls with tiny fungi. Cognac *is* cognac, from the tractor driver and pruning-knife wielder to the manufacturer of corks, bottles and cartons. Untouched by recession (eighty percent of production is exported), it is likely to thrive as long as the world has sorrows to drown – a sunny, prosperous, respectable, self-satisfied little place.

Arrival and information

From the very industrial **gare SNCF**, to get to the central place François-I, go down rue Mousnier, right on rue Taransaud, past the PTT and up rue du 14-Juillet. The square is dominated by an equestrian statue of the king rising from a bed of begonias; in fine weather the cafés here teem with locals. The **tourist office** is on rue du 14-Juillet at no. 16 (July & Aug Mon–Sat 9am–7pm,

Sun 10am–4pm; Sept–June Mon–Sat 10am–5pm; ☎05.45.82.10.71, ⓦwww
.tourism-cognac.com), where you can ask about visiting the various *chais*, as
well as get information on river trips.

Accommodation

The town **campsite** (☎05.45.32.13.32; May to mid-Oct) is next to the river
on boulevard de Chatenay, while **internet access** is available at Je Console,
24 allée de la Corderie (€3.50 per hour).

Hotels

Le Cheval Blanc 6 place Bayard
☎05.45.82.09.55, ⓦwww.hotel-chevalblanc.fr.
Not a huge amount of character, but good-value
rooms, fully equipped with flat-screen TVs, a/c and
wireless internet, mostly in one-storey buildings
surrounding a quiet patio. ❸
Héritage 25 rue d'Angoulême ☎05.45.82.01.26,
ⓦwww.hheritage.com. A creative hotel in the
middle of the traffic-free old town. Each room is
decorated according to a different theme; African,
Chinese, pink and so on. The restaurant also
deserves a mention for its outside seating on an

eighteenth-century arcaded terrace (menus from
€18). ❹
L'Oliveraie 6 place de la Gare ☎05.45.82.04.15,
ⓦwww.oliveraie-cognac.com. Opposite the station,
quiet rooms in a villa-style outbuilding are spacious
for the price and have a/c. ❸
Les Pigeons Blancs 110 rue Jules-Brisson
☎05.45.82.16.36, ⓦwww.chateauxhotels.com
/pigeonsblancs. 20min walk from the town centre,
set in lovely open grounds on top of a hill. Rooms
are luxurious and there is a high-quality restaurant
(around €30). ❺

The Town

Cognac has a number of medieval stone and half-timbered buildings in the
narrow streets of the old town, of which rue Saulnier and rue de l'Isle-d'Or
make atmospheric backdrops for a stroll, while picturesque **Grande-Rue** winds
through the heart of the old quarter to the *chais*, down by the river, with the
attractive Hôtel de Ville set in pleasant gardens just to the East.

The most appealing of the famous cognac houses to visit is **Otard** (guided
tours; April–Oct daily 11am–5pm; Nov–Dec Mon–Fri; ⓦwww.otard.com; €7)
whose cellars are located in the castle where François I was born in 1494. Indeed,
the building was only saved from anti-royalist revolutionaries when the far-
sighted Baron Otard purchased it in 1795, having realized that its thick walls and
high humidity provided perfect conditions for maturing the spirits which are
blended to make cognac. The lively guided tour recounts some history of the
place, before explaining the general principles (though no closely guarded
secrets) of cognac production. A tasting at the end allows you to test your nose
and compare different vintages.

Eating

For **eating** out, relaxed *La Bonne Goule*, 42 allée de la Corderie (from €11;
☎05.45.82.06.37; closed Sun & Mon), serves up excellent Charentais specialities at low prices and boasts a good list of local wines. Another possibility is *Le
Patio*, 42 avenue Victor-Hugo (☎05.45.32.40.50), with a range of steak and
duck dishes and a menu for €18.

Around Cognac

The area around Cognac is gentle enough for some restful walks, taking in some
pretty little Charentais villages. The tourist office sells large-scale maps of the
best possibilities for €2.30. Particularly pleasant is the towpath or *chemin de*

▲ Cognac cellar

halage that follows the south bank of the Charente upstream to Pont de la Trâche, then on along a track to the village of **BOURG-CHARENTE** (about 8km in all), with an excellent **restaurant** called ♯ *La Ribaudière* (☎05.45.81.30.54, ⓦ www.laribaudiere.com; closed Sun evening, Mon & Tues lunch; menus €40–76), where you should most definitely try their speciality, *matelote d'anguilles* – eels cooked in wine sauce. From there, you can amble to the village's interesting castle and Romanesque church. Alternatively, follow the GR4 the other way to the hamlet of **RICHEMONT**, 5km northwest of Cognac, where you can swim in the pools of the tiny River Antenne below an ancient church on a steep bluff lost in the woods.

Further afield, 18km northwest of Cognac between the villages of Migron and Authon, there's the fascinating **Écomusée du Cognac** (mid-June to mid-Sept daily 10am–12.30pm & 2.30–6.30pm; rest of year by reservation; ☎05.46.94.91.16; €4), which illustrates the history of the distillation process and the various tools involved, finishing off with a tasting of cognacs, liqueurs and cocktails; follow the D731 to St-Jean-d'Angély for 13km as far as Burie, then turn right onto the D131, 4km from Migron.

A particularly beautiful excursion is upstream to **Jarnac**, from where you can take boat trips on the Charente from €7.50, arranged by the tourist office (May–Sept; ☎05.45.82.09.35, ⓦ www.jarnac-tourisme.com). In the town, the late President Mitterrand's modest grave has become a place of pilgrimage for elderly left-wingers, and you can also visit the **Musée François-Mitterrand**, 10 quai de l'Orangerie (July & Aug daily 10am–12.30pm & 2.30–6.30pm; Jan–June, Sept & Oct Wed–Sun 2–6pm; closed Nov–Dec; ☎05.45.81.38.88; €5), which houses a permanent exhibition on the public works carried out during Mitterrand's two terms of office.

Angoulême and around

The charming cathedral city of **ANGOULÊME** used to be dominated by paper mills that employed thousands of workers and bolstered the city's prosperity. The industry collapsed in the 1980s, and today only a couple of small, specialized mills still function. Since then the economy has picked up again, especially the tourist industry, and it's now a moderately prosperous place.

In the past, however, the former capital of the Angoumois province was a much-coveted city politically, being heavily fought over during the fourteenth-century Anglo–French squabbles and again in the sixteenth century during the Wars of Religion, when it was a Protestant stronghold. After the revocation of the Edict of Nantes, a good proportion of its citizens – among them many of its skilled papermakers – emigrated to Holland, never to return.

Arrival and information

Angoulême is easily accessible by **train** from Cognac, Limoges and Poitiers. From the **gare SNCF**, avenue Gambetta leads uphill to the town centre through place Pérot, a fifteen-minute walk. Buses leave from either the train station or place Bouillaud, at the top of the hill, while the **tourist office**, 7 rue du Chat (July & Aug Mon–Sat 9.30am–6.30pm, Sun 10am–1pm; Sept–June Mon–Sat 9.30am–12.30pm & 1.30–5.30pm; ☎05.45.95.16.84, ⓦwww.angouleme-toursime.com), is on place des Halles, opposite the large covered market (daily 7am–1pm). **Internet** access is available at 14 Boulevard Pasteur (Mon–Sat noon–8pm).

Accommodation

The tourist office can help with **accommodation**; but if you go it alone you'll find a clutch of cheap hotels around the station and some more attractive options nearer the town centre.

Hotels

Le Crab 27 rue Kléber ☎05.45.93.02.93, Ⓔlecrab.angouleme@orange.fr. In a quiet backstreet, clearly signed from the station, the spotless rooms here are good value, as are the simple daily menus at the restaurant downstairs (€12; closed weekends). ❷–❸

HI Hostel parc des Bourgines ☎05.45.92.45.80. A very basic hostel with breakfast but no kitchens. Nicely situated, though, on an island in the Charente. Dorm beds €12.

D'Orléans 133 av Gambetta ☎05.45.92.07.53. Freshly renovated, but still the cheapest in town. Rooms are identical and soulless, but all have TV, shower and wireless internet. ❶

Du Palais 4 place Francis-Louvel ☎05.45.92.54.11, ⓦwww.hotel-angouleme.fr. A unique and charming hotel in an elegantly preserved former convent. The recent brightly coloured revamp has preserved the building's authenticity, with exposed beams and ancient stone a feature in most rooms. Those on higher floors have balconies which look out onto the central square. ❺

La Palma 4 rampe d'Aguesseau ☎05.45.95.22.89, ⓦwww.restaurant-hotel-palma .com. Friendly and helpful hotel with brand new, a/c rooms. There are only nine of them, so it's important to reserve. ❹

The Town

The **old town** occupies a high steep-sided plateau overlooking a bend in the Charente, a natural fortress. It has many charms, if few notable sights. The labyrinthine streets to the north of the delightful **place Louvel** and the massive Hôtel de Ville have been largely restored and pedestrianized. It's here that the restaurants and bars are concentrated, while the eastern section, down rue Marango and rue St-Martial, has become the main commercial centre. On the southern edge of the plateau stands the **cathedral**, whose west front – like Notre-Dame at Poitiers – is a fascinating display board for some expressive and lively twelfth-century sculpture, culminating in a Risen Christ with angels and clouds about his head, framed in the usual blaze of a halo. The lively frieze beneath the tympanum to the right of the west door commemorates the

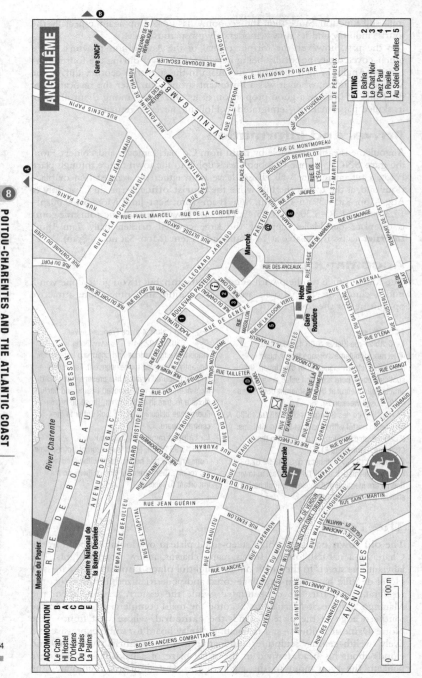

ANGOULÊME

ACCOMMODATION
Le Crab   B
HI Hostel   A
D'Orléans   C
Du Palais   D
La Palma   E

EATING
Le Bahia   2
Le Chat Noir   3
Chez Paul   4
La Ruelle   1
Au Soleil des Antilles   5

0   100 m

Musée du Papier
River Charente
Centre National de
la Bande Dessinée

Gare SNCF

recapture of Spanish Zaragoza from the Moors, showing a bishop transfixing a Moorish giant with his lance and Roland killing the Moorish king.

In one area at least, Angoulême is a world leader: **comic books**. Every year in the last weekend of January the city hosts the massively popular **Festival de la Bande Dessinée**, when thousands come to see the latest developments in what is most certainly regarded as a serious art form. "BDs", as they are known, are also permanently represented by the **Cité Internationale de la Bande Dessinée** (Ⓦ www.cnbdi.fr), which owns a vast collection of original drawings, tracing the development of the comic over 150 years. Astérix, Peanuts, Tintin and many other characters and artists are represented, and there's also a vast library, much of it in English, where you're welcome to relax on cushions and have a read. At the time of writing, the collection was due to move into attractive new buildings on the banks of the Charente on rue de Bordeaux, so check at the tourist office for new opening times and prices.

Another riverfront museum close by is the **Musée du Papier** (July & Aug noon–6.30pm; Sept–June Tues–Sun 10am–noon & 2–6pm; free), a tribute to the declining industry, appropriately located in an old paper mill, through which the waters of the Charente still gush impressively.

Eating

Angoulême has some wonderful **restaurants**, the best areas to look being rue de Genève, offering both traditional French and international options, and the narrow, pedestrianized rue Massillon.

Le Bahia 13 place des Halles ℡05.45.95.94.55. A South American-themed brasserie opposite the market. Sangria and bottled Mexican beers are on offer, as is a more conventional French *plat du jour* for €8.90. There are salsa nights every Thurs out of season, and live music in summer. Closed Sun.

Le Chat Noir 24 rue de Genève ℡05.45.95.26.27. Popular for its great-value salads and omelettes at lunchtime, and for its prize bruschetta (€7) and relaxed atmosphere in the evenings. On Thurs nights in summer there is live music out front which is middle-of-the-road in every sense. Closed Sun.

Chez Paul 8 place Francis-Louvel ℡05.45.90.04.61. A high-class restaurant serving bistro-style dishes with a modern twist (menus from €21), with a large terrace and garden. Inside there is a rather trendy bar which stays open until midnight.

La Ruelle 6 rue 3 Notre-Dame ℡05.45.95.15.19. A really fine restaurant, with impeccable service and some of the best food to be found in the region, combining local staples with exotic delicacies. So you might have, for example, Canadian lobster followed by beef in a red Bordeaux sauce. Menus from €22, closed Sun & Mon.

Au Soleil des Antilles 19 rue des 3 Notre-Dame ℡05.45.94.70.15. For something a bit different, try the tropical house cocktails and delicious creole menus (from €13) at this laid-back restaurant. On Fri & Sat the chef leaves the kitchen after dinner to offer some musical accompaniment. Closed Sun & Mon.

Around Angoulême

LA ROCHEFOUCAULD, 22km east of Angoulême, is the site of a huge Renaissance **château** on the banks of the River Tardoire, which still belongs to the family that gave its name to the town a thousand years ago. The stately pile, although still lived in, opens its elaborate portals to the public (Easter–Nov daily except Tues 10am–7pm; €8). In August it stages a massive son et lumière with a brigade-sized cast. If you want to **stay**, try the lovely old *Auberge de la Carpe d'Or* at 1 rue de Vitrac (℡05.45.62.02.72, Ⓕ05.45.63.01.88; ❷).

Further east, the country becomes hillier and more wooded, with buttercup pastures grazed by liver-coloured Limousin cattle. One place to aim for is the beautiful, if now rather touristy little town of **CONFOLENS**, about 40km northeast of La Rochefoucauld. Its ancient houses are stacked up a hillside above a broad brown sweep of the river Vienne, here crossed by a long narrow medieval bridge.

Having come this far, it's worth continuing the extra 6km to the minuscule village of **St-Germain-de-Confolens**, huddled by the riverside beneath the romantic towers of its ruined castle.

Aquitaine

In Roman times, **Bordeaux** was capital of the province of Aquitania Secunda. With the marriage of Eleanor of Aquitaine and King Henry II of England in 1152, it quickly became the principal English foothold for their three-hundred-year Aquitanian adventure, and it was to their presence, and particularly their taste for its red wines – imported back to England and termed "claret" – that the region owed its first great economic boom. The second boom, which financed the building of the gracious eighteenth-century centre of Bordeaux, came with the expansion of colonial trade.

The surrounding countryside is more notable for its wines and **vineyards** than its scenery, though the hills of **Entre-Deux-Mers** and the pretty town of **St-Émilion** are worth visiting in their own right. Quite different are the vast pine-covered expanse of **Les Landes** and the huge, wild Atlantic beaches of the **Côte d'Argent** to the south, but it's not a landscape that charms. Its appeal is more in its size and uniqueness – and you need your own transport to explore it fully.

Bordeaux

The city of **BORDEAUX** is stunning when approached from the south along the river. It's big, with a population of over half a million, and obviously rich – as it has been since the Romans set up a lively trading centre here; even today it still functions as the regional transport hub for Aquitaine. Especially attractive is the relatively small eighteenth-century centre, which has only been improved by the city's space-age tram network, which gives it a modern, electric feel that juxtaposes nicely with its classical architecture. Aside from the aesthetic appeal of its old centre, some excellent museums, some even finer restaurants and a fantastic nightlife make Bordeaux an absorbing town, well worth a few days of anybody's time.

Arrival and information

Bordeaux-Mérignac **airport** is 12km west of the city and is connected by shuttle buses (every 45min; €7) to the main tourist office. Arriving by **train**, you'll find yourself at the *gare St-Jean*, with its own small tourist office (May–Oct Mon–Sat 9am–noon & 1–6pm, Sun 10am–noon & 1–3pm; Nov–April Mon–Fri 9.30am–12.30pm & 2–6pm; ☎05.56.91.64.70), right at the heart of

▲ Tram outside Grand Theatre, Bordeaux

a somewhat insalubrious area, nearly 3km south of the city centre; bus #16 and tramline C run into the centre. There's no central **gare routière**, but the hub of bus transport is the south side of the esplanade des Quinconces, on allées de Munich, where you'll also find the information centre (℡05.57.57.88.88, Ⓦwww.infotbc.com) for all local transport. Troublesome exceptions are buses to Blaye, which leave from "Buttinière" (take tram line A), and buses to Margaux and Pauillac, which leave from "place Ravezies" (tram line C).

Tram services operate on the three lines frequently from 5am to midnight, and extend several kilometres into Bordeaux's suburbs. There are also frequent electric *navette* buses running between the two city-centre poles of Quinconces and Victoire. You can purchase either single-ride tickets (€1.30) or carnets of ten (€10), available from the machines at tram stops (coins only) or at *tabacs* all over the city. Though the city is certainly walkable, some sights are a fair distance away from each other, and if you're going to be here for a few days, it pays to buy an **unlimited-use pass**, available for between one and seven days.

For **car** drivers, there should be ample parking in the numerous underground car parks in the town centre, though it's cheaper to use the car parks next to the tram stations on the east bank of the Garonne: buy a round-trip park-and-ride ticket (€2.60), and hop on a tram into the centre.

Bordeaux's main **tourist office**, near the Grand Théâtre on 12 cours du 30-Juillet (May–Oct Mon–Sat 9am–7pm, Sun 9.30am–6.30pm; Nov–April Mon–Sat 9am–6.30pm, Sun 9.45am–4.30pm; ℡05.56.00.66.00, Ⓦwww .bordeaux-tourisme.com), can book accommodation free of charge, and it has useful information on the city and surrounding vineyards, to which it also arranges tours (see box, p.596).

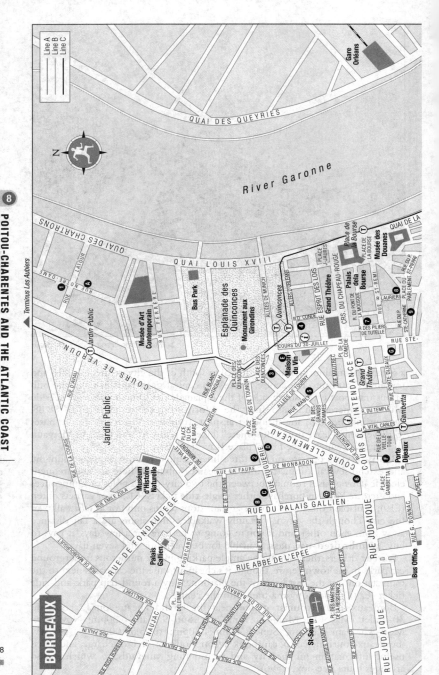

BORDEAUX

Line A
Line B
Line C

N

River Garonne

QUAI DES QUEYRIES

Gare Orléans

QUAI DES CHARTRONS

Terminus Les Aubiers

QUAI LOUIS XVIII

Jardin Public

Musée d'Art Contemporain

Bus Park

Esplanade des Quinconces

Monument aux Girondins

Place de la Bourse

Palais de la Bourse

Musée des Douanes

QUAI DE LA

RUE NOTRE-DAME

RUE LATOUR

RUE FERRÈRE

COURS DE VERDUN

Jardin Public

RUE D'AVIAU

RUE DE LA COURSE

Museum d'Histoire Naturelle

RUE EMILE ZOLA

RUE DE FONDAUDEGE

RUE DE MARGAUX-ROSE

Palais Gallien

RUE MAILLERE

RUE PAULIN

R. NAUJAC

RUE LIFFEACE

RUE ROSA BONHEUR

RUE FONDAUDEGE

RUE DELERME

RUE E. FOURCAND

PL. DE LA VILLE

R. D. LA VILLE DE MIRONNAC

RUE DU CH. DE MARS

PLACE DU CH. DE MARS

PLACE DES QUINCONCES

PLACE DES QUINCONCES

CRS DE TOUNON

RUE BLANC DUTROUILH

RUE HUSTIN

PLACE TOURNY

ALLÉES DE TOURNY

RUE MABLY

ALLEES DE MUNICH

ALLEES D'ORLEANS

R.D. CONDE

COURS DU 30-JUILLET

Maison du Vin

RUE ESPRIT DES LOIS

Grand Théâtre

CRS. DU CHAPEAU-ROUGE

Quinconces

Place de la Comédie

RUE MAUTREC

Grand Théâtre

R DES PILIERS DE TUTELLE

R. DU PONT DE LA MOUSQUE

R. ST-REMI

R DES LAURIERS

RUE DU PARLEMENT ST-PIERRE

PLACE DE LA BOURSE

RUE DU P.

RUE STE-CATHERINE

RUE STE-

COURS DE L'INTENDANCE

RUE PORTE DIJEAUX

PLACE DES GRANDS HOMMES

PL. DES GRANDS HOMMES

RUE DU TEMPLE

RUE DE MONTESQUIEU

RUE VITAL CARLES

RUE DE LA VIEILLE-TOUR

Porte Dijeaux

Gambetta

PLACE GAMBETTA

RUE HUGUERIE

RUE LA FAURE

RUE DE MONBADON

RUE TURENNE

RUE SAINT-FORT

RUE THIAC

RUE DU PALAIS GALLIEN

RUE ROLLAND

COURS CLEMENCEAU

RUE ABBE DE L'EPEE

RUE THIAC

RUE CASTEJA

RUE E. FOURCAND

RUE RODRIGUES PEREIRE

RUE DURANTELEU

RUE DE TURENNE

R. DE TURENNE

RUE SAINTE-LUCE

RUE GEORGES BONNAC

RUE ROYA

RUE VINDERMALE

RUE CASTELNAUD

PL. DES MARTYRS DE LA RÉSISTANCE

St-Seurin

RUE G. BONNAC

MICHELET

RUE JUDAIQUE

RUE JUDAIQUE

Bus Office

R. ROGA BONHEUR

A
B
C
D
E
F
G
1
2
3
4
5
6
7
8
9

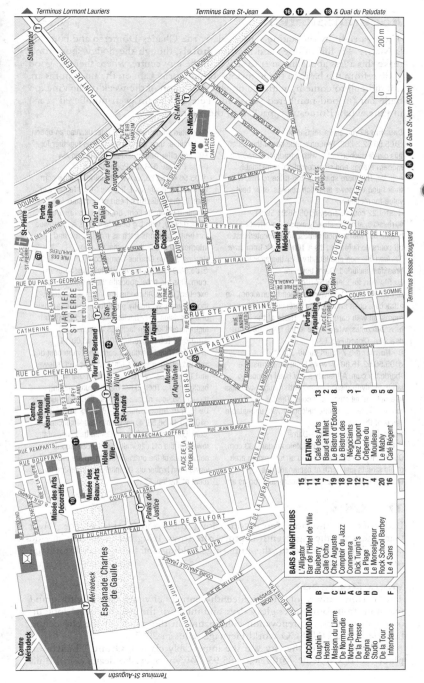

Accommodation

The area right by the station – particularly rue Charles–Domercq and cours de la Marne – is full of one- and two-star **hotels**, though the dodgy shop fronts make this a less appealing area to stay than the city centre, where there's a good choice, from the basic to the luxurious, though prices are on the up. Rooms are not difficult to come by, with the notable exception of the week of the Vinexpo trade fair (in odd-numbered years) and Fête du Vin (in even-numbered years) in June, when Bordeaux is packed to the gunnels.

Dauphin 82 rue du Palais Gallien ℡05.56.52.24.62. Though a little out of the action, this old-fashioned hotel, with a traditional decor but modern fittings and soundproofing, is justifiably popular. The more spacious, top-price rooms, with their huge windows and high ceilings, offer best value for money. ❸

Hostel 22 cours Barbey ℡05.56.91.59.51, ✉resa@bxaj.au. A slightly expensive private hostel, but with a good atmosphere. Located just off cours de la Marne, it's a 10min walk from *gare St-Jean*. Kitchen and laundry facilities available, breakfast included. Dorm beds are €21.

La Maison de Lierre 57 rue Huguerie ℡05.56.51.92.71, ⓦwww.maisondulierre.com. An attractive, quiet and friendly hotel with twelve rooms, all with parquet floors. Those at the front have balconies, while those at the back are more peaceful. Closed Feb. ❺

De Normandie 7 cours du 30-Juillet ℡05.56.52.16.80, ⓦwww.hotel-de-normandie -bordeaux.com. A friendly luxury hotel proposing large, nicely furnished rooms with minibar, wireless internet and all other mod cons. The top-floor rooms (❽) boast private balconies with unbeatable views of the city. ❺

Notre-Dame 36 rue Notre-Dame ℡05.56.52.88.24, ⓦwww.hotelnotredame33.com. Quiet, refined establishment in an interesting area of old streets just north of esplanade des Quinconces. A/c comes as standard, and rooms are

decorated with posters of Bordeaux. Also an option for families; they will put two rooms together for €90 and offer free breakfast to children. ❸

De la Presse 6–8 rue Porte Dijeaux ℡05.56.48.53.88, ⓦwww.hoteldelapresse.com. With very friendly staff, this well-kept family-run hotel in the pedestrian heart of Bordeaux is excellent value. Its light, bright rooms are well proportioned, with big beds to match, and provide three-star comforts such as minibar, a/c and internet access in the rooms. ❹

Regina 34 rue Charles-Domercq ℡05.56.91.66.07, ⓦwww.hotelreginabordeaux .com. This old hotel opposite the station offers excellent value. All rooms are in good condition, though you pay slightly more for en-suite facilities or a television. Very backpacker-friendly, with left-luggage and kitchen facilities thrown in. ❶

Studio 26 rue Huguerie ℡05.56.48.00.14, ✉studio@hotel-bordeaux.com. Easily the best deal in town, offering simple single rooms with shower and TV for a paltry €19, so very popular with backpackers. There's not much soundproofing though, so your night's sleep is slightly pot luck. ❶

De la Tour Intendance 14–16 rue de la Vieille-Tour ℡05.56.44.56.56, ⓦwww.hotel-tour-intendance .com. Located just off place Gambetta in one of the towers of the old city wall, the standard rooms are nothing out of the ordinary, but there are excellent views from higher up. Definitely worth asking for a room at the top. ❺

The City

Bordeaux is reasonably spread out along the western side of the River Garonne, with the eighteenth-century **old town** lying between the place de la Comédie to the north, the imposing buildings of the riverbank and the cathedral to the west.

Vieux Bordeaux

The narrow streets of the eighteenth-century city are lined with grand mansions from Bordeaux's glory days, and much of the area has been done up over recent years, the renovation culminating in the whole of the city centre being awarded UNESCO World Heritage status in 2007.

The social heart of the city was the impeccably classical **Grand Théâtre** on **place** de la Comédie (℡05.56.00.85.95, ⓦwww.opera-bordeaux.com). Built on the site of a Roman temple by the architect Victor Louis in 1780, this lofty building is faced with an immense colonnaded portico topped by twelve Muses and Graces. Inside, the interior is likewise opulently decorated with trompe l'oeil paintings; the best way to see it is to attend one of the operas or ballets staged throughout the year, with seats in the gods from as little as €8, or ask at the tourist office about the guided tours they offer from time to time (€6). Smart streets radiate from here: the city's main shopping street, **rue Ste-Catherine**, running south and partially pedestrianized to ease the consumer flow; the ritzy cours de l'Intendance running west; and the sandy, tree-lined allées de Tourny running northwest, commemorating the Marquis Louis Aubert de Tourny – the eighteenth-century administrator who was prime mover of the city's "Golden Age" and supervized much of the rebuilding. Back in the narrow streets of the old town, the harmonious **place du Parlement** and **place St-Pierre** are both lined with typical Bordelais mansions and peppered with wrought-iron balconies and arcading, making impressive examples of town planning.

The riverfront was also given the once-over by early eighteenth-century planners, with the imposing **place de la Bourse** creating a focal point on the quayside. Further south along the riverbank, the fifteenth-century **Porte Cailhau** takes its name from the stones (*cailloux – cailhaux* in dialect) unloaded on the neighbouring quay to be used as ballast for boats. Crossing the river just south of here, the only testimony to a nobler past is the impressive **Pont de Pierre** – "Stone Bridge", though in fact it's mostly brick – built at Napoleon's command during the Spanish campaigns, with seventeen arches in honour of his victories. The views of the river and quays from here are memorable, particularly when floodlit at night.

Place Gambetta, the cathedral and around

Cours de l'Intendance, a street lined with chic shops, links place de la Comédie with **place Gambetta**, a pivotal square for the city's museums, shops and the cathedral. In the middle of place Gambetta's arcaded house fronts, a valiant attempt at an English garden adds some welcome relief, belying the fact that the guillotine lopped three hundred heads off here at the time of the Revolution. In one corner stands the eighteenth-century arch of the **Porte Dijeaux**, an old city gate.

South of place Gambetta is the **Cathédrale St-André** (closed Mon morning), whose most eye-catching feature is the great upward sweep of the twin steeples over the north transept, an effect heightened by the adjacent but separate bell tower, the fifteenth-century **Tour Pey-Berland** (daily 10am–1.15pm & 2–6pm; €5). The interior of the cathedral, begun in the twelfth century, is vast and impressive, even if there's not much of artistic interest apart from the choir, which provides one of the few complete examples of the florid late Gothic style known as Rayonnant, and the north transept door and the Porte Royale to the right, which feature some fine carving.

The cream of Bordeaux's museums is to be found scattered in the streets around the cathedral. Directly behind the classical Hôtel de Ville, formerly Archbishop Rohan's palace, the **Musée des Beaux-Arts** (daily except Tues 11am–6pm; free) has a small but star-studded selection of European fine art, featuring works by Titian and Rubens among others, and often hosts imaginative or distinguished temporary exhibitions (usually €5). More engaging, however, is the **Musée des Arts Décoratifs** (daily except Tues 2–6pm; free), two blocks north on rue Bouffard and housed in a handsome eighteenth-century house. The exhibits are fine paintings, porcelain and furniture, arranged into a series of beguiling eighteenth- and nineteenth-century salons.

Continuing to circle clockwise round the cathedral, you'll pass the **Centre National Jean-Moulin** (Tues–Sun 2–6pm; free), an interesting museum dedicated to the local Resistance, featuring a history of the occupation of Bordeaux and a harrowing permanent exhibit of Holocaust-inspired paintings by French artist J.J. Morran, before reaching the imaginatively laid-out **Musée d'Aquitaine**, on cours Pasteur (Tues–Sun 11am–6pm; free), one of the city's best museums, tracing its development since Roman times through a variety of objects and art. If archeological bric-a-brac is not your bag you might want to move swiftly through the ground floor, but the upstairs is more varied, including a section on the wine trade and some documentary films with old footage of pre-war Aquitaine life.

North of the centre

North of the Grand Théâtre, cours du 30-Juillet leads into the bare, gravelly – and frankly unattractive – expanse of the **esplanade des Quinconces**, said to be Europe's largest municipal square. At the quayside end are two tall columns, erected in 1829 and topped by allegorical statues of Commerce and Navigation; at the opposite end of the esplanade is the **Monument aux Girondins**, a glorious *fin-de-siècle* ensemble of statues and fountains built in honour of the influential local deputies to the 1789 Revolutionary Assembly, later purged by Robespierre as moderates and counter-revolutionaries. During World War II, in a fit of anti-French spite, the occupying Germans made plans to melt the monument down, only to be foiled by the local Resistance, who got there first and, under cover of darkness, dismantled it piece by piece and hid it in a barn in the Médoc for the duration of the war.

To the northwest is the beautiful formal park, the **Jardin Public**, containing the city's botanical gardens as well as a small **natural history museum** (Mon & Wed–Fri 11am–6pm, Sat & Sun 2–6pm; temporary exhibitions €5). Behind it, to the west and north, lies a quiet, provincial quarter of two-storey stone houses. Concealed among the narrow streets, on rue du Dr-Albert-Barraud, is a large chunk of brick and stone masonry, the so-called **Palais Gallien**, in fact a third-century arena that's all that remains of Burdigala, Aquitaine's Roman capital. Nearby, on place Delerme, the unusual round **market hall** makes a focus for a stroll through the quarter.

To the east of the gardens, closer to the river, the **Musée d'Art Contemporain** on rue Ferrère (Tues & Thurs–Sun 11am–6pm, Wed 11am–8pm; €5) occupies a converted nineteenth-century warehouse for colonial imports. The vast, arcaded hall provides a magnificent setting for the mostly post-1960 sculpture and installation-based work by artists such as Richard Long, Daniel Buren and Sol LeWitt. Few pieces from the permanent collection are on display at any one time, the main space being filled by temporary exhibitions, so it's hit and miss as to whether you'll like what's on offer. However, there's a superb collection of glossy art books in the library and an elegant café-restaurant on the roof (lunch only).

Eating and drinking

Bordeaux is packed with **restaurants**, many of them top-notch, and due to its position close to the Atlantic coast, fresh seafood features prominently on many a Bordelais menu. The best place to look for a place to eat is around place du Parlement and place St-Pierre, undoubtedly touristy but usually good value and guaranteed to be lively. A plethora of modern, upmarket brasseries reflects the slick rich chic of part of the population, but you'll also find some wonderfully traditional old restaurants just off the main thoroughfares. For those on a tight budget, there are numerous sandwich bars and fast-food outlets at the south end of rue Ste-Catherine and spilling into place de la Victoire. For **picnic fodder**, there's a marvellous, round **market** in the place des Grands-Hommes, and on rue de Montesquieu, just off the square, Jean d'Alos runs the city's best *fromagerie*, with dozens of farm-produced cheeses.

The student population ensures a collection of young, lively **bars**, a host of which are found on and around place de la Victoire. Several offer live music and all are packed on Thursday nights. There's also a clutch of English, Irish and antipodean **pubs** in Bordeaux and a low-key **gay scene** concentrated at the south end of rue des Remparts and around the town hall.

Cafés and restaurants

Café des Arts 138 cours Victor-Hugo. This café-brasserie on the corner of rue Ste-Catherine is one of the city's few old-style cafés, its unique ambience created from faded relics of the 1940s and jazz music often playing in the background. The food is good, too, with a *plat du jour* for around €12, and the kitchens stay open till 1am.

Baud et Millet 19 rue Huguerie ☎ 05.56.79.05.77. The ultimate cheese-and-wine feast consumed around a few tables at the back of a wine shop where you choose your own bottle from the shelves. Portions are generous and the food rich, so one dish goes a long way. You can have a platter of cheese and cold meat with wine for €12.50, while *raclette* is another option. Closed Sun.

Le Bistrot d'Édouard 16 place du Parlement ☎ 05.56.81.48.87. In a great position on a lovely square, with outdoor seating in summer, this is as good value as you'll find anywhere. There is a three-course menu for €13.50, with lots of choice – their salads are particularly worth trying.

Le Bistrot des Négociants 4 place des Quinconces ☎ 05.56.52.84.56. Popular, modern brasserie. In fine weather locals vie for the outdoor tables, in a great spot facing the fountains. The modern, eclectic *carte* includes oysters and steak tartare and dishes cost roughly €16.

Chez Dupont 45 rue de Notre-Dame ☎ 05.56.81.49.59. Bustling, old-fashioned restaurant in the Chartrons district, with wooden floors, old posters and waiters sporting colourful waistcoats. Prices are very reasonable, with a *plat du jour*, fresh from the market, on the slate for €8.50.

Crêperie du Moulleau 20 rue du Parlement Ste-Catherine ☎ 05.56.51.65.79. A lively restaurant whose kitchen is in one corner of the dining room. It also has seats outside on a pleasant pedestrian street. *Galettes* are €8 or you could go for the lunchtime menu for €9.

Le Mably 12 rue Mably ☎ 05.56.44.30.10. Informal, friendly and popular restaurant with a warm, homely atmosphere. The food is of excellent quality and very traditional, most dishes featuring either duck or rabbit. Menus from €22. Closed Sun, Mon & three weeks in August.

Café Régent 46 place Gambetta. Certainly the place to be seen in Bordeaux, the interior is all sparkling mirrors and starched white tablecloths. A good place to have a drink and feel the city's pulse, but the food is a perhaps a touch expensive, with the cheapest menu now at €23.

Bars

L'Alligator 3 place du Général-Sarrail. Out of season, this bar is full to the rafters with student-types enjoying the party atmosphere, with a dancefloor downstairs. In summer, it's more chilled out; the music gets turned down a few notches and the terrace is a great place to enjoy a drink in the sun.

Calle Ocho 24 rue des Piliers-de-Tutelle. Bordeaux's best-known salsa bar has an unrivalled party atmosphere and is packed out most nights till 2am. They serve real Cuban rum and *mojitos*, and the self-inebriating bar staff frequently showers the crowds with water sprayed from the bar tap.

Chez Auguste Place de la Victoire. Friendly bar with plenty of outside seating on the sunny side of the square, occupied by a young crowd enjoying a cocktail list as long as your arm.

Connemara 18 cours d'Albret ⊛ www.connemara -pub.com. For the homesick pining for a pint of Guinness, this is Bordeaux's most active Irish pub, with free concerts (Sat), open mic nights (Tues) and a good atmosphere for sporting events. They also do reasonably priced pub food. Happy hour is 6–8pm daily.

Dick Turpin's 72 rue du Loup. Opposite the wisteria-filled courtyard of the municipal archives, this is a pretty good rendition of an English town pub with a quiet, relaxed atmosphere and an international clientele. There's the standard range of beers – Guinness, Bass and Newcastle Brown. Happy hour 5–8.30pm.

Nightlife and entertainment

Since Bordeaux's **clubs** are constantly changing it's best to ask around for the latest hotspots. There are one or two discos in the city centre, such as *Le Monseigneur*, at 42 allées d'Orléans, next to the tourist office, but the majority of clubs are spread out along southerly quai du Paludate, where things don't really get going until one in the morning and continue till closing time at four. Not all the clubs have very friendly atmospheres, but one safe bet is *La Plage* at no. 40, a fun, if slightly cheesy, disco in a tropical-beach setting. For alternative music (mainly electro and techno), your best option is *Le 4 Sans* at 40 rue d'Armagnac, which often hosts good DJs (Ⓦwww.le4sans.com).

The best **publication** on music is *Clubs & Concerts*, a monthly low-down revealing what's on in the most significant clubs and venues. The tourist office also issues *Bordeaux Magazine*, a free monthly in French with coverage of more highbrow cultural events around town. To buy **tickets** for city and regional events, contact the venue direct or head for the Box Office (Ⓣ05.56.48.26.26, Ⓦwww.box-office.fr) in the nineteenth-century Galerie Bordelaise arcade, wedged between rue Ste-Catherine and rue des Piliers-de-Tutelle. Virgin Megastore (Ⓣ05.56.56.05.55) on place Gambetta also has a ticket outlet, as does the FNAC on rue Ste-Catherine (Ⓣ05.56.00.21.30).

Jazz and blues fans should head south down the river to the respected *Comptoir du Jazz*, 57 quai de Paludate (Ⓣ05.56.85.98.85), or the less formal *Blueberry*, 61 rue Sauvageau (Ⓣ05.56.94.16.87). There's no shortage of more **contemporary music**, either. Bordeaux's home of rock music is the *Rock School Barbey*, 18 cours Barbey (Ⓦwww.rockschool-barbey.com), which hosts recognized international bands quite regularly.

Listings

Airlines Air France Ⓣ36.54; British Airways Ⓣ08.25.82.54.00; Bmibaby Ⓣ08.90.71.00.81; Easyjet Ⓣ08.99.65.00.11.

Bike hire Liberty Cycles (Ⓣ05.56.92.77.18; closed Sat afternoon & Sun) at 104 cours d'Yser is the best value of the various possibilities, renting out bikes from €9 per day. Another option is Station Vélo Services, just down the road at 48 cours d'Yser. Both shops also do repairs.

Books and newspapers Presse Gambetta, on place Gambetta, sells all the main English-language papers in addition to some regional guides and maps, while Bordeaux's largest bookstore, Mollat, 15 rue Vital Carles, has a better selection. They also stock a few English-language titles, though there's more choice at helpful Bradley's Bookshop, 8 cours d'Albret.

Car rental Numerous rental firms are located in and around the train station, including Europcar Ⓣ05.56.33.87.40; Hertz Ⓣ05.57.59.05.95; and National/Citer Ⓣ05.56.92.19.62. They all have outlets at the airport as well.

Cinema You're most likely to find original-language (*version originale* or *v.o.*) films at the wonderful art-house cinema Utopia, 5 place Camille-Jullian (Ⓣ05.56.52.00.03, Ⓦwww.cinemas-utopia.org), in a converted church. For more standard fare, there's the vast, seventeen-screen Megarama (Ⓣ08.92.69.33.17, Ⓦwww.megarama.fr) across the Pont de Pierre in the old Gare d'Orléans. The free weekly *Bordeaux Plus* has details of other cinemas and full programmes.

Consulates UK, 353 bd du Président-Wilson Ⓣ05.57.22.21.10; USA, 10 place de la Bourse Ⓣ05.56.48.63.80.

Emergencies To call an ambulance, phone SAMU on Ⓣ15.

Hospital Centre Hospitalier Pellegrin-Tripode, place Amélie-Raba-Léon (Ⓣ05.56.79.56.79), to the west of central Bordeaux.

Internet Internet cafés abound throughout the city. You'll find fast connections and long opening hours at Iphone, 24 rue du Palais Gallien (daily 10am–midnight), or La Cyb, 23 cours Pasteur (daily), though the latter has the disadvantage of crowds of enthusiastic internet gamers.

Money exchange American Express, 11 cours de l'Intendance (Mon–Fri 9.30am–5.55pm), handles most traveller's cheques and foreign currencies.

The main banks along cours de l'Intendance also offer exchange facilities and 24hr ATMs.

Police Commissariat Central, 23 rue François-de-Sourdis (☎05.57.85.77.77 or ☎17 in emergencies).

The Bordeaux wine region

Touring the **vineyards** and sampling a few local wines is one of the great pleasures of the Bordeaux region. The wine-producing districts lie in a great semicircle around the city, starting with the **Médoc** in the north, then skirting east through **St-Émilion**, before finishing south of the city among the vineyards of the **Sauternes**. In between, the less prestigious districts are also worth investigating, notably those of **Blaye**, to the north of Bordeaux, and **Entre-Deux-Mers**, to the east.

There's more to the region than its wine, however. Many of the Médoc's eighteenth-century châteaux are striking buildings in their own right, while the town of Blaye is dominated by a vast fortress, and there's a far older, more ruined castle at Villandraut on the edge of the Sauternes. St-Émilion is by far the prettiest of the wine towns, and has the unexpected bonus of a cavernous underground church. For scenic views, however, you can't beat the green, gentle hills of Entre-Deux-Mers and its ruined abbey, **La Sauve-Majeur**.

The main towns are well served by **public transport**, but to fully explore the region and its châteaux it's worth considering hiring a car (see listings opposite). There are train lines from Bordeaux running north through the Médoc to Margaux and Pauillac, and south along the Garonne valley to St-Macaire and La Réole. St-Émilion, meanwhile, lies on the Bordeaux–Sarlat line, but the station is a couple of kilometres out of town. In addition, there's a very comprehensive regional bus network for which you can pick up timetables from the office on allées de Munich in Bordeaux. Buses are operated by several different companies, the largest being Citram Aquitaine (☎05.56.43.68.43). **Cycling** is yet another option, as many of the towns are interconnected by well-marked, clean, blacktop footpaths that wend their way through the woods.

The Médoc

The landscape of **the Médoc**, a slice of land northwest of Bordeaux wedged between the forests bordering the Atlantic coast and the Gironde estuary, is itself rather monotonous: its gravel plains, occupying the west bank of the brown, island-spotted estuary, rarely swell into anything resembling a hill. Paradoxically, however, this poor soil is ideal for viticulture – vines root more deeply if they don't find the sustenance they need in the topsoil and, firmly rooted, they are less subject to drought and flooding. The D2 wine road, heading off the N15 from Bordeaux, passes through Margaux, St-Julien, Pauillac and St-Estèphe and, while the scenery might not be stunning, the many famous – albeit mostly inaccessible – châteaux are.

The problem of accommodation is much worse in the Médoc than in the rest of the wine region, but it's possible to visit the area on a day-trip from Bordeaux.

Château Margaux and Fort Médoc

Easily the prettiest of the Bordeaux châteaux, **Château Margaux** (by appointment only Mon–Fri; closed Aug and during harvest; ☎05.57.88.83.83, ⓦwww.chateau-margaux.com; free) is an eighteenth-century villa in extensive,

The wines of Bordeaux

With Burgundy and Champagne, the **wines of Bordeaux** form the "Holy Trinity" of French viticulture. Despite producing as many whites as reds, it is the latter – known as claret to the British – that have graced the tables of the discerning for centuries. The countryside that produces them encircles the city, enjoying near-perfect climatic conditions and soils ranging from limestone to sand and pebbles. It's the largest quality wine district in the world, turning out around 500 million bottles a year – over half the country's quality wine output and ten percent, by value, of the world's wine trade. While the niche market of the big names is largely immune to economic factors, smaller châteaux have been feeling the squeeze of competition from the new world in recent years and have been forced to be more inventive. One result is a growing fashion for "green" or organic wines.

The Gironde estuary, fed by the Garonne and the Dordogne, determines the lie of the land. The **Médoc** lies northwest of Bordeaux between the Atlantic coast and the River Gironde, with its vines deeply rooted in poor, gravelly soil, producing good, full-bodied red wines; the region's **eight appellations** are Médoc, Haut Médoc, St-Estèphe, Pauillac, St-Julien, Moulis en Médoc, Listrac-Médoc and Margaux. Southwest of Bordeaux are the vast vineyards of **Graves**, producing the best of the region's dry white wines, along with some punchy reds, from some of the most prestigious communes in France – Pessac, Talence, Martillac and Villenave d'Ornon among them. They spread down to Langon and envelop the areas of **Sauternes** and **Barsac**, whose extremely sweet white dessert wines are considered among the world's best.

On the east side of the Gironde estuary and the Dordogne, the **Côtes de Blaye** feature some good-quality white table wines, mostly dry, and a smaller quantity of reds. The **Côtes de Bourg** specialize in solid whites and reds, spreading down to the renowned **St-Émilion** area. Here, there are a dozen producers who have earned the accolade of **Premiers Grands Crus Classés**, and their output is a full, rich red wine that doesn't have to be kept as long as the Médoc wines. Lesser-known neighbouring areas include the vineyards of **Pomerol**, **Lalande** and **Côtes de Francs**, all producing reds similar to St-Émilion but at more affordable prices.

Between the Garonne and the Dordogne is **Entre-Deux-Mers**, an area which yields large quantities of inexpensive, drinkable table whites, mainly from the Sauvignon grape. Stretching along the north bank of the Garonne, the vineyards of the **Côtes de Bordeaux** feature fruity reds and a smaller number of dry and sweet whites.

The **classification** of Bordeaux wines is an extremely complex affair. Apart from the usual *appellation d'origine contrôlée* (AOC) labelling – guaranteeing origin but not quality – the wines of the Médoc châteaux are graded into five crus, or growths. These were established as long ago as 1855, based on the prices the wines had fetched over the last few hundred years. Four were voted the best or **Premier Grand Cru Classé**: Margaux, Lafitte, Latour and Haut-Brion. With the exception of Château Mouton-Rothschild, which moved up a class in 1973 to become the fifth *Premier Grand Cru Classé*, there have been no official changes, so divisions between the crus should not be taken too seriously.

If you're interested in **buying wines**, it's best all to do it at the châteaux themselves, where you'll get the best price and the opportunity to sample and receive expert advice before purchasing. In Bordeaux, the best place to go is La Vinotèque (Mon–Sat 10am–7.30pm), next to the tourist office, which always has a couple of wines on offer for tasting.

To **visit the châteaux**, ask at the Maison du Vin in each wine-producing village. In Bordeaux itself, enquire at the tourist office, which also organizes a variety of **guided tours**, covering all the main wine areas (from €28 per person). Generally interesting and informative, the guide translates the wine-maker's commentary into English and answers any questions. Tastings are generous, and expert tuition on how to go about it is part of the deal.

sculpture-dotted gardens close to the west bank of the Gironde, some 20km north of Bordeaux. Its wine, a classified *Premier Grand Cru* and world-famous in the 1940s and 1950s, went through a rough patch in the two succeeding decades but improved in the 1980s after the estate was bought by a Greek family. The château does not offer tastings or sell directly, but you can visit the grounds if you book a couple of weeks in advance.

In the small village of **MARGAUX** itself, there's an unusually friendly **Maison du Vin** (June–Sept Mon–Sat 10am–7pm, Sun 11am–1pm & 2–5pm; Oct–May Mon–Fri 10am–noon & 2–6pm; ℡05.57.88.70.82) that can help find accommodation and advise on visits to the *appellation*'s châteaux. At the other end of the village, the enterprising and inviting cellar La Cave d'Ulysse (daily 9am–7pm, closed Sun in winter; ⓦwww.caveulysse.com) provides free tastings from a variety of Margaux châteaux, giving you a chance to try and buy (and ship, if you need) some very good wines. Prices range from a €5 run-of-the-mill Médoc to €2400 for a delicate, rare 1990 Petrus. Margaux has a very comfortable **hotel**, *Le Pavillon de Margaux* (℡05.57.88.77.54, ⓦwww.pavillondemargaux.com; ❺), with a fine restaurant offering a good-value lunch for €15. Otherwise, try the *chambre d'hôte Le Domaine les Sapins* (℡05.56.58.18.26; ❷) in Moulis, a few kilometers to the west.

The seventeenth-century **Fort Médoc**, off the D2 road between Margaux and St-Julien by the banks of the estuary, is a good place to tuck into a few purchases between châteaux. It was designed by the prolific military architect Vauban to defend the Gironde estuary against the British. The remains of the fort are scant but scrambleable, and in summer its Toytown aspect has a leafy charm, marred only by the view of a nuclear power station across the river to the north of Blaye. A little further south, **LAMARQUE** is a very pretty village, full of flowers and centred around a church with a distinctive, minaret-like tower. A couple of kilometers from the village is the port, from which you can take a ferry across the muddy Gironde to Blaye (4–9 daily; one way: passengers €3.10, cycles €1.60, cars €13). It's also a pleasant place to stop for refreshments, with a couple of café-restaurants with outside seating, including *L'Escale* (menus from €12; closed Tues & evenings off season).

Pauillac and around

PAUILLAC is the largest town in the Médoc region and central to the most important vineyards of Bordeaux: no fewer than three of the top five *grand cru* come from around here. It has grown rapidly in recent years and, while its little harbour and riverfront are pretty enough, they can't counteract the presence of the nuclear power plant across the Gironde.

Pauillac has a huge **Maison du Tourisme et du Vin** along the waterfront (July & Aug Mon–Sat 9.30am–7pm, Sun 10am–1pm & 2–6pm; Sept–June Mon–Sat 9.30am–12.30pm & 2–6pm, Sun 10.30am–12.30pm & 3–6pm; ℡05.56.59.03.08, ⓦwww.pauillac-medoc.com). It can provide you with a list of *gîtes* and, for a modest fee, make appointments for you to visit the surrounding châteaux. To explore the area by **bike**, head to Sport Nature, 6 rue Joffre (℡05.57.75.22.60), which has decent rates for full-or half-day rental, though it's best to reserve in advance. Pauillac itself is not a great **place to stay**, but should you wish to, try the *Hôtel de France et d'Angleterre*, opposite the little harbour (℡05.56.59.01.20, ⓦwww.hoteldefrance -angleterre.com; ❸; closed Christmas & New Year), with a good restaurant (closed Sun off season), or the welcoming riverfront **campsite** further south on route de la Rivière (℡05.56.59.10.03; April–Sept). Campsites are rare in the Médoc: the only other alternative is the three-star *Camping Le Paradis* at

ST-LAURENT-DE-MÉDOC (☎05.56.59.42.15, ⓦwww.leparadismedoc
.com; March–Oct).

The most famous of the **Médoc châteaux** – Château Lafite-Rothschild
(☎05.56.73.18.18), Château Latour (☎05.56.73.19.80) and Château Mouton-
Rothschild (☎05.56.73.21.29) – can be visited by appointment only, either
direct (all have English-speaking staff) or through the Maison du Vin. Their
vineyards occupy larger single tracts of land than elsewhere in the Médoc, and
consequently neighbouring wines can differ markedly: a good vintage Lafite is
perfumed and refined, whereas a Mouton-Rothschild is strong and dark and
should be kept for at least ten years. **Château Mouton–Rothschild** and its
wine **museum** (which can only be visited as part of the tour; €6 or €25 with
a tasting) is the most absorbing of the big houses: as well as the viticultural stuff,
you also get to see the Rothschilds' amazing collection of art treasures, all
loosely connected with wine.

St-Estèphe

North of Pauillac, the wine commune of **ST-ESTÈPHE** is Médoc's largest
appellation, consisting predominantly of *crus bourgeois* properties and growers
belonging to the local *cave coopérative*, **Marquis de St-Estèphe**, on the D2
towards Pauillac (tastings July & Aug daily 10am–noon & 2–6pm; Sept–June by
appointment; ☎05.56.73.35.30). One of the *appellation*'s five *crus classés* is the
distinctive **Château Cos d'Estournel**, with its over-the-top nineteenth-
century French version of a pagoda; the *chais* (warehouses) can be visited by
appointment (Mon–Fri; ☎05.56.73.15.50; English spoken, reserve a week
ahead). The village of St-Estèphe itself is a sleepy affair dominated by its
landmark, the eighteenth-century **church of St-Étienne**, with its highly
decorative interior. The small, homespun **Maison du Vin** (June & Sept Mon–
Fri 10am–5pm, Sat 1.30–5.30pm; July & Aug Mon–Sat 10am–7pm; Oct–May
Mon–Fri 10am–12.30pm & 1.30–5pm; ☎05.56.59.30.59, ⓦwww.vins-saint
-estephe.com) is hidden in the church square.

For an elegant place to **stay**, head for *Château Pomys* (☎05.56.59.73.44,
ⓦwww.chateaupomys.com; ⑤), just south of the village, a mansion set in its
own park. There are also several good *chambres d'hôtes* in the area – ask at the
tourist office for a list.

Blaye

The green slopes north of the Garonne, the **Côtes de Bourg** and **Côtes de
Blaye**, were home to wine production long before the Médoc was planted. The
wine is a rather heavier, plummier red, and cheaper than anything found on the
opposite side of the river, and the **Maison du Vin des Premières Côtes de
Blaye** on cours Vauban (Mon–Sat 8.30am–12.30pm & 2–6.30pm), the main
street of the pretty little town of **BLAYE**, serves a representative selection of
the local produce, with some ridiculously inexpensive wines – you can get a
good bottle for around €5.

Blaye has long played a strategic role defending Bordeaux, and was fortified
by Vauban in the seventeenth century. The **citadelle** deserves a wander: people
still live here, and it's a strange combination of peaceful village and tourist
attraction. A beautiful spot, it has grass, trees, birds and a spectacular view over
the Gironde estuary. Blaye is also the last resting place of the heroic paladin
Roland, whose body was brought here in 778 after the battle of Roncevaux.
However, his mausoleum is now no more than a heap of rocks.

The **tourist office**, at 33 allées Marines (daily 9.30am–12.30pm & 2–5pm;
closed Sun Oct–March; ☎05.57.42.12.09, ⓦwww.tourisme-blaye.com), is

really helpful and can reserve rooms and give out details on wine tasting. If you fancy **staying** here, try the outstanding ⚜ *Auberge du Porche*, 5 rue Ernest-Régnier (☎05.57.42.22.69, ⓦwww.auberge-du-porche.com; ❸), which has finely decorated rooms in an old building on the riverfront. It also has a high-quality but unpretentious restaurant with seasonal menus for €22.50 and an excellent local wine list. Alternatively, there's the more expensive *Hôtel La Citadelle* within the old fort with views over the Garonne and a swimming pool (☎05.57.42.17.10, ⓦwww.hotel-la-citadelle.com; ❺, half board required July & Aug; restaurant from €25). Finally, there's a small municipal **campsite** within the citadelle (☎05.57.42.00.20; May–Sept).

St-Émilion

ST-ÉMILION, 35km east of Bordeaux, and a short train trip, is well worth a visit. The old grey houses of this fortified medieval town straggle down the south-hanging slope of a low hill, with the green froth of the summer's vines crawling over its walls. Many of the growers still keep up the old tradition of planting roses at the ends of the rows, which in pre-pesticide days served as an early-warning system against infection, the idea being that the commonest bug, *oidium*, went for the roses first, giving three days' notice of its intentions.

Arrival, information and accommodation

The super-efficient **tourist office** on place des Créneaux by the belfry (daily: June–Sept 9.30am–7/8pm; Oct–May 9.30am–12.30pm & 1.45–6/6.30pm; ☎05.57.55.28.28, ⓦwww.saint-emilion-tourisme.com) is a good source of information and organizes bilingual (French and English) vineyard tours in season (June–Sept; €10). They also have **bikes** for rent (€14.70 per day or €142 per month).

If you're short of funds or without your own transport, St-Émilion is best seen as a day-trip from Bordeaux, as there's a chronic shortage of budget **accommodation** within the town. However, the tourist office can furnish you with an extensive list of *chambres d'hôtes* in the area, many of which are very reasonably priced (from €40). Within the town itself, the two-star *Auberge de la Commanderie* on rue des Cordeliers (☎05.57.24.70.19, ⓦwww.aubergedelacommanderie .com; ❹; closed mid-Dec to mid-Feb) offers the cheapest option, although its starkly modernist decor won't be to everybody's taste. Two kilometres northwest on the road to Montagne, there's a fantastic three-star campsite, *La Barbanne* (☎05.57.24.75.80, ⓦwww.camping-saint-emilion.com; April–Sept), with several heated swimming pools.

The Town

The town's **belfry** belongs to the rock-hewn subterranean **Église Monolithe** beneath it, which can be visited only on a **guided tour** from the tourist office (daily every hour 10am–5pm; €6.50). The tour starts in a dark hole in someone's back yard, supposedly the cave where St Émilion lived a hermit's life in the eighth century. A rough-hewn ledge served as his bed and a carved seat as his chair, where infertile women reputedly still come to sit in the hope of getting pregnant.

Above is the half-ruined thirteenth-century **Trinity Chapel**, which was built in honour of St Émilion and converted into a cooperage during the Revolution; some strikingly well-preserved frescoes are still visible, including a kneeling figure who is thought to be the saint himself. On the other side of the yard, a passage tunnels beneath the belfry to the **catacombs**, where three chambers dug out of the soft limestone were used as ossuary and cemetery from the eighth to the eleventh centuries.

Below, the ninth- and twelfth-century **church** itself is an incredible place. Simple and huge, the entire structure – barrel-vaulting, great square piers and all – has been hacked out of the rock. The impact has been somewhat diminished, however, by the installation of massive metal supports after cracks were discovered in the bell tower above in 1990. The whole interior was painted once, but only faint traces survived the Revolution, when a gunpowder factory was installed here. These days, every June, the wine council – *La Jurade* – assembles in the church in distinctive red robes to evaluate the previous season's wine and decide whether each *viticulteur's* produce deserves the *appellation contrôlée* rating.

Behind the tourist office, the town comes to an abrupt end with a grand view of the **moat** and old **walls**. To the right is the twelfth-century **collegiate church**, with a handsome but badly mutilated doorway and a lovely fourteenth-century **cloister**, accessed via the tourist office (same hours; free).

You should take advantage of the produce of this well-respected wine region, ideally by visiting one of the local vineyards for a tasting: Château Fonplegade (℡05.57.74.43.11) is friendly and convenient from the train station, if a bit expensive, while Château Canon (℡05.57.55.23.45; by appointment only), just west of the town, has impressive buildings and respected wines. The **Maison du Vin**, opposite the tourist office in St-Émilion (daily 10am–12.30pm & 2–6pm; Ⓦwww.vins-saint-emilion.com), can advise further on which vineyards to visit as well as itself selling wine from the region at excellent prices.

Eating and drinking

You should try the town's other speciality while you're here: **macaroons** were devised here by the Ursuline sisters in 1620, and the one authentic place to buy them is at the Fabrique de Macarons, 9 rue Guadet, where the tiny melt-in-the-mouth biscuits are baked to the original recipe. An excellent place for a **meal** is the relaxed contemporary-style bistro *L'Envers du Décor* (closed Sun Nov–April) on rue du Clocher, with a creative menu for €29 and local wine by the glass. Alternatively, try the homely looking *Les Giron Dines* at 5 rue des Girondins, which has a fine menu for €19.50.

Entre-Deux-Mers

The landscape of **Entre-Deux-Mers** (literally "between two seas") – so called because it's sandwiched between the tidal waters of the Dordogne and Garonne – is the prettiest of the Bordeaux wine regions, with its gentle hills and scattered medieval villages. Its wines, including the *Premières Côtes de Bordeaux*, are mainly dry whites produced by over forty *caves coopératives*, and are regarded as good but inferior to the Médocs or super-dry Graves to the south. It's a region which can be explored, at least in part, by public transport.

La Sauve-Majeure

The one place you should really try to see is the ruined **Abbey** (June–Sept daily 10am–6pm; Oct–May Tues–Sun 10.30am–1pm & 2.30–5.30pm; €6.50) at **LA SAUVE-MAJEURE**, some 25km east of Bordeaux, an important stop for pilgrims en route to Santiago de Compostela in Spain. It was once all forest here, the abbey's name being a corruption of the Latin *silva major* (big wood). Founded in 1079, the treasures of what remains are the twelfth-century Romanesque apse and apsidal chapels and the outstanding sculpted capitals in the chancel. The finest are the ones illustrating stories from the

Walking in France

France is quite simply a walker's paradise. It has some 60,000km of long-distance footpaths, known as GRs (*sentiers de grande randonnée*), not to mention thousands of shorter routes (PRs, or *sentiers de promenade et de randonnée*), all well maintained and signposted. They take you through the best of France's beautiful and varied landscape, including the majestic Alps in the east, the volcanic plugs of the Massif Central and the lofty Pyrenees in the south.

The Alps

For sheer mountain grandeur the northern Alps are unbeatable. The area has over a hundred peaks topping 3000m – including the highest, Mont Blanc (4807m) – glaciers, soaring pinnacles, high Alpine meadows and rich flora and fauna. The two main areas for walking are the Chamonix valley, which offers plenty of impressive views of Mont Blanc, and the Parc National de la Vanoise, created to protect the wild ibex; you'll stand a good chance of seeing these wild goats on one of the spectacular high-level hikes through the park.

The southern Alps are generally more accessible to less experienced walkers; a good introduction to the area is the Parc Naturel Régional du Vercors, criss crossed with around 2850km of waymarked paths. At its heart is the impressive Vercors plateau, edged with craggy limestone cliffs and riven with deep gorges. More Mediterranean in appearance is the Parc Naturel Régional du Queyras, with its meadows of violets, orchids and pinks.

The Pyrenees

Generally less formidable than the Alps, the Pyrenees are still serious mountains, with a number of peaks topping 3000m, and offer some of France's finest walking. The classic long-distance path is the GR10, which traverses the whole range from west to east and is about 800km long. There are plenty of shorter walks too, the best of which are to be found in the central Ariège region, characterized by steep lush-green valleys, meadows full of wild flowers and abundant wildlife, including vultures – lammergeiers and griffon vultures – and marmots.

Wild flowers of the Pyrenees ▲

Ibex, Chamonix ▼

The Auvergne and Cévennes

At the heart of France lies the sparsely populated **Auvergne** region of the Massif Central. It's wild and rugged terrain, formed by three volcanic mountain chains, the Monts-Dore, Monts du Cantal and the smaller Monts-Dômes. The biggest draw for walkers is the jagged Puy de Sancy (1885m), the source of the Dordogne River.

Just south of the Auvergne, the **Cévennes** region is a picturesque one of deep valleys clothed with chestnut trees, high limestone plateaux and soft rounded granite peaks. A number of long-distance paths wind their way through the area, the best known of which is the GR70, the route famously described by R.L. Stevenson in his book *Travels with a Donkey*.

Provence

This most beguiling region, with its lovely warm light and Mediterranean colours and scents, has numerous walking possibilities. You could hike through the dramatic and vast Gorges du Verdon, or ramble among the gentle hills and lavender fields of the Luberon. Towards the Italian border is the Parc National du Mercantour, an unspoilt Alpine wilderness, sheltering chamois, golden eagles and rare species of flowers.

Corsica

Corsica offers some of the most adventurous walking in France. Scores of footpaths give access to spectacular coastline, rocky gorges and mountainous peaks.

▲ Walking in the Pyrenees

▲ Hiking in the Livradois-Forez Park, Auvergne

▼ Donkey trails in the Cévennes

Restonica valley, Corsica ▲

Vercors Natural Park, Alps ▼

Ten top walks in France

▶▶ **Northern Alps:** The classic Tour du Mont Blanc which crosses French, Italian and Swiss terrain and takes eight to ten days. See p.906.

▶▶ **The Chemin de Saint-Jacques,** the ancient pilgrimage route that starts in Le-Puy-en-Velay and ends at Santiago de Compostela in Spain (see p.856). To hike the whole thing would take weeks, but you could do just a section, such as the six-day stretch between Figeac and Moissac through the Lot valley.

▶▶ **A two-day loop walk above** Cauterets in the Pyrenees: Pont d'Espagne–Vallée du Gaube–Vallée de Lutour–Pont d'Espagne. See p.717.

▶▶ **The Crête d'Iparla,** one of the best ridge walks in the Pyrenees (a day-hike along the GR10). See p.693.

▶▶ **Corsica's two-hundred-kilometre-long GR20,** possibly Europe's most testing walk. See p.1119.

▶▶ **The Côte de Granit Rose** (see p.433). This attractive stretch of Brittany coast is dotted with sculpted pink granite rocks. One of the best stretches is from Trégastel to Tréguier (a three-day hike) along the GR34.

▶▶ **The ninety-minute walk up and** down the rocky headlands from Cassis, on the Côte d'Azur, to the Calanque d'En Vau, with its beautifully secluded beach. See p.1036.

▶▶ **The circuit of the southern Alps'** Parc National des Écrins (along the GR54), hard to beat for the grandeur of its scenery. See p.881.

▶▶ **The Canyon du Verdon:** the seven-hour walk from La Maline to the Point Sublime is by far the best way to explore the canyon. See p.1007.

▶▶ **The GR7 "Stevenson trail",** which takes about a fortnight to walk, passing through the rugged Gévaudan highlands and the bare hilltops of Mont Lozère. See p.848.

Old and New Testaments (Daniel in the lions' den, Delilah shearing Samson's hair and so on), while others show fabulous beasts and decorative motifs. There is a small **museum** at the entrance, with some excellent photos of the ruins, along with keystones from the fallen roofs. But what makes the visit so worthwhile is not just the capitals themselves, but the remote, undisturbed nature of the site.

St-Macaire and La Réole

If you're heading south through Entre-Deux-Mers, Langon is the first town of any size you come to. But **ST-MACAIRE**, across the Garonne, is far better for a rest or food stop. The village still has its original **gates** and **battlements** and a beautiful medieval church, the **Église-Prieuré**, with significant wall paintings which are in the process of being restored. The **tourist office**, 8 rue Canton (June–Sept daily 10am–1pm & 3–7pm; April & May Tues–Sun same hours; March & Oct Tues–Fri 2–6pm, Sat & Sun 10am–noon & 2–6pm; Nov–Feb same hours, also closed Tues; ℡05.56.63.32.14), also hosts a boutique of regional produce, which here means honey and wine. Staff can help arrange visits to the *chais*, and in season (July & Aug daily) they organize tastings hosted by various local winemakers. Good value accommodation is offered by *Les Tilleuls* (℡05.56.62.28.38, ⓦwww.tilleul-medieval.com; ❷), based just outside the medieval city, which owns studio apartments in various buildings within the walls. More elegant, though, is *Les Feuilles d'Acanthe* (℡05.56.62.33.75, ⓦwww .feuilles-dacanthe.fr; closed mid-Dec to mid-Jan; ❺), opposite the tourist office, whose very agreeable, stone-walled, wooden-beamed rooms offer some fine views out over the rooftops. As well as a Jacuzzi and south-facing terrace, the hotel also boasts one of the town's best **restaurants**, which serves traditional meaty dishes with menus from €21.

 LA RÉOLE, on the north bank 18km further east, boasts a wealth of medieval architecture along a walk through its narrow, hilly streets – pick up a map from the tourist office on place Richard-Coeur-de-Lion. France's oldest **town hall**, constructed for Richard the Lionheart in the twelfth century, and the well-preserved simple **Abbaye des Bénédictins** – with a fantastic view over the River Garonne and the surrounding countryside – reward a stroll through the town, although little remains of the fortified **castle**.

Sauternes and around

The **Sauternes** region, which extends southeast from Bordeaux for 40km along the left bank of the Garonne, is an ancient wine-making area, originally planted during the Roman occupation. The distinctive golden wine of the area is certainly sweet, but also round, full-bodied and spicy, with a long aftertaste. It's not necessarily a dessert wine, either: try it with some Roquefort cheese. Gravelly terraces with a limestone subsoil help create the delicious taste, but mostly it's due to a peculiar microclimate of morning autumn mists and afternoons of sun and heat which causes *Botrytis cinerea* fungus, or "noble rot", to flourish on the grapes, letting the sugar concentrate and introducing some intense flavours. When they're picked, they're not a pretty sight: carefully selected by hand, only the most shrivelled, rotting bunches are taken. The wines of Sauternes are some of the most highly sought-after in the world, with bottles of **Château d'Yquem**, in particular, fetching thousands of euros. Sadly that particular château does not offer tastings, but you can at least have a wander around its attractive buildings and grounds, two minutes' drive north of Sauternes.

SAUTERNES itself is a sleepy little village surrounded by vines and dominated by the ✈ **Maison du Sauternes** (Mon–Fri 9am–7pm, Sat & Sun 10am–7pm; ☎05.56.76.69.83, ⓦwww.maisondusauternes.com) at one end of the village, with a pretty church at the other. The *maison* is a room full of treasures, the golden bottles with white and gold labels being quite beautiful objects in themselves. A non-profit organization, it offers tastings, expert advice and unbeatable prices.

For a luxurious place to **stay**, try the sumptuous *Relais du Château d'Arche*, on the D125 just outside Sauternes heading north (☎05.56.76.67.67, ⓦwww.chateaudarche-sauternes.com; ➐). The seventeenth-century estate was recently restored to its original lustre and has been refurbished with near-period styling and paraphernalia; many rooms look directly onto the vineyard, the best views being from those in the towers.

A good place to **eat** in Sauternes is the *Auberge Les Vignes*, by the church (☎05.56.76.60.06; closed Sun & Mon evening & Feb), a typical country restaurant with regional specialities like *grillades aux Sauternes* (meats grilled over vine clippings), a great wine list and a lunch menu at €13.

Ten kilometres south of Sauternes, the ruinous curtain walls and corner towers of a colossal moated **château** (July & Aug daily 10am–7pm; Sept–June 2–6pm; €3.50) still dominate **VILLANDRAUT**. The castle was built by Pope Clement V, a native of the area who caused a schism by moving the papacy to Avignon in the fourteenth century. You can visit his tomb in the even smaller village of **UZESTE** en route to **BAZAS**, 15km east, which has a laid-back, southern air. Bazas' most attractive feature is the wide, arcaded place de la Cathédrale, overlooked by the grey, lichen-covered **Cathédrale St-Jean-Baptiste**, which displays a harmonious blend of Romanesque, Gothic and classical styles in its west front.

Two other excellent reasons to include Bazas in your itinerary are its **restaurants**. *Bistrot St-Jean* (☎05.56.25.18.53), under the colonnades facing the decorative facade of the cathedral, has great lunch menus for €12 with generous helpings and friendly service (closed evenings except weekends in summer). In the evening, you should try *Les Remparts* (☎05.56.25.25.52; closed Sun evening and Mon), opposite, which has a good view from its terrace and more sophisticated, gastronomic fare on set menus for €25 or €50. On the southern outskirts of the town is a place to **stay** in pampered luxury: the *Domaine de Fompeyre* (☎05.56.25.98.00, ⓦwww.monalisahotels.com; ➏) has tempting rooms set in extensive grounds with a pool. For more modestly priced lodgings, ask at Bazas' tourist office (☎05.56.25.25.84, ⓦwww.ville-bazas.fr) for the list of *chambres d'hôtes* in the area, whose rates begin at around €45.

The Côte d'Argent

The **Côte d'Argent** is the long stretch of coast from the mouth of the Gironde estuary to Biarritz, which – at over 200km – is the longest, straightest and sandiest in Europe. The endless beaches are backed by high sand dunes, while behind lies the largest forest in western Europe, **Les Landes**. Despite these attractions, the lack of conventional tourist sights means that outside July and August the coast gets comparatively few visitors, and away from the main resorts it's still possible to find deserted stretches of coastline.

Arcachon

On summer weekends, the Bordelais escape en masse to **ARCACHON**, the oldest resort on the Côte d'Argent and a forty-minute train ride across flat, sandy forest from Bordeaux. The beaches of white sand are magnificent but can be crowded, and its central jetties are busy with boats going off on an array of cruises.

The seafront itself can feel a little tacky these days, especially in summer, but the sense of extravagance which built the town remains palpable in the rather exclusive **ville d'hiver** (winter town), whose wide shady streets are full of fanciful Second Empire mansions overlooking the seaside **ville d'été** (summer town). Well worth a wander, the area can be reached by following the lively pedestrianized and restaurant-filled rue de Maréchal-de-Lattre-de-Tassigny, running perpendicular to the seafront boulevard de la Plage; at the end of this mouthful of a street, a lift carries you up to the flower-filled, wooded **Parc Mauresque**), with the *ville d'hiver* beyond it. From the park, there are fine views over the seafront.

Practicalities

A well-stocked **tourist office**, on esplanade Georges-Pompidou (April–June & Sept Mon–Sat 9am–6.30pm, Sun 10am–1pm & 2–5pm; July & Aug daily 9am–7pm; Oct–March Mon–Fri 9am–6pm, Sat 9am–5pm; ☎05.57.52.97.97; ⓦwww.arcachon.com), can be reached by following avenue Gambetta back from seafront place Thiers. In summer, boats leave the jetties of Thiers and Eyrac on various **cruises**, including the Île aux Oiseaux (1hr 45min; €14), and an exploration of the Arcachon basin with a look at the Dune de Pyla (2hr 45min; €21). There's also a regular boat service from here to Cap Ferret on the opposite peninsula (30min; €11.50 return). Discounted tickets can be purchased for all excursions at the tourist office.

Be prepared to pay resort prices for **hotels** in summer. If you're determined to stay on the seafront, you could opt for the grand old *Hôtel Richelieu* (☎05.56.83.16.50, ⓦwww.grand-hotel-richelieu.com; ❺), right in the thick of the action at 185 boulevard de la Plage. Significantly more expensive rooms (❻) have balconies with sea views. An altogether better deal, however, is in the tranquil *ville d'hiver* at the friendly *Marinette* (☎05.56.83.06.67, ⓔhotelmarinette@aol .com; ❸), 800m from the beach at 15 allée José-Maria de Hérédia, with shady rooms in a villa-style building. Alternatively, the tourist office can give you a list of the many **holiday apartments** available to rent. **Camping** is another option, with plenty of sites around the Arcachon basin, though only the three-star *Le Camping Club*, allée de la Galaxie (☎05.56.83.24.15), is actually within the town; set in an expanse of bird-filled woodland beyond the *ville d'hiver*, it's worth the high summer prices.

The best **restaurant** for appreciating some seafood is *Chez Yvette*, 59 boulevard de Général-Leclerc, which offers dishes for around €20 or immense platters for €32.

Cap Ferret and the north coast

The Atlantic coast between the Bassin d'Arcachon and the Gironde has a wild, undeveloped feel and, despite its proximity to Bordeaux and Arcachon, is seldom crowded. No motorable road follows the coast for most of the way, which contributes to the relaxed nature of the place; instead a cycle path, built at the end of World War II, winds through more than 75km of pine-forested dunes from the low-key holiday village of **Cap Ferret** to the resort of Soulac in the north, from where trains run through the Médoc vineyards to Bordeaux or to the Pointe de Grave and Verdon for the ferry to Royan. Apart from the occasional surf shack or beach restaurant, the only settlement of any size is Lacanau-Ocean, 30km north of Cap Ferret, best avoided unless you're into overpriced hotels and golf courses. Cap Ferret can be reached by boat from Arcachon. There are a few places to **stay**, the best of which is the characterful ⚲ *Hotel des Pins* at 23 rue des Fauvettes (T 05.56.60.60.11, W www.hotel despins.eu; Feb to mid-Nov; ➎), overlooking the ocean and still decorated in the spirit of the 1920s, when it was built. It also has a restaurant with menus for €24. If funds are low, go for the youth hostel at 87 avenue de Bordeaux (T 05.56.60.64.62). Some 10km to the north there's a **campsite** at Grand Crohot, Bremontier (T 05.56.60.03.99; June to mid-Sept).

The Dune du Pyla and Le Teich

The Côte d'Argent's chief curiosity is the **Dune du Pyla**. At over 100m it's the highest sand dune in Europe – a veritable mountain of wind-carved sand, about 12km south of Arcachon. Bus #1 leaves from the *gare SNCF* in Arcachon every hour in July and August – two to five a day at other times. From bus stop "dune du Pilat" it's a fifteen-minute walk to the dune itself – if you're driving, it costs €2.30–3.05 to use the obligatory car park. There's the inevitable group of stands selling ice cream, *galettes* and junk, but from the top you get a superb view over the bay of Arcachon and the forest of the Landes stretching away to the south. It's a great sandy slide down to the sea (the sides are as steep as an Olympic ski-jump) and a long haul back up but well worth the effort.

At **LE TEICH**, about 14km east of Arcachon in the southeast corner of the Bassin d'Arcachon, one of the most important expanses of wetlands remaining in France has been converted into a bird sanctuary, the **Parc Ornithologique du Teich** (daily 10am–6pm; W www.parc-ornithologique-du-teich.com; €6.80), one of only two in the country. There's no **accommodation** in Le Teich beyond a couple of **campsites**, but you can easily come here on a day-trip by train from Arcachon or Bordeaux.

Les Landes

Travelling south from Bordeaux by road or rail, you pass for what seems like hours through an unremitting, flat, sandy pine forest known as **Les Landes**. Containing nearly 10,000 square kilometres of trees and designated a *parc naturel régional* since 1970, it is, in the main, a region for outdoor pursuits rather than cultural enrichment.

Mont de Marsan

The administrative centre of Les Landes, **MONT DE MARSAN**, 100km south of Bordeaux and served by regular trains, makes a good base for exploring the inland part of the region. The **tourist office** on place du Général-Leclerc (Mon–Sat: July & Aug 9am–6pm; Sept–June 9am–12.30pm & 1.30–5pm; T 05.58.05.87.37, W www.tourisme-montdemarsan.com) can provide you with large-scale maps of walking and cycling routes within easy reach (€1.50 each). Another outdoor activity on offer is canoeing on one of the three rivers whose confluence is at Mont de Marsan: Canoe Loisir (T 05.58.45.62.21, E canoe-loisir@orange.fr) is based at Latrillette, just off the N134 to the west of town, and offers half-day trips for €12 per person.

The town itself boasts various medieval remnants, most notably a **twelfth-century keep** which now contains a collection of work by two local sculptors (daily except Tues 10am–noon & 2–6pm; free). By far the most attractive part of the centre is the **Parc Jean Rameau**, on the north bank of the river Douze, where immaculately kept lawns and blooming flowerbeds, interwoven with shady paths, make a great spot to spend a hot afternoon watching the locals play *boules*.

If you're lucky enough to be in the area at the right time in summer, you should definitely make the effort to see the **festival** for which Mont de Marsan is best known. Les Fêtes Madeleine (mid-July; ⓦ www.fetesmadeleine.fr) consist of a week of parades, sports and carnival atmosphere, when the town's Basque identity is most tangible, with flamenco dancing and bullfighting playing a major role.

Apart from this period, **accommodation** shouldn't be hard to come by. You could have a reasonably priced luxury stay at *Le Renaissance*, 1km from the centre at 225 avenue de Villeneuve (ⓣ 05.58.51.51.51, ⓦ www.le-renaissance .com; ➎) with its own outdoor swimming pool and restaurant serving high quality seafood on a gastronomic menu for €51. Various cheaper and more central options are also available, another good bet being *Le Richelieu*, 3 rue Wlérick (ⓣ 05.58.06.10.20, ⓔ le.richelieu@orange.fr; ➌), which has comfortable, fully equipped rooms in the heart of the town. For **eating**, good-value brasseries line rue Gambetta, while the *Crêperie la Floralie* on rue Wlérick serves a slice of Brittany for as little as €8.50 at lunchtime.

The Écomusée de Marquèze

At **SABRES**, 30km north of Mont de Marsan on the N134, you can take a special train to the excellent **Écomusée de Marquèze** (trains depart every 40min April–May & mid-Sept to Oct Mon–Sat 2–4.40pm, Sun 10am–4.40pm; June to mid-Sept daily 10am–5.20pm; €13 including entrance; ⓦ www.parc-landes-de-gascogne.fr), set up by the park authorities to illustrate the traditional *landais* way of life, when shepherds used to clomp around the scrub on long stilts.

Travel details

Trains

Angoulême to: Bordeaux (20 daily; 1hr–1hr 30min); Limoges (6 daily; 1hr 30min–2hr); Poitiers (23 daily; 40min–1hr 10min); Royan (4 daily; 2hr).
Bordeaux to: Angoulême (17 daily; 1hr–1hr 30min); Arcachon (frequently; 40–45min); Bayonne (10–12 daily; 1hr 40min–2hr 10min); Bergerac (6–10 daily; 50min–1hr 30min); Biarritz (6–12 daily; 2hr–2hr 45min); Brive (1–2 daily; 2hr 15min); La Rochelle (6–8 daily; 2hr 20min); Lourdes (4–6 daily; 2hr 30min–3hr); Marseille (5–6 daily; 6–7hr); Mont de Marsan (4 daily; 1hr 30min); Nice (4 daily; 9–10hr); Paris-Montparnasse (8–10 daily; 3hr–3hr 30min); Périgueux (10–12 daily; 1hr–1hr 25min); Pointe de Grave (5 daily; 1hr 45min); Poitiers (8–15 daily; 1hr 45min); Saintes (7–14 daily; 1hr 30min); Sarlat (3–4 daily; 3hr); St-Émilion (3–6 daily; 40 min); St-Jean-de-Luz (8–12 daily; 2hr–2hr 40min); Toulouse (10–17 daily; 2hr–2hr 40min).
La Rochelle to: Bordeaux (6 daily; 2hr 20min); La Roche-sur-Yon (5 daily; 1hr); Nantes (4 daily; 1hr 50min); Paris-Montparnasse (8 daily; 3hr 10min); Rochefort (12 daily; 20min); Saintes (9 daily; 50min–1hr).
La Roche-sur-Yon to: Les Sables-d'Olonne (4 daily; 30min).
Les Sables-d'Olonne to: Nantes (8 daily; 1hr 30min).
Poitiers to: Angoulême (17 daily; 1hr); Bordeaux (3–15 daily; 1hr 45min); Châtellerault (12 daily; 20min); Dax (2–3 daily; 3–4hr); Hendaye (3 daily; 4–5hr); Irun (2 daily; 4–5hr); La Rochelle (12 daily; 1hr 45min); Limoges (4–6 daily; 2hr); Niort (4–12 daily; 45min); Paris-Montparnasse (frequently; 1hr 45min); Surgères (10 daily; 1hr).

Royan to: Angoulême (3–4 daily; 2hr); Cognac (3–4 daily; 1hr); Saintes (3–4 daily; 30min).

Saintes to: Angoulême (9 daily; 1hr); Cognac (9 daily; 20min); Rochefort (9 daily; 30min).

Buses

Bordeaux to: Blaye (4–10 daily; 1hr 30min); Cap Ferret (4–10 daily; 2hr); Lacanau (2 daily; 1hr 15min); La Sauve-Majeure (2–4 daily; 40min); Margaux (2–8 daily; 45min–1hr); Pauillac (2–8 daily; 1hr–1 20min).

La Rochelle to: St-Martin de Ré (6–16 daily; 1hr).

La Roche-sur-Yon to: Noirmoutier en l'Ile (2–4 daily; 2hr).

Les Sables-d'Olonne to: Luçon (4 daily; 2hr); Nantes (4 daily; 5hr 30min).

Mont de Marsan to: Sabres (3 per week; 1hr).

Parthenay to: Airvault (several daily; 25min); Niort (8 daily; 50min); Thouars (at least 10 daily; 1hr).

Poitiers to: Châteauroux (3–5 daily; 3hr); Chauvigny (3–5 daily; 45min); Le Blanc (3–5 daily; 1hr 25min); Limoges (daily; 3hr); Parthenay (6–10 daily; 1hr 30min); Ruffec (daily; 2hr 30min); St-Savin (3–5 daily; 1hr).

Rochefort to: Château d'Oléron (3–6 daily; 1hr); La Fumée-Île d'Aix (6–8 daily; 30min); Marennes (3–6 daily; 40min).

Saintes to: Rochefort (2 daily; 1hr 20min); St-Pierre d'Oléron (2 daily; 2hr).

9

The Limousin, Dordogne and Lot

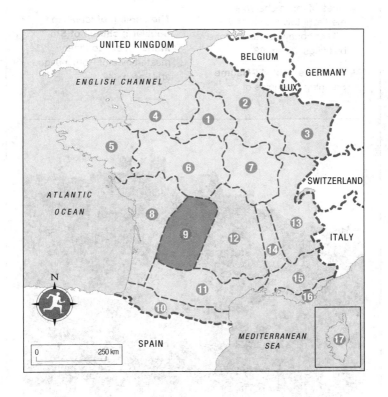

CHAPTER 9

Highlights

* **Cuisine** The Dordogne is the place to sample French country cooking at its best. See p.624

* **Monpazier** An almost perfectly preserved *bastide* (fortified town). See p.633

* **Sarlat** Wander the narrow lanes of this archetypal medieval town, with its *vielle ville* of honey-coloured stone buildings. See p.635

* **Grotte de Font-de-Gaume** Stunning examples of prehistoric cave-art, including the spectacular frieze of five bison. See p.639

* **Châteaux of Beynac and Castelnaud** Two of the region's most majestic castles eye each other across the Dordogne valley. See p.645

* **The carving of Isaiah in Souillac's church of Ste-Marie** An extraordinary masterpiece of Romanesque art. See p.647

▲ Bayeux and Castelnaud

9

The Limousin, Dordogne and Lot

The region covered in this chapter forms a rough oval bordered to the east by the uplands of the Massif Central and to the west by the Atlantic plains. It's the area which was most in dispute between the English and the French during the Hundred Years War, and has been most in demand among English visitors and second-home buyers in more recent times. Although it doesn't coincide exactly with either the modern French administrative boundaries or the old provinces of Périgord and Quercy, which constitute the core of the region, the land has a physical and geographical homogeneity thanks to its great rivers: the **Dordogne**, the **Lot** and the **Aveyron**, all of which drain westwards from the Massif Central into the mighty **Garonne**, which forms the southern limit covered by this chapter.

The wartime Resistance was very active in these out-of-the-way regions, and the roadsides are dotted with memorials to those killed in ambushes or shot in reprisals. There is also one monstrous monument to wartime atrocity: the ruined village of **Oradour-sur-Glane**, still as the Nazis left it after massacring the population and setting fire to the houses.

The landscapes themselves are surprisingly homogenous. From **Limoges** in the province of Limousin in the north to the Garonne valley in the south, the country is gently hilly, full of lush hidden valleys and miles of woodland, mainly oak. The northerly **Limousin** is slightly greener and wetter, the south more open and arid. But you can travel a long way without seeing a radical shift, except in the uplands of the **Plateau de Millevaches**, where the rivers plunge into gorges and the woods are beech, chestnut and conifer plantations. The other characteristic landscape is the *causses*, the dry scrubby limestone plateaux like the **Causse de Gramat** between the Lot and Dordogne and the **Causse de Limogne** between the Lot and Aveyron. Where the rivers have cut their way through the limestone, the valleys are walled with overhanging cliffs, riddled with fissures, underground streams and caves. And in these caves – especially in the valley of the Vézère around **Les Eyzies** – is some of the most awe-inspiring **prehistoric art** to be found anywhere in the world.

The other great artistic legacy of the area is the Romanesque sculpture, most notably adorning the churches at **Souillac** and **Beaulieu-sur-Dordogne**, but all modelled on the supreme example of the cloister of St-Pierre in **Moissac**. And the dearth of luxurious châteaux is compensated for by the numerous

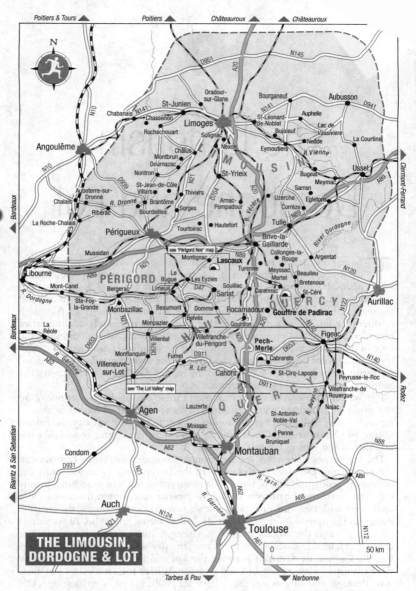

Map labels:

Poitiers & Tours · Poitiers · Châteauroux · Châteauroux

N

N145

D951

A20

N141

Oradour-sur-Glane

Bourganeuf

Aubusson

D941

St-Junien

N141

St-Léonard-de-Noblat

Auphelle

Lac de Vassivière

La Courtine

Chabanais · Chassenon

Rochechouart

Limoges

Solignac

Bujaleuf

Nedde

R.Vienne

Nexon

Angoulême

N10

N141

Châlus

Montbrun

Dournazac

Nontron

St-Jean-de-Côle

Villars

Thiviers

St-Yrieix

N21

Arnac-Pompadour

R. Vézère

Eymoutiers

Bugeat

Sarran

Meymac

Ussel

A89

Clermont-Ferrand

D79

Aubeterre-sur-Dronne

Chalais

R. Dronne

Brantôme

Bourdeilles

Sorges

Uzerche

Corrèze

Egletons

Riberac

La Roche-Chalais

Périgueux

Tourtoirac

Hautefort

Tulle

N89

N120

Mussidan

N21

see 'Périgord Noir' map

Montignac

Lascaux

Brive-la-Gaillarde

Collonges-la-Rouge

Argentat

River Dordogne

Libourne

A89

PÉRIGORD

Le Bugue

Les Eyzies

Turenne

Meyssac

Martel

Beaulieu

N120

Mont-Caret

R. Dordogne

Bergerac

Limeuil

D47

Souillac

Carennac

St-Céré

Bretenoux

Aurillac

Ste-Foy-la-Grande

Monbazillac

Beaumont

Domme

Sarlat

Rocamadour

Gouffre de Padirac

QUERCY

N122

La Réole

Monpazier

Belvès

HAUT

Gourdon

D20

N140

Figeac

D933

Monflanquin

Villeréal

Fumel

Villefranche-du-Périgord

D676

D911

Pech-Merle

D653

N140

R. Garonne

A62

Villeneuve-sur-Lot

see 'The Lot Valley' map

R. Lot

Cahors

Cabrerets

St-Cirq-Lapopie

Peyrusse-le-Roc

Rodez

Biarritz & San Sebastian

Agen

Lauzerte

D911

QUERC

A20

R. Aveyron

Villefranche-de-Rouergue

Najac

Moissac

St-Antonin-Noble-Val

N88

Condom

D931

N21

Penne

Bruniquel

Montauban

Albi

Auch

N21

A62

R. Tarn

N124

R. Garonne

A68

Toulouse

A61

N112

THE LIMOUSIN, DORDOGNE & LOT

0   50 km

Tarbes & Pau · Narbonne

splendid **fortresses** of purely military design, such as **Bonaguil**, **Najac**, **Biron**, **Beynac** and **Castelnaud**.

There are no great cities in the area: its charm lies in the landscapes and the dozens of harmonious small towns and villages. Some, like **Sarlat** and **Rocamadour**, are so well known that they are overrun with tourists. Others, like **Figeac**, **Villefranche-de-Rouergue**, **Gourdon**, **Montauban**, **Monflanquin** and the many *bastides* (fortified towns) that pepper the area between the

Lot and Dordogne, boast no single notable sight but are perfect organic ensembles.

For **getting around**, all the region's main towns are linked by rail and/or bus services, while a fair number of smaller places have sporadic public transport links. To really make the most of the area, though, particularly the Plateau de Millevaches, you'll need your own wheels.

The Limousin

The **Limousin** – the country around **Limoges** – is hilly, wooded, wet and not particularly fertile: ideal pasture for the famous Limousin breed of cattle. This is herdsman's country, from where the widespread use of the shepherd's cape known as a *limousine* gave its name to the big, wraparound, covered twentieth-century car.

The modern Limousin region stretches south to the Dordogne valley to include **Brive, Uzerche and Turenne.** But while these places, together with Limoges itself, are not without interest, the star of the show is the countryside – especially in the east on the **Plateau de Millevaches,** between **Eymoutiers** and **Meymac.** Walkers, cyclists and other outdoor sports enthusiasts are well catered for and there are plenty of small hotels, *gîtes* and campsites to accommodate the wanderer. Although the region is remote and sparsely populated, a mountain rail line still survives, connecting Limoges and Ussel.

Limoges

LIMOGES is a pleasant city, if not one that calls for a long stay. Its main draw is the craft industries that made the city a household name: enamel in the Middle Ages and, since the eighteenth century, china, including some of the finest ever produced. If these appeal, then the city's unique museum collections – and its Gothic cathedral – will reward a visit. But it has to be said that the porcelain industry today seems a spent tradition, hard hit by recession and changing tastes among the wealthy. The local *kaolin* (china clay) mines that gave Limoges china its special quality are exhausted, and the workshops survive mainly on the tourist trade, though some are now successfully diversifying into high-tech ceramics.

Arrival and information

Limoges' magnificent Art Deco **gare des Bénédictins** and neighbouring **gare routière** (☎05.55.45.10.72) lie slightly northeast of centre along avenue de-Gaulle, where you'll find **car rental** at ADA at no. 27 (☎05.55.79.61.12). The **tourist office** is on place Wilson (May–15 June & 15 Sept to 5 Oct Mon–Sat 9am–7pm; 16 June to 14 Sept Mon–Sat 9am–7pm, Sun 10am–5.30pm; Oct–April Mon–Sat 9.30am–6pm; ☎05.55.34.46.87, ⓦ www.tourismelimoges .com).You can get a cheap, fast **internet** connection at *Cybernaute Wilson*, place Wilson (Mon-Thur 8am–4am, Fri 8am–Mon 4am non-stop; €2.60 per hour).

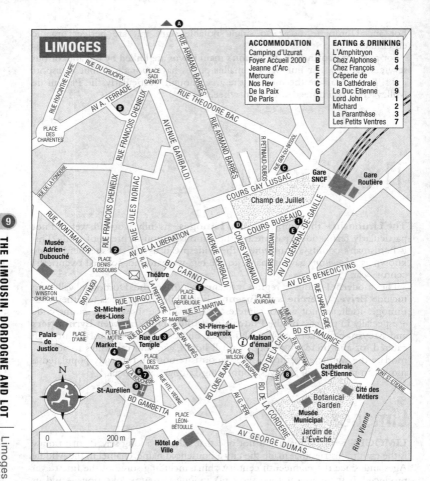

ACCOMMODATION

Camping d'Uzurat	A
Foyer Accueil 2000	B
Jeanne d'Arc	E
Mercure	F
Nos Rev	C
De la Paix	G
De Paris	D

EATING & DRINKING

L'Amphitryon	6
Chez Alphonse	5
Chez François	4
Crêperie de la Cathédrale	8
Le Duc Etienne	9
Lord John	1
Michard	2
La Paranthèse	3
Les Petits Ventres	7

Accommodation

Hotels

Jeanne d'Arc 17 av de-Gaulle ☎05.55.77.67.77, ⊛www.hoteljeannedarc-limoges.fr. The elegant entrance, tastefully decorated rooms and grand breakfast hall make this a more appealing option than the *Mercure* (below). Rooms with showers are on the small side, however – better to upgrade to one with a bath, and overlooking the interior courtyard. ➍

Mercure place de la République ☎05.55.34.65.30, ⊛www.mercure.com. The only hotel in the old quarter, this is a surprisingly unattractive, concrete affair, though the rooms are a decent size and boast three-star facilities, including room-service and wi-fi. More expensive rooms have a balcony looking over the square. ➎

Nos Rev 16 rue du Général-du-Bessol ☎05.55.77.41.43, ⊛www.hotelnos-rev.com. Contemporary decor, with strong reds and lime greens, make this tiny, recently renovated hotel stand out as a mid-range option. It's set back off a quietish street near the station. ➌

De la Paix 25 place Jourdan ☎05.55.34.36.00, ⊕05.55.32.37.06. A wonderful old hotel, doubling as a museum of gramophones, which decorate the breakfast room in all shapes and sizes. Bedrooms are not quite so characterful, but large and nicely furnished for the price. The cheapest have no en-suite toilet. ➋–➌

De Paris 5 cours Vergniaud ☎05.55.77. 56.96, ✉hoteldeparis4@orange.fr. You'll need to book ahead for this well-located budget hotel, where good size rooms – the cheapest with washbasin only – make up for the rather worn furnishings. ❶

Hostel and campsite

Foyer Accueil 2000 20 rue Encombe-Vineuse ☎ 05.55.77.63.97, ✉ fjt.accueil-2000@orange.fr. A

hike out on the north side of town, but you still need to book well ahead. €18 per night includes breakfast, and there is also a communal kitchen. **Camping d'Uzurat** ☎ 05.55.38.49.43, ✆ www .campinglimoges.fr. About 5km out of town in Limoges' northern suburbs; take bus #20 from the *gare SNCF*. March–Oct.

The City

The **Cathédrale St-Étienne**, a landmark for miles around, was begun in 1273 and modelled on the cathedral of Amiens, though only the choir, completed in the early thirteenth century, is pure Gothic. The rest of the building was added piecemeal over the centuries, the western part of the nave not until 1876. The most striking external feature is the sixteenth-century facade of the north transept, built in full flamboyant style with elongated arches, clusters of pinnacles and delicate tracery in window and gallery. At the west end of the nave, the tower, erected on a Romanesque base that had to be massively reinforced to bear the weight, has octagonal upper storeys, in common with most churches in the region. It once stood as a separate campanile and probably looked the better for it. Inside, the effects are much more pleasing. The sense of soaring height is accentuated by all the upward-reaching lines of the pillars, the net of vaulting ribs, the curling, flame-like lines, and, as you look down the nave, by the narrower and more pointed arches of the choir.

The best of the city's museums – with its showpiece collections of enamelware dating back to the twelfth century – is the **Musée Municipal de l'Évêché** in the old bishop's palace next to the cathedral. At the time of writing, the museum was closed for long-term renovation though due to reopen in 2010 with twice the amount of exhibition space, charting the progression from the simple, sober, Byzantine-influenced *champlevé* (copper filled with enamel), to seventeenth- and eighteenth-century work using a far greater range of colours and indulging in elaborate, virtuoso portraiture. Meanwhile, contemporary enamel work is on display at the nearby **Maison d'émail** at 18 boulevard de la Cité (Tues–Sat 10.30am–6.30pm; €2; ✆ www.maison-email.fr), which also runs introductory half-day classes (€40) if you'd like to try your hand.

Behind the cathedral, the well-laid-out **botanical garden** (daily sunrise to sunset; free) is an inviting prospect, descending gracefully towards the River Vienne. In the garden's northern corner an old refectory now houses the excellent **Cité des Métiers et des Arts** (Easter–May Wed, Sat & Sun 2–6pm; June, Sept & Oct daily 2–6pm; July & Aug daily 10.30am–1pm & 2.30–7pm; €5; ✆ www.cma-limoges.com) displaying pieces – mostly carpentry – by France's top crafts-guild members.

The best area for a relaxed stroll is the partly renovated **old quarter** of the town, over to the west, where you'll find rue de la Boucherie, for a thousand years the domain of the butchers' guild. The dark, cluttered **chapel of St-Aurélien** belongs to them, while one of their former shophouses makes an interesting little museum, the **Maison de la Boucherie**, at no. 36 (July–Sept daily 10am–1pm & 2–7pm; free). At the top of the street, the **market hall** is in place de la Motte and, to the right, partly hidden by adjoining houses, the fourteenth- and fifteenth-century **church of St-Michel-des-Lions**, named after the two badly weathered Celtic lions guarding the south door and topped by one of the best towers and spires in the region. The inside is dark and atmospheric, with two beautiful, densely coloured fifteenth-century windows either side of the choir.

Further east, the concrete swathes of place de la République conceal the fourth-century **crypt** of the long-vanished **Abbey of St-Martial** (July–Sept daily 9.30am–12pm & 2.30–7pm; free), containing the saint's massive sarcophagus, discovered during building work in the 1960s. Nearby is the **church of St-Pierre-du-Queyroix** under another typically Limousin belfry. The interior, partly twelfth-century, has the same slightly pink granite glow as the cathedral. There's more fine stained glass here, including an eye-catching window at the end of the south aisle depicting the Dormition of the Virgin, signed by the great enamel artist Jean Pénicault in 1510.

Limoges' renowned **porcelain** is best displayed in the **Musée Adrien-Dubouché** (daily except Tues 10am–12.25pm & 2–5.40pm; €4.50; Ⓦwww .musee-adriendubouche.fr), west of the old quarter on place Winston-Churchill. The well-presented collection is more interesting than you might expect, including samples of the local product and china displays from around the world, as well as various pieces from celebrity services ordered for the likes of Abraham Lincoln, Queen Elizabeth and sundry French royals.

Eating, drinking and festivals

Limoges has an abundance of good and not too expensive **places to eat**. For **drinks** at any time of the day, one option is the not very attractive place de la République; a slightly nicer choice is lively place Denis-Dussoubs, a short walk further west, where you'll find fine beers on tap at the *Michard* micro-brewery (closed Sun). *Le Duc Etienne*, at 19 rue de la Boucherie, is a relaxed, wood-timbered bar in the old quarter, while over on the other side of town the *Lord John* is a welcoming, British-style pub with concerts some weekends.

Restaurants

L'Amphitryon 26 rue de la Boucherie ☏05.55.33.36.39. There's no better place for a real treat of subtle and sophisticated cuisine, well deserving its Michelin star. You'll be offered a good choice of seafood as well as beef, veal and other local fare. The lunchtime *formule* is just €12, while three-course menus start at €25, or €42 in the evening. Closed Sun, Mon, two weeks in Aug/Sept & one week in Jan, March & May.

Chez Alphonse 5 place de la Motte ☏05.55.34.34.14. Welcoming and popular brasserie, complete with red-check cloths and bustling waiters, which specializes in local dishes such as pig's trotters and sweetbreads, plus a broader range of daily specials. Around €30 a head for three courses. Closed Sun.

🏃 **Chez François** place de la Motte. For a good-value lunch and a lively atmosphere, head straight to the central market hall to join the locals round communal tables. Colourful pictures of market life adorn the walls. Menus €10 & €17. If it's full, try the *Bistrot d'Olivier* next door. Closed Sun & Aug.

Crêperie de la Cathédrale 3 rue Haute-Cité. One of a cluster of brasseries with outside seating on this attractive pedestrian street by the cathedral. It's good value at lunchtime, with a *plat du jour*, dessert and drink for €10.

La Paranthèse cour du Temple. Tucked away in an attractive courtyard off rue du Temple, this is a great place for a light lunch or tea break. They offer various *formules* including a drink and one of their scrumptious deserts from €13.50, as well as good, fresh salads and a *plat du jour*. Closed evenings & Sun.

Les Petits Ventres 20 rue de la Boucherie ☏05.55.34.22.90. This surprisingly elegant restaurant in a timbered, seventeenth-century building will delight lovers of brain, brawn, tongue and other unmentionable cuts – though they also do plenty of more everyday dishes and even a vegetarian platter. You'll pay €14.50 for a lunchtime *formule*, while three-course menus start at €23.50. Closed Sun & Mon.

Festivals

In late September, there's an interesting and important gathering of writers, dramatists and musicians from other French-speaking countries at the **Festival**

International des Francophonies (Ⓦwww.lesfrancophonies.com). For one week in mid-August brass instruments take pride of place in the **Cuivres en Fête** music festival (Ⓦwww.epsilon.asso.fr), while gourmets of a certain persuasion should make sure their visit coincides with the third Friday in October for the **Frairie des Petits Ventres food fair**, when the entire population turns out to gorge on everything from pig's trotters to sheep's testicles in the rue de la Boucherie. Otherwise, there's **Urbaka**, a festival of street theatre held at the end of June (Ⓦwww.urbaka.com), and the **Danse Emoi** contemporary dance festival every two years in January, the next being in 2009 and 2011.

Around Limoges

There's a clutch of villages within a day's reach of Limoges. A route linking places of interest on the south bank of the Vienne, like the **châteaux** of **Rochechouart**, **Châlus**, **Montbrun** and **Nexon** is detailed in the *Route Richard-Coeur-de-Lion* leaflet (available at local tourist offices), so called because of its associations with the English king. The route also takes close to **Solignac**'s abbey church and the **Château de Châlucet**, now reduced to atmospheric ruins. North of the Vienne, the charred walls of **Oradour-sur-Glane** stand testimony to a World War II massacre, while east of Limoges, beyond the attractive market town of **St-Léonard-de-Noblat**, the master weavers of **Aubusson** have been producing tapestries for more than six hundred years, and carpets since 1743.

Visiting all these places really requires a car, but some are accessible by a combination of public transport, walking and patient hitching.

Oradour-sur-Glane

Twenty-five kilometres northwest of Limoges, the village of **ORADOUR-SUR-GLANE** stands just as the soldiers of the SS left it on June 10, 1944, after killing 642 of the inhabitants in reprisal for attacks by French *maquisards*. The entire village has been preserved both as a shrine and a chilling reminder of human brutality.

Before entering the village, the **Centre de la Mémoire**, immediately southeast of Oradour on the Limoges road (daily: Feb & Nov to 15 Dec 9am–5pm; March to 15 May & 16 Sept to Oct 9am–6pm; 15 May to 15 Sept 9am–7pm; closed 16 Dec–Jan; entry to village free, exhibition €7.50; Ⓦwww.oradour.org), sets the historical context and attempts to expalain how – and why – such acts of brutality took place.

From here an underground passage leads into the village itself, where a sign admonishes *Souviens-toi* ("Remember"), and the main street leads past roofless houses gutted by fire. Telephone poles, iron bedsteads and gutters are fixed in tormented attitudes where the fire's heat left them; prewar cars rust in the garages; cooking pots hang over empty grates; last year's grapes hang wizened on a vine whose trellis has long rotted away.

To the north of the village a dolmen-like slab on a shallow plinth covers a crypt containing relics of the dead, and the awful list of names, while to the southeast, by the stream, stands the church where the women and children – five hundred of them – were burnt to death.

There are **buses** from Limoges to Oradour, or alternatively you can take the train to **ST-JUNIEN** and pick up a bus there. The *Relais de Comodoliac*, 22 avenue Sadi-Carnot (℡05.55.02.27.26, Ⓦwww.comodoliac.com; ❸), about

1km northwest of the train station, with a garden and a popular restaurant (menus €16–37), makes a decent **place to stay** in St-Junien. There's also a **hostel**, 13 rue de St-Amand (ⓣ&ⓕ05.55.02.22.79), in an old abbey 500m further west along rue Henriette-Perucaud.

Rochechouart

ROCHECHOUART, a beautiful little walled town roughly 45km west of Limoges, has two claims to fame. Two hundred million years ago it was the site of one of the largest **meteorites** ever to hit earth, a monster 1.5km in diameter and weighing some 6 billion tonnes. The traces of this cosmic calamity still attract the curiosity of astronomers, though the only evidence that a layman might notice is the unusual-looking breccia stone many of the region's older buildings are made of: the squashed, shattered, heat-transformed and reconstituted result of the collision. A small museum in town, the **Espace Météorite**, 16 rue Jean Parvy (mid-June to mid-Oct & school holidays Mon–Fri 10am–noon & 2–6pm, Sat & Sun 2–6pm; rest of year Mon–Fri 2–6pm, though phone to be sure; €4; ⓣ05.55.03.02.70, ⓦwww.espacemeteorite.com), uncovers the history of the meteorite with interactive displays, models and videos.

One building using the stone from the impact is Rochechouart's other source of pride: the handsome **château** that stands at the town's edge. It started life as a rough fortress before 1000 AD, was "modernized" in the thirteenth century (the sawn-off keep and entrance survive from this period) and embellished with Renaissance additions in the fifteenth. Until it was acquired as the *mairie* in 1832, it had belonged to the de Rochechouart family for 800 years. Today it houses not only the town hall, but also the very well-regarded **Musée Départemental d'Art Contemporain** (daily except Tues: March–Sept 10am–12.30pm & 1.30–6pm; Oct to mid-Dec 10am–12.30pm & 2–5pm; closed mid-Dec to Feb; €4.60), with an important collection of works by the Dadaist Raoul Haussmanh, who died in Limoges in 1971. In another room decorated with its original sixteenth-century frescoes of the Labours of Hercules, the British artist Richard Long has created a special installation of white stones, while in the garden Guiseppe Penone's metal sculpture grapples with a tree.

The Rochechouart **tourist office** is at 6 rue Victor-Hugo (July & Aug daily 10am–noon & 2.30–6.30pm; Sept–June Mon–Sat 10am–noon & 2–5pm; ⓣ05.55.03.72.73). Should you wish to **stay**, there are two well-priced **hotels** on place Octave-Marquet: the *Hôtel de France* (ⓣ05.55.03.77.40, ⓦwww .hoteldefrance-rochechouart.fr; ❷), and the slightly smarter *Météorite* (ⓣ05.55.02.86.80, ⓦwww .hotel-lameteorite.fr; ❸; menus from €12).

Châlus and Nexon

The small town of **CHÂLUS**, 35km southwest of Limoges, is dominated by the ruined **Château de Châlus-Chabrol** (not open to the public), where in 1199 Richard the Lionheart was mortally wounded by an archer shooting from the still-extant keep. Richard, son of Eleanor of Aquitaine and as much French as English, was campaigning to suppress a local rebellion against English rule. Upon capturing the castle, Richard – by now on his deathbed – ordered all the rebels hanged save the archer, whom he pardoned. It was a short-lived reprieve; as soon as Richard was dead, the archer was flayed alive by the captain of the English troops.

Of several other castles around Châlus, the most rewarding is the medieval **Château de Montbrun** (mid-June to mid-Sept guided visits daily except

Thurs 2–6pm; €10; ⓦwww.montbrun.com), 8km to the southwest. The château, now a private home, has been beautifully restored and furnished, though its best attribute is perhaps its fairy-tale lakeside location – even more spectacular when floodlit at night.

Eighteen kilometres east in the village of **NEXON** you'll find a fine, heavily restored seventeenth-century **château** (now the *mairie*), whose gardens now host a summer **festival of circus arts** and occasional performances during the rest of the year (ⓦwww.cirquenexon.com).

Châlucet and Solignac

A dozen kilometres south of Limoges in the lovely wooded valley of the Briance, the Château de Châlucet and the church of **SOLIGNAC** make the most attractive day's outing from the city. There are **buses** and **trains** to Solignac-Le Vigen station, 1km away on the Limoges–Brive line, and occasional buses to Solignac itself, but beware that no combination allows you to see Solignac and get back in one day. There is, however, a comfortable **hotel** opposite the church, *Le St-Éloi* (ⓣ05.55.00.44.52, ⓦwww.lesainteloi.fr; ❸; closed three weeks in Jan, one in June & one in Sept; restaurant from €25; closed Sat lunch, Sun evening & Mon).

Approaching from Le Vigen you see Solignac's Romanesque **abbey church** ahead of you, simple and sturdy, with the tiled roofs of its octagonal apse and neat little brood of radiating chapels. The twelfth-century facade has little sculpture, as the granite is too hard to permit intricate carving. Inside it's beautiful, with a flight of steps leading down into the nave with a dramatic view of the length of the church. There are no aisles, just a single space roofed with three big domes – an absolutely plain Latin cross in design.

The **Château de Châlucet** is a good 5km up the valley of the Briance in the other direction. At the highest point of the climb there is a dramatic view across the valley to the romantic, ruined keep of the castle, rising above the woods. Built in the twelfth century, the château was in English hands during the Hundred Years War and, in the lawless aftermath, became the lair of a notorious local brigand, Perrot le Béarnais. Dismantled in 1593 for harbouring Protestants, it is now owned by the local authorities who are in the middle of major restoration works. It's still possible to visit, though you are restricted to safe areas along fenced-off paths. You can borrow an explanatory guide from the visitors' centre (daily: mid-March to mid-June & mid-Sept to mid-Nov 9.30am–12.30pm & 1.30–6pm; mid-June to mid-Sept 11am–6.30pm) on the path up to the ruins.

St-Léonard-de-Noblat

ST-LÉONARD-DE-NOBLAT, 20 minutes by train from Limoges or 30 minutes by bus, is an appealing little market town of narrow streets and medieval houses with jutting eaves and corbelled turrets. There's a very lovely eleventh- and twelfth-century church, with a six-storey tower, high dome and simple, barrel-vaulted interior – the whole in grey granite. A couple of kilometres northwest, on the banks of the Vienne, demonstrations of papermaking and printing are on offer at a lovingly restored fifteenth-century paper mill, the **Moulin du Got** (guided visits: May, June, Sept & school holidays Tues–Sat 2.30pm & 4pm; July & Aug Tues–Fri 10.30am, 2.15–5.15pm, Sat 2.15–5.15pm; rest of year Wed & Sat 2.30pm & 4pm; closed Jan; €6.50; ⓦwww.moulindugot.com). In the town centre, the **HistoRail museum**, on rue de Beaufort (July & Aug Mon–Fri 10am–noon & 2.30–7pm; €4.50; ⓦwww.historail.com), is also good fun, with some excellent, working model railways.

The **tourist office** on place du Champs-de-Mars (April–June & Sept Mon–Sat 10am–12.30pm & 2.30–5.30pm; July & Aug Mon–Sat 10am–1pm & 2.30–6.30pm, Sun 10am–12.30pm; Oct–March Mon–Sat 10am–12.30pm & 2.30–5pm; ☎05.55.56.25.06, ⓦwww.otsi-noblat.fr) offers ideas for local walks and will point you to *chambre d'hôte* possibilities round about. A good **place to stay** or **eat** is the *Relais St-Jacques* on the boulevard encircling the old town (☎05.55.56.00.25, ⓔle.relais.st.jacques@orange.fr; ❷; closed Sun evening & Mon lunchtime Oct–May; restaurant from €15), and you can also **eat** well just round the corner at the welcoming *Le Gay Lussac*, 18 rue Victor-Hugo, which offers great-value menus featuring local and seasonal produce (weekday lunches from €11.50, weekends & evenings from €18). There's a spruce **campsite**, the *Camping de Beaufort* (☎05.55.56.02.79, ⓦwww.campingdebeaufort.com; April–Sept), beside the river a couple of kilometres out of town on the D39.

Aubusson

AUBUSSON is 90km east of Limoges and served by regular buses and trains. A neat grey-stone town in the bottom of a ravine formed by the River Creuse, it's of no great interest in itself. What makes it unique is its reputation as a centre for weaving **tapestries**, second only to the Gobelins in Paris. The **Musée Départemental de la Tapisserie**, in avenue des Lissiers (July & Aug Mon & Wed–Sun 10am–6pm, Tues 2–6pm; Sept–June daily except Tues 9.30am–noon & 2–6pm; €5), traces the history of Aubusson tapestries over six centuries, up to the modern-day works of Jean Lurçat (see p.652). The **Maison du Tapissier** next to the tourist office (same hours as tourist office; €5) is also worth a quick look for its overview of weaving techniques and local history displayed in the sixteenth-century home of a master weaver.

For information about further exhibitions and workshop visits ask at the **tourist office** in rue Vieille (March–June, Sept & Oct Mon–Sat 9.30am–12.30pm & 2–6pm; July & Aug daily 9.30am–6pm; Nov–Feb Mon–Sat 10am–12.30pm & 3–5pm; ☎05.55.66.32.12, ⓦwww.ot-aubusson.fr). As for **hotels**, a reliable budget place is the *Chapitre*, on the main Grande-Rue above a bar at no. 53 (☎05.55.66.18.54, ⓦwww.hotellechapitre.com; ❶). For something smarter, try *Le France* at 6 rue des Déportés (☎05.55.66.10.22, ⓦwww.aubussonlefrance.com; ❸), with elegant rooms and a decent formal **restaurant** (menus from €20) plus a cheaper brasserie open for lunch only (closed Sun; *plat du jour* €9). The town's *La Croix Blanche* **campsite** (☎05.55.66.18.00, ⓔcamping23@orange.fr; April–Sept), is by the river on the Felletin road.

The Plateau de Millevaches

Millevaches, the plateau of a thousand springs, is undulating upland country 800–900m in altitude, on the northern edge of the Massif Central, with a wild and sparsely populated landscape and villages few and far between. Those that do exist appear small, grey and sturdy, inured to the buffeting of upland weather. It's a magnificent country of conifer plantations and natural woodland – of beech, birch and chestnut – interspersed with reed-fringed tarns, man-made lakes and pasture grazed by sheep and cows, much of it now designated a **natural regional park** (ⓦwww.pnr-millevaches.fr). It's an area to walk or cycle in, or at least savour at a gentle pace, stopping in the attractive, country inns scattered across the plateau.

The small towns, like **Eymoutiers** and **Meymac**, have a primitive architectural beauty and an old-world charm largely untouched by modern development. Not that the modern world has passed the area by. Near Eymoutiers, the **Lac de Vassivière** offers all sorts of sports activities and a beautiful setting for a contemporary art museum. Obviously, getting around by car is easiest, but there is access by public transport. Both Eymoutiers and Meymac lie on a cross-country rail line connecting Limoges and Ussel, while Meymac and Egletons are on the main line between Brive and Clermont-Ferrand.

Eymoutiers and around

EYMOUTIERS, 45km southeast of Limoges, is an upland town of tall, narrow stone houses crowding round a much-altered Romanesque **church**. Not interesting enough for a prolonged stay, it nonetheless makes an agreeable stopover, especially for campers, as it has a simple but magnificently sited municipal **campsite**, the *St-Pierre Château* (☎05.55.69.27.81, ⓦwww .mairie-eymoutiers.fr; June–Sept), on a hill 2km southeast of town off the Bugeat road. If you prefer a **hotel**, you'll find simple rooms and hearty food at *Le Ranch des Lacs* (☎05.55.69.15.66, ⓦwww.le-ranch-des-lacs.com; ❶; menus €12–35; closed 24 Dec to 26 Jan) about 7km northeast of Eymoutiers, signposted off the Bujaleuf road.

Eymoutiers is also the jumping-off point for the **Lac de Vassivière**. This 1000-hectare man-made lake, with 45km of indented shoreline, provides some lovely spots for walking and cycling – and no fewer than five **campsites**. In summer, the lake is also a popular destination for watersports enthusiasts, with opportunities for sailing, windsurfing and water skiing, among other activities. An island, accessed by a causeway, provides a wonderful home for the **Centre International d'Art et du Paysage** (July & Aug daily 11am–7pm; Sept–June Tues–Fri 2–6pm, Sat & Sun 11am–1pm & 2–6pm; exhibition hall €3; ⓦwww .ciapiledevassiviere.com), a contemporary art centre where many of the pieces lie scattered among the trees. There's also a hall hosting temporary exhibitions and a **café** where you can get light meals while admiring the views (April–Sept daily; Oct–March Sat & Sun only). The main **information** centre for the lake is the Maison de Vassivière (July & Aug daily 9am–1pm & 2–6pm; Sept–June Mon–Fri 9am–1pm & 2–5pm; ☎05.55.69.76.70, ⓦwww.vassiviere.com), at **AUPHELLE**, on the western shore.

Ten kilometres southwest of Eymoutiers, the small village of **NEDDE** nestles beside the Vienne river. The reason for coming here, particularly if you've got children in tow, is the **Cité des Insectes** (July & Aug daily 10.30am–7pm; April–Oct & school holidays Wed, Sat & Sun 10.30am–7pm; closed Nov–March; €6.50; ⓦwww.lacitedesinsectes.com), a couple of kilometres to the south. Exhibits trace the history of entomology and delve into their secret lives, ending with living examples of weird and wonderful insects from around the world. Nedde also boasts a welcoming little **hotel** and **crêperie**, *Le Verrou* (☎05.55.69.98.04, ⓦwww.leverrou.com; ❷–❸), where the more expensive rooms have been tastefully restored. Alternatively, head 15km further southwest to **TARNAC**, another mountain village, where the *Hôtel des Voyageurs* (☎05.55.95.53.12, ⓦwww.hotel-voyageurs-correze.com; ❷; closed mid-Dec to mid-Jan, last week in Feb and last week in June) is a simple but appealingly old-fashioned, country **hotel** with a good traditional **restaurant** to match (menus €16–30; closed Sun evening & Mon).

THE LIMOUSIN, DORDOGNE AND LOT | The Plateau de Millevaches

Meymac and around

Pepper-pot turrets and steep slate roofs adorn the ancient grey houses of **MEYMAC**, 50km southeast of Eymoutiers, on the southern fringes of the plateau. The village is packed tightly around its Romanesque church and the Benedictine **abbey**, whose foundation a thousand years ago brought the town into being. Part of the abbey now houses the innovative **Centre National d'Art Contemporain** (daily except Mon: July & Aug 10am–1pm & 2–7pm; Sept–June 2–6pm; closed Jan; €4), featuring changing exhibitions of young, local artists as well as big-name retrospectives. It's also worth popping into the adjacent **Musée de la Fondation Marius Vazeilles** (May to 14 June & 16 Sept to Oct Wed & Fri–Sun 2.30–6pm; 15 June to 15 Sept daily 3–7pm; Nov daily except Tues 3–5pm; closed Dec–April; €2.80) to learn about the history and traditions of the plateau.

Grande-Rue, the main street, ends in steps that climb past the round **bell tower**, the town's landmark, to a pretty square in front of the town hall. Here you'll also find the **tourist office** (July to 15 Sept daily 10am–12.30pm & 2–6.30pm; 16 Sept to June Mon–Fri 10am–noon & 2–4.30pm; ☎05.55.95.18.43, Ⓦwww.ot-meymac.visite.org), which has plenty of information on hiking among other things.

There's a reasonable two-star **hotel** on the main road, the *Limousin*, 76 avenue Limousine (☎05.55.46.12.11, Ⓦwww.logis-de-france.fr; ❷; closed Sat from Sept to June & Sun evening all year; restaurant from €11.50). Alternatively, book ahead for one of the four rooms in a sixteenth-century tower at *Chez Françoise*, up the hill from the tourist office (☎05.55.95.10.63, Ⓕ05.55.95.40.22; ❸). They also run a well-respected **restaurant** serving local specialities, with a vast wine list (closed Sun evening & Mon; menus €15–35). Finally, there's a municipal **campsite**, *La Garenne* (☎05.55.95.22.80, Ⓔmairie.meymac @orange.fr; mid-May to mid-Sept), close at hand on the Sornac road.

Egletons and around

Some 20km southwest of Meymac, the ancient market town of **EGLETONS** flourished during medieval times under the powerful dukes of Ventadour, whose twelfth-century **château** is now a magnificent ruin on a narrow spur about 6km southeast. The celebrated troubadour Bernard de Ventadour was born here, child of a castle servant. The site is now undergoing lengthy restoration work; you can get quite close but the ruins themselves are fenced off.

By way of contrast, the area's foremost sight is the **Musée du Président Jacques Chirac** (Feb–Dec daily 10am–12.30pm & 1.30–6pm; closed Jan; €4; Ⓦwww.museepresidentjchirac.fr) at **SARRAN**, where the Chirac's own a château, deep in the country around 10km west of Egletons. This quirky, ultra-modern and ever-expanding museum is a showcase of the gifts given to the president during state visits and other official duties. Look out for the natty cowboy boots (from then US President Bill Clinton), the stuffed coelacanth (a gift from the Comoros Islands for the man who has everything) and the delightful South African chess set in which the pieces are caricatures of Mandela, de Klerk, Archbishop Tutu and other famous personalities. Downstairs is a treasure-trove of some 1300 gifts from the archives, with interactive screens offering hours of fun finding who gave what outrageous gift.

Egletons has a clutch of **hotels**, of which the smartest is the *Ibis* on the main road 1.5km east of town (☎05.55.93.25.16, Ⓦwww.ibishotel.com; ❸; restaurant from €17). A simpler option is the *Borie* in the centre of town on avenue Charles-de-Gaulle (☎05.55.93.12.00, Ⓦwww.hotelrestaurantborie.com; ❷;

restaurant from €11.50, closed Sun evening & last two weeks in Aug). When it comes to **eating**, try *Le Jardin de Ventadour*, immediately north of the centre on place du Marchadial, which serves a range of imaginative dishes (closed Tues; menus €20–52).

Brive-la-Gaillarde and around

BRIVE-LA-GAILLARDE is a major rail junction and the nearest thing to an industrial centre for miles around. Nevertheless, it has an attractive old centre and makes an agreeable base for exploring the Corrèze *département* and its beautiful villages, as well as the upper reaches of the Vézère and Dordogne rivers.

Though it has no commanding sights, Brive does have a few distractions. At its centre is the much-restored **church of St-Martin**, originally Romanesque in style, though only the transept, apse and a few comically carved capitals survive from that era. St Martin himself, a Spanish aristocrat, arrived in pagan Brive in 407 AD on the feast of Saturnus, smashed various idols and was promptly stoned to death by the outraged onlookers.

Numerous streets fan out from the central square, place du Général-de-Gaulle, with a number of turreted and towered houses, some dating back to the thirteenth century. The most impressive is the sixteenth-century **Hôtel de Labenche** on boulevard Jules-Ferry, now housing the town's archeological finds as well as a collection of seventeenth-century tapestries in the **Musée Labenche** (daily except Tues: April–Oct 10am–6.30pm; Nov–March 1.30–6pm; €4.70; ⓦ www.musee-labenche.com). There's also the **Centre National d'Études Edmond Michelet** at 4 rue Champanatier (Mon–Sat 10am–noon & 2–6pm; free; ⓦ www.centremichelet.org), based in the former house of this minister of de Gaulle, and one of the town's leading *résistants*, with exhibitions portraying the occupation and Resistance through photographs, posters and objects of the time.

Practicalities

From the **gare SNCF**, it's a five-minute walk north along avenue Jean-Jaurès to the boulevard ringing the old town. The **tourist office** is outside the ring road to the north on place 14-Juillet (April–June & Sept Mon–Sat 9.30am–12.30pm & 1.30–6.30pm; July & Aug Mon–Sat 9am–7pm, Sun 10am–4pm; Oct–March Mon–Sat 9am–noon & 2–6pm; ☎05.55.24.08.80, ⓦ www .brive-tourisme.com), where you'll also find the modern market hall and the **gare routière**. The best place to go for **internet** access is the *Centre Culturel* at 31 avenue Jean-Jaurès (Mon, Tues & Thur–Sat 9am–noon & 2–7pm, Wed 9am–noon; €2 per hour).

There's a decent **HI hostel** a 25min walk across town at 56 avenue du Maréchal-Bugeaud (☎05.55.24.34.00, ✉brive@fuaj.org), while the best of the cheap **hotels** is *L'Andréa*, near the station at 39 avenue Jean-Jaurès (☎05.55.74.11.84, ℱ05.55.17.25.73; ❷), with pleasant rooms, a small garden-terrace and a bar. *Le Collonges*, on the ring road at 3 place Winston-Churchill (☎05.55.74.09.58, ⓦ www.hotel-le-collonges.com; ❸), is a welcoming, family-run place, nothing fancy but the rooms are perfectly acceptable. From there it's a big jump up to *La Truffe Noir*, 22 boulevard Anatole-France (☎05.55.92.45.00, ⓦ www.la-truffe -noire.com; ❻), Brive's grandest hotel. Despite the impressive lobby, the rooms are disappointingly ordinary, though they're well equipped and air-conditioned.

For **places to eat**, try the *Viviers St-Martin*, at 4 rue Traversière (closed two weeks each in March & late Sept; menus from €12), tucked down an alley near St-Martin, which serves brasserie-style food, including plenty of fish dishes. Though it doesn't look much from the outside, *Le Boulevard*, at 8 boulevard Jules-Ferry (℡05.55.23.07.13; closed Sun evening & Mon; menus from €14), hides a cosy dining room where locals come for dishes such as duck breast with local mustard. For something smarter, *La Crémaillère*, at 53 avenue de Paris (closed Sun; menus from €20), has a well-deserved reputation for its classic regional cuisine.

Uzerche and Arnac-Pompadour

A half-hour train ride north of Brive along the course of the bubbling River Vézère, **UZERCHE** is squeezed onto a rocky promontory high above the river. It's worth a passing visit as the town has several fine old buildings. The **tourist office** (15–30 June & 1–15 Sept daily 10am–noon & 2–6pm; July & Aug Mon–Fri 10am–12.30pm & 2.30–6.30pm; school holidays Mon–Fri 10am–noon & 2–5pm, Sat 10am–noon; rest of year Mon–Fri 10am–noon; ℡05.55.73.15.71, ⓦ www.pays-uzerche.com), behind the main church, provides a suggested walking route, but the town is so small you can easily find your own way around. If you need a **place to stay**, the *Hôtel Teyssier*, down by the river (℡05.55.73.10.05, ⓦ www.hotel-teyssier.com; ❸; restaurant menus €20 & €26) is the nicest option. There's also a three-star municipal **campsite** (℡05.55.73.12.75, ⓦ www.uzerche.fr; May–Sept) at the Minoterie leisure centre, 2km south along the river, from where you can rent **canoes** and **bikes** (℡05.55.73.02.84, ⓦ www.vezerepassion.com).

Roughly 20km west of Uzerche (40min by train, on a different line, from Brive) is **ARNAC-POMPADOUR**. It's a town dominated by its grey, turreted château, presented in 1745 by Louis XV to his mistress, Madame de Pompadour, though she never actually came here. The **château** is now home to one of France's best-known **stud farms** (*haras*), founded by Louis XV in 1761, where Anglo-Arabs were first bred. Only the gardens and a few rooms are open to the public (April–Oct & school holidays daily; rest of year daily except Sun; €5), but it's more interesting to visit the *écurie des étalons* where the stallions are kept (April–Oct & school holidays daily; rest of year daily except Sun; €6), across the square from the château. The mares live in the Jumenterie de la Rivière (afternoons only: April–June daily; July–Sept Tues, Thurs & Sat; €6), 4km away near the village of Beyssac. In each case you have to join a guided visit organized by Trois Tours de Pompadour, based at the entrance to the château (℡05.55.98.51.10, ⓦ www.les3tours-pompadour.com); times vary, so call ahead to be safe. From March to October there are frequent race meetings on the magnificent track in front of the château, plus events and open days, the biggest of which is the **Fête du Cheval** on August 15.

The **gare SNCF** is 500m southeast of the old town along the main D7 Vigeois road. There's a reasonable **place to stay** and **eat**, the *Hôtel du Parc* (℡05.55.73.30.54, ⓦ www.logis-de-france.fr; ❷; closed Christmas to mid-Jan; restaurant menus from €12), behind the château. Or you could try the modern *Auberge de la Mandrie*, 4km west on the D7, with chalet rooms around a heated pool (℡05.55.73.37.14, ⓦ www.la-mandrie.com; ❷; restaurant menus €12.50–40; closed Nov–Feb).

Turenne and Collonges-la-Rouge

TURENNE, just 16km south of Brive, was capital of the viscountcy of Turenne, whose most illustrious seigneur was Henri de la Tour d'Auvergne – the "Grand

Turenne", born 1611, whom Napoleon rated the finest tactician of modern times. Mellow stone houses crowd in the lee of the sharp bluff on whose summit sprout two towers, all that remains of the castle. One, known as **La Tour de César**, can be visited (April–June, Sept & Oct daily 10am–noon & 2–6pm; July & Aug daily 10am–7pm; Nov–March Sun 2–5pm; €3.80; ⓦwww.chateau-turenne.com) and is worth climbing for vertiginous views to the mountains of Cantal.

With its red-sandstone houses, pepper-pot towers and pink-candled chestnut trees, **COLLONGES-LA-ROUGE**, 7km east of Turenne, is the epitome of rustic charm – make sure you get here early in the day to avoid the crowds. Though small-scale, there's a certain grandeur about the place, befitting the status of the resident Turenne administrators. On the main square a twelfth-century **church** testifies to the imbecility of shedding blood over religious differences: here, side by side, Protestant and Catholic conducted their services simultaneously. Outside, the covered **market hall** still retains its old-fashioned baker's oven.

If you want to **stay**, it's best to head east 2km to **MEYSSAC**, a town built in the same red sandstone, though less grandly, to the very pleasant *Relais du Quercy* (ⓣ05.55.25.40.31, ⓦwww.relaisduquercy.com.fr; ❸; closed one week each in March & Nov; restaurant menus from €12). On the way you'll pass a three-star **campsite**, *Moulin de la Valanne* (ⓣ05.55.25.41.59, ⓦwww.meyssac.fr; May–Sept).

The Dordogne

To the French, the **Dordogne** is a river. To the British, it is a much looser term, covering a vast area roughly equivalent to what the French call Périgord. This starts south of Limoges and includes the Vézère and Dordogne valleys. The Dordogne is also a *département*, with fixed boundaries that pay no heed to either definition. The central part of the *département*, around Périgueux and the River Isle, is known as **Périgord Blanc**, after the light, white colour of its rock outcrops; the southeastern half around Sarlat as **Périgord Noir**, said to be darker in aspect because of the preponderance of oak woods. To confuse matters further, the tourist authorities have added another two colours to the Périgord patchwork: **Périgord Vert**, the far north of the *département*, so called because of the green of its woods and pastureland; and **Périgord Pourpre** in the southwest, purple because it includes the wine-growing area around Bergerac. This southern region is also known for its **bastides** – fortified towns – built during the turbulent medieval period when there was almost constant conflict between the French and English. In the reaches of the **upper Dordogne**, the colour scheme breaks down, but the villages and scenery in this less travelled backwater still rival anything the rest of the region has to offer.

Périgord Vert and Périgord Blanc

The close green valleys of **Périgord Vert** are very rural, with plenty of space and few people, large tracts of wood and uncultivated land. Less well known than the Périgord Noir, its largely granite landscape bears a closer resemblance to the neighbouring Limousin than to the rest of the Périgord. It's partly for

The food and wine of Périgord

The two great stars of Périgord cuisine are **foie gras** and **truffles** (*truffes*). Foie gras is best eaten either chilled in succulent, buttery slabs, or lightly fried and served with a fruit compote to provide contrasting sweetness and acidity. Truffle is often dished up in omelettes and the rich *périgourdin* sauces which accompany many local meat dishes, but to appreciate the delicate earthy flavour to the full, you really need to eat truffle on its own, with just a salad and some coarse, country bread.

The other mainstay of Périgord cuisine is the grey Toulouse **goose**, whose fat is used in the cooking of everything, including the flavourful potato dish, *pommes sarladaises*. The goose fattens well: *gavé* or crammed with corn, it goes from six to ten kilos in weight in three weeks, with its liver alone weighing nearly a kilo. Though some may find the process off-putting, small local producers are very careful not to harm their birds, if for no other reason than that stress ruins the liver. Geese are also raised for their meat alone, which is cooked and preserved in its own thick yellow grease as *confits d'oie*, which you can either eat on its own or use in the preparation of other dishes, like cassoulet. **Duck** is used in the same way, both for foie gras and *confits*. *Magret de canard*, or duck-breast fillet, is one of the favourite ways of eating duck and appears on practically every restaurant menu.

Another goose delicacy is *cou d'oie farci* – goose neck stuffed with sausage meat, duck liver and truffles; while a popular favourite salad throughout the region is made with warm *gésiers* or goose gizzards. Try not to be put off by fare such as this, or your palate will miss out on some delicious experiences – like *tripoux*, sheep's stomach stuffed with tripe, trotters, pork and garlic, which is really an Auvergnat dish but is quite often served in neighbouring areas like the Rouergue. Other less challenging specialities include stuffed *cèpes*, or wild mushrooms; *ballottines*, fillets of poultry stuffed, rolled and poached; the little flat discs of goat's cheese known as *cabécou* or *rocamadour*; and for dessert there's *pastis*, a light apple tart topped with crinkled, wafer-thin pastry laced with armagnac.

The **wines** should not be scorned, either. There are the fine, dark, almost peppery reds from Cahors, and both reds and whites from the vineyards of Bergerac, of which the sweet, white Monbazillac is the most famous. Pécharmant is the fanciest of the reds, but there are some very drinkable Côtes de Bergerac, much like the neighbouring Bordeaux and far cheaper. The same goes for the wines of Duras, Marmande and Buzet. If you're thinking of taking a stock of wine home, you could do much worse than make some enquiries in Bergerac itself, Ste-Foy, or any of the villages in the vineyard areas.

this reason that in 1998 the most northerly tip, together with the southwestern part of the Haute-Vienne, was designated as the **Parc Naturel Régional Périgord-Limousin** in an attempt to promote "green" tourism in this economically fragile and depopulated area.

Périgueux, in the centre of **Périgord Blanc**, is interesting for its domed cathedral and its Roman remains, whose existence is a reminder of how long these parts have been civilized. But it's in the countryside that the region's finest monuments lie. One of the loveliest stretches is the **valley of the Dronne**, from **Aubeterre** on the Charente border through **Brantôme** to the marvellous Renaissance château of **Puyguilhem** and the picture-postcard village of **St-Jean-de-Côle**, and on to the Limousin border, where the scenery becomes higher and less intimate. Truffle-lovers might like to take a look at **Sorges**, where there's a nature trail through truffle country and a museum to explain it all.

Périgueux

PÉRIGUEUX, capital of the *département* of the Dordogne and a central base for exploring the countryside of Périgord Blanc, is a small, busy and not particularly attractive market town for a province made rich by tourism and specialized farming. Its name derives from the Petrocorii, the local Gallic tribe, but it was the Romans who transformed it into an important settlement. A few Roman remains, as well as a medieval *vieille ville*, survive to this day.

Arrival and information

Périgueux's **gare SNCF** lies to the west of town at the end of rue des Mobiles-du-Coulmiers, the continuation of rue du Président-Wilson. Regional **buses** run by CFTA Périgord (℡05.53.08.43.13, ⊛www.cftaco.fr) stop at both the *gare SNCF* and on place Francheville, a wide, open square with underground parking. On the east side of this square, next to Tour Mataguerre, the last surviving bit of the town's medieval defences, you'll find the **tourist office** (June–Sept Mon–Sat 9am–7pm, Sun 10am–1pm & 2–6pm; Oct–May Mon–Sat 9am–1pm & 2–6pm; ℡05.53.53.10.63, ⊛www.tourisme-perigueux.fr), which organizes various guided visits on foot and by bike in summer. For **internet** access go to *Ouratech* on place du Général-Leclerc (Mon–Sat 10am–7pm; €3 per hour).

Accommodation

Hotels

Des Barris 2 rue Pierre-Magne ℡05.53.53.04.05, ⊛www.hoteldesbarris.com. With views across the river to the cathedral from some rooms, this small, city-centre hotel offers good value. Double-glazing cuts out the road noise, and there's a decent restaurant downstairs with a riverside terrace (menus €22–42). ❸

Bristol 37 rue Antoine-Gadaud ℡05.53.08.75.90, ⊛www.bristolfrance.com. A good find, in a quiet area 2min from the town centre. Rooms are large, and all have a/c and wireless internet. There is also free parking for guests. ❹

Mercure 7 pl Francheville ℡05.53.06.65.00, ⊛www.mercure.com. This new three-star on the main square offers spacious rooms decked out in earth tones. Facilities include secure parking, flat-screen satellite TVs and internet access. ❻

Le Midi 18 rue Denis-Papin ℡05.53.53.41.06, ⊛www.hotel-du-midi.fr. A decent budget hotel opposite the station, with a restaurant serving three-course menus from €14.50. The collection of toy cars on display downstairs is worth a visit in its own right. ❶–❷

Hostel

Résidence des Jeunes Travailleurs rue des Thermes-Prolongés ℡05.53.06.81.40, ⒺContact @fjt24.com. Very basic shared rooms are available here for €12.20 per person, including breakfast and the use of a communal kitchen.

The City

The main hub of the modern city's is the tree-shaded **boulevard Montaigne**, which marks the western edge of the *vieille ville*. At its southern end, a short walk along rue Taillefer brings you to the domed and coned **Cathédrale St-Front**, its square, pineapple-capped belfry surging far above the roofs of the surrounding medieval houses. It's no beauty, having suffered from the attentions of the nineteenth-century restorer Abadie, best known for the white elephant of Paris's Sacré-Coeur. The result is an excess of ill-proportioned, nipple-like projections: "a supreme example of how not to restore", Freda White tartly observed in her classic travelogue, *Three Rivers of France*. It's a pity, since when it was rebuilt in 1173 following a fire, it was one of the most distinctive Byzantine churches in France, modelled on St Mark's in Venice and the Holy Apostles in Constantinople. Nevertheless, the Byzantine influence is still evident in the interior in the Greek-cross plan – unusual in France – and in the massive clean curves of the

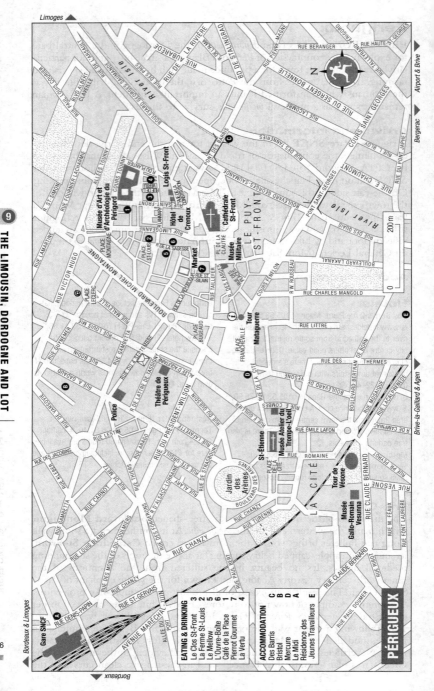

Limoges

Airport & Brive

Bergerac

Brive-la-Gaillard & Agen

Bordeaux

Bordeaux & Limoges

RIVER ISLE

River Isle

RUE BERANGER

RUE HAUTE S.-GEORGES

RUE DU SERGENT BONNELIE

RUE PIERRE-MAGNE

RUE DE L'ABBAYE

RUE DE LA RIVIÈRE

BD DE STALINGRAD

RUE DES PRÉS

RUE DE TALM

COURS SAINT GEORGES

RUE DU PONT JAPHET

RUE P. BLOY

RUE LACOMBE

RUE DE LASSERRE

BOULEVARD GEORGES SAUMANDE

RUE DES TANNERIES

PONT DES BARRIS

RUE E. CHAUMONT

BOULEVARD GEORGES SAUMANDE

RUE DE L'ABREUVOIR

RUE TALLEYRAND-PÉRIGORD

N

RUE ST-SIMON

ALLÉES TOURNY

COURS TOURNY

RUE FOURNIER LACHARME

COURS TOURNY

COURS MONTAIGNE

ALLÉES TOURNY

RUE SAINT-FRONT

PONT SAINT PONT

Logis St-Front

Musée d'Art et
d'Archéologie du
Périgord

Hôtel
de
Crenoux

Cathédrale
St-Front

LE PUY-
ST-FRONT

RUE LAMARTINE

RUE VICTOR HUGO

PLACE
MONTAIGNE

RUE LIMOGEANNE

PLACE ST-LOUIS

RUE DE LA SAGESSE

PLACE
DE LA
CLAUTRE

Market

Musée
Militaire

RUE TAILLEFER

RUE DES FARGES

PLACE DE LA
CLAUTRE

PLACE
LECLERC

BOULEVARD MICHEL MONTAIGNE

RUE MALEVILLE

RUE SALINIÈRE

RUE ST-
SILAIN

ALLÉE D'AQUITAINE

PLACE
BUGEAUD

PLACE
FRANCHEVILLE

Tour
Mataguerre

R. ROUSSEAU

RUE CHARLES MANGOLD

RUE LITTRÉ

RUE LOUIS MIE

RUE GOURNIER

RUE BODIN

RUE A. GADAUD

RUE GAMBETTA

RUE 4 SEPTEMBRE

ALLÉE DE TASSIGNY

ALLÉE D'AQUITAINE

RUE DU PRÉSIDENT-WILSON

RUE DE LA CITÉ

RUE DES
THERMES

BOULEVARD BERTRAN DE BORN

RUE DES VÉSONE

Théâtre de
Périgueux

Police

RUE LESTIN

RUE DES JACOBINS

RUE KLÉBER

RUE DES MOBILES DU COUMIERS

RUE LOUIS BLANC

RUE THIERS

RUE ARAGO

RUE SAINTE-URSULE

RUE DU GUESDE

RUE STE-LORRAINE

RUE SAINTE-MARTHE

BOULEVARD DES ARÈNES

Jardin
des
Arènes

PLACE
DE LA
CITÉ

St-Étienne

Musée Atelier du
Trompe-L'oeil

RUE DES
COMBES

RUE ÉMILE LAFON

RUE
ROMAINE

Tour de
Vésone

LA CITÉ

Musée
Gallo-Romain
Vesunna

RUE CLAUDE BERNARD

RUE VÉSONE

RUE LACAL PRENÈDE

RUE MOSAÏQUE

R DE CAMPNIAC

RUE PR PEYROT

RUE M. FÉAUX

RUE FONT LAURIÈRE

RUE M. FÉAUX

RUE BROT

RUE CLAUDE BERNARD

RUE PAUL DOUMER

RUE DE MEZ

RUE CARNOT

RUE GAMBETTA

RUE DES FORGERONS

RUE D'ALSACE-LORRAINE

RUE ALARY

RUE TURENNE

RUE CHANZY

RUE CHANZY

RUE PAUL BERT

RUE DENIS-PAPIN

RUE ST-GERVAIS

AVENUE MARÉCHAL JUIN

ALLÉE DU MARÉCHAL JUIN

Gare SNCF

PÉRIGUEUX

0   200 m

EATING & DRINKING
Le Clos St-Front   3
La Ferme St-Louis   2
Le Mellow   5
L'Ouvre-Boîte   6
Café de la Place   1
Pierrot Gourmet   7
La Vertu   4

ACCOMMODATION
Des Barris   C
Bristol   B
Mercure   D
Le Midi   A
Résidence des
Jeunes Travailleurs   E

domes and their supporting arches. The big Baroque altarpiece, carved in walnut wood in the gloomy east bay, is worth a look, too, depicting the Assumption of the Virgin, with a humorous little detail in the illustrative scenes from her life of a puppy tugging the infant Jesus' sheets from his bed with its teeth.

In front of the cathedral, there's a fresh produce market on Wednesday and Saturday mornings in **place de la Clautre**, at the heart of the renovated streets of the medieval town, the most attractive of which is the narrow **rue Limogeanne**, lined with Renaissance mansions, now turned into boutiques and delicatessens, intermingled with fast-food outlets. The surrounding streets are also scattered with fine Renaissance houses; particularly handsome are the **Logis St-Front**, 7 rue de la Constitution, and the more sedate **Hôtel de Crenoux** at no. 3. Another striking building is at 17 rue de l'Éguillerie, on the corner of the attractive **place St-Louis**, where a turreted watchtower leans out over the street.

At the northern end of rue Limogeanne, on tree-lined cours Tourny, the **Musée d'Art et d'Archéologie du Périgord** (April–Sept Mon & Wed–Fri 10.30am–5.30pm, Sat & Sun 1–6pm; Oct–March Mon & Wed–Fri 10am–5pm, Sat & Sun 1–6pm; €4) is best known for its extensive and important prehistoric collection and some beautiful Gallo-Roman mosaics. Exhibits include copies of a 70,000-year-old skeleton, the oldest yet found in France, and a beautiful engraving of a bison's head. More lively but of less general interest is the **Musée Militaire**, near the cathedral at 32 rue des Farges (Jan–March Wed & Sat 2–6pm; April–Dec Mon–Sat 2–6pm; €4), which contains some unusual exhibits, particularly relating to the French colonial wars in Vietnam.

Roman Périgueux, known as **La Cité**, lies to the west of the town centre towards the *gare SNCF*. The most prominent vestige is the high, brick **Tour de Vésone**, the last remains of a temple to the city's guardian goddess, standing in a public garden just south of the train tracks. Beside the tower, the foundations of an exceptionally well-preserved Roman villa form the basis of the **Musée Gallo-Romain Vesunna** (April–June & Sept Tues–Fri 9.30am–5.30pm, Sat & Sun 10am–12.30pm & 2.30–6pm; July & Aug daily 10am–7pm; Oct–March Tues–Fri 9.30am–12.30pm & 1.30–5pm, Sat & Sun 10am–12.30pm & 2.30–6pm; €5.50; ⓦ www.vesunna.fr). This was no humble abode: the villa, complete with under-floor heating, thermal baths and colonnaded walkways around the central garden with its cooling pond and fountains, boasted at least sixty rooms. Visitors can see the remains of first-century murals of river and marine life, the colours still amazingly vibrant, and here and there, graffiti of hunting scenes, gladiatorial combat and even an ostrich – no doubt the work of some bored Roman urchin.

Eating and drinking

The best place to look for **places to eat** is in the *vieille ville*, particularly around place St-Louis, place St-Silain and in the streets behind the tourist office. As for **cafés**, *Café de la Place*, on place du Marché-du-Bois, is a relaxed, traditional place with a shady terrace and good-value brasserie food. For the best of Périgueux's limited **nightlife**, head for rue de la Sagesse, where you'll find *Le Mellow* (Tues–Sat) and *L'Ouvre-Boîte* (Wed–Sun), both lively bars with music and cocktails.

Restaurants

Le Clos St-Front 5 rue de la Vertu ☎05.53.46.78.58. High-quality menus served in a leafy, walled courtyard or elegant dining rooms. You can eat for €25, but for the €60 set menu you get the best of the best and wine included. Sept–June closed Sun evening & Mon.

La Ferme St-Louis pl St-Louis ☎05.53.53.82.77. The most appealing of the many restaurants on the square, it has a small terrace and a homely, stone-walled interior. Food here can be much more local than the duck breast in a truffle-based sauce. You'll pay €19 for two courses at lunchtime and €25 in the evening. Closed Sun & Mon.

Pierrot Gourmet 6 rue de l'Hôtel-de-Ville. This gourmet deli has a few tables during the daytime where you can chose from a range of fresh, top quality dishes. A plateful of delicacies will cost around €10–12. Closed Sun.

La Vertu 11 rue Notre-Dame. A lively bar and restaurant, serving tapas and menus for €12 at lunch and dinner. It only opens in summer (June– Sept), when the salsa music and pitchers of sangria go down best.

Brantôme and the valley of the Dronne

Although **Brantôme** itself is very much on the tourist trail, the country to both the west and east of the town along the **River Dronne** remains largely undisturbed. It's tranquil and very beautiful, and best savoured at a gentle pace, perhaps by bike or even by canoeing along the river.

Brantôme

BRANTÔME, 27km north of Périgueux on the Angoulême road, sits on an island in the River Dronne, whose still, water-lilied surface mirrors the limes and weeping willows of the riverside gardens. On the north bank of the river are the church and convent buildings of the former **Benedictine abbey** that has been Brantôme's focus ever since it was founded, possibly by Charlemagne. The other big name associated with the abbey is that of its most notorious abbot, Pierre de Bourdeilles, the sixteenth-century author of scurrilous tales of life at the royal court. Brantôme's best architectural feature, however, is the Limousin-style Romanesque **belfry**, built into the cliff-face behind the church and only accessible on a guided tour arranged by the tourist office (15 June to 15 Sept; €6).

There are also pleasant views to be had wandering the nearby **gardens** and the balustraded riverbanks, while in summer you can take a leisurely **boat trip** on the river (Easter to mid-Oct; €7).

Five days a week (Mon, Wed & Fri–Sun), **buses** connect Brantôme with Périgueux and the TGV in Angoulême. The **tourist office** (May, June & Sept daily except Tues 10am–noon & 2–6pm; July & Aug daily 10am–6pm; Oct–April

▲ River Dronne at Brantôme

daily except Tues 10am–noon & 2–5pm; ☎05.53.05.80.52, ⓦwww
.ville-brantome.fr) is next to the abbey church. From April to September you
can rent **canoes** from Brantôme Canoë (☎05.53.05.77.24, ⓦwww.brantome
-canoe.com), on the east side of town on the road to Thiviers, while **bikes** are
available at *Spadzone,* 2 avenue des Martyrs (☎05.53.08.02.65, ⓦwww.spadzone
.com), north on the Angoulême road.

Cheapish **accommodation** is to be found at the friendly and recently
renovated *Hôtel Coligny,* 8 place de Gaulle, at the north end of town
(☎05.53.05.71.42; ❸; restaurant menus from €12; closed mid-Dec to March).
Moving up a notch, the *Hôtel Chabrol* across the river (☎05.53.05.70.15, ⓦwww
.lesfrerescharbonnel.com; ❸; closed Feb & mid-Nov to mid-Dec) boasts comfortable, pretty rooms and a gourmet restaurant (three-course menus €38–65; closed
Sun evening & Mon Oct–June). Another lovely place to stay is the *Maison Fleurie,*
an English-owned *chambre d'hôte* at 54 rue Gambetta (☎05.53.35.17.04, ⓦwww
.maison-fleurie.net; ❸), with a pool and quiet courtyard garden. Other good
eating options include *Les Jardins de Brantôme,* with an attractive garden, a short
walk north of town at 33 rue Pierre-de-Mareuil (closed Wed & Thurs; menus
€21–29), and *Au Fil de l'Eau,* on quai Bertin, which specializes in not too
expensive fish dishes (closed mid-Oct to Easter; menus from €24) and spreads
along the riverbank in fine weather. Campers should head for the *Le Peyrelevade*
campsite just east of Brantôme on the D78 Thiviers road (☎08.25.00.20.30,
ⓦwww.village-center.com; mid-May to mid-Sept).

Bourdeilles

BOURDEILLES, 16km down the Dronne from Brantôme by a beautiful back
road, is a sleepy backwater. The ancient village clusters round its **château** (Feb,
March, Nov & Dec Mon, Wed, Thurs & Sun 10am–12.30pm & 2–5.30pm;
April–June, Sept & Oct daily except Tues 10am–12.30pm & 2–6pm; July & Aug
daily 10am–7pm; €5.80; ⓦwww.semitour.com) on a rocky spur above the river.
The château consists of two buildings: one a thirteenth-century fortress, the
other an elegant Renaissance residence begun by the lady of the house as a
piece of unsuccessful favour-currying with Catherine de Médici – unsuccessful
because Catherine never came to stay and the château remained unfinished.
Climb the octagonal keep for a good view over the town's clustered roofs and
along the valley of the Dronne.

The château is now home to an exceptional collection of **furniture** and
religious statuary bequeathed to the state by its former owners. Among the
more notable pieces are some splendid Spanish dowry chests and a sixteenth-
century Rhenish Entombment with life-sized statues, embodying the very
image of the serious, self-satisfied medieval burgher. The *salon doré,* the room in
which de Médici was supposed to sleep, has also been preserved.

Lesser mortals wanting to **stay** the night could try the appealing *Hostellerie Le
Donjon* (☎05.53.04.82.81, ⓦwww.hostellerie-ledonjon.fr; ❸; menus €23 & €29;
closed mid-Nov to Easter), on the main street, or the more upmarket *Hostellerie
Les Griffons* (☎05.53.45.45.35, ⓦwww.griffons.fr; ❻; closed Nov–Easter) in a
sixteenth-century house beside the old bridge, with a restaurant serving top-
notch regional cuisine (menus from €33; closed lunchtime Tues & Wed).

Aubeterre-sur-Dronne and around

Rather touristy, but very beautiful with its ancient galleried and turreted houses,
AUBETERRE-SUR-DRONNE hangs on a steep hillside above the river
some 30km downstream of Ribérac. Its principal curiosity is the cavernous
Église Monolithe (daily 9.30am–12.30pm & 2–6pm; €4), carved out of the

soft rock of the cliff face in the twelfth century, with its rock-hewn tombs going back to the sixth. A (blocked-off) tunnel connects with the **château** on the bluff overhead. There's also the extremely beautiful church of **St-Jacques**, with an eleventh-century facade sculpted and decorated in the richly carved Poitiers style on the street leading uphill from the square.

The **tourist office** is beside the main car park (June & Sept Mon & Sat 2–6pm, Tues–Fri 10am–noon & 2–6pm; July & Aug Mon 2–7pm, Tues–Sun 10am–12.30pm & 2–7pm; Oct–May Mon–Fri 2–6pm; ☎05.45.98.57.18, ⓦaubeterresurdronne.free.fr). You'll find comfortable **accommodation** and a fine restaurant just below the village at the *Hostellerie du Périgord*, beside the bridge (☎05.45.98.50.46, ⓦwww.hostellerie-perigord.com; ❸; menus €16.50–43.50, closed Sun evening & Mon). There's also a **campsite** (☎05.45.98.60.17; May–Sept) across the other side of the river. An early-morning **bus** runs to Angoulême (Mon–Fri, also Sat in July & Aug), while Chalais, which is on the Angoulême train line, is only 12km away.

South of Aubeterre the country gradually changes. Farmland gives way to an extensive forest of oak and sweet chestnut, bracken and broom, interspersed with sour, marshy pasture, and is very sparsely populated. It's ideal cycling and picnicking country.

St-Jean-de-Côle and around

Twenty kilometres northeast of Brantôme, **ST-JEAN-DE-CÔLE** ranks as one of the loveliest villages in the Dordogne. Its ancient houses huddle together in typical medieval fashion around a wide sandy square dominated by the charmingly ill-proportioned eleventh-century **church of St-Jean-Baptiste** and the rugged-looking **Château de la Marthonie** (not open to the public). The château, which dates from the twelfth century, has acquired various additions in a pleasingly organic fashion.

The **tourist office** (mid-June to mid-Sept daily 10am–12.30pm & 2–6.30pm; mid-Sept to mid-June Thur–Sun 10am–1pm & 2–6pm; ☎05.53.62.14.15, ⓦwww.ville-saint-jean-de-cole.fr) is also on the square, as well as a couple of **restaurants**. However, for good traditional fare like truffle omelette, you can't beat the wisteria-covered *Hôtel St-Jean* (☎05.53.52.23.20, ⓕ05.53.52.44.55; ❶; menus from €23, closed Sun evening & Mon off season) on the main road through the village; it also offers a few simple but clean and comfortable **rooms**.

Around 10km west of St-Jean, just outside the village of **VILLARS**, the **Château de Puyguilhem** (May–Aug daily 10am–12.30pm & 2–6.30pm; Sept–April Wed–Sun 10am–12.30pm & 2–5.30pm; €5; ⓦpuyguilhem .monuments-nationaux.fr) sits on the edge of a valley backed by oak woods. It was erected at the beginning of the sixteenth century on the site of an earlier military fortress. With its octagonal tower, broad spiral staircase, steep roofs, magnificent fireplaces and false dormer windows, it's a perfect example of French Renaissance architecture. From the gallery at the top of the stairs you get a close-up of the roof and window decoration, as well as a view down the valley, which once was filled by an ornamental lake.

A short distance north of Villars, the **Grotte de Villars** (daily: April–June & Sept 10am–noon & 2–7pm; July & Aug 10am–7.30pm; Oct 2–6.30pm; closed Nov–March; €7; ⓦwww.grotte-villars.com) boasts a few prehistoric paintings – notably of horses and a still unexplained scene of a man and a bison. The main reason for coming here, however, is to see the impressive array of stalactites and stalagmites.

Thiviers and Sorges

If you're heading along the main N21 Périgueux–Limoges road, it's worth stopping off at the small market town of **THIVIERS**, which styles itself as the foie gras capital of the region. Its well-stocked **tourist office**, on the central square (Mon–Fri 10am–1pm & 2–6pm, Sat 9am–1pm & 3–6pm; July & Aug also open Sun 10am–1pm; ☏05.53.55.12.50, ⓦwww.thiviers.fr), makes the most of this with a small **museum** dedicated to the history and production of foie gras (same hours; €1.50). A particularly welcoming place to **stay** is the attractive and characterful *Hôtel de France et de Russie*, 51 rue du Général-Lamy (☏05.53.55.17.80, ⓦwww.thiviers-hotel.com; ❸), between the tourist office and the **gare SNCF**.

   SORGES, closer to Périgueux and strung out along the road, has less to offer aesthetically than Thiviers. However, the **tourist office** (March–May, Sept & Oct Tues–Sun 10am–noon & 2–5pm; July & Aug daily 9.30am–12.30pm & 2.30–6.30pm; Nov–Feb Tues–Sun 2–5pm; ☏05.53.05.90.11, ⓦwww.truffe-sorges.org) contains an informative **truffle museum** (same hours; €4), and staff can also direct you to a nature trail that gives an idea of how and where truffles grow.

Château de Hautefort

Forty kilometres east of Périgueux (take the D5 along the River Auvézère for the most attractive route), the **Château de Hautefort** (March & 1–11 Nov Sat & Sun 2–6pm; April & May daily 10am–12.30pm & 2–6.30pm; June–Sept daily 9.30am–7pm; Oct daily 2–6pm; closed 12 Nov to Feb; €8.50; ⓦwww.chateau-hautefort.com) enjoys a majestic position at the end of a wooded spur above its feudal village. A magnificent example of good living on a grand scale, the castle has an elegance that is out of step with the usual rough stone fortresses of Périgord. The approach is across a wide esplanade flanked by formal gardens, over a drawbridge, and into a stylish Renaissance courtyard, open to the south. In 1968 a fire gutted the castle, but it has since been meticulously restored using traditional techniques; it's all unmistakably new, but the quality of the craftsmanship is superb.

   Hautefort has a very pleasant **hotel**, the *Auberge du Parc* (☏05.53.50.88.98, ⓦwww.aubergeduparc-hautefort.fr; ❷; closed mid-Dec to Feb; restaurant menus €16.50–34; closed Sun evening & Wed), just beneath the castle walls.

Périgord Pourpre

The area known as the **Périgord Pourpre** takes its name from the wine-growing region concentrated in the southwest corner of the Dordogne *département*, most famous for the sweet white wines produced around **Monbazillac**. The only town of any size is **Bergerac**, which makes a good base for exploring the vineyards and the uplands to the south. These are peppered with *bastides*, medieval fortified towns (see box, p.633), such as the beautifully preserved **Monpazier**, and here also you'll find the **Château de Biron**, which dominates the countryside for miles around.

Bergerac and around

BERGERAC, "capital" of Périgord Pourpre, lies on the riverbank in the wide plain of the Dordogne. Once a flourishing port for the wine trade, it is still the main market centre for the surrounding maize, vine and tobacco farms. Devastated in the Wars of Religion, when most of its Protestant population fled overseas, Bergerac is now essentially a modern town with some interesting and attractive reminders of the past.

The compact **vieille ville** is a beguiling area to wander through, with numerous late-medieval houses and one or two beautiful squares. In rue de l'Ancien-Pont, the splendid seventeenth-century Maison Peyrarède houses an informative **Musée du Tabac** (15 March to 15 Nov Tues–Fri 10am–noon & 2–6pm, Sat 10am–noon & 2–5pm, Sun 2.30–6.30pm; 16 Nov to 14 March Tues–Fri 10am–noon & 2–6pm, Sat 10am–noon; €3.50), detailing the history of the weed, with collections of pipes and tools of the trade.

Bergerac has a couple of other museums, the best of which is the small **Musée du Vin et de la Batellerie** in rue des Conférences in the heart of the old town (Tues–Fri 10am–noon & 2–5.30pm, Sat 10am–noon; April–Oct also Sun 2.30–6.30pm; €2.50), focusing on viticulture, barrel-making and the town's once-bustling river-trade. Nearby, on the picturesque place de la Myrpe and further up the hill on place Pélissière, are two statues in honour of **Cyrano de Bergerac**, the town's most famous association. The big-nosed hero of Edmond Rostand's play, though fictional, was inspired by the seventeenth-century philosopher of the same name, who, sadly, had nothing to do with the town.

Wine-lovers should make a beeline for the **Maison des Vins**, down by the river on quai Salvette (Feb–June & Sept–Dec Tues–Sun 10.30am–12.30pm & 2–6pm; July & Aug daily 10am–7pm; closed Jan; ⓦwww.vins-bergerac.fr), which offers free tastings and beginners' courses in July and August (☏05.53.63.57.55; €8). It also sells a selection of local wines and provides information about visiting the surrounding vineyards.

Practicalities

The **gare SNCF** is at the end of cours Alsace-Lorraine, ten-minutes' walk north from the old town, while the **airport** (☏05.53.22.25.25) lies 5km southeast of Bergerac (roughly €13 by taxi). The main **tourist office** is at 97 rue Neuve-d'Argenson, two-minutes' walk northeast of the old town (July & Aug Mon–Sat 9.30am–7.30pm; Sept–June Mon–Sat 9.30am–1pm & 2–7pm; ☏05.53.57.03.11, ⓦwww.bergerac-tourisme.com), and a second office opens in summer behind the Maison des Vins in the Cloître des Récollets (July & Aug daily 10.30am–1pm & 2.30–7pm). You can rent motorbikes, scooters and **bicycles** and from Apolo Cycles (☏06.20.64.59.25, ⓦwww.apolo-cycles.com), which has an outlet by the port in summer (June–Sept) and otherwise will deliver to your hotel. A vast **market** takes place on Wednesday and Saturday mornings in the covered *halles* in the old town centre and around Notre-Dame church. If you're here in July, don't miss the magnificent La Table de Cyrano **food festival** in the week of July 14.

There's a decent range of **accommodation** to choose from. The best budget option is *Le Moderne*, opposite the station (☏05.53.57.19.62, ℉05.53.61.80.50; ❶), a welcoming, well-kept place with a brasserie (closed Sun; menus from €16.50). For something more comfortable, try one of the three-star hotels on place Gambetta between the station and the old town: the *France* (☏05.53.57.11.61, ⓦwww.hoteldefrance-bergerac.com; ❸), where the more expensive rooms have balconies and air conditioning, or the *Bordeaux* (☏05.53.57.12.83, ⓦwww.hotel-bordeaux-bergerac.com; ❸), with a marginally larger swimming pool and a bit of greenery. There's also a municipal **campsite**, *La Pelouse* (☏05.53.57.06.67, ⓔcamping@ville-bergerac.fr; mid-Feb to Oct), on the south bank of the river.

For **eating**, *Coté Noix*, on place Pélissière (closed Sun & Mon), makes a great pit-stop with its mouth-watering array of home-made cakes and light lunches, while *La Blanche Hermine*, beside the covered market (closed Sun & Mon), is a cheerful crêperie dishing up an imaginative range of buckwheat crêpes as well as copious salads – all at very reasonable prices. Nearby, *La Table du Marché*, 21 place de la Bardonnie (three courses €25; closed Wed & Thurs evening and Sun), offers innovative takes on classic dishes, such as cucumber gazpacho or prawn and mango ceviche.

Monpazier and around

MONPAZIER, founded in 1284 by King Edward I of England (who was also Duke of Aquitaine), is one of the most complete of the surviving *bastides*. Picturesque and placid though it is today, the village has a hard and bitter history, being twice – in 1594 and 1637 – the centre of peasant rebellions provoked by the misery following the Wars of Religion. Both uprisings were brutally suppressed: the 1637 peasants' leader was broken on the wheel in the

Bastides

From the Occitan word *bastida*, meaning a group of buildings, **bastides** were the new towns of the thirteenth and fourteenth centuries. Although they are found all over southwest France, from the Dordogne to the foothills of the Pyrenees, there is a particularly high concentration in the area between the Dordogne and Lot rivers, which at that time formed the disputed "frontier" region between English-held Aquitaine and Capetian France.

That said, the earliest *bastides* were founded largely for economic and political reasons. They were a means of bringing new land into production – in an era of rapid population growth and technological innovation – and thus extending the power of the local lord. But as tensions between the French and English forces intensified in the late thirteenth century, so the motive became increasingly military. The *bastides* provided a handy way of securing the land along the frontier, and it was generally at this point that they were fortified.

As an incentive, anyone who was prepared to build, inhabit and defend the *bastide* was granted various benefits in a founding charter. All new residents were allocated a building plot, garden and cultivable land. The charter might also offer asylum to certain types of criminal or grant exemption from military service, and would allow the election of consuls charged with day-to-day administration – a measure of self-government remarkable in feudal times. Taxes and judicial affairs, meanwhile, remained the preserve of the representative of the king or local lord under whose ultimate authority the *bastide* lay.

The other defining feature of a *bastide* is its layout. They are nearly always square or rectangular in shape and are divided by streets at right angles to each other to produce a chequerboard pattern. The focal point is the market square, often missing its covered *halle* nowadays, but generally still surrounded by arcades, while the church is relegated to one side.

The busiest *bastide* founders were Alphonse de Poitiers, on behalf of the French crown, after he became Count of Toulouse in 1249, and King Edward I of England (1272–1307), who wished to consolidate his hold on the northern borders of his Duchy of Aquitaine. The former chalked up a total of 57 *bastides*, including **Ville-neuve-sur-Lot** (1251) and **Monflanquin** (1252), while Edward was responsible for **Beaumont** (1272) and **Monpazier** (1284), among others. While many *bastides* retain only vestiges of their original aspect, both Monpazier and Monflanquin have survived almost entirely intact.

square. Sully, the Protestant general, describes a rare moment of light relief in the terrible wars, when the men of the Catholic *bastide* of Villefranche-du-Périgord planned to capture Monpazier on the same night as the men of Monpazier planned to capture Villefranche. By chance, both sides took different routes, met no resistance, looted to their hearts' content and returned home congratulating themselves on their luck and skill, only to find in the morning that things were rather different. The peace terms required that everything was returned to its proper place.

Monpazier follows the typical *bastide* layout, with a grid of streets built around a gem of a central square – sunny, still and slightly menacing. Deep, shady arcades pass under all the houses, which are separated from each other by a small gap to reduce fire risk; at the corners the buttresses are cut away to allow the passage of laden pack animals. There's also an ancient *lavoir* where women used to wash clothes, and a much altered church.

The **tourist office** is on the central square (July & Aug daily 10am–12.30pm & 2–7pm; Sept–June Tues–Sun 10am–12.30pm & 2–6pm; ℡05.53.22.68.59, ⓦwww.pays-des-bastides.com), where you'll also find reasonable **accommodation** and a good traditional **restaurant** at the *Hôtel de France*, 21 rue St-Jacques (℡05.53.22.60.06, ⓦwww.hoteldefrancemonpazier.fr; ❷; closed Nov–Easter; menus from €21, closed Tues evening & Wed, open daily July & Aug). A more luxurious option is the *Hôtel Edward 1er* (℡05.53.22.44.00, ⓦwww.hoteledward1er.com; ❺; closed mid-Nov to mid-March) at 5 rue St-Pierre, a few-minutes' walk from the main square, with its own swimming pool and a restaurant with menus from €28 (reservations required; closed Wed evening & mid-Nov to mid-March). The best of the local **campsites** is the luxurious *Moulin de David*, roughly 3km south on the road to Villeréal (℡05.53.22.65.25, ⓦwww.moulin-de-david.com; April to mid-Sept).

The Château de Biron

Eight kilometres south of Monpazier, the vast **Château de Biron** (Feb, March, Nov & Dec Tues–Thurs & Sun 10am–12.30pm & 2–5.30pm; April–June, Sept & Oct Tues–Sun 10am–12.30pm & 2–6pm; July & Aug daily 10am–7pm; €5.80; ⓦwww.semitour.com) was begun in the eleventh century and added to piecemeal afterwards. You can take a guided tour (in French only), but it's better to borrow the English-language translation and wander at will around the rooms and the grassy courtyard, where there is a restored Renaissance chapel and guardhouse with tremendous views over the roofs of the feudal village below.

A single street runs through the village of **BIRON**, past a covered **market** on timber supports iron-hard with age, and out under an arched gateway, where well-manured vegetable plots interspersed with iris, lily and Iceland poppies lie under the tumbledown walls. At the bottom of the hill, another group of houses stands on a small square with a well in front of the village **church**, its Romanesque origins hidden by motley alterations.

Périgord Noir

Périgord Noir encompasses the central part of the valley of the Dordogne, and the valley of the Vézère. This is the distinctive Dordogne country: deep-cut valleys between limestone cliffs, with fields of maize in the alluvial bottoms and dense oak woods on the heights, interspersed with patches of not very fertile farmland. Plantations of walnut trees (cultivated for their oil), flocks of

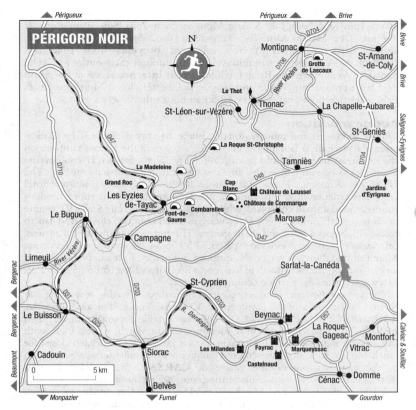

PÉRIGORD NOIR

N

Montignac

St-Amand
-de-Coly

Grotte
de Lascaux

Le Thot

Thonac

La Chapelle-Aubareil

St-Léon-sur-Vézère

St-Geniès

La Roque St-Christophe

Tamniès

La Madeleine

Grand Roc

Cap
Blanc

Château de Laussel

Jardins
d'Eyrignac

Les Eyzies
de-Tayac

Château de Commarque

Font-de-
Gaume

Combarelles

Le Bugue

Marquay

Campagne

Limeuil

Sarlat-la-Canéda

St-Cyprien

Le Buisson

Beynac

La Roque-
Gageac

Montfort

Cadouin

Les Milandes

Fayrac

Marqueyssac

Vitrac

Siorac

Castelnaud

Cénac

Domme

0   5 km

Belvès

9

low-slung grey geese (their livers enlarged for foie gras) and prehistoric-looking stone huts called *bories* are all hallmarks of Périgord Noir.

The well-preserved medieval architecture of **Sarlat**, the wealth of **prehistory** and the staggering cave paintings of the **Vézère valley**, and the stunning beauty of the château-studded **Dordogne** have all contributed to making this one of the most heavily touristed inland areas of France, with all the concomitant problems of crowds, high prices and tack. If possible, it's worth coming out of season, but if you can't, seek accommodation away from the main centres, and always drive along the back roads – the smaller the better – even when there is a more direct route available.

Sarlat and around

SARLAT-LA-CANÉDA, "capital" of Périgord Noir, lies in a hollow between hills 10km or so back from the Dordogne River. You hardly notice the modern town, as it's the mainly fifteenth- and sixteenth-century houses of the *vieille ville* in mellow, honey-coloured stone that draw the attention.

Arrival and information

The **gare SNCF** is just over 1km south of the old town, where on rue Tourny you'll find the **tourist office** (April & Sept–Nov Mon–Sat 9am–noon & 2–6pm, Sun 10am–1pm; May & June Mon–Sat 9am–6pm, Sun

10am–1pm & 2–5pm; July & Aug Mon–Sat 9am–7pm, Sun 10am–noon & 2–6pm; Dec–March Mon–Sat 9am–noon & 2–5pm; ☎05.53.31.45.45, Ⓦwww.sarlat-tourisme.com). You can rent **bicycles** from Bike Bus (☎06.08.94.42.01, Ⓦwww.multitravel.co.uk), through their outlet at Cycles Sarladais, avenue Aristide-Briand, while there is **internet** access at the Salon de Thés, opposite the *Mairie* on place de la Liberté (closed Mon, also Jan & Feb) – it's free if you eat there or €2.50 an hour otherwise.

Accommodation

One of the nicest and most reasonable **place to stay** in Sarlat is *La Couleuvrine* at 1 place de la Bouquerie, occupying a tower in the former ramparts on the northeast side of the old town (☎05.53.59.27.80, Ⓦwww.la-couleuvrine .com; ❸; closed end Jan), with a fine restaurant (three-course menu €21). The *Hôtel des Récollets*, 4 rue J.Rousseau (☎05.53.31.36.00, Ⓦwww.hotel -recollets-sarlat.com; ❸), is another good-value place, with more modern rooms around a small courtyard, while the three-star *Hôtel de Selves*, 93 avenue de Selves (☎05.53.31.50.00, Ⓦwww.selves-sarlat.com; ❺; closed mid-Jan to mid-Feb), boasts a pool and small garden. The nearest **campsite**, *Les Périères*, on Sarlat's northern outskirts (☎05.53.59.05.84, Ⓦwww.lesperieres.com; March to mid-Nov), is very well equipped but pricey; instead, try *Les Terrasses du Périgord*, about 2.5km north of Sarlat near Proissans village (☎05.53.59.02.25, Ⓦwww.terrasses-du-perigord.com; April–Sept).

Not far away there are some very pleasant alternatives to staying – or eating – in Sarlat. On the banks of the Dordogne at **VITRAC**, about 7km south of Sarlat, the 🎍 *Hôtel La Treille* (☎05.53.28.33.19, Ⓦwww.latreille-perigord.com; ❸; closed mid-Nov to mid-Dec, also Mon & Tues from Oct to March) is great value, with large rooms and an excellent restaurant (menus from €23; Oct–March closed for lunch Mon & Tues) in a vine-covered building with a sunny terrace. Some 5km to the east, just outside the village of **CARSAC**, the *La Villa Romaine* (☎05.53.28.52.07, Ⓦwww.lavillaromaine.com; ❼; menus from €29, evenings only; closed mid-Feb to mid-March & 2 weeks in Nov) offers extreme pampering in a cluster of attractive former farm buildings around a swimming pool.

The Town

The **vieille ville** is an excellent example of medieval organic urban growth. It was also the first town to benefit from culture minister André Malraux's law of 1962 which created the concept of a *secteur sauvegardé* (protected area), and boasts no fewer than 65 protected buildings and monuments. The old centre is violated only by the straight swath of the rue de la République which cuts through its middle. The west side remains relatively quiet the east side is where most people wander. Approaching from the south, rue Lakanal leads to the large and unexciting **Cathédrale St-Sacerdos**, mostly dating from its seventeenth-century renovation. Opposite stands the town's finest house, the **Maison de La Boétie** (not open to the public) where the poet and humanist Étienne de La Boétie was born in 1530, with its gabled tiers of windows and characteristic steep roof stacked with heavy limestone tiles (*lauzes*).

For a better sense of the medieval town, wander through the cool, shady lanes and courtyards – **cour des Fontaines** and **cour des Chanoines** – around the back of the cathedral. On a slope directly behind the cathedral stands the curious twelfth-century coned tower, the **Lanterne des Morts**, whose exact function has escaped historians, though the most popular theory is that it was built to commemorate St Bernard, who performed various miracles when he visited the town in 1147.

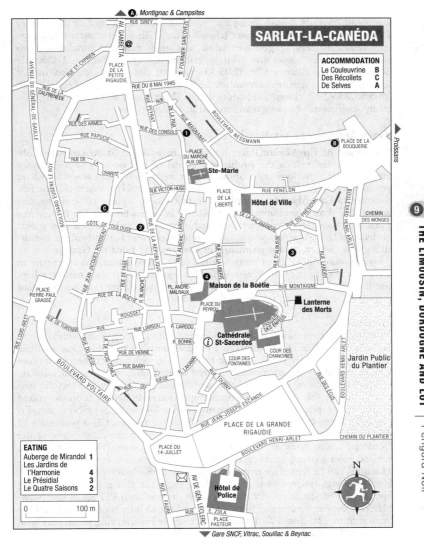

▲ ⒶMontignac & Campsites

SARLAT-LA-CANÉDA

ACCOMMODATION	
Le Couleuvrine	B
Des Récollets	C
De Selves	A

RUE SIREY

AV. GAMBETTA

RUE ST-CYPRIEN

AVENUE DU GÉNÉRAL-DE-GAULLE

RUE DE LA CALPRENEDE

PLACE DE LA PETITE RIGAUDIE

RUE DU 8 MAI 1945

R. FOURNIER-SARLOVEZE

BOULEVARD NESSMANN

Proissans ►

RUE DES ARMES

RUE PAPUCIE

RUE DE — LA CHARITÉ

BOULEVARD EUGÈNE LE ROY

RUE PÉTRAT

RUE DE LA PAIX

RUE MAGNANAT

RUE DES CONSULS ❶

PLACE DU MARCHÉ AUX OIES

Ste-Marie

PLACE DE LA BOUQUERIE ⒷB

BOULEVARD HENRI-ARLET

RUE VICTOR-HUGO

RUE FÉNELON

Hôtel de Ville

CHEMIN DES MONGES

CÔTE DE TOULOUSE ❷

ⒸC

PLACE DE LA LIBERTÉ

R. DE LA SALAMANDRE

RUE DU PRÉSIDIAL

❾9

RUE JEAN-JACQUES-ROUSSEAU

RUE DE LA RÉPUBLIQUE

RUE DE FAGE

RUE ALBÉRIC-CAHUET

RUE DE LA LIBERTÉ

❸

RUE LANDRY

RUE BLANCHET

RUE DE LA BOÉTIE

PL. ANDRÉ-MALRAUX ❹

Maison de la Boétie

RUE MONTAIGNE

Lanterne des Morts

PLACE PIERRE-PAUL GRASSÉ

ROUSSET

PLACE DU PEYROU

PASSAGE DES ENFEUS

RUE LOUIS-ARLET

RUE DE TURENNE

RUE DU TROIS CONILS

RUE LIARSOU

R. LIARSOU

R. BONNEL

Cathédrale St-Sacerdos ⓘ

COUR DES CHANOINES

Jardin Public du Plantier

RUE DE VIENNE

RUE BARRY

RUE DU SIEGE

R. LAKANAL

COUR DES FONTAINES

RUE TOURNY

BOULEVARD HENRI-ARLET

BOULEVARD VOLTAIRE

RUE DES ÉCUS

RUE JEAN-JOSEPH-ESCANDE

PLACE DE LA GRANDE RIGAUDIE

CHEMIN DU PLANTIER

PLACE DU 14-JUILLET

BOULEVARD HENRI-ARLET

EATING	
Auberge de Mirandol	1
Les Jardins de	
l'Harmonie	4
Le Présidial	3
Le Quatre Saisons	2

AV. DE GÉN. LECLERC

Hôtel de Police

RUE E. FAURE

RUE LECLERC

E. ZOLA

PLACE PASTEUR

N

0 ——— 100 m

THE LIMOUSIN, DORDOGNE AND LOT | Périgord Noir

▼ Gare SNCF, Vitrac, Souillac & Beynac

There are more wonderful old houses in the streets to the north, especially **rue des Consuls**, and up the slopes to the east. Eventually, though, Sarlat's labyrinthine lanes will lead you back to the central **place de la Liberté**, where the big Saturday **market** spreads its stands bearing foie gras, truffles, walnuts and mushrooms according to the season.

Eating and drinking

Many **restaurants** in Sarlat open only for the summer and standards vary enormously. Two safe choices are the *Auberge de Mirandol*, 7 rue des Consuls (menus from €13; closed Dec to mid-Feb), serving local delicacies in a fourteenth-century house, complete with its own cave, and ⚱ *Les Jardins d'Harmonie*, place André-Malraux (closed Mon & Tues), an attractive teashop-cum-restaurant serving gourmet salads and main dishes at lunchtime (two courses €19). For something a bit special, try *Le Quatre Saisons*, 2 Côte de Toulouse (three courses €28; ☎05.53.29.48.59; closed Tues & Wed out of season), with an interior courtyard, or *Le Présidial*, 6 rue Landry (menus €26–42; ☎05.53.28.92.47; closed Sun, Mon lunch, Thurs lunch & Nov–March), in a lovely seventeenth-century mansion and its walled garden.

The Vézère valley

The **valley of the Vézère** River between **Limeuil** and **St-Amand-de-Coly** justifiably styles itself as the **prehistory** capital of the world. The high, rocky outcrops which overlook acres of thick forest are riddled with caves which have provided shelter for humans for tens of thousands of years. It was here that the first skeletons of **Cro-Magnon people** – the first Homo sapiens, tall and muscular with a large skull – were unearthed in 1868 by labourers building the Périgueux–Agen train line. Since then, an incomparable wealth of archeological and artistic evidence of late Stone Age people has been revealed, most famously in the breath-takingly sophisticated **cave paintings** of Lascaux and **Font de Gaume**.

Away from the throngs of visitors at the caves, there is much to appreciate in the peace and quiet of the Vézère valley. It's best enjoyed from a **canoe**, where you'll often find yourself alone in a bend of the river, rather than part of a vast armada, as tends to be the case on the Dordogne.

Limeuil

Built into the steep slope at the confluence of the Dordogne and Vézère rivers, the beautiful village of **LIMEUIL** is a picturesque place to while away a couple of hours. From the riverbank – an ideal picnic spot, with a pebbly beach for those who fancy a dip – the narrow, cobbled rue du Port leads steeply uphill, winding in between medieval houses and through the old gateways. At the top, the best views out over the village and surrounding countryside have been monopolized by the rather pricey **Parc Panoramique** April–June & Sept–Nov Sun–Fri 10am–12.30pm & 2.30–6pm; July & Aug daily 10am–8pm; €5), a wilderness of trees, shrubs and crumbling stone walls. For an even more classic view of the Dordogne valley, however, head west on the D31 towards Trémolat to find a vantage point looking down on one of two huge meanders in the river.

Canoes can be rented for trips on either river at the "port" (☎05.53.63.38.73, ⓦ www.canoes-rivieres-loisirs.com), where there are also a couple of **eating** options: the bar-brasserie *A l'Ancre de Salut* (menus from €17.50; closed Nov–March & evenings except in July & Aug), and the slightly more formal *Le Chai* (menus from €21; closed Wed & mid Nov to early Feb), serving pizzas plus local cuisine and a vast range of ice creams and sorbets.

Les Eyzies-de-Tayac

The main base for visiting many of the prehistoric painted caves is **LES EYZIES-DE-TAYAC**, a one-street village completely dedicated to tourism. While you're here, though, visit the excellent **Musée National de Préhistoire** (June & Sept daily except Tues 9.30am–6pm; July & Aug daily 9.30am–6.30pm; Oct–May daily except Tues 9.30am–12.30pm & 2–5.30pm; €5; ⓦ www .musee-prehistoire-eyzies.fr), which contains many important prehistoric artefacts found in the various caves in the region. Look out for the oil lamp from Lascaux and the exhibits from La Madeleine, to the north of Les Eyzies, including a superb bas-relief of a bison licking its flank.

The **tourist office**, on Les Eyzies' one street (mid-March to June & Sept Mon–Sat 9am–noon & 2–6pm, Sun 10am–noon & 2–5pm; July & Aug Mon–Sat 9am–7pm, Sun 10am–noon & 2–6pm; Oct to mid-March Mon–Fri 9am–noon & 2–6pm, Sat 10am–noon & 2–5pm; ☎05.53.06.97.05, Ⓦwww .tourisme-terredecromagnon.com) offers **bike** rental, **internet** access and information on local *chambres d'hôtes* and *gîtes d'étape*, among other things. For **canoe** rental, try AVCK (☎05.53.06.92.92, Ⓦwww.vezere-canoe.com), which offers trips between Thonac and Le Bugue.

Hotels are pricey and may require half-board in high season, while most are closed in winter. A good-value option is *La Rivière*, in a quiet spot about 1km away on the Périgueux road, with a handful of bright, well-kept rooms (☎05.53.06.97.14, Ⓦwww.lariviereleseyzies.com; ❷; closed Nov–March; simple meals from €12). There is also a **campsite** here (April–Oct), under the same management. Moving up a notch, make sure you book well ahead for *Le Moulin de la Beune* (☎05.53.06.94.33, Ⓦwww.moulindelabeune.com; ❸; closed Nov–March), with an excellent restaurant (closed for lunch Tues, Wed & Sat; menus €32–48), in a lovely spot by a millrace just east of the centre. Back on the other side of town, beside the tiny railway station, *Les Glycines* (☎05.53.06.97.07, Ⓦwww.les-glycines-dordogne.com; ❺; three-course menus €28 & €49; closed Nov–March) offers three-star luxury plus a pool – it's worth upgrading to a bigger room with views over the spacious garden. Alternatively, you could stay in **CAMPAGNE**, a pretty village 6km downstream, where you'll find big, bright rooms and regional menus at the *Hôtel du Château* (☎05.53.07.23.50, Ⓔhotduchateau@aol.com; ❸; closed mid-Oct to Easter; restaurant from €20).

When it comes to **eating**, you're best off dining in one of the hotel restaurants mentioned above. Alternatively, there's a clutch of cheap-and-cheerful bar-brasseries around the tourist office, or you could take a picnic down to the river.

Around Les Eyzies

There are more **prehistoric caves** around Les Eyzies than you could possibly hope to visit in one day. Besides, the compulsory guided tours are tiring, so it's best to select just a couple of the ones listed below.

Most of these caves were not used as permanent homes, and there are various theories as to the purpose of such inaccessible spots. Most agree that they were sanctuaries and, if not actually places of worship, at least had religious signifi-cance. One suggestion is that making images of animals that were commonly hunted – like reindeer and bison – or feared – like bears and mammoths – was a kind of sympathetic magic intended to help men either catch or evade these animals. Another is that they were part of a fertility cult: sexual images of women with pendulous breasts and protuberant behinds are common. Others argue that these cave paintings served educational purposes, making parallels with Australian aborigines who used similar images to teach their young vital survival information as well as the history and mythological origins of their people. But much remains unexplained – the abstract signs that appear in so many caves, for example, and the arrows which clearly cannot be arrows, since Stone Age arrowheads looked different from these representations.

Grotte de Font-de-Gaume

Since its discovery in 1901, dozens of polychrome paintings have been found in the **Grotte de Font-de-Gaume** (daily except Sat: mid-May to mid-Sept 9.30am–5.30pm; mid-Sept to mid-May 9.30am–12.30pm & 2–5.30pm; €6.50; ☎05.53.06.86.00, Ⓔfontdegaume@monuments-nationaux.fr), 1.5km along the D47 to Sarlat. Be aware that only 180 people are allowed to visit the cave each day and tickets sell out fast. You are advised to book (by phone or email) at least a month ahead in high season and well in advance at other times. You have to pay at the same time (€1.50 reservation fee; credit cards accepted) and tickets cannot be cancelled, though you can change the date and time if necessary. If you want to chance it, fifty tickets are sold on the spot each day; start queuing early.

The **cave** was first settled by Stone Age people during the last Ice Age – about 25,000 BC – when the Dordogne was the domain of roaming bison, reindeer and mammoths. The entrance is no more than a fissure concealed by rocks and trees above a small lush valley, leading to a narrow twisting passage. The first painting you see is a frieze of bison, reddish-brown in colour, massive, full of movement and very far from the primitive representations you might expect. Further on comes the most miraculous image of all, a **frieze** of five bison discovered in 1966 during cleaning operations. The colour, remarkably sharp and vivid, is preserved by a protective layer of calcite. Shading under the belly and down the thighs is used to give three-dimensionality with a sophistication that seems utterly modern. Another panel consists of superimposed drawings, a fairly common phenomenon in cave painting, sometimes the result of work by successive generations, but here an obviously deliberate technique. A reindeer in the foreground shares legs with a large bison behind to indicate perspective.

Stocks of **artists' materials** have also been found: kilos of prepared pigments; palettes – stones stained with ground-up earth pigments; and wooden painting sticks. Painting was clearly a specialized, perhaps professional, business, reproduced in dozens of caves located in the central Pyrenees and northern Spain.

Grotte des Combarelles

The **Grotte des Combarelles** (same hours as Font-de-Gaume; €6.50; maximum six people per tour), 2km along the D47 towards Sarlat, was discovered in 1910. The innermost part of the cave is covered with **engravings** from the Magdalenian period (about 12,000 years ago). Drawn over a period of two thousand years, many are superimposed one upon another, and include horses, reindeer, mammoths and stylized human figures – among the finest are the heads of a horse and a lioness.

As with Font-de-Gaume, pre-booking is essential, especially in peak season (same phone and email); collect tickets from Font-de-Gaume.

Abri du Cap Blanc and the Château de Commarque

Not a cave but a natural rock shelter, the **Abri du Cap Blanc** (same hours as Font-de-Gaume, though phone to check in the off-season; ☎05.53.06.86.00; €6.50) lies on a steep wooded hillside about 7km east of Les Eyzies. The shelter contains a **sculpted frieze** of horses and bison dating from the Middle Magdalenian period, about 14,000 years ago. Of only ten surviving prehistoric sculptures in France, this is undoubtedly the best. The design is deliberate, with the sculptures polished and set off against a pockmarked background. But what makes this place extraordinary is not just the large scale, but the high relief of some of the sculptures. This was only possible in places where light reached in, which in turn brought the danger of destruction by exposure to the air. Cro-Magnon people actually lived in this shelter, and a female skeleton some two thousand years younger than the frieze was found here.

For a non-cave detour, continue a little further up the heavily wooded Beune valley to visit the romantic ruins of the **Château de Commarque** (daily: April 10am–6pm; May, June & Sept 10am–7pm; July & Aug 10am–8pm; €6;

@ www.commarque.com). Dating from the twelfth century, it was originally a **castrum**, a fortified village made up of six separate fortresses, each belonging to a different noble family. The ruins have now been made structurally sound and it's possible to climb the thirty-metre-high tower for views over the surrounding countryside. You can reach the château by a footpath starting below Cap Blanc. Cars have to approach from the south, following signs from the D47 Sarlat road.

Grotte du Grand Roc

As well as prehistoric cave paintings, you can see some truly spectacular **stalactites** and **stalagmites** in the area around Les Eyzies. Some of the best examples are off the D47 towards Périgueux, 2km north of Les Eyzies, in the **Grotte du Grand Roc** (daily: Easter–June, Sept–Nov & Christmas holidays 10am–6pm; July & Aug 9.30am–7pm; €7.50; @ www.grandroc.com), whose entrance is high up in the cliffs that line much of the Vézère valley. There's a great view from the mouth of the cave and, inside, along some eighty metre of tunnel, a fantastic array of rock formations.

La Roque St-Christophe

The enormous prehistoric dwelling site, **La Roque St-Christophe** (daily: Feb, March & Oct 10am–6pm; April–June & Sept 10am–6.30pm; July & Aug 10am–8pm; Nov–Jan 2–5pm; €7; @ www.roque-st-christophe.com), 9km northeast of Les Eyzies along the D706 to Montignac, is made up of about a hundred **rock shelters** on five levels, hollowed out of the limestone cliffs. The whole complex is nearly a kilometre long and about eighty metres above ground level, where the River Vézère once flowed. The earliest traces of occupation go back over 50,000 years. The view is pretty good, and the French guided tour instructive, but most of the finds are on display at the museum in Les Eyzies (see p.638).

Montignac

Some 26km up the Vézère valley, **MONTIGNAC** is the main base for visiting the Lascaux cave. It's a more attractive place than Les Eyzies, with several wooden-balconied houses leaning appealingly over the river, a good **market** (Wed & Sat) and a lively annual **arts festival** (third week of July), featuring international folk groups. The **tourist office** is on place Bertran-de-Born (Feb, March, Sept & Oct Mon–Sat 9am–noon & 2–6pm; July & Aug daily 9am–7pm; Nov–Jan Mon–Sat 10am–noon & 2–5pm; ☎05.53.51.82.60, @ www.bienvenue-montignac.com) and offers **internet** access. You can rent **canoes** from **Kanoak** (☎05.53.51.94.62 or 06.75.48.60.47, @ www.kanoak-vezere.com).

   Hotels, as everywhere around here, get booked up quickly in summer. The cheapest rooms on offer – but still nice and cheerful – are at *Le P'tit Monde*, just out of centre on the road to Sarlat (☎05.53.51.32.76, @ hotelrestaurant lepetitmonde@hotmail.fr; ❷; restaurant from €12). The nearby *Hôtel de la Grotte*, rue du 4-Septembre (☎05.53.51.80.48, @ hoteldelagrotte@orange.fr; ❸; restaurant menus from €16; closed Jan), is another good, reasonably priced option, with a small but pleasant garden beside a stream; ask for rooms off the main road. Then it's a big leap up to the three-star *Relais du Soleil d'Or*, also on the main rue du 4-Septembre (☎05.53.51.80.22, @ www.le-soleil-dor.com; ❹; closed two weeks in Feb), with its own pool and gourmet restaurant (menus from €28; Nov–March closed Sun evening & Mon), and the pretty, period rooms of the ivy- and wisteria-clad *Hostellerie de la Roseraie*, across the river in quiet place d'Armes (☎05.53.50.53.92, @ www.laroseraie-hotel.com; ❺; closed Nov–March; restaurant menus €22–48), also with a pool and flower-filled garden. Finally, there's a well-tended three-star **campsite**, *Le Moulin du Bleufond* (☎05.53.51.83.95, ⓦwww.bleufond.com; April to mid-Oct), on the riverbank 500m downstream.

Grotte de Lascaux and Lascaux II

The **Grotte de Lascaux** was discovered in 1940 by four boys who were looking for their dog and stumbled across a deep cavern decorated with marvellously preserved **paintings** of animals. Executed by Cro-Magnon people 17,000 years ago, the paintings are among the finest examples of prehistoric art in existence. There are five or six identifiable styles, and subjects include bison, mammoths and horses, plus the biggest known prehistoric drawing, of a 5.5-metre bull with astonishingly expressive head and face. In 1948, the cave was opened to the public, and over the course of the next fifteen years more than a million tourists came to Lascaux. Sadly, because of deterioration caused by the heat and breath of visitors, the cave had to be closed in 1963; now you have to be content with the replica known as **Lascaux II**, 2km south of Montignac on the D704 (Feb, March, Nov & Dec Tues–Sun 10am–12.30pm & 2–5.30pm; April–June & Sept daily 9am–6.30pm; July & Aug daily 9am–8pm; Oct daily 10am–12.30pm & 2–6pm; closed Jan; €8.30, combined ticket with Le Thot prehistoric theme park, €11.50; ⓦwww.semitour.com). There are two thousand tickets on sale each day but these go fast in peak season; you can buy them in person a day or so in advance, while telephone bookings are accepted only in July and August (☎05.53.51.96.23). Note also that in winter (Oct–Easter) tickets are normally on sale at the site, while in summer (Easter–Sept) they are only available from an office (daily: July & Aug 9am–7pm; Sept & Easter to June 9am–6pm) beside Montignac tourist office – the system and opening times are somewhat fickle, however, so it's safest to check in Montignac before heading up to the cave.

Opened in 1983, Lascaux II was the result of eleven years' painstaking work by twenty artists and sculptors, using the same methods and materials as the original cave painters. While the visit can't offer the excitement of a real cave, the reconstruction rarely disappoints the thousands who trek here every year. The guided tour lasts fourty minutes (commentary in French or English). If you have bought the joint ticket including **Le Thot** (Feb, March, Nov & Dec Tues–Sun 10am–12.30pm & 2–5.30pm; April–June & Sept daily 10am–6pm; July & Aug daily 10am–7pm; Oct daily 10am–12.30pm & 2–6pm; closed Jan; €5.80, €11.50 for joint ticket with Lascaux II; ⓦwww.semitour.com), 5km down the Vézère near **THONAC**, it's best to visit the park first for an enhanced appreciation of the cave itself, particularly if you have kids. The video showing the construction of Lascaux II is particularly interesting, and there are Disneyesque mock-ups of prehistoric scenes and live examples of some of the animals featured in the paintings: European bison, long-horned cattle and Przewalski's horses, rare and beautiful animals from Mongolia believed to resemble the prehistoric wild horse – notice the erect mane.

St-Amand-de-Coly

Nine kilometres east of Montignac, the village of **ST-AMAND-DE-COLY** boasts a superbly beautiful fortified Romanesque church, a magical venue for concerts in the summer. Despite its bristling military architecture, the twelfth-century church manages to combine great delicacy and spirituality, with its purity of line and simple decoration most evocative in the low sun of late afternoon or early evening. Its defences left nothing to chance: the walls are four metres thick, a ditch runs all the way round, and a passage once skirted the eaves, with numerous positions for archers to rain down arrows and blind stairways to mislead attackers. Near the church, the unpretentious *Hôtel Gardette* (T05.53.51.68.50, Wwww.hotel-gardette.com; ❶; restaurant menus from €17.50; closed Oct–March) makes it possible to stay overnight in this tiny, idyllic place.

The middle Dordogne valley

The most familiar images of the River Dordogne are those from around **Beynac** and **La Roque-Gageac**, where the scenery is at its most spectacular, with clifftop châteaux facing each other across the valley. The most imposing of these date from the Hundred Years War, when the river marked the frontier between French-held land to the north and English territory to the south. Further upstream, the hilltop *bastide* village of **Domme** offers stunning views, but is as crowded as Sarlat in summer.

Just south of the river, the **Abbaye de Cadouin** lies tucked out of harm's way in a fold of the landscape, hiding a lovely Gothic cloister. The train line from Bergerac to Sarlat runs along the river for this stretch, offering some wonderful views but unfortunately not stopping anywhere very useful; to appreciate the villages covered here, you need your own transport or, better still, a canoe.

The Abbaye de Cadouin

Before setting off up the Dordogne, it's worth taking a detour about 6km south of **LE BUISSON** to the twelfth-century Cistercian **Abbaye de Cadouin**. For eight hundred years until 1935 it drew flocks of pilgrims to wonder at a piece of cloth first mentioned by Simon de Montfort in 1214 and thought to be part of Christ's shroud. In 1935 the two bands of embroidery at either end were shown to contain an Arabic text from around the eleventh century. Since then the main attraction has been the finely sculpted but badly damaged capitals of the flamboyant Gothic **cloister** (Feb, March, Nov & Dec Mon, Wed, Thurs & Sun 10am–12.30pm & 2–5.30pm; April–June, Sept & Oct daily except Tues 10am–12.30pm & 2–6pm; July & Aug daily 10am–7pm; closed Jan; €5; Wwww.semitour.com). Beside it stands a Romanesque **church** with a stark, bold front and wooden belfry roofed with chestnut shingles (chestnut trees abound around here – their timber was used in furniture-making and their nuts ground for flour during frequent famines). Inside the church, the nave is slightly out of alignment; this is thought to be deliberate and perhaps a vestige of pagan attachments, as the three windows are aligned so that at the winter and summer solstices the sun shines through all three in a single shaft.

You can **stay** across the road at the *Restaurant de l'Abbaye* (T05.53.63.40.93, Edelpech@orange.fr; ❷; closed Sun evening & Mon), which has four simple en-suite rooms and serves reasonably priced meals (menus from €13.50), or in the monks' dormitories themselves, now an excellent HI **youth hostel** (T05.53.73.28.78, Ecadouin@fuaj.org; closed mid-Dec to Jan). There's also a small **campsite** in the village, *Les Jardins de l'Abbaye* (T05.53.61.89.30, Wwww.dordogne-perigord.com/jardins-abbaye; April–Oct).

Another possibility is to stay in the hilltop town of **BELVÈS**, some 15km further east along the D54. The *Hôtel Le Home*, on the through road at the top of the hill, provides good cheap **accommodation** and food (T05.53.29.01.65, Wwww.lehomedebelves.fr; ❶; restaurant menus €11–29; Oct–March closed Sun evening & Fri evening). Next door is the more upmarket *Belvédère* (T05.53.31.51.41, Ele.belvedere.perigord@orange.fr; ❷; restaurant €20–29; Nov–March closed

Wed & Thurs). The nearest **campsite** is the three-star *Les Nauves* (☎ 05.53.29.12.64, ⓦ www.lesnauves.com; April–Sept), 4.5km off the Monpazier road.

The châteaux of Les Milandes and Castelnaud

The first of the string of châteaux that line the Dordogne east of Le Buisson is **Les Milandes** (daily: April–June, Sept & Oct 10am–6.15pm; July & Aug 9.30am–7.30pm; €8; ⓦ www.milandes.com), perched high on the south bank. Built in 1489, it was the property of the de Caumont family until the Revolution, but its most famous owner was the Folies Bergères star, Josephine Baker (see box below), who lived here from 1936 to 1968. The stories surrounding the place are more intriguing than the château itself, which contains a motley collection of Ms Baker's effects. The garden, meanwhile, hosts daily displays by birds of prey.

Further along on the same side of the river, the **Château de Fayrac** was an English forward position in the Hundred Years War, built to watch over Beynac, on the opposite bank, where the French were holed up. All slated pepper-pot towers, it's unfortunately closed to the public, but you can visit the partially ruined **Château de Castelnaud** (daily: Feb, March & Oct 10am–6pm; April–June & Sept 10am–7pm; July & Aug 9am–8pm; Nov–Jan 2–5pm; €7.60, or €13 for a joint ticket with Marqueyssac; ⓦ www.castelnaud .com), a little to the south of Fayrac and the true rival to Beynac in terms of

---

Josephine Baker and the Rainbow Tribe

Born on June 3, 1906, in the black ghetto of East St Louis, Illinois, **Josephine Baker** was one of the most remarkable women of the twentieth century. Her mother washed clothes for a living, her father was a drummer who soon deserted his family, yet by the late 1920s Josephine was the most celebrated cabaret star in France, primarily due to her role in the legendary Folies Bergères show in Paris. On her first night, de Gaulle, Hemingway, Piaf and Stravinsky were among the audience, and her notoriety was further enhanced by her long line of illustrious husbands and lovers, which included the Crown Prince of Sweden and the crime novelist Georges Simenon. She also kept a pet cheetah called Mildred, with whom she used to walk around Paris. During the war, Baker was active in the Resistance, for which she won the Croix de Guerre, and later became involved in the civil rights movement in North America, where she insisted on playing to non-segregated audiences, a stance which got her arrested in Canada and tailed by the FBI in the US.

By far her most bizarre project was the château of **Les Milandes**, which she rented from 1936 and then bought in 1947, after she married the French orchestra leader Jo Bouillon. Having converted the place into two hotels with a mini-golf course, tennis court and an autobiographical wax museum, she opened the château to the general public as a model multicultural community, popularly dubbed the *"village du monde"*. In the course of the 1950s, she adopted babies (mostly orphans) of different ethnic and religious backgrounds from around the world, and by the end of the decade had twelve children at Les Milandes, including a black Catholic Colombian and a Buddhist Korean, along with her mother, brother and sister from East St Louis.

Over 300,000 people a year visited the château in the 1950s, but the conservative local population was never very happy about Les Milandes and what Josephine dubbed her "Rainbow Tribe". In the 1960s, Baker's financial problems, divorce and two heart attacks spelled the end for the project and, despite a sit-in protest by Baker herself (by then in her 60s), the château was sold off in 1968. Josephine died of a stroke in 1975 and was given a state funeral at La Madeleine in Paris, mourned by thousands of her adopted countryfolk.

impregnability – although it was successfully captured by the bellicose Simon de Montfort as early as 1214. The English held it for much of the Hundred Years War, and it wasn't until the Revolution that it was finally abandoned. Fairly heavily restored in recent years, it now houses a highly informative **museum of medieval warfare**. Its core is an extensive collection of original weaponry, including all sorts of bizarre contraptions, and a fine assortment of armour.

Beynac-et-Cazenac

Clearly visible on an impregnable cliff on the north bank of the river, the eye-catching village and castle of **BEYNAC-ET-CAZENAC** was built in the days when the river was the only route open to traders and invaders. By road, it's 3km to the **château** (daily: 10am–6pm; €7) but a steep lane leads up through the village and takes only 15 minutes by foot. It's protected on the landward side by a double wall; elsewhere the sheer drop of almost two hundred metres does the job. The flat terrace at the base of the keep, which was added by the English, conceals the remains of the houses where the beleaguered villagers lived. Richard the Lionheart held the place for a time, until a gangrenous wound received while besieging the castle of Châlus, north of Périgueux ended his term of blood-letting.

Originally, to facilitate defence, the rooms inside the keep were only connected by a narrow spiral staircase. The division of domestic space into dining rooms and so forth only came about when the advent of artillery made these old châteaux-forts militarily obsolete. From the roof there's a stupendous – and vertiginous – view upriver to the **Château de Marquey-ssac**, whose beautiful seventeenth- and nineteenth-century **gardens** extend along the ridge (same hours as Castelnaud; €7, or €13 for a joint ticket with Castelnaud).

For a different perspective of these châteaux, it's worth taking a **river cruise** with Gabarres de Beynac (April–Oct daily 10am–12.30pm & 2–6pm; €7.50; Ⓦ www.gabarre-beynac.com) on a replica *gabarre*, the traditional wooden river-craft. This is also classic **canoeing** country, with rental available from Copeyre Canoë (Ⓣ 05.53.28.95.01, Ⓦ www.canoe-copeyre.com), amongst numerous outlets along this stretch of river.

The best of Beynac's **hotels** is the *Hôtel du Château* (Ⓣ 05.53.29.19.20, Ⓦ www.hotelduchateau-dordogne.com; ❸; closed Dec to mid-Jan), with fresh, bright rooms, a small swimming pool and a good restaurant (menus from €16) with a terrace overlooking the river; though it's on the busy main road, rooms are double-glazed and some have air-conditioning. A little further east there's also a **campsite**, *Le Capeyrou* (Ⓣ 05.53.29.54.95, Ⓦ www.campinglecapeyrou .com; April–Sept).

La Roque-Gageac

The village of **LA ROQUE-GAGEAC** is almost too perfect, its ochre-coloured houses sheltering under dramatically overhanging cliffs. It inevitably pulls in the tourist buses, and since the main road separates the village from the river, the noise and fumes of the traffic can become oppressive. The best way to escape is to slip away through the lanes and alleyways that wind up through the terraced houses towards the ruins of some twelfth-century **fortifications** built into the cliff face (daily: July & Aug 10.30am–7pm; Sept–June 11am–5pm; €5). Alternatively, hop on a *gabarre* for a leisurely **river-trip** (daily: April–Sept 10am–6pm; Oct 2–5pm; €8.70; Ⓦ www.norbert.fr), or rent a **canoe** (Ⓣ 05.53.28.17.07, Ⓦ www.canoevacances.com) and paddle over to the opposite

Canoeing on the Dordogne and Vézère

Canoeing is hugely popular in the Dordogne, especially in summer, when the Vézère and Dordogne rivers are shallow and slow-flowing – ideal for beginners. There are rental outlets at just about every twist in both rivers, and a few are mentioned in the text. Although it's possible to rent one-person kayaks or two-person canoes by the hour, it's best to take at least a half-day or longer (some outfits offer up to a week's rental), and simply cruise downstream. The company you book through will either take you to your departure point or send a minibus to pick you up from your final destination. **Prices** vary according to what's on offer; expect to pay around €20–25 per person per day. Most places function daily in July and August, on demand in May, June and September, depending on the weather, and are closed the rest of the year. All companies must provide life jackets (*gilets*) and teach you basic safety procedures, most importantly how to capsize and get out safely. You must be able to swim.

bank, where you can picnic and enjoy a great view of the village, at its best in the burnt-orange glow of the evening sun.

Most people just come here for the afternoon, so there's usually space if you want to **stay** the night, most pleasantly at *La Belle Étoile* (℡05.53.29.51.44, ⓦwww.belleetoile.fr; ❸; closed Nov–March), whose restaurant serves good traditional cuisine (menus from €26, closed Mon & lunch Wed), and whose more expensive rooms have lovely views out over the river. Of the many **campsites** in the vicinity, *Le Beau Rivage* (℡08.25.00.20.30, ⓦwww.village -center.com; April–Sept), on the D703 towards Sarlat, is a good three-star choice with lots of activities.

Domme

High on a cliff on the river's south bank, **DOMME** is an exceptionally well-preserved *bastide*, now wholly given over to tourism. Its attractions, in addition to its position, include three original thirteenth-century **gateways** and a section of the old **walls**. From the northern edge of the village, marked by a drop so precipitous that fortifications were deemed unnecessary, you look out over a wide sweep of river country. Beneath the village is a warren of **caves** (daily: Feb to mid-Nov & Christmas holidays; contact the tourist office below for times & tickets; €6.50) in which the townspeople took refuge in times of danger. Unfortunately, the rock formations can't compare with the area's other caves; the only good point is the exit onto the cliff-face with a panoramic lift up to the top. The entrance to the complex is under the market hall, opposite the **tourist office** (Feb to June & Sept to mid-Nov daily 10am–noon & 2–6pm; July & Aug daily 10am–7pm; mid-Nov to Dec Mon–Fri 10am–12.30pm & 1.30–4.30pm; closed Jan; ℡05.53.31.71.00, ⓦwww.ot-domme.com).

The smartest **hotel** in town is *L'Esplanade*, right on the cliff edge (℡05.53.28.31.41, ⓦwww.esplanade-perigord.com; ❺; closed Nov–March), with a fine restaurant (menus €42–95; closed Mon & lunchtime Wed); note that rooms with a view are premium-rated. A cheaper alternative is *Le Nouvel Hôtel*, at the top of the Grand'rue (℡05.53.28.36.81, ⓦwww.domme-nouvel-hotel .com; ❷; closed mid-Nov to Easter), which has several simple, reasonably priced rooms above a restaurant (menus from €15). The closest **campsite** is the one-star municipal site (℡05.53.28.31.91, ⓔmairie.cenac@orange.fr; mid-June to mid-Sept) down by the river at **Cénac**.

The upper Dordogne

East of Sarlat and Domme, you leave the crowds of Périgord Noir behind, but the Dordogne valley retains all of its beauty and interest. **Martel** and **Carennac** are wonderfully preserved medieval villages, and there are exceptional examples of Romanesque sculpture in the churches at **Souillac** and **Beaulieu**. Travel is difficult without a car, but Souillac is reachable by train and has bus routes to Sarlat and Martel. Cyclists can follow the *"voie verte"*, a 23km-long cycle-route from Sarlat to Souillac along a decommissioned train.

Souillac

The first place of any size east of Sarlat is **SOUILLAC**, at the confluence of the Borrèze and Dordogne rivers and on a major road junction. Virginia Woolf stayed here in 1937, and was pleased to meet "no tourists ... England seems like a chocolate box bursting with trippers afterward". There are still few tourists, since Souillac's only real point of interest is the twelfth-century **church of Ste-Marie**, west of the main road. Roofed with massive domes like the cathedrals of Périgueux and Cahors, its spacious interior creates just the atmosphere for cool reflection on a summer's day. On the inside of the west door are some of the most wonderful Romanesque sculptures, including a seething mass of beasts devouring each other. The greatest piece of craftsmanship, though, is a **bas-relief of Isaiah**, fluid and supple, thought to be by one of the artists who worked at Moissac. Next to the church, the **Musée de l'Automate** (April, May & Oct Tues–Sun 10am–noon & 3–6pm; June & Sept daily 10am–noon & 3–6pm; July & Aug daily 10am–7pm; Nov–March Wed–Sun 2.30–5.30pm; €5.50) contains an impressive collection of nineteenth- and twentieth-century mechanical dolls and animals, which dance, sing and perform magical tricks; look out for the irresistible laughing man.

The **tourist office** (July & Aug Mon–Sat 9.30am–12.30pm & 2–7pm, Sun 10am–noon & 3–6pm; Sept–June Mon–Sat 10am–noon & 2–6pm; ☎05.65.37.81.56, ⓦwww.tourisme-souillac.com) is on the main boulevard Louis-Jean-Malvy. For **accommodation**, head to the old quarter, where you'll find beautifully renovated and not expensive rooms in the 16th-century *Pavillon St-Martin*, on place St-Martin in the shadow of the old belfry (☎05.65.32.63.45, ⓦhotel-saint-martin-souillac.com; ❷–❸). If they're full, try *La Vieille Auberge*, 1 rue de la Recège (☎05.65.32.79.43, ⓦwww.la-vieille-auberge.com; ❹; closed mid-Nov to mid-Dec), where guests have access to a pool and its best known for its excellent **restaurant** (menus €25–65; closed Sun evening & Mon). For simpler meals, head to *Le Beffroi* on place St-Martin (menus from €12; closed Sun evening & Mon), with its lovely, wisteria-shaded terrace. There's also a large riverside **campsite**, *Les Ondines* (☎05.65.37.86.44, ⓦwww.souillac.fr; May–Sept). You can rent **bicycles and canoes** from Copeyre Canoë (☎05.65.32.72.61, ⓦwww.copeyre.com), next to the campsite.

Martel

About 15km east of Souillac and set back even further from the river, **MARTEL** is a minor medieval masterpiece, built in a pale, almost white stone, offset by warm reddish-brown roofs. A Turenne-administered town (see p.622), its heyday came during the thirteenth and fourteenth centuries, when the viscounts established a court of appeal here.

The main square, **place des Consuls**, is mostly taken up by the eighteenth-century **market hall**, but on every side there are reminders of the town's illustrious past, most notably in the superb Gothic **Hôtel de la Raymondie**. Begun in 1280, it served as the Turenne law courts, though it doubled as the town's refuge, hence the distinctive corner turrets. Facing the hôtel is the **Tour des Pénitents**, one of the many medieval towers which gave the town its epithet, *la ville aux sept tours* ("the town with seven towers"). The Young King Henry, son of Henry II died in the striking **Maison Fabri**, in the southeast corner of the square. One block south, rue Droite leads east to the town's main **church**, St-Maur, built in a fiercely defensive, mostly Gothic style, with a finely carved Romanesque tympanum depicting the Last Judgement above the west door.

For somewhere to **stay**, it's a choice between the unpretentious *Auberge des 7 Tours* (☎05.65.37.30.16, Ⓦwww.auberge7tours.com; ❷; restaurant menus from €15, closed for Sun evening & Mon), or the luxurious rooms at the 🍴 *Relais Ste-Anne* (☎05.65.36.40.56, Ⓦwww.relais-sainte-anne.com; ❺; open March–Nov), in the ivy-covered buildings of a former religious school, surrounded by attractive gardens with a small pool. There's also a basic municipal **campsite**, *La Callopie* (☎05.65.37.30.03, ✉mairiedemartel@orange.fr; May–Sept), on the northern edge of town, and the more attractive riverside *Camping les Falaises* (☎05.65.37.37.78, Ⓕ05.65.41.05.32; mid-June to mid-Sept), 5km away in the village of **GLUGES**, where you can also rent **canoes and bikes** from Port-Loisirs down by the water (☎05.65.32.27.59, Ⓦwww.portloisirs.com).

Railway enthusiasts might be interested in the **steam tourist trains** (April–Sept; ☎05.65.37.35.81, Ⓦwww.trainduhautquercy.info), which run on a restored line between Martel and St-Denis. The return trip (€9.50) lasts about an hour as the train puffs along the edges of the cliffs overlooking the river valley.

Carennac and Castelnau-Bretenoux

CARENNAC is without doubt one of the most beautiful villages along this part of the Dordogne River. Elevated just above the south bank of the river, 13km or so east of Martel, it's best known for its typical Quercy architecture, its Romanesque priory, where the French writer Fénelon spent the best years of his life, and for its greengages.

Carennac's feature, as so often in these parts, is the Romanesque tympanum – in the Moissac style – above the west door of its church, the **Église St-Pierre**. Christ sits in majesty with the Book of Judgement in his left hand, with the apostles and adoring angels below him. Next to the church, don't miss the old **cloisters and chapterhouse** (April–June, Sept & Oct Mon–Sat 10am–noon & 2–6pm; July & Aug daily 10am–1pm & 2–7pm; Nov–March Mon–Fri 10am–noon & 2–5pm; €2.50), which contain an exceptionally expressive life-size *Entombment of Christ*.

Carennac's only **hotel**, the *Hostellerie Fénelon*, on the main street (☎05.65.10.96.46, Ⓦwww.hotel-fenelon.com; ❸; closed Jan to mid-March), has simple but perfectly adequate rooms, a pool and a good **restaurant** specializing in traditional regional cuisine (menus from €22.50, closed Fri & for lunch on Mon & Sat). There's also a welcoming *chambre d'hôte*, *La Petite Vigne* (☎05.65.50.25.84, Ⓦwww.lapetitevigne-carennac.com; ❹), on the east edge of Carennac, and a **campsite**, *L'Eau Vive*, 1km further east along the river (☎05.65.10.97.39, Ⓦwww.dordogne-soleil.com; May–mid-Oct).

Another 10km further upstream, the sturdy towers and machicolated red-brown walls of the eleventh-century **Château de Castelnau-Bretenoux** (May & June daily 10am–12.30pm & 2–6.30pm; July & Aug daily 10am–7pm;

Sept–April daily except Tues 10am–12.30pm & 2–5.30pm; €6.50; @www
.monuments-nationaux.fr) dominate a sharp knoll above the Dordogne. Most
of it has now been restored and refurnished.

Beaulieu-sur-Dordogne

In a picturesque spot on the banks of the Dordogne, 8km upriver from
Castelnau-Bretenoux, **BEAULIEU-SUR-DORDOGNE** boasts another of
the great masterpieces of Romanesque sculpture on the porch of the **church
of St-Pierre**. This doorway is unusually deep-set, with a tympanum presided
over by an oriental-looking Christ with one arm extended to welcome the
chosen. All around him is a complicated pattern of angels and apostles, executed
in characteristic "dancing" style, similar to that at Carennac. The dead raise the
lids of their coffins hopefully, while underneath a frieze depicts monsters
crunching heads. Take the opportunity also to wander north along rue de la
Chapelle past some handsome sculpted facades and down to the river.

The most appealing **hotel** is ✶ *Le Relais de Vellinus*, 17 place du Champ-de-
Mars (☎05.55.91.11.04, @www.vellinus.com; ❹; closed Christmas & New Year
holidays), imaginatively decorated in warm, contemporary colours. You'll find
the same attention to detail in its **restaurant**, which serves good-value lunch
menus from €15 and €26 in the evening. Another nice option, also with a
decent restaurant, is the riverside *Les Charmilles* (☎05.55.91.29.29, @www
.auberge-charmilles.com; ❸; menus from €19; Oct–April closed Wed). The
welcoming HI **hostel** is at the far end of rue de la Chapelle in a magnificent
half-timbered and turreted building, with surprisingly modern rooms inside
(☎05.55.91.13.82, @beaulieu@fuaj.org; closed Nov–March). There are river-
bathing and canoeing possibilities and a good riverside **campsite**, *Camping des
Îles*, close by (☎05.55.91.02.65, @www.campingdesiles.fr; mid-April to
mid-Oct).

South through the Lot

The core of this section is formed by the old provinces of **Haut Quercy** and
Quercy: the land between the Dordogne and the Lot rivers and between the
Lot and the Garonne, Aveyron and Tarn. While it largely corresponds to the
modern-day Lot *département*, we have extended it slightly eastwards to include
the gorges of the River **Aveyron** and Villefranche-de-Rouergue on the edge
of the province of Rouergue.

The area is hotter, drier, less well known and, with few exceptions, less
crowded than the Dordogne, though no less interesting. The cave paintings at
Pech-Merle are on a par with those at Les Eyzies. **Najac, Penne** and **Peyrusse**
have ruined castles to rival those of the Dordogne. Towns like **Figeac** and
Villefranche-de-Rouergue are without equal, as are villages like
St-Antonin-Noble-Val, and stretches of country like that below **Gourdon**,
around **Les Arques** where Osip Zadkine had his studio, and the **Célé valley**.

Again, without transport, many places are out of reach. Some consolation,
however, is the existence of the Brive–Toulouse train line that makes Figeac,

Villefranche-de-Rouergue and Najac accessible, while **Agen**, **Moissac** and **Montauban** are on the Bordeaux–Toulouse line.

Rocamadour and around

Halfway up a cliff in the deep and abrupt canyon of the Alzou stream, the spectacular setting of **ROCAMADOUR** is hard to beat. Since medieval times the town has been inundated by pilgrims drawn by the supposed miraculous ability of Rocamadour's Black Madonna. Nowadays, pilgrims are outnumbered by more secular-minded visitors, who fill the lanes lined with shops peddling incongruous souvenirs, but who come here mainly to wonder at the sheer audacity of the town's location, built almost vertically into its rocky backdrop.

Legend has it that the history of Rocamadour began with the arrival of **Zacchaeus**, a tax-collector in Jericho at the time of Christ. According to one legend he was advised by the Virgin Mary to come to France, where he lived out his years as a hermit. When in 1166 a perfectly preserved body was found in a grave high up on the rock, it was declared to be Zacchaeus, or **St Amadour**. The place soon became a major pilgrimage site and a staging post on the road to Santiago de Compostela in Spain. St Bernard, numerous kings of England and France and thousands of others crawled up the chapel steps on their knees to pay their respects and seek cures for their illnesses. Young King Henry, son of Henry II of England, was the first to plunder the shrine, but he was easily outclassed by the Huguenots, who tried in vain to burn the saint's corpse and finally resigned themselves simply to hacking it to bits. A reconstruction was produced in the nineteenth century, in an attempt to revive the flagging pilgrimage.

The area's other main sight is the **Gouffre de Padirac**, with its vast underground river system, which lies across open country to the northeast of Rocamadour. Further east again, the town of **St-Céré** is an attractive spot, best known for its museum dedicated to the twentieth-century artist Jean Lurçat.

▲ Rocamadour

The Town

Rocamadour is easy enough to find your way around. There's just one street, rue de la Couronnerie, strung out between two medieval gateways. Above it, the steep hillside supports no fewer than seven churches. There's a lift dug into the rock-face (€3 return), but it's far better to climb the 223 steps of the Via Sancta, up which the devout drag themselves on their knees to the little **Chapelle Notre-Dame** where the miracle-working twelfth-century Black Madonna resides. The tiny, crudely carved walnut statue glows in the mysterious half-light, but the rest of the chapel is unremarkable. From the rock above the entrance door hangs a rusty sword, supposedly Roland's legendary blade, Durandal.

The neighbouring **Musée d'Art Sacré**, which contains sacred art treasures, reliquaries and various historical documents, is closed for long-term restoration – check at the tourist office for the latest situation. However, you can still access the ancient **ramparts** (daily 8am–9pm; €2) higher above Rocamadour in **L'Hospitalet**. They're reached via a winding shady path, La Calvarie, past the Stations of the Cross – the effort is rewarded with vertiginous views across the valley. Alternatively, you can hop in another lift (€4 return) up to the top.

There are two different **wildlife centres** worth visiting in L'Hospitalet: the **Rocher des Aigles** (April–June & Sept Tues–Sun 2–5pm; 1–14 July daily 1–7pm; 15 July to Aug daily 11am–7pm; Oct to mid-Nov Tues, Thurs, Fri & Sun 2.30–5pm; closed mid-Nov to March; €8; @www.rocherdesaigles.com), a breeding centre for birds of prey – don't miss the demonstrations of the birds in flight; and the **Forêt des Singes**, off the D673 (April–June & first two weeks Sept daily 10am–noon & 1–5.30pm; July & Aug daily 9.30am–6.30pm; mid-Sept to Oct Mon–Fri 1–5pm, Sat & Sun 10am–noon & 1–5pm; €7.50; @www.la-foret-des-singes.com), where more than one hundred Barbary apes roam the plateau in relative freedom.

Practicalities

Getting to Rocamadour without your own transport is awkward unless you're prepared to walk or take a taxi the 4km from the Rocamadour-Padirac **gare SNCF** on the Brive–Capdenac line. If you arrive by car, you'll have to park in L'Hospitalet, on the hilltop above Rocamadour (which has the best view of the town), or else in the car park several hundred metres below. There are two **tourist offices**: the main one in l'Hospitalet (T05.65.33.22.00, @www.rocamadour.com), and a second next to the Hôtel de Ville, on rue de la Couronnerie. Inconveniently, the distribution of hours between the two offices changes significantly most years, though you're assured that at least one will be open on any given day.

Rocamadour's **hotels** close for the winter months, and you need to book early in summer. There's good value at the *Lion d'Or*, on rue de la Couronnerie (T05.65.33.62.04, @www.liondor-rocamadour.com; ❷; closed mid-Nov to Easter), plus a decent restaurant with menus from €13, and at *Le Terminus des Pèlerins*, at the bottom of the Via Sancta, with fine views of the valley (T05.65.33.62.14, @www.terminus-des-pelerins.com; ❷–❸; closed Nov to mid-March; restaurant from €17). For a night of luxury, try the *Beau Site*, also on rue de la Couronnerie (T05.65.33.63.08, @www.bestwestern.com; ❾; closed mid-Nov to early Feb), which has an excellent restaurant, the *Jehan de Valon* (lunch menus from €18), plus a cheaper bistrot (menus from €14) Up in L'Hospitalet, the *Belvédère* (T05.65.33.63.25, @www.lebelvedere-rocamadour.com; ❸–❹; closed Jan to mid-March) enjoys prime views from its more expensive rooms and from its more formal – and recommended – restaurant (menus from €17). **Campers** should head for the nearby three-star site, *Les Cigales* (☎05.65.33.64.44, Ⓦwww .camping-cigales.com; Easter–Sept). Apart from the hotels, a reliable **place to eat** is the homely *Chez Anne-Marie*, on rue de la Couronnerie (☎05.65.33.65.81), which offers good-value menus from €16.50. Or try *Les Jardins de la Louve*, at the far end of rue de la Couronnerie, with tables in the garden in fine weather (menus from €16; closed mid-Nov to Easter).

Gouffre de Padirac

The **Gouffre de Padirac** (daily guided tours: April–June 9.30am–5.30pm; July 9.30am–6pm; Aug 8.30am–6.30pm; Sept to mid-Nov 10am–5pm; €8.70; Ⓦwww.gouffre-de-padirac.com) is about 20km east of Rocamadour on the other side of the main Brive–Figeac road. An enormous limestone sinkhole, about 100m deep and over 100m wide, it gives access to an underground river system containing some spectacular rock formations and magical lakes, but is very, very popular. There is no system for reservations, so in summer you're advised to arrive before 10am. Visits are partly on foot, partly by boat, and the guided tours last an hour and a half. In wet weather you'll need a waterproof jacket.

St-Céré

East of Padirac and about 9km from **Bretenoux**, you come to the medieval town of **ST-CÉRÉ**, full of ancient houses crowding around place du Mercadial, and dominated by the brooding ruins of the **Château de St-Laurent-les-Tours**, whose two powerful keeps were once part of a fortress belonging to the Turenne. During World War II, the artist Jean Lurçat operated a secret Resistance radio post here; after the war he turned it into a studio, and it's now a **museum** of his work, with mainly huge tapestries but also sketches, paintings and pottery (daily: two weeks at Easter & mid-July to Sept 9.30am–noon & 2.30–6.30pm; €2.50). At over 200m altitude, the site is spectacular, with stunning views all around.

St-Céré has two very pleasant and reasonable **places to stay**: the *Hôtel Victor-Hugo*, avenue Victor-Hugo, by the river (☎05.65.38.16.15, Ⓦwww.hotel-victor-hugo.fr; ❸; closed two weeks in Feb & three in Oct/Nov; restaurant menus from €16, closed Sun evening and Mon), and the modern, more upmarket *Hôtel de France*, on avenue François-de-Maynard (☎05.65.38.02.16, Ⓦwww.lefrance-hotel.com; ❸; closed mid-Dec to Feb; restaurant menus from €24, evenings only), with a pool. Otherwise, there's *Le Soulhol* riverside **campsite** (☎05.65.38.12.37, Ⓦwww.campinglesoulhol.com; May–Sept) near the *Victor-Hugo*.

Bikes can be rented from Cycles St-Chamant, 45 rue Faidherbe (☎05.65.38.03.23) – one of the best trips you could do is to cycle to the extremely pretty little village of **AUTOIRE**, in a tight side valley about 10km to the west of St-Céré. Much hillier but glorious country lies to the east along the road to Aurillac via Sousceyrac and Laroquebrou.

Gourdon and around

GOURDON lies between Sarlat and Cahors, conveniently served by the Brive–Toulouse train line, and makes a quiet, agreeable base for visiting some of the major places in this part of the Dordogne and Lot. It's 17km south of the River Dordogne and pretty much at the eastern limit of the luxuriant woods and valleys of Périgord, which give way quite suddenly, at the line of the N20, to the arid limestone landscape of the **Causse de Gramat**.

In the Middle Ages, Gourdon was an important place, deriving wealth and influence from the presence of four monasteries. It was besieged and captured in 1189 by Richard the Lionheart, who promptly murdered its feudal lords. Legend has it that the archer who fired the fatal shot at Richard during the siege of Châlus was the last surviving member of this family. But more than anything it was the devastation of the Wars of Religion that dispatched the place into centuries of oblivion.

Gourdon is a striking town, its medieval centre of yellow-stone houses attached like a swarm of bees to a prominent hilltop, neatly ringed by modern boulevards containing all the commerce. The main street through the old town, with a fortified **gateway** at one end, is rue du Majou. It's lined all the way up with splendid stone houses, some, like the **Maison d'Anglars** at no. 17, dating back to the thirteenth century. At the top you emerge into a lovely, intimate square in front of the massive but not particularly interesting fourteenth-century **church of St-Pierre**. From the square, steps climb to the top of the hill, where the castle once stood and from where there is a superb view stretching for miles.

A couple of kilometres along the Sarlat road in the direction of Cougnac from Gourdon, are some interesting caves, the **Grottes de Cougnac**, discovered in 1949 (April–June & Sept daily 10–11.30am & 2.30–5pm; July & Aug daily 10am–6pm; Oct Mon–Sat 2–4pm; closed Nov–March; €6; ⓦ www.grottesdecougnac .com). Inside are beautiful rock formations as well as some fine prehistoric paintings rather similar to those at Pech-Merle and, intriguingly, sharing some of the same unexplained symbols.

Practicalities

Gourdon's **train station** lies roughly 1km northeast of the centre; from the station, walk south on avenue de la Gare, then turn right onto avenue Gambetta to reach the boulevard encircling the old town. Turn left here to find rue du Majou and the **tourist office** at no. 24 (March–June, Sept & Oct Mon–Sat 10am–noon & 2–6pm; July & Aug Mon–Sat 10am–7pm, Sun 10am–noon; Nov–Feb Mon–Sat 10am–noon & 2–5pm; ⓣ05.65.27.52.50, ⓦ www.tourisme -gourdon.com). **Bikes** can be rented from Nature Évasion, 73 avenue Cavignac (ⓣ05.65.37.65.12), out on the west side of town, while free **Internet** is available at Cyber Base, down towards the station on avenue Gambetta (closed Sun; phone for current hours ⓣ 05.65.37.10.22).

For an overnight **stay**, the *Hôtel de la Promenade*, on the northwest side of the ring road at 48 boulevard Galiot-de-Genouillac (ⓣ05.65.41.41.44,ⓦwww .lapromenadegourdon.fr; ❷; restaurant closed Sat lunch & Sun, menus from €12), is a cheerful place with well-priced rooms, though you have to put up with the clutter of English-pub-style tack downstairs. On the opposite side of town, tucked down a quiet cul-de-sac, is the agreeable *Hostellerie de la Bouriane*, place du Foirail (ⓣ05.65.41.16.37, ⓦwww.hotellabouriane.fr; ❹; closed Feb to mid-March & one week in Oct), with a fine, traditional restaurant (menus from €26; evenings only, closed Mon). There's a well-equipped **campsite**, *Domaine Le Quercy* (ⓣ05.65.41.06.19, ⓦwww.domainequercy .com; Easter to Sept), 1.5km north on the D704 Périgueux road.

In addition to the hotels above, you'll find cafés and **restaurants** scattered around the ring road.

Les Arques

Twenty-five kilometres southwest of Gourdon on the Fumel road, you come to a pretty but not remarkable *bastide* called **Cazals**. A left turn here takes you along the bottom of the valley of the Masse and up its left flank to the exquisite hamlet of **LES ARQUES**. This is quiet, remote, small-scale farming country, emptied of people by the slaughter of the two World Wars and by migration to the towns in search of jobs.

Les Arques' main claim to fame is the Russian Cubist/Expressionist sculptor Osip Zadkine, who bought an old house by the church here in 1934. Some of his sculptures are on display outside the church and in its lovely interior, and there's also a **museum** with a number of his works (Tues–Sun: April–Oct 10am–1pm & 3–7pm; Nov–March 2–6pm; closed Jan; €3).

The other reason to come here is the old village school, now transformed into a wonderful **restaurant**, ✲ *La Récréation* (℡05.65.22.88.08; closed Wed & Thurs, also Nov–Feb; reservations highly recommended), where you are served a copious and delicious meal beneath the chestnut trees of the school yard or in one of the converted classrooms for €20 at midday in July and August, or otherwise for €32. On a summer night, with the swifts flying overhead, it's idyllic.

On the other side of the valley, and well signposted, the tiny Romanesque **chapel of St-André-des-Arques** has some very lovely fifteenth-century frescoes discovered by Zadkine. The chapel is locked, but you can borrow the key from the museum in Les Arques (see above); you'll be asked for your passport, driving licence or other form of identification.

Cahors and around

CAHORS, on the River Lot, was the capital of the old province of Quercy. In its time, it has been a Gallic settlement; a Roman town; a briefly held Moorish possession; a town under English rule; a bastion of Catholicism in the Wars of Religion, sacked in consequence by Henri IV; a university town for 400 years; and birthplace of the politician Léon Gambetta (1838–82), after whom so many French streets and squares are named. Modern Cahors is a sunny southern backwater, with two interesting sights in its **cathedral** and the remarkable **Pont Valentré**.

While you're in the Cahors area, don't miss out on the local **wine**, heady and black but dry to the taste and not at all plummy like the Gironde wines from Blaye and Bourg, which use the same Malbec grape.

Arrival, information and accommodation

The **gare SNCF** is at the end of avenue Jean-Jaurès off rue du Président-Wilson. For further information on the area, make for the **tourist office** (Sept–June Mon–Sat 9am–12.30pm & 1.30–6pm; July & Aug, also Sun 10am–1pm; ℡05.65.53.20.65, ⊛www.mairie-cahors.fr/tourisme/page.html) on place François-Mitterrand in the town centre. You can get **internet** access at Cyber Caviole, 118 rue du Président-Wilson (Mon–Fri 8am–12.30pm & 1.30–5pm; €2 per hour). A leisurely way to enjoy some of the Lot's scenery is one of the **cruises** run by Croisières Fénelon (℡05.65.30.16.55, ℮bateaufenelon @orange.fr). They offer day-trips from around €31 in July and August, for example to St-Cirq-Lapopie, where the boat moors to allow you time to explore the village.

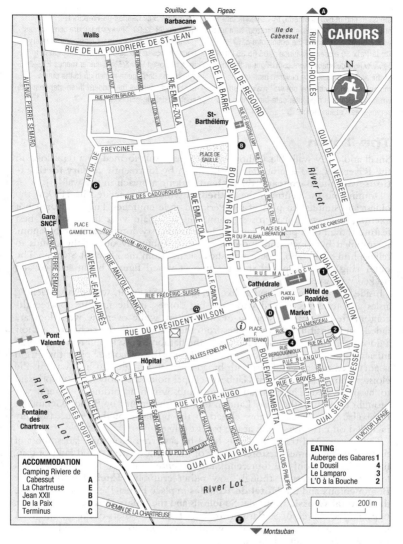

Souillac ▲▲ Figeac ▲▲ Ⓐ

Barbacane

Walls

Ile de
Cabessut

CAHORS

N

RUE DE LA POUDRIERE DE ST-JEAN

RUE DE LA BARRE

QUAI DE RÉGOURD

RUE LUDO-ROLLÈS

RUE DUTY-ZOLE

AVENUE PIERRE SEMARD

RUE FERNAND IMBERT

RUE MARTIN BAUDEL

RUE EMILE-ZOLA

RUE LÉON BLUM

RUE EMILE-ZOLA

St-
Barthélémy

RUE ST-BARTHÉLÉMY

QUAI DE LA VERRERIE

FREYCINET

AV CH DE

PLACE DE
GAULLE

Ⓑ

BOULEVARD GAMBETTA

RUE DES SOUBIROUS

River Lot

RUE DES CADOURQUES

Ⓒ

RUE EMILE-ZOLA

RUE CLÉ DU 06 PO

PONT DE CABESSUT

Gare
SNCF

PLACE
GAMBETTA

RUE JOACHIM-MURAT

R DU P. ALBAN

PLACE DE LA
LIBÉRATION

QUAI CHAMPOLLION

AVENUE PIERRE SEMARD

AVENUE JEAN-JAURÈS

RUE ANATOLE-FRANCE

R.J.F CANOLE

RUE MAL-FOCH

Ⓘ

RUE FRÉDÉRIC-SUISSE

Cathédrale

RUE JOFFRE

PLACE J.
CHAPOU

Hôtel de
Roaldès

Pont
Valentré

RUE DU PRÉSIDENT-WILSON

Ⓓ

Market

Ⓘ

RUE G. CLEMENCEAU

Ⓔ

Ⓐ

PLACE
F.
MITTERAND

RUE DE LASTE

QUAI SÉGUR D'AGUESSEAU

River Lot

ALLÉE DES SOUPIRS

RUE JULES MICHELET

RUE ST GÉRY

Hôpital

ALLÉES FÉNELON

Ⓓ

RUE
BERGOUGNIOUX

RUE BLANQUI

RUE E. BRIVES

RUE DES BADERNES

RUE NATIONALE

Fontaine
des
Chartreux

RUE DONADIEU

RUE SAINT-MAURICE

RUE HAUTESSERRE

RUE VICTOR-HUGO

RUE DES HORTES

RUE DES JARDINIERS

BOULEVARD GAMBETTA

R.VICTOR LAPAGE

RUE DU POT

RUE BINQUOU

QUAI CAVAIGNAC

PONT LOUIS PHILIPPE

ACCOMMODATION
Camping Riviere de
  Cabessut   **A**
La Chartreuse   **E**
Jean XXII   **B**
De la Paix   **D**
Terminus   **C**

EATING
Auberge des Gabares **1**
Le Dousil   **4**
Le Lamparo   **3**
L'O à la Bouche   **2**

0   200 m

CHEMIN DE LA CHARTREUSE

River Lot

Ⓔ

▼ Montauban

Cahors boasts several attractive, mid-range hotel options. There's less choice for those on a tight budget, beyond a riverside **campsite**, *Camping Rivière de Cabessut* (℡05.65.30.06.30, Ⓦ www.cabessut.com; April–Sept), across the Pont de Cabessut.

Hotels

La Chartreuse St-Georges ℡05.65.35.17.37, Ⓦ www.hotel-la-chartreuse.com. In a nice quiet spot on the south bank, over the river from the town centre, this modern, concrete hotel has a

small pool and a decent restaurant (menus from €16). Ask for a room overlooking the river. ❸

Jean XXII 2 rue Edmond-Albe ℡05.65.35.07.66, Ⓦ www.hotel-jeanxxii.com. Situated in the fourteenth-century buildings of the Palais Duèze, at the north end of bvd Gambetta, this small hotel offers comfortable rooms, all modernized, with free wi-fi internet access and the option of a/c. ❸ **De la Paix** 30 place St-Maurice ☏05.65.35.03.40, ☮www.hoteldelapaixcahors.com. Right in the thick of the action, opposite the covered market. The rooms are fairly functional but well maintained, while downstairs is a popular café-bar, which also serves meals at lunchtime. ❸

Terminus 5 av Charles-de-Freycinet ☏05.65.53.32.00, ☮www.balandre.com. Cahors' grandest hotel, in an elegant nineteenth-century house opposite the station, with a restaurant to match (closed Sun & Mon; dinner menus €52–88). The rooms don't quite match up to the public areas, but boast all the modern three-star comforts such as double-glazing and a/c. ❹

The Town

Small and easily walkable, Cahors sits on a peninsula formed by a tight loop in the River Lot, and is protected to the north by fourteenth-century **fortifications**, with the **Barbacane de St-Jean** making a breach in the walls.

Dominating the centre is the **cathedral** which, consecrated in 1119, is the oldest and simplest in plan of the Périgord-style churches. The exterior is not exciting: a heavy square tower dominates the plain west front, whose best feature is the north portal, where a Christ in Majesty dominates the tympanum, surrounded by angels and apostles, while cherubim fly out of the clouds to relieve him of his halo. Side panels show scenes from the life of St Stephen. The outer ring over the portal shows a line of naked figures being stabbed and hacked with axes.

Inside, the cathedral is much like Périgueux's St-Front, with a nave lacking aisles and transepts, roofed with two big domes; in the first are fourteenth-century frescoes of the stoning of St Stephen, while over the west door are faded but beautiful Creation scenes from the same era. To the right of the choir a door opens into a delicate **cloister** in the flamboyant style, still retaining some intricate, though damaged, carving. On the northwest corner pillar the Virgin is portrayed as a graceful girl with broad brow and ringlets to her waist. In the cloister's northeast corner St Gaubert's chapel holds the Holy Coif, a cloth said to have covered Christ's head in the tomb, which according to legend was brought back from the Holy Land in the twelfth century by Bishop Géraud de Cardaillac. The chapel is now closed to the public, though it is occasionally included on city tours – ask at the tourist office.

The area around the cathedral is filled by a warren of narrow lanes, most of them now handsomely restored. Many of the houses, turreted and built of thin, flat brick, date from the fourteenth and fifteenth centuries. It's worth taking a look at the impressive, though now rather crumbly, **Hôtel d'Issale** in rue Bergougnioux and the **Hôtel de Roaldès** in place Henri-IV; also of interest are the **Hôpital Grossia** in rue des Soubirous and the **Palais Duèze**, further north opposite the church of St-Barthélemy, built for the brothers of Pope John XXII in the fourteenth century. As you wander, look out for the many little "secret gardens" scattered round the town.

Immediately south of the cathedral, the lime-bordered **place Jean-Jacques-Chapou** commemorates a local trade unionist and Resistance leader, killed in a German ambush on July 17, 1944. Next to it is the covered **market** and a building still bearing the name Gambetta, where the family of the famous deputy of Belleville in Paris had their grocery shop.

The reason most people venture to Cahors, however, is the dramatic fourteenth-century **Pont Valentré**, one of the finest surviving medieval bridges. Its three powerful towers, originally closed by portcullises and gates, made it effectively an independent fortress, guarding the river crossing on the west side of town.

▲ Pont Valentré, Cahors

Eating and drinking

In addition to the hotel **restaurants** mentioned on pp.655–656, there are numerous brasseries along boulevard Gambetta. The 🅇 *Auberge des Gabares*, 24 place Champollion (☎05.65.53.91.47), serves excellent-value home-cooking on its wisteria-covered terrace overlooking the Lot – there's just one five-course menu, with a certain amount of choice, which changes daily (€14, Sat evening €21). *Le Lamparo* (☎05.65.35.25.93; menus from €16; closed Sun), on the south side of the market square, is a perennial favourite for its varied menus and generous portions, while for something more upmarket, try *L'O à la Bouche*, 124 rue St-Urcisse (☎05.65.35.65.69; menus from €26; closed Sun & Mon), for its nicely presented and imaginative dishes.

As for drinking, *Le Dousil*, a **wine bar** at 124 rue Nationale (closed Sun & Mon), is a great venue to sample the local reds. The food's not bad either: salads, open sandwiches and cheese and charcuterie platters from around €13.

St-Cirq-Lapopie

If you have your own transport you could easily make a side trip from Cahors to the village of **ST-CIRQ-LAPOPIE**, 30km to the east, perched high above the south bank of the Lot. The village was saved from ruin when poet André Breton came to live here in the early twentieth century, and though it's now an irresistible draw, with its cobbled lanes, half-timbered houses and gardens, it's still well worth the trouble, especially if visiting early or late in the day.

Public transport in the form of an SNCF bus will get you from Cahors to Gare-St-Cirq in the valley bottom at Tour-de-Faure, from where there's no alternative but to leg it up the steep hill for the final 2km. For **accommodation**, there's the pretty *Auberge du Sombral* on the central square (☎05.65.31.26.08, ℻05.65.30.26.37; ❸; closed mid-Nov to March; restaurant menus from €15, closed Thurs & evenings Sun–Wed), with plain but perfectly adequate rooms, or *La Pélissaria* (☎05.65.31.25.14, ℗pagesperso-orange.fr/hoteldelapelissaria; ❺; closed mid-Oct to April), in a sixteenth-century house perched on the cliff at

St-Cirq's eastern entrance. There's also a very comfortable *gîte d'étape* in the centre (T05.65.31.21.51, Emaisondelafourdonne46@orange.fr; closed Mon & mid-Nov to March), and a well-run **campsite**, *Camping de la Plage* (T05.65.30.29.51, Wwww.campingplage.com; open all year), down by the river, with various activities on offer, including swimming, canoeing and horseriding.

When it comes to **restaurants**, you can eat very well at *L'Oustal* (T05.65.31.20.17; closed Mon & Nov–March; menus from €12 at lunch, €17 evenings), tucked into a corner of rue de la Pélissaria just south of the church. At the top of the village, with views from its terrace over jumbled roofs, *Lou Bolat* serves a varied menu of salads, pizzas and regional dishes (closed mid-Nov to Feb, also Mon evening & Tues lunch; lunch menu €12, evenings €18).

For **canoeing**, from hourly rental to week-long expeditions on the Lot and Célé rivers, contact Kalapca Loisirs (T05.65.30.29.51, Wwww.kalapca.com), with a base below St-Cirq in July & August. At other times, they can be reached through the Bureau des Sports Nature, across the river at Conduché (see p.664).

Downstream from Cahors

West of Cahors the vine-cloaked banks of the Lot are dotted with ancient villages. The first of these, **Luzech** and the dramatic **Puy-l'Évêque**, are served by an SNCF bus that threads along the valley from Cahors via Fumel to Monsempron-Libos, on the Agen–Périgueux train line. You'll need your own transport, however, to reach the splendid **Château de Bonaguil**, in the hills northwest of Puy-l'Évêque, worth the effort for its elaborate fortifications and spectacular position. From here the Lot valley starts to get ugly and industrial, though **Villeneuve-sur-Lot** provides a pleasant enough base for exploring the villages around. Prettiest are **Pujols**, to the south, which also boasts a number of excellent restaurants, and **Penne-d'Agenais**, overlooking the Lot to the east. **Monflanquin**, a *bastide* to the north of Villeneuve, is also well worth a visit for its hilltop location and almost perfect arcaded central square.

Luzech, Puy-l'Évêque and the Château de Bonaguil

Twenty kilometres downriver from Cahors you come to **LUZECH**, with scant Gaulish and Roman remains of the town of L'Impernal, and the **Chapelle de Notre-Dame-de-l'Île**, dedicated to the medieval boatmen who transported Cahors wines to Bordeaux. The town stands in a huge river loop, overlooked by a thirteenth-century keep, with some picturesque alleys and dwellings in the quarter opposite place du Canal.

Several bends in the river later – 22km by road – **PUY-L'ÉVÊQUE** is probably the prettiest village in the entire valley, with many grand houses built in honey-coloured stone and overlooked by both a **church** and the **castle** of the bishops of Cahors. The best view is from the bridge across the Lot. For an overnight **stay**, the classy *Bellevue* (T05.65.36.06.60, Wwww.lot-hotel-bellevue.com; ❹; closed two weeks in Nov and four weeks in Jan/Feb), perched on the cliff edge, has stylish rooms and a good restaurant (menus from €29, or €14 in the brasserie; closed Sun & Mon). For something cheaper, at the bottom of the town, the *Henry* has excellent-value, air conditioner rooms (T05.65.21.32.24, Wwww.hotel-henry.com; ❶; closed two weeks in Jan), a garden and a good traditional restaurant (menus from €17; closed Sun evening), and there's a well-tended riverside

campsite, *Camping Les Vignes* (📞05.65.30.81.72, Ⓦwww.camping-les-vignes
.net; April–Sept), 3km to the south.

With your own transport, follow the Lot as far as Duravel and then cut across
country via the picturesque hamlet of St-Martin-le-Redon to reach the
Château de Bonaguil (Feb–May & Oct daily 10.30am–12.30pm & 2–5pm;
June & Sept daily 10am–12.30pm & 2–6pm; July & Aug daily 10am–7pm; Nov
Sat & Sun 10.30am–12.30pm & 2–5pm; Christmas holidays daily 2–5pm; €6;
Ⓦwww.bonaguil.org) some 15km later, spectacularly perched on a wooded
spur. Dating largely from the fifteenth and sixteenth centuries, with a double
ring of walls, five huge towers and a narrow boat-shaped keep designed to resist
artillery, Bonguil was the last of a dying breed, completed just when military
architects were abandoning such elaborate fortifications.

Villeneuve-sur-Lot and around

VILLENEUVE-SUR-LOT, 75km west and downstream from Cahors, is a
pleasant, workaday sort of town which makes a useful base. While there are no
very interesting sights, the handful of attractive timbered houses in the old town
and the arcaded central square go some way to compensate. If you're reliant on
public transport, note that SNCF runs regular bus services to Agen, on the
Bordeaux–Toulouse line.

The town's most striking landmark is the red-brick tower of the **church of
St-Catherine**, completed as late as 1937 in typically dramatic neo-Byzantine
style. A couple of towers alone survive from the fortifications of this originally
bastide town, and to the south the main avenue, rue des Cieutats, crosses
thirteenth-century **Pont des Cieutat**, resembling the Pont Valentré in Cahors
but devoid of its towers.

The helpful **tourist office**, 3 place de la Libération (July & Aug Mon–Sat
9.30am–12.30pm & 2.30–7pm, Sun 9.30am–1pm; Sept–June Mon–Sat 9am–
noon & 2–6pm; 📞05.53.36.17.30, Ⓦwww.cc-villeneuvois.fr/region.html),
lies just outside the town's northern gate; it also has one **internet** terminal
(€4 per hour). The best place to look for **accommodation** is around the
former train station, now the **gare routière**, five-minutes' walk south of
centre, where the welcoming *La Résidence*, 17 avenue Lazare-Carnot
(📞05.53.40.17.03, Ⓦwww.hotellaresidence47.com; ❶–❷), offers excellent
value for money. Closer to the centre, *Les Platanes*, 40 boulevard de la Marine
(📞05.53.40.11.40, Ⓦwww.hoteldesplatanes.com; ❸), offers unfussy but
spacious and well-kept rooms and a popular brasserie restaurant (lunchtime
formule €13). For **campers**, there's the *Camping du Rooy*, signed off the Agen
road 1.5km south of the centre (📞05.53.70.24.18; mid-April to Sept).

When it comes to **eating**, *Ze CuiZ'in*, north of Ste-Catherine's at 38 rue des
Frères-Clavet, attracts a lunchtime crowd with its scrumptious home-made tarts,
deserts and patisseries, plus a few daily dishes (three-course menu €14; closed
Sun). Basque cuisine is the order of the day at *L'Oustal*, a cheerful spot under
the arches on place Lafayette (lunch menus from €14, evenings from €20; closed
Sun), while for a more upmarket ambience and good-value regional cooking
you could try *L'Entracte* at 30 boulevard de la Marine (lunch menus from €14,
dinner €22; closed Wed), with a terrace under the plane trees. Alternatively, head
south to Pujols (see below).

Pujols

Three kilometres south of Villeneuve the tiny hilltop village of **PUJOLS** makes
a popular excursion, partly to see the faded Romanesque frescoes in the **church
of Ste-Foy** and partly for the views over the surrounding country. But the main

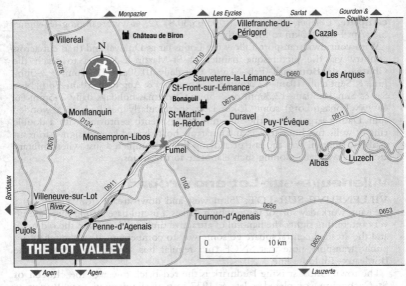

reason locals come here is for the quality of its **restaurants**. Top of the list is the excellent but expensive ⚜ *La Toque Blanche* (☎05.53.49.00.30, ⓦwww.la-toque -blanche.com; closed Sun evening to Tues lunch; menus €25–85), just south of Pujols with views back to the village. The panorama is even better, however, from their less formal outlet, *Lou Calel*, overlooking the Lot valley in Pujols itself, where you can sample beautifully cooked, traditional but light menus (☎05.53.70.46.14; closed Tues evening to Thurs lunch; menus from €22).

Monflanquin

Some 30km north of Villeneuve-sur-Lot, pretty **MONFLANQUIN**, founded by Alphonse de Poitiers in 1256, is another perfectly preserved *bastide* (see box, p.633), less touristy than Monpazier and even more impressively positioned on the top of a hill that rises sharply from the surrounding country. It conforms to the regular pattern of right-angled streets leading from a central square to the four town gates. The square – **place des Arcades** – with its distinctly Gothic houses, derives a special charm from being on a slope and tree-shaded. On the square's north side you'll find the informative **Musée des Bastides** (May, June, Sept & Oct Mon–Sat 10am–noon & 2–6pm, Sun 3–5pm; July & Aug daily 10am–7pm; Nov–April Mon–Sat 10am–noon & 2–5pm; €4), detailing the life and history of *bastides*.

The museum is above the **tourist office** (same hours as the Musée des Bastides; ☎05.53.36.40.19, ⓦwww.cc-monflanquinois.fr), which can furnish you with lists of *chambres d'hôtes*. The only hotel to speak of in Monflanquin is the modern and rather soulless *Monform*, in a housing estate just west of town (☎05.53.49.85.85, ⓦhotelrestaurantmonform.com; ❸; closed mid-Jan to mid-Feb), which doubles as a health centre with heated pool, sauna and gym. **Campers** are better served by the four-star *Camping des Bastides* (☎05.53.40.83.09, ⓦwww.campingdesbastides.com; mid-April to Sept), 10km east of Monflan-quin, near the village of Salles. For somewhere to eat, try one of the **cafés** and **restaurants** on place des Arcades: *La Grappe de Raisin* (menus at €15 and €20; closed Nov–March, also Sun evening & Mon) serves a varied menu of salads,

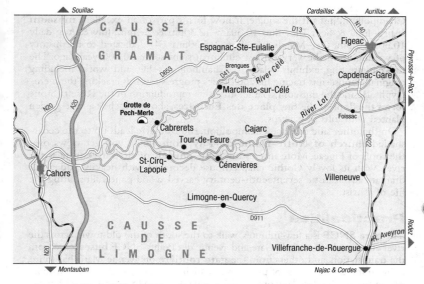

pizzas and local dishes, while across the square, the *Bistrot du Prince Noir* (April, May & Oct–Dec closed Tues & Wed; open daily June–Sept; closed Jan–March; lunch menus from €12, evenings from €26) offers traditional dishes and more unusual specialities like vegetable tempura with spicy Thai sauce.

Figeac and around

FIGEAC lies on the River Célé, 71km east of Cahors. It's a beautiful town with an unspoilt medieval centre not too encumbered by tourism. Like many other provincial towns hereabouts, it owes its beginnings to the foundation of an abbey in the early days of Christianity in France, one which quickly became wealthy because of its position on the pilgrim routes to both Rocamadour and Compostela. In the Middle Ages it became a centre of tanning, which partly accounts for why many houses' top floors have *solelhos*, or open-sided wooden galleries used for drying skins and other produce. Again, it was the Wars of Religion that pushed it into eclipse, for Figeac sided with the nearby Protestant stronghold of Montauban and suffered the same punishing reprisals by the victorious royalists in 1662.

In the old town centre, the **Hôtel de la Monnaie** surveys place Vival. It's a splendid building dating back to the thirteenth century, when the city's mint was located in this district. In the streets radiating off to the north of the square there's a delightful range of houses of the medieval and classical periods, both stone and half-timbered, adorned with carvings and colonnettes and interesting ironwork. At the end of these streets are the two adjacent squares of **place Carnot** and **place Champollion**, both of great charm. The former is the site of the old *halles*, under whose awning cafés now spread their tables.

Jean-François Champollion, who cracked Egyptian hieroglyphics by deciphering the triple text of the Rosetta Stone, was born at 4 impasse

Champollion, just off the square. It now forms part of an excellent **museum** (April–June & Sept Tues–Sun 10.30am–12.30pm & 2–6pm; July & Aug daily 10.30am–6pm; Oct–March Tues–Sun 2–5.30pm; €4) dedicated to the history of writing, from the very earliest cuniform signs some 50,000 years ago. The most interesting exhibits relate to Champollion's life and work, including original manuscripts tracing his and other's progress towards cracking the hieroglyphs. Beside the museum, a larger-than-life reproduction of the Rosetta Stone forms the floor of the tiny **place des Écritures**, above which is a little garden planted with tufts of papyrus.

On the other side of place Champollion, rue Boutaric leads up to the cedar-shaded **church of Notre-Dame-du-Puy**, from where you get views over the roofs of Figeac. More interesting is the **church of St-Sauveur**, near the river, with its lovely Gothic chapterhouse decorated with heavily gilded but dramatically realistic seventeenth-century carved wood panels illustrating the life of Christ.

Practicalities

The **gare SNCF** is a few-minutes' walk to the south of the old town, across the river at the end of rue de la Gare and avenue des Poilus. SNCF **buses** leave from the train station, and others from the **gare routière** on avenue Maréchal-Joffre, a few-minutes' walk west of place Vival, which is where you'll find the **tourist office** in the Hôtel de la Monnaie (May, June & Sept Mon–Sat 10am–12.30pm & 2.30–6pm, Sun 10am–1pm; July & Aug daily 10am–7pm; Oct–April Mon–Sat 10am–12.30pm & 2.30–6pm; ☎05.65.34.06.25, ⊛www.tourisme-figeac.com).

One of the nicest places to **stay** in Figeac is *Le Solielho*, 8 rue Prat (☎05.65.34.64.41, ⊛www.location-gites-lot.com; ❸), a stylish *chambre d'hôte* with four rooms in a fourteenth-century mansion near the St-Sauveur church. Among the hotels, the riverside *Des Bains*, 1 rue du Griffoul (☎05.65.34.10.89, ⊛www.hoteldesbains.fr; ❷; mid-Nov to Feb closed Fri–Sun, also closed Christmas & New Year), has simple but bright, well-kept rooms. The nearby *Pont d'Or*, 2 avenue Jean-Jaurès (☎05.65.50.95.00, ⊛www.hotelpontdor.com; ❺; restaurant menus from €15), is a smartish chain hotel with sauna, gym and rooftop pool. Or treat yourself to a night of pure luxury at the *Château du Viguier du Roy*, rue Émile-Zola (☎05.65.50.05.05, ⊛www.chateau-viguier -figeac.com; ❽; closed mid-Oct to mid-April), a fourteenth-century château with huge rooms, a cloister garden, small (unheated) pool and a gourmet restaurant (menus €30–75 closed Mon & lunchtime Sat).

There's also a well-equipped riverside **campsite**, *Les Rives du Célé* (☎05.61.64.88.54, ⊛www.lesrivesducele.com; April–Sept), just east of town, where you can rent **bikes** and **canoes** in summer; at other times contact the Office Intercommunal des Sports at 2 avenue de Gaulle (☎05.65.34.52.54).

Figeac boasts some excellent **restaurants**. One of the nicest is the elegant *La Cuisine du Marché*, 15 rue Clermont (☎05.65.50.18.55; closed Sun), just north of St-Sauveur church, offering a select range of well-prepared seasonal dishes on menus ranging from €19 to €48. Tucked off place Champollion, ✴ *Les Anges Gourmands*, 4 rue Séguier (open for lunch Tues–Sat & dinner Fri & Sat), is a funky little place dishing up tasty salads, open sandwiches and a couple of more substantial options, with ices or home-made cakes to follow; try one of their "medieval aperitifs". The *Pizzeria del Portal*, 9 rue Ortabadial (closed Sun lunch & Mon), is a convivial place serving an extensive menu of pizzas, salad platters, *moules* and the like, with the benefit of outside seating; most dishes are under €4.

Peyrusse-le-Roc

About 20km southeast of Figeac, following a series of beautiful lanes across the *causse*, you happen upon one of the most remarkable old villages in this corner of France, **PEYRUSSE-LE-ROC**. The "modern" village sits astride a ridge above a narrow wooded valley: a tiny huddle of long-eaved, half-timbered houses gathered round a seventeenth-century church. On the slopes below, hidden in the steep woods, lie the remains of a medieval stronghold, abandoned around 1700, that once stood guard over the silver-rich country round about. Cobbled paths connect the ruins of a Gothic church, a synagogue and a hospital, while a vertiginous ladder gives access to the twin towers of the old fort. The site is gradually being excavated and some of the buildings restored, but still remains a moving and atmospheric place.

The valley of the Célé

For the last stretch of its course from Figeac to Conduché, where it joins the Lot, the **River Célé** flows through a luxuriant canyon-like valley cut into the limestone uplands of the Causse de Gramat. A twisting minor road follows the river: a silent backwater of a place, hot in summer, frequented mainly by canoeists. The **GR651** follows the same route, sometimes close to the river, sometimes on the edge of the *causse* on the north bank.

Espagnac-Ste-Eulalie and Marcilhac-sur-Célé

Travelling downstream from Figeac, two villages in particular are worth a stop. The first is **ESPAGNAC-STE-EULALIE**, about 18km west of Figeac. It's a tiny and beautiful hamlet on the south bank of the river, reached across an old stone bridge, under the limestone outcrops of the *causse*. An eye-catching octagonal lantern crowns the belfry of the **church** (guided visits: daily 10.30am, 5pm & 6.30pm by appointment, call Mme Bonzani on ☎05.65.40.06.17; €2), and under a weathered tower next door, an ancient gateway houses a *gîte d'étape* (☎05.65.11.42.66; closed mid-Nov to March). There's an attractive and good-value *chambre d'hôte*, Les Anons du Célé, 2.5km north of Espagnac on the D41 (☎05.65.50.26.57, ⓦlesanonsducele.free.fr; ❸; dinner €17), and two quiet riverside **campsites** in the next hamlet, **Brengues**: Le Moulin Vieux (☎05.65.40.00.41, ⓦwww.brengues.com; April–Sept), and the smaller municipal site (☎05.65.40.06.82, ⓦwww.brengues.com; June–Sept).

The second village of real interest is **MARCILHAC-SUR-CÉLÉ**, 9km downstream of Brengues, whose partially ruined **abbey** (July & Aug visits at 5.30pm Mon, Wed & Fri; Sept–June by appointment – call ☎05.65.40.65.52; €3), with its gaping walls and broken columns, conjures a strongly romantic atmosphere. Very early and rather primitive ninth-century Carolingian sculpture decorates the lintel, and there are some handsome Romanesque capitals in the chapterhouse. In the damp interior are frescoes from around 1500 and old coats of arms of the local nobility, testimony to Marcilhac's once mighty power, when even Rocamadour was under its sway. During World War II, it was the scene of one of the *maquis'* first theatrical gestures of turning the tables on the occupier: on November 11, 1943 – Armistice Day – Jean-Jacques Chapou's group (see p.656) briefly occupied the village and laid a wreath at the war memorial.

There's a well-tended **campsite**, Pré de Monsieur, just north of the village (☎05.65.40.77.88, ⓦwww.camping-marcilhac.com; April to mid-Oct), with a decent little **restaurant** serving snacks, salads and main meals. Otherwise, the *Café de la Promenade*, on Marcilhac's main street, serves no-nonsense country cooking, with a four-course menu at €15 (closed Wed).

Grotte de Pech-Merle

Discovered in 1922, the **Grotte de Pech-Merle** (Easter to mid-Nov daily 9.30am–noon & 1.30–5pm; ☎05.65.31.27.05, ⓦwww.pechmerle.com; €7) is less accessible than the caves at Les Eyzies but still attracts sufficient visitors to warrant restricting numbers to seven hundred per day; it's advisable to book (by phone or online) at least five days ahead in July and August. The cave is well hidden on the scrubby hillsides above Cabrerets, which lies 15km from Marcilhac and 4km from Conduché. The cave itself is far more beautiful than those at Padirac or Les Eyzies, with galleries full of the most spectacular stalactites and stalagmites – structures tiered like wedding cakes, hanging like curtains, or shaped like discs or pearls.

The first **drawings** you come to are in the "Chapelle des Mammouths", executed on a white calcite panel that looks as if it's been specially prepared for the purpose. There are horses, bison – charging head down with tiny rumps and arched tails – and tusked, whiskery mammoths. Next comes a vast chamber where the glorious horse panel is visible on a lower level; it's a remarkable example of the way in which the artist used the relief of the rock to do the work, producing an utterly convincing mammoth in just two black lines. The ceiling is covered with finger marks, preserved in the soft clay. You pass the skeleton of a cave hyena that has been lying there for 20,000 years – wild animals used these caves for shelter and sometimes, unable to find their way out, starved to death. And finally, the most spine-tingling experience at Pech-Merle: the footprints of an adolescent preserved in a muddy pool.

The admission charge includes an excellent film and **museum**, where prehistory is illustrated by colourful and intelligible charts, a selection of objects (rather than the usual 10,000 flints), skulls and beautiful slides displayed in wall panels.

There's a **campsite**, *Le Cantal* (☎05.65.31.26.61, ⓕ05.65.31.20.47; April–Oct), close by at **CABRERETS**, a tiny place which also boasts a pair of two-star **hotels**: the spick-and-span *Auberge de la Sagne*, 1km outside the village on the road to Pech-Merle (☎05.65.31.26.62, ⓦwww.hotel-auberge-cabrerets .com; ❸; closed mid-Sept to mid-May), which has a pool and a good restaurant (evening only; menus €16 & €24); and the welcoming riverside *Les Grottes* (☎05.65.31.27.02, ⓦwww.hoteldesgrottes.com; ❷; closed Nov–Easter), also with a decent traditional restaurant (menus from €16) and a small pool. There's also pretty and well-equipped *chambre d'hôte* accommodation at *Un Jardin dans la Falaise* (☎05.65.30.85.35, ⓦwww.unjardindanslafalaise.com; ❸; closed mid-Nov to mid-Jan), perched above the village with wonderful views; meals available on request (€20).

For **canoes** and **bikes**, contact the Bureau des Sports Nature (☎05.65.24.21.01, ⓔbureau.sports.nature@orange.fr; April–Oct), a few kilometres further south at **Conduché**, where the Célé joins the Lot. It also organizes various other activities, including rock-climbing, caving and canyoning.

The valley of the Aveyron

Thirty-odd kilometres south of Figeac, **Villefranche-de-Rouerge** lies on a bend in the River Aveyron, clustered around its perfectly preserved, arcaded market square. From here the Aveyron flows south through increasingly deep, thickly wooded valleys, past the hilltop village of **Najac** and then turns abruptly west as it enters the **Gorges de l'Aveyron**. The most impressive stretch of this gorge begins just east of **St-Antonin-de-Noble-Val**, an ancient village caught between soaring limestone cliffs, and continues downstream to the villages of **Penne** and **Bruniquel**, perched beside their crumbling castles. Bruniquel marks the end of the gorges, as you suddenly break out into flat alluvial plains where the Aveyron joins the great rivers of the Tarn and Garonne.

Villefranche-de-Rouergue

No medieval junketing, barely a craft shop in sight, **VILLEFRANCHE-DE-ROUERGUE** must be as close as you can get to what a French provincial town used to be like, though it is not undiscovered. It's a small town, lying on a bend in the Aveyron, 35km due south of Figeac and 61km east of Cahors across the **Causse de Limogne**. Built as a *bastide* by Alphonse de Poitiers in 1252 as part of the royal policy of extending control over the recalcitrant lands of the south, the town became rich on copper from the surrounding mines and its privilege of minting coins. From the fifteenth to the eighteenth centuries, its wealthy men built the magnificent houses that grace the cobbled streets to this day.

Rue du Sergent-Bories and rue de la République, the main commercial street, are both very attractive, but they are no preparation for **place Notre-Dame**, the loveliest *bastide* square in the region. It's built on a slope, so the uphill houses are much higher than the downhill, and you enter at the corners underneath the buildings. All the houses are arcaded at ground-floor level, providing for a **market** (Thurs morning) where local merchants and farmers spread out their weekly produce – the quintessential Villefranche experience. The houses are unusually tall and some are very elaborately decorated, notably the so-called **Maison du Président Raynal** on the lower side at the top of rue de la République.

The square's east side is dominated by the **church of Notre-Dame** with its colossal porch and bell tower, nearly 60m high. The interior has some fine late fifteenth-century stained glass, carved choir stalls and misericords.

On the boulevard that forms the northern limit of the old town, the seventeenth-century **Chapelle des Pénitents-Noirs** (April–June Tues–Sat 2–6pm; July–Sept daily 10am–noon & 2–6pm; closed Oct–March; €4) boasts a splendidly Baroque painted ceiling and an enormous gilded retable. Another ecclesiastical building worth the slight detour is the **Chartreuse St-Sauveur** (same hours; €4), about 1km out of town on the Gaillac road. It was completed in the space of ten years from 1450, giving it a singular architectural harmony, and has a very beautiful cloister and choir stalls by the same master as Notre-Dame in Villefranche, which, by contrast, took nearly three hundred years to complete.

Practicalities

The **gare SNCF** lies a couple of minutes' walk south across the Aveyron from the old town. For information about buses, contact the **tourist office** just north of the river on promenade du Guiraudet (May–June & Sept Mon–Fri 9am–noon & 2–7pm, Sat 9am–noon & 2–6pm; July & Aug also open Sun 10am–12.30pm; Oct–April Mon–Fri 9am–noon & 2–6pm, Sat 9am–noon; ☎05.65.45.13.18, Ⓦwww.villefranche.com), beside the bridge. They also lay on guided tours of the town in summer, and can provide you with an audio-guide out of season.

The nicest place to **stay** is *Le Claux de la Bastide*, 8 rue Ste-Emile-de-Rodat (☎06.70.74.61.57, Ⓦwww.leclauxdelabastide.fr; ❹), a lovely *chambres d'hôte* in an elegant town house one block north of the tourist office. If you'd prefer a hotel, the *Aveyron*, near the station at 4 rue Lapeyrade (☎05.65.45.17.88, Ⓔhotel -restaurant.aveyron@orange.fr; ❷; closed Christmas & New Year holidays and weekends out of season), offers simple rooms and a decent restaurant (menu at €16; closed evenings & weekends). The other option is to head 3km north on the Figeac road to where *Le Relais de Farrou* (☎05.65.45.18.11, ⓦwww .relaisdefarrou.com; ❸) offers much more luxurious surroundings and a fine restaurant (menus from €22; closed Sat lunch, Sun evening & Mon), albeit in a rather unpromising location. Back in Villefranche, there's an excellent *Foyer de Jeunes Travailleurs* **HI hostel** (☎05.65.45.09.68, ⓔfjt.villefranche@orange.fr), next to the *gare SNCF*. There's also a *gîte d'étape* by the river at La Gasse (☎05.65.45.10.80; closed Nov to mid-April), 3km out of town on the D269 back road to La Bastide-L'Évêque, at the start of GR62b, plus a three-star **campsite**, the *Camping du Rouergue* (☎05.65.45.16.24, ⓦwww.campingdurouergue.com; mid-April to Sept), 1.5km to the south on the D47 to Monteil.

For **eating**, in addition to the two hotel restaurants mentioned above, the terrace of *Le Dali's*, on the cathedral square, has an unbeatable location, while the food is perfectly acceptable (menus €16–38; closed Nov, also evenings Mon–Fri & lunch Sat & Sun except July & Aug). You'll eat very well at the *Assiette Gourmande*, one block north of the cathedral on place André-Lescure (menus €15–33; closed Tues & Sun evening and Wed), which specializes in local cuisine, and at the aptly named *L'Epicurien* (☎05.65.45.01.12; closed Sun evening. Mon & Tues; menus €15–41.50), a gourmet establishment near the station on avenue Raymond-St-Gilles.

Najac

NAJAC occupies an extraordinary site on a conical hill isolated in a wide bend in the deep valley of the Aveyron, 25km south of Villefranche-de-Rouergue and on the Aurillac–Toulouse train line. Its magnificent castle, which graces many a travel poster, sits right on the peak of the hill, while the half-timbered and stone-tiled village houses tail out in a single street along the narrow back of the spur that joins the hill to the valley side.

The **château** (April, May, Sept & Oct 10am–12.30pm & 3–5.30pm; June daily to 6.30pm; July & Aug daily 10am–1pm & 3–7pm; closed Nov–March; €4) is a model of medieval defensive architecture and was endlessly fought over because of its impregnable position in a region once rich in silver and copper mines. In one of the chambers of the keep are sculpted portraits of St Louis, king of France, his brother Alphonse de Poitiers and Jeanne, the daughter of the count of Toulouse, whose marriage to Alphonse was arranged in 1229 to end the Cathar wars by bringing the domains of Count Raymond and his allies under royal control. It was Alphonse who "modernized" the castle and made the place we see today – a model in one of the turrets shows his fortifications as they were in the castle's prime in 1253. The main reason to visit, however, is the magnificent all-round view from the top of the keep, a full 200m above the river.

At the foot of the castle, in the centre of what was the medieval village, stands the sturdy **church of St-Jean** (April–Sept daily 10am–noon & 2–6pm; Oct Sun 10am–noon & 2–6pm; free), which the villagers of Najac were forced by the Inquisition to build at their own expense in 1258 as a punishment for their conversion to Catharism. In addition to a collection of reliquaries and an extraordinary iron cage for holding candles, the church has one architectural oddity: its windows are solid panels of stone from which the lights have been cut out in trefoil form. Below the church, a surviving stretch of **Roman road** leads downhill to where a thirteenth-century bridge spans the Aveyron.

Heading the other way, a narrow street overlooked by ancient houses leads from the castle to what is now the village centre, **place du Faubourg**, a sort of elongated square bordered by houses raised on pillars, like the central square of a *bastide*.

Here you'll find the **tourist office** (April–June & Sept Mon–Sat 9am–noon & 2.30–6pm; July & Aug also Sun 10am–1pm; Oct–March Mon–Fri 9am–noon & 2.30–5pm, Sat 9am–noon; ℡05.65.29.72.05, ℮otsi.najac@orange.fr) and a very comfortable **hotel**, *L'Oustal del Barry* (℡05.65.29.74.32, ⓦwww.oustaldelbarry .com; ❸; closed early Nov to mid-March), whose restaurant is renowned for its subtle and inventive cuisine (menus €19–44; closed Mon & Tues lunch except July & Aug). Another attractive option is the *Belle Rive* (℡05.65.29.73.90, ⓦwww .lebellerive.com; ❸; closed Nov–March), in a nice, peaceful spot down by the river, with a pool and a restaurant serving good-value regional cooking (menus €20–50). Nearby is a four-star **campsite**, *Le Païsserou* (℡05.65.29.73.96, or 05.65.47.45.72 off season, ℮cledelles.reservations@orange.fr; May–Sept), with a *gîte d'étape* (same contact details; open all year). You can also rent **canoes** and **bikes** down here (℡05.65.29.73.94, ⓦwww.aagac.com).

St-Antonin-Noble-Val

One of the finest and most substantial towns in the valley is **ST-ANTONIN-NOBLE-VAL**, 30km southwest of Najac. It sits on the bank of the Aveyron beneath the beetling cliffs of the Roc d'Anglars, and has endured all the vicissitudes of the old towns of the southwest: it went Cathar, then Protestant and each time was walloped by the alien power of the kings from the north. Yet, in spite of all this, it recovered its prosperity, manufacturing cloth and leather goods, and was endowed by its wealthy merchants with a marvellous heritage of medieval houses in all the streets leading out from the lovely **place de la Halle**. It's on this square that you'll find the town's finest building, the **Maison des Consuls**, whose origins go back to 1120. It now houses the town museum, **Musée du Vieux St-Antonin** (July & Aug daily except Tues 10am–1pm & 3–6pm; €1), with an uninspiring collection of objects illustrating the former life of the place, including various prehistoric finds.

The **tourist office** is in the "new" town hall next to the church (March & Oct Mon 2–5.30pm, Tues–Sun 10am–12.30pm & 2–5.30pm; April–June & Sept daily 9.30am–12.30pm & 2–6pm; July & Aug daily 9am–1pm & 2–7pm; Nov–March Mon & Sat 2–5pm, Tues–Fri 10am–12.30pm & 2–5pm; ℡05.63.30.63.47, ⓦwww.saint-antonin-noble-val.com), and will supply information about B&Bs, canoeing on the Aveyron and walks in the region. The nearest **hotel** is the very pleasant *Les Jardins des Thermes*, 7km upstream in the village of Féneyrols (℡05.63.30.65.49, ⓦwww.jardinsdesthermes.eu; ❷; closed early Nov to Feb), set in its own grounds and with a recommended restaurant (menus €19–50, closed Wed & Thurs except July & Aug). The closest of several **campsites** is the quiet and well-kept *Camping Le Ponget*, 500m north of the centre (℡05.63.28.21.13, ℮camping.leponget@orange.fr; May–Sept). As for **places to eat**, you'll find bar-brasseries on place de la Halle and on avenue Paul-Benet, to the north of the old centre. One of the nicest restaurants is the *Auberge Côté Pont*, 6 boulevard des Thermes (℡05.63.30.63.75; closed for lunch Mon & Tues & Sun eve; menu at €22), with an inventive and constantly changing menu. You'll also eat well across the river at *Le Festin de Babettte* (closed Wed), which offers good-value menus (€13–25) and lovely views.

Penne and Bruniquel

Twenty kilometres downstream of St-Antonin you come to the beautiful ridge-top village of **PENNE**, once a Cathar stronghold, with its ruined castle impossibly perched on an airy crag. Everything is old and leaning and bulging, but holding together nonetheless, with a harmony that would be impossible to create purposely.

BRUNIQUEL, a few kilometres further on, is another hilltop village clustered round its **castle** (daily: March–June, Sept & Oct 10am–6pm; July & Aug 10am–7pm; 1–11 Nov 10am–5pm; €2.50, or €3.50 including guided visit; Ⓦ www.bruniquel.org). You can also visit a handsome house in the village, the aristocratic **Maison des Comtes de Payrol** (April–Sept daily 10am–6pm; €3). If you want to **stay**, Marc de Badouin runs a good *chambre d'hôte* to the right of the church (Ⓣ 05.63.67.26.16, Ⓦ www.chambres-bruniquel.fr; ❸; meals around €20); he's also a keen mountain-biker and can advise on local trails and footpaths. There's also a small two-star **campsite**, *Le Payssel* (Ⓣ 05.63.67.25.95, Ⓔ gugu2@orange.fr; July–Sept), about 2km south on the D964 to Albi.

Montauban and around

MONTAUBAN today is a prosperous, provincial city, capital of the largely agricultural *département* of Tarn-et-Garonne. It lies on the banks of the River Tarn, 53km from Toulouse, close to its junction with the Aveyron and their joint confluence with the Garonne. It is also, conveniently, on the main road and railway between Toulouse and Bordeaux.

The city's **history** goes back to 1144, when the count of Toulouse decided to found a *bastide* here as a bulwark against English and French royal power. In fact, it's generally regarded as the first *bastide*, the model for those rationally laid-out medieval new towns, and that plan is still clearly evident in the old city centre.

Montauban has enjoyed periods of great prosperity, as one can guess from the proliferation of fine town houses. The first followed the suppression of the Cathar heresy and the final submission of the counts of Toulouse in 1229, and was greatly enhanced by the building of the Pont-Vieux in 1335, making it the best crossing-point on the Tarn for miles around. The Hundred Years War did its share of damage, as did Montauban's opting for the Protestant cause in the Wars of Religion, but by the time of the Revolution it had become once more one of the richest cities in the southwest, particularly successful in the manufacture of cloth.

Arrival, information and accommodation

At Montauban's centre lies the perfect **place Nationale**, with the cathedral five-minutes' walk to the south on the unattractive **place Roosevelt**. From here, rue de l'Hôtel-de-Ville leads directly to the Pont-Vieux and across the river to avenue de Mayenne, at the end of which is the **gare SNCF**. There's no central *gare routière*, so you'll need to ask for bus information at the **tourist office**, on the northern corner of boulevard Midi-Pyrénées (July & Aug Mon–Sat 9.30am–6.30pm, Sun 10am–noon; Sept–June Mon–Sat 9.30am–12.30pm & 2–6.30pm; Ⓣ 05.63.63.60.60, Ⓦ www.montauban-tourisme.com). **Internet** access is available at Arobaze, 112 faubourg Lacapelle (Tues–Thurs 10am–9pm, Fri & Sat 10am–11pm), on the southwest side of town.

Among a limited choice of **hotels**, the best deal is the attractive *Du Commerce*, 9 place Roosevelt (Ⓣ 05.63.66.31.32, Ⓦ www.hotel-commerce-montauban.com; ❸), near the cathedral. The *Mercure*, opposite at 12 rue Notre-Dame (Ⓣ 05.63.63.17.23, Ⓦ www.mercure.com; ❻; restaurant menus €15–35), offers larger rooms and three-star services, but less character. Otherwise, your best option is the *Hôtel d'Orsay*, 32 rue Salengro, opposite the train station (☎05.63.66.06.66, ⓦwww.hotel-restaurant-orsay; ❸; closed Sun), which has dated but comfortable rooms and an excellent restaurant (menus €24–58; closed Sun & lunchtime Mon & Sat).

The simplest way of finding a place to eat is to browse the cafés, bars and brasseries around **place Nationale**. For a light lunch along the lines of homemade quiche and salad (€8) or afternoon tea and cakes, head for ⚭ *Crumble Tea*, tucked in a courtyard at 25 rue de la République (☎ 05.63.20.39.43; closed Sun & eves) – it's a good idea to reserve at lunchtime. *Le Contre Filet*, just off place Nationale at 4 rue Princesse (closed Wed & Sun), serves tasty and inexpensive platters of local produce and excellent *faux filet* (lunch platters €12, two-course evening menu €15. Moving up a notch, *La Cave O Délices*, 10 place Roosevelt (closed Sun & lunchtime Sat & Mon), is building a reputation for its good quality traditional cooking (eve menu €23) while *Les Saveurs d'Ingres*, 13 rue de l'Hôtel-de-Ville (☎05.63.91.26.42; closed Sun & Mon), near the Musée d'Ingres, is one of Montauban's top restaurants. Its small, simple interior masks the highly sophisticated dishes on offer, like salmon smoked over vine clippings (menus €28–65).

The Town

Montauban couldn't be easier to find your way around. The greatest delight is simply to wander the streets of the compact city centre, with their lovely pink-brick houses. The finest point of all is **place Nationale**, the *bastide's* central square, rebuilt after a fire in the seventeenth century and surrounded on all sides by exquisite double-vaulted arcades with the octagonal belfry of St-Jacques showing above the western rooftops.

The adjacent **place du Coq** on rue de la République is also pretty, and if you follow the street down it brings you out by the **church of St-Jacques** (first built in the thirteenth century on the pilgrim route to Compostela) and the end of the **Pont-Vieux** with a wide view of the river. At the near end of the bridge, the former bishop's residence is a massive half-palace, half-fortress, begun by the Black Prince, the son of King Edward III of England, in 1363 but never finished because the English lost control of the town. It's now home to the **Musée Ingres** (July & Aug daily 10am–6pm; Sept–June Tues–Sun 10am–noon & 2–6pm; July & Aug €6, Sept–June €4), based on a collection of drawings and paintings that artist Jean-Auguste-Dominique Ingres, a native of Montauban, left to the city on his death. It's a collection the city is very proud of, though his supremely realistic, luminous portraits won't be to everyone's taste. The museum also contains a substantial collection of sculptures by another native, Émile-Antoine Bourdelle.

The **Cathédrale Notre-Dame**, ten-minutes' walk up rue de l'Hôtel-de-Ville, is a cold fish: an austere and unsympathetic building erected just before 1700 as part of the triumphalist campaign to reassert the glories of the Catholic faith after the cruel defeat and repression of the Protestants. Apart from being a rare example of a French cathedral built in the classical style, its most interesting features are the statues of the four evangelists which triumphantly adorn the facade. Those on show now are recent copies, but the weather-beaten originals can be seen just inside.

Lauzerte

As you head north from Montauban towards Cahors, leaving the wide flat valleys of the Tarn and Garonne behind you, the land rises gradually to gently undulating country, green and woody, cut obliquely by parallel valleys running down to meet the Garonne and planted with vines and sunflowers, maize, and apple and plum orchards. It's a very soft landscape, and villages are small and widely scattered. The pace of life seems about equal with that of a turning sunflower.

Should you find yourself taking this route, then the place to make a halt is **LAUZERTE**, one of Raymond of Toulouse's *bastides* and once of great military importance as it commanded the road to Cahors. The town is short on sights, but there are some old houses, a pretty arcaded central square and a good Baroque altarpiece in the church, as well as views of the countryside round about.

You'll find a very pleasant **hotel** at the entrance to the village: *Le Quercy* (T05.63.94.66.36, Ehotel.du.quercy@orange.fr; ❷), which also serves superb food, with lunch menus from €11.50 and dinner €18–28 (closed Sun evening & Mon).There's a **campsite** nearby, *Le Grenier des Cœurs* (T05.63.94.75.60, Wwww .camping-de-lauzerte.fr; April–Oct), and a *gîte d'étape* in the village for walkers on the GR65 to Compostella (T05.63.94.61.94, Eacceuil@lauzerte-tourisme.fr; March–Oct).

Moissac

There's nothing very memorable about the modern town of **MOISSAC**, 30km northwest of Montauban, largely because of the terrible damage done by the flood of March 1930, when the Tarn, swollen by a sudden thaw in the Massif Central, burst its banks, destroying 617 houses and killing 120 people.

Luckily, the one thing that makes Moissac a household name in the history of art survived: the cloister and porch of the **abbey church of St-Pierre**, a supreme masterpiece of Romanesque sculpture. Indeed, the fact that it has survived numerous wars, including siege and sack by Simon de Montfort senior in 1212 during the crusade against the Cathars, is something of a miracle. During the Revolution it was used as a gunpowder factory and billet for soldiers, who damaged many of the sculptures. In the 1830s it only escaped demolition to make way for the Bordeaux–Toulouse train line by a whisker.

Legend has it that Clovis the Frank first founded a monastery here, though it seems more probable that its origins belong in the seventh century, which saw the foundation of so many monasteries throughout Aquitaine. The first Romanesque church on the site was consecrated in 1063 and enlarged in the following century. The famous south **porch**, with its magnificent tympanum and curious wavy door jambs and pillars, dates from this second phase of building, and its influence can be seen in the decoration of porches on countless churches across the south of France. It depicts Christ in Majesty, right hand raised in benediction, the Book of Life in his hand, surrounded by the evangelists and the elders of the Apocalypse as described by St John in the Book of Revelation. There's more fine carving in the capitals inside the porch, and the interior of the church, which was remodelled in the fifteenth century, is interesting too, especially for some of the wood and stone statuary it contains.

The adjoining **cloister** (same hours as tourist office – see opposite; €5) is entered through the tourist office, and is most peaceful first thing in the morning. The cloister surrounds a garden shaded by a majestic cedar, and its pantile roof is supported by 76 alternating single and double marble columns. Each column supports a single inverted wedge-shaped block of stone, on which are carved with extraordinary delicacy all manner of animals and plant motifs, as well as scenes from Bible stories and the lives of the saints. An inscription on the middle pillar on the west side explains that the cloister was made in the time of Abbot Ansquitil in the year of Our Lord 1100.

Practicalities

The **tourist office** (April–June, Sept & Oct Mon–Fri 9am–12.30pm & 2–6pm, Sat & Sun 10am–12.30pm & 2–6pm; July & Aug daily 9am–7pm; Nov–March Mon–Fri 10am–noon & 2–5pm, Sat & Sun 2–5pm; ℡05.63.04.01.85, @www.moissac.fr) is next to the cloister, with the **gare SNCF** further west along avenue Pierre-Chabrié. There's a weekend **market** in place des Récollets at the end of rue de la République, which leads away from the abbey, a marvel of colour and temptation.

The *Moulin de Moissac* (℡05.63.32.88.88, @www.lemoulindemoissac.com; ❹; restaurant menus from €22, closed Sat lunch & Sun), occupying a former mill on the river, rates as Moissac's top **hotel**; the building is large and not particularly attractive, but the interior has been beautifully refurbished. Alternatively, *Le Chapon Fin*, on place des Récollets (℡05.63.04.04.22, @www.lechaponfin -moissac.com; ❸), has faded but comfortable rooms. For **campers**, there's a shady site across the river on the *Île du Bidounet* (℡05.63.32.52.52, @www.camping-moissac.fr; April–Sept), and for walkers a *gîte d'étape* at 5 sente du Calvaire (℡05.63.04.62.21, @accueil.cafmoissac@orange.fr) on the hill above town. The nicest **place to eat** is the magnolia-shaded *Auberge du Cloître* (℡05.63.04.37.50; closed Wed & Sun evenings and Mon; menus €13–32), beside the tourist office. Or, in summer, head to the river bank just up from the *Moulin de Moissac*, where the *Kiosque de l'Uvarium* has a large terrace and serves a varied menu of grills, salads, pasta and the like; you'll eat well for around €20 a head (closed Mon & Oct–April).

Agen and around

AGEN, capital of the Lot-et-Garonne *département*, is more pleasant than it first appears. It was quartered by modern boulevards in the nineteenth century in its own version of a Haussmann clean-up, and it's down these roads that you're funnelled into the centre, with the result that you see nothing of interest.

The town lies on the broad, powerful River Garonne halfway between Bordeaux and Toulouse, and lived through the Middle Ages racked by war with England and internecine strife between Catholics and Protestants. But it was able to extract some advantage from disputes as it seesawed between the English and French, gaining ever more privileges as the price of its loyalty – a tradition that it maintained during and after the Revolution by being staunchly republican (the churches still bear the legend: *Liberté, Fraternité, Égalité*). Its pre-Revolutionary wealth derived from the manufacture of various kinds of cloth and its thriving port on the Garonne, but the Industrial Revolution put paid to all that. Agen's prosperity now is based on agriculture – in particular, its famous prunes and plums, said to have been brought back from Syria during the Crusades.

The interesting part of Agen centres on **place Goya**, where boulevard de la République, leading to the river, crosses boulevard du Président-Carnot. The main shopping area is just to the south around place Wilson and rue Garonne, a left turn at the end of which brings you to the wide place du Dr–Esquirol and the **Musée Municipal des Beaux–Arts** (daily except Tues: May–Sept 10am–6pm; Oct–April 10am–12.30pm & 1.30–6pm; €4; ⓦwww.ville-agen/musee), housed in four adjacent sixteenth- and seventeeth-century mansions. The collections include a rich variety of archeological finds, Roman and medieval, and some fine paintings – among them five Goyas and a Tintoretto rediscovered in the basement in 1997.

South of here, rue Beauville, with heavily restored but beautiful medieval houses, leads to rue Richard-Coeur-de-Lion and the **Église des Jacobins**. This big, brick Dominican church of the thirteenth century, now forms an annexe of the Musée des Beaux-Arts and hosts temporary exhibitions (daily except Tues 2–6pm; prices vary). Beyond lie the river and the public gardens of **Le Gravier**, where a **market** is held every Saturday morning.

Opposite place Wilson on the north side of boulevard de la République, the arcaded rue Cornières leads to the **Cathédrale St–Caprais**, somewhat misshapen but with a finely proportioned Romanesque apse and radiating chapels still surviving. In nearby rue du Puits-du-Saumon is one of Agen's finest houses, the fourteenth-century **Maison du Sénéchal**, with an elaborate open loggia on the first floor.

Practicalities

From the central place Goya, boulevard du Président-Carnot leads to the **gares SNCF** and **routière**. The **tourist office** is at 38 rue Garonne (July & Aug Mon–Sat 9am–7pm, Sun 9.30am–12.30pm; Sept–June Mon–Sat 9am–12.30pm & 2–6.30pm; ☎05.53.47.36.09, ⓦwww.ot-agen.org). **Internet** access is available at *N@uteus Cybercafé*, 83 cours Victor-Hugo (Mon–Wed 10am–8pm, Thurs & Fri to 10pm, Sat & Sun 2–8pm; €3 per hour).

Agen has several reasonable **hotels**. Of those in the old centre, the best-value budget option is the aged but friendly and clean *Des Ambans*, 59 rue des Ambans (☎05.53.66.28.60, ☎05.53.87.94.01; ❶), near place Goya, where cheaper rooms share toilets. A more comfortable alternative is the *Régina*, round the corner at 139 boulevard Carnot (☎05.53.47.13.27, ⓦwww.hotelreginagen .com; ❶–❷), with reasonably spacious rooms; again, not all have en-suite toilets. For four-star luxury and buckets of atmosphere, head for the *Château des Jacobins*, in an elegant nineteenth-century town house beside the Jacobins church (☎05.53.47.03.31, ⓦwww.chateau-des-jacobins.com; ❼).

As far as **restaurants** are concerned, *La Cantine*, 25 rue des Cornières (open for lunch Mon–Sat and dinner on Sat & Sun), is known for its big, fresh salads and open sandwiches, with *formules* at around €10–15. ⚑ *La Part des Anges*, 14 rue Emile-Sentini (☎05.53.68.31.00; closed Mon; menus €18–35), is the place to go for well-prepared and presented local dishes, such as black Gascon pork, beef from the Duras and cheeses aged on the premises. More formal is the excellent *Mariottat*, 25 rue Louis-Vivent to the south of the Jacobins church, offering contemporary cuisine in a lovely stately house and garden (☎05.53.77.99.77; closed Sun evening. Mon & lunch Sat; menus €26–68).

Villascopia

For years farmers around the village of **CASTELCULIER**, 8km southwest of Agen, have been digging up Roman mosaics, coins and even marble statues. Eventually the archeologists got to work in 1986 and revealed the foundations of a vast Gallo-Roman villa of the second century AD. It covered 1.5 hectares at its largest extent, including among the largest thermal complexes so far discovered outside Italy. These, and the various treasures also unearthed, now form part of one of the region's more rewarding Gallo-Roman sites, **Villascopia** (Feb & May Tues–Sun 2–5pm; June & Sept Tues–Sun 10am–6pm; July & Aug daily 11am–8pm; Oct–Dec Wed, Sat & Sun 2–5pm; closed Jan; €6). The visit starts with a 3-D film depicting daily life in the villa, after which some of the finds – including a graceful statue of Minerva – are on display in a small museum. You finally get to walk among the foundations themselves, with the benefit of now being able to imagine the villa as it once was. Unfortunately, there's no English-language version of the film yet, but it's possible to follow the gist of the story.

Travel details

Trains

Agen to: Belvès (2–4 daily; 1hr–1hr 10min); Bordeaux (hourly; 1hr 10min–1hr 50min); Le Buisson (2–4 daily; 1hr 10min–1hr 30min); Les Eyzies (2–4 daily; 1hr 40min); Moissac (2–5 daily; 30min); Monsempron-Libos (4–7 daily; 35–45min); Montauban (1–2 hourly; 35–55min); Périgueux (2–4 daily; 2hr–2hr 20min); Toulouse (1–2 hourly; 1hr–1hr 20min).
Bergerac to: Bordeaux (7–10 daily; 1hr 10min–1hr 30min); Le Buisson (3–7 daily; 30–40min); St-Émilion (4–7 daily; 55min); Sarlat (3–7 daily; 1hr 30min).
Brive to: Bordeaux (1–2 daily; 2hr 15min–2hr 45min); Cahors (5–8 daily; 1hr 05min); Figeac (4–7 daily; 1hr 15min–1hr 30min); Gourdon (2–5 daily; 40min); Limoges (1–2 hourly; 1hr–1hr 20min); Meymac (4–6 daily; 1hr 30min); Montauban (3–6 daily; 1hr 50min); Paris-Austerlitz (6–8 daily; 4hr–4hr 30min); Périgueux (4–5 daily; 50min–1hr); Pompadour (3–7 daily; 40 min); Rocamadour-Padirac (4–7 daily; 40min); Souillac (2–5 daily; 25min); Toulouse (4–8 daily; 2hr–2hr 30min); Uzerche (4–8 daily; 25–30min).
Cahors to: Brive (8–9 daily; 1hr–1hr 10min); Montauban (6–9 daily; 40min); Toulouse (9–11 daily; 1hr–1hr 20min).
Figeac to: Brive (6–8 daily; 1hr 20min); Najac (4–6 daily; 50min); Rodez (5–7 daily; 1hr 20min); Toulouse (4–6 daily; 2hr 30min); Villefranche-de-Rouergue (4–6 daily; 40min).
Limoges to: Angoulême (3–6 daily; 2hr); Aubusson (1 daily except Sat; 1hr 45min); Bordeaux (3–5 daily; 2hr 30min); Brive (1–2 hourly; 1hr–1hr 50min); Eymoutiers (4–9 daily; 45min); Meymac (3–5 daily; 1hr 40min–2hr 15min); Nexon (1 hourly; 15min); Paris-Austerlitz (1–2 hourly; 3hr–3hr

30min); Périgueux (7–15 daily; 1hr–1hr 20min); Poitiers (3–6 daily; 2hr); Pompadour (1–2 daily; 1hr 10min); St-Junien (2–6 daily; 40min); St-Léonard (6–10 daily; 20min); Solignac-Le Vigen (1–3 daily; 10min); Thiviers (7–15 daily; 40–50min); Ussel (4–6 daily; 1hr 35min–2hr).
Montauban to: Agen (1–2 hourly; 35–55min); Bordeaux (hourly; 1hr 30min–2hr 15min); Moissac (5–7 daily; 15–20min); Toulouse (1–2 hourly; 25–35min).
Périgueux to: Agen (2–5 daily; 2hr–2hr 20min); Belvès (2–5 daily; 1hr–1hr 20min); Bordeaux (6–12 daily; 1hr 15min–1hr 45min); Brive (3–6 daily; 45min–1hr); Le Buisson (2–6 daily; 50min); Les Eyzies (2–6 daily; 35min); Limoges (6–12 daily; 1hr–1hr 30min); Monsempron-Libos (2–5 daily; 1hr 30min).
Sarlat to: Bergerac (5–8 daily; 1hr 10min–1hr 30min); Bordeaux (4–6 daily; 2hr 40min); Le Buisson (5–8 daily; 40min).

Buses

Agen to: Auch (7–10 daily; 1hr 20min); Condom (1–3 daily; 45 min–1hr); Villeneuve-sur-Lot (5–13 daily; 45min–1hr 15min).
Bergerac to: Périgueux (Mon–Fri 3–5 daily; 1hr).
Brive to: Arnac-Pompadour (Mon–Sat 1 daily; 1hr 45min); Beaulieu-sur-Dordogne (school term Mon–Sat 1–3 daily; July & Aug Mon, Tues & Thurs–Sat 1–2 daily; rest of year Tues, Thurs & Sat 1–2 daily; 1hr 20min); Collonges-la-Rouge (Mon–Sat 1–3 daily; 30min); Meyssac (Mon–Sat 1–3 daily; 35min); Montignac (school term Mon–Fri 1 daily; 1hr 15min); Turenne (school term Mon–Sat 1 daily; 20min); Uzerche (Mon–Sat 2 daily; 1hr).
Cahors to: Figeac (3–7 daily; 1hr 30min–2hr); Fumel (4–6 daily; 1hr 10min); Luzech (4–9 daily; 25min); Monsempron-Libos (4–6 daily; 1hr 15min);

Puy-l'Évêque (4–9 daily; 45min); Tour-de-Faure (3–6 daily; 35min).

Limoges to: Aubusson (1–4 daily; 1hr 40min); Châlus (Mon–Sat 3–6 daily; 1hr); Nexon (Mon–Sat 3–4 daily; 40min); Oradour-sur-Glane (Mon–Sat 2–3 daily; 30–40min); Rochechouart (Mon–Sat 3–4 daily; 1hr–1hr 30min); St-Junien (Mon–Sat 3–4 daily; 1hr); St-Léonard (2–4 daily; 35min); Solignac (Mon–Sat 1 daily; 30min); Le Vigen (Mon–Sat 2–4 daily; 30min).

Périgueux to: Angoulême (Mon, Wed, Fri, Sat & Sun 1–2 daily; 1hr 40min); Bergerac (Mon–Fri 3–5 daily; 1hr–1hr 30min); Brantôme (Mon, Wed, Fri, Sat & Sun 1–2 daily; 35min); Ribérac (Mon–Fri 3–4 daily; 1hr).

Souillac to: Martel (Mon–Sat 2–4 daily; 20min); Sarlat (2–4 daily; 50min).

10

The Pyrenees

✳ **Surfing the Côte Basque**
Catch a wave at Biarritz
or Anglet, Europe's top
destination for both boogie-
boarders and classic surfers.
See p.685 & p.687

✳ **Cauterets** Several lake-
spangled valleys above this
agreeable spa offer superb
trekking, whether modest day-
loops or more ambitious multi-
day traverses. See p.716

✳ **The Cirque de Gavarnie** A
vast alpine amphitheatre with
wind-blown cascades and
traces of glacier. See p.718

✳ **Niaux cave** The upper Ariège
valley hosts a cluster of
prehistoric caves painted by
Cro-Magnon humans over
10,000 years ago; Niaux
contains the best preserved
and most vivid of these
images. See p.728

✳ **L'Abbaye de St-Hilaire,
Aude** Its carved sarcophagus
of St-Sernin is considered
among the masterworks of
the mysterious twelfth-century
Maître de Cabestany.
See p.736

✳ **Cathar castles** The imposing
castles of the upper Aude
and Corbières region testify
to southwestern Languedoc's
era of independence.
See p.738

✳ **Musée d'Art Moderne, Ceret**
An astonishing collection
of paintings from the prime
movers of the early twentieth-
century avant garde.
See p.748

✳ **Petit Train Jaune** Rumble
up the dramatic Têt valley of
Roussillon in an open-car,
narrow-gauge train.
See p.752

▲ Cirque de Gavarnie

10

The Pyrenees

B asque-speaking, wet and green in the west; craggy, snowy, Gascon-influenced in the middle; dry, Mediterranean and Catalan-speaking in the east – the **Pyrenees** are physically beautiful, culturally varied and less developed than the Alps. The whole range is marvellous walkers' country, especially the central region around the **Parc National des Pyrénées**, with its 3000-metre-high peaks, streams, forests and wildlife. If you're a committed **hiker**, it's possible to traverse these mountains, usually from the Atlantic to the Mediterranean, along the **GR10** or the higher, more difficult **Haute Randonnée Pyrénéenne** (HRP). There are numerous spa resorts as well – **Cauterets**, **Luz-St-Sauveur**, **Barèges**, **Ax-les-Thermes** – with shorter hikes nearby to suit all abilities, as well as skiing opportunities in winter.

As for the more conventional tourist attractions, the **Côte Basque** is lovely, sandy but very popular, suffering from seaside sprawl and a surfeit of caravan-colonized campsites. **St-Jean-de-Luz** is arguably the prettiest of the resorts, while

---

Hiking in the Pyrenees

There are plenty of walkers' **guidebooks** to the area in both French and English (see p.1213), plus two series of widely available **maps**. The most detailed of the latter are the French IGN 1:25,000 "TOP 25" series (🌐www.ign.fr); #1547OT, #1647ET, #1647OT, #1748ET and #1748OT cover the Parc National des Pyrénées, while #1848OT covers the Luchon area. Less demanding walkers can make do with Rando Éditions' *Cartes de Randonnées*, which covers the range at 1:50,000 in eleven sheets numbered from west to east (#9 is out of print).

The **walking season** usually lasts from mid-June until late September; earlier in the year, few staffed refuges function, and you'll often find snow on parts of the GR10 (even more so the HRP) until early July. These are big mountains and should be treated with respect: tackling any of the main walks means **proper preparation**. Before setting out, check weather forecasts – posted at the local tourist office – and be properly equipped and provisioned. Above all, don't take chances: mountain conditions change very quickly: sunny, warm weather in the valley doesn't mean it will be the same higher up, three hours later. If you are not experienced, it's best not to embark on anything other than a well-frequented path unless you're accompanied by someone who does.

One kilometre in twelve minutes (5kph) is a rather brisk average **walking pace** for level ground; if you're going uphill, allow an hour for every 350m in elevation gained. If you're out of condition, or have a heavy pack, the same climb will take longer. Much terrain is so steep, and trail surface so uneven, that going downhill isn't any faster. Be mindful of the punishment your knees will take: bring or buy telescopic walking poles or a traditional walking stick.

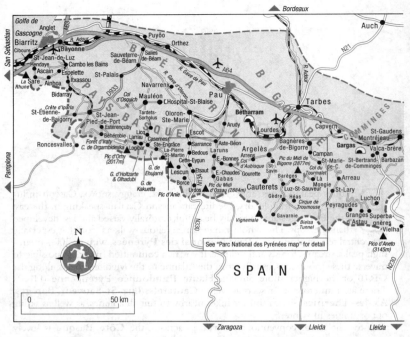

See "Parc National des Pyrénées map" for detail

0   50 km

S P A I N

once-elitist **Biarritz** is now enjoying a renaissance. **Bayonne**, just inland, is an attractive, if heavily touristed medieval town at the confluence of two broad rivers. The foothill towns are on the whole rather dull, although **Pau** merits at least a day, while monstrously kitsch **Lourdes** has to be seen whether you're a devout pilgrim or not. **Roussillon** in the east, focused on busy **Perpignan**, has beaches every bit as popular as those of the Côte Basque, nestled into the compact coves of its rocky coast, while its interior consists of craggy terrain split by spectacular canyons, sprouting a crop of fine Romanesque abbeys and churches – **St-Michel-de-Cuixà**, **St-Martin-de-Canigou** and **Serrabona** being the most dramatic – and a landscape bathed in Mediterranean light. Finally, the sun-drenched foothills just to the northwest harbour the famous **Cathar castles**, legacies of the once-independent and ever-rebellious inhabitants of southwestern Languedoc.

The Pays Basque

The three **Basque provinces** – Labourd (Lapurdi), Basse Navarre (Behe Nafarroa) and Soule (Zuberoa) – share with their Spanish neighbours a common language – Euskera – and a strong sense of distinct identity. The language is widely spoken, and Basques refer to their country as Euskal-herri (or, across the border in Spain, Euskadi). You'll see bilingual French/Euskera

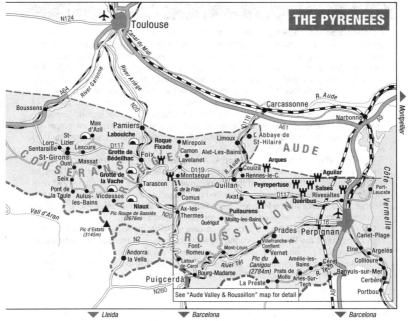

toponym signage and posters throughout the region (sometimes only in Euskera), so in this section we have given the Euskera for all locations in brackets after the French. Unlike some of their Spanish counterparts, few French Basques favour an independent state or secession from France, though a Basque *département* has been mooted (see below). For decades the French authorities turned a blind eye to the Spanish Basque terrorist organization ETA, which used the region as a safe haven and organizational base. Since the millennium, however, as France has extradited suspected terrorists to Spain, incidents of violence and vandalism associated with nationalists have increased, notably around Bayonne and Pau. Such events, however, are so exceptional as to not concern visitors.

Administratively, the three French Basque provinces were combined with the county of Béarn in the single *département* of Basses-Pyrénées (now Pyrénées-Atlantiques) after the 1789 Revolution, when the Basques' thousand-year-old *fors* (customary privileges) were abolished. It was a move designed to curtail their nationalism, but ironically has probably been responsible for preserving their unity. Of late there have been proposals to create a Pays-Basque *département*, hived off from the Pyrénées-Atlantiques, with its capital at Bayonne – a notion greeted with horror in the capital of such a centralized nation, but not so inconceivable now in an EU that gives increasing power to regions.

Apart from the language and the traditional broad beret, the most obvious manifestations of Basque national identity are the ubiquitous *trinquets* (enclosed) or *frontons* (open) concrete courts in which the national game of **pelota** is played. Pairs of players wallop a hard leather-covered ball, either with their bare hands or a long basket-work extension of the hand called a *chistera*

Although **Basque cooking** shares many of the dishes of the southwest and the central Pyrenees – in particular **garbure**, a thick potato, carrot, bean, cabbage and turnip soup enlivened with pieces of pork, ham or duck – it does have distinctive recipes. One of the best known is the Basque omelette, **pipérade**, made with tomatoes, peppers and often Bayonne ham, actually more like scrambled eggs. Another delicacy is sweet red peppers, or **piquillos**, stuffed whole with *morue* (salt cod). **Poulet basquaise** is also common, especially as takeaway food: pieces of chicken browned in pork fat and casseroled in a sauce of tomato, ground Espelette chillis, onions and a little white wine. In season there's a chance of **salmi de palombe**, an onion-and-wine-based stew of wild doves netted or shot as they migrate north over the Pyrenees.

With the Atlantic adjacent, **seafood** is also a speciality. The Basques inevitably have their version of fish soup, called *ttoro*. Another great delicacy is **elvers** or *piballes*, netted as they come up the Atlantic rivers. **Squid** are common, served here as *txiperons*, either in their own ink, stuffed and baked or stewed with onion, tomato, peppers and garlic. All the locally caught fish – tuna (*thon*), sea bass (*bor*), sardines (*sardines*) and anchovies (*anchois*) – are regular favourites, too.

Cheeses mainly comprise the delicious ewe's-milk *tommes* and *gasna* from the high pastures of the Pyrenees. Among sweets, ubiquitous is the **gâteau basque**, an almond-custard pie often garnished with preserved black cherries from Itxassou. As for alcohol, the only Basque AOC **wine** is the very drinkable Irouléguy – as red, white or rosé – while the local digestif **liqueur** is the potent green or yellow Izzara.

(in the variation known as *cesta punta*), against a high wall blocking one end of the court. It's extraordinarily dangerous – the ball travels at speeds of up to 200kph – and knockouts or worse are not uncommon. Trials of strength (*force Basque*), rather like Scottish Highland games, are also popular, including tugs-of-war, lifting heavy weights, turning massive carts and sawing or axing giant tree trunks.

The Côte Basque

Barely 30km long from the Spanish frontier to the mouth of the Adour, the **Basque coast** is easily accessible by air, bus and train, and reasonably priced accommodation is not difficult to find – except from mid-July through August, when space should be reserved at least six weeks in advance. **Bayonne**, slightly inland, is the cultural focus and only town with some life apart from tourism. **Biarritz**, the most prestigious and varied resort, is flanked by magnificent beaches but proves a rather noisy, congested place to stay in high season. Families manifestly prefer **St-Jean-de-Luz** to the south – an attractive and more manageable town in any case – or distinctly suburban **Anglet** just to the north, with even better beaches which attract surfers from near and far. At the border, **Hendaye** itself is rather dull but has another superb beach at the mouth of the Bidas(s)oa River.

Bayonne (Baïona)

BAYONNE stands back some 5km from the Atlantic, a position that until recently protected it from any real touristic exploitation. It bestrides the confluence of the River Adour, which rises near the Pic du Midi d'Ossau, and the much smaller Nive, whose source is the Basque Pyrenees above St-Jean-Pied-de-Port. Although purists dispute whether it's truly a Basque rather than a Gascon city (indeed street-signage is trilingual in Gascon, Euskera and French), Bayonne is effectively the economic and political capital of the Pays Basque. To the lay person, at least, its Basque flavour predominates, with tall half-timbered dwellings and woodwork painted in the traditional green and red. Here, too, Basques in flight from Franco's Spain came without hesitation to seek refuge among their own. For many years the Petit Bayonne quarter on the Nive's right bank was a hotbed of violent Basque nationalism, until the French government clamped down on such dangerous tendencies.

The city originated as the Roman fort of Lapurdum; this Latin name, corrupted to Labourd (Lapurdi), was subsequently extended to cover the whole of this westernmost of the three Basque provinces. For three centuries until 1453 and the end of the Hundred Years War, it enjoyed prosperity and security under English domination, and this wealth was consolidated when, in the sixteenth century, Sephardic Jews fleeing the Portuguese Inquisition arrived, bringing their chocolate-manufacturing trade with them. The city reached the peak of its commercial success in the eighteenth century, when it was also a centre of the armaments industry (it gave its name to the bayonet). More recent economic activity has included processing of by-products from the natural gas field at Lacq near Pau – although this is approaching exhaustion – electronics and aeronautical equipment.

These issues don't immediately impinge on the visitor, however, and first impressions are likely to be favourable. Despite forming, with Biarritz and Anglet, a conurbation of about 200,000 people, Bayonne is a small-scale, easily manageable city, at the hub of all major road and rail routes from the north and east. Although there are no great sights, it's a pleasure to walk the narrow streets of the old town, bisected by the River Nive and still wrapped in the fortifications of **Sébastien le Preste de Vauban**, Louis XIV's military engineer. The cathedral is on the west bank in **Grand Bayonne**, the museums east of the river in **Petit Bayonne**.

Arrival and information

From the **airport**, city buses #6 or C take you into town. The **gare SNCF** and **gare routière** for points in Béarn, Basse Navarre and Soule are next door to each other, just off place de la République on the north bank of the Adour, across the wide Pont St-Esprit from the city centre. In addition, **bus stops** in place des Basques on the Adour's south bank serve Biarritz and Anglet (though most of these lines stop at the *gare SNCF* too), as well as destinations in the Nive valley. The **tourist office** is also in place des Basques (July & Aug Mon–Sat 9am–7pm, Sun 10am–1pm; Sept–June Mon–Fri 9am–6.30pm, Sat 10am–6pm; ☎08.20.42.64.64, ⓦwww.bayonne-tourisme.com). All **car hire** outfits – for example Ada (☎05.59.50.37.10, ⓔada.bayonne@orange.fr) at 10 bis quai de Lesseps – are in the St-Esprit quarter, within sight of the *gare SNCF*.

Accommodation

The most agreeable budget **hotel** is the basic *Hôtel des Basques*, at the corner place Paul-Bert and rue des Lisses (☎05.59.25.59.03; ❶); a slight step up in comfort means pastel-hued, part-antique furnished *Hôtel des Arceaux* at 26 rue Port Neuf (☎05.59.59.15.53, ⓦwww.hotel-arceaux.com; ❸). Three-star alternatives include *Best Western Le Grand Hôtel*, at 21 rue Thiers (☎05.59.59.62.00, ⓦwww.bw-legrandhotel.com), with rooms (❺) and suites (❻) set in a nineteenth-century town house, and the *Hôtel Loustau*, on place de la République (☎05.59.55.08.08,

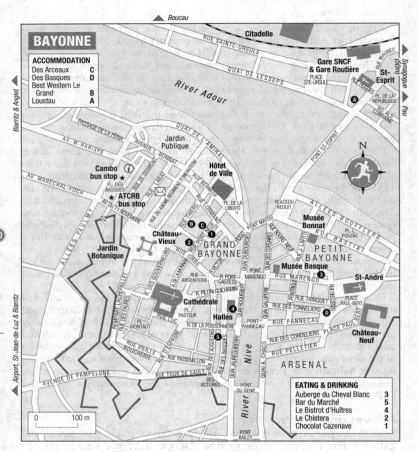

THE PYRENEES | The Côte Basque

10

BAYONNE

ACCOMMODATION
Des Arceaux	C
Des Basques	D
Best Western Le Grand	B
Loustau	A

Boucau

Citadelle

RUE SAINTE-URSULE

Gare SNCF & Gare Routière

QUAI DE LESSEPS

PLACE STE-URSULE

St-Esprit

RUE MAUBEC

RUE TUGES

PL. DE LA RÉPUBLIQUE

BD AL. LORRAINE

Synagogue (50m)

Pau

Biarritz & Anglet

River Adour

QUAI DE L'AMIRAL

PASSAGE DE LA FERIA

AV. M-HARISPE

AVENUE L. BONNAT

Jardin Publique

Hôtel de Ville

RUE BERNÈDE

PONT ST-ESPRIT

AV. MARÉCHAL-FOCH

AV. DU DR CAMBO bus stop (i)

PL. DES BASQUES

★ ATCRB bus stop

AV. DU 11 NOVEMBRE

RUE DE GRAMONT

RUE LABAT

RUE DU 49ÈME RÉGIMENT D'INFANTERIE

RUE ORBE

RUE THIERS

RUE ORMAND

PL. DE LA LIBERTÉ

PLACE DU RÉDUIT

ALLÉES BOUFFLERS

Musée Bonnat

PL. POLZAC

RUE BASTIAT

N

Château-Vieux

B

2

RUE DE LA PONT NEUF

GRAND BAYONNE

RUE HUGO

PONT MAYOU

RUE DES FRÈRES

RUE LAFFITTE

PETIT BAYONNE

ALLÉES PAULMY

Jardin Botanique

RUE DES GOUVERNEURS

RUE DE LA MONNAIE

RUE ARGENTERIE

R. VICTOR HUGO

QUAI DUBOURDIEU

QUAI DES CORSAIRES

Musée Basque

3

St-André

PLACE PAUL-BERT

RUE MARENGO

RUE TRINQUET

Cathédrale

PL. PASTEUR

R. PONT CASTETS

PONT MARENGO

RUE MARENGO

RUE GALUPERIE

RUE DES TONNELIERS

D

Château-Neuf

REMPART LACHEPAILLET

RUE DES FAURES

R. PILORI GUILHAMIN

RUE LUC

R. DE LA POISSONNERIE

Halles

4

QUAI ROQUEBERT

QUAI GALUPERIE

RUE PANNECAU

RUE DES CORDELIERS

PLACE PAUL-BERT

RUE PELLETIER

PL. MONTAUT

RUE D'ESPAGNE

RUE DES AUGUSTINS

PONT PANNECAU

PONT MAYOU

Nive

ARSENAL

RUE VIEILLE BOUCHERIE

RUE PASSEMILLON

RUE DES BASQUES

QUAI AMIRAL JAURÉGUIBERRY

QUAI CHACO

AVENUE DE PAMPELUNE

RUE TOUR DE SAULT

PL. DES VICTOIRES

PONT DU GÉNIE

Airport, St-Jean-de-Luz & Biarritz

River Nive

PONT BAILEY

0   100 m

EATING & DRINKING
Auberge du Cheval Blanc	3
Bar du Marché	5
Le Bistrot d'Huîtres	4
Le Chistera	2
Chocolat Cazenave	1

W www.hotel-loustau.com; ⑤), overlooking the river beside Pont St-Esprit, with a well-regarded restaurant.

Grand Bayonne

In Grand Bayonne, just up the avenue from the tourist office, stands the town's fourteenth-century **castle** (closed to the public except for an exclusive, by-appointment-only restaurant 3 nights weekly; booking info posted). The oldest part, the Château-Vieux, is a genuine example of no-nonsense late-medieval fortification; a plaque on the east wall lists some of the more famous willing or unwilling guests, including four French kings, the Black Prince, King Pedro the Cruel of Castile, and the notorious mercenary Bertrand de Guesclin. Just west lies the **Jardin Botanique** (April 15 to Oct 15 daily 9.30am–noon & 2–6pm; free), an enormous, well-designed garden with plants labelled in French, Basque and Latin.

Just around the corner on magnolia-shaded place Pasteur, the **Cathédrale Ste-Marie** (Mon–Sat 10–11.45am & 3–5.45pm, Sun 3.30–6pm), with its twin towers and steeple rising with airy grace above the houses, is best seen from across the grassy expanse of its own **cloister** (daily 9am–12.30pm & 2–5pm, closes 6pm May–Sept) on its south side, restored in 2008–09. Up close, the yellowish stone reveals bad weathering, with most decorative detail lost. Inside, its most impressive features are the height of the nave and some sixteenth-century glass (restored in 2002), set off by the prevailing gloom. Like other southern Gothic cathedrals of the period (around 1260), it was based on northern models, in this case Soissons and Reims.

The smartest, most commercial streets in town extend northeast from the cathedral: **rue Thiers** leading to the Hôtel de Ville, and **rue de la Monnaie**, leading into **rue Port-Neuf**, with its chocolate *confiseries* and restaurants. South and west of the cathedral, along **rue des Faures** and **rue d'Espagne**, there's exemplary half-timbering and a bohemian, artsy-craftsy feel, where antique shops and rare-book dealers alternate with the odd bar or restaurant.

Petit Bayonne and St-Esprit

East of the cathedral, the Nive's riverside **quays** are the city's most picturesque focus, with sixteenth-century arcaded houses on the Petit Bayonne side, the one at 37 quai des Corsaires containing the worthwhile **Musée Basque** (all year Tues–Sun 10am–6.30pm, July & Aug also Mon; free Wed 6.30–9.30pm; €5.50, €9 with Musée Bonnat; ⓦ www.musee-basque.com). Its exhibits (aside from temporary ones) illustrate traditional Basque life through farm implements such as solid-wheeled oxcarts and field rollers, as well as *makhilak* – innocent-looking carved, wooden walking sticks with a concealed steel spear tip at one end, used by pilgrims and shepherds for self-protection if need be. The seafaring gallery features a superb rudder handle carved as a sea-monster, a wood-hulled fishing boat, and a model of Bayonne's naval shipyards c.1805; Columbus's skipper was a Basque, as was Juan Sebastián de Elakano, who completed the first global circumnavigation in 1522.

The city's second museum, the nearby **Musée Bonnat** at 5 rue Jacques-Lafitte (daily except Tues & hols: May–Oct 10am–6.30pm; Nov–April 10am–12.30pm & 2–6pm; July–Aug open daily & also Weds to 9.30pm; €5.50, €9 with Musée Basque; ⓦ www.musee-bonnat.com), holds an unexpected treasury of art. Thirteenth- and fourteenth-century Italian painting is well represented, as are most periods before Impressionism. Highlights include Goya's *Self-Portrait* and *Portrait of Don Francisco de Borja*, Rubens' powerful *Apollo and Daphne* and *The Triumph of Venus*, plus works by Murrillo, El Greco and Ingrès. A whole gallery is devoted to high-society portraits by Léon Bonnat (1833–1922), whose personal collection formed the original core of the museum. There are also frequent, worthwhile temporary exhibits in the annexe at 9 rue Fredéric-Bastiat.

Apart from the view back across the river, there's relatively little on the northern bank of the Adour. A deliberately inconspicuous, early nineteenth-century **synagogue** at 33 rue Maubec is a legacy of Bayonne's Jewish community, which settled here on arrival from Portugal during the sixteenth century. St-Esprit in effect became their ghetto after an expulsion order in 1602, when Grand Bayonne was consecrated to the Virgin and off-limits to unbelievers. The **church of St-Esprit**, opposite the station, is all that remains of a hostel that once served Chemin de St-Jacques pilgrims – it's worth a peek inside for a fine fifteenth-century wood sculpture of the Flight into Egypt. Just above the station looms Vauban's massive **citadelle**; built in 1680 to defend the town against Spanish attack, it actually saw little action until the Napoleonic wars, when its garrison resisted a four-month 1813 siege by Wellington before falling the next year.

Eating, drinking and entertainment

The most popular areas for **eating** and **drinking** are along the right-bank Nive quay between Pont Marengo and Pont Pannecau, or along quai Jauréguiberry between Pont Pannecau and Pont du Genie on the Grand Bayonne side – though eateries there tend to be more notable for their number than their quality. The backstreets either side of the river can be rewarding, especially in Petit Bayonne or the area south and west of the *halles*.

Bayonne's biggest annual **festival** is the Fêtes de Bayonne, which usually starts on the last Wednesday in July and consists of five days and nights of continuous boozing and entertainment. There are *corridas* (bullfights) the last two days, plus a few more in the run-up to August 15. A well-established, three-day **jazz festival**, La Ruée au Jazz (W www.larueeaujazz.com), takes place in mid-July.

Auberge du Cheval Blanc 68 rue Bourg-Neuf, Petit Bayonne, (T 05.59.59.01.33.) is seafood-strong, formerly Michelin-starred, and considered the best in town. weekday lunch menu is offered, but assume €90 expenditure; booking essential. Closed part July, all Sun evening & Mon except Aug.

Bar du Marché 39 rue des Basques, Grand Bayonne. Despite the name, this begins serving food and drink – including good beer on tap – at 5am to market sellers and continues with good-value *plats du jour* at lunchtime. The decor is accented by posters for Basque-country beverages, and the San Fermín bull-running at Pamplona. Closed all evenings & all Sun.

Le Bistrot d'Huîtres Southeast corner of the *halle*. One of three such oyster bars based in the market, with a good-value €19 *formule*.

Le Chistera 42 rue Port-Neuf, Grand Bayonne. Doyenne of a row of three similar eateries under the arcades here, offering gazpacho, fish soup, *merlu*-based dishes, a few meat platters and good home-made desserts; best order à la carte (allow €27) and/or off the daily specials board rather than the dull menu. Closed Mon, part May, and Tues & Wed evenings except July & Aug.

Chocolat Cazenave 19 rue du Port-Neuf, Grand Bayonne. The local chocolate tradition is duly honoured with a handful of *chocalateries* on, or just off this street. This, the most famous one, serves hot whipped chocolate and cold cocoa-based desserts at tables under the arcade or in its Art Nouveau interior. Closed Sun.

Biarritz (Miarritze)

A few minutes by rail or road from Bayonne, **BIARRITZ** was, until the 1950s, the Monte Carlo of the Atlantic coast, transformed by Napoléon III during the mid-nineteenth century into a playground for monarchs, aristos and glitterati. With the 1960s rise of the Côte d'Azur, however, the place went into seemingly terminal decline, despite having been discovered by the first surfers in 1957. But from about 1994, Biarritz was rediscovered by Parisian yuppies, a new generation of the international surfing fraternity and a slightly alternative family clientele, who together have put the place back on the map.

Arrival, information and transportation

The **gare SNCF** lies 3km southeast of the centre at the end of avenue Foch/ avenue Kennedy in the *quartier* known as La Négresse (STAB bus #2 or B from or to square d'Ixelles). The **tourist office**, also selling tickets for local events and spectacles, is on square d'Ixelles (daily: July & Aug 8am–8pm; Sept–June Mon–Sat 10am–6pm, Sun 10am–5pm; T 05.59.22.37.00, W www.biarritz.fr). Alternatives to the STAB bus are basically fairly pricey hired **mountain bikes** or **scooters** (best rates from Cycle Océan at Carrefour d'Hélianthe, T 05.59.24.94.47, W www.cycleocean.com).

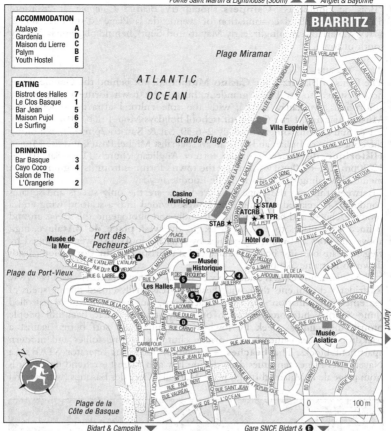

ACCOMMODATION
Atalaye   A
Gardenia   D
Maison du Lierre C
Palym   B
Youth Hostel   E

EATING
Bistrot des Halles 7
Le Clos Basque   1
Bar Jean   5
Maison Pujol   6
Le Surfing   8

DRINKING
Bar Basque   3
Cayo Coco   4
Salon de The
  L'Orangerie   2

BIARRITZ

Plage Miramar

ATLANTIC OCEAN

Grande Plage

Villa Eugénie

Casino Municipal

Musée de la Mer

Port dês Pecheurs

Plage du Port-Vieux

Hôtel de Ville

Musée Historique

Les Halles

Plage de la Côte de Basque

Musée Asiatica

Airport ▶

0   100 m

Accommodation

Accommodation is booked out weeks in advance during July and August, especially the more affordable choices. *Hôtel Palym* at 7 rue du Port-Vieux (☎05.59.24.16.56, ⓦwww.le-palmarium.com; ❷–❸), with a variety of old-fashioned rooms and a ground-floor bar-restaurant, is a solid budget option, though owing to nearby bars isn't suited for those after an early night. Nearby stands completely en-suite *Hôtel Atalaye*, 6 rue des Goélands (☎05.59.24:06.76, ⓦwww.hotelatalaye.com; ❸–❹), with the best rooms having balconies facing a quiet square and, obliquely, the sea. Even quieter, if inland, is popular, non-smoking *Hôtel Gardénia*, 19 avenue Carnot (☎05.59.24.10.46, ⓦwww.hotel -gardenia.com; ❸), with wi-fi signal, though not all rooms are en suite. For more comfort and character, *La Maison du Lierre* at 3 avenue du Jardin Public (☎05.59.24.06.00, ⓦwww.maisondulierre.com; ❺), offers good-sized, wood-floored rooms in a restored mansion.

The nearest **youth hostel** (☎05.59.41.76.07, Ⓔaubergejeune.biarritz @orange.fr) is 2km southwest of the centre on the shore of Lac Mouriscot, just walkable from the *gare SNCF*; otherwise take bus #2 or B from the centre, stop

"Bois de Boulogne". **Campers** should try *Biarritz Camping*, at 28 route d'Harcet, the inland continuation of avenue de la Plage (T05.59.23.00.12, Wwww.biarritz-camping.fr; early May to mid-Sept), behind plage de la Milady south of town.

The Town

The focus of Biarritz is the **Casino Municipal**, just behind the Grande Plage, now restored to its 1930s grandeur. Inland, the town forms a surprisingly amorphous, workaday sprawl, with the sole cultural attractions being the **Musée Asiatica**, 1 rue Guy-Petit (school holidays Mon–Fri 10.30am–6.30pm, Sat & Sun 2–7pm, otherwise daily 2–6.30, Sat & Sun to 7pm; €7), exhibiting the collection of Indian and Tibetan art specialist Michel Postel, and the **Musée Historique de Biarritz** in the former Anglican church (Tues–Sat 10am–12.30pm & 2–6.30pm; €4), tracing the town's fortunes from its beginnings as a medieval whaling station to its Belle Époque heyday.

Between this and the plage du Port-Vieux are the only streets and squares conducive to relaxed strolling. The **halles**, divided into a seafood wing and a produce, cheese and ham division, is friendly and photogenic, the streets around it lined with places to eat and drink. To the west, **place de l'Atalaye**, high above the port and named for a nearby whalers' lookout tower, is fringed by elegant mansions; just below, characterful if touristy **rue du Port-Vieux** leads down to its namesake beach.

The **ocean**, however, is undeniably beautiful – if not especially clean (Wwww .surfrider.fr documents this), with beaches occasionally closed during spells of extreme contamination – and also treacherous, thus heavily lifeguard-patrolled (June–Sept). White breakers crash on sandy strands, where beautiful people bronze their limbs cheek by jowl with families and surf bums, against a backdrop of ocean-liner hotels, ornate churches, Gothic follies and modern apartment blocks. The **beaches** – served by local bus operator STAB's La Navette des Plages ten times daily during July and August – extend northwards from plage de la Milady through plage Marbella, Côte des Basques (with several

▲ Surfers, Biarritz

surfing schools), plage du Port-Vieux, Grande Plage and plage Miramar to the Pointe St-Martin with its lighthouse. Most of the action takes place between the plage du Port-Vieux and the plage Miramar, overlooked by the huge **Hôtel du Palais** (formerly the Villa Eugénie), built by Napoléon III in the mid-nineteenth century for his wife, whom he met and courted in Biarritz.

Just beside the **plage du Port-Vieux**, the most sheltered and intimate of the beaches, a rocky promontory sticks out into the sea, ending in the **Rocher de la Vierge**, an offshore rock topped by a white statue of the Virgin, and linked to the mainland by an Eiffel-built iron catwalk. Around it are scattered other rocky islets where the swell heaves and combs. On the bluff above the Virgin stands the **Musée de la Mer** (daily: June & Sept 9.30am–7pm; July & Aug 9.30am–midnight; Oct–May 9.30am–12.30pm & 2–6pm; closed Jan 7–21 & Mon Nov–March; €7.80; ⓦ www.museedelamer.com), which contains interesting displays on the fishing industry and the region's birds, and an aquarium of North Atlantic fish as well as the obligatory seal tank with twice-daily feedings.

Just below is the picturesque **Port des Pêcheurs**, most easily approached by a switchback pedestrian lane. The fishermen are long gone, replaced by pleasure boats, two **scuba outfitters** (the more established being BAB, ⓣ 06.09.26.22.65, ⓦ www. babsub.fr) and pricey seafood restaurants. To the northeast lies the **Grande Plage**, an immaculate sweep of sand once dubbed the "Plage des Fous" after the 1850s practice of taking lunatics to bathe here as a primitive form of thalassotherapy.

Eating, drinking and nightlife

Away from the touristy snack bars on rue du Port-Vieux, it's possible to eat well for an affordable price, especially near the *halles*. Formal **nightlife** in the town centre includes *Cayo Coco*, a Cuban theme bar (Thurs–Sat eves) at 5 rue Jaulerry offering free salsa dance lessons, and *Bar Basque* at the start of rue du Port-Vieux, with the most buzzing-est crowd on this lane and reasonably priced Spanish-style *raciones*. Have a good start to the day at *Salon de Thé l'Orangerie* (closed Wed) at 1 rue Gambetta, serving forty varieties of tea and a reasonably copious breakfast.

Bar Jean 5 rue Halles. Semi-subterranean Spanish-theme outfit with tapas or seafood meals for about €25; also has side-walk tables.

Bistrot des Halles 1 rue du Centre ⓣ 05.59.24.21.22. Cosy place (thus groups should book) doing generously portioned, tasty fish or meat-under-sauce dishes. Menu at lunch only, allow €29–35 à la carte. Closed Sun evening except school holidays.

Le Clos Basque 12 rue Louis-Barthou ⓣ 05.59.24.24.96. Another favourite bistro –

booking mandatory even spring/autumn – with meaty, hearty fare. Menus at €24–26 give a wide choice. Closed Mon & low-season Sun evening.

Maison Pujol 1 rue du Centre. Basically a deli (specializing in foie gras) also doing very reasonable tapas, bigger platters of ham or seafood and wine in any measure at impromptu seating around barrel-tables out front.

Le Surfing Plage de Côte des Basques. A seaview shrine to the sport, festooned with antique boards and serving decent seafood grills and *frites*.

Anglet (Angelu)

Immediately north and east of Biarritz, resolutely residential **ANGLET** sprawls up the coast from the Pointe St-Martin to the mouth of the Adour at La Barre. Tourism revolves around a half-dozen contiguous, superb beaches, broader and wilder than any at Biarritz. The most frequented are **Chambre d'Amour**, so named for two lovers trapped in their trysting place by the tide, and adjacent **Sables d'Or** and **Marinella**, both much favoured by the surfers and with schools operating in season. On the downside, parking in season (even scooters) is hopeless and a sharp drop-off means bathers hug the shore.

The summertime Navette des Plages calls here, too, or you can walk from Biarritz in about thirty minutes, along avenue de l'Impératrice, avenue MacCroskey, then second left down to the seaside boulevard des Plages. Anglet has a **HI hostel** at 19 route des Vignes (T05.59.58.70.00; mid-Feb to mid-Nov; stop "Les Corsaires" on Navette des Plages or STAB bus #4 or C). Numerous snack bars flank the car parks, including *Havana Café* at Chambre d'Amour, serving *plats du jour* at lunch.

St-Jean-de-Luz (Donibane Lohitzun)

With its fine sandy bay – the most protected of the Basque beaches – and magnificent old quarter speckled with half-timbered mansions, **ST-JEAN-DE-LUZ** remains the most attractive resort on the Basque coast, despite being fairly overrun by families in peak season. As the only natural harbour between Arcachon and Spain, it has long been a major port, with whaling and cod-fishing the traditional occupations of its fleets. Even now, St-Jean remains one of Frances' busiest fisheries, and the principal one for landing anchovy and tuna.

Arrival, information and accommodation

St-Jean's **gare SNCF** is on the southern edge of the town centre, 500m from the beach, while **buses** arrive at the *halte routière* diagonally opposite. The **tourist office** (April–June & Sept Mon–Sat 9am–12.30pm & 2–7pm, Sun 10am–1pm; July & Aug Mon–Sat 9am–7.30pm, Sun 10am–1pm & 3–7pm; Oct–March Mon–Sat 9am–12.30pm & 1.30–6.30pm, Sun 10am–1pm; T05.59.26.03.16, Wwww.saint-jean-de-luz.com) stands opposite the fish market on the corner of boulevard Victor Hugo and rue Bernard Jaureguiberry.

Well-placed, good-value hotels include the *Hôtel Ohartzia* (T05.59.26.00.06, Wwww.hotel-ohartzia.com; ❹–❺), just inland from the beach at 28 rue Garat, with rear rooms overlooking the garden where breakfast is served, and the *Lafayette* (T05.59.26.17.74, Wwww.hotelpaysbasque.com; ❸–❹) at pedestrianized 18–20 rue de la République, the best rooms with balconies. Three-star comfort means quietly set ⚓ *Les Goëlands* at 4–6 avenue d'Etcheverry (T05.59.26.10.05, Wwww.hotel-lesgoelands.com; ❻; all year), which consists of two 2005-renovated *belle-époque* villas, with parking and a full-service restaurant (Easter–Oct; half board at ❽ obligatory mid-July to early Sept). There are numerous **campsites**, seaward of the N10 between St-Jean and Guéthary.

The Town

The wealth and vigour of St-Jean's seafaring and mercantile past is evident in surviving seventeenth- and eighteenth-century town houses. One of the finest, adjacent to the Hôtel de Ville on plane-tree-studded place Louis-XIV, is the turreted **Maison Louis XIV** (guided visits only: June & Sept 1 to Oct 15 11am, 3pm, 4pm, 5pm; July & Aug Mon–Sat 10.30am–12.30pm & 2.30–6.30pm; by appointment only otherwise; €5), built for the Lohobiague family in 1635, but renamed after the young King Louis stayed here for a month in 1660 during the preparations for his marriage to Maria Teresa, Infanta of Castile. She lodged in the equally impressive pink Italianate villa known as the **Maison de l'Infante** (June 15 to Oct 15 11am–12.30pm & 2.30–6.30pm; €3), overlooking the harbour on the eponymous quay.

The wedding of King Louis and Maria Teresa was *the* major event in local history, overshadowing the Spanish destruction of the town in 1558. The couple's sumptuous, nay extravagant, wedding took place in the **church of St-Jean-Baptiste** on pedestrianized **rue Gambetta**, the main shopping-and-tourism street today. Cardinal Mazarin alone presented the new queen with twelve thousand pounds of pearls and diamonds, a gold dinner service and a pair of carriages drawn by teams of six horses – all paid for by money made in the service of France. The door through which they left the church – right of the existing entrance – has been sealed up ever since. Even without this curiosity, the church deserves a look inside: the largest French Basque church, its barn-like nave roofed in wood and lined on three sides with tiers of dark oak galleries accessed by wrought-iron stairways. These are a distinctive feature of Basque churches, reserved for the men, while the women sat at ground level. Equally Basque is the elaborate gilded retable of tiered angels, saints and prophets behind the altar. Hanging from the ceiling is an *ex voto* model of the Empress Eugénie's paddle steamer, the *Eagle*, which narrowly escaped being wrecked outside St-Jean in 1867.

Ciboure (Ziburu), the harbour and Urrugne (Urruña)

On the far side of the harbour and Nivelle river mouth, **CIBOURE** seems a continuation of St-Jean but is in fact a separate community, terminating in the little fortress of **Socoa (Sokoa)**, today home to a sailing/windsurfing club and smaller beach (shuttle boat 9am–7pm from St-Jean beach, €2). Its streets are prettier (and emptier) than its neighbour's, especially waterfront **quai Maurice-Ravel** (the composer was born at no. 12) and the parallel **rue Pocolette** just inland, an exquisite terrace of wide-fronted, half-timbered, balconied town houses gaily painted in typical Basque colours. The octagonal tower protruding above the houses belongs to the sixteenth-century **church of St-Vincent**, where you'll find more characteristic Basque galleries, a Baroque altarpiece and yet another *ex voto* model ship; the entrance is via a paved courtyard with gravestones embedded in it. From either side of the Nivelle or the Pont Charles-de-Gaulle linking St-Jean and Ciboure, the **fishing harbour** dominates proceedings seaward, with most working tuna boats tied up on the quai de l'Infante or Ciboure's quai Pascal-Elisalt, cheek by jowl with pleasure craft.

Also worth considering is a visit to the **Château d'Urtubie** (guided tours April–Oct 10.30am–12.30pm & 2–6.30pm, July–Aug no lunchbreak; €6; Ⓦ www.chateaudurtubie.net) at **URRUGNE**, just outside Ciboure, 3km southwest of St-Jean-de-Luz, which has belonged to the same family since its construction as a fortified château in 1341. It was enlarged and gentrified during the sixteenth and eighteenth centuries, and provided hospitality for the French King Louis XI, as well as for Maréchal Soult and later Wellington during the Napoleonic Wars. If you fancy following in their footsteps, note that it's also a very upmarket **hotel** (Ⓣ05.59.54.31.15; ❻–❽); otherwise just visit and take tea in the salon afterwards for €4 extra.

Eating and drinking

Leading off place Louis-XIV – with its cafés, sidewalk artists and **free summer-time evening concerts** in the bandstand – rue de la République has several **restaurants**, including cheap-and-cheerful *La Ruelle* (closed Mon, also Tues low season) at no. 19, with two seafood menus (€18–23), though service is "relaxed" and drinks stiffly priced. The next street east, rue Tourasse, also offers possibilities, including durable *La Vieille Auberge* at no. 22 (closed Weds, & Tues lunch), with three menus (€14–27). Less scenically set but equally popular is friendly *Le Buvette des Halles* (lunch only to 3pm, closed Mon off season), on the corner of the market hall on boulevard Victor-Hugo, which serves impeccably fresh tuna, crab and sardines, plus *pipérade*, drink and dessert for around €22 (three courses), though portions could be more generous.

Hendaye (Hendaïa) and Château d'Abbadia

HENDAYE, 15km southwest of St-Jean-de-Luz, is the last French town before the Spanish frontier. Neither the town proper, **Hendaye-Ville**, nor the seaside quarter, **Hendaye-Plage**, is of much intrinsic interest, though the latter's narrow if long, safe beach is popular with Spaniards who reckon it better than anything on their side until reaching San Sebastián.

Hendaye-Ville, served by both the Paris–Bordeaux–Irún and Toulouse–Irún train lines, lies on the River Bida(s)soa estuary, which here forms the border with Spain. Just upstream, the tiny, wooded **Île des Faisans** was once used as a meeting place for the monarchs of the two countries. In 1659 it was venue for the signature of the Treaty of the Pyrenees, and the year after for the marriage contract between Louis XIV and Maria Teresa. The painter Velázquez, responsible for the decor of the negotiations chamber, apparently caught the cold here which resulted in his death. Another interesting encounter was between Hitler and Franco at Hendaye train station on October 23, 1940. The version promulgated by Franco and his publicists, long believed even by his enemies, had "El Caudillo" preserving Spanish neutrality by parrying the Führer's threats to annexe Spain; in fact Franco, dazzled by Hitler's early victories and the prospect of a greatly enlarged Spanish Morocco at the expense of France, begged to be allowed to fight alongside Germany. But Hitler – mindful of how much assistance the Spanish Nationalists had needed to win their civil war, and aware of Spain's dire economic state – considered the proposed alliance a liability and was having none of it.

The main local sight, just east, is the **Château d'Abbadia** (ⓦwww.academie -sciences.fr/Abbadia.htm), home of nineteenth-century Dublin-born explorer Antoine d'Abbadie, on the headland closing off Hendaye-Plage on the east, just off the route de la Corniche (Feb–May & Oct–Dec 15 Tues–Sat guided visits only 2–5pm; June–Sept Mon–Fri guided visits 10–11.30am & 2.30–6pm, without guide 12.30–2.30pm; Sat & Sun visit without guide 2–5.30pm; €5.50 unguided, €6.60 guided). After expeditions in Ethiopia and Egypt, d'Abbadie had the neo-Gothic château built between 1860 and 1870; the architect was Eugène Viollet-le-Duc, and the result a bizarre Franco-Hibernian folly with every surface painted, carved or fabric-covered, filled with objects collected by d'Abbadie on his travels. Visits take in the chapel, a ground-floor bedroom in red with Arabic calligraphy, upstairs rooms with Ethiopian inscriptions and a round reception room, blue-motifed like d'Abbadie's own quarters.

Practicalities

Hendaye's **tourist office** is at 67B boulevard de Mer in Hendaye-Plage (April–June & Sept–Oct Mon–Sat 9am–12.30pm & 2–6pm; July & Aug Mon–Sat 9am–7.30pm, Sun 10.30am–1pm; Nov–March Mon–Sat 9am–12.30pm & 2–5pm; ☎05.59.20.00.34, ⓦwww.hendaye.com). Ten local **campsites** are all found east of Hendaye-Plage, just off the Route de la Corniche; one of the more tent-friendly, and closest to the beach, is *Alturan* (☎05.59.20.04.55; June–Sept), on rue de la Côte. With room to spread out, apartments for seasonal occupancy are big, and many **hotels** have shut. Best of the survivors, both on boulevard de Mer are *Hôtel Uhainak* at no. 3 (☎05.59.20.33.63, ⓦwww.hotel -uhainak.com; Feb–Nov; ❹), and mock-Moorish *Hôtel Valencia* at no. 29 (☎05.59.20.01.62, ⓦwww.hotelvalencia.fr; most of year; ❹), with wi-fi and free parking (a big point as beachside street-parking is charged for all day). Independent **restaurants** are overwhelmingly fishy if not too numerous; cheap (because prosaically set by a car park) and popular is *La Petite Marée* at 2 avenue des Mimosas, one block inland. For a sea view, head west to the yacht and fishing port, where *La Cabane du Pêcheur* (closed Sun evening & Mon) does full seafood meals (weekday menus €25). Just around the corner at 4 rue des Orangers, ✷ *Le Parc à Huîtres* (closed Tues) is a superb oyster-bar-cum-takeaway-deli with seating outdoors and in; make a meal of it with salad, oysters or other tapas, desserts and oyster-compatible wines *en vrac* or by the bottle.

Inland: Labourd (Lapurdi) and Basse Navarre (Behe Nafarroa)

Without your own transport, the simplest forays into the soft, seductive landscapes of the Basque hinterland are along the **St-Jean-de-Luz–Sare bus route** or the **Bayonne–St-Jean-Pied-de-Port train line**. Both give a representative sample of the area.

La Rhune (Larrun) and Ascain (Azkaine)

The 905-metre cone of **La Rhune**, straddling the frontier with Spain, is the westernmost skyward thrust of the Pyrenees before they decline into the Atlantic. As *the* landmark of Labourd, in spite of its unsightly multipurpose antennae, and duly equipped with a rack-and-pinion rail service, it's a predictably popular a vantage point, offering fine vistas way up the Basque coast and east along the Pyrenees. Two or three **buses** a day (July–Aug Mon–Sat; Sept–June Mon–Fri), run by Le Basque Bondissant, ply the route from St-Jean-de-Luz, stopping also at Ascain, Col de St-Ignace and Sare.

ASCAIN, where Pierre Loti wrote his romantic novel *Ramuntcho*, is like so many Labourdan villages – postcard-perfect to the point of tweeness with its galleried church, *fronton* and polychrome, half-timbered houses. Loti's house on place du Fronton is now the central **hotel-restaurant** *De la Rhune* (☎05.59.54.00.04, ✉hoteldelarhune@orange.fr; ❹) with a garden at the back, one of several accommodation options in the village.

You could walk up La Rhune from here in about two and a half hours, or take the **rack-and-pinion tourist train** from **Col de St-Ignace** (March 18 to Nov 3; every 35min 9am–5pm peak season, much less otherwise; current fares/schedules at ⓦwww.rhune.com). The ascent takes 35 minutes, but you should allow up to two hours for the round trip. Be warned: it's massively popular in summer, with long queues and two snack bars near the base station taking full advantage of a captive clientele.

Sare (Sara) and Ainhoa

With or without the bus, it's worth continuing to **SARE**, another perfectly proportioned Basque knoll-top village ringed by satellite hamlets. You can either walk on the **GR10** from the intermediate station below the summit of La Rhune in about an hour and a quarter, or follow 3km of road from St-Ignace in rather less time. Several scattered **hotels** make for a more attractive overnight than Ascain; most central – and poshest – choice is the three-star *Arraya* on the village square (☎05.59.54.20.46, ⓦwww.arraya.com; April–Oct; ❺), a former hospice on the Santiago pilgrimage route. More affordable are the *Baratxartea*, 1km northeast in Ihalar hamlet (☎05.59.54.20.48, ⓦwww.hotel-baratxartea .com; March 15 to Nov 15; ❸), or the *Pikassaria* in Lehenbizkai 1.5km south of the square (☎05.59.54.21.51, ⓦwww.hotel-pikassaria.com; ❸), with a respected restaurant (supper only except Sun; *formules*/menus €16–22). The only independent **restaurant** is popular *Lastiry* opposite the *Arraya*, offering *nouvelle Basquaise* cuisine under the arcade (menus €23–33). The more consistently open of two **campsites** is *La Petite Rhune* (☎05.59.54.23.97; May–Sept), near *Hôtel Pikassaria*.

Instead of going back to St-Jean-de-Luz from Sare, an easy three- to four-hour stint on the GR10 brings you to **AINHOA**, another gem of a village. It consists of little more than a single street lined with substantial, mainly seventeenth-century houses, whose lintel plaques offer mini-genealogies as well as foundation dates. Take a look at the bulky towered **church** with its gilded Baroque altarpiece of prophets and apostles in niches, framed by Corinthian columns. Indoor **accommodation** is only for well-heeled trekkers (or drivers); best value among three pricey hotels is 2007-redone *Hôtel Oppoca* (☎05.59.29.90.72, ⓦwww.oppoca.com; mostly closed mid-Nov to April; ❺) with a good **restaurant** (closed Mon; menus €26–38). Otherwise it's *Camping Harazpy* near the village centre (☎05.59.29.89.38; mid-June to mid-Sept).

The valley of the Nive

The **River Nive** valley is the only public transport corridor southeast into the Basque hinterland, with several daily trains making the riverside journey from Bayonne to St-Jean-Pied-de-Port. The luminous green landscape on the approach to the mountains is scattered with peaceful villages untouched by speculative development.

Cambo-les-Bains (Kanbo)

The first major stop is **CAMBO-LES-BAINS**, an old spa resort whose favourable microclimate made it ideal for the treatment of tuberculosis in the nineteenth century; it's an attractive place, green and open, but suffers from the usual genteel stuffiness of spas. The "new" town, with its ornate houses and hotels, radiates out from the baths over the heights above the River Nive, while the old quarter of Bas Cambo lies beside the river and *gare SNCF*.

The main local sight is the **Villa Arnaga**, 1.5km northwest of town on the Bayonne road (guided or "free" visits: March 15–31 2.30–6pm; April–June & Sept 1 to Oct 15 10am–12.30pm & 2.30–7pm; July–Aug 10am–7pm; Oct 16 to Nov 9 2.30–6pm; €6), built for Edmond Rostand, author of *Cyrano de Bergerac*, who came here to cure his pleurisy in 1903. This larger-than-life Basque house, painted in deep-red trim, overlooks an almost surreal formal garden with discs and rectangles of water and segments of grass punctuated by blobs, cubes and cones of topiary box, with a distant view of green hills. Inside, it's very kitsch, with a minstrels' gallery, fake pilasters, allegorical frescoes, numerous portraits and various memorabilia.

The **tourist office** is at the start of the road down to Bas Cambo (July 14–Aug Mon–Fri 8.30am–6.30pm, Sat 8.30am–noon & 2–5.30pm, Sun 10am–12.30pm; Sept–July 13 Mon–Fri 8.30am–12.30pm & 2–6.30pm, Sat 8.30am–noon & 2–5.30pm; ☎05.59.29.70.25). For an overnight **stay**, try *Auberge de Tante Ursule* in Bas Cambo by the pelota court (☎05.59.29.78.23, ⓦwww.tante -ursule.com; ❷), with old-fashioned rooms upstairs from the sizeable, excellent

restaurant (menus €16–35). The nearest year-round **campsite** is *Ur-Hégia* on route des Sept-Chênes (☎05.59.29.72.03), also in Bas Cambo.

Espelette (Ezpeleta), Itxassou (Itsasu) and Laxia

Buses cover the 5km southwest from Cambo to **ESPELETTE**, a somewhat busy village of wide-eaved houses, with a **church** notable for its heavy square tower, painted ceiling (climb the triple gallery for a closer look) and keyhole-shaped, inscribed-slab gravestones (the oldest by the church, under the lime trees). The village's principal source of renown is its dark red **chilli peppers** – much used in Basque cuisine, hung to dry in summer on many housefronts – and its **pottok** markets. *Pottoks* are the indigenous Basque pony, once used in British coal mines but now reared mainly for meat and riding. The annual sales happen on the last Tuesday and Wednesday in January; the pepper jamboree takes place on the last Sunday in October. There's a very good **hotel–restaurant** in Espelette, *Euzkadi,* on the main street at the northeast edge of the village (☎05.59.93.91.88; ❸; restaurant closed Mon, & Tues low season), with calmer rear rooms facing a pool and three menus (€23–35) featuring hearty Basque country cooking.

About the same distance south from Cambo-les-Bains, next stop up the train line (though only one train a day stops here), is the delightful village of **ITXASSOU**, quieter than most of the others in the area, and surrounded by green wooded hills. The main point of interest is the little seventeenth-century **church of St-Fructueux**, about 1km out on the minor D349 road towards Pas de Roland and Laxia hamlet, its vast cemetery harbouring a significant collection of both modern and ancient keyhole-shaped gravestones; inside, its three-tiered wooden galleries and sumptuous retable are worth a quick look. Itxassou is a great base for a gentle recharge of the batteries, with about a half-dozen **hotel–restaurants** scattered locally. Best-value and quietest are – next to St-Fructueux – the ⚑ *Hôtel du Chêne* (☎05.59.29.75.01, ⓕ05.59.29.27.39; closed Dec 15 to Feb; ❸), with bright, often wood-floored rooms over two storey and a well-kept restaurant (closed Mon, also Tues low season) doing menus featuring *pipérade*, salad, game and dessert, and – at bucolic **LAXIA** – the *Hôtel Ondoria* (☎05.59.29.75.39, ⓦwww.ondoria.fr; closed Dec 15 to Jan & Mon; ❷), where meals are taken at a wisteria-festooned terrace overlooking the river.

Bidarray (Bidarrai) to St-Étienne-de-Baïgorry (Baigorri)

The GR10 from Ainhoa, the train line (station Pont-Noblia) and a perilously narrow road beyond Laxia all converge at **BIDARRAY**, which at first glance seems restricted to a few houses clustered around its medieval bridge over the Nive, the **Pont d'Enfer**. Further investigation, however, reveals the upper village, scattered appealingly on a ridge with superb views. On the way into the village on the GR10 is a *gîte d'étape* spread over two buildings, the *Auñamendi* (☎05.59.37.71.34), while the central place de l'Église is flanked by the charac-terful *Hôtel Barberaenea* (☎05.59.37.74.86, ⓦwww.hotel-barberaenea.fr; closed mid-Nov to mid-Dec), with a mix of sink-only rooms (❶) and en suites (❸), and a creditable **restaurant**. A short walk east, equidistant from upper and riverside quarters, lies refreshingly tent-only *Camping Errekaldia* (☎05.59.37.72.36).

Bidarray is the preferred starting point for the classic **ridge-trek** of the Basque country, the section of the GR10 running roughly south along the **Crête d'Iparla**, then descending east to St-Étienne-de-Baïgorry. It's seven hours' walking one way, and should only be attempted in settled conditions –

when bad weather closes in, you won't get its famous views and close-range sightings of vultures, and you'll be at risk from lightning strikes or falling from the mist-shrouded brink, both events killing hikers here regularly. Consult current SNCF schedules before setting out so that you coincide with one of the afternoon **rail-buses** that cover the eight kilometres between St-Étienne and the actual train station of Ossès-St-Martin-d'Arrossa, one stop above Pont-Noblia.

Like many other Basque villages, **ST-ÉTIENNE-DE-BAÏGORRY** is divided into distinct quarters, more like separate hamlets than a unified settlement. A prosperous, sleek place, its business is still predominantly agriculture rather than tourism, with the Pays Basque's only vineyards scattered around, producing the Irouléguy (Irulegi) wine named after the village 5km east; the vintner's on the D15 road offers *dégustation* and sales. The "sights" here comprise a seventeenth-century, barrel-vaulted **church** with a fine organ over the southwest door in addition to the usual galleries and altarpiece, plus a picturesque medieval bridge posing against a backdrop of the romantic Château de Etchauz and distant hills.

The **tourist office** is opposite the church (all year Mon–Fri 9am–noon & 2–6pm; ☎05.59.37.47.28). **Accommodation** includes the municipal **campsite** *Irouléguy* (☎05.59.37.43.96; March–Dec 15), opposite the swimming pool on the St-Jean road, plus *Hôtel-Restaurant Juantorena* on the through road in Bourg quarter (☎05.59.37.40.78; ❷), with a pleasant terrace and parking in the back. With transport, head for tranquil, stream-side *Hôtel Manechenea*, 5km north in the hamlet of **Urdos** (Urdoze) (☎05.59.37.41.68, ✉hotel-manechenea@orange.fr; ❸; closed Nov–March), with a decent restaurant (menu from €19).

St-Jean-Pied-de-Port (Donibane Garazi)

The old capital of Basse Navarre, **ST-JEAN-PIED-DE-PORT** lies in a circle of hills at the foot of the Bentarte pass into Spain. It owes its name to its position "at the foot of the *port*" – the pass leading into Spain. Only part of France since the 1659 Treaty of the Pyrenees, it was an important halt on the **pilgrimage to Santiago de Compostela** in the Middle Ages. The routes from Paris, Vézelay and Le Puy converged just northeast of here at Ostabat, before struggling over the ridge to the Spanish monastery of Roncesvalles (Roncevaux in French).

The town straddles the young River Nive, the old quarter enclosed by walls of pinky-red sandstone (which can be accessed for a partial walkaround). Above it rises a wooded hill crowned by the Richelieu-Vauban **Citadelle**, while on the east a further defensive system guards the road to Spain. The pleasant but unremarkable modern town spreads down across the main road onto lower ground. In season, all of it – except for the further reaches of the new quarter – is packed to the gills with visitors.

The old town consists essentially of a single cobbled street, first as **rue de la Citadelle**, running downhill from the fifteenth-century **Porte St-Jacques** – the gate by which pilgrims entered the town, St Jacques being French for Santiago – to the **Porte Notre-Dame**, commanding the bridge over the Nive, with a constantly photographed view of balconied houses overlooking the stream. A fourteenth-century Gothic church, **Notre-Dame-du-Bout-du-Pont**, stands just inside the Porte Notre-Dame and, opposite, short rue de l'Église leads through the **Porte de Navarre** to place du Général-de-Gaulle and the modern road; south of the Nive the same main thoroughfare continues, as **rue d'Espagne**, to the southerly **Porte d'Espagne**.

The final French leg of the **GR65** pilgrim route starts from St-Jean and follows the line of the old Roman road across to Roncesvalles in Spanish Navarra, a walk of 27km (allow 7–8hr). Follow characteristic star-ray yellow-on-blue signs south from the Porte d'Espagne, soon adopting the one-lane D428 with which you will stay for more than half the route; the typical yellow waymarks of the Chemin de St-Jacques guide you, as do newer red-and-white ones. Though the climb on tarmac is initially dull, there are attractive farmhouses to look at, with immensely broad roofs – one side short, the other long to cover stalls and tools – plus views out across the valleys east and west. After about ninety minutes you'll reach the tiny hamlet of **HONTO**, which for late starters in particular offers excellent *chambres d'hôte* (as well as cheaper dorm beds) and hearty evening meals at *Ferme Ithurburia* (T05.59.37.11.17; ❷; year round). Beyond Honto, the grade sharpens, but there's only one brief path short cut from the D428 before you arrive, an hour further along, at the well-sited *Refuge-Auberge Orisson* (T06.81.49.79.56, Ⓦwww.refuge-orissson.com; 18 bunks; March–Oct), your last chance for meals and shelter before Roncesvalles. After passing a pennant-festooned altar, you'll finally leave the D428 for a proper trail at Pic Urdanarré (1240m), some four hours along and just before the frontier and spring at Col de Bentarte (c.1340m), where sheep (and a few *pottoks*) are everywhere, and vultures gliding literally in your face.

The Chemin de St-Jacques was rerouted through the Col de Bentarte some years back, diverted from the Puerto de Ibañeta well inside Spain, to the annoyance of purists who were committed to the latter as the locale for the events related in the medieval **Chanson de Roland** (though Bentarte is just as likely a venue). Roland was a historical character, warden of the Breton marches, who in 778 accompanied Emperor Charlemagne on a campaign to support the Muslim ruler of Zaragoza in his war against the Emir of Córdoba. The mission degenerated into raids for booty, and on their way home the Franks sacked the Navarrese capital of Pamplona. In revenge, local Basques ambushed and massacred Charlemagne's rearguard, commanded by Roland, as it withdrew up the slopes beyond Roncevaux/Roncesvalles. The medieval romance describes how Roland sounded his horn for aid in vain, and "hewed and smote" various and sundry with his magical sword Durandal – and also paints the dastardly foe as infidel Saracens rather than fellow Christians. This bit of propaganda was concocted four hundred years later during the Crusades, in order to demonize the contemporary Muslim foe.

Practicalities

The **tourist office** is at 14 place du Général-de-Gaulle (July & Aug Mon–Sat 9am–7pm, Sun 9.30am–1pm & 2.30–5pm; Sept–June Mon–Sat 9am–noon & 2–6pm; T05.59.37.03.57, Ⓦwww.terre-basque.com), while a handful of newsagents and bookstores sell guides and IGN maps. The **gare SNCF** lies a ten-minute walk away at the end of avenue Renaud, north of the centre.

Chambres d'hôtes, particularly along rue de la Citadelle, are numerous. Among **hotels**, a budget choice is relatively quiet *Les Remparts*, 16 place Floquet (T05.59.37.13.79, Ⓦwww.touradour.com/hotel-remparts.htm; ❸; closed Nov–Feb 15), just before you cross the Nive coming into town on the Bayonne road. More comfortable are the *Ramuntcho*, just inside the walls at 1 rue de France (T05.59.37.03.91; ❹; closed Nov 26 to Jan 11, Tues–Wed low season), with some balconied rooms, parking near by and a popular, competent restaurat, (menus €16.50–31.50), and the *Central* on place du Général-de-Gaulle (T05.59.37.00.22; ❺; closed Dec–Feb, Tues low season; menu €19.50–45), with some river-view rooms and parking.

Dormitory lodgings for pilgrims and hikers include helpful *Gîte d'Étape Etchegoin* at 9 route d'Uhart, on the Bayonne road (T05.59.37.12.08; 12 bunks), and Dutch-volunteer-run, inexpensive ☀ *L'Esprit du Chemin*, 40 rue de la Citadelle (☎05.59.37.24.68, ⊛www.espritduchemin.org; April–Sept; 14 bunks), offering sound advice and moral support to walkers and pilgrims. The municipal **campsite**, *Plaza Berri* (☎05.59.37.11.19; Easter–early Nov), is on the south bank of the Nive, off avenue du Fronton.

Independent **restaurants** are mostly slapdash bistros and "café-snacks" aimed squarely at the day-tripper trade. Two exceptions are popular *Paxkal Oillarburu* at 8 rue de l'Église just inside the Porte de Navarre (closed Tues low season, book on ☎05.59.37.06.44 in summer), with a €21.50 menu where fair quality offsets small portions, and *Hurrup Eta Klik* at 3bis rue de la Citadelle (☎05.59.37.09.18; closed Wed), just inside the Porte Notre–Dame and serving country cooking and abundant measures of cider.

Estérençuby, Béhérobie and Les Sources de la Nive

From St-Jean, the D301 follows the deepening valley of the Nive to the southeast, past small farms and bucolic villages, while the GR10 stays well northeast of the river, first on paved lanes and then on track or trail along Handiamendi ridge. Both routes converge at **ESTÉRENÇUBY** (Ezterenzubi), 8km from St-Jean and an attractive spot. *Auberge Carricaburu* by the *fronton* is the most characterful **restaurant** (menus €18–22) and lively village bar, but sadly its upstairs rooms are currently inoperative, leaving only *Hôtel Andreinia-Larramendy* over the bridge (☎05.59.37.09.70, ⊛www.hotel-andreinia.com; closed Nov 11 to Dec 26, Wed low season; ❷), with 2005-remodelled bathrooms; they also run a 19-bunk *gîte d'étape* (March–Nov).

Beyond Estérençuby the valley-floor D428 road continues alongside the Nive, now no more than a mountain stream, tumbling down between steep green slopes, covered in hay and bracken. Some 4km from Estérençuby the road reaches tiny **Béhérobie** (Beherobia) before climbing up the border by the Col de Bentarte and looping back to St-Jean – an excellent bike-ride or drive. At Béhérobie the ☀ *Hôtel des Sources de la Nive* (☎05.59.37.10.57, ⊛www .hotel-sourcesdelanive.com; ❷–❺ half board; closed Jan to mid-Feb and Tues low season, booked out in Oct by pigeon-shooters), beside the stream, is ideal for a quiet stay despite the rooms being decidedly 1970s, with a restaurant where frog's legs, *cèpes*, trout, roebuck and pigeon feature on copious menus.

Just before the bridge at Béhérobie, a lane leads to the left, signposted to "**Sources de la Nive**". With a car, you can drive 400m to the asphalt's end, then continue on foot along the dirt track going left, not the one going over the bridge. After fifteen minutes, you'll reach the springs, where water percolates a thousand metres down through the karstic slopes to well up as surging rapids. Hidden in dense beech woods, it's a magic spot in any weather, with a faint mist often rising from the surface of the young stream.

Haute Soule

East of the Nive valley, you enter largely uninhabited country, the old Basque county known as the **Haute Soule**, threaded only by the GR10 and a couple of minor roads. The border between Basse Navarre and Soule skims the western edge of the **Forêt d'Iraty**, one of Europe's largest surviving beech woods, a popular summer retreat and winter cross-country skiing area. There are no shops or proper hotels until you reach **Larrau**, the only real village hereabouts, though the scattered hamlet of **Ste-Engrâce** in the east of the district has

Pastoralism in the Pyrenees

Like other shepherds in Mediterranean or southern Europe, the Basques are forced to take their flocks to high **mountain pastures** in summer in search of better grazing. A few shepherds still live with their dogs out on the treeless slopes in stone-hut sheepfolds called *cayolars*, milking the ewes twice a day and making the *fromage de brébis* whose soft and hard versions are a speciality throughout the pastoral Pyrenees. Most pastures today are accessible by pick-up or 4WD jeep, at least at the gentler Basque end of the Pyrenees, so a shepherd's life is not as harsh and isolated as it used to be – though there are still places accessible only by mule or pony. A measure of the former pre-eminence of sheep in the Basque economy is the Basque word for "rich", *aberats*, the literal meaning of which is "he who owns large flocks".

Much of the grazing land is owned by various *communes*, who over the centuries have made elaborate agreements (*faceries*) to ensure a fair shareout of the best pasture and avoid disputes. One of the oldest of these, concluded by the inhabitants of Spanish Roncal and French Barétous in 1326, is still in force and renewed each July 13 at the frontier **Col de la Pierre-St-Martin** on symbolic payment of three white heifers.

accommodation, as do **Licq** and **Tardets-Sorholus**, foothill settlements some way down the valley. There's even a downhill ski resort, the westernmost in the Pyrenees, at **La-Pierre-St-Martin**, technically just over the border in Béarn but included here for convenience.

Haute Soule is a land of open skies, where griffon vultures turn on the thermals high above countless flocks of sheep (their occasional corpses providing sustenance), with three vast gorges to explore. Although the beeline distance from the Nive valley to Béarn is not great, the slowness of the roads (there's no public transport) or the GR10 – it's two days' hiking from Estérençuby to Larrau – and the grandeur of the scenery seems to magnify it.

The Forêt d'Iraty (Irati)

To drive to the **Forêt d'Iraty**, follow the D301 east out of the Nive valley from the junction on the D428, where the forest is signposted. The road is steep, narrow and full of tight hairpins and ambling livestock – it's best avoided at night or in misty conditions – but as you climb up the steep spurs and around the heads of labyrinthine gullies, ever more spectacular views open out over the valley of the Nive, St-Jean and the hills beyond. Solar-powered sheep ranches abound, with cheese on sale. Beech copses fill the gullies, shadowing the lighter grass whose green is so intense it seems almost theatrical – an effect produced by a backdrop of purplish rock outcrops.

Once past the north flank of **Occabé** (Okabe; 1456m), you're in Haute Soule, and from here the road loops down to meet the D18 on the **plateau d'Iraty**, with its small lake and *Le Cayolar* snack bar. A minor road, soon a jeep track, leads south towards Ochagavia in Spain via *Chalet Pedro* (1km along), a basic hikers' *gîte* and comfier apartments sleeping eight (☎05.59.28.55.98, ⓦwww .chaletpedro.com/iraty/; 12 places, mid-June to Sept 1) as well as the best **restaurant** in the area (menus €23–29, featuring trout, *cèpes*, Iberian ham). The GR10 emerges from here its descent of flat-topped Occabé (75min up from here), with its Iron Age **stone circle** up top. Continuing east from the plateau, the D18 road enters the densest part of the forest, climbing past another small lake and a **campsite** half hidden in the magnificent beeches, to nine wooden chalets and a *gîte d'étape* at the **Col de Bagargi-Iraty (1327m)**. An **information** office here (open all year; ☎05.59.28.51.29) takes bookings for the chalets and the *gîte*; across the car park is a small shop and normally priced **restaurant**. From here you descend slightly to the nearby **Col d'Orgambidexka**, which is one of the prime viewing fields for the autumn bird migrations. As you emerge into the open beyond Orgambidexka, the ground drops sharply away on the left into the **Valleé de Larrau**, 600m lower.

Larrau (Larraiñe) to La-Pierre-St-Martin

The first thing you notice coming into **LARRAU** from the west is how different the architecture is. In contrast to the painted, half-timbered facades and tiled roofs of Labourd and Basse Navarre, the houses here are grey and stuccoed, with Béarnais-style, steep-pitched slate roofs to shed heavy snow. And, although it's the biggest place since St-Jean, it's nonetheless very quiet – almost dead out of season. There are two friendly **hotels**: the simple, old-fashioned *Hôtel Despouey* (☎05.59.28.60.82; ❷; closed mid-Nov to Easter), with a mix of shower-only and full-bathed rooms, and the fancier 🏃 *Hôtel-Restaurant Etchémaïté* (☎05.59.28.61.45, ⓦwww.hotel-etchemaite.fr; closed Jan & late Nov), with state-of-the-art rooms in three grades (❷–❸), half board urged at its excellent restaurant serving eels, *cèpes*, pigeon and decadent desserts, albeit in small portions (closed early Jan to mid-Feb; menus/*formules* €18–42).

There's one **campsite** in Larrau, the *Ixtila* (☎05.59.28.63.09; April to mid-Nov), and the *Auberge Logibar*, a *gîte d'étape* (☎05.59.28.61.14; 30 places) with a bar-restaurant (closed Dec–Feb) 3km away at **LOGIBAR**, close to the mouth of the **Gorges d'Holzarte**. This is one of several locally, cutting deep into northern slopes of the ridge that forms the frontier with Spain. A short track leads from Logibar across a lively, chilly stream to a car park, from where a steep, usually very busy path – a variant of the GR10 – climbs through beech woods in about 45 minutes to the junction of the Holzarte gorge with the **Gorges d'Olhadubi**. Slung across the mouth of the latter is a spectacular

▲ Gorges d'Olhadubi, Haute Saule

Himalayan-style **suspension bridge**, the *passerelle*, which bounces and swings alarmingly as you walk out over the 180-metre drop. You can continue along the **GR10** to Ste-Engrâce in seven hours, or down to the beginning of the Gorges de Kakuetta in about six; less ambitiously, the car-bound can fashion a very satisfying four-hour loop-hike taking in the entire Gorges d'Olhadubi by using the old GR10, which takes you over the *passerelle*, up along the west flank of the *gorges*, and then crosses it at the Pont d'Olhadubi before returning to Logibar. The route is obviously marked on *Carte de Randonnées* no. 2, "Pays Basque Est".

Licq and Tardets-Sorholus

The Gave (Stream) de Larrau and the Gave de Ste-Engrâce unite downstream from Logibar to form the Saison, the major river of Haute Soule. About 2km below this junction on the D26, the pleasant village of **LICQ** (Licq-Atherey on old maps; Ligi in Euskera) offers **accommodation** which, given the scarcity of indoor facilities in the area, could come in handy at high season, especially for those with transport: the rambling, old-style *Hôtel des Touristes-Bouchet* (℡05.59.28.61.01; closed Dec & Jan; ❸), with the best balconied rooms on the first floor and a grassy camping area down by the river. The restaurant is competent but surprisingly pricey; taking half board eases the pain. Just 6km north the small town of **TARDETS-SORHOLUS** has shops, bank ATMs and another **hotel**, the *Piellenia*, just off the main square (℡05.59.28.53.49; ❸), with a characterful ground-floor **bar-restaurant**.

The Gorges de Kakuetta and Gorges d'Ehujarré

Fifteen kilometres east of Larrau, well beyond the turning for Licq and Tardets, you reach the **Gorges de Kakuetta** (March 15 to Nov 15 8am–nightfall; €4.50), having veered off the D26 and onto the D113. About 4km along the latter, minuscule **CASERNES** hamlet offers a shop opposite the *mairie*, and the attractive riverside **campsite** *Ibarra* (℡05.59.28.73.59; Easter–Oct).

Kakuetta gorge is truly dramatic and, outside peak season, not crowded at all; allow about two hours to visit. It pays to be well shod – the metal catwalk or narrow path, by turns, are slippery in places and provided with safety cables where needed. The walls of the gorge rise up to 300m high and are scarcely more than 5m apart in spots, so little sunlight penetrates except at midday from May to July. The air hangs heavy with mist produced by dozens of seeps and tiny waterfalls, nurturing tenacious ferns, moss and other vegetation that thrives in the hothouse atmosphere. Within an hour, the path brings you to a small cave beyond which only technical climbers need apply; just before it a twenty-metre waterfall (which you can walk behind) gushes out of a hole in the rock.

There's another, scarcely visited gorge, the **Gorges d'Ehujarré**, a short distance east at Senta, the easternmost of the three hamlets that comprise Ste-Engrâce (see below). It's a straightforward walk up along the east flank – this route has been used for centuries for moving sheep up to the pastures of Pic Lakhoura – and then down along the gorge floor, a five-hour round trip.

Ste-Engrâce and La-Pierre-St-Martin

Le bout du monde – "the end of the earth" – is what they used to call tiny **STE-ENGRÂCE**, hidden in its cul-de-sac valley beneath the Spanish frontier at the easternmost extremity of the Basque country. And, although a road now runs through it to Béarn and La-Pierre-St-Martin, the place remains beautifully remote and peaceful. Life is not so idyllic for the locals – there's no work and the young don't stay – but for an outsider it has great charm.

Ste-Engrâce's hallmark is the eleventh-century Romanesque **church** in the hamlet of **SENTA**, which features in most coffee-table books about the Pyrenees. Focus of a popular **festival** the last two Sundays in July, it stands with heavily buttressed walls, belfry and assymetrical roof, a sharply defined and angular assertion of humanity against the often mist-shrouded bulwarks of the mountains behind. Inside, it has some excellent carved column capitals depicting among other things the Adoration of the Magi, lions devouring Christians, and King Solomon copulating with the Queen of Sheba. There's a 30-bunk **gîte d'étape** opposite the church, the *Auberge Elichalt* (T 05.59.28.61.63), with a few *chambres d'hôtes* (❸), a garden to camp and a café-bar serving light meals.

The road up to the ski resort of **LA-PIERRE-ST-MARTIN** (Arette-la-Pierre on old maps) gives fabulous views of the Ste-Engrâce valley, through magnificent forests of pine and beech, though if the cloud is down (it often is), you'll be lucky to see much at all. At a little col with a three-way junction, you're just inside the ancient county of Béarn, poised for the descent east into the Vallée d'Aspe. The upper, right-hand turning leads to La-Pierre, an ugly ski resort (18 pistes), and the excellent *Refuge Jeandel* (1670m; T 05.59.66.14.46; W www.refugejeandel.com; May 10 to Sept 30; 3- to 6-bunk dorms), serving trekkers on the GR10, with enthusiastic management, internet access and decent meals. La-Pierre skiing is better than you'd imagine for the modest altitude (2153m top point), owing to moist Atlantic exposure and some quite long runs for beginners and intermediates.

The Central Pyrenees

The **Central Pyrenees**, immediately east of the Pays Basque, hosts the range's highest mountain peaks, the most spectacular section by the border being protected within the **Parc National des Pyrénées**. Getting here by public transport is straightforward, at least as far as the foothill towns, served by frequent trains on the Bayonne–Toulouse line. But travelling uphill, and around once there, can be very slow. Buses – and most other traffic – keep mainly to the north–south valleys, making it difficult to switch from one valley system to the next without having to emerge from the mountains each time. The GR10 provides a good lateral link for hikers, and it's possible to hitch across the main passes such as the **Col d'Aubisque** and **Col du Tourmalet**, though you'll often get left on the top by drivers who come up for the view and go back the same way.

Highlights – apart from the lakes, torrents, forests and 3000-metre peaks around **Cauterets** – are the cirques of **Lescun**, **Gavarnie** and **Troumouse**, each with its distinctive character. And for less *sportif* interests, there's many a flower-starred mountain meadow accessible by car, especially near **Barèges** and **Luchon**, in which to picnic. The only real urban centres are **Pau**, a probable entry point to the area, dull **Tarbes** and the tacky pilgrimage target of **Lourdes**. Great man-made monuments – except for the fortified churches at **Luz-St-Sauveur**, **St-Savin** and **St-Bertrand-de-Comminges** – are equally scarce, though there are wonderful Romanesque carvings on smaller churches at **Oloron-Ste-Marie**, **St-Aventin** and **Valcabrère**.

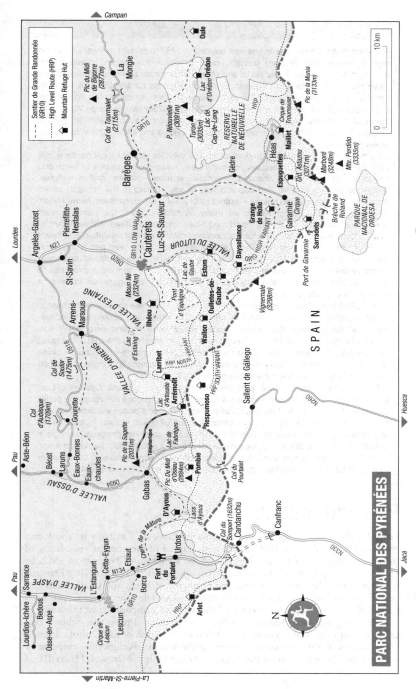

PARC NATIONAL DES PYRÉNÉES

Legend:
- - - Sentier de Grande Randonnée (GR10)
- - - High Level Route (HRP)
- ◈ ■ Mountain Refuge Hut

Scale: 0 — 10 km

Campan

Oule

La Mongie

Pic du Midi de Bigorre (2877m)

Col du Tourmalet (2115m)

GR10

Lac d'Orédon Orédon

Lac de Cap-de-Long

P. Néouvielle (3091m)

Turon (3035m)

RESERVE NATURELLE DE NÉOUVIELLE

HRP

Cirque de Troumouse

Pic de la Munia (3133m)

Barèges

Gèdre

Héas

Maillet

Espuguettes

Gavarnie Cirque

Grd. Astazou (3071m)

Marboré (3248m)

Mte. Perdido (3335m)

Sarradets

Brèche de Roland

PARQUE NACIONAL DE ORDESA

Pierrefitte-Nestalas

Argelès-Gazost

Lourdes

St-Savin

N21

D920

Cauterets

Luz-St-Sauveur

GR10 LOW VARIANT

Grange de Holle

Bayssellance

GR10 HIGH VARIANT

Moun Né (2324m)

VALLÉE D'ESTAING

Pont d'Espagne

Lac de Gaube

Estom

Oulettes-de-Gaube

Vignemale (3298m)

Port de Gavarnie

Arrens-Marsous

Ilhéou

Lac d'Estaing

VALLÉE D'ARRENS

Col de Soulor (1475m) D918

Larribet

Wallon

HRP NORD

SPAIN

Pau

Aste-Béon

Béost

Laruns

Gourette

Eaux-Bonnes

Eaux-chaudes

Col d'Aubisque (1709m)

Pic de la Sagette (2031m)

Téléphérique

Lac de Fabrèges

Arrémolit

Lac d'Artouste

HRP SOUTH VARIANT

Respumoso

Sallent de Gállego

N260

Huesca

Gabas

Pic Du Midi d'Ossau (2884m)

VALLÉE D'OSSAU

D934

Pombie

Col du Pourtalet

Lourdios-Ichère

Bedous

Osse-en-Aspe

Sarrance

L'Estanguet

Cette-Eygun

Etsaut

N134

Borce

Fort du Portalet

Urdos

VALLÉE D'ASPE

Cirque de Lescun

Lescun

GR10

chem. de la Mâture

D'Ayous

Lacs d'Ayous

Col du Somport (1632m)

Candanchu

Canfranc

N330

Jaca

Arlet

HRP

La-Pierre-St-Martin

N

Pau

Lourdes

Campan

The **Parc National des Pyrénées** was created in 1967 to protect at least part of the high Pyrenees from modern touristic development – ski resorts, paved roads, mountain-top restaurants, car parks and other inappropriate amenities. It extends for more than 100km along the Spanish border from Pic de Laraille (2147m), south of Lescun, in the west, to beyond Pic de la Munia (3133m), almost to the Aragnouet–Bielsa tunnel. Varying in altitude between 1070m and 3298m at the Pic de Vignemale, south of Cauterets, the park includes the spectacular Gavarnie and Troumouse cirques, as well as 220 lakes, more than a dozen valleys and about 400km of marked walking routes.

By the **banning of hunting** and all dogs and vehicles (except local herders), the park has also provided sanctuary for many rare, endangered species of birds and mammals. These include chamois, marmots, ermines, genets, griffon vultures, golden eagles, eagle owls and capercaillies, to say nothing of the rich and varied flora. The most celebrated animal – extinct as of 2004 – is the Pyrenean **brown bear**, whose pre-1940 numbers ran to as many as two hundred; the dozen current specimens are descended from introduced Slovenian brown bears. Although largely herbivorous, bears will take livestock opportunistically, and most mountain shepherds are their remorseless enemies. To appease them, local authorities pay prompt and generous compensation for any losses, but the restocking programme remains highly controversial, with pro- and anti-bear graffitti prominent on the road approaches to the park, and troublesome animals being shot illegally by aggrieved farmers or herders on a regular basis.

The **GR10** runs through the entire park on its 700-kilometre journey from coast to coast, starting at Banyuls-sur-Mer on the Mediterranean and ending at Hendaye-Plage on the Atlantic; the tougher **Haute Randonnée Pyrénéenne** (HRP) also finishes its course in Hendaye-Plage and runs roughly parallel to the GR10, but takes in more rugged, alpine terrain. While the Pyrenees have a modest maximum altitude by world-mountain standards, their climate can be as extreme as ranges twice their height – hikers should heed the warnings on p.677.

There are **Maisons du Parc** (park information centres) in Etsaut, Cauterets, Luz-St-Sauveur, Gavarnie, Laruns and Arrens-Marsous, giving information about the park's wildlife and vegetation and the best walks. There are over a dozen wardened refuges in *parc* territory and plenty of hotels, campsites and *gîtes* just outside it, listed in the text or highlighted on the map on p.701. Backcountry camping (*camping sauvage*) is forbidden in many areas, except for emergency bivouacs above 2000m elevation which must be disassembled by 9am. For an update on weather conditions in the *départe-ment* of Hautes-Pyrénées, telephone ☎08.92.68.02.65, or ☎3250, option 4.

Pau and around

From humble beginnings as a crossing on the Gave de Pau (*gave* is "mountain river" in Gascon dialect), **PAU** became the capital of the ancient viscountcy of Béarn in 1464, and of the French part of the kingdom of Navarre in 1512. In 1567 its sovereign, Henri d'Albret, married the sister of French King François I, Marguerite d'Angoulême, friend and protector of artists and intellectuals and herself the author of a celebrated Boccaccio-like tale (the *Heptameron*), who transformed the town into a centre of the arts and nonconformist thinking.

Their daughter was Jeanne d'Albret, a philistine Protestant, whose zeal offended her own subjects as well as attracting the wrath of the Catholic French king Charles X, thus embroiling Béarn in the Wars of Religion – temporarily resolved by the accession to the French throne of her own son, Henri III of

Navarre, in 1589. An adroit politician, he renounced his faith to facilitate his transformation into Henri IV of France, quipping that "Paris is worth a Mass" and then appeasing the regional sensibilities of his Béarnais subjects by announcing that he was giving France to Béarn rather than Béarn to France. He did not incorporate Béarn into the French state; that was left to his heir and successor, Louis XIII, in 1620. Pau's most famous son, Henri acquired a suitably colourful reputation, beginning with his traditional Béarnais baptism in the local Jurançon wine, his infant lips rubbed with garlic; in his adult life he was known as the *vert-galant* for his romantic prowess. He also gave France one of its more famous recipes, *poulet au pot* – chicken stuffed and boiled with vegetables; he reputedly said that he did not want anyone in his realm to be so poor as not to be able to afford the dish once a week.

The least-expected thing about Pau is its **English connection**, which dates from the arrival of Wellington and his troops after the defeat of Maréchal Soult at Orthez in 1814. Seduced by its climate and persuaded (mistakenly) of its curative powers by Scottish doctor Alexander Taylor, the English flocked to Pau throughout the nineteenth century, bringing along their cultural idiosyncrasies – fox-hunting, horse-racing, polo, croquet, cricket, golf (the first eighteen-hole course in continental Europe in 1860, and the first to admit women), tea salons and parks. When the railway arrived here in 1866, the French came, too: writers like Victor Hugo, Stendhal and Lamartine, as well as socialites. The first French rugby club opened here in 1902, after which the sport spread throughout the

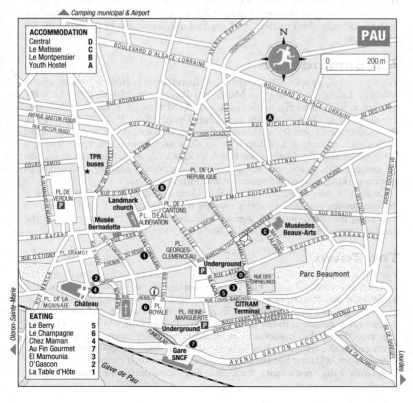

southwest. During the 1950s, natural gas was discovered at nearby Lacq, bringing new jobs and subsidiary industries, as well as massive sulphur-dioxide-based pollution, now reduced by filtration – and the imminent depletion of the gas field. In addition, there's a well-respected university, founded in 1972, whose 15,000 students give the town a youthful buzz.

Arrival and information

Pau's **airport** (☎05.59.33.33.00, ⓦwww.pau.aeroport.fr) is increasingly busy, with year-round no-frills arrivals from the UK and Holland. The *navette* service to the city centre is suspended as of writing; a taxi to town costs about €20. The **gare SNCF**, for both trains and SNCF buses, is on the southern edge of the city centre by the riverside. TPR buses leave from a terminal at 4 rue Lapouble, near place de Verdun, while CITRAM buses leave from a stop at the west end of the Parc Beaumont. Services run south down the Vallée d'Ossau and to Oloron-Ste-Marie, with onward connections from there to the Vallée d'Aspe. **Parking** (and driving) is predictably nightmarish; there are a few free spaces at the far west end of boulevard des Pyrénées and many more on place de Verdun, otherwise shell out for kerbside meters or use the giant underground car park at place Georges-Clemenceau.

A **free funicular** carries you up from the train station to the boulevard des Pyrénées, opposite place Royale. At the far end of the place is the **tourist office** (July & Aug Mon–Fri 9am–6.30pm, Sat 9am–6pm, Sun 9am–1pm & 2–6pm; Sept–June Mon–Sat 9am–6pm, Sun 9.30am–1pm; ☎05.59.27.27.08, ⓦwww .pau.fr). Librairie des Pyrénées at 14 rue St-Louis stocks books and maps on the mountains.

Accommodation

For a friendly and relatively quiet budget **hotel**, try the *Hôtel le Matisse*, 17 rue Mathieu-Lalanne, opposite the Musée des Beaux-Arts (☎05.59.27.73.80; ❶), all rooms with showers, some with toilets. Mid-range options include the excellent-value ⚕ *Central*, 15 rue Léon-Daran (☎05.59.27.72.75, ⓦwww .hotelcentralpau.com; ❸), with unusually tasteful room decor and wi-fi signal throughout. Among a half-dozen or so three-star contenders, most stylish is 2005-renovated *Le Montpensier* (☎05.59.27.42.72, Ⓔhotel.montpensier-pau @orange.fr; ❹), at 36 rue Montpensier, an eighteenth-century building with private parking, non-smoking rooms and internet access.

There is a **hostel** at 30 rue Michel-Hounau (☎05.59.11.05.05, ⓦwww .habitat-jeunes-pau-asso.fr), and a municipal **campsite**, *La Plaine des Sports* on boulevard du Cami-Salié, off avenue Sallenave towards the autoroute, on the northern edge of town (☎05.59.02.30.49; May to late Sept).

The Town

Pau has no must-see sights or museums, so you can enjoy its relaxed elegance without any sense of guilt. The parts to wander in are the streets behind the **boulevard des Pyrénées**, especially the western end, which stretches along the escarpment above the Gave de Pau, from the castle to the Palais Beaumont, now a convention centre, in the English-style **Parc Beaumont**. On a (rare) clear day, the view from the boulevard encompasses a broad sweep of the highest Pyrenean peaks, with the distinctive Pic du Midi d'Ossau slap in front of you.

In the narrow streets between the castle and ravine-bed chemin du Hédas are numerous cafés, restaurants, bars and boutiques, with the main Saturday market in the *halles* just northeast on place de la République. The **château** itself (exterior gardens free, unenclosed) is very much a landmark building, though not much remains of its original fabric beyond the southeasterly brick keep built by Gaston Fébus in 1370. The handsome Renaissance windows and other details on the inner courtyard were added by Henri d'Albret. Louis-Philippe renovated it in the nineteenth century after two hundred years of dereliction, and Napoléon III and Eugénie titivated it further with stellar vaulting, chandeliers and coffered ceilings. The **Musée National** inside is visitable by a skull-thumpingly boring, French-only, one-hour guided tour (daily: June 15 to Sept 15 9.30am–12.15pm & 1.30–5.45pm; Sept 16 to June 14 9.30–11.45am & 2–5pm; €5 except €3.50 Sun, free first Sun of month), but this is the only way to see the vivid eighteenth-century tapestries with their wonderfully observed scenes of rural life, or Henri IV memorabilia like the giant turtle shell that purportedly served as his cradle.

A short distance northeast of the château, the mildly interesting **Musée Bernadotte**, 6 rue Tran (Tues–Sun 10am–noon & 2–6pm; €3), is the birthplace of the man who, having served as one of Napoleon's commanders, went on to become Charles XIV of Sweden. As well as fine pieces of traditional Béarnais furniture, the house contains some valuable works of art collected over his lifetime. Pau's other museum, the **Musée des Beaux-Arts** in rue Mathieu-Lalanne (daily except Tues 10am–noon & 2–6pm; €3), has an eclectic collection of little-known works from European schools spanning the fourteenth to twentieth centuries; the only really world-class items are Rubens' *The Last Judgement* and Degas' *The Cotton Exchange*, a slice of finely observed *Belle-Époque* New Orleans life.

Eating and drinking

Pau's better **restaurants** are concentrated in the pedestrianized lanes around the château, on place Royal or in rue du Hédas, though there are a few choices elsewhere. **Bars**, many themed (Australian, Irish, etc), cluster immediately west of place Reine-Marguerite, about halfway along boulevard des Pyrénées.

Le Berry Rue Gachet, near corner rue Louis-Barthou. Less than brilliant siting, by the "rabbit hole" of the subterranean car park, but compensated for by excellent brasserie grub (*magret de canard*, Chateaubriand steaks). Expect a wait for interior tables; service until 11pm; budget €20–28 à la carte.

Le Champagne 5 place Royale. Popular, upscale brasserie with *carte* or five *formules* from €14.50 up – even the cheapest nets you a solid lamb-based main course, salad and dessert. There's been an establishment here since 1843, and the current interior with swirling fans and original art (larger parties can book the back room) vies for allure with tables on the *place* in fine weather. Service is consistently leisurely, however.

Chez Maman 6 rue de Château. Simple but palatable crêperie/*cidrerie* right opposite the castle, which doesn't unduly abuse its unbeatable position; a good option for vegetarians, with big salads – €20 will about cover two courses and a bit of cider. Tues–Sun 11am–midnight.

Au Fin Gourmet 24 av Gaston-Lacoste, opposite the *gare SNCF*. Trim, modern place with a few game-oriented lunch menus (pigeon, rabbit) from €19, but best allow €40-plus à la carte. Closed Sun eve–Tues lunch, plus 2 weeks in mid-summer.

El Mamounia 7 rue des Orphelines. Competent Moroccan eatery with upscale, not overly orientalized interior; lunch menus from €12, otherwise allow €19–27. Closed Sun, Mon lunch.

O'Gascon 13 rue du Château. The most popular and reasonable of the four non-pizzerias on this little *place*; their €29 *menu tradition* – big salad, stuffed quail, free dessert choice – is excellent. Supper only except Sun lunch.

La Table d'Hôte 1 rue du Hédas. Elegant bare-brick restaurant in a former warehouse, one of the first to colonize this trendy area and relying on duck, pork, foie gras and fish like *rouget* or *lotte*. Menus €18–31; service can be leisurely. Closed Sun, Mon.

Around Pau

One worthwhile excursion from Pau, particularly for families, is to the **Grottes de Bétharram** (Ⓦ www.grottes-de-betharram.com; guided visits only March 25 to Oct 25 daily 9am–noon & 1.30–5.30pm; Feb 11 to March 25 groups only Mon–Fri 2.30–4pm; €11.50, family/child concessions) at St-Pé-de-Bigorre, just off the D937 between Pau and Lourdes, 14km from the latter. Part of the eighty-minute tour around its spectacular stalactites and stalagmites takes place in a barge on an underground lake; the remaining kilometre is by miniature railway.

In the opposite direction from Pau lies tourist-board-dubbed **Béarn des Gaves**, so called because several *gaves* – de Pau, de Oloron, the Seleys and the Saison – slant across the landscape before mingling with each other or, ultimately, the Adour. The four major destinations here have strategic riverside locations, and three were traditional halts on the **Chemin de St-Jacques**, though the main variant of the modern GR65 traces a course across the southeast of the territory.

Orthez

Thirty kilometres northwest of Pau, **ORTHEZ** was the original capital of Béarn, its wealth due largely to a beautiful, still-surviving thirteenth-century **Pont-Vieux**, which controlled the most important commercial route across the Gave de Pau for English and Flemish textiles, Aragonese wool, olive oil and wine, as well as the Chemin de St-Jacques (there's still a pilgrims' hostel at 14 rue de l'Horloge, March–Nov). The town also serves as a gateway to Haute Soule in the Pays Basque: SNCF **buses** run from Puyôo, 12km west, to Salies-de-Béarn, Sauveterre-de-Béarn and Mauléon.

The **tourist office** (July–Aug Mon–Sat 9.30am–12.30pm & 2–6.30pm, Sun 9.30am–12.30pm; Sept–June Mon–Sat 9am–noon & 2–6pm; ☏ 05.59.69.37.50) occupies the sixteenth-century Maison Jeanne d'Albret on rue du Bourg-Vieux, which also hosts a **Musée de Protestantisme en Béarn** on the second floor (Mon–Sat 10am–noon & 2.30–6.30pm; €4.50), not quite worth the fee for the self-guiding tour-with-crib-sheet documenting Orthez's role as a Protestant stronghold and missionary tradition to Spain and Lesotho. Other fine old houses can be found in the town centre, especially along **rue Moncade**, the uphill continuation of rue du Bourg-Vieux, leading to five-sided, thirteenth-century **Tour Moncade** (June–Aug daily 10am–12.30pm & 3–7pm; Sept daily & May/Oct weekends 10am–12.30pm & 2.30–6.30pm; €3), all that remains of Orthez's castle, though the town retains some of its medieval walls. **Staying** overnight, your best option is historic *Hôtel Restaurant Au Temps de la Reine Jeanne*, opposite the tourist office at 42–44 rue du Bourg-Vieux (☏ 05.59.67.00.76; ❹), with a traditional-fare **restaurant** (menus from €13.50 lunch/€23 supper), sauna and in-house jazz events (March–May).

Salies-de-Béarn and Sauveterre-de-Béarn

Fifteen kilometres west from Orthez (TPR bus from Pau), **SALIES-DE-BÉARN** is a typical Béarnais village of winding lanes and flower-decked houses with brightly painted woodwork. The River Saleys, hardly more than a stream here, runs through the middle of it, separating the old village from the nineteenth-century quarter that sprang up to exploit the powerful saline spring for which it has long been famous. You can try the curative waters at the wonderful **thermal baths** (Ⓦ www.thermes-de-salies.com), in place Jardin Public, starting from €8 for a one-hour plunge in the outdoor, 32°C pool (daily May–Sept). The **tourist office** is 150m around the corner on rue des Bains (mid-June to mid-Sept Mon–Sat 9.30am–12.30pm & 3–7pm, Sun

9.30am–12.30pm; mid-Sept to mid-June Mon–Sat 9.30am–noon & 2–6pm; ☎05.59.38.00.33, ⓦwww.bearn-gaves.com). **Accommodation** includes the the economical but en-suite *Au Petit Béarn* (☎05.59.38.17.42, ⓕ05.59.65.01.75; ❶; restaurant closed Fri evening & Sat noon Oct–June) on rue Bellecave, off the road to Sauveterre. A plusher but good-value option is the *Helios* (☎05.59.38.37.59, ⓦwww.golf-salies .com; ❸–❹), on the northeastern outskirts of town, by the twelve-hole course. The closest local **campsite** is *Mosqueros*, 1km from the *thermes* (☎05.59.38.12.94; mid-March to Oct).

Heading south, the D933 winds over hilly farming country to **SAUVET-ERRE-DE-BÉARN**, another pretty country town beautifully set on a bluff high above the Gave d'Oloron, just before it mingles with the Saison. From the terrace by the thirteenth-century **church of St-André** – over-restored but still retaining a fine west-portal relief of Christ in Glory – you look down over the river and the remains of fortified, half-ruined **Pont de la Légende**, while at the west end of the compact *cité médiévale* stand the ruins of a Gaston Fébus **château**. A pedestrian-only lane leads down to the bridge and river, full of bathers (and **canoers/rafters**, see ⓦwww.aboste.com) on hot days despite its murky greenness; many come from the adjacent, tent-friendly *Camping du Gave* (☎05.59.38.53.30; mid-April to mid-Oct). Alluring indoor **accommodation** comprises *Auberge du Saumon* (☎05.59.38.53.20; closed mid-Jan to mid-Feb & Sat low season; ❷), an old coaching inn across the river on the road south out of town, and less remote *La Maison de Navarre* in quartier St-Marc (☎05.59.38.55.28, ⓦwww.lamaisondenavarre.com; closed Nov, restaurant closed Sun evening Sept–June & Wed; ❸), a converted garden-set mansion.

Navarrenx and L'Hôpital-S-Blaise

Just across the river, the D936 bears southeast along the flat valley bottom to **NAVARRENX**, 20km away on the Pau–Mauléon bus route, a sleepy, old-fashioned market town built as a *bastide* in 1316 and still surrounded by its medieval **walls**. Having crossed the medieval **bridge** over the Gave d'Oloron – claimed here as the salmon–fishing capital of France – you enter from the west by the fortified **Porte St-Antoine**. The friendly *Hôtel du Commerce* just inside on place des Casernes should make an agreeable place to **stay** (☎05.59.66.50.16, ⓦwww.hotel-commerce.fr; ❸; closed Jan) once its rooms get a badly needed refit in 2008–09; its restaurant opposite is already excellent, the basis of good half-board prices and a decent buffet breakfast. The only alternative is court-yarded *Le Relais du Jacquet* (☎06.75.72.89.33; ❷), a *chambre d'hôte* at 42 rue Saint-Germain, the main street. GR 65 pilgrims have a spartan *Gîte d'Étape Communal* entered from no. 41 of the same street, housed in a medieval arsenal (☎05.59.66.02.67; all year; 16 places), immediately behind the tourist office (daily except Sun pm/Mon am 9am–12.30pm & 2–6.30pm). There's also a riverside **campsite**, the *Beau Rivage*, in allée des Marronniers southwest of the ramparts (☎05.59.66.10.00, March 15 to Oct 15).

Just off the Navarrenx-Oloron highway on the road to Mauléon, **L'HÔPITAL-ST-BLAISE** (Ospitalepea) is named for its cross-in-square, twelfth-century central **church** (daily: 10am–7pm; 8-min audioguide with synchronized lighting for "donation"), all that remains of a vanished pilgrims' hospice. A Romanesque–Gothic–Islamic melange, it juxtaposes Basque features like a carved-wood gallery over the west door with Moorish-tracery windows and arches, plus stellar vaulting inside the octagonal dome. The surrounding valley-bottom hamlet offers two **hotel-restaurants**, *L'Auberge du Lausset* opposite the church (☎05.59.66.53.03; ❷) being more reliably open.

Lourdes

LOURDES, 37km southeast of Pau by either of two routes, has just one function. Over seven million Catholic pilgrims arrive here yearly, and the town is totally dedicated to looking after and exploiting them. Lourdes was hardly more than a village before 1858, when Bernadette Soubirous, 14-year-old daughter of a poor local miller, had the first of eighteen visions of the Virgin Mary in the Grotte de Massabielle by the Gave de Pau. Since then, Lourdes has become the most visited attraction in this part of France, many pilgrims hoping for a miraculous cure for conventionally intractable ailments.

The first large-scale **pilgrimage** took place in 1873, organized (once the local clergy had been sidelined) by a fundamentalist Catholic movement called the Assomptionistes, whose avowed purpose was to stem the advancing tide of republicanism and anti-clericism. Adroit propagandists and agitators, the Assomptionistes promoted their cause by publishing a cheap mass-circulation paper called *La Croix*, aimed at the poor and uneducated.

Myriad shops are devoted to the sale of unbelievable religious kitsch: Bernadette and/or the Virgin in every shape and size, adorning barometers, thermometers, plastic tree trunks, empty bottles that you can fill with holy water, bellows, candles and illuminated plastic grottoes. Clustered around the miraculous grotto are the churches of the Domaine de la Grotte, an annexe to the town proper that sprang up in the century following Bernadette's visions. The first to be built was an underground crypt in 1866, followed by the flamboyant double **Basilique du Rosaire et de l'Immaculée Conception** (1871–83), and then in 1958 by the massive subterranean **Basilique St-Pie-X**, which can apparently fit 20,000 people at a time. The **Grotte de Massabielle** itself is the focus of pilgrimage – a moisture-blackened overhang by the riverside with a marble statue on high of the Virgin, where pilgrims queue to circumambulate, stroking the grotto wall with their left hand. To one side are taps for filling souvenir containers with the holy spring water; to the other are the *bruloirs* or rows of braziers where enormous votive candles burn, prolonging the prayers of supplicants.

Lourdes' only secular attraction is its **château**, poised on a rocky bluff east of the Gave de Pau, guarding the approaches to the valleys and passes of the central Pyrenees. Briefly an English stronghold in the late fourteenth century, it later became a state prison. Inside, it houses the surprisingly excellent **Musée Pyrénéen** (ⓦ www.lourdes-visite.com; daily: April–Sept 9am–noon & 1.30–6.30pm, no lunchbreak July 14 to Aug 31; Oct–March daily 9am–noon & 2–6pm, 5pm on Fri; last entry 50min before closing; €5). Its collections include Pyrenean fauna, all sorts of fascinating pastoral and farming gear, and an interesting section on the history of Pyrenean mountaineering.

Practicalities

Tarbes-Ossun-Lourdes **airport** is finally being served by no-frills flights from Britain; there's no shuttle bus, and a taxi the 11km into Lourdes costs an inflated €22. Lourdes' **gare SNCF** is on the northeast edge of the town centre, at the end of avenue de la Gare; the **gare routière** is in central place Capdevieille, and the not terribly helpful **tourist office** is in place Peyramale (Easter–June & Sept to mid-Oct Mon–Sat 9am–7pm, Sun 11am–6pm; July & Aug Mon–Sat 9am–7pm, Sun 10am–6pm; mid-Oct to Easter Mon–Sat 9am–noon & 2–6pm; ⓣ 05.62.42.77.40, ⓦ www.lourdes-infotourisme.com).

Lourdes has more **hotels** than any city in France outside Paris, mostly modest establishments in the streets around the castle – however many of these are set to close by 2010 as they can't be made compliant with strict new fire laws. One such, though intending to keep its **restaurant** open for hearty meals including full breakfasts, is English-run *Le Menvielle* at 3 chaussée du Bourg. Another likely to survive, opposite the food *halles*, some 300m south of place Peyramale, is two-star *Hôtel d'Albret* (T05.62.94.75.00; ❸; closed mid-Nov to mid-March), with its ground-floor *Taverne de Bigorre* offering a range of menus (€22 gets you three hearty courses).

Tarbes

Twenty minutes away by train to the north, **TARBES** is a fairly dull town dominated by its history as a military stronghold (a paratroop regiment is still based here), but useful for launching into the mountains to the south. Tarbes' only real highlight is the Napoleonic stud farm, **Les Haras**, entered from chemin de Mauhourat (1hr guided visits only depart July–Aug & school holidays Mon–Fri at 2, 3 & 4pm; rest of year by appointment only; T05.62.56.30.80; €8), best known for the *cheval Tarbais*, bred from English, Basque and Arabian stock as a cavalry horse. Highlight of the horse-year is the late July/early August Equestria Festival (Wwww.festivalequestria.com).

The **gare SNCF** is on avenue Maréchal-Joffre, about 500m north of the centre, and the **gare routière** on the other side of town on place au Bois, off rue Larrey. The **tourist office** is near the central place de Verdun, at 3 cours Gambetta (Mon–Sat 9am–noon & 2–6pm; T05.62.51.30.31, Wwww.tarbes .com). One modestly priced **hotel** in the vicinity of the station is friendly *Hôtel de l'Avenue*, 80 avenue Bertrand-Barère (T05.62.93.06.36; ❶), though most people will probably only stop long enough for a **meal**. A bit out of the way, but worth the trek east of the oasis-like **Jardin Massey**, is ⚘ *Chez Patrick* at 6 rue Adolphe-d'Eichtal, a cheery working-class institution that fills by 12.30pm and features a sustaining five-course menu (€11 includes wine and coffee). In the centre, rue Abbé-Torné and perpendicular streets host many restaurants and bistros, in particular *L'Epicerie* at 1 rue de la Victoire, specializing in fish and *magret aux cèpes* (closed Sun, Sat lunch).

The valleys of the Aspe and Ossau

The parallel valleys of the **Aspe** and **Ossau** present the central Pyrenees at their most undeveloped, especially the Aspe, because inappropriate topography and unreliable snow conditions have precluded ski-resort construction – but what tourism has failed to do, a major road-building scheme threatens to achieve (see box, p.710). To see the best of the region you should get out a large-scale map and walk perpendicular to the north–south line of the valleys, using the handful of refuges or camping in permitted areas.

Oloron-Ste-Marie

The Vallée d'Aspe begins at the grey town of **OLORON-STE-MARIE**, 45km west of Lourdes and only 33km southwest of Pau, where the *gaves* of the Aspe and Ossau meet to form the Gave d'Oloron. It's served by train from Pau as well as by CITRAM buses, with SNCF buses rolling up the valley to Urdos, a few of these continuing as far as Canfranc in Spain. Oloron

Since the early 1990s, the **Aspe** has been the focus of bitter controversy between environmentalists, and officialdom plus local boosters of a multi-lane **autoroute** through the valley. This was part of a wider campaign for various tunnels under the middle Pyrenees, a strategy strongly advocated by Spain, keen to export heavy and/ or perishable goods as quickly and cheaply as possible to northern Europe.

An all-weather tunnel was finally opened in 2003 under the Col du Somport at the head of the valley, after years of delay from cost overruns and design changes required by the environmental litigants, organized as CSAVA. Locals at first bitterly resented now-defunct CSAVA and its flamboyant chief Eric Pétetin, seeing increased communications as the best hope of keeping valley communities alive, but since the tunnel has opened and the next project phase looms, there's been a change of heart as implications sink in. The slopes of the Aspe would be blasted to accommodate a six-lane highway carrying hundreds of articulated lorries daily, blighting the villages which were supposed to be rejuvenated. Bumper stickers with a terse "NON" and the silhouette of a truck in the middle of the "O" are now ubiquitous.

As a condition of the tunnel's construction, the long-abandoned trans-frontier railway was supposed to be rehabilitated to carry freight as well as passengers; although EU funding has been approved "in principle", there's been no tangible result as yet. Ironically, two factors may soon condemn the Somport tunnel to obsolescence: spiralling costs threaten to make the mega-motorway unfeasible, and the low-wage economies of the EU's Central European members will render Spanish exports uneconomical. The likely outcome may instead be massive expansion of port facilities around Perpignan and Bayonne, to take pressure off the hopelessly lorry-congested motorways there.

was long famous as the manufacturing centre for the famous woollen pancake-shaped *beret basque*, once the standard headgear for all French men but now seldom seen; the single surviving factory has had to branch out into more fashionable hats.

There is little here to detain the visitor other than the Romanesque **Cathédrale Ste-Marie** across the Gave d'Aspe, with its beautiful west portal in Pyrenean marble. In the upper arch, the elders of the Apocalypse play violins and rebecs, while in the second arch scenes from medieval life – a cooper, slaying wild boar, fishing for salmon – are represented. The gallant knight on horseback over the outer column on the right is Gaston IV, Count of Béarn, who commissioned the portal on his return from the first Crusade at the beginning of the twelfth century – hence the inclusion of Saracens in chains among the sculptures. Inside, well away from the main area of worship, stands a stoup reserved for use by the Cagots, a stark reminder of centuries-long persecution and segregation of this mysterious Pyrenean tribe, now thought to have been of Visigothic origin. Across the river in Oloron, hilltop **Sainte-Croix** is one of the oldest Romanesque structures in Béarn, its unusual interior vaulting created by thirteenth-century Spanish stonemasons in imitation of the Great Mosque in Córdoba.

Oloron's **tourist office** lies west of the Aspe in the Villa Bourdeu (July–Aug Mon–Sat 9am–7pm, Sun 10am–1pm; Sept–June Mon–Sat 9am–12.30pm & 2–6pm; ☎05.59.39.98.00, ⓦwww.tourisme-oloron.com). **Accommodation** includes *Hôtel de la Paix* at 24 avenue Sadi-Carnot opposite the train station (☎05.59.39.02.63; ❸), quiet despite the location and with easy parking. The closest **campsite** is *Camping du Stade*, on the D919 Arrette road (☎05.59.39.11.26; April–Sept). Independent **restaurants** are not especially numerous; try cheap and cheerful *La Cour des Miracles* (shut Sun) at 13 place de la Cathédrale, opposite the Romanesque portal, or *Samia*, a late-serving Moroccan eatery in Oloron on place Amédée-Gabe.

Along the Aspe valley

The narrow enclosed world of the valley proper, an important variant of the Chemin de St-Jacques, begins south of Oloron at **Escot**. South of there, the road follows the river through a narrow defile, past the attractive riverside village of **SARRANCE**, where the **Ecomusée du Vallée d'Aspe** (July–Sept daily 10am–noon & 2–7pm; Oct–June Sat & Sun 2–6pm; €4.50), devoted to local history, is less compelling than the ancient **monastic church of Notre-Dame-de-la-Pierre**, particularly its wonderfully rustic cloister with wood columns and pyramidal roofs over the upper gallery.

Some 7km further south is **BEDOUS**, the largest settlement in the valley, with a miniature château, arcaded *mairie* and the *gîte d'étape Le Mandragot* (℡05.59.34.59.33), all on or near place de l'Église. Just east of town on the road to Aydius is **Moulin d'Orcun**, the last stone-grinding flour mill in the area, now run as a museum (guided visits July–Aug daily 11am, 3pm, 4pm, 5pm & 6pm; Sept–June by appointment only on ℡05.59.34.74.91).

Lescun and its cirque

Six steep kilometres southwest of the N134 and valley floor at L'Estanguet, the ancient stone-and-stucco houses of **LESCUN** huddle on the northeast slopes of a huge and magnificent green **cirque**. The floor of the cirque and the lower slopes, dimpled with vales and hollows, have been gently shaped by generations of farming, while to the west it's overlooked by the great grey molars of **Le Billare**, Trois Rois and Ansabère, beyond which rises the storm-lashed bulk of the **Pic d'Anie** (2504m). Over 1km below the village by the stream draining the cirque, grassy *Camping Le Lauzart* (℡05.59.34.51.77; May–Sept) has a matchless position with unimpeded views of the peaks. Lescun itself has a lovely old antique-furnished **chambres d'hôtes**, the *Pic d'Anie* (℡05.59.34.71.54, ℻05.59.34.53.22; ❷–❸; April–Sept), with a restaurant (guests only) and co-managed *gîte d'étape* opposite.

The obvious local **walk** is along the GR10 in the direction of La-Pierre-St-Martin. From Lescun, the path keeps close to a minor road as far as the abandoned Refuge de Labérouat – around a ninety-minute walk – then crosses meadows before entering beech forest beneath the organ-pipe crags of **Les Orgues de Camplong**, with fantastic views of the pine-stippled ridges of Billare. It emerges above the tree line in a long, hanging valley by the primitive **Cabane d'Ardinet**, reaching the shepherds' hut at **Cap de la Baigt** (1689m) in another ninety minutes. From there you can either continue on the GR towards La-Pierre-St-Martin, or swing south for the Col des Anies and the Pic d'Anie itself – a good two and a half hours to the summit.

Cette-Eygun to the border

A couple of kilometres beyond the turn-off for Lescun, **CETTE-EYGUN** offers, in its upper Cette quarter, the excellent, welcoming ✻ *Au Château d'Arance* (℡05.59.34.75.50, ⓦwww.auchateaudarance.com; ❸), a converted twelfth-century manor made very contemporary with wi-fi signal; meals (menus €12–19) and leisurely breakfasts (7.30–11am) are served on a terrace with unbeatable views, while co-managed *Chambres d'Hôtes Pouquette* (❷) occupy a nearby house, next to the swimming pool.

Some 3.5km southeast at **ETSAUT**, the **Maison du Parc** (July–Aug only daily 10am–12.30pm & 2–6pm; ☎05.59.34.88.30) inhabits the old *gare SNCF*. There's a **gîte d'étape** beyond the church, *Auberge La Garbure* (☎05.59.34.88.98, ⓦwww .garbure.net), and a **hotel** on the square, *Des Pyrénées* (☎05.59.34.88.62; ❶; closed mid-Dec to mid-Jan) with a restaurant, though you may find the welcome warmer across the *place* at *Bar Tabac Le Randonneur*, which does *plats du jour* in the bar or full meals in the attractive diner upstairs, as well as offering wi-fi **signal**.

BORCE, a more attractive medieval village 1km away on the west flank of the valley, is home to more **gîtes**: *La Communal* (☎05.59.34.86.40; 18 places) in the centre, above the bar-*épicerie*, plus the historic *Hospitalet de Borce* (no phone; 6 places) on the north outskirts, next to the original pilgrims' church, which is now an annexe of the Ecomusée in Sarrance.

Further upstream at one of the narrowest, rockiest, steepest points of the Aspe – a serious challenge to would-be motorway builders (see box, p.710) – squats the menacing **Fort du Portalet** (privately owned), which served as a prison for 1930s Socialist premier Léon Blum under Pétain's Vichy government, and then for Pétain himself after the liberation of France. Just before the fort, the GR10 threads east along the **Chemin de la Mâture**, an eighteenth-century mule path hacked out of the sides of a dizzying ravine, facilitating the transport of tree trunks felled for use as ships' masts. The really spectacular part – which, however, has minimal exposure and attracts lots of young families – ends after about 45min from the upper parking area (1hr from the lower car park at Pont de Cebers south of Etsaut); the GR10 continues to the **Lacs d'Ayous refuge** (see p.714) opposite the Pic du Midi d'Ossau in five-plus hours, but by careful study of *Carte de Randonée* no. 3, "Béarn", it's easy to form a three-hour loop hike returning you to the Pont de Cebers parking area on local trails.

Less than 2km south of the fort, **URDOS** is the last village on the French side of the frontier, and has one of the best **hotel-restaurants** in the valley: ⚘ *Hôtel des Voyageurs* (☎05.59.34.88.05, ⓦwww.hotel-voyageurs-aspe.com; ❶–❷), which serves wonderful, four-course set menus (€20 & €28, own-label wine

▲ Ossau Valley

extra). From here, you (and the odd bus) can continue through the free tunnel under the **Col de Somport** and on to Canfranc in Spain, the terminus for trains from Jaca, though in fine weather the far more scenic, 2008-regraded road over the pass is not that strenuous a drive.

Along the Ossau valley

The **Ossau valley** is notable mainly for its distinctive **Pic du Midi**, around which are some beautiful lakes set in rugged country; the usual base for visiting is tiny **Gabas** hamlet. The main valley market town of **Laruns** is pleasant enough, and the route east via the spa of **Eaux-Bonnes** and the ski resort of **Gourette** has its appeal. Pic Bus runs two daily **bus services** during summer and winter peak seasons to the top of the valley via Laruns and Gabas, calling once in each direction at the trailhead for the most visited lakes, whilst CITRAM provides service most of the year to Eaux-Bonnes and Gourette.

Aste-Béon and Laruns

Between Pau and Laruns, few places compel a stop. One is **ASTE-BÉON**, home to **La Falaise aux Vautours** (ⓦwww.falaise-aux-vautours.com; April–May & Sept Mon–Fri 10am–noon & 2–6pm, Sat–Sun 2–5/6pm; June–Aug daily 10.30am–12.30pm & 2–6.30pm; rest of year except Jan school holidays only daily 2–5pm; €7), a vulture-watching installation where over a hundred breeding pairs and their chicks are observable nesting naturally.

Otherwise unremarkable **LARUNS**, on the valley bottom just before steep wooded heights rise towards the border, comes alive for its August 15 **festival**, with revellers in trad dress and live music. The **tourist office** on the main place de la Mairie (summer Mon–Sat 9am–12.30pm & 2–6.30pm, Sun 9am–1pm & 2–6pm; ⓣ05.59.05.31.41) stands back-to-back with a **Maison du Parc** (mid-June to mid-Sept daily 10am–1pm & 2–6.30pm; ⓣ05.59.05.41.59). **Accommodation** includes characterful *Hôtel de France*, at the eastern end of town opposite the disused *gare SNCF* (ⓣ05.59.05.33.71; ❷); more or less opposite stands pilgrim-friendly *Chalet-Refuge L'Embaradère* (ⓣ05.59.05.41.88; 28 places; cheap meals; closed Mon–Tues low season). Two of the few independent **restaurants** are on rue du Bourguet off the square: *L'Arrégalet* at no. 37 (closed lunch Mon & Tues; menus from €15), strong on local recipes, and *Auberge Bellevue* at no. 55 (closed Mon evening & all Tues low season), with varied menus from €13 and brasserie grub available between main-meal hours. Just across the river in **BÉOST**, *Auberge Chez Trey* is an excellent traditional grill.

Eaux-Chaudes and Gabas

The road to Gabas, 13km south, winds steeply into the upper reaches of the Gave d'Ossau valley, through **EAUX-CHAUDES** spa, whose few bright spots include the excellent ⭐ *Auberge La Caverne* (ⓣ05.59.05.36.40, ⓦaubergelacaverne.com; closed Oct–Nov), run by a hard-working couple who offer both dorms and en-suite doubles (❶) in an atmospheric old building, as well as very salubrious *table d'hôte* meals (€15–27.50 includes house wine and coffee). Another is the restored nineteenth-century **spa** itself (May–Oct 3.30–6.30pm; from €6) by the river.

Primarily a base for climbers and walkers, there's little to **GABAS** beyond a minuscule chapel and limited **accommodation** – which fills quickly in summer. The preferable of two hotels, at Gabas' north entrance, *Chez Vignau* (ⓣ05.59.05.34.06, ⓦwww.hotelvignau.fr; ❷) has basic rooms, some with toilets down the hall, plus a decent restaurant; as good or better is independent *Du Pic du Midi* up the road (menus €13–23). There's also the CAF *Chalet-Refuge*

(☎05.59.05.33.14; 46 places; open June–Sept & winter weekends except mid-Oct to mid-Nov) 700m above Gabas, with unusually good food.

Pic du Midi d'Ossau

The **Pic du Midi d'Ossau**, with its craggy, mitten-shaped summit (2884m), is a classic Pyrenean landmark, visible for kilometres around. From Gabas, it's a steep 4.5-kilometre climb on the D231 road (1 daily morning bus) to the artificial **Lac de Bious-Artigues**, so named because it flooded the *artigue* or "mountain pasture" that formerly existed here. Drivers will be directed by *parc national* wardens to one of two car parks, the higher one just above the dam. There are no longer any facilities of note here, so come prepared.

A hiking circuit of the peak, excluding the summit – the **Tour du Pic du Midi** – takes about six hours. It can be broken by a **stay** at the CAF *Refuge de Pombie* (☎05.59.05.71.78; open June–Sept, weekends May & Oct), below the southeast flank of the mountain. From Bious-Artigues, follow the GR10, initially a broad track, along the *gave*; at the turning right to the Lacs d'Ayous (see below), instead cross the Pont de Bious, following a signpost indicating "Pombie Par Peyreget", and continue upstream across an expanse of flat meadow. There follows a steepish zigzagging climb on a path to the junction with the HRP route, which takes you (1hr 30min from the dam) to the tiny **Lac de Peyreget**. Once over the **Col de Peyreget** (2320m), you descend east – with great views – to *Refuge de Pombie* (about 3hr 30min along). The path continues north via the **Col de Suzon**, then finally west back to Bious-Artigues.

The Tour des Lacs

Starting again from the Bious-Artigues trailhead, the **Tour des Lacs** (Ayous, Bersau and Castérau) is another popular classic loop, in some ways more impressive than circling the Pic du Midi d'Ossau itself, especially if you spend the night en route to get the quintessential dawn view of the peak silhouetted against the rising sun and reflected in the slaty waters of Lac Gentau.

Begin walking as for the Tour du Pic du Midi, but instead of crossing the Pont de Bious, stay on the GR10 (a sign says "Lacs d'Ayous 1hr 30min") to climb through pine and beech woods, with widening views of the valley dotted with herds of livestock. Near the top, you reach three small lakes, the third and largest being **Lac Gentau**; on its banks there's flat, soft meadow for camping, permitted here as it's just outside the PNP. Above looms the *Refuge d'Ayous* (1982m; ☎05.59.05.37.00; 47 places; mid-June to mid-Sept).

Continue south on the obvious path to **Lac Bersau**, dominated by the peaks – both nearly 2400m high – of Larry and Hourquette; it's a favourite picnicking spot and irresistible for a swim on a hot day. A col (2150m) just south is the high point of the *tour*, which now turns east under **Pic Castérau** (2227m) to pass the eponymous lake, and begins a sharp descent, with full-on views of the Pic du Midi. After passing some shepherds' *cabanes* – a path shortcuts the 4WD tracks serving them – you follow the *gave* northeast to the Pont de Bious and the car park. The circuit's basically four hours' walking, but allow six with stops; you can reverse these directions to arrive at the refuge for lunch.

Lac d'Artouste and Le Petit Train

Some 6.5km out of Gabas, the Pourtalet road passes the dammed **Lac de Fabrèges**, with an access drive around the east shore leading to a huge ski-chalet complex, among which is concealed the *billeterie* for a *télécabine*. This attains the base of **Pic de la Sagette** (2031m) to connect with **Le Petit**

Train, a miniature rail line running 10km southeast through the mountains to **Lac d'Artouste**. Built in the 1920s to service a hydroelectric project which raised this lake's level 25m, it was later converted for tourist purposes. Weather permitting, the train starts operating in late May and continues until late September (low season 8.30am–2.30pm, July–Aug 8am–4.30pm; reserve on ☎05.59.05.36.99 or Ⓦwww.train-artouste.com). It's a beautiful trip, lasting about four hours, including the *télécabine*; you've time to walk down to the lake and back (and to *Refuge Arrémoulit*; ☎05.59.05.31.79; 40 places) if you set a brisk pace. **Prices** are a stiff €21 return, €16 one-way (useful for trekkers). In **winter** the same lift gives access to the small downhill **ski centre** on northeast of the Col de la Sagette.

Eaux-Bonnes, Gourette and the road to the Gave de Pau

The only way of reaching the Gave de Pau by road without going back towards Pau is along the minor D918 east over the Col d'Aubisque, via Eaux-Bonnes and **Gourette**, 12km east of Laruns and the favourite **ski centre** of folk from Pau. The base development is ugly but the skiing, on 28 north-facing runs from a top point of 2400m, is more than respectable. You can of course stay here, but the Second Empire spa village of **EAUX-BONNES**, 8km below Gourette, is more elegant and pleasant. Here the old-fashioned *Hôtel de la Poste* on the central park-square (☎05.59.50.33.06, Ⓦwww.hotel-dela-poste.com; closed late spring & mid-Oct to Christmas; ❷) represents excellent value, especially at half-board rates with a four-course *table d'hôte* supper. About the only independent eatery is *La Farandole*, specializing in crêpes and fondue.

The **Col d'Aubisque** itself (1709m), a grassy saddle with a souvenir stall/café on top, usually sees the Tour de France come through, making the pass irresistible to any French cyclist worth his salt. Once over the next, lower Col de Soulor, the route descends, 18km in all, to attractive **ARRENS-MARSOUS**, at the head of the Val d'Azun. Despite being another gateway to the PNP, with **information** (including local walking guidebooks) from the Maison du Val d'Azun (☎05.62.97.49.49, Ⓦwww.valdazun.com; Mon–Sat 9am–noon & 3–6/7pm), **accommodation** is limited to *Gîte Camélat*, in a fine, rambling house from 1887 just off the central *place* (☎05.62.97.40.94, Ⓦwww.gite-camelat.com/; 50 places; all year) with both doubles (❷) and dorm space.

The Gave de Pau and around

From its namesake city, the **Gave de Pau** forges southeast towards the mountains, bending sharply south at Lourdes and soon fraying into several tributaries: the **Gave d'Azun**, the **Gave de Cauterets**, the **Gave de Gavarnie** (draining the eponymous cirque) and the **Gave de Bastan**, dropping from the Col du Tourmalet. All four valleys, and their villages, are served by SNCF buses from Lourdes or Argelès-Gazost. **Cauterets**, 30km due south of Lourdes, and **Gavarnie** 37km southeast of Argelès, are busy, established resorts on the edge of the PNP, but the countryside they adjoin is so spectacular that you forgive their deficiencies. If you want a smaller, more manageable base, then either **Barèges**, up a side valley from the spa resort of **Luz-St-Sauveur**, or Luz itself, are better bets. But pick your season – or even the time of day – right, and you can enjoy the most popular sites in relative solitude. At Gavarnie few people stay the night, so it's quiet early or late, and the **Cirque de Troumouse**, which is just as impressive (though much harder to get to without a car), has far fewer visitors. The spa-town of **Bagnères-de-Bigorre**, east of the *gave* within striking distance of Lourdes, is fairly dull, primarily a gateway to the Vallée de Campan.

St-Savin and Arcizans-Avant

Between Lourdes and Cauterets, some 3km southeast of the congested town of Argelès-Gazost, pleasant, sleepy **ST-SAVIN** merits a stop for its twelfth-century **abbey-church**, with later fortifications and a fine Romanesque portal. The interior (daily 9am–7pm) offers an amusing organ cabinet carved with three grotesque faces – supposedly those of damned souls – that were designed to grimace as the unbearable (for them) heavenly music played. The **treasury** (daily: April–June & Sept–Oct 2.30–6pm; July & Aug 10.30am–12.30pm & 2.30–6.30pm; €2), installed in the vaulted former chapterhouse, is home to a twelfth-century "black Madonna" which tradition holds was carried back from Syria by Crusaders. Also worth a visit is the little eleventh-century hilltop chapel of **Notre-Dame-de-Piétat** (April–Oct Sat–Sun & holidays 2.30–6pm but July–Aug daily same hours; free), 1km south of the village, which has an elaborately painted ceiling, where birds perch on floral motifs covering every available space.

St-Savin has a couple of hotels, but much the best-value **food** and **lodging** locally is 2km northwest at **ARCIZANS-AVANT**, where friendly *L'Escapade* (aka *Chez Michelle*; ☎05.62.90.36.16) at the central junction offers four no-nonsense menus (from €11 at lunch) and cheerful dormer rooms upstairs (❷).

Cauterets and around

CAUTERETS is a pleasant if unexciting little town that owes its fame and rather elegant Neoclassical architecture (especially on boulevard Latapie-Flurin) to its spa, and more recently to its role as one of the main Pyrenean ski and mountaineering centres. Cauterets originated with Count Raymond de Bigorre's grant of land to the monks of St-Savin in 945 AD. In the seventeenth century, Marguerite d'Angoulême came to take the waters and wrote her *Heptameron* here. The eighteenth and nineteenth centuries were its zenith, especially the latter with its Romantic worship of mountains. Hugo visited, as did Chateaubriand, Baudelaire, Debussy, Sarah Bernhardt, Edward VII and many other celebrities.

The town is small enough to present no difficulties in orientation; most of it is still squeezed between the steep wooded heights that close the mouth of the Gave de Cauterets valley. Next door to the **gare routière** on the north edge of the centre, where SNCF coaches stop, the **Maison du Parc** (daily 9.30am–noon & 3.30–7pm; ☎05.62.92.52.56) has a small display of flora and fauna. In the centre, five-minutes' walk distant, you'll find the **tourist office** in place Maréchal-Foch (Mon–Sat: July & Aug 9am–12.30pm & 2–7pm; Sept–June 9am–noon & 2–6pm; ☎05.62.92.50.50, ⊛www.cauterets.com).

Several well-equipped **campsites** line the road north of town, the closest being *La Prairie* (☎05.62.92.54.28; June–Sept). Inexpensive **hotels** include *Le Grum* at 4 rue Victor-Hugo, off rue de la Raillère (☎05.62.92.53.01; closed Oct 20 to Dec 10; ❷), with a mix of rooms en suite and not; and *Le Pas de l'Ours*, 21 rue de la Raillère (☎05.62.92.58.07, ⊛www.lepasdelours.com; all year; ❹), which also runs a **gîte**. For a more upmarket stay, try the atmospheric *Lion d'Or* at 12 rue Richelieu (☎05.62.92.52.87, ⊛www.liondor.eu; closed mid-Oct to Christmas & 3 weeks after Easter; ❺), or the elegant

Asterides-Sacca at 11 boulevard Latapie-Flurin (℡05.62.92.50.02; closed Oct 15 to Dec 15; ❻). As many hotels require half board in peak season, independent **restaurants** are thin on the ground.

Hikes around Cauterets

Most classic excursions around Cauterets begin from the **Pont d'Espagne** 7km south, where the Gave de Gaube and Gave du Marcadau hurtle together in a boiling spume of spray, before rushing down to Cauterets over a series of spectacular waterfalls. In season there are six daily *navettes* from the town to the giant visitor centre and car park (€4–6 per vehicle) here; purists can walk there in about two hours along an attractive, streamside trail, known first as the "Avenue Demontzey" and, once past the satellite spa of **La Raillère**, as the "Chemin des Cascades".

From Pont d'Espagne (1420m), you proceed southwest some two hours up the **Marcadau valley** to *Refuge Wallon* (1886m; ℡05.62.92.64.28; 115 places; open mid-May to Oct), poised between the HRP and GR10, and the base for numerous walks – the most popular being the five-hour loop north, then east, then back to the refuge via the **lakes of Nère**, **Pourtet** and **de l'Embarrat**.

Alternatively, head due south up into the alpine valley of the Gave de Gaube, with picturesque **Lac de Gaube** (1725m) backed by the snowy north face of **Vignemale** (3298m). A combined *télécabine/télésiège* (June–Sept; €7 return) spares you most of the ascent from Pont d'Espagne. Beyond the lake, a path continues to the *Refuge Oulettes-de-Gaube* at the base of Vignemale (℡06.64.45.41.46 or 05.62.92.62.97; 2151m; 120 places; open May–Oct 15; 3hr from Pont d'Espagne), from where you can return to La Raillère by one of two routes.

The HRP from *Refuge Oulettes* goes over a 2734-metre pass to *Refuge de Bayssellance* (℡05.62.92.40.25; 58 places; open June–Sept; weekends April & Oct weather permitting) and then loops broadly around to the *Refuge d'Estom* (℡05.62.92.74.86; 1804m; open June–Sept) in the beautiful and quieter **Lutour valley**; alternatively you can omit *Bayssellance* and head straight to *Estom* over the 2583-metre Col d'Arraillé, and then to La Raillère. Even with bus and *télécabine* rides at the start and using this lower route, you should allow eight hours for the walking day; if you take in the high country around *Bayssellance*, schedule an overnight at one of the three refuges.

A less subscribed walk from Cauterets goes to **Lac d'Ilhéou** along the **GR10** (about 3hr). To avoid the initial steep climb you can take another combined *télécabine/télésiege* (July 4 to Sept 7 only; €8 one way, €10 return; €15 return includes Pont d'Espagne service too), up to the 2300-metre contour under the Crêtes du Lys. From there's a 45-minute descent to popular but expensive *Refuge d'Ilhéou* (1988m; ℡05.62.92.52.38; open June–Sept) beside its lake, where ice floes drift on its still surface reflecting snow on surrounding peaks early in summer. From the refuge, you can either descend the Gave d'Ilhéou back to Cauterets or, more ambitiously, pop over the Col de la Haugade (2311m) into the Marcadau valley and thence back to Cauterets via the Val de Jéret.

Luz-St-Sauveur and Gèdre

The only road approach to the Gavarnie and Troumouse zones is through **LUZ-ST-SAUVEUR**, astride the GR10 and SNCF bus route from Lourdes. Like Cauterets, this was a nineteenth-century spa, patronized by Napoléon III and Eugénie, and elegant Neoclassical facades in the left-bank St-Saveur quarter date from them. The principal sight, at the top of Luz's medieval, right-bank quarter, is **St-André church** (daily May 15 to Sept 30 3–6pm; €2). Built in the late twelfth century, it was fortified in the fourteenth by the Knights of St John with a crenellated outer wall and two stout towers. The north entrance sports a handsome portal surmounted by a Christ in Majesty carved in fine-grained local stone.

The **tourist office** (all year minimum hours Mon–Sat 9am–7.30pm, Sun 9am–12.30pm & 4.30–7.30pm; ☎05.62.92.30.30, ⓦwww.luz.org), edges the central place du Huit-Mai. One worthwhile central **hotel** is *Les Templiers* (☎05.62.92.81.52, ⓦwww.hotellestempliers.com; closed April or May; ❷–❸), opposite the church with half board offered and pricier rooms with view. Best value for three-star comfort is in adjoining Esquièze-Sère village at 2007-redone ⚑ *Le Montaigu* (☎05.62.92.81.71, ⓔhotel.montaigu@orange.fr; ❺, half board ❼), with large balconied rooms and professional management. The better of two **campsites**, also with a *gîte* on site, is smallish *Les Cascades* (☎05.62.92.94.14; Dec–Sept), uphill from the church, with a pool. Stand-alone **restaurants** aren't numerous; two reliable ones are *La Tasca* on place St-Clement, tops for Spanish tapas and seafood, and ⚑ *Chez Christine* (daily summer & school hols, closed Nov & Sun–Wed low season) near the post office, specializing in pizzas, own-made pasta and desserts, plus locally sourced lamb and trout.

Eleven kilometres south, just before the Cirque de Troumouse turning, is tiny **GÈDRE**. This offers a comfortable **hotel-restaurant**, *La Brèche de Roland* (☎05.62.92.48.54, ⓦwww.pyrenees-hotel-breche.com; ❹, or half board ❻; May–Sept plus winter weekends/hols), with menus at €18 and €25), the cheaper getting you *garbure*, lamb stew and choice of dessert. Shame about the noisy road by outdoor seating – the dining room appeals more in winter. Cyclists, hikers and raptor-watchers will appreciate *Gîte d'Étape Le Saugué* (☎05.62.92.48.73; May–Oct; 25 places), alone in high hay meadows 9km south with unbeatable views of Gavarnie.

Gavarnie and its cirque

A further 8km up the ravine from Gèdre, **GAVARNIE** is connected with Luz-St-Sauveur by two daily **bus services** (July–Aug only; otherwise just 3 weekly, or a taxi from Luz). You can walk it on the higher variant of the GR10 from Cauterets in two days. If you drive in, a **parking** fee (July 1 to Sept 15 8am–5pm; €4) is charged; otherwise there is ample free parking around the shops and hotels. Once poor and depopulated, Gavarnie found the attractions of mass tourism – much of it excursions from Lourdes – too seductive to resist, and it's now an unattractive mess of souvenir shops and mediocre snack bars. As with other overly popular sites, visit in shoulder season and/or before 9am or after 5pm, to avoid the bus-borne hordes.

However, the **cirque** itself – Victor Hugo called it "Nature's Colosseum" – is magnificent, a natural amphitheatre scoured out by glaciers. Over 1500m high, it consists of three sheer bands of rock streaked by seepage and waterfalls, separated by sloping ledges covered with snow and glacier remnants. On the east, it's dominated by jagged **Astazou** and **Marboré** peaks, both over 3000m. In the middle, a cornice sweeps round to the **Brèche de Roland**, a curious vertical slash, 100m deep and about 60m wide, said to have been hewn from the ridge by Roland's sword, Durandal. In winter, there's good beginner-to-intermediate **skiing** at the nearby 24-run resort of **Gavarnie-Gèdre**, with great views of the cirque from the top point of 2400m.

Practicalities

La Bergerie (☎05.62.92.48.41; mid-May to Oct), on the east bank of the *gave* on the cirque side of the village, must be one of the most stunningly located Pyrenean **campsites**, with views compensating for exceedingly basic facilities for tents and vans. Otherwise, **dorm–type** accommodation is available at high-standard *Gîte Auberge Le Gypaëte* (☎05.62.92.40.61; 45 places; most of year), below the main car park.

Fair-value **hotel** options include en-suite *Le Taillon* (☎05.65.92.48.20, Ⓦwww.letaillon.com; closed Nov 1 to Dec 15; ❹), with a competent restaurant, and smallish *Hôtel Compostelle* by the church (☎05.62.92.49.43, Ⓦwww.compostellehotel.com; closed Oct to Christmas, part Jan; ❸), with most rooms facing the cirque. You can park next to, or near, both but the village is closed to traffic in high season 10am–6pm. Most idyllically set, by the *gave*, are two non-en-suite *chambres d'hôtes* at *La Chaumière* (☎05.62.92.48.08, Ⓦlachaumiere.gavarnie.free.fr; closed Oct–Christmas; ❶).

The best independent **restaurant** is duck and trout specialist ⚐ *Les Cascades*, next to the **Maison du Parc** (Mon–Sat 9am–noon & 1.30–6.30pm, Sun 10am–noon & 3–6pm; ☎05.62.92.42.48) on the north side of the village, with the top tables overlooking the cirque (best reserve on ☎05.62.92.40.17), a midday *formule*, good bulk wine and two menus (€18 & 30) – service is miraculously polite and efficient, the food accomplished. Other **information** sources include the tourist office by the car parks (daily summer 9am–noon & 1.30–7pm; ☎05.62.92.49.10, Ⓦwww.gavarnie.com), and the CRS mountain rescue unit opposite *La Bergerie*, for accurate snow and weather reports.

The cirque and around

It's an easy walk from Gavarnie into the cirque along the *gave* draining it, using either the main east-bank track or the longer, steeper west-bank trail. Luckily, the scale of the place is sufficient to dwarf humans, but for a bit of serenity it's still best to use the west-bank path, or go up early or late. The broad track ends after 45 minutes at the *Hôtel du Cirque et de la Cascade*, once a famous meeting place for mountaineers and now a popular, surprisingly reasonable snack bar in summer. To get to the foot of the cirque walls, you face a steeper, final half-hour on a dwindling, increasingly slippery path which ends in a spray-bath at the base of the **Grande Cascade**, fed by Lago Helado on the Spanish side, and at 423m the highest waterfall in Europe. This plummets and fans out in three stages down the rock faces – a fine sight in sunny weather, with rainbows in the wind-teased plumes.

If you don't want to retrace your steps, an enjoyable and not too demanding return to Gavarnie follows the path from the *Hôtel du Cirque* up the east flank of the valley to the **Refuge des Espuguettes** (2030m; ☎05.62.92.40.63; 60 places; daily May–Sept, Easter & Oct weekends; 2hr). It's a beautiful path, cut into rocky, pine-shaded slopes, with more fine views of the cirque; at the top, you emerge into open meadows tilting up to the refuge. Those staying overnight here may want to bag **Piméné** (2801m; 3hr 30min return), the bare peak above you, for unbeatable views over the Cirque d'Estaubé, and Monte Perdido in Spain. For Gavarnie, turn right (north) at the signposted trail fork below the refuge (allow 90min from there).

La Brèche de Roland

La Brèche de Roland is *the* walk to do in Gavarnie. It's high, and involves crossing a glacier with ice-axe and crampons. It is, however, extremely popular in summer, so there's a good chance of being able to team up with someone more experienced. The *brèche* is about forty minutes above the refuge described below, with the glacier crossing occupying the final moments.

There are three approaches to the *brèche*, all converging on the **Refuge des Sarradets/Brèche de Roland** (2587m; ☎06.83.38.13.24; 60 places; open June–Sept, Oct weekends); for which reservations are always necessary in high season. The easiest route is from the end of the road to the Port de Boucharo, where a clear path climbs under the north face of Le Taillon to join the footpath coming directly from Gavarnie (1hr-plus). The latter path starts beside the church, climbs steadily through the Pouey Aspé valley, then zigzags steeply up to join the first path on the flank of Sarradets peak (2hr 45min). From the junction of these two paths, it's half an hour to the refuge. The third route (4hr 30min from Gavarnie to the hut) is via the **Échelle des Sarradets/HRP** path above the *Hôtel du Cirque*, better than its IGN map-depiction suggests, though scrambling sections, slippery surfaces and cable-holds appear at several points.

The Cirque de Troumouse

Much bigger than Gavarnie and, in bad weather, rather intimidating, the **Cirque de Troumouse** lies up a wild valley whose only habitations are the handful of farmsteads and pilgrimage chapel with its ancient polychrome statuette of the Virgin and Child which make up the scattered hamlet of **HÉAS** – among the loneliest outposts in France before the road in was constructed. The only **rooms** are at *Auberge de la Munia* (☎05.62.92.48.39, ⓦwww.aubergedelamunia.com; closed Oct 15 to Dec 15; half board only ❹), by the chapel, though you've more choice in **meals** (eg, *Le Refuge* 400m along, menu €18.50), near which you can **camp**. By *Le Refuge* there's a **tollgate** (9am–6pm; €4 per car), after which the road climbs in tight hairpins 4km to the *Auberge du Maillet* (☎05.62.92.48.97; May 20 to Oct 10; 33 dorm places, also doubles half board only ❹), beside a small tarn at 1837m. Beyond, the road climbs again, even more steeply over 3km, beneath snow-streaked crags, to a car park at 2103m. Nearby, a prominent statue of the Vièrge d'Héas crowns a grassy knoll amid enough moorland pasture for thousands of animals, enclosed by the vast cirque. Beneath its eastern walls are scattered a half-dozen blue glacial lakelets, the **Lacs des Aires**. A *parc national* path arrives here, starting from just before the Héas tollboth (2.5hr uphill).

Vallée de Bastan and Barèges

Luz-St-Sauveur marks the start of climb east along the D918 through the **Vallée de Bastan**, culminating after 18km in the **Col du Tourmalet** (2115m), one of the major torments of the Tour de France and the fulcrum of a giant **skiing** *domaine*. North of the pass rises the landmark **Pic du Midi de Bigorre** (2877m), with its observatory reachable by funicular.

The only major village in between is **BARÈGES**, 7km along, served by SNCF bus (change at Pierrefite-Nestalas). An attractive if one-street place, Barèges has been a popular spa since 1677, when it was visited by Madame de Maintenon with her infant charge, the 7-year-old Duc de Maine, son of Louis XIV. A military hospital opened here in 1744, as its waters were efficacious in treating gunshot wounds, and a low-key army connection endures – a mountain warfare training centre and an R&R facility stand opposite each other. But today it's primarily a skiing, mountaineering and paragliding centre, and the most congenial, low-key resort around the Gave de Pau.

The central **tourist office** (July & Aug Mon–Sat 9am–12.30pm & 2–6.30pm, Sun 10am–noon & 4–6pm; Sept–June shorter afternoon hours; ☎05.62.92.16.00, ⓦwww.bareges.com) can supply accommodation lists and ski-lift plans. The

Skiing and hiking around Barèges

With its links to the adjacent, equal-sized *domaine* of **La Mongie** over 10km east on the far side of the Col du Tourmalet, Barèges offers access to the largest **skiing** area in the French Pyrenees, including downhill pistes totalling 125km (1850–2400m) and 31km of cross-country trails through the Lienz plateau forest (1350–1700m). Beginners' runs finishing in Barèges village are much too low (1250m) to retain snow, so all skiers usually have to start from the Tournaboup or Tourmalet zones. High-speed, state-of-the-art chair lifts are now the rule at Barèges, and runs have been regraded to make the resort more competitive, but La Mongie over the hill, despite its hideous purpose-built development, offers even higher, longer pistes. For more information consult ⓦwww.tourmalet.fr.

The **GR10** passes through Barèges on its way southeast into the lake-filled **Néouvielle Massif**, part of France's oldest (1935) natural reserve, and highly recommended as a hiking area. The best trailhead for **day-hikes**, with limited parking, lies 3km east at **Pont de la Gaubie** (1538m), from where the classic seven-hour day-loop takes in the Vallée des Aygues Cluses plus the lakes and peak of Madamète, followed by a descent via Lac Nère and Lac Dets Coubous back to Gaubie. For those **traversing** with full packs, a seven-hour walking day from Barèges via either the Col de Madamète or the Horquette d'Aubert brings you into the Néouvielle reserve for an overnight at either the mammoth, modernized *Chalet du Lac d'Orédon* (☎05.62.23.05.72.60; mid-June to mid-Sept; doubles ❷ & dorms), or the *Chalet-Hôtel de l'Oule* (☎05.62.98.48.62; 28 places; open early June to mid-Sept & ski season). Lakeside *Refuge de Bastan* (☎05.62.98.48.80; 24 places; June–Sept), over the Horquette Nère from Aygues Cluses, is also a tempting target, its young managing couple being excellent cooks.

through road (rue Ramond) is lined with a half-dozen **hotels**, all with a fairly similar summer opening season (May–Oct) and price (typically ❸); best value among these is *Hôtel La Montagne Fleurie* (☎05.62.92.68.50, ⓦwww.hotel -bareges.fr) at no. 21, renovated in 2007 without losing its charm, with a good restaurant and wi-fi signal. Equally distinctive are two high-quality, English-run *chambres d'hôtes*: 🎋 *Les Sorbiers* on the main street (☎05.62.92.86.68, ⓦwww .lessorbiers.co.uk; ❸; all year), offering vegetarian meals on request, and 🎋 *Mountain Bug* (☎05.62.92.16.39, ⓦwww.mountainbug.com; ❼ half board, 1-week bookings preferred) behind the butcher's, a superbly restored eighteenth-century farmhouse with modern bathrooms and tasteful wood-floored common areas; proprietors Robert and Emma are certified guides offering local walking holidays. The cosier of two **gîtes d'étape** is welcoming, Anglo–French-run *L'Oasis*, right behind the spa (☎05.62.92.69.47, ⓦwww.gite-oasis.com; 40 places; closed April & Oct), offering evening meals and reasonable half-board rates.

The Col du Tourmalet and the Pic du Midi de Bigorre

Some 3km out of Barèges, the D918 begins climbing in earnest over denuded slopes to the **Col du Tourmalet**, at 2115m the highest motorable pass in the French Pyrenees, only reliably open from late May/early June until the first snowdrifts (some time in November). Even in summer it's apt to be desolate and windy, flanked by a sleeker replacement of the rough-hewn, anatomically correct original cyclist-statue, commemorating the first passage of the Tour through here in 1910. The better of two **restaurants** here, off to the left just east of the col, is *Eric Le Berger*, open most of the year, tops for (his own-raised) lamb chops and once voted Best European On-Piste Eats in a *Sunday Times* poll.

By the statue, a dirt road meanders up towards the **Pic du Midi**, though you can no longer use this to drive to the summit observatory, but must visit either on foot or by **téléphérique** (June–Sept daily 9am–4.30pm; sporadic, complicated schedule otherwise; €34 adult, €84 family, includes admission to museum; ⓦwww.picdumidi.com) from La Mongie. The venerable observatory, continuously staffed since opening in 1880 and still a serious research facility, long resisted commercialization but has bowed to the inevitable with an **astronomical museum**, solar observatory, observation deck and restaurant (very popular for its monthly *soirée etoilée* dinners).

Vallée de Campan and Bagnères-de-Bigorre

From the col the road descends past La Mongie ski centre, down into the meadowy **Vallée de Campan**, whose architecture is distinct from the valleys to the west. Farm roofs are still slate, but house and barn are built in line as one building, with the balconied living quarters always to the right as you face the sun. The first proper village is **STE-MARIE-DE-CAMPAN**, where the preferable of two **accommodation** and **eating** choices is *Hôtel les Deux Cols* (☎05.62.91.85.60, Ⓕ05.62.91.85.31; closed mid-Oct to mid-Dec; ❶), with three hearty menus (€13–19.50) aimed at cyclists. The valley's "capital", 6.5km further, is **CAMPAN**, with its interesting sixteenth-century covered market, old houses and another curious-looking fortified church with a presumed Cagot door in the west wall.

Both villages have daily summer bus links down valley to **BAGNÈRES-DE-BIGORRE**, nearly equidistant from Tarbes and Lourdes, with buses from Tarbes calling at the **gare SNCF** on avenue de Belgique, 400m north of the town centre. It's yet another pleasant if nondescript Pyrenean spa town which has burnished its somewhat faded image with **Aquensis** (daily: school holidays 10.30am–8.30pm, otherwise 10.30am/1pm–8pm; ⓦwww.aquensis-bagneres .com), certainly the most striking thermal baths in the Pyrenees with the central pool overarched by a forest of cantilevered wood beams. The **tourist office** is at 3 allée Tournefort (all year: daily 9am–12pm & 2–6pm; ☎05.62.95.50.71, ⓦwww.bagneresdebigorre-lamongie.com), close to pedestrianized, central **place de Strasbourg** with its cafés and nearby *halles*.

Many **hotels** can be fusty and/or overpriced. Better-value choices, all with restaurants, include – just north of the *halles* on rue de l'Horloge 3bis – old-fashioned *Pension l'Horloge* (☎05.62.91.00.20; March–Nov; ❶); well-kept *Hôtel de la Paix* (☎05.62.95.20.60, ⓦwww.hotel-delapaix.com; closed Jan; ❸), with some rooms facing away from the noisy avenue; and (especially for drivers) rambling *Hôtel Tivoli* (☎05.62.91.07.13, ⓦwww.hoteltivoli.fr; all year; ❷), in its own grounds southwest of the centre on avenue du Salut. **Restaurants** aren't Bagnères' strong point, but it's got one goodie in ⍟*L'Annexe*, right opposite the *halles* door in an ex-butchers (look for the "Boucherie" sign), with a €16 menu or cheapish à la carte including duck, escargot, game and grilled camembert.

The Comminges

Stretching from **Luchon** almost to Toulouse, the **Comminges** is an ancient feudal county encompassing the upper Garonne River valley. It also hosts one of the finest buildings in the Pyrenees, magnificent **St-Bertrand-de-Comminges** cathedral, built over three distinct periods. The mountainous southern part is the most visited; access is via the unprepossessing little town of Montréjeau, from where there are daily bus and train services to Luchon.

Valcabrère

VALCABRÈRE, some 10km south of Montréjeau on the main Bayonne–Toulouse rail line, can be reached by SNCF bus (direction "Luchon") to the hamlet of Labroquère, by the Garonne, and then a short stroll across the river. It's a sleepy village of rough stone barns and open lofts for drying hay, with an exquisite Romanesque church, **St-Just** (daily 9am–noon & 2–7pm; €2), whose square tower rises above a cypress-studded cemetery. The north portal is girded by four elegant full-length sculptures and overtopped by a relief of Christ in Glory borne heavenward by angels. Between the altar and apse with its blind arches stands a carved Gothic shrine once containing saintly relics, which pilgrims could revere by means of the now off-limits stone staircase. Both interior and exterior are full of recycled masonry from the Roman **Lugdunum Convenarum**, whose remains are visible at the crossroads just beyond the village. Founded by Pompey in 72 BC, this had 60,000 inhabitants in its prime, making it one of the most important towns in Roman Aquitaine. Josephus, the Jewish first-century AD historian, says it was the place of exile of Herod Antipas and his wife Herodias, who had John the Baptist beheaded. Destroyed by Vandals in the fifth century and again by Burgundians in the sixth century, it remained deserted until Bishop Bertrand, the future saint, appeared toward the end of the eleventh century.

St-Bertrand-de-Comminges and around

Further southwest 2km is **ST-BERTRAND-DE-COMMINGES**, whose grey fortress-like **Cathedral** (Feb–April & Oct Mon–Sat 10am–noon & 2–6pm, Sun 2–6pm; May Mon–Sat 9am–6pm, Sun 2–6pm; June–Sept Mon–Sat 9am–7pm, Sun 2–7pm; Nov–Jan Mon–Sat 10am–noon & 2–5pm, Sun 2–5pm; admission to cloister and choir €4) commands the plain from the knoll ahead, the austere white-veined facade and heavily buttressed nave totally subduing the clutch of fifteenth- and sixteenth-century houses huddled at its feet. To the right of the west door a Romanesque twelfth-century cloister with carved capitals looks out across a lush valley to the foothills, haunt of Resistance fighters during World War II. In the aisleless interior, the church's great attraction is the central choir, built by Toulousain craftsmen and installed 1523–35. The 66 elaborately carved stalls, each one the work of a different craftsman, are a feast of virtuosity, mingling piety, irony and satire – though sadly roped off-limits and difficult to see in detail even from a metre away. Each of the gangways dividing the misericords has a representation of a cardinal sin on top of the end partition. By the middle gangway on the south side, for example, Envy is represented by two monks, faces contorted in hatred, engaged in a furious tug-of-war over the abbot's baton of office. The armrest south of the (locked) rood-screen entrance depicts the abbot birching a monk, while the bishop's throne has a fine back-panel in marquetry, depicting St Bertrand himself and St John. In the ambulatory a fifteenth-century shrine records scenes from St Bertrand's life, with the church and village visible in the top right panel.

Practicalities

Traffic into the old quarter is sporadically controlled, and **parking** (except for a few spaces near the cathedral) is restricted to two car parks at the south and southwest outskirts. During July and August the cathedral and St-Just in Valcabrère, both with marvellous acoustics, host the musical **Festival du Comminges** (Ⓦ www.festival-du-comminges.com). The **tourist office** is installed in the nineteenth-century Olivétain chapel and monastery on the cathedral square (Mon–Sat 10/11am–5/6/7pm; Ⓣ05.61.88.32.00 or 05.61.98.45.35), doubling as an adjunct festival box office.

Staying overnight is an attractive proposition, at least outside peak season. Opposite the cathedral, friendly *Hôtel du Comminges* (Ⓣ05.61.88.31.43, Ⓕ05.61.94.98.22; April–Sept; ❷–❸) makes a fine, slightly old-fashioned option, though only breakfast is served (outside in fine weather). **Restaurant** choices have improved lately, with *Vielle Auberge* in the lower town and friendly ❊ *Chez Simon* near the cathedral, the latter featuring duck, game, paté and regional dishes on a €16 menu or à la carte (allow €24); there's a lovely terrace or beam-ceilinged interior with fireplace.

The Grottes de Gargas

About 6km from St-Bertrand in the direction of St-Laurent, the **Grottes de Gargas** (half-hourly guided tours daily: July & Aug 10am–noon & 2–7pm; rest of year by prior arrangement, but reservations usually necessary Ⓣ05.62.39.72.39, Ⓦgrottesdegargas.free.fr/; €7) are renowned for their 231 prehistoric painted hand-prints. Outlined in black, red, yellow or white, they mostly seem deformed – perhaps the result of leprosy, frostbite or ritual mutilation, though no one really knows why. There are representations of large animals as well.

Luchon and around

There's none of the usual spa-town fustiness about **LUCHON** (formerly Bagnères de Luchon), long one of the focuses of Pyrenean exploration. The main **allées d'Étigny**, lined with cafés and brasseries, has a metropolitan elegance and bustle. There is not, however, much to see, apart from the **Musée du Pays de Luchon** (daily 9am–noon & 2–6pm; €1.60) next to the tourist office, containing an extraordinarily eclectic collection of engravings and travel posters, ancient climbing or skiing gear, and strange rural impedimenta, and the nineteenth-century **baths** (March–Oct Mon–Sat 7.30–11.45am, also Wed & Sat 5–7pm; Ⓦwww.thermes-luchon.fr) at the end of allées d'Étigny behind the **Parc des Quinconces** and its duck-lake. Luchon is best reckoned a comfortable base for exploring the surrounding mountains in summer, and for **skiing** at the nearby centres of Superbagnères and Peyragudes in winter. Because of the peculiar local topography, the valley here is also one of the major Pyrenean centres for **paragliding** and **light aviation**.

The area west of town, en route to the Col de Peyresourde along the D618, is also home to three Romanesque churches. The most accessible of these is **St-Aventin**, in the eponymous village 5km west of Bagnères. The south portal is completely surrounded by fine relief carving, including a fine Christ in Majesty, a Virgin and Child and the beheading of St-Aventin, followed by a bull discovering his grave. There are more carvings, and frescoes inside; a key can be borrowed from the *mairie* (Mon–Fri 9am–noon & 2–5pm).

Practicalities

The **gare SNCF**, also the **gare routière**, is in avenue de Toulouse across the River One in the northern part of the town. The **tourist office** is at 18 allée d'Étigny (daily: July–Aug & peak ski season 9am–7pm, rest of year same but closed for lunch; Ⓣ05.61.79.21.21, Ⓦwww.luchon.com), which stocks leaflets detailing lodging and currently operating activity outfitters.

There are several classic hikes south and southwest of Luchon, though there's no public transport to most of the various trailheads. The exception, 14km southwest of Luchon, is **Granges d'Astau**, jump-off point for the **Lac d'Oô**, served by two daily shuttle buses (July–early Sept). Here, you'll find the *Auberge d'Astau* (☎05.61.79.35.63; May–Oct; 16 places in dorms, also doubles ❷), with a restaurant, though many hikers prefer *Le Mailh d'Astau* next door for **meals**. From the car park here a busy section of the GR10 climbs an hour to the dammed lake, where the pricey *Refuge-Auberge du Lac d'Oô* (1504m; ☎05.61.79.12.29, ⓦwww.refuge-lac-oo.com; 26 places; May–Oct) perches beyond the west end of the dam. The onward path leads to the *Refuge d'Espingo* exactly an hour above Oô, just below the Col d'Espingo. This hut (1967m; ☎05.61.79.20.01; 70 places; June–Oct 15) overlooks beautiful, undammed **Lac d'Espingo**, and the frontier ridge; most day-trippers stop here, as the grade stiffens considerably beyond. You can also get here by taking the *télécabine* from Luchon up to Superbagnères (June 7–27 & Sept 1–28 weekends 1.30–6pm; June 28 to Aug 31, daily 9am–12.45pm & 2–6pm; €7.90 return, €5.90 one way), then continuing west on the GR10 to the *Refuge d'Espingo* (4hr 30min total).

Another possible walking route from Luchon involves following the Pique valley south 11km, partly on the D125, to the **Hospice de France** (1385m), originally founded by the Knights of St John and now being restored for 2009 opening as a refuge, from where a signposted path climbs a steep, narrow valley to the **Boums du Port** (just under 2hr with daypack), four small, scenic lakes; beside the middle one sits the small but welcoming *Refuge de Vénasque* (☎05.61.79.26.46; June 15 to Sept 15). Next you tackle the short, sharp path-climb to the notch on the frontier ridge known as the **Port de Vénasque** (3hr from Hospice de France), with superb views of the **Maladeta massif** and the **Pico d'Aneto**, highest summit of the Pyrenees (3404m). Return the same way, or fashion a classic loop taking in the frontier ridge to the east, then a descent of the Vallée de la Frèche back to the Hospice.

Luchon has two downhill **ski resorts** within striking distance, of which **Peyragudes** (ⓦwww.peyragudes.com) 15km west of Luchon overlooking each approach to Peyresourde, is much better. Its 43 runs, mostly of intermediate calibre and broad by Pyrenean standards, start from 2400m, with superb views of the frontier ridge and a decent lift system. Lower-altitude **Superbagnères** (ⓦwww.luchon.com), right above the town and accessible by a 15-kilometre road or the *télécabine* (included in ski pass), has 28 mostly beginnner-to-intermediate pistes lamentably exposed to morning sun and thus often mushy.

10

You're best off forsaking obvious **accommodation** on allées d'Étigny for better value in quieter side streets. Possibilities there include *Hôtel des Deux Nations* to the west at 5 rue Victor-Hugo (☎05.61.79.01.71, ⓦwww.hotel-des2nations.com; ❸), a popular choice with a busy downstairs restaurant and the best en-suite rooms on the lower two floors; east of the main street, *Hôtel la Petite Auberge*, 15 rue Lamartine (☎05.61.79.02.88; ❷), in a *belle-époque* mansion, with ample parking and a *table d'hôte* restaurant; and south, just over the municipal boundary in St-Mamet at 4 avenue de Gascogne, friendly, chalet-style ⚐ *Hôtel La Rencluse* (☎05.61.79.02.81, ⓦwww.hotel-larencluse.com; ❸), with the best, updated rooms in the attic, decent buffet breakfast and ample parking. There's no *gîte*, but the least cramped of eight **campsites** in the vicinity is *Camping La Lanette* (☎05.61.79.00.38; open mid-Dec to Oct), 1.5km down rue Lamartine) towards Montauban-de-Luchon.

As with lodging, the best **restaurant** prospects are some distance away from the allée d'Etigny. *Hôtel La Rencluse*'s diner is excellent, serving until 10pm or so without grumbling (unlike most town eateries), with four-course *table d'hôte* suppers at €14.50, plus palatable own-label wine. With transport and more funds, try *L'Auberge de Castel-Vielh*, 3km south on the D125 (April–Oct Wed–Sun; Nov–March weekends only; menus from €28), in a converted country house, purveying game and regional dishes, including snails, offal and trout; or – 7km west in **BILLIÈRE** village – ❧ *La Ferme d'Espiau* (book on ☎05.61.79.69.69, ⓦwww.restauant-luchon.com; 3 menus €17–30; closed Mon, also Tues–Wed low season; also *chambre d'hôte* at ➋), which excels at local meat or game and foie gras served amid antique rustic decor.

The Eastern Pyrenees

The dominant climatic influence of the **Eastern Pyrenees**, excluding the misty Couserans region, is the Mediterranean; the climate is warmer, the days sunnier, the landscape more arid. Dry-weather plants like cistus, broom and thyme make their appearance, and the foothills are planted with vines. The proximity of Spain is evident, with much of the territory definitively incorporated into France in 1659 belonging to historical Catalonia. As with the rest of the Pyrenees, the countryside is spectacular, and densely networked with hiking trails. Historical sights, with the exception of the painted caves of the **Ariège** and the Cathar castles and medieval towns of the **upper Aude**, are concentrated towards the coast in French Catalonia, comprising **Roussillon** and the Cerdagne (Rossilló and Cerdanya in Catalan).

The Ariège valley

Whether you're coming from the western Pyrenees or heading south from the major transport hub of Toulouse, the **Ariège valley** marks the start of the transition to the Mediterranean zone. The river, extending from high peaks along the Andorran border around the spa of **Ax-les-Thermes** down to agricultural plains north of **Foix**, forms the main axis of the eponymous *département*. In between lie a wealth of **caves**, most notably near **Tarascon** and **Mas d'Azil**. Transport is no problem as long as you stick to the valley, but for side trips into the **Couserans** region just west you really need a car or bicycle.

Foix and around

France's smallest *départemental* capital, **FOIX** lies 82km south of Toulouse on the Toulouse–Barcelona train line and the N20 road to Ax-les-Thermes and the Spanish border. It's an agreeable country town of narrow alleys and sixteenth- to seventeenth-century half-timbered houses, with an attractive old quarter squeezed between the rivers Ariège and Arget.

   Dominating all are the three distinctive hilltop towers of the **Château des Comtes de Foix**, which contains a dull handful of themed exhibits (May, June & Sept daily 9.45am–noon & 2–6pm; July & Aug daily 9.30am–6.30pm; Oct–April Wed–Sun 10.30am–noon & 2–5.30pm; €4.30) – though the views merit the climb. Determined opponents of the territorial ambitions of the Capetian kings of France and stout defenders of Catharism, the counts of Foix attracted the wrath of Simon de Montfort, who four times laid unsuccessful siege to the castle, though he did capture the town in 1211. Their resistance was finally broken in 1229 when Count Roger-Bernard was obliged to accept the suzerainty of the French king. Foix's age of glory came in 1290 when its counts married into the house of Béarn and later moved their court to Orthez in the fourteenth century. This was the start of a powerful Pyrenean mini-state – including the kingdom of Navarre – whose influence lasted three centuries, culminating in the 1589 coronation of Béarnais Henri IV as king of France.

The **gares SNCF and routière** are together on avenue de la Gare, off the N20 on the right (east) bank of the Ariège. The **tourist office** is on rue Théophile-Delcasse (July & Aug Mon–Sat 9am–7pm, Sun 10am–noon & 2–6pm; Sept–June Mon–Sat 9am–noon & 2–6pm; ☎05.61.65.12.12, ⓦwww .ot-foix.fr).

Most **accommodation** is found in the old town, on the left bank of the Ariège, though little of it is inspiring. The quietest and most comfortable option is three-star *Hôtel Lons*, on 6 place Duthil, near the Pont-Vieux (☎05.61.65.52.44, ⓦwww.hotel-lons-foix.com; ❸; closed late Dec to early Jan), with a respected restaurant. The 2005-upgraded *Eychenne* at 11 rue Noël-Peyrevidal (☎05.61.65.00.04, ⓦwww.hotel-eychenne.com; ❸) has a busy ground-floor café, but no restaurant. Opposite at no. 16, *Auberge Léo Lagrange* (☎05.61.65.09.04, ⓦwww.leolagrange-foix.com) is more an activity centre (rafting, etc) than hostel, but offers 74 bunks in doubles or quads, plus economical weekday lunches in its downstairs *foyer*.

A prime area for **eating** is rue de la Faurie and lanes leading off it, the old blacksmiths' bazaar at the heart of the old town. At no. 17, ⚵ *Le Jeu de l'Oie* does classic French country-bistro fare – *cassoulet*, duck dishes, *terrines*, offal, good desserts, Leffe draught beer – at friendly prices (*formules* and menus from under €10), which guarantees a lunch-time crush, though service doesn't suffer unduly. Also popular is *Les Quatres Saisons* at no. 11 (menus from €14; closed Sun–Thurs evening low season), whose speciality is *pierrade* – hot ceramic plates at your table to grill fish and meat. *Crêperie La Luciole* at 1 place Lazema, the west end of rue de la Faurie, is also well attended by civil servants at midday.

Labouiche and Mas d'Azil

Six kilometres northwest of Foix, the **underground river** at **Labouiche** (April–June & Sept daily 10–11.15am & 2–5.15pm; July & Aug daily 9.30am–5.15pm; Oct–Nov 11 weekends/hols 10am–11.15 & 2–4.30pm, expect a 15-minute wait; €7.50) is the longest navigable subterranean river in Europe. The visit consists of a barge trip (1hr 15min), along 1km of the river, 60m underground, to admire its stalactites and stalagmites.

Twenty-five kilometres west of Foix, the **Mas d'Azil** was one of the first prehistoric caves to yield evidence of human habitation, but its most impressive feature is a magnificent 500-metre-long natural tunnel, scoured by the River Arize, which now carries the D119 road from here towards Pamiers.

Secondary caves leading off the river-cavern are the focus of historical interest; they were inhabited in prehistoric periods for over 20,000 years and used as a refuge by Cathars and Protestants more recently. The most important galleries are sealed off, though this hasn't stopped damage from road pollution, and those caves you can visit are interesting mainly for their sheer size (March, Oct & Nov Sun 2–6pm; April–May Tues–Sat 2–6pm, Sun 10am–noon; June & Sept Tues–Sun

10am–noon & 2–6pm; July & Aug daily 10am–6pm; Christmas week admission 3pm & 4.15 only; €6.10, including museum entry).

A few animal bones and other artefacts found during excavation remain on view in glass cases in the caves, but the best pieces are now on display in the attractive, sleepy village of **LE MAS-D'AZIL**, 1km to the north, in the **Musée de la Préhistoire** (same hours and ticket as the cave). Among other engraved tools and weapons, the museum's most outstanding exhibit is the beautiful carved antler known as *le faon aux oiseaux* (fawn with birds), perhaps used as a spear-thrower. There's just one surviving **hotel** here on the central *place*, *Gardel* (☎05.61.69.90.05; ❷; closed mid-Nov to mid-March), as well as a municipal **campsite** (☎05.61.69.71.37; mid-June to mid-Sept) 1.5km away. The best of three spots to **eat** is *Le Jardin de Cadettou* (closed Sat lunch time, Sun evening. Mon, Dec 15 to April), with excellent regional menus (€16–26); they also have *chambres d'hôtes* (☎05.61.69.95.23; ❸).

Tarascon and around

TARASCON-SUR-ARIÈGE lies 17km south of Foix, where the N20 crosses the Ariège (a bypass diverts the worst of the traffic). Once a centre for the now-defunct iron-mining industry, it's a hot, unexciting little town enclosed by high wooded ridges. However, Tarascon is convenient for the nearby prehistoric caves, and more pleasant than first impressions suggest. From the east bank of the Ariège with its riverside cafés, narrow **rue de Barri** leads to St-Michel church in the old quarter, presiding over a partly arcaded square. Two items of the mostly razed medieval walls survive: the **Tour St-Michel** and the **Porte-d'Espagne**.

The combined **gare SNCF/halte routière** is a few-minutes' walk north from the centre, on the west bank. The **tourist office** is also just west of the bridge in the Éspace François Mitterrand (Mon–Sat 9am–1pm & 2–6pm, also Sun 9.30am–1pm peak summer/ski season; ☎05.61.05.94.94, ⓦwww.paysdetarascon.com). **Accommodation** options include quiet *Hôtel Confort* on riverside quai Armand-Sylvestre (☎&ⓕ05.61.05.61.90; closed Jan; ❶), with some rooms facing a courtyard; for rooms facing the river, try *Hostellerie de la Poste* (☎05.61.05.60.41, ⓦwww.hostellerieposte.com; all year; ❷), on the main street. This also has the town's best **restaurant** (closed Mon noon), with summer seating facing a lawn-garden and four menus (including one vegetarian) at €13–38. The **campsite**, *Pré Lombard* (☎05.61.05.61.94), is on the left bank of the river, ten-minutes' walk upstream from the bridge.

Niaux and other prehistoric caves

Just south of Tarascon, the D8 cuts up right into the green Vicdessos valley; the hamlet of **NIAUX** lies in the valley bottom, 4km along, hosting an interesting **Musée Pyrénéen** (daily: July & Aug 9am–8pm; Sept–June 10am–noon & 2–6pm; €8), with an unrivalled collection of tools, furnishings and old photos illustrating the vanished traditions of peasant Ariège.

But the real reason people descend on this little hamlet is for the **Grotte de Niaux**, a huge cave complex under an enormous rock overhang 2km north of the hamlet (45min guided tours: July–Sept daily 9am–5.45pm, English tours at 9am & 1pm; April–June & Oct 10.30am–5pm; Nov–Jan & March, tours at 11am, 2.30pm & 4.15pm; €9.40; max group size 20, advance reservations mandatory on ☎05.61.05.10.10). There are 4km of galleries in all, with paintings of the Magdalenian period (c.11,000 BC) scattered throughout, although tours see just a fraction of the complex, in particular paintings

▲ Niaux cave

adorning a vast chamber, a slippery 900-metre walk from the entrance of the cave along a subterranean riverbed. No colour is used to render the subjects – horses, ibex, stags and bison – just a dark outline and shading to give body to the drawings, executed with a "crayon" made of bison fat and manganese oxide. They present an extraordinary mix of bold impressionistic strokes and delicate attention to detail: nostrils, pupils and tendons are all drawn in.

The village of **ALLIAT**, right across the valley from Niaux, is home to the **Grotte de la Vache** (90min guided tours: April–June, Sept & school holidays 2.30 & 4pm; July & Aug daily 10am–5.30pm; otherwise by arrangement; ☏05.61.05.95.06, ⓦwww.grotte-de-la-vache.org; €9), a relatively rare example of an inhabited cave where you can observe hearths, embossed bones, tools and other remnants *in situ*. The area's third cave, the **Grotte de Bédeilhac** (same tour length and schedule as de la Vache, plus every Sun at 3pm; €8) above **BÉDEILHAC** village is reached by a different road out of Tarascon, the D618 towards Saurat; after 5km, the cave entrance yawns in the Soudour ridge. Inside are examples of every known technique of Paleolithic art; while not as immediately powerful as at Niaux, its diversity – including modelled stalagmites and mud reliefs of beasts – compensates.

Ax-les-Thermes

Twenty-six kilometres east of Tarascon, still on the banks of the Ariège, the spa town of **AX-LES-THERMES** is completely hemmed in by shaggy mountains, for which it's a good exploration base; Ax is the last sizeable place before the Andorran and Spanish frontiers. The town is small and agreeable enough, but there's little to see once you've wandered rue de l'École and rue de la Boucarie with their few medieval buildings in the quarter west of the N20, which (a bypass is due for completion late 2009) forms the main through road, avenue Delcassé. Above place du Breilh, the **church of St-Vincent** retains a Romanesque tower; on the *place* itself you can dangle your feet for free in the **Bassin des Ladres**, a pool of sulphurous water – one of forty local *sources* as hot as

77°C – which is all that remains of the hospital founded in 1260 by St Louis for soldiers wounded in the Crusades.

The **gare SNCF** is off avenue Delcassé on the northwest side of town. The **tourist office** (July & Aug daily 9am–1pm & 2–7pm; Sept–June 9am–noon & 2–6pm; ☏05.61.64.60.60, Ⓦwww.vallees-ax.com) is halfway through town on the north side of the main road. There's a **campsite**, *Le Malazéou* (☏05.61.64.09.14; closed Nov), on the riverbank 500m downstream from the *gare SNCF*. For indoor **accommodation**, a good budget choice at part-pedestrianized 6 place Roussel is *Hôtel Le P'tit Montagnard* (☏05.61.64.22.01, Ⓦwww.leptitmontagnard.fr; ❶–❷). Next niche up in standards is occupied by *Hôtel Restaurant Le Grillon* on rue St-Udaut, 300m southeast of place du Breilh (☏05.61.64.31.64, Ⓦwww.hotel-le-grillon.com; closed Easter to late May; ❷). But much the best deal in town is 🍴 *Hôtel Restaurant Le Chalet* at 4 avenue Turrel, opposite the *thermes* (☏05.61.64.24.31, Ⓦwww.le-chalet.fr; ❸), managed by a friendly, energetic young couple and thoroughly overhauled in 2006. All the airy rooms over two wings are unique, but share parquet floors and plasma TV, and most have balconies overlooking the river. You'll do best for full **meals** at *Le P'tit Montagnard* (menus €17–38), *Le Grillon* (weekday menu, otherwise à la carte), or at the riverside diner of *Le Chalet* (menus €18–45; closed Sun evening & Mon). For **snacks** and **drinks**, try *Crêperie L'Oiseau Bleu* behind *Le P'tit Montagnard*, or *Brasserie Le New Club* on place Roussel, which occasionally hosts live jazz.

Into the Couserans

Back at Niaux, the road continues along the valley, beneath the romantically pinnacled ruins of the **Château de Miglos** (unrestricted access), to Vicdessos and Auzat, the latter with an unsightly aluminium works. From Vicdessos, the stunning, summer-only D18 climbs the lush, largely abandoned **Vallée de Suc** to the pass at the **Port de Lers** (1517m) – from November to May only the D618, via Massat, is kept open. On the far side of the *porte*, cattle graze the alpine meadows down to the Étang de Lers. Then the road climbs again to another col overlooking the head of the beech-clogged **Vallée du Garbet**; directly south looms a high-walled crenellated cirque underlined by wedges of snow lying beneath their sheerest faces. From here west lies the **Pays de Couserans**, one of the poorest, least developed and most depopulated regions of the Pyrenees. Its villages, **Aulus-les-Bains** in particular, were once renowned for their bear-trainers, who toured the lowland towns with their performing beasts.

Aulus-les-Bains

Once in the Garbet valley, the road drops quickly west to **AULUS-LES-BAINS**, a remote spa-village surrounded by fragrant meadows and dramatic peaks; remote though it feels, Aulus has daily (Mon–Sat) bus links with St-Girons. Like other such spots, Aulus enjoyed its moment of glory and fell again into rustic somnolence, from which it is trying to resurrect itself once more. There's not much to do other than enjoy (and walk through) the scenery; the classic hike here involves heading south on a local path to the **Étang de Guzet** and then east to the **Cascade d'Ars** on a bit of the GR10, then returning to Aulus via the stream draining from it (round trip about 5hr). The 2006-renovated **thermal baths** (Ⓦwww.thermalisme-pyrenees.com) offer plunges and treatments from €11.50 (daily July–Aug 8am–1pm & 3–7pm; Easter & winter holidays 3–7pm).

For summer bike rental and information on other activities, consult the **tourist office** in allée des Thermes (daily: July & Aug 10am–1pm & 2–7pm; Sept–June 10am–noon & 2–6pm; ℡05.61.96.01.79). Two good-value **accommodation** choices are *Hôtel L'Oustalet* (℡05.61.96.00.90; closed Nov & Sun pm–Mon; ❶–❷), with the most reliable restaurant (menus €13–18.50), or studios and apartments in the converted former *Grand Hotel* opposite the spa (℡05.34.09.09.69; studio ❺, apartments ❻, weekly rates). The better of two **gîtes d'étape**, at the rear of the old casino, is *La Goulue* (℡05.61.66.53.01, ⓦwww.ariege.com/la-goulue/; May–Nov, Christmas, Feb hols; 16 places, some doubles ❶), offering meals and bike storage. *Le Couledous* (℡05.61.96.02.26; all year), 500m west along the river, is the local **campsite**.

St-Girons

With numerous SNCF buses a day from Boussens on the main Tarbes–Toulouse rail line, and onward connections to Aulus, Ustou, Massat and Seix, **ST-GIRONS** may be your first taste of the Couserans. Apart from its long reliance on cigarette-paper manufacture – there's one pulp mill at the outskirts towards Castillons, the paper plant itself looming just east in Eycheil – the most striking things about St-Girons are reddish-pink marble paving stones on many pavements. And although there are no other memorable sights, it's a pleasant town with a lively July **music festival**.

The handiest orientation point is the **Pont-Vieux**, just below picturesque rapids on the River Salat; the bridge points you into the old commercial town centre on the right bank, whose old-fashioned shops have alas largely succumbed to modern competitors. To the right, past the tiny cathedral, lies typically provincial **place des Poilus**, ringed by elegantly faded period-pieces. Beyond this square, along the river, asphalted, shady **Champ de Mars** hosts markets on the second and fourth Mondays of each month, plus every Saturday morning: herbs, honey, clothes, produce and Africana.

Buses arrive at place des Capots on the left (west) bank. The well-stocked **tourist office** is inside the Maison de Couserans (July & Aug Mon–Sat 9am–7pm, Sun 10am–1pm; Sept–June Mon–Sat 9am–noon & 2–6pm; ℡05.61.96.26.60, ⓦwww.ville-st-girons.fr), on the right bank, just downriver from the cathedral. An economical **accommodation** option is *Hôtel Restaurant La Flamme Rouge* (℡05.61.66.12.77, ⓦwww.hotel-la-flamme-rouge.com; ❷) on the west bank at 15 avenue Galliéni, with simple but cheerful rooms facing a rear garden, pool and secure parking. With transport, an excellent *chambre d'hôte* 13km south in **CASTILLON-EN-COUSERANS** is Anglo–French-run ⚘ *Le Clos Enchanté* (℡05.61.04.64.47, ⓦwww.jonathanstours.com; ❸) at no. 58 of the through road, ensconced in a rambling Napoleonic mansion whose gardens lead down to the river, with walking and snow-shoeing tours offered. For luxury, choose ⚘ *Château de Beauregard* (℡05.61.66.66.64, ⓦwww.chateaubeauregard.net; closed March) at the edge of St-Girons on the Seix road in a hilltop estate. This 2006–07-renovated nineteenth-century manor has a mix of upstairs rooms (❹) and suites (❺), a few with bathrooms in the turrets, plus a stunning on-site spa in the old barn. Their restaurant, *L'Auberge d'Antan* (eves only except Sat/Sun; closed Mon low season), offers a weekly changing, five-course menu for €35. The other recommendable local eatery, *Les Nourritures Terrestres* (closed Sat lunch, Sun; must book Fri/Sat pm on ℡05.61.96.75.40), specializing in fondue and *raclette* (allow €30), is in the far northwest of town at 17 avenue Fernand-Loubet.

St-Lizier

Historical hilltop **ST-LIZIER**, 2km downstream along the Salat, totally outclasses St-Girons in the tourism stakes: walled, arcaded, cobbled, cathedral-ed, half-timbered and fairly lifeless except in summer. Architecturally the most interesting building in town is the **Cathédrale de St-Lizier** (May–Oct daily 9am–noon & 2–7pm; Nov–April Mon–Sat 10am–noon & 2–6pm; free), with its distinctive octagonal tower posing photogenically against the mountains to the south. Inside – venue for a late-July-to-mid-August **classical music festival** – are some twelfth-century frescoes (including an improbably big-nosed Christ enthroned in a celestial Jerusalem in the conch) and a fine Romanesque cloister, also twelfth century, with an array of sculpted column capitals, mostly geometric but some with beings and beasts. The hilltop bishop's palace is home to the **Musée Départemental de l'Ariège** on the first floor (closed for works), which contains a permanent ethnographic collection devoted to the Vallée du Bethmale, not really worth it unless renovation improves the exhibits. It's worth walking up, though, for views over St-Lizier, and continuing on around the old **ramparts**.

The helpful **tourist office** is by the cathedral (same hours as at St-Girons; ☏05.61.96.77.77). There's just one place to **stay**, the *Hôtel de la Tour* (☏05.61.66.38.02; ❷–❸), in a remodelled old building down by the River Salat on rue du Pont, with pricier rooms overlooking the water. Their **restaurant** has four seafood-strong menus (€19–45), but quality varies. You'll have a consistently better feed 600m northwest, just over the municipal boundary in **LORP-SENTARAILLE**, at *La Petite Maison* (closed Mon & Tues; menus €20–46) on the main road, whose blank facade belies pleasant garden seating; the cuisine is small-portioned but highly creative.

The Pays de Sault

The Pays de Sault – a magnificent upland bounded by the rivers Ariège and Aude, and the D117 road from Foix to Quillan – marks the start of "Cathar country", approaching from the west. The first of their former strongholds encountered is **ROQUEFIXADE**, roughly 19km east of Foix on the D117 (or a bit less on the minor D9a); the ruinous (free, unenclosed) eleventh-century castle towers above the eponymous village, a thirteenth-century *bastide* with a country *gîte d'étape* (☏05.61.03.01.36; all year; 15 places) which does meals. The region's main town, Lavelanet, is a nondescript place on the banks of the River Touyre, 28km from Foix and 35km from Quillan, offering little beyond bus connections – including north to **Mirepoix**, covered on p.734 for convenience though not strictly in the *pays*.

Montségur

From Lavelanet, there's no public transport south towards Montségur, so whether you approach via Montferrier (12km) or via Bélesta and Fougax-et-Barrineuf (21km in all) is a matter of taste. The **village** of **MONTSÉGUR** straggles in long terraces at the foot of its castle-rock, a modified version of a *bastide* (the original settlement was up by the castle). Depopulated now except as a second-home venue, the place comes to life only with the influx of tourists, most of them day-trippers.

A footpath from the top of the village shortens the way up to the saddle of the hill and the **Prats des Cramats**, the field where the Cathar martyrs (see box p.733) were burnt. From here it's a steep, slick-when-wet, twenty-minute climb to the **Château de Montségur** (daily: Feb 10.30am–4pm; March 10am–5pm; April & Sept–Oct 9.30am–6pm; May–Aug 9am–7.30pm; Nov 10am–5.30pm; Dec 10.30am–4.30pm; €4), of which all that remain are the stout, now truncated curtain walls and keep. The space within is terribly cramped, and one can easily imagine the sufferings of the besieged. The walls are off-limits (a prohibition universally defied for postcard views over kilometres of forested hills and snowy peaks), though you can climb to the west keep.

There's a seasonal **tourist office** in the village (July–Sept daily 10am–1pm & 2–6pm; ☎05.61.03.03.03, ⊛www.montsegur.fr). Several **accommodation** options fill quickly in (and even out of) season; the least expensive hotel is the old-fashioned, partly en-suite *Couquet* (☎05.61.01.10.28; ❷), a rambling pension fronted by pollarded lime trees. An even homier option is ⚲ *Maison d'Hôte L'Oustal* at the north end of the village (☎05.61.02.80.70, ⓔserge .germa@orange.fr; ❷), with your extrovert hosts laying on a superb, four-course supper (€18); the four rooms, mostly triples/quads, share baths but there are extensive common areas. If Montségur is full and you've transport, consider another excellent *chambre d'hôte* 8km downhill in **FOUGAX-ET-BARRINEUF**, opposite the post office: English/Canadian-run ⚲ *Tindleys* (☎05.61.01.34.87, ⊛www.tindleys.com; ❸), with three restored rooms, a copious breakfast and supper on request. The region is deficient in stand-alone **restaurants**; one of the few to aim for is *Le Rendez Vouz* at the north edge of **MONTFERRIER** (menus from €13 at lunch, €20 at supper; closed Sun, Mon, Sat lunch).

The Gorges de la Frau

From either Montségur or Fougax-et-Barrineuf, you can take an impressive half-day walk through the **Gorges de la Frau**, emerging at Comus hamlet in the heart of the Pays de Sault. The route from Montségur initially follows the "Sentier Cathare" until linking up with the **GR107** (ex-GR7B) at Pelail in the valley of the Hers river, which has carved out the gorge. Starting from Fougax, just follow the minor D5 south along the Hers until, beyond Pelail, tarmac dwindles to a rough, steep track as you enter the *gorges* proper, where thousand-metre-high cliffs admit sunlight only at midday. The canyon bottom is densely wooded, though it is in fact a major pastoral-migratory route; each mid-October hundreds of cattle which have summered on the Sault plateau are driven down en masse. The defile ends some 3.5km before Comus, where the track broadens and the grade slackens. **COMUS** itself has a good *gîte d'étape* in the former school (☎04.68.20.33.69, ⊛www.gites-comus.com; 38 places, some doubles ❶); here you're just 2.5km shy of the D613 road between Ax-les-Thermes and Quillan, with a daily bus to the latter.

Mirepoix and Camon

Heading north from Lavelanet towards Carcassonne, it's definitely worth stopping in at **MIREPOIX**, a late thirteenth-century *bastide* built around one of the finest surviving arcaded market squares – **Les Couverts** – in the country. The square is bordered by houses dating from the thirteenth to the fifteenth centuries, and a harmonizing modern *halle* on one side, but its highlight is the medieval **Maison des Consuls** (council house), whose rafter-ends are carved with dozens of unique portrayals of animals, and monsters, and caricatures of medieval social groups and professions, as well as ethnic groups from across the world. Just south of Les Couverts, the early Gothic cathedral of **St-Maurice** is claimed to have the largest undivided nave in France, supported only by airy rib vaulting.

There's a **tourist office** in the main square (Mon–Sat 9.15am–12.15pm & 2–6pm; ☎05.61.68.83.76, ⊛www.tourisme-mirepoix.com). The best-value **accommodation** and **eating** – you often have to reserve a table – is at modest but salubrious ⋊ *Hôtel-Restaurant Le Commerce*, 20 cours Docteur-Chabaud by the cathedral (☎05.61.68.10.29, ⊛www.chez.com/lecommerce; ❷), where three generous, expertly prepared à la carte courses (*salade chèvre chaud* or *ariegeoise*, *filets de rougets* or fennel-grilled sea bass, sorbet) plus house wine won't much top €26 – menus are varied but not much cheaper. The next comfort-niche up, at no. 6 of the arcaded square, is occupied by *Maison des Consuls* (☎05.61.68.81.81, ⊛www.maisondesconsuls.com; all year; ❸), its plushly furnished units just above the carved rafters. There's a municipal **campsite** on the Limoux road (☎05.61.01.55.44; June–Sept).

Those with transport have another **accommodation** option 13km southeast in the medieval village of **CAMON**, easiest reached off the D625 Lavelanet-Mirepoix road. Here the twelfth- to fourteenth-century **fortified Benedictine abbey** at the summit of things has been transformed by English owners into *chambres d'hôtes* with a difference, ⋊ *L'Abbaye-Château de Camon* (☎05.61.60.31.23, ⊛www.chateaudecamon.com; closed early Jan to mid-March; ❼). There's a large pool, a part of the original cloister, eighteenth-century canvases in the lounge, a frescoed chapel, plus all the echoing galleries and spiral staircases you could want; the gourmet **restaurant** does supper for all comers (€38 *table d'hôte*).

Along the Aude

South of Carcassonne, the D118 and the (mostly disused) rail line both forge steadily up the twisting **Aude** valley between scrubby hills and vineyards, past **L'Abbaye de St-Hilaire** and its carved sarcophagus, river-straddling **Limoux** and sleepy **Alet-les-Bains**, before reaching **Quillan** where the topography changes. Now the route squeezes through awesome gorges either side of **Axat**

Legend:
- Sentier de Grande Randonnée (GR10)
- High Level Route (HRP)

N

10 km

0

Côte Vermeille

SPAIN

CORBIÈRES

CATHAR CASTLES

DONEZAN

MASSIF DU CANIGOU

CAPCIR

Narbonne

Narbonne

Limoux

Perpignan

Banyuls-sur-Mer
Cerbère
Port-Vendres
Collioure
Le Racou
Argelès-Plage
Argelès-sur-Mer
Elne
St-Cyprien Plage
Canet-Plage
Port-Leucate
Port-Barcarès

Musée Maillol

Forteresse de Salses
Rivesaltes

Château de Aguilar
Tuchan
Padern
Cucugnan
Château de Quéribus
Duilhac
Château de Peyrepertuse
Rouffiac-des-Corbières
Maury
St-Paul-de-Fenouillet
Gincla
Château de Puilaurens
Gorges de Galamus

Tautavel

River Agly
River Agly
River Têt
River Têt
River Tech
River Tech
River Aude
River Aude

Col du Perthus

Girona & Barcelona

Barcelona

Barcelona

Céret
PONT DU DIABLE
D115
Amélie-les-Bains
Arles-sur-Tech
La Preste
Prats-de-Mollo
Col d'Ares
Col Pregon

Roc de Frausa (1450m)

Boule-d'Amont
La Trinité
St-Marsal
Boulternère
Prieuré-de-Serrabona
Ille-sur-Têt

St-Michel-de-Cuixà
Eus
Cornellà-de-Conflent
Prades
Villefranche-de-Conflent
Molitg-les-Bains
St-Martin-du-Canigou
Vernet-les-Bains
Chalet des Cortalets
Pic du Canigou (2784m)
Grand Marailles
Gorges de la Fou

Gorges de la Carança
Ras de la Carança
St-Thomas
Thuès-entre-Valls
Pic de la Géant (2882m)
Roc Colom (2507m)
Col de Pailhères

Mosset
Sournia

Gorges de St-Georges
Gorges de l'Aude
Grotte de l'Aguzou
Axat
Escouloubre-les-Bains
La Glèbe (2024m)
Madres (2469m)
Pic de la Pelade (2370m)
Puig d'Escoutou (2292m)

Défilé de Pierre-Lys
Pont d'Alès
Quillan

Château d'Usson
Mijanès
Quérigut
Le Roc Blanc (2542m)
Pic de Bers (2532m)
Pic (2810m)
Forges d'Orlu
Pic Col Rouge (2835m)
Pic Carlit (2921m)
Etang de Lanoux
Lac des Bouillouses

Formiguères
Les Angles
Mont-Louis
Font-Romeu
Odello
Eyne
Saillagouse
Bourg-Madame
Llívia
Puigcerdà
Latour-de-Carol
Dorres
Ur
Enveitg

Belcaire
Espezel
Comus
Montaillou
Col de Pailhères (2132m)

Ax-les-Thermes
Montségur

D618
D117
D117
D117
D116
N116
N116
N114
N152
9
6N
6N
A9

735

before emerging near the river's headwaters on the Capcir plateau, east of the Carlit massif. It's a magnificent drive or slightly hair-raising cycle-ride up to isolated **Quérigut**, then easier going on to **Formiguères**.

Limoux and L'Abbaye de St-Hilaire

The first stop, 24km south of Carcassonne, **LIMOUX** is served regularly by **SNCF buses**; those arriving by car will find free **parking** on the riverbanks by the picturesque old bridge. The town straddles the Aude, for much of the year a powerful brownish-green flood of snowmelt. Life revolves around pretty **place de la République** in the heart of the old town, with its Friday market, brasseries and cafés, and the nineteenth-century **promenade du Tivoli**, in effect a bypass road on the west. Previously known for its wool and leather-tanning trades, Limoux's current claim to fame is the excellent regional sparkling wine, Blanquette de Limoux, cheaper than champagne, and easiest gotten from the Aimery-Sieur d'Arques Co-operative in avenue du Mauzac (daily 9am–noon & 2.30–7pm).

Blanquette was supposedly invented 11km northeast by minor road in 1531 at the **Abbaye de St-Hilaire**, which dominates the centre of the eponymous village. The Gothic cloister (always open) doubles as the village square, but the main attraction is the so-called **sarcophagus** in the south chapel of the thirteenth-century cathedral (daily: Nov–March 10am–noon & 2–5pm; April–June & Sept-Oct, same hours, closes 6pm; July–Aug 10am–7pm; €4). This is one of the masterpieces of the mysterious **Maître de Cabestany**, an itinerant sculptor whose work – found across the the eastern Pyrenees on both sides of the border – is distinguished by the elongated fingers, pleated clothing and cat-like, almond-eyed faces of the human figures. Here the arrest of evangelizing **St Sernin** (Saturnin), patron of Toulouse, his martyrdom through dragging by a bull, and burial by female disciples is portrayed on three intricately carved side panels of what's actually a twelfth-century marble reliquary too small to contain a corpse.

Limoux's **tourist office** is at promenade du Tivoli 32 (July–Aug daily 9am–7pm; Sept–June Mon–Fri 9am–noon & 2–6pm, Sat–Sun 10am–noon & 2–5pm; T04.68.31.11.82). The better value of two **hotel** choices is *Des Arcades*, north of St-Martin church at 96 rue St-Martin (T04.68.31.02.57; closed Dec 15 to Jan 1 & Wed; ❷). The municipal **campsite** (T04.68.31.13.63; mid-May to Oct) is on the east bank of the river, south of the old bridge. The best independent **restaurant** is *Maison de la Blanquette*, at 46bis promenade du Tivoli, which purveys regional dishes and wines (closed Tues; menus from €17.50; T04.68.31.01.63), more interesting than the merely sustaining fare (menus from €16) in *Des Arcades'* time-warped diner overlooking St-Martin church.

Alet-les-Bains, Arques and Rennes-le-Château

South of Limoux, the next place to halt is the thermal resort of **ALET-LES-BAINS**; the spa on the outskirts is incidental to the lovely half-timbered houses and arcaded *place* inside the fortifications. There's also a ruined Romanesque abbey, next to the tourist office which has the keys (daily: 10am–noon & 2.30–6pm), and an excellent **hotel** partly occupying the old bishop's palace, the *Hostellerie de l'Évêché* (T04.68.69.90.25, ⓦwww.hotel-eveche.com; April–Oct; ❸), by the abbey in its own vast park-like grounds. Their elegant **restaurant** (the only one here) has three menus (€26–42).

With transport, it's worth taking a detour left south of Alet at Couiza for 10km to twelfth-century **ARQUES** castle (closed Jan–Feb & Nov 15 to Dec 31; €5), just west of the eponymous village (one restaurant, one *chambre d'hôte*), perhaps the most domesticated of the Cathar castles (see p.738). Most of the curtain wall, except for the southwest tower, is gone, but the place's glory is its thirteenth-century central **donjon**, with four round corner *bartizans* (turrets), one containing the spiral staircase giving access to four upper storeys – and fine views to a wooded ridge.

Another road, the D52, climbs 4.5km southeast out of Couiza towards mountaintop **RENNES-LE-CHÂTEAU**. The views alone repay the effort, but the main reason for the jaunt is the mysterious **parish church** run by Abbé Bérenguer Saunière from 1885 until 1910, when he was defrocked by the bishop of Carcassonne for failing to explain how he financed his comfortable lifestyle and lavish redecoration of the fifteenth-century church (free admission). This is supposedly full of veiled symbols and codes, which – say some (others will see only lavish kitsch) – indicate that he had discovered Solomon's lost treasure, brought here by the Visigoths in the fifth century. This and other theories are explored in the **Musée Presbytère de l'Abbé** (daily: July–Aug 10am–6pm; March–June & Sept–Oct 10am–1pm & 2–5pm; Nov 1–Jan 10 Sat–Sun & holidays 2–4pm; @www.rennes-le-chateau.fr; €4.25) comprising Saunière's Villa Béthania – where he lived openly with his mistress Marie Denardaud – and its gardens.

Quillan and Axat

Back on the D118, pleasant little **QUILLAN**, 28km upstream from Limoux, is a useful staging post en route south into the mountains or east to the Cathar castles (see p.738). The only monument is the ruined castle, burnt by the Huguenots in 1575 and partly dismantled in the eighteenth century. The **gare SNCF** and **gare routière** sit together on the main bypass road, while the **tourist office** (June–Sept Mon–Sat 8am–noon & 2–7pm, Sun 9am–noon; Oct–May Mon–Fri 9am–noon & 2–6pm, Sat 9am–1pm; ☎04.68.20.07.78) stands opposite in the former Art Deco public baths. **Accommodation** options on the same (noisy) boulevard are the *Canal* at no. 36 (☎04.68.20.08.62; ❷) and the *Cartier* at no. 31 (☎04.68.20.05.14, @www.hotelcartier.com; ❷–❸; closed Jan 15 to Feb). A good independent **restaurant** is *Pizzeria des Platanes* at 2 avenue Pasteur, towards the river by the cinema, with seating outdoors under the namesake trees. The *Sapinette* **campsite** is at 21 rue René-Delpech (☎04.68.20.13.52; April–Oct).

Beyond Quillan, the road heads southeast 11km, through the narrow **Défilé de Pierre-Lys**, to **Pont d'Aliès**, where there's another campsite and a clutch of **river-rafting** outfitters, the Aude being a major venue for watersports. Just 1km south of the *pont* is **AXAT**, covering both banks of the river; you can **eat** (not Sun pm) at *Auberge La Petite Ourse*, no. 88 on the main highway, and **stay** at basic *Hôtel Axat* at no. 101 (☎04.68.20.93.76; ❷). Otherwise, Axat is the westerly terminus of the Train du Pays Cathare et du Fenouillèdes (see p.739), and the last town of any size before entering the rocky canyons to the south.

The Aude gorges, the Donezan and the Capcir

On its first 20km south of Axat, the D618 threads hazardously through two consecutive canyon systems: the **Gorges de St-Georges** and the **Gorges de l'Aude**. Beyond the second set of narrows is a magnificent cave, the **Grotte**

de l'Aguzou. It's expensive to visit (contact guide Philippe Moreno via Ⓦwww.grotte-aguzou.com; €60 full day, bring your own picnic), but – accoutred like a pro – as near to real speleology as you can get without being a caver. The closest indoor **accommodation** is 8km up the Aude at **ESCOU-LOUBRE-LES-BAINS**, where *Chambre d'Hôte Maison Roquelaure* (Ⓣ04.68.20.47.29, Ⓦwww.maison-roquelaure.com; ❶), in the old thermal establishment, makes evening meals for hikers and cyclists, and still has a spring-fed spa pool on the ground floor.

Upstream, the road divides just above abandoned Usson-les-Bains (the easterly fork goes to Escouloubre-les-Bains). On a shaggy bluff between the arms of the fork, dwarfed in turn by crags either side, stands forlornly ruined **Château d'Usson** (Feb & Easter hols, Sept 1–21 2–6pm, July–Aug daily 10am–1pm & 3–7pm; €4), allegedly the hiding place of the "Cathar treasure" after the siege of Montségur (see box, p.733). This is the gateway to the **Donezan** region, beautifully forested but the most neglected and depopulated corner of the Ariège. Passing the castle's base, the westerly road winds up to the attractive tiered houses of **MIJANÈS** – where there's a good **hotel–restaurant**, the *Relais de Pailhères* (Ⓣ04.68.20.46.97; ❷), the only local facility comparable in quality to *Maison Roquelaure*.

From Mijanès a road heads 8km up-valley to **QUÉRIGUT**, last settlement before the border with Roussillon and end of the infrequent summer bus line. The high, chilly village is guarded by the ruined **Château de Donezan**, last refuge of Cathars who held out for eleven years after the fall of Montségur. There's a single, central, skier/cyclist-friendly **hotel–restaurant**, *Auberge du Donezan* (Ⓣ04.68.20.42.40, Ⓦwww.auberge-du-donezan.com; ❷). Beyond Quérigut, it's 14km south through forest and meadowland on the D16 to Formiguères, chief village of the **Capcir** plateau, and as much again to Mont-Louis in the Cerdagne, with more facilities and public transport. **FORMIGUÈRES** is a pleasant upland village with a central **hotel–restaurant**, the *Picheyre*, by the church (Ⓣ04.68.04.40.07; closed April–May & Nov–Christmas; ❸).

The Cathar castles

Romantic and ruined, the medieval fortresses which pepper the hills between Quillan and Perpignan have become known as the **Cathar castles**, though many were built either before or after the Cathar era. Roussillon, Languedoc and the eastern Ariège was this twelfth-century sect's power-base; their name derives from the Greek word for "pure", *katharon*, as they abhorred the materialism and worldly power of the established Church, were initially pacifist and denied the validity of feudal vows or allegiances. While the Cathars probably never accounted for more than ten percent of the population, they included many members of the nobility and mercantile classes, which alarmed the powers that were.

Once disputational persuasion by the ecclesiastical hierarchy proved fruitless, Pope Innocent III anathemized the Cathars as heretics in 1208 and persuaded the French king to mount the first of many "Albigensian" crusades, so called after Albi, a Cathar stronghold. Predatory northern nobles, led for a decade by the notoriously cruel Simon de Montfort, descended on the area with their forces, besieging and sacking towns, massacring Cathar and Catholic civilians alike, laying waste or seizing the lands of local counts. The effect of this brutality was to unite both the Cathars and their Catholic neighbours in southern solidarity against the barbarous north. Though military defeat became inevitable with the capitulation of Toulouse in 1229 and the fall of Montségur (see box, p.733) in 1244, it took the informers and torturers of the Holy Inquisition another 180 years to root out Catharism completely.

The best of the castles stud the arid, herb-scented hills of the **Corbières** which separate Roussillon from Languedoc. **Walking** is the most direct way to experience them; the **GR36**, crossing from Carcassonne to St-Paul-de-Fenouillet, and the **Sentier Cathare**, traversing east to west from Port-la-Nouvelle to Foix, together cover most of the sites. The Sentier Cathare is described in *Le Sentier Cathare* Topo-guide (Rando Éditions).

Without transport or walking boots, the best way to tackle the castles is from the south, as the most spectacular ones are close to the **Quillan–Perpignan road**. This route is served by bus, but a better option is the narrow-gauge **Train du Pays Cathare et du Fenouillèdes** (℡04.68.59.96.18, Ⓦwww .tpcf.fr), which runs from Rivesaltes or Espira de Agly, just north of Perpignan, to Axat, stopping at the main towns along the way. The service (sometimes only St-Paul-de-Fenouillet to Axat) runs Sun–Wed in May, June, September and October, daily in July & August (adult fare €11–18 depending on direction and distance).

Puilaurens

The westernmost of the Fenouillèdes Cathar castles can be reached by road from Quillan or rail from Axat, from the Lapradelle station of the seasonal train noted above. Lapradelle (food and accommodation options), 6km east of Axat, is in turn 2km north of the turnings for dramatically sited **Château de Puilaurens** (daily: April–June & Sept 10am–6pm; July & Aug 9am–8pm; Oct 10am–5pm; Feb–March & Nov 1–15 Sat–Sun & holidays 10am–5pm; closed Nov 16 to Jan 31; €3.50). You can either drive up a 1500-metre side road starting 500m south of Puilaurens hamlet, or there's a shorter and fairly gentle path up from the hamlet through forest alive with cuckoos. The castle perches atop a hill at 700m, its fine crenellated walls sprouting organically from the rock outcrops. Originally the site of a Visigothic citadel, it was fortified to its present extent in the early thirteenth century, when it passed from the king of France to the count of Roussillon, and then to the king of Aragón. It sheltered many Cathars up to 1256, when Chabert de Barbera, the region's *de facto* ruler, was captured and forced to hand over this citadel and Quéribus further east to secure his release. The castle remained strategically important – being close to the Spanish border – until 1659, when France annexed Roussillon and the frontier was pushed south. Highlights of a visit are the **west donjon** and **southeast postern gate**, where you're allowed briefly on the curtain wall for views, and the **Tour de la Dame Blanche**, with a rib-vaulted ceiling.

▲ Château de Puilaurens

Quéribus, Cucugnan and Peyrepertuse

The **Château de Quéribus** (daily: Feb 10am–5.30pm; March 10am–6pm; Nov–Dec 10am–5pm; April–June & Sept 9.30am–7pm; July–Aug daily 9am–8pm; Oct 10am–6.30pm; closed most Jan; €5), 30km further east towards Perpignan, overlooks the vine-ringed village of Cucugnan (see below) from the ridge that marked the French–Spanish border until 1659. The history of Quéribus is similar to that of Puilaurens, holding out until 1255 or 1256; not reduced by siege, its role as a Cathar sanctuary ended with the capture of the luckless Chabert, though the garrison escaped to Spain.

Spectacularly situated above the Grau de Maury pass 6km north of the Quillan–Perpignan road, the castle balances on a storm-battered rock pinnacle above sheer cliffs – access is forbidden in bad weather. Because of the cramped topography, the space within the walls is stepped in terraces, linked by a single stairway and dominated by the polygonal keep. High point, in all senses, is the so-called **Salle du Pilier**, whose vaulted ceiling is supported by a graceful pillar sprouting a canopy of intersecting ribs. A spiral staircase leads to the roof terrace and fantastic views (best outside summer) in every direction, including Canigou, the Mediterranean and northwest to the next Cathar castle, Peyrepertuse.

A popular base for visiting Quéribus (and Peyrepertuse) is **CUCUGNAN**, in the valley roughly halfway between the two, its popularity such that in season you must **park** vehicles at the village outskirts. There's ample **accommodation** in *chambres d'hôtes* and hotels, the latter including central *Auberge du Vigneron* at 2 rue Achille-Mir (☏04.68.45.03.00; ❸; restaurant, menus from €22, closed Mon, also Nov 11–March 15) and the *Auberge de Cucugnan* (☏04.68.45.40.84 Ⓔ contact@auberge-cucugnan.com; closed Thur & Jan–March; ❸), with smallish rooms but a pleasant rear courtyard, and a very competent restaurant (menus from €18). Just downhill, the right transept of the **church** contains a very rare polychrome-and-gilt-wood statue, about 50cm high, of a **pregnant Virgin Mary**.

If you only have time for one of the Cathar castles, make it the **Château de Peyrepertuse** (daily: Feb, March & Nov to early Jan 10am–5pm; April–June & Sept 10am–7pm; July–Aug 9am–8pm; Oct daily 10am–6pm; closed 3 weeks in

Jan; €5), not only for the unbeatable site and stunning views, but also because it's unusually well preserved. The castle was obtained by treaty with the Kingdom of Aragón in 1258, and most of the existing fortifications were built afterwards, staying in use until 1789. The 3.5-km access road starts in Duilhac village or, alternatively, you can walk up from Rouffiac des Corbières village to the north via the GR36 – a tough, hot climb of over an hour. Either way the effort is rewarded, for Peyrepertuse is among the most awe-inspiring castles anywhere, draped the length of a jagged rock-spine with sheer drops at most points. Access is banned during fierce summer thunderstorms, when (as at Quéribus) the ridge makes an ideal lightning target.

Tickets are sold by the southerly car park, but you then walk fifteen minutes through thickets of box to the entrance on the north side. The bulkiest fortifications enclose the lower, eastern end of the ridge, with a **keep** and **barbican** controlling the main gate. Things get increasingly airier as you progress west along the ridge past and through various cisterns, chapels and bastions, culminating in a **stairway** of over a hundred steps carved into the living rock, which leads to a keep, tower and the **chapel of San Jordi** at the summit.

Rouffiac, Gorges de Galamus and Aguilar

In sleepy **ROUFFIAC-DES-CORBIÈRES**, 3km north, there's a **hotel**, the *Auberge de Peyrepertuse* (☏04.68.45.40.40; closed Dec 15 to Feb 1, plus Wed; ❷), with well-appointed en-suite rooms and a restaurant (menus from €17) very well attended at weekends despite small portions. The Sentier Cathare heads west-southwest from here towards Puilaurens, or generally east via the castles of Quéribus, Padern and Aguilar.

Moving on from Rouffiac by car or bike, you can return to St-Paul-de-Fenouillet, initially via the villages of Soulatgé and Cubières-sur-Cinoble, through the **Gorges de Galamus**, a short but impressive defile worn through the limestone ridge by the River Agly. From Cubières, a perilously narrow corniche road threads the gorge, with a limited number of turnouts and car parks, from one of which a path leads down ten minutes to the impressive cave-cleft **Ermitage de St-Antoine** (daily 10am–6pm) on the east flank of the ravine. This is a popular canyoning venue, though most just swim in river-pools below the *ermitage*.

Alternatively, the drive, cycle or hike east from Rouffiac offers, just east of Tuchan overlooking the Côtes de Roussillon-Villages wine *domaine*, the isolated, thirteenth-century **Château d'Aguilar** (daily: in theory April to Nov 12, 11am–5/7pm; €3.50, in practice unrestricted access). Perched at the end of a steep, one-lane drive, its hexagonal curtain wall shelters a keep with the chatelain's lodge on the top floor.

Roussillon

The area comprising the eastern fringe of the Pyrenees and the lowlands down to the Mediterranean is known as **Roussillon**, or **French Catalonia**. Catalan power first emerged in the tenth century under the independent counts of Barcelona, who then became kings of Aragón as well in 1163. They attempted to unify with Occitania under the counts of Toulouse, but that ended unhappily with the death of Pere II of Aragón at the battle of Muret in 1213, fighting with Raymond VI of Toulouse against anti-Cathar crusader Simon de Montfort. The Catalan zenith was reached during the thirteenth and fourteenth centuries, when the Franco–Catalan frontier traced the Corbières hills north of Perpignan. But Jaume I of Aragón and

> ## Intersite pass
>
> As with Aude's Passeport (see p.739), there's an **Intersite Pass** scheme for Roussillon, with the same rules and discounts. The 44 participating attractions include the abbeys of St-Martin-du-Canigou and St-Michel-de-Cuixà, the Palais des Rois de Majorque, the art museum in Céret and the cloister at Elne.

Valencia made the mistake of dividing his kingdom between his two sons at his death in 1276: the Roussillonais part became the kingdom of Mallorca under Jaume II with its mainland capital at Perpignan, but, coveted by the rival brother, King Pere III of Aragón, it immediately allied itself with the French kings, who saw this as a splendid opportunity to expand their southern territories, thus ensuring continuous see-saw battles and annexations that ended only with the Treaty of the Pyrenees, negotiated by Louis XIV and the Spanish king in 1659.

After the treaty, the French began a ruthless process of Frenchification, more successful in Perpignan where the bourgeoisie identified their commercial interests with a central power. The Pyrenean hinterland, however, was largely unaffected until the late nineteenth century, when the collapse of traditional agriculture, the introduction of compulsory education and phylloxera-devastated vineyards combined to depopulate the mountains – a continuing process.

Although there's no real separatist impetus among French Catalans today, their sense of identity remains strong: the language is very much alive (not least in bilingual place-signage), and their red-and-yellow flag is ubiquitous. The **Pic du Canigou**, which completely dominates Roussillon despite its modest (2784m) elevation, shines as a powerful beacon of Catalan nationalism, attracting hordes of Catalans from across the border to celebrate St John's Eve (June 23–24). At its feet the little town of **Prades**, place of exile from Franco's Spain of cellist Pablo (Pau) Casals, served as a focus of Catalan resistance until 1975.

Most of the region's attractions are easily reached by public transport from Roussillon's capital, **Perpignan**. The coast and foothills between it and the Spanish frontier are beautiful, especially at **Collioure**, though predictably crowded and in most places overdeveloped. You'll find the finest spots in the **Tech** and **Têt valleys** which slice southwest towards the high peaks, among them the Romanesque monasteries of **Serrabona**, **St-Michel-de-Cuixà** and **St-Martin-du-Canigou**, the world-class modern art museum at **Céret** and **Mont Canigou** itself, lapped by foothill orchards of peaches and cherries.

Perpignan

This far south, climate and geography alone would ensure a palpable Spanish influence. Moreover, a good part of **PERPIGNAN**'s population is of Spanish origin – refugees from the Civil War and their descendants. The southern influence is further augmented by a substantial contingent of North Africans, including both Arabs and white French settlers repatriated after Algerian independence in 1962.

Perpignan's glory days were the late thirteenth and early fourteenth centuries, when the kings of Mallorca held court here, and most of its historical interest derives from this period. Yet there are surprisingly few memorable monuments, and the city won't necessarily make a good first impression; street life ranges from the lively – flamenco buskers and such – to downright dirty and shabby, with numerous boarded-up business premises around the corner from chic boutiques. Few will want to stay more than a day or two; with your own transport, you may prefer to base yourself somewhere in the surrounding area.

Arrival, information and accommodation

From the **airport** at Rivesaltes, 6km north (no-frills flights from UK), there are up to six daily shuttle buses into town (€5), which call at the **gare routière** just off avenue Général-Leclerc, near the Pont Arago; a taxi will cost about three times as much. The **gare SNCF** is on avenue Général-de-Gaulle in the west of town. Both stations are a fifteen-minute walk from the **municipal tourist office** in the Palais des Congrès at the end of boulevard Wilson (mid-June to mid-Sept Mon–Sat 9am–7pm, Sun 10am–4pm; rest of year Mon–Sat 9am–6pm, Sun 9am–noon; ☎04.68.66.30.30, ⓦwww.perpignantourisme.com).

There's cheap **accommodation** near the *gare SNCF*, the best standard being the *Hôtel Terminus*, 2 avenue Général-de-Gaulle (☎04.68.34.32.54, ⓕ04.68.35.48.16; ❷), right opposite the station. In the town centre, best value is offered by *Hôtel de la Loge* at 1 Fabriques d'en Nabot (☎04.68.34.41.02,

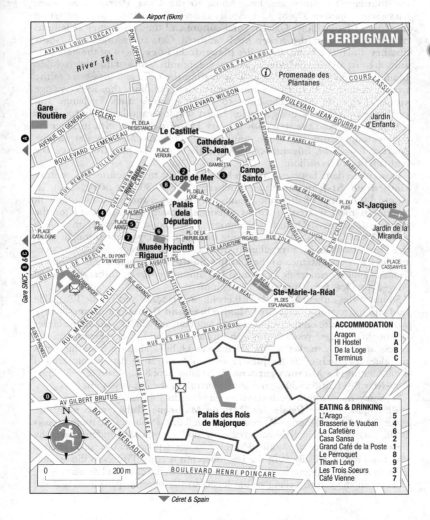

▲ Airport (6km)

PERPIGNAN

Promenade des Plantanes

Gare Routière

Le Castillet

Cathédrale St-Jean

Campo Santo

Loge de Mer

Palais dela Députation

Musée Hyacinth Rigaud

Ste-Marie-la-Réal

St-Jacques

Jardin de la Miranda

Palais des Rois de Majorque

ACCOMMODATION	
Aragon	D
HI Hostel	A
De la Loge	B
Terminus	C

EATING & DRINKING	
L'Arago	5
Brasserie le Vauban	4
La Cafetière	6
Casa Sansa	2
Grand Café de la Poste	1
Le Perroquet	8
Thanh Long	9
Les Trois Soeurs	3
Café Vienne	7

0   200 m

BOULEVARD HENRI POINCARE

▼ Céret & Spain

ⓦwww.hoteldelaloge.fr; ❸), a well-renovated medieval mansion with a central courtyard, on a quiet alley. A bit out of the way, but handy for the Palais des Rois de Majorque, is two-star *Hôtel d'Aragon* at 17 avenue Gilbert Brutus (ⓣ04.68.54.04.46, ⓦwww.aragon-hotel.com; ❸) with non-fusty rooms, wi-fi signal and parking just conceivable nearby. In addition, there is a welcoming, if somewhat traffic-noisy, **HI hostel** (ⓣ04.68.34.63.32, ⓦwww.fuaj.net /homepage/perpignan/; closed Nov 15 to March 18), behind the Parc de la Pépinière by Pont Arago (entrance from avenue de Grande-Bretagne), and the closer of two **campsites**, *La Garrigole* (ⓣ04.68.54.66.10), on rue Maurice-Lévy (take bus #19), 5km northwest.

The City

The best place to begin explorations is at **Le Castillet**, built as a gateway in the fourteenth century and now home to the **Casa Païral** (Wed–Mon: May–Sept 10am–6.30pm; Oct–April 11am–5.30pm; €4), an interesting museum of Roussillon's Catalan rural culture and the anti-French rebellions of 1661–74, when the tower held captured Catalan insurgents. A short distance down rue Louis-Blanc lies **place de la Loge**, focus of the pedestrianized heart of the old town, with a voluptuous Venus statue by Aristide Maillol (see p.747) in the centre. Dominating the cafés and brasseries of the narrow square is Perpignan's most interesting building, the 1397-vintage Gothic **Loge de Mer**. Designed to hold the city's stock exchange and maritime court, it features gargoyles, lancet windows and lacy balustrades up top. Adjacent stand the sixteenth-century **Hôtel de Ville**, with its magnificent wrought-iron gates and another Maillol (*La Méditerranée*) in the courtyard, and the fifteenth-century **Palais de la Députation**, once the parliament of Roussillon.

From place de la Loge, rue St-Jean leads northeast to the fourteenth-century **Cathédrale St-Jean** on place Gambetta (daily 7.30am–6.30pm; free), its external walls built of alternating bands of river stones and brick. The dimly lit interior is most interesting for its elaborate Catalan altarpieces and for the fourteenth-century, Rhenish polychrome Crucifixion known as the *Dévôt Christ*; it's in the fifth side chapel along the north wall, probably brought from the Low Countries by a travelling merchant. Out of the side door, a few steps on the left is the entrance to the **Campo Santo**, a vast enclosure that's one of France's oldest cemeteries, now used for summer concerts (otherwise closed May–Sept; Oct–April Tues–Sun 11am–5pm).

South of the cathedral, rue de la Révolution-Française and rue de l'Anguille lead into the teeming, dilapidated **Maghrebian and Romany quarters**, where women congregate on the secluded inner lanes but are seldom seen on the busier thoroughfares. Here you'll find North African shops and cafés, especially on rue Llucia, and a daily market on place Cassanyes. Uphill and north from this stands the elegant church of **St-Jacques** (Tues–Sun 11am–5pm) dating from around 1200, abutting **La Miranda gardens** (daily: June–Sept 8–11.45am & 2–5.45pm; Oct–May 8–11am & 3.30–6pm), atop a section of the old city walls.

A twenty-minute walk southwest through place des Esplanades brings you to the main entrance of the **Palais des Rois de Majorque** (daily: June–Sept 10am–6pm; Oct–May 9am–5pm; €4), crowning the hill that dominates the southern part of the old town. Although Vauban's walls surround it now, and it's suffered generally from ongoing military use until 1946, the two-storey palace and its partly arcaded courtyard date originally from the late thirteenth century. Thanks to the Spanish influence, there's a finesse to the Gothic-Moorish architecture and detailing – for instance in the carved ceiling of the loggia to the queen's apartments, and the

Islamic-influenced fresco fragments in the chapel – that you don't often find in heavier northern styles. There are frequent worthwhile temporary exhibits in the former king's apartments.

Finally, at 16 rue de l'Ange near place Arago, you'll find the **Musée Hyacinth Rigaud** (Wed–Mon: May–Sept noon–7pm; Oct–April 11am–5.30pm; €4). The collection is largely devoted to Catalan painters, most notably Minorcan-born **Pierre Daura** (1896–1976), a Republican and godson of Pablo Casals long exiled in the US, his sympathies evident in two symbolic canvases of the post-civil-war Republican refugee camps at nearby Argelès. One room has a few Maillol sketches and statues, and three portraits by Picasso.

Eating, drinking and entertainment

Full-service **restaurants** are thin on the ground in central Perpignan. A budget choice is popular *Le Perroquet*, near the station at 1 avenue de Gaulle, with a good selection of reasonably priced Catalan dishes (closed Wed Sept–April). For something smarter, head for *Casa Sansa*, 3 rue Fabriques-Couvertes, founded in 1846 and serving traditional Catalan cuisine amid bullfight posters and old photos; there's a seafood annexe adjacent. In the back streets at rue des Agustins 18, there's pretty authentic Vietnamese fare at *Thanh Long* from €8 for the *formule*.

You'll have better luck with **brasserie** fare or at **cafés**. Favourites include *L'Arago* (open until late), with big portions, and *Café Vienne*, on palm-shaded place Arago, or the Art Deco *Brasserie le Vauban* across the River Basse at 29 quai Vauban. On place Verdun, *Grand Café de la Poste* is great for people-watching, especially on summer evenings when the Catalan *sardana* dance might be spontaneously performed here. The best cup of coffee (both flavoured and premium grade) is obtainable right opposite the Hyacinth Rigaud museum at no. 17, at tiny *La Cafétière*.

The most reliable central **bar** is *Les Trois Sœurs*, 2 rue Fontfroide, with novelty acts and theme evenings (Wed–Sun). There's also **live street theatre**, **dance and music** in the city centre during the July Estivales. The Palais des Rois de Majorque's parkland is the venue for the Trobades festival (June 14–29), plus other events like the October-long Jazzèbre festival. But Perpignan's best-known spectacle is **La Procession de la Sanch**, the Good Friday procession of red-hooded penitents that goes from the church of St-Jacques to the cathedral between 3 and 5pm.

Around Perpignan: Salses to Elne

CANET-PLAGE, 12km east, is the closest place to Perpignan for a Mediterranean dip, although there's nothing to recommend the place except that its beach is wide and sandy and the sea is wet; take a CTP bus #1 from place Catalogne. Perhaps more interesting, 15km north and served by regular trains, is the late-fifteenth-century **Forteresse de Salses** (daily: June–Sept 9.30am–7pm; Oct–May 10am–12.15pm & 2–5pm; €6.50). This was one of the first forts to be designed with a ground-hugging profile to protect it from artillery fire, though higher up it exhibits the traits of a pre-cannon-age château.

Another place, with not much to see but interesting anthropologically, is vine-girt **TAUTAVEL**, 25km northwest off the St-Paul-de-Fenouillet road. In 1971 the remains of the oldest known European human being – dated to around 450,000 BC – were discovered in the nearby Caune d'Arago cave, and a reconstruction of the skull and other cave finds are displayed in the village's **Musée de la Préhistoire** (daily: April–June & Sept 10am–12.30pm & 2–6pm; July–Aug 10am–7pm; Oct–March 10am–12pm & 2–5pm; Ⓦ www.tautavel.com; €7).

Fourteen kilometres southeast of Perpignan, on the way to the Côte Vermeille resorts, lies **ELNE**. This small town once had the honour of seeing Hannibal camp below its walls en route to Rome, and used to be the capital of Roussillon. It was only eclipsed by Perpignan when the latter became the seat of the kings of Mallorca; Elne's decline accelerated in 1602 when the bishopric moved to Perpignan. Today, it's worth a stop for its fortified, partially Romanesque **cathedral of Ste-Eulalie** and extremely beautiful **cloister** (daily: April–May 9.30am–5.45pm; June–Sept 9.30am–6.45pm; Oct 9.30am–12.15pm & 2–5.45pm; Nov–March 9.30am–11.45pm & 2–4.45pm; €5). The four colonnades of the cloister ably demonstrate a gradual transition from Romanesque to Gothic styles, clockwise from the south bay (twelfth century) to the east bay (fourteenth), intricately carved with biblical and secular scenes, plus mythical creatures. It's the best possible introduction to Roussillon Romanesque, especially if you're planning to visit Serrabona and St-Michel-de-Cuixà further west. Around the cathedral are the strollable lanes of the old town, and a certain amount of **accommodation**, including pricey, 2006-renovated *Hôtel Restaurant Cara-Sol* at 10 boulevard Illibéris (☎04.68.22.10.42, ⓦwww.hotelcarasol .com; ❺); their somewhat more reasonable (menus €15–36), competent restaurant has seating with an unbeatable view on the ramparts outside.

The Côte Vermeille

The Côte Vermeille, where the Pyrenees meet the sea, is the last patch of French shoreline before Spain, its seaside villages once so remote that the Fauvist painters of the early 1900s hid out here. Mass tourism has ended any sense of exclusivity or unspoiltness, but in low season at least they remain attractive, and well served by public transport. **Argelès-Plage** is the first resort beyond Elne, but you're best off bypassing it in favour of the ports of **Collioure** and **Banyuls-sur-Mer**.

Collioure

Eleven kilometres southeast of Elne, **COLLIOURE** is achingly picturesque – and achingly expensive. Palm trees line the curving main beach of **Port d'Avall**, while slopes of vines and olives rise to ridges crowned with ruined forts and watchtowers. Its setting and monuments inspired Henri Matisse and André Derain to embark in 1905 on their explosive Fauvist colour experiments. Collioure is dominated by its twelfth-century **Château-Royal** (daily: June–Sept 10am–6/7pm; Oct–May 9am–5pm; €4), founded by the Templars and subject to later alterations by the kings of Mallorca and Aragón, and again after the Treaty of the Pyrenees gave Collioure to France. The mediocre permanent "collection" inside scarcely merits the entrance fee; attend instead a concert in the courtyard. Collioure's other landmark is the distinctive round belfry of the seventeenth-century **church of Notre-Dame-des-Anges** (daily 9am–noon & 2–6pm), formerly the harbour lighthouse. Behind it two small **beaches** (the northerly one naturist) are divided by a causeway leading to the **chapel of St-Vincent**, built on a former islet, while west from here a concrete path follows the rocky shore to the bay of **Le Racou**.

Just north of the château lies the **old harbour**, still home to a bare handful of brightly painted lateen-rigged fishing boats – now more likely used as pleasure craft – all that remains of Collioure's traditional fleet. Beyond this, the stone houses and sloping lanes of the old **Mouré** quarter are the main focus of interest. The **tourist office** is here on place de 18-Juin (July & Aug daily 9am–8pm; Sept–June Tues–Sat 9am–noon & 2–6.30pm; ☎04.68.82.15.47, ⓦwww.collioure.com).

The most central place to **stay** is atmospheric *Hostellerie des Templiers* (☎04.68.98.31.10, ⓦwww.hotel-templiers.com; closed parts Nov–Feb; ❸ annexes, ❺ main bldg) at 12 avenue Camille-Pelletan, crammed with artwork and housing overflow in various annexes. With a car (central **parking** is nightmarish) and/or desire for a sea view, opt instead for *Hôtel Triton*, Port d'Avall beach (☎04.68.98.39.39, Ⓦ www.hotel-triton-collioure.com; all year; ❷) or remoter *Hôtel Caranques* (☎04.68.82.06.68, Ⓦ www.les-caranque.com; Easter–Oct; ❹) at the east side of the bay on route de Port-Vendres, very friendly and with direct access to a lido from the terraced gardens. The best **campsite** is seaside, caravan-free *La Girelle* (☎04.68.81.25.56; April–Sept), at plage d'Ouille, west of town on the coastal path to Le Racou. Rue Camille-Pelletan and its perpendicular lanes have some cafés and **restaurants**, but you'll fork out well over the odds for listless grub. Get, at least, what you pay for at *Amphytrion* on Port d'Avall, crowded even off season for the sake of good-sized, seafood-based menus (€18–21).

Banyuls-sur-Mer

South towards **BANYULS-SUR-MER**, 10km further on from Collioure, both the main highway and minor D914 wind through attractive vineyards, with the Albères hills rising steeply on the right. The town itself, facing a broad sweep of pebble beach, is pleasant (and is where the GR10 meets the Mediterranean) but lacks the overt charm of Collioure. There are, however, several local attractions. One is the seafront **aquarium** of the Laboratoire Arago (daily: July–Aug 9am–1pm & 2–9pm; Sept–June 9am–noon & 2–6.30pm; €4.60; Ⓦ http://aquarium.obs-banyuls.fr), run by the Sorbonne's marine biology department, whose tanks contain a comprehensive collection of the region's submarine life; this is protected in a nearby *réserve marine*, France's best, which can be explored with local **scuba outfitters**. Also worth a look are the works of sculptor **Aristide Maillol** (1861–1944), who was born near Banyuls; they are best seen at the **Musée Maillol** (daily: May–Sept 10am–noon & 4–7pm; Oct–April 10am–noon & 2–5pm; €3.50), 4km outside the town in the Vallée de Roume, where he is buried under his statue *La Pensée*. You might also sample the dark, full-bodied Banyuls dessert **wine**, an *appellation* which applies only to the vineyards of the Côte Vermeille.

The **tourist office** stands diagonally opposite the *mairie* on the seafront (July & Aug daily 9.30am–12.30pm & 2.30–7pm; Sept–June Mon–Sat 9am–noon & 2–6pm; ☎04.68.88.31.58, Ⓦ www.banyuls-sur-mer.com). The only budget **hotel** is *Canal*, 9 rue Dugommmier a block inland (☎04.68.88.00.75; ❷–❸), basic but adequate and with wi-fi signal throughout, while with a bit more to spend try *Les Elmes* at the eponymous sandy cove 1.5km north (☎04.58.88.03.12, Ⓦ www.hotel-des-elmes.com; ❾), with quieter rear-facing rooms, or *Al-Fanal* (☎04.68.88.00.81, Ⓦ www.al-fanal.com; ❹) overlooking the yacht port, with parking. This also has its own seafood **restaurant**, but the best value in town – on an otherwise touristy street – is provided by seafood and shellfish specialists ⌘ *Les Canadells* opposite the *mairie*, with big portions and good own-label wine (the €24 menu will do for most). Also worth considering is *La Casa Miguel* at 3 rue St-Pierre, purveying abundant, savoury tapas; inside are original Maillol lithographs and photos of old Banyuls.

Céret and the valley of the Tech

The first tempting stop on the D115, the main road which follows the **Tech valley** inland all the way up to the Spanish border just past Prats-de-Mollo, is **CÉRET**, capital of the Vallespir region, served like the rest of the valley by regular buses from Perpignan. It's a delightful place, with a wonderfully shady old town overhung by huge plane trees; central streets are narrow and winding, opening onto small squares like the **Plaça de Nou Reigs** ("Nine Spouts" in Catalan), named after a currently missing central fountain; on avenue d'Espagne, two remnants of the medieval walls, the **Porte de France** and **Porte d'Espagne**, are visible. Céret is also known for cherries from surrounding orchards (June festival), plus July *corridas* (bullfights) and Pamplona-style running of bulls. Other annual events include the Easter Sunday procession of the Resurrected Christ, and an international *sardana* jamboree in July.

Céret's main sight, however, is the remarkable **Musée d'Art Moderne** (June 15–Sept 15 daily 10am–7pm; Feb 16 to Sept daily 10am–6pm; Oct–Feb 15 same hours; closed Tues; ⓦwww.musee-ceret.com; €8), at 8 boulevard Maréchal-Joffre. Between about 1910 and 1935, Céret's charms – coupled with the residence here of the Catalan artist and sculptor Manolo – drew a number of avant-garde artists to the town, including Matisse and Picasso, who personally dedicated a number of pictures to the museum. The holdings are too extensive to mount everything at once, but works on show should include canvases by Chagall, Miró, Pignon and Dufy, among others. Permanently displayed Picassos include a marvellous series of ceramic bowls illustrating bullfighting scenes, executed over just five days in April 1953. The upper floor has worthwhile temporary exhibits.

The **tourist office** is at 1 avenue Clemenceau (July & Aug Mon–Sat 9.30am–12.30pm & 2–7pm; Sept–May Mon–Fri 9am–noon & 2–5pm, Sat 9.30am–12.30pm; ☏04.68.87.00.53, ⓦwww.ceret.fr). There's no better **accommodation** than friendly ⚒ *Hôtel Vidal* at 4 place Soutine (☏04.68.87.00.85; closed Nov; ❷), a tastefully converted episcopal palace with variable-sized but salubrious en-suite rooms. Full-service **restaurant** options aren't abundant but include the Vidal's very own *El Bisbe* (closed Tues & Wed low season), with gourmet if sparing menus at €31; *Pizzeria Quattrocento* (shut Tues) on Plaça de Nou Reigs; and *Côte Jardin* at 12 rue St-Ferréol down from the museum, with a €16 lunch menu.

Arles-sur-Tech and Gorges de la Fou

West of Céret, past the single span of its fourteenth-century **Pont du Diable**, the view opens towards the towering eminence of the Canigou massif. Once past congested Amélie-les-Bains (8km), it's 4km further to **ARLES-SUR-TECH**, a more interesting proposition. The Carolingian origins of its Romanesque **Abbaye de Ste-Marie** (July–Aug 9am–7pm; Sept–June Mon–Sat 9am–noon & 2–6pm; also Sun April–Oct 2–5pm; €3.50) are thought to account for the back-to-front alignment of altar at the west end and entrance at the east. Entry is now via the pleasant thirteenth-century cloister, though it can't remotely compare in merit to Elne's or St-Michel-de-Cuixà's. The unique and compelling feature of the massive church interior is a band of still-vividly coloured twelfth-century **frescoes** high up in the apse of the eastern antichapel dedicated to St-Michel, appropriately featuring the archangel.

Outside the east facade – surmounted by an impressive Romanesque relief of Christ and the Tetramorphs – stands a very ancient (fourth- or fifth-century) sarcophagus, known as the **Sainte-Tombe**, which has the mysterious habit of slowly filling with very pure water. Every July 30, when Arles celebrates its *fête* dedicated to SS Abdon and Sennen (two Roman martyrs whose bones used to lodge inside), the water is siphoned out and distributed after Mass to worshipful pilgrims. The town's other festivals include the probably prehistoric **Fête de l'Ours**, devised to exorcize human fear of awakening bears, traditionally held in late February when hibernation ended; there's also a torchlit **Procession de la Sanch** at Easter. Arles is an important stage on the **GR10**, which from here heads northwest towards the Canigou massif or southeast towards Las Illas.

The **tourist office** (Mon–Sat 9am–noon & 2–6pm, Sun 2–6pm; ℡04.68.39.11.99, Ⓦwww.ville-arles-sur-tech.fr) also serves as the abbey ticket office. **Accommodation** is limited to the *Hôtel les Glycines* on rue du Jeu-de-Paume (℡04.68.39.10.09; Feb–Nov; ❷), with a terrace restaurant (from €18), and *Chambre d'Hôte La Couvent Sana* (℡04.68.83.92.90; ❷), on the edge of town. There's also a **campsite**, *Riuferrer* (℡04.68.39.11.06), on the west side of town.

Just west of Arles, on the road to Prats-de-Mollo, is the entrance to the **Gorges de la Fou**, 2km long, very narrow and up to 250m deep (April–Nov daily 10am–6pm weather permitting; €5). It's spectacular, but inevitably a tourist trap, with snack stalls and a metal catwalk all along the bottom.

Prats-de-Mollo

Beyond the gorge, the D115 climbs steadily, between valley sides thick with walnut, oak and sweet chestnut, 19km to **PRATS-DE-MOLLO**, end of the bus line. Prats is the last French town before the **Spanish frontier**, 13km beyond at Col d'Ares, but it has none of the usual malaise of border towns and is much the most attractive place in the valley since Céret. Hub of the newer quarter is **El Firal**, the huge square used for markets since 1308; the walled and gated **ville haute** just south makes for a wonderful wander, with steep cobbled streets and a weathered church with marvellous ironwork on the door. The old town's walls were rebuilt in the seventeenth century after the suppression of a local revolt against onerous taxation imposed by Louis XIV on his new, post-Treaty Pyrenees holdings. Vauban's **Fort Lagarde** (April–June & Sept–Oct Tues–Sun 2–6pm; July & Aug daily 11am–1pm & 5–7pm; guided visits only, apply to tourist office), on the heights above the town, also dates from this period, built to intimidate the local population as much as to keep the Spanish out.

The **tourist office** is on El Firal (July–Aug daily 9am–1pm & 2–7pm; Sept–June Mon–Fri 9am–noon & 2–6pm, Sat 9am–noon; ℡04.68.39.70.83). There's ample good-quality **accommodation**, which makes Prats a good base or transit stopover; in the walled quarter, go for *Hostellerie Le Relais* at 3 place Josep de la Trinxeria (℡04.68.39.71.30, Ⓦwww.hostellerie-le-relais.com; ❷), with cheerful pastel-hued rooms and a south-facing garden restaurant. Just outside, overlooking El Firal, is *Hôtel Le Bellevue* (℡04.68.39.72.48, Ⓦwww.lebellevue .fr.st; closed Dec to mid-Feb; ❸), with more old-fasioned rooms but modern baths, private parking and a restaurant (menu from €21).

Les Aspres: Trinité and Serrabona

The only direct route between the **valleys of the Tech and the Têt**, best covered with a small car or cycle, is the D618 from Amélie-les-Bains to Bouleternère, across the eastern spurs of Canigou. It's 44 slow kilometres of mountain road, twisting through hillside meadows and magnificent woods, past isolated *masies* (Catalan farmsteads), many now tenanted by foreigners or French *soixante-huitard* idealists drawn to **Les Aspres**, as this region is known. The only amenities en route, 20km along, are in tiny **ST-MARSAL** with its broad vistas, at *Hôtel Auberge de Saint-Marsal* (℡04.68.39.42.68, Ⓦwww.saintmarsal.net; ❶), a converted *mas*. Some 5km further, the Romanesque **Chapelle de la Trinité** stands by the road, opposite the *mairie* of Prunet-Belpuig. Inside (usually open) is a fine, serene *majestat*, the particularly Catalan wood-carved Crucifixions of the eleventh or twelfth centuries; most of the Spanish examples were destroyed in 1936.

From here the D618 descends into the Boulès valley, through the pretty hamlet of **Boule d'Amont**, before reaching the steep D84 side road climbing 4km to the remarkable, bluff-top **Prieuré de Serrabona** (formerly Serrabonne; daily except major holidays 10am–6pm; €3). One of the finest examples – arguably *the* finest – of Roussillon Romanesque, the interior of the church (consecrated 1151) is starkly plain, making the beautifully carved column-capitals of its rib-vaulted tribune even more striking: lions, centaurs, griffins and human figures with Asiatic faces and hairstyles – motifs brought back from the Crusades – executed in pink marble from Villefranche-de-Conflent, by students of the Maître d'Cabestany if not himself. The altar is made of the same stone, as are the pillars and equally elaborate capitals of the cloister, comprising just one row of columns because of the narrow site. Despite the rigours of monastic life here – long abandoned – the settlement was well developed, and the monks' terraces and irrigation system have been adapted to support a lush botanical garden.

The Têt valley and Canigou

The upper **Têt valley**, known as the **Pays de Conflent**, is utterly dominated by the **Pic du Canigou**. The valley bottoms are lush with fields and orchards, but the vast and uncompromising mountain presides over all. Continuing upstream, the valley narrows and steepens until you emerge onto the Cerdagne plateau.

Prades, Molitg-les-Bains and St-Michel-de-Cuixà

Chief valley town is **Prades**, easily accessible by train and bus on the Perpignan–Villefranche–Latour-de-Carol route, and the obvious starting point for all excursions in the Canigou region. Although there are no great sights beyond the **church of St-Pierre** in central place de la République, the town enjoys a status disproportionate to its size. This is largely thanks to Catalan cellist Pablo (Pau) Casals, who settled here as an exile and fierce opponent of the Franco regime in Spain. In 1950 he instituted the internationally renowned **chamber music festival** (ⓦwww.prades-festival-casals.com), held annually from late July to mid-August, the usual venue being the abbey of St-Michel-de-Cuixà (see below). Prades (or Prada) also hosts a Catalan university in mid-August and has the first Catalan-language primary school in France.

The **tourist office** is at 4 rue des Marchands (July & Aug Mon–Sat 9am–12.30pm & 2–7pm, Sun 9am–noon; Sept–June Mon–Fri 9am–noon & 2–6pm; ☏04.68.05.41.02, ⓦwww.prades-tourisme.com). Prades has two central hotels, but both have seen better days, and currently the best **accommodation** is just west of town on chemin de la Llitera: *Chambre d'Hôte Castell Rose* (☏04.68.96.07.57, ⓦwww.castellrose-prades.com; ❺–❻), in a converted manor house set in extensive grounds with a pool and tennis court. If that's beyond your budget, and you've transport, make for welcoming *Hôtel St Joseph*, 7km west across the river in gorge-set **MOLITG-LES-BAINS** (☏04.68.05.02.11, ⓔgerard.pommerol6yahoo.fr; all year; rooms ❶, studios ❷), though **eating**'s much better next door at *Royal*, where the €16 tasting menu (choice of meat mains) includes wine and coffee. Back in Prades, the best **restaurant** is *La Meridienne* at 20 rue des Marchands (book in season on ☏04.68.05.98.31), doing *nouvelle* Mediterranean cuisine as the name suggests, with menus from €16 (à la carte more generously portioned).

Three kilometres south of Prades stands one of the loveliest abbeys in France, originally eleventh-century **St-Michel-de-Cuixà** (May–Sept Mon–Sat 9.30–11.50am & 2–6pm, Sun 2–6pm; Oct–April Mon–Sat 9.30–11.50am & 2–5pm, Sun 2–5pm; €4). Although mutilated after the Revolution it is still beautiful, with its crenellated tower silhouetted against the wooded – sometimes snowy – slopes of Canigou. You enter via the labyrinthine, vaulted crypt, with a round central chamber, before proceeding to the church with its strange Visigothic-style "keyhole" arches. But the glory of the place is the **cloister** and its twelfth-century column capitals. Although most of the north and east bays were taken to the Cloisters Museum in New York early in the last century, the remaining west and south series – filled in with capitals from the vanished tribune in the church – rival Serrabona and Elne for virtuosity, sharing Serrabona's rose marble, and possibly artist (the Maître de Cabestany, or a disciple). They feature highly stylized figures strongly reminiscent of Sumerian, Assyrian or Persian relief art: often monsters, either alone or being grappled by human keepers displaying an array of Asiatic beards, exotic headgear and corpulent anatomies.

Vernet-les-Bains and St-Martin-du-Canigou

An innocuous little hillside spa, **VERNET-LES-BAINS**, 12km along the minor, foothill-skimming D27 from the abbey, has a **tourist office** in place de la Mairie (Mon–Fri 9am–noon & 2–6pm; ☎04.68.05.55.35, ⓦwww.vernet-les-bains.fr). Two of the best **hotels** are spa-affiliated *Les Sources* (☎04.68.05.52.84, ⓦwww .thermes-vernet.com; ❷) and the *Princess*, rue de Lavandiers (☎04.68.05.56.22, ⓦwww.hotel-princess.com; ❸). There are two **campsites** outside Vernet and a **gîte d'étape** (☎04.68.05.51.30) next to the municipal pool.

A half-hour mandatory walk (no car access) above the hamlet of Casteil, itself 2.5km south of Vernet, lies the stunning abbey of **St-Martin-du-Canigou**, founded in 1001. Resurrected from ruins between 1902 and 1982, and now occupied by a working religious community, the monastery at over 1000m altitude occupies a narrow promontory of rock surrounded by chestnut and oak woods, while above it rise the precipitous slopes of Canigou. Below, the ground drops sheerly into the ravine of the Cady stream rushing down from the Col de Jou. The place is visitable in French-narrated tours (year-round Mon–Sat 10am, 11am, 2pm, 3pm, 4pm; also June–Sept noon & 5pm; Sun/hols 10am & 12.30pm rather than 10am, 11am, noon; closed Jan & Mon Oct–May; €5). What you see is a beautiful little garden and cloister overlooking the ravine, a low-ceiling, atmospheric chapel beneath the church, and the main church itself.

From the monastery, a **path** leads up to a rocky viewpoint from which most photographs of the place are taken. This trail continues to meet the GR10 at the Col de Segalès, and from there to the *Refuge Grand Mariailles* (1718m; ☎04.68.04.49.86; 55 bunks; late May to early Oct) on Canigou's west flank. For a **day-loop** walk back to Casteil, another path drops down into the Cady ravine just at the start of the monastery buildings.

The Pic du Canigou

You can climb at least part way up the **Pic du Canigou** by vehicle, although given the roughness of the road you may not want to risk your own wheels. Sturdy **cars** (preferably 4WD) can get as far as the *Chalet des Cortalets* refuge either by the track from Clara-Villerach, near Taurinyà, or the even steeper and rougher mining road that begins by the *Al Pouncy* **campsite** near Fillols. Both routes take about an hour at the wheel. Alternatively, you could **rent a jeep** and driver from Ria (☎04.68.05.27.08) or Corbières Grand Raid (☎04.68.05.24.24) in Prades, plus Garage Villaceque (☎04.68.05.66.58) or Jean-Paul Bouzan (☎04.68.05.62.28) in Vernet-les-Bains. For **walkers**, the standard ascent is from Vernet on a path that begins about 700m along the road to Fillols, joining up with the **GR10** at the Refuge de Bonaigua (about 3hr) which you leave (about 1hr later) below the **Pic Joffre** to follow an HRP variant up the ridge to the summit (about 1hr). It's not for faint hearts or the inexperienced (some have fallen to their deaths), as the final ascent is rather exposed. An easier five-hour alternative starts from Casteil, passing the aforementioned *Refuge Grand Marialles*, then following the HRP for the last stretch via the unstaffed Arago hut.

From the *Chalet des Cortalets* (2150m; ☎04.68.96.36.19; 111 places; May 15 to Oct 15; doubles plus dorm bunks, restaurant), it's a straightforward, ninety-minute walk to the top in good weather. Strike west through the last trees, past a little lake, with a magnificent view into the cirque below the summit, round the back of the Pic Joffre, and along stony Crête de Barbet to the cross and Catalan flag marking the summit.

On the evening of June 23, Catalans from counties around, including seemingly half the population of Barcelona, head for Canigou to light the bonfire from which a flame is carried to kindle all the *focs de Sant Joan* of nearby villages – though the scene around the refuge can be pretty horrendous, with tents, sound sytems and litter galore.

Villefranche-de-Conflent and the Petit Train Jaune

A medieval garrison town suffering from arrested development, **VILLE-FRANCHE-DE-CONFLENT**, 6km up the Têt from Prades and a similar distance below Vernet-les-Bains, is today a tourist trap of the first order. Founded in 1092 by the counts of Cerdagne to block incursions from rivals in Roussillon, then remodelled by Vauban in the seventeenth century after annexation by France, its streets and fortifications have remained untouched by subsequent events, aside from becoming one giant, uninterrupted *tchatchka* stall. Worth a look is **St-Jacques church**, with a primitively carved thirteenth-century baptismal font just inside the door; you can also walk the perimeter of the **walls** (daily: Feb–May & Oct–Dec 10.30am–12.30pm & 2–5/6pm; June–Sept 10am–8pm; closed Jan; €4.50). If you do, you'll see why in 1681 Vauban constructed the **Château-Fort Libéria** on the heights above town to protect it from "aerial" bombardment. Getting up there (daily: June & Sept 9am–7pm; July–Aug 9am–8pm; Oct–May 10am–5/6pm; €6) involves taking the free minibus or jeep leaving from near the town's main gate; you can return to Villefranche by descending a subterranean stairway of a thousand steps, emerging at the end of rue St-Pierre.

The **tourist office** (Feb–Dec daily 10am–12.30pm & 2–5.30pm; ☎04.68.96.22.96) is in place d'Église. The best-value local **restaurant**, in the old town at 31 rue St-Jean, is *La Casa de la Nine* (most of year Wed–Sat pm & Sun lunch; menus €28–41), English-run but well respected by locals.

Villefranche is the terminus for main-line trains from Perpignan. From here up to La Tour-de-Carol on the Spanish frontier, transport is by SNCF bus, or – far nicer – the narrow-gauge, year-round **Petit Train Jaune**, which climbs along the Têt at a cyclist's pace allowing proximity to the scenery, especially in summer when some of the carriages are open-air (☎04.68.96.56.62, ⓦwww.trainstouristiques-ter.com). The summertime frequency of the trains makes it practical to hop off and on, allowing you to explore the areas around smaller, isolated stations, many of them *haltes facultatifs* (ask to be set down).

The upper Têt

The next sizeable village upstream from Villefranche, 10km along, is sleepy **OLETTE**, perched in tiers on the north flank of the Têt with an excellent, English-run **chambre d'hôte**, ⚑ *La Fontaine* (☎04.68.97.03.67, ⓦwww.olette66.com; closed Jan; ❸), with spare but very tasteful rooms (no. 4, with its old fireplace, best for couples) and good *table d'hôte* suppers (€16).

▲ Le Petit Train Jaune

Some 7km southwest of Olette on the south side of the valley, the wild, wooded **Gorges de Carança** cuts south through the mountains towards Spain. A clear path, with catwalks, follows the canyon to the GR10 at the basic *Refuge Ras de Carança* (3–4hr; 1831m; ℡04.68.04.13.18; 30 places; June–Sept 15). **THUÈS-ENTRE-VALLS** is the closest village to the *gorges* and its **car park** (€2), with a *halte facultatif* on the Petit Train Jaune, and Luk & Micheline Peters' unsigned **gîte** *Mas de Bordes* (℡04.68.97.05.00; most of year; doubles ❷, s/c family quads ❸, evening meal €15), up the single lane from the train line. This also offers dorms, a camping meadow and an on-site **hot spring** (free, 40°C) a 25-minute tough but scenic walk distant.

At **Fontpédrouse**, 4km beyond Thuès, a minor side road veers south across the river and up a grassy spur above the River Aigues towards the village of Prat-Balaguer. Bearing right instead at a fork leads, 3km from Fontpédrouse station, to the organized **Bains de St-Thomas** (daily 10am–7.40pm, last admission 8.40pm July/Aug; closed Nov 14 to Dec 5; €4.50), with open pools at a pleasant 37–38°C.

The Cerdagne

Another 10km up the N116 from Fontpédrouse, or three stops on the train, brings you onto the wide, grassy **Cerdagne** plateau, whose once-powerful counts controlled lands from Barcelona to Roussillon. It's a region that's never been sure whether it is Spanish or French. After the French annexation of Roussillon, it was partitioned, with Spain retaining – as it still does – the enclave of Lliva. The Petit Train Jaune snakes laboriously across the entire plateau, though stations aren't always convenient for the settlements they nominally serve.

Easterly gateway to the region is the little garrison town of **MONT-LOUIS**, built by Vauban in 1679–82; the top citadel is still a training school for paratroops and marines. There's not much to see other than the **ramparts** (guided visits only Mon–Sat 10am–2pm, enquire at tourist office; €4.50), but it is a far pleasanter place to stay than the monstrous ski resort of **Font-Romeu** just up the road, far from the best locally (that title is shared between Les Angles and Formiguères in the nearby Capcir). There's a **tourist office** (July & Aug daily 9.30am–noon & 2–7pm; Sept–June Mon–Sat 10am–noon & 2–6pm; ℡04.68.04.21.97, Ⓦwww.mont-louis.net), while the best **accommodation** is *Chambre d'Hôte La Volute* (℡04.68.04.27.21, Ⓦlavolute.monsite.orange.fr; ❹), both rooms and a family *gîte*, set in the seventeenth-century former governor's mansion, with a lawn-garden atop a section of the ramparts. The most popular **restaurant** is *Le Dagobert* at 8 boulevard Vauban, with a decent €15 menu (but exorbitant à la carte and mediocre desserts).

The Têt ultimately has its source in the Carlit massif, which looms above dammed **Lac des Bouillousses**, 13km northwest of Mont-Louis by the D60 and very busy in summer. Car access along this road is limited to a *navette* during peak season, or you can hike in along the GR10 from Mont-Louis in under four hours. On arrival you'll find a triple choice of **accommodation**; best of the three, east of the dam, is *Auberge du Carlit* (℡04.68.04.22.23; all year), with rooms (❺ half board) and a 32-bunk *gîte* in a separate building.

The Petit Train Jaune continues past Mont-Louis, though the drama of the ride is diminished compared with the lower Têt valley. A good intermediate spot to alight is **SAILLAGOUSE**, where dead-central *Hôtel Planes-Planotel* (℡04.68.04.72.08, Ⓦwww.planotel.fr; closed Nov 3 to Dec 19) offers **rooms** in the 1895-built *vieille maison* (❸) or a nearby modern annexe (❹), and excellent-value **meals** either in its brasserie or the full-on restaurant. Ur-les-Escaldes is the closest (5km) station to more hot springs in **DORRES**, the **Bains Romans** (daily 8.30/8.45am–7.40/8.15pm; €3.90), with open-air granite pools (39–40° C) at their best in ski season. End of the line is **LATOUR-DE-CAROL** with its fine old quarter 1km northwest of Enveitg station; on the main road the ⚵ *Auberge Catalane* (℡04.68.04.80.66, Ⓦwww.auberge-catalane.fr; ❸) has been going since 1929, with soundproofed rooms and a well-attended restaurant where menus (€18–40) encompass fish, foie gras, *gesiers* and *boudin noir*.

Travel details

Trains

Bayonne to: Biarritz (14 daily; 10min); Bordeaux (6–12 daily; 1hr 40min–2hr 10min); Boussens (7–8 daily; 3hr); Cambo-les-Bains (4–5 daily; 25min); Hendaye (14 daily; 35min); Lourdes (5–8 daily; 1hr 45min–2hr); Orthez (5–6 daily; 45min–1hr); Pau (7–8 daily; 1hr 15min); St-Gaudens (7–8 daily; 2hr 45min); St-Jean-de-Luz (16–20 daily; 25min); St-Jean-Pied-de-Port (4–5 daily; 1hr); Tarbes (7–8 daily; 2hr); Toulouse (7–12 daily; 3hr–3hr 30min).

Foix to: Ax-les-Thermes (11–13 daily, some on SNCF bus; 55min); Barcelona (3–4 daily; 5hr–5hr 30min); Latour-de-Carol (7 daily, some on SNCF bus; 1hr 45min–2hr); Tarascon-sur-Ariège (11–13 daily; 15–20min); Toulouse (11–13 daily; 1hr 20min–1hr 45min).

Luchon to: Montréjeau (5–6 daily; usually SNCF coach; 45–55min).

Pau to: Bordeaux (5–7 daily; 1hr 15min–2hr); Oloron-Ste-Marie (6–9 daily; 35min); Orthez (5–6 daily; 20min).

Perpignan to: Argelès-sur-Mer (8–12 daily; 20min); Banyuls-sur-Mer (8–12 daily; 30min); Cerbère (8–12 daily; 40min); Collioure (8–12 daily; 25min); Elne (8–12 daily; 10min); Narbonne (10–13 daily; 35–50min); Prades (5–8 daily; 45min); Salses (7–9 daily; 15min); Toulouse (10–12 daily; 2hr 30min–3hr); Villefranche-de-Conflent (5–8 daily; 55min).

Quillan to: Carcassonne (4–5 daily, SNCF coach except in summer; 55min–1hr 15min); Limoux (6–7 daily, SNCF coach; 30–40min).

St-Girons to: Boussens (6–8 daily on SNCF coach; 45min).

Tarbes to: Bordeaux (6–9 daily; 3hr 15min); Dax (6–9 daily; 1hr 50min); Lourdes (11–14 daily; 15min); Orthez (3–5 daily; 1hr 10min).

Villefranche-de-Conflent to: Latour-de-Carol (3–6 daily; 2hr 45min); Mont–Louis (4–7 daily; 1hr 35min).

Buses

Bayonne to: Ainhoa (2–3 daily; 30min); Biarritz (local transport; 15–20min); Cambo-les-Bains (several daily; 30–40min); Orthez (3 daily; 50min); Pau (2–3 daily; 1hr 10min); San Sebastian (2 daily Mon–Sat; 1hr 45min); St-Jean-de-Luz (5–7 daily; 40min).

Biarritz to: Hendaye (5–7 daily; 35min); Orthez (2–3 daily; 1hr 45min); Pau (2–3 daily; 2hr 30min); St-Jean-de-Luz (11–16 daily; 25min); Salies-de-Béarn (2 daily; 1hr 20min).

Foix to: Lavelanet (2–3 daily; 30min); Mirepoix (2–3 daily; 45min); Quillan (1 daily Mon–Sat; 1hr 30min).

Laruns to: Bious-Oumette trailhead (1 daily in morning, summer only; 40min); Fabrèges (2 daily summer and winter ski seasons; 55min); Gabas (2 daily summer and winter ski seasons; 25min).

Lourdes to: Bagnères-de-Bigorre (2–3 daily; 45min); Barèges, usually changing at Pierrefite-Nestalas (6–7 daily on SNCF coach or SALT bus; 1hr 10min); Cauterets, changing at Pierrefitte-Nestalas (4–7 daily; 50min); Gavarnie, changing at Luz-St-Sauveur (July–Aug 2 daily, otherwise 3 weekly; 1hr 15min); Luz-St-Sauveur (5–7 daily; 45min); Pau (4–8 daily; 1hr 15min).

Oloron-Ste-Marie to: Bedous (4–6 daily on SNCF coach; 30min); Urdos (4–6 daily; 50min) 3–4 continue to Canfranc, Spain).

Pau to: Agen (1–2 daily; 3hr); Bayonne (3–4 daily on TPR; 2hr 15min); Biarritz (2–3 daily on TPR; 2hr 30min); Eaux-Bonnes (3–4 daily on CITRAM; 1hr 15min); Gourette (2 daily on CITRAM; 1hr 30min); Laruns (5–8 daily via Buzy; 1hr 10min); Oloron-Ste-Marie (2–3 daily on CITRAM; 45min); Orthez (2–3 daily; 45min); Salies-de-Béarn (3 daily; 1hr 10min).

Perpignan to: Arles-sur-Tech (6 daily; 1hr 15min); Axat (2 daily, 1hr 40min); Banyuls-sur-Mer (3 daily; 1hr 10min); Céret (14 daily; 55min); Collioure (3 daily; 45min); Latour-de-Carol (2–3 daily; 3hr); Mont-Louis (3–4 daily; 2hr 15min); Prades (7 daily; 1hr); Prats-de-Molló (6 daily; 1hr 40min); Villefranche-le-Conflent (7 daily; 1hr 15min).

Prades to: Molitg-les-Bains (4–5 daily; 10min).

Quillan to: Axat (2 daily; 20min); Carcassonne (2 daily; 1hr 20min); Comus (1–2 daily; 1hr 5min); Perpignan (1 daily; 1hr 30min); Quérigut (3 weekly in summer; 1hr 30min).

St-Girons to: Aulus-les-Bains (Mon–Sat 1–2 daily; 45min); Boussens (Mon–Sat 7 daily, Sun 5 on SNCF coach; 40min); Foix (4 daily; 1hr); Toulouse (2–3 daily; 2hr).

St-Jean-de-Luz to: Cambo-les-Bains (2–4 daily; 45min); Espelette (2 daily; 35min); Hendaye (9–17 daily; 20min); Sare (2–3 daily; 30min).

Tarbes to: Auch (2–6 daily; 1hr 40min); Bagnères-de-Bigorre (4–6 daily by SNCF coach; 40min); Lourdes (hourly; 30min); Luz-St-Sauveur (5–7 daily on SALT bus; 1hr); Pau (6 daily; 1hr).

11

Languedoc

UNITED KINGDOM
BELGIUM
GERMANY
LUX.
ENGLISH CHANNEL
SWITZERLAND
ATLANTIC
OCEAN
ITALY
N
SPAIN
MEDITERRANEAN
SEA
0
250 km
1
2
3
4
5
6
7
8
9
10
11
12
13
14
15
16
17

CHAPTER 11

Highlights

* **Bulls** Whether in the ring or on your plate as a succulent *boeuf à la gardienne*, the *taureaux* of the plains of Languedoc are famous. See p.763

* **Pont du Gard** This graceful aqueduct is an emblem of southern France and a tribute to Roman determination. See p.766

* **Carcassonne** The Middle Ages come alive in this walled fortress town. See p.767

* **Water-jousting** A Setois tradition, in which teams of rowers charge at each other in gondolas. See p.774

* **St-Guilhem-le-Désert** The ancient Carolingian monastery and the tiny hamlet at its feet present a quintessential Occitan panorama. See p.777

* **The Canal du Midi** Cycling, walking or drifting along this tree-shaded canal is the most atmospheric way of savouring France's southwest. See p.789

* **Les Abattoirs** This former slaughterhouse in Toulouse contains an important collection of modern and contemporary art. See p.799

* **Albi's Toulouse-Lautrec** The most comprehensive collection of Toulouse-Lautrec's work is in the former Bishop's Palace of his home town. See p.804

▲ The Canal du Midi

Languaedoc

anguedoc is more an idea than a geographical entity. The modern *région* covers only a fraction of the lands where Occitan or the *langue d'oc* – the language of *oc*, the southern Gallo-Latin word for *oui* – once dominated. These stretched south from Bordeaux and Lyon into Spain and northwest Italy. The heartland today is the Bas Languedoc – the coastal plain and dry, stony vine-growing hills between Carcassonne and Nîmes. It's here that the **Occitan** movement has its power base, demanding recognition of its linguistic and cultural distinctiveness. A good part of its character derives from resentment of political domination by remote and alien Paris, aggravated by the area's traditional poverty. In recent times this has been focused on Parisian determination to drag the province into the modern world, with massive tourist development on the coast and the drastic transformation of the cheap wine industry. It is also mixed up in a vague collective folk memory with the brutal repression of the Protestant Huguenots around 1700, the thirteenth-century massacres of the Cathars and the subsequent obliteration of the brilliant *langue d'oc* troubadour tradition. It is a hostility that has made an essentially rural and conservative population vote traditionally for the Left – at least until the elections of 2002, which saw wide support for Le Pen's resurgent Front National. Although a sense of Occitan identity remains strong in the region, it has very little currency as a spoken or literary language, despite the popularity of university-level language courses and the foundation of Occitan-speaking elementary schools.

Toulouse, the cultural capital of medieval and modern Languedoc, lies outside the administrative *région* but is included in this chapter and is a high point among numerous other attractions. There are great stretches of dramatic landscape and river gorges, from the **Cévennes** foothills in the east to the **Montagne Noire** and **Corbières** hills in the west. There's ecclesiastical architecture in **Albi** and **St-Guilhem-le-Désert**, and medieval towns at **Cordes** and **Carcassonne**, which also provides access to the unforgettably romantic Cathar castles to the south. **Montpellier**'s university ensures it has an exciting cultural vibe which outstrips the city's modest size. **Nîmes** has extensive Roman remains, and there are great swathes of **beach** where – away from the major resorts – you can still find a kilometre or two to yourself.

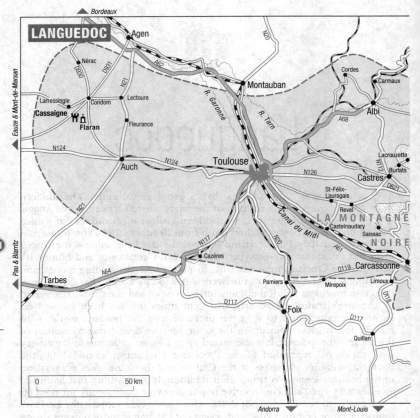

Within the map:

LANGUEDOC

Bordeaux

Agen

Nérac

D931

D930

D21

Larressingle

Cassaigne

Condom

Lectoure

Flaran

Fleurance

N124

Auch

N124

Toulouse

Montauban

R. Garonne

R. Tarn

A62

N20

Cordes

Carmaux

Albi

A68

Lacrouzette

N112

Burlats

Castres

N126

St-Félix-Lauragais

Revel

LA MONTAGNE

Castelnaudary

Saissac

NOIRE

Canal du Midi

D621

Carcassonne

A61

D119

N117

Cazères

N20

A64

Tarbes

Pamiers

Mirepoix

Limoux

D118

D117

Foix

D117

Quillan

0   50 km

Andorra   Mont-Louis

Eauze & Mont-de-Marsan

Pau & Biarritz

Eastern Languedoc

Heading south from Paris via Lyon and the Rhône valley, you can go one of two ways: east to Provence and the Côte d'Azur – which is what most people do – or west to **Nîmes**, **Montpellier** and the comparatively untouched northern Languedoc coast. Nîmes itself, while not officially in the administrative *région*, makes a good introduction to the area, a hectic modern town impressive for its Roman past and for some scattered attractions, such as the **Pont du Gard** nearby. **Montpellier** is also worth a day or two, not so much for historical attractions as for a heady vibrancy and easy access to the ancient villages, churches and fine scenery of the upper **Hérault valley**. This part of Languedoc was most affected by the spread of Protestantism in the sixteenth century, which has marked the region's character more than any other. The Protestants, with their attachment to rationality and self-improvement, espoused the cause of French over Occitan, supported the Revolution and the Republic, fought Napoléon III's coup against the 1848 Revolution and adhered to the anticlerical and socialist movement under the Third Republic. They dominated

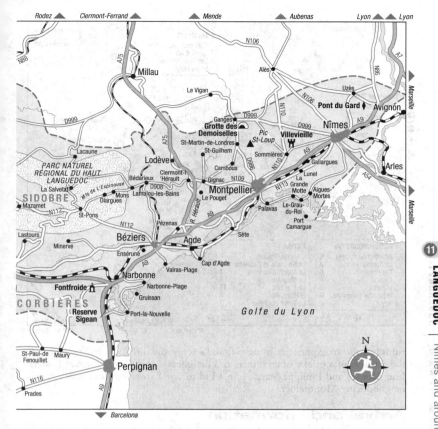

the local textile industry in the nineteenth century and were extremely active in the Resistance to the Nazis.

They also suffered a great deal for their cause, as did the whole region. After the Revocation of the Edict of Nantes in 1685 – the treaty which granted religious toleration at the end of the sixteenth century – persecution drove their most committed supporters, especially in the Cévennes to the north, to form clandestine *assemblées du Désert*, and finally, in 1702, to take up arms in the first guerrilla war of modern times, La Guerre des Camisards, conflicts which still resonate in the minds of both Huguenot and Catholic families.

Nîmes and around

On the border between Provence and Languedoc, the name of **NÎMES** is inescapably linked to two things – denim and Rome. The latter's influence resulted in some of the most extensive Roman remains in Europe, while the former (*de Nîmes*), equally visible on the backsides of the populace, was first manufactured in the city's textile mills, and exported to the southern USA in the nineteenth century to clothe slaves. The city is worth a visit, in part for the

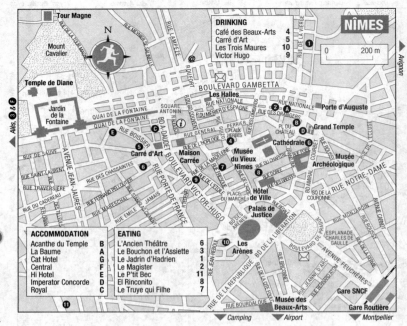

NÎMES

Tour Magne
Mount
Cavalier
Temple de Diane
Jardin
de la
Fontaine

DRINKING
Café des Beaux-Arts	4
Carré d'Art	5
Les Trois Maures	10
Victor Hugo	9

0   200 m

Avignon

Alès, 3 & F

QUAI DE LA FONTAINE
QUAI DE LA FONTAINE
RUE BOISSIER
RUE DE SALVE
AVENUE JEAN-JAURÈS
RUE SAINT-LAURENT
RUE DES CHASSAINTES
RUE TRAVERSIÈRE
RUE DU CADEREAU
RUE FERNAND PELLOUTIER
RUE MABESCHAL
RUE ÉMILE JAMAIS
RUE DE L'HORLOGE
BD A-DAUDE
BOULEVARD GAMBETTA
Les Halles
RUE NATIONALE
RUE DUME/RIEUD'ESPAGNE
SQUARE
ANTONIN
RUE GÉNÉRAL
Carré d'Art
Maison
Carrée
BOULEVARD VICTOR-HUGO
RUE PORTE DE FRANCE
Musée
du Vieux
Nîmes
RUE DES ORANGERS
RUE NATIONALE
Porte d'Auguste
PERRIER
RUE DES HALLES
PL. DU
CHÂTEAU
Grand Temple
Cathédrale
Musée
Archéologique
RUE NOTRE-DAME
RUE DE L'ÉTOILE
PLACE
DU MARCHÉ
Hôtel
de Ville
RUE DORÉE
BD AMIRAL COURBET
SQ DE LA
COURONNE
Palais de
Justice
Les
Arènes
BD DE LA LIBÉRATION
BOULEVARD GAULLE
ESPLANADE
CHARLES DE
GAULLE
AVENUE FEUCHÈRES
RUE JEAN-REBOUL
RUE DE LA RÉPUBLIQUE
RUE BROCONNIE
RUE JEANNE D'ARC
Gare SNCF
RUE BOURDALOUE
Musée des
Beaux-Arts
Gare Routière

ACCOMMODATION		EATING	
Acanthe du Temple	B	L'Ancien Théâtre	6
La Baume	A	Le Bouchon et l'Assiette	3
Cat Hotel	G	Le Jadrin d'Hadrien	1
Central	F	Le Magister	2
Hi Hotel	E	Le P'tit Bec	11
Imperator Concorde	D	El Rinconito	8
Royal	C	Le Truye qui Filhe	7

▼ Camping   ▼ Airport   ▼ Montpellier

ruins but also to experience its new-found energy and direction, having enlisted the services of a galaxy of architects and designers – including Norman Foster, Jean Nouvel and Philippe Starck – in a bid to wrest southern supremacy from neighbouring Montpellier.

Arrival and information

The Camargue **airport**, shared by Nîmes and Arles, lies 20km southeast of the city. A shuttle service links it to the town centre (2–4 daily, timed with flights; ☎04.66.29.27.29; "Gambetta" or "Imperator" stop; €5). By taxi, the trip will cost at least €30 (€35 at night). The **gare SNCF** is ten-minutes' walk southeast of the city centre at the end of avenue Feuchères, with the **gare routière** (☎04.66.29.52.00) just behind (access through the train station). The main **tourist office** is at 6 rue Auguste, by the Maison Carrée (Mon–Fri 8.30am– 6.30/7/8pm, Sat 9am–6.30/7pm & Sun 10am–5/6pm; ☎04.66.58.38.00, Ⓦwww.ot-nimes.fr).

Accommodation

There are several decent **hotels** in Nîmes, located in two main zones: a cluster north of the train station and in the old city. An attractive **HI hostel** with tent space can be found on chemin de la Cigale, 2km northwest of the centre (☎04.66.68.03.20, Ⓦwww.fuaj.org; July & Aug membership required; Sept– June no curfew; €10); take bus #2 direction "Alès/ Villeverte" from the *gare SNCF* to stop "Stade" – the last bus goes at 8pm. The municipal **campsite** (☎04.66.62.05.82, Ⓦwww.camping-nimes.com; year-round) is on route de Générac, 5km south of the city centre, beyond the modern Stade Costières and the autoroute.

Acanthe du Temple 1 rue Charles Babout ☎04.66.67.54.61, ⓦwww.hotel-temple.com. A clean and economical hotel, with friendly staff, good amenities and 24-hour access. This is one of the old town's best bargains. Closed Jan. ❸

La Baume 21 rue Nationale ☎04.66.76.28.42, ⓦwww.new-hotel.com. Set in a renovated mansion, with a courtyard dining area, and appointed with tasteful restraint. The best in this range, with excellent location and price (and off-season reductions). ❼

Cat Hotel 22 bd Amiral Courbet ☎04.66.67.22.85, ⓔcathotelnimes@orange.fr. A budget travellers' favourite, with excellent amenities for its price; a simple but all-you-can eat continental breakfast is available for €3.50. ❶

Central 2 place du Château ☎04.66.67.27.75, ⓦwww.hotel-central.org. Set on the edge of the historic centre in an eighteenth-century building, this hotel is excellent value for money. ❷

Imperator Concorde Quai de la Fontaine ☎04.66.21.90.30, ⓦwww.hotel-imperator.com. The city's finest choice, and a favourite of Hemingway's, located by the Jardin de la Fontaine. The luxuriously appointed rooms have a/c and satellite TV, the service is excellent and there is private parking. ❼

Royal 3 bd Alphonse-Daudet ☎04.66.58.28.27, ⓦwww.royalhotel-nimes.com. Atmospheric mid-market hotel near the Maison Carrée, equipped with all mod cons. Also has a good restaurant, with an excellent selection of tapas. ❸

The City

Most of what you'll want to see is contained within the boulevards de la Libération, Amiral-Courbet, Gambetta and Victor-Hugo, and there's much pleasure to be had from wandering the narrow lanes that they enclose, discovering unexpected squares with fountains and cafés.

Les Arènes

The focal point of the city is a first-century Roman arena, known as **Les Arènes** (March & Oct 9.30am–6pm; April, May & Sept 9am–6.30pm; June–Aug 9am–7pm; Nov–Feb 9.30am–5pm; closed during special events; €7.70), at the junction of boulevards de la Libération and Victor-Hugo. One of the best-preserved Roman arenas in the world, its arcaded two-storey facade conceals massive interior vaulting, riddled with corridors and supporting raked tiers of seats with a capacity of more than 20,000 spectators, whose staple fare was the blood and guts of gladiatorial combat. When Rome's sway was broken by the barbarian invasions, the arena became a fortress and eventually a slum, home to an incredible

The bullfight

Nîmes' great passion is **bullfighting**, and its *ferias* are acknowledged and well attended by both aficionados and fighters at the highest level. The wildest and most famous is the Feria de Pentecôte, which lasts five days over the Whitsun weekend. A couple of million people crowd into the town (hotel rooms need to be booked a year in advance), and seemingly every city native opens a bodega at the bottom of the garden for dispensing booze. There are *corridas*, which end with the killing of the bull, *courses* where *cocards* are snatched from the bull's head, and semi-amateur *courses libres* when a small posse of bulls is run through the streets and the daring try to snatch the *cocards* from their heads. In 1996, Nîmes witnessed the acclamation of the first-ever woman matador, Cristina Sanchez, though she took early retirement in 1999, blaming the profession's machismo. Recently events have been marked by small but vocal protests and in 2006 several organizers of the local *tauromachie* world were injured by letter bombs. Two other *ferias* take place: one at carnival time in February, when the inflatable roof of the Arènes is pulled over for protection from the weather; the other in the third week of September at grape-harvest time, the Feria des Vendanges. The **tourist office** can supply full details and advise about accommodation if you want to visit at *feria* time.

2000 people when it was cleared in the early 1800s. Today it has recovered something of its former role, with passionate summer crowds still turning out for some blood-letting – Nîmes has the premier bullfighting scene outside Spain.

If you're planning on making the rounds of museums and monuments, opt for the Billet Nîmes Romaine and Forfait Musée (from the tourist office; €9.80, for the Roman ruins, €7.50 for the museums).

The Hôtel de Ville and Museums

Just to the north of the Roman arena lies the warren of narrow streets that makes up Nîmes' compact old town. Among the mostly seventeenth- and eighteenth-century mansions you'll find the **Hôtel de Ville**, set between rue Dorée and rue des Greffes, the interior of which has been redesigned by the architect Jean-Michel Wilmotte to combine high-tech design with classical stone. Look out for the stuffed crocodiles suspended from chains above the stairwells – a gift from wealthy and contented eighteenth-century burghers. At the eastern end of rue des Greffes is the combined **Musée Archéologique** and **Muséum d'Histoire Naturelle** (daily 10am–6pm, Nov–May closed Mon; free); housed in a seventeenth-century Jesuit chapel at no. 13, they are full of Roman bits and bobs, assorted curios, and stuffed animals.

The Cathédrale Notre-Dame-et-St-Castor and Porte d'Auguste

Banned from public office, the Protestants put their energy into making money. The results of their efforts can be seen in the seventeenth- and eighteenth-century *hôtels* they built in the streets around the cathedral – rues de l'Aspic, Chapitre, Dorée and Grand'Rue, among others. At the end of Grand'Rue, the former bishop's palace is now the **Musée du Vieux Nîmes** (daily 10am–6pm, Nov–May closed Mon; free), with displays of Renaissance furnishings and decor and documents to do with local history. Opposite, the **Cathédrale Notre-Dame-et-St-Castor** sports a handsome sculpted frieze on the west front, illustrating the story of Adam and Eve, and a pediment inspired by the Maison Carrée. It's practically the only existing medieval building in town, as most were destroyed in the turmoil that followed the Michelade, the St Michael's Day massacre of Catholic clergy and notables by Protestants in 1567. Despite brutal repression in the wake of the Camisard insurrection of 1702, Nîmes was, and remains, a doggedly Protestant stronghold. Apart from that, the cathedral is of little interest, having been seriously mutilated in the Wars of Religion and significantly altered in the nineteenth century. The author Alphonse Daudet was born in its shadow, as was Jean Nicot – a doctor, no less – who introduced tobacco into France from Portugal in 1560 and gave his name to the world's most widely consumed drug.

North of the cathedral stands Nîmes' surviving Roman gate, **Porte d'Auguste** at the end of rue Nationale, the former Roman main street. Already a prosperous city on the Via Domitia, the main Roman road from Italy to Spain, Nîmes did especially well under Augustus. He gave the city its walls, remnants of which surface here and there, and its gates, as the inscription on the Porte records. He is also responsible for the chained crocodile, which figures on Nîmes' coat of arms. The device was copied from an Augustan coin struck to commemorate his defeat of Antony and Cleopatra after he settled veterans of that campaign on the surrounding land.

The Maison Carrée and the Carrée d'Art

Meandering west from the cathedral are the narrow lanes of the medieval city, at the heart of which is the delightful **place aux Herbes**, with two or three cafés and bars and a fine twelfth-century house on the corner of rue de la Madeleine. Heading west along **rue de l'Horloge** will take you to the city's other famous landmark, the **Maison Carrée** (March & Oct 10am–6.30pm; April, May & Sept 10am–7pm; June–Aug 10am–7.30pm; Nov–Feb 10am–1pm & 2–5pm; €4.50), a neat, jewel-like temple celebrated for its integrity and harmonic proportions. Built in 5 AD, it's dedicated to the adopted sons of Emperor Augustus – all part of the business of inflating the imperial personality cult. No surprise, then, that Napoleon, with his love of flummery and tendency to ennoble his cronies to boost his own legitimacy, took it as the model for the Madeleine church in Paris. The temple stands in its own small square opposite rue Auguste, where the Roman forum used to be, with pieces of Roman masonry scattered around. On the west side of place de la Maison Carrée, there's a gleaming example of French architectural boldness, the **Carrée d'Art**, by British architect Norman Foster. In spite of its size, this box of glass, aluminium and concrete sits modestly among the ancient roofs of Nîmes, its slender portico echoing that of the Roman temple opposite. Light pours in through the walls and roof, giving it a grace and weightlessness that makes it not in the least incongruous. Housed within the Carrée d'Art is the excellent **Musée d'Art Contemporain** (daily 10am–6pm; Nov–May closed Mon; €5.10), containing an impressive collection of French and Western European art from the last four decades. There's a roof-terrace café at the top, overlooking the Maison Carrée.

Beyond the old town

Perhaps the most refreshing thing you can do in Nîmes is head east of the centre to the **Jardin de la Fontaine**, France's first public garden, created in 1750. Behind the formal entrance, where fountains, nymphs and formal trees enclose the **Temple de Diana**, steps climb the steep wooded slope, adorned with grottoes and nooks and artful streams, to the **Tour Magne** (March & Oct 9.30am–1pm & 2–6pm; April, May & Sept 9.30am–6.30pm; June–Aug 9.30am–7pm; Nov–Feb 9.30am–1pm & 2–4.30pm; €2.70). The 32-metre tower, left over from Augustus' city walls, gives terrific views over the surrounding country – as far, it is claimed, as the Pic du Canigou on the edge of the Pyrenees. At the foot of the slope flows the gloriously green and shady **Canal de la Fontaine**, built to supplement its rather unsteady supply of water from the *fontaine*, the Nemausus spring, whose presence in a dry, limestone landscape gave Nîmes its existence.

The city's remaining sights lie south of the Arènes. The **Musée des Beaux-Arts**, in rue de la Cité-Foulc (daily 10am–6pm, Nov–May closed Mon; €5.10), prides itself on a huge Gallo-Roman mosaic showing the Marriage of Admetus, but is otherwise pretty ordinary. Further afield, out on the southern edge of town, you'll find examples of the revolutionary civic architecture for which Nîmes was once famed. Jean Nouvel's pseudo-Mississippi-steamboat housing project, named **Nemausus** after the deity of the local spring that gave Nîmes its name, squats off the Arles road behind the *gare SNCF*, and the magnificent sports stadium, the **Stades des Costières**, by Vittorio Gregotti, looms close to the autoroute along the continuation of avenue Jean-Jaurès.

Eating and drinking

The best places to hang out for **coffee and drinks** are the numerous little squares scattered through the old town: place de la Maison-Carrée, place du

Marché and place aux Herbes (breakfast here early at the *Café des Beaux-Arts* to watch the sun creep up behind the cathedral tower). *Les Trois Maures*, in boulevard des Arènes, is a classic Nîmes café. For a quiet evening, head to *Carrée d'Art* piano bar on rue Gaston-Bossier, near the canal and the post-modern place d'Assas, while the *Victor Hugo*, a music-bar at 36 boulevard Victor-Hugo attracts a younger, livelier crowd.

For **eating**, boulevard de la Libération and boulevard Amiral-Courbet harbour a stock of reasonably priced brasseries and pizzerias, and the squares are full of possibilities.

Restaurants

L'Ancien Théâtre 4 rue Racine ☏ 04.66.21.30.75. A short stroll from the Maison Carrée, offering zippy Mediterranean cuisine from €17. Closed Sat noon, Sun & Mon.

Le Bouchon et l'Assiette 5bis rue de Sauve, ☏ 04.66.62.02.93. Serves elaborate *gastronomique* variations on traditional Tarnaise themes; menus €17–45. Closed Tues & Wed.

Le Jardin d'Hadrien 111 rue Enclos-Rey ☏ 04.66.21.86.65. Inventive southeastern Gardoise cuisine with both fish and beef-based *plats* such as *boeuf à la gardienne* at reasonable prices. Menus at €15–44. Closed Wed out of season, Sun & Mon in season.

Le Magister 5 rue Nationale ☏ 04.66.76.11.00. Affordable and daringly *gastronomique* restaurant, with €26–36 menus and a pricier *carte*. Closed Sat noon & Sun.

Le P'tit Bec 87bis rue de la République ☏ 04.66.38.05.83. The best mid-range place for typical Gardoise cuisine (€18–42), such as *boeuf à la gardienne*. Closed Sun, Mon & Wed evening & mid-Aug to mid-Sept.

El Rinconcito 7 rue des Marchands ☏ 04.66.76.17.30. Friendly Chilean restaurant which provides a welcome break from the local fare (lunch menu from €12; €28 for dinner). Closed Sun & Mon & mid-Jan to mid-March.

La Truye qui Filhe 9 rue Fresque. Attractive self-service, where you can eat for around €9. Lunch-times only, closed Sun & Aug.

The Pont du Gard and Uzès

Some twenty kilometres northeast from Nîmes, the **Pont du Gard** is the greatest surviving stretch of a fifty-kilometre-long Roman aqueduct built in the middle of the first century AD to supply fresh water to the city. With just a seventeen-metre difference in altitude between start and finish, the aqueduct was quite an achievement, running as it does over hill and dale, through a tunnel, along the top of a wall, into trenches and over rivers; the Pont du Gard carries it over the River Gardon. Today the bridge is a UNESCO World Heritage Site and something of a tourist trap, but is nonetheless a supreme piece of engineering and a brilliant combination of function and aesthetics; it made the impressionable Rousseau wish he'd been born Roman.

Three tiers of **arches** span the river, with the covered water conduit on the top, rendered with a special plaster waterproofed with a paint apparently based on fig juice. A visit here used to be a must for French journeymen masons on their traditional tour of the country, and many of them have left their names and home towns carved on the stonework. Markings made by the original builders are still visible on individual stones in the arches, such as "FR S III – frons sinistra", front side left no. 3. The Pont du Gard has recently undergone a massive restoration programme and now features an extensive multimedia complex, the **Site de Pont du Gard**, which includes a state-of-the-art **musuem** (daily May–Sept 9am–7pm; Oct–April 9.30am–5.30pm; €7; ⓦ www .pontdugard.fr), botanical **gardens**, and a range of regular children's activities. With the swimmable waters of the Gardon and ample picnic possibilities available, you could easily spend a day here.

Uzès

Seventeen kilometres further on, near the start of the aqueduct and served by daily buses from Nîmes, **UZÈS** is a lovely old town perched on a hill above the River Alzon. Half a dozen medieval towers – the most fetching is the windowed Pisa-like **Tour Fenestrelle**, tacked onto the much later cathedral – rise above its tiled roofs and narrow lanes of Renaissance and Neoclassical houses. The latter were the residences of the seventeenth- and eighteenth-century local bourgeoisie, who had grown rich, like their fellow Protestants in Nîmes, on textiles. From the mansion of Le Portalet, with its view out over the valley, walk past the Renaissance church of **St-Étienne** and into the medieval place aux Herbes, where there's a Saturday morning market, and up the arcaded rue de la République. The Gide family used to live off the square, the young André spending summer vacations with his granny there. To the right of rue de la République is the **castle of Le Duché** (1hr 30min guided tours: July & Aug 10am–12.30pm & 2–6.30pm; Sept to June 10am–noon & 2–6pm; €14), still inhabited by the same family a thousand years on, and dominated by its original keep, the **Tour Bermonde** (tower only €9). Today, there are guided tours around the castle, exhibits of local history and vintage cars. Opposite, the courtyard of the eighteenth-century **Hôtel de Ville** holds summer concerts.

For details of these and other summer events, including more bull-running, consult the **tourist office** in place Albert-1ᵉʳ on boulevard Gambetta (June–Sept Mon–Fri 9am–6/7pm, Sat & Sun 10am–1pm & 2–7pm; Oct–May Mon–Fri 9am–12.30pm & 2–6pm, Sat 10am–1pm; ☎04.66.22.68.88, ⓦwww .uzes-tourisme.com). The **gare routière** (☎04.66.22.00.58) is further west on avenue de la Libération. Should you need **accommodation**, head for the friendly *Hostellerie Provençal* in two old row houses at 1 rue Grand Bourgade, south of the church of St-Étienne (☎04.66.22.11.06, ⓦwww.hostellerieprovencale.com; ❺), or the attractively renovated ⚵ *La Taverne* (☎04.66.22.13.10, ⓕ04.66.22.45.90; ❸) a small and welcoming hotel with good amenities (including wi-fi) set behind the tourist office at 4 rue Xavier-Sigalon, and with a good *terroir* restaurant up the road at no. 7 (€20). The town's de luxe option is the *General d'Entraigues*, 8 rue de la Calade (☎04.66.22.32.68, ⓦwww.leshotelsparticuliers.com; ❸–❽), in a converted fifteenth-century mansion opposite the cathedral. Alternatively, there's a municipal **campsite** off avenue Maxime-Pascal (mid-June to mid-Sept; ☎04.66.22.38.55) on the Bagnols-sur-Cèze road running northeast of town.

The Via Domitia and Sommières

About 25km west of Nîmes, off the Sommières road out of Lunel and close to the A9 autoroute, the Roman **Via Domitia** crosses the vineyards from the village of Gallargues to the bank of the River Vidourle, where one isolated arch of the original **Roman bridge** remains. On the west bank, a fine stretch of the old **cobbled way** is visible climbing the slopes of the former Roman settlement of **Ambrussum**, a fortified staging post on the road. From the top of the hill you can look down on international traffic still passing the same way on the autoroute and parallel rail line.

About 10km to the north, 28km from Nîmes and still on the Vidourle, the little medieval town of **SOMMIÈRES**, with a much-modified Roman bridge, is where author Lawrence Durrell spent his last years. The town itself boasts no major sights, though it's well preserved and atmospheric. However, a visit to the **castle of Villevieille** (April–June & Oct Sat & Sun 2–7pm; July–Sept daily 2–8pm; €8), on the hillside 3km above Sommières, should not be missed. Owned by the same family for nearly eight hundred years, it is full of exquisite antique furniture. There are daily **buses** to Sommières from Nîmes; for **accommodation**, try the *L'Estelou* (☎04.66.77.71.08, ⓦwww.hoteldelestelou.free.fr; ❸), an arty hotel set in the town's old *gare*, or the *chambre d'hôte*, *La Mas Fontclaire* in 8 avenue Émile-Jamais (☎04.66.77.78.69, ⓦmasfonclair.free.fr; English spoken; ❹). There's also a municipal **campsite** on rue Eugène-Rouch.

Montpellier

A thousand years of trade and intellectual activity have made **MONTPELLIER** a teeming, energetic city. Benjamin of Tudela, the tireless twelfth-century Jewish traveller, reported its streets crowded with traders from every corner of Egypt, Greece, Gaul, Spain, Genoa and Pisa. After the king of Mallorca sold it to France in 1349 it became an important university town in the 1500s, counting the radical satirist François Rabelais among its alumni. Periodic setbacks, including almost total destruction for its Protestantism in 1622, and depression in the wine trade in the early years of the twentieth century, have done little to dent its progress. Today it vies with Toulouse for the title of the most dynamic city in the south. The reputation of its university especially, founded in the thirteenth century and most famous for its medical school, is a long-standing one: more than sixty thousand students still set the intellectual and cultural tone of the city, the average age of whose residents is said to be just 25. In many senses the best time to visit is during the academic year (October to June), when the city teems with students looking for stimulation of every kind.

Montpellier is renowned for its **cultural life**, and hosts a number of annual **festivals**: Le Printemps des Comédiens (mid-June to mid-July) is a theatre festival; Montpellier Danse (June) is for dance; there's also a music festival, Le Festival de Radio-France et de Montpellier (second half of July); and the Festival du Cinéma Méditerranéen (second half of Oct, early Nov). The tourist office provides information about programmes and booking.

Arrival and information

The **gare SNCF** (☎04.99.74.15.10) and **gare routière** (☎04.67.92.01.43) are next to each other at the opposite end of rue Maguelone from the central place de la Comédie. The **airport**, Montpellier-Méditerranée (☎04.67.20.85.00, ⓦwww.montpellier.aeroport.fr), is 8km to the southeast beside the Étang de Mauguio; from here a **navette** (timed for flights; 15min €4.90) runs to the stop on rue de Crète (by the Léon Blum tramstop); it will cost you €15–32 by **taxi** depending on the time of day and traffic conditions. Much of the city centre is pedestrianized, but you can street park outside the centre and there are many well-signed municipal garages.

The **tourist office** (daily: Mon–Fri 9am–7.30pm, Sat 9.30am–6pm, Sun & public holidays 9.30am–1pm & 2.30–6pm; ☎04.67.60.60.60, ⓦwww.ot-montpellier.fr), which has money exchange facilities, lies at the east end of place de la Comédie, opposite the Polygone shopping centre. They also sell the one-, two- and three-day City Card, which includes public transport, free admission to many sites and other discounts. TAM **city buses** run between the stations and outer districts (as far as coastal Palavas), while the Petibus crosses the city centre – tickets cost €1.30 (day ticket for €3.20) and cover both services for one hour, including transfers. The green transport policies of Montpellier have also resulted in the construction of a **tramway**,

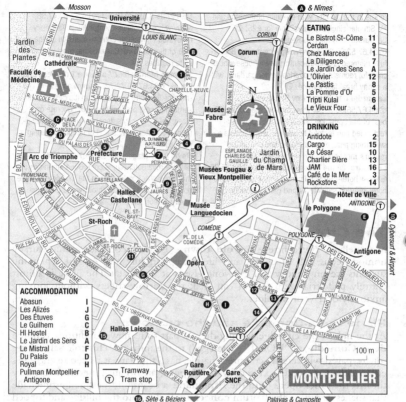

Inside the map:

▲ Mosson   ▲ ❹ & Nîmes

Université

Jardin des Plantes

LOUIS BLANC   CORUM

Corum

Cathédrale

Faculté de Médecine

Musée Fabre

N

Arc de Triomphe

Préfecture

Esplanade Charles de Gaulle

Jardin du Champ de Mars

Musées Fougau & Vieux Montpellier

Halles Castellane

Musée Languedocien

St-Roch

Hôtel de Ville

le Polygone

ANTIGONE

Antigone

COMÉDIE

PL. DE LA COMÉDIE

Opéra

⟶ ❿, Cybersurf & Airport

11

LANGUEDOC | Montpellier

Halles Laissac

Gare Routière   Gare SNCF

MONTPELLIER

ACCOMMODATION
Abasun	I
Les Alizés	J
Des Étuves	G
Le Guilhem	C
HI Hostel	B
Le Jardin des Sens	A
Le Mistral	F
Du Palais	D
Royal	H
Pullman Montpellier Antigone	E

— Tramway
Ⓣ Tram stop

EATING
Le Bistrot St-Côme	11
Cerdan	9
Chez Marceau	1
La Diligence	7
Le Jardin des Sens	A
L'Olivier	12
Le Pastis	8
La Pomme d'Or	5
Tripti Kulai	6
Le Vieux Four	4

DRINKING
Antidote	2
Cargo	15
Le César	10
Charlier Bière	13
JAM	16
Café de la Mer	3
Rockstore	14

0   100 m

▼ ⓰, Sète & Béziers   Palavas & Campsite ▼

---

sweeping across town from northwest to southeast, as well as over 120km of **bike paths** running throughout the city and to the sea.

Accommodation

Most hotel **accommodation** is conveniently concentrated in the streets between the train station and place de la Comédie, or in the nearby centre of the old town. There's a well-equipped **hostel** in a renovated old building in impasse Petite Corraterie, off rue des Écoles Laïques (closed mid-Dec to mid-Jan; ℡04.67.60.32.22, ⓦwww.fuaj.org; bus #6 "Ursulines"; ❶), plus several **campsites** around Montpellier, particularly in nearby Palavas (bus #28); the most central and expensive is *L'Oasis Palavasienne* (℡04.67.15.11.61, ⓦwww.oasis-palavasienne.com; April–Sept), just south of town on the D21 (to Palavas; bus #28), which also has a waterpark.

Hotels

Abasun 13 rue Maguelone ℡04.67.58.36.80, ⓦwww.abasunhotelmontpellercentre.com. On a busy street a stone's throw from the train station, this recently renovated hotel is clean, if somewhat basic – a good option for budget-conscious travellers. ❷

Les Alizés 14 rue Jules-Ferry ℡04.67.12.85.35, ⓔcouleurs.suds@club-internet.fr. Perhaps overpriced, but convenient, with a station-side location. Amenities include en-suite bath, satellite TV in every room, and a restaurant serving from 5am–1am. ❸

Des Étuves 24 rue des Étuves ℡04.67.60.78.19, ⓦwww.hoteldesetuves.fr. No-nonsense, spotless

769

rooms in the old city, with en-suite bathrooms and TV. Simpler singles are available for €25. ❶

Le Guilhem 18 rue J.J.-Rousseau ☎04.67.52.90.90, ⒲www.leguilhem.com. Beautifully restored sixteenth-century town house whose cheerful rooms mostly overlook quiet gardens, with a sunny breakfast terrace. ❺

Le Jardin des Sens 11 av St-Lazare ☎04.67.58.38.38, ⒲www.jardindessens.com. The best of the upmarket hotels and the epitome of restrained and tasteful luxury, *Le Jardin* boasts a swimming pool, elegant rooms and one of the region's most acclaimed restaurants. ❻

Le Mistral 25 rue Boussairolles ☎04.67.58.45.25, ⒲www.hotel-le-mistral.com. Decent, comfortable hotel, offering satellite TV and garage parking (€5 extra). ❷

Du Palais 3 rue du Palais ☎04.67.60.47.38, ⒲www.hoteldupalais-montpellier.fr. Tastefully renovated eighteenth-century mansion on the west side of the old town. Cosy rooms, most with en-suite facilities. ❹

Pullman Montpellier Antigone 1 rue des Pertuisanes ☎04.67.99.72.72, ⒲www.sofitel-montpellier.com. Suitably futuristic design, with a somewhat cold predominance of concrete over glass, set in the city's flagship Antigone development. Four-star service and amenities including a pool. ❽

Royal 8 rue Maguelone ☎04.67.92.13.36, ⒲www.royalhotel-nimes.com. Good amenities in this three-star hotel between the Comédie and the *gare* – excellent value with old-world ambience at a very reasonable price. ❹

The City

Montpellier's city centre – the **old town** – is small, compact, architecturally homogeneous, full of charm and life, except in July and August when the students are on holiday and everyone else is at the beach. The place is almost entirely pedestrianized, so you can walk the narrow streets without looking anxiously over your shoulder.

Place de la Comédie and the old town

At the hub of the city's life, joining the old part to its newer additions, is **place de la Comédie**, or "L'Oeuf" ("the egg") to the initiated. This colossal, oblong square, paved with cream-coloured marble, has a fountain at its centre and cafés either side. One end is closed by the **Opéra**, an ornate nineteenth-century theatre; the other end opens onto the **Esplanade**, a beautiful tree-lined promenade that snakes its way to the Corum **concert hall**, dug into the hillside and topped off in pink granite, with splendid views from the roof. South of the Corum, the city's most trumpeted museum, the **Musée Fabre** (Tues, Thurs & Fri 10am–6pm, Wed 1–9pm, Sat & Sun 11am–6pm; €6), has reopened after a major renovation. Its huge collection features seventeenth- to nineteenth-century European painting, including works by Delacroix, Zurabaran, Raphael, Jan van Steen and Veronese, as well as ceramics and contemporary art.

From the north side of L'Oeuf, **rue de la Loge** and **rue Foch**, opened in the 1880s in Montpellier's own Haussmann-izing spree, slice through the heart of the old city. Either side of them, a maze of narrow lanes slopes away to the encircling modern boulevards. Few buildings survive from before the 1622 siege, but the city's busy bourgeoisie quickly made up for the loss, proclaiming their financial power through austere seventeenth- and eighteenth-century mansions. Known as "Lou Clapas" (rubble), the area is rapidly being restored and gentrified. It's a pleasure to wander through and come upon secretive little squares like the places St-Roch, St-Ravy and de la Canourgue.

First left off rue de la Loge is **Grande-Rue Jean-Moulin**, where Moulin, hero of the Resistance, lived at no. 21. To the left, at no. 32, the present-day chamber of commerce is located in one of the finest eighteenth-century *hôtels*, the Hôtel St-Côme, originally built as a demonstration operating theatre for medical students. On the opposite corner, rue de l'Argenterie forks up to **place Jean-Jaurès**. This square is a nodal point in the city's student life: early on fine evenings you get the impression that half the population is sitting here and in the adjacent place du Marché-aux-Fleurs. Through the Gothic doorway of no. 10 is the so-called palace of the kings of Aragon, named after the city's thirteenth-century rulers. Also on the square, the **Musée de l'Histoire de Montpellier** (Tues–Sat enter 10.30–11.50am & 1.30–5.20pm), housed in an ancient crypt, offers reconstructions of the city's past. Close by is the **Halles Castellane**, a graceful, iron-framed market hall.

A short walk from place Jean-Jaurès, the Hôtel de Varenne, on place Pétrarque, houses two local history museums of somewhat specialized interest and a rather paltry range of artefacts; the **Musée du Vieux Montpellier** (Tues–Sat 10.30am–12.30pm & 1.30–5pm; free) concentrates on the city's history, and the more interesting, private **Musée Fougau** on the top floor (Wed & Thurs 3–6pm; free) deals with the folk history of Languedoc and things Occitan. Off to the right, the lively little rue des Trésoriers-de-France has one of the best seventeenth-century houses in the city, the **Hôtel Lunaret**, at no. 5, while round the block on rue Jacques-Coeur you'll find the **Musée Languedocien** (Mon–Sat 2/3–5/6pm; €5), which houses a mixed collection of Greek, Egyptian and other antiquities.

Jardin des Plantes and around

On the hill at the end of rue Foch, from which the royal artillery bombarded the Protestants in 1622, the formal gardens of the **Promenade du Peyrou** look out across the city and away to the Pic St-Loup, which dominates the hinterland behind Montpellier, with the distant smudge of the Cévennes beyond. At the farther side a swagged and pillared water tower marks the end of an eighteenth-century aqueduct modelled on the Pont du Gard. Beneath the grand sweep of its double-tiered arches is a daily fruit and veg market and a huge Saturday **flea market**. At the city end of the promenade, the vainglorious **Arc de Triomphe** shows Louis XIV as Hercules, stomping on the Austrian eagle and English lion, forcefully reminding the locals of his victory over their Protestant "heresy".

Lower down the hill, on boulevard Henri-IV, the lovely but slightly run-down **Jardin des Plantes** (July & Aug daily noon–8pm; Sept–June daily 2–5pm; free), with avenues of exotic trees, is France's oldest botanical garden, founded in 1593. Across the road is the long-suffering **cathedral**, with its massive porch, sporting a patchwork of styles from the fourteenth to the nineteenth centuries. Inside is a memorial to the bishop of Montpellier, who sided with the half-million destitute vine-growers who came to demonstrate against their plight in 1907 and were fired on by government troops. Above the cathedral, in the university's prestigious medical school on rue de l'École-de-Médecine, the **Musée Atger** (Mon, Wed & Fri 1.30–5.45pm; free) has a distinguished academic collection of French and Italian drawings, while the macabre **Musée d'Anatomie** (daily 2.30–5pm; free) displays revolting things in bottles.

Antigone

South of place de la Comédie stretches the controversial quarter of **Antigone**, a chain of post-modern squares and open spaces designed to provide a mix of fair-rent housing and offices, aligned along a monumental axis from the place du Nombre-d'Or, through place du Millénaire, to the glassed-in arch of the Hôtel de la Région. It's more interesting in scale and design than most attempts at urban renewal, but it has failed to attract the crowds away from the place de la Comédie and is often deserted. The enclosed spaces in particular work well, with their theatrical references to classical architecture, like oversized cornices and columns supporting only sky. The more open spaces are, however, disturbing, with something totalitarian and inhuman about their scale and blandness.

Eating, drinking and entertainment

Montpellier's year-round vitality supports a variety of **restaurants** and **bars** to suit all budgets and tastes. **Cafés** line every square while some of the more expensive restaurants use the city's ancient interiors to stunning effect. And Montpellier's youthful population ensures an energetic bar and **nightclub** scene right through to the early hours.

There's always plenty of **drinking** activity in the place de la Comédie, place du Marché-aux-Fleurs and place Jean-Jaurès, and two very different options are *Charlier Bière*, a grungy beer bar at 22 rue Olivier, and *Antidote*, a snappy cocktail joint on place de la Canourgue, which attracts the arty set. The *Café de la Mer*, at 5 place de Marché-aux-Fleurs, is a popular, gay-friendly establishment with a busy terrace. The old perennial for late-night dancing and live gigs is the *Rockstore*, near the station at 20 rue de Verdun (⊛ www.rockstore.fr), while *JAM*, at 100 rue Ferdinand-Lesseps, and *Cargo*, on place St-Denis, offer jazz and blues respectively. In addition to its clubs, bars and live music, Montpellier has a very lively **theatre scene**, as well as a tradition of engaging *café-littéraires* on a variety of themes; *Le César* at 17 place Nombre-d'Or (☎ 04.67.20.27.02) hosts two such gatherings, the *café des femmes* and the *café des arts* – check for days and times. For what's on at the various venues, look for posters around town or check the free weekly listings magazines, *Le Sortir* and *Olé*. The best central food **markets** are Halles Castellane, on rue de la Loge, and Laissac, place A. Laissace (daily 7.30am–1pm).

Restaurants and cafés

Le Bistrot St-Côme 2 place St-Côme. The best of a phalanx of open-air eateries dominating the south side of place St-Côme, offering a range of menus and standard but dependable French fare (€14–22). Service from noon till 11.30pm.

Cerdan 8 rue Collot ☎ 04.67.60.86.96. High-quality cuisine combining Norman and Algerian specialities, just off of the place de la Comédie. Lunch from €10 and dinners €14–36. Closed Sun & noon Mon.

Chez Marceau 7 place de la Chapelle Neuve ☎ 04.67.66.08.09. Excellent-value Languedocian cuisine (both inland and coastal varieties) with a wonderful shaded terrace. The *pâtés de canard* are particularly delicious. Menus €200 at lunch and dinner. Closed Sun & Wed low season.

La Diligence 2 place Pétrarque ☎ 04.67.66.12.21. *La Diligence* boasts an atmospheric, vaulted medieval setting perfect for a good-value dip into the finest French cuisine. Menus €20–61. Closed Sat lunch, Sun & Mon lunch.

Le Jardin des Sens 11 av St-Lazaire ☎ 04.67.79.63.38. Located just north of Le Corum and run by the Pourcel twins, scions of a local vinter family renowned for their

gastronomique creativity, this is one of the highest-rated restaurants in Languedoc. The ever-changing *carte* features excellent terroir-based creations ranging from pigeon pie to stuffed squid, served in elegant surroundings. Menus from €65. Closed Sun, Mon, Tues & Wed lunch.

L'Olivier 12 rue Aristide-Olivier ☎ 04.67.92.86.28. Pretty little restaurant north of the station offering excellent-value traditional French cuisine. Menus at €32–47. Closed Sun & Mon, and Aug.

Le Pastis 3 rue Terral ☎ 04.67.02.78.59. Great southern French cooking in a fine old mansion. Menus €21–32. Closed Sat.

La Pomme d'Or 23 rue du Palais des Guilhem ☎ 04.67.52.82.62. Arty restaurant-bar with a predominantly gay clientele. A very wide selection of inventive menus at €18.

Tripti Kulai 20 rue Jacques-Coeur. Quirky, friendly women-run vegetarian restaurant. Dishes with oriental-influenced flair, including a good choice of salads, start at €12. Closed Sun.

Le Vieux Four 59 rue de l'Aiguillerie ☎ 04.67.60.55.95. Meat-eaters should head for this cosy, candlelit place specializing in *grillades au feu de bois*. Menus €14–25. Evenings only.

Listings

Bike rental Bikes can be rented at Vill'a Vélo at the *gare routière* (T 04.67.92.92.67).

Books English books at: As You Like It, 8 rue du Bras de Fer; Book Shop, 4 rue de l'Université. Travel books at: Les Cinq Continents, 20 rue Jacques-Coeur.

Internet There are lots of cybercafés around town; try *Cybersurf*, 22 place du Millénaire in Antigone (Mon–Fri 8am–9pm, Sat & Sun 10am–6pm).

Medical emergencies T 04.67.22.81.67 or T 15; Centre Hospitalier de Montpellier, 555 rte de Ganges (T 04.67.33.93.02) – take bus #16 from the gare to "Route de ganges" or the tram to "Hôpital Lapeyronie" and walk.

Post office The main office is on place Rondelet, 34000 Montpellier (Mon–Fri 9am–7pm, Sat 9am–noon).

Shopping The most convenient place is the Polygone mall, which contains a FNAC and Galeries Lafayette.

Swimming The nearest beaches for a dip are at Palavas (tram direction "Odysseum" to Port Marianne, then bus #28), but the best are slightly to the west of the town.

The coast: Aigues-Mortes to Agde

On the face of it, the **Languedoc coast** isn't particularly enticing, lined with bleak beaches and treeless strands, often irritatingly windswept and cut off from the sea by marshy *étangs* (lagoons). The area does, however, have long hours of sunshine, 200km of only sporadically populated sand and relatively unpolluted water. Resorts – mostly geared towards families who settle in for a few weeks at a time – have sprung up, sometimes engulfing once quiet fishing towns, but there's still enough unexploited territory to make this coast a good getaway from the crowds, and many of the old towns have managed to sustain their character and traditions despite the summer onslaught.

La Grande-Motte, Le Grau-du-Roi and Aigues-Mortes

The oldest of the new resorts, on the fringes of the Camargue, **LA GRANDE-MOTTE** is a 1960s vintage beach-side Antigone – a "futuristic" planned community which has aged as gracefully as the bean bag and eight-track tape. In summer, its seaside and streets are crowded with semi-naked bodies; in winter, it's a depressing, wind-battered place with few permanent residents. If you plan on **staying**, both *Camping Louis Pibols* (T 04.67.56.50.08; April–Oct) and *Camping le Garden* (T 04.67.56.50.09; March–Oct) offer excellent facilities and are just a couple of minutes' walk from the beach. The most appealing among the town's dozen or so near-identical **hotels** is the *Azur* (T 04.67.56.56.00, W www.hotelazur.net; ❹), set dramatically on the extremity of the town's quay.

A little way east are Port-Camargue, with a sprawling, modern marina, and **LE GRAU-DU-ROI**, which manages to retain something of its character as a working fishing port. Tourist traffic still has to give way every afternoon at 4.30pm when the swing bridge opens and lets in the trawlers to unload the day's catch onto the quayside, from where it's whisked off to auction – *la criée* – now conducted largely by electronic means rather than harsh-voiced shouting. For a reasonable place to **stay**, try the *Bellevue et d'Angleterre*, quai Colbert (closed Jan; T 04.66.51.40.75, W www.hotelbellevueetdangleterre .com; ❹), or the huge *Camping L'Eden* (April–Oct; T 04.66.51.49.81, W www .campingleden.fr), just east of town.

Eight kilometres inland lies the appealingly named town of **AIGUES-MORTES** ("dead waters"), built as a fortress port by Louis IX in the thirteenth century for his departure on the Seventh Crusade. Its massive walls and towers remain virtually intact. Outside the ramparts, amid drab modern development, flat salt pans lend a certain otherworldly appeal, but inside all is geared to the tourist. If you visit, consider a climb up the **Tour de Constance** on the northwest corner of the town walls (daily: May–Aug 10am–7pm; Sept–April 10am–5.30pm; €6.50), where Camisard women were imprisoned (Marie Durand was incarcerated for 38 years), and a walk along the wall, where you can gaze out over the weird mist-shrouded flats of the Camargue.

Sète

Some 28km southeast of Montpellier, twenty minutes away by train, **SÈTE** has been an important port for three hundred years. The upper part of the town straddles the slopes of the Mont St-Clair, which overlooks the vast Bassin de Thau, a breeding ground of mussels and oysters, while the lower part is inter-sected by waterways lined with tall terraces and seafood restaurants. It has a lively workaday bustle in addition to its tourist activity, at its height during the summer *joutes nautiques* (see box below).

Arrival, information and accommodation

The **gare routière** is awkwardly placed on quai de la République, and the **gare SNCF** further out still on quai Maréchal-Joffre – though it is on the main bus route, which circles Mont St-Clair (last bus about 7pm). **Ferries** for Morocco (1–2 weekly) and Mallorca (1–3 weekly) depart from the *gare maritime* at 4 quai d'Alger (℡04.67.46.68.00). The **tourist office**, at 60 Grand'Rue Mario-Roustan (April–June & Sept–Oct daily 9.30am–6pm; July & Aug daily 9.30am–7.30pm; Nov–March Mon–Fri 9.30am–6pm, Sat & Sun 9.30am–12.30pm & 2–5.30pm; ℡04.67.74.71.71, Ⓦwww.ot-sete.fr), has a good array of English-language information.

For **accommodation**, a great option is the *belle-époque* splendour of the *Grand Hôtel*, 17 quai de Lattre-de-Tassigny (℡04.67.74.71.77, Ⓦwww.legrandhotelsete .com; ❻), which also has apartments (€220), and ⚞ *L'Orque Bleu* at 10 quai Aspirant-Herber (℡04.67.74.72.13, Ⓦwww.hotel-orqueblueu-sete.com; ❹), which offers an equally charming alternative at a lower price. The **HI hostel** (mid-Jan to mid-Dec; ℡04.67.53.46.68, Ⓦwww.fuaj.org; €15,50 or ❶) is high up in the town on rue Général-Revest. Campers should ask the tourist office for details of the numerous campsites in the area.

The Town

Sète's crowded and vibrant pedestrian streets are scattered with café tables. A short climb up from the harbour is the **cimetière marin**, the sailors' cemetery, where poet Paul Valéry is buried. Adjacent to the cemetery, the small **Musée Paul Valéry**, in rue Denoyer (July & Aug daily 10am–noon & 2–6pm; Sept–June Wed–Mon 10am–noon & 2–6pm; €4), opposite the cemetery, and the

Éspace Brassens (June–Sept daily 10am–noon & 2–7pm; Oct–May Tues–Sun 10am–noon & 2–6pm; €5), dedicated to a locally born singer-songwriter, will be of scarce interest to non-fans. More interesting is the **Musée International des Arts Modestes** (July & Aug daily 10am–noon & 2–6pm; Sept–June daily except Tues 10am–noon & 2–6pm; €5) at 23 quai Maréchal-Lattre, containing a collection of art made from cast-off goods and spinning on popular culture themes. For €6 you can get the "Pass Musée" for all three museums.

Eating and drinking

There's a barrage of **restaurants** along quai Général-Duran, from the Pont de la Savonnerie right down to the fish market at the mouth of the pleasure port, all offering seafood in the €15–35 bracket. Local favourite ☎ *La Palangrotte* (☎04.67.74.80.35; closed Sun evening & Mon & Wed off season), at 1 rampe Paul-Valéry, is famous for its mussels and bouillabaisse (€23–36) and solid wine list. Another good choice is *La Galinette*, 26 place des Mouettes (closed lunch July–Sept, Oct–Dec closed evenings Sun–Thurs & lunch Fri & Sat; ☎04.67.51.16.77), on the north side of town.

Agde and around

Midway between Sète and Béziers, at the western end of the Bassin de Thau, **AGDE** is the most interesting of the coastal towns. Originally Phoenician, and maintained by the Romans, it thrived for centuries on trade with the Levant. Outrun as a seaport by Sète, it later degenerated into a sleepy fishing harbour.

Today, it's a major tourist centre with a good deal of charm, notably in the narrow back lanes between rue de l'Amour and the riverside, where fishing boats tie up. There are few sights apart from the impressively fortified **cathedral**, though the **waterfront** is attractive, and by the bridge you can watch the Canal du Midi slip modestly into the River Hérault on the very last leg of its journey from Toulouse to the Bassin de Thau and Sète.

The **tourist office** (July & Aug 10am–7pm; noon & 2–6pm; Sept–June Mon & Wed–Sat 9am–noon & 2–5/6pm, Sun 2–5/6pm; ☎04.67.01.04.04, ⓦwww .capdagde.com) for the old town of Agde (the *cité*) and nearby Cap d'Agde and Grau d'Agde is unmissable, set on the roundabout at the entrance to Cap, travelling from the *cité*. The pick of the town's **hotels** is ☎ *La Galiote* (☎04.67.94.45.58, ⓦwww.lagaliote.fr; ❺), located in the old bishop's palace on place J.-Jaurès, with its excellent service and restrained elegance while *Le Donjon* (☎04.67.94.12.32, ⓦwww.hotelledonjon.com; ❹) in another atmospheric old building next door, comes a close second. Aside from the numerous places to **eat** around La Promenade, a good bet is *La Fine Fourchetté Libanaise* (☎04.67.94.49.56; Sept–June closed Sun) at 2 rue du Mont-Saint-Loup, featuring a delightful *carte* (menus from €10) of Middle Eastern dishes. One of the area's best restaurants is at *Le Jardin de Beaumont* (☎04.67.21.19.23; closed Sept–June Thurs–Sat evening & Sun noon), set in a wine *domaine* 3km north of town, where you can dine on tapas and excellent wines indoors or out (starting for as little as €10).

An hourly **bus service** operates between the town and the sea at **Cap d'Agde** (see below); you can pick it up at the *gare* SNCF at the end of avenue Victor-Hugo, at the bridge and on La Promenade. Should you want to explore the Canal du Midi, **boat trips** are organized by Bateaux du Soleil, 6 rue Chassefières (☎04.67.94.08.79).

Cap d'Agde

CAP D'AGDE lies to the south of Mont St-Loup, 7km from Agde. The largest (and by far the most successful) of the newer resorts, it sprawls out from the volcanic mound of St-Loup in an excess of pseudo-traditional modern buildings that offer every type of facility and entertainment – and are all expensive. It is perhaps best known for its colossal **quartier naturiste** (Ⓦ www.villagenaturiste-agde.com), one of the largest in France, with the best of the beaches, space for 20,000 visitors, and its own restaurants, banks, post offices and shops. Access is possible if you're not actually staying there (€12 per car, €5 on foot; both until 8pm only).

If you have time to fill, head for the **Musée de l'Éphèbe** (Mon & Wed–Sat 9am–noon & 2–6pm & Sun 2–6pm; €8.50), which displays antiquities discovered locally, many of them from the sea. Alternatively, the **Fort de Brescou** (July–Sept; €3), which dates back to 1680, lies on a rocky, seagull-infested island just offshore; it can be reached by ferries from the centre port at Cap d'Agde and Grau d'Agde (April & early Sept Wed & Thurs 2.30pm; late June daily 2.30pm; July & Aug daily 2.30 & 4.30pm; Sept 2.30pm; €6 & €7).

Inland from Montpellier

For getting out into the country of the Bas Languedoc, there are two good routes from Montpellier, both served by regular buses: the D986 to **Ganges** and the N109 to **Lodève**. This out-of-the-way corner of Languedoc is best for its relatively untouristed villages, as well as excellent hiking and rafting opportunities.

The Ganges route

The Ganges road weaves north across the Plateau des Garrigues, a landscape of scrubby trees, thorns and fragrant herbs cut by torrent beds. The plateau is dominated by the high limestone ridge of the **Pic St-Loup** until you reach a lovely little town of arcaded houses, **ST-MARTIN-DE-LONDRES**, an excellent place to stretch one's legs.

Further north, through dramatic river gorges almost as far as Ganges, you reach the **Grotte des Demoiselles** (March & Oct daily 10–11am & 2–4.30pm; April–June & Sept daily 10am–5.30pm; July & Aug daily 10am–6pm; Nov–Feb

---

The Camisards

By issuing the Revocation of the Edict of Nantes in 1685, Louis XIV ended religious freedom in France, outlawing the Calvinist Protestantism of the Hugenots. Some five hundred thousand chose to flee the country, including many merchants and textile workers, while those who remained were subjected to **oppression**; some feigned conversion, some were deported to the colonies, and others fled to the "desert" – the wild and isolated hills of the Cévennes. It was here that they staged the **Camisard** revolt, so-called for the shirts they wore as a sign of recognition (from "chemise", French for shirt).

In July 1702, the parish priest of Chayla arrested a small group of fugitive Protestants, and was killed in the ensuing struggle. Knowing that retribution would be swift and cruel, Protestants across the Cévennes began a guerrilla war which pitted their forces, numbering between three and five thousand, against some thirty thousand royal troops. Unable to conclude the struggle militarily against the rebel guerrillas, the French army succeeded in bribing one of the leaders to change sides, precipitating the defeat of the movement in 1704.

Sun 10–11am & 2–4pm; ⓦwww.demoiselles.com; €8.70), the most spectacular of the region's many caves: a set of vast cathedral-like caverns hung with stalactites descending with millennial slowness to meet the limpid waters of eerily still pools. Located deep inside the mountain, it's reached by funicular (hourly departures).

Ganges

GANGES itself, 46km from Montpellier and connected by regular buses (which continue to Le Vigan on the southern edge of the Cévennes), is a rather nondescript but busy market town (Friday's the day), whose old quarter is notable for its vaulted alleys, designed for defence in the Wars of Religion. It was here that the last-ditch revolt of the Camisards (see box opposite) earned its name; the rebels sacked and pillaged a shirt factory and went off wearing the shirts (*chemises/camises*). Heading north from Ganges on your own steam will lead you deeper into Protestant territory, to the Huguenot villages around Le Vigan (see p.851).

The **tourist office** (July & Aug Mon–Sat 9am–noon & 2–7pm & Sun 10am–noon; Sept–June Mon–Fri 9am–noon & 2–6pm & Sat 9.30am–12.30pm; ☏04.67.73.00.56, ⓦwww.ot-cevennes.com) is on plan de l'Ormeau. On the same square you'll find the basic *De la Poste* (☏04.67.73.85.88, ⓦwww.hoteldelaposteganges.com; closed Jan; ❷), which is the best overnight choice in town and has family-sized rooms. West of town, on the road towards Navacelles, is the splendid *Château de Madières* (closed Nov–March; ☏04.67.73.84.03, ⓦwww.chateau-madieres.fr; ❽), a renovated fourteenth-century castle. The municipal **campsite** (mid-June to Aug; ☏04.67.57.92.97) is along the river at the southern end of town.

The Lodève route

The second inland route runs due west from Montpellier, passing **Gignac** – the turn-off for the spectacular **Gorges de l'Hérault** and **St-Guilhem-le-Désert** – before reaching **Clermont-l'Hérault**, a transport hub from where you can access the Haut Languedoc to the west or the old cathedral town of **Lodève** further north.

St-Guilhem-le-Désert and around

The small town of **Gignac** lies amid vineyards 30km west of Montpellier. It is here that buses turn off for the glorious abbey and village of **ST-GUILHEM-LE-DÉSERT**, which lies in a side ravine, 6km further north up the Hérault beyond the famed medieval Pont du Diable. A ruined castle spikes the ridge above, and the ancient tiled houses of the village ramble down the banks of the rushing Verdus, which is everywhere channelled into carefully tended gardens. The grand focus is the tenth- to twelfth-century **abbey church** (daily 8am–12.10pm & 2.30–6.20pm; free), founded at the beginning of the ninth century by St Guilhem, comrade-in-arms of Charlemagne. The church is a beautiful and atmospheric building, though architecturally impoverished by the dismantling and sale of its cloister – now in New York – in the nineteenth century. It stands on place de la Liberté, surrounded by honey-coloured houses and arcades with traces of Romanesque and Renaissance domestic styles in some of the windows. The interior of the church is plain and somewhat severe compared to the warm colours of the exterior, best seen from rue Cor-de-Nostra-Dama/Font-du-Portal, where you get the classic view of the perfect apse.

In season the village is on every tour operator's route, making early mornings and late afternoons better for visiting. The best **hotel** is *Le Guilhaume d'Orange* (☏04.67.57.24.53, ⓦwww.guilhaumedorange.com; ❸), while budget

▲ The abbey church of St-Guilhem-le-Désert

travellers should head to the English-speaking *Gîte de la Tour* (T&F04.67.57.34.00; ❶). The nearest **campsite** is *Le Moulin de Siau* (T04.67.57.51.08, Wwwwcamping-moulin-de-siau.com), near Aniane on the road back down to Gignac; currently being renovated it is set to reopen in 2009. Nearby, cave enthusiasts will enjoy the **Grotte de Clamouse** (Feb, May & Oct 10am–5pm; June–Sept daily 10am–6/7pm; €8.50). This extensive and beautiful stalactite cave is entered along a subterranean river and opens up into three expansive grottoes.

Clermont-l'Hérault

Eight kilometres west of Gignac, the market town of **CLERMONT-L'HÉRAULT** (bus from Montpellier) is a dull little cantonal capital, whose only recommendation is that it is a good jumping-off point for visiting the area around **Lac Salagou** to the west, an attractive man-made reservoir sited amid striking iron-rich terrain. The sole interesting site in town is a thirteenth-century **church**, fortified in the fourteenth century to defend it against the English.

The **tourist office** (Mon–Fri 9am–12.30pm & 2–7pm, Sat 9am–noon & 2–5/6pm; plus July & Aug Sun 10am–noon; T04.67.96.23.86, Wwww .clermont-l-herault.com) is at 9 rue René-Gosse, close to the cathedral. By far the best **place to stay** is *Le Terminus*, on allées Roger-Salengro near the old station (T04.67.88.45.00, Wpagesperso-orange.fr/leterminus; ❷). If you're **camping**, head for the year-round site *Le Salagou* (T04.67.96.13.13), northwest of Clermont near the lake. Reasonable meals, including African specialities, can be had at Clermont-l'Hérault at *Yellba a l'Arlequin*, tucked under the south wall of the church on place St-Paul (closed Sat noon, Sun evening & Mon; menus from €15).

Around Clermont-l'Hérault

Three kilometres west from Clermont-l'Hérault, along the main road to Bédarieux, lies **VILLENEUVETTE**. This model factory and workers' settlement was created in the seventeenth century for the production of high-quality wool for sale in the Mediterranean. Initially successful, the factory eventually closed down in 1954, but the settlement still boasts 85 inhabitants. There's a very nice, and reasonably priced, **hotel** tacked on to the village walls – *La Source* (closed Jan to mid-Feb & late Nov; ☎04.67.96.05.07, ⓦ www.hoteldelasource .com; English spoken; ❸), with a good restaurant (€19–36), pool and garden. Eight kilometres further west just off the Bédarieux road, in the picturesque little village of **MOURÈZE**, you'll find an alternative hotel, *Les Hauts de Mourèze* (☎04.67.96.04.84, ⒻHGFE04.67.96.25.85; closed Nov–March; ❸).

On to Lodève

Heading north from Clermont to **LODÈVE**, 19km away, the swift A75 autoroute brings heavy traffic down from Clermont-Ferrand. It passes through countryside further scarred by uranium mining – the area around the village of St-Martin-du-Bosc has some of the highest soil concentration of radioactivity in the world.

Lodève, entirely enclosed by vine-terraced hills at the confluence of the Lergues and Soulondres rivers, is almost in the shadow of the **Causse de Larzac**. There are no real sights here, but it's a pleasant, old-fashioned place to pause on your way up to Le Caylar or La Couvertoirade on the *causse*. The **cathedral** – a stop on the pilgrim route to Santiago de Compostela – is worth a look, as is the unusual World War I **Monument aux Morts**, in the adjacent park, by local sculptor Paul Dardé. This spooky *mise en scène* of civilians mourning a soldier fall on the field is a departure from the usual stiff commemorations of the "Morts pour la France". More of his work is displayed at the town **museum** in the Hôtel Fleury (Tues–Sun 9.30am–noon & 2–6pm; €7) and the **Halle Dardé** (daily 9am–7pm; free) in the place du Marché. With a bit of organizing it's also possible to visit the **Atelier National de Tissage de Tapis** (Tues–Thurs 2.30pm; €3.20; arrange visit through tourist office), on the outskirts of Lodève, where priceless Gobelins tapestries are woven.

The **tourist office** is at 7 place de la République (Mon–Fri 9.30am–noon & 2.30–6pm, Sat 9.30am–noon; ☎04.67.88.86.44, ⓦ www.lodeve.com), next door to the **gare routière**, where you can catch buses to Montpellier, Béziers, Millau, Rodez and St-Afrique. The best place to **stay** in town is the *Hôtel du Nord* (☎04.67.44.10.08, ⓦ www.hotellodeve.com; ❸) at 18 boulevard de la Liberté, or the family-run *Hôtel de la Paix* (☎04.67.44.07.46, ⓦ www.hotel-dela-paix.com; ❸; closed Jan & Feb) on 11 boulevard Montalangue. There's a big **market** on Saturdays, and local farmers bring in their produce three times a week in summer.

Southern Languedoc

Southern Languedoc presents an exciting and varied landscape, its coastal flats stretching south from the mouth of the Aude towards Perpignan, interrupted by occasional low, rocky hills. Just inland sits **Béziers**, its imposing cathedral set high above the languid River Orb, girded in the north by the amazingly preserved Renaissance town of **Pézenas** and in the south by the pre-Roman settlement of the **Ensérune**. It's also a gateway to the spectacular uplands of the **Monts de l'Espinouse** and the **Parc Naturel Régional du Haut Languedoc**, a haven for ramblers. Just south of Béziers, the ancient Roman capital of **Narbonne** guards the mouth of the Aude. Following the course of this river, which is shadowed by the historic **Canal du Midi**, you arrive at the quintessential medieval citadel, the famous fortress-town of **Carcassonne**. Once a shelter for renegade **Cathar** heretics, Carcassonne is also a fine departure point for the Cathar castles – a string of romantically ruined castles covered on p.738.

Béziers and around

Though no longer the rich city of its nineteenth-century heyday, **BÉZIERS** has risen out of its recent dreariness with admirable panache. The town is the capital of the Languedoc **wine** country and a focus for the **Occitan** movement, as well as being the birthplace of Resistance hero **Jean Moulin**. The fortunes of the movement and the vine have long been closely linked; Occitan activists have helped to organize the militant local vine-growers, and there were ugly events during the mid-1970s, when blood was shed in confrontations with the authorities over the import of cheap foreign wines and the low prices paid for the essentially poor-grade local product. Things are calmer now, the conservatism of Languedoc farmers giving way to more modern attitudes in the face of public demand for something better than the traditional table wine. As a result, some of the steam has also gone out of the movement; interest today is more in the culture than in anti-Paris separatist feelings. The town is also home to two great Languedocian adopted traditions: English **rugby** and the Spanish **corrida**, both of which are followed with a passion. The best time to visit is during the mid-August **feria**, a raucous four-day party that can be enjoyed even if bullfighting isn't to your taste.

The City

The finest view of the old town is from the west, as you come in from Carcassonne: crossing the willow-lined River Orb by the Pont-Neuf, you can look upstream at the sturdy arches of the **Pont-Vieux**, above which rises a steep-banked hill crowned by the **Cathédrale St-Nazaire** which, with its crenellated towers, resembles a castle more than a church. The best approach to the cathedral is up the medieval lanes at the end of Pont-Vieux, rue Canterelles and passage Canterellettes. Its architecture is mainly Gothic, the original building having been burnt in 1209 during the sacking of Béziers, when Armand Amaury's crusaders massacred some seven thousand people at the church of the Madeleine for refusing to hand over about twenty Cathars. "Kill them all", the pious abbot is said to have ordered, "God will recognize his own!"

From the top of the cathedral **tower**, there's a superb view out across the vine-dominated surrounding landscape. Keep an eye on small kiddies, however, lest they slip through the potentially perilous gaps in the wall. Next door, you can wander through the ancient **cloister** (free) and out into the shady **bishop's garden** overlooking the river. In the adjacent **place de la Révolution**, a monument commemorates the people who died resisting Napoléon III's coup d'état in 1851 and their leader, Mayor Casimir Péret, who was shipped off to Cayenne where he drowned in a *Papillon*-style escape attempt. Also on the square, the Hôtel Fabrégat houses a **Musée des Beaux-Arts** (Tues–Sun: July & Aug 10am–6pm; Sept–June 9am–noon & 2–5/6pm; €3) which, apart from an interesting collection of Greek Cycladic vases, won't keep you long. Nearby, **Hôtel Fayet**, at 9 rue Capus (same hours and ticket), has been pressed into service as an annexe to the museum, though it's as much of interest for its period interiors as its collection of nineteenth- and early twentieth-century art and works by local sculptor Jean-Antoine Injalbert.

The city's other museum, the **Musée du Biterrois** (same hours; €3), in the old St-Jacques barracks on avenue de la Marne near the train station, displays a variety of entertaining exhibits, ranging from Greek amphorae and nineteenth-century door knockers to distilling manuals, clogs and winepresses. You might also take a look at the modest remains of the **Roman amphitheatre** two streets to the north of the museum off rue St-Jacques, which at the time of writing was being developed as an open-air museum. It once had a capacity of over thirteen thousand spectators, and its stones were used to construct the medieval walls.

Away from the medieval streets round the cathedral, the centre of life in Béziers is the **allées Paul-Riquet**, a broad, leafy esplanade lined with cafés, crêpe stalls, restaurants, banks and shops; it's named after the seventeenth-century tax collector who lost health and fortune in his obsession with building the Canal du Midi to join the Atlantic and Mediterranean. The *allées* runs from an elaborate nineteenth-century theatre on place de la Victoire to the gorgeous little park of the **Plateau des Poètes**, whose ponds, palms and lime trees were laid out in the so-called English manner by the man who created the Bois de Boulogne in Paris.

Practicalities

From the **gare SNCF** on boulevard Verdun, the best way into town is through the landscaped gardens of the Plateau des Poètes opposite the station entrance and up the allées Paul-Riquet. The **gare routière** is in place de Gaulle, at the northern end of the *allées*, while the **tourist office** is in the new Palais des Congrès at 29 avenue Saint-Saëns (July & Aug Mon–Sat 9am–6.30pm, Sun 9.30am–1pm & 3–6pm; Sept–June Mon–Sat 9am–noon/12.30pm & 2–6/6.30pm; ☏04.67.76.84.00, ⓦwww.beziers-tourisme.fr).

For a central place to **stay**, try the *Hôtel des Poètes*, 80 allées Paul-Riquet (☏04.67.76.38.66,ⓦwww.hoteldespoetes.net;❷), at the southern end overlooking the gardens, or the *France* (☏04.67.28.44.71, Ⓔfrancehotel@orange.fr; ❸) at 36 rue Boiëdieu. The town's deluxe option, *Hôtel Imperator* (☏04.67.49.02.25, ⓦwww.hotel-Imperator.fr; ❹), at 28 allées Paul-Riquet, is a notch above the rest but won't break the bank. There's no **campsite** in Béziers, but you can head to *Les Berges du Canal* (☏04.67.39.36.09, ⓦwww.lesbergesducanal.com; mid-April to mid-Sept) in Villeneuve-lès-Béziers, about 4km southeast of the town centre, or 6km east to *Clariac* (☏04.67.76.78.97; April–Sept).

A string of **restaurants** with patios are lined along the west side of allées Paul-Riquet, serving the usual *steak-frites*-type menus for about €14. Better fare can be found in the old quarter; rue Viennet has a good choice of places. The best choice is probably 🍴 *Le Cep d'Or*, at no. 7, a bistro with a charming old-fashioned air, serving mostly seafood (menus at €15–23; closed Sun evening & Mon out of season), while *Les Deux Lombard*, at no. 32, is more upmarket, with menus from €30. Lighter fare can be found at *La Table Bretonne* (closed Mon), at no. 21, an airy crêperie with a large street-side patio where savoury or sweet pancakes start at €11. *L'Ambassade* (closed Sun & Mon; ☏04.67.76.06.24), at 22 boulevard de Verdun is one of the town's best places, its cuisine a local favourite.

Béziers has one of the star **rugby** clubs in France, A.S.B.H., based at the Stade de la Méditerranée in the eastern suburbs (☏04.67.11.03.76, ⓦwww.asbh.net). If you fancy pottering along the Canal du Midi, you can rent **bikes** at La Maison du Canal (☏04.67.62.18.18) beside the Pont-Neuf, south of the *gare SNCF*.

Pézenas

PÉZENAS lies 18km east of Béziers on the old N9. Market centre of the coastal plain, it looks across to rice fields and shallow lagoons, hazy in the heat and dotted with pink flamingos. The town was catapulted to glory when it became the seat of the parliament of Languedoc and the residence of its governors in 1465, and reached its zenith in the late seventeenth century when the prince Armand de Bourbon made it a "second Versailles". The legacy of this illustrious past can be seen in the town's exquisite array of fourteenth- to seventeenth-century mansions.

The town also plays up its association with **Molière**, who visited several times with his troupe in the mid-seventeenth century, when he enjoyed the patronage of Prince Armand. He put on his plays at the **Hôtel d'Alfonce** on rue Conti, including the first performance of *Le Médecin Volant*, according to local tradition. The building is now privately owned, and closed to visitors. When in town, he lodged at the Maison du Barbier-Gély in the unspoiled **place Gambetta**. Although Molière features in the eclectic **Musée Vulliod St-Germain** (Tues–Sun: mid-Feb to May & Oct to mid-Nov 10am–noon & 2–5.30pm; June–Sept 10am–noon & 3–7pm plus Tues & Thurs 9–11pm; €2.50), housed in a sixteenth-century palace just off the square, it's the grand salon, with its Aubusson tapestries and collection of seventeenth- and eighteenth-century furniture, that steals the show.

The **tourist office** (July & Aug Wed & Fri 9am–10pm, Sat & Sun 10am–7pm, rest of week 9am–7pm; Sept–June Mon–Sat 9am–noon & 2–6pm, Sun 10am–noon & 2–5/6pm; ☏04.67.98.36.40, ⓦwww.pezenas-tourisme.fr), set in place des Etats du Languedoc at the main entrance to the old town, distributes a guide to all the town's eminent houses, taking in the former **Jewish ghetto** on rue des Litanies and rue Juiverie, but you can just as easily follow the explanatory plaques posted all over the centre, starting at the east end of rue François-Outrin where it leaves the town's main square, place du 14-Juillet.

Practicalities

The **gare routière** is on the opposite side of the square on the riverbank, with buses to Montpellier, Béziers and Agde, while an enormous **market** takes place each Saturday on cours Jean-Jaurès, a five-minute walk away.

There are two **hotels** in old Pézenas: *Genieys*, at 9 rue Aristide-Briand (☏04.67.98.13.99, ⓦwww.hotel-restaurant-genieys.fr.st; ❸), and the splendid *Molière*, 18 place du 14-Juillet (☏04.67.98.14.00, ⓦwww.hotel-le-moliere .com; ❹). There are plenty of **restaurants** to choose from, most with menus for under €20. *Le Pomme d'Amour* (March–Dec; closed Mon evening & Tues in winter), on rue Albert-Paul-Alliés, has good duck dishes, and *Le Conti*, 27 rue Conti (closed Sun & out of season Mon), is a popular pizzeria. The best spot, however, is *Les Palmiers* on 50 rue de Mercière (☏04.67.09.42.56; June–Sept only), a beautiful and welcoming establishment featuring inventive Mediterranean-style cuisine from about €28. Those with a sweet tooth should sample two local delicacies: flavoured sugar-drops called *berlingots*, and *petits pâtés* – bobbin-shaped pastries related to mince pies, reputedly introduced by the Indian cook of Clive of India, who stayed in Pézenas in 1770.

Narbonne and around

On the Toulouse–Nice main train line, 25km west of Béziers, is **NARBONNE**, once the capital of Rome's first colony in Gaul, Gallia Narbonensis, and a thriving port in classical times and the Middle Ages. Plague, war with the English and the silting-up of its harbour finished it off in the fourteenth century, though a tentative prosperity returned in the late nineteenth century with the birth of the modern wine industry. Today, despite the ominous presence of the Malvesi nuclear power plant just 5km out of town, it's a pleasant provincial city with a small but well-kept old town, dominated by the great truncated choir of its cathedral and bisected by a grassy esplanade on the banks of the Canal de la Robine.

In the early 1990s Narbonne acquired notoriety as a flash point in France's continuing problems with its ethnic minorities, as the Harkis – Algerians who had enlisted in the French forces and fought with them against their own people in the Algerian war of independence in the late 1950s – began angrily to protest official neglect of their community. The discontent has rumbled on, and the Harkis have organized a political group, the Mouvement Harki, to counter the city's far-right municipal administration.

The Town

One of the few Roman remnants in Narbonne is the **Horreum**, at the north end of rue Rouget-de-l'Isle (April–Sept 9.30am–12.15pm & 2–6pm; Oct–March Tues–Sun 10am–noon & 2–5pm; €3.70 or €5.20 for a pass to the town's four museums), an unusual underground grain store divided into a series of small chambers leading off a rectangular passageway. At the opposite end of the same street, close to the attractive tree-lined banks of the **Canal de la Robine**, is Narbonne's other principal attraction, the enormous Gothic **Cathédrale St-Just-et-St-Pasteur**. With the Palais des Archevêques and its forty-metre high keep, it forms a massive pile of masonry that completely dominates the restored lanes of the old town, and – like the cathedral of Béziers – can be seen for kilometres around. In spite of its size, it's actually only the choir of a much more ambitious church, whose construction was halted to avoid wrecking the city walls. The immensely tall interior has some beautiful fourteenth-century stained glass in the chapels on the northeast side of the apse and imposing Aubusson tapestries – one of the most valuable of these is kept in the **Salle du Trésor** (July–Sept Mon–Sat 11am–6pm & Sun 2–6pm; Oct–June daily 2–6pm; €2.50), along with a small collection of ecclesiastical treasures.

The adjacent **place de l'Hôtel-de-Ville** is dominated by the great towers of St-Martial, the Madeleine and Bishop Aycelin's keep. From there the passage de l'Ancre leads through to the **Palais des Archevêques** (Archbishops' Palace), housing a fairly ordinary **museum of art** and a good **archeology museum** (both museums have the same hours and price as the Horreum), whose interesting Roman remains include a massive 3.5-metre wood and lead ship's rudder, and a huge mosaic. Across into the southern part of the town, beyond the bisecting Canal de la Robine and the built-over Pont des Marchands, the small early Christian crypt of the church of **St-Paul**, off rue de l'Hôtel-Dieu (Mon–Sat 9am–noon & 2–6pm & Sun 9am–noon; free), is worth a quick look, as is the deconsecrated church of **Notre-Dame-de-Lamourguié**, which now houses a collection of Roman sculptures and epigraphy (same hours and cost as the Horreum).

Practicalities

The **gare routière** and the **gare SNCF** are next door to each other on avenue Carnot on the northwest side of town. The **tourist office** is on place Salengro, next to the cathedral (mid-June to mid-Sept daily 9am–7pm; rest of year Mon–Sat 10am–12.30pm & 1.30–6pm, Sun 10am–5pm; ℡04.68.65.15.60, Ⓦwww .mairie-narbonne.fr).

The best budget **accommodation** is the modern and friendly *MJC Centre International de Séjour*, in place Salengro (℡04.68.32.01.00, Ⓦwww.cis-narbonne .com; ❶). Two of the more reasonable hotels are *Will's Hotel*, 23 avenue Pierre-Sémard (℡04.68.90.44.50, Ⓦwww.willshotel-narbonne.com; ❸), a homely backpackers' favourite near the station, and the spruce *Hôtel de France*, 6 rue Rossini (℡04.68.32.09.75, Ⓦwww.hotelnarbonne.com; ❸), beside the attractive market hall. A fancier option is the plush *La Résidence*, 6 rue du 1ᵉʳ-Mai (℡04.68.32.19.41, Ⓦwww.hotelresidence.fr; ❹), in a nineteenth-century renovated house, but best is ⚑ *Grand Hôtel du Languedoc*, 22 boulevard Gambetta (℡04.68.65.14.74, Ⓦwww .hoteldulanguedoc.com; ❸), set in a dignified nineteenth-century house. The nearest **campsite** is *Les Folralys* (℡04.68.32.65.65, Ⓦwww.lesfloralys.com), on the route de Gruissan to the south of town (take bus #2 from the Hôtel de Ville).

As for **food**, you'll find a string of alfresco snack bars and brasseries along the terraces bordering the Canal de la Robine in the town centre, while *L'Estagnol* (℡04.68.65.09.27; closed Sun & Mon eve; menus €15–30), across the canal on Cours Mirabeau, attracts the crowds with its simple, good-value fare. ⚑ *L'Ecrevisse Alsace*, at 2 avenue Pierre-Sémard (℡04.68.65.10.24; closed Sun evening & Wed) is Narbonne's best restaurant, hands down, featuring mammoth servings of excellent *terroir* and northeastern French dishes, plus local seafood dishes (€15–35) – baked sea wolf is the house speciality.

Fontfroide

For a side trip from Narbonne – only 15km southwest, but nigh impossible without transport of your own – the lovely **abbey** of **FONTFROIDE** enjoys a beautiful location, tucked into a fold in the dry cypress-clad hillsides. The extant buildings go back to the twelfth century, with some elegant seventeenth-century additions in the entrance and courtyards, and were in use from their foundation until 1900, first by Benedictines, then Cistercians. It was one of the Cistercian monks, Pierre de Castelnau, whose murder as papal legate set off the Albigensian Crusade against the Cathars in 1208.

Visits to the restored abbey are only possible on a **guided tour** (daily: 10am–noon & 2–4pm on the hour; €9). Star features include the cloister, with its marble pillars and giant wisteria, the church itself, some fine ironwork and a rose garden. The stained glass in the windows of the lay brothers' dormitory consists of fragments from churches in north and eastern France damaged in World War I.

Parc Naturel Régional du Haut Languedoc

Embracing Mont Caroux in the east and the Montagne Noire in the west, the **Parc Naturel Régional du Haut Languedoc** is the southernmost extension of the Massif Central. The west, above Castres and Mazamet, is Atlantic in feel and climate, with deciduous forests and lush valleys, while the east is dry, craggy and calcareous. Except in high summer you can have it almost to yourself. Buses serve the **Orb valley** and cross the centre of the park to **La Salvetat** and **Lacaune**, but you really need transport of your own to make the most of it.

Bédarieux to St-Pons: the valleys of the Orb and Jaur

Some 34km north of Béziers, the pleasant if unremarkable town of **BÉDARIEUX** lies on the edge of the park. Served by buses from both Béziers and Montpellier, and by train from Béziers, it makes a good base for entering the park, especially as the bus service continues along the Orb and Jaur valleys to St-Pons beneath the southern slopes of the Monts de l'Espinouse.

The best part of town is to the east of the river, where the tall, crumbly old houses are redolent of a rural France long since vanished in more prosperous areas. You'll find the **tourist office** on place aux Herbes (June–Aug Mon–Sat 9am–noon & 2–6pm, Sun 3–6pm; Sept–May Mon–Fri 9am–noon & 2–6pm, Sat 2–6pm, Sun 3–6pm; ☎04.67.95.08.79, ⓦwww.bedarieux.fr). The town's only **hotel**, *Hôtel de l'Orb* (☎04.67.23.35.90, ⓦwww.hotel-orb.com; ❷), is on route de St-Pins, near the station, and there's a municipal **campsite** on boulevard Jean-Moulin (☎04.67.23.30.19; closed Oct to mid-June). The best **restaurant** deal can be had at *Le Rapier*, by the Hôtel de Ville on rue de la République, where a four-course meal including dessert, coffee and wine runs to around €20.

The Orb valley and Mons

Continuing west, the D908 (on the Bédarieux bus route) moves through spectacular scenery, with the peaks of the Monts de l'Espinouse rising up to 1000m on your right. The spa town of **LAMALOU-LES-BAINS**, 8km on, is notably livelier than neighbouring settlements, boasting the attraction of **recuperative springs** where the likes of André Gide and crowned heads of Spain and Morocco soothed their aches and pains. At the west end of the town by the main road, the **cemetery** is an untypically grand necropolis crowned with ornate mausoleums, while the ancient **church** on the north side of town contains carvings left by Mozarab (Christian) refugees from Moorish Spain.

Seven or eight kilometres further along the D908 is **MONS**, which features a comfortable B&B, *Manoir le Trivalle* (☎04.67.97.85.56, ⓦwww.monslatrivalle .com; ❸). From Mons a road climbs 5km up the dramatic **Gorges d'Héric** to the hamlet of Héric, with the Gorges de l'Orb winding their way southwards back to Béziers along the D14.

Olargues and St-Pons-de-Thomières

Five kilometres after Mons, you reach the medieval village of **OLARGUES**, scrambling up the south bank of the Jaur above its thirteenth-century single-span bridge. The steep twisting streets, presumably almost unchanged since the bridge was built, lead up to a thousand-year-old belfry crowning the top of the hill. With the river and gardens below, the ancient and earth-brown farms on the infant slopes of Mont Caroux beyond, and swifts swirling round the tower in summer, you get a powerful sense of age and history. There's a tiny **tourist office** on rue de la Place near the church (June Tues–Sat 9.30am–12.30pm & 2–6pm; July & Aug Tues–Sun 9.30am–12.30pm & 4–7pm; ☎04.67.97.71.26, ⓦwww.olargues.org), as well as an old train station now served only by SNCF **buses**. There is a deluxe country **hotel**, the *Domaine de Rieumégé*

(T 04.67.97.73.99, W www.domainederieumege.fr; ©), just outside the town on the St-Pons road, but a better deal is the homely *Les Quatr' Farceurs* in rue de la Comporte (T 04.67.97.81.33, W www.olargues.co.uk; ©), which also serves huge meals with free-flowing wine for €20. **Campers** should head for *Camping Le Baous*, down by the river (mid-April to mid-Sept; T 04.67.97.71.50).

ST-PONS-DE-THOMIÈRES, 18km further west, is a little larger and noisier: it's on the Béziers–Castres and Béziers–La Salvetat bus routes, as well as the Bédarieux–Mazamet route. This is the "capital" of the park, with the **Maison du Parc** housed in the local **tourist office** (July & Aug Mon–Sat 9.20am–1pm & 2–7pm & Sun 9.30am–1pm; Sept–June Tues–Sat 10am–noon & 2–6pm; T 04.67.97.06.65, W www.saint-pons-tourisme.com) on place du Forail. Sights include the **cathedral** – a strange mix of Romanesque and classical – and a small and reasonably interesting **Musée de la Préhistoire** (March to mid-June & mid-Sept to Oct Tues & Thurs–Sun 3–6pm, Wed 10am–noon & 3–6pm; mid-June to mid-Sept Tues–Sun 10am–noon & 3–6pm; €3.50), across the river from the tourist office.

If you need to **stay**, try the basic *Le Somail* (T 04.67.97.00.12; ①). The municipal **campsite** (T 04.67.97.34.85) is on the main road east to Bédarieux. Deluxe accommodation can be found at the *Bergeries de Ponderach* 1km east of town (T 04.67.97.02.57, W bergeries-ponderach.com; ©), a luxurious seventeenth-century country estate with a fine **restaurant**. Head north up the D907 and you'll reach the Col du Cabaretou and the stunningly situated *Relais du Cabaretou* (T 04.67.95.31.62, E esseguier2@orange.fr; ©; closed mid-Jan to mid-Feb), with a *terroir* restaurant serving menus starting at €12. North of here the D907 leads to La Salvetat in the heart of the park.

The park's uplands

The uplands of the park are a wild and little-travelled area, dominated by the towering peak of **Mont Caroux** and stretching west along the ridge of the **Monts de l'Espinouse**. This is prime hiking territory, where thick forest of stunted oak alternates with broad mountain meadows, opening up on impressive vistas. Civilization appears again to the west in the upper Agout valley, where **Fraïsse** and **La Salvetat** have become thriving bases for outdoor recreation, and to the north, at the medieval spa town of **Lacaune**. There's no transport crossing the uplands, but the D180 takes you from Le Poujol-sur-Orb, 2km west of Lamalou-les-Bains, to Mont Caroux and L'Espinouse.

Into the Agout valley

The D180 is the most spectacular way to climb into the park. Soon after leaving the main highway, you'll pass the **Forêt des Écrivains–Combattants**, named after the French writers who died in World War I. Just above the hamlet of Rosis, the road levels out in a small mountain valley, whose slopes are brilliant yellow with broom in June. Continuing north, the D180 climbs another 12km above deep ravines, offering spectacular views to the summit of **L'Espinouse**. The Col de l'Ourtigas is a good place to stretch your legs and take in the grandeur surrounding you. Here the landscape changes from Mediterranean cragginess to marshy moor-like meadow and big conifer plantations, and the road begins to descend west into the valley of the River Agout. It runs through tiny Salvergues, with plain workers' cottages and a striking fortress-church; Cambon, where the natural woods begin; and postcard-pretty **FRAÏSSE-SUR-AGOUT** – where you can **stay** at the homely *Auberge de l'Espinouse* (T 04.67.95.40.46, W aubergespinouse.net; ©), which also has a good *terroir* **restaurant** (May–Nov; menu €20).

Next, you'll reach **LA SALVETAT-SUR-AGOUT**, another attractive mountain town built on a hill above the river, with car-wide streets and houses clad in huge slate tiles, situated between the artificial lakes of La Raviège and Laouzas. It's usually half-asleep except at holiday time, when it becomes a busy outdoor activities centre. With several **campsites**, including *La Blaquière* (July & Aug; ☎04.67.97.61.29, ⓦ www.blaquiere.fr.st) on allée St-Étienne de Cavall just north of the centre, and the pleasantly rustic *Auberge la Resse* (☎04.67.97.53.97, ⓦ www.aubergelaresse.com; ❷) a short walk west of the town centre, it's a convenient stopover for the centre of the park. There's a **tourist office** in place des Archers at the top of the hill (July & Aug Mon–Sat 9am–1pm & 2–7pm, Sun 10am–1pm; Sept–June Mon–Fri 9am–noon & 2–6pm, Sat 10am–noon & 2–5pm, Sun 10am–noon; closed Sat Nov–Mar & Sun mid-Sept to mid-June; ☎04.67.97.64.44, ⓦ www.lasalvetatot.com).

Lacaune

Twenty kilometres further north, **LACAUNE** makes another agreeable stop if you're heading for Castres. Surrounded by rounded wooded heights, it's very much a mountain town and one of the centres of Protestant Camisard resistance at the end of the seventeenth century, when its inaccessibility was ideal for clandestine worship.

The air is fresh, and the town, though somewhat grey in appearance because of the slates and greyish stucco common throughout the region, is cheerful enough. For a place to **stay**, try *Fusiés*, an erstwhile coaching inn opposite the church on rue de la République (☎05.63.37.02.03, ⓦ www.hotelfusies.fr; ❹), offering old-fashioned class, or the simpler *Hôtel Calas*, up the hill (☎05.63.37.03.28, ⓦ www.pageloisirs.com/calas; ❶; closed mid-Dec to mid-Jan), which has a good **restaurant** (menus €11–35). There are **bus** connections most days – inconveniently afternoon or very early morning – to Castres, Albi and Bédarieux.

From here to Castres the most agreeable route is along the wooded **Gijou valley**, following the now defunct train track, past minuscule Gijounet and **LACAZE**, where a nearly derelict **château** strikes a picturesque pose in a bend of the river.

Carcassonne and around

Right on the main Toulouse–Montpellier train link, **Carcassonne** couldn't be easier to reach. For anyone travelling through this region it is a must – one of the most dramatic, if also most-visited, towns in the whole of Languedoc. Carcassonne owes its division into two separate "towns" to the wars against the Cathars. Following Simon de Montfort's capture of the town in 1209, its people tried in 1240 to restore their traditional ruling family, the Trencavels. In reprisal King Louis IX expelled them from the **Cité**, only permitting their return on condition they built on the low ground by the River Aude – what would become the **ville basse**.

Arrival and information

Arriving by **train**, you'll find yourself in the *ville basse* on the north bank of the Canal du Midi at the northern limits of the town. To reach the **centre** from the train station, cross the canal bridge by an oval lock, pass the Jardin Chénier and follow rue Clemenceau, which will take you through the central **place Carnot** and out to the exterior boulevard on the southern side of town (a fifteen-minute walk). The **gare routière** (in fact a series of bus stops with no actual building) is on boulevard de Varsovie on the northwest side of town, south of the canal, while the **airport** (T04.68.71.96.46, Wwww.carcassonne.cci.fr) lies just west of the city. A *navette* service (€5; timed to coincide with flights) leaves from outside the terminal and stops at the *gare SNCF*, square Gambetta and the Cité; a taxi to the centre will cost €10–18. If you are planning on visiting other medieval sites in the vicinity of Carcassonne (including the Cathar castles), you might purchase the Intersite Card, which gives you a discounted admission price to many castles and monuments (see p.742 for details).

The **tourist office** is at 28 rue Verdun (July–Aug daily 9am–7pm; Sept–June Mon–Sat 9am–6pm, Sun 9am–noon/1pm; T04.68.10.24.30, Wwww .carcassonne-tourisme.com), west of square Gambetta, where the main road from Montpellier enters the town across the Pont-Neuf and the River Aude. There's also an annexe (daily: April–Sept 9am–6/7pm; Oct–March 9am–5pm) just inside the main gate to the medieval Cité, Porte Narbonnaise. For information on the **Cathars**, consult the Centre National d'Études Cathares, 53 rue de Verdun (T04.68.47.24.66), while bookshops offer plenty of Cathar literature and souvenir picture books.

Accommodation

With the exception of the modern, clean, but frequently booked-up **HI hostel** on rue Trencavel (T04.68.25.23.16, Wwww.fuaj.org), which offers beds for €16.60, the price of staying in the Cité can be high. If you don't mind paying, you can stay at the ⚔ *Hôtel de la Cité* (T04.68.71.98.71,

CARCASSONNE: VILLE BASSE

EATING
La Divine Comédie   1
L'Ecurie   2

ACCOMMODATION
La Bastide   B
Montségur   C
Du Soleil Terminus   A

⑪

Canal du Midi

The **Canal du Midi** runs for 240km from the River Garonne at Toulouse via Carcassonne to the Mediterranean at Agde. It was the brainchild of Pierre-Paul Riquet, a minor noble and tax collector, who succeeded in convincing Louis XIV (and more importantly, his first minister, Colbert) of the merits of linking the Atlantic and the Mediterranean via the Garonne.

The work, begun in 1667, took fourteen years to complete, using tens of thousands of workers. The crux of the problem from the engineering point of view was how to feed the canal with water when its high point at Naurouze, west of Carcassonne, was 190m above sea level and 58m above the Garonne at Toulouse. Riquet responded by building a system of reservoirs in the Montagne Noire, channelling run-off from the heights down to Naurouze. He spent the whole of his fortune on the canal and, sadly, died just six months before its inauguration in 1681.

The canal was a success and sparked a wave of prosperity along its course, with traffic increasing steadily until 1857, when the Sète–Bordeaux railway was opened, reducing trade on the canal to all but nothing. Today, the canal remains a marvel of engineering and beauty, incorporating no fewer than 99 locks (*écluses*) and 130 bridges, almost all of which date back to the first era of construction. A double file of trees lines most of its length, giving it a distinctive "Midi" look and impeding loss of water through evaporation, while the greenery is enhanced in spring by the bloom of yellow irises and wild gladioli. With all of this and the occasional glimpses afforded of a world beyond – a distant smudge of hills and the towers of Carcassonne – the canal is a pleasure to travel. You can follow it by road, and many sections have foot or bicycle paths, but the best way to travel it, of course, is by boat.

Outfits in all the major ports rent houseboats and barges, and there are many cruise options to choose from as well. For **boat rental and cruises**, contact Crown Blue Line, Le Grand Bassin, BP1201, 11492 Castelnaudary (℡04.68.94.52.94, ⓦwww .crownblueline.fr), or Locaboat, in Négra (℡05.61.81.36.40, ⓦwww.locaboat.com), both of which have a number of branches in Languedoc and the Midi; or Nautic in Carcassonne (℡04.68.71.88.95, ⓕ04.67.94.05.91). Canal **information** can be found at the port offices of Voies Navigables de France, at 2 Port St-Étienne in Toulouse (℡05.61.36.24.24, ⓦwww.vnf.fr), who also have English-speaking offices at the major canal ports. For a quicker taste of the locks, the cruise barge *Lou Gabaret* does ninety-minute and longer excursions; contact Allan Millian, 27 rue des 3 Couronnes, Carcassonne (℡04.68.71.61.26).

ⓦwww.hoteldelacite.com; ❾), which offers rooms and suites in the opulent surroundings of a medieval manor house, with a heated swimming pool and stunning views from the battlemented walls. *Le Donjon*, 2 rue Comte-Roger (℡04.68.11.23.00, ⓦwww.hotel-donjon.fr; ❻), is more economical, but still luxurious. *Hôtel Espace Cité*, just outside the main gate at 132 rue Trivalle (℡04.68.25.24.24, ⓦwww.hotelespacecite.fr; ❸), has all mod cons and efficient service at reasonable prices.

There are, however, some very well-priced hotels in the *ville basse*. Pride of place goes to the *Hôtel du Soleil Terminus*, at 2 avenue de Maréchal-Joffre (℡04.68.25.25.00, ⓦsoleilvacances.com; ❹), a station-side hotel of decaying steam-age luxury, with a splendid *fin-de-siècle* facade. The *Montségur*, 27 allée d'Iéna (℡04.68.25.31.41, ⓦwww.hotelmontsegur.com; ❺), is a comfortable nineteenth-century town house, with ample-size rooms, but quite far from the Cité. A good economy option is the surprisingly well-equipped *La Bastide*, at 81 rue de la Liberté (℡04.68.71.96.89, ⓦwww.hotel-bastide.fr; ❷).

There's a **campsite**, *La Cité*, on route St-Hilaire (℡04.68.25.11.77, ⓦwww .campeoles.com; mid-March to mid-Oct), with good shady sites, a shop and some bungalows. Tucked off among parkland to the south of town, it can be reached by local bus (line 8) or by foot (about 20min) from the Cité.

The Cité

The attractions of the well-preserved and lively *ville basse* notwithstanding, what everybody comes for is the **Cité**, the double-walled and turreted fortress that crowns the hill above the River Aude. From a distance it's the epitome of the fairy-tale medieval town. Viollet-le-Duc rescued it from ruin in 1844, and his "too-perfect" restoration has been furiously debated ever since. It is, as you would expect, a real tourist trap. Yet, in spite of the chintzy cafés, crafty shops and the crowds, you'd have to be a very stiff-necked purist not to be moved at all.

To reach the Cité from the *ville basse*, take bus #2 from outside the station, or a *navette* from square Gambetta. Alternatively, you can walk it in under thirty minutes, crossing the Pont-Vieux and climbing rue Barbacane, past the church of St-Gimer to the sturdy bastion of the **Porte d'Aude**. This is effectively the back entrance – the main gate is **Porte Narbonnaise**, on the east side.

There is no charge for admission to the streets or the grassy *lices* – "lists" – between the walls, though cars are banned from 10am to 6pm. However, to see the inner fortress of the **Château Comtal** and walk the walls, you'll have to join a **guided tour** (daily April–Sept 9.30am–6.30pm; Oct–March 9.30am–5pm; 35–40min; €7.50). These – including several per day in English (June–Sept) – assume some knowledge of French history, and point out the various phases in the construction of the fortifications, from Roman and Visigothic to Romanesque and the post-Cathar adaptations of the French kings.

In addition to wandering the narrow streets, don't miss the beautiful **church of St-Nazaire** (mid-June to mid-Sept Mon–Fri 9–11.45am & 1.45–6pm, Sun 9–10.45am & 2–4.30pm; rest of year closes at 5pm), towards the southern corner of the Cité at the end of rue St-Louis. It's a serene combination of nave with carved capitals in the Romanesque style and a Gothic choir and transepts, along with some of the loveliest stained glass in Languedoc. In the south transept is a tombstone believed to belong to Simon de Montfort. You can also climb the **tower** (same hours; €1.50), for spectacular views over the Cité.

Eating, drinking and entertainment

With over fifty **restaurants** within its walls, the Cité is a good place to look for somewhere to eat, though it tends to be expensive. First choice is the *Auberge de Dame Carcas*, 3 place du Château (☎04.68.71.23.23; closed Sun evening. Mon lunch & Feb; menu at €14.50), a traditional bistro offering cassoulet and other regional dishes. Otherwise try the *Jardin de la Tour*, 11 rue Porte d'Aude (open evenings only Tues–Sat; closed Nov), with outside tables, or the smart *Brasserie du Donjon*, in the hotel of the same name; serving *terroir* menus from €24 and €16 respectively.

There's greater variety of affordable places in the *ville basse*: among these the brasserie of the *Soleil Terminus*, which has menus from €12.50. Nearby, at 29 boulevard Jean-Jaurès, the *Divine Comédie* serves a varied menu of pasta, pizzas and regional dishes in generous portions (closed Sun; from €14). For something more sophisticated, try ⚓ *L'Écurie* (☎04.68.72.04.04) at 43 boulevard Barbès, offering local cuisine with adventurous touches, such as roast lamb with thyme and garlic (menus €15–30; closed Sun evening & Wed). For picnic provisions, head for the market on place Carnot (Tues, Thurs & Sat mornings).

Carcassonne hosts two major festivals: the month-long **Festival de la Cité** in July, with dance, theatre and music, the highpoint of which is the mammoth

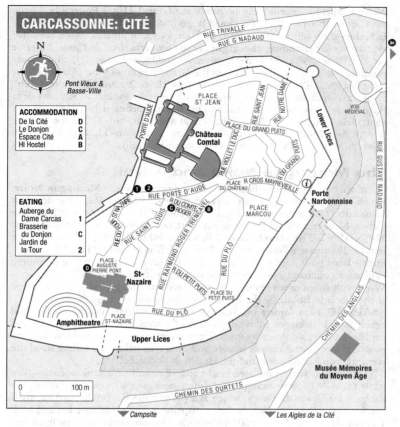

CARCASSONNE: CITÉ

N

Pont Vieux &
Basse-Ville

RUE TRIVALLE
RUE G NADAUD

RUE NOTRE DAME

VOIE
MÉDIÉVAL

ACCOMMODATION
De la Cité   D
Le Donjon   C
Éspace Cité   A
HI Hostel   B

PLACE
ST JEAN

RUE SAINT JEAN

PLACE DU GRAND PUITS

**Château
Comtal**

PORTE D'AUDE

RUE VIOLLET LE DUC

Lower Lices

RUE GUSTAVE NADAUD

EATING
Auberge du
  Dame Carcas   1
Brasserie
  du Donjon   C
Jardin de
  la Tour   2

RUE PORTE D'AUDE
R CROS MAYREVIEILLE
PLACE
DU CHÂTEAU

R DU COMTE
ROGER

RUE DU GRAND PUITS

**Porte
Narbonnaise**

RUE SAINT LOUIS

R DU COMTE
ROGER

RUE RAYMOND ROGER TRENCAVEL

PLACE
MARCOU

RUE DU PLO

PLACE
AUGUSTE
PIERRE PONT

**St-
Nazaire**

R DU PETIT PUITS

PLACE DU
PETIT PUITS

RUE DE L'EAU

CHEMIN DES ANGLAIS

Amphitheatre

PLACE
ST-NAZAIRE

RUE DU PLO

Upper Lices

0   100 m

**Musée Mémoires
du Moyen Âge**

CHEMIN DES OURTETS

▼ Campsite

▼ Les Aigles de la Cité

11

LANGUEDOC | Carcassonne and around

---

fireworks display on Bastille Day (July 14); and the elaborate medieval pageant,
Les Médiévales, held in the first fortnight of August.

Castelnaudary

Thirty-six kilometres west of Carcassonne, on the main road from Toulouse,
CASTELNAUDARY is one of those innumerable French country towns that
boast no particular sights but are nonetheless a pleasure to spend a couple of
hours in, having coffee or shopping in the market. Today it serves as an
important commercial centre for the rolling Lauragais farming country hereabouts, as it once was for the traffic on the Canal du Midi. In fact, the most
flattering view of the town is still that from the canal's **Grand Bassin**, which
makes it look remarkably like a Greek island town, with its ancient houses
climbing the hillside from the water's edge.

In town you'll find some fine old **mansions**, a restored **windmill** and an
eighteenth-century **semaphore** tower. However, Castelnaudary's chief claim to
fame is as the world capital of **cassoulet**, which, according to tradition, must be
made in an earthenware pot from Issel (a *cassolo*) with beans grown in Pamiers
or Lavelanet, and cooked in a baker's oven fired with rushes from the Montagne

791

Noire. Authentic cassoulet can be had at the **Grand-Hôtel Fourcade**, 14 rue des Carmes (☎04.68.23.02.08; closed Jan; ❶), where you can gorge yourself for €15, then sleep off the after-effects by taking a room upstairs. More attractive alternatives for **spending the night** are the modern *Hôtel du Canal*, 2 avenue Arnaut-Vidal (☎04.68.94.05.05, ⓦwww.hotelducanal.com; ❹), in a shady position beside the canal just west of the Grand Bassin, and the *Hôtel du Centre et du Lauragais* (☎04.68.23.25.95, Ⓕ04.68.94.01.66; ❹; closed Jan to mid-Feb), a converted nineteenth-century house that's centrally located at 31 cours de la République, close to the post office. The **tourist office** is in Castelnaudary's central Halle aux Grains (April–June & Sept Mon–Sat 9am–12.30pm & 2–6pm; July & Aug Mon–Sat 9am–1pm & 2–7pm, Sun 10am–12.30pm & 3–6pm; ☎04.68.23.05.73, ⓦwww.castelnaudary-tourisme.com).

The Montagne Noire and Revel

There are two good routes from Carcassonne north into the **Montagne Noire**, which forms the western extremity of the Parc Naturel Régional du Haut Languedoc: Carcassonne–Revel and Carcassonne–Mazamet by the valley of the Orbiel. Neither is served by public transport, but both offer superlative scenery. NPINDENT **The Revel route** follows the N113 out of Carcassonne, then the D629 through Montolieu (17km) and Saissac. **MONTOLIEU**, semi-fortified and built on the edge of a ravine, has set itself the target of becoming France's secondhand book capital (a conscious imitation of Wales's Hay-on-Wye), with shops overflowing with dog-eared and antiquarian tomes. Drop in at the Librairie Booth, by the bridge over the ravine, for English titles.

SAISSAC, 8km further on, is much more an upland village. Conifers and beech wood, interspersed with patches of rough pasture, surround it, and gardens are terraced down its steep slopes. Remains of towers and fortifications poke out among the ancient houses, and on a spur below the village stand the romantic ruins of its castle and the church of St-Michel.

If you wish to **stay** in the area, head north of town to *Domaine du Lampy-Neuf* (☎04.68.24.46.07, ⓦwww.domainedulampy-neuf.com; ❶), a *chambre d'hôte* by the banks of the Bassin du Lampy, which as a *gîte* and also has family-sized rooms. If you have your own transport, the best **campsite**, and an experience in itself, is the *Camping du Bout du Monde* (☎04.68.94.95.96, ⓦwww.leboutdumonde.fr; all year round), a beautiful tumbledown farm near Verdun-en-Lauragais, 5km west of Saissac, which also has a *gîte* and restaurant (from €22).

Some 14km west of Saissac on the D103 (or just a few kilometres southwest of the *Bout du Monde* campsite), the ancient village of **ST-PAPOUL**, with its walls and Benedictine **abbey**, makes for a gentle side trip. The abbey is best known for the sculpted corbels on the exterior of the nave, executed by the "Master of Cabestany". These can be viewed free at any time, although the interior of the church and its pretty fourteenth-century cloister (daily April–June, Sept, Oct 10–noon & 2–5/6pm; July & Aug 10am–7pm; Nov, Dec, Feb & March Sat, Sun & holidays 10–noon & 2–6pm; €3.50) are also worth a peek.

Back on the "main" D629, the road winds down through the forest, past the Bassin de St-Férréol, constructed by Riquet to supply water to the Canal du Midi, and on to **REVEL**. Revel is a *bastide* dating from 1342, featuring an attractive arcaded central square with a superb wooden-pillared medieval *halle* in the middle. Now a prosperous market town (Saturday is market day), it makes an agreeably provincial stopover. The *Auberge du Midi* at 34 boulevard Gambetta (closed late Nov to early Dec; ☎05.61.83.50.50, ⓦwww.logis-de-france.fr; ❸) is set in a refined old nineteenth-century mansion, and also has the town's best **restaurant** (menus €23–45). Close by at 7 rue de Taur, is the *Commanderie Hôtel* (05.34.66.11.24;

@lacommanderie@yahoo.fr; closed part Feb, part June, part Sept; ❸), a good second choice, with an old timber-frame facade and a remodelled interior.

Lastours and the valley of the Orbiel

The alternative route from Carcassonne into the Montagne Noire takes you through the region known as the **Cabardès**. Cut by the deep ravines of the Orbiel and its tributary streams, it's covered with Mediterranean scrub lower down and forests of chestnut and pine higher up. The area is extremely poor and depopulated, with rough stone villages and hamlets crouching in the valleys. Until relatively recently, its people lived off beans and chestnut flour and the meat from their pigs, and worked in the region's copper, iron, lead, silver and gold mines. Nothing now remains save for the gold mine at Salsigne, a huge and unsightly open pit atop a bleak windswept plateau.

The most memorable site in the **Orbiel valley** is the **Châteaux de Lastours** (Feb, March, Nov & Dec Sat, Sun & holidays 10am–5pm; April–June & Sept daily 10am–6pm; July & Aug daily 9am–8pm; Oct daily 10am–5pm; €5), the most northerly of the Cathar castles (see p.738), 16km north of Carcassonne. As the name suggests, there is more than one castle – four in fact, their ruined keeps jutting superbly from a sharp ridge of scrub and cypress that plunges to rivers on both sides. The two oldest castles, Cabaret (mid-eleventh century) and Surdespine (1153), fell into de Montfort's hands in 1211, after their lords had given shelter to the Cathars. The other two, Tour Régine and Quertinheux, were added after 1240, when the site became royal property, and a garrison was maintained here as late as the Revolution. Today, despite their ruined state, they look as impregnable and beautiful as ever. A path winds up from the roadside, bright in early summer with iris, cistus, broom and numerous others.

About 7km upriver from Lastours, the road and river divide. The left fork leads to the village of **Mas-Cabardès**, hunkered down defensively in the river bottom. The right goes to **Roquefère**, whose ancient château hosts a summer-time theatre. From here a steep, serpentine road winds up through magnificent scenery to the tiny hamlet of **Cupservies**, balanced on the edge of a sudden and deep ravine where the Rieutort stream drops some 90m into the bottom. A couple of kilometres further, by the crossroads at **Caninac**, there's a tenth-century chapel, **St-Sernin**, in the middle of the woods. To get here without transport, there's a marked footpath from Roquefère, which then returns via Labastide-Esparbairenque (a 4hr 30min round trip).

Toulouse and western Languedoc

With its sunny, cosmopolitan charms, **Toulouse** is a very accessible kick-off point for any destination in the southwest of France. Of the immediately surrounding places, **Albi**, with its highly original cathedral and comprehensive collection of Toulouse-Lautrec paintings, is the number-one priority. Once you've made it that far, it's worth the extra hop to the well-preserved medieval town of **Cordes**. West of Toulouse the land opens up into the broad plains of the **Gers**, a sleepy and rather dull expanse of wheat fields and rolling hills. Those in search of a solitary little-visited France will enjoy its uncrowded monuments, especially lovers of rich terrines and Armagnac.

Toulouse

TOULOUSE, with its beautiful historic centre, is one of the most vibrant and metropolitan provincial cities in France. This is a transformation that has come about since World War II, under the guidance of the French state, which has poured in money to make Toulouse the think-tank of high-tech industry and a sort of premier trans national Euroville. Long an **aviation** centre – St-Exupéry and Mermoz flew out from here on their pioneering airmail flights over Africa and the Atlantic in the 1920s – Toulouse is now home to Aérospatiale, the driving force behind Concorde, Airbus and the Ariane space rocket. The national Space Centre, the European shuttle programme, the leading aeronautical schools, the frontier-pushing electronics industry – it's all happening in Toulouse, whose 110,000 students make it second only to Paris as a **university** centre. But it's not to the burgeoning suburbs of factories, labs, shopping and housing complexes that all these people go for their entertainment, but to the old **Ville Rose** – pink not only in its brickwork, but also in its politics.

This is not the first flush of pre-eminence for Toulouse. From the tenth to the thirteenth centuries the counts of Toulouse controlled much of southern France. They maintained the most resplendent court in the land, renowned especially for its troubadours, the poets of courtly love, whose work influenced Petrarch, Dante and Chaucer and thus the whole course of European poetry. The arrival of the hungry northern French nobles of the Albigensian Crusade put an end to that; in 1271 Toulouse became crown property.

Arrival and information

The **gare SNCF** (better known to locals as **gare Matabiau**) and **gare routière** (℡05.61.61.67.67) stand side by side in boulevard Pierre-Sémard on the bank of the tree-lined Canal du Midi. This is where you might find yourself if you arrive by air as well – the **airport shuttle** (every 20min; €4) puts you down at the bus station (with stops in allées Jean-Jaurès and at place Jeanne-d'Arc). It's also the best spot to aim for if you're in a car: leave the **boulevard périphérique** at exit 15.

To reach the city centre from the train station takes just five minutes by **métro** to Capitole (€1.30, covering one hour's transport by métro and Tisseo-Connex city buses within the city centre), or twenty minutes on foot. Turn left out of the station, cross the canal and head straight down allées Jean-Jaurès, through place Wilson and on into place du Capitole, the city's main square. Just before it lie the shady and much-frequented gardens of the square Charles-de-Gaulle, where the main **tourist office** (June–Sept Mon–Sat 9am–7pm, Sun 10.30am–5.15pm; Oct–May Mon–Fri 9am–6pm, Sat 9am–12.30pm & 2–6pm, Sun 10am–12.30pm & 2–5pm; ℡05.61.11.02.22, Ⓦwww.ot-toulouse.fr) is housed in a sixteenth-century tower that has been restored to look like a castle keep; the Capitole métro stop is right outside. To save on admissions, buy a pass valid for three or six of the city's museums (€6 and €9); in addition, the

TOULOUSE

N20 & Camping Pont-du-Rupé

Albi

Aerospatiale, Auch, Camping,

Place St-Cyprien, Les Abattoirs & Arènes

Foix

Joliment

Cité de l'Espace & Castres

George-Labit Museum

Montpellier

DRINKING

L'Ambassade	12
Le Café des Artistes	15
Bibent	9
Bodega-Bodega	7
Le Chat d'Oc	20
Erich Coffie	21
Le Florida	8
The Frog & Rosbif	6
Hey Joe	2
Jour de Fête	4
Le Petit Voisin	19
Le Shanti	18
L'Ubu	14

EATING

Les Abbatoirs Chez Carmen	16
Atilla	5
La Bascule	22
Benjamin	13
Au Chat Dingue	19
Faim des Haricots	17
Les Jardins de l'Opéra	10
Michel Sarran	11
Au Pois Gourmand	1
Le Sept Place St-Sernin	3

0   200 m

ACCOMMODATION

Albert 1er	H	Grand Hôtel de l'Opéra	L
Des Ambassadeurs	B	Mermoz	A
Des Arts	M	Ours Blanc	G
Beausejour	F	St-Sernin	D
Castellane	K	Terminus	C
Le Clochez de Rodez	E	Wilson Square	J
France	I		

"Toulouse en liberté" card (€10) offers discounts at a range of hotels, museums, cultural events and shops.

The top guides to **what's on** in and around the city – and usually there is a lot, from opera to cinema – are the weekly listings magazines *Toulouse Hebdo* (€0.50) and *Flash* (€1). More highbrow interests are covered in the free monthly *Toulouse Culture*, available from the tourist office, among other places.

Accommodation

The best place to **stay** is in the city centre, where there are a number of excellent-value hotels, as well as many more upmarket establishments. The area around the train station, though charmless and still retaining some of its red-light seediness, has a few acceptable options. There's no hostel, but there are a number of accommodation centres for visitors who plan on staying for more than a few days: the CRIJ (☎05.61.21.20.20, ⓦ www.crij.org) can provide details. The closest **campsite** is *Camping de Rupé*, chemin du Pont du Rupé (☎05.61.70.07.35, ⓔ campinglerupe31@orange.fr; bus #59, stop "Rupé").

Hotels

Albert 1er 8 rue Rivals ☎05.61.21.17.91, ⓦ www.hotel-albert1.com. This small, comfortable and good-value establishment is set in a quiet side street just off the Capitole and close to the central market in place Victor-Hugo. Check for special weekend deals. ➍

Des Ambassadeurs 68 rue Bayard ☎05.61.62.65.84, ⓦ www.hotel-des-ambassadeurs .com. Very friendly little hotel just down from the station. All rooms have TV, en-suite bath and phone – a surprisingly good deal given the price. ➋

Des Arts 1bis rue Cantegril ☎05.61.23.36.21, ⓕ 05.61.12.22.37. On a corner diagonally opposite the Augustins museum, this is a top choice in the lower price range, with large, quirky rooms (some with a fireplace) in a superb old building. ➋

Beausejour 4 rue Caffarelli ☎05.61.62.77.59, ⓔ hotelbeausejour@cegetel.net. Basic, but dirt-cheap and with a great copper-balconied facade and soundproofed rooms. Best of the hotels in the slightly dodgy but engagingly gritty neighbourhood around place de Belfort. ➊

Castellane 17 rue Castellane ☎05.61.62.18.82, ⓦ www.castellanehotel.com. A cheerful hotel with a wide selection of room types and sizes – most of which are bright and quiet. One of the few wheelchair-accessible hotels in this price range. ➍

🏃 **Le Clochez de Rodez** 14 de Jeanne-d'Arc ☎05.61.62.42.92, ⓦ www.hotel-clochez -toulouse.com. Comfortable and central, with secure parking and all mod cons. Despite its size, it exudes a very personal hospitality. ➋

France 5 rue d'Austerlitz ☎05.61.21.88.24, ⓦ www .hotel-france-toulouse.com. One of the better options in the rue d'Austerlitz/place Wilson area. Clean rooms with cable television and a/c. ➌

Grand Hôtel de l'Opéra 1 place du Capitole ☎05.61.21.82.66, ⓦ www.grand-hotel-opera.com. The grand dame of Toulouse's hotels presides over the place du Capitole in the guise of a seventeenth-century convent. The rich decor, peppered with antiques and artwork, underlines the atmosphere of sophistication. Has a fitness centre for working off that second helping of foie gras. ➑

Mermoz 50 rue de Matabiau ☎05.61.63.04.04, ⓦ www.hotel-mermoz.com. Immaculate, comfortable rooms in a 1930s Art Deco-style hotel close to the station. Also has wheelchair access and parking. ➐

Ours Blanc 25 place de Victor-Hugo ☎05.61.21.62.40, ⓦ www.hotel-ours-blanc.com. Right by the covered market and steps from the Capitole, this welcoming hotel is one of the city's better bargains. Recently redecorated, each room now has TV, a/c, wi-fi and telephone, as well as a private bath. ➍

St-Sernin 2 rue St-Bernard ☎05.61.21.73.08, ⓦ www.hotelstsernin.com. Well-renovated old hotel in one of the best districts of the old town, around the basilica – close to all the action, but far enough away to provide peace in the evening. ➍

Terminus 13 bd Bonrepos ☎05.61.62.44.78, ⓦ www.terminus31.com. This old three-star station-side hotel has large, reconditioned rooms that make it worth the price, and there are special room prices for off-season weekends. Parking and buffet breakfast (€8) available; however, it is rather far from the sights. ➍

Wilson Square 12 rue d'Austerlitz ☎05.61.21.67.57, ⓦ www.hotel-wilson.com. Clean and well-kept place at the top end of rue Austerlitz, with TV, a/c and a lift. Also has a great patisserie at street level. ➍

The City

The part of the city you'll want to see forms a rough hexagon clamped round a bend in the wide, brown River Garonne and contained within a ring of nineteenth-century boulevards, including Strasbourg, Carnot and Jules-Guesde. The Canal du Midi, which here joins the Garonne on its way from the Mediterranean to the Atlantic, forms a further ring around this core. Old Toulouse is effectively quartered by two nineteenth-century streets: the long shopping street, **rue d'Alsace-Lorraine/rue du Languedoc**, which runs north–south; and **rue de Metz**, which runs east–west onto the Pont-Neuf and across the Garonne. It's all very compact and easily walkable, and the city's métro is of little use for getting to sites of interest.

In addition to the general pleasure of wandering the streets, there are three very good museums and some real architectural treasures in the churches of St-Sernin and Les Jacobins and in the magnificent Renaissance town houses – *hôtels particuliers* – of the merchants who grew rich on the woad-dye trade. This formed the basis of the city's economy from the mid-fifteenth to the mid-sixteenth century, when the arrival of indigo from the Indian colonies wiped it out.

Place du Capitole is the centre of gravity for the city's social life. Its smart cafés throng with people at lunchtime and in the early evening, when the dying sun flushes the pink facade of the big town hall opposite. This is the scene of a mammoth Wednesday **market** for food, clothes and junk, and a smaller organic food market on Tuesday and Saturday mornings. From place du Capitole, a labyrinth of narrow medieval streets radiates out to the town's other squares, such as place Wilson, the more intimate place St-Georges, the delightful triangular place de la Trinité and place St-Étienne, in front of the cathedral.

For green space, you have to head for the sunny banks of the Garonne or the lovely formal gardens of the **Grand-Rond** and **Jardin des Plantes** in the southeast corner of the centre. A less obvious but attractive alternative is the towpath of the Canal du Midi; the best place to join it is a short walk southeast of the Jardin des Plantes, by the neo-Moorish pavilion of the Georges-Labit Museum, which houses a good collection of Egyptian and Oriental art.

The Capitole and the hôtels particuliers

Occupying the whole of the eastern side of the eponymous square, the **Capitole** has been the seat of Toulouse's city government since the twelfth century. In medieval times it housed the *capitouls*, who made up the oligarchic and independent city council from which its name derives. This institution, under the name of *consulat*, was common to other Languedoc towns and may have been the inspiration for England's first parliamentary essays, often attributed to Simon de Montfort, son of the general who became familiar with these parts in the course of his merciless campaigns against the Cathar heretics in the early 1200s. Today, these medieval origins are disguised by an elaborate pink and white classical facade (1750) of columns and pilasters, from which the flags of Languedoc, the Republic and the European Union are proudly flown. If there are no official functions taking place, you can peek inside (Mon–Fri 9am–5pm, Sat 9am–1pm; free) the Salle des Illustres and a couple of other rooms covered in flowery, late nineteenth-century murals and some more subdued Impressionist works by Henri Martin.

Many of the old *capitouls* built their **hôtels** in the dense web of now mainly pedestrianized streets round about. The material they used was almost exclusively the flat Toulousain brick, whose rosy colour gives the city its nickname of *Ville Rose*. It is an attractive material, lending a small-scale, detailed finish to otherwise plain facades, and setting off admirably any wood- or stonework. Although many of the hôtels survive, they are rarely open to the public, so you have to do a lot of nonchalant sauntering into courtyards to get a look at them. The best known, open to visitors thanks to its very handsome Bemberg collection of paintings, is the **Hôtel d'Assézat**, at the river end of rue de Metz (Tues–Sun 10am–12.30pm & 1.30–6pm, Thurs until 9pm; €4.60, ⓦwww .fondation-bemberg.fr). Started in 1555 under the direction of Nicolas Bachelier, Toulouse's most renowned Renaissance architect, and never finished, it is a sumptuous palace of brick and stone, sporting columns of the three classical orders of Doric, Ionic and Corinthian, plus a lofty staircase tower surmounted by an octagonal lantern. The paintings within include works by Cranach the Elder, Tintoretto and Canaletto as well as moderns like Pissarro, Monet, Gauguin, Vlaminck, Dufy and a roomful of Bonnards. From April to October there's also a *salon de thé* in the entrance gallery.

Other fine houses exist just to the south: on rue Pharaon, in place des Carmes, on rue du Languedoc and on rue Dalbade, where the Hôtel Clary (also known as de Pierre) at no. 25 is unusual for being built of stone. To the north, it's worth wandering along rue St-Rome, rue des Changes, rue de la Bourse and rue du May, where the Hôtel du May at no. 7 houses the **Musée du Vieux-Toulouse** (Mon–Sat 2–6pm; €2.20), a rather uninspiring museum of the city's history.

The Musée des Augustins, the cathedral and the riverside

Right at the junction of rue de Metz and rue d'Alsace-Lorraine stands the **Musée des Augustins** (Thurs–Tues 10am–6pm, Wed 10am–9pm; ⓦwww .augustins.org; €3). Outwardly unattractive, the nineteenth-century building incorporates two surviving cloisters of an Augustinian priory (one now restored as a monastery garden) and contains outstanding collections of Romanesque and medieval sculpture, much of it saved from the now-vanished churches of Toulouse's golden age. Many of the pieces form a fascinating, highly naturalistic display of contemporary manners and fashions: merchants with forked beards touching one another's arms in a gesture of familiarity, and the Virgin represented as a pretty, bored young mother looking away from the Child who strains to escape her hold.

To the south of the museum, just past the Chambre de Commerce, **rue Croix-Baragnon**, full of smart shops and galleries, opens at its eastern end onto the equally attractive **place St-Étienne**, which boasts the city's oldest fountain, the Griffoul (1546). Behind it stands the lopsided **cathedral of St-Étienne**, whose construction was spread over so many centuries that it makes no architectural sense at all. But there's ample compensation in the quiet and elegant streets of the quarter immediately to the south, and in the **Musée Paul-Dupuy**, a few-minutes' walk away along rue Tolosane and rue Mage at 13 rue de la Pléau (Wed–Mon 10am–5pm; June–Sept until 6pm; €3), which has a beautifully displayed and surprisingly interesting collection of clocks, watches, clothes, pottery and furniture from the Middle Ages to the present day, as well as a good display of religious art.

If you follow the rue de Metz westward from the Musée des Augustins, you come to the **Pont-Neuf** – begun in 1544, despite its name – where you can cross over to the **St-Cyprien quarter** on the left bank of the Garonne. At the end of the bridge on the left, an old water tower, erected in 1822 to supply clean water to the city's drinking fountains, now houses the **Galerie Municipale du Château d'Eau** (Tues–Sun 1–7pm; €2.50), a small but influential photography exhibition space and information centre, with frequently changing exhibitions. Next door in the old hospital buildings there's a small **medical museum** (Thurs, Fri & some Sundays 11am–5pm; free), housing a selection of surgical instruments and pharmaceutical equipment.

But the star of the left bank is undoubtedly Toulouse's contemporary art gallery, **Les Abattoirs**, at 76 allées Charles-de-Fitte (Wed–Sun 11am–7pm; €6, ⓦ www.lesabattoirs.org). This splendid venue is not only one of France's best contemporary art museums, but an inspiring example of urban regeneration, constructed in a vast brick abattoir complex dating from 1828. The space itself is massive, with huge chambers perfectly suited to display even the largest canvases. The collection comprises over two thousand works (painting, sculpture, mixed- and multimedia) by artists from 44 countries; the most striking piece is undoubtedly Picasso's massive 14m by 20m theatre backdrop, *La dépouille du Minotaure en costume d'Arlequin*, painted in 1936 for Romain Rolland's *Le 14 Juillet*, which towers over the lower gallery.

The churches of Les Jacobins and St-Sernin

A short distance west of place du Capitole, on rue Lakanal, you can't miss the **church of the Jacobins**. Constructed in 1230 by the Order of Preachers (Dominicans), which St Dominic had founded here in 1216 to preach against Cathar heretics, the church is a huge fortress-like rectangle of unadorned brick, buttressed – like Albi cathedral – by plain brick piles, quite unlike what you'd normally associate with Gothic architecture. The interior is a single space divided by a central row of ultra-slim pillars from whose minimal capitals spring an elegant splay of vaulting ribs – 22 from the last in line – like palm fronds. Beneath the altar lie the bones of the philosopher St Thomas Aquinas. On the north side, you step out into the calming hush of a **cloister** with a formal array of box trees and cypress in the middle, and its adjacent art **exhibition hall** (daily 9am–7pm; €3). Nearby, at the corner of rue Gambetta and rue Lakanal, poke your nose into the stone-galleried courtyard of the **Hôtel de Bernuy**, one of the city's most elaborate Renaissance houses.

From the north side of place du Capitole, **rue du Taur** leads past the belfry wall of **Notre-Dame-du-Taur**, whose diamond-pointed arches and decorative motifs – the acme of Toulousain bricklaying skills – to place St-Sernin. Here you're confronted with the largest Romanesque church in France, the **basilica of St-Sernin**, begun in 1080 to accommodate the passing hordes of Santiago pilgrims, and one of the loveliest examples of its genre. Its most striking external features are the octagonal brick belfry with rounded and pointed arches, diamond lozenges, colonnettes and mouldings picked out in stone, and the apse with nine radiating chapels. Entering from the south, you pass under the Porte Miégeville, whose twelfth-century carvings launched the influential Toulouse school of sculpture. Inside, the great high nave rests on brick piers, flanked by double aisles of diminishing height, surmounted by a gallery running right around the building. The fee for the **ambulatory** (daily 10am–6pm; €2) is worth it for the exceptional eleventh-century marble reliefs on the end wall of the choir and for the extraordinary wealth of reliquaries in the spacious **crypt**.

Right outside St-Sernin is the city's archeological museum, **Musée St-Raymond** (June–Sept 10am–7pm; Oct–May 10am–6pm; €3), housed in what remains of the block built for poor students of the medieval university and containing a large collection of objects ranging from prehistoric to Roman, as well as an excavated necropolis in the basement. On Sunday mornings the whole of place St-Sernin turns into a marvellous, teeming **flea market**.

The suburbs

To see something of the modern face of Toulouse, it's necessary to venture out into the suburbs, where you can visit a high-tech amusement park and a specialized but surprisingly interesting aircraft assembly plant. The first of these is the **Cité de l'Espace** (early Feb to late April daily 9.30am–5/6pm; late April to Aug daily 9.30am–5/6/7pm; Sept to early Jan Tues–Sun 9.30am–5/6pm; Ⓦwww.cite-espace.com; €19.50, children under 5 free), beside exit 17 of the A612 *périphérique* on the road to Castres, or take bus #19 from place Marengo (school holidays only). The theme is space and space exploration, including satellite communications, space probes and, best of all, the opportunity to walk inside a mock-up of the Mir space station – fascinating, but chilling. Many of the exhibits are interactive and, though it's a bit on the pricey side, you could easily spend a half-day here, especially with children in tow.

In 1970 Toulouse became home to **Aérospatiale**, which, along with the aerospace industries of Germany, Britain and Spain, now manufactures Airbus passenger jets. The planes are assembled, painted and tested in a vast hangar, L'Usine Clément Ader, before taking their maiden flights from next-door Blagnac airport. Members of the public are allowed inside the plant on a highly informative guided tour (Ⓣ05.34.39.42.00, Ⓦwww.taxiway.fr; €14; normally in French), but you need to apply at least two weeks before with your passport details, or a few days before for citizens of EU-member countries. After a brief bus tour round the site and a short PR film, you climb high above the eerily quiet assembly bays where just one hundred people churn out five planes a week, ably assisted by scores of computerized robots. Look out for the latest Airbus, the A380, a two-storey superliner which dwarfs even the Jumbo.

Eating, drinking and entertainment

Regular daytime **café-lounging** can be pursued around the popular student-arty hangout of place Arnaud-Bernard, while place du Capitole is the early evening meeting place. Place St-Georges remains popular, though its clientele is no longer convincingly bohemian, and place Wilson also has its enthusiasts.

For lunch, a great informal option is the row of five or six small restaurants jammed in line on the mezzanine floor above the gorgeous **food market** in place Victor-Hugo, off boulevard de Strasbourg. They only function at midday, are all closed on Monday, and cost as little as €12 for market-fresh menus. Both food and atmosphere are perfect.

Cafés

Le Café des Artistes Place de la Daurade. Lively young café overlooking the Garonne. A perfect spot to watch the sun set on warm summer evenings, as floodlights pick out the brick buildings along the *quais*.

Bibent 5 place du Capitole. On the south side of the square, this is Toulouse's most distinguished café, with exuberant plasterwork, marble tables and cascading chandeliers.

Le Florida 12 place du Capitole. Relaxed café with a retro air. One of the most pleasant places to hang out on the central square.

Jour de Fête 43 rue de Taur. Trendy tearoom and brasserie with a small street-side patio. Friendly service and a young university-set crowd.

Le Shanti 21 rue Peyrolières. A funky "Indian" tea house where you can enjoy a narghile (Arab water-pipe).

Restaurants

Les Abbatoirs Chez Carmen 97 allée Charles-de-Fitte Ⓣ05.61.42.04.95. Family-run for two generations, this is one of the last of the traditional slaughterhouse-side meat emporia, with a reputation for top-of-the-line intestinal delicacies, such as calves' brains and pigs' feet. Menus from €19. Closed Sun, Mon & Aug.

Atilla Market, place Victor-Hugo. The best of the market restaurants, this no-nonsense lunchtime establishment is also one of Toulouse's best options for seafood – their Spanish *zarzuela* stew is a fish-lover's dream. Menus from €15. Closed Mon & part Aug.

La Bascule 14 av Maurice-Hauriou ☎05.61.52.09.51. A Toulouse institution. Its chromey interior is pure Art Deco and the food well prepared and presented. The menu includes regional dishes like cassoulet, *foie de canard* and oysters from the Bay of Arcachon. Expect to spend €16 or more. Closed Sat lunch & Sun.

Benjamin 7 rue des Gestes ☎05.61.22.92.66. A long-standing institution for economical *terroir* food; service is pleasant and professional, although the atmosphere is somewhat anonymous. There's a wide selection of duck-based lunch and dinner menus from €11.50 and €19. Open daily.

Au Chat Dingue 40bis rue Peyrolières. Small, hip bistro with cool blue decor across from the *Petit Voisin* bar. The selection is not overly imaginative, with a solid southern French base and occasional Italian incursions (usually in the form of pasta). Menus start at €18, but considerably more à la carte. Closed Sun.

Faim des Haricots 3 rue de Puits Vert ☎05.61.22.49.25. Toulouse's best vegetarian option, with generous *formules* starting at €11. Open Mon–Sat lunch & Thurs–Sat dinner; closed first half Aug.

Les Jardins de l'Opéra 1 place du Capitole ☎05.61.21.05.56. The *Grand Hôtel*'s restaurant is Toulouse's best and most luxurious. If you fancy a splurge you will pay for it – a basic menu starts at €29 – but the food is outstanding. Closed Sun, Mon & part Aug.

Michel Sarran 21 bd Armand-Duportal ☎05.61.12.32.32. Justifiably renowned *gastronomique* restaurant, a fifteen-minute walk from the place du Capitole (follow rue des Lois and rue des Salenques to the end, and turn left). Imaginative dishes with a strong Mediterranean streak are served with style and warmth. Menus from €48 at lunch and €98 at dinner. Closed Wed noon, Sat, Sun & part Aug.

Au Pois Gourmand 3 rue Émile-Heybrard ☎05.34.36.42.00. Great location in a riverside nineteenth-century house with a beautiful patio. The quality French cuisine does not come cheap here (menus €35–39), but is of a predictably high standard, and the *carte* presents a pleasant

departure from purely regional dishes. Bus #66 or #14 from métro St-Cyprien-République. Closed Sat & Mon lunch & Sun.

Le Sept Place St-Sernin 7 place St-Sernin ☎05.62.30.05.30. A small house behind the basilica conceals a lively and cheerful restaurant serving inventive and original cuisine with a constantly changing *carte*, followed by dazzling desserts. Menus €18–60. Closed Sat lunch & Sun.

Bars and clubs

L'Ambassade 22 bd de la Gare. Downbeat club where funk and soul rule. Live jazz on Sun nights. Mon–Fri 7pm–2am, Sat & Sun 7pm–5am.

Bodega-Bodega 1 rue Gabriel-Péri. The old *Telegraph* newspaper building makes a superb venue for this bar-restaurant, with its hugely popular disco after 10pm. Daily 7pm–2am, till 4am on Sat.

Le Chat d'Oc 7 rue de Metz. Hip bar near the Garonne, attracting a mixed crowd which gets younger as the night progresses. Nightly animations include DJs and occasional live acts. Mon–Fri 7am–2am, Sat 9am–5am.

Erich Coffie 9 rue Joseph-Vié ☎05.61.42.04.27. Just west of the river in the quartier St-Cyprien, this is one of the city's liveliest and most enjoyable music bars (food available), with an eclectic music policy. Live bands most evenings. Open Tues–Sat from 10pm.

The Frog & Rosbif 14 rue de l'Industrie. Stop by this friendly British pub & micro-brewery, just off bd Lazare-Carnot, for a pint of Darktagnan stout, or one of their other excellent home-brews. Quiz nights, football and fish and chips draw a surprisingly international crowd. Mon–Fri & Sun 5.30pm–2am, Sat 2pm–4am. Closed part Aug.

Hey Joe Place Héraclès. Popular disco with theme nights on Thurs. Men pay €8, women get in free; happy hour midnight–1am. Open daily 11pm–5am.

Le Petit Voisin 37 rue Peyrolières. A neighbourhood place, just like the name says, laid-back during the day, and with DJs at night. Open Mon–Fri 7.30am–2am, Sat 8am–4am. Closed mid-Aug.

L'Ubu 16 rue St-Rome ☎05.61.23.26.75. Long-standing pillar of the city's dance scene, which remains as popular as ever. Mon–Sat 11pm till dawn.

Film, theatre and live music

Drinking and dancing aside, there's plenty to do at night in Toulouse. Several **cinemas** regularly show *v.o.* films, including: ABC, 13 rue St-Bernard (☎05.61.29.81.00, 🕸www.abctoulouse.net); Cinémathèque, 68 rue de Taur (☎05.62.30.30.10, 🕸www.lacinemathequedetoulouse.com); Cratere, 95 Grande-Rue St-Michel (☎05.61.52.50.53); and Utopia, 24 rue Montardy

(☎05.61.23.66.20, 🌐www.cinemas-utopia.org). There's also an extremely vibrant **theatre** culture here. The tourist office can give you a full list of venues, which range from the official Théâtre de la Cité, 1 rue Pierre-Baudis (☎05.34.45.05.05, 🌐www.tnt-cite.com), to the workshop Nouveau Théâtre Jules-Julien, 6 avenue des Écoles-Jules-Juliens (Mon–Fri 9am–noon & 2–5pm; ☎05.61.25.79.92). The larger venues, such as Odyssud, 4 avenue du Parc Blagnac (☎05.61.71.75.15; bus #66), feature both theatre and **opera**, while the Orchestre National du Capitole has its base in the Halle aux Grains on place Dupuy (☎05.61.99.78.00, 🌐www.onct.mairie-toulouse.fr). The city's biggest **concert venue** (9000 seats), specializing in rock, is Zénith, at 11 avenue Raymond Badiou (☎05.62.74.49.49; métro Arènes), while Cave-Poesie at 71 rue de Taur (☎05.61.23.62.00) is home to literary workshops and gatherings of a decidedly bohemian spirit.

Listings

Airport Aéroport Toulouse-Blagnac ☎05.61.42.44.00 and 05.24.61.80.00, 🌐www .toulouse.aeroport.fr; for shuttle bus information ☎05.34.60.64.00.

Bike rental The municipal bike co-op Movimento (Mon–Fri 8am–7pm, Sat & Sun 10am–7pm; 🌐movimento.coop) has branches at square Charles-de-Gaulle (opposite the tourist office) and 5 Port Saint-Saveur. Holiday Bikes, 9 bd des Minimes (☎05.34.25.79.62, ✉toulouse@holiday-bikes.com) also has scooters and motorcycles.

Books For English-language books, Books and Mermaides, 3 rue Mirepoix, specializes in second-hand tomes and will exchange, while The Bookshop, 17 rue Lakanal, stocks new titles. There are book markets on Thursday mornings in place Arnaud-Bernard, and all day Saturday in place St-Étienne.

Car hire A2L, 81 bd Déodat-de-Séverac ☎05.61.59.33.99; Avis, *gare SNCF* ☎05.61.63.71.71; Budget, 49 rue Bayard ☎05.61.63.18.18; Europcar, 15 bd Bonrepos ☎05.61.62.52.89; Hertz, *gare SNCF* ☎05.61.62.94.12.

Consulates Canada, 10 rue Jules de Resseguier ☎05.61.52.19.06, ✉consulat.canada.toulouse @orange.fr; USA, 25 allées Jean-Jaurès ☎05.34.41.36.50, 🌐www.amb-usa.fr; the closest British Consulate is in Bordeaux at 353 bd Wilson (☎05.57.22.21.10); there is an Honorary Consulate in Toulouse (☎05.61.30.37.91).

Gay and lesbian For information contact the gay and lesbian students' group Jules et Julies (Comité des Étudiants, Université du Mirail, 5 allée Machado, 31058) or Gais et Lesbiennes en Marche (☎06.11.87.38.81, ✉gelem@altern.org).

Internet Cyber Media-Net, 19 rue de Lois (Mon–Fri 9am–11.30pm, Sat 10am–midnight), or @fterbug, 12 place St-Sernin (Mon–Fri noon–2am, Sat noon–5am, Sun 2.30–10.30pm).

Pharmacy The Pharmacie de Nuit, 70–76 allées Jean-Jaurès (entry on rue Arnaud-Vidal) is open 8pm–8am.

Police 23 bd de l'Embouchure ☎05.61.12.77.77.

Taxi Capitole ☎05.34.25.02.50; Taxi Radio Toulou-sain ☎05.61.42.38.38. For taxis to the airport call ☎05.61.30.02.54.

Albi and Cordes

ALBI, 77km and an hour's train ride northeast of Toulouse, is a small industrial town with two unique sights: a museum containing the most comprehensive collection of Toulouse-Lautrec's work (Albi was his birthplace); and one of the most remarkable Gothic cathedrals you'll ever see. Its other claim to fame comes from its association with Catharism; though not itself an important centre, it gave its name – Albigensian – to both the heresy and the crusade to suppress it.

The town hosts three good **festivals** over the course of the year: jazz in May, theatre at the end of June and beginning of July, and classical music at the end of July and beginning of August. During July and August there are also free organ recitals in the cathedral (Wed 5pm & Sun 4pm).

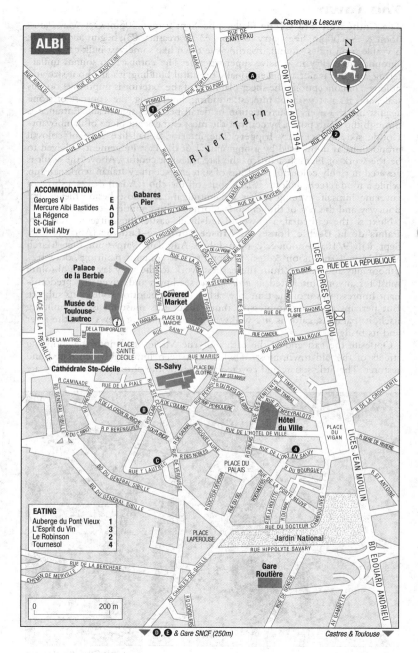

Castelnau & Lescure

ALBI

River Tarn

PONT DU 22 AOÛT 1944

N

LANGUEDOC

RUE DE CANTEPAU
RUE STE MARIE
RUE PERROTY
RUE PORTA
RUE PORTA
RUE DU PORT
RUE RINALDI
RUE DE LA MADELEINE
RUE RINALDI
RUE DU TENDAT
RUE PONT-VIEUX
RUE EDOUARD BRANLY
R. BASSE DES MOULINS
RUE DE LA RIVIÈRE
SENTIER DES BERGES DU TARN
QUAI CHOISEUL
RUE DE LA GRD CÔTE
RUE EMILE GRAND
RUE DE LA VIGNE
RUE AFRIC
LICES GEORGES POMPIDOU
RUE DE LA RÉPUBLIQUE

Gabares Pier

ACCOMMODATION
Georges V	E
Mercure Albi Bastides	A
La Régence	D
St-Clair	B
Le Vieil Alby	C

Palace de la Berbie

Musée de Toulouse-Lautrec

RUE DE LA SOUQUE
RUE DE LA RUADE
R ST ÉTIENNE
R D FOISSANS
RUE STE CLAIRE
BONNE-CAMBE D'ELBENE
PL STE CLAIRE
RUE DE
RHONEL

Covered Market

PLACE DU MARCHÉ
RUE DE LA TEMPORALITÉ
R D FARGUES
RUE SAINT JULIEN
RUE CANDEIL
RUE AUGUSTIN MALROUX

PLACE DE LA TRÉBAILLE
R DE LA MAITRISE
PLACE SAINTE CÉCILE

Cathédrale Ste-Cécile

RUE MARIES
St-Salvy
PLACE DU CLOITRE
IMP STE MARIE

R. CAMINADE
RUE DE LA PIALE
RUE STE CÉCILE
R DE L'OULMET
RUE PEYROLIÈRE
R DU PUITS DE LA GRACE
RUE DES PÉNITENTS
IMP TIMBAL
IMP TIMBAL
RUE TIMBAL
R DE LA CROIX VERTE

BD GÉNÉRAL SIBILLE
R D PRESSE
R DE LA CROIX BLANCHE
R ST CÉCILE
R P BERENGUIER
R D'OUR AMOSS
RUE SKINNA
R ROQUE AURE
RUE DE L'HÔTEL DE VILLE
RUE D'EMPEYRALOTS

Hôtel du Ville

PLACE DU VIGAN
LICES JEAN MOULIN
R SÈRE DE RIVIÈRE

R DU C BROT
RUE T LAUTREC
R DES NOBLES
R VÉROUSSE
R V OCTAVE DEVOIR
RUE DU SEL
RUE DE L'ORT EN SALVY
R DU BOURGUET
R ST ANTOINE

PLACE DU PALAIS

EATING
Auberge du Pont Vieux	1
L'Esprit du Vin	3
Le Robinson	2
Tournesol	4

BD DU GÉNÉRAL SIBILLE
BD DU GÉNÉRAL SIBILLE
RES METIERS
RUE DE LA VIOLETTE
RUE DU MAL
RUE DE LA PORTE NEUVE
RUE DU DOCTEUR CAMBOULIVES

PLACE LAPEROUSE
Jardin National
RUE HIPPOLYTE SAVARY

RUE DE LA BERCHÈRE
CHEMIN DE MERVILLE
RUE DE LA BERCHÈRE
AV CHARLES-DE-GAULLE
R D CORDELIERS
RUE DE GENÈVE

Gare Routière

BD EDOUARD ANDRIEU
AV GAMBETTA

0	200 m

D, E & Gare SNCF (250m)

Castres & Toulouse

803

The Town

The **Cathédrale Ste-Cécile** (daily: June–Sept 9am–6.30pm; Oct–May 9am–noon & 2–6.30pm; free; entry to choir €3, to treasury €3), begun about 1280, is visible from miles around, dwarfing the town like some vast bulk carrier run aground, the belfry its massive superstructure. The comparison sounds unflattering, and this is not a conventionally beautiful building; it's all about size and boldness of conception. The sheer plainness of the exterior is impressive on this scale, and it's not without interest: arcading, buttressing, the contrast of stone against brick – every differentiation of detail becomes significant. Entrance is through the south portal, by contrast the most extravagant piece of flamboyant-Gothic sixteenth-century frippery. The interior, a hall-like nave of colossal proportions, is dominated by a huge mural of the Last Judgement, believed to be the work of Flemish artists in the late fifteenth century. Above, the vault is covered in richly colourful paintings of sixteenth-century Italian workmanship, while a rood screen, delicate as lace, shuts off the choir: Adam makes a show of covering himself, evening strikes a flaunting model's pose beside the central doorway, and the rest of the screen is adorned with countless statues.

Next to the cathedral, a powerful red-brick castle, the thirteenth-century **Palais de la Berbie**, houses the **Musée Toulouse-Lautrec** (April–June & Sept daily 9/10am–noon & 2–6pm; July & Aug daily 9am–6pm; Oct–March Wed–Mon 10am–noon & 2–5/5.30pm; €5). It contains paintings, drawings, lithographs and posters from the earliest work to the very last – an absolute must for anyone interested in *belle-époque* seediness and, given the predominant Impressionism of the time, the rather offbeat painting style of its subject. But perhaps the most impressive thing about this museum is the building itself, its parapets, gardens and walkways giving stunning views over the river and its bridges.

Opposite the east end of the cathedral, rue Mariés leads into the shopping streets of the old town, most of which has been impeccably renovated and restored. The little square and covered passages by the **church of St-Salvy** are

▲ Albi's Cathédrale Ste-Cécile

worth a look as you go by. Eventually you come to the broad **Lices Georges Pompidou**, the main thoroughfare of modern Albi, which leads down to the river and the road to Cordes. Less touristy, this is the best place to look for somewhere to eat and drink.

Practicalities

From the **gare SNCF** on place Stalingrad it's a ten-minute walk into town along avenues Maréchal-Joffre and de-Gaulle; you'll see the **gare routière** on your right in place Jean-Jaurès as you reach the limits of the old town. The **tourist office** is in one corner of the Palais de la Berbie (July & Aug Mon–Sat 9am–7pm, Sun 10am–12.30pm & 2.30–6.30pm; Sept–June Mon–Sat 9am–12.30pm & 2–6/6.30pm, Sun 10am–12.30pm & 2.30–5pm; ℡05.63.49.48.80, ⓦwww.albi-tourisme.fr); ask for a copy of their English-language leaflet describing three walking tours round Albi. Also recommended is the "Albi Pass" (€6.50) which gives free or discounted admission to the town's sights.

There are two attractive **hotels** near the station on avenue Maréchal-Joffre which have now merged: *La Régence*, at no. 27, and the *Georges V*, at no. 29 (℡05.63.54.24.16, ⓦwww.laregence-georgev.fr; ❷). On the opposite side of the town, on the north bank of the river, you'll find the luxurious *Mercure Albi Bastides* (℡05.63.47.66.66, Ⓔmercure.albi@orange.fr; ❺) at 41 rue Porta. In the heart of old Albi near the cathedral, the *Hôtel St-Clair*, 8 rue St-Clair (℡05.63.54.25.66, ⓦwww.andrieu.michele.free.fr; ❷) is a good bargain, but A *Le Vieil Alby*, 25 rue Toulouse-Lautrec (℡05.63.54.14.69, Ⓔlevieilalby @orange.fr; ❷) is a real find – cheap and comfortable, with a friendly owner and excellent home-cooked food available. Otherwise, there's a caravan and **campsite** (℡05.63.60.37.06; April–Oct) in the Parc de Caussels, about 2km east on the D999 Millau road.

Albi's cuisine is predominantly *terroir* – local cooking notable only for *lou tastou*, the local version of tapas. One of the best *terroir* **restaurants** is *Auberge du Pont Vieux*, at 98 rue Porta (℡05.63.77.61.73; closed Oct–May & Wed lunch & Thurs outside midsummer; from €17), on the north bank of the Tarn. *Le Robinson*, at 142 rue Edouard Branly (℡05.63.46.15.69; Tues & Wed off season & Nov-Mar; from €18), is set apart by its park-like surroundings, while *L'Esprit du Vin*, 11 quai Choiseul (℡05.63.54.60.44; closed Sun, Mon & mid-Feb to May; from €30), has imaginative *gastronomique* cuisine. *Tournesol*, off place du Vigan (℡05.63.38.38.14; open Tues–Sat lunch only & Fri dinner), is Albi's vegetarian option (from about €16).

Cordes

One of the region's "don't miss" sights is **CORDES**, perched on a conical hill 24km northwest of Albi, from which it's a brief trip by train (as far as Cordes-Vindrac, 5km away, with bike rental from the station) or bus (daily except Sun). Founded in 1222 by Raymond VII, Count of Toulouse, Cordes was a **Cathar** stronghold, and the ground beneath the town is riddled with tunnels for storage and refuge in time of trouble. As one of the southwest's oldest and best-preserved *bastides*, complete with thirteenth- and fourteenth-century houses climbing steep cobbled lanes, Cordes is inevitably a major tourist attraction: medieval banners flutter in the streets and artisans practise their crafts. The **Musée Charles–Portal** (July & Aug daily 2–6pm; €4) depicts the history of the town. Also of interest is the **Musée d'Art Moderne et Contemporain** (daily: April–May & Oct 11am–12.30pm & 2–6.30pm; June–Sept 11am–12.30pm & 2–7pm; Nov–March 2–5pm; €3.50), which features works by the figurative painter Yves Brayer, who lived in Cordes from 1940. The best **hotel** in town is the splendid ✦ *Grand Écuyer* (☎05.63.53.79.50, Ⓦwww.thuries.fr; closed mid-Oct to Easter; ⑥) – from its gargoyle-studded facade to the ponderous stone of the interior, this former palace of Count Raymond VII of Toulouse is an evocative combination of medieval atmosphere and modern amenities. Just down the street, the *Vieux Cordes* (closed Jan; ☎05.63.53.79.20, Ⓦwww.thuries.fr; ②) is housed in a medieval building. There's also a **campsite** (☎05.63.56.11.10, Ⓦwww.campingmoulindejulien.com); closed Oct–March) 1km southeast down the Gaillac road.

Castres

In spite of its industrial activities, **CASTRES**, 40km south of Albi and 55km east of Toulouse, has kept a lot of its charm, in the streets on the right bank of the Agout and, in particular, the riverside quarter where the old tanners' and weavers' houses overhang the water. The centre is a bustling, businesslike sort of place, with a big morning **market** on Saturdays on place Jean-Jaurès. By the rather unremarkable old cathedral, the former bishop's palace holds the Hôtel de Ville and Castres' **Musée Goya** (July & Aug daily 10am–6pm; Sept–June Tues–Sun 9am–noon & 2–5/6pm; €2.30), home to the biggest collection of Spanish paintings in France outside the Louvre. Goya is represented by some lighter political paintings and a large collection of

Jean Jaurès

Jean Jaurès, the nineteenth-century labour activist, politician and martyr, was born in Castres in 1859, showed exceptional promise as a student and won a scholarship to complete his studies in Paris. After graduating, rather than stay in the capital he returned to his home *département* of Tarn and taught philosophy in Albi, while lecturing at the University of Toulouse. But the miserable living and working conditions of his working-class neighbours drew him out of the academy. At the young age of 26 Jaurès was elected a legislative representative. Under his guidance the glass-workers at Albi founded the collectively run VOA. bottle factory, which still operates today. In 1893, as socialist deputy for Carmaux, he supported the miners' struggle, and his renown as a social reformer began to spread.

However, Jaurès' desire for reform was not limited to local causes, and in 1898 he joined other liberals, including Zola, in defence of the Jewish army captain, Alfred Dreyfus, convicted on unfounded charges of espionage, and helped to obtain his eventual pardon. The patriotically charged issue temporarily cost Jaurès his popularity, but he was soon back, founding the Communist daily *L'Humanité* in 1904 (still one of France's major newspapers; Ⓦwww.humanite.fr) and helping found the socialist SFIO party. With the dawn of World War I, Jaurès' internationalism was manifested in an outspoken and unpopular pacifist stand which led to his assassination in Paris by a nationalist extremist called Villain in July 1914. He was hailed as a martyr, and became the hero of the Tarn – a local politician who fought for this marginalized region, and who wasn't afraid to take on the political establishment of Paris in order to defend a higher justice.

There could be no better epitaph than his own last article in *L'Humanité*, in which he wrote: "The most important thing is that we should continue to act and to keep our minds perpetually fresh and alive ... That is the real safeguard, the guarantee of our future."

engravings, and there are also works by other famous Iberian artists, like Murillo and Velázquez.

Castres' other specialist museum is the **Musée Jean–Jaurès** (July & Aug daily 10am–noon & 2–6pm; Sept–June Tues–Sun 9am–noon & 2–5/6pm; €1.50), dedicated to its famous native son (see box opposite). It's located in place Pélisson, and getting to it takes you through the streets of the old town, past the splendid seventeenth-century **Hôtel Nayrac**, on rue Frédéric-Thomas. The museum was opened in 1988 by President Mitterrand – appropriately enough, because Mitterrand's Socialist Party is the direct descendant of Jaurès' SFIO, founded in 1905, which split at the Congress of Tours in 1920, when the "Bolshevik" element left to form the French Communist Party. The slightly hagiographic museum nonetheless pays well-deserved tribute to one of France's boldest and best political writers, thinkers and activists of modern times.

Practicalities

Arriving from Toulouse by train, you'll find the **gare SNCF** a kilometre southwest of the town centre on avenue Albert-1er. The **gare routière** is on place Soult, with bus services to Mazamet and Lacaune. The **tourist office** stands beside the Pont Vieux at 3 rue Milhau-Ducommun (July & Aug daily 9.30am–12.30pm & 1.30–6.30pm; otherwise Mon–Sat 9.30am–12.30pm & 2–6pm; ☎05.63.62.63.62, ⓦwww.ville-castres.fr).

Castres has two marvellous seventeenth-century mansions converted into luxurious but affordable **hotels**: the marginally more deluxe ⚥ *Renaissance* is at 17 rue Victor-Hugo (☎05.63.59.30.42, ⓦwww.hotel-renaissance.fr; ❸); and the *Rivière*, 10 quai Tourcaudière (☎05.63.59.04.53, ⓔhotelriviere @orange.fr; ❶), has pleasant views over the Agout and helpful staff. The nicely sited *Miredames*, at 1 place Roger Salengro (☎05.63.71.38.18, ⓦwww.hotel-miredames.com; ❷), is a bargain. The municipal **campsite** (☎05.63.59.33.51, ⓦwww.campingdegourjade.com; closed Oct–March) is in a riverside park 2km northeast of town on the road to Roquecourbe, which you can also reach by river-taxi (round trip €5).

For simple, inexpensive **meals**, you can't beat the upstairs dining room in the *Brasserie des Jacobins*, on place Jean-Jaurès. In the evening, the best bet is the *Renaissance* (see above) which offers all-you-can eat buffets for €12.

The Gers

West of Toulouse, the *département* of **Gers** lies at the heart of the historic region of Gascony. In the long struggle for supremacy between the English and the French in the Middle Ages it had the misfortune to form the frontier zone between the English base at Bordeaux and the French at Toulouse. The attractive if unspectacular rolling agricultural land is dotted with ancient, honey-stoned farms. Settlement is sparse and – with the exception of **Auch**, the capital – major monuments are largely lacking, which keeps it well off the beaten tourist trails.

The region's traditional sources of renown are its stout-hearted mercenary warriors – of whom Alexandre Dumas' d'Artagnan and Edmond Rostand's Cyrano de Bergerac are the supreme literary exemplars – its rich cuisine and its **Armagnac**. The food and brandy still flourish: Gers is the biggest producer of **foie gras** in the country.

Auch

The sleepy provincial capital of the Gers, **AUCH** is most easily accessible by rail from Toulouse, 78km to the east. The old town, which is the only part worth exploring, stands on a bluff overlooking the tree-lined River Gers, with the cathedral towering dramatically over the town.

It is this building – the **Cathédrale Ste-Marie** – which makes a trip to Auch worthwhile. Although not finished until the latter part of the seventeenth century, it is built in broadly late Gothic style, with a classical facade. Of particular interest are the choir stalls (daily: July & Aug 8.30am–6.30pm; Sept–June 8.30am–noon & 2–5/6pm; closed during services; €2) and the stained glass; both were begun in the early 1500s, though the windows are of clearly Renaissance inspiration, while the choir remains Gothic. The stalls are thought to have been carved by the same craftsmen who executed those at St-Bertrand-de-Comminges, and show the same extraordinary virtuosity and detail. The eighteen windows, unusual in being a complete set, parallel the scenes and personages depicted in the stalls. They are the work of a Gascon painter, Arnaud de Moles, and are equally rich in detail.

Immediately south of the cathedral, in the tree-filled place Salinis, is the forty-metre-high **Tour d'Armagnac**, which served as an ecclesiastical court and prison in the fourteenth century. Descending from here to the river is a **monumental stairway** of 234 steps, with a statue of d'Artagnan gracing one of the terraces. From place de la République, in front of the cathedral's main west door, rue d'Espagne connects with rue de la Convention and what is left of the narrow medieval stairways known as the **pousterles**, which give access to the lower town. On the north side of place de la République, the tourist office inhabits a splendid half-timbered fifteenth-century house on the corner with rue Dessoles, a pedestrianized street boasting an array of fine buildings. Just down the steps to the east of rue Dessoles, on place Louis-Blanc, the former convent, now the **Musée des Jacobins** (April–Oct daily 10am–noon

---

Armagnac

Armagnac is a dry, golden brandy distilled in the district extending into the Landes and Lot and Garonne *départements*, divided into three distinct areas: Haut-Armagnac (around Auch), Ténarèze (Condom) and Bas-Armagnac (Éauze), in ascending order of output and quality. Growers of the grape like to compare brandy with whisky, equating malts with the individualistic, earthy Armagnac distilled by small producers, and blended whiskies with the more consistent, standardized output of the large-scale houses. Armagnac grapes are grown on sandy soils and, importantly, the wine is distilled only once, giving the spirit a lower alcohol content but more flavour. Aged in local black oak, Armagnac matures quickly, so young Armagnacs are relatively smoother than corresponding Cognacs.

Distilled originally for medicinal reasons, Armagnac has many claims made for its efficacy. Perhaps the most optimistic are those of the priest of Éauze de St-Mont, who held that the eau de vie cured **gout** and hepatitis. More reasonably, he also wrote that it "stimulates the spirit if taken in moderation, recalls the past, gives many joy above all else, conserves youth. If one retains it in the mouth, it unties the tongue and gives courage to the timid."

Many of the producers welcome visitors and offer tastings, whether you go to one of the bigger *chais* of Condom or Éauze, or follow a faded sign at the bottom of a farm track. For more **information**, contact the Bureau National Interprofessionnel de l'Armagnac, place de la Liberté, 32800 Éauze (☎05.62.08.11.00, ⊛www.cognacnet .com/armagnac).

& 2–6pm; rest of the year Mon–Fri 2–5pm & Sat & Sun 10am–noon & 2–5pm; €3) houses one of the best collections of pre-Columbian and later South American art in France, left to the town by an adventurous son, M. Pujos, who had lived in Chile in the last years of the nineteenth century. Also of interest is its small collection of traditional Gascon furniture, religious artefacts and Gallo-Roman remains.

Practicalities

The **tourist office** (mid-July to mid-Aug Mon–Sat 9.30am–6.30pm & Sun 10am–12.15pm & 3–6.15pm; mid-Aug to mid-July Mon–Sat 9.15am–noon & 2–6/6.30pm; also open Sun 10am–12.15pm May–Oct; ℡05.62.05.22.89, Ⓦwww.mairie-auch.fr) stands at the corner of place de la République and rue Dessoles. West of here, place de la Libération leads to the allées D'Étigny, with the **gare routière** off to the right.

In terms of accommodation, the only choice in the centre is the relatively luxurious *Hôtel de France* at 2 place de la Libération (℡05.62.61.71.71, Ⓦwww .hoteldefrance-auch.com; ❺), right by the *mairie* and only a few-minutes' walk west of the cathedral. The best hotel is 2km northwest of the town centre: the *Château les Charmettes* (℡05.62.10.10; ❼). An economical alternative is the *Hôtel de Paris*, 38 avenue de la Marne (℡05.62.63.26.22, Ⓕ05.62.60.04.27; ❸; closed Nov). To get there from the **gare SNCF**, turn right on avenue de la Gare, follow it to the end, then turn left. Otherwise, the municipal **campsite** (℡05.62.05.00.22; mid-April to mid-Sept) is beside the river on the south side of town.

Avenue d'Alsace, in the lower town, is the best place to look for inexpensive places to **eat**. Alternatively, up by the cathedral, place de la République and place de la Libération boast a fair selection of cafés and brasseries; try *Café Daroles* by the fountain (menus from €17.90 or €10.55 at lunch). For something traditional, *La Table d'Oste*, off rue Dessoles at 7 rue Lamartine, offers good Gascon fare from €16 (closed Sat–Mon, depending on season). The well-regarded restaurant of the *Hôtel de France* has menus from €15, although à la carte will set you back considerably more.

Travel details

Trains

Béziers to: Agde (18 daily; 45min); Arles (10–14 daily; 2hr 10min); Avignon (4–10 daily; 2hr); Bédarieux (4–8 daily; 40min); Carcassonne (22 daily; 45min–1hr 45min); Clermont-Ferrand (3 daily; 6–7hr); Marseille (8 daily; 3hr 10min); Millau (4–6 daily; 2hr); Montpellier (26 daily; 45min); Narbonne (18 daily; 14min); Nîmes (20 daily; 1hr 15min); Paris (30 daily; 4hr 30min–12hr); Perpignan (18 daily; 40min–1hr); Sète (23 daily; 25min).

Carcassonne to: Arles (4–8 daily; 2hr 40min–3hr 30min); Béziers (22 daily; 45min–1hr 45min); Bordeaux (18–22 daily; 3hr 20min–4hr 30min); Limoux (16 daily; 25min); Marseille (12–18 daily; 3hr 20min–5hr 30min); Montpellier (18 daily; 1hr

30min–4hr); Narbonne (22 daily; 35min); Nîmes (26 daily; 2hr 5min–3hr 10min); Quillan (6 daily; 1hr 15min); Toulouse (22 daily; 45min–1hr).

Montpellier to: Arles (10–14 daily; 1hr 20min); Avignon (22 daily; 1hr 15min–2hr); Béziers (18 daily; 40min); Carcassonne (22 daily; 1hr 15min); Lyon (18 daily; 1hr 40min–3hr 30min); Marseille (18–22 daily; 2hr 20min); Mende (18 daily; 3hr 40min–4hr 30min); Narbonne (26 daily; 45min–1hr 15min); Paris (16 daily; 3hr 15min–6hr); Perpignan (12 daily; 2hr 15min); Sète (22 daily; 15–20min); Toulouse (18 daily; 2hr 15min–2hr 55min).

Narbonne to: Arles (18–22 daily; 2hr); Avignon (4–8 daily; 2hr 10min); Béziers (18 daily; 14min); Bordeaux (18–22 daily; 3hr 45min–6hr); Carcas- sonne (22 daily; 35min); Cerbère (12–16 daily;

1hr–1hr 30min); Marseille (20 daily; 2hr 40min–3hr 30min); Montpellier (26 daily; 45min–1hr 15min); Nîmes (20 daily; 1hr 45min); Perpignan (24 daily; 36–45min); Sète (23 daily; 45min); Toulouse (18 daily; 1hr 30min).

Nîmes to: Arles (22 daily; 30–40min); Avignon (14–18 daily; 30min); Béziers (36 daily; 1hr 15min); Carcassonne (26 daily; 2hr 5min–3hr 10min); Clermont-Ferrand (12–16 daily; 5–6hr); La Bastide-St-Laurent (6–8 daily; 1hr 45min–2hr 40min); Marseille (20 daily; 40min–1hr 15min); Montpellier (26 daily; 30min); Narbonne (20 daily; 1hr 45min); Paris (23 daily; 3–9hr 30min); Perpignan (12 daily; 2hr 45min); Sète (22 daily; 48min).

Toulouse to: Albi (17 daily; 1hr); Auch (18–20 daily; 1hr 15min–2hr 30min); Ax-les-Thermes (6 daily; 1hr 55min); Bayonne (18–22 daily; 2hr 25min–3hr 45min); Bordeaux (18–22 daily; 2hr 30min); Castres (11 daily; 1hr 5min); Foix (13 daily; 47min–1hr 15min); La-Tour-de-Carol (6 daily; 2hr 30min); Lourdes (8–16 daily; 1hr 40min); Lyon (14–18 daily; 4–6hr); Marseille (22 daily; 3hr 30min–6hr); Mazamet (11 daily; 1hr 30min–1hr 55min); Pamiers (13 daily; 50min–1hr 10min); Paris (13 daily; 5hr 20min–6hr 45min); Pau (6–10 daily; 2hr–2hr 30min); Tarascon-sur-Ariège (13 daily; 1hr 20min); Tarbes (6–13 daily; 1hr 45min).

Buses

Albi to: Cordes-sur-Ciel (2 daily; 35min).
Auch to: Agen (6–10 daily; 1hr 30min); Bordeaux (1 daily; 3hr 40min); Condom (1–2 daily; 40min); Lectoure (4–8 daily; 40min); Montauban (0–3 daily; 2hr); Tarbes (3–4 daily; 2hr); Toulouse (1–4 daily; 1hr 30min).

Bédarieux to: Olargues (1–2 daily; 40min); St-Pons-de-Thomières (3 daily; 1hr 20min).
Béziers to: Agde (2 daily & 4–6 in summer; 25min); Bédarieux (0–2 daily; 1hr); Castres (2 daily; 2hr 50min); La Salvetat (0–2 daily; 2hr 10min); Mazamet (2 daily; 2hr); Pézenas (4–11 daily; 32min); St-Pons-de-Thomières (4 daily; 1hr 20min).
Carcassonne to: Castelnaudary (3–5 daily; 45min); Quillan (2 daily; 1hr 20min).
Montpellier to: Aigues-Mortes (2–4 daily; 1hr); Bédarieux (3–4 daily; 1hr 35min); Clermont-l'Hérault (3–4 daily; 1hr); Ganges (4–5 daily; 1hr 15min); Gignac (for St-Guilhem: 6–8 daily; 40min); La Grande-Motte (8–12 daily; 1hr 5min; hourly in summer); Grau-du-Roi (4–8 daily; 1hr 10min); Le Vigan (3–5 daily; 1hr 40min); Lodève (4 daily; 1hr 15min); Millau (2–8 daily; 2hr 20min); Palavas (local service); Rodez (1–3 daily; 3hr 55min); St-Martin-de-Londres (2–4 daily; 50min); St-Pons-de-Thomières (1–3 daily; 2hr 55min); Viols-le-Fort (2–9 daily; 40min).
Narbonne to: Gruissan (3–6 daily; 45min); Narbonne-Plage (2–8 daily; 45min).
Nîmes to: Aigues-Mortes (17 daily; 55min); Ganges (2–3 daily; 1hr 30min); La Grande-Motte (2–9 daily; 1hr 30min); Le Grau-du-Roi (12–18 daily; 1hr 15min); Le Vigan (3–5 daily; 1hr 50min); Pont du Gard (8 daily; 45min); Sommières (8 daily; 45min); Uzès (8–12 daily; 30min–1hr).
Sète to: Montpellier (3–15 daily; 1hr 5min).
Toulouse to: Albi (12–16 weekly; 2hr 40min); Carcassonne (1 daily; 2hr 20min); Castres (8–12 weekly; 1hr 40min–2hr); St-Girons (3 daily; 2hr 30min).

12

The Massif Central

CHAPTER 12 | # Highlights

* **Cheese** The pasture lands of France's central region produce some of its best cheeses: Roquefort, Laguiole and St Nectaire. **See p.815**

* **Puy de Dôme** Four hundred metres above Clermont-Ferrand, this long-extinct volcano offers staggering vistas of the Massif Central. **See p.820**

* **Conques** Modern pilgrims trek to this monastery town, once an important way-station on the medieval Chemin de St-Jacques, for the church's Romanesque facade and treasury of early medieval reliquaries. **See p.839**

* **Canoeing** The river gorges of the Tarn, Lot and Ardèche provide near limitless opportunities for kayaking and canoeing. **See pp.846 & 854**

* **Cirque de Navacelles** Cutting 150m down into the limestone *causse*, the River Vis doubles back on itself, leaving a tiny island that was capped centuries ago by a farming hamlet. **See p.847**

* **Gorges de l'Ardèche** From the natural bridge at Pont d'Arc, the rushing Ardèche has carved out a dramatic descent through wooded and cave-riddled cliffs. **See p.854**

▲ Le Puy de Dôme

12

The Massif Central

One of the loveliest spots on earth ... a country without roads, without guides, without any facilities for locomotion, where every discovery must be conquered at the price of danger or fatigue ... a soil cut up with deep ravines, crossed in every way by lofty walls of lava, and furrowed by numerous torrents.

hus one of George Sand's characters described the Haute-Loire, the central *département* of **the Massif Central**, and it's a description that could still be applied to some of the region. Thickly forested and sliced by numerous rivers and lakes, these once volcanic uplands are geologically the oldest part of France and culturally one of the most firmly rooted in the past. Industry and tourism have made few inroads here, and the people remain rural and somewhat taciturn, with an enduring sense of regional identity.

The Massif Central takes up a huge portion of the centre of France, but only a handful of towns have gained a foothold in its rugged terrain: **Le Puy**, spiked with theatrical pinnacles of lava, is the most compelling, with its steep streets and majestic cathedral; the spa town of **Vichy** has an antiquated elegance and charm; even heavily industrial **Clermont-Ferrand**, the capital, has a certain cachet in the black volcanic stone of its historic centre and its stunning physical setting beneath the **Puy de Dôme**, a 1464-metre-high volcanic plug. There is pleasure, too, in the unpretentious provinciality of **Aurillac** and in the untouched medieval architecture of smaller places like **Murat, Besse, Salers, Orcival, Sauveterre-de-Rouergue**, and **La Couvertoirade**, and in the hugely influential abbey of **Conques**. But, above all, this is a country where the sights are landscapes rather than towns, churches and museums.

The heart of the region is the **Auvergne**, a wild and unexpected scene of extinct volcanoes (*puys*), stretching from the grassy domes and craters of the **Monts-Dômes** to the eroded skylines of the **Monts-Dore**, and deeply ravined **Cantal mountains** to the rash of darkly wooded pimples surrounding Le Puy. It's one of the poorest regions in France and has long remained outside the main national lines of communication: much of it is above 1000m in height and snowbound in winter. However, the new Clermont–Montpellier *autoroute* now provides a convenient means of travel from the capital to the gorges of the Tarn and Ardèche. There's little arable land in the region, just thousands of acres of upland pasture, traditionally grazed by sheep brought up from the southern lowlands for the summer. Nowadays, cows far outnumber the sheep, some raised for beef and some still for the production of Auvergne's four great cheeses (see box, p.815). The **population** has emigrated for generations, especially to Paris, where the café and restaurant trade has long been in the hands of Auvergnats. The same flight of population has affected the equally infertile but beautiful and

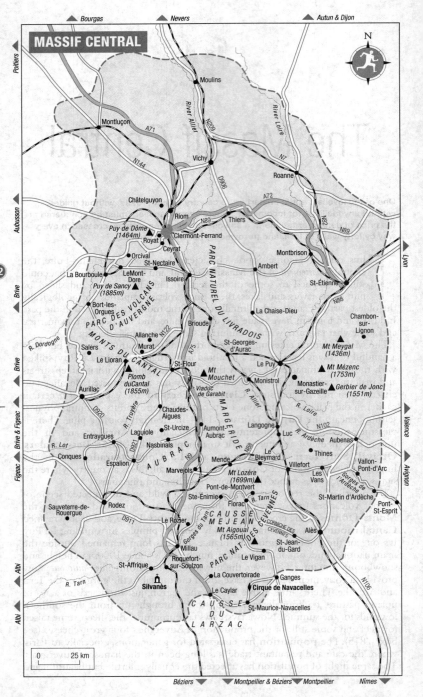

N

Poitiers

Moulins

Montluçon

A71

River Allier

N209

River Loire

Vichy

N144

D906

N7

Roanne

A72

Aubusson

Châtelguyon

Riom

N89

Thiers

N82

N89

Puy de Dôme (1464m)
Royat

Clermont-Ferrand

Ceyrat

Montbrison

Lyon

Orcival

St-Nectaire

La Bourboule

LeMont-Dore

Puy de Sancy (1885m)

Issoire

Ambert

St-Étienne

PARC NATUREL DU LIVRADOIS

Brive

Bort-les-Orgues

PARC DES VOLCANS D'AUVERGNE

N88

La Chaise-Dieu

Chambon-sur-Lignon

R. Dordogne

MONTS DU CANTAL

Allanche

N122

Brioude

St-Georges-d'Aurac

Mt Meygal (1436m)

Brive

Salers

Murat

Le Lioran

St-Flour

Le Puy

Mt Mézenc (1753m)

Monastier-sur-Gazeille

Gerbier de Jonc (1551m)

Aurillac

Plomb duCantal (1855m)

Mt Mouchet

Monistrol

A75

Viaduc de Garabit

MARGERIDE

R. Allier

R. Loire

D920

Chaudes-Aigues

R. Truyère

Laguiole

St-Urcize

Aumont-Aubrac

Langogne

Luc

N102

R. Ardèche

Aubenas

Valence

D921

Entraygues

Nasbinals

N9

Mende

Le Bleymard

Villefort

Thines

Vallon-Pont-d'Arc

Avignon

Figeac

Brive & Figeac

R. Lot

Conques

Espalion

AUBRAC

Marvejols

Mt Lozère (1699m)

Les Vans

Gorges de l'Ardèche

St-Martin d'Ardèche

Pont-St-Esprit

Sauveterre-de-Rouergue

Rodez

D911

Pont-de-Montvert

Ste-Énimie

Florac

R. Tarn

CAUSSE MEJEAN

Gorges du Tarn

CORNICHE DES CÉVENNES

Alès

Le Rozier

PARC NAT DES CÉVENNES

Mt Aigoual (1565m)

St-Jean-du-Gard

Albi

Millau

Roquefort-sur-Soulzon

Le Vigan

St-Affrique

Silvanès

La Couvertoirade

Ganges

Cirque de Navacelles

N106

Albi

R. Tarn

Le Caylar

St-Maurice-Navacelles

CAUSSE DU LARZAC

0   25 km

12

THE MASSIF CENTRAL

Don't expect anything very refined from the cuisine of the Auvergne and Massif Central: it's solid peasant fare as befits a poor and rugged region. The best-known dish is **potée auvergnate**, basically a kind of cabbage soup, easy to make and very nourishing. The ingredients – potatoes, pork or bacon, cabbage, beans, turnips – though added at different intervals, are all boiled up together. Another popular cabbage dish is **chou farci**, cabbage stuffed with pork and beef and cooked with bacon.

Two potato dishes are very common – **la truffade** and **l'aligot**. For *truffade*, the potatoes are sliced and fried in lard, then fresh Cantal cheese is added; for an *aligot*, the potatoes are puréed and mixed with cheese. Less palatable for the squeamish is **tripoux**, usually a stuffing of either sheep's feet or calf's innards, cooked in a casing of stomach lining. **Fricandeau**, a kind of pork pâté, is also wrapped in sheep's stomach.

By way of dessert, **clafoutis** is a popular fruit tart in which the fruit is baked with a batter of flour and egg simply poured over it. The classic fruit ingredient is black cherries, though pears, blackcurrants or apples can also be used.

The Auvergne and the Ardèche in the east produce some wines, though these are not of any great renown. **Cheese**, however, is a different story. In addition to the four great cow's milk cheeses – St-Nectaire (see p.827), Laguiole, Cantal, Fourme d'Ambert and Bleu d'Auvergne – this region also produces the prince of all cheeses, **Roquefort**, made from sheep's milk at the edge of the Causse du Larzac (see p.847).

more Mediterranean southern part of the region: the hills and valleys of the **Cévennes**, where Robert Louis Stevenson and his donkey made one of the more famous literary hikes in 1878.

Many of France's greatest rivers rise in the Massif Central: the **Dordogne** in the Monts-Dore, the **Loire** on the slopes of the Gerbier de Jonc in the east, and in the Cévennes the **Lot** and the **Tarn**. It is these last two rivers which create the distinctive character of the southern parts of the Massif Central, dividing and defining the special landscapes of the *causses*, or limestone plateaux, with their stupendous gorges. This is territory tailor-made for walkers and lovers of the **outdoors**, and everywhere you go tourist offices will supply ideas and routes for walks and bike rides.

The Parc des Volcans d'Auvergne

The **Parc Naturel Régional des Volcans d'Auvergne** encompasses the whole of the western edge of the Massif Central, from **Vichy** in the north to **Aurillac** in the south. It consists of three groups of extinct volcanoes – the **Monts-Dômes**, the **Monts-Dore** and the **Monts du Cantal** – linked by the high plateaux of Artense and the Cézallier. It's big, wide-open country, sparsely populated and with largely treeless pasture grazed by the cows whose milk produces Cantal and St-Nectaire cheese.

The park organization, whose headquarters are at the **Maison du Parc**, Château de Montlosier, 20km southwest of Clermont-Ferrand just off the Mont-Dore road (Feb–April & Nov–Dec Fri–Mon 9am–12.30pm & 1.30–5/6pm; May, June, Sept & Oct Mon–Sat 9am–12.30pm & 1–6pm; July & Aug daily 8am–12.30pm & 1.30–7pm; ☎04.73.65.64.00, ⓦwww.parc-volcans-auvergne.com), oversees various subsidiary *maisons du parc*, each a kind of museum devoted to different themes or activities: fauna and flora, shepherd life, peat bogs and so on.

The best way to understand the park, its landscapes and activities is to walk or bike around it. Four **GR footpaths** cross or make circuits within the park. The **GR40** runs from north to south. The **GR441** makes a circuit round the Monts-Dômes, called the **Tour de la Chaîne des Puys**. The **GR400** encircles the Cantal mountains, and the **GR30** the lakes of the Artense plateau and Cézallier, under the title **Tour des Lacs d'Auvergne**. There are also lots of shorter walks; ask at local tourist offices for more information, and for details of mountain bike rental.

If only because of the practicalities of transport, you will likely pass through **Clermont-Ferrand**, the capital of the *départment*. Given its rather dramatic historical associations – it was the site of Pope Urban II's speech which launched the Crusades in 1095 – the city may disappoint, but nonetheless the town is worth an afternoon's rambling. Otherwise, the towns in the area are few and of secondary interest, although **Orcival**, **Murat** and **Salers** are unexpectedly attractive; **St-Nectaire** contains an exceptionally beautiful small church in the distinct Auvergne version of Romanesque; and **St-Flour** and **Aurillac** have an agreeable provincial insularity.

Clermont-Ferrand and around

CLERMONT-FERRAND lies at the northern tip of the Massif Central. Although its situation is magnificent, almost encircled by the wooded and grassy volcanoes of the **Monts-Dômes**, it has for over a century been a typical smoke-stack industrial centre, the home base of Michelin tyres, which makes it a rather incongruous capital for the rustic and isolated province of the Auvergne.

Its roots, both as a spa and a communications and trading centre, go back to Roman times. It was just outside the town, on the plateau of Gergovia to the south, that the Gauls under the leadership of **Vercingétorix** won their only victory against Julius Caesar's invading Romans. In the Middle Ages, the rival towns of Clermont and Montferrand were ruled respectively by a bishop and the count of Auvergne. Louis XIII united them in 1630, but it was not until the rapid industrial expansion of the late nineteenth century that the two really became indistinguishable.

Michelin came into being thanks to the inventions of Charles Mackintosh, the Scotsman of raincoat fame. His niece married Edouard Daubrée, a Clermont sugar manufacturer, and brought with her some ideas about making rubber goods that she had learnt from her uncle. In 1889, the company became Michelin and Co, just in time to catch the development of the automobile and the World War I aircraft industry. The family ruled the town and employed 30,000 of its citizens until the early 1980s, when the industry went into decline. In the years since, the workforce has been halved, causing rippling unemployment throughout Clermont's economy.

As in many other traditional industrial towns hit by recession and changing global patterns of trade, Clermont has had to struggle to reorientate itself, turning to service industries and the creation of a university of 34,000 students. Nonetheless, many people have moved elsewhere in search of work, reducing

CLERMONT-FERRAND

Musée Roger I.-Quillot & ▲

Airport, Gare SNCF, ③ & ▲

ACCOMMODATION

Albert Elisabeth	C
Des Deux Avenues	A
Foch	E
Inter-hôtel des Puys	B
Ravel	D
Regina	F

EATING & DRINKING

L'Alambic	1
Chez Flo	8
Hôtel des Commerçants	3
Emmaneul Hodencq	5
Garden Ice Café	11
Gérard Anglard	10
Les Goûters de Justine	4
Le Magma Café	9
Mai Lan	6
Pescajoux	2
Petit Bonneval	12
Le 1513	7

the population by nearly a tenth. The town has changed physically, too, as many of the old factories have been demolished. Despite all of this, the old centre has a surprisingly hip and youthful feel, with pavement bars packed out in the evenings as the boutiques and galleries which have sprung up wind down for the day.

Arrival and information

The **gare SNCF** is on avenue de l'Union Soviétique, from where it is a ten-minute bus journey to place de Jaude, at the western edge of the cathedral hill. The **gare routière** (℡04.73.35.05.62) is on boulevard François-Mitterrand, with a city transport information kiosk called Boutique T2C at 24 boulevard Charles-de-Gaulle (℡04.73.28.70.00). The city **airport** (℡04.73.62.71.00, ⓦwww.clermont-fd.cci.fr) is at Aulnat, 7km east; mainly internal flights, but in summer flights to London as well. A *navette* (€4 one way) connects the airport with the train and bus stations.

The main **tourist office** is opposite the cathedral in place de la Victoire (May–Sept Mon–Fri 9am–7pm, Sat & Sun 10am–7pm; Oct–April Mon–Fri 9am–6pm, Sat 10am–1pm & 2–6pm, Sun 9.30am–12.30pm & 2–6pm; ℡04.73.98.65.00,

@www.ot-clermont-ferrand.fr), and there's another conveniently placed annexe immediately to the left outside the train station exit (June–Sept Mon–Sat 9.15–11.30am & 12.15–5pm; Oct–May closed Sat; ℡04.73.91.87.89). At the main office you can pick up a *Passe Découverte* (€8) which will admit you once to each of the town's museums. The **departmental office** is on place de la Bourse (℡04.73.42.22.50, @planetepuydedome.com), and the **regional office** at 44 avenue des États-Unis (℡04.73.29.49.49, @www.auvergne-tourisme.info). Specific hiking or mountain-bike information is available from Chamina, 5 rue Pierre-le-Vénérable (℡04.73.92.81.44). Bikes are available from the SNCF, at the main station and at a central office at 20 place Remoux (℡04.73.14.12.36). For **Internet** access *CyberStrike* at 31 avenue de Grande-Bretagne (Mon–Sat 10am–2am, Sun noon–2am; ℡04.73.92.96.78) has the best hours.

Accommodation

Most of Clermont's **hotels** are concentrated just off the lively place de Jaude, close to the town's main shops, and around the rather characterless station area. There's not a tremendous choice, but they are generally good value. Campers will find municipal **campsites** at Royat (*L'Indigo Royat*), 4km to the southwest (℡04.73.35.97.05; closed mid-Sept to early April; bus #41); Ceyrat (*Le Chanset*), 5km to the south (℡04.73.61.30.73; bus #4C & #41, stop "Preguille"); and Cournon (*Le Pré des Laveuses*), 10km to the east, on the River Allier (April–Oct; ℡04.73.84.81.30; bus #3, stop "Plaine de jeux").

Albert Elisabeth 37 av Albert-Elisabeth ℡04.73.92.47.41, @www.hotel-albertelisabeth .com. Well-run family hotel, with pastel-decorated rooms; handy for the train station. ❷
Des Deux Avenues 4 av de la République ℡04.73.92.37.52, @www.hotel-2avenues.fr. This funky hotel near place Delille is the best option in town and offers clean airy rooms at budget rates; about 5min walk from the station. Family rooms also available. ❶
Foch 22 rue Maréchal-Foch ℡04.73.93.48.40, @www.hotel-foch-clermont.com. Tucked away down a side street off place de Jaude, this is a good-value budget hotel, with bright, summery rooms. ❷
Inter-hôtel des Puys 16 place Delille ℡04.73.91.92.06, @www.hoteldespuys.com.

A modern, top-of-the-range hotel, offering spacious rooms, some with balconies. Its first-rate gourmet restaurant has splendid views of the town and Le Puy de Dôme (menus €14.50–44). ❹
Ravel 8 rue de Maringues ℡04.73.91.51.33, @hotelravel63@orange.fr. Opposite the old Marché St-Joseph, this friendly hotel offers attractive rooms, with sunny Mediterranean decor and good value for money. The proximity to the train and bus stations makes it convenient for travellers passing through. Closed Jan. ❷
Regina 14 rue Bonnabaud ℡04.73.93.44.76, @www.hotel-foch-clermont.com. A little grubby outside, but inside an elegant spiral staircase leads up to fresh, clean rooms. ❷

The City

The most dramatic and flattering approach to Clermont is from the Aubusson road or along the scenic rail line from Le Mont-Dore, both of which cross the chain of the Monts-Dômes just north of the Puy de Dôme. This way you descend through the leafy western suburbs with marvellous views over the town, dominated by the black towers of the cathedral sitting atop the volcanic stump that forms the hub of the old town.

The Cathédrale Notre-Dame and around

Clermont's reputation as a *ville noire* becomes immediately understandable when you enter the appealing medieval quarter, clustered in a characteristic muddle around the cathedral. The colour is due not to industrial pollution but to the black volcanic rock used in the construction of many of its buildings. The

Cathédrale Notre-Dame stands at the centre and highest point of the old town, with its dark and sombre walls, build from local lava. Begun in the mid-thirteenth century, it was not finished until the nineteenth, under the direction of Viollet-le-Duc, who was the architect of the west front and those typically Gothic crocketed spires, whose too methodically cut stonework at close range betrays the work of the machine rather than the mason's hand. The interior is swaddled in gloom, illuminated all the more startlingly by the brilliant colours of the rose windows in the transept and the stained-glass windows in the choir, most dating back to the fourteenth century. Remnants of medieval frescoes survive, too: a particularly beautiful Virgin and Child adorns the right wall of the Chapelle Ste-Madeleine and an animated battle scene between the crusaders and Saracens unfolds on the central wall of the Chapelle St-Georges.

On a fine day it's worth climbing the **Tour de la Bayette** (Mon–Fri 10am–5.15pm, Sun 3–6pm; €1.50) by the north transept door: you look back over the rue des Gras to the Puy de Dôme looming dramatically over the city, with white morning mist retreating down its sides like seaweed from a rock.

Northeast of the cathedral, down the elegant old rue du Port, stands Clermont's other great church, the Romanesque **Basilique Notre-Dame-du-Port** – a century older than the cathedral and in almost total contrast both in style and substance, built from softer stone in pre-lava-working days and consequently corroding badly from exposure to Clermont's polluted air. For all that, it's a beautiful building in pure Auvergnat Romanesque style, featuring a Madonna and Child over the south door in the strangely stylized local form, both figures stiff and upright, the Child more like a dwarf than an infant. It was here in all probability that Pope Urban II preached the First Crusade in 1095 to a vast crowd who received his speech with shouts of *Dios lo volt* (Occitan for "God wills it"), which became the battle-cry of the crusaders.

For general animation, shopping, drinking and eating, the streets between the cathedral and place de Jaude are best, with the main morning market taking place in the conspicuously modern **place St-Pierre** just off rue des Gras. **Place de Jaude** remains another monument to planners' deviation in spite of the shops, the cafés well placed to take in the morning sun and an attempt to make it more attractive with trees and a fountain. Smack in the middle of the traffic, the Romantic equestrian statue of Vercingétorix stands vigil, his sword raised dramatically in salute of the Puy de Dôme.

Outside the city centre

Away from these central streets, there are a few concrete sights to tempt the pedestrian. Among these are **rue Ballainvilliers**, whose eighteenth-century facades recall the sombre elegance of Edinburgh and lead to the **Musée Bargoin** (Tues–Sat 10am–noon 1–5pm, Sun 2–7pm; €4.20), with displays of archeological finds. These include an array of fascinating domestic bits: Roman shoes, baskets, bits of dried fruit, glass and pottery, as well as a remarkable burial find from nearby Martres-de-Veyre dating back to the second century AD. There is also a diverse collection of tapestries and textiles. Though not of great interest, the **Musée Lecoq**, directly behind the Musée Bargoin (Tues–Sat 10am–noon & 2–5/6pm, Sun 2–6pm; €4.20), is devoted mainly to natural history – and named after the gentleman who also founded the public garden full of beautiful trees and formal beds just across the street.

Clermont-Ferrand's most impressive museum, the **Musée d'Art Roger-Quillot** (Tues–Sun 10am–6pm; €4.20), is situated on place Louis-Deteix in **Monteferrand**, some 2.5km northeast of the centre (bus #1, #9 or #16 from place de Jaude). Housed in a daringly renovated eighteenth-century Ursuline convent, this museum holds a broad collection of over two thousand works of art from the medieval to the contemporary. Notable pieces include a collection of carved capitals and a stunning enamelled reliquary of Thomas Becket. Montferrand is today little more than a suburb of larger Clermont, standing out on a limb to the north – if you journey out for the museum you should take time to stroll around. Built on the *bastide* plan, its principal streets, rue de la Rodade and rue Jules-Guesde (the latter named after the founder of the French Communist Party, as Montferrand was home to many of the Michelin factory workers), are still lined with the fine town houses of its medieval merchants and magistrates.

Eating and drinking

For a daytime drink, *Garden Ice Café*, on the corner of place de Jaude, is one of the most popular places to hang out. More unusual is *Les Goûters de Justine,* a *salon de thé*, tucked away in old rue Pascal and furnished with antique chairs, old sofas and oriental carpets. At night one of the most fashionable places is *Le Magma Café* on place de la Victoire.

Restaurants

Le 1513 3 rue des Chaussetiers. Sited opposite the cathedral, this is the best of the cheaper places and very popular. The restaurant occupies a superb Renaissance mansion built in 1513. Lunchtime menu €9.50.

Hôtel des Commerçants Opposite the station. Inexpensive and very friendly, with a terrace at the back (closed Sun; menus from €14).

L'Alambic 6 rue Ste-Claire ☎04.73.36.17.45. A good-value *terroir* restaurant with an upper-end feel, excellent food and service with mid-range prices. Menus from €26. Closed Mon & Wed lunch & Sun.

Emmaneul Hodencq 6 place St-Pierre ☎04.73.31.23.23. The city's finest *gastronomique* has a pleasantly airy dining room and a *carte* ranging lobster through truffle ravioli (expect to spend €70+). Closed Sun & Mon lunch.

Chez Flo 18 rue des Cheval Blanc. A basic brasserie with excellent value local cuisine. Menus from €13.50. Closed Sat evening.

Gérard Anglard 17 rue Lamartine, off place de Jaude ☎04.73.93.52.25. Provides a specialized gastronomic experience, with refined and inventive cooking. The lunchtime menu starts at €29. Closed Sun & first two weeks Aug.

Mai Lan 41 bd Trudaine. Serves first-class Vietnamese cooking for around €18 (€9 at lunch). Closed Mon lunch & Sun.

Pescajoux 13 rue du Port. A good place for a quick snack with a lunch crêpe-menu starting from €11 (closed Sat noon, Sun & Mon)

Petit Bonneval 5km southeast off the N9 Issoire road at Pérignat-lès-Sarliève ☎04.73.79.11.11. A delicious stop for dinner on a summer evening; menus from €26. Also a hotel (❸). Closed Sun evening.

The Puy de Dôme

Visiting Clermont without going to the top of the **Puy de Dôme** (1464m) would be like visiting Athens without seeing the Acropolis. And if you choose your moment – early in the morning or late in the evening – you can easily avoid the worst of the crowds.

Clearly signposted from place de Jaude, it's about 15km from the city centre by the D941. The last 6.5km is a private road (March, April, Oct & Nov 8am–sunset; May–Sept 7am–sunset); there is also a shuttle bus (10am–6pm: May–June & Sept Sat & Sun; July–Aug daily; €4.20) serving the route when the road is closed to vehicles. If you're driving, make sure to pump your brakes on the descent; otherwise you may find yourself waiting for a long time before driving off, while your brakes cool down. Alternatively, you can leave the car at the **Col de Ceyssat** and climb the Puy on foot in about an hour. The route is reserved for cyclists in summer (May–Sept Wed & Sun 7–9am).

The result of a volcanic explosion about 10,000 years ago, the Puy is an abrupt 400m from base to summit. Although the weather station buildings and enormous television mast are pretty ugly close up, the staggering views and sense of airy elevation more than compensate. Even if Mont Blanc itself is not always visible way to the east – it can be if conditions are favourable – you can see huge distances, all down the Massif Central to the Cantal mountains. Above all, you get a bird's-eye view of the other volcanic summits to the north and south, largely forested since the nineteenth century and including the perfect one hundred-metre-deep grassy crater of the **Puy de Pariou**.

Immediately below the summit are the scant remains of a substantial **Roman temple** dedicated to Mercury (free entry), some of the finds from which are displayed in the Musée Bargoin in Clermont-Ferrand. Beside it is a memorial commemorating the exploits of Eugène Renaux, who landed a plane here in 1911 in response to the offer of a 100,000-franc prize by the Michelin brothers. Today's aviators are hang-gliders and paragliding enthusiasts, taking advantage of the updrafts and the stunning scenery.

Riom

Just 15km north of Clermont-Ferrand, **RIOM** is sedate and provincial. One-time capital of the entire Auvergne, its Renaissance architecture, fashioned out of the local black volcanic stone, now secures the town's status as a highlight of the northern Massif. In 1942, just before the first trains of Jewish deportees were shipped to Nazi Germany, Léon Blum, Jewish prime minister and architect of the Socialist Popular Front government, was put on trial in Riom by Marshal Pétain, France's collaborationist ruler, in an attempt to blame the country's defeat in 1940 on the Left. Defending himself, Blum turned the trial into an indictment of collaboration and Nazism. Under pressure from Hitler, Pétain called it off, but nonetheless deported Blum to Germany, an experience which he survived, to give evidence against Pétain after the war.

You may only want to spend a morning here, but Riom does provide a worth-while stopover for lunch if you're on the way up to Vichy. It's an aloof, old-world kind of place, still Auvergne's judicial capital, with a nineteenth-century **Palais de Justice** that stands on the site of a grand palace built when the dukes of Berry controlled this region in the fourteenth century. Only the Gothic **Ste-Chapelle** survives of the original palace, with fine stained-glass windows taking up almost the entirety of three of the walls (July & Aug Mon–Fri 11.30am–4.30pm; €0.50; Sept–June guided tours Tues & some Weds 4.30pm; €2.60).

The best way to admire the town's impressive ensemble of basalt-stone houses, with their red-tiled roofs, is to climb up to the viewing platform of the sixteenth-century **clock tower**, at 5 rue de l'Horloge, off the main street, rue du Commerce (May, June & Sept Mon & Sun 2–6pm, Tues–Sat 10am–noon & 2–6pm; July & Aug daily 10am–noon & 2–6pm; €0.50). There's an interesting museum on the region's folk traditions at 10bis rue Delille, the **Musée Régional d'Auvergne** (daily except Mon: April–June & Sept 10am–noon & 2–5.30pm; July & Aug 10am–6pm; €3, or €6 joint ticket with the Musée Mandet; free on Wed), with the **Musée Mandet**'s displays of Roman finds and bland paintings not far away at 4 rue de l'Hôtel-de-Ville (same hours; €3, free on Wed). At 44 rue du Commerce, the **church of Notre-Dame-du-Marthuret** holds Riom's most valued treasures, two statues of the Virgin and Child – one a Black Madonna, the other, the so-called *Vierge à l'Oiseau*, a touchingly realistic piece of carving that portrays the young Christ with a bird fluttering in his hands. A copy stands in the entrance hall of the church (its original site), where you can see it with the advantage of daylight.

Practicalities

Riom's **tourist office** is at 27 place de la Federation (July & Aug Mon–Sat 9.30am–1pm & 2–6.30pm, Sun 10am–1pm; Sept–June Mon–Sat 9.30am–12.30pm & 2–6pm; ☎04.73.38.59.45, Ⓦwww.tourisme-riomlimagne.fr). There's little **hotel** selection in town, but the best is *Le Pacifique* (☎04.73.38.15.65, Ⓦwww.hotel-lepacifique-riom.com; ❸), a box-like modern, structure on the edge of town. *Le Magnolia*, at 11 avenue du Commandant Madeline, is one of Riom's finest **restaurants** for local cuisine (open Tues–Fri, Sat evening. Sun lunch; menus €18–42). Alternatively follow the locals to *Ane Gris* at 13 rue Gomot (Tues evening to Sat), which has *terroir* menus from €12.50. For internet access go to *Clic et tel* at 19 rue Hyppolite Gomot (Mon–Sat 9am–9pm & Sun 2–9pm) or use the wi-fi at *Le Pacifique*.

Vichy

VICHY is famous for two things: its World War II puppet government under Marshal Pétain, and its curative sulphurous springs, which attract thousands of ageing and ailing visitors, or *curistes*, every year. There's no mention of Pétain's government in town, but the fact that Vichy is one of France's foremost spa resorts colours everything you see here. The town is almost entirely devoted to catering for its largely elderly, genteel and rich population, which swells several-fold in summer; they come here to drink the water, wallow in it, inhale its steam or be sprayed with it. An attempt is now being made to rejuvenate the image of Vichy by appealing to a younger, more fitness-conscious generation.

The Town

All of this makes Vichy seem unappealing, and yet it has a certain element of charm. There's a real *fin-de-siècle* atmosphere about the place and a curious fascination in its continuing function. The town revolves around the **Parc des Sources**, a stately tree-shaded park that takes up most of the centre. At its north end stands the **Hall des Sources**, an enormous iron-framed greenhouse in which people sit and chat or read newspapers, while from a large tiled stand in the middle the various waters emerge from their spouts, beside the just-visible remains of the Roman establishment. The *curistes* line up to get their prescribed cupful, and for a small fee you can join them. The Célestins is the only one of

---

Volvic to Laschamp walk

For a good day's walk and a thorough exploration of the *puys*, take the train from Clermont to Volvic-Gare. Follow the D90 road beside the train line for about 1km until you join up with the **GR441** path, where the road turns right under the track. Keep along your side of the train track for a few minutes longer and follow the GR441 round to the left, almost doubling back southwest along the line of the wooded Puys Nugères, Jumes and Coquille to the northern foot of the Puy de Chopine (2–3hr). Here you join up with the **GR4** and follow the combined GR4–441 across the Orcines–Pontgibaud road to the summit of the Puy de Dôme (about 2hr 30min from the road). From the Puy, descend to the Col de Ceyssat in half an hour (good chance of a lift back to Clermont), or continue to **Laschamp** (50min), where there is a **gîte d'étape** (7–8hr, 6hr for a very fit walker).

You should not set off without either the relevant section of the GR4 Topo-guide or, preferably, the IGN 1:25,000 map, the *Chaîne des Puys*, which also marks the GR441 from Volvic-Gare. If you don't feel up to a walk, you should investigate the beautiful train ride from Clermont to the town of Le Mont-Dore, which follows the chain of the *puys*.

the springs that is bottled and widely drunk: if you're into a taste experience, try the remaining five. They are progressively more sulphurous and foul, with the Source de l'Hôpital, which has its own circular building at the far end of the park, an almost unbelievably nasty creation. Each of the springs is prescribed for a different ailment and the tradition is that, apart from the Célestins, they must all be drunk on the spot to be efficacious – a dubious but effective way of drawing in the crowds.

Although all the springs technically belong to the nation and treatment is partially funded by the state, they are in fact run privately for profit by the Compagnie Fermière, first created in the mid-nineteenth century to prepare for a visit by the Emperor Napoléon III, whose interest in the waters brought Vichy to public notice. The Compagnie not only has a monopoly on selling the waters but also runs the casino and numerous hotels – it even owns the chairs conveniently dotted around the Parc des Sources.

Directly behind the Hall des Sources, on the leafy **Esplanade Napoléon III**, is the enormous, Byzantine-style **Grand Établissement Thermal**, the former thermal baths, decorated with Moorish arches, gold-and-blue domes and blue ceramic panels of voluptuous mermaids. All that remains inside of the original baths is the grand entrance hall, with its fountain and two beautiful murals, *La Bain* and *La Source*, painted by Osberd in 1903. The arcades leading off either side of the hall, once the site of gyms and treatment rooms, now house expensive boutiques.

To provide distraction for the *curistes*, a grand **casino** and **opera house** were built at the southern end of the Parc des Sources. From May to September the opera house is the venue for regular concerts and opera productions, while lighter music oompahs out from the open-air bandstand in the park behind it.

After the waters, Vichy's curiosities are limited. There's a pleasant, wooded riverside in the **Parc de l'Allier**, also created for Napoléon III. And, not far from here, the old town boasts the strange **church of St-Blaise**, actually two churches in one, with a 1930s Baroque structure built onto the original Romanesque one – an effect that sounds hideous but is rather imaginative. Inside, another Auvergne Black Virgin, Notre-Dame-des-Malades, stands surrounded by plaques offered by the grateful healed who stacked their odds with both her and the sulphur.

Practicalities

Vichy's **gare SNCF** is about a ten-minute walk from the centre, on the eastern edge of the city centre at the end of rue de Paris. The **gare routière** sits on the corner of rue Doumier and rue Jardet, by the central place Charles-de-Gaulle, and there's a public transport information line on ☎04.70.30.17.30. The building that used to house the wartime Vichy government at 19 rue du Parc is now home to the **tourist office** (April–June & Sept Mon–Sat 9am–12.30pm & 1.30–7pm, Sun 9.30am–12.30pm & 3–7pm; July & Aug 9am–7pm, Sun 9.30am–12.30pm & 3–7pm; Oct–March Mon–Fri 9am–noon & 1.30–6pm, Sat 9am–noon & 2–6pm, Sun 2.30–5.30pm; ☎04.70.98.71.94, ⓦwww.vichy -tourisme.com). Internet access is available at *Echap Internet Café* (12 rue Source de l'Hôpital, Tues–Sat noon–midnight, Sun 2pm–midnight).

There is an abundance of hotels and finding a place to stay is not difficult. You'll find several around the station, but the most pleasant is the friendly, grand neo-Baroque *Midland*, 4 rue de l'Intendance, in a quiet street off rue de Paris (☎04.70.97.48.48, ⓦwww.hotel-midland.com; ❹; closed mid-Oct to mid-April; good restaurant with menus from €25). An excellent budget option is the clean but simple *Hôtel Cognac* (☎04.70.32.15.58; ❶). There's a municipal

campsite, *La Gravière*, at the Centre Omnisports (℡04.70.59.21.00; closed Oct to late May).

For **eating**, apart from the hotel-restaurants listed above, the simplest solution is to head for the area around the junction of rue Clemenceau and rue de Paris, where there are several brasseries and cafés. To do so, however, would be to miss out on the best that Vichy has to offer – a surprising range of top-notch restaurants. Two of the best include the frenetically eclectic *Jacques Decoret* on 7 avenue de Gramont (℡04.70.97.65.06; closed Tues & Wed & Aug), which has menus drawing on flavours from places as jarringly diverse as Oaxaca and Marseille at €40–160, and the more affordable and less daring *La Table d'Antoine* at 8 rue Burnol (℡04.70.98.99.71; closed Sun lunch & Mon; from €21).

The Monts-Dore

The **Monts-Dore** lie about 50km southwest of Clermont. Also volcanic in origin – the main period of activity was around five million years ago – they are much more rugged and more obviously mountainous than their gentler, younger neighbours, the Monts-Dômes. Their centre is the precipitous, plunging valley of the River Dordogne, which rises on the slopes of the **Puy de Sancy**, at 1885m the highest point in the Massif Central, just above the little town of **Le Mont-Dore**.

In spite of their relative ruggedness, there are few crags or rock faces and their upper slopes, albeit steep, are grassy and treeless for miles and miles. They are known as *montagnes à vaches* – mountains for cows – as they traditionally provided summer pasture land for herds of cows, raised above all for their milk and the production of **St-Nectaire** cheese. The herdsmen who milked them and made the cheese set up their primitive summer homes in the dozens of (now mainly ruined) stone huts, or *burons*, that scatter the landscape.

Le Mont-Dore and the Puy de Sancy

Squeezed out along the narrow wooded valley of the infant Dordogne, grey-slated **LE MONT-DORE**, 50km southwest of Clermont, is a long-established spa resort, with Roman remnants testifying to just how old it is. Its popularity goes back to the eighteenth century, when metalled roads replaced the old mule paths and made access possible, but reached its apogee with the opening of the rail line around 1900. It is an altogether wholesome and civilized sort of place.

The **Établissement Thermal** – the baths, which give the place its *raison d'être* – are in the middle of town and are certainly worth visiting (30min guided tours Mon–Sat: mid-May to mid-Oct on the hour; €2). Early every morning, the *curistes* stream into its neo-Byzantine halls – an extravaganza of tiles, striped columns and ornate ironwork – hoping for a remedy in this self-proclaimed "world centre for treatment of asthma". For many Parisians, of all ages and walks of life, this is their annual mecca: whiling away their days sniffing sulphur from bunsen burner tubes, and sitting in thick steam.

Walkers also frequent the town, the principal attraction being the **Puy de Sancy** (1885m), whose jagged skyline blocks the head of the Dordogne valley, 3km away (mid-May to Sept; 4 buses per day, 1 on Wed & Sun, from the tourist office; €3.50). Accessible by *téléphérique* (May–Sept; €7.30 return) since the 1930s, it's one of the busiest tourist sites in the country. As a result, the path from the *téléphérique* station to the summit has had to be railed and paved with baulks of timber to prevent total erosion. Combined with the scars of access tracks for the ski installations, this has done little for its beauty.

Practicalities

Without a car, Le Mont-Dore is most easily accessible by train from Clermont. The **train** and **bus stations** are at the entrance to the town. A ten-minute walk down avenue Michelet takes you to the centre, where the **tourist office** sits in the park on avenue de la Libération (April–June daily 9/10am–noon/12.30pm & 1.30/2–5/6pm; July & Aug Mon–Sat 9am–7pm, Sun 9am–noon & 2–6pm; ☎04.73.65.20.21, ⓦwww.sancy.com); the helpful staff will advise about other walking and cycling possibilities (VTT rental), as well as day excursions to otherwise rather inaccessible places in the area. The web page also lists the schedule of the *navettes* which regularly serve the surrounding villages and connect them to Clermont-Ferrand. Internet access can be found at *Sancyber* at 4 rue Georges-Lagaye (daily 10am–midnight).

Accommodation is not hard to come by, as the town is brimming with hotels. Close to the baths, at 8 rue Favart, *Hôtel aux Champs d'Auvergne* (☎04.73.65.00.37, ⓦwww.auxchampsdauvergne.com; ❶; closed Nov to mid-Dec; half-*pensions* available) is very welcoming and serves copious breakfasts, while the stately nineteenth-century *Grand Hôtel*, nearby on rue Rigny (☎04.73.65.02.64, ⓦwww.hotel-mont-dore.com; ❸), is excellent value. One of the best deals, with mod cons at a bargain price, is the *Beau Site* at 17 rue des Déportés (☎04.73.65.05.51, ⓦwww.beau-site.com; ❷; closed Nov–Feb; restaurant from €15), beside the main baths. There's an efficient modern **hostel** on the Puy de Sancy road, with a stunning view of the mountains (☎04.73.65.03.53, ⓔle-mont -dore@fuaj.org; closed mid-Nov to mid-Dec), and a very cheap *gîte*, *Les Hautes Pierres* (☎04.73.65.25.65, ⓦwww.gite-les-hautes-pierres.com; Jan–Oct or by request), on chemin de Vergnes. The municipal **campsite**, *Les Crouzets* (☎04.73.65.21.60, ⓔcamping.crouzets@orange.fr; closed mid-Oct to mid-Dec), is nearby, opposite the station. The other municipal campsite is *L'Esquiladou* (☎04.73.65.23.74, ⓔcamping.esquiladou@orange.fr; closed Nov–April), off to the right on the road to La Bourboule.

As far as **eating** is concerned, there are large numbers of brasseries and cafés in the centre offering *plats* for €8–10. A particularly pleasant place is rustic *Le Bougnat*, 23 avenue Clemenceau, which serves various Auvergnat traditional dishes, as well as *raclette* and fondue (☎04.73.65.28.19; closed Mon; menus from €18). A great place for a **drink** is the atmospheric, 1940s-style *Café de Paris*, located on rue Jean-Moulin.

La Bourboule

LA BOURBOULE is just 7km down the road from Le Mont-Dore. Known as the sister to Le Mont-Dore, it's another traditional spa – the "capital of allergies" – but with a more open feel and, with its lower altitude, temperatures are a degree or two warmer. The big **casino**, the domed **Grands Thermes baths** and several other *belle-époque* buildings which once housed privately run baths are ornate, gilded and wonderfully vulgar, with a faded, permanently off-season look to them, though the town has a certain Parisian flair that sets it apart from the smaller more provincial towns in the region. All in all, it's a cool, tranquil place to unwind: as the tourist office's leaflet says, "You will be able to put your vital node to rest in La Bourboule".

Behind the Hôtel de Ville, the large wooded **Parc Fenestre** has a *télécabine* taking you right up to **Plateau de Charlannes** (1300m), where it's possible to stroll in the woods or ski in winter; the **tourist office** in the Hôtel de Ville on place de la République (May–June & Sept daily 9/10am–noon & 1.30/2–6pm; July & Aug Mon–Sat 9am–7pm & Sun 9am–noon & 2–6pm; Oct Mon–Sat 9am–noon & 1.30–6pm; ☎04.73.65.57.71, ⓦwww.sancy.com) sells a booklet of local walks.

Hotels here are plentiful, three good bargains being the *Aviation Hôtel*, in rue de Metz (☎04.73.81.32.32, ⓦwww.aviation.fr; ❸; closed Oct–Dec 20; restaurant from €8), with indoor pool; the welcoming, Art Deco-style *Le Pavillon*, 209 avenue d'Angleterre (☎04.73.65.50.18, ⓦwww.hotelpavillon. fr; ❸; closed Feb; restaurant from €16); and the more basic *Les Fleurs* on avenue de Mussy (☎04.73.81.09.44, ⓦwww.hotellesfleurs.com; ❷; closed Nov & Dec; vegetarian restaurant €21–25). There's also a good selection of **campsites**, with the *camping municipal* on avenue Maréchal Lattre-de-Tassigny (☎04.73.81.10.20, ⓔville-labourboule@orange.fr), and another at Murat-le-Quaire, 4km away, along the Mont-Dore road (☎04.73.65.54.81, ⓔcampinglescouderts@orange.fr).

Orcival

Twenty-seven kilometres southwest of Clermont and about 20km north of Le Mont-Dore, lush pastures and green hills punctuated by the abrupt eruptions of the *puys* enclose the small village of **ORCIVAL**, the home town of ex-President Valéry Giscard d'Estaing. A pretty, popular, place, founded by the monks of La Chaise-Dieu in the twelfth century, it makes a suitable base for hiking in the region.

Orcival is dominated by the stunning Romanesque **church of Notre-Dame** (daily 8am–noon & 2–7pm), built of the same dark-grey volcanic stone as the cathedral in Clermont and topped with a spire and fanned with tiny chapels. Once a major parish, it counted no fewer than 24 priests in the mid-1200s, and the ironwork on the north door, with its curious forged human head motif, dates from that era. Inside, attention focuses on the choir, neatly and harmoniously contained by the semicircle of pillars defining the ambulatory. Mounted on a stone column in the centre is the celebrated **Virgin of Orcival**, a gilded and enamelled twelfth-century statue in typical Romance style; the object of a popular cult since the Middle Ages and still carried through the streets on Ascension Day.

There's no public transport to Orcival itself; the nearest **bus station** is at Rochefort-Montagne, 6km away, served by buses from Clermont-Ferrand. There

---

Walking and skiing around La Bourboule

Fit and serious walkers may want to conquer the **Puy de Sancy**, a six-hour hike south of La Bourboule on the GR30–41, passing after about two hours the two fine waterfalls of the **Cascade de la Vernière** and **Plat à Barbe** – themselves a satisfying destination. For the summit of Puy de Sancy, see the account of Le Mont-Dore, p.824. An easier walk out of La Bourboule is to the summit of the **Banne d'Ordanche** (1500m): pick up the GR path to the east of the town where it crosses the D130 road and the train line, then take the signposted GR41 where it diverges from the GR30. During winter months, both Le Mont-Dore and La Bourboule double as ski resorts – centres of a **ski-de-fond** (cross-country) network of circular pistes, some over 20km long, and there is limited downhill skiing as well, although at a maximum of 1150m this is not a resort for enthusiasts. Skiable paths also connect La Bourboule to other ski centres in the locality – Sancy, Besse, Chastreix and Picherande.

Walking possibilities from Orcival include trips to **Lac de Servières** and **Lac de Guéry**. The first takes two and a half hours, the second some five hours. For Lac de Servières, follow the **GR141–30** south through the woods above the valley of the Sioule. The lake is a beauty; it's 1200m up, with gently sloping shores surrounded by pasture and conifers. You can either head southeast to the **gîte d'étape** at Pessade (℡04.73.79.31.07), or continue to the larger Lac de Guéry, lent a slightly eerie air by the black basalt boulders strewn across the surrounding meadows, where there's a romantically situated lakeside hotel, the *Lac de Guéry* (℡04.73.65.02.76, Ⓦwww .auberge-lac-guery.fr; ❸; closed mid-Oct to mid-Jan; restaurant from €18).

If you're driving to Le Mont-Dore, only 9km further on from here, just before the Lac de Guéry, the road takes you round the head of the **Fontsalade valley**, where two prominent rocks composed of banks of basalt organ-pipes rise spectacularly from the woods: the **Roche Tuilière** and the **Roche Sanadoire**. A footpath takes you on a two-hour walk round the valley, starting from the roadside belvedere overlooking Sanadoire. A little higher up, on the bare slopes of the **Puy de l'Aiguiller**, a roadside memorial commemorates some English airmen killed in an accident while making a parachute drop to the maquis in March 1944.

A detailed Topo-guide to the region is available from both the Orcival and Bourboule tourist offices (€6).

is, however, a helpful **tourist office** (July & Aug daily 10am–noon & 2–7pm; rest of year holiday periods only Tues–Sat 2–5pm; ℡04.73.65.89.77, Ⓦwww .terresdomes-sancy.com), just below the church. Modest **accommodation** can be found at the *Hôtel des Touristes* (℡04.73.65.82.55, Ⓦwww.hotel-les-toursistes .com; ❶; closed mid-Nov to mid-Feb; restaurant from €12.50) near the church. There's a lakeside **campsite**, *Camping de l'Étang de Fléchat* (℡04.73.65.82.96, Ⓦwww.campingdeflechat.com; closed Nov–May), 2km outside Orcival, but a better bet is the municipal site at St-Bonnet, 5km to the north of the village (℡04.73.65.83.32, Ⓦwww.camping-auvergne.info; closed Oct–April), on a hillside with wonderful views of the surrounding mountains.

St-Nectaire and around

ST-NECTAIRE lies some way to the southeast of Orcival, midway between Le Mont-Dore and Issoire. It comprises the tiny spa of **St-Nectaire-le-Bas**, whose main street is lined with grand but fading *belle-époque* hotels, which was added on to the old village of **St-Nectaire-le-Haut**, overlooked by a magnificent Romanesque **church** (daily April–Oct 9am–7pm & Nov–March 9.30am–12.30pm & 2–6pm). Like the church in Orcival and Notre-Dame-du-Port in Clermont, this is one of the most striking examples of the Auvergne's Romanesque architecture. The carved capitals around the apse retain the tantalizing hues of the paint which once covered the whole interior, while the church's treasures are guarded in the north transept and include a magnificent gilded bust of St Baudime (the third-century missionary of the Auvergne and parish-founder), a polychrome *Virgin in Majesty*, and two enamelled plaques, all dating from the twelfth century. Among the town's other curiosities are a couple of caverns, the spa (a two-hour basic session from €12.90), and the **Maison du St-Nectaire** where you'll find an exhibition on the cheese-making process and a chance to visit a cheese-ripening cellar. The surrounding countryside is notable for its menhirs and other pre historic megaliths; the tourist office has information on how to find them.

The **tourist office** (July & Aug 9.30am–12.15pm & 2–6.45pm; Sept–June Mon–Sat 9.30–11.45am & 2–4.45/5.45pm; ℡04.73.88.50.86, Ⓦwww .ville-saint-nectaire.fr) is located in the "Grandes Thermes" complex on the main road and has information on six different circuit walks of various lengths that take from two to five hours to complete. For a **place to stay**, *Hotel de la Paix*, situated at the base of the GR30 footpath below the church, offers comfortable rooms and a reasonably priced restaurant (℡04.73.88.49.07, Ⓔhotelpaix63710@aol.com; ❷; menus from €15; closed Nov to mid-Dec). Greater comfort can be found at the *Mercure*, near the town centre, a converted spa renovated as a hotel (℡04.73.88.57.00, Ⓦwww.hotel-bains -romains.com; ❺; closed Nov, Dec & part Jan & March), also with a fine restaurant (menu €23). The best-value campsite is the *Clé des Champs* (℡04.73.88.52.33, Ⓦwww.campingcledeschamps.com) located on the D996 on the right when heading in the direction of Champeix. For walkers, the GR30 heads north from here to Lac Aydat in five hours, or west to the forest-girt **Lac Chambon** in three hours via Murol. There's a *gîte* on the way at Phialeix (℡04.73.79.32.43; closed Nov–March).

For shorter walks out of St-Nectaire, take the D150 past the church through the old village towards the **Puy de Mazeyres** (919m), and turn up a path to the right for the final climb to the summit (1hr), where you get a superb aerial view of the surrounding country. Alternatively, follow the D966 along the Couze de Chambon valley to **SAILLANT**, where the stream cascades down a high lava rock face in the middle of the village.

Murol

MUROL, 6km west of St-Nectaire by road (July & Aug twice-daily bus to Clermont) or 5.5km by footpath, is an attractive, sleepy little place best known for its powerful medieval **château**, dramatically situated on top of a basalt cone commanding the approaches for kilometres around (April–June & Sept daily 10am–noon & 1.30–6pm; July & Aug daily 10am–7pm; Oct–March Sat, Sun & holidays 2–5pm; €4). In summer, a local organization re-enacts the medieval life of the castle in costume (€7.50).

There are several small family-run **hotels** here; the *Hôtel de Paris*, on place de l'Hôtel-de-Ville (℡04.73.88.60.09 *50 les pins*, Ⓦwww.hoteldeparis-muriol .com; ❷; May–Sept), is the best value. Of the **campsites**, the best value is the *Ribeyre*, a short distance away at **JASSAT** (℡04.73.88.64.29, Ⓦlaribeyre.free.fr; closed mid-Sept to April).

Besse

Eleven kilometres due south of Murol, **BESSE** is one of the prettiest and oldest villages in the region. Its fascinating winding streets of noble lava-built houses – some fifteenth-century – sit atop the valley of the Couze de Pavin, with one of the original fortified town **gates** still in place at the upper end of the village.

Its wealth was due to its role as the principal market for the farms on the eastern slopes of the Monts-Dore, and its co-operative is still one of the main producers of St-Nectaire cheese (see box opposite). The annual **festivals** of the Montée and Dévalade, marking the ascent of the herds to the high pastures in July and their descent in autumn, are still celebrated by the procession of the Black Virgin of Vassivière from the **church of St-André** in Besse to the chapel of **La Vassivière**, west of **Lac Pavin**, and back again in autumn (July 2 & first Sun after Sept 21).

Lac Pavin lies 5km west of the village, on the way to the purpose-built downhill ski resort of **SUPER-BESSE** (both are connected to Besse by an hourly *navette*). It's a perfect volcanic lake, filling the now wooded crater. The **GR30** goes through, passing by the **Puy de Montchal**, whose summit (1407m) gives you a fine view over several other lakes and the rolling plateau south towards **ÉGLISENEUVE-D'ENTRAIGUES**, 13km by road, where the Parc des Volcans' **Maison du Fromage** gives a detailed account of the making of the different cheeses of Auvergne (daily: mid-May to June & Sept 2–6pm; July & Aug 10am–12.30pm & 2.30–7pm; €3.50).

Besse's **tourist office** is next to the church on place du Dr-Pipet (July & Aug Mon–Sat 9–7pm, Sun 10am–noon & 2–6pm; Sept–June Mon–Sat 10am–noon & 2–6pm, Sun 10am–noon 2–4pm; ☎04.73.79.52.84, ⓦwww.sancy.com), and will provide information and advice about walking, mountain biking and skiing. Good, simple fare can be had next door at the *Le Sancy*, which has a *plat du jour* for €7.50. For a place to **stay**, the old *Hostellerie du Beffroy*, 24 rue Abbé-Blot (☎04.73.79.50.08, ⓦwww.lebeffroy.com; ❸), whose restaurant has an excellent but pricey *carte* (menu €45), is worth a try.

The Monts du Cantal

The **Cantal Massif** forms the most southerly extension of the Parc des Volcans. Still nearly 80km in diameter and once 3000m in height, it is one of the world's largest (albeit extinct) volcanoes, shaped like a wheel without a rim. The hub is formed by the three great conical peaks that survived the erosion of the original single cone: **Plomb du Cantal** (1855m), **Puy Mary** (1787m) and **Puy de Peyre-Arse** (1686m).

From this centre a series of deep-cut wooded valleys radiates out like spokes. The most notable are the **valley of Mandailles** and the **valleys of the Cère and Alagnon** in the southwest, where the road and rail line run, and in the north the **valleys of Falgoux and the Rhue**. Between the valleys, especially on the north side, are huge expanses of gently sloping grassland, including the **Plateau du Limon**, and it's these which for centuries have been the mainstay of life in the Cantal: summer pasture for the cows whose milk makes the firm yellow Cantal cheese, pressed in the form of great crusty drums. But this traditional activity has long been in serious decline; as elsewhere, many of the herds are now beef cattle. And tourism is on the increase, in particular walking, horseriding and skiing.

You can trace the circumference of the Massif by car, following the sinuous and spectacular **Route des Crêtes**. But, be warned, if you hit a period of bad weather, you'll drive a long way seeing no more than white banks of mist illumined by your headlight. The main centres within the massif lie on the N122 between Murat and Aurillac: **LE LIORAN**, where the road and rail tunnels begin, and **SUPER-LIORAN**, the downhill and cross-country ski centre, with many hotels, including the rustic and comfortable *Rocher de Cerf* (T04.71.49.50.14, Wwww.lerocherducerf.com; summer obligatory half-*pension*, for two ❺ otherwise ❷) and several *gîtes d'étape*, as well as a tourist office (April–Aug daily 9.30am–12.30pm & 1.30–5/6pm; except mid-July to mid-Aug 9am–6pm; Sept–Christmas Mon–Sat 9.30am–12.30pm & 1.30–5.30pm; Christmas–March daily 9am–6pm; T04.71.49.50.09, Wwww.lelioran.com). **THIEZAC**, 10km south, also has a tourist office (June & Sept Mon–Fri 3–6pm; July & Aug Mon–Sat 3–6.30pm; T04.71.47.03.50), as well as the *Hôtel Elancèze et la Belle Vallée* (T04.71.47.00.22, Wwww.elanceze.com; ❸; closed Nov–Dec 20; restaurant €15–32), three *gîtes d'étape* and a municipal campsite, *La Bedisse* (T04.71.47.00.41; closed mid-Sept to May). Further south at **VIC-SUR-CÈRE** there's a tourist office (July & Aug daily 9.30am–12.30pm & 2.30–7.30pm; June & Sept daily 9.30–noon & 2–6pm; T04.71.47.50.68), and accommodation at the *Hôtel des Bains*, 9 avenue de la Promenade (T04.71.47.50.16, Wwww.arvernehotel.com; ❷; closed mid-Oct to mid-April; restaurant from €14), and the riverside municipal **campsite** (T04.71.47.54.18, Wwww.camping-la-pommeraie.com; closed mid-Sept to April).

Aurillac

AURILLAC, the provincial capital of the Cantal, lies on the west side of the mountains, 98km east of Brive and 160km from Clermont-Ferrand. In spite of its good main-line train connections and the fact that its population has almost doubled in the last forty years to around 30,000, it remains one of the most out-of-the-way French provincial capitals. It was until recently a major manufacturer of umbrellas, though that seems doomed to eventual extinction, like its older traditional lace-making and tanning industries. It is now mainly an administrative and commercial centre, with important cattle markets in the suburb of Sistrières on Mondays.

The most interesting part of town is the kernel of old streets, now largely pedestrianized and full of good shops, just to the north of the central **place du Square**. **Rue Duclaux** leads through to the attractive **place de l'Hôtel-de-Ville**, where big markets are held (Wed & Sat) in the shadow of the handsome grey-stone **Hôtel de Ville**, built in restrained Republican-classical style in 1803. Beyond it, the continuation of **rue des Forgerons** leads to the beautiful little **place St-Géraud**, with a round twelfth-century fountain overlooked by a Romanesque house that was probably part of the original abbey guesthouse, and the externally rather unprepossessing **church of St-Géraud**, which nonetheless has a beautifully ribbed late Gothic ceiling.

At the back of the church, past a delightful small garden, **rue de la Fontaine** comes out on the riverbank by the Pont du Buis, with a shady walk back along cours d'Angoulême on the other side to the Pont-Rouge and **place Gerbert**, where there is an ancient *lavoir*, or washing place. On a steep bluff overlooking this end of town towers the eleventh-century keep of the Château St-Étienne, containing the town's only worthwhile museum, the **Muséum des Volcans** (Tues–Sat 2–6pm; €4), with a good section on volcanoes and a splendid view over the mountains to the east.

Practicalities

The **gare SNCF** and **gare routière** are together on place Sémard, a ten-minute walk from the central place du Square along avenue de la République and rue de la Gare. The **tourist office** occupies a small kiosk on the downhill side of place du Square (Easter–June & Sept Mon–Sat 9am–noon & 2–6.30pm, Sun 9am–2pm; July & Aug daily 9am–7pm; Oct–Easter Mon–Sat 9am–noon & 2–6.30pm; ☎04.71.48.46.58, ⓦwww.iaurillac.com). There's **internet** access at the Absolut Games cyber café, 1 place du Buis.

For a **place to stay** in the centre of town, try the smart and comfortable *Le Square*, 15 place du Square (☎04.71.48.24.72, ⓦwww.cantal-hotel.com; ❸–❹), with a restaurant whose stuffed cabbage has won several prizes (from €15). Rather more de luxe accommodation and attentive service can be found at the *Grand Hotel de Bordeaux* at 2 avenue République (☎04.71.48.01.84, ⓦwww .hotel-de-bordeaux.fr; ❼), set in a nineteenth-century mansion.

There are a number of **restaurants** where you can sample Auvergnat specialities. Two of the most popular are the atmospheric *Le Terroir du Cantal*, 5 rue du Buis (closed Sun lunch & Mon; from €17), with its rough-stone walls and wooden benches, and *Poivre et Sel*, 4 rue du 14-Juillet (closed Sun & Mon; menus from €15), featuring classic dishes such as *magret de canard*. The pretty, riverside *Birland*, by the Pont-Rouge, done out in the French version of pub style, serves pizzas for around €8.50 and menus for €12–17 (closed Sun); if you're looking for **nightlife**, note that the *Le Bateau Lavoir* disco is part of the same establishment (Thurs–Sun 11pm–4/5am; €10). Finally, Aurillac's most unexpected event is an annual international **street theatre festival** (ⓦwww .aurillac.net), which lasts for one week in August, attracting performers from all over Europe and filling the town with rather more exotic characters than are normally to be seen in these provincial parts.

Salers

SALERS lies 42km north of Aurillac, at the foot of the northwest slopes of the Cantal and within sight of the Puy Violent. Scarcely altered in size or aspect since its sixteenth-century heyday, it remains an extraordinarily homogeneous example of the architecture of that time. If things appear rather grand for a place so small, it's because the town became the administrative centre for the highlands of the Auvergne in 1564 and home of its magistrates. Exploiting this past is really all it has left, but Salers still makes a very worthwhile visit.

If you arrive by the Puy Mary road, you'll enter town by the **church**, which is worth a look for the super-naturalistic statuary of the Entombment of Christ (1496), hidden in a side chapel near the entrance. In front of you, the cobbled **rue du Beffroi** leads uphill, under the massive clock tower, and into the central **place Tyssandier-d'Escous**. It is a glorious little square, surrounded by the fifteenth-century mansions of the provincial aristocracy with pepper-pot turrets, mullioned windows and carved lintels, among them the sturdy **Maison du Bailliage**, and, nearby, the **Maison des Templiers**, housing the small Musée de Salers (April–Sept daily 10.30am–noon & 2–7.30pm; closed Tues except July & Aug; €3). Though the museum itself is rather dull, with exhibitions on the Salers cattle breed, traditional costumes and the local cheese-making industry, it's worth having a look at the vaulted ceiling of the entrance passageway, with its carved lions and heads of saints, such as St John the Baptist, framed by wild flowing hair. Before you're done, be sure to make your way to the **Promenade de Barrouze** for the view out across the surrounding green hills and the Puy Violent.

The **tourist office** is in place Tyssandier-d'Escous (July & Aug 10am–7pm; Sept–June Tues–Sun 10am–noon & 2–6pm; ☎04.71.40.70.33, Ⓦwww.pays-de -salers.com). If you want to **stay**, try the *Hôtel des Remparts*, near the Promenade de Barrouze (☎04.71.40.70.33, Ⓦwww.salers-hotel-remparts.com; ❸; closed mid-Oct to mid-Dec), whose restaurant specializes in Auvergnat cuisine (from €12.50), or the more luxurious *Le Gerfaut* in route du Puy-Mary (☎04.71.40.75.75, Ⓦwww.salers-hotel-gerfaut.com; ❸; closed Nov–Easter). There's a municipal **campsite**, *Le Mouriol*, on the Puy Mary road (☎04.71.40.73.09, Ⓔmairie.salers@orange.fr; closed mid-Oct to April).

Murat

MURAT, on the eastern edge of the Cantal, is the closest town to the high peaks and a busy little place, its cafés and shops bustling uncharacteristically for the region. It is also the easiest to access, lying on the N122 road and main train line, about 12km northeast of Le Lioran. Rather than any particular sight, it's the ensemble of grey-stone houses that attracts, many dating from the fifteenth and sixteenth centuries. Crowded together on their medieval lanes, they make a magnificent sight, especially as you approach from the St-Flour road, with the backdrop of the steep basalt cliffs of the **Rocher Bonnevie**, once the site of the local castle and now surmounted by a huge white statue of the Virgin Mary. Facing the town, perched on the distinctive mound of the **Rocher Bredons**, on your left as you approach, there's the lovely Romanesque **Église de Bredons** (July & Aug daily 10am–noon & 2.30–6.30pm), containing some fine eighteenth-century altarpieces. One of the finest of the old houses is now open to the public as the **Maison de la Faune** (July & Aug Mon–Sat 10am–12.30pm & 2–7pm, Sun 10am–noon & 3–7pm; Sept–June Mon–Sat 10am–noon & 2–5pm, Sun 2–5pm; €4.30), full of stuffed animals and birds illustrating the wildlife of the Parc desVolcans.

The **monument** to deportees on place de l'Hôtel-de-Ville and the name of the **avenue des 12-et-24-Juin-1944**, opposite the tourist office, both commemorate one of the blackest days in Murat's recent history. On June 12, 1944, a local Resistance group interrupted a German raid on the town and killed a senior SS officer. In reprisal, the Germans burnt several houses down on June 24 and arrested 120 people, 80 of whom died after deportation. Near the river, below the Rocher Bredons, a stone with an inscription marks the spot where the villagers were assembled before being deported.

Practicalities

The **tourist office** is at 2 rue du Faubourg Notre-Dame (July & Aug Mon–Sat 9am–12.30pm & 1.30–7pm, Sun 9.30am–12.30pm & 2.30–6.30pm; Sept–June Mon–Sat 9am–noon & 2–6pm & Sun 10am–noon; ☎04.71.20.09.47, Ⓦwww .paysdemurat.fr/tourisme), and you can rent **mountain bikes** from La Godille, opposite, or from Bernard Escure, in place Gandilhon-Gens-d'Armes.The **gare SNCF** is on the main road, avenue du Dr-Mallet, where there are also some good **places to stay**.The most comfortable is the *Hôtel des Breuils*, a handsome, ivy-covered bourgeois house at no. 34 (☎04.71.20.01.25, Ⓦwww.hostellerie -les-breuils.com; ❹; closed Nov–Christmas & April), with a heated indoor pool and sauna. A few doors down at no. 18, *Les Messageries* (☎04.71.20.04.04, Ⓦwww.hotel-les-messageries.com; ❷) has somewhat clinical rooms, but the restaurant (from €14–37) serves good hearty meals, including home-made terrines and fruit tarts. The town's **campsite**, *Les Stalapos*, is southwest of the centre in rue du Stade (May–Sept; ☎04.71.20.01.83, Ⓦwww.murat.fr).

St-Flour and the Margeride

Seat of a fourteenth-century bishopric, **ST-FLOUR** stands dramatically on a cliff-girt basalt promontory above the River Ander, 92km west of Le Puy and 92km south of Clermont-Ferrand. Prosperous in the Middle Ages because of its strategic position on the main road from northern France to Languedoc and the proximity of the grasslands of the Cantal whose herds provided the raw materials for its tanning and leather industries, it fell into somnolent decline in modern times, only partially reversed in the last thirty-odd years.

While the lower town that has grown up around the station is of little interest, the wedge of old streets that occupies the point of the promontory surrounding the cathedral has considerable charm. The best time to come is on a Saturday morning when the old town is filled with market stalls selling sausages, cheese and other local produce. If you're in a car, leave it in the car park in the chestnut-shaded square, **Les Promenades**. One end of the square is dominated by the **memorial** to Dr Mallet, his two sons and other hostages and assorted citizens executed in reprisals by the Germans during World War II.

The narrow streets of the old town lead off here and converge on the **place d'Armes**, where the fourteenth-century **Cathédrale St-Pierre** stands, backing onto the edge of the cliff, with a terrace giving good views out over the countryside. From the outside, the plain grey volcanic rock of the cathedral makes for a rather severe and uninspiring appearance; it's an impression that's partly mitigated inside by the fine vaulting of the ceiling and a number of works of art, most notably a carved, black-painted walnut figure of Christ with a strikingly serene expression, dating from the thirteenth century.

Facing the cathedral on the place d'Armes are some attractive old buildings, housing a couple of cafés under their arcades, while at the north and south extremities of the square stand the town's two museums. At the north end, the fine fourteenth-century building that was once the headquarters of the town's consuls contains the **Musée Alfred Douët**'s somewhat ragbag collections of furniture, tapestries and paintings (mid-April to mid-Oct daily 9am–noon & 2–6pm; mid-Oct to mid-April closed Sun; €3.30, joint ticket with Haute-Auvergne museum €3.40); the view from the cliffs behind the museum gives a sense of the impregnable position of the town. At the south end of the square, the current Hôtel de Ville, formerly the bishop's palace built in 1610, houses the more interesting **Musée de la Haute-Auvergne** (mid-April to mid-Oct daily 10am–noon & 2–6pm; mid-Oct to mid-April closed Sun; same prices as above), whose collections include some beautifully carved Auvergnat furniture and exquisitely made traditional musical instruments, such as the *cabrette*, a kind of accordion peculiar to the Auvergne.

Practicalities

The **gare SNCF** is on avenue Charles-de-Gaulle in the lower town. A few trains from Clermont-Ferrand and Aurillac stop here, but most journeys involve changing at Neussargues onto a SNCF bus, which can drop you off on the Promenades in the old town, saving you the walk up. The **tourist office** is on the Promenades, opposite the memorial (May–June & Sept Mon–Sat 9am–12.30pm & 2–6.30pm, Sun 10am–12.30pm & 2.30–5.30pm; July & Aug Mon–Sat 9am–12.30pm & 1.30–7pm, Sun 10am–12.30pm & 2.30–5.30pm; Oct–April Mon–Sat 9am–noon & 2–6pm; ☎04.71.60.22.50, ⓦwww.saint-flour.com). **Internet** access can be found at *Cg-Net* on rue Marchande (daily 9.30am–9pm).

The best deal for **accommodation** in the atmospheric upper town is the magnificent, old-style *La Maison des Planchettes* at 7 rue des Planchettes

(☎04.71.60.10.08, ⓦwww.maison-des-planchettes.com; ❶), which has half-*pensions* for as low as €31 and a *terroir* restaurant with menus from €12.90. Another great option is the *Hotel de France*, 28 rue de Lacs (☎04.71.60.04.75, ⓦwww.saint-flour-hoteldefrance.com; ❶), a welcoming, family-run establishment. The town's municipal **campsite**, *Les Orgues*, is off avenue des Orgues in the old town (June to mid-Sept; ☎04.71.60.44.01). The best place for both local cuisine and *cuisine gastronomique* is *Le Nautilus* on 23 avenue Charles-de-Gaulle (☎04.71.60.11.36; closed Oct–May) with menus around €19–25. The *Viking* bar and brasserie next to the *de France* has a good-value *carte* and stunning views of the valley.

The Margeride

South and east of St-Flour stretch the wild, rolling, sparsely populated wooded hills of the **Margeride**, one of the strongholds of the wartime Resistance groups. If you have your own transport, the D4 makes a slow but spectacular route east (92km) to Le Puy, crossing the forested heights of **Mont Mouchet**, at 1465m the highest point of the Margeride. A side turning, the D48 (signposted), takes you to the national Resistance **monument** by the woodman's hut that served as HQ to the local Resistance commander during the June 1944 battle to delay German reinforcements moving north to strengthen resistance to the D-day landings in Normandy. There's an **eco-museum** here (La Tour, Ruynes-en-Margeride; daily: July & Aug 10am–7pm, Sept–June 2–6pm; €4), sketching the progression of the Resistance movement in the area. The views back west from these heights to the Cantal are superb.

Further south, the modern *autoroute* crosses the gorge of the River Truyère beside the delicate steel tracery of the **Viaduc de Garabit**, built by Gustave Eiffel (of Tower fame) in 1884 to carry the newly constructed rail line – experience he put to important use in the Tower. Not far away, about 20km south of St-Flour and perched above the waters of the lake created by the damming of the Truyère for hydroelectric power, are the romantic ruins of the keep of the **Château d'Alleuze**, stronghold in the 1380s of one Bernard de Garlan, a notorious leader of lawless mercenaries employed by the English in the Hundred Years War to sow panic and destruction in French-held parts of the country.

The southwest: Aubrac and Rouergue

In the southwest corner of the Massif Central, the landscapes start to change and the mean altitude begins to drop. The wild, desolate moorland of the **Aubrac** is cut and contained by the savage gorges of **the Lot and Truyère rivers**. To the south of them, the arid but more southern-feeling plateaux of the *causses* form a sort of intermediate step to the lower hills and coastal plains of Languedoc. And they in turn are cut by the dramatic trenches formed by the **gorges of the Tarn, Jonte** and **Dourbie**, along with the spectacular caves of the **Aven Armand** and **Dargilan**. These are places best avoided at the height of the holiday season, when they turn into overcrowded outdoor playgrounds for amateur canoeists, parties of schoolchildren, motorists and campers.

The bigger towns, like **Rodez** and **Millau** in the old province of The **Rouergue**, also have much more of a southern feel. Both are worth a visit, though their attractions need not keep you for more than half a day. Rodez has a fine cathedral and Millau is worth considering as a base for exploring the *causses* and river gorges of the Tarn and Jonte.

The two great architectural draws of the area are **Conques**, with its medieval village and magnificent abbey, which owes its existence to the Santiago pilgrim route (now the GR65), and the perfect little *bastide* town of **Sauveterre-de-Rouergue**.

The mountains of Aubrac

The **Aubrac** lies to the south of St-Flour, east of the valley of the River Truyère and north of the valley of the Lot. It's a region of bleak, windswept uplands with long views and huge skies, dotted with glacial lakes and granite villages hunkered down out of the weather. The highest points are between 1200m and 1400m, and there are more cows up here than people; you see them grazing the boggy, peaty pastures, divided by dry-stone walls and turf-brown streams. There are few trees: a scatter of willow and ash and the occasional stand of hardy beeches on the tops, and only abandoned shepherds' huts testify to more populous times. It's an area that's invisible in bad weather, but which, in good conditions, has a bleak beauty, little disturbed by tourism or modernization.

Aumont-Aubrac and Aubrac

The waymarked **Tour d'Aubrac** footpath does a complete circuit of the area in around ten days, starting from the town of **AUMONT-AUBRAC**, where you'll find *Chez Camillou* at 10 rue Languedoc (☎04.66.42.80.22, ⓦwww.hotel-camillou.com; ❸; restaurant from €17; periodic closings mid-Nov to mid-Feb), the *Relais de Peyre*, across the street at no. 9 (☎04.66.42.85.88, ⓦwww.lerelaisdepeyre.com; ❶; closed Jan; restaurant €15–25), and a municipal **campsite** (☎04.66.42.80.02). The **tourist office** is on a small side street to the right of the town hall (Mon–Sat 9am–12.30pm & 2–7pm, Sun 9.30am–12.30pm & 3–6pm; ☎04.66.42.88.70, ⓦwww.ot-aumont-aubrac.fr). There is also a daily train connection on the Millau–St-Flour line.

The marathon **GR65** from Le Puy to Santiago de Compostela in Spain also crosses the area from northeast to southwest en route to Conques. In fact, the tiny village of **AUBRAC**, which gave its name to the region, owes its existence to this Santiago pilgrim route; around 1120, a way-station was opened here for the express purpose of providing shelter for the pilgrims on these inhospitable heights. Little remains of it today, beyond the windy **Tour des Anglais**, into which is incorporated the friendly *Hôtel de la Dômerie* (☎05.65.44.28.42, ⓦwww.hoteldomerie.com; ❸; closed mid-Nov to April; restaurant €20–39).

St-Urcize and Nasbinals

This is the wildest and most starkly beautiful part of the Aubrac. The close-huddled village of **ST-URCIZE**, 13km north of the town of Aubrac, hangs off the side of the valley of the River Lhère, with a lovely Romanesque church at its centre and a World War I **memorial**, with so many names on it you wouldn't have thought it possible such a small place could furnish so much cannon fodder. The village is ghostly out of season, with most of the unspoiled granite houses owned by people who live elsewhere. Should you wish to **stay**, there's a campsite and the welcoming *Hôtel Remise* (T04.71.23.20.02, F04.71.23.20.02; ❷; excellent food for around €17; closed Jan). On the other hand, if you can afford it, it would be a shame to pass up *Guy Prouhèze*, on 2 route de Languedoc (T04.66.42.80.07, Wwww.prouheze.com; closed Nov–March; ❹), a hotel featuring a famed *gastronomique* restaurant (menu €56; closed Sun noon & Mon) as well as a good *terroir* restaurant (€21), *Le Compostelle*. Those on a budget can enjoy a gourmet experience at *L'Ousta Bas* (T04.66.42.87.44; closed off season Tues & Wed and weekdays Nov–March), which has *terroir* menus from €17.

NASBINALS, 8km to the southeast, is rather bigger and livelier, and something of a cross-country ski resort in winter. It, too, has a beautiful small-scale **church** of the twelfth century, joined onto the adjacent house with a round fortified tower incorporated in the transept wall by the entrance. Just above the building, the *Hôtel de La Route d'Argent* (T04.66.32.50.03, F04.66.32.56.77; ❷) provides comfortable accommodation and good food (from €18). The friendly **tourist office** is on the other side of the road (Mon–Sat: July & Aug 9.30am–12.30pm & 2.30–5.30pm; Sept–June Mon–Sat 9.30am–12.30pm & 3–6pm; T04.66.32.55.73, Wwww.nasbinals-tourisme.fr). For internet access there's a computer at *Café du Foirail* on place du Foirail on the edge of town. A **campsite** (T04.66.32.50.17) and **gîte d'étape** (T04.66.32.50.65; meals available) are located on the St-Urcize road.

Laguiole

Seventeen kilometres west of St-Urcize and 24km north of Espalion, **LAGUIOLE** passes for a substantial town in these parts. Derived from the Occitan word for "little church", it's a name that now stands for knives and cheese. The **knives**, which draw hordes of French to the town's many shops, are characterized by a long, pointed blade and bone handle that fits the palm; the genuine article should bear the effigy of a bee stamped on the clasp that holds the blade open. It's an industry that started in the nineteenth century, then moved to industrial Thiers, outside Clermont-Ferrand, before returning to Laguiole in 1987, when the Société Laguiole (the only outlet for the genuine article) opened a factory designed by Philippe Starck on the St-Urcize road, with a giant knife projecting from the roof of the windowless all-aluminium building. They have a shop on the main through-road, on the corner of the central marketplace (Wwww.forge-de-laguiole.com). Laguiole's **cheese-making** tradition dates back to the twelfth century; unpasteurized cow's milk is formed into massive cylindrical cheeses, and aged up to eighteen months. The hard, tangy result is a world apart from neighbouring Roquefort; to sample or buy, the factory outlet on the north edge of town is the best bargain.

The **tourist office** is in place du Mairie (July & Aug Mon–Sat 9.30am–1pm & 2–7pm, Sun 10.30am–12.30pm & 2–5pm; Sept–June Mon–Sat 10am–12.30pm & 2–5pm; T05.65.44.35.94, Wwww.laguiole-online.com). For first-class **accommodation**, *Michel Bras*, a highly rated **hotel** (T05.65.51.18.20, Wwww.michel-bras.fr; ❾) with one of the country's finest restaurants (menus €113–180), is located just outside of town on the route d'Auibrac. For something less extravagant there are several hotels on the main street. Try the *Aubrac* opposite the marketplace (☎05.65.44.32.13, ⓦwww.hotel-aubrac.fr; ❷; restaurant from €11.50), or the *Grand Hôtel Auguy* (early April to mid-Nov; ☎05.65.44.31.11, ⓦwww.hotel-auguy.fr; ❹), 2 allée de l'Amicale, with a good restaurant with *terroir* menu at €58. For more economical accommodation try the tiny *Hotel Noù 4* on rue Bardière, a cosy cross between a café-restaurant, boutique and hotel (☎05.65.51.68.30, ⓦwww.nou4.com; ❷). There is a municipal **campsite** (☎05.65.44.39.72; closed mid-Sept to mid-May) on the St-Urcize road. Communications, however, are not good, and if you don't have a car your only chance of getting in or out of town is the daily bus to Rodez.

Rodez and the upper valley of the Lot

A particularly beautiful and out-of-the-way stretch of country lies on the southwestern periphery of the Massif Central, bordered roughly by the valley of the **River Lot** in the north and the **Viaur** in the south. The upland areas are open and wide, with views east to the mountains of the Cévennes and south to the Monts de Lacaune and the Monts de l'Espinouse. **Rodez**, capital of the Rouergue, with a fine cathedral, is the only place of any size, accessible on the main train and bus routes. But the most dramatic places are in the river valleys, in particular the great abbey of **Conques** and the small towns of **Entraygues** and **Estaing**.

Rodez

Until the 1960s, **RODEZ** and the Rouergue were synonymous with backcountry poverty and underdevelopment. Today it's an active and prosperous provincial town with a charming, renovated centre, even though the approach, through spreading commercial districts, is uninspiring.

Built on high ground above the River Aveyron, the **old town**, dominated by the massive red-sandstone **Cathédrale Notre-Dame**, is visible for kilometres around. No matter from what direction you approach, you'll find yourself in the **place d'Armes**, where the cathedral's plain, fortress-like west front and the seventeenth-century bishop's palace sit side by side – both buildings were incorporated into the town's defences. The Gothic cathedral, its plain facade relieved only by an elaborately flowery rose window, was begun in 1277 and took three hundred years to complete. Towering over the square is the cathedral's 87-metre **belfry**, decorated with pinnacles, balustrades and statuary almost as fantastical as that of Strasbourg cathedral. The impressively spacious interior, architecturally as plain as the facade, is adorned with a magnificently extravagant seventeenth-century walnut organ loft and choir stalls that were crafted by André Sulpice in 1468.

Leaving by the splendid south porch, you find yourself in the tiny place Rozier in front of the fifteenth-century **Maison Cannoniale**, whose courtyard is guarded by jutting turrets. From the back of the cathedral to the north and the south, a network of well-restored medieval streets connects place de-Gaulle, place de la Préfecture and the attractive place du Bourg, with its fine sixteenth-century houses. In place Foch, just south of the cathedral, the Baroque chapel of the old **lycée** is worth a look for its amazing painted ceiling, while in place Raynaldy, the modern **Hôtel de Ville** and the **médiathèque** are interesting examples of attempts to graft modern styles onto old buildings.

Practicalities

The **tourist office** is situated on place Foch, just off boulevard Gambetta and the place d'Armes, near the cathedral (June to mid-July & mid-Aug to Sept Mon–Sat 9am–12.30pm & 1.30–6.30pm; mid-July to mid-Aug Mon–Sat 9am–6.30pm & Sun 10am–noon; Oct–May Mon 2.30–6pm, Tues–Fri 9am–12.30pm & 1.30–6pm, Sat 9.30am–12.30pm & 2.30–6pm; ☎05.65.75.76.77, Ⓦwww.ot-rodez.fr).The **gare routière** is on avenue V.-Hugo (☎05.65.68.11.13), and the **gare SNCF** on boulevard Joffre, on the northern edge of town.

For reasonable hotel **accommodation**, try the *Hôtel du Clocher*, off the east end of the cathedral at 4 rue Séguy (☎05.65.68.10.16, Ⓦwww.hotel-clocher .com; ❸). More upmarket is *La Tour Maje*, on boulevard Gally behind the tourist office (☎05.65.68.34.68, Ⓦwww.hotel-tour-maje.fr; ❸), a modern building tacked onto a medieval tower. *Hotel Le Broussy*, recognizable by its beautiful Art Deco facade on avenue Victor-Hugo next to the cathedral, provides stylish accommodation and a leisurely *terrasse* restaurant (☎05.65.68.18.71, Ⓦhotel .broussy.monsite.orange.fr; ❸; menus from €11). Rodez' municipal **campsite** (☎05.65.67.09.52; closed Oct–May) is on the riverbank in the quartier Layoule, about 1km from the centre.

As for **eating**, one of the best places to sample local cuisine is *La Taverne*, 23 rue de l'Embergue (closed Sun & Mon lunch; menus from €18), with an attractive terrace at the back, while the place to go for more gourmet food is the classy *Goûts et Couleurs*, 38 rue Bonald (closed Sun & Mon), where menus start at €34. *Le Bistroquet*, 17 rue du Bal, off place d'Olmet (closed Sun & Mon), does good salads and grills for around €14. For a **drink**, head for the *Café de la Paix*, on place Jean-Jaurès, or *Au Bureau*, in the Tour Maje. The most central **internet** access, Resolument Plus Net, is at 11 rue Béteille (☎05.65.75.66.87; Tues–Thurs 11am–10pm, Fri–Sat 11am–midnight).

Sauveterre-de-Rouergue and the gorges of the Viaur

Forty kilometres southwest of Rodez and 6.5km northwest of Naucelle, **SAUVETERRE-DE-ROUERGUE** makes the most rewarding side trip in this part of the Rouergue. It is a perfect, otherworldly *bastide*, founded in 1281, with a large, wide central square, part cobbled, part gravelled, and surrounded by stone and half-timbered houses built over arcaded ground floors. Narrow streets lead off to the outer road, lined with stone-built houses the colour of rusty iron. On summer evenings, *pétanque* players come out to roll their *boules* beneath chestnut and plane trees, while swallows and swifts swoop and dive overhead.

In summer, a **bus** runs once a weekday here in the late afternoon from Rodez. The **tourist office** is in the main square (June–Sept Mon–Sun 10am–1pm & 2.30–7pm, Fri until 9pm; ☎05.65.72.02.52, Ⓦwww.sauveterre-de-rouergue .eu). There are several agreeable **hotels**, including the cheap and charming ⚑*Hôtel La Grappe d'Or*, on the outer road (☎05.65.72.00.62; ❶), whose restaurant (closed Oct–April) offers an excellent menu at €12, with dishes like *gésiers chauds*, *tripoux*, cheese, ice cream and *fouace* (a kind of sweet cake). More upmarket is the *Sénéchal*, at the entrance to the village (☎05.65.71.29.00, Ⓦwww.hotel-senechal.fr; ❻; closed Jan to mid-March), with an indoor pool and an excellent restaurant (closed Mon plus Tues lunch; menus €27–120). There's also a **campsite**, just off the D997 (☎05.65.47.05.32).

The country round about, known as the **Ségala**, is high (around 500m) and wide, cut by sudden and deep river valleys full of lush greenery. The most spectacular of these is the valley of the **River Viaur** to the south and west of Sauveterre, where a car is essential. If you're heading west towards Najac, there's a marvellous backcountry route through La Salvetat, crossing the Viaur at Belle-combe and again at Moulin-de-Bar, where there's a riverside **campsite**, *Le Gomvassou*. The wartime Resistance was very active hereabouts and there are numerous memorials to the Resistance fighters who lost their lives in the aftermath of the D-Day landings. There is a particularly interesting one beside the tiny church in **Jouqueviel**, further downstream, dedicated to a unit of Polish volunteers and 161 escaped Soviet POWs.

Conques

CONQUES, 37km north of Rodez, is one of the great villages of southwest France. It occupies a spectacular position on the flanks of the steep, densely wooded gorge of the little **River Dourdou**, a tributary of the Lot. For all its glory, Conques is not easy to get to. The only public transport to the village is a seasonal bus that runs up the Tarn valley from Entraygues via Vieillevie and as far as St-Geniez d'Olt. The shuttle makes one run in each direction (June & Sept Mon; July & Aug Tues, Thurs & Sat; confirm departure times with the tourist office at Conques), allowing you to visit Conques and return the same day.

It's the abbey which brought the village into existence. Its origins go back to a hermit called Dadon who settled here around 800 AD and founded a community of Benedictine monks, one of whom pilfered the relics of the martyred girl, Ste Foy, from the monastery at Agen. Known for her ability to cure blindness and liberate captives, Ste Foy's presence brought the pilgrims flocking to Conques in ever-increasing numbers, earning the abbey a prime place on the pilgrimage route to Compostela.

▲ Reliquary statue of Ste Foy in the church of Ste-Foy, Conques

The abbey church

At the village's centre, dominating the landscape, stands the renowned Roman-esque **church of Ste-Foy**, whose giant pointed towers are echoed in those of the medieval houses that cluster tightly about it. Begun in the eleventh century, its plain fortress-like facade rises on a small cobbled square beside the tourist office and pilgrims' fountain, the slightly shiny silver-grey schist prettily offset by the greenery and flowers of the terraced gardens.

In startling contrast to this plainness, the elaborately sculpted *Last Judgement* in the **tympanum** above the door admonishes all who see it to espouse virtue and eschew vice (ask at the tourist office for guided tours of the tympanum and the tribunes; 45min; €3.30). Christ sits in judgement in the centre, with the chosen on his right hand, among them Dadon the hermit and the emperor Charlemagne, while his left hand directs the damned to Hell, as usual so much more graphically and interestingly portrayed with all its gory tortures than the boring bliss of Paradise, depicted in the bottom left panel.

The **inside** of the church was designed to accommodate the large numbers of pilgrims and channel them down the aisles and round the ambulatory. From here they could contemplate Ste Foy's relics displayed in the choir, encircled by a lovely wrought-iron screen, still in place. There is some fine carving on the capitals, especially in the triforium arches, too high up to see from the nave: you need to climb to the organ loft, which gives you a superb perspective on the whole interior. This is also a good place to admire the windows, designed by the abstract artist Pierre Soulages, which consist of plain plates of glass that subtly change colour with the light outside.

The unrivalled asset of this church is the survival of its medieval treasure of extraordinarily rich, bejewelled **reliquaries**, including a gilded statue of Ste Foy, bits of which are as old as the fifth century, and one known as the *A of Charlemagne*, because it is thought to have been the first in a series given as presents by the emperor to monasteries he founded. Writing in 1010, a cleric named Bernard d'Angers gave an idea of the effect of these wonders on the medieval pilgrim: "The crowd of people prostrating themselves on the ground was so dense it was impossible to kneel down. ... When they saw it for the first time [Ste Foy], all in gold and sparkling with precious stones and looking like a human face, the majority of the peasants thought that the statue was really looking at them and answering their prayers with her eyes." The treasure is kept in a room adjoining the now ruined cloister (daily: April–Sept 9.30am–12.30pm & 2–6.30pm; Oct–March 10am–noon & 2–6pm; €6.20); the second part of the Conques museum, displayed on three floors of a house on the cathedral square, consists of a miscellany of sixteenth-century and later tapestries, furnishings and assorted bits of medieval masonry.

By far the best way to experience the beauty of Conques is by visiting the church at around 9.30pm on a summer evening for the **Nocturne des Tribunes**. The church is opened to the public and is beautifully illuminated while an organist or pianist fills it with music (€5).

The Village

The **village** of Conques is very small, largely depopulated and mainly contained within the medieval **walls**, parts of which still survive, along with three of its **gates**. The houses date mainly from the late Middle Ages. The whole ensemble of cobbled lanes and stairways is a pleasure to stroll through. There are two main streets, the old **rue Haute**, or "upper street", which was the route for the pilgrims coming from Estaing and Le Puy and passing onto

Figeac and Cahors through the **Porte de la Vinzelle**; and the lane, now **rue Charlemagne**, which leads steeply downhill through the **Porte de Barry** to the river and the ancient **Pont Romain**, with the little **chapel of St-Roch** off to the left, from where you get a fine view of the village and church. Better still: climb the road on the far side of the valley. The rather grandiose-sounding **European centre for medieval art and civilization**, hidden in a bunker right at the top of the hill (9am–noon & 2–6pm), sometimes has exhibitions and displays. Throughout August, the village hosts a prestigious **classical music festival**, most of the concerts taking place at the abbey church; contact the tourist office for more information.

Practicalities

The **tourist office** is on the square beside the church (daily: April–Sept 9.30am–12.30pm & 2–6.30pm; Oct–March 10am–noon & 2–6pm; ☎08.20.82.08.03, Ⓦwww.conques.fr; internet access available) and can provide information on local walks. For somewhere central to **stay**, the *Auberge St-Jacques* (☎05.65.72.86.36, Ⓦwww.aubergestjacques.fr; ❸), near the church, provides good-value, old-fashioned accommodation and also has a popular restaurant, with menus from €18 and *plats du jour* at €8–11. A good alternative is the *Auberge du Pont Romain*, on the main road below the hill on which Conques stands (☎05.65.69.84.07, Ⓕ05.65.69.85.12; ❶; closed first two weeks Nov; menus from €14) – it's a twenty-minute walk from here to the church. A little way upstream, the attractive *Moulin de Cambelong* (☎05.65.72.84.77, Ⓦwww.moulindecambelong.com; ❻) offers more comfort – some rooms have spacious wooden balconies with great views of the river – and a first-rate restaurant, specializing in duck dishes (à la carte from €55).

There are several **campsites** in Conques: try *Beau Rivage* (☎05.65.69.82.23, Ⓔcamping.conques@orange.fr; closed Oct–March), on the banks of the Dourdou, just below the village, *St-Cyprien-sur-Dourdou* (☎05.65.72.80.52, Ⓔmairie-stcyprien12@orange.fr), 7km to the south, or *Le Moulin* (☎05.65.72.87.28, Ⓦwww.camping.du.moulin.free.fr; closed Nov–March), at Grand-Vabre, 5km downstream. Walkers can use sections of the **GR65** and **GR62**, both of which pass through the village; the tourist office will provide information about shorter local walks.

The upper valley: Grand-Vabre to Entraygues

The most beautiful stretch of the **Lot Valley** is the 21.5km between the bridge of Coursavy, below **Grand-Vabre**, just north of Conques, and **Entraygues**: deep, narrow and wild, with the river running full and strong, as yet unaffected by the dams higher up, with scattered farms and houses high on the hillsides among long-abandoned terracing. The shady, tree-tunnelled road is level and not heavily used, making it ideal for cycling.

There is a good hotel 6.5km east in **VIEILLEVIE**, where canoe rental is also available: the *Hôtel de la Terrasse* (☎04.71.49.94.00, Ⓦwww.hotel-terrasse.com; ❸; closed mid-Nov to April; restaurant €22–40). A further possibility is the delightful *Auberge du Fel*, some 10km further on, high on the north slopes of the valley in the hamlet of **LE FEL** (☎05.65.44.52.30, Ⓦwww.auberge-du-fel .com; ❸; closed mid-Nov to March; excellent restaurant with menus at €20–40), which by an unexpected quirk of climate produces a little local wine. There is also a beautifully sited municipal **campsite** high on the hillside (☎05.65.44.51.86; closed Oct–May).

Entraygues and around

ENTRAYGUES, with its riverside streets and attractive grey houses, has an airy, open feel that belies its mountain sleepiness. It lies right in the angle of the junction of the Lot with the equally beautiful River Truyère. The brown towers of a thirteenth-century **château** overlook the meeting of the waters, and a magnificent four-arched **bridge** of the same date crosses the Truyère a little way upstream, alongside the ancient tanners' houses.

The **tourist office** is on place de la République (April–June & Sept Mon–Sat 10am–12.15pm & 2–6pm, Sun 10am–12.15pm; July & Aug Mon–Sat 9.30am–12.30pm & 3–7pm, Sun 10am–12.30pm; Oct–March Mon 2–6pm, Tues–Fri 10am–12.15pm & 2–5/6pm; ☎05.65.44.56.10, ⓦwww.tourisme-entraygues.com). It frequently remains open outside of its official hours and will provide information about walking, mountain biking and canoeing in the area. Reasonable **places to stay** include the *Hôtel Le Centre*, on the main street (☎05.65.44.51.19, Ⓕ05.65.48.63.09; ❷; menus €11.50–29), and the *Lion d'Or*, on the corner of the main street and the bank of the Lot (☎05.65.44.50.01, ⓦwww.hotel-lion-or.com; ❸), with a covered swimming pool and garden and attached restaurant (from €15). There's also a **campsite**, *Le Val-de-Saures* (☎05.65.44.56.92; closed Oct–April), on the GR65 at **GOLINHAC**, about 7km south of Entraygues on the other side of the Lot. There is a **bus** to Aurillac (Tues–Fri 12.50pm from the post office) in the north and Rodez (Mon–Sat) to the south.

There are further accommodation options at **ESTAING**, another beautiful village huddled round a rocky bluff and castle in a bend of the Lot about 10km beyond Golinhac. The *Hôtel aux Armes d'Estaing*, named after the family who occupied the castle for five hundred years, offers attractive rooms and very good food in the centre of the village (☎05.65.44.70.02, ⓦwww.estaing.net; ❸; closed mid-Nov to mid-March; meals €11–40). There's also a municipal **campsite** (☎05.65.44.72.77; closed Oct–April) and **gîte d'étape** on the GR65 (☎05.65.44.71.74). A date to watch out for is the first Sunday in July when the place fills up with people, many in medieval dress, who come to honour the relics of **St Fleuret**, bishop of Clermont, who died here in 621 AD and is buried in the fifteenth-century church by the castle.

Espalion

The substantial little town of **ESPALION** lies in a mild, fertile opening in the valley of the Lot, 10km from Estaing and 32km northeast of Rodez. It was the "first smile of the south" to the muleteers, pilgrims and other travellers coming down from the rude heights of the Massif Central and places north.

The only interesting part of town is the **riverside quarter**, with its galleried and balconied old houses, once used as tanneries, hanging over the water. The finest view of the area is from the Pont Neuf, where the main road to Rodez crosses the Lot, as just upstream there's a lovely red sandstone packhorse **bridge** with the domed and turreted château dating from 1572 right behind it.

Don't miss the glorious little twelfth-century Romanesque **church of St-Hilarion de Perse**, built on the spot, so the story goes, where, in the reign of Charlemagne, the Saracens lopped off the head of St Hilarion. It sits on the edge of the cemetery, about fifteen-minutes' walk to the left of the bridge on the château side of the river, past the campsite. Built in red sandstone, with a wall belfry and wide porch with sculpted tympanum and dozens of figures adorning the corbel ends of the apse, it's a delight.

Also well worth a visit is the **Château de Calmont d'Olt** (daily: May, June & Sept 10am–noon & 2–6pm; July & Aug 10am–7pm; school holidays 2–6pm; €7.50 in summer, otherwise €5; ⓦwww.chateaucalmont.org), for its unbeatable views of the town and the country beyond. It's a rough and atmospheric old fortress dating from the eleventh century, on the very peak of an abrupt bluff, 535m high and a stiff 1km climb above the town on the south bank. Particularly good for children is a regular programme of activities throughout the day (afternoon only out of season), including demonstrations of medieval siege engines and artillery.

Practicalities

The **tourist office** is just across the Pont Vieux in rue St-Antoine (May, June & Sept Mon–Fri 10am–noon & 2–6pm & Sat 10am–noon & 2.30–5.30pm; July & Aug Mon–Fri 9.30am–1pm & 2–7pm, Sat 9.30am–1pm & 2–6pm, Sun 10am–12.30pm; Oct–May Tues–Fri 10am–noon & 2–6pm, Sat 10am–noon & 2.30–5.30pm; ☎05.65.44.10.63, ⓦwww.ot-espalion.fr). For **accommodation**, there's no better place to stay than the *Hôtel Moderne* on the crossroads in the middle of town at 27 boulevard de Guizard (☎05.65.44.05.11, Ⓔhotelmoderne12@aol.com; ❷; closed part-Jan & part-March). The rooms are comfortable but, more importantly, its restaurant is first-rate, especially for river fish (menus €12–42). There's also a municipal **gîte** (☎05.65.51.10.30) at 5 rue St-Joseph. A riverside **campsite**, Roc de l'Arche, sits behind the château (March to mid-Nov; ☎05.65.44.06.79, ⓦperso.orange.fr/camping-rocdelarche).

Espalion has a second superb **restaurant**, *Méjane*, by the old bridge (☎05.65.48.22.37; closed March & Sun evening. & Mon lunch & Wed, in July & Aug Sun evening. & Mon; menus €16–53), specializing in regional cuisine with a post-*nouvelle* influence, while for uncomplicated eating, there are several brasseries on the main through-street.

Millau, Roquefort and the Gorges du Tarn

MILLAU, now bypassed by the spectacular Millau viaduct (see below), occupies a beautiful site in a bend of the River Tarn at its junction with the Dourbie. It's enclosed on all sides by impressive white cliffs, formed where the rivers have worn away the edges of the *causses*, especially on the north side, where the spectacular table-top hill of the **Puech d'Andan** stands sentinel over the town. From medieval until modern times, thanks to its proximity to the sheep pastures of the *causses*, the town was a major manufacturer of leather goods, especially gloves. Although outclassed by cheaper producers in the mass market and suffering serious unemployment as a result, Millau still leads in top-of-the-range goods.

In recent years the town hit the headlines with the construction of the astonishing **Grand Viaduc du Millau** in 2004, a 2.5-kilometre bridge supported by seven enormous pillars that, at times, puncture through the cloud level (the tallest is 326m high, taller than the Eiffel tower). Designed by British architects Foster and Partners (of Sir Norman Foster fame), French engineer Michel Virbgeux (whose previous credits include the wonderful Pont de Normandie) and Eiffage, a construction firm that traces its heritage back to Gustave Eiffel, it is as much a work of art as it is a vital new link from Paris to the Languedoc coast.

Arrival, information and accommodation

From the **bus and train stations** it's about a ten-minute walk down rue Alfred-Merle to the main square, place du Mandarous. The **tourist office** is on place du

Beffroi in the centre of the old town (July & Aug Mon–Sat 9am–7pm, Sun 9.30am–4pm; Sept–June Mon–Fri 9am–12.30pm & 2–6.30pm, Sat 9am–6.30pm, Sun 9.30am–4pm; ℡05.65.60.02.42, ⓌMwww.ot-millau.fr). **Bikes and outdoor equipment** can be rented from Roc et Canyon, 55 avenue Jean-Jaurès.

The best-value **hotel** is *Des Causses*, set in an attractive building on the N9 at 56 avenue Jean-Jaurès (℡05.65.60.03.19, Ⓦwww.hotel-des-causses.com; ❷), and with a reasonable restaurant (la carte from €30). Even more atmospheric is the *Emma Calvé* at 28 rue Jean-Jaurès (℡05.65.60.13.49, Ⓦwww.millau-hotel -emmacalve.com; ❸), once home of the popular nineteenth-century singer of that name and with decor and furnishings evocative of the old bourgeousie. Though modern and characterless, *Hotel de la Capelle* (℡05.65.60.14.72, Ⓦwww.hotel-millau-capelle.com; ❶), overlooking the Puech d'Andan at 7 place de la Fraternité, is a good-value option, especially for groups of four. There are several **gîtes**, and over half a dozen **campsites**. The riverside *Les Erables* (℡05.65.59.15.13, Ⓦwww.campingleserables.fr; closed Oct to late April) on avenue de Millau Plage is shady and not overly crowded. For internet access, *Cyber-café* at 5 rue Droite is the most central option (Mon–Sat 10am–8pm).

The Town

Millau is a very pleasant, lively provincial town whose clean and well-preserved old streets have a summery, southern charm. It owes its original prosperity to its position on the ford where the Roman road from Languedoc to the north crossed the Tarn, marked today by the truncated remains of a medieval **bridge** surmounted by a watermill jutting out into the river beside the modern bridge.

Whether you arrive from north or south, you'll find yourself sooner or later in **place du Mandarous**, the main square, where avenue de la République, the road to Rodez, begins. South of here, the **old town** is built a little way back from the river to avoid floods and contained within an almost circular ring of shady boulevards. The rue Droite cuts through the centre, linking the three squares: place Emma-Calvé, place des Halles and place Foch. The prettiest by far is **place Foch**, with its cafés, shaded by two big plane trees and bordered by houses supported on stone pillars; some are twelfth century. In one corner, the **church of Notre-Dame** is worth a look for its octagonal Toulouse-style belfry, originally Romanesque. In the other, there's the very interesting **Musée de Millau** (May–Sept daily 10am–noon & 2–6pm; July & Aug 10am–6pm; Oct–March closed Sun; €5), housed in a stately eighteenth-century mansion. Its collections revolve around the bizarre combination of archeology and gloves, and include the magnificent red pottery of the Graufesenque works (see below), as well as a complete 180-million-year-old plesiosaurus. Millau's other two squares have been the subject of some rather questionable attempts at reconciling old stones and Richard Rogers-inspired contemporary urban design. Off one of these, place Emma-Calvé, the **clock tower** (June & Sept Mon–Sat 10–11.30am & 3–5.30pm; July & Aug daily 10am–noon & 3.30–6pm; €3) is worth a climb for the great all-round view. Take a look also in the streets off the square – rue du Voultre, rue de la Peyrollerie and their tributaries – for a sense of the old working-class and bourgeois districts.

Clear evidence of the town's importance in Roman times is to be seen in the **Graufesenque pottery works** archeology museum, just upstream on the south bank (Tues–Sun: May–June & Sept 10am–12.30pm & 2–7pm; July & Aug 10am–noon & 2–7pm; Oct–April 10am–noon & 2–6pm; €4), whose renowned red terracotta ware (*terra sigillata*) was distributed throughout the Roman world. A pass (€12) is available for entry into all of the towns sights and museums.

Eating and drinking

For a quick **meal**, you'll find numerous brasseries and cafés on place du Mandarous. But for something more traditional, dine in the magnificent surroundings of ✷ *La Mustardière* at 34 avenue de la République (℡05.65.60.20.63; closed Dec–Feb; €33–50) which serves excellent *gastronomique* and *terroir* specialities, or the less upmarket *La Braconne*, on place Foch (℡05.65.60.30.93; closed Sun evening & Mon; from €19), offering high-calorie fare such as stuffed goose and pork with juniper berries. Alternatively, head for boulevard de la Capelle on the northeast side of the old town, where two good establishments spread their tables under the trees: *La Mangeoire*, at no. 8 (℡05.65.60.13.16; closed Mon; menu from €22), which serves grilled fish, meat and game dishes; and next door, *La Marmite du Pêcheur*, featuring menus from €18, including *aligot*. A popular place for a **drink** is *La Locomotive*, at 33 avenue Gambetta (till 2am), which has live music on summer evenings.

Roquefort-sur-Soulzon and the Abbey of Silvanès

Twenty-one kilometres south of Millau, the little village of **ROQUEFORT-SUR-SOULZON** has nothing to say for itself except cheese, and almost every building is devoted to the cheese-making process. What gives the cheese its special flavour is the fungus, *penicillium roqueforti*, that grows exclusively in the fissures in the rocks created by the collapse of the sides of the valley on which Roquefort now stands. Legend has it that once upon a time a local shepherd one day forgot his lunch of bread and cheese, and found it some months later, covered with mould. He bit tentatively and discovered to his surprise that instead of ruining the cheese, the mould had much improved its taste.

While the sheep's milk used in the making of the cheese comes from different flocks and dairies as far afield as the Pyrenees, the crucial fungus is grown here, on bread. Just 2g of powdered fungus are enough for 4000 litres of milk, which in turn makes 330 Roquefort cheeses; they are matured in Roquefort's many-layered cellars, first unwrapped for three weeks and then wrapped up again. It takes three to six months for the full flavour to develop.

Two of the cheese manufacturers have organized **visits**: **Société** (daily: July & Aug 9.30am–6.30pm; Sept–June 9.30/10am–noon & 1.30–4.30/5pm; €3) and **Papillon** (April–June & Sept daily 9.30–11.30am & 1.30–5.30pm; July & Aug daily 9.30am–6.30pm; Oct–March Mon–Fri 9.30–11.30am & 1.30–4.30pm; free). Each visit consists of a short film, followed by a tour of the cellars and tasting – not, in fact, very interesting, except to hard-core cheese fans.

Some 25km further south, deep in the isolation of the *causses*, squats the twelfth-century **Cistercian Abbey of Silvanès** (daily July & Aug 9.30am–1pm & 2–7pm; Sept–June 9.15am–12.30pm & 2–6pm; closed Sat & Sun Dec–Feb; €2), founded in 1137 and the first Cistercian house in the region. Having largely survived the depredations of war and revolution, the abbey serves today as a centre for sacred music and dance from the world over. Although you'll have to manage your own transport, it's worth visiting not only for the evocative setting, but also for the excellently preserved thirteenth-century church as well as the surviving monastic buildings, including a refectory and scriptorium dating back to the 1100s. There are a couple of **hotels** in the village by the abbey, but only 4km from the monastery you can stay at the magnificent sixteenth-century *Château de Gissac* (℡05.65.98.14.60, ⊛www.chateau.gissac.com; ❹), which also offers half and full *pensions*.

The Gorges du Tarn

Jampacked with tourists in July and August, but absolutely spectacular nonetheless, the **Gorges du Tarn** cuts through the limestone plateaux of the Causse de Sauveterre and the Causse Méjean in a precipitous trench 400–500m deep and 1000–1500m wide. Its sides, cloaked with woods of feathery pine and spiked with pinnacles of eroded rock, are often sheer and always very steep, creating within them a microclimate in sharp distinction to the inhospitable plateaux above. The permanent population is tiny, though there's plenty of evidence of more populous times in abandoned houses and once-cultivated terraces. Because of the press of people and the subsequent overpricing of **accommodation**, the best bet, if you want to stay along the gorge, is to head up onto the Causse Méjean, where there are several small family-run hotels and *chambres d'hôte*, among which is the attractively sited *Auberge de la Cascade* in St-Chély-du-Tarn (T04.66.48.52.82, Wwww.aubergecascade.com; ❸; closed Nov–March; menu for €34).

The most attractive section of the gorge runs northeast for 53km from the pretty village of **LE ROZIER**, 21km northeast of Millau, to **ISPAGNAC**. If you want to stay in Le Rozier, good accommodation can be found at the *Grand Hôtel Voyageurs* (T05.65.62.60.09, Wwww.grandhoteldesvoyageurs.fr; ❷; menu from €20; closed Nov–Easter) and there's a municipal **campsite** (T05.65.62.63.98, F05.65.62.60.83; closed Oct–April). A better bet, however, is *Le Vallon* (T04.66.44.21.24, Wwww.hotel-vallon.com; ❶) in Ispagnac, a small hotel with an excellent *terroir* restaurant (from €16) and which has family-size rooms and good-value half-*pensions*.

A narrow and very twisty road follows the right bank of the river from Le Rozier, but it's not the best way to see the scenery. For the car-borne, the best views are from the road to St-Rome-de-Dolan above Les Vignes, and from the roads out of La Malène and the attractive **STE-ÉNIMIE**, where you'll find a well-informed **tourist office** (Easter–June & Sept–Oct Mon–Fri 9.30am–12.30pm & 1.30–5.30pm, Sat 9am–12.30pm & 2–5.30pm; July & Aug Mon–Sat 9am–7pm & Sun 9am–12.30pm; Nov–Easter Mon–Fri 9.30am–12.30pm & 1.30–5.30pm; T04.66.48.53.44, Wwww.gorgesdutarn .net). La Malène has a municipal **campsite** (T04.66.48.58.55, Ela.malene .mairie@orange.fr; closed mid-Oct to March) and *La Blanquière* site (T04.66.48.54.93, Ecamping.blaquière@orange.fr; closed mid-Sept to May), which is beautifully sited on the main road towards Les Vignes some 6km from town. But it's best to walk if possible, or follow the river's course by boat or canoe. There are dozens of places to rent canoes (€15 per person for 2–3hr, plus pick-up), and maps for various walking routes can be downloaded from the Ste-Énimie website (look under "*téléchargements*").

Also eminently worth seeing are two beautiful **caves** about 25km up the Jonte from Le Rozier. **Aven Armand** (daily: mid-March to June & Sept–Oct 10am–noon, 1.30–5pm; July & Aug 10am–6pm; €8.50), on the edge of the Causse Méjean, which is fitted with a funicular, claims the world's tallest stalagmite towering 30m above the cave floor. The **Grotte de Dargilan** (daily: April–June & Sept 10am–noon & 2–5.30pm; July & Aug 10am–6.30pm; Oct 10am–noon & 2–4.30pm; €8.50), on the south side of the river on the edge of the Causse Noir, known as the "pink cave" from the colour of its rock, is known as one of the country's most beautiful stalactite caverns. **HYELZAS**, near the Aven Armand cave, has a *gîte*, *Du Four à Pain* (T04.66.45.61.64, Wmonsite .orange.fr/gitedufourapain; ❷).

South of Millau

Heading south from Millau the autoroute skirts the barren and windswept Causse du Larzac. Two sights lie not far off the highway, but neither is served by public transport. **LA COUVERTOIRADE**, 5km off the main road (parking €3), is billed as a perfect "Templar" village, although its present remains postdate the dissolution of that Order in the late thirteenth century. Yet, it is a striking site, still completely enclosed by its towers and walls and almost untouched by renovation. Its forty remaining inhabitants live by tourism, and you have to pay to walk around the **ramparts** (daily: March–June & Sept to mid-Nov 10am–noon & 2–5/6pm; July & Aug 10am–7pm; €3, or €6 including a video presentation; English audio-guide available). Just outside the walls on the south side is a *lavogne*, a paved water hole of a kind seen all over the *causse* for watering the flocks, whose milk is used for Roquefort cheese. If you want to stay, there's the municipal **gîte d'étape** (☎05.65.58.17.75 or 06.12.50.09.86; ❶) in the far corner from the entrance, serving the GR71 and GR71C. A bus from Millau (Mon, Wed & Fri) serves the village during July and August.

A further 5km south, turn off at **Le Caylar** for the stunning road to **ST-MAURICE-NAVACELLES**. Wild box grows along the lanes, often meticulously clipped into hedges. Here and there among the scrubby oak and thorn, or driving along the road at milking time, you pass flocks of sheep. Occasional farmhouses materialize, like *Les Besses* – one of the few still in use – huge, self-contained and fortress-like, with the living quarters upstairs and the sheep stalls down below. St-Maurice-Navacelles, on the GR7 and GR74, is a small and sleepy hamlet with a fine World War I memorial by Paul Dardé at its centre. Its services include a summer-only shop and a *gîte* (☎04.76.44.62.55) which also does meals. There's no official **campsite**, but if you ask they'll direct you to a grassy place by the cemetery, where a traditional *glacière* – a stone-lined pit for storing snow for use as ice before the days of refrigerators – has been restored. Its chief advantage is as a base for visiting the **Cirque de Navacelles**, 10km north on the D25 past the beautiful ruined seventeenth-century sheep farm of *La Prunarède*. The cirque is a widening in the 150-metre deep trench of the Vis *gorges*, formed by a now dry loop in the river that has left a neat pyramid of rock sticking up in the middle like a wheel hub. An ancient and scarcely inhabited hamlet survives in the bottom – a bizarre phenomenon in an extraordinary location, and you get literally a bird's-eye view of it from the edge of the cliff above. Both road and GR7 go through. Continuing to Le Vigan via Montdardier, you pass a prehistoric **stone circle** on the left of the road, a silent and evocative place, especially in a close *causse* mist.

The Cévennes and Ardèche

The **Cévennes** mountains and River **Ardèche** form the southeastern defences of the Massif Central, overlooking the Rhône valley to the east and the Mediterranean littoral to the south. The bare upland landscapes of the inner or western edges are those of the central Massif. The outer edges, Mont Aigoual and its radiating valleys and the tributary valleys of the Ardèche, are distinctly Mediterranean: deep, dry, close and clothed in forests of sweet chestnut, oak and pine.

Remote and inaccessible country until well into the twentieth century, the region has bred rugged and independent inhabitants. For centuries it was the most resolute stronghold of Protestantism in France, and it was in these valleys that the persecuted Protestants put up their fiercest resistance to the tyranny of Louis XIV and Louis XV. In World War II, it was heavily committed to the Resistance, while in the aftermath of 1968, it became the promised land of the hippies – *zippies*, as the locals called them; they moved into the countless abandoned farms and hamlets, whose native inhabitants had been driven away by hardship and poverty. The odd hippy has stuck it out, true to the last to the alternative life. In more recent times, it has been colonized by Dutch and Germans.

The author Robert Louis Stevenson crossed it in 1878 with Modestine, a donkey he bought in Le Monastier-sur-Gazeille, near **Le Puy** and sold at journey's end in the former Protestant stronghold of **St-Jean-du-Gard**, a now-famous route described in *Travels with a Donkey* (see p.1209).

The Parc National des Cévennes

The **Parc National des Cévennes** was created in 1970 to protect and preserve the life, landscape, flora, fauna and architectural heritage of the Cévennes. North to south, it stretches from **Mende** on the Lot to **Le Vigan** and includes both **Mont Lozère** and **Mont Aigoual**. Access, to the periphery at least, is surprisingly easy, thanks to the Paris–Clermont–Alès–Nîmes train line and the Montpellier–Mende link.

Numerous walking routes crisscross the area: **GR 6**, **GR 7** and **GR 60** cross all or part of the range, and other paths complete various circuits. The **GR66** does the tour of Mont Aigoual in 78.5km, the **GR68** of Mont Lozère in 110km. Another good route is the 130-kilometre **Tour des Cévennes** on the **GR67**. If you do go off hiking, remember that these are proper mountains for all their southerly latitude. You need good hiking boots, warm and weatherproof clothing, emergency shelter, adequate food, maps and guidebooks. The current weather situation is obtainable on: ☎07.08.36.68.02 (Ardèche); ☎08.36.68.02.30 (Gard); and ☎08.36.68.02.48 (Lozère).

The **main information office** for the park is at Florac (see p.850). It publishes numerous leaflets on the flora, fauna and traditions of the park, plus activities and routes for walkers, cyclists, canoeists and horse riders. It also provides a list of **gîtes d'étape** in the park and can provide information for those following Stevenson's route, including where to hire a donkey. In July and August, it's wise to book ahead for accommodation; otherwise you could find yourself sleeping out.

Mende and Mont Lozère

Capital of the Lozère *département*, **MENDE** lies well down in the deep valley of the Lot at the northern tip of the Parc des Cévennes, and 40km north of Florac, with train and bus links to the Paris–Nîmes and Clermont–Millau lines. It's an attractive southern town, though much of its charm is lost in the newly commercialized streets of the city centre. What Mende lacks in authenticity it makes up for in practicality: it's a great place to purchase last-minute supplies before you head off to the mountains.

Standing against the haze of the mountain background, the town's main landmark, the **cathedral**, owes its construction to Pope Urban V, who was born locally and wished to give something back to his native soil. Although work began in 1369, progress was hampered by war and natural disasters and the building wasn't completed until the end of the nineteenth century. The most obvious signs of its patchy construction are the two unequal towers that frame the front entrance, from where there's a fine view back along the pine-clad Lot valley. Inside is a handsome choir, and, suspended from the clerestory, eight great Aubusson tapestries, depicting the life of the Virgin. She's also present in one of the side chapels of the choir in the form of a statue made from olive wood, thought to have been brought back from the Middle East during the crusades.

Aside from the cathedral, most pleasure resides in a quiet wander in the old town's minuscule squares and narrow medieval streets, with their houses bulging outwards, as though buckling under the weight of the upper storeys. In **rue Notre-Dame**, which separated the Christian from Jewish quarters in medieval times, the thirteenth-century house at no. 17 was once a synagogue. If you carry on down to the river, you'll see the medieval packhorse bridge, the **Pont Notre-Dame**, with its worn cobbles.

Practicalities

The **tourist office** is on place du Foirail located at the southern end of boulevard Henri-Bourrillon, the ring road that encircles the city centre (July & Aug Mon–Sat 9am–12.30pm & 2–7pm, Sun 10am–noon & 3–5pm; Sept–June Mon–Fri 9am–12.30pm & 2–6pm, Sat 9am–noon; ☎04.66.94.00.23, ⓦwww .ot-mende.fr). The **gare SNCF** (☎04.66.49.00.39) lies across the river, north of the centre. **Buses** depart from either the station or place du Foirail.

For a place to **stay**, the best choice is the *Lion d'Or* at 12–14 boulevard Britexte (☎04.66.49.16.46, ⓔlion-dor48@orange.fr; ❸), set in a beautiful, renovated old building and featuring an excellent *terroir* restaurant (from €18). Another good choice is the pretty *Hôtel de France* on boulevard Lucien-Arnault, the northern part of the inner ring road (☎04.66.65.00.04, ⓦwww.hotel defrance-mende.com; ❹; closed Dec & Jan; menu from €28). Slightly further out of town, on the river at 2 avenue du 11-Novembre, the classy *Hôtel Pont-Roupt* (☎04.66.65.01.43, ⓦwww.hotel-pont-roupt.com; ❹) offers such luxuries as an indoor pool, terrace and good restaurant; dishes include *truite au lard* and *salade au Roquefort* (menus €25–60). The best **restaurant** in town is *La Safranière* in Chabrits (☎04.66.49.31.54), which daringly blends *terroir* and *gastronomique* styles (menus €20–44). Another good choice is *Le Mazel* (☎04.66.65.05.33; closed Mon evening & Tues; from €14.50), though the setting – in the only modern square in the old town – is a little disappointing.

Mont Lozère

Mont Lozère is a windswept and desolate barrier of granite and yellow grassland, rising to 1699m at the summit of **Finiels**, still grazed by herds of cows, but in nothing like the numbers of bygone years when half the cattle in Languedoc came up here for their summer feed. Snowbound in winter and wild and dangerous in bad weather, it has claimed many a victim among lost travellers. In some of the squat granite hamlets on the northern slopes, like Servies, Auriac and Les Sagnes, you can still hear the bells, known as *clochers de tourmente*, that tolled in the wind to give travellers some sense of direction when the cloud was low.

If you're travelling by car from Mende, the way to the summit is via the village of **LE BLEYMARD**, about 30km to the east on the bank of the infant River Lot, with accommodation in the form of the comfortably rustic *Hôtel La Remise* (☎04.66.48.65.80, ⓦwww.hotel-laremise.com; ❷–❹; *terroir* restaurant from €16). From here, the D20 winds 7km up through the conifers to another country-style hotel/*gîte* and restaurant, the *Chalet-Hotel du Mont Lozère* (℡04.68.48.62.84, Ⓦwww.chaletdumontlozere.fr; ➊), where it's joined by the GR7, which has taken a more direct route from Le Bleymard. This is the route that Stevenson took, waymarked as the "Tracé Historique de Stevenson". Road and footpath run together as far as the **Col de Finiels**, where the GR7 strikes off on its own to the southeast. The source of the River Tarn is about 3km east of the col, the summit of Lozère 2km to the west. From the col, the road and Stevenson's route drop down in tandem, through the lonely hamlet of **FINIELS** to the pretty but touristy village of **LE PONT-DE-MONTVERT**.

At Le Pont, a seventeenth-century **bridge** crosses the Tarn by a stone tower that once served as a tollhouse. In this building in 1702, the Abbé du Chayla, a priest appointed by the Crown to reconvert the rebellious Protestants enraged by the revocation of the Edict of Nantes, set up a torture chamber to coerce the recalcitrant. Incensed by his brutality, a group of them under the leadership of one Esprit Séguier attacked and killed him on July 23. Reprisals were extreme; nearly 12,000 were executed, thus precipitating the Camisards' guerrilla war against the state (see p.776).

At the edge of the village, there's also an *écomusée* on the life and character of the region, the **Maison du Mont Lozère** (daily: April–May & Oct 3–6pm; June–Sept 10.30am–12.30pm & 2.30–6.30pm, Nov–March Sun only 3–6pm; €3.50). If you're tempted to **stay**, there's the small and atmospheric *Auberge des Cévennes* (℡04.66.45.80.01; ➊; closed mid-Nov to March; restaurant from €16.50), overlooking the bridge.

Florac and Mont Aigoual

Situated 39km south of Mende, **FLORAC** lies in the bottom of the trench-like valley of the Tarnon just short of its junction with the Tarn. Behind the village rises the steep wall that marks the edge of the Causse Méjean. When you get here, you will have already passed the frontier between the northern and Mediterranean landscapes; the dividing line seems to be the **Col de Montmirat** at the western end of Mont Lozère. Once you begin the descent, the scrub and steep gullies and the tiny abandoned hamlets, with their eyeless houses oriented towards the sun, speak clearly of the south.

The village, with some two thousand inhabitants, is strung out along the left bank of the Tarnon and the main street, **avenue Jean–Monestier**. There's little to see, though the close lanes of the village up towards the valley side have their charms, especially the plane-shaded **place du Souvenir**. It is worth visiting on a Thursday during summer for the **market**, when you'll find the tiny streets packed with merchants and local produce. A red-schist castle stands above the village, housing the **Centre d'Information du Parc National des Cévennes** (July & Aug daily 9am–6.30pm; Easter–Sept daily 9.30am–12.30pm & 1.30–6pm; Oct–Easter Mon–Fri 9.30am–12.30pm & 1.30–6pm; ℡04.66.49.53.01, Ⓦwww.pnc.fr). The **tourist office** is on avenue Jean-Monestier (Mon–Sat 9am–noon & 2–6pm; ℡04.66.45.01.14, Ⓦwww.mescevennes.com); they provide details on the year-round "Festival of Nature" programme, with guided treks around the national park. **Mountain bike rental** is available from Cévennes Evasion, in place Boyer (℡04.66.45.18.31).

The **accommodation** on offer is not fantastic. The best place is the *Grand Hôtel du Parc* on avenue Jean-Monestier (℡04.66.45.03.05, Ⓦwww.grand hotelduparc.fr; ➌; closed Dec–March; restaurant €15–36), with pleasant gardens and a pool. *Les Gorges du Tarn* at 48 rue de Pecheur (℡04.66.45.00.63, Ⓦwww.hotel-gorgesdutarn.com; ➋) is the most comfortable option, while

L'Esplanade, a restaurant in the middle of the Esplanade, has six simple rooms (☎04.66.47.45.15; ❶) and an economical restaurant (menus €9.50–16). The best-value **campsite** is the municipal one at Le Pont-du-Tarn out on the road towards Ispagnac (April to mid-Sept; ☎04.66.45.18.26,ⓦwww.causses -cevennes.com/erebuissonniere).

Florac's Esplanade is a good place to look for somewhere to **eat**, otherwise the *Adonis* restaurant in the *Les Gorges* hotel serves high-quality local cuisine (menus €17–55; closed Sun lunch), while another good choice is the riverside *La Source du Pêcher* at 1 rue de Rémuret in the old town (☎04.66.45.03.01; menus €15–35; closed Nov–Easter). **Internet** access can be found on rue du Pêcher at *Florac-Online* (Tues–Sat 9.30am–12.30pm & 3–7pm).

Mont Aigoual

It's 24km by road up the beautiful valley of the Tarnon to the **Col de Perjuret**, where a right turn will take you on to the **Causse Méjean** and to the strange rock formations of **Nîmes-le-Vieux**, and a left turn along a rising ridge a further 15km to the 1565-metre summit of **Mont Aigoual** (GR6, GR7, GR66). From the latter, it is said that you can see a third of France, from the Alps to the Pyrenees, with the Mediterranean coast from Marseille to Sète at your feet. It's not a craggy summit, although the ground drops away pretty steeply into the valley of the River Hérault on the south side, but the view and the sense of exposure to the elements is dramatic enough. At the summit is an **observatory** which has been in use for over a century. A small but interesting **exhibition** (May–Sept daily 10am–6pm; free) shows modern weather-forecasting techniques alongside displays of old barometers and weather vanes. The observatory also harbours a CAF refuge and *gîte d'étape* (☎04.67.82.62.78; closed Oct–April).

The descent to Le Vigan by the valley of the Hérault is superb; a magnificent twisty road follows the deepening ravine through dense beech and chestnut woods, to come out at the bottom in rather Italianate scenery, with tall, close-built villages and vineyards beside the stream. The closest accommodation to the summit is the *Hôtel du Touring* (☎04.67.82.60.04, ⓦwww.hotel-restaurant -touring.com; ❸; restaurant menus €11–21; closed April & Nov to mid-Dec) at **L'ESPÉROU**, a rather soulless mountain resort just below the summit. Better to go down to the charming village of **VALLERAUGUE**, with its brown-grey schist houses and leafy riverside setting. There are a number of hotels here, including the pleasantly sited *Les Bruyères* (☎&Ⓕ04.67.82.20.06; ❷; menus €16–35).

Le Vigan and the Huguenot strongholds

Only 64km from Montpellier and 18km from Ganges, **LE VIGAN** makes a good starting point for exploring the southern part of the Cévennes. It's a leafy, cool and thoroughly agreeable place, at its liveliest during the **Fête d'Isis** at the beginning of August and the colossal fair that takes over the Parc des Châtaigniers on September 9 and 22.

The prettiest part of the town is around the central **place du Quai**, shaded by lime trees and bordered by cafés and brasseries. From here it's only a two-minute walk south, down rue Pierre-Gorlier, to reach the gracefully arched **Pont Vieux**. Beside it stands the **Musée Cévenol** (April–Oct daily except Tues 10am–noon & 2–6pm; Nov–March Wed only 10am–noon & 2–6pm; €4.50), a well-presented look at traditional rural occupations in the area, including the woodcutter, butcher, shepherd and wolf-hunter. There's also a room devoted to the area's best-known twentieth-century writer, André Chamson, noted for his novels steeped in the traditions and countryside of the Cévennes. Interestingly, Coco Chanel also features in the museum: she had local family connections and it seems found inspiration for her designs in the *cévenol* silks.

The **tourist office** occupies a modern block in the centre of the place du Marché, at the opposite end of the place du Quai from the church (July & Aug Mon–Sat 8.30am–12.30pm & 1.30–7pm, Sun 10am–1pm; Sept–June Mon–Fri 9.30am–12.30pm & 2–6pm, Sat 8.30am–1pm; ☎04.67.81.01.72, ⓦwww .cevennes-meridionales.com). For somewhere to **stay**, try the simple but attractive *Hôtel du Commerce*, with its wisteria-covered balcony and little garden, at 26 rue des Barris (☎04.67.81.43.20, Ⓔsarreboubee.serge@orange.fr; ❶; closed mid-Oct to mid-Nov). The best alternative is a couple of kilometres out of town, south towards Montdardier on the D48: the handsome old *Auberge Cocagne* in the village of **AVÈZE** (☎04.67.81.02.70, ⓦwww.auberge-cocagne -cevennes.com; ❷; closed mid-Nov to mid-Feb; restaurant from €11). There is also a **campsite**, the well-shaded riverside Val de l'Arre (☎04.67.81.02.77, ⓦwww.valdelarre.com; closed Oct–March), 2km upriver from Le Vigan, on the opposite bank. One of the best places to eat in Le Vigan is *Le Jardin* (closed Mon), in place du Terral, just off the main square; menus start at €19 and feature French classics with a local twist, such as *filet mignon* with a chestnut sauce. From Le Vigan, or more particularly from the Pont de l'Hérault bridge, a beautiful lane (D153) slowly winds around 45km northeast through typical south Cévennes landscape – deep valleys thick with sweet chestnut and thinly peopled with isolated farms half-buried in greenery – from Sumène to St-Jean-du-Gard.

St-Jean-du-Gard and around

Thirty-two kilometres west of Alès, **ST-JEAN-DU-GARD** was the centre of Protestant resistance during the Camisard war in 1702–04 (see p.776). It straggles along the bank of the River Gardon, crossed by a graceful, arched, eighteenth-century bridge, with a number of picturesque old houses still surviving in the main street, **Grande-Rue**. One of them contains the splendid **Musée des Vallées Cévenoles** (April–Oct daily 10am–12.30pm & 2–7pm; July & Aug 10am–7pm; Nov–March Tues–Sat 9am–noon & 2–6pm, Sun 2–6pm; €4.50), a museum of local life with displays of tools, trades, furniture, clothes, domestic articles and a fascinating collection of pieces related to the silk industry. The work of spinning the silk was done by women in factories and lists of regulations and rules on display give some idea of the tough conditions in which they had to work.

The **tourist office** is just off the main street by the post office (July & Aug Mon & Wed–Fri 9am–1pm & 3–6pm, Tues & Sat 9am–7pm, Sun 10am–noon; Sept–June Mon–Fri 9am–12.30pm & 1.30–5pm, Sat 10am–12.30pm; ☎04.66.85.32.11, ⓦotsi.st.jeandugard.free.fr). They can advise you about the times of the **steam train** that operates between St-Jean and Anduze (April to early Sept daily; early Sept to Oct Tues–Sun; €12 return). There's a big **market** all along Grande-Rue on Tuesday mornings.

The best bet for **accommodation** is *Auberge du Peras* on route de Nîmes (☎04.66.85.35.94, ⓦwww.aubergeduperas.com; ❸; good restaurant from €11). There's a *gîte d'étape* 3km north on the D907 at **LE MOULINET**; contact Mme Laurtay on ☎04.66.85.10.98.

The Musée du Désert

Signposts at St-Jean direct you to the museum at **MAS SOUBEYRAN**, a minuscule hamlet of beautiful rough-stone houses in a gully above the village of Mialet, about 12km east. The **Musée du Désert** (daily: March–June & Sept–Nov 9.30am–noon & 2–6pm; July & Aug 9.30am–7pm; €4.50) is in the house that once belonged to Rolland, one of the Camisards' self-taught but most successful military leaders, and it remains much the same as it would have been in 1704, the year of his death. It catalogues the appalling sufferings and sheer dogged heroism of the Protestant Huguenots in defence of their freedom of conscience; and the "desert" they had to traverse between the Revocation of the Edict of Nantes in 1685 and the promulgation of the Edict of Tolerance in 1787, which restored their original rights (full emancipation came with the Declaration of the Rights of Man in the first heady months of the Revolution in 1789). During this period, they had no civil rights, unless they abjured their faith. They could not bury their dead, baptize their children or marry. Their ministers were forced into exile on pain of death. The recalcitrant were subjected to the infamous *dragonnades*, which involved the forcible billeting of troops on private homes at the expense of the occupants. As if this were not enough, the soldiers would beat their drums continuously for days and nights in people's bedrooms in order to deprive them of sleep. Protestants were also put to death or sent to the galleys for life and their houses were destroyed.

Not surprisingly, such brutality led to armed rebellion, inspired by the prophesying of the lay preachers who had replaced the banished priests, calling for a holy war. The rebels were hopelessly outnumbered and the revolt was ruthlessly put down in 1704 (see box, p.776). On display are documents, private letters and lists of those who died for their beliefs, including the names of five thousand who died as galley slaves (*galériens pour la foi*) and the women who were immured in the Tour de Constance prison in Aigues-Mortes. Also on show are the chains and rough uniform of a *galérien*.

Prafrance and the Mine Témoin

Twelve kilometres southeast of St-Jean in the direction of Anduze, **PRAFRANCE** is noteworthy for **La Bambouseraie** (March to mid-Nov daily 9.30am to closing time dependent on season and weather; €7.50), an extraordinary and appealing garden consisting exclusively of bamboos of all shapes and sizes; the project was started in 1855 by local entrepreneur Eugène Mazel. An easy way to get here is to take the steam train (see opposite) from St-Jean-du-Gard; it takes just ten minutes.

If you want to leave the area by main-line train, the place to head for is **ALÈS** on the Nîmes–Paris line. This was a major coal-mining centre, though 25,000 jobs have been lost and all but two open-cast pits closed in the last four decades. Today, it has a superb museum on the history and techniques of coal-mining, known as the **Mine Témoin**, in the underground workings of a disused mine on chemin de la Cité Ste-Marie in the Rochebelle district (French-only guided tours daily: June 10am–6.30pm; July & Aug 9am–7.30pm; Sept–May 9am–12.30pm & 2–5.30pm; €7.50; last visit 1hr 30min before closing).

Aubenas and the northern Cévennes

A small but prosperous and surprisingly industrial town of around twelve thousand, **AUBENAS** sits in the middle of the southern part of the Ardèche *département*, high up on a hill overlooking the middle valley of the River Ardèche. Located 91km southeast of Le Puy and 42km west of Montélimar, the town, with a character and non-tourist-dependent economy of its own, makes a much better base than overly crowded places further downstream around Vallon-Pont-d'Arc.

The central knot of streets with their cobbles and bridges, occupying the highest point of town around **place de l'Hôtel-de-Ville**, have great charm, particularly towards place de la Grenette and place 14-Juillet. Place de l'Hôtel-de-Ville is dominated by the eleventh-century **château**, from which the local *seigneurs* ruled the area right up until the Revolution (90-min guided tours: April–June & Sept Tues & Thurs–Sat 10.30am & 2pm; July & Aug daily 11am, 2pm & 5pm; Oct & Dec–March Tues, Thurs & Sat 2pm; closed on hols; €3.50). Other sights include the heavily restored thirteenth-century **St-Laurent church**, which has the curious seventeenth-century hexagonal **Dôme Bênoit chapel** (July & Aug Mon–Fri 5pm; €3.50). There's a magnificent view of the Ardèche snaking up the valley from under an arch beside the castle, as there is from the end of boulevard Gambetta 200m downhill, where the **tourist office** is located on the main square (July & Aug Mon–Sat 9am–12.30pm & 2–7pm, Sun 9am–1pm; Sept–June Mon–Sat 9am–noon & 2–6pm; ☎04.75.89.02.03, ⊛www.aubenasvals.com). To use the **internet** go to Espace Informatique at 10 boulevard Saint-Didier (Mon noon–7pm, Tues–Sat 10am–7pm).

For somewhere to **stay**, the budget choice is the *Hôtel Le Provence* on boulevard de Vernon (☎04.75.35.28.43, ⊛hotelleprovence.free.fr; ❶) which has clean simple rooms. At the top end of the scale the 5-room *La Bastide du Soleil* (☎04.75.36.91.66, ⊛www.bastidesoleil.com; ❻; closed Dec–Jan) offers a splendid blend of antique charm and modern convenience (restaurant menus €18–30). There are many campsites to choose from in between Aubenas and Vallon. Cafés and brasseries line boulevard de Vernon on the south side of town; the best place for both food and atmosphere is *Le Fournil*, 34 rue du 4-Septembre, set in a fifteenth-century house at the end of Béranger-de-la-Tour, in the heart of the old town (closed Sun & Mon; menus €21–39), or *Le Coyote*, 13 boulevard Jean-Mathon (☎04.75.35.01.28; menus from €17), whose specialities are fish and foie gras.

The Gorges de l'Ardèche

The **Gorges de l'Ardèche** begin at the **Pont d'Arc**, a very beautiful arch that the river has cut for itself through the limestone, just downstream from **VALLON**, itself 39km south of Aubenas. They continue for about 35km to **ST-MARTIN-D'ARDÈCHE** in the valley of the Rhône.

The fantastic gorges wind back and forth, much of the time dropping 300m straight down in the almost dead-flat scrubby Plateau des Gras. Unfortunately they are also an appalling tourist trap; the road following the rim, with spectacular viewpoints marked out at regular intervals, is jammed with traffic in summer. The river, down in the bottom, which is where you really want to be to appreciate the grandeur of the canyon, is likewise packed with canoes in high season. It is walkable, depending on the water level, but you would need to bivouac midway at either Gaud or Gournier. The problem with the gorges is that they are so popular. If you go in season, be prepared for heavy traffic, and book accommodation well ahead.

The plateau itself is riddled with caves. **Aven Marzal**, a stalactite cavern north of the gorge (daily 11.30am–5pm; €8.40, joint ticket with zoo €14.40), has a prehistoric **zoo**, which consists of reconstructions of dinosaurs and friends (Feb, March, Oct & Nov Sun & school holidays 10.30am–6pm; April–Sept daily

11.30am–5pm; €8.40), but the frequency of visits to the cave depends on the number of visitors waiting – they are approximately every twenty minutes in July and August, falling to four per day in other months. Best of the area's caves is the **Aven Orgnac**, to the south of the gorge (90-min tour daily: Feb, March, Nov & Dec holidays 10.30am–4.45pm; April, June & Sept 10am–5.30pm; July & Aug 10am–6.30pm; Oct 10am–5.15pm; €9.70), one of France's most spectacular and colourful stalactite formations. In addition to the normal tours, you can also opt for the "*visites spéléologiques*" hard-core caving tours; they last three and eight hours respectively (reserve two weeks ahead; ☎04.75.38.65.10). There's also a very good prehistory **museum** (daily: March–June & Sept to mid-Nov 10am–noon & 2–6pm; July & Aug 10am–6pm; €5, joint ticket with Aven Orgnac €9.70).

Further upstream near Vallon-Pont-d'Arc, a complex series of cave paintings was discovered in December 1994, after being left untouched for 30,000 years, making the **Chauvet-Pont d'Arc** cave the oldest-known decorated cave in the world (closed to public). However, there is a small but rewarding **exhibition** on the cave complex at Vallon, behind the *mairie*. The highlight is a video taken inside the caves, showing many of the paintings close up (Tues–Sun: mid-March to May & Sept to mid-Nov 10am–noon & 2–5.30pm; June–Aug 10am–1pm & 3–7pm; €5).

Practicalities

Accommodation in the area can be a problem during the high season. By far the best is *Le Manoir du Raveyron*, rue Henri-Barbusse (☎04.75.88.03.59, ✉le .manoir.du.raveyron@orange.fr; ❹–❼; closed Oct to mid-March), with a good restaurant from €20, while another good option is the *Hôtel du Tourisme*, on rue du Miarou in Vallon (☎04.75.88.02.12, ⓦwww.hotel-tourisme-pont -darc.com; closed Dec–Feb; ❹). The river is lined with **campsites**, the cheapest being the municipal one (☎04.75.88.04.73, ⓦwww.municipalvallon.com; closed Oct–March). There's a **gîte d'étape** on place de la Mairie (☎04.75.88.07.87, ⓦwww.escapade-loisirs.com), and a **tourist office** on the south side of town (April & Oct Mon–Sat 9am–noon & 2–5pm, Sat closed at 4pm; May, June & Sept Mon–Sat 9am–noon & 2–6pm, Sat closed at 5pm, Sun 9.30am–12.30pm; July & Aug Mon–Sat 9am–1pm & 3–7pm, Sun 9.30am–12.30pm; Nov–March Mon–Fri 9am–noon & 2–5pm, Sat 9am–noon; ☎04.75.88.04.01, ⓦwww.vallon-pont-darc.com).

The valley of the Chassezac and the Corniche du Vivarais

Between Aubenas and Les Vans, 27km to the southwest, several wild mountain streams flow out of the northern part of the Cévennes to join the Ardèche. One of the most beautiful is the **Chassezac**, which rises north of Villefort and carves a dry, twisting ravine covered with pine, bracken and sweet chestnut down to **LES VANS**.

The centre of the town is occupied by the wide and cheerful **place Léopold-Ollier**. Nearby you'll find the comfortable *Viverais* (☎04.75.37.22.73, ⓦwww .le-vivarais-hotel.com; ❶; closed mid-Sept to April), which has a *terroir* restaurant (menus €14) and offers full *pensions*. Worth seeking out, however, is the beautifully renovated former convent, *Le Carmel*, at 7 montée Carmel (☎04.75.94.99.60, ⓦwww.le-carmel.com; ❹; closed mid-Dec to Feb), home to one of the area's best restaurants (€25). You must book either place well in advance in high season. Other attractions are the remains of the old town and, just outside, the bizarre rock formations of the **Bois de Paiolive**. There's a **gîte d'étape** across the river at Chambonas (☎04.75.37.24.99).

Le Puy-en-Velay and the northeast

Right in the middle of the Massif Central, 78km from St-Étienne and 132km from Clermont, **LE PUY-EN-VELAY**, often shortened to Le Puy, is one of the most remarkable towns in the whole of France, with a landscape and archi-tecture that are totally theatrical. Slung between the higher mountains to east and west, the countryside erupts in a chaos of volcanic acne: everywhere is a confusion of abrupt conical hills, scarred with dark outcrops of rock and topknotted with woods. Even in the centre of the town, these volcanic thrusts burst through.

In the past, Le Puy enjoyed influence and prosperity because of its ecclesiastical institutions, which were supported in part by the production of the town's famous green lentils. It was – and in a limited way, still is – a centre for pilgrims embarking on the 1600-kilometre trek to Santiago de Compostela. The specific starting point is place du Plot (also the scene of a lively Saturday market) and rue St-Jacques. History has it that Le Puy's Bishop Godescalk, in the tenth century,

was the first pilgrim to make the journey. During the Wars of Religion the town managed to resist the Protestant fervour of much of the Massif Central. Recently, however, it has fallen somewhat on hard times, and its traditional industries – tanning and lace – have essentially gone bust. Even today Le Puy is somewhat inaccessible for the capital of a *département*: the three main roads out all cross passes more than 1000m high, which causes problems in winter.

Arrival and information

If you arrive at the **gare SNCF** or **gare routière** (T04.71.09.25.60), facing each other in place Maréchal-Leclerc, you'll find yourself barely a ten-minute walk from the central place du Clauzel and the **tourist office** (Easter–June & Sept–Oct Mon–Sat 8.30am–noon & 1.30–6.15pm, Sun 9am–noon & 2–6pm; July & Aug daily 8.30am–7.30pm; Nov–Easter Mon–Sat 8.30am–noon & 1.30–6.15pm, Sun 10am–noon; T04.71.09.38.41, Wwww.ot-lepuyenvelay.fr). The town hall at 1 place Monsiegneur de Galard is home to the **Comité Départemental du Tourisme** (June–Aug Mon–Sat 8.30am–7.30pm, Sun 9am–noon & 2–6pm; Sept–May Mon–Sat 8.30am–noon & 2–6pm; T04.71.07.41.54, Wwww.mididelauvergne.com). Here you'll find information useful for venturing into the countryside. There are quite a few places to access the **internet**, the best option being *Cyb'Aire* at 17 rue Général-Lafayette (Mon–Thurs 9am–9pm, Fri–Sat 9am–midnight, Sun 3–7pm).

Accommodation

Le Puy doesn't have a superabundance of **hotels**, so it's wise to book ahead in peak season. The budget options include the very well-equipped *Dyke Hôtel*, at no. 37 (T04.71.09.05.30, Wwww.dykehotel.fr; ❶), and the basic *Régional*, at no. 36 (T04.71.09.37.74, F04.71.02.47.50; ❶), both on boulevard Maréchal-Fayolle, the main boulevard connecting the station and place du Clauzel. On the same street but more luxurious is *Regina*, the renovated old mansion at no. 34 (T04.71.09.14.71, Wwww.hotelrestregina.com; ❸–❻; restaurant €16.50–56.50). Best of all is ⚑ *Le Bristol*, 7 avenue Foch (T04.71.09.13.38, Wwww .hotelbristol-lepuy.com; ❷), set in one of the area's oldest buildings, a former pilgrim's hostel, with a restaurant offering an excellent regional set menu from €11. For those on a tight budget, there's a good **HI hostel**, the attractive *Centre Pierre-Cardinal* at 9 rue Jules-Vallès (T04.71.05.52.40, Wwww.mairie-le-puy -en-velay.fr; closed weekends Oct–March), just off rue Lafayette, in the heart of the old town. **Campers** should head for the municipal *Camping d'Audinet* (April–Sept; T04.71.09.10.18, Wwww.brives-charensac.fr), near the River Loire in the northeast corner of town.

The Town

It would be hard to lose your bearings in Le Puy, for wherever you go there's no losing sight of the colossal, brick-red statue of the Virgin and Child that towers above the town on the **Rocher Corneille**, 755m above sea level and 130 abrupt metres above the lower town. The Virgin is cast from 213 guns captured at Sebastopol and painted red to match the tiled roofs below. You can climb up to the statue's base and, irreverent though it may seem, even up inside it (daily: mid-March to April 9am–6pm; May–June & Sept 9am–7pm; July & Aug 9am–7.30pm; Oct to mid-March 10am–5pm; €3). From here you get stunning views of the city, the church of St-Michel atop its needle-pointed pinnacle a few hundred metres northwest, and the surrounding volcanic countryside.

▲ Le Puy-en-Velay

In the maze of steep cobbled streets and steps that terrace the Rocher, lace-makers – a traditional, though now commercialized, industry – do a fine trade, with doilies and lace shawls hanging enticingly outside souvenir shops. The main focus here, in the **old town**, is the Byzantine-looking **Cathédrale Notre-Dame-de-France**, begun in the eleventh century and decorated with multi-coloured layers of stone and mosaic patterns and roofed with a line of six domes. It's best approached up the rue des Tables, where you get the full theatrical force of its five-storeyed west front towering above you. In the rather exotic eastern gloom of the interior, a black-faced Virgin in spreading lace and golden robes stands on the main altar, the copy of a revered original destroyed during the Revolution; the copy is still paraded through the town every August 15. Other lesser treasures are displayed at the back of the church in the sacristy, beyond which is the entrance to the exceptionally beautiful eleventh- and twelfth-century **cloister** (daily: June & Sept 9am–noon & 2–6.30pm; July & Aug 9am–6.30pm; Oct–March 9am–noon & 2–5pm; €5), with its carved capitals, cornices and magnificent views of the cathedral and the towering Virgin and Child overhead. The passageway to the cloisters takes you past the so-called **Fever Stone**, whose origins may have been as a prehistoric dolmen and which was reputed to have the power of curing fevers. The surrounding ecclesiastical buildings and the **place du For**, on the south side of the cathedral, all date from the same period and form a remarkable ensemble.

It's a ten-minute walk from the cathedral to the **church of St-Michel** (signposts lead the way), perched atop the 82-metre needle-pointed lava pinnacle of the **Rocher d'Aiguilhe**. The little Romanesque church, built on Bishop Godescalk's return from his pilgrimage and consecrated in 962, is a beauty in its own right, and its improbable situation atop this striking pinnacle of rock is quite extraordinary – it's a long haul up 265 steps to the entrance (daily: Feb to mid-March 2–5pm; mid-March to April & Oct to mid-Nov 9.30am–noon & 2–5.30pm; May–Sept 9am–6.30pm; €2.75).

The new town and Pagès Verveine distillery

In the new part of town, beyond the squat **Tour Pannessac**, which is all that remains of the city walls, **place de Breuil** joins **place Michelet** and forms a social hub backed by the spacious Henri Vinay public gardens, where the **Musée Crozatier** (10am–noon & 2–6pm: May to mid-June & late Sept Wed–Mon; mid-June to mid-Sept daily; mid-Sept to Apr closed Tues & Sun am; free) is best known for its collections relating to the region's traditional lace-making activities. Busy boulevard Maréchal-Fayolle converges with place Cadelade, where there's another of Le Puy's crazier aspects: the extraordinary bulbous tower of what used to be the **Pagès Verveine distillery**. The *verveine* (verbena) plant is normally used to make *tisane* (herb tea), but in this region provides a vivid green, powerful digestive liqueur instead.

Eating and drinking

For a city its size, Le Puy has an impressive array of fine yet economical **restaurants**, so there is little need to resort to the row of anonymous brasseries on the main street. The best of the eateries is the creative cuisine of the ⚜ *François Gagnaire Restaurant* at 4 avenue Charbonnier (☎04.71.02.75.55, Ⓦ www.francois -gagnaire-restaurant.com; closed Sun evening. Mon and Tues lunch, July & Aug closed Sun, Mon, Tues lunch; menus €25–90); try the *Saint-Jacques* with green lentils. Other good choices include *Restaurant Tournayre*, set in a seventeenth-century building at 12 rue Chènebouterie (☎04.71.09.58.94; closed Sun & Wed evening. Mon & Jan), specializing in the regional fare (menus €21–65), and the *gastronomique Lapierre* at 6 rue Capucins (☎04.71.09.08.44; closed Dec & Jan, Sun out of season & Sat) with menus from €20. For salads and crêpes, *Le Croco* on 5 rue Chaussade is a local favourite (closed Sun, menus from €13).

For a **drink** or light snack, the terrace of *Le Petit Gourmande*, at the bottom of rue des Tables, makes a pleasant stop in summer (closed Wed; *galettes* for €5, à la carte from €13). Though lacking atmosphere, the large *La Distillerie* pub on place du Breuil has an impressive selection of regional speciality beers and liqueurs. *Le Bistrot* at 7 place de la Halle is a lively place for an evening drink. Try the local green lentil beer which is available in many of Le Puy's pubs.

North of Le Puy

North of Le Puy, the D906 crosses a vast and terminally depopulated area of pine-clad uplands – now the Parc Naturel Régional Livradois-Forez – and continues all the way to Vichy, via the historic town of **La Chaise-Dieu** and the old industrial centres of **Ambert** and **Thiers**.

La Chaise-Dieu

After 42km you come to the little town of **LA CHAISE-DIEU**, renowned for the **abbey church of St-Robert** (daily: June & mid-Aug to Sept 9am–noon & 2–6/7pm; July to mid-Aug 9am–7pm; Oct–May 10am–noon & 2–5pm; €3.70), whose square towers dominate the town. Founded in 1044 and restored in the fourteenth century at the expense of Pope Clement VI, who had served as a monk here, the church was destroyed by the Huguenots in 1562, burnt down in 1692, and remained unfinished when the Revolution brought a wave of anticlericalism. It was only really finished in the twentieth century. Its interior contains the tomb of Clement VI, some magnificent Flemish tapestries of Old and New Testament scenes hanging in the choir, which also boasts some fine Gothic stalls, and a celebrated fresco of the **Danse Macabre**, depicting Death plucking at the coarse plump bodies of 23 living figures, representing the different classes of society. "It is yourself", says the fifteenth-century text below, as indeed it might easily have been in an age when plague and war were rife.

Nearby on the place de l'Echo, the **Salle de l'Echo** (10am–6pm, until 5pm Nov–April; free) is another product of the risk of contagion – if not from plague, then from leprosy. For in this room, once used for hearing confession from the sick and dying, two people can turn their backs on each other, stand in opposite corners and still have a perfectly audible conversation just by whispering.

A **classical music festival** takes place here in late August and early September, details of which are available from the **tourist office**, on place de la Mairie (Easter–June & Sept Tues–Sun 10am–noon & 2–6pm; July & Aug daily 9am–12.30pm & 1.30–7pm; Oct–March Tues–Sat 10am–noon & 2–6pm; ⓣ04.71.00.01.16, ⓦwww.la-chaise-dieu.info). The *Hôtel Monastère et Terminus*, on avenue de la Gare (ⓣ04.71.00.00.73, ⓦwww.hmt43.com; ❷; closed Nov–March; menus at €15–19), and *De La Casadei*, in place l'Abbaye (ⓣ04.71.00.00.58; ❹; restaurant from €17), offer reasonable comfort for a night's stay. There's also a municipal **campsite**, *Les Parades*, on the Vichy side of the D906 (ⓣ04.71.00.07.88; closed Oct–May).

Ambert

Twenty-five kilometres north of La Chaise-Dieu, the little town of **AMBERT** was, from the fourteenth to eighteenth centuries, the centre of papermaking in France. It especially supplied the printers of Lyon, a connection that brought the region into contact with new ideas, in particular the revolutionary teachings of the Reformed Church. Although those small-scale operations have long since been sidelined, there is still a **paper mill** in operation at Richard-de-Bas just east of the town, with its **Musée Historique du Papier** (daily: July & Aug 9.30am–7pm; Sept–June 9.30am–12.30pm & 2–6pm; €6.50), featuring exhibits and explanations from papyrus to handmade samples from medieval days. In the town itself, there's a small **museum** (July & Aug daily 9am–noon & 2–7pm; Sept–June Tues & Thurs–Sat 9am–noon & 2.30–7pm; €4) devoted to the manufacture of the soft blue Fourme d'Ambert cheese, the region's speciality. An old diesel *train panoramique* runs between Ambert and **Sembadel** stopping at La Chaise-Dieu on the way (€14 return); a leisurely way to see the region. There is also an authentic steam train named "Picasso" that will take you from Ambert to **Olliergues** (€12 return).

East of Le Puy

East of Le Puy lies the barrier of the mountains of the Vivarais, rounded and wooded with beech, pine and fir, interspersed with open cow pastures. The highest points are the **Gerbier de Jonc** (1551m) and **Mont Mézenc** (1753m), with long views west across the whole of the Massif Central.

The Gerbier is a curious wooded mound rising out of the otherwise flattish surrounding uplands, about 50km southeast of Le Puy, with the River Loire rising on its upper slopes – home to a bucolic and still-isolated countryside. To get out there, take the D535 through **MONASTIER-SUR-GAZEILLE**, where R.L. Stevenson bought his donkey and started his famous journey. Although the village is pretty, with a particularly lovely church, there's something forlorn and unfriendly about it. The rather bleak *Hôtel Le Provence* above the village would do for a night's stay (ⓣ04.71.03.82.37, ⓦwww .le-provence.com; ❷; restaurant €12–25). The riverside municipal **campsite** (May–Sept; ⓣ04.71.03.82.24) and **gîte d'étape** (ⓣ04.71.03.84.74) are more welcoming. From here, thirty kilometres of winding lanes lead to the summit itself.

St-Étienne

ST-ÉTIENNE, 78km northeast of Le Puy, was until recently a particularly bland town. Almost unrelievedly industrial, it was a major armaments manufacturer, enclosed for kilometres around by mineworkings, warehouses and factory chimneys. Like so many other industrial centres, it fell on hard times, and the demolition gangs have moved in to raze its archaic industrial past. Only in recent years has an equilibrium been restored thanks to a concerted programme to revitalize the town.

The centre is now quite cheerful, buoyed by a collection of small new museums, the best of which is the **Musée d'Art Moderne** at La Terrasse (La Terrasse station is served by frequent trains from St-Étienne's central station, Châteaucreux), in the north of the city (Wed–Mon 10am–6pm; €4.70). This justifies a detour for anyone with an interest in twentieth-century art – a quite unexpected treasure house of contemporary work, both pre- and post-World War II, with a good modern American section, in which Andy Warhol and Frank Stella figure prominently, along with work by Rodin, Matisse, Léger and Ernst, and rooms filled entirely with French art, imaginatively laid out to exciting effect. The **Musée d'Art et d'Industrie**, 2 place Louis-Comte, is also good on St-Étienne's industrial background, including the development of the revolutionary Jacquard loom, and an impressive exhibition of arms and armour (Wed–Mon 10am–6pm, closed on Mon 12.30–2.30pm; €4.50).

St-Étienne's small airport (T 04.77.55.71.71, W www.saint-etienne.aeroport .fr) is mainly used for internal flights to and from Paris. The **tourist office** on 16 avenue de la Liberation (Mon–Fri 9am–1pm & 2–6/7pm, Sun 9am–noon; T 08.92.70.05.42, W www.tourisme-st-etienne.com) is around ten-minutes' walk from Châteaucreux train station along avenue D.-Rochereau. If you decide to stay, try *Hôtel de la Tour*, 1 rue Mercière (T 04.77.32.28.48, W hoteldelatour.fr; ❶), *Le Cheval Noir*, 11 rue François-Gillet (T 04.77.33.41.72, W www.hotel-chevalnoir .com; ❶) or *Hôtel Terminus du Forez*, 29–31 avenue D.-Rochereau (T 04.77.32.48.47, W www.hotel-terminusforez.com; ❸). For a truly fine meal dine at *La Bouche Pleine* at 2 place Chavanelle (T 04.77.33.92.47; closed Sat & Sun in Aug; menus from €20).

Travel details

Trains

Alès to: Nîmes (6–9 daily; 35min); Villefort (6–8 daily; 1hr).
Aurillac to: Brive (4 daily; 1hr 40min); Le Lioran (3–5 daily; 40min); Murat (3–5 daily; 50min); Neussargues (3–5 daily; 1hr); Toulouse (3–7 daily; 2hr 40min); Vic-sur-Cère (3–5 daily; 15min).
Clermont-Ferrand to: Aurillac (4–6 daily; 2hr 30min–5hr); Béziers (3 daily; 6–7hr); Brive (3 daily; 3hr 40min); La Bourboule (4 daily; 1hr 20min); Le Lioran (3–4 daily; 2–4hr); Le Mont-Dore (4 daily; 1hr 30min); Limoges (4 daily; 3hr 30min–4hr); Lyon (12–18 daily; 2hr 45min–3hr 30min); Marvejols (4 daily; 2hr 15min–3hr); Millau (1 daily; 4hr 15min); Murat (5–7 daily; 1hr 40min); Neussargues (12–14 daily; 1hr 30min–3hr 30min); Nîmes (12–16 daily;

5–6hr); Paris (5–10 daily; 2–5hr); Riom (12–14 daily; 10min); St-Étienne (2–3 daily; 2hr 10min); St-Flour (4 daily; 1hr 20min–2hr); Thiers (6 daily; 35min); Vic-sur-Cère (5–7 daily; 2hr 15min); Vichy (12–14 daily; 40min); Volvic (5 daily; 24min).
Le Puy to: St-Étienne (8 daily; 1hr 20min).
Mende to: La Bastide-Puylaurent (2–3 daily; 50min); Marvejols (3–5 daily; 40min); Montpellier (16–20 daily; 3hr–4hr 30min); Nîmes (16–20 daily; 2hr 30min–4hr); St-Flour (1–2 daily; 1hr 40min).
Millau to: Aumont-Aubrac (4 daily; 1hr 30min); Béziers (3 daily; 2hr); Marvejols (5 daily; 1hr 10min); Paris (2 daily direct; 8hr–9hr 30min).
Rodez to: Millau (7 daily; 1hr 10min–2hr 30min).
St-Étienne to: Clermont-Ferrand (3–6 daily; 2hr 40min); Lyon (3 daily; 45min); Paris (3 daily; 2hr 50min); St-Germain-des-Fosses (2 daily; 3hr).

St-Flour to: Neussargues (2–3 daily; 25min).

Vichy to: Clermont-Ferrand (12–14 daily; 40min); Nîmes (12–16 daily; 7–9hr); Paris (4 daily; 3hr 30min).

Buses

Ambert to: St-Étienne (1 daily; 2hr).

Aubenas to: Alès (2–3 daily; 2hr 10min); Entraygues (1–4 daily; 1hr); Les Vans (4 daily; 1hr 10min); Valence (7 daily; 2hr); Vallon-Pont-d'Arc (1–2 daily; 45min).

Aurillac to: Brommat, changing at Mur-de-Barrez (3 weekly; 2hr); Carlat (3–4 daily; 30min); Entraygues (1 daily; 1hr 30min); Mandailles (1 daily; 1hr 20min); Murat (1 daily; 1hr 40min); St-Flour (1 daily; 2hr 10min); Super-Lioran (1 daily; 1hr 20min); Vic-sur-Cère (2–3 daily; 40min).

Clermont-Ferrand to: Ambert (1–2 daily; 1hr 40min); Aydat (1–2 daily; 40min); Besse (July & Aug 2 daily; 1hr 35min); La Chaise-Dieu (1 Mon; 2hr); Le Puy (1 daily; 2hr 15min); Lyon (daily; 4hr); Mauriac (1–2 daily; 2hr 45min); Moulins (4 daily; 2hr 30min); Murol (July & Aug 2 daily; 1hr 10min); Riom (2 daily; 40min); St-Flour (2 weekly; 2hr); St-Nectaire (July & Aug 2 daily; 1hr); Superbesse (July & Aug 2 daily; 1hr 45min); Thiers (several daily; 1hr); Vichy (5 daily; 1hr 45min).

Conques to: Entraygues (June & Sept Tues, July & Aug Tues, Thurs & Sat 1 daily; 35min); Espalion (June & Sept Tues, July & Aug Tues, Thurs & Sat 1 daily; 1hr 20min); Najac (June & Sept Tues, July & Aug Tues & Fri 1 daily; 2hr 30min); St-Geniez-d'Olt (June & Sept Tues, July & Aug Tues, Thurs & Sat 1 daily; 2hr 15min).

La Bourboule to: Le Mont-Dore (3–5 daily; 10min); Le Sancy (3–5 daily; 35min).

Le Puy to: Aubenas (2 weekly; 3hr 15min); Clermont-Ferrand (1 daily; 3hr); La Chaise-Dieu (2 daily; 1hr); St-Étienne (4 daily; 2hr 10min).

Le Vigan to: Ganges (1–6 daily; 25min); Montpellier (3 daily; 2hr); Nîmes (3–5 daily; 1hr 50min); Valleraugue (July & Aug 1 daily; 30min).

Mende to: Le Puy (2 daily; 2hr); Marvejols (3 daily; 50min); St-Chély (1 daily; 1hr 10min); St-Étienne (1 daily; 3hr).

Millau to: Aven Armand (July & Aug daily; 1hr 45min); Le Caylar (2–6 daily; 40min); Le Rozier (1–4 daily; 40min); Montpellier (3–8 daily; 2hr 20min); Rodez (4 daily; 1hr 30min); Roquefort (July & Aug 3 weekly; 30min); St-Affrique (3–6 daily; 45min); Ste-Énimie (July & Aug daily; 2hr 25min); Toulouse (2 daily; 4hr).

Neussargues to: Allanche (2–3 daily; 20min); Condat (2–3 daily; 30min); Riom-ès-Montagnes (2–3 daily; 1hr 15min); St-Flour (2 daily; 30min).

Riom to: Volvic (4–8 daily; 25min).

Rodez to: Albi (3 daily; 2hr); Conques (1 daily; 1hr); Entraygues (1–2 daily; 2hr); Espalion (3–4 daily; 45min); Laguiole (1 daily; 1hr 45min); Le Caylar (1–4 daily; 2hr 40min); Mende (1 daily; 3hr 30min); Millau (3–8 daily; 1hr 40min); Montauban (1 daily; 3hr 15min); Montpellier (1–4 daily; 3hr 55min); Mur-de-Barrez (1 daily; 2hr 45min); Sauveterre-de-Rouergue (5 weekly; 55min); Séverac-le-Château (several daily; 45min); Toulouse (2–4 daily; 3hr 30min); Villefranche-de-Rouergue (1–2 daily; 1hr 30min).

St-Chély-d'Aubrac to: Espalion (1 daily; 30min).

St-Flour to: Laguiole (Tues, Thurs & Sat 1 daily; 3hr).

St-Martin-d'Ardèche to: Avignon (1 daily; 1hr 40min); Pont St-Esprit (2 daily; 15min); Vallon-Pont-d'Arc (2 daily; 1hr 10min).

Vichy to: Ambert (4 daily; 2hr 10min); La Chaise-Dieu (daily; 2hr 45min); Thiers (several daily; 40min).

Villefranche-de-Rouergue to: Conques (July & Aug Tues & Fri 1 daily; 2hr); Najac (July & Aug Tues & Fri 1 daily; 30min).

The Alps and Franche-Comté

CHAPTER 13

Highlights

* **Chartreuse** Indulge in this famous green liquer known as "the elixir of life" made by the Carthusian monks since since the seventeenth century. See p.875

* **Skiing and snowboarding** Test your skills from December to April in the world-class resorts of Chamonix, Méribel and Val d'Isère. See p.877

* **Parc Naturel Régional du Queyras** Walk or drive through the empty mountain landscapes of the Queyras to St-Véran, one of the highest villages in Europe. See p.882

* **Annecy** Admire the beauty of Annecy's fairy-tale location beside the Lac d'Annecy and in the midst of spectacular mountains. See p.895

* **Aiguille du Midi** Brave one of the world's highest cable-car ascents for a spectacular view of Mont Blanc, the highest peak in Europe. See p.903

* **Lake Geneva** Enjoy the sedate pleasures of spa towns like Évian on the French side of this huge and beautiful lake, or hop on one of the frequent ferries to Switzerland. See p.909

* **Besançon** Explore the imposing Citadelle, the well-preserved Roman ruins and the inviting cafés of the capital of Franche-Comté. See p.913

▲ Chamonix

The Alps and Franche-Comté

Far, far above, piercing the infinite sky,
Mont Blanc appears – still, snowy, and serene –
Its subject mountains their unearthly forms
Pile around it, ice and rock; broad vales between
Of frozen floods, unfathomable deeps,
Blue as the overhanging heaven...

Percy Bysshe Shelley, *Lines written in the Vale of Chamouni* (1817)

These lines were written by Shelley less than fifty years after Mont Blanc, the highest peak in Europe at 4807 metres, had first been successfully climbed, and they reflect the "unfathomable" and yet still "serene" qualities of the French Alps which have fascinated travellers in both Shelley's age and our own.

The present appearance of the Alps is the result of both the collision of continental tectonic plates over tens of millions of years, and the eroding actions of multiple glaciers and fast-flowing rivers. The mountain range contains some of Europe's most stunning mountain landscapes and picturesque rural settlements, while also providing plenty of fun outdoor pursuits. Although you have to walk a long distance or, in winter, ski (see p.877) to see the more remote parts of these landscapes, there are also many beautiful routes open to car-drivers and cyclists. Perhaps the most famous is the **Route des Grandes Alpes**, which crosses all the major mountain massifs from Thonon-les-Bains on Lake Geneva to Menton on the Mediterranean Sea.

The region of Franche-Comté to the north is often bypassed by tourists, but the mountains, forests and pastures which you will find here are beautifully tranquil, and nestled among them are some of the prettiest villages in the country. One great way to explore this region is through walking on the **GR** (Grande Randonnée) footpaths, the network of long-distance trails that connect France with its European neighbours. Notable paths which pass through Franche-Comté include the marathon GR5 from the Netherlands to the Mediterranean, and the GR9, which snakes its way through the Parc Régional du Haut-Jura.

With regard to **transport**, the more remote areas of the Alps and Jura **are difficult to reach without a car**, but are best explored once you're there on foot or by bicycle. Nonetheless, there are frequent trains between the

Langres

N19

Combeaufontaine

Vesoul
N19   Lure

Mulhouse

Belfort

Basel

FRANCHE-COMTÉ

Gray

Dijon

Besançon

Doubs

Dole

Beaune

Ornans

la Chaux-
de-Fonds

Villers-
le-Lac

Neuchâtel

BERN

Chalon-
sur-Saône

R Love

Levier

Pontarlier

Lac de Neuchâtel

Arbois

Poligny

Château
de Joux

Lons-le-
Saunier

Château
Chalon

Champagnole

Cascades
du Hérisson

St-Laurent

Clairvaux-
les-Lacs

Morez

SWITZERLAND

Lausanne

St-Claude

Col de la
Faucille

Lake Geneva (Lac Leman)

PARC
HAUT JURA

Gex

Yvoire

Evian-
les-Bains

St-Gingolph

Sion

Rhône

Bourg-
en-Bresse

Oyonnax

Nantua

Annemasse

Geneva

Thonon-
les-Bains

Abondance

Morzine

Samoëns

Sixt

Martigny

Cluses

Flaine

le Buet

la Roche-
sur-Foron

SAVOIE

Gorges
du Fier

Annecy   La Clusaz

St-Gervais

Chamonix

Mont Blanc
Tunnel

Lyon

Menthon-St-Bernard

Crêt de Châtillon

Talloires   Megève

Courmayeur

Abbaye de
Hautcombe

Duingt

Lac d'Annecy

Doussard

Ugine

Mont Blanc
(4807m)

Aosta

Aix-les-Bains

Lac du
Bourget

Mt Revard

PARC DES
BAUGES

Albertville

Petit
St-Bernard

Séez

Chambéry

Aime

Bourg St-Maurice

PARC DE
CHARTREUSE

Grande Chartreuse
Monastery

la Plagne

Moûtiers

Tignes

Val d'Isère

St-Pierre-de-Chartreuse

Voiron

MASSIF DE
LA
CHARTREUSE

Méribel

PARC DE
LA VANOISE

Col d'Iseran

Bonneval-sur-Arc

Lanslebourg

Bessans

Grenoble

St-Michel

Modane

ITALY

Lans-en-Vercors

Pic Blanc
(3330m)

Col de
Galibier

Valloire

Fréjus
Tunnel

Villard-
de-Lans

l'Alpe-
d'Huez

la Grave

Col du
Lautaret

le Bourg-
d'Oisans

Névache

Turin

Valence

les Deux-Alpes

le-Monêtier-
les-Bains

Serre Chevalier

PARC
VERCORS

Mt Pelvoux
(3946m)

Col de Montgenèvre

Briançon

Col d'Izoard

Col de Rousset

Châtillon-
en-Diois

Die

PARC
DES
ECRINS

Vallouise

Argentière

l'Échalp

Château Ville-Vieille

DAUPHINÉ

Mont Dauphin

St-Véran

PARC DU
QUEYRAS

Lac de
Serre-Ponçon

Guillestre

0   25 km

Gap

Embrun

Savines-le-Lac

Durance

**THE ALPS &
FRANCHE-COMTÉ**

N

THE ALPS AND FRANCHE-COMTÉ

St-Étienne

Milan

Milan

13

major towns and resorts, while during the skiing season of December–April and the summer months of July and August, more bus services become available. Car-drivers should remember that some high passes in the east of the region, including the Col du Galibier and the Col de l'Iseran, can remain closed well into June. This can force you to make long detours into Italy via expensive Alpine tunnels. As for accommodation, the **hotels** are often seasonal (closed in late spring and late autumn) and over-priced; it's always worth booking ahead to get the best deals and nicest spots. If you're on a budget, then campsites provide the cheapest and most numerous places to stay, although there are also hostels and *refuges* (huts) for those who don't want to carry camping equipment.

The **towns** in the Alps and Franche-Comté offer an excellent base to explore the surrounding countryside, but they also have many notable attractions of their own. Grenoble, the economic capital of the Alps, has a vibrant nightlife and lively cultural scene; **Annecy** is a town whose picturesque streets match the beauty of its lakeside setting; **Besançon**, the capital of Franche-Comté, and **Briançon**, the highest town in Europe, are still dominated by formidable fortresses that reflect the tumultuous past of this region on France's eastern frontier. The website ⓦ www.rhonealpes -tourisme.com and the information on the Alps and Jura at ⓦ www .franceguide.com are both excellent introductions to this "serene" and "unfathomable" corner of France.

Hiking and Climbing in the Alps and Franche-Comté

There are seven national or regional parks in the area covered by this chapter: Vanoise, Chartreuse, Bauges, Écrins, Queyras, Vercors and Haut Jura. All of these contain gentle day-walks and more demanding treks – not least classic long distance paths like the Tour du Mont Blanc – which require one or two weeks' walking. Most of these routes are clearly marked and equipped with *refuge* huts; the routes are also described in high detail by the Topo-guides guidebooks (see Basics, p.54). Nonetheless, even the most experienced walkers or skiers treat these mountains and their unpredictable weather conditions with due respect. Even low-level walks in the Alps during summer often require a good level of fitness and specialist equipment like crampons or ice axes. You should take due account of the weather conditions (which can vary considerably between the valleys and peaks), of the potentially debilitating effects of high altitude, and of the serious danger of avalanches.

The Alps was the first great centre for European rock climbers in the nineteenth century and still offers countless routes which can be enjoyed by both novices and world-class climbers. A more recent development has been the creation of Via Ferrata courses, in which wires and ladders are bolted on to the rock so that even inexperienced climbers (wearing harnesses and ropes) can make ascents which would otherwise be impossible for them. There are Via Ferrata courses being developed across the whole region, but at present two of the largest centres for this popular sport are at Serre Chevalier and in the Parc National des Écrins.

The **Bureau Info Montagne** office in Grenoble and the **Office de Haute Montagne** in Chamonix can provide information on the best guides and the most up-to-date information on all the **GR paths** and the best **Via Ferrata** courses, while local tourist offices often produce detailed maps of walks in their own areas.

The Alps

Europe's highest mountain range offers a plethora of exciting outdoor activities, ranging from extreme skiing to the most gentle of Valley walks. Yet you'll also find plenty of charming villages and towns to explore, not least Grenoble, the small city which is the easiest point to access the region by car, train or plane.

Grenoble

While it has its fair share of the grey, concrete apartment blocks which blight the outskirts of many a French city, **GRENOBLE**, the self-styled "capital of the Alps", has a colourful and quirky maze of streets at its centre, where modern and medieval buildings are packed close together. Beautifully situated at the confluence of the Drac and Isère rivers, the city is also home to a vibrant student population of over

---

Food and drink in the Alps and Franche-Comté

Indulging in an evening **feast** after a long day in the mountains is one of the greatest pleasures of travelling in the Alps and Franche-Comté, and it is a pleasure that can most often be attributed to the quality of the local ingredients – of the various cheeses, fish and herbs in particular – rather than to any great innovation in the cookery itself.

Nonetheless, it is the liberal amounts of the cheese made from the local cows, ewes and goats that most characterizes Alpine cuisine. The *fromageries* of Franche-Comté and the Northern Alps are full of cheeses like Roblochon, Emmental, Chèvre, Comté and Beaufort. These are found not just in the famous fondue, but also the lesser-known *raclette* and *tartiflette* (both cheese-based dishes served with ham and potatoes). Further south, the spicy and dry goat's cheese Picodon is another intriguing variety for cheese-lovers to sample.

Many restaurants feature **fish** (notably salmon and trout) from the Alpine lakes and use locally grown herbs, like savory, thyme, basil and rosemary. These herbs are particularly in evidence in the Southern Alps around Briançon, where they are often used to flavour the *saucisson* (cured sausage) which you'll find in many a morning shopping market.

If you are looking for some "gastronomique" fireworks, then the best place to head for is **Grenoble**, where plenty of local chefs combine the local produce into creative dishes, often with an Eastern or Mediterreanean feel to them.

The region produces many light and fruity varieties of **wine**, of which the most popular is the dark red Mondeuse, with its faint taste of raspberries and strawberries. By contrast, the *vin jaune* from the Jura is a potent, golden wine, made from Sauvignon grapes with a fermentation process similar to that of sherry – it remains in the cask for 6–10 years before being bottled. Vin Jaune is a favourite accompaniment for the local cheeses of Franche-Comté, as well as in other speciality dishes like *poulet au vin jaune* (chicken and morels in a creamy sauce flavoured by the wine). In the towns of Franche-Comté, especially Belfort, you'll find ample amounts of excellent German beers, but for a more local beverage, it's worth sampling some **liquers**. The most famous of these is undoubtedly **Chartreuse**, the drink produced by Carthusian monks since the sixteenth century, which contains 130 different herbs and is known as the "elixir of life".

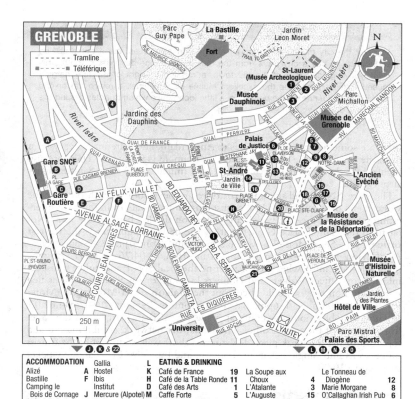

ACCOMMODATION			EATING & DRINKING						
Alizé	A	Gallia	L	Café de France	19	La Soupe aux		Le Tonneau de	
Bastille	F	Hostel	K	Café de la Table Ronde	11	Choux	4	Diogène	12
Camping le		Ibis	H	Café des Arts	1	L'Atalante		Marie Morgane	8
Bois de Cornage	J	Institut	D	Caffe Forte	5	L'Auguste	15	O'Callaghan Irish Pub	6
Citôtel de Patinoire	N	Mercure (Alpotel)	M	Chez la Mère Ticket	20	Le Bagatel	14	Pizzeria des Halles	17
Des Alpes	E	Park	O	Ciao a Te	18	Le Chasse Spleen	7	Shaman	9
D'Angleterre	I	Residhotel		Kaméléon	21	Le Couche Tard	10	Styx	13
Du Moucherotte	G	Central'Gare	B	La Luna	22	Le Mont Liban	2	Tarteline	16
		Terminus	C						

50,000 and a lively cultural scene which attracts young clubbers, actors and musicians from across the whole region. Grenoble was only annexed by France in the fourteenth century, and the atmosphere of this city in the mountains is quite unique. It was here after all, far from Paris, that a local uprising in 1788 (known as the Journée des Tuiles) initiated the French Revolution. The prosperity of the city was originally founded on glove-making, but in the nineteenth century its economy diversified to include industries as diverse as mining and hydroelectric power, while more recently it has forged a reputation as a centre for scientific research in the electronic and nuclear industries. Grenoble's **Musée de Grenoble**, packed with paintings by notable nineteenth-and twentieth-century artists, is the region's outstanding art gallery, while the restaurants and cafés of the town provide relaxing spots in which to sit and admire the grandeur of this fantastic mountain setting.

Arrival and information

The Grenoble-Isère airport (☎04.76.65.48.48, ⓦwww.grenoble-airport.com) lies some 45km to the north west of the city. It is served by several low-cost airlines; most of the flight connections are with Britain and Ireland, although

Many of the city museums no longer charge admission fees, but it could still be economical to buy a **city pass** from the tourist office (one-day pass €12.50). This gives you a guided tour of the old town, admission to eight of the fee-charging museums (which includes the excellent Musée de Grenoble), a return trip on the *téléférique* and a ride on the *petit train*, a little locomotive which trundles around the city and is often a hit with kids.

there are some less frequent services to Amsterdam. There are buses every hour from the airport to the **gare routière** in Grenoble (45min; €4). There are also regular buses between the *gare routière* and the (much larger) Lyon Saint Exupéry airport (1 hr; €20).

The **gare SNCF** and the **gare routière** are next door to each other at the western end of avenue Félix-Viallet, just ten-minutes' walk from the most interesting sections of the city, which are mainly on the left bank of the Isère. Not far from the central place Grenette, at 14 rue de la République, is the **tourist office** (May–Sept Mon–Sat 9am–6.30pm, Sun 10am–1pm & 2–5pm; Oct–April Mon–Sat 9am–6.30pm, Sun 10am–1pm; ☎04.76.42.41.41, ⓦwww .grenoble-isere.info), where you'll also find the local SNCF and public transport information offices. Walkers and climbers looking for suggestions and detailed information on *refuges* should check out the **Maison de la Montagne** (Mon–Fri 9am–12.30pm & 1–6pm, Sat 10am–1pm & 2–5pm; ☎04.76.44.67.03, ⓦwww.grenoble-montagne.com), at 3 rue Raoul-Blanchard, across the street from the rear of the tourist office. The **transport** network, combining bus and tram routes, has the bleak place de Verdun (a short walk southeast of the tourist office) as its hub. Single tickets for both bus and tram cost €1.30 and ten-ticket strips cost €10.90.

Accommodation

There is no shortage of **hotels** – the good, the bad and the ugly – in Grenoble, but the city is busy from September to June with conferences and graduations, so it's worth booking ahead. The Tourist Office also provides an online booking service (see ⓦwww.grenoble-resatourisme.com).

Hotels

Alizé 1 rue Amirai Courbet ☎04.76.43.12.91, ⓦwww.hotelalize.com. You'll only find the most basic facilities at this hotel, but it's the cheapest place in the centre. ❶

Des Alpes 45 av Félix-Viallet ☎04.76.87.00.71, ⓦwww.hotel-des-alpes.fr. If you can bear the 1960s-style interior decor, then this hotel close to the station is a good one to head for. ❸

D'Angleterre 5 place Victor-Hugo ☎04.76.87.37.21, ⓦwww.hotel-angleterre-grenoble.com. Here you'll find well-equipped rooms (DVD players are standard) and free overnight parking. ❻

Bastille 25 av Felix Viallet ☎04.76.43.10.27, ⓦwww.hotel-bastille.fr. Situated on this busy central Avenue, *Bastille* is well placed near the main bus and train lines, but the rooms can get noisy. ❸

Citôtel de Patinoire 12 rue Marie-Chamoux ☎04.76.44.43.65, ⓦwww.hotel-patinoire.com. Located to the southeast of the city centre, this is an excellent mid-range option with a generous breakfast at €6.50. ❸

Gallia 7 bd du Maréchal Joffre ☎04.76.87.39.21, ⓦwww.hotel-gallia.com. While the rooms here lack any individual character, they do have satellite TV and there is a gym to help blow away the cobwebs. ❸

Ibis 5 rue de Miribel ☎04.76.47.48.49, ⓦwww .ibishotel.com. You'll get all the usual mod cons at this chain hotel, but there's also a good-value restaurant and substantial discounts (up to one-third of the room price) available at weekends. ❺

Institut 10 rue Barbillon ☎04.76.46.36.44, ⓦwww.institut-hotel.fr. This colourful little two-star

hotel provides friendly service, internet connection and satellite TV.
Mercure (Alpotel) 12 bd du Maréchal Joffre ☎04.76.87.88.41, ⓦwww.mercure.com. One of three *Mercure* hotels in Grenoble, this place has comfortable (if pricey) rooms and a good restaurant. **❼**
Du Moucherotte 1 rue Auguste Gaché ☎04.76.54.61.40. This hotel is an inexpensive option with clean, bright rooms (TVs included). **❷**
Park 10 place Paul-Mistral ☎04.76.85.81.23, ⓦwww.park-hotel-grenoble.fr. A luxury four-star hotel with rooms that are elegantly decorated and which come with excellent facilities. **❾**

🛏 **Residhotel Central'Gare** 8 place de la Gare, 38000 Grenoble ☎04.76.50.77.88, ⓦwww.residhotel.com/en/business/grenoble/central-gare. These studios and apartments for 2 or 4 people are ideal for anyone looking for a longer spell in the area. They are close to the station, and you get private kitchen facilities, in addition to all the usual mod cons, for the same price as a good hotel room. **❺**

Terminus 10 place de la Gare ☎04.76.87.24.33, ⓦwww.terminus-hotel-grenoble.fr. This flash 3-star hotel has soundproof, air-conditioned rooms opposite the *gare SNCF*. **❺**

Campsite and hostel

Camping Le Bois de Cornage Chemin du Camping, Vizille ☎06.83.18.17.87, ⓦwww.campingvizille.com. Open May–September. Situated 15km from the city centre, this three-star campsite has a swimming pool and restaurant on site. Take bus #3000 from the *gare routière* in Grenoble and get off at stop "Place du Chateau" in Vizille. €13.90 for a two-person tent.
Hostel 10 av de Gresivaudan ☎04.76.09.33.52, ⒺⒺ grenoble@fuaj.org. A recently renovated hostel which provides simple meals, but also has good kitchen facilities and is near a supermarket. It's 5km south of the city centre in Echirolles; you can take bus #1 to the "Quinzaine" stop or tram A to "La Rampe". €17.60 including breakfast.

The City

The best way to start your tour is to take the **téléférique** (☎04.76.44.33.65, ⓦwww.bastille-grenoble.com) or cable car from the riverside quai Stéphane-Jay to **Fort de la Bastille** on the steep slopes above the northern bank of the Isère. It's best to check the complicated opening times before arrival, but the cable car is open roughly every day at the following times: March–Sept 9.30am–midnight; Nov–Feb 11am–6.30pm. The ride is hair-raising, as you're whisked steeply and swiftly into the air in a sort of transparent egg, which allows you to see very clearly how far you would fall in the event of an accident. If you don't like the sound of the cable car, you can climb the steep but pleasant footpath from the St-Laurent church on the northern bank of the Isère.

Although the nineteenth-century fortifications on the hill have been well preserved, the site's chief draw is the view. At your feet, the Isère flows under old bridges which join the St-Laurent quarter (a home for Italian immigrants in the later 1800s) on the northern bank of the river to the nucleus of the medieval town. Even this far south, if you look northeast on a clear day you can see the distant white peaks of Mont Blanc further up the deep valley of the Isère. To the east, snowfields gleam in the high gullies of the Belledonne massif (2978m). To the southeast is the peak of Le Taillefer (2807m), while further to the south you can make out the mountain pass which the famous Route Napoléon crosses on its way northwards from the Mediterranean. This was the road towards Paris that Napoleon took after his escape from Elba in March 1815; he crossed these Alpine valleys and peaks triumphantly, only to meet his final defeat three months later at Waterloo. Finally, to the west you can admire Moucherotte (1901m), the highest peak of the Vercors massif, and the mountain which most seems to dominate the city beneath. For heading back into town, a path down through the public gardens offers an alternative to the cable car.

▲ Place Grenette, Grenoble

The northern bank of the Isère

On the same northern side of the Isère as La Bastille is the **Église St-Laurent** on place St-Laurent. This former church contains archaeological excavations which have shown evidence of pagan and Christian places of worship dating from the fourth century, as well as an eighth-century crypt and a high medieval cloister. Unfortunately, the museum on the site is closed for the foreseeable future (check Ⓦ www.musee-archeologique-grenoble.com for the latest information). One museum that is open, however, is the **Musée Dauphinois**, 30 rue Maurice-Gignoux (June–Sept everyday except Tues 10am–7pm; Oct–May 10am–6pm; free), which lies up a steep cobbled path opposite the St-Laurent footbridge further west of the city. Located in a former convent, this museum is devoted to the history, arts and crafts of the Dauphiné province. In the basement, there's a Baroque chapel with grey and gold wall paintings depicting episodes from the New Testament and scenes from the life of St-François-de-Sales, the founder of the convent in the seventeenth century. In the museum proper, there's plenty of information on the lives of the rugged and self-sufficient Dauphinois mountain people, but perhaps the most memorable exhibit details the evolution of skiing in the area over the last four thousand years, right through to the modern winter sports that came to Grenoble when it hosted the 1968 Winter Olympics.

The Old Town

The narrow streets of the Old Town on the southern bank of the Isère, particularly around places Grenette, Vaucanson, Verdun and Notre-Dame, make up the liveliest and most colourful quarter of the city. Near the bustling place Notre-Dame, on the riverbank at 5 place de Lavalette, is the **Musée de Grenoble** (daily except Tues 10am–6.30pm; €5), a modern complex that houses a large gallery of paintings ranging from the sixteenth century to the present day. Of particular note are the rooms filled with paintings from the last two hundred years – including works by Chagall, Gauguin, Léger and Matisse – although there are also paintings by Rubens and Caravaggio, as well as a large set of Egyptian antiquities.

On the eastern side of place Notre-Dame is the **Musee de l'Ancien Évêché** (daily except Tues and Sun 9am–6pm, Tues 1.30-6pm, Sun 10am–7pm; free). Housed in the old bishop's palace, the museum offers a brisk tour through Grenoble's history from the Stone Age to the twentieth century. The remains of the Roman town walls and a fifth-century **baptistry** are on show in the basement, while upstairs you will find sets of Neolithic flint tools, weapons made by the Celts and many Roman artefacts, including a colourful mosaic floor panel, decorated with a pair of parrots.

To the east of the *téléférique* station on the southern bank of the Isère is the sixteenth-century **Palais de Justice** (open to the public), with place St-André and the **church of St-André** behind. Built in the thirteenth century, the church once served as the palace chapel of the princes of Dauphiné, though it has been heavily restored since.

To the south of the Old Town

A few blocks to the south at 14 rue Hébert is the **Musée de la Résistance et de la Déportation de l'Isère** (open daily except Tues: July & Aug 10am–7pm; Sept–June 9am–6pm; Tues 1.30-6pm;), which is full of both high-tech audiovisual exhibits and simpler, more poignant types of wartime memorabilia. The subject is the brutal Nazi occupation of the Dauphiné and the bravery of the members of the Resistance who fought against the Germans and laid the seeds for France's eventual liberation. All the captions are translated into English.

Eating, drinking and nightlife

Eating in Grenoble is a pleasure; it's less expensive than nearby Lyon but just as creative. There are a wide variety of **restaurants** catering to all budgets and tastes; it's worth booking ahead at the restaurants listed below, especially in the evenings.

Restaurants

L'Atalante 87 rue St. Laurent ℡04.76.01.85.16. A popular restaurant which has a bohemian feel thanks to the pictures of French musicians and actors on the walls. The cuisine centres on some excellent steak dishes (€13). Closed Sun.

L'Auguste 6 rue Auguste Gaché ℡04.76.51.36.96. One of the more refined establishments in town, *L'Auguste* has an extensive wine list (€20–49 for a bottle) and serves creative meat dishes which include some local sausage varieties. Closed Sat–Mon.

Le Chasse Spleen 6 place de Lavallette ℡04.38.37.03.52. This place serves up dishes featuring a mix of local and more exotic ingredients (€16–22) such as duck fillets in pomegranate sauce. Mon–Fri noon–2pm & 7–11pm.

Chez La Mère Ticket 13 rue Jean-Jacques Rousseau ℡04.76.44.45.40. A friendly little family-run restaurant serving traditional local specialities like *poulet aux écrevisses* (chicken with crayfish) for reasonable prices (€15–18). Mon–Sat noon–2pm & 7–10pm.

Ciao A Te 2 rue de la Paix ℡04.76.42.54.41. This hole-in-the-wall Italian place whips up classic pasta dishes (around €15) as well as innovative seafood (€25). Tues–Sat noon–2pm & 7.30–11pm. Closed in Aug.

Le Mont Liban 50 quai Xavier Jouvin ℡04.76.51.25.75. An inauspicious exterior masks the quality of this award-winning Lebanese restaurant, which provides three-course meals for €22. Closed Sun.

Pizzeria des Halles 2 rue Auguste Gaché ℡04.76.54.06.23. A very cosy Italian restaurant where you can watch your pizzas (€10) cooking in the fireplace. Closed Sat evening.

Shaman 1 place Notre-Dame ℡04.38.37.23.56. The decoration here is straight from the Indian subcontinent, but you'll find meals and wines from several different continents. The sushi meals (€10–16) are a particular highlight. Closed Sun evening.

Cafés, bars and nightlife

It's also easy to find quirky, atmospheric places in Grenoble to drink a coffee or something more alcoholic, particularly in the lively squares of Grenette, St-André and Notre-Dame, and the maze of tiny streets around them. Grenoble's large student population means that the **nightlife** is never dull, although it does tend to centre around bars rather than nightclubs. A few central places worth trying out if you want live music include *Styx*, 6 place de Claveyson (Tues–Sun, 6pm–1am), a trendy bar with occasional DJs; the small club *Kaméléon*, 5 place Vaucanson (11pm–5.30am), which churns out punk music for the local rock fans; and *La Soupe aux Choux*, 7 route du Lyon (Fri & Sat 8pm–1am), the place to go if you want to hear some brilliant live jazz. Further out, *La Luna*, 94 cours Jean Jaurès (Thurs–Sun 11pm–5.30am), is a gay-friendly dance club.

Café des Arts 36 rue St. Laurent ☎04.76.54.65.31. Situated on the northern bank of the river, *Café des Arts* has live music (including jazz, blues, folk and South American music) on Fri & Sat nights. Mon–Sat 8pm–midnight.

Le Bagatel 7 place St. Andre ☎04.76.51.77.83. A down-to-earth brasserie offering much better-value meals than the more famous *De la Table Ronde* nearby, not least with its range of filling salads (€4–9). Open daily 7am–1am. Closed in Aug.

Le Couche Tard 1 rue du Palais ☎04.76.44.18.79. The liveliest pub in the old town. During the happy hours of 7–9pm, you can indulge in cheap beers and cocktails (€2.50–3) without lightening your wallet too much. Mon–Sat 7pm–2am. Closed in Aug.

Caffe Forte 4 place Lavallette ☎04.76.03.22.83. A popular and intimate café with innovative Mediterranean-style dishes (€12–16). Closed Tues.

Café de France 17 rue Bayard ☎04.76.54.53.83. This unassuming, traditional bar has a 1930s style interior and provides light meals. The menu is €10. Closed Sun.

Marie Morgane 3 rue Frédéric Taulier ☎04.38.37.03.74. A delightful crêperie with an interior inspired by the ships of yesteryear and a wide range of sweet crêpes and savoury *galettes* (€5–10). The selection of ice creams (€6) is also well worth sampling. Closed Sun.

O'Callaghan Irish Pub 2 place de Bérulle ☎04.76.01.05.66. Are you desperate for a pint of the black stuff and an "authentic Irish pub" experience? If so, then head to O'Callaghan, where you can get a pint of Guinness for €5.70. Open daily 3pm–1am.

Café de La Table Ronde 7 place St- Andre ☎04.76.44.51.41. This café has been a hotspot for writers, artists and tourists since it opened in 1739, perhaps more due to its bohemian layout and good coffee than the fairly uninspiring food menu. Closed on Tues & Sun evenings in winter.

Tarteline 6 Grande Rue ☎04.76.51.53.86. An irresistible bakery-cum-café with a €12 menu that gives you a tasty mix of the home-made products: a quiche, salad and cake. Closed Sun & Mon.

Le Tonneau de Diogène 6 place Notre-Dame ☎04.76.42.38.40. The favourite haunt of the local literary elite. Bring a book or newspaper if you want to look suitably intellectual as you tuck into one of the tasty house omelettes (€5–8). Open daily 11am–midnight.

Listings

Bike rental Metrovelo in the underpass of the *gare SNCF*, place de la Gare ☎04.76.59.59.59, ⓦwww.metrovelo.fr. €3 for 5hr.

Bookshop Librarie des Alpes, 1 rue Casimier Perier, has an excellent collection of coffee-table books on the Alps, although few of these have English captions.

Car hire Several of the larger agencies have kiosks in or around the *gare SNCF* (closed on Sun): AVIS, *gare SNCF* ☎08.20.61.16.51; Europcar, *gare SNCF* ☎08.25.88.70.90; Hertz, *gare SNCF* ☎04.76.86.55.80; Rent-a-Car, 10 place de la Gare ☎04.76.86.27.60.

Internet Pl@net On-Line, 1 place Vaucanson (Mon–Sat 9am–midnight).

Medical emergencies Centre Hospitalier Universitaire (CHU) ☎04.76.76.50.25; ambulance Alp'Azur (a private ambulance company) ☎04.76.21.11.11.

Pharmacy There are several large pharmacies in the centre which have long opening hours. Pharmacie Victor Hugo, 2 bd Agutte Sembat (open everyday 8am–8pm) ☎04.76.46.04.15.

Police 36 bd Maréchal-Leclerc ☎04.76.60.40.40.

Taxi Grenoblois, 14 rue de la République ☎04.76.54.42.54 provides a 24hr radio taxi service.

Around Grenoble

To the southwest of Grenoble, the limestone plateau of ridges and valleys that comprise the **Vercors massif** offer plenty of gentle hiking trails, which can be easily accessed from the villages of Lans-en-Vercors or Villard-de-Lans. These villages are only a 10–15km journey on the D531 road; if you don't have a car, you can get there by catching the #5100 bus, which leaves several times a day from the *gare routière* in Grenoble.

Of the mountain ranges that lie close to Grenoble, however, it is the **Chartreuse massif** to the north which packs the most highlights for travellers. It is a relatively gentle mountain range, making it an ideal area for less experienced walkers. The massif is not heavily populated, and the lack of industry makes it popular with all types of energetic outdoor enthusiasts, from cavers to mountain bikers. The lack of large settlements, however, also means that the range is not easy to visit without your own vehicle.

The Chartreuse massif

The Chartreuse massif, designated in 1995 as the **Parc Naturel Régional de Chartreuse** (ⓦ www.parc-chartreuse.net), is a place of spectacular landscapes, including sharp limestone peaks, mountain pastures and large areas of pine forest. The Grenoble **Maison de la Montagne** office (see p.870) publishes descriptions of the various hiking routes in the area.

The Grande Chartreuse Monastery and Voiron

The massif's main local landmark is the **Grande Chartreuse Monastery**, situated up the narrow Gorges des Guiers Morts, southeast of St-Laurent-du-Pont, and some 35km from Grenoble, one of nineteen Carthusian monasteries still functioning worldwide. Carthusian monks and nuns seek a life of contemplation following the example of their founder, the eleventh-century monk St Bruno, a life which involves long periods of solitude, silence, work and prayer everyday. Members of the order live in cells and meet only for Mass and a weekly communal meal, eaten in silence. Since 1605, however, the Carthusians have also become famous as the producers of various **Chartreuses**. These powerfully alcoholic herbal elixirs range from the better-known green and yellow variants to a number of gentler fruit liqueurs. The monastery is not open to the public, but near the village of **ST-PIERRE-DE-CHARTREUSE**, 5km back on the Grenoble road, you can visit the **Musée de la Grande Chartreuse**, formerly La Correrie monastery, which illustrates the life of the Carthusian Order (daily April, Oct & early Nov 10am–noon & 4–6pm; May 9.30am–noon & 2–6.30pm; June–Sept 9.30am–6.30pm; €4; ⓦ www.musee-grande-chartreuse.fr).

For those less interested in religious austerity and more interested in those mysterious liqueurs, a visit to **VOIRON**, 30km west of the park and on the train line from Grenoble to Lyon, is in order. The **Caves de la Chartreuse** on boulevard Edgar-Kofler (Apr–Oct 9–11.30am & 2–6.30pm; Nov–March Mon–Fri 9–11.30am & 2–5.30pm; free) are where the "elixir of life" is now bottled. The tour takes you through the world's largest liqueur cellars, and includes a splendidly corny 3-D film on the history of the monastery and the secret manuscript with the recipe of the original liquer. The undoubted highlight of the tour, however, is a tasting of one of the alcoholic beverages themselves. There's not much else to see in Voiron, but if you're looking for a **hotel**, try the small but comfortable *La Chaumière* (☏ 04.76.05.16.24, ⓦ www .hotel-lachaumiere-voiron.com; ➌).

Southwest of Grenoble: the road to Briançon

Connecting Grenoble to Briançon, the **N91** twists through the precipitous valley of the Romanche and over the **Col du Lautaret** (2058m), which is kept open all year round and crossed at least a couple of times a day (and more often during the skiing season) by the Grenoble–Briançon bus. As well as being an exciting taste of the high mountain scenery to come, this route offers the opportunity for some worthwhile detours, including the climb across the **Col du Galibier** to **Valloire** and some fine mountain hikes above the modern ski resort of **L'Alpe d'Huez**, which is perched on the northern slopes of the Romanche valley above the attractive town of **Le Bourg-d'Oisans**. On the southern slopes is the sprawling village of **Les Deux-Alpes**, which has been wholly subsumed by the skiing industry, while close to Briançon another modern resort, **Serre Chevalier**, has been created around five farming hamlets.

Le Bourg-d'Oisans

The first major settlement on the route, **LE BOURG-D'OISANS** (known as "Le Bourg"), 20km southeast of Grenoble, is of no great interest in itself, but it sits in a beautiful position in the valley and is a good base for summer sports. You can pick up information on hiking routes from the **tourist office**, on quai Girard, by the river in the middle of town (July & Aug 9am–7pm; Sept–June Mon–Sat 9am–noon & 2–6pm; ☎04.76.80.03.25, ⊛www.bourgdoisans.com), and the **Maison du Parc National des Écrins** on rue Gambetta (July & Aug 8am–noon & 3–7pm; Sept–June Mon–Fri 8am–noon & 2–5.30pm; ☎04.76.80.00.51). There are some good-value **hotels** here, among them *L'Oberland*, on avenue de la Gare (☎04.76.80.24.24, ⊛www.hoteloberland .com; ❹), and the *Hôtel Le Florentin* at 8 rue Thiers (☎04.76.80.01.61, ⊛www .le-florentin.com; ❸), which has a pleasant garden to relax in. For **camping**, a good option is *La Cascade*, 1.5km outside town on the Route de l'Alpe d'Huez (☎04.76.80.02.42, ⊛www.lacascadesarenne.com; open mid-Dec to Sept; €19). Bourg-d'Oisans is a hotspot for cyclists, many of whom you'll see relaxing at the end of the day in popular central restaurants like *La Romanche*, avenue Docteur Louis Faure (€16.50–20 for a hearty pizza) and *La Crepizza*, place Marche (€16 menu of crêpes and pizza or pasta). The Tourist Office and the website ⊛www .bikes-oisans.com can provide you with information on plenty of routes, both in the mountains surrounding the town and on more gentle tracks in the valley. Bikes can be rented for €25 at Cycles et Sports, place du Docteur Faure.

L'Alpe d'Huez and around

One cycling route that can only be recommended for the fittest travellers is the road up from Bourg-d'Oisans to the ski resort of **L'ALPE D'HUEZ**. The resort is situated more than a vertical kilometre above the valley floor, and the eleven-kilometre road, which crawls up the valley side, is often used as a stage in the Tour de France. As you ascend through the 21 hairpins, there's a fine view of the acutely crumpled strata of rock exposed by passing glaciers on the south side of the Romanche valley. During the winter, the extensive network of *télécabines* and *téléphériques* whisks skiers to the **Pic Blanc** (3330m), at the bottom of the Chaîne des Rousses ridge, from which two mammoth black runs (over two kilometres in length) descend. Yet while it is undoubtedly a skier's paradise in winter, the purpose-built resort itself has little character in July and August.

L'Alpe d'Huez's **tourist office** in the Maison de l'Alpe, place Paganon (May–June & Sept–Nov daily 9am–12.30pm & 2.30–6pm; Dec–April & July–Aug daily 9am–7pm; ☎04.76.11.44.44, ⓦwww.alpedhuez.com), provides detailed walking and mountain biking maps; the Maison also houses the **ESF ski school** office (☎04.76.80.31.69, ⓦwww.esf-alpedhuez.com). The hotels in the main village are generally expensive and unremarkable; one three-star hotel that provides excellent facilities and a central location near the pistes is *Le Dome*, Place du Cognet (☎04.76.80.32.11, ⓦwww.dome-alpedhuez.com; ❽). A cheaper, if less convenient, option is to stay in one of the *chambres d'hôtes* in Huez en Oisans, just below the main village. One of the best is *Florineige* (☎04.76.80.94.89, ⓦwww.hebergement-florineige.com; ❺), which is run by Yves and Sylvie Forestier, both of whom are ski instructors and they are very knowledgeable about walking and cycling in the area.

La Grave and the Col du Lautaret

Continuing on the N91 towards La Grave past the modern ski resort of **Les Deux-Alpes**, you'll pass two waterfalls issuing from the north side of the valley:

Skiing in the Alps

With their long and varied runs, extensive lift networks, and world-renowned après-ski, the French Alps offer some of the best skiing in Europe. Skiing first became a recreational sport in the early 1900s but the industry really began to boom in the Alps during the 1960s with the construction of dozens of high-altitude, purpose-built resorts that ensured good lasting snow cover. Some of the resorts have their detractors: the modern architects often created sprawling concrete settlements that had little in common with the traditional farming villages lower in the valleys, and in so doing they earned France a lasting reputation for "ski factories". Nonetheless, few can knock the efficiency of these resorts. They have an abundance of hotels, equipment outlets and ski schools, while at many you can simply clip your skis on at the hotel door and be skiing on some of the most challenging pistes on earth within minutes. If you are looking for more peaceful accommodation options, the villages at the foot of the valleys are now often linked to the major resorts by fast, modern lifts.

Unsurprisingly given the size of the French Alps, you'll find opportunities for many different kinds of skiing. **Downhill skiing** is the most common form of the sport at all the resorts, but **cross-country or nordic skiing** has become increasingly popular on gentler slopes (particularly around Morzine and in the Parc Naturel Régional du Queyras), although the real magnet for cross-country skiers lies further to the north in Franche-Comté (see the "Cross-country skiing in Franche-Comté" box on p.921). Back in the Alps, there are also several famous routes for **ski touring** (a form of cross-country skiing with uphill sections and across much longer distances), not least the **Haute Route** between Chamonix and Zermatt (Switzerland) and the Grande Traversée des Alps, which leads south from Thonon-les-Bains on Lake Geneva through several national parks. There are also plenty of opportunities for **snowboarding**; many of the resorts now have snowparks expressly designed for snowboarders to refine their jumping technique.

The ski **season** runs from December to late April, with high season over Christmas and New Year, February half-term and (to a lesser extent) Easter; the weekends are also busy with crowds descending on resorts close to big urban centres and those with short airport transfers. During the summer more and more resorts are trying to attract **mountain bikers** and **hikers**; many ski lifts stay open during the summer, which makes many hiking and VTT (*velo tout terrain*) biking trails more accessible. For advice on which ski resort to choose for your holiday, see the "Alpine ski resorts at a glance" box, p.904–905.

early summer run-off enhances the three hundred-metre plume of the **Cascade de la Pisse** (the source of many a snigger by schoolboys from across Europe), while, 6km further on, the near-vertical fall of churning whitewater called the **Saut de la Pucelle** ("the virgin's leap") is a breathtaking sight.

LA GRAVE, 18km on from the Barrage du Lac du Chambon, lies at the foot of the Col du Lautaret, facing the majestic glaciers of the north side of **La Meije** (3984m). While it lies at the heart of a large and testing ski area, La Grave, with its small collection of stone buildings, could not be a more different environment than Les Deux-Alpes.

In addition to the skiing opportunities, it's also a good base for walkers and climbers; the **GR54** passes to the northwest of the village, and there are also two equipped Via Ferrata courses nearby (an easier one at Arsine and a tougher course at the Mines du Grand Clot) which can be accessed for free. The **Bureau des Guides**, place du Téléphérique (T 04.76.79.90.21, W www.guidelagrave .com), provides guides for the different hiking paths in the area.

If you don't want to walk, then an easier way of appreciating the stunning vistas is provided by the *télécabine* (mid-June to early Sept & late Dec to early May; €18 return), which rises sharply from the centre of the village to the 3200-metre summit of **Le Rateau**, just west of La Meije. The 35-minute ride is very good value for money considering that the view of the barely accessible interior of the Écrins is normally seen only by the most intrepid mountaineers. The lift also provides access to acres of off-piste skiing, and the freezing conditions of the mountain's northerly face make it ideal for ice climbing. The **tourist office**, near the *télécabine* (T 04.76.79.90.05, W www.lagrave-lameije.com), has plenty of information about the best areas for skiing and walking, as well as a host of other activities, like rafting and climbing on Via Ferrata.

For **accommodation**, a good-value central option is *Hotel Castillan* (T 04.76.79.90.04, W http://perso.orange.fr/castillan; open Jan–Sept; ❸), where you'll find a swimming pool, bar and some good views out to La Meije. The best nearby campsite is *Le Gravelotte* (T 04.76.79.93.14, W www.camping-le -gravelotte.com; open June–Sept; €12.10 for a two-person tent).

From La Grave it's only 11km to the top of the **Col du Lautaret**, a pass which is important enough to be generally kept clear for traffic during the winter months, despite its high altitude (2057m). The Roman road from Milan to Vienne crossed this col; the name Lautaret emanates from the small temple (*altaretum*) the Romans built to placate the deity of the mountains. Around the col is a huge expanse of meadow long known to botanists for its glorious variety of Alpine flowers (especially the narcissi and anemones), which are seen at their best in mid-July. You'll also find **Le Jardin Botanique Alpin du Lautaret**, founded in 1899 and maintained by the University of Grenoble (June–Sept daily 10am–6pm; €5); it displays plants from mountain ranges throughout the world.

The Col du Galibier and Serre Chevalier

Turn north at Lautaret and you're on your way to the even higher **Col du Galibier** (no public transport), which is closed by snow from mid-October to mid-June. A monument on the south side of the col commemorates Henri Desgranges, the editor of the newspaper *L'Auto* who founded the Tour de France in 1903. Crossing the col is one of the most gruelling stages in the race, and is often made more difficult for the cyclists because of the snow and ice that can linger even in July and August.

On the other hand, if you turn southwest at the Col du Lautaret, you stay on the main N91 road heading towards Briançon. Nine kilometres before reaching that town, you'll come to the skiing area of **SERRE CHEVALIER**, a name given to five traditional farming hamlets whose old wooden chalets have now been surrounded by small hotels and holiday homes.

This area is Skiing Central for the Southern Alps. In total, there's access to around 250km of ski runs with various degrees of difficulty, and you can generally guarantee good weather: the resort has an average of three hundred days of sunshine a year. The hamlets of Saint-Chaffrey and Chantemerle form Serre Chevalier 1350 (named for its altitude of 1350m); Villeneuve and La-Salle-les-Alpes make up Serre Chevalier 1400; and Le Monêtier-les-Bains is Serre Chevalier 1500. Each area is linked by a series of **ski lifts** and pistes which climb and descend the north-facing slopes of the valley, and there are ESF ski school offices in all three areas (W www.esf-serrechevalier.com), as well as plenty of shops from which to rent equipment. Of all these settlements it is **Le Monêtier-les-Bains**, with its narrow streets that weave between old stone houses and rickety wooden balconies, which is arguably the prettiest. The village has been a thermal spa since Roman times, with two hot-water springs. You can now partake of this ancient mode of relaxation in the thoroughly modern surroundings of *Les Grands Bains* (€20; 3hr ticket), one of the largest spa complexes in Europe, which comes with a plethora of pools, steam rooms and fitness centres.

The **tourist office** for the whole of Serre Chevalier is located in the centre of Villeneuve (T 04.92.24.98.98, W www.serre-chevalier.com), while Le Monêtier-les-Bains in particular offers a range of modern and more traditional places to stay. *Auberge du Choucas* (T 04.92.24.42.73, W www.aubergeduchoucas .com; closed May & Nov; ❼) is a beautiful old house with an excellent gourmet restaurant. A cheaper option close to the village at Pont de l'Alp is the *Auberge Les Amis* (T 04.92.24.44.24, W www.aubergelesamis.com; open mid-Dec to Oct; ❹ including breakfast). There's also a **hostel** at Le Bez (T 04.92.24.74.54, E serre-chevalier@fuaj.org; open mid-Dec to April & mid-June to Aug; €12.90 for a dorm bed), 500m from the centre of Serre Chevalier 1400, where you'll find friendly staff and very basic kitchen facilities.

The Hautes-Alpes: Briançon, the Écrins and the Queyras

The **Hautes-Alpes** are the area of high mountains to the southwest of Grenoble and south of the Massif de la Vanoise. To the east lies the Italian border and to the south, the Alpes de Provence. The region is sliced in two by the Durance valley with the **Parc National des Écrins** lying on the western side of the divide and the **Parc Naturel Régional du Queyras** on the eastern. At the head of the Durance valley, where the Guisane and Durance rivers converge, the ancient fortified city of **Briançon** makes an excellent base for exploring the surrounding region.

Briançon

Located 100km east of Grenoble along the N91, **Briançon** is the capital of the Écrins and one of Europe's highest towns at 1,350 metres above sea level. An imposing citadel, it looms on the cusp of a rocky outcrop high above the Durance and Guisane valleys. Fortified originally by the Romans to guard the road from Milan to Vienne, the town is encircled by lofty ramparts and sheer walls constructed by the French architect and soldier, Sébastien Le Preste de Vauban in the seventeenth century (see box opposite). Today, despite its apparent remoteness, Briançon has a surprisingly cosmopolitan feel thanks to the mix of students, military personnel and tourists who populate the town.

The steep, narrow streets of the **ville haute**, high above the urban spread of the modern town, are the main focus of interest. There are four **gates**: portes Dauphine and Pignerol lie to the north, porte d'Embrun to the southwest and porte de la Durance to the east. If you come by car the best option is to park at the **Champ de Mars** at the top of the hill and enter the town through the porte Pignerol. From here the narrow main street – known as the *grande gargouille* because of the "gurgling" stream running down the middle – tips steeply downhill, bordered by mostly eighteenth-century houses. To the right is the sturdy plain **collegiate church**, designed under the supervision of Vauban, again with an eye to defence. Beyond it, there's a fantastic **view** from the walls, especially on a clear starry night, when the snows on the surrounding barrier of mountains give off a silvery glow.

Vauban's **citadelle**, the highest point of the fortifications, can be visited for free in July and August, and by guided tour during the rest of the year. These tours usually start at 3pm from the porte Pignerol and cost €5.15; there are English-language tours on Fridays at 3pm. The fortified keep, designed by Vauban, looks over the strategic intersection of five valleys and guards the start of the climb to the desolate and windswept **Col de Montgenèvre**, one of the oldest and most important passes into Italy.

Down in the *ville basse*, the **Télécabine de Prorel** shoots up from avenue René-Froger and links Briançon with the Serre Chevalier skiing resort area. It also provides a head start to mountain walkers (€5.30 return trip).

Practicalities

The **gare SNCF** is along avenue de la République in the *ville basse*, 1.5km south of the old city. Local **buses** #1, #2 and #3 link the station and the Champ de Mars. Briançon's **tourist office** is in the place du Temple close to the porte Pignerol gateway (Mon–Sat 8.30am–noon & 1.30–6.30pm, Sun 10am–12.30pm & 2.30–6pm; ☎04.92.21.08.50, ⓦwww.briancon.com). For the best information about outdoor activities in the mountains, head for the **Bureau des Guides** in Parc Chancel (July & Aug 10am–noon & 3–7pm; Sept–May 5–7pm; ☎04.92.20.15.73, ⓦwww.guides-briancon.fr). The **Maison du Parc National des Écrins**, place Médecin-Général-Blanchard (☎04.92.21.42.15, ⓦwww.les-ecrins-parc-national.fr), provides maps for those venturing into the nearby Écrins massif.

There's a range of inexpensive **hotels** in the town. At the upper end of the scale for luxury is the *Vauban*, 13 avenue du Général De Gaulle (☎04.92.21.12.11, ⓦwww.hotel-vauban.fr; ❹), which comes with spacious rooms, a gym and sauna. You can find perfectly comfortable if rather characterless rooms at the Parc, Central Parc (☎04.92.20.37.47; ❹), which is also in the *ville basse*. Partway up the hill towards the *ville haute* is the *Edelweiss*, 32 avenue de la République (☎04.92.21.02.94, ⓦwww.hotel-edelweiss-briancon.fr; ❸), which has a colourful interior and rooms with satellite TV. The cheapest hotel in town is the *Pension des Remparts*, which is in the citadelle itself at 14 avenue de Vauban (☎&ⓕ04.92.21.08.73; ❷; closed Nov). The nearest **campsite** is the three-star *Camping des Cinq Vallées* at St-Blaise (☎04.92.21.06.27, ⓦwww.camping5vallees.com; open June–Sept; €14 for a two-person tent), 2km to the south of the town.

The *ville haute* is full of hole-in-the-wall cafés and restaurants serving both local and many Italian dishes. On a sunny afternoon, you can enjoy the pleasant outdoor seating of *Les Templiers*, next to the tourist office in place du Temple (☎04.92.20.29.04), which has some large fondues on offer for €14–23. For some exceptionally tasty and good-value traditional dishes, try out ♣ *Le Passé Simple 1200* at 3 rue Porte Méane (☎04.92.21.37.43), where desserts like the *fromage blanc gateau*, served with walnuts and red berries, are a particular delight (menus are €23–38). If you're looking for live music, then the trendy *Duo Restolounge* at 8 place du Général Eberlé (☎04.92.21.09.18; open from lunchtime onwards) plays host to DJs at the weekend.

The Parc National des Écrins

The small towns of the Écrins are of little interest in themselves, especially in comparison with the architecture and culture of the Queyras and the nightlife in Chamonix, but the national park is worth a trip for the sheer variety of sports that it offers in a much less crowded setting than Mont Blanc. The best base for exploring the park is the village of **Vallouise**, which lies to the southwest of Briançon on the D902. From Vallouise, there are several excellent shorter walks that take you into the heart of the Écrins or you can follow the GR54, which makes a circuit of the park and passes through the village. There's a tourist office in place de l'Église (daily except Sun & Mon 9am–noon & 2–6pm; ☎04.92.23.36.12, ⓦwww.paysdesecrins.com), and a Bureau des Guides hut in the main car park (☎04.92.23.32.29, ⓦwww.guides-ecrins.com). The Maison du Parc des Écrins provides hiking information (☎04.92.23.32.31).

Reaching Vallouise by **public transport** is difficult: there are several trains and SCAL buses that go between the *gare SNCF* in Briançon and Argentière, from which there are buses to Vallouise and the surrounding villages. It's best to contact the Vallouise tourist office for the latest transport information.

Vallouise has a handful of **gîtes and hotels**: the pick of the bunch is *Hôtel Les Vallois* (☎04.92.23.41.37, ⓦwww.lesvallois.com; open all year; ❸), where you can enjoy pleasant rooms and a garden with swimming pool. *Le Baoüti* (☎04.92.23.46.50, ⓦwww.gite-le-baouti.com; €13.50 per person per night) is a **gîte** with rooms for up to six people, a large common room and self-catering facilities. All rooms in the village are likely to be full in July and August unless you book. For simple but filling meals try the *Brasserie AlpHand* on place du Village (☎04.92.23.20.00; closed May to mid-June; dishes for €12–25), which also brews its own excellent beers.

Briançon to the Queyras

The direct road from Briançon to Queyras (the D902) is a beautiful route that ascends steeply to the 2360m **Col d'Izoard** before descending into the **Casse**

Déserte, a wild, desolate region with an abundance of scree running down from the peaks above. If the Col d'Izoard is closed (or if you don't fancy driving on the high, winding mountain roads), then the Queyras can be reached from the north or the south on the N94. From Briançon, the River Durance meanders leisurely through a wide valley, following the N94, until some 50km later it reaches **EMBRUN**, a beautiful little town of narrow streets on a rocky bluff above the Durance and an important base if you want to spend a longer time exploring the Parc du Queyras. Embrun has been a fortress town for centuries. Hadrian made it the capital and main religious centre for this part of the Alps, and from the third century to the Revolution it was the seat of an important archbishopric. The chief sight is its twelfth-century cathedral, which has inspired numerous imitations throughout the region. The **tourist office**, in a former chapel of the Cordeliers on place Général-Dosse (Mon–Sat 9am–noon & 1.30–6pm; ℡04.92.43.72.72, ⓦwww.ot-embrun.fr), can provide information on nearby walking routes, as well as on the wide range of other outdoor activities (including rafting, sailing and climbing) which are organized in the area south of Embrun.

A vehicle is very helpful for exploring the remoter areas of the Queyras, but there are also several **trains** daily from Briançon to Embrun, as well as Guillestre (see below) and Mont-Dauphin. For **accommodation**, the most agreeable option in town is the flower-decked *Hôtel de la Mairie* on the central place de la Mairie (℡04.92.43.20.65, ⓦwww.hoteldelamairie.com; ❸; closed Oct–Nov), which also has a restaurant (from €15) that serves tasty local specialities, including some excellent foie gras. There are also several **campsites**; at the southern end of town, *La Vielle Ferme* (℡04.92.43.04.08, ⓦwww.campingembrun.com; open May–Sept; €23 for a two-person tent) has the most convenient location and the best facilities. Some 10km south of Embrun, you'll come to **SAVINES-LE-LAC**, a town that was moved from what is now the bottom of the **Lac de Serre-Ponçon** to its current location. This wide expanse of water was created by the damming of the Durance during the 1950s and 1960s, and is still one of the largest man-made lakes in Europe. If you're looking for a cheap place to stay near the Queyras, but lack camping facilities, then your best option is the **hostel** which overlooks this lake (℡04.92.44.20.16, Ⓔsavines@fuaj.org; mid-Jun to Aug; €15.20 for a dorm bed). Savines is on the bus route between Marseille and Briançon; there are also several trains daily from Briançon to Embrun and Mont-Dauphin.

Parc Régional du Queyras

Spreading southeast of Briançon to the Italian border, the **Parc Régional du Queyras** (ⓦwww.queyras.com) is much more Mediterranean in appearance than the mountains to the north, with only shallow soils and low scrub covering the mountainsides. The open land along the park's rolling roads makes it particularly enjoyable to spend a few hours driving up to **St-Véran**, an Alpine village near the Italian border. There are some good walking opportunities: the **GR58** or **Tour du Queyras** path runs through St-Véran on its circuit of the park, and the **GR5** passes Ceillac and Arvieux on its way from Briançon towards Embrun.

Guillestre and Château-Ville-Vieille

The road into the Queyras park follows the River Guil from Mont-Dauphin. The first stop is **GUILLESTRE**, a pretty mountain village that only really comes to life in summer. Its houses, in typical Queyras style, have open granaries

Vallée de la Clarée & Névache
Turin & Milan
Col de Montgenèvre
Sestrière
Grenoble
N91
N94
N94
ITALY
Briançon
D902
Bric Froid
(3302m)
Le Laus
GR5
Pic de Rochebrune
(3320m)
GR58
Col d'Izoard
(2360m)
Casse Déserte
Aiguilles
Brunissard
La Chalp
D947
Abriès
Arvieux
Château-Queyras
River Guil
L'Échalp
Château-Ville-Vieille
GR58
GR5
Molines-en-Queyras
GR5B
D5
D205
Grand Queyras
(3114m)
Mt. Granero
(3179m)
N94
Mont-Dauphin
GR58
St-Véran
Col Agnel
(2741m)
COMBE DU QUEYRAS
D902
D60
Notre-Dame-de-Clausis
Ceillac
Mt. Viso
(3841m)
Guillestre
Gap & Embrun
Font Sancte
(3387m)
ITALY
D902
Col de Vars
(2111m)
GR5

PARC NATUREL RÉGIONAL DU QUEYRAS

0   10 km

N

13

THE ALPS AND FRANCHE-COMTÉ | The Hautes-Alpes

on the upper floors and its sixteenth-century church has an intriguing porch (reminiscent of the cathedral at Embrun) with squatting lions carved from limestone. Continuing along the D947 from Guillestre, you'll come to the fortress of **Château-Queyras** (another product of Vauban's military and engineering savvy) which bars the way so completely that there's scarcely room for the road to squeeze around its base. Just beyond is **Ville-Vieille**, a small village with only a few old houses and church still intact. A right turn here takes you towards St-Véran, but if you stay on the road parallel to the river Guil, you will pass through the villages of Aiguilles, Abriès and L'Échalp (all with *gîtes d'étape*), to the **Belvédère du Viso**, close to the Italian border and the **Monte Viso**, at 3841m the highest peak in the area.

St-Véran

Seven kilometres south of Château-Ville-Vieille lies **ST-VÉRAN**, which at 2042m is one of the highest villages in Europe. As with many high Alpine villages, the traditional farming that once provided a livelihood for the people here has now largely died out and today the principal economic activity for the 280 permanent inhabitants is entertaining tourists.

St-Véran's houses are part stone and part timber, and there are several refurbished old drinking fountains, made entirely of wood. The seventeenth-century **Eglise d'St-Véran** stands prettily on the higher of the two streets, with its white tower silhouetted against the bare crags on the other side of the valley. The **GR58** passes just south of the village; waymarked and easy to follow, this path eventually turns right down to the river, before continuing up the opposite bank through woods of pine and larch as far as the chapel of Notre-Dame-de-Clausis. There, above the line of trees, it crosses to the right bank of the stream and winds up damp grassy slopes to the **Col de Chamoussière** (2884m), about three and a half hours from St-Véran. The ridge to the right of the col marks the frontier with Italy. In early July, there are glorious flowers – violets, Black Vanilla orchids, pinks and gentians – in the meadows leading up to the col.

St-Véran's very accommodating **tourist office** is halfway down the main high street (Mon–Sat 9am–12.30pm & 2–5.30pm; also open Sun in high season; ℡04.92.45.82.21, Ⓦ www.saintveran.com). There's **internet access** available in the library (Mon, Wed & Fri 4.30–6.30pm) at the entrance to the village. During July to Aug, there are *Petit Mathieu* **buses** (℡04.92.46.71.56, Ⓔ cars .petitmathieu@orange.fr) that come here from the *gare SNCF* in Guillestre, although it's best to contact the tourist office about the latest times and the potential need to reserve a place. One of the most tranquil places to stay is 🎿 *Les Chalets du Villard*, 05350 St-Véran (℡04.92.45.86.22, Ⓦ www.leschaletsduvillard .fr; open from mid-Dec to April & June to mid-Sept; ❹), which has spacious studio-apartments with kitchen facilities and private terraces.

North of Grenoble: Chambéry and around

Nestling in a valley to the north of the Chartreuse Massif, the town of **Chambéry** commands the entrance to the mountain passes which lead towards Italy, and has thus held an important strategic position for the various armies, merchants and artists who have crossed the Alps over the centuries. Perhaps unsurprisingly, the town is now a diverse mix of cultural influences, and it is this diversity that makes Chambéry's streets themselves (rather than its museums or churches) the highlight of any city tour.

Around 13km north of Chambéry is the spa resort of **Aix-les-Bains**, with its famous thermal baths, as well as the **Lac du Bourget**, the largest natural lake in France and one of the best sites in the country for watersports.

Chambéry

CHAMBÉRY grew up around the château built by Count Thomas of Savoie in 1232, and became the Savoyard capital, enjoying a golden age in the fourteenth and fifteenth centuries. Although superseded as capital by Turin in 1562, it remained an important commercial and cultural centre, and the philosopher Rousseau spent some of his happiest years in the town during the 1730s. Only incorporated into France in 1860, modern Chambéry is a bustling provincial town with a wealth of grand Italianate architecture and a strong sense of its regional identity, which can be discerned thorough the colourful red-and-white flags and the "Savoie Libre" car-bumper stickers which you'll see throughout the town.

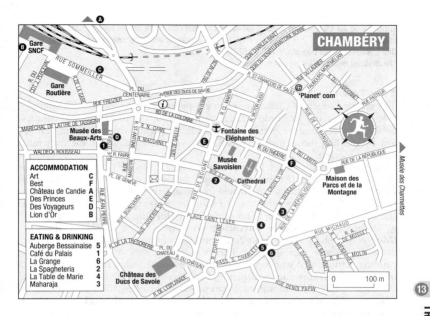

Map caption / labels:

CHAMBÉRY

Gare SNCF
Gare Routière
Musée des Beaux-Arts
Fontaine des Eléphants
Musée Savoisien
Cathedral
'Planet' com
Maison des Parcs et de la Montagne
Château des Ducs de Savoie
Musée des Charmettes

ACCOMMODATION

Art	C
Best	F
Château de Candie	A
Des Princes	E
Des Voyageurs	D
Lion d'Or	B

EATING & DRINKING

Auberge Bessainaise	5
Café du Palais	1
La Grange	6
La Spagheteria	2
La Table de Marie	4
Maharaja	3

0   100 m

Arrival and information

The **gare SNCF** is on rue Sommeiller, 500m north of the old town, with the **gare routière** just outside in place de la Gare. Five-minutes' walk away at no. 24 boulevard de la Colonne, where all the **city buses** stop, is the **tourist office** (July & Aug Mon–Sat 9am–6pm, Sun 10am–1pm; Sept–June Mon–Sat 9am–noon & 1.30–6pm; ☎04.79.33.42.47, ⓦwww.chambery-tourisme.com), which can also provide maps and information about the Bauges and Vanoise massifs if you intend to explore them. There's **internet access** at the tourist office (same hours apply) or in the eastern part of the town centre at the internet shop Planet'Com, 9 Faubourg Montmélian (☎04.79.71.96.50), as well as several other internet shops on the same street.

Accommodation

There's plenty of inexpensive **accommodation** scattered around the centre of Chambéry, but you can also enjoy some real luxury without lightening your wallet to the same extent as you would in Chamonix or Annecy. Most of the hotels stay open all year.

Art 154 rue Sommeiller ☎04.79.62.37.26, ⓦwww.arthotel-chambery.com. This place is close to the railway station and has pleasantly decorated rooms with satellite TV. ❸

Best 9 rue Denfert Rochereau ☎04.79.85.76.79, ⓦwww.besthotel.fr. The more expensive apartments here have balconies overlooking the Place du Theatre, but all the rooms are soundproofed, stylishly decorated and have all the mod cons. ❸

Château de Candie rue du Bois de Candie ☎04.79.96.63.00, ⓦwww.chateaudecandie .com. You'll find elegant rooms and an excellent

restaurant in this château that lies a few km to the north of the town. ❼

Lion d'Or 1 av de la Boisse ☎04.79.44.32.75, ⓦwww.liondor73.com. Located directly opposite the *gare SNCF*, this place has clean, basic rooms with a brasserie serving filling meals next door. ❸

Des Princes 4 rue de Boigne, 73000 Chambéry ☎04.79.33.45.36, ⓦwww .hoteldesprinces.eu. There is a sense of colonial grandeur in the Indian-themed decor of this refined hotel, where the rooms are cosy and

stylish, while the €9 breakfast buffet is excellent value. ⑤
Des Voyageurs 3 rue Doppet ☎ 04.79.33.57.00. The cheapest beds in town are perched above a lively café on the ground floor; the communal bathrooms aren't the cleanest and it can get noisy in the evening. ①

The Town

The restored streets of Chambéry's densely-packed centre abound with fashionable boutiques and streetside cafés, as well as groups of musicians and dancers performing on summer evenings. Alongside the sights which you can admire just by strolling through these streets, however, there are also some museums worth exploring.

Halfway down the broad, leafy boulevard de la Colonne is Chambéry's most famous monument, the extravagant and bizarrely off-scale **Fontaine des Éléphants**. The fountain was erected in homage to Général Comte de Boigne (1751–1830), a local boy who amassed a fortune working as a mercenary in India and subsequently used much of his vast wealth to fund major urban developments in his home town. **Musée Savoisien**, on nearby square de Lannoy-de-Bissy (Mon & Wed–Sun 10am–noon & 2–6pm; €3), chronicles the history of Savoie from the Bronze Age onwards. There's a diverse mix of exhibits: medieval paintings and painted wooden statues from various churches in the region; a set of thirteenth-century murals depicting battle-scenes and life at the royal court; and a collection of traditional local craft products, including tools and furniture.

Next to the museum in place de la Métropole is the **cathedral**, which dates from the 1400s but has an interior decorated in elaborate nineteenth-century trompe l'oeil. From here a passage leads to the fine old street of the **rue de la Croix-d'Or**, the hub of aristocratic Chambéry in the seventeenth century and now home to numerous restaurants. A few blocks to the south of here is the **rue de la République**, where there are several large public buildings, as well as the **Maison des Parcs et de la Montagne** (Tues–Sat 10am–noon and 2–7pm; free), which has a fun little museum with multimedia exhibits concerning the local mountains and lakes.

Heading west from the **rue de la Croix-d'Or** along the long, rectangular **place St-Léger** (home to Jeans-Jacques Rousseau in 1735) and the smart **rue de Boigne**, you will soon find yourself facing the **Château des Ducs de Savoie**. A massive and imposing structure, the Château was once the main home of the dukes of Savoie, and is now occupied by the prefecture; the interior is only accessible by guided tours, which begin from the adjacent place du Château (May, June & Sept daily 2.30pm; July & Aug Mon–Fri 10.30am, 2.30, 3.30 and 4.30pm; Oct–Dec Mon–Fri 2.30pm; €4). A short walk north from the castle exit along rue Jean Pierre Veyrat brings you to the **Musée des Beaux-Arts** on place du Palais de Justice (Mon & Wed–Sun 10am–noon & 2–6pm; €3), which is largely devoted to works by lesser-known Italian artists from the Renaissance; the pride of the collection is the fifteenth-century *Portrait of a Young Man,* attributed to Paolo Uccello.

Two kilometres south of town on the rustic chemin des Charmettes is Rousseau's other Chambéry address, **Les Charmettes**. This country cottage is now home to the **Musée des Charmettes** (April–Sept daily except Tues 10am–noon & 2–6pm; Oct–March daily except Tues 10am–noon & 2–4.30pm; free), a museum focused on Rousseau's writing and domestic life. The house is beautifully furnished in the style of the day, with eighteenth-century furniture like the philosopher's old writing desk on display; you can also admire the lovely formal gardens outside, which are laid out just as Rousseau would have remembered them.

Eating and drinking

Tasty meals at decent prices are not hard to find in Chambéry. The town is an excellent place to indulge in some local Savoyard dishes, including fondues and fresh fish from the local lakes and rivers.

Restaurants

Auberge Bessainaise 28 place Monge ☎04.79.33.40.37. You can find traditional Savoyard fondues here, but the chef's real speciality are the large omelettes, in particular the *omelette aux truffles* (€15). Closed Mon–Tues & Jan.

La Grange 33 place Monge ☎04.79.85.60.31. There are plenty of inexpensive regional dishes on offer here, and some of the best feature the local salmon (€13–14). Closed Wed & Sun.

Maharaja 4 rue de Roche ☎04.79.70.65.04. Here you'll find some quirky variants of classic Indian cuisine, including some vegetarian options. Menus are €13–26. Closed Mon.

La Spagheteria 43 rue St Réal ☎04.79.33.27.62. Situated on a busy street, this Italian restaurant serves home-made pizzas and pastas. The menus are €15–20. Closed Sun.

Bars and cafés

Café du Palais 5 place du Palais de Justice ☎04.79.33.75.12. A traditional café that overlooks the modern square, and is popular with the locals for an evening beer (€3–4) or coffee (€1.35). Open daily noon–midnight.

La Table de Marie 193 rue de la Croix d'Or, 73000 Chambéry ☎04.79.85.99.76. If you're missing tea, cakes and scones, then *La Table de Marie*, a café which also serves some large evening meals, is the place for you. The full evening menu (which includes meat dishes like *saucisson*) is €15. Open Mon–Sat noon–3pm & 7–11pm.

Aix-les-Bains and the Lac du Bourget

13km north of Chambéry is **AIX-LES-BAINS**, one of France's premier spa resorts since the eighteenth century. The town's waters have been famous for their healing qualities since Roman times, but the streets are chiefly composed of the elegant buildings that date from the *belle époque* of the late 1800s, when the members of European high society dropped by to relax and take the waters. These days, Aix-les-Bains is a sedate and genteel place, with thousands of French pensioners descending on the town throughout the year for state-funded thermal treatments. This is a good spot for a mud bath, but there are also some Roman ruins to explore in the old town. It's also the best base for enjoying the sights and outdoor activities at the nearby **Lac du Bourget**.

Arrival, information and accommodation

The **gare SNCF** of Aix-les-Bains is on the southern side of the town centre on boulevard Président-Wilson, and from here it's a brief stroll northwards up avenue Charles-de-Gaulle to the central place Maurice-Mollard. The **tourist office** (daily: June–Aug 9am–6.30pm; Sept–May 9am–noon & 2–6pm; ☎04.79.88.68.00, ⒲www.aixlesbains.com) is on the north side of this square. It's only 2km from the town centre to the Grand Port on the Lac du Bourget, but you can take bus #2 from the bus stop close to the tourist office if you don't want to walk.

Aix-les-Bains has almost a hundred **hotels**, but they are busy year-round so advance bookings are advisable. The four-star *Radisson SAS*, avenue. Charles De Gaulle (☎04.79.34.19.19, ⒲www.aixlesbains.radissonsas.com; ➐), is close to the *gare SNCF* and has excellent facilities, including a restaurant, pool and fitness centre. At the eastern end of the town centre, the *Agora* at 1 avenue Marlioz (☎04.79.34.19.19, ⒲www.hotel-agora.com; ➎) also has a pool and large, comfortable rooms. The nearby *Grand Hotel du Parc*, 28 rue de Chambéry (☎04.79.61.29.11, ⒲www.grand-hotel-du-parc.com; ➌), is a cheaper option with bright, airy rooms. However, you'll find very affordable rooms with far more character than any of these options at the *Savoy*, 21 avenue Charles de Gaulle (T 04.79.35.13.33, E hotelsavoyaixlesbains@orange.fr). This hotel (undergoing restoration; due for completion in 2009) is in a charming nineteenth-century building and provides some basic but clean and tidy rooms with communal bathrooms (€17), but the highlight are the larger rooms with balconies (③) overlooking the town centre.

Closer to the Lake itself, the Aix-les-Bains hostel is at Promenade du Sierroz (T 04.79.88.32.88, E aix-les-bains@fuaj.org; open Feb–Oct; €17.60 for a dorm bed). There are several **campsites** close to this; a good mid-range option is *Camping du Sierroz*, boulevard Robert Barrier (T 04.79.61.21.43, W www .aixlesbains.com/campingsierroz; €14 for a two-person tent).

The Town
The activities and sights of the town are focused around place Maurice-Mollard, where the most eye-catching landmark is **Arc de Campanus**, a Roman arch erected in the first century BC as a funerary monument. The large Roman baths that once stood near here are said to have incorporated over 24 kinds of marble; of the surviving ruins in the square (some of which back on to the *mairie*). The most intact is the Temple du Diane, a rectangular monument which now houses the **Musée Lapidaire** (daily 10am–noon, 1.30–6pm; closed Tues pm; €5), where there's a small collection of Gallo-Roman ceramics and statues.

A short walk north from here is the uber-modern spa centre **Les Thermes d'Aix-les-Bains** (open daily 10am–7.45pm; T 08.10.44.33.32, W www .thermaix.com; €18 per day), one of the best places to experience the healing qualities of the local sulphurous water. Also north of the place Maurice-Mollard, at 10 boulevard Côtes, is the **Musée Faure** (daily except Tues 10am–noon & 1.30–6pm; €4.40), an elegant house with a small but impressive collection of nineteenth-century art. It includes paintings from Impressionists like Cézanne, Pissaro and Sisley, as well as some lovely Degas pastels.

Lac de Bourget
Connected to the River Rhône by the Canal de Savières, the **Lac du Bourget** is a place of great beauty, a protected wildlife reserve and home to the now scarce European beaver. "Nowhere could one find such perfect concord between water, mountains, earth and sky", enthused the nineteenth century French writer Balzac, and it's clear what attracted him and so many other poets and artists to this place. The lake's "Côte Sauvage" rises precipitously above the sparkling blue water on its western bank, which is dominated at its southern end by the looming presence of the **Dent du Chat** (1390m). There are daily sightseeing **cruises** on the lake between March and November (1–2hr; €12–15), as well as

---

Watersports on the Lake

Whatever your favourite watersport, the Lac du Bourget is likely to have a club and good facilities available. For sailing, you can visit the **Club Nautique Voile d'Aix** on boulevard Barrier at the Grand Port (T 04.79.34.10.74, W www.cnva.com; 5 half-day sessions for €140). Water-skiers should contact the **Ski Club Nautique**, at the Plage Municipale to the east of the Petit Port (T 06.18.24.64.59, W www.club-ski-nautique .com; €32 for a lesson). There's kayaking and rowing on offer at the **Club d'aviron d'Aix-les-Bains**, 22 avenue Daniel Rops (T 04.79.88.12.07, W http://aviron.ena.free .fr; €12 for a 2hr session).

more expensive lunch, dinner and evening cruises. Contact the Bateaux du Lac du Bourget office at the Grand Port in Aix-les-Bains (☎04.79.88.92.09, ⓦwww .gwel.com).

There are also daily cruises (30min) to the picturesque **Abbaye d'Hautecombe** (audioguide tours in English and other languages; daily except Tues 10–11.15am & 2–5pm; €3) on the western side of the lake. The abbey is the final resting place of many members of the Savoie royals, including the last king and queen of Italy, Umberto II de Savoie and his wife Marie-José. The Abbaye lies close to the village of St-Pierre de Curtille, and is also accessible to cars via the D18 road.

Eating and drinking

There's a broad range of **restaurants** and **cafés** to choose from. *La Rotonde* (☎04.79.35.00.60) has a pleasant setting in the Parc Thermal, near to the Place Maurice-Mollard, live music on Fridays and Saturdays, and provides some excellent fondues for €16–19. *Le Nelson* (☎04.79.35.11.32) in passage Boccara is a central bar which offers outdoor seating for a drink or croissant. ⚛ *La Palette des Saveurs*, 1 place de Carnot, 73100 Aix-les-Bains (☎04.79.88.37.11), has an array of inventive ice cream (€4–8); if you want to sample a local product, try the Chartreuse flavour. Next to the lake at the Grand Port, you'll find the friendly *Skiff Pub* (☎04.79.63.41.00; closed Tues), which serves fish from the lake, as well seafood dishes like oysters, king prawns and lobsters.

The Isère valley and the Vanoise

The **Massif de la Vanoise**, a rugged set of mountains further to the west of Chambéry, rises to heights of over 3500m, and offers challenging routes for skiers, particularly along the steep slopes of the Isère valley. The glacier-capped southeast quadrant of the Vanoise forms the **Parc National de la Vanoise**, where hikers will find some of the most spectacular GR trails in France. The easiest road access to the Massif is from Chambéry or Grenoble, although driving the winding and precipitous old highways from Annecy or Chamonix is an adventure in itself.

The Isère valley

The A43 from Chambéry cuts between the Massif des Bauges to the north and the Vanoise to the south, following the path of the lower **Isère River** as it flows down from the industrial town Albertville. Following the river by road from here involves a 180-kilometre journey south, north and south again back to its source high in the mountains near the **Col de l'Iseran** (2770m), close to the Italian frontier. From Albertville, whose edge-of-town hypermarkets make it a useful place for stocking up, the N90 climbs southeast along the bends of the Isère River for 50km to Moûtiers, the turn-off for the massive **Les Trois Vallées** ski region. At Moûtiers, the river course swings northeast and following it will lead you to **Bourg–St–Maurice**, the town at the midpoint of the upper Isère valley. At Séez, a couple of kilometres further east, the road comes to an important junction: the N90 continues to climb steeply towards the **Col du Petit St–Bernard** (2188m), following the path of the ancient Roman Way (now a classic touring route into the Italian Val d'Aosta), while the D902 heads south towards the famous resort of **Val d'Isère**.

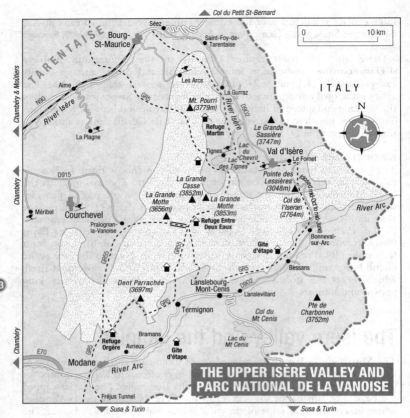

The following labels appear on the map:

Col du Petit St-Bernard

Séez

Bourg-St-Maurice

Saint-Foy-de-Tarentaise

T A R E N T A I S E

Chambéry & Moûtiers

Les Arcs

La Gurraz

Aime

N90

River Isère

GR5

Mt. Pourri (3779m)

River Isère

D902

ITALY

N

Le Grande Sassière (3747m)

Refuge Martin

Val d'Isère

La Plagne

Tignes

Lac du Chevril

Le Fornet

Lac des Tignes

D915

Chambéry

Méribel

Courchevel

La Grande Casse (3852m)

La Grande Motte (3656m)

La Grande Motte (3853m)

Pointe des Lessières (3048m)

Col de l'Iseran (2764m)

(closed mid-Oct to mid-June)

River Arc

Pralognan-la-Vanoise

GR55

Refuge Entre Deux Eaux

Gîte d'étape

Bonneval-sur-Arc

GR55

GR5

Bessans

Chambéry

Dent Parrachée (3697m)

GR5

Lanslebourg-Mont-Cenis

Lanslevillard

D902

Pte de Charbonnel (3752m)

Termignon

Col du Mt Cenis

Bramans

Lac du Mt Cenis

Refuge Orgère

Avrieux

Gîte d'étape

E70

Modane

River Arc

THE UPPER ISÈRE VALLEY AND PARC NATIONAL DE LA VANOISE

Fréjus Tunnel

Susa & Turin

Susa & Turin

0   10 km

Méribel and Les Trois Vallées

Just off the N90, south of the industrial town of Moûtiers, **Les Trois Vallées** (Ⓦ www.les3vallees.com) is one of the world's largest linked skiing areas, with an ingenious lift network that makes skiing from village to village easy, and near endless off-piste possibilities awaiting the intrepid. There are several component resorts: expensive and luxurious Courchevel (Ⓦ www.courchevel.com); ugly and family-oriented Les Menuires (Ⓦ www.lesmenuires.com), which has a number of cheap hotels; and lively Val Thorens (Ⓦ www.valthorens.com), popular with younger crowds and the snowboard set. However, the main focus of interest of Les Trois Vallées is **MÉRIBEL**, a resort established in 1938 by the Scottish Colonel Peter Lindsay and traditionally dominated by British tourists, which now offers a good range of cheap accommodation and après-ski activities. There are plenty of pubs and other British imports, but the small wooden chalets which climb the eastern side of the valley also manage to give the resort a traditional Savoyard feel. At the bottom of the valley is the large **Olympic Park** (Dec–April, July & Aug daily 11am-7.45pm), which includes a swimming pool (€4.60) and ice rink (€4.30).

Practicalities

Méribel's **tourist office** (daily 9am–noon & 3–7pm; ℡04.79.08.60.01, ⓦwww.meribel.net), at the top of the route de la Monte in the village centre, provides information on mountain biking and walking in summer, as well as **internet** access. In summer, it's worth enquiring about the **Meripass** card at the tourist office; this card (valid for six days; €60) gets you free access to both the Olympic park and to the ski lifts in the area.

There are many ski shops in Méribel that sell and rent out skis and snowboards during the winter, while the ESF ski school office (℡04.79.08.60.31) is in the tourist office. In summer, the tourist office produces a useful "Guide to Walks" (€6.50) in the local area, as well as maps with the best local biking trails. The **Bureau des Guides** (℡04.79.00.30.38) is also located in the tourist office; the guides organize a wide variety of walks in the area (€25 per person per day).

Though most local **accommodation** is based on the fixed packages of British tour companies, there are a few independent guesthouses and hotels. *Hôtel Doron* (℡04.79.08.60.02, ⒺŁdoron@mountaintradingco.com; open Dec–April & July–Aug; ❺) has simple, affordable rooms as well as a central location. For something a little more luxurious but still close to the centre, try the *Chalet Hôtel Marie Blanche* on route de la Renard (℡04.79.08.65.55, ⓦwww.marie-blanche.com; ❼) featuring cosy rooms and an excellent restaurant serving tasty dishes of lamb, veal and duck.

Bourg-St-Maurice and around

A pleasant if unremarkable town situated at the roaring confluence of the Isère and Chapieux rivers, **BOURG-ST-MAURICE** is mainly of interest for British tourists because of its direct Eurostar train link with London during Dec–Apr (10hr journey; from €125). It also has some good shops – including a large Intersport (which rents out and sells ski gear) and a couple of supermarkets – which are useful for stocking up before heading up to the resorts. The **tourist office** (Mon–Fri 9am–noon & 2–7pm, Sat 8.30am–7pm, Sun 9am–12.30pm & 3.30–7pm; ℡04.79.07.04.92) is across the main road from the building which incorporates both the **gare SNCF** and the **gare routière**. In winter, there are regular bus services to Les Arcs and Val d'Isere, but in summer, these are reduced to one or two a day. If you don't have a car and want to get to the resorts, you may have to pay an expensive taxi fare or hitch a ride.

There are a few reasonable **places to stay** in Bourg-St-Maurice. Located in a pretty, forested setting at 69 route Hauteville, *L'Autantic* (℡04.79.07.01.70, ⓦwww.hotel-autantic.fr; rooms €40–130), is a modern chalet with a pool and sauna, while *Arolla*, 192 avenue du Centenaire (℡04.79.07.01.78, ⓦwww.hotel-arolla.fr; ❷), has cheaper rooms in the centre of town. The nearest **HI hostel**, *La Verdache* (℡04.79.41.01.93, Ⓔseez-les-arcs@fuaj.org; open June to mid-Sept & mid-Dec to April; €16.70 for a dorm bed), lies 4km away outside Séez among beautiful Alpine woods, and has pleasant bedrooms but no kitchen facilities. A good **campsite** is *Camping Le Reclus* in Seez (℡04.79.41.01.05, ⓦwww.campinglereclus.com; €12.90 for a two-person tent). From Bourg-St-Maurice, you can take any bus towards Val d'Isere and ask to get off near the campsite or the hostel.

There are several major ski resorts in the mountains around Bourg-St-Maurice. On the northern slopes above the town, **Paradiski** (ⓦwww.paradiski.com) is a ski area that was formed in 2003 when the resorts of La Plagne and Les Arcs were joined by a giant double-decker *téléphérique* that swings over the Ponthurin valley in a single bound. **Les Arcs** (Ⓦ www.lesarcs .com), to the southeast of Bourg-St-Maurice and accessible from the town via a funicular railway, comprises four villages of varying altitude; while the resort has excellent snow and terrain for all levels, it also has a decidedly mellow après-ski scene and the villages lack atmosphere. **La Plagne** (Ⓦ www.la-plagne.com) is a huge ski station made up of ten resorts high above the Isère valley, with plenty of opportunities for both beginners and more advanced skiers. The most attractive (and exclusive) of these purpose-built resorts is **Belle Plagne**; be warned that here again the nightlife is not anywhere near as lively as that which you'll find in Val d'Isere.

Bourg-St-Maurice to Val d'Isère

Beyond Bourg-St-Maurice and the road junction at Séez, the D902 follows the path of the Isère as it climbs towards Val d'Isère. After around 12km, the road brings you to the artificial **Lac de Chevril**, which sits below another popular and purpose-built ski resort: **Tignes**. The resort is not attractive, and in summer has little to offer aside from a handful of lifts open for glacier skiing, yet in winter, the slopes nearby become irresistible for expert skiers. From Tignes, you can easily access 130km of pistes which pass over or around the 3656-metre **Grand Motte** to Val d'Isère (see below); these are collectively known as the **Espace Killy**, named after French downhill legend Jean-Claude Killy. The resort is usually filled with package-holidayers, but independent travellers can stay at the **HI hostel** Les Clarines (Ⓣ 04.79.41.01.93, Ⓔ tignes@fuaj.org; open mid-June to Aug & Oct–April; €16.70 for a dorm bed). If you're looking for something a little more upmarket, then the resort's **tourist office** (Ⓣ 04.79.40.04.40, Ⓦ www.tignes.net) can help book hotel accommodation (Ⓣ 04.79.40.03.03, Ⓦ www.tignesreservation.net).

Val d'Isère

Once a tiny mountain village, **VAL D'ISÈRE** is now a sprawling mass of cafés, supermarkets, chalets and bars. Because of its distance from Bourg-St-Maurice and the larger towns to the west, the resort almost completely closes down in the off season, with only one or two hotels remaining open in May. Nonetheless, Val d'Isere does make a convenient centre for walking in the summer, and you can ski year-round on the glacier.

The **skiing** around Val d'Isère is varied and demanding; many international experts never ski anywhere else. There are two beginner's slopes, one close to the resort centre and the other in nearby **Le Daille**. Of the three major skiing areas, **Le Fornet** provides the best slopes for novices, but it is also relatively undeveloped, and there are some narrow, unkept pistes. The **Solaise** area provides easily accessible sheltered skiing between larch trees during bad weather, and has two free beginners' lifts near its swimming pool and ice-skating complex. **Le Rocher de Bellevard** is home to the Olympic downhill and its east-facing slopes (site of the 1992 Olympics and the 2009 World Championships) are reserved for the most accomplished skiers.

Practicalities

The **tourist office** (daily 8.30am–7.30pm; Ⓣ 04.79.06.06.60, Ⓦ www .valdisere.com) is next to the *mairie* in the centre of the resort and has **internet access** at a pricey €9/hr. There is a **Bureau des Guides** (Ⓣ 06.14.62.90.14, Ⓦ www. guide-montagne-tarentaise.com) information desk in the Killy Sport Shop next to the tourist office; here you can find information and guides for the various climbs, Via Ferrata courses and hiking trails in the area, including those which are in the nearby **Parc National de la Vanoise** (see box below).

There are several **ski schools** in the town. The tried-and-trusted ESF has an office (☏04.79.06.02.34, ⊛www.esfvaldisere.com; €30 for a morning lesson in a group) in the centre at the Carrefour des Dolomites, while Misty Fly (☏04.79.40.08.74, ⊛www.mistyflyvaldisere.com; €38 for a morning lesson in a group) has a fun-loving, young set of instructors. Misty Fly also sells and rents ski and snowboard gear; it is situated opposite the tourist office.

Staying in Val d'Isère will certainly lighten your wallet. One of the most convenient and comfortable **accommodation** options is the *Mercure* (☏04.79.06.12.03, ⓔhotel@mercurevaldisere.com; ❾), right in the centre of town. One of the more affordable hotels in town is the two-star *La Bailletta* (☏04.79.06.02.06, ⊛http://lerelaisduski.valdisere.com; open Dec to early May; ❽), where you'll find a restaurant, rooms with a TV and private bathroom, and a garage. On the same site is another slighter cheaper hotel, *Le Relais du Ski*, which is operated by the same owners; it has rooms without TV and more basic facilities. The cheapest spot in Val d'Isère, however, is unsurprisingly the **campsite**: *Camping Les Richardes* (☏04.79.06.26.60, ⊛http://campinglesrichardes.free.fr; open mid-June to mid-Sept; €13 for a two-person tent) is 1km from the centre of the resort at Le Laisinant.

As with the hotels, the resort's **restaurants** are mostly closed except in winter; they also have a tendency to burn a hole in your wallet without providing anything more refined than what you can find in Chambéry for half the price. If you feel like trying a place which aims to produce "*cuisine gastronomique*", the best option is *Le Savoyard*, which has set menus from €43 and a particularly good cheeseboard. Much cheaper are crêperies like *Crêpe Val's* (☏04.79.41.14.62), which serves both sweet crêpes and savoury *galettes* for €3–7, while there are also several popular restaurants serving uncomplicated dishes at the Rond Pont des Pistes, the site of many of the resort's ski lifts: at *Le Bananas* (☏04.79.06.04.23), for example, you can enjoy the "Tex-Mex" menu, which includes a filling *chilli con carne* (€18).

When it comes to the resort's **nightlife**, the most popular spot is just down from the Rond Pont, where *Dick's Tea Bar* provides a mix of local bands and UK DJs until the early hours. Just round the corner from here is the *La Foret* bar, which has Guinness on tap and a decent array of cocktails (€8–10). During the winter, many of the bars close at 4am and open again just four hours later as the early-morning skiers hit the slopes. However, most bars shut down outside of the peak skiing season of Nov–April.

The Parc National de la Vanoise

The **Parc National de la Vanoise** (⊛www.vanoise.com) occupies the eastern end of the Vanoise Massif. It's extremely popular, with over 500km of marked paths, including the **GR5**, **GR55** and **GTA** (Grande Traversée des Alpes), and numerous *refuges* along the trails. For in-depth information on the various routes, head for the tourist offices in Val d'Isère, Bourg-St-Maurice and Méribel.

To cross the park, you can take the **GR55** from the Lac de Tignes and over the **Col de la Vanoise**. You can then connect with the **GR5**, which brings you out at the southern end of the park in the town of Modane. There are countless shorter but equally beautiful walks in the park. Settlements in the Arc Valley like Bessans are good bases to start exploring the park, but even the so-called ski resorts of Tignes, Val d'Isère and Méribel are good starting-points.

The Col de l'Iseran

From Val d'Isère, both the **D902** veers south from the river and climbs towards the **Col de l'Iseran** (2770m), the highest pass with a paved road in the Alps. Despite the dangers of weather and the arduous climb, the pass has been used for centuries, mainly because it is by far the quickest route between the remote upper valleys of the Isère and Arc. In the distant past, the volume of road traffic was too small to disturb the small communities that eked out an existence in this harsh, high-altitude landscape, but twentieth-century roads and the development of winter sports have changed all that. From October to June, the pass is blocked by snow, but in summer, it's a must-see sight for tourists with cars, who have the option of moving on to the much less touristy villages of the **Arc Valley** that lie beyond the pass. If the weather is good and you are reasonably fit, you should consider walking from here along a steep path to the **Pointe des Lessières** (3041m), which offers beautiful views of the Vanoise Massif, as well as the fearsome Italian side of Mont Blanc.

Annecy and around

Lying 60km to the south of Lake Geneva, **ANNECY** is one of the most beautiful and popular resort towns of the French Alps. It enjoyed a brief moment of political and religious importance in the early sixteenth century, when Geneva opted for the Reformation and François de Sales, a fugitive Catholic bishop, decamped here with a train of ecclesiastics and a prosperous, cultivated elite.

Annecy has never been so influential a political centre in the succeeding centuries, but for most visitors, that is nothing to lament over. The delights of the town nowadays lie not just in its historical monuments, like the imposing Chateâu on the hill or the fort of the Palais d'Île closer to the lake, but also in the stunning scenery which can be admired from various points around the town. Surrounded by spectacular mountains and located on the banks of a sparkling turquoise lake, Annecy is about as close to a fairy-tale city as it is possible to get except in a children's story.

Arrival and information

The **gare SNCF** and **gare routière** complex is northwest of the town centre. The **tourist office** (Mon–Sat 9am–12.30pm & 1.45–6pm; Jun–Aug also open Sun at the same times; ☎04.50.45.00.33, ⓦwww.annecytourisme.com) is housed in Centre Bonlieu, a modern shopping centre on rue Pâquier, near the lake. For cheap, fast **internet service**, head for the internet shop Planète Telecom at 2 rue Jean Jaurès. There's **bike rental** from Roul' ma poule at 4 rue des Marquisats (☎04.50.27.86.83).

Accommodation

Annecy has a number of good **hotels**, but these fill quickly during both the winter ski season and in July and August, so it's always good to reserve a bed well in advance. If you have a car, it's also worth calling ahead to check about parking; several of the hotels offer free parking in the centre, which can substantially cut the price of your stay.

ANNECY

ACCOMMODATION

Allobroges	B
Camping le Belvedere	J
Carlton	F
Central	D
Les Jardins du Château	I
Hostel	A
L'Imperial Palace	E
Nouvel	G
Palais de L'Isle	C
Splendid	C

EATING & DRINKING

Auberge de Savoie	4
Brasserie des Européens	3
Bull	7
Da Pietro	1
Finn Kelly's	8
L'Etage	2
Le Munich	5
Le Petit Zinc	6

Hotels

Allobroges 11 rue Sommeiller ☎ 04.50.45.03.11, ⓦ www.allobroges.com. Tastefully decorated and comfortable rooms + free internet access + free breakfast = an excellent value three-star hotel. ❺

Carlton 5 rue des Glières ☎ 04.50.10.09.09, ⓦ www.bestwestern-carlton.com. This place provides large, modern and fairly unoriginal rooms for a mainly business clientele. ❻.

Central 6 rue Royale ☎ 04.50.45.05.37, ⓦ www .hotelcentralannecy.com. While the exterior of this one-star hotel is not promising, you will find bright, colourful rooms which look out over a quiet courtyard or one of the town's canals. ❷

L'Imperial Palace allée de l'Imperial ☎ 04.50.09.30.00, ⓦ www.imperial-annecy.com. Undoubtedly the most prestigious hotel in town, *L'Imperial Palace* boasts an excellent restaurant, casino, beauty centre and a beautiful position on the lakeside. Doubles are €300–375.

🏃 **Les Jardins du Château** place du Château ☎ 04.50.45.72.28. Situated right next to the Château, this *chambre d'hôte* provides apartments with small kitchens for up to five people. There's a leafy little garden, a terrace overlooking the city, and you can rent bikes. ❹

Nouvel 37 rue Vaugelas ☎ 04.50.45.05.78, ⓦ www.nouvelhotel.com. Situated close to the *gare SNCF*, the *Nouvel* has 1930s-style decor but thoroughly modern rooms with satellite TV. ❹

Palais de l'Isle 13 rue Perrière ☎ 04.50.45.86.87, ⓦ www.hoteldupalaisdelisle.com. Location, location, location. The position of the *Palais*, just off the lively quai Perrière, is its main attraction, although the rooms also come with all the mod cons. ❻

Splendid 4 quai Eustache Chappuis ☎ 04.50.45.20.00, ⓦ www.splendidhotel.fr. Well placed opposite the grassy expanse of the Champ de Mars, the *Splendid* has spacious rooms with satellite TV and a/c. ❼

Campsite and Hostel

Camping Le Belvedere 8 route du Semnoz ☎ 04.50.45.48.30, ⓔ camping@ville-annecy.fr. The municipal campsite is just 10min walk from the Old Town; there's a bar and laundry on site. €14.20 for a two-person tent.

Hostel 4 route du Semnoz ☎ 04.50.45.33.19, ⓔ annecy@fuaj.org. This hostel can get crowded and is 2km away from the *gare SNCF*, but has good facilities, including internet access and kitchens. Open mid-Jan to Nov. €17.60 for a dorm bed.

The Town

The old town of Annecy is a bewitching warren of passages and arcaded houses which date from the sixteenth century and are divided by peaceful little branches of the **Canal du Thiou**. Many of the houses here are ringed by canalside railings that overflow with geraniums and petunias in summer; added to the cool shade offered by the arcades, these flowers make the town's pedestrianized streets a particular delight to wander around on a sunny afternoon.

From rue de l'Île on the canal's south bank, the narrow rampe du Château leads up to the **Château**, the former home of Genevois counts and the dukes of Nemours, a junior branch of the house of Savoy. There has been a castle on this site since the eleventh century, but the Nemours found the old fortress a little too rough for their taste and added more refined living quarters in the sixteenth century. These now house the collections of the **Musée-Château** and **Observatoire Régional des Lacs Alpins** (Jun–Sept daily 10.30am–6pm; Oct–May daily except Tues 10am–noon & 2–5pm; €4.80). In the latter, there are some intriguing exhibits about the geology and marine life of the local lakes, while the former contains folk art and handicrafts from across the region. The main attractions, however, are the castle itself and the views it provides of the lake beneath: both make paying the entrance fee worthwhile.

At the base of the château is **rue Ste-Claire**, the main street of the old town, with arcaded shops and houses. At no. 18 is the **Hôtel Favre**. It was here in 1606 that Antoine Favre, an eminent lawyer, and Bishop de Sales founded the group of literary intellectuals known as the Académie Florimontane in the belief that "the Muses thrive in the mountains of Savoie". The Académie, which

▲ Palais de l'Isle, Annecy

aims to encourage the study of the Savoyard region, is still active in the twenty-first century.

Running parallel to rue Ste-Claire, on the other side of the canal, rue J.-J.-Rousseau passes the city's **cathedral**, where Rousseau once sang as a chorister. It was in Annecy that Rousseau met Madame de Warens and eventually converted to Catholicism.

Nearby, to the east, you'll find the **Palais de l'Île**, a small twelfth-century fort, beautifully constructed out of the local stone, which served in turn as a palace, mint, court and prison (the latter as late as World War II). It now houses the **Centre d'interprétation de l'Architecture et du Patrimoine de l'Agglomération d'Annecy** (June–Sept daily 10.30am–6pm; Oct–May daily except Tues 10am–noon & 2–5pm; €3.40), a museum with several French-language audiovisual presentations on urban environments in the region.

A few blocks to the north, the fifteenth-century **church of St-Maurice** conceals some excellent fifteenth- and sixteenth-century religious art. Across the lakeside road from here are the extensive lawns of the **Champ de Mars**; the quai Napoleon III skirts this area, and it is from here that boats leave on **cruises around the lake**.

From the Hôtel de Ville a stroll south on rue des Marquisats leads along the lake to the free grassy **plage de Marquisats**, while a slightly longer walk in the other direction around the lake past the casino reaches the **plage d'Albigny**. Several years ago, there was an outbreak of so-called "swimmers itch" (*puces de canard*) as a result of swimming in the lake. The main symptom was itchy skin, and it came mainly as the result of an immune reaction to

The **International Animated Film Festiival** (🖳 www.annecy.org) which takes place in Annecy each June should appeal to far more than just fans of old Disney movies. It's a renowned showcase for a wide range of French and global animated films, which increasingly displays the influence of Bollywood and Chinese film-makers. It's also great fun for kids, with many of the films using special effects and 3-D glasses. A bus runs from the Centre Bonlieu to several venues around the town. Contact the tourist office for the latest details and programme.

parasites carried by ducks. The authorities have spent much time and money eradicating the problem and cases now are rare. If the symptoms are noted, then the best course of action is to shower and dry thoroughly straight after swimming.

Eating and drinking

There are plenty of **bars and cafés** in Annecy from which you can admire the local architecture with a beverage in hand, but the **restaurants** tend to churn out rather unimaginative fare to feed the tourist crowds. You'll find a string of inexpensive places to eat overlooking the canal along quai Perrière and rue Ste-Claire.

Restaurants

Auberge de Savoie 1 place St-François ☎ 04.50.45.03.05. A step above the usual tourist fare, this place serves an excellent range of white-fish and shellfish dishes, which include sea urchin (*langues d'Oursin*) and lobster (*homard*). Closed Tues & Wed. Menus are €21–57.

Brasserie des Européens place de l'Hôtel de Ville ☎ 04.50.45.00.81. The seafood here is also wonderfully fresh (look out for the display of fish and crabs in the window) and there's an extensive list of French wines. Open daily. Mains are €17–24.

Da Pietro 23 rue Sommeiller ☎ 04.50.51.30.70. Situated north of most of the tourist restaurants, *Da Pietro* provides some excellent pizzas for €8–12, although the chef's specialities are his steaks (€18). Closed Sun.

L'Etage 13 rue du Paquier ☎ 04.50.45.03.28. There's a good range of traditional Savoyard fondues, *raclettes* and *tartiflettes* on offer here for reasonable prices (€13–20). Open daily noon–11pm.

Le Petit Zinc 11 rue Pont Morens ☎ 04.50.51.12.93. This popular little bistro serves up tasty Savoyard favourites, including excellent local sausages (€17–21). Open daily noon–3pm & 7–11pm.

Bars and cafés

Finn Kelly's 10 Faubourg des Annonciades ☎ 04.50.51.29.40. This Irish pub is the best place in town for watching live sport and you can get 50cl of Guinness for €6. It's also next door to *Bull*, one of the few central nightclubs (Wed–Sat 9pm–5am).

Le Munich 1 quai Perrière ☎ 04.50.45.02.11. *Le Munich* is a hotspot for fans of German beer, with favourites like Leffe on tap (€5–6 for 50cl). Closed Mon.

Around Annecy

While the tourist crowds which flock to Annecy in the summer high season may only be bearable for a day or two, there are plenty of places around the lake to escape and run wild. As well as **boat tours**, **cycling** is an especially enjoyable means of appreciating the beauty of the Lac d'Annecy. Cycling the 40km road circuit of the lake is a very popular Sunday morning activity among sporty Annéciens; a traffic-free cycle route follows the west shore of the lake. The surrounding hills offer walking and mountain-biking excursions to suit all levels of ability and fitness. Experienced walkers should enjoy the relatively undemanding ascent of **La Tournette** (2351m) on the eastern side of the lake, while gentler walks and cycle routes are to be found in the forested **Semnoz mountains** on the lake's west side. The tourist office sells a detailed guidebook to hiking trails in the area (€6), and can provide information about the best guides and maps. Ten kilometres to the west of Annecy, the **Gorges du Fier** are some of the most spectacular and beautiful natural gorges in France.

Around the lake

It's an obvious choice, but a **lake cruise** is still the most peaceful way of covering the distance between Annecy and the other settlements around the lake. Compagnie des Bateaux, 2 place aux Bois (℡04.50.51.08.40, ⓦwww .annecy-croisieres.com), runs several boats daily from the Quai Napoleon III which stop off at various points around the lake; the price for a full circuit is €14.60. The Compagnie also runs 2–3hr cruises which include lunch or dinner (as well as dancing in the evening) on the MS *Libellule*; prices start at €50.

Close to the village of **MENTHON-ST-BERNARD** on the eastern shore of the lake is the grand, turreted **Château de Menthon** (May, June & Sept Fri–Sun & holidays 2–6pm; July & Aug daily noon–6pm; €7, €8 at weekends). The fortress has been inhabited since the twelfth century and was the birthplace of St Bernard, the patron saint of mountaineers. In the nineteenth century, however, it was extensively renovated in the romantic Gothic revival style and now possesses an impressive library (containing some 12,000 books) which dates from the mid-1800s, as well as fine views across the lake back to Annecy.

The village itself has a few places to stay. One rather opulent and expensive **hotel** is the *Palace de Menthon*, 665 Route des Bains (℡04.50.64.83.00, ⓦwww .palacedementhon.com; ❽), which offers bright rooms overlooking the lake and an excellent restaurant. There are more options a few kilometres down the road at the lovely lakeside village of **TALLOIRES**, whose eleventh-century Benedictine abbey has been converted into the luxurious *Hôtel de l'Abbaye de Talloires* on chemin des Moines (℡04.50.60.77.33, ⓦwww.abbaye-talloires .com; open Feb to mid-Nov; €230–310 for a double room).

On the west side of the lake, the village of **DUINGT** occupies a peninsula which juts out into the narrowest point of the lake. There are two thousand-year-old **châteaux** here, one in ruins and the other partly rebuilt, which are unfortunately not open for visitors. Like Menthon-St-Bernard and Talloires, Duingt has a small beach, with the opportunity to rent pleasure craft. The hotels are much cheaper on this side of the lake, but most still provide comfortable rooms with lakeside views. The **hotel** *Le Clos Marcel*, allée de la Plage (℡04.50.68.67.47, ⓦwww.clos-marcel.com; open April–Oct; ❹), also has a large garden and direct access to the lake.

If you want to explore these lakeside villages without using a car or boat, note that Transdev Crolard (℡04.50.45.08.12, ⓦwww.voyages-crolard.com) has buses leaving the *gare routière* in Annecy several times a day which pass down each side of the lake.

The Gorges du Fier

West of Annecy, the River Fier has cut a narrow crevice through the limestone rock at the **Gorges du Fier** (open daily; mid-March to mid-June & mid-Sept to mid-Oct 9.15am–6pm; mid-June to mid-Sept 9am–7pm; €4.90), which is signposted off the D14 at Lovagny. Once you are inside the three-hundred-metre-long gorge, you traverse a high-level walkway pinned to the gorge side.

The crevice is so narrow that when it rains heavily, the water can rise by around 25 metres in just a few hours.

Mont Blanc

Fifty kilometres to the west of Annecy on the Swiss and Italian borders looms **Mont Blanc** (4807m), Western Europe's highest peak. First climbed in 1786 by Jacques Balmat and Michel-Gabriel Paccard, two intrepid gentlemen from Chamonix, the mountain and its surrounding valleys are now the biggest tourist draw to the Alps.

The closest airport is in Geneva, but if you're coming from France then Annecy (see p.895) is the easiest city from which to approach the mountain, and, of the two road routes, the one east via the Megève is the more picturesque. The two main approach roads to Mont Blanc come together at Le Fayet, a village just outside **St-Gervais-les-Bains**, where the **Tramway du Mont Blanc** begins its 75-minute haul to the **Nid d'Aigle** (2375m), a vantage point on the northwest slope (Ⓦwww.compagniedumontblanc.com; €24.50 return). Experienced mountaineers can press on from here along the famous Goûter ridge to the summit of Mont Blanc itself.

It is the resort of **Chamonix-Mont Blanc**, however, which is the primary French base camp for outdoor activities on or around Mont Blanc. "Cham" throngs with visitors throughout the year, but even the tourist hordes cannot diminish the grandeur of the Mont Blanc Massif, and if you're walking in the area, you can soon get away from the crowds.

Chamonix-Mont Blanc

The bustling, cosmopolitan town of **CHAMONIX** (known officially as Chamonix Mont-Blanc) may have long since had its village identity submerged in a sprawl of tourist development, flashy restaurants and boutiques, but the stunning backdrop of glaring snowfields, eerie blue glaciers and ridges of shark-toothed *aiguilles* that surround Mont Blanc are ample compensation.

Arrival and information

The **gare SNCF** and **gare routière** are a short walk to the south of place du Triangle-de-l'Amitié, where the **tourist office**, at no. 85 (daily: 8.30am–7pm; Ⓣ04.50.53.00.24, Ⓦwww.chamonix.com), publishes a map of summer walks in the area (€4). The Chamonix multipass (see p.903) and other mountain lift passes can also be purchased here, as well as at the foot of each cable-car ascent. The **websites** Ⓦwww.chamonix.net and Ⓦwww.chamonixexperience.com are also good sources of information on the town.

Near the tourist office, the **Maison de la Montagne** houses the **Compagnie des Guides** (daily: 8.30am–noon and 3.30–7.30pm; Ⓣ04.50.53.00.88, Ⓦwww.chamonix-guides.com) which runs lessons in rock- and ice-climbing, as well as providing guides for those who don't want to ski off-piste or hike unaccompanied. The same building houses the **Office de Haute Montagne** (Mon–Sat 9am–noon & 3–6pm, also open on Sun in July & Aug; Ⓣ04.50.53.22.08, Ⓦwww.ohm-chamonix.com), which can give advice on *refuges* in addition to up-to-the-minute information on the weather in the mountains, and the details of countless local hiking routes, which you can photocopy. There's an **internet** café in the centre at *Mojo's* sandwich café,

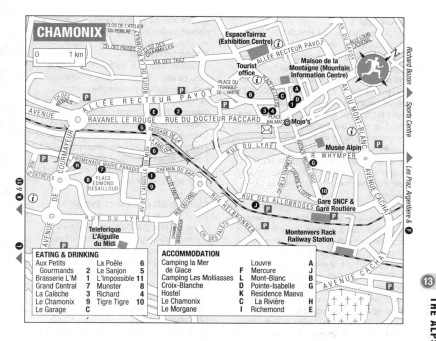

CHAMONIX

0   1 km

CLOS DE L'ATELIER
DU PEINTRE
CH. DES PAUSES
CLOS DES
CHARMILLES
VIA DES TRAZ
ROUTE DE LA ROUMMAZ
ALLÉE RECTEUR PAVOT
AV. DU SAPIN
ALLÉE LOUIS LACHENAL

EspaceTairraz
(Exhibition Centre) ⓘ

Maison de la
Montagne (Mountain
Information Centre)

Tourist
office ⓘ

PLACE DU
TRIANGLE-
DE-L'AMITIÉ

ALLÉE   RECTEUR   PAYOT

AVENUE
RAVANEL LE ROUGE   RUE DU DOCTEUR PACCARD

PLACE
BALMAT @ Mojo's

PASSAGE DE LA
LA VARLOPE
RUE   DU   LYRET

RUE DU DOCTEUR PACCARD

Musée Alpin
R. WHYMPER

AV. DU MONT-BLANC
AVENUE   CACHAT

RUE DE LA TOURNETTE
CHEMIN DU TOUR
RUE DE LA MOLLARD

RUE DES ALLOBROGES

Gare SNCF &
Gare Routière

AVENUE
DE   COURMAYEUR
PROMENADE MARIE PARADIS
CHEMIN DU SAPI

PLACE
EDMOND
DESAILLOUD

RUE   DU   LYRET

Teleferique
L'Aiguille
du Midi

CHAMP
DU MOULIN
RUE DU LYRET
AV. DE L'AIGUILLE
RUE DES ALLOBROGES
RUE   HELBRONNER
CH. DES PALÉIS

Montenvers Rack
Railway Station

Richard Bozon ▶ Sports Centre   ▶ Les Praz, Argentière & ⓕ

◀ K & ⓐ
ⓘ
ⓔ

AVENUE   CACHAT

13

EATING & DRINKING			
Aux Petits		La Poêle	6
Gourmands	2	Le Sanjon	5
Brasserie L'M	1	L'Impossible	11
Grand Central	7	Munster	8
La Calèche	3	Richard	4
Le Chamonix	9	Tigre Tigre	10
Le Garage	C		

ACCOMMODATION			
Camping la Mer		Louvre	A
de Glace	F	Mercure	J
Camping Les Molliasses	L	Mont-Blanc	B
Croix-Blanche	D	Pointe-Isabelle	G
Hostel	K	Residence Maeva	
Le Chamonix	C	La Rivière	H
Le Morgane	I	Richemond	E

place Balmat (daily 9am–8pm), as well as at *Grand Central* café further to the south in Chamonix Sud (see p.903).

There are plenty of **ski schools** in the town centre which provide lessons for skiers and snowboarders, as well as guides. The ESF office (☎04.50.53.22.57, ⓦ www.esf-chamonix) is situated in the Maison de la Montagne; the guides here hold special lessons on the famous runs of the Vallee Blanche. Ski Sensations, 120 place de Poilu (☎04.50.53.56.46, ⓦ www.ski-sensations.com), also runs heliskiing trips; using helicopters to transport skiers is illegal in France, but this company takes clients over the border into Italy where they can explore some very remote slopes.

Accommodation

One of the biggest headaches in and around Chamonix is finding a bed, especially if, as a walker or climber, you're having to sit out bad weather while waiting to get into the hills. All hotels need booking in advance and tend to be expensive; however, there's also a good supply of *gîte* accommodation, as well as a clean and comfortable HI hostel a few kilometres to the west of the town centre. The tourist office also offers a **reservation service** (☎04.50.53.23.33, ⓦ http://reservation.chamonix.com), which can find you a room at even the busiest times. **High season** in Chamonix is February to March and July and August, with the summer season being less expensive; many establishments close in May and October. If you're staying in a Chamonix hotel or at the hostel, then you should receive a free *Carte d'Hôte* on arrival; this guest card entitles you to free transport on the resort's public buses and on the SNCF train line between Servoz and Vallorcine.

THE ALPS AND FRANCHE-COMTÉ | Mont Blanc

Hotels

Le Chamonix 11 rue d l'Hôtel de Ville ℡ 04.50.53.11.07, Ⓦ www.hotel-le-chamonix.com. This central hotel has wood-panelled rooms set above the lively hotel bar. It's within stumbling distance of the central restaurants and bars. ❺

Croix-Blanche 81 rue Vallot ℡ 04.50.53.00.11, Ⓦ www.bestmontblanc.com. The oldest surviving hotel in Chamonix, the *Croix-Blanche* dates from 1793; its rooms combine an old-fashioned elegance with all the mod cons. ❼

Louvre 95 impasse de l'Androsace ℡ 04.50.53.00.51, Ⓦ www.hoteldulouvre.fr. The *Louvre* offers simple but clean rooms, free parking and a central location. It's excellent value for money. ❸

Mercure 39 rue des Allobroges ℡ 04.50.53.07.56, Ⓦ www.mercure.com. This outlet of the hotel chain is situated close to the *gare SNCF* and it provides spacious rooms, all of which have balconies. ❼

Mont-Blanc 62 allée du Majestic ℡ 04.50.53.05.64, Ⓦ www.bestmontblanc.com. You'll find both friendly service and beautifully decorated rooms at this central four-star hotel, which also has a gourmet restaurant. Doubles are €228–304 (including breakfast).

Le Morgane 145 av de l'Aiguille du Midi ℡ 04.50.53.57.15, Ⓦ www.morgane-hotel-chamonix.com. This stylish hotel has rooms designed in a minimalist (but very comfortable) fashion, and there's a pool, spa and an excellent bistro on site. ❾

Pointe-Isabelle 165 av Michel Croz ℡ 04.50.53.12.87. The *Pointe-Isabelle* has inexpensive rooms with TV and balconies close to the *gare SNCF*. ❺

Richemond 228 rue Docteur Paccard ℡ 04.50.53.08.85, Ⓦ www.richemond.fr. Set back from the busy rue Paccard, the *Richemond* has a pleasant garden, as well as spacious, airy rooms. ❻

Apartments

Résidence Maeva La Rivière 187 promenade Marie Paradis ℡ 08.25.07.25.39, Ⓦ www.maeva.com. Maeva, which provides apartments throughout France, has three sets of apartments in Chamonix. The pick of these are the La Rivière apartments located to the southwest of the town centre, which are designed for 4–6 people and include kitchens, a terrace or balcony and a TV. A 4-person suite costs €500–690 per week in the winter high-season, but the price falls to a third of this at other times of the year.

Campsites and hostel

Camping La Mer de Glace 200 chemin de la Bagna, Les Praz ℡ 04.50.53.44.03, Ⓦ www.chamonix-camping.com. A pleasant, unflashy campsite with good facilities (including free internet access) that is 2km northeast of Chamonix. Open May–Sept. €21 for a two-person tent.

Camping Les Molliasses chemin à Batioret ℡ 04.50.53.16.81, Ⓦ www.campingmolliasses.com. Located at the southern end of Chamonix, *Les Molliasses* also has a good range of basic facilities and a restaurant. Open June to mid-Sept. €17.50 for a two-person tent.

Hostel 127 montée Jacques-Balmat, Les-Pèlerins-en-Haut ℡ 04.50.53.14.52, Ⓔ chamonix@fuaj.org. This hostel lacks a communal kitchen, but otherwise has good facilities and provides cheap, filling meals in the evening. It's 2.5km out of the town centre; catch the #5 bus to the "Les Pelerins – Auberge" stop. Open mid-May to Sept & Dec–Apr. €16.60 for a dorm bed.

The Town

The mountains provide the main sights and activities, but on days when the bad weather sets in, there are a few things to do in town. The **Musée Alpin**, off avenue Michel-Croz in the town centre (daily: 3–7pm; €5), is full of exhibits which detail the life of the valley since the first tourists began to arrive in the eighteenth century and will be of particular interest to mountaineers, who can see the development of equipment throughout the period. The **Espace Tairraz** (same hours and ticket as the Musée Alpin) is an exhibition centre close to the tourist office in the Esplanade Saint-Michel; it hosts temporary photography exhibitions of the mountains, as well as a permanent collection of crystals. The **Richard Bozon Sports Centre**, to the west of the town centre at 214 avenue de la Plage, has ice-skating, a pool, sauna and hamam, a climbing wall and tennis courts (hours vary; ℡ 04.50.53.09.07).

Eating, drinking and nightlife

The choice of **bars**, **cafés and restaurants** reflects not only Chamonix's geographical location, with Swiss and Italian culinary influences, but also the tastes of the cosmopolitan mix of visitors. Vietnamese, fusion and hamburger places share the food scene with more traditional Savoyard restaurants, pizzerias and *haute* French cuisine. Rue Joseph-Vallot has plenty of gourmet **food shops** with local cheeses and other Alpine delicacies, and there are several well-stocked supermarkets in town for making a picnic. If you're after some **live music**, then either head for the rue des Moulins, which is packed from end to end with English-speaking pubs and nightclubs, or Chamonix Sud, where there's a good range of popular bars filled by mountaineers and skiers of every nationality. The best **nightclub** in town is *Le Garage* at 213 avenue de l'Aiguille-du-Midi (open daily 1–4am), which regularly hosts top international DJs.

Restaurants

Brasserie L'M 87 rue Vallot ☎04.50.53.48.83. The multicoloured outdoor seating is the most striking feature of this central brasserie, but its tapas meals (€1.50–3.50 per dish) are also worth sampling; they include fish, cheese and sausages. Open daily 11am–midnight.

La Calèche 18 rue Docteur Paccard ☎04.50.55.94.68. This place is a good central option which serves some hearty fondues and *raclettes* (€22) to fill hungry tourist tummies. Closed mid-Nov to early Dec.

L'Impossible 9 chemin du Cry ☎04.50.53.20.36. With a cosy farmhouse interior, some delicious dishes of grilled meats (€20–30), and an exceptional wine list (€12–40 for most bottles), *L'Impossible* is worth the 10min walk from the town centre. Closed Nov & Tues in May–Jun & Sept–Oct.

La Poêle 79 av de l'Aiguille-du-Midi ☎04.50.55.96.13. The speciality of the chef here are his omelettes. There's a large set of options in terms of size, ingredients (including sausages, mushrooms, anchovies and salmon) and price (€7–20). Open daily noon–3pm & 6–11pm.

Le Sanjon 5 av Ravanel-le-Rouge ☎04.50.53.56.44. This homely little restaurant produces traditional Savoyard favourites, not least the delicious beef, veal and duck which you cook yourself on a *pierre chaud* (hot stone) for €20. Closed Sun–Mon.

Tigre Tigre 239 av Michel Croz ☎04.50.55.33.42. British-style Indian meals like chicken tikka masala

(€15) are on offer here, as well as some intriguing salads with curry sauces (€9.50–12.50). Open daily 4pm–2am.

Bars and cafés

Grand Central 62 promenade Marie Paradis, Chamonix Sud 74000 Chamonix ☎04.50.54.04.91. This little internet café offers a "healthy fresh alternative" to the average tourist grub you'll find in Cham, with fresh fruit smoothies, healthy sandwiches and (if you are feeling indulgent) some tasty little cakes (€2–6). Open daily 8am–7.30pm.

Le Chamonix 11 rue de l'Hotel de Ville ☎04.50.53.11.07. This hotel bar has several beers on tap (50cl is €5–7) and provides a nice spot to watch the world go by in the adjacent place de l'Eglise. Closed Sun.

Munster 25 place Edmond Desailloud, Chamonix Sud ☎04.50.18.46.38. A traditional pub devoted to Munster rugby club, this place is the best place in town to sit back with a Guinness (50cl is €5) and watch some live sport. Open daily 4pm–2am.

Aux Petits Gourmands 168 rue Docteur Paccard ☎04.50.53.01.59. A delightful bakery-cum-café, where you'll find plenty of alluring coffees and hot chocolate drinks (€1.50–5), as well as a mouth-watering array of pastries (€1–3). Closed Sun.

Richard 10 rue Docteur Paccard ☎04.50.53.56.88. A popular central bakery which draws in the summer tourists with the tastiest ice-cream selection in town (four scoops for €6). Open daily 10am–9pm.

Excursions in the Chamonix Valley

Alongside the walking and skiing opportunities around Chamonix, there are several exhilarating excursions that can be made using the various ski lifts and mountain railways; it may be worth getting a **multipass** that covers all the lifts in the area (starting at €47 for 24 hours, €53 for two consecutive days).

The ski lifts and mountain railways

The most famous excursion is the very expensive, and often very crammed, **téléférique** (May–Sept 8am–5pm; mid-Dec to April 8.30am–4.30pm;

The association of the major French ski resorts, Ski France (Association Nationale des Maires des Stations de Montagne – ANMSM), 9 rue de Madrid, Paris (℡01.47.42.23.32, ⊛www.skifrance.fr), can provide the latest information on the different resorts.

Resort name	Altitude	Towns	KM of Piste	Cross-country	Ski lifts
Alpe d'Huez	1500–3330m	Alpe d'Huez	249km	50km	84
Chamonix Valley	1035–3842m	Chamonix, Argentière, Les Houches	155km	48km	43
Deux-Alpes	1300–3669m	Les Deux-Alpes, La Grave	225km	20km	52
Espace Killy	1550–3456m	Val d-Isère, Tignes	300km	44km	90
Grand Massif	700–2480m	Samoëns, Flaine	265km	109km	78
Massif des Aravis	1200–2470m	La Clusaz	220km	86km	94
Megève	1150–2350m	Megève, St-Gervais	325km	73km	83
Paradiski	1200–3250m	Les Arcs, La Plagne	425km	158km	144
Portes du Soleil	900–2350m	Morzine, Avoriaz, Châtel-les-Gets	650km	200km	200
Serre Chevalier	1350–2830m	Serre Chevalier	250km	35km	66
Trois Vallées	1300–3266m	Méribel, Courchevel, Val Thorens	600km	130km	185

€38 return, advance reservations €2; call ℡08.92.68.00.67) to the **Aiguille du Midi** (3842m), one of the longest cable-car ascents in the world, rising no fewer than 3000m above the valley floor in two extremely steep stages. Penny-pinching by buying a ticket only as far as the Plan du Midi is a waste of money: go all the way or not at all. If you do go up, make the effort to be on your way before 9am, as the summits tend to cloud over towards midday, and huge crowds may force you to wait for hours if you try later. Take warm clothes – even on a summer's day it'll be below zero at the top – and sunblock is also advisable to protect against the glare off the snow. You need a steady head, too: the drop beneath the little bubble of steel and glass reaches a nerve-jangling five hundred metres at one stage.

The Aiguille is an exposed granite pinnacle on which a restaurant and the *téléférique* dock are precariously balanced. The view is incredible. At your feet is

Six-day pass	Round-up	Page
€198.50	A purpose-built resort with good skiing for all levels and extensive slopes (including La Sarenne, the longest in the world). The resort is dominated by French, rather than foreign, tourists.	p.876
€225	A strung-out set of resorts that ascend into the high mountains and offer superb off-piste adventures for advanced skiers. The lively après-ski underlines the reputation of the area for high-adrenaline entertainment.	p.906
€172	The intermediate slopes of Deux-Alpes are popular with snowboarders, while La Grave has more difficult slopes that often require a guide. These resorts have the best nightlife you'll find in the French Alps.	p.877
€208.50	Though these high-altitude resorts are a delight for advanced skiers, and have a lively après-ski scene, they are not the prettiest or the most easily accessible.	p.892
€187.20	The pretty, low-altitude village of Samoëns has no direct ski access, while the higher resort of Flaine is full of unattractive, ski-in-ski-out apartment blocks. The skiing is best suited for intermediate and novice skiers.	p.908
€158	To the west of Chamonix; the villages here are pretty, traditional and offer good value, especially for families. However, the nightlife is muted and the low altitude means that snow conditions are uncertain.	
€171	The Monaco of skiing: poodles with fur coats, de luxe chalets, gentle slopes for intermediate skiing, and the stunning view of Mont Blanc on the horizon.	p.907
€237	These purpose-built resorts lack the charm or the lively nightlife of other ski areas, but they do provide plenty of varied pistes.	p.891
€237	An area extending across twelve resorts into Switzerland. Morzine is an expensive but elegant resort, while Avoriaz is higher and has tougher slopes. There's excellent skiing for all, but low snow cover can be a problem.	
€181	A set of pretty villages, with beautiful scenery, varied slopes and sunny weather for an average of 300 days per year. However, the relatively low altitude often results in a lack of snow.	p.879
€220	A massive ski area with skiing for all abilities, but it is also overpriced and usually crowded. It lacks the charm of the more traditional resorts.	p.890

the snowy plateau of the **Col du Midi**, with the glaciers of the Vallée Blanche and Géant sloping down the mountainside. From the Aiguille, the Three Monts Route takes mountaineers up the steep snowfield and exposed ridge to the summit of Mont Blanc with its final cap of ice, what Coleridge once called "thy bald awful head, O sovran Blanc!" On the horizon lies rank upon rank of snow- and ice-capped monsters receding into the distance. Perhaps most impressive of all is the view from east to south, in which the Aiguille Verte, Triollet and the Jorasses, with the Matterhorn and Monte Rosa, form a cirque of needle-sharp peaks and sheer crags. After looking at these peaks, no one will be surprised that the Alps are still considered to be one of the most prestigious and most lethal of testing grounds for climbers.

If you have not tired of superb panoramic views, you can make for the **Montenvers rack railway** (May–Sept 8.30am–5pm; Oct to mid-Nov &

mid-Dec to April 10am–4pm; €17 return), a train service which has been running up from Chamonix to the Mer de Glace on the flanks of Mont Blanc since 1908. At the top you have the option of walking for twenty minutes or of taking a short cable-car ride (an additional €4) down into an **ice cave** carved out of the Mer de Glace every summer.

Hiking and climbing

There are countless excellent **shorter walks** around Chamonix, including many on the northern side of the valley amidst the lower but nonetheless impressive peaks of the **Aiguilles Rouges**. One easy, picturesque trail takes you from the village of Les Praz (just to the northeast of Chamonix itself) to **Lac Blanc**. Take the *téléférique* from Les Praz to Flégère and then the gondola to L'Index (a combined ticket is €19). The walk to the lake and back from L'Index takes around 2hr 30min and requires good walking boots.

Climbing Mont Blanc should not be undertaken lightly. It is a semi-technical climb and fast-changing weather conditions mean that a guide is essential. There are several different routes, the most popular of which is the **Gouter** ridge route (three days); this ascends from the Nid d'Aigle at the top of the Tramway du Mont Blanc. The best season for climbing the mountain is mid-June to Sept, but even in this period the ascent should only be attempted by fit, acclimatized and well-prepared mountaineers.

Skiing

Despite its fame, Chamonix is not the most user-friendly of ski resorts and access to the slopes relies on shuttle buses, trains or a car. For advanced skiers, however, it's probably one of the best places in the Alps since it offers an impressive range of challenging runs and off-piste itineraries. It's not so much a single resort as a chain of unconnected ski areas set along both sides of the Chamonix valley and dominated by Mont Blanc. The **Brévent** and **Flégère** areas on the southern slopes both have a good variety of pistes and provide some fine views of the Mont Blanc massif across the valley, while **Argen-tière–Les Grands Montets** is a colder, north-facing area that is well suited to advanced skiers. The famous **Vallée Blanche** can be accessed by cable car from the Aiguille du Midi; skiing here involves a twenty-kilometre descent which passes many crevasses and is not patrolled, so a guide is strongly recommended. Closer to Chamonix itself, the **Les Planards** and **Le Savoy** areas

The Tour du Mont Blanc

The classic way for walkers to admire Mont Blanc without putting themselves through the dangers of an ascent is to undertake the **Tour du Mont Blanc**, the trail which makes a 250km circuit of the mountain across French, Swiss and Italian terrain. The trail normally takes eight to twelve days, during which you can either camp or stay at the *refuges* (€20–25) en route. Many of the *refuges* provide food and other supplies, but it's worth checking the latest details with the **Office de Haute Montagne** in Chamonix, which can also provide maps of the route. Even in early July, many of the passes on the route can still be covered in snow, so walkers should carry crampons and heavy-duty waterproofs.

Several tour companies in Chamonix can provide guides for the walk. The Compagnie des Guides (see p.900) is the oldest (it was established in 1821) and still the most recommended; a twelve-day hike, in which food and guides are provided and a minibus can transport luggage between *refuges*, costs €1150.

require artificial snow and snow cannons to stay open, but they are good spots for beginners to hone their technique.

The road to Italy

If you want to head into Italy from Chamonix, then the most direct road is the N205, which takes you south out of Chamonix, then through the 11.6km **Mont Blanc Tunnel** (one way €33.20, return journey €41.40), and finally brings you out on the road to Aosta and Milan. There is often a waiting-time of an hour or more on either side of the Tunnel due to its narrowness.

Megève

It is the stunning views of Mont Blanc, added to an almost tangible sense of old-world charm, that make **MEGÈVE**, 15km to the west of Chamonix, one of the most beautiful French ski resorts. At the heart of the village is the traffic-free place de l'Église, a square surrounded by buildings dating from the eighteenth century, and there's also a fine medieval church. Combined with these carefully restored examples of older architecture, however, are the exclusive modern hotels, designer boutiques and smart ski-rental shops that lend Megève its rather chic ambiance.

While once Megève could guarantee snow during the winter, global warming has taken its toll; the resort's relatively low altitude now means that snow cannons are often required to give adequate snow cover. There are, however, plenty of higher pistes nearby, which are quite gentle in comparison with those in Val d'Isère and Chamonix.

In summer, the Compagnie des Guides (☎04.50.21.55.11, ⓦwww.guides -megeve.com) provides guides for hikes in the area, as well as for rock climbing and mountain biking. The Compagnie has an office in the Maison de la Montagne at no. 76 on rue Ambroise Martin. There's also a sports centre, the Palais des Sports et des Congrès, on the north side of the town centre on the Route du Palais des Sports. Here you'll find a climbing wall, swimming pool and ice rink, and outdoor tennis courts (hours vary; ☎04.50.21.15.71).

The **tourist office** is on rue Monseigneur Conseil (April to mid-June & Sept to mid-Dec 9am–12.30pm & 2–6.30pm; rest of year 9am–7pm; ☎04.50.21.27.28 ⓦwww.megeve.com).

Upmarket **hotels** include the luxurious *Le Fer à Cheval*, 36 route du Cret d'Arbois (☎04.50.21.30.39, ⓦwww.feracheval-megeve.com; doubles are €400– 600), which has a spa and gourmet restaurant. A cheaper but still central option hotel is *La Chaumine*, 36 chemin des Bouleaux (☎04.50.21.37.05, ⓦwww .hotel-lachaumine-megeve.com; ❸), while *Les Cimes*, 341 rue Charles Feige (☎04.50.21.11.13, ⓦwww.hotellescimes.info; ❹), provides cosy rooms and a communal terrace just a few minutes' walk out of town. Some of the best-value accommodation is in **chambres d'hôtes**; one excellent choice is *Les Oyats*, 745 chemin de Lady (☎04.50.21.11.56, ⓦwww.lesoyats.fr; ❺), which lies 1.5km out of town; here you'll find lovely wood-panelled rooms with a shared kitchen in an old farmhouse. Situated 3km out of Megève at 57 route du Grand Bois is the local **campsite**, *Camp Bornand* (☎04.50.93.00.86, ⓦwww.camping-megeve .com; open May–Aug; €12 for a two-person tent).

Megève has some of the most swish and refined gourmet restaurants around; head for the Michelin two-star restaurant *Flocons de Sel*, 75 rue St Franois (☎04.50.21.49.99), which serves some wonderfully inventive fish dishes (menus €35–65). Yet you'll also find some fun, cheaper eating places in the town:

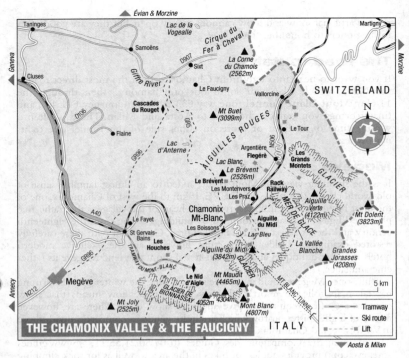

Labels within map:
Évian & Morzine
Taninges
Lac de la Vogealle
Samoëns
Cirque du Fer à Cheval
Martigny
Geneva
D907
Sixt
La Corne du Chamois (2562m)
SWITZERLAND
N
Cluses
Giffre River
Le Faucigny
Vallorcine
Morzine
D106
Cascades du Rouget
GR5
Mt Buet (3099m)
Flaine
Le Tour
AIGUILLES ROUGES
Lac d'Anterne
GR96
Argentière
Flegère
N506
Les Grands Montets
GLACIER
Lac Blanc
Le Brévent (2526m)
Le Brévent
Les Montenvers
Rack Railway
Les Praz
MER DE GLACE
Aiguille Verte (4122m)
Mt Dolent (3823m)
A40
Le Fayet
Chamonix Mt-Blanc
Les Boissons
Aiguille du Midi
Lac Bleu
St Gervais-Bains
Les Houches
TRAMWAY DU MONT-BLANC
Aiguille du Midi (3842m)
GLACIER
La Vallée Blanche
Grandes Jorasses (4208m)
MT BLANC TUNNEL
GR96
Megève
Annecy
N212
Le Nid d'Aigle
GLACIER DE BIONNASSAY
Mt Maudit (4465m)
4052m
4304m
Mont Blanc (4807m)
0   5 km
Mt Joly (2525m)
THE CHAMONIX VALLEY & THE FAUCIGNY
ITALY
Tramway
Ski route
Lift
Aosta & Milan

13

THE ALPS AND FRANCHE-COMTÉ | Mont Blanc

Bouddha Moor, 158 route Edmond de Rothschild (☎04.50.90.17.69), serves an eclectic range of Asian dishes in a chilled-out, oriental atmosphere, while *Chez Tante Marie*, 66 rue Ambroise Martin (☎04.50.57.71.31), has a more traditional Savoyard menu (€28) and live jazz on some evenings.

The Faucigny and the Cirque du Fer-à-Cheval

To the north of Chamonix is the **Faucigny**, a region of wide glacial valleys, gentle forested slopes and peaceful little villages that seem a world away from the high-octane atmosphere of the resorts further south. **Samoëns**, lying 15km away from Chamonix, is one such village; despite its relatively low altitude, it has become popular with **skiers** thanks to a short transfer time from Geneva and its proximity to the Grand Massif ski area (particularly the purpose-built resort of **Flaine**) via the Express du Grand Massif, a *télécabine* to the south of the village.

If you head east from Samoëns along the D907, you follow the valley as it narrows into the Gorges des Tines before opening out again at another delightful little village, **SIXT-FER-À-CHEVAL**. This pretty village lies on the confluence of two branches of the river Giffre: the Giffre-Haut, which comes down from Salvagny, and the Giffre-Bas, which flows all the way from the **Cirque du Fer-à-Cheval**. The cirque is a horseshoe-shaped ridge which has been admired by travellers for the rugged beauty of its cliffs and waterfalls since at least the Middle Ages, and it is this which makes the journey away from Chamonix truly memorable.

The cirque begins about 6km from Sixt and you can reach it easily via the footpath on the left bank of the Giffre-Bas. It is a vast semicircle of limestone walls, up to 700m in height and 4–5km long, from which spring countless waterfalls, particularly in the summer months. The left-hand end of the cirque is dominated by a huge spike of rock known as La Corne du Chamois (The Goat's Horn). At its foot the valley of the Giffre bends sharply north to its source in the glaciers above the Fond de la Combe. The bowl of the cirque is thickly wooded except for a circular meadow in the middle where the road ends.

There's a **tourist office** and a park office in the place de la Gare of Sixt-Fer-à-Cheval (Mon–Sat 9am–noon & 3–6.30pm; ☎04.50.34.49.36, ⓦwww.sixteracheval.com). The park office produces a useful and well-illustrated folder of walks in the region. The village has a pleasant chalet-style **hotel**, *Le Petit Tetras* (☎04.50.34.42.51, ⓦwww.le-petit-tetras.fr; open late Dec to March & June to mid-Sept; €265–285 per person for a week's stay), with an outdoor pool and bar. The closest accommodation to the Cirque itself is in the **campsite**, *Le Pelly* (☎04.50.34.12.17; open June–Aug; €11 for a two-person tent). If you're struggling for accommodation, be aware that there are plenty of rooms available in Samoëns, although most are at the more expensive end of the scale. One of the best-value options in Samoëns is *Hôtel Edelweiss* (☎04.50.34.41.32, ⓦwww.edelweiss-samoens.com; ❹), a chalet-style hotel with beautiful views from the terrace and an excellent restaurant.

Lake Geneva

The crescent-shaped expanse of **Lake Geneva** (known as Lac Léman in France) is over 70km long, 14km wide and an impressive 310m deep; it has always been a natural border with Switzerland to the north. Even in summer, the lake is subject to violent storms, yet the experience of sailing across its waters on a calm day is delightful, and should not be missed. On the French side of the lake, the spa resort of **Évian-les-Bains** (of bottled water fame) and the picturesque village of **Yvoire** are the main sites of interest. **Thonon-les-Bains**, a larger town situated between these two landmarks, is the starting point of the renowned touring route, the **Route des Grandes Alpes**, and a gateway to the beautiful Chablais region to the south of the lake.

Évian-Les-Bains

ÉVIAN is a pleasant and peaceful spa resort, although there isn't a great deal to see or do other than simply to enjoy a stroll along the waterfront, or take leisurely trips on the lake. The waterfront is elegantly laid out with squares of immaculately mown grass, colourful flower beds and exotic trees; there are also mini-golf, water slides and other peaceful ways of amusing oneself if you need them.

Évian is an excellent base for exploring other towns around the lake, thanks to the Compagnie General de Navigation (CGN) **Ferries** (☎00.41.84.81.18.48, ⓦwww.cgn.ch) that depart from the port here everyday. These head towards several destinations, including Lausanne (16 daily; €45 return) and Geneva (2 daily; €41.60 return) in Switzerland, as well as Yvoire (3 daily; €27.10 return) and Thonon-les-Bains (4 daily; €15.50 return) on the French side.

Situated by the lake on the town's western outskirts and accessible only by a boat that leaves from the centre of Évian are the **Pré-Curieux** water gardens (ⓦwww.precurieux.com; three boats daily, 10am, 1.45pm, 3.30pm in July–Aug;

May, June and Sept boats run at the same times but only Wed–Sun; €10 for boat and tour of gardens).These picturesque lakeside gardens are divided into various water-based ecosystems (including ponds, marshes and a waterfall), which each exhibit different forms of plant and animal life. Tickets for the gardens are available at the small chalet in front of the casino and boats leave from the nearby quay.

If you're looking to exploit the famous healing properties of the local water, then head for **Les Thermes Évian**, place de la Libération (T04.50.75.02.30, Wwww.lesthermesevian.com; one-day programmes start at €45), where you'll find a range of spa treatments, which offer everything from weight-loss sessions to specific programmes for senior citizens.

The mineral water for which Évian is famous is now bottled at an industrial estate in Amphion, 3km along the lakeside (reserve at the tourist office for one of the four daily tours; T04.50.26.80.29; €2), but you can admire the **Source Cachat** on avenue des Sources which gushes away behind the Évian company's Art Nouveau offices on rue Nationale.

Practicalities

The **tourist office** is on place de la porte d'Allinges (June–Sept Mon–Fri 9am–noon & 4–7pm, Sat 9am–noon & 3–7pm, Sun 10am–noon & 3–6pm; Oct–May Mon–Fri 8.30am–noon & 2–6pm, closes at 5pm on Sat; T04.50.75.04.26, Wwww.eviantourism.com).The **gare SNCF** lies on the hill to the southwest of the town centre on avenue de la Gare; the **gare routière**, from which you can catch buses to Thonon-les-Bains and Yvoire, is next to the tourist office on the lakeside street, quai Baron de Blonay.

The town has a few top-notch four-star **hotels**.The best option if you're after some full-on luxury is the *Évian Royal Palace* (T04.50.26.85.00, Wwww .evianroyalresort.com; rooms start from €350 per night), which is part of a luxury resort outside the town, and has gorgeously decorated rooms, a gourmet restaurant, spa and a beautiful golf course nearby.There are also many affordable hotels in the town itself. In the centre of town at place Charles Cottet, *Le Bourgogne* (T04.50.75.01.05, Wwww.hotel-evian-bourgogne.com; closed in Jan; ❹) has spacious (if slightly dull) rooms and a fitness centre. Even cheaper is *Hôtel du Palais*, 69 rue Nationale (T04.50.75.00.46, Wwww.hoteldupalaisevian.com; ❸), which provides modern, simple rooms with TV.The *Terminus*, at 32 avenue de la Gare (T04.50.75.15.07, Wwww.hotel-terminus-evian.com; ❹), also has basic rooms (some with balconies) directly across from the *gare SNCF*.

There are some excellent **chambres d'hotes** which offer a very comfortable stay. Located on the heights above the resort and 10min from the town centre at 437 avenue du Flon, *Le Clos Gemme* (T04.50.75.15.75, Wwww .gemme-plus.com; ❼) provides a pool, sauna and hammam, as well as a cocktail service. Rather less salubrious but perfectly convenient and clean is the private **hostel** *Côté Lac Évian* (T04.50.75.35.87, Wwww.cotelacevian. com; €54 for a double room with shower) which lies at the top of a steep climb on avenue de Neuvecelle.There's a four-star **campsite**, *Camping de la Plage*, 304 rue de la Garenne (T04.50.70.00.46, Wwww.camping-dela-plage. com; open late Dec to Oct; €22 for a two-person tent), at 304 rue de la Garenne in nearby Amphion.

For eating, the cheapest option for budget travellers are the local pizzerias, where you'll generally find simple but tasty and home-made Italian grub; *La Pizza*, 4 place Charles De Gaulle (T04.50.75.05.36) is one of the better options (pizzas are €13). *Entre Nous* (T04.50.70.76.88), is a good mid-price

The Route des Grandes Alpes

Winding its way over mountain passes and secluded valleys all the way from Thonon-les-Bains to Menton on the Mediterranean coast is the most renowned tourist route of the French Alps, the 684km **Route des Grandes Alpes**. The route crosses six Alpine passes over 2000m, three of which – the Col de la Cayolle, the Col de l'Izoard and the Col de Vars – were only paved in 1934. The complete route opened in 1937 and has been a popular touring route for drivers, walkers and cyclists ever since. It can be covered in a couple of days by car, but only by rushing through the stunning mountain landscapes and intriguing settlements (including Morzine, Valloire, Briançon and Barcelonnette) which line the route.

restaurant at no. 69 on the bustling Rue Nationale; it dishes up excellent fish courses, with the perch caught fresh from the lake (€21) being especially tasty. If you're looking for a more upmarket menu, it's worth making a trip to the restaurants at the *Évian Royal Resort*. *Le Gourmandin* (☎04.50.26.85.54) at the *Royal Ermitage* hotel serves delicious fish courses (€60 menu).

Yvoire

Situated some 25km to the west of Évian **YVOIRE** is a pretty medieval village famous for its colourful flowers, which seem to abound on every street corner during the summer. The narrow cobbled lanes are choked with hordes of day-trippers in July and August, but you can still find some peace and quiet next to the lake even in those months. The main attraction for the aforementioned hordes is the **Labyrinthe-Jardin des Cinq Sens**, just off rue du Lac in the centre of the village(Daily: April 11am–6pm; May to mid-Sept 10am–7pm; mid-Sept to Oct 1–5pm; €10). These immaculate formal gardens are designed to appeal to each of the five senses: strawberries and raspberries tempt your tastebuds; the foliage in the Jardin des Textures encourages you to touch; geraniums provide vivid colours to delight your eyes; lilies and honeysuckle produce a memorable aroma; and finally, in the central aviary, birds' twitters provide a little melody for your ears. The **castle** and two stone gateways, both dating from the fourteenth century, are within easy walking distance of the gardens in the village's centre. Guided visits of the medieval part of the village can be organized at the tourist office.

The **tourist office** is on place de la Mairie (Oct–March Mon–Fri 9.30am–12.30pm & 1.30–5pm; April–June Mon–Sat 9.30am–12.30pm & 1.30–5pm, Sun noon–4pm; July–Aug daily 9.30am–12.30pm & 1.30–6pm; ☎04.50.72.80.21, ⓦwww.yvoiretourism.com). Finding **accommodation** in the village can be difficult, especially in high season, but the quality is high. ⚐ *Le Vieux Logis* on the Grande Rue (04.50.72.80.24, ⓦwww.levieuxlogis.com; open Feb–Dec; ❹) is a beautiful hotel and restaurant in the heart of the medieval village. *Les Flots Bleus* (☎04.50.72.80.08, ⓦwww.flotsbleus-yvoire.com; open April–Oct; ❺) is located to the west of the main village in Port de Plaisance, and has spacious, stylish rooms with balconies or terraces.

Finding somewhere to **eat** is rather easier, with several rustic harbour-side restaurants serving the tourist crowds. *La Vielle Porte* in the place de la Mairie (☎04.50.72.80.14) has an especially creative menu (€35), featuring plenty of fresh lake fish.

THE ALPS AND FRANCHE-COMTÉ | Lake Geneva

⑬

Franche-Comté

The region of **Franche-Comté** (Ⓦ www.franche-comte.org), which lies to the northwest of Lake Geneva, was once ruled by the Grand Dukes of Burgundy and has only been formally a part of France since the late seventeenth century. Within the four *départements* of Franche-Comté – the Territoire de Belfort, the

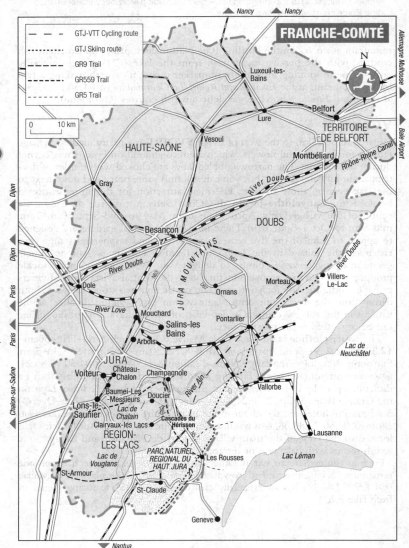

Haute-Saône, the Doubs and the Jura – you will find settlements that are far more tranquil and less touristy than those in the Alps. Foremost among these is the region's capital, **Besançon**, an attractive town built around an imposing set of fortifications which were developed by the French military engineer Vauban (see the box on p.881) during the late 1600s.

Lying in the rich agricultural valley to the south of **Besançon**, the quiet town of **Lons-le-Saunier** provides a gateway to the Jura mountains to the east. Composed of gentle, forested slopes in the west, of more sheer crags in the east and of high-forested plateaux in between, these mountains have long been considered as being well suited to cross-country skiing, but the varied terrain also provides plenty of good trails for hikers. Readers should note that the official *département* of Jura in the south of Franche-Comté does not contain the whole of the mountain range commonly known as the Jura; these mountains stretch northward into the Doubs *département* as well. A particular highlight in these mountains is the **Region des Lacs**, which possesses beautiful lakes, pine forests and small farming communities as well as ski resorts.

Across Franche-Comté as a whole, there are hundreds of square kilometres of some of France's most undisturbed woodland, lake and pasture which are just waiting to be explored. Some of the most picturesque landscapes are to be found just to the north of Lons-le-Saunier, where pretty medieval villages lie among vineyards that have been producing unusual wines since the Middle Ages.

Besançon and around

The capital of Franche-Comté, **BESANÇON**, is an attractive town of handsome stone buildings that sits between the northern edge of the Jura mountains and a loop of the wide River Doubs. It is this natural defensive position that has defined the town's history. Besançon was briefly a Gallic fortress before Caesar smashed the Gauls' resistance in 58 BC to make it into a Roman one. Strong outer walls were developed during the Middle Ages and the indefatigable military engineer Vauban added the still-extant Citadelle in the seventeenth century in order to guard the natural breach in the river. A large French army presence remained in the area until well into the twentieth century, but Besançon is more than just a barracks town or military outpost. The old town, lying on the southern side of the Doubs, has a wealth of good museums, intriguing ruins and delightful cafés which make it a pleasure to explore. The modern town has sprawled to the north of the Doubs, and it is here that you will find important facilities like the *gare SNCF* and the tourist office.

Arrival and information

The **gare SNCF** is at the end of avenue Maréchal-Foch, 10min walk to the north of the old town. There is an extensive **bus network** in the town, with several major bus stops, including one at the *gare SNCF*. The Ginkobus office at no. 4 in the central place du 8 Septembre (Mon–Sat 10am–7pm; ☎08.25.00.22.44, ⓦwww.ginkobus.com) offers information and timetables for buses departing to Ornans, Belfort or other towns in the area. The **tourist office** is on the northern bank by the Pont de la République at place de la Première Armée Française (Mon 10am–7pm, Tues–Sat 9.30am–7pm, Sun 11am–1pm; ☎03.81.80.92.55, ⓦwww.besancon-tourisme.com). There's high-speed **internet access** available in the tourist office, but there are no internet cafés in the old town. On the other side of the Pont de la République

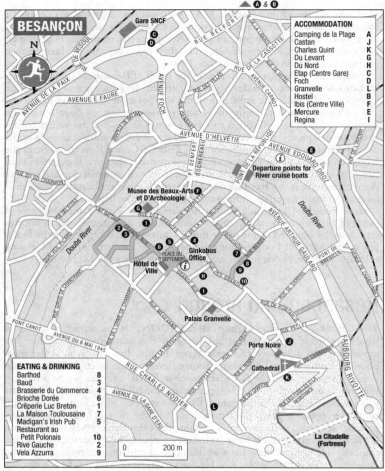

BESANÇON

N

Gare SNCF

ACCOMMODATION

Camping de la Plage	A
Castan	J
Charles Quint	K
Du Levant	G
Du Nord	H
Etap (Centre Gare)	C
Foch	D
Granvelle	L
Hostel	B
Ibis (Centre Ville)	F
Mercure	E
Regina	I

RUE BELFORT

RUE DE LA LIBERTÉ

RUE DE LA CASSOTTE

RUE DE VITEL

AVENUE CARNOT

RUE DE VESOUL

AVENUE DE LA PAIX

AVENUE E FAURE

AVENUE FOCH

RUE ISENBART

RUE DES VILLAS

AVENUE D'HELVÉTIE

PT DE DENFERT ROCHEREAU

AVENUE DE LA RÉPUBLIQUE

AVENUE EDOUARD DROZ

E

Departure points for
River cruise boats

RUE DU GD CHARMONI

PONT BATTANT

RUE GAMBETTA

RUE DE POLIPONE

Doubs River

AVENUE ARTHUR GAULARD

Musee des Beaux-Arts
et D'Archeologie **F**

G

RUE DES GRANGES

GRANDE RUE

QUAI VEIL PICARD

Doubs River

RUE D'ALSACE

RUE PROUDHON

RUE BERSOI

PONT DE BRESILLE

AVENUE DE CHARDONNET

1

2 3

6 5

4

Ginkobus
Office
(i)

7

PLACE DU
8 SEPTEMBRE

Hôtel de
Ville

8

RUE DE LA RÉPUBLIQUE

H

9

10

RUE DU SARRAIL

PONT CANOT

RUE BRICQ DE CHANTRANS

GRANDE RUE

RUE DES GRANGES

RUE DE PONTARLIER

I

AVENUE DU 8 MAI 1945

RUE DE L'ORME DE CHAMARS

RUE MEGEVAND

RUE DE LA PRÉFECTURE

Palais Granvelle

RUE RONCHAUX

RUE PÉCLET

FAUBOURG RIVOTTE

RUE CHARLES NODIER

AVENUE DE LA GARE D'EAU

RUE CHIFFLET

RUE RONJON

Porte Noire J

Cathedral

K

RUE DU CHAMBRIER

RUE DE MIDI

RUE DE LA RÉSISTANCE

L

**La Citadelle
(Fortress)**

0   200 m

EATING & DRINKING

Barthod	8
Baud	3
Brasserie du Commerce	4
Brioche Dorée	6
Crêperie Luc Breton	1
La Maison Toulousaine	7
Madigan's Irish Pub	5
Restaurant au Petit Polonais	10
Rive Gauche	2
Vela Azzurra	9

13

THE ALPS AND FRANCHE-COMTÉ | Besançon and around

from the tourist office is the departure point for the **bateaux-mouches** or cruise boats (four times daily July & Aug; €9.50), which follow the Doubs on its course around the outer limits of the town centre. The biggest **cultural event** of the year is the **Festival de Besançon**, a classical music festival which takes place in early September. The highlight is the international young conductors' competition.

Accommodation

There is a wide variety of both older and more modern **hotels** to choose from in the town centre, although you will have to look further outside the centre for the cheaper options. If you have a car, it is worth calling ahead at all hotels to check about parking. Many have some parking spaces, but they tend to be limited and may charge a small fee for an overnight stay. Most also close for an extended period over the winter when demand is low.

Hotels

Castan 6 square Castan ☎ 03.81.65.02.00, ⓦ www.hotelcastan.fr. Situated close to the Roman ruins in a rustic eighteenth-century house, the *Castan* provides luxurious rooms and a filling breakfast (€10–14). Open June–Oct. ❼

🏃 **Charles Quint** 3 rue du Chapître, ☎ 03.81.82.05.49, ⓦ www .hotel-charlesquint.com. This delightful hotel is also set in an eighteenth-century building and is next to the Cathedral St-Jean and close to the Citadelle. There are large, comfortable rooms, a beautiful garden with a small swimming pool and very friendly service. ❺

Etap (Centre Gare) 5 av Maréchal Foch ☎ 08.92.68.11.86, ⓦ www.etaphotel.com. Here you'll find spacious (if also a little uninspiring and bare) rooms with cable TV. It's also close to the *gare SNCF*. ❷

Foch 7 av Foch ☎ 03.81.80.30.41, ⓦ www .hotel-foch-besancon.com. Another hotel close to the *gare SNCF*, *Foch* has cosy rooms (some with good views of the city) behind the rather depressing concrete exterior. ❸

Granvelle 13 rue du General Lecourbe, ☎ 03.81.81.33.92, ⓦ www.hotel-granvelle.fr. Despite their slightly dated decoration, the rooms here are pleasant enough, with a/c and cable TV in a quieter part of the old town. ❸

Ibis (Centre Ville) 21 rue Gambetta ☎ 03.81.81.02.02, ⓦ www.ibishotel.com. A central and affordable option, with large rooms full of mod cons (including cable TV) that will hold few surprises for the business travellers who make up most of the customers. ❹

Du Levant 9 rue des Boucheries ☎ 03.81.81.07.88. Placed above a busy restaurant, these rooms are dark and the building is a little rickety, but they are also the cheapest rooms that you'll find in the centre. ❷

Mercure 3 av Edouard Droz ☎ 03.81.40.34.34, ⓦ www.mercure.com. Situated on the far bank of the river from the old town, the *Mercure* is not cheap or central, but it has spacious, quiet rooms and all the facilities you'll need. ❼

Du Nord 8 rue Moncey ☎ 03.81.81.34.56, ⓦ www .hotel-du-nord-besancon.com. A central hotel with wi-fi access and satellite TV, as well as an elegant lounge-bar. ❸

Regina 91 Grande Rue ☎ 03.81.81.50.22, ⓦ www .besancon-regina.fr. Located right in the heart of town, the *Regina* manages to still feel quite private by being set back from the road. The rooms do not have the fanciest decoration but they still come with TVs and bathrooms. ❸

Campsite and hostel

Camping de la Plage 12 route du Belfort, Chalezeule ☎ 03.81.88.04.26, ✉ laplage .besancon@ffcc.fr. Open April–Sept. Located 5km out of town, this campsite has a restaurant, pool and plenty of opportunities for various sporting activities. €13 for a two-person tent.

Hostel 48 rue des Cras ☎ 03.81.40.32.00, ✉ fjtlesoiseaux@yahoo.fr. This hostel offers free internet access and hire of nearby tennis court (€5 per hr), but there are no communal kitchens and the free breakfast ends early (8am). It's a 15min walk from the *gare SNCF* along rue de Belfort, but difficult to find; head for the tourist office, where you can catch the #5 bus and get off at the "Les Oiseaux" stop, which is next to the hostel. There are no dorms; a double room costs €37.

The Old Town

The old town of Besançon, with its pedestrianized streets and narrow walkways, is much more pleasant to navigate by walking or cycling than by driving. From the tourist office on the far side of the river, the **rue de la République** leads across the pont de la Republique and into the heart of the old town, to the central **place du 8-Septembre** and the sixteenth-century **Hôtel de Ville**.

The Grand-Rue

The principal street, **Grande-Rue**, cuts across the square along the line of an old Roman road. At its northwestern end is another bridge, the **Pont Battant**, which is now a fairly uninspiring concrete construction; this spot, however, was also the position of the original Roman bridge into the city, which (in a testament to Roman engineering) survived until 1953. Just before the bridge is the liveliest and most modern part of town, with fancy boutiques, clothing shops and inviting cafés everywhere to be seen. In the nearby place de la

Révolution, you'll find the **Musée des Beaux-Arts et d'Archéologie** (daily except Tues 9.30am–noon & 2–6pm; €5, free Sun). The most attractive feature of this museum is the diversity of its exhibits: Egyptian sarcophagi, Gallo-Roman mosaics and a fine European art collection (including works by Rembrandt and Bonnard) are just a few noteworthy examples.

Midway down Grande-Rue, the fine sixteenth-century **Palais Granvelle**, which contains the **Musée du Temps** (Closed Mon & Tues; May–Sept, 1–7pm; Oct–May, 1–6pm; €5, free Sun), a museum packed with interactive and multimedia exhibits that pay homage to the clock-making which was a major industry in the town from the seventeenth century onwards. Continuing up the street, you pass place Victor-Hugo (he was born at no. 140) and arrive at the **Porte Noire**, a lofty and well-preserved Roman arch built in the second century AD in honour of the Emperor Marcus Aurelius. The arch is undergoing restoration due for completion in 2009. Beyond the arch is the eighteenth-century **Cathédrale St-Jean** (closed Tues); the principal interest here is the **Horloge Astronomique** (hourly guided visits in French: Feb–Dec Mon & Thurs–Sun 9.50–11.50am & 2.50–5.50pm; €2.50), a remarkable astronomical clock built in 1858–60 which contains some 30,000 parts and indicates over a hundred terrestrial and celestial positions.

The Citadelle

The spectacular **citadelle** (April–June & Sept to early Nov, daily 9am–6pm; July & Aug, daily 9am–7pm; early Nov to April 10am–5pm, closed Tues; €7.80) is a steep fifteen-minute climb from the cathedral. From this higher ground, there is a superb view of the old town and the meander in the river which contains it. It's not hard to see why a military engineer like Vauban would have considered the area as a good position for a fortification; indeed, Hitler's retreating German army were still defending the area as late as September 1944. The citadelle itself is in good condition and you can spend a fascinating hour or so exploring the walls, turrets and ditches that Vauban left as traps for any potential assailant. There are also several museums that are well worth visiting, all of which have the same opening hours as the citadelle. The **Musée d'Histoire Naturelle** contains an aquarium, insectarium and zoo, while the **Musée Comtois** has collections of pottery, furniture and a good nineteenth-century marionettes. Best of all, however, is the **Musée de la Résistance et de la Déportation**, which details the activities of the wartime Résistance both locally and throughout France. English audio commentary is available.

Eating, drinking and entertainment

While the Old Town does not have the most lively nightlife of any French city, you'll find plenty of popular and inexpensive **bars, cafés and restaurants** that offer an excellent variety of drinks and meals.

Restaurants

Barthod 20–24 rue Bersot ☎03.81.82.27.14. Behind its small, inauspicious entrance, the *Barthod* is a refined spot. There's an extensive wine list and some delicious steak and duck main courses to enjoy on the quiet inner terrace. €20–28 main courses. Closed Sun–Mon.

Brasserie du Commerce 31 rue des Granges ☎03.81.81.33.11. Open since 1873, *Du*

Commerce is another local old-timer. It boasts extravagant interior decor (including a grand chandelier) and the menu features plenty of steak (€14–19). Open daily noon–2.30pm & 7–10.30pm.

Crêperie Luc Breton 7 rue Luc Bretton ☎03.81.81.13.45. This stylish central crêperie provides an innovative set of *galettes* as well as plenty of crêpes for those with a sweet tooth. €5–11 for a crêpe. Closed Sun.

La Maison Toulousaine 1 rue Proudhon ☏03.81.81.22.93. A popular restaurant with the locals, which specializes in innovative duck dishes. Try the duck burger, or the multiple varities of foie gras. €16–35 menus. Open daily noon–2.30pm & 7–11pm.

Restaurant au Petit Polonais 81 rue des Granges ☏ 03.81.81.23.67. Founded in 1870, this restaurant provides a small but tasty range of standard brasserie-type fare (hamburger and fries is a popular choice and costs €15). Closed Sat evening & Sun.

Vela Azzurra 16 rue Bersot ☏03.81.82.81.42. There's no danger of going hungry at this Italian restaurant on the popular pedestrian rue Bersot. The large pizzas are €9–12, but it's also worth sampling the fish menu; the delicious salmon, pesto and asparagus option is just €15.50. Closed Sun.

Bars and cafés

Baud 4 Grand-Rue ☏03.81.81.20.12. This *choco-latier*-cum-café provides an irresistible array of nugget-sized chocolates (€10 for 150g) to nibble on, as well as coffee and other hot drinks. Closed Sun.

Brioche Dorée 1 place du 8 septembre ☏03.81.82.21.40. This branch of the national *Brioche Dorée* café chain provides a handy takeaway service on the street, as well as a good strong cup of coffee. The real thing that makes it special, however, are the tempting and often monster-sized pastries; the dimensions and the taste of the *pain au chocolate* (€1.65) are especially notable. Closed Sun.

Madigan's Irish Pub 17 place du 8 septembre ☏03.81.81.33.11. You'll find a super range of beers in this traditional pub. 50cl of Guinness is €6, but there are lots of Irish and continental options, as well as plenty of whiskies (€4.50–9).

Rive Gauche 2 quai Vauban ☏03.81.61.99.57. There's some pleasant outdoor seating at this riverside café, in addition to a small but high-quality range of meals. The salads (€8–11), which are made with local cheeses and ham, are particularly good. Closed Sun–Mon.

Around Besançon: Ornans and the valley of the Loue

Lying around 10km to the southeast of Besançon (roughly halfway between the regional capital and the large border town of Pontarlier), the sleepy settlement of **ORNANS** looks and feels like the picture-postcard Franche-Comté village. The town is best appreciated from its numerous footbridges, where you can watch the river Loue as it flows by numerous medieval balconied houses. The sixteenth-century **Eglise d'St Laurent** has a beautiful gothic interior and a fine belfry. The church was the subject of many paintings by Gustave Courbet, who was born here in 1819, and his old house is now the **Musée de la Maison Natale de Gustave Courbet**. The Museum houses a large collection of his paintings, sculptures and drawings, and is currently under renovation and due to reopen at the end of 2010.

Ornans is the main base for tourists looking to explore the beautiful **valley of the Loue**. The source of the river is a spring that lies a couple of kilometres above the village and from this source you can continue on foot down the valley, which is a popular summer walking route thanks to the densely wooded limestone cliffs and string of pretty villages that you pass along the way.

The Ornans **tourist office** is at 7 rue Pierre-Vernier (April–June, Sept, Oct & school holidays Mon–Sat 9.30am–noon and 2–6pm; July & Aug Mon–Sat 9am–7pm, Sun 10am–noon & 3–6pm; Nov–March Mon–Fri 10am–noon & 3–5pm; ☏03.81.62.21.50, ⓦwww.ornans.fr) and it can provide details about the local walking routes. In the town itself, there are a few **hotels** offering pleasant places to stay. An excellent hotel in the town centre is the three-star *Hôtel de France*, 51–53 rue Pierre-Vernier (☏03.81.62.24.44, ⓦwww.hotel defrance-ornans.com; ❺), which occupies the site of a sixteenth-century coaching inn, but which also provides stylish modern rooms and a pleasant garden to relax in. The *Hôtel Restaurant La Table de Gustave* at 11 rue Jacques-Gervais (☏03.81.62.16.79; ❸) is on the eastern side of the town centre; the rooms here are simpler, but still comfortable. There's a four-star **campsite**, *Le Chanet*, a couple of kilometres to the west of the town centre at 9 chemin du Chanet (☏03.81.62.23.44, ⓦwww.lechanet.com; open Mar–Oct; €17.40 for a two-person tent) where you'll find a small swimming pool and a snack bar.

If you're on the lookout for **places to eat**, note that both the hotels mentioned above have good restaurants serving traditional regional cuisine, with menus costing from €20. Another cheap and friendly restaurant with a terrace overlooking the river is the *Pizzeria Le Chavot* on 24 rue Pierre-Vernier (☏03.81.62.25.23), which serves some home-made and very filling pizzas (€7–10).

Lons-le-Saunier and around

Rising up from the shores of Lake Geneva, the Jura landscape ascends into a broad plateau of mountains that form the northern border with Switzerland. To the west of this central plateau, the spa town and departmental capital of **LONS-LE-SAUNIER** has grown wealthy over the centuries through the rich agricultural produce of the surrounding countryside. While the town was once the site of a Neolithic settlement, most of the remaining ruins (as well as its medieval centre) were destroyed by a fire in the early seventeenth century. What remains today mainly dates from the 1700s, and a wander around the town is still an agreeable way to spend an afternoon.

The central **place de la Liberté** is a good place to start your tour of the town. Should you happen to be in the square on the hour, the **theatre clock** at the eastern end will chime a familiar half-dozen notes from *La Marseillaise* to honour Lons' most famous citizen, Rouget de Lisle; he composed the anthem during his time as a campaigner in the French revolutionary army during the early 1790s. Running north from the square is the attractive, colonnaded thoroughfare of **rue du Commerce**, where some of Lons' oldest buildings line the street. No. 24 on this street is the house where de Lisle was born; now the **Musée Rouget de Lisle** (open Jun–Sept; Mon & Wed–Fri 10am–noon & 2–6pm, Sat & Sun 2–5pm; €2), it is mainly of interest for its fine eighteenth-century interior and furniture.

At the northern end of rue du Commerce in place Philibert Chalon, you'll find the **Musée des Beaux Arts** (Mon & Wed–Fri 10am–noon & 2–6pm, Sat & Sun 2–5pm; €2), which houses a fine display of nineteenth-century sculptures, including those of the local artist Jean-Joseph Perraud. If you return south along rue Richebourg to avenue Jean-Moulin, you come to a statue of de Lisle himself. It was created by Frédéric Bartholdi, a sculptor whose work is now rather more well known than Perraud's: Bartholdi went on to refine de Lisle's stirring pose on a much grander scale in the Statue of Liberty.

A left turn here leads to the pleasant **Parc Edouard Guenon**, where you'll find the delightfully ornate *fin-de-siècle* building of the **Thermes Ledonia**, or mineral baths. The baths are now run by **Thermes Valvital** (open Mon–Fri 11am–8pm, Sat 9am–6pm, Sun 9am–2pm; ☏03.84.24.38.18, ⓦwww.valvital.eu; one-day spa treatments start from €40), and come lavishly equipped with a sauna, Turkish bath and Jacuzzi. The high salt content of the water here is said to soothe the usual aches and pains, and is also renowned for its ability to cure bed-wetting.

Practicalities

Lons' **gare SNCF** is a ten-minute walk south of place de la Liberté; just head straight down avenue Aristide Briand (opposite the station entrance) to get into the centre. There are a couple of very helpful information points in the town.

The **tourist office** (Mon–Sat 9am–noon & 2–6pm, closes at 5pm on Sat; ☎03.84.24.65.01, ⓦwww.ville-lons-le-saunier.fr) is in the same building as the theatre on place du 11 Novembre, and there's cheap, fast **internet access** on the first floor. The **Comité Départemental du Tourisme de Jura**, 8 rue Louis-Rousseau (Mon–Fri: April–Nov 8.30am–12.30pm and 2–6pm; Dec–March 8.30am–6pm; ☎03.84.87.08.88, ⓦwww.jura-tourism.com), can provide information about the Jura mountains. There are no particularly upmarket **hotels** in the centre of Lons, but plenty of good-value, mid-range options. The *Au Terminus*, 37 avenue Aristide-Briand, (☎03.84.24.41.83, ⓦwww.hotel-terminus-lons.com; ❸), has bright, stylish rooms close to the *gare SNCF*. Another good two-star hotel is the *Nouvel*, 50 rue Lecourbe (☎03.84.47.20.67, ⓦwww.nouvel-hotel-lons.fr; ❸), situated just to the west of the place de la Liberté; here you'll find cosy rooms with satellite TV. Budget travellers might choose to head for the *Hotel Restaurant des Sports*, 21 rue Saint Désiré (☎03.84.24.04.42; ❶), where the rooms are placed above a lively café; these rooms are dark and small but are also the cheapest in town.

For a delicious **meal** in a charming setting, pay a visit to *La Comedié*, 65 rue de l'Agriculture (☎03.84.24.20.66; closed on Sun & Mon; €18–32 menus); the fish (including salmon and crayfish) and wide range of cheeses are particularly noteworthy. The most popular and vibrant **café** in town is *De Strasbourg*, situated next to the tourist office on place du 11 Novembre, which is a great place for sitting out with a beer or coffee, and has an eclectic menu: you can get anything from steak frites (€12.50) to more creative salads filled with local ham and cheese.

The Région des Lacs

If you drive east for 20km along the N78 road from Lons, you'll enter the **Région des Lacs**, an area of woods, pastures and lakes strung out along the valley of the River Ain. During the journey, the road begins to ascend to the peaks and gorges that define the border with Switzerland. With each bend in the climbing road, the views down to the tiny villages, often huddled around churches with ornate mosaic domes, become all the more impressive. Some of the lakes charge parking fees during the day, but after 6pm, when the crowds and swimming supervisors have gone home, they are deserted and serenely peaceful – the perfect place for an evening picnic watching the sunset.

The region's main resort town is **CLAIRVAUX-LES-LACS**. It's here that the River Ain flows into the northern tip of the serpentine **Lac de Vouglans**, which is dammed 25km downstream. The **Grand Lac**, just south of town, is the focus of summer resort activity, with a beach area and water sports facilities. It's calm and scenic, in spite of all the camping activity going on around it. The **Office du Tourisme du Pays des Lacs**, 36 Grande-Rue (Mon–Fri 9am–noon & 2–6pm, Sat 9am–noon; July & Aug also Sun 10am–noon; ☎03.84.25.27.47, ⓦwww.juralacs.com), is the place to find information about the region and outdoor activities such as boat and bike rental. For **hiking**, the tourist office sells an €8 guide with maps and descriptions of 46 hikes of varying levels of difficulty in the local area. There's a good-value **hotel** on the Grand Lac, *La Chaumière du Lac* (☎03.84.25.81.52, ⓦwww.juralacs.com/adherents/lachaumiere.htm; open Apr–Sept; ❸), which provides simple rooms but also a cosy, fire-lit restaurant serving local fish and cheese (€15–35 menus).

The Cascades du Hérisson

Some 16km north of Clairvaux, near the village of **DOUCIER** and surrounded by hills, **Lac de Chalain**, is a much more impressive setting. It's also a very popular spot for **camping**, hence the prices can be high. Of the **campsites** by the lake, the *Le Grand Lac* (℡03.84.25.26.19, ⓦwww.relaisoleiljura.com; open Jun to early Sept; €21 for a two-person tent), located on the lake at Chemin du langard, offers the best combination of good facilities (including a pool, snack bar and a games area for kids) and value for money. Run by the same company, the nearby campsite *Le Fayolan* (same contact details; open May to mid-Sept; €36 for a two-person tent), is pricier, but provides a sauna and hammam, as well as more sporting activities and a restaurant.

One reason for the popularity of this area for campers is its proximity to the **Cascades du Hérisson**, the septet of waterfalls that has become one of the Jura's best-known natural spectacles. **If you are driving**, you can reach the main car park for the Cascades by passing through Val-Dessous, a village just to the southeast of Doucier, and then heading for the Parking de l'Eventail. A well-signposted path takes you from the car park to the highest of the falls, which descend a breathtaking 255m over just 7km. A gentle walk of around ten minutes from the car park leads to the prettiest of the falls, the **Éventail**. If you continue upstream, you'll shake off most of the other casual spectators and, after passing through woods of wild oak (and lovely daffodils in spring), will arrive at the **Grand Saut** fall, where the water plummets down a sheer drop of some sixty metres.

If you follow the pathway behind the waterfall, you can then ascend a steep trail as it leads past several smaller springs as well as a drinks kiosk; this kiosk intersects with another path that leads south to the village of Bonlieu. Finally, the path ends at the uppermost fall, which is known as **Saut Girard** and which lies close to the village of **ILAY**. In all, the walk should take around three hours for most walkers, taking into account the odd stop at each viewpoint which deserves a photograph. There's a choice of restaurants in Ilay, but only one **hotel**, the *Auberge du Hérisson*, 5 rue des Lacs (℡03.84.25.58.18, ⓦwww .herisson.com; ❷; closed Nov–Jan; restaurant menus €15–40), where you can expect fairly simple, small rooms but also some friendly owners who can provide useful information about the area.

Les Rousses

A couple of kilometres before the frontier with Switzerland, **LES ROUSSES** is a resort which seems to exist mainly for skiers, and for a select band at that: this is an outstanding area for cross-country skiing (see cross-country skiing box opposite). Yet the skiers don't have it all their own way; Les Rousses also holds a very useful position for hikers looking to explore the **Parc Naturel Regional du Haut-Jura** (ⓦwww.parc-haut-jura.fr), the regional park which runs south from Champagnole across the southern Jura mountains. There are several **GR** footpaths which can be accessed from Les Rousses. **GR9** passes through here as it moves along the crest of the ridge towards the Col de la Faucille; the **GR559**, a route which takes you on a tour of the lakes of Franche-Comté, begins here and ends in Lons-le-Saunier; even the much longer **GR5** passes within a few kilometres of the resort.

The **tourist office**, 495 rue Pasteur (℡03.84.60.04.31, ⓦwww.lesrousses .com), can provide information on the local skiing conditions. The ESF is also based in the tourist office (℡03.84.60.01.61); the ESF ski instructors organize lessons that can focus specifically on cross-country skiing technique.

There are plenty of **hotels** in Les Rousses: *Le Lodge*, 309 rue Pasteur (℡03.84.60.50.64, ⓦwww.hotellelodge.com; ❺), offers rustic, cosy rooms in an old cottage in the centre; *Le Village*, just down the road at 344 rue Pasteur (℡03.84.34.12.75, ⓦwww.hotelvillage.fr; ❸), is a cheaper option but the rooms are comfortable and the continental breakfast (€6.50) agreeably large. To the east

The high plateaux of the Jura mountains guarantee good snow cover in winter, but they also lack the steep gradients of the Alpine peaks further to the south; it is this high but level terrain which has made the Jura into France's most popular destination for **cross-country skiing**, or *ski de fond*. The goal of any superfit *fondeur* is the 175-kilometre Grande Traversée du Jura (GTJ), which crosses the high plateau from Villers-le-Lac to Giron, a town in the south of the Parc Naturel Régional Haut Jura.

The same gentle topography and established infrastructure that enable cross-country skiing have made this region an ideal high-summer venue for **mountain biking**, with hundreds of waymarked cross-country skiing pistes used out of season as trails for adventuresome mountain bikers. The 360-kilometre **GTJ–VTT**, which starts near Montbéliard (just to the south of Belfort), has become the greatest long-distance biking challenge in the area. Many people cycle on the road; there aren't many cars, so if you can handle the hills, then go for it.

The headquarters of the departmental tourist board, the **Comité Départemental du Tourisme de Jura** in Lons-le Saunier (T03.84.87.08.88, W www.jura-tourism .com), can supply plenty of information, maps and literature (in English as well as French) on outdoor leisure opportunities of all kinds in the Jura.

of the village and close to the ski slopes is *Le Chamois*, 230 montée le Noirmont (T03.84.60.01.48, W www.lechamois.org; ❸), which has spacious rooms with all the mod cons, as well as a gourmet restaurant on site. 3.5km outside Les Rousses at Bief-de-la-Chaille is a **HI hostel** located in an old, red-shuttered farmhouse by a stream (T03.84.60.02.80, €les-rousses@fuaj.org; open late-Dec to March & mid-May to mid-Sept; €17 for a dorm bed). To book a stay between December and March, it is necessary to contact the hostel directly and reserve a bed.

For a good-quality **meal** featuring local trout and cheeses, try the restaurant at the *Hotel Gai Pinson*, 1465 route Blanche (T03.84.60.02.15; closed Sun evenings & mid-Nov to mid-Dec; €25 menu). There are also plenty of cafés and pizzerias in the town.

To the North of Lons-le-Saunier: Poligny, Arbois and the surrounding villages

The journey north of Lons on the N83 road towards Besançon is known with good reason as the **Route des Vins du Jura**, for it passes through miles of pretty countryside filled with vineyards. The idyllic villages that you'll find here often have their own vintages, which provide an excellent excuse for prolonging your stay.

Château-Chalon and Baume les Messieurs

10km to the north of Lons on the N83 road towards Besançon, the route known locally as the Route des Vins du Jura, you come to a turn-off on the D120 for **Voiteur**. This is an unremarkable provincial town, but just beyond it is one of the prettiest villages that you will find in Franche-Comté, if not the whole country. **CHÂTEAU-CHALON** is a delight to wander around, a settlement with a beautiful church, the twelfth-century **Eglise Saint Pierre**, and a medieval keep that are all that remain of the grand Benedictine Abbey which once stood here. As well as holding a stunning position on top of a high rocky outcrop, the village is also noted for the unique variety of *vin jaune* that it has produced ever since Roman times, and there are several vineyards still operating around the town. A good choice if you want to sample a range of local and regional wines is the

▲ Vineyard near Lons-le-Saunier

vineyard of Jean Berthet-Bondet on the rue de la Tour (℡03.84.33.60.48, ⓦwww.berthet-bondet.net; contact the vineyard to organize a tour), which provides tasting sessions. The **tourist office** in Voiteur (℡03.84.44.62.47, ⓦwww.hauteseille.com) can provide the latest details about these cellars and the local accommodation options. *La Maison d'Eusebia* (℡03.84.44.92.10, ⓦwww .eusebia.fr; ❻) provides comfortable rooms in the village, along with a superb restaurant serving creative local and seasonal food (€27–54 menus).

If at Voiteur you turn southwards instead of heading north towards Chateau-Chalon and Besançon, then after 4km you'll reach another pretty hamlet, **BAUME LES MESSIEURS**. Nestling in the narrow intersection of three valleys and sitting underneath some sheer two-hundred-metre high cliffs, this village boasts spectacular views as well as some fascinating buildings and medieval streets. The main attraction is the **Imperiale Abbey** (guided visits in mid-May to Sept 10am–noon & 2–6pm; ℡03.84.44.95.45; €3.60), a monastery originally founded in the sixth century, but which now is composed of sections built later in the Middle Ages. Inside, you can admire various striking pieces of Christian art, with the sixteenth-century Flemish triptych altarpiece, a depiction of the Passion, being perhaps the most impressive.

There are a few small *chambres d'hôtes* in the village which can offer a pleasant night's stay; the pick of the bunch is *La Grange à Nicolas*, 5 rue Saint Jean (℡03.84.85.20.39, ⓦwww.lagrangeanicolas.com; ❺), which has cosy, intimate rooms with some elegant eighteenth-century furniture.

Poligny and Arbois

After Voiteur, around 10km further along the N83 road, you reach the attractive medieval town of **POLIGNY**, at the southern end of the Culée de Vaux valley. The town is worth a stop for its well-preserved buildings from the early Middle Ages, as well as for the **Maison du Comté** (guided tours every 30min; April & Oct Tues–Sun 2–5pm; May, June & Sept daily 2–6pm; July & Aug daily 10am–noon & 2–6pm; ℡03.84.37.78.40; €4) on avenue de la Résistance. This old *fromagerie* is now the headquarters of the Comité Interprofessional du Gruyère du Comté, France's favourite cheese, and it includes a centre with films, models and tasting sessions that are "dedicated to awakening your senses".

If you are a wine-lover, however, it is **ARBOIS**, 10km to the north of Poligny, that should be your main port of call in the area. Glittering wine emporia line the central place de la Liberté, all of which seem to entreat you to sample the unusual local reds, whites and rosés that are placed in the shop windows. Of these local wines, the sweet *vin de paille* is the rarest; the name derives from its grapes, which are dried on beds of straw during the production process, thus giving the wine a strong aftertaste. The *chocolatier* **M. Hirsinger** has even developed a range of chocolates to eat with wines, especially the Jura's own *vin jaune*. A visit to the Hirsinger chocolate shop on place de la Liberté should be on the itinerary of every visitor to Arbois, as much for its delicious ice cream as the chocolate itself.

A few kilometres south of town on the D469 is the Château Pécauld, where you'll find the **Musée de la Vigne et du Vin** (March–June, Sept & Oct daily except Tues 10am–noon & 2–6pm; July & Aug daily 10am–12.30pm & 2–6pm; Nov–Feb daily except Tues 2–6pm; €3.50), which details the development and production of wine in the Jura. The château also has wine-tasting sessions, which must be organized in advance (T03.84.66.40.53, Wwww.chateaupecauld.com).

The **Arbois tourist office** is at 10 rue de l'Hôtel-de-Ville (July & Aug Mon–Sat 9am–12.30pm & 2–6.30pm, Sun 10am–noon & 2–5pm; Sept–June Mon 3–6pm, Tues–Sat 9am–noon & 2–6pm; T03.84.66.55.50, Wwww.arbois .com); it can provide details of vineyards in the area which offer opportunities for tourists to sample the local wine.

If you're **staying** overnight and fancy sleeping in a spacious room adorned with lots of bright and colourful modern paintings, try out the three-star *Hôtel Jean Paul Jenet* (T03.84.66.05.67, Wwww.jeanpauljeunet.com; ⑥). If you would like cheaper rooms, however, then it's best to head instead for the *Hôtel Des Messageries*, 2 rue de Courcelles (T03.84.66.15.45, Wwww.hoteldesmessageries.com; ❸), which is located in an old stone town house full of character and atmosphere. The **municipal campsite**, *Les Vignes*, on avenue Général-Leclerc (T03.84.66.14.12, Wwww.camping.arbois.fr; open May–Sept; €17 for a two-person tent), is 1km east of the centre; it has a grocery store, snack bar and swimming pool.

Of the **restaurants** in town, the *Jean Paul Jenet* is the best; the €39 menus include some delicious traditional dishes with a twist. Another good option is *La Balance Mets et Vins*, 47 rue de Courcelles (T03.84.37.45.00; closed on Tues & Wed; €20–40 menus), which serves many classic local specialities, as well as some creative vegetarian dishes.

Salins-les-Bains

One final town between Besançon and Lons that is an attractive stop for many tourists (especially those after a taste of the finer things in life) is the spa resort of **SALINS-LES-BAINS**. The **Thermes de Salins** (T03.84.73.04.63, Wwww .thermes-salins.com; open Feb–Dec Mon–Sat 2–6.30pm, Sun 10–11.45am & 2–5.30pm; a day's treatment costs from €9) exploit the surrounding valley's salt springs; specific treatments for rheumatism are on offer, as well as a salt-water pool, Jacuzzi, hammam and beauty centre for casual tourists.

For those curious about the saline content of the local water, one illuminating visit would be to the **Salines** (saltworks) which are home to a series of underground tunnels with Roman art and a hydraulic pumping system that was developed in the eighteenth century (guided visits; open at weekends from Nov to mid-March, open daily from mid-March to Oct, contact the office about times; T03.84.73.01.34, Wwww.salinesdesalins.com; €4.70). The salines only stopped producing salt commercially in 1962.

There are several excellent **places to stay** in the town that aren't overly expensive, not least the *Residence Charles Sander*, 26 rue de la République

(03.84.73.36.40, ⓦwww.residencesander.com; ❹), which has bright, stylish rooms and a lovely patio where you can enjoy your morning breakfast. Rather less salubrious but a bit cheaper is the *Hotel des Deux Forts* in place du Vigneron (ⓣ03.84.73.70.40, ⓦhttp://pagesperso-orange.fr/hoteldesdeuxforts; ❷).

Northern Franche-Comté: Belfort

Nestled in the gap between two mountain ranges – the Vosges to the north and the Jura to the south – lies **BELFORT**, a town assured of a place in French hearts for its history as an insurmountable stronghold on this obvious route for invaders. The town is remembered particularly for its long resistance to a siege during the 1870 Franco–Prussian War; it was this resistance that spared it the humiliating fate of being annexed into the German empire, the fate suffered by much of neighbouring Alsace-Lorraine. The commanding officer at the time was one Colonel Denfert-Rochereau (known popularly as the "Lion of Belfort"), who earned himself the honour of numerous street names throughout the country, as well as that of a Parisian square and métro station. These days it's a town that exudes both French and German influences with regard to its architecture, cuisine and the cheery demeanour of many of its inhabitants.

Arrival, information and accommodation

The **gare SNCF** and departure point for local **buses** are at the end of Faubourg-de-France, the main shopping street in the new town. The **tourist office** (mid-June to mid-Sept Mon–Sat 9am–7pm; mid-Sept to mid-June Mon–Sat 9am–12.30pm & 1.45–6pm; ⓣ03.84.55.90.90, ⓦwww.ot-belfort.fr) is at 2 rue Clemenceau. The office can also help find the best hiking trails in the southern Vosges if you are heading north into Alsace and Lorraine (see "Hiking in the southern Vosges" section, p.281). You can reach the tourist office from the *gare SNCF* by walking for ten minutes down Faubourg-de-France as far as the river, then turning left and walking along quai Charles-Vallet until you reach rue Clemenceau. Cheap and high-speed **internet access** is available at Dina Telecom (ⓣ03.84.21.00.02) just south of the *gare SNCF* at 27 avenue Wilson.

There is an excellent choice of **hotels** in Belfort, but watch out for Eurock-éennes (see below) and the other music festivals which take place here; these events make beds very difficult to find. It's also worth calling ahead for the latest prices, as the Belfort hotels change these substantially from day to day, especially during July and August. On the northern edge of the old town, the *ATRIA Novotel*, avenue de l'Esperance (ⓣ03.84.58.85.00, ⓦwww.novotel .com: ❽), is a large, three-star hotel in a stylish glass and steel building; the rooms have excellent facilities and there's a gym and restaurant on site. Just across the river at 4 rue du Magasin, *Le Vauban* (ⓣ03.84.21.59.37, ⓦwww .hotel-vauban.com; ❹) is a little different: the building dates from 1902, and the cosy rooms are full of character, charm and the colourful paintings of the owner. In the centre of the old town, the *Grand Hôtel du Tonneau d'Or*, 1 rue Général Reiset (ⓣ03.84.58.57.56, ⓦwww.tonneaudor.fr; ❼), is also in a building that dates from 1902, yet the rooms here are spacious and packed with all the mod cons expected of a three-star hotel. In the new town, *Boreal*, 2 rue du Comte de la Suze (ⓣ03.84.22.32.32, ⓦwww.hotelboreal.com; ❺), offers some functional if rather uninspiring rooms. Belfort's **hostel**, *Résidence Madrid*, is 1km west of the railway line at 6 rue de Madrid (ⓣ03.84.21.39.16, ⓔfjt .belfort@orange.fr; open all year; €11.90 for a dorm bed). The best local

campsite, *Camping International de l'Étang des Forges*, is a few kilometres north of the old town on rue du Général-Béthouart (☎03.84.22.54.92, ⓦwww .camping-belfort.com; open April–Sept; €14.50 for a two-person tent); here you'll find a grocery store, swimming pool and bar.

The Town

Finding your way around Belfort is easy enough. The town is sliced in two by the River Savoureuse: the **new town** to the west is the commercial hub; lying beneath the impressive edifice of the red **Citadelle** on the eastern side is the quieter **old town**. This fortress was built by Vauban on the site of a medieval keep, of which only a single tower to the north of the castle remains. Even if you are not a fan of visiting castles, it is worth making the trip simply for the excellent views of Belfort's old town and of the surrounding countryside. In the course of his work here, Vauban did not just build the Citadelle, he was also responsible for a new set of fortifications surrounding Belfort, and from the castle you can see how these moulded the old town into a pentagonal shape. The street plan is still largely unchanged.

The Citadelle now houses the **Musée d'Art et d'Histoire** (daily except Tues: April–June & Sept 10am–noon & 2–6pm; July & Aug 10am–6pm; Oct–March 10am–noon and 2–5pm; ☎03.84.54.25.50; €2.95). The museum contains some exhibits on the town's former military heroes, as well as many Bronze and Iron Age artefacts (including painted pottery, jewellery and tools), which were found in a cave at Cravanche, 5km to the north, in 1876. For art-lovers, however, the highlight of the museum's collection is likely to be the paintings of Dürer and Doré on display.

Belfort's excellent Modern Art museum, the **Donation Maurice Jardot** (daily except Tues; Oct–March 10am–noon & 2–5pm; April–June & Sept 10am–noon & 2–6pm; July & Aug 10am–6pm; €3.95), lies on the northern edge of the new town at 8 rue de Mulhouse. The museum was founded at the behest of Maurice Jardot, an associate of Daniel-Henry Kahnweiler, one of the most noted art dealers of the twentieth century; when Jardot died in 1997, he left 110 works of art to the town, including some by Chagall, Léger and Picasso.

The most famous (and photographed) phenomenon in town is an eleven-metre-high red sandstone **lion** carved out of the rock-face that you pass on the way up to the castle. It was designed by Frédéric Bartholdi, a sculptor from Colmar whose main claim to fame is a certain statue currently standing in the harbour of New York city, as a monument to commemorate the 1870 siege.

Belfort becomes a hotspot for **rock music** fans on the first weekend of July each year, when the **Eurockéennes** festival (ⓦwww.eurockeennes.fr) takes place at the nearby Malsaucy lake. If shopping in a **market** is more your idea of a good time, then you can visit the vibrant flea market (featuring over two hundred local artisans and antique-dealers) which takes place in the old town on the first Sunday of every month between March and December.

Eating and drinking

Belfort's **bars and cafés** tend to have a good selection of German beers, which reflects the history of the town on the frontier with the Germanic lands to the east. *Brasserie des Halles*, close to the river at 2 rue Docteur Perry (☎03.84.21.66.90), is a magnet for all kinds of sports fans, who can enjoy a cheap beer (€2.50 for 25cl) and an interior covered in sporting memorabilia. ⚹ *Bistrot des Moines*, 22 rue Dreyfus Schmidt (☎03.84.21.86.40), is a popular central pub with a circular bar displaying a fine array of German and Irish beers (€6.30 for 50cl) and some hearty pub grub. *Café du Commerce*, 6 Faubourg de France (T03.84.28.29.41), is the best place in town to sit down, chill out with a coffee (€2) and watch the world go by on the main pedestrian street. Located near to the *gare SNCF* at 60 Faubourg de France, *Kleiber Chocolatier* (T03.84.21.31.85) provides indoor seating for you to enjoy some delicious little chocolates or ice-creams (€2.50–4.50).

With regard to **restaurants**, one of the grandest places to dine in town is the restaurant at the *Tonneau d'Or* (see the hotels above; closed Sat–Sun & Aug; lunch menu is €13.90; evening menus cost from €24), where you can enjoy some delicious local specialities. The *Brasserie de la Gare*, opposite the station at 11 avenue Wilson (T03.84.28.74.82; closed Sun), provides good-quality steaks and salads for very reasonable prices (€8–14), but there are also several good restaurants offering more inventive cuisine. *Au Palais de Chine*, 62 Faubourg de France (T03.84.22.71.25), is a cosy hole in the wall that serves an excellent range of Chinese and Vietnamese cuisine (€25 menu).

Travel details

Trains

Annecy to: Aix-les-Bains (frequent; 25min); Chambéry (frequent; 40min); Chamonix via St Gervais (4 daily; 3hr); Grenoble (hourly; 2hr); Lyon (hourly; 2hr); Paris-Lyon (several daily; 3hr 40min).
Annemasse, near Geneva to: Annecy (several daily; 1hr); Évian (frequent; 35min); Paris-Lyon via Bellegarde (4 daily; 4hr).
Belfort to: Basel via Mulhouse (several daily; 1hr 15min); Besançon (every hour; 1hr 15min); Montbéliard (frequent; 15min); Mulhouse (8 daily; 30min); Paris-Est (2 daily; 4hr); Strasbourg (3 daily; 1hr 30min).
Besançon to: Bourg-en-Bresse (4 daily; 1hr 30min); Dijon (several daily; 1hr); Morez via Dole Ville (2 daily; 2hr 30min); Paris-Lyon (5 daily; 2hr 30min).
Briançon to: Grenoble (2 daily; 4hr); Marseille via Valence (2 daily; 6hr).
Chambéry to: Aix-les-Bains (frequent; 10min); Annecy (frequent; 45min); Bourg St Maurice (several daily; 2hr); Geneva (3 daily; 1hr 30min); Grenoble (frequent; 45min); Lyon (frequent; 1hr 20min); Paris-Lyon (several daily; 3hr).
Évian to: Geneva via Annemasse (several daily; 1hr); Thonon-les-Bains (frequent; 10min).
Grenoble to: Annecy (hourly; 2hr); Briançon, changing at Gap (6 daily; 4hr 20min); Chambéry (hourly; 1hr); Lyon (frequent; 1hr 30min); Paris-Lyon (3 daily; 3hr).
Lons-le-Saunier to: Annecy via Lyon (5 daily; 3hr 30min); Belfort (4 daily; 2hr); Besanon (every hour; 1hr); Geneva via Bourg-en-Bresse (3 daily; 2hr 30min); Paris-Lyon via Bourg-en-Bresse (4 daily; 3hr).

Buses

Annecy to: Geneve (2 daily; 1hr 15min); Lyon (5 daily; 2hr).
Besançon to: Ornans (3 daily; 40min).
Bourg-St-Maurice to: Aosta, Italy (1 daily in July & Aug; 2hr 30min); Les Arcs (4 on Sat only in July & Aug; 1hr); Tignes (2–3 daily; 1hr 15min); Val d'Isère (2–3 daily; 45min).
Briançon to: Col du Lautaret (3 daily; 50min); La Grave (3 daily; 1hr 10min); Le Monêtier-les-Bains (3 daily; 45min); St-Véran via Guillestre (1–2 daily; 1hr 40min); Vallouise via Argentière (1 daily; 2hr).
Chambéry to: Meribel, depart from the airport (2 daily; 1hr).
Chamonix to: Geneva (2 daily; 2hr); other resorts in the Chamonix-Mont Blanc area: Argentiere (12 daily; 20 min); Les Houches (frequent; 20min).
Grenoble to: L'Alpe d'Huez (1–2 daily; 40min); Le Bourg-d'Oisans (7 daily; 1hr); Briançon (3 daily; 2hr 40min); Chambéry (9 daily; 2hr); Col du Lautaret (3 daily; 1hr 50min); La Grave (3 daily; 1hr 30min); Le Monêtier-les-Bains (3 daily; 2hr 10min); St-Pierre-de-Chartreuse (at least 1 daily; 1hr); Villard-de-Lans and other towns in the Vercors (6 daily; 1hr).
Thonon-les-Bains to: Évian (several daily; 25min); Yvoire (3–4 daily; 20min).

The Rhône valley

CHAPTER 14

Highlights

* **Traboules** Follow in the footsteps of the plucky Resistance fighters, and explore Lyon's dark and winding *traboules*, hidden away behind large, hulking doorways. See p.938

* **Lyon's bouchons** Meat-lovers will be in heaven in the city famous for its earthy *bouchons* and award-winning chefs. See p.941

* **Pérouges** A short train's ride from Lyon, this is an impeccably preserved medieval hill-top village made up of sunkissed cobbled lanes and quaint houses. See p.944

* **Musée Internationale de la Chaussure** Fascinating historical museum in Romans-sur-Isère, displaying the world's wackiest designs in footwear – from early Egyptian sandals and tiny Chinese slippers to the latest Jimmy Choos. See p.948

* **Montelimar nougat** Without doubt, the best place to gorge on the moreish *bonbon* made of sweet honey and crunchy nuts. See p.951

▲ Pérouges

The Rhône valley

T
he **Rhône valley** stretches down from the compelling city of Lyon, the
second biggest city in France, to just north of Orange, in Provence. The
north–south route of ancient armies, medieval traders and modern rail
and road, the valley is now as industrialized as the least attractive parts
of the north. Though the river is still a means of transport, its waters now also
cool the reactors of the Marcoule and Tricastin nuclear power station between
Montélimar and Avignon and act as a dumping ground for the heavy industries along its banks. Following the River Rhône holds few attractions, with
the exceptions of the scenic stretch of **vineyards** and fruit orchards between
the Roman city of **Vienne** and the distinctly southern city of **Valence**. But
the big magnet is, of course, the gastronomic paradise of **Lyon**, with its
hundreds of sophisticated bars and restaurants.

Lyon and around

Viewed at high speed from the Autoroute du Soleil, the first impression of
LYON is of a major confluence of rivers and roads, around which only petrochemical industries thrive. In fact, from the sixteenth century right up until the
postwar dominance of metalworks and chemicals, silk was the city's main
industry, generating the wealth which left behind a multitude of Renaissance
buildings. But what has stamped its character most on Lyon is the commerce
and banking that grew up with its industrial expansion. Today, with its eco-
friendly tram system, high-tech industrial parks home to international
companies, Lyon is certainly a modern city *par excellence*.

Most French people find themselves here for business rather than for
recreation: it's a get-up-and-go place, not a lie-back-and-rest one, with an
almost Swiss sense of cleanliness, order and efficiency. But as a wonderfully
manageable slice of urban France, Lyon certainly has its charms. Foremost
among these is **gastronomy**; there are more restaurants per Gothic and
Renaissance square metre of the old town than anywhere else on earth, and
the city could form a football team with its superstars of the international
chef circuit. While the **textile museum** is the second famous reason for
stopping here, Lyon's nightlife, cinema and theatre (including the famous
Lyonnais puppets), its antique markets, music and other cultural festivities
might tempt you to stay at least a few days. As if that weren't enough, Lyon's
distinctive older quarters and its winding, secret *traboules* are an urban explorer's paradise.

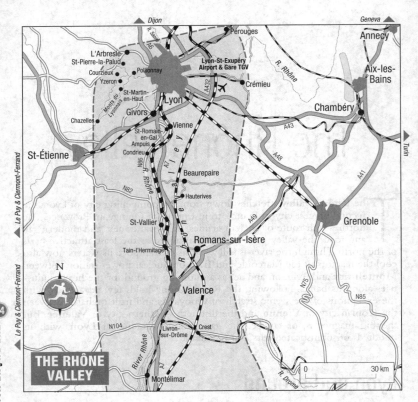

THE RHÔNE VALLEY

Lyon is organized into nine arrondissements. A visit to the city will take you into the Presqu'île (1er and 2e arrondissements), the area between the rivers Saône and Rhône, and you're likely to spend some time in Vieux Lyon (5e) on the west bank of the Saône, as well as the east bank of the Rhône (3e), including the modern development known as La Part-Dieu.

Arrival, information and city transport

The **Lyon-St Exupéry international airport** (☎08.26.80.08.26, ⓦwww .lyon.aeroport.fr) and the **TGV station** are off the Grenoble autoroute, 25km to the southeast of the city, with a fifty-minute Satobus bus link to the town centre (every 20min 6am–11.40pm; €8.60).

Central Lyon has two train stations: the **Gare de Perrache** on the Presqu'île is used mainly for ordinary trains rather than TGVs, and has the **gare routière** alongside; and **La Part-Dieu TGV station** is in the 3e arrondissement to the east of the Presqu'île. Some TGV trains from Paris give the option of getting off at either station, so ask when buying your ticket. Central Lyon is linked to the suburbs by an efficient **métro**, as well as trolleybuses and a slick **tram** system.

There's a **Bureau d'Information** in the Centre Perrache at the station (Mon–Fri 7.30am–6.30pm, Sat 9am–noon & 1.45–5pm; ⓦwww.tcl.fr), where you can pick up a métro, tram, bus and funicular map; or it's just two stops on the métro to place Bellecour, where the **central tourist office** stands on the southeast corner (daily 9am–5pm; ☎04.72.77.69.69, ⓦ www.lyon-france.com). The tourist office organizes and sells tickets for a number of **guided tours** that focus on different aspects of the city; the silk tour, for example, explores the Croix-Rousse, where many silk workers used to live, before visiting a silk-printing workshop; another tour delves into the complex web of Lyon's famous *traboules*. Tours last either 1hr 30min, 2hr or 3hr and cost €9–12, depending on duration and theme.

At métro stations or the city transport TCL offices, the cheapest way to buy **tickets** is in a carnet of ten (€12.80), or there's the *Ticket Liberté*, valid for 24hr (€4.40). Ordinary tickets (€1.60) are flat-rate within an hour's duration and limited to a single one-way journey, with changes allowed. The métro runs 5am–12.30am, though some bus lines close as early as 8pm. The **bureau de guides**, situated next to the Vieux Lyon metro station, on Avenue Adolphe-Max, has information on other tourist-friendly tickets offering discounts on travel round the city.

Accommodation

As a result of Lyon's commercial pre-eminence, hotel **rooms** can be a problem to find, particularly on weekdays. If you don't book ahead, you could end up paying well over the odds for inferior accommodation. Hotels in Perrache (2ᵉ) and Bellecour (2ᵉ) fill up quickly, but you may be luckier around Terreaux (1ᵉʳ). If you're stuck, the tourist office offers a reservation service, though you'll have to stump up your room desposit then and there.

If you're on a real budget, stop by the CROUS offices, 59 rue de la Madeleine, 7ᵉ (☎04.72.80.17.70, ⓦ www.crous-lyon.fr; Mᵒ Jean-Macé), or CRIJ offices, 10 quai Jean Moulin, 2ᵉ (☎04.72.77.00.66; Mᵒ Bellecour), both of which may be able to fix you up in student lodgings or residences closer to the centre during vacation time.

Hotels

Alexandra 49 rue Victor-Hugo, 2ᵉ ☎04.78.37.75.79, ⓦ www.hotel-alexandra-lyon.fr; Mᵒ Ampère Victor-Hugo. Well-run old hotel overlooking place Ampère, a lively pedestrian zone. Parking available. ❸

Des Artistes 8 rue Gaspard-Andre, 2ᵉ ☎04.78.42.04.88, ⓦ www.hotel-des-artistes.fr; Mᵒ Bellecour. Smart hotel situated on the lovely Place des Celestins. Bathrooms are sparkling and fresh, the beds are comfortable and there's an elegant dining room downstairs. ❼

Hotel d'Azur 64 rue Victor Hugo, 2ᵉ ☎04.78.42.51.26, ⓦ www.hotelazurlyon.com; Mᵒ Ampere-Hugo. Double-glazed windows seal out the noise from the pedestrianized Victor-Hugo, while the cheerful yellow and blue tones of this pleasant hotel can't help but lift your mood. ❸

🏃 **Le Boulevardier** 5 rue de la Fromagerie, 1ᵉʳ ☎04.78.28.48.22, ⓦ www.le boulevardier.fr; Mᵒ Cordeliers. Despite its central location on a main pedestrian street and the popular jazz club downstairs, this place exudes an extraordinary sense of calm and peace. You can admire the stonework of the church of St-Nizier from your bedroom window, you're that close. Fantastic value and very friendly management. ❸

🏃 **College** 5 place St-Paul, 5ᵉ ☎04.72.10.05.05, ⓦ www.college-hotel.com; Mᵒ Vieux-Lyon. Imaginative decor on a "school" theme: there's a library, aged black and white prints of students in the lift and a reception consisting of school gym equipment. Rooms are clean, white and coolly minimalist. ❽

Cour des Loges 2–8 rue du Boeuf, 5ᵉ ☎04.72.77.44.44, ⓦ www.courdesloges.com; Mᵒ Vieux-Lyon. Lyon's finest hotel, set in a seventeenth-century former Jesuit college, with a stunning dining area in the glazed atrium. ❾

Globe et Cécil 21 rue Gasparin, 2ᵉ ☎04.78.42.58.95, ⓦ www.globeetcecilhotel.com; Mᵒ Bellecour. Attractive, central and upmarket place with impeccable, attentive service. The comfortable rooms are all individually decorated. ❾

De la Marne 78 rue de la Charité, 2ᵉ ☎04.78.37.07.46, ⓦ www.hoteldelamarne.fr; Mᵒ Perrache. Conveniently located a few minutes' walk from the Musée des Arts Décoratifs, this

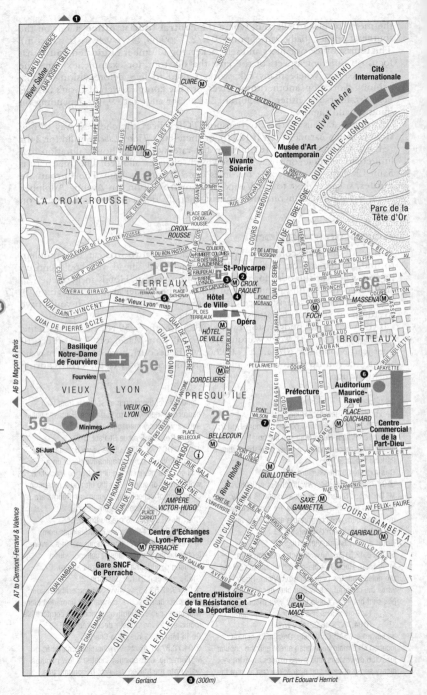

▲ ❶

River Saône

QUAI DU COMMERCE

QUAI JOSEPH GILLET

RUE PHILIPPE DE LASSALLE

RUE HENRI GORJUS

RUE HÉNON

HÉNON Ⓜ

LA CROIX-ROUSSE

4e

BOULEVARD DE LA CROIX-ROUSSE

RUE DENFERT ROCHEREAU

RUE DE BELFORT

RUE D'IVRY

RUE DE LA CROIX ROUSSE

GRANDE RUE DE LA CROIX ROUSSE

BOULEVARD DES CANUTS

RUE CLAUDE BAUDRAND

CUIRE Ⓜ

RUE COSTE

Cité
Internationale

COURS ARISTIDE BRIAND

River Rhône

Musée d'Art
Contemporain

PL WINSTON CHURCHILL

QUAI ACHILLE-LIGNON

Parc de la
Tête d'Or

BOULEVARD DES BELGES

Vivante
Soierie

PLACE DE LA
CROIX-
ROUSSE

CROIX
ROUSSE

PL.
COLBERT

RUE JOSEPH SERLIN

COURS D'HERBOUVILLE

PT DE LATTRE
DE TASSIGNY

AV DE GD BRETAGNE

AVENUE MAL FOCH

RUE DUQUESNE

RUE MONTGOLFIER

RUE SULLY

BOULEVARD DE LA CROIX ROUSSE

RUE P. DUPONT

COURS GÉNÉRAL GIRAUD

1er

TERREAUX

PLACE
FERNAND RUE

PLACE
SATHONAY

R DU BON PASTEUR

RUE IMBERT COLOMES

RUE BURDEAU

RUE IRÉNE LEYNAUD

RUE DES CAPUCINS

RUE STE CLAUDINE

St-Polycarpe

❷

Ⓜ CROIX
PAQUET

❸

❹

6e

RUE TRONCHET

COURS FR. ROOSEVELT

MASSENA Ⓜ

RUE VITTON

FOCH Ⓜ

RUE CUVIER

RUE BUGEAUD

RUE VAUBAN

BROTTEAUX

QUAI SAINT-VINCENT

QUAI DE PIERRE SCIZE

See 'Vieux Lyon' map

Hôtel
de Ville

PL DES
TERREAUX

Ⓜ
HÔTEL
DE VILLE

Opéra

QUAI DE SERBIE

PONT
MORAND

QUAI GAL. SARRAIL

RUE DE LA RÉPUBLIQUE

QUAI SAINT-ANTOINE

Basilique
Notre-Dame
de Fourvière

5e

VIEUX   LYON

Fourvière

VIEUX Ⓜ
LYON

Minimes

St-Just

5e

QUAI DE BONDY

QUAI DE LA PÊCHERIE

CORDELIERS Ⓜ

PRESQU'ÎLE

2e

QUAI DES CELESTINS

QUAI ROMANIN ROLLAND

RUE SAINTE-HÉLÈNE

RUE SALA

PLACE
BELLECOUR

BELLECOUR Ⓜ

ⓘ

PT LA FAYETTE

COURS

PONT
WILSON

❼

QUAI VICTOR AUGAGNEUR

COURS DE LA LIBERTÉ

Préfecture

Auditorium
Maurice-
Ravel

❻

LAFAYETTE

PLACE
GUICHARD Ⓜ

Centre
Commercial
de la
Part-Dieu

RUE GARIBALDI

RUE PAUL-BERT

RUE DE LA GUILLOTIÈRE

RUE VICTOR-HUGO

AMPÈRE
VICTOR-HUGO Ⓜ

PLACE
CARNOT

Centre d'Echanges
Lyon-Perrache

Ⓜ PERRACHE

Gare SNCF
de Perrache

QUAI RAMBAUD

QUAI PERRACHE

COURS CHARLEMAGNE

QUAI DE TILSIT

PONT DE LA
GUILLOTIÈRE

PONT DE
L'UNIVERSITÉ

River Rhône

QUAI CLAUDE-BERNARD

RUE DE MARSEILLE

RUE DE L'UNIVERSITÉ

RUE PASTEUR

PONT GALLIÉNI

AVENUE BERTHELOT

AV LECLERC

GUILLOTIÈRE Ⓜ

RUE SÉBASTIEN GRYPHE

RUE DE L'UNIVERSITÉ

SAXE
GAMBETTA Ⓜ

COURS GAMBETTA

RUE D'ARMÉNIE

AVENUE JEAN-JAURÈS

RUE CHEVREUL

JEAN Ⓜ
MACÉ

7e

GARIBALDI Ⓜ

RUE DE LA GUILLOTIÈRE

AV FÉLIX- FAURE

RUE GARIBALDI

Centre d'Histoire
de la Résistance et
de la Déportation

▲ A6 to Mâcon & Paris

▲ A7 to Clermont-Ferrand & Valence

▼ Gerland   ▼ ❽ (300m)   ▼ Port Edouard Herriot

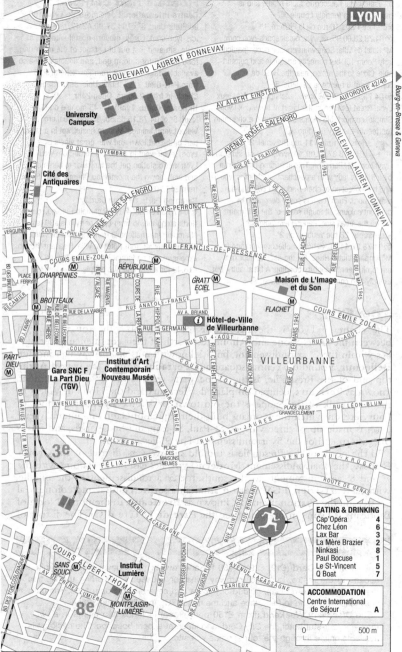

University Campus

BOULEVARD LAURENT BONNEVAY

AV. ALBERT EINSTEIN

AVENUE ROGER SALENGRO

AUTOROUTE 42/46

Bourg-en-Bresse & Geneva

BD DU 11 NOVEMBRE

BOULEVARD LAURENT BONNEVAY

RUE DES ANTONINS

RUE DE LA FILATURE

RUE DE CHATEAU-GA

RUE DU 8 MAI 1945

Cité des Antiquaires

AVENUE ROGER SALENGRO

RUE EDOUARD VAILANT

RUE DES BIENVENUS

RUE ALEXIS-PERRONCEL

BD DE STALINGRAD

VERGUIN

COURS A.-PHILIP

RUE FRANCIS-DE-PRESSENSE

RUE FLACHET

RUE GREUZE

RUE DU 8 MAI 1945

BD DE BROTTEAUX

PLACE J. FERRY

CHARPENNES

COURS EMILE-ZOLA

RUE D'ALSACE

RUE MAGENTA

RÉPUBLIQUE

COURS DE LA RÉPUBLIQUE

RUE DEDIEU

GRATT ECIEL

Maison de L'Image et du Son

RECAMIER

BROTTEAUX

AVENUE THIERS

RUE DE LA VIABERT

RUE DE BELLECOMBE

RUE HIPPOLYTE KAHN

RUE ANATOLE-FRANCE

AV A. BRIAND

GERMAIN

Hôtel-de-Ville de Villeurbanne

FLACHET

COURS ÉMILE ZOLA

RUE 1ER MARS 1943

RUE DU 4-AOÛT

PART DIEU

COURS LAFAYETTE

RUE DU 4-AOÛT

RUE CLÉMENT MICHUT

RUE CAMILE KOECHLIN

VILLEURBANNE

BD MARIUS VIVIER MERLE

Gare SNCF La Part Dieu (TGV)

Institut d'Art Contemporain Nouveau Musée

AVENUE GEROGES-POMPIDOU

COURS TOLSTOÏ

PLACE JULES GRANDCLEMENT

RUE LÉON-BLUM

RUE PAUL-BERT

AV. MARC-SANGLIER

PLACE DES MAISONS NEUVES

RUE JEAN-JAURÈS

AVENUE PAUL-KRÜGER

AV. FÉLIX-FAURE

ROUTE DE GENAS

3e

AVENUE LACASSAGNE

RUE SAINT-ISIDORE

RUE BONNARD

N

COURS ALBERT-THOMAS

SANS SOUCI

AV. DE FRÈRES LUMIÈRE

Institut Lumière

RUE FEUILLAT

RUE DU PROFESSEUR ROCHAIX

AVENUE LACASSAGNE

RUE DU PROFESSEUR FLORENCE

BD DES TCHÉCOSLOVAQUES

MONTPLAISIR-LUMIÈRE

RUE TRARIEUX

8e

EATING & DRINKING	
Cap'Opéra	4
Chez Léon	6
Lax Bar	3
La Mère Brazier	2
Ninkasi	8
Paul Bocuse	1
Le St-Vincent	5
Q Boat	7

ACCOMMODATION	
Centre International de Séjour	A

0   500 m

Venissieux, A ▼ St Exupéry Airport, TGV Station & Grenoble

pleasant hotel has comfortable rooms and is managed by a friendly couple. ❹

Hôtel de Paris 16 rue de la Platiere, 1ᵉʳ ☎04.78.28.00.95, ⓦ www.hoteldeparis-lyon.com; Mᵒ Hotel de Ville. Somewhat eclectic decor (particularly Room 10), but perfectly adequate and comfortable. Close to the action, near the Hotel de Ville. ❹

Saint Paul 6 rue de la Lainerie, 5ᵉ ☎04.78.28.13.29, ⓦ www.hotelstpaul.fr; Mᵒ Vieux Lyon. Great location in the heart of the Vieux Lyon. Simple, comfortable rooms built around a charming fourteenth-century building. ❺

🏃 **Hotel Simplon** 11 rue Duhamel, 2ᵉ ☎04.78.37.41.00, ⓦ www.hotel-du-simplon -lyon.com; Mᵒ Perrache. This appealing hotel is run by a friendly lady with a penchant for cherries; you'll find her collection of cherry-adorned *objets* in the dining room. Each room is cosily decorated in different colours, although some of the bathrooms are on the small side. Parking available. ❹

Vaubecour 28 rue Vaubecour, 2ᵉ ☎04.78.37.44.91, Ⓔ hotelvaubecour@orange.fr; Mᵒ Ampère Victor-Hugo. On the second floor of a grand nineteenth-century building. A bit shabby, but friendly and comfortable for the price. ❸

Hostels and campsite

Centre International de Séjour de Lyon 103 bd États-Unis, 8ᵉ ☎04.37.90.42.42, ⓦ www .cis-lyon.com. Large, modern hostel with lots of beds, situated just out of earshot of the main ring road €18.70 for a dorm bed, and doubles are also available. Take bus #32 from Perrache or #36 from Part-Dieu, stop "États-Unis-Beauvisage". Check-in from 2.30pm. Open 24hr.

HI hostel (Vieux Lyon) 41–45 montée du Chemin Neuf, 5ᵉ ☎04.78.15.05.50, Ⓔ lyon@fuaj.org; Mᵒ Vieux-Lyon/Minimes. Modern hostel, set in a steep part of the old town and with great views over Lyon. If you want to avoid the climb from Vieux Lyon métro station get the funicular to Minimes and walk down the montée du Chemin Neuf. Beds from €15.70.

Camping Porte de Lyon Dardilly ☎04.78.35.64.55, ⓦ www.camping-indigo.com. North along the A6 from Lyon or by bus #89 (stop "Camping International") from the gare de Vaise. Alternatively #3 from Hôtel de Ville. Pleasant though expensive, with a tourist information bureau. €18.40 for a tent and two people.

The City

The centre of Lyon is the **Presqu'île**, or "peninsula", the tongue of land between the rivers Saône and Rhône, just north of their confluence. Most of it lies within the 2ᵉ arrondissement, but it's known by its *quartiers*, which include **Bellecour**, around the central square, and **Perrache**, around the station. At the top end of the Presqu'île, as the Saône veers west, is the 1ᵉʳ arrondissement, known as **Terreaux**, centred on place des Terreaux and the Hôtel de Ville. On the west bank of the Saône is the old town, or **Vieux Lyon**, at the foot of Fourvière, on which the Romans built their capital of Gaul, Lugdunum. Vieux Lyon is made up of three villages: St-Paul, St-Jean and St-Georges, and forms the eastern end of the 5ᵉ arrondissement. The 9ᵉ lies to its north.

To the north of the Presqu'île is the old silk-weavers' district of **La Croix-Rousse**, the 4ᵉ arrondissement. **Modern Lyon** lies east of the Rhône, with the 7ᵉ and 8ᵉ arrondissements to the south, the 3ᵉ arrondissement in the middle, with **La Part-Dieu TGV station** amid an assertive cultural and commercial centre, and the 6ᵉ arrondissement, known as **Brotteaux**, to the north. North of Brotteaux is Lyon's main open space, the **Parc de la Tête d'Or**. The district of

---

Lyon City Card and Discovery Weekend

The **Lyon City Card** (€19, €29 or €39 for one, two or three days) grants unlimited access to the métro, bus and tramway, nineteen museums (including the Roman ruins in St-Romain-en-Gal), guided city tours and several short boat trips. The card is available from the tourist office and the major TCL (public transit) offices.

The **Discovery Weekend** (from €150 per person) includes two nights in a two-, three- or four-star hotel, the City Card, and lunch at a local *bouchon*. The package is available online through the tourist office website.

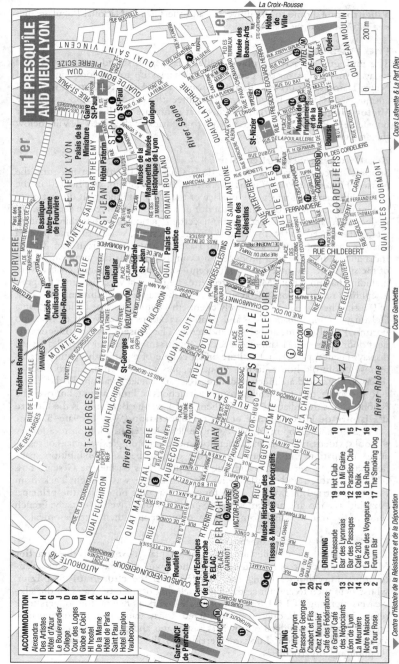

Villeurbanne, home to the university and the Théâtre National Populaire, lies east of the 6ᵉ and the park.

The Presqu'île

The pink gravelly acres of **place Bellecour** were first laid out in 1617, and today form a focus on the peninsula, with views up to the looming bulk of Notre-Dame-de-Fourvière. Running south, **rue Auguste-Comte** is full of antique shops selling heavily framed eighteenth-century art works, and **rue Victor-Hugo** is a pedestrian precinct that continues north of place Bellecour on rue de la République all the way up to the back of the Hôtel de Ville below the area of La Croix-Rousse.

South of place Bellecour

South of place Bellecour at 34 rue de la Charité is Lyon's best museum, the **Musée Historique des Tissus** (Tues–Sun 10am–5.30pm; €6), housed in the eighteenth-century former town palace of the Duke of Villeroy. It doesn't quite live up to its claim to cover the history of decorative cloth through the ages, but it does have brilliant collections from certain periods, notably third-century Greek-influenced and sixth-century Coptic tapestries, woven silk and painted linen from Egypt as well as silks from Baghdad and carpets from Iran, Turkey, India and China. The stuff produced in Lyon itself reflects the luxurious nature of the silk trade: seventeenth- to nineteenth-century hangings and chair covers, including hangings from Marie-Antoinette's bedroom at Versailles, from Empress Josephine's room at Fontainebleau and from the palaces of Catherine the Great of Russia. There are also some lovely twentieth-century pieces – including Sonia Delaunay's *Tissus Simultanés* – and couture creations from Worth to Mariano Fortuny, Paco Rabanne and Christian Lacroix. The **Musée des Arts Décoratifs** next door (Tues–Sun 10am–noon & 2–5.30pm; same ticket as Musée des Tissus) displays faïence, porcelain, furniture and a couple of eighteenth-century rooms removed from old houses in the Presqu'île, plus a collection of superb modern silverware by noted architects, including Richard Meier and Zaha Hadid.

To the south, the station area around Perrache is of little interest, but over the Rhône, across the adjacent pont Gallieni, at 14 avenue Berthelot, is the **Centre d'Histoire de la Résistance et de la Déportation** (Wed–Fri 9am–5.30pm, Sat & Sun 9.30am–6pm; €4; Mº Perrache/Jean-Macé). In addition to a library of books, videos, memoirs and other documents recording experiences of resistance, occupation and deportation to the camps, there's an exhibition space housed over the very cellars and cells in which Klaus Barbie, the Gestapo boss of Lyon, tortured and murdered his victims. Barbie was brought back from Bolivia and tried in Lyon in 1987 for crimes against humanity; the principal "exhibit" is a moving and unsettling 45-minute video (five shows daily; French only) of the trial in which some of his victims recount their terrible ordeal.

North of place Bellecour

To the north of place Bellecour at the top of quai St-Antoine is the **quartier Mercière**, the old commercial centre of the town, with sixteenth- and seventeenth-century houses lining rue Mercière, and the **church of St-Nizier**, whose bells used to announce the nightly closing of the city's gates. In the silk-weavers' uprising of 1831 (see box opposite), workers fleeing the soldiers took refuge in the church, only to be massacred. Today, traces of this working-class life are almost gone, edged out by bars, restaurants and designer shops, the latter along rue du Président Edouard-Herriot and the long pedestrian rue de la République in particular.

Further north is the monumental nineteenth-century **fountain** in front of the even more monumental **Hôtel de Ville** on place des Terreaux. It was designed by Bartholdi, of Statue of Liberty fame, although the rows of watery leaks that sprout up unexpectedly across the rest of the square are a modern addition. Opposite is the large bulk of the **Musée des Beaux-Arts** (Mon–Thurs, Sat & Sun 10am–6pm; Fri 10.30am–6pm; €6), housed in a former Benedictine abbey and whose collections are second in France only to those in the Louvre. The museum is organized roughly by genre, with nineteenth- and twentieth-century sculpture in the ex-chapel on the ground floor. There's a fine collection of medieval French, Dutch, German and Italian woodcarving on the first floor along with antiquities, coins and *objets d'art*. Twentieth-century painting includes works by Picasso and Matisse, and there are also Braques, a brace of typically domestic Bonnards and a gory Francis Bacon. The nineteenth century is represented by the Impressionists and their forerunners, Corot and Courbet; there are works by the Lyonnais artists Antoine Berjon and Fleury Richard, and from there you can work your way back through Rubens, Zurbarán, El Greco, Tintoretto and a hundred others.

Behind the Hôtel de Ville, on the edge of several linked squares, stands Lyon's **opera house** (tours every other Sat at 1pm; €9, book through the tourist office on place Bellecour). Radically redesigned in 1993 by the architect Jean Nouvel, its original Neoclassical elevations are now topped by a huge glass Swiss roll of a roof, and the interior is now entirely black with silver stairways climbing into the darkness.

La Croix-Rousse

La Croix-Rousse is the old silk-weavers' district and spreads up the steep slopes of the hill above the northern end of the Presqu'île. It's still a working-class area, but barely a couple of dozen people operate the modern high-speed computerized looms that are kept in business by the restoration and mainte-nance of France's palaces and châteaux. You can see an authentic silk worker's

The silk strike of 1831

Though the introduction of the Jacquard loom of 1804 made it possible for one person to produce 25cm of silk in a day instead of taking four people four days, **silk workers**, or *canuts* – whether masters and apprentices, or especially women and child workers – were badly paid whatever their output. Over the three decades following the introduction of the Jacquard, the price paid for a length of silk fell by over fifty percent. Attempts to regulate the price were ignored by the dealers, even though hundreds of skilled workers were languishing in debtors' jails.

On November 21, 1831, the *canuts* called an all-out **strike**. As they processed down the Montée de la Grande Côte with their black flags and the slogan "Live working or die fighting", they were shot at and three people died. After a rapid retreat uphill they built barricades, assisted by half the National Guard, who refused to fire cannon at their "comrades of Croix-Rousse". For three days the battle raged on all four banks, the silk workers using sticks, stones and knives to defend themselves, and the bourgeoisie running scared, with only the area between the rivers, place des Terreaux and just north of St-Nizier still under their control. Unfortunately for the *canuts*, their employers were able to call on outside aid, and 30,000 extra troops arrived to quash the rebellion. Some 600 people were killed or wounded, and in the end the silk industrialists were free to pay whatever pitiful fee they chose, but the uprising was one of the first instances of organized labour taking to the streets during the most revolutionary fifty years of French history.

atelier at the **Soierie Vivante**, 21 rue Richan (Tues 2–6.30pm, Wed–Sat 9am–noon & 2–6.30pm; M° Croix-Rousse; €4), while at **Passage Thiaffait** on rue Réné-Leynaud one of the original **traboules** – alleyways and tunnelled passages originally built to provide shelter from the weather for the silk-weavers as they moved their delicate pieces of work from one part of the manufacturing process to another – has been refurbished to provide premises for young couturiers.

The streets running down from **boulevard de la Croix-Rousse**, as well as many across the river in Vieux Lyon, are intersected by these *traboules*. Normally hidden by plain doors, they are impossible to distinguish from normal entryways; hence they proved an indispensable escape network for prewar gangsters, wartime Resistance fighters and, more recently, for anarchists, who used them in thwarting police efforts to capture them during the 2005 riots, forcing the authorities to resort to temporary curfews. The *traboules* are indicated by subtle signs on the walls: try going up **rue Réné-Leynaud**, passing St-Polycarpe on your right, then take rue Pouteau via a *passage*. Turn right into **rue des Tables Claudiennes**, and enter no. 55 emerging opposite 29 rue Imbert-Colomes. Climb the stairs into 14bis, cross three more courtyards and trek up some steps, where you finally emerge at **place Colbert**.

Officially the *traboules* of La Croix-Rousse and Vieux-Lyon are public thoroughfares during daylight hours, but you may find some closed for security reasons, especially as the area is gradually being gentrified. The long climb up the part-pedestrianized **Montée de la Grande Côte**, however, still gives an idea of what the *quartier* was like in the sixteenth century, when the *traboules* were first built. Take a look at the pretty **place Sathonay** at the bottom, where a public garden and a lively local café are overlooked by Croix-Rousse Mairie.

Vieux Lyon

Reached by one of the three *passerelles* (footbridges) crossing the Saône from Terreaux and the Presqu'île, **Vieux Lyon** is made up of the three villages of St-Jean, St-Georges and St-Paul at the base of the hill overlooking the Presqu'île.

South of place St-Paul, the streets of Vieux Lyon, pressed close together beneath the hill of **Fourvière**, form a backdrop of Renaissance and medieval facades, bright night-time illumination and a swelling chorus of well-dressed Lyonnais in search of supper or a midday splurge.

A short way south of the Hôtel Paterin, the **Musée Historique de Lyon**, on the ground floor of a fifteenth-century mansion on place du Petit-Collège, examines various decorative features found all around Lyon and on its buildings, but was closed for major refurbishment at the time of writing (check with tourist office for information). The entertaining **Musée de la Marionnette** is also housed here, on the first floor, and shows off the eighteenth-century Lyonnais creations, Guignol and Madelon – the French equivalents of Punch and Judy.

If you're *traboule*-hunting in Vieux Lyon, two of the best can be found on two streets leading south from place du Petit-Collège: the long, dark winding passage behind the door at 27 rue de Boeuf, and that at 28 rue St-Jean, which leads to the serene courtyard of a fifteenth-century palace. The central pedestrianized **rue St-Jean** ends at the twelfth- to fifteenth-century **Cathédrale St-Jean** (Mon–Fri 8am–noon & 2–7.30pm; Sat, Sun & holidays 8am–noon & 2–5pm). Though the west facade lacks most of its statuary as a result of various wars and revolutions, it's still impressive, and the thirteenth-century stained glass above the altar and in the rose windows of the transepts is in perfect condition.

In the northern transept is a fourteenth-century astronomical clock, its mechanism cloaked by a beautiful Renaissance casing: it's capable of computing moveable feast days (such as Easter) till the year 2019, and most days on the strike of noon, 2pm, 3pm and 4pm the figures of the Annunciation go through an automated set piece, heralded by the lone bugler at the top of the clock.

Just beyond the cathedral, opposite avenue Adolphe-Max and pont Bonaparte, is the **gare funicular** and the Vieux Lyon métro, from where you can ascend to the town's Roman remains (direction "St-Just", stop "Minimes"). The antiquities consist of two ruined **theatres** dug into the hillside (entrance at 6 rue de l'Antiquaille; mid-April to mid-Sept 7am–9pm; mid-Sept to mid-April 7am–7pm; free) – the larger of which was built by Augustus and extended in the second century by Hadrian to seat 10,000 spectators – and an underground museum of Lyonnais life from prehistoric times to 7 AD, the **Musée de la Civilisation Gallo-Romaine**, 17 rue Cléberg (Tues–Sun 10am–6pm; €3.80). The fragments of a fine bronze engraving of a speech by the Lyon-born Emperor Claudius, as well as the sheer number and splendour of the mosaics here, serve to underline Roman Lyon's importance. Nowadays, the ancient theatres are the focal point for the **Nuits de Fourvière** music and film festival that takes place annually in the summer (☏04.72.32.00.00, Ⓦ www.nuitsdefourviere.fr).

From the museum, it's just a moment's walk to the **Basilique Notre-Dame de Fourvière**, a fussily ornamented wedding cake of a church built, like the Sacré-Coeur in Paris, in the aftermath of the 1871 Commune to emphasize the defeat of the godless socialists. And like the Sacré-Coeur, its hilltop position has become an almost defining element in the city's skyline. At the time of writing, the cathedral was undergoing restoration, rendering its **Tour de l'Observatoire** inaccessible. Trips up to the rooftop are an adequate and vertigo-worthy replacement, however (tours 2.30pm & 4pm: April, May, Oct Wed & Sun; June–Sept daily; Nov 2.30pm & 3.30pm; 1hr 15min; €5). The Basilique is also accessible direct from the Vieux Lyon funicular station: if you arrive by this route, it's worth walking down along the **montée St-Barthélémy** footpath, which winds back to Vieux Lyon through the hanging gardens below the church.

Modern Lyon

On the skyline from Fourvière, you can't miss the gleaming pencil-like skyscraper that belongs to Lyon's home-grown Crédit Lyonnais bank. This is the centrepiece of **La Part-Dieu**, a business-culture-commerce conglomerate which includes one of the biggest public libraries outside Paris, a mammoth concert hall and a busy shopping centre (Mᵒ Part-Dieu). The elegant tower aside, it's all rather lumpen and unfriendly to look at. Penetrate the exterior of the main Halles market at 102 cours Lafayette, however, and you'll discover a gastronomic wonderland within, with superb seafood, poultry, cheese and charcuterie stalls (Tues–Sat 7am–noon & 3–5pm, Sun 7am–noon).

For a break from city buildings head north to the **Parc de la Tête d'Or** (Mᵒ to Masséna, then walk up rue Masséna), where there are ponds and rose gardens, botanical gardens, a small zoo and lots of amusements for kids. It's overlooked by the bristling antennae of the international headquarters of Interpol, part of a **Cité Internationale**, which is made up of glass-heavy luxury apartments, slick restaurants, the **Palais des Congres** conference centre and the enormous Amphitheatre. The complex is also home to the **Musée d'Art Contempo-rain**, at 81 quai Charles-de-Gaulle (Wed–Sun 10am–5pm; Ⓦ www.moca-lyon .org; €8; Line B to Mᵒ Saxe-Gambetta or Mᵒ Place Guichard then bus #4, stop

"Musée d'Art Contemporain"). The museum hosts excellent temporary exhibitions as well as the Lyon art biennial. Designed by Renzo Piano, it's a grand, white building, fronted by an imposing Neoclassical facade. The whole area looks good, if a little artificial and immaculate behind its security barriers. To the east, dividing the park and the university, is boulevard de Stalingrad, where antique-fanciers can browse in the **Cité des Antiquaires** arcades at 117 boulevard de Stalingrad (Thurs–Sun 10am–5pm).

In Villeurbanne, not far to the east of Part-Dieu, is the **Institut d'Art Contemporain**, 11 rue Dr-Dolard (Wed & Fri 1–6pm, Thurs 1–8pm, Sat & Sun 1–7pm; ℡04.78.03.47.00; €4; bus #C3, stop "Institut d'Art Contemporain"), where thought-provoking and engaging exhibitions by contemporary artists question the function of art and architecture and their relation to society. It's also worth looking out for exhibitions at Villeurbanne's **Maison du Livre de l'Image et du Son**, to the east on avenue Émile-Zola (Mon 2–7pm, Tues–Fri 11am–7pm, Sat 10am–6pm; M° Flachet), which might feature anything from medieval illuminations to CD-ROMs.

Further south, on the edge of the 8ᵉ arrondissement, is the enlightening **Institut Lumière**, 25 rue du Premier-Film (Tues–Sun 11am–6.30pm; ⊛www.institut-lumiere.org; €6; M° Monplaisir-Lumière). The building was the home of Antoine Lumière, father of Auguste and Louis, who made the first films, and the exhibits feature early magic lanterns and the cameras used by the brothers, along with touching family photographs. The Institut also shows several different films nightly; check their website for the schedule.

Right down in the south of the city, in the **Gerland quartier** (7ᵉ), is a developed area with a marina and a park on the Rhône's east bank, while across the bridge from the southern tip of the Presqu'île, just off place Docteurs Charles et Christophe Mérieux, squats the massive **Tony Garnier Hall** (M° Debourg), a former abbatoir, whose 17,000 cubic metres is completely free of roof-supporting columns. Its massive space lends itself freely to music concerts, conventions and sporting events; ask at the tourist office for what's on.

Eating and drinking

You'll find **restaurants** offering dishes from every region of France and overseas in Lyon. Vieux Lyon is the area with the greatest concentration of eateries, though you'll find cheaper and less busy ones between place des Jacobins and place Sathonay at the top of the Presqu'île, with a particularly dense and atmospheric concentration in rue Mercière.

Restaurants

L'Amphitryon 33 rue St-Jean, 5ᵉ ℡04.78.37.23.68; M° Vieux-Lyon. Usually packed restaurant serving Lyonnais specialities; menus from €15. Service till midnight.

Brasserie Georges 30 cours de Verdun, 2ᵉ ℡04.72.56.54.54; M° Perrache. Bright, buzzing Art Deco brasserie originally founded in 1836. *Choucroutes* are the speciality, and the local pork and pistachio sausages are good too. Menus from €20.

Chabert et Fils 11 rue des Marronniers, 2ᵉ ℡04.78.37.01.94; M° Bellecour. *Bouchon* offering the ubiquitous *quenelle* and *andouillette* (offal sausage) specialities, along with other first-rate dishes. Menus from €17.50.

Chez Léon Halles de la Part-Dieu, 102 cours Lafayette, 3ᵉ ℡04.78.62.30.28; M° Part-Dieu. Tiny, bustling oyster bar in the market halls. Around €20 for lunch. Closed outside the oyster season, which usually means May–Aug.

Chez Mounier 3 rue des Marronniers, 2ᵉ ℡04.78.37.79.26; M Bellecour. Good-value menus from €11 at this unpretentious *bouchon*. Serves imaginative dishes, such as tripe and cognac soufflé.

Café des Fédérations 8 rue du Major-Martin, 1ᵉʳ ℡04.78.28.26.00; M° Hôtel-de-Ville. Typical *bouchon* serving the earthiest of Lyonnais specialities (marinated tripe and black pudding). Cheerful green and white checked tables are complemented

The **bouchon**, the traditional Lyonnais eating establishment, is the best place to eat *quenelles*, sausages, tripe and the like. Its name derives either from *bouchon* (cork), or *bouchonner* (to rub down). One popular theory has it that wine bottles were lined up as the evening progressed, and at the end of the night the bill was determined by measuring from the first cork to the last. Another explanation, however, is that inns serving wine would attach small bundles of straw to their signs, indicating that horses could be cared for (*bouchonnés*) while the coachmen went inside to have a drink. Wandering around Vieux Lyon, you'll come across many bouchons – we've listed a few special ones on below.

by rough wooden floorboards and jovial pictures on the walls. Menu at €25 for dinner. Closed Sun.

Le Grand Café des Négociants 1 place Francisque Regaud, 1er ☎04.78.42.50.05; M Cordeliers. Despite a position on a busy road, this place attracts the punters for its sumptuous cuisine and sophisticated decor. Meat dishes go for up to €38 but pasta is cheaper at €14.

Léon de Lyon 1 rue Pléney, 1er ☎04.72.10.11.12; Mo Hôtel-de-Ville. Sophisticated and delicious food, with original culinary creations as well as traditional Lyonnais recipes in this upmarket brasserie. Closed first three weeks in Aug.

La Mère Brazier 12 rue Royale, 1er ☎04.78.28.15.49; Mo Croix-Paquet. A beautiful setting complements the excellent food at this restaurant, still run by Mme Brazier, the granddaughter of the couple who founded it in 1921. Closed Sat lunch, Sun, Tues & Aug.

La Meunière 11 rue Neuve, 1er ☎04.78.28.62.91; Mo Hôtel-de-Ville. Booking is essential at this excellent *bouchon*. Dishes include skate wings in nut butter sauce with capers (€16). Closed Sun, Mon & mid-July to mid-Aug.

Notre Maison 2 rue de Gadagne, 1er ☎04.72.41.78.48; M Vieux Lyon. "Salad is for goats", or so this *bouchon* claims. Expect meat, meat and more meat, with a bit of fish thrown in there. Menus from €19.

Paul Bocuse 40 rue de la Plage, Collonges-au-Mont-d'Or ☎04.72.42.90.90. Lyon's most famous restaurant, named after its celebrity chef-owner, is 9km north of the city, on the west bank of the Saône. Traditional French gastronomy is the bill of fare, with menus from €125 upwards.

Le St-Vincent 6 place Fernand-Rey, 1er ☎04.72.07.70.43; Mo Hôtel-de-Ville. A dozen tables in a quiet, arty square shaded by mimosas. Very popular with locals. Lunch €12.50, evening menu €23. Closed Sun.

La Tour Rose 22 rue du Boeuf, 5e ☎04.78.92.69.10; Mo Vieux-Lyon. Gastronomic place with concoctions like fig caviar with a fricassee of mushrooms and John Dory with creamed Jersualem artichokes. Menus from €29. Closed Sun.

Nightlife and entertainment

Lyon is almost as good a place for **nightlife** and **entertainment** as it is for eating, with a good range of clubs, cinema, opera, jazz, classical music concerts and theatre. The best places to wander if you are looking for a **bar** are rue Mercière, the area around place des Terreaux and the Opéra (where most of Lyon's **lesbian and gay** scene is also found) and, most particularly, the streets of Vieux Lyon. Make a point of crossing the river by the *passerelles*; the whole district looks magnificent at night.

For **listings**, pick up a free copy of the free weekly newspaper *Le Petit Bulletin* from tourist offices and outlets citywide. Alternatively buy a copy of the weekly *Lyon Poche*, available from newsagents (every Wed; €1), or look online at Ⓦ www.lyonpoche.com.

Bars and clubs

L'Ambassade 4 rue Stella, 2e ; M Cordliers. One of the best and hippest places to party in Lyon; this

funky club features top DJs bashing out heavy house beats, hip-hop and some soul. Wed–Sat from 10.30pm.

▲ Rue des Marronniers, Lyon

Bar des Lyonnais 1 quai des Celestins, 2ᵉ; Mᵒ Bellecour. Right next to the river, this popular bar has a terrace for sunny weather, and a cosy and funky bar inside. Also serves food. Closed Mon.

🏃 **Bar des Passages** 8 rue du Platre, 1ᵉʳ; Mᵒ Hotel-de-Ville. Gorgeous, intimate wine bar adorned with candles and soft red lights. A glass of wine can be anything from €4 to €15 although in such luxurious surroundings you may be tempted to splash out on champagne. Closed Sun & Mon.

Café 203 9 rue du Garet, 1ᵉʳ; Mᵒ Hôtel-de-Ville. Lively bar that takes it name from the classic Peugeots parked out the front. Cheap *plats du jour* all day. Daily 7am–2am.

La Cave des Voyageurs 7 place Saint-Paul, 5ᵉ; Mᵒ Vieux Lyon. Small wine bar serving 450 varieties of wine that you can taste and take away. Serves plates of *charcuterie* to share. Closed Sun & Mon.

Hot Club 26 rue du Lanterne, 1ᵉʳ ☎04.78.39.54.74, Ⓦwww.hotclubjazz.com; Mᵒ Hôtel-de-Ville. A variety of great jazz jam sessions and concerts in a vaulted cellar. Tues–Sat 9pm–1am; closed July & Aug.

La Mi Graine 11 place St-Paul, 5ᵉ; Mᵒ Vieux-Lyon. Welcoming small café on a sun-drenched square. Enjoy a drink and a sunbathe while listening to the café's relaxing jazz soundtrack. Mon–Sat 11.30am–3am, Sun 3–9pm.

Ninkasi 267 rue Marcel Mérieux, 7ᵉ; Mᵒ Gerland. Lyon's own microbrewery, with salads and burgers upstairs, bar, DJs and live music downstairs. Mon–Wed 10–1am, Thurs 10–2am, Fri 10–3am, Sat 10–4am & Sun 4pm–midnight.

Paradiso Club 24 rue Pizay, 1ᵉʳ; Mᵒ Hôtel-de-Ville. Wild and funky place with transvestite or burlesque shows often entertaining the crowds. Daily 10pm–dawn.

Q Boat 21 quai Augagneur, 3ᵉ; Mᵒ Guillotière. The name gives it away – a big boat moored on the River Saone draws in a young, fashionable crowd with its pumping house tunes. Open til late Thurs, Fri & Sat.

The Smoking Dog 16 Rue Lainerie, 5ᵉ; M Vieux Lyon. Very popular English-run pub with a large TV screen showing sports. Pleasant and cosy decor, with the book-filled shelves lining the walls. Daily 2pm–1am.

Lesbian and gay bars and clubs

Cap'Opéra 2 place Louis-Pradel, 1ᵉʳ; Mᵒ Hôtel-de-Ville. Trendy, officially "mixed" (but really mostly gay) DJ bar close to the opera house. Mon–Sat 2pm–3am.

Forum Bar 15 rue des Quatre-Chapeaux, 2ᵉ; Mᵒ Cordeliers. Convivial men's bar with bearish decor and clientele, down an alley just north of the places des Jacobins and de la République. Mon–Thurs 5pm–2am, Fri & Sat 5pm–3am.

Lax Bar 2 rue Coysevox, 1ᵉʳ; Mᵒ Hôtel-de-Ville. As much a youth club as a bar, with internet access, pool table and giant video screen. Mixed, but it tends to be gayer later. Open 4pm–3am.

Oblik 26 rue Hippolyte-Flandrin, 1ᵉʳ; Mᵒ Hôtel-de-Ville. Relaxed café/bar popular with gay men and lesbians. Tues–Sat 5pm–1am.

La Ruche 22 rue Gentil. Lyon's busiest and most famous gay bar, with a lively atmosphere, an international crowd and a heavy emphasis on drag. Mon–Sun 5pm–3am.

Theatre, music and film

Look out for **stage productions** by the Théâtre National Populaire (TNP), located at 24 rue Emile-Decorps (☎04.78.03.30.00; M° Laurent Bonnevay). Less radical stuff is shown at the city's gilded Théâtre des Célestins, in place des Célestins, 2ᵉ (☎04.72.77.40.00, ⓦwww.celestins-lyon.org; M° Bellecour). The **opera house**, one of the best in France, is on place de la Comédie, 1ᵉʳ (☎08.26.30.53.25, ⓦwww.opera-lyon.com; M° Hôtel-de-Ville), with cheap tickets sold just before performances begin. For avant-garde, classic and obscure **films**, usually in their original language, check the listings for the cinemas CNP Terreaux, Bellecour, Fourmi Lafayette, Opéra and Ambiance, as well as the Institut Lumière. Also, look out for the Lyon dance biennial, which brings in hundreds of artists and troupes from around the world (last three weeks of Sept in even-numbered years; ⓦwww.biennale-de-lyon.org).

Listings

Bike rental Holiday Bikes, 199 rue Vendome, 3ᵉ ☎04.78.60.11.10, ⓦwww.holiday-bikes.com.
Boat trips Société Naviginter, 13bis quai Rambaud, 2ᵉ ☎04.78.42.96.81. Leaving from quai des Célestins, boats run up the Saône or down to the confluence with the Rhône at the Île Barbe (April & Sept–Oct Tues–Sun, May–Aug daily; €9). The same company offers lunch and dinner cruises from €44.
Car rental Europcar, 40 rue de la Villette, 3ᵉ ☎08.25.00.25.22; Hertz, 40 rue Villette, 3ᵉ ☎04.72.33.89.89; Avis, Gare Part-Dieu, 3ᵉ ☎04.72.33.37.19. All the above also have offices at the airport and at the Perrache centre.
Consulates Canada, 21 rue Bourgelat, 2ᵉ ☎04.72.77.64.07; UK, 24 rue Childebert, 2ᵉ ☎04.72.77.81.70; USA, 16 rue République, 2ᵉ ☎04.78.38.36.88.
Disabled travellers For information on facilities for the disabled contact Délégation Départementale APF, 73ter, rue Francis de Pressensé, Villeurbanne ☎04.72.43.01.01, Ⓕ04.78.93.61.99.
Emergencies Samu – emergency medical attention ☎15; Police ☎17; SOS Médecins ☎04.78.83.51.51. Hospitals: Croix-Rousse, ☎04.72.07.10.46; Hôpital

Edouard-Herriot, place d'Arsonval, 3ᵉ (☎04.72.11.69.53). For house calls contact the medical referral centres (☎04.72.33.00.33).
Internet Planète Net Phone, 21 rue Romarin, 1ᵉʳ (Mon–Fri 10am–10pm, Sat til 9pm), has plenty of terminals; Raconte Moi de la Terre, 38 rue Thomassin, 2ᵉ (Mon–Sat noon–7.30pm) also serves snacks.
Lesbian and gay info ARIS (Accueil Rencontres Informations Services), 13 rue des Capucins (☎04.78.27.10.10), is a gay and lesbian centre organizing various activities and producing a useful scene guide. État d'Esprit, 19 rue Royale (☎04.78.27.76.53, ⓦwww.etatdesprit.free.fr), is a gay and lesbian bookstore that also holds cultural events. Online listings and activities are posted at the Forum Gai et Lesbien (ⓦwww.fgllyon.org). Lyon celebrates lesbian and gay pride in mid-June.
Pharmacy Blanchet, 5 place des Cordeliers, 2ᵉ ☎04.78.42.12.42. Daily till midnight.
Police The main commissariat is at 47 rue de la Charité, 2ᵉ ☎04.78.42.26.56.
Post office PTT, place Antonin-Poncet, Lyon 69002.
Taxis ☎04.78.28.23.23 or 04.72.10.86.10.

Around Lyon

Within easy reach of the city, the **Monts du Lyonnais** to the south and west of Lyon may not reach spectacular heights, but they offer quiet and solitude among steep, forested hills and unassuming villages surrounded by cherry orchards, the region's main source of income. Tourism is low-key, but finding food and accommodation in the hostels of the mountain villages is rarely a problem for visitors to the area's parks and museums. **Bus** services from the main *gare routière* and the western *gare de Gorge du Loup* (M° Gorge-du-Loup; 9ᵉ) to the larger villages are reasonably frequent. The medieval town of **Pérouges** is particularly special, and deserves at least a half-day visit. It can be reached by train and bus from Gare de Part Dieu (M° Part-Dieu).

Pérouges

Twenty-nine kilometres northeast of Lyon, on the N84, **PÉROUGES** (Ⓦ www.perouges.org) is a lovely village of cobbled alleyways and ancient houses. By train from Lyon, you will arrive at the station in Meximieux where the tourist office on 1 rue de Geneve (Ⓣ04.74.23.36.72, Ⓦ www .mairie-meximieux; Tues & Thurs 9.30am–noon & 3–6pm, Wed 9.30am–noon, Fri & Sat 2.30–6pm), will equip you with a choice of three walking routes to medieval Pérouges, perched high on a hill. Each route takes 30min and requires sturdy shoes; route 2 is perhaps the most scenic, skirting a fishing pond and traversing narrow stone bridges.

Pérouges' charm has not gone unnoticed by the French film industry – historical dramas like *The Three Musketeers* and *Monsieur Vincent* were filmed within its fortifications – nor by some of the residents, who have fought long and hard for preservation orders on its most interesting buildings. The result is an immaculate, if perhaps rather stifling, work of conservation. Local traditional life is also thriving in the hands of a hundred or so workers who still weave locally grown hemp.

No particular monument stands out, but the central square, the **place du Halle**, and its main street, the **rue du Prince**, have some of the best-preserved French medieval remains, while the beautifully plain Church Fortress stands serenely near the main gate. The **lime tree** on place du Halle is a symbol of liberty, planted in 1792. The place both to **stay** and eat in Pérouges, if you can afford it, is the *Ostellerie du Vieux Pérouges* (Ⓣ04.74.61.00.88, Ⓦ www.ostellerie.com; ❾), in a medieval town house fronting the square; its **restaurant** serves traditional mountain dishes of duck and carp, with menus at €40 and €61. Those with a more modest wallet should head for *Auberge du Coq*, rue des Rondes (Ⓣ04.74.61.05.47), where menus from €15.90 feature Lyonnais delights such as snail casserole and *coq au vin*. Pérouges' speciality is a delicious, sugary **galette**, washed down with cider; make for the *galette* shop just up from *Auberge du Coq*, on rue des Rondes.

Vienne and around

Heading south from Lyon on the A7, a twenty-kilometre stretch of oil refineries, steel, chemical and paper works, cement, fertilizer and textile factories, all spewing plumes of grey and orange pollution into the air, may well tempt you to make a bee-line for the lavender fields of Provence further south. However, a short detour off the autoroute brings you to **VIENNE**, which, along with **St-Romain-en-Gal**, across the river, makes for the most interesting stop on the Rhône before Orange.

With their riverside positions, Vienne and St-Romain prospered as Rome's major wine port and *entrepôt* on the Rhône, and many Roman monuments survive to attest to this past glory. Several important churches recall Vienne's medieval heyday as well: it was a bishop's seat from the fifth century and the home town of twelfth-century Pope Calixtus II. Today, the compact old quarter is crisscrossed with pedestrian precincts that make for enjoyable wandering, and there's a feeling that despite the distant rumble of the autoroute calling you to sunnier climes, the town has maintained its character and sense of purpose.

Arrival and information

The cours Brillier runs down from the **gare SNCF** to the river, with the **tourist office** (Mon–Sat 9am–noon & 1.30–6pm, Sun 10am–noon & 2–5pm; Ⓣ04.74.53.80.30, Ⓦ www.vienne-tourisme.com) at no. 3, near quai Jean-Jaurès, next to the pretty Jardin du 8 Mai 1945. Halfway up the cours, rue Boson leads up to the west front of the cathedral. For **internet** access, go to *World of Gamers Cybercafé*, 22 rue de la Table Ronde (Mon–Thurs 9.30am–6.45pm, Fri 9.30am–9.30pm, Sat 2–11pm), which also serves snacks and drinks.

Accommodation

Hotels

Hotel Central 7 rue de l'Archevêché ☎04.74.85.18.38, ⓦwww.hotel-central-vienne .com. Acceptable, although rather gloomy, hotel in a great, central location. ❹

Château des Sept Fontaines 7km northwest on the N7 at Seyssuel ☎04.74.85.25.70, ⓦwww .hotel7fontaines.com. If you have your own transport, this is the place to stay. Lovely house surrounded by a large garden; comfortable, luxurious rooms and a good restaurant (closed Sun Oct–April). ❺

Ibis ☎04.74.78.41.11, ⓦwww.ibishotel.com. Budget option near the *gare routière* in place

Camille-Jouffray, just down from the tourist office. ❹

Poste 47 cours Romestang ☎04.74.85.02.04, ⓦwww.hotel-vienne.fr. Decent rooms overlooking a pretty, tree-lined *cours*. ❸

Hostel

HI hostel 11 quai Riondet ☎04.74.53.21.97, ⒻF04.74.31.98.93. Not far from the centre of town on the other side of the gardens from the tourist office. €9.10 per person. Open for reservations Mon–Thurs 5–8pm, Fri 8am–noon.

The Town

Roman monuments are scattered liberally around the streets of Vienne; the magnificently restored **Temple d'Auguste et de Livie**, a perfect, scaled-down version of Nîmes' Maison Carrée, on place du Palais, and the bulky remains of the **Théâtre de Cybèle**, off place de Miremont. The **Théâtre Antique**, off rue du Cirque at the base of Mont Pipet to the north (Tues–Sun 9.30am–5pm; €2.20, or €6 combined ticket), is a bit of trek up a hill but it's definitely worth the effort for the view of the town and river from the very top seats. The theatre hosts a large number of concerts throughout the summer, climaxing in a much-celebrated **international jazz festival** in the first two weeks of July (☎08.92.70.20.07, ⓦwww.theatreantiquvienne.com). An **audioguide** (available in English, from the tourist office; €5) will give you more information on the city's glorious past at each of the main temples and ruins.

The **Église-Musée St-Pierre** (April–Oct Tues–Sun 9.30am–1pm & 2–6pm; Nov–March Tues–Fri 9.30am–12.30pm & 2–5pm, Sat & Sun 2–6pm; €2.20 or €6 combined ticket with other museums) stands on the site of one of France's first cathedrals. Since its origins in the fifth century, the building has suffered much reconstruction and abuse, including a stint as a factory in the nineteenth century, though the monumental portico of the former church is still striking. Today it has something of the atmosphere of an architectural salvage yard, housing substantial but broken chunks of Roman columns, capitals and cornices. Close by is the most prominent – and vaunted – of Vienne's monuments, the **Cathédrale St-Maurice** (daily 8am–6pm; free), whose unwieldy facade, a

Vienne museum pass

The Théâtre Antique, Église and Cloître de St-André-le-Bas, Musée des Beaux-Arts et d'Archéologie and Église-Musée St-Pierre can be visited on a **single ticket** (€6), which can be picked up at any of the sites and is valid for 48 hours.

combination of Romanesque and Gothic, appears as if its upper half has been dumped on top of a completely alien building. The interior, with its ninety-metre-long vaulted nave, is impressive though, spare and elegant, with some modern stained-glass windows and traces of fifteenth-century frescoes.

The **Église** (visits by arrangement; enquire at the cloister; or €2.30) and **Cloître de St-André-le-Bas** (same hours and ticket as St-Pierre) on place du Jeu de Paume, a few streets north of the cathedral, date from the ninth and twelfth centuries. The back tower of the church, on rue de la Table Ronde, is a remarkable monument, studded with tiny carved stone faces, while the cloister, entered through a space where temporary exhibits are held, is a beautiful little Romanesque affair, whose walls are decorated with local tombstones, some dating from the fifth century.

The major museum in Vienne is the **Musée des Beaux-Arts et d'Archéologie** on place de Miremont (same hours and ticket as St-Pierre), with a preponderance of eighteenth-century French pottery, but also some attractive pieces of third-century Roman silverware. More enlightening is the small textile museum, the **Musée de la Draperie** (mid-April to mid-Sept Wed–Sun 2–6pm; €2.30), in the Espace St-Germain to the south of the centre off rue Vimaine, which, with the aid of videos, working looms and weavers, illustrates the complete process of cloth-making as it was practised in the city for over two hundred years.

Eating

Le Bec Fin 7 place St-Maurice ☎04.74.85.76.72. Classy and welcoming restaurant offering filling Lyonnais menus at €22 and €58. Closed Sun & Wed evening & Mon.

Le Cloître 2 rue des Cloitres ☎04.74.31.93.57. Nice position, tucked in next to the Cathedral St Maurice. Serves French dishes such as foie gras (€21.90) and *crème brulée* (€8.50). Closed Sat & Sun lunch.

L'Estancot 4 rue de la Table Ronde ☎04.74.85.12.09. Cheery and inexpensive, this place does good seafood for under €20. Closed early to mid-Sept.

La Mariniere 6 rue de la Table Ronde ☎04.74.85.19.77. One of the best deals in town; *moules frites* for €12. Closed Sun & Mon.

La Pyramide 14 bd Fernand-Point ☎04.74.53.01.96. If you fancy a splurge, head for the superlative restaurant with exquisite menus from €61 to €161; going à la carte starts at €49. Closed Tues & Wed.

St-Romain-en-Gal

Facing Vienne across the Rhône, several hectares of Roman ruins constitute the site of **ST-ROMAIN-EN-GAL**, also the name of the modern town surrounding it. The excavations (still ongoing), just across the road bridge from Vienne, attest to a significant community dating from the first century BC to the third AD, and give a vivid picture of the daily life and domestic architecture of Roman France. You enter through the excellent and child-friendly **Musée Archéologique de St-Romain-en-Gal** (site & museum Tues–Sun: March–Oct 10am–6pm; Nov–Feb 10am–5pm; €3.80), which displays frescoes, superb mosaics and other objects recovered from the site, along with explanatory models. The ruins themselves are clearly laid out, and be sure to check out the Romans' lavishly decorated marble public toilets, by the entry ramp to the dig.

Between Vienne and Valence

Between Vienne and Valence are some of the oldest, most celebrated **vineyards** in France: the renowned Côte Rotie, Hermitage and Crozes-Hermitage *appellations*. If you've got any spare luggage space, it's well worth stopping to pick up a bottle from the local co-op; even their *vin ordinaire* is superlative and unbelievably cheap, considering its quality. Just south of Ampuis on the west bank, 8km south of Vienne, is the tiny area producing one of the most exquisite and oldest French white wines, Condrieu, and close by one of the most exclusive –Château-Grillet – an *appellation* covering just this single château (by appointment; ☎04.74.59.51.56).

Between **St-Vallier** and **Tain l'Hermitage**, the Rhône becomes quite scenic, and after Tain you can see the Alps. In spring you're more likely to be conscious of orchards everywhere rather than vines. Cherries, pears, apples, peaches and apricots, as well as bilberries and strawberries, are cultivated in abundance.

Tain-l'Hermitage

TAIN-L'HERMITAGE, accessible from both the N7 and the A7, is unpretentious and uneventful, but if you have a weakness for wine or chocolate, you'll love this place. There are cellars all over town where you can taste and buy wine but, for ease and expertise, head to the Cave de Tain-l'Hermitage at 22 route de Larnage (daily: 9am–12.30pm & 2–6.30pm; mid-May to mid-Sept & mid-to end Dec 9am–12.30 & 1.30–7pm; ☎04.75.08.20.87, Ⓦ www.cavedetain.com), walking distance from the *gare SNCF*, where they have all the wines of the distinguished Hermitage and Crozes-Hermitage *appellations* you'll ever need. If your visit happens to fall on the last weekend in February you can try out wines from 78 vineyards in the Foire aux Vins des Côtes du Rhône Septentrionales, and on the third weekend of September, the different wine-producing villages celebrate their cellars in the **Fête des Vendanges**. But at any time of the year you can go bottle-hunting along the N86 for some 30km north of Tain along the right bank, following the *dégustation* signs then crossing back over between Serrières and Chanas.

The famous Tain **chocolates** are made by Valrhona and are available at the shop (Mon–Fri 9am–7pm, Sat 9am–6pm; ☎04.75.07.90.62) at 14 avenue du Président-Roosevelt (the RN7), past the junction with the RN95 as you're heading south.

Practicalities

On the RN7 further north from the chocolaterie, the **tourist office** at place du 8-mai-1945 (Sept–May Mon–Sat 9am–noon & 2–6pm; June–Aug Mon–Sat 9am–5pm, Sun 9.30am–noon; ☎04.75.08.06.81, Ⓦ www.tain-tourisme .com) can provide you with lists of vineyard addresses. For accommodation, try the pleasant *Pavillon de l'Ermitage* at 69 avenue Jean Jaures, just down from the *gare* (☎04.75.08.65.00, Ⓦ www.pavillon-ermitage.com; ❺), which has family rooms and a pool. *Les 2 Côteaux* (☎04.75.08.33.01, Ⓦ www.hotel-les -2-coteaux.com; ❸) is a smarter choice situated at 18 Joseph-Péala, next to the rather splendid pedestrian suspension bridge). For cheap **food**, try the creperie *Oh! Sucré Salé* at 8 place Taurobole, where crêpes go for as little as €2.50. *Le Mangevins* (☎04.75.08.00.76; closed Sun & Mon), just opposite *Pavillon de l'Ermitage* at 6 avenue du Docteur Paul-Durand is a cute little wine bar serving reasonably priced meals; succulent roast sea bream, for example, is €12. The most upmarket choice, however, is *Le Quai* (☎04.75.07.05.90), opposite *Les 2 Côteaux*, at 17 rue Joseph-Péala. Delicious, inventive cuisine includes gnocchi in garlic cream with snails and duck with minted quinoa (both €17).

Hauterives

HAUTERIVES, 25km northeast of Tain, is a small village with a remarkable creation – a manic, surreal **Palais Idéal** (daily: Jan & Dec 9.30am–12.30pm & 1.30–4.30pm; Feb, March, Oct & Nov 9.30am–12.30pm & 1.30–5.30pm; April–June & Sept 9am–12.30pm & 1.30–6.30pm; July & Aug 9am–12.30pm & 1.30–7pm; ⓦ www.facteurcheval.com; €5.30) built by a local postman by the name of Ferdinand Cheval (1836–1912). The house is truly bizarre, a bubbling frenzy reminiscent of the *modernista* architecture of Spain, with features that recall Thai or Indian temples. The eccentric building took thirty years to carve, and Cheval designed an equally bizarre tombstone which can also be seen. Various Surrealists have paid homage to the building and psychoanalysts have given it much thought, but it defies all classification. The *palais* is a tourist magnet, reached along a lane cluttered with shops hawking assorted trinkets. The rest of the village, however, is relatively unspoilt. If you want to **stay** here, you have the choice of the *Camping du Château* on the edge of town on the N538 (ⓣ 04.75.68.80.19, Ⓕ 04.75.68.90.94; open April to mid-Oct; €8.60 per person) or a **hotel**, *Le Relais* (ⓣ 04.75.68.81.12, ⓦ www.hotel-relais-drome.com; ❹; closed mid-Jan to Feb), opposite the village church.

Romans-sur-Isère

Despite its bustle, **ROMANS-SUR-ISÈRE**, south of Hauterives and 15km east of the Rhône at Tain, isn't the most exciting of towns. The main attraction is a fascinating museum specializing in the town's principal and most-established industry: shoemaking. The **Musée International de la Chaussure** is in the former Convent of the Visitation at 2 rue Ste-Marthe (Jan–April & Oct–Dec Tues–Sat 10am–5pm; May, June & Sept Tues–Sat 10am–6pm; July & Aug Mon–Sat 10am–6pm; €4.50, or joint ticket with Palais Idéal at Hauterives, see above, €7; ⓣ 04.75.05.51.81) and also includes a permanent exhibition on the Resistance. Your toes will curl in horror at the extent to which women have been immobilized by their footwear from ancient times to the present on every continent, while at the same time you can't help but admire the craziness of some of the creations. If inspired to replenish your own shoe stock, drop in to the Charles Jourdan factory shop at 1 boulevard Voltaire or the large shopping outlet, Marques Avenue, along avenue Gambetta.

The old town is pleasant enough, peppered with the inevitable shoe shops as well as establishments offering Roman's two other specialities – this time gastronomic: *pogne*, a ringed spongy bread flavoured with orange water, and *ravioles*, cornflour-based ravioli with an eggy, cheesy, buttery filling.

Practicalities

The **tourist office** is on place Jean-Jaurès (April–Oct Mon–Fri 9am–7pm, Sat 9am–6pm, Sun 9.30am–12.30pm; Nov–March Mon–Sat 9am–6pm, Sun 9.30am–12.30pm; ⓣ 04.75.02.28.72, ⓦ www.ville-romans.com), housed in an ugly grey building opposite the church, Notre Dame de Lourdes; look for the peach-coloured tower. **Hotels** include the lovely ⚐ *L'Oree du Parc* (ⓣ 04.75.70.26.12, ⓦ www.hotel-oreeparc.com; ❺) at 6 avenue Gambetta, a short walk from the main town. Housed in a 1920s mansion, the stylish rooms are immaculate and restful, and there's an inviting pool and terrace in the leafy back garden. A cheaper alternative is the decent *Cendrillon* on place Carnot by the station (ⓣ 04.75.02.83.77, ⓦ www.hotelcendrillon.com; ❷).

The municipal **campsite**, *Les Chasses* (☎04.75.72.35.27; €7 for two people and a tent; open April–Oct), is 1km off the N92 northeast of the city, next to the aerodrome.

Agreeable places to **eat** include *Le Chevet de St-Barnard* (☎04.75.05.04.78; closed Sun evening. Tues evening. Wed & mid-July to Aug) on pretty little place aux Herbes, next to the cathedral; traditional *ravioles* here are €11. *La Cassolette* (☎04.75.02.55.71; closed Sun & Mon) at 16 rue Rebatte, just off place Jacque-mart, also serves delicious *ravioles* (€8) in a beautiful old stone house. Along with cafés/bar around place Charles de Gaulle, a popular place to have a **drink** is the daytime only *Comptoir des Loges* on 76 rue Nicolas (☎04.75.45.40.92; closed Mon), which also does inexpensive meals.

Valence

At an indefinable point along the Rhône, there's an invisible sensual border, and by the time you reach **VALENCE**, you know you've crossed it. The quality of light is different and the temperature higher, bringing with it the scent of eucalyptus and pine, and the colours and contours suddenly seem worlds apart from the cold lands of Lyon and the north. Valence is the obvious place to celebrate your arrival in the **Midi** (as the French call the south), with plenty of good bars and restaurants in the old town, though little else.

Arrival and information

To the southeast of the old town are the **gare routière**, the **gare SNCF** and the **tourist office** on parvis de la Gare (June–Aug Mon–Sat 9.30am–6.30pm, Sun 10am–1pm; Sept–May Mon–Fri 9.30am–12.30pm & 1.30–6pm, Sat 9.30am–12.30pm & 1.30–5pm; ☎08.92.70.70.99, ⓦwww.tourisme-valence .com). The **TGV** station is 10km northeast, along the autoroute to Romans. There are regular shuttles and trains (daily 6.30am–10.50pm; €2.20) which connect the *gare TGV* with the *gare SNCF*.

Accommodation

Hotel de France 16 General de Gaulle ☎04.75.43.00.87, ⓦwww.hotel-valence.com. The decor is a touch corporate, perhaps, but this hotel enjoys a great position near Vieux Valence. Comfortable beds and clean bathrooms. ❸
De Lyon 23 av Pierre-Semard ☎04.75.41.44.66, ⓦwww.hoteldelyon.com. A decent two-star located just opposite the station. White walls and bright colours give it a bit of a chain feel and some of the bathrooms are absurdly small. ❷
Les Négociants 27 av Pierre-Semard ☎04.75.44.01.86, ⓦwww.hotel -lesnegociantsvalence.com. Clean lines,

minimalist furniture and probably an orchid on your bedside table. ❷
Pic 285 av Victor-Hugo ☎04.75.44.15.32, ⓦwww.pic-valence.com. Fifteen incredibly luxurious rooms in an old coach house, along with a gastronomic restaurant and less expensive, but as fantastic, brasserie (see p.950). Rooms range between €280 and €880. ❾
Yan's quartier Maninet, route de Montéleger ☎04.75.55.52.52, ⓦwww.yanshotel.com. Spacious rooms in a stylish modern building with park and pool, southeast of the city on the route de Montéléger. ❺

The Town

Valence is, for the most part, a spruce town basking in its new-found cleanliness and space: road work continues in a vigorous effort to give the town back to the pedestrians as cars are forced out to suburban car parks. The result is a town made up of tidy boulevards, large public areas and fresh-looking facades as well as a very pleasant old section, Vieux Valence.

Vieux Valence

The focus of Vieux Valence, the **Cathédrale St-Apollinaire**, was consecrated in 1095 by Pope Urban II (who proclaimed the First Crusade), and largely reconstructed in the seventeenth century. More work was carried out later, including the horribly mismatched nineteenth-century tower, but the interior still preserves its original Romanesque grace – especially the columns around the ambulatory.

Between the cathedral and **Église de St-Jean** at the northern end of Grande-Rue, which has preserved its Romanesque tower and porch capitals, are some of the oldest and narrowest streets of Vieux Valence. They are known as **côtes**: côte St-Estève just northwest of the cathedral; côte St-Martin off rue du Petit-Paradis; and côte Sylvante off rue du Petit-Paradis' continuation, rue A.-Paré. Diverse characters who would have walked these steep and crooked streets include Rabelais, a student at the university founded here in 1452 and suppressed during the Revolution, and the teenage Napoleon Bonaparte, who began his military training as a cadet at the artillery school.

Though Valence lacks the cohesion of the medieval towns and villages further south, it does have several vestiges of the sixteenth-century city, most notably the Renaissance **Maison des Têtes** at 57 Grande-Rue. Be sure if you can to look at the ceiling in the passageway here (office hours only), where sculpted roses transform into the cherub-like heads after which the palace is named. Also worth a look is the **Maison Dupré-Latour**, on rue Pérollerie, which has a superbly sculptured porch and spiral staircase. On Sunday a **bric-a-brac market** fills the streets with stalls selling everything from underwear to oranges.

At sunset, Parc Jouvet is definitely the best place to be in the city – a tranquil oasis away from the town's bustle – with a bottle of Cornas or sparkling St-Peray from the vineyards across the water. It's even better at dawn.

Eating and drinking

Café Bancel 7 bd Bancel ☎ 04.75.78.35.98. Black and chrome decor sets the tone for this slick, modern restaurant, which serves imaginative dishes like tuna with lime sorbet and parmesan (€19).

Le Bistrot des Clercs 48 Grande-Rue ☎ 04.75.55.55.15. An old-fashioned brasserie with a wide range of dishes and prices. The *formule Bistrot* is €20 and *andouillette* goes for €15.

Divinus 4 av Andre Lacroix ☎ 04.75.56.86.64. Fantastically inventive, good-value, cuisine – think lamb tagine with strawberries and almond milk (€15) – served on a pretty little terrace adorned with flowers and lanterns.

L'Épicerie 18 place Belat ☎ 04.75.42.74.46. One of the most congenial places to eat, overlooking a market place. Soft, restful decor and wonderful food – go for one of their excellent seafood platters – on menus from €25 to €68. Closed Sat lunch & Sun.

Le Marché 6 place des Clercs ☎ 04.75.42.17.78. Funky bar in the heart of the action surrounded by restaurants and overlooked by the cathedral. Six different beers (€3/pint) on tap.

Le Milou 10 place de la Pierre ☎ 04.75.43.12.77. On a lovely, peaceful square, this joint dishes up Lyonnais classics for around €17 and is a great drinking spot.

Pic 285 av Victor-Hugo ☎ 04.75.44.15.32, ⊛ www.pic-valence.com. The city's top restaurant, but expect a wallet-bashing – there's a menu here for €325 (*plats* average €80). More affordable is *Bistrot7* par Anne Sophie Pic (the granddaughter of the restaurant's founder), which offers a menu with delights such as pigeon with blackcurrant and mushrooms, and dreamy *moelleux aux chocolat* with chantilly mousse. Closed Sun evening & Mon; *Bistro7* open daily.

Montélimar

If you didn't know it before, you'll soon pick up what makes the town of **MONTÉLIMAR**, 40km south of Valence, tick: nougat. Shops and signs everywhere proclaim the glory of the stuff, which has been made here for centuries. The *vieille ville* is made up of narrow lanes that radiate out from the main street, **rue Pierre-Julien**, which runs from the one remaining medieval **gateway** on the nineteenth-century ring of boulevards at place St-Martin, south past the **church of Sainte-Croix**, and on to place Marx-Dormoy.

Make sure you stop by the fascinating **Musée de la Miniature** (July & Aug daily 10am–6pm; Sept–June Wed–Sun 2–6pm; €4.90), at 19 rue Pierre Julien, opposite the post office. You have to look through a microscope to see many of these tiny exhibits, the most incredible of which are the minute necklaces and earrings, a caravan of twelve camels traipsing through the eye of a needle, and an amusing pair of mosquitoes playing mini chess. Above the old town to the east is the impressive **Château des Adhémar** on rue du Château (daily 9.30am–noon & 2–6pm; closed Tues Nov–March; €3.50). Originally belonging to the family after whom the town ("Mount of the Adhémars") was named, the castle is mostly fourteenth century, but also boasts a fine eleventh-century chapel and twelfth-century living-quarters.

If you're overwhelmed by the number of establishments offering nougat, visit the **Fabrique et Musée d'Arnaud Soubeyran** in the Zone Commerciale Sud (Mon–Sat 9am–7pm, Sun 10am–noon & 2.30–5pm; free; bus line 1 from outside the train station towards Soleil Levant; stop A. Pontaimery) where they'll show you how they concoct the sweet treat; there's also a fun museum outlining its history. The shop sells many flavours of nougat, including delicious orange and lavender.

To escape the heat of the streets and burn off all that nougat, head for **Base Nautique**, a 20min walk from the centre of town; there's swimming (supervised July & Aug), mini-golf and pétanque, among other activities, as well as a pleasant picnic area.

Practicalities

The **gare SNCF** is on the western corner of town, with the **tourist office** across the Jardin Public on the Allees Provençales (Mon–Sat 9am–12.15pm & 2–5.30pm; ☎04.75.01.00.20, ⓦwww.montelimar-tourisme.com).

There are plenty of **hotels** around the boulevards, including the very pleasant *Sphinx*, in a seventeenth-century town house at 19 boulevard Marre-Desmarais (☎04.75.01.86.64, ⓦwww.sphinx-hotel.fr; ❸; closed mid-Dec to mid-Jan) and the smart *Le Relais de l'Empereur* at the southern end of town on place Marx Dormoy (☎04.75.01.32.21, ⓦwww.relaisdeleempereur; ❸). In the old town the *Pierre*, 7 place des Clercs (☎04.75.01.33.16; ❶), is, despite the unpromising exterior, comfortable and very peaceful, apart from the nearby bell of Sainte-Croix tolling the hours. The **campsite**, *L'Île Blanc* (☎04.75.51.20.05, ⓦwww.camping-montelimar.com; €4.50 per person), is at Montélimar-Ancône, 5km northwest of the town.

The best place to enjoy a **drink** or snack is along the Allées from the tourist office to the Théâtre Municipal, or down Boulevard Menot, opposite *Le Relais de l'Empereur*, which itself serves good, quite pricey, **food** in its restaurant; rump of lamb, shared between two people, is €55, while fresh salmon steak is €25. Better, though, is *Don Camilo* at 9 boulevard Desmarais (☎04.75.01.80.04), an elegant restaurant serving generous salads (€15) and a fantastic nougat glacé with fruit coulis (€6).

Travel details

Trains

Lyon (La Part-Dieu or Perrache) to: Arles (7 daily; 2hr 40min); Avignon (15 daily; 2hr–2hr 40min); Avignon TGV (16 daily; 1hr 10min); Bourg-en-Bresse (9 daily; 1hr); Clermont-Ferrand (12 daily; 2hr 20min–2hr 50min); Dijon (1–3 hourly; 2hr); Grenoble (every 30min; 1hr 15min); Lille-Europe (8 daily; 3hr 10min); Marseille (frequent; 1hr 40min–3hr 45min); Montélimar (12 daily; 1hr 35min); Orange (11 daily; 2hr 5min); Paris (every 30min; 2hr); Paris CDG Airport (8 daily; 2hr 10min); Meximieux (for Perouges) (6 daily; 30min); Roanne (1–3 hourly; 1hr 20min); Tain l'Hermitage (hourly; 1hr); Valence (frequent; 1hr 10min); Valence TGV (11–18 daily; 35min); Vienne (frequent; 20–40min).

Lyon St-Exupéry TGV to: Paris (9 daily; 1hr 50min).

Valence to: Gap (5 daily; 2hr 20min–2hr 40min); Grenoble (frequent; 1hr–1hr 40min); Lyon (hourly; 1hr 10min); Montélimar (frequent: approx hourly at peak times; 30min); Tain l'Hermitage (frequent; 12min).

Buses

Lyon to: Bourg-en-Bresse (27 daily; 1hr 10–1hr 30min); Meximieux (for Pérouges 6 daily; 1hr); Vienne (20 daily; 1hr 10min).

Provence

UNITED KINGDOM

BELGIUM

GERMANY

LUX

ENGLISH CHANNEL

SWITZERLAND

ATLANTIC
OCEAN

ITALY

N

MEDITERRANEAN
SEA

SPAI

0   250 km

CHAPTER 15

Highlights

* **Roman remains** Impressive arenas in Orange and Arles host summer festivals and concerts. See pp.959 & 985

* **Medieval hilltop villages** Les Baux and Gordes are the most famous, but there are many others equally picturesque, and much less frequented. See p.963

* **Avignon** The former city of popes has spectacular monuments and museums to go along with the annual Festival d'Avignon. See p.966

* **La Camargue** The marshland of the Rhône delta is home to white horses, flamingos and unearthly landscapes. See p.987

* **Aix** The most beautiful of Provence's major cities is a wonderful place for café idling and has the region's most vibrant markets. See p.997

* **Les Gorges du Verdon** The largest canyon in Europe, with stunning views and a full range of hikes. See p.1007

* **Haute-Provence** The Parc National du Mercantour and the Vallée des Merveilles are Alpine gems off the beaten path. See p.1013

▲ Gorges du Verdon

Provence

O f all the areas of France, **Provence** is the most irresistible. Geographically ranging from the snow capped mountains of the **southern Alps** to the delta plains of the **Camargue**, it boasts Europe's greatest canyon, the **Gorges du Verdon**. Fortified towns guard its old borders; countless villages perch defensively on hilltops; and its great cities – **Aix-en-Provence** and **Avignon** – are full of cultural glories. The sensual inducements of Provence include sunshine, food and wine, and the heady perfumes of Mediterranean vegetation. Along with its coast – which is covered in the following chapter – the region has attracted the rich and famous, the artistic and reclusive, and countless arrivals who have found themselves unable to conceive of life elsewhere.

Provençal food and drink

The food of Provence is some of the most appetizing in the whole of France. It has many Mediterranean influences, such as the heavy use of **olives**: accompanying the traditional Provençal aperitif of *pastis,* they appear in sauces and salads, on tarts and pizzas, and mixed with capers in a paste called *tapenade* to spread on bread or biscuits. **Garlic** is another Provençal classic, used in *pistou*, a paste of olive oil, garlic and basil, and aïoli, the name for both a garlic mayonnaise and the dish in which it's served with salt cod.

Vegetables – tomatoes, capsicum, aubergines, courgettes and onions – are often made into **ratatouille**, while **courgette flowers** *(fleurs de courgettes farcies)*, stuffed with *pistou* or tomato sauce, are one of the most exquisite Provençal delicacies.

Sheep, taken up to the mountains in the summer months, provide the staple **meat**, of which the best is *agneau de Sisteron*, often roasted with Provençal herbs as *gigot d'agneau aux herbes*. But it's **fish** that features most on traditional menus, with freshwater trout, salt cod, anchovies, sea bream, monkfish, sea bass and whiting all common, along with wonderful seafood such as clams, periwinkles, sea urchins and oysters.

Sweets include almond *calissons* from Aix and candied fruit from Apt, while the **fruit** – melons, white peaches, apricots, figs, cherries and Muscat grapes – is unbeatable. **Cheeses** are invariably made from goat's or ewe's milk. Two famous ones are Banon, wrapped in chestnut leaves and marinated in brandy, and the aromatic Picadon, from the foothills of the Alps.

The best **wines** come from around the Dentelles, notably Gigondas, and from Châteauneuf-du-Pape. To the west are the light, drinkable, but not particularly special wines of the Côtes du Ventoux and the Côtes du Lubéron *appellations*. With the exception of the Côteaux des Baux around Les Baux, and the Côtes de Provence in the Var *département*, the best wines of southern Provence come from along the coast.

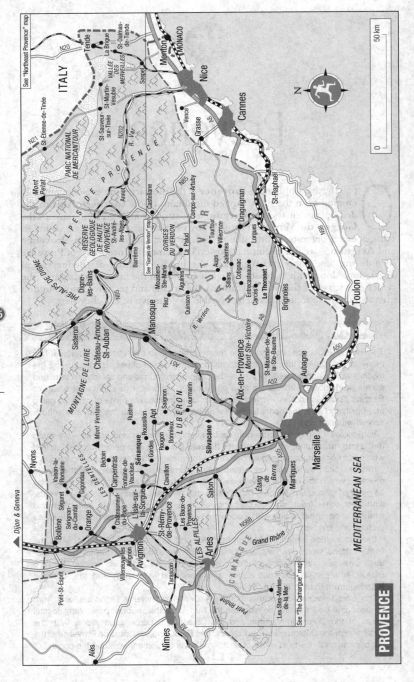

PROVENCE

50 km

0

N

MEDITERRANEAN SEA

ITALY

See "Northeast Provence" map

Tende

La Brigue

St-Dalmas-de-Tende

N20

VALLÉE DES MERVEILLES

Menton

Sospel

St-Martin-Vésubie

MONACO

St-Sauveur-sur-Tinée

N202

St-André-les-Alpes

Nice

St-Étienne-de-Tinée

N21

PARC NATIONAL DE MERCANTOUR

Vence

Cannes

Mont Pelat

Annot

Grasse

A L P E S   D E   P R O V E N C E

Castellane

Comps-sur-Artuby

N85

St-Raphaël

N98

RÉSERVE GÉOLOGIQUE DE HAUTE PROVENCE

Digne-les-Bains

Barrême

See "Gorges de Verdon" map

GORGES DU VERDON

Tourtour

Draguignan

Moustiers-Ste-Marie

La Palud

Villecroze

Lorgues

P R É - A L P E S   D E   D I G N E

N85

Riez

Aups

Salernes

Colignac

Entrecasteaux

A8

Château-Arnoux St-Auban

Aiguines

Sillans

Cotignac

Le Thoronet

Sisteron

Manosque

Quinson

R. Verdon

Brignoles

H A U T   V A R

Toulon

MONTAGNE DE LURE

A51

Rustrel

Apt

Salignon

Lourmarin

Mont Ste-Victoire

A8

St-Maximin-de-la-Ste-Baume

A50

Mont Ventoux

Bédoin

Roussillon

Bonnieux

L U B E R O N

Aix-en-Provence

Aubagne

Nyons

Séguret

Gigondas

LES DENTELLES

Fontaine-de-Vaucluse

Gordes

Roujon

Silvacane

A52

Vaison-la-Romaine

Carpentras

Cavaillon

A7

Sénanque

Marseille

Dijon & Geneva

Bollène

Sérignan-du-Comtat

Orange

Châteauneuf-du-Pape

L'Isle-sur-la-Sorgue

Salon

Étang de Berre

A55

Pont-St-Esprit

Villeneuve-lès-Avignon

St-Rémy-de-Provence

Martigues

Avignon

Les Baux-de-Provence

LES ALPILLES

N568

Tarascon

Arles

Grand Rhône

C A M A R G U E

Nîmes

A9

Petit Rhône

Alès

Les Stes-Maries-de-la-Mer

See "The Camargue" map

In appearance, despite the throngs of foreigners and French from other regions, **inland Provence** remains remarkably unscathed. The history of its earliest known natives, of the Greeks, then Romans, raiding Saracens, schismatic popes, and shifting allegiances to different counts and princes, is still in evidence. Provence's complete integration into France dates only from the nineteenth century and, though the Provençal language is only spoken by a small minority, the accent is distinctive even to a foreign ear. In the east the rhythms of speech become clearly Italian.

Unless you're intending to stay for months, the main difficulty in visiting Provence is choosing where to go. In the west, along the **Rhône valley**, are the Roman cities of **Orange**, **Vaison-la-Romaine**, **Carpentras** and **Arles**, and the papal city of **Avignon**, with its fantastic summer festival. **Aix-en-Provence** is the mini-Paris of the region and was home to Cézanne, for whom the **Mont Ste-Victoire** was an enduring subject; Van Gogh's links are with **St-Rémy** and Arles. The **Gorges du Verdon**, **the Parc National du Mercantour** along the Italian border, **Mont Ventoux** northeast of Carpentras, and the flamingo-filled lagoons of the **Camargue** are just a selection of the diverse and stunning landscapes of this region.

Western Provence

The richest area of Provence, the Côte d'Azur apart, is the **west**. Most of the large-scale production of fruit, vegetables and wine is based here in the low-lying plains beside the Rhône and the Durance rivers. The only heights are the rocky outbreaks of the **Dentelles** and the **Alpilles**, and the narrow east–west ridges of **Mont Ventoux**, the **Luberon** and the **Mont Ste-Victoire**. The two dominant cities of inland Provence, **Avignon** and **Aix**, both have rich histories and contemporary fame for their festivals of art; **Arles**, **Orange** and **Vaison-la-Romaine** have impressive Roman remains. Around the Rhône delta, the **Camargue** is a unique self-contained region, as different from the rest of Provence as it is from anywhere else in France.

Orange and around

ORANGE was the former seat of the counts of Orange, a title created by Charlemagne in the eighth century and passed to the Dutch crown in the sixteenth century. The family's most famous member was Prince William, who ascended the English throne with his consort Mary in the 1688 "Glorious Revolution". Today the town is best known for its spectacular **Roman theatre**, which hosts the important summer Chorégies **music festival**. While the rest of Orange is certainly attractive, there's not a lot to detain you once you've visited the theatre and adjacent museum and taken a quick look at the Roman triumphal arch at the northern approach to the town centre, so a two- or three-day visit should suffice.

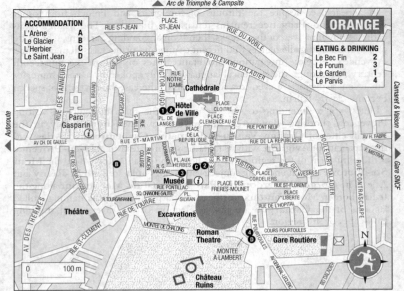

Arrival and information

The **gare SNCF** is about 1.5km east of the centre, at the end of avenue Frédéric-Mistral. Taxis into town are outside the station. The **tourist office** (April–June & Sept Mon–Sat 9am–6.30pm, Sun 10am–1pm & 2–6.30pm; July–Aug Mon–Sat 9am–7.30pm, Sun 10am–1pm & 2–7pm; Oct–March Mon–Sat 10am–1pm & 2–5pm; ☎04.90.34.70.88, ⓦwww.otorange.fr) is at the opposite end from the Théâtre Municipal on cours Aristide Briand, and there's a **seasonal tourist office** facing the Théâtre Antique (July–Aug only, same hours as main office). The **gare routière** is close to the centre on boulevard Edouard-Daladier.

Accommodation

The tourist office can provide lists of hotels and *chambres d'hôtes* based outside of Orange, but to get a real sense of the old town, it's best to stay in the centre. The hotels below all have private parking.

L'Arène place de Langes ☎04.90.11.40.40, ⓦwww.hotel-arene.fr. Smart hotel with spacious rooms and all mod cons. ❺
Le Glacier 46 cours Aristide-Briand ☎04.90.34.02.01, ⓦwww.le-glacier.com. Comfortable, cosy Provençal-style rooms – think yellows and blues with pretty quilts and floral curtains. ❸
L'Herbier 8 place aux Herbes ☎04.90.34.09.23, ⓦwww.lherbierdorange .com. Fabulous location right by the Théâtre Antique, with pleasant rooms set in a seventeenth-century house. ❷

Le Saint Jean 1 cours Pourtoules ☎04.90.51.15.16, ⓦwww.hotelsaint-jean.com. Very homely place with rambling corridors and a sunny terrace at the front. ❹

Campsite

Le Jonquier rue Alexis-Carrel ☎04.90.34.49.48, ⓦwww.campinglejonquier.com. 1.5km northwest of town. Popular campsite equipped with tennis courts, mini-golf and a pool. €24 for two people and a tent. Open mid-March to Sept.

The Town

Days off in Orange c.55 AD were most entertainingly spent from dawn to dusk watching farce, clownish improvisations, song and dance, and occasionally, for the sake of a visiting dignitary, a bit of Greek tragedy in Latin at the huge Roman **theatre** (daily: March & Oct 9.30am–5.30pm; April, May & Sept 9am–6pm; June–Aug 9am–7pm; Nov–Feb 9.30am–4.30pm; €7.70, including audioguide and combined ticket with museum), built into the hill which squats on the south side of the old town. Despite its impressive dimensions, the theatre was by no means exceptional for a city of Orange's size, but today it's the best-preserved example in Europe, and makes for a stimulating visit. The excellent audioguide (in English) paints an evocative picture of the theatre and its 10,000-strong audience, while clearly taking you through the various statues and pillars on the inside of the stage wall.

The best view of the theatre in its entirety is from St-Eutrope hill. You can follow a path up the hill either from the top of cours Aristide-Briand (montée P. de Chalons) or from cours Pourtoules (montée Albert-Lambert) until you are looking directly down onto the stage. The ruins around your feet are those of the short-lived seventeenth-century castle of the princes of Orange. Louis XIV had it destroyed in 1673 and the principality of Orange was officially annexed to France forty years later.

The **municipal museum** (same hours and ticket as theatre) might seem like small fry compared to the theatre just opposite, but it does house some worthwhile Roman artefacts, taken from the theatre: fragments of land registries, a couple of sphinxes and a mosaic floor. The two upper levels are dedicated to the Gasparin family, who promoted the safeguarding of Roman Orange, and are filled with family portraits, mementoes and a reconstructed *salon*.

Orange's old town is very small, hemmed in between the theatre and the River Meyne and shelters some pretty fountain-adorned squares and houses with ancient porticoes and courtyards. Don't miss the town's second major Roman monument, the **Arc de Triomphe**, situated to the north of town at the bottom of Avenue de l'Arc de Triomphe. Built around 20 BC, its intricate frieze and relief celebrate imperial victories of the Roman Second Legion against the Gauls.

Eating and drinking

Sun-drenched **brasseries** and **bars** are situated in place de la Republique; some are also in place Clemenceau, but these are slightly more touristy.

Le Bec Fin rue Segond Weber ☎04.90.34.05.10. Down a narrow street with equally narrow views of the Théâtre Antique, this place serves hearty salads and tasty pizzas (both €9.50).

Le Forum 3 rue du Mazeau ☎04.90.34.01.09. Small, intimate restaurant near the Théâtre. Menus (from €22) revolve around seasonal ingredients; in January, truffles feature heavily, while in May, it's asparagus. Often booked up, so reserve ahead. Closed Mon, Sat lunch & Sun evening.

Le Garden 6 place de Langes ☎04.90.34.63.47. Well-regarded restaurant where you can expect fresh, interesting dishes, such as lamb with sautéed asparagus and potatoes with grilled almonds (€22). Closed Sun lunch & Mon.

Le Parvis 55 cours Pourtoules ☎04.90.34.82.00. The best food in Orange. Straight from the market, ingredients are whipped up into tempting, good-value dishes (€17) – marlin with butter beans, peas and chorizo, for example. Menus up to €33.50. Closed Sun evening & Mon.

Entertainment

Orange's main festival is the **Chorégies**, a programme of opera, oratorios and orchestral concerts in July – details and tickets from the Bureau des Chorégies,

18 place Silvain (☎04.90.34.24.24, ⓦwww.choregies.asso.fr). The theatre is also used throughout the year for jazz, film, folk and rock concerts. Details of ticket prices from the Service Culturel de la Ville, 14 place Silvain (☎04.90.51.57.57). Tickets for all events can be bought from FNAC shops in all big French cities, and at the theatre box office in Orange.

Sérignan-du-Comtat

The village of **SÉRIGNAN-DU-COMTAT**, 8km northeast of Orange (around six buses daily from Orange and Avignon, very limited service Sun), was the home of **Jean-Henri Fabre**, a remarkable self-taught scientist, famous for his insect studies, who also composed poetry, wrote songs and painted his specimens with artistic brilliance as well as scientific accuracy. In the 1860s he had to resign from his teaching post at Avignon because parents and priests thought his lectures on the fertilization of flowering plants were licentious, if not downright pornographic. His beautiful **house**, *Harmas* (mid-March to mid-Oct 10am–12.30pm & 2.30-6pm; €5), lies a two-minute walk from the *mairie*, back towards Orange, and contains his study filled with rock and insect specimens as well as a collection of his watercolours. At the front of his house is a lovely jungle-like garden, providing a tranquil oasis away from the hustle and bustle of Orange.

Châteauneuf-du-Pape

If you're heading down to Avignon, the slower route through **CHÂTEAUNEUF-DU-PAPE** exerts a strong pull. The village takes its name from the summer palace of the Avignon popes, but neither the views down the Rhône valley towards Avignon from the ruins of the fourteenth-century **château** (freely accessible) nor the medieval streets around **place du Portail** – the hub of the village – give Châteauneuf its special appeal. Rather it's the wines produced by the local vineyards, warmed at night by the large pebbles that cover the ground and soak up the sun's heat during the day, that are its real attraction. The rich ruby red is one of France's most renowned, but the white, too, is exquisite.

The *appellation* Châteauneuf-du-Pape does not, alas, come cheap. A first stop, for those who want to learn how these famous wines are made, should be the Musée du Vin on Avenue Pierre-de-Luxembourg (daily May to mid-Oct 9am–1pm & 2–7pm; end-Oct to April 9am–noon & 2–6pm; free), where they also do free tastings. Before you tackle the multitude of *caves* in and around town, pick up a list of all the producers at the **tourist office** (☎04.90.83.71.08) on place du Portail (Sept–May 9.30am–12.30pm & 2–6pm, Mon, Tues, Thurs–Sat closed Wed & Sun; June–Aug Mon, Tues, Thurs, Fri & Sun 9.30am–6pm, Wed & Sat 9.30am–noon 2–6pm).

If wine isn't sweet or strong enough for you, head to A. Blachère, 3km out of town towards Avignon, which has been producing a very powerful **brandy**, Réserve des Légats, for fifteen years. The **chocolaterie**, Bernard Castelain, is next door, and offers free tastings and a shop stuffed full of gastronomic delights.

Accommodation is confined to four very pleasant but small hotels: *La Garbure*, 3 rue Joseph-Ducos (☎04.90.83.75.08, ⓦwww.la-garbure.com; ❹); the four-star *Hostellerie du Château des Fines Roches*, on route d'Avignon (☎04.90.83.70.23, ⓦwww.chateaufinesroches.com; ❻); *La Mère Germaine*, on avenue Cdt-Lemaître (☎04.90.83.54.37, ⓦwww.lameregermaine.com; ❹); and *La Sommellerie*, 3km north of the village on route de Roquemaure (☎04.90.83.50.00, ⓦwww.la-sommellerie.fr; ❻, closed Jan to mid-Feb).

▲ Châteauneuf du Pape

You can **eat** well at the brasserie *La Mule du Pape* (☎04.90.83.79.22), 2 rue de la République; salads are €9.50, while pizza is €8.50. *Le Verger des Papes* (☎04.90.83.50.40; closed Sun evening) right next to the chateau on the top of the hill, serves traditional food on its peaceful terrace (menus €19.50 & €29). *La Mère Germaine* (see opposite), dishes up well-crafted but more expensive Provençal cuisine, and *La Sommellerie* (see opposite; closed Sat & Mon lunchtime; menus €30–62) is one of the top restaurants in the area, producing exquisite dishes such as grilled lamb with garlic, rosemary and tapenade.

Vaison-la-Romaine and around

VAISON-LA-ROMAINE lies 27km northeast of Orange and hit the headlines in 1992 when the River Ouvèze, which divides the medieval and eighteenth-century towns, burst its banks, destroying riverside houses, the modern road bridge and an entire industrial quarter. The town has recovered remarkably, and now its pleasant streets are flanked by souvenir shops and cafés, each plying their trade to tourists eager to visit the medieval **haute ville** across the **Pont Romain**, which stubbornly held out against the floods. The modern town itself is equipped with the extensive remains of two **Roman districts**, as well as a cloistered former cathedral. Vaison-la-Romaine is surrounded by a number of stunning **hill-top villages**, each lending itself to peaceful wandering.

Arrival and information

Buses to and from Carpentras, Orange and Avignon stop at the **gare routière** on avenue des Choralies near the junction with avenue Victor-Hugo, east of the town centre on the north side of the river. The **tourist office** (April–June & Sept to mid-Oct Mon–Sat 9am–noon & 2–5.45pm; mid-Oct to March Mon–Sat 9am–noon & 2–5.45pm; July–Aug 9–12.30pm & 2–6.45pm; ☎04.90.36.02.11, ⓦwww.vaison-la-romaine.com) is between the two archeological sites in the north of the modern town.

Accommodation

Vaison makes a lovely base for exploring the surrounding area, mostly because of its wonderful **hotels**. Make sure you book the following well in advance.

Le Beffroi rue de l'Evêché, *haute ville*
⊤ 04.90.36.04.71, ⊛ www.le-beffroi.com.
Beautiful, luxurious rooms in a sixteenth-century residence. Has a pool, a great restaurant and unsurpassable views over the valley. Closed mid-Jan to March. **⑤**

Hotel Burrhus 2 place Montfort ⊤ 04.90.36.00.11, ⊛ www.burrhus.com. Located in the heart of the town, this cool, contemporary hotel is adorned with an eclectic mix of retro furniture. **③**

L'Évêché rue de l'Evêché, *haute ville*
⊤ 04.90.36.13.46, ⊛ www.eveche-vaison .com. B&B with a lovely, homely atmosphere. You can enjoy coffee and croissants on the little terrace at the back. **④**

La Fête en Provence place du Vieux Marché, *haute ville* ⊤ 04.90.36.36.43, ⊛ www.hotellafete -provence.com. Gorgeous, comfortable rooms and apartments surrounding a pool and flower-decked patio. Also has a restaurant (see opposite). **④**

Campsite

Camping du Théâtre Romain Chemin du Brusquet, off av des Choralies, quartier des Arts ⊤ 04.90.28.78.66, ⊛ www.camping-theatre.com. Located 500m from the centre of town, this campsite is popular in summer, so reserve ahead. Open mid-March to mid-Nov. €8 per tent.

The Town

The **haute ville** lies on the south side of the river, with **rue du Pont** climbing up towards place des Poids and the fourteenth-century **gateway** to the town. More steep zigzags take you past the Gothic gate and overhanging portcullis of the **belfry** and into the heart of this sedately quiet, uncommercialized and rich *quartier.* There's an almost unavoidable pull to the top of the hill with its **ruined castle** and remarkable views over the valley and to the mountains beyond; the climb to the top is quite steep and stoney, so wear good shoes.

On the north bank from the Pont Romain, Grande-Rue leads up to the central streets of rue de la République and cours Henri-Fabré, after which it becomes avenue Général-de-Gaulle. The two excavated **Roman residential districts** lie to either side of this avenue: **Puymin** to the east (April & May 9.30am–6pm; June–Sept 9.30am–6.30pm; March & Oct 10am–12.30pm; Nov, Dec & Feb 10am–noon & 2–5pm) and **La Villasse** to the west (April & May 10am–noon & 2.30–6pm; June–Sept 10am–noon & 2.30–6.30pm; March & Oct 10am–12.30pm & 2–5.30pm; Nov, Dec & Feb 10–noon & 2–5pm). **Tickets** for both, plus Puymin museum and cathedral cloisters, cost €8 and can be bought at the Puymin entrance just by the tourist office or in the cloisters.

The Puymin excavations contain the theatre, several mansions and houses, a colonnade known as the *portique de Pompée* and a museum of all the items discovered. The excavations of La Villasse reveal a street with pavements and gutters with the layout of a row of arcaded shops running parallel, more patrician houses (some with mosaics still intact), a basilica and the baths. La Villasse's theatre still seats seven thousand people during the July festival.

Most of the detail and decoration of the buildings are displayed in the **museum** in the Puymin district (same hours as Puymin archeological site). Tiny fragments of painted plaster have been jigsawed together with convincing reconstructions of how whole painted walls would have looked. There are mirrors of silvered bronze, lead water pipes, taps shaped as griffins' feet, dolphin door knobs, weights and measures, plus impressive busts and statues.

The former **Cathédrale Notre-Dame**, west down chemin Couradou, runs along the south side of La Villasse. The apse of the cathedral is a confusing overlay of sixth-, tenth- and thirteenth-century construction, using pieces quarried from the Roman ruins. The **cloisters** are fairly typical of early medieval workmanship – pretty enough but not wildly exciting. The only surprising feature is the large inscription visible on the north wall of the cathedral, a convoluted precept for the monks.

Eating and drinking

Vaison has a large number of good **restaurants**, on both sides of the river. For a more local feel, stick to the modern town, particularly around place de Montfort and cours Taulignan, but the places in the haute ville cannot be beaten for their lovely views.

L'Auberge de Bartavelle 12 place Sus-Auze ☎04.90.36.02.6. A lively place in the modern town; food is decent and affordable (*plats* €20) and there are fun black and white photos on the wall honouring the playwright and filmmaker, Marcel Pagnol. Closed Mon, Fri lunch & Jan.
Le Bateleur 1 place Théodore-Aubanel ☎04.90.36.28.04. Situated on the approach to the *haute ville*, punters come here for hearty meat dishes at decent prices (menus from €29; *plats* around €19). Try the marinated beef with pureéd

field mushrooms. Closed Mon, Thurs evening & Sat lunch.
Le Bistrot d'Ou rue du Château, *haute ville* ☎04.90.41.72.90. Popular, sophisticated restaurant serving refined bistro dishes. The *menu ardoise* (€27) includes a beautiful *soupe de fraises* with grapefruit sorbet. Closed Sun & Mon lunch.
La Fête en Provence place du Vieux Marché, *haute ville* ☎04.90.36.36.43. Classic Provençal dishes at affordable prices, such as guinea fowl with black olive sauce (€15). Easter–Nov closed Wed.

Hill-top villages

The tourist office in Vaison can supply you with a map and guide to the **hill-top villages** in the area: all are worth visiting in their own right and possess their own particular charm, especially tiny, hill-top **LE CRESTET**. South of Vaison, the village is 3.5km down the Malaucène road, and off to the right. There's not a lot to do other than wander the steep and picturesque cobbled streets, earning a refreshment break at the restaurant at the top.

MONT VENTOUX, whose outline repeatedly appears upon the horizon from the Rhône and Durance valleys, rises some 20km east of Vaison. White with snow, black with storm-cloud shadow or reflecting myriad shades of blue, the barren pebbles of the uppermost 300m are like a weathervane for all of western Provence. Winds can accelerate to 250km per hour around the meteorological, TV and military masts and dishes on the summit, but if you can stand still for a moment the view in all directions is unbeatable. A road, the D974, climbs all the way to the top, though no buses go there. The road up the northern face from Malaucène is wider, straighter, and better surfaced than the southern ascent.

If you want to make the ascent on foot, the best path is from Les Colombets or Les Fébriers, two hamlets off the D974, east of **BEDOIN**, whose **tourist office** on the espace M.-L.-Gravier (mid-June to Oct Mon–Sat 9–12.30pm & 2–6pm, Sun 9.30am–12.30pm; Nov to mid-June Mon–Fri 9–12.30pm & 2–6pm, Sat 9.30am–12.30pm; ☎04.90.65.63.95) can give details of routes (including a once a week night-time ascent in July & Aug), plus addresses of campsites and *gîtes ruraux*.

Mont Ventoux is one of the challenges of the Tour de France. Within sight of the stony summit is a memorial to the British cyclist Tommy Simpson, who died here from heart failure on one of the hottest days ever recorded in the race; according to race folklore his last words were "Put me back on the bloody bike."

The Dentelles and around

The **Dentelles**, a row of jagged limestone pinnacles, run across an arid, windswept and near-deserted upland area, the **Massif Montmirail–St-Amand**, just south of Vaison-la-Romaine. Their name refers to lace – the limestone protrusions were thought to resemble the contorted pins on a lace-making board – though the word's alternative connection with teeth (*dents* means "teeth") is equally appropriate.

The area is best known for its wines. On the western and southern slopes lie the wine-producing villages of **Gigondas**, **Séguret**, **Beaumes-de-Venise**, **Sablet**, **Vacqueyras** and, across the River Ouvèze, **Rasteau**. Each one carries the distinction of having its own individual *appellation contrôlée* within the Côtes du Rhône or Côtes du Rhône Villages areas: in other words, their wines are exceptional. It's best to have your own wheels, as **public transport** is less than comprehensive.

Séguret

Nine kilometres southwest of Vaison-la-Romaine is the magnificent town of **SÉGURET**, whose name comes from the Latin word, *securitas*. It is indeed a secure little place, hemmed in by its ramparts and large stone gateways, which manages to avoid feeling overrun by tourists, despite its popularity. The centre of town is entirely pedestrianized (free parking at the bottom of town) while souvenir-shops and cafés sympathetically blend into the classic, Provençal mix of sand-and-peach-coloured roofs.

There's a **hotel** at the top of town, *La Table du Comtat*, (☎04.90.46.91.49, ⓦwww.table-comtat.fr; ❺), which has decent rooms and even better views. For food, there's *Le Mesclun* on rue des Poternes (☎04.90.46.93.43; closed Mon & Tues out of season), which has classy menus at €33 and 40; *plats* such as roasted scallops with a *pistou* vinagrette are around €18. At the foot of the town is the gorgeous *Le Bastide Bleue*, route de Sablet (☎04.90.46.83.43; closed Sun, plus Jan & Feb; open evenings only), which serves fresh Provençal food out on its pretty rose-draped terrace or in its rustic, characterful dining room. They also have seven comfortable **rooms** (❹). For those equipped with a tent, there's a **campsite** (☎04.90.46.82.5; €14.50 for two people and a tent) at Sablet, 3km south of Séguret, on the way to Gigondas.

Gigondas

Gigondas, 14km southwest of Seguret, is another worthwhile stop in the Dentelles area, its main draw being its exquisite **red wine**, which is strong with an aftertaste of spice and nuts. You can taste the produce from forty different *domaines* at the **Caveau du Gigondas** on place de la Mairie in the village (daily 10am–noon & 2–6.30pm). Besides *dégustation* and bottle-buying, you can go for long **walks** in the area, stumbling upon mysterious ruins or photogenic panoramas of Mont Ventoux and the Rhône valley.

The pinnacles are favourite scaling faces for apprentice rock-climbers – though their wind-eroded patterns can be appreciated just as well without risking your neck on an ascent. Information on walking and climbing is available from Gigondas' **tourist office** on place du Portail (June–Sept Mon–Fri 10am–12.30pm & 2.30–6pm; Oct–May Mon–Fri 10am–noon & 2–5pm; ☎04.90.65.85.46), which also sells a local footpath map for €2.50.

Hotel options around Gigondas include the very pleasant *Les Florets*, 2km from the village along the route des Dentelles (☎04.90.65.85.01, ⓦwww.hotel-lesflorets.com; ❺), and the peaceful *Hôtel Montmirail*, which you reach via

Vacqueyras (☎04.90.65.84.01, Ⓦwww.hotelmontmirail.com; ❺; open June–Oct). **Restaurants** include the pricey *L'Oustalet* (☎04.90.65.85.30; lunchtime menu €35, evening menus €47 & €59), in the heart of the village at place Gabriel-Andéol and which serves hearty and delicious fare; cheaper meals, such as pizza and salads, are on offer at *Les Copains d'Abord* on rue Eugene Raspail (☎04.90.63.71.36).

Carpentras

With a population of around 30,000, **CARPENTRAS** is a substantial city for this part of the world. It's also a very old one, its known history commencing in 5 BC as the capital of a Celtic tribe. The Greeks who founded Marseille came to Carpentras to buy honey, wheat, goats and skins, and the Romans had a base here. For a brief period in the fourteenth century, it became the papal headquarters and gave protection to Jews expelled from France. Today, the town is in the throes of gradual refurbishment, so that immaculately restored squares and fountains alternate with gently decayed streets of seventeenth- and eighteenth-century houses, some forming arcades over the pavement.

The erotic fantasies of a seventeenth-century cardinal frescoed by Nicolas Mignard in the **Palais de Justice**, formerly the episcopal palace, were effaced by a later incumbent. The *palais* is attached to the dull **Cathédrale St-Siffrein**, behind which, almost hidden in the corner, stands a **Roman arch** inscribed with scenes of prisoners in chains. Fifteen hundred years after its erection, Jews – coerced, bribed or otherwise persuaded – entered the cathedral in chains to be unshackled as converted Christians. The door they passed through, the **Porte Juif**, is on the southern side and bears strange symbolism of rats encircling and devouring a globe. The **synagogue** (Mon–Thurs 10am–noon & 3–5pm, Fri 10am–noon & 3–4pm; closed Jewish feast days; free), near the Hôtel de Ville, is a seventeenth-century construction on fourteenth-century foundations, making it the oldest surviving place of Jewish worship in France.

Carpentras cheers up every Friday for the **market**, which from the end of November to early March specializes in truffles, and during **festival** time in the second half of July. The town is very proud of its sweet speciality of **berlingots** (you'll see them on signs, in shops, and at the end of your meal, as an accompaniment to your bill), small, striped *bonbons* made from fruit syrup – the mint flavour is the most famous, but the coffee one is absolutely delicious.

Practicalities

Buses (trains are freight only) arrive either on avenue Victor-Hugo or place Terradou, a short walk away from place Aristide-Briand, where the **tourist office** is located (Mon–Sat 9.30am–12.30pm & 2–6pm; July & Aug plus Sun 9.30am–1pm; ☎04.90.63.00.78, Ⓦwww.carpentras-ventoux.com). **Accommodation** options include the drab but adequate *Univers*, 110 place A.-Briand (☎04.90.63.00.05, Ⓦwww.hotel-univers.com; ❷) and the pleasant *Forum* at 24 rue du Forum (☎04.90.60.57.00, Ⓦwww.hotel.forum-provence.com; ❹). For something grander with greater character, try *Le Fiacre*, 153 rue Vigne (☎04.90.63.03.15, Ⓦwww.hotel-du-fiacre.com; ❹), an eighteenth-century town house; the owners are extremely friendly and can help plan walking and cycling tours in the surrounding area. The local four-star **campsite**, *Lou*

Comtadou (☎04.90.67.03.16; open Feb–Oct; price for two people starts at €15), is 1km from town on Route de Saint Didier.

The Friday market and seasonality influence the **restaurant** menus. The cheery *La Petite Fontaine* (☎04.90.60.77.83; closed Wed & Sun) is, as the name suggests, situated next to a little fountain on place du Colonel Mouret, and serves delicious, fresh food, with a menu at €25. Another restaurant worth trying is *La Fraisiere* at 125 boulevard Alfred Rogier (☎04.90.67.06.39; closed Wed), draped in lush foliage, which cooks up superb dishes like beef grilled in thyme (€15). Traditional bistro fare is on offer at the sleek *Chez Serge*, 90 rue Cottier (☎04.90.63.21.24; closed Sun; menu €35). Once the sun goes down, the best place for café or **bar** crawling is place Aristide-Briand.

Avignon

Twenty-five kilometres southwest of Carpentras **AVIGNON**, great city of the popes, and for centuries one of the major artistic centres of France, can be dauntingly crowded in summer and stiflingly hot. Away from the main tourist drag the old town is often remarkably unkempt and somewhat intimidating, with a laissez-faire approach to rubbish collection at odds with its UNESCO World Heritage status and an intrusive graffiti problem that leaves even the prettiest facades disfigured. But it's worth persevering for its spectacular monuments and museums, countless impressively decorated buildings, ancient churches, chapels and convents. During the **Festival d'Avignon** in July and the beginning of August, it is *the* place to be.

Central Avignon is still enclosed by its medieval walls, built in 1403 by the antipope Benedict XIII, the last of nine **popes** who based themselves here

The Festival of Avignon

Unlike most provincial festivals of international renown, the **Festival d'Avignon** is dominated by theatre rather than classical music, though there's also plenty of that, as well as lectures, exhibitions and dance. It uses the city's great buildings as backdrops to performances, and takes place every year for three weeks from the second week in July. During festival time everything stays open late and everything gets booked up; there can be up to 200,000 visitors, and getting around or doing anything normal becomes virtually impossible.

Originally created in 1947 by actor-director **Jean Vilar**, over the years programmes have included theatrical interpretations as diverse as Molière, Euripides and Chekhov, performed by companies from across Europe. While big-name directors (Jacques Lasalle, Alain Françon) draw the largest crowds to the main venue, the Cour d'Honneur in the Palais des Papes, there's more than enough variety in all the smaller productions, dance performances and lectures to keep everyone sufficiently entertained.

The main **festival programme**, with details of how to book, is available from the second week in May from the Bureau du Festival d'Avignon, 20 rue du portail Boquier (ⓦwww.festival-avignon.com), or from the tourist office. Tickets (€13–36) go on sale from the second week in June. As well as phone sales (9am–1pm & 2–5pm; ☎04.90.14.14.14), they can be bought from FNAC shops in all major French cities and via the FNAC website. During the festival, tickets are available until three hours before the performance. The Festival Off programme is available from Avignon Public Off, 5 rue Ninon Vallin (ⓦwww.avignonleoff.com). Ticket prices range from €10 to €20 and a *Carte Public Adhérent* for €13 gives you thirty percent off all shows.

throughout most of the fourteenth century. The first pope to come to Avignon was Clement V in 1309, who was invited over by the astute King Philippe le Bel ("the Good"), ostensibly to protect Clement from impending anarchy in Rome. In reality, Philip saw a chance to extend his power over the Church by keeping the pope in the safety of Provence, during what came to be known as the Church's "Babylonian captivity". Clement's successors were a varied group, from the villainous John XXII (of Umberto Eco's *The Name of the Rose* fame), to the dedicated Urban V, and later Gregory XI, who managed to re-establish the papacy in Rome in 1378. However, this was not the end of the papacy here – after Gregory's death in Rome, dissident local cardinals elected their own pope in Avignon, provoking the Western Schism: a ruthless struggle for the control of the Church's wealth, which lasted until the pious Benedict fled Avignon for self-exile near Valencia in 1409.

As home to one of the richest courts in Europe, fourteenth-century Avignon attracted hordes of princes, dignitaries, poets and raiders, who arrived to beg from, rob, extort and entertain the popes. According to Petrarch, the overcrowded, plague-ridden papal entourage was "a sewer where all the filth of the universe has gathered". Burgeoning from within its low battlements, the town must have been a colourful, frenetic sight.

Arrival and information

Both the **gare SNCF** on boulevard St-Roch and the adjacent **gare routière** are close to Porte de la République, on the south side of the old city. The **TGV** station is near the hospital 2km south of the city centre; regular shuttles connect the TGV station with the bus stop on avenue President Kennedy (daily 5.38am–11.20pm; €2.50); passengers are picked up or dropped off next to the post office, a short walk from the main tourist office. The city's main **local bus** information centre can be found at 1 avenue de Lattre de Tassigny, a two-minute walk from Porte de la République. From Cité Administrative all buses go to place de l'Horloge. Tickets may be bought from drivers and at TCRA (Transports en Commun de la Région d'Avignon; Ⓦwww.tcra.fr) kiosks throughout town (€1.10 each; €9.40 for a book of ten). Driving into Avignon involves negotiating a nightmare of junctions and one-way roads. The best **parking** option is the free, guarded car park on the Île de Piot, between Avignon and Villeneuve; a free shuttle runs every 10min (Mon–Fri 7.30am–8.30pm, Sat 1.30–8.30pm; during festival daily 7.30am–2.30am; end of festival to mid-Aug daily 7.30am–8.30pm) between the car park and Porte de l'Oulle; otherwise parking inside the city walls is expensive and often full, starting at €1.50 for 1hour.

Cours Jean-Jaurès runs into the old city from the Porte de la République, with the main **tourist office** a little way up on the right at no. 41 (Easter–Oct Mon–Sat 9am–6pm, till 7pm in July, Sun 9.45am–5pm; Nov–Easter Mon–Fri 9am–6pm, Sat 9am–5pm, Sun 10am–noon; Ⓣ04.32.74.32.74, Ⓦwww .avignon-tourisme.com).

Accommodation

Even outside festival time, finding a **room** in Avignon can be a problem: cheap hotels fill fast, so book in advance. Remember, too, that Villeneuve-lès-Avignon is only just across the river and may have rooms when its larger neighbour is full. Between the two, the Île de la Barthelasse is an idyllic spot for **camping**, and you may find the odd farmhouse advertising rooms. The tourist office can also help you find accommodation.

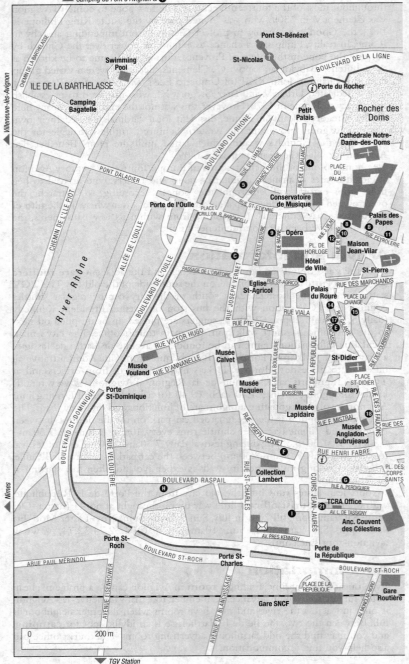

Camping du Pont d'Avignon & ❶

Pont St-Bénézet

St-Nicolas

BOULEVARD DE LA LIGNE

Swimming Pool

(i) Porte du Rocher

ILE DE LA BARTHELASSE

Camping Bagatelle

Petit Palais

Rocher des Doms

Cathédrale Notre-Dame-des-Doms

PLACE DU PALAIS

BOULEVARD DU RHONE

RUE DE L'IMAS

RUE DE LA BALANCE

RUE GRANDE FUSTERIE

PONT DALADIER

❺

❹

Conservatoire de Musique

Porte de l'Oulle

PLACE CRILLON R. BARONCELLI

RUE ST-ETIENNE

RUE PETITE FUSTERIE

RUE VILAR

RUE RACINE

❾ Opéra

❽

B

Palais des Papes

❿

RUE PEYROLERIE

⓫

River Rhône

CHEMIN DE L'ILE PIOT

ALLÉE DE L'OULLE

BOULEVARD DE L'OULLE

C

PASSAGE DE L'ORATOIRE

RUE JOSEPH VERNET

RUE ST-AGRICOL

⓬ RUE DE MONS

Maison Jean-Vilar

Hôtel de Ville

St-Pierre

Eglise St-Agricol

Palais du Roure

RUE DES MARCHANDS

PLACE DU CHANGE

RUE VIALA

⓮

⓯

RUE PTE. CALADE

RUE VICTOR HUGO

RUE GALANTE

⓱ E

RUE BANCASSE

RUE DES TEINTURIERS

RUE D'ANNANELLE

Musée Vouland

Musée Calvet

RUE DE LA BOULQUERIE

RUE DE LA RÉPUBLIQUE

St-Didier

Porte St-Dominique

Musée Requien

RUE BOISSERIN

PLACE ST-DIDIER

Library

BOULEVARD ST-DOMINIQUE

RUE VELOUTERIE

Musée Lapidaire

RUE F. MISTRAL

⓲

RUE DES 3 FAUCONS

RUE DES

Musée Angladon-Dubrujeaud

RUE JOSEPH VERNET

F

RUE HENRI FABRE

(i)

PL. DES CORPS SAINTS

Collection Lambert

BOULEVARD RASPAIL

RUE ST-CHARLES

H

G

RUE A. PERDIGUIER

TCRA Office

COURS JEAN-JAURÈS

❶

㉑

AV. L. DE TASSIGNY

Anc. Couvent des Célestins

Porte St-Roch

ARUE PAUL MÉRINDOL

AVENUE EISENHOWER

AV. PRES KENNEDY

BOULEVARD ST-ROCH

Porte St-Charles

Porte de la République

BOULEVARD ST-ROCH

Gare Routière

AVENUE DU BLANCHISSAGE

PLACE DE LA RÉPUBLIQUE

AV. MONCLAR NORD

Gare SNCF

0   200 m

TGV Station

968

Villeneuve-lès-Avignon

Nîmes

⓯ PROVENCE

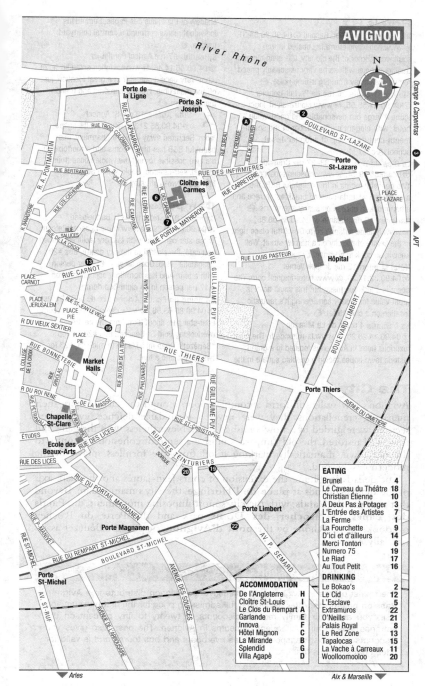

River Rhône

N

Porte de
la Ligne

Porte St-
Joseph

RUE TROIS COLOMBES

RUE PALAPHARNERIE

R. A. PONTMARTIN

RUE BERTRAND

RUE JJ PILA'S

RUE ST-CATHERINE

R BANASTERIE

R. SALUCES

RUE DE LA CROIX

P. DES CARMES

RUE LEDRU-ROLLIN

RUE CAMPANE

RUE PORTAIL MATHERON

RUE DES INFIRMIÈRES

RUE CARRETERIE

BOULEVARD ST-LAZARE

Porte St-
Joseph

Porte
St-Lazare

PLACE
ST-LAZARE

Cloître les
Carmes

6

7

A

RUE SIREAU

RUE CREMADE

R. DE L'AMOUIER

RUE LOUIS PASTEUR

RUE GUILLAUME PUY

Hôpital

13

RUE CARNOT

PLACE
CARNOT

PLACE
JERUSALEM

RUE ST-JEAN LE VIEUX

PLACE
PIE

R DU VIEUX SEXTIER

PLACE
PIE

16

RUE BONNETERIE

R. COLLEGE
DE LA CROIX

RUE GRIVOLAS

RUE ANGLADE

Market
Halls

RUE DU FOUR DE LA TERRE

RUE PHILONARDE

RUE THIERS

RUE PAUL-SAIN

BOULEVARD LIMBERT

Porte Thiers

AVENUE DU CIMETIERE

RUE DU ROI RENE

R. PETRAMALE

Chapelle
St-Clare

ÉTUDES

Ecole des
Beaux-Arts

RUE DES LICES

RUE DES LICES

R. DE LA MASSE

RUE ST-CHRISTOPHE

RUE GUILLAUME PUY

RUE DES TEINTURIERS

SORGUE

20

19

RUE DU PORTAIL MAGNANEN

Porte Limbert

Porte Magnanen

22

AV. P. SEMARD

RUE ST-MANUEL

Porte
St-Michel

BOULEVARD ST-MICHEL

RUE DU REMPART ST-MICHEL

AVENUE DES SOURCES

AVENUE DE L'ARROSAGE

AV. ST-RUF

RUE P. MANIVET

Arles

Aix & Marseille

Orange & Carpentras

3

APT

15

PROVENCE

969

2

EATING	
Brunel	4
Le Caveau du Théâtre	18
Christian Étienne	10
A Deux Pas à Potager	3
L'Entrée des Artistes	7
La Ferme	1
La Fourchette	9
D'ici et d'ailleurs	14
Merci Tonton	6
Numero 75	19
Le Riad	17
Au Tout Petit	16

DRINKING	
Le Bokao's	2
Le Cid	12
L'Esclave	5
Extramuros	22
O'Neills	21
Palais Royal	8
Le Red Zone	13
Tapalocas	15
La Vache à Carreaux	11
Woolloomooloo	20

ACCOMMODATION	
De l'Angleterre	H
Cloître St-Louis	I
Le Clos du Rempart	A
Garlande	E
Innova	F
Hôtel Mignon	C
La Mirande	B
Splendid	G
Villa Agapè	D

Hotels

De l'Angleterre 29 bd Raspail ☎04.90.86.34.31, ⓦwww.hotelangleterre.fr. Located in the southwest corner of the old city, this is an old and traditional hotel with some very reasonably priced rooms, well away from night-time noise. ❷

Cloître St-Louis 20 rue de Portail-Boquier ☎04.90.27.55.55, ⓦwww.cloitre-saint-louis .com. A large but personable and good-value hotel, with elegant modern decor in the seventeenth-century setting of a former Jesuit school. A/c. ❽

Le Clos du Rempart 33–37 rue Cremade ☎04.90.86.39.14, ⓦwww.closdurempart.com. Two peaceful rooms in this delightful B&B; there's a wonderful wisteria-covered breakfast terrace and a hammock to doze in on sunny afternoons. ❼

Garlande 20 rue Galante ☎04.90.85.08.85, ⓦwww.hotelgarlande.com. Delightful place right in the centre of the city on a narrow street. Well known, so book in advance. ❹

Hôtel Mignon 12 rue Joseph Vernet ☎04.90.82.17.30, ⓦwww.hotel-mignon.com. The decor is a little too fussy, but this small hotel is great value for money considering it's fantastic location on a chic street. ❸

La Mirande 4 place de La Mirande ☎04.90.14.20.20, ⓦwww.la-mirande.fr. The most luxurious hotel in Avignon is located in a grand historic town house facing a cobbled square in the shadow of the Palais des Papes. Sumptuous individual rooms surround a central courtyard garden. ❾

Splendid 17 rue Agricol Perdiguier ☎04.90.86.14.46, ⓦwww.avignon-splendid-hotel .com. Very decent one-star in a great location, just off the main drag. Fresh bathrooms and friendly management. ❸

Villa Agapè 13 rue St Agricol ☎04.90.85.21.92, ⓦwww.villa-agape .com. Secreted away above a pharmacy, this beautiful B&B has three rooms and a rooftop pool. It's also possible to rent the whole house (four rooms), self-catered. Book well in advance. Minimum two-night stay. ❻

Campsites

Camping Bagatelle Île de la Barthelasse ☎04.90.86.30.39, ⓦwww.campingbagatelle.com. Three-star campsite, with laundry facilities, a shop and café; the closest to the city centre. Bus #20 "Bagatelle" stop. Open all year. €14 per person with a tent. Also has dormitory accommodation (€17 per person in an eight-bed dorm).

Camping du Pont d'Avignon Île de la Barthelasse ☎04.90.80.63.50, ⓦwww.camping-avignon.com. Four-star site, about 3km from the centre, overlooking Pont St-Bénézet. Bus #20 to stop "Bénézet". Open mid-March to mid-Oct. €23 for two people and a tent.

The City

Avignon's low walls still form a complete loop around the city. Despite their menacing crenellations, they were never a formidable defence, even when sections were girded by a now-vanished moat. Nevertheless with the gates and towers all restored, the old ramparts still give a sense of cohesion and unity to the old town, dramatically marking it off from the formless sprawl of the modern city beyond.

Rue de la République, the extension of cours Jean-Jaurès and the main axis of the old town, ends at **place de l'Horloge**, the city's main square. Beyond that is **place du Palais**, with the city's most imposing monument, the **Palais des Papes**, the **Rocher des Doms** park and the Porte du Rocher, overlooking the Rhône by the **pont d'Avignon**, or pont St–Bénézet as it's officially known.

Avignon Passion passports

The tourist offices in Avignon and Villeneuve-lès-Avignon distribute free **Avignon Passion passports**. After paying the full admission price for the first museum you visit, you and your family receive discounts of twenty to fifty percent on the entrance fees of all subsequent museums in Avignon. The pass also gives you discounts on tourist transport (such as riverboats and bus tours), and is valid for fifteen days after its first use

The Palais des Papes

Rising high above the east side of place du Palais is the vast **Palais des Papes** (daily: summer 9am–7pm; winter 9.30am–6.30pm, subject to variations; last ticket 1hr before closing; €9.50, €11.50 for palace and the Pont, €7.50 with the Avignon Passion passport; ticket includes an audioguide; guided tours on request). With its massive stone vaults, battlements and sluices for pouring hot oil on attackers, the palace was built primarily as a fortress, though the two pointed towers that hover above its gate are incongruously graceful. Inside the palace, so little remains of the original decoration and furnishings that you can be deceived into thinking that all the popes and their retinues were as pious and austere as the last official occupant, Benedict XIII. The denuded interior leaves hardly a whiff of the corruption and decadence of fat, feuding cardinals and their mistresses, the thronging purveyors of jewels, velvet and furs, musicians, chefs and painters competing for patronage, the riotous banquets and corridor schemings.

The visit begins in the **Pope's Tower**, otherwise known as the Tower of Angels. You enter the **Treasury** where the serious business of the church's deeds and finances went on. Four large holes found in the floor (covered over) of the smaller downstairs room served as safes. The same cunning storage device was used for the chamberlain who lived upstairs in the **Chambre du Camérier** (just off the Jesus Hall), where the safes have been revealed. As he was the Pope's right-hand man, the quarters would have been lavishly decorated, but successive occupants have left their mark, most recently military whitewash, and what is now visible is a confusion of layers. The other door in this room leads into the **Papal Vestiary**, where the Pope would dress before sessions in the consistory. He also had a small library here and could look out onto the gardens below.

A door on the north side of the Jesus Hall leads to the **Consistoire** of the **Vieux Palais**, where sovereigns and ambassadors were received and the canonizations examined and proclaimed. The room was damaged by fire in 1413, and the only decoration that remains are fragments of frescoes moved from the cathedral, and a nineteenth-century line-up of the popes, in which all nine look remarkably similar thanks to the artist using the same model for each portrait. As you cross from the Vieux Palais to the **Palais Neuf**, Clement VI's bedroom and the Chambre du Cerf – his study – are further evidence of this pope's secular concerns, the walls in the former adorned with wonderful entwined oak and vine leaf motifs, the latter with superb hunting and fishing scenes. But austerity resumes in the cathedral-like proportions of the **Grande Chapelle**, or Chapelle Clementine, and in the **Grande Audience**, its twin in terms of volume on the floor below.

Around the Palais des Papes

Next to the Palais des Papes, the **Cathédrale Notre-Dame-des-Doms** might once have been a luminous Romanesque structure, but the interior has had a bad attack of Baroque, and the result is a stifling clutter. There's greater reward behind, in the peaceful **Rocher des Doms** park, which has fountains, ducks and views over the river to Villeneuve and beyond, along with a little café.

The **Petit Palais** (daily except Tues: June–Sept 10am–1pm & 2–6pm; Oct–May 9.30am–1pm & 2–5.30pm; €6), not far from the park's main entrance, contains a daunting collection of first-rate thirteenth- to fifteenth-century painting and sculpture, most of it by masters from northern Italian cities. As you progress through the collection, you can watch as the masters wrestle with and finally conquer the representation of perspective – a revolution from medieval art, where the size of figures depended on their importance rather than position.

▲ Palais des Papes, Avignon

Behind the Petit Palais, and well signposted, is the half-span of Pont St-Bénézet, or the **Pont d'Avignon** (same hours as Palais des Papes; €4, €11.50 combined ticket with Palais des Papes, audioguide in English included), canonized in the famous song "Sur le pont d'Avignon". One theory has it that the lyrics say "*Sous le pont*" (under the bridge) rather than "*Sur le pont*" (on the bridge) because they refer to the thief and trickster clientele of a tavern on the Île de la Barthelasse (which the bridge once crossed on its way to Villeneuve) who danced with glee at the arrival of more potential victims. Keeping the bridge in repair from the ravages of the Rhône was finally abandoned in 1660, three and a half centuries after it was built, and only four of the original 22 arches remain, but the bridge's failure over the centuries to withstand the rigours of its function didn't stop its builder, Bénézet, from becoming the patron saint of architects.

Around place de l'Horloge

The café-lined **place de l'Horloge**, frenetically busy most of the time, is the site of the city's imposing **Hôtel de Ville** and **clock tower**, and the **Opéra**. Around the square, on rues de Mons, Molière and Corneille, famous faces appear in windows painted on the buildings. Many of these figures from the past were visitors to Avignon, and of those who recorded their impressions of the city it was the sound of over a hundred bells ringing that stirred them most. On a Sunday morning, traffic lulls permitting, you can still hear myriad different peals from churches, convents and chapels in close proximity.

To the south, just behind rue St-Agricol on rue Collège du Roure, is the beautiful fifteenth-century **Palais du Roure**, a centre of Provençal culture. The gateway and the courtyard are definitely worth a look; there may well be temporary art exhibitions, and if you want a rambling tour through the attics to see Provençal costumes, publications and presses, photographs of the Camargue in the 1900s and an old stagecoach, you need to turn up at 3pm on Tuesday (€4.60).

To the west of place de l'Horloge are the most desirable Avignon addresses – both now and three hundred years ago – and it's below the mellow stone facades along **rue Joseph–Vernet** and **rue Petite-Fusterie** that you'll find Avignon's most luxurious shops.

Musée Calvet and around

The excellent, airy **Musée Calvet** is housed in a lovely eighteenth-century palace at 65 rue Joseph-Vernet (daily except Tues: June–Sept 10am–6pm; Oct–May 10am–1pm & 2–6pm; €6). The collection includes a wonderful **Galerie des Sculptures** made up of a handful of languorous nineteenth-century marble sculptures, including Bosio's *Young Indian*. The gallery also houses the Puech collection with a large selection of silverware, Italian and Dutch paintings. Upstairs you'll find works by Soutine, Manet and Joseph Vernet, as well as the subtle, moving *Death of Young Barra* by Jacques-Louis David and Géricault's *Battle of Nazareth*.

Avignon's remaining museums are considerably less compelling. Next door to the Musée Calvet is the **Musée Requien** (Tues–Sat June–Sept 10am–6pm; Oct–May 10am–1pm & 2–6pm; free); its subject is natural history and its sole advantage is in being free and having clean toilets. With little more to recommend it is the **Musée Lapidaire**, a museum of Roman and Gallo-Roman stones housed in the Baroque chapel at 27 rue de la République (same hours as Musee Requien; €2). Finally, at the **Musée Vouland**, at the end of rue Victor-Hugo near Porte St-Dominique (Tues–Sat: May–Oct noon–6pm; Nov–April 2–6pm; €6), you can feast your eyes on the fittings, fixtures and furnishings that French aristocrats enjoyed both before and after the Revolution. Just west of the tourist office, down rue Violette, is the **Collection Lambert** (Tues–Sun: July & Aug 11am–7pm; Sept–June 11am–6pm; €5.50), Avignon's only attempt at a contemporary art gallery, which shows off works by the likes of Cy Twombly, Jasper Johns and Nan Goldin, and has three temporary exhibitions each year.

Rue de la République to place Pie

Between the chainstore blandness of rue de la République and the hideous modern **market hall** on **place Pie** (mornings Tues–Sun) is the main pedestrian precinct, centring on **place de la Principale**. **Rue des Marchands** and **rue du Vieux-Sextier** have their complement of chapels and late medieval mansions, in particular the **Hôtel des Rascas** on the corner of rue des Marchands and rue Fourbisseurs, and the **Hôtel de Belli** on the corner of rue Fourbisseurs and rue du Vieux-Sextier. The Renaissance **church of St-Pierre** on place St-Pierre has superb doors sculpted in 1551, and a retable dating from the same period. More Renaissance art is on show in the fourteenth-century **church of St-Didier** (daily 8am–6.30pm), chiefly *The Carrying of the Cross* by Francesco Laurana, commissioned by King René of Provence in 1478. There are also fourteenth-century frescoes in the left-hand chapel.

Rue de la République to rue des Teinturiers

Between rue de la République and place St-Didier, on rue Labourer, is the worthwhile **Musée Angladon** (Wed–Sun 1–6pm, plus Tues in high season; €6), displaying the remains of the private collection of Jacques Doucet. The upper floor houses cosy rooms filled with Doucet's most-cherished pieces, with further rooms dedicated to Renaissance art, seventeenth and eighteenth-century art (including an orientalist room), showing items collected by Doucet's great nephew, Jean Angladon. The paintings here are alone worth the admission price, and include Modigliani's *The Pink Blouse*, various Picasso and Cezanne still lives, along with Van Gogh's *The Railroad Cars*, the only painting from Van Gogh's stay in Provence to be on permanent display in the region.

Through the park by the tourist office (where there's an old British red phone box) you come to **place des Corps-Saints**, a lively area of cafés and restaurants whose tables fill the square. Just to the north, rue des Lices runs eastwards, past the École des Beaux-Arts, to **rue des Teinturiers**, the city's most atmospheric street. Its name refers to the eighteenth- and nineteenth-century business of calico printing. The cloth was washed in the Sorgue canal which still runs alongside the street, turning the wheels of long-gone mills, and, although the water is fairly murky and sometimes smelly, this is still a great street for evening strolls, with a large number of cheap restaurants.

The Banasterie and Carmes quartiers

The **quartier de la Banasterie**, lying immediately east of the Palais des Papes and north of place Pie, is almost solid seventeenth and eighteenth century, and the heavy wooden doors, with their highly sculptured lintels, today bear the nameplates of lawyers, psychiatrists and doctors. Here, tourist-oriented commercialism is kept in check, and at night in particular this is an atmospheric and beautiful part of the city.

Between Banasterie and **place des Carmes** are a tangle of tiny streets guaranteed to get you lost. Pedestrians have priority over cars on many of them, and there are plenty of tempting café or restaurant stops.

Eating and drinking

Avignon has a huge selection of **restaurants**, ranging from the expensive, gastronomic types to cheap, fast food eateries. The large terraced café-brasseries on place de l'Horloge and rue de la République all serve quick, if not necessarily memorable, meals. Rue des Teinturiers is good if you're on a budget, and the streets between place Crillon and place du Palais are full of temptation if you're not.

Restaurants and cafés

A Deux pas à potager 46 rue Edmond Delteil, around 2km east of Avignon ☎04.90.85.46.41. The name means "Two steps from the kitchen garden" and indeed, everything that the outstandingly friendly chef, Didier Mariani, cooks up at this beautiful, tiny restaurant is as fresh as can be. Menus range from €29–82; expect sublime dishes like green lentils with foie gras vinaigrette and crunchy pancetta. Closed Sun evening & Mon.

Brunel 46 rue Balance ☎04.90.85.24.83. Superb regional dishes; *plat du jour* for €11. Closed Sun & Mon & first half of Aug.

Le Caveau du Theatre 16 rue des Trois Faucons ☎04.90.82.60.91. Expect incredibly delicious dishes such as market-fresh fish with an artichoke and champagne reduction (€13). Pretty painted walls, jolly red tables and occasional jazz.

Christian Étienne 10 rue de Mons ☎04.90.86.16.50. One of Avignon's best restaurants, housed in a fourteenth-century mansion and offering mouthwatering delights such as whole lobster with ginger, asparagus and sesame seeds followed by orange and carrot macaroons

with almond sorbet. Menus €35–120. Closed Sun & Mon.

L'Entrée des Artistes 1 place des Carmes ☎04.90.82.46.90. Cool, small bistro serving traditional French dishes; €26 menu. No bank cards. Closed Sun & Mon.

La Fourchette 17 rue de Racine ☎04.90.85.20.93. Popular, refined restaurant serving classic and sophisticated fish and meat dishes. Try the tasty sardines marinated in coriander. Closed Sat & Sun.

D'ici et d'ailleurs 4 rue Galante ☎04.90.14.63.65. Tasteful modern surroundings, inexpensive Provençal dishes from "here", international flavours from "there". Mains around €16. Service until 11pm; closed Sun & Mon.

Merci Tonton 21 place des Carmes ☎04.32.70.02.34. Cute, down-to-earth restaurant serving traditional French food on its atmospheric terrace or in the funky little garden out the back.

Numero 75 75 rue Guillaume Puy, ☎04.90.27.16.00. In a beautiful mansion, *Numero 75* is a smart, sophisticated restaurant serving menus from €30.

Le Riad 17 rue Galante ☎04.90.82.10.85. The best couscous (€13) in the city. Also does delicious tagine (€13) in an airy restaurant decorated with Moroccan rugs.
Au Tout Petit 4 rue d'Amphoux ☎04.90.82 38.86. This tiny, unpretentious place stuck down a side alley near Les Halles doesn't look like much, but the food served here is imaginative, fresh and unbeatable. Two courses around €16.

Bars and clubs

Le Bokao's 9bis St-Lazare ☎04.90.82.47.95. Eclectic mix of music styles including house and techno at the weekends in a converted barn. Wed–Sat 10pm–5am.
Le Cid 11 place de l'Horloge ☎04.90.82.30.38. Trendy mixed gay/straight bar and terrace that stays open long after the rest of place de l'Horloge has closed for the night.
L'Esclave 12 rue du Limas ☎04.90.85.14.91. Avignon's gay and lesbian bar, with regular DJs, drag shows and karaoke nights. Tues–Sun from 11pm.
Extramuros 44 bd Saint-Michel ☎04.32.74.22.22, ⓦwww.extramuros.fr. As the name suggests, this cool, laidback bar lies just outside Avignon's walls.

Look out for the wall made of real Provençal soaps in the toilets. Closed Sat lunch.
O'Neill's 38 cours Jean Jaures ☎04.32.76.33.40. Extremely popular Irish pub serving the inevitable Guinness for the crowds that spill out onto the pavement.
Palais Royal place de l'Amirande ☎04.90.14.02.54. Large, buzzing bar-restaurant decorated with gold-embellished mirrors and chandeliers. Music shows Thurs–Sat; drag-queen acts on Sun.
Le Red Zone 25 rue Carnot ☎04.90.27.02.44. Bar with DJs and weekly concerts. Daily 9pm–3am.
Tapalocas 15 rue Galante ☎04.90.82.56.84. Tapas and spanish music, sometimes live, in a large, atmospheric bar. Daily noon–1am.
🏃 **Le Vache à Carreaux** 14 rue Peyrolerie ☎04.90.80.09.05. Intimate, homely wine bar that serves food and stays open till 1am.
🏃 **Woolloomooloo** 16bis rue des Teinturiers ☎04.90.85.28.44. An old printshop with all the presses still in place that oozes a relaxed vibe, with fairy lights and candles completing the boho look. Also serves food. Occasional theme nights. Closed Mon.

Theatre, music and film

There's a fair amount of nightlife and cultural events in Avignon: the **Opéra**, on place de l'Horloge (☎04.90.82.81.40, ⓦwww.operatheatredavignon.fr), mounts a good range of productions; Le Chêne Noir, 8bis rue Ste-Catherine (☎04.90.86.58.11, ⓦwww.chenenoir.fr), is a theatre company worth seeing, with mime, musicals or Molière on offer; and plenty of **classical concerts** are performed in churches, usually for free. Cinéma Utopia, at La Manutention, 4 rue Escalier Ste-Anne (☎04.90.82.65.36), shows films in *version originale* (undubbed); the same complex houses the *AJMI Jazz Club* (☎04.90.86.08.61), which hosts live jazz and features major acts and some adventurous new groups. To find out what's on, get hold of the tourist office's free monthly calendar *Rendez-Vous*. They may also have the arts, events and music magazine *César* (free), which is otherwise found in arts centres.

Listings

Bike rental Provence Bike, 52 bd St-Roch ☎04.90.27.92.61 (also scooters and motorbikes).
Boat trips Grands Bateaux de Provence, allée de l'Oulle ☎04.90.85.62.25, ⓦavignon-et-provence .com/mireio. Offering year-round trips upstream towards Châteauneuf-du-Pape and downstream to Arles; two-week advance booking recommended.
Books Shakespeare, 155 rue Carreterie. English bookshop and *salon de thé*. Closed Sun, Mon & evenings.

Car rental National/Citer, *gare TGV* ☎04.90.27.30.07; Rent a Car, 130 av Pierre-Sémard ☎04.90.88.08.02; Sixt Eurorent, 3 av St-Ruf ☎04.90.86.06.61.
Emergencies Doctor/ambulance ☎15; hospital, Centre Hospitalier H.-Duffaut, 305 rue Raoul-Follereau ☎04.32.75.33.33; night chemist, call police ☎04.90.85.13.13 for addresses.
Internet W@M 34 rue de la Bonneterie; Webzone 3 rue St-Jean-le-Vieux/place Pie.

15

PROVENCE | Avignon

Laundry 9 rue du Chapeau-Rouge; 27 rue Portail-
Magnanen; 113 av St-Ruf.
Police ☎17.
Post office Poste, cours Président-Kennedy,
Avignon 84000.

Swimming pool Piscine Jean Clement, Chemin de
la Martelle, ☎04.90.31.38.73
Taxis place Pie ☎04.90.82.20.20. Velocité (bicycle
taxis €1 per km) ☎06.37.36.48.89.

Villeneuve-lès-Avignon

Well-to-do **VILLENEUVE-LÈS-AVIGNON** rises up a rocky escarpment
above the west bank of the Rhône, looking down on its older neighbour from
behind far more convincing fortifications. Historically, Villeneuve operated
largely as a suburb of Avignon, with palatial residences constructed by the
cardinals and a great monastery founded by Pope Innocent VI.

To this day, Villeneuve is technically a part of Languedoc and not Provence,
and would score better in the hierarchy of towns to visit were it further from
Avignon, whose monuments it can almost match for colossal scale and impres-
siveness. Despite the closeness of its relationship with Avignon it is, however, a
very different – and really rather sleepy – kind of place, and as such retains a
repose and a sense of timelessness that bustling Avignon inevitably lacks. In
summer it provides venues for the Avignon Festival as well as alternatives for
accommodation overspill, and it's certainly worth a day, whatever time of year
you visit.

Arrival and information

From Avignon's post office on cours Président-Kennedy, across the way from the
gare SNCF, the half-hourly #11 bus (take care not to go in the direction "Les
Angles–Villeneuve") runs direct to place Charles-David ("Office du Tourisme"
stop) taking less than ten minutes, or five if you catch it from Porte d'Oulle. After
7.30pm you'll have to take a taxi or walk – it's only 3km. Place Charles-David
is where you'll find both the **tourist office** (Mon–Sat 9am–12.30pm & 2–6pm;
July Mon–Fri 10am–7pm, Sat & Sun 10am–1pm & 2.30–7pm; ☎04.90.25.61.33,
ⓦ www.villeneuvelezavignon.fr/tourisme), and a food **market** on Thursday
morning and bric-a-brac on Saturday morning. A little south of the square rue
Farigoule runs west to rue de la République, the main street, which runs due
north past place Jean-Jaurès. It's here you'll find what limited restaurant and bar
life there is.

Accommodation

L'Atelier 5 rue de la Foire ☎04.90.25.01.84,
ⓦ www.hoteldelatelier.com. A sixteenth-century
house with a central stone staircase bathed in light,
with huge open fireplaces and a shady walled
garden. ❹
Les Écuries des Chartreux 66 rue de la République ☎04.90.25.79.93, ⓦ www.ecuries-des
-chartreux.com. B&B in a light and airy rustic
house with exposed stone walls and antique
furniture. ❹
Jardin de la Livrée 4bis rue Camp de Bataille
☎04.90.26.05.05, ⓦ www.la-livree.oxatis.com.
B&B in an old house in the centre of the village

with comfortable rooms around a swimming pool;
also has a good-value restaurant. ❺
Le Prieuré 7 place du Chapitre ☎04.90.15.90.15,
ⓦ www.leprieure.com. The first choice if money is
no object. An old priory surrounded by a peaceful
garden full of flowers. The restaurant serves
Provençal cuisine with a gourmet twist. Rooms
from €205; apartment from €410. ❾

Hostel and campsite
YMCA hostel 7bis chemin de la Justice
☎04.90.25.46.20, ⓦ www.ymca-avignon.com.
Beautifully situated overlooking the river by Pont

du Royaume, with balconied rooms for one to four people (€23 for dorm bed) and an open-air swimming pool (stop "Pont d'Avignon" on Avignon–Villeneuve bus or "Gabriel Péri" on the Villeneuve–Avignon bus).

Camping Municipal de la Laune chemin St-Honoré ℡04.90.25.76.06. A three-star site off the D980, near the sports stadium and swimming pools. €5.50 per person. Open mid-March to mid-Oct.

The Town

For a good overview of Villeneuve – and Avignon – make your way to the **Tour Philippe-le-Bel** at the bottom of montée de la Tour (bus stop "Philippe-le-Bel"). This tower was built to guard the French end of Avignon's Pont St-Bénézet (or Pont d'Avignon), and a rather tricky climb to the top (April–Sept 10am–12.30pm & 2–6.30pm; Oct–March 10am–noon & 2–5.30pm; closed Mon & Dec–Feb; €2) will be rewarded with stunning views.

Even more indicative of French distrust of its neighbours is the enormous **Fort St-André** (daily: April–Sept 10am–1pm & 2–6pm; Oct–March 10am–1pm & 2–5pm; €5), whose bulbous double-towered gateway and vast walls loom over the town. Inside, refreshingly, there's not a hint of a postcard stall or souvenir shop – just tumbledown houses and the former **abbey**, with its gardens of olive trees, ruined chapels, lily ponds and dovecotes (Tues–Sun: July & Aug 10am–12.30pm & 2–6pm; Sept–June 10am–noon & 2–5pm; €4). You can reach the approach to the fortress, montée du Fort, from place Jean-Jaurès on rue de la République, or by the "rapid slope" of **rue Pente-Rapide**, a cobbled street of tiny houses leading off rue des Récollets on the north side of place Charles-David.

Almost at the top of rue de la République, on the right, allée des Muriers leads from place des Chartreux to the entrance of **La Chartreuse du Val de Bénédiction** (daily: April–Sept 9.30am–6pm; Oct–March 9.30am–5pm; €8). This Carthusian monastery, one of the largest in France, was founded by the sixth of the Avignon popes, Innocent VI (pope 1352–62). The buildings, which were sold off after the Revolution and gradually restored last century, are totally unembellished. With the exception of the Giovanetti frescoes in the chapel beside the refectory, all the paintings and treasures of the monastery have been dispersed, leaving you with a strong impression of the austerity of the Carthusian order. You're free to wander around unguided, through the three cloisters, the church, chapels, cells and communal spaces, which have little to see but plenty of atmosphere to absorb. It's one of the best venues in the Festival of Avignon.

Another festival venue is the fourteenth-century **Église Collègiale Notre-Dame** and its cloister on place St-Marc close to the *mairie* (April–Sept 10am–12.30pm & 2–6.30pm; Oct–March daily 10am–noon & 2–5pm; free). Notre-Dame's most important treasure is a rare fourteenth-century smiling Madonna and Child made from a single tusk of ivory, now housed, along with many of the paintings from the Chartreuse, in the **Musée Pierre-de-Luxembourg**, just to the north along rue de la République (same hours as Église Collègiale Notre-Dame; €3), which is itself given over to the most stunning painting in the collection – *The Coronation of the Virgin*, painted in 1453 by Enguerrand Quarton as the altarpiece for the church in the Chartreuse.

Eating and drinking

Aubertin 1 rue de l'Hôpital ℡04.90.25.94.84. In the shade of the old arcades by the Collègiale Notre-Dame. Simple local dishes followed by fabulous desserts: try the chocolate and raspberry tart. €40 menu. Closed Sun & Mon.

La Banaste 28 rue de la République ℡04.90.25.64.20. Serves plentiful *terroir* meals. Menus from €33. Closed Thurs low season.

La Cigale 38 rue de la Republique ℡04.32.70.22.34. Inexpensive restaurant

specializing in fish dishes. *Plats* around €10.
Closed Wed.

La Magnanerie 37 rue Camp de Bataille
☎04.90.25.11.11. For blowout posh nosh off rue
de la République, with an evening menu for €33 (à
la carte over €33).

Le Prieuré 7 place du Chapitre ☎04.90.15.90.15.
Luxurious restaurant serving fresh, simple dishes
such as saddle of rabbit with asparagus and, for
after, pear meringue. Menus from €40.

St-Rémy-de-Provence and the Alpilles

The watery and intensely cultivated scenery of the Petite Crau plain south of
Avignon changes abruptly with the eruption of the **Chaîne des Alpilles**,
whose peaks look like the surf of a wave about to engulf the plain. At their
northern foot nestles **ST-RÉMY-DE-PROVENCE**, a lovely, dreamy place
whose busy boulevards contain an old town no more than half a kilometre in
diameter.

The best time to visit St-Rémy is during the **Fête de Transhumance** on Whit
Monday (around mid- to late-May), when a two thousand-strong flock of sheep,
accompanied by goats and donkeys, does a tour of the town before being packed
off to the Alps for the summer. Another good time to come is for the **Carreto
Ramado**, on August 15, a harvest thanksgiving procession in which the religious
or secular symbolism of the floats reveals the political colour of the various village
councils, while a pagan rather than workers' **May Day** is celebrated with donkey-
drawn floral floats on which people play fifes and tambourines.

Arrival and information

There's no train station in St-Rémy; **buses** from Avignon, Aix and Arles drop you
in place de la République, the main square abutting the old town on the east. The
tourist office, at place Jean-Jaurès (Easter to Oct Mon–Sat 9am–12.30pm &
2–7pm, Sun 10am–noon; Nov to Easter Mon–Sat 9am–noon & 2–6pm;
☎04.90.92.05.22, ⓦwww.saintremy-de-provence.com) has excellent free guides
to **cycling and walking routes** in and around the Alpilles and can provide
addresses for **horse riding** stables. If you want to rent a **bike**, try Telecycles
(☎04.90.92.83.15, ⓦwww.telecycles-location.com). Without a car, it's difficult to
get to Glanum or Les Baux except by foot or taxi (☎06.09.52.71.54 or
04.90.92.46.92).

Accommodation

Accommodation in St-Remy is of a high standard, and it's all fairly pricey.

Le Castellet des Alpilles 6 place Mireille
☎04.90.92.07.21, ⓦwww.castelet-alpilles.com.
Pleasant, traditional rooms in a hotel situated on
the road up towards Glanum. Open March–Nov. ⑤

Le Soleil 35 av Pasteur ☎04.90.92.00.63,
ⓦwww.hotelsoleil.com. Welcoming place with a
pool and private parking. ③

Hotel Sous Les Figuiers at 3 av Taillandier
☎04.32.60.15.40, ⓦwww.hotel-charme
-provence.com. Gorgeous place run by a creative
team of photographer and painter; there are
thirteen delightful rooms centring on a peaceful
fig-tree orchard. ⑥

Campsites

Le Mas de Nicolas 800m from the centre on a
turning off the route de Mollèges
☎04.90.92.27.05, ⓦmasdenicolas.celeonet.fr.
Municipal campsite offering plenty of activities
including table tennis and pétanque. €19 for two
people. Open mid-March to mid-Oct.

Monplaisir 1km from the centre on chemin de
Monplaisir ☎04.90.92.22.70, ⓦwww.camping
-monplaisir.fr. Family-run, five-acre campsite with a
pool and snack facilities. €19.50 for two people;
open March–Oct.

The Town

To reach the old town from place de la République, take avenue de la Résistance, which runs alongside the town's imposing main church, the **Collégiale St-Martin**, and wander up the boutique-adorned alleyways into tranquil, leafy squares. For an introduction to the region, a good first visit would be to the **Musée des Alpilles** on place Favier, housed in the Hôtel Mistral de Mondragon (daily: Feb–Nov 10am–noon & 2–6pm; Dec–Jan 2–5pm; €3). The museum features interesting displays on folklore, festivities and traditional crafts, plus some intriguing local landscapes, creepy portraits by Marshal Pétain's first wife and souvenirs of local boy Nostradamus.

On rue Hoche is the birthplace of Michel de Nostredame – aka **Nostradamus** – the well-known physician and astrologer. Today he is most often given credit for predicting the rise of Napoleon and Hitler, and major catastrophes such as the Great Fire of London in 1666. The facade of the house is contemporary with the savant, however the building is not open for visits. The Hôtel d'Estrine, 8 rue Estrine, houses the **Centre d'Art Présence Van Gogh** (April to mid-Oct Tues–Sun 10.30am–1pm & 3–7pm; mid-Oct to Dec Tues–Sun 10.30am–12.30pm & 2–6pm; €3.20), which hosts contemporary art exhibitions and has a permanent exhibition of Van Gogh reproductions and extracts from letters, as well as audiovisual presentations on the painter.

Eating and drinking

You'll find plenty of **brasseries** and **restaurants** in and around old St-Rémy, the best of them on rue Carnot and on boulevards Mirabeau and Gambetta.

L'Aile ou la Cuisse 5 rue de la Commune ☎04.32.62.00.2. Offers posh picnic items, as well as delectable jams and olive oils; lunch and à la carte dinner is around €23. Closed Sun & Mon.
Divin 12 bd Gambetta. Bang next to the Café du Lezard – they share the same address – this cool bar is decked out in dark, saloon-like wood.
Grain de Sel 25 bd Mirabeau ☎04.90.92.00.89. Chic restaurant serving menus from €27, which include fantastic desserts such as rhubarb compote with frozen almond milk. Closed Sat & Sun in low season, Wed evening in high season.
Le Jardin de Frederic 8 bd Gambetta ☎04.90.92.27.76. Lovely, flower-decked restaurant serving interesting, fresh dishes like home-smoked salmon with vodka cream (€12.50). Closed Mon.
Café du Lezard 12 bd Gambetta. Very much a local watering hole, so if you want to escape the tourists, head here. Funky, eclectic décor.

South of St-Rémy

The four main sites south of St-Rémy, **St-Paul-de-Mausole**, **Mas de la Pyramid**, **Les Antiques** and **Glanum** are perfectly walkable at about 1.5km. Parking can be tricky, so get there early; it costs €4.

St-Paul-de-Mausole

The old monastery **St-Paul-de-Mausole** was home to **Vincent Van Gogh**, in 1889-1890 after he requested he be put under medical care for several months. He was living in Arles at the time, and his friends chose this monastery for him; it remains a psychiatric clinic today. Although the regime was more prison than hospital, Van Gogh was allowed to wander out around the Alpilles and painted prolifically during his twelve-month stay. *The Oliviers' Fields*, *The Reaper*, *The Enclosed Field* and *The Evening Stroll* are among the 150 canvases of this period. The **church**, **cloisters** and the enlightening reconstruction of Van Gogh's **room** can be visited (April–Sept 9.30am–7pm; Oct–March 10.15am–5pm; €4): take avenue Edgar-Leroy or allée St-Paul from avenue Vincent-Van-Gogh, go past the main entrance of the clinic and into the gateway on the left at the end of the wall.

Mas de la Pyramide

Not very far beyond the hospital is a signposted farm called **Mas de la Pyramide** (daily: July & Aug 9am–noon & 2–7pm; Sept–June 9am–noon & 2–5pm; €4). It's an old troglodyte farm in the Roman quarries for Glanum with a lavender and cherry orchard surrounded by cavernous openings into the rock filled with ancient farm equipment and rusting bicycles. The farmhouse is part medieval and part Gallo-Roman, with pictures of the owner's family who have lived there for generations.

Les Antiques

Opposite the exit to St Paul-de-Mausole is **Les Antiques** (free access), a triumphal arch supposedly celebrating the Roman conquest of Marseille, and a mausoleum thought to commemorate two grandsons of Augustus. Save for a certain amount of weather erosion, the mausoleum is perfectly intact, while on the arch you can still make out the sculptures of fruits and leaves representing the fertility of "the Roman Province" (hence "Provence"), and the figures of chained captives, symbolizing Roman might.

Glanum

One of the most impressive ancient settlements in France, **Glanum**, 500m south of Les Antiques (daily: April–Aug 10am–6.30pm; Sept–March Tues–Sun 10.30am–5pm; €6.50), was dug out from alluvial deposits at the very foot of the Alpilles. The site was originally a Neolithic homestead; then, between the second and first centuries BC, the Gallo-Greeks, probably from Massalia (Marseille), built a city here, on which the Gallo-Romans, from the end of the first century BC to the third century AD, constructed yet another town.

Though Glanum is one of the most important archeological sites in France, it can be very difficult to get to grips with. Not only were the later buildings moulded onto the earlier, but the fashion at the time of Christ was for a Hellenistic style. You can distinguish the Greek levels from the Roman most easily by the stones: the earlier civilization used massive hewn rocks while the Romans preferred smaller and more accurately shaped stones. The leaflet at the admission desk is very helpful.

The site is bisected by a road running from north to south, with several **Hellenic houses** to the northwest. East of here are the **Thermes**, a complex of furnaces, bathing chambers and pools. A **forum** dating from Roman times is south of here, near a restored **theatre** and the superb sculptures on the Roman **Temples Geminées** (Twin Temples). As the site narrows in the ravine at the southern end, you'll find a Grecian edifice around a **sacred spring** – the feature that made this location so desirable. Steps lead down to a pool, with a slab above for the libations of those too disabled to descend. An inscription records that Agrippa was responsible for restoring it in 27 BC and dedicating it to Valetudo, the Roman goddess of health.

Les Baux and the Val d'Enfer

At the top of the Alpilles ridge, 7km southwest of St-Rémy, lies the distinctly unreal fortified village of **LES BAUX-DE-PROVENCE**, where the ruined eleventh-century citadel is hard to distinguish from the edge of the plateau,

▲ Fortress at Les Baux

whose rock is both foundation and part of the structure. Within walking distance of Les Baux, along the D27 leading northwards, is the valley of quarried and eroded rocks named the **VAL D'ENFER** – the Valley of Hell.

Once, Les Baux lived off the power and widespread possessions in Provence of its medieval lords, who owed allegiance to no one. When the dynasty died out at the end of the fourteenth century, however, the town, which had once numbered six thousand inhabitants, passed to the counts of Provence and then to the kings of France. In 1632 Richelieu razed the feudal citadel to the ground and fined the population into penury for their disobedience. From that date until the nineteenth century, both citadel and village were inhabited almost exclusively by bats and crows. The discovery in the neighbouring hills of the mineral bauxite (whose name derives from "Les Baux") brought back some life to the village, and tourism has more recently transformed the place. Today the population stays steady at around four hundred, while the number of visitors exceeds 1.5 million each year. Day-tripping crowds thin rapidly in Les Baux after around 5pm so, depending on the season, it can be worthwhile turning up rather late and enjoying the splendid castle in relative peace.

The castle site

Following the signs to the château from the town will bring you to the entrance to the now-abandoned **castle site**, the main reason for coming to Les Baux (daily: March–June 9am–6.30pm; July & Aug 9am–8.30pm; Sept–Nov 9.30am–6pm; Dec–Feb 9am–5pm; €7.60 audioguide in English available, in exchange for ID) and where you can find ruins and several more museums. The most impressive ruins are those of the feudal castle demolished on Richelieu's orders; there's also the partially restored **Chapelle Castrale** and the **Tour Sarrasine**, ruined houses half carved out of the rocky escarpment and some spectacular views, the best of which is out across the Grande Crau from beside the statue of Provençal poet Charloun Riev at the southern edge of the plateau where you will also find replicas of medieval catapults and battering rams.

The Val d'Enfer

The **Val d'Enfer** gets its name from Dante's description of "Hell" in his *Divine Comedy*, which was inspired by this very place. One quarry has been turned into an audiovisual experience under the title of the **Cathédrale des Images** (daily 10am–6pm; €7), signposted to the right downhill from Les Baux's car park. The projection is continuous, so you don't have to wait to go in. You're surrounded by images projected all over the floor, ceilings and walls of these vast rectangular caverns, and by music that resonates strangely in the captured space. The content of the show, which changes yearly, doesn't really matter (recent shows include one on Van Gogh); it's an extraordinary sensation, wandering on and through the shapes and colours. As an erstwhile work site put to good use, it couldn't be bettered.

Practicalities

The **tourist office** is at the beginning of Grande-Rue (daily: July & Aug 9am–7pm; Sept–June 9am–6pm; ℡04.90.54.34.39, Ⓦwww.lesbauxdeprovence.com). You have to park – and pay – before entering the village. Nothing in Les Baux comes cheap, least of all **accommodation.** Try the B&B *Le Prince Noir*, in an artist's house on rue de l'Orme, which has bags of character (℡04.90.54.39.57, Ⓦwww.leprincenoir.com; ❺). If you're feeling rich and fancy a treat, head for the luxurious hotel-restaurant *Oustau de Baumanière*, just below Les Baux to the west on the road leading down to the Val d'Enfer (℡04.90.54.33.07, Ⓦwww.oustaudebaumaniere.com; ❾).

Arles

ARLES is a major town on the tourist circuit, its fame sealed by the extraordinarily well-preserved Roman arena, **Les Arènes**, at the city's heart, and backed by an impressive variety of other stones and monuments, both Roman and medieval. It was the key city of the region in Roman times, then, with Aix, main base of the counts of Provence before unification with France. For centuries it was Marseille's only rival, profiting from the inland trade route up the Rhône whenever the enemies of France were blocking Marseille's port. Arles declined when the railway put an end to this advantage, and it was an inward-looking depressed town that **Van Gogh** came to in the late nineteenth century. Today it's a staid and conservative place with an unmistakable small-town feel, but comes to life for the **Saturday market**, which brings in throngs of farmers from the surrounding countryside, and during the various **festivals** of *tauromachie* between Easter and All Saints, when the town's frenzy for bulls rivals that of neighbouring Nîmes.

Arrival and information

Arriving by train eases you gently into the city, with the **gare SNCF** conveniently located a few blocks to the north of the Arènes. Most buses also arrive here at the

Museum passes

The **Pass Monuments** (€15) grants free admission to all of Arles' museums and monuments, and is available either from the tourist office or at the sites themselves.

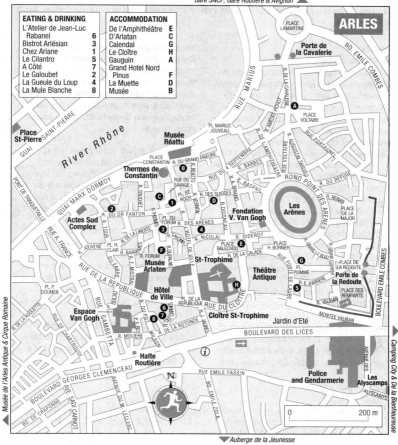

ARLES

15 PROVENCE | Arles

EATING & DRINKING	
L'Atelier de Jean-Luc Rabanel	6
Bistrot Arlésian	3
Chez Ariane	1
Le Cilantro	5
A Côté	7
Le Galoubet	2
La Gueule du Loup	4
La Mule Blanche	8

ACCOMMODATION	
De l'Amphithéâtre	E
D'Arlatan	C
Calendal	G
Le Cloître	H
Gauguin	A
Grand Hotel Nord Pinus	F
La Muette	D
Musée	B

Musée de l'Arles Antique & Cirque Romaine

Camping City & De la Bienheureuse

Auberge de la Jeunesse

unstaffed adjacent **gare routière**, though some, including all local buses, stop on the north side of boulevard Georges-Clemenceau just east of rue Gambetta. Rue Jean-Jaurès, with its continuation rue Hôtel-de-Ville, is the main axis of old Arles. At the southern end it meets boulevard Georges-Clemenceau and boulevard des Lices, with the **tourist office** directly opposite (March–Sept daily 9am–6.45pm; Oct–April Mon–Sat 9am–4.45pm, Sun 10am–1pm; ☎04.90.18.41.20, ⓦwww .arlestourisme.com); there's also an annexe in the *gare SNCF* (April–Sept Mon–Fri 9am–1.30pm & 2.30–4.45pm). You can rent **bikes** from Arles VAE, 65 avenue Paulin Talabot (☎04.90.43.33.14), or Europbike, 1 rue Philippe-Lebon (☎06.85.55.44.71), and cars from Europcar (☎04.90.93.23.24), Eurorent (☎04.90.93.50.14) or Hertz (☎04.90.96.75.23), all on avenue Victor-Hugo. For **internet**, head for *Cyber City*, 41 rue du 4 septembre.

Accommodation

There's little shortage of **hotel** rooms at either end of the scale. The best place to look for cheap rooms is in the area around Porte de la Cavalerie near the station. If you get stuck, the tourist office will find you accommodation for a €1 fee.

Hotels

De l'Amphithéâtre 5–7 rue Diderot
ⓣ04.90.96.10.30, ⓦwww.hotelamphitheatre.fr.
Situated close to Les Arènes, this place has plenty of warm colours, tiles and wrought ironwork. ❹
D'Arlatan 26 rue du Sauvage ⓣ04.90.93.56.66,
ⓦwww.hotel-arlatan.fr. A luxurious and good-value place, set in a beautiful old fifteenth-century mansion and decorated with antiques. Closed Jan. ❺
Calendal 5 rue Porte de Laure ⓣ04.90.96.11.89,
ⓦwww.lecalendal.com. Pleasant, welcoming hotel with generous rooms overlooking a garden. Closed Jan. ❺
🏃 **Le Cloître** 16 rue du Cloître
ⓣ04.90.96.29.50, ⓦwww.hotelcloitre .com. Rambling hotel in a lovely location overlooking the cloister of St Tromphime. Closed Nov to mid-March. ❸
Gauguin 5 place Voltaire ⓣ04.90.96.14.35,
ⓕ04.90.18.98.87. Comfortable, cheap and well run. Advisable to book. ❶
Grand Hotel Nord Pinus place du Forum
ⓣ04.90.93.44.44, ⓦwww.nord-pinus.com. Chic rooms in a grand old house, located at the head of a pretty, lively square in the heart of the old town. ❽
🏃 **La Muette** 13 rue des Suisses
ⓣ04.90.96.15.39, ⓦwww.hotel-muette .com. Tranquil rooms decked out in beiges and creams, along with soft, modern uplighting. Copious buffet breakfast, and friendly management. ❸
Musée 11 rue du Grand-Prieuré
ⓣ04.90.93.88.88, ⓦwww.hoteldumusee.com. Small, good-value, family-run place in a quiet location opposite Musée Réattu, with a pretty, flower-filled terrace. ❸

Hostel and campsites

Auberge de Jeunesse 20 av Maréchal Foch
ⓣ04.90.96.18.25, ⓔarles@fuaj.org. Old-style hostel with dormitory accommodation only. Bus #4 from town, direction "Fourchon"; alight at stop "Fournier". From €15.40 per bed. Open mid-June to mid-Dec.
De la Bienheureuse 7km out on the N453 at Raphèles-les-Arles ⓣ04.90.98.48.06,
ⓦwww.labienheureuse.com. Best of Arles' half-dozen campsites; the restaurant here is furnished with pieces similar to those displayed in the Musée Arlaten and full of pictures of popular Arlesian traditions. Regular buses from Arles. €13.80 for two people and a tent. Open all year.
City 67 rte de Crau ⓣ04.90.93.08.86, ⓦwww .camping-city.com. The closest campsite to town on the Crau bus route. €16 for two people and a tent. Open April–Sept.

The City

The centre of Arles fits into a neat triangle between boulevard E.-Combes to the east, boulevards Clemenceau and des Lices to the south, and the Rhône to the west. The **Musée de l'Arles Antique** is southwest of the expressway by the river, not far from the end of boulevard Clemenceau; **Les Alyscamps** is down across the train lines to the southeast. But these apart, all the **Roman and medieval monuments** are within easy walking distance in this very compact city centre.

Roman Arles

Roman Arles provided grain for most of the western empire and was one of the major ports for trade and shipbuilding. Under Constantine it became the capital of Gaul and reached its height as a world trading centre in the fifth century. Once the empire crumbled, however, Arles found itself isolated between the Rhône, the Alpilles and the marshlands of the Camargue – an isolation that allowed its Roman heritage to be preserved.

A good place to start any tour of Roman Arles is the **Musée de l'Arles Antique** (daily: April–Oct 9am–7pm; Nov–March 10am–5pm; €5.50), southwest of the town centre. It's housed in a resolutely contemporary building positioned on the axis of the second-century **Cirque Romaine**, an enormous chariot racetrack that stretches 450m from the museum to the town side of the expressway. The airy, spacious museum covers the prehistory of the area, then

Bullfighting, or more properly *tauromachie* (roughly, "the art of the bull"), comes in two styles in Arles and the Camargue. In the local **courses camarguaises**, which are held at fêtes from late spring to early autumn (the most prestigious of which is Arles' Cocarde d'Or in early July), *razeteurs* run at the bulls in an effort to pluck ribbons and cockades tied to the bulls' horns, cutting them free with special barbed gloves. The drama and grace of the spectacle is in the stylish way the men leap over the barrier away from the bull, and in the competition for prize money between the *razeteurs*. In this gentler bullfight, people are rarely injured and the bulls are not killed.

More popular, however, are the brutal Spanish-style **corridas** (late April, early July & Sept, at Arles), consisting of a strict ritual leading up to the all-but-inevitable death of the bull. After its entry into the ring, the bull is subjected to the *bandilleros* who stick decorated barbs in its back, the *picadors*, who lance it from horseback, and finally, the *torero*, who endeavours to lead the bull through as graceful a series of movements as possible before killing it with a single sword stroke to the heart. In one *corrida* six bulls are killed by three *toreros*, for whom injuries (sometimes fatal) are not uncommon. Whether you approve or not, *tauromachie*, which has a history of some centuries here, is your best way of taking part in local life and of experiencing the Roman arena in Arles (€6 per seat). The tourist office, local papers and publicity around the arena will give you the details, or call the Bureau des Arènes ☏04.90.96.03.70.

takes you through the five centuries of Roman rule, from Julius Caesar's legionary base through Christianization to the period when spices and gems from Africa and Arabia were being traded here. Fabulous mosaics are laid out with walkways above; and there are numerous sarcophagi with intricate sculpting depicting everything from music and lovers to gladiators and Christian miracles.

Back in the centre of Arles, the most impressive Roman monument is the amphitheatre, known as **Les Arènes** (daily 9am–6.30pm; €5.50, or covered by Pass Monuments – see box, p.982), dating from the end of the first century. To give an idea of its size, it used to shelter over two hundred dwellings and three churches built into the two tiers of arches that form its oval surround. This medieval quarter was cleared in 1830 and the Arènes was once more used for entertainment. Today, though missing its third storey and most of the internal stairways and galleries, it's still a very dramatic structure and a stunning venue for performances, seating twenty thousand spectators.

The **Théâtre Antique** (daily: March, April & Oct 9–11.30am & 2–5.30pm; May–Sept 9am–6pm; Nov–Feb 10–11.30am & 2–4.30pm; €3), just south of Les Arènes, comes to life during July, with the Fête du Costume in which local folk groups parade in traditional dress, and the Mosaïque Gitane Romany festival. The theatre is nowhere near as well preserved as the arena, with only one pair of columns standing, all the statuary removed and the sides of the stage littered with broken bits of stone.

At the river end of rue Hôtel-de-Ville, the **Thermes de Constantin** (daily: March, April & Oct 9–11.30am & 2–5.30pm; May–Sept 9am–noon & 2–6pm; Nov–Feb 10–11.30am & 2–4.30pm; €5.50), which may well have been the biggest Roman baths in Provence, are all that remain of the emperor's palace that extended along the waterfront. The Roman forum was up the hill on the site of **place du Forum**, still the centre of life in Arles. You can see the pillars of an ancient temple embedded in the corner of the *Nord-Pinus* hotel.

The Romans had their burial ground southeast of the centre, and it was used by well-to-do Arlesians well into the Middle Ages. Now only one alleyway, foreshortened by a train line, is preserved. To reach **Les Alyscamps** (daily: March, April & Oct 9–11.30am & 2–5.30pm; May–Sept 9am–6pm; Nov–Feb 10–11.30am & 2–4.30pm; €3.50), follow avenue des Alyscamps from the east end of boulevard des Lices. Sarcophagi still line the shaded walk, whose tree trunks are azure blue in Van Gogh's rendering. This walk is quite special, and heads to the twelfth-century Romanesque St-Honorat's church, wonderfully simple and cool on a hot day.

Medieval Arles and beyond

The doorway of the **Cathédrale St-Trophime** on Arles' **central place de la République** is one of the most famous examples of twelfth-century Provençal stonecarving in existence. It depicts the Last Judgement, trumpeted by angels playing with the enthusiasm of jazz musicians while the damned are led naked in chains down to hell and the blessed, all draped in long robes, process upwards. Begun in the ninth century, the cathedral was largely completed by the twelfth century. Today the nave is decorated with d'Aubusson tapestries, while there is lovely Romanesque and Gothic stonecarving in the beautiful **cloisters**, accessible from place de la République to the right of the cathedral (same hours as Les Arènes; €3.50).

Across place de la République from the cathedral stands the palatial seventeenth-century **Hôtel de Ville**, inspired by Versailles. You can walk through its vast entrance hall, with its flattened vaulted roof designed to avoid putting extra stress on the spooky **Cryptoporticus du Forum** (closed for restoration at the time of writing; ask at tourist office) below. This is a huge, dark, dank and wonderfully spooky three-sided underground gallery, built by the Romans, possibly as a food store, possibly as a barracks for public slaves.

In case you feel that life stopped in Arles, if not after the Romans, then at least after the Middle Ages, head for the **Musée Arlaten** on rue de la République (daily: April, May & Sept 9.30am–12.30pm & 2–6pm; June–Aug 9.30am–1pm & 2–6.30pm; Oct–March 9.30am–12.30pm & 2–5pm; €1). The museum was set up in 1896 by Frédéric Mistral, the Nobel Prize-winning novelist who was responsible for the turn-of-the-twentieth-century revival of interest in all things Provençal and shows off an illuminating collection of costumes, documents, tools, pictures and paraphernalia of Provençal life.

Opposite the Thermes (see p.985) is the **Musée Réattu** (Tues–Sun 10am–7pm; €7), housing an engrossing collection of photographs documenting Arles' development throughout the eighteenth and nineteenth century. There are "donations" by Picasso, including his *Woman with Violin* sculpture and 57 ink-and-crayon sketches made in Arles between December 1970 and February 1971.

Van Gogh in Arles

At the back of the Réattu museum, lanterns line the river wall where **Van Gogh** used to wander, wearing candles on his hat, watching the night-time light: *The Starry Night* is the Rhône at Arles. The café painted in *Café de Nuit* still stands in place du Forum, and the distinctive Pont Langlois drawbridge painted by the artist in March 1888 can be seen on the southern edge of the town (poorly signposted off the D35). Van Gogh had arrived by train in February 1888 to be greeted by snow and a bitter mistral wind. But he started painting straight away, and in this period produced such celebrated canvases as *The Sunflowers*, *Van Gogh's Chair*, *The Red Vines* and *The Sower*. Van Gogh found few kindred souls in

Arles and finally managed to persuade Gauguin to join him in mid-autumn. Although the two were to influence each other substantially in the following weeks, their relationship quickly soured as the increasingly bad November weather forced them to spend more time together indoors. According to Gauguin, Van Gogh, feeling threatened by his friend's possible departure, finally succumbed to a fit of psychosis and attacked first Gauguin and then himself. He was packed off to the Hôtel-Dieu hospital on rue du Président-Wilson down from the Musée Arlaten, now the **Espace Van Gogh**, an academic and cultural centre with arty shops in its arcades and courtyard flower beds re-created according to Van Gogh's painting and descriptions of the hospital garden.

Arles has none of the artist's works but the **Fondation Vincent Van Gogh** (April–June daily 10am–6pm; July–Sept daily 10am–7pm; Oct–March Tues–Sun 11am–5pm; €7), facing the Arènes at 26 rond-point des Arènes, exhibits works by contemporary artists inspired by Van Gogh, including Francis Bacon and David Hockney.

Eating and drinking

Arles has a good number of excellent-quality and cheap **restaurants**. Place du Forum is the centre of **café** life, particularly at the young and noisy *Bistrot Arlésien*. Nevertheless, don't be surprised to discover that most of Arles packs up for the night around 10.30pm.

L'Atelier de Jean Luc Rabanel 7 rue des Carmes ☎04.90.91.07.69, ⊛www.rabanel.com.The top restaurant in Arles – the renowed Rabanel offers menus from €45, involving seven delectable *amuse bouches,* to the gastronomic thirteen bites for €140. A fantastic culinary experience. Closed Mon & Tues.

Chez Ariane 2 rue Dr-Fanton ☎04.90.52.00.65. The eccentric Ariane rules the roost at this inexpensive restaurant serving unpretentious home cooking and fabulous organic wines. Closed Mon & Tues.

Le Cilantro 31 rue Porte de Laure, ☎04.90.18.25.05. A calm, serene place where you can dine on beautifully executed, imaginative dishes. The young chef prepares excellent *plats,* such as pikeperch in a truffle crust for around €30. Closed Sat lunch, Sun & Mon.

A Coté 21 rue des Carmes ☎04.90.47.61.13. The cheaper sister to *L'Atelier,* but as gastronomically satisfying. Mouth-watering tapas includes aubergine caviar (€6.50). Open daily until midnight.

Le Galoubet 18 rue du Dr-Fanton ☎04.90.93.18.11. Pleasant, vine-covered terrace and elegant dining room in which to taste the modern Provençal cuisine on a good-value €25 menu. Closed Sun & Mon lunch.

La Gueule du Loup 39 rue des Arènes ☎04.90.96.96.69. Cosy restaurant serving traditional dishes, with menus from €22. Closed Mon lunch.

La Mule Blanche 9 rue du Président Wilson ☎04.90.93.98.54. Affordable, delicious food served in a laidback atmosphere; salads are €10 and *plats* around €15. Occasional jazz. Closed Sun.

The Camargue

The boundaries of the **CAMARGUE** are not apparent until you come upon them. Its shimmering horizons are infinite because land, lagoon and sea share the same horizontal plain. Both wild and human life have traits peculiar to this drained, ditched and now protected delta land. Today, the whole of the Camargue is a Parc Naturel Régional, with great efforts made to keep an equilibrium between tourism, agriculture, industry and hunting on the one hand, and the indigenous ecosystems on the other.

After World War II, the northern marshes were drained and re-irrigated with fresh water. The main crop planted was rice, and so successful was it that by

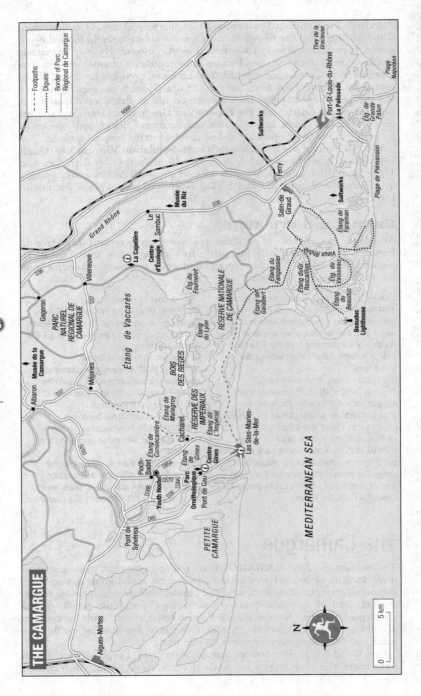

THE CAMARGUE

Footpaths
Digues
Border of Parc
Regional de Camargue

N

0   5 km

MEDITERRANEAN SEA

the 1960s the Camargue was providing three-quarters of all French consumption of the grain. Vines were also reintroduced – in the nineteenth century they had survived the disease that devastated every other wine-producing region because their stems were under water. There are other crops – wheat, rapeseed and fruit orchards – as well as trees in isolated clumps. To the east, along the last stretch of the Grand Rhône, the chief business is the production of salt, which was first organized in the Camargue by the Romans in the first century AD.

Though the Étang du Vaccarès and the central islands are out of bounds, there are paths and sea dykes from which their inhabitants can be watched, and special nature trails (see below). The ideal months for birdwatching are the mating period of April to June, with the greatest number of flamingos present between April and September.

The only town, or rather overgrown village, and the main resort, is **Stes-Maries-de-la-Mer** on the sea close to the mouth of the Petit Rhône.

Getting around the Camargue

Fairly frequent **buses** run between Arles and Stes-Maries (6 daily), where you can rent **bikes** at Le Vélociste on place Mireille in the centre of town (℡04.90.97.83.26), and at Le Vélo Saintois on avenue de la République (℡04.90.97.74.56). **Canoes** are also available from Kayak Vert in Sylvéréal, on RD38 direction Aigues-Mortes (℡04.66.73.57.17). There are around thirty farms that offer **horseriding** by the hour, half-day or day. The tourist office in Stes-Maries (see p.990) has a complete list.

For transport as an end in itself, there's the **paddle steamer** *Le Tiki III*, which leaves for river trips from the mouth of the Petit Rhône, off the route d'Aigues-Mortes, 2.5km west of Stes-Maries (mid-March to mid-Nov; ℡04.90.97.81.68; 1hr 30min), and the *Camargue*, which leaves from the port in Stes-Maries (mid-March to mid-Oct; ℡04.90.97.84.72; 1hr 30min). Finally, *Camargue Safaris Gallon* in avenue Van-Gogh in Stes-Maries (℡04.90.97.86.93) offers jeep safaris, sometimes in combination with horseriding or cycle riding.

Be wary of taking your car or bike along the **dykes**: although maps and road signs show which routes are closed to vehicles and which are accessible only at low tide, they don't warn you about the road surface. The other problem is **theft** from cars. There are well-organized gangs of thieves with a particular penchant for foreign licence plates.

Camarguais wildlife

The Camargue is home to **bulls** and the **white horses** that the region's *gardiens* (herdsmen) ride. Neither beast is truly wild, though both run in semi-liberty. The Camargue horse is a distinct breed, born dark brown or black and turning white around its fourth year. It is never stabled, surviving the humid heat of summer and the wind-racked winter cold outdoors. The *gardiens* likewise are a hardy community. Their traditional homes, or *cabanes*, are thatched and windowless one-storey structures, with bulls' horns over the door to ward off evil spirits. They play a major role in guarding Camarguais traditions: throughout the summer they put on spectacles involving bulls and horses, and the work carries local glamour. Winter is a good deal harder, with fewer and fewer Camarguais property owners able to afford the extravagant use of land that bull-rearing requires.

Other Camargue **wildlife** includes flamingos, marsh and sea birds, waterfowl and birds of prey; wild boars, beavers and badgers; tree frogs, water snakes and pond turtles; and a rich flora of reeds, wild irises, tamarisk, wild rosemary and juniper trees.

The tourist office in Stes-Maries-de-la-Mer will be able to help you with **walking routes** around the Camargue. Be warned that **mosquitoes** are rife from March through to November; you'll need serious chemical weaponry. Biting flies are also prevalent and can take away much of the pleasure of this hill-less land for bicycling. The other problem is the **winds**, which in autumn and winter can be strong enough to knock you off your bike. Conversely, in summer the weather can be so hot and humid that the slightest movement is an effort. There's really no ideal time for visiting the area.

Les Stes-Maries-de-la-Mer

LES STES-MARIES-DE-LA-MER is best known for its annual festival on May 24–25, when the town is swamped with Romanies celebrating their patron Ste-Sarah. It's a time for weddings and baptisms as well as music, dancing and fervent religious observance. The rest of the year it's unmistakably and unashamedly a holiday resort: unobtrusive white houses with tiled roofs line a tidy grey sandy beach with countless bucket-and-spade shops, fish restaurants with neon signs and ice-cream parlours. It makes good base from which to explore the Camargue, with plenty of reasonably priced accommodation and restaurants.

On the way there you could drop in on the **Musée de la Camargue** (April–June & Sept daily 9.15am–5.45pm; July & Aug 9.15am–6.45pm; Oct–March daily except Tues 10.15am–4.45pm; €5), halfway between Gimeaux and Albaron, which documents the traditions and livelihoods of the Camarguais people in the nineteenth and twentieth centuries. Just down the road at Pont du Garc, 4km from Stes-Maries, is the engrossing **Parc Ornithologique** (daily: April–Sept 9am–sunset; Oct–March 10am–sunset; €7), with some of the less easily spotted birds kept in aviaries, plus trails across a twelve-hectare marsh and a longer walk with vantage points, all with ample signs and information.

Arrival and information

There's good, secure parking on the seafront in Stes-Maries at the Police Municipale, close to the **tourist office** on avenue Van-Gogh (daily: Jan, Feb, Nov & Dec 9am–5pm; March & Oct 9am–6pm; April–June & Sept 9am–7pm; July & Aug 9am–8pm; ⓣ04.90.97.82.55, ⓦwww.saintesmaries.com). There's a lively **market** on place Gitan on Monday and Friday mornings.

Accommodation

From April to October **rooms** in Stes-Maries should be booked in advance, and for the Romany festival, several months before. Prices go up considerably during the summer and outlying *mas* (farmhouses) renting out rooms tend to be quite expensive. **Camping** on the beach is not officially tolerated, but even at Stes-Maries people sleeping beneath the stars rarely get told to move on. The fifteen-kilometre seaside plage de Piemanson, also known as the plage d'Arles, south of Salin-de-Giraud, 10km east of Stes-Maries, is a favoured venue for *camping sauvage* in summer.

Hotels

Hostellerie du Pont de Gau rte d'Arles, Pont de Gau, 4km north of Stes-Maries, between the Maison du Parc and the Parc Ornithologique ⓣ04.90.97.81.53, ⓦwww.pontdegau.com. Old-fashioned Camarguais decor, pleasant rooms and a good restaurant (see opposite). Closed Jan to mid-Feb. ❸

Mangio Fango rte d'Arles ⓣ04.90.97.80.56, ⓦwww.hotelmangiofango.com Situated 600m from Stes-Maries, overlooking the Étang des Launes. A peaceful farmhouse with a Meditterean twist; stylish, comfortable rooms and a pool surrounded by lush green foliage. ❺

Mistral ☎04.90.97.82.09, 🌐www
.mediterraneehotel.com. Decked out in jolly flowers, this welcoming hotel has pretty Provençal rooms and is in the heart of the town, seconds from the sea. ❷
Hotel Le Neptune 14 rue Jean Aicard
☎04.90.97.83.95. Traditional seaside hotel, with fresh, white rooms. ❸
Des Rièges rte de Cacharel ☎04.90.97.85.07, 🌐www.hoteldesrieges.com. An upmarket hotel in a cluttered old farmhouse, with swimming pool and garden. Down a track signed off the D85a at the edge of Stes-Maries. Closed mid-Nov to mid-Feb. ❹

Hostel and campsites

Hostel on the Arles–Stes-Maries bus route, 10km north of Stes-Maries in the hamlet of Pioch-Badet ☎04.90.97.51.72, Ⓕ04.90.97.54.88. Bike rental, horserides and other excursions. Open all year, but you must make reservations. €29 (half-board only).
Camping La Brise rue Marcel-Carrière ☎04.90.97.84.67, 🌐www.camping-labrise.fr. A three-star site, with a pool and laundry facilities, and tents, mobile homes or bungalows for rent. €20.50 for two people and a tent.
Camping Le Clos du Rhône at the mouth of the Petit Rhône, 800km from the centre of town on the rte d'Aigues-Mortes ☎04.90.97.85.99, 🌐www .campingleclos.fr. Easily reached via a seaside path, this is a busy four-star site with a pool, laundry and shop. Open mid-March to Oct. €23.50 for two people and tent.

The Town

Stes-Maries is a neat and pleasant, if excessively commercialized town, in size scarcely more than a large village. It exploits its monopoly as the only Camargue resort and every leisure activity is catered for, to excess. There are kilometres of **beach**; a pleasure port with boat trips to the lagoons; horses or bikes to ride; watersports; the *arènes* for bullfights, cavalcades and other entertainment (events are posted on a board outside); and flamenco guitarists playing on the restaurant and café terraces – it can all be very good fun.

As for sights, the fortified **church of Stes-Maries** allows a look at Sarah's tinselled and sequinned statue, which is carried into the sea each year. It's at the back of the crypt on the right, and always surrounded by candles and abandoned crutches and callipers from the miraculously cured. The church **tower** (hours erratic – ask at the tourist office; €2) has one of the best possible views over the Camargue; it's the tallest thing for miles.

A few steps south of the church on rue Victor-Hugo, the **Musée Baroncelli** (closed at the time of writing; ask at tourist office; €2) is named after the man who, in 1935, was responsible for initiating the Romanies' procession down to the sea with Sarah. The museum covers this event, other Camarguais traditions and the region's fauna and flora.

Eating and drinking

With so much trade, many of the restaurants in Stes-Maries are undeservedly pricey, and not particularly memorable. On the main drag, avenue Frederic Mistral, try the decent *Le Romarin* (☎04.90.96.37.73) at no. 31, while facing the harbour at 34 rue Theodore Aubanel is the popular *Jardin des Delices* (☎04.90.97.91.83; closed mid-Nov to mid-Jan), serving great seafood; you can make up your own platter of favourite shellfish (from €18.50). Out of town is the warm and inviting hotel-restaurant *Pont de Gau* (see opposite); while even further from town on route du Sambuc, 12km from Arles, is the exquisite 🎋 *La Chassagnette* (☎04.90.97.26.96; closed Wed). There's a beautiful outdoor terrace, a cosy, contemporary indoor restaurant serving organic produce. Unforgettable menus from €34; *plats* from €26.

From Avignon to the Luberon

Heading east from Avignon to the Luberon, worthwhile stops include pretty **Isle-sur-la-Sorgue**, the third largest centre for antiques in France, and **Fontaine-la-Vaucluse**, home to the source of the Sorgue – one of the most powerful natural springs in the world. It's a romantic spot, yet deluged by tourists much of the time. Approximately six buses daily shuttle between the two towns; on Sundays, there's a reduced service.

Isle-sur-la Sorgue

Isle-sur-la-Sorgue, 30km east of Avignon, is also known as "Provençal Venice", for its little canals and waterways running around and through the centre. In the past, fishing was the town's major industry, along with silk and paper manufacturing; the mills still churn the waters today, although now they are more pretty than perfunctory. The town is a major centre for **antiques**; most dealers are open from Friday afternoon until Monday morning so if you're a keen hunter, be sure to turn up then. Le Patio (☎04.90.38.63.63), at 15 esplanade Robert Vasse, has thirty or so dealers set in a lovely, peaceful courtyard. There's also a large antiques market all over town on Sunday morning.

Two museums worth popping into are the little **Musée du Jouet et de la Poupée Ancienne** (☎04.90.20.97.31; daily 10.30am–6pm; €3.50), which shows off a private collection of remarkably intact dolls dating from 1880 to 1920, and the **Maison René Char** housed in the elegant Hotel Donadei de Campredon on 20 rue Docteur Tallet (☎04.90.38.17.41; daily 10am–12.30pm & 2–5.30pm; €6.20), where the poet, and part-time surrealist, René Char was born in 1907. The ground floor of the hôtel holds temporary art exhibitions while upstairs you'll find the *ecrivain's* writing desk and various documents *du jour*.

Practicalities

The **tourist office** (Mon–Sat 9am–12.30pm & 2.30–6pm, Sun 9am–12.30pm; ☎04.90.38.04.78, ⊛www.oti-delasorgue.fr) is situated next to the church. For somewhere to **stay** in town, you could try the charming hotel-restaurant *Le Prevôté* (☎04.90.38.57.29, ⊛www.la-prevote.fr; ❼) at 4 rue J.J Rousseau; the cosy rooms are decked out in beautiful terracotta tiles, wooden beams and Provençal quilts, while the small, superb restaurant, serving gastronomic menus from €26, is housed downstairs in the old sacristy. A cheaper alternative is the decent *La Gueulardière* at 1 cours René Char (☎04.90.38.10.52, ⊛www.gueulardiere.com; ❸). For a gastronomic feast, head for the delightful *Le Vivier* (☎04.90.38.52.80; menu €34; closed lunchtime Fri & Sat, Sun evening & Mon) at 800 cours Fernande Peyre. Approximately 1.5km out of town at 147, chemin du Bosquet is the lovely *L'Oustau de l'Isle* (☎04.90.20.81.36; closed Tues & Wed) set in a beautiful country house. Less exciting and more affordable places back in town are dotted along the waterside quai Jean Jaurès.

Fontaine-de-Vaucluse

Lying 7km east of Isle-sur-la-Sorgue, **FONTAINE-DE-VAUCLUSE** invariably draws large crowds of visitors who trudge the ten-minute walk up to the top of the gorge above the village, where a mysterious tapering fissure and a calm azure-blue pool signals, beguilingly, France's most powerful spring.

The town was once a rustic backwater where the fourteenth-century poet Petrarch pined for his Laura. To learn a little more about this lovelorn rhymester, drop into the **Musée de Pétrarque** through an alleyway just over the river (daily except Tues: April–May 10am–noon & 2–6pm; June–Sept 10am–12.30pm & 1.30–6pm; Oct 10am–noon & 2–5pm; €3.50). The museum shows off beautiful books dating back to the fifteenth century and pictures of Petrarch, his beloved Laura and Fontaine, where he passed sixteen years of his unrequited passion.

The **tourist office** is on chemin de la Fontaine (daily 10am–1pm & 2–6pm; ☎04.90.20.32.22). Ignoring its uninspiring exterior, the most luxurious place to **stay** here is *L'Hotel du Poète* (☎04.90.20.34.05, ⓦwww.hoteldupoete.com; ➎) down the road to the right as you approach the town, with large, comfortable rooms and a pool. Alternatively, there's the cheaper *Hôtel les Sources* (☎04.90.20.31.84, ⓦwww.hoteldessources.com; ➍), and a pleasant **hostel** on chemin de la Vignasse, 1km south on the road to Lagnes (☎04.90.20.31.65, Ⓔfontaine@fuaj.org; open Jan to mid-Nov; €16.20 per bed). The **campsite**, *Les Prés* (☎04.90.20.32.38; all year), is 500m downstream from the village, equipped with swimming pool. For **food**, you have a choice of several reasonably priced restaurants in town, including *Lou Fanau* (☎04.90.20.31.90; closed Wed; menus from €14.50) and *Petrarque et Laure* (☎04.90.20.31.48; closed Mon; menus from €11.80).

The Luberon

Lying east of Avignon and north of Arles, **the Luberon** valley has long been escape country for well-heeled Parisians, Dutch and British, but has also attracted a good number of artists to its beautiful wine-growing, lavender-carpeted countryside. The Luberon's northern face is damper, more alpine in character than the southern area and extremely cold in winter. The southern slopes, by contrast, are Mediterranean in scent and feel. It's almost all wooded, except for the summer sheep pastures at the top, and there's just one main route across, the Combe de Lourmarin. The Luberon is home to many small **villages** clinging stubbornly to the foothills – with their history, beauty and individuality, they make wonderful days out and even better places to stay.

A large section of the area has been designated the **Parc Naturel Régional du Luberon** (ⓦwww.parcduluberon.com), with the aim of conserving the natural fauna and flora and limiting development. The park is administered by the **Maison du Parc**, 60 place Jean-Jaurès in Apt (Mon–Fri 8.30am–noon & 1.30–6pm; April–Aug also Sat 8.30am–noon; ☎04.90.04.42.00), which is the place to go for information about every aspect of the Luberon.

Given the region's general dearth of public transport, the only practical and pleasurable way to explore the park without a car is by hiking or cycling. The organization **Vélo Loisir en Luberon** (☎04.92.79.05.82, ⓦwww.veloloisir luberon.com) is a consortium of hotels, campsites and cycle hire and repair shops, which promotes cycle tourism throughout the region. In Apt, bikes can be **hired** from Luberon Cycles at 86 quai du Général Leclerc (☎04.90.74.17.16).

Apt

The sole town base for exploring the Luberon is **APT**, though it's not much of a town for sightseeing, nor is it renowned for the charm and friendliness of its people. Its large confectionery factory spews mucky froth into the concrete-channelled River Coulon and the streets are far from immaculate. You won't want to stay long, but it's worth visiting on a Saturday for the lively **market** when, as well as every imaginable Provençal edible, there are barrel organs, jazz musicians and stand-up comics on show.

Practicalities

Arriving by bus – Apt's *gare SNCF* is freight-only – you'll be dropped at place de la Bouquerie, the main square lined with cafés and restaurants, or at the **gare routière** on avenue de la Libération at the eastern end of the town on avenue Saignon. The **tourist office** is at 20 avenue Philippe-de-Girard (July & Aug daily 9am–7pm; rest of year Mon–Sat 9am–noon & 2–6pm, Sun 9.30am–12.30pm; ⓣ04.90.74.03.18, ⓦwww.luberon-apt.fr), just up to the left from place de la Bouquerie as you face the river. The best place to **stay** in town is *Auberge du Luberon*, 8 place du Faubourg du Ballet (ⓣ04.90.74.12.50, ⓦwww.auberge-luberon-peuzin.com.com; ❺), a traditional French hotel with restful rooms and a gastronomic restaurant serving *plats* such as monkfish studded with candied orange peel (€28) and menus from €29. A cheaper alternative is the central but rather dingy *Le Palais*, at 24 place Gabriel-Péri (ⓣ04.90.04.89.32, ⓔhotel-le-palais@orange.fr; ❸; closed mid-Nov to March). *Camping Les Cèdres* on avenue deViton (ⓣ&ⓕ04.90.74.14.61; open mid-Feb to Dec; €14.50 for two people and a tent) is across the bridge from place St-Pierre, within easy walking distance of the town.

If you haven't stuffed yourself with chocolates and candied fruit (Apt's speciality), you can get cheap and decent **meals** at the *Bistrot le France* (ⓣ04.90.74.22.01), 61 place de la Bouquerie, where they serve generous platters of cheese, ham and salad (€16). *Le Plantane*, 25 place Jules Ferry (ⓣ04.90.04.74.36; closed Sun), is worth trying for its traditional, Mediterranean-inspired menus (€26) on its pretty little terrace.

The Luberon villages

In many ways, the **villages** that dot the Luberon valley epitomize the true beauty of Provence: impossibly narrow, cobbled streets, tumbledown houses strewn with flowers and sun-baked *places*. As they don't possess many specific sights in themselves, many of the villages warrant just half a day's exploration. The best time to visit is on **market** day, when the whole village turns up to buy their baguettes, fruit and vegetables.

Getting from village to village is pretty impossible without your own wheels. Around eleven buses daily (reduced service Sun) leave from Avignon to Apt, stopping off at Bonnieux en route, while from Aix-en-Provence there are just two daily. The tourist office in Apt can supply you with a skeleton bus timetable, but be aware that this is infrequently updated. Don't forget that there are many *mas* and B&Bs surrounding these villages; check out ⓦwww.provenceweb.fr for a list.

Ménerbes

Situated around 23km west of Apt, surrounded by sweeping countryside and perched on a hill, **MENERBES** boasts a fine collection of medieval and Renaissance-era houses and a dominant sixteenth-century citadele. If you're feeling overwhelmed by the multitude of Luberon road signs directing you to various wine-tasting *caves* or *châteaux*, Ménerbes is the place to head for: the elegant **Maison de la Truffe et des Vins** (April–Oct daily 10am–12.30pm & 2.30–6.30pm; ⓣ04.90.72.38.37, ⓦwww.vin-truffe-luberon.com) on place de l'Horloge, houses wines from all three of Luberon's *appellations* and from over sixty vineyards, selling them for the same price as at the wholesalers. They arrange wine and truffle-tasting, and also act at the **tourist office** (same hours). **Market** day is Thursday.

Accommodation in Ménerbes includes the luxurious *Mas du Magnolia* (ⓣ04.90.72.48.00, ⓦwww.masdumagnolia.com; ❼), just outside town on the

D103, and the cheaper *Les Douze Oliviers* (☎04.90.72.23.80, ⓦwww
.les-douze-oliviers.com; ❺), at the foot of town in Quartier Gaujas. To practise
your newly acquired wine expertise, head for the popular **restaurant** *Le
Gaboulet*, on avenue. Marcellin Poncet (☎04.90.72.36.08; closed Wed), which
serves good-quality, traditional Provençal dishes (*plats* €18), while the smarter
Café Veranda (☎04.90.72.33.33; closed Mon) next door offers much the same,
at higher prices (menu for €39).

Gordes and around

Not far from Ménerbes, on the north side of the D22, lies **Gordes**, an incredibly
picturesque Provençal village much favoured by Parisian media personalities, film
directors, artists and the like. This might prompt you to give it a miss but there
are good reasons for its popularity with the rich and famous: the cluster of
magnificent, honey-coloured buildings clinging on to a sheer rockface is a
spectacular sight. At the top of the village, a church and houses surround a
mighty twelfth- to sixteenth-century **château**, housing the contemporary
paintings of the Flemish artist Pol Mara (daily 10am–noon & 2–6pm; €4).
Market day is Tuesday.

The **tourist office** is in the château (Mon–Sat 9am–noon & 2–6pm, Sun
10am–noon & 2–6pm; ☎04.90.72.02.75, ⓦwww.gordes-village.com). For
somewhere to **stay**, the most reasonably priced hotel within the village is the
decent *Le Provençal* (☎04.90.72.10.01, ⓦwww.le-provencal.fr; ❸) while a more
luxurious option is the *La Bastide de Gordes* in the old village (☎04.90.72.12.12,
ⓦwww.bastide-de-gordes.com; ❾), built into the old ramparts; some of the
rooms have vaulted ceilings and the terrace boasts impressive views. Opposite
the hotel is the cute and unpretentious ⚑*Mon Mari était Patissier* (☎06.37.38.25.34;
closed Mon), which serves fabulous **food** on a tiny terrace with a cool jazz
soundtrack; menus are around €29 and feature dishes like aubergine *gâteau* with
tomato compôte and strawberry crumble to finish. Alternatively, *Les Cuisines du
Château* on place du Château (☎04.90.72.01.31; closed Mon & Jan–Feb) serves
à la carte dishes from €22.

▲ Gordes

Village des Bories

The **Village des Bories** (daily 9am–sunset; €5.50), 3.5km east off the D2 towards Cavaillon, comprises a collection of peculiar dry-stone dwellings; buildings like these were first constructed in the Bronze Age but in fact most of the constructions here – sheep-pens, wine vats, bread-ovens and the like – date from the eighteenth century and were inhabited until a hundred years ago. It's easiest to get here with your own car, although buses going to Cavaillon drop visitors off 1.7km from the village.

Abbaye de Sénanque

Four kilometres north of **Gordes**, set amid lavender fields in a deep cleft in the hills, stands the twelfth-century Cistercian **Abbaye de Sénanque** (visits by 1hr guided tour only, in French; ☎04.90.72.05.72 or enquire at abbey shop; €7). It's still in use as a monastery and you can visit the church, cloisters and all the main rooms of this substantial and austere building; a shop sells the monks' produce, including liqueur, honey and lavender essence.

Roussillon and around

The houses in the village of **ROUSSILLON**, 10km east of Gordes, radiate all the different shades of the seventeen ochre tints once quarried here. As colourful as an artist's palette itself, the town attracts a multitude of painters, potterers and sculptors, whose works are on show and for sale throughout the town. If you want to find out more about the ochre industry, head to the **Conservatoire des Ocres et des Pigments Appliqués** (☎04.90.05.66.69; Tues–Sun 9am–1pm & 2–6pm; guided tour €5). **Market** day is Thursday.

The **tourist office** (☎04.90.05.60.25, ⓦwww.roussillon-provence.com) is on place de la Poste, just down from the swanky **hotel**-restaurant *Le Clos de la Glycine* (☎04.90.05.60.13, ⓦwww.luberon-hotel.com; ❼), whose sumptuous rooms have fabulous views over the valley. A cheaper, more charming option is *Les Reves d'Ocres* on the route de Gordes (☎04.90.05.60.50, ⓦwww.hotel-revesdocres.com; ❹). For **food**, the top restaurant is *Restaurant David* (part of *Le Clos de la Glycine*), which has a €48 menu. A close second and much more affordable restaurant is *Le Piquebaure* (☎04.90.05.79.65; closed Mon & Tues), route de Gordes, serving *plats* for €12 and menus from €34. Otherwise, there are plenty of inexpensive cafés and bistros dotted around town.

The Sentiers des Ocres and The Colorado Provençal

To further admire the lovely ochre hues of the Luberon – and to stretch your legs – head for the **Sentiers des Ocres**, a pretty natural park full of colourful and oddly shaped rocks and pinnacles. The entrance is next to Roussillon's cemetery, and you can follow the sandy, colour-coded walks (€2). The **Colorado Provençal** is a more dramatic valley, lying just outside the village of **Rustrel**, 9km northeast of Apt and is signed off the D22 towards Gignac. You have to pay to park, either in the municipal car park (€2) or in a private car park (€6; map included) and then you're free to wander around the weird, fiery-red landscape.

Saignon

Four kilometres from Apt, tiny, immaculate **Saignon** is perhaps the most enchanting of Luberon's villages, and remains somewhat undiscovered on the tourist circuit. For a breathtaking overview of the town and its surrounding splendour, head up to **Le Rocher** (signs from the centre of town).

The best **hotel** in the village is *Auberge du Presbytère* (☎04.90.74.11.50, ⓦwww.auberge-presbytere.com; ❹) on the dreamy, rose-covered place de la

Fontaine; its sixteen lovely rooms are cosy and comfortable, and there's a rather pricey, but good, restaurant (menu €38; closed Wed). For something more rural and a bit less expensive, *La Bastide du Jas* (℡04.90.04.88.27, ⓦwww.labastidedujas; ❹), at the bottom of the village among rambling gardens, has glorious, homely rooms and studios (two-bed studio €1200 per week), along with a swimming pool. Another **restaurant** worth trying here is *La Cave Gourmande* (℡04.90.71.60.81; closed Mon; menus from €13), featuring dishes such as Provençal lamb with olives, served on a snug terrace.

Bonnieux

Built on several interlocking levels, it's very easy to get lost among the narrow, twisting lanes of Bonnieux, 12km southwest of Apt, but if all else fails, head to the top of the hill and dinky twelfth-century **église haute** where there are marvellous views across the valley. **Market** day is Friday.

If you can afford it, the place to stay and eat is *La Bastide du Capelongue* (℡04.90.75.89.78, ⓦwww.capelongue.com; ❾), located at the top of the village, an incredibly luxurious hotel filled with beautiful bedrooms, sitting rooms, terraces and pool. The chef, Edouard Loubet, has received two Michelin stars and concocts fabulous dishes, such as duck breast with cauliflower mousse, at rather exorbitant prices. For more down-to-earth accommodation, try 🦋 *Le Mas del Sol*, an immaculate B&B with a pool, run by a friendly young couple. From the *pain au chocolat* to the jams and pear compote, the breakfasts are all home made, and the rooms are extremely comfortable and homely. They also prepare delicious dinners on request (€34). For inexpensive fodder in town, head for the relaxed *St André* (℡04.90.75.11.72), serving salads (€10) and delicious apple tart (€5).

The Abbaye de Silvacane

If you're heading for Aix-en-Provence from Apt, you'll pass close to another ancient Cistercian abbey contemporary with Sénanque, 29km south of Apt, just across the Durance. After a long history of abandonment and evictions, the **Abbaye de Silvacane** (June–Sept daily 10am–6pm; Oct–May daily except Tues 10am–1pm & 2–5pm; €6.50) is once again a monastic institution. Isolated from the surrounding villages on the bank of the Durance, its architecture has hardly changed over the last seven hundred years; you can visit the stark, pale-stoned splendour of the church, its cloisters and surrounding buildings.

Aix-en-Provence and around

AIX-EN-PROVENCE would be the dominant city of central Provence were it not for the great metropolis of Marseille, just 25km away. Historically, culturally and socially, the two cities are moons apart and the tendency is to love one and hate the other. Aix is complacently conservative and a pretty place, its riches based on landowning and the liberal professions. The youth of Aix dress immaculately; hundreds of foreign students, particularly Americans, come to study here; and there's a certain snobbishness, almost of Parisian proportions.

Arrival and information

Cours Mirabeau, which replaced the town's old southern fortifications, is the main thoroughfare of Aix, with the multi-fountained place Général-de-Gaulle,

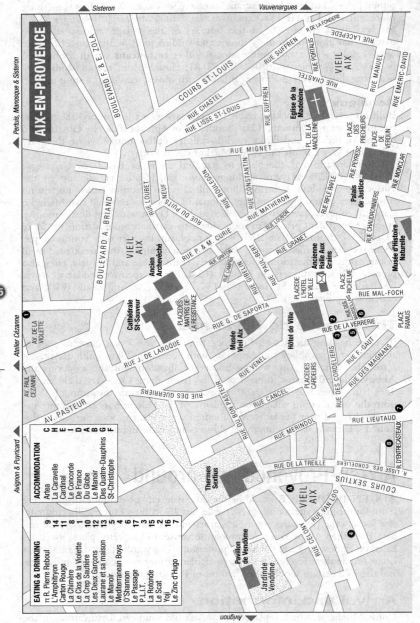

AIX-EN-PROVENCE

▲ Sisteron
Vauvenargues ▲

◄ Pertuis, Manosque & Sisteron

◄ Atelier Cézanne

◄ Avignon & Puyricard

▼ Avignon

ACCOMMODATION

Artea	C
La Caravelle	H
Cardinal	E
Le Concorde	I
De France	D
Du Globe	A
Le Manoir	B
Des Quatre-Dauphins	G
St-Christophe	F

EATING & DRINKING

Tï R. Pierre Reboul	9
L'Amphitryon	14
Carton Rouge	11
La Chimère	8
Le Clos de la Violette	1
La Crep Sautière	10
Les Deux Garçons	12
Laurane et sa maison	13
Le Manoir	4
Mediterranean Boys	6
O'Shannon	17
Le Passage	3
P.L.I.T.	15
La Rotonde	2
Le Scat	16
Yoji	7

Thermes Sextius

Pavillon de Vendôme

Jardin de Vendôme

Cathédrale St-Sauveur

Ancien Archevêché

Musée Vieil Aix

Hôtel de Ville

Ancienne Halle Aux Grains

Eglise de la Madeleine

Palais de Justice

Musée d'Histoire Naturelle

VIEIL AIX

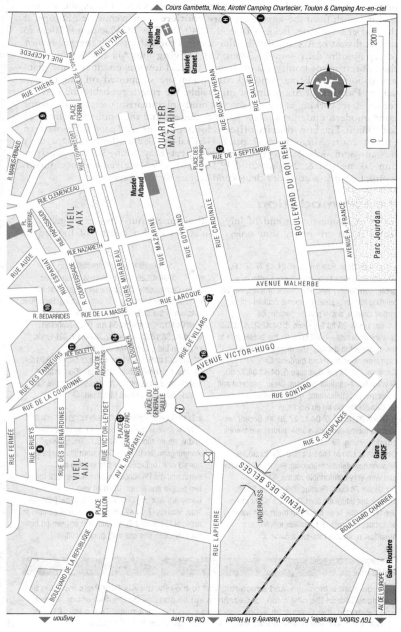

St-Jean-de-Malte

Musée Granet

QUARTIER MAZARIN

RUE D'ITALIE

RUE DE L'OPÉRA

RUE LACÉPÈDE

RUE THIERS

R. MARIUS-REINAUD

PLACE FORBIN

RUE TOURNEFORT

RUE ROUX-ALPHÉRAN

RUE SALLIER

Musée Arbaud

RUE CLEMENCEAU

VIEIL AIX

PL. ALBERTAS

RUE PAPASSAUDI

RUE NAZARETH

RUE ESPARIAT

R. COURTEISSADE

COURS MIRABEAU

RUE MAZARINE

RUE GOYRAND

RUE CARDINALE

PLACE DES 4 DAUPHINS

RUE DE 4 SEPTEMBRE

BOULEVARD DU ROI RENÉ

AVENUE A.-FRANCE

Parc Jourdan

RUE AUDE

R. BEDARRIDES

RUE DE LA MASSE

RUE LAROQUE

AVENUE MALHERBE

RUE DES TANNEURS

RUE ISOLETTE

RUE P. DOUMER

PLACE DES AUGUSTINS

RUE DE VILLARS

AVENUE VICTOR-HUGO

RUE GONTARD

RUE DE LA COURONNE

PLACE DU GENERAL DE GAULLE

RUE FERMÉE

RUE BRUEYS

RUE DES BERNARDINES

RUE VICTOR-LEYDET

AV. N. BONAPARTE

PLACE JEANNE D'ARC

VIEIL AIX

RUE G.-DESPLACES

Gare SNCF

PLACE NIOLLON

BOULEVARD DE LA RÉPUBLIQUE

RUE LAPIERRE

UNDERPASS

AVENUE DES BELGES

BOULEVARD CHARRIER

AV. DE L'EUROPE

Gare Routière

PROVENCE

15

0   200 m

N

or La Rotonde, at its west end, the main point of arrival. The **gare SNCF** is on rue Gustavo-Desplace at the end of avenue Victor-Hugo, the avenue leading south from the square; the **gare routière** is on avenue de l'Europe, at the end of avenue des Belges (℡08.91.02.40.25). The **TGV** station is 10km to the southwest of Aix; regular shuttles connect the station with the *gare routière* (every 30 min: daily 4am–11.30pm; €5). **Driving** into Aix can be confusing: the entire ring of boulevards encircling the old town is essentially one giant roundabout, circulating anticlockwise; hotels are signposted off this ring in yellow. **Parking** in Aix is almost impossible; the ring is probably the best bet for on-street parking as the old town is pretty nightmarish; there are also some good, modern underground car parks dotted around the boulevards (from €1 for 40min). The busy **tourist office** is located on the *rond point* at the western end of cours Mirabeau at 2 place Général-de-Gaulle (June & Sept daily 8.30am–8pm; July & Aug 8.30am–9pm; Sept–May Mon–Sat 8.30am–7pm, Sun 10am–1pm & 2–6pm; ℡04.42.16.11.61, ⊛www.aixenprovencetourism .com), between avenue des Belges and avenue Victor-Hugo.

Accommodation

From mid-June to the end of July (festival time) your chances of getting a **hotel** room are pretty slim unless you've reserved a couple of months in advance at least.

Artea 4 bd de la Republique ℡04.42.27.36.00, ⊛www.hotel-artea-aix-en-provence.com. In a great position very near the centre of town, this old building has forty pleasant rooms decked out in muted colours, and a private garage. ❻

La Caravelle 29 bd Roi-René ℡04.42.21.53.05, ⊛www.lacaravelle-hotel.com. By the boulevards to the southeast of the city. The more expensive rooms overlook courtyard gardens. ❹

Cardinal 22–24 rue Cardinale ℡04.42.38.32.30, ⊛www.hotel-cardinal-aix.com. Clean, peaceful and welcoming establishment; great value. ❹

Le Concorde 68 bd du Roi Rene ℡04.42.26.03.95, ℻04.42.27.38.90. Decent two-star; its rooms overlook a little garden and there's private parking. ❸

De France 63 rue Espariat ℡04.42.27.90.15, ⊛www.hoteldefrance-aix.com. Right in the centre and with very comfortable rooms. ❹

Du Globe 74 cours Sextius ℡04.42.26.03.58, ⊛www.hotelduglobe.com. There's a slight chain-like feel to this large hotel, but the rooms are very adequate, and cater for families too. Modern breakfast room and roof-top terrace. ❹

Le Manoir 8 rue d'Entrecasteaux ℡04.42.26.27.20, ⊛www.hotelmanoir .com. Comfortable and characterful old hotel in a central but discreet location with parking. Breakfast is taken in the sixteenth-century cloister. ❸

Des Quatre-Dauphins 54 rue Roux-Alphéran ℡04.42.38.16.39, ℻04.42.38.60.19. Old-world charm in the *quartier* Mazarin. ❹

St-Christophe 2 av Victor-Hugo ℡04.42.26.01.24, ⊛www.hotel-saintchristophe.com. Comfortable 1920s-style place above a popular brasserie, close to the station and cours Mirabeau. ❺

Hostels and campsites

Airotel Camping Chantecler 41 av du Val St-André, rte de Nice ℡04.42.26.12.98, ⊛www .campingchantecler.com. 3km from the centre on bus #3 or #10. Expensive site in a big park surrounding a Provençal country house. €22 for two people and a tent. Open all year.

Camping Arc-en-Ciel 45 av Malacrida, Pont des Trois Sautets ℡04.42.26.14.28, ⊛www.campinga rcenciel.fr. Located 2km southeast of town on bus #3, this clean site has very good facilities,

Visa pass

If you want a thorough, and structured, visit to the city, the **Aix City Pass** includes a guided tour of the city, a tour of Cezanne's studio and Jas de Bouffan estate as well as entry to the Granet Museum and a tour on the mini-train. The pass (€15) is available from the tourist office, and is valid for five days from first use.

including a pool. €6.20 per person. Closed Oct–March.

HI hostel 3 av Marcel-Pagnol ℗04.42.20.15.99, ℗04.42.59.36.12. Located 2km west of the centre, this hostel has small dorm rooms (€17.50), a

restaurant, baggage deposit, tennis and volleyball courts, as well as sought-after parking. Take bus #4, direction "La Mayanelle", stop "V. Vasarély". Open Feb–Christmas.

The City

The whole of the **old city of Aix**, clearly defined by its ring of boulevards and the majestic plane tree-lined cours Mirabeau, is the great monument here, far more compelling than any one single building or museum within it. With so many streets alive with people, so many tempting restaurants, cafés and shops, plus the best markets in Provence, it's easy to pass several days wandering around without the need for any itinerary or destination.

Vieil Aix

To explore the network of jumbled little lanes and narrow roads that make up the heart of Aix, wander north from leafy **cours Mirabeau** to anywhere within the ring of *cours* and boulevards. The layout of **Vieil Aix** is not designed to assist your sense of direction, but it hardly matters when there's a fountained square to rest at every 50m and a continuous architectural backdrop of treats from the sixteenth and seventeenth centuries. On Saturdays, and to a lesser extent on Tuesdays and Thursdays, the centre is taken up with various **markets**.

On the central place des Prêcheurs is the **church of the Madeleine**, decorated with paintings by Rubens and Van Loo (who was born in Aix in 1684), and a three-panel medieval *Annunciation*. The **Hôtel de Ville** on place de l'Hôtel-de-Ville displays perfect classical proportions and embroidery in wrought iron above the door; rue Gaston-de-Saporta takes you up from place de Hôtel-de-Ville to the **Cathédrale St-Sauveur** (daily: 8am–noon & 2–6pm), a conglomerate of fifteenth- to sixteenth-century buildings, full of medieval art treasures. The best of these is a triptych commissioned by King René in 1475, *Le Buisson Ardent*. It is currently undergoing a lengthy restoration; there's a small copy in its place.

A short way down from the cathedral, through place des Martyrs-de-la-Résistance, is the former bishop's palace, the **Ancien Archevêché**, housing the not particularly inspiring **Musée des Tapisseries** (daily except Tues 10am–12.30pm & 1.30–6.45pm; €2.50), while the slightly more detaining **Musée du Vieil Aix** at 17 rue Gaston-de-Saporta (Tues–Sun: 10am–noon & 2.30–6pm; €4) possesses a set of religious marionettes and a huge collection of *santons* (Provençal crib figures).

Quartier Mazarin

Aix's other central museums are in the **quartier Mazarin**, south of cours Mirabeau, a peaceful mid-seventeenth-century residential district built on the orders of an archbishop, around the four-dolphin fountain of place des Quatre-Dauphins at its heart. On place St-Jean-de-Malte the most substantial of all Aix's museums, the **Musée Granet** (Wed–Mon 11am–6pm; €10), covers art and archeology. Finds from the Oppidum d'Entremont (see p.1002) are displayed in the basement, and there's a commemorative exhibition marking one hundred years since the death of the most famous Aixois painter, **Paul Cézanne**, on the first floor. Those on permanent display are a less impressive handful of minor canvases such as *Bathsheba*, *The Bathers* and *Portrait of Madame*. There are also two of his student drawings from when he studied on the ground floor of the building, at that time the art school Granet. The rest of the museum's paintings are a mixed, rather uninspiring, bag – Italian, Dutch, French, mostly seventeenth to nineteenth century.

Cezanne in Aix-en-Provence

Cézanne used many studios in and around Aix but he finally had a house built for the purpose in 1902 at what is now 9 avenue Paul-Cézanne, overlooking Aix from the north. It was here that he painted the *Grandes Baigneuses*, the *Jardinier Vallier* and some of his greatest still lifes. The **Atelier Cézanne** (April–June & Sept 10am–noon & 2–6pm; July & Aug daily 10am–noon & 2–6pm; Oct–March 10am–noon & 2–5pm; €5.50; bus #20, stop "P. Cézanne") is exactly as it was at the time of his death in 1906: coat, hat, wineglass and easel, the objects he liked to paint, his pipe, a few letters and drawings … everything save the pictures he was working on.

To unearth more of Cezanne's life, visit the **Jas de Bouffan** (open when there are tours, reserve at the tourist office; 1hr compulsory guided tour €5.50, English spoken; bus #6 "Corsy" stop) westward on the route de Galice (D64). This elegant, though now rather shabby, Provençal manor was bought by Cezanne's father when the artist was 20 years old, and remained in the family for forty years. Somewhat reluctantly, Cezanne senior. gave his son free rein to paint the walls of the drawing room, all traces of which have now been removed and dispersed about France's museums. As part of the guided tour, though, an excellent, and illuminating, projectory video gives a good idea of what it used to look like. Outside are the rambling gardens and duck-filled pond that were often subject to Cezanne's paintbrush.

Beyond the centre

If you feel the need to escape the sometimes cloying grandeur of seventeenth-century Aix, check out the extraordinary **Fondation Vasarély** on avenue Marcel-Pagnol in Jas-de-Bouffan, 4km west of the city centre (Tues–Sat 10am–1pm & 2–6pm; €7; bus #4, stop "V. Vasarély"). There are innumerable sliding showcases, showing images related to all the themes of architect/artist Vasarély's work, including his "plastic alphabet" and designs for apartment buildings.

The **Oppidum d'Entremont** (daily except Tues 9am–noon & 2–6pm; free; take bus #20 from cours Sextius), 2.5km from the centre of Aix, is the excavated site of the Gallic settlement that preceded the foundation of the town, predating the Roman conquest by more than two hundred years. You'll find the remains of a fortified enclosure, as well as excavations of the residential and commercial quarters of the town. Statues and trinkets unearthed at the site are displayed in the Musée Granet (see p.1001).

Eating

Aix is stuffed full of **restaurants** of every price and ethnic origin. Place des Cardeurs, just northwest of the Hôtel de Ville, is nothing but restaurant, brasserie and café tables, while rue de la Verrerie running south from the Hôtel de Ville and place Ramus have an immense variety of Indian, Chinese and North African restaurants. Rue des Tanneurs is a good street for low budgets. More expensive are Aix's soft biscuits, the elliptical candied-fruit and almond-flavoured *calissons*. Local gourmet *chocolatier* Puyricard has a shop at 7 rue Rifle-Rafle.

Cafés and restaurants

L'Amphitryon 2–4 rue Paul-Doumer
☎04.42.26.54.10. Eclectic cuisine with market-fresh ingredients, served on a flower-drenched terrace in historical old Aix. An excellent restaurant, which won't break the bank. Menu from €26. Closed Sun, Mon & second half Aug.

Le Carton Rouge 7 rue Isolette,
☎04.42.91.41.75. Cute little bistrot serving traditional, home-made food (*plats* €22); the owner will help you choose delectable wines to complement your food. Closed Sun & Mon.

La Chimère 15 rue Brueys ☎04.42.38.30.00. New spin on French standards, with dishes like salad of octopus with Provençal herbs or roast sea bream with lemon, *tian* of vegetables and *sauce vierge*. Menu €26.50. Closed Sun.

Le Clos de la Violette 10 av de la Violette ☎04.42.23.30.71. Aix's most renowned restaurant serves unsurpassable gastronomic delights such as fillet of duck with cherries and poached rhubarb. Puddings are equally appealing – tiramisu cream with lemon and olive oil with a warm madeleine cake. Lunch menu €50, otherwise menus start at €90 and if you're going à la carte, the *plats* alone start around €40. Closed Sun & Mon & Wed lunch & middle 2 weeks of Aug.

La Crep Sautière 18 rue Bedarrides ☎04.42.27.91.00. Delicious, fresh crêpes (from €5) to take away or enjoy squashed into the cosy, vaulted and often packed restaurant. Open til late.

Les Deux Garçons 53 cours Mirabeau. The erstwhile haunt of Camus is done up in faded 1900s style and still attracts a motley assortment of literati. Good brasserie food, but not cheap (from €28). Service daily till midnight.

 Laurane et sa Maison 16 rue Victor Leydet ☎04.42.93.02.03. Cool, eclectic restaurant with a garden out the back; there's a large variety of classic dishes – from simple sandwiches to hearty risotto (€10). Fancier dishes, such as succulent tuna with lime and coriander salsa, are more expensive (€15).

Le Passage 10 rue Villars ☎04.42.37.09.00, ⊛www.le-passage.fr. Modern, airy three-storey restaurant serving a wide range of traditional Provençal dishes such as mustard-marinated rabbit (from €15). Jazz every evening; and two-hour cooking courses (check out online).

πR Pierre Reboul 11 petite rue Saint Jean ☎04.42.20.58.26. One of the top restaurants in Aix; Michelin-starred Reboul serves impeccable, and expensive, cuisine in his slick, contemporary restaurant. Menus at €75 and €110.

Yoji 7 av Victor Hugo ☎04.42.38.48.76. Extremely popular Japanese restaurant serving sushi (from €3.70) and sashimi (from €12) as well as generous menus from €23. Closed Sun & Mon lunchtime.

La Zinc d'Hugo 22 rue Lieutaud ☎04.42.27.69.69. Snug wine bar with inventive cuisine; try the tuna steak with raspberry balsamic vinegar, shellfish pate and honey glazed carrots (€24). Closed Sun & Mon.

Drinking and nightlife

Aix is too pretty to have gritty, urban **nightlife**. Students tend to congregate around the fountains and cafés near cours Mirabeau until midnight when the bars on rue Verrerie get going; as a warm-up, try the cool *La Rotonde* (☎04.42.91. 61.70) at 2 place Jeanne d'Arc, for potent cocktails and hard disco beats. For **jazz** there's the cave-like *Le Scat* at no. 11 (☎04.42.23.00.23), *Le Passage* (see above) and *Hot Brass*, chemin d'Eguilles-Celony (☎04.42.23.13.12, ⊛www.hotbrassaix.com). Cheesy tunes blast out of the **disco**, *P.L.I.T.* at no. 24 rue Verrerie (☎06.12.58.86.79), and for **pubs** with live music or DJs try *Le Manoir* and *O'Shannon* at nos. 25 and 30 respectively. Aix's **gay** bar is *Mediterranean Boys*, 6 rue de la Paix.

Festivals

During the annual **music festivals**, Aix en Musique (June; ☎04.42.21.69.69) and the Festival International d'Art Lyrique (opera and classical concerts; last two weeks of July; ☎04.42.17.34.34), the alternative scene – of street theatre, rock concerts and impromptu gatherings – turns the whole of Vieil Aix into one long party. Tickets for events range from €12 to €185 and can be obtained, along with programmes, from La Boutique du Festival at Espace Forbin, 11 rue Gaston de Saporta (☎04.42.17.34.34, ⊛www.festival-aix.com). Details of the Danse à Aix international dance festival (two weeks in mid-July) are available from 1 place Rewald off cours Gambetta (☎04.42.96.05.01).

Listings

Bike rental Cycles Zammit, 27 rue Mignet ☎04.42.23.19.53.

Books Paradox Bookstore, 15 rue du 4-Septembre, or Book in Bar, 1bis rue Cabassol, for English books; Vents du Sud, 7 rue Maréchal-Foch, is the best French bookshop.

Car rental ADA Location, 1 av Henri-Mouret ☎04.42.52.36.36; Avis, 11 bd Gambetta ☎04.42.21.64.16; Europcar, 55 bd de la République ☎08.25.89.69.76; Hertz 43 av Victor Hugo ☎04.42.27.91.32.

Cinema The Cézanne, rue Marcel-Guillaume, sometimes screens English or American films in *version originale*, ie with the original soundtrack.

Emergencies Centre Hospitalier, av des Tamaris ☎04.42.33.90.28; SOS Médecins

☎04.42.26.24.00; for a late-night pharmacy, ring the *gendarmerie* on ☎04.42.26.31.96.

Internet *Le Hublot*, 17 rue Paul-Bert; Progamers, 14 Forum des Cardeurs; Cyber@Vanloo, 20 rue Van Loo.

Laundry 15 rue Jacques de la Roque; 5 rue de la Fontaine; 60 rue Boulegon; 36 cours Sextius.

Police 2 cours des Minimes, ☎04.42.91.91.11.

Post office 2 rue Lapierre.

Taxis Central Radio Taxi ☎04.42.21.61.61; Association des Taxis Radio Aixois ☎04.42.27.71.11 (24hr).

Mont Ste-Victoire

Mont Ste-Victoire, a rough pyramid whose apex has been pulled off-centre, lies 10km east of Aix. Ringed at its base by the dark green and orange-brown of pine woods and cultivated soil, the limestone rock reflects light, turning blue, grey, pink or orange. In the last years of his life **Cézanne** painted and drew Ste-Victoire more than fifty times, and, as part of his childhood landscape, it came to embody the incarnation of life within nature.

If you are interested in climbing Mont Ste-Victoire, hiking on the Mont, and many other summits in the area, is forbidden from July to mid-September. The southern face has a sheer five hundred-metre drop, but from the north the two-hour walk requires nothing more than determination. The **GR9**, also called the Chemin des Venturiers, leaves from a small car park on the D10 just before **VAUVENARGUES**, 14km east of Aix. Having reached the 945-metre ridge, marked by a monumental nineteenth-century cross that doesn't figure in any of Cézanne's pictures, you can follow the path east along the ridge to the summit of the massif and then descend south to **PUYLOUBIER** (about 15km from the cross; reckon on four and a half hours). Bring plenty of water and protection against the sun if walking in hot weather. Much of the walk was affected by forest fires in 1989 and, to guard against erosion, you're urged to stick to the path.

At Vauvenargues (several buses daily from the Aix *gare routière*), a perfect weather-beaten, red-shuttered fourteenth-century **château** (not open to the public) stands just outside the village, with nothing between it and the slopes of Ste-Victoire. **Picasso** bought the château in 1958, lived there until his death and now lies buried in the gardens, his grave adorned with his sculpture *Woman with a Vase*. There is a friendly, good-value hotel in the village, *Au Moulin de Provence*, 33 rue des Maquisards (☎04.42.66.02.22; ❷), whose owners speak English.

Central Provence

In **central Provence**, it's the landscapes – not the towns – that dominate. The gentle hills and tranquil villages of the **Haut-Var** make for happy exploration by car or bike, before the foothills of the Alps gradually close in around the citadelle town of **Sisteron** and further east, around **Dignes-les-Bains**. In the heart of Provence, the most exceptional geographical feature is undoubtedly the

Gorges du Verdon – Europe's answer to the Grand Canyon. As long's you have your own transport, good bases for exploring the majestic peaks, cliffs and lakes of this spectacular area are the small market town of **Aups**, to the south of the gorges, and to the northeast, **Castellane**, the place to go for Gorges-based sports and activities.

Aups

Charming and peaceful, **AUPS** is scarcely more than a village. On **place Martin-Bidauré**, which, along with **place Frédéric-Mistral** (Wed & Sat market), makes up the leafy open space before the start of the old town. The town's speciality is truffles; a marvellous **truffle market** takes place on Thursdays between November and mid-March.

Surprisingly for such a small place, Aups has a museum of modern art, the **Musée Simon Segal** in the former chapel of a convent on avenue Albert-1er (July & Aug daily 10am–noon & 4–7pm; €2.30). The best works are those by the Russian-born painter Simon Segal, but there are interesting local scenes in the other paintings, such as the Roman bridge at Aiguines, now drowned beneath the artificial lake of Sainte-Croix. Just outside Aups, 3.5km along the Tourtour road, is a sculpture park by local artist Maria de Faykod (daily except Tues: June 2–7pm; July & Aug 10am–noon & 3–7pm; Sept, Oct & Dec–May 2–6pm; closed Nov; €6), with dramatic human forms in marble.

Practicalities

The **tourist office** is part of the *mairie* on place Frédéric-Mistral (April–June & Sept Mon–Sat 8.30am–noon & 2–5pm; July & Aug daily Mon–Sat 8.30am–12.30pm & 3.30–7pm, Sun 9am–noon; Oct–March Mon–Sat 9am–noon & 2–5pm; ☎04.94.84.00.69, ⊛ www.aups-tourisme.com). All the **hotels** are good value: *Le Provençal* on place Martin-Bidauré (☎04.94.70.00.24, ⓕ04.94.84.06.25; ❸) and the *Auberge de la Tour* on rue J.P. Aloisi (☎04.94.70.00.30, ⊛www.aubergedelatour.com; ❸) are both good, inexpensive options, as is St-Marc (☎04.94.70.06.08, ⊛www.lesaintmarc.com; closed three weeks in Nov; ❷). The closest **campsite** to town is the two-star *Camping Les Prés*, to the right off allée Charles-Boyer towards Tourtour (☎04.94.70.00.93, ⓕ04.94.70.14.41; open all year; €12.50), with bikes to rent nearby.

As for **restaurants**, try the cheerful *L'Aiguière*, 6 place Maréchal Joffre (☎04.94.70.12.40; closed Sun evening & Mon), which serves delicious seafood and an impeccable scrambled eggs with truffle (€20), the truffle-obsessed *Restaurant des Gourmets* (☎04.94.70.14.97; *plats* around €22) on 5 rue Voltaire, or the popular *Le St-Marc* (see above), which has a delectable *marmite du chalutier* (fisherman's casserole) for €28; pre-order only.

Haut-Var villages

The little **villages** in the Haut-Var are some of the prettiest in all of Provence, It's essential to have your own wheels to be able to explore them all. Bask in their tranquility and beauty, wander the maze-like lanes and admire the glorious, verdant landscape – this is rural Provence at its best. The main historical sight in the area is the serene and substantial **Abbaye de Thoronet**, between the villages of Cabasse and Carcès, off the D79.

Around 18km southeast of Aups is lovely **LORGUES**, blessed with a serious gourmet **restaurant**, *Chez Bruno* (T04.94.85.93.93; closed Mon & Sun evening out of season; seasonal truffle menu at €130, à la carte around €59), on route de Vidauban, where the truffle reigns supreme, appearing in myriad forms, even in desserts. Heading 14km west, **ENTRECASTEAUX** has an ancient stone **laundry** by the river that's still used, and a very beautiful seventeenth-century **château** (tours Easter–Oct; ring in advance on T04.94.04.43.95). **COTIGNAC**, 9km west of Entrecasteaux, is the Haut-Var village *par excellence*, with a shaded main square for *pétanque* and passages and stairways bursting with begonias, jasmine and geraniums leading through a cluster of medieval houses. More gardens sprawl at the foot of the bubbly rock cliff that forms the back wall of the village, threaded with troglodyte walkways. If you fancy lunch or a reviving cup of tea, head for the quaint, flower-bedecked *Le Temps de Pose* (T04.94.77.72.07) on 11 place de Mairie; tasty, fresh sandwiches and quiches are around €6.

Six kilometres north of Cotignac is **SILLANS-LA-CASCADE**, which has a beautiful walk, signposted off the main road, to an immense waterfall and aquamarine pool (about 20min). **VILLECROZE** (15km) and **TOURTOUR** (21km) further northeast are both suitably picturesque and worth a wander. Between the two villages is an extremely popular, and highly regarded **restaurant**, *Les Chênes Verts* (T04.94.70.55.06; closed Tues, Wed, June & July), with a *menu dégustation* at €55.

Abbaye de Thoronet

East of the **Lac de Carcès** lies the last of the three great Cistercian monasteries of Provence. Even more so than Silvacane and Sénanque, the **Abbaye du Thoronet** (April–Sept Mon–Sat 10am–6.30pm, Sun 10am–noon & 2–6.30pm; Oct–March Mon–Sat 10am–1pm & 2–5pm, Sun 10am–noon & 2–5pm; €6.50) has been unscathed by the vicissitudes of time, and during the Revolution was kept intact as a remarkable monument of history and art; today it is occasionally used for concerts. It was first restored in the 1850s, while a more recent campaign has brought it to clear-cut perfection. As with the other two abbeys, its interior spaces, delineated by walls of pale rose-coloured stone, are inspiring.

Northwest of Aups

Two little towns worth visiting before embarking on the Gorges du Verdon are situated northwest of Aups: **Quinson**, which marks the start of the Basses Gorges du Verdon, and workaday **Riez**, with its smattering of Roman remains. One bus daily runs the 35min journey between the two towns.

Quinson

Around 20km west of Aups lies the small village of **QUINSON**. The chief attraction here is the **Musée du Préhistoire des Gorges du Verdon**, route de Montmeyan (Feb, March & Oct–Dec daily except Tues 10am–6pm; April–June & Sept daily except Tues 10am–7pm; July & Aug daily 10am–8pm; T04.92.74.09.59; €7), designed by the British architect Sir Norman Foster in a clean and sympathetic modern style, so that despite its immense size it does not dominate the village. It's the largest museum of human prehistory in Europe, and charts one million years of human habitation in Provence. The museum arranges hikes lasting three and a half hours to the **cave of Baume Bonne** (guided visits by arrangement; €4), the most important of the sixty or so archeological sites around Quinson. Excavations here have traced human habitation back 400,000 years. Less strenuous is a visit to the Prehistoric village and Neolithic Garden, set on the bank of the river (guided tours offered, reserve ahead; €4).

Riez

Fifteen kilometres west of Moustiers is bustling **RIEZ**, where the main business is derived from the lavender fields that cover this corner of Provence. The antiquity of the town soon becomes clear: standing in a field just off avenue Frederic Mistral at the bottom of allées Louis-Gardiol are four stately **Roman columns**, while over the river on the left of the road are the disappointing scant remains of a sixth-century **cathedral** (freely visited). If you fancy a **walk** with good views over the town, head first for the clock tower above Grande-Rue and then go up the steps past the cemetery where a stoney, curving path brings you to a cedar-shaded platform on the hilltop where the pre-Roman Riezians lived. The only building now occupying the site is the eighteenth-century Chapelle Ste-Maxime, with a gaudily patterned interior. Finally, it's well worth popping into the **Maison de l'Abeille** (10am–12.30pm & 2.30–7.30pm; closed Mon am; ☎04.92.77.84.15) 1km along the road to Digne, which has a small museum explaining how honey is made – along with two hives of the honey-makers themselves. There's the opportunity to taste and purchase the wonderful variety of produce, including the local speciality, lavender honey.

The **tourist office** is on place de la Marie (Mon–Sat 8.30am–12.15pm & 1–5pm; ☎04.92.77.99.09, ⓦwww.ville-riez.fr). Given the general lack of accommodation in Riez and its environs, it's best to just stop by for a day visit. For a long, relaxing **lunch** stop, try *Le Rempart* (☎04.92.77.89.54) on 17 rue du Marché; the Provençal and Italian *plats* (around €15) are superb, and a two- to three-hour meal for most diners seems to be the norm. If you're more pushed for time, *L'Art des Mets* at 26 allee Louis Gardiol (☎04.92.77.82.60) serves great salads and pizzas for €10.

The Gorges du Verdon and around

The **Gorges du Verdon** is also labelled the Grand Canyon du Verdon, and although on a much smaller scale, the breathtaking drama and beauty of the French landscape isn't far off its American counterpart. Peppered with spectacular viewpoints, plunging crevisses up to 700m deep, and glorious azure-blue lakes, the area is absolutely irrestible; you shouldn't leave Provence without spending at least a day here. The river falls from Rougon at the top of the gorge, disappearing into tunnels, decelerating for shallow, languid moments and finally exiting in full, steady flow at the **Pont de Galetas**, next to the huge artificial **Lac de Sainte-Croix**, which is great for swimming when the water levels are high; otherwise the beach becomes a bit sludgy.

West of the gorge

A convenient starting point to a trip round the Gorges, **MOUSTIERS-STE-MARIE** is a glorious place – and the number of tourists swamping the cobbled streets and little squares during the summer attest its beauty. Its loveliness is almost absurd: the backdrop of sheer cliffs and the single star suspended high above the village (don't forget to look up) being the sort of view that launched a thousand calendars. The town is mostly famous for its pretty, pastel faïence – virtually every house sells the stuff. You can best escape the shoppers by making the steep ascent to the **church of Notre Dame de Beauvoir**.

The **tourist office** is on place de l'Eglise (T04.92.74.67.84, Www.moustiers .fr). A more picturesque place to **stay** would be hard to find: try the very central *Le Relais* (T04.92.74.66.10, Www.lerelais-moustiers.com; open March to mid-Oct; ➍) on place du Couvert, or the four fresh and spacious rooms at the B&B, *Clerissy* (T04.92.74.62.67, Www.clerissy.fr; ➋; open Easter–Nov), place du Chevalier de Blacas. If you feel the need for some proper pampering, there's the famed hotel-restaurant *La Bastide de Moustiers* (T04.92.70.47.47, Www.bastide-moustiers.com; ➒), situated just below the village and run by celebrity chef Alain Ducasse; sophisticated menus start at €48. For cheaper **food**, try the *Coté Jardin* (T04.92.74.68.91; open Feb–Oct) on rue de Lérins, which has a shady terrace looking out over the valley; classic Provençal *plats* are around €18.

North of the gorge

Along the northern rim, the two most-visited towns are **LA PALUD-SUR-VERDON**, where the Route de Cretes begins and ends (see box below) and **ROUGON**, 8km to the east. Peace, tranquility and breathtaking scenery reign supreme here – whether you're staying for a while or just passing through, take the time to wander around the narrow, rambling streets and enjoy a meal or drink at a traditional restaurant or café.

Getting round the Gorges

With so many hairpin bends and twisting, narrow roads, it takes a full, rather exhausting day to get right round the Gorges; the entire circuit is 130km long and it's cycling country solely for the preternaturally fit.

Routes
Beginning at Moustiers-Ste-Marie or Lac-Ste-Croix, it's possible to drive along the **North Rim** (D952) or the **South Rim** (D71). The North Rim runs 31km east, all the way to Pont de Soleils, passing La Palud-sur-Verdon and Rougon, while the more protracted South Rim goes through Aiguines, Trigance and then on to the Pont de Soleils. Both routes have their share of spectacular lookout points – particularly the Balcons de la Mescla on the South Rim – and breathtaking scenery. Altenatively, you may prefer the more dramatic, looping **Routes des Crêtes** (D952) – on some of the highest stretches there's nothing to stop you driving straight off into the abyss – but it's not so consistently scenic, even though at some points you look down a sheer 800m drop to the sliver of water below. The mid-section of the Route des Crêtes is one way (westbound only), so if you want to do it all you'll have to start from the more scenic eastern end. It closes each winter from November 15 to March 15.

Public transport
Public transport around the canyon is less than comprehensive. One bus daily runs from Riez–Roumoles–Moustiers-Ste-Marie–la Palud-sur-Verdon–Rougon–Pont de Soleil–Castellane and back again (July–Aug Mon–Sat; April & Sept–Oct Mon, Wed & Sat; Nov–March Sat only on reservation T04.42.54.72.82).

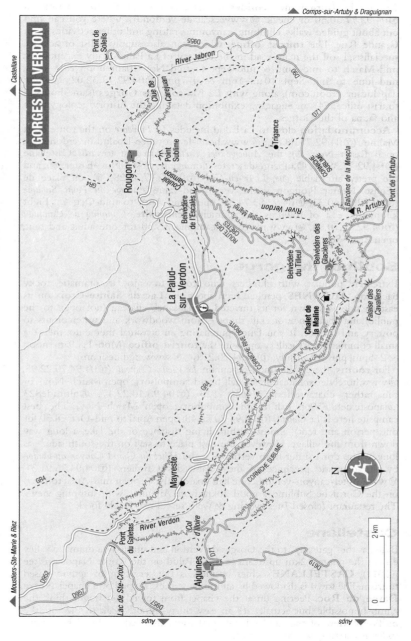

GORGES DU VERDON

Pont de
Soleils

River Jabron

D955

D90

D71

Clue de
Carejuan

Trigance

CORNICHE
SUBLIME

Point
Sublime

Balcons de la Mescla

Rougon

GR4

Couloir Samson

Pont de l'Artuby

R. Artuby

River Verdon

Belvédère
de l'Escalès

ROUTE DES CRÊTES

Sentier Martel

D90

Belvédère des
Glacières

Belvédère
du Tilleul

GR49

La Palud-
sur-Verdon

Falaise des
Cavaliers

CORNICHE DROITE

Chalet de
la Maline

GR4

CORNICHE SUBLIME

Mayreste

N

GR4

River Verdon

Col
d'Illoire

Pont
du Galetas

D19

D71

Aiguines

0   2 km

D952

D957

D957

Lac de Ste-Croix

D619

▼ Aups

▼ Aups

15

PROVENCE

La Palud is the place to go for information on **sports and activities** in the Gorges: the **Bureau des Guides** (hours erratic – call for information on ☎04.92.77.30.50 or check ⓦwww.escalade-verdon.fr), where you can find out about guided walks, climbing, canyoning, rafting and other activities, is on Grande Rue. The **tourist office**, which can also supply a list of activity specialists, is off the main road in the château of La Palud (daily except Tues: mid-March to mid-June & mid-Sept to mid-Nov 10am–noon & 4–6pm; mid-June to mid-Sept 10am–1pm & 4–7pm; ☎04.92.77.32.02, ⓦwww .lapaludsurverdon.com), along with **La Maison des Gorges** (same hours as tourist office; €4), an engaging exhibition detailing the history, geology, flora and fauna of the Gorges.

Accommodation close to La Palud includes *Le Provence* on the route de la Maline (☎04.92.77.38.88, ⓦwww.hotel-le-provence-lapaludsurverdon.com; open Easter–Nov; ❹); the *Auberge des Crêtes*, 1km east towards Castellane (☎04.92.77.38.47, ⓔaubergesdescretes@orange.fr; closed Nov–Easter; ❹); and the pretty, affordable *gîte*, *L'Arc-en-Ciel* (☎04.92.77.32.28; ❶), on place de l'Eglise. Nearer Rougon is the very good-value *Auberge du Point Sublime* (☎04.92.83.60.35, ⓕ04.92.83.74.31; open mid-April to mid-Oct; ❸). Eight kilometres east of town is the municipal **campsite**, *Camping de Carajuan* (☎04.92.83.70.94, ⓦwww.rougon.fr/camping; €5.30 for one adult and tent; open April–Sept).

South of the gorge

Extremely popular with climbers who come to enjoy its dramatic, rocky backdrop, **AIGUINES**, perched high above the **Lac de Sainte-Croix** on its eastern side, is known for its turreted Renaissance château (not open to the public) and abundance of craft shops – from woodwork and watercolours to pottery and faïence. If you fancy purchasing an artisinial memento, there's a small commerical art gallery opposite the **tourist office** (Mon–Fri 9am–noon & 2–5pm, plus Sat in July; ☎04.94.70.21.64, ⓦwww.aiguines.com).

For **rooms**, there's the hotel-restaurant *Le Vieux Château* (☎04.94.70.22.95, ⓦwww.hotelvieuxchateau.fr; ❹, half board compulsory; open March–Nov), or the rather characterless *Altitude 823* (☎04.98.10.22.17, ⓔaltitude823 @laposte.net; €59pp half board compulsory; open March–Nov). The best campsite here is *Le Galetas* (☎04.94.70.20.48; open April to mid-Oct; €8.30 for one person and tent), almost within diving distance of the lake, a long way down from the village. However, the best place to stay on the south side – as long as you don't suffer from vertigo – is the *Hôtel du Grand Canyon du Verdon* by the dramatic precipice of the Falaise des Cavaliers (☎04.94.76.91.31, ⓦwww.hotel-canyon-verdon.com; half board only; ❼; open mid-April to Nov) on the Corniche Sublime, a good 20km from Aiguines, with stunning views. The restaurant (closed Tues evening & Wed) serves reasonable food.

Castellane

Billed as the "gateway" to the Gorges du Verdon and sitting in a dramatic valley east of the gorge, 12km upstream from La Palud on the Route Napoleon (see p.1011), **CASTELLANE**'s chief business is the servicing of activity-based tourism. The town is shadowed by an immense rock, topped by a chapel, **Notre Dame du Roc**. Peering up at the chapel from town, you might think the climb impossible, but actually it's an easy thirty-minute walk to the top: the bird's-eye view of the jumbled medieval town huddled in the rich, verdant valley is certainly worth the effort.

The **tourist office**, at the top of rue Nationale (Mon–Sat 9.30am–noon & 2.30am–5.30pm; Sun 10am–noon; ☎04.92.83.61.14, ⓦwww.castellane.org), can provide a full list of the **hotels** and campsites in the village and its environs. An old-fashioned, and very comfortable, cheapie is the hotel-restaurant *Ma Petite Auberge* (☎04.92.83.62.06, ⓦwww.mapetiteauberge.com; ❸; open Feb–Nov), overlooking the main square at 8 boulevard de la Republique, while the three-star *Hôtel du Commerce* on place de l'Église (☎04.92.83.61.00, ⓦwww.hotel -fradet.com; ❹; open Feb–Nov) is the swanky option. The closest **campsite** to town, a mere hundred metres off place Marcel-Sauvaire on boulevard Frédéric-Mistral, is *Le Frédéric Mistral* (☎04.92.83.62.27). The town isn't blessed with superb **restaurants**, but you can get a very decent meal at *La Voute* (☎04.92.83.10.59), on rue du Mitan. Steaks (€15), aubergine gratin (€10) and creamy yogurt with honey (€6) are all on the menu.

Castellane is packed with adventure activity specialists offering everything from **canyoning** to **canoeing** and **mountain biking** in the Gorges du Verdon: Sports Passion (☎04.92.83.64.06, ⓦwww.sports-passion-verdon.com) at 9 rue du Mitan, Aqua Verdon at 9 rue Nationale (☎04.92.83.72.75, ⓦwww .aquaverdon.org), Aboard Rafting (☎04.92.83.76.11, ⓦwww.aboard-rafting .com) on place de l'Église, to name but a few.

Alpes de Haute-Provence

North of Castellane, the **Route Napoléon** passes through the barren scrubby rocklands of some of the most obscure and empty parts of Provence, the **Alpes de Haute-Provence**. The road was built in the 1930s to commemorate the great leader's journey north through Haute-Provence on return from exile on Elba in 1815, in the most audacious and vain recapture of power in French history. Using mule paths still deep with winter snow, Napoleon and his seven hundred soldiers forged ahead towards **Digne-les-Bains** and **Sisteron** on their way to Grenoble – a total of 350km – in just six days. One hundred days later, he lost the battle of Waterloo and was permanently incarcerated on the island of St Helena.

Digne-les-Bains

Possessing a rather unlikely connection with Tibet, **DIGNE-LES-BAINS** is the chief town of the Alpes-de-Haute-Provence *département*. The surrounding area has particular attractions for geologists: covering over 150,000 hectares to the north and east of the town, the **Réserve Naturelle Géologique de Haute-Provence** is the largest geological reserve in Europe, with fossils dating back 300 million years. To learn a little more about these, visit the ammonite-laden

The Chemin de Fer de la Provence

To see some of the most breathtaking scenery – glittering rivers, lush dark-green forests, dramatic cliff faces, plunging gorges – in the region, take a trip on the narrow-gauge **Chemin de Fer de la Provence**, also known as the **Train des Pignes** (named after the pinecones that were originally used as fuel). The line runs between Dignes-les-Bains and Nice; other stations en route are Annot and St-André-les-Alpes. A single ticket from Dignes to Nice is €17.50 per person, and the journey takes around three hours. For more information, see ⓦwww.trainprovence.com.

Musée-Promenade (April–Oct daily 9am–noon & 2–5.30pm, closes Fri 4.30pm; July–Aug Mon–Fri 9am–1pm & 2–7pm, Sat & Sun 10.30am–12.30pm & 2–7pm; Nov–March Mon–Fri 9am–noon & 2–5.30pm; €4.60; ℡04.92.36.70.70) just north of the city, down to the left after the bridge across the river on the Barles road.

If you only have time to see one museum, make sure it's the **Musée Alexandra David–Neel** at 27 avenue du Maréchal-Juin (guided visits daily 10am, 2pm & 3.30pm; free; ℡04.92.31.32.38) – the reason for the town's link to Tibet. Dedicated solely to the memory of this extraordinary, tenacious explorer who spent over fourteen years travelling the length and breadth of Tibet, the museum is where David-Neel lived out the remainder of her life, eventually dying at the age of 101. The house is stuffed full of fascinating photographs tracing her journeys, old Tibetan ornaments, masks and paintings. Paling in comparison, but still worth a visit for its interesting temporary exhibitions, is the municipal museum, **Musée Gassendi** at 64 boulevard Gassendi (daily except Tues: April–Sept 11am–7pm; Oct–March 1.30–5.30pm; €4), which holds some sixteenth- to nineteenth-century paintings and pays homage to local seventeenth-century mathematician and savant Pierre Gassendi.

The **tourist office** is on the *rond point* du 11-Novembre-1918 (June–Sept Mon–Sat 8.45am–12.30pm & 2–6.30pm, Sun 10am–noon; Oct–May Mon–Sat 8.45am–noon & 2–6pm; ℡04.92.36.62.62, ⓦ www.ot-dignelesbains.fr), with the **gare routière** adjacent. The **gare Chemins de Fer de la Provence** is to the west over the river on avenue Pierre-Sémard (see box, p.1011). **Hotel** options include the central *Hotel Julia*, on place Pied deVille (℡04.92.32.22.96, ⓔjuliacharmer@orange.fr; ❷), and the much more luxurious *Le Grand Paris*, 19 boulevard Thiers (℡04.92.31.11.15, ⓦ www.hotel-grand-paris.com; ❺; open March–Nov), which has an expensive, semi-gastronomic restaurant (closed Mon, Tues & Wed lunchtime out of season; menus from €32), along with a surprising menagerie in the reception. For cheaper food, go for the modern *La Taverne*, 36 boulevard Gassendi (℡04.92.31.30.82; closed Sun), which serves *raclette* (€16) and traditional menus from €18.

Sisteron

The Route Napoléon leads eventually to **SISTERON**, 25km northwest of Digne, and the most important mountain gateway to Provence. The site has been fortified since time immemorial and even now, half destroyed by the Anglo-American bombardment of 1944, its citadel stands as a fearsome sentinel over the city and the solitary bridge across the River Durance.

Even the quickest of visits should include a trip up to the magnificent **citadelle** (April–Nov daily 9am–dusk; €5); the views from the remparts are breath-taking. A small **historical museum** with a room dedicated to Napoleon lies just inside the walls, and further up is the vertiginous late-medieval chapel, **Notre-Dame-du-Château**, restored to its Gothic glory and equipped with lovely stained-glass windows, added in the 1970s. It was here that the future king of Poland, Jan Kazimierz, was imprisoned in 1639; there's a stuffed model of the unfortunate royal, and a reconstruction of his room, in the main tower. In July and August, the festival, the Nuits de la Citadelle, takes place; there are open-air performances of music, drama and dance in the citadel grounds.

Back in Sisteron's old town, you'll see three large **towers**, which belonged to the citadelle ramparts, built in 1370. Beside them is the **Cathédrale Notre-Dame-des-Pommiers** (daily 3–6pm), a cool and well-proportioned twelfth-century church. From the cathedral, rue Deleuze leads to **place de l'Horloge**, where the

Wednesday and Saturday **market** is held and where, on the second Saturday of every month, there's a fair. If you fancy a **swim**, take a dip in the large artificial lake between the allée de Verdon and the river (summer only).

Practicalities

Arriving by train at Sisteron, turn right out of the **gare SNCF** along avenue de la Libération until you reach place de la République, where you'll find the **tourist office** (July–Aug Mon–Sat 9am–7pm, Sun 10am–1pm; Sept–June Mon–Sat 9am–noon & 2–6pm; ☎04.92.61.36.50, ⓦwww.sisteron.fr) and the **gare routière**. The genteel and old-fashioned *Grand Hôtel du Cours* on allée de Verdon (☎04.92.61.04.51, ⓦwww.hotel-lecours.com; ❹; open March–Dec), is the best **hotel** in town. For cheap, clean rooms with great views of the imposing landscape, head for *La Citadelle* (☎04.92.61.13.52, ⓦwww.hotel-lacitadelle .com; ❷) at 126 rue Saunerie. Sisteron's four-star **campsite**, *Les Prés Hauts*, is across the river and 2km along the D951 (☎04.92.61.19.69; open March–Oct; €13.50 for two people and a tent).

Don't expect much from Sisteron's **restaurants**: *Le Cours* (see above) serves traditional *plats* for around €20, including the renowned *gigot d'agneau de Sisteron*, while *Les Becs Fins* (☎04.92.61.12.04; closed Sun evening & Mon out of season), 16 rue Saunerie, is a decent place to sample pricey fish dishes; *plats* go for €20.

Northeast Provence

Depending on the season, the **northeastern corner of Provence** is two different worlds. In winter, the sheep and shepherds find warmer pastures, leaving the snowy heights to horned mouflons, chamois and the perfectly camouflaged ermine. The villages where shepherds came to summer markets are battened down for the long, cold haul, while modern conglomerations of Swiss-style chalet houses, sports shops and discotheques come to life around the ski lifts. The seasonal dichotomy is particularly evident in towns like **Colmars-les-Alpes** and **Barcelonnette**.

The **Alpes-Mairitimes** make up much of northeastern Provence, encompassing a large amount of the magnificent **Parc National du Mercantour** (see box, p.1014), which runs south of Barcelonnette to the Italian border villages of Tende, Breil-sur-Roya and Sospel. Base yourself in one of the small Alpes-Maritime towns, which include **St-Étienne-de-Tinée**, **St-Martin-Vésubie**, **St-Sauveur-sur-Tinée** and from the **upper Roya valley**.

Colmars-les-Alpes

On the western periphery of the Parc National du Mercantour is the charming village of **Colmars-les-Alpes**; and if you're driving northwards on the D908 towards Barcelonnette, it makes an ideal journey's break, even out of season, when it's spookily empty. Secreted away in a valley behind imposing, honey-coloured walls and large seventeenth-century *portes*, the place comes to life in winter as a base for skiers, and during the summer festivals (third week in July and second Sunday in August).

The **tourist office** (℡04.92.83.41.92, ⓦwww.colmars-les-alpes.fr) is situated just outside the walls in the *Ancienne Auberge Fleurie*. There's one **hotel**, the *Hôtel Le France* (℡04.92.83.42.93, ⓦwww.hotel-lefrance-colmars.com; ❸), which also has apartments (one bedroom, from €450 for seven nights). There are few **restaurants**; you could try the *Le Lezard* on place Neuve, 2km from the town (℡04.92.83.64.41), the pizzeria of the hotel or cobble together a picnic from the summer **market** (Tues & Fri). Out of season, you'll be restricted to the bakeries near the tourist office.

Barcelonnette

Forty-four kilometres north of Colmars, and surrounded by majestic snow-capped mountains, attractive **Barcelonnette** teems with skiiers in the winter and is packed with party-goers during the August Mexican festival; the rest of the year it's pretty dead.

The town has an unlikely link with Mexico: in the late nineteenth and twentieth centuries, there was a mass migration to the Americas, and those who came back years later brought with them wealth and many Mexican habits and customs. If you want to learn more about this connection, head for the **Musée de la Vallée**, which is housed in an elegant Mexican-style villa at 10 avenue de la Libération (Wed–Sat 2.30–6pm; June–Sept Tues–Sat 2.30–7pm; July 11 to Aug 28 daily 10am–noon & 2.30–7pm; €3.30). There are engrossing photographs, letters, clothes and various other objects pertaining to the mass exodus. La Maison du Parc (℡04.92.81.21.31, ⓦwww.mercantour .eu) for the Mercantour shares the premises.

Practicalities

Barcelonnette's **tourist office** is on place Frédéric-Mistral (Mon–Sat 9am–noon & 2–6pm; ℡04.92.81.04.71, ⓦwww.barcelonnette.com). The top **hotel** is the Mexican-style *Azteca* on rue François-Arnaud (℡04.92.81.46.36, ⓦwww.azteca-hotel.fr; ❹), while the traditional *Le Cheval Blanc*, 12 rue Grenette (℡04.92.81.00.19, ⓦwww.chevalblancbarcelonnette.com; ❸), is a cheaper option. There are three **campsites**, the closest being the three-star *Du Plan* at 52 avenue E.-Aubert (℡04.92.81.08.11, ⓦwww.campingduplan.fr; closed late Sept to mid-May; €12 for two people and a tent).

The Parc National du Mercantour

The 685km **Parc National du Mercantour** is a long, narrow band of mountainland running for 75km close to the Italian border, from south of Barcelonnette to Sospel, 16km north of the Mediterreanean. The area is a haven for wildlife, with colonies of chamois, mouflon, ibex and marmots, breeding pairs of golden eagles and other rare birds of prey, great spotted woodpeckers and hoopoes, blackcocks and ptarmigan. In recent years grey wolves have begun returning to the area from neighbouring Italy, since disappearing in the 1930s. The flora too is very special, with many unique species of lilies, orchids and Alpine plants, including the rare multi-flowering saxifrage.

The park is crossed by numerous paths, including the GR5 and GR52, with *refuge* huts providing basic food and bedding for hikers. For more detailed information, contact the **Maisons du Parc** in Barcelonnette, St-Étienne-de-Tinée or St-Martin-Vésubie, which can provide maps and accommodation details as well as advice on footpaths and weather conditions. Camping, lighting fires, picking flowers, playing radios or doing anything that might disturb the delicate environment is strictly outlawed.

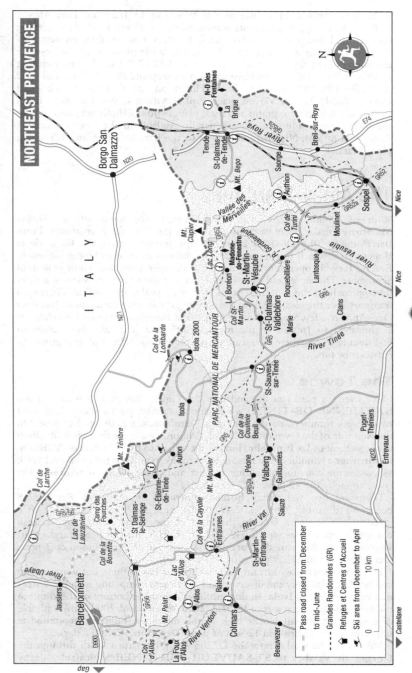

N

ITALY

Borgo San Dalmazzo

N20

N21

Col de la Lombarde

Col de Larche

River Ubaye

Jausiers

Barcelonnette

Col de la Bonette

Camp des Fourches

Lac de Lauzanier

GR5/56

GR56

Mt. Pelat

La Foux d'Allos

Col d'Allos

River Verdon

Allos

Lac d'Allos

Ratery

Colmars

Beauvezer

Castellane

St Dalmas-le-Selvage

St-Étienne-de-Tinée

Auron

Mt. Ténibre

Isola 2000

Isola

PARC NATIONAL DE MERCANTOUR

Col de la Cayolle

Entraunes

St-Martin-d'Entraunes

Mt. Mounier

GR52a

Péone

Col de la Couillole

Beuil

Valberg

Guillaumes

Sauze

River Var

Puget-Théniers

Entrevaux

N202

St-Sauveur-sur-Tinée

Marie

Clans

River Tinée

GR5

St-Dalmas-Valdeblore

Col St-Martin

Le Boréon

St-Martin-Vésubie

Madone-de-Fenestre

Lac Long

Mt. Clapier

Vallée des Merveilles

Mt. Bégo

N-D des Fontaines

La Brigue

Tende

St-Dalmas-de-Tende

GR52

River Roya

Breil-sur-Roya

E74

GR52

Saorge

Sospel

Nice

Nice

GR52a

GR52

Moulinet

Col de Turini

Authion

r. Gordolasque

Roquebillière

Lantosque

River Vésubie

GR5

15

PROVENCE

1015

== Pass road closed from December to mid-June

--- Grandes Randonnées (GR)

Ⓘ Refuges et Centres d'Accueil

Ski area from December to April

0   10 km

Gap

Gap

The best **restaurant** in the area is 9km east in **Jausiers**: *Villa Morella* (☏04.92.84.67.78, ⓦwww.villa-morelia.com) is a Mexican place serving sophisticated nouvelle cuisine (menu €68). Back towards Barcelonnette, try the cosy *Le Refuge des Marmottes* at Le Pied de la Maure, opposite the bowling alley about 2km southwest of town (☏04.92.32.17.71) for hearty, warming cuisine. In Barcelonnette itself, sample some cheap and cheerful Mexican food at *Adelita* (☏04.92.81.16.12; closed Thurs) on rue Donnadieu, while *La Plancha* (☏04.92.81.12.97) on place Paul Reynaud serves mountain dishes such as *tartiflette*, potato gratin and meat platters from €15. Be sure also to taste the local juniper liquor, *Genepy*, generally available in the town on market days (Wed & Sat). **Nightlife** is limited to the bars *St-Tropez* and *Chocas* on place Manuel.

The Alpes-Maritimes

With an economy driven mostly by tourism, the towns of the **Alpes-Maritimes** make great bases for exploring the Parc du Mercantour. From Barcelonnette (the D64) it's a breathtaking journey across the Cime de la Bonette pass, which reaches over 2800m and is is claimed to be the highest in Europe. It's only open for three months of the year, from the end of June until September. The air is cold even in summer and the green and silent spaces of the approach to the summit, circled by barren peaks, are magical. There's no transport over the pass, but from Barcelonnette you can take a *navette* (Sat only Dec–April & a few weekly July & Aug; ask at Barcelonnette's tourist office for a timetable) to Jausiers at the route's north end, and hike from there to St-Étienne, from where you can then connect to Nice and the points in between by bus.

The Towns

Once over the pass, you descend into the Tinée valley and its highest town, **ST-ÉTIENNE-DE-TINÉE**, which springs awake for its sheep fairs, held twice every summer, and the Fête de la Transhumance at the end of June. On the west side of the town off boulevard d'Auron, a cable car then chair lift climb to the summit of **La Pinatelle**, linking the village to the ski resort of **AURON**. In **summer** a handful of the lifts are open to hikers and mountain bikers (check ⓦwww.auron.com for telephone contact and tarifs) while in **winter** skiers come to enjoy the 42 *pistes* (€27.80 a day).

There are two welcoming **hotel-restaurants** on offer: the *Regalivou*, 8 boulevard d'Auron (☏04.93.02.49.00; ❷), and *Des Amis*, 1 rue Val-Gélé (☏&ⓕ04.93.02.40.30; ❷). On the edge of the village, you'll find a small **campsite** (open June–Sept; ☏04.93.02.41.57; €8.50 for two people and a tent) adjacent to the **Maison du Parc** (July & Aug daily 9.30am–noon & 2–6pm; Oct–May open until 5.30pm; ☏04.93.01.42.27).

The next stretch downstream from St-Étienne has nothing but white quartz and heather, with only the silvery sound of crickets competing with the water's roar before reaching **Isola**, an uneventful village at the bottom of the climb to the purpose-built ski resort of **ISOLA 2000** (ⓦwww.isola2000.com), a jumble of concrete apartment blocks high in the mountain, built to accommodate skiers using the 22 lifts and 120km of piste (Dec–April; €27.80 a day).

After Isola, the road – now the D2205 – and river turn south through the **Gorges de Valabre** to **ST-SAUVEUR-SUR-TINÉE**, a pleasantly sleepy place, with a boulangerie on place de la Mairie selling general provisions (daily except Tues in winter 1–4pm). Shifting east to the Vésubie valley, you come to the lovely little town of **ST-MARTIN-VÉSUBIE** where a cobbled, narrow street with a channelled stream runs through the old quarter beneath the overhanging roofs and balconies of Gothic houses. The **tourist office** on place Félix-Faure (July–Aug daily 9am–1pm & 2.30–7pm; Sept–June Mon–Sat 9am–noon & 2–6pm, Sun 10am–noon; ☎04.93.03.21.28, Ⓦwww.saintmartinvesubie.fr) provides details on walks and *gîtes/refuges* in the vicinity as well as information on the wolf reserve, **Alpha** (summer daily 10am–7pm; winter Wed, Sat & Sun 10am–4.30pm; ☎04.93.02.33.69, Ⓦwww.alpha-loup.com; €10) – in spring, you can see newborn wolf puppies from three observation points.

If you're **staying**, try the cute *Hôtel Gélas* (☎04.93.03.21.81, Ⓦwww.hotel -gelas.com; ❹) or *Edward's et la Châtaigneraie* (☎04.93.03.21.22, Ⓦwww .raiberti.com; half board compulsory; €52 per person for two people; open June–Sept), on allées de Verdon, with a swimming pool. The closest **campsite** is the *Ferme St-Joseph* (☎04.93.03.20.14; all year; €10.80 for two people and a tent), on the route de Nice by the lower bridge over La Madone. The **restaurant** to go for is the unpretentious and inexpensive *La Treille* (☎04.93.03.30.85) at 68 rue Docteur Cagnoli.

The Roya valley

The thickly forested **Roya valley** – made up of the **upper** and **lower** parts – runs from Col de Tende on the French–Italian border down to Breil-sur-Roya. The major highlight in the upper valley is the **Vallée des Merveilles**, a jumble of lakes and tumbled rocks situated on the western flank of Mont Bego; the first person to stumble on the area was a fifteenth-century traveller who had lost his way. He described it as "an infernal place with figures of the devil and thousands of demons scratched on the rocks": a pretty accurate description, except that some of the carvings are of animals, tools, people working and mysterious symbols, dated to some time in the second millennium BC. In the lower valley, head for the sleepy Italianate town of **Sospel**.

Getting around the region is relatively time-consuming; the roads are narrow and steep so driving can be slow, and the once-daily **Train des Merveilles** (departs Nice 9am; €22 return), with an English commentary (May–Oct), trundles along the Nice–Cuneo line at a leisurely pace. There are also normal trains running along the same line, for those who want a later start.

The upper Roya valley

Near the end of the Train des Merveilles line is **TENDE**, where the French spoken has a distinctly Italian accent. The old town is fun to wander through, looking at the symbols of old trades on the door lintels, the overhanging roofs and multiple balconies, and there's a beautifully designed **Musée des Merveilles** (May to mid-Oct daily 10am–6.30pm; mid-Oct to April daily except Tues 10am–5pm; free; tour by appointment on ☎04.93.04.32.50; €22.85), on avenue du 16-Septembre-1947, where you can check out reproductions of the engravings on the Vallée des Merveilles. The **tourist office** is at 103 avenue 16-Septembre-1947 (daily 9am–noon & 2–6pm, Oct–May until 5.30pm; ☎04.93.04.73.71, Ⓦwww.tendemerveilles.com). For **accommodation**, there's the basic *Du Centre* on place de la République

(☎04.93.04.62.19; ❶; closed two weeks in Nov). Tende has plenty of shops and restaurants located on avenue du 16-Septembre-1947, though nothing very special on the gourmet front.

One stop south from Tende is pretty **LA BRIGUE**, which makes a good base for the Vallée des Merveilles. While you're here, make the trip 4km east of town to the sanctuary of **Notre-Dame-des-Fontaines** (May–Sept daily 10am–noon & 2–5.30pm; €1.50; tours possible, ask at the tourist office), whose frescoes were executed by one Jean Canavéso. The frescoes, which cover the entire building, are akin to an arcade of video nasties – the goriest detail is a devil extracting Judas's soul from his disembowelled innards. The **tourist office** is on place St-Martin (April–Oct daily 9am–noon & 2–5.30pm; winter Tues–Sat 9.30am–12.30pm & 1.30–4.30pm; ☎04.93.79.09.34, ⓦwww .labrigue.fr; closed mid-Jan to mid-Feb). The three **hotels** in La Brigue are *Le and Mirval*, rue Vincent-Ferrier (☎04.93.04.63.71, ⓦwww.lemirval.com; ❷). *Auberge St-Martin* (☎04.93.04.62.17, ⓦwww.auberge-st-martin.fr; ❸) and the *Fleurs des Alpes* (☎04.93.04.61.05, ⓔhotel.fleurdesalpes@tiscali.fr; ❸), both on place St-Martin. They all have decent restaurants serving inexpensive, traditional cuisine.

The Vallée des Merveilles is best approached from **ST-DALMAS-DE-TENDE** one stop south of La Brigue. The easiest route into the valley is the ten-kilometre hike (5–7hr there and back) that starts at *Les Mesches Refuge*, about 8km west of St-Dalmas-de-Tende, on the D91. The engravings are beyond the *Refuge des Merveilles*. Note that certain areas are out of bounds unless accompanied by an official guide – and remember that blue skies and sun can quickly turn into violent hailstorms and lightning, so go prepared, properly shod and clothed, and take your own food and water. **Guided walks** around the area depart from the *refuge* and last between 2hr 30min and 3hr 30min (June weekends only; Sept Fri–Wed 8am & 1pm; July–Aug daily 8am, 11am, 1pm, 3pm; €10; contact Maison du Mercantour in Tende ☎04.93 04.73.71, or local tourist offices).

The lower Roya valley

The best place to spend a relaxed day, or couple of days, in the lower Roya valley is **SOSPEL**, situated three stops south of St-Dalmas-de-Tende. You may find it over-tranquil after the excitements of the high mountains or the flashy speed of the Côte d'Azur, but it can make a pleasant break.

Sospel

Sospel's main street, avenue Jean-Médecin, follows the river on its southern bank; halfway down is the **Vieux Pont**, built originally in the thirteenth century to link the town centre on the south bank with its suburb across the river. The town centre is made up of dark, narrow lanes, with its heart at **place St-Michel**, a riot of colourful Baroque facades and arcaded houses, dominated by the large Cathedrale St-Michel. For something a little more contemporary, head ten minutes out of town, left along boulevard de Verdun to the **Musée du Fort St-Roch**, a resistance museum (☎04.93.04.15.80; April–May & Oct Sat & Sun 2–6pm; June–Sept Tues–Sun 2–6pm; €3) housed in an imposing concrete bunker, reaching at times depths of 30m.

The best view of the town is reached via a relatively easy three-hour **hike** up Col d'Agaisen, starting from the Pont de la Liberation and walking away from the old town. The tourist office (see opposite) has a map of the route, and there are plenty of signs to point you in the right direction.

Practicalities

The **gare SNCF** is southeast of the town on avenue A.-Borriglione, which becomes avenue des Martyrs-de-la-Résistance, before leading down to the park on place des Platanes opposite place St-Pierre. The friendly **tourist office**, is at 19 avenue Jean-Médecin (mid-June to mid-Sept Mon–Sat 9.30am–6.30pm; mid-Sept to mid-June 10am–12.30pm & 1.30–5pm; ☏04.93.04.15.80, ⓦwww.sospel -tourisme.com). The two hotels to go for are next to each other on boulevard de Verdun: at no. 9 is the cheaper *Hôtel de France*, (☏04.93.04.00.01, ⓦwww.hotel defrance-sospel.com; ❷), with comfortable, colourful rooms, while *Hotel des Etrangers* (☏04.93.04.00.09, ⓦwww.sospel.net; ❹), at no. 7, is smarter and has a pool and a good restaurant (à la carte €16). There are three **campsites** around Sospel, the closest of which is *Le Mas Fleuri* in *quartier* La Vasta (☏04.93.04.03.48, ⓦwww.camping-mas-fleuri.com; €15.50 for two people and a tent), with its own pool, 2km along the D2566 to Moulinet, following the river upstream.

As for **restaurants**, there's *Le Relais du Sel* (☏04.93.04.00.43; closed Fri out of season) on boulevard de Verdun, serving very affordable and good-quality dishes (menus from €22) – the home-made profiteroles are particularly special (€10). If you find it open – the hours can be unreliable – *Sout'a Laupia* (☏04.93.04.00.43) at 13 rue St-Pierre serves delicious traditional cuisine, from rabbit with *cepes* (€14.50) and basil-infused trout (€13) to generous salads and pasta (€10).

Travel details

Trains

Aix-en-Provence to: Marseille (every 30min; 30–45min).
Aix-en-Provence TGV to: Avignon TGV (17 daily; 20min); Lille-Europe (5 daily; 4hr 30min); Lyon (10 daily; 1hr 30min); Marseille (frequent daily; 15min); Paris (8 daily; 3hr); Paris CDG Airport (4 daily; 3hr 30min); Valence TGV (3 daily; 50hr).
Arles to: Avignon (11–16 daily; 20min); Avignon TGV (4 daily; 40min); Lyon (7–9 daily; 2hr 45min); Marseille (frequent; 45min–1hr).
Avignon to: Arles (hourly; 20–45min); Cavaillon (9–14 daily; 35min); Lyon (frequent daily; 2hr 30min); Marseille (14 daily; 1hr 5min); Orange (17 daily; 15min); Valence (half-hourly at peak times; 1hr 20min).
Avignon TGV to: Aix-en-Provence TGV (22 daily; 20min); Lille-Europe (5 daily; 4hr 30min); London St. Pancras (summer 1 on sat only: 5hr 53min; Lyon (14 daily; 1hr 10min); Marseille (frequent; 30min); Paris (17 daily; 2hr 40min); Paris CDG Airport (5 daily; 3hr 30min); Valence TGV (9 daily; 30–40min).
Digne to: Nice, via Aix en Provence (4 daily; 6hr).
Orange to: Paris (2 daily; 2hr 30min).
Sospel to: La Brigue (1–3 daily; 50min); Nice (4 daily; 50min); St-Dalmas-de-Tende (3 daily; 45min); Tende (3 daily; 55min).

Valence TGV to: Aix-en-Provence TGV (5 daily; 1hr); Avignon TGV (11 daily; 35min); Lyon (11–19 daily; 35min); Marseille (10 daily; 1hr 5min); Paris (10 daily; 2hr 15min).
Vienne to: Lyon (frequent; 20–30min); Valence (frequent; 50min).

Buses

Aix-en-Provence to: Apt (2 daily; 1hr 50min); Arles (7 daily; 1hr 15min); Avignon (6 daily; 1hr 15min); Bonnieux (2 daily; 1hr 30min); Carpentras (3–4 daily; 1hr 30min); Cavaillon (4 daily; 1hr 20min); Marseille (frequent; 30–50min); Sisteron (3 daily; 2hr).
Apt to: Aix en Provence (1 daily; 2 hr); Bonnieux (3 daily; 20min).
Arles to: Aix (3 daily; 1hr 15min); Avignon (7 daily; 1hr 15min); Avignon TGV (5 daily; 35–40min); Cavaillon (3 daily; 1hr 20min); Stes-Maries-de-la-Mer (4–7 daily; 55min); St-Rémy (4 daily; 25–30min).
Aups to: Aiguines (1 daily; 35min); Cotignac (3 daily; 25min).
Avignon to: Aix (6 daily; 1hr 15min); Apt (7 daily; 1hr 10min–1hr 30min); Arles (10 daily; 50min); Carpentras (frequent; 35–45min); Cavaillon (9 daily; 35min); Digne (3–4 daily; 3hr–3hr 30min); Fontaine-de-Vaucluse (4 daily; 55min); L'Isle-sur-la-Sorgue (10 daily; 40min); Orange (daily

every 30–45min); St-Rémy (8 daily; 40min); Vaison (3 daily; 1hr 25min).

Barcelonnette to: Digne (2 daily; 1hr 45min); Gap (3 daily; 1hr 20min); Marseille (2 daily; 3hr 50min).

Carpentras to: Aix (3–4 daily; 1hr 25min–1hr 50min); Avignon (4 daily; 1hr); Cavaillon (2–5 daily; 45min); Gigondas (1–3 daily; 30min); L'Isle-sur-la-Sorgue (5 daily; 20min); Marseille (3 daily; 1hr 15min–2hr 5min); Orange (3 daily; 40–45min); Vaison (4 daily; 45min).

Cavaillon to: Gordes (3–4 daily; 30min).

Digne to: Aix (4 daily; 2hr); Avignon (3 daily; 3hr 30min); Barcelonnette (2 daily; 1hr–1hr 30min); Marseille (4 daily; 2hr–2hr 20min); Nice (2 daily; 3hr–3hr 15min); Riez (3 daily; 1hr 15min); Sisteron (3 daily; 1hr 15min).

Gigondas to: Carpentras (1–3 daily; 30min).

Gordes to: Cavaillon (3 daily; 30min).

Isle-sur-la-Sorgue to: Carpentras (2–5 daily; 45min).

Isola 2000 to: Nice (3–6 daily; 2hr 30min); St-Sauveur-sur-Tinée (3–6 daily; 45min).

Orange to: Avignon (frequent; 50min); Carpentras (3 daily; 40–45min); Châteauneuf-du-Pape (1 Thurs; 30min); Séguret (2 daily; 40min); Sérignan (7 daily; 15min); Vaison (2 daily; 40–50min).

Quinson to: Riez (1 daily; 35min).

St-Rémy to: Les Baux (4 daily; 15–20min).

Riez to: Digne-les-Bains (3 daily; 1hr 15min); Moustiers-Ste-Marie (2 daily; 20min); Quinson (1 daily; 35min).

Sisteron to: Digne (2 daily; 1hr 15min).

16

The Côte d'Azur

CHAPTER 16

Highlights

* **Vieux Port, Marseille** The gritty port, with its bars, cafés and restaurants, attracts the most colourful characters in southern France. **See p.1028**

* **Les Calanques** The limestone cliffs between Marseille and Cassis make for excellent hikes leading to isolated coves in which to go swimming. **See p.1036**

* **Îles de Port-Cros and St-Honorat** These well-preserved islands offer a glimpse of what much of the coast must have looked like a hundred years ago. **See pp.1043 & 1064**

* **Massif des Maures** This undeveloped range of hazy coastal hills is a world apart from the glitz and glamour of the Côte. **See p.1046**

* **Fondation Maeght** Modern art, architecture and landscape fuse to create a stunning visual experience. **See p.1072**

* **Nice** The Riviera's capital of street life is laid back, surprisingly cultured and easy to enjoy, whatever your budget. **See p.1074**

▲ Vieux port, Marseille

The Côte d'Azur

The **Côte d'Azur** polarizes opinion like few places in France. To some, it remains the ultimate Mediterranean playground, while for others it has become an overdeveloped victim of its own hype. But in the gaps between the urban sprawl, on the islands, in the remarkable beauty of the hills, the scent of the plant life, the mimosa blossom in February and the impossibly blue water after which the coast is named, the Côte d'Azur remains undeniably captivating. The chance to see the work of artists seduced by the land and light also justifies the trip: Cocteau in **Menton** and **Villefranche**, Matisse and Chagall in **Nice** and **Vence**, Léger in **Biot**, Picasso in **Antibes** and **Vallauris**, and Fauvists and Impressionists at St-Tropez and Hauts-de-Cagnes. And while you'll either love or hate **Monaco** and **Cannes**, they certainly have entertainment value, and the great cities of **Marseille** and Nice possess their own special magnetism.

Food and wine of the Côte d'Azur

The **Côte d'Azur**, as part of Provence, shares its culinary fundamentals of olive oil, garlic and the herbs that flourish in dry soil, its gorgeous vegetables and fruits, plus Menton's lemons, the goat's cheeses and, of course, the predominance of fish.

The fish soups of **bouillabaisse**, famous in Marseille, and **bourride**, accompanied by a garlic and chilli-flavoured mayonnaise known as *rouille*, are served all along the coast, as are **fish** covered with Provençal herbs and grilled over an open flame. **Seafood** – from spider crabs to clams, sea urchins to crayfish, crabs, lobster, mussels and oysters – are piled onto huge *plateaux de mer*, which don't necessarily represent Mediterranean harvest, more the luxury associated with this coast.

The **Italian influence** is strong, with delicate ravioli stuffed with spinach, prawns, wild mushrooms or *pistou*, pizzas with wafer-thin bases and every sort of pasta as a vehicle for anchovies, olives, garlic and tomatoes. **Nice** has its own specialities, such as *socca*, a chickpea flour pancake, *pissaladière*, a tart of fried onions with anchovies and black olives, *salade niçoise* and *pan bagnat*, both of which combine egg, olives, salad, tuna and olive oil, and *mesclum*, a salad of bitter leaves including dandelion: consequently, Nice is about as good a spot to enjoy cheap street food as you'll find. *Petits farcies* – stuffed aubergines, peppers or tomatoes – are a standard feature on Côte d'Azur menus.

As for **wine**, the rosés of Provence might not have great status in the viniculture hierarchy, but for baking summer days they are hard to beat. The best of the Côte wines come from Bandol: Cassis too has its own *appellation*, and around Nice the Bellet wines are worth discovering. Fancy cocktails are a Côte speciality, and *pastis* is the preferred thirst quencher at any time of the day.

THE CÔTE D'AZUR

Genoa ▲

Corsica ▲

N

0 ___ 25 km

ITALY

San Remo
Ventimiglia
Menton
Roquebrune
MONACO
Monte Carlo
La Turbie
Èze
Beaulieu
Villefranche
Cap Ferrat *(see "The Corniches" map)*

Turin ▲
Tende ▲

Nice
St-Paul
Vence
Cagnes
Antibes
Biot
Juan-les-Pins
Vallauris
Cannes
Îles de Lérins

Grasse

N202

N85

Sisteron, Grenoble & Lyon ▲

ESTÉREL

St-Raphaël
Fréjus
A8
N98
Ste-Maxime
St-Tropez
Grimaud
Gassin
Ramatuelle
Cogolin
La Croix-Valmer
Cap Camarat
Cavalaire
Cap Lardier
Le Rayol
La Garde-Freinet
Collobrières
Le Lavandou
Bormes
Cabasson

M A S S I F   D E S   M A U R E S

Chartreuse
de la Verne

A57
Brégançon

Hyères
Îles d'Hyères
Île du Levant
Île de Port-Cros
Île de
Porquerolles

Corsica & Sardinia ▶

Presqu'île
de Giens

Toulon
Ollioules
Bandol
St-Cyr-sur-Mer
Le Castellet
Le Brusc
Cap Sicié
I. des
Embiez

Sisteron ▲

A51
A50
A52
D7N

Aubagne
La Ciotat
I. Verte
Cassis
Les Calanques

Aix-en-Provence

Marseille
Château
d'If

N7

Avignon ▼
Nîmes ▼
Tunisia & Spain ▼
Corsica, Sardinia, Algeria, ▼

The months to avoid are July and August, when hotels are booked up, overflowing campsites become health hazards, the locals get short-tempered, and the vegetation is at its most barren, and November, when many museums, hotels and restaurants close and the weather is wet.

From Marseille to Toulon

From the vast and wonderful scruffiness of **Marseille** to the utilitarian naval base of **Toulon**, this stretch of the Mediterranean is not what most people think of as the Côte d'Azur. There is no continuous corniche, few villas are in the grand style, and work is geared to an annual rather than summer cycle. **Cassis** is the exception, but the overriding attraction here is Marseille – a city that couldn't be confused with any other.

Marseille

The most renowned and populated city in France after Paris, **MARSEILLE** has prospered and been ransacked over the centuries. It has lost its privileges to sundry French kings and foreign armies, recovered its fortunes, suffered plagues, religious bigotry, republican and royalist Terror and had its own Commune and Bastille-storming. It was the presence of so many Marseillaise revolutionaries marching from the Rhine to Paris in 1792 that gave the *Hymn of the Army of the Rhine* its name of *La Marseillaise*, later to become the national anthem.

In recent years Marseille has undergone a renaissance, shaking off much of its old reputation for sleaze and danger to attract a wider range of visitors taking advantage of the TGV link from the north. The march of progress is not, however, relentless: too often last year's prestige civic project becomes this year's broken, bottle-strewn fountain. But that's Marseille. If you don't like your cities gritty, it may not be for you. See past its occasional squalor, though, and chances are you will warm to this down-to-earth, cosmopolitan, vital metropolis.

Arrival, information and city transport

The city's **airport**, the Aéroport Marseille-Provence (☎04.42.14.14.14, ⓦwww.mrsairport.com), is 20km northwest of the city, linked to the *gare SNCF* by bus (every 20min 6.15am–8.50pm; later buses meet flights; €8.50). The **gare SNCF St-Charles** (☎3635) is on the northern edge of the 1ᵉʳ arrondissement on square Narvik with the new **gare routière** alongside at 3 rue Honnorat (☎08.91.02.40.25). From the *gare SNCF*, a monumental staircase leads down to boulevard d'Athènes and thence to La Canebière, Marseille's main street. The **tourist office** is at 4 La Canebière (Mon–Sat 9am–7pm, Sun & public holidays 10am–5pm; ☎04.91.13.89.00, ⓦwww.marseille-tourisme .com), down by the Vieux Port.

Marseille has an efficient **bus** and **métro** network, supplemented by two gleaming new **tram** lines, scheduled to be fully operational by summer 2009.

MARSEILLE

MONTAGNE DE MARSEILLEVEYRE

Musée de la Faïence

MAC

Château Borély

Parc Borély

Port de Plaisance de la Pte Rouge

LA MADRAGUE

Unité d'Habitation

Plage du Prado

PROMENADE POMPIDOU

AVENUE DU PRADO

Football Stadium

ROND-POINT DU PRADO

AVENUE DE PRADO

Basilique Notre-Dame-de-la-Garde

MALMOUSQUE

Rade d'Endoume

Îles d'Endoume

Palais Longchamp

Gare SMCF

LE PANIER

Avant Port Nord

Anse des Auffes

Rochers de Pendus

See 'Marseille: Le Vieux Port map'

Hôtel du Département

Les Docks

Gare Maritime

Rade de Marseille

Digue du Large

ACCOMMODATION

Le Corbusier	B
Edmond-Rostand	C
HI Youth Hostel	A
Bois Luzy	
HI Youth Hostel	A
Bonneveine	D

EATING, DRINKING & ENTERTAINMENT

L'Abri Côtié	10
Aux 3G	3
Bar Le Petit Nice	4
Chez Fonfon	9
Les Docks des Suds	7
La Maronaise	11
L'Intermédiare	6
New Cancan	5
Le Poste à Galène	2
Le Red Lion	8
Trash	1

— Tramway

1 km

N

The métro runs from 5am until 10.30pm on weekdays and until after midnight at weekends; trams run from 5am to after midnight. Night buses run from 9.30pm to around 12.30am. You can get a plan of the transport system from RTM at 6 rue des Fabres (Mon–Fri 8.30am–6pm, Sat 9am–12.30pm, 2–5.30pm; Ⓦwww.rtm.fr), one street north of La Canebière near the Bourse. **Tickets** are flat rate for buses, trams and the métro and can be used for journeys combining all three as long as they take less than one hour. You can buy individual tickets (€1.70) from bus and tram drivers, and from métro ticket offices, or **multi-journey** *Cartes Libertés* (in increments of €6 and €12), which are valid for five and ten journeys respectively; these can be bought from métro stations, RTM kiosks and shops displaying the RTM sign. You should also consider the good-value one-day *Carte Journée* (€4.50) or three-day *Carte 3 Jours* (€10). Tickets must be punched in the machines on the bus, on tramway platforms or at métro gates.

Accommodation

Since Marseille is not a great tourist city, **finding a room** in July or August is no more difficult than at any other time. Hotels are plentiful, though if you get stuck the tourist office offers a same-day **accommodation hotline**, Allotel (Ⓣ08.26.88.68.26; premium rates apply). The cheapest options are the city's **hostels**, both quite a way from the centre.

Hotels

Alizé 35 quai des Belges, 1ᵉʳ Ⓣ04.91.33.66.97, Ⓦwww.alize-hotel.com. Comfortable, freshly renovated and soundproofed rooms, with the more expensive ones looking out onto the Vieux Port. ❹–❺

Le Corbusier Unité d'Habitation, 280 bd Michelet, 8ᵉ Ⓣ04.91.16.78.00, Ⓦwww.hotellecorbusier.com. Stylish hotel on the third floor of the renowned architect's iconic high-rise; book in advance. ❺

Edmond-Rostand 31 rue Dragon, 8ᵉ Ⓣ04.91.37.74.95, Ⓦwww.hoteledmondrostand .com. Comfortable, recently revamped and friendly, and well known, so book in advance. ❹

Etap Hotel Vieux Port 46 rue Sainte, 1ᵉʳ Ⓣ08.92.68.05.82, Ⓦwww.etaphotel.com. Big branch of the comfortable budget chain in a superb location close to the Vieux Port. Situated in a historic building, some of the rooms have timber beams; it's incredibly popular so book ahead. ❸

Lutétia 38 allée Léon-Gambetta, 1ᵉʳ Ⓣ04.91.50.81.78, Ⓦwww.hotelmarseille.com. Right in the thick of things with pleasant, sound-proofed and a/c rooms. ❹

Du Palais 26 rue Breteuil 6ᵉ Ⓣ04.91.37.78.86, Ⓦwww.hotelmarseille.com. Very smart three-star in a great location a short walk from the Vieux Port. ❺

Radisson SAS 38–40 quai de Rive Neuve, 7ᵉ Ⓣ04.88.92.19.50, Ⓦmarseille.radissonsas.com. Beautiful, primarily business-oriented new luxury hotel on the Vieux Port, with the most competitive deals at weekends and during holiday periods. ❾

St Ferréol 19 rue Pisançon, corner of rue St-Ferréol, 1ᵉʳ Ⓣ04.91.33.12.21, Ⓦwww.hotel saintferreol.com. Pretty decor and marble baths with Jacuzzis, in a central pedestrianized area. ❺

Sylvabelle 63 rue Sylvabelle, 6ᵉ Ⓣ04.91.37.75.83, Ⓦwww.hotel-bearn.com. A bit shabby, but comfortable, friendly and close to the centre – and they plan to renovate. ❷

Vertigo 42 rue des Petites Maries, 1ᵉʳ Ⓣ04.91.91.07.11, Ⓦwww.hotelvertigo.fr. Wonderfully funky new budget hotel and hostel near the train and bus stations, with simple but stylish decor, friendly, youthful staff, and dorm beds from €23.90. ❸

Hostels

HI Youth Hostel 76 allée des Primevères, 12ᵉ Ⓣ04.91.49.06.18, Ⓦwww.fuaj.org. Bus #8 from Metro Chartreux (direction "St-Julien", stop "Bois Luzy"). Cheap, clean youth hostel in a former château a long way out from the centre. Reception 7.30–noon & 5–10.30pm. Dorm bed €11.

HI Youth Hostel Bonneveine impasse Bonfils, av J.-Vidal, 8ᵉ Ⓣ04.91.17.63.30, Ⓦwww.fuaj.org. Mᵒ Rd-Pt-du-Prado, then bus #44 (direction "Floralia Rimet", stop "Place Bonnefon") or night bus #583 from Vieux Port. Recently renovated hostel just 200m from the beach, with internet access. Reception 7am–noon, 2–10pm. Dorm bed €17.10. Closed mid-Dec to mid-Jan.

The City

Marseille is divided into fifteen arrondissements which spiral out from the focal point of the city, the **Vieux Port**. Due north lies the old town, **Le Panier**, site of the original Greek settlement of Massalia, and beyond that the rapidly regenerating area of **Les Docks**. The wide boulevard leading from the head of the Vieux Port, La Canebière is the central east–west axis of the town. The **Centre Bourse** and the little streets of **quartier Belsunce** border it to the north, while the main shopping streets lie to the south. The main north–south axis is **rue d'Aix**, becoming cours Belsunce then rue de Rome, avenue du Prado and finally boulevard Michelet. The lively, youngish quarter around place Jean-Jaurès and cours Julien lies east of rue de Rome. From the headland west of the Vieux Port, the **corniche** heads south past the city's most favoured residential districts towards the **beaches** and promenade nightlife of the **Plage du Prado**.

The Vieux Port

The cafés around the east end of the **Vieux Port** indulge the sedentary pleasures of observing street life, despite the fumes of exhausts and of fish sold straight off the boats on quai des Belges. Prime afternoon café lounging spot is the north (Le Panier) side, where the terraces are sunnier and the views better.

Two **fortresses** guard the harbour entrance. **St-Jean**, on the north side, dates from the Middle Ages when Marseille was an independent republic, and is currently undergoing conversion to create a new national Musée des Civilisations d'Europe et de la Méditerranée; an eye catching new building alongside the fort is part of the project, due to be completed in 2012. The Fort St-Jean's enlargement in 1660 and the construction of **St-Nicolas** on the south side of the port, represent the city's final defeat as a separate entity. Louis XIV ordered the new fort to keep an eye on the city after he had sent in an army, suppressed the city's council, fined it, arrested all opposition and – in an early example of rate-capping – set ludicrously low limits on Marseille's subsequent expenditure and borrowing. The best view of the Vieux Port is from the **Palais du Pharo**, on the headland beyond Fort St-Nicolas, or, for a wider angle, from **Notre-Dame-de-la-Garde** (daily: summer 7am–7pm; winter 7am–6.30pm; bus #60 or tourist train from Vieux Port), the city's Second Empire landmark atop the hill south of the harbour. Crowned by a monumental gold Virgin that gleams to ships far out at sea, it's the most distinctive of all Marseille landmarks. Inside, model ships hang from the rafters while the paintings and drawings displayed are by turns kitsch, unintentionally comic or deeply moving, as they depict the shipwrecks, house fires and car crashes from which the Virgin has supposedly rescued grateful believers.

A short way inland from the Fort St-Nicolas, above the Bassin de Carénage, is Marseille's oldest church, the **Basilique St-Victor** (daily 9am–7pm; €2 entry to crypt). Originally part of a monastery founded in the fifth century on the burial site of various martyrs, the church was built, enlarged and fortified – a vital requirement given its position outside the city walls – over a period of two hundred years from the middle of the tenth century. It looks and feels like a

Marseille City Pass

If you're going to be visiting several of Marseille's museums it may be worth considering the **Marseille City Pass**, which for €20 or €27 for one or two days respectively includes free admission to museums, city guided tours, entry to the Château d'If and free use of the métro and bus system.

fortress, though the interior has an austere power and the **crypt** is a fascinating, crumbling warren containing several sarcophagi, including one with the remains of St Maurice.

Le Panier and les Docks

To the north of the Vieux Port is the oldest part of Marseille, **Le Panier**, where, up until the last war, tiny streets, steep steps and houses of every era formed a *vieille ville* typical of the Côte. In 1943, however, with Marseille under German occupation, the quarter became an unofficial ghetto for *Untermenschen* of every sort, including Resistance fighters, Communists and Jews. The Nazis gave the twenty thousand inhabitants one day's notice to quit; many were deported to the camps. Dynamite was laid, and everything from the waterside to rue Caisserie was blown sky-high, except for three old buildings that appealed to the fascist aesthetic: the seventeenth-century **Hôtel de Ville**, on the quay; the **Hôtel de Cabre**, on the corner of rue Bonneterie and Grande-Rue; and the **Maison Diamantée**, on rue de la Prison, which houses the **Musée de Vieux Marseille** (June–Sept Tues–Sun 11am–6pm; Oct–May Tues–Sun 10am–5pm; €2), whose collections cover the lifestyles and maritime history of Marseille from the seventeenth century to the present day.

After the war, archeologists reaped some benefits from this destruction when they discovered the remains of a Roman dockside warehouse, equipped with vast food-storage jars, which can be seen *in situ* at the **Musée des Docks Romains**, on place de Vivaux (Tues–Sun: June–Sept 11am–6pm; Oct–May 10am–5pm; €2).

At the junction of rue de la Prison and rue Caisserie, the steps of montée des Accoules lead up to **place de Lenche**, site of the Greek *agora* and a good café stop. What's left of old Le Panier is above montée des Accoules, though many of the tenements have been demolished. At the top of rue du Réfuge stands the restored **Hospice de la Vieille Charité**, a seventeenth-century workhouse with a gorgeous Baroque chapel surrounded by columned arcades; only the tiny grilled exterior windows recall its original use. It's now a cultural centre, and alarmingly empty except during its major temporary exhibitions – usually brilliant – and evening concerts. It also houses two museums (both Tues–Sun: June–Sept 11am–6pm; Oct–May 10am–5pm; €2; combined ticket for entire complex €4.50): the **Musée d'Archéologie Méditerranéenne** with some very beautiful pottery and glass and an Egyptian collection with a mummified crocodile; and the dark and spooky **Musée des Arts Africains, Océaniens et Amérindiens**.

The expansion of Marseille's **Joliette docks** started in the first half of the nineteenth century. Like the new cathedral, wide boulevards and Marseille's own Arc de Triomphe – the **Porte d'Aix** at the top of **cours Belsunce**/rue d'Aix – the docks were paid for with the profits of military enterprise, most significantly the conquest of Algeria in 1830. Anyone fascinated by industrial architecture should visit the mammoth old warehouse building, **Les Docks** (follow rue de la République to the end), now restored as part of the ambitious **Euroméditerranée** regeneration scheme. Alongside the docks looms the town's massive late nineteenth-century **Cathédrale de la Nouvelle Major**, architecturally a blend of neo-Romanesque and neo-Byzantine, with a distinctive pattern of alternating bands of stone.

La Canebière

La Canebière, the occasionally tatty boulevard that runs for about a kilometre down to the port, is the city's hub, though it's more a place to move through

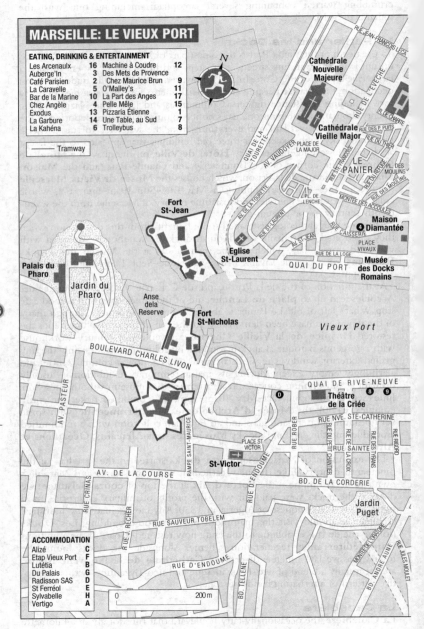

MARSEILLE: LE VIEUX PORT

EATING, DRINKING & ENTERTAINMENT

Les Arcenaulx	16	Machine à Coudre	12
Auberge'In	3	Des Mets de Provence	9
Café Parisien	2	Chez Maurice Brun	
La Caravelle	5	O'Malley's	11
Bar de la Marine	10	La Part des Anges	17
Chez Angèle	4	Pelle Mêle	15
Exodus	13	Pizzaria Étienne	1
La Garbure	14	Une Table, au Sud	7
La Kahéna	6	Trolleybus	8

―――― Tramway

N

RUE JEAN-FRANÇOIS LECA

Cathédrale Nouvelle Majeure

RUE DE L'EVECHE

R. DE CHARITE

QUAI DE LA TOURETTE

AV. VAUDOYER

PLACE DE LA MAJOR

Cathédrale Vieille Major

RUE DES P. PUITS

RUE DU THIER

LE PANIER

RUE STE-FRANÇOISE

RUE REFUGE

PL. DES MOULINS

RUE DES MOULINS

AV. DE LA TOURETTE

PL. DE LENCHE

MONTÉE DES ACCOULES

Maison Diamantée

RUE ST-LAURENT

AV. ST-JEAN

RUE CAISSERIE

PLACE VIVAUX

Fort St-Jean

Eglise St-Laurent

RUE DE LA LOGE

QUAI DU PORT

Musée des Docks Romains

Palais du Pharo

Jardin du Pharo

Anse de la Reserve

Fort St-Nicholas

Vieux Port

BOULEVARD CHARLES LIVON

QUAI DE RIVE-NEUVE

Théâtre de la Criée

8 9

AV. PASTEUR

RUE NVE. STE-CATHERINE

RUE ROBER

RUE DU PETIT CHANTIER

RUE DE LA CROIX

RUE SAINTE

RUE DES THANS

RUE RIGORD

RAMPE SAINT-MAURICE

PLACE ST VICTOR

RUE D'ENDOUME

St-Victor

BD. DE LA CORDERIE

AV. DE LA COURSE

Jardin Puget

RUE CRINAS

RUE J. RECHER

RUE SAUVEUR TOBELEM

MONTÉE DE L'ORIFLAMME

RUE JULES MOULET

BD. ANDRE AUNE

RUE D'ENDOUME

BD. TELLENE

ACCOMMODATION

Alizé	C
Etap Vieux Port	F
Lutétia	B
Du Palais	G
Radisson SAS	D
St Ferréol	E
Sylvabelle	H
Vertigo	A

0   200 m

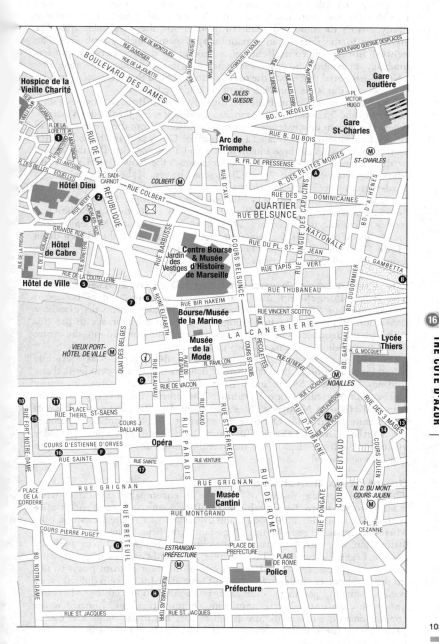

than to linger. It takes its name from the hemp (*canabê*) that once grew here and provided the raw materials for the town's rope-making trade. La Canebière neatly divides the moneyed southern *quartiers* and the ramshackle **quartier Belsunce** to the north – an extraordinary, dynamic, mainly Arab area. The **central library** on cours Belsunce is another of the regeneration projects gradually supplanting the dilapidated tenements, its slick modernity softened by a beaux-arts portal that recalls the old Alcazar music hall that it replaced – where the likes of Tino Rossi and Yves Montand once performed.

Immediately west of cours Belsunce, the ugly **Centre Bourse** provides a stark contrast to the dynamic, mainly Arab area. Behind it is the **Jardin des Vestiges**, where the ancient port extended, curving northwards from the present quai des Belges. Excavations have revealed a stretch of the Greek port and bits of the **city wall** with the bases of three square towers and a gateway, dated to the second or third century BC. Within the Centre Bourse, the **Musée d'Histoire de Marseille** (Mon–Sat noon–7pm; €2) presents the rest of the finds, including a third-century wreck of a Roman trading vessel. Back at the Vieux Port end of La Canebière is the **Musée de la Marine** (daily 10am–6pm; €2), housed in the Neoclassical stock exchange and with a superb collection of shipbuilders' models, including the legendary 1930s liner *Normandie* and Marseille's own prewar queen of the seas, the *Providence*. Further up at no. 11, the **Musée de la Mode** (Tues–Sun: June–Sept 11am–6pm; Oct–May 10am–5pm; €3) displays fashion from 1945 to the present day.

The Palais Longchamp and the Hôtel du Département

The **Palais Longchamp**, 2km east of the port at the end of boulevard Longchamp (bus #8, or M° Longchamp–Cinq-Avenues), forms the grandiose conclusion of an aqueduct that brought water from the Durance to the city. Although the aqueduct is no longer in use, water is still pumped into the centre of the colonnade connecting the two palatial wings.

The palace's north wing is the city's **Musée des Beaux-Arts** (currently closed for renovation), with a fair share of delights, including works by Rubens, Jordaens, Corot and Signac and a room devoted to the nineteenth-century satirist from Marseille, Honoré Daumier. The other wing is occupied by the **Musée d'Histoire Naturelle** (Tues–Sun 10am–5pm; €4), and its collection of stuffed animals and fossils. Opposite the palace, at 140 boulevard Longchamp, is the **Musée Grobet-Labadi** (Tues–Sun: June–Sept 11am–6pm; Oct–May 10am–5pm; €2) an elegant late-nineteenth-century town house filled with exquisite *objets d'art*.

South of La Canebière

The prime shopping district of Marseille is encompassed by three streets running **south from La Canebière**: rue Paradis, rue St-Ferréol and **rue de Rome**. The most elegant boutiques and galleries cluster in the area around the **Musée Cantini**, 19 rue Grignan (Tues–Sun: June–Sept 11am–6pm; Oct–May 10am–5pm; €3), with Fauvists and Surrealists well represented, plus works by Matisse, Léger, Picasso, Ernst, Le Corbusier, Miró and Giacometti.

A few blocks east of rue de Rome is one of the most pleasant places to idle in the city, **cours Julien** (M° Notre-Dame-du-Mont–Cours-Julien), with pools, fountains, pavement cafés and boutiques, populated by Marseille's bohemian crowd and diverse immigrant community, all of it buried under copious quantities of graffiti. Streets full of bars and music shops lead east to **place Jean-Jaurès**, locally known as "la Pleine", where the market is a treat, particularly on Saturdays.

The corniche, beaches and Parc Borély

The most popular stretch of sand close to the city centre is the **plage des Catalans**, a few blocks south of the Palais du Pharo. This marks the beginning of Marseille's **corniche**, avenue J.-F.-Kennedy, which follows the cliffs past the dramatic statue and arch that frames the setting sun of the **Monument aux Morts des Orients**. South of the monument, steps lead down to an inlet, **Anse des Auffes**, which is the nearest Marseille gets to being picturesque, with small fishing boats beached on the rocks and narrow stairways leading nowhere. The corniche then turns inland, bypassing the **Malmousque peninsula**, whose coastal path gives access to tiny bays and beaches – perfect for swimming when the mistral wind is not inciting the waves.

The corniche ends at the **Plage du Prado**, the city's main sand beach. A short way up **avenue du Prado**, avenue du Park-Borély leads into the city's best green space, the **Parc Borély**, with a boating lake, rose gardens, palm trees and a botanical garden (Tues–Fri 10am–5/6pm; Sat & Sun 11am–5/6pm; €3) The quickest way to the park and the beaches is by bus #19 from métro Rd-Pt-du-Prado; for the corniche, take bus #83 from the Vieux Port.

The Château d'If

The **Château d'If** (May to mid-Sept daily 9am–6pm; mid-Sept to March Tues–Sun 9am–5.15pm; April daily 9am–5.30pm; €5) on the tiny island of If is best known as the penal setting for Alexandre Dumas' *The Count of Monte Cristo*. Having made his watery escape after fourteen years of incarceration as the innocent victim of treachery, the hero of the piece, Edmond Dantès, describes the island thus: "Blacker than the sea, blacker than the sky, rose like a phantom the giant of granite, whose projecting crags seemed like arms extended to seize their prey". The reality, for most prisoners, was worse: they went insane or died (and sometimes both) before reaching the end of their sentences. Only the nobles living in the less fetid upper-storey cells had much chance of survival. The sixteenth-century castle and its cells are horribly well preserved, and the views back towards Marseille are fantastic. **Boats** for If leave regularly from the quai des Belges in the Vieux Port (every 30–45min in summer; less frequent in winter; €10), with the last boat back timed to coincide with the château's closing time; the journey takes twenty minutes.

The Musée de la Faïence, MAC and the Cité Radieuse

From the plage du Prado the promenade continues all the way to the suburb of **Montredon**, where the nineteenth-century Château Pastré, set in a huge park, contains the **Musée de la Faïence** (Tues–Sun: June–Sept 11am–6pm; Oct–May 10am–5pm; €2). The eighteenth- and nineteenth-century ceramics, most produced in Marseille, are of an extremely high quality, and a small collection of novel modern and contemporary pieces is housed on the top floor. The entrance to the park (free) is at 157 avenue de Montredon (bus #19 from Mº Rd-Pt-du-Prado, stop "Montredon-Chancel"). Along the coast from here are easily accessible *calanques* (rocky inlets), ideal for evening swims and supper picnics as the sun sets.

Between Montredon and **boulevard Michelet**, the main road out of the city, is the contemporary art museum, **MAC** (Tues–Sun: June–Sept 11am–6pm; Oct–May 10am–5pm; €3), at 69 avenue d'Haïfa (bus #23 or #45 from Mº Rd-Pt-du-Prado, stop "Haïfa Marie-Louise"). The permanent collection includes works from the 1960s to the present day by Buren, Christo, Klein, Niki de Saint-Phalle, Tinguely and Warhol, as well as Marseillais artists César and Ben.

Set back just west of boulevard Michelet stands a building that broke the mould, Le Corbusier's seventeen-storey block of flats, the **Unité d'Habitation**, designed in 1946 and completed in 1952. The Cité Radieuse, as it's also known, only fails to amaze now because so many architects the world over have tried to imitate its revolutionary example, but up close the difference in quality between this and what followed is apparent. At ground level the building is decorated with Le Corbusier's famous human figure, the Modulor; on the third floor there is a hotel (see p.1027) and café. Not all of the iconic rooftop recreation area can be visited, though a circuit of the running track is essential. To reach the Unité, take bus #21 from Mº Rd-Pt-du-Prado to "Le Corbusier".

Eating and drinking

Fish and **seafood** are the mainstay of Marseille's diet, and the superstar of dishes is Marseille's own **bouillabaisse**, a saffron- and garlic-flavoured soup with bits of fish, croutons and *rouille* thrown in; theories conflict as to which fish should be included, but one essential is the *rascasse* or scorpion fish. The other speciality is *pieds et paquets* – mutton or lamb belly and trotters.

Good **restaurant** hunting grounds include cours Julien or place Jean-Jaurès (international options), the Vieux Port (touristy and fishy), the Corniche and plage du Prado (glitzy and pricey). Rue Sainte is good for smart, fashioniable dining close to the opera and Vieux Port.

Cafés and bars

Aux 3G 3 rue St-Pierre, 5ᵉ. Marseille's most popular lesbian bar, regularly packed at weekends. Open Thurs & Sun 7pm–midnight, Fri & Sat until 2am.

Bar de la Marine 15 quai de Rive-Neuve, 1ᵉʳ. A favourite bar for Vieux Port lounging, and inspiration for Pagnol's celebrated Marseille trilogy. Open daily.

O'Malley's Irish Pub 9 quai de Rive Neuve, 1ᵉʳ. A wildly popular Vieux Port boozer with the usual "Irish" trimmings, including Kilkenny and Guinness, and live music on Wed.

Café Parisien 1 place Sadi-Carnot, 2ᵉ. Very stylish mix of old elegance and modern chic, with pasta dishes from around €10 and meat mains from €15 up. Closed Sun.

Bar Le Petit Nice 26 place Jean-Jaurès, 1ᵉʳ. The place to head for on Saturday morning during the market, with an interesting selection of beers. Open Mon–Sat from 6.30am.

Le Red Lion 231 av Pierre-Mendès-France, 8ᵉ. Large, raucous, British-style pub close to plage Borély, with eleven beers on draught. Open until 4am Fri & Sat.

Trash 28 rue du Berceau, 5ᵉ. Slick, cruisy gay men's bar with DJ, live entertainment and plenty of dark corners. Open daily 9pm–2am.

Restaurants

L'Abri Côtié bd des Baigneurs, plage du Fortin, 8ᵉ ☎04.91.72.27.29. Smart beachside restaurant in Montredon, serving fish, meat and pasta. It's a block

or so down from the boulevard and a little tricky to find, despite the many signs. *Plats* around €20.

Les Arcenaulx 25 cours d'Estienne-d'Orves, 1ᵉʳ ☎04.91.59.80.30. Lovely, atmospheric intellectual haunt that is also a bookshop and *salon de thé*; there's a light €27 menu, otherwise €36 and €55. Last orders 11pm. Closed Sun.

Auberge'In 25 rue du Chevalier-Roze, 2ᵉ ☎04.91.90.51.59. Health-food shop and restaurant on the edge of Le Panier, with a vegan and vegetarian *menu fixe* for €14.50. Open for lunch Mon–Sat, dinner Fri & Sat only.

Chez Angèle 50 rue Caisserie, 2ᵉ ☎04.91.90.63.35. Packed Le Panier local, dishing up fresh pasta and pizza. Closed lunchtimes Sat & Sun.

Chez Fonfon 140 Vallon des Auffes, 7ᵉ ☎04.91.52.14.38. There's no debate about the quality of the bouillabaisse here, for this chic restaurant overlooking a small fishing harbour is one of an elite band of restaurants guarding the true recipe of the dish. Expect to pay €46; closed Sun, Mon lunch and Jan.

La Garbure 9 cours Julien, 6ᵉ ☎04.91.47.18.01. Rich specialities from southwest France, including Bresse chicken. Lunch menu €24; dinner menus from €35. Closed Sat midday & Sun.

La Kahena 2 rue de la République, 2ᵉ ☎04.91.90.61.93. Popular Moroccan restaurant near the Vieux Port, with grills and couscous from €9. Open daily.

Des Mets de Provence Chez Maurice Brun 18 quai de Rive-Neuve, 7ᵉ ☎04.91.33.35.38. A

Marseille institution with authentic Provençal cooking in a pretty dining room at the top of a steep staircase. Lunch menu €40, including wine, otherwise €60. Closed lunchtime Sat–Mon.

La Part des Anges 33 rue Sainte, 1ᵉʳ ☎04.91.33.55.70. Wonderful *cave de vins* serving hearty food to mop up the classy alcohol; *plats* around €14. Open daily.

Pizzaria Étienne 43 rue Lorette, 2ᵉ. An old-fashioned Le Panier pizzeria; hectic, cramped and crowded.
Une Table, au Sud 2 quai du Port, 2ᵉ ☎04.91.90.63.53. Stylish restaurant *gastronomique* overlooking the Vieux Port, where chef Lionel Lévy's contemporary take on Provençal cooking includes the likes of bouilla-baisse milkshake. Menus €37, €52, €74. Closed Sun, Mon and Aug.

Nightlife and entertainment

Marseille's **nightlife** has something for everyone, with plenty of live rock and jazz, nightclubs and discos, as well as theatre, opera and classical concerts. Theatre is particularly innovative and lively in Marseille. The Virgin Megastore at 75 rue St-Ferréol, the book- and record shop FNAC in the Centre Bourse and the tourist office's ticket bureau are the best places to go for **tickets and information**. Virgin also stocks English books and has a café, open, like the rest of the store, Monday to Saturday until 8.30pm and on Sundays until 8pm. There is a free weekly **listings** mag, *Ventilo*, and a monthly, *César*, which you can pick up from FNAC, Virgin, tourist offices, museums and cultural centres.

Live music and clubs

La Caravelle 34 quai du Port, 2ᵉ. Prewar cabaret on the first floor of the *Hôtel Bellevue* with portside views. Free plates of tapas 6–9.30pm; live jazz weekends. Daily till 2am.
Les Docks des Suds 12 rue Urbain V, 3ᵉ ☎04.91.99.00.00. Vast warehouse that serves as the venue for Marseille's annual Fiesta des Suds world-music festival and is a regular live venue.
Exodus 9 rue des Trois Mages, 1ᵉ ☎04.91.42.02.39. Small performance space between cours Julien and place Jean-Jaurès, presenting world music and theatre with a strong focus on Africa and Asia. Live events usually start at 8.30pm.
L'Intermédiare 63 place Jean-Jaurès, 6ᵉ ☎04.91.47.01.25. Loud, hip, smoky bar with a variety of live bands, from rock to jazz and world music, plus old-skool DJ nights. Mon–Sat 6pm–2am.
Café Julien 39 cours Julien, 6ᵉ ☎04.91.24.34.10. Lively bar with mixed clientele, part of the Espace Julien arts centre. Regular live rock and reggae music; performances start 8.30–10pm.
Machine à Coudre 6 rue Jean-Roque, 1ᵉ ☎04.91.55.62.65. Music café hosting alternative rock, hip-hop and reggae acts. Small entry charge depending on act; some free events. Open Thurs–Sat.
La Maronaise Rte de la Maronaise, Les Goudes, 8ᵉ ☎06.27.01.03. 23. From May–Sept this open air disco in a wild setting by the sea is the most alluring place to dance in Marseille. Open 11–5; weekends only in May but daily from June onwards.
New Cancan 3 rue Sénac, 1ᵉʳ ☎04.91.48.59.76. It's pretty cheesy, but the New Cancan is neverthe-less Marseille's best-known and longest running gay disco, with regular Sunday night cabaret. Open Thurs–Sun 11pm–dawn; Fri & Sat entry charges are steep.
Pelle Mêle 8 place aux Huiles, 1ᵉʳ ☎04.91.54.85.26. Intimate, smart and lively jazz bistro and piano bar. Open 5pm–2am Tues–Sat.
Le Poste à Galène 103 rue Ferrari, 5ᵉ ☎04.91.47.57.99. Live pop, rock and electro plus 1980s nights and a bar. Entry price varies depending on event; opening times also vary.
Trolleybus 24 quai de Rive-Neuve, 7ᵉ ☎04.91.54.30.45. Atmospheric bar, club and live music venue in a series of vaulted rooms; house, pop, electro, hip-hop, reggae and techno. Closed Sun–Tues.

Film, theatre and concerts

Alhambra 2 rue du Cinéma, 16ᵉ ☎04.91.03.84.66. Art house cinema occasionally showing undubbed English-language films (v.o).
Ballet National de Marseille 20 bd Gabès, 8ᵉ ☎04.91.32.72.72. The home venue of the famous dance company, founded in 1972 by Roland Petit.
La Friche la Belle de Mai 41 rue Jobin, 3ᵉ ☎04.95.04.95.04. Interdisciplinary arts complex occupying a former industrial site in the north of the city, hosting theatre, dance, live music and arts exhibitions.

Opéra 2 rue Moliére, 1ᵉʳ ☏04.91.55.11.10.
Symphony concerts and operas in a magnificent
setting, part Neoclassical, part Art Deco.
Théâtre National la Criée 30 quai de Rive-Neuve,
7ᵉ ☏04.91.54.70.54. Home of the Théâtre National
de Marseille and Marseille's best theatre.

Les Variétés 37 rue Vincent Scotto, 1ᵉʳ
☏04.96.11.61.61. Downtown cinema offering v.o.
films.

Listings

Airlines Air France, 14 La Canebière, 1ᵉʳ ☏36.54.
Bike rental Blue bicycles belonging to Le Vélo
scheme can be rented from 80 self-service rental
points throughout the city using a bank card (€1
for first half hour then €1 for each additional half
hour). Mountain bikes can be rented from Cycles
Ulysse, 3 av du Parc Borély ☏04.91.77.14.51;
and Tandem, 16 av du Parc Borély
☏04.91.22.64.80.
Bookstore Virgin, 75 rue St-Ferréol, 1ᵉʳ, has an
English books section; Maupetit, 140 La Canebière,
1ᵉʳ, is a good general French bookshop.
Car hire Avis, Gare St-Charles ☏08.20.61.16.36;
National Citer, 20 bd Schloessing, 8ᵉ
☏04.91.83.05.05; Europcar, 59 allées Léon
Gambetta, 1ᵉʳ ☏04.91.10.74.91. These and others
also have head offices at the airport.
Consulates UK, 24 av du Prado, 6ᵉ
☏04.91.15.72.10; USA, place Varian Fry, 6ᵉ
☏04.91.54.92.00.

Emergencies Ambulance ☏15; SOS Médecins
☏04.91.52.91.52; 24hr casualty departments at
La Conception, 144 rue St-Pierre, 5ᵉ
☏04.91.38.36.52; and SOS Voyageurs, Gare
St-Charles, 3ᵉ ☏04.91.62.12.80.
Ferries SNCM (61 bd des Dames ☏32.60,
Ⓦwww.sncm.fr) runs ferries to Corsica, Tunisia
and Algeria.
Internet Info-Café, 1 quai du Rive Neuve, 1ᵉʳ
☏04.91.33.74.98.
Lost property 41 bd de Briançon, 3ᵉ
☏04.91.14.68.97.
Pharmacy Pharmacie du Vieux Port, 4 quai du Port
(open daily) ☏04.91.91.63.10.
Police Commissariat Central, 2 rue Antoine-Becker,
2ᵉ (24hr; ☏04.91.39.80.00).
Post office 1 place de l'Hôtel-des-Postes, 1ᵉʳ.
Taxis Taxi Radio Marseille ☏04.91.02.20.20; Taxi
Radio Tupp ☏04.91.05.80.80; Taxi Plus
☏04.91.03.60.03.

Cassis, Le Ciotat and Bandol

Between Marseille and the sprawling naval port of Toulon, scenic splendours –
notably in the Calanques and along the spectacular Route des Crêtes – alternate
with small, unspoilt coastal towns like **Cassis**, **La Ciotat** and **Bandol**, which
may lack the glitter of the more famous resorts to the east but make up for it
with their low-key charm, good food and wine and easy access to the sea.

Cassis

Many people rate **CASSIS** the best resort this side of St-Tropez; hemmed in
by cliffs, its development has been necessarily modest. Portside posing and
sunbathing aside, the main thing to do is to take a boat trip to the **calanques**
(from around €13) – fjord-like inlets that cut deep into the limestone cliffs.
Several companies operate from the port, but check if they let you off or just
tour in and out, and be prepared for rough seas. If you're feeling energetic,
follow the well-marked footpath from the route des Calanques behind the
western beach; it's about ninety-minutes' walk to the furthest and best
calanque, **En Vau**, where you can reach the shore. The water is deep blue and
swimming between the cliffs is an experience not to miss. In summer the fire
risk is high; smoking and fires are prohibited and you're advised not to head
inland off the coastal path if the wind is high. There are no refreshment stops,
so take water.

You can hire kayaks or boats in Cassis, sometimes including a skipper, and there are a couple of diving outfits; the tourist office has details. The spectacular clifftop **route des Crêtes** links Cassis with La Ciotat; regular belvederes allow you to stop and take the perfect shot of distant headlands receding into the sunset – vertigo permitting. The route is closed during high winds.

Practicalities

Buses from Marseille arrive at rond point du Gendarmerie from where it's a short walk to the port and beach. The **gare SNCF** is 3km from town, connected by bus (Mon–Fri & Sat am; 15min). The **tourist office** is on the port at quai des Moulins (March–June, Sept & Oct Mon–Fri 9am–12.30pm & 2–6pm, Sat 9.30am–12.30pm & 2–5.30pm, Sun 10am–12.30pm; July & Aug Mon–Fri 9am–7pm, Sat & Sun 9.30am–12.30pm & 3–6pm; Nov–Feb Mon–Fri 9.30am–12.30pm & 2–5.30pm, Sat 10am–12.30pm & 2–5pm, Sun 10am–12.30pm; ℡08.92.25.98.92, ⓦwww.ot-cassis.com).

Cassis is small, so demand for cheaper **rooms** in high season is intense. Cheap options include *Le Commerce*, 12 rue St-Clair (℡04.42.01.09.10, ⓦwww.hotel-lecommerce.fr; ❶–❷; closed mid-Nov to mid-Jan), and *Le Provençal*, 7 avenue Victor-Hugo (℡04.42.01.72.13, ⓦwww.cassis-le-provencal.fr; ❸), close to the port. For a little more money, and a view over the port, try *Le Golfe*, place du Grand-Carnot (℡04.42.01.00.21, ⓦwww.legolfe-cassis.fr; ❺; closed Nov–March). Further out, there's also *Le Joli Bois*, route de la Gineste (℡04.42.01.02.68; ⓦwww.hotel-du-joli-bois.com; ❷), just off the Marseille road, 3km from Cassis and with few amenities. Far more isolated is the gorgeously scenic but basic **hostel**, *La Fontasse*, in the hills above the *calanques* west of Cassis (℡04.42.01.02.72, ⓦwww.fuaj.org; mid-March to Dec; €10.70 per night; reception 8–10.30am & 5–9pm). The **campsite**, *Les Cigales* (℡04.42.01.07.34, ⓦwww.campingcassis.com; closed mid-Nov to mid-March; €16.60 for car, tent and two people), is just off the D559 from Marseille.

Restaurants are abundant along the port. The ratatouille and fresh fish at *Chez Gilbert*, 19 quai Baux (℡04.42.01.71.36; menu €27; closed Tues evening & Wed out of season), are hard to beat. *El Sol*, at no. 23 (℡04.42.01.76.10; closed Mon all day & Tues lunch), with *terroir* fare, costs a bit less. In the backstreets, *Le Clos des Arômes* at 10 rue Abbé Paul-Mouton (℡04.42.01.71.84; closed Mon, Tues & Wed lunch; menu €26) is well regarded and has a pretty garden.

La Ciotat

Cranes still loom over the little port of **LA CIOTAT**, where vast oil tankers were once built. Today, the town relies on tourism and yachting, yet it remains pleasantly unpretentious, less a place for museum visits or sightseeing than one in which to relax, with excellent beaches and a lively waterfront.

In 1895, **August and Louis Lumière** filmed the first moving pictures here, including the arrival of a train at the *gare SNCF*, which had Parisians jumping out of their seats in fright when it was premiered there. The world's oldest movie house, the **Eden Cinema**, still stands on the corner of boulevard A.-France and boulevard Jean-Jaurès; you can view the interior through glass and there's a permanent exhibition there (Mon–Sat 10am–6pm; free). The town has an annual film festival; the brothers are also commemorated by a monument on plage Lumière.

The streets of the old town, apart from rue Poilus, are uneventful, though the increasing numbers of boutiques and *immobiliers* reflect the change from shipyard to pleasure port. Île Verte Navette (℡04.42.83.11.44) makes the crossing to the islet of Île Verte daily, while Catamaran Le Citharista

(☎06.09.35.25.68) runs trips to the *calanques* of Cassis and Marseille (€19–25) from quai Ganteaume.

Alternatively, take a walk through the **Parc du Mugel** (daily: April–Sept 8am–8pm; Oct–March 9am–6pm; bus #30, stop "Mugel"), with its strange cluster of rock formations on the promontory beyond the shipyards. A path leads up through overgrown vegetation to a narrow terrace overlooking the sea. If you continue on bus #30 to Figuerolles you can reach the **Anse de Figuerolles** *calanque* down the avenue of the same name, and its neighbour, the **Gameau**.

Practicalities

The **gare SNCF** is 5km from the town but bus #10 is frequent at peak times and gets you to the Vieux Port in around fifteen minutes. The old town and port look out across the Baie de la Ciotat, whose inner curve provides the beaches and resort lifestyle of La Ciotat's modern extension, **La Ciotat-Plage**. The **gare routière** is at the end of boulevard Anatole-France by the Vieux Port right beside the **tourist office** (June–Sept Mon–Sat 9am–8pm, Sun 10am–1pm; Oct–May Mon–Sat 9am–noon & 2–6pm; ☎04.42.08.61.32, ⓦwww.tourisme-laciotat.com). **Bikes** can be hired from Cycle Lleba at 1b avenue F.-Mistral (☎04.42.83.60.30).

For **hotels**, the best cheapies are *La Marine*, 1 avenue Fernand Gassion (☎&Ⓕ04.42.08.35.11; ❷), and *La Rotonde*, 44 boulevard de la République (☎04.42.08.67.50, Ⓕ04.42.08.45.21; ❸), both on the fringes of the old town. In La Ciotat-Plage, *Miramar*, 3 boulevard Beaurivage (☎04.42.83.33.79, Ⓦwww .miramarlaciotat.com; ❼), is right on the palm-fringed seafront, while across the bay, on Corniche du Liouquet, you can stay in little villas in a park at *Ciotel Le Cap* (March to mid-Dec; ☎04.42.83.90.30, Ⓦwww.leciotel.com; ❽). La Ciotat has five **campsites**, of which *Le Soleil*, (avenue Emile Bodin (☎04.42.71.55.32, Ⓦwww.camping-dusoleil.com; €17 for tent and two people in high season), is about the most central.

La Ciotat's best **restaurant** is *La Sardine*, 18 rue des Combattants (☎04.42.08.00.60; closed Sun evening & Mon), mixing Japanese and Provençal influences with a menu at €29. Otherwise, *Coquillages Franquin*, 13 boulevard Anatole-France (☎04.42.83.59.50), serves fish on an €18.50 menu, and there are plenty of cafés and brasseries around the port.

Bandol to Toulon

Across La Ciotat bay are the fine sand and shingle beaches of the family resort of **LES LECQUES**, an offshoot of the inland town of **St-Cyr-Sur-Mer**, to which it is fused by modern suburbs. The **train station** is in St-Cyr, but the tourist office (July & Aug Mon–Sat 9am–7pm, Sun 10am–1pm & 4–7pm; March–June & Sept–Oct Mon–Fri 9am–6pm, Sat 9am–noon & 2–6pm; Nov–Feb Mon–Fri 9am–5pm, Sat 9am–noon & 1–5pm; ☎04.94.26.73.73, Ⓦwww .saintcyrsurmer.com) is on place de l'Appel du 18 Juin, on the seafront in Les Lecques. Most **accommodation** is in two-star hotels clustered near the sea in Les Lecques. A ten-kilometre **coastal path** (signposted) runs from the east end of Les Lecques' beach through a stretch of secluded beaches and *calanques* to the unpretentious resort of **BANDOL**, while inland *dégustation* signs announce the *appellation* Bandol, whose **vineyards** produce some of the best wines on the Côte. The reds are highly reputed; the pale rosé is sublime on a warm summer's evening.

In Bandol there are several reasonable **hotels** near the centre, including *Hôtel Florida*, 26 impasse de Nice (☎04.94.29.41.72, Ⓦwww.villaflorida.fr; ❺), and *La Cigale Bleue* at 177 avenue de la Gare (☎04.94.29.41.40; ❷). The very pleasant *Golf*

Hotel (☎04.94.29.45.83, ⓦwww.golfhotel.fr; open mid–March to end Oct; ❹) is right on Rénecros beach, west of the town centre. The **tourist office**, on allée Vivien by the quayside (late June & early Sept Mon–Sat 9.30am–noon & 2–6pm; July & Aug daily 9.30am–6.30pm; Sept–June Mon–Fri 10am–noon & 2–5pm, Sat 10am–noon; ☎04.94.29.41.35, ⓦwww.bandol.fr), will help if you're stuck during the high season and there's a live accommodation search facility on their website.

The other stretch of **coastal path** this side of Toulon is along the southern edge of the **Sicié peninsula** from Le Brusc, thickly forested and inaccessible in summer to cars due to the fire risk. The path climbs up to the sturdy clifftop chapel of Notre-Dame-du-Mai, which affords fantastic views of the coast and hinterland. The chapel is only open on the first Saturday morning of the month, and on certain religious holidays.

The central resorts and islands

Out of season, the coast between **Hyères** and **Fréjus/St-Raphaël** and its backdrop of wooded hills hold their own against the cynicism engendered by tourist brochure overkill. The magic lies in the scented Mediterranean vegetation, silver beaches, secluded islands and medieval hilltop villages.

Sedate Hyères, flashy St-Raphaël and historic Fréjus are the only significant towns, though the urban sprawl around the erstwhile fishing villages of **Le Lavandou**, **Cavalaire-sur-Mer** and **Ste-Maxime** keeps any sense of wilderness at bay. But there are moments when it's almost possible to imagine the coastline of old: near the **Cap de Bregançon** south of **Bormes**, between **Le Rayol** and Cavalaire, in the **Domaine de Rayol gardens**, and around the southern tip of the **St-Tropez peninsula**. Offshore on the **Îles d'Hyères** you can experience unspoilt landscapes with some of the best fauna and flora in Provence. **La Croix-Valmer** is probably the most pleasant of the resorts, while overhyped **St-Tropez** – where the summer crush really can be unbearable – is a must if only for a day-trip. Inland, amid the dense wooded hills of the **Massif des Maures**, are the gorgeous villages of **Collobrières** and **La Garde-Freinet**.

Transport is the main problem in the area. There is a regular bus service along the coast, but traffic is extremely slow in high season, and cycling doesn't get you very far unless you're Tour de France material.

Hyères

HYÈRES is the oldest resort on the Côte, listing Queen Victoria and Tolstoy among its early admirers, but the lack of a central seafront meant it lost out when the foreign rich switched from winter convalescents to quayside strollers, and today it has the rare distinction of not being totally dependent on the summer influx; it exports cut flowers and exotic plants – the most important being the date palm, which graces every street – and it's a garrison town, the home of the French army's 54th artillery regiment.

Arrival, information and accommodation

The **gare SNCF** is on place de l'Europe, 1.5km south of the centre, with frequent buses (#29, #39 or #67) to the **gare routière** on place Mal-Joffret, two blocks south of the entrance to the old town (℡08.25.00.06.50, ⓦwww.reseaumistral.com). Hyères-Toulon **airport** (℡08.25.01.83.87, ⓦwww.toulon-hyeres.aeroport.fr) is between Hyères and Hyères-Plage, 3km from the centre, to which it's connected by an infrequent bus service. The **tourist office** is at the Forum du Casino, 3 avenue Ambroise Thomas (July & Aug daily 8.30am–7.30pm; Sept–June Mon–Fri 9am–6pm, Sat 10am–4pm; ℡04.94.01.84.50, ⓦwww.hyeres-tourisme.com). **Bikes** and **mopeds** can be hired from Holiday Bikes, 10 rue Jean d'Agrève, near port Saint-Pierre (℡04.94.38.79.45, ⓦwww.holiday-bikes.com).

Hotels in the old town include the *Hôtel du Soleil*, on rue du Rempart (℡04.94.65.16.26, ⓦwww.hoteldusoleil.com; ④), in a renovated house at the foot of the parc St-Bernard, and the smaller *Le Portalet*, 4 rue de Limans (℡04.94.65.39.40, ⓦwww.hyeres-hotel-portalet.com; ⑤). Overlooking the port at Ayguade is *La Reine Jane* (℡04.94.66.32.64, ⓦwww.reinejane.com; ④). There are plenty of **campsites** on the coast. Two smaller ones are *Camping-Bernard*, a two-star in Le Ceinturon (℡04.94.66.30.54, ⓕ04.94.66.48.30; closed Oct–Easter; €15.90), and *Clair de Lune*, avenue du Clair de Lune (℡04.94.58.20.19, ⓦwww.campingclairedelune.com; closed mid-Nov to Jan; €21), a three-star one on the Presqu'Île de Giens.

The Town

Walled and medieval **old Hyères** perches on the slopes of Casteou hill, 5km from the sea; below it lies the **modern town**, with avenue Gambetta the main north–south axis. At the coast, the **Presqu'Île de Giens** is leashed to the mainland by an isthmus, known as **La Capte**, and a parallel sand bar enclosing the salt marshes and a lake.

From place Clemenceau, a medieval gatehouse, the **Porte Massillon**, opens into the old town on rue Massillon, lined with tempting shops selling fruit and vegetables, chocolate, soaps, olive oil and wine. It ends at **place Massillon**, a perfect Provençal square with terraced cafés overlooking the twelfth-century **Tour des Templiers**, the remnant of a Knights Templar fort elegantly converted into exhibition space for contemporary art (April–Oct daily except Tues 10am–noon & 4–7pm; Nov–March Wed–Sun 10am–noon & 2–5pm; free). Behind the tower, rue Ste-Catherine leads uphill to place St-Paul, from which you have a panoramic view over the Golfe de Giens.

Wide steps fan out from the Renaissance door of the former collegiate **church of St-Paul** (April–Sept daily except Tues 10am–noon & 4–7pm; Oct–March Wed–Sun 10am–noon & 2–5.30pm), whose distinctive belfry is pure Romanesque, as is the choir, though the simplicity of the design is masked by the collection of votive offerings hung inside.

To the right of St-Paul, a Renaissance house bridges rue St-Paul, its turret supported by a pillar rising beside the steps. Through this arch you can head up rue Ste-Claire to the entrance of **Parc Ste-Claire** (daily 8am–5/7pm; free), the exotic gardens around **Castel Ste-Claire**, once home to the American writer

Edith Wharton and now the offices of the Parc National de Port-Cros. Cobbled paths lead up the hill towards the **Parc St-Bernard** (daily 8am–5/7pm; free), full of almost every Mediterranean flower known. At the top, above montée des Noailles (which by car you reach from cours Strasbourg and avenue Long), is the **Villa Noailles**, a Cubist mansion enclosed within part of the old citadel walls, designed by Mallet-Stevens in the 1920s and a home to all the luminaries of Dada and Surrealism. It now hosts contemporary art exhibitions (daily 10am–noon & 1–4.30pm; free). To the west of the park and further up the hill are the immaculate remains of the eleventh-century **castle**, whose keep and ivy-clad towers give stunning views out to the Îles d'Hyères and east to the Massif des Maures.

The switch from medieval to eighteenth- and nineteenth-century Hyères at **avenue des Îles-d'Or** and its continuation, **avenue Général-de-Gaulle**, is abrupt, with wide boulevards, opulent villas and palms creating a spa town atmosphere. If you're keen on the ancient history of this coast, the **Site Archéologique d'Olbia** in Almanarre (closed for conservation at the time of writing) is worth a visit: the remains of the fortified Greek trading post are supplemented by later Roman and medieval remains, including those of the abbey of Saint-Pierre de l'Almanarre. An alternative pastime is to wander around the spectacular array of cacti and palms in the **Jardins Olbius-Riquier**, just to the southeast of avenue Gambetta (daily 7.30am–6/8pm; free). It has a small zoo and miniature train to keep kids happy. Hyères' coastal suburbs have plenty of **beaches**, but can be subject to mosquito plagues in spring and summer. Alternatively, take the **route du Sel** to the **Presqu'Île de Giens** (closed mid-Nov to mid-April) for a glimpse of the saltworks and flamingoes on the adjoining lake.

Eating and drinking

For **eating and drinking**, place Massillon is the obvious place: filled with restaurant tables and with an unmistakably Mediterranean atmosphere in the evening. Of its restaurants ✻ *Le Bistrot de Marius*, 1 place Massillon (☎04.94.35.88.38; closed Mon in July & Aug), is perhaps the most tempting, with plenty of fish on its €18–32 menus. In the new town, *Les Jardins de Bacchus*, 32 avenue Gambetta (☎04.94.65.77.63; menus from €32; closed Sat lunch, Sun dinner & Mon), serves novel concoctions with panache, while *Les Jardins de Saradam*, 35 avenue de Belgique (☎04.94.65.97.53; closed Sun evening & Mon out of season; evenings only July & Aug), is a reliable North African restaurant with a pretty garden and filling couscous and tagines from around €13.

The Îles d'Hyères

A haven from tempests in ancient times, then the peaceful home of monks and farmers, the **Îles d'Hyères** became, from the Middle Ages onwards, the target of piracy and coastal attacks. The three main islands, **Porquerolles**, **Port-Cros** and **Levant**, are covered in half-destroyed, rebuilt or abandoned forts, dating from the sixteenth century, when François I started a trend of under-funded fort building, up to the twentieth century, when the German gun positions on Port-Cros and Levant were put out of action by the Americans. Porquerolles and Levant are not yet free of garrisons, thanks to the knack of the French armed forces for securing prime beauty sites for their bases. Their presence has helped prevent development and, in the non-military areas, the islands' very fragile environment is protected by the Parc National de Port-Cros and the Conservatoire Botanique de Porquerolles. The fire risk in summer is extreme: at times large sections of the islands are therefore closed off and visitors must stick to marked paths.

The islands' wild, scented greenery and fine sand beaches are a reminder of what much of the mainland was like forty years ago. To **stay** on them, the only reasonable option is Levant, though you must book months in advance. Accommodation on Porquerolles is limited, expensive and needs reserving in advance; on Port-Cros it's almost nonexistent. All visitors should observe signs forbidding smoking (away from the ports), flower-picking and littering.

Île de Porquerolles

The most easily accessible of the islands is **Porquerolles**, whose permanent village, also called **PORQUEROLLES**, has a few hotels and restaurants, plenty of cafés, a market and interminable games of *boules*. It dates from a nineteenth-century military settlement, and the village still focuses around the central **place d'Armes**, the erstwhile military exercise ground. In summer its population explodes to over ten thousand, but there is some activity all year round. This is the only cultivated island of the three, with a few olive groves and three Côtes de Provence *domaines* that can be visited.

Porquerolles is big enough to find yourself alone amid its stunning landscapes. The **lighthouse** (April–Nov 11am–noon & 2.30–4pm weather permitting), due south of the village, and the **calanques** to its east make good destinations for an hour's walk, though the southern shoreline is all cliffs, with scary paths meandering close to the edge through heather and exuberant maquis scrub. Just off the path to the lighthouse at the southern end of the village is the **Maison du Parc** (Mon–Fri & Sun: July & Aug 9.30am–12.30pm & 2.30–6.30pm; April–June, Sept & Oct 9.30am–12.30pm & 1.30–5.15pm) with a garden of palms from around the world, information on the national park's activities and tours of the nearby Mediterranean botanic garden of

▲ Plage d'Argent, Île de Porquerolles

Le Hameau. The longest beach is the **plage Notre-Dame**, 3km northeast of the village just before the *terrain militaire* on the northern tip. The nearest beach to the village is the **plage d'Argent**, 1km away (continue west from the port past the Arche de Noë and take the first, well-signed right). This 500m strip of white sand fringes a curving bay backed by pine forests, and has a pleasant **restaurant**, *La Plage d'Argent* (☎04.94.58.32.48; closed Oct–March; lunchtime *plat du jour* €14–24).

Practicalities

There's a small **information centre** by the harbour (daily: April–Sept 9am–5.30pm; Oct–March 9am–12.30pm; ☎04.94.58.33.76, ⓦwww.porquerolles.com) where you can get basic maps. You can hire **bikes** from several outlets: La Bécane (☎06.74.64.94.26) and L'Indien (☎04.94.58.30.39) are both on place d'Armes.

Expect to pay upwards of €100 a night for **hotel** accommodation in Porquerolles in season; marginally cheaper is the *Relais de la Poste*, place d'Armes (☎04.98.04.62.62, ⓦwww.lerelaisdelaposte.com; ❺; closed Oct–March). Otherwise, you might try *Les Mèdes*, rue de la Douane (☎04.94.12.41.24, ⓦwww.hotel-les-medes.fr; ❼; closed Jan to mid-March & early Nov to late Dec), or *Villa Sainte-Anne*, on place d'Armes (☎04.98.04.63.00, ⓦwww.sainteanne.com; ❻; closed early Nov to mid-Feb), which has the most character. There's no campsite and *camping sauvage* is strictly forbidden, so don't miss the last ferry to the mainland.

Most of the cafés and **restaurants** in the village are pure tourist fodder; if you want gourmet fare you'll need to make the trek to the idyllic *Le Mas du Langoustier* (☎04.94.58.30.09, closed early October to late April) in the west of the island to feast on the likes of roast turbot on menus starting from €55. You can buy sandwiches and *pan bagnat* on the place d'Armes for around €4, and there's also a supermarket and fruit and vegetable stall here.

Île de Port-Cros

The dense vegetation and mini-mountains of **Port-Cros** (ⓦwww.portcros parcnational.fr) make its exploration much tougher than Porquerolles, though it's less than half the size. Aside from ruined forts and the handful of buildings around the port, the only intervention is the classification labels on some of the plants and the extensive network of paths; you're not supposed to stray from these and it would be difficult to do so given the thickness of the undergrowth. The entire island is a protected zone, and has the richest fauna and flora of all the islands. Kestrels, eagles and sparrowhawks nest here; there are shrubs that flower and bear fruit at the same time, and more common species like broom, lavender, rosemary and heather flourish. One kilometre from the port (and a 45min walk) is the nearest beach, **plage de la Palud**; it takes rather longer to reach Mont Vinaigre, the island's highest point, via the **Vallon de la Solitude** – a three-hour round trip. From here there are views over the island's south coast and the islet of Gabinière. Except for those close to the beaches, the island's 30km of paths are all liable to closure during times of high fire risk.

There are two **hotels**: *Le Manoir d'Hélène* (T04.94.05.90.52, Wmonsite .orange.fr/hotelmanoirportcros; ❽ half-board; closed Oct to mid-April; menus €43) books up fast; there are five half-board rooms at the restaurant, *Hostellerie Provençale* (T04.94.05.90.43, Wwww.hostellerie-provencale.com; ❼; closed mid-Oct to Easter). Almost as expensive is dining in the few **restaurants** around the port, though you can get a sandwich or a slice of pizza. Once you leave the village, however, there's nothing; at the very least, walkers should be sure they carry enough water. Again, camping is forbidden.

Île du Levant

The **Île du Levant** – ninety percent military reserve – is almost always humid and sunny. Cultivated plant life goes wild, with the result that giant geraniums and nasturtiums climb three-metre hedges, overhung by gigantic eucalyptus trees and yuccas. The tiny bit of the island spared by the military is the **nudist colony** of **HELIOPOLIS**, set up in the 1930s. About sixty people live here all year round, joined by thousands who come for the summer, and by tens of thousands of day-trippers, who are treated as voyeurs; if you **stay**, even for one night, you'll receive a friendlier reception. The most reasonable **hotels** are *Chez Valéry* (T04.94.05.90.83, F04.94.05.92.95; ❺; closed Oct–March) and *Gaëtan* (T04.94.05.91.78, Wwww.hotelgaetan.com; ❸; closed Oct–March). There are two **campsites**: *Le Colombero* (T04.94.05.90.29; closed Oct–March) and *La Pinède* (T04.94.05.92.81, Wwww.campingdulevant.free.fr, closed Oct–March).

Levant has a better choice of **restaurants** than Port-Cros, though price and quality still don't match; *Le Minimum* and *La Pomme d'Adam* are among the cheaper options.

The Corniche des Maures

The Côte really gets going with the resorts of the **Corniche des Maures**, as multimillion-dollar residences lurk increasingly in the hills, luxurious yachts moor in the bays, and seafront prices become alarming. Douglas Fairbanks Jr, the late Grand Duke of Luxembourg and sundry other titled names have pushed this coastline into legend.

The Corniche des Maures has beaches that shine silver (from the mica crystals in the sand), tall dark pines, oaks and eucalyptus to shade them, glittering rocks of purple, green and reddish hue and chestnut-forested hills keeping winds away.

Bormes-les-Mimosas and around

Seventeen kilometres east of Hyères, chic **BORMES–LES–MIMOSAS** is medieval in flavour, with a ruined but restored **castle** at the summit of its hill, protected by spiralling lines of pantiled houses backing onto immaculately restored flights of steps. The mimosas here, and all along the Côte d'Azur, are no more indigenous than the people passing in their Porsches: the tree was introduced from Mexico in the 1860s, but the town still has some of the most luscious climbing flowers of any Côte town, and in summer, the displays of bougainvillea and oleander are impressive.

To the southwest of Bormes is one of those rare unbuilt-up stretches of coast around **BREGANÇON** and **CABASSON**, good wine-growing terrain, harbouring a presidential residence in the castle at **Cap de Bregançon**. Access to the sea is heavily controlled, with three **beaches** charging parking fees (€7) and a small fee to cyclists and walkers. The beach by the castle past Cabasson is the best.

Two **hotels** worth trying in old Bormes are the simple but attractive *Bellevue*, on place Gambetta (℡04.94.71.15.15, ⊛bellevuebormes.fr.st; ❸; closed mid-Nov to Jan), or the fancier *Hostellerie du Cigalou* opposite (℡04.94.41.51.27, ⊛www.hostellerieducigalou.com; ❻). In Cabasson, the attractive and peaceful *Les Palmiers*, 240 chemin du Petit-Fort (℡04.94.64.81.94, ⊛www.hotel lespalmiers.com; ❽; closed mid-Dec to Jan; half board compulsory in summer), has its own path to the beach. All **campsites** are just below the main road or in La Favière, closer to Le Lavandou than to Bormes. One of the best is *Clau-Mar-Jo* at 895 chemin de Bénat (℡04.94.71.53.39, ⊛www.camping-clau-mar -jo.fr; €27 for two people; closed mid-Oct to mid-March). The **tourist office** in Bormes is on place Gambetta (April–Sept daily 9am–12.30pm & 2.30–6.30pm; Oct–March Mon–Sat 9am–12.30pm & 1.30–5.30pm; ℡04.94.01.38.38, ⊛www.bormeslesmimosas.com). Good **restaurants** include *La Tonnelle* on place Gambetta (℡04.94.71.34.84; closed mid-Nov to mid-Dec; lunch menus from €27), specializing in local recipes including *daube de boeuf*; *La Cassole* at 1 ruelle du Moulin (℡04.94.71.14.86; menus from €26), which serves Provençal specialities in unpretentious surroundings, and *Pâtes…et Pâtes*, on place du Bazar (℡04.94.64.85.75; closed Tues), which serves the best pasta in town from around €9.

Le Lavandou to La Croix-Valmer

LE LAVANDOU, a few kilometres east of Bormes, is a pleasantly unpretentious seaside town known for its good, sandy beaches. Its name derives from *lavoir* or "wash-house" rather than "lavender". From the central promenade of quai Gabriel-Péri the sea is all but invisible thanks to the pleasure boats moored at the three harbours; demand from restaurateurs also keeps a few fishing boats in business. If you want to indulge in watersports or nightlife, the **tourist office** on quai Gabriel-Péri (May–Sept Mon–Sat 9am–12.30pm & 2.30–7pm, Sun 10am–noon & 4–6pm; Nov–March Mon–Sat 9am–noon & 2.30–6pm; ℡04.94.00.40.50, ⊛www.ot-lelavandou.fr) will happily advise. For **accommodation**, try the *Hôtel L'Oustaou*, 20 avenue Général-de-Gaulle (℡04.94.71.12.18, ⊛www.lavandou-hotel-oustaou.com; ❷), a clean, family-run place in the town centre.

The town beach at Le Lavandou is quite broad and sandy, but if you're after the fabled silver beaches you need to head out of town and east along the corniche to **Cavalière**, **Pramousquier**, **Le Canadel** and **Le Rayol**. It's hardly countryside, but you can explore the Pointe du Layet headland just east of

Cavalière, follow the sinuous D27 up to the **Col du Canadel** for breathtaking views and beautiful cork-oak woodland, and, in **Le Rayol**, visit a superb garden, the **Domaine de Rayol** (daily: summer 9.30am–7.30pm; spring & autumn 9.30am–6.30pm; winter 9.30am–5.30pm; €8) which has plants from differing parts of the world that share the Mediterranean climate.

Beyond Le Rayol the corniche climbs away from the coast through 3km of open countryside, scarred almost every year by fires. As abruptly as this wilderness commences, it ends with the sprawling family resort of **Cavalaire-sur-Mer**. From here another exceptional stretch of coastline, dressed only in its natural covering of rock and woodlands, is visible across the Baie de Cavalaire. This is the **Domaine de Cap Lardier**, a wonderful coastal conservation area around the southern tip of the St-Tropez peninsula, easily accessible from **LA CROIX-VALMER**. The resort's centre is 2.5km from the sea; some of the land in between is taken up by vineyards producing a very decent Côte de Provence.

La Croix-Valmer's **tourist office** is at Esplanade de la Gare (mid-June to mid-Sept Mon–Sat 9.15am–12.30pm & 2.30–7pm, Sun 9am–1pm; mid-Sept to mid-June Mon–Fri 9.15am–noon & 2–6pm, Sat & Sun 9.15am–noon; ℡04.94.55.12.12, ⓦwww.lacroixvalmer.fr), just up from the junction of the D559 and D93. A good-value **hotel** is *La Bienvenue* on rue L.-Martin (℡04.94.17.08.08, ⓦwww.hotel-la-bienvenue.com; ❸; closed Nov–Feb) in the village centre. One of the cheapest options near the beach is the family-run *Hostellerie La Ricarde*, plage du Débarquement (℡04.94.79.64.07, ⓦwww .hotel-la-ricardecom; ❸; closed Oct–March), while at the other end of the scale is *Le Château de Valmer*, on route de Gigaro (℡04.94.55.15.15, ⓦwww .chateauvalmer.com; ❾; closed Nov to early April), a luxurious old mansion within walking distance of the sea. You can **camp** at the four-star *Sélection*, on boulevard de la Mer (℡04.94.55.10.30, ⓦwww.selectioncamping.com; €31.50 per tent; closed mid-Oct to mid-March; booking advisable), 400m from the sea and with excellent facilities. Good pizzas are guaranteed (from €10) at *L'Italien* (℡04.94.79.67.16) on plage de Gigaro, just before the conservation area. Two other good but expensive **restaurants** on this beach are *La Brigantine* and *Souleïas*.

The Massif des Maures

The secret of the Côte d'Azur is that however vulgar the coast, Provence is still just behind – sparsely populated, village-oriented and exploiting the land for produce, not real estate. The most bewitching hinterland is the **Massif des Maures**, stretching from Hyères to Fréjus. The highest point of these hills stops short of 800m, but the quick succession of ridges, the sudden drops and views, and the curling, looping roads, are pervasively mountainous. In spring, the sombre forest is enlivened by millions of wild flowers and the roads are busy with cyclists; in winter, this is the haunt of hunters. Amid the brush crawl the last of the Hermann's tortoises, which once could be found along the whole of the northern Mediterranean coast.

Much of the Massif is inaccessible even to walkers. However, the **GR9 footpath** follows the highest and most northerly ridge from Pignans on the N97 past Notre-Dame-des-Anges, La Sauvette, **La Garde-Freinet** and down to the head of the Golfe de St-Tropez. If you're **cycling**, the D14 that runs for 42km through the middle, parallel to the coast, from Pierrefeu-du-Var, north of

Hyères, to **Cogolin** near St-Tropez, is manageable and stunning, climbing from 150m to 411m above sea level.

Collobrières and La Chartreuse de la Verne

At the heart of the Massif is the ancient village of **COLLOBRIÈRES**, reputed to have been the first place in France to learn from the Spanish that a certain tree plugged into bottles allows a wine industry to grow. From the Middle Ages until supplanted by the sweet chestnut, cork production was the major business of the village. The church, the *mairie* and houses don't seem to have been modernized for a century, but the 🌰 **Confiserie Azurienne** on boulevard Koenig (9.30am–12.30pm & 1.30–6.30pm) exudes efficiency and modern business skill in the manufacture of all things chestnut: ice cream, jam, nougat, purée and *marrons glacés*. There's also a small outdoor café there where you can enjoy the delicious ice cream.

Collobrières' **tourist office** on boulevard Charles-Caminat (Tue, Wed, Fri & Sat 10am–noon & 2–5.30pm; ☎04.94.48.08.00, ⓦ www.collobrieres-tourisme .com; not always open during its published opening hours) can supply details of walks in the surrounding hills. There are two **hotels**: *Notre-Dame*, 15 avenue de la Libération (☎04.94.48.07.13, ⓕ04.94.48.05.95; ❶; closed mid-Dec to Jan), and the equally excellent-value *Hôtel des Maures*, 19 boulevard Lazare Carnot (☎04.94.48.07.10, ⓕ04.94.48.02.73; ❶). There are also some great **chambres d'hôtes**, including Loïc and Andrée de Saleneuve's *La Bastide de La Cabrière*, 6km in the direction of Gonfaron on the D39 (☎04.94.48.04.31, ⓦ www .saleneuve.com; ❹). A municipal **campsite** (☎04.94.28.15.72; bookings through the tourist office), the *St-Roch*, south of the village near place Charles-de-Gaulle, is open in July and August. *Camping sauvage* is forbidden; one stray spark and you could be responsible for a thousand acres of burnt forest.

For food other than chestnuts, the **restaurant** *La Petite Fontaine*, 6 place de la République (☎04.94.48.00.12; closed Sun evening & Mon), is congenial and affordable, with menus from €25, but books up fast. If you want to buy some local **wines**, visit Les Vignerons de Collobrières close to the *Hôtel Notre-Dame* at the western entrance to the village. **Market** days are Thursday and Sunday.

Hidden in the forest, 12km from Collobrières off the D14 towards Grimaud, is a huge and now largely restored twelfth-century monastery, **La Chartreuse de la Verne** (daily except Tues: Feb–May & Oct–Dec 11am–5pm; June–Sept 11am–6pm; €6), abandoned at the time of the Revolution. These days it looks a little too pristine, though there's no denying the wonder of its setting. The access road deteriorates into a rutted track for the last 500m.

Grimaud

GRIMAUD, 25km east of Collobrières along the twisting D14 and more easily reached from St-Tropez or La Croix Valmer, is a film set of a *village perché*. The cone of houses enclosing the eleventh-century church and culminating in the ruins of a medieval castle appears as a single, perfectly unified entity, though the effect of timelessness is undermined by the glass lift that whisks visitors up into the village from the main road. The most vaunted street is the arcaded **rue des Templiers**, which leads up to the pure Romanesque **Église de St-Michel** and a house of the Knights Templar, while the view from the **castle** ruins is superb. Grimaud's celebrated coastal extension, **PORT GRIMAUD**, stands at the head of the Golfe de St-Tropez, just north of La Foux. Created in the 1960s with waterways for roads and yachts everywhere, it's exquisitely tasteful, though the complex is surrounded by car parks rather than fields of lavender and there's an inevitable air of theme-park artificiality. The inhabitants include a certain Joan Collins. The main entrance is well signed off the N98. You don't have to pay to get in, but you can't explore all the islands without hiring a boat (€20 for 30min) or joining a crowded boat tour (€4).

Grimaud's **tourist office** is at 1 boulevard des Aliziers (Mon–Sat: April–June & Sept 9am–12.30pm & 2.30–6.15pm; July & Aug 9am–12.30pm & 3–7pm; Oct–March Mon–Sat 9am–12.30pm & 2.15–5.30pm; ☎04.94.55.43.83, ⓦwww.grimaud-provence.com), just off the main road which passes by the old village and the little folk museum, the **Musée des Arts et Traditions** (May–Sept Mon–Sat 2.30–6pm; Oct–April Mon–Sat 2–5.30pm; free). Excellent, if pricey, **menus** from €45 are offered at *Le Coteau Fleuri*, place des Pénitents (☎04.94.43.20.17, ⓦwww.coteaufleuri.fr; closed Tues except July & August), which also has fourteen **rooms** (❹–❻).

La Garde-Freinet

The attractive village of **LA GARDE-FREINET**, 10km northwest of Grimaud, was founded in the late twelfth century by people from the nearby villages of Saint Clément and Miremer. The original fortified settlement sat further up the hillside, and the foundations of the fortress are still visible above the village beside the ruins of a fifteenth-century castle (take the path from La Planette car park at the northwestern end of the village). These days a note of St-Tropez trendiness is creeping in, but it still feels that it belongs to the locals, thanks in part to the regeneration of forestry business around cork and chestnut. It also has medieval charm; easy walks to stunning panoramas; markets twice a week (Wed & Sun); a chestnut cooperative on the northern approach to the village; tempting food shops selling organic produce and good local wines; and very reasonable accommodation.

The **tourist office** operates from the Chapelle St Jean, on place de l'Hôtel de Ville (April–June & Sept Mon–Sat 9.30am–12.30pm & 3.30–5.50pm; July–Aug Mon–Sat 9.30am–1pm & 4–6.30pm, Sun 9.30am–12.30pm; Oct–March Tues–Sat 9.30am–12.30pm & 2–5pm; ☎04.94.43.67.41, ⓦwww .lagardefreinet-tourisme.com), and will provide details for the entire Maures region, including suggesting **walks** and hikes such as the spectacular 21km GR9 route des Crêtes. The danger of forest fires is particularly high here; the current risk level is posted up outside the tourist office in summer. Next door is the **Conservatoire du Patrimoine** (Tues–Sat 10am–12.30pm & 3–6pm; free), which organizes guided walks on various local topics and has exhibits on local sericulture and a model of the old fortress.

For **rooms**, *La Claire Fontaine* on place Vieille (☎&ⓕ04.94.43.63.76; ❸) and *Le Fraxinois* on place Neuve (☎04.94.43.62.84, ⓕ04.94.43.69.65; ❹) are incredibly good value. There's also a campsite, *La Ferme de Bérard*, 5km along the D558 towards Grimaud (☎04.94.43.21.23, ⓕ04.94.43.32.33; €12.10 for two adults, car and tent; closed Nov–Feb).

The place to be of an evening is *Le Carnotzet* bar, art gallery and **restaurant**, on the exquisite place du Marché (☎04.94.43.62.73; *plats du jour* from €15; occasional live music). *La Colombe Joyeuse*, on place Vieille (☎04.94.43.65.24; closed Tues in winter; menu from €14.50), has pigeon as its speciality, while *La Faucado*, on the main road (☎04.94.43.60.41; closed Tues in winter; à la carte around €60), is overpriced, but serves beautiful dishes from local produce in a pretty garden setting.

St-Tropez and its peninsula

The origins of **ST-TROPEZ** are unremarkable: a fishing village that grew up around a port founded by Marseille's Greeks, destroyed by Saracens in 739 and finally fortified in the late Middle Ages. Its sole distinction was its inaccessibility: stuck on a small peninsula that never warranted proper roads, St-Tropez could only easily be reached by boat. This held true as late as the 1880s, when the novelist Guy de Maupassant sailed into the port during his final high-living binge before the onset of syphilitic insanity.

Soon after, the painter Paul Signac was sailing down the coast when bad weather forced him to moor in St-Tropez. He promptly decided to build a house there, to which he invited his friends. Matisse was one of the first to accept, with Bonnard, Marquet, Dufy, Dérain, Vlaminck, Seurat and Van Dongen following suit, and by the evening of World War I St-Tropez was an established bohemian hangout. The 1930s saw a new influx, of writers as much as painters: Cocteau, Colette and Anaïs Nin, whose journal records "girls riding bare-breasted in the back of open cars". In 1956, Roger Vadim filmed Brigitte Bardot in *Et Dieu… Créa la Femme*; the international cult of Tropezian sun, sex and celebrities promptly took off and the place has been groaning under the weight of visitors ever since.

As the summer playground of Europe's youthful rich, St-Tropez remains undeniably glamorous, its oversized yachts and infamous champagne "spray" parties creating an air of hedonistic excess. Unless you have the holiday budget of a supermodel or Formula One racing driver, however, it can feel like a party you're not invited to.

Arrival and information

Infrequent buses run between the main coast road at **La Foux** and St-Tropez, 5.5km away, dropping you at the **gare routière** on avenue Général-de-Gaulle. From here it's a short walk along avenue du 8-Mai-1945 to the **Vieux Port**, where you'll find the **tourist office** on quai Jean-Jaurès (daily: April–June & Sept–Oct 9.30am–12.30pm & 2–7pm; July & Aug 9.30am–8pm; Nov–March 9.30am–12.30pm & 2–6pm; ℡04.94.97.45.21, ⓦwww.ot-saint-tropez.com). **Bikes** and **motorbikes** can be rented at Holiday Bikes, 12 avenue G.-Leclerc (℡04.88.91.56.10, ⓦwww.holiday-bikes.com).

Accommodation

Accommodation is a problem; between April and September you'll be lucky to find a room unless you've booked in advance or are prepared to pay exorbitant prices. The tourist office can help with reservations, but, transport permitting, you might be better off staying in La Croix-Valmer or even Sainte-Maxime, from which you can get to St-Tropez by sea. Many hotels close out of season. **Camping** near St-Tropez can be expensive, with many sites more geared towards chalet lets than providing emplacements for tents. The nearest sites are the two on the plage du Pampelonne, which charge extortionate rates and are massively crowded in summer. Otherwise, within a three-kilometre radius of the nearby village of Ramatuelle are *Les Tournels* on route de Camarat (℡04.94.55.90.90, ⓦwww.tournels.com; closed Jan to mid-March; €42 per tent in high season) and *La Rouillère* in quartier la Rouillère (℡04.94.79.21.42, ⓦwww.camping-larouillere; €30 in high season; closed Nov–March). Overnighting in vehicles is not permitted.

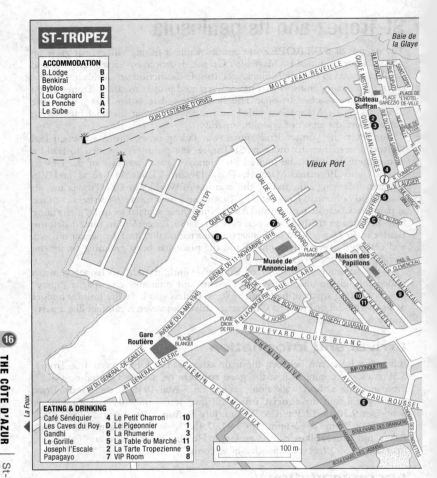

ST-TROPEZ

ACCOMMODATION

B.Lodge	**B**
Benkiraï	**F**
Byblos	**D**
Lou Cagnard	**E**
La Ponche	**A**
Le Sube	**C**

Baie de la Glaye

QUAI F. MISTRAL
RUE SAINT-ESPRIT
RUE DUPLAN
MOLE JEAN REVEILLE
PLACE DE L'HOTEL-DE-VILLE
PLACE GAREZZIO
L'HOTEL-DE-VILLE
Château Suffran
QUAI D'ESTIENNE D'ORVES
RUE DU CEDRON SIMMARTIN
RUE DE LA PONCHE
RUE DE LA MISERICORDE
QUAI JEAN-JAURÈS
Vieux Port
R.V. LAUGIER
RUE SIBILLI
RUE FRANÇOIS
QUAI SUFFREN
PAS. D'YTROIT
QUAI DE L'EPI
QUAI DE L'EPI
QUAI DE L'EPI
QUAI H. BOUCHARD
AVENUE DU 11-NOVEMBRE-1918
PLACE GRAMMONT
RUE GEORGES CLEMENCEAU
PAS. G. CLEMENCEAU
Musée de l'Annonciade
Maison des Papillons
RUE PISTE DE LA
RUE ALLARD
RUE DE LA CITADELLE
RUE ETIENNE BERNY
RUE DES TISSERANDS
RUE DES FÉNIERS
RUE BOUTIN
R. DE LA CROIX DE FER
RUE JOSEPH QUARANTA
B.J. AICARD
AVENUE DU 3-MAI-1945
PLACE CROIX DE FER
BOULEVARD LOUIS BLANC
AV DU GENERAL-DE-GAULLE
Gare Routière
PLACE BLANQUI
AV GENERAL LECLERC
CHEMIN PRIVE
IMP. CONQUETTES
CHEMIN DES AMOUREUX
AVENUE PAUL ROUSSEL
CHEMIN DES CONQUETTES
BD. DES AMANDIERS
BOULEVARD DES ORANGERS
BOULEVARD DES JASMINS

EATING & DRINKING

Café Sénéquier	**4**	Le Petit Charron	**10**
Les Caves du Roy	**D**	Le Pigeonnier	**1**
Gandhi	**6**	La Rhumerie	**3**
Le Gorille	**5**	La Table du Marché	**11**
Joseph l'Escale	**2**	La Tarte Tropezienne	**9**
Papagayo	**7**	VIP Room	**8**

0 — 100 m

B. Lodge 23 rue de l'Aïoli ☏04.94.97.06.57, ⓦwww.hotel-b-lodge.com. Overlooking the citadel, not the bargain it once was but quieter than hotels in the centre and with stylish decor. **7**

Benkiraï 11 chemin du Pinet ☏04.94.97.04.37, ⓦwww.hotel-benkirai.com. Trendy newcomer with decor by a young associate of Philippe Starck and doubles from €450 in summer. **9**

Byblos av Paul-Signac ☏04.94.56.68.00, ⓦwww.byblos.com. The perennial favourite if money really is no object and you need to be with the in-crowd, with doubles over €500 a night in July and Aug. **9**

Lou Cagnard 18 av Paul-Roussel ☏04.94.97.04.24, ⓦwww.hotel-lou-cagnard.com. One of the best cheaper options, in a central yet relatively peaceful location and with a decent garden. **4**

La Ponche 3 rue des Remperts ☏04.94.97.02.53, ⓦwww.laponche.com. An old block of fishermen's houses with a host of famous arty names in its guest book. Closed Nov to mid-Feb. **9**

Le Sube 15 quai Suffren ☏04.94.97.30.04, ⓦwww.hotel-sube.com. Right in the thick of it, with some rooms offering unique views over the port. **7**

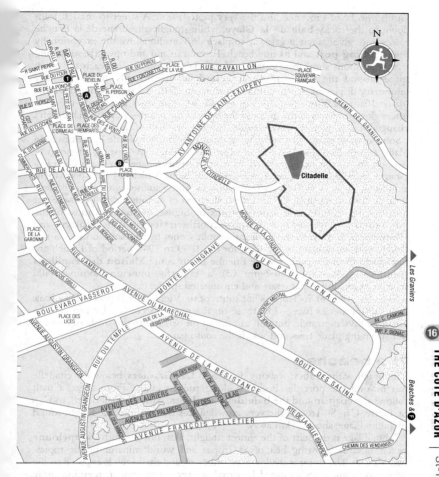

Citadelle

Les Graniers

Beaches & F

16

THE CÔTE D'AZUR | St-Tropez and its peninsula

The Town

Beware of St-Tropez in high summer. Even getting to it is an ordeal, unless you waft in by helicopter, yacht or on the ferry from Sainte-Maxime, for the traffic jams can be appalling. The people jams around the port are little better, and the beaches aren't the cleanest. Save your visit for a spring or autumn day and you'll understand better why this place has had such hype.

The **Vieux Port**, rebuilt after its destruction in World War II, is where you'll get the classic St-Tropez experience: the quayside café clientele *face-à-face* with the yacht-deck Martini sippers and the latest fashions parading in between, defining the French word *frimer*, which means to stroll ostentatiously in places like St-Tropez. It's all highly theatrical, if more than a little vulgar – a sort of human zoo where celebrities, millionaires and their hangers-on are the willing exhibits. You'll either love it or hate it.

Up from the port, at the end of quai Jean-Jaurès, you enter place de l'Hôtel-de-Ville, with the **Château Suffren**, originally built in 980 by Count

1051

Guillaume 1er of Provence, and the very pretty *mairie*. A street to the left leads down to the rocky **baie de la Glaye**, while straight ahead rue de la Ponche passes through an ancient gateway to place du Revelin above the exceptionally pretty **fishing port** and its tiny beach. Turning inland and upwards, struggling past continuous shop fronts, stalls and café tables, you finally reach the open space around the sixteenth-century **citadelle**. It currently houses an arty temporary display of its scheduled reopening in 2010 as a **maritime museum** (daily: 10am–12.30pm & 1.30–5.30pm; €2.50). The walk round the ramparts offers glorious views of the gulf and the back of the town – views which haven't changed much since they were painted in the first half of the last century.

Some of these paintings you can see at the marvellous **Musée de l'Annonciade** (daily except Tues: July–Sept 10am–1pm & 3–7pm; Oct–June 10am–noon & 2–6pm; €5) in the deconsecrated sixteenth-century chapel on place Georges-Grammont, right on the port. It was originally Signac's idea to have a permanent exhibition space for the neo-Impressionists and Fauvists who painted here, though it was not until 1955 that the collections of various individuals were put together. The Annonciade features works by Signac, Matisse and most of the other artists who worked here: grey, grim, northern views of Paris, Boulogne and Westminster, and then local, brilliantly sunlit scenes by the same brush – a real delight and unrivalled outside Paris for the 1890 to 1940 period of French art. Just inland from the port at 9 rue Etienne Berny is the **Maison des Papillons** (April–Oct Mon–Sat 2.30–6pm; €3), a butterfly museum housing 4500 specimens including many rare and endangered species.

The other pole of St-Tropez's life, south of the Vieux Port, is **place des Lices**. The café-brasseries have – like those on the port – become a bit too like the Champs-Elysées in style, but you can still sit on benches in the shade of decayed but surviving plane trees and watch the *boules* games.

The beaches

The beach within easiest walking distance is **Les Graniers**, below the citadelle just beyond the port des Pêcheurs along rue Cavaillon. From there, a path follows the coast around the **baie des Canebiers**, with its small beach, to Cap St-Pierre, Cap St-Tropez, the very crowded **Les Salins** beach and right round to Tahiti-Plage, about 11km away.

Tahiti-Plage is the start of the almost straight, 5km north–south **Pampelonne** beach, famous bronzing belt of St-Tropez and world initiator of the topless bathing cult. The water is shallow for 50m or so, and the beach is exposed to the wind, and sometimes scourged by dried sea vegetation, not to mention more distasteful garbage. But spotless glitter comes from the unending line of **beach bars** and restaurants, all with patios and sofas, serving cocktails, gluttonous ice creams and full-blown meals. *Le 55* on boulevard Patch (℡04.94.55.55.55) is the original and most famous; *Maison Ocoa*, also on boulevard Patch (℡04.94.79.89.80), is *über*-trendy, almost a nightclub on the beach; and *Nikki Beach*, route de l'Epi (℡04.94.79.82.04), is *the* current celebrity hangout.

Transport from St-Tropez is provided by a frequent **minibus** service (June–Sept only) from place des Lices to Salins, or bus #106 to Ramatuelle (Tuesdays and Saturdays), which runs along the route de Pampelonne. If you're driving, you'll have to pay high parking charges at all the beaches, or to leave your car or motorbike some distance from the sea and easy prey to thieves.

Eating and drinking

Restaurants in St-Tropez obsess as much over how stylish they (and their customers) look as over the quality of the food, and budget offerings are distinctly in the minority. You should reckon on paying quite a bit more than in comparable places in other resorts in the Var, and be aware that price doesn't necessarily correspond to quality.

Gandhi 3 quai de l'Epi ☎04.94.97.71.71. Curries and tandoori, with a good selection of fish and shellfish on the menu. Lunch menu from €18.50 and dinner from €21. Closed all day Wed out of season.
Le Gorille 1 quai Suffren. Straightforward steak and burger fare on the port, for around €15.
Joseph l'Escale 9 quai Jean-Jaurès ☎04.94.97.00.63. Slick quayside restaurant that is rather more affordable than its sister restaurant around the corner, with cheaper *plats du jour* from around €14; otherwise, menu at €39.
Le Petit Charron 6 rue des Charrons ☎04.94.97.73.78. Tiny terrace and dining room serving beautifully cooked Provençal specialities. Around €40 for what? A meal? A set menu? A dish? Please clarify – a meal. Closed first two weeks in Aug, plus two weeks in Nov & Jan.
La Rhumerie quai Jean-Jaurès ☎04.94.97.31.58. Just about the cheapest proper meals on the port,

with pasta dishes from €8.60 and *plats du jour* around €15.
Café Sénéquier 90 quai Jean-Jaurès. The top quayside café, open from breakfast; vast and expensive – horribly so for drinks – but it sells sensational nougat (also on sale from the shop in place aux Herbes at the back).
La Table du Marché 38 rue Georges Clemenceau ☎04.94.97.85.20. Smart deli, restaurant and *salon de thé* with plenty of healthy salads, pasta and fish, plus a €29 menu.
La Tarte Tropezienne 36 rue G.-Clemenceau. Patisserie claiming to have invented the rather sickly eponymous sponge and custard cake, though you no longer have to come to St-Tropez to sample it – the company is now a chain with branches the length of the Côte.

Nightlife

In season St-Tropez stays up late. You can spend the evening trying on clothes in the couturier shops; the *boules* games on place des Lices continue well after dusk; and the portside spectacle doesn't falter till the early hours. If you're rich or mad enough to want to see – and be seen with – the **nightlife** creatures of St-Tropez, clubs include: *Les Caves du Roy*, in the *Hôtel Byblos* on rue Paul-Signac (the most expensive and exclusive); *Papagayo*, on the port, which has a restaurant terrace overlooking the yachts; and the *VIP Room* on the Nouveau Port. There's also a gay club, *Le Pigeonnier*, in rue de la Ponche.

Gassin and Ramatuelle

In delightful contrast to the overcrowded coast, the interior of the **St-Tropez peninsula** remains undeveloped, thanks to government intervention, complex ownerships and the value of some local wines. The best view of this richly green countryside is from the hilltop village of Gassin, its lower neighbour Ramatuelle, or the tiny road between them, the dramatic route des Moulins de Paillas, where three ruined windmills could once catch every wind.

GASSIN is the shape and size of a small ship perched on a summit; once an eighth-century Muslim stronghold, it's an excellent place for a big dinner, sitting outside by the village wall with a spectacular panorama east over the peninsula. Of the handful of **restaurants**, *Bello Visto*, 9 place des Barrys (☎04.94.56.17.30, ⓦwww.bellovisto.eu; closed Nov–March), has very acceptable Provençal specialities on a €30 menu, plus nine rooms at excellent prices for this brilliant setting (❸).

RAMATUELLE is bigger, though just as old, and is surrounded by some of the best Côte de Provence vineyards. The twisting, arcaded streets are full of arts and crafts of dubious talent, but it's all very pleasant. The most beautiful French actor ever to have appeared on screen, Gérard Philippe (1922–59), is buried in Ramatuelle's **cemetery**. His ivy-covered tomb, shaded by a rose bush, is set against the wall on the right as you look down. Hotels worth trying are the fairly basic *Chez Tony*, 31 rue Clemenceau (℡04.94.79.20.46; ❸), and the more attractive *L'Écurie du Castellas*, route des Moulins de Paillas (℡04.94.79.20.67, ⓦwww .lecurieducastellas.com; ❺). For **food**, great pasta dishes are to be had at *Au Fil à la Pâte*, 7 rue Victor-Léon (℡04.94.79.16.40; closed mid-Oct to Feb), with *plats du jour* at €12.

Ste-Maxime and around

Facing St-Tropez across its gulf, **STE-MAXIME** is the perfect Côte stereotype: palmed corniche and enormous pleasure-boat harbour, beaches crowded with bronzed windsurfers and water skiers, and estate agents outnumbering any other businesses by something like ten to one. It sprawls a little too much – merging with its northern neighbours to create a continuous suburban strip all the way to Fréjus. But though hardly as colourful as St-Tropez, it's less pretentious and the beaches are cleaner.

If your budget denies you the pleasures of water skiing, wet-biking and windsurfing, you might find Ste-Maxime a little lacking in diversions. You can, at least, eat at reasonable cost, since there are plenty of crêperies, *glaciers* and snack places along the central avenue Charles-de-Gaulle.

For the spenders, the east-facing plage de la Nartelle, 2km east from the centre towards Les Issambres, is the strip of sand to head for. Here, at **Barco Beach** and its seven neighbours, you'll pay for shaded cushioned comfort, you can enter the water on a variety of different vehicles, eat grilled fish, have drinks brought to your mattress and listen to a piano player as dusk falls. A kilometre or so further on, **plage des Éléphants** recalls the town's link to Jean de Brunhoff, creator of Babar the elephant, who had a holiday home in Ste-Maxime.

Ste-Maxime's *vieille ville* has several good **markets**: a covered flower and food market on rue Fernand-Bessy (June–Sept daily 7.30am–1pm & 4–8pm; Oct–May Tues–Sun same hours); a Thursday morning food market on and around place du Marché; bric-a-brac every Friday morning on place Jean-Mermoz; and arts and crafts in the pedestrian streets (mid-June to mid-Sept daily 5–11pm).

High up in the Massif des Maures on the road to Le Muy, some 10km north of Ste-Maxime, the marvellous **Musée du Phonographe et de la Musique Mécanique**, in the parc St-Donat (Easter to October Wed–Sun 10am–noon; July & Aug also 4–6.30pm; €3), is the result of one amazing woman's forty-year obsession with collecting audio equipment, amassing a wide selection of automata, musical boxes and pianolas, plus one of Thomas Edison's "talking machines" dating from 1878.

Practicalities

Buses into town stop outside the **tourist office** on the promenade Simon-Lorière (June & Sept Mon–Sat 9am–noon & 2–7pm; July & Aug Mon–Sat 9am–8pm, Sun 10am–noon & 4–7pm; Oct–May Mon–Sat 9am–noon & 2–6pm; ℡04.94.55.75.55, ⓦwww.ste-maxime.com), which can give you information on trips and advice on hotel vacancies – once again, rare in summer. If you're heading for St-Tropez from Ste-Maxime, an alternative to the bus is to go by **boat**; the twenty-minute service from Ste-Maxime's *gare maritime* on the port (€12 return) runs from February to early November and again over Christmas and New Year, with more frequent crossings in July and August. Bikes can be rented at **1max2Velos**, 28 route du Plan de la Tour (T04.94.43.49.54).

The best of the cheaper **hotels** is the welcoming *Auberge Provençale*, 19 rue Aristide-Briand (T04.94.55.76.90, F04.94.55.76.91; ❸), with its own restaurant; or there's the small *Castellamar*, 8 avenue G.-Pompidou (T04.94.96.19.97; ❸; closed Oct–March), on the west side of the river but still close to the centre and the sea. For more comfortable surroundings, try the central *Hôtellerie de la Poste*, 11 boulevard Frédéric-Mistral (T04.94.96.18.33, Wwww.hotelleriedusoleil.com; ❻), a modern but attractive hotel with very nice rooms. For camping, *Les Cigalons*, in quartier de la Nartelle, is the two-star seaside option (T04.94.96.05.51, Wwww.campingcigalon.com; closed mid-Oct to March; €21). It also rents out holiday bungalows.

For non-beach **eating**, the *Hostellerie de la Belle Aurore*, 5 boulevard Jean-Moulin (T04.94.96.02.45; closed Wed Sept–June; weekday menu €38), offers gourmet food on a sea-view terrace; less expensive is the classic French cuisine at *La Table des Gémeaux*, 33 rue des Maures (T04.94.49.16.54; menus start at €28).

Fréjus and St-Raphaël

The major conurbation of **St-Raphaël** on the coast and Fréjus, 3km inland, has a history dating back to the Romans. Fréjus was established as a naval base under Julius Caesar and Augustus, St-Raphaël as a resort for its veterans. The ancient port at Fréjus, or Forum Julii, had 2km of quays and was connected by a walled canal to the sea, which was considerably closer then. After the battle of Actium in 31 BC, the ships of Antony and Cleopatra's defeated fleet were brought here.

The area between Fréjus and the sea is now the suburb of **Fréjus-Plage** with a vast 1980s marina, **Port-Fréjus**. Both Fréjus and Fréjus-Plage merge with St-Raphaël, which in turn merges with **Boulouris** to the east.

Despite the obsession with facilities for the seaborne rich this is not a bad place for a stopover. There's a wide range of hotels and restaurants in St-Raphaël, reasonable sandy beaches, good transport links and some interesting sightseeing to be done in Fréjus.

Fréjus

The population of **FRÉJUS**'s *vieille ville*, which lies within the Roman perimeter, was greater in the first century BC than it is today. Little remains of the Roman walls that once circled the city, and the harbour that made Fréjus an important Mediterranean port silted up and was finally filled in after the Revolution. It's the **medieval centre**, as much as the classical remnants, that evokes the antiquity of this ancient town.

Arrival, information and accommodation

Up to thirteen eastbound and nine westbound trains a day stop at Fréjus' **gare SNCF**, just five to eight minutes away from St-Raphaël. Trains to St-Raphaël itself are much more frequent, and it's usually easiest to alight there and then take the #1, #3, #4, #5, #6, #7 or #10 Agglobus, which run frequently between the two towns. The **gare routière** is on the east side of the town centre on place Paul-Vernet (T04.94.53.78.46), opposite which is the **tourist office**, at 325 rue Jean-Jaurès (April & May Mon–Sat 9.30am–6pm, Sun 9am–noon; June–Sept daily 9am–7pm; Oct–March Mon–Sat 9.30am–noon & 2–6pm, Sun 9.30am–noon; T04.94.51.83.83, Wwww.frejus.fr). If you're planning to visit most of Fréjus's sights it may be worth getting a **Fréjus'Pass** (€4.60), which is valid for seven days and includes access to the amphitheatre, Roman theatre and Musée Archéologique. You can pick up the pass at the sights themselves. Cycles Patrick Béraud at 337 rue de Triberg (ⓣ04.94.51.20.20), and Holiday Bikes, 238 avenue de Verdun (ⓣ04.94.64.06.40, ⓦwww.holiday-bikes.com), have **bikes** for hire.

Three central **hotels** worth trying are the plush *Aréna*, 145 rue de Général-de-Gaulle (ⓣ04.94.17.09.40, ⓦwww.arena-hotel.com; ◑), with pretty, if rather small rooms and a pool; *Le Bellevue*, place Paul-Vernet (ⓣ04.94.17.12.20; ❶), fairly basic but in a central though not particularly quiet location; and *La Riviera*, 90 rue Grisolle (ⓣ04.94.51.31.46, ⓕ04.94.17.18.34; ❶), small and not very modern, but clean and acceptable. There's an **HI hostel** 2km northeast from the centre at 675 chemin du Counillier (ⓣ04.94.53.18.75, ⓦwww.fuaj .org; reception 8–11am & 5.30–8.30pm; dorm bed €13.50); take bus #10 from St Raphaël *gare routière*. There are many **campsites** in the Fréjus area, mostly west of the town, some of them extremely large. One of the more moderate-sized sites is *Les Acacias*, 370 rue Henri-Giraud (ⓣ04.94.53.21.22, ⓦwww .acacias.net; April–Oct; €29 for tent, car & two people), 2.5km from the centre.

The Roman town

A tour of the Roman remains will give you a good idea of the extent of Forum Julii, but they are scattered throughout and beyond the town centre and take a full day to get around. Turning right out of the *gare SNCF* and then right down boulevard Severin-Decuers brings you to the **Butte St-Antoine**, against whose east wall the waters of the port would have lapped, and which once was capped by a fort. It was one of the port's defences, and one of the ruined **towers** may have been a lighthouse. A path around the southern wall follows the quayside (some stretches are visible) to the medieval **Lanterne d'Auguste**, built on the Roman foundations of a structure marking the entrance of the canal into the ancient harbour.

In the other direction from the station, past the Roman **Porte des Gaules** and along rue Henri-Vadon, you come to the **amphitheatre** (Tues–Sun: May–Oct 9.30am–12.30pm & 2–6pm; Nov–April 9.30am–12.30pm & 2–5pm; €2, or covered by the Fréjus'Pass, see above), smaller than those at Arles and Nîmes, but still able to seat around ten thousand. Today it's used for bullfights and concerts. Its upper tiers have been reconstructed in the same greenish local stone used by the Romans, but the vaulted galleries on the ground floor are largely original. The Roman **theatre** (same hours and prices) is north of the town, along avenue du Théâtre-Romain, its original seats long gone, though again it's still used for shows in summer. Northeast of it, in the parc Aurelienne at the far end of avenue du XVème-Corps-d'Armée, six arches are visible of the forty-kilometre **aqueduct**, once as high as the ramparts. Closer to the centre, on rue des Moulins, are the arcades of the **Porte d'Orée**, positioned on the former harbour's edge alongside what was probably a **bath complex**.

The medieval town

The **Cité Episcopale**, or cathedral close, takes up two sides of **place Formigé**, the marketplace and heart of both contemporary and medieval Fréjus. It comprises the **cathedral** (8am–noon & 2.30–6.30pm; free), flanked by the fourteenth-century bishop's palace (now the Hôtel de Ville), the baptistry, chapterhouse, cloisters and archeological museum. Visits to the cloisters and baptistry are guided (June–Sept daily 9am–6.30pm; Oct–May Tues–Sun 9am–noon & 2–5pm; €5).

The oldest part of the complex is the **baptistry**, built in the fourth or fifth century and so contemporary with the decline of the city's Roman founders. Its two doorways are of different heights, signifying the enlarged spiritual stature of the baptized. Bits of the early Gothic **cathedral** may belong to a tenth-century church, but its best features, apart from the bright diamond-shaped tiles on the spire, are Renaissance: the choir stalls, a wooden crucifix on the left of the entrance and the intricately carved doors with scenes of a Saracen massacre, protected by a wooden cover and only opened for the guided tours. The most engaging component of the whole ensemble, however, is the **cloisters**. In a small garden of scented bushes around a well, slender twelfth-century marble columns support a fourteenth-century ceiling painted with apocalyptic creatures. The treasures of the **Musée Archéologique** (same hours and prices as amphitheatre) on the upper storey of the cloisters include a complete Roman mosaic of a leopard and a copy of a double-headed bust of Hermes.

Eating, drinking and entertainment

One of the best **restaurants** in the old town is the tiny *Les Potiers*, 135 rue des Potiers (℡04.94.51.33.74; closed all day Tues & Wed lunch), which has menus of fresh seasonal ingredients from €23. The rather more expensive restaurant at *L'Aréna* hotel is excellent for fish and seafood, with a €26 lunch menu and evening menus at €45. Cheaper eats can be found on place Agricola, place de la Liberté and the main shopping streets. *Cadet Rousselle*, at the top of place Agricola (℡04.94.53.36.92), is a crêperie with a €13 menu that includes three crêpes. Equally good value are the massive salads at the *Brasserie Hermès* (℡04.94.17.26.02) opposite the cathedral at 15 place Formigé. At Fréjus-Plage there's a string of eating options, though menus are monotonously alike, with more upmarket *plateau des fruits de mer* outlets at Port-Fréjus. The main **market days** are Wednesday and Saturday. If you happen to be in town during the August **Féria**, you can take in a Spanish-style **bullfight**, plus the associated entertainment – flamenco and the like.

Around Fréjus

Unlikely remnants of the more recent past come in the shape of a Vietnamese pagoda and an abandoned mosque, both built by French colonial troops. The **Mosquée Missiri de Djenné** is on the left off the D4 to Bagnols, in the middle of an army camp 2km from the RN7 junction. A strange, guava-coloured, fort-like building, it's a replica of a Sudanese mosque in Mali, sadly fenced off, though much of the interior is visible from outside. The **pagoda Hong Hien** (daily: summer 9am–7pm; winter 9am–5pm; €2), still maintained as a Buddhist temple, is on the crossroads of the RN7 to Cannes and the D100, about 2km out of Fréjus. Alongside it is the massive memorial to the dead of the Indo–Chinese wars of the 1940s and 1950s (daily except Tues 10am–5.30pm). It is inscribed with the name of every fallen Frenchman; the sheer length of the lists suggesting the years 1950–54 were the most bloody. Just off the RN7 at La Tour de Mare is the last of Jean Cocteau's artistic landmarks, the chapel of **Notre-Dame-de-Jerusalem** (same hours and prices as amphitheatre). Conceived as the church for a failed artistic community, the octagonal building was not completed until after Cocteau's death in 1963, and the interior was completed to Cocteau's plans by Edouard Dermit. The Last Supper scene inside includes a self-portrait of Cocteau; the building's exterior is covered in elegantly simple mosaics and its floors with vibrant blue tiles.

There are a number of **mountain biking** trails which start in the Base Nature, just west of Port-Fréjus along the coast, and head up into the forested hills of the **Massif de l'Esterel** to the northeast of the town. The trails range from a flat, five-kilometre ride around a marsh to more serious 35-kilometre rides in the massif; call the Point Accueil VTT for more information (T04.94.51.91.10). The tourist office in St Raphaël sells a **walking** guide to the surrounding district for €7.80.

For children, there's a **zoo** in Le Capitou, close to exit 38 on the D4 heading north (daily: March–May & Sept–Oct 10am–5pm; June–Aug 10am–6pm; Nov–Feb 10.30am–4.30pm; €13, children aged 3–9 €9; bus #1 or #2), and a water amusement park, **Aqualand** (daily from mid-June to mid-Sept: 10am–6pm, 7pm in July & Aug; €24, children under 12 €17.50; bus #9), off the RN98 to St-Aygulf.

St-Raphaël

ST-RAPHAËL became fashionable at the turn of the twentieth century, but lost many of its seafront *belle-époque* mansions and hotels to World War II bombardment; the tourist office organizes guided visits to the survivors. The **old town** beyond place Carnot on the other side of the railway line is pleasantly low-key, no longer the commercial focus of the town but a good place to stroll and browse. On rue des Templiers a crumbling fortified Romanesque church has fragments of the Roman aqueduct that brought water from Fréjus in its courtyard, along with a local history and underwater archeology **museum** (Tues–Sat 9am–noon & 2–6pm; entry to church and museum free).

The **beaches** stretch between the Jardin Bonaparte at the entrance to the old port and the modern **Marina Santa Lucia**, with opportunities for every kind of watersport. You can also take boat trips to St-Tropez, the Îles d'Hyères and the much closer *calanques* of the Esterel coast from the quai Nomy on the south side of the Vieux Port. When you're tired of sea and sand you can lose whatever money you have left at the **casino** (daily 10am–dawn) on Square de Gand overlooking the Vieux Port, or there are plenty of snooty discotheques.

Practicalities

St-Raphaël's **gare SNCF**, in the centre of town, is the main station for the Marseille–Ventimiglia line; the **gare routière** is on square du Dr-Régis, across the rail line behind the *gare SNCF*. Information on the surrounding region is available from the **tourist office**, facing the Vieux Port at quai Albert-1ᵉʳ (July & Aug daily 9.30am–7.30pm; Sept–June Mon–Sat 9am–12.30pm & 2–6.30pm; T04.94.19.52.52, Wwww.saint-raphael.com). Car hire outlets cluster around the *gare SNCF*. **Bikes** can be rented from Patrick Moto, 280 avenue Général-Leclerc (T04.94.53.65.99).

Seafront **accommodation** in St-Raphaël is available on promenade René-Coty at the elegant old *Excelsior* (T04.94.95.02.42, Wwww.excelsior-hotel.com; ❸), whose rooms are luxurious and well equipped. *Bellevue*, 22 boulevard Félix-Martin (T04.94.19.90.10, Wwww.hotelbellevue.150m.com; ❹), is good value for its central location; and the *Provencal*, 197 rue de la Garonne (T04.98.11.80.00, Wwww.hotel-provencal.com; ❺), is a smart two-star hotel close to the old port. East of the centre, the *Hôtel du Soleil*, 47 boulevard du Domaine du Soleil, off boulevard Christian-Lafon (T04.94.83.10.00, Wperso.orange.fr/hotel.du.soleil; ❹), is a small, pretty villa with its own garden. There's a two-star **campsite** close to the beach, *Camping de L'Ile d'Or*, on the N98 in Boulouris (T&F04.94.95.52.13), which is open from late March until the end of October.

Food markets are held every day except Monday on place Victor-Hugo and place de la République. You'll find reasonably priced cafés and brasseries around these, and plenty of pizzerias, crêperies and restaurants of varying quality around the Vieux Port, Port Santa Lucia and along the promenades. Of the more expensive establishments, one of the best is *Le Sirocco*, 35 quai Albert-1ᵉʳ (☎04.94.95.39.99), a smart restaurant specializing in fish (menus €19.50–39.50) with a view of the port; alternatively, try *L'Arbousier* on the corner of rue Marius Allongue in the old town (☎04.94.95.25.00) where Philippe Troncy's innovative cooking is available on a €30 lunchtime menu or from €44 in the evening.

For **drinking**, try the selection of beers at the *Blue Bar* on promenade René-Coty, plage du Veillat (open till 4am in summer); *Aux Ambassadeurs*, a brasserie in the Casino complex that attracts a young crowd (till around midnight); the *Coco-Club* at Port Santa Lucia (till 5am) for more expensive cocktails; or one of the beachfront discos like *La Réserve* on promenade René Coty or *L'Odysée* or *La Playa* in Fréjus-Plage. There's also one gay club, *La Gaymence*, on rue Charabois behind the mairie.

The Riviera

The **Riviera**, the seventy-odd kilometres of coast between **Cannes** and **Menton** by the Italian border, was once an inhospitable shore with few natural harbours, its tiny communities preferring to cluster round feudal castles high above the sea. It wasn't until the nineteenth century that the first foreign aristocrats began to winter in the region's mild climate. In the interwar years the aristocrats were gradually supplanted by new elites – film stars, artists and writers – and the democratization of the Riviera began when French workers were granted paid holidays by Léon Blum's socialist government in 1936. But the real transformation came in the 1950s and after, as films like Alfred Hitchcock's *To Catch a Thief* and Roger Vadim's *et Dieu... Créa la Femme* generated an image of elegance and excitement. Nowadays, it's an almost uninterrupted promenade, lined by palms and megabuck hotels, with speeding sports cars on the Corniche and yachts like ocean liners moored at each resort.

Attractions, however, still remain, most notably in the legacies of the artists who stayed here: Picasso, Léger, Matisse, Renoir and Chagall. **Nice**, too, has real substance as a major city.

Cannes and around

With its immaculate seafront hotels and exclusive beach concessions, glamorous yachts and designer boutiques, **CANNES** is in many ways the definitive Riviera resort of popular fantasy. It's a place where appearances count, especially during the film festival in May, when the orgy of self-promotion reaches its annual peak. The ugly seafront Palais des Festivals is the heart of the film festival but also hosts conferences, tournaments and trade shows throughout the year. Despite its glittery image Cannes works surprisingly well as a big seaside resort, with plenty of free, sandy public beaches away from the famed plage de la Croisette, and if it all gets too much the **Îles de Lérins**, just offshore, offer a sublime contrast. Alternatively, you can escape the glitz of present-day Cannes by exploring the

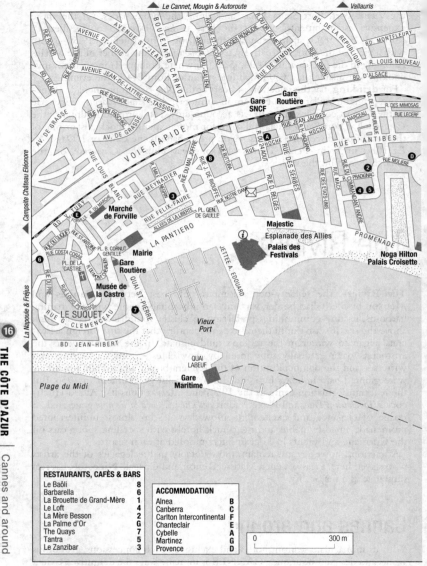

Le Cannet, Mougin & Autoroute

Vallauris

Gare
SNCF

Gare
Routière

RUE JEAN JAURES

RUE D'ANTIBES

Marché
de Forville

Majestic

Esplanade des Allies

Palais des
Festivals

Noga Hilton
Palais Croisette

PROMENADE

Mairie

Gare
Routière

Musée de
la Castre

LE SUQUET

JETTÉE A. EDOUARD

Vieux
Port

BD. JEAN-HIBERT

QUAI
LABEUF

Gare
Maritime

Plage du Midi

RESTAURANTS, CAFÈS & BARS

Le Baôli	8
Barbarella	6
La Brouette de Grand-Mère	1
Le Loft	4
La Mère Besson	2
La Palme d'Or	G
The Quays	7
Tantra	5
Le Zanzibar	3

ACCOMMODATION

Alnea	B
Canberra	C
Carlton Intercontinental	F
Chanteclair	E
Cybelle	A
Martinez	G
Provence	D

0   300 m

nineteenth-century glitz of La Croix des Gardes and La Californie, the aristocratic suburbs once populated by Russian and British royals.

Arrival, information and transport

The **gare SNCF** is on rue Jean-Jaurès, five blocks north of the concrete Palais
des Festivals on the seafront. There are **tourist offices** at the train station

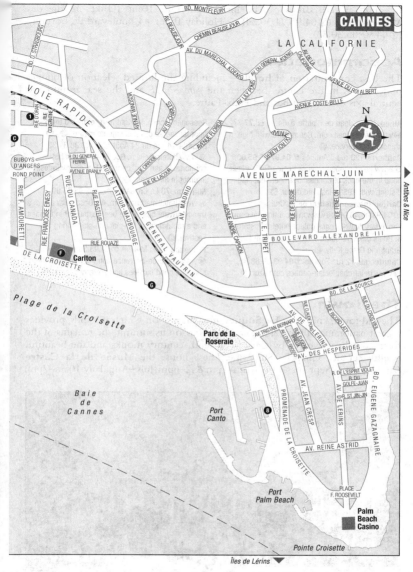

CANNES

LA CALIFORNIE

BD. MONTFLEURY

CHEMIN BEAUSEJOUR

AV. BEAUSEJOUR

AV. DU MARECHAL KOENIG

AV. DU GENERAL KOENIG

AV. DE LA CALIFORNIE

AVENUE DU ROI ALBERT

AVENUE COSTE-BELLE

AV. LILY PONS

VOIE RAPIDE

BD. DE STRASBOURG

RUE D'ORAN

RUE COSENTINE

BUBOYS D'ANGERS

ROND POINT

R DU GENERAL FERRIE

AVENUE BRANLY

AVENUE WINDSOR

AV. ST-CHARLES

AV. FLORIDA

RUE GIRODE

RUE DE LACOUR

AVENUE MARECHAL-JUIN

▶ Antibes & Nice

RUE F. AMOURETTI

RUE FRANCOISE EINESY

RUE DU CANADA

RUE PASTEUR

RUE DE LA TOUR-MAUBOURGE

RUE ROUAZE

AV. MADRID

AVENUE ANDRE CAPRON

BD. GENERAL VAUTRIN

BD. E. TRIPET

RUE DE RUSSIE

RUE FENELON

BOULEVARD ALEXANDRE III

F **Carlton**

DE LA CROISETTE

G

BD. DE LA SOURCE

RUE DU LYCEE V.I.

RUE RICORD LATTY

RUE CALEX PONS LERINS

Plage de la Croisette

Parc de la Roseraie

AV. TRISTAN BERNARD

AV. DE PONS LERINS

AV. LOUIS GRISSO

AV. EUGENE

AV. DES HESPERIDES

R. DE L'ESPRIT VIOLET

R. DU GOLFE-JUAN

AV. ST-JIN-JIN

AV. DE LERINS

BD. EUGENE GAZAGNAIRE

Baie de Cannes

Port Canto

8

PROMENADE DE LA CROISETTE

AV. JEAN CRESP

AV. REINE ASTRID

Port Palm Beach

PLACE F. ROOSEVELT

Palm Beach Casino

Pointe Croisette

Îles de Lérins ▼

16

THE CÔTE D'AZUR | Cannes and around

(Mon–Sat 9am–7pm; ☎04.93.99.19.77); at the Palais des Festivals (daily 9am–7/8pm; ☎04.92.99.84.22, ⓦwww.cannes.com); and at 1 avenue Pierre-Sémard in Cannes-La Bocca (Tues–Sat 9am–noon & 2.30–6.30pm; ☎04.93.47.04.12). There are two **gares routières**: one on place B.-Cornut-Gentille between the *mairie* and Le Suquet, serving coastal destinations; and the other next to the *gare SNCF* for buses inland to places such as Grasse. Bus Azur runs 24 lines and five night buses, serving all of Cannes and the surrounding area (☎08.25.82.55.99;

€1 single ticket). **Bikes** can be hired from Elite Rent a Bike, 32 rue des Maréchal Juin (☎04.93.94.30.34) or Holiday Bikes, 44 boulevard de Lorraine (☎04.97.06.30.63).

Accommodation

The best concentration of **hotels** – including the limited selection of budget options – is in the centre, between the *gare SNCF* and the sea, around the central axis of rues Antibes and Félix-Faure.

Alnea 20 rue Jean de Riouffe ☎04.93.68.77.77, ⓦwww.hotel-alnea.com. Central and with high standards of service. **④**

Canberra 120 rue d'Antibes ☎04.97.06.95.00, ⓦwww.hotel-canberra-cannes.cote.azur.fr. Classy hotel in the thick of Cannes' designer shopping district, with 1950s-inspired decor. **⑧**

Carlton Intercontinental 58 La Croisette ☎04.93.06.40.06, ⓦwww.intercontinental.com. Legendary *belle-époque* palace hotel that starred in Hitchcock's *To Catch a Thief*, along with Cary Grant and Grace Kelly. **⑨**

Chanteclair 12 rue Forville ☎04.93.39.68.88, ⓦwww.hotel-chanteclair-cannes.cote.azur.fr.

Reasonable cheapie, right next to the old town, approached across a private courtyard. **③–④**

Cybelle 14 rue du 24 Août ☎04.93.38.31.33, ⓦwww.hotelcybelle.fr. Good value, plain but comfortable and very central. They offer wireless internet in all rooms. **③**

Martinez 73 La Croisette ☎04.92.98.73.00, ⓦwww.hotel-martinez.com. Art Deco palace with a trendy private beach, the best restaurant in Cannes and a reputation as the place to stay during the Festival. **⑨**

Provence 9 rue Molière ☎04.93.38.44.35, ⓦwww.hotel-de-provence.com. Comfortable three star with good facilities and a pretty garden. **⑤**

The Town

The old town, known as **Le Suquet** after the hill on which it stands, provides a great panorama of the 12km beach, and has, on its summit, the remains of the fortified priory lived in by Cannes' eleventh-century monks and the beautiful twelfth-century Chapelle Ste-Anne. These house the **Musée de la Castre** (April–June & Sept Tues–Sun 10am–1pm & 2–6pm; July–Aug daily 10am–7pm;

▲ Carlton Intercontinental, Cannes

Oct–March Tues–Sun 10am–1pm & 2–5pm; €3.20), which has an extraordinary collection of musical instruments from all over the world, along with pictures and prints of old Cannes and an ethnology and archeology section. Just a few hundred metres to the west of Le Suquet on avenue du Dr-Raymond-Picaud in La Croix des Gardes is the **Château Eléonore**, the villa built by the retired British Chancellor Lord Brougham after his enforced stay in the then-unknown village of Cannes in 1834; he couldn't reach Nice because of a cholera epidemic but, liking what he found in Cannes, he built his villa here and laid the foundations for Cannes' development as an aristocratic resort.

You'll find the non-paying **beaches** to the west of Le Suquet towards the suburb of **La Bocca** along the **plages du Midi**, though there's also a tiny public section of beach on **La Croisette**, just east of the Palais des Festivals. La Croisette is certainly the sight to see, with its palace hotels on one side and private beaches on the other. It's possible to find your way down to the beach without paying, but not easy (you can of course walk along it below the rows of sun beds). The beaches, owned by the deluxe *palais-hôtels* – the *Martinez, Carlton* and *Noga Hilton* – are where you're most likely to spot a face familiar in celluloid or a topless hopeful, especially during the film festival, though you'll be lucky to see further than the sweating backs of the paparazzi. Alternative entertainment can be had buying your own food in the **Forville covered market** two blocks behind the *mairie,* or by wandering through the day's flower shipments on the allées de la Liberté, just back from the Vieux Port.

Eating, drinking and nightlife

Cannes has hundreds of **restaurants** catering for every budget, with Rue Meynadier, Le Suquet and quai St-Pierre being good places to look. As ever in the south of France, pasta and pizza are the best bet for a cheap, filling meal; for more substantial but still affordable fare, try *La Mère Besson,* 13 rue des Frères Pradignac (☎04.93.39.59.24; closed sun), with menus at €28 and €33, or *La Brouette de Grand-Mère,* 9bis rue d'Oran (☎04.93.39.12.10; evenings only, closed Sun), which has a single, very filling €35 menu including wine. If you'd just won a film festival prize the place to celebrate would be *La Palme d'Or* in the *Hôtel Martinez,* 73 La Croisette (☎04.92.98.74.14; menus at €79, €104, €155 and €180; closed Sun and Mon). *Barbarella,* 16 rue Saint Dizier in Le Suquet (☎04.92.99.17.33; Tues–Sun, evenings only, daily during festival; menus from €30), is rather more affordable but still stylish and fun, with a Japanese-influenced fusion menu.

Cannes abounds with trendy, exclusive **bars** and **clubs**, especially in the grid of streets bounded by rue Macé, rue V. Cousin, rue Dr G.-Monod and rue des Frères Pradignacs. Smart, trendy bars to try include *Le Loft* and *Tantra*, both on rue Dr-Gérard-Monod and open until 2.30am; if you want to rub shoulders with celebrities the place to head is *Le Baôli* at Port Pierre Canto (open daily from 8pm), an exotic outdoor disco–restaurant with palms, tented pavilions and Asian food. For something more straightforward, *The Quays,* 17 quai St-Pierre, is the inevitable Irish pub, open until well after midnight and with live music on Thursdays and Saturdays. Cannes has one of the oldest **gay** bars in France, *Le Zanzibar,* 85 rue Félix-Faure (6pm–4am).

Îles de Lérins

The **Îles de Lérins** would be lovely anywhere, but at fifteen minutes' ferry ride from frantic Cannes, they're not far short of paradise. **Boats** for both islands leave from the quai des Îles at the seaward end of the quai Max-Laubeuf. **St-Honorat**

is served by Compagnie Planaria (T04.92.98.71.38, Wwww.cannes-ilesdelerins
.com; summer 10 daily, winter 7 daily; €11); the last boat back to Cannes leaves
at 5pm in winter & 6pm in summer. There are regular services to **Ste-Margue-**
rite run by two companies, S.A.R.L. Horizon (hourly; winter 10am–4.15pm,
summer 9am–5.30pm; T04.92.98.71.36; €11) and Trans Côte d'Azur
(T04.92.98.71.30, Wwww.trans-cote-azur.com; up to 16 departures 7.30am–
4pm; €11); the last boats back to Cannes leave Ste-Marguerite at 4.30pm 5pm
or 6pm, depending on the operator, season and weather. Taking a picnic is a good
idea, particularly out of season, though there are reasonably priced snack stalls on
Ste-Marguerite during the summer months.

Ste-Marguerite

Ste-Marguerite is more touristy than its neighbour, St-Honorat. It's still
beautiful, though, and large enough for visitors to find seclusion by following
the trails that lead away from the congested port, through the Aleppo pines and
woods of evergreen oak that are so thick they cast a sepulchral gloom. The
western end is the most accessible, but the lagoon here is brackish, so the best
places to swim are along the rocky southern shore, reached most easily along
the **allée des Eucalyptus**. The channel between Ste-Marguerite and
St-Honorat is however a popular anchorage for motor yachts, so you're unlikely
to find real solitude.

The dominating structure of the island is the **Fort Ste-Marguerite** (April–
May & mid- to late Sept Tues–Sun 10.30am–1.15pm & 2.15–5.45pm; June–Sept
daily 10am–5.45pm; Oct–March Tues–Sun 10.30am–1.15pm & 2.15–4.45pm;
€3.20), a Richelieu commission that failed to prevent the Spanish occupying
both of the Lérin islands between 1635 and 1637. Later, Vauban rounded it off,
presumably for Louis XIV's *gloire* – since the strategic value of greatly enlarging
a fort facing your own mainland without upgrading the one facing the sea is
pretty minimal. There are cells to see, including the one in which Dumas' *Man
in the Iron Mask* is supposed to have been held, and the **Musée de la Mer** (same
hours and ticket as fort), containing mostly Roman local finds but also remnants
of a tenth-century Arab ship.

Ste-Honorat

Owned by monks almost continuously since its namesake and patron founded
a monastery here in 410 AD, **St-Honorat**, the smaller southern island, was
home to a famous bishops' seminary, where St Patrick trained before setting out
for Ireland. The present **abbey** buildings date mostly from the nineteenth
century, though some vestiges of the medieval and earlier constructions remain
in the austere church and the cloisters. You can visit the church, but there is no
access to the residential part of the monastery unless you're staying there on a
spiritual retreat. A shop sells the sought-after white wine and liqueurs produced
by the 28 Cistercian brothers of the monastic community. Behind the cloisters
on the sea's edge stands the eleventh-century fortified monastery.

There's one small restaurant near the landing stage (open April–Oct only), but
no bars, hotels or cars: just vines, lavender, herbs and olive trees mingled with
wild poppies and daisies, and pine and eucalyptus trees shading the paths beside
the white rock shore.

Vallauris

Pottery and Picasso are the twin attractions of **VALLAURIS**, an otherwise
unremarkable town in the hills above Golfe-Juan, 6km east of Cannes. It was
here that Picasso first began to use clay, thereby reviving one of the traditional

Festive France

The French celebrate everything, from saints' days to cinema, from *saucisson* to wine. While summer is the prime festive season, even in winter you'll be able to track down some festival or other. Indeed, the calendar is so packed full of events, it's hard to know which to plump for. What follows is a round-up of some of the best, the most famous and the relatively undiscovered. For websites – and further ideas – see Basics, pp.50–51

Traditional Breton costumes ▲

Gypsy festival, Les Stes-Maries-de-La-Mer ▼

Cannes Film Festival ▼

Nationwide celebrations

France's independence day, Bastille Day (July 14), is celebrated with firework displays and dances countrywide. On the more formal side, there's a military parade in Paris and the president addresses the nation.

Music-lovers are in for a treat with the Fête de la Musique (June 21), which marks the summer solstice. All manner of musical events take place, including many free concerts, which may be amateur or professional, spontaneous or programmed. And it keeps getting bigger and better each year.

Religious and folk festivals

Catholicism is deeply ingrained in rural culture and religious feast days still bring people out in all their finery. Among the most famous are the Breton *pardons* (June–Sept), when processions wind through the countryside; the biggest takes place in the Morbihan (July 26). Another annual event with deep historical roots is the great gypsy gathering at Les Stes-Maries-de-la-Mer in the Camargue (May 24 and 25) held in honour of their patron saint, the mysterious, black-faced Sara-la-Kâli, while the Festival Inter-Celtic (early Aug) in Brittany attracts thousands of musicians, dancers, writers and scholars from around the world.

Music and cinema

Classical music lovers will be hard pressed to choose from the tremendous variety of festivals on offer, from sacred music to comic opera, almost nonstop throughout the year. In the depths of winter, Nantes hosts La Folle Journée (late Jan), in which dozens of concerts take place over five packed days, with a different theme each year. If you've got the energy, you'll find theatre performances, films and conferences. Prices are very affordable.

In July and August jazz fills the air of many French towns and villages. Fans flock to the big-name concerts at Jazz à Vienne (first two weeks of July), but there are plenty of more intimate events, too. Jazz in Marciac (early Aug), for example, set in a little market town in the heart of Gascony, still retains the atmosphere of a local fete.

Intimate is not how you'd describe the Festival des Vieilles Charrues, a pop fest held at Carhaix in Brittany (mid-July). This is one of France's largest annual

▲ Carhaix pop festival

▼ Choregies d'Orange opera festival

Fest-Noz and Fest-Diez

Brittany boasts a particularly rich and vibrant cultural calendar, with the liveliest events being the hugely popular summer **dance festivals**, Fest-Noz (held at night) and Fest-Diez (in the daytime). These ancient folk festivals originally celebrated a marriage or the end of the harvest, but today they're just an excuse for partying; thousands of people gather to dance, eat, drink and make merry to the accompaniment of traditional Breton music. It's infectious stuff, played on bagpipes, *bombarde* (a high-pitched flute), and increasingly nowadays violins and other musical instruments. Dancers follow simple steps, usually linking hands to form a chain or circle – everyone is welcome to join in. Dates of upcoming events are listed on Ⓦwww.fest-noz.net.

Fest-Diez, Brittany ▲

Performance art in Avignon ▼

bashes, attracting over 200,000 revellers to hear the likes of Johnny Hallyday and Madness, Iggy Pop and Vanessa Paradis play the massive open-air stages. Side events feature local Breton bands and electronic music.

Everyone's heard of Cannes international film festival (May), but the French passion for cinema is reflected in dozens of smaller events throughout the year. There's a festival of animated films at Annecy (June; Ⓦ www.annecy.org), another devoted to women's film at Créteil (March; Ⓦ www .filmsdefemmes.com), near Paris, even a festival of detective movies at Cognac (April; Ⓦ www.festival.cognac.fr). And that's only scratching the surface.

Performance arts

Contemporary performance arts are alive and kicking in France. The highlight is probably Avignon's packed programme of avant-garde theatre, dance and music (July). Directed by a different guest artist each year, and featuring many new productions, it's a veritable showcase for up-and-coming talent, with performances taking place in the Pope's Palace as well as churches, school halls and even a stone quarry.

It's also worth catching one of the growing number of street theatre festivals. At Aurillac's four-day festival (mid-Aug), for example, some five hundred companies from around the world come together in a frenzy of creativity. You'll also find contemporary circus – acrobatic theatre rather than performing lions – well represented at the aptly named Festival Furies (early June) at Châlons-en-Campagne. Anarchic, provocative and endlessly entertaining, the Furies kicks off with a performance by the graduation class at Châlons' national school for circus arts.

crafts of this little town. Today the main street, **avenue Georges-Clemenceau**, sells nothing but pottery, much of it garish bowls or figurines that could feature in souvenir shops anywhere. Picasso used to work in the **Madoura workshop** on avenue des Ancien-Combattants-d'AFN, to the left as you ascend avenue Georges-Clemenceau; it still has sole rights on reproducing his designs, which it sells, at a price, in the shop on avenue Suzanne & Georges Ramié (Mon–Fri 10am–12.30pm & 3–6pm; closed Sat, Sun & Nov).

The bronze statue of **Man with a Sheep**, Picasso's gift to the town, stands in the main square, place Paul Isnard, beside the church and castle. The local authorities also suggested he should decorate the deconsecrated early medieval **chapel** in the castle courtyard (daily except Tues: July & August 10am–7pm; Sept to June 10am–12.15pm & 2–5pm; €3.25), which he finally did in 1952; his subject was war and peace. The space is tiny, with the architectural simplicity of an air-raid shelter, and at first it's easy to be unimpressed by the painted panels covering the vault – as many critics still are – since the work looks mucky and slapdash, with paint-runs on the plywood panel surface. But stay a while and the passion of this violently drawn display of pacifism slowly emerges. The ticket for the chapel also gives admission to the **Musée de la Céramique/Musée Magnelli** in the castle (same hours and ticket), which exhibits Picasso's and other ceramics.

Regular buses from Cannes and from Golfe-Juan SNCF arrive at the rear of the château. The **tourist office** is at the bottom of avenue Georges-Clemenceau on square du 8-Mai-1945 (July & Aug daily 9am–7pm; Sept–June Mon–Sat 9am–12.15pm & 1.45–6pm; ☎04.93.63.82.58, 🖥www.vallauris-golfe-juan.fr), which is where you'll also find the main tourist **car park**. One worthwhile lunch stop in Vallauris is *Café Llorca*, (place Paul Isnard (☎04.93.64.30.42; open daily, *plats du jour* from €10), which is celebrity chef Alain Llorca's simple, modern version of a traditional café, complete with Provencal food, patisserie and shady terrace.

Grasse

GRASSE, 16km inland from Cannes and with some stunning views over the Côte, is the world capital of *parfumiers* and has been for almost three hundred years. These days it promotes a perfumed image of a medieval hill town surrounded by scented flowers, though in truth its outskirts sprout boxy suburban villas with rather more luxuriance. Making perfumes is presented as a mysterious process, an alchemy, turning the soul of the flower into a liquid of luxury and desire, and the industry is at pains to keep quiet about modern innovations and techniques. Grasse is the official starting point of the Route Napoléon but is equally easy to visit as a day-trip from the coast.

Arrival, information and accommodation

Grasse's **gare routière** is north of the old town at place de la Buanderie. Head downhill on avenue Thiers, which becomes boulevard du Jeu de Ballon (where there's an annexe of the tourist office) and you'll find the major museums fronting place du Cours, with the main **tourist office** on cours Honoré-Cresp (July–Sept Mon–Sat 9am–7pm, Sun 9am–1pm & 2–6pm; Oct–June Mon–Sat 9am–12.30pm & 2–6pm; ☎04.93.36.66.66, 🖥www.grasse-riviera.com).

Accommodation options at the budget end of the market are limited, though it might be worth considering one of the tourist office's selection of *chambres* *d'hôtes*. Affordable but comfortable hotels include the *Panorama*, on place du Cours (☎04.93.36.80.80, ⓦwww.hotelpanorama-grasse.com; ❹), whose rooms boast views and all mod cons. Even more comfortable, if less well located, is the *Charm Hôtel du Patti*, place du Patti (☎04.93.36.01.00, ⓦwww.hotelpatti.com;❺), with pretty, Provençal-style rooms including three adapted for wheelchair users.

The Town

Even when Grasse was part of the aristocratic tourist boom of the late nineteenth century, the desirable addresses, Queen Victoria's among them, were all east of **Vieux Grasse**, and in recent years the pretty *vieille ville* degenerated into little more than a picturesque slum. But after years of peeling into oblivion, Vieux Grasse is now changing rapidly as an energetic programme of restoration – and, inevitably, of gentrification – kicks in.

Place aux Aires, at the top of the town, is the main meeting point and the venue for the daily flower and vegetable **market**. It's ringed by arcades of different heights and the elegant wrought-iron balcony of the *Hôtel Isnard* at no. 33, and at one time was the exclusive preserve of the tanning industry. At the opposite end of Vieux Grasse lie the **cathedral** – containing various paintings, including one by local boy Jean-Honoré Fragonard, three by Rubens and a wondrous triptych by the sixteenth-century Niçois painter Louis Bréa – and the **bishop's palace**, now the Hôtel de Ville, both built in the twelfth century.

Grasse has several engrossing small museums. The **Musée d'Art et d'Histoire de Provence**, 2 rue Mirabeau (June–Sept daily 10am–6.30pm; Oct & Dec–May Wed–Mon 10am–12.30pm & 2–5.30pm; €4), is housed in a luxurious town house commissioned by Mirabeau's sister as a place to entertain. As well as all the gorgeous fittings and an eighteenth-century kitchen, the collections are highly eclectic and include eighteenth- to nineteenth-century faïence from Apt and Le Castellet, Mirabeau's death mask, a tin bidet and six prehistoric bronze leg bracelets. The fascinating **Musée International de la Parfumerie**, 8 place du Cours (same hours and price as Musée d'Histoire), displays perfume bottles from the ancient Greeks via Marie-Antoinette to the present, and has a reconstruction of a perfume factory.

You can see more works by Jean-Honoré Fragonard in the **Villa–Musée Fragonard** at 23 boulevard Fragonard (same hours and price as Musée d'Histoire), where the celebrated Rococo painter returned to live after the Revolution. The staircase is impressive wall paintings by his son Alexandre-Evariste, while the salon is graced by copies of *Love's Progress in the Heart of a Young Girl*, which Jean-Honoré painted for Madame du Barry.

The perfume factories

There are thirty-odd **parfumeries** in and around Grasse, most of them making not perfume but essences-plus-formulas which are then sold to Dior, Lancôme, Estée Lauder and the like, who make up their own brand-name perfumes. One litre of pure rose essence can cost as much as €19,000; perfume contains twenty percent essence (eau de toilette and eau de Cologne considerably less). The major cost in this multibillion-dollar business is marketing. The grand Parisian couturiers, whose clothes, on strictly cost-accounting grounds, serve simply to promote the perfume, go to inordinate lengths to sell their latest fragrance, spending millions of euros a year on advertising alone.

The ingredients that the "nose" – as the creator of the perfume's formula is known – has to play with include resins, roots, moss, beans, bark, civet (extract of cat genitals), ambergris (intestinal goo from whales), bits of beaver and musk from Tibetan goats. If that hasn't put you off, you can visit the various

showrooms, with overpoweringly fragrant shops and free guided tours, in English, of the traditional perfume factory set-up (the actual working industrial complexes are strictly out of bounds). These visits are free and usually open daily without interruption in summer; a few to choose from are: **Fragonard**, 20 boulevard Fragonard (Feb–Oct daily 9am–6pm; Nov–Jan Mon–Sat 9am–12.30pm & 2–6.30pm; Ⓦwww.fragonard.com); **Galimard**, 73 route de Cannes (guided visits daily: summer 9am–6.30pm; winter 9am–12.30pm & 2–6pm; Ⓦwww.galimard.com); and **Molinard** at 60 boulevard Victor-Hugo (April–Sept daily Mon–Fri 9am–6.30pm; Oct–March Mon–Fri 9am–12.30pm & 2–6pm, Sat 9am–noon & 2-6pm; Ⓦwww.molinard.com).

Eating and drinking

Compared with the coastal towns Grasse isn't terribly well endowed with **restaurants**. The best in town is *La Bastide Saint Antoine*, 48 rue Henri-Dunant (☎04.93.70.94.94), which serves *cuisine gourmande* with a Provençal twist (lunch menus €59; otherwise menus from €145). Alternatively, *Lou Fassum*, southeast of town at 381 route de Plascassier (☎04.93.60.14.44; closed Tues in July & Aug; menu €38), is a traditional Provençal restaurant serving specialities from the pays de Grasse. For drinks, the bars on place aux Aires are friendly. At *Maison Venturini*, 1 rue Marcel-Journet (☎04.93.36.20.47; closed Sun & Mon), you can buy sweet *fougassettes* – a local pastry, flavoured with the Grasse speciality of orange blossom – to take away.

Antibes and around

Graham Greene, who lived in **Antibes** for more than twenty years, considered it the only place on this stretch of coast to have preserved its soul. And although Antibes and its twin, **Juan-les-Pins**, have not completely escaped the overdevelopment that blights much of this region, they have avoided its worst excesses. Antibes itself is a pleasing old town, extremely animated, with one of the finest **markets** on the coast and the best **Picasso collection** in its ancient seafront castle; and the southern end of the Cap d'Antibes still has its woods of pine, in which some of the most exclusive mansions on the Riviera hide.

Arrival and information

Antibes' **gare SNCF** lies north of the old town at the top of avenue Robert-Soleau. Turn right out of the station and three-minutes' walk along avenue R.-Soleau will bring you to place de Gaulle. The **tourist office** is on this square, at no. 11 (July & Aug daily 9am–7pm; Sept–June Mon–Fri 9am–12.30pm & 1.30–6pm, Sat 9am–noon & 2–6pm; additionally Sun 10am–noon during April–June & Sept; ☎04.97.23.11.11, Ⓦwww.antibesjuanlespins.com). The **gare routière** is east of here on place Guynemer with frequent buses to and from the *gare SNCF*. Bus #2 goes to Cap d'Antibes, bus #3 to Juan-les-Pins and #10 to Biot. **Bikes** can be hired from Holiday Bikes, 122 boulevard Wilson in Juan les Pins (☎04.93.20.90.20). Heidi's English Bookshop at place Audiberti in Antibes is the cheapest English **bookshop** on the coast.

Accommodation

The cheapest **hotels** in the Antibes-Juan les Pins area cluster around avenue de l'Estérel in Juan-les-Pins – try *Hôtel Parisiana*, 14, avenue de l'Estérel

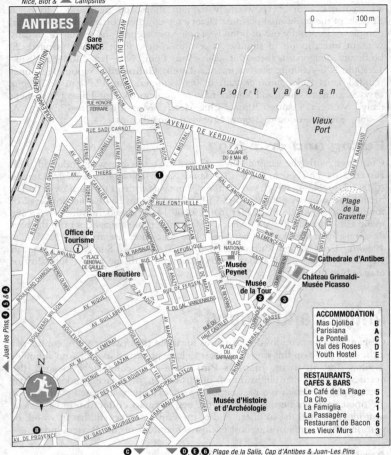

Map labels (Antibes):

ANTIBES

Nice, Biot & ▲ Campsites

Gare SNCF

Port Vauban

Vieux Port

0 ———— 100 m

AVENUE DU 11 NOVEMBRE

AV. DE LA LIBERATION

RUE HONORE FERRARE

RUE SADI CARNOT

AVENUE DE VERDUN

BOULEVARD GENERAL VAUTRIN

Plage de la Gravette

QUAI RAMBAUD

SQUARE DU 8 MAI 45

BOULEVARD DUGOMMIER

AVENUE THIERS

AVENUE DU GRAND CAVALIER

AVENUE PASTEUR

AVENUE TOURNELLI

AVENUE MIRABEAU

AV. SAINT ROCH

AV. F. MISTRAL

BOULEVARD D'AGUILLON

B.D D'ANDROSSY

RUE FONTVIEILLE

RUE MACE

RUE VAUBAN

RUE LACAN

RUE ROSTAN

RUE CHAMPIONNET

AV. P. DOUMER

RUE THURET

RUE G. CLEMENCEAU

RAMP. DES TEMPLIERS

RUE ALBERTI

Office de Tourisme

PLACE GENERAL DE GAULLE

AV. DE L'ARMEE

AV. ROBERT SOLEAU

AV. GAMBETTA

RUE DE LA REPUBLIQUE

R. JAMES CLOSE

R. M. RAYBAUD

RUE DE LA RACHE

PLACE NATIONALE

RUE SADE

COURS MASSÉNA

Cathedrale d'Antibes

Château Grimaldi-Musée Picasso

BD D'ALGER

AVENUE CHANCEL

BOULEVARD WILSON

BOULEVARD MARECHAL LECLERC

LEMERAY

AV. DE FREJUS OLIVIER

Gare Routière

RUE DE FERSEN

R. DU 24 AOUT

AV. NIQUET

AV. GUILLABERT

BOULEVARD ALBERT 1ER

RUE D. MARC

R. DU GAL. VANDENBERG

RUE DE REYMES

Musée Peynet

Musée de la Tour

RUE DU HAUT CASTELET

PLACE DU SAFRANIER

TOURRAQUE

PROMENADE AMIRAL DE GRASSE

AV. PRINCIPAL PASTEUR

AV. GAZAN

AVENUE FOCH

AV. DES FRERES ROUSTAN

AV. GENERAL MAIZIERES

BARQUIER

Musée d'Histoire et d'Archéologie

AV. DE PROVENCE

AV. GASTON BOURGEOIS

N

ACCOMMODATION

Mas Djoliba	B
Parisiana	A
Le Ponteil	C
Val des Roses	D
Youth Hostel	E

RESTAURANTS, CAFÉS & BARS

Le Café de la Plage	5
Da Cito	2
La Famiglia	1
La Passagère	4
Restaurant de Bacon	6
Les Vieux Murs	3

Juan les Pins ◀ ❹ ❺ & A

THE CÔTE D'AZUR | Antibes and around

❶ ❷ ❸

C ▼ D, E, 6, Plage de la Salis, Cap d'Antibes & Juan-Les-Pins

(☏04.93.61.27.03, ⓦ www.hotel-le-parisiana.fr; ❸). For greater comfort, there's the *Mas Djoliba*, 29 avenue de Provence (☏04.93.34.02.48, ⓦ www.hotel-djoliba.com; closed Nov–Feb; ❺, but half board obligatory May–Sept), between the old town and the beach, or *Le Ponteil*, 11 impasse Jean-Mensier (☏04.93.34.67.92, ⓦ www.leponteil.com; ❻; closed mid-Nov to Feb), in a quiet location at the end of a cul-de-sac close to the sea. For something secluded and elegant, *Val des Roses* (☏06.85.06.06.29, ⓦ www.val-des-roses .com; ❽), an upmarket **chambre d'hôte** on chemin des Lauriers just off the plage de la Salis, fits the bill.

There's a **hostel** on Cap d'Antibes, the *Relais International de la Jeunesse* on boulevard de la Garoupe (☏04.93.61.34.40, ⓦ www.clasjud.fr; closed Oct–Mar; €17; bus #2 stops right outside), which needs booking well in advance. All of Antibes' **campsites** are 3–5km north of the city in the *quartier* of La Brague (bus #10 or one train stop to "Gare de Biot"). The three-star *Logis de La Brague* (☏04.93.33.54.72, ⓦ www.camping-logisbrague.com; closed Oct–April; €13.50

16

1068

for tent and two people) is closest to the station, while the small two-star *Idéal-Camping* (℡04.93.74.27.07; closed Oct–April) is south of the station; both are on the route de Nice and close to the sea.

The Town

Lording it over the Antibes ramparts and the sea, the sixteenth-century **Château Grimaldi** is a beautifully cool, light space, with hexagonal terracotta floor tiles, windows over the sea and a terrace garden with sculptures by Germaine Richier, Miró, César and others. In 1946 Picasso was offered the dusty building – by then already a museum – as a studio. Several extremely prolific months followed before he moved to Vallauris, leaving all his Antibes output to what is now the **Musée Picasso** (mid-June to mid-Sept Tues–Sun 10am–6pm, Wed & Thurs in July & Aug until 8pm; mid-Sept to mid-June 10am–noon & 2–6pm; €6). Although Picasso donated other works later on, the bulk of the collection belongs to this one period. Picasso himself is the subject of works here by other painters and photographers, including Man Ray, Hans Hartung and Bill Brandt; there are also several anguished canvases by Nicolas de Staël, who stayed in Antibes for a few months from 1954 to 1955. Alongside the castle is the **cathedral**, built on the site of an ancient temple. The choir and apse survive from the Romanesque building that served the city in the Middle Ages while the nave and stunning ochre facade are Baroque. Inside, in the south transept, is a sumptuous medieval altarpiece surrounded by immaculate panels of tiny detailed scenes.

One block inland, the morning **covered market** (June–Aug daily 6am–1pm; Sept–May Tues–Sun 6am–1pm) on cours Masséna overflows with Provençal goodies and cut **flowers**, the traditional and still-flourishing Antibes business. In the afternoons, a **craft market** (June–Sept Tue & Thurs–Sun; Oct–May Fri, Sat & Sun only, from 3pm weekdays, 4.30pm Sat) takes over, and when the stalls pack up, café tables take their place.

Cap d'Antibes

Plage de la Salis, the longest Antibes beach, runs along the eastern neck of Cap d'Antibes, with no big hotels squatting its sands – an amazing rarity on the Riviera. To the south, at the top of chemin du Calvaire, you have superb views from the **Chapelle de la Garoupe** (daily 10am–noon & 2.30–5pm), which contains Russian spoils from the Crimean War and hundreds of *ex votos*. To the west, on boulevard du Cap between chemins du Tamisier and G.-Raymond, you can wander around the **Jardin Thuret** (Mon–Fri: summer 8am–6pm, winter 8.30am–5.30pm; free; guided tours on request to ℡04.97.21.25.00), botanical gardens belonging to a national research institute. Back on the east shore, further south, lies a second public beach, **plage de la Garoupe**. From here a footpath follows the shore to join the chemin des Douaniers. At the southern end of the Cap d'Antibes, on avenue L.D. Beaumont, stands the grandiose **Villa Eilenroc** (gardens Tues, Wed & Sat; open 9am–5pm; villa Wed 9am–noon & 1.30–5pm; closed in July & Aug; free), designed by Charles Garnier, architect of the casino at Monte-Carlo, and surrounded by lush gardens. There are more sandy coves and little harbours along the western shore, where you'll also find the **Musée Napoléonien** (Tues–Sat: mid-June to mid–Sept 10am–6pm; mid-Sept to mid-June 10am–4.30pm; €3), at the end of avenue J.-F.-Kennedy. This documents the great man's return from Elba along with the usual Bonaparte paraphernalia of hats, cockades and signed commands. Much of the southern tip of the *cap* is a warren of private roads, including the area around the fabled *Hotel du Cap Eden Roc* and the so-called "bay of millionaires".

Juan-les-Pins

JUAN-LES-PINS, less than 2km from the centre of Antibes, had its heyday in the interwar years, when the summer season on the Riviera first took off and the resort was the haunt of film stars like Charlie Chaplin, Maurice Chevalier and Lilian Harvey, the polyglot London-born 1930s musical star who lingered here until 1968, long after her fame had faded. Juan-les-Pins isn't as glamorous as it once was either, though it still has a casino and a certain cachet, the beaches are sand, and there are haunting reminders of its glory days, including the Art Deco bulk of the long-derelict **Hotel Provençal**, which looms over the town from the eastern side of boulevard Baudoin and is now being converted to apartments.

Juan's **international jazz festival** – known simply as Jazz à Juan – takes place in the middle two weeks of July. It's the best in the region and is held in the central pine grove, the **Jardin de La Pinède** (known simply as La Pinède), and **square Gould** above the beach by the casino. A Hollywood-style walk of fame immortalizes various jazz greats at la Pinede, set into the pavement.

Eating and drinking

Place Nationale and cours Masséna are lined with **cafés**; rue James-Close is nothing but **restaurants**, while there's a smattering of big pubs and ethnic eateries close to the port. For pizzas, there's *Da Cito* in the covered market, and *La Famiglia*, a cheap, family-run outfit at 34 avenue Thiers (closed Wed, Sat & Sun lunch). *Les Vieux Murs*, near the castle at avenue Amiral-de-Grasse (℡04.93.34.06.73; closed Mon all day & Tues lunch out of season; lunch menu €34, €42 or dinner menu €60), serves very classy food, such as king crab with *niçois* ratatouille or scallops with orange butter in a perfect setting on the ramparts. For excellent fish and a view of the sea, *Restaurant de Bacon*, boulevard de Bacon, Cap d'Antibes (℡04.93.61.50.02; closed Mon, Tues lunch & Nov–March), is renowned locally, with menus from €49.

La Passagère at the *Hotel Belles Rives* (℡04.93.61.02.79) serves up modern Mediterranean delights in lovely, restored Art Deco surroundings, with menus at €70, €90 and €95. The terrace has wonderful views over the bay. That apart, Juan-les-Pins is not blessed with particularly memorable restaurants, so take pot luck from the countless menus on offer on the boulevards around La Pinède. *Le Café de la Plage*, at 1 boulevard Edouard-Baudouin (℡04.93.61.37.61; lunchtime *plats* €12), is a good bet, serving seafood, cocktails and ice cream with sea views, while several beach concessions offer classy *plats du jour* and home comforts along promenade du Soleil in the summer. Juan-les-Pins still cuts a dash in the nightlife stakes. The fads and reputations of the different **discos** may change, but in general opening hours are midnight to dawn, and you can count on searching appraisal of your attire and on paying around €16 for entrance plus your first drink. Some of the current hotspots include *Whisky a Gogo* on rue Jacques-Leonetti, *Le Milk* on avenue G.-Gallice and *Minimal* on boulevard Wilson. The perennially popular **live music** venue *Le Pam-Pam*, 137 boulevard Wilson, often has Brazilian bands, but you'll need to go early to get a seat.

Biot

Frequent buses connect Antibes with **BIOT**, 8km to the north, where Fernand Léger lived for a few years at the end of his life. A stunning collection of his intensely life-affirming works, created between 1905 and 1955, can be seen at the purpose-built **Musée Fernand Léger** (daily except Tues: June–Oct 10am–6pm; Nov–May 10am–5pm; €4.50). The museum is just east of the village on the chemin du Val de Pome, stop "Fernand Léger" on the Antibes bus, or a rather unpleasant and dangerous thirty-minute walk from Biot's *gare SNCF*.

The village itself is beautiful (if rather self-consciously so) and oozes with art in every form – architectural, sculpted, ceramic, jewelled, painted and culinary. The **tourist office**, 46 rue Saint Sebastien, at the western entrance to the village (July & Aug Mon–Fri 10am–7pm, Sat & Sun 2.30–7pm; Sept–June Mon–Fri 9am–noon & 2–6pm, Sat & Sun 2–6pm; ☎04.93.65.78.00, ⓦwww .biot.fr) can provide a map showing the various glassworks – the traditional industry that brought Léger here, and which produces the famous hand-blown **bubble glass**.

If you book well in advance you could stay at the very reasonable *Hôtel des Arcades*, 16 place des Arcades (☎04.93.65.01.04, ⓕ04.93.65.01.05; ⓽), full of old-fashioned charm and with huge rooms in the medieval centre of the village. Its **café-restaurant**, which doubles as an art gallery, serves delicious Provençal food (closed Sun evening & Mon; *plats du jour* around €16), or try the delightful *salon de thé*, *Le Mas Des Orangers*, at 3 rue des Roses.

Above the Baie des Anges

Between Antibes and Nice, the **Baie des Anges** laps at a long stretch of undistinguished twentieth-century resorts. At Villeneuve-Loubet-Plage the vast concrete sails of the Marina Baie des Anges rise above strip-mall squalor: drive-in restaurants, furniture stores and car dealerships.

The old towns and softer visual stimulation lie inland. **Cagnes** is another artists' town – associated in particular with Renoir – as is **St-Paul-de-Vence**, which houses the wonderful modern art collection of the Fondation Maeght. Vence has a small chapel decorated by Matisse, and is a relaxing place to stay, if quiet in the evenings.

Cagnes

CAGNES is a confusing agglomeration, made up of the seaside district of Cros-de-Cagnes, the immaculate medieval village of Haut-de-Cagnes overlooking the town from the northwest, and Cagnes-sur-Mer, the traffic-choked town centre wedged between the two. The three busy coastal roads slicing through the town don't add to its appeal.

At the top of place de-Gaulle, the main square in **Cagnes-sur-Mer**, avenue Auguste-Renoir runs right and crosses the road to La Gaude. A short way further on, chemin des Collettes leads off to the left up to **Les Collettes**, the house that Renoir had built in 1908 and where he spent the last twelve years of his life. It's now a **museum** (daily except Tues: May–Sept 10am–noon & 2–6pm; Oct–April 10am–noon & 2–5pm; check with museum for dates of annual winter closure; €3), and you can wander around the house and through the olive and rare orange groves that surround it. One of the two studios in the house – north-facing to catch the late afternoon light – is arranged as if Renoir had just popped out. Albert André's painting, *A Renoir Painting*, shows the ageing artist hunched over his canvas, plus there's a bust of him by Aristide Maillol, and a crayon sketch by Richard Guido. Bonnard and Dufy were also visitors to Les Collettes; Dufy's *Hommage à Renoir*, transposing a detail of *Le Moulin de la Galette*, hangs here. Renoir's own work is represented by several sculptures, some beautiful watercolours and ten paintings from his Cagnes period.

Arty **Haut-de-Cagnes** lives up to everything dreamed of in a Riviera *village perché*. The ancient village backs up to a crenellated feudal **château** (daily except Tues: May–Sept 10am–noon & 2–6pm; Oct–April 10am–noon & 2–5pm; €3; shuttle bus from bus station June–Sept, or by foot, the steep ascent along rue Général-Bérenger and montée de la Bourgade), with a stunning Renaissance interior, housing museums of local history, olive cultivation, the **donation Solidor** – a diverse collection of paintings of the famous cabaret artist Suzy Solidor – plus an **olive museum** and exhibition space for **contemporary art**.

Practicalities

The **gare SNCF** Cagnes-sur-Mer (one stop from the *gare SNCF* Cros-de-Cagnes) is southwest of the centre alongside the autoroute; turn right on the northern side of the autoroute along avenue de la Gare to head into town. The sixth turning on your right, rue des Palmiers, leads to the **tourist office** at 6 boulevard Maréchal-Juin (July–Aug Mon–Fri 9am–12.30pm & 2–6pm, Sat 9am–12.30pm; Sept–June Mon–Fri 9am–noon & 2–6pm, Sat 9am–noon; ☎04.93.20.61.64, ⓦwww.cagnes-tourisme.com). Buses #42, #49 and #56 all make the short run from the *gare SNCF* to the **gare routière** on square Bourdet.

Cros de Cagnes has the largest choice of **hotels** but also – despite recent traffic calming efforts – plenty of traffic: *Beaurivage*, 39 boulevard de la Plage on the seafront (☎04.93.20.16.09, ⓦwww.beaurivage.biz; ④), has very pleasant rooms with views of the sea, or there's *Le Turf*, 13 rue des Capucines (☎04.93.20.64.00, ⓦwww.turfhotel.com; ④), set back slightly from the seafront. If you're feeling extremely flush, you could try *Le Cagnard* on rue Sous Barri (☎04.93.20.73.21, ⓦwww.le-cagnard.com; ⑨), the ancient guard room for the castle, with a top-notch restaurant. **Campsites** are plentiful, and mostly in wooded locations inland; the two-star *Le Val Fleuri*, approximately 4km north of Cros-de-Cagnes at 139 chemin Vallon des Vaux (☎04.93.31.21.74, ⓦwww.campingvalfleuri.fr; €19.50 per tent; closed Nov–Jan), has a pool, bar and free wireless internet.

The best places to **eat** are in Haut-de-Cagnes, and, for café lounging, place du Château or place Grimaldi, to either side of the castle, are the obvious spots. *Fleur de Sel* at no 85 montée de la Bourgade (☎04.92.20.33.33; closed Wed & Thurs lunch) serves octopus salad and *bourride de lotte*, with menus starting at €32. *Le Cagnard* hotel has a predictably smart restaurant (☎04.93.20.73.21; menus from €55; closed mid-Nov to mid-Dec), or there's *Josy-Jo*, 2 rue du Planastel (☎04.93.20.68.76; around €29; closed Sat lunch & Sun) with Provençal delicacies dished up in the space that served as Soutine's workshop in the interwar years.

In summer there are free **jazz concerts** on place du Château and, at the end of August, a bizarre **square boules** competition takes place down montée de la Bourgade.

St-Paul-de-Vence: the Fondation Maeght

Further into the hills, the fortified village of **ST-PAUL-DE-VENCE** is home to yet another artistic treat, and one of the best in the whole region: the remarkable **Fondation Maeght** (daily: July–Sept 10am–7pm; Oct–June 10am–6pm; €11), created in the 1950s by Aimé and Marguerite Maeght, art collectors and dealers who knew all the great artists who worked in Provence. The Nice–Vence **bus** has two stops in St-Paul: alighting at the Village-Fondation Maeght stop, the first on the way up from Nice, the Fondation is a left turn up the hill from the roundabout; from the village centre, head uphill along the steep street opposite the entrance to the village itself. By **car** or **bike**, follow the signs just before you reach the village, off the D7 from La-Colle-sur-Loup or the D2 from Villeneuve.

Once through the gates, any idea of dutifully seeing the catalogue of priceless museum pieces crumbles; this, instead, is a sublime fusion of art, modern architecture and landscape. Alberto Giacometti's *Cat* is sometimes stalking along the edge of the grass; Miró's *Egg* smiles above a pond; it's hard not to be bewitched by the Calder mobile swinging over watery tiles, by Léger's *Flowers, Birds and a Bench* on a sunlit rough stone wall, or by the clanking tubular fountain by Pol Bury. The building itself is superb: multi-levelled, flooded with daylight and housing a fabulous collection of works by Braque, Miró, Chagall, Léger and Matisse, among others. Not everything is exhibited at any one time, and during the summer, when the main annual exhibition is mounted, none are on show, apart from those that make up the decoration of the building.

The other famous sights are in the extremely busy but beautiful *vieux village*. The hotel-restaurant **La Colombe d'Or** on place du Général-de-Gaulle (☎04.93.32.80.02, ⓦ www.la-colombe-dor.com; ◉; *plats du jour* from around €25; closed Nov to late Dec) is celebrated not for its food but for the art on its walls, donated in lieu of payment for meals by the then-impoverished Braque, Picasso, Matisse and Bonnard in the lean years following World War I. Rather fewer visitors make the pilgrimage to the simple grave of **Marc Chagall** on the right-hand side of the little **cemetery** (summer 7.30am–8pm; winter 8am–5pm) at the southern end of the village, running the gauntlet of the boutiques and galleries on rue Grande to get there.

Vence

A few kilometres north, with abundant water and the sheltering pre-Alps behind, **VENCE** has always been a town of some significance. The old town is blessed with numerous ancient houses, gateways, fountains, chapels and a **cathedral** containing Roman funeral inscriptions and a Chagall mosaic. In the 1920s it became yet another haven for painters and writers: André Gide, Raoul Dufy, D.H. Lawrence (who died here in 1930 while being treated for tuberculosis contracted in England) and Marc Chagall were all long-term visitors, along with **Matisse** whose work is the reason most people come here.

Towards the end of World War II, Matisse moved to Vence to escape the Allied bombing of the coast, and his legacy is the town's most famous and exciting building, the **Chapelle du Rosaire**, at 466 avenue Henri-Matisse (Tues & Thurs 10–11.30am & 2–5.30pm, Mon, Wed, Fri & Sat 2–5.30pm; closed mid-Nov to mid-Dec; €3), off the road to St-Jeannet, which leaves the town from carrefour Jean-Moulin at the top of avenue des Poilus. The chapel was his last work – consciously so – and not, as some have tried to explain, a religious conversion. "My only religion is the love of the work to be created, the love of creation, and great sincerity", he said in 1952 when the five-year project was completed.

The drawings on the chapel walls – black outline figures on white tiles – were executed by Matisse with a paintbrush fixed to a two-metre-long bamboo stick specifically to remove his own stylistic signature from the lines. He succeeded in this to the extent that many people are bitterly disappointed, not finding the "Matisse" they expect. Yet it is a total work – every part of the chapel is Matisse's design – and one that the artist was content with.

Vieux Vence has its share of chic boutiques and arty restaurants, but it also has an everyday feel about it, with ordinary people and run-of-the-mill cafés. On place du Frêne, by the western gateway, the fifteenth-century **Château de Ville-neuve Fondation Emile Hugues** (Tues–Sun: 10am–12.30pm & 2–6pm; €5) provides a beautiful temporary exhibition space for the works of artists such as Matisse, Dufy, Dubuffet and Chagall.

Practicalities

Arriving by bus, you'll be dropped close to the **tourist office** on place du Grand-Jardin (July–August Mon–Sat 9am–7pm, Sun 10am–6pm; March–June & Sept–Oct Mon–Sat 9am–6pm; Nov–Feb Mon–Sat 9am–5pm; ℡04.93.58.06.38, Ⓦwww.ville-vence.fr). You can rent **bikes** at Vence Motos on avenue Henri Isnard, just behind the tourist office.

Vence has some affordable **places to stay**, such as the soundproofed, very central *La Victoire*, on place du Grand Jardin (℡04.93.24.15.54, Ⓦwww .hotel-victoire.com; ❸); otherwise try the welcoming and peaceful *La Closerie des Genêts*, 4 impasse Maurel (℡04.93.58.33.25, Ⓕ04.93.58.97.01; ❷), off avenue M.-Maurel to the south of the old town, and *Le Provence*, 9 avenue M.-Maurel (℡04.93.58.04.21, Ⓦwww.hotelleprovence.com; ❷), with a pleasant garden. A little more luxury, including a pool, is available at *La Villa Roseraie*, avenue Henri-Giraud (℡04.93.58.02.20, Ⓦwww.villaroseraie.com; ❺–❼). There's a **campsite**, *La Bergerie* (€21.50 for two people and a tent), 3km west off the road to Tourettes-sur-Loup (℡04.93.58.09.36, Ⓦwww.camping -domainedelabergerie.com; closed mid-Oct to late March).

For a special, excellent-value **meal**, try *La Farigoule*, 15 avenue Henri-Isnard (℡04.93.58.01.27; menus from €22). For more run-of-the-mill fare, try the astounding choice of pizzas from €8 at *Le Pêcheur du Soleil*, 1 place Godeau. *Le Clemenceau*, on place Clemenceau, is the big café-brasserie-glacier.

Nice

The capital of the Riviera and fifth largest city in France, **NICE** lives off a glittering reputation, its former glamour now gently faded. First popularized by English aristocrats in the eighteenth century, Nice reached its zenith in the *belle époque* of the late nineteenth century, an era that left the city with several extraordinary architectural flights of fancy. Today, more than a quarter of Nice's residents are over 60, their pensions and investments contributing to the high ratio of per capita income to economic activity.

Far too large to be considered simply a beach resort, Nice has all the advantages and disadvantages of a major city: superb culture, wonderful street life and excellent shopping, eating and drinking, but also a high crime rate, graffiti and horrendous traffic, all set against a backdrop of blue skies, sparkling sea and sub-tropical greenery kept lush by sprinklers.

Nice's charm is at odds with its history of reactionary **politics**. For decades municipal power was the monopoly of a dynasty whose corruption was finally

---

Chemin de Fer de Provence

The **Chemin de Fer de Provence** runs one of France's most scenic and fun railway routes, from the Gare de Provence on rue Alfred-Binet (4 daily; 3hr 25min). The line runs up the Var valley into the hinterland of Nice to Digne-les-Bains, and climbs through some spectacular scenery as it goes. The return fare to Digne is €35.30 (for more information call ℡04.97.03.80.80 or check online at Ⓦwww.trainprovence.com).

exposed in 1990, when Mayor Jacques Médecin fled to Uruguay, only to be extradited and jailed. From his prison cell, he backed Jacques Peyrat, a former Front National member and friend of Jean-Marie Le Pen, in the 1995 local elections. Peyrat won with ease and retained the mayoralty until 2008, when he was defeated by Christian Estrosi, the locally born son of Italian parents and the candidate of the mainstream centre-right Nice Ensemble.

Nice has retained its historical styles almost intact: the medieval rabbit warren of **Vieux Nice**, the Italianate facades of **modern Nice** and the rich exuberance of **fin-de-siècle residences** dating from when the city was Europe's most fashionable winter retreat. It has also retained mementos from its ancient past, when the Romans ruled the region from here, and earlier still, when the Greeks founded the city. Nice's many museums are a treat for art lovers: within France the city is second only to Paris for art.

Of late the city has been smartening up its act with extensive **refurbishment** of its public spaces and the construction of a new **tramway**. Conservative it may be, but Nice does not rest on its laurels.

Arrival and information

From the **airport**, two fast buses connect with the city: #99 goes to the **gare SNCF** on avenue Thiers (25–30min; €4 day pass required) and #98 to the **gare routière** (20–35min; €4 day pass) on boulevard Jean-Jaurès. The regular bus #23 (40min; €1) also serves the *gare SNCF* from the airport. **Taxis** are plentiful at the airport and will cost about €21–31 into town.

The main **tourist office** is beside the *gare SNCF* on avenue Thiers (June–Sept Mon–Sat 8am–8pm, Sun 9am–7pm; Oct–May Mon–Sat 8am–7pm, Sun 10am–5pm; ☎08.92.70.74.07, ⓌWwww.nicetourisme.com). It's one of the most helpful in the region – though it can be a nightmare trying to get through by phone – and has annexes at 5 promenade des Anglais (June–Sept Mon–Sat 8am–8pm, Sun 9am–6pm; Oct–May Mon–Sat 9am–6pm), and at terminal 1 of the airport (June–Sept daily 8am–9pm; Oct–May Mon–Sat 8am–9pm).

Buses are frequent and run until early evening (roughly 7.30–9pm), after which five Noctambus night buses serve most areas from Station Bermand close to place Masséna until 1.10am. Fares are flat rate and you can buy a single ticket (€1), a Multi+ carnet of twenty tickets (€20), or a day pass (€4) on the bus; a ten-journey multipass (€10) and seven-day passes (€15) are available from *tabacs*, kiosks, newsagents and from Ligne d'Azur, the transport office, at 3 place Masséna, where you can also pick up a free route map. One line of the long-heralded **tramway** system is now in operation, though it's of relatively limited relevance to visitors as the route concentrates on linking the inland suburbs with the city centre; trams run until 1.35am.

Taxis around town are scarce, and cost €1.62 per kilometre by day; night rates (7pm–7am and all day at weekends) are €2.16 per kilometre. There are various surcharges. Scams are not unknown: if a restaurant or bar calls a cab for you, it's possible you'll enjoy a luxurious ride home in a top of the range Mercedes – with a hefty bill at your journey's end. **Bicycles**, **mopeds** and **motorbikes** can be rented from Holiday Bikes at 23 rue de Belgique just by the *gare SNCF* (☎04.93.16.01.62).

Accommodation

Before hunting for **accommodation**, it's worth taking advantage of the **online reservation service** (ⓌWwww.niceres.com) operated by the tourist office. The area around the station teems with cheap hotels, some of them seedy,

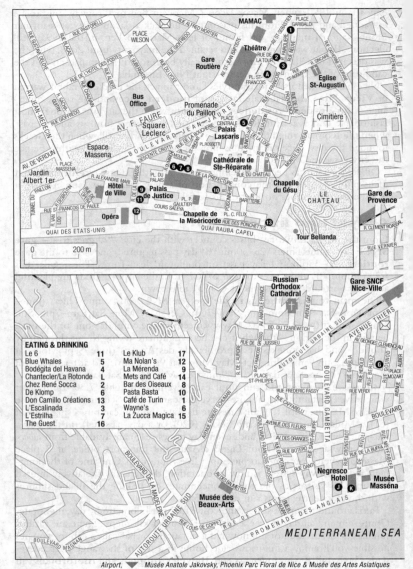

MAMAC

Théâtre

Gare
Routière

Eglise
St-Augustin

Cimitière

Bus
Office

Promenade
du Paillon

Palais
Lascaris

Espace
Massena

Cathédrale de
Ste-Réparate

Jardin
Albert 1er

Hôtel
de Ville

Palais
de Justice

Chapelle
du Gésu

LE
CHATEAU

Gare de
Provence

Opéra

Chapelle de
la Miséricorde

Tour Bellanda

0   200 m

Russian
Orthodox
Cathedral

Gare SNCF
Nice-Ville

EATING & DRINKING
Le 6	11	Le Klub	17
Blue Whales	5	Ma Nolan's	12
Bodégita del Havana	4	La Mérenda	9
Chantecler/La Rotonde	L	Mets and Café	14
Chez René Socca	2	Bar des Oiseaux	8
De Klomp	6	Pasta Basta	10
Don Camillo Créations	13	Café de Turin	1
L'Escalinada	3	Wayne's	6
L'Estrilha	7	La Zucca Magica	15
The Guest	16		

Musée des
Beaux-Arts

Negresco
Hotel

Musée
Masséna

MEDITERRANEAN SEA

PROMENADE DES ANGLAIS

Airport,   Musée Anatole Jakovsky, Phoenix Parc Floral de Nice & Musée des Artes Asiatiques

though there are a few gems. Sleeping on the beach is illegal and impractical: the promenade des Anglais is brightly illuminated.

Hotels

Cronstadt 3 rue Cronstadt ☎04.93.82.00.30, ⓦ www.hotelcronstadt.com. Hidden in the shady courtyard of a big residential block,

tranquil and near the sea, with clean, comfortable rooms. ⑤

Le Floride 52 bd de Cimiez ☎04.93.53.11.02, ⓦ www.hotel-floride.fr.

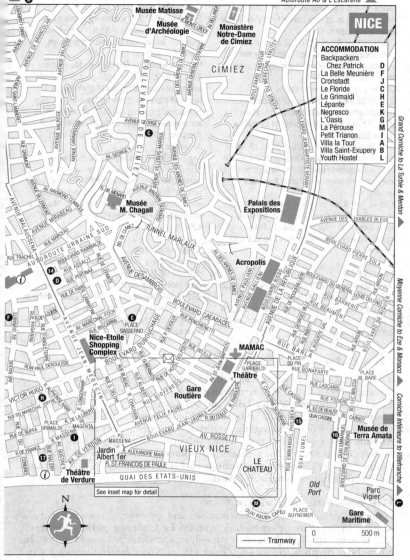

CIMIEZ

Musée Matisse

Musée
d'Archéologie

Monastère
Notre-Dame
de Cimiez

ACCOMMODATION	
Backpackers	
Chez Patrick	D
La Belle Meunière	F
Cronstadt	J
Le Floride	C
Le Grimaldi	H
Lépante	E
Negresco	K
L'Oasis	G
La Pérouse	M
Petit Trianon	I
Villa la Tour	A
Villa Saint-Exupéry	B
Youth Hostel	L

Musée M. Chagall

Palais des
Expositions

AVENUE DES DIABLES BLEUS

TUNNEL MARLAUX

Acropolis

Nice-Etoile
Shopping
Complex

MAMAC

Théâtre

Gare
Routière

VIEUX NICE

Musée de
Terra Amata

Jardin
Albert 1er

Théâtre
de Verdure

QUAI DES ETATS-UNIS

LE
CHÂTEAU

Old
Port

Parc
Vigier

See inset map for detail

Gare
Maritime

PLACE
GUYNEMER

N

Tramway

0   500 m

Charming small hotel in Cimiez, close to the Chagall museum, with some cheap singles. Free private parking. ❸

Le Grimaldi 15 rue Grimaldi ☎04.93.16.00.24, ⓦwww.le-grimaldi.com. Highly regarded, smart and central, with chic, individually designed rooms. ❻

Lépante 6 rue Lépante ☎04.93.62.20.55, ⓦwww.hotellepante.com. Smart, comfortable and gay-friendly, with a convenient, central location, wireless internet and air-conditioning. ❺

Negresco 37 promenade des Anglais ☎04.93.16.64.00, ⓦwww.hotel-negresco-nice.com. This legendary, somewhat eccentric seafront palace hotel is a genuine one-off, with two top-class restaurants, its own private beach and all the luxury you'd expect. ❾

L'Oasis 23 rue Gounod ℡04.93.88.12.29, ⓦwww .hoteloasis-nice.com. In a quiet and leafy setting, with small, modern rooms. In summer breakfast is served in the garden. ❺

La Pérouse 11 quai Rauba-Capeu ℡04.93.62.34.63, ⓦwww.hotel-la-perouse.com. The best-situated hotel in central Nice, at the foot of Le Château. Wonderfully peaceful for such a central location. ❾

Petit Trianon 11 rue Paradis ℡04.93.87.50.46, ⓔhotel.nice.lepetittrianon@orange.fr. Cheerful if basic hotel close to place Masséna and the *vieille ville*, with free internet and good front door security. ❷

Villa la Tour 4 rue de la Tour ℡04.93.80.08.15, ⓦwww.villa-la-tour.com. A good, if potentially noisy, location in Vieux Nice, with double glazing and individually designed rooms at various price levels. ❸

Hostels

🏃 **Backpackers Chez Patrick** First floor, 32 rue Pertinax ℡04.93.80.30.72, ⓦwww .backpackerschezpatrick.com. Friendly & funky air conditioned hostel close to the station, with eating facilities and no curfew. €22.

La Belle Meunière 21 av Durante ℡04.93.88.66.15, ⓦwww.bellemeuniere.com. Efficiently run backpacker hotel in a lovely old bourgeois house, with the bonus of a garden. Closed Dec and Jan. €17.

HI Youth Hostel rte Forestière du Mont-Alban ℡04.93.89.23.64, ⓦwww.fuaj.org. Four kilometres out of town. Take bus #14 from Station J.C. Bermond (direction "place du Mont-Boron", stop "L'Auberge"); the last bus that runs as far as the hostel leaves at 7.35pm. €16.20 per dorm bed. Reception 6.30am–noon & 5–9.30pm. Open June–Sept.

🏃 **Villa Saint-Exupery** 22 av Gravier ℡04.93.84.42.83, ⓦwww.vsaint.com. Impressively well-equipped modern hostel, some way out of central Nice, with internet, kitchen and laundry facilities. Tram from Place Masséna direction Las Planas, stop "Comte de Falicon". €25.

Campsite

Camping Terry 768 rte de Grenoble, St-Isidore ℡04.93.08.11.58. The only campsite anywhere near Nice, 6.5km north of the airport on the D6202; take the #59 bus from the *gare routière* to "Saint Isidore" stop (or ask the driver to drop you at the site), or the Chemins de Fer de la Provence train to "Bellet".

The City

It doesn't take long to get a feel for the layout of Nice. Shadowed by mountains that curve down to the Mediterranean east of its port, it still breaks up more or less into old and new. **Vieux Nice**, the old town, groups about the hill of **Le Château**, its limits signalled by **boulevard Jean-Jaurès**, built along the course of the River Paillon. Along the seafront, the celebrated **promenade des Anglais** runs a cool 5km until forced to curve inland by the sea-projecting runways of the airport. The central square, **place Masséna**, is at the bottom of the modern city's main street, **avenue Jean-Médecin**, while off to the north is the exclusive hillside suburb of **Cimiez**.

The château and Vieux Nice

For initial orientation, with fantastic sea and city views, fresh air and the scent of Mediterranean vegetation, head for **Le Château park** (daily: April, May & Sept 9am–7pm; June–Aug 9am–8pm; Oct–March 10am–5.30pm). It's where Nice began as the ancient Greek city of Nikea, hence the mosaics and stone vases in mock Grecian style. There's no château to see, just wonderful views over the scrambled rooftops and gleaming mosaic tiles of Vieux Nice and along the sweep of the promenade des Anglais. To reach the park, you can take the lift by the Tour Bellanda (€2) at the eastern end of quai des États-Unis, or climb the steps from rue de la Providence or montée du Château in the old town.

   Vieux Nice has been greatly gentrified in recent years, but the expensive shops, smart restaurants and art galleries still coexist with humbler shops, there's washing strung between the tenements overhead, and away from the showpiece squares a certain shabbiness lingers. Tourism now dominates Vieux Nice: throbbing with life day and night in August, much of it seems deserted in November. It is best explored on foot.

The central square is **place Rossetti**, where the soft-coloured Baroque **Cathédrale de Ste-Réparate** (Mon–Sat 9am–noon & 2–6pm, Sun 3–6pm) just manages to be visible in the concatenation of eight narrow streets. There are two cafés to relax in, with the choice of sun or shade, and a magical ice-cream parlour, *Fenocchio*, with an extraordinary choice of flavours. The real magnet of the old town, though, is **cours Saleya** and the adjacent place Pierre-Gautier and place Charles-Félix. These are wide-open, sunlit spaces alongside grandiloquent municipal buildings and Italianate chapels, and are the site of the city's main **market**. Every day except Monday from 6am to 1.30pm there are gorgeous displays of fruit, vegetables, cheeses and sausages, plus cut flowers and potted roses, mimosa and other scented plants displayed till at least 5.30pm (except Sunday afternoons); on Monday the stalls sell bric-a-brac and secondhand clothes (5.30am–6pm). Café and restaurant tables fill the *cours* on summer nights.

To feast your eyes on Baroque splendour, pop into the **chapels** and **churches** of Vieux Nice: La Chapelle de la Miséricorde, on cours Saleya (Tues 2.30–5pm); L'Église du Gesu, on rue Droite (open Thurs pm, Sat am & Sun evening); or L'Église St-Augustin, on place St-Augustin (Tues–Sun 8am–noon & 2–6pm), which also contains a fine pietà by Louis Bréa. For contemporary graphic and photographic art, check out the best **art galleries** (all Tues–Sat 10am–6pm; free) in Vieux Nice, which include: Galerie Espace Ste-Réparate, 4 rue Ste-Réparate; Galerie Municipale Renoir, 8 rue de la Loge; and Galerie du Château, 14 rue Droite.

Also on rue Droite is the **Palais Lascaris** (daily except Tues 10am–6pm; free), a seventeenth-century palace built by the Duke of Savoy's Field-Marshal, Jean-Paul Lascaris, whose family arms, engraved on the ceiling of the entrance hall, bear the motto "Not even lightning strikes us". It's all very sumptuous, with frescoes, tapestries and chandeliers, along with a collection of porcelain vases from an eighteenth-century pharmacy.

Place Masséna and around

The stately, largely pedestrianized **place Masséna** is the hub of the new town, built in 1835 across the path of the River Paillon, with good views north past fountains and palm trees to the mountains. A balustraded terrace and steps on the south of the square lead to Vieux Nice; the new town lies to the north. A short walk to the west lie the **Jardins Albert 1ᵉʳ**, where the Théâtre de Verdure occasionally hosts concerts.

The covered course of the Paillon northeast of place Masséna is the site of the city's more recent prestige projects. Most appealing of these is the marble **Musée d'Art Moderne et d'Art Contemporain**, or MAMAC (Tues–Sun 10am–6pm; ⓦ www.mamac-nice.org; free), with rotating exhibitions of avant-garde French and American movements from the 1960s to the present. New Realism (smashing, burning, squashing and wrapping the detritus or mundane objects of everyday life) and Pop Art feature strongly with works by Warhol, Klein, Lichtenstein, César, Arman and Christo.

Running north from place Masséna, **avenue Jean-Médecin** is the city's nondescript main shopping street, cheered up slightly by the revamped Nice-Étoile **shopping complex** between rue Biscarra and boulevard Dubouchage; there are branches of FNAC and Virgin nearby for books, CDs and concert tickets. **Couturier** shops are to be found west of place Masséna on rue du Paradis and rue Alphonse Karr. Both these streets intersect with the pedestrianized **rue Masséna** and the end of **rue de France** – true holiday territory, all ice-cream parlours and big brasseries, and always crammed.

Western Nice is chiefly memorable for its flamboyant and exotic flights of architectural fancy, like the **Russian Orthodox Cathedral** (daily except Sun morning: mid-Feb to April & Oct 9.15am–noon & 2.30–5.30pm; May–Sept 9am–noon & 2.30–6pm; Nov to mid-Feb 9.30am–noon & 2.30–5pm; €3), at the end of avenue Nicolas-II, which runs off boulevard Tsaréwitch, reached by bus #14 or #17 (stop Tzaréwitch).

The promenade des Anglais and the beaches

The point where the Paillon flows into the sea marks the beginning of the **promenade des Anglais**, created by nineteenth-century English residents for their afternoon strolls along the Mediterranean shore. Today it's more or less a permanent traffic jam, still bordered by some of the most fanciful turn-of-the-twentieth-century architecture on the Côte d'Azur. At nos. 13–15, the Palais de la Méditerranée is once again a luxurious casino, though the splendid Art Deco facade is all that remains of the 1930s original.

Most celebrated of all is the opulent, vaguely eccentric **Negresco Hotel** at no. 37 (see p.1077), built in 1906, and occupying the block between rues de Rivoli and Cronstadt. Provided you're wearing *tenue correcte* you can try wandering in to see the Salon Louis XIV and the Salon Royale. The first, on the left of the foyer, has a seventeenth-century painted oak ceiling and mammoth fireplace, plus royal portraits, all from various French châteaux. The Salon Royale, in the centre of the hotel, is a vast domed oval room, decorated with 24-carat gold leaf and the biggest carpet ever to have come out of the Savonnerie workshops. The chandelier is one of a pair commissioned from Baccarat by Tsar Nicholas II – the other hangs in the Kremlin.

Just before the *Negresco*, with its entrance at 65 rue de France, stands the **Musée Masséna** (open daily except Tues 10am–6pm), the city's art and history museum, which charts the city's development from Napoleonic times up to the 1930s. The fascinating pictures of old Nice aside, it's also worth a visit to see the sumptuous internal proportions of a grand old Nicois villa.

A kilometre or so down the promenade and a couple of blocks inland at 33 avenue des Baumettes lies the **Musée des Beaux-Arts** (Tues–Sun 10am–6pm; free; bus #38, stop "Chéret"), where the chief glory is the collection of 28 works by Raoul Dufy, who is intimately connected with the visual image of Nice. Continuing southwest along the promenade des Anglais towards the airport, you'll find the **Musée International d'Art Naïf Anatole Jakovsky** (daily except Tues 10am–6pm; free), home to a refreshingly different and surprisingly good collection of amateur art from around the world.

The **beach** below the promenade des Anglais is all pebbles and mostly public, with showers provided. It's not particularly clean and you need to watch out for broken glass. There are fifteen private beaches, clustering at the more scenic, eastern end of the bay close to Vieux Nice. If you don't mind rocks, you might want to try the string of coves beyond the port that starts with the **plage de la Réserve**, opposite Parc Vigier (bus #20 or #30).

On the far side of the castle sits the **old port**, flanked by gorgeous red and ochre eighteenth-century buildings and headed by the Neoclassical Notre-Dame du Port; it's full of yachts but has little quayside life despite the restaurants along quai Lunel. On the hill to the east, prehistoric life in the region has been reconstructed on the site of an excavated fossil beach in the **Musée de Terra Amata**, 25 boulevard Carnot (Tues–Sun 10am–6pm; free; bus #81 or 100, stop "Gustavin").

Cimiez

The northern suburb of **Cimiez** has always been posh. The approach up boulevard de Cimiez is punctuated by vast *belle-époque* piles, many of them former hotels: at the foot of the hill stands the gargantuan *Majestic*, while the summit is dominated by the equally vast *Hôtel Régina*, built for a visit by Queen Victoria. The heights of Cimiez were the social centre of the local elite some 1700 years ago, when the town was capital of the Roman province of Alpes-Maritimae. Part of a small amphitheatre still stands, and excavations of the **Roman baths** have revealed enough detail to distinguish the sumptuous and elaborate facilities for the top tax official and his cronies, the plainer public baths and a separate complex for women. All the finds, plus an illustration of the town's history up to the Middle Ages, are displayed in the **Musée d'Archéologie**, 160 avenue des Arènes (daily except Tues 10am–6pm; free; bus #17 or #22, stop "Arènes").

The seventeenth-century villa between the excavations and the arena is the **Musée Matisse** (daily except Tues 10am–6pm; Ⓦ www.musee-matisse-nice .org; free). Matisse spent his winters in Nice from 1916 onwards, staying in hotels on the promenade – from where *A Storm at Nice* was painted – and then from 1921 to 1938 renting an apartment overlooking place Charles-Félix. It was here that he painted his most sensual, colour-flooded canvases of odalisques posed against exotic draperies. As well as the Mediterranean light, Matisse loved the cosmopolitan aspect of Nice and the presence of fellow artists Renoir, Bonnard and Picasso in neighbouring towns. He died in Cimiez in November 1954, aged 85.

The Roman remains and the Musée Matisse back onto an old olive grove, one of the best open spaces in Nice and venue for the July **jazz festival**. At its eastern end are the sixteenth-century buildings and exquisite gardens of the **Monastère Notre-Dame de Cimiez** (Mon–Sat 10am–noon & 3–6pm; free); the oratory has brilliant murals illustrating alchemy, while the church houses three masterpieces of medieval painting by Louis and Antoine Bréa.

At the foot of Cimiez hill, just off boulevard Cimiez on avenue du Docteur-Menard, **Chagall's Biblical Message** is housed in a **museum** (daily except Tues: July–Sept 10am–6pm; Oct–June 10am–5pm; €6.50, €8.50 during temporary exhibitions; bus #22, stop "Musée Chagall") built specially for the work and opened by the artist in 1972. The rooms are light, white and cool, with windows allowing you to see the greenery of the garden beyond the indescribable shades between pink and red of the *Song of Songs* canvases. The seventeen paintings are all based on the Old Testament and complemented with etchings and engravings.

The Phoenix Parc Floral de Nice

Right out by the airport, the **Phoenix Parc Floral de Nice**, 405 promenade des Anglais (daily: April–Sept 9.30am–7.30pm; Oct–March 9.30am–6pm; €2; exit St-Augustin from the highway or bus #9, #10 or #23 from Nice), is a cross between a botanical garden, aviary and tacky theme park. The best reason to visit is to see the **Musée Départemental des Arts Asiatiques** (daily except Tues: May to mid-Oct 10am–6pm; mid-Oct to April 10am–5pm; Ⓦ www.arts-asiatiques.com; free), housed in a beautiful building designed by Japanese architect Kenzo Tange. It houses a collection of ethnographic artefacts, including silk goods and pottery, as well as traditional and contemporary art.

Eating, drinking and entertainment

Nice is a great place for **eating**, whether you're picnicking on market fare, snacking on Niçois specialities or dining in the palace hotels. The Italian influence is strong, with pasta on every menu; seafood is also a staple. For **snacks**, many of the cafés sell sandwiches with typically Provençal fillings such as fresh basil, olive oil, goat's cheese and *mesclum*, the unique green salad mix of the region. If you want to buy the best bread or croissants in town, seek out Espuno, 35 rue Droite, in the old town.

Despite the usual fast-food chains and tourist traps dotted around, most areas of Nice have plenty of reasonable restaurants. Vieux Nice has a dozen on every street catering for a wide variety of budgets; the port quaysides have good, but pricey, fish restaurants. In summer it's wise to book tables or turn up before 8pm, especially in Vieux Nice.

Vieux Nice is also the centre of Nice's lively **pub** and **club** scene, much of it anglophone in character. A good place to set out is along rue Central in the old town, where many pubs have early evening happy hours. Many Vieux Nice bars boast huge selections of beers and spirits and offer regular live music. As for Niçois nightclubs, bouncers judging your wallet or exclusive membership lists are the rule.

Nice's **lesbian and gay** nightlife scene is surprisingly active given the city's reactionary reputation, and for lesbian and gay visitors the city has a relaxed feel. The annual Pink Parade takes place in early summer.

For festivals, the **Mardi Gras Carnival** opens the year's events in Nice in February (Ⓦ www.nicecarnaval.com), with the last week of July taken up by the **Nice Jazz Festival** in the Parc de Cimiez (Ⓦ www.nicejazzfestival.fr for info, or contact the main tourist office in May/June).

Cafés

Cave de la Tour 3 rue de la Tour ☎ 04.93.80.03.31. Local *bar à vins* that serves wine from the bottle or, for the more daring, straight from huge vats.

Nocy-be 4–6 rue Jules-Gilley. This New-Agey tea house has a cushioned interior which evokes a Bedouin tent. Countless varieties of organic teas and infusions. Mon–Sat until 12.30am.

Le Café du Palais place du Palais. A prime al-fresco lounging spot on the handsome square by the Palais de Justice.

Les Ponchettes and **La Civette du Cours** cours Saleya. At Le Château end of the marketplace, neighbouring cafés with cane seats fanning out a good 50m from the doors. Open late in summer.

Restaurants

Chantecler and **La Rotonde** Hôtel Negresco, 37 promenade des Anglais ☎ 04.93.16.64.00. *Chantecler* is the best restaurant in Nice, seriously expensive à la carte, but chef Bruno Turbot provides a lunchtime menu, including wine and coffee, for €55, which will give you a good idea of how sublime Niçois food is at its best. At *La Rotonde* you can taste less fancy but still mouth-watering dishes on the €34 menu. Closed Mon, Tues & Jan 6 to Feb 7.

Chez René Socca 2 rue Miralhéti, off rue Pairolière. The cheapest meal in town: you can buy helpings of *socca, pissaladière*, stuffed peppers, pasta or calamares at the counter and eat with your fingers; the bar opposite serves the drinks. Closed Mon & Jan.

Don Camillo Créations 5 rue des Ponchettes ☎ 04.93.85.67.95. Elegant modern restaurant with contemporary Niçois/Italian cooking on a €40 menu. Closed Sun & Mon.

L'Escalinada 22 rue Pairolière ☎ 04.93.62.11.71. Good Niçois specialities on a €24 menu – *pissaladière* to start, then you help yourself to chickpea salad from a huge pot. The location is pretty, at the foot of a stepped side street. Open daily; closed mid-Nov to mid-Dec.

L'Estrilha 13 rue de l'Abbaye ☎ 04.93.62.62.00. Reservations essential in summer for this popular restaurant that serves bourride, civet de lapin and *daube niçoise*. Closed Mon.

La Mérenda 4 rue Raoul Bosio. Courgette fritters, *tripe à la niçoise* and the like from Dominic le Stanc, former chef at *Chantecler*. À la carte only, around €30. No phone, no smoking, no credit cards. Closed Sat & Sun.

Mets and Café 28 rue Assalit ☎04.93.80.30.85. Busy budget brasserie close to many of the backpacker hostels, with a €10.50 menu and no shortage of custom. Closed Sun.

🏃 Pasta Basta 18 rue de la Préfecture ☎04.93.80.03.57. Excellent fresh pasta and sauce from around €7 – the choice is bewildering – and they hand you the block of parmesan to grate yourself. Inexpensive pizza and bruschetta too.

Café de Turin 5 place Garibaldi ☎04.93.62.29.52. Queues around the block for the spectacular seafood at this restaurant on the edge of Vieux Nice. *Plateaux de fruits de mer* from just over €20. There are seafood stalls in the street outside should you get tired of waiting.

La Zucca Magica 4bis quai Papacino ☎04.93.56.25.27. Long-established, homely Italian vegetarian restaurant on the port, with a sound reputation but a tendency to overdo the cheese. Around €29. Closed Sun & Mon.

Bars, clubs and live entertainment

Blue Whales 1 rue Mascoïnat. Intimate venue with a friendly atmosphere and live music on Fri. Open daily till 4.30am.

Bodéguita del Havana 14 rue Chauvain. Wildly popular Cuban salsa bar with DJs and live music. Open Tues–Sun until 2.30am. Smart dress required.

De Klomp 6 rue Mascoïnat. Dutch-style brown café with big selection of beers and whiskies and regular live music. Mon–Sat 5.30pm–2.30am.

The Guest 5 quai des Deux-Emmanuel. Very stylish portside bar and dance club, attracting a slightly older crowd and with expensive cocktails.

Le Klub 6 rue Halévy. Nice's largest and best gay club attracts a young, stylish crowd including women and some heteros. Open Wed–Sun; entry charge varies according to night.

Ma Nolan's 2 rue St-François de Paul. Vast Irish pub with regular live music, televized Irish and British sport plus Murphy's and Guinness on draught. Popular with a younger expat crowd.

Bar des Oiseaux 5 rue St-Vincent. Eccentric cabaret bar named for the birds that fly down from their nests in the loft and the pet parrot and screeching mynah bird that perch by the door. Live jazz, chanson and the like, open lunchtimes Mon–Fri and evenings Thurs–Sat.

Le 6 6 rue Raoul Bosio. Smart lesbian and gay music bar, with regular live entertainment including drag, rai (Algerian funk/rap music) and karaoke. Tues–Sun from 10pm.

Wayne's 15 rue de la Préfecture. Big, popular rock bar on the edge of Vieux Nice, with regular live British bands. Still the lynchpin of the area's nightlife despite its vaguely Neanderthal sexual politics. Open daily.

Listings

Airlines Aer Lingus ☎08.21.23.02.67; Air Transat ☎08.25.12.02.48; BMI Baby ☎08.90.71.00.81; British Airways ☎08.25.82.54.00; British Midland ☎01.41.91.87.04; Delta ☎08.11.64.00.05; Easyjet ☎08.26.10.33.20.

Airport information ☎08.20.42.33.33, ⍟www .nice.aeroport.fr.

Books The Cat's Whiskers, 30 rue Lamartine, sells English-language books.

Car rental Major firms have offices at the airport and/or at the *gare SNCF* on av Thiers. Try also: Avis, 2 av Phocéens ☎04.93.80.63.52; Europcar, 3 av Gustave-V ☎08.25.82.76.74; or Hertz, 9 av Gustav-V ☎04.93.87.11.87.

Cinema Rialto, 4 rue de Rivoli (☎08.92.68.00.41) shows subtitled films in the original language *(v.o.)*.

Consulates Canada, 10 rue Lamartine ☎04.93.92.93.22; UK, 22 av Notre Dame ☎04.93.62.94.95; USA, 7 av Gustave-V, 3rd floor ☎04.93.88.89.55.

Disabled access Transport for people with reduced mobility ☎04.97.11.40.53.

Emergencies SAMU ☎15; SOS Médecins ☎08.10.85.01.01; Riviera Medical Services (English speaking doctors) ☎04.93.26.12.70; Hôpital St-Roch, 5 rue Pierre-Dévoluy ☎04.92.03.33.75; SOS Dentaire ☎04.93.76.53.53.

Ferries SNCM gare maritime, quai du Commerce ☎04.93.13.66.99, ⍟www.sncm.fr; Corsica Ferries, quai Amiral-Infernet ☎08.25.09.50.95.

Internet Internet Café, 30 rue Pertinax; Taxi Phone Internet, 10 rue de Belgique and at 25 rue Paganini.

Laundry Best One, 16 rue Pertinax; Lavomatique, corner of rue Lamartine and Pertinax; du Mono, 8 rue de Belgique.

Lost property 1 rue Raoul Bosio ☎04.97.13.44.10.

Money exchange American Express, Airport; Travelex, 13 av Thiers.

Pharmacy 7 rue Masséna ☎04.93.87.78.94; 66 av Jean Médecin ☎04.93.62.54.44.

16

Police Commissariat Central de Police, 1 av
Maréchal Foch ☎ 04.92.17.22.22.
Post office 21 av Thiers.

Taxis ☎ 04.93.13.78.78.
Trains General information and reservations
☎ 36.35.

The Corniches

Three **corniche roads** run east from Nice to the independent principality of Monaco and to Menton, the last town of the French Riviera. Napoleon built the **Grande Corniche** on the route of the Romans'Via Julia Augusta, and the **Moyenne Corniche** dates from the first quarter of the twentieth century, when aristocratic tourism on the Riviera was already causing congestion on the lower, coastal road, the **Corniche Inférieure**. The upper two are the classic location for car commercials, and for movie car crashes. Real deaths occur too – most notoriously Princess Grace of Monaco, who died as she descended from La Turbie to the Moyenne Corniche – a bitter irony, since the corniches had been the backdrop to one of her greatest film successes, *To Catch a Thief*.

Buses take all three routes; the **train** follows the lower corniche, and all three are superb means of seeing the most mountainous stretch of the Côte d'Azur. **Hotel** rooms between Nice and Menton are relatively scarce and frequently expensive; it probably makes more sense to base yourself in Nice.

The Corniche Inférieure

VILLEFRANCHE-SUR-MER is on the far side of Mont Alban from Nice. The cruise liners attracted by the deep-water anchorage in its beautiful bay ensure a steady stream of tour buses climbing the hill from the port, but as long as your visit doesn't coincide with shore excursions, the old town, with its fishing boats, sixteenth-century citadelle and the covered medieval rue Obscure running beneath the houses, is a charming place to while away an afternoon.

The tiny harbour is overlooked by the medieval **Chapelle de St-Pierre** (Tues–Sun: spring & summer 10am–noon & 3–7pm; autumn & winter 10am–noon & 2–6pm; €2), decorated by Jean Cocteau in 1957 in shades he described as "ghosts of colours". The drawings portray scenes from the life of St Peter and homages to the women of Villefranche and the gypsies. The chapel is used just once a year, on June 29, when fishermen celebrate the feast day of St Peter and St Paul with a Mass.

On the main road along the neck of the **Cap Ferrat peninsula**, between Villefranche and Beaulieu, stands the **Villa Éphrussi** (Feb–June & Sept–Oct daily 10am–6pm; July & Aug daily 10am–7pm; Nov–Jan Mon–Fri 2–6pm, Sat & Sun 10am–6pm; €10, €3 extra to visit first-floor collections). Built in 1912 for a Rothschild heiress, it overflows with decorative art, paintings, sculpture and artefacts ranging from the fourteenth to the nineteenth centuries, and from European to Far Eastern origins. The villa is surrounded by elaborate gardens.

Attractive, *belle-époque* **BEAULIEU** overlooks the pretty Baie des Fourmis, sheltered by a ring of hills that ensure some of the highest temperatures on the Côte. Its main attraction is the **Villa Kérylos** (mid-Feb to June & Sept–Oct daily 10am–6pm; July & Aug daily 10am–7pm; Nov–Feb weekdays 2–6pm, Sat & Sun 10am–6pm; €8.50), a near-perfect reproduction of an ancient Greek villa, east of the casino on avenue Gustav-Eiffel. Théodore Reinach, the archeologist who had it built in 1900, lived here for twenty years, eating, dressing and acting like an Athenian citizen, taking baths with his male friends and assigning separate suites to women. The villa is five-minutes' walk from the **gare SNCF**.

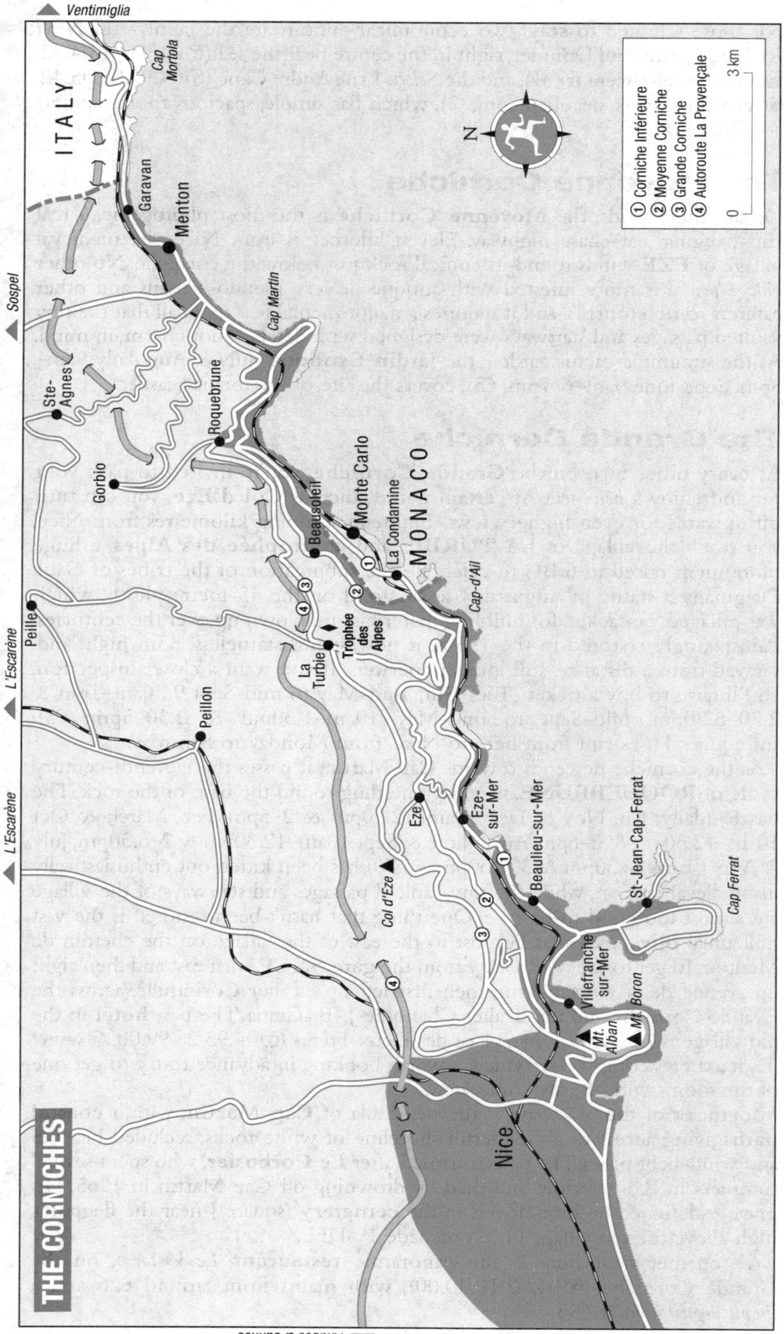

THE CORNICHES

①	Corniche Inférieure
②	Moyenne Corniche
③	Grande Corniche
④	Autoroute La Provençale

0   3 km

N

Ventimiglia

ITALY

Cap Mortola

Garavan

Menton

Cap Martin

Sospel

Ste-Agnes

Roquebrune

Gorbio

Beausoleil

Monte Carlo

La Condamine

MONACO

Peille

L'Escarène

Cap-d'Ail

L'Escarène

La Turbie

Trophée des Alpes

Peillon

Eze

Col d'Eze

Eze-sur-Mer

Beaulieu-sur-Mer

St-Jean-Cap-Ferrat

Villefranche-sur-Mer

Cap Ferrat

Mt. Alban

Mt. Boron

Nice

Antibes & Cannes

For those tempted to **stay**, two economical options are the family-run *Hôtel Riviera* at 6 rue Paul Doumer, right in the centre near the sea (℡04.93.01.04.92, Ⓦwww.hotel-riviera.fr; ➌), and the *Select*, 1 rue André Cane (℡04.93.01.05.42, Ⓦwww.hotelelect-beaulieu.com; ➎), which has simple, spacious rooms and air conditioning.

The Moyenne Corniche

Of the three roads, the **Moyenne Corniche** is the most photogenic, a real cliff-hanging, car-chase highway. Eleven kilometres from Nice, the medieval village of **EZE** winds round its conical rock just below the corniche. No other *village perché* is more infested with antique dealers, pseudo-artisans and other caterers to rich tourists, and it requires a major mental feat to recall that the tiny vaulted passages and stairways were designed with defence, not charm, in mind. At the summit, a cactus garden, the **Jardin Exotique** (July & Aug daily 9am–8pm; Sept–June 9am–6/7pm; €5), covers the site of the former castle.

The Grande Corniche

At every other turn on the **Grande Corniche**, you're invited to park your car and enjoy a *belvédère*. At certain points, such as **Col d'Eze**, you can turn off upwards for even higher views. Eighteen stunning kilometres from Nice, you reach the village of **LA TURBIE** and its **Trophée des Alpes**, a huge monument raised in 6 BC to celebrate the subjugation of the tribes of Gaul. Originally a statue of Augustus Caesar stood on the 45-metre plinth, which was pillaged, ransacked for building materials and blown up over the centuries. Painstakingly restored in the 1930s, it now stands statueless, 35m high, and, viewed from a distance, still looks imperious. If you want a closer inspection, you'll have to buy a ticket (Tues–Sun: mid-May to mid-Sept 9.30am–1pm & 2.30–6.30pm; mid-Sept to mid-May 10am–1.30pm & 2.30–5pm; €5). Infrequent buses run from here to Nice, from Monday to Saturday.

As the corniche descends towards Cap Martin, it passes the eleventh-century castle of **ROQUEBRUNE**, its village nestling round the base of the rock. The **castle** (daily: Jan, Nov & Dec 10am–12.30pm & 2–5pm; Feb, March & Oct 10am–12.30pm & 2–6pm; April–June & Sept 10am–12.30pm & 2–6.30pm; July & Aug 10am–12.30pm & 3–7.30pm; €3.70) has been kitted out enthusiastically in medieval fashion, while the tiny vaulted passages and stairways of the village are almost too good to be true. One thing that hasn't been restored is the vast millennial **olive tree** that lies just to the east of the village on the chemin de Menton. To get to the *vieux village* from the **gare SNCF**, turn east and then right up avenue de la Côte d'Azur, then first left up escalier Corinthille, across the Grande Corniche and up escalier Chanoine-J.-B.-Grana. The best **hotel** in the old village is *Les Deux Frères*, place des Deux-Frères (℡04.93.28.99.00, Ⓦwww.lesdeuxfreres.com; ➍–➏), which is worth booking in advance to try to get one of the rooms with the awesome view.

Southeast of the old town is the peninsula of **Cap Martin**, with a **coastal path** giving access to a wonderful shoreline of white rocks, secluded beaches and wind-bent pines. The path is named after **Le Corbusier**, who spent several summers in Roquebrune and died by drowning off Cap Martin in 1965. His grave – designed by himself – is in the **cemetery** (section J near the flagpole), high above the old village on promenade 1ᵉʳ-DFL.

A gourmet treat here is the panoramic **restaurant** *Le Vistaero*, on the Grande Corniche (℡04.92.10.40.00), with mains from around €26 and a *menu dégustation* at €85.

Monaco

Viewed from a distance, there's no mistaking the cluster of towers that is **MONACO**. Rampant development in the 1960s and 1970s rescued the tiny principality from postwar decline but elbowed aside much of its old prettiness, leaving it looking like nowhere else on the Riviera. Not for nothing was **Prince Rainier**, who died in 2005, known as the Prince Bâtisseur ("Prince Builder").

Though it may have lost its looks, this tiny state, no bigger than London's Hyde Park, retains its comic opera independence. It has been in the hands of the autocratic Grimaldi family since the thirteenth century, and in theory Monaco would become part of France were the royal line to die out. It remains home to six thousand well-heeled British expats – including Roger Moore and Shirley Bassey – out of a total population of 32,000.

Along with its wealth, Monaco latterly acquired an unwelcome reputation for wheeler-dealer **sleaze**. On his accession in 2005, the US-educated Prince Albert II set about trying to get the principality off an OECD list of uncooperative tax havens, declaring he no longer wished Monaco to be known – in the words of Somerset Maugham – as "a sunny place for shady people". One time to avoid Monaco – unless you're a motor-racing enthusiast – is the end of May, when racing cars burn around the principality for the Formula 1 **Monaco Grand Prix**. Every space in sight of the circuit is inaccessible without a ticket, making sightseeing or sneaky free views of the race impossible.

Arrival, information and accommodation

The **gare SNCF** is wedged between boulevard Rainier III and avenue Prince Pierre in La Condamine, with several exits: signs for Le Rocher-Fontvieille will deposit you at the end of avenue Prince Pierre above place d'Armes; directions for Monte-Carlo lead to place Sainte Dévote. Municipal buses ply the length of the principality from 7am to 9pm (€1 single; ten-trip card €6). Buses following the lower corniche stop at place d'Armes; other routes have a variety of stations; most also stop in Monte-Carlo. Local buses #1 & #2 run to the "Casino-Tourisme" stop, close to the **tourist office** at 2a boulevard des Moulins (Mon–Sat 9am–7pm, Sun 10am–noon; ☎92.16.61.16, ⓦ www.visitmonaco .com), with an annexe at the *gare SNCF* (daily 9am–7pm). Clean and efficient **lifts** link the lower and higher streets (marked on the tourist office map). **Bicycles** can be hired from Monte-Carlo-Rent, quai des États-Unis (☎99.99.97.79) on the port.

The best area for budget **hotels** is Beausoleil, just across the border in France, where you'll find the pleasant *Villa Boeri* at 29 boulevard du Général-Leclerc (☎04.93.78.38.10, ⓦ www.hotelboeri.com; ❹) and the comfortable, if slightly gloomy, *Hotel Diana* at no. 17 (☎04.93.78.47.58, ⓦ www.monte-carlo.mc /hotel-diana-beausoleil; ❷–❹), both a couple of minutes' walk from Monte-Carlo centre. In La Condamine you could try the *Hôtel de France*, at 6 rue de la Turbie (☎93.30.24.64, ⓦ www.monte-carlo.mc/france; ❺). If you want luxury

---

Phoning Monaco

Monaco phone numbers have only eight digits and no 04 French area code. If you are phoning from France you must dial Monaco's international code, 00377, then the number (leaving out the first 0).

without the steep prices of the palace hotels, *Columbus*, 23 avenue des Papalins (℡92.05.90.00, Ⓦ www.columbushotels.com; ❾), is a stylish boutique hotel in Fontvieille with sea views. Monaco has no campsite, and caravans are illegal – as are bathing costumes, bare feet and chests once you step off the beach. Camper vans have to be parked at the Parking des Écoles, in Fontvieille, and even then not overnight.

The Principality

The oldest part of the miniscule state is **Monaco-Ville**, around the palace on the rocky promontory, with the new marina of **Fontvieille** in its western shadow. **La Condamine** is the old port on the other side of the promontory; the ugly bathing resort of **Larvotto** extends to the eastern border; and **Monte-Carlo** is in the middle.

Monte-Carlo

Monte-Carlo is the area of Monaco where the real money is flung about, and its famous **casino** (Ⓦ www.casinomontecarlo.com; bus #1, #2 or #6) demands to be seen. Entrance is restricted to over-18s and you may have to show your passport; dress code is rigid, with shorts and T-shirts frowned upon, though most visitors are scarcely the last word in designer chic. Skirts, jackets and ties are obligatory for the more interesting sections. Bags and large coats are checked at the door.

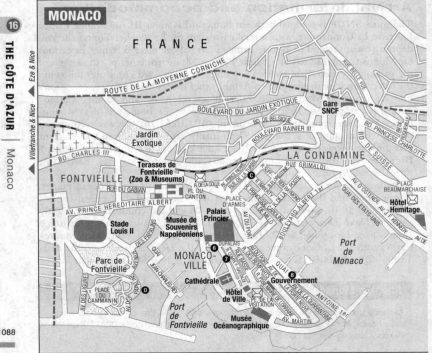

The first gambling hall is the **Salons Européens** (open from 2pm; €10) where slot machines surround the American roulette, craps and blackjack tables, the managers are Vegas-trained, the lights low and the air oppressively smoky. Above this slice of Nevada, however, the decor is *fin-de-siècle* Rococo extravagance, while the ceilings in the adjoining Pink Salon Bar are adorned with female nudes smoking cigarettes. The heart of the place is the **Salons Privés** (Mon–Fri from 4pm, Sat & Sun from 3pm), through the Salles Touzet. To get in, you have to look like a gambler, not a tourist (no cameras), and dispense with €20 at the door. Rather larger and more richly decorated than the European Rooms, its early afternoon or out-of-season atmosphere is that of a cathedral.

Adjoining the casino is the gaudy **opera house**, and around the palm-tree-lined place du Casino are more casinos plus the city's palace-hotels and *grands cafés*. The American Bar of the **Hôtel de Paris** is *the* place for the elite to meet, while the turn-of-the-twentieth-century **Hermitage** has a beautiful Gustave Eiffel iron-and-glass dome.

Monaco-Ville, Fontvieille and Larvotto

After the casino, the amusements of **Monaco–Ville** (bus #1 or #2) are less exciting, though the old town is the one part of the principality to have been spared the developer's worst. You can take a self-guided tour around the Lilliputian **Palais Princier** (daily: April 10.30am–6pm; May–Sept 9.30am–6.30pm; Oct 10am–5.30pm; closed Nov–March; €7); look at Napoleonic relics at the

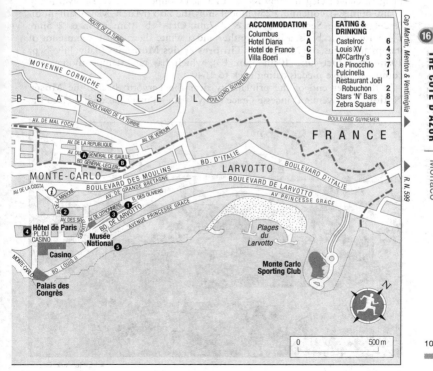

Musée des Souvenirs Napoléoniens et Collection des Archives Historiques du Palais, place du Palais (mid-Dec to May Tue–Sun 10.30am–12.30pm & 2–5pm; June–Sept daily 9.30am–6.30pm; Oct to mid-Nov daily 10am–5pm; €4); see the tombs of Prince Rainier and Princess Grace in the nineteenth-century **cathedral** (daily 8.30am–6.45pm) on rue Colonel; and even watch "Monaco the movie", at the **Monte-Carlo Story**, parking des Pecheurs (Jan–June & Sept–Oct 10am, 11am & 2–5pm; July & Aug 10am, 11am & 2–6pm; €7).

If you've had your fill of Grimaldis, check out the **Musée de la Chapelle de la Visitation** on place de la Visitation (Tues–Sun 10am–4pm; €3), displaying part of Barbara Piasecka Johnson's collection of religious art, a small but exquisite collection including works by Zurbarán, Rubens and Vermeer.

One of Monaco's best sights is the aquarium in the imposing **Musée Océanographique** (April–June & Sept 9.30am–7pm; July & Aug 9.30am–7.30pm; Oct–March 10am–6pm; €12.50), where the fishy beings outdo the weirdest Kandinsky or Hieronymus Bosch creations. Less exceptional but still peculiar, cactus equivalents can be viewed in the **Jardin Exotique**, on boulevard du Jardin Exotique high above Fontvieille (mid-May to mid-Sept 9am–7pm; mid-Sept to mid-May 9am–6pm or dusk; €6.90; bus #2).

There are more museums in **Fontvieille**, below the rock of Monaco-Ville. They include the **Collection de Voitures Anciennes de SAS le Prince de Monaco** (daily 10am–6pm; €6), an enjoyable miscellany of old and not-so-old cars, with everything from a 1928 Hispano-Suiza worthy of Cruella de Ville to Princess Grace's elegant 1959 Renault Florida Coupé; the **Musée Naval** (daily 10am–6pm; €4), containing 250 model ships; the **zoo** (March–May 10am–noon & 2–6pm; June–Sept 9am–noon & 2–7pm; Oct–Feb 10am–noon & 2–5pm; €4), with exotic birds, a black panther and a white tiger; and the museum of stamps and coins, the **Musée des Timbres et des Monnaies** (daily: July–Sept 10am–6pm; Oct–June 10am–5pm; €3), which has rare stamps, money and commemorative medals dating back to 1640.

At the other end of the principality near the Larvotto beach, the **Musée National**, 17 avenue Princesse Grace (daily 10am–6pm; €6), is dedicated to the

▲ Monte Carlo Casino

history of **dolls and automata**, and is better than you would think: some of the dolls' house scenes and the creepy automata are quite surreal and fun.

Eating and drinking

La Condamine and the old town are replete with **restaurants**, but good food and reasonable prices don't exactly match; prices near the casino can be absurd. The best-value cuisine is Italian, notably ⅄ *Le Pinocchio*, at 30 rue Comte-F.-Gastaldi (☎93.30.96.20; closed Dec), with *plats du jour* from €12, and *Pulcinella*, 17 rue du Portier in Monte-Carlo (☎93.30.73.61), offering à la carte around €30, *plats* from €12. Alternatively, try *Castelroc* (☎93.30.36.68; closed Sat), in the old town on place du Palais, which serves fish and Monegasque specialities. It's not worth going upmarket in Monaco unless you're prepared to pay €90 and more per head, in which case there are some worthy places: Alain Ducasse's *Louis XV* (☎98.06.88.64; closed Tues, Wed & Dec) in the *Hôtel de Paris*, or the *Restaurant Joël Robuchon* at the *Hotel Métropole*, 4 avenue de la Madone (☎93.15.15.10), where the cooking is under the aegis of one of France's most respected chefs.

Your best bet for non-casino **nightlife** is *Stars 'N' Bars* on the quai Antoine 1ᵉʳ, packed out on Fridays and Saturdays, with a lively club upstairs, or the ubiquitous Irish pub, *McCarthy's*, 7 rue du Portier, for Guinness and occasional live music. For something a little more flash, try *Zebra Square* atop the Grimaldi Forum, open until 2.30am and with regular DJs.

Menton

Of all the Côte d'Azur resorts, **MENTON** is the warmest and most Italianate, being right on the border. In 1861 a British doctor, James Henry Bennet, published a treatise on the benefits of Menton's mild climate to tuberculosis sufferers, and soon thousands of well-heeled invalids were flocking here in the vain hope of a cure. Menton is ringed by protective mountains, so hardly a whisper of wind disturbs this suntrap of a city; you'll notice the difference in winter, when you'll need a change of clothes between here and the exposed central resorts.

Arrival and information

Roquebrune and Cap Martin merge into Menton along the 3km shore of the Baie du Soleil. The modern town is arranged around three main streets parallel to the sea. The **gare SNCF** is on the top one, rue Albert-1ᵉʳ, from which a short walk to the left brings you to the north–south avenue de Verdun and avenue Boyer divided by the Jardins Biovès – central location for citrus sculptures during February's **Fête du Citron**. The **tourist office** is at 8 avenue Boyer (mid-June to mid-Sept daily 9am–7pm; mid-Sept to mid-June Mon–Fri 8.30am–12.30pm & 1.30–6pm, Sat 9am–noon & 2–6pm; ☎04.92.41.76.76, Ⓦwww.menton.fr), in the Palais de l'Europe, a former casino. The **gare routière** and the **urban bus station** are between the continuation of the two avenues north of the train line on the avenue de Sospel. Local bus lines (€1) all pass through the *gare routière*.

Accommodation

Menton is no less popular than the other major resorts, so in summer you should reserve **accommodation** in advance, which you can do online through the tourist office website.

Hotels

L'Aiglon 7 av de la Madonne ℡04.93.57.55.55, ⓦwww.hotelaiglon.net. Spacious rooms in a nineteenth-century residence surrounded by a large garden. **❼**

Beauregard 10 rue Albert-1ᵉʳ ℡04.93.28.63.63, ⓦwww.hotelmenton.com. Traditionally furnished rooms and a relaxed atmosphere. **❷**

Moderne 1 cours George-V ℡04.93.57.20.02, ⓦwww.hotel-moderne-menton.com. Good-value modern, central hotel; many rooms have balconies. **❺**

M. Paul Gazzano 151 rte de Castellar ℡04.93.57.39.73. *Chambre d'hôte* 2km from Menton; a delightful house with a terrace looking down over the wooded slopes to the sea. **❸**

Napoléon 29 porte de France, Garavan ℡04.93.35.89.50, ⓦwww.napoleon-menton .com. Elegantly modern seafront hotel with pool and garden. Mountain or sea views from the rooms. **❻**

Hostel and campsite

HI hostel plateau St-Michel ℡04.93.35.93.14, ⓦwww.ajmenton.com. Up a gruelling flight of steps (signposted *Camping St-Michel*) from the northern side of the railway to the east of the station, or take bus #6 from the *gare routière*. Reception open summer 7–noon & 6pm–midnight; winter 7–10am, 6–10pm. Curfew. Closed Nov–Jan. €16.

Camping St-Michel rte des Ciappes ℡04.93.35.81.23, ⓦwww.menton.fr/camping. Reasonably priced campsite in the hills above the town, with plenty of shade and good views; follow directions for youth hostel. Closed mid-Oct to March except for Fête du Citron. Around €19.40 with car, tent, electricity and tax.

The Town

The **promenade du Soleil** runs along the pebbly beachfront of the Baie du Soleil, stretching from the quai Napoléon-III past the casino towards Roque-brune. The most diverting building on the front is a seventeenth-century fort by the quai Napoléon-III south of the old port, now the **Musée Jean Cocteau** (daily except Tues 10am–noon & 2–6pm; €3), set up by the artist himself. It contains pictures of his Mentonaise lovers in the *Inamorati* series, a collection of delightful *Fantastic Animals* and the tapestry of *Judith and Holofernes* telling the sequence of seduction, assassination and escape. There are also photographs, poems, ceramics and a portrait by his friend Picasso.

As the *quai* bends around the western end of the Baie de Garavan from the Cocteau museum, a long flight of pebbled steps leads up into the **vieille ville** to the **Parvis de la Basilique**, an attractive Italianate square hosting concerts in summer and giving a good view out over the bay. The frontage of the **Église St-Michel** (Mon–Fri 10am–noon & 3–5.15pm, Sat & Sun 3–5.15pm) proclaims its Baroque supremacy in perfect pink-and-yellow proportions; a few more steps up will reward you with the beautiful facade of the **chapel of the Pénitents-Blancs** (Mon & Wed 3–5pm) in apricot and white. The crumbly **cemetery**, at the top of the old town on the site once occupied by the town's château, is hauntingly sad – many of the young tuberculosis sufferers who ended their days in Menton are buried here – but also bewitchingly beautiful, with views along the coast into Italy.

In the middle of the modern town, the **Salles des Mariages** (Mon–Fri 8.30am–12.30pm & 2–5pm; €1.50), or registry office, forms part of the **Hôtel de Ville** on place Ardoiono and was decorated in inimitable style by Jean Cocteau in 1957.

On avenue de la Madone, at the other end of the modern town, an impressive collection of paintings from the Middle Ages to the twentieth century can be seen in the **Palais Carnolès** (daily except Tues 10am–noon & 2–6pm; free; bus #7), the old summer residence of the princes of Monaco. Of the early works, the *Madonna and Child with St Francis* by Louis Bréa is exceptional. The most recent include canvases by Graham Sutherland, who spent some of his last years in Menton.

If it's cool enough, the gardens of **Garavan**'s villas make a change from shingle beaches. The best is **Les Colombières**, just north of boulevard de Garavan and designed by the artist Ferdinand Bac between 1918 and 1927, but it's privately owned; check for information on occasional guided visits with the tourist office. Alternatively, try the **Jardin Exotique Val Rameh** (daily except Tues: April–Sept 10am–12.30pm & 3–6pm; Oct–March 10am–12.30pm & 2–5pm; €4) below boulevard de Garavan or **Fontana Rosa** (guided visits Friday at 10am; €5) on avenue Blasco-Ibañez, the former home of the Spanish author Vincente Blasco-Ibañez and bright with ceramic decoration. From here it's a short walk up rue Webb-Ellis and chemin Wallaya behind the Garavan *gare SNCF* to the villa **Isola Bella**, the former home of author Katherine Mansfield, though it is not open to the public.

Eating and drinking

Menton's **restaurants** tend towards the informal and touristy; the pedestrianized rue St-Michel is promising ground for cheap eats, and in summer there is no shortage of swanky places along the promenade de la Mer in which to get a **drink** or **meal** on the beach, either. If you're after something more ambitious, *La Lyre* on the port at 15 quai Bonaparte (☎04.93.35.39.25) serves excellent calamares and other Italian dishes, while the stylish modern *Mirazur* at 30 avenue Aristide Briande (☎04.92.41.86.86) flies the flag for French gastronomy close to the border with Italy, with menus from €35 at lunchtime.

Travel details

Trains

Cannes to: Antibes (approx. every 20min peak time; 10–15min); Biot (approx. every 20min–1hr; 17min); Cagnes-sur-Mer (every 20min peak time; 20min); Golfe Juan-Vallauris (approx. every 20 min–1hr; 7min); Juan-les-Pins (approx. every 20min–1hr; 11min); Marseille (every 30min–1hr; 2hr); Nice (approx. every 20min peak time; 25–59min); St-Raphaël (every 20min–1hr; 32min–40min); Villeneuve-Loubet-Plage (approx. every 20min–1hr; 21min).

Marseille to: Arles (up to 26 daily; 50min); Avignon (12–14 daily; 1hr 10min); Bandol (approx. every 30min–1hr 30min; 42min); Cannes (approx. hourly; 2hr); Cassis (approx. every 30min–1hr 30min; 23min); Cavaillon (2–5 daily; 55min–1hr 15min); Hyères (1–5 daily; 1hr 20min); La Ciotat (approx. every 30min–1hr 30min; 30min); Les Arcs-Draguignan (7–15 daily; 1hr 20min–2hr); Lyon (up to 12 daily; 3hr 40min); Menton (1–2 daily; 3hr 6min); Nice (hourly at peak times; 2hr 30min); Paris (8 daily; 3hr 15min); St-Cyr/Les Lecques (approx. every 30min–1hr 30min; 35–45min); St-Raphaël (every 30 min–1hr 30min; 1hr 30min–1hr 45min); Salon (2–5 daily; 40–55min); Toulon (every 20min at peak times; 40min–1hr 3min).

Nice to: Beaulieu (every 15–30min; 11min); Cannes (every 20min at peak times; 25–40min); Cap Martin–Roquebrune (every 35min–1hr; 30min); Digne (4 daily; 3hr 25min); Èze-sur-Mer (every 35min–1hr; 15min); Les Arcs-Draguignan (approx. half hourly at peak times; 1hr 10min); Marseille (every 30min–1hr 30min; 2hr 30min); Menton (every 15–35min; 25–40min); Monaco (every 15–35min; 20–25min); Paris (7 daily; 5hr 40min); St-Raphaël (approx. half hourly at peak times; 55min–1hr 30min); Sospel (6 daily; 53min); Tende (2 daily; 1hr 46min); Villefranche (every 15–45min; 8min).

St-Raphaël to: Cannes (every 20–55min; 25–40min); Nice (every 20–55min; 50min–1hr 25min).

Buses

Antibes to: Biot (approx. every 30min; 15min); Cannes (every 15min; 30min); Juan-les-Pins (every 20–30min; 8min); Nice (every 15min; 50–55min); Nice Airport (every 15–30min; 20–47min).

Cannes to: Antibes (every 15min; 35min); Cagnes (every 15min; 45min–1hr); Grasse (every 20min 40–50min); Nice (every 15min; 1hr 25min–1hr 45min); Nice Airport (every 30min; 50min); St Raphael (2 daily; 1hr 5min); Vallauris (hourly; 15min).

Grasse to: Cagnes (every 25–50min; 40min); Cannes (every 15–30min; 40–55min); Nice (every 25–50min; 1hr 30min).

Hyères to: Bormes (approx. hourly; 25min); La Croix-Valmer (8 daily; 1hr 20min); Le Lavandou (approx. hourly; 25min); Le Rayol (8 daily; 55min); St-Tropez (6 daily; 1hr 45min–1hr 50min); Toulon (every 25–45min; 35min–1hr 10min).

Le Lavandou to: Bormes (approx. hourly; 8); Hyères (approx. hourly; 25min); La Croix-Valmer (8 daily; 45min); Le Rayol (8 daily; 20min); St-Tropez (6 daily; 1hr 15min); Toulon (approx. hourly; 1hr 10min).

Marseille to: Aix (every 5min at peak times; 30–50min); Barcelonnette (1–2 daily; 4hr); Carpentras (2–3 daily; 2hr–2hr 20min); Cassis (2–4 daily; 45min); Digne (3–7 daily; 2hr 15min–2hr 40min); Grenoble (1 daily; 4hr 25min); La Ciotat (approx. hourly; 45min); Manosque (3 daily; 1hr 30min); Sisteron (2–4 daily; 2hr 10min–2hr 45min).

Menton to: Monaco (every 10–15min; 30–42min); Nice (every 10–15min; 1hr–1hr 25min).

Monaco to: Èze (7 daily; 15min); La Turbie (3–6 daily; 30min); Menton (every 10–15min; 40min); Nice (every 10–15min; 40–50min).

Nice to: Aix (3–5 daily; 2hr 40min–3hr 50min); Antibes (every 15min; 55min–1hr 20min); Beaulieu (every 10–15min; 15–18min); Cagnes-sur-Mer (every 15min; 47min); Cannes (every 15min; 1hr 25min–1hr 50min); Digne (2 daily; 3hr–3hr 15min); Èze-Village (7 daily; 20min); Grasse (every 25–35 min; 1hr 20min–1hr 35min); Grenoble (1 daily; 6hr 10min); La Turbie (5 daily; 40min); Marseille (3–5 daily; 3hr 5min–4hr 25min); Menton (every 10–15min; 1hr–1hr 25min); Monaco (every 10–15min; 35–52min); Roquebrune

(every 10–15min; 45min–1hr 10min); St-Paul (every 30–45min; 55min–1hr); Sisteron (2 daily; 3hr 40min–4hr); Vence (every 30–45min; 1hr–1hr 15min); Villefranche (every 10–15min; 10–15min).

St-Raphaël to: Cannes (2 daily; 1hr 10min); Fréjus (frequent; 20min); Grimaud (6 daily; 50min–1hr); La Foux (6 daily; 1hr 15min); Ste-Maxime (11 daily; 30–35min); St-Tropez (10 daily; 1hr 10min–1hr 25min).

St-Tropez to: Bormes (6 daily; 1hr 5min–1hr 15min); Gassin (2 weekly; 30min); Grimaud (7 daily; 20min); Hyères (8 daily; 1hr 40min–1hr 50min); Hyères airport (2 daily; 1hr); La Croix-Valmer (8 daily; 18min); La Garde-Freinet (1–2 daily; 50min); Le Lavandou (8 daily; 1hr); Ramatuelle (4 daily; 37min); Ste-Maxime (10 daily; 40–55min); St-Raphaël (10 daily; 1hr 10min–1hr 30min); Toulon (8 daily; 2hr–2hr 20min).

Toulon to: Aix (2–5 daily; 1hr 15min); Collobrières (2 daily; 1hr 20min–1hr 30min); Hyères (every 15–45min; 55min–1hr 5min); La Croix-Valmer (8 daily; 1hr 55min); Le Lavandou (approx. hourly; 55 min–1hr 15min); St-Tropez (7 daily; 2hr 10min–2hr 30min).

Vence to: Cagnes (every 45min; 22–30min); Nice (every 45min; 50min–1hr 10min); St-Paul-de-Vence (every 45min; 5min)

Ferries

For Îles d'Hyères and Îles de Lérins services, see p.1043 & p.1063.

Marseille to: Corsica (1–6 daily; 8hr 45min–12hr).

Nice to: Corsica (summer 4–6 daily; winter 1 weekly; 3hr–5hr 45min).

Toulon to: Corsica (summer 2–4 daily; 7hr 30min).

Corsica

CHAPTER 17

Highlights

* **Plage de Saleccia** Soft white shell sand, turquoise water and barely a building in sight. See p.1113

* **Calvi** Corsica's hallmark resort, framed by snow peaks and a spectacular blue gulf. See p.1115

* **The GR20** Gruelling 170km footpath, which takes in spectacular mountain scenery – but is only for the fit. See p.1119

* **Girolata** The only fishing village on the island still inaccessible by road, set against a backdrop of red cliffs and dense maquis. See p.1120

* **Les Calanches de Piana** A mass of porphyry, eroded into dogs' heads, witches and devils. See p.1123

* **Filitosa menhirs** Among the Western Mediterranean's greatest archeological treasures, unique for their carved faces. See p.1134

* **Boat trips from Bonifacio** Catch a navette from the harbour visited by Odysseus for imposing views of the famous chalk cliffs and haute ville. See p.1143

* **Corte** A nationalist stronghold, with loads of eighteenth-century charm and a rugged mountain setting. See p.1146

▲ Calvi

Corsica

Nearly two-and-a-half million people visit **Corsica** each year, drawn by the mild climate and some of the most diverse landscapes in all Europe. Nowhere in the Mediterranean has beaches finer than the island's perfect half-moon bays of white sand and transparent water, or seascapes more dramatic than the red porphyry Calanches of the west coast. Even though the annual visitor influx now exceeds the island's population seven or eight times over, tourism hasn't spoilt the place: there are a few resorts, but overdevelopment is rare and high-rise blocks are confined to the main towns.

Bastia, capital of the north, was the principal Genoese stronghold, and its fifteenth-century citadelle has survived almost intact. Of the island's two large towns, this is the more purely Corsican, and commerce rather than tourism is its main concern. Also relatively undisturbed, the northern Cap Corse harbours inviting sandy coves and fishing villages such as **Macinaggio** and **Centuri-Port**. Within a short distance of Bastia, the fertile region of the Nebbio contains a scattering of churches built by Pisan stoneworkers, the prime example being the cathedral of Santa Maria Assunta at the appealingly chic little port of **St-Florent**.

To the west of here, **L'Île-Rousse** and **Calvi**, the latter graced with an impressive citadelle and fabulous sandy beach, are major targets for holiday-makers. The spectacular **Scandola nature reserve** to the southwest of Calvi is most easily visited by boat from the tiny resort of **Porto**, from where walkers can also strike into the wild **Gorges de Spelunca**. **Corte**, at the heart of Corsica, is the best base for exploring the mountains and gorges of the interior which form part of the **Parc Naturel Régional** that runs almost the entire length of the island.

Sandy beaches and rocky coves punctuate the west coast all the way down to **Ajaccio**, Napoleon's birthplace and the island's capital, where pavement cafés and palm-lined boulevards are thronged with tourists in summer. Slightly fewer make it to nearby **Filitosa**, greatest of the many prehistoric sites scattered across the south. **Propriano**, the town perhaps most transformed by the tourist boom, lies close to stern **Sartène**, former seat of the wild feudal lords who once ruled this region and still the quintessential Corsican town.

More megalithic sites are to be found south of Sartène on the way to **Bonifacio**, a comb of ancient buildings perched atop furrowed white cliffs at the southern tip of the island. Equally popular, **Porto-Vecchio** provides a springboard for excursions to the amazing beaches of the south. The eastern plain has less to boast of, but the Roman site at **Aléria** is worth a visit for its excellent museum.

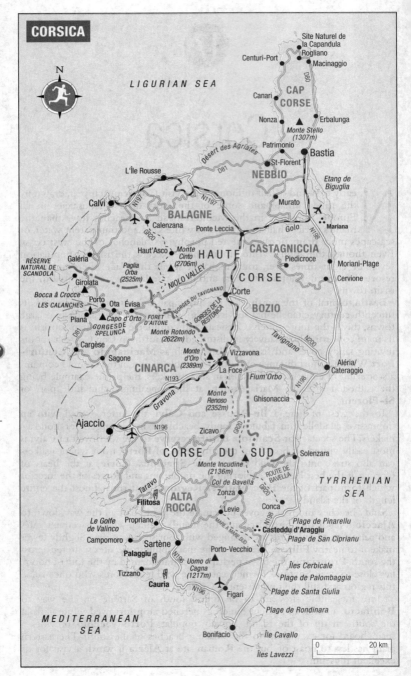

Some history

Set on the western Mediterranean trade routes, Corsica has always been of strategic and commercial appeal. Greeks, Carthaginians and Romans came in successive waves, driving native Corsicans into the interior. The Romans were ousted by Vandals, and for the following thirteen centuries the island was attacked, abandoned, settled and sold as a nation-state, with generations of islanders fighting against foreign government. In 1768 France bought Corsica from Genoa, but over two hundred years of French rule have had a limited effect and the island's Baroque churches, Genoese fortresses, fervent Catholic rituals and a Tuscan-influenced indigenous language and cuisine show a more profound affinity with Italy.

Corsica's uneasy relationship with the mainland has worsened in recent decades. Economic neglect and the French government's reluctance to encourage Corsican language and culture spawned a nationalist movement in the early 1970s, whose clandestine armed wing – the FLNC (Fronte di Liberazione Nazionale di a Corsica) – and its various off-shoots have been engaged ever since in a bloody conflict with the central government. The violence seldom affects tourists but signs of the "troubles" are everywhere, from the graffiti-sprayed roadsigns to the bullet holes plastering public buildings.

Relations between the island's hard-line nationalists and Paris may be perennially fraught, but there's little support among ordinary islanders for total independence. Bankrolled by Paris and Brussels, Corsica is the most heavily subsidized region of France. Moreover, Corsicans are exempt from social

---

The food of Corsica

It's the herbs – thyme, marjoram, basil, fennel and rosemary – of the maquis (the dense, scented scrub covering lowland Corsica) that lend the island's cuisine its distinctive aromas.

You'll find the best **charcuterie** in the hills of the interior, where pork is smoked and cured in the cold cellars of village houses – it's particularly tasty in Castagniccia, where wild pigs feed on the chestnuts which were once the staple diet of the locals. Here you can also taste chestnut fritters (*fritelli a gaju frescu*) and chestnut porridge (*pulenta*) sprinkled with sugar or eau de vie. **Brocciu**, a soft mozzarella-like cheese made with ewe's milk, is found everywhere on the island, forming the basis for many dishes, including omelettes and cannelloni. *Fromage corse* is also very good – a hard **cheese** made in the sheep- and goat-rearing central regions, where *cabrettu à l'istrettu* (kid stew) is a speciality.

Game – mainly stews of hare and wild boar but also roast woodcock, partridge and wood pigeon – features throughout the island's mountain and forested regions. Here blackbirds (*merles*) are made into a fragrant pâté, and eel and trout are fished from the unpolluted rivers. **Sea fish** like red mullet (*rouget*), bream (*loup de mer*) and a great variety of shellfish is eaten along the coast – the best crayfish (*langouste*) comes from around the Golfe de St-Florent, whereas oysters (*huîtres*) and mussels (*moules*) are a speciality of the eastern plain.

Corsica produces some excellent, and still little-known, **wines**, mostly from indigenous vinestocks that yield distinctive, herb-tinged aromas. Names to look out for include: Domaine Torraccia (Porto-Vecchio); Domaine Fiumicicoli (Sartène); Domaine Saparale (Sartène); Domaine Gentille (Patrimonio); Domaine Leccia (Patrimomio); and Venturi-Pieretti (Cap Corse). In addition to the usual whites, reds and rosés, the latter also makes the sweet muscat for which Cap Corse was renowned in previous centuries. Another popular aperitif is the drink known as Cap Corse, a fortified wine flavoured with quinine and herbs. Note that **tap water** is particularly good quality in Corsica, coming from the fresh mountain streams.

17

CORSICA

security contributions and the island as a whole enjoys preferential tax status, with one-third of the permanent population an employee of the state. Increasingly, nationalist violence is seen as biting the hand that feeds it.

Opinion, however, remains divided on the best way forward for Corsica. In 2003, a package of radical devolutionary measures was narrowly rejected in a referendum, a decision which the then-interior Minister, Nicholas Sarkozy, condemned as a "wasted opportunity". A massive crackdown on corruption and organized crime was ordered soon after, to which the paramilitaries responded with a renewed bombings, machine gun and rocket attacks on State symbols.

Corsica practicalities

Getting to Corsica

One French company, SNCM – along with its freight subsidiary CMN – dominates **ferry** services to Corsica. In addition, an Italian operator, Corsica Ferries, has superfast services from **Nice** to Calvi and Bastia. Crossings take between seven and twelve hours on a regular ferry, and from two and a half to three and a half hours on the giant hydrofoil ("NGV", or *navire à grande vitesse*). The cost depends on the season, with the lowest between October and May; during July and August fares quadruple. A one-way crossing costs anything from €15 to €120 per person, plus €50 to €250 per vehicle, depending on the date of the journey.

Regular ferries run all year round to various ports around the island from **Marseille**, **Toulon** and **Nice**. You can **book** SNCM and CNM tickets via their central reservation desk (☎ 08.36.67.95.00, ⊛ www.sncm.fr). For Corsica Ferries contact ☎ 04.92.00.42.93, ⊛ www.corsicaferries.fr. Note that reservations are essential for journeys in July and August.

Direct **flights** to Corsica depart from most major French cities with charters cheaper than scheduled services. The largest operator is Air France (☎ 08.20.82.08.20, ⊛ www.airfrance.fr), whose fourteen-day advance fares from Paris rise to €450 return in July and August, dropping to €160 out of season. Compagnie Corse Méditerranée (☎ 08.02.80.28.02, ⊛ www.ccm-airlines.com) offers routes from a range of mainland airports. Their fares from the Côte d'Azur vary little: €125–260 return depending on season.

Getting around

With public transport woefully inadequate, the most convenient way of getting around Corsica is by **rental car**. All the big firms (see Basics p.39) have offices at airports and towns across the island, allowing you to collect and return vehicles in different places. Even if your budget won't stretch to a week, it's worth renting for a couple of days to explore the back roads of the interior.

Bus services are fairly frequent between Bastia, Corte and Ajaccio, and along the east coast from Bastia to Porto-Vecchio and Bonifacio. Elsewhere in the island, services tend to peter out in the winter months or are relatively infrequent. Getting accurate timetable information for bus services can also be difficult – the best way to check information is at a tourist office or, better still, online at ⊛ www.corsicabus.org. See "Travel details" at the end of this chapter for a roundup of routes and frequencies.

Corsica's diminutive **train**, the *Micheline* or *Trinighellu* (little train; ⊛ www.ter-sncf .com), rattles through the mountains from Ajaccio to Bastia via Corte, with a branch line running northwest to Calvi. The route's had a major upgrade recently, and is a notch quicker than the bus – plus it takes you through some stupendous scenery. Again, current timetable information and fares may be viewed online at ⊛ www .corsicabus.org.

Then, in 2006, with Sarkozy bound for the Elysée Palace, the focus of nationalist ire shifted to French-owned second homes on the island – a reaction against the recent tide of middle-class buyers from the continent, who have pushed up property prices beyond the reach of the average islander. By the summer, ten holiday houses per week were being blown up.

A perennial vote winner for the island's paramilitaries, the campaign against "foreign-owned" holiday villas has succeeded in rallying public opinion behind the nationalist cause, at a time when the Sarkozy administration seems clueless about what to do with Corsica in the long term. Other than sporadic reports of bombings, the only time the island has hit the headlines over the past couple of years was when a TV telephone hoaxer pretending to be the Quebecois premier got presidential candidate Ségolène Royal to agree that "Corsica should be independent". Sarkozy responded by saying that "for me, Corsica isn't a joke ... It's the Republic" – a statement of platitudinous resolve that encapsulates current government thinking on the thorny *"problème corse"*.

Bastia and around

The dominant tone of Corsica's most successful commercial town, **BASTIA**, is one of charismatic dereliction, as the city's industrial zone is spread onto the lowlands to the south, leaving the centre of town with plenty of aged charm. The old quarter, known as the Terra Vecchia, comprises a tightly packed network of haphazard streets, flamboyant Baroque churches and lofty tenements, their crumbling golden-grey walls set against a backdrop of maquis-covered hills. Terra Nova, the historic district on the opposite side of the old port, is a tidier area that's now Bastia's trendy quarter.

The city dates from Roman times, when a base was set up at Biguglia to the south, beside a freshwater lagoon. Little remains of the former colony, but the site merits a day-trip for the well-preserved pair of Pisan churches at Mariana, rising from the southern fringes of Poretta airport. Bastia began to thrive under the Genoese, when wine was exported to the Italian mainland from Porto Cardo, forerunner of Bastia's Vieux Port, or Terra Vecchia. Despite the fact that in 1811 Napoleon appointed Ajaccio capital of the island, initiating a rivalry between the two towns which exists to this day, Bastia soon established a stronger trading position with mainland France. The Nouveau Port, created in 1862 to cope with the increasing traffic with France and Italy, became the mainstay of the local economy, exporting chiefly agricultural products from Cap Corse, Balagne and the eastern plain.

Arrival and information

Bastia's Poretta **airport** (℡04.95.54.54.54, Ⓦwww.bastia.aeroport.fr) is 16km south of town, just off the Route Nationale (N193). **Shuttle buses** into the centre coincide with flights, dropping passengers at the north side of the main square, place St-Nicolas, and terminating at the train station for €8.50 (one way). **Taxis** from the airport cost €40/50 (day/night). **Ferries** arrive at the **Nouveau Port**, just a five-minute walk from the centre of town. Bastia doesn't have a proper bus station, which can cause confusion, with services arriving and departing from different locations around the north side of the main square. A summary of times and departure points is available at the **tourist office**, at the north end of place St-Nicolas (June to mid-Sept daily 8am–8pm; mid-Sept to May Mon–Sat 8am–6pm, Sun 9am–1pm; ℡04.95.54.20.40, Ⓦwww.bastia-tourisme.com).

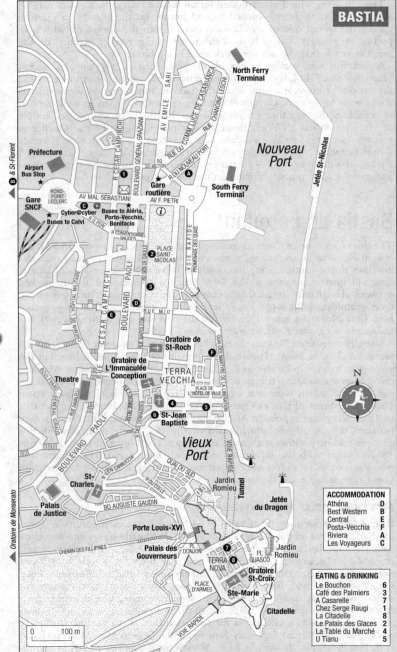

Camping Casanova & Cap Corse

BASTIA

North Ferry Terminal

Nouveau Port

Jetée St-Nicolas

Préfecture

Airport Bus Stop

Gare SNCF

RÔND-POINT LECLERC

Cyber@cyber

Buses to Calvi

AV MAL SÉBASTIANI

R CÉSAR CAMPINCHI

BOULEVARD GÉNÉRAL GRAZIANI

AV ÉMILE SARI

RUE DU COMMT LUCE DE CASABIANCA

RUE CHANOINE LESCHI

RUE DU NOUVEAU PORT

SQ ST-VICTOR

Gare routière

AV F. PIETRI

Buses to Aléria, Porto-Vecchio, Bonifacio

R G PERI

R CONVENTIONNEL SALICETI

PLACE SAINT-NICOLAS

BD GEN DE GAULLE

VOIE RAPIDE

PROMENADE DES QUAIS

South Ferry Terminal

BOULEVARD PAOLI

R CÉSAR CAMPINCHI

CHEMIN DE L'HÔPITAL MILITAIRE

RUE MIOT

RUE NAPOLÉON

Oratoire de St-Roch

QUAI DES MARTYRS DE LA LIBÉRATION

Theatre

Oratoire de L'Immaculée Conception

RUE DES TERRASSES

TERRA VECCHIA

PLACE DE L'HÔTEL DE VILLE

St-Jean Baptiste

BOULEVARD PAOLI

BOULEVARD GÉNÉRAL GIRAUD

RUE FAVALELLI

St-Charles

R GEN CARBUCCIA

Vieux Port

QUAI DU SUD

VOIE RAPIDE

Palais de Justice

BD AUGUSTE GAUDIN

R DU COLLE

Jardin Romieu

Tunnel

Jetée du Dragon

Oratoire de Monserato

Porte Louis-XVI

CHEMIN DES FILLIPINES

Palais des Gouverneurs

PL DONJON

TERRA NOVA

PL GUASCO

Jardin Romieu

Oratoire St-Croix

PLACE D'ARMES

Ste-Marie

Citadelle

VOIE RAPIDE

0   100 m

ACCOMMODATION
Athéna	**D**
Best Western	**B**
Central	**E**
Posta-Vecchia	**F**
Riviera	**A**
Les Voyageurs	**C**

EATING & DRINKING
Le Bouchon	**6**
Café des Palmiers	**3**
A Casarelle	**7**
Chez Serge Raugi	**1**
La Citadelle	**8**
Le Palais des Glaces	**2**
La Table du Marché	**4**
U Tianu	**5**

B & St-Florent

N

La Marana, Étang de Biguglia, Poretta Airport, Corte, Porto-Vecchio, Bonifacio & Ajaccio

Accommodation

The choice of **hotels** is not great, particularly at the budget end the scale, and rooms tend to be booked well in advance, especially on weekends. The most pleasant and convenient **campsite** if you're relying on public transport is the *Casanova* (℡04.95.33.24; open April–Oct) at Miomo, 5km north (frequent buses leave from the top of place St-Nicolas opposite the tourist office).

Hotels

Athéna 2 rue Miot ℡04.95.34.88.40. Modern hotel close to the ports and central *place*, with light, airy rooms at various rates. Go for the pricier ones if space is an issue (the cheaper ones are quite small). ❺

Best Western av Zuccarelli ℡04.95.55.05.10, ⓦwww.bestwestern-corsica-hotels.com. Hardly the most characterful option, but rates are highly competitive, the location (on the hill above town) attractive, and rooms spacious for the price. Central a/c. ❺

🏃 **Central** 3 rue Miot ℡04.95.31.71.12, ⓦwww.centralhotel.fr. Eighteen pleasantly furnished rooms (plus a handful of larger studios), with textured walls and sparkling bathrooms, just off the southwest corner of place St-Nicolas. By far the most pleasant and best-value place to stay in the centre. Advance reservation essential. ❻

Posta-Vecchia quai-des-Martyrs-de-la-Libération ℡04.95.32.32.38, ⓦwww.hotel-postavecchia .com. The only hotel in the Vieux Port, and good value, with views across the sea from the (pricier) rooms at the front. There are smaller, cheaper rooms in the old block across the lane (❸); all have a/c. ❹

Riviera 1 bis, rue du Nouveau-Port ℡04.95.31.07.16, ⓦwww.corsehotelriviera.com. Basic and a bit noisy, with recently renovated rooms behind a period façade, but very near the harbour. ❹

Les Voyageurs 9 av Maréchal-Sébastiani ℡04.95.34.90.80, ⓦwww.hotel-lesvoyageurs .com. Smart three-star near the train station, done out in pale yellow and with two categories of rooms: the larger, pricier ones have tubs instead of showers. No views to speak of, but fine for a night or two. Secure parking and central a/c. ❺

The Town

The centre of Bastia is not especially large, and all its sights can easily be seen in a day without the use of a car. The spacious **place St-Nicolas** is the obvious place to get your bearings: open to the sea and lined with shady trees and cafés, it's the main focus of town life. Running parallel to it on the landward side are boulevard Paoli and rue César-Campinchi, the two main shopping streets, but all Bastia's historic sights lie within **Terra Vecchia**, the old quarter immediately south of place St-Nicolas, and **Terra Nova**, the area surrounding the Citadelle. Tucked away below the imposing, honey-coloured bastion is the much-photographed **Vieux Port**, with its boat-choked marina and crumbling eighteenth-century tenement buildings. By contrast, the **Nouveau Port**, north of the *place*, is bland and modern.

Terra Vecchia

From place St-Nicolas the main route into Terra Vecchia is **rue Napoléon**, a narrow street with some ancient offbeat shops and a pair of sumptuously decorated chapels on its east side. The first of these, the **Oratoire de St-Roch**, is a Genoese Baroque extravagance, reflecting the wealth of the rising bourgeoisie. Built in 1604, it has walls of finely carved wooden panelling and a magnificent gilt organ.

A little further along stands the **Oratoire de L'Immaculée Conception**, built in 1611 as the showplace of the Genoese in Corsica, who used it for state occasions. The austere facade belies the flamboyant interior, where crimson velvet draperies, a gilt and marble ceiling, frescoes and crystal chandeliers create the ambience of an opera house.

Just behind the oratoire, the place de l'Hôtel-de-Ville is commonly known as **place du Marché** after the lively farmers' market that takes place here each morning, from around 7am until 2pm. Dominating the south end of the square is the **church of St-Jean-Baptiste**, an immense ochre edifice that dominates the Vieux Port. Its twin campaniles are iconic of the city, but the interior – a hideous Rococo overkill of multicoloured marble – is less impressive.

Around the church extends the oldest and most photgenic part of Bastia, the **Vieux Port** – a secretive zone of dark alleys, vaulted passageways and seven-storey houses. Site of the original Roman settlement of Porto Cardo, the harbour later bustled with Genoese traders, but since the building of the ferry terminal and commercial docks to the north it has become a backwater. The most atmospheric time to come here is early evening, when huge flocks of swifts swirl in noisy clouds above the harbour. Things liven up after sunset, with the glow and noise from the waterside bars and restaurants, which continue round the north end of the port along the wide **quai des-Martyrs-de-la-Libération**, where live bands clank out pop covers for the tourists in summer.

Terra Nova

The military and administrative core of old Bastia, **Terra Nova** (or the citadelle) is focused on **place du Donjon**, which gets its name from the squat round tower that formed the nucleus of Bastia's fortifications: it was used by the Genoese to incarcerate Corsican patriots, among them the nationalist rebel Sampiero Corso in 1657, who was held in the dungeon for four years.

Facing the *place* is the impressive fourteenth-century **Palais des Gouverneurs**. With its great round tower, arcaded courtyard and peach-coloured paintwork, the building has a distinctly Moorish feel. Originally built for the Genoese governor and bishop, it became a prison after the French transferred the capital to Ajaccio, and was then destroyed during a British attack of 1794 (in which an ambitious young captain named Horatio Nelson played a decisive part). The subsequent rebuilding was not the last, as parts of it were mistakenly blown up by American B-52s in the bungled attack of 1943 – which devastated the city centre on the day after the island's liberation. A massive renovation project started a decade ago to restore the building to its former glory, but has been bogged down for years in financial disputes. If and when it is ever completed, the site's centrepiece will be the **Musée d'Ethnographie** (timings not yet available at time of writing; admission around €5), presenting the history of Corsica from prehistoric times to the present day. Star exhibits of the collection include a diminutive Roman sarcophagus decorated with hunting scenes, busts of famous Corsicans and an original 1755 Flag of Independence, with its distinctive Moorish emblem.

Back in place du Donjon, if you cross the square and follow rue Notre-Dame you come out at the **Église Ste-Marie**. Built in 1458 and overhauled in the seventeenth century, it was the cathedral of Bastia until 1801, when the bishopric was transferred to Ajaccio. Inside, the church's principal treasure is a small silver statue of the Virgin (housed in a glass case on the right wall as you face the altar), which is carried through Terra Nova and Terra Vecchia on August 15, the Festival of the Assumption. Immediately behind Ste-Maire in rue de l'Évêché stands the **Oratoire Sainte-Croix**, a sixteenth-century chapel decorated in Louis XV style, with lashings of rich blue paint and gilt scrollwork. It houses another holy item, the *Christ des Miracles*, a blackened oak crucifix much venerated by Bastia's fishermen, which in 1428 was discovered floating in the sea surrounded by a luminous haze. A festival celebrating the miracle takes place in Bastia annually on May 3, when local fishing families carry the crucifix around Terra Nova.

L'Oratoire de Monserato

One of Bastia's most extraordinary monuments, the **Oratoire de Monserato**, lies a pleasant two-kilometre walk from the town centre. From Terra Nova, leave the citadelle through its main (northern) gateway next to the Palais des Gouverneurs and follow the chemin des Fillipines (a stepped lane starting on the opposite side of the main road) uphill for ten minutes. When you reach a road at the top turn left and keep going for another 300m until you see a lane leading left to the Oratoire. The building itself looks unremarkable from the outside, but its interior houses the much revered **Scala Santa**, a replica of the Holy Steps of the Basilica of Saint John of Lateran in Rome. Penitents who ascend it on their knees as far as its high altar may be cleansed, or so it is believed, of all sins, without the intercession of a priest.

Eating and drinking

Lively **place St-Nicolas**, lined with smart café-restaurants, is the place to be during the day, particularly between noon and 3pm, when the rest of town is deserted. Along **boulevard Paoli** and **rue César-Campinchi**, chi-chi *salons de thé* offer elaborate patisseries, local chestnut flan and doughnuts (*beignets*). Late-night clubbers can revive themselves with an early coffee and a pain au chocolat at one of the three cafés in **place de l'Hôtel-de-Ville**, which open at 4.30am for the market traders. There are also numerous **pizza vans** scattered about town until about 9pm.

Drinking is serious business in Bastia. The **Casanis** pastis factory is on the outskirts in Lupino, and this is indisputably the town's drink – order a "*Casa*" and you'll fit in well.

Nightclubs are few and far between in Corsica, and the only *boîte* of note in the Bastia area is *L'Apocalypse* (☎04.95.33.36.83, ⓦwww.apocalypse-bastia .com; closed Mon & Tues), 10km south of Bastia on the route de La Marana, Biguglia. It attracts a mainly teenage crowd, and you'll need a car to get there. Entry is free and drinks extortionate.

Bars and cafés

Le Bouchon 4 bis, rue St-Jean, Vieux Port. Occupying a prime position on the quayside, this easy-going wine bar serves local and continental French wines by the glass (€6.50), as well as variously priced gastro-tapas on slate platters. Closed Wed and Sun.

Chez Serge Raugi 2 bis, rue Capanelle, off bd Général Graziani, at the north end of place St-Nicolas. Arguably Corsica's greatest ice-cream maker, from an illustrious line of local *glaciers*. Tables on a cramped pavement terrace or upstairs on an even smaller mezzanine floor. In winter, they also do a legendary chickpea tart to take away.

La Citadelle In front of the Palais des Gouverneurs, Terra Nova. Basically a sandwich and ice-cream bar that would have little to recommend it were it not for the superb location overlooking the Vieux Port.

Café des Palmiers place St-Nicolas. One of several cafés along this stretch, with comfy wicker chairs which catch the sun at breakfast time, plus delicious fresh patisseries and attentive service.

Restaurants

🦞 **A Casarelle** 6 rue Ste-Croix
☎04.95.32.02.32. Innovative Corsican–French cuisine (lamb *noisettes* in Pietra beer and maquis-herb sauce, for example) served on a terrace on the edge of the citadelle. The chef's specialities are traditional dishes of the Balagne, such as *casgiate* (nuggets of fresh cheese baked in fragrant chestnut leaves) or the rarely prepared *storzapretti* – balls of *brocciu*, spinach and herbs in tomato sauce. Menu at €29 for lunch, or €35 for dinner. Closed Sat lunchtime and all day Sun.

Le Palais des Glaces place St-Nicolas ☎04.95.35.05.01. One of the few dependable lunch spots on the main square, frequented as much by Bastiais as visitors. Their good-value €25 menu, served under swish awnings beneath the plane trees, often includes the house favourite: fish bruschettas.

La Table du Marché place du Marché ☎04.95.31.64.25. Offering far better value than most places on the nearby Vieux Port, this smart terrace restaurant serves a tempting €27.50 *menu* regional featuring local crayfish, east-coast oysters and *filets du St Pierre*. The à la carte menu is dominated by fancier gastro seafood, and is much more expensive. Closed Sun.

U Tianu 4 rue Rigo ☎04. 95. 31. 36. 67. Tiny, family-run restaurant with lots of atmosphere, hidden in a narrow backstreet behind the Vieux Port. Their limited but excellent-value menus (€22–27) change daily but feature typical country dishes such as *figatellu* pâté, blackbird terrine, chickpeas with anchovies, mutton and lentil stew, sardines stuffed with *brocciu*, and *fiadone* soaked in home-made eau de vie.

Listings

Bike rental Locacycles, behind the Palais de Justice (☎04.95.32.30.64), rents out bicycles by the day (€18) or for longer periods, as does Objectif Nature, rue Notre Dame-de Lourdes (☎04.95.32.54.34, ⓦwww.objectif-nature-corse.com).

Car rental ADA, 35 rue César-Campinchi ☎04.95.31.48.95, airport ☎04.95.54.55.44; Avis (Ollandini), 40 bd Paoli ☎04.95.31.95.64, airport ☎04.95.54.55.46; Europcar, 1 rue du Nouveau-Port ☎04.95.31.59.29, airport ☎04.95.30.09.50; Hertz, square St-Victor ☎04.95.31.14.24, airport ☎04.95.30.05.00; Rent-a-Car, Poretta airport ☎04.95.54.55.11.

Ferry offices Corsica Ferries, 5 bis, rue Chanoine-Leschi ☎00-33/4.92.00.43.76, ⓦwww.corsicaferries.com; Mobylines, Sarl Colonna D'Istria & Fils, 4 rue Luce de Casablanca, just behind the Nouveau Port ☎ 49-611/14020, ⓦwww.mobylines.com; SNCM, Nouveau Port ☎00-33/8.25.88.80.88, ⓦwww.sncm.fr.

Internet access Café Albert, at 11 bd Général de Gaule.

Laundry Lavoir du Port (daily 7am–9pm), two doors down from the big Esso petrol station, opposite the ferry dock's north terminal.

Left luggage Bags can be left for €3/day at Objectif Nature, rue Notre Dame-de Lourdes.

Post office The central post office is on av Maréchal-Sebastiani, between the train station and place St-Nicolas.

La Marana, Mariana and the Étang de Biguglia

Traditionally the summer haunt of prosperous Bastia families, the sixteen-kilometre littoral known as **LA MARANA** lies a few kilometres south of Bastia. The beach here offers shady pine woods, restaurants and bars, though the sea is quite polluted. The whole of this part of the coast is divided into holiday residences or sections of beach attached to bars, the latter freely open to the public.

Fed by the rivers Bevinco and Golo, the **Étang de Biguglia** is the largest lagoon in Corsica, and one of its best sites for rare migrant birds. The Roman town of **MARIANA**, just south of the *étang*, can be approached by taking the turning for Poretta airport, 16km along the N193, or the more scenic coastal route through **La Marana**. It was founded in 93 BC as a military colony, but today's houses, baths and basilica are too ruined to be of great interest. It's only the square baptistry, with its remarkable mosaic floor decorated with dancing dolphins and fish looped around bearded figures representing the four rivers of paradise, that is worth seeking out.

Adjacent to Mariana stands the **church of Santa Maria Assunta**, known as **La Canonica**. Built in 1119 close to the old capital of Biguglia, it's the finest of around three hundred churches built by the Pisans in their effort to evange-lize the island. Modelled on a Roman basilica, the perfectly proportioned edifice is decorated outside with Corinthian capitals plundered from the main Mariana site and with plates of Cap Corse marble. Marooned amid muddy fields about 300m to the south of La Canonica is another ancient church, **San Parteo**, built in the eleventh and twelfth centuries over the site of a pagan burial ground. A smaller edifice than La Canonica, it displays some elegant arcading and fine sculpture.

Cap Corse

Until Napoléon III had a coach road built around **Cap Corse** in the nineteenth century, the promontory was effectively cut off from the rest of the island, relying on Italian maritime traffic for its income – hence its distinctive Tuscan dialect. Many Capicursini later left to seek their fortunes in the colonies of the Caribbean, which explains the distinctly ostentatious mansions, or *palazzi*, built by the successful émigrés (nicknamed "les Américains") on their return. For all the changes brought by the modern world, Cap Corse still feels like a separate country, with wild flowers in profusion, vineyards and quiet, traditional fishing villages.

Forty kilometres long and only fifteen across, the peninsula is divided by a spine of mountains called the Serra, which peaks at **Monte Stello**, 1307m above sea level. The coast on the east side of this divide is characterized by tiny ports, or *marines*, tucked into gently sloping rivermouths, alongside coves which become sandier as you go further north. The villages of the western coast are sited on rugged cliffs, high above the rough sea and tiny rocky inlets that can be glimpsed from the corniche road.

The main villages on Cap Corse are connected to Bastia's *gare routière* by **bus**. Services are fairly frequent during the summer, but drop off considerably between October and May. Running up the east coast to Pietracorbara, the Bastia municipal bus company, SAB (☎04.95.31.06.65, ⓦwww.bastiabus .com), lays on between six and nine services from Monday to Saturday in June–Sept, the first departing at 6.30am. Transports Micheli (☎04.95.35.14.64) also runs two daily services all the way Macinaggio. It's advisable to check all timings before departure via the Bastia tourist office or online at ⓦwww .corsicabus.org.

Erbalunga

Built along a rocky promontory 10km north of Bastia, the small port of **ERBALUNGA** is the highlight of the east coast, with aged, pale buildings stacked like crooked boxes behind a small harbour and ruined Genoese watchtower. A little colony of French artists lived here in the 1920s, and the village has drawn a steady stream of admirers ever since. Come summer it's transformed into something of a cultural enclave, with concerts and art events adding a spark to local nightlife. The town is most famous, however, for its Good Friday procession, known as the **Cerca** (Search), which evolved from an ancient fertility rite. Hooded penitents, recruited from the ranks of a local religious brotherhood, form a spiral known as a *Granitola*, or snail, which unwinds as the candlelit procession moves into the village square.

A port since the time of the Phoenicians, Erbalunga was once a more important trading centre than Bastia or Ajaccio. In the eleventh century, with the increasing exportation of wine and olive oil, it became the capital of an independent village-state, ruled by the da Gentile family, who lived in the **palazzu** that dominates place de-Gaulle.

The one **hotel**, the gorgeous *Castel Brando* (☎04.95.30.10.30, ⓦwww .castelbrando.com; April to mid-Oct; ❼), stands at the entrance to the *place*, shaded by a curtain of mature date palms, like the backdrop to a classic Visconti movie. It's an elegant, old, stone-floored *palazzu* with a lovely pool and its own car park. Pick of the harbourside **restaurants** is the renowned *A Le Pirate* (☎04. 95. 33. 24. 20, ⓦwww.restaurantlepirate.com; open Easter–Oct), for whose *haute gastronomie* well-heeled Bastiais flock here throughout the year. Local seafood and meat delicacies, such as braised *cabri* (suckling kid) or lobster tagliatelli served with wild asparagus, dominate their menu (€29–35/€60–90 for lunch/dinner); à la carte courses range from €26 to €75. A more affordable option is *A Piazzetta* (T04. 95. 33. 28. 69), in the tiny square behind the harbour, which does quality pizzas, veal in Cap Corse, excellent *moules-frites* and possibly Corsica's best sorbets; count on €20–25 for three courses, plus wine.

Macinaggio

A port since Roman times, well-sheltered **MACINAGGIO**, 20km north of Erbalunga, was developed by the Genoese in 1620 for the export of olive oil and wine to the Italian peninsula. The Corsican independence leader, Pascal Paoli, landed here in 1790 after his exile in England, whereupon he kissed the ground and uttered the words "*O ma patrie, je t'ai quitté esclave, je te retrouve libre*" ("Oh my country, I left you as a slave, I rediscover you a free man") – a plaque commemorating the event adorns the wall above the ship chandlers. There's not much of a historic patina to the place nowadays, but with its packed **marina** and line of colourful seafront awnings, Macinaggio has a certain appeal, made all the stronger by its proximity to some of the wildest landscape on the Corsican coast. Daily **boat trips** from the marina on board the *San Paulu* (T04.95.35.07.09; €19.50) transport visitors to some of the best of them, as well as the remote islands off the north coast of the cape. Another reason to linger is to sample the superb **Clos Nicrosi** wines, grown in the terraces above the village, which you can taste at the domaine's little shop on the north side of the Rogliano road, opposite the *U Ricordu* hotel.

The least expensive **accommodation** in Macinaggio is the *Hôtel des Îles*, opposite the marina (T04.95.35.43.02; ❸), which also has a serviceable restaurant on its ground floor. All the rooms, though tiny, have showers and toilets; those at the front of the building overlook the port but get noisy at night. Otherwise try the more modern *U Libecciu*, down the lane leading from the marina to the plage de Tamarone (T04.95.35.43.22, Wwww.u-libecciu.com; open April–Oct; ❻); or the pricier three-star *U Ricordu*, on the south side of the road to Rogliano (T04.95.35.40.20, Wwww.hotel-uricordu.com; open March–Sept; ❽), is the most luxurious option hereabouts, with a swimming pool, sauna and tennis courts.

Macinaggio's only **campsite**, *U Stazzu*, lies 1km north of the harbour and is signposted off the Rogliano road (T04. 95. 35. 43. 76; open May to mid-Sept). The ground is like rock, but it's cheap and there's ample shade and easy access to the nearby **beach**; the site's little café-pizzeria serves particularly good breakfasts and pizzas.

Besides the hotel **restaurants** listed above, commendable places to eat in Macinaggio include the *Pizzeria San Columbu*, at the end of the port facing out to sea, which does a tasty seafood pizza for under €10. For a taste of local seafood, you won't do better than *Le Vela d'Oro* (T04.95.35.41.46), tucked away down a narrow alleyway running off the little square opposite the marina. Offering menus at around €15–20, they serve mainly capsorsin seafood specialities – such as local crayfish in home-made spaghetti – in a cosy dining room decorated with old nautical maps. The other place worth a try is *Osteria di u Portu* (T04.95.35.40.49; open April–Sept), facing the marina, where you can dine on fish straight off local boats, suckling lamb stew and tender free-range veal – at honest prices.

North of Macinaggio: Site Naturel de la Capandula

North of the town lie some beautiful stretches of sand and clear sea – an area demarcated as the **Site Naturel de la Capandula**. A marked footpath, known as **Le Sentier des Douaniers** because it used to be patrolled by customs officials, threads its way across the hills and coves of the reserve, giving access to an area that cannot by reached by road. The **Baie de Tamarone**, 2km along this path, is a good place for diving and snorkelling. Just behind the beach, the *piste* forks: follow the left-hand track for twenty minutes and you'll come to a stunning arc of turquoise sea known as the **rade de Santa Maria**, site of the isolated Romanesque **Chapelle Santa-Maria**. The bay's other principal landmark is the huge **Tour Chiapelle**, a ruined three-storeyed watchtower dramatically cleft in half and entirely surrounded by water. The **tourist office** in Macinaggio will furnish you with a free **map** and route description of the path. Otherwise get hold of a copy of IGN #4347 OT, which covers the entire route to Centuri-Port (7–8hr).

Centuri-Port

When Dr Johnson's biographer, James Boswell, arrived here from England in 1765, the former Roman settlement of **CENTURI-PORT** was a tiny fishing village, recommended to him for its peaceful detachment from the dangerous turmoil of the rest of Corsica. Not much has changed since Boswell's time: Centuri-Port exudes tranquillity despite a serious influx of summer residents, many of them artists who come to paint the fishing boats in the slightly prettified harbour, where the grey-stone wall is highlighted by the green serpentine roofs of the encircling cottages, restaurants and bars. The only drawback is that you'll find the small beach disappointingly muddy and not ideal for sunbathing (although it is an excellent spot for snorkelling).

Centuri-Port has more **hotels** than anywhere else on Cap Corse. *Hôtel-Restaurant du Pêcheur* (☎04.95.35.60.14; Easter to mid-Nov; ❹), the pink building in the harbour, is among the most pleasant and has a popular restaurant. If it's full, try *Hôtel La Jetée*, to the left on the road as you arrive in Centuri (☎04.95.35.64.46; April–Sept; ❹), whose rooms are ordinary and for the most part without sea views, but the cheapest in the village during high season. The *Vieux Moulin* (☎04.95.35.60.15, ⓦwww.le-vieux-moulin.net; March–Oct; ❺), opposite, is the most stylish option: a converted *maison d'Américain* with a wonderful terrace and attractively furnished en-suite rooms. For **campers**, choice is limited to the rather scruffy *Camping l'Isolettu*, 400m south along the D35 (☎04.95.35.62.81; May–Oct).

Nonza

Set high on a black rocky pinnacle that plunges vertically into the sea, the village of **NONZA**, 18km south of Centuri, is one of the highlights of the Cap Corse shoreline. It was formerly the main stronghold of the da Gentile family, and the remains of their **fortress** are still standing on the overhanging cliff.

The village is also famous for **St Julia**, patron saint of Corsica, who was martyred here in the fifth century. The story goes that she had been sold into slavery at Carthage and was being taken by ship to Gaul when the slavers docked. A pagan festival was in progress, and after Julia refused to participate she was crucified; the gruesome legend relates that her breasts were then cut off and thrown onto a stone, from which sprang two springs, now enshrined in a chapel by the beach. To get there, follow the sign on the right-hand side of the road before you enter the square, which points to **La Fontaine de Ste-Julia**, down by the rocks. Reached by a flight of six hundred steps, Nonza's long grey **beach** is discoloured as a result of pollution from the now disused asbestos mine up the coast. This may not inspire confidence, but the locals insist it's safe (they take their own kids there in summer), and from the bottom you get the best view of the tower, which looks as if it's about to topple into the sea.

The village has two **accommodation** options: a stylish little B&B called *Casa Maria* (℡04.95.37.80.95, Ⓦwww.casamaria-corse.com; ➎), in restored schist house above the square; and the *Casa Lisa* (℡04.95.37.83.52, Ⓦcasalisa .free.fr; ➍), further down the hillside at the bottom fringes of the village, which has equally gorgeous rooms with exposed beams, original tiled floors and shuttered windows looking across the gulf to the Désert des Agriates.

The Nebbio (U Nebbiu)

Taking its name from the thick mists that sweep over the region in winter, the **Nebbio** has for centuries been one of the most fertile parts of the island, producing honey, chestnuts and some of the island's finest wine. Tourism, has so far made little impact on this depopulated area, which comprises the amphitheatre of rippled hills, vineyards and cultivated valleys that converge on St-Florent, half an hour's drive west over the mountain from Bastia. Aside from EU subsidies, the major money earner here is viticulture: the village of **Patrimonio** is the wine-growing hub, with *caves* offering *dégustations* lined up along its main street.

A bishopric until 1790, **St-Florent** is nowdays a chic coastal resort at the base of Cap Corse. It remains the Nebbio's chief town, and is the obvious base for day-trips to the beautifully preserved Pisan church of Santa Maria Assunta, just outside the town, and the **Désert des Agriates**, a wilderness of parched maquis-covered hills whose rugged coastline harbours one of Corsica's least accessible, but most picturesque, beaches.

The principal **public transport** serving the Nebbio is the twice-daily bus from Bastia to St-Florent, operated by Transports Santini (℡04.95.37.02.98). Timings can be checked at Ⓦwww.corsicabus.org, or at the tourist office in St-Florent.

St-Florent and around

Viewed from across the bay, **ST-FLORENT** (San Fiurenzu) appears as a bright line against the black tidal wave of the Tenda hills, the pale stone houses seeming to rise straight out of the sea, overlooked by a squat circular citadelle. It's a relaxing town, with a decent beach and a good number of restaurants, but the key to its success is the **marina**, which is jammed with expensive boats throughout the summer. Neither the tourists, however, nor indeed St-Florent's proximity to Bastia, entirely eclipse the air of isolation conferred on the town by its brooding backdrop of mountains and scrubby desert.

Arrival and information

Bus times vary a little from year to year, but can be checked at the **tourist office**, at the top of the village (July & Aug Mon–Fri 8.30am–12.30pm & 2–7pm, Sat & Sun 9am–noon & 3–6pm; Sept–June Mon–Fri 9am–noon & 2–5pm, Sat 9am–noon; ℡&℻04.95.37.06.04) in the same building as the **post office**, 100m north of place des Portes. There's a small **cyber café** just off the square, on the left (north) side of the road leading to Santa Maria Assunta. The photography shop opposite turning also offers internet access.

Accommodation

St-Florent is a popular resort, and **hotels** fill up quickly, especially at the height of summer when prior booking is essential. A fair number of **campsites** are dotted about the coast, but are packed in August and closed out of season. *Camping Kallisté*, route de la Plage (☎04.95.37.03.08, ⓦwww.camping-kalliste .com; closed Oct–May), is the closest to town and most congenial.

Du Centre rue de Fornellu ☎04.95.37.00.68, ⓕ04.95.37.41.01. Refreshingly unpretentious, old-fashioned place of a kind that's fast disappearing on the island. The modest rooms, all en suite and with showers, are kept impeccably clean by the feisty Mme Casanova. Ask for "*côté jardin*". ❺
De l'Europe place des Portes ☎04.95.37.00. 33, ⓦwww.hotel-europe2.com. Simply refurbished old building in the village centre next to the square, with original flagstone floors and modern comforts. Rooms are on the small side, but all are en suite and well aired, and some overlook the marina. ❺–❻

Maloni On the Bastia road, 2km northeast of town ☎04.95.37.14.30, ⓦwww.malonihotel.com. An excellent little budget hotel, especially popular with bikers, with simple but pleasant en-suite rooms opening on to a leafy garden. The whole place is slightly frayed around the edges, but the tariffs are the lowest for miles. ❸
Maxime route d'Oletta, just off place des Portes ☎04.95.37.05.30, ⓕ04.95.37.13.07. Bright, modern hotel in the centre. Rooms to the rear of the building have French windows and little balconies overhanging a small water channel. No credit cards. ❺

The Town

In Roman times, a settlement called Cersunam – referred to as Nebbium by chroniclers from the ninth century onwards – existed a kilometre east of the present village. Few traces of it remain, and in the fifteenth century it was eclipsed by the port that developed around the new Genoese citadelle. St-Florent prospered as one of Genoa's strongholds, and it was from here that Paoli set off for London in 1796, never to return.

Place des Portes, the centre of town life, has café tables facing the sea in the shade of plane trees, and in the evening fills with strollers and pétanque players. In rue du Centre, which runs west off the square, parallel to the seafront and marina, you'll find some restaurants, a few shops and a couple of wine-tasting places – be sure to sample the sweet, maquis-scented muscat made around here. The fifteenth-century circular **citadelle** can be reached on foot from place Doria at the seafront in the old quarter. Destroyed by Nelson's bombardment in 1794, it was renovated in the 1990s and affords superb views from its terrace.

Just a kilometre to the east of the town off a small road running off place des Portes, on the original site of Cersanum, the **church of Santa Maria Assunta** – the so-called "cathedral of the Nebbio" – is a fine example of Pisan Romanesque architecture. Built of warm yellow limestone, the building has a distinctly barn-like appearance – albeit a superlatively elegant one. Gracefully symmetrical blind arcades decorate the western facade, and at the entrance twisting serpents and wild animals adorn the pilasters on each side of the door. The interior, too, appears deceptively simple. Carved shells, foliage and animals adorn the capitals of the pillars dividing the nave where, immediately to the right, you'll see a glass case containing the mummified figure of St Flor, a Roman soldier martyred in the third century.

Eating

St-Florent is renowned for the seafood from its gulf and there's no better location to enjoy it than down on the quayside, where a handful of swish gourmet places stand alongside standard pizzerias and tourist **restaurants**. With menus from €38, *La Rascasse* (☏04.95.37.06.99) has become renowned for its imaginative spins on local seafood: cream of ray's wing, mussel and chestnut fritters, and lobster sautéed in cured ham with tartlets of warm *brocciu*. In a similar price bracket is the nearby *La Gaffe* (☏04.95.37.00.12; closed Tues, except in July & Aug), where you can order sumptuous devilfish stew on a bed of tagliatelle, with menus at €30 and €40.

Patrimonio (Patrimoniu)

Leaving St-Florent by the Bastia road, the first village you come to, after 6km, is **PATRIMONIO**, centre of the first Corsican wine region to gain *appellation contrôlée* status. Apart from the renowned local muscat, which can be sampled in the village or at one of the *caves* along the route from St-Florent, Patrimonio's chief asset is the sixteenth-century **church of St-Martin**, occupying its own little hillock and visible for kilometres around. The colour of burnt sienna, it stands out vividly against the rich green vineyards. In a garden 200m south of the church stands a limestone **statue–menhir** known as U Nativu, a late megalithic piece dating from 900–800 BC. A carved T-shape on its front represents a breastbone, and two eyebrows and a chin can also be made out.

U Nativu takes pride of place next to the stage at Patrimonio's annual open-air **guitar festival** (🌐www.festival-guitare-patrimonio.com), held in the last week of July next to the church, when performers and music aficionados from all over Europe converge on the village.

The Désert des Agriates

Extending westwards from the Golfe de St-Florent to the mouth of the Ostriconi River, the **Désert des Agriates** is a vast area of uninhabited land, dotted with clumps of cacti and scrub-covered hills. It may appear inhospitable

▲ Patrimonio

now, but during the time of the Genoese this rocky moonscape was, as its name implies, a veritable breadbasket (*agriates* means "cultivated fields"). In fact, so much wheat was grown here that the Italian overlords levied a special tax on grain to prevent any build-up of funds that might have financed an insurrection. Fires and soil erosion eventually took their toll, however, and by the 1970s the area had become a total wilderness.

Numerous crackpot schemes to redevelop the Désert have been mooted over the years – from atomic weapon test zones to concrete Club-Med-style resorts – but during the past few decades the government has gradually bought up the land from its various owners (among them the Rothschild family) and designated it as a protected nature reserve. Nevertheless, species such as the Agriates' rare wild boar remain under threat, mainly from trigger-happy hunters and bush fires.

A couple of rough pistes wind into the desert, but without some kind of 4WD vehicle the only feasible way to explore the area and its rugged coastline, which includes two of the island's most beautiful **beaches**, is by foot. From St-Florent, a pathway winds northwest to **plage de Perajola**, just off the main Calvi highway (N1197), in three easy stages. The first takes around five hours, 30 minutes, and leads past the famous **Martello tower** and much-photographed **plage de Loto** to **plage de Saleccia**, a huge sweep of soft white sand and turquoise sea that was used as a location for the invasion sequences in the film *The Longest Day*. There's a seasonal **campsite** here, *U Paradisu* (℡04.95.37.82.51; mid-June to Sept only). From plage de Saleccia, it takes around three hours to reach the second night halt, **plage de Ghignu**, where a simple *gîte d'étape* (℡04.95.37.09.86) provides basic facilities for €12 per night. The last stretch to Perajola can be covered in under s ix hours.

Note that the only water sources along the route are at Saleccia and Ghignu, so take plenty with you. It's also worth knowing that between May and October, **excursion boats**, leaving throughout the day from the jetty in St-Florent marina (€12 return), ferry passengers across the gulf to and from plage de Loto. If you time your walk well, you can pick one up for the return leg back to town.

The Balagne (A Balagna)

The **Balagne**, the region stretching west from the Ostriconi valley as far as the red-cliffed wilderness of Scandola, has been renowned since Roman times as "Le Pays de l'Huile et Froment" (Land of Oil and Wheat). Backed by a wall of imposing, pale grey mountains, the characteristic outcrops of orange granite punctuating its spectacular coastline shelter a string of idyllic beaches, many of them sporting ritzy marinas and holiday complexes. These, along with the region's two honeypot towns, **L'Île Rousse** and **Calvi**, get swamped in summer, but the scenery more than compensates. In any case, Calvi, with its cream-coloured citadelle, breathtaking white-sand bay and mountainous backdrop, should not be missed.

L'Île Rousse

Developed by Pascal Paoli in the 1760s as a "gallows to hang Calvi", the port of **L'ÎLE ROUSSE** (Isula Rossa) simply doesn't convince as a Corsican town, its palm trees, smart shops, neat flower gardens and colossal pink seafront hotel creating an atmosphere that has more in common with the French Riviera. Pascal Paoli had great plans for his new town on the Haute-Balagne coast, which was laid out from scratch in 1758 as a port to export the olive oil produced in the region. A large part of the new port was built on a grid system, featuring lines of straight parallel streets quite at odds with the higgledy-piggledy nature of most Corsican villages and towns. Thanks to the busy trading of wine and oil, it soon began to prosper and, two and a half centuries later, still thrives as a successful port. These days, however, the main traffic consists of holiday-makers, lured here by brochure shots of the nearby beaches. This is officially the hottest corner of the island, and the town is thus deluged by German and Italian sun-worshippers in July and August. Given the proximity of Calvi, and so much unspoilt countryside, it's hard to see why you should want to stop here for more than a couple of hours.

Arrival and information

The **train station** (T04.95.60.00.50) is on route du Port, 500m south of where the ferries arrive. The Bastia–Calvi **bus** stops just south of place Paoli in the town's main thoroughfare, avenue Piccioni. The CFC office is on avenue J. Calizi (T04.95.60.09.56), and the **tourist office** on the south side of place Paoli (April–June & Sept–Oct Mon–Fri 9am–noon & 2–5pm; July & Aug daily 9am–1pm & 2.30–7.30pm; T04.95.60.04.35, Wwww.ot-ile-rousse.fr). For **internet** access, go to Movie Stores (Mon–Sat 10am–2am), diagonally opposite the supermarket on the crossroads where the Route Nationale cuts through the centre of town.

Accommodation

L'Île Rousse fills up early in the year and it can be difficult to find a **hotel** at any time from May to October. Most places are modern buildings, more functional than personable. The town has two main **campsites**: *Les Oliviers*, 1km east (T04.95.60.19.92), and *Le Bodri* (T04.95.16.19.70, Wwww.campinglebodri .com), 3km west off the main Calvi road. The latter site, which is slap on a beach, can be reached direct by rail – ask for "l'arrêt Bodri".

Hotels

Le Grillon 10 av Paul-Doumer T04.95.60.00.49, F04.95.60.43.69. The best cheap hotel in town, just 1km from the centre on the St-Florent/Bastia road. Nothing special, but quiet and immaculately clean. April–Oct. **4**

De la Puntella rte du Port T04.95.60.04.34, F04.95.60.40.87. Smart little "studios" (rooms with four beds, kitchenette and bathroom), which are usually booked on a weekly basis during Aug; particularly good value for families. Ample parking too. **5**

Santa Maria rte du Port T04.95.63.05.05, Wwww.hotelsantamaria.com. Next to the ferry port, this is one of the larger and best-value three-star places. Their recently refurbished, a/c rooms have small balconies or patios opening onto a garden and pool, and there's exclusive access to a tiny pebble beach. **6**

Splendid 4 bd Valéry-François T04.95.60.00.24, Wwww.le-splendid-hotel.com. Well-maintained, 1930s-style building with a small swimming pool and some sea views from upper floors; very reasonable tariffs, given the location. April to mid-Nov. **6**

The town and beaches

All roads in L'Île Rousse lead to **place Paoli**, a shady square that's open to the sea and has as its focal point a fountain surmounted by a bust of "U Babbu di u Patria" (Father of the Nation), one of many local tributes to Pascal Paoli. There's a Frenchified covered **market** at the entrance to the square, which hosts a popular artisan-cum-antiques sale on Saturday mornings, while on the west side rises the grim facade of the **church of the Immaculate Conception**.

To reach the **Île de la Pietra**, the islet that gives the town its name, continue north, passing the station on your left. Once over the causeway connecting the islet to the mainland, you can walk through the crumbling mass of red granite as far as the lighthouse at the far end, from where the view of the town is spectacular, especially at sundown, when you get the full effect of the red glow of the rocks.

Immediately in front of the promenade, the **town beach** is a crowded Côte d'Azur-style strand, blocked by ranks of sun loungers and parasols belonging to the row of lookalike café-restaurants behind it.

Eating and drinking

Though there's an abundance of mediocre **eating** places in the narrow alleys of the old town, a few restaurants do stand out, some offering classic gourmet menus and others serving superb fresh seafood. The best cafés are found under the plane trees lining the southern side of place Paoli.

L'Escale rue Notre Dame ☎04.95.60.10.53. Giant fresh mussels, prawns and crayfish from the east coast *étangs* are the thing here, served in various *formules* and menus (€15–25) on a spacious terrace looking across the *micheline* line to the bay. Brisk, courteous service, copious portions and for once the house white (by the glass or *pichet*) is palatable. The *menu pêcheur* (a mixed platter) is especially good value.

L'Ostéria place Santelli ☎04.95.60.08.39. On a quiet backstreet in the old quarter, this established Corsican speciality restaurant offers an excellent set

menu (€18), featuring delicious courgette fritters, *soupe de nos villages*, tarragon-scented *gratin d'aubergines*, stuffed sardines and fresh pan-fried prawns. You can sit in a vaulted room adorned with farm implements or on the shaded terrace.

U Libecciu Rue Notre Dame, just behind the covered market ☎04.95.60.13.82, ⊛www .ulibecciu.com. Trendsetting designer decor and gourmet cuisine to match, served in a little bar-restaurant just off the square. Specialities include king prawns in house pasta and seafood *feuillté* – and there's even a chocolate fountain. Count on €30–50 per head for three courses.

Calvi

Seen from the water, **CALVI** is a beautiful spectacle, with its three immense bastions topped by a crest of ochre buildings, sharply defined against a hazy backdrop of mountains. Twenty kilometres west along the coast from L'Île Rousse, the town began as a fishing port on the site of the present-day *ville basse* below the citadelle, and remained just a cluster of houses and fishing shacks until the Pisans conquered the island in the tenth century. Not until the arrival of the Genoese, however, did the town become a stronghold when, in 1268, Giovaninello de Loreto, a Corsican nobleman, built a huge citadelle on the windswept rock overlooking the port and named it Calvi. A fleet commanded by Nelson launched a brutal two-month attack on the town in 1794; he left saying he hoped never to see the place again, and very nearly didn't see anywhere else again, having sustained the wound that cost him his sight in one eye.

The French concentrated on developing Ajaccio and Bastia during the nineteenth century, and Calvi became primarily a military base, used as a point for smuggling arms to the mainland in World War II. A hangout for European glitterati in the 1950s, the town these days has the ambience of a slightly kitsch Côte d'Azur resort, whose glamorous marina, souvenir shops and fussy boutiques jar with the down-to-earth villages of its rural hinterland. It's also an important base for the French Foreign Legion's parachute regiment, the 2ᵉ REP, and immaculately uniformed legionnaires are a common sight around the bars lining avenue de la République.

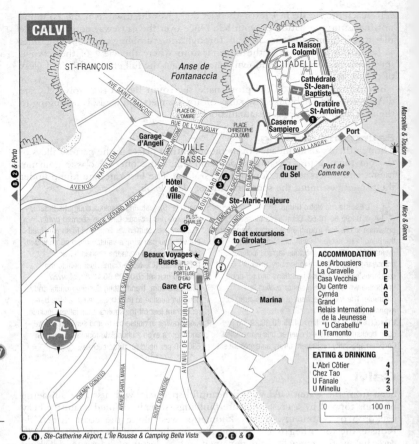

CALVI

ST-FRANÇOIS

Anse de
Fontanaccia

La Maison
Colomb

CITADELLE

Cathédrale
St-Jean-
Baptiste

Oratoire
St-Antoine

Caserne
Sampiero

Port

AVE SAINT-FRANÇOIS

PLACE DE
L'OMBRE

RUE DE L'URUGUAY

PLACE
CHRISTOPHE
COLOMB

R. COLOMB

Garage
d'Angeli

VILLE
BASSE

QUAI LANDRY

AVENUE NAPOLÉON

Hôtel
de
Ville

BOULEVARD WILSON

Tour
du Sel

Port de
Commerce

AVENUE GÉRARD MARCHÉ

Ste-Marie-Majeure

QUAI LANDRY

RUE CLÉMENCEAU

PL. ST-
CHARLES

RUE CLÉMENCEAU

Boat excursions
to Girolata

Beaux Voyages
Buses

PL.
DE LA
PORTEUSE
D'EAU

Gare CFC

Marina

AVENUE SANTA MARIA

AVENUE SANTA MARIA

AVENUE DE LA RÉPUBLIQUE

CHEMIN DONATEO

ROUTE DE SANTORE

N

Marseille & Toulon

Nice & Genoa

B, 2 & Porto

ACCOMMODATION
Les Arbousiers   F
La Caravelle   D
Casa Vecchia   E
Du Centre   A
Cyrnéa   G
Grand   C
Relais International
  de la Jeunesse
  "U Carabellu"   H
Il Tramonto   B

EATING & DRINKING
L'Abri Côtier   4
Chez Tao   1
U Fanale   2
U Minellu   3

0   100 m

G, H, Ste-Catherine Airport, L'Île Rousse & Camping Bella Vista ▼ D, E & F

Arrival and information

Ste-Catherine airport lies 7km south of Calvi (℡04.95.65.88.88, ⓦwww
.calvi.aeroport.fr); the only public transport into town is by **taxi**, which
shouldn't cost more than €17 weekdays (or €22 on weekends). The **train
station** (℡04.95.65.00.61) is on avenue de la République, close to the marina,
where you'll find the **tourist office** on quai Landry (mid-June to Sept daily
9am–7pm; Oct to mid-June Mon–Fri 9am–noon & 2–5.30pm, Sat 9am–noon;
℡04.95.65.16.67, ⓦwww.balagne-corsica.com). **Buses** from Bastia and towns
along the north coast stop outside the train station on place de la Porteuse
d'Eau, whereas those from Porto pull in behind the marina.

Ferries, including NGV hydrofoils, dock at the Port de Commerce at the
foot of the citadelle. Tramar (aka "CCR"), agents for **SNCM**, are on the quai
Landry (℡04.95.65.01.38); Corsica Ferries' office is over in the Port de
Commerce (℡04.95.65.43.21). You can **rent bicycles** from Garage d'Angeli,
rue Villa-Antoine, on the left just west of place Christophe-Colomb
(℡04.95.65.02.13, ⓦwww.garagedangeli.com) from €13 per day. Take along
your credit card or passport, which they'll need to secure the deposit.

Accommodation

Accommodation is easy to find in Calvi except during the jazz festival (third week of June). Hotels range from inexpensive pensions to luxury piles with pools and sweeping views of the bay. If you're on a tight budget, take your pick from the town's two excellent **hostels**, or the dozen **campsites** within walking distance of the centre.

Hotels

Les Arbousiers route de Pietra-Maggiore ☎04.95.65.04.47, ℻04.95.65.26.14. Large, fading pink place set back from the main road, 1km south of town and 150m from the beach, with rooms ranged around a quiet courtyard. ❹

La Caravelle Marco Plage, 1km south of centre ☎04.95.65.95.50, ⓦwww.hotel-la-caravelle.com. An impeccably clean, modern hotel virtually on the beach, with ground floor rooms set around a garden; those on the first floor are more luxurious. Buffet breakfasts served on a sunny patio, and there's a nice bar-restaurant. Good value considering the location, quality of the property and service. ❼

Casa Vecchia route de Santore ☎04.95.65.09.33, ⓦwww.hotel-casa-vecchia.com. Small chalets set in a leafy garden, 500m east of town, and 200m from the beach. Half board obligatory in July & Aug. Friendly management. Open May–Sept. ❹

Du Centre 14 rue Alsace-Lorraine ☎04.95.65.02.01. Old-fashioned *pension*, with a welcoming owner, occupying a former police barracks in a narrow, pretty street near Église Ste-Marie-Majeure and harbourside. Its rooms are large for the price, but plain with shared WC. The cheapest option in town by a long chalk. ❷

Cyrnea route de Bastia ☎04.95.65.03.35, ⓦwww.hotelcyrnea.com. Large budget hotel, a twenty-minute walk south of town, and 300m from the beach. Good-sized rooms for the price, all with bathrooms and balconies (ask for one with "*vue montagne*" to the rear). Outstanding value for money, especially in high season. Open April–Nov. ❹

Grand 3 bd Wilson ☎04.95.65.09.74, ⓦwww.grand-hotel-calvi.com. Wonderful old luxury hotel in the centre of town, with original *fin-de-siècle* furniture and fittings. The rooms, though somewhat dowdy and in need of a lick of paint, are huge, and many have good views (as does the breakfast salon, which looks over the rooftops of the old quarter). Smaller-than-average tariff increases in high season. April–Oct. ❺

Il Tramonto rte de Porto ☎04.95.65.04.17, ⓦwww.hotel-iltramonto.com. Another excellent little budget hotel, with clean, comfortable and light rooms. Definitely try for one with "*vue mer*", which have little terraces and superb views over Punta de la Revellata. ❸

Hostels and campsites

Relais International de la Jeunesse "U Carabellu" 4km from the centre of town on rte Pietra-Maggiore ☎04.95.65.14.16 or 04.93.81.27.63. Follow the N197 for 2km, turn right at the sign for Pietra-Maggiore, and the hostel – two little houses with spacious, clean dormitories at €16 per bed (or €25 with breakfast), looking out over the gulf – is in the village another 2km further on (along a track that's impassable for cars). Phone ahead to make sure it's open. May–Oct.

Camping Bella Vista rte de Pietra-Maggiore, 1km southeast of the centre (700m inland from the beach) ☎04.95.65.11.76, ⓦwww.camping-bellavista.com. The best option for backpackers as it's much closer to the centre of town than the competition – though you pay a couple of euros per night extra for the privilege. Plenty of shade, nice soft ground and clean toilet blocks. Closed Nov–March.

The town and citadelle

Social life in Calvi focuses on the restaurants and cafés of the **quai Landry**, a spacious seafront walkway linking the marina and the port. This is the best place to get the feel of the town, but the majority of Calvi's sights are found within the walls of the **citadelle**.

"Civitas Calvis Semper Fidelis" – always faithful – reads the inscription of the town's motto, carved over to the ancient gateway into the fortress. Once through the entrance you come immediately to the enormous **Caserne Sampiero**, formerly the governor's palace. Built in the thirteenth century, when the great round tower was used as a dungeon, the castle is currently used for military purposes, and therefore closed to the public. The best way of seeing the rest of the citadelle is to follow the ramparts, which connect the three immense bastions. From each bastion the views across the sea, the Balagne and the Cinto Massif are magnificent.

Within the walls the houses are tightly packed along tortuous stairways and narrow passages that converge on the place d'Armes. Dominating the square is the **Cathédrale St-Jean-Baptiste**, set at the highest point of the promontory. This chunky ochre edifice was founded in the thirteenth century, but was partly destroyed during the Turkish siege of 1553 and then suffered extensive damage twelve years later, when the powder magazine in the governor's palace exploded. It was rebuilt in the form of a Greek cross. The church's great treasure is the **Christ des Miracles**, housed in the chapel on the right of the choir; this crucifix was brandished at marauding Turks during the 1553 siege, an act which reputedly saved the day.

To the north of place d'Armes in rue de Fil stands **La Maison Colomb**, the shell of a building which Calvi believes – as the plaque on the wall states – was Christopher Columbus's birthplace, though the claim rests on pretty tenuous, circumstantial evidence. The house itself was destroyed by Nelson's troops during the siege of 1794, but as recompense a statue was erected in 1992, the 500th anniversary of Columbus's "discovery" of America; the date of this historic landfall, October 12, is now a public holiday in Calvi.

Calvi's outstanding **beach** sweeps right round the bay from the end of quai Landry, but most of the first kilometre or so is owned by bars which rent out sun loungers for a hefty price. To avoid these, follow the track behind the sand, which will bring you to the start of a more secluded stretch. The sea might not be as sparklingly clear as at many other Corsican beaches, but it's warm, shallow and free of rocks.

Eating and drinking

Eating is a major pastime in Calvi, and you'll find restaurants and snack bars on almost every street. Fish restaurants predominate in the marina, where – at a price – you can eat excellent seafood fresh from the bay. **Cafés**, fronted with fashionable parasols and teak furniture, line the marina, becoming more expensive the nearer they are to the foot of the citadelle.

Cafés and bars

Chez Tao rue St-Antoine, in the citadelle ☎04.95.65.00.73. Legendary nightclub, opened in the wake of the Bolshevik Revolution by a Muslim White Russian, and long the haunt of the Riviera's glitterati. Now turned into a pricey piano bar serving fussy nouvelle cuisine and local fish dishes, costing around €30–35 à la carte. June–Sept 7pm–midnight.

Restaurants

L'Abri Côtier On quai Landry, but entrance on rue Joffre ☎04.95.65.12.76. Mostly seafood dishes (such as sea bass with fennel) and pizzas (from €13), served on a lovely terrace looking out to sea. Their set menus (€23–35) and *suggestions du jour* are invariably the best deals.

U Fanale rte de Porto, just outside the centre of town on the way to Punta de la

Revellata ☎04.95.65.18.82. Worth the walk out here for their delicious, beautifully presented Corsican specialities – mussels or lamb simmered in ewe's cheese and white wine, a fine *soupe Corse*, and melt-in-the-mouth *fiadone* (traditional flan). Menus €25 plus a full à la carte choice, and pizzas from €10. You can dine outside in the garden or inside their *salle panoramique*, with views across the bay to Punta de la Revellata.

U Minellu Off bd Wilson, nr Ste-Marie-Majeure. Wholesome Corsican specialities served in a narrow stepped alley, or on a shady terrace with pretty mosaic tables. Their menu features baked lamb, *cannelloni al brocciu*, spider crab dressed "*à la Calvaise*", and a cheese platter – good value at €22.

Winding some 170km from Calenzana (12km from Calvi) to Conca (22km from Porto-Vecchio), the **GR20** is Corsica's most demanding long-distance footpath. Only one-third of the estimated 17,000 hikers who start it each season complete all sixteen stages (*étapes*), which can be covered in ten to twelve days if you're in good physical shape – if you're not, don't even think about attempting this route. Marked with red-and-white splashes of paint, it comprises a series of harsh ascents and descents, sections of which exceed 2000m and become more of a scramble than a walk, with stanchions, cables and ladders driven into the rock as essential aids. The going is made tougher by the necessity of carrying a sleeping bag, all-weather kit and two or three days' food with you. That said, the rewards more than compensate. The GR20 takes in the most spectacular mountain terrain in Corsica and along the way you can spot the elusive mouflon (mountain sheep), glimpse lammergeier (a rare vulture) wheeling around the crags, and swim in ice-cold torrents and waterfalls.

The first thing you need to do before setting off is get hold of the Parc Régional's indispensable **Topo-guide**, published by the Fédération Française de la Randonnée Pédestre, which gives a detailed description of the route, along with relevant sections of IGN contour maps, lists of refuges and other essential information. Most good bookshops in Corsica stock them, or call at the park office in Ajaccio (see p.1126).

The route can be undertaken in either **direction**, but most hikers start in the north at Calenzana, tackling the most demanding *étapes* early on. The hardship is alleviated by extraordinary mountainscapes as you round the Cinto massif, skirt the Asco, Niolo, Tavignano and Restonica valleys, and scale the sides of Monte d'Oro and Rotondo. At Vizzavona on the main Bastia–Corte–Ajaccio road, roughly the halfway mark, you can call it a day and catch a bus or train back to the coast, or press on south across two more ranges to the needle peaks of Bavella. With much of the forest east of here blackened by fire, hikers in recent years have been leaving the GR20 at Zonza, below the Col de Bavella (served by daily buses to Ajaccio and Porto-Vecchio), and walking to the coast along the less arduous Mare a Mare Sud trail.

Accommodation along the route is provided by **refuges**, where, for around €11–12, you can take a hot shower, use an equipped kitchen and bunk down on mattresses. Usually converted *bergeries*, these places are staffed by wardens during the peak period (June–Sept). Advance reservation is not possible; beds are allocated on a first-come-first-served basis, so be prepared to bivouac if you arrive late. Another reason to be on the trail soon after dawn is that it allows you to break the back of the *étape* before 2pm, when clouds tend to bubble over the mountains and obscure the views.

The **weather** in the high mountains is notoriously fickle. A sunny morning doesn't necessarily mean a sunny day, and during July and August violent storms can rip across the route without warning. It's therefore essential to take good wet-weather gear with you, as well as a hat, sunblock and shades. In addition, make sure you set off on each stage with adequate **food** and **water**. At the height of the season, many *refuges* sell basic supplies (*alimentation*), but you shouldn't rely on this service; ask hikers coming from the opposite direction where their last supply stop was and plan accordingly (basic provisions are always available at the main passes of Col de Vergio, Col de Vizzavona, Col de Bavella and Col de Verde). The refuge wardens (*gardiens*) will be able to advise you on how much water to carry at each stage.

Finally a word of **warning**: each year, injured hikers have to be air-lifted to safety off remote sections of the GR20, normally because they strayed from the marked route and got lost. Occasionally, fatal accidents also occur for the same reason, so always keep the paint splashes in sight, especially if the weather closes in – don't rely purely on the many cairns that punctuate the route, as these sometimes mark more hazardous paths to high peaks.

The Réserve Naturel de Scandola and Girolata

The **Réserve Naturel de Scandola** takes up the promontory dividing the Balagne from the Golfe de Porto, its name derived from the wooden tiles (*scandules*) that cover many of the island's mountain houses. But the area's roof-like rock formations are only part of its amazing geological repertoire: its stacked slabs, towering pinnacles and gnarled claw-like outcrops were formed by Monte Cinto's volcanic eruptions 250 million years ago, and subsequent erosion has fashioned shadowy caves, grottoes and gashes in the rock. Scandola's colours are as remarkable as the shapes, the hues varying from the charcoal grey of granite to the incandescent rusty purple of porphyry.

The headland and its surrounding water were declared a nature reserve in 1975 and now support significant colonies of sea birds, dolphins and seals, as well as 450 types of seaweed and some remarkable fish such as the grouper, a species more commonly found in the Caribbean. In addition, nests belonging to the rare Audouin's gull are visible on the cliffs, and you might see the odd fish eagle (*Balbuzard pêcheur*) – there used to be only a handful of nesting pairs at one time, but careful conservation has increased their numbers considerably over the past two decades.

Scandola is off-limits to hikers and can be viewed only by **boat** (Colombo Lines ☎04.95.62.32.10, ⓦwww.colombo-line.com), which means taking one of the daily excursions from Calvi or Porto. These leave morning and afternoon from Calvi, and from Porto at various intervals throughout the daytime and early evening (April–Oct), the first two stopping for two hours at Girolata (see below) and returning in the late afternoon. It's a fascinating journey and well worth the steep fare, although it's a good idea to take a picnic if you're on a tight budget, as the restaurants in Girolata are very pricey.

Girolata

Connected by a mere mule track to the rest of the island (1hr 30min on foot from the nearest road), the tiny fishing haven of **GIROLATA**, immediately east of Scandola, has a dreamlike quality that's highlighted by the vivid red of the surrounding rocks. A short stretch of stony beach and a few houses are dominated by a stately watchtower, built by the Genoese later in the seventeenth century in the form of a small castle on a bluff overlooking the cove. For most of the year, this is one of the most idyllic spots on the island, with only the odd yacht and party of hikers to threaten the settlement's tranquillity. From June through September, though, daily boat trips from Porto and Calvi ensure the village is packed during the middle of the day, so if you want to make the most of the scenery and peace and quiet, walk here and stay a night in one of the *gîtes*.

The head of the Girolata trail is at **Bocca â Crocce** (Col de la Croix), on the Calvi–Porto road, from where a clear path plunges downhill through dense maquis and forest to a flotsam-covered cove known as **Cala di Tuara** (30min). The more rewarding of the two tracks that wind onwards to Girolata is the more gentle one running left around the headland, but if you feel like stretching your legs, follow the second, more direct route uphill to a pass.

In Girolata, *La Cabane du Berger* (☎04.95.20.16.98; May–Oct; €36 per person for dorm bed, half board) offers a choice of **accommodation** in dorms or small wood cabins in the garden behind (these accommodate two people); you can also put your tent up here. Meals are served in their quirky wood-carved bar, but the food isn't up to much. The same is true of the other *gîte*, *Le Cormorant*, among the houses at the north end of the cove (☎04.95.20.15.55; July & Aug; €36; half board obligatory), which has eighteen dorm spaces and a small restaurant overlooking the boat jetty. Unless you're staying at one of the *gîtes*, you'll be better off paying a little extra to eat at one of the two restaurants just up the steps. With a terrace overlooking the beach, *Le Bel Ombra* is the pricier of the pair, offering local seafood specialities, including fresh Scandola lobster. *Le Bon Espoir*, next door, is marginally cheaper. Note that neither restaurant accepts credit cards.

Porto (Portu) and around

The overwhelming proximity of the mountains, combined with the pervasive eucalyptus and spicy scent of the maquis, give **PORTO**, 30km south of Calvi, a uniquely intense atmosphere that makes it one of the most interesting places to stay on the west coast. Except for a watchtower erected here by the Genoese in the second half of the sixteenth century, the site was only built upon with the onset of tourism since the 1950s; today the village is still so small that it can become claustrophobic in July and August, when overcrowding is no joke. Off season, the place becomes eerily deserted, so you'd do well to choose your times carefully; the best months are May, June and September.

The crowds and traffic jams tend to be most oppressive passing the famous **Calanches**, a huge mass of weirdly eroded pink rock just southwest of Porto, but you can easily sidestep the tourist deluge in picturesque **Piana**, which overlooks the gulf from its southern shore, or by heading inland from Porto through the **Gorges de Spelunca**. Forming a ravine running from the sea to the watershed of the island, this spectacular gorge gives access to the equally grandiose **Forêt d'Aïtone**, site of Corsica's most ancient Laricio pine trees and a deservedly popular hiking area. Throughout the forest, the river and its tributaries are punctuated by strings of *piscines naturelles* (natural swimming pools) – a refreshing alternative to the beaches hereabouts, which tend to be crammed in peak season. If you're travelling between Porto and Ajaccio, a worthwhile place to break the journey is the clifftop village of **Cargèse** where the two main attractions are the Greek church and spectacular beach.

Arrival and information

Buses from Calvi, via Galéria, and from Ajaccio, via Cargèse, pull into the junction at the end of route de la Marine, opposite the Banco supermarket, en route to the marina. Timetables are posted at the stops themselves, and at the **tourist office**, down in the marina (May, June & Sept daily 9am–6pm; July & Aug daily 9am–7pm; Oct–April Mon–Fri 9am–5pm; ☎04.95.26.10.55, ⓦwww.porto-tourisme.com), where you can buy *Topoguides* and brochures for hikes in the area. Timetable information and tickets for the **boat excursions** to Scandola, the Calanches and Girolata are available in advance from the operators at their counters around the marina.

Accommodation

Competition between **hotels** is more cut-throat in Porto than in any other resort on the island. During slack periods towards the beginning and end of the season, most places engage in a full-on price war, pasting up cheaper tariffs than their neighbours – all of which is great for punters. In late July and August, however, the normal high rates prevail. Photos of all the hotels listed below are posted on the local tourist office website (see "Arrival and information", above).

Hotels

Le Belvédère Porto marina ☎ 04.95.26.12.01, ⓦ www.hotel-le-belvedere.com. This three-star is the smartest of the hotels overlooking the marina, with great views from its comfortable rooms and terraces of Capo d'Orto. Reasonable rates given the location. ❹

Brise de Mer On the left of rte de la Marine as you approach tower from the village, opposite the telephone booths ☎ 04.95.26.10.28, ⓦ www .brise-de-mer.com. A large, old-fashioned place with very friendly service and a congenial terrace restaurant. Rooms at the back have the best views. April to mid-Oct. ❺

Le Colombo At the top of the village opposite the turning for Ota ☎ 04.95.26.10, ⓦ www.hotelle colombo.com. An informal, sixteen-room hotel overlooking the valley, imaginatively decorated in sea-blue colours with driftwood and flotsam sculpture. ❼

Le Golfe At the base of the rock in the marina ☎ 04.95.26.13.33. Small, cosy and unpretentious;

every room has a balcony with a sea view. Among the cheapest at this end of the village. May–Oct. ❹

Le Maquis At the top of the village just beyond the Ota turning ☎ 04.95.26.12.19, ⓦ www.hotel-lemaquis.com. A perennially popular, well-maintained budget hotel; rooms are basic, but comfortable enough, and they give good off-season discounts. Advance booking recommended; half board obligatory July and Aug. ❺

Campsites

Camping Les Oliviers ☎ 04.95.26.14.49, ⓦ www.camping-oliviers-porto.com. Top-notch two-star site, boasting a huge multi-layered pool. April–Nov.

Camping Sol e Vista At the main road junction near the supermarkets ☎ 04.95.26.15.71, ⓦ www .camping-sol-e-vista.com. A superb location on shady terraces ascending a steep hillside with a small café at the top. Great views of Capo d'Orto cliffs opposite, and immaculate toilet blocks. April–Nov.

The Town

Eucalyptus-bordered **route de la Marine** links the two parts of the resort. The village proper, known as **Vaïta**, comprises a strip of supermarkets, shops and hotels 1km from the sea, but the main focus of activity is the small **marina**, located at the avenue's end. Overlooking the entrance to the harbour is the much-photographed **Genoese Tower** (May–Sept daily 9am–8.45pm; €2.50, or €6.50 for combined entry with the aquarium, see below), a square chimney-shaped structure that was cracked by an explosion in the seventeenth century, when it was used as an arsenal. An awe-inspiring view of the crashing sea and maquis-shrouded mountains makes it worth the short climb. Occupying a converted powder house down in the square opposite the base of the tower is the newly established **Aquarium de la Poudrière** (June–Aug daily 10am–10pm; Sept–May Mon–Sat 10am–7pm; €5.50, or €6.50 for combined ticket with the tower), where you can view the various species of sea life that inhabit the gulf, including grouper, moray eels and sea horses.

The **beach** consists of a pebbly cove south beyond the shoulder of the massive rock supporting the tower. To reach it from the marina, follow the little road that skirts the rock, cross the wooden bridge which spans the River Porto on your left, then walk through the car park under the trees. Although it's rather rocky and exposed, and the sea very deep, the great crags overshadowing the shore give the place a vivid, wild atmosphere.

Eating and drinking

The overall standard of restaurants in Porto is pitiably poor, with overpriced food and indifferent service the norm, particularly during high season. There are, however, a couple of exceptions. At the budget end, *le Maquis*, in the hotel of the same name, serves honest, affordable home cooking in a cosy bar or on a tiny terrace that hangs over the valley. Their good-value €20 menu includes delicious scorpion fish in mussel sauce. Down in the port, *La Mer*, opposite the tower (☎04.95.26.11.27), is the posh option, and one of the finest seafood restaurants in the area, with fish fresh from the gulf, imaginatively prepared and served in an ideal setting. Menus start at €22 and it's best to reserve early for a seat with a view.

The Calanches

The UNESCO-protected site of the **Calanches**, 5km southwest of Porto, takes its name from *calanca*, the Corsican word for creek or inlet, but the outstanding characteristics here are the vivid orange and pink rock masses and pinnacles which crumble into the dark blue sea. Liable to unusual patterns of erosion, these tormented rock formations and porphyry needles, some of which soar 300m above the waves, have long been associated with different animals and figures, of which the most famous is the Tête de Chien (Dog's Head) at the north end of the stretch of cliffs. Other figures and creatures conjured up include a Moor's head, a monocled bishop, a bear and a tortoise.

One way to see the fantastic cliffs of the Calanches is by boat from Porto; excursions leave daily in summer, cost €25 and last about an hour. Alternatively, you could drive along the corniche road which weaves through the granite archways on its way to Piana. Eight kilometres along the road from Porto, the *Roches Bleues* café is a convenient landmark for walkers.

Piana

Picturesque **PIANA** occupies a prime location overlooking the Calanches, but for some reason does not suffer the deluge of tourists that Porto endures. Retaining a sleepy feel, the village comprises a cluster of pink houses ranged around an eighteenth-century church and square, from the edge of which the panoramic views over the Golfe de Porto are sublime.

If you want to **stay**, head straight for *Les Roches Rouges* (☎04.95.27.81.81, Ⓦwww.lesrochesrouges.com; April–Oct; ❺), an elegant old *grand hôtel* rising from the eucalyptus canopy on the outskirts. Having lain empty for two decades, the turn-of-the-century building was restored with most of its original fittings and furniture intact, and possesses loads of *fin-de-siècle* style. The rooms are huge and light, with large shuttered windows, but make sure you get one facing the water. Non-residents are welcome to drop in for a sundowner on the magnificent terrace, or for a meal in the fresco-covered restaurant, whose *menus gastronomiques* (€32, €36 and €68), dominated by local seafood delicacies, are as sophisticated as the ambience. A cheaper alternative is the *Continental*, an old house with high wooden ceilings, stripped wood floors and a leafy garden, on the right as you leave Piana for Porto (☎04.95.27.89.00, Ⓦwww.continentalpiana.com; ❸).

The Gorges de Spelunca

Spanning the 2km between the villages of Ota and Évisa, a few kilometres inland from Porto, the **Gorges de Spelunca** are a formidable sight, with bare orange granite walls, 1km deep in places, plunging into the foaming green torrent created by the confluence of the rivers Porto, Tavulella, Onca, Campi and Aïtone. The sunlight, ricocheting across the rock walls, creates a sinister effect that's heightened by the dark jagged needles of the encircling peaks. The

The rock formations visible from the road are not a patch on what you can see from the waymarked **trails** winding through the Calanches, which vary from easy ambles to strenuous stepped ascents. An excellent leaflet highlighting the pick of the routes is available free from tourist offices. Whichever one you choose, leave early in the morning or late in the afternoon to avoid the heat in summer, and take plenty of water.

The most popular walk is the one to the **Château Fort** (1hr), which begins at a sharp hairpin in the D81, 700m north of the *Café Roches Rouges* (look for the car park and signboard at the roadside). Passing the famous **Tête de Chien**, it snakes along a ridge lined by dramatic porphyry forms to a huge square chunk of granite resembling a ruined castle. Just before reaching it there's an open platform from where the views of the gulf and Paglia Orba, Corsica's third highest mountain, are superb – one of the best sunset spots on the island – but bring a torch to help find the path back.

For a more challenging extension to the above walk, begin instead at the **Roches Rouges café**. On the opposite side of the road, two paths strike up the hill: follow the one on your left nearest the stream (as you face away from the café), which zigzags steeply up the rocks, over a pass and down the other side to rejoin the D81 in around 1hr 15min. About 150m west of the spot where you meet the road is the trailhead for the Château Fort walk, with more superb views.

A small oratory niche in the cliff by the roadside, 500m south of *Café Roches Rouges*, contains a Madonna statue, Santa Maria, from where the wonderful **sentier muletier** (1hr) climbs into the rocks above. Before the road was blasted through the Calanches in 1850, this old paved path, an extraordinary feat of workmanship supported in places by dry-stone banks and walls, formed the main artery between the villages of Piana and Ota. After a very steep start, the route contours through the rocks and pine woods above the restored mill at Pont de Gavallaghiu, emerging after one hour back on the D81, roughly 1.5km south of the starting point. Return by the same path.

most dramatic part of the gorge can be seen from the road, which hugs the edge for much of its length.

ÉVISA's bright orange roofs emerge against a lush background of chestnut forests about 10km from Ota, on the eastern edge of the gorge, and the village makes the best base for hiking in the area. Situated 830m above sea level, it caters well for hikers and makes a pleasant stop for a taste of mountain life – the air is invariably crisp and clear, and the food particularly good.

The best **place to stay** is the rambling *La Châtaigneraie*, on the west edge of the village on the Porto road (T 04.95.26.24.47, W www.hotel-la -chataigneraie.com; April–Oct; ❷). Set amid chestnut trees, this traditional schist and granite building has a dozen smart, cosy rooms (with and without toilets) in an annexe around the back of the main building. On the front side, a pleasant little restaurant serves mountain cooking such as wild boar stew with *pulenta* made from local chestnuts. The young *patronne* is American, so English is spoken. At the other end of the village, *L'Aïtone* (T 04.95.26.20.04, W www.hotel-aitone.com; ❷) is a large country hotel with a wide range of differently priced rooms, a swimming pool and relaxing bar-restaurant that enjoys a reputation both for gastronomic prowess and for its fine views. For **campers**, the *Camping Acciola* (T 04.95.26.23.01), a small site with a café-bar and great panorama over the mountains, lies roughly 3km out of Evisa: take the D84 for 2km, and turn right at the T-junction towards Cristinacce; the site lies another 400m on your left.

Forêt d'Aïtone

Thousands of soaring Laricio pines, some of them as much as 50m tall, make up the **Forêt d'Aïtone**, just a few kilometres east of Évisa. The most beautiful forest in Corsica, it extends over ten square kilometres between Évisa and the Col de Verghio (1477m), the highest point in Corsica traversable by road. Well-worn tourist paths cross the forest at various points, but local wildlife still thrives here.

Some of the oldest pines in the forest are approaching five hundred years old. Fine-grained, strong and very resistant to weathering, the Laricio was highly valued by the Genoese for ships' masts and furniture, and it was they who first built a road down the valley to the coast.

One of the most popular short **walks** goes to the **Belvédère**, a great natural balcony giving magnificent views across the copper-tinted rocks of the Spelunca gorge. To reach it, look for the wide lay-by on the left-hand side of the road, 5km northeast of Evisa. Following the unsurfaced forest track that peels left a little further up the main road, you can also drop down to the **piscine naturelle d'Aïtone**, one of the more accessible bathing spots in the forest, where the river crashes through a series of idyllic pools and falls.

Cargèse (Carghjese)

Sitting high above a deep blue bay on a cliff scattered with olive trees, **CARGÈSE**, 20km southwest of Porto, exudes a lazy charm that attracts hundreds of well-heeled summer residents to its pretty white houses and hotels. The full-time locals, half of whom are descendants of Greek refugees who fled the Turkish occupation of the Peloponnese in the seventeenth century, seem to accept with nonchalance this inundation – and the proximity of a large Club Med complex – but the best times to visit are May and late September, when Cargèse is all but empty.

Two churches stand on separate hummocks at the heart of the village, a reminder of the old antagonism between the two cultures (resentful Corsican patriots ransacked the Greeks' original settlement in 1715 because of the newcomers' refusal to take up arms against their Genoese benefactors). The **Roman Catholic church** was built for the minority Corsican families in 1828 and is one of the latest examples of Baroque with a trompe l'oeil ceiling. The **Greek church**, however, is the more interesting of the two: a large granite neo-Gothic edifice built in 1852 to replace a building that had become too small for its congregation. Inside, the outstanding feature is an unusual iconostasis, a gift from a monastery in Rome, decorated with uncannily modern-looking portraits. Behind it hang icons brought over from Greece with the original settlers – the graceful Virgin and Child, to the right-hand side of the altar, is thought to date as far back as the twelfth century.

The best beach in the area, **plage de Pero**, is 2km north of the village – head up to the junction with the Piana road and take the left fork down to the sea.

Practicalities

There's a **tourist office** on rue Dr-Dragacci (daily: July–Sept 9am–noon & 4–7pm; Oct–June 3–5pm; ☎04.95.26.41.31, ⓦwww.cargese.net), which can help find accommodation and sells tickets for summer boat trips to the Calanches, costing €45. **Buses** for Ajaccio and Porto stop outside the tiny main square in the centre of the village.

There are plenty of hotels to choose from in Cargèse. Overlooking the crossroads at the top of the village, two comfortable midscale options are *Le Continental*

(T04.95.26.42.24; ⑥) and *St Jean* (T04.95.26.46.68, Wwww.lesaintjean
.com; ④). Better still, head down the lane dropping from opposite these last two
places to the wonderful plage de Pero beach, where you'll find the beautifully
situated *Les Lentisques* (T04.95.26.42.34, Wwww.leslentisques.com; ⑥), a
congenial, family-run three-star with a large, breezy breakfast hall and ten simple
rooms (fully en suite and sea-facing). The nearest **campsite**, *Camping Torraccia*
(T04.95.26.42.39), is 4km north of Cargèse on the main road.

A fair number of **restaurants** are scattered about the village, as well as the
standard crop of basic pizzerias, but the most tempting places to eat are down
in the harbour. On a raised deck overlooking the jetty, *Le Cabanon de Charlotte*
serves local seafood in a wooden cabin, with menus at €15–40, or you can go
for their fresh fish of the day.

Ajaccio (Aiacciu)

Edward Lear claimed that on a wet day it would be hard to find so dull a place
as **AJACCIO**, a harsh judgement with an element of justice. The town has none
of Bastia's sense of purpose and can seem to lack a definitive identity of its own,
but it is a relaxed and good-looking place, with an exceptionally mild climate,
and a wealth of smart cafés, restaurants and shops.

Although it's an attractive idea that Ajax, hero of the Trojan War, once
stopped here, the name of Ajaccio actually derives from the Roman *Adjaccium*
(place of rest), a winter stop-off point for shepherds descending from the
mountains to stock up on goods and sell their produce. This first settlement
was destroyed by the Saracens in the tenth century, and modern Ajaccio grew
up around the citadelle founded in 1492. **Napoleon** gave the town international fame, but though the self-designated *Cité Impériale* is littered with
statues and street names related to the Bonaparte family, you'll find the

▲ Fromage Corse

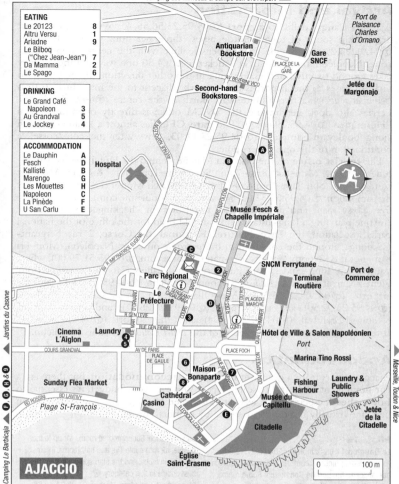

EATING

Le 20123	8
Altru Versu	1
Ariadne	9
Le Bilboq ("Chez Jean-Jean")	7
Da Mamma	2
Le Spago	6

DRINKING

Le Grand Café Napoleon	3
Au Grandval	5
Le Jockey	4

ACCOMMODATION

Le Dauphin	A
Fesch	D
Kallisté	B
Marengo	G
Les Mouettes	H
Napoleon	C
La Pinède	F
U San Carlu	E

Antiquarian Bookstore

Gare SNCF

PLACE DE LA GARE

AV BEVERINI VICO

Second-hand Bookstores

Port de Plaisance Charles d'Ornano

Jetée du Margonajo

Hospital

N

Musée Fesch & Chapelle Impériale

Parc Régional

Le Préfecture

SNCM Ferrytanée

Terminal Routière

PLACE DU MARCHÉ

Port de Commerce

Cinema L'Aiglon

Laundry

Hôtel de Ville & Salon Napoléonien

Port

Marina Tino Rossi

COURS GRANDVAL

AV DE PARIS

PLACE DE GAULE

Maison Bonaparte

Fishing Harbour

Laundry & Public Showers

Sunday Flea Market

Cathédral

Musée du Capitellu

Jetée de la Citadelle

Casino

Plage St-François

Citadelle

Jardins du Casone

Camping Le Barbicaja

Marseille, Toulon & Nice

17

CORSICA | Ajaccio (Aiacciu)

Église Saint-Érasme

AJACCIO

0   100 m

Napoleonic cult has a less dedicated following here than you might imagine: the emperor is still considered by many Ajacciens as a self-serving Frenchman rather than as a Corsican.

Since the early 1980s, Ajaccio has gained an unwelcome reputation for nationalist violence. The most infamous terrorist atrocity of recent decades was the murder, in February 1998, of the French government's most senior official on the island, Claude Erignac, who was gunned down as he left the opera. However, separatist violence rarely (if ever) affects tourists, and for visitors Ajaccio remains memorable for the things that have long made it attractive – its battered old town, relaxing cafés and the encompassing view of its glorious bay.

Arrival and information

Ajaccio's Campo dell'Oro **airport** (℡04.95.23.56.56, ⓦwww.ajaccio.aeroport .fr) is 6km south of town; shuttle buses (three per hour 6.30am–10.45pm; ℡04.95.23.29.41) provide an inexpensive link with the centre, stopping on cours Napoléon, the main street – tickets cost €4.50 one way, and the journey takes around twenty minutes. Heading in the other direction, the best place to pick up buses to the airport is the car park adjacent to the main **bus station** (*terminal routière*), a five-minute walk north of the centre (℡04.95.51.55.45). Ferries also dock nearby, and the SNCM office is directly opposite at quai l'Herminier (℡04.95.29.66.99). The **gare CFC** lies almost a kilometre north along boulevard Sampiero (℡04.95.23.11.03, ⓦwww.ter-sncf.com/corse), a continuation of the quai l'Herminier.

The **tourist office** on the place du Marché, behind the Hôtel de Ville (April–June & Sept Mon–Sat 8am–7pm, Sun 9am–1pm; July & Aug Mon–Sat 8am–8.30pm, Sun 9am–1pm & 4–7pm; Oct–March Mon–Fri 8.30am–6pm, Sat 8.30am–noon; ℡04.95.51.53.03, ⓦwww.ajaccio-tourisme.com), hands out large free glossy maps and posts transport timetables for checking departure times. Anyone planning a long-distance hike should head for the office of the national parks association, the **Parc Naturel Régional de Corse**, 2 rue Sergeant-Casalonga, around the corner from the *préfecture* on cours Napoléon (Mon–Fri 8am–noon & 2–6pm; ⓦwww.parc-naturel-corse.com; ℡04.95.51.79.00), where you can buy Topo-guides, maps, guidebooks and leaflets. Cars can be rented from: Rent-a-Car, at the *Hôtel Kalliste*, 51 cours Napoléon (℡04.95.51.34.45) and the airport (℡04.95.23.56.36); Avis-Ollandini, 1 rue Colonna d'Istria (℡04.95.23.92.50) and the airport (℡04.95.21.28.01); and Hertz-Locasud, 8 cours Grandval (℡04.95.21.70.94) and the airport (℡04.95.23.57.04). **Internet access** is free in the lobby of the *Hotel Kalliste* on cours Napoléon.

Accommodation

Ajaccio suffers from a dearth of inexpensive **accommodation**, but there are a fair number of mid- and upscale places. Whatever your budget, it's essential to **book ahead**, especially for weekends between late May and September, when beds are virtually impossible to come by at short notice.

Hotels

Le Dauphin 11 bd Sampiero ℡04.95.21.12.94, ⓦwww.ledauphinhotel.com. No-frills place above a bar, opposite the port de Commerce. Some rooms are on the grotty side for the price, but their budget options in an adjacent building (with shared showers and toilets) are among the cheapest beds in town. Includes breakfast. ➍

Fesch 7 rue Cardinal-Fesch ℡04.95.51.62.62, ⓦwww.hotel-fesch.com. One of the oldest-established hotels in Ajaccio, and famous as the site of a (bloodless) armed siege in 1980, when it was occupied by fugitive nationalist guerrillas and their French secret service hostages. All rooms are bright and modern with repro antique furniture, a/c and TVs; balconies cost extra. ➎

Kalliste 51 cours Napoléon ℡04.95.51.34.45, ⓦwww.hotel-kalliste-ajaccio.com. Revamped three-storey hotel right in the centre, with plenty of parking space. Soundproofed rooms for up to four people, all with cable TVs and bathrooms. Internet facilities in lobby, and the staff speak English. The best choice in this category. ➎

Marengo 12 bd Mme-Mère ℡04.95.21.43.66, ⓦwww.hotel-marengo.com. A ten-minute walk west of the centre, up a quiet side street off bd Mme-Mère. Slightly boxed in by tower blocks, but it's a secluded, quiet and pleasant small hotel (with only 16 rooms) away from the city bustle. Open mid-March to mid-Nov. ➌

Les Mouettes 9 Cours Lucien-Bonapartere ℡04.95.50.40.40, ⓦwww.hotellesmouettes.fr. Luxuriously renovated nineteenth-century villa off the Routes des Sanguinaires, shaded by mature palms and pines, with direct access to its own private cove. The pricier rooms, facing the pool and sun terrace, enjoy expansive views of the bay and have well shaded balconies. ➏

Napoleon 4 rue Lorenzo-Vero ☏04.95.51.54.00, ⓦwww.hotelnapoleonajaccio.com. Dependable mid-scale hotel slap in the centre of town, up a side road off cours Napoléon, in a recently revamped Second Empire style. Comfortable, very welcoming and good value for the location. ❻

La Pinède rte des Sanguinaires ☏04.95.52.00.44, ⓦwww.la-pinede.com. Most secluded and peaceful of the swish hotels, 4km west of the town centre. It's 300m from the beach (up a narrow lane signposted right off the main road as you head out of town), but with great views of the gulf, a large pool and tennis court. ❼–❽

U San Carlu 8 bd Danielle-Casanova ☏04.95.21.13.84, ⓦwww.hotel-sancarlu.com. Sited opposite the citadelle and close to the beach, this three-star hotel is the poshest option in the old town, with sunny, well-furnished rooms, all fully air-conditioned, and a special suite for disabled guests in the basement – but no parking. ❻

Campsites

Le Barbicaja 4.5km west along the rte des Sanguinaires ☏04.95.52.01.17. Crowded site, but close to the beach and easier to reach by bus (#5 from place de Gaulle) than *Les Mimosas*. Open April–Oct.

Les Mimosas 3km northwest of town ☏04.95.20.99.85, ⓦwww.camping-lesmimosas .com. A shady and well-organized site with clean toilet blocks, friendly management and fair rates. It's a fair trudge if you're loaded with luggage. Open May–Oct.

Napoleon and Corsica

Napoleon Bonaparte was born in Ajaccio in 1769, a year after the French took over the island from the Genoese. They made a thorough job of it, crushing the Corsican leader Paoli's troops at Ponte Nuovo and driving him into exile. Napoleon's father Carlo, a close associate of Paoli, fled the scene of the battle with his pregnant wife in order to escape the victorious French army. But Carlo's subsequent behaviour was quite different from that of his former leader – he came to terms with the French, becoming a representative of the newly styled Corsican nobility in the National Assembly, and using his contacts with the French governor to get a free education for his children.

At the age of 9, Napoleon was awarded a scholarship to the **Brienne military academy**, an institution specially founded to teach the sons of the French nobility the responsibilities of their status, and the young son of a Corsican Italian-speaking household used his time well, leaving Brienne to enter the exclusive **École Militaire** in Paris. At the age of 16 he was commissioned into the artillery. When he was 20 the Revolution broke out in Paris and the scene was set for a remarkable career.

Always an ambitious opportunist, he obtained leave from his regiment, returned to Ajaccio, joined the local Jacobin club and – with his eye on a colonelship in the Corsican militia – promoted enthusiastically the interests of the Revolution. However, things did not quite work out as he had planned, for Pascal Paoli had also returned to Corsica.

Carlo Bonaparte had died some years before, and Napoleon was head of a family that had formerly given Paoli strong support. Having spent the last twenty years in London, **Paoli** was pro-English and had developed a profound distaste for revolutionary excesses. Napoleon's French allegiance and his Jacobin views antagonized the older man, and his military conduct didn't enhance his standing at all. Elected second-in-command of the volunteer militia, Napoleon was involved in an unsuccessful attempt to wrest control of the citadelle from royalist sympathizers. He thus took much of the blame when, in reprisal for the killing of one of the militiamen, several people were gunned down in Ajaccio, an incident which engendered eight days of civil war. In June 1793, Napoleon and his family were chased back to the mainland by the Paolists.

Napoleon promptly renounced any special allegiance he had ever felt for Corsica. He Gallicized the spelling of his name, preferring Napoléon to his baptismal Napoleone. And, although he was later to speak with nostalgia about the scents of the Corsican countryside, he put the city of his birth fourth on the list of places he would like to be buried.

The Town

The core of the **old town** – a cluster of ancient streets spreading north and south of **place Foch**, which opens out to the seafront by the port and the marina – holds the most interest in Ajaccio. Nearby, to the west, **place de Gaulle** forms the modern centre and is the source of the main thoroughfare, **cours Napoléon**, which extends parallel to the sea almost 2km to the northeast. West of place de Gaulle stretches the modern part of town fronted by the **beach**, overlooked at its eastern end by the citadelle.

If you're intending to work your way around all of the town's museums and galleries, it's worth investing in a **Passemusée**. Costing €10, the pass covers all the museums (except A Bandera) and is valid for seven days from the time of your first visit; you can buy them at the tourist office and at the admission desks of the museums themselves.

Around place de Gaulle and the new town

Place de Gaulle (otherwise known as place du Diamant, after the Diamanti family who once owned much of the property in Ajaccio) is the most useful point of orientation, even if it's not much to look at – just a windy concrete platform surrounded by a shopping complex. The only noteworthy thing on the square is the huge, bronze equestrian statue, a pompous lump commissioned by Napoléon III in 1865 showing the first Napoleon in Roman attire, surrounded by his four brothers.

Devotees of Napoleon should take a stroll 1km up **cours Grandval**, the wide street rising west of place de Gaulle and ending in a square, the **Jardins du Casone**, where gaudily spectacular son et lumière shows and costumed re-enactments take place throughout the tourist season. An impressive monument to Napoleon dominates the square, standing atop an appropriately huge, proto-Fascist pedestal inscribed with the names of his battles. Behind the monument lies a graffiti-bedaubed cave where Napoleon is supposed to have frolicked as a child.

Place Foch

Once the site of the town's medieval gate, **place Foch** lies at the heart of old Ajaccio. A delightfully shady square sloping down to the sea, it gets its local name – place des Palmiers – from the row of palms bordering the central strip. Dominating the top end, a fountain of four marble lions provides a mount for the inevitable statue of Napoleon. A humbler effigy occupies a niche high on the nearest wall – a figurine of Ajaccio's patron saint, **La Madonnuccia**, dating from 1656, a year in which Ajaccio's local council, fearful of infection from plague-struck Genoa, placed the town under the guardianship of the Madonna in a ceremony conducted on this spot.

At the northern end of place Foch stands the **Hôtel de Ville** of 1826. Its first-floor is given over to the **Salon Napoléonien** (mid-June to mid-Sept Mon–Sat 9–11.45am & 2–5.45pm; mid-Sept to mid-June Mon–Fri 9–11.45am & 2–4.45pm; €2.80), which contains a replica of the ex-emperor's death mask, along with a solemn array of Bonaparte family portraits and busts. A smaller medal room has a fragment from Napoleon's coffin and part of his dressing case, plus a model of the ship that brought his body back from St Helena.

South of place Foch

The south side of place Foch, standing on the former dividing line between the poor district around the port and the bourgeoisie's territory, gives access to **rue Bonaparte**, the main route through the latter quarter. Built on the promontory rising to the citadelle, the secluded streets in this part of town – with their dusty buildings and hole-in-the-wall restaurants lit by flashes of sea or sky at the end of the alleys – retain more of a sense of the old Ajaccio than anywhere else.

Napoleon was born in what's now the colossal **Maison Bonaparte**, on place Letizia (May–Sept Mon 2–6pm, Tues–Fri 9am–noon & 2–6pm, Sat 9–11.45am & 2–6pm, Sun 9am–noon; Oct–April Mon 2–6pm, Tues–Sat 10am–noon & 2–5pm, Sun 10am–noon; €4), off the west side of rue Napoléon. The house passed to Napoleon's father in the 1760s and here he lived, with his wife and family, until his death. But in May 1793, the Bonapartes were driven from the house by Paoli's partisans, who stripped the place down to the floorboards. Requisitioned by the English in 1794, Maison Bonaparte became an arsenal and a lodging house for English officers until Napoleon's mother Letizia herself funded its restoration. Owned by the state since 1923, the house now bears few traces of the Bonaparte family's existence. One of the few original pieces of furniture left in the house is the wooden sedan chair in the hallway – the pregnant Letizia was carried back from church in it when her contractions started. The up floors house an endless display of portraits, miniatures, weapons, letters and documents.

Napoleon was baptized in 1771 in the **cathedral** (Mon–Sat 8am–1.30pm & 2.30–6pm; no tourist visits on Sun), around the corner in rue Forcioli-Conti. Modelled on St Peter's in Rome, it was built in 1587–93 on a much smaller scale than intended, owing to lack of funds – an apology for its diminutive size is inscribed in a plaque inside, on the wall to the left as you enter. Inside, to the right of the door, stands the font where he was dipped at the age of 23 months; his sister, Elisa Baciochi, donated the great marble altar in 1811. Before you go, take a look in the chapel to the left of the altar, which houses a gloomy Delacroix painting of the Virgin.

A left turn at the eastern end of rue Forcioli-Conti brings you onto boulevard Danielle-Casanova. Here, opposite the citadelle, an elaborately carved capital marks the entrance to the **Musée du Capitellu** (May–Oct Mon–Sat 10am–noon & 2–6pm, Sun 10am to noon; €4), a tiny museum mainly given over to offering a picture of domestic life in nineteenth-century Ajaccio. The house belonged to a wealthy Ajaccien family, the Baciochi, who were related to Napoleon through his sister's marriage. Amid the watercolour landscapes and marble busts, the glass display cases hold the most fascinating exhibits, including a rare edition of the first history of Corsica, written by Agostino Giustiniani, a bishop of the Nebbio who drowned in 1536, and the 1769 Code Corse, a list of laws set out by Louis XV for the newly acquired Corsica.

Opposite the museum, the restored **citadelle**, a hexagonal fortress and tower stuck out on a wide promontory into the sea, is occupied by the military and usually closed to the public. Founded in the 1490s, the fort wasn't completed until the occupation of Ajaccio by Sampiero Corso and the powerful Marshal Thermes in 1553–58. The building overlooks the town **beach**, plage St-François, a short curve of yellow sand which faces the expansive mountain-ringed bay. Several flights of steps lead down to the beach from boulevard Danielle-Casanova.

A little further along the promenade, the car park in front of the municipal sports centre hosts a weekly **flea market** each Sunday morning, starting at around 9am. For the nicest beach within easy walking distance of the town, press on past the exercise area and gendarmerie to **plage Trottel**, which is larger and much cleaner than plage St-François.

North of place Foch

The dark narrow streets backing onto the port to the north of place Foch are Ajaccio's traditional trading ground. Each weekday and Saturday morning (and on Sundays during the summer), the square directly behind the Hôtel de Ville hosts a small **fresh produce market** – a rarity in Corsica – where you can browse and buy top-quality fresh produce from around the island, including myrtle liqueur, wild-boar sauces, ewe's cheese from the Niolo valley and a spread of fresh vegetables, fruit and flowers.

Behind here, the principal road leading north is **rue Cardinal-Fesch**, a delightful meandering street lined with boutiques, cafés and restaurants. Halfway along the street, set back from the road behind iron gates, stands Ajaccio's best gallery, the **Musée Fesch** (July & Aug Mon 1.30–6pm, Tues–Thurs 9am–6.30pm, Fri & Sat 10.30am–12.15pm, Sun 10.30am–6pm; Sept–June Mon 1–5.15pm, Tues–Sun 9.15am–12.15pm & 2.15–5.15pm; €5.35). Cardinal Joseph Fesch was Napoleon's step-uncle and bishop of Lyon, and he used his lucrative position to invest in large numbers of paintings, many of them looted by the French armies in Holland, Italy and Germany. His bequest to the town includes seventeenth-century French and Spanish masters, but it's the Italian paintings that are the chief attraction: Raphael, Titian, Bellini, Veronese and Botticelli all have a place here.

You'll need a separate ticket for the **Chapelle Impériale** (same hours; €1.50), which stands across the courtyard from the museum. With its gloomy monochrome interior the chapel itself is unremarkable, and its interest lies in the crypt, where various members of the Bonaparte family are buried. It was the cardinal's dying wish that all the Bonaparte family be brought together under one roof, so the chapel was built in 1857 and the bodies – all except Napoleon's – subsequently ferried in.

Eating, drinking and nightlife

At mealtimes, the alleyways and little squares of Ajaccio's old town become one large, interconnecting **restaurant** terrace lit by rows of candles. All too often, however, the breezy locations and views of the gulf mask indifferent cooking and inflated prices. With the majority of visitors spending merely a night or two here in transit, only those places catering for a local clientele attempt to provide real value for money. **Bars** and **cafés** jostle for pavement space along cours Napoléon, generally lined with people checking out the promenades, and on place de Gaulle, where old-fashioned cafés and *salons de thé* offer a still more sedate scene. If you fancy a view of the bay, try one of the flashy cocktail bars that line the seafront on boulevard Lantivy, which, along with the casino, a few cinemas and a handful of overpriced clubs, comprise the sum total of Ajaccio's **nightlife**.

Bars and cafés

Le Grand Café Napoleon 10 cours Napoléon, opposite the *préfecture*. Allegedly the oldest café in town, with Second Empire decor and a *troisième âge* clientele. The bar inside was the scene of a famous shootout during World War II, when a cell of key Resistance members was disturbed by the Italian *caribinieri* and forced to flee, guns blazing. The €16 lunch menu ranks among the best midday meal deals in town.

Au Grandval 4 rue Maréchal-Ornano. Lively neighbourhood bar that's famous for its collection of antique photos of Ajaccio (mostly evocative portraits). Only a couple of doors down from *Le Jockey*, which stays open later.

Le Jockey 1 rue Maréchal-Ornano. An Ajaccien institution, renowned above all for its extraordinary list of wines, which you can order by the glass or bottle: Saint Amar, Cantemerle, Morgon, Sancerre, Chasse-Spleen, Châteauneuf du Pâpe and all the local stars. The decor's a quirky but cosy hotch-potch of ephemera and old memorabilia, with a soundtrack to match.

Restaurants

Le 20123 2 rue Roi-de-Rome ☎04.95.21.50.05, ⓦwww.20123.fr. Decked out like a small hill village, complete with *fontaine* and parked Vespa, the decor here's a lot more frivolous than the food: serious Corsican gastronomy featured on a single €34 menu. Top-notch cooking, and organic AOC wine. Closed Mon, except in July & Aug.

Altru Versu 2 rue Jean-Baptiste Marcaggi ☎04.95.50.05.22. Classy Corsican speciality place hosted by one of the island's top young chefs. The menu's mouthwatering array of traditional fare given a gourmet twist: seabass soufflé with *brocciu* and fresh mint, chestnut tagliatelle. À la carte only (count on €45–50 per head, plus wine). Live Corsican music on Fri & Sat. Closed Sun.

Ariadne rte des Sanguinaires, near *Barbicaja* campsite ☎04.95.52.09.63. The oldest and most cheerful of Ajaccio's many beachside *paillotes*, with a terrace opening straight on to the sand. World cuisine dominates the menu and there's usually live music (salsa/reggae/soukous) from 8.30pm. Most main courses €17–27. Open Easter–Oct Tues–Sun. You can get there from place de Gaulle on bus #5.

Le Bilboq ("Chez Jean-Jean") av des Glacis, just off place Foch ☎04.95.51.35.40. The eponymous *patron* (a former fisherman and boxer) of this legendary seafood joint is Ajaccio's undisputed "lobster king", and there's no point in coming here to eat anything but local *langouste*, served grilled with spaghetti. You can dine al fresco on a narrow alley terrace, or inside, regaled by Tino Rossi music (which, unlike the lobster, is definitely an acquired taste). Count on €32 per head for three courses, plus wine.

Da Mamma passage Guinghetta ☎04.95.21.39.44. Tucked away down a narrow passageway connecting cours Napoléon and rue Cardinal-Fesch. Authentic but affordable Corsican cuisine – such as *cannelloni al brocciu*, roast kid and seafood – on set menus from €14 to €29 served in a stone-walled dining room or under a rubber tree in a tiny courtyard.

Le Spago 1bis, Rue Emmanuel Arene ☎04.95.21.15.71. Thanks largely to its idiosyncratic designer decor, this funky little lounge restaurant has become one of Ajaccio's hippest places to eat. Techno DJs and local bands frequently ENLIVEN meals, and the modern Corsican is reasonably priced. Try their tasty *raclette*, or Bonifacien-style baked aubergine; and leave room for one of the tempting desserts. Most mains around €20.

Le Golfe de Valinco

From Ajaccio, the vista of whitewashed villas and sandy beaches lining the opposite side of the gulf may tempt you out of town when you first arrive. On closer inspection, however, **Porticcio** turns out to be a faceless string of leisure settlements for Ajaccio's smart set, complete with tennis courts, malls and flotillas of jet-skis. Better to skip this stretch and press on south along the Route Nationale (RN194) which, after scaling the **Col de Celaccia**, winds down to the stunning **Golfe de Valinco**. A vast blue inlet bounded by rolling, scrub-covered hills, the gulf presents the first dramatic scenery along the coastal highway. It also marks the start of militant and Mafia-ridden south Corsica, more closely associated with vendetta, banditry and separatism than any other part of the island. Many of the mountain villages glimpsed from the roads hereabouts are riven with age-old divisions, exacerbated in recent years by the spread of organized crime and nationalist violence. But the island's seamier side is rarely discernible to the hundreds of thousands of visitors who pass through each summer, most of whom stay around the small port of **Propriano**, at the eastern end of the gulf. In addition to offering most of the area's tourist amenities, this busy resort town lies within easy reach of the menhirs at **Filitosa**, one of the western Mediterranean's most important prehistoric sites.

The Golfe de Valinco region is reasonably well served by public **transport**, with buses running four times per day between Ajaccio and Bonifacio, via Propriano and Sartène. Note, however, that outside July and August there are no services along this route on Sundays.

Propriano (Pruprià)

Tucked into the narrowest part of the Golfe de Valinco, the small port of **PROPRIANO**, 57km southeast of Ajaccio, centres on a fine natural harbour that was exploited by the ancient Greeks, Carthaginians and Romans, but became a prime target for Saracen pirate raids in the eighteenth century, when it was largely destroyed. Redeveloped in the 1900s, it now boasts a thriving marina, and handles ferries to Toulon, Marseille and Sardinia. During the summer, tourists come here in droves for the area's **beaches**. The nearest of these, **plage de Lido**, lies 1km west, just beyond the Port de Commerce, but it's nowhere near as pretty as the coves strung along the northern shore of the gulf around **Olmeto plage**, where an abundance of campsites are on offer (see below). You can reach Olmeto on the three daily buses from Propriano to Porto.

Practicalities

Ferries from the mainland and Sardinia dock in the Port de Commerce, ten-minutes' walk from where the **buses** stop at the top of rue du Général-de- Gaulle, the town's main street. The SNCM office is on quai Commandant-L'Herminier (℡04.95.76.04.36), while the **tourist office** is down in the harbour-master's office in the marina (June & Sept Mon–Sat 9am–noon & 3–7pm; July & Aug daily 8am–8pm; Oct–May Mon–Fri 9am–noon & 2–6pm; ℡04.95.76.01.49, ⓦwww.propriano.net).

There's a reasonable choice of **hotels** in the centre of town, including the high-tech *Loft*, 3 rue Camille-Pietri (℡04.95.76.17.48; ❹), directly behind the port; and the *Bellevue* on avenue Napoléon (℡04.95.76.01.86, ⓦwww .hotels-propriano.com; ❸), overlooking the marina and with the cheapest central rooms. If you have a car, one other place worth trying is the *Arcu di Sole*, 3km northeast on the route de Baracci (℡04.95.76.05.10, ⓦwww .arcudisole.fr.st; ❹), which has a pool and gourmet restaurant; note that half board (€150 for two) is obligatory in July and August.

Campers are well provided for, although the best sites are well out of town: for the best facilities go to *Camping Colomba* (℡04.95.76.06.42, ⓦwww .camping-colomba.com), 3km north along route de Baracci, which has a swimming pool.

Cafés and **restaurants** are concentrated along the marina's avenue Napoléon. For fresh seafood, you can't beat *Terra Cotta*, at 29 avenue Napoléon (℡04 95 74 23 80) – the town's swankiest restaurant, with tables in a cool, Moroccan-style bistrot, or out on a seafront terrace. *Formules* at lunchtime start at €20; count on €50–60 à la carte. A less pricy option is *U Famale*, a funky little pizzeria on the plage du Phare (℡04 95 76 43 06), which occupies a great spot facing the beach and gulf. They do a reasonably priced €24 menu featuring *mussels à la crème*, fish of the day and various *grillades* (or *croustillant d'aubergines* for veggies), and host live Corsican music most evenings.

Filitosa

Set deep in the countryside of the fertile Vallée du Taravo, the extraordinary **Station Préhistorique de Filitosa** (Easter–Oct 9am–sunset, out of season by arrangement only; ℡04.95.74.00.91; €5), 17km north of Propriano, comprises a wonderful array of statue-menhirs and prehistoric structures encapsulating some eight thousand years of history. There's no public transport to the site; vehicles should be parked in the small car park five-minutes' walk from the entrance in the village.

Filitosa was settled by Neolithic farming people who lived here in rock shelters until the arrival of navigators from the east in about 3500 BC. These invaders were the creators of the menhirs, the earliest of which were possibly phallic symbols worshipped by an ancient fertility cult. When the seafaring people known as the Torréens (after the towers they built on Corsica) conquered Filitosa around 1300 BC, they destroyed most of the menhirs, incorporating the broken stones into the area of dry-stone walling surrounding the site's two *torri*, or towers, examples of which can be found all over the south of Corsica. The site remained undiscovered until a farmer stumbled across the ruins on his land in the late 1940s.

Filitosa V looms up on the right shortly after the main entrance to the site. The largest statue-menhir on the island, it's an imposing spectacle, with clearly defined facial features and a sword and dagger outlined on the body. Beyond a sharp left turn lies the *oppidum* or central monument, its entrance marked by the **eastern platform**, thought to have been a lookout post. The cave-like structure sculpted out of the rock is the only evidence of Neolithic occupation and is generally agreed to have been a burial mound. Straight ahead, the Torréen **central monument** comprises a scattered group of menhirs on a circular walled mound, surmounted by a dome and entered by a corridor of stone slabs and lintels. Nobody is sure of its exact function.

Nearby **Filitosa XIII** and **Filitosa IX**, implacable lumps of granite with long noses and round chins, are the most impressive of the menhirs. Filitosa XIII is typical of the figures made just before the Torréen invasion, with its vertical dagger carved in relief – **Filitosa VII** also has a clearly sculpted sword and shield. **Filitosa VI**, from the same period, is remarkable for its facial detail. On the eastern side of the central monument stand some vestigial Torréen houses, where fragments of ceramics dating from 5500 BC were discovered; they represent the most ancient finds on the site, and some of them are displayed in the museum.

The **western monument**, a two-roomed structure built underneath another walled mound, is thought to have been some form of Torréen religious building. A flight of steps leads to the foot of this mound, where a footbridge opens onto a meadow that's dominated by five statue-menhirs arranged in a semicircle beneath a thousand-year-old olive tree. A bank separates them from the quarry from which the megalithic sculptors hewed the stone for the menhirs – a granite block is marked ready for cutting.

The **museum** is a downbeat affair, but the artefacts themselves are fascinating. The major item here is the formidable **Scalsa Murta**, a huge menhir dating from around 1400 BC and discovered at Olmeto. Like other statue-menhirs of this period, this one has two indents in the back of its head, which are thought to indicate that these figures would have been adorned with headdresses. Other notable exhibits are **Filitosa XII**, which has a hand and a foot carved into the stone, and **Trappa II**, a strikingly archaic face.

Sartène (Sartè) and around

Prosper Mérimée famously dubbed **SARTÈNE** *"la plus corse des villes corses"* (the most Corsican of Corsican towns), but the nineteenth-century German chronicler Gregorovius put a less complimentary spin on it when he described it as a "town peopled by demons". Sartène hasn't shaken off its hostile image, despite being a smart, better groomed place than many small Corsican towns. The main square doesn't offer many diversions once you've explored the enclosed old town, and the only time of year Sartène teems with tourists is at Easter for **U Catenacciu**, a Good Friday procession that packs the main square with onlookers.

Close to Sartène are some of the island's best-known **prehistoric sites**, most notably Filitosa, the megaliths of **Cauria** and the **Alignement de Palaggiu** – Corsica's largest array of prehistoric standing stones.

Arrival, information and accommodation

Arriving in Sartène by **bus**, you'll be dropped either at the top of avenue Gabriel-Péri or at the end of cours Général-de-Gaulle. The **tourist office**, on cours Soeur Amélie (summer only Mon–Fri 9am–noon & 2.30–6pm; ⊤04.95.77.15.40), can help find accommodation in the area if the hotels listed below are full. The only **hotel** in Sartène itself is *Les Roches* on avenue Jean-Jaurès, a large family-run place just below the old town (⊤04.95.77.07.61, Ⓦ www.sartenehotel.fr; ❺); it commands panoramic views of the Vallée du Rizzanese and has a restaurant that serves hearty Corsican food. Otherwise try the swanky, Swiss-owned *U San Damianu* (⊤04.95.70.55.41, Ⓦ www .sandamianu.fr; ❻), just across the bridge from the *vielle ville*, beneath the convent of the same name. A three-star occupying a plum spot with spectacular views over the town, it offers all the comforts and amenities you'd expect for a hotel in this class, although it's a bit bland. With a car, the best **B&B** option in the area is the *Domaine de Croccano*, 3km down the D148 (⊤04.95.77.11.37, Ⓦ www.corsenature.com; ❺), a gorgeous eighteenth-century farmhouse hidden in a fold of the Rizzanese Valley, with panoramic views over the Sartenais from its vine-covered terraces. The welcoming hosts also offer horseriding and guided walks. The nearest **campsite**, the very pleasant and friendly *U Farrandu*, lies 1km down the main Propriano road (⊤04.95.73.41.69; closed Nov–April).

The Town

Place Porta – its official name, place de la Libération, has never caught on – forms Sartène's nucleus. Once the arena for bloody vendettas, it's now a well-kept square opening onto a wide terrace. Flanking the north side is the **church of Ste-Marie**, built in the 1760s but completely restored to a smooth granitic appearance. Inside the church, the most notable feature is the weighty wooden cross and chair carried through the town by hooded penitents during the Easter **Catenacciu** procession.

A flight of steps to the left of the **Hôtel de Ville**, formerly the governor's palace, leads past the post office to a ruined **lookout tower**, which is all that remains of the town's twelfth-century ramparts. This apart, the best of the old town is to be found behind the Hôtel de Ville in the **Santa Anna** district, a labyrinth of constricted passageways and ancient fortress-like houses that rarely give any signs of life. Featuring few windows and often linked to their neighbours by balconies, these houses are entered by first-floor doors which would have been approached by ladders – dilapidated staircases have replaced these necessary measures against unwelcome intruders. To the left of rue des Frères-Bartoli are the strangest of all the vaulted passageways, where outcrops of rock block the paths between the ancient buildings.

Sartène's only other cultural attraction is **Musée de la Préhistoire Corse** (closed at time of writing, pending a move to new premises across town, scheduled for 2009; check with the tourist office for timings), Corsica's centre for archeological research. If the old museum was anything to go by, the exhibits will comprise mostly Neolithic and Torréen pottery fragments, with some bracelets from the Iron Age and painted ceramics from the thirteenth to sixteenth centuries.

Eating

For **restaurants**, a dependable choice is the *Restaurant du Cours ("Chez Jean")* at 20 cours Soeur Amélie (℡04.95.77.19.07), which serves wholesome, honest *cuisine sartenaise* (pork stews, stuffed courgettes and local liver sausage grilled over an open fire), as well as inexpensive pizzas, in a stone-walled inn. The house menus are priced around €22. For more refined local gastronomy, head down the mountainside to the *Auberge Santa Barbara* (℡04.95.77.09.66), 2km out of town on the Propriano road, where you can enjoy fine, authentic Sartenais dishes from both the coast and interior, served in a lovely garden. Seafood lovers should try the bream with aubergine caviar or cuttlefish in red wine; and leave room for the *flan grandemère*. **Cafés** cluster around place Porta, and are great places for crowd-watching.

The megalithic sites

Sparsely populated today, the rolling hills of the southwestern corner of Corsica are rich in prehistoric sites. The megaliths of **Cauria**, standing in ghostly isolation 10km southwest from Sartène, comprise the Dolmen de Fontanaccia, the best-preserved monument of its kind on Corsica, while the nearby alignments of **Stantari** and **Renaggiu** have an impressive congregation of statue-menhirs.

More than 250 menhirs can be seen northwest of Cauria at **Palaggiu**, another rewardingly remote site. Equally wild is the coast hereabouts, with deep clefts and coves providing some excellent spots for diving and secluded swimming.

Cauria

To reach the **Cauria megalithic site**, you need to turn off the N196 about 2km outside Sartène, at the Col de l'Albitrina (291m), taking the D48 towards Tizzano. Four kilometres along this road a left turning brings you onto a winding road through maquis, until eventually the **Dolmen de Fontanaccia** comes into view on the horizon, crowning the crest of a low hill amidst a sea of maquis. A blue sign at the parking space indicates the track to the dolmen, a fifteen-minute walk away.

Known to the locals as the **Stazzona del Diavolu** (Devil's Forge), a name that does justice to its enigmatic power, the Dolmen de Fontanaccia is in fact a burial chamber from around 2000 BC. This period was marked by a change in burial customs – whereas bodies had previously been buried in stone coffins in the ground, they were now placed above, in a mound of earth enclosed in a stone chamber. What you see today is a great stone table, comprising six huge granite blocks nearly 2m high, topped by a stone slab that remained after the earth eroded away.

The twenty "standing men" of the **Alignement de Stantari**, 200m to the east of the dolmen, date from the same period. All are featureless, except two which have roughly sculpted eyes and noses, with diagonal swords on their fronts and sockets in their heads where horns would probably have been attached.

Across a couple of fields to the south is the **Alignement de Renaggiu**, a gathering of forty menhirs standing in rows amid a small shadowy copse, set against the enormous granite outcrop of Punta di Cauria. Some of the menhirs have fallen, but all face north to south, a fact that seems to rule out any connection with a sun-related cult.

Palaggiu

To reach the **Alignement de Palaggiu**, the largest concentration of menhirs in Corsica, regain the D48 and head southwards past the Domaine la Mosconi vineyard (on your right, 3km after the Cauria turn-off), 1500m beyond which a green metal gate on the right side of the road marks the turning. From here a badly rutted dirt track leads another 1200m to the stones, lost in the maquis, with vineyards spread over the hills in the half-distance. Stretching in straight lines across the countryside like a battleground of soldiers, the 258 menhirs include three statue-menhirs with carved weapons and facial features – they are amid the first line you come to. Dating from around 1800 BC, the statues give few clues as to their function, but it's a reasonable supposition that proximity to the sea was important – the famous Corsican archeologist Roger Grosjean's theory is that the statues were some sort of magical deterrent to invaders.

Bonifacio (Bonifaziu)

BONIFACIO enjoys a superbly isolated location at Corsica's southernmost point, a narrow peninsula of dazzling white limestone creating a town site unlike any other. The much-photographed **haute ville**, a maze of narrow streets flanked by tall Genoese tenements, rises seamlessly out of sheer cliffs that have been hollowed and striated by the wind and waves, while on the landward side the deep cleft between the peninsula and the mainland forms a perfect natural harbour. A haven for boats for centuries, this inlet is nowadays a chic marina that attracts yachts from around the Med. Separated from the rest of the island by a swathe of dense maquis, Bonifacio has maintained a certain temperamental

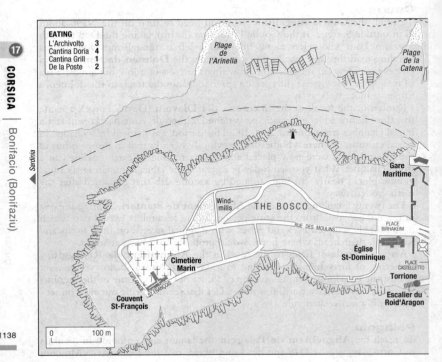

EATING
L'Archivolto 3
Cantina Doria 4
Cantina Grill 1
De la Poste 2

Plage de l'Arinella

Plage de la Catena

Gare Maritime

Windmills

THE BOSCO

RUE DES MOULINS

PLACE BIRHAKEIM

Cimetière Marin

Église St-Dominique

PLACE CASTELLETTO

Torrione

Couvent St-François

Escalier du Roi d'Aragon

ESPLANADE ST-FRANÇOIS

0   100 m

detachment from the rest of Corsica, and is distinctly more Italian than French in atmosphere. The town retains Renaissance features found only here, and its inhabitants have their own dialect based on Ligurian, a legacy of the days when this was practically an independent Genoese colony.

Such a place has its inevitable drawbacks: exorbitant prices, overwhelming crowds in August and a commercial cynicism that's atypical of Corsica as a whole. However, the old town forms one of the most arresting spectacles in the Mediterranean, easily transcending all the tourist frippery that surrounds it, and warrants at least a day-trip. If you plan to come in peak season, try to get here early in the day before the bus parties arrive at around 10am.

Arrival and information

Figari **airport**, 17km north of Bonifacio (℡04.95.71.10.10), handles flights from mainland France and a few charters from the UK. There's a seasonal **bus** service operated by Transports Rossi (℡04.95.71.00.11) that in theory should meet incoming flights, stopping at Bonifacio en route to Porto-Vecchio; otherwise, your only option is to take a taxi into town – around €45–50. If you're coming by bus from other parts of the island you'll be dropped at the car park by the marina, close to most of the hotels. The **tourist office** is up in the *haute ville*, in the Fort San Nicro at the bottom of rue F. Scamaroni (July–Sept daily 9am–8pm; Oct–June Mon–Fri 9am–12.30pm & 2–5.15pm; ℡04.95.73.11.88, ⓦwww.bonifacio.fr); they can check for you which hotels have vacancies. **Cars** may be rented from Avis, quai Banda del Ferro (℡04.95.73.01.28); Citer, quai

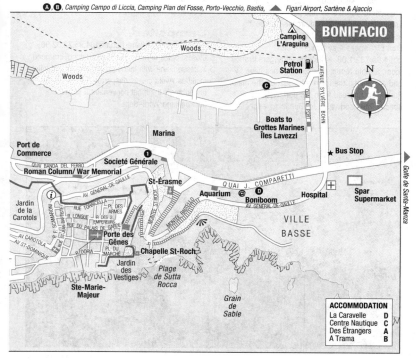

Ⓐ,Ⓑ, Camping Campo di Liccia, Camping Pian del Fosse, Porto-Vecchio, Bastia, ▲ Figari Airport, Sartène & Ajaccio

BONIFACIO

Golfe de Santa-Manza

ACCOMMODATION
La Caravelle   D
Centre Nautique   C
Des Étrangers   A
A Trama   B

Noel-Beretti (☎04.95.73.13.16); Hertz, quai Banda del Ferro (☎04.95.73.06.41). All of the above also have branches at the airport. If you need to change money, note that Bonifacio's only **ATM**, at the Société Générale on the quai J. Comparetti, frequently runs out of cash, so get there early in the day or you'll be at the mercy of the rip-off bureaux de change dotted around the town. *Bomiboom.com*, also on quai Comparetti, offers pricey **internet** access.

Accommodation

Finding a **place to stay** can be a chore, as Bonifacio's hotels are quickly booked up in high season; for a room near the centre, reserve well in advance. Better still, save yourself the trouble, and a considerable amount of money, by finding a room somewhere else and travelling here for the day; tariffs in this town are the highest on the island. The same applies to the large campsites dotted along the road to Porto-Vecchio, which can get very crowded.

Hotels

La Caravelle 35 quai J. Comparetti ☎04.95.73.00.03, ⓦwww.hotel-caravelle-corse .com. Long-established place in prime location on the quayside, whose standard rooms are on the small side for the price. ❼

Centre Nautique on the marina ☎04.95.73.02.11, ⓦwww.centre-nautique.com. Chic but relaxed hotel on the waterfront, fitted out with mellow wood and nautical charts. All rooms are tastefully furnished and consist of two storeys connected with a spiral staircase. The best upmarket option in town. ❾

Des Étrangers 4 av Sylvère-Bohn ☎04.95.73.01.09, ⓦhoteldesetrangers.ifrance .com. Simple rooms (the costlier ones have TV and a/c) facing the main road, just up the main Porto-Vecchio road from the port. Nothing special, but good value for Bonifacio, especially in July & Aug, when rooms go for under €50. April–Oct. ❷

A Trama 1.5km from Bonifacio along the route de Santa Manza ☎04 95 73 17 17, ⓦa-trama.com. Discreet three-star, hidden behind a screen of maquis, palms, pines and dry-stone chalk walls. The rooms, all with private terraces, are grouped around a garden and pool, and there's a classy restaurant (*Le Clos Vatel*). Expensive in high summer, but more affordable off season. Open all year. ❽

Campsites

L'Araguina av Sylvère-Bohn ☎04.95.73.02.96. Closest place to town, but unwelcoming, cramped in season, and with inadequate washing and toilet facilities. Avoid unless desperate. That said, it's undoubtedly the most convenient if you're backpacking. April–Sept.

▲ Haute ville, Bonifacio

Campo di Liccia 3km north towards Porto-Vecchio, ☎04.95.73.03.09. Well shaded and large, so you're guaranteed a place. April–Oct.
Pian del Fosse 4km out of town on the rte de Santa Manza ☎04.95.73.16.34. Big three-star site

that recently had a makeover. Very peaceful and quiet in June & September, and well placed for the beaches. April to mid-Oct.

The Town

Apart from the cafés, hotels and restaurants of **quai Comparetti**, the only attraction in the **ville basse** is the marina's **aquarium** (daily: May, June, Sept & Oct 10am–8pm; July & Aug 10am–midnight; €4), where a solitary blue lobster is the star attraction. At the far end lies the **port commercial**, where ferries leave for Sardinia, and, in between, a cluster of restaurants and shops at the foot of **Montée Rastello**, the steps leading up to the **haute ville**.

Many of the houses on the edge of the citadelle are bordered by enormous battlements which, like the tenements themselves, have been rebuilt many times after various sieges. The climb to the top of the montée Rastello is rewarded by a magnificent view of the white limestone cliffs tapering to Capu Persutau, and the huge lump of fallen rock-face called the Grain de Sable. The tiny **Chapelle St-Roch**, at the head of steps, was built on the spot where the last plague victim died in 1528; another, narrower stone staircase twists down to the tiny beach of **Sutta Rocca**.

Montée St-Roch takes you up the final approach to the citadelle walls, entered via the great **Porte des Gênes**, once the only gateway to the *haute ville*. It opens on to the place des Armes, where you can visit the **Bastion de l'Étendard** (April–June & Sept Mon–Sat 11am–5.30pm; July & Aug daily 10am–9pm; €2.50), sole remnant of the fortifications destroyed during a siege in 1554. While exploring the narrow streets, look out for flamboyant marble escutcheons above the doorways and double-arched windows separated by curiously stunted columns. Many of the older houses did not originally have doors; the inhabitants used to climb up a ladder which they would pull up behind them to prevent a surprise attack.

Cutting across rue du Palais de Garde brings you to the church of **Ste-Marie-Majeure**, originally Romanesque but restored in the eighteenth century, though the richly sculpted belfry dates from the fourteenth century. The facade is hidden by a loggia where the Genoese municipal officers used to dispense justice in the days of the republic. The church's treasure, a fragment of the True Cross, was saved from a shipwreck in the Straits of Bonifacio; for centuries after, the citizens would take the relic to the edge of the cliff and pray for calm seas whenever storms raged. It is kept under lock and key in the sacristy, along with an ivory cask containing relics of St Boniface.

Heading south, rue Doria leads towards the Bosco (see below); at the end of this road a left down rue des Pachas will bring you to the **Torrione**, a 35-metre-high lookout post built in 1195 on the site of Count Bonifacio's castle. Descending the cliff from here are the **Escalier du Roi d'Aragon**'s 187 steps (June–Sept daily 11am–5.30pm; €2), which were said to have been built in one night by the Aragonese in an attempt to gain the town in 1420, but in fact they had already been in existence for some time and were used by the people to fetch water from a well.

The Bosco

To the west of the tower lies the **Bosco**, a quarter named after the wood that used to cover the far end of the peninsula in the tenth century. In those days a community of hermits dwelt here, but nowadays the limestone plateau is open and desolate. The entrance to the Bosco is marked by the **church of St-Dominique**, a rare example of Corsican Gothic architecture – it was built in 1270, most probably by the Templars, and later handed over to the Dominicans.

Beyond the church, rue des Moulins leads on to the ruins of three **mills** dating from 1283, two of them decrepit, the third restored. Behind them stands a memorial to the 750 people who died when a troopship named *Sémillante* ran aground here in 1855, on its way to the Crimea, one of the many disasters wreaked by the notoriously windy straits.

The tip of the plateau is occupied by the **Cimetière Marin**, its white crosses standing out sharply against the deep blue of the sea. Open until sundown, the cemetery is a fascinating place to explore, with its flamboyant mausoleums displaying a jumble of architectural ornamentations: stuccoed facades, Gothic arches and classical columns. Next to the cemetery stands the **Couvent St-François**, allegedly founded after St Francis sought shelter in a nearby cave – the story goes that the convent was the town's apology to the holy man, over whom a local maid had nearly poured a bucket of slops. Immediately to the south, the **Esplanade St-François** commands fine views across the bay to Sardinia.

Eating, drinking and nightlife

Eating possibilities in Bonifacio might seem unlimited, but it's best to avoid the chintzy restaurants in the marina, few of which merit their exorbitant prices – the places in the *haute ville* are less pretentious. For a snack, try the boulangerie-patisserie Faby, 4 rue St-Jean-Baptiste, in the *haute ville*, a tiny local bakery serving Bonifacien treats such as *pain des morts* (sweet buns with walnuts and raisins) and *migliacis* (buns made with fresh ewe's cheese), in addition to the usual range of spinach and *brocciu bastelles*, baked here in the traditional way – on stone. For a scrumptious Bonifacien breakfast you can buy a *pain de morts* warm out of the oven at the *Patisserie Sorba* (follow the smell of baking bread to the bottom of the Montée Rastello steps) and take it to *Bar du Quai* a couple of doors down.

The **bars** and **cafés** further along quai Comparetti are the social focus for the town and what little nightlife there is revolves around the terraces here. Bonifacio's only nightclub was blown up by nationalist bombers a couple of years back, so for a real *nuit blanche* you'll have to head for Porto-Vecchio.

Restaurants

L'Archivolto rue de l'Archivolto ☏ 04.95.73.17.48. With its candlelit, antique- and junk-filled interior, this would be the most commendable place to eat in the *haute ville* were the cooking a little less patchy and the prices fairer. But it still gets packed out – advance reservation is recommended. Lunch menus around €16–20; evening à la carte only, around €30–35 for three courses. Open Easter–Oct.

Cantina Doria 27 rue Doria ☏ 04.95.73.50.49. Down-to-earth Corsican specialities at down-to-earth prices. Their popular three-course €18 menu – which includes the house speciality, aubergines *à la bonifacienne* – offers unbeatable value for the *haute ville*, though you'll soon bump up your bill if you succumb to the temptations of the excellent wine selection.

Cantina Grill quai Banda del Ferro ☏ 04.95.70.49.86. Same *patron* as the popular *Cantina Doria* in the citadelle, but down in the marina and with a better choice of seafood (octopus risotto, swordfish steaks, fish soup). They also do succulent *grillades* with a selection of different sauces. The food is dependably fresh, well prepared and presented, and the prices great value.

De la Poste 6 rue Fred-Scamaroni. A cheap and cheerful pizza place serving oven-baked lasagne, *spaghetti al brocciu*, stuffed mussels and delicious pizzas (€9–12). Particularly good-value *formules* and *menus fixes* from €13.50.

Around Bonifacio

There are impressive views of the citadelle from the **cliffs** at the head of the montée Rastello (reached via the pathway running left from the top of the steps), but they're not a patch on the spectacular panorama to be had from the sea. Throughout the day, a flotilla of excursion **boats** ferries visitors out to the best vantage points, taking in a string of caves and other landmarks only accessible by water en route, including the **Îles Lavezzi**, the scattering of small islets where the troop ship *Sémillante* was shipwrecked in 1855, now designated as a nature reserve. The whole experience of bobbing around to an amplified running commentary is about as touristy as Bonifacio gets, but it's well worth enduring just to round the mouth of the harbour and see the *vieille ville*, perched atop the famous chalk cliffs. The Lavezzi islets themselves are surrounded by wonderfully clear sea water, offering Corsica's best snorkelling. On your way back, you skirt the famous **Île Cavallo**, or "millionaire's island", where the likes of Princess Caroline of Monaco and other French and Italian glitterati have luxury hideaways. The boats leave from the east side of the marina: tickets cost €12–15 for trips to the caves, and around €23–27 for the longer excursions to Lavezzi.

The **beaches** within walking distance of Bonifacio are generally smaller and less appealing than most in southern Corsica. For a dazzling splash of turquoise, you'll have to follow the narrow, twisting lane east of town in the direction of Pertusatu lighthouse, turning left when you see signs for the **plage de Sperone**, a pearl-white cove with calm, shallow water that's ideal for kids. If it's busy, venture further north to **Calalonga**, reached via the D58: take the first turning right, on to the D258, after around 3km.

By far the most photogenic beach in this area, though, is **Rondinara**, a perfect shell-shaped cove of turquoise water enclosed by dunes and a pair of twin headlands. Located 10km north (east of N198), it's sufficiently off the beaten track to remain relatively peaceful (outside school holidays). Facilities are minimal, limited to a smart wooden beach restaurant, paying car park and campsite, the *Camping Rondinara* (☏04.95.70.43.15, ⓦwww.rondinara.fr; open mid-May to Sept). Shade is at a premium, so come armed with a parasol.

Porto-Vecchio and around

Set on a hillock overlooking a beautiful deep blue bay, **PORTO-VECCHIO**, 25km north of Bonifacio, was rated by James Boswell as one of "the most distinguished harbours in Europe". It was founded in 1539 as a second Genoese stronghold on the east coast, Bastia being well established in the north. The site was perfect: close to the unexploited and fertile plain, it benefited from secure high land and a sheltered harbour, although the mosquito population spread malaria and wiped out the first Ligurian settlers within months. Things began to take off mainly thanks to the cork industry, which still thrived well into the twentieth century. Today most revenue comes from tourists, the vast majority of them well-heeled Italians who flock here for the fine outlying **beaches**: spectacular stretches of shoreline lie to the south, with Palombaggia the most popular and Golfe de Santa Giulia coming a close second, while to the north, the deep inlet of the Golfe de Porto-Vecchio boasts some fine pine-backed strands. To the northwest, the little town of **Zonza** makes a good base for exploring the dramatic forest that surrounds the **route de Bavella**.

Around the centre of town there's not much to see, apart from the well-preserved **fortress** and the small grid of **ancient streets** backing onto the main place de la République. East of the square you can't miss the **Porte Génoise**, which frames a delightful expanse of sea and salt pans and through which you'll find the quickest route down to the modern marina, lined with cafés and restaurants.

Practicalities

Porto-Vecchio doesn't have a **bus** station; instead, the various companies who come here stop and depart outside their agents' offices on the edge of the old town. From the bus stops it's a five-minute walk to the main square, place de l'Hôtel-de-Ville, site of the efficient **tourist office** (June & Sept Mon–Sat 9am–1pm & 3–6pm; July & Aug Mon–Sat 9am–8pm, Sun 9am–1pm; Oct–May Mon–Fri 9am–noon & 2–6pm, Sat 9am–noon; ☎04.95.70.09.58, Ⓦwww .ot-portovecchio.com).

Accommodation is easy to come by except in high summer. One of the least expensive places is the *Panorama*, 12 rue Jean-Nicoli, just above the old town (☎04.95.70.07.96; ❹), which isn't all that well maintained but offers the cheapest beds in the centre of town. Moving up a couple of brackets, the *San Giovanni* (☎04.95.70.22.55, Ⓦwww.hotel-san-giovanni.com; ❼), a couple of kilometres south of Porto-Vecchio on the D659 towards Arca, has thirty comfortable chalet-style rooms set in landscaped gardens, with a pool and tennis courts. It's well run, peaceful and good value for money.

Of the many **campsites** in the area, *Matonara* (☎04.95.70.37.05, Ⓦwww .lamatonara.com), just north of the centre at the Quatre-Chemins intersection, is the most easily accessible. Lying within easy reach of the "Hyper U" supermarket, it's large and shaded by stands of cork trees.

For quality local **food**, try *U Sputinu*'s copious *grande assiette* – a selection of quality charcuterie, cheese, spinach pasties (*chaussons herbes*), savoury fritters (*migliacciu*) and mint omelettes (€15) – served on rustic wooden tables in the little square in front of the church. Plenty of other places to eat are clustered around the marina and *port de commerce*, but none can rustle up pizzas more delectable than those served at *U Corsu* (☎04.95.70.13.91). Reserve early for a sea view on their *pieds dans l'eau* terrace.

Golfe de Porto-Vecchio

Much of the coast of the **Golfe de Porto-Vecchio** and its environs is characterized by ugly development and hectares of swampland, yet some of the clearest, bluest sea and whitest beaches on Corsica are also found around here. The most frequented of these, Palombaggia and Santa Giulia, can be reached by **bus** from the town in summer, timetables for which are posted in the tourist office (see above) and online at Ⓦwww.corsicabus.org; at other times you'll need your own transport. The same applies to the **Casteddu d'Araggiu**, one of the island's best-preserved Bronze Age sites, which stands on a ledge overlooking the gulf to the north of town.

Heading south of Porto-Vecchio along the main N198, take the turning signposted for **Palombaggia**, a golden semicircle of sand edged by short twisted umbrella pines that are punctuated by fantastically shaped red rocks. This might be the most beautiful beach on the island were it not for the crowds, which pour on to it in such numbers that a wattle fence has had to be erected to protect the dunes. A few kilometres further along the same road takes you to **Santa Giulia**, a sweeping sandy bay backed by a lagoon. Despite the presence of several sprawling holiday villages, crowds are less of a problem here, and the shallow bay is an extraordinary turquoise colour.

North of Porto-Vecchio, the first beach worth a visit is **San Ciprianu**, a half-moon bay of white sand, reached by turning left off the main road at the Elf petrol station. Carry on for another 7km, and you'll come to the even more picturesque beach at **Pinarellu**, an uncrowded, long sweep of soft white sand with a Genoese watchtower and, like the less inspiring beaches immediately north of here, benefiting from the spectacular backdrop of the Massif de l'Ospédale.

The coast between Porto-Vecchio and Solenzara is also strewn with **prehistoric monuments**. The most impressive of these, Casteddu d'Araggiu, lies 12km north along the D759. From the site's car park (signposted off the main road), it's a twenty-minute stiff climb through maquis and scrubby woodland to the ruins. Built in 2000 BC, the *casteddu* consists of a complex of chambers built into a massive circular wall of pink granite from the top of which the views over the gulf are superb.

The route de Bavella

Starting from the picture-postcard-pretty mountain village of **ZONZA**, 40km northwest of Porto-Vecchio, and running northeast towards the coast, the D268 – known locally as the **route de Bavella** – is perhaps the most dramatic road in all Corsica. Well served by buses, it also affords one of the simplest approaches to the spectacular landscapes of the interior. The road penetrates a dense expanse of old pine and chestnut trees as it rises steadily to the **Col de Bavella** (1218m), where a towering statue of **Notre-Dame-des-Neiges** marks the windswept pass itself. An amazing panorama of peaks and forests spreads out from the col: to the northwest the serrated granite ridge of the Cirque de Gio Agostino is dwarfed by the pink pinnacles of the Aiguilles de Bavella; behind soars Monte Incudine.

Just below the pass, the seasonal hamlet of **BAVELLA** comprises a handful of congenial cafés, corrugated-iron-roofed chalets and hikers' hostels from where you can follow a series of waymarked **trails** to nearby viewpoints. Deservedly the most popular of these is the two-hour walk to the **Trou de la Bombe**, a circular opening that pierces the Paliri crest of peaks. From the car park behind the *Auberge du Col* follow the red-and-white waymarks of GR20 for 800m, then head right when you see orange splashes.

From Bavella, it's a steep descent through what's left of the **Forêt de Bavella**, which was devastated by fire in 1960 but still harbours some huge Laricio pines. The winding road offers numerous breathtaking glimpses of the Aiguilles de Bavella and plenty of places to pull over for a swim in the river.

The best **place to stay** locally is Zonza, which has a cluster of hotels, all with more than decent restaurants, such as *Le Tourisme*, set back on the west side of the Quenza road north of the village (℡04.95.78.67.72, www.hoteldu tourisme.fr; ❼; April–Oct), or *L'Aiglon* in the village centre (℡04.95.78.67.72, www.aiglonhotel.com; ❹; April–Dec).

Aléria

Built on the estuary at the mouth of the River Tavignano on the island's east coast, 40km southeast of Corte along the N200, **ALÉRIA** was first settled in 564 BC by a colony of Greek Phoceans as a trading port for the copper and lead they mined and the wheat, olives and grapes they farmed. After an interlude of Carthaginian rule, the Romans arrived in 259 BC, built a naval base and re-established its importance in the Mediterranean. Aléria remained the east coast's principal port right up until the eighteenth century. Little is left of the historic town except Roman ruins and a thirteenth-century Genoese fortress, which stands high against a background of chequered fields and green vineyards. To the south, a strip of modern buildings straddling the main road makes up the modern town, known as **Cateraggio**, but it's the village set on the hilltop just west of here that holds most interest. Aléria/Cateraggio can be reached on any of the daily **buses** running between Bastia and the south of the island via the east coast.

To sample the famous Nustale oysters hauled fresh each day from the nearby Étang de Diane lagoon, head 1.2km north and look for a signboard on the right (east) side of the road pointing the way down a surfaced lane to the *Aux Coquillages de Diane* **restaurant** (℡04.95.57.04.55). Resting on stilts above the water, it serves a great-value €23 seafood platter, featuring clams, mussels and a terrine made from dried mullet's eggs called *poutargue* – the kind of food one imagines the Romans must have feasted on when they farmed the *étang* two millennia ago.

The Site

Before looking around the ruins of the ancient city, set aside an hour for the **Musée Jerôme Carcopino** (mid-May to Sept daily 8am–noon & 2–7pm; Oct to mid-May Mon–Sat 8am–noon & 2–5pm; €2), housed in the Fort Matra. It houses remarkable finds from the **Roman site**, including Hellenic and Punic coins, rings, belt links, elaborate oil lamps decorated with Christian symbols, Attic plates and a second-century marble bust of Jupiter Ammon. Etruscan bronzes fill another room, with jewellery and armour from the fourth to the second century BC.

A dusty track leads from here to the Roman site itself (closes 30min before museum; same ticket), where most of the excavation was done as recently as the 1950s. Most of the site still lies beneath ground and is undergoing continuous digging, but the balneum (bathhouse), the base of Augustus's triumphal arch, the foundations of the forum and traces of shops have already been unearthed.

Some traces of the **Greek settlement**, comprising the remains of an acropolis, have been discovered further to the east. It's believed that the main part of the town would have extended from the present site over to this acropolis and down to the Tavignano estuary. The port was located to the east of the main road, where the remnants of a second-century bathhouse have been found.

Corte (Corti)

Stacked up the side of a wedge-shaped crag against a spectacular backdrop of granite mountains, **CORTE** epitomizes *l'âme corse*, or "Corsican soul" – a small town marooned amid a grandiose landscape, where a spirit of dogged patriotism is never far from the surface. Corte has been the home of Corsican nationalism since the first National Constitution was drawn up here in 1731, and was also where **Pascal Paoli**, "U Babbu di u Patria" (Father of the Nation), formed the island's first democratic government later in the eighteenth century. Self-consciously insular and grimly proud, it can seem an inhospitable place at times,

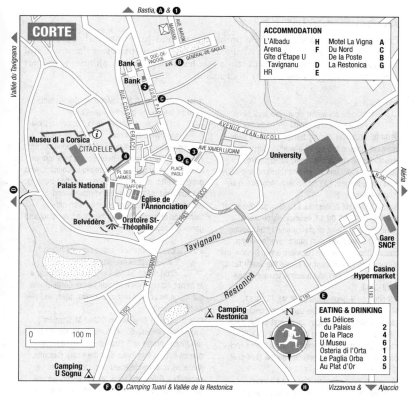

ACCOMMODATION

L'Albadu	H	Motel La Vigna	A
Arena	F	Du Nord	C
Gîte d'Étape U		De la Poste	B
Tavignanu	D	La Restonica	G
HR	E		

EATING & DRINKING

Les Délices du Palais	2
De la Place	4
U Museu	6
Osteria di l'Orta	1
Le Paglia Orba	3
Au Plat d'Or	5

although the presence of the island's only university lightens the atmosphere noticeably during term-time, when the bars and cafés lining its long main street fill with students. For the outsider, Corte's charm is concentrated in the tranquil *haute ville*, where the forbidding **citadelle** – site of the island's premier **museum** – presides over a warren of narrow, cobbled streets. Immediately behind it, the Restonica and Tavignano gorges afford easy access to some of the region's most memorable mountain scenery, best enjoyed from the marked trails that wind through them.

Arrival and information

Buses from Ajaccio and Bastia stop in the centre of town on avenue Xavier-Luciani; the **gare CFC** (☎04.95.46.00.97) is at the foot of the hill near the university, a ten-minute walk from the centre and campsites. If you're driving, the best place to **park** is at the top of avenue Jean-Nicoli, the road which leads into town from Ajaccio. Corte's **tourist office** is situated just inside the main gates of the citadelle, near the museum (Jan–May & Oct–Dec Mon–Fri 9am–noon & 2–6pm, plus Sat in May; June & Sept Mon–Sat 9am–1pm & 2–7pm; July & Aug daily 9am–8pm; ☎04.95.46.26.70, ⓦwww.corte-tourisme.com). In the same building is the information office of the **Parc Régional** (same hours and phone number).

Accommodation

Finding a **place to stay** can be a problem from mid-June until early September, when it's advisable to book in advance. With three **campsites** in the town, and a couple a short drive away, tent space is at less of a premium, although the sites across the river get crowded in high season.

Hotels

L'Albadu ancienne rte d'Ajaccio, 2.5km southwest of town ☎04.95.46.24.55, ⒻEquipment04.95.46.13.08. Simply furnished rooms with showers (shared toilets) on a working farm-cum-equestrian centre. Warm family atmosphere, beautiful horses, fine views and Corsican speciality food (for a bargain €42 half board). Advance reservation essential. ②

Arena Vallée de la Restonica, 2.5km southwest of town ☎04.95.46.09.13, ⓦwww.hotel-arena-lerefuge.com. Cosy, unpretentious hotel-restaurant at the roadside, with rooms overlooking a stream (the ones at the back are a touch noisy in spring, when the snowmelt raises the water level, but fine in summer) and a sunny terrace. Open April–Sept. ⑥

HR allée du 9-Septembre ☎04.95.45.11.11, ⓦwww.hotel-hr.com. This converted concrete-block *gendarmerie*, 200m southwest of the *gare CFC*, looks grim from the outside, but its 125 rooms are comfortable enough and its rates rock-bottom; bathroom-less options are the best deal. No credit cards. ②

Motel La Vigna chemin de Saint-Pancrace ☎04.95.46.02.19. Tucked away on the leafy edge of town, this small but rather swish students' hall of residence is vacated between early June and the end of September and converted into a motel. The rooms are simple and lacking character by Corte standards, but clean and all en suite, with balconies. Open June–Sept. ③

Du Nord 22 cours Paoli ☎04.95.46.00.33, ⓦwww.hoteldunord-corte.com. Pleasant, clean place right in the centre. Despite recent renovation, the building has oodles of charm and the (variously priced) rooms are large for the tariffs. ⑤

De la Poste 2 place du Duc-de-Padoue ☎04.95.46.01.37. The cheapest rooms in the centre, in a huge old building that opens onto a quiet square just off the main drag. Comfortable enough, but on the gloomy side. ②

La Restonica Vallée de la Restonica, 2km southwest from town ☎04.95.46.09.58, ⓦwww.aubergerestonica.com. Sumptuous comfort in a wood-lined riverside hotel set up by a former French-national footballer, Dominique Colonna, who bought it after winning the lottery. Hunting trophies, old paintings, salon with open fireplace and leather-upholstered furniture create an old-fashioned atmosphere, and there's a large pool and garden terrace. ⑦

Hostels and campsites

L'Albadu 2.5km southwest of town ☎04.95.46.24.55. Perfect little *camping à la ferme*, situated on a hillside above Corte. Basic, but much nicer than any of the town sites, and well worth the walk.

Gîte d'Étape U Tavignanu ("Chez M. Gambini") behind the citadelle ☎04.95.46.16.85. Run-of-the-mill hikers' hostel with small dorms and a relaxing garden terrace that looks over the valley. Peaceful, secluded, and the cheapest place to stay after the campsites. Follow the signs for the Tavignano trail (marked with orange spots of paint) around the back of the citadelle. €17 per bed (includes breakfast).

Tuani vallée de la Restonica, 7km southeast ☎04.95.46.11.62. Too far up the valley without your own car, but the wildest and most atmospheric of the campsites around Corte, overlooking a rushing stream, deep in the woods. Ideally placed for an early start on Monte Rotondo. Basic facilities, although they do have a cheerful little café serving good *bruschettas* and other hot snacks.

U Sognu rte de la Restonica ☎04.95.46.09.07. At the foot of the valley, a 15min walk from the centre. Has a good view of the citadelle, plenty of poplar trees for shade, and toilets in a converted barn. There's also a small bar and restaurant (in summer).

The Town

Corte is a very small town whose centre effectively consists of one street, **cours Paoli**, which runs from place Paoli at the southern end, a tourist-friendly zone packed with cafés, restaurants and market stalls, to **place du Duc-de-Padoue**, an elegant square of *fin-de-siècle* buildings.

The old **haute ville** is next to the cours Paoli, reached by climbing one of the cobbled ramps on the west side of the street or by taking the steep rue

Scoliscia from place Paoli. **Place Gaffori**, the hub of the *haute ville*, is dominated by a statue of General Gian-Pietru Gaffori pointing vigorously towards the church. On its base a bas-relief depicts the siege of the Gaffori house by the Genoese, who attacked in 1750 when the general was out of town and his wife Faustina was left holding the fort. Their house stands right behind, and you can clearly make out the bullet marks made by the besiegers.

For the best view of the citadelle, follow the signs uphill to the viewing platform, the **Belvédère**, which faces the medieval tower, suspended high above the town on its pinnacle of rock and dwarfed by the immense crags behind. The platform also gives a wonderful view of the converging rivers and encircling forest – a summer bar adds to the attraction.

Just above the place Gaffori, left of the gateway to the citadelle, stands the **Palais National**, a great, solid block of a mansion that's the sole example of Genoese civic architecture in Corte. Having served as the seat of Paoli's government for a while, it became the Università di Corsica in 1765, offering free education to all (Napoleon's father studied here). The university closed in 1769 when the French took over the island after the Treaty of Versailles, not to be resurrected until 1981. Today several modern buildings have been added, among them the Institut Universitaire d'Études Corses, dedicated to the study of Corsican history and culture.

The Museu di a Corsica and citadelle

The monumental gateway just behind the Palais National leads from place Poilu into Corte's Genoese citadelle, whose lower courtyard is dominated by the modern buildings of **Museu di a Corsica** (April to June 19 & Sept 20–Oct daily except Tues 10am–6pm; June 20 to Sept 19 daily 10am–8pm; Nov–March Tues–Sat 10am–6pm; €5.50), a state-of-the-art museum inaugurated in 1997 to house the collection of ethnographer Révérend Père Louis Doazan, a Catholic priest who spent 27 years amassing a vast array of objects relating to the island's traditional transhumant and peasant past: principally old farm implements, craft tools and peasant dress.

The museum's entrance ticket also admits you to Corte's principal landmark, the **citadelle**. The only such fortress in the interior of the island, the Genoese structure served as a base for the Foreign Legion from 1962 until 1984, but now houses a pretty feeble exhibition of nineteenth-century photographs. It's reached by a huge staircase of Restonica marble, which leads to the medieval tower known as the **Nid d'Aigle** (Eagle's Nest). The fortress, of which the tower is the only original part, was built in 1420, and the barracks were added during the mid-19th century. These were later converted into a prison, in use as recently as World War II, when the Italian occupiers incarcerated Corsican Resistance fighters in tiny cells. Adjacent to the cells is a former **watchtower** which at the time of Paoli's government was inhabited by the hangman.

Eating and drinking

Corte has only four **restaurants** worthy of note, plus the usual handful of pizzerias and crêperies. As a rule of thumb, avoid anywhere fronted by gaudy food photographs and multilingual menus; their dishes may be cheap, but they offer poor value for money – for not much more you'll eat a lot better in one of the places listed below.

Cafés and bars

Les Délices du Palais cours Paoli. Frilly little crêperie-cum-*salon-de-thé* whose bakery sells a selection of delicious Corsican patisserie: try their *colzone* (spinach pasties) or *brocciu* baked in flaky chestnut-flour pastry.

De la Place place Paoli. On the shady side of the main square, this is the place to hole up for a spot of crowd-watching over a *barquettes de frites* (a pile of chips) and draught Pietra.

Restaurants

🏃 **Osteria di l'Orta** Casa Guelfucci, Pont de l'Orta, ☎04.95.61.06.41, ⓦwww .osteria-di-l-orta.com. The only *ferme auberge* on the island located in a town. Served in a stone-walled annexe tacked on to the family's 18th-century mansion, the food is honest, fragrant and traditional. House specialities include veal with figs, char-grilled lamb fillets and – the dessert *de résist-ance* – chestnut mousse. *Formules* €20–35. Head 500m north of the place du Duc de Padoue, and take the first right after the Pont de l'Orta – it's the grand, five-storey house painted bright blue.

Le Paglia Orba 1 av Xavier-Luciani ☎04.95.61.07.89. Quality Corsican cooking at very reasonable prices, served on a raised terrace overlooking the street. Most people come for their succulent pizzas (€6–8), but there is also plenty of choice à la carte, particularly for vegetarians. Pan-fried veal served with *stozapreti* (nuggets of *brocciu* and herbs) is their *plat de résistance*. Menus from €16.

Au Plat d'Or place Paoli ☎04.95.46.27.16. The classiest option in Corte: Corsican specialities made from locally produced ingredients, and served under awnings on the shady side of place Paoli. Meat and seafood dishes are their forte, but they also do pizzas, pastas and home-made desserts. Menu for €23 (four courses). Closed Sun.

🏃 **U Museu** rampe Ribanelle in the *haute ville* at the foot of the citadelle, 30m down rue Colonel-Feracci ☎04.95.61.08.36. Congenial and well-situated place. Try the €17 *menu corse*, featuring lasagne in wild boar sauce, trout, and *tripettes* (imaginatively translated as "trips"). Their hot goat's cheese (*chèvre chaud*) salad, filling enough for two, comes on a groaning bed of richly flavoured potatoes. Great value for money, atmospheric terrace and the house wines are local AOC.

Central Corsica

Central Corsica is a nonstop parade of stupendous scenery, and the best way to immerse yourself in it is to get onto the region's ever-expanding network of trails and forest tracks. The ridge of granite mountains forming the spine of the island is closely followed by the epic **GR20** footpath, which can be picked up from various villages and is scattered with refuge huts, most of them offering no facilities except shelter. For the less active there also are plenty of roads penetrating deep into the **forests** of Vizzavona, La Restonica and Rospa Sorba, crossing lofty passes that provide exceptional views across the island.

The most popular attractions in the centre, though, are the magnificent **gorges** of La Restonica and Tavignano, both within easy reach of Corte.

Gorges du Tavignano

A deep cleft of ruddy granite beginning 5km to the west of Corte, the **Gorges du Tavignano** offers one of central Corsica's great walks, marked in yellow paint flashes alongside the broad cascading River Tavignano. You can pick up the trail from opposite the Chapelle Sainte-Croix in Corte's *haute ville* and follow it as far as the Lac de Nino, 30km west of the town, where it joins the GR20. There's a very well set up **refuge**, *A Sega* (dorm beds €11, bivouac €5; advance reservation essential: ☎06.10.71.77.26), situated at the halfway point, which serves filling breakfasts and evening meals (half board €30 to bivouac or €52 in a dorm), and can supply packed lunches (€7).

Gorges de la Restonica

The glacier-moulded rocks and deep pools of the **Gorges de la Restonica** make the D936 running southwest from Corte the busiest mountain road in Corsica – if you come in high summer, expect to encounter traffic jams all the way up to the car park at the **Bergeries de Grotelle**, 15km from Corte. **Minibuses** run from Corte to the Bergeries, costing €12; taxis charge around €35. The gorges begin after 6km, just beyond where the route penetrates the **Forêt de la Restonica**, a glorious forest of chestnut, Laricio pine and the tough maritime pine endemic to Corte. Not surprisingly, it's a popular place to walk, picnic and bathe in the many pools fed by the cascading torrent of the River Restonica, easily reached by scrambling down the rocky banks.

From the *bergeries*, a well-worn path winds along the valley floor to a pair of beautiful glacial lakes. The first and larger, **Lac de Melo**, is reached after an easy hour's hike through the rocks. One particularly steep part of the path has been fitted with security chains, but the scramble around the side of the passage is perfectly straightforward, and much quicker. Once past Lac de Melo, press on for another forty minutes along the steeper marked trail over a moraine to the second lake, **Lac de Capitello**, the more spectacular of the pair. Hemmed in by vertical cliffs, the deep turquoise-blue pool affords fine views of the Rotondo massif on the far side of the valley, and in clear weather you can spend an hour or two exploring the surrounding crags.

Travel details

Note that the details apply to June–Sept only; during the winter both train and bus services are considerably scaled down. Current timetables for all public transport services on the island can be viewed online at Ⓦ www.corsicabus.org.

Trains

Ajaccio to: Bastia (4 daily; 3hr 20min); Calvi (2 daily; 3hr 40min); Corte (4 daily; 2hr 5min); L'Île Rousse (2 daily; 4hr).
Bastia to: Ajaccio (2–4 daily; 3hr 50min); Biguglia (2–4 daily; 20min); Calvi (2 daily; 3hr 10min); Corte (2–4 daily; 1hr 50min); L'Île Rousse (2 daily; 2hr 30min).
Calvi to: Ajaccio (2 daily; 4hr 45min); Bastia (2 daily; 3hr 5min); Corte (2 daily; 2hr 40min); L'Île Rousse (2–10 daily; 30min).
Corte to: Ajaccio (4 daily; 2hr); Bastia (4 daily; 1hr 40min); Calvi (2 daily; 2hr 30min); L'Île Rousse (2 daily; 1hr 50min).
L'Île Rousse to: Ajaccio (2 daily; 4hr 5min); Bastia (2 daily; 2hr 30min); Corte (2 daily; 2hr 5min).

Buses

Ajaccio to: Bastia (2 daily; 3hr); Bonifacio (3 daily; 4hr); Cargèse (2–3 daily; 1hr 10min); Corte (2 daily; 1hr 45min); Évisa (1–3 daily; 2hr); Porto (1–2 daily;

2hr 10min); Porto-Vecchio (2–5 daily; 3hr 10min–3hr 45min); Propriano (2–6 daily; 1hr 50min); Sartène (2–6 daily; 2hr 15min); Zonza (3 daily; 2hr 15min–3hr).
Aléria to: Bastia (2 daily; 1hr 30min); Corte (3 weekly; 1hr 25min); Porto-Vecchio (2 daily; 1hr 20min).
Bastia to: Ajaccio (2 daily; 3hr); Bonifacio (2–4 daily; 3hr 50min); Aléria/Cateraggio (2 daily; 1hr 30min); Calvi (2 daily; 2hr 20min); Centuri (3 weekly; 2hr); Corte (2–3 daily; 1hr 15min); Erbalunga (hourly; 30min); L'Île Rousse (2 daily; 1hr 40min); Porto-Vecchio (2 daily; 3hr); St-Florent (2 daily; 1hr).
Bonifacio to: Ajaccio (2 daily; 3hr 30min–4hr); Bastia (2–4 daily; 3hr 35min); Porto-Vecchio (1–4 daily; 30min); Propriano (2–4 daily; 1hr 40min–2hr 10min); Sartène (2 daily; 1hr 25min–2hr).
Calvi to: Bastia (1 daily; 2hr 15min); L'Île Rousse (2 daily; 40min); Porto (1 daily; 2hr 30min); St-Florent (1 daily; 1hr 20min).
Cargèse to: Ajaccio (1–2 daily; 1hr 10min); Porto (2–3 daily; 1hr).

Corte to: Ajaccio (2 daily; 2hr); Bastia (2 daily; 1hr 15min); Évisa (4 daily; 2hr); Porto (4 daily; 2hr 30min).

Évisa to: Ajaccio (1–3 daily; 1hr 45min).

Porto to: Ajaccio (1–2 daily; 2hr); Calvi (1 daily; 3hr); Cargèse (2–3 daily; 1hr 15min).

Porto-Vecchio to: Ajaccio (2–4 daily; 3hr 30min); Bastia (2 daily; 3hr); Bonifacio (1–4 daily; 30min); Propriano (2–4 daily; 2hr 10min); Sartène (2–4 daily; 40min).

Propriano to: Ajaccio (2–4 daily; 1hr 35min–1hr 50min); Bonifacio (2–4 daily; 2hr 15min); Porto-Vecchio (2–4 daily; 2hr 10min); Sartène (2–4 daily; 20min).

Ferries

Marseille to: Ajaccio (4–7 weekly; 11–12hr overnight, or 4hr 30min NGV); Bastia (2–4 weekly; 10hr); L'Île Rousse (1–4 weekly; 11hr 30min overnight); Porto-Vecchio (2–5 weekly; 14hr overnight); Propriano (1 weekly; 12–13hr overnight).

Nice to: Ajaccio (1–5 weekly; 12–13hr overnight); Bastia (1–12 weekly; 6hr, or 2hr 30min NGV); Calvi (2–5 weekly; 2hr 40min NGV); L'Île Rousse (1–3 weekly; 7hr overnight, or 2hr 50min NGV).

Toulon to: Ajaccio (2–4 weekly; 10hr overnight); Bastia (2–4 weekly; 8hr 30min–9hr overnight).

Contexts

Contexts

History

E ver since Julius Caesar observed that "Gaul" was divided into quite distinct parts, and then conquered and unified the country, France has been perceived as both a nation and a collection of fiercely individualistic *pays*, or localities. The two Frances have often come into conflict. Few countries' governments have centralized as energetically, or have imposed such radical change from above. Equally, few peoples have been so determined to hold on to their local traditions. Charles de Gaulle famously complained that it was impossible to govern a country with 246 different kinds of cheeses. Yet each of those cheesemaking regions, as de Gaulle was well aware, was proud to belong to the kind of impossibly, quarrelsomely traditional nation that could have so many cheeses.

The themes of nationalism and localism, of central control and popular resistance, of radicalism and conservatism, continue to define France today. What follows is necessarily a brief account of major events in the country's past. For more in-depth coverage see the recommendations given in "Books", p.1209.

Mousterians, Cro-Magnons, Celts and Gauls

Traces of human existence are rare in France until about 50,000 BC. Thereafter, beginning with the stone tools of the Neanderthal "Mousterian civilization", they become ever more numerous, with an especially heavy concentration of sites in the Périgord region of the Dordogne, where, near the village of Les Eyzies, remains were discovered in 1868 of a late Stone Age people, subsequently dubbed "Cro-Magnon". Flourishing from around 25,000 BC, these cave-dwelling hunters seem to have developed quite a sophisticated culture, the evidence of which is preserved in the beautiful paintings and engravings on the walls of the region's caves.

By 10,000 BC, human communities had spread out widely across the whole of France, and by about 7000 BC, **farming and pastoral communities** had begun to develop. By 4500 BC, the first **dolmens** (megalithic stone tombs) showed up in Brittany, while dugout canoes dating back to the same epoch have been unearthed in Paris. It seems that a thriving trade followed the rivers, while the land between was heavily forested.

By 1800 BC, the **Bronze Age** had arrived in the east and southeast of the country, and trade links had begun with Spain, central Europe, southern Britain and around the Mediterranean – **Greek colonists** founded Massalia (Marseille) in around 600 BC.

The first Celts made an appearance in around 500 BC. Whether these were the same people known to the Romans as "long-haired" Gauls isn't certain. Either way, the inhabitants of France were far from shaggy-haired barbarians. The Gauls, as they became known, invented the barrel and soap and were skilful manufacturers and prolific traders – as was proved by the "chariot tomb" of **Vix**, where the burial goods included rich gold jewellery, a metal-wheeled cart and elaborate Greek vases.

Roman Gaul

By 100 BC the **Gauls** had established large **hilltop towns with merchant communities**. The area equivalent to modern **Provence** – became a Roman colony in 118 BC and, in 58 BC, **Julius Caesar** arrived to complete the Roman conquest of Gaul, there were perhaps fifteen million people living in the area now occupied by modern France. **Tribal rivalries** made the Romans' job of conquering the north fairly easy, and when the Gauls finally united under **Vercingétorix** in 52 BC, it only made their defeat at the battle of **Alésia** more final.

This **Roman victory** was one of the major turning points in the history of France, fixing the frontier between Gaul and the Germanic peoples at the Rhine, saving Gaul from disintegrating because of internal dissension and made it a Roman province. During the five centuries of peace that followed, the Gauls farmed, manufactured and traded, became urbanized and educated – and learnt Latin. The emperor Augustus founded numerous cities – including Autun, Limoges and Bayeux – built roads and settled Roman colonists on the land. Vespasian secured the frontiers beyond the Rhine, thus ensuring a couple of hundred years of peace and economic expansion.

Serious **disruptions** of the Pax Romana only began in the third century AD. Oppressive aristocratic rule and an economic crisis turned the destitute peasantry into gangs of marauding brigands – precursors of the medieval *jacquerie*. But most devastating of all, there began a series of incursions across the Rhine frontier by various restless **Germanic tribes**, the first of which, the Alemanni, pushed down as far as Spain, ravaging farmland and destroying towns.

In the fourth century the reforms of the emperor **Diocletian** secured some decades of respite from both internal and external pressures. Towns were rebuilt and fortified, foreshadowing feudalism and the independent power of the nobles. By the fifth century, however, the Germanic invaders were back: **Alans**, **Vandals** and **Suevi**, with **Franks** and **Burgundians** in their wake. While the Roman administration assimilated them as far as possible, granting them land in return for military duties, they gradually achieved independence from the empire.

The Franks and Charlemagne

By 500 AD, the **Franks**, who gave their name to modern France, had become the dominant invading power. Their most celebrated king, **Clovis**, consolidated his hold on northern France and drove the Visigoths out of the southwest into Spain. In 507 he made the until-then insignificant little trading town of Paris his capital and became a Christian, which inevitably hastened the **Christianization** of Frankish society.

Under the succeeding **Merovingian** dynasty the kingdom began to disintegrate until, in 732 **Charles Martel**, reunited the kingdom and saved western Christendom from the northward expansion of Islam by defeating the Spanish Moors at the **battle of Poitiers**.

In 754 Charles's son, Pepin, had himself crowned king by the pope, thus inaugurating the **Carolingian dynasty** and establishing for the first time the principle of the divine right of kings. His son was **Charlemagne**, who extended Frankish control over the whole of what had been Roman Gaul, and far beyond. On Christmas Day in 800, he was crowned emperor of the **Holy Roman Empire**, though the kingdom again fell apart following his death in squabbles over who was to inherit various parts of his empire. At the Treaty of Verdun in 843, his grandsons agreed on a division of territory that corresponded roughly with the extent of modern France and Germany.

Charlemagne's administrative system had involved the royal appointment of counts and bishops to govern the various provinces of the empire. Under the destabilizing attacks of Norsemen/Vikings (who evolved into the Normans) during the ninth century, Carolingian kings were obliged to delegate more power and autonomy to these **provincial governors**, whose lands, like **Aquitaine** and **Burgundy**, already had separate regional identities as a result of earlier invasions.

Gradually the power of these governors overshadowed that of the king, whose lands were confined to the Île-de-France. When the last Carolingian died in 987, it was only natural that they should elect one of their own number to take his place. This was Hugues Capet, founder of a dynasty that lasted until 1328.

The rise of the French kings

The years 1000 to 1500 saw the gradual extension and consolidation of the power of the **French kings**, accompanied by the growth of a centralized administrative system and bureaucracy. Foreign policy was chiefly concerned with restricting papal interference in French affairs and checking the English kings' continuing involvement in French territory. Conditions for the overwhelming majority of the population, meanwhile, remained remarkably unchanged.

Surrounded by vassals much stronger than themselves, **Hugues Capet** and his successors remained weak throughout the eleventh century, though they made the most of their feudal rights.

At the beginning of the twelfth century, having successfully tamed his own vassals in the Île-de-France, Louis VI had a stroke of luck. **Eleanor**, daughter of the powerful duke of Aquitaine, was left in his care on her father's death, so he promptly married her off to his son, the future Louis VII, though the marriage ended in divorce and in 1152, Eleanor married Henry of Normandy, shortly to become **Henry II** of England. Thus the **English** crown gained control of a huge chunk of French territory, stretching from the Channel to the Pyrenees. Though their fortunes fluctuated over the ensuing three hundred years, the English rulers remained a perpetual thorn in the side of the French kings, with a dangerous potential for alliance with any rebellious French vassals.

Philippe Auguste (1179–1223) made considerable headway in undermining English rule by exploiting the bitter relations between Henry II and his three sons, one of whom was Richard the Lionheart. By the end of his reign Philippe had recovered all of Normandy and the English possessions north of the Loire.

For the first time, the royal lands were greater than those of any other French lord. The foundations of a systematic administration and civil service had been established in **Paris**, and Philippe had firmly and quietly marked his independence from the papacy by refusing to take any interest in the **crusade** against the heretic Cathars of Languedoc. When Languedoc and Poitou came under royal control in the reign of his son Louis VIII, France was by far the greatest power in western Europe.

The Hundred Years War

In 1328 the Capetian monarchy had its first succession crisis, which led directly to the ruinous **Hundred Years War** with the English. Charles IV, last of the line, had only daughters as heirs, and when it was decided that France could not be ruled by a queen, the English king, **Edward III** claimed the throne of France for himself – on the grounds that his mother was Charles's sister.

The French chose **Philippe, Count of Valois**, instead, and Edward acquiesced for a time. But when Philippe began whittling away at his possessions in Aquitaine, Edward renewed his claim and embarked on war. With its population of about twelve million, France was the far richer and more powerful country, but its army was no match for the superior organization and tactics of the English. Edward won an outright victory at **Crécy** in 1346 and seized the port of Calais as a permanent bridgehead. Ten years later, his son, the Black Prince, actually took the French king, Jean le Bon, prisoner at the **battle of Poitiers**.

Although by 1375 French military fortunes had improved to the point where the English had been forced back to Calais and the Gascon coast, the strains of war and administrative abuses, as well as the madness of Charles VI, caused other kinds of damage. In 1358 there were **insurrections** among the Picardy peasantry (the *jacquerie*) and among the townspeople of Paris under the leadership of Étienne Marcel. Both were brutally repressed, as were subsequent risings in Paris in 1382 and 1412.

When it became clear that the king was mad, two rival camps began to vie for power: the **Burgundians**, led by the king's cousin and Duke of Burgundy, Jean sans Peur, and the **Armagnacs**, who gathered round the Duke of Orléans, Charles' brother. The situation escalated when Jean sans Peur had Orléans assassinated, and when fighting broke out between the two factions, they both called on the English for help. In 1415 Henry V of England inflicted another crushing defeat on the French army at **Agincourt**. The Burgundians seized Paris, took the royal family prisoner and recognized Henry as heir to the French throne. When Charles VI died in 1422, the English and their Burgundian allies assumed control of much of France, leaving the young French heir, the Dauphin Charles, barely clinging on to a rump state around the Loire Valley.

The French state might well have been finally exterminated had it not been for the arrival at court, in 1429, of Joan of Arc, a peasant girl who promised divine support for an aggressive military campaign. The English were driven back from their siege of Orléans, the Dauphin crowned as Charles VII at Reims in July 1429, Paris was retaken in 1436 and the English finally driven from France altogether (except for a toehold at Calais) in 1453. Joan's own end was less triumphant: she fell into the hands of the Burgundians and was burnt at the stake in 1431.

From the 1450s, court life was centred on pleasure-seeking in the Loire valley. Even for the **peasantry** life grew less hard. The threats of war and plague steadily receded, and from 1450 the harvests did not fail for seventy unbroken years. The population began to grow again, and a kind of peasant aristocracy took shape in the form of the smallholder *fermiers*. In the towns, meanwhile, the *aisés*, or well-to-do merchants and artisans, began to form the basis of what would become the bourgeoisie.

By the end of the fifteenth century, **Dauphiné**, **Burgundy**, **Franche-Comté** and **Provence** were under royal control, and an effective standing army had been created. The taxation system had been overhauled, and France had emerged from the Middle Ages a rich, powerful state, firmly under the centralized authority of an absolute monarch.

The Wars of Religion

After half a century of self-confident but inconclusive pursuit of military glory in Italy, brought to an end by the **Treaty of Cateau–Cambrésis** in 1559, France was plunged into another period of devastating internal conflict. The **Protestant** ideas of Luther and Calvin had gained widespread adherence among all classes of society, despite sporadic brutal attempts by François I and Henri II to stamp them out.

Catherine de Médicis, acting as regent for her son, later Henri III, implemented a more tolerant policy, provoking violent reaction from the ultra-Catholic faction led by the **Guise** family. Their massacre of a Protestant congregation coming out of church in March 1562 began a civil **War of Religion** that, interspersed with ineffective truces and accords, lasted for the next thirty years.

Well organized and well led by the Prince de Condé and Admiral Coligny, the **Huguenots** – French Protestants – kept their end up very successfully, until Condé was killed at the battle of Jarnac in 1569. Three years later came one of the blackest events in the memory of French Protestants, even today: the **massacre of St Bartholomew's Day**. Coligny and three thousand Protestants who had gathered in Paris for the wedding of Marguerite, the king's sister, to the Protestant Henri of Navarre were slaughtered at the instigation of the Guises, and the bloodbath was repeated across France, especially in the south and west where the Protestants were strongest.

In 1584 Henri III's son died, leaving his brother-in-law, **Henri of Navarre**, heir to the throne, to the fury of the Guises and their Catholic league, who seized Paris and drove out the king. In retaliation, Henri III murdered the Duc de Guise, and found himself forced into alliance with Henri of Navarre, whom the pope had excommunicated. In 1589 Henri III was himself assassinated, leaving Henri of Navarre to become Henri IV of France. It took another four years of fighting and the abjuration of his faith for the new king to be recognized. "Paris is worth a Mass," he is reputed to have said.

Once on the throne, Henri IV set about reconstructing and reconciling the nation. By the **Edict of Nantes** of 1598, the Huguenots were accorded freedom of conscience, freedom of worship in certain places, the right to attend the same schools and hold the same offices as Catholics, their own courts and the possession of a number of fortresses as a guarantee against renewed attack, the most important being La Rochelle and Montpellier.

Kings, cardinals and absolute power

The main themes of the seventeenth century, when France was largely ruled by just two kings, **Louis XIII** (1610–43) and **Louis XIV** (1643–1715), were, on the domestic front, the strengthening of the centralized state embodied in the person of the king; and in external affairs, the securing of frontiers in the Pyrenees, on the Rhine and in the north, coupled with the attempt to prevent the unification of the territories of the Habsburg kings of Spain and Austria. Both kings had the good fortune to be served by capable, hard-working ministers dedicated to these objectives. Louis XIII had **Cardinal Richelieu** and Louis XIV had cardinals **Mazarin** and **Colbert**. Both reigns were disturbed in their early years by the inevitable aristocratic attempts at a coup d'état.

Having crushed revolts by Louis XIII's brother Gaston, Duke of Orléans, Richelieu's commitment to extending royal absolutism brought him into renewed conflict with the Protestants. Believing that their retention of separate fortresses within the kingdom was a threat to security, he attacked and took La Rochelle in 1627. Although he was unable to extirpate their religion altogether, Protestants were never again to present a military threat.

The other important facet of Richelieu's domestic policy was the promotion of economic self-sufficiency – **mercantilism**. To this end, he encouraged the growth of the luxury craft industries, especially textiles, in which France was to excel right up to the Revolution. He built up the navy and granted privileges to companies involved in establishing **colonies** in North America, Africa and the West Indies.

In pursuing his foreign policy objectives, Richelieu adroitly kept France out of actual military involvement by funding the Swedish king and general, Gustavus Adolphus, to make war against the Habsburgs in Germany. When in 1635 the French were finally obliged to commit their own troops, they made significant gains against the Spanish in the Netherlands, Alsace and Lorraine, and won Roussillon for France.

The Sun King

Richelieu died just a few months before Louis XIII in 1642. As Louis XIV was still an infant, his mother, Anne of Austria, acted as regent, served by Richelieu's protégé, **Cardinal Mazarin**, who was hated just as much as his predecessor by the traditional aristocracy and the *parlements*. They considered him an upstart and were anxious that their privileges, including the collection of taxes, would be curtailed. Spurred by these grievances, which were in any case exacerbated by the ruinous cost of the Spanish wars, various groups in French society combined in a series of revolts, known as the **Frondes**.

The first Fronde, in 1648, was led by the *parlement* of Paris, which resented royal oversight of tax collection. It was quickly followed by an aristocratic Fronde, supported by various peasant risings round the country. All were suppressed easily enough. These were not so much revolutionary movements but, rather, the attempts of various groups to preserve their privileges in the face of the growing power of the state.

In 1659 Mazarin successfully brought the Spanish wars to an end. Two years later, **Louis XIV** came of age, declaring that he would rule without a first minister. He embarked on a long struggle to modernize the administration. The war ministers, Le Tellier and his son Louvois, provided Louis with a well-equipped and well-trained professional army that could muster some 400,000 men by 1670. But the principal reforms were carried out by **Colbert**, who tackled corruption, set up a free-trade area in northern and central France, established the French East India Company, and built up the navy with a view to challenging the commercial supremacy of the Dutch.

Alongside his promotion of wise governance, Louis XIV certainly liked to gild his own throne, earning himself the title Le Roi Soleil, the "**Sun King**". His grandiosity was expressed in two ruinously expensive forms: his extravagant new royal palace at Versailles and incessant military campaigns. His war against the Dutch, in 1672, ultimately resulted in the acquisition of Franche-Comté and a swathe of Flanders, including the city of Lille. In 1681 he simply grabbed Strasbourg, and got away with it.

In 1685, under the influence of his very Catholic mistress, Madame de Maintenon, the king removed all privileges from the **Huguenots** by revoking the Edict of Nantes. The result was devastating. Many of France's most skilled artisans, its wealthiest merchants and its most experienced soldiers were Protestants, and they fled the country in huge numbers – over 200,000 by some estimates. Protestant countries promptly combined under the auspices of the League of Augsburg to fight the French. Another long and exhausting war followed, ending, most unfavourably for Louis XIV, in the **Peace of Rijswik** (1697).

No sooner was this concluded than Louis became embroiled in the question of who was to succeed the moribund Charles II of Spain as ruler of the Hapsburg domains in Europe. William of Orange, now king of England as well as ruler of the Dutch United Provinces, organized a Grand Alliance against Louis. The so-called **War of the Spanish Succession** broke out and went badly for the French. A severe winter in 1709 compounded the hardships with famine and riots at home, causing Louis to seek negotiations. The terms were too harsh for him and the war dragged on until 1713, leaving the country totally impoverished. The Sun King, finally, was eclipsed. He died in 1715, after ruling for 72 years over a country that had grown to dominate Europe, and had become unprecedentedly prosperous, largely because of colonial trade. Louis XIV's power and control, however, had masked growing tensions between central government and traditional vested interests.

Louis XV and the parlements

Louis XIV had outlived both his son and grandson. His successor, **Louis XV**, was only 5 when his great-grandfather died. During the **Regency**, the traditional aristocracy and the *parlements*, who for different reasons hated Louis XIV's advisers, scrambled – successfully – to recover a lot of their lost power and prestige. An experiment with government by aristocratic councils failed, and attempts to absorb the immense national debt by selling shares in an overseas trading company ended in a huge collapse. When the prudent and reasonable **Cardinal Fleury** came to prominence upon the regent's death in 1726, the nation's lot began to improve. The Atlantic seaboard towns grew rich on slavery and trade with the American and Caribbean colonies, though industrial production did not improve much and the disparity in wealth between the countryside and the growing towns continued to increase.

In mid-century there followed more disastrous military ventures, including the **War of Austrian Succession** and the **Seven Years War**, both of which were in effect contests with England for control of the colonial territories in America and India – contests that France lost. The need to finance the wars led to the introduction of a new tax, the Twentieth, which was to be levied on everyone. The *parlement*, which had successfully opposed earlier taxation and fought the Crown over its religious policies, dug its heels in again, leading to renewed conflict over Louis' pro-Jesuit religious policy.

The division between the *parlements* and the king and his ministers continued to sharpen during the reign of **Louis XVI**, which began in 1774. Attempts by the enlightened finance minister Turgot to cooperate with the *parlements* and introduce reforms to alleviate the tax burden on the poor produced only short-term results. Ironically, the one radical attempt to introduce an effective and equitable tax system led directly to the Revolution. Calonne, finance minister in 1786, tried to get his proposed tax approved by an **Assembly of Notables**, a device that had not been employed for more than a hundred years. His purpose was to bypass the *parlement*, which could be relied on to oppose any radical proposal. The attempt backfired, the *parlement* demanding a meeting of the **Estates–General**, representing the nobles, the clergy and the bourgeoisie – this being the only body competent to discuss such matters. As law and order began to break down, the king gave in and agreed to summon the Estates-General on May 17, 1789.

Revolution

Against a background of deepening economic crisis and general misery, the **Estates–General** proved unusually radical. On June 17, 1789, the Third Estate – the representatives of the bourgeoisie – seized the initiative and declared itself the National Assembly, joined by some of the lower clergy and liberal nobility. Louis XVI appeared to accept the situation, and on July 9 the National Constituent Assembly declared itself. However, the king then called in troops, unleashing the anger of the people of Paris, the *sans-culottes* (literally, "without trousers").

On July 14 the *sans-culottes* stormed the fortress of the **Bastille**, symbol of the oppressive nature of the king's "*ancien régime*". Throughout the country, peasants attacked landowners' châteaux, destroying records of debt and other symbols of oppression. On the night of August 4, the Assembly abolished the feudal rights and privileges of the nobility – a momentous shift of gear in the Revolutionary process. Later that month they adopted the **Declaration of the Rights of Man**. In December church lands were nationalized.

Bourgeois elements in the Assembly tried to bring about a compromise with the nobility, with a view to establishing a constitutional monarchy, but these overtures were rebuffed. Émigré aristocrats were already working to bring about foreign invasion to overthrow the Revolution. In June 1791 the king was arrested trying to escape from Paris. The Assembly, following an initiative of the wealthier bourgeois **Girondin** faction, decided to go to war to protect the Revolution.

On August 10, 1792, the *sans-culottes* set up a **Revolutionary Commune** in Paris and imprisoned the king, marking a radical turn in the Revolution. A new National Convention was elected and met on the day the ill-prepared Revolutionary armies finally halted the Prussian invasion at Valmy. A major rift swiftly developed between the more moderate **Girondins** and the **Jacobins** and *sans-culottes* over the abolition of the monarchy. The radicals carried the day, and, in January 1793, Louis XVI was executed. By June, the Girondins had been ousted.

Counter–Revolutionary forces were gathering in the provinces and abroad. A Committee of Public Safety was set up as chief organ of the government. Left-wing popular pressure brought laws on general conscription and price controls and a deliberate policy of secularization, and **Robespierre** was pressed onto the Committee as the best hope of containing the pressure from the streets, marking the beginning of the **Terror**.

As well as ordering the death of the hated queen, Marie-Antoinette, Robespierre felt strong enough to guillotine his opponents on both Right and Left. But the effect of so many rolling heads was to cool people's faith in the Revolution; by mid-1794, Robespierre himself was arrested and executed, and his fall marked the end of radicalism. More conservative forces gained control of the government, deregulating the economy, limiting suffrage and establishing a five-man executive Directory, in 1795.

Napoleon

In 1799, **General Napoleon Bonaparte**, who had made a name for himself as commander of the Revolutionary armies in Italy and Egypt, returned to France and took power in a coup d'état. He became First Consul, with power to choose officials and initiate legislation. He redesigned the tax system, created the Bank of France, replaced the power of local institutions by a corps of *préfets* answerable to himself, and made judges into state functionaries – in short, laid the foundations of the modern French administrative system.

Although alarmingly revolutionary in the eyes of the rest of Europe, Napoleon was no Jacobin. He restored unsold property to émigré aristocrats, reintroduced slavery in the colonies, and recognized the Church once more. The authoritarian, militaristic nature of his regime, meanwhile, became more and more apparent. In 1804 he crowned himself **emperor** in the presence of the pope.

The tide began to turn in 1808. Spain, which was then under the rule of Napoleon's brother, rose in revolt, aided by the British, and in 1812, Napoleon threw himself into the disastrous **Russian campaign**. He reached Moscow, but the long retreat in terrible winter conditions annihilated his veteran Grande Armée. The nation was now weary of the burden of unceasing war and in 1814 Napoleon was forced to abdicate by a coalition of European powers. They installed **Louis XVIII**, brother of the decapitated Louis XVI, as monarch. In a last effort to recapture power, Napoleon escaped from exile in Elba and reorganized his armies, only to meet final defeat at **Waterloo** on June 18, 1815. Louis XVIII was restored to power.

Restorations and revolutions

The years following Napoleon's downfall were marked by a determined campaign, including the **White Terror**, on the part of those reactionary elements who wanted to wipe out all trace of the Revolution and restore the *ancien régime*. **Louis XVIII** resisted these moves and was able to appoint a moderate royalist minister, Decazes, under whose leadership the liberal faction that wished to preserve the Revolutionary reforms made steady gains. This process, however, was wrecked by the assassination of the Duc de Berry in an attempt to wipe out the Bourbon family. In response to reactionary outrage, the king dismissed Decazes. An attempted liberal insurrection was crushed and the four Sergeants of La Rochelle were shot by firing squad. Censorship became more rigid and education was once more subjected to the authority of the Church.

In 1824, Louis was succeeded by the thoroughly reactionary **Charles X**, who pushed through a law indemnifying émigré aristocrats for property lost during the Revolution. When the opposition won a majority in the elections of 1830, the king dissolved the Chamber and restricted the already narrow suffrage.

Barricades went up in the streets of Paris. Charles X abdicated and parliament was persuaded to accept **Louis–Philippe**, Duc d'Orléans, as king. On the face of it, divine right had been superseded by popular sovereignty as the basis of political legitimacy. The **1814 Charter**, which upheld Revolutionary and Napoleonic reforms, was reaffirmed, censorship abolished, the tricolour restored as the national flag, and suffrage widened.

However, the **Citizen King**, as he was called, had somewhat more absolutist notions about being a monarch. In the 1830s his regime survived repeated challenges from both attempted coups by reactionaries and some serious labour unrest in Lyon and Paris. The 1840s were calmer under the ministry of **Guizot**, the first Protestant to hold high office, and it was at this time that **Algeria** was colonized.

Guizot, however, was not popular. He resisted attempts to extend the vote to enfranchise the middle ranks of the bourgeoisie. In 1846, economic crisis brought bankruptcies, unemployment and food shortages. Conditions were appalling for the growing urban working class, whose hopes of a more just future received a theoretical basis in the **socialist writings** and activities of Blanqui, Fourier, Louis Blanc and Proudhon, among others.

1848 and the Second Republic

In February 1848 the government banned an opposition *banquet* – the only permissible form of political meeting – prompting workers and students to take to the streets. When the army fired on a demonstration and killed forty people, civil war appeared imminent. The Citizen King fled to England, a provisional government was set up and a **republic** proclaimed. The government issued a right-to-work declaration, set up national workshops to relieve unemployment and extended the vote to all adult males – an unprecedented move for its time.

All was not plain sailing, though. By the time elections were held in April, a new tax designed to ameliorate the financial crisis had antagonized the countryside. A massive conservative majority was re-elected, to the dismay of the radicals. Three days of bloody street fighting at the barricades followed, when General Cavaignac, who had distinguished himself in the suppression of Algerian resistance, turned the artillery on the workers. More than 1500 were killed and 12,000 arrested and exiled.

A reasonably democratic constitution was drawn up and elections called to choose a president. To everyone's surprise, Louis-Napoléon, nephew of the emperor, romped home. In spite of his liberal reputation, he restricted the vote again, censored the press and pandered to the Catholic Church. In 1852, following a coup and further street fighting, he had himself proclaimed Emperor Napoléon III.

Empire and Commune

Napoléon III ran an authoritarian regime whose most notable achievement was a rapid growth in industrial and economic power. When he came to power, the vast majority of the population lived in conditions that the post-Revolutionary years had done little to change. Over half the country depended on the land (a figure down from three-quarters at the Revolution). Two-thirds of road traffic took the form of a mule and France itself remained a semi-continent made up as much of wilderness – forests, mountains, moorlands and grassy wastes – as land under cultivation. The peasant population was overwhelmingly enmired in debt, poverty and hunger: in 1865, life expectancy for those who made it to 5 years old was 51 years.

Industrialization, however, was now under way, and the emperor's economic **liberalization** began to bite. Other reforms included the right to strike and form trade unions, an extension of public education and the lifting of censorship. The explosive expansion of the railways, meanwhile, began to lift the provinces out of their previous isolation. By 1888, 22,000 miles of track had been laid.

Disaster, however, was approaching in the shape of the **Franco–Prussian** war. Involved in a conflict with Bismarck and the rising power of Germany, Napoléon III declared war. The French army was quickly defeated and the emperor himself taken prisoner in 1870. The result at home was a universal demand for the proclamation of a **third republic**. The German armistice agreement insisted on the election of a national assembly to negotiate a proper peace treaty. France lost Alsace and Lorraine and was obliged to pay hefty war reparations.

Outraged by the monarchist majority re-elected to the new Assembly and by the attempt of its chief minister, Thiers, to disarm the National Guard, the people of Paris created their own municipal government known as the **Commune**. However, it had barely existed two months before it was savagely crushed. On May 21, the "*semaine sanglante*" began in which government troops fought with the Communards street by street, massacring around 25,000, the last of them lined up against the wall of Père Lachaise cemetery and shot. It was a brutal episode that left a permanent scar on the country's political and psychological landscape.

The Third Republic

In the wake of the Commune, competing political factions fought it out for control. Legitimists supported the return of a Bourbon to the throne, while Orléanists supported the heir of Louis-Philippe. Republicans, of course, would have none of either. Thanks in part to the intransigence of the Comte de Chambord, the Bourbon claimant who refused to accept a constitutional role – and in part to a corruption scandal surrounding the first President of the Third Republic, himself a monarchist – it was the Radicals and Socialists who came out on top. Minister Jules Ferry set out laws for free, secular education in 1881 and 1882, and the Crown Jewels were sold off in 1885.

From 1894, the **Dreyfus Affair** dramatically widened the split between right and left. Captain Dreyfus was a Jewish army officer convicted of spying for the Germans and shipped off to the penal colony of Devil's Island. It soon became clear that he had been framed – by the army itself – yet they refused to reconsider his case. The affair immediately became an issue between the anti-Semitic, Catholic Right and the Republican Left, with Radical statesman Clemenceau, Socialist leader Jean Jaurès and novelist Émile Zola coming out in favour of Dreyfus. Charles Maurras, founder of the fascist Action Française – precursor of Europe's Blackshirts – took the part of the army.

Dreyfus was officially rehabilitated in 1904, but in the wake of the affair the more radical element in the Republican movement began to dominate the administration, bringing the army under closer civilian control and dissolving most of the religious orders. In 1905 the Third Republic affirmed its anticlerical roots by introducing a law on the **separation of church and state**.

In the years preceding **World War I**, the country enjoyed a period of renewed prosperity. Yet the conflicts in the political fabric of French society remained unresolved. With the outbreak of war in 1914, France found itself swiftly overrun by Germany and its allies, and defended by its old enemy, Britain. The cost of the war was even greater for France than for the other participants because it was fought largely on French soil. Over a quarter of the eight million men called up were either killed or injured; industrial production fell to sixty percent of the prewar level. This – along with memories of the Franco–Prussian war of 1870 – was the reason that the French were more aggressive than either the British or the Americans in seeking war reparations from the Germans.

In the **postwar struggle for recovery** the interests of the urban working class were again passed over, save for Clemenceau's eight-hour-day legislation in 1919. As the **Depression** deepened in the 1930s and Nazi power across the Rhine became more menacing, fascist thuggery and antiparliamentary activity increased in France, culminating in a pitched battle outside the Chamber of Deputies in February 1934. The effect of this fascist activism was to unite the Left, including the Communists, in the **Front Populaire** – which won the 1936 elections with a handsome majority. **Léon Blum** became France's first socialist and first Jewish Prime Minister. He pushed through progressive reforms, including capping the working week at forty hours and nationalizing the arms industry. Following challenges from the Senate, however, his government fell; the Left would remain out of power until 1981.

World War II

The agonies of **World War II** were compounded for France by the additional traumas of **occupation**, **collaboration** and **Resistance** – in effect, a civil war.

After the lightning defeat of the Anglo-French forces in May–June 1940, **Maréchal Pétain**, a cautious and conservative veteran of World War I, emerged from retirement to sign an armistice with Hitler and head the collaborationist **Vichy government**, which ostensibly governed the southern part of the country, while the Germans occupied the strategic north and the Atlantic coast. Pétain's prime minister, Laval, believed it was his duty to adapt France to the new authoritarian age heralded by the Nazi conquest of Europe.

There has been endless controversy over who collaborated, how much and how far it was necessary in order to save France from even worse sufferings. One thing at least is clear: Nazi occupation provided a good opportunity for out-and-out French fascists to track down Communists, Jews, Resistance fighters, freemasons – all those who they considered "alien" bodies in French society.

While some Communists were involved in the **Resistance** right from the start, Hitler's attack on the Soviet Union in 1941 brought them into the movement on a large scale. Resistance numbers were further increased by young men taking to the hills to escape conscription as labour in Nazi industry. General de Gaulle's radio appeal from London on June 18, 1940, resulted in the Conseil National de la Résistance, unifying the different Resistance groups in May 1943.

Although British and American governments found him irksome, **de Gaulle** was able to impose himself as the unchallenged spokesman of the Free French, and to insist that the voice of France be heard as an equal in the Allied councils of war. Even the Communists accepted his leadership. Representatives of his provisional government moved into liberated areas of France behind the Allied advance after D-Day, thereby saving the country from

▲ General de Gaulle at Bayeux, June 14, 1944

localized outbreaks of civil war – and saving France, in de Gaulle's view, from the threat of Communist uprising.

The aftermath of war

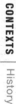

France emerged from the war demoralized, bankrupt and bomb-wrecked. Almost half its population were peasants, living off the land, and its industry was in ruins. The only possible provisional government in the circumstances was de Gaulle's **Free French** and the Conseil National de la Résistance, which meant a coalition of Right and Left. As an opening move to deal with the mess, coal mines, air transport and Renault cars were nationalized. But a new constitution was required and elections, in which **French women** voted for the first time, resulted in a large Left majority in the new Constituent Assembly – which, however, soon fell to squabbling over the form of the new constitution. De Gaulle resigned in disgust.

The constitution finally agreed on, with little enthusiasm in the country, was not much different from the discredited Third Republic. In the shadow of Vichy, the presidency was a weak institution, and the new **Fourth Republic** began its life with a series of short-lived coalitions. Nevertheless, the foundations for welfare were laid, banks nationalized and trade union rights extended. And thanks in part to American aid in the form of the Marshall Plan, France achieved enormous industrial **modernization and expansion** in the 1950s, its growth rate even rivalling that of West Germany at times. France opted to remain in the US fold, but at the same time aggressively and independently pursued **nuclear technology**, finally detonating its own atom bomb in early 1960. France also took the lead in promoting closer **European integration**, a process culminating in 1957 with the creation of the European Economic Community.

Colonial wars

On the surrender of Japan to the Allies in 1945, **Vietnam**, the northern half of the French Indochina colony, came under the control of Ho Chi Minh and his Communist organization, Vietminh. An eight-year armed struggle ended with French defeat at Dien Bien Phu and partition of the country at the Geneva Conference in 1954 – at which point the Americans took over in the south, with well-known consequences.

In the same year the **Algerian war of liberation began**. The French government was legally, economically and, it felt, morally committed to maintaining its rule over Algeria. Legally, the country was a *département*, an integral part of France, and the million-odd settlers, or *pieds noirs*, were officially French. And there was oil in the south. By 1958, half a million troops, most of them conscripts, had been committed to a bloody and brutal war that cost some 700,000 lives.

By 1958, it began to seem as if the government would take a more liberal line towards Algeria. In response, hard-line Rightists among the settlers and in the army staged a putsch and threatened to declare war on France. General de Gaulle let it be known that in its hour of need and with certain conditions – ie stronger powers for the president – the country might call upon his help. Thus, on June 1, 1958, the National Assembly voted him full powers for six months and the Fourth Republic came to an end.

De Gaulle's presidency

As prime minister, then president of the **Fifth Republic** – with powers as much strengthened as he had wished – **de Gaulle** wheeled and dealed with the *pieds noirs* and Algerian rebels, while the war continued. In 1961, a General Salan staged a military revolt and set up the OAS (Secret Army Organization) to prevent a settlement. When his coup failed, his organization made several attempts on de Gaulle's life – thereby strengthening the feeling on the mainland that it was time to be done with Algeria.

The high-water mark of the violence occurred in Paris, in the same year – though the extraordinary incident was covered up and censored until the 1990s. Following a peaceful demonstration against police powers to impose a curfew on any place in France frequented by North Africans, between seventy and two hundred French Algerians were killed by the police in Paris in a **"secret massacre"**. The police shot into crowds, batoned protesters and even threw their bodies into the Seine. For weeks corpses were recovered, but the French media remained silent.

Eventually, in 1962, a referendum gave an overwhelming yes to **Algerian independence**, and *pieds noirs* refugees flooded into France. As the rest of the French colonial empire had achieved independence by this time, the succeeding years saw a resurgence of fascist and racist activity. From the mid-1950s to the mid-1970s a French labour shortage led to massive recruitment campaigns for workers in North Africa, Portugal, Spain, Italy and Greece. People were promised housing, free medical care, trips home and well-paid jobs. When they arrived in France, however, these **immigrants** found themselves under-paid, ill-housed and discriminated against both socially and officially: they had no vote, no automatic permit renewal, and were subject to frequent racial abuse and assault.

De Gaulle's leadership was haughty and autocratic in style, more concerned with *gloire* and grandeur than the everyday problems of ordinary people. His quirky strutting on the world stage irritated France's partners. He blocked British entry to the European Economic Community, cultivated the friendship of the Germans, rebuked the US for its imperialist policies in Vietnam, withdrew from NATO, refused to sign a nuclear test ban treaty and called for a "free Québec".

May 1968

At home, discontent was bubbling under a suspiciously calm surface. The sudden over-boiling of **May 1968** took everyone by surprise. Beginning with protests against the paternalistic nature of the education system by students at the University of Nanterre, the movement of revolt rapidly spread to the Sorbonne and out into factories and offices.

On the night of May 10, barricades went up in the streets of the Quartier Latin in Paris, and the CRS (riot police) responded by wading in with determined ferocity. A **general strike** followed, and within a week more than a million people were out, with many factory occupations and professionals joining in with students and workers to march under radical slogans. Rather than demanding specific reforms, there was a general feeling that all French institutions – French society itself – needed overhauling.

De Gaulle seemed to lose his nerve and on May 27 he vanished from the scene. It turned out he had gone to assure himself of the support of the commander of the French army of the Rhine. On his return he appealed to the nation to elect him as the only effective barrier against left-wing dictatorship, and dissolved parliament. The "silent majority", frightened and shocked by *les événements* – "the events", as they were nervously called – voted massively in his favour. When the smoke cleared, the formal, paternalistic and often authoritarian structures and institutions of France remained in place.

Pompidou and Giscard

Having petulantly staked his presidency on the outcome of yet another referendum (on a couple of constitutional amendments) and lost, de Gaulle once more took himself off to his country estate and retirement. He was succeeded as president by his business-oriented former prime minister, **Georges Pompidou**.

The new regime was devotedly capitalist, and Pompidou hoped to eradicate the memory of 1968 in the creation of wealth, property and competition. His visions, however, had little time to attain reality. Having survived an election in 1972, Pompidou died, suddenly. His successor – and the 1974 presidential election winner by a narrow margin over the socialist François Mitterrand – was the former finance minister **Valéry Giscard d'Estaing**.

Having announced that his aim was to make France "an advanced liberal society", Giscard opened his term of office with some spectacular media coups, inviting Parisian trash collectors to breakfast, visiting prisons in Lyon and addressing the nation on television from his living room every evening. But, aside from reducing the voting age to 18 and liberalizing divorce laws, the advanced liberal society did not make a lot of progress. In the wake of the 1974 oil crisis the government introduced economic austerity measures. Giscard fell out with his ambitious prime minister, **Jacques Chirac**, who set out to challenge the leadership with his own RPR Gaullist party. And in addition to his superior, monarchical style, Giscard further compromised his popularity by accepting diamonds from the (literally) child-eating emperor of the Central African Republic, Bokassa, and by involvement in various other scandals.

The Left seemed well placed to win the coming 1978 elections, when the fragile union between the Socialists and Communists cracked, the latter fearing their roles as the coalition's junior partners. The result was another right-wing victory, with Giscard able to form a new government, with the grudging support of the RPR. Law and order and immigrant controls were the dominant features of Giscard's second term.

The Mitterrand Era, 1981–95

When **François Mitterrand** won the presidential elections over Giscard in 1981, inaugurating the first Socialist government for decades, hopes and expectations were sky high. The government pledged to increase state control over industry, introduce higher taxes for the rich, devolve more power to local government, raise the living standards of the least well-off and pursue European integration. By 1984, however, the flight of capital, inflation and budget deficits had forced a complete turnaround. Prime minister **Laurent Fabius** presided over a cabinet of centrist to conservative "socialist" ministers, clinging desperately to power. The 1986 parliamentary election saw the Right, under Jacques Chirac, winning a clear majority in parliament, so beginning *cohabitation* – the head of state and head of government belonging to opposite sides of the political fence. As Prime Minister, Chirac embarked on a policy of privatization and monetary control.

The 1980s ended with the most absurd blow-out of public funds ever – the **bicentennial celebrations of the French Revolution**. They symbolized a culture industry spinning mindlessly around the vacuum at the centre of the French vision for the future. And they highlighted the contrast between the unemployed and homeless begging on the streets and the limitless cash available for prestige projects.

During this period, Jean-Marie Le Pen, extreme right-winger and leader of the racist Front National, began to attract support. In 1991, Mitterrand sacked Socialist prime minister Michel Rocard, and appointed **Édith Cresson** as France's first woman prime minister. Her brand of left-wing nationalist rhetoric combined with centrist pragmatism made her highly unpopular at home and abroad.

In 1992, Mitterrand staked his reputation on the **Maastricht referendum** on creating closer political union in Europe, as well as economic. The vote was carried by a narrow margin in favour. On the whole, poorer rural areas voted "No" while rich urbanites and political parties voted "Yes". Only the extreme end of the political spectrum, the Communists and the Front National remained determinedly anti-Europe.

Scandals over cover-ups and corruption culminated in the rout of the Socialists in the 1993 parliamentary elections, and the mysterious suicide a few months later of their last prime minister, **Pierre Bérégovoy**. Ushering in another period of *cohabitation*, **Edouard Balladur**, a fresh and fatherly face from the Right, was appointed prime minister. His government carried out a new privatization programme but soon lost the respect of its natural supporters after a series of U-turns following demonstrations by Air France workers, teachers, farmers, fishermen and school pupils, and the state's rescue of the Crédit Lyonnais bank after spectacular losses.

Mitterrand tottered on to the end of his presidential term, looking less and less like the nation's favourite uncle. Two months after Bérégovoy's suicide, Réné Bousquet, head of police in the Vichy government and responsible for the rounding up of Jews in 1942, was murdered. A personal friend of Mitterrand's, he was thought to have carried shady secrets about the president to his grave. A biography of Mitterrand, *Le Grand Secret*, stirred up further controversy about the president's war record as an official in the Vichy regime before he joined the Resistance.

Allegations of **corruption** against politicians and leading figures in industry were becoming an almost weekly occurrence. Several mayors ended up in jail, but it seemed as if the Paris establishment was above the law. Meanwhile, the country's profile abroad was also suffering, nowhere more so than in **Rwanda**, whose genocidal government had been supported and armed by France.

By the time Mitterrand finally stepped down, he had been the French head of state for fourteen years, during a period when crime rose and increasing numbers of people found themselves excluded from society by racism, poverty and homelessness. Corruption scandals touched the president, politicians of all parties and business chiefs and, as faith in old left-wing certainties foundered, support for extreme Right policies propelled the Front National from a minority faction to a serious electoral force. Despite this, when he died in January 1996, Mitterrand was genuinely mourned as a man of culture and vision, a supreme political operator, and an unwavering supporter of a united Europe.

Chirac's presidency

Elected as president in 1995 and winning a second mandate in 2002, Chirac showed himself every bit as astute a politician as Mitterand, and no less prone to scandal and controversy. An early sign of the rocky road ahead came when his Prime Minister, Alain Juppé, introduced **austerity measures**, designed to prepare France for European monetary union. Reforms to pensions and healthcare spending provoked a series of damaging strikes in 1995 and 1996, and led to growing popular disenchantment with the idea of closer European integration.

The **Front National** played up their image of standing up for the small man against the corrupt political establishment, and at municipal elections in June 1995 gained control of three towns, including the major port of Toulon. The **Algerian bomb attacks** which rocked Paris in the mid-1990s – designed to punish France for supporting Algeria's anti-Islamist military government – further played into the hands of the far Right and diminished public confidence in the government as guardian of law and order. The interior minister, **Charles Pasqua**, tapped into the general feelings of insecurity and stepped up anti-immigration measures.

Feeling increasingly beleaguered and unable to deliver on the economy, Chirac called a snap parliamentary election in May 1997. His gamble failed spectacularly, and he was forced into a weak *cohabitation* with a Socialist parliament headed by **Lionel Jospin**, who promptly introduced the 35-hour working week, a 50:50 gender quota for representatives of political parties and, in 1999, the **Pacs** or Pacte Civile de Solidarité, a contract giving cohabiting couples, particularly gay couples, almost the same rights as married people.

Skeletons in the mayoral cupboard

The most persistent **corruption scandals** focused on the finances of the Paris town hall, dating back to the 1980s. In 1995 it was revealed that Alain Juppé had rented a luxury flat in Paris for his son at below-market rates, and in 1998 the conservative Paris mayor **Jean Tiberi** was implicated in a scam involving subsidized real-estate and fake town-hall jobs – with real salaries – for party activists and relatives. Prosecutors edged ever closer to Chirac himself. In 2001 the president was accused of using some three million francs in cash from illegal sources to pay for luxury holidays, and in 2003 it was revealed that in eight years in office as mayor of Paris he and his wife had run up grocery bills of 2.2 million euros – over half of which had been reimbursed in cash. When investigating magistrates tried to question Chirac he claimed presidential immunity, a position that was upheld by France's highest court. (It seems unlikely he will be called to account, even now that he is out of office.)

The election earthquake

In the run-up to the **presidential elections of 2002**, everyone in France assumed that the race was between Jacques Chirac and his Socialist rival, Lionel Jospin. The far left was as divided as ever, while the far-right vote had been damagingly split since 1996 – and Front National leader, **Jean-Marie Le Pen**, had lost much support for punching a woman Socialist candidate in 1998.

Lionel Jospin's hopes had been bolstered by the election of Socialist **Bertrand Delanoë** as Mayor of Paris in March 2001 – the first time that the Socialists had won control of the capital since the bloody uprising of the Paris Commune in 1871. In the run-up to the elections, however, the economy began to falter, unemployment was once more on the rise and fears over crime were widespread. Chirac's campaign began mirroring that of his far-right rival, talking up issues of immigration and law and order. The results of the first round came through on the evening of April 21. Jospin had been beaten into third place by Le Pen – leaving Chirac and Le Pen to stand against each other in the final run-off in May.

The result, widely referred to as an "earthquake", sent shockwaves throughout the country and abroad. Widespread **voter apathy** and disillusionment were blamed. Many voters had abstained or voted for marginal candidates as a protest against the mainstream parties. Le Pen himself had fought a canny campaign, toning down his racist rhetoric and making capital out of the mainstream parties' sleaze and remoteness from ordinary people. On May 1, however, 800,000 people packed the boulevards of Paris to protest against Le Pen and his anti-immigration policies, in the biggest **demonstration** the capital had seen since the student protests of 1968. The Socialists called on their supporters to vote for Chirac in order to keep Le Pen out – and Chirac duly swept the board.

In the **ensuing parliamentary elections**, Chirac's supporters rallied round to create an umbrella grouping of right-wing parties, called the **Union for a Presidential Majority**. The Right swept to power with 369 of the 577 seats in the National Assembly. In an attempt to address widespread concerns about lack of representation and government accountability, one of Chirac's first measures was a **devolution** bill, giving more power to 26 regional assemblies and ending centuries of central government steadily accruing power to itself.

Iraq, Muslims and climate change

In 2003, a reinvigorated Chirac thrust himself into the international spotlight by adopting a remarkably intransigent stance over the **Iraq war**. As self-appointed spokesman for the no-sayers, Chirac declared in early March that he would wield France's Security Council veto if the US tried to table a resolution that contained an ultimatum leading to war. It was a bravura performance to an approving domestic crowd, the nationalist Right admiring Chirac's Gaullist flexing of France's international muscles and the Left reluctantly applauding his jaw-jutting opposition to American imperialism. Internationally, some interpreted France's stance as a principled defence of the UN and international law; others saw it as a test of the EU's diplomatic clout, and an assertion of France's power within Europe. Others still saw Chirac's actions as cynical political posturing.

Whether blamed on US bullishness or French pig-headedness, the result was an almighty farmyard scrap that left the US-led "coalition of the willing" exposed in Iraq without the diplomatic cover of definitive UN sanction. On either side of the Atlantic, the cherished Franco–American relationship suffered its worst spat ever. In France, American tourist numbers plummeted, and the nation indulged itself in an orgy of anti-Americanism.

One thing France's tough stance wasn't based on was any particularly pro-Arab or pro-Islamic bias, despite the presence of 5 million or more **Muslims** in France – the largest community in Europe. During 2003, Chirac presided over a government setting expulsion targets for illegal immigrants and enacting a hugely controversial bill – though it was backed by almost two-thirds of the population and passed in parliament by 494 votes to 36 – banning "ostensibly religious" signs, notably Islamic headscarves, from schools and hospitals. Proposing the measure in December 2003, Chirac avowed that "Secularity is one of the republic's great achievements ... We must not allow it to be weakened."

In 2003 **climate change** also bludgeoned its way onto the headlines, by indirectly causing the deaths of some 15,000 people over the norm. In Paris, temperatures in the first half of August were the hottest ever recorded, regularly topping 40°C (104°F) – more than ten degrees above the average maximum for that time of year. The authorities blamed lack of air-conditioning and the duration of the heatwave; the opposition blamed an ill-prepared health ministry. No one seemed willing to take responsibility for doing anything about it.

Reform and revolt

Faced with an ageing population, unemployment flatlining at around ten percent and a budget deficit persistently exceeding the eurozone's three-percent ceiling, the newly confident Right decided it would take on the public sector once and for all. Dubbed Agenda 2006, the **reform programme**'s targets were loathed by economic liberalizers and loved by most of the French public in equal measure. First to go under the knife would be the state's generous pensions and unemployment benefits, then worker-friendly hiring and firing rights, and finally the world-leading health service.

Most of France saw the programme less as prudent milk-rationing and more as getting their sacred cows ready to be sent off to slaughter. In the spring of 2003 the country suffered wave after wave of public-sector strikes and marches rolled through the streets. By mid-May, two million workers were out on strike; and on May 26 half a million protested in the streets of Paris. And this was only in defence of pensions.

By 2004, the government had curbed its ambitions, while still insisting that reform was essential. The slick and ambitious new finance minister, **Nicolas Sarkozy**, set out a programme of privatizations and public-sector parsimony. The health-care budget would be trimmed, but so would the defence budget, and the electorate would be further mollified by consumer-focused tax breaks. The public response was unequivocal. In the regional elections of March 2004 just one of the 22 mainland regional councils remained in the control of the centre-right. Overnight, the electoral map had turned a furious pink.

The electorate's anger was not aimed solely at the Right. In the referendum of May 2005, 55 percent of French voters rejected the proposed new EU constitution when all the major political parties had urged them to vote "Yes". Opponents of the draft constitution saw it as wedding France to an "Anglo-Saxon" Europe, on the neoliberal economic model. Many were voting against globalization or political paternalism as much as against the constitution itself.

Civil unrest…

Nicolas Sarkozy had hardly got himself nominated as the new leader of Chirac's UMP party, and acquired a new job as Interior Minister, when **civil unrest** swept France's urban areas. The initial cause was the accidental deaths of two teenagers in October 2005, electrocuted while running from police in a run-down area of the Paris *banlieue* – the swathes of impoverished, disenfranchised housing estates surrounding Paris. Local anger led to numerous **car-burnings** and confrontations with police, and before a week was out rioting had spread to Dijon, Rouen and Marseille. Night after night, youths torched cars, buses, schools and even police and power stations – anything associated with the state.

The hardline response of "Sarko", as the Interior Minister was now dubbed, was to call the rioters *racailles* (a rabble) and to demand the neighbourhoods were cleaned with power-hoses. A state of emergency was declared and after three weeks, the *banlieue* seemed to have burned itself out. Almost 9000 vehicles and property worth €200 million had gone up in smoke, right across France, and almost over 2900 people had been arrested.

The causes of the unrest were hotly debated. A complete breakdown of relations between disaffected young people and the police was certainly the major factor. Young people who actually lived in the "hot" suburbs saw the main causes as anger at **racism** and exclusion from society, including exclusion from employment. Many of the worst-affected areas are home to communities of largely African or North-African origin, where youth unemployment runs as high as fifty percent – double the already high average among young people.

…and youth protest

Even as the *banlieue* burned, the more prosperous towns and suburbs were becoming uncomfortably hot. Prime Minister Dominique de Villepin attempted to tackle the problem of youth unemployment and economic stagnation by giving small companies the right to dismiss new employees without having to give cause. Labour-market flexibility and economic growth were the goals. This looked suspiciously like an attack on the cherished **French exception** – the political status quo whereby the state protects workers' rights, the national agricultural and industrial base, and French culture generally. It looked dangerously like neoliberal or

"Anglo-Saxon" capitalism. On 5 October, 2005, a million workers across the country marched against the new labour law, and polls showed that three-quarters of the population supported them.

In 2006, the laws were to be extended to all companies employing workers under the age of 26, as part of the *Contrat première embauche* (**CPE**), or first employment contract. The law was supposed to encourage firms to hire young people. Students and the young wondered why they, uniquely, should be denied the rights their elders took for granted. In March, students in Paris **occupied the Sorbonne**, in conscious imitation of May 1968. Once again, they were brutally driven out by riot police. And just as in 1968, people protested across France in their millions – only this time in the hope not that France would radically change, but that everything would stay the same. A notorious survey at this time concluded that the most desired job among young people in France was not that of film director or political activist, but of civil servant. *Casseurs*, or hooligans, blended in and sometimes clashed with the protestors – who seemed determined to back down. On April 10, Dominique de Villepin withdrew the law.

Super Sarko?

In the wake of the CPE debacle, Nicolas Sarkozy was confirmed as the UMP's candidate for the 2007 presidential election. His Socialist rival, **Ségolène Royal**, occupied a Blairite centre ground previously unknown in French politics. The electorate was unconvinced, choosing to trust instead the apparent dynamism of a man who promised to renew the country by completing the radical reforms that strike after strike had previously defeated. On May 6 Sarkozy was duly elected President – the first to have been born after the end of World War II.

The fairly narrow margin of Sarkozy's victory may have been one reason for his conciliatory choice of cabinet: half his ministers were women, his foreign minister was a left-winger while his Justice Minister, Rachida Dati, was of north African descent. The new Prime Minister, François Fillon, however, was a pure-blooded conservative. He had been the driving force behind the pension **reforms** of the early 2000s. This time, however, the government vowed to finish the job.

Half of France was equally determined it wouldn't. By November 2007, civil servants and other workers were on the streets. In May 2008, the government was beset by general strikes against the notion of raising the retirement age by one year, accompanied by yet more rioting in the Paris *banlieue*. Cracks were appearing in the government. Matters weren't helped by a President who appeared distracted by **media attention**, and who had responded to his wife's departure by pursuing a whirlwind romance with a high-profile former model, Carla Bruni. Amid accusations of Berlusconi-like hubris, narcissism and media control, Sarkozy's ratings plummeted.

By the summer of 2008, the reforming zeal of "Super Sarko", as he was ironi-cally dubbed, didn't look as if it would survive to the end of his term. He had instituted modest **constitutional changes**, strengthening parliament and reducing the power of the presidency. He had trimmed the state-sector payroll and reduced taxes, especially for the upper middle classes. He had promised to increase France's reliance on nuclear energy – which was already producing 87 percent of France's electricity – and cut carbon emissions. Real, radical reform, however – the dream of generations of French politicians and thinkers – seemed as impossible as ever.

The prospects of Sarkozy's presidency were sharply revived by the developing financial crisis of the autumn. French banks had long been derided internationally for their caution, with credit cards barely in circulation and household debt running at less than half the level in the UK. The French government, similarly, was traditionally scorned for its excessive enthusiasm for regulation: its supposedly hidebound unwillingness to participate in the economic miracle of liberal capitalism. As banks around the world teetered on the edge of collapse, however, French doubts about the sustainability of the debt-heavy "Anglo-Saxon" economic model suddenly looked entirely reasonable. As the holder of the European Union Presidency during the initial stages of the developing crisis, Sarkozy was able to reap political profit from the energetic leadership he so eagerly displayed: calling European summits and announcing package after package of measures designed to stimulate the domestic economy. Whether his efforts could do anything to shore up France's slow slide into recession, however, was less than clear.

Art

Since the Middle Ages, France has held – with occasional gaps – a leading position in the history of European painting, with Paris, above all, attracting artists from the whole continent. The story of French painting is one of richness and complexity, partly due to this influx of foreign painters and partly due to the capital's stability as an artistic centre.

Beginnings

In the late Middle Ages, the itinerant life of the nobles led them to prefer small and transportable works of art; splendidly **illuminated manuscripts** were much praised and the best painters, usually trained in Paris, continued to work on a small scale until the fifteenth century. Many illuminators were also panel painters, and foremost among them was **Jean Fouquet** (c.1420–81). Born in Tours in the Loire valley he became court painter to Charles VIII, drawing from both Flemish and Italian sources and utilizing the new fluid oil technique that had been perfected in Flanders. His feeling for volume and ordered geometric shapes laid down principles that became intrinsic to French art for centuries to come, from Poussin to Seurat and Cézanne.

Two other fifteenth-century French artists could be said to represent distinctive northern and southern strands. **Enguerrand Quarton** (c.1410–c.1466) was the most famous Provençal painter of the time. His *Coronation of the Virgin*, which hangs at Villeneuve-lès-Avignon, ranks as one of the first city/landscapes in the history of French painting: Avignon itself is faithfully depicted and the Mont Ste-Victoire, later to be made famous by Cézanne, is recognizable in the distance. The **Master of Moulins**, active in the 1480s and 1490s, was noticeably more northern in temperament, painting both religious altarpieces and portraits commissioned by members of the royal family or the fast-increasing bourgeoisie.

Mannerism and Italian influence

At the end of the fifteenth and the beginning of the sixteenth centuries, the French invasion of Italy brought both artists and patrons into closer contact with the Italian Renaissance.

The most famous of the artists who were lured to France was **Leonardo da Vinci**, spending the last three years of his life (1516–19) at the court of François 1ᵉʳ. From the Loire valley, which until then had been his favourite residence, the French king moved nearer to Paris, where he had several palaces decorated. Italian artists were once again called upon, and two of them, **Rosso** and **Primaticcio**, who arrived in France in 1530 and 1532, respectively, were to shape the artistic scene in France for the rest of the sixteenth century.

Both artists introduced to France the latest Italian style, **Mannerism**, a sometimes anarchic derivation of the High Renaissance of Michelangelo and Raphael. Mannerism, with its emphasis on the fantastic, the luxurious and the large-scale decorative, was eminently compatible with the taste of the court, and it was first put to the test in the revamping of the old Château de Fontainebleau. Most French artists worked at Fontainebleau at some point in their career, or were influenced by its homogeneous style, leading to what was subsequently called the **School of Fontainebleau**.

Antoine Caron (c.1520–1600), who often worked for Catherine de Médicis, the widow of Henri II, contrived complicated allegorical paintings in which elongated figures are arranged within wide, theatre-like scenery packed with ancient monuments and Roman statues. Even the Wars of Religion, raging in the 1550s and 1560s, failed to rouse French artists' sense of drama, and representations of the many massacres then going on were detached and fussy in tone.

Portraiture tended to be more inventive, and very French in its general sobriety. The portraits of **Jean Clouet** (c.1485–1541) and his son **François** (c.1510–72), both official painters to François 1er, combined sensitivity in the rendering of the sitter's features with a keen sense of abstract design in the arrangement of the figure, conveying with great clarity social status and giving clues to the sitter's profession.

The seventeenth century

In the **seventeenth century**, Italy continued to be a source of inspiration for French artists, most of whom were drawn to Rome – at that time the most exciting artistic centre in Europe, dominated by Italian painters such as Michelangelo Merisi da Caravaggio and Annibale Carracci.

Some French painters like **Moise Valentin** (c.1594–1632) worked in Rome and were directly influenced by Caravaggio; others, such as the great painter from Lorraine, **Georges de la Tour** (1593–1652), benefited from his innovations at one remove, gaining inspiration from the Utrecht Caravaggisti who were active at the time in Holland. Starting with a descriptive realism in which naturalistic detail made for a varied painted surface, La Tour gradually simplified both forms and surfaces, producing deeply felt religious paintings in which figures appear to be carved out of the surrounding gloom by the magical light of a candle. Sadly, his output was very small – just some forty or so works in all.

Lowlife subjects and attention to naturalistic detail were also important aspects of the work of the **Le Nain brothers**, especially **Louis** (1593–1648), who depicted with great sympathy, but never with sentimentality, the condition of the peasantry. He chose moments of inactivity or repose within the lives of the peasants, and his paintings achieve timelessness and monumentality by their very stillness. The other Italian artist of influence, the Bolognese **Annibale Carracci** (d. 1609), impressed French painters not only with his skill as a decorator but, more tellingly, with his ordered, balanced landscapes, which were to prove of prime importance for the development of the classical landscape in general, and in particular for those painted by **Claude Lorrain** (1604/5–82). Born in Lorraine, he studied and travelled in Italy, which would provide him with subjects of study for the rest of his life. His landscapes are airy compositions in which religious or mythological figures are lost within an idealized, Arcadian nature, bathed in tranquil light.

Landscapes, harsher and even more ordered, but also recalling the Arcadian mood of antiquity, were painted by the other French painter who elected to make Rome his home, **Nicolas Poussin** (1594–1665). Like Claude, Poussin selected his themes from the rich sources of Greek, Roman and Christian myths and stories; unlike Claude, however, his figures are not subdued by nature but rather dominate it, in the tradition of the masters of the High Renaissance, such as Raphael and Titian, whom he greatly admired. Poussin only briefly returned to Paris, called by the king, Louis XIII, to undertake some large decorative works quite unsuited to his style or character. Back in Rome he refined a style that became increasingly classical and severe.

Many other artists visited Italy, but most returned to France, the luckiest to be employed at the court to boost the royal images of Louis XIII and XIV and the egos of their respective ministers, Richelieu and Colbert. **Simon Vouet** (1590–1649), **Charles Le Brun** (1619–90) and **Pierre Mignard** (1612–95) all performed that task with skill, often using ancient history and mythology to suggest flattering comparisons with the reigning monarch.

The official aspect of their works was paralleled by the creation of the new **Academy of Painting and Sculpture** in 1648, an institution that dominated the arts in France for the next few hundred years, if only by the way artists reacted against it. **Philippe de Champaigne** (1602–74), a painter of Flemish origin, alone stands out at the time as remotely different, removed from the intrigues and pleasures of the court and instead strongly influenced by the teaching and moral code of Jansenism, a purist and severe form of the Catholic faith. But it was the more courtly, fun-loving portraits and paintings by such artists as Mignard that were to influence most of the art of the following century.

The early eighteenth century

The semi-official art encouraged by the foundation of the Academy became more frivolous and light-hearted in the **eighteenth century**. The court at Versailles lost its attractions, and many patrons now were to be found among the hedonistic bourgeoisie and aristocracy living in Paris. History painting, as opposed to genre scenes or portraiture, retained its position of prestige, but at the same time the various categories began to merge and many artists tried their hands at landscape, genre, history or decorative works, bringing aspects of one type into another. **Salons**, at which painters exhibited their works, were held with increasing frequency and bred a new phenomenon in the art world – the art critic. The philosopher **Diderot** was one of the first of these arbiters of taste, doers and undoers of reputations.

Possibly the most complex personality of the eighteenth century was **Jean-Antoine Watteau** (1684–1721). Primarily a superb draughtsman, Watteau's use of soft and yet rich, light colours reveals how much he was struck by the great seventeenth-century Flemish painter Rubens. The open-air scenes of flirtatious love painted by Rubens and by the fifteenth/sixteenth-century Venetian Giorgione provided Watteau with precedents for his own subtle depictions of dreamy couples, often seen strolling in delicate, mythical landscapes. In these "*Fêtes Galantes*" Watteau conveyed a mood of melancholy and poignancy which was largely lacking in the works of followers such as Nicolas Lancret and J.-B. Pater.

The work of **François Boucher** (1703–70) was probably more representative of the eighteenth century: the pleasure-seeking court of Louis XV found the lightness of morals and colours in his paintings immensely congenial. Boucher's virtuosity is seen at its best in his paintings of women, always rosy, young and fantasy-erotic.

Jean-Honoré Fragonard (1732–1806) continued this exploration of licentious themes but with an exuberance, a richness of colour and a vitality (*The Swing*) that was a feast for the eyes and raised the subject to a glorification of love. Far more restrained were the paintings of **Jean-Baptiste-Siméon Chardin** (1699–1779), who specialized in homely genre scenes and still lifes, painted with a simplicity that belied his complex use of colours, shapes and space to promote a mood of stillness and tranquillity. **Jean-Baptiste Greuze** (1725–1805) chose stories that anticipated reaction against the laxity of the times; the moral, at times sentimental, character of his paintings was all-pervasive, reinforced by a stage-like composition well suited to cautionary tales.

Neoclassicism

This new seriousness became more severe with the rise of **Neoclassicism**, a movement for which purity and simplicity were essential components of the systematic depiction of edifying stories from the classical authors. Roman history and legends were the most popular subjects, and though **Jacques-Louis David** (1748–1825), a pupil of an earlier exponent of Neoclassicism, J.M. Vien, conformed to that to a certain extent, he was different in that he was also keenly sensitive to the changing mood and philosophies of his time and to the reaction against frivolity and self-indulgence. Many of his paintings are reflections of republican ideals and of contemporary history, from the *Death of Marat* to events from the life of Napoleon, who was his patron. For the emperor and his family, David painted some of his most successful portraits – *Madame Recamier* is not only an exquisite example of David's controlled use of shapes and space and his debt to antique Rome, but can also be seen as a paradigm of Neoclassicism.

Two painters, **Jean-Antoine Gros** (1771–1835) and **Baron Gérard** (1770–1837), followed David closely in style and in themes (portraits, Napoleonic history and legend), but often with a touch of softness and heroic poetry that pointed the way to Romanticism.

Jean-Auguste-Dominique Ingres (1780–1867) was a pupil of David; he also studied in Rome before coming back to Paris to develop the purity of line that was the essential and characteristic element of his art. His effective use of it to build up forms and bind compositions can be admired in conjunction with his recurrent theme of female nudes bathing, or in his magnificent and stately portraits that depict the nuances of social status.

Romanticism

Completely opposed to the stress on drawing advocated by Ingres, two artists created, through their emphasis on colour, form and composition, pictures that look forward to the later part of the nineteenth century and the Impressionists. **Théodore Géricault** (1791–1824), whose short life was still dominated by the heroic vision of the Napoleonic era, explored dramatic themes of human suffering in such paintings as *The Raft of the Medusa*, while his close contemporary, **Eugène Delacroix** (1798–1863), epitomized the **Romantic movement** – its search for emotions and its love of nature, power and change.

Delacroix was deeply aware of tradition, and his art was influenced, visually and conceptually, by the great masters of the Renaissance and the seventeenth and eighteenth centuries. In many ways he may be regarded as the last great religious and decorative French painter, but through his technical virtuosity, freedom of brushwork and richness of colours, he can also be seen as the essential forerunner of the Impressionists.

Other painters working in the Romantic tradition were still haunted by the Napoleonic legends, as well as by North Africa (Algeria) and the Middle East, which had become better known to artists and patrons alike during the Napoleonic wars. These were the subjects of paintings by **Horace Vernet** (1789–1863), **Jean-Louis-Ernest Meissonier** (1815–91) and **Théodore Chassériau** (1819–56).

Among their contemporaries was **Honoré Daumier** (1808–79): very much an isolated figure, influenced by the boldness of approach of caricaturists, he was content to depict everyday subjects such as a laundress or a third-class rail car – caustic commentaries on professions and politics that work as brilliant observations of the times.

Landscape painting and realism

The first part of the **nineteenth century** saw nature, in its true state, unadorned by conventions, became a subject for study, and running parallel to this was the realization that painting could be the visual externalization of the artist's own emotions and feelings. These two aspects, which until this time had only been very tentatively touched upon, were now more fully explored and led directly to the innovations of the Impressionists and later painters.

Jean-Baptiste-Camille Corot (1796–1875) started to paint landscapes that were fresh, direct and influenced as much by the unpretentious and realistic country scenes of seventeenth-century Holland as by the balanced compositions of Claude. His loving and attentive studies of nature were much admired by later artists, including Monet.

At the same time, a whole group of painters developed similar attitudes to landscape and nature, helped greatly by the practical improvement of being able to buy oil paint in tubes rather than as unmixed pigments. Known as the **Barbizon School** after the village on the outskirts of Paris around which they painted, they soon discovered the joy and excitement of *plein-air* (open-air) painting.

Théodore Rousseau (1812–67) was their nominal leader, his paintings of forest undergrowth and forest clearings displaying an intimacy that came from the immediacy of the image. **Charles-François Daubigny** (1817–78), like Rousseau, often infused a sense of drama into his landscapes.

Jean-François Millet (1814–75) is perhaps the best-known associate of the Barbizon group, though he was more interested in the human figure than simple nature. Landscapes, however, were essential settings for his figures; indeed, his most famous pictures are those exploring the place of people in nature and their struggle to survive. *The Sower*, for instance, reflected a typical Millet theme, suggesting the heroic working life of the peasant. As is so often the case for painters touching on new themes or on ideas that are uncomfortable to the rich and powerful, Millet enjoyed little success during his lifetime, and his art was only widely appreciated after his death.

The moralistic and romantic undertone in Millet's work was something that **Gustave Courbet** (1819–77) strove to avoid. After an initial resounding success in the Salon exhibition of 1849, he endured constant criticism from the academic world and patrons alike, his scenes of ordinary life regarded as unsavoury and wilfully ugly. Breaking with the Salon tradition, Courbet put on a private exhibition of some forty of his works. Inscribed on the door in large letters was one word: "**Realism**".

Impressionism

Like Courbet, **Edouard Manet** (1832–83) was strongly influenced by Spanish painters. Unlike Courbet, however, he never saw himself as a rebel or avant-garde painter – yet his technique and his themes were both new and shocking. Manet used bold contrasts of light and very dark colours, giving his paintings a forcefulness that critics often took for a lack of sophistication. And his detractors saw much to decry in his reworking of an old subject originally treated by the sixteenth-century Venetian painter, Giorgione, *Le Déjeuner sur l'Herbe*. Manet's version was shocking because he placed naked and dressed figures together, and because the men were dressed in the costume of the day, implying a pleasure party too specifically contemporary to be "respectable".

Manet was not interested in painting moral lessons, however, and some of his most successful pictures are reflections of ordinary life in bars and public places, where respectability, as understood by the late nineteenth-century bourgeoisie, was certainly lacking. To Manet, painting was to be enjoyed for its own sake and not as a tool for moral instruction – in itself an outlook on the role of art that was quite new, not to say revolutionary, and marked a definite break with the paintings of the past. With Manet, the basis of our present expectations and understanding of modern art was established.

From the 1870s, Manet began to adopt the **Impressionist** techniques of painting out-of-doors, and his work became lighter and freer. Although it is doubtful whether Manet either wanted or expected to assume the role of leader, he found himself a much-admired member of that group of painters, one of whom was **Claude Monet** (1840–1926). Born in Le Havre, Monet came into contact with **Eugène Boudin** (1824–98), whose colourful beach scenes anticipated the way the Impressionists approached colour. He then went to Paris to study under Charles Gleyre, a respected teacher in whose studio he met many of the people with whom he formulated his ideas. Monet soon discovered that, for him, light and the way in which it builds up forms and creates an infinity of colours was the element that governed all representations. Under the impact of Manet's bright hues and his unconventional attitude ("art for art's sake"), Monet soon began using pure colours side by side, blended together to create areas of brightness and shade.

In 1874, a group of thirty artists exhibited together for the first time. Among them were some of the best-known names of this period of French art: Degas, Monet, Renoir, Pissarro. One of Monet's paintings was entitled *Impression: Sun Rising*, a title that was singled out by the critics to ridicule the colourful, loose and unacademic style of these young artists. Overnight they became, derisively, the "**Impressionists**".

Camille Pissarro (1830–1903) was slightly older than most of them and seems to have played the part of an encouraging father-figure, always keenly aware of any new development or new talent. Not a great innovator himself, Pissarro was a very gifted artist whose use of Impressionist technique was supplemented by a lyrical feeling for nature and its seasonal changes. But it was really with **Monet** that Impressionist theory ran its full course: he painted and repainted the same motif under different light conditions, at different times of

▲ Two Blue Dancers by Edgar Degas

the day, and in different seasons, producing whole series of paintings such as *Grain Stacks*, *Poplars* and, much later, his *Waterlilies*.

Auguste Renoir (1841–1919), who started life as a painter of porcelain, was swept up by Monet's ideas for a while, but soon felt the need to look again at the old masters and to emphasize the importance of drawing to the detriment of colour. Renoir regarded the representation of the female nude as the most taxing and rewarding subject that an artist could tackle. Like Boucher in the eighteenth century, Renoir's nudes are luscious, but rarely, if ever, erotic. They have a healthy, uncomplicated quality that was, in his later paintings, to become cloyingly, almost overpoweringly, sickly and sweet. Better were his portraits of women fully clothed, both for their obvious and innate sympathy and for their keen sense of design.

Edgar Degas (1834–1917) was yet another artist who, although he exhibited with the Impresssionists, did not follow their precepts very closely. The son of a rich banker, he was trained in the tradition of Ingres: design and drawing were an integral part of his art, and, whereas Monet was fascinated mainly by light, Degas wanted to express movement in all its forms. His pictures are vivid expressions of the body in action, usually straining under fairly exacting circumstances – dancers and circus artistes were among his favourite subjects, as well as more mundane depictions of laundresses and other working women.

Like so many artists of the day, Degas had his imagination fired by the discovery of **Japanese prints**, which could for the first time be seen in quantity.

These provided him with new ideas of composition, not least in their asymmetry of design and the use of large areas of unbroken colour. **Photography**, too, had an impact, if only because it finally liberated artists from the task of producing accurate, exacting descriptions of the world.

Degas' extraordinary gift as a draughtsman was matched only by that of the Provençal aristocrat **Henri de Toulouse-Lautrec** (1864–1901). Toulouse-Lautrec, who had broken both his legs as a child, was unusually small, a physical deformity that made him particularly sensitive to free and vivacious movements. A great admirer of Degas, he chose similar themes: people in cafés and theatres, working women and variety dancers all figured large in his work. But, unlike Degas, Toulouse-Lautrec looked beyond the body, and his work is scattered with social comment, sometimes sardonic and bitter. In his portrayal of Paris prostitutes, there is sympathy and kindness; to study them better he lived in a brothel, revealing in his paintings the weariness and sometimes gentleness of these women.

Post-Impressionism

Though a rather vague term, as it's difficult to date exactly when the backlash against Impressionism took place, **Post-Impressionism** represents in many ways a return to more formal concepts of painting – in composition, in attitudes to subject and in drawing.

Paul Cézanne (1839–1906), for one, associated only very briefly with the Impressionists and spent most of his working life in relative isolation, obsessed with rendering, as objectively as possible, the essence of form. He saw objects as basic shapes – cylinders, cones, and so on – and tried to give the painting a unity of texture that would force the spectator to view it not so much as a representation of the world but rather as an entity in its own right, as an object as real and dense as the objects surrounding it. It was this striving for pictorial unity that led him to cover the entire surface of the picture with small, equal brush strokes which made no distinction between the textures of a tree, a house or the sky.

The detached, unemotional way in which Cézanne painted was not unlike that of the seventeenth-century artist Poussin, and he found a contemporary parallel in the work of **Georges Seurat** (1859–91). Seurat was fascinated by current theories of light and colour, and he attempted to apply them in a systematic way, creating different shades and tones by placing tiny spots of pure colour side by side, which the eye could in turn fuse together to see the colours mixed out of their various components. This **pointillist** technique also had the effect of giving monumentality to everyday scenes of contemporary life.

While Cézanne, Seurat and, for that matter, the Impressionists sought to represent the outside world objectively, several other artists – the **Symbolists** – were seeking a different kind of truth, through the subjective experience of fantasy and dreams. **Gustave Moreau** (1840–98) represented, in complex paintings, the intricate worlds of the romantic fairy tale, his visions expressed in a wealth of naturalistic details. The style of **Puvis de Chavannes** (1824–98) was more restrained and more obviously concerned with design and the decorative. And a third artist, **Odilon Redon** (1840–1916), produced some weird and visionary graphic work that especially intrigued Symbolist writers; his less frequent works in colour belong to the later part of his life.

The subjectivity of the Symbolists was of great importance to the art of **Paul Gauguin** (1848–1903). He started life as a stockbroker who collected

Impressionist paintings, a Sunday artist who gave up his job in 1883 to dedicate himself to painting.

During his stay in Pont-Aven in Brittany, Gauguin worked with a number of artists who called themselves the **Nabis**, among them **Paul Sérusier** and **Émile Bernard**. He began exploring ways of expressing concepts and emotions by means of large areas of colour and powerful forms, and developed a unique style that was heavily indebted to his knowledge of Japanese prints and of the tapestries and stained glass of medieval art. His search for the primitive expression of primitive emotions took him eventually to the Pacific, where, in Tahiti, he found some of his most inspiring subjects.

A similar derivation from Symbolist art and a wish to exteriorize emotions and ideas by means of strong colours, lines and shapes underlies the work of **Vincent Van Gogh** (1853–90), a Dutch painter who came to live in France. Like Gauguin, with whom he had an admiring but stormy friendship, Van Gogh started painting relatively late in life, lightening his palette in Paris under the influence of the Impressionists, and then heading south to Arles where, struck by the harshness of the Mediterranean light, he turned out such frantic expressionistic pieces as *The Reaper* and *Wheatfield with Crows*. In all his later pictures the paint is thickly laid on in increasingly abstract patterns that follow the shapes and tortuous paths of his deep inner melancholy.

Édouard Vuillard (1868–1940) and **Pierre Bonnard** (1867–1947) explored the Nabi artists' interest in Japanese art and in the decorative surface of painting. They produced intimate images in which figures and objects blend together in complicated patterns. In the works of Bonnard, in particular, the glowing design of the canvas itself becomes as important as what it's trying to represent.

Fauvism, Cubism, Surrealism

The **twentieth century** kicked off to a colourful start with the **Fauvist** exhibition of 1905, an appropriately anarchic beginning to a century which, in France above all, was to see radical changes in attitudes towards painting. The painters who took part in the exhibition included, most influentially, **Henri Matisse** (1869–1954), **André Derain** (1880–1954), **Georges Rouault** (1871–1958) and **Albert Marquet** (1875–1947), and they were quickly nicknamed the Fauves (Wild Beasts) for their use of bright, wild colours that often bore no relation whatsoever to the reality of the object depicted. Skies were just as likely to be green as blue since, for the Fauves, colour was a way of composing, of structuring a picture, and not necessarily a reflection of real life. Raoul Dufy (1877–1953) used Fauvist colours in combination with theories of abstraction to paint an effervescent industrial age.

Fauvism was just the beginning: the first decades of the twentieth century were times of intense excitement and artistic activity in Paris, and painters and sculptors from all over Europe flocked to the capital to take part in the liberation from conventional art that individuals and groups were gradually instigating. This loose, cosmopolitan grouping of artists gradually became known as the **École de Paris**, though it was never a "school" as such. **Pablo Picasso** (1881–1973) was one of the first to arrive in Paris – from Spain, in 1900. He soon started work on his first Blue Period paintings, which describe the sad and squalid life of itinerant actors in tones of blue. Later, while Matisse was experimenting with colours and their decorative potential, Picasso came under the sway of Cézanne and his organization of forms into geometrical shapes. He also learned from so-called "primitive", and especially African, sculpture, and out of these studies came a painting that heralded a definite new direction, not only for Picasso's own style but for the whole of modern art – *Les Demoiselles d'Avignon*. Executed in 1907, this painting combined Cézanne's analysis of forms with the visual impact of African masks.

It was from this semi-abstract picture that Picasso went on to develop the theory of **Cubism**, inspiring artists such as **Georges Braque** (1882–1963) and **Juan Gris** (1887–1927), another Spaniard, and formulating a whole new movement. The Cubists' aim was to depict objects not so much as they saw them but rather as they knew them to be: a bottle and a guitar were shown from the front, from the side and from the back as if the eye could take in all at once every facet and plane of the object. Braque and Picasso first analysed forms into these facets (analytical Cubism), then gradually reduced them to series of colours and shapes (synthetic Cubism), among which a few recognizable symbols such as letters, fragments of newspaper and numbers appeared. The complexity of different planes overlapping one another made the deciphering of Cubist paintings sometimes difficult, and the very last phase of Cubism tended increasingly towards abstraction.

Spin-offs of Cubism were many: such movements as **Orphism**, headed by **Robert Delaunay** (1885–1941) and **Francis Picabia** (1879–1953), who experimented not with objects but with the colours of the spectrum. **Fernand Léger** (1881–1955), one of the main exponents of the so-called School of Paris, exploited his fascination with its smoothness and power to create geometric and monumental compositions of technical imagery that were indebted to both Cézanne and Cubism.

The war, meanwhile, had affected many artists: in Switzerland, **Dada** was born out of the scorn artists felt for the petty bourgeois and nationalistic values that had led to the bloodshed. It was best exemplified in the work of the Frenchman **Marcel Duchamp** (1887–1968), who selected everyday objects ("ready-mades") and elevated them, without modification, to the rank of works of art simply by putting them on display – his most notorious piece was a urinal which he called *Fontaine* and exhibited in New York in 1917. His conviction that art could be made out of anything would be hugely influential.

Dada was a literary as well as an artistic movement, and through one of its main poets, André Breton, it led to the inception of **Surrealism**. It was the unconscious and its dark unchartered territories that interested the Surrealists: they derived much of their imagery from Freud and even experimented in words and images with free-association techniques. Strangely enough, most of the "French" Surrealists were foreigners, primarily the German **Max Ernst** (1891–1976) and the Spaniard **Salvador Dalí** (1904–89), though Frenchman **Yves Tanguy** (1900–55) also achieved international recognition. Mournful landscapes of weird, often terrifying images evoked the landscape of nightmares in often very precise details and with an anguish that went on to influence artists for years to come. **Picasso**, for instance, shocked by the massacre at the Spanish town of Guernica in 1936, drew greatly from Surrealism to produce the disquieting figures of his painting of the same name.

Towards Nouveau Réalisme

At the outbreak of **World War II** many artists emigrated to the US, where the economic climate was more favourable. France was no longer the artistic melting pot of Europe, though Paris itself remained full of vibrant new work. Sculptors like the Romanian **Brancusi** (1876–1957) and the Swiss **Giacometti** (1886–1966) lived most of their lives in city. Reacting against the rigours of Cubism, many French artists of the 1940s and 1950s opened themselves instead to the language and methods of American Abstract Expressionism, emanating from a vibrant New York. French painters such as **Pierre Soulages** (b.1919) and **Jean Dubuffet** (1901–85) pursued **Tachisme**, also known as **l'Art informel**. Dubuffet was heavily influenced by **Art Brut** – that is, works created by children, prisoners or the mentally ill. He produced thickly textured, often childlike paintings, pioneering the depreciation of traditional artistic materials and methods, fashioning junk, tar, sand and glass into the shape of human beings. His work (which provoked much outrage) influenced the French-born American, **Arman** (1928–2005), and **César** (1921–98), both of whom made use of scrap metals – their output ranging from presentations of household debris to towers of crushed and compressed cars.

These artists, among others, began to constitute what would be seen as the last coherent French art movement of the century: **Nouveau Réalisme**. A phenomenon largely of the late 1950s and 1960s, this movement rejected traditional materials and artistic genres, and concentrated instead on the distortion of the objects and signs of contemporary culture. It is often compared to Pop Art. Nouveau Réaliste sculpture is best represented by the works of the Swiss **Jean Tinguely** (1925–91), whose work was concerned mainly with movement and the machine, satirizing technological civilization. His most famous work, executed in collaboration with **Niki de Saint-Phalle** (1926–2002), is the exuberant fountain outside the Pompidou Centre, featuring fantastical birds and beasts shooting water in all directions.

Loosely associated with the Nouveaux Réalistes, though resisting all classification, **Yves Klein** (1928–1962) laid the foundations for several currents in contemporary art. He is seen as a precursor of Minimalism thanks to his exhibition "Le Vide" in 1958, in which he redefined the void and the immaterial as having a pure energy. He was fascinated by the colour blue, which he considered to possess a spiritual quality. He even patented his own colour, International Klein Blue, employing it in a series of "body prints" in which he covered female models with paint, thus prefiguring performance art.

Conceptual and contemporary

The chief legacy of Surrealism in 1960s France was the way avant-garde artists regularly banded together – and often quickly disbanded – around ideological or conceptual manifestos. These groups were not art schools as such, more conscious experiments in defining and limiting what art could be, in the search for political or theoretical meaning – in search, some would say, of coherence. One of the first such self-constituted groups of the 1960s, **GRAV** (Groupe de recherche d'art visuel) played with abstraction in the form of mirrors, visual tricks and **kinetic art** – which had a strong heritage in France from Duchamp and Alexander Calder. Among the leading figures were **François Morellet** (b.1926), who focused on geometric works, and the Argentine-born **Julio Le Parc** (b.1928). GRAV's goal, as its 1963 *Manifesto* declared, was to demystify art by tricking the spectator into relaxing in front of the artwork.

Perhaps the most significant group launched itself in January 1967, when Daniel Buren, Olivier Mosset, Michel Parmentier and Niele Toroni removed

their own works from the walls of the Salon de la Jeune Peinture, in protest
against the reactionary nature of painting itself – and, paradoxically, to reaffirm
the relevance of painting as an art form existing in itself, without interpretation.
It was an early taste of the politics of 1968. The works of **BMPT** – the name
was taken from the four men's surnames – focused on abstract colour, often in
regular patterns. The best-known of the four, **Daniel Buren** (b.1938), caused a
furore in 1985–6 with his installation in the courtyard of the Palais Royal
consisting of numerous black-and-white, vertically striped columns of differing
heights. Now, however, this one-time *enfant terrible* has become one of France's
most respected living artists.

Following BMPT's lead, the geometrically abstract **Supports-Surfaces**
group emerged in Nice in 1969, founded by the likes of **Daniel Dezeuze**
(b.1942), **Jean-Pierre Pincemin** (1944–2005) and **Claude Villat** (b.1936).
The group stressed the importance of the painting as object – as paint applied
to a surface. As Viallat put it, "Dezeuze painted stretchers without canvases, I
painted canvases without stretchers."

The 1977 opening of the Musée Nationale d'Art Moderne, in Paris's
Pompidou Centre, was a sign of the increased state support that French contemporary art was beginning to attract – a support that would be hugely boosted
in the early 1980s by the active buying policy of the Socialist government. The
landmark Pompidou exhibition of 1979, *Tendances de l'art en France*, showed
artists in three groupings. The first was broadly abstract, the second, figurative.
It was the third, however, which would look most prophetic of future directions;
it focused on **conceptual artists**, many of them working with unconventional
materials. This third group included the BMPT iconoclasts, along with three
artists who would become landmark figures in French contemporary art:
Christian Boltanski (b.1944) and **Annette Messager** (b.1943) – who were
then husband and wife – and **Bertrand Lavier** (b.1949). All three work with
found objects: Boltanski's often harrowing work has even employed personal
property lost in public places, while Messager has drawn on toys and needle-
work to create unsettling works, often challenging perceptions of women.
Lavier, meanwhile, is best known for playing with art and reality – principally
by applying paint to industrial objects.

A quintessentially French reaction to minimalist and conceptual art emerged
in 1981 with **Figuration Libre**, a movement which absorbed comic-strip art
and graffitti in an explosion of punk creativity. Among the key figures were
Jean-Charles Blais (b.1956), **Robert Combas** (b.1957), **François Boisrond**
(b.1959) and **Herve di Rosa** (b.1959). Despite such breakout movements, the
juggernaut of conceptual art continued to roll on through the last two decades.
Large-scale installation has become important, particularly in the works of
Jean-Marc Bustamante (b.1952) and **Jean-Luc Vilmouth** (b.1952), who
have been known to co-opt buildings themselves, resulting in a blurring of the
aesthetic and the functional. Artists crossing and recrossing generic boundaries
is another ongoing theme. Bustamante, for example, also works with photography, and in the early 1980s he collaborated for three years with the sculptor
Bernard Bazile (b.1952) under the name **Bazile Bustamante**.

A new generation of artists is using non-traditional media, including video,
photography, electronic media and found objects. Recent work could hardly
be more diverse, but a common thread seems to be the use of films and installations which explore the relationships between reality and fiction, between
interiority and the exterior world – ideas which resonate in the films, puppet
shows and "public interventions" of **Pierre Huyghe** (b.1962). Huyghe is
often associated with – and has worked with – the Algerian-born **Philippe**

Parreno (b.1964), who in 2006 released a feature film which followed the footballer Zinédine Zidane for ninety minutes of relentless close-up. Two other associated artists are **Dominique Gonzalez-Foerster** (b.1965), who works with films, photographs, installations and even métro stations and shop windows to create worlds where fantasy and reality seem to overlap, and **Claude Closky** (b.1963), whose "books" and videos restructure everyday flotsam and jetsam. Closky has declared, "My work bears on all that daily life has made banal, on things that are never called into question." Similarly eclectic in his choice of media is **Fabrice Hybert** (b.1961), who has created the world's largest-ever bar of soap (at 22 tons) and a working television studio. His playful, interactive work taps into what he describes as the "enormous reservoir of the possible". **Sophie Calle** (b.1953) blends texts and photographs; among her most publicized works have been her intimate documentations of the lives of both strangers and – after she asked her mother to hire a private detective for the purpose – Calle herself.

In such a multimedia milieu, some critics have claimed that actual painting is moribund in France. Bucking this trend is the celebrated Lyonnais painter **Marc Desgrandchamps** (b.1960). He may work with traditional oils, but Desgrandchamps is hardly a traditionalist. His figures often appear partially transparent, or are presented as fragments, thus overlaying doubt and disquiet over the perception of reality.

Architecture

France's architectural legacy is rich and important, reflecting the power and personality of successive kings, the Church and the state, vying to outdo their peers with bold, lavish statements in brick and stone. Many architectural trends filtered into France from Italy – Romanesque, Renaissance and Baroque – but they have been refined and developed by the French. Rococo grew from Baroque, Neoclassicism came from the Renaissance, and Art Nouveau was a brilliant, confused jumble of Baroque features combined with the newly developed cast-iron industry. Architecture in the twentieth century produced two great names – Auguste Perret and Le Corbusier – but France's contemporary scene is still thriving, with a host of new developments throughout the country.

The Romans

The **Romans**, who had colonized the south of France by around 120 BC, were fine town-planners, linking complexes of buildings with straight roads punctuated by decorative fountains, arches and colonnades. They built essentially in the Greek style, and their large, functional buildings were concerned more with strength and solidity than aesthetics. A number of substantial Roman building works survive: in **Nîmes** you can see the Maison Carrée, the best-preserved Roman temple still standing, and the Temple of Diana, one of just four vaulted Roman temples in Europe. Gateways remain at **Autun**, **Orange**, **Saintes** and **Reims**, and largely intact amphitheatres can be seen at Nîmes and **Arles**. The **Pont du Gard** aqueduct outside Nîmes is still a magnificent and ageless monument of civil engineering, built to carry the town's fresh water over the gorge, and Orange has its massive theatre, with Europe's only intact Roman facade. There are excavated archeological sites at **Glanum** near St-Rémy, **Vienne**, **Vaison-la-Romaine** and **Lyon**.

Romanesque

Charlemagne's ninth-century **Carolingian dynasty** attempted to revive the symbols of civilized authority by recourse to Roman models. Of this era, very few buildings remain, though the motifs of arch and vault and the plan of semicircular apse and basilican nave and aisles would be hugely influential.

The style later dubbed "**Romanesque**" (*Roman* in French, as opposed to *Romain* which, confusingly, means Roman/classical) only really developed from the eleventh century onwards. Classical Roman architecture was not so much a direct model as a distant inspiration, filtered partly through the Carolingian heritage and partly through Byzantine models – as imported by returning crusaders and arriving artisans from Italy. The new style was also shaped by the particular needs of monastic communities, which began to burgeon in the period, and the requirements of pilgrims, who began to tour shrines in ever-greater numbers.

The key characteristics of Romanesque are thick walls with small windows, round arches on Roman-style piers and columns, and a proliferation of stone sculpture and wall paintings – these last often being the first victims of wear-and-tear and iconoclasm. Romanesque is as diverse as the various regions of France. In the south, the classical inheritance of Provence is strong, with stone barrel vaults, aisleless naves and domes. **St–Trophime** at Arles (1150) has a porch directly derived from Roman models and, with the church at St-Gilles nearby, exhibits a delight in carved ornament peculiar to the south at this time. The presence of the wealthy and powerful Cluniac order, in Burgundy, made this region a veritable powerhouse of architectural experiment, while the south was the readiest route for the introduction of new cultural developments. The pointed arch and vault are probably owed to Spanish Muslim sources, and appear first in churches such as **Notre–Dame** at Avignon, Notre-Dame-la-Grande at Poitiers, the cathedral at **Autun** and **Ste–Madeleine** at Vézelay (1089–1206).

In Normandy, the nave with aisles is more usual, capped by twin western towers. The emphasis in general is on mass and size, and geometrical design is favoured over figurative sculpture. The **Abbaye aux Hommes** at Caen (1066–77) is typical – and also contains many of the elements later identified as "Gothic", notably ribbed vaults and spires.

Gothic

The reasons behind the development of the **Gothic style** (twelfth to sixteenth centuries) lie in the pursuit of the sublime; to achieve great height without apparent great weight would seem to imitate religious ambition. Its development in the north is partly due to the availability of good building stone and soft stone for carving, but perhaps more to the growth of royal aspiration and power based in the Île de France, which, allied with the papacy, stimulated the building of the great **cathedrals** of Paris, Bourges, Chartres, Laon, Le Mans, Reims and Amiens in the twelfth and thirteenth centuries.

The Gothic phase is said to begin with the building of the choir of the **abbey of St–Denis** near Paris in 1140. In France, the style reigned supreme until the end of the fifteenth century. Architecturally, it encompasses the development of spacious windows of coloured glass and the flying buttress, a rib of external stone that resists the outward push of the vaulting. But, above all, French Gothic is characterized by verticality.

In the south, as at Albi and Angers, the great churches are generally broader and simpler in plan and external appearance, with aisles often almost as high as the nave. Many secular buildings survive – some of the most notable in their present form being the work of Viollet-le-Duc, the pre-eminent nineteenth-century restorer – and even whole towns, for example **Carcassonne** and **Aigues Mortes**; **Avignon** has the bridge and the papal palace.

Even castles began to lend themselves to the disappearing walls of the Gothic style, as windows steadily increased in size in response to more settled times. Fine Gothic stone-carving was applied to doors and windows, and roofscapes came alive with balustrades, sculpted gables and exquisite leadwork finials and ridges. Some of the most elaborate châteaux, as at **Châteaudun** and **Saumur**, in the Loire valley, were veritable palaces. Yet they still incorporated the old defensive feudal tower in their design, perhaps in the form of a elaborately sculpted open staircase. In the Dordogne region, an series of colonial settlements, the **bastides**, or fortified towns, are a refreshing antidote to triumphal French bombast.

Renaissance

French military adventures in Italy in the early sixteenth century hastened the arrival of a new style borrowing heavily from the Italian **Renaissance**. The persistence of Gothic traditions, however, and the necessity of steep roofs and tall chimneys in the more northerly climate, gave the newly luxurious castles, or châteaux, a distinctively French emphasis on the vertical line, with an elaboration of detail on the facade at the expense of the clear modelling of form.

Gradually, these French forms were supplanted by a purely classical style – a development embodied by the **Louvre** palace, which was worked over by all the grand names of French architecture from Lescot in the early sixteenth century, via François Mansart and Claude Perrault in the seventeenth, to the later years of the nineteenth century.

At Blois and **Maisons Lafitte** (1640), Mansart began to experiment with a new suavity and elegance, attitudes that appear again in the eighteenth century in the town houses of the Rococo period. On the other hand, **Claude Perrault** (1613–88), who designed the great colonnaded east front of the Louvre, gives an austere face to the official architecture of despotism, magnificent but far too imperial to be much enjoyed by common mortals. The high-pitched roofs, which had been almost universal until then, are replaced here by the classical balustrade and pediment, the style grand but cold and supremely secular. Art and architecture were at the time organized by boards and academies, including the Académie Royale d'Architecture, and style and employment were strictly controlled by royal direction. With such a limitation of ideas at the source of patronage, it's hardly surprising that there was a certain dullness to the era.

Baroque

In a similar way to the preceding century, the churches of the **seventeenth and eighteenth centuries** have a coldness quite different from the German, Flemish and Italian **Baroque**. When the Renaissance style first appeared in the early sixteenth century, there was no great need for new church building, the country being so well endowed from the Gothic centuries. **St-Étienne-du-Mont** (1517–1620) and **St-Eustache** (1532–89), both in Paris, show how old forms persisted with only an overlay of the new style.

It was with the Jesuits in the seventeenth century that the Church embraced the new style to combat the forces of rational disbelief. In Paris the churches of the **Sorbonne** (1653) and **Val-de-Grâce** (1645) exemplify this, as do a good number of other grandiose churches in the **Baroque** style, through **Les Invalides** at the end of the seventeenth century to the **Panthéon** of the late eighteenth century. Here is the Church triumphant, rather than the state, but no more beguiling.

The architect of Les Invalides was **Jules Hardouin Mansart**, a product of the Académie Royale d'Architecture, which harked back to the ancient, classical tradition. Mansart also greatly extended the palace of **Versailles** and so created the Cinemascope view of France with that seemingly endless horizon of royalty. As an antidote to this pomposity, the **Petit Trianon** at

Versailles is as refreshing now as it was to Louis XV, who had it built in 1762 as a place of escape for his mistress. This is even more true of that other pearl formed of the grit of boredom in the enclosed world of Versailles – **La Petite Ferme**, where Marie-Antoinette played at being a milkmaid, which epitomizes the Arcadian and "picturesque" fantasy of the painters Boucher and Fragonard.

The lightness and charm that was undermining official grandeur with Arcadian fancies and **Rococo** decoration was, however, snuffed out by the Revolution. There's no real Revolutionary architecture, as the necessity of order and authority soon asserted itself and an autocracy every bit as absolute returned with Napoleon, drawing on the old grand manner but with a stronger trace of the stern old Roman.

In Paris it was not the democratic Doric but the imperial Corinthian order that re-emerged triumphant in the church of the **Madeleine** (1806) and, with the **Arc de Triomphe** like some colossal paperweight, reimposed the authority of academic architecture in contrast to the fancy-dress structures of contemporary Regency England.

The nineteenth century

The restoration of legitimate monarchy after the **fall of Napoleon** stimulated a revival of interest in older Gothic and early Renaissance styles, which offered a symbol of dynastic reassurance not only to the state but also to the newly rich. So in the private and commercial architecture of the nineteenth century these earlier styles predominate – in mine-owners' villas and bankers' headquarters.

From 1853, the overgrown and insanitary medieval capital was ruthlessly transformed into an urban utopia. In half a century, half of Paris was rebuilt. Napoléon III's authoritarian government provided the force – land was compulsorily purchased and boulevards bulldozed through old quarters – while banks and private speculators provided the cash. The poor, meanwhile, provided the labour – and were shipped out to the suburban badlands in their tens of thousands to make way for richer tenants. The presiding genius was Napoléon III's architect-in-chief, **Baron Haussmann** (1809–91). In his brave new city, every apartment building was seven storeys high. Every facade was built in golden limestone, often quarried from under the city itself, with unobtrusive Neoclassical details sculpted around the windows. Every second and fifth floor had its wrought-iron balcony and every lead roof sloped back from the streetfront at precisely 45 degrees.

Competing with Haussmann's totalitarian sobriety was a voluptuous, exuberant **neo-Baroque** strain, exemplified by Charles Garnier's Opéra in Paris (1861–74), and a third, engineering-led approach, embodied in the official **School of Roads and Bridges**. The teachings of Viollet-le-Duc, the great restorer who reinterpreted Gothic style as pure structure, led to the development of new techniques out of which "modern" architectural style was born. Iron was the first significant new material, often used in imitation of Gothic forms and destined to be developed as an individual architectural style in America. In the enormously controversial **Eiffel Tower** (1889), France set up a potent symbol of things to come.

Le Corbusier to Art Déco

Towards the end of the century, France pioneered the use of reinforced concrete, most notably in buildings by **Auguste Perret**, whose 1903 apartment house at 25 rue Franklin in Paris turns the concrete structure into a visible virtue and breaks with conventional facades. Perret and other **modernists** designed gigantic skyscraper avenues and suburban rings, which now look like totalitarian horror-movie sets.

The greatest proponent of the super New York scale was **Le Corbusier**. His stature may now appear diminished by the ascendancy of a blander style in concrete boxing, as well as by the significant technical and social failures of his buildings – not to mention his total disregard for historic streets and monuments – but he remains France's most influential modern architect. Surprisingly few of his works were ever built, but the Cité **Radieuse** in Marseille and plenty of lesser examples in Paris bear witness to the ideas of the man largely responsible for changing the face and form of buildings throughout the world.

One respect in which Paris at the turn of the century lagged behind London, Glasgow, Chicago and New York was in **underground transport**. First proposed in the 1870s, it took twenty years of furious debate before the Paris métro was finally realized in 1900. The design of the entrances was as controversial as every other aspect of the system, but the first commission went to **Hector Guimard**, renowned for his variations on the then-current fashion in style. The whirling metal railings, Art Nouveau lettering and bizarre antennae-like orange lamps were his creation. Conservatives were less amused when it came to sites such as the Opéra. **Charles Garnier**, architect of that edifice, demanded classical marble and bronze porticoes for every station, and his line was followed, on a less grandiose scale, wherever the métro steps surfaced by a major monument, putting Guimard out of a job. Some of the early ones remain (**Place des Abbesses** is one), as do some of the white-tiled interiors, replaced after World War II in central stations by bright paint with matching seats and display cases.

Art Nouveau designs also found their way onto buildings – the early department stores in Paris, such as Printemps and La Samaritaine, are the best examples – but the new materials and simple geometry of the modern or International Style favoured the **Art Deco** look; again, you're most likely to come across them in the capital.

Contemporary

The miserable 1950s and 1960s buildings found all over the country are probably best skipped over. From the 1970s onwards, however, France again established itself as one of the most exciting patrons of international **contemporary architecture**. The **Pompidou Centre**, by **Renzo Piano** and **Richard Rogers**, derided, adored and visited by millions, maximizes space by putting the service elements usually concealed in walls and floors on the outside. It is one of the great contemporary buildings in western Europe – for its originality, popularity and practicality.

Paris remained the focus of more innovative and exciting architecture in the 1980s with President Mitterand's *grands projets* ("grand projects"). One of the most ambitious was to extend the grand axis from the Louvre to the Arc de Triomphe westwards with the **Grande Arche de la Défense**, symbol of the new La Défense business district. Designed by Von Spreckelsen, it isn't really an arch but a huge hollow cube, conceived as an open gateway to the world. Mitterand also left his stamp at the other end of the grand axis with Ieoh Ming Pei's glass **pyramid** in the Cour Napoléon, the main entrance to the Louvre. Hugely controversial at first, it's now widely accepted and admired.

As part of the wider reorganization of the Louvre, the **Ministry of Finance** decamped to a new building in **Bercy** designed by Paul Chemetov and nicknamed the "steamboat" because of its titanic length and its anchoring in the Seine. Formerly full of wine warehouses, Bercy is now extensively redeveloped. The centrepiece is the Parc de Bercy, lined with neo-Haussmannian buildings and containing Frank Gehry's (architect of Bilbao's Guggenheim Museum) free-form, exuberant **American Centre**.

The **Cité de la Musique** concert hall and conservatoire complex was designed by acclaimed architect Christian de Portzamparc to be like a symphony, its various sections creating a harmonious ensemble. The Cité is the finishing touch to the **Parc de la Villette** complex which was built under Giscard d'Estaing on the site of an old abattoir, and which also houses the Cité des Sciences and Bernard Tschumi's 21 "*folies*" of urban life.

Perhaps the most outstanding of Mitterand's grands travaux is the **Institut du Monde Arabe** by **Jean Nouvel**, France's most eminent contemporary architect, with a design which ingeniously marries high-tech architecture and motifs from traditional Arabic culture. In a reference to the decorative wooden sunscreens used in Islamic countries, the facade is patterned with geometric metal screens punctured with apertures that are supposed to work a bit like a camera lens, opening and closing in response to the amount of sunlight received.

Mitterand's last project was the **Bibliothèque Nationale**. Designed by Dominique Perrault, it's made up of four L-shaped tower blocks, resembling four open books, set around an inaccessible sunken garden. This apparently facile design is made up for by the complexity (and expense) of the detail, in aluminium and rare woods.

Paris continues to find space for new architecture. The futuristically twisting double-ribbon of the **Passarelle Simone de Beauvoir** now bridges the Seine opposite Perrault's Bibliothèque. Upstream, the **Paris Rive Gauche** project occupies the formerly industrial southern part of the 13th arrondissement, alongside the river. It is edging towards completion. The University Paris 7 is now installed in the massive **Grands Moulins de Paris** and **Halle aux Farines**, and a new school of architecture – appropriately enough – resides in the handsomely arched, late nineteenth-century **SUDAC** building.

In Marseille there's Will Alsop's mammoth seat of regional government, while the first cathedral to be built in France since the nineteenth century, the **Cathédrale d'Évry**, masterminded by Swiss Mario Botta and finished in 1995, is a huge cylindrical red-brick tower which, besides being a place of worship, houses an art centre, concert hall and cinema screen. The new **European Parliament** building in Strasbourg, designed by the Architecture Studio group, was finished in 1997. A huge, boomerang-shaped structure with a glass dome and metal tower, it sits across the river from the eccentric, high-tech Richard Rogers-designed **European Court of Human Rights**.

Museums across the country continue to attract innovative architects. In Nîmes, Norman Foster's **Carré d'Art** modern art museum (1993) is character-ized by its simple transparent design, while his **Musée de Préhistoire des**

Gorges du Verdon (2001) in Provence uses local materials – part of the museum is folded into the landscape and blends on one side into an existing stone wall, while the entrance hall resembles the very caves the museum celebrates. Jean Nouvel's curving, light-filled **Quai Branly** museum (2006), on the banks of the Seine beside the Eiffel Tower, traverses over a lush garden designed by Gilles Clément, who landscaped the Parc André Citroën.

The country's ever-advancing transport network has fuelled some of the most state-of-the-art design and engineering in Europe, as in **Roissy**, around the Charles-de-Gaulle airport, and at **Euralille**, the large complex around Lille's TGV/Eurostar station, masterminded by Dutch architect Rem Koolhaas. Most dramatic of all is the **Millau Viaduct**, a bridge so huge in scale and ambition that its impact could almost be described as geographical. Designed by engineer Michel Virlogeux and Norman Foster's firm, and opened in December 2004, its sleekness belies its size: the largest of its soaring white pylons is actually taller than the Eiffel Tower.

The French are also very good at preserving the past – too good, some would say. A passion for restoring "*la patrimoine*" results in many fine old buildings being practically rebuilt – the dominant restoration theory in France is to restore to perfection rather than halt decay. More often than not, restoration is carried out by the **Maisons de Compagnonage**, the old craft guilds, which have maintained traditional building skills, handing them down as of old from master to apprentice (and never to women), while also taking on new industrial skills.

As regards the future, three landmark projects are already under way in Paris. Frank Gehry's **Fondation Louis Vuitton pour la Création** is taking shape in the Jardin d'Acclimation, in the Bois de Boulogne. Judging by the plans, Gehry's fantasy looks like nothing less than a lunatic glass armadillo which has burst out of its own skin. A new and boldly curvaceous eco-scraper, the Tour Phare, is planned for the Défense business district. Far more significant, if less self-promoting, will be the newly made-over Les Halles, in the heart of Paris. The glazed arcades which poured into a pit of a 1970s shopping centre are being transformed by architect David Mangin into light-filled spaces under a giant glass roof.

Cinema

The first (satisfied) cinema audience in the world was French. Screened to patrons of the Grand Café, on Paris's boulevard des Capucines, in December 1895, Louis **Lumière**'s single-reelers may have been jerky documentaries, but they were light-years ahead of anything that had come before. Soon after, Georges Méliès' magical-fantastical features were proving a big hit with theatre audiences, and the twin cinematic poles of Realism and Surrealism had been established. France took to cinema with characteristic enthusiasm and seriousness. Ciné-clubs were formed all over the country, journals were published, critics made films and film-makers became critics. The avant-garde wing of French cinema acquired the moniker of **French Impressionism**, a genre characterized by experimental directors such as Louis Delluc, Jean Epstein and Abel Gance, who used experimental, highly visual techniques to express altered states of consciousness. It was only a short step from here to the all-out **Surrealism** of the artist-polymath Jean Cocteau, and the Spanish director Luis Buñuel.

Towards the end of the 1920s, histrionic adaptations of novels, epic historical dramas and broad comedies attracted mass audiences, but the silent heyday ended abruptly with the advent of sound in 1929. Most silent stars faded into obscurity, but a number of directors successfully made the transition, notably Jean Renoir, the son of the painter, René Clair, Julien Duvivier, Jean Gremillon and Abel Gance. Among the newcomers were Jean Vigo, who died young in 1934, and Marcel Carné, who worked with the powerful scripts of the poet Jacques Prévert. The film-makers of the 1930s developed a bold new style, dubbed **Poetic Realism** for its pessimism, powerful visual aesthetic – high-contrast, often nocturnal – and devotion to "realistic", usually working-class, settings.

In 1936 the collector Henri Langlois set up the **Cinémathèque Française**, devoted to the preservation and screening of old and art films – an indication of the speed with which the "*septième art*" had found its niche within the pantheon of French culture. Langlois played an important role in saving thousands of films from destruction during the war, but the Occupation had surprisingly little effect on the industry. Renoir and Clair sought temporary sanctuary in Hollywood, and domestic production dipped, but hundreds of films continued to be made in Vichy France at a time when audiences sought the solace and comfort of the cinema in record numbers.

Post-war and pre-television, the late 1940s and early 1950s was another boom time for French cinema. Poetic Realism morphed into **film noir**, whose emphasis on darkness and corruption gave birth in turn to the thriller, a genre exemplified by the films of Henri-Georges Clouzot and Jean-Pierre Melville. During this period the mainstream cinema industry became highly organized and technically slick, older directors such as Clair, Renoir and Jacques Becker making superbly controlled masterpieces spanning genres as diverse as thrillers, comedies and costume dramas.

The first shot of the coming revolution – a warning shot only – was fired by the acerbic young critic François Truffaut, writing in the legendary film magazine, **Les Cahiers du cinéma**, in the mid-1950s. In opposition to what he and fellow critics dubbed *la tradition de qualité*, Truffaut envisaged a new kind of cinema based on the independent vision of a writer-director, an *auteur* (author), who would make films in a purer and more responsive manner. Directors such as Melville and Louis Malle – who made his first film with the diver Jacques Cousteau – were beginning to make moves in this direction, but Truffaut's vision was only fully realized towards the end of the decade, when the **Nouvelle Vague** ("New Wave") came rolling in. Claude Chabrol's *Les Cousins*, Truffaut's own *Les Quatre-cents coups*, Eric Rohmer's *Le Signe du lion*, Alain Resnais' *Hiroshima, mon amour* and Jean-Luc Godard's *À Bout de souffle* were all released in 1959. The trademark freedom of these *auteur*-directors' films – loosely scripted, highly individualistic and typically shot on location – ushered in the modern era.

The 1960s was the heyday of the *auteur*. Truffaut established his pre-eminent status by creating an extraordinary oeuvre encompassing science fiction, thriller, autobiography and film noir, all his films characteristically elegant and excitingly shot. But the "new wave" hadn't carried all before it: René Clément, Henri-Georges Clouzot and even Jean Renoir were still working throughout the decade, Jean-Pierre Melville continued shooting his characteristically noir **films policiers** (crime-thrillers), and the Catholic director Robert Bresson carried on making films on his favourite theme of salvation. And Jacques Tati, the maverick genius behind the legendary comic character M. Hulot, made two of his greatest and most radical quasi-silent films, *Playtime* and *Trafic*, at either end of the 1960s.

The 1970s is probably the least impressive decade in terms of output, but a shot in the arm was delivered in the 1980s by the **Cinéma du Look**, a genre epitomized in the films of Jean-Jacques Beineix, Luc Besson and Leos Carax. Stylish, image-conscious and postmodern, films such as *Diva* or *Betty Blue* owed much to the look of American pulp cinema and contemporary advertising. Meanwhile, throughout the 1980s and into the 1990s, high-gloss costume dramas – historical or adaptations of novels – were the focus of much attention. Often called **Heritage Cinema**, the best films of this genre are the superbly crafted creations of Claude Berri, though Jean-Pierre Rappeneau's *Cyrano de Bergerac* is probably the internationally recognized standard-bearer. At the other end of the scale lies **cinéma beur**: naturalistic, socially responsible and low-budget films made by French-born film-makers of North African origin – *les beurs* in French slang. The newest trends in contemporary art cinema follow a related path of social realism. In recent years, a number of younger directors, notably Mathieu Kassovitz, have made films set in the deprived suburbs (*la banlieue*), creating a number of sub-genres that have been acclaimed variously as **New Realism**, **cinéma de banlieue** and **le jeune cinéma** ("young cinema").

Today, France remains the second-largest exporter of films in the world. The industry's continued health is largely due to the intransigence of the French state, which continues to protect and promote domestic cinema as part of its policy of **l'exception culturelle** – despite the complaints of the free-marketeers who would have the French market "liberalized". Half of the costs of making a feature film in France are paid for by state subsidies, levied on television stations, box-office receipts and video sales. Currently, American-made films capture around fifty percent of the French market, while home-grown productions make up around forty percent. But the future looks promising: recent years have seen the number of films made in France rise to almost two hundred a year, most of them domestically funded.

Note that the **films reviewed below** are only intended to point out a few landmarks of French cinema; we can't review every Godard film nor cover every significant director. As such, they can all be considered as highly recommended. Alternative English titles are given for those films renamed for the main foreign release.

L'Atalante Jean Vigo, 1934. Aboard a barge, a newly married couple struggle to reconcile themselves to their new situation. Eventually, the wife, Juliette, tries to flee, but is brought back by the unconventional deck-hand, Père Jules, superbly portrayed by the great Michel Simon. This sensual and naturalistic portrait of a relationship was made just before Vigo died, and is his only feature film.

La Belle équipe/They Were Five Julien Duvivier, 1936. A group of unemployed workers wins the lottery and sets up a cooperative restaurant. The version with an upbeat conclusion was a huge hit with contemporary audiences; Duvivier himself preferred his darker ending. Jean Gabin stars as the defeated hero, as in Duvivier's other greats, *La Bandéra* (1935) and the cult classic, *Pépé-le-Moko* (1937).

Un Chien andalou/An Andalusian Dog Luis Buñuel, 1929. Made in collaboration with Salvador Dali, this short opens with a woman's eye being cut into with a razorblade. While it doesn't get any less weird or shocking for the rest of its twenty-minute length, it's surprisingly watchable – when it came out, it was a big hit at Paris's Studio des Ursulines cinema. Buñuel further developed his Surrealist techniques in the feature-length talkie *L'Age d'or* (1930).

Les Enfants du Paradis Marcel Carné, 1945. Probably the greatest of the collaborations between Carné and the poet–script-writer, Jacques Prévert, this film is set in the low-life world of the popular theatre of 1840s Paris. Beautiful and worldly actress Garance (the great Arletty) is loved by arch-criminal Lacenaire, ambitious actor Lemaître, and brilliant, troubled mime Baptiste – unforgettably played by the top mime of the 1940s, Jean-Louis Barrault. The outstanding character portrayals and romantic, humane ethos are reminiscent of a great nineteenth-century novel.

Le Jour se lève/Daybreak Marcel Carné, 1939. This brooding classic from the Poetic Realist stable has Jean Gabin, the greatest star of the era, playing another of his iconic working-class hero roles. After shooting his rival, the villainous old music-hall star Valentin, François (Gabin) is holed up in a hotel bedroom. In the course of the night, he recalls the events that led up to the murder. Also stars the great female idol of the 1930s, Arletty, and a superb script by the poet Jacques Prévert. Carné's *Hôtel du Nord* (1938) and *Quai des brumes* (1938) are in a similar vein.

Le Million René Clair, 1931. In 1930 Clair had made the first great French talkie, *Sous les toits de Paris*, but it wasn't until *Le Million* that the true musical film was born. A hunt for a lost winning lottery ticket provides plenty of opportunity for madcap comedy, suspense and romance.

La Règle du jeu/The Rules of the Game Jean Renoir, 1939. Now hailed as the foremost masterpiece of the prewar era, this was a complete commercial failure when it was released. The Marquis de la Chesnaye invites his wife, mistress and a pilot friend to spend a weekend hunting and partying in the countryside. Matching the four are a group of four servants with similarly interweaved love lives. Renoir himself plays Octave, who moves between the two groups. A complex, almost farcical plot based around misunderstanding and accusations of infidelity moves inexorably towards disaster.

Ascenseur pour l'échafaud/ Elevator to the Gallows/Frantic Louis Malle, 1957. This thriller is Louis Malle's remarkable debut. Two lovers (Jeanne Moreau and Maurice Ronet) murder the woman's husband but get trapped by a series of unlucky coincidences. Beautifully shot – especially when Jeanne Moreau wanders through the streets of Paris, accompanied by Miles Davis' superb original score – and as breathtaking as any Hitchcock film.

La Belle et la bête/Beauty and the Beast Jean Cocteau, 1946. Cocteau's theatrical rendition of the "Beauty and the Beast" tale teeters on the edge of the surreal, but the pace is as compelling as any thriller. *Orphée* (1950) is more widely considered to be Cocteau's masterpiece, a surreal retelling of the Orpheus tale in a setting strongly redolent of wartime France.

Casque d'or/Golden Marie Jacques Becker, 1952. Becker's first great film depicts the ultimately tragic romance between a gangster and a beautiful, golden-haired prostitute, portrayed with legendary seductiveness by Simone Signoret. Underneath the love story lurks the moral corruption of a brilliantly re-created turn-of-the-century Paris. Becker went on to make the seminal crime thriller, *Touchez pas au grisbi/ Honour Among Thieves* (1953).

Un Condamné à mort s'est échappé/A Man Escaped Robert Bresson, 1956. A prisoner, Fontaine (François Leterrier), calmly plans his escape from prison, working with a painstaking slowness that is brilliantly matched by the intensely absorbed camerawork. Working with real locations and amateur actors, Bresson echoed the work of the Italian Neo-realists, and foreshadowed the work of the Nouvelle

Vague directors. Sometimes entitled *Le Vent souffle où il veut*.

Et ... Dieu créa la femme/And God Created Woman Roger Vadim, 1956. This film should be called "And Roger Vadim created Brigitte Bardot", as its chief interest is not its harmless plot – love and adultery in St-Tropez – but its scantily clad main actress, who spends most of the time sunbathing and dancing in front of fascinated males. Deemed "obscene" by the moralizing authorities of the time, it helped liberate the way the body was represented in film.

Les Jeux interdits René Clément, 1952. A small Parisian girl loses her parents and her dog in a Stuka attack on a column of refugees, and is rescued and befriended by a peasant boy. Together, they seek solace from the war by building an animal cemetery in an abandoned barn. This moving meditation on childhood and death extracted two remarkable performances from the child actors.

Le Salaire de la peur/The Wages of Fear Henri-Georges Clouzot, 1953. This is the tensest, most suspense-driven of all the films made by the "French Hitchcock", focusing on four men driving an explosive-laden lorry hundreds of miles to a burning, third-world oil field. Tight and shatteringly sustained right up to the magnificent finale.

Les Vacances de Monsieur Hulot/Mr Hulot's Holiday Jacques Tati, 1951. The slapstick comic mime Jacques Tati created his most memorable character in Hulot, the unwitting creator of chaos and nonchalant hero of this gut-wrenchingly funny film. So full of brilliantly conceived and impeccably timed sight gags that you hardly notice the innovative absence of much dialogue or plot. Groundbreaking cinema, and superlative entertainment. The later

Mon oncle (1958) has an edgier feel, adopting a distinctly critical attitude to modern life.

The Nouvelle Vague

A Bout de souffle/Breathless Jean-Luc Godard, 1959. This is the film that came nearest to defining the Nouvelle Vague: insolent charm, cool music and sexy actors. Jean-Paul Belmondo is a petty criminal, Michel, while Jean Seberg plays Patricia, his American girlfriend. The film's revolutionary style, with its jerky, unconventional narrative, abrupt cuts and rough camerawork, proved one of the most influential of the twentieth century.

Les Cousins/The Cousins Claude Chabrol, 1959. The Balzac-inspired

plot centres around Charles (Gérard Blain), an earnest provincial student, who comes to live in Neuilly with his glamorous cousin Paul (Jean-Claude Brialy). A near-caricature of the Nouvelle Vague – idle students in the Quartier Latin, extravagant parties, convertible cars and exciting music.

Hiroshima, mon amour Alain Resnais, 1959. On her last days of shooting a film in Hiroshima, a French actress (Emmanuelle Riva) falls in love with a Japanese architect (Eiji Okada). Gradually, she reveals the story of her affair with a

▲ A Bout de souffle film poster

German soldier during the Occupation, and her subsequent disgrace. Based on an original script by Marguerite Duras, Resnais' first film masterfully weaves together past and present in a haunting story of love and memory.

Ma Nuit chez Maude/My Night at Maud's Eric Rohmer, 1969. Rohmer's career-long obsessions with sexuality, conversation, existential choices and the love triangle are given free rein in this moody, lingering portrait of a flirtation. Jean-Louis Trintignant plays a handsome egotist who, during the course of one long night, is drawn into a strange and inconclusive relationship with his friend's friend, the hypnotically attractive Maude (Françoise Fabian).

Les Quatre-cents coups/ The 400 Blows François Truffaut, 1959. A young *cinéphile* and critic turned film-maker, François Truffaut triumphed at the 1959 Cannes film festival with this semi-autobiographical film, showing a Parisian adolescent (Jean-Pierre Léaud) trying to escape his lonely, loveless existence, and slowly drifting towards juvenile delinquency. Léaud's poignant performance, and Truffaut's sensitive, sympathetic observation, make this one of the most lovable films of the Nouvelle Vague.

Comedies

Belle de jour Luis Buñuel, 1966. Catherine Deneuve plays Séverine, who lives out her sexual fantasies and obsessions in a brothel. At first sight, this is a far cry from Buñuel's prewar collaborations with Dalí, though the film moves away from the initial acerbic comedy towards surrealism.

La Cage aux folles/Birds of a Feather Edouard Molinaro, 1978. Renato runs a cabaret nightclub at which his boyfriend, Albin, is the headlining drag act. When Renato's son, Laurent, decides to get married, the couple are drawn into an escalating farce as they try to present themselves as a conventional mother-and-son couple to Laurent's conservative in-laws. A supremely camp international hit.

Le Fabuleux destin d'Amélie Poulain/Amélie Jean-Pierre Jeunet, 2001. This sentimental, feel-good portrait of a youthful ingenue wandering around a romanticized Montmartre was a worldwide hit. Amélie (Audrey Tatou) is on a mission to help the world find happiness; her own is harder to fix up.

La Grande vadrouille Gérard Oury, 1966. Head and shoulders the biggest blockbuster in French cinema history, "The Big Jaunt" stars Bourvil and Louis de Funès as a conductor and a decorator. Set in wartime Paris, the comic plot sees three Allied soldiers parachuting down on the hapless pair. In their desperation to be rid of the parachutists, they end up leading them to the free zone.

Playtime Jacques Tati, 1967. Tati once more plays Hulot, cinema's most radical slapstick creation. From a simple premise – he is showing a group of tourists round a futuristic Paris – he creates an intimately observed and perfectly controlled farce. Just as the city has somehow been transformed into a refined and faceless world of glass and steel, Tati's comedy has become infinitely subtle and reflective.

Les Visiteurs/The Visitors Jean-Marie Poiré, 1993. A medieval knight and his squire are transported to present-day France, where they discover their castle has been turned into a country hotel by their descendants. The earthily comic encounters between time-travellers and modern middle-classes make for an extremely funny comedy of manners. French audiences so loved being sent up that this became the third most successful film in French history.

Zazie dans le métro/Zazie Louis Malle, 1960. In one of his few comedies, Malle successfully rendered novelist Raymond Queneau's verbal experiments by using cartoon-like visual devices. 12-year-old Catherine Demongeot is perfect as the delightfully rude little girl driving everybody mad; and the film offers some great shots of Paris, climaxing in a spectacular scene at the top of the Eiffel Tower.

Thrillers/films policiers

L'Armée des ombres/The Army in the Shadows Jean-Pierre Melville, 1969. A small group of Resistance fighters, played by Yves Montand, Simone Signoret and Jean-Pierre Meurisse, are betrayed, questioned and then released. The tight, minimalist style creates a suffocating tension which culminates in an unforgettable conclusion.

Le Boucher/The Butcher Claude Chabrol, 1969. A young schoolteacher in a tiny southwest village lives in an apartment above her school. Her loneliness is eased by a surprising fledgling romance with the local butcher – a kindly yet sinister figure – until a sequence of schoolgirl murders sows doubt in her mind. This would be gripping as a portrayal of village life even without the underlying tension and lurking violence.

Caché/Hidden Michael Haneke, 2005. The smooth bourgeois life of literary TV presenter Georges (Daniel Auteuil) and his wife Anne (Juliette Binoche) is disrupted when they receive a chillingly innocuous videotape of their own home under surveillance. In what has been widely read as a metaphor for France's attitude to its own colonial past, Georges is forced to confront a childhood friend, Majid (Maurice Bénichou), and his own troubled conscience.

Coup de Torchon/Clean Slate Bertrand Tavernier, 1981. The setting is colonial West Africa, 1938. Ineffective, humiliated police chief Cordier (Philippe Noiret) decides to take murderous revenge on his wife, her lover, his mistress's husband and the locals he views as uniformly corrupt. As much an extremely black comedy as a true thriller.

Irréversible Gaspar Noé, 2002. One of the more disturbing films ever made: not just for the nightmarish rape and murder scenes but for the evisceration of the most terrifying elements of the male sexual psyche. A giddy, swooping camera traces the events of one night backwards in time from a brutal murder to a post-coital couple (Vincent Cassel and Monica Bellucci) getting ready for a party.

Monsieur Hire Patrice Leconte, 1989. A slow-moving, unsettlingly erotic psychological thriller. Michel Blanc plays the spookily impassive Monsieur Hire, a voyeur who witnesses his neighbour's boyfriend commit a murder, and becomes the prime suspect.

Ne le dis à personne/Tell No one Guillaume Canet, 2006. Disturbing psycho-thriller in which a doctor who is slowly rebuilding his life after the murder of his wife, eight years earlier, is suddenly implicated in two fresh murders. To complicate matters further, he is sent evidence that his wife is still alive. As much *Mulholland Drive* as *Frantic*, and more exciting than either.

🏃 **Pierrot-le-fou** Jean-Luc Godard, 1965. Godard's fascination with American pulp fiction is most brilliantly exploited in this highly charged and deeply sophisticated thriller. Accidentally caught up in a murderous gangland killing, Ferdinand (Jean-Paul Belmondo) flees with his babysitter (Godard's then-wife, Anna Karina) to the apparent safety of a Mediterranean island. The bizarre and tragic denouement is one of the great scenes of French cinema.

Films d'amour

🏃 **L'Ami de mon amie/ Boyfriends and Girlfriends** Eric Rohmer, 1987. Two glossy young women in a flashy new town outside Paris – Cergy-Pontoise – become friends. While Blanche is away, Léa falls in love with Blanche's boyfriend Alexandre; when Blanche comes back, she in turn falls in love with Léa's boyfriend, Fabien. Behind the light comedy and seemingly inconsequential dialogue lurks a profound film about love and free will.

Baisers volés/Stolen Kisses François Truffaut, 1968. The third of Truffaut's five-part semi-autobiographical sequence, which began with *Les Quatre-cents coups*, is probably the simplest and most delightful. Returning from military service, idealistic young Antoine Doinel (Jean-Pierre Léaud) mooches about Paris while working variously as a hotel worker, private detective and TV repairman. Through various amorous and bizarre adventures he slowly finds his way back towards the girl he loved and left behind.

La Belle noiseuse Jacques Rivette, 1991. "The beautiful troublemaker" originally stretched to four hours, though the more commonly screened "Divertimento" cut is half that length. A washed-out painter (the splendidly stuttering Michel Piccoli) lives in the deep south with his wife (Jane Birkin). An admiring younger painter offers his beautiful girlfriend (Emmanuelle Béart) as a nude model. Her fraught sittings become the catalyst for all the latent tensions in the two relationships to quietly explode.

Un Coeur en hiver/A Heart in Winter/A Heart of Stone Claude Sautet, 1992. In this thoughtful, fresh *ménage à trois* scenario, violinist Camille (Emmanuelle Béart) is paired first with Maxime (André Dussolier), a violin shop owner, and then with loner Stéphane (Daniel Auteuil), the chief craftsman. As the title "A Heart in Winter" suggests, this is a moody but ultimately sentimental film about love, and the fear of love.

Le Dernier métro/The Last Metro François Truffaut, 1980. This huge commercial success stars Catherine Deneuve and Gérard Depardieu as two actors who fall in love while rehearsing a play during the German Occupation. Wartime Paris is evoked through lavish photography and a growing feeling of imprisonment inside the confined space of the theatre. Swept the Césars that year, for Best Film, Director, Actor and Actress.

🏃 **Le Mari de la coiffeuse/ The Hairdresser's Husband** Patrice Leconte, 1990. Leconte's film about a man who grows up obsessed with hairdressers, and ends up marrying one, epitomizes the best in French romantic film-making. A quirky, subtle and engagingly twisted portrait of an obsessive relationship.

Les Parapluies de Cherbourg/ The Umbrellas of Cherbourg Jacques Demy, 1964. Demy's most successful film also gave Catherine Deneuve one of her first great roles. It is an extraordinarily stylized musical, shot in bright, artificial-looking colours, and entirely sung rather than spoken. Demy disturbingly twists the traditional cheerfulness of the musical genre to give a dark, bitter ending to this story of love and abandonment, set during the Algerian war.

Quand j'étais chanteur/The Singer Xavier Giannoli, 2006. Tender vehicle for Gérard Dépardieu as a failing provincial crooner who won't stop trying to live as if the plots of his romantic pop songs were realistic. The realistic portrait of life

in and around Clermont-Ferrand keeps it far above mere shlock.

Trois Couleurs: Rouge/ Three Colours: Red Krzysztof Kieslowski, 1994. The final part of Polish-born director's Kieslowski's "tricolore" trilogy is perhaps the most satisfying, though to get the most out of the powerful denouement, in which all the strands are pulled together through a series of chances and accidents, you really need to have watched *Bleu* and *Blanc* as well. A young model, Valentine (Irène Jacob), runs over a dog and traces its owner, a reclusive retired judge (Jean-Louis Trintignant) who assuages his loneliness by tapping his neighbours' phone calls. The film's "colour" is expressed through presiding red-brown tones and the theme of *fraternité*, the third principle of the French Republic.

Heritage cinema

Cyrano de Bergerac Jean-Paul Rappeneau, 1990. It's hard to know what's finest about this extravagantly romantic film: Rostand's original story, set in seventeenth-century France, or Gérard Dépardieu's landmark performance as the big-nosed swashbuckler-poet, Cyrano, who hopelessly loves the brilliant and beautiful Roxanne. The film's panache is matched by the verse dialogue – brilliantly rendered into English subtitles by Anthony Burgess. Hilarious, exciting and sublimely weepy.

Jean de Florette Claude Berri, 1986. This masterful adaptation of Marcel Pagnol's novel created the rose-tinted genre, *cinema du patrimoine*. In the gorgeous setting of inland, prewar Provence, Gérard

Depardieu plays a deformed urban refugee struggling to create a rural utopia. He is opposed by the shrewd peasant Papet (Yves Montand) and a simpleton, Ugolin (Daniel Auteuil), who dreams of giant fields of carnations. The excellent sequel, *Manon des Sources* (1987), launched the stellar career of the improbably pouting Emmanuelle Béart.

Au Revoir les enfants/Goodbye, Children Louis Malle, 1987. Malle's autobiographical tale is one of the finest film portraits of the war, and of school life in general. It is minutely observed, and desperately moving without being unduly sentimental. Three Jewish boys are hidden among the pupils at a Catholic boys' boarding school. Eventually, the Gestapo discover the ruse.

Cinéma du look

🏃 **37°2 le matin/Betty Blue** Jean-Jacques Beineix, 1986. Pouty Béatrice Dalle puts on a compellingly erotic performance as

Betty, a free-thinking girl who lives in a beach house with struggling writer Zorg. The film opens in romantic mood with a sustained

France in literature

▲ Marcel Proust

Listed below is a highly selective recommendation of works – mostly novels – that are rooted in the various French regions, and which would make good holiday reading.

Paris and around
Honoré de Balzac *Old Goriot*
Muriel Barbery *The Elegance of the Hedgehog*
Steven Barclay (ed) *A Place in the World Called Paris*
Charles Baudelaire *Baudelaire's Paris*, trans Laurence Kitchen
André Breton *Nadja*
Blaise Cendrars *To the End of the World*
Helen Constantine (ed) *Paris Tales*
Didier Daeninckx *Murder in Memoriam*
Gustave Flaubert *A Sentimental Education*
André Gide *The Counterfeiters*
Faiza Guène *Kif Kif Demain/Just Like Tomorrow*
Ernest Hemingway *A Moveable Feast*
Victor Hugo *Les Misérables*
Jack Kerouac *Satori in Paris*
Anaïs Nin *Journals 1917–1974*
George Orwell *Down and Out in Paris and London*
Daniel Penac *Monsieur Malaussène*
Georges Perec *Life: A User's Manual*
Marcel Proust *Remembrance of Things Past*
Paul Rambali *French Blues*
Jean Rhys *Quartet, Good Morning Midnight*
Jean-Paul Sartre *Roads to Freedom* trilogy
Georges Simenon Any Maigret thriller
Michel Tournier *The Golden Droplet*
Émile Zola *Nana, L'Assommoir, La Bête Humaine, La Curée, Le Ventre de Paris*

The north
Sebastian Faulks *Birdsong*
Julien Gracq *A Balcony in the Forest, The Opposing Shore*
Irène Nemirovsky *All Our Worldly Goods*
Émile Zola *Germinal, La Débâcle, La Terre*

Alsace, Franche-Comté and Jura
John Berger *Pig Earth*
Bernard Clavel *The Spaniard*
Colette *My Mother's House*
Pierre Gascar *Women and the Sun*
Stendhal *Scarlet and Black*

and passionate sex scene but rapidly spirals towards its disturbing ending. The film's intense and sometimes weird stylishness, along with its memorable score, made it an international hit.

Les Amants du Pont-Neuf Léos Carax, 1991. Homeless painter Michèle (Juliette Binoche) is losing her sight. One day, on Paris's Pont-Neuf, she meets an indigent, fire-eating acrobat (Denis Lavant), and they tumble

Normandy and Brittany
Honoré de Balzac *Les Chouans, Modeste Mignon*
Colette *Ripening Seed*
Gustave Flaubert *Madame Bovary*
André Gide *Strait is the Gate*
Pierre Loti *Pêcheur d'Islande*
Guy de Maupassant *Selected Short Stories*
Jean Rouard *Fields of Glory, Of Illustrious Men*
Jean-Paul Sartre *La Nausée*

The Loire
Honoré de Balzac *Eugénie Grandet*
Alain Fournier *Le Grand Meaulnes*
Joanne Harris *Five Quarters of the Orange*
George Sand *The Devil's Pool*

Burgundy
Gabriel Chevallier *Clochemerle, Atlantic Coast*
François Mauriac *Thérèse*

The Pyrenees
Pierre Loti *Ramuntcho*

Languedoc
Hannah Closs *High Are the Mountains*

Rhône valley and Provence
Lawrence Durrell *The Avignon Quintet*
Jean Giono *The Horseman on the Roof, The Man Who Planted Trees, Joy of Man's Desiring*
Marcel Pagnol *Jean de Florette, Manon des Sources*
Émile Zola *Fortune of the Rougons*

Côte d'Azur
Colette *Collected Stories*
Alexandre Dumas *The Count of Monte Cristo*
F. Scott Fitzgerald *Tender is the Night*
Graham Greene *Loser Takes All, May We Borrow Your Husband?*
Katherine Mansfield *Selected Short Stories*
Françoise Sagan *Bonjour Tristesse*

Corsica
Prosper Mérimée *Colomba*

together into a consuming love, madly played out against the background of their life on the streets. An intense and beautiful film.

🏃 **Delicatessen** Jean-Pierre Jeunet/Marc Caro, 1991. Set in a crumbling apartment block in a dystopian fantasy city – Occupation Paris meets comic book – a grotesque local butcher murders his assistants and sells them as human meat, until his daughter falls in love with the latest butcher boy and the subterranean vegetarian terrorists

find out. Hilarious and bizarre in equal measure, with superb cameos from the neighbours.

Subway Luc Besson, 1985. The favoured urban-nocturnal setting of the *cinéma du look* is given its coolest expression in *Subway*. A hock-headed Christophe Lambert is hunted by police and criminals alike for a cache of documents he shouldn't have. He hides out in the Paris métro where he manages to form a rock band – before being found by Isabelle Adjani. Film noir meets MTV.

New realism: beur, banlieue and jeune

Comme une image/Look at Me Agnès Jaoui, 2004. Agnès Jaoui manages to be both sensitive and hard-hitting in this exploration of the dysfunctional relationship between a self-conscious, under-confident daughter (Marilou Berry) and her monstrously egotistical, literary lion of a father – a role played superbly by Jean-Pierre Bacri, who co-wrote the script with Jaoui.

La Haine/Hate Mathieu Kassovitz, 1995. The flagship film of the *cinéma de banlieue*, films of the tough suburbs, centres on three friends: Hubert, of black African origin; Saïd, a *beur* (from North Africa); and Vinz, who has white Jewish roots – and a gun. They spend a troubled night wandering Paris before heading back to the *banlieue* and a violent homecoming. Brilliantly treads the line between gritty realism and street cool – the fact that it's shot in black-and-white helps, as does the soundtrack from French rapper MC Solaar, among others.

Hexagone Malik Chibane, 1991. Shooting in just 24 days, and using amateur actors, Chibane somehow pulled off exactly what he planned: to raise the profile of the new gener-ation of *beurs*. The story is a simple enough rite-of-passage tale focused on five young friends who get in

trouble, but the recurring motif of the sacrifice of Abraham gives it a thoughtful twist. The street-slang peppered script and cinematography – strong on handheld shots of the inner city landscape – are superb.

Le Thé à la menthe Abdelkrim Bahloul, 1984. In this funny and ultimately touching film, an Algerian immigrant living in the Barbès quarter of northern Paris writes home to his mother to let her know how successful he has become in his new life. In fact, he struggles to get by on minor scams and chancey ventures. When his mother makes a surprise visit, he foolishly tries to carry on the pretence – to comic effect.

🏃 **La Ville est tranquille/The Town Is Quiet** Robert Guédiguian, 2000. Notwithstanding its title, this harrowing film describes the dysfunctional society of a far-from-quiet city – Marseille – focusing on the hardships of Michèle (Ariane Ascaride), a 40-year-old woman working in a fish factory while fighting to save her heroin-addict daughter. After a series of light, happy tales, Robert Guédiguian magnificently turns here to a more realistic and political tone.

James McConnachie and Eva Lœchner

Books

Publishers are detailed below in the form of British publisher/American publisher, where both exist. Where books are published in one country only, UK or US follows the publisher's name. Books marked 🎿 are highly recommended. Abbreviations: UP (University Press).

Travel

🎿 **Marc Augé** *In the Metro* (University of Minnesota Press, 2002). A philosophically minded anthropologist descends deep into metro culture and his own memories of life in Paris. Brief and brilliant.

🎿 **Walter Benjamin** *The Arcades Project* (Harvard, 2002). An all-encompassing portrait of Paris from 1830 to 1870, in which the *passages* are used as a lens through which to view Parisian society. Never completed, Benjamin's magnum opus is a kaleidoscopic assemblage of essays, notes and quotations, gathered under such headings as "Baudelaire", "Prostitution", "Mirrors" and "Idleness".

🎿 **Adam Gopnik** *Paris to the Moon* (Vintage/Random House). Intimate and acutely observed essays from the Paris correspondent of the New Yorker on society, politics, family life and shopping.

Julien Green *Paris* (Marion Boyars, 2005). A collection of very personal sketches and impressions of the city, by an American who has lived all his life in Paris, writes in French, and is considered one of the great

French writers of the century. Bilingual text.

Richard Holmes *Footsteps* (Flamingo, 2004/Vintage, 1996). A marvellous mix of objective history and personal account, such as the tale of the author's own excitement at the events of May 1968 in Paris, which led him to investigate and reconstruct the experiences of the British in Paris during the 1789 Revolution.

Michael de Larrabeiti *French Leave* (Robert Hale, 2003). In the summer of 1949, aged just 15, Michael de Larrabeiti set off on his own by bicycle to Paris from the UK. This book provides a wonderfully evocative testimony to his love of France as he looks back over fifty years of working and travelling throughout the country.

Robert Louis Stevenson *Travels with a Donkey* (Penguin/Echo, 2006). Mile-by-mile account of Stevenson's twelve-day trek in the Haute Loire and Cévennes uplands with the donkey Modestine. His first book, *Inland Voyage*, took him round the waterways of the north.

History

General

Colin Jones *The Cambridge Illustrated History of France* (CUP, 1999). A political and social history of France from prehistoric times to the mid-1990s, concentrating on issues of regionalism, gender, race and class.

Good illustrations and a friendly, non-academic writing style.

Colin Jones *Paris: Biography of a City* (Penguin, 2006). Jones focuses tightly on the actual life and growth of the city, from the Neolithic past to the future. Five hundred pages flow by easily, punctuated by thoughtful but accessible "boxes" on characters, streets and buildings whose lives were especially bound up with Paris's, from the Roman arènes to Zazie's métro. The best single book on the city's history.

Graham Robb *The Discovery of France* (2007). Captivating, brilliant study of France which makes a superb antidote to the usual narratives of kings and state affairs. With affection and insight, and in fine prose, Robb describes a France of vast wastes inhabited by "faceless millions" speaking mutually unintelligible dialects, and reveals how this France was gradually discovered and, inevitably, "civilized".

Robert Tombs & Isabelle Tombs *That Sweet Enemy: The British and the French from the Sun King to the Present* (Pimlico/Arrow, 2007). A fascinating, original and mammoth study of a strangely intimate relationship. The authors are a French woman and her English husband, and they engage in lively debate between themselves. Covers society, culture and personalities, as well as politics.

Theodore Zeldin *A History of French Passions: 1848–1945* (OUP, 1993). Brilliant and original set of books tackling French history by theme. Volume 1 covers Ambition and Love, Volume 2 Intellect and Pride, and so on. Highly readable and unusually stimulating.

The Middle Ages and Renaissance

Natalie Zemon Davis *The Return of Martin Guerre* (Harvard UP, 1984). A vivid account of peasant life in the sixteenth century and a perplexing and titillating hoax in the Pyrenean village of Artigat.

J.H. Huizinga *The Waning of the Middle Ages* (Dover, 1999). Primarily a study of the culture of the Burgundian and French courts – but a masterpiece that goes far beyond this, building up meticulous detail to re-create the whole life and mentality of the fourteenth and fifteenth centuries.

R.J. Knecht *The French Renaissance Court* (Yale, 2008). The definitive work by a genuine authority. Not exactly a racy read, but successfully mixes high politics with sharp detail on life at court life, backed up by plentiful illustrations.

Marina Warner *Joan of Arc* (UCal Press, 2000). Brilliantly places France's patron saint and national heroine within historical, spiritual and intellectual traditions.

Eighteenth and nineteenth centuries

Vincent Cronin *Napoleon* (Harper-Collins, UK, 1990). Enthusiastic and accessible biography.

Christopher Hibbert *The French Revolution* (Penguin, 1982/Harper, 1999). Well-paced and entertaining narrative treatment by a master historian.

Alistair Horne *The Fall of Paris* (Pan, 2002). A very readable and humane account of the extraordinary period of the Prussian siege of Paris in 1870 and the ensuing struggles of the Commune.

Ross King *The Judgement of Paris: The Revolutionary Decade That Gave the World Impressionism* (Pimlico/Walker, 2006). Lively account of the stormy early years when the Impressionists were refused entry to official exhitions.

Lucy Moore *Liberty: The Lives and Times of Six Women in Revolutionary France* (HarperCollins, 2006). This engaging and original book follows the lives of six influential – and very different women – through the Revolution, taking in everything from sexual scandal to revolutionary radicalism.

Ruth Scurr *Fatal Purity: Robespierre and rhe French Revolution* (Chatto & Windus/Metropolitan, 2006). This myth-busting biography of the "remarkably odd" figure of the man they called The Incorruptible, and who went on to orchestrate the notorious Terror, ends up being one of the best books on the Revolution in general.

Twentieth century

Marc Bloch *Strange Defeat* (Norton, 1999). Moving personal study of the reasons for France's defeat and subsequent caving-in to fascism. Found among the papers of this Sorbonne historian after his death at the hands of the Gestapo in 1942.

Carmen Callil *Bad Faith: A Forgotten History of Family and Fatherland* (Vintage/Knopf, 2006). This quietly angry biography of the loathsome Louis Darquier, the Vichy state's Commissioner for Jewish Affairs, reveals the banality of viciousness in wartime France.

Geoff Dyer *The Missing of the Somme* (Weidenfeld, 2001). Structured round the author's visits to the war graves of northern France, this is a highly moving meditation on the trauma of World War I and the way its memory has been perpetuated.

Irène Nemirovsky *Suite Française* (Vintage, 2007/Knopf, 2006). The author was transported to Auschwitz, where she died. Before she left, she deposited the notebooks containing these two extraordinary novellas with her daughter. They were only published in 2004. This, the first part, details the flight from Paris in June 1940; the second depicts life in a provincial town under German occupation.

Ian Ousby *Occupation: The Ordeal of France 1940–1944* (Pimlico, 1999/Cooper Square, 2000). Revisionist 1997 account which shows how relatively late resistance was, how widespread collaboration was, and why.

Barbara Tuchman *The Proud Tower* (Ballantine, 1996). A portrait of England, France, the US, Germany and Russia in the years 1890–1914. Written in Tuchman's inimitable and readable style, it includes superb chapters on the extraordinary passions and enmities of the Dreyfus Affair.

Society and politics

John Ardagh *France in the New Century: Portrait of a Changing Society* (Penguin, 2000). Long-time writer on France gets to grips with the 1980s and 1990s. Attempts to be a comprehensive survey, but gets rather too drawn into party politics and statistics.

Julian Barnes *Something to Declare* (Picador/Knopf, 2002). This journalistically highbrow collection of essays on French culture – films, music, the Tour de France, and of course Flaubert – wears its French-style intellectualism on its sleeve, but succeeds in getting under the skin anyway.

🏃 **Roland Barthes** *Mythologies* (Vintage, 1993; Hill & Wang, 1972). *Mythologies* is a brilliant and witty structuralist critique on the socio-historical importance of myth and its signs in France today, based on a series of quirky examples.

Mary Blume *A French Affair: The Paris Beat 1965–1998* (Plume, 2000). Incisive and witty observations on contemporary French life by the *International Herald Tribune* reporter who was stationed there for three decades.

🏃 **Jonathan Fenby** *On the Brink* (Abacus, 2002/Arcade, 2000). While France isn't perhaps quite as endangered as the title suggests, this provocative book takes a long, hard look at the problems facing contemporary France. Somewhat dated, but the issues have changed surprisingly little.

🏃 **Mark Girouard** *Life in the French Country House* (Knopf, 2000). Girouard meticulously re-creates the social and domestic life that went on between the walls of French châteaux, starting with the great halls of early castles and ending with the commercial marriage venues of the twentieth century.

Tim Moore *French Revolutions: Cycling the Tour De France* (Vintage,

2002/St Martin's, 2003). A whimsical bicycle journey along the route of the Tour by a genuinely hilarious writer. Lots of witty asides on Tour history and French culture.

Jim Ring *Riviera: The Rise and Rise of the Cote d'Azur* (John Murray, 2005). A fascinating portrait of France's most anomalous region, taking in its discovery by aristocratic pleasure-seekers in the nineteenth century, the golden years of the 1920s when it was the playgroud of artists, film stars and millionaires, and the inevitable fall from grace.

🏃 **Charles Timoney** *Pardon My French: Unleash Your Inner Gaul* (Penguin, UK, 2007). Incisive and often very droll dissection of contemporary culture through the words and phrases that the French use all the time. Looks and maybe sounds like a gift book, but it's rather brilliant.

Gillian Tindall *Célestine: Voices from a French Village* (Minerva, UK, 1996). Intrigued by some nineteenth century love letters left behind in the house she has bought in Chassignolles, Berry, Tindall researches the history of the village back to the 1840s. A brilliant piece of social history.

🏃 **Theodore Zeldin** *The French* (Harvill UK, 1997). A wise and original book that attempts to describe a country through the prism of the author's intensely personal conversations with a fascinating range of French people. Chapter titles include "How to be chic" and "How to appreciate a grandmother".

Art, architecture and poetry

Philip Ball *Universe of Stone: Chartres Cathedral and the Triumph of the Medieval Mind* (The Bodley Head, UK, 2008). Ball gets hopelessly sidetracked

into potted histories of all kinds of aspects of medieval life, but at the core of this book is a fascinating letter of love to an extraordinary building.

André Chastel *French Art* (Flammarion, France, 1995–96). Authoritative, three-volume study by one of France's leading art historians. Discusses individual works of art in some detail in an attempt – from architecture to tapestry, as well as painting – to locate the Frenchness of French art. With glossy photographs and serious-minded but readable text.

David Cairns *Berlioz: The Making of an Artist 1803–1832* (Penguin, 2000). The multiple-award winning first volume of Cairns' two-part biography is more than just a life of the passionate French composer, it's an extraordinary evocation of post-Napoleonic France and its burgeoning Romantic culture.

John Richardson *The Life of Picasso* (Pimlico/Random House, various dates). No twentieth-century artist has ever been subjected to as much scrutiny as Picasso receives in Richardson's brilliantly illustrated biography. Three of an expected four volumes have been published to date.

Stephen Romer (editor) *20th-Century French Poems* (Faber, 2002). A collection of around 150 French poems spanning the whole of the century. Although there's no French text, many of the translations are works of art in themselves, consummately rendered by the likes of Samuel Beckett, T.S. Eliot and Paul Auster.

Rolf Toman (editor) *Romanesque: Architecture, Sculpture, Painting*. Huge, sumptuously illustrated volume of essays on every aspect of the genre across Europe, with one chapter specifically devoted to France.

Guides

Glynn Christian *Edible France* (Interlink, 1998). A guide to food rather than restaurants: regional produce, local specialities, markets and best shops for buying goodies to bring back home. Dated, but still reliable for the provinces, if not Paris.

Cicerone Walking Guides (Cicerone, UK). Neat, durable guides with detailed route descriptions. Titles include *Tour of Mont Blanc*; *Chamonix-Mont Blanc*; *Tour of the Oisans* (GR54); *French Alps* (GR5); *The Way of Saint James* (GR65); *Tour of the Queyras*; *The Pyrenean Trail* (GR10); *Walks and Climbs in the Pyrenees*; *Walking in the Alps*.

Philippe Dubois *Where to Watch Birds in France* (Helm, 2006). Maps, advice on when to go, habitat information, species' lists – everything you need.

David Hampshire *Living and Working in France* (Survival Books, 2007). An invaluable guide for anyone considering residence or work in France; packed with ideas and advice on job hunting, bureaucracy, tax, health and so on. Usually updated every two years.

Richard Holmes *Fatal Avenue: A Traveller's History of the Battlefields of France and Flanders 1346–1945* (2008). Excellent combination of guidebook and storytelling from a renowned military historian.

Language

Language

French

rench can be a deceptively familiar language because of the number of words and structures it shares with English. Despite this, it's far from easy, though the bare essentials are not difficult to master and can make all the difference. Even just saying "Bonjour Madame/Monsieur" and then gesticulating will usually get you a smile and helpful service. People working in tourist offices, hotels and so on almost always speak English and tend to use it when you're struggling to speak French – be grateful, not insulted.

Pronunciation

One easy rule to remember is that **consonants** at the ends of words are usually silent: the most obvious example is Paris, pronounced "Paree", while the phrase *pas plus tard* (not later) sounds something like "pa–plu–tarr". The exception is when the following word begins with a vowel, in which case you generally run the two together: *pas après* (not after) becomes "pazaprey". Otherwise, consonants are much as in English, except that: *ch* is always "sh", *c* is "s", *h* is silent, *th* is the same as "t", *ll* is like the "y" in yes, *w* is "v", and *r* is growled (or rolled).

Vowels are the hardest sounds to get exactly right, but they rarely differ enough from English to make comprehension a problem. The most obvious differences are that *au* sounds like the "o" in "over"; *aujourd'hui* (today) is thus pronounced "oh-jor-dwi". Another one to listen out for is *oi*, which sounds like "wa"; *toi* (to you) thus sounds like "twa". And "u" as in *tu* (you) is said

Phrasebooks and courses

Breakthrough French (Palgrave Macmillan). One of the best teach-yourself courses, with three levels to choose from. Each comes with a book and CD-ROM.

The Complete Merde! The Real French You Were Never Taught at School (HarperCollins). More than just a collection of swearwords, this book is a passkey into everyday French, and a window into French culture.

Get Into French Course Pack (BBC Worldwide). Comes with an audio CD, a book and a CD-ROM which allows you to set up your own role-play situations. The BBC offers a whole range of French learning products – see ⓦ www.bbc.co.uk/languages/french, which also offers a basic "Quick Fix", with free MP3 downloads, and a free, 24-part, online audio course: "French Steps".

Harrap's French Mini Dictionary (Harrap). This relatively comprehensive French–English and English–French dictionary also has a brief grammar and pronunciation guide.

Pardon My French (Penguin). See review on p.1212.

Rough Guide French Phrasebook (Rough Guides). Mini dictionary-style phrasebook with both English–French and French–English sections, along with cultural tips and a menu reader.

with much more pursed lips than in English. Lastly, adding "m" or "n" to a vowel, as in *en* or *un*, adds a nasal sound, as if you said just the vowel with a cold.

Basic words and phrases

French nouns are divided into masculine and feminine. This causes difficulties with adjectives, whose endings have to change to suit the nouns they qualify – you can talk about *un château blanc* (a white castle), for example, but *une tour blanche* (a white tower). If you're not sure, stick to the simpler masculine form – as used in this glossary.

Essentials

hello (morning or afternoon)	bonjour	big	grand
		small	petit
hello (evening)	bonsoir	more	plus
good night	bonne nuit	less	moins
goodbye	au revoir	a little	un peu
thank you	merci	a lot	beaucoup
please	s'il vous plaît	cheap	bon marché
sorry	pardon/Je m'excuse	expensive	cher
excuse me	pardon	good	bon
yes	oui	bad	mauvais
no	non	hot	chaud
OK/agreed	d'accord	cold	froid
help!	au secours!	with	avec
here	ici	without	sans
there	là	entrance	entrée
this one	ceci	exit	sortie
that one	celà	man	un homme
open	ouvert	woman (pronounced "fam")	une femme
closed	fermé		

Numbers

1	un	12	douze
2	deux	13	treize
3	trois	14	quatorze
4	quatre	15	quinze
5	cinq	16	seize
6	six	17	dix-sept
7	sept	18	dix-huit
8	huit	19	dix-neuf
9	neuf	20	vingt
10	dix	21	vingt-et-un
11	onze	22	vingt-deux

30	trente	100	cent
40	quarante	101	cent-et-un
50	cinquante	200	deux cents
60	soixante	300	trois cents
70	soixante-dix	500	cinq cents
75	soixante-quinze	1000	mille
80	quatre-vingts	2000	deux milles
90	quatre-vingt-dix	5000	cinq milles
95	quatre-vingt-quinze	1,000,000	un million

Time

today	aujourd'hui	now	maintenant
yesterday	hier	later	plus tard
tomorrow	demain	at one o'clock	à une heure
in the morning	le matin	at three o'clock	à trois heures
in the afternoon	l'après-midi	at ten-thirty	à dix heures et demie
in the evening	le soir	at midday	à midi

Days and dates

January	janvier	Sunday	dimanche
February	février	Monday	lundi
March	mars	Tuesday	mardi
April	avril	Wednesday	mercredi
May	mai	Thursday	jeudi
June	juin	Friday	vendredi
July	juillet	Saturday	samedi
August	août	August 1	le premier août
September	septembre	March 2	le deux mars
October	octobre	July 14	le quatorze juillet
November	novembre	November 23	le vingt-trois novembre
December	décembre	2009	deux mille neuf

Talking to people

When addressing people a simple *bonjour* is not enough; you should always use *Monsieur* for a man, *Madame* for a woman, *Mademoiselle* for a young woman or girl. This isn't as formal as it seems, and it has its uses when you've forgotten someone's name or want to attract someone's attention.

Do you speak English?	Parlez-vous anglais?	... English	... anglais[e]
How do you say it in French?	Comment ça se dit en français?	... Irish	... irlandais[e]
		... Scottish	... écossais[e]
What's your name?	Comment vous appelez-vous?	... Welsh	... gallois[e]
		... American	... américain[e]
My name is ...	Je m'appelle ...	... Australian	... australien[ne]
I'm ...	Je suis ...	... Canadian	... canadien[ne]

... a New Zealander	... néo-zélandais[e]	I don't know	Je ne sais pas
... South African	... sud-africain[e]	Let's go	Allons-y
I understand	Je comprends	See you tomorrow	À demain
I don't understand	Je ne comprends pas	See you soon	À bientôt
Can you speak slower?	S'il vous plaît, parlez moins vite	Leave me alone (aggressive)	Fichez-moi la paix!
How are you?	Comment allez-vous?/ Ça va?	Please help me	Aidez-moi, s'il vous plaît
Fine, thanks	Très bien, merci		

Finding the way

bus	autobus/bus/car	I'm going to ...	Je vais à ...
bus station	gare routière	I want to get off at ...	Je voudrais descendre à ...
bus stop	arrêt		
car	voiture	the road to ...	la route pour ...
train/taxi/ferry	train/taxi/bac	near	près/pas loin
boat	bâteau	far	loin
plane	avion	left	à gauche
shuttle	navette	right	à droite
train station	gare (SNCF)	straight on	tout droit
platform	quai	on the other side of	à l'autre côté de
What time does it leave?	Il part à quelle heure?	on the corner of	à l'angle de
		next to	à côté de
What time does it arrive?	Il arrive à quelle heure?	behind	derrière
		in front of	devant
a ticket to ...	un billet pour ...	before	avant
single ticket	aller simple	after	après
return ticket	aller retour	under	sous
validate your ticket	compostez votre billet	to cross	traverser
valid for	valable pour	bridge	pont
ticket office	vente de billets	town centre	centre ville
how many kilometres?	combien de kilomètres?	all through roads (road sign)	toutes directions
how many hours?	combien d'heures?	other destinations (road sign)	autres directions
hitchhiking	autostop		
on foot	à pied	upper town	ville haute/haute ville
Where are you going?	Vous allez où?	lower town	ville basse/basse ville
		old town	vieille ville

Questions and requests

The simplest way of asking a question is to start with *s'il vous plaît* (please), then name the thing you want in an interrogative tone of voice. For example:

Where is there a bakery?	S'il vous plaît, la boulangerie?	Can we have a room for two	S'il vous plaît, une chambre pour deux?
Which way is it to the Eiffel Tower?	S'il vous plaît, la route pour la tour Eiffel?	Can I have a kilo of oranges?	S'il vous plaît, un kilo d'oranges?

where?	où?
how?	comment?
how many/how much?	combien?
when?	quand?
why?	pourquoi?
at what time?	à quelle heure?
what is/which is?	quel est?

Accommodation

a room for one/two persons	une chambre pour une/deux personne(s)
a double bed	un grand lit/un lit matriomonial
a room with two single beds/twin	une chambre à deux lits
a room with a shower	une chambre avec douche
a room with a bath	une chambre avec salle de bain
for one/two/three nights	pour une/deux/trois nuits
Can I see it?	Je peux la voir?
a room on the courtyard	une chambre sur la cour
a room over the street	une chambre sur la rue
first floor	premier étage
second floor	deuxième étage
with a view	avec vue
key	clef
to iron	repasser
do laundry	faire la lessive
sheets	draps
blankets	couvertures
quiet	calme
noisy	bruyant
hot water	eau chaude
cold water	eau froide
Is breakfast included?	Est-ce que le petit déjeuner est compris?
I would like breakfast	Je voudrais prendre le petit déjeuner
I don't want breakfast	Je ne veux pas de petit déjeuner
bed and breakfast	chambre d'hôte
Can we camp here?	On peut camper ici?
campsite	camping/terrain de camping
tent	tente
tent space	emplacement
hostel	foyer
youth hostel	auberge de jeunesse

Driving

service station	garage
service	service
to park the car	garer la voiture
car park	un parking
no parking	défense de stationner/ stationnement interdit
petrol/gas station	poste d'essence
fuel	essence
unleaded	sans plomb
leaded	super
diesel	gazole
(to) fill it up	faire le plein
oil	huile
air line	ligne à air
put air in the tyres	gonfler les pneus
battery	batterie
the battery is dead	la batterie est morte
plugs	bougies
to break down	tomber en panne
gas can	bidon
insurance	assurance
green card	carte verte
traffic lights	feux
red light	feu rouge
green light	feu vert

L

LANGUAGE | Basic words and phrases

Health matters

doctor	médecin
I don't feel well	Je ne me sens pas bien
medicines	médicaments
prescription	ordonnance
I feel sick	Je suis malade
I have a headache	J'ai mal à la tête
stomach ache	mal à l'estomac
period	règles

pain	douleur
it hurts	ça fait mal
chemist/pharmacist	pharmacie
hospital	hôpital
condom	préservatif
morning-after pill /emergency contraceptive	pilule du lendemain
I'm allergic to ...	Je suis allergique à ...

Other needs

bakery	boulangerie
food shop	alimentation
delicatessen	charcuterie, traiteur
cake shop	pâtisserie
cheese shop	fromagerie
supermarket	supermarché
to eat	manger
to drink	boire
tasting, eg wine tasting	dégustation
camping gas	camping gaz

tobacconist	tabac
stamps	timbres
bank	banque
money	argent
toilets	toilettes
police	police
telephone	téléphone
cinema	cinéma
theatre	théâtre
to reserve/book	réserver

Restaurant phrases

I'd like to reserve a table	Je voudrais réserver une table
for two people, at eight thirty	pour deux personnes, à vingt heures et demie

I'm having the €30 set menu	Je prendrai le menu à trente euros
Waiter!	monsieur/madame!/ s'il vous plaît!
the bill/check please	l'addition, s'il vous plaît

Food and dishes

Basic terms

l'addition	bill/check
beurre	butter
bio or biologique	organic
bouteille	bottle
carafe d'eau	jug of water
la carte	the menu
chauffé	heated

couteau	knife
cru	raw
cuillère	spoon
cuit	cooked
emballé	wrapped
à emporter	takeaway
entrée	starter

formule	lunchtime set menu	pimenté	spicy
fourchette	fork	plat	main course
fumé	smoked	poivre	pepper
gazeuse	fizzy	salé	salted/savoury
lait	milk	sel	salt
le menu	set menu	sucre	sugar
moutarde	mustard	sucré	sweet
oeuf	egg	table	table
offert	free	verre	glass
pain	bread	vinaigre	vinegar

Snacks

un sandwich/une baguette	a sandwich	oeufs	eggs
au jambon	with ham, no butter	au plat	fried
jambon beurre	with ham and butter	à la coque	boiled
au fromage	with cheese, no butter	durs	hard-boiled
mixte	with ham and cheese	brouillés	scrambled
au pâté (de campagne)	with pâté (country-style)	omelette	omelette
		nature	plain
croque-monsieur	grilled cheese and ham sandwich	aux fines herbes	with herbs
		au fromage	with cheese
panini	toasted Italian sandwich	salade de tomates	tomato salad
tartine	buttered bread or open sandwich, often with jam	salade vert	green salad

Pasta (pâtes), pancakes (crêpes), tartes and couscous

nouilles	noodles	couscous	steamed semolina grains, usually served with meat or veg, chickpea stew and chilli sauce
pâtes fraîches	fresh pasta		
crêpe au sucre/aux oeufs	pancake with sugar/ eggs		
galette	buckwheat pancake		
pissaladière	tart of fried onions with anchovies and black olives	couscous Royale	couscous with spicy Merguez sausage, chicken and beef or lamb kebabs
tarte flambée	thin pizza-like pastry topped with onion, cream and bacon		

Soups (soupes)

bisque	shellfish soup	bouillon	broth or stock
bouillabaisse	soup with five fish	bourride	thick fish soup

consommé	clear soup		rouille	red pepper, garlic and saffron mayonnaise served with fish soup
garbure	potato, cabbage and meat soup		soupe à l'oignon	onion soup with rich cheese topping
pistou	parmesan, basil and garlic paste added to soup		velouté	thick soup, usually fish or poultry
potage	thick vegetable soup			
potée auvergnate	cabbage and meat soup			

Starters (hors d'œuvres)

assiette anglaise	plate of cold meats		hors d'oeuvres	combination of the above often with smoked or marinated fish
assiette composée	mixed salad plate, usually cold meat and veg			
crudités	dressed raw vegetables			

Fish (poisson), seafood (fruits de mer) and shellfish (crustaces or coquillages)

anchois	anchovies		homard	lobster
anguilles	eels		huîtres	oysters
barbue	brill		langouste	spiny lobster
baudroie	monkfish or anglerfish		langoustines	saltwater crayfish (scampi)
bigourneau	periwinkle		limande	lemon sole
brème	bream		lotte de mer	monkfish
cabillaud	cod		loup de mer	sea bass
calmar	squid		maquereau	mackerel
carrelet	plaice		merlan	whiting
claire	type of oyster		moules (marinière)	mussels (with shallots in white wine sauce)
colin	hake			
congre	conger eel		oursin	sea urchin
coques	cockles		palourdes	clams
coquilles	scallops St-Jacques		poissons de roche	fish from shoreline rocks
crabe	crab			
crevettes grises	shrimp		praires	small clams
crevettes roses	prawns		raie	skate
daurade	sea bream		rouget	red mullet
éperlan	smelt or whitebait		saumon	salmon
escargots	snails		sole	sole
flétan	halibut		thon	tuna
friture	assorted fried fish, often like whitebait		truite	trout
			turbot	turbot
gambas	king prawns		violet	sea squirt
hareng	herring			

Fish dishes and terms

aïoli	garlic mayonnaise served with salt cod and other fish	grillé	grilled
		hollandaise	butter and vinegar sauce
anchoïade	anchovy paste or sauce	à la meunière	in a butter, lemon and parsley sauce
arête	fish bone		
assiette de pêcheur	assorted fish	mousse/mousseline	mousse
beignet	fritter	pané	breaded
darne	fillet or steak	poutargue	mullet roe paste
la douzaine	a dozen	quenelles	light dumplings
frit	fried	raïto	red wine, olive, caper, garlic and shallot sauce
friture	deep-fried small fish		
fumé	smoked		
fumet	fish stock	thermidor	lobster grilled in its shell with cream sauce
gigot de mer	large fish baked whole		

Meat (viande) and poultry (volaille)

agneau (de pré-salé)	lamb (grazed on salt marshes)	langue	tongue
		lapin/lapereau	rabbit/young rabbit
andouille	cold pork and tripe sausage	lard/lardons	bacon/diced bacon
		lièvre	hare
andouillette	hot, cooked tripe sausage	merguez	spicy, red sausage
		mouton	mutton
bavette	flank-like steak	museau de veau	calf's muzzle
bifteck	steak	oie	goose
boeuf	beef	onglet	tasty, flank-like steak
boudin blanc	sausage of white meats	os	bone
		poitrine	breast
boudin noir	black pudding	porc	pork
caille	quail	poulet	chicken
canard	duck	poussin	baby chicken
caneton	duckling	rillettes	pork mashed with lard and liver
contrefilet	sirloin roast		
coquelet	cockerel	ris	sweetbreads
la cuisson?	how would sir/madam like his/her steak done?	rognons	kidneys
		rognons blancs	testicles
		sanglier	wild boar
dinde/dindon	turkey	steak	steak
entrecôte	rib steak	tête de veau	calf's head (in jelly)
faux filet	sirloin steak	tournedos	thick slices of fillet
foie	liver	tripes	tripe
foie gras	(duck/goose) liver	tripoux	mutton tripe
gibier	game	veau	veal
gigot (d'agneau)	leg (of lamb)	venaison	venison
grenouilles (cuisses de)	frogs' (legs)		

Meat and poultry dishes and terms

aïado	roast shoulder of lamb stuffed with garlic and other ingredients
aile	wing
blanquette, daube, estouffade, hochepôt, navarin, ragoût	types of stew
blanquette de veau	veal in cream and mushroom sauce
boeuf bourguignon	beef stew with Burgundy, onions and mushrooms
carré	best end of neck, chop or cutlet
cassoulet	casserole of beans, sausages and duck/ goose
choucroute	sauerkraut with peppercorns, sausages, pork and ham
civet	game stew
confit	meat preserve
coq au vin	chicken slow-cooked with wine, onions and mushrooms
côte	chop, cutlet or rib
cou	neck
cuisse	thigh or leg
en croûte	in pastry
épaule	shoulder
farci	stuffed

au feu de bois	cooked over wood fire
au four	baked
garni	with vegetables
gésier	gizzard
grillade	grilled meat
grillé	grilled
hâchis	chopped meat or mince hamburger
magret de canard	duck breast
marmite	casserole
médaillon	round piece
mijoté	stewed
pavé	thick slice
pieds et paques	mutton or pork tripe and trotters
poêlé	pan-fried
poulet de Bresse	chicken from Bresse
râble	saddle
rôti	roast
sauté	lightly fried in butter
steak au poivre (vert/rouge)	steak in a black pep percorn sauce (green/red peppercorn)
steak tartare	raw chopped beef, topped with a raw egg yolk
tagine	North African casserole
tournedos rossini	beef fillet with foie gras and truffles
viennoise	fried in egg and bread crumbs

Terms for steaks

bleu	almost raw
saignant	rare
à point	medium rare

bien cuit	well done
très bien cuit	very well done/ruined
brochette	kebab

Garnishes and sauces

américaine	sauce of white wine, cognac and tomato
arlésienne au porto	with tomatoes, onions, aubergines, potatoes and rice in port

auvergnat	with cabbage, sausage and bacon
béarnaise	sauce of egg yolks, white wine, shallots and vinegar

beurre blanc	sauce of white wine and shallots, with butter	diable	strong mustard seasoning
bonne femme	with mushroom, bacon, potato and onions	façon	in the style of ...
		forestière	with bacon and mushroom
bordelaise	in a red wine, shallot and bone-marrow sauce	fricassée	rich, creamy sauce
		mornay	cheese sauce
		pays d'auge	cream and cider
boulangère	baked with potatoes and onions	périgourdine	sauce with foie gras and possibly truffles
bourgeoise	with carrots, onions, bacon, celery and braised lettuce	piquante	with gherkins or capers, vinegar and shallots
chasseur	sauce of white wine, mushrooms and shallots	provençale	sauce of tomatoes, garlic, olive oil and herbs
		savoyarde	with gruyère cheese
châtelaine	with artichoke hearts and chestnut purée	véronique	sauce of grapes, wine and cream

Vegetables (légumes), grains (grains), herbs (herbes) and spices (épices)

ail	garlic	épinard	spinach
anis	aniseed	estragon	tarragon
artichaut	artichoke	fenouil	fennel
asperge	asparagus	férigoule	thyme (in Provençal)
avocat	avocado	fèves	broad beans
basilic	basil	flageolets	flageolet beans
betterave	beetroot	gingembre	ginger
blette/bette	Swiss chard	haricots	beans
cannelle	cinnamon	verts	green beans
capre	caper	rouges	kidney beans
cardon	cardoon, a beet related to artichoke	laurier	bay leaf
		lentilles	lentils
carotte	carrot	maïs	maize (corn)
céleri	celery	menthe	mint
champignons, cèpes, ceps, girolles, chanterelles, pleurotes	mushrooms	moutarde	mustard
		oignon	onion
		panais	parsnip
		pélandron	type of string bean
chou (rouge)	(red) cabbage	persil	parsley
choufleur	cauliflower	petits pois	peas
concombre	cucumber	piment rouge/vert	red/green chilli pepper
cornichon	gherkin	pois chiche	chickpeas
échalotes	shallots	pois mange-tout	mange-tout
endive	chicory	pignons	pine nuts

poireau	leek	riz	rice
poivron (vert, rouge)	sweet pepper (green, red)	safran	saffron
		sarrasin	buckwheat
pommes de terre	potatoes	tomate	tomato
primeurs	spring vegetables	truffes	truffles
radis	radish		

Vegetable dishes and terms

à l'anglaise	boiled	mousseline	mashed potato with cream and eggs
beignet	fritter		
duxelles	fried mushrooms and shallots with cream	à la parisienne	sautéed potatoes, with white wine and shallot sauce
farci	stuffed		
feuille	leaf	parmentier	with potatoes
fines herbes	mixture of tarragon, parsley and chives	petits farcis	stuffed tomatoes, aubergines, courgettes and peppers
gratiné	browned with cheese or butter		
à la grecque	cooked in oil and lemon	râpée	grated or shredded
		à la vapeur	steamed
jardinière	with mixed diced vegetables	en verdure	garnished with green vegetables

Fruit (fruit) and nuts (noix)

abricot	apricot	mangue	mango
acajou	cashew nut	marron	chestnut
amande	almond	melon	melon
ananas	pineapple	mirabelle	small yellow plum
banane	banana	myrtille	bilberry
brugnon, nectarine	nectarine	noisette	hazelnut
cacahouète	peanut	noix	walnuts; nuts
cassis	blackcurrant	orange	orange
cérise	cherry	pamplemousse	grapefruit
citron	lemon	pastèque	watermelon
citron vert	lime	pêche	peach
datte	date	pistache	pistachio
figue	fig	poire	pear
fraise (de bois)	strawberry (wild)	pomme	apple
framboise	raspberry	prune	plum
fruit de la passion	passion fruit	pruneau	prune
grenade	pomegranate	raisin	grape
groseille	redcurrant	reine-claude	greengage

Fruit dishes and terms

agrumes	citrus fruits
beignet	fritter
compôte	stewed fruit
coulis	sauce of puréed fruit
crème de marrons	chestnut purée
flambé	set aflame in alcohol

fougasse	bread flavoured with orange-flower water or almonds (can be savoury)
frappé	iced

Desserts (desserts or entremets) and pastries (pâtisserie)

bombe	moulded ice-cream dessert
brioche	sweet breakfast roll
charlotte	custard and fruit in lining of almond fingers
clafoutis	heavy custard and fruit tart
crème Chantilly	vanilla-flavoured and sweetened whipped cream
crème fraîche	sour cream
crème pâtissière	thick, eggy pastry-filling
crêpe suzette	thin pancake with orange juice and liqueur
fromage blanc	cream cheese
gaufre	waffle
glace	ice cream
Île flottante/oeufs à la neige	whipped egg-white floating on custard
macaron	macaroon

madeleine	small sponge cake
marrons Mont Blanc	chestnut purée and cream on a rum-soaked sponge cake
mousse au chocolat	chocolate mousse
omelette norvégienne	baked alaska
palmier	caramelized puff pastry
parfait	frozen mousse, sometimes ice cream
petit-suisse	a smooth mixture of cream and curds
petits fours	bite-sized cakes/pastries
poires belle hélène	pears and ice cream in chocolate sauce
tarte tatin	upside-down apple tart
tarte tropezienne	sponge cake filled with custard cream, topped with nuts
yaourt/yogourt	yoghurt

Glossary of architectural terms

These are either terms you'll come across in the Guide, or come up against while travelling around.

abbaye abbey

ambulatory passage round the outer edge of the choir of a church

apse semicircular termination at the east end of a church

Baroque mainly seventeenth-century style of art and architecture, distinguished by ornate Classicism

basse ville lower town

bastide walled town

capital carved top of a column

Carolingian dynasty (and art, sculpture etc) named after Charlemagne; mid-eighth to early tenth centuries

château mansion, country house, castle

château fort castle

chevet east end of a church

choir the eastern part of a church between the altar and nave, used by the choir and clergy

Classical architectural style incorporating Greek and Roman elements: pillars, domes, colonnades, etc, at its height in France in the seventeenth century and revived, as Neoclassical, in the nineteenth century

clerestory upper storey of a church, incorporating the windows

donjon castle keep

église church

flamboyant florid, late (c.1450–1540) form of Gothic

Gallo-Roman from the Roman era in France

Gothic late-medieval architectural style characterized by pointed arches, verticality and light

haute ville upper town

hôtel (particulier) mansion or town house

Merovingian dynasty (and art etc) ruling France and parts of Germany from sixth to mid-eighth centuries

narthex entrance hall of church

nave main body of a church

porte gateway

Renaissance Classically influenced art/ architectural style imported from Italy to France in the early sixteenth century

retable altarpiece

Roman Romanesque (easily confused with Romain, which means Roman)

Romanesque early medieval architecture distinguished by squat, rounded forms and naive sculpture, called Norman in Britain

stucco plaster used to embellish ceilings etc

tour tower

transepts transverse arms of a church

tympanum sculpted panel above a church door

voussoir sculpted rings in arch over church door

Travel store

Africa & Middle East
Cape Town &
  the Garden Route
Dubai **D**
Egypt
Gambia
Jordan
Kenya
Marrakesh **D**
Morocco
South Africa, Lesotho
  & Swaziland
Tanzania
Tunisia
West Africa
Zanzibar

Travel Specials
First-Time Africa
First-Time Around
  the World
First-Time Asia
First-Time Europe
First-Time Latin
  America
Make the Most of
  Your Time on Earth
Travel with Babies &
  Young Children
Travel Online
Travel Survival
Ultimate Adventures
Walks in London
  & SE England
World Party

Maps
Algarve
Amsterdam
Andalucia
  & Costa del Sol
Argentina
Athens
Australia
Barcelona
Berlin
Boston & Cambridge
Brittany
Brussels
California
Chicago
Chile
Corsica
Costa Rica
  & Panama
Crete

Croatia
Cuba
Cyprus
Czech Republic
Dominican Republic
Dubai & UAE
Dublin
Egypt
Florence & Siena
Florida
France
Frankfurt
Germany
Greece
Guatemala & Belize
Iceland
India
Ireland
Italy
Kenya & Northern
  Tanzania
Lisbon
London
Los Angeles
Madrid
Malaysia
Mallorca
Marrakesh
Mexico
Miami & Key West
Morocco
New England
New York City
New Zealand
Northern Spain
Paris
Peru
Portugal
Prague
Pyrenees & Andorra
Rome
San Francisco
Sicily
South Africa
South India
Spain & Portugal
Sri Lanka
Tenerife
Thailand
Toronto
Trinidad & Tobago
Tunisia
Turkey
Tuscany

Venice
Vietnam, Laos
  & Cambodia
Washington DC
Yucatán Peninsula

Phrasebooks
Croatian
Czech
Dutch
Egyptian Arabic
French
German
Greek
Hindi & Urdu
Italian
Japanese
Latin American
  Spanish
Mandarin Chinese
Mexican Spanish
Polish
Portuguese
Russian
Spanish
Swahili
Thai
Turkish
Vietnamese

Computers
Blogging
eBay
FWD this link
iPhone
iPods, iTunes
  & music online
The Internet
Macs & OS X
MySpace
PlayStation Portable
Website Directory

Film & TV
American
  Independent Film
British Cult Comedy
Chick Flicks
Comedy Movies
Cult Movies
Film
Film Musicals
Film Noir
Gangster Movies
Horror Movies

Sci-Fi Movies
Westerns

Lifestyle
Babies
Ethical Living
Pregnancy & Birth
Running

Music Guides
The Beatles
The Best Music
  You've Never Heard
Blues
Bob Dylan
Book of Playlists
Classical Music
Elvis
Frank Sinatra
Heavy Metal
Hip-Hop
Led Zeppelin
Opera
Pink Floyd
Punk
Reggae
The Rolling Stones
Soul and R&B
Velvet Underground
World Music

Popular Culture
Classic Novels
Conspiracy Theories
Crime Fiction
Cult Fiction
The Da Vinci Code
Graphic Novels
His Dark Materials
Poker
Shakespeare
Superheroes
Tutankhamun
Unexplained
  Phenomena
Videogames

Science
The Brain
Climate Change
The Earth
Genes & Cloning
The Universe
Weather

ROUGH GUIDES

Small print and

Index

A Rough Guide to Rough Guides

Published in 1982, the first Rough Guide – to Greece – was a student scheme that became a publishing phenomenon. Mark Ellingham, a recent graduate in English from Bristol University, had been travelling in Greece the previous summer and couldn't find the right guidebook. With a small group of friends he wrote his own guide, combining a highly contemporary, journalistic style with a thoroughly practical approach to travellers' needs.

The immediate success of the book spawned a series that rapidly covered dozens of destinations. And, in addition to impecunious backpackers, Rough Guides soon acquired a much broader and older readership that relished the guides' wit and inquisitiveness as much as their enthusiastic, critical approach and value-for-money ethos.

These days, Rough Guides include recommendations from shoestring to luxury and cover more than 200 destinations around the globe, including almost every country in the Americas and Europe, more than half of Africa and most of Asia and Australasia. Our ever-growing team of authors and photographers is spread all over the world, particularly in Europe, the USA and Australia.

In the early 1990s, Rough Guides branched out of travel, with the publication of Rough Guides to World Music, Classical Music and the Internet. All three have become benchmark titles in their fields, spearheading the publication of a wide range of books under the Rough Guide name.

Including the travel series, Rough Guides now number more than 350 titles, covering: phrasebooks, waterproof maps, music guides from Opera to Heavy Metal, reference works as diverse as Conspiracy Theories and Shakespeare, and popular culture books from iPods to Poker. Rough Guides also produce a series of more than 120 World Music CDs in partnership with World Music Network.

Visit www.roughguides.com to see our latest publications.

Rough Guide travel images are available for commercial licensing at www.roughguidespictures.com

Rough Guide credits

Text editor: Róisín Cameron, Emma Gibbs, Christina Valhouli and Alison Murchie
Layout: Sachin Tanwar
Cartography: Rajesh Mishra
Picture editor: Emily Taylor
Production: Rebecca Short
Proofreaders: Susannah Wight
Cover design: Chloë Roberts
Photographers: David Abram, Marc Dubin, Lydia Evans, Jean-Christophe Godet, Michelle Grant, James McConnachie and Greg Ward
Editorial London: Ruth Blackmore, Andy Turner, Keith Drew, Edward Aves, Alice Park, Lucy White, Jo Kirby, James Smart, Natasha Foges, Emma Traynor, Kathryn Lane, Monica Woods, Mani Ramaswamy, Harry Wilson, Lucy Cowie, Helen Ochyra, Amanda Howard, Alison Roberts, Joe Staines, Peter Buckley, Matthew Milton, Tracy Hopkins, Ruth Tidball, Kate Berens; **Delhi** Madhavi Singh, Karen D'Souza, Lubna Shaheen
Design & Pictures: London Scott Stickland, Dan May, Diana Jarvis, Mark Thomas, Nicole Newman, Sarah Cummins; **Delhi** Umesh Aggarwal, Ajay Verma, Jessica Subramanian, Ankur Guha, Pradeep Thapliyal, Anita Singh, Nikhil Agarwal

Production: Vicky Baldwin
Cartography: London Maxine Repath, Ed Wright, Katie Lloyd-Jones; **Delhi** Rajesh Chhibber, Ashutosh Bharti, Animesh Pathak, Jasbir Sandhu, Karobi Gogoi, Alakananda Bhattacharya, Swati Handoo, Deshpal Dabas
Online: London George Atwell, Faye Hellon, Jeanette Angell, Fergus Day, Justine Bright, Clare Bryson, Áine Fearon, Adrian Low, Ezgi Celebi, Amber Bloomfield; **Delhi** Amit Verma, Rahul Kumar, Narender Kumar, Ravi Yadav, Debojit Borah, Rakesh Kumar, Ganesh Sharma, Shisir Basumatari
Marketing & Publicity: London Liz Statham, Niki Hanmer, Louise Maher, Jess Carter, Vanessa Godden, Vivienne Watton, Anna Paynton, Rachel Sprackett, Libby Jellie, Laura Vipond, Vanessa McDonald; **New York** Katy Ball, Judi Powers, Nancy Lambert; **Delhi** Ragini Govind
Manager India: Punita Singh
Reference Director: Andrew Lockett
Operations Manager: Helen Phillips
PA to Publishing Director: Nicola Henderson
Publishing Director: Martin Dunford
Commercial Manager: Gino Magnotta
Managing Director: John Duhigg

Publishing information

This eleventh edition published May 2009 by
Rough Guides Ltd,
80 Strand, London WC2R 0RL
14 Local Shopping Centre, Panchsheel Park, New Delhi 110017, India
Distributed by the Penguin Group
Penguin Books Ltd,
80 Strand, London WC2R 0RL
Penguin Group (USA)
375 Hudson Street, NY 10014, USA
Penguin Group (Australia)
250 Camberwell Road, Camberwell, Victoria 3124, Australia
Penguin Group (Canada)
195 Harry Walker Parkway N, Newmarket, ON, L3Y 7B3 Canada
Penguin Group (NZ)
67 Apollo Drive, Mairangi Bay, Auckland 1310, New Zealand
Cover concept by Peter Dyer.

Typeset in Bembo and Helvetica to an original design by Henry Iles.
Printed in Italy by L.E.G.O. S.p.A, Lavis (TN)
© Rough Guides 2009

1256pp includes index
A catalogue record for this book is available from the British Library
ISBN: 978-1-84836-029-7

1 3 5 7 9 8 6 4 2

SMALL PRINT

Help us update

We've gone to a lot of effort to ensure that the eleventh edition of **The Rough Guide to France** is accurate and up to date. However, things change – places are "discovered", opening hours are notoriously fickle, restaurants and rooms raise prices or lower standards. If you feel we've got it wrong or left something out, we'd like to know, and if you can remember the address, the price, the hours, the phone number, so much the better.

Please send your comments with the subject line "**Rough Guide France Update**" to ©mail @roughguides.com. We'll credit all contributions and send a copy of the next edition (or any other Rough Guide if you prefer) for the very best emails.
Have your questions answered and tell others about your trip at
®community.roughguides.com

Acknowledgements

Brian Catlos: Thanks to Mélissa Buttelli (OT Toulouse), Núria Silleras-Fernández and Hélène Aznar.

Marc Dubin: Thanks to Jonathan and Myriam Peat in Castillons-en-Couserans, and Mark Stickland and Julia Stagg in Castet d'Aleu.

Samantha Cook would like to thank Greg Ward, for lighting up Paris and so much more besides; Ruth Blackmore and James McConnachie; and Róisín Cameron for a brilliant editing job.

Alexander Larman: Thanks to Thierry & Yolaine Auger, Gloria & Bob Belknap, Peggy Boutin,

Frédérique Colin, Elisabeth Donetti, Amanda Monroe, Anne & Xavier Olivereau.

James McConnachie would like to thank David and Kate Hunt.

Kate Turner would like to thank Charlynne and Lottie for their company and their opinions.

Lucy White: Thanks to Richard and Lucine at *Mas del Sol* for putting me up for a few days; thanks also to Anna for her marvellous pancake place, and to Christopher and family for constant moral support.

Readers' letters

Thanks to all the readers who have taken the time to write in with comments and suggestions (and apologies if we've inadvertently omitted or misspelt anyone's name):

Lynne Alderson, Stephen Bach, Amanda Baltazar, Jim Berry, Chris Bethell, Robert Buckle, Chris Burin, Mary Burnett, Allan Cameron, Mrs AT Canton, Hélene Carleschi, Clare and Gerald Chapman, Stuart Connell, Judy Consden, Sandy Cordone, Mike Cowley, Jeremy Cutler, Pierre Delomenede, Hans Deseure, Claire Dorfan, Vivian & Ann Dunn, Caroline Edelin, Stuart Elliott, Nedellec Elvira, Emmanuelle, Jan Engmann, Mike Evans, Richard Fearn, Huw Foxall, Julia Gasper, Per Goller, David Goodacre, Andrew Hambleton, Elaine Hansen, Sam Hardie, Felicity Harvest, Laura Henderson, Ian Holtam, Dr. Britt Hornei & Wolfgang Prämassing, Dr Jörg W Huber, Richard and Gaynor Hudson, Helen Keightley, Simon and Maggie Krabbendam,

Leo Lacey, Phillippe Lecerf, Helen Lewis, Peter & Charlotte Malcolm, Kevin Mulshine, James Muller, Sue and Chris Nurse, Antonia Owen, E. Phillips, Gwerfyl Price, Sue Procter, Keith Resnick, Kenneth Richardson, Carol Robinson, Sue Rodgers, Kevin Rogers, John Ronaghan, Alison and Ivor Rowe, Eric & Sally Rowland, Peter Ryan, Pavel Sarek, Gisele Shaw, Peter Shepherd, Mr & Mrs SL Strack, Fiona Relf, Derek Robinson, Steve Rock, Frank Paul Silye, Alison Sinclair, Steve Soper, Michael & Victoria Steward, Geoff Taylor, Titi, Nancy Trasande, Mark Trumper, Peter Townsend, Rankin Weir, Ulrika Wernmark, Frank Wernicke, Edwin Whitaker, Matt Wiles, Rhea Williams.

SMALL PRINT

Photo credits

All photos © Rough Guides except the following:

Title page
Rows of purple lavender on farm in Provence
 © Chad Ehlers/Tips Images

Introduction
Cobblestone Street, Rue Du Jerzual, Dinan,
 Brittany © Chris Parker/Axiom
Combatants in the serious ball game of boules
 © Barry Mason /Alamy

Things not to miss
01 Gorges du Verdon, Provence © Tom Mackie/
 Pictures Colour Library
03 Vine in autumn, St. Emilion, Bordeaux © Adam
 Woolfitt/Robert Harding/Jupiter Images
04 Interior Amiens Cathedral © David Carton/
 Fotolibra
05 View of Annecy from Perriere bridge © PNS/
 Tips Images
06 The Nativity of the Antonins of Isenheim
 © The Print Collector/Alamy
08 Colours of France over the Arc de Triomphe
 during the annual Bastille © Reuters/Corbis
11 The Tour de France © Gerard Vandystadt/Tips
 Images
12 Carnac, megalithic site of Kermario © Hemis/
 Axiom
14 Gorges de l'Ardeche © AgenceImages/Jupiter
 Images
16 Bayeux Tapestry © Miles Kelly/Fotolibra
17 Open-air dining in Lyon © Jon Hicks/Corbis
18 Park of the Abbey Fontenay, Burgundy
 © Dieterich, W/Tips Images
21 Bottles of champagne in the cellars of Moet,
 Epernay © Harald Koch/Rex Features
22 Gravestones at Ryes Military war cemetery,
 Normandy © ICP-FR/Alamy
23 Châteaux of the Loire © James McConnachie
25 Medieval walled city of Carcassonne
 © Imagestate/Tips Images
28 Snowboarding in the Alps © Denkou Image/
 Tips Images

**Bars, Bistros and Brasseries colour
section**
French menu board © Foodfolio/Pictures Colour
 Library

Walking in France colour section
Chamonix, randonneurs devant le Mont-Blanc
 © PNS/Tips Images
Ibex on a rock in the Alps © macumazahn /iStock
 Images
Hiking in Livradois-Forez park, Auvergne
 © S.Picavet/Jupiter Images
Donkey trail in the Cevennes mountains
 © Hemis/Alamy
Vercours, Le Mont Aiguille © PNS/Tips Images

Flora in the French Pyrenees © Michelle Bhatia
Hiking in the Pyrenees © Michelle Bhatia

Festive France colour section
Fireworks bursting over the Eiffel Tower on
 Bastille Day © Reuters/Corbis
Roma gather for the annual pilgrimage to
 Les-Saintes-Maries-de-la-Mer in the Camargue
 © Sygma/Corbis
Girls in traditional costume wearing lace
 headdress, Breton © Steve Vidler/eStock Photo
Film premiere at the 61st Cannes Film Festival
 © James McCauley/Rex Features
Orange Festival opening © Sipa Press/Rex
 Features
Pop Fest in Carhaix-Plouguer © Fred Tanneau/
 Getty Images
Dancers perform on stage in Avignon, as part of
 the theatre festival © AFP/Getty Images
Folklore festival © Francois Le Divenah/
 Photononstop/Photolibrary

Black and whites
p.182 Palace of Versailles © Bernard Dupont/Tips
 Images
p.205 Nausicáa National Centre of the sea in
 Boulogne © David Jones/Alamy
p.217 Grand Place, Lille © PNS/Tips
p.227 Canadian national memorial at Vimy Ridge
 © Alan Orr/Alamy
p.244 Champagne © Stefano Torrione/Axiom
 Photographic
P.256 Hôtel de Ville © Wilmar Photography/
 Alamy
p.267 Traditional restaurant Bierstub/Winstub,
 Strasbourg © Ingolf Pompe 5/Alamy
p.276 Haut-Koenigsbourg castle © PNS/Tips
 Images
p.282 Cité de l'Automobile, Mulhouse © courtesy
 of C. Recoura /Cité de l'Automobile
p.291 Saint-Étienne Cathedral © PNS/Tips
 Images
p.362 Art exhibition, elephant-shaped machine,
 Nantes © Alain Le Bot/PNS/Tips Images
p.463 Blois, the Garden of Bishop's Palace,
 Loir-et-Cher © Sunset/Tips Images
p.476 Amboise © AgenceImages/Jupiter Images
p.487 Saumur, Champagne grape harvest
 © Hemis/Alamy
p.500 Ancy-le-Franc, Chambre des Arts
 © AJ Cassaigne/PNS/Tips Images
p.515 Semur-en-Auxois © Yves Talensac/PNS/
 Tips Images
p.545 Charollais cattle and vineyard below the
 chateau of Pierreclos © Mick Rock/Photolibrary
p.548 Punting, Marais Poitevin © Hugh Cleary
p.565 La Rochelle Harbour © Jean-Paul Garcin/
 Photononstop/Photolibrary

Selected images from our guidebooks are available for licensing from:
ROUGHGUIDESPICTURES.COM

Index

Map entries are in colour.

I

INDEX

INDEX | I

INDEX

1249

W

Y

Z

INDEX

Map symbols

maps are listed in the full index using coloured text

– – –	Chapter division boundary	★	Bus stop
▪–▪▪–▪▪	International boundary	⛽	Fuel station
▪ ▪–	Regional boundary	♦	Point of interest
▬▬▬	Autoroute	@	Internet café
═══	Major road	ⓘ	Tourist office/information point
══	Minor road	⊠	Post office
▬▬	Pedestrianized street	⊞	Hospital
⊓⊓⊓⊓	Steps	◉	Accommodation
]┈┈[	Tunnel	⚠	Campsite
▬▬	Railway	⛺	Gîte d'Étape/Mountain refuge
▬▪▬	TGV line	⌂	Cave
┉┉┉┉	Funicular railway	∴	Ruin
– – – –	Footpath	♜	Fort
────	River	⚔	Battlefield
— —	Ferry	↑	Lighthouse
────	Wall/fortification	⊛	Swimming pool
⊠–⊠	Gate	⊙	Statue/memorial
)(	Bridge/mountain pass	⛪	Monastery/abbey
↟↟↟↟↟	Cutting	⛫	Château
⋀⋀	Mountain range	▭	Market
▲	Mountain peak	▬	Building
ⶥ	Rocks	⊞	Church
⩫	Swamp	⬭	Stadium
⩘	Viewpoint	⊞	Cemetery
✈	Airport	▨	Park
Ⓡ	RER station	▨	Beach
Ⓜ	Métro station		
Ⓣ	Tram stop